Roger Ebert's Movie Home Companion
1992 Edition

Merry Christmas, Bob
from your
Movie & Home Companion
Love,
Pat

Other Books by Roger Ebert

An Illini Century
A Kiss Is Still a Kiss
Two Weeks in the Midday Sun: A Cannes Notebook

With Daniel Curley
The Perfect London Walk

With Gene Siskel
The Future of the Movies: Interviews with Martin Scorsese,
   Steven Spielberg, and George Lucas

ROGER EBERT'S
MOVIE HOME COMPANION
1992
EDITION

ANDREWS AND McMEEL
A UNIVERSAL PRESS SYNDICATE COMPANY
KANSAS CITY

Library of Congress Cataloging-in-Publication Data

Ebert, Roger.
    Roger Ebert's movie home companion.

    "Reviews in this book originally appeared in the Chicago
sun-times."—T.p. verso.
    Includes index.
    1. Moving-pictures—Reviews.   2. Video recordings—
Reviews.   I. Title.   II. Title: Movie home companion.
PN1995.E318   1987   791.43'75   88-646878
ISBN 0-8362-6242-5 (pbk.)

All the reviews in this book originally appeared in
the *Chicago Sun-Times*.

Attention: Schools and Businesses

Andrews and McMeel books are available at quantity discounts
with bulk purchase for educational, business, or sales promotional use.
For information, please write to:
Special Sales Department, Andrews and McMeel,
4900 Main Street, Kansas City, Missouri 64112.

This book is dedicated to
Robert Zonka, 1928–1985.
God love ya.

Acknowledgments

Donna Martin, editor and friend, was instrumental in the conception of this book. The design is by Cameron Poulter, a fellow Chicagoan. My thanks to Patty Donnelly, who keyboards the reviews, and Dorothy O'Brien, who assembles the book. Their help has been invaluable. I have been blessed with the unfailingly expert and discriminating copy-editing of Lon Grahnke, Lynn Roberts, Laura Emerick, Joe Pixler, Jeff Johnson, and Jennifer Steinbeck at the *Chicago Sun-Times*, Kate McMahon at the *New York Daily News*, and Sue Roush at Universal Press Syndicate. Many thanks are also due to the production staff at "Siskel & Ebert," and to Marsha Jordan, my producer at WLS-TV. A special word of gratitude is due to Sally Sinden, my expert, cheerful, and patient assistant for eight years.

ROGER EBERT

Key to Symbols

★ ★ ★ ★   A great film
★ ★ ★   A good film
★ ★   Fair
★   Poor

G, **PG**, **PG-13**, **R**, **NC-17**: Ratings of the Motion Picture Association of America

G	indicates that the movie is suitable for general audiences
PG	suitable for general audiences but parental guidance is suggested
PG-13	recommended for viewers 13 years or above; may contain material inappropriate for younger children
R	recommended for viewers 17 or older
NC-17	intended for adults only

141 m.   Running time

1983   Year of theatrical release

Contents

Introduction to the 1992 Edition

This seventh annual edition of the *Movie Home Companion* represents the second year of Cameron Poulter's handsome new design, which adds a third column to a slightly wider page so that we can continue to expand the word count of the book while still keeping it convenient to handle.

For 1992 I've added some 150 new reviews, bringing the total number of films reviewed to over one thousand. Other new material this year includes the "Film Clips" section, wherein we talk to some of the directors and actors who made notable films during the year, and also pay homage to David Lean and Martin Ritt, who died during 1991. The section includes what has become a treasured tradition, an annual conversation with Woody Allen.

There are new topical articles about film issues, including the rising tide of violence in American films, and the continuing puzzle about why the Motion Picture Academy is unable to bring itself to vote an Oscar to the best living American director, Martin Scorsese.

I have also added a section commemorating the fiftieth anniversary of Orson Welles's *Citizen Kane*, believed by many to be the greatest film ever made. There is "A Viewer's Guide to *Citizen Kane*" that discusses many of the specific visual and production details you may want to look for while watching the movie. *Citizen Kane* was voted first among all films in 1962, 1972, and 1982 in *Sight & Sound* magazine's decennial poll of the world's film experts, and in anticipation of the fortieth anniversary of the *S&S* poll in 1992 I list and discuss my own revised choices of the "Ten Greatest Films of All Time." Of course, such lists are of questionable significance, which adds to the fun of drawing them up.

Readers sent in many new suggestions for the "Glossary of Movie Terms," which is much expanded and improved as a result. I have given credit where due. Send your contributions to me in care of the publisher. There are also many new entries in the "Movie Lover's Source List," which includes mail-order houses that rent and sell videos, as well as the names of several invaluable magazines and catalogs. With the continuing trend toward a hit-oriented policy at many video stores, this list provides you with a way to get your hands on hard-to-find movies.

The section "How to Attend a Film Festival," which was new last year, was well received by many readers. I would like to emphasize that you are welcome at almost all of the world's film festivals, which indeed exist to attract you. Only a handful of festivals—Cannes at the head of the list—are primarily for professionals only in the film trades. The rest are public events. I suggest you plan a vacation around one of them. Write for literature and spend your holiday in darkened theaters, instead of exposed to dangerous solar radiation.

* * *

Thoughts and second thoughts, applause and outrage, inspired by events of the past year:

• **The NC-17 Rating, or, the X in Sheep's Clothing.** By all rights I should be rejoicing that in the year since the last edition, the Motion Picture Association of America has revised the movie rating system, by renaming the dreaded X rating as the more innocuous-sounding NC-17. Reform of the rating system has been a crusade of mine for years, and faithful readers will know that I've long advocated the addition of an A-for-Adult rating, to be positioned between the R and the X. The NC-17 did not accomplish that, and instead only renamed the X in an attempt to avoid some of the rating's negative associations.

In May of 1990, at the Cannes Film Festival, David Lynch's *Wild at Heart* won the Palme d'Or and yet was widely rumored to be headed for an X from the MPAA. "The betting at Cannes," I wrote at the time, "is that by autumn the MPAA rating system will be revised." I received a copy of this article in the mail from Jack Valenti, the capable head of the MPAA, with the words "Wanna bet?" written across it. By autumn, I was wishing I had taken his bet, since NC-17 was announced in September.

The sad fact, however, is that America still remains one of the only nations with no such thing as an ordinary adults-only category. NC-17 is still stigmatized as a haven for porno flicks, and big national video chains like Blockbuster refuse to handle movies with the rating. Valenti has been successful in encouraging newspapers and broadcast outlets to accept ads for NC-17 movies, on a case-by-case basis, but the big Hollywood studios are still reluctant to permit directors to make them—the lost video revenue is too important—and most of the NC-17 movies have been released by independent distributors like Miramax.

My feeling is *still* that the MPAA should add an A rating, which simply states that the movie is not suitable for those under seventeen, and should retain NC-17 as an open-ended category for hard-core pornography. When I repeated this opinion in an article in 1991, I received another note from Valenti, who sighed, "Roger, Roger, Roger," and then asked me how many times he needed to remind me that, in the opinion of MPAA counsel, such a category would invite lawsuits from those excluded from it. Jack, Jack, Jack, then why don't they sue when they're excluded from the R category?

The fact is that the NC-17 is a cop-out, and the MPAA, hand in hand with the theater owners, is against an A rating because it would involve the nightmare of refusing admission to paying customers. As long as the "respectable" NC-17 movies continue to be art films in art houses, the rating has no practical effect on the American box office.

• **High-Def Is Now Maybe Four Years Away.** Everybody knows that high-def TV is on the way. The joke in the industry is that it's five years in the future—and always will be. Maybe it's creeping closer.

I saw the most impressive demonstration yet of HDTV in December 1990 during the Hawaii International Film Festival. It took place in the chapel of a community college. Resting complacently on the altar of the old clapboard church, the machine looked like a conventional TV, except for the wide screen. The shape of a conventional TV screen has become so ingrained in our expectations that this screen seemed somehow like a mutation. When it came to life, it showed an image so crisp and detailed, with colors so subtle and lifelike, that some of the viewers applauded.

Shohachi Sakai beamed. He runs the High Definition Software Center of the Sony corporation in Tokyo, and he and a delegation from Sony had come to Honolulu to unveil a new 36-inch Sony high-def TV monitor at the film festival. They had not picked an ideal place to look at a TV picture, because bright sunlight streamed in through the tall old windows of the chapel. Sakai warned his guests that the picture would look better in a darker room. But he thought it would look OK even in the brightness.

He was right. High-def TV puts 1,125 lines of picture detail on the screen. The set in your living room supplies only 525. The difference in picture quality is astonishing. Bright reds and oranges no longer bleed. Blacks are deep and solid, not grayish areas with white speckles. Lettering is crisp and reflects typographical nuances. The picture is so clear that deep focus works well, and you can see details in the backgrounds of shots—backgrounds that conventional TV might have avoided in preference to the medium shots and close-ups that carry better on 525-line

TV. There is the illusion that you are looking at a small movie screen, and not at TV at all.

"By 1995," Sakai said, "these sets will be affordable enough for many consumers."

What does affordable mean? A thirty-six-inch set is for sale today in Tokyo, he said, for about forty thousand dollars. "It is primarily for industrial use," he said—used, for example, as a monitor for technicians editing high-def television. "But the funny thing is, we are sold out," he added. "As many as we make, we sell. Japanese are eager to have the latest technology."

Sony believes the set cannot be sold through general consumer outlets, however, until the price comes down to around eight thousand dollars, he said. That will be in 1995. And of course the price will keep coming down, until someday a high-def television will be in the same price range as today's best conventional sets.

• **Why High-Def Looks Better.** As I mentioned before, conventional TV does not do a good job with the dark areas of the screen; true black is hard to obtain, except with laserdiscs. Another problem with conventional TV is that there is very little flexibility in the "gray areas," as the picture shades from light to dark. Ordinary celluloid movie film has an infinite series of gradations from white to dark. But conventional TV exists mostly in the middle of the color and intensity range, with a quick drop-off at either end of the spectrum. High-def television is considerably more versatile and subtle.

Many of the scenes in the demonstration film took place in darkened rooms. Others took place at night, or in candlelight. Watching material like this on a conventional TV would be a nightmare; scenes would either be too dark to see, or lost in a blur of light speckles. Yet even in the Hawaiian sunlight, the high-def TV was able to make the shadows rich and evocative. Ironically, since high-def's strong point is its subtle colors, the picture made me eager to see a black-and-white *film noir* on the high-def screen.

The wide screen ratio of high-def will be another gain for movie lovers. Current TV has a screen ratio of about four to three, meaning that movies shot in a wider format have to be cropped or letterboxed. High-def TV has a ratio of about nine to five, so that many wide-screen movies can be entirely contained within the shape of its screen, and even those shot in an extremely wide ratio—*Lawrence of Arabia*, for example—can be accommodated with much more moderate letterboxing.

Because a high-def picture contains so much more visual information, it is more "projectable" than conventional television, Sakai said. Sony is experimenting with a five-hundred-inch screen in Tokyo, and for home use, front projection screens of one hundred or two hundred inches will be quite practical (if you have a gigantic living room, that is). A high-def projector will mount under the ceiling or on a coffee table, projecting its picture into a screen on a wall, giving consumers (very affluent ones at first) their own home projection rooms.

How will high-def first begin to enter the lives of the average American consumer? Exactly the same way television itself did—in bars and restaurants. Just as the early, primitive front-projection Advent systems began to show up in sports bars ten years ago (and just as TV itself turned up in bars in the late 1940s), high-def TV will start appearing at your friendly local in maybe three years. At first there may not be much programming available for it, although the networks will begin to simulcast and most cable systems will have at least one high-def channel. But the quality of the picture will whet people's appetites. Maybe not at eight thousand dollars. But sooner or later.

• **The Super Shield and Why You Need One.** Last year in this space I wrote about the Super Shield, a clear sheet of a Plexiglas-type material that is custom mounted to fit over the screen of your large-screen rear-projection TV. The Super Shield is sold primarily as a screen protector, since (as viewers with small children will know) little nicks and scratches on the fragile plastic screen turn into marks that are easily visible when you're watching TV.

Some viewers, watching their TVs through a Super Shield, thought they actually detected an improvement in picture quality; I was among them. It seemed to me that some optical property of the Shield smoothed out the lines of the TV images and made them look glossier and more movie-like. This is a subjective opinion, however, and whether or not you make the same discovery, I recommend the Super Shield to preserve your rear-projection set. For information, call Fred and John Ananian in Laguna Beach, California (1-800-888-4406, or in California 714-364-4396; their fax number is 714-364-5854).

• **Laservision.** Until the day when high-def is a reality, no higher quality home video delivery system exists than Laservision, which continues to win fans now that the new "combi" players accept not only movies on disc, but also audio compact discs. Several manufacturers have introduced budget-priced Laservision players in the four-hundred-dollar to six-hundred-dollar range.

The installed base of Laservision players increased substantially as a result of a major media ad campaign by Pioneer for the Christmas season. Although Laservision still represents only a small portion of the home video market compared to VCRs, the share is growing because more and more people are buying big-screen TVs. Anyone who has a TV with a screen larger than twenty-five inches needs Laservision.

People who live in smaller cities find it harder to buy or rent laserdiscs locally. Although there are more than five thousand movies available in the format, most stores don't stock that many, and many collectors use mail-order sup-

pliers (a list of several good dealers is in this book's "Movie Lover's Source List"). Most discs are still sold, not rented, but the good news is that many laserdiscs are cheaper than tapes. In the summer of 1990, Blockbuster Video launched a test program to rent laserdiscs in some of its stores.

The most important source of innovative Laservision software is the Voyager Company, whose Criterion Collection includes collectors' editions of classic films, many of them with outtakes, interviews, still photos, original screenplays, or parallel sound tracks on which the movies are discussed shot-by-shot by their directors or other experts. (Of special interest: The new Criterion edition of *Taxi Driver*, with voice-overs by director Martin Scorsese and writer Paul Schrader, and a separate track for the Bernard Hermann score.) Other distributors are following Criterion's lead and adding supplementary material to their discs. Voyager now sells a Hypercard program for the Macintosh that allows you to use the computer to control a Laservision player and edit and play back the discs as you please.

• **Restoration.** It is a continuing source of amazement that the major studios pay so little attention to preserving their primary asset, their film libraries. In 1991, Stanley Kubrick's *Spartacus* was restored and re-released (see my review), after the expert attentions of Robert Harris, the same man who revived *Lawrence of Arabia* a year earlier. But less acclaimed films still rot and crumble in Hollywood's vaults.

The Film Foundation has been started by George Lucas, Martin Scorsese, Steven Spielberg, and other major directors to work with the studios on a consistent and coordinated plan of film preservation. Gene Siskel and I did a television special on which we interviewed those three directors, and the interviews are now available in book form in *The Future of the Movies*, published by Andrews and McMeel.

• **Letterboxing.** This format is now established in the video marketplace as a viable alternative to the chopped, panned and scanned versions of wide-screen movies that were once standard. Viewers are now accustomed to the format, which uses black bands at the top and bottom of the TV screen so that the remaining picture area will duplicate the screen ratio of wide-screen movies. Even some broadcast and cable stations are now using letterboxing, and MTV videos use it constantly, maybe because rock stars think it makes their videos look more like real movies.

• **Movies on Cable TV.** I remain a faithful fan of American Movie Classics, which is included as part of the basic service on many cable systems. If your local cable system doesn't offer it, call them up and ask them why. AMC controls a huge library, including hundreds of titles from RKO Radio Pictures, 20th Century-Fox, and many British sources. Many of their movies are not available on home video. They're especially strong in *film noir* and musicals, and between the movies they show classic short subjects and newsreels. The service is hosted by Bob Dorian, an actor who is also a film buff and spins lore about the making of all of the films. His guests have included such immortals as Douglas Fairbanks, Jr., and Joan Fontaine.

American Movie Classics sets a standard for the rest of cable by adhering to inflexible guidelines involving movie standards. The channel refuses to show films that have been colorized, trimmed, or subjected to that weird process known as "time compression," in which a movie is squeezed into a time slot by being played at a slightly faster speed.

Ted Turner's TNT cable channel also shows great old movies, many of them actually in black and white, and deserves special mention for its Sunday night Foreign Film Festival, which not only shows foreign-language classics with subtitles but also places great emphasis on obtaining the best available prints. The Bravo channel, unfortunately not available in many areas, specializes in film-buff material such as foreign films and documentaries, as well as more adventuresome English-language features.

• **The Academy's Attention Span.** Every year at Oscar time, movies and performances from the first nine months of the year are routinely ignored. To be perfectly honest, the Academy should award its Oscars to the "best films of the autumn."

For two years, I've been proposing a change in the Academy's rules. On the first of July, a "summer sweep" for nominations should be held, focusing on the films of the first six months of the year. The nominations would be kept secret in the fabled vaults of Price, Waterhouse. Then, at the end of the year, a second sweep would take place. The Academy would announce ten "finalists" in each category, from which five nominees would be selected, and then the voting would proceed in the usual fashion. This would be a procedural way to assure that films from earlier in the year would not be so unfairly overlooked.

• **Content Information.** From time to time, I receive letters from readers who wish that I would include information on the possibly objectionable contents of movies. They want to know why a movie has been rated "R," and would like a sentence mentioning any nudity, profanity, violence, or whatever. I have never provided this information in my reviews, and I do not plan to start now. The MPAA rating system itself is designed to provide such

guidelines to parents, and it is administered by experts. If they rate a movie "R," take their word for it—they think those under 17 should probably not see it.

There's another reason why I don't include "objectionable content" information. I think such an approach is an insult to the art form of the motion picture. From their earliest days, movies have somehow been considered an "occasion of sin" in our society, perhaps because they have such a powerful emotional appeal. Otherwise sensible newspapers go along with this prudery. It would be unthinkable for a serious newspaper to tack a paragraph onto the end of a book or theater review, evaluating the "objectionable" content—and yet they do it to movie reviews. I have never supplied such information in my movie reviews, and when such paragraphs appear at the end of my reviews in the two hundred papers which carry my column, they have been written by the editors, not by me.

For parents who want informed guidance on the content of movies, I recommend *The Movie Guide for Puzzled Parents* (Delta) by Lynn Minton.

* * *

This *Companion* is not intended as a comprehensive listing of every movie available on video, but as a collection of essays on about a thousand of the best, most popular, most important, or even worst movies since 1970. The supplementary material—interviews, essays, polemics—changes every year. For an exhaustive guide to some eighteen thousand movies on TV and video, I recommend Leonard Maltin's guide, which has become a standard.

Several readers have asked that I include a "basic library" of books on the movies. I can do no better than to recommend the collected works of Pauline Kael, Stanley Kauffmann, Dwight Macdonald, Manny Farber, and James Agee. François Truffaut's classic book-length interview with Alfred Hitchcock is back in paperback and belongs on every movie lover's shelf. David Thomson's *A Biographical Dictionary of Film* (Morrow) contains concise and intelligent essays on the key actors and directors. Douglas Pratt's *The Laser Video Disc Companion* (New York Zoetrope) is a virtuoso guide, strong on the technical standards of the discs.

Thanks to the many readers who have enjoyed the book, who have written me on various issues, and who have caught errors. Corrections and suggestions from readers continue to be welcomed, and can be addressed to me c/o my faithful and patient publishers, Andrews and McMeel, 4900 Main Street, Kansas City, Missouri 64112.

ROGER EBERT

A

About Last Night . . . ★ ★ ★ ★
R, 116 m., 1986

Rob Lowe (Danny), Demi Moore (Debbie), James Belushi (Bernie), Elizabeth Perkins (Joan), George DiCenzo (Mr. Favio), Michael Alldredge (Mother Malone), Robin Thomas (Steve), Joe Greco (Gus). Directed by Edward Zwick and produced by Jason Brett and Stuart Oken. Screenplay by Tim Kazurinsky and Denise DeClue.

If one of the pleasures of moviegoing is seeing strange new things on the screen, another pleasure, and probably a deeper one, is experiencing moments of recognition—times when we can say, yes, that's exactly right, that's exactly the way it would have happened. *About Last Night . . .* is a movie filled with moments like that. It has an eye and an ear for the way we live now, and it has a heart, too, and a sense of humor.

It is a love story. A young man and a young woman meet, and fall in love, and over the course of a year they try to work out what that means to them. It sounds like a simple story, and yet *About Last Night . . .* is one of the rarest of recent American movies, because it deals fearlessly with real people, instead of with special effects.

If there's anyone more afraid of a serious relationship than your average customer in a singles bar, it's a Hollywood producer. American movies will cheerfully spend millions of dollars on explosions and chases to avoid those moments when people are talking seriously and honestly to one another. After all, writing good dialogue takes some intelligence.

And intelligence is what sparkles all through *About Last Night . . .*—intelligence and a good, bawdy comic sensibility. The movie stars Rob Lowe as a salesman for a Chicago grocery wholesaler, and Demi Moore as an art director for a Michigan Avenue advertising agency. They meet at a softball game in Grant Park. Their romance blossoms in the singles bars of Rush Street, with a kindly bartender as father figure. At first they are attracted mostly by biological reasons (they belong to a generation that believes it's kind of embarrassing to sleep with someone for the first time after you know them too well). Then they get to like each other. Then it is maybe even love, although everyone tap-dances around that word. Commitment, in their world, is the moment when Lowe offers Moore the use of a drawer in his apartment. Her response to that offer is one of the movie's high points.

Meanwhile, there is counterpoint, too. Lowe's best friend is his partner at work, played by James Belushi. Moore's best friend is Elizabeth Perkins, her roommate and fellow warrior on the singles scene. While Lowe and Moore start getting really serious about each other, Belushi and Perkins grow possessive—and also develop a spontaneous dislike for one another.

The story is kind of predictable in *About Last Night . . .*, if you have ever been young and kept your eyes open. There are only a limited number of basic romantic scenarios for young people in the city, and this movie sees through all of them. What's important is the way the characters look and sound, the way they talk, the way they reveal themselves, the way they grow by taking chances. Time after time, there are shocks of recognition, as the movie shows how well it understands what's going on.

Lowe and Moore, members of Hollywood's "Brat Pack," are survivors of 1985's awful movie about yuppie singles, *St. Elmo's Fire*. This is the movie *St. Elmo's Fire* should have been. The 1985 movie made them look stupid and shallow. *About Last Night . . .* gives them the best acting opportunities either one has ever had, and they make the most of them. Moore is especially impressive. There isn't a romantic note she isn't required to play in this movie, and she plays them all flawlessly.

Belushi and Perkins are good, too, making us realize how often the movies pretend that lovers live in a vacuum. When a big new relationship comes into your life, it requires an adjustment of all the other relationships, and a certain amount of discomfort and pain. Belushi and Perkins provide those levels for the story, and a lot of its loudest laughs, too.

The movie is based on *Sexual Perversity in Chicago*, a play by David Mamet. The screenplay by Tim Kazurinsky and Denise DeClue smooths out Mamet's more episodic structure, and adds three-dimensional realism. It's a wonderful writing job, and Edward Zwick, directing a feature for the first time, shows a sure touch. His narrative spans an entire year, and the interest never lags.

Why is it that love stories are so rare from Hollywood these days? Have we lost faith in romance? Is love possible only with robots and cute little furry things from the special-effects department? Have people stopped talking? *About Last Night . . .* is a warmhearted and intelligent love story, and one of 1986's best movies.

Above the Law ★ ★ ★
R, 97 m., 1988

Steven Seagal (Nico Toscani), Henry Silva (Zagon), Pam Grier (Delores Jackson), Sharon Stone (Sara Toscani), Joe Greco (Father Gennaro), Jack Wallace (Uncle Branca), Daniel Faraldo (Salvano), Ronnie Barron (Bartender), Ron Dean (Lukich), Joseph Kosala (Strozah), Chelcie Ross (Fox), John Drummond (TV Reporter). Directed by

Andrew Davis and produced by Steven Seagal and Davis. Screenplay by Steven Pressfield, Ronald Shusett, and Davis, from a story by Davis and Seagal.

Some people in Hollywood think Steven Seagal is the heir to Eastwood and Bronson, contemporary of Stallone, Norris, and Schwarzenegger. His stats: He's 6-foot-4, with a sixth-degree black belt in aikido, and he ran his own martial arts school in Japan before returning to Los Angeles, where he worked as an aikido instructor and bodyguard (it says in his bio) for stars and heads of state. He's married to actress Kelly LeBrock, the one with the great lips. A studio executive was quoted as saying Seagal has "extraordinary" screen magnetism.

With a buildup like that, doesn't Seagal's first movie almost have to be anticlimactic? And yet the curious thing is, Seagal more or less deserves the buildup. He does have a strong and particular screen presence. It is obvious that he is doing a lot of his own stunts, and some of the fight sequences are impressive and apparently unfaked. He isn't just a hunk, either. He can play tender and he can play smart, two notes often missing on the Bronson and Stallone accordions. His aquiline face and slicked-back, slightly receding hairline accentuate the macho exterior. He moves around too much in close-ups, but then he moves around a lot anyway, seeming restless on screen, sometimes swaggering instead of walking.

His first movie is *Above the Law*, and it is nothing if not ambitious; it contains fifty percent more plot than it needs, but that allows it room to grow in areas not ordinarily covered in action thrillers. When was the last time you saw Norris or Schwarzenegger in a film where they ran cars through walls and killed people with their bare hands *and* went to Mass, stood up at baptisms, meditated, hugged their wives, kidded their partners, and made speeches about the need for a free and open society? If this film is an audition, it demonstrates that Seagal is willing to try anything.

The movie costars Pam Grier, who plays Seagal's partner but not his squeeze (he's a happily married father). She was one of the most intriguing action stars of the 1970s, before the collapse of the black film market took her down with it. Seagal and Grier play plainclothes Chicago police detectives who engineer a major drug bust, only to find that their arrests have been quashed by the FBI

and they've been ordered to stay away from a cocaine kingpin. Why should this guy be immune?

In a less ambitious picture, we'd find out about a payoff, blackmail, or extortion. *Above the Law* does not lack ambition. We get flashbacks to the hero's service in the CIA in Vietnam, where he first stumbled across evidence that a CIA official (Henry Silva, venomous and sleek) was using the agency as a cover for drug smuggling. Now there's another element involved: Central American political refugees have taken sanctuary in the basement of Seagal's church, and their priest has information about Silva's plan to assassinate a senator.

The movie was cowritten and directed by Andrew Davis, whose *Code of Silence* remains the best movie Chuck Norris has ever made, and contains the best use of Chicago locations I've seen. *Above the Law* also exploits great locations, from the unexpected (a vast old Catholic church) to the bizarre (there's a struggle to the death on the roof of the Executive House). Davis also seems concerned to create a community around the Seagal character, and so we spend time in well-written scenes with his wife (Sharon Stone), his priest (Joe Greco), his uncle (Jack Wallace), and a tough cop (Joseph Kosala, a real Chicago cop). As in his previous film, Davis gets mileage out of supporting players who do not look or sound like professional actors, and so add a level of realism to the action.

Seagal doesn't look or sound like a professional actor, either, but he's effective in his film debut. His voice has a certain quality to it, like Richard Gere's, that suggests he would sometimes rather keep talking after he barks out typical action dialogue. He is physical enough to create a believable menace in the violent scenes, and yet we can believe that sensitivity coexists with brutality in his makeup. Is he indeed Hollywood's hottest action star? Who knows. But he has the stuff.

Absence of Malice ★ ★ ★
PG, 116 m., 1981

Paul Newman (Michael Gallagher), Sally Field (Megan Carter), Bob Balaban (Rosen), Melinda Dillon (Teresa), Wilford Brimley (Official), John Harkins (Libel Lawyer). Directed and produced by Sydney Pollack. Screenplay by Kurt Luedtke.

There are at least two ways to approach

Absence of Malice, and I propose to take the second. The first approach, no doubt, would be to criticize this film's portrait of an investigative newspaper reporter—to say that no respectable journalist would ever do the things that Sally Field does about, to, and with Paul Newman in this movie. She is a disgrace to her profession. What journalistic sins does she commit in this film? She allows the facts of a secret investigation to be leaked to her. She prints an unattributed story about the investigation. Then she becomes "personally involved with the subject of the investigation," as they say. In other words, she falls in love with Paul Newman. Then she prints another story she should never have printed, and as a result an innocent bystander commits suicide. Then . . .

But you get the idea. Would real investigative reporters actually commit Field's mistakes, improprieties, misjudgments, indiscretions, and ethical lapses? Generally speaking, no, they wouldn't. And if they did, they shouldn't have. And furthermore, their editors would never let them get away with it. (The unbelievable laxity of the editors in *Absence of Malice* creates the movie's greatest credibility gap.) But let's face it: Sometimes reporters *do* commit acts such as Sally Field allows herself in this movie. Sometimes news of an investigation is printed without official attribution. And so on.

One of my colleagues cornered me at the water fountain to say indignantly that, whatever else you might think about this movie, you'd have to admit that no reporter would *ever* sleep with a news source.

"Oh yeah?" asked a woman who was standing by. "Who was the news source?"

"Paul Newman," I said.

"I'd sleep with that news source in a second," she said.

And that leads us out of the first, or socially responsible, approach to *Absence of Malice*, and into the second, or romantic, approach. I not only liked this movie despite its factual and ethical problems—I'm not even so sure they matter so much to most viewers. In the newspaper business we're quick to spot the errors in movies about newspaper reporters, but where were we when the archaeologists squirmed over Harrison Ford's barbaric conduct in *Raiders of the Lost Ark?* The fact is, this movie is *really* about a woman's spunk and a common man's sneaky revenge. And on that level it's absorbing and entertaining. Sally Field's newspaper reporter is created through a quietly original performance that is *not* Norma Rae with a pencil behind her ear, but is an earnest, nervous, likable young woman who makes mistakes when she listens too closely to her heart, her ambition, or her editor (which of us cannot admit the same?).

Paul Newman's character is a liquor distributor who is (presumably) totally innocent of the murder for which he is being investigated. But because his father was a Mafioso, he finds his name being dragged through the press, and he achieves a vengeance that is smart, wicked, appropriate, and completely satisfying to the audience. Besides these two performances, there are some other good ones, most notably one by Wilford Brimley, as a lawman who takes brusque command of an informal hearing and reduces everyone but Newman to quivering surrender, and another by John Harkins, as a newspaper libel lawyer who is able to make the restraints (and freedoms) of libel law clear not only to Sally Field but even to us.

There's a story about a legendary Chicago editor who was presented with a major scoop obtained by dubious means. First he convinced himself the story was factually sound. Then he issued the classic instruction: "Print it tonight, and call the lawyers in the morning." Now there's an editor who might have enjoyed *Absence of Malice*. He would not have approved of what Sally Field does in this movie. But he would have understood it.

The Accidental Tourist ★ ★ ★ ★
PG, 121 m., 1988

William Hurt (Macon Leary), Kathleen Turner (Sarah, His Wife), Geena Davis (Muriel Pritchett), Amy Wright (Rose Leary), David Ogden Stiers (Porter Leary), Ed Begley, Jr. (Charles Leary), Bill Pullman (Julian), Robert Gorman (Alexander), Bradley Mott (Mr. Loomis). Directed by Lawrence Kasdan and produced by Kasdan, Charles Okun, and Michael Grillo. Screenplay by Frank Galati and Kasdan.

"Yes, that is my son," the man says, identifying the body in the intensive care unit. Grief threatens to break his face into pieces, and then something closes shut inside of him. He has always had a very controlled nature, fearful of emotion and revelation, but now a true ice age begins, and after a year, his wife tells

him she wants a divorce. It is because he cannot seem to feel anything.

The Accidental Tourist begins on that note of emotional sterility, and the whole movie is a journey toward a smile at the end. The man's name is Macon Leary (William Hurt), and he writes travel books for people who detest traveling. He advises his readers on how to avoid human contact, where to find "American food" abroad, and how to convince themselves they haven't left home. His own life is the same sort of journey, and maybe it began in childhood; his sister and two brothers still live together in the house where they were born, and any life outside of their routine would be unthinkable.

Macon's wife (Kathleen Turner) moves out, leaving him with the dog, Edward, who does like to travel, and is deeply disturbed by the curious life his masters have provided for him. He barks at ghosts and snaps at strangers. It is time for Macon to make another one of his overseas research trips, so he takes the dog to be boarded at a kennel, and that's where he meets Muriel Pritchett (Geena Davis). Muriel has Macon's number from the moment he walks in through the door. She can see he's a basket case, but she thinks she can help. She also thinks her young son needs a father.

Macon isn't so sure. He doesn't use the number she gives him. But later, when the dog trips him and he breaks his leg, he takes Edward back to the kennel, and this time he submits to a little obedience training of his own. He agrees to acknowledge that Muriel exists, and before long they are sort of living together (lust still exists in his body, but it lurks so far from the center of his feelings that sex hardly seems to cheer him up).

The peculiarity about these central passages in the film is that they are quite cheerful and sometimes even very funny, even though Macon himself is mired in a deep depression. Geena Davis, as Muriel, brings an unforced wackiness to her role in scenes like the one where she belts out a song while she's doing the dishes. But she is not as simple as she sometimes seems, and when Macon gets carried away with a little sentimental generalizing about the future, she warns him, "Don't make promises to my son that you are not prepared to keep."

There is also great good humor in the characters in Macon's family: brothers Porter (David Ogden Stiers) and Charles (Ed Begley, Jr.) and sister Rose (Amy Wright), a matriarch who feeds the family, presides over

their incomprehensible card games, and supervises such traditional activities as alphabetizing the groceries on the kitchen shelves. One evening Macon takes his publisher, Julian (Bill Pullman), home to dinner, and Julian is struck with a thunderbolt of love for Rose. He eventually marries her, but a few weeks later Julian tells Macon that Rose has moved back home with the boys; she was concerned that they had abandoned regular meals and were eating only gorp.

This emergency triggers the movie's emotional turning point, which is subtle but unmistakable. Nobody knows Rose as well as Macon does, and so he gives Julian some very particular advice: "Call her up and tell her your business is going to pieces. Ask if she could just come in and get things organized. Get things under control. Put it that way. Use those words. 'Get things under control,' tell her."

In context, this speech is hilarious. It is also the first time in the film that Macon has been able to extend himself to help anybody—and it starts him on the road to emotional growth. Clinging to the sterility and loneliness that has been his protection, he doesn't realize at first that he has turned the corner. He still doubts that he needs Muriel, and when she buys herself a ticket and follows him to Paris, he refuses to have anything to do with her. When his wife also turns up in Paris, there is a moment when he thinks they may be able to patch things together again, and then finally Macon arrives at the sort of moment he has been avoiding all of his life: He has to make a choice. But by then the choice is obvious; he has already made it by peeking so briefly out of his shell.

The screenplay for *The Accidental Tourist*, by Lawrence Kasdan and Frank Galati, is able to reproduce a lot of the tone and dialogue of the Anne Tyler novel without ever simply being a movie version of a book. The textures are too specific and the humor is too quirky and well-timed to be borrowed from anywhere; the filmmakers have reinvented the same story in their own terms. The movie is a reunion for Kasdan, Hurt, and Turner, who all three put their careers on the map with *Body Heat* (1981). Kasdan used Hurt again in *The Big Chill* (1983), and understands how to employ Hurt's gift for somehow being likable at the same time he seems to be withdrawn.

What Hurt achieves here seems almost impossible: He is depressed, low-key, and intensely private through most of the movie, and yet somehow he wins our sympathy. What Kasdan achieves is just as tricky; I've never seen a movie so sad in which there was so much genuine laughter. *The Accidental Tourist* was one of the best films of 1988.

The Accused ★ ★ ★
R, 110 m., 1988

Kelly McGillis (Kathryn Murphy), Jodie Foster (Sarah Tobias), Bernie Coulson (Kenneth Joyce), Ann Hearn (Sally Frazer), Steve Antin (Bob Joiner), Leo Rossi (Cliff Albrecht), Carmen Argenziano (District Attorney Rudolph), Terry David Mulligan (Detective Duncan), Woody Brown (Danny Rudkin), Peter Van Norden (Ted Paulson). Directed by Jonathan Kaplan and produced by Stanley R. Jaffe and Sherry Lansing. Screenplay by Tom Topor.

The Accused demonstrates that rape victims are often suspects in their own cases. Surely they must have been somehow to blame. How were they behaving at the time of the crime? How were they dressed? Had they been drinking? Is their personal life clean and tidy? Or are they sluts who were just asking for it?

I am aware of the brutal impact of the previous sentence. But the words were carefully chosen because sometimes they reflect the unspoken suspicions of officials in the largely male criminal justice system. *The Accused* is a movie about Sarah Tobias, a young woman who is not a model citizen. One night she has a fight with her live-in boyfriend, who is a drug dealer. She goes to a sleazy bar and has too much to drink, and does a provocative dance to the jukebox, and begins to flirt with a man in the bar's back room.

And then things get out of hand. The man, also drunk, picks her up and lays her down on top of a pinball machine, and begins to assault her. Two other men hold her down, helpless. The music pounds. The other guys in the back room begin to cheer and chant and egg him on, and when he is finished they push another guy forward, and then another. Finally she escapes and runs weeping out onto the highway, crying for help.

The film shows most of this sequence only later, in a flashback. Its opening scenes deal with the immediate aftermath of the rape, as the woman (Jodie Foster) is moved through the emergency care and legal systems, where she meets professionals who are courteous and efficient, but not overly sympathetic. Then she meets Kathryn Murphy (Kelly McGillis), the assistant district attorney who will handle her case. McGillis is not impressed with some of the things she discovers, such as Tobias's previous conviction on drug possession charges, or her drinking on the night of the crime. And one of the rape suspects is a young fraternity man whose parents hire a good lawyer. In conference, the assistant D.A. agrees to reduce charges to "aggravated assault."

Sarah Tobias feels betrayed. She was raped, brutally, repeatedly, in front of many witnesses. It was not "aggravated assault." And the argument of the movie is that although a young woman may act improperly, even recklessly, she should still have the right to say "no" and be heard. This is something the McGillis character has difficulty in understanding at first; she is so comfortable within the informal compromises of the criminal justice system that she has lost some of her capacity for outrage.

In a sense, the movie is about the relationship between these two women, one an articulate lawyer, the other an inarticulate, angry alcoholic who sometimes lacks the words for the things she feels. One of the interesting choices in the screenplay by Tom Topor was to make it so hard for the Foster character to express herself, so that when she speaks we can almost feel each word being wrung out of her emotions. During the course of the film, the woman attorney comes to identify some of her client's feelings as actual experiences, not simply legal evidence. And the rape victim begins to see herself as others see her; we feel it is possible that the relationship between the two women will eventually lead the Foster character to clean up her act, stop drinking, and start taking responsibility for herself.

The other current in the film is equally interesting. This is the first film I can remember that considers the responsibility of bystanders in a rape case. The drunken fraternity boys and townies who climb on the furniture and chant and cheer are accessories to rape, although our society sometimes has difficulty in understanding that. When the McGillis character finally decides to bring some of them to trial, she gets no support at all from the chief district attorney, and many of her colleagues feel she's lost her mind. Assistant D.A.s are supposed to try cases they can win, not go looking for lost causes. But the lesson learned in the movie's second trial may be the most important message this movie has to offer.

I wonder who will find the film more uncomfortable—men or women? Both will recoil from the brutality of the actual scenes of the assault. But for some men, the movie will reveal a truth that most women already know. It is that verbal sexual harassment, whether crudely in a saloon back room or subtly in an everyday situation, is a form of violence—one that leaves no visible marks but can make its victims feel unable to move freely and casually in society. It is a form of imprisonment.

The Adventures of Baron Munchausen ★ ★ ★
PG, 126 m., 1989

John Neville (Baron Munchausen), Eric Idle (Desmond/Berthold), Sarah Polley (Sally Salt), Oliver Reed (Vulcan), Charles McKeown (Rupert/Adolphus), Winston Dennis (Bill/Albrecht), Valentina Cortese (Queen/Violet), Robin Williams (King of the Moon), Sting (Heroic Officer). Directed by Terry Gilliam and produced by Thomas Schuhly. Screenplay by Charles McKeown and Gilliam.

"I have ever confined myself to facts."
—Attributed to Baron Munchausen

There really was a Baron Munchausen. His full name was Karl Friedrich Hieronymus, Freiherr von Munchausen, and he lived from 1720 to 1797 and fought for the Russians against the Turks. He was, it is said, in the habit of embellishing his war stories, and in 1785 a jewel thief from Hanover named Rudolph Erich Raspe published a book in England that claimed to be based on the baron's life and times.

The real von Munchausen apparently did not complain about this book that made free with his reputation, even though it included such tall stories as the time the baron tethered his horse to a "small twig" in a snowstorm, and discovered when the snow melted that the twig was actually a church steeple.

I remember the illustration that appeared with that story when I read it as a child: The baron on the ground, looking up in perplexity at his horse, which was still hanging from the steeple. I remember asking my father how the horse was going to get down, and my father speculating that he would have to wait until it snowed again, which seemed like a bleak prospect for the horse. And so I asked if the baron could feed his horse in the meantime by climbing up the steeple with hay. The mind of a child is wonderfully literal. And one of the charms of seeing *The Adventures of Baron Munchausen* is to see some of the baron's other impossible adventures looking for all the world as if they had really happened, thanks to extraordinary special effects.

For adults, this is a "special effects movie," and we approach it in that spirit, also appreciating the sly wit and satire that sneaks in here and there from director Terry Gilliam and his collaborators, who were mostly forged in the mill of Monty Python. They have not made a "children's movie," but children may find it fascinating, because these adventures involve castles and sultans and horses and knights and the man in the moon—subjects that seem fresh, now that the high-tech hardware of outer space is taken for granted by most kids.

Terry Gilliam's film is, in itself, a tribute to the spirit of the good baron. Gilliam must have had to embellish a few war stories himself, to get Columbia Pictures to spend a reported $46 million on this project, which is one of the three or four most expensive films ever made. The special effects are astonishing, but so is the humor with which they are employed. It is not enough that one of the baron's friends is the fastest runner in the world. He must run all the way to Spain and back in an hour to fetch a bottle of wine and save the baron's neck. And he must be able to outrun a speeding bullet, stop it, and redirect it back toward the man who fired it.

These adventures, and others, are told with a cheerfulness and a light touch that never betray the time and money it took to create them. It's one thing to spend $46 million; it's another to spend it insouciantly. The movie begins when the baron indignantly interrupts a play that is allegedly based on his life, and continues as he tells the "real" story of his travels—which took him not merely to Turkey but also to the moon, to the heart of a volcano, and into the stomach of a sea monster so big that people actually lived there quite comfortably, once they had been swallowed.

The baron (John Neville) is accompanied on some of these adventures by his friends, including not only the world's fastest man, but also the world's strongest man, the man with the best hearing in the world, and

another friend who does not have great eyesight, but owns glasses that allow him to see almost any distance. Even when he is separated from these comrades, the baron travels in good company; when a Venus appears from a seashell, she is played by Uma Thurman, the young innocent from *Dangerous Liaisons*, and when the King of the Moon appears, he is Robin Williams, with a detachable head that is able to spin off into the night on its own.

Some of the effects in this movie are actually quite wonderful, as when the baron and a friend return from the moon by climbing down two lengths of the same rope again and again, while the markings of a celestial globe apportion the sky behind them. In another scene, a giant feather falls softly onto a vast plain, while the baron tries to understand what strange new world he has found. Neville, a veteran of the Stratford, Canada, Shakespeare festival, keeps his composure in the midst of these special effects, and seems sensible and matter-of-fact, as anyone would if he had spent a lifetime growing accustomed to the incredible.

The wit and the spectacle of *Baron Munchausen* are considerable achievements. I wish only that Gilliam, who co-wrote the screenplay as well as directed, had been able to edit his own inspiration more severely as he went along. The movie is slow to get off the ground (the prologue goes on forever before we discover what it's about), and sometimes the movie fails on the basic level of making itself clear. We're not always sure who is who, how they are related, or why we should care. One of the things you have to do, when you fill a movie with extravagant fantasies, is to explain the story in clear and direct terms, so it doesn't fly apart with intoxication at its own exuberance.

I was confused sometimes during *Baron Munchausen*, and bored sometimes, but this is a vast and commodious work, and even allowing for the unsuccessful passages, there is a lot here to treasure. Gilliam said it was the third part of a trilogy. His first film, *Time Bandits*, was about childhood. His second, *Brazil*, was about adulthood. *Baron Munchausen* is about old age. He may have been telling us the truth. He may also have been telling us he tethered his film to a twig in a snowstorm.

The Adventures of Ford Fairlane ★
R, 100 m., 1990

Andrew Dice Clay (Ford Fairlane), Wayne Newton (Julian Grendel), Priscilla Presley (Colleen Sutton), Morris Day (Don Cleveland), Lauren Holly (Jazz), Maddie Corman (Zuzu Petals), Gilbert Gottfried (Johnny Crunch), David Patrick Kelly (Sam). Directed by Renny Harlin and produced by Joel Silver and Steve Perry. Screenplay by Daniel Waters and James Cappe.

The Adventures of Ford Fairlane is a movie about a hero I didn't like, chasing villains I didn't hate, in a plot I didn't understand. It is also loud, ugly, and mean-spirited. That makes it the ideal vehicle for Andrew Dice Clay, a comedian whose humor is based upon hating those not in the room for the entertainment of those present.

The story involves Clay as a "rock 'n' roll detective," whose beat is the music business and whose name and image come from one of those 1962 Fords with the retractable hardtops. He has an office up on Sunset Boulevard, and he roams the nightclubs and rock concerts in search of clients, suspects, and action. He gets a lot of action; one of the motifs of the movie is how he gobbles up women, usually two at a time, and spits them out the next morning.

True to the stereotyped movie private eyes he's inspired by, Ford Fairlane has a faithful Girl Friday (Lauren Holly) who waits patiently in the office, taking phone calls and telling lies. He also has the ability, common to so many movie detectives, of acting as the narrator, and so we hear his weathered voice on the sound track, describing with appropriate cynicism the dog-eared world he inhabits.

The movie begins with the spectacular onstage death of a heavy-metal singer, and Fairlane, investigating the case, gets drawn into a plot involving Wayne Newton, as a corrupt music executive, Morris Day (funny in *Purple Rain* but muted here) as a record producer, and Maddie Corman as the bubble-gumblowing teen-ager whose abduction concerns her dad (Gilbert Gottfried), a shock-jock whose on-the-air murder sounds at first like just another one of his schticks.

The cast is crawling with walk-throughs, some of whom (like Sheila E. can barely be recognized). Others are Robert Englund, who plays Freddy in the *Nightmare on Elm Street* series, and Priscilla Presley, attractive in the underwritten role of a seductress who Fairlane discovers astraddle his investigation.

The movie is cheap, but it wasn't inexpensive. The director is Renny Harlin, who also directed *Die Hard 2*, and he shoots mostly at night in a neon world of hundreds of bizarre extras. Through this human shrubbery strides Fairlane, a cigarette always dangling from his mouth. (He must get through cartons every day, since he never smokes more than the first half-inch and lights some cigarettes just so he can disdainfully throw them away.) Fairlane, like Clay himself, uses the language of insult and aggression, and the screenplay's uncounted obscenities bark out of his mouth as if he were an angry dog—a dog that can only say the same thing over and over again and hope that you will understand him.

For a movie about the music business, *The Adventures of Ford Fairlane* has surprisingly little music in it. Of course, there's the wall-to-wall background score by Yello, but there's little in the way of performance; Sheila E. and Motley Crue's Vince Neil get one song phrase apiece on camera, and Clay himself belts out half of a rock 'n' roll number, but Harlin never lets loose with a real rock production number. Odd, in a movie where every scene seems to be the introduction to one.

Clay's challenge in the movie is to somehow maintain his stage and club image while presenting himself as a halfway plausible hero. He does this by being nice to his secretary on occasion, by befriending a lonely little boy, and by making fun of some of his own mannerisms (he lights a cigarette with a bewildering series of choreographed tics, jerks, and spasms).

Is the movie any good? No. Does Andrew Dice Clay have a future in the movies? As an actor, yes. He has a strong screen presence and he's at home and confident. But his persona is going to get very old very fast, because it's not likable to begin with, and there's nowhere he can go with it. In a club or on a stage, foul-mouthed and race-baiting, he implicates the audience, and they laugh in order to exclude themselves as his targets (anyone who doesn't laugh is by definition an asshole). But a movie audience is more separate, more contemplative—and, sitting in the dark, watching him, more likely to be appalled than entertained. If he wants a future in the movies, Andrew Dice Clay is going to have to play somebody other than himself.

After Hours ★ ★ ★ ★
R, 96 m., 1985

Griffin Dunne (Paul Hackett), Rosanna Arquette (Marcy), Linda Fiorentino (Kiki), Verna Bloom (June), Thomas Chong (Pepe), Teri Garr (Julie), John Heard (Bartender), Catherine O'Hara (Gail). Directed by Martin Scorsese and produced by Amy Robinson, Griffin Dunne, and Robert F. Colesberry. Screenplay by Joseph Minion.

Martin Scorsese's *After Hours* is a comedy, according to the strict definition of that word: It ends happily, and there are indications along the way that we're not supposed to take it seriously. It is, however, the tensest comedy I can remember, building its nightmare situation step by insidious step until our laughter is hollow, or defensive. This is the work of a master filmmaker who controls his effects so skillfully that I was drained by this film—so emotionally depleted that there was a moment, two-thirds of the way through, when I wondered if maybe I should pause and gather my thoughts and come back later for the rest of the "comedy."

The movie tells the story of a night in the life of Paul Hackett (Griffin Dunne), a midtown Manhattan word processing specialist who hates his job and his lonely private life. One night in a restaurant he strikes up a conversation with a winsome young woman (Rosanna Arquette). They seem to share some of the same interests. He gets her telephone number. He calls her, she suggests he come downtown to her apartment in Soho, and that is the beginning of his Kafkaesque adventure.

The streets of Soho are dark and deserted. Clouds of steam escape from the pavement, as they did in Scorsese's *Taxi Driver*, suggesting that Hades lurks just below the field of vision. The young woman is staying for a few days in the apartment of a friend (Linda Fiorentino), who makes bizarre sculptures, has kinky sexual tastes, and talks in a strange, veiled way about being burned. In Arquette's bedroom, Dunne makes the usual small talk of a first date, and she gushes that she's sure they'll have a great time, but then everything begins to fall apart.

At first, we think perhaps Dunne is the victim of random bad luck, as he is confronted with nightmares both tragic and trivial: Ominous strangers, escalating subway fares, a shocking suicide, sadomasochistic sexual practices, a punk nightclub where he

almost has his head shaved, a street mob that thinks he is a thief. Only later, much later, on this seemingly endless night, do we find how everything is connected—and even then, it doesn't make any logical sense. For Paul Hackett, as for the Job of the Old Testament, the plague of bad luck seems generated by some unexplained divine wrath.

And yet Scorsese does not simply make a horror movie, or some kind of allegory of doom. Each of his characters is drawn sharply, given quirky dialogue, allowed to be offbeat and funny. Teri Garr has a scene as a waitress who has tried to make sense of New York for so long that it has driven her around the bend. Fiorentino has a dry, sardonic angle on things. Arquette speaks wonderingly of a lover who was so obsessed by *The Wizard of Oz* that he always called her Dorothy in bed. John Heard is a bartender who has seen everything walk in through the doors of his all-night saloon and has lost the capacity for astonishment.

After Hours is another chapter in Scorsese's continuing examination of Manhattan as a state of mind; if he hadn't already used the title *New York, New York*, he could have used it this time. The movie earns its place on the list with his great films *Mean Streets*, *Taxi Driver*, and *Raging Bull*. For New Yorkers, parts of the film will no doubt play as a documentary. In what other city is everyday life such an unremitting challenge?

After Hours is a brilliant film, one of the year's best. It is also a most curious film. It comes after Scorsese's *The King of Comedy*, a film I thought was fascinating but unsuccessful, and continues Scorsese's attempt to combine comedy and satire with unrelenting pressure and a sense of all-pervading paranoia. This time he succeeds. The result is a film that is so original, so particular, that we are uncertain from moment to moment exactly how to respond to it. The style of the film creates, in us, the same feeling that the events in the film create in the hero. Interesting.

After the Rehearsal ★ ★ ★ ★
R, 72 m., 1984

Erland Josephson (Henrik Vogler), Ingrid Thulin (Rakel), Lena Olin (Anna Egerman), Nadja Palmstjerna-Weiss (Anna at Twelve). Directed by Ingmar Bergman and produced by Jorn Donner. Screenplay by Bergman.

Ingmar Bergman's *After the Rehearsal* seems to be as simple and direct as a tape recording of actual conversations, and yet look at the thickets of interpretation it has inspired in its critics. After seeing it, I thought I understood the film entirely. Now I am not so sure. Like so many of Bergman's films, and especially the spare "chamber films" it joins *(Winter Light, Persona)*, it consists of unadorned surfaces concealing fathomless depths.

It is safest to begin with the surfaces. All of the action takes place on a stage prepared for a production of Strindberg's *A Dream Play*. An aging director sits among the props, and every chair and table reminds him of an earlier production. The rehearsal has ended some time ago, and now the director simply sits, as if the stage were his room. A young actress returns to the stage for a missing bracelet. But of course the bracelet is an excuse, and she wants to talk to the great man, and perhaps to begin a relationship with him (as, perhaps, she has heard that many other actresses have done over the years). The old director was once the lover of the girl's mother. It is even possible that this girl is his daughter. They talk. Then an older actress enters. She has a few lines in the play, and wants to know—frankly, brutally—if her career as a leading actress is really over because she is known as a drunk. She cries, she rants, she bares her breasts to show the old man that her body is still sound, if sodden. The director is tempted: He was once this woman's lover, and perhaps her daughter is his.

The young girl stays on stage during the extraordinary display of the older actress. When the older woman leaves, the director and ingenue talk again, and this time the old man, who has been through the turmoil of love too many times, talks her through their probable future: We could make love, we could have an affair, we would call it part of our art, you would be the student, I would be the teacher, I would grow tired, you would feel trapped, all our idealism would turn into ashes. Since the relationship is foredoomed, why bother with it?

Just in terms of these spare passages of dialogue and passion, *After the Rehearsal* is an important and painful confessional, for the old director, of course, bears many points of resemblance to Bergman, whose lovers have included his actresses Harriet Andersson, Bibi Andersson, and Liv Ullmann, among others, and whose daughter by Ullmann appeared in *Face to Face*. But the film is not a scandalous revelation: It is actu-

ally more of a sacramental confession, as if Bergman, the son of a Lutheran bishop, now sees the stage as his confessional and is asking the audience to bless and forgive him. (His gravest sin, as I read the film, is not lust or adultery, but the sin of taking advantage of others—of manipulating them with his power and intellect.)

If that were the extent of *After the Rehearsal*, it would be deep enough. But Bergman has surrounded the bare bones of his story with mystifying problems of interpretation. Just as in *Persona* he included scenes in which his characters exchanged personalities and engaged in scenes that might have or might not have been fantasies and dreams, so here, too, he gives us things to puzzle over. Reading the earlier reviews of the film, I discover that one critic realized only belatedly that the younger actress, Anna, was onstage the whole time the older actress, Rakel, poured out her heart. Strange, and yet another critic thought the whole scene with Rakel was the director's own dream. Yet another suggested that Anna represents not only herself but also Rakel's absent daughter. And another theory is that Anna is the daughter of the director and Rakel, and is brought into being by the residual love between them, as a sort of theatrical Holy Spirit. The age of Anna has been variously reported as ranging from twelve to twenty, with one critic reporting that both ages of the character are represented.

Which is the correct interpretation? They are all correct. Each and every one is equally correct; otherwise what is the use of a dream play? The point is not to find the literal meaning, anyway, but to touch the soul of the director, and find out what still hurts him after all these years. After all the sex and all the promises, all the lies and truths and messy affairs, there is still one critical area where he is filled with guilt and passion. It is revealed when Anna tells him she is pregnant. He is enraged. How could she, a young actress given the role of a lifetime, jeopardize her career and his play by getting pregnant? Then she tells him she has had an abortion, for the sake of the play. And then he really is torn in two, for he does not believe, after all, that a play—not even his play—is worth the sacrifice of a life. What we are left with at the end of *After the Rehearsal*, however, is the very strong sense of an artist who has sacrificed many lives for the sake of his art, and now wonders if perhaps one of those lives was his own.

Against All Odds ★ ★ ★
R, 128 m., 1984

Rachel Ward (Jessie Wyler), Jeff Bridges (Terry Brogan), James Woods (Jake Wise), Alex Karras (Hank Sully), Jane Greer (Mrs. Wyler), Richard Widmark (Ben Caxton). Directed by Taylor Hackford and produced by Hackford and William S. Gilmore. Screenplay by Eric Hughes.

There have been too many sweet girls in thrillers. What we need are more no-good, double-dealing broads who can cross their legs and break your heart. *Against All Odds* has a woman like that, and it makes for one of the most intriguing movie relationships in a long time; in thirty-five years, to be exact, which is when they told this story for the first time. You may remember the original movie. It was called *Out of the Past*. It starred Robert Mitchum and Kirk Douglas, and it was the greatest cigarette-smoking movie of all time. Mitchum and Douglas smoked all the way through every scene, and they were always blowing sinister, aggressive clouds of smoke at each other. The movie was shot so there was always a lot of light on the place in midair where their smoke was aimed. The only drawback to the fact that smoking is no longer fashionable in movies is that we don't get any great smoking scenes anymore. Anyway, if you remember that movie, you remember that Kirk Douglas was a hoodlum and Robert Mitchum was a guy who would take a job for a buck, and Douglas hired Mitchum to track down his missing girlfriend, who was played by Jane Greer. After Mitchum found Greer, they had a big love affair—or so Mitchum thought. But Greer, that no-good, two-timing, double-crossing broad, liked security more than passion.

Against All Odds is not really a remake of *Out of the Past*. The only similarity between the two movies is in the cynical love triangle. And it was a real inspiration to tell that story again, since it makes for an intriguing, complicated, interesting romance. This time, the bad guy is a gambler, played by James Woods. His girlfriend (Rachel Ward) is the daughter of the owner of a pro-football team (played by Jane Greer, of all people). And the guy who tracks her down (Jeff Bridges), is a team player who's just been fired after a knee injury.

There is a lot of plot in this movie—probably too much. The best thing to do is to accept the plot, and then disregard it, and pay attention to the scenes of passion. They really work. Bridges and Ward have an interesting sexual tension in *Against All Odds*, since their relationship is not simply sweetness and light, but depends upon suspicion, dislike, and foul betrayal. That's ever so much more interesting than just falling in love. And the situation liberates Ward from the trap she'd been in; the trap of playing attractive, sexy, strong heroines. This time, as a complicated schemer, she's fascinating.

The movie has a lot of muted social criticism in it, involving professional sports and ecology. The Jane Greer character has a plan to destroy several beautiful canyons to build houses. The Bridges character is a victim of unfair labor practices. And so on. Sometimes we get the idea we're watching a clone of *Chinatown*—but not with that jealous triangle. Woods is the villain, so he does smoke, of course. But Bridges and Ward are so consumed with passion, they don't even need to.

Airplane! ★ ★ ★
PG, 88 m., 1980

Lloyd Bridges (McCroskey), Peter Graves (Captain Oveur), Kareem Abdul-Jabbar (Murdock), Julie Hagerty (Elaine), Robert Hays (Ted Striker), Leslie Nielsen (Dr. Rumack), Howard Jarvis (Man in Taxi), Ethel Merman (Lieutenant Hurwitz). Directed and written by Jim Abrahams, David Zucker, and Jerry Zucker and produced by Howard W. Koch.

Airplane! is a comedy in the great tradition of high school skits, the Sid Caesar TV show, *Mad* magazine, and the dog-eared screenplays people's nephews write in lieu of earning their college diplomas. It is sophomoric, obvious, predictable, corny, and quite often very funny. And the reason it's funny is frequently *because* it's sophomoric, predictable, corny, etc. Example:

Airplane Captain (Peter Graves): Surely you can't be serious!

Doctor (Leslie Nielsen): Of course I am! And stop calling me Shirley!

This sort of humor went out with Milton Berle, Jerry Lewis, and knock-knock jokes. That's why it's so funny. Movie comedies these days are so hung up on being contemporary, radical, outspoken, and cynically satirical that they sometimes forget to be funny. And they've lost the nerve to be as corny as *Airplane!*—to actually invite loud

groans from the audience. The flop *Wholly Moses*, for example, is no doubt an infinitely more intelligent comedy—but the problem was, we didn't laugh.

Airplane! has a couple of sources for its inspiration. One of them is obviously *Airport* (1970) and all of its sequels and rip-offs. The other might not come immediately to mind unless you're a fan of the late show. It's *Zero Hour!* (1957), which starred the quintessential 1950s B-movie cast of Dana Andrews, Linda Darnell, and Sterling Hayden. *Airplane!* comes from the same studio (Paramount) and therefore is able to cheerfully borrow the same plot (airliner is imperiled after the crew and most of the passengers are stricken with food poisoning). The *Zero Hour!* crisis situation (how to get the airplane down) was also borrowed for the terrible *Airport 1975*, in which Karen Black played a stewardess who tried to follow instructions radioed from the ground.

Airplane! has two desperate people in the cockpit: Julie Hagerty, as the stewardess, and Robert Hays, as a former Air Force pilot whose traumatic war experiences have made him terrified of flying. (The cockpit also contains a very kinky automatic pilot . . . but never mind.)

The movie exploits the previous films for all they're worth. The passenger list includes a little old lady (like Helen Hayes in *Airport*), a guitar-playing nun (like Helen Reddy in *Airport 1975*), and even a critically ill little girl who's being flown to an emergency operation (Linda Blair played the role in *Airport 1975*). Predictable results occur, as when the nun's guitar knocks loose the little girl's intravenous tubes, and she nearly dies while all the passengers sing along inspirationally.

The movie's funniest scene, however, occurs in a flashback explaining how the stewardess and the Air Force pilot first met and fell in love years ago. The scene takes place in an exotic Casablanca-style bar, which is miraculously transformed when somebody's hurled at the jukebox and it starts playing "Stayin' Alive" by the Bee Gees. The scene becomes a hilarious send-up of the disco scenes in *Saturday Night Fever*, with the young pilot defying gravity to impress the girl.

Airplane! is practically a satirical anthology of classic movie clichés. Lloyd Bridges, as the ground-control officer, seems to be satirizing half of his straight roles. The opening titles get an enormous laugh with an unexpected reference to *Jaws*. The neurotic

young pilot is talked back into the cockpit in a scene from *Knute Rockne, All American*. And the romantic scenes are played as a soap opera. None of this really adds up to great comic artistry, but *Airplane!* compensates for its lack of original comic invention by its utter willingness to steal, beg, borrow, and rewrite from anywhere.

Airport ★ ★
G, 137 m., 1970

Burt Lancaster (Mel Bakersfield), Dean Martin (Vernon Demerest), Jean Seberg (Tanya), Jacqueline Bisset (Gwen Meighen), George Kennedy (Patroni), Helen Hayes (Ada Quonsett), Van Heflin (D.O. Guerrero). Directed by George Seaton and produced by Ross Hunter. Screenplay by Seaton.

On some dumb fundamental level, *Airport* kept me interested for a couple of hours. I can't quite remember why. The plot has few surprises (you know and I know that no airplane piloted by Dean Martin ever crashed). The gags are painfully simpleminded (a priest, pretending to cross himself, whacks a wise guy across the face). And the characters talk in regulation B-movie clichés like no B-movie you've seen in ten years. Example: A bomb blows a hole in the airplane and weakens the tail structure. Martin's co-pilot says: "Listen, Vern, I want you to know that if there's anything I can do. . . ." What's he talking about? Martin's girl.

The movie has a lot of expensive stars, but only two (Helen Hayes and Van Heflin) have wit enough to abandon all pretense of seriousness. Even Martin, who can be charming in a movie when he relaxes, plays a straight hero-type this time. Burt Lancaster is even straighter and more heroic, as needs be, since he has to run the airport, supervise George Kennedy in pulling out a stuck Boeing 707, and decide to divorce his wife, all at the same time.

But Miss Hayes and Heflin apparently realized early on that *Airport* was going to be a deadly dull affair, and they went about salvaging their own roles, at least. Miss Hayes milks her role of a little-old-lady stowaway for all it's conceivably worth, and I have a suspicion she wrote some of her own dialogue. It's warmer and more humorous than the stiff lines everyone else has to recite, and she won an Oscar for the role.

Heflin, as the guy with the bomb in his briefcase, is perhaps the only person in the cast to realize how metaphysically absurd *Airport* basically is. The airplane already has a priest, two nuns, three doctors, a stowaway, a customs officer's niece, a pregnant stewardess, two black GIs, a loudmouthed kid, a henpecked husband, and Dean Martin aboard, right? So obviously the bomber has to be typecast, too. Heflin sweats, shakes, peers around nervously, clutches his briefcase to his chest, refuses to talk to anybody, and swallows a lot. The customs officer sees him going on the plane and notices "something in his eyes." Also in his ears, nose, and throat. What Heflin does is undermine the structure of the whole movie with a sort of subversive overacting. Once the bomber becomes ridiculous, the movie does, too. That's good, because it never had a chance at being anything else.

Airport 1975 ★ ★ ½
PG, 106 m., 1974

Charlton Heston (Murdock), Karen Black (Nancy), George Kennedy (Patroni), Efrem Zimbalist, Jr. (Stacy), Susan Clark (Mrs. Patroni), Helen Reddy (Sister Ruth). Directed by Jack Smight and produced by William Frye. Screenplay by Don Ingalls.

The original *Airport* was never one of my favorite movies, but I had to admire the slick, competent way it worked us over for two hours. Its clichés were ancient and its typecasting was relentless, but it didn't bore us. *Airport 1975*, a reworking of the same good old ingredients happens, by some happy chance, to be better than the original.

The story is familiar to anyone. A private plane crashes into the flight deck of a 747, killing or disabling its crew. A stewardess pilots the plane by following radioed instructions, and then a rescue pilot (Charlton Heston, inevitably) is lowered from an Air Force helicopter into the gaping hole in the plane. Meanwhile, a young kidney patient grows weaker, a drunk accosts the pilot, and Gloria Swanson dictates the finishing touches on her autobiography ("I never did want the damn thing published while I was alive, anyway").

What makes this work so well is that the screenplay and direction concentrate on the action, instead of getting bogged down in so many subplots, as *Airport* did. It can't be helped, I suppose, that Heston and the brave stewardess (Karen Black) have been having an affair for six years, or that the airline vice president (George Kennedy, promoted from his operations command in *Airport*) has a wife and daughter on the crippled plane, or that we have the usual ecumenical mixture of stereotypes, racial groups, ages, sexes, and occupants on board. That's all part of the formula.

But at least *Airport 1975* introduces its characters quickly and without fuss, and then gets on with the business at hand. And after the midair collision (which has been telegraphed for at least twenty minutes), the movie's excellent special effects become really gripping. With *Airport*, you never quite felt those people were on a real plane. The exterior shots looked faked. *Airport 1975* has a much more plausible look and a lot of effective aerial photography.

It also gives us a compelling performance by Karen Black, the stewardess. She's probably too good an actress for a role like this, but she makes it real. (And who could ever quite believe Dean Martin as the pilot in *Airport?*) The only quarrel I have with the role is that it falls into the trap of assuming she's incompetent because she's a woman. Her lip quivers, her eyes well up with tears, she's indecisive at key moments. The men on the ground decide they have to get a real pilot on board. My notion is that a real stewardess, faced with such an unlikely situation, would respond professionally and coolly.

No matter. While the wind rips into the plane and the passengers bundle up with blankets and the mountains loom up ahead and the first rescue pilot falls to his death and Gloria Swanson remembers her first flight ("It was in 1917, Cecil B. DeMille was the pilot, and we flew nonstop from Los Angeles to Pasadena"). *Airport 1975* is good, exciting, corny escapism and the kind of movie you would *not* want to watch as an in-flight film.

Alex in Wonderland ★ ★ ★ ★
R, 109 m., 1971

Donald Sutherland (Alex), Ellen Burstyn (Beth), Meg Mazursky (Amy), Glenna Sergent (Nancy), Viola Spolin (Mother), Paul Mazursky (Hal Stern). Directed by Paul Mazursky and produced by Larry Tucker. Screenplay by Mazursky and Tucker.

"Who are you," said the Caterpillar.
This was not an encouraging opening for a conversation. Alice replied rather shyly. "I—hardly know, Sir, just at present—at least I know who I was when I got up this morning, but I think I must have changed several times since then."

That was exactly the case in Hollywood in the early seventies. Works of genius were showered on us by bright, radical, young, etc., filmmakers who announced their intention to overturn the Hollywood establishment. Occasionally one of their films did make it very big, as *Easy Rider* did. Within weeks, the Hollywood hills were jammed with other would-be geniuses, shooting nihilistic cycle flicks with pseudo-Dylan lyrics. Meanwhile, the original boy wonders . . . have got to make themselves another film. That was the situation for Paul Mazursky and Larry Tucker, who wrote, produced, and directed *Bob & Carol & Ted & Alice*. That movie was an artistic and financial success. It was chosen to open the New York Film Festival. It was argued about in all the best publications. Elliott Gould became a star. Natalie Wood made her comeback. Tucker and Mazursky got rich. The whole enchilada, baby.

Alex in Wonderland was their response to that situation; it's a movie about a director whose first movie is a success and who's at a loss for another project. In this sense, it's autobiographical; not in the details of life, but in the crises. Mazursky himself even appears, as Hal Stern, the doggedly mod movie producer who hopes to interest Donald Sutherland in *Don Quixote* as a Western? Or maybe . . .?

If the director's dilemma sounds familiar, perhaps you're reminded of Fellini's *8½*. Mazursky and Tucker were. The blocked director's daughter even asks why he doesn't do a movie about not knowing what to do next, and he says, no, Fellini already did that. *Alex in Wonderland* is a deliberately Felliniesque movie, all the same, and all the more fun for that. Fellini himself appears briefly, to no special purpose, and Fellini trademarks like parades, circuses, and clowns keep turning up in the hero's daydreams.

If *Alex* had been left just on this level, however, it would have been of little interest. What makes it so good is the gift Mazursky, Tucker, and their actors have of fleshing out the small scenes of human contact that give the movie its almost frightening resonance.

Sutherland, as the director, has trouble handling his success. His uncertainty about what to do next spills over into aloofness, even cruelty, toward his wife (Ellen Burstyn) and mother (Viola Spolin). A short scene in a car with his mother, and a long scene in a kitchen with his wife, actually make the rest of the movie work, because they give the character a depth that sticks even through the superficial dream sequences.

And beyond these intimate scenes, there are icily observant portraits of the "new Hollywood." Of aimless "idealistic" arguments on the beach, of luncheon meetings, of idle people trying somehow to be idly committed. These scenes are the 1970 equivalent of Fitzgerald's *The Last Tycoon* or Nathanael West's *The Day of the Locust*: Unforgivingly accurate studies of the distance between America and the filmmakers who would be "relevant" about it.

The Fellini elements are laid onto the film and don't quite sink in (although buffs will enjoy them just as parody). But the human story does work, remarkably well, and if the movie doesn't hold together we're not disposed to hold that against it. Half an enchilada is better than none.

Alice ★ ★ ★
PG-13, 106 m., 1990
(See related Film Clip, p. 693.)

Joe Mantegna (Joe), Mia Farrow (Alice), William Hurt (Doug), Cybill Shepherd (Nancy Brill), Gwen Verdon (Alice's Mother), Bernadette Peters (Muse). Directed by Woody Allen and produced by Robert Greenhut. Screenplay by Allen.

Woody Allen's *Alice* snatches its heroine out of the cradle of luxury and takes her on a dizzying tour of the truths in her life, fueled by the mysterious herbal teas of an enigmatic acupuncturist. It's a strange, magical film, in which Allen uses the arts of the ancient Chinese healer as a shortcut to psychoanalysis; at the end of the film, which covers only a few days, Alice has learned truths about her husband, her parents, her marriage, her family, and herself, and has undergone a profound conversion in values. Because this is a Woody Allen film, a lot of that metaphysical process is funny.

Mia Farrow stars as Alice, who has no apparent relationship to Alice in Wonderland, but finds her own looking glass in the dingy walk-up offices of the highly recommended Dr. Yang, in New York's Chinatown. He asks her to gaze into a spinning wheel while he hypnotizes her, and then he discovers, as he suspected all along, that her pains are not in her back, as she claims, but in her heart.

She leads a comfortable life, cut off from all sources of suffering and, therefore, also of joy. She and her husband (William Hurt) live in a Manhattan apartment that has been interior-designed to within an inch of its life. Also occupying their home, in supporting roles, are a cook ("I couldn't get free-range chickens today!"), a nanny, and, of course, their small assortment of two children. It's the kind of house where support personnel are constantly ringing the doorbell: Here comes the trainer now.

Alice has been married for sixteen affluent years to Doug, a stockbroker played by Hurt as a kind of human deflecting machine, whose physical and verbal postures seem designed to avoid any kind of actual contact. He's always changing the subject, usually into silence.

One day Alice is taking the kids to school and drops a book on the stair, and the book is returned by a dark, handsome stranger (Joe Mantegna), and instantly she begins thinking about having an affair. The very notion shocks and thrills her, and after Dr. Yang (Keye Luke) discovers her secret, he gives her various herbal potions, including one to make her invisible and another that gives her the knack of talking seductively.

What Dr. Yang has really done is to release her from all inhibitions, psychological and physical, so she's free to range widely through her current and past life. She confronts her sister. She has an imaginary conversation with her husband. She levels with her mother. She is even taken on a flight over Manhattan by the ghost of a former boyfriend. The movie uses Allen's unique style of off-center, fast-thinking dialogue, with throwaway lines and quick topical references. Everyone in the story is fairly smart, although some are in over their heads, like the Mantegna character, who cannot quite understand why this strange woman is first seducing, then abandoning him. A lot of the material in the film spins out of Alice's childhood Catholicism; perhaps she still clings to a notion that someday she might become a nun, instead of a parasitic consumer of goods.

The world of *Alice* is the rich world of Manhattan, where the homeless and the poor are seldom seen. This is a world inhabited by countless stars in supporting roles, including Blythe Danner, Judy Davis, Keye Luke, Bernadette Peters, Cybill Shepherd, and Gwen Verdon. (The old boyfriend is played by Alec Baldwin, who is transparent in every scene. It is somehow typical of Woody Allen

to obtain the latest box office superstar for his cast, and then neglect to make him opaque.)

The women in this world are intimate with boutiques, hair salons, chic restaurants, and the interiors of limousines. Yet Alice can somehow not get the image of Mother Teresa out of her mind. Perhaps if she went to Calcutta, if she became a follower of Mother Teresa, then these vague stirrings of unease would stop tormenting her. In a Woody Allen picture all such developments and U-turns are, of course, eminently thinkable, and one of the best things about *Alice* is that the characters are not linear creatures, hell-bent on moving in a straight line from the beginning of the movie to the end.

Alice lacks the philosophical precision of Allen's *Crimes and Misdemeanors* and the psychological messiness of *Hannah and Her Sisters*, and it also lacks the rigorous self-discovery of his underrated *Another Woman*. It's in the tradition of his more whimsical films like *A Midsummer Night's Sex Comedy*. And yet lurking in the shadows are some seductive questions. Wouldn't it be wonderful if there *were* a man like Dr. Yang, a *deus ex machina* to drop into our lives with his herbs and paraphernalia, and lift the scales from our eyes, and free us from our petty routines and selfishness, and allow us to practice the sainthood we have always suspected lies buried deep inside?

Alice Doesn't Live Here Anymore
★ ★ ★ ★
PG, 113 m., 1974

Ellen Burstyn (Alice Hyatt), Kris Kristofferson (David), Billy Green Bush (Donald), Diane Ladd (Flo), Alfred Lutter (Tommy), Harvey Keitel (Ben). Directed by Martin Scorsese and produced by David Susskind and Audrey Maas. Screenplay by Robert Getchell.

Martin Scorsese's *Alice Doesn't Live Here Anymore* opens with a parody of the Hollywood dream world little girls were expected to carry around in their intellectual baggage a generation ago. The screen is awash with a fake sunset, and a sweet little thing comes strolling along home past sets that seem rescued from *The Wizard of Oz*. But her dreams and dialogue are decidedly not made of sugar, spice, or anything nice: This little girl is going to do things her way.

That was her defiant childhood notion, anyway. But by the time she's thirty-five,

Alice Hyatt has more or less fallen into society's rhythms. She's married to an incommunicative truck driver, she has a precocious twelve-year-old son, she kills time chatting with the neighbors. And then her husband is unexpectedly killed in a traffic accident and she's left widowed and—almost worse than that—independent. After all those years of having someone there, can she cope by herself?

She can, she says. When she was a little girl, she idolized Alice Faye and determined to be a singer when she grew up. Well, she's thirty-five, and that's grown-up. She has a garage sale, sells the house, and sets off on an odyssey through the Southwest with her son and her dreams. What happens to her along the way provides one of the most perceptive, funny, occasionally painful portraits of an American woman I've seen.

The movie has been both attacked and defended on feminist grounds, but I think it belongs somewhere outside ideology, maybe in the area of contemporary myth and romance. There are scenes in which we take Alice and her journey perfectly seriously, there are scenes of harrowing reality and then there are other scenes (including some hilarious passages in a restaurant where she waits on tables) where Scorsese edges into slight, cheerful exaggeration. There are times, indeed, when the movie seems less about Alice than it does about the speculations and daydreams of a lot of women about her age, who identify with the liberation of other women, but are unsure on the subject of themselves.

A movie like this depends as much on performances as on direction, and there's a fine performance by Ellen Burstyn (who won an Oscar for this role) as Alice. She looks more real this time than she did as Cybill Shepherd's available mother in *The Last Picture Show* or as Linda Blair's tormented mother in *The Exorcist*. It's the kind of role she can relax in, be honest with, allow to develop naturally (although those are often the hardest roles of all). She's determined to find work as a singer, to "resume" a career that was mostly dreams to begin with, and she's pretty enough (although not good enough) to almost pull it off. She meets some generally good people along the way, and they help her when they can. But she also meets some creeps, especially a deceptively nice guy named Ben (played by Harvey Keitel, the autobiographical hero of Scorsese's two films set in Little Italy). The singing jobs

don't materialize much, and it's while she's waitressing that she runs into a divorced young farmer (Kris Kristofferson).

They fall warily in love, and there's an interesting relationship between Kristofferson and Alfred Lutter, who does a very good job of playing a certain kind of twelve-year-old kid. Most women in Alice's position probably wouldn't run into a convenient, understanding, and eligible young farmer, but then a lot of the things in the film don't work as pure logic. There's a little myth to them, while Scorsese sneaks up on his main theme.

The movie's filled with brilliantly done individual scenes. Alice, for example, has a run-in with a fellow waitress with an inspired vocabulary (Diane Ladd, an Oscar nominee for this role). They fall into a friendship and have a frank and honest conversation one day while sunbathing. The scene works perfectly. There's also the specific way her first employer backs into offering her a singing job, and the way Alice takes leave from her old neighbors, and the way her son persists in explaining a joke that could only be understood by a twelve-year-old. These are great moments in a film that gives us Alice Hyatt: female, thirty-five, undefeated.

Alien Nation ★ ★
R, 96 m., 1988

James Caan (Matthew Sykes), Mandy Patinkin (Sam Francisco), Terence Stamp (William Harcourt), Kevyn Major Howard (Kipling), Leslie Bevis (Cassandra), Peter Jason (Fedorchuk), George Jeneky (Quint), Jeff Kober (Josh Strader), Rober Aaron Brown (Bill Tuggle), Tony Simotes (Wiltey). Directed by Graham Baker and produced by Gale Anne Hurd and Richard Kobritz. Screenplay by Rockne S. O'Bannon.

Alien Nation takes place in the near future, a few years after an alien spaceship wanders off course, lands on earth, and deposits 100,000 extraterrestrials in our midst. These visitors, known as the Newcomers, have been created by genetic engineering to be good slaves; they're smart, strong, and adaptable. But there is no slavery on earth, and so the aliens are slowly absorbed into Southern California society, where some become cops, some become robbers, and some operate convenience stores. There is some prejudice against them, of course, and

they look a little odd with their bulbous heads, but they fit in fairly well. The only question is—are they keeping any secrets?

This plot contains the elements of a good idea, but it does so little with it, and is so cheerfully willing to recycle an absolutely standard story, that the idea is finally just frustrating—the movie would have been more fun if it had just gone ahead and admitted it was a Creature Feature. The film has high technical qualities and a prestigious cast, and so during the opening scenes I couldn't believe it was simply another police action potboiler. I was waiting for subtle hints of deeper meanings, of surprises lurking beneath the surface. But there weren't any. This is sea-level filmmaking: What you see is all you get.

The movie stars James Caan as a police detective in a situation we've seen several dozen times before. His partner is killed in a shoot-out with Newcomer stickup men, and the chief wants him to accept a new partner—a Newcomer, of course. At first Caan is reluctant. But then he figures the Newcomer can give him entry into his people's underworld, so that he can revenge the death of his partner.

This story has been recycled so often, we can recite the dialogue right along with the characters, but we're thinking, maybe the aliens will provide a new angle. The filmmakers couldn't think of one, alas, but I'm happy to offer several: (a) The Newcomers have a secret agenda they're concealing from humans; (b) this is *Invasion of the Body Snatchers* all over again, except that the pod people are operating in plain sight this time; (c) the race that bred the Newcomers to be slaves sends its warships to recapture them, and humans and Newcomers fight side-by-side to repel them; (d) this is a political satire on the role of minority groups in Los Angeles.

Alien Nation takes none of these approaches, or any other interesting approach, because it is so pleased with its almost pathetically thin opening premise. Once we understand that the movie takes place in the near future and has aliens who are being integrated into human society, everything else is an assembly-line cop picture. They've just taken the standard cop/buddy/drug lord routine and changed some of the makeup. The Newcomers have no surprises. This is especially disappointing since Gale Anne Hurd, the film's coproducer, has demonstrated she does know how to invest aliens with fascination; her credits include *Aliens* and *The Terminator.* Compared to them, this film is minor league.

Consider, for example, how *Alien Nation* introduces its villain, a Newcomer played by Terence Stamp. How do we immediately know he is a villain? Because he is the featured speaker at a charity banquet honoring his good works, but he talks coldly and doesn't seem amused when he laughs. Since we are familiar with the Law of Economy of Characters, we know this guy isn't *really* being honored for his civic achievements, because that would be a waste of screen time. Nope, he's a seemingly respectable businessman who is actually manufacturing and selling a drug that his people get high on. There is not a person who watches this movie that could not have written this plot—and many of them probably have.

A feeble attempt is made to invest the Newcomers with interest, by having them get drunk on sour milk instead of booze, and depriving them of any sense of humor. Mandy Patinkin, a good actor, has the thankless role of playing "Sam Francisco," the Newcomer who is Caan's partner, and so he gets to drink the milk and puzzle over the jokes. All of the Newcomers, by the way, were given human names by U.S. immigration officers, none of whom seem to have heard of the First Law of Funny Names: "Funny names, in general, are a sign of desperation at the screenplay level."

Alien Nation was not an inexpensive movie. The makeup took trouble, the photography looks good, the cast and technical credits are top-drawer. So what went wrong? The movie is simply a failure of imagination. Nobody looked at the screenplay and observed that it didn't try hard enough, that it had no surprises, that it didn't attempt to delight its audiences with twists and turns on the phoned-in plotline. *Alien Nation* feels like a movie made by people who have seen a lot of movies, but don't think the audience has.

Aliens ★ ★ ★ ½
R, 135 m., 1986

Sigourney Weaver (Ripley), Carrie Henn (Newt), Michael Biehn (Corporal Hicks), Paul Reiser (Burke), Lance Henriksen (Bishop), Jenette Goldstein (Private Vasquez). Directed by James Cameron and produced by Gale Anne Hurd. Screenplay by Cameron.

This movie is so intense that it creates a problem for me as a reviewer: Do I praise its craftsmanship, or do I tell you it left me feeling wrung out and unhappy? When I walked out of the theater, there were knots in my stomach from the film's roller-coaster ride of violence. This is not the kind of movie where it means anything to say you "enjoyed" it.

Aliens is a sequel to the very effective 1979 film, *Alien,* but it tells a self-contained story that begins fifty-seven years after the previous story ended. The first time around, you may recall, Sigourney Weaver and a shipload of her fellow space voyagers were exploring a newly discovered planet when they found an abandoned spaceship. Surviving in the ship was an alien life-form that seemed to consist primarily of teeth. The aliens were pure malevolence; their only function was to attack and eat anything that was warm and moved. And they incubated their young inside the bodies of their victims.

Weaver was the only survivor of that first expedition, and after saving her ship by expelling an alien through the air lock into deep space, she put herself into hibernation. She is found fifty-seven years later by a salvage ship, and when she awakes she is still tormented by nightmares. (The script does not provide her, however, with even a single line of regret after she learns that fifty-seven years have passed and everyone she knew is dead.)

A new expedition is sent back to the mystery planet. Weaver is on board. She knows what the aliens are like and thinks the only sane solution is to nuke them from outer space. But in the meantime, she learns to her horror that a human colony has been established on the planet and billions of dollars have been invested in it. Now Earth has lost contact with the colony. Has it been attacked by aliens? Are there stars in the sky?

The crew is made up of an interesting mixed bag of technicians and military personnel. My favorites were Lance Henriksen as a loyal android, Jenette Goldstein as a muscular marine private, and Michael Biehn as the uncertain Corporal Hicks. Also on board is the slimy Burke (Paul Reiser), who represents the owners of the planet's expensive colony and dreams of making millions by using the aliens as a secret weapon.

The movie gives us just enough setup to establish the characters and explain the situation. Then the action starts. The colony has, of course, been overrun by the aliens, all except for one plucky little girl (Carrie Henn) who has somehow survived by hiding in the air ducts. The marines explore the base on foot, which seems a little silly in view of the great speed with which the aliens attack. Nobody seems very interested in listening to Weaver's warnings. After all, she's only the one person who has seen an alien, so what does she know? And then the movie escalates into a nonstop war between human and alien.

It's here that my nerves started to fail. *Aliens* is absolutely, painfully, and unremittingly intense for at least its last hour. Weaver goes into battle to save her colleagues, herself, and the little girl, and the aliens drop from the ceiling, pop up out of the floor, and crawl out of the ventilation shafts. (In one of the movie's less plausible moments, one alien even seems to know how to work the elevator buttons.) I have never seen a movie that maintains such a pitch of intensity for so long; it's like being on some kind of hair-raising carnival ride that never stops.

I don't know how else to describe this: The movie made me feel bad. It filled me with feelings of unease and disquiet and anxiety. I didn't want to talk to anyone. I was drained. I'm not sure *Aliens* is what we mean by entertainment. Yet I have to be accurate about this movie: It is a superb example of filmmaking craft.

The director, James *(The Terminator)* Cameron, has been assigned to make an intense and horrifying thriller, and he has delivered. Weaver, who is onscreen almost all the time, comes through with a very strong, sympathetic performance: She's the thread that holds everything together.

The supporting players are sharply drawn. The special effects are professional. I'm giving the movie a high rating for its skill and professionalism and because it does the job it says it will do. I am also advising you not to eat before you see it.

All Dogs Go to Heaven ★ ★ ★
G, 87 m., 1989

With the voices of: Burt Reynolds (Charlie B. Barkin), Dom De Luise (Itchy), Vic Tayback (Carface), Judith Barsi (Anne-Marie), Charles Nelson Reilly (Killer), Melba Moore (Whippet Angel), Loni Anderson (Flo). Directed by Don Bluth, codirected by Dan Kuenster and Gary Goldman, and produced by Morris F. Sullivan and George A. Walker. Screenplay by David Weiss.

The first thing I noticed about Don Bluth's *All Dogs Go to Heaven* was the colors, the rich, saturated colors I identify with the early days of animated features. When Technicolor shut down its classic color operation and led the movie world to an inferior but cheaper system, animated films suffered more than live-action movies because their bright primary colors were essential to their overall effect. Most movies made from the early 1960s to the late 1970s have suffered serious fading—but the animated movies looked a little pale even to begin with.

Now Technicolor is back with an improved color system, and in *All Dogs Go to Heaven* it permits such a voluptuous use of color that the movie is an invigorating bath for the eyes. The bright palette is used to paint animated characters who are also a treat, because in his latest animated feature Don Bluth has allowed his characters to look and behave a little more strangely. There is a lot of individualism in this movie, both in the filmmaking and in the characters themselves.

Bluth is the former Disney animator who led a group of artists away from the studio during its doldrums in 1979 and set up his own animation operation. His feature credits so far include *The Secret of NIMH*, the dinosaur adventure *The Land Before Time*, and *An American Tail*—the story of an immigrant mouse that set box-office records for an animated film. Now here he is with a fantasy about canine lowlife in New Orleans.

The movie involves the adventures of Charlie B. Barkin (who has not only the voice of Burt Reynolds but even some of the mannerisms). Barkin is a professional criminal who has teamed up in the past with a pit bull named Carface, but now Carface has Barkin rubbed out, and he finds himself in heaven, which should not be a surprise if he has read the title of his movie. Bent on revenge, Barkin returns to earth, and then the main story of the movie begins as he makes friends with a little girl who has an amazing knack for predicting winners out at the track.

The movie tells its story with several timeouts for song and dance numbers, notably one in which an alligator does an Esther Williams imitation. The plot is not particularly inventive (all but the younger viewers should be able to call most of the big surprises), but the style and tone of the movie are fresh. Although Walt Disney's very earliest movies had a lot of fun playing around with animation, most modern animated characters seem to come out of the same image bank. They look more or less like residents of the same reality level. What Bluth

has done in *All Dogs Go to Heaven* is to allow the characters to be drawn in a more parodistic, even slightly bizarre way, so that their very shapes seem to change to echo their moods. It's fun.

All of Me ★ ★ ★ ½
PG, 93 m., 1984

Steve Martin (Roger Cobb), Lily Tomlin (Edwina Cutwater), Victoria Tennant (Terry Hoskins), Madolyn Smith (Peggy), Richard Libertini (Prahka Lasa), Jason Bernard (Tyrone Wattel). Directed by Carl Reiner. Screenplay by Phil Alden Robinson.

All of Me shares with a lot of great screwball comedies a very simple approach: Use absolute logic in dealing with the absurd. Begin with a nutty situation, establish the rules, and follow them. The laughs happen when ordinary human nature comes into conflict with ridiculous developments.

We can identify with almost all of the motives of the characters in *All of Me*. There is, for example, the millionaire spinster Edwina Cutwater (Lily Tomlin), who wants to live forever and thinks she has found a way to do that. There is the unhappy lawyer Roger Cobb (Steve Martin), who is desperately unhappy with his work and will do anything to get a promotion—even cater to nutcase clients like Edwina. There is the evil Terry Hoskins (Victoria Tennant), who plans to cruelly deceive Edwina, and there is the beatific Prahka Lasa (Richard Libertini), who hopes to transfer Edwina's soul into a brass pot, and then insert it in Miss Hoskins's body. There is, however, a terrible psychic miscalculation, and when Edwina dies, she transmigrates instead into Cobb's body. When I heard *All of Me* described, I couldn't think of any way this plot could possibly work. To begin with, why put one of my favorite comedians, Tomlin, inside Martin, a man whose movies I have not admired? And yet it does work. The moment it starts to work is the first time Martin has to deal with this alien female entity inside his brain. He retains control of the left side of his body. She controls the right. They are trying to cross the sidewalk together, each in their own way, and this sets up a manic tug-of-war that is one of the funniest scenes I've seen in a long time.

There are other great scenes, some of them probably obligatory, as when Martin has to go to the bathroom. The movie doesn't

just go for obvious physical jokes, however; it scores a lot of points by speculating on the ways in which a man and a woman could learn to coexist in such close quarters. Against all the odds, a certain tenderness and sweetness develops by the end of the film. Although it is Tomlin who disappears into Martin's body, she does not disappear from the movie. For one thing, her reflection can be seen in mirrors, and there is some exquisite timing involved in the way they play scenes with each other's mirror images. For another thing (and this is really curious), there is a real sense of her presence even when Martin is alone on the screen: The film's premise, which seems so unlikely, begins to work.

The movie is filled with good supporting performances. My favorites are Richard Libertini, as the guru of transmigration, who speaks incomprehensible words in a tone of complete agreement, and Jason Bernard, as a black musician who is Martin's friend and partner during several tricky scenes of bodysnatching and brain-grabbing. *All of Me* is in a class with *Ghostbusters*, and for some of the same reasons.

All the President's Men ★ ★ ★ ½
PG, 135 m., 1976

Robert Redford (Bob Woodward), Dustin Hoffman (Carl Bernstein), Jack Warden (Harry Rosenfeld), Martin Balsam (Howard Simons), Hal Holbrook (Deep Throat), Jason Robards (Ben Bradlee), Jane Alexander (Bookkeeper), Stephen Collins (Hugh Sloan), Robert Walden (Donald Segretti), Frank Wills (Frank Wills). Directed by Alan J. Pakula and produced by Walter Coblenz. Screenplay by William Goldman.

All the President's Men is truer to the craft of journalism than to the art of storytelling, and that's its problem. The movie is as accurate about the processes used by investigative reporters as we have any right to expect, and yet process finally overwhelms narrative—we're adrift in a sea of names, dates, telephone numbers, coincidences, lucky breaks, false leads, dogged footwork, denials, evasions, and sometimes even the truth. Just such thousands of details led up to Watergate and the Nixon resignation, yes, but the movie's more about the details than about their results. That's not to say the movie isn't good at accomplishing what it sets out to do. It provides the most observant study of working journalists we're ever likely to see in a feature film (Bob Woodward and Carl Bernstein may at last, merciful God, replace Hildy Johnson and Walter Burns as career models). And it succeeds brilliantly in suggesting the mixture of exhilaration, paranoia, self-doubt, and courage that permeated the *Washington Post* as its two young reporters went after a presidency.

Newspaper movies always used to play up the excitement and ignore the boredom and the waiting. This one is all about the boredom and the waiting and the tireless digging; it depends on what we already know about Watergate to provide a level of excitement. And yet, given the fact that William Goldman's screenplay is almost all dialogue, almost exclusively a series of scenes of people talking (or not talking) to each other, director Alan J. Pakula has done a remarkable job of keeping the pace taut. Who'd have thought you could build tension with scenes where Bernstein walks over to Woodward's desk and listens in on the extension phone? But you can. And the movie's so well paced, acted, and edited that it develops the illusion of momentum even in the scenes where Woodward and Bernstein are getting doors slammed in their faces.

When Robert Redford announced that he'd bought the rights to *All the President's Men*, the joke in the newsroom was about reporters becoming movie stars. What in fact has happened is that the stars, Redford as Woodward and Dustin Hoffman as Bernstein, became reporters: They sink into their characters and become wholly credible. There's not a false or "Hollywood" note in the whole movie, and that's commendable— but how much authenticity will viewers settle for? To what secret and sneaky degree do they really want Redford and Hoffman to come on like stars?

There must have been a temptation to flesh out the Woodward and Bernstein characters, to change the pace with subplots about their private lives, but the film sticks resolutely to its subject. This is the story of a story: of two reporters starting with an apparently minor break-in and following it, almost incredulously at times, as it finally leads all the way to the White House. At times the momentum of Watergate seems to propel Woodward and Bernstein, instead of the other way around. It must have occasionally been like that at the time, and it's to the movie's credit that it doesn't force its characters into the center of every scene.

All the President's Men doesn't dwell on the private lives of its characters, but it does have a nice touch with their professional lives, and especially with their relationships with editors. The Watergate story started as a local story, not a national one, and it was a continuing thorn in the side of the *Post*'s prestigious national staff as Woodward and Bernstein kept it as their own. We meet the *Post* metro editor, Harry Rosenfeld (Jack Warden), defending and badgering "Woodstein" as the team came to be known. Martin Balsam plays Howard Simons, the managing editor, and Jason Robards is Benjamin Bradlee, the executive editor. All three are well cast; they may never have been in a newspaper office before, but they've learned the correct tone, they carry on a news conference as if they've held one before, and they even exhibit typical shadings of office fashion—the closer in time you are to having once covered a daily beat, the more you're permitted to loosen your tie and have baggy pants.

The movie has dozens of smaller character roles, for all the people who talked to Woodstein, or who refused to, and there's one cameo from real life: Frank Wills, the Watergate guard who found the fateful tape on the lock, plays himself. Some of the other roles tend to blend into one faceless Source, but Robert Walden makes a memorable Donald Segretti, playing the "dirty tricks" expert with bravado shading into despair. And two of the key informants are portrayed in interestingly different ways. Jane Alexander is a bookkeeper who gives the team some of their best leads, and is plain, honest, and scared; Hal Holbrook, as the mysterious "Deep Throat," the source inside the administration, is disturbingly detached, almost as if he's observing the events with a hollow laugh.

All of these elements in *All the President's Men* are to be praised, and yet they don't quite add up to a satisfying movie experience. Once we've seen one cycle of investigative reporting, once Woodward and Bernstein have cracked the first wall separating the break-in from the White House, we understand the movie's method. We don't need to see the reporting cycle repeated several more times just because the story grows longer and the sources more important. For all of its technical skill, the movie essentially shows us the same journalistic process several times as it leads closer and closer to an end we already know. The film is long, and

would be dull if it weren't for the wizardry of Pakula, his actors, and technicians. What saves it isn't the power of narrative, but the success of technique. Still, considering the compromises that could have been made, considering the phony "newspaper movie" this could have been, maybe that's almost enough.

All the Right Moves ★ ★ ★
R, 91 m., 1983

Tom Cruise (Stef), Craig T. Nelson (Nickerson), Lea Thompson (Lisa). Directed by Michael Chapman and produced by Stephen Deutsch. Screenplay by Michael Kane.

I started on newspapers as a sportswriter, covering local high school teams. That was a long time ago, and I had almost forgotten, until I saw *All the Right Moves*, how desperately important every game seemed at the time. When the team members and the fans are all teen-agers, and when a school victory reflects in a significant way upon your own feelings of worth, when "We won!" means that we won, a football game can take on aspects of Greek tragedy.

All the Right Moves remembers the strength of those feelings, but does not sentimentalize them. The movie stars Tom Cruise (from *Risky Business*) as a high school football player in a small Pennsylvania mill town where unemployment is a way of life. His ticket out of town is a football scholarship to a good engineering school. The high school football coach (Craig T. Nelson) also is looking for a ticket, to an assistant coaching job in a college. On the night of the big game, these two people get into a position where each one seems to have destroyed the hopes of the other.

The movie plays this conflict against an interesting background. This isn't another high school movie with pompon girls and funny principals and weirdo chem teachers. The movie gets into the dynamics of the high school student body and into the tender, complicated relationship between the Cruise character and his girlfriend (Lea Thompson).

After all the junk high school movies in which kids chop each other up, seduce the French teacher, and visit whorehouses in Mexico, it is so wonderful to see a movie that remembers that most teen-agers are vulnerable, unsure, sincere, and fundamentally decent. The kid, his girlfriend, and all of their friends have feelings we can recognize as real. The plot feels real, too, because it centers around those kinds of horrible misunderstandings and mistakes that we all remember from high school. A lot of teenagers walk around all day feeling guilty, even if they're totally innocent. Get them into a situation that gives them the appearance of guilt and they're in trouble. And it is so easy to get into trouble when you are old enough to do wrong but too young to move independently to avoid it. A lot of kids who say they were only along for the ride are telling the simple truth.

The movie frames the Cruise character in a situation like that, one we can identify with. And then it does an interesting thing. Instead of solving the problem with a plot twist, it solves it through the exercise of genuine human honesty: Two people finally tell each other the truth. This is, of course, an astonishing breakthrough in movies about teen-agers, and *All the Right Moves* deserves credit for that achievement.

Allegro non Tropo ★ ★ ★ ½
NO MPAA RATING, 75 m., 1977

An animated feature by Bruno Bozzetto.

Classical music illustrated with animated fantasies! What an inspiration! The impresario in the vast old Italian opera house can hardly contain himself. He bustles about the stage, confiding his plans: He'll have an animator as his chief soloist. A full orchestra of little old ladies. A selection from the greatest symphonic works of all time. . . .

The telephone rings. It's Hollywood calling. The impresario can't believe his ears. It's been done already! Somebody had the same idea years ago—somebody named, ah, Prisney. Something like that. No matter. He'll do it anyway! His little old ladies arrive in a horse-drawn wagon guided by the impresario himself. Did that Prisney, or whatever his name is, give you stuff like this?

And so Bruno Bozzetto introduces his *Allegro non Tropo*, a tribute to Walt Disney's *Fantasia* and at the same time a delightfully original animated feature itself. The two movies show how limitless the possibilities are: Animation, which has few boundaries, reveals none here.

Bozzetto's animated fantasies are funny and sad, erotic and the opposite, pessimistic and visionary. He selects such familiar symphonic works as Stravinsky's *Firebird*, Sibelius's *Valse Triste*, Vivaldi's *Concerto in C*, Debussy's *Prelude to the Afternoon of a Faun*, and Ravel's *Bolero*, and then he finds ways of illustrating them that are inspired, and amusing, and somehow just right.

Take *Bolero*, for example, that majestic progression to larger and larger statements. How would you visualize it? Bozzetto begins with an empty Coke bottle, tossed from a spaceship visiting a barren planet. The bottle comes to rest just as the spaceship departs. There's a little Coke left in the bottom of it. And as Ravel's music relentlessly builds, the stuff in the bottle ferments. Simple forms of life become more complex. Weird and wonderful shapes form, and try to crawl up the side of the bottle, and fail. And then finally one succeeds. And Bozzetto marches through the stages of a strange evolution, as bizarre monsters struggle across the barren landscape, learning very suddenly to fly, and swim, and do the other things to keep from becoming meals.

The Sibelius is illustrated with an affecting idea: A scrawny house cat wanders forlorn through the streets of a city destroyed by war. No people live there anymore, but some ancient racial cat memory inhabits the ruins with dream-images of people: with quiet domestic scenes that evaporate, one after another, leaving the cat alone, lonely and afraid. An idea like this is in Loren Eiseley's biography, *All the Strange Hours*. He wonders if the dogs and cats that cast their lot with us so many tens of thousands of years ago will remember us uneasily for a few generations after we've annihilated ourselves; Bozzetto illustrates the idea beautifully.

And then there's his version of Stravinsky's *Firebird*, in which the serpent in the Garden of Eden eats the apple himself and has a very hard time of it as a result. And the aging, self-deluded rake in *Prelude to the Afternoon of a Faun*, trying to make himself look younger in his doomed pursuit of a nymph. And the busy little bee in Vivaldi's *Concerto in C*, who sets her table at one promising flower after another, only to be disturbed by two vulgar, gigantic humans who insist on making love in her meadow.

Bozzetto, one of the best animators now at work, has been making shorts for years. *Allegro non Tropo*, his first feature, is a treasure. It deserves its place beside *Fantasia*, is as delightful and inspired, and will no doubt be around as long. Even what's-his-name, Prisney, would agree.

Almost an Angel ★ ★ ½
PG, 97 m., 1990

Paul Hogan (Terry Dean), Elias Koteas (Steve), Linda Kozlowski (Rose Garner), Doreen Lang (Mrs. Garner), Robert Sutton (Guido), Sammy Lee Allen (Bubba). Directed and produced by John Cornell. Screenplay by Paul Hogan.

Paul Hogan is an unlikely movie star, with his Australian twang and his quizzical grin and his air of being constantly a little surprised to find himself at the center of attention. But he does indeed have a genuine star quality, and I found myself meditating on that quality while watching *Almost an Angel*.

This is, on the face of it, the kind of movie I cannot abide—a soppy fable in which a crook does a good deed and is almost killed, then goes to heaven and is told by God (who looks remarkably like Charlton Heston) that he is being given a chance to redeem himself—that he's an angel on probation. And then the guy comes back to Earth and befriends a man in a wheelchair and falls in love with his sister, who runs a center for homeless kids, and *come on*, enough already.

So why was I watching the movie with interest and amusement, instead of cynical detachment? In large part, I believe, because Paul Hogan and the other actors in the story were able to project complete sincerity, and at the same time, a subtle sense of humor and an enormous feeling of good will. There is something so unstudied and likable about Hogan that he can inhabit material like this and not come across as an insufferable goody-two-shoes.

Part of that quality comes because Hogan is innately a comedian. If he were not in show business, he would probably be regaling his buddies down at the bar, or emceeing the banquet for his bowling league. He possesses an instinctive good humor.

That comes across in the funny opening scenes of *Almost an Angel*, when he is discharged from prison—having wired every lock, gate, and alarm in the joint to his portable channel-changer. Hogan is an expert on security systems—so good the cops can easily spot his trademark jobs. So he changes professions, going in for bank robbery, and for his first two jobs he disguises himself as Willie Nelson and Rod Stewart. Sounds contrived, I know, but it's funny the way the movie handles it, and the cops even get into an argument about Willie's last album.

Then comes the heroic stunt that sends Hogan to heaven—or what he thinks is heaven—and brings him back to Earth again much chastened and determined to wreak goodness upon his fellow men. That's when he meets the man in the wheelchair (Elias Koteas), and makes him a friend by challenging him to a fight ("We'll both sit down"), and gets taken home, and meets his sister (perennial Hogan costar Linda Kozlowski), and gets involved with helping out at the center for street kids. So once again he's the helpful stranger, an angel doubling as "Crocodile" Dundee.

The movie's plot is not exactly sophisticated, and some of the sequences are so naive they seem borrowed from old grade-B Westerns—the one, for example, where Hogan convinces a couple of tough guys that he is being backed up by an invisible posse. But the movie's low-key charm and good will make up for a lot. And so does Hogan's natural, entertaining screen presence.

I cannot, however, much as I'd like to, quite recommend this movie—the going gets a little too thick at the end, and some of the plot developments are pretty dumb. I'd like the ending better if it hadn't pulled out every possible stop. But that isn't to say I'm scornful of the special qualities in the film, and its gentle good humor.

Altered States ★ ★ ★ ½
R, 103 m., 1980

William Hurt (Eddie Jessup), Blair Brown (Emily Jessup), Bob Balaban (Arthur Rosenberg), Charles Haid (Mason Parrish), Thaao Penghlis (Eccheverria), Miguel Godreau (Primal Man). Directed by Ken Russell and produced by Howard Gottfried. Screenplay by Sidney Aaron.

Altered States is one hell of a movie—literally. It hurls its characters headlong back through billions of years to the moment of creation and finds nothing there except an anguished scream of "No!" as the life force protests its moment of birth. And then, through the power of the human ego to insist on its own will even in the face of the implacable indifference of the universe, it turns "No!" into "Yes!" and ends with the basic scene in all drama, the man and the woman falling into each other's arms.

But hold on just a second here: I'm beginning to sound like the movie's characters, a band of overwrought pseudo-intellectuals

who talk like a cross between Werner Erhard, Freud, and Tarzan. Some of the movie's best dialogue passages are deliberately staged with everybody talking at once: It doesn't matter what they're saying, only that they're incredibly serious about it. I can tell myself intellectually that this movie is a fiendishly constructed visual and verbal roller coaster, a movie deliberately intended to overwhelm its audiences with sensual excess. I know all that, and yet I *was* overwhelmed, I *was* caught up in its headlong energy.

Is that a worthy accomplishment for a movie? Yes, I suppose it is, if the movie earns it by working as hard as *Altered States* does. This is, at last, the movie that Ken Russell was born to direct—the same Ken Russell whose wretched excesses in the past include *The Music Lovers, The Devils,* and *Lisztomania.* The formula is now clear. Take Russell's flair for visual pyrotechnics and apocalyptic sexuality, and channel it through just enough scientific mumbo jumbo to give it form. The result may be totally meaningless, but while you're watching it you are not concerned.

The movie is based on a Paddy Chayevsky novel, which was, in turn, inspired by the experiments of Dr. John Lilly, the man who placed his human subjects in total immersion tanks—floating them in total darkness so that their minds, cut off from all external reality, could play along the frontiers of sanity. In *Altered States,* William Hurt plays a Harvard scientist named Jessup who takes such an experiment one step further, by ingesting a drug made from the sacred hallucinatory mushrooms of a primitive tribe. The strange thing about these mushrooms, Hurt observes in an easily missed line of dialogue in the movie, is that they give everyone who takes them the same hallucinatory vision. Perhaps it is our cellular memory of creation: There is chaos, and then a ball of light, and then the light turns into a crack, and the crack opens onto Nothing, and that is all there was and all there will be, except for life, which has its only existence in the mind.

Got that? It hardly matters. It is a breathtaking concept, but *Altered States* hardly slows down for it. This is the damnedest movie to categorize. Just when it begins to sound like a 1960s psychedelic fantasy, a head trip—it turns into a farce. The scientist immerses himself in his tank for too long, he regresses to a simian state, physically turns into some kind of ape, attacks the campus

security guards, is chased by a pack of wild dogs into the local zoo, and kills and eats a sheep for his supper before turning *back* into the kindly Professor Jessup, the Intellectual Hulk.

The movie splits up into three basic ingredients: The science, the special effects, and the love relationship between the professor and his wife. The science is handled deliciously well. We learn as much as we need to (that is, next to nothing) about total immersion, genetics, and the racial memory. Then come the special effects, in four long passages and a few short bursts. They're good. They may remind you at times of the sound-and-light extravaganza toward the end of 2001, but they are also supposed to evoke the birth of the universe in a pulsating celestial ovum. In the center of this vision is Dr. Jessup, his body pulsing in and out of an ape-shape, his mouth pulled into an anguished "O" as he protests the hell of being born. These scenes are reinforced by the music and are obviously intended to fuel the chemically altered consciousness of the next generation of movie cultists.

But then there is the matter of the love relationship between the professor and his wife (Blair Brown), and it is here that we discover how powerful the attraction of love really is. During the professor's last experiment, when he is disappearing into a violent whirlpool of light and screams on the laboratory floor, it is his wife who wades into the celestial mists, gets up to her knees in eternity, reaches in, and pulls him out. And this is despite the fact that he has filed for divorce. The last scene is a killer, with the professor turning into the protoplasm of life itself, and his wife turning into a glowing shell of rock-like flesh, with her inner fires glowing through the crevices (the effect is something like an overheated Spiderman). They're going through the unspeakable hell of reliving the First Moment, and yet as the professor, as Man, bangs on the walls and crawls toward her, and she reaches out, and the universe rocks, the Man within him bursts out of the ape-protoplasm, and the Woman within her explodes back into flesh, and they collapse into each other's arms, and all the scene really needs at that point is for him to ask, "Was it as good for you as it was for me?"

Altered States is a superbly silly movie, a magnificent entertainment, and a clever and brilliant machine for making us feel awe, fear, and humor. That is enough. It's pure movie and very little meaning. Did I like it? Yeah, I guess I did, but I wouldn't advise trying to think about it very deeply.

Always ★ ★
PG, 121 m., 1989

Richard Dreyfuss (Pete Sandich), Holly Hunter (Dorinda Durston), Brad Johnson (Ted Baker), John Goodman (Al Yackey), Audrey Hepburn (Hap), Roberts Blossom (Dave), Keith David (Powerhouse), Ed Van Nuys (Nails), Marg Helgenberger (Rachel). Directed by Steven Spielberg and produced by Spielberg, Frank Marshall, and Kathleen Kennedy. Screenplay by Jerry Belson.

Sometimes there are movies that strike you in a certain way, that haunt your memory and provide some of the terms with which you view your own life. For Steven Spielberg and Richard Dreyfuss *A Guy Named Joe* must have been a movie like that. Released in 1944, it starred Spencer Tracy as a pilot who dies in combat and is assigned by heaven to return to earth to inspire the younger pilot (Van Johnson) who will take his place. The kicker is that Tracy also has to stand by helplessly and watch while Johnson falls in love with Tracy's girlfriend (Irene Dunne).

Richard Dreyfuss says he has seen *A Guy Named Joe* at least thirty-five times. Steven Spielberg watched it again and again on the late show when he was a kid, and it was one of the films that inspired him to become a movie director. When Spielberg and Dreyfuss were making *Jaws* in 1974, they quoted individual shots from the movie to each other, and finally, in 1989, they got to make it themselves. The remake is called *Always*, and it takes place now instead of then, and the pilots are fighting forest fires instead of enemy planes, but the basic ideas are all still in place. They do not, unfortunately, add up to much; this is Spielberg's weakest film since *1941*.

Dreyfuss stars as a guy named Pete, who fights fires in the Pacific Northwest and spends his off-duty hours romancing a cute forest service air traffic controller played by Holly Hunter. Pete is a guy who likes to take chances, and there are cliff-hanging scenes early in the movie where he runs out of gas and glides to a landing and another when he nearly crashes into a blazing forest fire. His best pal is a pilot named Al (John Goodman), who also likes to take chances and crashes into some burning trees one day, setting his plane on fire. Pete the daredevil goes into a dive and puts out the fire on Goodman's plane by dumping chemicals all over it, but then Pete's own plane crashes, and he wakes up in a heavenly forest grove presided over by an angel (Audrey Hepburn).

That sets up the second act of the movie, in which poor Pete has to come back to earth and be an invisible inspiration for the youngster (Brad Johnson) who has replaced him. And he has to watch, impotently, as the kid and Pete's former girl fall in love. There is a lot of pathos to be exploited here somewhere, but I didn't feel much; my reaction to this version resembled the critic James Agee's merciless review of the 1944 film, which he admired a good deal less than Spielberg and Dreyfuss. "Joe's affability in the afterlife is enough to discredit the very idea that death in combat amounts to anything more than getting a freshly pressed uniform," he wrote, adding that Tracy "is so unconcerned as he watches Van Johnson palpitate after Irene Dunne that he hardly bothers to take the gum out of his mouth."

One of the problems with *Always* is that the cause itself seems less urgent. It's one thing to sacrifice your life for a buddy in combat and quite another to run unnecessary risks while fighting forest fires. Another problem seems to stem from Spielberg's love of spectacular special effects. The airplanes in this movie—World War II surplus bombers modified to dump chemicals on fires—seem to crash and bludgeon their way through acres of blazing treetops. You'd think a collision with just one of these trees would cause a plane to crash, but the fire fighters in *Always* mow through the woods like airborne Lawnboys. The effects are so spectacular they're not believable. All the movie's risks seem to be same—laughable.

The best casting in the movie is Holly Hunter, as the air traffic controller, bringing some of the same urgency and hard-bitten impatience that made her right for *Broadcast News*. She has a no-nonsense approach that works better than the derring-do and unflappability of Dreyfuss and Goodman. The scenes where the angelic Dreyfuss watches while Hunter and Johnson fall in love are the most awkward in the film; the screenplay gives Dreyfuss flip lines like "That's my girl, pal!" when maybe a hurt look or a silent turn away would have been more effective.

The film's most curious quality, given the fact that it was directed by Spielberg, is a lack of urgency. Even though pilots are flying into the jaws of hell, they have an insouciance, a devil-may-care attitude, that undermines the drama. The feeling of the film is more 1940s than 1980s, which is no doubt what Spielberg was hoping for, but I'm not sure it works. Some of the dialogue seems dated, too, and a lot of it sounds "written" instead of "spoken"—as if these guys learned to talk by studying old pulp magazines. The result is a curiosity: a remake that wasn't remade enough.

Amadeus ★ ★ ★ ★
PG, 158 m., 1984

F. Murray Abraham (Salieri), Tom Hulce (Mozart), Elizabeth Berridge (Constanze), Simon Callow (Emanuel Schikaneder), Roy Dotrice (Leopold Mozart), Christine Ebersole (Katerina Cavalieri), Jeffrey Jones (Joseph I). Directed by Milos Forman and produced by Saul Zaentz. Screenplay by Peter Shaffer.

Milos Forman's *Amadeus* is one of the riskiest gambles a filmmaker has taken in a long time—a lavish movie about Mozart that dares to be anarchic and saucy, and yet still earns the importance of tragedy. This movie is nothing like the dreary educational portraits we're used to seeing about the Great Composers, who come across as cobwebbed profundities weighed down with the burden of genius. This is Mozart as an eighteenth-century Bruce Springsteen, and yet (here is the genius of the movie) there is nothing cheap or unworthy about the approach. *Amadeus* is not only about as much fun as you're likely to have with a movie, it also is disturbingly true. The truth enters in the character of Salieri, who tells the story. He is not a great composer, but he is a good enough composer to know greatness when he hears it, and that is why the music of Mozart breaks his heart. He knows how good it is, he sees how easily Mozart seems to compose it, and he knows that his own work looks pale and silly beside it.

The movie begins with the suggestion that Salieri might have murdered Mozart. The movie examines the ways in which this possibility might be true, and by the end of the film we feel a certain kinship with the weak and jealous Salieri—for few of us can identify with divine genius, but many of us probably have had dark moments of urgent self-contempt in the face of those whose effortless existence illustrates our own inadequacies. Salieri, played with burning intensity by

F. Murray Abraham, sits hunched in a madhouse confessing to a priest. The movie flashes back to his memories of Wolfgang Amadeus Mozart, the child genius who composed melodies of startling originality and who grew up to become a prolific, driven artist.

One of the movie's wisest decisions is to cast Mozart not as a charismatic demigod, not as a tortured superman, but as a goofy, immature, likable kid with a ridiculous laugh. The character is played by Tom Hulce, and if you saw *Animal House*, you may remember him as the fraternity brother who tried to seduce the mayor's daughter, while an angel and a devil whispered in his ears. Hulce would seem all wrong for Mozart, but he is absolutely right, as an unaffected young man filled with delight at his own gifts, unaware of how easily he wounds Salieri and others, tortured only by the guilt of having offended his religious and domineering father.

The film is constructed in wonderfully well-written and acted scenes—scenes so carefully constructed, unfolding with such delight, that they play as perfect compositions of words. Most of them will be unfamiliar to those who have seen Peter Shaffer's brooding play, on which this film is based; Shaffer and Forman have brought light, life, and laughter to the material, and it plays with grace and ease. It's more human than the play; the characters are people, not throbbing packages of meaning. It centers on the relationships in Mozart's life: with his father, his wife, and Salieri. The father never can be pleased, and that creates an undercurrent affecting all of Mozart's success. The wife, played by delightful, buxom Elizabeth Berridge, contains in one person the qualities of a jolly wench and a loving partner: She likes to loll in bed all day, but also gives Mozart good, sound advice and is a forceful person in her own right. The patrons, especially Joseph II, the Austro-Hungarian emperor, are connoisseurs and dilettantes, slow to take to Mozart's new music but enchanted by the audacity with which he defends it. And then there is Salieri (F. Murray Abraham), the gaunt court composer whose special torture is to understand better than anybody else how inadequate he is, and how great Mozart is.

The movie was shot on location in Forman's native Czechoslovakia, and it looks exactly right; it fits its period comfortably, perhaps because Prague still contains so

many streets and squares and buildings that could be directly from the Vienna of Mozart's day. Perhaps his confidence in his locations gave Forman the freedom to make Mozart slightly *out* of period. Forman directed the film version of *Hair*, and Mozart in this movie seems to share a spirit with some of the characters from *Hair*. Mozart's wigs do not look like everybody else's. They have just the slightest suggestion of punk, just the smallest shading of pink. Mozart seems more a child of the 1960s than of any other age, and this interpretation of his personality—he was an irreverent proto-hippie who trusted, if you will, his own vibes—sounds risky, but works.

I have not mentioned the music. There's probably no need to. The music provides the understructure of the film, strong, confident, above all, *clear* in a way that Salieri's simple muddles only serve to illustrate. There are times when Mozart speaks the words of a child, but then the music says the same things in the language of the gods, and all is clear.

Amadeus is a magnificent film, full and tender and funny and charming—and, at the end, sad and angry, too, because in the character of Salieri it has given us a way to understand not only greatness, but our own lack of it. This movie's fundamental question, I think, is whether we can learn to be grateful for the happiness of others, and that, of course, is a test for sainthood. How many movies ask such questions and succeed in being fun, as well?

Amarcord ★ ★ ★ ★
R, 127 m., 1974

Magali Noel (Gradisca), Bruno Zamin (Titta), Pupella Maggio (His Mother), Armando Drancia (His Father), Giuseppe Lanigro (His Grandfather), Nando Orfei (Pataca), Chiccio Ingrassia (Uncle Teo), Luigi Rossi (Lawyer). Directed by Federico Fellini and produced by Iranco Cristaldi. Screenplay by Fellini.

Federico Fellini's *Amarcord* takes us back to the small Italian town of his birth and young manhood, and gives us a joyful, bawdy, virtuoso portrait of the people he remembers there. He includes a character undoubtedly meant to be young Federico—earnest, awkward, yearning with all the poignancy of adolescent lust after the town beauties. But the movie's not an autobiography of a character. It's the story of the town itself.

We see it first when the dandelion seeds

blow in from the fields, signaling the arrival of spring. The townspeople gather in the piazza to build a ceremonial bonfire and burn the witch of winter, and as they dance around the flames in one of Fellini's beloved processions, we get to know them.

They're of all sizes, sexes, and ages, but they're bound together by their transparent simplicity and a strain of cheerful vulgarity. Fellini likes their weaknesses as much as their virtues, and gives us the pompous lawyer, the egotistical theater owner (who cultivates a resemblance to Ronald Colman), the buxom beautician Gradisca flaunting her delightful derrière, and especially the lustful adolescents and their tormenting fantasies.

Fellini also gives us, in a much more subtle way, some notion of the way fascist Italy of the early 1930s helped to shape these people. In an authoritarian system, the individual has fewer choices to make, and there's a temptation to surrender the responsibilities of freedom. The townspeople are almost children in their behavior, taking delight in the simple joys of eating and making love and parading around the square and gossiping about each other and about the hypnotic Gradisca. Fellini implies that this simple behavior is nourished by a system that encourages a mindless going along—but *Amarcord* isn't a political movie. It is a memory, fond but merciless, of how it was in Italy at a certain time.

It's also absolutely breathtaking filmmaking. Fellini has ranked for a long time among the five or six greatest directors in the world, and of them all, he's the natural. Bergman achieves his greatness through thought and soul-searching, Hitchcock built with meticulous craftsmanship, and Bunuel used his fetishes and fantasies to construct barbed jokes about humanity. But Fellini . . . well, moviemaking for him seems almost effortless, like breathing, and he can orchestrate the most complicated scenes with purity and ease. He's the Willie Mays of movies.

He did hit upon hard critical times, though. After the towering success of *La Dolce Vita* and *8½*, and such 1950s landmarks as *La Strada* and *I Vitelloni*, he began to indulge himself (his critics said). *Juliet of the Spirits* was too fantastical and structureless, and *Satyricon* was an exercise in excess, and *The Clowns* was really only a TV show, and *Fellini Roma* was episodic—a great director spinning out sequences that contained brilliance, yes, but no purpose or direction.

I couldn't agree with those criticisms. I find Fellini's magic spellbinding even when he's only marking time, as he was to some extent in *Roma*. But now, with *Amarcord*, Fellini returns to the very top of his form. And he has the last laugh on the critics of his "structureless" films. Because *Amarcord* seems at first to be a series of self-contained episodes and then reveals a structure so organic and yet so effortless that at its end, we can only marvel at this triumph over ordinary movie forms.

And we can marvel, too, at how universal *Amarcord* is. This is a movie for everybody, even those who hardly ever see foreign or "art" films. Fellini's greatest achievement, in my opinion, was *8½*. But that was a difficult film that revealed its meaning only after a good deal of thought and repeated viewings.

Amarcord, on the other hand, is a totally accessible film. It deals directly, hilariously, and sometimes poignantly with the good people of this small town (actually Fellini's birthplace, Rimini). It's no more complicated than they are, it understands them inside-out, and the audiences I've seen it with (three times) have been moved to horse-laughs, stilled by moments of beauty, and then brought back almost to tears. It's not only a great movie, it's a great joy to see.

Someone once remarked that Fellini's movies are filled with symbols, but they're all obvious symbols. At the beginning of *La Dolce Vita*, for example, he wanted to symbolize the gulf between modern, decadent Rome and its history as the center of the Church, so he gave a statue of Christ being helicoptered by pilots who wave and whistle at girls sunning themselves in bikinis. The scene says everything it needs to say, openly and with great economy.

Amarcord is obvious in that way, with a showman's flair for the right effect. There is a night, for example, when all the people of the town get into their boats and sail out to wait for the great new Italian liner to pass by. And when it comes, it towers hundreds of feet above the waves and has thousands of portholes—and is, of course, only a prop built by the special-effects men. It drifts away into invisibility like a candle dying out. The image is of Italy itself in the 1930s: all grandeur and pomp and nationalism, but with an insubstantial soul.

The movie is filled with moments like that, and they're just right. But then there are moments of inexplicable, almost mystical beauty, as when the dandelion seeds drift in on the wind, or when an old lady sweeps up the ashes of the bonfire, or when a peacock spreads its tail feathers in the snow. At moments like that we're almost blinded with delight. Hitchcock once said he wanted to play his audiences like a piano. Fellini requires the entire orchestra.

American Flyers ★ ★ ½
PG-13, 113 m., 1985

Kevin Costner (Marcus), David Grant (David), Rae Dawn Chong (Sarah), Alexandra Paul (Becky), Janice Rule (Mrs. Sommers), John Amos (Dr. Conrad), Doi Johnson (Randolph), Luca Bercovici (Muzzin). Directed by John Badham and produced by Gareth Wigan and Paula Weinstein. Screenplay by Steve Tesich.

American Flyers tells the story of a grueling bicycle race named "The Hell of the West" and of the grueling relationships within a sick family. That is apparently too much for the movie to deal with, and so we get a bike race surrounded by giant unanswered questions. This is one of those stories timed so that all of the personal crises come to a climax at the finish line, and maybe the approach would work if there weren't so many enormous inconsistencies and loose ends and puzzlements.

The movie stars David Grant as an eighteen-year-old in St. Louis who trains on his bicycle every day, hoping someday to be as good a racer as his older brother. Kevin Costner is the big brother, a doctor in Madison, and Janice Rule is their mother. A painful dinner scene at the beginning of the movie sets up the conflict in the family, caused because the father died painfully and the mother apparently did nothing during his last two weeks on earth to make his passing less painful. The movie never spells out what she didn't do, but that's only the first of many mysteries.

The father died of a stroke from a weakened blood vessel in the brain. Now Costner fears that Grant may have the same condition. He takes him to Madison and runs him through a series of tests, which do indeed indicate the family condition. Then he decides not to tell him, and the two brothers set out by van to compete in the Hell of the West race, in Colorado. Meanwhile, we meet Costner's girlfriend (Rae Dawn Chong), and along the way they pick up a hitchhiker (Alexandra Paul) who pairs off with Grant.

The race then becomes several showdowns. The brothers must compete against the other racers, and also against the shadow of death. Their main competition comes from a mean SOB named Muzzin (Luca Bercovici), who used to be married to Rae Dawn Chong. The race is run in three stages, and in the second stage, the older brother begins to bleed from the nose and lose his orientation. So then it's up to the kid brother to win the race.

That leaves us with certain problems.

1. Does the older brother have the family condition, or only a nosebleed? I ask because after the frightening scene where he loses control and almost dies, he is taken, not to a hospital, but to his hotel room.

2. Is Muzzin as mean as he seems? I ask because he is cruel to Chong prior to the race and threatens to make her boyfriend "bleed." Then, after Costner's illness, he is tender toward Chong and she is sweet toward him. Then he tries to kill Grant.

3. What's with the mother? Since we never know what she did, or didn't, do during her husband's last weeks, we don't know how to read her. But she turns up for the finish of the race, and there is a reconciliation which is happy or not, depending on issues we don't understand.

Against these large and troubling matters, which probably indicate that many key scenes were cut from the movie, there are several good things to consider. The bicycle race is brilliantly photographed, and very exciting, despite the fact that we can easily guess who will win. The performances are all interesting, especially Rae Dawn Chong's sweet patience as the girlfriend. There are some great supporting characters, including John Amos as Grant's trainer and Doi Johnson as his chubby teen-age son who hates to exercise and dreams of being the first black bowling star. But the movie is shaky at the core, because it tries to tap-dance around its own central issues.

American Gigolo ★ ★ ★ ½
R, 117 m., 1980

Richard Gere (Julian), Lauren Hutton (Michelle), Hector Elizondo (Sunday), Nina Van Pallandt (Anne), Bill Duke (Leon Jaimes), Brian Davies (Stratton). Directed by Paul Schrader and produced by Jerry Bruckheimer. Screenplay by Schrader.

The bare outline of its plot makes *American Gigolo* sound like a fairly sleazy package: A

Hollywood male prostitute is framed in a kinky murder case, tracks down the pimp who's responsible for the framing, watches in horror as the pimp himself is killed, and then finds himself faced with prison unless the wife of a senator provides him with an alibi. This is strong stuff—almost sensational enough for daytime soap opera.

But the film *American Gigolo* is a stylish and surprisingly poignant handling of this material. The experiences in the film may be alien to us, but the emotions of the characters are not: Julian Kay, the gigolo of the title, is played by Richard Gere as tender, vulnerable, and a little dumb. We care about him. His business—making love to rich women of a certain age—allows him to buy the baubles by which Beverly Hills measures success, and he has his Mercedes, his expensive wardrobe, his antique vases, his entrée to country clubs.

But he says he's in business for reasons other than money, and we believe him, if only because he hardly seems to value his possessions as anything other than props. He feels a sense of satisfaction when he makes a middle-aged woman happy, he says. He seems to see himself as a cross between a sexual surrogate and a therapist, and the movie does, too: Why, he's hardly a whore at all, not even counting his heart of gold.

The movie sentimentalizes on this point, setting up the character of Julian Kay as so sympathetic that we forgive him his profession. That's a tactic that *American Gigolo*'s writer and director, Paul Schrader, is borrowing from one of his own heroes, the French director Robert Bresson, whose *Pickpocket* makes a criminal into an antihero. Schrader is setting the stage for the key relationship in the film, between Julian and the senator's wife (Lauren Hutton).

He tries to pick her up in an exclusive restaurant, but breaks off their conversation when he decides she's not a likely client. But she is all *too* likely, and tracks him down to his apartment. They fall in love, at about the time he's being framed for the murder of a Palm Springs socialite, and the movie wants us to believe in the power of love to redeem both characters: Julian learns to love unselfishly, without money, and the woman learns to love honestly, without regard for her husband's position.

This business of redemption would work better if *American Gigolo* had at least a few more scenes developing the relationship between Gere and Hutton: Her character, so central to the movie's upbeat conclusion, isn't seen clearly enough. We aren't shown the steps by which she moves from sex to love with him (unless she's simply been won over by the old earth-shaking orgasm ploy). We aren't given enough detail about their feelings.

That's a weakness, but not a fatal one, because when Schrader cuts away from their relationship, it's to develop a very involving story about the murder, the framing, and the police investigation. The movie has an especially effective performance by Hector Elizondo as a cigar-chomping vice detective who cheerfully admits he thinks Gere is guilty as sin.

Gere tries to find out who's framing him by descending into the Los Angeles sexual underground. Schrader explored this same universe in his previous film, *Hardcore*, but this time he seems more restrained: The sexual netherlands seem less lurid, more commonplace and sad.

The whole movie has a winning sadness about it; take away the story's sensational aspects and what you have is a study in loneliness. Richard Gere's performance is central to that effect, and some of his scenes—reading the morning paper, rearranging some paintings, selecting a wardrobe—underline the emptiness of his life. We leave *American Gigolo* with the curious feeling that if women weren't paying this man to sleep with them, he'd be paying them: He needs the human connection and he has a certain shyness, a loner quality, that makes it easier for him when love seems to be just another deal.

American Graffiti ★ ★ ★ ★
PG, 112 m., 1973

Ron Howard (Steve), Cindy Williams (Laurie), Richard Dreyfuss (Curt), Paul Le Mat (John), Mackenzie Phillips (Carol), Charles Martin Smith (Terry), Candy Clark (Debbie), Wolfman Jack (Disc Jockey). Directed by George Lucas and produced by Francis Ford Coppola. Screenplay by Lucas, Gloria Katz, and Willard Huyck.

My first car was a '54 Ford and I bought it for $435. It wasn't scooped, channeled, shaved, decked, pinstriped, or chopped, and it didn't have duals, but its hubcaps were a wonder to behold.

On weekends my friends and I drove around downtown Urbana—past the Princess Theater, past the courthouse—sometimes stopping for a dance at the youth center or a hamburger at the Steak 'n' Shake ("In Sight, It Must Be Right"). And always we listened to Dick Biondi on WLS. Only two years earlier, WLS had been the Prairie Farmer Station; now it was the voice of rock all over the Midwest.

When I went to see George Lucas's *American Graffiti* that whole world—a world that now seems incomparably distant and innocent—was brought back with a rush of feeling that wasn't so much nostalgia as culture shock. Remembering my high school generation, I can only wonder at how unprepared we were for the loss of innocence that took place in America with the series of hammer blows beginning with the assassination of President Kennedy.

The great divide was November 22, 1963, and nothing was ever the same again. The teen-agers in *American Graffiti* are, in a sense, like that cartoon character in the magazine ads: the one who gives the name of his insurance company, unaware that an avalanche is about to land on him. The options seemed so simple then: to go to college, or to stay home and look for a job and cruise Main Street and make the scene.

The options were simple, and so was the music that formed so much of the way we saw ourselves. *American Graffiti*'s sound track is papered from one end to the other with Wolfman Jack's nonstop disc jockey show, that's crucial and absolutely right. The radio was on every waking moment. A character in the movie only realizes his car, parked nearby, has been stolen when he hears the music stop: He didn't hear the car being driven away.

The music was as innocent as the time. Songs like "Sixteen Candles" and "Gonna Find Her" and "The Book of Love" sound touchingly naive today; nothing prepared us for the decadence and the aggression of rock only a handful of years later. The Rolling Stones of 1972 would have blown WLS off the air in 1962.

American Graffiti acts almost as a milestone to show us how far (and in many cases how tragically) we have come. Stanley Kauffmann, who liked it, complained in the *New Republic* that Lucas had made a film more fascinating to the generation now between thirty and forty than it could be for other generations, older or younger.

But it isn't the age of the characters that matters; it's the time they inhabited. Whole cultures and societies have passed since

1962. *American Graffiti* is not only a great movie but a brilliant work of historical fiction; no sociological treatise could duplicate the movie's success in remembering exactly how it was to be alive at that cultural instant.

On the surface, Lucas has made a film that seems almost artless; his teen-agers cruise Main Street and stop at Mel's Drive-In and listen to Wolfman Jack on the radio and neck and lay rubber and almost convince themselves their moment will last forever. But the film's buried structure shows an innocence in the process of being lost, and as its symbol Lucas provides the elusive blonde in the white Thunderbird—the vision of beauty always glimpsed at the next intersection, the end of the next street.

Who is she? And did she really whisper "I love you" at the last traffic signal? In 8½, Fellini used Claudia Cardinale as his mysterious angel in white, and the image remains one of his best; but George Lucas knows that for one brief afternoon of American history angels drove Thunderbirds and could possibly be found at Mel's Drive-In tonight . . . or maybe tomorrow night, or the night after.

An American Werewolf in London ★ ★
R, 95 m., 1981

David Naughton (David), Griffin Dunne (Jack), Jenny Agutter (Alex), John Woodvine (Dr. Hirsch). Directed by John Landis and produced by George Folsey, Jr. Screenplay by Landis.

An American Werewolf in London seems curiously unfinished, as if director John Landis spent all his energy on spectacular set pieces and then didn't want to bother with things like transitions, character development, or an ending. The movie has sequences that are spellbinding, and then long stretches when nobody seems sure what's going on. There are times when the special effects almost wipe the characters off the screen. It's weird. It's not a very good film, and it falls well below Landis's work in the anarchic *National Lampoon's Animal House* and the rambunctious *Blues Brothers*. Landis never seems very sure whether he's making a comedy or a horror film, so he winds up with genuinely funny moments acting as counterpoint to the gruesome undead. Combining horror and comedy is an old tradition (my favorite example is *The Bride of Franken-*

stein), but the laughs and the blood coexist very uneasily in this film.

One of the offscreen stars of the film is Rick Baker, the young makeup genius who created the movie's wounds, gore, and werewolves. His work is impressive, yes, but unless you're single-mindedly interested in special effects, *American Werewolf* is a disappointment. And even the special effects, good as they are, come as an anticlimax if you're a *really* dedicated horror fan, because if you are, you've already seen this movie's high point before: the onscreen transformation of a man into a werewolf was anticipated in *The Howling*, in which the special effects were done by a Baker protegé named Rob Bottin.

The movie's plot involves two young American students (David Naughton and Griffin Dunne), who are backpacking across the English moors. They stumble into a country pub where everyone is ominously silent, and then one guy warns them to beware the full moon and stick to the road. They don't, and are attacked by werewolves. Dunne is killed, Naughton is severely wounded, and a few days later in the hospital Naughton is visited by the decaying cadaver of Dunne—who warns him that he'll turn into a werewolf at the full moon. Naughton ignores the warning, falls in love with his nurse (Jenny Agutter), and moves in with her when he's discharged from the hospital. Then follows a series of increasingly gruesome walk-ons by Dunne, who begs Naughton to kill himself before the full moon. Naughton doesn't, turns into a werewolf, and runs amok through London. That gives director Landis his chance to stage a spectacular multi-car traffic accident in Piccadilly Circus; crashes have been his specialty since the homecoming parade in *Animal House* and the nonstop carnage in *Blues Brothers*.

The best moments in *American Werewolf* probably belong to Dunne, who may be a decaying cadaver but keeps right on talking like a college student: "Believe me," he says at Naughton's bedside, "this isn't a whole lot of fun." The scene in which Naughton turns into a werewolf is well done, with his hands elongating and growing claws, and his face twisting into a snout and fangs. But it's as if John Landis thought the technology would be enough. We never get a real feeling for the characters, we never really believe the places (especially that awkwardly phony pub and its stagy customers), and we are particularly

disappointed by the ending. I won't reveal the ending, such as it is, except to say it's so sudden, arbitrary, and anticlimactic that, although we are willing for the movie to be over, we still can't quite believe it.

Angel Heart ★ ★ ★ ½
R, 113 m., 1987

Mickey Rourke (Harry Angel), Robert De Niro (Louis Cyphre), Lisa Bonet (Epiphany Proudfoot), Charlotte Rampling (Margaret Krusemark), Brownie McGhee (Toots Sweet), Stocker Fontelieu (Ethan Krusemark). Directed by Alan Parker and produced by Alan Marshall and Elliott Kastner. Screenplay by Parker.

After everything is all over and the dust has settled and the blood has dried, it is possible to unsort the plot of *Angel Heart* and see that it's really fairly simple. But it doesn't feel that way at the time. It has the unsettled logic of a nightmare, in which nothing fits and everything seems inevitable and there are a lot of arrows in the air and they are all flying straight at you.

The movie stars Mickey Rourke as Harry Angel, an unwashed private eye who works out of an office that looks like Sam Spade gave it to the Goodwill. He gets a call to visit some kind of devil-worship cult in Harlem, where a strange man wants to talk to him. The man's name is Louis Cyphre (Robert De Niro), and he wants Angel to track down a missing person for him. Angel takes the case for five grand and follows a trail that is littered with stale leads and fresh corpses.

This sounds like a million other private-eye movies, and, in a way, it is. A few things make it different: a sly sense of humor, good acting and directing, and a sudden descent into the supernatural as Harry Angel discovers the horrifying true nature of his investigation.

The movie is by Alan Parker, a director who has vowed to work in every genre before he dies. After *Angel Heart*, he can cross two off his list: private-eye movies and supernatural horror films. Parker's films are always made with great gusto, as if he were in up to his elbows and taking no hostages.

He enjoys what timid folks might call stylistic excess, and that's what got him in trouble with the MPAA ratings board over a scene involving Rourke and Lisa Bonet, who plays a young Louisiana woman who holds the secrets of the past. They meet in a leaky hotel room during a rainstorm, and while they make love the raindrops from the ceiling turn to blood. In the context of the movie, the blood makes perfect sense, although the scene had to be trimmed to qualify the movie for an R rating. It has been reinstated, however, in an unrated version of the video.

The scene is consistent with the whole film, which is sensuous and depraved. The De Niro character sets the tone, with his sharp, pointed fingernails and his elegant black suits. De Niro must have had fun preparing for the character: He uses a neatly trimmed black beard, slicked-back hair, and tricks of lighting and makeup to make himself look uncannily like Martin Scorsese, his favorite director. Given what we eventually discover about the character, it's a wicked homage.

Rourke occupies the center of the film like a violent unmade bed. No other actor, with the possible exception of France's Gerard Depardieu, has made such a career out of being a slob. He looks unshaven, unwashed, hungover, and desperate, and that's at the beginning of the film, before things start to go wrong. By the end, he is a man whose nerves are screaming for help.

His odyssey in *Angel Heart* takes him from New York to Algiers, Louisiana, a town across from New Orleans that makes the fleshpots of Bourbon Street look like Disneyland. He is advised to go back home by a crusty old blues player (played by the fast-talking Brownie McGhee in a performance that proves Dexter Gordon wasn't the only old musician who could act). But he doesn't listen and gets drawn deeper into bayou country, where he spies on the forbidden rituals of a voodoo cult.

Bonet is the priestess of the cult and plays the role with an abandoned sexuality that you wouldn't have expected after watching her on the "Cosby Show." She was probably right to take this controversial role as her movie debut; it was such a stretch from the Cosby character that it established her as a plausible movie actress.

The movie's final revelations make a weird sense, once we figure them out. This is one of those movies where you rerun the plot in your head, re-interpreting the early scenes in terms of the final shocking revelations. *Angel Heart* is a thriller and a horror movie, but most of all it's an exuberant exercise in style, in which Parker and his actors have fun taking it to the limit.

Angelo My Love ★ ★ ★ ½
R, 91 m., 1983

Angelo Evans, Michael Evans, Steve Tsigonoff, Millie Tsigonoff. Written and directed by Robert Duvall. Associate producer, Gail Youngs.

The late Italian director Vittorio De Sica once said that anyone can play at least one role—himself—better than anybody else possibly could. De Sica illustrated that belief in his late-1940s neo-realist films like *Bicycle Thief*, and now the American actor Robert Duvall proves it again, in a wonderful and unique movie he has written and directed, named *Angelo My Love*. Here is a movie that could not exist without the people who are in it—and of how many movies is that true? The film is about the lives, feuds, rivalries, and dreams of a group of New York Gypsies, and Duvall has recruited real Gypsies to play themselves. His inspiration for the movie came when he saw a young Gypsy boy named Angelo Evans conning a much older woman during an argument on a Manhattan sidewalk.

Duvall thought Angelo belonged in the movies. Having seen the movie, I agree. Here is a street-smart, inventive kid of about eleven or twelve who has some of the moves and some of the cynicism of an experienced con man. ("He's got his tiny macho moves down so pat," David Anson wrote in *Newsweek*, "he's like a child impersonator.") Angelo is the product of a culture that has taught him that the world owes him a living, and he cheerfully agrees. What we sometimes almost forget is that Angelo is also a child, vulnerable and easily wounded, and that a lot of his act is a veneer.

Duvall weaves his story around Angelo. We meet his mother, father, sister, and girlfriend, and a couple of villainous Gypsies who steal a ring that Angelo had intended to present to his future bride. All of these people play themselves, more or less. Angelo's family really is his family; the villains are played by a brother and sister, Steve and Millie Tsigonoff, whom Duvall met in Los Angeles. Although the movie's plot is basically a device for letting us watch the lives of the characters, it's the kind of plot, I suspect, that Gypsies might be able to identify with—involving theft, pride, thwarted justice, and revenge. After the Tsigonoffs steal the ring, there's an ill-advised chase to Canada to get it back (and a wonderful set piece

in a Gypsy camp supposedly under attack by ghosts). Then there's a trial scene in the backroom of an Irish-American bar in Brooklyn. It's all done with great energy and seriousness, even though by the movie's end the ring hardly seems to matter.

Angelo also stars in several fairly self-contained scenes that abundantly illustrate why Duvall found him so fascinating. He makes a defiant mess of his one day in school. He attempts to pick up a pretty country singer who is at least ten years older than he is. He and his sister engage in a long, ingratiating conversation with an old lady in a cafeteria; they want to inveigle her into their mother's fortune-telling parlor, but the lady is a New Yorker and wasn't born yesterday.

All of these scenes have a special magic because we sense that they're real, that they come out of people's lives. *Angelo My Love* is technically a fictional film, but Duvall has worked so close to his sources that it has the conviction of a documentary. Maybe because he's such a good actor, Duvall has been able to listen to his characters, to really see *them* rather than his own notion of how they should move and behave. There are moments in this movie when the camera lingers for an extra moment, and scenes that do not quite dovetail into everything else, and we sense that Duvall left them in because they revealed something about his Gypsies that he had observed and wanted to share.

At the end of the movie we ask ourselves a question the movie does not attempt to answer: What will become of Angelo in the years to come? It's one thing to be a cute, street-wise kid. It's another thing to try to carry that role on through life with you. Angelo might be able to pull it off, but the movie doesn't try to sell us that romanticized hope. Instead, Duvall seems to be suggesting that Angelo is more than a colorful Gypsy kid; that he has real potential as a person, if he can grow out of the trap of his glib mannerisms and is not too badly scarred by his upside-down childhood. Who knows? One day ten years from now, there might be a movie named *Angelo My Friend*.

Annie ★ ★ ★
PG, 128 m., 1982

Aileen Quinn (Annie), Albert Finney (Daddy Warbucks), Carol Burnett (Miss Hannigan), Bernadette Peters (Lily), Ann Reinking (Grace Farrell), Tim Curry (Rooster), Geoffrey Holder (Punjab), Edward Herrmann (F.D.R.).

Directed by John Huston and produced by Ray Stark. Screenplay by Carol Sobieski.

In the abstract, *Annie* is fun. It has lots of movement and color, dance and music, sound and fury. In the particular, it has all sorts of problems, and I guess the only way to really enjoy the movie is to just ignore the particulars. I will nevertheless mention a few particulars. One is the story itself, about how Little Orphan Annie is rescued from a cruel orphanage by a billionaire who wants a Rent-An-Orphan for Christmas. This is said to be a universal story. Critics have written that you just can't help cheering for Annie as she faces the cold world with pluck and courage. I didn't find myself cheering much, though, since Annie didn't seem to need the encouragement; as played by the feisty young Aileen Quinn, she is the sort of child who makes adults run for the hills.

The adventures she gets herself into are likewise questionable. I've never thought of *Oliver!* as a particularly realistic musical, but at least when its little hero said "Please, sir, more food?" there was a hint of truth. *Annie* has been plunged into pure fantasy, into the mindless sort of musical boosterism that plays big for Broadway theater parties but almost always translates to the movie screen as sheer contrivance. *Annie* is not *about* anything. It *contains* lots of subjects (such as cruel orphanages, the Great Depression, scheming conmen, heartless billionaires, and President Franklin Delano Roosevelt) but it isn't *about* them. It's not even really about whether Annie will survive her encounters with them, since the book of this musical is so rigorously machine-made, so relentlessly formula, it's one of those movies where you can amaze your friends by leaving the auditorium, standing blindfolded in the lobby and correctly predicting the outcome.

And yet I sort of enjoyed the movie. I enjoyed the energy that was visible on the screen, and the sumptuousness of the production numbers, and the good humor of several of the performances—especially those by Albert Finney, as Daddy Warbucks, and Carol Burnett, as the wicked orphanage supervisor, Miss Hannigan. Aileen Quinn sort of grew on me, too. She cannot be said to really play a child—at least not the sort of plausible flesh-and-blood child that Henry Thomas creates in *E.T.* But Quinn is talented, can dance well and sing passably, and does not seem to be an overtrained puppet like, say, Ricky Schroeder. She seems more like the kind of kid who will get this acting out of her system and go on to be student body president.

If there is a center to the film, it belongs to Albert Finney. He has a thankless task: He must portray Daddy Warbucks as a self-centered, smug rich man who has everything in the world, except love, and who learns to love through the example of a little girl. This is the sort of role actors kill over—to avoid playing. Albert Finney has the true grit. He's gone through this personality transformation twice; he starred in *Scrooge* in 1970. This time, he even pulls it off, by underplaying. He isn't too aloof at the beginning, and he's not too softhearted at the end. He has a certain detachment. Annie may win his heart, but she'll still have to phone for an appointment.

Will kids like the movie? I honestly don't know. When I was a kid, I didn't much like movies about other kids, maybe because I was jealous (why does *that* kid get to ride a horse in the Derby?). The movie was promoted as a family entertainment, but was it really a family musical, even on the stage? I dunno. I think it was more of a product, a clever concoction of nostalgia, hard-sell sentiment, small children, and cute dogs. The movie is the same mixture as before. It's like some kind of dumb toy that doesn't do anything or go anywhere, but it is fun to watch as it spins mindlessly around and around.

Annie Hall ★ ★ ★ ½
PG, 95 m., 1977

Woody Allen (Alvy Singer), Diane Keaton (Annie Hall), Tony Roberts (Rob), Carol Kane (Allison), Paul Simon (Tony Lacey), Shelley Duvall (Pam), Janet Margolin (Robin), Colleen Dewhurst (Mom Hall). Directed by Woody Allen and produced by Charles H. Joffe. Screenplay by Allen and Marshall Brickman.

Woody Allen's *Annie Hall* explores new dimensions of the persona Allen has constructed in movies, on the stage, and even in a comic strip. We're all familiar by now with "Woody," the overanxious, underachieving intellectual with the inept social life. We've watched him develop from bits in a stand-up comedy routine to a fully developed comic character in the tradition of Chaplin's tramp or Fields's drunk. We know how "Woody" will act in so many situations that we're already laughing before the punch line. Maybe nobody since Jack Benny has been so hilariously predictable.

And yet there's always the realization that "Woody" is a projection of a real Woody Allen. That beneath the comic character is a certain amount of painful truth. That just as W.C. Fields really *was* a drunk, so Woody Allen perhaps really is insecure about his height, shy around girls, routinely incompetent in the daily joust with life.

It's not that the "real" Woody Allen is as hapless as his fictional creation, but that the character draws from life by exaggerating it. *Annie Hall* is the closest Allen has come to dealing with that real material. It's not an autobiography, but we get the notion at times that scenes in the movie have been played before, slightly differently, for real.

Allen plays Alvy Singer, stand-up comic and incurable combination of neurotic and romantic. He's self-consciously a New Yorker, a liberal, a Jew, an intellectual, a seeker after the unattainable, and an expert at *making* it unattainable. One of Alvy Singer's problems is that he understands this all so well. He's not a victim of forces beyond his control, but their author.

And one of the problems he keeps providing for himself is the problem of love. He falls in love too easily, to girls who are right for him in all the little ways and incompatible in all the big ones. His girls tend to reflect the stages he's going through. When he's an Adlai Stevenson liberal in the late 1950s, he marries another one. When he's a romantic ten or fifteen years later, he finds another one, a kookier one. His only trouble is that women are people, not stages.

The movie dares to go into this material a little more seriously and cohesively than is usually the case in an Allen film. *Annie Hall* is a comedy, yes, and there are moments in it as funny as anything Woody has done, but the movie represents a growth on Allen's part. From a filmmaker who would do anything for a laugh, whose primary mission seemed to be to get through the next five minutes, Allen has developed in *Sleeper*, *Love and Death*, and this film into a much more thoughtful and (is it possible?) more mature director.

Maybe that's why *Annie Hall* is called a "nervous romance": because Allen himself is a little nervous about this frankly nostalgic, romantic, and sentimental material. He throws in a few gags (like the hilarious walk-on by Marshall McLuhan) almost to reassure his old fans that all's well at the laugh works.

But he wants to do a lot more this time than just keep us laughing. By looking into some of his own relationships, some of his own patterns, he wants to examine how a personality works.

And so there are two Woody Allens here: Our old pal the original Woody, who's given to making asides directly into the camera, and a new Allen who creates Alvy Singer in his own image and then allows him to behave consistently, even sometimes at the cost of laughs. It's this new Woody who has the nervous romance, the complicated relationship with the would-be nightclub singer Annie Hall (played by Diane Keaton with an interesting mixture of maternal care, genuine love, and absolute craziness).

At the end of the affair, we've learned only two things for certain: That enduring relationships are very likely impossible in this time and place (i.e., New York City during Woody Allen's lifetime), and that life without the search for relationships is unthinkable. In the movie, Woody quotes Groucho Marx's statement that he'd never belong to any club that would accept someone like him as a member. Then Allen muses that maybe he should never get into a relationship in which one of the partners is himself. Tricky, isn't it? And in *Annie Hall* he makes it very funny, and sad, and tricky indeed.

Another 48 HRS ★ ★
R, 102 m., 1990

Eddie Murphy (Reggie Hammond), Nick Nolte (Jack Cates), Brion James (Ben Kehoe), Kevin Tighe (Blake Wilson), Ed O'Ross (Frank Cruise), David Anthony Marshall (Willy Hickok), Andrew Divoff (Cherry Ganz). Directed by Walter Hill and produced by Lawrence Gordon and Robert D. Wachs. Screenplay by John Fasano, Jeb Stuart, and Larry Gross.

You know how sometimes in a dream you'll see these familiar scenes and faces floating in and out of focus, but you're not sure how they connect? *Another 48 HRS* is a movie that feels the same way. The broad outlines are familiar from the original *48 HRS*, and the villains and cops are all basic movie stereotypes. But what exactly is happening here?

Everybody seems to be looking for the Iceman. The Iceman is the criminal mastermind in control of all drug traffic in the San Francisco Bay area. A cop named Cates (Nick Nolte) has been on his trail for years—but every time he gets close, the Iceman slips away. Meanwhile, a convict named Hammond (Eddie Murphy) is about to be released from prison. Maybe he knows who the Iceman is. Maybe he can help Cates. On the other hand, maybe he can't. He sure doesn't want to.

Watching the movie, I was trying to remember the details of the earlier 1982 film. In that one, Nolte was on the trail of some cop killers and he sprung Murphy from prison for forty-eight hours to help him out. They turned into quite a team—the hungover cop and the confident young black man, both suspicious of each other, both learning to be friends. The movie contained the scene that made Murphy into a star, a scene where he walked into a redneck bar, impersonated a police officer, and intimidated everyone with the sheer force of his personality.

In *Another 48 HRS*, years have passed. Nolte has stopped drinking (and also apparently lost his long-suffering girlfriend). Murphy is back in prison, but Nolte is holding $500,000 for him, for when he gets out. Meanwhile, in a shoot-out during a motorcycle race, Nolte kills a man who fired at him. But the other guy's gun disappears, and with no evidence apart from Nolte's troublesome personnel record, his badge is lifted and he's charged with manslaughter.

Meanwhile, there are a bunch of long-haired, leather-jacketed, tattooed motorcycle gang members who cruise the desert blowing people away. They apparently work for a young black man who works for the Iceman. They want Murphy dead—so badly that they try to kill him by opening fire on the prison bus that's returning him to civilization. You might ask why the bus driver couldn't simply push them off the road during the high-speed chase, but that would be too logical a question for this movie, which specializes in confusing and endless action scenes.

There's one crucial difference between this movie and the original: We never get much of an idea of the friendship and camaraderie between Murphy and Nolte. Their idea of friendship boils down to hitting each other as hard as they can, "to even the score." They have no dialogue scenes together of any depth. The plot they're in is so confusing that at one point they simply go back to the prison and ask a long-timer (Bernie Casey) to identify the guy they're after.

He gives them the man's name and address. How does he know all this stuff? Don't even ask.

Meanwhile, back at police headquarters, the cop plot is recycled from dozens of other movies. How often do we have to sit through that scene where the Internal Affairs guy makes the hero hand over his badge and gun? Leaving all the other movies out of it, this was the second time in a few months that Nike Nolte personally had to go through that scene (after *Q & A*). And when the big secret of the Iceman's identity is finally revealed, ask yourself this question: Would the drug kingpin of the entire Bay Area really need to keep the daytime job?

Another 48 HRS was directed by Walter Hill, who also did the previous movie, and who knows how to shoot violence so it looks convincing, although here he stages a scene which sets some kind of indoor record for the amount of glass that is broken. Hill and his writers, John Fasano, Jeb Stuart, and Larry Gross, have not exactly extended themselves to create a new and original story for this movie, and the big set piece once again involves Murphy and Nolte inside a redneck bar. It's an aimless scene with a lot of loose ends, a reminder of how well the earlier scene worked.

What holds the movie together to some extent is the simple star presence of Murphy and Nolte, who are not given great dialogue or much of a plot, but who have a certain magnetism that's interesting to watch. Murphy in particular needed this movie, I think, as a corrective after his unfortunate *Harlem Nights*—a movie that was seen by a great many people, many of whom didn't enjoy it all that much. If it does nothing else, *Another 48 HRS* reminds us that Murphy is a big, genuine talent.

Another Woman ★ ★ ★ ★
PG, 81 m., 1988

Gena Rowlands (Marion), Philip Bosco (Sam), Betty Buckley (Cathy), Martha Plimpton (Laura), Blythe Danner (Lydia), Sandy Dennis (Claire), Mia Farrow (Hope), Gene Hackman (Harry), John Houseman (Marion's Father), Ian Holm (Ben). Written and directed by Woody Allen. Produced by Robert Greenhut.

Film is the most voyeuristic medium, but rarely have I experienced this fact more sharply than while watching Woody Allen's

Another Woman. This is a film almost entirely composed of moments that should be private. At times, privacy is violated by characters in the film. At other times, we invade the privacy of the characters. And the central character is our accomplice, standing beside us, speaking in our ear, telling us of the painful process she is going through.

This character is named Marion Post (Gena Rowlands), and she is the kind of woman who might feel qualified to advise the rest of us how to organize our lives by "balancing" the demands of home, job, spouse, and friends. She is fearsomely self-contained, well-organized, sane, efficient, and intelligent. *Another Woman* is about the emotional compromises she has had to make in order to earn that description.

She is the head of a university department of philosophy. She is married to a physician, and, childless, has a good relationship with her husband's teen-age daughter from an earlier marriage. She dresses in a fashion that is so far above criticism as to almost be above notice. She is writing a book, and to find a place free of distractions, she rents an office in a downtown building. She tells us some of these details on the sound track, describing her life with a dry detachment that seems to hide an edge of concern.

The office is in one of those older buildings with a tricky ventilation system. Sitting at her desk one day, Marion discovers that she can hear every word of a therapy session taking place in the office of the psychiatrist who has his office next door. At first she blocks out the sound by placing pillows against the ventilation outlet. Then, frankly, she begins to listen.

While he is establishing this device of the overheard conversations, Allen does an interesting thing. Not only can Marion Post (and the rest of us) easily eavesdrop on the conversations, but when the pillows are placed against the air shaft, they completely block out every word. The choice—to listen, or not to listen—is presented so clearly that it is unreal. It's too neat, comprehensive, final. Although most of the scenes in *Another Woman* are clearly realistic, I think the treatment of sound in the office is a signal from Allen that the office is intended to be read in another way—as the orderly interior of Marion Post's mind, perhaps. And the cries coming in through the grillwork on the wall are the sounds of real emotions that she has put out of her mind for years. They are her nightmares.

During the course of the next few weeks, Marion Post will find the walls of her mind tumbling down. She will discover that she intimidates people, and that they do not love her as much as she thinks, nor trust her to share their secrets. She will find that she knows little about her husband, little about her own emotions, little about why she married this cold, adulterous doctor instead of another man who truly loved her.

If this journey of discovery sounds familiar, it is because *Another Woman* has a great many elements in common with Ingmar Bergman's *Wild Strawberries*, the story of an elderly doctor whose day begins with a nightmare and continues with a voyage of discovery. The doctor finds that his loved ones have ambiguous feelings about him, that his "efficiency" is seen as sternness, and that he made a mistake when he did not accept passionate love when it was offered to him. Allen's film is not a remake of *Wild Strawberries* in any sense, but a meditation on the same theme—the story of a thoughtful person, thoughtfully discovering why she might have benefited from being a little less thoughtful.

There is a temptation to say that Gena Rowlands has never been better than in this movie, but that would not be true. She is an extraordinary actor who is usually this good, and has been this good before, especially in some of the films of her husband, John Cassavetes. What is new here is the whole emotional tone of her character.

Great actors and great directors sometimes find a common emotional ground, so that the actor becomes an instrument playing the director's song. Cassavetes is a wild, passionate spirit, emotionally disorganized, insecure, and tumultuous, and Rowlands has reflected that personality in her characters for him—white-eyed women on the edge of stampede or breakdown. Allen is introspective, considerate, apologetic, formidably intelligent, and controls people through thought and words rather than through physicality and temper. Rowlands now mirrors that personality, revealing in the process how the Cassavetes performances were indeed *acting* and not some kind of ersatz documentary reality. To see *Another Woman* is to get an insight into how good an actress Rowlands has been all along.

I have not said much about the movie's story. I had better not. More than with many thrillers, *Another Woman* depends upon the audience's gradual discovery of what happens. There are some false alarms along the way. The patient in the psychiatrist's office (Mia Farrow), pregnant and confused, turns up in the "outside" world of the Rowlands character, and we expect more to come of that meeting than ever does. Some critics have asked why the Rowlands and Farrow characters did not interact more deeply—but the whole point is that the philosopher has suppressed everything inside of her that could connect to that weeping, pregnant other woman.

There is also an actual "other woman" in the film, as well as a dry, correct performance by Ian Holm as a man who must have a wife so he can be unfaithful to her. Gene Hackman is precisely cast as the earlier lover whose passion was rejected by Marion, and there is another of Martha Plimpton's bright, somehow sad, teen-agers. In the movie's single most effective scene, Betty Buckley plays Holm's first wife, turning up unexpectedly at a social event and behaving "inappropriately," while Holm firmly tries to make her disappear (this scene is so observant of how people handle social embarrassment that it plays like an open wound).

In this last performance before his death, John Houseman finally cut loose from all the appearances of robust immortality and allowed himself to be seen as old, feeble, and spotted—and with immense presence. (In a scene involving the character when he was younger, David Ogden Stiers makes an uncanny Houseman double.)

Another Woman ends a little abruptly. I expected another chapter. And yet I would not have enjoyed a tidy conclusion to this material, because the one thing we learn about Marion Post is that she has got her package so tightly wrapped that she may never live long enough to rummage through its contents. At least by the end of the film she is beginning to remember what it was that she boxed up so carefully, so many years before.

Apocalypse Now ★ ★ ★ ★
R, 139 m., 1979

Marlon Brando (Colonel Kurtz), Robert Duvall (Lieutenant Colonel Kilgore), Martin Sheen (Captain Willard), Frederic Forrest (Chef), Albert Hall (Chief), Sam Bottoms (Lance), Larry Fishburne (Clean), Dennis Hopper (Photographer). Directed and produced by Francis Ford Coppola. Screenplay by John Milius and Coppola.

In his book *The Films of My Life*, the French director François Truffaut makes a curious statement. He used to believe, he says, that a successful film had to simultaneously express "an idea of the world and an idea of cinema." But now, he writes: "I demand that a film express either the joy of making cinema or the agony of making cinema. I am not at all interested in anything in between; I am not interested in all those films that do not pulse."

It may seem strange to begin a review of Francis Coppola's *Apocalypse Now* with those words, but consider them for a moment and they apply perfectly to this sprawling film. The critics who rejected Coppola's film mostly did so on Truffaut's earlier grounds: They had arguments with the ideas about the world and the war in *Apocalypse Now*, or they disagreed with the very idea of a film that cost $31 million to make and was then carted all over the world by a filmmaker *still* uncertain whether he had the right ending.

That "other" film on the screen—the one we debate because of its ideas, not its images—is the one that caused so much controversy about *Apocalypse Now*. We all read that Coppola took as his inspiration the Joseph Conrad novel *Heart of Darkness*, and that he turned Conrad's journey up the Congo into a metaphor for another journey up a jungle river, into the heart of the Vietnam War. We all read Coppola's grandiose statements (the most memorable: "This isn't a film about Vietnam. This film *is* Vietnam."). We heard that Marlon Brando was paid $1 million for his closing scenes, and that Coppola gambled his personal fortune to finish the film, and, heaven help us, we even read a journal by the director's wife in which she disclosed her husband's ravings and infidelities.

But all such considerations are far from the reasons why *Apocalypse Now* is a good and important film—a masterpiece, I believe. Now, when Coppola's budget and his problems have long been forgotten, *Apocalypse* stands, I think, as a grand and grave and insanely inspired gesture of filmmaking—of moments that are operatic in their style and scope, and of other moments so silent we can almost hear the director thinking to himself.

I should at this moment make a confession: I am not particularly interested in the "ideas" in Coppola's film. Critics of *Apocalypse* have said that Coppola was foolish to translate *Heart of Darkness*, that Conrad's vision had nothing to do with Vietnam, and that Coppola was simply borrowing Conrad's cultural respectability to give a gloss to his own disorganized ideas. The same objection was made to the hiring of Brando: Coppola was hoping, according to this version, that the presence of Brando as an icon would distract us from the emptiness of what he's given to say.

Such criticisms are made by people who indeed are plumbing *Apocalypse Now* for its ideas, and who are as misguided as the veteran Vietnam correspondents who breathlessly reported that *The Deer Hunter* was not "accurate." What idea or philosophy could we expect to find in *Apocalypse Now*—and what good would it really do, at this point after the Vietnam tragedy, if Brando's closing speeches *did* have the "answers"? Like all great works of art about war, *Apocalypse Now* essentially contains only one idea or message, the not-especially-enlightening observation that war is hell. We do not see Coppola's movie for that insight—something Coppola, but not some of his critics, knows well.

Coppola also well knows (and demonstrated in the *Godfather* films) that movies aren't especially good at dealing with abstract ideas—for those you'd be better off turning to the written word—but they *are* superb for presenting moods and feelings, the look of a battle, the expression on a face, the mood of a country. *Apocalypse Now* achieves greatness not by analyzing our "experience in Vietnam," but by re-creating, in characters and images, something of that experience.

An example: The scene in which Robert Duvall, as a crazed lieutenant colonel, leads his troops in a helicopter assault on a village is, quite simply, the best movie battle scene ever filmed. It's simultaneously numbing, depressing, and exhilarating: As the rockets jar from the helicopters and spring through the air, we're elated like kids for a half-second, until the reality of the consequences sinks in. Another wrenching scene—in which the crew of Martin Sheen's Navy patrol boat massacres the Vietnamese peasants in a small boat—happens with such sudden, fierce, senseless violence that it forces us to understand for the first time how such things could happen.

Coppola's *Apocalypse Now* is filled with moments like that, and the narrative device of the journey upriver is as convenient for him as it was for Conrad. That's really why he uses it, and not because of literary cross-references for graduate students to catalog. He takes the journey, strings episodes along it, leads us at last to Brando's awesome, stinking hideaway . . . and then finds, so we've all heard, that he doesn't have an ending. Well, Coppola *doesn't* have an ending, if we or he expected the closing scenes to pull everything together and make sense of it. Nobody should have been surprised. *Apocalypse Now* doesn't tell any kind of a conventional story, doesn't have a thought-out message for us about Vietnam, has no answers, and thus needs no ending. The way the film ends now, with Brando's fuzzy, brooding monologues and the final violence, feels much more satisfactory than any conventional ending possibly could.

What's great in the film, and what will make it live for many years and speak to many audiences, is what Coppola achieves on the levels Truffaut was discussing: the moments of agony and joy in making cinema. Some of those moments come at the same time; remember again the helicopter assault and its unsettling juxtaposition of horror and exhilaration. Remember the weird beauty of the massed helicopters lifting over the trees in the long shot, and the insane power of Wagner's music, played loudly during the attack, and you feel what Coppola was getting at: Those moments as common in life as art, when the whole huge grand mystery of the world, so terrible, so beautiful, seems to hang in the balance.

See also Hearts of Darkness, *a documentary on the making of* Apocalypse Now.

The Applegates ★ ★
R, 90 m., 1991

Ed Begley, Jr. (Dick Applegate), Stockard Channing (Jane Applegate), Dabney Coleman (Aunt Bea), Bobby Jacoby (Johnny Applegate), Cami Copper (Sally Applegate), Glenn Shadix (Greg Samson). Directed by Michael Lehmann and produced by Denise Di Novi. Screenplay by Redbeard Simmons and Michael Lehmann.

The Applegates is yet another attempt to find humor behind the façade of middle-class suburbia, by revealing that a normal family is secretly bizarre. For some reason these movies almost always center around eating habits. In *Parents*, the parents ate human flesh; in *Mermaids*, Mom prepared marshmallow-kabobs; and in *Edward Scissorhands*, the hero had lots of trouble picking up his food.

Now we have a family of insects in human form. "Clean up your sugar," Mom tells the kids, "and for dessert you can have some rancid trash I found in a dumpster behind the 7-11."

The Applegates, we learn, are insects from deep in the Amazon rain forest—a rare species that can mimic the forms and customs of their hosts, while dining off their garbage. They are such consummate masters of disguise, indeed, that even their pet is special; it's an insect that can assume the shape of a dog.

The movie involves the attempts of the Applegates to blend into suburban life, despite the suspicions of their next-door neighbor, an exterminator. Like the pod people in *Invasion of the Body Snatchers*, they presumably have plans to take over society, replacing one family at a time until everyone is an insect and the charade can be discontinued.

Dick Applegate is played by Ed Begley, Jr.—tall, blond, and vaguely Gary Cooperish—who is always being cast as a typical American in movies where the typical is bizarre. Remember him as one of Kathleen Turner's goofy brothers-in-law in *The Accidental Tourist*, or Roseanne Barr's husband in *She-Devil*? This time he's a stern team leader who delivers dinnertime lectures on the correct mispronunciation of "nuclear." Jane Applegate is Stockard Channing in a perky blond wig, like Doris Day with a nasty little secret. Dabney Coleman makes a cameo appearance as "Aunt Bea," an insect who disguises itself as a woman, but forgets that human women do not have Dabney Coleman moustaches.

The Aunt Bea joke gets old in a hurry, and indeed *The Applegates* is a one-joke movie. If you think it is funny that insects would serve a large bar of chocolate in place of a pot roast, then you will laugh, once, when they do so, but as the same kinds of jokes are replayed over and over; the movie gradually grows dispiriting.

The Applegates does, however, raise a larger question: Why is it that so many filmmakers have assumed that the most grotesque and unspeakable practices go on behind the drawn blinds of suburbia? Are these movies being made for suburban high school kids, many of whom have probably always suspected that their neighborhoods are populated by insects in disguise? Who do we have to thank for the vision behind, or beneath, this movie?

The answer, I am afraid, is that David Lynch has indirectly inspired many dirty-secrets-of-suburbia movies with *Blue Velvet*, a movie that—whatever you thought of it—was at least original, and with "Twin Peaks," a TV series that—whatever you may have thought of it—was Lynch repeating himself. He at least had some kind of point he was trying to make (I think it was that the Troy Donahue and Sandra Dee romantic comedies were encoded calls of despair), but movies like *The Applegates* exist all on one level; the most shallow.

Is there a satirical point here? Parallels we can draw with real life? Lessons to learn? *Invasion of the Body Snatchers* was widely read as a social commentary in which individualism was under attack by sinister foreign forces. But this movie doesn't even seem to have a point of view—unless it's something on the level of Stupid Pet Tricks, in which human behavior becomes funny when it's mimicked by life forms that do not quite understand what they're doing.

The Apprenticeship of Duddy Kravitz
★ ★ ★
PG, 121 m., 1974

Richard Dreyfuss (Duddy), Micheline Lanctot (Yvette), Jack Warden (Max), Randy Quaid (Virgil), Joseph Wiseman (Uncle Benjy), Denholm Elliott (Friar), Henry Ramar (Dingleman), Joe Silver (Farber). Directed by Ted Kotcheff and produced by John Kemeny. Screenplay by Mordecai Richler.

Duddy Kravitz has grown up hearing about the Boy Wonder. The Wonder, real name Dingleman, started out in life picking up bus transfers from the street and selling them for three cents. When he had a quarter, he got into a gin game and ran it up to ten dollars. With that as a nest egg, the Wonder parlayed a string of poker games and fly-by-night investments into a fortune, and returned home (according to legend) in a chauffeured limousine and with his own string of racehorses. And all from a handful of lousy three-cent bus transfers!

Duddy thinks he can do better than that. When we meet him, he's a sixteen-year-old Jewish kid from Montreal whose mother is dead and whose father drives a cab and does a little part-time pimping to send the older son through medical school. The Boy Wonder was a boyhood friend of Duddy's father; the story, whether true or not, has been told so many times that Duddy naturally assumes he will be a millionaire, or something, by the time he's twenty. And he's right. By the time he's twenty, he's something.

The Apprenticeship of Duddy Kravitz is a movie that somehow manages to be breakneck and curiously touching at the same time. It's a story of ambition and greed, with a hero that will stop at almost nothing (by the movie's end, Duddy has succeeded in alienating the girl who loves him, has lost all his friends, has brought his grandfather to despair, and has paralyzed his most loyal employee). And yet we like Duddy, with a kind of exasperation, because we get some notion of the hungers that drive him, and because nobody suffers at his hands more than he does himself.

The movie's a sort of Canadian *What Makes Sammy Run?* Duddy Kravitz even gets into the movie business, as Budd Schulberg's hero did. But Duddy doesn't exactly get to Hollywood. He runs across a blacklisted, alcoholic American director, in exile from Hollywood during the dark days of McCarthyism (the film is set somewhere in the late 1940s and early 1950s).

Duddy forms a movie production company (Dudley Kane Productions, inevitably), hires the director, and produces films of bar mitzvahs. Their first production, shown in its entirety, is a lunatic montage of off-the-wall images that have no perceptible relevance to the bar mitzvah itself; the director arguably got himself drunk and spliced together stock footage (after the opening temple scenes played over Beethoven's Fifth). But Duddy's client is (somewhat dazedly) pleased by the film, and Duddy is off and running.

His ambition is to own land. "A man without land is a nobody," his grandfather has told him. During a summer spent as a waiter at a resort, he finds a beautiful, half-hidden lake. He determines to buy it and develop it, and his dream is shared by a plain-pretty French Canadian girl who is a maid at the resort. They fall into love. Or, more precisely, she loves him and Duddy loves a prospect of his future life which includes her, slightly to one side of center. The ways in which he finally succeeds in driving her away, the ways in which he makes himself miserable before he is even twenty-one, are played against his own series of get-rich-fast schemes (during which he not only succeeds in meeting the real Boy Wonder but even unknowingly smuggles heroin over the border for him).

The movie is based on a Mordecai Richler novel and was the most popular film to have come out of Canada through the early seventies (that country which, in cinema as in other things, remains more foreign for many Americans than any place in Europe). It was filmed on location with a great sense of life and energy and with details seen as Duddy sees them. It's populated with an incredible gallery of character roles (I've only suggested a few of them). It's a little too sloppy, and occasionally too obvious, to qualify as a great film, but it's a good and entertaining one, and it leaves us thinking that Duddy Kravitz might amount to something after all, should he ever grow up.

Arachnophobia ★ ★ ★
PG-13, 103 m., 1990

Jeff Daniels (Ross Jennings), Harley Jane Kozak (Molly Jennings), John Goodman (Delbert McClintock), Julian Sands (Dr. James Atherton), Stuart Pankin (Sheriff Parsons), Brian McNamara (Chris Collins). Directed by Frank Marshall and produced by Kathleen Kennedy and Richard Vane. Screenplay by Don Jakoby and Wesley Strick.

Spiders are among the most elegant of God's creatures, with their delicate, spindly legs and infinite patience. Contained in their tiny memories is the geometry for a million webs, and when you see a web wet with dew in the morning sunlight, you know there is order in the universe, because the spider has found it and didn't even know what it was looking for.

Cockroaches, now, are another matter. They are fearsome, ugly little amphibious vehicles that lurk under the sink and eat anything, even Brillo pads. A horror movie based on roaches would be almost unbearable, and indeed I remember with revulsion an episode from George Romero's *Creepshow* in which a man was covered with a swarm of roaches and eaten alive.

Compared to such loathsome horrors, *Arachnophobia* is a relatively benign thriller, in which spiders kill a few people and scare a lot more, but never get really disgusting the way cockroaches would. The movie begins in the mysterious rain forests of South America, where a new species of spider is discovered. It's a formidable beast, about the size of a baseball mitt, and it has a deadly bite. It kills one of the expedition members

and then hitches a ride back to California inside his coffin. Once it arrives in a bucolic rural town, it crossbreeds with a domestic spider and starts lurking in the shoes and toilet bowls of the locals.

The movie's plot includes the elements common to all titles in this genre: (a) the old fuddy doctor who refuses to accept the alarming evidence, (b) the narrow-minded local policeman who resents outsiders, (c) the bright young doctor whose warnings are ignored, (d) the loyal wife and kids, (e) the plain-spoken local woman who sticks up for the new doc, and, of course, (f) the scientist, called in at the crisis to shake his head gravely and announce that a deadly infestation seems to be at hand. There are also, of course, the usual cats and dogs, necessary for the obligatory scene in which they can sense something even when the humans can't.

The bright young doctor, hero of the movie, is played by Jeff Daniels as a man who literally has a paralyzing fear of spiders. He moves with his wife (Harley Jane Kozak) and their kids into one of those charming little Victorians you find only on the back lots of movie studios. It has a barn, suitable for spiders' nests, and a cellar filled with places you wouldn't want to stick your hand into if you thought there might be a deadly arachnoid the size of a coffee cake in there.

Soon bad things start to happen. The kindly local widow bites the dust. A young football player topples over dead. The old-fogey doctor refuses to order an autopsy, but then events conspire to prove him wrong, and soon the spider man (Julian Sands) has been called in from the university and is shaking his head in the approved manner.

You wouldn't think spiders would be good visual elements for a movie. Remember that awful horror movie *The Swarm*, in which killer bees completely failed to make an impression? But the spiders in *Arachnophobia* are wonderfully photogenic, partly because the director, Frank Marshall, is good at placing them in the foreground, shooting them in close-up, and allowing their shadows to cast alarming images when the characters aren't looking. He's also clever at establishing where the spiders are, and then allowing us to cringe as the people in the movie do exactly the wrong thing. The toilet seat scene is a splendid case in point.

And yet for all of the creepy-crawly shocks in the film, *Arachnophobia* never goes over the edge into sheer disgusting horror. It maintains a certain humorous edge—espe-

cially in the scenes involving John Goodman as the friendly local exterminator who knows a big spider when he sees one, throws away his biodegradable and ecologically sound chemicals, and gets out the dangerous stuff. This is the kind of movie where you squirm out of enjoyment, not terror, and it's probably going to be popular with younger audiences—it doesn't pound you over the head with violence. Like the spider itself, it has a certain respect for structure.

Aria ★ ★ ★
R, 90 m., 1988

Produced by Don Boyd, with segments directed by Robert Altman, Bruce Beresford, Bill Bryden, Jean-Luc Godard, Derek Jarman, Franc Roddam, Nicolas Roeg, Ken Russell, Charles Sturridge, and Julien Temple.

Aria could be described, somewhat disrespectfully, as an operatic hit parade. The film is a labor of love by a British producer named Don Boyd, who convinced ten different directors to interpret ten famous arias in any style they chose. The result is uneven, of course, but stimulating and sometimes outrageous, as such diverse talents as Robert Altman, Ken Russell, and Jean-Luc Godard go to work.

None of the directors chose to just go ahead and film his aria in a straightforward, traditional way; Bill Bryden comes closest, with a wraparound segment starring John Hurt as a has-been virtuoso remembering his happier days. His story continues between each of the other arias, and finally he stands alone on stage and sings the famous aria from *I Pagliacci*, an opera about a man who found he could smile through his sadness. (John Hurt did not learn to sing for the movie; he mimes Caruso, and indeed all the segments feature prerecorded performances.)

Of the ten segments, I particularly enjoyed Franc Roddam's interpretation of *Liebestod*, from Wagner's *Tristan und Isolde*. He uses Bridget Fonda and James Mathers as young lovers who arrive in Las Vegas, drive slowly and (given the music) sadly down Glitter Gulch, check into a cheap hotel room, make love, and kill themselves. Despite, or perhaps because of, the unlikely setting, the episode is truly poignant in its portrait of the two doomed lovers.

Among the other segments, Nicolas Roeg's vision of Verdi's *Un Ballo in Mas-*

chera, stars his wife, Theresa Russell, made up as a man, in a story based on the attempted assassination of King Zog of Albania in 1931 (you see how fanciful the directors were allowed to become). Charles Sturridge begins with Verdi's *La Vergine Degli Angeli*, from *La Forza del Destino*, and illustrates it with the story of three teenagers who skip school and end up in a traffic accident. Godard uses Lully's *Armide* as an excuse for a segment about bodybuilders. Julien Temple, the brash young British director, shoots his illustration of Verdi's *Rigoletto* in the famous Madonna Inn in San Luis Obispo, California, and stars Buck Henry as a movie producer who sneaks away with Beverly D'Angelo to the very hotel where his wife has also repaired with her lover.

Robert Altman's segment on Rameau's *Abaris ou les Boreades* re-creates the Parisian opening night in 1734 at the Ranelagh Theater, where he imagines the audience as being filled with a raffish and perhaps diseased assortment of lowlifes and the decadent. Bruce Beresford re-creates the seemingly dead city of Bruges, Belgium, to illustrate Korngold's *Die Tote Stadt*. Ken Russell chooses Puccini's *Turandot*, and uses the British pinup model Linzi Drew as his subject. She imagines her body is being adorned by jewels, but wakes up in an operating room where she is receiving emergency care after a car crash. The mixture is typical of Russell's taste for exoticism and sensation. The final segment by Derek Jarman shows a veteran opera singer at her last performance, intercut by 8mm home movies of an early love affair.

At the end of *Aria* one must decide, I suppose, what it all means. I am not sure that any indispensable statement about opera has been made here, and purists will no doubt recoil at the irreverence of some of the images. But the film is fun almost as a satire of itself; as a project in which the tension between the directors and their material allows them to poke a little fun at their own styles and obsessions. It's the first MTV version of opera.

Ariel ★ ★ ★
NO MPAA RATING, 74 m., 1990

Turo Pajala (Taisto Kasurinen), Susanna Haavisto (Irmeli), Matti Pellonpaa (Mikkonen), Eetu Hilkamo (Riku), Erkki Pajala (Miner), Matti Jaaranen (Mugger). Directed and produced by Aki Kaurismaki. Screenplay by Kaurismaki.

Ingmar Bergman made a film at the dawn of his career named *It Rains on My Future*, and I thought of that title while I was watching *Ariel*. This is the new film by Aki Kaurismaki, the director from Finland whose work has been winning festivals and inspiring articles in the film magazines calling him the best young director from Europe. I went expecting to see the new Fassbinder or Herzog or Almodovar, and what surprised me was how traditional the film is; it's a despairing *film noir* with a "happy" ending that taunts us with its irony.

The story involves Taisto, a miner from northern Finland who loses his job when the mine closes. He sits in a café with a depressed friend who gives him his old Cadillac convertible and then walks into the men's room and blows his brains out. Taisto drives the convertible to southern Finland, where he is quickly relieved of his life savings by muggers. He gets a day-labor job, gets a bed in a skid row mission, and then strikes up an instant romance with a meter maid, who throws away her parking tickets and goes for a ride in the Cadillac.

Meeting the meter maid is a stroke of luck for Taisto, but life is not going to be kind to him, and the plot of *Ariel* involves one crushing misfortune after another. It's like one of those 1940s B movies—*Detour*, maybe—where the hero tells you on the sound track that his luck is always rotten, and the story proves that he's right.

One of the special qualities of the movie is the physical clumsiness of most of the characters. They move like real people, not like the smoothly choreographed athletes we see on TV and in American movies. When the hero runs, he looks like he's not accustomed to running. When cops race up to nab somebody, they run flat-footed and grab him in an awkward and uncoordinated tussle.

A similar clumsiness adds conviction to the action. Events occur in a stark and naive way. A bank robbery ends with money being dropped all over the sidewalk. Conversations are blunt. Motives are simple. The movie's lack of physical and social finesse is a positive quality; it makes the characters seem touchingly real. Watching their clumsiness, I became aware of how actions sometimes don't seem spontaneous in Hollywood films. Nobody ever seems to be performing an action for the first time, and the moves all seem practiced and familiar.

The hero of *Ariel* is played by Turo Pajala, an actor who bears a passing resemblance to Bruno S., the star of Herzog's *Kasper Hauser*. He projects the qualities of a congenital victim, a man so overwhelmed by the relentless malice of the universe that he's punch-drunk with bad luck. The movie surrounds him with people who are on the same wavelength. Misfortune is their companion. The strongest character in the movie is the meter maid's young son, who keeps his nose stuck in comic books and accepts his roller-coaster life with stoic calm.

Ariel is the first film of Kaurismaki's I've seen, and on the basis of it, I want to see more. He has a particular vision. It isn't the vision of a flashy stylist with fashionable new attitudes, but the vision of a man who has found a filmmaking rhythm that suits his own bruised sensibility. *Ariel* speaks for the dispossessed with a special conviction because it isn't even angry. It's too tired to be angry. It's resigned. The more you think about it, the last scene, the "happy" ending, may be the only really angry scene in the movie.

Arthur ★ ★ ★ ½
PG, 97 m., 1981

Dudley Moore (Arthur Bach), Liza Minnelli (Linda Marolla), John Gielgud (Hobson), Geraldine Fitzgerald (Martha Bach), Jill Eikenberry (Susan), Stephen Elliott (Burt), Tod Ross (Bitterman), Barney Martin (Linda's Father). Directed and written by Steve Gordon. Produced by Robert Greenhut.

Only someone with a heart of stone could fail to love a drunk like Arthur Bach, who spends his wasted days in a poignant search for someone who will love him, will care for him, will inflame his passions, and soothe his pain, and who, most of all, will laugh at his one-liners. Arthur is such a servant of humanity that he even dedicates himself to thinking up new one-liners and holding them in reserve, lest he be unprepared if someone walks into his life and needs a laugh, quick.

Arthur, played by Dudley Moore, is the alcoholic hero of *Arthur*, a comedy about a man who is worth $750 million and who would never think of trying to buy anyone's love with his money. Arthur is like the woman in the poem by Yeats, who spent her days in innocent good will, and her nights in argument, till her voice grew shrill. Arthur, God love him, is a drunk. He slips into his bath of a morning, and his butler brings him a martini. After he completes his bath, Arthur sets about the day's business, which consists of staying drunk, and being driven about Manhattan in a limousine in his endless quest for love.

Now the problems with searching for love while you are drunk are many. They include (a) no one will want to love you while you are drunk, (b) you are not at your best while you are drunk, so they won't know what they're missing, (c) you may be too drunk to notice it if someone does finally fall in love with you, and (d) if you survive all of these pitfalls, you will nevertheless wake up hung over, and scientific studies prove that hangovers dissolve love. All of these things having been said, Arthur, against all odds, does find love. He finds it in the person of Linda (Liza Minnelli), a smart cookie who doesn't care about his money but is overwhelmed by the dimensions of his needs. Arthur would like to marry Linda. But his billionaire father insists that he marry a perfectly boring WASP (Jill Eikenberry) whose idea of a good holiday is probably the January white sales.

Arthur turns for help to his loyal butler, Hobson, who is played by John Gielgud with an understated elegance and a naughty tongue. Hobson is dying. But Hobson wishes to see Arthur prevail, for once, against Arthur's father, a sadistic puppetmaster. So Hobson subtly manipulates the situation so that the lovers are thrown together at the party announcing Arthur's engagement to the WASP. That inspires a rupture within the family, and a very drunken odyssey by Arthur, who wants to press $100,000 upon Linda, and visits her at home. When Linda turns him down, her father (Barney Martin) becomes a grown man who sheds tears, creating perhaps the funniest moment in the movie.

Dudley Moore became a star, of course, with *10*, playing a man who became obsessed with Bo Derek, and who could blame him? In *Arthur*, he makes his bid for world-class status as a comic character actor. He brings a wonderful intensity to scenes like the one near the beginning of the film where he has invited a hooker to dinner at the Plaza and then forgotten who she is, and what she is, or why he is with her. It is marvelous to see him try to focus his attention, which he seems to

believe is all concentrated in his eyebrow muscles.

Apart from Moore, the treasure of *Arthur* is in its many supporting performances, especially Gielgud's, although everyone in this movie has great moments. You might be tempted to think that *Arthur* would be a bore, because it is about a drunk who is always trying to tell you stories. You would be right if *Arthur* were a party and you were attending it. But *Arthur* is a movie. And so its drunk, unlike real drunks, is more entertaining, more witty, more human, and more poignant than you are. He embodies, in fact, all the wonderful human qualities that drunks fondly, mistakenly believe the booze brings out in them.

The Assault ★ ★ ★
NO MPAA RATING, 149 m., 1987

Derek de Lint (Anton Steenwijk), Marc van Uchelen (Anton as a Boy), Monique van de VenCor (Truus Coster), John Kraaykamp (Takes). Directed and produced by Fons Rademakers. Screenplay by Gerard Soeteman.

The Assault, which won the 1987 Academy Award as best foreign film, begins in Nazi-occupied Holland in the bitter late days of World War II. On a quiet suburban street, a Dutch collaborator is shot to death by partisans. From behind their curtains, the fearful residents peek out into the night, certain that the Nazis will perform dreadful reprisals. Shadowy figures dart out and drag the body to the front of the house next door, and then the movie is the story of the rest of the life of Anton Steenwijk, the young boy who lived in that house.

His family is taken away by the Nazis. All of them disappear, apparently liquidated, except for Anton, who is spared through a combination of bureaucratic oversights and lucky chances. After the war, Anton goes to college, marries, and becomes successful in his profession. Always his life is haunted by the aftermath of that terrible night.

But there are two other families also scarred by the assault. One is the family of the murdered Nazi collaborator. Anton runs across the collaborator's son a few years later and finds that he has become a bitter young right-winger, a youth whose father's political choice made him into an outsider and menial laborer who was scorned after the war.

Even later, in a 1960s ban-the-bomb parade, Anton meets the woman who lived next door on that night and learns why her father dragged the dead body to the front of his house, assuring that another family would be punished by the Nazis. He had his reasons. Perhaps they were good. Of course, from the point of view of a man who lost his entire family because of those reasons, they were not good enough.

The Assault is like a fictional footnote to *Shoah*, the great documentary that also asked difficult, perhaps unanswerable, questions about guilt and blame in the Holocaust. It also is a little like *Rashomon*, the Japanese film that looked at the same crime from many different viewpoints and discovered many different versions of the truth.

A terrible thing happened on that night. Lives were destroyed. For those who survived, each one had to deal with the guilt in a different way. Even Anton had guilt, because he was spared when all of his family was murdered. The truest and most painful moment in the film takes place at a time about twenty years after the night of the assault. Anton—happily married, a father, successful, content—is suddenly visited by a great devastation. To call it a depression would be too mild. He is overcome with a crushing awareness of the fact that utter injustice exists in our world, that evil is real, that death is irrevocable. In a way, this movie is about how he is able to continue his life in the face of that realization.

Although *The Assault* is a film that asks important questions and examines them fearlessly, it is not as effective as it could be. The film covers nearly forty years, and that is a weakness as well as a strength. The power of the film is that it shows how one night of tragedy has echoed down the decades, affecting many lives for years afterward. Multiply this assault by the millions of others, and you have some measure of the devastation caused by the war.

Yet at the same time, by covering so many lives for so many years, the film loses something in energy and focus. The canvas is too large. The moments I will remember best are the small ones, one in particular: On the night of the assault, Anton is comforted in a jail cell by the young woman partisan who committed the murder that led to his family's death. Years later, through a coincidence, he is able to meet her partner and tell the man, now old and ill, something he never knew: that she loved him.

At Close Range ★ ★ ★ ½
R, 115 m., 1986

Sean Penn (Brad, Jr.), Christopher Walken (Brad, Sr.), Mary Stuart Masterson (Terry), Christopher Penn (Tommy), Millie Perkins (Julie), Eileen Ryan (Grandma). Directed by James Foley and produced by Elliott Lewitt and Don Guest. Screenplay by Nicholas Kazan.

Here is a spare, violent, unforgiving story of a boy's need for a father who does not love him and who would, if necessary, murder him. It is also a story with passages of love and adventure and cheerfulness, as a teenager grows up in the hills of rural Pennsylvania. The way that the two sides of the story grow together creates a tragedy that reminds me of myth, of the ancient stories of children betrayed by their parents, and yet *At Close Range* is based on a true story. It happened in 1978.

The movie stars Sean Penn, probably the best of the younger actors, as Bradford Whitewood, Jr. He lives with his divorced mother and grandmother and half-brother in a setting of shabby poverty, nonstop TV watching, and boredom. Once in a while, his father, Brad Senior, appears out of nowhere and throws money on the table. Then Brad Senior drives away in a fast car with a pretty girl. The kid would like a taste of his father's life. It looks a lot better than what he has.

The father is played by Christopher Walken, in one of the great hateful performances of recent years. Walken is a strange actor, hard to pin down, but when he is given the right role (as he is here, and in *Dead Zone* and *The Deer Hunter*), there is nobody to touch him for his chilling ability to move between easy charm and vile evil. In the movie, he's the leader of a gang of professional thieves who have recently been specializing in stealing tractors. He likes to play the big shot, and in a way he enjoys the fact that his young son has started to idolize him.

Penn, as Brad Junior, isn't really criminal material, but he's a misfit and an outcast and absolutely nothing is happening for him in his own life. He drifts into the orbit of his father, looking for love but also looking for action. He's the leader of a young gang of his own, and his father assigns the kids to a couple of easy jobs—getting them ready for the big time. But when the big time turns dangerous, and it looks as if the gang might be busted, the Walken character is absolutely prepared to save his own skin, even at the cost of betraying his own child.

At Close Range is not a pleasant movie. Few recent films have painted such a bleak picture of human nature. The Walken character is pure evil, wrapped in easy charm, and most of the other characters in the film are weak, or deprived, or lacking in the ability to see beyond their own immediate situation. That's especially true of Brad Junior's mother (Millie Perkins) and grandmother (Eileen Ryan), who sit endlessly around the house, their eyes straying away from every conversation, toward the TV set. Only Brad Junior and his local girlfriend (Mary Stuart Masterson) have a chance of breaking free, and their love affair is on a collision course with Brad Senior.

Because this film is violent and cruel and very sad, why would you want to see it? For a couple of reasons, perhaps. One might be to watch two great actors, Penn and Walken, at the top of their forms, in roles that give them a lot to work with. Another might be to witness some of the dynamics of a criminal society, some of the forces that push criminals further than they intend to go. It's the same dynamic you could see in the great crime film *In Cold Blood* (1967)—seemingly ordinary people whose moral sense is missing, and who drift into actions so evil that perhaps even they are appalled.

Au Revoir les Enfants ★ ★ ★ ★
PG, 103 m., 1988

Gaspard Manesse (Julien Quentin), Raphael Fejto (Jean Bonnet), Francine Racette (Madame Quentin), Stanislas Carre de Malberg (Francois Quentin), Philippe Morier-Genoud (Father Jean), Francois Berleand (Father Michel), Francois Negret (Joseph), Peter Fitz (Muller). Directed, written, and produced by Louis Malle.

Which of us cannot remember a moment when we did or said precisely the wrong thing, irretrievably, irreparably? The instant the action was completed or the words were spoken, we burned with shame and regret, but what we had done could never be repaired. Such moments are rare, and they occur most often in childhood, before we have been trained to think before we act. *Au Revoir les Enfants* is a film about such a moment, about a quick, unthinking glance that may have cost four people their lives.

The film was written and directed by Louis Malle, who based it on a childhood memory. Judging by the tears I saw streaming down his face on the night the film was shown at the Telluride Film Festival, the memory has caused him pain for many years. His story takes place in 1944, in a Catholic boarding school in Nazi-occupied France. At the start of a new semester, three new students are enrolled, and we realize immediately that they are Jews, disguised with new names and identities in an attempt to hide them from the Nazis.

To Julien Quentin (Gaspard Manesse), however, this is not at all obvious. Julien, who is intended as Malle's autobiographical double, does not quite understand all of the distinctions involving Jews and gentiles in a country run by Nazis. All he knows is that he likes one of the new boys, Jean Bonnet (Raphael Fejto), and they become friends. Bonnet is not popular with the other students, who follow the age-old schoolboy practice of closing ranks against newcomers, but then Julien is not very popular either; the two boys are a little dreamy and thoughtful—absorbed in themselves and their imaginations, as bright adolescents should be. Malle's film is not filled with a lot of dramatic incidents. Unlike such roughly comparable Hollywood films as *The Lords of Discipline*, it feels no need for strong plotting and lots of dramatic incidents leading up to the big finale. Instead, we enter the daily lives of these boys. We see the classroom routine, the air-raid drills, the way each teacher has his own way of dealing with problems of discipline. More than anything else, we get a feeling for the rhythm of the school. Malle has said that when, years later, he visited the actual site of the boarding school he attended, he found that the building had disappeared and the school was forgotten. But to a student enrolled in such a school, the rules and rituals seem timeless, handed down by innumerable generations and destined to survive forever. A schoolboy cannot be expected to understand how swiftly violence and evil can strike out and change everything.

Julien and Jean play together, study together, look at dirty postcards together. One day, one of those cold early spring days when the shadows seem ominous and there is an unsettling wind in the trees, they go exploring in a nearby forest, and darkness falls. They get lost, or almost lost, and they weather this adventure and become even closer friends. One day, Julien accidentally discovers that "Jean Bonnet" is not his friend's real name. A few days later, when Julien's mother comes to visit, he invites Jean to join them at lunch in a local restaurant, and they witness an anti-Semitic incident as a longtime local customer is singled out because he is Jewish.

That is about all the input that Julien receives, and it is hard to say exactly what he knows, or suspects, about Jean. But when Nazis visit the school, Julien performs in one tragic second an action that will haunt him for the rest of his days. Malle has said that the incident in *Au Revoir les Enfants* does not exactly parallel whatever happened in real life, but the point must be the same: In an unthinking moment, action is taken that can never be retrieved.

Is the film only about guilt? Not at all. It is constructed very subtly to show that Julien only half-realized the nature of the situation, anyway. It isn't as if Julien knew absolutely that Jean was Jewish. It's more as if Julien possessed a lot of information that he had never quite put together, and when the Nazis came looking for hidden Jews, Julien suddenly realized what his information meant. The moment in which he makes his tragic mistake is also, perhaps, the moment when he comprehends for the first time the shocking fact of racism.

Autumn Sonata ★ ★ ★ ★
PG, 97 m., 1978

Ingrid Bergman (Charlotte), Liv Ullmann (Eva), Lena Nyman (Helena), Halvor Bjork (Viktor), Georg Lokkeberg (Leonardo), Knut Wigert (The Professor). Directed by Ingmar Bergman. Screenplay by Bergman.

Ingrid Bergman was certainly one of the most beautiful women to ever appear in a film, but that is not the source of her mysterious appeal. There is something there, in that voice and those eyes and in the way her mouth thinks words before she says them, that is, quite simply, unduplicated in the movies. It took Ingmar Bergman thirty-five years to finally cast her in one of his films, and then, in her fortieth year as an actress, Ingrid Bergman called *Autumn Sonata* her last film. Sweden's two most important film artists finally worked together.

The movie is a historic event, taking us back to so many different areas of our memories. We remember Ingrid Bergman from some of the basic cinematic artifacts of all

time, movies like *Casablanca* and *Notorious*. But we've never seen her really pushed, really tested, by a director whose commitment to honesty is nothing short of merciless.

Ingmar Bergman didn't cast her for reasons of nostalgia, or sentiment: He cast her because he had an idea for a role she could brilliantly contain and that would contain her, and in *Autumn Sonata* she gives nothing less than the performance of her lifetime. We can only be quietly grateful that she performs opposite Liv Ullmann, who is herself good enough to meet her on the same very high level.

They play mother and daughter. The mother is an internationally famous pianist (and we remember Ingrid Bergman's first great success, as the pianist in *Intermezzo*). She has not seen her daughter for seven years. She's too busy and always traveling and booked up almost every night of the week . . . and, not incidentally, terrified of confronting her daughter.

There are, in fact, two daughters: The one played by Ullmann, who is serious and introspective and filled with guilt and blame and love, and then the other daughter (Lena Nyman), who lives with her, and who suffers from a degenerative nerve disease. The mother's solution to this daughter's illness was to place her in a "home;" Ullmann has taken her out of the institution and brought her home to live with her.

On the morning when the mother arrives for her long-delayed visit, she has no idea that the sick daughter will be there. Her response, on learning that her other daughter is upstairs, is dismay. She's never been able to deal with the illness—but, then, she's never been able to deal at all with the fact of being a mother. She doesn't merely reject the responsibility; she flees from it.

Autumn Sonata then gives us a sort of long day's journey into night in which the pleasantries of the opening hours give way to deeper and deeper terrors and guilts, accusations and renunciations, cries and whispers. And Ingmar Bergman, standing apart from this material and regarding it with clarity and detachment, refuses to find any solutions. There are none, I suppose. A lesser filmmaker would have resolved everything at the end in some sort of neat Freudian bookkeeping, but Bergman finds in his story only two people, each demanding love from the other, each doomed by the past to fall just short of the ability to love.

This is excruciatingly difficult material. Ingrid Bergman and Liv Ullmann confront it with a courage and skill that is astonishing. We've always known that Liv Ullmann was a great actress (that is one of the givens of film in the past two decades), and we've known, too, that Ingrid Bergman was a great movie star. But how important that in her sixties, acting in her native language for the first time in four decades, working with one of the supreme film directors, Bergman was able to use not only her star qualities but also every last measure of her artistry and her humanity. It is not just that *Autumn Sonata* was Ingrid Bergman's last film. It's that she knew she had to make it before she died.

Avalon ★ ★ ★ ½
PG, 126 m., 1990

Leo Fuchs (Hymie Krichinsky), Eve Gordon (Dottie Kirk), Lou Jacobi (Gabriel Krichinsky), Armin Mueller-Stahl (Sam Krichinsky), Elizabeth Perkins (Ann Kaye), Joan Plowright (Eva Krichinsky), Kevin Pollak (Issy Kirk), Aidan Quinn (Jules Kaye). Directed by Barry Levinson and produced by Mark Johnson and Levinson. Screenplay by Levinson.

"All happy families are alike but an unhappy family is unhappy after its own fashion."
—Tolstoy

This is one of the most familiar quotations in literature for the excellent reason that it states a truth everyone can recognize. The strength of Barry Levinson's *Avalon* is that it starts as a movie about a happy family and shows why it became unhappy after its own fashion. During the first half hour of the film, my heart sank because it seemed to be another of those potted biopics about an immigrant family's legends and eccentricities, all three times as colorful as life. Then the colors began to darken and the mood began to change, and the film deepened into the story of many American families that have grown apart over the generations.

Consider for a moment the term "nuclear family." It reflects a goal we aspire to in our society: mom and dad and all the kids gathered around the hearth with the family dog and the television set. But there is something missing from the picture: grandparents, uncles, aunts, cousins, in-laws. We call such a family nuclear because it revolves around the nucleus of a single family home. But it is also nuclear because it flies in a lonely orbit of its own.

Levinson's *Avalon* is inspired by the experiences of his own family. His grandparents came to America from Russia, part of a large Jewish family that pooled its resources and brought over one relative after another until at last the five Krichinsky brothers had all settled in Baltimore. They were musicians—violinists, available by hire—but during the week they worked as paper-hangers. They worked hard and raised large families and their extended family was the center of their social life. They lived near to one another, held family councils, and pooled their money for charitable giving and to help out family members in need. And they had glowing ambitions for their children. One parent tells his son he will never teach him how to hang wallpaper, because "it is not a job you should grow up to do." Notes like this are struck with absolute accuracy; I remember my own father refusing to teach me his trade for the same reason.

The world of Baltimore in the first half of the century is re-created by the film with an unforced, but rich detail. The clothes and cars are just right, of course, but so are the values. We understand how for some of the brothers, especially Gabriel (Lou Jacobi), family traditions are sacred. He objects when one of his brothers moves to the suburbs after the war. He complains that he cannot find the suburbs, that it is too far a drive—but his real complaint is that the family is flying apart and losing its solidarity. This process is dramatized in the film's central scene, a Thanksgiving dinner where Gabriel and his wife arrive late and the family has already cut the turkey.

It is a trivial incident, perhaps, but it symbolizes a much larger event, the cutting of the family's close ties. Each generation is a little more alienated from the sense of community that the first generation brought over from Russia. Each new family drifts a little further from the center of the family circle. This is a process that may have something to do with the nature of American society. Europeans are vertically conformist; they want to do things as their ancestors did. Americans are horizontally conformist; we want to do things as our neighbors do. This process breaks down the richness of ethnic heritage and creates a bland Middle American who, in a way, is from nowhere—who was invented in TV commercials.

Television gets a lot of the blame from Levinson for the breakdown of the family. At first the whole family gathers around the first set they've seen, staring in fascination at the test patterns. Later the big, loud family meals are replaced by smaller groups eating off of TV trays, looking at prime time.

Meanwhile, material success comes quickly to some of the Krichinskys. Issy and Jules (Kevin Pollak and Aidan Quinn), two cousins of the second generation, "Americanize" their surnames to Kirk and Kaye and open a big appliance store. They advertise on TV in hambone commercials that have the customers lined up around the block. They expand and eventually take over a big warehouse, opening the first discount department store in Baltimore. Things are going well when two of their children—including a character probably meant to be Levinson himself—do something I will not reveal here, but which is told with such empathy, with such a memory for how young children do and remember things, that it becomes the other central pillar of the film.

In a way, the kids do what they do because of what they've seen on television. The result, indirectly, is that one of their fathers gets a job selling advertising time on TV. Television is a thread all through the movie. It's a socially divisive force, but it's also an entertainment, a hypnotic pastime, an occupation, an influence, a presence. Levinson seems to feel that TV is a disastrous invention that has cut our human society off from its roots. That may be true (although it will not, of course, prevent the eventual sale of this film to television).

Avalon is often a warm and funny film, but it is also a sad one, and the final sequence is heartbreaking. It shows the way in which our modern families, torn loose of their roots, have left old people alone and lonely—warehoused in retirement homes. The story of the movie is the story of how the warmth and closeness of an extended family is replaced by alienation and isolation. The title of the film comes from the name of the Baltimore neighborhood where the family first settled. In Celtic mythology, Avalon was an island of blessed souls, an earthly paradise somewhere in the western seas. Who would think, sailing for it, that they would fall off the edge of the Earth?

Awakenings ★ ★ ★ ★
PG-13, 121 m., 1990

Robert De Niro (Leonard Lowe), Robin Williams (Dr. Malcolm Sayer), Julie Kavner (Eleanor Costello), Ruth Nelson (Mrs. Lowe), John Heard (Dr. Kaufman), Anne Meara (Miriam), Lolly Esterman (Lolly), Penelope Ann Miller (Paula). Directed by Penny Marshall and produced by Walter F. Parkes and Lawrence Lasker. Screenplay by Steven Zaillian.

We do not know what we see when we look at Leonard. We think we see a human vegetable, a peculiar man who has been frozen in the same position for thirty years, who neither moves nor speaks. What goes on inside his mind? Is he thinking in there? Of course not, a neurologist says, in Penny Marshall's film *Awakenings*. Why not? "Because the implications of that would be unthinkable." Ah, but the expert is wrong, and inside the immobile shell of his body, Leonard is still there. Still waiting.

Leonard is one of the patients in the "garden," a ward of a Bronx mental hospital that is so named by the staff because the patients are there simply to be fed and watered. It appears that nothing can be done for them. They were victims of the great "sleeping sickness" epidemic of the 1920s, and after a period of apparent recovery they regressed to their current states. It is 1969. They have many different symptoms, but essentially they all share the same problem: They cannot make their bodies do what their minds desire. Sometimes that blockage is manifested through bizarre physical behavior, sometimes through apparent paralysis.

One day, a new doctor comes to work in the hospital. He has no experience in working with patients; indeed, his last project involved earthworms. Like those who have gone before him, he has no particular hope for these ghostly patients, who are there and yet not there. He talks without hope to one of the women, who looks blankly back at him, her head and body frozen. But then he turns away, and when he turns back she has changed her position—apparently trying to catch her eyeglasses as they fell. He tries an experiment. He holds her glasses in front of her, and then drops them. Her hand flashes out quickly and catches them.

Yet this woman cannot move through her own will. He tries another experiment, throwing a ball at one of the patients. She catches it. "She is borrowing the will of the ball," the doctor speculates. His colleagues will not listen to this theory, which sounds suspiciously metaphysical, but he thinks he's on to something. What if these patients are not actually "frozen" at all, but victims of a stage of Parkinson's disease so advanced that their motor impulses are canceling each other out—what if they cannot move because all of their muscles are trying to move at the same time, and they are powerless to choose one impulse over the other? Then the falling glasses or the tossed ball might be breaking the deadlock!

This is the great discovery in the opening scenes of *Awakenings*, preparing the way for sequences of enormous joy and heartbreak, as the patients are "awakened" to a personal freedom they had lost all hope of ever again experiencing—only to find that their liberation comes with its own cruel set of conditions. The film, directed with intelligence and heart by Penny Marshall, is based on a famous 1972 book by Oliver Sacks, the British-born New York neurologist whose *The Man Who Mistook His Wife for a Hat* is a classic of medical literature. These were his patients, and the doctor in the film, named Malcolm Sayer and played by Robin Williams, is based on him.

What he discovered in the summer of 1969 was that L-dopa, a new drug for the treatment of Parkinson's disease, might, in massive doses, break the deadlock that had frozen his patients into a space-time lock for endless years. The film follows some fifteen of those patients, particularly Leonard, who is played by Robert De Niro in a virtuoso performance. Because this movie is not a tearjerker but an intelligent examination of a bizarre human condition, it's up to De Niro to make Leonard not an object of sympathy, but a person who helps us wonder about our own tenuous grasp on the world around us.

The patients depicted in this film have suffered a fate more horrible than the one in Poe's famous story about premature burial. If we were locked in a coffin while still alive, at least we would soon suffocate. But to be locked inside a body that cannot move or speak—to look out mutely as even our loved ones talk about us as if we were an uncomprehending piece of furniture! It is this fate that is lifted, that summer of 1969, when the doctor gives the experimental new drug to his patients, and in a miraculous rebirth their bodies thaw and they begin to move and talk once again, some of them after thirty years of self-captivity.

The movie follows Leonard through the stages of his rebirth. He was (as we saw in a prologue) a bright, likable kid, until the disease took its toll. He has been on hold for three decades. Now, in his late forties, he is filled with wonder and gratitude to be able to move around freely and express himself. He cooperates with the doctors studying his case. And he finds himself attracted to the daughter (Penelope Ann Miller) of another patient. Love and lust stir within him for the first time.

Dr. Sayer, played by Williams, is at the center of almost every scene, and his personality becomes one of the touchstones of the movie. He is shut off, too, by shyness and inexperience, and even the way he holds his arms, close to his sides, shows a man wary of contact. He really was happier working with those earthworms. This is one of Robin Williams's best performances, pure and uncluttered, without the ebullient distractions he sometimes adds—the schtick where none is called for. He is a lovable man here, who experiences the extraordinary professional joy of seeing chronic, hopeless patients once again sing and dance and greet their loved ones.

But it is not as simple as that, not after the first weeks. The disease is not an open-and-shut case. And as the movie unfolds, we are invited to meditate on the strangeness and wonder of the human personality. Who are we, anyway? How much of the self we treasure so much is simply a matter of good luck, of being spared in a minefield of neurological chance? If one has no hope, which is better: to remain hopeless, or to be given hope and then lose it again? Oliver Sacks's original book, which has been reissued, is as much a work of philosophy as of medicine. After seeing *Awakenings*, I read it, to know more about what happened in that Bronx hospital. What both the movie and the book convey is the immense courage of the patients and the profound experience of their doctors, as in a small way they re-experienced what it means to be born, to open your eyes, and discover to your astonishment that "you" are alive.

B

Baby Boom ★ ★ ★
PG, 110 m., 1987

Diane Keaton (J.C. Wiatt), Sam Shepard (Dr. Jeff Cooper), Harold Ramis (Steven Buchner), Sam Wanamaker (Fritz Curtis), James Spader (Ken Arrenberg), Pat Hingle (Hughes Larrabee), Kristina and Michelle Kennedy (Baby Elizabeth). Directed by Charles Shyer and produced by Nancy Meyers. Screenplay by Shyer and Meyers.

Baby Boom tells the story of a yuppie who receives the ultimate toy, a cute little baby daughter. At first she doesn't want to play with it, but eventually it grows on her, and even provides the inspiration for her to acquire other toys, such as a farm in Vermont, a baby-food company, and a handsome veterinarian.

This story could have been told as a satire, but the filmmakers aren't quite sure. They see a lot of humor in the yuppie's lifestyle, but they love the baby so much that the movie finally turns into a sweet romance. I guess that's all right. It sure is a cute baby.

The yuppie is played by Diane Keaton, whose Annie Hall more or less created the category. As the film opens, she is a hard-driving Manhattan business executive who works hard and takes no hostages. The opening narration by Linda Ellerbee supplies some details: She has a salary in six figures, a corner apartment in the right part of town, and a live-in lover (Harold Ramis) who is her perfect match because he, too, is a workaholic.

Then two of Keaton's long-lost relatives die in a traffic accident in Britain, and she inherits their pride and joy, a baby girl named Elizabeth (played by twins, Kristina and Michelle Kennedy). There is, of course, no question of her raising the baby herself. After all, she's just had a partnership dangled in front of her. She copes with the kid as best she can for a few days, feeding it gourmet pasta and checking it in a restaurant cloakroom during a power lunch. Then she takes it to be adopted, but finds she just can't part with this sweet little girl.

Right then is when the movie changes tone. Up until Keaton's decision to keep the child, *Baby Boom* has been a hard-edged satire (the dialogue between Keaton and the hat-check attendant is an example, as Keaton thrusts the squawling infant across the counter and promises "a big, big tip"). But after the film's turning point, it turns from a satire into an escapist fantasy, a harmless one, in one of those worlds where everything turns out more or less right, because folks are more or less nice.

The film is careful never to confront the Keaton character with any of the real messiness of the world, such as poverty, illness, and catastrophe. After she quits her job, she has enough money in the bank to buy a sixty-two-acre home in Vermont for herself and baby Elizabeth. And when the money runs low, she starts a gourmet baby-food company that is worth millions within a few months. She also discovers companionship up there in the woods, from Sam Shepard, the local vet and only person under sixty in the immediate surrounding area.

All of this is too good to be true, of course, but that's why I enjoyed it. *Baby Boom* makes no effort to show us real life. It is a fantasy about mothers and babies and sweetness and love, with just enough wicked comedy to give it an edge. The screenplay by Nancy Meyers and Charles Shyer has some of the same literate charm as their previous film, *Irreconcilable Differences*, and some of the same sly observation of a generation that wages an interior war between selfishness and good nature.

The flaw in *Baby Boom* is that the Keaton character ends up not having sacrificed a single thing by leaving the business world to become a mom. In fact, she becomes a millionaire as a direct result of keeping the baby. It doesn't often happen that way, but, of course, it should. Like a Frank Capra film, *Baby Boom* shows us a little of the darkness and a lot of the dawn.

Baby, It's You ★ ★ ★
R, 105 m., 1983

Rosanna Arquette (Jill), Vincent Spano (Sheik), Joanna Merlin (Mrs. Rosen), Jack Davidson (Dr. Rosen). Directed by John Sayles and produced by Griffin Dunne and Amy Robinson. Screenplay by Sayles.

Rosanna Arquette has a way about her. She's a natural actress, and by that I don't mean she was born talented (although perhaps she was), but that she is able to appear onscreen with such an unaffected natural quality that I feel as if I'm looking past the script and direction and actually experiencing the life of her character. That's the feeling I got during *Baby, It's You*, a sometimes very good, sometimes disappointingly uneven movie that she carries from beginning to end. Even when her scenes aren't working, her character is, and we're getting to know this young woman she plays, this Jill Rosen, who turns from an uncommonly engaging high school student to a scared-stiff college freshman.

The movie is by John Sayles, who has built a career for himself out of the carefully observed events that make up ordinary lives. His first film was *Return of the Secaucus Seven*, about some thirty-fiveish survivors of the 1960s. Then he made *Lianna*, about a thirty-fiveish faculty wife who discovers, with fear and some anticipation, that she is a lesbian. Now here is Jill Rosen, a high school student from the 1960s who could, we suspect, easily grow up to be any of the women in Sayles's first two films.

Jill is smart and pretty, especially when she smiles. Her brains and her smile are only the half of it. She's also got a personal style. She has this way of letting you know she's listening, even when she seems to be ignoring you. A way of caring for you, even when she's mad at you. You get the feeling this is a woman whose love would be a very important thing for you to count on. And that's certainly the opinion of the Sheik (Vincent Spano), a semi-greaser who is consumed by his desire to be exactly like Frank Sinatra. The Sheik and (actually) a lot of this movie seem to belong more to the fifties than the sixties—but never mind. Here is a kid who's a sharp dresser, has a lot of apparent self-confidence, and doesn't mind that he stands out like a sore thumb with his brazen ways and his Sinatra wardrobe. He's a rebel with ambitions. Jill loves him, but when she leaves Trenton, New Jersey, and enters the uncertain world of Sarah Lawrence College, the Sheik doesn't fit in.

Baby, It's You does two things with this material. First, it remembers it accurately, right down to the irritating mannerisms of preppy college boys with too much unearned self-confidence. Then, it uses it as a meditation on growing up—which means learning to listen to your heart as well as to your ambitions. The movie works best in its high school segments, and the opening hour is wonderful. Then the infuriating stuff begins, when this movie that has been so surefooted loses its way in the college scenes, and allows us to wonder at times what we're supposed to be thinking. Rosanna Arquette is equally good, however, in the good parts and the disappointing ones.

Bachelor Party ★ ★ ★
R, 100 m., 1984

Tom Hanks (Rick), Tawny Kitaen (Debbie), Adrian Zmed (Jay), George Grizzard (Mr. Thompson), Robert Prescott (Cole). Directed by Neal Israel and produced by Ron Moler and Bob Israel. Screenplay by Neal Israel and Pat Proft.

Bachelor Party is 1984's version of the Annual Summer Food Fight Movie. With a movie like this, it doesn't really matter whether anyone actually throws mashed

potatoes across the room; what matters is whether the movie is faithful to the spirit of Blotto Bluto in *Animal House* when he yelled "Food fight!" and the madness began. The story this time is about this guy who decides to get married, and his friends decide to throw him a bachelor party. That's about it. The first half of the movie sets up the party and the second half of the movie is the party. Both halves of the movie are raunchy, chaotic, and quite shameless in aiming at the lowest possible level of taste, of course.

The bachelor in the movie is played by Tom Hanks. He was the guy from *Splash* who the mermaid fell in love with. I didn't think he was all that terrific in *Splash*—I thought he was miscast, and they should have gone for somebody who was less of a conventional leading man—but in *Bachelor Party* he's a lot more funny and I enjoyed the performance. He plays the kind of guy who goes over to his fiancée's house for dinner and drops table scraps onto the floor in *case* they have a dog. He has a great one-liner when he has to introduce himself to his fiancée's nerdy ex-boyfriend: "The name is Bond. James Bond." During the chaos of the party itself, one of his primary roles is simply to direct traffic.

The idea during the party, I think, is to approximate the spirit of one of those Jack Davis drawings in *Mad* magazine, where dozens of people are running around like crazy, and down in the corners you can see strange little figures doing inexplicable things. Most of the gags depend on varieties of public embarrassment and some of them are pretty funny, especially when the women decide to have their revenge by visiting a male go-go bar.

Is *Bachelor Party* a great movie? No. Why do I give it three stars? Because it honors the tradition of a reliable movie genre, because it tries hard, and because when it is funny, it is very funny. It is relatively easy to make a comedy that is totally devoid of humor, but not all that easy to make a movie containing some genuine laughs. *Bachelor Party* has some great moments and qualifies as a raunchy, scummy, grungy Blotto Bluto memorial.

Back to School ★ ★ ★
PG-13, 94 m., 1986

Rodney Dangerfield (Thornton Melon), Sally Kellerman (Diane), Burt Young (Lou), Keith Gordon (Jason Melon), Robert Downey, Jr. (Derek), Paxton Whitehead (Philip Barbay), M. Emmet Walsh (Coach Turnbull), Ned Beatty (Dean Martin). Directed by Alan Metter and produced by Chuck Russell. Screenplay by Steven Kampmann, Will Porter, Peter Torokvei, and Harold Ramis.

Rodney Dangerfield has given many interviews on the subject of his loneliness. Why, he asks, should a guy like him, who is able to fill up giant concert halls and pull down millions of dollars a year, be condemned to go through life without the love of a woman? This is not the sort of thing you want to hear from a comedian. You want him to be zany and madcap, to stand astride the problems of the mundane world and laugh at them.

Yet in Dangerfield, there has always been something else in addition to the comedian. This is a man who has failed at everything, even comedy. Rodney Dangerfield is his third name in show business; he flopped under two earlier names as well as his real name. Who is really at home inside that red, sweating face and that knowing leer?

The most interesting thing about *Back to School*, which is otherwise a pleasant but routine comedy, is the puzzle of Rodney Dangerfield. Here is a man who reminds us of some of the great comedians of the early days of the talkies—of Groucho Marx and W. C. Fields—because, like them, he projects a certain mystery. Marx and Fields were never just being funny. There was the sense that they were getting even for hurts so deep that all they could do was laugh about them. It's the same with Dangerfield.

He plays Thornton Melon, a millionaire clothing manufacturer who owns a chain of Tall & Fat Shops. His father was a penniless Italian immigrant who took him into the family business as a child. He never had the opportunity to get an education. Now he is rich, his second wife is an obnoxious bauble, and all he cares about is his son, Jason, who is a college student.

Dangerfield fondly believes Jason is a fraternity member and a star of the diving team. But actually Jason is the campus wimp, the team's towel boy, and, naturally, he gets no respect. When Dangerfield discovers the truth, he decides to enroll in the university as a freshman so he can teach his son the ropes. Of course, there's resistance to this plan, but not after Dangerfield endows the Melon School of Business Administration.

The campus characters are predictable, but well-cast. Sally Kellerman is the sexy English teacher, Paxton Whitehead is the Anglophile business teacher, and Ned Beatty is the venal administrator, always referred to as Dean Martin. Dangerfield takes the "drinks for everybody" approach, throwing his money around and hiring expensive coaches to help him pass his classes. Kurt Vonnegut, Jr., turns up as a paid expert on his own work. Meanwhile, young Jason learns how to be a big man on campus.

This is exactly the sort of plot Marx or Fields could have appeared in. Dangerfield brings it something they might also have brought along: a certain pathos. Beneath his loud manner, under his studied obnoxiousness, there is a real need. He laughs that he may not cry.

Back to the Beach ★ ★ ★ ½
PG, 94 m., 1987

Frankie Avalon (The Big Kahuna), Annette Funicello (Annette), Lori Loughlin (Sandi), Tommy Hinkley (Michael), Demian Slade (Bobby), Connie Stevens (Connie). Directed by Lyndall Hobbs and produced by Frank Mancuso, Jr. Screenplay by Peter Krikes, Steve Meerson, and Christopher Thompson.

This movie absolutely blind-sided me. I don't know what I was expecting from *Back to the Beach*, but it certainly wasn't the funniest, quirkiest musical comedy since *Little Shop of Horrors*. Who would have thought Frankie Avalon and Annette Funicello would make their best beach party movie twenty-five years after the others?

For those who have never seen them, a description is probably better than the actual experience: The beach party movies were a series of chaste comedies in which Frankie and Annette and the gang hung out on the beach, rode the big waves, necked a little, and tried to defend their lifestyle against the old fogeys who were always trying to ban rock & roll. The movies were a tie between harmless and brainless.

Back to the Beach is a wicked satire that pokes fun at Frankie, Annette, and the whole genre, but does it with a lot of good humor and with the full cooperation of the victims. Avalon and Funicello do a better job of satirizing themselves than anyone else possibly could.

The story: Frankie and Annette have gotten married and moved to Ohio, where Frankie sells cars on television, riding a phony surfboard in his sharkskin suit, while Annette prepares endless meals of peanut butter sandwiches. They have two children: a daughter who has moved to Malibu and a young teen-age son who is a punk, wears leather, flicks his switchblade, and mercilessly attacks the inane banality of his parents.

The kid (Demian Slade) almost steals the opening scenes of the movie. He has spray-painted graffiti on the fireplace in the living room, he practices karate moves on the family dog, and when Frankie and Annette exchange empty-headed clichés, he's ironic: "This is the sort of conversation you'd hear at the Kissingers.'"

The three of them head to Hawaii on vacation but get sidetracked to Malibu, where Frankie is horrified to learn that his daughter has shacked up with a beach bum (in the beach party movies, the sexes always were strictly segregated at bedtime). Meanwhile, he and Annette discover that some of the old gang still is hanging out at the beach, including Connie Stevens, Miss Lip Gloss of 1962, who still looks luscious.

Frankie flirts with Connie. Annette pouts. There is a confrontation between the clean-cut surfers and the punk surfers. There's a surfing competition, and Frankie comes out of retirement to win it. Annette sings a reggae song. Frankie sings a few rock songs. So does Connie Stevens. And at one point, Pee-wee Herman jets in from nowhere, does a virtuoso version of "Surfin' Bird," and disappears.

All of this sounds, I suppose, like the kind of movie you could afford to miss, because a plot summary only suggests the elements of the movie, not the style. Director Lyndall Hobbs, an Australian making her feature debut, has a good eye and a good ear, and the movie is filled with satirical angles from beginning to end. It's a quirky little gem filled with good music, a lot of laughs, and proof that Annette still knows how to make a polka-dot dress seem ageless.

Back to the Future ★ ★ ★ ½
PG, 116 m., 1985

Michael J. Fox (Marty McFly), Christopher Lloyd (Dr. Brown), Lea Thompson (Lorraine Baines), Crispin Glover (George McFly), Thomas F. Wilson (Biff Tannen), Claudia Wells (Jennifer Parker). Directed by Robert Zemeckis and produced by Bob Gale and Neil Canton. Screenplay by Zemeckis and Gale.

One of the things all teen-agers believe is that their parents were never teen-agers. Their parents were, perhaps, children once. They are undeniably adults now. But how could they have ever been teen-agers, and yet not understand their own children? This view is actually rather optimistic, since it assumes that you can learn something about teen-agers by being one. But *Back to the Future* is even more hopeful: It argues that you can travel back in time to the years when your parents were teen-agers and straighten them out right at the moment when they need help the most.

The movie begins in the present, with a teen-ager named Marty (Michael J. Fox). His parents (let's face it) are hopeless nerds. Dad tells corny jokes and Mom guzzles vodka in the kitchen and the evening meal is like feeding time at the fun house. All that keeps Marty sane is his friendship with the nutty Dr. Brown (Christopher Lloyd), an inventor with glowing eyes and hair like a fright wig.

Brown believes he has discovered the secret of time travel, and one night in the deserted parking lot of the local shopping mall, he demonstrates his invention. In the long history of time-travel movies, there has never been a time machine quite like Brown's, which resembles nothing so much as a customized DeLorean.

The gadget works, and then, after a series of surprises, Marty finds himself transported back thirty years in time, to the days when the shopping mall was a farmer's field (there's a nice gag when the farmer thinks the DeLorean, with its gull-wing doors, is a flying saucer). Marty wanders into town, still wearing his 1985 clothing, and the townsfolk look at his goose-down jacket and ask him why he's wearing a life preserver.

One of the running gags in *Back to the Future* is the way the town has changed in thirty years (for example, the porno house of 1985 was playing a Ronald Reagan movie in 1955). But a lot of the differences run more deeply than that, as Marty discovers when he sits down at a lunch counter next to his dad— who is, of course, a teen-ager himself. Because the movie has so much fun with the paradoxes and predicaments of a kid meeting his own parents, I won't discuss the plot in any detail. I won't even get into the horrifying moment when Marty discovers his mother "has the hots" for him. The movie's surprises are one of its great pleasures.

Back to the Future was directed by Robert (*Romancing the Stone*) Zemeckis, who shows not only a fine comic touch but also some of the lighthearted humanism of a Frank Capra. The movie, in fact, resembles Capra's *It's a Wonderful Life* more than other, conventional time-travel movies. It's about a character who begins with one view of his life and reality, and is allowed, through magical intervention, to discover another. Steven Spielberg was the executive producer, and the movie's world view (smart kid in Yuppie suburb redefines reality for his parents) is part of the basic Spielberg approach. This time it comes with charm, brains, and a lot of laughter.

Back to the Future Part II ★ ★ ★
PG, 108 m., 1989

Michael J. Fox (Marty McFly, Marty McFly, Jr., and Marlene McFly), Christopher Lloyd (Dr. Emmett Brown), Lea Thompson (Lorraine), Thomas F. Wilson (Biff Tannen and Griff), Harry Waters, Jr. (Marvin Berry), Charles Fleischer (Terry), Elisabeth Shue (Jennifer), Jeffrey Weissman (George McFly). Directed by Robert Zemeckis and produced by Bob Gale and Neil Canton. Screenplay by Gale.

Back to the Future Part II is an exercise in goofiness, an excursion into various versions of the past and future that is so baffling that even the characters are constantly trying to explain it to each other. I should have brought a big yellow legal pad to the screening, so I could take detailed notes just to keep the time lines straight. And yet the movie is fun, mostly because it's so screwy.

Any story involving travel through time involves the possibility of paradoxes, which have provided science-fiction writers with plots for years. What happens to you, for example, if you kill your grandfather? What do you say if you meet yourself? In one famous S-F story, a time traveler to the dis-

tant past steps on a single bug, and wipes out all the life forms of the future.

Back to the Future Part II is the story of how the heroes of the first movie, Marty McFly and Doc Brown, try to manipulate time without creating paradoxes, and how they accidentally create an entirely different future—one in which Marty's beloved mother is actually married to his reprehensible enemy, Biff Tannen. McFly and Brown are played again this time by Michael J. Fox and Christopher Lloyd, the stars of the 1985 box-office hit, and they not only made *Part II* but went ahead and filmed *Part III* at the same time.

The script conferences on the set of this movie must have been utterly confusing, as director Bob Zemeckis and writer Bob Gale tried to find their way through the labyrinth they had created. The movie opens in 1985. McFly has just returned from his previous adventure when Doc Brown appears once again in that souped-up DeLorean. He's breathless with urgency, and wants McFly to join him on a trip to the year 2015, where absolutely everything has gone wrong and McFly is needed to save his own son from going to jail.

The city of Hill Valley in the year 2015 looks like the cover of an old pulp magazine; the town square we remember from the previous film has been transformed with ramps heading for the skies, and jet-powered vehicles cruise through the clouds. The kids even have skateboards that operate on the same principle as hovercraft, which leads to one of the movie's best special-effects numbers when McFly tries to evade a gang of rowdies. He more or less accomplishes his mission in 2015, but makes the mistake of buying a sports almanac that has all of the scores from the years 1950 to 2000 in it.

The almanac and the DeLorean are stolen by Biff, who travels back in time to give them to himself, so that he can place lots of winning bets and become a billionaire. In the process, Hill Valley in the future turns into a hellhole lorded over by the evil billionaire who is produced by this scheme, and so McFly and Doc travel back to 1955 to try to steal the almanac away from Biff, and if you are following all of this, you are a very clever reader. I won't even begin to try to explain the ways in which the various parents and children of the main characters also get involved in the story, or what happens when McFly very nearly attends a high school dance on a double date with himself, or how

Fox plays three roles including his own daughter.

What's entertaining about *Back to the Future Part II* is the way Christopher Lloyd, as Doc, breathlessly tries to figure out what's happening as he flies through time trying to patch everything together again. At one point he even finds a blackboard and delivers a lecture to the baffled McFly. The flaw in his reasoning, of course, is his assumption that he knows which is the correct time line that *should* be restored. How does he know that the "real world" of the first movie was not itself an alternate time line? It's a job for God.

One thing I'd better make clear is that *Part II*, for all its craziness, lacks the genuine power of the original film. The story of the 1985 film has real heart to it: If McFly didn't travel from 1985 to 1955 and arrange for his parents to have their first date, he might not even exist. The time travel in that film involved his own emotional confrontation with his own parents as teen-agers. *Part II*, on the other hand, is mostly just zaniness and screwball jokes. But on that level, it's fun.

Back to the Future Part III ★ ★ ½
PG, 120 m., 1990

Michael J. Fox (Marty/Seamus McFly), Christopher Lloyd (Dr. Emmett Brown), Mary Steenburgen (Clara Clayton), Thomas F. Wilson (Buford "Mad Dog" Tannen, Biff Tannen), Lea Thompson (Maggie McFly, Lorraine McFly), Elisabeth Shue (Jennifer). Directed by Robert Zemeckis and produced by Bob Gale and Neil Canton. Screenplay by Gale.

One of the delights of the first two *Back to the Future* movies was the way the story moved dizzyingly through time. Paradoxes piled on top of paradoxes, until we had to abandon any attempt to follow the plot on a rational level, and go with the temporal flow. That looking-glass quality is missing, alas, from *Back to the Future Part III*, which makes a few bows in the direction of time-travel complexities, and then settles down to be a routine Western comedy.

The movie was shot back-to-back with *Back to the Future Part II*, which, you will recall, took Marty McFly (Michael J. Fox) forward to a thoroughly depressing future which he had created by meddling around in the immediate future. He had to travel back in time in order to undo his damage, so that the eventual future would be a nicer place to live.

Now comes *Back to the Future Part III*, in which Marty receives a letter from the past—a letter written by his old friend Doc Brown (Christopher Lloyd) from a century ago, explaining that he has traveled back to the Old West and is generally happy there, and asking Marty to simply leave him alone. This letter, of course, has taken a hundred years to arrive.

Doc Brown does, however, reveal where he hid the DeLorean time-travel machine, in an abandoned mine near town. McFly does some historical research and discovers to his horror that Doc Brown was killed only a week after writing the letter, so he determines to venture back in time, whatever the risk, to rescue his friend. He goes looking for the machine in the old mine and finds it still there, and it even starts after a century, which is more than you can say for most cars after a month in the garage. McFly travels back into time, and, unfortunately, once he gets there he mostly stays there.

The Old West of *Back to the Future Part III* might have been interesting if it had been an approximation of the real Old West—the one we saw in *McCabe and Mrs. Miller,* say. But this movie's West is unfortunately a sitcom version that looks exactly as if it were built on a back lot somewhere. The movie is so filled with old Western clichés that the regulars in the bar even include Pat Buttram. Now don't get me wrong: I was delighted to see Buttram again (he was Gene Autry's sidekick in the old days) and even happier to hear that his voice is still in need of oiling. But the town in *Future III* is made up of lots of pieces from old movies, including even a shoot-out on Main Street and the usual troubles with the local sheriff.

One element of the Old West story is sweet and entertaining: The romance between the eccentric Doc Brown and a local woman named Clara (Mary Steenburgen). They fall in love at first sight, and then Doc gets to thinking about his duty to the future and mankind, and he grows depressed about the mischief he has wrought in the world by inventing time travel, and he decides it is his duty to return to the time he came from, and leave poor Clara behind.

This is easier said than done, since no gasoline exists in the past and McFly has ruptured the fuel line of the DeLorean, a development that leads Doc Brown to an ingenious scheme to get the car up to time-travel velocity (88 mph) by having it pushed by a train. All of this is sort of fun (the movie did not stint on its budget), but it's somehow too linear. It's as if Robert Zemeckis, who directed, and Bob Gale, who wrote, ran out of time-travel plot ideas and just settled into a standard Western universe.

The one thing that remains constant in all of the *Back to the Future* movies, and which I especially like, is a sort of bittersweet, elegiac quality involving romance and time. In the first movie, McFly went back in time to be certain his parents had their first date. The second involved his own romance. The third involves Doc Brown and Clara. In all of these stories, there is the realization that love depends entirely on time; lovers like to think their love is eternal, but do they ever realize it depends entirely on temporal coincidence, since if they were not alive at the same time romance would hardly be feasible?

Backdraft ★ ★ ★
R, 132 m., 1991

Kurt Russell (Stephen McCaffrey), William Baldwin (Brian McCaffrey), Robert De Niro (Donald Rimgale), Donald Sutherland (Ronald Bartel), Jennifer Jason Leigh (Jennifer Vaitkus), Scott Glenn (John Adcox), Rebecca De Mornay (Russell's Wife). Directed by Ron Howard and produced by Richard B. Lewis, Pen Densham, and John Watson. Screenplay by Gregory Widen.

Ron Howard's *Backdraft* is a movie half in love with fire, a film like *Fahrenheit 451* that finds something seductive in tendrils of smoke and boiling cauldrons of flame. Never before in the movies have I seen fire portrayed by such convincing, encompassing special effects. Unfortunately, they are at the service of an unworthy plot. If the story of this movie had risen to the level of the production values, it might really have amounted to something.

The movie grafts no less than three formulas onto its wonderful action scenes. We get brothers who are rivals, two broken couples trying to find love again, and a crooked politician who may be behind a series of crimes. Each of these formulas unwinds with relentless conventionality.

The movie takes place in Engine Company 17, based in Chicago's Chinatown, where Kurt Russell is the grizzled veteran and William Baldwin is his kid brother, a rookie fresh from the Fire Academy. Many years before, their father died as a hero in a fire, and Baldwin, then a small boy, made the cover of *Life* magazine as he grasped his dad's blackened helmet while tears ran down his face. The two brothers have been rivals ever since—Russell trying to prove he is the true heir to the family's tradition of heroism; Baldwin trying to prove himself as a man. These character traits have probably not been explored in the movies more than several thousand times.

Russell lives the life of an untidy bachelor in his dad's old boat, permanently aground. He and his wife, played by Rebecca De Mornay, are still really in love with one another, but have separated because she can't count on him to be there when she needs him, because fire fighting comes first in his life, and she can no longer bear the fear of what could happen to him, she loves him too much to lose him, etc. De Mornay brings more intelligence to this situation than the screenplay deserves.

Meanwhile, Baldwin's former girlfriend (Jennifer Jason Leigh) now works as the aide to a powerful alderman (J.T. Walsh), who is running for mayor, apparently on a platform of slashing the budget of the fire department. And a series of mysterious fires have broken out. The canny veteran fire inspector (Robert De Niro) has determined that they were set by an expert, to create a backdraft that would instantly kill their victims with such force that they would then blow themselves out.

If you were not born yesterday, you can probably take this information and correctly predict how everything in the movie turns out. The producers did not get their money's worth from the screenplay by Gregory Widen—unless, of course, all they wanted was a clothesline from which to hang their special effects. That's all they got. We know that the director, Ron Howard, can handle more truthful and complex plots, because he has made *Parenthood* and *Cocoon*. Maybe this time he deliberately chose to make a no-brainer.

But then you have the scenes involving fire. They're so good they make me recommend the movie anyway, despite its brain-damaged screenplay. With special effects and pyrotechnics coordinated by Allen Hall, a battalion of stunt men and visual experts allow the camera to plunge into the center of roaring fires so convincingly that there is never a moment's doubt that we are surrounded by flames.

What is particularly impressive is the way the filmmakers are able to convince us the stars are in the middle of the action. A conventional fire scene uses doubles and stand-ins, over-the-shoulder shots, and other evasive tricks, for brief scenes showing men in the middle of a fire. Then they use close-ups of the actors in front of a back-projection screen filled with flames.

Similar techniques may have been used here, but they are not detectable. It actually looks as if Russell, Baldwin, and the others are right there in the center of blazing tenements and exploding factories, hanging by their fingernails over boiling balls of flame. I personally doubt that anyone, even an expert fireman, could actually survive in such conditions for more than a moment or two. And Russell's exploits are especially dubious, since he prefers not to wear a mask and likes to run bare-faced into hell, in search of heroism. But it sure plays well.

Bad Boys ★ ★ ★ ½
R, 123 m., 1983

Sean Penn (Mick O'Brien), Reni Santoni (Ramon Herrera), Esai Morales (Paco Moreno), Jim Moody (Gene Daniels), Eric Gurry (Horowitz), Clancy Brown (Viking Lofgren). Directed by Richard Rosenthal and produced by Robert Solo. Screenplay by Richard Di Lello.

Bad Boys tells the story of some tough Chicago street-gang kids who get in a lot of trouble, get sent to a juvenile correctional institution, and get in a lot more trouble once they're inside. Following the tradition governing such movies, the story eventually comes to a moral crossroad at which a bad boy has to decide whether to become a good man—and that's too bad, because until the movie turns predictable it is very, very good. The acting, the direction, and the sense of place in *Bad Boys* is so strong that the movie deserves more than an obligatory fight scene for its conclusion.

The movie stars Sean Penn as Mick O'Brien, a teen-age Irish-American hood and Esai Morales as Paco, a Latino hood. They are both tough, mean, anti-social kids; this movie doesn't sentimentalize street gangs. Their paths cross in connection with a drug deal that Paco is doing with a black gang. There's a misunderstanding, a sudden, shocking exchange of gunfire, and Paco's kid brother is dead. Mick killed him.

Mick is sent to prison, and then Paco has his revenge by raping Mick's girlfriend (Ally Sheedy). Paco is caught and sent to the same prison where Mick is being held. Mick already has learned the ropes, and Paco learns them quickly: The prison guards preside sincerely but ineffectually over a reign of terror enforced by the toughest kids in the prison. Violence and sexual crimes are commonplace. The strongest survive. This situation is complicated, of course, by the fact that everyone in the prison immediately knows that Mick and Paco will have to fight to the death over the feud of honor.

And it's at precisely that moment, when the two kids are being set up for an eventual showdown, that *Bad Boys* begins to unwind. The first hour of this movie is so good it's scary; Penn and Morales and the supporting actors are completely convincing, and *Bad Boys* is the first movie I've seen in which the street gangs are not glamorized *(West Side Story)*, stylized *(The Warriors)*, or romanticized *(The Wanderers)*. We believe, watching *Bad Boys*, that we are observing an approximation of the real thing. The direction, by Richard Rosenthal, is sure-footed, confident, and fluid; we are in the hands of a fine director, even if he *did* make *Halloween II*. Sean Penn is mean and defiant in a real star performance, and the other kids in the prison include such inimitable characters as Horowitz (Eric Gurry), a bright kid who invents things and talks casually of his arson conviction; Viking (Clancy Brown), the hard but vulnerable boss of the prisoners; and Tweety (Robert Lee Rush), who rules at Viking's side.

These performances are good. That's why it's such a disappointment when the movie allows itself to become just another prison picture. Although the second half of the movie continues its close, convincing observations of everyday life in the youth prison, the story structure begins to feel programmed: We know we're heading for a big fight, we think we know who'll win—and what is this, anyway? They've *already* made *Rocky* three times. *Bad Boys* misses its chance at greatness, but it's saying something that this movie *had* a chance. It stands as one of those benchmark movies that we'll look back at for the talent it introduced. On the basis of their work here, Penn, Morales, and Rosenthal prove they have important careers ahead of them, and some of the supporting actors do, too. This movie's not a complete success, but it's a damned good try.

Bad Influence ★ ★ ★
R, 100 m., 1990

James Spader (Michael Boll), Rob Lowe (Alex), Lisa Zane (Claire), Christian Clemenson (Pismo Boll), Kathleen Wilhoite (Leslie). Directed by Curtis Hanson and produced by Steve Tisch. Screenplay by David Koepp.

Bad Influence is like one of those old Charles Atlas ads, where the bullies on the beach kicked sand into the eyes of the ninety-nine-pound weakling, until Atlas came along and showed the wimp how to build some muscle. The primary difference between the ads and this thriller is that the role of Atlas is now filled by a sadistic sociopath. He walks into the life of a cowardly financial analyst and treats him to some assertiveness training that is more than he bargained for.

The analyst is played by James Spader, whose cool diffidence is just right for the early scenes, in which the office bully hacks into the computer system and hides three months' worth of Spader's work. In response, Spader does what any normal coward would do, and walks across the street to a bar to have a beer. It isn't his day. In the lounge, a big guy is having a fight with his girlfriend, and when Spader looks at him wrong, he gets his face mashed into the bar.

That's when Rob Lowe comes in, breaks a beer bottle off at the neck, and has a few words with the bully while waving the jagged edge at his face. The bully leaves. Spader is grateful, and over the next few days he becomes friends with this mysterious stranger, who offers to teach him how to stand up for himself. At first the lessons are innocuous, as Spader outsmarts his rival in the office. Then they get more troublesome, and finally they get deadly.

Bad Influence reminded me a little of *Strangers on a Train*, the 1951 Hitchcock movie where Robert Walker offers to trade murders with Farley Granger—his father for Granger's wife—so they can both be rid of people they hate. Granger doesn't take him seriously, but Walker is very serious indeed. In *Bad Influence*, Lowe has the smooth Walker role, but the difference is, Spader has no idea he's made a bargain until it's much too late.

The movie sneaks up on you. At first you're not even sure where it's going: Maybe this will be the story of a creepy relationship between Spader, who is a born innocent, and

Lowe, who likes to change identities and accents every night while he's picking up girls in the Los Angeles underground bar scene. Lowe is slick and likable, and very attractive except for those sinister shadows that always seem to be playing over his eyes.

There's a hint of homosexuality in their relationship; Spader clearly likes Lowe, who seduces him with compliments and friendship. "Tell me what you really desire, and what you really fear," Lowe tells Spader one night when they're both looped. Spader says he fears marriage, even though he is engaged to a rich girl, the kind who pecks her future hubby on the cheek as if she were a bird and he were a mirror. Lowe is able to end the unwanted engagement with a spectacular act of social embarrassment, by infiltrating a party given by the future in-laws, and showing a home video of Spader having sex with another woman.

This scene, and another one with Lowe in bed with two girls, will no doubt stir memories of his celebrated scandal involving a videotape. Indeed, the parallels between *Bad Influence* and the Lowe videotape incident are so numerous that I would almost believe him if he claimed to have been doing research. Believers in coincidence can also savor the fact that this is Spader's first big role since *sex, lies, and videotape*—which would have made an excellent title for *Bad Influence*. The movie is strong enough and the performances so convincing, however, that echoes from real life never distracted me.

Like many thrillers that begin with an intriguing premise, *Bad Influence* is more fun in the setup than in the payoff. For at least the first hour, we are not quite sure what game Lowe is playing, and the full horror of his plan is only gradually revealed. The climax of the movie discharges a lot of the suspense by turning into a more conventional cat-and-mouse game. But I was grateful for the final shots, which played fair with the logic of the plot and didn't try to sneak in the cheap surprise I was waiting for.

Movies like this do raise a few questions, and one I kept asking was, how does Spader do it? As a broker based in Los Angeles, he has to be at work when the New York markets open, and there is indeed one scene where he's at his desk at 5:30 A.M. Since he spends night after night with Lowe, turning into a zombie in one bar after another, how does he manage to hit the deck every morning looking like a preppie fresh from busi-

ness school? On one occasion, he is drunk enough to stick up some convenience stores after the clubs close, and sober enough to be horrified at his behavior only a few hours later.

Bad Influence was written by David Koepp and directed by Curtis Hanson, and is a much superior exploitation of a theme that Koepp used in his screenplay for his previous *Apartment Zero:* A passive hero falls for the spell of a virile man who enters his life under false and deadly pretenses. *Apartment Zero* was lurid and overwrought, almost a self-parody, while Hanson's direction of *Bad Influence* makes it into a somber, introspective study of the relationship. Perhaps it says something about our times that when strangers meet in movies these days, one of them is almost always operating out of some kind of secret depravity.

Badlands ★ ★ ★ ★
PG, 94 m., 1974

Martin Sheen (Kit), Sissy Spacek (Holly), Warren Oates (Holly's Father), Ramon Bieri (Cato), Ramon Vint (Deputy). Directed, produced, and written by Terence Malick.

They meet for the first time when she is in her front yard practicing baton-twirling. He has just walked off his job on a garbage truck. She thinks he is the handsomest man she's ever seen—he looks just like James Dean. He likes her because he never knew a fifteen-year-old who knew so much: "She could talk like a grown-up woman, without a lot of giggles." Within a few weeks, they will be the targets of a manhunt after he has shot down half a dozen victims.

Terence Malick's *Badlands* calls them Kit and Holly, but his characters are inspired, of course, by Charles Starkweather and Caril Ann Fugate. They went on a wild ride in 1958 that ended with eleven people shot dead. The press named him the Mad Dog Killer, and Sunday supplement psychoanalysts said he killed because the kids at school kidded him about his bowlegs. Starkweather got the electric chair on June 25, 1959. From time to time a story appears about Caril Fugate's appeals to her parole board. She was sentenced to life.

She claimed she was kidnapped and forced to go along with Starkweather. When they first were captured, he asked the deputies to leave her alone: "She didn't do nothing." Later, at his trial, he claimed she was

the most trigger-happy person he ever knew, and was responsible for some of the killings. It is a case that is still not closed, although *Badlands* sees her as a child of vast simplicity who went along at first because she was flattered that he liked her: "I wasn't popular at school on account of having no personality and not being pretty."

The film is tied together with her narration, written like an account of summer vacation crossed with the breathless prose style of a movie magazine. Some of the dialogue is loosely inspired by a book written by James Reinhardt, a criminologist who interviewed Starkweather on death row. Starkweather was offended by his death sentence. He viewed his crimes with total uninvolvement and asked how it was fair for him to die before he'd even been to a big city, or eaten in a fine restaurant, or seen a major-league game. That's what the movie captures, too: The detachment with which Kit views his killings, as Holly eventually draws away from him. He gets no pleasure from killing. He sees it only as necessary. He offers explanations which satisfy her for a while: "I killed them because they was bounty hunters who wanted the reward money. If they was policemen, just being paid for doing their job, that would have been different."

The movie makes no attempt to psychoanalyze its Kit Carruthers, and there are no symbols to note or lessons to learn. What comes through more than anything is the enormous loneliness of the lives these two characters lived, together and apart. He is ten years older than she is, but they're both caught up in the same adolescent love fantasy at first, as if Nat King Cole would always be there to sing "A Blossom Fell" on the portable radio while they held their sweaty embrace. He would not. To discourage his daughter from seeing "the kind of a man who collects garbage," her father punishes her by shooting her dog. She is "greatly distressed."

Kit is played by Martin Sheen, in one of the great modern film performances. He looks like James Dean, does not have bowlegs, and plays the killer as a plain and simple soul who has somehow been terribly damaged by life (the real Starkweather, his father explained at the time, was never quite right after being hit between the eyes with a two-by-four). Holly is played by the freckle-faced redhead Sissy Spacek. She takes her schoolbooks along on the murder spree so as not to get behind. She is in love with Kit at first, but there is a stubborn logic in her makeup and she eventually realizes that Kit means trouble. "I made a resolution never again to take up with any hell-bent types," she confides.

After the first murder and their flight, they never have any extended conversations about anything, nor are they seen to make love, nor is their journey given any symbolic meaning. They hope to reach refuge in the "Far North," where Kit might find employment as a mounted policeman. They follow their case in the newspapers, become aware of themselves as celebrities, and, in a brilliant scene at the end, the captured Kit hands out his comb, his lighter, and his ballpoint pen as souvenirs to the National Guardsmen who had been chasing him.

The movie is very reserved in its attitude toward the characters. It observes them, most of the time, dispassionately. They are strange people, as were their real-life models; they had no rationalizations like Dillinger's regard for the poor or Bonnie and Clyde's ability to idealize themselves romantically. They were just two dumb kids who got into a thing and didn't have the sense to stop. They're something like the kids in Robert Altman's *Thieves Like Us* and the married couple in *The Sugarland Express*. They are in over their heads, incapable of understanding murder as a crime rather than a convenience, inhabitants of lives so empty that even their sins cannot fill them.

Bagdad Cafe ★ ★ ★ ½
PG, 91 m., 1988

Marianne Sägebrecht (Jasmine), CCH Pounder (Brenda), Jack Palance (Rudi Cox), Christine Kaufmann (Debby), Monica Calhoun (Phyllis), Darron Flagg (Sal, Jr.), George Aquilar (Cahuenga), G. Smokey Campbell (Sal), Alan S. Craig (Eric). Written, produced, and directed by Percy Adlon. Also written and produced by Eleonore Adlon.

The heavy-set German lady, her body and soul tightly corseted, her hair sprayed into rocklike permanence, is having a fight with her husband, right there in the Mohave Desert. They are in the middle of some kind of miserable vacation, touring America as a version of hell. She can take no more. She grabs her suitcase and stalks away from their Mercedes, and he drives away into the red, dusty sky, and she walks to a miserable truck stop and asks for a room.

An opening like that makes you stop and think, doesn't it, about how cut-and-dried most Hollywood movies are. There would seem to be no place in today's entertainment industry for movies about fat German ladies and homesick truck stops, and yet *Bagdad Cafe* sets us free from the production line of Hollywood's brain-damaged "high concepts," and walks its own strange and lovely path. There is poetic justice in the fact that this movie, shot in English in America by a German, was one of the biggest box-office successes in recent European history.

The German woman is named Jasmine (Marianne Sägebrecht), and she is appalled by the conditions she finds at the Bagdad Cafe. It is simply not being run along clean and efficient German lines. The proprietor is a free-thinking black woman named Brenda (CCH Pounder—yes, CCH Pounder), who shares the premises with her teen-age children, a baby, a bewildered Italian cook, a tattoo artist, and a shipwrecked former Hollywood set painter who is played by Jack Palance as if he had definitely painted his last set.

Jasmine sets to work. She gets a mop and a pail and begins to clean her room, while the motel regulars look on in amazement. Back and forth she goes, like some kind of natural force that has been set into implacable motion against dirt. Gradually her sphere extends to other rooms in the motel, and to the public areas, and she gives Brenda little lectures about cleanliness and the importance of maintaining high standards for the public.

Day by day, little by little, however, Jasmine herself is changed by this laid-back desert environment. Her too-tight hausfrau dresses give way to a blouse that billows outside her slacks. A stray wisp of hair escapes from the glistening spray, and then finally her hair comes tumbling down in windswept freedom. And she reveals that she can do magic tricks.

Yes, magic tricks. After she whips the cook into shape and the truck stop's restaurant begins to do some business, she starts entertaining some of the customers with close-up illusions, which eventually grow in scale until the Bagdad Cafe is presenting its own cabaret night after night, with all the regulars pressed into the act.

All of this sounds rather too nice, I suppose, and so I should add that Percy Adlon, the director, maintains a certain bleak undercurrent of despair, of crying babies and

unpaid bills, and young people who have come to the ends of their ropes.

He is saying something in this movie about Europe and America, about the old and the new, about the edge of the desert as the edge of the American Dream. I am not sure exactly what it is, but that is comforting; if a director could assemble these strange characters and then know for sure what they were doing in the same movie together, he would be too confident to find the humor in their situation. The charm of *Bagdad Cafe* is that every character and every moment is unanticipated, obscurely motivated, of uncertain meaning, and vibrating with life.

Bambi ★ ★ ★ ½
G, 69 m., 1942

In the annals of the great heartbreaking moments in the movies, the death of Bambi's mother ranks right up there with the chaining of Mrs. Jumbo and the moment when E.T. seems certainly dead. These are movie moments that provide a rite of passage for children of a certain age: You send them in as kids, and they come out as sadder and wiser preteen-agers.

Seeing *Bambi* again, I was reminded of the strength of the movie's most famous scene. I was sitting behind a four-year-old who asked his mother, "Where's Bambi's mom?" during that long, sad passage before Bambi's father comes along to explain the facts of death. How do you answer a question like that? For some kids, *Bambi* probably represents their first exposure to the existence of death.

And there are other moments in the movie almost as momentous. *Bambi* exists alone in the Disney canon. It is not an adventure and not a "cartoon," but an animated feature that describes with surprising seriousness the birth and growth of a young deer. Everybody remembers the cute early moments when Bambi can't find his footing and keeps tripping over his own shadow. Those scenes are among the most charming the Disney animators ever drew.

But in the course of little more than an hour, those funny moments are followed by Bambi's exposure to man, his first experience with guns and killing, the death of his mother, and the destruction of the forest by fire. By then the deer has grown to young adulthood, and finds that he must battle another stag for the favors of the female deer he fancies.

The movie ends after Bambi has become a father. Do you remember the last shot? It shows Bambi and his own father, two proud stags silhouetted against the sky. Meanwhile, Bambi's mate takes care of raising his child. This is as it should be in the world of Bambi; the hero is raised by his own mother, while his father poses on the mountaintop.

Bambi is essentially a fable about how children are born, raised, and come of age in a hard, cruel world. Its messages are many. Young viewers learn that fathers are absent and mysterious authority figures, worshiped and never blamed by mothers, who do all the work of child-raising. They learn that you have to be quick and clever to avoid being killed deliberately—and that even then, you might easily be killed accidentally. They learn that courtship is a matter of "first love" and instant romance with no communication, and that the way to win the physical favors of the desired mate is to beat up all the other guys who want to be with her. And they learn that after you've grown to manhood and fathered a child, your role is to leave home and let your mate take care of the domestic details.

Hey, I don't want to sound like an alarmist here, but if you really stop to think about it, *Bambi* is a parable of sexism, nihilism, and despair, portraying absentee fathers and passive mothers in a world of death and violence. I know the movie's a perennial classic, seen by every generation, remembered long after other movies have been forgotten. But I am not sure it's a good experience for children—especially very young and impressionable ones.

We forget how real animated cartoons seem to small children. Think back. When you were very young, didn't you always consider the cartoons to be more real than the live-action features, because the colors were brighter, the edges were sharper, and the motives and behavior were easier to understand? That's how I felt, and for me, *Snow White* and *Pinocchio* and *Dumbo* were not fantasies but realities. There's a tradition in our society of exposing kids to the Disney classics at an early age, and for most kids and most of the Disney movies, that's just fine. But *Bambi* is pretty serious stuff. I don't know if some little kids are going to be ready for it.

Bang the Drum Slowly ★ ★ ★ ★
PG, 98 m., 1973

Michael Moriarty (Henry Wiggen), Robert De Niro (Bruce Pearson), Vincent Gardenia (Dutch Schnell), Phil Foster (Joe), Ann Wedgeworth (Katie), Patrick McVey (Mr. Pearson). Directed by John Hancock and produced by Maurice and Lois Rosenfield. Screenplay by Mark Harris.

Bang the Drum Slowly is the ultimate baseball movie—and, despite what a plot summary might suggest, I think it's more about baseball than death. It takes place during the last season on this Earth of one Bruce Pearson, an earnest but dumb catcher from Georgia who learns, in the movie's first scene, that he is suffering from an incurable disease. The movie is about that season and about his friendship with Henry Wiggen, a pitcher, who undertakes to see that Bruce at least lives his last months with some dignity, some joy, and a few good games.

On the surface, then, the movie seems a little like *Brian's Song*. But it's not: It's mostly about baseball and the daily life of a major league club on the road. The fact of Bruce's approaching death adds a poignancy to the season, but *Bang the Drum Slowly* doesn't brood about death and it isn't morbid. In its mixture of fatalism, roughness, tenderness, and bleak humor, indeed, it seems to know more about the ways we handle death than a movie like *Love Story* ever guessed. The movie begins at the Mayo Clinic, follows the team through spring training, and then carries it through a season that feels remarkably like a Chicago Cubs year: a strong start, problems during the hot weather, dissension on the team, and then a pennant drive that (in the movie, anyway) is successful. There isn't a lot of play-by-play action, only enough to establish the games and make the character points. So when the team manager and the pitcher conspire to let Bruce finish his last game, despite his illness, the action footage is relevant and moving.

Bang the Drum Slowly was adapted for the screen by Mark Harris, from his observant 1955 novel. He seems to understand baseball players, or at least he can create convincing ones; if real baseball players aren't like the ones in this movie, somehow they should be. The director, John Hancock, is good with his actors and very good at establishing a lot of supporting characters without making a

point of it (in this area he reminds me of Robert Altman's shorthand typecasting in *M*A*S*H* and *McCabe and Mrs. Miller*). Some of the best scenes are in the clubhouse, an arena of hope, despair, anger, practical jokes, and impassioned speeches by the manager.

He's played by Vincent Gardenia as a crafty, tough tactician with a heart of gold he tries to conceal. ("When I die," he says during one pre-game pep talk, "in the newspapers they'll write that the sons of bitches of this world have lost their leader.") He knows Bruce and Henry are concealing something, but he doesn't know what, and his efforts to find out are hilariously frustrated. At various times, the midwinter visit to the Mayo Clinic is explained as a fishing trip, a hunting trip, a wenching trip, and a secret mission to rid Bruce of the clap.

Gardenia, as the manager, is the third angle of a triangle that includes very good acting by Michael Moriarty, as Henry, and Robert De Niro, as Bruce. Henry is the All Star with the $70,000 contract and Bruce is a mediocre catcher who is constantly being ragged by his teammates. Henry's his only friend, until somehow when the team comes together for the pennant stretch, Bruce starts playing the best ball in his life, and the club (somewhat predictably) accepts him.

Hancock and Harris avoid any temptation to structure *Bang the Drum Slowly* as a typical sports movie. Although the team does win the pennant, not much of a point is made of that. There are no telegraphed big moments on the field, when everything depends on a strikeout or a home run or something. Even Bruce's last big hit in his last time at bat is limited, tactfully, to a triple.

Instead of going for a lot of high points, the movie paints characters in their everyday personalities. We get some feeling of life on the road as Henry talks with a hotel telephone operator who's a baseball fanatic, and Bruce moons over the prostitute he's in love with. Phil Foster has a great cameo role as a first-base coach with a genius for luring suckers into card games with remarkably elastic rules. Occupying the background in a lot of shots is the team's Cuban third baseman, who has it written into his contract that he be provided with a translator. And then, as the movie's shape begins to be visible, we realize it's not so much a sports movie as a movie about those elusive subjects, male bonding and work in America. That the males play baseball and that sport is their work is what makes this the ultimate baseball movie; never before has a movie considered the game from the inside out.

Barfly ★ ★ ★ ★
R, 110 m., 1987

Mickey Rourke (Henry), Faye Dunaway (Wanda Wilcox), Alice Krige (Tully), Jack Nance (Detective), J.C. Quinn (Jim), Frank Stallone (Eddie), Gloria LeRoy (Grandma Moses). Directed by Barbet Schroeder and produced by Schroeder, Fred Roos, and Tom Luddy. Screenplay by Charles Bukowski.

Louis Armstrong was trying to explain jazz one day, and he finally gave up and said, "There are some folks that, if they don't know, you can't tell 'em." The world of Charles Bukowski could be addressed in the same way. Bukowski is the poet of Skid Row, the Los Angeles drifter who spent his life, until age fifty, in an endless round of saloons and women, all of them cheap, expensive, bad, or good in various degrees. *Barfly*, based on his original screenplay, is a grimy comedy about what it might be like to spend a couple of days in his skin—a couple of the better and funnier days, although they aren't exactly a lark.

The movie takes place in a gutbucket bar down on the bad side of town, where the same regulars take up the same positions on the same bar stools every day. Your private life is nobody's business, but everybody in the joint knows all about it. To this bar, day after day, comes Henry (Mickey Rourke), a drunk who is sometimes also a poet. The day bartender hates him, probably for the same reason all bartenders in gutter saloons hate their customers: It's bad enough that they have to serve these losers, without taking a lot of lip from them, too.

Henry and the bartender head for the back alley to have a fight. Henry is beaten to a pulp. Hawking up spit and blood, he tosses down another drink and heads off for the hovel he calls his room. Another day, another adventure. One day he looks up from his drink and sees, sitting at the other end of the bar, a woman named Wanda (Faye Dunaway). She looks like she belongs in the place, and she doesn't look like she belongs in the place, you know? She looks like a drunk, all right, but she's still kind of classy. Henry and Wanda strike up a conversation, and, seeing that Henry is broke, Wanda invites him home.

The dialogue scenes between Rourke and Dunaway in this movie are never less than a pleasure, but their exchanges on that first night are poetry. She explains that if a guy comes along with a fifth, she is likely to leave with that guy, since when she drinks she always makes bad decisions. He nods. What other kinds of decisions are there when you're drunk? They drink, they talk, they flirt, they coexist. Another day, another adventure.

One day a beautiful rich girl with long hair (Alice Krige) comes to the bar looking for Henry. She publishes a literary magazine and has purchased some of Henry's stuff. He likes this development. They go to her house and drink, talk, flirt and coexist. The next time she turns up in the bar, Wanda is already there. The rich girl and Wanda do not coexist.

That's basically what the movie is about. *Barfly* is not heavy on plot, which is correct, since in the disordered world of the drinker, one thing rarely leads to another through any visible pattern. Each day is a window that opens briefly after the hangover and before the blackout, and you can never tell what you'll see through that window.

Barfly was directed by Barbet Schroeder, who commissioned the original screenplay by Bukowski and then spent eight years trying to get it made. (At one point, he threatened to cut off his fingers if Cannon Group president Menahem Golan did not finance it; the outcome of the story can be deduced by the fact that this is a Cannon release.) Rourke and Dunaway take their characters as opportunities to stretch as actors, to take chances and do extreme things. Schroeder never tries to impose too much artificial order on the events; indeed, he committed to filming Bukowski's screenplay exactly as written, in all its rambling but romantic detail.

The result is a truly original American movie, a film like no other, a period of time spent in the company of the kinds of characters Saroyan and O'Neill would have understood, the kinds of people we try not to see, and yet might enjoy more than some of our more visible friends. *Barfly* was one of 1987's best films.

Bat 21 ★ ★ ★
R, 104 m., 1988

Gene Hackman (Col. Hambleton), Danny Glover (Birddog), Jerry Reed (Col. Walker), David Marshall Grant (Ross Carver), Clayton Rohner (Sgt. Rumbaugh), Erich Anderson (Major Scott). Directed by Peter Markle and produced by David Fisher, Gary A. Neill, and Michael Balson. Screenplay by William C. Anderson and George Gordon.

Bat 21 is the kind of lean, no-nonsense war film Hollywood used to make back before the subject became burdened with metaphysical insights. It's the story of a middle-aged Air Force colonel's attempt to survive behind enemy lines, where he has no business being in the first place, and about how a stubborn spotter pilot returns time and again in a light aircraft to keep his spirits up. The movie could have been about any modern war, and in Gene Hackman it has its everyman.

Hackman's character is inspired by the real-life adventures of Lt. Col. Iceal Hambleton, a World War II and Korean veteran who held a high-level desk job in Vietnam. After reports were received of a jungle highway carrying a major troop movement, Hambleton decided one day to go along on a mission and have a look. His plane was shot down, he parachuted, and was stranded in the jungle with a survival kit, a pistol, and a radio.

Because Hambleton had access to high-level secrets, his rescue became more than usually important, and the movie is the story of how the Air Force tries to get him out despite weather, bad luck, and its impending plans to carpet-bomb the troop movements in the immediate vicinity. The story is told in a straightforward way as the relationship between a nearly hopeless man on the ground, and the pilot of a Cessna Skymaster who returns day and night to maintain radio contact until a helicopter rescue mission can be mounted.

Because this is essentially a two-character story, it's the kind of movie the studios used to shoot in the jungles on their back lots. *Bat 21* was shot on location in Malaysia, however, and it looks authentic and gets us involved through the energy of its performances. Hackman plays a thoroughly ordinary man, not a hero with special jungle survival skills, and there are times when we despair of him. Why, for example, does he use his radio so freely when nearby enemy troops could possibly hear it? That's so dumb, it's the sort of thing we'd do.

The spotter pilot, called "Birddog," is played by Danny Glover as another veteran, an extraordinarily skilled light aircraft pilot who swoops low over the treetops and keeps up a running commentary on Hambleton's chances. He disobeys orders in order to fly at night and in bad weather to keep Hambleton's spirits up, and the rescue becomes a personal obsession with him.

Because Hambleton is concerned that the enemy may be eavesdropping on his radio frequency, he comes up with a code for discussing his movements with Birddog. Hambleton's a fanatic golfer, and he imagines various military golf courses he has played and then places it in the jungle so that he can describe his movements as drives on various fairways of the course. This is such a goofy strategy that it is probably based on real life; it is, in any event, true to the war movie tradition of naming operations after silly details from civilian life (remember Tom, Dick, and Harry? Those were the names of the three tunnels in *The Great Escape).*

Although they meet face-to-face only once in the film, Hackman and Glover work well together, as two men who come to share a common, stubborn determination. And Hackman's colonel is different from his other military characters; Hambleton isn't a fighting man but a desk officer who takes a cup of coffee along on his foolhardy mission and is sipping it when the missiles strike his airplane. He has no combat experience, has never gotten close to the front lines, and is horrified by his encounter with a Vietnamese family that leads him to kill for the first time. This is not a combat movie but the story of a man who spent almost his entire career keeping war at arm's length, until it reached out and grabbed him.

Batman ★ ★
PG-13, 126 m., 1989

Jack Nicholson (The Joker/Jack Napier), Michael Keaton (Batman/Bruce Wayne), Kim Basinger (Vicki Vale), Robert Wuhl (Alexander Knox), Pat Hingle (Police Commissioner Gordon), Billy Dee Williams (District Attorney Harvey Dent), Michael Gough (Alfred), Jerry Hall (Alicia), Jack Palance (Carl Grissom). Directed by Tim Burton and produced by Jon Peters and Peter Guber. Screenplay by Sam Hamm and Warren Skaaren.

The Gotham City created in *Batman* is one of the most distinctive and atmospheric places I've seen in the movies. It's a shame something more memorable doesn't happen there. *Batman* is a triumph of design over story, style over substance—a great-looking movie with a plot you can't care much about. All of the big moments in the movie are pounded home with ear-shattering sound effects and a jackhammer cutting style, but that just serves to underline the movie's problem, which is a curious lack of suspense and intrinsic interest.

Batman discards the recent cultural history of the Batman character—the camp 1960s TV series, the in-joke comic books—and returns to the mood of the 1940s, the decade of *film noir* and fascism. The movie is set at the present moment, more or less, but looks as if little has happened in architecture or city planning since the classic DC comic books created that architectural style you could call Comic Book Moderne. The streets of Gotham City are lined with bizarre skyscrapers that climb cancerously toward the sky, held up (or apart) by sky-bridges and steel struts that look like webs against the night sky.

At street level, gray and anonymous people scurry fearfully through the shadows, and the city cancels its two-hundredth-anniversary celebration because the streets are not safe enough to hold it. Gotham is in the midst of a wave of crime and murder orchestrated by The Joker (Jack Nicholson), and civilization is defended only by Batman (Michael Keaton). The screenplay takes a bow in the direction of the origin of the Batman story (young Bruce Wayne saw his parents murdered by a thug and vowed to use their fortune to dedicate his life to crime-fighting), and it also explains how The Joker got his fearsome grimace. Then it turns into a gloomy showdown between the two bizarre characters.

Nicholson's Joker is really the most important character in the movie—in impact and screen time—and Keaton's Batman and Bruce Wayne characters are so monosyllabic and impenetrable that we have to remind ourselves to cheer for them. Kim Basinger strides in as Vicki Vale, a famous photographer assigned to the Gotham City crime wave, but although she and Wayne carry on a courtship and Batman rescues her from certain death more than once, there's no chemistry and little eroticism. The strangest scene in the movie may be the one where Vicki is

brought into the Batcave by Alfred, the faithful valet, and realizes for the first time that Bruce Wayne and Batman are the same person. How does she react? She doesn't react. The movie forgets to allow her to be astonished.

Remembering the movie, I find that the visuals remain strong in my mind, but I have trouble caring about what happened in front of them. I remember an astonishing special-effects shot that travels up, up to the penthouse of a towering, ugly skyscraper, and I remember the armor slamming shut on the Batmobile as if it were a high-tech armadillo. I remember The Joker grinning beneath a hideous giant balloon as he dispenses free cash in his own travesty of the Macy's parade, and I remember a really vile scene in which he defaces art masterpieces in the local museum, before Batman crashes in through the skylight.

But did I care about the relationship between these two caricatures? Did either one have the depth of even a comic-book character? Not really. And there was something off-putting about the anger beneath the movie's violence; this is a hostile, mean-spirited movie about ugly, evil people, and it doesn't generate the liberating euphoria of the *Superman* or *Indiana Jones* pictures. It's rated PG-13, but it's not for kids.

Should it be seen, anyway? Probably. Director Tim Burton and his special-effects team have created a visual place that has some of the same strength as Fritz Lang's *Metropolis* or Ridley Scott's futuristic Los Angeles in *Blade Runner.* The gloominess of the visuals has a haunting power. Jack Nicholson has one or two of his patented moments of inspiration—although not as many as I would have expected. And the music by Prince, intercut with classics, is effectively joined in the images. The movie's problem is that no one seemed to have any fun making it, and it's hard to have much fun watching it. It's a depressing experience. Is the opposite of comic book "tragic book"?

Beaches ★ ★ ¹/₂
PG-13, 123 m., 1988

Bette Midler (CC Bloom), Barbara Hershey (Hillary Whitney), John Heard (John Pierce), Spalding Gray (Dr. Milstein), Lainie Kazan (Leona Bloom), James Read (Michael Essex). Directed by Garry Marshall and produced by Bonnie Bruckheimer-Martell and Bette Midler. Screenplay by Mary Agnes Donoghue.

Maybe the problem is with the flashbacks. Maybe if the whole story had simply been told from beginning to end, it would have felt less like one of those 1950s tearjerkers with the rain blowing in through the window and getting the curtains all wet. But *Beaches* begins on a note of impending doom, and that colors everything else with an undertone of bittersweet poignancy, and, believe me, there is only so much bittersweet poignancy I can take in any one movie.

The film opens with CC Bloom (Bette Midler), a pop star, rehearsing for a big concert at the Hollywood Bowl. Then she gets an urgent message, and suddenly the concert seems unimportant and she has to drop everything and race to San Francisco. Well, of course there's bad weather and the planes are all grounded, and so she sets off through the night in a rental car, raindrops on the windshield and tears in her eyes.

The movie then flashes back to an event some years earlier on the Boardwalk in Atlantic City, where young CC first meets a playmate named Hillary Whitney. CC is a trouper even at the age of twelve, and we follow her through a show-biz audition in which her mother (Lainie Kazan) cheerleads from the front of the stalls. She doesn't get the job, but she does make a friend in Hillary, and of course this friendship is to endure all during the lives of these two quite different women, all the way up until the tragedy that is foreshadowed in the opening scenes.

What happens in the first half hour of *Beaches* is sort of discouraging. The story is set up so completely in terms of ancient movie cliches that we know we can relax; nothing unexpected is going to happen. We're way ahead of the characters on the screen. We know that the two women will meet again as young adults, that they will fall in love with the same man, that one will love him and the other leave him, that they'll have some big fights but their friendship will endure. We also know, of course, that some sort of movie disease will strike Hillary—because why else is CC driving all night through the rain?

Hillary Whitney is played in the movie by Barbara Hershey, as a rich WASP to Midler's irreverent Jewish girl. Various men and marriages drift in and out of view, and we see John Heard as a hot young theater director and Spalding Gray as a supercilious doctor, but the important thing is that Hillary has a child (Grace Johnston). CC, of course, has never had a child and is not sure she likes this

one, and the suspicion is mutual, so we know—we simply *know*—that the Hershey character will die and that there will be a big heart-tugging scene at the end where CC and the kid decide to plug on through life, side by side.

I have no doubt that the people who made this film approached it with great sincerity, and that there were long conversations about what CC "would" do and how Hillary "would" act in such-and-such a situation. But *Beaches* lacks the spontaneity of life. This is a movie completely constructed out of other movies—out of cliches and archetypes that were old before most of the cast members were born. It is difficult for a filmgoer of reasonable intelligence to care about characters whose lives are reenactments of cliches: If these people are as smart as they think, why can't they see that their lives are a bad B movie?

Maybe, in a strange way, one of the problems is Midler herself. She has a reputation for intelligence and irreverence that is mostly deserved, and so when we go to see her in a movie we don't expect her to be portraying a character completely dictated by convention. We expect a little spin on the ball. *Beaches* gives us nothing that can't be spotted coming a mile down the road.

The Bear ★ ★ ★
PG, 93 m., 1989

Bart (Kaar), Douce (Youk), Jack Wallace (Bill), Tcheky Karyo (Tom), Andre Lacombe (The Dog Handler). Directed by Jean-Jacques Annaud and produced by Claude Berri. Screenplay by Gerard Brach.

I was out at the zoo the other day, gawking through a plate-glass window at a family of gorillas who were going about their business with sublime indifference to mine. One fellow over in the corner was meticulously sorting through a pile of straw, looking for something he had mislaid. Two adolescents were tumbling over each other in rough play. It was a touching domestic scene, until without any warning the big male gorilla came charging directly at me and slammed against the glass with a fearsome roar.

The glass was thick, the incident was over in a moment, but for the length of that moment I felt the kind of instinctual response that has been bred into us from prehistory. I knew fear, because a wild beast wanted to kill me. And it is respect for that

reality that is at the heart of *The Bear*, a movie about the first year of a bear cub's lifetime.

This is not a cute fantasy in which bears ride tricycles and play house. It is about life in the wild, and it does an impressive job of seeming to show wild bears in their natural habitat. I write "seeming" because I know that the movie was made with trained bears, and that parts of certain scenes were even fabricated using animated models. But film is an art of illusion, and the illusion in *The Bear* is that we are seeing the real thing.

The movie was directed by Jean-Jacques Annaud, whose *Quest for Fire* (1982) was an effective film recreating man's earliest days. He used little language in that movie, and in *The Bear* he uses almost none—except for the brief statements of two hunters, whose words are not meant to be language, but simply the sounds made by the animal named man.

The movie opens with the birth of a bear cub. It follows the cub through the traumatic experience of the death of its mother, and then it shows the cub being adopted by an adult male grizzly, who protects it and endures it during the first summer of its growth.

The animals live in a high range of mountain pastures (the film was shot in the Dolomites and the Canadian Arctic). We are always aware of the vast sweep of nature, of the fact that the grizzly is the most deadly animal for hundreds of miles—except, of course (as Bambi's mother once warned), for man. Two hunters penetrate into this wilderness, encounter the bears, and in a very quiet scene of great drama, arrive at a kind of truce. The actors have little to do in a traditional theatrical sense, but the presence of the lead hunter (Jack Wallace) is fully convincing in the movie's key scene.

Other scenes in the movie are more everyday. I am sure it took great patience on the part of the filmmakers to obtain the shots of the bears fishing for trout, but the scene plays like a moment stolen from life. Other scenes—of horseplay and genuine struggles—gradually build up our sense of the personalities of these animals. There is always a temptation to interpret the behavior of animals in terms of human personality, and *The Bear* indulges that temptation, but there are also moments to remind us that these are wild beasts for whom killing, and being killed, is a fact of life.

Beetlejuice ★ ★
PG, 105 m., 1988

Alec Baldwin (Adam), Geena Davis (Barbara), Michael Keaton (Betelgeuse), Jeffrey Jones (Charles), Catherine O'Hara (Delia), Winona Ryder (Lydia), Sylvia Sidney (Juno). Directed by Tim Burton and produced by Michael Bender, Larry Wilson, and Richard Hashimoto. Screenplay by Michael McDowell and Warren Skaaren.

Beetlejuice gets off to a start that's so charming it never lives it down. The movie is all anticlimax once we realize it's going to be about gimmicks, not characters. During the enchanted opening minutes of the film, we meet a young married couple who have just moved into a strange new house, and we're introduced to some of the local townspeople. All of these characters have an offhand, unforced innocence, and no wonder: The movie was directed by Tim Burton, who created a similar feeling in *Pee Wee's Big Adventure*.

It's hard to describe what makes the opening scenes so special. Alec Baldwin and Geena Davis, as the young couple, seem so giddy, so heedlessly in love, that they project an infectious good cheer. The local folks are so gosh-darn down-home they must have been sired by L.L. Bean out of the *Prairie Home Companion*. The movie is bathed in a foolish charm. And, fool that I am, I expected that note to be carried all the way through the film. But it was not to be.

The young couple die in a silly accident. But they still live in the same house. The only problem is, there's nothing outside the door except for a strange science-fiction landscape that looks borrowed from Paul Schrader's *Cat People*. It takes them a while to figure out they're dead, and even longer to realize what has happened: Their fate is to remain in their former home as ghosts, while it is sold to a New York family (Jeffrey Jones and Catherine O'Hara, and Winona Ryder as their daughter) who have big plans for remodeling it.

This is all, I guess, a fairly clever idea. And the movie is well-played, especially by Davis (the girlfriend in *The Fly*) and Jones (the emperor in *Amadeus*, the principal in *Ferris Bueller's Day Off*). But the story, which seemed so original, turns into a sitcom fueled by lots of special effects and weird sets and props, and the inspiration is gone.

To be sure, there has never before been a

movie afterworld quite like this one. Heaven, or whatever it is, seems a lot like a cruise ship with a cranky crew. The "newlydeads" find a manual that instructs them on how to live as ghosts, and they also find an advertisement from a character named Betelgeuse (Michael Keaton), who specializes in "exorcisms of the living." They enlist him to try to scare the New Yorkers out of the house, but he turns out to be a cantankerous demon, and a lot more trouble than he's worth.

The best thing about the movie, apart from the opening, is the set design by Bo Welch. Both he and Burton seem inspired by the spirit of "Pee Wee's Playhouse" and *Pee Wee's Big Adventure*, in which objects can have lives of their own, and architectural details have an unsettling way of rearranging themselves. The look of the film might be described as cartoon surrealistic. But the film's dramatic method isn't nearly as original.

One of the problems is Keaton, as the exorcist. Nearly unrecognizable behind pounds of makeup, he prances around playing Betelgeuse as a mischievous and vindictive prankster, but his scenes don't seem to fit with the other action, and his appearances are mostly a nuisance. It's also a shame that Baldwin and Davis, as the ghosts, have to spend most of their time playing tricks on Jones and O'Hara and winning the sympathy of their daughter; I would have been more interested if the screenplay had preserved their sweet romanticism and cut back on the slapstick.

Being There ★ ★ ★ ★
PG, 130 m., 1980

Peter Sellers (Chance), Shirley MacLaine (Eve Rand), Melvyn Douglas (Ben Rand), Jack Warden (President), Richard Dysart (Dr. Allenby), Richard Basehart (Skrapinov). Directed by Hal Ashby and produced by Andrew Braunsberg. Screenplay by Jerzy Kosinski.

There's an exhilaration in seeing artists at the very top of their form: It almost doesn't matter what the form is, if they're pushing their limits and going for broke and it's working. We can sense their joy of achievement—and even more so if the project in question is a risky, off-the-wall idea that could just as easily have ended disastrously.

Hal Ashby's *Being There* is a movie that

inspires those feelings. It begins with a cockamamie notion, it's basically one joke told for two hours, and it requires Peter Sellers to maintain an excruciatingly narrow tone of behavior in a role that has him onscreen almost constantly. It's a movie based on an idea, and all the conventional wisdom agrees that emotions, not ideas, are the best to make movies from. But *Being There* pulls off its long shot and is a confoundingly provocative movie.

Sellers plays a mentally retarded gardener who has lived and worked all of his life inside the walls of an elegant Washington town house. The house and its garden are in a decaying inner-city neighborhood, but what goes on outside is of no concern to Sellers: He tends his garden, he watches television, he is fed on schedule by the domestic staff, he is content.

Then one day the master of the house dies. The household is disbanded. Sellers, impeccably dressed in his employer's privately tailored wardrobe, wanders out into the city. He takes along the one possession he'll probably need: His remote-control TV channel switcher. He uses it almost immediately; surrounded by hostile street kids, he imperturbably tries to switch channels to make them go away. He hasn't figured out that, outside his garden, life isn't television.

And that is the movie's basic premise, lifted intact from a Jerzy Kosinski novel. The Sellers character knows almost nothing about real life, but he has watched countless hours of television and he can be pleasant, smile, shake hands, and comport himself; he learned from watching all those guests on talk shows. He knows nothing about *anything*, indeed, except gardening. But when he stumbles into Washington's political and social upper crust, his simple truisms from the garden ("Spring is a time for planting") are taken as audaciously simple metaphors. This guy's a Thoreau! In no time at all, he's the closest confidant of a dying billionaire industrialist (Melvyn Douglas)—and the industrialist is the closest confidant of the president.

This is, you can see, a one-joke premise. It has to be if the Sellers performance is to work. The whole movie has to be tailored to the narrow range within which Sellers's gardener can think, behave, speak, and make choices. The ways in which this movie could have gone out of control, could have been relentlessly boring on the one hand, or manic with its own audacity on the other, are endless. But the tone holds. That's one of the most exhilarating aspects of the joy you can sense, as Ashby pulls this off: Every scene needs the confidence to play the idea completely straight.

There are wonderful comic moments, but they're never pushed so far that they strain the story's premise. Some of them involve: a battle between the CIA and the FBI as to which agency destroyed the gardener's files; Shirley MacLaine unsuccessfully attempts to introduce Sellers to the concept of romance; Sellers as a talk-show guest himself (at last!), and Sellers as the hit of a Washington cocktail party. The movie also has an audacious closing shot that moves the film's whole metaphor into a brand-new philosophical arena.

What is *Being There* about? I've read reviews calling it an indictment of television. But that doesn't fit; Sellers wasn't warped by television, he was retarded to begin with, and has TV to thank for what abilities he *has* to move in society. Is it an indictment of society, for being so dumb as to accept the Sellers character as a great philosophical sage? Maybe, but that's not so fascinating either. I'm not really inclined to plumb this movie for its message, although I'm sure that'll be a favorite audience sport. I just admire it for having the guts to take this weird conceit and push it to its ultimate comic conclusion.

Best Boy ★ ★ ★ ★
NO MPAA RATING, 111 m., 1980

A documentary produced, directed, and edited by Ira Wohl.

Sometimes there are movies that absorb you so completely that you forget you're watching them: They're simply happening to you. Ira Wohl's *Best Boy* is a movie like that. To see it is to participate in the lives of other people and to learn just a little more about being human. *Best Boy*, which won the 1980 Academy Award as best documentary, is the story of an only son named Philly, whose parents have always been too protective of him. But as the movie opens, it is time for Philly to go out a little more on his own—to go down to the corner for an ice cream cone, for example, or to look forward to his first day of school. Philly is fifty-two years old. He is mentally retarded, but otherwise, as a psychiatrist explains in the film, "quite normal." He is also warm and lovable, and when Wordsworth wrote that heaven was all about

us when we were children, did he guess that would also be true for someone like Philly, who will never really leave childhood?

Best Boy deals intelligently with real people and their problems. It is not simply a documentary; it contains the surprises of true drama, and it is put together so thoughtfully that it takes what could have been a case study and turns it into a cliffhanger. That is largely due to the complete access that the filmmaker, Ira Wohl, had to his subject. Philly is Wohl's cousin, and Philly's parents are Wohl's aunt and uncle. All the time he was growing up, Ira knew Philly—he played with him, presumably, when he was four or five and Philly seemed to be about the same age. Philly stayed four or five. As Wohl grew older, he realized that sooner or later Philly's parents would die, and that Philly's total dependence on them would leave him defenseless.

Philly had been at home almost all his life. The movie begins as his parents make the first reluctant, tentative steps to allow him a little more independence—to set him free. *Best Boy* moves very delicately around this subject, and with good reason: As we watch it, we realize that the parents have come to depend on Philly, too. He provided them with a rationale for their own lives and choices. He is their crutch as well as their burden. And there is yet another drama that unfolds within the film—unfolds so subtly we barely realize it is there, and yet concludes so inevitably that it casts a light back on all the scenes that went before. Philly's father is dying. There is a time in the film when the father clearly knows that and no one else in the film does, but we, strangers, share his secret with him.

You see what I mean when I say *Best Boy* isn't a case study. It's not about what should be done with Philly, and it has little to do with the "problem" of mental retardation. It is so specifically about Philly and his family and their daily choices in life that we almost feel adopted into the family. And we get to like Philly so much! He is sweet and cheerful, patient and good-humored, with a child's logic that cuts right through so much of the confusion adults surround him with. There is a wonderful scene with a psychiatrist, who is trying to administer a series of questions Philly obviously feels are silly. There is a visit to the theater, where Philly is allowed backstage to meet Zero Mostel, and they sing "If I Were a Rich Man" together. Why is it, the movie asks but never answers,

that Philly can remember songs better than speech?

Best Boy suffers, I suppose, from being labeled a documentary: Some small-minded people make it a policy never to watch one. But at the Toronto Festival of Festivals, where the patrons are asked to vote for their favorite film, it astonished everyone by defeating all the features in the festival and placing first. It's a wonderfully positive experience.

Betrayal ★ ★ ★ ★
R, 95 m., 1983

Jeremy Irons (Jerry), Ben Kingsley (Robert), Patricia Hodge (Emma). Directed by David Jones and produced by Sam Spiegel. Screenplay by Harold Pinter.

Love stories have beginnings, but affairs . . . affairs have endings, too. Even sad love stories begin in gladness, when the world is young and the future reaches out cheerfully forever. Then, of course, eventually you get Romeo and Juliet dead in the tomb, but that's the price you have to pay. Life isn't a free ride. Think how much *more* tragic a sad love story would be, however, if you could see into the future, so that even *this* moment, *this* kiss, is in the shadow of eventual despair.

The absolutely brilliant thing about *Betrayal* is that it is a love story told backward. There is a lot in this movie that is wonderful—the performances, the screenplay by Harold Pinter—but what makes it all work is the structure. When Pinter's stage version of *Betrayal* first appeared, back in the late 1970s, there was a tendency to dismiss his reverse chronology as a gimmick. Not so. It is the very heart and soul of this story. It means that we in the audience know more about the unhappy romantic fortunes of Jerry and Robert and Emma at *every moment* than they know about themselves. Even their joy is painful to see.

Jerry is a youngish London literary agent, clever, good-looking, confused about his feelings. Robert, his best friend, is a publisher. Robert is older, stronger, smarter, and more bitter. Emma is Robert's wife and becomes Jerry's lover. But that is telling the story chronologically. And the story begins at the end, with Robert and Emma fighting, and with Robert slapping her, and with Emma and Jerry meeting in a pub for a painful reunion two years after their affair is over. Each additional scene takes place further back in time, and the sections have uncanny titles: Two years earlier. Three years earlier. We aren't used to this. At a public preview of the film, some people in the audience actually *resisted* the backward timeframe, as if the purpose of the playwright was just to get on with the story, damn it all, and stop this confounded fooling around.

The *Betrayal* structure strips away all artifice. It shows, heartlessly, that the very capacity for love itself is sometimes based on betraying not only other loved ones, but even ourselves. The movie is told mostly in encounters between two of the characters; all three are not often on screen together, and we never meet Jerry's wife. These people are smart and they talk a lot—too much, maybe, because there is a peculiarly British reserve about them that sometimes prevents them from quite saying what they mean. They lie and they half-lie. There are universes left unspoken in their unfinished sentences. They are all a little embarrassed that the messy urges of sex are pumping away down there beneath their civilized deceptions.

The performances are perfectly matched. Ben Kingsley (of *Gandhi*) plays Robert, the publisher, with such painfully controlled fury that there are times when he actually is frightening. Jeremy Irons, as Jerry, creates a man whose desires are stronger than his convictions, even though he spends a lot of time talking about his convictions, and almost none acknowledging his desires. Patricia Hodge, as Emma, loves them both and hates them both and would have led a much happier life if they had not been her two choices. But how could she know that when, in life, you're required by the rules to start at the beginning?

Betrayed ★ ★
R, 123 m., 1988

Debra Winger (Katie Phillips/Cathy Weaver), Tom Berenger (Gary Simmons), John Heard (Michael Carnes), Betsy Blair (Gladys Simmons), John Mahoney (Shorty), Ted Levine (Wes), Jeffrey DeMunn (Flynn), Albert Hall (Al Sanders), David Clennon (Jack Carpenter), Robert Swan (Dean). Directed by Costa-Gavras and produced by Irwin Winkler. Written by Joe Eszterhas.

Betrayed is a film that left me in turmoil, torn between the strong sympathies I felt for the characters, and the fundamental doubts I had about the plot. Here were people I believed in, involved in a story that no one could believe in—and that kind of conflict raises basic questions, such as how could the characters themselves, who seem so intelligent, believe their own story? That's the trickiest thing about creating movie characters who can think for themselves.

The movie opens in harvest season, with Debra Winger as an itinerant farm laborer who gets a few days' work running the combine on a big Iowa farm owned by a divorced man, played by Tom Berenger. There is a certain chemistry between them right from the start, and when she establishes a rapport with his two children, they begin to fall in love. Berenger asks Winger to stay on his farm when the harvest is over, and she does.

But *Betrayed* is not a love story. It is an undercover thriller, and we quickly learn that Winger is an FBI agent and that Berenger is suspected of being part of a secret right-wing terrorist organization that is responsible for the murder of a left-wing Chicago talk show host. How can this be true? How can this honest, open-faced farmer from a world of Sunday church services and apple pie be a neo-Nazi killer?

At first Winger herself doesn't believe it, and she tells her FBI contacts that they are after the wrong man. But then, after she falls more deeply in love with Berenger, he decides to trust her with his secrets. His first wife left because she could not endure his world of secret paranoia, but he realizes he must be honest with Winger because he loves her. His desire to share his hidden life creates some of the weirdest scenes in the film, because there is such an ironic tension between the ultra-right paramilitary organization he belongs to, and the pop psychology of his language when he explains that they must be open with each other and share the things that are important.

The plot, as it unfolds, is cleverly constructed by writer Joe Eszterhas (who crafted the diabolical double-reverses in *Jagged Edge*) and director Costa-Gavras (who has specialized in clandestine right-wing groups in movies like *Z* and *Missing*). Winger and Berenger form a sympathetic couple right from the start, and even well into the story there is a residual feeling that this Iowa farmer cannot be as two-faced and racist as he seems. Then, as the film's center of gravity shifts, it becomes mostly Winger's story, and she is wonderful at creating sympathy as Costa-Gavras turns up the heat, trapping her between love and danger.

This is essentially the same dilemma that Eszterhas created for Glenn Close in *Jagged Edge*. Can she trust the man she loves, or is he, as all evidence seems to indicate, a two-faced killer? In that film, the audience did not know the answer until the last moment, but in *Betrayed*, the answer is obvious from fairly early on (even the title is a giveaway). The thriller doesn't hinge on Berenger's behavior, but on how Winger will save herself from almost certain exposure. And as that level of the plot unfolded, I began to have problems.

I know that there are right-wing paramilitary groups in America. I know that members of one of them were convicted of the murder of Alan Berg, the liberal Denver talk show host whose murder inspired this story. I didn't question that level of the story, and even when *Betrayed* went out of its way to exaggerate the contradictions in the Berenger character, I accepted that as part of the job of thriller-making.

What bothered me were two other elements. One was the heavy-handed way in which the plot sets up Winger for danger. An FBI man, played by John Heard, becomes adept at being in the wrong place at the wrong time and acting carelessly, and the stupidity of his character would have been irritating even if the movie didn't also reveal an old romance between Winger and Heard, so that jealousy could be added to police work. Over and over, I found myself asking why the Winger character, who is so intelligent, makes such stupid decisions in the film, inspiring her own betrayal.

Another element that bothered me much more was a particularly disgusting and violent scene in which Berenger and his right-wing buddies capture a black man and then stage a "hunt" in which they chase him through the forest at night and finally kill him. It is reprehensible to put a sequence like that in a film intended as entertainment, no matter what the motives of the characters or the alleged importance to the plot. This sequence is as cynical as anything I've seen in a long time—a breach of standards so disturbing that it brings the film to a halt from which it barely recovers. I imagine that Costa-Gavras, whose left-wing credentials are impeccable, saw this scene as necessary to his indictment of the racist underworld he was exposing. But *Betrayed* is not a small, brave, political statement like *Z*; it is a Hollywood entertainment with big stars, and vile, racist manhunts have no place in it.

More than anything else, *Betrayed* is finally just very deeply confused. Costa-Gavras must have considered it a political film, Eszterhas undoubtedly saw it as a thriller, and Winger and Berenger, to give them full credit, interpret it as the complicated human stories of their characters. That's why the film creates its turmoil; in the center of confusion, sloppy plot developments and the conflicting motivations of the filmmakers, there are two performances of such power that the characters become real, and sympathetic, despite everything.

Betsy's Wedding ★ ★
R, 97 m., 1990

Alan Alda (Eddie Hopper), Joey Bishop (Eddie's Father), Madeline Kahn (Lola Hopper), Anthony LaPaglia (Stevie Dee), Catherine O'Hara (Gloria Henner), Joe Pesci (Oscar Henner), Molly Ringwald (Betsy Hopper), Ally Sheedy (Connie Hopper), Burt Young (Georgie), Julie Bovasso (Grandma). Directed by Alan Alda and produced by Martin Bregman and Louis A. Stroller. Screenplay by Alda.

Betsy's Wedding assembles all of the materials for a human comedy and then seems unconvinced by them. It's the story of a wedding that brings together—in one way or another—three families. The bride's father is in construction. The groom's father is in high finance. And the bride's sister falls in love with the nephew of a Mafia kingpin. The Mafia gets involved after the bride's father goes to his rich brother for a loan to pay for the wedding, and the payback involves hiring the nephew of the brother's Mafioso investor, if you can follow that.

This material could move in a number of directions: toward sitcom, toward satire, even toward a tear-jerking slice of life. But Alan Alda, who wrote and directed it and plays the proud father of the bride, prefers to play it mostly placid and even pedestrian. There have been two movies recently about inter-ethnic romances (*Spike of Bensonhurst* and *True Love*), and they were both more alive than this movie, more willing to take chances. *Betsy's Wedding* is awfully safe.

One of the strange things about the movie is that the bride-to-be, played by Molly Ringwald, is a relatively insignificant character in the movie. More screen time is devoted to her sister Connie (Ally Sheedy), a policewoman who falls in love with Stevie Dee, the Mafioso nephew. He's played by Anthony LaPaglia in a performance that provides the movie's best moments.

He's an earnest, curiously formal young man who wears his hair slicked into a glistening black helmet and is constantly adjusting the lapels of his suit, perhaps because he carries a gun in a shoulder holster. He first sees Connie, the cop, when she comes to visit her dad on a construction site. Stevie Dee's job on the site is to "observe," at $2,000 a week, but when he observes the Ally Sheedy character, all other thoughts fly from his mind, and he can think only of her.

She goes out with him on a few dates, but tries to explain that they were simply not meant to be: "I'm a cop, and you're . . . not." But then he kisses her goodnight, and he's a really great kisser, and despite everything she falls for him. Their relationship, and especially LaPaglia's performance, are the bright spots I kept hoping for the movie to return to.

Not much else is that entertaining. There is the business of how much will be spent on the wedding, and the business of how a wedding ceremony can be cobbled together out of bits of the Jewish, Catholic, agnostic, and vegetarian traditions, and, of course, the big set piece: the wedding reception at which all issues get resolved. Isolated lines are funny (as when Connie explains that she loves being a cop because arresting men gets her high). But the movie has a low-key, almost low-energy approach to its material; Alda should have turned up the juice.

The supporting cast looks promising on paper. Burt Young plays LaPaglia's uncle, Joe Pesci is Alda's rich brother, and Catherine O'Hara has some fun as his wife (she eavesdrops on his real estate deals, then buys the property he's after and resells it to him). There are a couple of good lines delivered with comic conviction by Julie Bovasso, who plays Alda's mother (she was John Travolta's mother in *Saturday Night Fever*). But seeing these interesting actors and hearing two or three good lines from them, we want more. And the movie never really cranks itself up. It's nice enough, it's sweet, I loved LaPaglia's work, but there's nothing compelling here.

Beverly Hills Cop ★ ★ ¹/₂
R, 105 m., 1984

Eddie Murphy (Axel Foley), Judge Reinhold (Detective Billy Rosewood), John Ashton (Sergeant Taggart), Lisa Eilbacher (Jenny), Ronny Cox (Lieutenant Bogomil). Directed by Martin Brest and produced by Don Simpson and Jerry Bruckheimer. Screenplay by Daniel Petrie.

Eddie Murphy looks like the latest victim of the Star Magic Syndrome, in which it is assumed that a movie will be a hit simply because it stars an enormously talented person. Thus it is not necessary to give much thought to what he does or says, or to the story he finds himself occupying. *Beverly Hills Cop* is a movie with an enormously appealing idea—a tough black detective from Detroit goes to Beverly Hills to avenge the murder of a friend—but the filmmakers apparently expected Murphy to carry this idea entirely by himself.

Murphy plays a street-wise rebel who is always getting in trouble with his commanding officer because he does things his own way. The movie opens with an example of that: Murphy is single-handedly running a sting operation when the cops arrive unexpectedly, setting off a wild car-truck chase through the city streets. Even while we're watching the thrilling chase, however, stirrings of unease are beginning to be felt: Any movie that *begins* with a chase is not going to be heavy on originality and inspiration. Then Murphy's old friend comes to town, fresh from a prison term and six months of soaking up the rays in California. The friend has some negotiable bonds with him, and then some friends of the guy who owns the bonds turn up and murder Murphy's friend. That makes Eddie mad, and he drives his ancient beater out to Beverly Hills, where it sort of stands out among the Porsches and Mercedeses. He also meets a childhood friend (Lisa Eilbacher) who now works for an art dealer.

At this point, the movie can go in one of two directions. It can become a perceptive and pointed satire about American attitudes, showing how the ultrachic denizens of Beverly Hills react to this black cop from Detroit. Or it can go for broad, cheap laughs, and plug into a standard plot borrowed from countless TV crime shows. *Beverly Hills Cop* doesn't pause a moment before taking the low road. We figure that out right away, when Murphy tries to register in a hotel and is told there isn't any room. He loudly pulls both ranks and race, claiming to be a correspondent from *Rolling Stone* and accusing the desk clerk of racism. This is (a) not funny, and (b) not convincing, because Beverly Hills desk clerks were not born yesterday. If the people who made this movie had been willing to listen to the ways that real people really talk, they could have made the scene into a jewel instead of an embarrassment.

Meanwhile, the plot thickens. It turns out that the killers of Eddie's friend were employees of the evil Victor Maitland (Steven Berkoff), a Beverly Hills criminal whose art gallery—where Eilbacher works—is a front for cocaine smuggling. When Murphy tries to move against Maitland, he comes up against the Beverly Hills Cops, including an Abbott and Costello team that supplies unnecessary pratfalls, successfully undermining the credibility of any police scene that threatens to work. But wait a minute. What's this movie about, anyway? Is it a comedy or an action picture? Audiences may expect a comedy, but the closing shoot-out seems inspired by the machine gun massacre at the end of Brian De Palma's *Scarface*, and the whole business with the cocaine is so very, very tired that when we see the boss and his henchmen in the warehouse, we feel like we've switched to another movie—maybe a dozen other movies. Murphy is one of the smartest and quickest young comic actors in the movies. But he is not an action hero, despite his success in *48 HRS*, and by plugging him into an action movie, the producers of *Beverly Hills Cop* reveal a lack of confidence in their original story inspiration. It's like they had a story conference that boiled down to: "Hey gang! Here's a great idea! Let's turn it into a standard idea and fill it with clichés, and take out the satire and put in a lot of machine guns!"

Beverly Hills Cop II ★
R, 105 m., 1987

Eddie Murphy (Axel Foley), Judge Reinhold (Detective Rosewood), Brigitte Nielsen (Karla Fry), Dean Stockwell (Chip Cain), John Ashton (Sergeant Taggart). Directed by Tony Scott produced by Don Simpson and Jerry Bruckheimer. Screenplay by Larry Ferguson and Warren Skaaren.

Something has gone terribly wrong here.

They've made the wrong sequel. The original *Beverly Hills Cop* was a screenplay written for Sylvester Stallone, but filmed by Eddie Murphy. After it was such a big hit, the theory was that *Beverly Hills Cop II* would be a *real* Eddie Murphy movie, with more comedy and fewer guns and chases.

Alas, Part Two seems even more like a Stallone vehicle than the first movie. I'm not even sure it's intended as a comedy. It's filled wall-to-wall with the kind of routine action and violence that Hollywood extrudes by the yard and shrink-wraps to order. But it makes no particular effort to be funny, and actually seems to take its ridiculous crime plot seriously—as if we cared.

There's another problem, too. A big one. Eddie Murphy is not likable in this movie. He comes across as a loud, arrogant boor; a little of him goes a long way. Somehow they've lost track of their original appealing idea, which was that a smart, funny street cop from Detroit would waltz into Beverly Hills and deflate the Porsche and sunglasses set.

Doesn't work that way this time. Murphy's idea of a comic scene in this movie is to shout endlessly at people in a shrill, angry voice. There's a scene where he visits the Playboy mansion and shouts at the receptionist, and you want to crawl under your seat in embarrassment. Murphy comes across as the problem rather than the solution.

What is comedy? That's a pretty basic question, I know, but *Cop II* never thought to ask it. Doesn't comedy usually center around a series of surprises based on insights into human nature? Let's assume that everyone in Beverly Hills is obsessed with money, power, possessions, and social status. Let's further assume that a black cop from Detroit rides into town and doesn't give a damn for their effete values and conspicuous consumption, and cuts through the crap like a knife through butter. That would be funny. It is, however, an idea which this series has been unable to fully exploit after two tries. Instead, Murphy and his associates make the fatal error of assuming that the way you deal with jerks is to be a bigger jerk.

For what they probably paid for the screenplay for this movie, they should have been able to buy a new one. The plot of *Cop II* is recycled right out of every other brainless, routine modern high-tech crime picture. It's not really even a plot; it's a series of standard sequences, involving the Chase, the

Powerful Men of Evil, the Sexy Bitch-Goddess, the Hit Men, and the Shoot-Out. (The chase involves a cement truck, and proves definitely that cement trucks do not work very well in chases.)

On a good day Eddie Murphy is capable of being funnier than anybody else in the movies. I was one of the admirers of *The Golden Child*, which plugged him into a cheerfully ridiculous plot, and made him a lovable character who was doggedly trying to endure a series of exotic dangers. I also like Murphy when he's street-smart and capable, as in *48 HRS*.

What I don't like is the unstated assumption, in *Cop II* and the awful *Harlem Nights*, that he is funny by definition, and that anybody who gets in his way is a fool. Maybe Murphy should study some of those old "I Love Lucy" episodes where Lucy gets into situations she can't handle—she's up against a snooty headwaiter in a stuck-up restaurant, let's say. What does she do? Scream at the guy? No, she always finds a way to deflate the guy simply by remaining true to her own character and insisting on being treated as a human being. That's what's missing in *Cop II*.

Big ★ ★ ★
PG, 102 m., 1988

Tom Hanks (Josh Baskin), Elizabeth Perkins (Susan Lawrence), Robert Loggia (MacMillan), Jared Rushton (Billy Kopeche). Directed by Penny Marshall and produced by James L. Brooks and Robert Greenhut. Screenplay by Anne Spielberg and Gary Ross.

Sooner or later, they're going to get this right. *Big* was no less than the fourth almost simultaneous variation on the same theme—a kid trapped in an adult body. How did four Hollywood studios simultaneously find themselves making essentially the same story? I guess each one thought its was the best, and refused to back down. And so we got *Like Father, Like Son* and *Vice Versa* and *18 Again* and now *Big*, which is a streamlined edition.

Instead of having a father and son exchange bodies, this one does away with the second character and simply gives us a thirteen-year-old who wishes he was big, and gets his wish. That's a useful inspiration, because it spares the filmmakers from the task of cutting back and forth between two different stories (dad in kid's body goes out with teen-age girl while kid in dad's body dates sexpot). Instead, we follow one character on his journey across the generation gap, and because there's more time to develop his dilemma, the movie is more persuasive.

Big describes the adventures of Josh Baskin, who, in a brief opening sequence, is a normal, pint-sized adolescent. He has a crush on one of the girls in his class—a girl who stands a head taller than he does. I had forgotten (or repressed) my memories of those strange days in the seventh grade when all the girls suddenly become amazons, but they all came crashing back during the movie's most poignant scene. In a carnival, Josh manages to stand in line next to the girl of his dreams, and it looks like he'll be able to sit next to her on the ride—but when they get to the front of the line, the carnival guy tells him he's not tall enough to go on the ride.

This is a species of humiliation beyond the limits of human endurance. As the girl gets on the ride with a taller boy, Josh wanders off forlorn and lonely, to a remote corner of the midway where he finds a strange fortune-telling machine. He puts in a quarter, wishes he were big, and wakes up the next morning as Tom Hanks.

Hanks carries most of the movie, and does it well; as a thirteen-year-old in a thirty-year-old body, he is able to suggest such subtle things as a short attention span, a disregard for social niceties, and an ability to hop, skip, and jump through an office lobby. Through a stroke of good luck, he gets hired by a toy company, where his childlike innocence soon gets him a promotion to vice president in charge of product development. He and the company president (Robert Loggia) are the only two guys in the place who really like to play with toys, and there is a brilliant comic sequence where the two of them play "Chopsticks" by dancing on a giant computerized piano keyboard.

The movie is never quite able to deal successfully with the fact that the kid's mother thinks he has been kidnapped—it's cruel the way that plot thread is left dangling. But as Hanks slowly adjusts to his incredible good fortune, he attracts the attention of Elizabeth Perkins, a company executive who falls genuinely in love with his childlike innocence, little realizing it is real.

Big is a tender, soft-hearted, and cheerful movie, well-directed by Penny Marshall and with a script by Anne Spielberg and Gary Ross that has a lot of fun with simple verbal misunderstandings. (When the kid says, "What's a market research report?" Loggia nods and barks, "Exactly!") Hanks finds a vulnerability and sweetness for his character that's quite appealing.

In the sweepstakes of generation-gap movies, *Big* is not as funny as *Vice Versa*, and Hanks does not have as much fun with physical humor as Judge Reinhold did in that movie. But both films are way ahead of the other two contenders, and this one may be the only one of the four that could really be identified with by a thirteen-year-old kid.

The Big Bang ★ ★ ★
R, 82 m., 1990

Emma Astner (The Girl), Missy Boyd (The Mother), Max Brockman (The Boy), Darryl Dawkins (The Basketball Star), Eugene Fodor (The Violinist), Polly Frost (The Artist). Directed by James Toback and produced by Joseph H. Kanter.

One of the great luxuries of life is to pontificate. Rare is the person who feels he has no wisdom on the nature of existence, and even if his truths are third-hand, he is greatly cheered by having shared them. One of the purposes of children is to serve as a captive audience for such lessons.

Try engaging someone in a relaxed conversation and steer it around to the meaning of life—easier than it seems. Ask what it's all about. Chances are your victim's first answer will be weary and cynical. But keep pushing and eventually almost everyone will be revealed as a closet romantic, one who has thought from time to time about the immensity of the universe and his own role as a mote in the nose of God.

The Big Bang is a movie filled with such conversations. People are asked what they think is the meaning of existence. Invariably they respond with grace, humor, and surprising honesty. In real life we generally save such insights for rare moments involving love and death, and so the experience of hearing strangers share them during an entire film is rather moving.

The Big Bang was directed by James Toback, a man of great intensity and drive, whose feature films (*Fingers*, *Exposed*), whatever else they have sometimes lacked, have never wanted for passion. He conceived the idea for this film during a conversation on an airplane with Joseph Kanter, a Florida investor, who has dabbled in film production. In one of the film's early scenes, we hear Kanter asking to be reminded once again why he should invest his money in such a cockamamie idea. And Toback replies that long after Kanter's banking and real estate triumphs have been forgotten, this film will endure—it's his chance at immortality.

It is an argument to sway a Medici. Cities were built on the same premise. The pyramids were constructed because some glib Egyptian sat next to a pharoah on a long chariot ride. One of the most powerful desires in this life is to be remembered after we have left it. Most people are not remembered very long, but we all hope to be—if only because we won the lottery or went over Niagara in an inner tube.

In *The Big Bang* we hear from people who have survived the Holocaust and others who know they are dying. We hear from the young and the old, from black and white, from artists and those who envy artists. What they say is often very interesting, but the real point of the film is simply that they are saying it. Their eyes turn inward and there is a certain wonderment in their voices, and we realize that they are being photographed in the moment of turning away from petty matters and thinking about what it means to be alive.

My disappointment with Toback is that he did not cast his net a little wider. Most of the people he talks to are the sorts of people a movie director might meet in the course of an ordinary lifetime. A violinist and a basketball star. An author and an artist. A mother and a daughter. I wish the approach had been extended to encompass more of the family of man: the very, very old, for example. The very poor. People from other lands and cultures. *The Big Bang* may be a sketch when a mural is called for, but it is a challenging sketch, the kind of movie you want to see with a friend and then sit down afterward for a good long talk.

Big Business ★ ★
PG, 94 m., 1988

Bette Midler (Sadie Shelton/Ratliff), Lily Tomlin (Rose Shelton/Ratliff), Fred Ward (Roone Dimmick), Edward Herrmann (Graham Sherbourne), Michele Placido (Fabio Alberici), Daniel Gerroll (Chuck), Barry Primus (Michael). Directed by Jim Abrahams and produced by Steve Tisch and Michael Peyser. Screenplay by Dori Pierson and Marc Rubel.

Big Business opens with a scene in which two sets of twins are mixed up, so that in later life each set will contain one Bette Midler and one Lily Tomlin. This ought to have inspired a funny movie, but instead, what it inspires is an endless and dreary series of scenes in which the various twins just barely miss running into each other in the Plaza Hotel. You can picture the scenes. The elevator doors close on one Bette Midler just as the other Bette Midler comes running down the hallway.

This is not funny. It is never funny, in this movie or any other movie. People running into each other can be funny, but when they just miss, what are we supposed to do? Slap our knees and say, "Lord a-mighty, they dern near ran into each other and wouldn't *that* have been funny!" Early in the production history of this movie, somebody should have made the following observation: Scenes of people barely missing one another in hotels are not amusing.

In its presentation of the two sets of non-twins, the movie backs genetics rather than environment as the prime formative factor in human development. Both Bette Midlers are conniving and materialistic, and both Lily Tomlins are flutter-brained and well-meaning. But the Midler/Tomlin team from down South in Jupiter Hollow is a little nicer. They work in the local factory, which has manufactured porch swings from time immemorial.

Meanwhile, the New York Midler wants to sell out the factory and the town to a shifty Italian investor who wants to strip-mine the whole county right off the map. The impending sale inspires the Jupiter Hollow women to travel up north to New York for the annual stockholders' meeting of the company controlled by the Manhattan women. Both sets of women check into the Plaza Hotel at the same time, inspiring numerous flat and tedious scenes that are structured as if they were intended to be slapstick.

The life all seems to have escaped from this movie. Midler and Tomlin can be funny actors, but here they both seem muted and toned down in all of the characters they play. The most promising character is probably Sadie Shelton, Midler's New York company executive, who has the potential to be a bitch on wheels but never realizes it. The Jupiter Hollow Midler seems unfocused, and both Tomlins seem to be the same rather vague woman who has trouble with her shoulder pads.

The fundamental problems of the movie can all be traced, I suspect, back to the screenplay. After the babies have been switched and the premise has been set up, far too much time is spent with the futile manipulation of the four characters in the Plaza Hotel. One begins a breakfast and the other finishes it. One doesn't recognize the Italian, but the other one does. In the least amusing of several would-be running gags, a bum outside the hotel does double takes when he thinks he's seeing double. All of these scenes are givens—and should have been given away, to make room for laughs that could come from character, dialogue, and conflict.

In a movie of disappointments, the major disappointment is a shocker. What have we been waiting for through the whole movie? For the moment when the four women all meet in the same place at the same time, right? So what happens when they do? After the first shocked moment of mutual recognition—*nothing* happens! The movie cuts to the next scene. There is *no* scene in which the women reconstruct what must have happened, and deal with their new reality. No scene in which the two nice Tomlins gang up on the two bitchy Midlers. If there's anything worse than a long, slow, boring buildup to a payoff, it's the buildup without the payoff. This movie doesn't feel finished.

The Big Chill ★ ★ ¹/₂
R, 108 m., 1983

Tom Berenger (Sam), Glenn Close (Sarah), William Hurt (Nick), Jeff Goldblum (Michael), Meg Tilly (Chloe), Kevin Kline (Harold), Mary Kay Place (Meg), JoBeth Williams (Karen). Directed by Lawrence Kasdan. Screenplay by Kasdan and Barbara Benedek.

I was going through some old papers the other night, from cardboard boxes that were packed at the end of college and have followed me around ever since. To open them up was like walking into a time capsule. There they were, the little campus literary magazines and the yellowing issues of the University of Illinois' *Daily Illini*, and a photo of a political demonstration on the steps of the student union.

On the other hand, I was going through my mail the next day and I got a letter from a teen-ager who wanted to know why they were making so many movies about the 1960s. "Who cares what happened in the olden days?" I think "olden days" was an attempt at humor.

I wrote back that the 1960s were big in the movies right now because the people who make the movies were students in the 1960s, and that the teen-agers of 2001 would no doubt be sick and tired of the olden days of the 1980s. And then I thought about *The Big Chill*, a movie in which survivors of the 1960s ask themselves how they could possibly be in their thirties. This is the second movie on almost exactly the same theme—a weekend reunion among college friends from the 1960s, during which they relive the past, fear the present, and regret the interim. They could have called it *Son of the Return of the Secaucus Seven*.

It's a good movie. It's well acted, the dialogue is accurately heard, and the camera is extremely attentive to details of body language. It observes wonderfully well how its veterans of the 1960s have grown up into adulthood, consumerhood, parenthood, drunkenhood, adulteryhood, and regrethood. These people could all be wearing warm-up jackets with *poignancy* stenciled on the backs.

The movie begins at a funeral. One of the old college friends has killed himself, for reasons that never become clear. The others gather for his funeral and stay for a weekend in a big old summer house. We get to meet them: the intellectual, the failed writer, the confused TV star, the woman who wants to have a baby and can't tear her eyes away from the biological clock. They eat, they drink, they pair up in various combinations, and they ask themselves questions like, Who were we? Who are we now? What happened to us? What will happen to us?

Because they are all graduates of the University of Michigan at Ann Arbor, they phrase these questions with style, of course. The dialogue sounds like a series of bittersweet captions from *New Yorker* cartoons. And at the end, of course, nothing is really discovered, nothing is really settled, and they go back into holding patterns until the next funeral.

The Big Chill is a splendid technical exercise. It has all the right moves. It knows all the right words. Its characters have all the right clothes, expressions, fears, lusts, and ambitions. But there's no payoff and it doesn't lead anywhere. I thought at first that was a weakness of the movie. There also is the possibility that it's the movie's message.

The Big Easy ★ ★ ★ ★
R, 106 m., 1987

Dennis Quaid (Remy McSwain), Ellen Barkin (Anne Osborne), Ned Beatty (Jack Kellom), John Goodman (Andre De Soto), Lisa Jane Persky (McCabe), Ebbe Roe Smith (Ed Dodge), Tom O'Brien (Bobby McSwain), Charles Ludlam (Lamar Parmentel). Directed by Jim McBride and produced by Stephen Friedman. Screenplay by Daniel Petrie, Jr.

The Big Easy happens to be a great thriller. I say "happens," because I believe the plot of this movie is only an excuse for its real strength: the creation of a group of characters so interesting, so complicated, and so original that they make a lot of other movie people look like paint-by-number characters.

The movie takes place in New Orleans, that most mysterious of American cities, a city where you have the feeling you will never really know what goes on down those shadowy passages into those green and humid courtyards so guarded from the street. The heroes of the film are two law enforcement officials: Remy (Dennis Quaid), a homicide detective, and Anne (Ellen Barkin), a special prosecutor for the D.A. They meet after the death of a Mafia functionary, and of course they are immediately attracted to each other.

So far, no surprises. But when they go out to dinner and the restaurant owner won't think of accepting their money, Anne accuses Remy of being on the take and he accuses her of not understanding how the system operates. Later we learn more about the system in New Orleans and come to understand more about Remy. He is an honest cop in the ways that really count and a dishonest cop in small ways he has been able to rationalize. He doesn't have a problem, for example, with the department's illegal "widows and orphans fund," because he's using the money to send his kid brother through college.

There are more killings. There also is, between Anne and Remy, one of the most erotic love scenes I have ever seen in a movie—all the more erotic because the two lovers do not perform like champions in the sexual Olympics, but come to bed with all the insecurity of people who are almost afraid to believe it could, this time, be for real.

The background of their story is populated with characters so well-drawn and with character actors so finely chosen that the movie is fascinating from moment to moment, even when nothing much seems to be happening.

My favorite supporting performance in the movie is by Charles Ludlam, as a defense attorney, impeccable in his Panama hat and summer suit, talking a mile a minute in a shrill Cajun shriek, like a cross between Truman Capote and F. Lee Bailey. Another slick Southerner is created by Ned Beatty, in his finest performance in years, as the police captain who sincerely wants to do the right thing and sincerely cannot.

All of these characters inhabit the most convincing portrait of New Orleans I've ever seen. The authentic local Cajun music on the sound track and the instinctive feel for the streets and alleys, the lives and the ways of doing business, the accents and the evasions, make the city itself into a participant in what happens.

In the middle of this riotous gumbo of colorful life, Quaid and Barkin construct a relationship that, by itself, would be enough for a whole movie. They love each other. They are disillusioned. They face each other as enemies in court. They eye each other warily in a wonderful scene at a fish boil and Cajun hootenanny thrown by Quaid's friends.

The movie indeed ends with the obligatory scene of climactic violence that is required in all thrillers, but it's well-handled and the actions at least do seem to be consistent with the characters.

The movie was directed by Jim McBride, whose previous film was *Breathless*, with Richard Gere, a high-style pastiche of 1940s crime movies and 1980s art direction. *The Big Easy* seems to be by a different man, a director not only in full mastery of his materials but in full sympathy with his characters. Forget it's a thriller. See it because you want to meet these people.

The Big Red One ★ ★ ★
PG, 113 m., 1980

Lee Marvin (Sergeant), Mark Hamill (Griff), Robert Carradine (Zab), Bobby Di Cicco (Vinci), Kelly Ward (Johnson), Siegfried Rauch (Schroeder), Stephanie Audran (Walloon). Directed and written by Samuel Fuller and produced by Gene Corman.

Sam Fuller's *The Big Red One* is a lot of war stories strung together in a row, almost as if the director filmed it for the thirty-fifth reunion of his old Army outfit, and didn't want to leave anybody out. That's one of the most interesting things about it—the feeling that the movie's events are included, not because they help the plot or make a point, but just because they happened.

Some of them happened to Fuller himself, he tells us, and there's a kid in the movie who's obviously supposed to be young Sam. Other scenes are based on things Fuller heard about. Some of them are brutal and painful, some of them are romantic, a lot of them are corny. The movie takes no position on any of them: This movie is resolutely nonpolitical, is neither pro- nor anti-war, is deliberately just a record of five dogfaces who found themselves in the middle of the action.

The movie's title refers to the U.S. Army's First Infantry Division, and the action follows one rifle squad through the entire war. The squad leader is a hard-bitten sergeant, played by Lee Marvin with the kind of gravel-voiced, squint-eyed authority he had more than a decade before in *The Dirty Dozen*. His four squad members are kids in their teens, and his job is to whip them into shape. He does. The squad is so efficient, or competent, or just plain lucky, that it survives to see action in half the major theaters of the war in Europe. At a rough count, they fight in North Africa, Tunis, Sicily, Normandy, Omaha Beach, rural France, Belgium, Czechoslovakia, and Germany. Halfway through this litany, we begin to suspect that *The Big Red One* is supposed to be something more than plausible.

The squad fights in so many places, stays together in one piece for so long, experiences so many of the key events of World War II (from the invasion of Europe to the liberation of the Nazi death camps) that of course these characters are meant to be symbols of all the infantrymen in all the battles. But Fuller, who fought in the First Division, seems determined to keep his symbols from illustrating a message. They fight. They are frightened. Men kill, other men are killed. What matters is if you're still alive. "I don't cry because that guy over there got hit," Fuller said in an interview, "I cry because I'm gonna get hit next."

This leads to a deliberately anecdotal structure for the film. One battle ends, another begins. A little orphan kid appears out of the smoke, is befriended, braids flowers into the netting of a helmet, is forgotten for the rest of the film. What we have is a series of experiences so overwhelming that the characters can't find sense or pattern in them, and so simply try to survive them through craft and experience.

Is this all Fuller got out of the war? He seems to believe it's all anybody really gets, that the vast patterns of war's meaning are really just the creations of novelists, film-makers, generals, and politicians, and that for the guy under fire there is no pattern, just the desperately sincere desire to get out in one piece.

The Big Red One is Sam Fuller's first film in more than a decade, and by far the most expensive and ambitious film he's ever made. It's like a dream come true, the cap-stone of a long career. Fuller began as a news-paperman in New York, he fought in the war, he went to Hollywood and he directed a lot of B-action pictures that are considered by con-noisseurs to be pulp landmarks: *I Shot Jesse James, Pickup on South Street, Hell and High Water, Shock Corridor.* His previous film, hardly seen in this country, was a 1972 West German production with the marvelous title *Dead Pigeon on Beethoven Street.*

While this is an expensive epic, he hasn't fallen to the temptations of the epic form. He doesn't give us a lot of phony meaning, as if to justify the scope of the production. There aren't a lot of deep, significant speeches. In the ways that count, *The Big Red One* is still a B-movie—hard-boiled, filled with action, held together by male camaraderie, directed with a lean economy of action. It's one of the most expensive B-pictures ever made, and I think that helps it fit the subject. "A" war movies are about War, but "B" war movies are about soldiers.

The Big Town ★ ★ ★ ½
R, 110 m., 1987

Matt Dillon (J.C. Cullen), Diane Lane (Lorry Dane), Tommy Lee Jones (George Cole), Bruce Dern (Mr. Edwards), Lee Grant (Ferguson Edwards), Tom Skerritt (Phil Carpenter), Suzy Amis (Maggie Donaldson), Del Close (Deacon Daniels). Directed by Ben Bolt and produced by Martin Ransohoff. Screenplay by Robert Roy Pool.

This story has been told a hundred times, and yet, when it is told well, it is always fun to watch it being told again. The kid comes from the small town to the big city. He has a gift. He signs up as a professional, working for some pretty tough people. He meets a

good girl. He meets a bad girl. He meets a villain. He wants more independence than his employers will give him. At the end of the story, we don't have to be movie producers to know that he will reject the bad girl, embrace the good girl, defeat the villain, triumph in his big test, and win his independence.

This story could be about baseball, jazz, open-heart surgery, computer program-ming, tap-dancing, or mind-reading. In *The Big Town*, it's about gambling. Matt Dillon plays the farm boy from Iowa who keeps winning at the crap tables because he knows the odds cold, and also because he has amaz-ing good luck. Suzy Amis is the good girl, a waitress supporting her small son. Diane Lane plays the bad girl, a stripper who is married to Tommy Lee Jones, who is the vil-lain. The employers are Lee Grant and Bruce Dern, a married couple who are pro-fessional gamblers with a string of dice-play-ers, or "arms," under contract.

Add a few character touches and you've got it. For example, Dern was blinded by acid years ago, and is looking for the man who did it—a man with a heart tattooed on the inside of his wrist. Lane married Jones because she thought she'd get control of half of his business, but she was wrong. And Lee Grant used to be in love with the Iowa gambler who sent Matt Dillon to the big city to work for her.

Why am I persisting in describing so much of the plot? So you can see that the story has little to do with the brilliance of this film. *The Big Town* is compulsively watch-able not because of its plot, which is predict-able down to the smallest detail, but because of its acting, its direction, and its style. This is a great-looking movie that never steps wrong, and Matt Dillon uses it to demon-strate once again that he is a master of unforced, natural acting. In a 1950s period film that's wall-to-wall with clichés, he never seems less than absolutely at home.

Dillon has some kind of spontaneous rap-port with the camera. He never seems aware of it, never seems aware that he's playing a character; his acting is graceful and fluid, and his scenes always seem to start before the first shot, so that we see him in the middle of a motion. *The Big Town* requires Dillon to spend a lot of time shooting craps, and you wouldn't think it would be possible to bring anything new to the sight of a man throwing dice onto a table, but Dillon does it. He has little moves, subtle small touches of body language, that make every throw important.

(That's a neat trick, since he hardly ever loses.)

The actors around him also are good, especially Tommy Lee Jones as the evil vice boss, who has his best moments when he simply stands and looks at Dillon with eyes filled with hate. Suzy Amis, a newcomer, is fresh and appealing as the waitress who loves this small-town boy, and Diane Lane is able to seem sincere to Dillon while letting us know she's calculating every move.

The look of the movie is effective in its studied artificiality. It's set in Chicago's South Loop, under the el tracks, in a series of exteriors and sets that are supposed to repre-sent both sides of only a block or two—this is the 1950s backlot look, brought to a location. The photography and the wall-to-wall period music on the sound track (Ivory Joe Hunter, Big Joe Turner, Little Willie John, Ray Charles, Red Sovine) get the right bal-ance between the wickedness of the big city and the dreams of the small-town kid. The story is predictable, but the style had me on the edge of my seat.

Billy Jack ★ ★ ½
PG, 112 m., 1971

Tom Laughlin (Billy Jack), Delores Taylor (Jean), Clark Howat (Sheriff), Julie Webb (Barbara). Directed and produced by T.C. Frank (Tom Laughlin). Screenplay by Frank and Teresa Christina.

Billy Jack was not only the first film by Tom Laughlin and Delores Taylor since *Born Losers* (1967), but in many respects the same film, with the same hero and the same theme. Both films were directed by Laughlin himself, using the pseudonym of T.C. Frank, and they represent a passionate obsession with the role of violence in society. Laughlin and Taylor surface so rarely because their movies are personal ventures, financed in unorthodox ways and employing the kind of communal chance-taking that Hollywood finds terrifying. The chances they take sometimes create flaws in their films, but flaws that suggest they were trying to do too much, never too little.

What I find interesting is that they de-cided, in effect, to remake their earlier film: not to copy it, but to grapple again with the same identities and ideas. Both films are about a character named Billy Jack (Laugh-lin), who is a returned Vietnam hero, half-Indian, a master of karate, who takes the law into his own hands because he believes that's the only way to obtain justice.

In *Born Losers* an outlaw motorcycle gang terrorizes a community and its sheriff's office. When they brutally beat a teen-ager, Billy Jack steps in and shoots one of them. He gets ninety days. The gang members get a slap on the wrist for assault. But when he gets out of jail he finds the police powerless and the community terrified. So, because he feels he must, he fights them again, using karate, gasoline, Indian tricks, and his rifle.

In *Billy Jack*, the same character has become more mythic and supernatural. "We don't know how to contact Billy Jack," one of his friends says. "We communicate with him Indian-style; when we need him, somehow he's there." And indeed he is, riding his horse or motorcycle out of the woods, an almost supernatural presence. This time the town is terrorized, not by a bike gang, but by a brutal local businessman and his half-crazy sadomasochistic son. With the exception of the sheriff himself, who has good intentions but is ineffectual, the local law officers are on the side of evil against good.

"Good" is represented by a freedom school run by Delores Taylor, "where children can come when they have no place else to go." The townspeople (who are conveniently represented as hateful, violent, and prejudiced) resent the "hippie school," but it's on an Indian reservation and thus accountable only to federal law.

The daughter of a deputy sheriff runs away after a beating and is hidden at the school, and this provides the food for the plot: The deputy and the other bad guys go after Billy Jack, who single-handedly cuts them down with karate blows, etc. The kids and staff at the school are all pacifists, but Billy Jack can't buy that. His morality is a simple Old Testament one, an eye for an eye.

There are a lot of things in *Billy Jack* that are seriously conceived and very well-handled. Some of the scenes at the school, for example, with real kids experimenting with psychodrama, are interesting. Some of the action scenes are first-rate. There's a lot of dialogue, mostly involving putdown of the older generation.

But the movie has as many causes in it as a year's run of the *New Republic*. There's not a single contemporary issue, from ecology to gun control, that's not covered, and toward the movie's end you're wondering how these characters—who are just ordinary folks in a small Southwestern town—managed to confront every single ethical hurdle in a few weeks of living. It's possible, I guess, but it would keep you awfully busy, and then there are always the Jews in the Soviet Union to think about, and the Pakistan refugees.

I'm also somewhat disturbed by the central theme of the movie. *Billy Jack* seems to be saying the same thing as *Born Losers*, that a gun is better than a constitution in the enforcement of justice. Is democracy totally obsolete, then? Is our only hope that the good fascists defeat the bad fascists? Laughlin and Taylor are still asking themselves these questions, and *Billy Jack* arrives at a conclusion that is only slightly more encouraging.

Bird ★ ★ ★ ½
R, 160 m., 1988

Forest Whitaker (Charlie "Bird" Parker), Diane Venora (Chan Parker), Michael Zelniker (Red Rodney), Samuel E. Wright (Dizzy Gillespie), Keith David (Buster Franklin), Michael McGuire (Brewster), James Handy (Esteves), Damon Whitaker (Young Bird), Morgan Nagler (Kim), Arlen Dean Snyder (Mr. Heath). Produced and directed by Clint Eastwood. Written by Joel Oliansky.

In two documentaries about Charlie Parker I haven't seen a lot of Parker. In an age when archives are filled with newsreel footage and videotape on even the most obscure of public figures, Parker seems always to have been somewhere else when the cameras were on. There is a shot of him accepting a Downbeat award at a banquet, where the master of ceremonies solemnly informs him that jazz is colorblind (if so, then why the reassurance?), and another brief clip of him playing with Dizzy Gillespie. There are a few minutes of silent footage, too, and that's it. No complete performances on film. No interviews. No home movies.

That's one reason why Clint Eastwood's *Bird*, a musical biography of Charlie Parker, is so valuable. It supplies us with images to go with the music, and it provides an idea of the man, more than thirty years after his death. If we are to judge by Forest Whitaker's substantial performance, Parker was a large, warm, gentle man who was comfortable with himself and loved his work. He was haunted all of his days by drug addiction—he got hooked as a teen-ager and never got off—but for many years he doesn't seem to have been filled with the rages of most addicts. He seems to have regarded addiction as a burden to carry, and been resigned to carrying it while not wishing it on anybody else. He carried on as long and as well as he could, and only in the last years was he finally overcome with despair. But addiction took a dreadful physical toll. When he died, a coroner estimated his age at sixty-five. He was thirty-four.

Bird is a long, complex, ambitious movie, and it contains a lot of great music. Charles (Bird) Parker was one of the great fountainheads of jazz, a creator of bebop whose improvisations and joyful discoveries on the saxophone created a sound that is absolutely distinctive. He stood as a bridge between the swing era and the cool modern jazz of the 1950s, and even as his career collapsed into disarray, his influence continued to grow. At the end, Bird was denied a cabaret license because of his drug use, and couldn't even play in Birdland, the famous club named after him. But wherever and whenever he did play, other musicians gathered, because he taught them what they were working for.

Eastwood might seem like an unlikely choice to direct this film, but not if you consider his origins as a West Coast kid, growing up in the 1940s and buying into the Parker legend. Two of the themes running through much of Eastwood's work—and especially the fourteen films he has directed—are a love of music and a fascination with characters who are lonely, heroic drifters. There is a connection between the Charlie Parker of *Bird* and the alcoholic guitar player in *Honkytonk Man*. They are both men who use music as a way of insisting they are alive and can feel joy, in the face of the daily depression and dread they draw around themselves.

The film follows the general drift of Charlie Parker's life, but does not pay much attention to specific details (it glosses over all but his last marriage, for example). It shows the kid growing up in love with jazz, and sneaking in to hear his heroes play. It shows the almost overnight acceptance given to Parker's talent. It shows him joining bands, forming bands, taking delight in stunts like the time he toured the South with a band including Red Rodney, a white sideman who was passed off as "Albino Red" because integrated bands were forbidden. It shows him touring the West Coast and hearing some simple truths one night from Dizzy Gillespie, who told him that the difference between them was that Diz took care of business, and Charlie took care of screwing up. And it shows his relationship with Chan Parker, a white woman who loved jazz and understood Parker enough to be the best of his enablers—all of those who cared so much for Parker that they were willing to coexist with his drugs.

If Clint Eastwood were not a major movie star, he would be known as one of the most successful American directors of recent years (since *Play Misty for Me*, in 1971). His films are often bittersweet, and most at home in poverty. His heroes, usually played by himself, are loners who depend upon a strong personal code in the face of an uncaring world. The difference between Charlie Parker and the other Eastwood protagonists is that Parker was an artist, and so, on top of all the other adventures and struggles, there is the music, which comes from somewhere inside and is inexplicable.

Bird wisely does not attempt to "explain" Parker's music by connecting experiences with musical discoveries. This is a film of music, not about it, and one of the most extraordinary things about it is that we are really, literally, hearing Charlie Parker on the sound track. Eastwood and Lennie Niehaus, his music coordinator, began with actual Parker recordings, some of them from Chan Parker's private collection. They isolated the Parker tracks, scrubbed them electronically, recombined them with contemporary sidemen, and created a pure, clean, new stereophonic sound track on which Charlie Parker's saxophone is unmistakably present.

The movie is all of a piece—the music, the visual look, the tone of Forest Whitaker's performance. Eastwood has gone for a mostly somber, indoor, nighttime look, with a lot of shadows and warm, muted lighting. This is a world where breakfast is a meal held in the late afternoon, where hotel rooms are home, where work is play, and everything else is work. Whitaker occupies this world as a large, friendly, sometimes taciturn man who tries to harm nobody and who cannot understand why the world would not let him play his music. Neither can we.

Bird on a Wire ★ ★ ¹/₂
PG-13, 111 m., 1990

Mel Gibson (Rick Jarmin), Goldie Hawn (Marianne Graves), David Carradine (Eugene Sorenson), Bill Duke (Albert Diggs), Stephen Tobolowsky (Joe Weyburn), Joan Severance (Rachel Varney), Harry Caesar (Marvin), Jeff Corey (Lou Baird). Directed by John Badham and produced by Rob Cohen. Screenplay by David Seltzer, Louis Venosta, and Eric Lerner.

My guess is they screened a lot of Hitchcock movies before they made *Bird on a Wire*, and the parts they liked the best were where Hitch placed his couples in situations that were dangerous and picturesque at the same time—scenes like the Mount Rushmore climax in *North by Northwest*. That was a delicate balancing act when Hitchcock did it; the locations, sensational as they were, couldn't be allowed to upstage the thrills. In *Bird on a Wire*, the act loses its balance.

Mel Gibson stars in the movie as another of his likable, good-humored heroes who can get tough if he needs to. When we first meet him, he's working in a gas station in Detroit, and we learn that it's the latest in a long string of jobs and identities he's held since he joined the Federal Witness Protection Program. He testified against some government narcs fifteen years ago, and they've been looking for him ever since.

Into his lonely life comes love, the second time around, in the person of Goldie Hawn as a tough New York lawyer. She drives into the station by accident, recognizes him, and doesn't believe him when he says he's never seen her before. So she drives back out to the station that night, just in time to save Gibson from being killed by the guys who are looking for him. In a few words of breathless dialogue we learn the two were lovers fifteen years ago, until Gibson suddenly disappeared. Now she knows why.

Up until about this point, the movie is hard-edged and convincing. But all attempts at realism are thrown overboard during a car chase where Hawn mans the wheel while Gibson, upside-down, pushes down hard on the accelerator with his hand. It's one of those slapstick chases that tells you nothing else in the movie needs to be plausible, either.

The movie then develops into a cross between the Idiot Plot and the Hitchcockian search for colorful locations. The key mistake made by the characters—who join up together and flee from the killers who are after them—is to keep phoning their whereabouts to the FBI. How long can it possibly take them to discover that the FBI's security has been compromised—that the killers are getting regular updates from the bureau? In real life it would take them one call, I imagine, but in this movie they never quite figure that one out.

Gibson and Hawn are attractive actors, and they're both good at the kind of light comedy this movie needs. But the plot

doesn't exploit the fact that Hawn is allegedly a powerful, aggressive lawyer. She keeps talking about how she's going to call her office and get money and help, but what actually happens is that she stops being a lawyer and becomes yet one more dizzy and hapless blonde who is pulled through the movie by a resourceful male.

The final scene is shot in a zoo—inside of those gigantic "natural habitats" where tigers and alligators and snakes roam unmolested, and the deer and the antelope play. This is the setup for an ambitious chase sequence that involves snapping alligator jaws and the roars of the big cats and, of course, the obligatory suspension-bridge scene in which the strands of the ropes snap away one at a time, while danger lurks below and the bad guys are holding target practice.

We never really expect the bad guys to hit anyone, because the unspoken rule in a movie like this is that the bad guys fire thousands of rounds and never hit anyone who is even remotely a movie star. What we do expect is some kind of spatial orientation so we can understand where Gibson and Hawn are in relation to the killers. But the scene has been blocked and edited so confusingly that all we know is that danger surrounds them.

I don't know how Hitchcock did it, but somehow he managed to keep us caring about his characters even when they were crawling up the nostrils of the presidents on Mount Rushmore. In *Bird on a Wire*, director John Badham doesn't pay the dues before he brings in the exotic locations. We don't believe the characters, and so the elaborate chases and escapes and stunts and special effects are all affectations.

Birdy ★ ★ ★ ★
R, 120 m., 1985

Nicolas Cage (Al), Matthew Modine (Birdy). Directed by Alan Parker and produced by Alan Marshall. Screenplay by Sandy Kroopf and Jack Behr.

The strangest thing about *Birdy*, which is a very strange and beautiful movie indeed, is that it seems to work best at its looniest level, and is least at ease with the things it takes most seriously. You will not discover anything new about war in this movie, but you will find out a whole lot about how it feels to be in love with a canary.

The movie is about two friends from South Philadelphia. One of them, Al, played by Nicolas Cage, is a slick romeo with a lot of self-confidence and a way with the women. The other, nicknamed Birdy (Matthew Modine), is goofy, withdrawn, and absolutely fascinated with birds. As kids, they are inseparable friends. In high school, they begin to grow apart, separated by their individual quests for two different kinds of birds. But they still share adventures, as Birdy hangs upside-down from elevated tracks to capture pigeons, or constructs homemade wings that he hopes will let him fly. Then the war comes. Both boys serve in Vietnam and both are wounded. Cage's face is disfigured, and he wears a bandage to cover the scars. Modine's wounds are internal: He withdraws entirely into himself and stops talking. He spends long, uneventful days perched in his room at a mental hospital, head cocked to one side, looking up longingly at a window, like nothing so much as a caged bird.

Because *Birdy* is not told in chronological order, the story takes a time to sort itself out. We begin with an agonizing visit by the Cage character to his friend Birdy. He hopes to draw him out of his shell. But Birdy makes no sign of recognition. Then, in flashbacks, we see the two lives that led up to this moment. We see the adventures they shared, the secrets, the dreams. Most importantly, we go inside Birdy's life and begin to glimpse the depth of his obsession with birds. His room turns into a birdcage. His special pets—including a cocky little yellow canary—take on individual characteristics for us. We can begin to understand that his love for birds is sensual, romantic, passionate. There is a wonderful scene where he brushes his fingers against a feather, showing how marvelously it is constructed, and how beautifully.

Most descriptions of *Birdy* tend to dwell on what seems to be the central plot, the story of the two buddies who go to Vietnam and are wounded, and about how one tries to help the other return to the real world. I felt that the war footage in the movie was fairly routine, and that the challenge of dragging Birdy back to reality was a good deal less interesting than the story of how he arrived at the strange, secret place in his mind. I have seen other, better, movies about war, but I have never before seen a character quite like Birdy.

As you may have already guessed, *Birdy* doesn't sound like a commercial blockbuster. More important are the love and care

for detail that have gone into it from all hands, especially from Cage and Modine. They have two immensely difficult roles, and both are handicapped in the later scenes by being denied access to some of an actor's usual tools; for Cage, his face; for Modine, his whole human persona. They overcome those limitations to give us characters even more touching than the ones they started with.

The movie was directed by Alan Parker. Consider this list of his earlier films: *Bugsy Malone, Fame, Midnight Express, Shoot the Moon, Pink Floyd: The Wall.* Each one coming out of an unexpected place, and avoiding conventional movie genres. He was the man to direct *Birdy,* which tells a story so unlikely that perhaps even my description of it has discouraged you—and yet a story so interesting it is impossible to put this movie out of my mind.

The Black Marble ★ ★ ★ ½
PG, 110 m., 1980

Robert Foxworth (Sergeant Valnikov), Paula Prentiss (Sergeant Zimmerman), Harry Dean Stanton (Philo Skinner), Barbara Babcock (Madeline Whitfield), John Hancock (Clarence Cromwell), Raleigh Bond (Captain Hooker), Judy Landers (Pattie Mae), Pat Corley (Itchy Mitch). Directed by Harold Becker and produced by Frank Capra, Jr. Screenplay by Joseph Wambaugh.

The Black Marble is a delightfully twisted comedy, backing into itself, starting out in one direction, ending up somewhere else, constantly surprising us with its offbeat characters. It's so many things at once it's a juggling act: It's a police movie with lots of authentic details; it's a bizarre comedy about a kidnapped prize dog; it's a shaggy romance; it's got the most excruciating chase sequence I can remember; it's goofy, but it moves us.

The movie centers around several days in the life of a Los Angeles police sergeant named Valnikov (Robert Foxworth), an incurably romantic Russian who has been drinking too much since his partner's suicide. He gets a new partner, Sgt. Natalie Zimmerman, played by Paula Prentiss as a combination of Sally Kellerman and Lucille Ball. His new partner thinks Valnikov is insane. Maybe she's right.

The case they begin working on together involves a prize bitch that has been kid-

napped and is being held for $85,000 ransom. Valnikov goes to interview the kidnapped dog's grieving owner, an attractive woman of a certain age. And, in a delightful scene that illustrates the movie's gift of being able to slide ever so lightly from drama into cheerful comedy, he winds up on the sofa with the woman, drying her tears and vowing, "Don't worry; I promise I'll get your doggie back."

The dry tone Foxworth brings to the pronunciation of such lines is one of the movie's charms. He is mustachioed, mournful-eyed, usually hung over, and filled with ancient Russian dreams and curses. It is inevitable, of course, that he and the sexy Zimmerman fall in love, and they have a wonderful seduction scene in his apartment. He puts sweepingly romantic Russian folk music on his stereo. They dance. "Translate the lyrics for me!" she whispers into his ear. He does. It does not bother either of them that there *are* no lyrics since the song is instrumental.

Meanwhile, a parallel plot involves the evil dog kidnapper, played by that uniquely malevolent character actor Harry Dean Stanton, who looks and talks like Robert Mitchum's mean kid brother. Stanton is a veterinarian who has never hurt a dog in his life. But he needs the ransom to pay a gambling debt before he is killed. Coughing, wheezing, and spitting through an endless chain of cigarettes, he makes telephone threats to the dog's owner, who counters with descriptions of her own financial plight, unpaid bills, and tax problems.

When Valnikov and the kidnapper finally meet face to face, they get into what is undoubtedly the most painful chase sequence I can remember, a chase that requires them to climb mesh fences separating a series of savage and terrified dogs that snap maniacally at their legs. The chase is another scene illustrating the curious way in which *The Black Marble* succeeds in being funny, painful, and romantic, sometimes simultaneously. The movie's not altogether a comedy, although we laugh; it's a love story that kids itself and ends up seriously; it contains violence but is not really violent. What it always does is keep us off balance. Because we can't anticipate what's going to happen next, the movie has a persistent interior life; there's never the sense that a scene is included because it's expected.

The performances go to show you that a good actor in a bad film can have a very hard time appearing to be any good. Foxworth's previous screen credits include *The Omen, Part II* and *Prophecy.* Neither film gave me the slightest reason to look forward to him in *The Black Marble,* but he's wonderful here. He gives his character weariness and craziness and then covers them both with warmth. He and Prentiss have so much fun with the long seduction scene that we can sense the joy of acting craftsmanship going into it.

The movie's the second production by Joseph Wambaugh, the L.A. cop who became a best-selling novelist only to see Hollywood doing terrible things to his novels. Wambaugh vowed to produce his own books. The industry had its doubts, especially when Wambaugh hired a little-known British director, Harold Becker, to direct his first project, *The Onion Field.* But that was a strong, edgy, effective movie, and now Wambaugh and Becker are back with this unusual and distinctive comedy. Because it is uneven and moves so easily among its various tones and moods, it's possible, I suppose, to fault it on form: This isn't a seamless piece of work, but it's infectious and charming.

Black Rain ★ ★
R, 125 m., 1989

Michael Douglas (Nick Conklin), Andy Garcia (Charlie Vincent), Ken Takakura (Masahiro Matsumoto), Kate Capshaw (Joyce Kingsley), Yusaku Matsuda (Sato), Tomisaburo Wakayama (Sugai), Shigeru Koyama (Ohashi), Yuya Uchida (Nashida), Miyuki Ono (Miyuki). Directed by Ridley Scott and produced by Stanley R. Jaffe and Sherry Lansing. Screenplay by Craig Bolotin and Warren Lewis.

The grim specter of Osaka dominates *Black Rain* the same way Gotham City looms over *Batman.* It's a vast, dingy, polluted, and cheerless metropolis, with hideous neon advertisements climbing up into the sulphurous skies. Down below where the people live, there are nightclubs like burrows, where evil men plot and scheme. The movie sends two New York cops on a mission into this vision of hell—they have to recapture a vicious gangster who has disappeared into the underworld of the yakuza—the Japanese Mafia.

I've seen Osaka in a lot of movies, but it's never looked quite like this before, not even in violent thrillers. The director, Ridley Scott, must have been bewitched by memories of the futuristic Los Angeles he created

for his *Blade Runner* (1982). The difference is that in *Blade Runner* the characters inhabited their city, and in *Black Rain* they are crushed by it. The production design (by Norris Spencer) is so overwhelming that the characters seem lost and upstaged; frequently the humans are not even the most interesting things on the scene.

The film stars Michael Douglas as a detective with questionable ethics who captures a Japanese gangster after he commits a bloody double murder in New York. Douglas and his partner (Andy Garcia) are assigned to escort the killer (Yusaku Matsuda) back to Osaka, where they ineptly hand him over to his fellow gangsters, disguised as cops. Determined to recapture the man, they team up with an Osaka cop (Ken Takakura), after which the plot settles down into a predictable routine.

The story of *Black Rain* is thin and prefabricated, and doesn't stand up to much scrutiny—so Scott distracts us with overwrought visuals. After a motorcycle chase underneath a New York expressway, there's a foot chase through a meat locker, and then, in Japan, chases through underground parking garages and rain-swept plazas, before a gangster summit meeting is held in the fiery dungeon of a steel mill. (The opening motorcycle chase is the setup for another one at the end of the film, of course; the screenplay seems to have been manufactured out of those Xeroxed outlines they pass out in film school.)

I would probably have enjoyed the visuals if they served any purpose in the movie (I admired the look of *Blade Runner*), but they're just show-off virtuosity. Other elements also seem shoehorned into the movie for dubious reasons—for example, the major supporting role for Kate Capshaw, as an Osaka bartender who apparently knows most of the secrets of the gangsters and feeds them to Douglas one at a time. I don't know whether to be annoyed by the implausible way in which an American woman has been slipped into a Japanese role, or relieved that the movie spares us yet another set of geisha clichés. I doubt strongly, however, whether a blonde from Chicago would know many yakuza secrets, even after eight years of Osaka bartending.

As a general rule, the logic in thrillers should be clear and lean, so that we can understand the reasons for the action. In addition to the unlikely Capshaw character, however, *Black Rain* also asks us to believe

(1) that a Japanese man who has murdered two top mafiosi and machine-gunned a restaurant would be sent back to Osaka instead of being charged in New York; (2) that a cop under investigation for graft by the Internal Affairs Division would be assigned to accompany the killer to Japan; and (3) that the Japanese police would be waiting at one door of an airplane while unaware that gangsters, disguised as police, were waiting at another. The movie ends with a scene where Douglas gives his Japanese partner a gift that, given the logic of the movie, he could not possibly have obtained.

Even given all of its inconsistencies, implausibilities, and recycled clichés, *Black Rain* might have been entertaining if the filmmakers had found the right note for the material. But this is a designer movie, all look and no heart, and the Douglas character is curiously unsympathetic. He plays it so cold and distant that the heartfelt scenes ring false. And the colors in the movie—steel grays, gloomy blues, and wet concrete, occasionally illuminated by neon signs, showers of sparks, and exploding automobiles—underline the general gloom.

Black Rain ★ ★ ★ ¹/₂
NO MPAA RATING, 113 m., 1990

Yoshiko Tanaka (Yasuko), Kazuo Kitamura (Shigematsu), Etsuko Ichihara (Shigeko), Shoichi Ozawa (Shokichi), Norihei Miki (Kotaro), Keisuke Ishida (Yuichi). Directed by Shohei Imamura and produced by Hisa Iino. Screenplay by Toshiro Ishido and Imamura.

Black Rain is by Japan's great director Shohei Imamura, who shoots in a beautifully textured black and white to tell the story of survivors of the Hiroshima atomic bomb who were contaminated by the fallout. For years after the terrible day of the attack, they lived in fear of developing radiation poisoning or cancer—and finally, one by one, many of them did. The mushroom cloud hovered over every day of their lives.

This is not, however, an antinuclear message movie. It is a film about how the survivors of that terrible day internalized their experiences, how they came to see themselves as flawed because they carried the seeds of radiation sickness. Only a Japanese—perhaps only Imamura—could have made a film in which the bomb at Hiroshima is simply the starting point for an unforgiving critique of Japanese society itself.

His story, based on the novel by Masuji Ibuse, involves Yasuko, a young woman, on the day the bomb falls. She suffers no obvious or visible effects from the blast, but like everyone in her village—across a wide bay from Hiroshima—she has been touched by fallout from the mushroom cloud. And as time passes, the radiation poisoning ticks inside of her like a time bomb.

Imamura's depiction of the day of the blast itself is sudden, graphic, and unforgiving. It is an ordinary day in the isolated community where the story takes place, and then it becomes extraordinary as the sky fills with the light of a thousand suns. We see a railroad car literally blown apart by the force of the blast, and then there are shots of survivors, wandering dazedly among the wreckage of a once-familiar world. The immediate impulse of the Japanese in the aftermath of such a cataclysm, Imamura shows in his film, is to reestablish the rhythms and values of traditional life. By returning to old ways, the wound can be healed and even denied.

That process would assume that Yasuko, who is of the appropriate age, would find the right man and marry. Her family tries to help arrange this process. But it is not so simple, since eligible men do not want a bride who may be infected with the lingering aftereffects of the fallout. Yasuko's uncle produces a document that allegedly certifies that the young woman is healthy, but, of course, what was really known about fallout in those days? Prudent would-be grooms take no chances with a woman whose health may be suspect.

As Yasuko grows older and is still unmarried, she becomes an affront to her family and community; the area is still very much bound by traditional beliefs, including the one that women of such an age should not be single. She does have a suitor, a young man she loves, and who loves her, but he is not of the right class or background to be an appropriate husband. Yet this is a delicate matter: Does the fact of her radiation poisoning "devalue" her to such an extent that they are more equal in status? And how long can her aunt and uncle maintain the fiction that she was not harmed by the blast?

Societies all over the world have sometimes blamed sick people for their illnesses; Susan Sontag's book *Illness as Metaphor* explores the ways in which we sometimes believe people get the diseases they deserve. Imamura's anger in *Black Rain* is directed not so much at those who dropped the bomb

on Hiroshima as at the way his Japanese characters immediately started behaving as if somehow it had been their own fault. Some of the characters in this movie seem almost to be apologizing for having been beneath the fallout, and that makes Imamura angry—provides him, indeed, with the impulse for this film.

Black Rain premiered at the Cannes Film Festival in May 1989, but was released more than a year later in the U.S., perhaps to avoid confusion with the 1989 Michael Douglas thriller of the same name. There is irony in the fact that both movies concern Japan, Douglas's showing it as a canny, aggressive society with criminals who are up-to-date by anybody's standards, Imamura's concerned with ancient traits in the collective national personality.

It must have taken no small amount of courage for Imamura to make this film, which carries an insight many Japanese may not want to heed and many foreigners may not be able to believe. It's also interesting that he chose to shoot in black and white. He made that decision, I think, because the scenes of the atomic bomb explosion and its immediate aftermath would have been so gory in color that they would have wiped out all the subtlety of what he wanted to say. This is a film, after all, about people who want to conduct their lives and businesses as usual, to deal with the atomic holocaust by denying it. Imamura's message is that—do what you will—it cannot be denied.

The Black Stallion ★ ★ ★ ★
G, 120 m., 1980

Kelly Reno (Alec Ramsey), Mickey Rooney (Henry Dailey), Teri Garr (Alec's Mother), Clarence Muse (Snoe), Hoyt Axton (Alec's Father), Michael Higgins (Neville). The black stallion is portrayed by Cass-ole, owned by San Antonio Arabians. Directed by Carroll Ballard and produced by Francis Ford Coppola, Fred Roos, and Tom Sternberg. Screenplay by Melissa Mathison, Jeanne Rosenberg and William D. Wittliff.

The first half of *The Black Stallion* is so gloriously breathtaking that the second half, the half with all the conventional excitement, seems merely routine. We've seen the second half before—the story of the kid, the horse, the veteran trainer, and the big race. But the first hour of this movie belongs among the

great filmgoing experiences. It is described as an epic, and earns the description.

The film opens at sea, somewhere in the Mediterranean, forty or so years ago, on board a ship inhabited by passengers who seem foreign and fearsome to a small boy. They drink, they gamble, they speak in foreign tongues, they wear caftans and beards and glare ferociously at anyone who comes close to their prize possession, a magnificent black stallion.

The boy and his father are on board this ship for reasons never explained. The father gambles with the foreigners and the boy roams the ship and establishes a shy rapport with the black stallion, and then a great storm sweeps over the ocean and the ship catches fire and is lost. The boy and the stallion are thrown free, into the boiling sea. The horse somehow saves the boy, and in the calm of the next morning they both find themselves thrown onto a deserted island.

This sequence—the storm, the ship's sinking, the ordeal at sea—is a triumphant use of special effects, miniature models, back projection, editing, and all the tricks of craft that go into the filming of a fantasy. The director, Carroll Ballard, used the big water tank at Cinecitta Studios in Rome for the storm sequences; a model ship, looking totally real, burns and sinks headfirst, its propellers churning slowly in the air, while the horse and boy struggle in the foreground.

The horse in this film (its name is Cass-ole) is required to perform as few movie horses ever have. But its finest scene is the quietest one, and takes place on the island a few days after the shipwreck. Ballard and his cinematographer, Caleb Deschanel, have already established the mood of the place, with gigantic, quiet, natural panoramas. The boy tries to spear a fish. The horse roams restlessly from the beaches to the cliffs. And then, in a single shot that is held for a long time, Ballard shows us the boy inviting the horse to eat out of his hand.

It is crucial here that this action be seen in a *single* shot; lots of short cuts, edited together, would simply be the filmmakers at work. But the one uninterrupted shot, with the horse at one edge of the screen and the boy at the other, and the boy's slow approach, and the horse's skittish advances and retreats, shows us a rapport between the human and the animal that's strangely moving.

All these scenes of the boy and horse on the island are to be treasured, especially a montage photographed underwater and showing the legs of the two as they splash in the surf. There are also wonderfully scary sequences, such as one in which the boy awakens to find a poisonous snake a few feet away from him on the sand. This scene exploits the hatred and fear horses have for snakes, and is cut together into a terrifically exciting climax.

But then, as all good things must, the idyll on the island comes to an end. The boy and the horse are rescued. And it's here that the film, while still keeping our interest, becomes more routine. The earlier passages of the film were amazing to look at (they were shot, with great difficulty and beauty, on Sardinia). Now we're back to earth again, with scenes shot around an old racetrack in Toronto.

And we've seen the melodramatic materials of the movie's second half many times before. The boy is reunited with his mother, the horse returns home with him, and the boy meets a wise old horse trainer who admits that, yes, that Arabian can run like the wind—but the fool thing doesn't have any papers. The presence of Mickey Rooney, who plays the trainer, is welcome but perhaps too familiar. Rooney has played this sort of role so often before (most unforgettably in National Velvet) that he almost seems to be visiting from another movie. His Academy Award nomination for the performance is probably a recognition of that.

Still, the melodrama is effective. Everything depends on the outcome of the big race at the film's end. The young boy, of course, is the jockey (the Elizabeth Taylor role, so to speak). Ballard and Deschanel are still gifted at finding a special, epic look for the movie; one especially good scene has the stallion racing against time, in the dark before dawn, in the rain.

The Black Stallion is a wonderful experience at the movies. The possibility remains, though, that in these cynical times it may be avoided by some viewers because it has a G rating—and G movies are sometimes dismissed as being too innocuous. That's sure not the case with this film, which is rated G simply because it has no nudity, profanity, or violence—but it does have terrific energy, beauty, and excitement. It's not a children's movie; it's for adults and for kids.

Blade Runner ★ ★ ★
R, 114 m., 1982

Harrison Ford (Deckard), Rutger Hauer (Batty), Sean Young (Rachel), Edward James Olmos (Gaff), M. Emmet Walsh (Bryant), Daryl Hannah (Pris). Directed by Ridley Scott and produced by Michael Deeley. Screenplay by Hampton Fancher and David Peoples.

The strangest thing about the future is that this is now the future that was once foretold. Twenty years ago, we thought of "now" as "the year 1987," and we wondered what life would be like. Little could we have guessed that there would be no world government, that the cars would look like boxes instead of rocket ships, and that there would still be rock 'n' roll on the radio. Blade Runner asks us to imagine its own future, in "the year 2020." The movie takes place in a Los Angeles that looks like a futuristic Tokyo, with gigantic billboards showing smiling Japanese girls drinking Coca-Cola. I would have predicted L.A. would be Hispanic, but never mind, it looks sensational. The city is dominated by almost inconceivably huge skyscrapers. People get around in compact vehicles that fly, hover, climb, and swoop. (In a lot of fictional futures, people seem to zip around the city in private aircraft; can you imagine the traffic problems?) At ground level, however, the L.A. of the future is an urban jungle.

The movie stars Harrison Ford as a cop who moves confidently through the city's mean streets. He is laconic, cynical, competent. He has a difficult assignment. A group of "replicants," artificial people who seem amazingly human, have escaped from "off-world," and are trying to inflict themselves on Earth. Ford's job is to track them down and eliminate them. Anyone who has read this far can predict what happens next: He falls in love with one of the replicants. She may not be quite human, but, oh, you kid.

This basic story comes from a Philip K. Dick novel with the intriguing title, Do Androids Dream of Electric Sheep? The book examined the differences between humans and thinking machines, and circled warily around the question of memory: Does it make an android's personal memories less valid if they are inspired by someone else's experiences—especially if the android does not know that? Ford says he originally signed on for Blade Runner because he found such questions intriguing. For director Ridley

Scott, however, the greater challenge seemed to be creating that future world. Scott is a master of production design, of imagining other worlds of the future (Alien) and the past (The Duellists). He seems more concerned with creating his film worlds than populating them with plausible characters, and that's the trouble this time. Blade Runner is a stunningly interesting visual achievement, but a failure as a story.

The special effects were supervised by Douglas Trumbull, whose credits include 2001 and Silent Running, and who is about as good as anyone in the world at using miniatures, animation, drawings, optical effects, and other ways of tricking the eye. The visual environments he creates for this film are wonderful to behold, and there's a sense of detail, too; we don't just get the skyways and the monolithic skyscrapers and the sky-taxis, we also get notions about how restaurants, clothes, and home furnishings will look in 2020 (not too different). Blade Runner is worth seeing just to witness this artistry. The movie's weakness, however, is that it allows the special-effects technology to overwhelm its story. Ford is tough and low-key in the central role, and Rutger Hauer and Sean Young are effective as two of the replicants, but the movie isn't really interested in these people—or creatures. The obligatory love affair is pro forma, the villains are standard issue, and the climax is yet one more of those cliffhangers, with Ford dangling over an abyss by his fingertips. The movie has the opposite trouble as the replicants: Instead of flesh and blood, its dreams are of mechanical men.

Note: Reader Richard Doerflinger writes to observe that the movie reverses the original vision of Philip K. Dick's novel, which was about an under-populated future. In a world short of humans, the hero might well be attracted to androids, but "Scott reverses the premise that makes the story coherent."

Blaze ★ ★ ★ ½
R, 120 m., 1989

Paul Newman (Earl K. Long), Lolita Davidovich (Blaze Starr), Jerry Hardin (Thibodeaux), Gailard Sartain (LaGrange), Jeffrey DeMunn (Tuck), Garland Bunting (Doc Ferriday), Richard Jenkins (Picayune), Brandon Smith (Arvin Deeter), Jay Chevalier (Wiley Braden). Directed by Ron Shelton and produced by Gil Friesen and Dale Pollock. Screenplay by Shelton.

Toward the end of *Blaze*, the following exchange takes place between the film's two central characters:

Earl K. Long: "Would you still love me just as much if I wasn't the fine governor of the great state of Louisiana?"

Blaze Starr: "Would you still love *me* if I had little tits and worked in a fish house?"

The true and final answer to this question is withheld by the makers of *Blaze* almost until the movie's last scene; "love" is a big word, after all. But right from the opening passages of the film we can tell that these two characters like each other an awful lot: Earl, the boozy, wheeler-dealer governor of Louisiana, and Blaze, the hillbilly girl who became a famous stripper. They like each other for several reasons, including the obvious ones (she likes his power; he likes her body), but also because they are alike in so many ways. They're students of human nature who were born honest and have had to struggle with the consequences of that misfortune ever since.

Blaze is based on the autobiography of Blaze Starr, who can still to this day be glimpsed in Baltimore, where she remains, the movie's closing credits inform us, "a part of the local cultural scene." It is a good question whether she was ever as naive, or her career ever as simple, as this movie makes it look. But never mind. The heart of the movie is a public relationship between a woman who was not respectable and a man who didn't give a damn what people said.

Paul Newman is an ideal choice to play Earl K. Long. Portraying the fine governor of the great state with his hair a little mussed, his gut sticking out over his belt buckle, and his voice a little slurred by large amounts of bourbon, he seems completely at home. The role fits him like an old flannel shirt. After the disappointment of *Fat Man and Little Boy*, in which Newman seemed vaguely out of focus as a military man, *Blaze* shows him as the kind of instinctively humorous man he plays the best, the kind of man whose response to hypocrisy is a delighted horse-laugh, because he has been proven right once again in his theory that his enemies are full of it.

Although Newman is a delight, the best surprise in the movie is the performance of a new actress named Lolita Davidovich, who plays Blaze Starr. She has a comfortability in the role that is just right. Unlike a lot of new or beginning actors who project tension or concentration or a sense of how important they think every scene has to be, Davidovich acts like she's inside that flannel shirt along with Newman. It's important that she have that quality because *Blaze* is not by its nature a tense, wound-up story. It's about a couple of slightly frayed people who were a little peculiar, but who were not dumb, and who insisted on surviving on their own terms. The movie was directed by Ron Shelton, whose previous film was *Bull Durham*, and there is a similar sensibility in both films: Shelton's characters define their identities through their eccentricities.

During the course of the movie, the hillbilly girl who took the name Blaze Starr makes her way through a series of striptease parlors to the big time on Bourbon Street in New Orleans, where one night the long black limousine of the fine governor of the great state pulls up outside the club where she's working. The governor is instantly captivated by Blaze, but he doesn't know how much he likes her until she turns down his offer of a date: "Damn, but I'm attracted to strong-willed women," he tells one of his cronies. Blaze's mother has advised her never to believe it when a man says, "Trust me." She asks Earl if she can trust him. "Hell, no," he says. And so she does.

The development of their relationship is seen against a backdrop of Louisiana state politics in the late 1950s, as Long tries to hold together the populist, working-class, Democratic Party coalition first cobbled together by his late brother, Huey ("Every man a king") Long. The great threat to Earl's sovereignty is the "votin' rights bill" for blacks, which his cronies fear he will support in the legislature. They think it could lead to the destruction of their power base. Earl indeed favors the bill, and has long had his own peculiar and indirect ways of supporting the black cause; there is a scene in the movie where he creates jobs for black doctors and nurses in a state hospital by pretending to be shocked that black patients are being cared for by whites. Long is not a great reformist crusader, but within the realpolitik of the segregated South, he was a pragmatist who contributed to progress.

He was also a man constantly under indictment on tax charges, constantly under suspicion of "payrolling" and graft, and denounced from the pulpits of the state for his immoral liaison with Blaze Starr. He never bothered to deny his friendship with Blaze, and indeed often seemed to confuse his politics and sexuality (as in a wonderful scene where he is stricken temporarily impotent and admonishes his disobedient member to "stop acting like a payroller").

Blaze is the affectionate story of two colorful people who had the nerve to stick together even though that didn't suit everybody's notions of propriety. Whether it tells the whole story of their relationship is an open question; I imagine Blaze Starr could write a second volume of autobiography if she had a mind to. But this is a movie made up of feelings and moments, and not a work of political history. Newman and Davidovich create their characters with a rough affection that shines through, and by the end of the film we are prepared to concede that, yes, they might have loved each other even if she'd been a skinny waitress and he not the fine governor of the great state.

Blood Simple ★ ★ ★
R, 96 m., 1985

John Getz (Ray), Frances McDormand (Abby), Dan Hedaya (Julian Marty), M. Emmet Walsh (Detective), Samm-Art Williams (Meurice). Directed by Joel Coen and produced by Ethan Coen. Screenplay by Coen and Coen.

A lot has been written about the visual style of *Blood Simple*, but I think the appeal of the movie is more elementary. It keys into three common nightmares: (1) You clean and clean, but there's still blood all over the place; (2) You know you have committed a murder, but you are not sure quite how or why; (3) You know you have forgotten a small detail that will eventually get you into a lot of trouble. *Blood Simple* mixes those fears and guilts into an incredibly complicated plot, with amazingly gory consequences. It tells a story in which every individual detail seems to make sense, and every individual choice seems logical, but the choices and details form a bewildering labyrinth in which there are times when even the murderers themselves don't know who they are.

Because following the plot is one of this movie's most basic pleasures, I will not reveal too much. The movie begins with a sleazy backwoods bar owner's attempt to hire a scummy private detective to murder his wife. The private eye takes the money and then pulls a neat double-cross, hoping to keep the money and eliminate the only witness who could implicate him. Neat. And then it *really* gets complicated.

The movie has been shot with a lot of style, some of it self-conscious, but deliberately so. One of the pleasures in a movie like this is enjoying the low-angle and tilt shots that draw attention to themselves, that declare themselves as being part of a movie. The movie does something interesting with its timing, too. It begins to feel inexorable. Characters think they know what has happened; they turn out to be wrong; they pay the consequences, and it all happens while the movie is marching from scene to scene like an implacable professor of logic, demonstrating one fatal error after another.

Blood Simple was directed by Joel Coen, produced by his brother, Ethan, and written by the two of them. It's their first film, and has the high energy and intensity we associate with young filmmakers who are determined to make an impression. Some of the scenes are virtuoso, including a sequence in which a dead body becomes extraordinarily hard to dispose of, and another one in which two people in adjacent rooms are trapped in the same violent showdown. The central performance in the movie is by the veteran character actor M. Emmet Walsh, who plays the private eye like a man for whom idealism is a dirty word. The other actors in the movie are all effective, but they are obscured, in a way, by what happens to them: This movie weaves such a bloody web that the characters are upstaged by their dilemmas.

Is the movie fun? Well, that depends on you. It is violent, unrelenting, absurd, and fiendishly clever. There is a cliché I never use: "Not for the squeamish." But let me put it this way. *Blood Simple* may make you squeam.

Blow Out ★ ★ ★ ★
R, 107 m., 1981

John Travolta (Jack), Nancy Allen (Sally), John Lithgow (Burke), Dennis Franz (Manny Karp), Peter Boydon (Sam), Curt May (Donohue). Directed by Brian De Palma and produced by George Litto. Screenplay by De Palma.

There are times when *Blow Out* resembles recent American history trapped in the "Twilight Zone." Episodes are hauntingly familiar, and yet seem slightly askew. What if the "grassy knoll" recordings from the police radio in Dallas had been crossed with Chappaquiddick and linked to Watergate? What if Jack Ruby had been a private eye specializing in divorce cases? What if Abraham Zapruder—the man who took the home

movies of President John F. Kennedy's death—had been a sound-effects man? And what if Judith Exner—remember her?—had been working with Ruby? These are some of the inspirations out of which Brian De Palma constructs *Blow Out*, a movie which continues his practice of making cross-references to other movies, other directors, and actual historical events, and which nevertheless is his best and most original work.

The title itself, of course, reminds us of *Blow Up*, the 1966 film by Michelangelo Antonioni in which a photographer saw, or thought he saw, a murder—and went mad while obsessively analyzing his photographs of the "crime." *Was* there a dead body to be found on that fuzzy negative? Was there even such a thing as reality? In *Blow Out*, John Travolta plays the character who confronts these questions. He's a sound man for a sleazy Philadelphia B-movie factory. He works on cheap, cynical exploitation films. Late one night, while he's standing on a bridge recording owls and other night sounds, he becomes a witness to an accident. A car has a blowout, swerves off a bridge, and plunges into a river. Travolta plunges in after it, rescues a girl inside (Nancy Allen), and later discovers that the car's drowned driver was a potential presidential candidate. Still later, reviewing his sound recording of the event, Travolta becomes convinced that he can hear a gunshot just before the blowout. Was the accident actually murder? He traces down Nancy Allen, discovers that she was part of a blackmail plot against the candidate, and then comes across the trail of a slimy private eye (Dennis Franz) who wanted to cause a blowout, all right, but didn't figure on anybody getting killed.

The plot thickens beautifully. De Palma doesn't have just a handful of ideas to spin out to feature length. He has an abundance. We meet a gallery of violent characters, including Burke (John Lithgow), a dirty-tricks specialist who seems inspired by G. Gordon Liddy. The original crime is complicated by a series of other murders, designed to lay a false trail and throw the police off the scent of political conspiracy.

Meanwhile, the Travolta character digs deeper. For him, it's a matter of competence, of personal pride. Arguing with a cop about his tapes, Travolta denies that he's just imagining things: "I'm a *sound* man!" He stumbles across a series of photos of the fatal accident. In a brilliantly crafted sequence, we follow every step as he assembles the film

and his recording into a movie of the event, doggedly extracting what seem to be facts from what looks like chaos.

De Palma's visual images in *Blow Out* invite comparison to many Alfred Hitchcock films, and indeed De Palma invited such comparisons when the posters for *Dressed to Kill* described him as "Master of the Macabre." In *Blow Out* there are such Hitchcock hallmarks as a shower scene (played this time for laughs rather than the chills of *Dressed to Kill*), several grisly murders in unexpected surroundings, violence in public places, and a chase through Philadelphia on the anniversary of the ringing of the Liberty Bell. This last extended chase sequence reminds us of two Hitchcock strategies: His juxtaposition of patriotic images and espionage, as in *North by Northwest* and *Saboteur,* and his desperate chases through uncaring crowds, reminders of *Foreign Correspondent* and *Strangers on a Train.*

But *Blow Out* stands by itself. It reminds us of the violence of *Dressed to Kill,* the startling images of *The Fury,* the clouded identities of *Sisters,* the uncertainty of historical "facts" from *Obsession,* and it ends with the bleak nihilism of *Carrie.* But it moves beyond those films, because this time De Palma is more successful than ever before at populating his plot with three-dimensional characters. We believe in the reality of the people played by John Travolta, Nancy Allen, John Lithgow, and Dennis Franz. They have all the little tics and eccentricities of life. And although they're caught in the mesh of a labyrinthine conspiracy, they behave as people probably would behave in such circumstances—they're not pawns of the plot.

Best of all, this movie is inhabited by a real cinematic intelligence. The audience isn't condescended to. In sequences like the one in which Travolta reconstructs a film and sound record of the accident, we're challenged and stimulated: We share the excitement of figuring out how things develop and unfold, when so often the movies only need us as passive witnesses.

Blue Collar ★ ★ ★ ★
R, 114 m., 1978

Richard Pryor (Zeke), Harvey Keitel (Jerry), Yaphet Kotto (Smokey), Ed Begley, Jr. (Bobby Joe), Harry Bellaver (Eddie Johnson), George Memmoli (Jenkins). Directed by Paul Schrader and produced by Don Guest. Screenplay by Paul and Leonard Schrader.

Detroit. Dawn. The next shift arrives for work. On the sound track, music of pounding urgency, suggesting the power of the machines that stamp out car doors from sheets of sheel. The camera takes us into the insides of an automobile factory, takes us close enough to almost smell the sweat and shield our eyes against the sparks thrown off by welding torches.

Blue Collar is about life on the Detroit assembly lines, and about how it wears men down and chains them to a lifetime installment plan. It is an angry, radical movie about the vise that traps workers between big industry and big labor. It's also an enormously entertaining movie; it earns its comparison with *On the Waterfront*. And it's an extraordinary directing debut for Paul Schrader, whose credits include *Taxi Driver* and *Rolling Thunder.*

Schrader tells the story of three workers, buddies on and off the job, who are all more or less in the same boat. They work, they drink after work in the bar across the street, they go home to mortgages or bills or kids who need braces on their teeth. One day they get fed up enough to decide to rob the safe in the office of their own union. What they find there is only a few hundred bucks—and a ledger that seems to contain the details of illegal loans of union funds.

The three guys are played by Richard Pryor, Harvey Keitel, and Yaphet Kotto, and they're all three at the top of their forms. Pryor, in particular, is a revelation: He's been good in a lot of movies, but almost always as himself, fast-talking, wise-cracking, running comic variations on the themes suggested by his dialogue. This time, held in rein by Schrader, he provides a tight, convincing performance as a family man.

Yaphet Kotto plays his opposite, an ex-con who likes to throw all-night parties with lots of sex, booze, and grass. And Harvey Keitel is their white friend, always behind on his loan company payments, who comes home one day to discover that his daughter has tried to bend paper clips over her teeth to convince her friends at school that she's got the braces she should have.

Schrader goes for a nice, raunchy humor in the scenes involving the three guys: The movie is relaxed and comfortable with itself, and we get the precise textures and tones of the society they live in. We understand their friendship, too, because it defies one of the things the movie passionately charges: That unions and management tacitly collaborate

on trying to set the rich against the poor, the black against the white, the old against the young, to divide and conquer.

The burglary caper begins innocently enough with Pryor's demand, at a union meeting, that the company repair his locker: He's cut his hand trying to get the damn thing open. But the union representatives seem indifferent to Pryor and just about everyone else, and so Pryor marches into the office of the shaggy, white-maned union leader who was a radical himself, once, back in the 1930s. And while the great statesman is feeding him several varieties of lies, Pryor sees the office safe and gets his idea.

The burglary itself finds the right line between humor and suspense, and then the movie's anger begins to burn. Because when the three men discover that the ledger may be more important than any money in the safe, they're torn between using it for blackmail, or using it to expose the corruption of their own union. Schrader gradually reveals his total vision in the film's second hour: A friendship that was sound and healthy suddenly goes sour. The system drives a wedge between them, as Pryor is offered a union job, Keitel becomes an FBI informer, and Kotto is killed in a scene of great and gruesome power.

It took a measure of courage to make *Blue Collar,* and especially to follow its events through to their inevitable conclusion. The movie could have copped out in its last thirty minutes, and given us a nice, safe Hollywood ending. Instead, it makes criticisms of mass production that social critics like Harvey Swados and Paul Goodman might have agreed with. This isn't a liberal movie but a radical one, and one I suspect a lot of assembly-line workers might see with a shock of recognition.

It took courage to make the movie that honest. But it also took a special filmmaking gift to make it burst with humor, humanity, and suspense as well. Like *On the Waterfront,* it's both an indictment and an entertainment, working just as well on its human levels as with its theoretical concerns. Paul Schrader has been a Hollywood wonder kid ever since negotiating a $450,000 deal for his first screenplay, *The Yakuza.* After *Taxi Driver* and *Obsession,* he was able to demand that he direct his own work, and *Blue Collar* is a stunning debut, taking chances and winning at them.

The Blues Brothers ★ ★ ★
R, 133 m., 1980

John Belushi (Jake Blues), Dan Aykroyd (Elwood Blues), Ray Charles (Ray), Aretha Franklin (Waitress), James Brown (Rev. James), Cab Calloway (Curtis), Charles Napier (Good Ol' Boy), Henry Gibson (Nazi), John Candy (Burton Mercer), Murphy Dunne (Piano Player), Carrie Fisher (Mystery Lady). Directed by John Landis and produced by Robert K. Weiss. Screenplay by Dan Aykroyd and Landis.

The Blues Brothers is the Sherman tank of musicals. When it was being filmed in Chicago in 1979—with dozens of cars piling up in intersections, caroming down Lake Shore Drive and crashing through the Daley Center—it seemed less like a film than a war. The movie feels the same way. It's a big, raucous powerhouse that proves against all the odds that if you're loud enough, vulgar enough, and have enough raw energy, you can make a steamroller into a musical, and vise versa.

This is some weird movie. There's never been anything that looked quite like it; was it dreamed up in a junkyard? It stars John Belushi and Dan Aykroyd as the Blues Brothers, Jake and Elwood, characters who were created on "Saturday Night Live" and took on a fearsome life of their own. The movie tells us something of their backgrounds: They were reared in a sadistic West Side orphanage, learned the blues by osmosis, and, as the movie opens, have teamed up again after Jake's release from the Joliet pen.

The movie's plot is a simple one, to put it mildly. The brothers visit their old orphanage, learn that its future is in jeopardy because of five thousand dollars due in back taxes, and determine to raise the money by getting their old band together and putting on a show. Their odyssey takes them to several sleazy Chicago locations, including a Van Buren flophouse, Maxwell Street, and lower Wacker Drive. They find their old friends in unlikely places, like a restaurant run by Aretha Franklin, a music shop run by Ray Charles, and a gospel church run by James Brown.

Their adventures include run-ins with suburban cops, good ol' boys, and Nazis who are trying to stage a demonstration. One of the intriguing things about this movie is the way it borrows so freely and literally from news events. The plot develops into a sort of musical *Mad Mad Mad Mad World,* with the Blues Brothers being pursued at the same time by avenging cops, Nazis, and an enraged country and western band led by Charles Napier, that character actor with the smile like Jaws. The chase is interrupted from time to time for musical numbers, which are mostly very good and filled with high-powered energy.

Aretha Franklin occupies one of the movie's best scenes, in her South Side soul food restaurant. Cab Calloway, as a sort of road manager for the Blues Brothers, struts through a wonderful old-style production of *Minnie the Moocher*. The Brothers themselves star in several improbable numbers; the funniest has the band playing in a country and western bar where wire mesh has been installed to protect the band from beer bottles thrown by the customers.

I was saying the musical numbers interrupt the chases. The fact is, the whole movie is a chase, with Jake and Elwood piloting a used police car that seems, as it hurdles across suspension bridges from one side to the other, to have a life of its own. There can rarely have been a movie that made so free with its locations as this one. There are incredible, sensational chase sequences under the elevated train tracks, on overpasses, in subway tunnels under the Loop, and literally through Daley Center. One crash in particular, a pileup involving maybe a dozen police cars, has to be seen to be believed: I've never seen stunt coordination like this before.

What's a little startling about this movie is that all of this works. *The Blues Brothers* cost untold millions of dollars and kept threatening to grow completely out of control. But director John Landis (of *Animal House*) has somehow pulled it together, with a good deal of help from the strongly defined personalities of the title characters. Belushi and Aykroyd come over as hard-boiled city guys, total cynics with a world-view of sublime simplicity, and that all fits perfectly with the movie's other parts. There's even room, in the midst of the carnage and mayhem, for a surprising amount of grace, humor, and whimsy.

Blue Steel ★ ★ ★
R, 95 m., 1990

Jamie Lee Curtis (Megan Turner), Ron Silver (Eugene Hunt), Clancy Brown (Nick Mann), Elizabeth Pena (Tracy Perez), Louise Fletcher (Shirley Turner), Philip Bosco (Frank Turner). Directed by Kathryn Bigelow and produced by Edward R. Pressman and Oliver Stone. Screenplay by Bigelow and Eric Red.

Squint a little to see the structure lurking beneath the details, and *Blue Steel* is a sophisticated update of *Halloween*, the movie that first made Jamie Lee Curtis a star. She plays the competent, strong woman who finally has to defend herself because nobody else can. Her life is endangered by a man who seems unstoppable, unkillable: No matter what happens to him, he picks himself up, pulls himself together, and continues his inexorable pursuit.

Curtis plays a New York cop who graduates from the police academy in the pretitle sequence, and the movie's villain is Ron Silver, a commodities broker who goes off the deep end. The plot is a little of *Fatal Attraction*, a little of *Jagged Edge*, and a little of *Wall Street*. It works because it's so audacious in combining elements that don't seem to belong together.

As the movie opens, Curtis shoots and kills a stickup man on her first day on the job. As the man drops dead in a supermarket, his gun spins out of control over the tile floor and is picked up and pocketed by Silver—a customer who hit the deck when the shooting started. He is already a deeply troubled man, and the sight of Curtis—a uniformed female cop—shooting a man dead is the image that pushes him over the edge.

It goes without saying that Curtis gets in trouble with her superiors at the department (the only reason commanding officers appear in cop movies is to wrongheadedly strip the heroes of their badges and guns). In the meantime, however, her social life picks up: Silver arranges to meet her "by accident," and they begin to date. She really likes the guy. And of course she never suspects that he was present in the supermarket or has a weirdo reason for being attracted to her—not even when dead people begin turning up around New York with her name engraved on the bullets they were shot with.

The movie is not simply a series of violent encounters—not at first, anyway. There's a half-realized subplot involving Curtis's parents (Louise Fletcher and Philip Bosco), and some vague psychological hints about why Bosco hates the idea of his daughter becoming a cop. The movie's weakest scene is the one where Curtis and her father leave his home for the sole purpose of not being there when Silver arrives, so she can be chilled when she finds him there on her return. The manipulation here is so awkward the scene should have been rewritten on the spot.

Other moments are much more convincing. What happens is that no one—especially not the men of the police department—believes Curtis's version of events. Nor do they believe that a respectable commodities broker could possibly be a mass murderer. The Silver character is intelligent enough to set up situations so that Curtis is seen in the worst possible way, until finally she seems to be the killer herself. But what does Silver want? In a truly diabolical twist, it appears that he wants to be murdered by this woman cop; he was truly unhinged by the experience in the supermarket. Silver does a good job of gradually revealing the demented depths of his character.

Blue Steel was directed by Kathryn Bigelow, whose previous credit was the well-regarded *Near Dark*. Does that make it a fundamentally different picture than if it had been directed by a man? Perhaps, in a way. The female "victim" is never helpless here, although she is set up in all the usual ways ordained by male-oriented thrillers. She can fight back with her intelligence, her police training, and her physical strength. And there is an anger in the way the movie presents the male authorities in the film, who are blinded to the facts by their preconceptions about women in general and female cops in particular.

The bottom line, however, is that *Blue Steel* is an efficient thriller, a movie that pays off with one shock and surprise after another, including a couple of really serpentine twists and a couple of superior examples of the killer-jumping-unexpectedly-from-the-dark scenes. I always feel dumb after I jump during one of those scenes. But I always jump.

Blue Velvet ★
R, 120 m., 1986

Kyle MacLachlan (Jeffrey Beaumont), Isabella Rossellini (Dorothy Valiens), Dennis Hopper (Frank Booth), Laura Dern (Sandy Williams), Hope Lange (Mrs. Williams), Dean Stockwell (Gar), George Dickerson (Detective Williams). Directed by David Lynch and produced by Richard Roth. Screenplay by Lynch.

Blue Velvet contains scenes of such raw emotional energy that it's easy to understand why some critics have hailed it as a masterpiece. A film this painful and wounding has to be given special consideration. And yet those very scenes of stark sexual despair are the tip-off to what's wrong with the movie. They're so strong that they deserve to be in a movie that is sincere, honest, and true. But *Blue Velvet* surrounds them with a story that's marred by sophomoric satire and cheap shots. The director is either denying the strength of his material or trying to defuse it by pretending it's all part of a campy in-joke.

The movie has two levels of reality. On one level, we're in Lumberton, a simple-minded small town where people talk in television clichés and seem to be clones of 1950s sitcom characters. On another level, we're told a story of sexual bondage, of how Isabella Rossellini's husband and son have been kidnapped by Dennis Hopper, who makes her his sexual slave. The twist is that the kidnapping taps into the woman's deepest feelings. She finds that she is a masochist who responds with great sexual passion to this situation.

Everyday town life is depicted with a deadpan irony; characters use lines with corny double meanings and solemnly recite platitudes. Meanwhile, the darker story of sexual bondage is told absolutely on the level in cold-blooded realism.

The movie begins with a much-praised sequence in which picket fences and flower beds establish a small-town idyll. Then a man collapses while watering the lawn, and a dog comes to drink from the hose that is still held in his unconscious grip. The great imagery continues as the camera burrows into the green lawn and finds hungry insects beneath—a metaphor for the surface and buried lives of the town.

The man's son, a college student (Kyle MacLachlan), comes home to visit his dad's bedside and resumes a romance with the daughter (Laura Dern) of the local police detective. MacLachlan finds a severed human ear in a field, and he and Dern get involved in trying to solve the mystery of the ear. The trail leads to a nightclub singer (Rossellini) who lives alone in a starkly furnished flat.

In a sequence that Hitchcock would have been proud of, MacLachlan hides himself in Rossellini's closet and watches, shocked, as she has a sadomasochistic sexual encounter with Hopper, a drug-sniffing pervert. Hopper leaves. Rossellini discovers MacLachlan in the closet and, to his astonishment, pulls a knife on him and forces him to submit to her seduction. He is appalled but fascinated; she wants him to be a "bad boy" and hit her.

These sequences have great power. They make *9½ Weeks* look rather timid by comparison, because they do seem genuinely born from the darkest and most despairing side of human nature. If *Blue Velvet* had continued to develop its story in a straight line, if it had followed more deeply into the implications of the first shocking encounter between Rossellini and MacLachlan, it might have made some real emotional discoveries.

Instead, director David Lynch chose to interrupt the almost hypnotic pull of that relationship in order to pull back to his jokey, small-town satire. Is he afraid that movie audiences might not be ready for stark S&M unless they're assured it's all really a joke?

I was absorbed and convinced by the relationship between Rossellini and MacLachlan, and annoyed because the director kept placing himself between me and the material. After five or ten minutes in which the screen reality was overwhelming, I didn't need the director prancing on with a top hat and cane, whispering that it was all in fun.

Indeed, the movie is pulled so violently in opposite directions that it pulls itself apart. If the sexual scenes are real, then why do we need the send-up of the "Donna Reed Show"? What are we being told? That beneath the surface of Small Town, U.S.A., passions run dark and dangerous? Don't stop the presses.

The sexual material in *Blue Velvet* is so disturbing, and the performance by Rossellini is so convincing and courageous, that it demands a movie that deserves it. American movies have been using satire for years to take the edge off sex and violence. Occasionally, perhaps sex and violence should be treated with the seriousness they deserve. Given the power of the darker scenes in this movie, we're all the more frustrated that the director is unwilling to follow through to the consequences of his insights. *Blue Velvet* is like the guy who drives you nuts by hinting at horrifying news and then saying, "Never mind."

There's another thing. Rossellini is asked to do things in this film that require real nerve. In one scene, she's publicly embarrassed by being dumped naked on the lawn of the police detective. In others, she is asked to portray emotions that I imagine most actresses would rather not touch. She is degraded, slapped around, humiliated, and undressed in front of the camera. And when you ask an actress to endure those experiences, you should keep your side of the bargain by putting her in an important film.

That's what Bernardo Bertolucci delivered when he put Marlon Brando and Maria Schneider through the ordeal of *Last Tango in Paris*. In *Blue Velvet*, Rossellini goes the whole distance, but Lynch distances himself from her ordeal with his clever asides and witty little in-jokes. In a way, his behavior is more sadistic than the Hopper character.

What's worse? Slapping somebody around, or standing back and finding the whole thing funny?

Blume in Love ★ ★ ★ ★
R, 116 m., 1973

George Segal (Blume), Susan Anspach (Nina), Kris Kristofferson (Elmo), Marsha Mason (Arlene), Shelley Winters (Mrs. Cramer), Donald F. Muhich (Analyst), Paul Mazursky (Hellman). Directed, produced, and written by Paul Mazursky.

Paul Mazursky's *Blume in Love* begins with a busted-up Southern California marriage.

The marriage belonged to Blume, divorce lawyer, and his wife Nina, a social worker. It busted up all of a sudden one weekday afternoon when Nina came home with a cold and found Blume in bed with his secretary. Why, you may ask (Blume certainly does), could his wife not forgive this indiscretion—especially as Blume is madly in love with Nina and must have her back or die? ("And I don't want to die," he reasons, "so I have to get her back.")

Well, maybe Nina was sort of halfway ready for the marriage to end. She's into her own brand of self-improvement and women's lib, and isn't sure she approves of marriage anymore. She takes up with an out-of-work (for twelve years) musician who lives in a VW truck with his dreams. She gets into yoga and learns to play the guitar and to rely on herself instead of men.

Little good that does Blume, whose love for her becomes a consuming passion. It is complicated by the fact that he gets to like the musician, too: thinks, in fact, that the bearded Elmo is the nicest man he has ever met. Blume even goes so far as to start a beard himself. But nothing will work for him, because of the fact he refuses to accept: Nina simply does not love him anymore. Does not. Period. Blume is driven into a frenzy of love, desire, frustration.

This material, so far, doesn't exactly

sound like the stuff of a great film. It sounds more like the brainy, funny dissections of California dreamin' that Mazursky carried out in three previous films, *I Love You, Alice B. Toklas, Bob & Carol & Ted & Alice*, and *Alex in Wonderland*. Those were all fine films—Mazursky is one of the best directors of comedy in Hollywood—but they were all more concerned with the laugh than with reality.

With *Blume in Love*, however, he seems to have pulled off what everybody is always hoping for from Neil Simon: a comedy that transcends its funny moments, that realizes we laugh so we may not cry, and that finally is about real people with real desperations. He's done that in a number of scenes, and yet somehow even during the movie's gloomiest moments he keeps some sort of hope alive. That's probably because Blume is played by the charming George Segal, who seems intrinsically optimistic. No matter what Nina says, he cannot quite give up on her, because he knows she must eventually love him again—because he loves her.

He carries this hope with him on a trip to Venice, which is where the film opens; she's asked him to go away somewhere for a couple of weeks, while she thinks. They had their first and second honeymoons in Venice, but now Blume wanders through Piazza San Marco in the autumn, stranded with a few other lonely tourists looking for love. The story is told in flashbacks from Venice, and it ends there. It ends with a note so unashamedly romantic that Mazursky gets away with "Tristan and Isolde" as his sound-track music. He's right. The ending would not be believable at all, except as hyperbole.

Nina—thin, earnest, determined to do the right thing and no longer be mastered by mere emotion—is played with a very complex charm by Susan Anspach. We have to like her even though she doesn't like Blume, whom we're cheering for. We do, and we like her boyfriend as much as Blume does. The itinerant musician is played by Kris Kristofferson, who gives evidence once again that he has a real acting talent—particularly in the scene where he hits Segal and then bursts into tears, and in the scene where he tells Segal he's hitting the road again.

Blume in Love has a quality that's hard to analyze but impossible to miss: It sets up an intimate rapport with its audiences.

Body Double ★ ★ ★ ½
R, 110 m., 1984

Craig Wasson (Jake), Melanie Griffith (Holly), Gregg Henry (Sam), Deborah Shelton (Gloria). Directed and produced by Brian De Palma. Screenplay by Robert H. Averch and De Palma.

Body Double is an exhilarating exercise in pure filmmaking, a thriller in the Hitchcock tradition in which there's no particular point except that the hero is flawed, weak, and in terrible danger—and we identify with him completely. The movie is so cleverly constructed, with the emphasis on visual storytelling rather than dialogue, that we are neither faster nor slower than the hero as he gradually figures out the scheme that has entrapped him. And the casting of a Hitchcockian average guy also helps.

The movie stars Craig Wasson, an openfaced actor with an engaging smile, as its hero, an unemployed actor named Jake. He isn't smart, he isn't dumb, he isn't perfect, he isn't bad. He is an ideal choice to set up as a witness to a murder. Jake needs a place to stay, and another actor (Gregg Henry) offers him a job house-sitting in a weird, modernistic home on stilts up in the hills above Los Angeles. The other actor also points out all the sights—including a shapely neighbor who does a nightly striptease dance in front of her open window. Jake is only human. For two nights, he uses a telescope to watch the striptease. He also begins to suspect that the woman may be in danger. In sequences inspired by *Rear Window*, he begins to follow the woman (Deborah Shelton), but he keeps his distance because he's caught in the same dilemma as Jimmy Stewart was in the Hitchcock picture: He is, after all, technically a Peeping Tom, and he wouldn't know the woman was in danger if he hadn't been breaking the law.

Since the plot is so important in *Body Double*, and because the movie contains so many nice surprises, I won't reveal very much more of the story. Let me describe in a carefully vague way, however, some of the pleasures of the movie. After a murder does indeed seem to have been committed, Jake's path leads him into the world of pornographic filmmaking. He wants to meet and hire a porno superstar (Melanie Griffith) who he thinks can help him figure out the mystery. His attempts lead to a series of very funny conversations, as the blond porno actress talks to him with a Runyonesque mixture of jaded sophistication and startling ignorance. The speech in which she explains exactly what she will, and will not, do in a movie is shocking, sad, and curiously moving. *Body Double*'s excursion into the world of pornography (we see some fairly mild porno scenes, shot by De Palma himself) is part of a veritable anthology of styles in this movie. The film opens with a satire on vampire movies, includes a Hitchcockian catand-mouse sequence, and even borrows some of the clichés of 1940s thrillers, including a detailed recapitulation at the end, complete with flashbacks. There is also a sharp 1940s look to the cinematography, which uses dramatic lighting, tilted cameras, and carefully constructed shots to make the style part of the story.

But the movie is not just an exercise in style. It is also a genuinely terrifying thriller, in which an almost clockwork plot brings the hero and the killer together without a single logical glitch. De Palma is at home in this genre. Although his *Scarface* was more of a serious social commentary, thrilling suspense movies are his specialty, and his credits include *Carrie*, *Obsession*, and *Dressed to Kill*. With *Body Double*, he has his most airtight plot. He also has, once again, his almost unique courage to go over the top—to push scenes beyond the edge of common sense and into cheerfully heightened and impassioned overkill. The burial sequence next to the Hollywood reservoir, for example, or the photography in the tunnel during one of Jake's attacks of claustrophobia, are so uninhibited that they skirt the dangerous edge of being ridiculous. But because the story's so strong, they're not. They work.

Bolero ½★
NO MPAA RATING, 105 m., 1984

Bo Derek, George Kennedy, Andrea Occhipinti. Directed by John Derek.

Bolero is a film starring Bo Derek as a woman who believes that the cure for a man's impotence is for his woman to train as a bullfighter. "Bolero" is also the name of the composition by Ravel which Dudley Moore played in *10* while making love with Derek. So much we already know. Also, let's see here, paging through the old dictionary . . . a bolero is a Spanish dance, characterized by sharp turns and revolutions of the body and stamping of the feet, and it also is a jacket of waist-length or shorter, usually worn open. So *that* explains the jacket of waist-length or shorter, usually worn open, which is Bo Derek's only item of clothing during one scene in the movie! It also explains the sharp turns and revolutions of her body during the same scene, although there is no stamping of the feet, except by the viewer.

But I am still a little confused by the relationship between Derek and the bull-fighter who is her lover. If you have not seen the movie, let me explain. Derek has graduated from a fancy women's boarding school, and after mooning her professors she departs in search of a tall, dark, and handsome lover. First she meets a sheik, but he turns out to be a dud, maybe because he spends too much time inhaling the magic fumes of his hookah.

So Bo goes to Spain, where she meets this all-around guy who herds cattle on a mountaintop, owns a winery, and is a bullfighter. If he also was an investment banker whose last book read was *The Prophet*, he could be a Dewar's Profile. Bo and the guy make love at sunrise. Unfortunately, the sun rises directly into the camera at crucial moments. Then her lover goes into the ring to fight with the bull, and is gored in that portion of his anatomy he could least afford to spare in any continuing relationship with Derek. He is brave. While doctors fight to save his life, his only thought is for his dog. He asks Bo to be sure that the dog gets home safely.

Before long, Bo is observing that her lover is acting depressed and distant. Could this possibly be because of his horrible injuries? You would think so, and I would think so, but Bo tells him it doesn't matter, and then she vows that he will live to fight again another day, so to speak. Then she starts taking bullfighting lessons. Oh, but I almost forgot. The Arab sheik tears himself away from his hookah long enough to fly to Spain and kidnap her. She is tied up in his open biplane, but manages to untie herself and jump over the edge. Then Bo is immediately back in her lover's hacienda again. How did she get to the ground? For anyone with Bo's faith, all is possible, and I think this is a real good omen for the lover. If she can get down in one piece, think what he might be able to do.

Let's face it. Nobody is going to *Bolero* for the plot anyway. They're going for the Good Parts. There are two Good Parts, not counting her naked ride on horseback, which was the only scene in the movie that had me wondering how she did it. The real future of

Bolero is in home cassette rentals, where your fast forward and instant replay controls will supply the editing job the movie so desperately needs.

The Boost ★ ★ ★ ½
R, 95 m., 1988

James Woods (Lenny), Sean Young (Linda), John Kapelos (Joel), Steven Hill (Max), Kelle Kerr (Rochelle), John Rothman (Ned), Amanda Blake (Barbara), Grace Zabriskie (Cheryl). Directed by Harold Becker and produced by Daniel H. Blatt. Screenplay by Darryl Ponicsan.

The Boost is not simply about drugs. It is also about the hedonistic lifestyles of the 1980s, especially in go-go areas like the Los Angeles real estate market, in which fortunes are won and squandered in a matter of months and there is unspeakable pressure to keep up appearances. The movie is a modern-day version of *Death of a Salesman*, with James Woods selling leveraged tax shelters. He's out there on a smile, a shoeshine, and a line of cocaine.

Woods is one of the most intense, unpredictable actors in the movies today. You watch his characters because they seem capable of exploding—not out of anger, but out of hurt, shame, and low self-esteem. They're wounded, but they fight back by being smarter than anyone else, and using jokes and sarcasm to keep people at arm's length. That's the case with Lenny, the guy he plays in this movie. Lenny doesn't care if you like him or not, just so long as you see that he has a big house, an expensive car, and a wife so beautiful that—in his words—"How did she wind up with a runt like me?"

As the movie opens, Lenny is calling names in the phone book to peddle some kind of half-baked "investment opportunity." He meets a pleasant enough young prospect, invites him to dinner, and then explodes halfway through the meal, all of his resentments pouring out. Lenny hurts. But one day he meets a kind, philosophical older man (Steven Hill) who hires him to come out to L.A. and sell tax shelters to people with windfall profits.

Lenny is an overnight success. All he needed was the veneer of respectability—the expensive suits, the Mercedes—to cover his desperation. He's flying high. When he decides to invest in some cockamamie Mexican nightclub, his wife, Linda (Sean

Young), cautions him that they are overextended. He doesn't care. He's rich and the money is pouring in and he's invincible, and then Congress changes the tax laws and his business evaporates overnight.

It's at that point that he tries cocaine for the first time. He's given his first taste by a free-spending friend (John Kapelos) who owns a chain of car washes. He likes it. It puts him back on top of the world. And as Lenny and Linda hit the skids, they're looking up all the way down. Cocaine makes their failures seem like temporary setbacks in a master plan. It makes them feel great. They never figure out the truth in George Carlin's famous line: "What does cocaine make you feel like? It makes you feel like having some more cocaine."

As Lenny and Linda head for the bottom, the movie turns into one of the most convincing and horrifying portraits of drug addiction I've ever seen. The director, Harold Becker, has directed Woods in two of his best movies (*The Onion Field* and *The Black Marble*). In this even darker story, he never insists too much; he simply observes. Lenny and Linda lose their expensive house. They move out of their middle-class high-rise apartment. They spend some time working in a sporting-goods store on the beach, trying to go straight and dry out. Lenny attends some kind of a rehabilitation program (off-screen) and comes back temporarily sober, but he's walking a tightrope.

"I've got the problem," he says. "Linda was only keeping me company." Linda thinks the same thing—and so when the car-wash king and his wife visit her at the beach, she tries a line of cocaine, gets stoned, falls down some stairs, and has a miscarriage. And then they really hit the skids. The movie portrays with almost effortless conviction the world of apartments-by-the-week in the seamy neighborhoods of Hollywood, where everybody has two occupations—the one he hopes someday to work at, and dealing drugs. Lenny, who was born desperate, becomes completely strung out, disoriented, paranoid. And *still* he clings to the delusion that he'll be back on top someday, that drugs are somehow the answer.

I received a letter the other day from a documentary filmmaker who is working on a TV program about mystical experiences. "Alcoholism and drug addiction in the twentieth century," he wrote, "may be related to the human desire for transcendence." Yes, and in other centuries, too, but in a reverse sort of way: If you're a drunk or an addict, you've got to transcend that before you can move along to other kinds of transcendence. Lenny's problem, in the closing scenes of *The Boost*, is that every detail of his life is governed in one way or another by his need to drink or take drugs. He's not transcending. He's maintaining. All he can hope for is a miracle.

Born on the Fourth of July ★ ★ ★ ★
R, 144 m., 1989

Tom Cruise (Ron Kovic), Willem Dafoe (Charlie), Kyra Sedgwick (Donna), Raymond J. Barry (Mr. Kovic), Jerry Levine (Steve Boyer), Frank Whaley (Timmy), Carolina Kava (Mrs. Kovic), Abbie Hoffman (Strike Organizer), Oliver Stone (News Reporter), Tom Berenger (Recruiting Sergeant), Rob Camilletti (Tommy Finnelli), Sean Stone (Young Jimmy). Directed by Oliver Stone and produced by A. Kitman Ho and Stone. Screenplay by Stone and Ron Kovic.

For some time we've been reading in the papers about public apologies by governments of the Eastern bloc. The Russians admit they were wrong to invade Afghanistan and Czechoslovakia. The East Germans tear down the wall and denounce the secret luxuries of their leaders. The Poles and Hungarians say Marxism doesn't work very well. There is a temptation for an American reading these articles to feel smug. And yet—hold on a minute here. We had our own disastrous foreign policy mistake: the war in Vietnam. When is anybody going to get up before Congress and read an apology to the Vietnamese?

Never, is the obvious answer. We hail the Soviet bloc for its honesty but see no lessons for ourselves. And yet we have been issuing our own apologies, of a sort. A film like Oliver Stone's *Born on the Fourth of July* is an apology for Vietnam uttered by Stone, who fought there, and Ron Kovic, who was paralyzed from the chest down in Vietnam. Both of them were gung-ho patriots who were eager to answer their country's call to arms. When they came back home, they were still patriots—hurt and offended by the hostility they experienced from the antiwar movement.

Eventually both men turned against the war, Kovic most dramatically. He and his wheelchair were thrown out of the 1972 Republican convention, but in 1976 he addressed the Democratic convention, and if

you want to you could say his 1976 speech was the equivalent of one of those recent breast-beatings in the Supreme Soviet. We do apologize for our mistakes in this country, but we let our artists do it, instead of our politicians.

Kovic came back from the war with a shattered body, but it took a couple of years for the damage to spread to his mind and spirit. By the time he hit bottom he was a demoralized, spiteful man who sought escape in booze and drugs and Mexican whorehouses. Then he began to look outside of himself for a larger pattern to his life, the pattern that inspired his best-selling autobiography, *Born on the Fourth of July*.

The director, Oliver Stone, who based his earlier film *Platoon* on his own war experiences, has been trying to film the Kovic book for years. Various stars and studios were attached to the project, but it kept being canceled, and perhaps that's just as well, because by waiting this long Stone was able to use Tom Cruise in the leading role. Nothing Cruise has done earlier will prepare you for what he does in *Born on the Fourth of July*. He has been hailed for years now as a great young American actor, but only his first film, *Risky Business*, found a perfect match between actor and role. *Top Gun* overwhelmed him with a special-effects display, *The Color of Money* didn't explain his behavior in crucial final scenes, *Cocktail* was a cynical attempt to exploit his attractive image. Almost always he seemed to be holding something in reserve, standing back from his own presence. In *Born on the Fourth of July*, his performance is so good that the movie lives through it—Stone is able to make his statement with Cruise's face and voice and doesn't need to put everything into the dialogue.

The movie begins in the early 1960s, indeed with footage of John Kennedy on the television exhorting, "Ask not what your country can do for you; ask what you can do for your country." Young Ron Kovic, football star and high-school hero, was the kind of kid waiting to hear that message. And when the Marine recruiters came to visit his high school, he was ready to sign up. There was no doubt in his mind: There was a war in Vietnam, and his only worry was that he would miss the action. He knew there was a danger of being wounded or killed, but hell, he wanted to make a sacrifice for his country.

His is the kind of spirit all nations must have from time to time. The problem with

the Vietnam War is that it did not deserve it. There was no way for a patriotic small-town kid to know that, however, and so we follow young Kovic through boot camp and into the battlefield. In these scenes, Cruise still looks like Cruise—boyish, open-faced—and I found myself wondering if he would be able to make the transition into the horror that I knew was coming. He was.

Oliver Stone was in combat for a year. In *Platoon*, he showed us firefights so confused we (and the characters) often had little idea where the enemy was. In *Born on the Fourth of July*, Stone directs a crucial battle scene with great clarity so that we can see how a mistake was made by Kovic. That mistake, which tortures him for years afterward, probably produced the loss of focus that led to his crippling injury.

The scenes which follow, in a military hospital, are merciless in their honesty. If you have even once, for a few hours perhaps, been helpless in a sickbed and unable to summon aid, all of your impotent rage will come flooding back as the movie shows a military care system that is hopelessly overburdened. At one point, Kovic screams out for a suction pump that will drain a wound that might cost him his leg. He will never have feeling in the leg—but, God damn it, he wants to keep it all the same. It's his. And a hospital orderly absentmindedly explains about equipment shortages and "budget cutbacks" in care for the wounded vets.

Back in civilian life, Kovic is the hero of a Fourth of July parade, but there are peaceniks on the sidewalks, some of them giving him the finger. He feels more rage. But then his emotional tide turns one night in the backyard of his parents' home. He gets drunk with a fellow veteran and finds they can talk about things nobody else really understands. It is from this scene that the full power of the Cruise performance develops. Kovic's life becomes a series of confusions—bar brawls, self-pity, angry confrontations with women he will never be able to make love with in the ordinary way. His parents love him but are frightened of his rage. Eventually it is suggested that he leave home.

In a scene of Dantean evil, Stone shows Kovic in Mexico with other crippled veterans, paying for women and drugs to take away the pain, and finally, shockingly, abandoned in the desert with another veteran with no way to get back to their wheelchairs or to town. It's the sort of thing that happens to people who make themselves unbearable to other people who don't give a damn about them. (In a nod toward *Platoon*, the other crippled veteran in the desert is played by Willem Dafoe, costar of that film; the other costar, Tom Berenger, is the Marine who gives the recruitment speech in the opening scenes.)

Born on the Fourth of July is one of those films that steps correctly in the opening moments and then never steps wrongly. It is easy to think of a thousand traps that Oliver Stone, Ron Kovic, and Tom Cruise could have fallen into with this film, but they fall into none of them.

Although this film has vast amounts of pain and bloodshed and suffering in it, and is at home on battlefields and in hospital wards, it proceeds from a philosophical core—it is not a movie about battle or wounds or recovery, but a movie about an American who changes his mind about the war. The filmmakers realize that is the heart of their story and are faithful to it, even though they could have spun off in countless other directions. This is a film about ideology, played out in the personal experiences of a young man who paid dearly for what he learned. Maybe instead of anybody getting up in Congress and apologizing for the Vietnam War, they could simply hold a screening of this movie on Capitol Hill and call it a day.

The Bonfire of the Vanities ★ ★ ½
R, 126 m., 1990

Tom Hanks (Sherman McCoy), Bruce Willis (Peter Fallow), Melanie Griffith (Maria Ruskin), Kim Cattrall (Judy McCoy), Saul Rubinek (Jed Kramer), Morgan Freeman (Judge White), Alan King (Arthur Ruskin). Directed and produced by Brian De Palma. Screenplay by Michael Cristofer.

Tom Wolfe's saga about Sherman McCoy has by now become one of America's favorite urban legends, a cautionary tale about a "master of the universe" who was earning millions on Wall Street and enjoying the pleasures of his wife, his mistress, and his seductive lifestyle, when he made one fatal wrong turn off the expressway and found himself in the South Bronx.

There, in a ludicrous comedy of errors, his mistress ran their car into a black youth she thought was attacking them. The youth died, and the case became an overnight sensation. Sherman, whose life was graced with every

material and sensual excess, found himself plunged into a publicity circus, suffered the indignity of being jailed, and became the target of white political opportunists and black self-promoters who saw him as a convenient and hateful symbol.

The Bonfire of the Vanities, Wolfe's novel about McCoy, was savage and sarcastic, especially in the way it dissected the motives of every single character. Brian De Palma's movie is lacking in just that quality; it is not subtle or perceptive about the delicate nuances of motive that inspire these people. My notion is that Wolfe sees every single one of his characters in exactly the same light, as selfish, grasping swine who want to get their hands on everything they can, and whose approaches are suggested by the opportunities they find around them in whatever walk of life they occupy. The movie doesn't seem to despise anyone all that much.

Sherman McCoy, who makes millions and lives in a Park Avenue duplex, is no less selfish than the others in the novel, but he is not much of a survivor. He does well on the sedate battlefield of Wall Street, but when he runs into *real* fighters—cops, neighborhood activists, politicians, newspaper reporters, publicity hounds, ambulance-chasing lawyers, and his neighbors on the co-op board—he finds he's no match.

The Wolfe novel goes inside the characters' minds and lifestyles, showing how they think and what they value. The movie sees mostly the exteriors, and although it is narrated by one of the characters—Peter Fallow, the journalist, played by Bruce Willis—he provides few insights and little verbal grace, serving mostly just to hurry the story along. And yet it is enough of a story, and the actors are colorful enough in their different ways, that *The Bonfire of the Vanities* is an entertaining film, even if it misses the droll qualities of the book.

Tom Hanks stars as Sherman McCoy, but is more acted upon than acting in this movie. He has two typical expressions here: crafty cunning and disbelief shading into horror. He is never really developed as a character we feel we know, and he seems to inhabit his lifestyle rather than possess it. He generates no sympathy—but then he isn't supposed to. Much more interesting is Melanie Griffith, as Maria, his sexy mistress, who is utterly carnal, self-serving, and shameless.

The weakest character in the movie is Fallow, the journalist, played by Willis. He is supposed to be a drunk, and so the movie

opens with him waving a bottle as he emerges from a limousine. But the movie makes no attempt to turn him into an interesting character with a personality—he doesn't have the moxie or the smarts to be the kind of reporter he's representing. He just mopes about, sighing and shrugging and raising his eyebrows. The Fallow created by Wolfe in the book was a great fictional character, a shameless, freeloading con artist who uses the McCoy story as a ploy to keep his job.

Other important characters are glimpsed as if at a distance. It helps to have read the book to understand the motives of the white lawyer who suddenly materializes at the side of the victim's grieving mother. And without having read the book, it is impossible to know the true motives of the two black youths who materialize in the shadows of the expressway and strike terror into the hearts of Sherman and Maria; they are played simply as menacing symbols. De Palma misses a bet, too, with the character of the black minister and community leader—obviously inspired by Al Sharpton—by making him a comic blowhard rather than the scheming, intelligent grafter of the Wolfe novel. One of the more effective characters is played by Morgan Freeman, pounding away on his gavel as Sherman's angry judge. He has a delicious final speech that is filled with irony—he has arrived at the right verdict, but because of Sherman's lies about a crucial piece of evidence.

If *The Bonfire of the Vanities* lacks the texture and detail that would make it realistic, at least it does work well in a certain glossy way. Sharp satirical points are made, often as throwaways, and there are little moments of truth, as when Fallow takes Ruskin (Alan King), Maria's husband, out to dinner. Kim Cattrall goes way over the top as Sherman's wife, Judy, but sometimes that works, as when she tries to give a dinner party while her world crumbles around her. (A famous scene from the book, in which she explains to their child that daddy makes his millions by taking crumbs from other people's cakes, is overplayed and underlined until it dies.)

What we have here, I think, is a movie that will be enjoyed most by those who haven't read the Tom Wolfe novel. In its glittering surfaces and snapshot performances, it provides a digest version of the Wolfe story, filled with obvious ironies and easy targets. Those who have read the book will be constantly distracted because they know so much more than the movie tells them about the characters. The beauty of the Wolfe book was the way it saw through its time and place, dissecting motives and reading minds. The movie sees much, but it doesn't see through.

The Bostonians ★ ★ ★
PG, 120 m., 1984

Christopher Reeve (Basil Ransom), Vanessa Redgrave (Olive Chancellor), Madeleine Potter (Verena Tarrant), Jessica Tandy (Mrs. Birdseye), Nancy Marchand (Mrs. Burrage). Directed and produced by Ismail Merchant, James Ivory, and Ruth Prawer Jhabvala. Screenplay by Merchant, Ivory, and Jhabvala.

One of the qualities I like best in the novels of Henry James is the way his characters talk and talk about matters of passion and the heart, and never quite seem to act. One of his favorite words, in many of his books, is "intercourse," by which, significantly, he seems to mean conversation, although you can never quite be sure. James's novels run long and deep, and because he was writing for a 19th century that was not always open to the kinds of passions felt by his characters, he beat a lot, if you will, around the bush, so to speak, with lots of commas and asides and subtle hints of unspeakable practices.

The Bostonians is a novel with a lot of asides, and hundreds of pages of hints. We can summarize it boldly: It is about a sweet and somewhat inconsequential young woman who has inspired crushes in two of her admirers. One of her would-be lovers is a straight-spoken lawyer from the South, who wants to sweep her off her feet and make her his wife. The other is a woman, who does not seem quite in touch with the true nature of her feelings; today she would know she was a lesbian, but in the world of James it is necessary for her to displace her feelings—to convince herself that she is in love with the young woman's politics. Those politics are mostly secondhand, made up of things the young woman has been told by others. The story is set at the birth of the suffragette movement, and women meet in each others' homes to talk about the right to vote and, by extension, the right to lead full lives. *The Bostonians* shows us several of those women, including the veteran leader Mrs. Birdseye (wonderfully played by Jessica Tandy) and the younger firebrand Olive Chancellor (Vanessa Redgrave).

Chancellor is in love with Verena Tarrant (Madeleine Potter). That is clear to us, but not as clear to Chancellor. She promotes the young woman as a lecturer and campaigner, filled with visions of her role in social reform—a role that will necessarily require her to become Chancellor's associate, and have little to do with men. Then the tall Southern lawyer (Christopher Reeve) arrives on the scene, and the movie turns into a tug-of-war in which nobody is quite frank about the real nature of the battle.

The Bostonians is by the veteran producer-director-writer team of Ismail Merchant, James Ivory, and Ruth Prawer Jhabvala, who collaborated on a 1979 film version of Henry James's *The Europeans*. This is a much better film, intelligent and subtle and open to the underlying tragedy of a woman who does not know what she wants, a man who does not care what he wants, and a girl who does not need what she wants.

The Bounty ★ ★ ★ ★
PG, 130 m., 1984

Anthony Hopkins (Captain William Bligh), Mel Gibson (Fletcher Christian), Tevaite Vernette (Mauatua), Laurence Olivier (Admiral Hood), Edward Fox (Captain Greetham), Daniel Day Lewis (Fryer). Directed by Roger Donaldson and produced by Bernard Williams. Screenplay by Robert Bolt.

The relationship between Fletcher Christian and Captain William Bligh is one of the most familiar in the movies: We've seen it acted between Clark Gable and Charles Laughton, and between Marlon Brando and Trevor Howard, but it's never before been quite as intriguing as in *The Bounty*, the third movie based on the most famous mutiny in the history of the sea. The movie suggests that Bligh and Christian were friends, of all things, and that Bligh—far from being the histrionic martinet of earlier movies—was an intelligent, contemplative man of great complications. The story is well-known, and simple: *HMS Bounty* sets sail for the South seas, has a difficult voyage that frays everyone's tempers, and then anchors at a Polynesian island. During the trip, the original first mate has been replaced by the young Fletcher Christian, whom Bligh decides to trust. But Christian tires of the voyage and of the dangers and probable death that lie ahead. He falls in love with a native girl and leads a mutiny of sailors who choose to stay on their island paradise.

Bligh is played by Anthony Hopkins in one of the most interesting performances of 1984: He is unyielding, but not mindlessly rigid; certain he is right, but not egotistical; able to be realistic about his fate and his chances, and yet completely loyal to his ideas of a British naval officer's proper duties. When Fletcher Christian leads a mutiny against his command, it is not seen simply as a revolt against cruel authority (as in the earlier movies) but as a choice between a freer lifestyle, and Bligh's placing of duty above ordinary human nature.

Every *Bounty* movie seems to shape its Fletcher Christian somewhat to reflect the actor who plays him. Gable's Christian was a man of action, filled with physical strength and high spirits. Brando's was introverted and tortured. Mel Gibson's is maybe the hardest to figure of the three. He is a man of very few words (the screenplay gives him little to say, and almost no philosophizing), quiet, observant, an enigma. Only in the arms of the woman he comes to love, the Tahitian girl Mauatua, does he find the utter simplicity that perhaps he was looking for when he went to sea. It is a decision of some daring to give Gibson so noticeably little dialogue in this movie, but it works.

This *Bounty* is not only a wonderful movie, high-spirited and intelligent, but something of a production triumph as well. Although this third *Bounty* film was originally conceived as a big-budget, two-part epic to be directed by David *(Doctor Zhivago)* Lean, the current version was prepared and directed after only a few months' notice by a talented young New Zealander named Roger Donaldson, whose previous credits included the brilliant *Smash Palace*, a critical hit and commercial failure. What's interesting is that Donaldson's film doesn't feel like a secondhand treatment; he directs with flair and wit, and the spectacular scenes (like a stormy crossing of the Cape) never allow the special effects to steal the film away from the actors.

The sea voyage is done with the sort of macho confidence that a good sea movie needs, and the land portions do an interesting job of contrasting the proper, civilized British (represented by Laurence Olivier, as an admiral) with the cheerful absolute freedom of Polynesia. The romance between Gibson and the beautiful Tevaite Vernette, as his island lover, is given time to develop instead of just being thrown in as a plot point. And the Polynesians, for once, are all allowed to go topless all the time (the movie nevertheless gets the PG rating, qualifying under the *National Geographic* loophole in which nudity doesn't count south of the equator). *The Bounty* is a great adventure, a lush romance, and a good movie.

The Boy Who Could Fly ★ ★ ★
PG, 114 m., 1986

Lucy Deakins (Milly), Jay Underwood (Eric), Bonnie Bedelia (Charlene), Fred Savage (Louis), Colleen Dewhurst (Mrs. Sherman), Fred Gwynne (Uncle Hugo), Louise Fletcher (Psychiatrist). Directed by Nick Castle and produced by Gary Adelson. Screenplay by Castle.

Here is a sweet and innocent parable about a boy who could fly—and about a girl who could fly, too, when the boy held her hand. The lesson the girl learns in this film is that anything is possible, if only you have faith. The movie could have been directed fifty years ago by Frank Capra, except that in the Capra version, the boy wouldn't have been autistic and the girl wouldn't have been grieving because of the recent suicide of her father, who was dying of cancer. Parables have harder edges these days.

The movie takes place in a small town with picket fences, shade trees, and mean boys who won't let little kids ride their tricycles around the block. Into a run-down house on one of these streets, a small family moves: a mother, teen-age daughter, and little brother. The girl looks out her bedroom window to the house next door, and there she sees, poised on the roof, a teen-age boy with his arms outstretched, poised to fly.

She learns his story. When he was five, his parents died in an airplane crash. At the exact moment of the crash, he started to try to fly, as if he could have saved them. But can he really fly? The boy lives with an alcoholic uncle, who swears he has seen the kid fly. But the uncle sees a lot of things, not all of them real.

The Boy Who Could Fly surrounds this situation with small stories of everyday life. The mother (Bonnie Bedelia) goes back to her old job in the insurance industry and discovers she has to learn to use a computer. Her daughter (Lucy Deakins) goes to high school and makes friends with an understanding teacher (Colleen Dewhurst). The little brother (a small, fierce tyke named Fred Savage) plots to overcome the bullies who live around the corner. And next door, the

strange boy (Jay Underwood) lives in his world of dreams and silence.

Can anything break through to him? Yes, as it turns out, one power on Earth is strong enough to penetrate his autism, and that power is adolescent love.

He gets a crush on his new neighbor. She cares for him. One day, he saves her life. She believes he can really fly, but nobody else does, and then the kid is taken away from his drunken uncle and placed in an institution, which could crush his spirit.

The movie develops along lines that we can more or less anticipate, and it ends on a note of high sentimentality. What's good about it are the performances, especially by Deakins, a warm and empathetic teen-ager, Savage, a plucky little kid who could play Dennis the Menace, and Bedelia, a widow still mourning her husband.

Movies like this can be insufferable if they lay it on too thick. *The Boy Who Could Fly* finds just about the right balance between its sunny message and the heartbreak that's always threatening to prevail.

Boyfriends and Girlfriends ★ ★ ★
PG, 102 m., 1988

Emmanuelle Chaulet (Blanche), Sophie Renoir (Lea), Anne-Laure Meury (Adrienne), Eric Viellard (Fabien), Francois-Eric Gendron (Alexandre). Written and directed by Eric Rohmer and produced by Margaret Menegoz.

Paris is not all crowded together into a cozy warren of colorful streets nestled on the banks of the Seine. And Parisians are not all colorful intellectuals, bohemians, artists, and tradesmen, so authentic they make you feel like a stage American. France, in fact, is not all like France. Parts of it are glossy new architectural enclaves where young yuppies meet to chirp and preen. That is the France of Eric Rohmer's film, *Boyfriends and Girlfriends*. The movie takes place in a modern suburb of Paris, so close you can sometimes see the Eiffel Tower in the distance, so far away it is almost another country. This is a clean, well-lighted environment, in which all the fixtures of a Paris neighborhood have been picked up, shaken well, dusted, sterilized, painted, and set down again. The sidewalk cafes, for example, have just the right little porcelain sugar bowls and round white chairs. All they lack is a sidewalk.

In this environment, Rohmer places several young professionals, who range in age

from, say, twenty-four to thirty-two. One woman works in a social agency. Another works in a travel bureau. The men have more abstract jobs that require them to venture into Paris itself. But their true home is here in this brand-new environment that seems designed to set off their new slacks and sweaters without throwing too much light on their opinions.

Boyfriends and Girlfriends is one of a series of "proverbs" that Rohmer has been working through, after his earlier series of six "moral tales" such as *My Night at Maud's* and *Claire's Knee*. The moral tales presented their characters with actual and tricky moral dilemmas (for example, should one act selfishly on a desire to touch Claire's knee if that indulgence would interfere with Claire's otherwise happily innocent existence?). The proverbs, on the other hand, are skimpier affairs, lightweight little whimsies designed to illustrate some sort of everyday truth in an ironic way.

The proverb that inspired *Boyfriends and Girlfriends* is "The friends of my friends are my friends" (which in French was the original title of the movie, and in English would make a more intriguing one than *Boyfriends and Girlfriends*).

The movie is essentially about bad timing. Two young women are friends. Not deep, lifelong soul sisters, to be sure, but friends. They see a handsome young man. One likes him, the other gets him, and then, in a sense, they trade, with an additional boyfriend and a few other friends thrown into the mixture. All of the permutations are unimportant because we are not dealing with the heart here, but with fashion.

There is a sense in which none of these characters can feel deeply, although they can admittedly experience transient periods of weeping and moaning over their cruel fates. That's because their relationships are based essentially on outward appearances; they choose lovers as fashion accessories. In conversation, they find they have "a lot in common," but that's easy to explain: They all hold exactly the same few limited opinions.

When one girl thinks she has a boy and another girl gets him, there is a sense of betrayal, all right, but it's not the kind of passionate betrayal that leads to murder or suicide. It's the kind of betrayal that leads to dramatic statements like "I'm not ever going to speak to you again!"

Rohmer knows exactly what he is doing here. He has no great purpose, but an interesting small one: He wants to observe the everyday behavior of a new class of French person, the young professionals whose values are mostly materialistic, whose ideas have been shaped by popular culture, who do not read much, or think much about politics, or have much depth. By the end of this film, you may know his characters better than they will ever know themselves. In *My Night at Maud's*, a man sat by the bedside of a woman all night long while they talked and talked and talked. The sad thing about the people in *Boyfriends and Girlfriends*, we sense, is that in such a situation they would have little to talk about. And if the boy actually got into the bed, even less.

Brazil ★ ★
R, 130 m., 1985

Jonathan Pryce (Sam Lowry), Robert De Niro (Tuttle), Katherine Helmond (Ida Lowry), Ian Holm (Kurtzmann), Bob Hoskins (Spoor), Michael Palin (Jack Lint). Directed by Terry Gilliam and produced by Arnon Milchan. Screenplay by Tom Stoppard, Charles McKeown, and Gilliam.

Just as Orwell's *1984* is an alternative vision of our times, so *Brazil* is an alternative to Orwell. The movie happens in a time and place that seem vaguely like our own, but with different graphics, hardware, and politics. Society is controlled by a monolithic organization, and citizens lead lives of paranoia and control. Thought police are likely to come crashing through the ceiling and start bashing at dissenters. Life is mean and grim.

The hero of *Brazil* is Sam Lowry (Jonathan Pryce), a meek, desperate little man who works at a computer terminal all day. Occasionally he cheats; when the boss isn't looking, he and his fellows switch the screens of their computers to reruns of exciting old TV programs. Sam knows his life is drab and lockstep, but he sees no way out of it, and his only escape is into his fantasies—into glorious dreams of flying high above all the petty cares of the world, urged on by the vision of a beautiful woman.

His everyday life offers no such possibilities. Even the basic mechanisms of life support seem to be failing, and one scene early in the movie has Robert De Niro, in a walk-on, as an illegal free-lance repairman who defies the state by fixing things. De Niro makes his escapes by sliding down long cables to freedom, like Spider-Man. For Sam, there seems to be no escape.

But then he gets involved in an intrigue that involves the girl of his dreams, the chief executive of the state, and a shadowy band of dissenters. All of this is strangely familiar; the outlines of *Brazil* are much the same as those of *1984*, but the approach is different. While Orwell's lean prose was translated, last year, into an equally lean and dour film, *Brazil* seems almost like a throwback to the psychedelic 1960s, to an anarchic vision in which the best way to improve things is to blow them up.

The other difference between the two worlds—Orwell's, and the one created here by director and co-writer Terry Gilliam—is that Gilliam has apparently had no financial restraints. Although *Brazil* has had a checkered history since it was made (for a long time, Universal Pictures seemed unwilling to release it), there was a lot of money available to make it, and the movie is awash in elaborate special effects, sensational sets, apocalyptic scenes of destruction, and a general lack of discipline. It's as if Gilliam sat down and wrote out all of his fantasies, heedless of production difficulties, and then they were filmed—this time, heedless of sense.

The movie is very hard to follow. I have seen it twice, and am still not sure exactly who all the characters are, or how they fit. Perhaps I am not supposed to be clear; perhaps the movie's air of confusion is part of its paranoid vision. There are individual moments that create sharp images (shock troops drilling through a ceiling, De Niro wrestling with the almost obscene wiring and tubing inside a wall, the movie's obsession with bizarre ductwork), but there seems to be no sure hand at the controls.

The best scene in the movie is one of the simplest, as Sam moves into half an office and finds himself engaged in a tug-of-war over his desk with the man through the wall. I was reminded of a Chaplin film like *Modern Times*, and reminded, too, that in Chaplin economy and simplicity were virtues, not the enemy.

The Breakfast Club ★ ★ ★
R, 95 m., 1985

Emilio Estevez (Andrew Clark), Anthony Michael Hall (Brian Johnson), Judd Nelson (John Bender), Molly Ringwald (Claire Standish), Ally Sheedy (Allison Reynolds), Paul Gleason (Teacher), John Kapelos (Janitor). Directed by John Hughes and produced by Ned Tanen and Hughes. Screenplay by Hughes.

The Breakfast Club begins with an old dramatic standby. You isolate a group of people in a room, you have them talk, and eventually they exchange truths about themselves and come to new understandings. William Saroyan and Eugene O'Neill have been here before, but they used saloons and drunks. *The Breakfast Club* uses a high school library and five teen-age kids.

The movie takes place on a Saturday. The five kids have all violated high school rules in one way or another, and they've qualified for a special version of detention, all day long, from eight to four, in the school library. They arrive at the school one at a time. There's the arrogant, swaggering tough guy (Judd Nelson). The insecure neurotic (Ally Sheedy) who hides behind her hair and her clothes. The jock from the wrestling team (Emilio Estevez). The prom queen (Molly Ringwald). And the class brain (Anthony Michael Hall). These kids have nothing in common, and they have an aggressive desire *not* to have anything in common. In ways peculiar to teen-agers, who sometimes have a studious disinterest in anything that contradicts their self-image, these kids aren't even curious about each other. Not at first, anyway. But then the day grows longer and the library grows more oppressive, and finally the tough kid can't resist picking on the prom queen, and then there is a series of exchanges.

Nothing that happens in *The Breakfast Club* is all that surprising. The truths that are exchanged are more or less predictable, and the kids have fairly standard hang-ups. It comes as no surprise, for example, to learn that the jock's father is a perfectionist, or that the prom queen's parents give her material rewards but withhold their love. But *The Breakfast Club* doesn't need earthshaking revelations; it's about kids who grow willing to talk to one another, and it has a surprisingly good ear for the way they speak. (Ever notice the way lots of teen-age girls, repeating a conversation, say "she goes . . ." rather than "she says . . ."?)

The movie was written and directed by John Hughes, who also made 1984's *Sixteen Candles*. Two of the stars of that movie (Ringwald and Hall) are back again, and there's another similarity: Both movies make an honest attempt to create teen-agers who might seem plausible to other teen-agers. Most Hollywood teen-age movies give us underage nymphos or nostalgia-drenched memories of the 1950s. The performances are wonderful, but then this is an all-star cast, as younger actors go; in addition to Hall and Ringwald from *Sixteen Candles*, there's Sheedy from *WarGames* and Estevez from *Repo Man*. Judd Nelson is not yet as well known, but his character creates the strong center of the film; his aggression is what breaks the silence and knocks over the walls. The only weaknesses in Hughes's writing are in the adult characters: The teacher is one-dimensional and one-note, and the janitor is brought onstage with a potted philosophical talk that isn't really necessary. Typically, the kids don't pay much attention.

Note: The "R" rating on this film refers to language; I think a PG-13 rating would have been more reasonable. The film is certainly appropriate for thoughtful teen-agers.

Breakin' 2—Electric Boogaloo ★ ★ ★
PG, 94 m., 1984

Adolfo "Shabba-Doo" Quinones (Ozone), Michael "Boogaloo Shrimp" Chambers (Turbo), Lucinda Dickey (Kelly). Directed by Sam Firstenberg and produced by Menachem Golan and Yoram Globus. Written by Jan Ventura and Julie Reichert.

Movie musicals used to be allowed to be goofy and lightweight, but in recent years they've turned into ponderous, overbudget-ed artifacts that take themselves so seriously you feel guilty if you're having a good time. Remember all the self-importance of *Annie*? That's why a modest, cheerful little movie like *Breakin' 2—Electric Boogaloo* is so refreshing. Here is a movie that wants nothing more than to allow some high-spirited kids to sing and dance their way through a silly plot just long enough to make us grin.

The movie is a sequel to 1983's very successful *Breakin'*. I guess that explains the ungainly title. It involves the same actors, including a team of street-dance artists named Shabba-Doo Quinones and Boogaloo Shrimp Chambers, who more or less seem to be playing themselves. The plot is so familiar that if you're a fan of Mickey Rooney musicals or even the Beach Party movies, you may start rubbing your eyes. But the movie is a lot of fun.

Familiar? Try this plot out on your nearest trivia expert. A bunch of kids get together to turn a run-down old theater into a community center. The center is run by a nice old guy (who is not, for some reason, called "Pops"), and the ringleaders are Shabba-

Doo and Boogaloo. In the last movie, they formed a dance team with a rich girl (Lucinda Dickey), and as this movie opens she visits their center and decides to stay and pitch in, despite the opposition of her WASP parents, who want her to enroll in an Ivy League university. Then the plot thickens, when an evil real estate developer wants to tear down the center and put up a big retail development. With just a few minor modifications, this story could be about Mickey and Judy, or Frankie and Annette. But what does it matter, when the whole point of the enterprise is to provide an excuse for song and dance? Quinones, Chambers, and Dickey can indeed dance, very well, and there are a lot of other street dancers in the movie, but what's interesting is the way the traditions of street dancing are combined in this movie with the older traditions of stage dancing and chorus lines. The big extravaganza at the end (a benefit to save the center, needless to say) is a unique hybrid of old and new dance styles.

Electric Boogaloo is not a great movie, but it's inexhaustible, entertaining, and may turn out to be influential. It could inspire a boomlet of low-priced movie musicals—movies not saddled with multimillion dollar budgets, Broadway connections, and stars who are not necessarily able to sing and dance. And at a time when movie musicals (as opposed to movie sound tracks) are seriously out of touch with the music that is really being played and listened to by teenagers, that could be a revolutionary development.

Breaking Away ★ ★ ★ ★
PG, 100 m., 1979

Dennis Christopher (Dave), Dennis Quaid (Mike), Daniel Stern (Cyril), Jackie Earle Haley (Moocher), Paul Dooley (Dad), Barbara Barrie (Mom), Robyn Douglass (Katherine). Directed and produced by Peter Yates. Screenplay by Steve Tesich.

Here's a sunny, goofy, intelligent little film about coming of age in Bloomington, Indiana. It's about four local kids, just out of high school, who mess around for one final summer before facing the inexorable choices of jobs or college or the Army. One of the kids, Dave (Dennis Christopher), has it in his head that he wants to be a champion Italian bicycle racer, and he drives his father crazy with opera records and ersatz Italian.

His friends have more reasonable ambitions: One (Dennis Quaid) was a high school football star who pretends he doesn't want to play college ball, but he does; another (Jackie Earle Haley) is a short kid who pretends he doesn't want to be taller, but he does; and another (Daniel Stern) is one of those kids like we all knew, who learned how to talk by crossing Eric Sevareid with Woody Allen.

There's the usual town-and-gown tension in Bloomington, between the jocks and the townies (who are known, in Bloomington, as "cutters"—so called after the workers in the area's limestone quarries). There's also a poignant kind of tension between local guys and college girls: Will a sorority girl be seen with a cutter? Dave finds out by falling hopelessly in love with a college girl named Kathy (Robyn Douglass), and somehow, insanely, convincing her he's actually an Italian exchange student.

The whole business of Dave's Italomania provides the movie's funniest running joke: Dave's father (Paul Dooley) rants and raves that he didn't raise his boy to be an Eye-talian, and that he's sick and tired of all the eenees in the house: linguini, fettucini . . . even Jake, the dog, which Dave has renamed Fellini. The performances by Dooley and Barbara Barrie as Dave's parents are so loving and funny at the same time that we remember almost with a shock, that *every* movie doesn't have to have parents and kids who don't get along.

The movie was directed as a work of love by Peter Yates, whose big commercial hits have included *Bullitt* and *The Deep*. The Oscar-winning original screenplay was written by Steve Tesich, who was born in Yugoslavia, was moved to Bloomington at the age of thirteen, won the Little 500 bicycle race there in 1962, and uses it for the film's climax. Yates has gone for the human elements in *Breaking Away*, but he hasn't forgotten how to direct action, and there's a bravura sequence in which Dave, on a racing bicycle, engages in a high-speed highway duel with a semitrailer truck.

In this scene, and in scenes involving swimming in an abandoned quarry, Yates does a tricky and intriguing thing: He suggests the constant possibility of sudden tragedy. We wait for a terrible accident to happen, and none does, but the hints of one make the characters seem curiously vulnerable, and their lives more precious.

The whole movie, indeed, is a delicate balancing act of its various tones: This movie could have been impossible to direct, but Yates has us on his side almost immediately. Some scenes edge into fantasy, others are straightforward character development, some (like the high school quarterback's monlogue about his probable future) are heartbreakingly true. But the movie always returns to light comedy, to romance, to a wonderfully evocative instant nostalgia.

Breaking Away is a movie to embrace. It's about people who are complicated but decent, who are optimists but see things realistically, who are fundamentally comic characters but have three full dimensions. It's about a Middle America we rarely see in the movies, yes, but it's not corny and it doesn't condescend. Movies like this are hardly ever made at all; when they're made this well, they're precious cinematic miracles.

Breaking In ★ ★ ★
R, 94 m., 1989

Burt Reynolds (Ernie), Casey Siemaszko (Mike), Sheila Kelley (Carrie), Lorraine Toussaint (Delphine), Albert Salmi (Johnny Scat), Harry Carey (Shoes), Maury Chaykin (Tucci), Steve Tobolowsky (D.A.). Directed by Bill Forsyth and produced by Harry Gittes. Screenplay by John Sayles.

Bill Forsyth is the master of the small gesture, closely observed, which reveals the personalities of his characters. He doesn't deal in big-scale plots and actors who shout a lot, and goes instead for the comedy that can be found in the way people cover up their weaknesses and distrust their strengths.

Forsyth's *Local Hero*—that understated little masterpiece about a small Scottish town and a big American oil company—was voted one of the top ten films of the 1980s, in a poll in *Premiere* magazine. *Breaking In* is not that good, but it has some of the same qualities, especially in the way the characters play their own games by their own rules.

The movie stars Burt Reynolds as a sixtyish house burglar who works alone, quietly and competently. One night while he is attacking the wall safe in a prosperous suburban home, he meets another break-in artist: A teen-age kid (Casey Siemaszko) who came in through the upstairs window simply so he could raid the refrigerator, look through people's mail, and watch a little TV.

In the Forsyth universe, people don't question reality. They accept a situation and begin to see what they can get out of it. Reyn-

olds thinks he may be able to use the kid in a big job he's been considering—a burglary of the entire Fourth of July haul at an amusement park. The kid thinks, hey, why not? So they become partners.

Breaking In has received publicity because Reynolds plays an older man for the first time, but his age isn't really relevant, and he doesn't seem all that elderly, anyway. What's important is that he is a loner, a disciplined professional who has his hands full with this goofy kid.

Siemaszko, as the kid, doesn't so much steal the picture (Reynolds is very engaging) as benefit from the fact that his character is really the story's center of gravity. He has an infectious screen presence, and the kind of off-balance line readings that sound like he's making up his lines as he goes along.

The two thieves form a partnership and knock over some smaller targets while preparing their big Fourth of July heist, and it becomes clear that they have two different ideas about how to spend the money. Reynolds lives in an ordinary house on a run-down street, and plays poker with his pals. Siemaszko moves into a luxurious high-rise and pays the rent with cash. Reynolds tries to teach the disciplines of thievery. Siemaszko glories in the rewards.

The actual caper in *Breaking In* is not particularly elaborate or surprising, but then this isn't a caper film, it's a character film. And the characters are revealed almost tenderly in the closing scenes, which had best not be revealed.

Breaking In was billed as a comeback for Reynolds, but maybe it's simply a well-written, well-directed picture. Reynolds has a comfortable screen presence and can act, when that seems appropriate, but he derailed his career with a series of lamebrained action comedies directed by and costarring his pals. This time, in the Forsyth universe, he shows the warmth and quirkiness that made him fun to watch in the first place.

Bright Lights, Big City ★ ★ ★ 1/2
R, 107 m., 1988

Michael J. Fox (Jamie), Kiefer Sutherland (Tad), Phoebe Cates (Amanda), Swoosie Kurtz (Megan), Frances Sternhagen (Clara), Tracy Pollan (Vicky), John Houseman (Mr. Vogel), Charlie Schlatter (Michael), Jason Robards (Alex Hardy), Dianne Wiest (Mother). Directed by James Bridges and produced by Mark Rosenberg and Sydney Pollack. Screenplay by Jay McInerney.

What does cocaine make you feel like? It makes you feel like having some more cocaine.
—George Carlin

And that is what Jamie Conway feels like, all day, every day. The chasm between his professional existence and his private life is laughable, and it's growing impossible to keep up the charade that he even cares about the things he's supposed to be doing. He works for a high-powered New York magazine, and the only two things that keep him on the job are guilt and the need for money. He needs the money because he puts it into his nose. He needs the guilt because it's his only link to his ambitions.

Bright Lights, Big City is the record of Jamie's search for the bottom. It takes place over the course of a week or so, a chaotic week in which people, events, and even whole days drift in and out of focus. He is completely out of control. The irony is that he still looks halfway okay, if you don't look too hard. He's together enough to sit in a club and drink double vodkas and engage in absentminded conversation with transparent people. He drinks prodigious amounts of booze, punctuated by cocaine.

It's hard to classify a guy like this. Is he (a) an alcoholic, using the coke so he can stay awake and drink more? Or (b) a cokehead, using the booze to level off? Those are the two choices on Jamie's multiple-part exam. There are no other parts of his life worth serious discussion. His "life" consists, in fact, of the brief window that opens every day between his hangover and oblivion.

Jamie is played by Michael J. Fox, red-eyed and puffy-faced, and trembling with fear every morning when the telephone rings. He once lived in Kansas City and dreamed of becoming a writer, and it was there he met and married Amanda (Phoebe Cates), his pretty young wife. They met in a bar. The movie deliberately never makes clear what, if anything, they truly had to share. In New York, she finds overnight success as a model, and drifts away from him. That's no surprise; the movie makes it pretty clear that Jamie is the kind of port where the tide is always going out.

Now Jamie hauls himself, filled with nausea and self-loathing, into the magazine office every day. He works as a fact-checker. He could care less. He had dreams once. He can barely focus on them. One day he's cornered at the water cooler by the pathetic old drunk Alex Hardy (Jason Robards), who once wrote good fiction and knew Faulkner, and now exists as the magazine's gin-soaked fiction editor.

Alex drags Jamie out to a martini lunch, where the conversation is the typical alcoholic mixture of resentment against those who have made it, and self-hatred for drinking it all away. Jason Robards has always been a great actor, but there is a fleeting moment in this scene that is as good as anything he has ever done. It is a totally blank look. A moment when we can look into the face and eyes of his character and see that nobody, literally nobody, is at home. It's as if his mind has stalled. By supplementing booze with cocaine, Jamie is going to be able to reach Alex's state of numbed incomprehension decades more quickly.

There is one glimmer of hope in Alex's life. He has dinner one night with a bright college student (Tracy Pollan) who is the cousin of his drinking buddy (Kiefer Sutherland). At a restaurant, he goes into the toilet and then decides not to use cocaine: "Let's see if I can get through one evening without chemicals," he muses. He likes her. She is intelligent and kind. Several days later, at the end of a lost weekend of confusion and despair, he looks at himself in a mirror and says, "I need help." He telephones her in the middle of the night. His conversation is disconnected and confused, but what he is really doing is calling for help.

Maybe she can help him, maybe not. The movie ends with Jamie staggering out into the bright dawn of a new day and, in a scene a little too contrived for my taste, trading his dark glasses for a loaf of bread. *Bright Lights, Big City* is a *Lost Weekend* for the 1980s, a chronicle of wasted days and misplaced nights. It was directed by James Bridges, whose *Urban Cowboy* was in many ways an earlier version of the same story. Fox is very good in the central role (he has a long drunken monologue that is the best thing he has ever done in a movie). To his credit, he never seems to be having fun as he journeys through clubland. Few do, for long. If you know someone like Jamie, show him this movie, and don't let him go to the john.

Bring Me the Head of Alfredo Garcia
★ ★ ★ ★
R, 112 m., 1974

Warren Oates (Bennie), Isela Vega (Elita), Kris Kristofferson (Paco), Gig Young (Killer). Directed by Sam Peckinpah and produced by Martin Baum. Screenplay by Gordon T. Dawson and Peckinpah.

Sam Peckinpah's *Bring Me the Head of Alfredo Garcia* is a weird, horrifying film that somehow transcends its unlikely material. It's the story of a drunken and violent odyssey across Mexico by a dropout bartender who, if he returns Alfredo Garcia's head, stands to be paid a million dollars. The head accompanies him in a burlap bag, tossed into the front seat of a beat-up old Ford convertible, and it gathers flies and symbolic meaning at about the same pace.

The movie is some kind of bizarre masterpiece. It's probably not a movie that most people would like, but violence, with Peckinpah, sometimes becomes a psychic ballet. His characters don't look for it, they don't like it, and they negotiate it with weariness and resignation. They're too beat up by life to get any kind of exhilaration from a fight. They've been in far too many fights already, and lost most of them, and the violence they encounter is just another cross to bear.

That's the case with Bennie, the antihero of *Bring Me the Head of Alfredo Garcia*. He's played by Warren Oates, one of that breed of movie actors who attract us, somehow, through their negative qualities. He's like some of the characters played by Jack Nicholson or Bruce Dern; we like him because he's suffered so much more than we ever will (we hope) that no matter what horrors he goes through, or inflicts, we still care about him.

Bennie is a bartender and plays a little piano, and he hears about the head of Alfredo Garcia from a couple of bounty hunters who pass through his saloon. They're played, by the way, by the unlikely team of Gig Young and Robert Webber, who between them define dissipation. Garcia's head is worth a million bucks because Garcia, it turns out, has impregnated the daughter of a rich Mexican industrialist. The millionaire is almost a caricature of macho compulsiveness; he simultaneously puts a price on the head of the culprit, and looks forward with pride to the birth of a grandson.

Bennie sees the million dollars as his ticket out of hell, and on the way to finding it he runs across Alfredo Garcia's former lover, Elita (Isela Vega, looking as moistly erotic as anyone since young Anna Magnani). They fall in love, or something; their relationship is complicated by Bennie's crude shyness and her own custom of being abused by men. The most perversely interesting relationship

in the movie, however, is the friendship that grows between Bennie and Alfredo's head, once Bennie has gotten possession of it. That's made somewhat easier by the fact that Alfredo, it turns out, is already dead. But there is a gruesome struggle over his grave, and once Bennie finally gets the head he has to kill to protect his prize. His drive across Mexico is fueled by blood and tequila, and about halfway through it we realize why Peckinpah set his movie in the present, instead of in the past; this same material wouldn't have worked as a historical Western. The conventions of the genre would have insulted us from the impact of what happens. There would have been horses and watering holes and clichés. Instead, we get unforgettable scenes of Warren Oates with that grisly burlap bag and the bottle next to him in the front seat, and the nakedness of his greed is inescapable.

Somewhere along the way Oates, as Bennie, makes a compact with the prize he begins to call "Al." They both loved the same woman, they are both being destroyed by the same member of an upper class, they're both poor bastards who never asked for their grief in life. And slowly, out of the haze of the booze and the depths of his suffering, Bennie allies himself with Al and against the slob with the money. *Bring Me the Head of Alfredo Garcia* is Sam Peckinpah making movies flat out, giving us a desperate character he clearly loves, and asking us to somehow see past the horror and the blood to the sad poem he's trying to write about the human condition.

Broadcast News ★ ★ ★ ★
R, 125 m., 1987

William Hurt (Tom Grunick), Albert Brooks (Aaron Altman), Holly Hunter (Jane Craig), Lois Chiles (Jennifer Mack), Joan Cusack (Blair Litton), Robert Prosky (Bureau Chief). Directed, produced, and written by James L. Brooks.

Broadcast News is as knowledgeable about the TV news-gathering process as any movie ever made, but it also has insights into the more personal matter of how people use high-pressure jobs as a way of avoiding time alone with themselves. The movie was described as being about a romantic triangle, but that's only partly true. It is about three people who toy with the idea of love, but are obsessed by the idea of making television.

Deadline pressure attracts people like that. The newspapers are filled with them, and also ad agencies, brokerages, emergency rooms, show business, sales departments, and police and fire stations. There's a certain adrenaline charge in delivering on a commitment at the last moment, in rushing out to be an instant hero or an instant failure. There's a kind of person who calls you up to shout into the phone, "I can't talk to you now—I'm busy!" This kind of person is always busy, because the lifestyle involves arranging things so you're always behind. Given plenty of time to complete a job, you wait until the last moment to start—guaranteeing a deadline rush.

I know all about that kind of obsession (you don't think I finished this review early, do you?). *Broadcast News* understands it from the inside out, and perhaps the most interesting sequence in the whole movie is a scene where a network news producer sweats it out with a videotape editor to finish a report that is scheduled to appear on the evening news in fifty-two seconds. In an atmosphere like that, theoretical questions get lost. The operational reality, day after day, is to get the job done and beat the deadline and make things look as good as possible. Positive feedback goes to people who deliver. Yesterday's job is forgotten. What have you got for me today?

Right at the center of *Broadcast News* is a character named Jane Craig (Holly Hunter), who is a newswriter-producer for the Washington bureau of one of the networks. She is smart and fast and cherishes certain beliefs about TV news—one of them being that a story should be covered by the person best-qualified to cover it. One of her best friends is Aaron Altman (Albert Brooks), a bright, aggressive reporter. He's one of the best in the business, but he's not especially good on camera. During a trip south she meets Tom Grunick (William Hurt), a sportscaster who cheerfully admits he has little education, is not a good reader, and doesn't know much about current events. But he has been hired for the Washington bureau because he looks good and has a natural relationship with the camera.

The Hunter character is only human. She is repelled by this guy's credentials, but she likes his body. After he comes to Washington, he quickly gains the attention of the network brass, while the Brooks character goes into eclipse. Hunter is torn between the two men: Brooks, who says he loves her and is the better reporter, and Hurt, who says he wants to learn, and who is sexier.

The tricky thing about *Broadcast News*—the quality in James L. Brooks's screenplay that makes it so special—is that all three characters have a tendency to grow emotionally absentminded when it's a choice between romance and work. Frankly, they'd rather work. After Hunter whispers into Hurt's earpiece to talk him through a crucial live report on a Middle East crisis, he kneels at her feet and says it was like sex, having her voice inside his head. He never gets that excited about sex. Neither does she.

Much of the plot of *Broadcast News* centers around a piece that Hurt reports about "date rape." Listening to one woman's story, he is so moved that a tear trickles down his cheek. It means a great deal to Hunter whether that tear is real or faked. Experienced TV people will question why Hunter, a veteran producer, didn't immediately notice the detail that bothers her so much later on. But in a way, *Broadcast News* is not about details, but about the larger question of whether TV news is becoming show business.

Jack Nicholson has an unbilled supporting role in the movie as the network's senior anchorman, an irascible man who has high standards himself, but is not above seeing his ratings assisted by coverage that may be questionable. The implication is that the next anchor will be a William Hurt-type, great on camera, but incapable of discerning authenticity from fakery. Meanwhile, the Albert Brooks types will end up doing superior journalism in smaller "markets" (the TV word for "cities"), and the Holly Hunter types will keep on fighting all the old deadlines, plus a new one, the biological clock.

Broadcast News has a lot of interesting things to say about television. But the thing it does best is look into a certain kind of personality and a certain kind of relationship. Like *Terms of Endearment*, the previous film by James Brooks, it does not see relationships as a matter of meeting someone you like and falling in love. Brooks, almost alone among major Hollywood filmmakers, knows that some people have higher priorities than love, and deeper fears.

Broadway Danny Rose ★ ★ ★ ½
PG, 86 m., 1984

Woody Allen (Danny Rose), Mia Farrow (Tina Vitale), Nick Apollo Forte (Lou Canova). Directed by Woody Allen and produced by Robert Greenhut and Charles H. Joffe. Screenplay by Allen.

The first time we see him, he's talking fast, and his arms are working like a guy doing an imitation of an air traffic controller. His hands keep coming in for landings. This is Broadway Danny Rose, the most legendary talent agent in New York, the guy who will represent you after you've been laughed off every stage in the Catskills. He represents blind xylophonists, piano-playing birds, and has-been crooners with drinking problems. He's the kind of guy that comics sitting around on their day off tell stories about. He also is Woody Allen, but he is less like Woody Allen than some of the other characters Allen has played. After the autobiography of *Stardust Memories*, after the whimsy of *A Midsummer Night's Sex Comedy*, and the antiseptic experimentation of *Zelig*, this movie has Allen creating a character and following him all the way through a crazy story. After a period when Allen seemed stuck in self-doubt and introspection, he loosens up and has a good time.

Broadway Danny Rose, like all of Allen's best movies, is a New York movie. It starts at the Carnegie Deli, with comedians sitting around a table trading Danny Rose stories, and then it flashes back to the best Danny Rose story of them all, about how Danny signed up this has-been alcoholic tenor and carefully nurtured his career back to the brink of stardom. Riding the nostalgia boom, Danny takes the guy and books him into Top Forty concerts, until finally he gets him a date at the Waldorf—and Milton Berle is in the audience, looking for guests for his TV special. Except the crooner has a complicated love life. He has a wife, and he also has a girlfriend. He wants Danny Rose to be the "beard" and take the girlfriend to the concert. Otherwise he won't feel right. But then the crooner and the girl have a fight, and the girl goes back to her Mafioso boyfriend, and Danny Rose winds up at a mob wedding with a gun in his face.

All of this is accomplished with wonderfully off-the-wall characterizations. Allen makes Danny Rose into a caricature, and then, working from that base, turns him back into a human being: By the end of the film, we see the person beneath the mannerisms. Nick Apollo Forte, an actor I've never seen before, plays the has-been crooner with a soft touch: he's childish, he's a bear, he's loyal, he has a monstrous ego. The real treasure among the performances, however, is Mia Farrow's work as Tina Vitale, the crooner's girlfriend. You would think that Mia Farrow would be one of the most instantly recognizable actresses in the movies with those finely chiseled features and that little-girl voice. But here she is a chain-smoking, brassy blonde with her hair piled up on top of her head, and a pair of fashionable sunglasses, and dresses that look like they came from the boutique in a Mafia resort hotel.

Broadway Danny Rose uses all of the basic ingredients of Damon Runyon's Broadway: the pathetic acts looking for a job, the guys who get a break and forget their old friends, the agents with hearts of gold, the beautiful show girls who fall for Woody Allen types, the dumb gangsters, big shots at the ringside tables (Howard Cosell plays himself). It all works.

The Brother from Another Planet
★ ★ ★ ½
PG, 110 m., 1984

Joe Morton (The Brother), Maggie Renzi (Noreen), Fisher Stevens (Card Trickster), John Sayles (Man in Black). Directed by John Sayles and produced by Sayles and Maggie Renzi. Screenplay by Sayles.

When the movies started to talk, they began to lose the open-eyed simplicity with which they saw the world. *The Brother from Another Planet* tells the story of a man who cannot talk, but who can read minds, listen carefully, look deep into eyes, and provide a sort of mirror for our society. That makes it sound serious, but like all the most serious movies, it's a comedy.

The film stars Joe Morton as a visitor from outer space, who looks like a black human being, unless you look carefully at the three funny toes on his feet. He arrives on Earth in a spaceship that looks borrowed from the cheapest B space operas from the 1950s, swims ashore, and finds himself on Manhattan Island. At first he is completely baffled. Before long, everyone he meets is just as baffled. It is strange to deal with people who confound all your expectations: It might even force you to reevaluate yourself.

The brother is not looking for trouble, is not controversial, wants only to make sense of this weird new world. Because his instinctive response to most situations is a sort of blank reserve, people project their own feelings and expectations upon him. They tell him what he must be thinking, and behave as if they are right. He goes along.

The movie finds countless opportunities for humorous scenes, most of them with a quiet little bite, a way of causing us to look at our society. The brother runs into hookers and connivers, tourists from Indiana, immigrant shopkeepers, and a New York weirdo who, in one of the movie's best scenes, shows him a baffling card trick, and then demonstrates another trick that contains a cynical grain of big-city truth. The brother walks through this menagerie with a sometimes bemused, sometimes puzzled look on his face. People seem to have a lot of problems on this planet. He is glad to help out when he can; for example, curing video games by a laying on of hands. His right hand contains the power to heal machines, and it is amazing how quickly people accept that, if it is useful to them.

The Brother from Another Planet was written and directed by John Sayles, who is a one-man industry in the world of the American independent film. His credits include *Return of the Secaucus Seven*, *Lianna*, and *Baby, It's You*, and in this film—by using a central character who cannot talk—he is sometimes able to explore the kinds of scenes that haven't been possible since the death of silent film. There are individual moments here worthy of a Keaton, and there are times when Joe Morton's unblinking passivity in the midst of chaos really does remind us of Buster.

There is also a curious way in which the film functions as more subtle social satire than might seem possible in a low-budget, good-natured comedy. Because the hero, the brother, has literally dropped out of the skies, he doesn't have an opinion on anything. He only gradually begins to realize that on this world he is "black," and that his color makes a difference in some situations. He tries to accept that. When he is hurt or wronged, his reaction is not so much anger as surprise: It seems to him so unnecessary that people behave unkindly toward one another. He is a little surprised they would go to such an effort. His surprise, in its own sweet and uncomplicated way, is one of the most effective elements in the whole movie.

The Buddy Holly Story ★ ★ ★ ½
PG, 113 m., 1978

Bill Jordan (Riley Randolph), Maria Richwine (Maria Elena Holly), Conrad Janis (Ross Turner), Dick O'Neill (Sol Zuckerman), Gary Busey (Buddy Holly), Don Stroud (Jesse), Charles Martin Smith (Ray Bob). Directed by Steve Rash and produced by Fred Bauer. Screenplay by Robert Gittler.

On February 3, 1959, a small plane crashed outside Mason City, Iowa, killing Buddy Holly, Ritchie Valens, and J.P. (The Big Bopper) Richardson. Don McLean sang about that day in "American Pie." He called it the day the music died.

Walking out of *The Buddy Holly Story*, you wonder if maybe he wasn't right. It's no use trying to guess how things might have turned out if Holly hadn't been on that flight. He might have continued to develop as the most original rock and roll artist of his generation. He might, on the other hand, have gradually become a Paul Anka or a Barry Manilow, a polished performer of comfortably mainstream pop. The movie makes a pretty good case for the first possibility.

It also involves us as show-biz biographies rarely do. This is one rock and roll movie with a chance of being remembered, one with something to say and the style and energy to say it well. That's partly because it had good material to start with; Holly's life provides a microcosm of rock and roll's transformation into the dominant music of the last decades. But it's also because of Gary Busey's remarkable performance as Buddy Holly. If you're a fan of Holly and his music, you'll be quietly amazed at how completely Busey gets into the character. His performance isn't an imitation, a series of "impressions." It's a distillation of how Holly *seemed*, and how he sounded. That's all the more impressive because the movie doesn't use dubbing from the original records: Busey himself sings Holly's arrangements. And the movie's many concert scenes don't use post-dubbing, which almost always result in a flat and unconvincing sound. Busey did the material live.

That's crucial, in a way, because if *The Buddy Holly Story* doesn't convince (or remind) us that Holly's music was good, and important, the movie itself fails. Busey and the filmmakers do convince us, without even seeming to try. Walking out of the theater, I overheard a teen-age couple expressing surprise that Holly had composed "It's So Easy to Fall in Love." They thought it was a Linda Ronstadt original.

More performers than Ronstadt learned from Holly. All the important rockers of the last thirty years, and particularly the Beatles, benefited from Holly's fusion of basic rock and roll, deeper musical sophistication, and lyrics that came with a sincere intensity ("I *was* Buddy Holly," John Lennon once said.) Most albums cut in 1958 or 1959 sound dated today, even the good ones. Holly's old albums still sound fresh.

The movie follows the events of Holly's life, more or less, from his beginnings in Lubbock, Texas, through his early hit records, his quick national fame, his performances on "The Ed Sullivan Show," his marriage, his death. Rock historians have pointed out the ways in which the screenplay alters the facts (Holly's parents were not opposed to his musical career; his romance with his wife, Maria, was whirlwind, not the stubborn courtship in the movie; the decision to take a plane that last night was made, not because the bus broke down, but because Holly and the others wanted to get their laundry done).

Details like that don't matter much. The movie gets the feel right, and there's real energy in the concert scenes, especially the tricky debut of Buddy Holly and the Crickets as the first white act in Harlem's famous Apollo Theater. And the supporting performances are convincing; they're not walkons, as they tend to be in show biz movies. Don Stroud and Charles Martin Smith are just right as the down-home Crickets. Maria Richwine brings a sweetness, an understanding to the role of Holly's wife, and Gloria Irricari, as her aunt, steals a wonderful scene. And Dick O'Neill, as the white booker who thought Holly was black when he booked him into the Apollo, does an inspired double-take.

When all of this has been said, there are still the songs to be considered. "That'll Be the Day." "Peggy Sue." "Oh, Boy!" "Words of Love." "True Love Ways." "It's So Easy." "It Doesn't Matter Anymore." Gary Busey sings them with a style that does Holly justice. And that's saying something. They live, and the movie's concert sequences have the immediacy and energy of documentary footage—which is essentially what they are.

Bugsy Malone ★ ★ ★ ½
G, 94 m., 1976

Jodie Foster (Nightclub Singer), Scott Baio (Bugsy Malone), John Cassisi (Boss), Paul Murphy (Hit Man). Directed by Alan Parker and produced by Alan Marshall. Screenplay by Parker.

At first the notion seems alarming: a gangster movie cast entirely with kids. Especially when we learn that *Bugsy Malone* isn't intended as a kid's movie so much as a cheerful comment on the childlike values and behavior in classic Hollywood crime films. What are kids doing in something like this? But then we see the movie and we relax. *Bugsy Malone* is like nothing else. It's an original, a charming one, and it has yet another special performance by Jodie Foster, who at thirteen was already getting the roles that grown-up actresses complained weren't being written for women anymore. She plays a hard-bitten nightclub singer and vamps her way through a torch song by Paul Williams with approximately as much style as Rita Hayworth brought to *Gilda*. She starts on stage, drifts down into the audience, arches her eyebrows at the fat cats (all about junior high school age), and, in general, is astonishingly assured. And her performance seems just right in the film; *Bugsy Malone* depends almost totally on tone, and if you put kids in these situations and directed them just a little wrongly the movie would be offensive. But it's not, and it's especially right with Foster.

It tells a gangster story we know almost by heart, about the tough new gang that wants to take over the territory. Da Boss (a kid named John Cassisi who looks like he was born wearing a carnation in the lapel of his pinstripe) recruits hired guns to help protect his turf. Bugsy Malone (Scott Baio in training for John Garfield) is the guy he's gotta have. But maybe even Bugsy can't help, because the other gang has a dreaded new weapon. In Al Capone's day, it was machine guns. In Bugsy's movie, it's marshmallow guns. They open up on you with one of these, and you got more than egg on your face. Old-fashioned weapons like custard pies are useless in a one-on-one situation.

Halfway through *Bugsy Malone*, I started wondering how anyone ever came up with this idea for a movie. Alan Parker, who wrote and directed it, claims his inspiration came while he was watching *The Godfather*. I dunno, I think the movie has more insights into kids than into gangsters.

When kids play, it's real. That's one of the things we lose when we grow up: the ability to turn the backyard into the OK Corral. The kids in *Bugsy Malone* don't behave as if the material is camp or a put-on. For them, it's real—especially the indignity of catching a marshmallow in your ear. And so in an uncanny way the movie works as a gangster movie and we remember that the old Bogart and Cagney classics had a childlike innocence, too. The world was simpler then. Now it's so complicated maybe only a kid can still understand the Bogart role.

Bull Durham ★ ★ ★ ½
R, 108 m., 1988

Kevin Costner (Crash Davis), Susan Sarandon (Annie Savoy), Tim Robbins ("Nuke" LaLoosh), Trey Wilson (Skip), Robert Wuhl (Larry), William O'Leary (Jimmy). Directed by Ron Shelton and produced by Thom Mount and Mark Burg. Screenplay by Shelton.

"Some days, you win. Some days, you lose. And some days, it rains."—Baseball proverb

Bull Durham is a baseball version of *Wall Street*, in which everybody's takeover bid is for someone else's heart. The movie was promoted as a romantic comedy, but Susan Sarandon has a great scene right at the outset where she corrects that notion. She holds a little meeting between two of the new members of the local minor league ball club and explains that every year she chooses one player to spend the season with, and they are the two current finalists. The rest of the movie involves, in one way or another, a three-way contest to see (a) who really loves whom, (b) who really can trust whom, and (c) whether the answers to (a) and (b) involve the same two persons.

A lot of baseball is played along the way. *Bull Durham* was written and directed by Ron Shelton, who spent some time in the minor leagues, and this is a sports movie that knows what it is talking about. There are quiet little scenes that have the ring of absolute accuracy, as when a player is called into the office and told his contract is not being picked up, and the blow is softened by careful mention of a "possibility of a coaching job in the organization next season . . ." And there probably isn't a coaching job and nobody wants it anyway, but by such lies can sad truths be told.

The movie stars Kevin Costner as Crash Davis, an aging catcher and minor league veteran who knows the ropes, and Tim Robbins as "Nuke" LaLoosh, a hot young pitcher who has one hell of a fastball but no control and no maturity. Costner has been brought to the club to provide some seasoning for the rookie, and so inevitably they get into a fight before they've even been introduced. Costner has observed that Robbins has great control—unless he thinks about what he's doing. One moment of thought, and the ball gets pitched into the stands. So Costner stands outside a bar and taunts Robbins to hit him in the chest with his best fastball—something, of course, that once he starts thinking about it, Robbins is absolutely unable to do.

That kind of baseball philosophy provides a sound background for the movie, which has its foreground in Susan Sarandon's bedroom. I don't know who else they could have hired to play Annie Savoy, the Sarandon character who pledges her heart and her body to one player a season, but I doubt if the character would have worked without Sarandon's wonderful performance. Annie could have been portrayed as a lot of things—as a tramp, maybe, or a pathetic case study—but Sarandon portrays her as a woman who, quite simply, loves baseball and baseball players and wants to do her thing for the home team. Why does she limit her love affairs to one season? Anyone who has ever been a minor league baseball fan knows the answer to that one: Anybody who's any good goes up to the big leagues after a year, and Annie, of course, is only interested in the best players.

The romantic triangle unfolds during a season in which it never seems to matter very much how well the Durham Bulls are doing. They lose, they win, they spend a lot of time on buses and in hotel rooms, and meanwhile, Sarandon and Costner begin to realize that she is more than a groupie and he is more than a catcher. They find each other dropping the names of writers and making references to things they should not necessarily know, and finally one day Costner explodes in frustration: "Who *are* you, anyway?" Perhaps he suspects that if he finds the answer to that question, she will steal his heart away.

The kid pitcher is a lot less subtle about all of this. He enjoys being Annie's lover, for a time, but when he gets to a winning streak, he starts believing all those old stories about conserving your precious bodily fluids, and he becomes chaste as a monk. Costner, of course, is feeding him the stories. Meanwhile, we're getting to know some of the other members of the team and management, in a low-key, Altman-style directorial approach that fills up the background with a lot of atmosphere and action. *Bull Durham* is a treasure of a movie because it knows so much about baseball and so little about love. The movie is a completely unrealistic romantic fantasy, and in the real world the delicate little balancing act of these

three people would crash into pieces—but this is a movie, and so we want to believe in love, and we want to believe that once in a while lovers can get a break from fate. That's why the movie's ending is so perfect. Not because it seems just right, but because it seems wildly impossible and we want to believe it anyway.

The 'Burbs ★ ★
PG, 105 m., 1989

Tom Hanks (Ray Peterson), Bruce Dern (Mark Rumsfield), Carrie Fisher (Carol Peterson), Rick Ducommun (Art Weingartner), Corey Feldman (Ricky Butler), Wendy Schaal (Bonnie Rumsfield), Henry Gibson (Dr. Werner Klopek), Brother Theodore (Uncle Reuben Klopek), Courtney Gains (Hans Klopek), Gale Gordon (Walter). Directed by Joe Dante and produced by Michael Finnell and Larry Brezner. Written by Dana Olsen.

The 'Burbs tries to position itself somewhere between *Beetlejuice* and *The Twilight Zone,* but it lacks the dementia of the first and the wicked intelligence of the second, and turns instead into a long shaggy-dog story. It's about a group of nosy neighbors who grow concerned when a strange new family moves into their neighborhood, and settles into a crumbling Gothic house that seems as out of place in the split-level suburbs as a tarantula on an angel food cake.

Who are these people? They're never seen in the daylight, but at night their basement windows flash and crackle with giant discharges of electricity, and sometimes they can be seen out in their back yard, digging holes. For what? Corpses? Loot? They're like the Addams Family, ghoulish and aloof. They look like they were born under rocks and have never seen the light of day.

It would be wrong to say the neighbors are annoyed. Actually, they seem cheered by this sinister visitation in their midst: It gives them something to think about other than mowing the lawn or walking the dog. The hero of the film, Ray Peterson (Tom Hanks) has started his vacation just as the story begins, and instead of going fishing he elects to stay home and spy on the neighbors. His wife (Carrie Fisher) thinks this is childish behavior, but his neighbors (Bruce Dern and Rick Ducommun) are overgrown boys who enter enthusiastically into the enterprise.

Meanwhile, the film provides lots of little vignettes of suburban life, involving such

staples as the neighbor who allows his dog to poop on other people's lawns, and the housewife who likes to do her yard work in the briefest of halter tops. None of this material is as funny as it might have been, partly because it seems recycled out of fairly ancient ideas of what the suburbs are really like (I kept expecting to see Dennis the Menace or Mr. Wilson wandering down the street).

The movie was directed by Joe Dante, who contributed that eerie segment to *The Twilight Zone* movie in which the people in an isolated farmhouse all seemed to coexist in a comic-book dimension (they were the original Toons). This time, with a related idea at feature length, he seems to have run out of inspiration. One of the things he could have exploited was the very falseness of the suburban sets he uses. The street he shoots on may, for all I know, actually exist somewhere, but it looks for all the world like that permanent small-town set they drive you through on the Universal Tour.

It's hard to put your finger on exactly what's missing from the movie. The actors do what they can with the material, and the special effects are ambitious, but somehow the film fails to rouse itself into any real conviction. It's cut and dried; we anticipate the major events in the story and we're right. And when the explanation for the strange family's behavior finally arrives, it's not much of a surprise.

That family is led, by the way, by a small, pale, fish-faced doctor played by Henry Gibson (the Oscar nominee from *Nashville*). Watching him in the final scenes of the movie, I realized his character was more interesting than the suburbanites we'd been following all along. Maybe that's what the movie was missing: A comic inversion to undermine all of our expectations. What if the typical suburbanites had all been undernourished geeks, and the sinister new family had moved in looking all-American? Only asking.

Burden of Dreams ★ ★ ★ ★
NO MPAA RATING, 94 m., 1982

Featuring Werner Herzog, Klaus Kinski, Claudia Cardinale, Jason Robards, and Mick Jagger. Directed and produced by Les Blank, with Maureen Gosling.

Les Blank's *Burden of Dreams* is one of the most remarkable documentaries ever made about the making of a movie. There are at least two reasons for that. One is that the movie being made, Werner Herzog's *Fitzcarraldo*, involved some of the most torturous and dangerous on-location shooting experiences in film history. The other is that the documentary is by Les Blank, himself a brilliant filmmaker, who is unafraid to ask difficult questions and portray Herzog, warts and all.

The story of Herzog's *Fitzcarraldo* is already the stuff of movie legend. The movie was shot on location deep within the rain forests of South America, one thousand miles from civilization. When the first version of the film was half-finished, its star, Jason Robards, was rushed back to New York with amoebic dysentery and forbidden by his doctors to return to the location. Herzog replaced Robards with Klaus Kinski (star of his *Aguirre, the Wrath of God*), but meanwhile, co-star Mick Jagger left the production because of a commitment to a concert tour. Then the Kinski version of *Fitzcarraldo* was caught in the middle of a border war between tribes of Indians. The whole production was moved twelve hundred miles, to a new location where the mishaps included plane crashes, disease, and attacks by unfriendly Indians. And all of those hardships were on top of the incredible task Herzog set himself to film: He wanted to show his obsessed hero using teams of Indians to pull an entire steamship up a hillside using only block and tackle!

Blank and his associate, Maureen Gosling, visited both locations of Herzog's film. Their documentary includes the only available record of some of the earlier scenes with Robards and Jagger. It also includes scenes in which Herzog seems to be going slowly mad, blaming the evil of the jungle and the depth of his own compulsions. In *Fitzcarraldo*, you can see the incredible strain as men try to pull a steamship up a sharp incline, using only muscle power and a few elementary principles of mechanics. In *Burden of Dreams*, Blank's camera moves back one more step, to show the actual mechanisms by which Herzog hoped to move his ship. A giant bulldozer is used to augment the block-and-pulley, but it proves barely equal to the task, and at one point the Brazilian engineer in charge of the project walks off, warning that lives will be lost.

What drives Herzog to make films that test his sanity and risk his life and those of his associates? Stanley Kauffmann, in the *New Republic*, argued that, for Herzog, the purpose of film is to risk death, and each of his films is in some way a challenge hurled at the odds. Herzog has made films on the slopes of active volcanoes, has filmed in the jungle and in the middle of the Sahara, and has made films about characters who live at the edges of human achievement. *Burden of Dreams* gives us an extraordinary portrait of Herzog trapped in the middle of one of his wildest dreams.

Buster ★ ★ ★
R, 93 m., 1988

Phil Collins (Buster Edwards), Julie Walters (June Edwards), Larry Lamb (Bruce), Stephanie Lawrence (Granny), Ellen Beaven (Nicky), Michael Attwell (Harry), Ralph Brown (Ronnie), Martin Jarvis (Inspector Mitchell), Anthony Quayle (Sir James McDowell). Directed by David Green and produced by Norma Heyman. Screenplay by Colin Shindler.

Two of the key words in *Buster* are spoken softly, almost as an aside, and might be easy to miss. Spoken by one criminal to another, they are, "No shooters!" A "shooter" is Cockney slang for a gun, and the words come during the preparations for the crime that came to be known as the Great Train Robbery. The fact that Britain's crime of the century was carried out by unarmed men has contributed to its place in folklore, and helps to set the mood for this almost elegiac crime story.

The Royal Mail train from London to Glasgow was stopped and robbed on the night of Aug. 8, 1963, by a group of fifteen men who took loot that would be valued today at $35 million. The crime has inspired several earlier movies, notably *Robbery* (1967), a superior thriller starring Stanley Baker. All of the men were eventually captured except for one, Ronnie Biggs, who now enjoys a life of exile in Brazil. *Buster* tells the story of one of the more obscure Great Train Robbers, Ronnie (Buster) Edwards, who was safely in exile in Mexico but came back home to face the music because he missed his wife. The movie is a love story.

Buster, like *Robbery*, opens with the logistics of the robbery. But it sees it almost entirely through the eyes of Buster Edwards, who lives with his wife, June, and their little daughter in a flat that rents for three pounds a week. June would like them to have a nice bungalow of their own, but Buster doesn't have the money. "You could always borrow it from a bank," she suggests. "That's what I do for a living," he says. "I meant legally," she says.

Buster is played with surprising effectiveness by the rock star Phil Collins, who looks and sounds like a gentler Bob Hoskins. In the movie's opening sequence, he throws a garbage can through the window of a clothing store in order to steal a mannequin that is wearing a suit he fancies. This seems like a reckless act, but Buster seems to believe he is protected by a cloak of invulnerability. As his wife (Julie Walters) tells her mother, he's led a life of crime and served only two weeks in jail.

Yes, but he's never felt the heat the way it comes down after the Great Train Robbery. The papers are full of the crime, and the Conservative government of the day, still smarting from the Profumo Affair, is eager to bring the robbers to justice. Buster and June go into hiding in a series of "safe houses" and have a series of close calls before finally fleeing to Mexico with their daughter. Meanwhile, Buster's share of the loot dwindles as a series of middlemen and payoff artists take their shares.

The center of the movie is occupied, not by the crime, but by the relationship between Buster and June, and we are inclined to believe him when he says he has done everything just for the love of his family. They come closest to breaking apart under the pressure in Mexico, where life in the sun makes June desperately homesick. Faced with a menu of Mexican food, she yearns for steak and fries, and wistfully observes, "We never used to be able to afford it." Now that they can, they're in the wrong country to order it.

June eventually returns to England, and Buster eventually follows. One of the last scenes in the film shows them kissing hungrily before he walks out the door to be handcuffed and led away. A coda at the end of the film might seem corny to some audiences. It shows Buster and June, years later, running a flower stall in London, having retired from crime. The scene may be corny, but it is true, and the next time you go to London, if you stop at the flower kiosk outside Waterloo Station, you can buy a bouquet from Buster Edwards. Be sure to count your change.

Buster and Billie ★ ★ ★
R, 100 m., 1974

Jan-Michael Vincent (Buster), Joan Goodfellow (Billie), Pamela Sue Martin (First Girlfriend). Directed by Dan Petrie and produced
by Ron Silverman. Screenplay by Ron
Turbeville.

The problem with a lot of nostalgia is that it
captures the surface sound and style of a decade with an appreciation that works only
with hindsight. People didn't spend all their
time listening to Elvis, lowering their
Chevys, and scuffing their white bucks in
the fifties. Adolescence then, as now, was a
time of uncertainty and confusion, and the
surface stuff often only concealed the kids
inside. *The Lords of Flatbush* did a good job
of seeing past its black leather jackets and
into the hearts of the essentially immature
and unsure people who wore them, as does
Buster and Billie with a memory of what it
might have been like to go to high school in
the South, circa 1948.

The movie's no masterpiece, but it's an
affecting story well told, it observes its teen-
age characters with a fine insight, and it
almost earns its tragic ending. Happy endings used to be Hollywood clichés; now, if we
ever got one, it would almost feel original.

The story gives us some ordinary high
school kids growing up in a pleasant semirural
section of Georgia. They drive around in cars
and pickup trucks, they go to dances, they
study, and when the guys hang around with
the guys and the girls hang around with the
girls, the subject of conversation is, always and
eternally, the mysteries of the opposite sex.
Nobody knows much about sex, period,
much less the opposite one, but there's a lot of
big talk and an insatiable curiosity.

Curiosity is satisfied, however, for some of
the guys through the friendliness of Billie, a
shy, pretty girl who lives with subliterate parents and who is so lacking in self-confidence
that she seeks to find acceptance by, as the fine
old phrase has it, putting out. Several guys in
the school have been with Billie, or say they
have, or mean to, or in any event may.

But not Buster, who is your typical high
school jock and a little something more. He
knows his own mind, is independent, is
admired, and has a much larger measure of
compassion than his friends. He's engaged to
marry an insipid girl, the kind who wins the
Homecoming Queen title and believes the
momentum will carry her straight through

life. But Buster becomes intrigued with Billie. He senses something about her that has
value; he seems to instinctively understand
why she behaves as she does, and (more
importantly) why she doesn't have to.

Most of the movie is about the love that
slowly grows up between them as Buster
wins Billie's trust and helps her to develop
self-confidence. The fact that Buster would
be seen publicly with Billie (would, indeed,
take her to Sunday church) causes indignation within the cliquish high school crowd he
runs with, and especially among Billie's
numerous former boyfriends.

What's good about the movie—what you'll
remember—are the tender and rather lovely
scenes between Buster and Billie, and the
strength with which Buster faces down the
disapproval of his friends. What doesn't
work, for me, anyway, is the violent and tragic
ending. It's not that the ending isn't plausible;
indeed, as it's presented, it seems inevitable
enough. It's just that somehow the human values in the film should have been developed
more fully, so that at the end we could have
some sort of resolution based on changes in the
characters, rather than on their violent acts.

Much of the movie's affecting quality
comes from fine performances by Jan-Michael
Vincent and Joan Goodfellow, as the young
lovers. There's a scene showing their first
date, with the girl too shy, almost, to talk, and
it's so quiet and warm we can really understand how these two kids feel. There's a scene
where Buster defends Billie to his parents,
and another one in a pool room where he faces
his friends. This kind of movie, honestly
examining the bonds of both friendship and
cruelty that hold together adolescent peer
groups, is a lot more accurate about the old
days than any number of golden-oldie sound
tracks and gee-whiz sock hops.

Bye Bye Brazil ★ ★ ★ ★
NO MPAA RATING, 100 m., 1979

Jose Wilker (Lord Gypsy), Betty Faria
(Salome), Fabio Junior (Cico), Zaira Zambelli
(Desdo), Principe Nabor (Swallow). Directed
by Carlos Diegues and produced by L.C.
Barreto. Screenplay by Diegues.

It's rare to come across truly great movie
images, and we share them like treasured souvenirs—images like Jack Nicholson in the
football helmet in *Easy Rider*, the bone turning into a spaceship in *2001*, the peacock
spreading its feathers in the snow in *Amarcord*,
and the helicopter assault in *Apocalypse Now*.

To the short list of great images, a film
named *Bye Bye Brazil* adds one more. A
small, raggedy troupe of traveling entertainers is putting on a show in a provincial
Brazilian town. The townspeople sit packed
together in a sweaty, smoky room, while the
magician creates for brief moments the illusion that both he and his audience are more
sophisticated than they are. It is time for the
climax of his act, and he springs a completely
unexpected image on his audience, and on
us: Bing Crosby sings "White Christmas"
while it snows on his amazed patrons.

That moment provides more than an
image. It provides a neatly summarized little
statement about *Bye Bye Brazil*, a film which
exists exactly on the fault line between Brazil's modern civilization and the simple backwaters of its provinces. The film sees Brazil
as a nation where half-assimilated Western
culture (in the form of Bing Crosby, public
address systems, and politicians) coexists
with poverty, superstition, simple good nature, and the permanent fact of the rain forest.

The movie is about the small troupe of
entertainers, who travel the backroads in a
truck that contains living quarters, a generator, and the props for their nightly shows.
The troupe is led by Lord Gypsy, a young
man who is half-hippie, half-nineteenth-cen-
tury medicine show huckster. At his side is
Salome, a damply sultry beauty who is his
assistant but also has a tendency to do business on her own. Swallow, a strongman, doubles as crew and supporting act.

These three pick up two hitchhikers, a
young accordion player and his pregnant
wife. And then *Bye Bye Brazil* tells the story
of the changing relationships among the five
people, and their checkered success with
roadshow vaudeville.

Having said that, I've conveyed almost no
notion of this movie's special charms. It
shows us a society that most American
audiences never have seen in the movies, the
world of very old, very small Brazilian towns
perched precariously along the roads that
link them to far-away, half-understood cities.

Television has not come to most of these
towns. Electricity is uncertain. The traveling
entertainers provide more than music and
magic; they provide a link with style that is
more fascinating to the audiences than the
magician's tricks. People do not pay to see
the show, so much as to wonder at these
strange performers who speak the same language but could be from another planet.

C

Cabaret ★ ★ ★ ½
PG, 119 m., 1972

Liza Minnelli (Sally Bowles), Michael York (Brian Roberts), Joel Grey (Master of Ceremonies), Helmut Griem (Maximillian von Heune), Fritz Wepper (Fritz Wendel). Directed by Bob Fosse and produced by Cy Feuer. Screenplay by Jay Allen.

Cabaret explores some of the same kinky territory celebrated in Visconti's *The Damned*. Both movies share the general idea that the rise of the Nazi party in Germany was accompanied by a rise in bisexuality, homosexuality, sadomasochism, and assorted other activities. Taken as a generalization about a national movement, this is certainly extreme oversimplification. But taken as one approach to the darker recesses of Nazism, it may come pretty close to the mark. The Nazi gimmicks like boots and leather and muscles and racial superiority and outdoor rallies and Aryan comradeship offered an array of machismo-for-rent that had (and has) a special appeal to some kinds of impotent people.

Cabaret is about people like that, and it takes place largely in a specific Berlin cabaret, circa 1930, in which decadence and sexual ambiguity were just part of the ambience (like the women mud-wrestlers who appeared between acts). This is no ordinary musical. Part of its success comes because it doesn't fall for the old cliché that musicals have to make you happy. Instead of cheapening the movie version by lightening its load of despair, director Bob Fosse has gone right to the bleak heart of the material and stayed there well enough to win an Academy Award for Best Director.

The story concerns one of the more famous literary inventions of the century, Sally Bowles, who first came to life in the late Christopher Isherwood's *Berlin Stories*, and

then appeared in the play and movie *I Am a Camera* before returning to the stage in this musical, and then making it into the movies a second time—a modern record, matched only by Liza Doolittle, I'd say.

Sally is brought magnificently to the screen in an Oscar-winning performance by Liza Minnelli, who plays her as a girl who's bought what the cabaret is selling. To her, the point is to laugh and sing and live forever in the moment; to refuse to take things seriously—even Nazism—and to relate with people only up to a certain point. She is capable of warmth and emotion, but a lot of it is theatrical, and when the chips are down she's as decadent as the "daringly decadent" dark fingernail polish she flaunts.

Liza Minnelli plays Sally Bowles so well and fully that it doesn't matter how well she sings and dances, if you see what I mean. In several musical numbers (including the stunning finale *Cabaret* number), Liza demonstrates unmistakably that she's one of the great musical performers of our time. But the heartlessness and nihilism of the character is still there, all the time, even while we're being supremely entertained.

Sally gets involved in a triangular relationship with a young English language teacher (Michael York) and a young baron (Helmut Griem), and if this particular triangle didn't exist in the stage version, that doesn't matter. It helps define the movie's whole feel of moral anarchy, and it is underlined by the sheer desperation in the cabaret itself.

Here the festivities are overseen by a master of ceremonies (Joel Grey, whose performance received an Oscar for Best Supporting Actor) whose determination to keep the merriment going, at whatever psychic cost, has a poignant compulsiveness. When the song *Cabaret* comes at the end, you realize for

the first time that it isn't a song of happiness, but of desperation. The context makes the difference. In the same way, the context of Germany on the eve of the Nazi ascent to power makes the entire musical into an unforgettable cry of despair.

Cactus ★ ★ ★
NO MPAA RATING, 95 m., 1987

Isabelle Huppert (Colo), Robert Menzies (Robert), Norman Kaye (Tom), Monica Maughan (Bea), Banduk Marika (Banduk), Sheila Florance (Martha). Directed by Paul Cox and produced by Jane Ballantyne and Cox. Screenplay by Cox, Norman Kaye, and Bob Ellis.

One of the first shots in *Cactus* is a long, unbroken take in which the camera pans from a veranda across a lush landscape, all green and semi-tropical, while on the sound track we hear the loud cry of an exotic bird. The sound seems too loud, somehow, but what is being set up here is the condition of blindness, in which sounds take on an extraordinary importance.

The heroine of the film is a young French woman (Isabelle Huppert), who has come out to Australia on holiday. There is the suggestion that she has left an unhappy marriage behind in France. She has an accident, loses the sight of one eye, and is threatened with the loss of the other. The doctors offer her a choice. If she has the bad eye removed, the remaining eye may retain its function. Otherwise, "sympathetic blindness" may occur, and she will be totally blind.

No matter how this sounds, *Cactus* is not a docudrama, not a movie about medical problems. It is a movie about how we see, and what we choose to see. While she is trying to decide what to do, Huppert meets a young man who is blind. They talk, they understand each other, they fall in love. She seriously considers the option of choosing blindness, so that she will be able to share the world of her lover.

These episodes take place within the arms of a large, sheltering family. The woman's friends are middle-aged, literate, political. There are moments that have little to do with the movie's central problem; moments when friends gather to drink, talk, and listen to music. During those scenes, *Cactus* has an interesting, subtle technique. The visuals are always alive and inviting—rooms filled with unusual objects, landscapes jammed with life. And the sound track is filled, too, with words and music. Both senses, sight and sound, are calling out to be recognized.

Cactus was directed by Paul Cox, who is not one of the best-known of the new generation of Australian filmmakers, but in many ways is the most inventive, the most individual. His films are always about people who are cut off from normal relationships, and who try to improvise substitutes.

Lonely Hearts (1981) was about two people who met through a singles group, and found out why each was single. *Man of Flowers* (1983) was about a lonely, reclusive millionaire who paid a young woman to pose for him, so that he could fill his empty room with company. *My First Wife* (1984) was about a woman who decided that she could scarcely be lonelier outside marriage than inside it.

Cactus is not as satisfying as those three films, perhaps because its themes are not as clear. I was so distracted by the reality of the woman's choice—sight or blindness—that I found it hard to pull back to the larger question of how she should choose to communicate with the man she loved. In a way, the woman's choice is one we all have to make. Because there is such a gulf between all people, to bridge it we have to take on some of the blindness of others, and they have to share ours; two people who see things exclusively their own way may never be able to share the world. That is the issue in *Cactus*; the blindness is simply the way Cox chooses to dramatize it.

Although the movie is less than completely satisfying, it is worth seeing, as everything by Cox is worth seeing, because there is always the sense in his films of an active intelligence at work. He doesn't make routine genre pictures; he begins with complicated people and watches them as they live.

Sometimes he seems as mystified by the results as we are.

Caddyshack ★ ★ ½
R, 99 m., 1980

Chevy Chase (Ty Webb), Rodney Dangerfield (Al Czervik), Ted Knight (Judge Smails), Michael O'Keefe (Danny), Bill Murray (Carl), Sarah Holcomb (Maggie). Directed by Harold Ramis and produced by Douglas Kenney. Screenplay by Brian Doyle-Murray, Ramis, and Kenney.

Caddyshack never finds a consistent comic note of its own, but it plays host to all sorts of approaches from its stars, who sometimes hardly seem to be occupying the same movie. There's Bill Murray's self-absorbed craziness, Chevy Chase's laid-back bemusement, and Ted Knight's apoplectic overplaying. And then there is Rodney Dangerfield, who wades into the movie and cleans up.

To the degree that this is anybody's movie, it's Dangerfield's—and he mostly seems to be using his own material. He plays a loud, vulgar, twitching condo developer who is thinking of buying a country club and using the land for housing. The country club is one of those exclusive WASP enclaves, a haven for such types as the judge who founded it (Knight), the ne'er-do-well club champion (Chase), and the manic assistant grounds keeper (Murray).

The movie never really develops a plot, but maybe it doesn't want to. Director Harold Ramis brings on his cast of characters and lets them loose at one another. There's a vague subplot about a college scholarship for the caddies, and another one about the judge's nubile niece, and continuing warfare waged by Murray against the gophers who are devastating the club. But Ramis is cheerfully prepared to interrupt everything for moments of comic inspiration, and there are three especially good ones: The caddies in the swimming pool doing a Busby Berkeley number, another pool scene that's a scatalogical satire of *Jaws*, and a sequence in which Dangerfield's gigantic speedboat devastates a yacht club.

Dangerfield is funniest, though, when the movie just lets him talk. He's a Henny Youngman clone, filled with one-liners and insults, and he's great at the country club's dinner dance, abusing everyone and making rude noises. Surveying the crowd from the bar, he uses lines that he has, in fact, stolen

directly from his nightclub routine ("This steak still has the mark of the jockey's whip on it"). With his bizarre wardrobe and trick golf bag, he's a throwback to the Groucho Marx and W.C. Fields school of insult comedy; he has a vitality that the movie's younger comedians can't match, and they suffer in comparison.

Chevy Chase, for example, has some wonderful moments in this movie, as a studiously absent-minded hedonist who doesn't even bother to keep score when he plays golf. He's good, but somehow he's in the wrong movie: His whimsy doesn't fit with Dangerfield's blatant scenery-chewing or with the Bill Murray character. Murray, as a slob who goes after gophers with explosives and entertains sexual fantasies about the women golfers, could be a refugee from *Animal House*.

Maybe one of the movie's problems is that the central characters are never really involved in the same action. Murray's off on his own, fighting gophers. Dangerfield arrives, devastates, exits. Knight is busy impressing the caddies, making vague promises about scholarships, and launching boats. If they were somehow all drawn together into the same story, maybe we'd be carried along more confidently. But *Caddyshack* feels more like a movie that was written rather loosely, so that when shooting began there was freedom—too much freedom—for it to wander off in all directions in search of comic inspiration.

Cadillac Man ★ ★
R, 95 m., 1990

Robin Williams (Joey O'Brien), Tim Robbins (Larry), Pamela Reed (Tina), Fran Drescher (Joy Munchack), Zack Norman (Harry Munchack), Annabella Sciorra (Donna). Directed by Roger Donaldson and produced by Charles Roven and Donaldson. Screenplay by Ken Friedman.

It all comes down to which kind of movie you'd really rather see. Given the choice, would you prefer a movie about a hotshot car salesman so shameless he'd try to sell a car to a widow at her husband's funeral? Or would you rather see a movie about how the salesman tries to talk a suicidal husband out of killing himself and everybody else in the dealership?

If *Cadillac Man* had been the second movie from beginning to end, I have a feeling I might have enjoyed it more. But it started as the first movie and then turned into the second, leaving me frustrated and a little disoriented: What happened to all the setups in the first hour? Were they going to be left hanging?

The movie stars Robin Williams as Joey O'Brien, the car salesman, who addresses the audience in confidential asides like Tom Jones or Alfie. He has a lot of problems, most of them centering around women. He likes women, he has trouble resisting them, and he spends a lot of money on them. That means he's usually broke, and if he doesn't sell a dozen cars at the dealership's big moving sale this Sunday, he may lose his job.

We meet some of the women in his life, especially his mistress (Fran Drescher) and his ex-wife (Pamela Reed), and we also get a look at the sexpot Donna (Annabella Sciorra), who works in the dealership's front office. Everybody on the sales force feels libidinous about her, except for the super-saleswoman Molly (Lori Petty), who leads the staff in sales, perhaps because she has one less distraction.

Up until this point, the movie seems to be a setup for a big sales contest in which lies will be told and dirty tricks pulled. But then Donna's husband (Tim Robbins) comes crashing in through the plate-glass window on his motorcycle, waving a machine gun and threatening to kill everyone. The movie becomes an extended dialogue between Williams and Robbins, as the salesman tries to do the best selling job of his life on the distraught husband.

Williams and Robbins (who played the young pitcher in *Bull Durham*) are convincing in this long sequence, which is built by director Roger Donaldson and writer Ken Friedman into a series of peaks and valleys, complicated by the arrival of the husband of Williams's mistress. But somehow I kept waiting for the movie to get back on track— to get back to the zany comedy I thought I'd been promised. My problems with *Cadillac Man* were probably inspired more by false expectations than by anything on the screen, and maybe if Robbins had come crashing in through the window in the first scene I would have liked it more.

One footnote: Two scenes in the movie feature Lauren Tom as the waitress at the nearby Chinese restaurant. You've met waitresses like this before: small women who take a delight in talking back to their clients and banging them on the head with the menu when they order the wrong thing. Miss Tom steals both scenes with a performance that's funnier than anything else in the movie. Sometimes TV sitcoms are spun out of characters like hers, and I'd love to see them try one this time.

California Split ★ ★ ★ ★
R, 109 m., 1974

George Segal (Bill Denny), Elliott Gould (Charlie Waters), Ann Prentiss (Barbara Miller), Gwen Welles (Susan Peters), Edward Walsh (Lew), Joseph Walsh (Sparkle), Bert Remsen ("Helen Brown"). Directed by Robert Altman and produced by Altman and Joseph Walsh, based on a screenplay by Walsh.

They meet in a California poker parlor. One wins, despite a heated discussion with a loser over whether or not a dealt card hit the floor. They drink. They become friends after they are jointly mugged in the parking lot by the sore loser.

They did not know each other before, and they don't know much about each other now, but they know all they need to know: They're both compulsive gamblers, and the dimensions of the world of gambling equal the dimensions of the world they care anything about. It is a small world and a flat one, like one of those maps of the world before Columbus, and they are constantly threatened with falling over the edge.

They're the heroes (or at least the subjects) of *California Split*, the magnificently funny, cynical film by Robert Altman. Their names are Bill and Charlie, and they're played by George Segal and Elliott Gould with a combination of unaffected naturalism and sheer raw nervous exhaustion. We don't need to know anything about gambling to understand the odyssey they undertake to the tracks, to the private poker parties, to the bars, to Vegas, to the edge of defeat, and to the scene of victory. Their compulsion is so strong that it carries us along. The movie will be compared with *M*A*S*H*, the first big hit by Altman (who is possibly our best and certainly our most diverting American director). It deserves that comparison, because it resembles *M*A*S*H* in several big ways: It's funny, it's hard-boiled, it gives us a bond between two frazzled heroes trying to win by the rules in a game where the rules require defeat. But it's a better movie than *M*A*S*H* because here Altman gets it all together. Ever since *M*A*S*H*, he's been trying to make a kind of movie that would function like a comedy but allow its laughs to dig us deeper and deeper into the despair underneath.

Bill and Charlie are driven. We laugh at their hangovers, their bruises (treated with hot shaving cream), the kooky part-time prostitutes who serve them breakfasts of Froot Loops and beer. We move easily through the underworld of their friends, casually introduced through Altman's gift of overlapping dialogue and understated visual introductions, so that we're not so much shown a new character as encouraged to assume we knew him all along. And because Joseph Walsh's screenplay is funny and Segal and Gould are naturally engaging, we have a good time.

But then there are moments that take on bleaker meanings. At one point, for example, at the ragged edge of sleep, boozed out, defeated, Bill and Charlie cling desperately to a bar and very seriously bet with each other on the names of the Seven Dwarfs (There was Droopy . . . Sleepy . . . Dumbo?). And at another time, cornered with their winnings in still another parking lot by still another mugger, this one armed, they hand over half their winnings and bet him that's all they have.

He takes it and runs; they win; they could have been killed but their gambler's instinct forced them to make the try. At the end of *California Split* we realize that Altman has made a lot more than a comedy about gambling; he's taken us into an American nightmare, and all the people we met along the way felt genuine and looked real. This movie has a taste in its mouth like stale air-conditioning, and no matter what time it seems to be, it's always five in the morning in a second-rate casino.

As always, Altman fills his movie with quirky supporting roles—people who have somehow become caricatures of themselves. At the private poker game, Segal stands at the bar, surveys the table, and quietly describes every player. He's right about them, although he (and we) have never seen them before. We know he's right because these people wear their styles and destinies on their faces.

So do the hookers (played with a kind of tart-next-door wholesomeness by Ann Prentiss and Gwen Welles). So does "Helen Brown," one of their customers who's a middle-aged man who likes drag as much as he's terrified of the cops (inspiring a scene of true tragicomedy). Altman's movies always seem full, somehow; we don't have the feeling of an empty screen into which carefully drawn characters are introduced, but of a camera plunging into a boiling sea of frenzied human activity.

What Altman comes up with is sometimes almost a documentary feel; at the end of *California Split* we know something about organized gambling in this country we didn't know before. His movies always seem perfectly at home wherever they are, but this time there's an almost palpable sense of place. And Altman has never been more firmly in control of his style. He has one of the few really individual visual styles among contemporary American directors; we can always see it's an Altman film. He bases his visual strategies on an incredibly attentive sound track, using background noises with particular care so that our ears tell us we're moving through these people—instead of that they're lined up talking to us. *California Split* is a great movie and it's a great experience, too; we've been there with Bill and Charlie.

Camille Claudel ★ ★ ★ ½
R, 149 m., 1989

Isabelle Adjani (Camille Claudel), Gerard Depardieu (Auguste Rodin), Laurent Grevill (Paul), Alain Cuny (Camille's father), Madeleine Robinson (Camille's mother), Katrine Boorman (Jessie Lipscomb), Daniele Lebrun (Rose Beuret). Directed by Bruno Nuytten and produced by Bernard Artigues. Screenplay by Nuytten and Marilyn Goldin.

She is above all a lonely woman, because she chooses to do with her life what her society says no decent woman should do. She chooses to love whom she will, and she wants to be an artist—to create sculptures out of clay, just as if she were a man. It is hard to say which of her choices is the most offensive. And when she goes mad, it is impossible to say whether the seeds of madness were there from the beginning. Or whether she was driven to madness by a society that could not accept a woman who lived for herself.

Camille Claudel has until now occupied only the footnotes of late nineteenth-century art. She was one of the mistresses of Auguste Rodin, the willful sculptor who is known to everyone if only for "The Thinker." She was often his model, and for a time she worked as his collaborator.

She left behind many sculptures, which

can be seen here or there, not much remarked, while Rodin's work has been enshrined in the pantheon. She spent the last thirty years of her life in a madhouse.

The film *Camille Claudel* is more concerned with her personality and passions than with her art, and so it is hard to judge, from the evidence on the screen, how good a sculptor she really was. This is not a movie about sculpture. Those who have seen her work report that some of it has a power that is almost disturbing—that there is an urgency in her figures suggesting she was not simply shaping them but using them to bring her own emotions to life.

Certainly the pressures against an independent woman artist were sufficient in her late nineteenth-century Paris that she would not have bothered to be a sculptor unless she absolutely had to.

The first time we see her she is grubbing in the dirt of a Paris construction site, down there in a ditch like a burrowing animal, looking for good clay that she can use in her work. She straightens up and, as she rubs the sweat from her face with a filthy hand, we see her as a very young woman with eyes that see more than this ditch she stands in: She sees, already, the figures she will mold from this clay.

Camille is played by Isabelle Adjani, who was nominated for an Academy Award for her work, and one of the mysteries of this performance is how Adjani, now in her thirties, is able so convincingly to span this woman's lifetime and seem to be the right age at all times. She is certainly convincing in the early scenes as a young, open, determined woman who has somehow got it into her head that not only men should be sculptors.

As an academy student seeking a new teacher, she meets Auguste Rodin (Gerard Depardieu), who looms like a colossus over the art world of his time, not least because of his ability at self-promotion; Rodin was one of the inventors of the artist as celebrity, rejecting the myth of the lonely recluse in the wretched garret and consciously occupying the spotlight. At first he pays little attention to her, even though he has a reputation as a womanizer. She observes his longtime mistress, Rose Beuret (Daniele Lebrun), and wonders if they are married. She works on a piece of marble he has given her and creates a foot, a wonderful foot that he acknowledges as well-made. They fall into each other's orbit, he is bewitched, they make love, she becomes pregnant, he will not leave Rose,

and she begins the long descent into madness.

Rodin is simply not capable of being faithful to one woman. Nor is he much interested in a woman who dares to think of herself as his artistic rival. Such a woman can be allowed to grow only so far, to be encouraged so much, before she must be slapped back down into her place in his bed. Is this rejection what drives Camille mad, or is it the fundamental contradiction between what she is and the time she lives in? We follow her gradual decay as she moves into shabby lodgings and goes without food or fuel to pay for her art. This behavior concerns her parents, who begin to wonder if she has lost her senses, especially when she begins to drink and to neglect the impression she makes on people.

Adjani is possessed in this movie. It is not one of those leisurely costume dramas in which people in beautiful clothing move through elegant rooms. Her eyes always look haunted, and even in the moments of luxury and romance there is the suggestion in her body language of that feral creature down in the ditch, grubbing for clay. She makes sculptures because she must—because the figures in her work are trapped within her, and if she does not release them she will burst.

Depardieu plays a Rodin who is genial, assured, and malevolent. He will go only so far for a woman before he must pull back and be sure that his ego is served.

Has there ever been another actor, in any language, who seems so unself-consciously assured in such a variety of roles? Depardieu works all the time, always well, and just within the last few years he has been not only Rodin but also the hunchback peasant of *Jean de Florette* and the love-struck car salesman of *Too Beautiful for You*.

Artistic biographies are notoriously difficult to film because what an artist does takes place within his mind, and the camera can see only the outside. Sculptors are at least a little easier to deal with than writers or musicians; instead of Balzac or Mozart furiously scribbling on a piece of paper, we can at least see the knife shaping the block of clay. But *Camille Claudel* is not really about sculpture anyway. It is about a woman who tried to place sculpture before everything until she met a man who did the same thing.

Car Wash ★ ★ ★ ¹/₂
PG, 97 m., 1976

Franklin Ajaye (T.C.), Sully Boyer (Mr. B.),
Richard Brestoff (Irwin), George Carlin (Taxi
Driver), Prof. Irwin Corey (Mad Bomber), Ivan
Dixon (Lonnie), Richard Pryor (Daddy Rich).
Directed by Michael Schultz and produced by
Art Linson and Gary Stromberg. Screenplay
by Joel Schumacher.

The boss is named Mr. B. and he walks
around with a dead cigar stuck in his face,
pleading "Wash the cars! Wash the cars!"
But that's the last thing they get around to in
Car Wash, a sunny, lively comedy. The movie
covers a day in the life of the DeLuxe Car
Wash, down from the Strip in Los Angeles,
and by actual count only three totally sane
people stop by all day. We meet the rest in a
dizzying, nonstop kaleidoscope of cars, soul
music, characters, crises, crazy kids on
skateboards, hookers, television preachers,
and lots of suds and hot wax—not to mention
the Mad Pop Bottle Bomber, whose bottle
turns out to be a cruel disappointment. The
movie's put together with a manic energy, we
never even quite get introduced to half the
people in the cast, but by the movie's end we
know them, and what they're up to, and we
like them.

We meet the employees of the car wash in
the locker room, as they're putting on their
work clothes. Floyd and Lloyd enter doing
their James Brown imitation. T.C. is convinced he'll be the lucky caller to win the free
concert tickets in a radio station giveaway.
Lindy, probably the first drag queen employed full-time by a car wash, corrects his
makeup. Lonnie, the straw boss, provides an
element of sanity, but he's outnumbered.

Sooner or later during the day, everyone
seems to come through the car wash. While
Floyd and Lloyd, as the steam men, practice
their stage act on astonished customers, we
watch the parade go by. George Carlin plays a
bewildered taxi driver. Professor Irwin
Corey is briefly mistaken for the Mad Pop
Bottle Bomber. A limousine a yard long
wheels up and discharges Richard Pryor, as
Daddy Rich, the famous television evangelist. He has his backup singers with him:
the Pointer Sisters, who do a number right in
front of the gas pumps.

The movie looks like joyful chaos on the
surface, but there are several stories running
through it. One involves Bill Duke as a
young Black Muslim with fierce resentments. Another—delicately handled involves
a young black hooker who changes clothes in
the rest room and then hangs around the
corner all day lonely and lost. Another is the
relationship between Mr. B. and Lonnie—
Mr. B. tense and worried, Lonnie filled with
ideas he can't get an audience for.

The car wash seems almost a natural
gathering place. The kid on the skateboard
whizzes past on a regular schedule. Wives
and girlfriends of the workers stop by for
brief sessions of fighting and making up. A
guy named Kenny, who looks like he stepped
out of the fashion ads, stops in and gets a date
with the office girl. A man in a head-to-toe
cast goes through the wash, considerably
shaken. So does a little boy who first throws
up on his mother's Mercedes and, when it's
been washed, throws up on her.

All of this is held together by the music,
which is nearly wall-to-wall, and by the picture's tremendous sense of life. It's one thing
to have an idea like this—a zany, sometimes
serious day in the life of a car wash—and
another thing to make it work. But the
screenplay and the direction juggle the characters so adroitly, this is almost a wash-and-
wax *M*A*S*H*.

Carmen ★ ★ ★ ★
R, 95 m., 1983

Antonio Gades (Antonio), Laura Del Sol
(Carmen), Paco De Lucia (Paco), Cristina
Hoyos (Cristina). Sung by Regina Resnik and
Maria Del Monaco. Directed by Carlos Saura
and produced by Emiliano Piedra. Screenplay
by Saura and Antonio Gades.

Carlos Saura's *Carmen* is an erotic roller
coaster of a movie, incorporating dance into
its story more effectively than any other
movie I can remember. It isn't a "ballet
movie," and it's not like one of those musicals where everybody is occasionally taken
with the need to dance. It's a story of passion
and jealousy—the story of Bizet's *Carmen*—
with dance as part and parcel of its flesh and
blood. The movie is based on the opera by
Bizet, keeping the music and the broad outlines of the story of a poor girl whose fierce
romantic independence maddens the men
who become obsessed with her. Everything
else is new. Saura, the greatest living Spanish
film director, has collaborated with Antonio
Gades, the Spanish dancer and choreographer, to make this *Carmen* into a muscular,
contemporary story. Their strategy is to

make a story within a story. The film begins
with Gades as a dance teacher who is looking
for the "perfect" Carmen. He finds one in a
flamenco dancing school, and as he attempts
to mold her into Carmen, their relationship
begins to resemble the story of the opera.

Given this approach, *Carmen* could easily
have turned into an academic exercise, one of
those clever movies in which all the pieces fit
but none of them matter. That doesn't happen, and one of the reasons it doesn't is the
casting of a young woman named Laura Del
Sol as Carmen. She is a twenty-one-year-old
dancer who combines convincing technique
with a healthy, athletic sexiness, and her
dance duets (and duels) with Gades are bold,
erotic, and uninhibited. What's fascinating
is the way Saura is able to blend the dance,
the opera, and the "modern" story. For
example, Del Sol and Gades use dance to
create a scene that begins as an argument,
develops into fierce declarations of independence, and then climaxes in passionate
romance. In another scene, a routine day in a
dance studio becomes charged by the unexpected appearance of Carmen's other lover,
an ex-convict.

I have an ambivalence about dance on
film. I begin with the assumption that the
ideal way to see dance is live, on a stage.
Everything in dance begins with the fact that
the dancers are physically present and are
using their bodies to turn movement into art.
Movies, with their complete freedom over
time and space, break that contract between
real time and the dancer. Dances can be constructed out of many different shots and even
out of the work of more than one dancer (see
Flashdance). If I can't see dancing on a stage,
then, my preference is for classical movie
dancing, by which I mean frankly artificial
constructions of the Astaire and Rogers variety. Serious dance on film usually feels like a
documentary. The great achievement of *Carmen* is that it takes serious dance and music,
combines them with a plausible story, suspends our disbelief, and gives us a mesmerizing, electric experience.

Carmen ★ ★ ★ ★
PG, 152 m., 1984

Julia Migenes-Johnson (Carmen), Placido
Domingo (Don Jose), Ruggero Raimondi
(Escamillo), Faith Esham (Micaela), Jean-
Philippe Lafont (Dancairo). Directed by
Francesco Rosi and produced by Patrice
Ledoux.

Bizet's *Carmen* is what movies are all about. It's one of the few modern movies that requires one of those legendary Hollywood advertising men who'd cook up copy like, for example . . .

Cheer! As Bizet's towering masterpiece blazes across the screen! Cry bravo! To passion, romance, adventure! From the bullrings of Spain to the innermost recesses of her gypsy heart, Carmen drives men mad and immortalizes herself as a romantic legend! Thrill! To the golden voice of Placido Domingo, and the tempestuous screen debut of the smouldering Julia Migenes-Johnson!

The temptation, of course, is to approach, a film like this with hushed voice and bended knee, uttering reverent phrases about art and music. But to hell with it: This movie is the *Indiana Jones* of opera films, and we might as well not beat around the bush. *Carmen* is a Latin soap opera if ever there was one, and the sheer passionate joy of Bizet's music is as vulgar as it is sublime, as popular as it is classical. *Carmen* is one of those operas ideally suited to the movies, and this version by Francesco Rosi is exciting, involving, and entertaining.

You are doubtless already familiar with the music. The sound track was recorded in Paris with Lorin Maazel conducting the National Orchestra of France. Placido Domingo is in great voice, and a relatively unknown American soprano named Julia Migenes-Johnson not only can sing the title role but, perhaps just as importantly, can look it and act it. There is chemistry here, and without the chemistry—without the audience's belief that the scornful gypsy Carmen could enslave the soldier Don Jose—there would only be an illustrated sound track. After the recording was completed, the movie was shot on locations in Spain by Francesco Rosi, the Italian director of *Three Brothers* and *Christ Stopped at Eboli*. He has discovered lush, sun-drenched villages on hillsides, and a bullring of such stark Spanish simplicity that the ballet within the ring for once seems as elegant as the emotions it is reflecting. He also has found moonlight, rich firelight, deep reds and yellows—colors so glowing that the characters seem to warm themselves at his palette.

Opera films are traditionally not successful. They play in festivals, they find a small audience of music lovers, maybe they make some money in Italy. Domingo broke that pattern with his *La Traviata* (1983), directed by Franco Zeffirelli. It had good

long runs around the United States, and even broke through to audiences beyond the core of opera lovers. But we Americans are so wary of "culture." Opera for many of us still consists of the fat lady on "The Ed Sullivan Show." And for many of the rest, it is something that inhabits a cultural shrine and must be approached with reverence. Maybe it takes the movies, that most popular of art forms, to break that pattern. Rosi, Domingo, and Migenes-Johnson have filmed a labor of love.

Carnival of Souls ★ ★ ★
NO MPAA RATING, 80 m., 1962

Candace Hilligoss (Mary Henry), Sidney Berger (John Linden), Frances Feist (Landlady), Herk Harvey ("The Man"), Stanley Leavitt (Doctor), Art Ellison (Minister), Tom McGinnis (Boss). Directed and produced by Harold "Herk" Harvey. Screenplay by John Clifford.

Carnival of Souls is an odd, obscure horror film that was made in a low budget in 1962 in Lawrence, Kansas, and still has an intriguing power. Like a lost episode from *The Twilight Zone*, it places the supernatural right in the middle of everyday life and surrounds it with ordinary people. In 1989 the movie was revived in art houses around the country, and it's possible that it plays better today than when it was released. It ventures to the edge of camp, but never strays across the line, taking itself with an eerie seriousness.

The movie stars Candace Hilligoss, one of those worried blondes like Janet Leigh in *Psycho*, as a young woman who goes along for the ride when two hot-rodders hold a drag race. On a narrow wooden bridge, one of the cars crashes through a railing and plunges into the flooded river below. Police and volunteers search for the wreckage in vain—and then Hilligoss appears on a sandbar, dazed and covered with mud.

What happened to the others? How did she escape? She doesn't know. Indeed, she doesn't care. She's a brittle, cynical woman who works as a church organist but doesn't take religion seriously. That's despite the fact that the organ seems to be trying to tell her something. There is a sensational overhead shot in an organ factory, looking down past the steep, angled pipes to her diminutive figure far below, and another effective moment when she's in a car on a deserted highway and the radio picks up only organ music.

A few days after she crawls out of the river, the woman leaves town for a job playing the organ in Utah, and in one of the movie's best shots, a cadaverous face appears in the car window. It's the face of a ghostly figure who will follow her to Utah (the figure is played by the film's director, Harold "Herk" Harvey. In Utah, she checks into one of those B-movie boarding houses, presided over by the cherubic Frances Feist. There's one other boarder, a Mr. Linden (Sidney Berger), who is a definitive study of a nerd in lust.

Unlike most of today's horror movies, *Carnival of Souls* has few special effects—some wavy lines as we pass through various levels of existence and that's it. Instead, it depends on crisp black-and-white photography, atmosphere, and surprisingly effective acting. It's impossible to know whether this movie was seen by such directors as David Lynch or George Romero, but in the way it shows the horror beneath the surface of placid small-town life, it suggests *Blue Velvet*, and a shot of dead souls at an abandoned amusement park reminded me of the lurching undead in *Night of the Living Dead*.

Carrie ★ ★ ★ ½
R, 98 m., 1976

Sissy Spacek (Carrie), William Katt (Her Prom Date), Piper Laurie (Her Mother). Directed by Brian De Palma and produced by Paul Monash. Screenplay by Lawrence D. Cohen.

Brian De Palma's *Carrie* is an absolutely spellbinding horror movie, with a shock at the end that's the best thing along those lines since the shark leaped aboard in *Jaws*. It's also (and this is what makes it so good) an observant human portrait. This girl Carrie isn't another stereotyped product of the horror production line; she's a shy, pretty, and complicated high school senior who's a lot like kids we once knew. There is a difference, though. She has telekenesis, the ability to manipulate things without touching them. It's a power that came upon her gradually, and was released in response to the shrill religious fanaticism of her mother. It manifests itself in small ways. She looks in a mirror, and it breaks. Then it mends itself. Her mother tries to touch her and is hurled back against a couch. But then, on prom night . . .

Well, what makes the movie's last twenty minutes so riveting is that they grow so relentlessly, so inevitably, out of what's gone before. This isn't a science-fiction movie with a tacked-on crisis, but the study of a character we know and understand. When she fully uses (or is used by) her strange power, we know why. This sort of narrative development hasn't exactly been De Palma's strong point, but here he exhibits a gift for painting personalities; we didn't know De Palma, ordinarily so flashy on the surface, could go so deep. Part of his success is a result of the very good performances by Sissy Spacek, as Carrie, and by Piper Laurie, as Carrie's mother. They form a closed-off, claustrophobic household, the mother has translated her own psychotic fear of sexuality into a twisted personal religion. She punishes the girl constantly, locks her in closets with statues of a horribly bleeding Christ, and refuses to let her develop normal friendships.

At school, then, it's no wonder Carrie is so quiet. She has long blond hair but wears it straight and uses it mostly to hide her face. She sits in the back of the room, doesn't speak up much, and is the easy butt of jokes by her classmates. Meanwhile, the most popular girl in the class devises a truly cruel trick to play on Carrie. It depends on Carrie being asked to the senior prom by the popular girl's equally popular boyfriend—he's one of your average Adonises with letters in every sport. He's not in on the joke, though, and asks Carrie in all seriousness.

And then De Palma gives us a marvelously realized scene at the prom—where Carrie does, indeed, turn out to be beautiful. There's a little something wrong, though, and De Palma has an effective way to convey it: As Carrie and her date dance, the camera moves around them, romantically at first, but then too fast, as if they're spinning out of control.

I wouldn't want to spoil the movie's climax for you by even hinting at what happens next. Just let me say that *Carrie* is a true horror story. Not a manufactured one, made up of spare parts from old Vincent Price classics, but a real one, in which the horror grows out of the characters themselves. The scariest horror stories—the ones by M.R. James, Edgar Allan Poe, and Oliver Onions—are like this. They develop their horrors out of the people they observe. That happens here, too. Does it ever.

Casualties of War ★ ★ ★
R, 120 m., 1989

Michael J. Fox (Eriksson), Sean Penn (Meserve), Don Harvey (Clark), John C. Reilly (Hatcher), John Leguizamo (Diaz), Thuy Thu Le (Oahn), Erik King (Brown), Jack Gwaltney (Rowan), Ving Rhames (Lieutenant Reilly), Dan Martin (Hawthorne). Directed by Brian De Palma and produced by Art Linson. Screenplay by David Rabe.

Casualties of War is a film based, we are told, on an actual event. A five-man patrol of American soldiers in Vietnam kidnapped a young woman from her village, forced her to march with them, and then raped her and killed her. One of the five refused to participate in the rape and murder, and it was his testimony that eventually brought the others to a military court-martial and prison sentences. The movie is not so much about the event as about the atmosphere leading up to it—the dehumanizing reality of combat, the way it justifies brute force, and penalizes those who would try to live by a higher standard.

The film begins as Eriksson, a young infantryman (Michael J. Fox), arrives in Vietnam and is assigned to a unit filled with veterans. They've been in combat, on and off, for months, and Meserve, the sergeant (Sean Penn), is a short-timer with less than a month to go before he can return home. Meserve is a good soldier, strong, violent, and effective. He is capable of heroism and has leadership ability. But he has lost, or he never had, the fundamental moral standards that most of us would like to believe are a product of his, and our, civilization.

On the night before he is scheduled to lead his men on a long-range reconnaissance patrol, Meserve is prevented by the MPs from going to a nearby village where he plans to visit a prostitute. Enraged, he involves his men in a plan to enter the village secretly and kidnap a young woman (not a prostitute), who will be brought along on the mission to service the sexual needs of all five men. When he explains this plan, Eriksson, the Fox character, doesn't believe he really means it. But he means it, all right.

In the field, the five men break into two groups: Eriksson and Diaz, who make a private agreement to "support" each other in refusing to go along with the rape, and the other three men, who are gung ho in favor of it. Meserve is the ringleader and is played by

Sean Penn with such raw, focused power that it is easy to see how a weak person would be intimidated by him. Penn has a denial system that allows him to describe the kidnapped girl as a "Viet Cong prisoner," but actually he isn't even very concerned about justifying what he's doing. "What happens in the bush stays in the bush," one of the group members says.

When the actual moment of the gang rape arrives, Eriksson refuses to go along. He tries, in a tentative and agonizing way, to argue that "this isn't what it's supposed to be about over here." Meserve lashes him verbally: He is not loyal to the group, he loves the Cong, he's probably a queer, and so on. Diaz, hearing this, caves in and refuses to support Eriksson's stand. Four of the men rape the girl, and later the same four pump bullets into her.

This whole sequence of scenes is harrowing because it makes it so clear how impotent Eriksson's moral values are in the face of a rifle barrel. The other men either never had any qualms about what they are doing, or have lost them in the brutalizing process of combat. They will do exactly what they want to do, and Eriksson is essentially powerless to stop them. The movie makes it clear that when a group dynamic of this sort is at work, there is perhaps literally nothing that a "good" person can do to interrupt it. And its examination of the realities of the situation is what's best about the movie.

What is not so good are the scenes before and after the powerful central material. The movie begins and ends some time after the war, with the Fox character on a train—where he sees an Asian woman who reminds him of the victim. The dialogue he has with this woman in the movie's last scene is so forced and unnatural, and tries so hard to cobble an upbeat ending onto a tragic story, that it seems to belong in another movie. I also felt that the aftermath of the crime—Eriksson's attempts to bring charges—developed unevenly. Confrontations with two commanding officers are effective (they explain, obscenely and profanely, why he has no business pressing charges), but then the outcome seems sketchy and tacked on. Perhaps the movie would have been more effective if it had just recorded the incident, and ended as the group returned to base. That much would have contained everything important that the movie has to say; the narrative sandwich around it is simply distracting.

Casualties of War, written by the playwright David Rabe, is the first film by director Brian De Palma since *The Untouchables*. More than most films, it depends on the strength of its performances for its effect—and especially on Sean Penn's performance. If he is not able to convince us of his power, his rage, and his contempt for the life of the girl, the movie would not work. He does, in a performance of overwhelming, brutal power. Michael J. Fox, as his target, plays a character most of us could probably identify with, the person to whom rape or murder is unthinkable, but who has never had to test his values in the crucible of violence. The movie's message, I think, is that in combat human values are lost and animal instincts are reinforced. We knew that already. But the movie makes it inescapable, especially when we reflect that the story is true, and the victim was real.

Cat People ★ ★ ★ ½
R, 118 m., 1982

Nastassja Kinski (Irena Gallier), Malcolm McDowell (Paul Gallier), John Heard (Oliver Yates), Annette O'Toole (Alice Perrin), Ruby Dee (Female), Ed Begley, Jr. (Joe Creigh). Directed by Paul Schrader and produced by Charles Fries. Screenplay by Alan Ormsby.

It is a preposterous idea. Untold centuries ago, when all the world was a desert of wind-whipped, blood-orange sand, and leopards lounged lazily in barren trees and arrogantly ruled all they could see, a few members of the puny race of human beings made their own accommodation with the fearsome beasts. They sacrificed their women to them. And the leopards did not kill the women, but mated with them. From those mists of pre-history, the race they created lives even today: The Cat People.

These people have had a hard time of it. They have the physical appearance of ordinary humans, except for something feline around the eyes and a certain spring in their step. They have all the mortal appetites, too, but there are complications when they make love, because in the heat of orgasm they are transformed into savage black leopards and kill their human lovers. They should mate only with their own kind. But as our story opens, there are only two Cat People—and, like their parents before them, are brother and sister.

This is the stuff of audacious myth, com-bining the perverse, the glorious, and the ridiculous. The movies were invented to tell such stories. Paul Schrader's *Cat People* moves boldly between a slice-of-life in present-day New Orleans and the windswept deserts where the Cat People were engen-dered, and his movie creates a mood of doom, predestination, forbidden passion, and, to be sure, a certain silliness. It's fun in the way horror movies should be fun; it's totally unbelievable in between the times it's scaring the popcorn out of you.

Nastassja Kinski stars as the young sister, Irena. She is an orphan, reunited in New Orleans with her long-lost brother, Paul (Malcolm McDowell). She also is a virgin, afraid of sex and liquor because they might unleash the animal inside of her. (Little does she suspect that is literally what would hap-pen.) She is tall, with a sensual mouth, wide-set green eyes, and a catlike walk. She catches the attention of the curator at the New Orleans zoo (John Heard). He senses danger in her. He also senses that this is the creature he has been waiting for all his life—waiting for her as the leopards in their cells wait, expecting nothing, ready for anything.

We have here, then, a most complex love triangle. Kinski fears her brother because she fears incest. She fears the curator but loves him. To love him is, eventually, to kill him. The curator is in love with the idea of her threat, but does not realize she *really* will turn into a leopard and rend his flesh. There are some supporting characters: Annette O'Toole is the sensible friend who senses danger, and Ed Begley, Jr. is the lackadaisical custodian whose arm is ripped from its socket. You shouldn't mess with leopards.

Schrader tells his story in two parallel nar-ratives. One involves the deepening rela-tionships among the sister, the brother, and the curator. The other, stunningly pho-tographed, takes place in an unearthly ter-rain straight from Frank Herbert's Dune books. The designer, Ferdinando Scarfiotti, and the veteran special-effects artist, Albert Whitlock, have created a world that looks completely artificial, with its drifting red sands and its ritualistic tableau of humans and leopards—and yet looks realistic in its fantasy. In other words, you know this world is made up, but you can't see the seams; it's like the snow planet in *The Empire Strikes Back*.

Cat People moves back and forth between its mythic and realistic levels, held together primarily by the strength of Kinski's per-formance and John Heard's obsession. Kin-ski is something. She never overacts in this movie, never steps wrong, never seems ridiculous; she just steps onscreen and con-vincingly underplays a leopard. Heard also is good. He never seems in the grip of an ordi-nary sexual passion, but possesses one of those obsessions men are willing (and often are called upon) to die for. *Cat People* is a good movie in an old tradition, a fantasy-hor-ror film that takes itself just seriously enough to work, has just enough fun to be entertain-ing, contains elements of intrinsic fascina-tion in its magnificent black leopards, and ends in one way just when we were afraid it was going to end in another.

Chances Are ★ ★ ★ ½
PG, 108 m., 1989

Cybill Shepherd (Corinne Jeffries), Robert Downey, Jr. (Alex Finch), Ryan O'Neal (Philip Train), Mary Stuart Masterson (Miranda), Christopher McDonald (Louie Jeffries), Josef Sommer (Judge Fenwick), Henderson Forsythe (Ben Bradlee), Lester Lanin (Con-ductor). Directed by Emile Ardolino and produced by Mike Lobell. Screenplay by Perry and Randy Howze.

Chances Are comes from the same gene bank as all the other mind-swap and reincarnation movies, but it's smart and entertaining. It proves the underlying thesis of all film criti-cism, which is that movies are not about their stories, they're about *how* they're about their stories. Plots are easy. Style is every-thing. *Chances Are* is a lighthearted romance about reincarnation told with wit and a cer-tain irony.

Movies like this depend to a great degree on the personal styles of their actors: If we don't warm to the people on the screen and care about their feelings, then the plot is just the clanking and grinding of vast inter-changeable machines. All four of the leading actors in *Chances Are* devote themselves to the material as if they really believed in it, and that's why this silly story works yet once again. The difference between good and bad acting in a romantic comedy is that in the good performances the characters somehow convince us that their hearts are actually at risk.

Cybill Shepherd stars in *Chances Are* as a Washington, D.C., professional woman whose husband is killed in a traffic accident in the early 1960s. She never quite gets over that loss. Years pass, and then decades, and she still treasures her love in her heart. She was pregnant when she became a widow, and she raises her daughter (Mary Stuart Masterson) and leads her life and never remarries. Her love is so constant that she remains oblivious to the fact that the family's best friend (Ryan O'Neal) has always been in love with her.

Meanwhile, we get another one of those standard movie fantasies of Heaven, in which everyone walks around on white clouds and speaks English and looks like someone painted by Norman Rockwell. And we discover that it's time for the soul of Shepherd's dead husband to be recycled back to earth again. Through a heavenly mix-up, however, the soul is not inoculated with a special forgetfulness serum, and so the scene is set for the reincarnated husband to recognize his wife again.

When we meet the reborn husband (Robert Downey, Jr.), he is a student at Yale, where Shepherd's daughter also goes to school, of course. (Why don't they ever try a variation on this theme, and have the reborn husband come back as a yak breeder from Tibet?) Downey and Masterson start dating, she brings him home to meet her mom, and, of course, suddenly all of his memories come flooding back and he realizes that Shepherd is his wife and he is her reincarnated husband.

It's really at this point that the movie begins; everything earlier has just been laying the foundations. It is also at this point that I had better stop describing the details, because *Chances Are* has a lot of fun with the implications of its plot. If Downey is indeed the reborn husband, for example, then he is dating his own daughter. If he is not, then Shepherd will be guilty of stealing her daughter's boyfriend. And so on. Director Emile Ardolino (*Dirty Dancing*) approaches these paradoxes in a time-honored way, with lots of swinging bedroom doors and mistaken identities under the covers.

Although Cybill Shepherd gets top billing, and deserves it, in a way this movie belongs to Robert Downey, Jr. He is at the center of the action, trying to juggle the emotions of both women (while O'Neal stands on the sidelines, in love with Shepherd but still upstaged, after all these years, by the dead husband). If Downey were not able to bring a certain weight and conviction to his performance, everything else in the movie would

collapse, but Downey is convincing and good.

His career before this movie was uneven, ranging from a strong, harrowing dramatic performance as a self-destructive cocaine addict in *Less Than Zero* to an obnoxious goofball in *The Pickup Artist*. He costars with James Woods in *True Believer*, where he is almost acted off the screen by Woods, but then here he is filled with confidence at the emotional center of *Chances Are*. He's uneven, but he's got the stuff.

The movie itself is surprisingly affecting, perhaps because Shepherd never goes for easy laughs but plays her character seriously: This Yale student, after all, may actually harbor the soul of her late husband, and that is an awesome possibility. By the end of the movie, all of the confusing possibilities have been sorted out with impeccable romantic logic, and the movie somehow provides a happy ending for everyone. (Of course it does. Just once, couldn't the yak dealer from Tibet be killed in a second traffic accident, leaving the widow to discover him a third time, reborn as a canasta player in a New Jersey retirement home?)

Chapter Two ★ ★
PG, 124 m., 1980

James Caan (George), Marsha Mason (Jennie), Joseph Bologna (Leo), Valerie Harper (Faye), Alan Fudge (Lee), Judy Farrell (Gwen). Directed by Robert Moore and produced by Ray Stark. Screenplay by Neil Simon.

After the early loss of his first wife, playwright Neil Simon married again soon afterwards. Six months after the death, he fell in love at first sight with actress Marsha Mason, and they were married after a romance of only twenty-two days. Simon transformed those events of 1973 into an autobiographical play that opened in 1977, and now this film stars Mason in a role that is based, we guess, more or less upon herself.

Simon says the story isn't an actual record of what happened, but was just loosely inspired by his remarriage. There is no way for us to know. What we can say, on the basis of *Chapter Two*, is that if the key dialogue between husband and new wife wasn't taken from life, it is possibly taken from that wonderful category of what they *should* have said. And there is a great deal that they should have said. Simon is usually the most quick-

footed and -witted of dialogue writers, but this time he gives us more than two hours of discussions, arguments, debates, reconciliations, and accusations that quickly become tedious.

The conversations in his screenplay are too long and too literal to begin with, but they suffer from two additional handicaps: (a) They do not take place between two characters whose motives have been well established, and (b) they have the misfortune to involve James Caan, who is so tense, uptight, and verbally constipated that it's a trial to wait out his speeches.

Caan plays the Simon-like character, a writer and new widower who is inconsolable in his grief until Mason happens along. Caan has previously survived a series of blind dates with the usual assortment of hopeless choices, and so Mason enchants him: She's outspoken, direct, spunky. Their first "trial date" lasts five minutes (one of those standard Hollywood "meet cutes"), and in no time at all they're in Bermuda on their honeymoon.

So far, not so bad. This is all the stuff of dependable romantic comedy, and we know where we stand. But we are about to find ourselves at sea for the rest of the movie, because the Caan character suddenly has agonizing second thoughts . . . his new bride gets on his nerves . . . he doesn't know what's bugging him . . . he's hurtful . . . he splits. The movie never really bothers itself with *why* he behaves this way, unless we're supposed to supply our own instant Freudian analysis. Caan is awkward all through this movie (he never seems happy playing this part), but he's never more lost than when he undergoes this dramatic character transformation. And you can't really blame him: Simon just hasn't given him the words or actions to make himself clear.

After the split, the rest of the movie is devoted to attempts by first one and then the other of the newlyweds to figure out what went wrong. Their scenes are so tediously top-heavy with dialogue that we can barely stand to listen. And then there's the added distraction of a parallel plot involving an affair between their best friends (Valerie Harper and Joe Bologna).

There is absolutely no rational reason why this subplot is in the movie. Maybe it made sense in the mechanics of the stage play, but it doesn't belong here. And it's all the more distracting because, whatdaya know, Bologna and Harper are much better than

Caan and Mason at conjuring up the romantic and comic juices of a love affair. Their scenes are meaningless and unnecessary, but at least they're alive, and just when they get their emotional rhythm flowing, the movie cuts back to the nonstop marriage counseling session that occupies the main plot.

Chapter Two is called a comedy, maybe because that's what we expect from Neil Simon. It's not, although it has that comic subplot. It's a middlebrow, painfully earnest, overwritten exercise in pop sociology. I'm not exactly happy describing Neil Simon's semi-real-life in those terms, but then those are the terms in which he's chosen to present it. My notion is that Simon would have been wiser to imagine himself writing about another couple, and writing for another actress than his own wife; that way maybe he wouldn't have felt it so necessary to let both sides have the last word.

Chariots of Fire ★ ★ ★ ★
PG, 123 m., 1981

Ben Cross (Harold Abrahams), Ian Charleson (Eric Liddell), Nigel Havers (Lord Andrew Lindsay), Ian Holm (Coach Mussabini), Sir John Gielgud (Master of Trinity), Lindsay Anderson (Master of Caius), David Yelland (Prince of Wales), Nicholas Farrell (Aubrey Montague). Directed by Hugh Hudson and produced by David Puttnam. Screenplay by Colin Welland.

This is strange. I have no interest in running and am not a partisan in the British class system. Then why should I have been so deeply moved by *Chariots of Fire*, a British film that has running and class as its subjects? I've toyed with that question since I first saw this remarkable film in May 1981 at the Cannes Film Festival, and I believe the answer is rather simple: Like many great films, *Chariots of Fire* takes its nominal subjects as occasions for much larger statements about human nature.

This is a movie that has a great many running scenes. It is also a movie about British class distinctions in the years after World War I, years in which the establishment was trying to piece itself back together after the carnage in France. It is about two outsiders—a Scot who is the son of missionaries in China, and a Jew whose father is an immigrant from Lithuania. And it is about how both of them use running as a means of asserting their dignity. But it is about more

than them, and a lot of this film's greatness is hard to put into words. *Chariots of Fire* creates deep feelings among many members of its audiences, and it does that not so much with its story or even its characters as with particular moments that are very sharply seen and heard.

Seen, in photography that pays grave attention to the precise look of a human face during stress, pain, defeat, victory, and joy. Heard, in one of the most remarkable sound tracks of any film in a long time, with music by the Greek composer Vangelis Papathanassiou. His compositions for *Chariots of Fire* are as evocative, and as suited to the material, as the different but also perfectly matched scores of such films as *The Third Man* and *Zorba the Greek*. The music establishes the tone for the movie, which is one of nostalgia for a time when two young and naturally gifted British athletes ran fast enough to bring home medals from the 1924 Paris Olympics.

The nostalgia is an important aspect of the film, which opens with a 1979 memorial service for one of the men, Harold Abrahams, and then flashes back sixty years to his first day at Cambridge University. We are soon introduced to the film's other central character, the Scotsman Eric Liddell. The film's underlying point of view is a poignant one: These men were once young and fast and strong, and they won glory on the sports field, but now they are dead and we see them as figures from long ago.

The film is unabashedly and patriotically British in its regard for these two characters, but it also contains sharp jabs at the British class system, which made the Jewish Abrahams feel like an outsider who could sometimes feel the lack of sincerity in a handshake, and placed the Protestant Liddell in the position of having to explain to the peeved Prince of Wales why he could not, in conscience, run on the Sabbath. Both men are essentially proving themselves, their worth, their beliefs, on the track. But *Chariots of Fire* takes an unexpected approach to many of its running scenes. It does not, until near the film's end, stage them as contests to wring cheers from the audience. Instead, it sees them as *efforts*, as endeavors by individual runners—it tries to capture the exhilaration of running as a celebration of the spirit.

Two of the best moments in the movie: A moment in which Liddell defeats Abrahams, who agonizingly replays the defeat over and

over in his memory. And a moment in which Abrahams' old Italian-Arabic track coach, banned from the Olympic stadium, learns who won his man's race. First he bangs his fist through his straw boater, then he sits on his bed and whispers, "My son!"

All of the contributions to the film are distinguished. Neither Ben Cross, as Abrahams, nor Ian Charleson, as Liddell, are accomplished runners but they are accomplished actors, and they *act* the running scenes convincingly. Ian Holm, as Abrahams' coach, quietly dominates every scene he is in. There are perfectly observed cameos by John Gielgud and Lindsay Anderson, as masters of Cambridge colleges, and by David Yelland, as a foppish, foolish young Prince of Wales. These parts and others make up a greater whole.

Chariots of Fire is one of the best films of recent years, a memory of a time when men still believed you could win a race if only you wanted to badly enough.

Chattahoochee ★ ★ ½
R, 94 m., 1990

Gary Oldman (Emmett Foley), Dennis Hopper (Walker Benson), Frances McDormand (Mae Foley), Pamela Reed (Earlene), Ned Beatty (Dr. Harwood), M. Emmet Walsh (Morris), William De Acutis (Missy), Lee Wilkof (Vernon). Directed by Mick Jackson and produced by Aaron Schwab and Faye Schwab. Screenplay by James Hicks.

I know how I'm expected to feel when informed that a movie has been "based on a true story." I'm supposed to feel solemn in the presence of a real person's real experiences—which are, it is somehow implied, more significant and more authentic than the fictional adventures usually retailed on the screen. And yet such words as "This is a true story" make my heart sink, because the movies so often use truth as a substitute for invention. When a story sags or a character seems unlikely, the excuse of the "true story" is always the same: This really happened!

Yes, but we are not at the movies because it really happened. Unless we are members of Emmett Foley's family, for example, how interested are we, really, in the fact that he was unjustly held in a mental hospital and courageously helped to expose its injustices? Not enough, I imagine, to set aside an evening of our time and several dollars for the ticket—unless, of course, the movie made of Foley's experience is a good one. But its quality has nothing to do with its being based on "a true story."

What does it mean, anyway, "a true story"? Emmett Foley is not Gary Oldman, who stars in *Chattahoochee*. His wife was not Frances McDormand and his sister was not Pamela Reed, and it is quite likely that less than 5 percent of the dialogue in this movie was actually said in exactly the way the movie represents it. Nor can the events of many years be compressed into less than two hours without great liberties being taken with the "truth."

And yet I have little doubt that Mick Jackson, who directed the movie, and James Hicks, who wrote it, did a lot of research on the Foley case and scouted locations and hired people to make sure the women's dresses reflected just what Southern women were wearing on those summer afternoons in the 1950s. The result is a movie that looks and feels authentic. And the performances—especially by Oldman, McDormand, and Reed—are strong and well-textured.

The Emmett Foley story begins in shabbiness, climbs to defiance, and ends in heroism. He was a Korean War veteran who became depressed by unemployment and decided to shoot up the neighborhood in the hopes that the cops would kill him, and his wife could collect the insurance. Instead, the cops captured him (SWAT teams were not such good shots in those days), and he was sent to Chattahoochee, a prison for the mentally ill that was also used as a catch-basin for the overflow from the regular prison population.

Conditions inside are reflected with gruesome faithfulness: the filth, the cockroaches, the illnesses, the beatings, the lack of any focus for a man's hopes. At first Foley wants only to sink into oblivion. Then he gets mad, and with the encouragement of a friend (Dennis Hopper) he starts writing letters to the authorities, protesting conditions in the institution. When they take away his writing privileges (a denial of his constitutional rights), he starts recording outrages in the chapters of his Bible and slips it to his sister during a visit.

The outcome is more predictable than stirring: A state commission is formed, hearings are held, outrage is stirred, Foley is vindicated, and the evil prison functionaries get their comeuppance. We know this will happen because it has happened before, in various ways, in movies like *The Snake Pit, One Flew Over the Cuckoo's Nest*, and the Henry Fonda made-for-TV movie *Gideon's Trumpet*.

Isn't it strange how real-life stories somehow seem to shape themselves into the form of fictional clichés? How, for example, Foley's letters to the outside and Gideon's letters to the outside would end in similar hearings? Here are some fictional accounts of prison life: Kafka's *In the Penal Colony*, Dostoyevsky's *The House of the Dead*, Cummings's *The Enormous Room*, and Bresson's film *A Man Escaped*. Perhaps because they are fiction, they contain truth in every word. They were not required to compromise in obedience to the facts.

Child's Play ★ ★ ★
R, 87 m., 1988

Catherine Hicks (Karen Barclay), Chris Sarandon (Mike Norris), Alex Vincent (Andy Barclay), Brad Dourif (Charles Lee Ray), Dinah Manoff (Maggie Peterson), Tommy Swerdlow (Jack Santos). Directed by Tom Holland and produced by David Kirschner. Screenplay by Don Mancini, John Lafia, and Holland.

What is it about dolls that makes them seem so sinister? Why is it that kids in the movies always seem to share some evil secret with their dolls? And why is it that when you see a doll on a shelf, its eyes seem to move by themselves? I think that when we were kids, we all secretly believed our dolls were up to something while we were asleep. And the movies can exploit that fear, because most of us are not aware that we carry it around as part of the subconscious trauma that makes life so interesting.

Child's Play is a cheerfully energetic horror film of the slam-bang school, but slicker and more clever than most, about an evil doll named Charles Lee Ray, or "Chuckie." This doll has been possessed by the mind and soul of the Lake Shore Strangler, a Chicago mass murderer who studied voodoo from a black magician. After the strangler is shot by a cop and left for dead in a toy store, he gathers enough energy to utter a voodoo incantation, after which ominous clouds roll in the sky and lightning strikes the store, causing one of the several large explosions in this movie.

Cut to Karen Barclay (Catherine Hicks), a widow who works as a salesclerk at Carson, Pirie, Scott. Her kid wants a new kind of doll he's seen advertised on TV, but she can't afford the $100 price tag, so she buys one cheap from a peddler in the alley. No prizes for guessing if the Lake Shore Strangler has possessed this doll. Once Chuckie the Doll is home, he stays quiet around the adults but strikes up a friendship with Karen's son, Andy (Alex Vincent). Chuckie gets Andy to do favors for him, like carrying him into the living room so he can see the toy store explosion on the late news. And when the babysitter gets nosy, Chuckie plants a claw hammer between her eyebrows and sends her crashing through a window to the ground far below.

Film Note: The claw hammer scene is a case study of the False Alarm, a basic device in all horror movies of the Mad Slasher subgenre. Whenever there is a scare, and the scare turns out to amount to nothing, the movie takes a beat and *then* hits with the *real* scare. What's that noise behind the plant stand? Let's creep over and see. Gently . . . ah, nothing there! Relief. And then comes the Whammo! Moment. The next time you see one of these movies, wait for the False Alarm, and then start the countdown at the exact moment you hear the sigh of relief. The Whammo! Moment usually comes on the count of four. *Child's Play* is better than the average False Alarm movie because it is well-made, contains effective performances, and has succeeded in creating a truly malevolent doll. Chuckie is one mean SOB. The movie also has an intriguing plot device, which is that of course nobody will believe that the doll is alive. Little Andy tries to tell them, but they won't believe him. Then his mom realizes that Chuckie is moving and talking even though his batteries were not included. They won't believe her. After the police detective (Chris Sarandon) is nearly strangled by the little demon, who wrecks his squad car, he finally believes that Chuckie is for real. (Curiously, in the next scene, he meets with the mom but doesn't even mention what has just happened to him; in a movie like this, it takes a lot to hold your attention.)

Second Film Note: The movie ends with superb demonstrations of two other conventions in all Mad Slasher movies. The first is that once you kill the monster, he is never really dead. He looks dead, he's burned to a crisp and riddled with bullet holes, but then at a moment of peace and quiet we get another Whammo! Moment, and the godawful thing is still alive. The second convention of these movies is that the door is always left open for a sequel. *Child's Play* handles that with an ironic touch. The movie's last shot is of an open door.

The China Syndrome ★ ★ ★ ★
PG, 122 m., 1979

Jane Fonda (Kimberly Wells), Jack Lemmon (Jack Godell), Michael Douglas (Richard Adams), Scott Brady (Herman DeYoung), James Hampton (Bill Gibson), Peter Donat (Don Jacovich), Wilford Brimley (Ted Spindler). Directed by James Bridges and produced by Michael Douglas. Screenplay by Mike Gray, T.S. Cook, and Bridges.

The China Syndrome is a terrific thriller that incidentally raises the most unsettling questions about how safe nuclear power plants really are. It was received in some quarters as a political film, and the people connected with it make no secret of their doubts about nuclear power. But the movie is, above all, entertainment: well-acted, well-crafted, scary as hell.

The events leading up to the "accident" in *The China Syndrome* are indeed based on actual occurrences at nuclear plants. Even the most unlikely mishap (a stuck needle on a graph causing engineers to misread a crucial water level) really happened at the Dresden plant outside Chicago. And yet the movie works so well not because of its factual basis, but because of its human content. The performances are so good, so consistently, that *The China Syndrome* becomes a thriller dealing in personal values. The suspense is generated not only by our fears about what might happen, but by our curiosity about how, in the final showdown, the characters will react.

The key character is Godell (Jack Lemmon), a shift supervisor at a big nuclear power plant in Southern California. He lives alone, quietly, and can say without any self-consciousness that the plant is his life. He believes in nuclear power. But when an earthquake shakes his plant, he becomes convinced that he felt an aftershock—caused not by an earthquake but by rumblings deep within the plant.

The quake itself leads to the first "accident." Because a two-bit needle gets stuck on a roll of graph paper, the engineers think they need to lower the level of the water shield over the nuclear pile. Actually, the level is already dangerously low. And if the pile were ever uncovered, the result could be the "China syndrome," so named because the superheated nuclear materials would

melt directly through the floor of the plant and, theoretically, keep on going until they hit China. In practice, there'd be an explosion and a release of radioactive materials sufficient to poison an enormous area.

The accident takes place while a TV news team is filming a routine feature about the plant. The cameraman (Michael Douglas) secretly films events in the panicked control room. And the reporter (Jane Fonda) tries to get the story on the air. Her superiors refuse, influenced by the power industry's smoothly efficient public relations people. But the more Fonda and Douglas dig into the accident, the less they like it.

Meanwhile, obsessed by that second tremor, Lemmon has been conducting his own investigation. He discovers that the X-rays used to check key welds at the plant have been falsified. And then the movie takes off in classic thriller style: The director, James Bridges, uses an exquisite sense of timing and character development to bring us to the cliffhanger conclusion.

The performances are crucial to the movie's success, and they're all the more interesting because the characters aren't painted as anti-nuclear crusaders, but as people who get trapped in a situation while just trying to do their jobs. Fonda is simply superb as the TV reporter; the range and excellence of her performance are a wonder. Douglas is exactly right as the bearded, casually anti-establishment cameraman. And Jack Lemmon, reluctant to rock the boat, compelled to follow his conscience, creates a character as complex as his Oscar-winning businessman in *Save the Tiger*.

Chinatown ★ ★ ★ ★
R, 131 m., 1974
(See also *The Two Jakes*.)

Jack Nicholson (J.J. Gittes), Faye Dunaway (Evelyn Mulwray), John Huston (Noah Cross), Perry Lopez (Escobar), John Hillerman (Yelburton), Darrell Zwerling (Hollis Mulwray), Diane Ladd (Ida Sessions), Roman Polanski (Man with Knife). Directed by Roman Polanski and produced by Robert Evans. Screenplay by Robert Towne.

Roman Polanski's *Chinatown* is not only a great entertainment, but something more, something I would have thought almost impossible: It's a 1940s private-eye movie that doesn't depend on nostalgia or camp for its effect, but works because of the enduring

strength of the genre itself. In some respects, this movie actually could have been made in the 1940s. It accepts its conventions and categories at face value and doesn't make them the object of satire or filter them through a modern sensibility, as Robert Altman did with *The Long Goodbye*. Here's a private-eye movie in which all the traditions, romantic as they may seem, are left intact.

At its center, of course, is the eye himself: J.J. Gittes, moderately prosperous as a result of adultery investigations. He isn't the perenially broke loner like Philip Marlowe, inhabiting a shabby office and buying himself a drink out of the office bottle. He's a successful investigator with a two-man staff, and he dresses well and is civilized and intelligent. He does, however, possess the two indispensable qualities necessary for any traditional private eye. He is deeply cynical about human nature, and he has a personal code and sticks to it.

There is also, of course, the woman, who comes to the private eye for help but does not quite reveal to him the full dimensions of her trouble. And there are the other inevitable ingredients of the well-crafted private-eye plot, as perfected by Raymond Chandler and Dashiell Hammett and practiced by Ross Macdonald. There's the woman's father, and the skeletons in their family closet, and the way that a crime taking place now has a way of leading back to a crime in the past.

These plots work best when they start out seeming impossibly complicated and then end up with watertight logic, and Robert Towne's screenplay for *Chinatown* does that with consummate skill. But the whole movie is a tour de force; it's a period movie, with all the right cars and clothes and props, but we forget that after the first ten minutes. We've become involved in the movie's web of mystery, as we always were with the best private-eye stories, whether written or filmed. We care about these people and want to see what happens to them.

And yet, at the same time, Polanski is so sensitive to the ways in which 1930s' movies in this genre were made that we're almost watching a critical essay. Godard once said that the only way to review a movie is to make another movie, and maybe that's what Polanski has done here. He's made a perceptive, loving comment on a kind of movie and a time in the nation's history that are both long past. *Chinatown* is almost a lesson on how to experience this kind of movie.

It's also a triumph of acting, particularly

by Jack Nicholson, who is one of the most interesting actors now working and who contributes one of his best performances. He inhabits the character of J. J. Gittes like a second skin; the possession is so total that there are scenes in the movie where we almost have telepathy; we *know* what he's thinking, so he doesn't have to tell us. His loyalty is to the woman, but on several occasions, evidence turns up that seems to incriminate her. And then he must pull back, because his code will not admit clients who lie to him. Why he's this way (indeed, even the fact that he's this way) is communicated by Nicholson almost solely in the way he plays the character; dialogue isn't necessary to make the point.

The woman is Faye Dunaway, looking pale and neurotic and beautiful, and justifying for us (if not always for him) J. J.'s trust in her. And then there are all the other characters, who revolve around a complicated scheme to float a bond issue and build a dam to steal water from Los Angeles, in a time of drought. Because the film depends so much on the exquisite unraveling of its plot, it would be unfair to describe much more; one of its delights is in the way that dropped remarks and chance clues gradually build up the portrait of a crime.

And always at the center, there's the Nicholson performance, given an eerie edge by the bandage he wears on his nose after it's slit by a particularly slimy character played by Polanski himself. The bandage looks incongruous, we don't often see a bandaged nose on a movie private eye, but it's the kind of incongruity that's creepy and not funny. The film works similar ground: Drifting within sight of parody every so often, it saves itself by the seriousness of its character.

Chocolat ★ ★ ★ ★
PG-13, 105 m., 1989

Isaach De Bankole (Protee), Giulia Boschi (Aimee Dalens), Francois Cluzet (Marc Dalens), Cecile Ducasse (France Dalens [Child]), Jean-Claude Adelin (Luc Segalen), Kenneth Cranham (Jonathan Boothby). Directed by Claire Denis and produced by Alain Belmondo and Gerard Crosnier. Screenplay by Claire Denis and Jean-Pol Fargeau.

Of all the places I have visited, Africa is the place where the land exudes the greatest sadness and joy. Outside the great cities, the savannah seems ageless, and in the places where man has built his outposts, he seems to huddle in the center of a limitless space.

The land seems smaller at night than during the day. The horizon draws closer, containing strange rustlings and restlessness and the coughs of wild beasts, and voices carry a great distance—much farther than the lights from the verandah.

Chocolat evokes this Africa better than any other film I have ever seen. It knows how quiet the land can be, so that thoughts can almost be heard—and how patient, so that every mistake is paid for sooner or later. The film is set in a French colony in West Africa in the days when colonialism was already doomed but did not yet realize it. At an isolated outpost of the provincial government, a young girl lives with her father and mother and many Africans, including Protee, the houseboy, who embodies such dignity and intelligence that he confers status upon himself in a society that will allow him none.

The story is told partly through the eyes of the young girl, and the film opens in the present, showing her as an adult in 1988, going back to visit her childhood home. But what is most important about the story are the things the young girl could not have known, or could have understood only imperfectly. And the central fact is that Protee is the best man, the most capable man, in the district—and that her mother and Protee feel a strong sexual attraction to one another.

Protee moves through the compound almost silently, always prompt, always courteous, always tactful. He sees everything. His mistress is a French woman in her thirties, attractive, slender, with a few good dresses and the ability to provide a dinner party in West Africa with some of the chic of Paris. She has a workable marriage with her husband, whom she loves after the fashion of a dutiful bourgeois wife. But when the husband goes away on government business, the silence in the compound seems charged with tension; the man and woman who are left in charge become almost painfully aware of each other.

Daily life for the young girl is a little lonely for a child, but she shares secrets with Protee, too, and as she moves around the compound she has glimpses of a vast, unknown reality reaching out in all directions from the little patch of alien French society which has been planted there.

One day there is great excitement. An airplane makes an emergency landing in the district, bearing various visitors who seem exotic in this quiet place. One of them, young and bold, makes an implied proposition to the Frenchwoman. She is not interested, and yet there is a complicated dynamic at work here: She is drawn to Protee, yet cannot have him because of the racist basis of her society. And as is often the case, the master resents the servant, as if prejudice and segregation were the fault of the class that is discriminated against. In a way so subtle that some viewers of the film may miss it, the French woman behaves with the visiting male in such a way as to take revenge on Protee, whom she taunts because she cannot embrace.

Chocolat is a film of infinite delicacy. It is not one of those steamy, melodramatic interracial romances where love conquers all. It is a movie about the rules and conventions of a racist society, and how two intelligent adults, one black, one white, use their mutual sexual attraction as a battleground on which, very subtly, to hurt each other. The woman of course has the power; all of French colonial society stands behind her. But the man has the moral authority, as he demonstrates in the movie's most important scene, which is wordless, brief, and final.

Chocolat is one of those rare films with an entirely mature, adult sensibility; it is made with the complexity and subtlety of a great short story, and it assumes an audience that can understand what a strong flow of sex can exist between two people who barely even touch each other. It is a deliberately beautiful film—many of the frames create breathtaking compositions—but it is not a travelogue and it is not a love story. It is about how racism can prevent two people from looking each other straight in the eyes, and how they punish each other for the pain that causes them.

Choose Me ★ ★ ★ ½
R, 106 m., 1984

Genevieve Bujold (Dr. Love), Keith Carradine (Mickey), Lesley Ann Warren (Eve), Patrick Bauchau (Zack), Rae Dawn Chong (Pearl). Directed by Alan Rudolph and produced by Carolyn Pfeiffer and David Blocker. Screenplay by Rudolph.

Apart from its other qualities, which are many, Alan Rudolph's *Choose Me* is an audaciously intriguing movie. Its main purpose, indeed, may be to intrigue us—as other films aim to thrill or arouse or mystify. There is hardly a moment in the whole film when I knew for sure what was going to happen next, yet I didn't feel manipulated; I felt as if the movie were giving itself the freedom to be completely spontaneous.

The movie begins with strangers talking to each other. One of the strangers is a radio talk show host. Her name is Dr. Love, and she gives advice to the lovelorn over the radio (most of her advice seems to be variations on "That's not my problem"). One of her regular callers, we learn, is a woman named Eve who owns a bar. One day a mental patient named Mickey, a guy whose past seems filled with mysterious connections to the CIA, the space program, and the Russians, walks out of a closed ward and into the bar and meets Eve. A few days later, Dr. Love, hoping to do some research into the ways that we ordinary folk live, adopts an assumed name and goes looking for a roommate. She finds Eve and moves in with her, and neither woman knows who the other woman really is. They also don't make the connection that Eve is a regular caller to the radio program (highly unlikely, since Dr. Love speaks with an accent). None of this is really as hard to follow as it sounds. And since one of the pleasures of this movie is the leisurely and logical way it explores the implications of mistaken identity, I'm not going to write another word about the confusions the characters get involved in.

Choose Me is a deliberate throwback to the *film noir* of the 1940s—to those movies made up of dark streets and wet pavements, hookers under streetlamps, pimps in shiny postwar Studebakers, and people who smoke a lot. It's also about lonely people, but it's not one of those half-witted TV movies about singles bars and single women. It's about smart, complicated people who are trying to clear a space for themselves and using romance as an excavating tool. The performances are key to this strategy. The best thing in the movie is Genevieve Bujold's performance as Dr. Love. She is interesting, if detached, as the radio personality, but when love finally does touch her life, she is so unabashedly open and confessional and red-faced and sincere that we want to hug her. Bujold just gets better and better; coming so soon after her good work in *Tightrope*, this is a reminder of how many different kinds of roles she can play so well.

Keith Carradine is the drifter with the dangerous past. We are never quite sure how seriously to take him, and that's the idea behind his performance, I think: He is able to quite sincerely tell two different women he loves them and wants to marry them, and the funny thing is, we believe him, both times. Eve, the former hooker who owns a bar, is played by Lesley Ann Warren. It's another good performance, nervous and on-edge; she's the kind of woman who seeks a different man every night as a protection against winding up with the same guy for a whole lifetime in a row. There are other intriguing characters in this story, most notably Rae Dawn Chong as a cute young alcoholic with a weird marriage, a naive way of trusting strangers, and dreamy plans of becoming a poet someday. Her husband (Patrick Bauchau) begins to get real tired of seeing the Carradine character, who through a series of misunderstandings seems to specialize in robbing him of poker pots, dates, and the attentions of his wife.

All of these people interact throughout the whole movie without *Choose Me* ever settling into familiar patterns. It's as if Rudolph wanted to tell a story as it might actually have happened, with coincidental meetings, dumb misunderstandings, random chance, and the endless surprises of human nature. At the end of the movie we haven't learned anything in particular, but we have met these people and their loneliness and punch-drunk optimism, and we have followed them a little time through the night.

A Chorus Line ★ ★ ★ ½
PG-13, 117 m., 1985

Michael Blevins (Mark), Yamil Borges (Morales), Sharon Brown (Kim), Gregg Burge (Richie), Michael Douglas (Zack), Cameron English (Paul), Tony Fields (Al), Nicole Fosse (Kristine), Vicki Frederick (Sheila), Jan Gan Boyd (Connie), Michelle Johnston (Bebe), Janet Jones (Judy), Pam Klinger (Maggie), Audrey Landers (Val), Terrence Mann (Larry), Charles McGowan (Mike), Alyson Reed (Cassie), Justin Ross (Greg), Blane Savage (Don), Matt West (Bobby). Directed by Richard Attenborough and produced by Cy Feuer and Ernest Martin. Screenplay by Arnold Schulman.

Show business is the only business that reminds us there is no business like it. And it never tires of that message. If there were as many books about books as there are musicals about musicals, there wouldn't be room on the shelf for books about anything else. *A Chorus Line* is the quintessential backstage musical, a celebration of the lives and hard times of the gypsy dancers who turn up by the hundreds to audition for a handful of jobs on Broadway. It takes years of brutal hard work to become a good enough dancer to dare go to an audition, and then the reward is usually a brusque "thank you" and a sweaty ride home on the subway. In order to succeed as a Broadway dancer, applicants need a limitless capacity to absorb rejection, and *A Chorus Line* celebrates that masochism in song and dance.

A Chorus Line has spent more than a decade on stages all over the world; its story is by now well known. A choreographer is casting eight dancers for a new musical he hopes to stage, and during one long and truthful day he auditions dozens of dancers before he makes his final selection. Richard Attenborough's film treatment of this story sticks to the outlines of the stage version, by and large, although he leaves the stage to fill in the details of the choreographer's old romance, and he leaves out some of the original songs to make room for some new ones.

The result may not please purists who want a film record of what they saw on stage, but this is one of the most intelligent and compelling movie musicals in a long time— and the most grown-up, since it isn't limited, as so many contemporary musicals are, to the celebration of the survival qualities of geriatric actresses.

Most of the scenes take place inside a theater. Zack (Michael Douglas), the choreographer, sits behind a writing platform somewhere out there in the darkness. Occasionally he lights a cigarette, and the ash glows as he takes the measure of the dancers on the stage. He can see them. They can't see him. He communicates by microphone. They step hesitantly to the edge of the stage, blinded by the spotlight, and talk into the void. Well, if that isn't the life they wanted, why did they volunteer for it?

Platoons of dancers are brought on stage, winnowed, dismissed. Finally there are sixteen left, and Zack asks each one of them to talk on a personal level—talk about when they were born, and where, and what their lives have been like, and what their dreams are. Many of the dancers have the most extraordinary difficulties in doing this, and one of them is frank: "Give me the lines, and I can play anybody. Just don't ask me to talk about myself."

Meanwhile, backstage drama is taking shape. An unexpected dancer has appeared for the auditions—Cassie (Alyson Reed), Zack's former girlfriend. They met in the theater, courted in the theater, broke up because Zack's job left no time for a personal life. Cassie was a star, but now she simply needs a job.

The movie opens up the play by going offstage for flashbacks to their affair, but the flashbacks are notable mostly for the way they focus on the theatrical lives of this couple—the way their private lives seem valid only to the degree that they reflect acceptance from the audience. The underlying tension in the movie circles around Zack's eventual decision: Will his heart or his profession make the eventual decision about Cassie? Douglas plays Zack on a staccato, harsh note; this is a workaholic who walks around with a lot of anger. That makes it all the more effective when he occasionally relents and gives one of the dancers a break; softening momentarily before putting his mask on again.

I thought Zack's most revealing moment came when he made the cut from sixteen dancers to eight, reading out eight names and then, when the eight were assembled downstage with smiles on their faces, thanking them and dismissing them; he had chosen the eight he did not name. Was this a misguided attempt to tell the rejected eight that they were also winners? Or was it simply cruelty? We are left to answer for ourselves.

Such questions are intercut with song and dance, with virtuoso solo numbers (my favorite was Charles McGowan's "I Can Do That!") and ensemble production numbers, leading up to a big and splashy finale, in which all of the dancers who originally auditioned are back on stage, together once again.

That leads to my one major difference with Attenborough's approach. Since *A Chorus Line* is a musical about itself, and since the whole hard, bitter, romantic truth of the story is that many are called but few are chosen, the roll call at the end strikes a false note of triumph. Better, perhaps, to have eight dancers on stage, and then cut to the others putting on their street clothes, waiting at bus stops, explaining to friends how they didn't get the job, or going to their dance classes yet again. I think the message of the play is that you don't get called back for a grand finale; you simply go to another audition.

Christiane F. ★ ★ ★ ½
R, 130 m., 1981

Natja Brunkhorst (Christiane), Thomas Haustein (Detlev), Jens Kuphal (Axel), Reiner Wolk (Leiche). Directed by Ulrich Edel and produced by Bernd Eichinger and Hans Weth.

This is one of the most horrifying movies I have ever seen. The fact that it's based on actual events makes it heartbreaking. *Christiane F.* is the portrait of a young girl who between her thirteenth and fifteenth years went from a fairly average childhood into the horrors of drug addiction, prostitution, and life on the brink of death.

The movie has become notorious in Europe, where both the film and book versions of Christiane's adventures have been bestsellers. The real Christiane first came to light as a witness in the trial of a man accused of having sex with minors. A reporter at the trial was intrigued by her appearance on the witness stand and tracked her down. His tape-recorded interviews with her became the basis for a twelve-part series in *Stem*, the German news magazine, which inspired the movie.

It is one of the most unremittingly grim portraits of drug addiction ever filmed. The only American equivalent that comes to mind is Shirley Clarke's *The Connection* (1961), but in that film the hell of heroin addiction was tempered by the story construction of the film, which evolved as a well-told play. *Christiane F.* simply evolves as one lower plateau of suffering after another, until Christiane hits a low bottom.

The movie opens with Christiane as an unexceptional young teen-ager, given to such minor vices as playing rock records too loud and staying out too late. She lives in an apartment with her mother and resents the regular presence of her mother's boyfriend. With friends, she experiments with alcohol and pot, and then, after a rock concert (David Bowie, playing himself), she sniffs some heroin, "just out of curiosity." She likes the feeling it gives her. She tries to get it again. She has young friends who are already junkies, but she disregards their warnings that she'll get hooked. She mindlessly repeats the addict's ageless claim: "I can't get hooked if I just use a little, only once in a while. I can control my using." She cannot. Before long, she's shooting heroin, and not much longer after that she is selling her body to buy it.

This is a common story in the big cities of

the world. It is relatively unusual among girls as young as Christiane (I hope), but even more unusual is the fact that she finds her own way into the heroin-and-hooker underground, without being enslaved by a pimp. The movie is relentless in depicting the drug culture of West Berlin. We see unspeakable sights: a junkie leaping over a toilet stall to yank the needle from Christiane's arm and plunge it into his own, stealing her fix; Christiane and her boyfriend trying to withdraw cold turkey and vomiting all over one another; the discovery of dead overdose victims, and, unforgettably, the pale, sad faces of the junkies lined up in a subway station, all hope gone from their once-young eyes.

Christiane F. made lots of the "best ten" lists of European critics in 1982, but I found it hard to judge its artistic quality because of the shockingly bad dubbing job. The film has been dubbed into mid-Atlantic British, by voices that are often clearly too old and in slang that is ten to fifteen years out of date. New World should ask for its money back from the dubbers. And yet—the movie still works. After a time we forget the bad dubbing, because the images are so powerful, the horrors so strong and the performances (by a cast of young unknowns) so utterly, bleakly, realistic. This is a movie of hell.

Christine ★ ★ ★
R, 110 m., 1983

Keith Gordon (Arnie), John Stockwell (Dennis), Alexandra Paul (Leigh), Robert Prosky (Garage owner), Harry Dean Stanton (Junkins). Directed by John Carpenter and produced by Richard Kobritz. Screenplay by Bill Phillips.

I've seen a lot of movies where the teen-age guy parks in a car with the girl he loves. This is the first one where he parks with a girl in the car he loves. I knew guys like this in high school. They spent their lives customizing their cars. Their girlfriends were accessories who ranked higher, say, than foam-rubber dice, but lower than dual carbs.

The car is named *Christine*. It's a bright red 1958 Plymouth Fury, one of those cars that used to sponsor the "Lawrence Welk Show," with tail fins that were ripped off for the *Jaws* ad campaign. This car should have been recalled, all right—to hell. It kills one guy and maims another before it's off the assembly line. Its original owner comes to a sad end in the front seat. And later, when

Christine is twenty-one years old and rusting away, Arnie buys her. Arnie is a wimp. He's the kind of guy you'd play jokes on during lunch period, telling him the class slut wanted to talk to him, and then hiding his lunch tray while she was telling him to get lost. The kind of guy who was always whining, "Come on, guys—the joke's over!" But after Arnie buys Christine, he undergoes a strange metamorphosis. He becomes cool. He starts looking better. He stops with the greasy kid stuff. He starts going out with the prettiest girl in the school. That's where he makes his mistake. Christine gets jealous.

The entire movie depends on our willingness to believe that a car can have a mind of its own. I have believed in stranger things in the movies. Christine can drive around without a driver, play appropriate 1950s rock songs, lock people inside, and repair its own crushed fenders. The car is another inspiration from Stephen King, the horror novelist who specializes in thrillers about everyday objects. We saw his *Cujo*, about a rabid St. Bernard, and any day now I expect him to announce *Amityville IV: The Garage Door-Opener.*

Christine is, of course, utterly ridiculous. But I enjoyed it anyway. The movies have a love affair with cars, and at some dumb elemental level we enjoy seeing chases and crashes. In fact, under the right circumstances there is nothing quite so exhilarating as seeing a car crushed, and one of the best scenes in *Christine* is the one where the car forces itself into an alley that's too narrow for it.

Christine was directed by John Carpenter, who made *Halloween*, and his method is to take the story more or less seriously. One grin and the mood would be broken. But by the end of the movie, Christine has developed such a formidable personality that we are actually taking sides during its duel with a bulldozer. This is the kind of movie where you walk out with a silly grin, get in your car, and lay rubber halfway down the freeway.

A Christmas Story ★ ★ ★
PG, 94 m., 1983

Melinda Dillon (Mrs. Parker), Darren McGavin (The Old Man), Peter Billingsley (Ralphie). Directed by Bob Clark and produced by Rene Dupont and Clark. Screenplay by Jean Shepherd, Leigh Brown, and Clark.

Of course. That's what I kept saying during

A Christmas Story, every time the movie came up with another one of its memories about growing up in the 1940s. Of course, any nine-year-old kid in the '40s would passionately want, for Christmas, a Daisy Brand Red Ryder repeating BB carbine with a compass mounted in the stock. Of course. And of course, his mother would say, "You'll shoot your eye out." That's what mothers always said about BB guns. I grew up in downstate Illinois. The hero of this film, Ralphie, grew up in Gary, Ind. Looking back over a distance of more than thirty years, the two places seem almost identical—Middle American outposts where you weren't trying to keep up with the neighbors, you were trying to keep up with Norman Rockwell.

The movie is based on a nostalgic comic novel named *In God We Trust, All Others Pay Cash*, by Jean Shepherd, the radio humorist, who also narrates it. He remembers the obvious things, like fights with the bullies at school, and getting into impenetrable discussions with younger kids who do not quite know what all the words mean. He remembers legendary schoolteachers and hiding in the cupboard under the sink and having fantasies of defending the family home with a BB gun.

But he also remembers, warmly and with love, the foibles of parents. The Old Man in *A Christmas Story* is played by Darren McGavin as an enthusiast. Not an enthusiast of anything, just simply an enthusiast. When he wins a prize in a contest, and it turns out to be a table lamp in the shape of a female leg in a garter, he puts it in the window, because it is the most amazing lamp he has ever seen. Of course. I can understand that feeling. I can also understand the feeling of the mother (Melinda Dillon), who is mortified beyond words.

The movie's high point comes at Christmastime, when Ralphie (Peter Billingsley) goes to visit Santa Claus. Visits to Santa Claus are more or less standard in works of this genre, but this movie has the best visit to Santa I've ever seen. Santa is a workaholic, processing kids relentlessly. He has one helper to spin the kid and deposit him on Santa's lap, and another one to grab the kid when the visit is over, and hurl him down a chute to his parents below. If the kid doesn't want to go, he gets Santa's boot in his face. Of course.

Chuck Berry Hail! Hail! Rock 'n' Roll
★ ★ ★ ★
PG, 120 m., 1987

Featuring Chuck Berry, Keith Richards, Eric Clapton, Robert Cray, Etta James, Johnnie Johnson, Julian Lennon, and Linda Ronstadt. Directed by Taylor Hackford and produced by Stephanie Bennett. Music produced by Keith Richards.

I expected *Chuck Berry Hail! Hail! Rock 'n' Roll!* to be a great concert film, and it is. What I did not expect was that it would also be a tantalizing mystery, a study of Chuck Berry that makes him seem as shrouded and enigmatic as Charles Foster Kane. Here is a sixty-year-old man singing *Sweet Little Sixteen*, and he sings it with total conviction, and we have no idea what he means, or ever meant, by it.

The argument of this film is that Chuck Berry was a crucial figure in the development of rock 'n' roll, that fusion of black gospel and rhythm and blues with mainstream pop and teen-age trauma. A good case is made, especially when Eric Clapton and Keith Richards explain precisely which chords and guitar strategies Berry used, and how you can still hear them today. There is a moment in the film when Berry and Richards are rehearsing, and Berry makes Richards do the same passage over and over again until he duplicates an effect that was first heard on records thirty years ago. It still sounds exactly right.

The film is a documentary about the sixtieth birthday concert that Berry performed in his hometown of St. Louis in 1987. The concert was the inspiration of Richards, lead guitarist for The Rolling Stones, who says he wanted to repay Berry for all the things the Stones and other rock groups have stolen from him. The way he wanted to do that was by producing a concert in which Berry would be backed by Richards and—for once—a first-rate, well-rehearsed band.

We quickly learn that this is not the way Berry has been operating in recent years. In testimony from Bruce Springsteen (who once opened for Berry) and in documentary footage of Berry himself, we learn that Berry has reduced his public appearances to an absolute routine. He travels alone, arrives backstage minutes before showtime, requires a local back-up band that knows his hit songs, walks onstage, does his thing, collects his money, and gets out of town.

Money seems to be very important to Berry. He discusses his original decision to become a full-time musician entirely in terms of money; he describes his guitar as "tax-deductible," and he shows off some vintage Cadillacs that he refuses to sell until he gets his price. He never discusses his music with a tenth of the interest he has for his bank account.

And yet the man is a terrific musician, and his songs retain an elemental, driving power that defines rock 'n' roll. There is a lot of concert footage in the film, and the audience I saw it with was rocking in their seats. Although Berry is a tough customer during the rehearsals (at one point, he shouts at Richards, "I been doin' it my way for sixty years"), the concert is a magnificent celebration of Berry's work as a composer and performer.

Berry is all over the stage, doing his famous duck walk, assaulting the microphone, nailing the beat, exuding the kind of forbidden anarchic sexuality that startled the bland teen-agers of the 1950s. He sings, he says, about the things that mattered to kids: school, romance, and cars.

Berry is backed up onstage by a band including Johnnie Johnson, the piano player who led the original trio where Berry got his start. There is some speculation that Johnson may have helped originate Berry's style, but he seems happier in the background, pounding out the beat. Richards oversees the band and plays lead guitar to Berry's rough rhythm, and there are several guest artists including Clapton, Julian Lennon, Robert Cray, Linda Ronstadt, and, stealing the show, Etta James.

It's one hell of a concert, a joyous celebration of the music, yet always lurking just offstage is the sense of Berry's obsessive privacy about his personal life. One of the movie's quietest moments is unforgettable. We see Berry's wife on camera. She introduces herself. She is asked a question. We hear Berry's voice from off camera: "OK, that's enough." The screen goes black, and we never see her again. Behind the man who helped create a music that let it all hang out, there is another man who plays it all very close to the vest.

Cinderella ★ ★ ★
G, 74 m., 1950

Voices by Ilene Woods, Eleanor Audley, Verna Felton, Claire Dubrey, Helene Stanley, Luis Van Rooten, Don Barclay, Rhoda Williams, and James MacDonald. Directed by Wilfred Jackson, Hamilton Luske, and Clyde Geronimi. Directing animators: Eric Larson, Milt Kahl, Frank Thomas, John Lounsbery, Wolfgang Reitherman, Ward Kimball, Ollie Johnston, Marc Davis, Les Clark, and Norm Ferguson.

Walt Disney's *Cinderella* is considered by the studio to be a perennial that blooms every seven years or so, just in time for a new generation of kids. It has been several generations since I saw it as a kid, although when I saw it again recently, it was clear that it hadn't changed that much in thirty-eight years, and neither, in certain ways, had I.

This time around I was more aware of the power of the full-animation techniques, and I appreciated Disney's policy of using unfamiliar voices for the dubbing, instead of the studio's guess-that-voice derbies of recent years. But in other ways the movie still worked for me just as it had the first time. When those little mice bust a gut trying to drag that key up hundreds of stairs in order to free Cinderella, I don't care how many Kubrick pictures you've seen, it's still exciting.

You doubtless remember the original story. You may not—as I did not—remember how much the Disney studio expanded and supplemented it. Disney's most valuable and original contribution to the *Cinderella* tale was the addition of dozens of animals to the story. The screen fairly bursts with little birds helping Cinderella to dress, little mice helping her to plot, a dog to leap to the rescue, and an evil cat named Lucifer to chase the birds, pounce on the mice, spit at the dog, and do its best to come between Cinderella and Prince Charming.

These animals serve very much the same function as the Seven Dwarfs (and assorted birds and forest animals) did in *Snow White*. They provide a chorus, moral support, additional characters to flesh out a thin story, and a kaleidoscope of movement on the screen. When one of the little birds creeps under Cinderella's pillow to awaken her in the morning, it doesn't matter that I was aware of the shameless manipulation of the animators; I grinned anyway.

Using the traditional techniques of full animation, the Disney artists provided each animal with a unique flavor and personality. What they also did (as Richard Schickel observed in *The Disney Version*) was shamelessly wag the buttocks of all the animals as

a way of making them seem even livelier; a Disney quadruped has its center of gravity somewhere below its navel and its pivot point right beneath the wallet. With all that action going on, no wonder they never wore pants.

If there is an obvious difference between *Cinderella* and such predecessors as *Pinocchio* and *Snow White*, it's in the general smoothing-out of the central characters' appearances. Snow White herself looked fairly bland, but the other characters in the first decade of Disney animation had a lot of personality in their faces. They were allowed to look odd. *Cinderella* seems to come right out of its time, the bland postwar 1950s. Cinderella looks like the Draw Me girl, Prince Charming has all of the charm of a department-store dummy, and even the wicked stepsisters seem petulant rather than evil. Only the old king, his aide, and a few of the mice look bright enough to split a ticket.

Yet the movie works. There are dozens of little dramas played out for a minute or two by the mice, who must outsmart the cat and alert the dog. There are touching moments involving the king, who wants an heir more than anything, and looks on glumly as his son rejects all the women in the kingdom—except for one. And then there is that thrilling montage at the end, while the stepsisters desperately try to get the glass slipper to fit, while the mice sneak the key to Cinderella. You've got to hand it to her: The kid still has life. Another seven years, anyway.

Cinema Paradiso ★ ★ ★ ½
NO MPAA RATING, 123 m., 1989

Philippe Noiret (Alfredo), Jacques Perrin (Salvatore), Salvatore Cascio (Salvatore as a child), Marco Leonardi (Salvatore as an adolescent), Agnese Nano (Elena), Antonella Attili (young Maria), Isa Danielli (Anna), Pupella Maggio (old Maria), Leopoldo Trieste (Father Adelfio). Directed by Giuseppe Tornatore and produced by Franco Cristaldi. Screenplay by Tornatore.

There is a village priest in *Cinema Paradiso* who is the local cinema's most faithful client. He turns up every week, like clockwork, to censor the films. As the old projectionist shows the movies to his audience of one, the priest sits with his hand poised over a bell, the kind altar boys use. At every sign of carnal excess—which to the priest means a kiss—the bell rings, the movie stops, and the projectionist snips the offending footage out of the film. Up in the projection booth, tossed in a corner, the lifeless strips of celluloid pile up into an anthology of osculation, an anthology that no one will ever see, not in this village, anyway.

Giuseppe Tornatore's *Cinema Paradiso*, which won the Oscar for best foreign language film, takes place in Sicily in the final years before television. It has two chief characters: old Alfredo (Philippe Noiret), who rules the projection booth, and young Salvatore (Salvatore Cascio), who makes the booth his home away from an indifferent home. As the patrons line up faithfully, night after night, for their diet of films without kisses, the boy watches in wonder as Alfredo wrestles with the balky machine that throws the dream images on the screen. At first Alfredo tries to chase Salvatore away, but eventually he accepts his presence in the booth and thinks of him almost as his child. Salvatore certainly considers the old man his father and (this is the whole point) the movies his mother.

I wonder if a theater has ever existed that showed such a variety of films as the Cinema Paradiso does in this movie. Giuseppe Tornatore tells us in an autobiographical note that the theater in his hometown, when he was growing up, showed everything from Kurosawa to the Hercules movies, and in *Cinema Paradiso*, we catch glimpses of Charlie Chaplin, John Wayne, and, of course, countless Hollywood melodramas in which men and women look smolderingly at one another, come closer, seem about to kiss, and then (with the jerk of a jump cut) are standing apart, exchanging a look of deep significance.

We become familiar with some of the regular customers at the theater. They are a noisy lot—rude critics, who shout suggestions at the screen and are scornful of heroes who do not take their advice. Romances are launched in the darkness of the theater, friendships are sealed, wine is drunk, cigarettes smoked, babies nursed, feet stomped, victories cheered, sissies whistled at, and God only knows how this crowd would react if they were ever permitted to see a kiss.

The story is told as a flashback; it begins with a prominent film director (Jacques Perrin) learning in Rome that old Alfredo is dead and making a sentimental journey back to his hometown. Then we see the story of the director's childhood (he is portrayed by Cascio) and his teen-age years, where he is played by Marco Leonardi. The earliest parts of the movie are the most magical.

Then things grow predictable: There are not many rites of passage for an adolescent male that are not predictable, and not many original ways to show the death of a movie theater, either.

Tornatore's movie is a reminder of the scenes in Truffaut's *Day for Night*, where the young boy steals a poster of *Citizen Kane*. We understand that the power of the screen can compensate for a deprived life, and that young Salvatore is not apprenticing himself to a projectionist, but to the movies. Once that idea has been established, the film begins to reach for its effects, and there is one scene in particular—a fire in the booth—that has the scent of desperation about it, as if Tornatore despaired of his real story and turned to melodrama.

Yet anyone who loves movies is likely to love *Cinema Paradiso*, and there is one scene where the projectionist finds that he can reflect the movie out of the window in his booth and out across the town square, so that the images can float on a wall, there in the night above the heads of the people. I saw a similar thing happen one night in Venice in 1972 when they showed Chaplin's *City Lights* in the Piazza San Marco to more than ten thousand people, and it was then I realized the same thing this movie argues: Yes, it is tragic that the big screen has been replaced by the little one. But the real shame is that the big screens did not grow even bigger, grow so vast they were finally on the same scale as the movies they were reflecting.

City Slickers ★ ★ ★ ½
PG-13, 108 m., 1991

Billy Crystal (Mitch Robbins), Daniel Stern (Phil Berquist), Bruno Kirby (Ed Furillo), Patricia Wettig (Barbara Robbins), Helen Slater (Bonnie Rayburn), Jack Palance (Curly). Directed by Ron Underwood and produced by Irby Smith. Screenplay by Lowell Ganz and Babaloo Mandel.

City Slickers comes packaged as one kind of movie—a slapstick comedy about white-collar guys on a dude ranch—and it delivers on that level while surprising me by being much more ambitious, and successful, than I expected. This is the proverbial comedy with the heart of truth, the tear in the eye along with the belly laugh. It's funny, and it adds up to something.

The movie opens with three professional guys mired in their discontent. Billy Crystal plays Mitch, who sells time for a radio station, and is happy, more or less, although his wife tells him he has lost his smile. Daniel Stern labors for his father-in-law's supermarket, and is married to a woman so insufferable that he has developed psychosomatic narcolepsy as a form of dealing with her. Bruno Kirby, the third pal, is obsessed with the passage of time and proves himself by pursuing young women and egging his pals on to harebrained vacation ideas.

It's his notion that this year they should try a dude ranch—but a "real one," where along with other city slickers they'll be cowboys for a couple of weeks, and move a real herd of real cattle across real plains to Colorado, also real. The setup of the movie—the three buddies and their various forms of misery—is funny, but the dude ranch possesses a certain mythic quality, reinforced by the theme from *The Magnificent Seven*, which plays under the Western action, sometimes ironically, sometimes even heroically.

The city slickers are choosing, half ironically, to follow in the footsteps of the great movie cattle rides of the past. They're fans of *Red River*, the John Wayne classic where the Duke shouts "Move 'em out!" and the cowboys are seen in a montage, waving their hats and shouting with glee. The herd at this dude ranch exists solely for the purpose of being moved back and forth by tenderfoots, but the trail boss does indeed seem like a survivor from an earlier time. He's Curly (Jack Palance), with a cigarette permanently pasted into his mug.

The plot unfolds along fairly predictable lines. The three city dudes meet up with their fellow urban cowboys, including two black Baltimore dentists and a good-looking blonde who has been abandoned by her boyfriend. They ride out one morning at dawn, saddle sore but plucky, and along the way there are the obligatory showdowns with macho professional cowboys, stubborn cattle, and nature.

What brings these scenes to life is the quality of the dialogue, by Lowell Ganz and Babaloo Mandel (*Parenthood*), with additional lines that sound a lot like Crystal. There are moments of insight, of secrets sincerely shared, of the kind of philosophical speculation that's encouraged by life on the range. (What do guys talk about when they're on a cattle drive to Colorado? How to program the VCR, of course.)

Ron Underwood's direction is professional and focused; all of the subplots, like

Crystal's love for a baby calf he helps deliver, pay off at the end. There is also the kind of crazy heroism that can be indulged in only by guys who don't understand the real dangers they're in, and the dreamy nights around the campfire when they stand back and look at their lives, their marriages, and the meaning of it all.

City Slickers is like *Parenthood* in the way it deals with everyday issues of living in an unforced way that doesn't get in the way of the humor, and yet sets the movie up for a genuine emotional payoff at the end. And the male bonding among Crystal, Stern, and Kirby is unforced and convincing. There are so many ways this movie could have gone wrong—with gratuitous action scenes, forced dialogue, or contrived showdowns—that it's sort of astonishing, how many ways it finds to go right.

Claire's Knee ★ ★ ★ ★
PG, 103 m., 1971

Jean-Claude Brialy (Jerome), Aurora Cornu (Aurora), Beatrice Romand (Laura), Laurence de Monaghan (Claire). Directed by Eric Rohmer and produced by Pierre Cottrell. Screenplay by Rohmer.

Now if I were to say, for example, that *Claire's Knee* is about Jerome's desire to caress the knee of Claire, you would be about a million miles from the heart of this extraordinary film. And yet, in a way, *Claire's Knee* is indeed about Jerome's feelings for Claire's knee, which is a splendid knee.

Jerome encounters Claire and the other characters in the film during a month's holiday he takes on a lake between France and Switzerland. He has gone there to rest and reflect before he marries Lucinda, a woman he has loved for five years. And who should he run into but Aurora, a novelist who he's also been a little in love with for a long time.

Aurora is staying with a summer family that has two daughters: Laura, who is sixteen and very wise and falls in love with Jerome, and Claire, who is beautiful and blonde and full of figure and spirit. Jerome and Aurora enter into a teasing intellectual game, which requires Jerome to describe to Aurora whatever happens to him during his holiday. When they all become aware that Laura has fallen in love with the older man, Jerome encourages her in a friendly, platonic way. They have talks about love and the nature of life, and they grow very fond of

each other, although of course the man does not take advantage of the young girl.

But then Claire joins the group, and one day while they are picking cherries, Jerome turns his head and finds that Claire has climbed a ladder and he is looking directly at her knee. Claire herself, observed playing volleyball or running, hand-in-hand, with her boyfriend, is a sleek animal, and Jerome finds himself stirring with desire.

He doesn't want to run away with Claire, or seduce her, or anything like that; he plans to marry Lucinda. But he tells his friend Aurora that he has become fascinated by Claire's knee; that it might be the point through which she could be approached, just as another girl might respond to a caress on the neck, or the cheek, or the arm. He becomes obsessed with desire to test this theory, and one day has an opportunity to touch the knee at last.

As with all the films of Eric Rohmer, *Claire's Knee* exists at levels far removed from plot (as you might have guessed while I was describing the plot). What is really happening in this movie happens on the level of character, of thought, of the way people approach each other and then shy away. In some movies, people murder each other and the contact is casual; in a work by Eric Rohmer, small attitudes and gestures can summon up a university of humanity.

Rohmer has an uncanny ability to make his actors seem as if they were going through the experiences they portray. The acting of Beatrice Romand, as sixteen-year-old Laura, is especially good in this respect; she isn't as pretty as her sister, but we feel somehow she'll find more enjoyment in life because she is a . . . well, a better person underneath. Jean-Claude Brialy is excellent in a difficult role. He has to relate with three women in the movie, and yet remain implicitly faithful to the unseen Lucinda. He does, and since the sexuality in his performance is suppressed, it is, of course, all the more sensuous. *Claire's Knee* is a movie for people who still read good novels, care about good films, and think occasionally.

Clash of the Titans ★ ★ ★ ½
PG, 118 m., 1981

Harry Hamlin (Perseus), Judi Bowker (Andromeda), Burgess Meredith (Ammon), Laurence Olivier (Zeus), Maggie Smith (Thetis), Neil McCarthy (Calibos). Directed by Desmond Davis and produced by Charles H. Schneer and Ray Harryhausen, with special effects created by Harryhausen.

Clash of the Titans is a grand and glorious romantic adventure, filled with grave heroes, beautiful heroines, fearsome monsters, and awe-inspiring duels to the death. It is a lot of fun. It was quite possibly intended as a sort of Greek mythological retread of *Star Wars* (it has a wise little mechanical owl in it who's a third cousin of R2-D2), but it's also part of an older Hollywood tradition of special-effects fantasies, and its visual wonderments are astonishing.

The story, on the other hand, is robust and straightforward. Perseus (Harry Hamlin) is locked into a coffin with his mother and cast into the sea, after she has angered the gods. But Zeus (Laurence Olivier) takes pity and sees that the coffin washes ashore on a deserted island, where Perseus grows to manhood and learns of his mission in life. The mission, in a nutshell, is to return to Joppa and rescue Andromeda (Judi Bowker) from a fate worse than death: marriage to the hideously ugly Calibos, who was promised her hand in marriage before he was turned into a monster by the wrath of the gods. Calibos lives in a swamp and dispatches a gigantic, scrawny bird every night to fetch him the spirit of the sleeping Andromeda in a gilded cage. If Perseus is to marry Andromeda, he must defeat Calibos in combat and also answer a riddle posed by Cassiopeia, Andromeda's mother. Those who answer the riddle incorrectly are condemned to die. Love was more complicated in the old days.

There are, of course, other tests. To follow the bird back to the lair of Calibos, the resourceful Perseus must capture and tame Pegasus, the last of the great winged horses. He must also enter the lair of Medusa, who turns men to stone with one glance, and behead her so that he can use her dead eyes to petrify the gargantuan monster Kraken, who is unchained from his cage on the ocean floor so that he can ravish Joppa in general and Andromeda in particular.

All of this is gloriously silly. But because the movie respects its material, it even succeeds in halfway selling us this story; movies that look like *Clash of the Titans* have a tendency to seem ridiculous, but this film has the courage of its convictions. It is also blessed with a cast that somehow finds its way past all the monsters and through all the heroic dialogue and gets us involved in the characters. Harry Hamlin is a completely satisfactory Perseus, handsome and solemn and charged with his own mission. Judi Bowker is a beautiful princess and a great screamer, especially in the scene where she's chained to the rock and Kraken is slobbering all over her. Burgess Meredith has a nice little supporting role as Ammon, an old playwright who thinks he may be able to turn all of this into a quick epic. And Laurence Olivier is just as I have always imagined Zeus: petulant, but a pushover for a pretty face.

The real star of the movie, however, is Ray Harryhausen, who has worked more than forty years as a creator of special effects. He uses combinations of animation, miniatures, optical tricks, and multiple images to put humans into the same movie frames as the most fantastical creatures of legend, and more often than not, they look pretty convincing: when Perseus tames Pegasus, it sure looks like he's dealing with a real horse (except for the wings, of course).

Harryhausen's credits include *Mighty Joe Young, Jason and the Argonauts*, and *The Golden Voyage of Sinbad*, but *Clash of the Titans* is his masterwork. Among his inspired set-pieces: the battle in the Medusa's lair, with her hair writhing with snakes; the flying-horse scenes; the gigantic prehistoric bird; the two-headed wolf-dog, Dioskilos; the Stygian witches; and, of course, Kraken, who rears up from the sea and causes tidal waves that do a lot of very convincing damage to a Greek city that exists only in Harryhausen's art. The most lovable special-effects creation in the movie is little Bubo, a golden owl sent by the gods to help Perseus in his trials. Bubo whistles and rotates his head something like R2-D2 in *Star Wars*, and he has a similar personality, too, especially at the hilarious moment when he enters the film for the first time.

Clash of the Titans is a family film (there's nothing in it that would disturb any but the most impressionable children), and yet it's not by any means innocuous: It's got blood and thunder and lots of gory details, all presented with enormous gusto and style. It has faith in a story-telling tradition that sometimes seems almost forgotten, a tradition depending upon legends and myths, magical swords, enchanted shields, invisibility helmets, and the overwhelming power of a kiss.

Class Action ★ ★ ★
R, 110 m., 1991

Gene Hackman (Jedediah Tucker Ward), Mary Elizabeth Mastrantonio (Maggie Ward), Colin Friels (Michael Grazier), Joanna Merlin (Estelle Ward), Larry Fishburne (Nick Holbrook), Donald Moffat (Quinn), Jan Rubes (Dr. Pavel). Directed by Michael Apted and produced by Ted Field, Scott Kroopf, and Robert W. Cort. Screenplay by Carolyn Shelby, Christopher Ames, and Samantha Shad.

It's a strange thing about the coming attractions trailers they show before a movie comes out. Most of them promise more than the movie delivers. Michael Apted's *Class Action* is an exception; the trailer seems to promise a formula plot—a father and his daughter, both lawyers, are on opposing sides in court, trading legal arguments and clichés. The movie is indeed about the father and the daughter, but in ways we didn't anticipate, with surprising intelligence and empathy.

The movie stars Gene Hackman as an aging radical who shaped his politics in the 1950s (he proposed to his wife after spotting her mouthing "McCarthy is a weasel" in the gallery of the Army-McCarthy hearings). He specializes in defending underdogs and attacking the establishment. His daughter, played by Mary Elizabeth Mastrantonio, is a child of more materialist decades, and wants to become a partner in a big corporate law firm. Father and daughter find themselves on opposing sides in a case involving a giant automaker whose 1985 wagons have an unfortunate tendency to explode.

If that were all there was to the screenplay, *Class Action* would no doubt march down familiar corridors worn smooth by countless other movies about the law. But this is a very particular movie, where the details about the lawsuit are secondary to an ethical struggle that takes place between father and daughter. He believes she has sold out to heartless big business. She believes he is a showboating hypocrite who stuck up for the little guy, all right, but mostly for self-aggrandizement, while he was cheating on her mother and discarding former clients who needed him.

Both of them are right, and both of them are flawed, and the movie is about the inexact process by which both characters are able to forgive and change. That's what's interesting about it—that, and the surprising power of the performances, not only from the leads

but also from Joanna Merlin as Hackman's wife, who long ago made her accommodation with his faults; Donald Moffat, as the taciturn, utterly pragmatic head of the giant law firm; Jan Rubes as an aging engineer who is sure he remembers all the important things; and Colin Friels as a corporate lawyer who is both Mastrantonio's supervisor and her lover. Hackman is wonderful (one is tempted to add "of course"). But Mastrantonio is really at the center of the film and supports it with fierce energy. She has quiet authority and projects both her character's strong self-image and deepest resentments; this is a grown-up portrait of a woman still growing up.

The screenplay by Carolyn Shelby, Christopher Ames, and Samantha Shad contains dialogue scenes so well-heard and written it's hard to believe this is a Hollywood movie, with Hollywood's tendency to have characters underline every emotion so the audience won't have to listen so carefully. There's a scene, for example, where father and daughter are preparing dinner together, and their civility gradually collapses into anger and tearful recrimination. And other scenes, deliberately of few words, in which lawyers try to say things without saying them—to imply what must be done without being trapped into actually issuing unethical orders.

The details involving the exploding gas tanks are, in a way, the least important parts of the film, although they're sure to gladden Ralph Nader. What I liked best was the way the whole legal case and all of its twists and turns were used to force the Hackman and Mastrantonio characters into learning things about themselves. Apted is a director whose films have often been about people in a process of self-discovery (his credits include *Coal Miner's Daughter, Continental Divide, Gorillas in the Mist*, and the great continuing documentary *28 Up*), and that's what this film is really about, and why it's so much more interesting than the ads might have you believe.

The Class of 1984 ★ ★ ★ ½
R, 93 m., 1982

Perry King (Andy Norris), Timothy Van Patten (Stegman), Roddy McDowall (Terry Corrigan). Directed by Mark Lester and produced by Lester and Merrie Lynn Ross. Screenplay by Lester, John Saxton, and Tom Holland.

Movies like this either grab you, or they

don't. *The Class of 1984* grabbed me. I saw it for the first time at the 1982 Cannes Film Festival, where I wandered into the theater expecting to find the dog of the week and wandered out two hours later, a little dazed and sort of overwhelmed. *The Class of 1984* is not a great movie but it works with quiet, strong efficiency to achieve more or less what we expect from a movie with such a title. It is violent, funny, scary, contains boldly outlined characters, and gets us involved. It also has a lot of style. One of the reasons for the film's style may be that it was made by people who knew what they were doing. The whole Dead Teen-ager genre has been seriously weakened in the last several years by wave upon wave of cheap, idiotic tax-shelter films from Canada and elsewhere: films in which a Mad Slasher and a lot of screaming adolescents have been substituted for talent, skill, and craft—movies such as *Prom Night* and *Terror Train* and *The Burning*.

Mark Lester's *The Class of 1984* stands head and shoulders above movies like that. It tells a strong, simple story. It is acted well. It is not afraid to be comic at times and, even better, it's not afraid at the end to pull out all the stops and give us the sort of Grand Guignol conclusion that the slasher movies always botch. You may or may not think it's any good, but you'll have to admit that it works.

The movie stars Perry King, a skilled actor who has survived a lot of junk, as a music teacher who takes a job at a big city high school. The first day he walks into class, he faces trouble, and trouble is personified by Stegman (Timothy Van Patten), the brilliant but crazed leader of the high school gang. Stegman dresses as a cross between a punk rocker and a Hell's Angel. He terrorizes half the school with his violence and mesmerizes the other half with his charisma. He also happens to be a brilliant musician. King tries to deal with him, reason with him, outthink him, and even outmuscle him, but the kid is strong, smart, and mean. The other teachers and the school officials have mostly surrendered to the reign of terror. A few put up a fight, most memorably the biology teacher, played by Roddy McDowall. He has one of the great scenes in the movie as he pulls a gun on his class and invites them to share with him the joys of education, or else.

The movie builds toward one of those nightmarish conclusions where everything's happening at once. While the teacher prepares to lead his school orchestra in a concert, the thugs terrorize his helpless wife at home. The teacher turns the baton over to his best student, a shy young girl, and goes off to do battle with the punks. After a great deal of blood has been shed, the teacher and the gang leader are finally face to face, high in the wings over the high school auditorium stage, and the climax is a cross between *The Hunchback of Notre Dame* and *Beyond the Valley of the Dolls*.

The Class of 1984 has received some really savage criticism. Newsweek called it "*The Class of 1982* with herpes." What does that mean? I dunno. I guess it means the critic found the movie so hateful that it wasn't worth anything more than cheap wisecracks. But unless we can accept talent wherever we find it in the movies, and especially in smaller genre movies without big stars, we're going to be left with nothing but overpriced lead balloons and delicate little exercises in sensibility. *The Class of 1984* is raw, offensive, vulgar, and violent, but it contains the sparks of talent and wit, and it is acted and directed by people who cared to make it special.

Class of 1999 ★ ★
R, 98 m., 1990

Bradley Gregg (Cody Culp), Tracy Lin (Christie Langford), Malcolm McDowell (Dr. Miles Langford), Stacy Keach (Dr. Bob Forrest), Patrick Kilpatrick (Mr. Bryles), Pam Grier (Ms. Connors), John P. Ryan (Mr. Hardin), Darren E. Burrows (Sonny), Joshua Miller (Angel). Directed and produced by Mark L. Lester. Screenplay by C. Courtney Joyer.

The year is 1999. In the major American cities, gangs have taken control of the high schools and rule the neighborhoods around them with a reign of terror. Police no longer venture into these areas, which have been designated "Free Fire Zones."

It is clearly time for something like the Department of Educational Defense, which is run by Stacy Keach, wearing a white hairpiece with blank eyeballs to match. The DED, as it is inevitably acronymed, has purchased war-surplus androids to teach in the schools. They are robots who look like humans but have torch guns and rocket launchers concealed in their arms: just the thing to restore order in the classroom.

There are all sorts of ironic possibilities for social commentary here, and some of them are realized. But the strength of *Class of 1999* is in special effects and violence.

There are long stretches here where we're looking at virtuoso filmmaking on a technical level, but the story never matches up. We're amazed, we're impressed, but at the level of the characters we simply don't care.

The movie was produced and directed by Mark L. Lester, whose 1982 film *The Class of 1984*, starring Perry King, was one of the best action-genre movies of recent years. It told a strong story, with characters we got to know and conflicts we could understand. *Class of 1999* dissipates into a fantasy world of youth gangs and large collections of unidentified stuntmen who crash through windows on their motorcycles but serve no other particular purpose.

The film's hero is Cody (Bradley Gregg), a high-school student who has been released from prison and wants to go straight, if the rival gangs will let him. Back in school, he and his classmates are confronted by three androids who have been hired as teachers and law-enforcers. They're played by Patrick Kilpatrick, Pam Grier, and John P. Ryan (Grier's character is named "Ms. Connors"; apparently by 1999 even androids object to Miss and Mrs.). The trouble is, the androids get out of line and start shooting rockets through the school. Cody thinks capital punishment is a little stiff for crimes like talking in class, and the movie ends in an apocalyptic confrontation between the androids and the youth gangs, who have settled their differences and banded together for the occasion.

The closing scenes are incredibly violent (how does a movie like this get an R rating when *The Cook, the Thief, His Wife and Her Lover* doesn't?). But they are well-done, especially the sequences involving the androids. Sometimes we're looking at the actors, sometimes at robots constructed by Eric Allard (who made the robot in *Short Circuit*) and makeup wizard Rick Stratton (*Fright Night*).

So much work went into this film, indeed, that it's strange how little lasting effect it has. The fault may be with the screenplay by C. Courtney Joyer, which seldom pauses to make any of the characters believable. They're simply pawns pushed around for the convenience of the special effects. Bad guys become good guys on a moment's notice, motivation is nonexistent, and (in a real difference from *The Class of 1984*) the school itself never seems remotely real. This is a superior exercise in action and violence, but not much more.

Clean and Sober ★ ★ ★ ½
R, 124 m., 1988

Michael Keaton (Daryl Poynter), Kathy Baker (Charlie Standers), Morgan Freeman (Craig), M. Emmet Walsh (Richard Dirks), Tate Donovan (Donald Towle), Henry Judd Baker (Xavier), Claudia Christian (Iris), J. David Krassner (Miller), Dakin Matthews (Bob), Mary Catherine Martin (Cheryl Ann), Pat Quinn (June). Directed by Glenn Gordon Caron and produced by Tony Ganz and Deborah Blum. Written by Tod Carroll.

It's the kind of thing that could happen to anybody. Just plain rotten luck, really. He picks up a girl in a bar, and they do some cocaine together, and the next morning when he wakes up, she's dead. She had a heart attack or something. How was it his fault? What happens to the hero of *Clean and Sober* during the next several weeks of his life is that he decides that although it could have happened to anyone, he doesn't want it to happen to himself anymore.

The guy is named Daryl Poynter, and he is played by Michael Keaton with a kind of wound-up, edgy tension that is just right for the character. He's a hotshot Philadelphia real estate salesman, but by the time the movie opens there is nothing in his life of any importance, really, but cocaine. He doesn't even question the fact. It's not that he needs cocaine to function—because he doesn't function, really, he just goes through the motions—but that he needs cocaine to still himself from the savage, restless angers of his need for the drug.

It doesn't go over very well that the girl woke up dead in his bed. The police are interested. Even though it was her "fault" ("I didn't give her cocaine; she gave me cocaine," he argues), the girl's father plasters his neighborhood with posters branding him as a murderer. At work, things are not too good, either, because he has borrowed $92,000 from an escrow account and invested it in the market, hoping to make a lot of money. He has lost most of the money, instead.

So he needs a place to hide out, and when he hears on the radio about a confidential, anonymous drug rehabilitation program, he figures that might be a good place to disappear into. What he doesn't count on is that the program is run by a hard-headed counselor (Morgan Freeman) who has heard everybody's story before, and sees right through him.

Clean and Sober is the story of how the Keaton character is forced to look at the fact that his life is wildly out of control, and that cocaine addiction is the cause, not the solution. He fights this discovery every step of the way, and is far from being a model client in the rehab center. He steals phone calls to ask friends to send him cocaine in overnight Federal Express packages; he slips out of the center on wild, undefined missions; and, of course, he thinks he's God's gift to women—especially to one of his cute fellow patients.

She's played by Kathy Baker, as a woman who has two addictions, one to booze, the other to the man she lives with, who beats her and then comes whining to her for forgiveness, telling her he's nothing without her. Her self-esteem has been so seriously wounded by her alcoholism that she clings to this relationship, perhaps believing that this loser is the only man who will accept her.

In his first few days in the center, Keaton finds himself at war with Morgan Freeman, the counselor. This is because Freeman has met so many, many others just like him, and knows the alibis and evasions, and knows that unless this guy gets serious, he is going to go right back out and get screwed up again. The relationships between the counselor and the patients are at the heart of the central portion of the movie, which also shows Keaton going to an Alcoholics Anonymous meeting and trying, on Freeman's orders, to get himself a "sponsor"—a veteran AA member who will advise and help him. Of course, Keaton goes for the prettiest woman at the meeting, but eventually he winds up with wise, lethargic M. Emmet Walsh, who looks at him quizzically because he knows what a lost cause he could easily be.

Clean and Sober is not the story of an ideal recovery from drug or alcohol addiction, because Keaton is not an ideal candidate for recovery. He tells too many lies, especially to himself, and he doesn't much like to accept advice. He is still somewhat seduced by the notion that he can do some repairs on his old lifestyle and it will still work. But by the end of the movie there is some hope that he may be able to get straight.

The subject matter of this film is commonplace in our society—for every celebrity who checks into the Betty Ford Center, there are thousands of ordinary people who check in somewhere else, or who pick up the phone and call AA. Everybody knows somebody like this. But the actual process of surrender and recovery is hardly ever the subject of

films, maybe because it seems too depressing. One of the strengths Michael Keaton brings to *Clean and Sober* is his wild, tumultuous energy, which makes his character seem less a victim than an accident causing itself to happen. Surrounded by superb supporting performances—especially by Kathy Baker, who also costarred with Morgan Freeman as the prostitute in *Street Smart*—Keaton makes this general story into a particular one, and a touching one.

Close Encounters of the Third Kind: The Special Edition ★ ★ ★ ★
PG, 152 m., 1980

Richard Dreyfuss (Roy Neary), Francois Truffaut (Claude Lacombe), Teri Garr (Ronnie Neary), Melinda Dillon (Jillian Guiler). Directed and written by Steven Spielberg and produced by Julia Phillips and Michael Phillips.

Close Encounters of the Third Kind: The Special Edition is the movie Steven Spielberg wanted to make in the first place. The changes Spielberg has made in his original 1978 film are basic and extensive, adding up to essentially a new moviegoing experience. Spielberg's changes fall into four categories:

• He's provided an entirely new conclusion, taking us inside the alien spaceship that visits at the end of the film.

• He's provided more motivation for the strange behavior of the Richard Dreyfuss character—who is compelled by "psychic implanting" to visit the Wyoming mountain where the spaceship plans to land.

• He's added additional manifestations of UFO intervention in earthly affairs—including an ocean-going freighter deposited in the middle of the Gobi Desert.

• In addition to the sensational ending, he's added more special effects throughout the film. One shot seems like a lighthearted quote from Spielberg's own *Jaws*. In that film, a high-angle shot showed the shadow of the giant shark passing under a boat. In this one, a high-angle shot shows the shadow of a giant UFO passing over a pickup truck.

Spielberg's decision to revise the original version of *Close Encounters* is all but unprecedented. Some directors have remade their earlier films (Hitchcock did British and American versions of *The Man Who Knew Too Much*), and others have thought out loud about changes they'd like to make (Robert Altman wanted to edit a nine-hour version of

Nashville for TV). And countless directors, of course, have given us sequels—"part two" of their original hits.

Spielberg's *Special Edition* is sort of a *Close Encounters: Part 1½*. It is also a very good film. I thought the original film was an astonishing achievement, capturing the feeling of awe and wonder we have when considering the likelihood of life beyond the Earth. I gave that first version a four-star rating. This new version gets another four stars: It is, quite simply, a better film—so much better that it might inspire the uncharitable question, "Why didn't Spielberg make it this good the *first* time?"

His changes fall into three categories. He has (1) thrown away scenes that didn't work, like the silly sequence in which Dreyfuss dug up half of his yard in an attempt to build a model of the mountain in his vision; (2) put in scenes he shot three years ago but did not use, such as the Gobi sequence and Dreyfuss flipping out over the strange compulsion that has overtaken him, and (3) shot some entirely new scenes.

The most spectacular of these is the new ending, which shows us what Dreyfuss sees when he enters the spacecraft. He sees a sort of extraterrestrial cathedral, a limitless interior space filled with columns of light, countless sources of brilliance, and the machinery of an unimaginable alien technology. (The new special effects were designed by the underground artist R. Cobb, I understand; no credit is given.) This new conclusion gives the movie the kind of overwhelming final emotional impact it needed; it adds another dimension to the already impressive ending of the first version.

The movie gains impact in another way. Spielberg has tightened up the whole film. Dead ends and pointless scenes have been dropped. New scenes do a better job of establishing the characters—not only of Dreyfuss, but also of Francois Truffaut, as the French scientist. The new editing moves the film along at a faster, more absorbing pace to the mind-stretching conclusion. *Close Encounters*, which was already a wonderful film, now transcends itself; it's one of the great moviegoing experiences. If you've seen it before, I'm afraid that now you'll have to see it again.

Coal Miner's Daughter ★ ★ ★
PG, 125 m., 1980

Sissy Spacek (Loretta Lynn), Tommy Lee Jones (Mooney Lynn), Beverly D'Angelo (Patsy Cline), Levon Helm (Ted Webb), Phyllis Boyens (Clara Webb). Directed by Michael Apted and produced by Bernard Schwarts. Screenplay by Tom Rickman.

What improbable lives so many Americans lead, compared to the more orderly and predictable careers of the Swedes, say, or the French. It's not just that we're the most upwardly mobile society in history, we're the most mobile, period: We go to ruin as swiftly and dramatically as we hit the jackpot. No wonder one of our favorite myths involves a rags-to-riches story in which success then destroys the hero.

Look at country music star Loretta Lynn. If we can believe *Coal Miner's Daughter* (and I gather that, by and large, we can), here's a life which began in the poverty of the coalfields of Kentucky and led almost overnight to show-business stardom. And what's astonishing is that it wasn't even really planned that way: Loretta learned to play on a pawnshop guitar, her husband thought she could sing, and one day she just sorta found herself on stage. The movie's about Loretta Lynn's childhood, her very early marriage, her quick four kids, her husband's move to Washington State looking for a job, her humble start in show business, her apparently quick rise to stardom, and then the usual Catch-22 of self-destructivenss.

We're not surprised, somehow, that right after the scenes where she becomes a superstar, there are scenes where she starts using pills, getting headaches, and complaining that everybody's on her case all the time. We fiercely want to believe in success in this country, but for some reason we also want to believe that it takes a terrible human toll. Sometimes it does—and that always makes for a better story. Straightforward success sagas, in which the heroes just keep on getting richer, are boring. We want our heroes to suffer. We like to identify—it makes stars more human, somehow, if they get screwed by Valium, too.

What's refreshing about *Coal Miner's Daughter* is that it takes the basic material (rags to riches, overnight success, the onstage breakdown, and, of course, the big comeback) and relates them in wonderfully human terms. It's fresh and immediate.

That is due most of all to the performance by Sissy Spacek as Loretta Lynn. With the same sort of magical chemistry she's shown before, when she played the high school kid in *Carrie*, Spacek at twenty-nine has the ability to appear to be almost any age onscreen. Here she ages from about fourteen to somewhere in her thirties, always looks the age, and never seems to be wearing makeup. I wonder if she does it with her posture; early in the film, as a poor coal miner's kid, she slouches and slinks around, and then later she puts on dignity with the flashy dresses she wears onstage.

The movie is mostly about Lynn's relationships with her husband, Mooney (played by Tommy Lee Jones), and her first close show-business friend and mentor, Patsy Cline (Beverly D'Angelo). Both of these relationships are developed in direct, understated, intelligent ways; we are spared, for example, a routine portrait of Mooney Lynn as Official Show Biz Husband, and given instead a portrait of a recognizable human being who is aggressive, confident, loving, and fallible. The fact that this movie felt free to portray Mooney as hard-nosed is one of the most interesting things about it: Loretta Lynn, who had a certain amount of control over the project, obviously still has her feet on the ground and didn't insist that this movie be some kind of idealized fantasy.

We are left to speculate, of course, on whether Lynn's rise to stardom was really as picaresque as *Coal Miner's Daughter* suggests. She seems to get on the Grand Ole Opry mighty fast, and Patsy Cline seems to adopt her almost before she knows her. But then the amazing thing about Loretta Lynn's life seems to be how fast everything happened, and how wide open the avenues to success are in this country—if you're talented and, of course, lucky.

The most entertaining scenes in the movie are in the middle, after the coal mines and before the Top 40, when Loretta and Mooney are tooling around the back roads trying to convince country disc jockeys to play her records. The scene with Mooney taking a publicity photo of Loretta is a little gem illustrating the press agent that resides within us all.

So, anyway . . . how good *is* this movie? I think it's one of those films people like so much while they're watching it that they're inclined to think it's better than it is. It's warm, entertaining, funny, and centered around that great Sissy Spacek performance, but it's essentially pretty familiar material (not that Loretta Lynn can be blamed that Horatio Alger wrote her life before she lived it). The movie isn't great art, but it has been made with great taste and style; it's more intelligent and observant than movie biographies of singing stars used to be. That makes it a treasure to watch, even if we sometimes have the feeling we've seen it before.

Cocktail ★ ★
R, 103 m., 1988

Tom Cruise (Brian Flanagan), Bryan Brown (Doug Coughlin), Elisabeth Shue (Jordan Mooney), Lisa Barnes (Connie), Laurence Luckinbill (Mr. Mooney), Kelly Lynch (Jerry Coughlin), Ron Dean (Uncle Pat). Directed by Roger Donaldson and produced by Ted Field and Robert W. Cort. Screenplay by Heywood Gould.

Cocktail tells the story of two bartenders and their adventures in six bars and several bedrooms. What is remarkable, given the subject, is how little the movie knows about bars or drinking.

Early in the film, there's a scene where the two bartenders stage an elaborately choreographed act behind the bar, in which they juggle bottles in unison; one spins ice cubes into the air and the other one catches them, and then they flip bottles at each other like a couple of circus jugglers. All of this is done to rock & roll music, and it takes them about four minutes to make two drinks. They get a roaring ovation from the customers in their crowded bar, which is a tip-off to the movie's glossy phoniness. This isn't bartending, it's a music video, and real drinkers wouldn't applaud, they'd shout, "Shut up and pour!"

The bartenders in the film are played by Tom Cruise, as a young ex-serviceman who dreams of becoming a millionaire, and Bryan Brown, as a hard-bitten veteran who has lots of cynical advice. Brown advises Cruise to keep his eyes open for a "rich chick," because that's his ticket to someday opening his own bar. Cruise is ready for this advice. He studies self-help books and believes that he'll be rich someday, if only he gets that big break. The movie is supposed to be about how he outgrows his materialism, although the closing scenes leave room for enormous doubts about his redemption.

The first part of the movie works the best. That's when Cruise drops out of school, becomes a full-time bartender, makes Brown

his best friend, and learns to juggle those bottles. In the real world, Cruise and Brown would be fired for their time-wasting grandstanding behind the bar, but in this movie they get hired to work in a fancy disco, where they have a fight over a girl, and Cruise heads for Jamaica.

There, as elsewhere, his twinkling eyes and friendly smile seem irresistible to the women on the other side of the bar, and he lives in a world of one-night stands. That's made possible by the fact that no one in this movie has ever heard of AIDS, not even the rich female fashion executive (Lisa Barnes) who picks Cruise up and takes him back to Manhattan with her.

What do you think? Do you believe a millionaire Manhattan woman executive in her thirties would sleep with a wildly promiscuous bartender she picks up on the beach? Not unless she was seriously drunk. And that's another area this movie knows little about: the actual effects of drinking. Sure, Cruise gets tanked a couple of times and staggers around a little and throws a few punches. But given the premise that he and Brown drink all of the time, shouldn't they be drunk or hung over at least most of the time? Not in this fantasy world.

If the film had stuck to the relationship between Cruise and Brown, it might, however, have had a chance. It makes a crucial error when it introduces a love story involving Cruise and Elisabeth Shue, as a vacationing waitress from New York. They find true love, which is shattered when Shue sees Cruise with the rich Manhattan executive. After the executive takes Cruise back to New York and tries to turn him into a pampered stud, he realizes his mistake and apologizes to Shue, only to discover, of course, that she is pregnant—and rich.

The last stages of the movie were written, directed, and acted on automatic pilot, as Shue's millionaire daddy tries to throw Cruise out of the penthouse, but love triumphs. There is not a moment in the movie's last half-hour that is not borrowed from other movies, and eventually even the talented and graceful Cruise can be seen laboring with the ungainly reversals in the script. Shue, who does whatever is possible with her role, is handicapped because her character is denied the freedom to make natural choices; at every moment, her actions are dictated by the artificial demands of the plot.

It's a shame the filmmakers didn't take a longer, harder look at this material. The

movie's most interesting character is the older bartender, superbly played by Bryan Brown, who never has a false moment. If the film had been told from his point of view, it would have been a lot more interesting, but box-office considerations no doubt required the center of gravity to shift to Cruise and Shue.

One of the weirdest things about *Cocktail* is the so-called message it thinks it contains. Cruise is painted throughout the film as a cynical, success-oriented, 1980s materialist who wants only to meet a rich woman and own his own bar. That's why Shue doesn't tell him at first that she's rich. Toward the end of the movie, there's a scene where he allegedly chooses love over money, but then, a few months later, he is the owner and operator of his own slick Manhattan singles bar.

How did he finance it? There's a throwaway line about how he got some money from his uncle, a subsistence-level bartender who can't even afford a late-model car. Sure. It costs a fortune to open a slick singles bar in Manhattan, and so we are left with the assumption that Cruise's rich father-in-law came through with the financing. If the movie didn't want to leave that impression, it shouldn't have ended with the scene in the bar. But then, this is the kind of movie that uses Cruise's materialism as a target all through the story, and then rewards him for it at the end. The more you think about what really happens in *Cocktail*, the more you realize how empty and fabricated it really is.

Cocoon ★ ★ ★
PG-13, 115 m., 1985

Wilford Brimley (Ben), Steve Guttenberg (Jack), Brian Dennehy (Walter), Hume Cronyn (Joe), Don Ameche (Art), Maureen Stapleton (Mary), Jessica Tandy (Alma), Jack Gilford (Bernie), Tahnee Welch (Kitty). Directed by Ron Howard and produced by Richard D. Zanuck, David Brown, and Lili Fini Zanuck. Screenplay by Tom Benedek.

Cocoon is one of the sweetest, gentlest science-fiction movies I've seen, a hymn to the notion that aliens might come from outer space and yet still be almost as corny and impulsive as we are. It is also the first film since *On Golden Pond* to deal at length with old people, and you can tell by their performances that these older actors have been waiting a long time to get something nice and meaty and silly to sink their choppers into.

The movie opens with the suggestion that aliens have landed on Earth. Then we see apparently normal human beings renting a boat and a beachfront estate. Meanwhile, in a nearby retirement home, three of the old guys have started sneaking onto the estate to take illegal swims in a big enclosed pool. One day, they discover some large, mossy rocks on the bottom of the pool. That doesn't stop them. They dive in, and before long they feel terrific—and curiously youthful.

The rocks are actually cocoons collected from the bottom of the sea by aliens, who left them behind 10,000 years ago when they were forced to evacuate Atlantis in a hurry. The pool has been charged with a life force to reawaken the cocoons, and the force works on elderly humans, too. When the leader of the aliens (Brian Dennehy) finds the old guys in the pool, he doesn't zap them with extraterrestrial weaponry. He smiles and tells them to go ahead and keep using the pool—but not to tell anyone else.

That's impossible. The old guys can't keep a secret long in a retirement home, and before long this literal fountain of youth has totally changed the lifestyles of the senior citizens. The old guys are played by three wonderful actors: Hume Cronyn, Don Ameche, and, best of all, Wilford Brimley, who has a way of investing each word with such simple truth that his dialogue seems more weighted, more real, than the other dialogue in the movie.

Brimley is sort of a ringleader. He is also a homespun philosopher, who goes fishing with his grandson and talks about the meaning of life and death. Others in the retirement home are not so serene, especially the stubborn Jack Gilford, who does not want to feel young and does not want to go swimming and thinks we should all be satisfied with the time allotted us on this planet. The introduction of the mysterious pool and its life force tests Gilford's friendships with the others, and it also puts strains on the marriage between Cronyn and Jessica Tandy. The scenes involving these characters are the best scenes in the movie.

But I also liked the treatment of the aliens, especially the Dennehy character, who observes that every 10,000 years he's entitled to do something silly. Dennehy eventually offers the old folks eternal life, under certain rather difficult conditions, and the way they consider his offer is rather thought-provoking—especially in the scenes between Brimley and his grandson. That's really the payoff of the movie, right there, but the ending is too drawn-out. We could also do without the romance between the boat's human captain (Steve Guttenberg) and the beautiful alien (Tahnee Welch). But the good parts in *Cocoon* are warm and sort of tender.

Cocoon: The Return ★ ★ ¹/₂
PG, 116 m., 1988

Don Ameche (Art Selwyn), Wilford Brimley (Ben Luckett), Courteney Cox (Sara), Hume Cronyn (Joe Finley), Jack Gilford (Bernie Lefkowitz), Steve Guttenberg (Jack Bonner), Barret Oliver (David), Maureen Stapleton (Mary Luckett), Elaine Stritch (Ruby), Jessica Tandy (Alma Finley), Gwen Verdon (Bess McCarthy), Tahnee Welch (Kitty), Tyrone Power, Jr. (Pillsbury), Mike Nomad (Doc). Directed by Daniel Petrie and produced by Richard D. Zanuck, David Brown, and Lili Fini Zanuck. Screenplay by Stephen McPherson.

At the end of *Cocoon*, a group of senior citizens were lifted into the sky by a beam of light from a hovering spacecraft, and taken to live on a planet where nobody ever got tired, and nobody ever grew old. Now they are back on earth. Why did they return from their other-worldly paradise? It is too easy to give the cynical answer—because they were needed for the sequel—but I am afraid the movie comes up with no better justification.

The central weakness of *Cocoon: The Return* is that the film lacks any compelling reason to exist. Yes, it is a heartwarming film. Yes, the performances are wonderful, and yes, it's great to see these characters back again. But that's about it. If you've seen *Cocoon*, the sequel gives you the opportunity to see everybody saying good-bye for the second time.

The locale, once again, is a retirement community in Florida. Steve Guttenberg, as the skipper who fell in love with an alien being (Tahnee Welch) in the previous movie, is still chugging around on his glass-bottom boat casting winsome glances at the sky. In the bedroom of one of the local Little Leaguers, a strange event takes place. The kid tries to turn off his TV set, but the screen remains bright—and then suddenly he sees his grandfather (Wilford Brimley), one of the old-timers who disappeared into space. He's coming back for a visit, Gramps says.

If you want to get technical about it, there is a motive for the spacecraft's return: The "cocoons" that were deposited on the bottom of the bay have been discovered by oceanographers and are being disturbed. While an alien team sets about recovering one of their kidnapped fellows, we see a series of reunions between the human travelers and those they left behind.

In the process, all of the same problems, questions, and dilemmas that concerned the characters in the first movie are taken out and dusted off again. For example, which is better, to live forever on another world, or get sick and die on this one, but at least get to see your grandson playing baseball? To see the familiar sunsets over the tacky but comfortable retirement villages of the Florida coast, or live forever in a silver city beneath three alien moons? In a way, both *Cocoon* pictures consider the same dilemma that the angels struggled with in Wim Wenders's *Wings of Desire:* Is it better to live forever as a spirit who can feel nothing, or for a finite time as a creature who can breathe and hurt and die?

My answer would be, take me to the silver city and I'll think it over for a few thousand years. Dying now would be a permanent solution to a temporary problem. But the folks in *Cocoon: The Return* don't all see it that way, and each couple makes up its own mind. Don Ameche wants to get back on the spaceship, for example, because, to his wonderment, he and his middle-aged wife (Gwen Verdon) are expecting a child, and he wants to live long enough to see it grow up. Jessica Tandy, on the other hand, would rather stay here on earth and take a job as a teacher in a day-care center—"the first job anybody has ever offered me."

While these decisions are being arrived at, the movie provides a series of love affairs, misunderstandings, philosophical conversations, and tragedies small and large. There is also a subplot involving the kidnapped alien, who has fun at first with its captors, but was "awakened" too soon, and begins to pine away and die. Also, of course, there is another opportunity for Guttenberg and Welch to share the strange experience of "merging," which not only passes for sex on the other planet, but replaces it—with no complaints, by all accounts.

The last half of the movie feels kind of strange. It's all so elegiac, so filled with farewells and bittersweet moments of philosophy. The movie lacks the creative energy of the first one, in which the discovery of the alien "cocoons" created genuine tension, and there was such joy in the scenes where the old men (Brimley, Ameche, and Hume Cronyn) were suddenly made young again. This time, once again, we are invited to share the victory of the elderly cast over the effects of aging, and the best thing in the movie is probably the vitality of the actors. But at the end of the film, as those who wish to leave are carried up once more into the sky, we on earth are left with the question, was this trip necessary?

Code of Silence ★ ★ ★ ½
R, 102 m., 1985

Chuck Norris (Eddie Cusack), Henry Silva (Luis Comacho), Bert Remsen (Commander Kates), Mike Genovese (Tony Luna), Molly Hagan (Diana Luna), Nathan Davis (Felix Scalese), Ralph Foody (Cragie). Directed by Andy Davis and produced by Raymond Wagner. Screenplay by Michael Butler, Dennis Shryack, and Mike Gray.

Chuck Norris is often identified with grade-zilch karate epics, but *Code of Silence* is a heavy-duty thriller—a slick, energetic movie with good performances and a lot of genuine human interest. It grabs you right at the start with a complicated triple-cross, and then it develops into a stylish urban action picture with sensational stunts. How sensational? How about an unfaked fight on top of a speeding elevated train, ending when both fighters dive off the train into the Chicago River? The stunts are great, but not surprising; Chuck Norris is famous for the stunts he features in all of his movies. What is surprising is the number of interesting characters in *Code of Silence*. The screenplay doesn't give us the usual cardboard clichés; there's a lot of human life here, in a series of carefully crafted performances. For once, here's a thriller that realizes we have to care about the characters before we care about their adventures.

Norris stars as a veteran Chicago vice cop named Cusack. He's a straight arrow, an honest cop that his partners call a "one-man army." As the film opens, he's setting up a drug bust, but an Italian-American gang beats him to it, stealing the money and the drugs and leaving a roomful of dead gangsters. That sets off a Chicago mob war between the Italian-American factions, and as bodies pile up in the streets, Cusack begins to worry about the daughter of a Mafia chieftain—a young artist named Diana (Molly Hagan) who wants nothing to do with her father's business, but finds she can't be a bystander. After an elaborate cat-and-mouse chase through the Loop, she's kidnapped and Cusack wants to save her.

Meanwhile, the movie has an interesting subplot about a tired veteran cop (Ralph Foody) who has mistakenly shot and killed an Italian-American kid while chasing some mobsters through a tenement. The veteran's young partner (Joseph Guzaldo) watches him plant a gun on the dead kid and claim that the shooting was in self-defense. It's up to the freshman, backed up by Cusack, to decide what he'll say at the departmental hearing.

The movie has a knack for taking obligatory scenes and making them more than routine. Among the small acting gems in the movie is the performance of Chicago actor Nathan Davis as Felix Scalese, a wrinkled, wise old Mafia godfather who sits on his yacht and counsels against a mob war—to no avail. Mike Genovese plays the mob chief whose daughter is kidnapped, and his first scene, as he wishes his wife a happy birthday while hurrying out the door to go do battle, is wonderfully timed. Foody has some nice scenes as the tired old cop, hanging around a bar talking big and looking scared.

Holding all of the performances together is Norris's work as Cusack. Bearded, dressed in jeans for undercover street duty, and driving a battered old beater, Norris seems convincing as a cop—with, of course, the degree of heroic exaggeration you need in a role like this. By the end of the film, when he is reduced to functioning as a one-man army, we can't really believe the armored robot tank that he brings into action, but, what the hell, we accept it. Norris resembles Clint Eastwood in his insistence on the barest minimum of dialogue; there's a scene where he quietly, awkwardly tries to comfort the mobster's daughter, and it rings completely true. He also seems to be doing a lot of his own stunts, and although the credits list a lot of stuntmen and they were all obviously kept busy, it looks to me like that's really Norris on top of that elevated train.

The movie was directed by Andy Davis, who was a cinematographer on Haskell Wexler's 1968 Chicago film *Medium Cool*, and returned to some of the same locations to film this picture. Davis's directorial debut was the low-budget *Stony Island* (1977), which had moments of truth and insight but nothing like the assurance he shows this time; *Code of Silence* is a thriller so professional that it has the confidence to go for drama and humor as well as thrills. It may be the movie that moves Norris out of the ranks of dependable action heroes and makes him a major star.

The Color of Money ★ ★ ½
R, 119 m., 1986

Paul Newman (Eddie), Tom Cruise (Vincent), Mary Elizabeth Mastrantonio (Carmen), Helen Shaver (Janelle), John Turturro (Julian), Bill Cobbs (Orvis). Directed by Martin Scorsese and produced by Irving Axelrad and Barbara De Fina. Screenplay by Richard Price.

If this movie had been directed by someone else, I might have thought differently about it because I might not have expected so much. But *The Color of Money* is directed by Martin Scorsese, the most exciting American director now working, and it is not an exciting film. It doesn't have the electricity, the wound-up tension of his best work, and as a result I was too aware of the story marching by.

Scorsese may have thought of this film as a deliberately mainstream work, a conventional film with big names and a popular subject matter; perhaps he did it for that reason. But I believe he has the stubborn soul of an artist, and cannot put his heart where his heart will not go. And his heart, I believe, inclines toward creating new and completely personal stories about characters who have come to life in his imagination—not in finishing someone else's story, begun twenty-five years ago.

The Color of Money is not a sequel, exactly, but it didn't start with someone's fresh inspiration. It continues the story of "Fast Eddie" Felson, the character played by Paul Newman in Robert Rossen's *The Hustler* (1961). Now twenty-five years have passed. Eddie still plays pool, but not for money and not with the high-stakes, dangerous kinds of players who drove him from the game. He is a liquor salesman, a successful one, judging by the long, white Cadillac he takes so much pride in. One night, he sees a kid playing pool, and the kid is so good that Eddie's memories are stirred.

This kid is not simply good, however. He is also, Eddie observes, a "flake," and that gives him an idea: With Eddie as his coach, this kid could be steered into the world of big-money pool, where his flakiness would throw off the other players. They wouldn't be inclined to think he was for real. The challenge, obviously, is to train the kid so he can turn his flakiness on and off at will—so he can put the making of money above every other consideration, every other lure and temptation, in the pool hall.

The kid is named Vincent (Tom Cruise), and Eddie approaches him through Vincent's girlfriend, Carmen (Mary Elizabeth Mastrantonio). She is a few years older than Vince and a lot tougher. She likes the excitement of being around Vince and around pool hustling, but Eddie sees she's getting bored. He figures he can make a deal with the girl; together, they'll control Vince and steer him in the direction of money.

A lot of the early scenes setting up this situation are very well handled, especially the moments when Eddie uses Carmen to make Vince jealous and undermine his self-confidence. But of course these scenes work well, because they are the part of the story that is closest to Scorsese's own sensibility. In all of his best movies, we can see this same ambiguity about the role of women, who are viewed as objects of comfort and fear, creatures that his heroes desire and despise themselves for desiring. Think of the heroes of *Mean Streets*, *Taxi Driver*, and *Raging Bull* and their relationships with women, and you sense where the energy is coming from that makes Vincent love Carmen, and distrust her.

The movie seems less at home with the Newman character, perhaps because this character is largely complete when the movie begins. "Fast Eddie" Felson knows who he is, what he thinks, what his values are. There will be some moments of crisis in the story, as when he allows himself, to his shame, to be hustled at pool. But he is not going to change much during the story, and maybe he's not even free to change much, since his experiences are largely dictated by the requirements of the plot.

Here we come to the big weakness of *The Color of Money*: It exists in a couple of time-worn genres, and its story is generated out of standard Hollywood situations. First we have the basic story of the old pro and the talented youngster. Then we have the story of the kid who wants to knock the master off the throne. Many of the scenes in this movie are almost formula, despite the energy of Scorsese's direction and the good performances. They come in the same places we would expect them to come in a movie by anybody else, and they contain the same events.

Eventually, everything points to the ending of the film, which we know will have to be a showdown between Eddie and Vince, between Newman and Cruise. The fact that the movie does not provide that payoff scene is a disappointment. Perhaps Scorsese thought the movie was "really" about the personalities of his two heroes, and that it was unnecessary to show who would win in a showdown. Perhaps, but then why plot the whole story with genre formulas and only bail out at the end? If you bring a gun onstage in the first act, you've gotta shoot somebody by the third.

The side stories are where the movie really lives. There is a warm, bittersweet relationship between Newman and his long-time girlfriend, a bartender wonderfully played by Helen Shaver. And the greatest energy in the story is generated between Cruise and Mastrantonio—who, with her hard edge and her inbred cynicism, keeps the kid from ever feeling really sure of her. It's a shame that even the tension of their relationship is allowed to evaporate in the closing scenes, where Cruise and the girl stand side by side and seem to speak from the same mind, as if she were a standard movie girlfriend and not a real original.

Watching Newman is always interesting in this movie. He has been a true star for many years, but sometimes that star quality has been thrown away. Scorsese has always been the kind of director who lets his camera stay on actors' faces, who looks deeply into them and tries to find the shadings that reveal their originality. In many of Newman's close-ups in this movie, he shows an enormous power, a concentration and focus of his essence as an actor.

Newman, of course, had veto power over who would make this movie (because how could they make it without him?), and his instincts were sound in choosing Scorsese. Maybe the problems started with the story, when Newman or somebody decided that there had to be a young man in the picture; the introduction of the Cruise character opens the door for all of the preordained teacher-pupil clichés, when perhaps they should have just stayed with Newman, and let him be at the center of the story. Then Newman's character would have been free (as the Robert De Niro characters have been free in other Scorsese films) to follow his passions, hungers, fears, and desires wherever they led him—instead of simply following the story down a well-traveled path.

The Color Purple ★ ★ ★ ★
PG-13, 155 m., 1985

Danny Glover (Mister), Whoopi Goldberg (Celie), Margaret Avery (Shug Avery), Oprah Winfrey (Sofia), Willard Pugh (Harpo), Akosua Busia (Nettie), Adolph Caesar (Old Mister), Rae Dawn Chong (Squeak), Dana Ivey (Miss Millie). Directed by Steven Spielberg and produced by Kathleen Kennedy, Frank Marshall, Quincy Jones, and Spielberg. Screenplay by Menno Meyjes.

There is a moment in Steven Spielberg's *The Color Purple* when a woman named Celie smiles and smiles and smiles. That was the moment when I knew this movie was going to be as good as it seemed, was going to keep the promise it made by daring to tell Celie's story. It is not a story that would seem easily suited to the movies.

Celie is a black woman who grows up in the rural South in the early decades of this century, in a world that surrounds her with cruelty. When we first see her, she is a child, running through fields of purple flowers with her sister. But then she comes into clear view, and we see that she is pregnant, and we learn that her father has made her pregnant, and will give away the child as he has done with a previous baby.

By the time Celie is married—to a cruel, distant charmer she calls only "Mister"—she will have lost both her children and the ability to bear children, will have been separated from the sister who is the only person on Earth who loves her, and will be living in servitude to a man who flaunts his love for another woman.

And yet this woman will endure, and in the end she will prevail. *The Color Purple* is not the story of her suffering but of her victory, and by the end of her story this film had moved me and lifted me up as few films have. It is a great, warm, hard, unforgiving, triumphant movie, and there is not a scene that does not shine with the love of the people who made it.

The film is based on the novel by Alice Walker, who told Celie's story through a series of letters, some never sent, many never received, most addressed to God. The letters are her way of maintaining sanity in a world where few others ever cared to listen to her. The turning point in the book, and in the movie, comes after Celie's husband brings home the fancy woman he has been crazy about for years—a pathetic, alcoholic juke-joint singer named Shug Avery, who has been ravaged by life yet still has an indestructible beauty.

Shug's first words to Celie are: "You are as ugly as sin." But as Shug moves into the house, and Celie obediently caters to her husband's lover, Shug begins to see the beauty in Celie, and there is a scene where they kiss, and Celie learns for the first time that sex can include tenderness, that she can dare to love herself. A little later, Celie looks in Shug's eyes and allows herself to smile, and we know that Celie didn't think she had a pretty smile until Shug told her so. That is the central moment in the movie.

The relationship between Shug and Celie is a good deal toned down from the book, which deals in greater detail with sexual matters. Steven Spielberg, who made the movie, is more concerned with the whole world of Celie's life than he is with her erotic education. We meet many members of the rural black community that surrounds Celie. We meet a few of the local whites, too, but they are bit players in this drama.

Much more important are people like Sofia (Oprah Winfrey), an indomitable force of nature who is determined to marry Harpo, Mister's son by a first marriage. When we first see Sofia, hurrying down the road with everyone trying to keep up, she looks like someone who could never be stopped. But she is stopped, after she tells the local white mayor to go to hell, and the saddest story in the movie is the way her spirit is forever dampened by the beating and jailing she receives. Sofia is counterpoint to Celie: She is wounded by life, Celie is healed.

Shug Avery is another fascinating character, played by Margaret Avery as a sweet-faced, weary woman who sings a little bit like Billie Holiday and has long since lost all of her illusions about men and everything else. Her contact with Celie redeems her; by giving her somebody to be nice to, it allows her to get in touch with what is still nice inside herself.

Mister, whose real name is Albert, is played by Danny Glover, who was the field hand in *Places in the Heart*. He is an evil man, his evil tempered to some extent by his ignorance; perhaps he does not fully understand how cruel he is to Celie. Certainly he seems outwardly pleasant. He smiles and jokes and sings, and then hurts Celie to the quick—not so much with his physical blows as when he refuses to let her see the letters she hopes are coming from her long-lost sister.

And then, at the center of the movie, Celie is played by Whoopi Goldberg in one of the most amazing debut performances in movie history. Goldberg has a fearsomely difficult job to do, enlisting our sympathy for a woman who is rarely allowed to speak, to dream, to interact with the lives around her. Spielberg breaks down the wall of silence around her, however, by giving her narrative monologues in which she talks about her life and reads the words in the letters she composes.

The wonderful performances in this movie are contained in a screenplay that may take some of the smoking edges off Walker's novel, but keeps all the depth and dimension. The world of Celie and the others is created so forcibly in this movie that their corner of the South becomes one of those movie places—like Oz, like Tara, like Casablanca—that lay claim to their own geography in our imaginations. The affirmation at the end of the film is so joyous that this is one of the few movies in a long time that inspires tears of happiness, and earns them.

Colors ★ ★ ★
R, 120 m., 1988

Sean Penn (Danny McGavin), Robert Duvall (Bob Hodges), Maria Conchita Alonso (Louisa Gomez), Randy Brooks (Ron Delaney), Grand Bush (Larry Sylvester), Don Cheadle (Rocket). Directed by Dennis Hopper and produced by Robert H. Solo. Screenplay by Michael Schiffer.

There are many good moments in *Colors*, but the one I will remember the longest is in the scene where a group of Los Angeles gang members is trying to explain why the gang is so important to them. Talking to a social worker, they describe the feeling of belonging—of feeling for the first time in their lives that they were part of a "family" that cared for them and was ready to die for them.

The product of their family is, of course, tragic. Their gang deals in drugs, defends its turf, and uses murder to enforce its authority. Sometimes innocent bystanders are shot dead in the middle of a party, or while standing on their own lawns. Because the gangs represent a good deal of what little authority and structure survives in their neighborhoods, they help to set the tone for a segment of society—a tone of desperation, despair, and reckless, doomed grandiose gestures. Because there are so many gangs, so well-

entrenched, the police are all but helpless to bring about any fundamental change in the situation.

That helplessness of the police is the central subject of Dennis Hopper's *Colors*, which stars Sean Penn and Robert Duvall as two cops, one newly assigned to the gang unit, one a veteran. But what makes *Colors* special is not the portraits of the cops, but the movie's willingness to look inside the gangs. Almost without exception, American movies about gangs have either romanticized them in fantasies (*West Side Story, Warriors*) or viewed them from outside, as a monolithic, dangerous unit. This movie tries to understand a little of the tragic gang dynamic, to explain why in some devastated inner-city neighborhoods they seem to offer the only way for young men to find power and status.

The story of the two cops, on the other hand, is not exactly new. We have the street-smart veteran (Duvall), who has a realistic assessment of the situation and knows that he sometimes has to bend the rules to get results. And then we have the hotheaded younger cop (Penn), who has a simplistic us-against-them mentality, and wants to bust heads and make arrests. That leads into scenes where the cops come dangerously close to losing their street authority because they're fighting with each other instead of presenting a unified front to the gangs.

If the situation is not new, it is redeemed by the performances. Robert Duvall and Sean Penn are two of the best actors in America, bringing a flavor and authority to their roles that make them specific. A lot of their acting in this movie is purely physical, as when Penn disarms, frisks, and handcuffs a suspect, seeming sure and confident at every moment. Other moments, when the two actors are talking to each other, contain that electricity that makes you think these words are being said for the first time.

The plot involves the attempts of the two cops to come to terms with a gang that is involved, we discover, in dealing drugs. During the course of the film they follow the brief life of the younger brother of one of the gang members, who seems for a time to have a chance to escape gang society. And there is a brief, doomed romance between Penn and Maria Conchita Alonso, as a Chicano who loves him but cannot reconcile his status as a cop and her perception of how cops like Penn treat her people.

The movie has some flaws. The story is

needlessly complicated, and at times we're not sure who is who on the gang side. And some of the action seems repetitious; Hopper, trying to show the routine, makes it feel routine. But *Colors* is a special movie: Not just a police thriller, but a movie that has researched gangs and given some thought to what it wants to say about them.

Coma ★ ★ ★
PG, 113 m., 1978

Genevieve Bujold (Dr. Susan Wheeler), Michael Douglas (Dr. Mark Bellows), Elizabeth Ashley (Mrs. Emerson), Rip Torn (Dr. George), Richard Widmark (Dr. Harris), Lois Chiles (Nancy Greenly). Directed by Michael Crichton and produced by Martin Erlichman. Screenplay by Crichton.

They're always writing about the great movie kisses, and the great movie chase scenes, and the great movie saloon brawls. But what about the great movie surgical incisions? Just about every movie even remotely involved with medicine has at least one moment when the surgeon says "Scalpel, please," and chicken-hearts like me close our eyes.

A lot of movie fans, though, seem to live for the moment of incision. *Coma* must be a godsend for them; it has more hypodermic needles than your average junkie movie, and more kidneys and livers than your local meat counter. In the midst of the gruesome and the gory, though, there's a pretty good thriller here. *Coma* was written by Robin Moore, a doctor, and directed by Michael Crichton, who graduated from Harvard Medical School, and it takes place almost entirely within a hospital. The feeling of reality is inescapable, as when a veteran anesthetist lectures two students on what can go wrong during an operation, and we get the creepiest feeling that those very things are about to go wrong.

There seems to be a lot wrong with the surgical procedures, in fact, at "Boston Memorial," the (thank God) fictional hospital where *Coma* is set. Just in the last year, twelve perfectly healthy young people have gone into irreversible comas during minor operations. When the best friend of a spunky young resident doctor (Genevieve Bujold) goes into a coma, that's one too many. Bujold tries to find a pattern in the deaths, which involve many different doctors, anesthetists, and operations . . . but always the same operating room.

Everybody thinks she's crazy. Michael Douglas does. He's her boyfriend, but if he can't keep her in line he'll lose his shot at becoming chief resident. Richard Widmark does. He's the chief-of-staff, constantly on the phone to senators and presidents. The hospital's resident shrink does. And so does the guy hired to kill Bujold (she outsmarts him in an especially creepy scene in the anatomy department's cold room, burying him under corpses).

Movies like this have a way of turning silly, of producing a lot of unintentional laughs. But *Coma* really works pretty well, partly because Crichton is a competent technician who knows his subject matter first hand, but mostly because of Genevieve Bujold. She's a fine craftsman of an actress, playing her big scenes straight and seriously, selling us the material by getting so involved in it herself.

Thirty years ago, the Bujold role might have been played by a man. Now we seem to have entered an era of big female roles, and so the doctor's a woman. That gives the movie an opportunity to add one more interesting level to the ready-made thriller material: No one will quite take her seriously. The psychiatrist says she's hysterical because of the death of her friend. "She's a little paranoid," Douglas offhandedly explains to Widmark. Women have a tendency to get all emotional, y'know.

When she comes up with absolute proof that Operating Room No. 8 is about as safe as an airplane crash, all Douglas does is call the hospital, presumably so the fellows with the butterfly nets can hurry over. Such oversights have their advantages, though, giving us that terrific final sequence with Bujold, drugged and helpless, being rolled into the fatal operating room—desperately trying to get Douglas to believe her *now,* anyway . . . while Widmark pronounces those magic words, "Nurse? Scalpel, please . . ."

Come Back to the 5 & Dime, Jimmy Dean, Jimmy Dean ★ ★ ★
PG, 109 m., 1982

Sandy Dennis (Mona), Cher (Sissy), Karen Black (Joanne), Sudie Bond (Juanita), Kathy Bates (Stella Mae), Marta Heflin (Edna). Directed by Robert Altman and produced by Scott Bushnell. Screenplay by Ed Graczyk.

If Robert Altman hadn't directed this movie, the reviews would have described it as Altmanesque. It's a mixture of the bizarre and the banal, a slice of lives that could never have been led, a richly textured mixture of confessions, obsessions, and surprises.

The movie takes place in a worn-out Woolworth's in a small Texas town not far from the locations where James Dean shot *Giant* in 1955. The story begins twenty years later, at a reunion of the local James Dean fan club; the members swore a solemn vow to get together after two decades, and they drift in one by one, greeted by the tired waitress who's still on duty. There's Sandy Dennis, the flaky, visionary local woman who's convinced that she bore a son by James Dean. Then Cher walks in—looking not like the glamorous Cher of television, but like a small-town sexpot unsure of her appeal. The last arrival is Karen Black, who drove in all the way from California, and is not surprised when nobody recognizes her at first.

The fan club members and a few local good ol' girls join in a long afternoon of memories, nostalgia, self-analysis, accusation, shocking revelations, and anger, while heat-lightning flickers offscreen. And their memories trigger flashbacks to the time twenty years earlier when the proximity of James Dean served as a catalyst in all of their lives, giving some the courage to realize their dreams and others, the timid ones, the courage at least to dream them.

Jimmy Dean was a Broadway play before it was a movie, and Altman, who directed it first on stage, stays pretty close here to Ed Graczyk's script. He works just as closely with David Gropman's extraordinary stage set, on which the movie was shot. Gropman has actually created two dime stores, one a mirror-image of the other. They're separated by a two-way mirror, so that at times we're looking at the reflection of the "front" store, and at other times, the glass is transparent and we see the second store. Altman uses the front as the present and the back as the past, and there are times when a foreground image will dissolve into a background flashback. In an age of sophisticated optical effects, this sort of dissolve looks routine—until you learn that Altman isn't using optics, he's actually shooting through the two-way mirror. His visual effects sometimes require fancy offscreen footwork for his actors to be in two places during the same shot.

Jimmy Dean's script also requires some fancy footwork, as we reel beneath a series of predictable revelations in the last twenty minutes. This is not a great drama, but two things make the movie worth seeing: Altman's visual inventiveness and the interesting performances given by everyone in the cast. Although Sandy Dennis and Karen Black in many ways have more difficult roles, Cher is the one I watched the most because her performance here is a revelation. After years and years of giving us "Cher," she gives us a new character here, in a fine performance that creates sympathy for a sexpot who doubts her own sensuality.

Come See the Paradise ★ ★ ★
R, 133 m., 1991

Dennis Quaid (Jack McGurn), Tamlyn Tomita (Lily Kawamura), Sab Shimono (Mr. Kawamura), Shizuko Hoshi (Mrs. Kawamura), Stan Egi (Charlie Kawamura), Ronald Yamamoto (Harry Kawamura). Directed and written by Alan Parker.

Here is a movie about people who insist they are Americans, even when small and evil-minded people in power would treat them as if they were not. Most of the characters in *Come See the Paradise* are Japanese-Americans who were thrown into prison camps at the outset of World War II, even though there was no evidence that they were less patriotic, less "American," than members of other ethnic groups such as the Germans or the Italians. Their imprisonment was essentially racist, translated into laws that said they were not entitled to the same constitutional rights as their fellow citizens.

Another character in the film is an Irish-American who is a left-wing labor organizer. He gets involved in a stupid and illegal action against a movie theater chain, flees from the East to the West Coast, and changes his name. But he cannot change his ideas, and after he gets a job in a fish cannery, he is soon supporting the right of his fellow workers to strike. That means he, too, is not an "American"—at least not in the eyes of the company goons.

Although we make much of our traditions of freedom in this country, we are not so clever at understanding what freedom really means. Even George Bush, for example, cannot understand that among the rights symbolized by the American flag is the right to burn it—or honor it, if that is our choice. I have always wondered why the people who call themselves "American" most loudly are often the ones with the least understanding of the freedoms that word should represent.

When the country is threatened, our civil liberties are among the first casualties—as if we can fight the enemy by taking away our own freedoms before the enemy has a chance to. That is what happened in the early days of World War II, when a wave of racism swept the Japanese-Americans out of their homes and businesses, confiscated their savings and investments, and shipped them away in prison trains to concentration camps that were sometimes no more than barns and stables. Later on, some of these same Japanese-Americans fought with valor in the same war, perhaps because they understood better than their captors what they were fighting for.

Come See the Paradise tells a story of this period in terms of a romance between the labor organizer and a young Japanese-American woman. Her name is Lily (Tamlyn Tomita), and she is the daughter of a businessman who runs a little chain of Japanese-language movie theaters. When the Irishman, Jack McGurn (Dennis Quaid), flees to San Francisco after getting in trouble in New York, he finds a job as a projectionist in one of the theaters, and then he meets the daughter and they fall in love with each other almost immediately. (On their first date, he leans across the table and asks to kiss her, and she gives permission. It's a sweet scene, reminiscent of some of the Hollywood movies being made at about the same time.)

Lily's father, of course, opposes the marriage. Jack goes to confront him, in one of the movie's strongest scenes, and when the old man remains inflexible, the two young people run away to get married out of state (marriages between members of different races were illegal in California at the time). In a scene that is gloriously romantic and highly improbable, they find themselves at someone else's wedding party, where they dance the night away.

Then Pearl Harbor is attacked and war is declared. By executive order of Franklin Roosevelt, Lily, her family, and everyone they know find themselves herded away to prison camps. One of her brothers later volunteers for the U.S. Army and another becomes militantly pro-Japanese, but the saddest figure is the father, who is accused by his own people of being a spy, and literally fades away into death, sitting sadly in a chair and gazing at nothing.

Lily and Jack have had a daughter, who goes into the camp with her mother, while Jack goes into the Army, but not before one of the most lacerating scenes in the film, when Jack takes his little daughter to meet Santa Claus, and Santa refuses to let the child sit on his lap. "She's an American," Jack informs Santa, grabbing him, "and you will sit here and listen to what she wants for Christmas or I will kill you."

Come See the Paradise has been criticized in a few places because it uses a technique that is common in movies about minority groups: A convenient Caucasian provides the point of view, so that the audience will have someone to identify with. I didn't appreciate that approach in *Glory*—why couldn't the story of these black Civil War soldiers be seen through their own eyes, rather than through the eyes of their white commanding officer? But with *Come See the Paradise* the introduction of the Quaid character seemed somewhat less contrived because the film's director, Alan Parker, is making a statement not limited to the story of his Japanese-American characters. The theme of the whole movie is that all of its characters are Americans, too. That people of various colors and political beliefs are all equally Americans, and if there is not room for them here, then there is no purpose for this society. By adding the Quaid character, he is able to show in one story how eager we sometimes are to deprive people of their rights for both racial and political reasons.

The story itself is rather sweet, when it is not angry. It's told in a flashback from shortly after the war, when Lily is describing the events of those days to her daughter, now just barely old enough to ask questions. The love affair between Jack and Lily is tender and romantic, and if Lily's father dies after he loses all pride and self-esteem, at least her mother lives long enough to finally accept and embrace her little half-Japanese granddaughter. *Come See the Paradise* is a fable to remind us of how easily we can surrender our liberties, and how much we need them.

The Comfort of Strangers ★ ★ ½
R, 105 m., 1991

Christopher Walken (Robert), Natasha Richardson (Mary), Rupert Everett (Colin), Helen Mirren (Caroline). Directed by Paul Schrader and produced by Angelo Rizzoli. Screenplay by Harold Pinter.

"My father was a very big man. And he wore a black mustache. When he grew older and it grew gray, he colored it with a pencil. The kind women use. Mascara."

This is, at first glance, a fairly insignificant phrase, idle chatter between strangers who meet in Venice. But the man who says it repeats it two more times, until it becomes clear that these precise words are some kind of a fetish for him, that they suggest depths familiar only to him.

The speaker is an odd, polite man in a white suit, who lives in a luxurious Venetian palazzo with his wife. He speaks the words to a young couple, British tourists whom he rescues one night after they wander off the beaten path and get lost in the city's dark labyrinths. He buys them a drink and sees them back to their hotel. They will meet him again.

The young couple are Mary and Colin (Natasha Richardson and Rupert Everett), and they have come to Venice for a few days to repair their relationship—to discover, if they can, why all of the passion has disappeared. The older couple are Robert and Caroline (Christopher Walken and Helen Mirren), and they are spiders, twitching their net, waiting for the right victims to come along. At Mary and Colin, they pounce.

The Comfort of Strangers contains the elements to be a violent crime story, or a lurid horror film. Paul Schrader, who directed it, is not interested in such a mundane approach. He sees the story as literate, elegant eroticism. It is based on a novel by Ian McEwan, the best-selling British novelist of the perverse, and the screenplay is by Harold Pinter, so expert at suggesting the terrifying depths beneath innocent words. The actors are well-chosen for this material, particularly Walken, who can project decadence and danger without doing anything in particular to call attention to his methods.

Yet the movie is ultimately not quite successful; when it was over, I felt there was some additional payoff or explanation still due. Perhaps the arbitrary, unfinished nature of the story is part of its purpose. But I felt that characters this interesting should not be allowed to remain complete ciphers. Still, in individual moments, *The Comfort of Strangers* has an eerie, atmospheric charm.

There is, for example, the episode when Robert and Caroline invite Colin and Mary around to their palazzo for a drink. The older man is standing next to the younger man, the very model of urbanity, when suddenly . . . but I must not reveal what comes as a dramatic surprise. Or there is the moment when

Mary and Colin awaken from their nap, only to discover . . .

Venice is, of course, the correct city for this material. There is always the sense there of a corner not turned, a passage left unexplored, a lost building, a hidden place where unspeakable practices take place. The city is so old, so twisted in upon itself, that it has not been tamed and aired and sanitized. It is possible, we feel, that a Robert and Caroline could be living there somewhere, lazily, in languor, venturing out occasionally to the piazzas and cafés to strike up a conversation with pleasant young strangers.

And what of the father? And the father's mustache? The father was a very big man, we know, and he wore a black mustache. And when he grew older and it grew gray, he colored it with a pencil. The kind women use. Mascara. That much we definitely know.

Coming Home ★ ★ ★ ★
R, 127 m., 1978

Jane Fonda (Sally Hyde), Jon Voight (Luke Martin), Bruce Dern (Bob Hyde), Robert Carradine (Bill Munson), Penelope Milford (Vi Munson), Robert Ginty (Sergeant Mobley). Directed by Hal Ashby and produced by Jerome Hellman. Screenplay by Waldo Salt and Robert C. Jones.

Sally Hyde makes an ideal wife for a Marine: She is faithful, friendly, sexy in a quiet way, and totally in agreement with her husband's loyalties. Since his basic loyalty is to the Marine Corps, that presents difficulties at times. ("You know what they tell them," a girlfriend says. "'If the Marine Corps had wanted you to have a wife, they would have issued you one.'") Still, she's reasonably happy in the spring of 1968, as her husband prepares to ship out for a tour of duty in Vietnam. There's every chance he'll get a promotion over there. And the war, of course, is for a just cause, isn't it? It has to be, or we wouldn't be fighting it.

That is the Sally Hyde at the beginning of Hal Ashby's *Coming Home*, an extraordinarily moving film. The Sally Hyde at the end of the film—about a year later—is a different person, confused in her loyalties, not sure of her beliefs, awakened to new feelings within her. She hasn't turned into a political activist or a hippie or any of those other radical creatures of the late 1960s. But she is no longer going to be able to accept anything simply because her husband, or anybody else, says it's true.

Coming Home considers a great many subjects, but its heart lies with that fundamental change within Sally Hyde. She is played by Jane Fonda as the kind of character you somehow wouldn't expect the outspoken, intelligent Fonda to play. She's reserved, maybe a little shy, of average intelligence and tastes. She was, almost inevitably, a cheerleader in high school. She doesn't seem to have a lot of ideas or opinions. Perhaps she even doubts that it's necessary for her to have opinions—her husband can have them for her.

When her husband (Bruce Dern) goes off to fight the war, though, she finds herself on her own for the first time in her life. There's no home, no high school, no marriage, no Officers' Club to monitor her behavior. And she finds herself stepping outside the role of a wife and doing . . . well, not strange things, but things that are a little unusual for her. Like buying a used sports car. Like renting a house at the beach. Like volunteering to work in the local Veterans' Administration hospital. That's where she meets Luke (Jon Voight), so filled with his pain, anger, and frustration. She knew him vaguely before; he was the captain of the football team at her high school. He went off to fight the war, came home paralyzed from the waist down, and now, strapped on his stomach to a table with wheels, uses canes to propel himself furiously down hospital corridors. In time, he will graduate to a wheelchair. He has ideas about Vietnam that are a little different from her husband's.

Coming Home is uncompromising in its treatment of Luke and his fellow paraplegics, and if that weren't so the opening sequences of the film wouldn't affect us so deeply. Luke literally runs into Sally on their first meeting, and his urine bag spills on the floor between them. That's the sort of embarrassment he has to learn to live with—and she too, if she is serious about being a volunteer.

She is, she finds. Luke in the early days is a raging troublemaker, and the hospital staff often finds it simpler just to tranquilize him with medication. Zombies are hardly any bother at all. Sally tries to talk to Luke, gets to know him, invites him for dinner. He begins to focus his anger away from himself and toward the war; he grows calmer, regains maturity. One day, softly, he tells her: "You know there's not an hour goes by that I don't think of making love with you."

They do eventually make love, confronting his handicap in a scene of great tenderness, beauty, and tact. It is the first time Sally has been unfaithful. But it isn't really an affair; she remains loyal to her husband, and both she and Luke know their relationship will have to end when her husband returns home. He does, too soon, having accidentally wounded himself, and discovers from Army Intelligence what his wife has been up to. The closing scenes show the film at its most uncertain, as if Ashby and his writers weren't sure in their minds how the Dern character should react. And so Dern is forced into scenes of unfocused, confused anger before the film's not very satisfying ending. It's too bad the last twenty minutes don't really work, though, because for most of its length *Coming Home* is great filmmaking and great acting.

And it is also greatly daring, since it confronts the relationship between Fonda and Voight with unusual frankness—and with emotional tenderness and subtlety that is, if anything, even harder to portray.

Consider. The film has three difficulties to confront in this relationship, and it handles all three honestly. The first is Voight's paralysis: "You aren't one of these women that gets turned on by gimps?" he asks. She is not. The second is the sexual and emotional nature of their affair, an area of enormous dramatic danger, which the movie handles in such a straightforward way, and with such an obvious display of affection between the characters, that we accept and understand.

The third is the nature of the *friendship* between Voight and Fonda, and here *Coming Home* works on a level that doesn't depend on such plot elements as the war, the husband, the paralysis, the time and place, or anything else. Thinking about the movie, we realize that men and women have been so polarized in so many films, have been made into so many varieties of sexual antagonists or lovers or rivals or other couples, that the mutual human friendship of these two characters comes as something of a revelation.

The Competition ★ ★ ★
PG, 125 m., 1981

Richard Dreyfuss (Paul Dietrich), Amy Irving (Heidi Schoonover), Lee Remick (Greta Vandemann), Sam Wanamaker (Erskine). Directed and written by Joel Oliansky and produced by William Sackheim.

The Competition is a cornball, romantic, old-fashioned, utterly predictable movie—and enormously entertaining. It's the kind of movie where you speculate on what's going to happen next, and usually you're right. When you're wrong, somehow *that's* predictable, too, as in the big international piano competition that ends the movie. We think we know who's going to win, but the surprise ending is a built-in convention of this kind of movie.

The movie's about a big international competition in San Francisco among six world-class pianists who are fighting for a $20,000 first prize and a two-year concert contract. The movie has two counterpoints to its main theme. One involves a love affair between two of the finalists, Richard Dreyfuss and Amy Irving. The other one, ridiculous but forgivable, involves a Russian piano teacher who defects to the United States, creating an international incident that causes the competition to be postponed a week.

Both of these story lines are somehow time-honored, once we realize that *The Competition* is not intended as a deadly serious treatise on big-league pianists, but as an off-beat love story. Dreyfuss and Amy Irving have a real charm and rapport as the two lovers, especially in the scenes where they argue that love has absolutely no place in a piano competition—not if it's being used as a psychological weapon to undermine one of the competitors. That's exactly what Amy Irving's piano coach (Lee Remick) thinks the dastardly Dreyfuss is trying to do.

There are three areas that the movie gets into, superficially but earnestly. One has to do with the competition itself—with the idea of artists competing with one another. Another has to do with relationships between men and women: Will the love affair between Amy and Richard be destroyed if she should win? How will his fragile male ego be able to take that? The third has to do with the idea of the artist's career, and here Remick has several good scenes and intelligently written speeches, as she tries to explain the realities of a concert career to Irving.

There is, of course, a lot of music in this movie, in addition to all the scenes of romance, backstage butterflies, international intrigue, and self-examination. And *The Competition* does an extraordinary job of persuading us that the actors are really playing their own pianos. They're not. Stay for the credits if you want the names of the real pianists on the sound track. But Dreyfuss, Irving, and the rest really *look* as if they're playing, and it took them four months of daily rehearsal to learn to fake it so well.

The Competition isn't a great movie, but it's a warm, entertaining one. It has the nerve to tell a story about serious, interesting, complicated people, who are full of surprises, because Joel Oliansky, the writer-director, has thought about them and cared enough about them to let their personalities lead him down unexpected avenues. There's only one major lapse: the inclusion, after two hours of great piano compositions, of Lalo Schifrin's dreadful song, "People Alone," sung by Randy Crawford over the end titles as if none of those great composers should be allowed to rest in peace.

Conan the Barbarian ★ ★ ★
R, 129 m., 1982

Arnold Schwarzenegger (Conan), James Earl Jones (Thulsa Doom), Max von Sydow (King Osric), Sandahl Bergman (Valeria), Ben Davidson (Rexor). Directed by John Milius and produced by Buzz Feitshans and Raffaella de Laurentiis. Screenplay by Milius and Oliver Stone.

Not since Bambi's mother was killed has there been a cannier movie for kids than *Conan the Barbarian*. It's not supposed to be just a kids' movie, of course, and I imagine a lot of other moviegoers will like it—I liked a lot of it myself, and with me, a few broadswords and leather jerkins go a long way. But *Conan* is a perfect fantasy for the alienated preadolescent. Consider: Conan's parents are brutally murdered by the evil Thulsa Doom, which gets *them* neatly out of the way. The child is chained to the Wheel of Pain, where he goes around in circles for years, a metaphor for grade school. The kid builds muscles so terrific he could be a pro football player. One day he is set free. He teams up with Subotai the Mongol, who is an example of the classic literary type—the Best Pal—and with Valeria, Queen of Thieves, who is a *real* best pal.

Valeria is everything you could ever hope for in a woman, if you are a muscle-bound preadolescent, of course. She is lanky and muscular and a great sport, and she can ride, throw, stab, fence, and climb ropes as good as a boy. Sometimes she engages in sloppy talk about love, but you can tell she's only kidding, and she quickly recovers herself with cover-up talk about loyalty and betrayal—emotions more central to Conan's experience and maturity.

With the Mongol and the Queen at his side, Conan ventures forth to seek the evil Thulsa Doom and gain revenge for the death of his parents. This requires him to journey to the mysterious East, where he learns a little quick kung-fu, and then to the mountainside where Doom rules his slave-priests from the top of his Mountain of Power. There are a lot of battles and a few interesting nights at crude wayside inns and, in general, nothing to tax the unsophisticated. *Conan the Barbarian* is, in fact, a very nearly perfect visualization of the Conan legend, of Robert E. Howard's tale of a superman who lived beyond the mists of time, when people were so pure, straightforward, and simple that a 1930s pulp magazine writer could write about them at one cent a word and not have to pause to puzzle out their motivations.

The movie's casting is ideal. Arnold Schwarzenegger is inevitably cast as Conan, and Sandahl Bergman as Valeria. Physically, they look like artist's conceptions of themselves. What's nice is that they also create entertaining versions of their characters; they, and the movie, are not without humor and a certain quiet slyness that is never allowed to get out of hand. Schwarzenegger's slight Teutonic accent is actually even an advantage, since Conan lived, of course, in the eons before American accents.

The movie is a triumph of production design, set decoration, special effects and makeup. At a time when most of the big box-office winners display state-of-the-art technology, *Conan* ranks right up there with the best. Ron Cobb, the sometime underground cartoonist who did the production design on this film (and on *Alien*) supervises an effort in which the individual frames actually do look like blowups of panels from the Marvel Comics "Conan" books. Since this Conan could have so easily looked ridiculous, that's an accomplishment.

But there is one aspect of the film I'm disturbed by. It involves the handling of Thulsa Doom, the villain. He is played here by the fine black actor James Earl Jones, who brings power and conviction to a role that seems inspired in equal parts by Hitler, Jim Jones, and Goldfinger. But when Conan and Doom meet at the top of the Mountain of Power, it was, for me, a rather unsettling image to see this Nordic superman confronting a black, and when Doom's head was sliced off and contemptuously thrown down

the flight of stairs by the muscular blond Conan, I found myself thinking that Leni Reifenstahl could have directed the scene, and that Goebbels might have applauded it.

Am I being too sensitive? Perhaps. But when Conan appeared in the pulps of the 1930s, the character suggested in certain unstated ways the same sort of Nordic superrace myths that were being peddled in Germany. These days we are more innocent again, and Conan is seen as a pure fantasy, like his British cousin, Tarzan, or his contemporary, Flash Gordon. My only reflection is that, at a time when there are *no* roles for blacks in Hollywood if they are not named Richard Pryor, it is a little unsettling to see a great black actor assigned to a role in which he is beheaded by a proto-Nordic avenger.

That complaint aside, I enjoyed *Conan*. Faithful readers will know I'm not a fan of Sword & Sorcery movies, despite such adornments as Sandahl Bergman—having discovered some time ago that heaving bosoms may be great, but a woman with a lively intelligence and a sly wit is even greater.

The problem with *Conan* is the problem with all S & S movies. After the initial premise (which usually involves revenge) is established, we suspect there's little to look forward to *except* the sets, special effects, costumes, makeup, locations, action, and surprise entrances. Almost by definition, these movies exclude the possibility of interesting, complex characters. I'd love to see them set loose an intelligent, questing, humorous hero in one of these prehistoric sword-swingers. Someone at least as smart as, say, Alley Oop.

Conan the Destroyer ★ ★ ★
PG, 103 m., 1984

Arnold Schwarzenegger (Conan), Grace Jones (Zula), Wilt Chamberlain (Bombaata), Mako (The Wizard), Tracey Walter (Malak), Sarah Douglas (Queen). Directed by Richard Fleischer and produced by Raffaella de Laurentiis. Screenplay by Stanley Mann.

What you can see in *Conan the Destroyer*, if you look closely, is the beginning of a movie dynasty. This is the film that points the way to an indefinite series of Conan adventures—one that could even replace Tarzan in supplying our need for a noble savage in the movies. Tarzan was more or less stuck in Africa;

Conan can venture wherever his sword and sorcery can take him. The first Conan movie, *Conan the Barbarian*, was a dark and gloomy fantasy about the shadows of prehistory. This second film is sillier, funnier, and more entertaining. It doesn't take place before the dawn of time, but instead in that shadowy period of movie history occupied by queens and monsters, swords and castles, warriors and fools. There's more Prince Valiant and King Arthur than *Quest for Fire*.

And Conan is defined a little differently, too. He doesn't take himself as seriously. He's not just a muscle-bound superman, but a superstitious half-savage who gets very nervous in the presence of magic. Arnold Schwarzenegger, who plays Conan again, does an interesting job of defining his pop hero: Like James Bond, Conan now stands a little aside from the incessant action around him, and observes it with a bit of relish. The story this time involves the usual nonsense. Conan is recruited by an imperious queen (Sarah Douglas, looking vampirish) to take a virgin princess (Olivia D'Abo) on a mission to an enchanted crystal palace guarded by a monster, etc. He will be joined on his quest by the head of the queen's palace guard (Wilt Chamberlain). And along the way he rescues a savage woman warrior (Grace Jones) and earns her undying gratitude.

Let's face it. The Conan series does not require extraordinary acting ability, although Schwarzenegger provides a sound professional center to the story, and the film would be impossible if he couldn't carry off Conan. The characters around him, however, are basically atmosphere, and that frees the filmmakers to abandon the usual overexposed Hollywood character actors and go for really interesting types like Chamberlain and Jones. And Grace Jones is really sensational. She has all the flash and fire of a great rock stage star, and it fits perfectly into her role as Zula, the fierce fighter. Sarah Douglas provides the necessary haughty iciness as the queen, Chamberlain gives a good try at the thankless role of the turncoat guard, and only D'Abo is a disappointment: Her princess seems to have drifted in from a teen-age sitcom.

Conan the Destroyer is more entertaining than the first Conan movie, more cheerful, and it probably has more sustained action, including a good sequence in the glass palace. Compared to the first Conan movie, which was rated R for some pretty gruesome violence, this one is milder. That's part of the idea, I think: They're repackaging Conan as your friendly family barbarian.

Continental Divide ★ ★ ★
PG, 103 m., 1981

John Belushi (Souchak), Blair Brown (Nell), Allen Goorwitz (Howard), Carlin Glynn (Sylvia), Tony Ganios (Possum), Val Avery (Yablonowitz). Directed by Michael Apted and produced by Bob Larson. Written by Lawrence Kasdan.

Here is a movie that is supposed to be about a newspaperman—a columnist for the *Chicago Sun-Times*, in fact—who is like no newspaperman I know, but exactly like every newspaperman would like to be. In my opinion, that makes it accurate. *Continental Divide* stars John Belushi as the journalist, obviously inspired by Mike Royko. He likes to walk along the lakeshore with the towers of the city outlined behind him against the lonely sky at dusk, a notebook stuck in his pocket and a cigarette stuck in his mug, on his way to rendezvous with stoolie aldermen and beautiful women.

The movie takes this character, played by Belushi with a surprising tenderness and charm, and engages him in an absolute minimum of newspaper work before spiriting him off to the Rocky Mountains for what the movie is *really* about, a romance with an eagle expert. The movie opens as if it's going to be a tough Chicago slice-of-life, with Belushi getting tips from an insider about city graft and payola, but then the columnist is beaten up by a couple of cops on an alderman's payroll. The managing editor suggests this might be a good time for Belushi to spend a few weeks out of town, and so the columnist heads for the Rockies to get an interview with a mysterious and beautiful woman (Blair Brown) who has generated worldwide curiosity by becoming a hermit to spy on the habits of bald eagles.

The whole center section of the movie takes place in the mountains, and if nothing very original happens there, we are at least reminded of several beloved movie clichés that seemed, until this film, to belong exclusively in the comedies that Katharine Hepburn and Spencer Tracy used to make together. After the city slicker Belushi crawls wearily up a mountainside (losing his booze and cigarette supply in the process), he meets the beautiful birdwatcher and falls instantly in love. She's having none of it.

She's one of those independent women who marches from crag to aerie in her L.L. Bean boots and designer wardrobe.

Because Belushi's grizzled mountain guide already has disappeared down the mountain, the two of them are destined to spend the next two weeks together in a cabin. This sets up a classic situation in which the girl talks tough but starts to fall for the big lunkhead. And there are the obligatory switches on male-female roles as Brown climbs mountains and Belushi stays home and makes goulash. Occasionally, a mountain lion attacks.

This all sounds predictable, of course, and yet this movie's predictability is one of its charms. It's rare these days to find a film that is basically content to be about a colorful man and an eccentric woman who are opposites and yet fall madly in love. It is even rarer to find a movie cast with performers who are offbeat and appealing and do not have obvious matinee-idol appeal. Belushi's character in this movie is quite unlike his self-destructive slob in *National Lampoon's Animal House;* it shows the gentleness and vulnerability that made him so appealing in some of Second City's quieter skits. Brown is also a revelation. She has been in several other movies without attracting a great deal of attention, but here she is unmistakably and wonderfully a star, a tousled-haired, big-eyed warm person who does not project sex appeal so much as warmth and humor. In other words, she has terrific sex appeal.

One of Belushi's special qualities was always an underlying innocence. Maybe he created his Blues Brothers persona in reaction to it. He's an innocent in this movie, an idealist who's a little kid at heart and who wins the love of Brown not by seducing her but by appealing to her protective qualities. That's the secret of the character's appeal. We're cheering for the romance because Belushi makes us protective, too, and we want him to have a woman who'd be good for him.

What about the movie's view of journalism? It's really just a romanticized backdrop, *The Front Page* crossed with "Lou Grant" and modernized with a computerized newsroom. The newspaper scenes in the movie were shot on location in the *Sun-Times* features department, and one of the quietly amusing things about *Continental Divide*'s view of newspaper life is that in the movie it's more sedate and disciplined than the real thing. In the "real" *Sun-Times* fea-

tures department, there's a lot of informality and chaos and good-natured confusion and people shouting at one another and eating lunch at their desks. In the movie, the extras (recruited from the *Sun-Times* staff) forget about real life and sit dutifully at their video display terminals, grinding out the news.

The newspaper's managing editor is played by Allen Goorwitz, a gifted character actor who usually plays manic overcompensators, but who this time is reasonable, calm, civilized, compassionate, and understanding, just like my boss. The movie's city of Chicago is populated by colorful old newsstand operators, muggers who apologize before taking your watch, and city council bosses who make sure their shady deals don't get into the official transcript. The newsies and muggers are fiction. The movie itself is fun: goofy, softhearted, fussy, sometimes funny, and with the sort of happy ending that columnists like to find for their stories and hardly ever find themselves.

The Conversation ★ ★ ★ ★
PG, 113 m., 1974

Gene Hackman (Harry Caul), John Cazale (Stan), Allen Garfield (Bernie Moran), Frederic Forrest (Mark), Cindy Williams (Ann), Michael Higgins (Paul). Directed by Francis Ford Coppola and produced by Fred Roos. Screenplay by Coppola.

As he is played by Gene Hackman in *The Conversation*, an expert wiretapper named Harry Caul is one of the most affecting and tragic characters in the movies; he ranks with someone like Willy Loman in *Death of a Salesman* or the pathetic captives of the middle class in John Cassavetes's *Faces*. Hackman is such a fine actor in so many different roles, from his action roles like *The French Connection* to this introverted, frightened, paranoid who is "the best bugger on the West Coast." He is, indeed, maybe the best wiretapper in the country, but he hasn't gone back to the East Coast since a bugging assignment there led to the deaths of three people. He tries to force himself not to care. He goes to confession and begs forgiveness for not paying for some newspapers, but not for bringing about a murder—because the murder, you see, was none of his business. He is only a professional. He does his job and asks no questions: doesn't *want* to know the answers.

His latest job has been a tactical masterpiece. The assignment: Bug a noon-hour conversation between two young people as they walk in a crowded plaza. He does it by tailing them with a guy who's wired for sound, and also by aiming parabolic microphones at them from buildings overlooking the plaza. This gives him three imperfect recordings of their conversation, which he can electronically marry into one fairly good tape. He is a good craftsman, and, although the film doesn't belabor his techniques, it does show us enough of how bugging is done to give us a cynical education.

It's a movie not so much about bugging as about the man who does it, and Gene Hackman's performance is a great one. He does not want to get involved (whenever he says anything like that, it sounds in italics)—but he does. After he has recorded the conversation, he plays it again and again and becomes convinced that a death may result from it, if he turns the tape in. The ways in which he interprets the tape, and the different nuances of meaning it seems to contain at different moments, remind us of Antonioni's *Blow Up*. Both movies are about the unreality of what seems real: We have here in our hands a document that is maddeningly concrete and yet refuses to reveal its meaning. And the meaning seems to be a matter of life and death.

The movie is a thriller with a shocking twist at the end, but it is also a character study. Hackman plays a craftsman who has perfected his skill at the expense of all other human qualities; he lives in paranoia in a triple-locked apartment, and is terrified when it turns out his landlady has a key. She explains she might have to get in case of some emergency—his furniture might burn up or something. He explains that none of his possessions is important to him—except his keys.

He has no friends, but he does have acquaintances in the bugging industry, and they're in town for a convention. One of them (played by Allen Garfield) is a truly frightening character. He's the one who talks about the three murders, and he's the one whose hateful envy reveals to us how good Harry Caul really is. A boozy scene in Harry's workshop, with some colleagues and their random dates, provides a perfect illustration of the ways in which even Harry's pathetically constrained social life is expressed through his work.

The Conversation is about paranoia, invasion of privacy, bugging—and also about the bothersome problem of conscience. The Watergate crew seems, for the most part, to have had no notion that what they were doing was objectively wrong. Harry wants to have no notion. But he does, and it destroys him.

The Cook, the Thief, His Wife and Her Lover ★ ★ ★ ★
NO MPAA RATING, 120 m., 1990

Richard Bohringer (Richard), Michael Gambon (Albert), Helen Mirren (Georgina), Alan Howard (Michael), Tim Roth (Mitchel), Ciaran Hinds (Cory), Gary Olsen (Spangler), Ewan Stewart (Harris). Directed by Peter Greenaway and produced by Kees Kasander. Screenplay by Greenaway.

Rarely has a movie title been more—or less—descriptive than Peter Greenaway's *The Cook, the Thief, His Wife and Her Lover*. On one level you can describe the movie simply in terms of the characters and the lustful and unspeakable things they do to one another. On another level, there is no end to the ideas stirred up by this movie, which was threatened with an X rating in America while creating a furor in Great Britain because of its political content. So, which is it? Pornographic, a savage attack on Margaret Thatcher, or both? Or is it simply about a cook, a thief, his wife, and her lover?

The thief's thuggish personality stands astride the movie and browbeats the others into submission. He is a loud, large, reprehensible criminal, played by Michael Gambon as the kind of bully you can only look at in wonder that God does not strike him dead. He presides every night over an obscene banquet in a London restaurant, where the other customers exhibit remarkable patience at his hoglike behavior. He surrounds himself with his cronies, hit men, and hangers-on, and with his long-suffering wife (Helen Mirren), for whom martyrdom has become a lifestyle. No behavior is too crude for the thief, who delights in making animal noises, who humiliates his underlings, who beats and degrades his wife, and whose treatment of the chef in the opening scene may send some patrons racing for the exits before the real horror show has even begun.

At another table in the restaurant sits the lover (Alan Howard), a book propped up so that he can read while he eats. He ignores the crude displays of the thief; his book distracts him. Then one night his eyes meet the eyes of the thief's wife. Lightning strikes, and within seconds they are making passionate love in the ladies' room. The sex scenes in this movie are as hungry and passionate as any I have seen, and yet they are upstaged by the rest of the film, which is so uncompromising in its savagery that the sex seems tranquil by comparison.

Night after night the charade goes on—the thief acting monstrously, the cook being humiliated, the wife and her lover meeting to make love in the toilet, the kitchen, the meat room, the refrigerator, anywhere that is sufficiently inappropriate and uncomfortable. (Greenaway gives a nightmare tinge to these scenes by using a different color scheme for every locale—red for the dining room, white for the toilets—and having the color of the character's costumes change as they walk from one to another.) Then the thief discovers that he is a cuckold, and in a rage orders his men to shove a book on the French Revolution down the lover's throat, one page at a time. That is the prelude to the movie's conclusion, which I will merely describe as cannibalism, to spare your feelings.

So. What is all this about? Greenaway is not ordinarily such a visceral director, and indeed his earlier films (*The Draughtsman's Contract*, *A Zed and Two Noughts*, *In the Belly of the Architect*) have specialized in cerebral detachment. What is his motivation here? I submit it is anger—the same anger that inspired large and sometimes violent British crowds to demonstrate against Margaret Thatcher's poll tax that whipped the poor and coddled the rich. Some British critics read the movie this way:

Cook = Civil servants, dutiful citizens.

Thief = Thatcher's arrogance and support of the greedy.

Wife = Britannia.

Lover = Ineffectual opposition by leftists and intellectuals.

This provides a neat formula and allows us to read the movie as a political parable. (It is easily as savage as Swift's "modest proposal" that if the Irish were starving and overcrowded, they could solve both problems by eating their babies.) But I am not sure Greenaway is simply making an Identikit protest movie, leaving us to put the labels on the proper donkeys. I think *The Cook, the Thief, His Wife and Her Lover* is more of a meditation on modern times in general. It is about the greed of an entrepreneurial class that takes over perfectly efficient companies and steals their assets, that marches roughshod over timid laws in pursuit of its own aggrandizement, that rapes the environment, that enforces its tyranny on the timid majority—which distracts itself with romance and escapism to avoid facing up to the bullyboys.

The actors in this movie exhibit a rare degree of courage. They are asked to do things that few human beings would have the nerve or the stomach for, and they do them because they believe in the power of the statement being made. Mirren, Gambon, and Howard are three of the most distinguished actors in Britain—among them, they've played most of the principal roles in Shakespeare—and here they find the resources to not only strip themselves of all their defenses, but to do so convincingly.

This isn't a freak show; it's a deliberate and thoughtful film in which the characters are believable and we care about them. Gambon makes the thief a study in hatefulness. At the end of the film, I regretted it was over because it let him too easily off the hook. Mirren's character transformation is almost frightening—she changes from submissive wife to daring lover to vicious seeker of vengeance. And watch the way she and Howard handle their sex scenes together, using sex not as joy, not as an avenue to love, but as sheer escapism; lust is their avenue to oblivion.

The Cook, the Thief, His Wife and Her Lover is not an easy film to sit through. It doesn't simply make a show of being uncompromising—it is uncompromised in every single shot from beginning to end. Why is it so extreme? Because it is a film made in rage, and rage cannot be modulated. Those who think it is only about gluttony, lust, barbarism, and bad table manners will have to think again. It is a film that uses the most basic strengths and weaknesses of the human body as a way of giving physical form to the corruption of the human soul.

Cookie ★ ★
R, 93 m., 1989

Peter Falk (Dino), Dianne Wiest (Lenore), Emily Lloyd (Cookie), Michael V. Gazzo (Carmine), Brenda Vaccaro (Bunny), Adrian Pasdar (Vito), Lionel Stander (Enzo Della Testa), Jerry Lewis (Arnold Ross), Ricki Lake (Pia). Directed by Susan Seidelman and produced by Laurence Mark. Screenplay by Nora Ephron and Alice Arlen.

Cookie brings with it a strange sense of déjà vu, as if we'd seen this film on some earlier occasion, maybe when we weren't quite paying attention. It's the kind of pleasant, sometimes funny, fairly entertaining film that you can never quite remember very well, because even the filmmakers themselves haven't seen it very clearly.

The story stars Peter Falk as Dino Capisco, a middle-level mobster who is just winding up thirteen years in prison. He has a daughter named Cookie, played by Emily Lloyd, whose mother (Dianne Wiest) has been his mistress for years. He also has a wife, Bunny (Brenda Vaccaro), who is not supposed to know about the mistress or the daughter.

Cookie is an unconventional misfit of a teen-ager whose manners annoy her father. But when he gets out of prison, he wants to do the right thing by her, and so, after a couple of other bright ideas don't pan out, he hires her as his chauffeur. Eavesdropping on everything, she quickly discovers that her father has been swindled by his old partner in crime (Michael V. Gazzo), and is in danger of getting killed if he complains too much.

Know these facts, and the movie holds few surprises. It's the fourth recent movie about Italian-American family life and the Mafia, and the least successful. After the rich details in *Married to the Mob*, *Wise Guys*, and *Spike of Bensonhurst*, this one has the fewest surprises. It's all plot and behavior, and short on juice.

There is by now a visual landscape that we come to look for in these mafioso comedies, a landscape painted in our imaginations by the films of Coppola, Scorsese, and De Palma. We know about the big cars and the Mafia restaurants and the expensive suits and the urban wastelands and industrial parking lots where illicit meetings take place. We know the interiors of the homes will be garishly decorated and that the women will all look like they bought their wardrobes in the dress shops of Atlantic City casinos.

All of this stuff is just atmosphere, but in *Cookie* it's made to count for a lot, because the characters don't seem to vibrate with lives of their own. They all seem at the service of the plot. (If you want to see Italian-Americans filled with life and played convincingly, check out the movie *True Love*.)

That isn't to say that the performances are bad—just that they're thinly written. Peter Falk gives us a version of the character he's been playing for years, with no major varia-

tions. Emily Lloyd, as his daughter, lacks the absolute originality she brought to her movie debut in *Wish You Were Here*, but that's because she's been forced into a movie teenager mold instead of having a truly original character written for her. We can anticipate the trajectory of her role almost from the first few scenes.

The originality in the movie comes from the two supporting women, Dianne Wiest as the mistress and Brenda Vaccaro as the wife. Perhaps because these characters were closest to the hearts of the director, Susan Seidelman, and screenwriters Nora Ephron and Alice Arlen, they're seen with more detail and given more quirks and tics and eccentricities. Wiest is especially funny as she tries to incorporate the role of a Mafia mistress into the profoundly middle-class values of her character.

The last act of the movie is all plot and event, which betrays how thinly the main characters have been written. The giveaway is when what happens in the story becomes more important than what happens to the personalities of the characters. By the last twenty minutes, the Falk character is on autopilot, and his daughter is orchestrating an impossible series of surprises and coincidences. What actually happens seems kind of hazy, but then the whole movie is hazy. We never feel that the filmmakers knew their characters; they seem to have learned about them from movies.

Cop ★ ★ ★
R, 110 m., 1988

James Woods (Lloyd Hopkins), Lesley Ann Warren (Kathleen McCarthy), Charles Durning (Dutch), Charles Haid (Whitey Haines), Raymond J. Barry (Gaffney), Randi Brooks (Joanie), Steven Lambert (Bobby Franco), Christopher Wynne (Jack Gibbs), Jan McGill (Jen Hopkins), Vicki Wauchope (Penny Hopkins). Directed by James B. Harris and produced by Harris and James Woods. Screenplay by Harris.

Anyone without a history of watching James Woods in the movies might easily misread *Cop*. They might think this was simply a violent, sick, contrived exploitation picture—and that would certainly be an accurate description of its surfaces. But Woods operates in this movie almost as if he were writing his own footnotes. He uses his personality, his voice, and his quirky sense of humor to undermine the material and comment on it, until *Cop* becomes an essay on this whole genre of movie. And then, with the movie's startling last shot, Woods slams shut the book.

The film stars Woods, who is the most engaging and unconventional of leading men, as a brilliant but twisted cop. He's a lone ranger, and he likes to shoot first and ask questions later. In the movie's unsettling opening scene, he kills a man who is possibly innocent, and then lets his partner clean up the mess while he tries to pick up the dead man's date. No wonder Woods is considered a danger to public safety, even by his own superiors. He makes Dirty Harry look cool and reflective.

Before long a plot begins to emerge. A dead body has been discovered, and Woods, working backward from the date of the crime and piecing together apparently unrelated clues, becomes convinced that the dead woman is the latest of a long string of murders by the same serial killer. His superiors don't want to hear about it. The last thing Los Angeles needs is another mass murderer.

But Woods persists. He interviews a kinky cop, and cross-examines a feminist bookstore owner (Lesley Ann Warren) whose high school yearbook may contain the clue to the mystery. Can it be that events fifteen years ago in high school have triggered a series of killings which have continued ever since? It can in Woods's mind, and he stays on the case even after the department has stripped him of his badge and gun because of . . . well, because basically he represents a danger to the community.

The screenplay of *Cop* was based by the director, James B. Harris, on a thriller by James Ellroy. It contains echoes of the great *film noir* stories of the 1940s, where the supporting cast is filled with various sleazebags and weirdos who are ticked off, one by one, by the hero. The difference this time is that Woods is as sleazy and weird as any of them, and not above breaking and entering and stealing evidence and making love to potential witnesses in order to get information (or, for that matter, simply in order to get laid). He wants to solve this case, but not so much because he wants to punish evildoing as because he is one stubborn S.O.B. and he doesn't like to be told not to do something.

James Woods was born to play this role. He uses a curious and effective technique to get laughs, of which the movie has plenty.

Instead of saying funny things, he knows how to throw in a pause, just long enough for the audience to figure out what he's really thinking, so that when he says a straight line, it's funny. The result is creepy; he invites us into his mind, and makes us share his obsession.

Cop is a very violent movie, all the more so because it is so casual about the violence most of the time. It sees its events through the mind of a man who should never have been a cop, and who has been a cop much too long. Yet the Woods character is not stupid and not brutal, just several degrees off from normal.

As we follow him through his "case of the yearbook murders," we can figure out the clues and sometimes arrive at conclusions before he does, but we can never quite figure out what is driving him on this case. There are strange psychological clues, as in the unforgettable scene where he tells his little daughter a bedtime story that's based on straight police procedure, but by the end, the character still remains an enigma. It's as if Woods and Harris watched a Dirty Harry movie one night and decided to see what would happen if Harry were *really* dirty.

The Cotton Club ★ ★ ★ ★
R, 121 m., 1984

Richard Gere (Dixie Dwyer), Gregory Hines (Sandman Williams), Diane Lane (Vera Cicero), Lonette McKee (Lila Rose Oliver), Bob Hoskins (Owney Madden), James Remar (Dutch Schultz), Fred Gwynne (Frenchy). Directed by Francis Ford Coppola and produced by Robert Evans. Screenplay by William Kennedy and Coppola.

After all the rumors, all the negative publicity, all the stories of fights on the set and backstage intrigue and imminent bankruptcy, Francis Ford Coppola's *The Cotton Club* is, quite simply, a wonderful movie. It has the confidence and momentum of a movie where every shot was premeditated—and even if we know that wasn't the case, and this was one of the most troubled productions in recent movie history, what difference does that make when the result is so entertaining?

The movie takes place in New York in the 1920s and 1930s, where Irish and Jewish gangsters battled the Italians for the rackets. Most of their intrigues were played out in public, in flashy settings like the Cotton

Club, a Harlem nightclub that featured the nation's most talented black entertainers on stage—playing before an all-white audience. By telling us two love stories, Coppola shows us both sides of that racial divide. He begins by introducing Dixie Dwyer (Richard Gere), a good-looking young musician who saves the life of a gangster and is immediately recruited into the hood's inner circle. There he meets the gangster's teen-age girlfriend (Diane Lane), and they immediatley fall in love—but secretly, because they'll live longer that way. Then we meet Sandman Williams (Gregory Hines), a black tap dancer who dreams of appearing at the Cotton Club, and falls in love with a member of the chorus line (Lonette McKee), a mulatto who talks about her secret life among people who think she is white.

The two love stories are developed against a background of a lot of very good jazz, some great dancing, sharply etched character studies of the gang bosses, and a couple of unexpected bursts of violence that remind us, in their sudden explosion, of moments in Coppola's *Godfather* films. Indeed, there's a lot of *The Godfather* in *The Cotton Club*, especially in the movie's almost elegiac sadness: We get the feeling of time passing, and personal histories being written, and some people breaking free and other people dying or surrendering to hopelessness.

There's another reminder of *The Godfather* movies, and that's in the brilliant, in-depth casting. There's not an uninteresting face or a boring performance in this movie, but two supporting characters really stand out: Bob Hoskins, as a crooked club owner named Madden, and Fred Gwynne, as a towering hulk named Frenchy. They are friends. They also are criminal associates. Hoskins is a bantamweight filled with hostility; Gwynne is a giant with a deep voice and glowering eyes. After Gwynne is kidnapped and Hoskins pays the ransom, the scene between the two of them begins as a routine confrontation and unfolds into something surprisingly funny and touching.

Coppola has a way, in this film, of telling all the different stories without giving us the impression he's jumping around a lot. Maybe the music helps. It gives the movie a continuity and an underlying rhythm that makes all of the characters' lives into steps in a sad ballet. We like some of the characters, but we don't have much respect for them, and the movie doesn't bother with clear distinctions between good and evil. *The Cotton*

Club is a somewhat cynical movie about a very cynical time, and along with the music and the romance there is racism, cruelty, betrayal, and stunning violence. Romance with a cutting edge.

The performances are well-suited to the material. Richard Gere is especially good as Dixie Dwyer, maybe because the camera has a way of seeing him off-balance, so that he doesn't dominate the center of each shot like a handsome icon; Coppola stirs him into the action. Diane Lane, herself still a teen-ager, is astonishing as the party girl who wants to own her own club. Gregory Hines and his brother, Maurice, create a wonderful moment of reconciliation when they begin to tap dance and end by forgiving each other for a lifetime's hurts. And Hoskins, the British actor who played the unforgettable mob chief in *The Long Good Friday*, is so wound-up and fierce and funny as the mobster that he takes a cliché and turns it into an original.

The Cotton Club took months to shoot, and they claim they have another 200,000 feet of footage as good as this movie. I doubt it. Whatever it took to do it, Coppola has extracted a very special film out of the checkered history of this project.

Country ★ ★ ★ ½
PG, 108 m., 1984

Jessica Lange (Jewell Ivy), Sam Shepard (Gil Ivy), Wilford Brimley (Otis Stewart), Matt Clark (Tom McMullen), Therese Graham (Marlene Ivy), Levi L. Knebel (Carlisle Ivy). Directed by Richard Pearce and produced by William D. Wittliff and Jessica Lange. Screenplay by Wittliff.

The opening moments of *Country* show a woman frying hamburgers and wrapping them up and sending them out to her men, working in the fields. The movie is using visuals to announce its intentions: It wants to observe the lives of its characters at the level of daily detail and routine, and to avoid pulling back into "Big Country" cliché shots. It succeeds. This movie observes ordinary American lives carefully, and passionately. The family lives on a farm in Iowa. Times are hard, and times are now. This isn't a movie about symbolic farmers living in some colorful American past. It is about the farm policies of the Carter and Reagan administrations, and how the movie believes that those policies are resulting in the destruction of family farms. It has been so long since I've

seen a Hollywood film with specific political beliefs that a funny thing happened: The movie's anger moved me as much as its story.

The story is pretty moving, too. We meet the members of the Ivy family: Jewell Ivy (Jessica Lange), the farm wife; her husband, Gil (Sam Shepard); her father, Otis (Wilford Brimley); and the three children, especially Carlisle (Levi L. Knebel), the son who knows enough about farming to know when his father has given up. The movie begins at the time of last year's harvest. Some nasty weather has destroyed part of the yield. The Ivys are behind on their FHA loan. Ordinarily, that would be no tragedy; farming is cyclical and there are good years and bad years, and eventually they'll catch up with the loan. But this year is different. An FHA regional administrator, acting on orders from Washington, instructs his people to enforce all loans strictly, and to foreclose when necessary. He uses red ink to write his recommendation on the Ivys' loan file: *Move toward voluntary liquidation.* Since there is no way the loan can be paid off, the Ivys will lose the land that Jewell's family has farmed for one hundred years. The farm agent helpfully supplies the name of an auctioneer.

All of this sounds just a little like the dire opening chapters of a story by Horatio Alger, but the movie never feels dogmatic or forced because *Country* is so clearly the particular story of these people and the way they respond. Old Otis is angry at his son-in-law for losing the farm. Jewell defends her husband, but he goes into town to drink away his impotent rage. There are loud fights far into the night in a house that had been peaceful. The boy asks, "Would somebody mind telling me what's going on around here?"

The movie's strongest passages deal with Jewell's attempts to enlist her neighbors in a stand against the government. The most touching scenes, though, are the ones showing how abstract economic policies cause specific human suffering, cause lives to be interrupted, and families to be torn apart, all in the name of the balance sheet. *Country* is as political, as unforgiving, as *The Grapes of Wrath*.

The movie has, unfortunately, one important area of weakness, in the way it handles the character of Gil (Shepard). At the beginning we have no reason to doubt that he is a good farmer. Later, the movie raises questions about that assumption, and never clearly answers them. Gil starts drinking heavily, and lays a hand on his son, and leaves

the farm altogether for several days. The local farm agent tells him, point blank, that he's a drunk and a bad farmer. Well, is he? In an affecting scene where Gil returns and asks for the understanding of his family, his drinking is not mentioned. It's good that the movie tries to make the character more complex and interesting—not such a noble hero—but if he really is a drunk and a bad farmer, then maybe that's why he's behind on the loan. The movie shouldn't raise the possibility without dealing with it.

In a movie with the power of *Country*, I can live with a problem like that because there are so many other good things. The performances are so true you feel this really is a family; we expect the quality of the acting by Lange, Shepard, and gruff old Brimley, but the surprise is Levi L. Knebel, as the son. He is so stubborn and so vulnerable, so filled with his sense of right when he tells his father what's being done wrong, that he brings the movie an almost documentary quality; this isn't acting, we feel, but eavesdropping.

Coupe de Ville ★ ½
PG-13, 98 m., 1990

Patrick Dempsey (Bobby), Arye Gross (Buddy), Daniel Stern (Marvin), Annabeth Gish (Tammy), Rita Taggert (Betty Libner), Joseph Bologna (Uncle Phil), Alan Arkin (Fred Libner). Directed by Joe Roth and produced by Larry Brezner and Paul Schiff. Screenplay by Mike Binder.

Coupe de Ville has a good heart and some nice moments, and would no doubt mean something to that hypothetical viewer who has never seen a movie like this before. But spare me. There is something deadening about the kind of formula picture where you know with absolute certainty what is going to happen and how and why. And *Coupe de Ville* is composed of so many formulas that they must have a template for it in screenwriting school.

This is a movie about how three brothers pick up a classic old car and drive it cross-country from Detroit to Florida so they can deliver it to their dad, who is living in retirement and wants it as a surprise present for his wife. The car is a 1954 Cadillac, but never mind; any old car will do for a cross-country odyssey of self-discovery, as they proved with the Buick in *Rain Man* and the pink Cadillac in the movie of the same name.

When I see an old car at the center of a movie, warning signals go up. What does the car mean and to whom? Usually it means that the filmmakers are eager to add instant nostalgia to their film, to lend it the psychic weight of an old car so that the journey can take on mythic proportions. The new cars get better mileage but, let's face it, there is something diminishing about the notion of driving cross-country on an odyssey of self-discovery in an Escort.

The movie's opening scenes show the three Libner brothers in the 1950s, at earlier ages. Already they're fighting all the time: Marvin (Daniel Stern), the oldest, a would-be disciplinarian; Buddy (Arye Gross), in the middle, the dreamer and clown; and Bobby (Patrick Dempsey), the youngest, the rebel. Then we flash forward to 1963. Marvin has just been discharged from the Air Force and has returned home to pick up a 1954 Coupe de Ville and deliver it to Florida. His father (Alan Arkin) anxiously barks instructions into the phone—he wants the car to arrive without a scratch on it. And then it gradually develops that all three brothers will be going along on the trip.

Why all three? Because wise old Arkin hopes that on the trip they will bury the hatchet, learn to accept each other's differences, and start to love their brothers. And why is Arkin so concerned that this will happen? If there is one thing I know about a movie like this, it's that when a character pronounces the word "doctor," he's got a dread disease and only months to live.

The structure of the movie is standard, basic Road Picturese, with colorful characters encountered along the way. There is a romance (between Buddy and the delightful Annabeth Gish) and an encounter with a crafty old auto repairman (James Gammon, in the movie's most entertaining performance), and a lot of fights, among themselves and with others. But mostly what I remember is Daniel Stern shouting at the top of his voice. The family fights get tiresome in this movie, particularly since we know they're obligatory warm-ups for the eventual reconciliation.

For a road picture, *Coupe de Ville* has a particularly uninspired visual style. The shots are there simply to photograph the actors and locales and further the plot. No thought it given to making them intrinsically interesting—to developing a visual strategy for the movie. And even the backgrounds could use more variety. We don't get a real sense of traveling cross-country; the film feels more like Southern locations dressed up with out-of-state road signs.

Cousins ★ ★ ★ ½
PG-13, 110 m., 1989

Ted Danson (Larry Kozinski), Isabella Rossellini (Maria Hardy), William Petersen (Tom Hardy), Sean Young (Tish Kozinski), Norma Aleandro (Edie), Lloyd Bridges (Larry's Father), Keith Coogan (Larry's Son), Gina DeAngelis (Aunt Sofia). Directed by Joel Schumacher and produced by William Allyn. Screenplay by Stephen Metcalfe.

Cousins is a celebration of carnal desire, wrapped up in a comedy so that nobody is too badly hurt. In the real world, this kind of fooling around would turn family reunions into emotional bloodbaths—but here everybody smiles, and the sun always seems to be shining. When it's over, you start asking yourself what it was really about. But while it's playing you don't think in those terms because you're having too much fun.

The movie centers around three weddings, where a big, boisterous American family gets together for dancing, drinking, gossip, and shoving matches. At the first wedding, two distant relatives (William Petersen and Sean Young) sneak off for a little hanky-panky in the middle of the afternoon. They return long after the party's over, with some lame excuse about the car breaking down.

Their disappearance has given time for their spouses (Isabella Rossellini and Ted Danson) to meet each other, and to start to like each other. Danson is a job-hopper who teaches ballroom dancing, lives upstairs over a Chinese restaurant, and isn't too concerned about his wife's possible infidelity: "Everybody has to do what they feel they have to do." But Rossellini does take it seriously, and the next day she tracks Danson down at his work to ask him if he thinks her husband and his wife are having an affair. This is, of course, the beginning of their own affair—although they're not ready to admit that for a while.

The movie is intelligently directed by Joel Schumacher, who places these two affairs in the center of a lot of detail; this isn't one of those shallow movies that's about nothing except love, and instead we get inside the lives of these people—Petersen as the womanizing BMW salesman, Rossellini as the woman who has stopped loving him but wants to be faithful to him, Danson as a warmhearted misfit, Young as a woman who wandered into the wrong marriage by mistake.

And there are some other family members who are very important to the action, especially Danson's gruff old codger of a father (Lloyd Bridges), who has most of the best one-liners in the movie, and Danson's punkster son from an earlier marriage (Keith Coogan). Acting as kind of a chorus in the background are Rossellini's mother (Norma Aleandro), who loses one husband and gains another during the course of the movie, and Aunt Sofia (Gina DeAngelis), who is perfect as the bitter relative who attends every family event and mutters darkly in the background about everything she sees there ("That dress, you would wear to a hooker's wedding").

Rossellini and Danson are at the center of the story, however, because theirs is the romance based on true love, and they try, up to a point, to deny their feelings. And Rossellini is the key to everything. She is so huggable in this movie, so funny, so sweet, that she brings sunshine into scenes that might otherwise seem contrived. She has one moment almost impossible to describe, when she and Danson have agreed to meet "accidentally" at a restaurant by bringing their families along. And as she looks up and is "surprised" to see Danson there, her joy and embarrassment and good humor all bubble up at once, and she almost breaks out laughing as she tries to go through with the charade.

Rossellini has the role in *Cousins* that was played by Marie-Christine Barrault in *Cousin, Cousine*, the warmhearted 1975 French comedy that inspired this Hollywood remake. Both actresses share some of the same qualities: sunny good humor and instinctive warmth in a merry, *zaftig* package. And they both have particularly winning smiles. Rossellini has previously been in only six or seven movies, and the one that made the biggest impression (the gothic comedy *Blue Velvet*) was scarcely designed to bring out her warmth. But in *Cousins* she has the kind of qualities that viewers really respond to.

Danson is less perfectly cast as her lover; this is his most believable and likable role, and yet there is a certain reserve about him that never quite seems to lift, and maybe William Petersen, who plays the other man, would have seemed warmer. Still, the material is so strong that we're inclined to believe that if Rossellini likes him, she must know what she's doing. Petersen is very good as the womanizing salesman, tormented by guilt but a sinner anyway. Sean Young, as Danson's wife, is brittle and distant; we never really get to know her.

We do, though, have a lot of fun with Lloyd Bridges and Keith Coogan, as Danson's father and son. Bridges has three or four lines that are explosively funny, and Coogan, a self-styled "video performance artist," makes an avant-garde version of a wedding movie that brings things to a screeching halt.

Cousins is basically a rambling, warm-hearted but artificial construction that seems more convincing because of the riot of life that surrounds the manipulated central characters. We don't really believe what's happening—adultery is never this simple, and seldom this life-affirming—but the movie gets away with murder because it's funny; because the dialogue has been written with an ear for the funny things people say, especially when they're being serious; and because of Rossellini.

Crazy People ★ ★
R, 92 m., 1990

Dudley Moore (Emory Leeson), Daryl Hannah (Kathy Burgess), Paul Reiser (Stephen Bachman), Mercedes Ruehl (Dr. Elizabeth Baylor), J.T. Walsh (Charles F. Drucker), Ben Hammer (Dr. Horace Koch), Dick Cusack (Mort Powell), Alan North (Judge), David Paymer (George Cartelli), Danton Stone (Saabs). Directed by Tony Bill and produced by Tom Barad. Screenplay by Mitch Markowitz.

I wonder if they have a squad out in Hollywood named the Movie Police, who swoop down on screenplays and enforce all of the obligatory clichés and story formulas. Every once in a while you find a movie that has the spark of inspired craziness in it, that has a few scenes that tell you the people who wrote the movie were nutty but brilliant. And then, just when your hopes are beginning to stir—the Movie Police strike.

"Excuse me, sir. Movie Police here. Do you have a love story in this movie?"

"Uh, afraid not. There's no need for one."

"But who is the female lead?"

"There isn't any."

"And the heartwarming romantic conclusion?"

"Are you kidding? This is a cynical satire about advertising."

"And do you have a lot of lovable, huggable goofballs in supporting roles?"

"Only the usual demented creative types who work in any ad agency."

"Then I'm afraid you'll have to come down to the studio with us. What you've done is against . . . Movie Law!"

Why do I get the feeling a scene like this was played at some point early in the history of *Crazy People*? Because the two halves of the movie fit together so uneasily. On the one hand, we have Dudley Moore, demented and crazed advertising genius, who gets fed up with the hypocrisy of routine advertising and creates his own campaigns, campaigns that tell the literal, brutal, sacrilegious truth. On the other hand, we have a subplot involving his romance with a sweet girl he meets in an insane asylum, and, yes, there is a crowd of lovable, huggable goofballs who are vindicated in the relentlessly upbeat ending.

Moore plays Emory Leeson, ad man. The unorthodox campaigns he creates for his clients can mostly not be quoted here because they deal in very direct sexual imagery. Let it be said, however, that many of the campaigns inspire loud and delighted laughter from the audience. *Crazy People*, in fact, has more really big laughs in it than any other unsuccessful comedy I've seen. What's especially fun is when the campaigns are printed by mistake, and we see the reactions of a public exposed for the first time to things they have secretly believed for a long time.

The ad campaigns are rude, obscene, and hilarious. The rest of the story is sappy, as Moore's colleagues have him committed to a mental institution. At first he protests that he doesn't belong there, but then he begins to like the place, to enjoy the competent care of the psychiatrist (Mercedes Ruehl), and the soothing tenderness of a beautiful blond patient (Daryl Hannah). Before long, and without any preparation or particular justification for such a miracle, Moore and Hannah are in love. And Moore doesn't ever want to leave this wonderful place—especially not if it means returning to the real madhouse of the ad agency.

There is nothing really wrong with the scenes in the institution, except that they're in the wrong movie. Daryl Hannah is warm and engaging as the girl who loves Moore (I like her better in these everyday roles than

when she gets saddled with weirdos), and Mercedes Ruehl (the mobster's wife in *Married to the Mob*) avoids all of the usual psychiatrist clichés. The other patients in the institution turn out, inevitably, to be natural-born advertising geniuses, of course. (One of the basic Movie Police Laws is that crazy people are always more sane than the rest of us.)

My question is, what's this sweet, sunny story doing in the same movie with all of those cheerfully offensive ads? Why couldn't the movie have followed its first instincts and been a hard-edged, cynical social satire? A few weeks before this film was released, Michael Caine starred in *A Shock to the System*, a movie that *did* have the courage of its dark convictions and followed them through to the end. Now here is a movie that has never asked itself this basic question: Why would the kind of people who would laugh at the rude ads in this movie be interested in its cutesy-poo subplot?

Creepshow ★ ★ ★
R, 129 m., 1982

Hal Holbrook (Henry Northrup), Adrienne Barbeau (Wilma Northrup), Fritz Weaver (Dexter Stanley), Leslie Nielsen (Richard Vickers), Carrie Nye (Sylvia Graham), E.G. Marshall (Upson Pratt), Viveca Lindfors (Aunt Bedelia). Directed by George A. Romero and produced by Richard P. Rubinstein. Screenplay by Stephen King.

Creepshow plays like an anthology of human phobias. What could be more horrifying that sticking your hand into a long-forgotten packing crate and suddenly feeling teeth sink into you? Unless it would be finding yourself buried up to the neck on the beach, with the tide coming in? Or trapped in an old grave, with the tombstone toppling down on top of you? Or having green stuff grow all over you? Or how about being smothered by cockroaches?

The horrors in *Creepshow* are universal enough, and so is the approach. These stories have been inspired, right down to the very camera angles, by the classic EC Comics of the early 1950s—titles like "Tales from the Crypt," which curdled the blood of Eisenhower-era kids raised on such innocent stuff as Captain Marvel, and appalled their elders. (EC Comics almost single-handedly inspired the creation of the Comics Code Authority.) The filmmakers of *Creepshow* say they were raised on those old comics, and it would appear that their subsequent careers were guided by the Ol' Crypt-Keeper's bag of tales. The movie's director is George A. Romero, whose most famous credit is *Night of the Living Dead,* and the original screenplay is by Stephen King, who wrote *Carrie* and *The Shining.* What they've done here is to recapture not only the look and the storylines of old horror comics, but also the peculiar feeling of poetic justice that permeated their pages. In an EC horror story, unspeakable things happened to people—but, for the most part, they deserved them.

The five stories told in this film often center around a fatal flaw. Upson Pratt, for example, the hero of the fifth story, is a compulsively neat and tidy man who lives in a hermetically sealed command center, much like Howard Hughes. What could be more suitable than an invasion of his stronghold by cockroaches? The professors in the story about the thing in the box have spent their lives collecting old facts: how perfect that one long-collected piece of evidence should still bite back!

Romero and King have approached this movie with humor and affection, as well as with an appreciation of the macabre. They create visual links to comic books by beginning each segment with several panels of a comic artist's version of the story, and then dissolving from the final drawn panel to a reality that exactly mirrors it. The acting also finds the right note. Such veterans of horror as Hal Holbrook, E.G. Marshall, and Adrienne Barbeau know how to paint their personalities broadly, edging up to caricature. Nobody in this movie is a three-dimensional person, or is meant to be. They are all types. And their lives are all object lessons.

The original full name of EC Comics was "Educational Comics," and you got an education, all right. You learned it was unwise to stick your hand into a box labeled "Danger—Do Not Open." It was unwise to speak ill of the dead. And it was quite unwise to assume that cockroaches would never decide to gang up and fight back.

Cries and Whispers ★ ★ ★ ★
R, 106 m., 1973

Harriet Andersson (Agnes), Kari Sylwan (Anna), Ingrid Thulin (Karin), Liv Ullmann (Maria), Erland Josephson (Lakaren), Henning Moritzen (Joakim). Directed, produced, and written by Ingmar Bergman.

Cries and Whispers is like few movies we'll ever see. It is hypnotic, disturbing, frightening. It envelops us in a red membrane of passion and fear, and in some way that I do not fully understand, it employs taboos and ancient superstitions to make its effect. We slip lower in our seats, feeling claustrophobia and sexual disquiet, realizing that we have been surrounded by the vision of a filmmaker who has absolute mastery of his art. *Cries and Whispers* is about dying, love, sexual passion, hatred, and death—in that order.

The film inhabits a manor house set on a vast country estate. The rooms of the house open out from each other like passages in the human body; with the exception of one moment when Agnes, the dying woman, opens her window and looks at the dawn, the house offers no views. It looks in upon itself.

Three women stay in the house with Agnes (Harriet Andersson), waiting for her to die. She is in the final stages of cancer and in great pain. The women are Karin and Maria, her sisters, and Anna, the stout, round-cheeked servant. In elliptical flashbacks (intended to give us emotional information, not to tell a story), we learn that the three sisters have made little of their lives. Karin (Ingrid Thulin) is married to a diplomat she despises. Maria (Liv Ullmann) is married to a cuckold, and so she cuckolds him (what is one to do?). Agnes, who never married, gave birth to a few third-rate watercolors. Now, in dying, she discovers at last some of the sweetness of life.

The sisters remember that they were close in childhood, but somehow in growing up they lost the ability to love, to touch. Only Anna, the servant, remembers how. When Agnes cries out in the night, in fear and agony, it is Anna who cradles her to her bosom, whispering soft endearments. The others cannot stand to be touched. In a moment of conjured nostalgia, Maria and Karin remember their closeness as children. Now, faced with the fact of their sister's death, they deliberately try to synthesize feeling and love. Quickly, almost frantically, they touch and caress each other's faces, but their touching is a parody and by the next day they have closed themselves off again.

These two scenes—of Anna embracing Agnes, and of Karin and Maria touching like frightened kittens—are two of the greatest Bergman has ever created. The feeling in these scenes—I should say, the way they force us to feel—constitutes the meaning of this film. It has no abstract message; it communicates with us on a level of human feeling so deep that we are afraid to invent words for the things found there.

The camera is as uneasy as we are. It stays at rest mostly, but when it moves it doesn't always follow smooth, symmetrical progressions. It darts, it falls back, is stunned. It lingers on close-ups of faces with the impassivity of God. It continues to look when we want to turn away; it is not moved. Agnes lies thrown on her deathbed, her body shuddered by horrible, deep gasping breaths, as she fights for air, for life. The sisters turn away, and we want to, too. We know things are this bad—but we don't want to know. Bergman's camera stays and watches.

The movie is drenched in red. Bergman has written in his screenplay that he thinks of the inside of the human soul as a membranous red. Color can be so important; in *Two English Girls,* a movie about the absence of passion, Francois Truffaut kept red out of his compositions until the movie's one moment of unfeigned feeling, and then he filled his screen with red.

All of *Cries and Whispers* is occupied with passion—but the passion is inside, the characters can't get it out of themselves. None of them can, except Anna (Kari Sylwan). The film descends into a netherworld of the supernatural; the dead woman speaks (or is it only that they think they hear her?). She reaches out and grasps for Karin (or does Karin move the dead arms?—Bergman's camera doesn't let us see).

The movie, like all supernatural myths, like all legends and fables (and like all jokes—which are talismans to take the pain from truth) ends in a series of threes. The dead woman asks the living women to stay with her, to comfort her while she pauses within her dead body before moving into the great terrifying void. Karin will not. Maria will not. But Anna will, and makes pillows of her breasts for Agnes. Anna is the only one of them who remembers how to touch and love. And she is the only one who believes in God.

We saw her in the morning, praying. We learned that she had lost her little daughter, but is resigned to God's will. Is there a God in Bergman's film, or is there only Anna's faith? The film ends with a scene of astonishing, jarring affirmation: We see the four women some months earlier, drenched with the golden sun, and we hear Anna reading from Agnes's diary: "I feel a great gratitude to my life, which gives me so much." And takes it away.

Crimes and Misdemeanors ★ ★ ★ ★
PG-13, 107 m., 1989

Caroline Aaron (Barbara), Alan Alda (Lester), Woody Allen (Cliff Stern), Claire Bloom (Miriam Rosenthal), Mia Farrow (Halley Reed), Joanna Gleason (Wendy Stern), Anjelica Huston (Dolores Paley), Martin Landau (Judah Rosenthal), Jenny Nichols (Jenny), Jerry Orbach (Jack Rosenthal), Sam Waterston (Ben). Directed by Woody Allen and produced by Robert Greenhut. Screenplay by Allen.

Woody Allen's *Crimes and Misdemeanors* is a thriller about the dark nights of the soul. It shockingly answers the question most of us have asked ourselves from time to time: Could I live with the knowledge that I had murdered someone? Could I still get through the day and be close to my family and warm to my friends knowing that because of my own cruel selfishness, someone who had loved me was lying dead in the grave?

This is one of the central questions of human existence, and society is based on the fact that most of us are not willing to see ourselves as murderers. But in the world of this Woody Allen film, conventional piety is overturned, and we see into the soul of a human monster. Actually, he seems like a pretty nice guy.

He's an eye doctor with a thriving practice, he lives in a modern home on three acres in Connecticut, he has a loving wife and nice kids and lots of friends, and then he has a mistress who is going crazy and threatening to start making phone calls and destroy everything. This will not do. He has built up a comfortable and well-regulated life over the years and is respected in the community. He can't let some crazy woman bring a scandal crashing around his head.

Crimes and Misdemeanors tells his story with what Allen calls realism, and what others might call bleak irony. He also tells it with a great deal of humor. Who else but Woody Allen could make a movie in which virtue is punished, evildoing is rewarded, and there is a lot of laughter—even subversive laughter at the most shocking times?

Martin Landau stars in the film as the opthalmologist who has been faithful to his wife (Claire Bloom) for years—all except for a passionate recent affair with a flight attendant (Anjelica Huston). For a few blessed months he felt free and young again, and they walked on the beach, and he said things

that sounded to her like plans for marriage. But he is incapable of leaving his wife, and when she finally realizes that she becomes enraged.

What can the doctor do? It's a *Fatal Attraction* situation, and she's sending letters to his wife (which he barely intercepts) and calling up from the gas station down the road threatening to come to his door and reveal everything. In desperation, the doctor turns to his brother (Jerry Orbach), who has Mafia connections. And the brother says that there's really no problem, because he can make one telephone call and the problem will go away.

Are we talking . . . murder? The doctor can barely bring himself to say the word. But his brother is more realistic and certainly more honest, and soon the doctor is forced to ask, and answer, basic questions about his own values. Allen uses flashbacks to establish the childhood of both brothers, who grew up in a religious Jewish family with a father who solemnly promised them that God saw everything, and that, even if He didn't, a good man could not live happily with an evil deed on his conscience.

The story of the doctor's dilemma takes place at the center of a large cast of characters—the movie resembles Allen's *Hannah and Her Sisters* in the way all of the lives become tangled. Among the other important character are Allen himself, as a serious documentary filmmaker whose wife's brother (Alan Alda) is a shallow TV sitcom producer of great wealth and appalling vanity. Through his wife's intervention, Allen gets a job making a documentary about the Alda character—and then both men make a pass at the bright, attractive production assistant (Mia Farrow). Which will she choose? The dedicated documentarian or the powerful millionaire?

Another important character is a rabbi (Sam Waterston), who is going blind. The eye doctor treats him and then turns to him for moral guidance, and the rabbi, who is a good man, tells him what we would expect to hear. But the rabbi's blindness is a symbol for the dark undercurrent of *Crimes and Misdemeanors*, which seems to argue that God has abandoned men, and that we live here below on a darkling plain, lost in violence, selfishness, and moral confusion.

Crimes and Misdemeanors is not, properly speaking, a thriller, and yet it plays like one. In fact, it plays a little like those *film noir* classics of the 1940s, like *Double Indemnity*,

in which a man thinks of himself as moral, but finds out otherwise. The movie generates the best kind of suspense, because it's not about what will happen to people, it's about what decisions they will reach. We have the same information they have. What would we do? How far would we go to protect our happiness and reputation? How selfish would we be? Is our comfort worth more than another person's life? Woody Allen does not evade this question, and his answer seems to be, yes, for some people. Anyone who reads the crime reports in the daily papers would be hard put to disagree with him.

Crimes of Passion ★ ½
R, 107 m., 1984

Kathleen Turner (Joanne/China Blue), Anthony Perkins (Shayne), John Laughlin (Grady), Annie Potts (Amy). Directed by Ken Russell and produced by Barry Sandler. Screenplay by Sandler.

I like what George Burns said about his sex life: "I got more laughs in bed than I ever got in vaudeville." Sex is an activity of great and serious importance to its participants, but as a spectator sport it has a strange way of turning into comedy. Look, for example, at Ken Russell's overwrought film *Crimes of Passion*, in which good performances and an interesting idea are metamorphosed into one of the silliest movies in a long time.

Part of the fault for that lies with Russell. A great deal of the fault no doubt lies with the movie rating system, which required massive cuts in the movie before it could qualify for an R rating, and with New World Pictures, which was too chicken to release the movie with an X.* But some of the fault also lies with the subject of sex itself, because there is nothing quite so ridiculous as someone else's sexual fantasies, and nothing as fascinating as our own.

The movie stars Kathleen Turner in a performance which must have taken a great deal of nerve and curiosity. She plays a woman with a dual identity: by day, she's a sophisticated fashion designer named Joanne, and by night she's a kinky hooker named China Blue. The psychological reasons behind this double existence are dished up out of the usual Freudian stew. Turner's day work is photographed in a matter-of-fact way. The nighttime street scene is seen by Russell, however, as a lurid *film noir* world of flashing red neon signs, garter belts, squirming sadomasochists, and perverts like the one played by Anthony Perkins, who proves in this movie that there is probably no role he would turn down because it would be bad for his image. Perkins plays a demented street preacher who sniffs uppers, hangs out in peep shows, and brandishes a murder weapon that looks like *Jaws* crossed with the latest electronic sex toy.

Perkins is just one of the clients who enlivens Turner's evenings. Others are more poignant as when Turner is hired by the wife of a dying man, who wants her husband to feel like a man for one last time. She enters the man's room, and as they begin to talk, a touchingly authentic atmosphere is established.

The purpose of *Crimes of Passion* was apparently to explore the further shores of sexual behavior. Because of the double standard of the movie ratings system, which prizes violence more highly than sex, a great deal of the behavior is missing from the movie, and what is left is a steamy, bloody thriller. I'm not sure that's what Russell had in mind. Anthony Perkins distorts most of the scenes he's in, with overacting so blatant that the plausibility of the whole movie is undermined. Turner tries. So does John Laughlin, as a square young husband who learns a lot from her about sex and love. but when *Crimes of Passion* is over, what's left? Not much. You know you're in trouble in a sex movie when you spend more time thinking about the parts they left out than the parts they put in.

*The videocassette version restores some of the excised footage.

Critters ★ ★ ★
PG-13, 97 m., 1986

Dee Wallace Stone (Helen), M. Emmet Walsh (Harv), Billy Green Bush (Jay Brown), Scott Grimes (Brad Brown), Nadine Van Der Velde (April Brown), Don Opper (Charlie McFadden), Terrence Mann (Johnny Steele). Directed by Stephen Herek and produced by Rupert Harvey. Screenplay by Herek and Domonic Muir.

If perfect fools can hold driver's licenses, why can't creatures from outer space be just as dumb? And if they *are* bounty hunters, why shouldn't they be trigger-happy—firing at everything that moves, like a television set,

for example? We always assume that visitors from other worlds will be far more intelligent than we are, but maybe they'll just turn out to have faster means of intergalactic travel.

In the opening scenes of *Critters*, a spaceship is approaching a barren asteroid which has been converted into a prison. It carries on board several of the dreaded Cripes, who are furry little bowling balls with dozens of rows of sharp teeth. The Cripes escape, take over the ship, and land on earth. And bounty hunters follow them here, while the nasty little critters are terrorizing the countryside.

What this gives us is a truly ambitious rip-off of not one but four recent science-fiction movies: *Gremlins, E.T., The Terminator,* and *Starman.* We get the critters from the first and the hunters from the third, and from *Starman* the notion that an alien can assume the outward appearance of a human being. (That is a particularly attractive quality for an alien to have, especially in a low-budget picture, because then you can hire an actor and claim he is inhabited by an alien, and you can save a lot of money on special effects.) From *E.T.,* there is Dee Wallace Stone, who played Henry Thomas's mother in that film and is now the equally dubious and harried mother of young Scott Grimes, a plucky kid who goes into battle against the invaders.

The movie takes place in a small town and the surrounding countryside, where the vicious little furballs start attacking everything that moves. They have a lot of tricks at their command: They can eat you like a piranha, shoot darts at you from their foreheads, and curl up into a ball and roll away. That leads up to the big scene in the bowling alley, where we expect that someone's going to reach down and pick up a critter instead of a ball, but as it turns out, that scene contains other surprises.

We meet the folks in the area. There's the friendly farmer (Billy Green Bush), his wife (Stone), son (Grimes), and daughter (Nadine Van Der Velde). They live on a farm that gives the critters their first haven, and there's the obligatory scary scene where the father goes down in the basement with his flashlight to see what's making the noise.

Meanwhile, the local lawman (that dependably slimy character actor M. Emmet Walsh) notices that strange things are happening in his territory. Two strangers from out of town have turned up and started to blast everybody away, and dang if one of them doesn't look exactly like the local min-

ister! The other one soon assumes the outward appearance of the village idiot.

All of these plot threads move inexorably toward the final showdown, but what's interesting is the way the movie refuses to be just a thriller. The director, Stephen Herek, likes to break the mood occasionally with a one-liner out of left field, and he gives the critters some of the funniest lines. What makes *Critters* more than a rip-off are its humor and its sense of style. This is a movie made by people who must have had fun making it.

Crocodile Dundee ★ ★
PG-13, 98 m., 1986

Paul Hogan (Mike Dundee), Linda Kozlowski (Sue Charlton), John Meillon (Wally), Michael Lombard (Sam Charlton), Mark Blum (Richard). Directed by Peter Faiman and produced by John Cornell. Screenplay by Hogan, Ken Shadie, and Cornell.

They made this kind of movie better in the 1930s, when audiences were more accustomed to the reliable old story line: Aggressive female newspaper reporter from New York tracks down legendary wilderness guide in Outback, is saved from crocodiles, falls in love, asks living legend to return with her to New York, there to meet her millionaire daddy and her fiancé, a wimp. Clark Gable and Carole Lombard could have made this movie. Maybe they did.

Crocodile Dundee knows the words to this story, but not the music. All of the clichés are in the right places, and most of the gags pay off, and there are moments of real amusement as the Australian cowboy wanders around Manhattan as a naive sightseer. The problem is, there's not one moment of chemistry between the two stars—Paul Hogan as "Crocodile" Dundee and Linda Kozlowski as the clever little rich girl. The movie feels curiously machine-made, as if they had all the right ingredients and simply forgot to add the animal magnetism.

The movie got a lot of attention because of Paul Hogan, a former truck driver who has become one of Australia's top TV stars, and is known over here for those Australian tourism commercials where he reminds us about who won the 1986 America's Cup. He's a lean, tanned, weathered man with a perpetual squint, and he looks right at home when he's stabbing crocodiles and strangling snakes. His co-star is not as well cast; Linda Kozlowski always looks a little too made up, a little too formal, to be able to really unwind and accept this sweaty folk hero. When she smiles at him, it's politely, not passionately. Maybe she's downwind.

The story begins with a New York newspaper sending her on assignment to interview Dundee, who allegedly lost a leg to a crocodile and then crawled for hundreds of miles through the Outback. She spends more money on this story than most newspapers earmark for a gubernatorial election. She hires a helicopter, pays a $2,500 fee to Dundee's partner, and later—after she brings the Croc back to New York—puts him in a $900-a-day suite at the Plaza. What she doesn't do is get the story.

The Manhattan scenes are the best, as Dundee scares off muggers, unmasks transvestites, hitches rides with mounted policemen, and sleeps on the floor of his hotel room. Many of the best scenes have the same whimsical quality as *The Gods Must Be Crazy*, in which a character with a truly direct and open mind is able to see right through the strange conventions of civilization.

What doesn't work is the love story. If we don't believe in the chemistry between Crocodile and the woman reporter, we certainly don't believe her fiancé, a simpering and supercilious jerk who tries to pull the old foreign language menu trick on the guy from the sticks. The ending of the movie (which I would not dream of revealing) involves a love scene on a subway platform. If these were two lovers we really cared about, the scene, as written, could have had the impact of that moment in *An Officer and a Gentleman* where Richard Gere carries Debra Winger off the factory floor. As it's acted in this movie, alas, the scene is so unconvincing that the lovers are upstaged by the other people on the train platform.

Crossing Delancey ★ ★ ¹/₂
PG, 97 m., 1988

Amy Irving (Isabella Grossman), Peter Riegert (Sam Posner), Reizl Bozyk (Bubbie Kantor), Jeroen Krabbe (Anton Maes), Sylvia Miles (Hannah Mandelbaum). Directed by Joan Micklin Silver and produced by Michael Nozik. Screenplay by Susan Sandler.

Crossing Delancey makes the mistake of creating characters who are interesting enough to make us care for them—and then denying them freedom of speech. The people in this movie have intelligence in their eyes, but their words are defined by the requirements of formula comedy. If this had been a European film, the same plot would have been populated with adults, and the results might have been magical.

The film tells the story of Isabella (Amy Irving), a Jewish girl from New York in her early thirties, who works for a literary bookstore. In her work she gets to meet lots of interesting people—mad poets, bohemian book lovers, literary lions—and she considers herself to be part of the scene. She does not quite understand, or admit, that many of the shaggy intellectual giants she meets are attracted not by her mind but by her beauty. She has not fully accepted the fact that some men, on one level or another, are thinking of sex when they talk to a pretty girl, no matter how they may flatter her intelligence.

As the movie opens, Isabella is offered a job as the personal secretary of a self-important European poet (Jeroen Krabbe). This is the last job she needs. It is instantly obvious to the audience that her duties will be more personal than secretarial, and that the poet is an inflated, lying phony.

Meanwhile, Isabella's grandmother (Reizl Bozyk), known as "Bubbie," is concerned for her welfare. Why doesn't this nice young lady have a husband and a few babies? She engages the services of a matchmaker (Sylvia Miles) who produces a prime matrimonial candidate: Sam, the pickle man, who has inherited his father's pickle store on the Lower East Side.

To please Bubbie, Isabella agrees to dinner with the matchmaker and the pickle man (Peter Riegert). But she's an uptown girl now, moving in circles where she discusses novels, not pickles, and the whole world of her grandmother and matchmakers and pickle men seems hopelessly antiquated.

So, of course, we all know what happens next. The poet turns out to be a rat. The pickle man turns out to be sweet and sensitive, just the man for Isabella, and he only agreed to the matchmaker's offer because he'd had his eye on Isabella for months. It is inevitable that Isabella will marry into pickles, but first there has to be manufactured suspense, based on her own intractable nature. Sam turns up for dates, but Isabella doesn't. Things are said that are misunderstood. The whole relationship almost breaks down before it gets started. The usual stuff.

I think I could enjoy a movie about a book lover and a pickle man, if only the two characters were allowed to talk openly and deeply about their two different worlds. I would not even require them to talk seriously; they could be in a romantic comedy, if they were allowed to be articulate. But the characters in *Crossing Delancey* talk almost exclusively in terms of the movie's standard plot construction. And the character of the pickle man is so seriously underwritten that he is literally given only one speech of any substance. The rest of the time he is simply a story device. It is hard to believe these two people could, or should, fall in love because they have no communication of any depth or wit.

That leaves Bubbie and Hannah Mandelbaum, the matchmaker. Both characters are straight out of musical comedy by way of the TV sitcom, but at least they are acted with great joy by Bozyk and Miles, so they're fun to watch and listen to. They have the spontaneity of life and the gift of gab.

I suppose that some people watching this movie could get so caught up in the energy of the two older ladies that they'd go along with the conspiracy and try to cheer Isabella and Sam into marriage. But, hey, is it a good idea to get married simply because the rules of plot construction call for it? In life, maybe that would be OK, but it's not good enough for a movie.

Crossover Dreams ★ ★ ★
PG-13, 85 m., 1985

Ruben Blades (Rudy Veloz), Shawn Elliott (Orlando), Tom Signorelli (Lou Rose), Elizabeth Pena (Liz Garcia), Frank Robles (Ray Solo), Joel Diamond (Neil Silver). Directed by Leon Ichaso and produced by Manuel Arce. Screenplay by Ichaso and Arce.

Crossover Dreams does not begin with an original idea. It shows the rise and fall of a musician whose talent takes him to the top, and whose ego and weaknesses pull him back to the bottom again. The first time I saw this story, it was about Gene Krupa, and in his big comeback concert in Carnegie Hall, he dropped his drumsticks and had to find the courage to start again. I've seen the same story countless times again, translated into the idioms of jazz, country, rock, and classical, and now here is the salsa version, starring Ruben Blades.

The story isn't new, but it sure does wear well. Maybe that's because Blades is such an engaging performer, playing a character who is earnest and sincere when he needs to be, but who always maintains a veil over his deepest secrets. The story is formula, but the film's treatment of it is fresh and perceptive, and there's an exhilarating energy level. The opening shots, in fact, reminded me of the extraordinary opening of Martin Scorsese's first film, *Who's That Knocking at My Door?* Music pounds on the sound track, as young men race around the streets of New York, filled with their own life and importance.

The movie takes place largely in Spanish Harlem, where the Blades character, Rudy Veloz, makes the rounds of Latino nightclubs, working with a band of old friends and mentors. He dreams of "crossing over," of breaking out of the Latino circuit and making it downtown, to the world of national TV, music videos, and record contracts. And for a moment it looks as if he might.

He meets a shabby Broadway talent agent, who fails to impress him (but who gives him some of the most realistic advice he'll receive in this movie). Then he's "discovered" by a record producer, who picks him up out of his life, briefly shines the spotlight on him, and then throws him back into obscurity again. The movie's most convincing and painful scenes come after Veloz's brief moment of fame, when he has to return to his friends and try to conceal the extent of his failure.

Against this serious undertone, the movie hurls a lot of good music. Blades, the Panamanian salsa star who has crossed over, is not only a good singer but a surprisingly versatile actor who never seems to be straining for an effect, never seems to stray outside his character, and will probably get some more serious acting jobs after this debut.

Crossroads ★ ★ ★ ½
R, 98 m., 1985

Ralph Macchio (Eugene Martone), Joe Seneca (Willie Brown), Jami Gertz (Frances), Joe Morton (Scratch's Assistant), Robert Judd (Scratch), Harry Carey, Jr. (Bartender). Directed by Walter Hill and produced by Mark Carliner. Screenplay by John Fusco.

Crossroads borrows so freely and is a reminder of so many other movies that it's a little startling, at the end, to realize how effective the movie is and how original it manages to feel despite all the plunderings. The movie stars Ralph Macchio as a bright teen-ager

who studied classical guitar at Juilliard and worships as his heroes the great old blues musicians of the 1930s and 1940s. One day he tracks down a survivor of that era, a harmonica player named Willie Brown (Joe Seneca) in a nursing home. Macchio helps him escape, and they hit the road, hoboing their way down South to a crossroads where Seneca once made a deal with the devil.

With the devil? You bet. *Crossroads* is a cheerful cross between a slice of life and a supernatural fable. And at the end, it's up to the kid to pick up his guitar and outplay the devil's man, to save Seneca's soul. This story is a combination of no less than two reliable genres. It borrows, obviously, from Macchio's 1984 *The Karate Kid*, which was also the story of a young man's apprenticeship with an older master. It also borrows from the countless movies in which everything depends on who wins the big fight, match, game, or duel in the last scene. The notion of the showdown with the devil may have been suggested by the country song "Devil Went Down to Georgia."

And yet the remarkable thing is how fresh all this material seems, and how entertaining it is. Just when I'm ready to despair of a movie coming up with a fresh plot, a movie like *Crossroads* comes along to remind me that acting, writing, and direction can redeem any plot, and make any story new. The foundation for *Crossroads* is the relationship between the boy and the old man, and here we have two performances that are well suited to one another. Macchio, once again, as in *The Karate Kid*, has an unstudied, natural charm. A lot of young actors seem to take themselves seriously, but not many have Macchio's gift of seeming to take other things seriously. We really believe, in this movie, that he is a fanatic about the blues, and has read all the books and listened to all the records.

Seneca does a terrific job as a rock-solid, conniving, no-nonsense old man who doesn't take this kid seriously at first, and uses him as a way to get out of the nursing home and back down South to the crossroads, where he has a longstanding rendezvous. The kid knows that Willie was a partner of the legendary blues musician Robert Johnson and he makes a deal with the old man. He'll help him return to that crossroads if the old man will teach him a lost Johnson song.

Along the way, the two men pick up a third partner, a tough young runaway named

Frances (Jami Gertz), and there is a brief, sweet romance between the two young people before she leaves one morning, perhaps because it is better for the old man and the young one to move on toward their mutual destiny.

Gertz is a newcomer: this was her second major movie in 1985, after a somewhat thankless role in *Quicksilver*, in which she worked for a bicycle messenger service. She's just right for this movie, with the toughness required by the character, and yet with the tenderness and the romantic notes that remind us that this is really a myth. Another good performance in the movie is by Joe Morton, who played *The Brother from Another Planet* and this time is the devil's assistant, sinister and ingratiating.

The film was directed by Walter Hill, who specializes in myths, in movie characters who seem to represent something greater than themselves. Detailed character studies are not his strong point; he makes movies like *The Warriors*, *48 HRS*, and *Streets of Fire*, in which the characters seem made out of the stuff of legend. In *48 HRS*, though, he also found the human qualities in the Nick Nolte and Eddie Murphy characters, and he does that again this time, making Seneca and Macchio so individual, so particular, that we aren't always thinking that this movie is really about an old man and a boy and the devil.

A word about the music. Ry Cooder did most of the sound track, drawing from many blues scores, and the movie is wonderful to listen to: confident and sly and not all tricked up for Hollywood. The closing scene, the dueling guitars, presents a challenge that perhaps no film composer could quite solve (what's the right approach to music as a weapon?), but somehow Cooder actually does pull off the final showdown.

Crusoe ★ ★ ★ ½
PG-13, 95 m., 1989

Aidan Quinn (Crusoe), Ade Sapara (Warrior), Elvis Payne (Runaway Slave), Richard Sharp (Colcol), Colin Bruce (Clerk), William Hootkins (Auctioneer), Shane Rimmer (Mr. Mather), Jimmy Nail (Tarik), Patrick Monkton (Cook), James Kennedy (Captain Harding). Directed by Caleb Deschanel and produced by Andrew Braunsberg. Screenplay by Walon Green.

Crusoe is a film with a few important things to say and a magnificent way of saying them.

It is a big, bold production, with the width of vision that sometimes develops when the director has a background in cinematography; Caleb Deschanel, who made it, needs few spoken words to tell his story, and probably could have done with less.

The film takes place in the slave-trading days of the 19th century, when a Southern aristocrat in need of money (Aidan Quinn) sets off on a risky venture to bring back slaves from Africa. His ship is caught in a mountainous storm at sea, and he is shipwrecked on an uncharted island where at first he believes he is alone—all except for a small dog who has also been thrown ashore. The dog becomes his link with society. The animal may not be able to speak, but at least it can listen, and recognize his voice, and care about him. He needs the dog very much, he discovers, and when it dies, the scene is poignant and truthful.

In both the storm scene and the sequences with the dog, Deschanel seems inspired somewhat by Carroll Ballard's *The Black Stallion*, a film he photographed. The sea, the island, and the communion between man and beast are at least spiritually similar. But then the film takes a turn toward a more obvious meaning, as the man (named Crusoe, but not Robinson) finds that there are other humans on the island.

They are "savages." That is how he thinks of them. They conduct pagan ceremonies and would gladly kill him if they were given the opportunity. Spying on their rituals of human sacrifice, he saves an intended victim, nicknames him "Lucky," and finds him dead in the morning. A few days later, Crusoe himself is captured in a snare set by another native, and that begins the real business of the movie.

This warrior (Ade Sapara) does not necessarily want to kill Crusoe. He simply wants some of his geese. But Crusoe is able to place only one interpretation on the situation, and escapes to begin fighting the man. Their fight would lead to the death, but instead leads to a pit of quicksand, where the warrior must make a choice not determined entirely by his own lust for victory.

As a relationship gradually grows up between the two men, each one learns to accept the other as more or less his equal (prejudices die hard on both sides). And then a ship arrives from "civilization," and Crusoe must make his choice. And that is all, really, that *Crusoe* contains: a journey, a shipwreck, the death of a dog, two encounters,

and a choice. Yet in telling this simple story at feature length, Deschanel never seems to pad, and indeed uses a lean, economical storytelling strategy.

His secret is that he can see. Many directors grow uneasy when long silences develop in their films. They feel something has to be happening every moment. There has to be a "plot." Artificial climaxes must be contrived, leading to phony resolutions. Life becomes busier than is humanly possible. Deschanel, on the other hand, allows himself time to establish the mystery and isolation of his island, and to show us the personalities of his characters, rather than have them impatiently describe themselves. The story takes on the weight and importance of something that has been really thought about, and that is why the ending has such meaning. The film has earned it.

Cry-Baby ★ ★ ★
PG-13, 85 m., 1990

Johnny Depp (Cry-Baby), Amy Locane (Allison), Susan Tyrrell (Ramona), Polly Bergen (Mrs. Vernon-Williams), Iggy Pop (Belvedere), Ricki Lake (Pepper), Traci Lords (Wanda), Kim McGuire (Hatchet-Face). Directed by John Waters and produced by Rachel Talalay. Screenplay by Waters.

It is only now that I am in a condition to appreciate the 1950s. At the time, I was too cynical. I read *Mad* magazine and listened to Stan Freberg and Bob & Ray, and viewed all manifestations of 1950s teen-age culture with the superiority of one who had read *Look Homeward, Angel* and knew, even then, that you could not go home again.

Now things are different. Battered and weary after the craziness of the 1960s, the self-righteousness of the 1970s, and the greed of the 1980s, I want to go home again, oh, so desperately—home to that land of drive-in restaurants and Chevy Bel-Airs, making out and rock 'n' roll and drag races and Studebakers, Elvis and James Dean and black leather jackets. Not that I ever owned a black leather jacket. Even today, I do not have the nerve. Black leather suggests a degree of badness I could never aspire to.

Feelings like these are what John Waters's *Cry-Baby* is about. The movie takes place in 1954 in Baltimore, at the dawn of rock 'n' roll (one is reminded of the opening scenes of *2001*, at the dawn of man, an event less

remarked at the time). The teen-age culture is divided into three camps: the drapes, the squares, and the nerds. The drapes slick their hair into ducktails and wear black leather jackets and are proud to be juvenile delinquents. The squares wear crew cuts and want to go to college. The nerds are not made much of in *Cry-Baby*, but in my memory they were the kids who wore slide rules in their pockets and collected science-fiction magazines and grew up, one suspects, to be John Waters.

The movie tells the story of Cry-Baby himself, played by teen idol Johnny Depp as a juvenile delinquent who forever has a tear sliding halfway down his cheek, a reminder of a grief he will live with forever, a teen-age tragedy that has left its mark on his soul, a lost romance. Into his life comes Allison (Amy Locane), the good girl who has a crush on Cry-Baby and feels strange stirrings in her loins from the promise that he is as bad as they say. The movie's bad guy is the good guy, Baldwin (Stephen Mailer), who loves Allison in the right way, which is to say he loves her so boringly he might as well not love her at all.

The movie's very large cast (large enough to accommodate Polly Bergen and Traci Lords, David Nelson and Iggy Pop) includes Cry-Baby's grandparents (Iggy Pop and Susan Tyrrell), a rockabilly family that lives on the wrong side of the tracks and includes musicians who seem to be on the edge of inventing rock 'n' roll, if someone does not invent it for them. It also includes various parents, schoolmates, local tramps and sluts, and the straight-arrow types without which the 1950s would have lost their point of reference.

If there is one constant in recent social history, it is that we feel nostalgia for yesterday's teen-age badness even while we fear today's. As I was reading an alarmist newsweekly cover story on rap music recently, I found myself wishing that the hysterical old maids who wrote it could have been taken first to see *Cry-Baby* so that they could gain some insight into themselves.

In every generation teen-agers find a way to express themselves and annoy adults. And the adults of that generation find in this teen-age behavior alarming signs of the collapse of civilization as they know it. *Cry-Baby*, which is a good many things (including a passable imitation of a 1950s teen-age exploitation movie), is above all a reminder of that process. Today's teen-agers will grow up to be tomorrow's adults, and yet in every generation teen-agers and adults seem to have as little knowledge of that ancient fact as the caterpillar has of the butterfly. It is an additional irony that in human culture we have learned little from the insects, and the butterflies turn into the worms.

Cry Freedom ★ ★ ¹/₂
PG, 154 m., 1987

Kevin Kline (Donald Woods), Penelope Wilton (Wendy Woods), Denzel Washington (Steve Biko), John Thaw (Kruger), Sophie Mgcina (Evalina), Joseph Marcell (Moses). Directed and produced by Richard Attenborough. Screenplay by John Briley.

Cry Freedom begins with the story of a friendship between a white liberal South African editor and an idealistic young black leader who later dies at the hands of the South African police. But the black leader is dead and buried by the movie's halfway point, and the rest of the story centers on the editor's desire to escape South Africa and publish a book.

You know there is something wrong with the premise of this movie when you see that the actress who plays the editor's wife is billed above the actor who plays Biko. This movie promises to be an honest account of the turmoil in South Africa, but turns into a routine cliff-hanger about the editor's flight across the border. It's sort of a liberal yuppie version of that Disney movie where the brave East German family builds a hot-air balloon and floats to freedom. The problem with this movie is similar to the historic dilemma in South Africa: Whites occupy the foreground and establish the terms of the discussion while the eighty percent non-white majority remains a shadowy, half-seen presence in the background.

Yet *Cry Freedom* is a sincere and valuable movie, and despite my fundamental reservations about it, I think it probably should be seen. Although everybody has heard about apartheid, and South Africa remains a favorite subject of campus protest, few people have an accurate mental picture of what the country actually looks like and feels like. It is a place, not an issue, and *Cry Freedom* helps to visualize it. The movie was mostly shot across the border in Zimbabwe, the former nation of Southern Rhodesia, which serves as an adequate stand-in; we see the manicured lawns of the whites, who seem to live in

country club suburbs, and the jerry-built "townships" of the blacks, and we sense the institutional racism of a system where black maids call their employers "master," and even white liberals accept that without a blink.

The film begins with the story of Donald Woods, editor of the *East London* (South Africa) *Daily Dispatch*, and Steve Biko, a young black leader who has founded a school and a clinic for his people, and continues to hold out hope that blacks and whites can work together to change South Africa. In the more naive days of the 1960s and 1970s, Biko's politics are seen as "black supremacy," and Woods writes sanctimonious editorials describing Biko as a black racist. Through an emissary, Biko arranges to meet Woods, and eventually the two men become friends and Woods sees black life in South Africa at first hand (something few white South Africans have done).

Although Biko is played with quiet power by Academy Award-nominee Denzel Washington, he is seen primarily through the eyes of Woods (Kevin Kline). There aren't many scenes in which we see Biko without Woods, and fewer still in which his friendship with Woods isn't the underlying subject of the scene. No real attempt is made to show daily life in Biko's world; although we move into the Woods home, meet his wife, children, maid, and dog, and share his daily routine, there is no similar attempt to portray Biko's daily reality.

There is a reason for that. *Cry Freedom* is not about Steve Biko. It is Donald Woods's story from beginning to end, describing how he met Biko, how his thinking was changed by the man, how he actually witnessed black life at first hand (by patronizing a black speakeasy in a township and having a few drinks), and how, after he was placed under house arrest by the South African government, he engineered the escape from South Africa. The story has a happy ending: Donald Woods and his family made it safely to England, where he was able to publish two books about his experience. (The bad news is that Steve Biko was killed.)

For the first half of this movie, I was able to suspend judgment. Interesting things were happening, the performances were good, and it is always absorbing to see how other people live. Most of the second half of the movie, alas, is taken up with routine cloak-and-dagger stuff, including Woods's masquerade as a Catholic priest, his phony

passport, and his attempt to fool South African border officials. These scenes could have been recycled out of any thriller from any country in any time, right down to the ominous long shots of the men patroling the border bridge, and the tense moment when the guard's eyes flick up and down from the passport photo.

Cry Freedom is not really a story of today's South Africa, and it is not really the story of a black leader who tried to change it. Like *All the President's Men*, it's essentially the story of heroic, glamorous journalism. Remember, *Ace in the Hole*, that Kirk Douglas movie where the man was trapped in the cave, and Douglas played the ambitious reporter who prolonged the man's imprisonment so he could make his reputation by covering the story? I'm not saying the Donald Woods story is a parallel. But somehow the comparison did arise in my mind.

A Cry in the Dark ★ ★ ★
PG-13, 120 m., 1988

Meryl Streep (Lindy Chamberlain), Sam Neill (Michael Chamberlain), Charles "Bud" Tingwell (Muirhead), Bruce Myles (Parker), Dennis Miller (Sturgess), Neil Fitzpatrick (Phillips). Directed by Fred Schepisi and produced by Veriuty Lambert. Screenplay by Robert Caswell and Schepisi.

I had an argument about capital punishment with some friends, and I wish I could have taken them to see this movie. I was against the death penalty in principle, of course, but what really bothered me was the thought that a convicted person could be put to death on the basis of circumstantial evidence. There's just too much that can go wrong—as *A Cry in the Dark* and another 1988 movie, *The Thin Blue Line*, both demonstrate.

A Cry in the Dark takes place in Australia, and is based on the famous recent case of Lindy Chamberlain, the mother who said her baby daughter had been dragged away and killed by one of the wild Australian dogs named dingoes. No one else saw the tragic event take place, and the initial rush of sympathy for the parents was replaced, after a few weeks, by a malicious whispering campaign.

Did Lindy Chamberlain in fact murder her own baby and only then blame the dogs? The evidence against her began to pile up. A mark on a cloth looked like her bloody handprint. Blood was found sprayed all over the underside of the dashboard on the family car. A dingo was not big enough to carry away a human baby. Worst of all, Lindy Chamberlain did not seem sufficiently distraught by the death. Charges were eventually filed against her, she was found guilty and sentenced to life in prison, and she served three and a half years behind bars—even giving birth to another child there—before she was released. An appeals court quashed her conviction on September 15, 1988, declaring it a miscarriage of justice.

Why was Mrs. Chamberlain compelled to maintain her composure—even an icy facade—in press interviews and on TV? Why didn't she weep for her baby? There is the implication in *A Cry in the Dark* that if Lindy had behaved "correctly" in the media, the investigation that led to her conviction might never have been carried forward. In trying to help us understand Mrs. Chamberlain, Meryl Streep, the star of the movie, faces the formidable challenge of making an unlikable woman seem sympathetic. It appears that Mrs. Chamberlain was not naturally prone to outbursts of emotion in public. She kept things bottled up. After she was charged with murdering her child, anger took over, filling her with a deep bitterness that was evident in her face and voice.

And there was another matter, the matter of the religious beliefs of Lindy and Michael Chamberlain (who is solidly played by Sam Neill). They were Seventh-day Adventists in a country where that religion is in a small minority and widely misunderstood. While they spoke of reconciling themselves to the will of God, the public maliciously whispered that she had sacrificed her child in some sort of cult ceremony—an event that is unthinkable in terms of the Adventist religion. Whatever she did, she and her husband were religious, emotional, and social outsiders, and the press and the law were after them like a pack of dingoes.

A Cry in the Dark takes the time to marshal the case against Lindy Chamberlain, and the time to destroy it. The blood under the dashboard proved to be rust-proofing. Dingoes could indeed kill and carry a human baby. And additional physical evidence (the coat the baby was wearing when she disappeared) turned up years later, and corroborated Mrs. Chamberlain's story.

Fred Schepisi, who directed and cowrote the film, has used Australian public opinion as a sort of Greek chorus in the background. He cuts away to tennis games, saloons, filling stations, and dinner parties where the Australian public tries Lindy and finds her guilty (one hostess finally bans the subject at her dinner table, declaring that the case is not going to ruin another one of her parties). Schepisi is successful in indicting the court of public opinion, and his methodical (but absorbing) examination of the evidence helps us understand the state's circumstantial case.

In the lead role, Meryl Streep is given a thankless assignment: to show us a woman who deliberately refused to allow insights into herself. She succeeds, and so, of course, there are times when we feel frustrated because we do not know what Lindy is thinking or feeling. We begin to dislike the character, and then we know how the Australian public felt. Streep's performance is risky, and masterful.

The final point of the movie, I suppose, is that when passions run high enough, a court is likely to decide almost anything about anybody—especially an unlikable, unpopular member of a minority group who is charged with an unspeakable crime. When you combine that possibility with the uncertainty of circumstantial evidence and the human lust for revenge, you get a situation in which the death penalty can result in irrevocable tragedy. Lindy Chamberlain spent three and a half years in prison for a murder she did not commit, but at least she did not die for it.

Cyborg ★
R, 86 m., 1989

Jean-Claude Van Damme (Gibson Rickenbacker), Deborah Richter (Nady Simmons), Vincent Klyn (Fender Tremolo), Alex Daniels (Marshall Strat), Dayle Haddon (Pearl Prophet), Blaise Loong (Furman Vox), Rolf Muller (Brick Bardo), Haley Peterson (Haley), Terrie Batson (Mary), Jackson "Rock" Pinckney (Tytus). Directed by Albert Pyun and produced by Menahem Golan and Yoram Globus. Screenplay by Kitty Chalmers.

I am not sure I remember the opening words of *Cyborg* exactly, but I believe they were, "After the plague, things really got bad." I do remember laughing heartily at that point, about thirty seconds into the movie. Few genres amuse me more than postapocalyptic fantasies about supermen fighting for survival. *Cyborg* is one of the funniest examples of this category, which crosses *Escape From New York* with *The Road Warrior* but cheats on the budget.

The movie takes place in a future world in which all civilization has been reduced to a few phony movie sets. Leather-clad neo-Nazis stalk through the ruins, beating each other senseless and talking in Pulpspeak, which is like English, but without the grace and modulation. It's cold in the future, and it's wet, but never so cold or wet that the costumes do not bare the arm muscles of the men and the heaving bosoms of the women.

The plot of *Cyborg* is simplicity itself. The movie's heroine (Dayle Haddon) is half-woman, half-robot, and wears a computer under her wig. Her knowledge may include the solution to the plague that threatens to destroy mankind, but first she must somehow return to headquarters in Atlanta. Her enemy, Fender Tremolo (Vincent Klyn), wants to destroy her because he believes that if anarchy is unleashed upon the world, he can rule it. The hero, Gibson Rickenbacker (Jean-Claude Van Damme), is on a mission to escort her safely to Atlanta.

(If you look at the names "Fender Tremolo" and "Gibson Rickenbacker" and wonder why they set off strange stirrings in your subconscious, it is because both characters, according to the movie's press book, "are named after equipment and techniques associated with electric guitars." This rule presumably also applies to the characters Furman Vox, Nady Simmons, and Roland Pick.)

Once we know the central players, the movie turns into a sadomasochistic passion play, in which the villain tries out varieties of unspeakable tortures on the hero, including crucifixion, before the formula is (of course) delivered safely after all. The movie reduces itself to a series of smoking, smoldering cityscapes (which look a lot like urban neighborhoods slated for renewal), and the Pulpspeak is the usual combination of vaguely Biblical formalisms, spiced with four-letter words and high-tech gibberish.

Movies like this work if they're able to maintain a high level of energy and invention, as the Mad Max movies do. They do not work when they lower their guard and let us see the reality, which is that several strangely garbed actors feel vaguely embarrassed while wearing bizarre costumes and reciting unspeakable lines.

Cyrano de Bergerac ★ ★ ★ ½
PG, 138 m., 1990

Gerard Depardieu (Cyrano de Bergerac), Anne Brochet (Roxanne), Vincent Perez (Christian de Neuvillette), Jacques Weber (Comte De Guiche), Roland Bertin (Raguenea), Philippe Morier-Genoud (Le Bret). Directed by Jean-Paul Rappeneau and produced by Rene Cleitman and Michel Seydoux. Screenplay by Jean-Claude Rappeneau and Jean-Claude Carriere.

It is entirely appropriate that Cyrano—whose very name evokes the notion of grand romantic gestures—should have lived his life bereft of romance. What is romanticism, after all, but a bold cry about how life should be, not about how it is? And so here is Cyrano de Bergerac, hulking, pudding-faced, with a nose so large he is convinced everyone is laughing at him—yet he dares to love the fair Roxanne. I have made it one of my rules in life never to have anything to do with anyone who does not instinctively love Cyrano, and I am most at home with those who identify with him.

The "real" Cyrano, if there was such a creature beneath the many layers of myth that have grown up around the name, lived in France from 1619 to 1655, and wrote stories about his magnificent voyages to the moon and the sun. He inspired the Cyrano we love, a more modern creation, the work of Edmond Rostand, who wrote a play in 1897 that may not have been great literature, but has captured the imagination of everyone who has read it and has been recycled countless times.

Steve Martin and Daryl Hannah starred in the wonderful modern-dress comedy *Roxanne* (1987), inspired by the outlines of Rostand's story, and now here is a magnificently lusty, brawling, passionate, and tempestuous classical version, directed by Jean-Paul Rappeneau. Cyrano is played by Gerard Depardieu, the most popular actor in France, who won the best actor award at the 1990 Cannes festival for his work.

You would not think he would be right for the role. Shouldn't Cyrano be smaller, more tentative, more pathetic—instead of this outsize, physically confident man of action? Depardieu is often said to be "wrong" for his roles. His physical presence makes a definite statement on the screen, and then his acting genius goes to work and transforms him into whatever is required for the role—into a spiritual priest, a hunchbacked peasant, a Medieval warrior, a car salesman, a businessman, a sculptor, a gangster.

Here he plays Cyrano, gadfly and rabble-rouser, man about town, friend of some, envied by many, despised by a powerful few, and hopelessly, oh, most painfully and endearingly, in love with Roxanne (Anne Brochet). But his nose is too large. Not quite as long as Steve Martin's was, perhaps, but long enough that when he looks in the mirror he knows it would be an affront to present the nose anywhere in the vicinity of the fair Roxanne with an amorous purpose attached to it.

Now here is the inoffensive clod Christian de Neuvillette (Vincent Perez), Cyrano's friend. He is a romantic, too, but not in Cyrano's league. For him, love is a fancy. For Cyrano, a passion. Yet, if Cyrano cannot have Roxanne, then he will help his friend, and so he ghost-writes letters and ghost-recites speeches in the moonlight, and because Roxanne senses that the words come from a heart brave and true, she pledges herself to Christian. The irony—which only the audience can fully appreciate—is that anyone with a heart so pure she could love a cheesy lump like Christian because of his language could certainly love a magnificent man like Cyrano for the same reason, and regardless of his nose.

The screenplay by Rappeneau and the skilled veteran Jean-Claude Carriere spins this love story in a web of court intrigue and scandal, with Cyrano deeply involved on the wrong (that is, the good) side. And all leads up to the heartbreaking final round of revelations and truth-telling, and at last to Depardieu's virtuoso dying scene, which has to be seen to be believed.

What other actor would have had the courage to go with such determination so far over the top, to milk the pathos so shamelessly, to stagger and groan and weep and moan until it would all be funny, if it were not, paradoxically, so very effective and sad? Only the French could conceive and write, and perhaps only Depardieu could deliver, a dying speech that rises and falls with pathos and defiance for so long, only to end with the assertion that when he is gone, he will be remembered for . . . what? His heart? Courage? Bravery? No, of course not. Nothing half so commonplace: for his panache.

Cyrano de Bergerac is a splendid movie not just because it tells its romantic story and makes it visually delightful and centers it on Depardieu, but for a better reason: The movie acts as if it believes this story. Depardieu is not a satirist—not here, anyway. He plays Cyrano on the level, for keeps. Of course, the material is comic. But it is the frequent mistake of amateurs to play comedy for laughs, when the great artists know there is only one way to play it, and that is very seriously indeed. But with panache.

D

D.A.R.Y.L. ★ ★ ★
PG, 99 m., 1985

Barret Oliver (Daryl), Mary Beth Hurt (Joyce Richardson), Michael McKean (Andy Robinson), Daniel Bryan Corkill (Turtle), Josef Sommer (Dr. Stewart), Kathryn Walker (Ellen Lamb). Directed by Simon Wincer and produced by John Heyman and Burtt Harris. Screenplay by David Ambrose.

They know there is something odd about the kid when he starts doing his own laundry. That's not natural for a grade-schooler. Daryl has some other strange attributes. He is unfailingly polite, obsessively honest, and bats 1.000 in Little League. Finally his friend, Turtle, pulls him aside and explains that adults don't like it when a kid is too perfect. It makes them nervous. They need to connect with him so they can relax around him. Daryl nods gravely, and his next time at bat, he strikes out.

Daryl's history is strange. He was discovered by the side of the road, a neatly dressed little boy with amnesia. He didn't know who his parents were, or what his last name was, or where he lived. He is placed with a foster family, and by halfway through the movie *D.A.R.Y.L.* he is beginning to develop into a more typical kid, with real human emotions. That is against the game plan, unfortunately, because Daryl is both more and less than human. He is a prototype of a secret government attempt to combine a computer brain with a genetically cloned body, creating a humanoid who can use his five senses as input for his silicon mind.

D.A.R.Y.L. is sort of *Charly* in reverse. Instead of a retarded man who is allowed, through science, to have a brief glimpse of what it would be like to be normal, what we have here is a super-intelligent thinking machine who gets a taste of being a real little

boy. It's an intriguing premise, and the movie handles it with skill. The boy is played by Barret Oliver with an earnest, touching solemnity. The people around him (including his foster parents, Mary Beth Hurt and Michael McKean) are out of a Norman Rockwell drawing: loving, generous, loyal. His best friend Turtle (Daniel Bryan Corkill) is tactful in trying to get this odd kid to act normal.

Tacked onto this small-town story, the details of the intrigue seem almost unnecessary. The movie contains the usual hardnosed military men, visionary scientists, and officious cops. They've lost track of their expensive *D.A.R.Y.L.*, and want to find him and deprogram him. Daryl fights back by borrowing a supersecret fighter plane (as the movie is borrowing its ending from Clint Eastwood's *Firefox*), and the ending is really sort of neat; it's high-tech and heartwarming at the same time.

D.A.R.Y.L. is a good movie that could have been better. Maybe they should have screened *Charly* before making it. That would have reminded them that the scientific parts of their story are more or less predictable, and that the human elements are what keep us involved.

Dad ★ ★
PG, 115 m., 1989

Jack Lemmon (Jake Tremont), Ted Danson (John Tremont), Olympia Dukakis (Bette Tremont), Kathy Baker (Annie), Kevin Spacey (Mario), Ethan Hawke (Billy). Directed by Gary David Goldberg and produced by Goldberg and Joseph Stern. Screenplay by Goldberg.

Dad is a case of a movie with too much enthusiasm for its own good. If the filmmakers had

only been willing to dial down a little, they would have had the materials for an emotionally moving story, instead of one that generates incredulity and disbelief. The proof of the movie's promise is in the opening scenes, which work powerfully. The film doesn't go bad all at once; it derails about halfway through.

The story involves an elderly married couple (Jack Lemmon and Olympia Dukakis) whose lives have settled into a rigid routine. She does everything—even squeezing the toothpaste onto his brush in the morning—and he has grown completely dependent on her. Then one day, during their ritualistic trip to the supermarket, she has a heart attack and is rushed to the hospital. Suddenly Dad is on his own.

The kids doubt if he can cope with daily life. There's a sister (Kathy Baker) who still lives in the hometown, and a son (Ted Danson) who is a banker in the big city and has grown so remote from his family that he can't even remember if he was home last Christmas or the year before. Danson returns for a few days and tries to train his helpless Dad to do simple household tasks. He has a system of color-coded file cards, for example, with instructions like "(1) Fill sink with warm water. (2) Squeeze in liquid soap."

The amazing thing is that Dad turns out to be more resilient than anyone would have guessed. As played by Lemmon, he seems at the beginning of the movie to be tottering on the edge of senility, allowing himself to be treated almost as a baby. But gradually he improves. And gradually the bond between father and son, which had almost been severed, reestablishes itself.

Danson returns to work briefly, taking his dad along to a board meeting at the bank. But then tragedy strikes: Dad turns out to have a virulent form of cancer. Danson goes on leave from his job and returns indefinitely to his small town, where he now finds himself acting as parent to his parents. This is a role many people are playing these days, and *Dad* might have had something useful to say about it—but it's at just this point that the movie loses its wits and becomes unbelievable.

What are we to make, for example, of the scene where Danson grows angry with the hospital treatment Dad is receiving, and literally picks up his father and carries him out of the hospital and takes him home? The filmmakers no doubt thought this would be an emotionally shattering scene, but they got carried away by their own zeal. No one who has seen an elderly parent through major surgery could believe the scene for a moment; such an experience would cause the patient excruciating pain, and might kill him.

But Dad is a tough old bird—and, played by Lemmon, maybe too tough. With a sentence of death, he takes a new lease on existence and decides to taste joy and spontaneity for the first time in his life. To hell with what people think: He's going to trust his feelings! It's a good inspiration, but the movie takes it and goes berserk with it, turning into a silly sitcom just when we want to believe it the most.

I could believe, for example, the scene where Dad takes Mom (now mending from her heart attack) to visit the neighbors they've never met. This scene, played in a low key, is effective. But what about the absurd scene where Dad visits a used-clothing store at the beach and comes back with what must have been a carload of purchases—since he stages a costume party in the living room? As Lemmon pops through the doorway in a series of quick cuts, wearing funny hats and silly shirts, I wanted to get out my scissors and go to work on the movie. The sequence is disastrous. And it ushers in a series of scenes that seem more inspired by sitcoms than by real life.

What went wrong? Why couldn't the filmmakers tell their story simply and truthfully? *Dad* is based on a novel by William Wharton (who also wrote *Birdy*), and was written and directed by Gary David Goldberg. It's his first feature, after years of directing TV's *Family Ties*. Did he stop to reflect that movies allow their makers the freedom to be more thoughtful and observant, to take risks instead of treating the audience like simpletons? From the moment Danson carries his father out of the hospital, *Dad* abandons a realistic setup and flies off

into fantasy. *Dad* plays a dirty trick on the audience by getting us to care more deeply about the characters than it has the courage itself to care.

Daddy Nostalgia ★ ★ ★ ½
PG, 105 m., 1991

Dirk Bogarde (Daddy), Jane Birkin (Caroline), Odette Laure (Miche), Emmanuelle Bataille (Juliette), Charlotte Kady (Barbara). Directed by Bertrand Tavernier and produced by Adolphe Viezzi. Screenplay by Colo Tavernier O'Hagan.

The operation has been a success from the surgeon's point of view, but that leaves little consolation for the patient who knows he is going to die soon. All he can hope for are a few weeks or months of respite from pain. He is a British businessman somewhere in his sixties, who lives with his French wife in a retirement apartment on the Riviera, and he returns there to die.

Then something remarkable happens. His daughter arrives from England. They have not been close over the years, and often he was too distracted to really notice her. But now, as they begin to talk, the seasons of his life begin to take shape in her mind. They begin to know one another.

This is a wonderful story, but *Daddy Nostalgia* is not a very good title for it. I like the British title better: *These Foolish Things*. That refers to the song that haunts the movie, with some of the most bittersweet lyrics ever written, about how these foolish things remind me of you. Bertrand Tavernier's whole movie is told in the tone of that song, as a fond, elegiac memory.

The father is played by Dirk Bogarde. This is his first screen appearance in at least ten years, and he says it will be his last. He began in movies as a brash young man, but has aged into the perfect person to play this role. As in such movies as *Death in Venice* and *Providence*, he is a gentle man, a little regretful of lost opportunities, sentimental, and quietly brave. The daughter is Jane Birkin, angular and quick, a British actress who has long lived in Paris. Both she and Bogarde are fluent in French, which in the movie is sort of a joke between them; English people with a private language.

And then there is another character in the movie who is at the heart of what *Daddy Nostalgia* is really about, even though she doesn't speak much at all. This is Bogarde's wife and

Birkin's mother, played by Odette Laure as a stolid, resigned woman who sits in the kitchen and smokes endless cigarettes and drinks a lot of Coca-Cola and is deeply bitter. If you think enough about this character, the entire message of *Daddy Nostalgia* begins to shift.

It is easy enough to describe it as the leave-taking between two people who finally get to know one another: The father and daughter who allowed great silences to grow up in their lives, and who now cross those silences and become friends at the end. But what about the wife? In flashbacks from Birkin's point of view, we see a quiet, shy little daughter, sitting on the stairs as her glamorous parents whisk past on their way to parties and dinners. She was neglected then. But at some point, the Bogarde character lost interest in his wife. For years they have not really spoken to one another. And now this autumn relationship with his daughter is a flirtation of sorts—she is another young woman he wants to charm, even now, when he is about to die.

Tavernier directed this film from a screenplay by his former wife, Colo Tavernier O'Hagen. There must be elements of autobiography in it for both of them—especially when you remember his two earlier films, *A Week's Vacation* (1982) and *Sundays in the Country* (1989). Both told of children going to visit their fathers with a mixture of love and anger, and both showed fathers who were admirable and lovable but also self-centered and flawed.

It's that extra complication that makes *Daddy Nostalgia* so much more than just a sweet leave-taking. The movie knows that even as we die, we hang onto our weaknesses as fondly as our strengths. That dying people are selfish, all the more so because their resources are dwindling, and that even some of their good, generous, loving actions are done with complex motives. On one level, this is a heart-warming movie. On another, it is a wise and even a bitter one.

Dance With a Stranger ★ ★ ★ ★
R, 102 m., 1985

Miranda Richardson (Ruth Ellis), Rupert Everett (David Blakely), Ian Holm (Desmond Cussen), Matthew Carroll (Andy), Tom Chadbon (Anthony Findlater), Jane Bertish (Carole Findlater). Directed by Mike Newell and produced by Roger Randall Cutler. Screenplay by Shelagh Delaney.

Ruth Ellis and David Blakely were a tragedy waiting to happen. She was a B-girl, pouring drinks and massaging men's egos in a sleazy little 1950s London nightclub. He was a rich young brat, whose life centered around his career as a race driver. They met one boozy night in the club, and there was an instant spark of lust between them—Ruth, whose profession was to keep her distance from men, and David, who had never felt love in his life.

Dance With a Stranger is the story of their affair, which led to one of the most famous British murder trials of the decade. After Ellis shot Blakely dead in the street outside a pub, she was brought to trial, convicted, and executed with heartless speed; her trial began on June 20, 1955, and she was hanged on July 19—the last woman to receive the death penalty in England.

In the thirty years since Blakely and Ellis died, the case has fascinated the British, perhaps because it combines sexuality and the class system, two of their greatest interests. Blakely was upper-class, polished, affected, superior. Ellis was a working-class girl who made herself up to look like Marilyn Monroe and used the business of bar hostess as a way to support her young son and maintain her independence from men. Ironically, she was finally undone by her emotional dependence on Blakely, who gave and then withdrew his affection in a way that pushed her over the edge.

Their story is told by Mike Newell in a film of astonishing performances and moody, atmospheric visuals. Ruth Ellis is the emotional center of the film, and she is played by a newcomer, Miranda Richardson, as a woman who prides herself on not allowing men to hurt her, and who almost to the end cannot believe that the one man she loves would hurt her the most.

We see her first in the nightclub, where her blond Monroe looks supply the only style in the whole shabby room. We meet her regular "friends," including Desmond Cussen (Ian Holm), a quiet, loyal bachelor who adores her in an unpossessive way. Then Blakely (played by Rupert Everett) walks into her life, and in an instant there is erotically charged tension between them; the way they both flaunt their indifference is a clue. Their relationship falls into a pattern: lust, sex, tears, quarrels, absences, and then lust and sex again. Newell tells the story only in terms of the events and characters themselves. There are no detours into shallow

psychology; just the patterns of attraction and repulsion.

For Ruth Ellis, a woman living at a time when women's options were cruelly limited, the obsession with Blakely becomes totally destructive. She loses her job. She grows more dependent as he grows more cold and unpredictable, and everything is complicated by their mutual alcoholism. Cussen, the inoffensive, long-suffering admirer, takes her in, and she makes an effort to shape up, but Blakely sounds chords in her that she cannot ignore.

By the end of the movie, Blakely has done things to her that she cannot forgive. And they are not the big, melodramatic things like the violence that breaks out between them. They are little unforgivable things, as when he raises her hopes and then disappoints her. By the end, he is hardly even hurting her intentionally. He drinks in the company of fawning friends, he ignores responsibilities, he disappears into his own drunken absent-mindedness, and forgets her. And then one night outside a pub, she reminds him, once and for all.

Dances With Wolves ★ ★ ★ ★
PG-13, 181 m., 1990

Kevin Costner (Lieutenant Dunbar), Mary McDonnell (Stands With a Fist), Graham Greene (Kicking Bird), Rodney A. Grant (Wind in His Hair), Floyd Red Crow Westerman (Ten Bears), Tantoo Cardinal (Black Shawl), Annie Costner (Christine). Directed by Kevin Costner and produced by Jim Wilson and Costner. Screenplay by Michael Blake.

They meet at first in the middle of the prairie, holding themselves formally and a little awkwardly, the infantry officer and Sioux Indians. There should be instant mistrust between them, but they take each other's measure and keep an open mind. A civilized man is a person whose curiosity outweighs his prejudices, and these are curious men.

They know no words of each other's languages. Dunbar, the white man, tries to pantomime a buffalo. Wind in His Hair, the chief, looks at the charade and says, "His mind is gone." But Kicking Bird, the holy man, thinks he understands what the stranger is trying to say, and at last they exchange the word for "buffalo" in each other's languages. These first halting words are the crucial mo-

ments in Kevin Costner's *Dances With Wolves*, a film about a white man who goes to live with Indians and learns their civilization at first hand.

In real life, such contacts hardly ever took place. The dominant American culture was nearsighted, incurious, and racist, and saw the Indians as a race of ignorant, thieving savages, fit to be shot on sight. Such attitudes survived until so recently in our society—just look at the B Westerns of the 1940s—that we can only imagine how much worse they were one hundred years ago. In a sense, *Dances With Wolves* is a sentimental fantasy, a "what if" movie that imagines a world in which whites were genuinely interested in learning about a Native American culture that lived more closely in harmony with the natural world than any other before or since. But our knowledge of how things turned out—of how the Indians were driven from their lands by genocide and theft—casts a sad shadow over everything.

The movie, which won the Academy Award as the best picture of 1990, is a simple story, magnificently told. It has the epic sweep and clarity of a Western by John Ford, and it abandons the contrivances of ordinary plotting to look, in detail, at the way strangers get to know one another. The film is seen from the point of view of Dunbar (Costner), a lieutenant in the Union Army, who runs away from a field hospital as his foot is about to be amputated and invites death by riding his horse in a suicidal charge at the Confederate lines. When he miraculously survives, he is decorated and given his choice of any posting, and he chooses the frontier, because "I want to see it before it's gone."

He draws an isolated outpost in the Dakotas, where he is the only white man for miles around. He is alone, but at first not lonely; he keeps a journal and writes of his daily routine, and after the first contact with the Sioux, he documents the way they slowly get to know one another. Dunbar possesses the one quality he needs to cut through the entrenched racism of his time: He is able to look another man in the eye, and see the man, rather than his attitudes about the man.

As Dunbar discovers the culture of the Sioux, so do we. The Indians know the white man is coming, and they want to learn more about his plans. They have seen other invaders in these parts: the Spanish, the Mexicans, but they always left. Now the Indians fear the white man is here to stay. They want Dunbar to share his knowledge, but at first he holds back. He does not wish to discourage them. And when he finally tells how many whites will be coming ("As many as the stars in the sky"), the words fall like a death knell.

At first, Dunbar and the Indians meet on the open prairie. One day they bring along Stands With a Fist (Mary McDonnell), a white woman who as a girl came to live with the tribe after her family was killed. She remembers a little English. With a translator, progress is quicker, until one day Dunbar comes to live with the tribe, and is eventually given the name Dances With Wolves.

There are some of the plot points we would expect in a story like this. The buffalo hunt (thrillingly photographed). A bloody fight with a hostile tribe. The inevitable love story between Dunbar and Stands With a Fist. But all is done with an eye to detail, with a respect for tradition, and with a certain sweetness of disposition. The love story is especially delicate; this isn't one of those exercises in romantic cliché, but a courtship conducted mostly through the eyes, through these two people looking at one another. There is a delicate, humorous sequence showing how the tribe observes and approves of the romance when the chief's wife, Black Shawl (Tantoo Cardinal), tells her husband it is time for Stands With a Fist to stop mourning her dead husband and accept this new man into her arms.

Meanwhile, we get to know many members of the Sioux tribe, most especially Kicking Bird (Graham Greene), Wind in His Hair (Rodney A. Grant), and the old wise man Ten Bears (Floyd Red Crow Westerman). Each has a strong personality; these are men who know exactly who they are, and at one point, after Dunbar has killed in battle beside them, he realizes he never knew who "John Dunbar" was, but he knows who Dances With Wolves is. Much of the movie is narrated by Dunbar, and his speech at this point is a center for the film: He observes that the battle with the enemy tribe was not fought for political purposes, but for food and land, and it was fought to defend the women and children who were right there in the midst of battle. The futility he felt on his suicidal day as a Union officer has been replaced by utter clarity: He knows why he was fighting, and he knows why he was willing to risk losing his life.

Dances With Wolves has the kind of vision and ambition that is rare in movies today. It is not a formula movie, but a thoughtful, carefully observed story. It is a Western at a time when the Western is said to be dead. It asks for our imagination and sympathy. It takes its time, three hours, to unfold. It is a personal triumph for Kevin Costner, the intelligent young actor of *Field of Dreams*, who directed the film and shows a command of story and of visual structure that is startling; this movie moves so confidently and looks so good it seems incredible that it's a directorial debut. Costner and his cinematographer, Dean Semler, are especially gifted at explaining things visually. Many of their most important points are made with a glance, a close-up, a detail shot.

In 1985, before he was a star, Costner played a small role in a good Western called *Silverado* simply because he wanted to be in a Western. Now he has realized his dream by making one of the best Westerns I've seen. The movie makes amends, of a sort, for hundreds of racist and small-minded Westerns that went before it. By allowing the Sioux to speak in their own tongue, by entering their villages and observing their ways, it sees them as people, not as whooping savages in the sights of an infantry rifle.

Dangerous Liaisons ★ ★ ★
R, 120 m., 1988

Glenn Close (Marquise de Merteuil), John Malkovich (Vicomte de Valmont), Michelle Pfeiffer (Madame de Tourvel), Swoosie Kurtz (Madame de Volanges), Keanu Reeves (Chevalier Danceny), Mildred Natwick (Madame de Rosemonde), Uma Thurman (Cecile de Volanges). Directed by Stephen Frears and produced by Norma Heyman and Hank Moonjean. Screenplay by Christopher Hampton.

Dangerous Liaisons is a story of two people who lack the courage to admit they love each other, and so spend their energies destroying the loves of others. They describe as cynicism what is really depravity, and are so hardened to the ordinary feelings of life that only one emotion can destroy them. That emotion is love, of course.

The two people live in 18th-century France, at a time just before the Revolution, when the decadence of the aristocracy has become an end in itself. The Marquise de Merteuil lives in a world of drawing rooms and boudoirs, where she swoops down like a hawk upon the innocent and the naive, wrecking their idealism with a triumphant laugh to herself. Her partner and confidant is the Vicomte de Valmont, who was once her lover and is now her weapon against young women presumptuous enough to love. In their private scorekeeping, nothing counts more than a heart destroyed, and hopes laid to waste.

One day the Marquise (Glenn Close) comes to the Vicomte (John Malkovich) with an assignment. She has lost a lover, who has left her to marry an innocent young woman named Cecile (Uma Thurman). She wishes the Vicomte to seduce the young woman before she can bear her virginity to the marital bed. The Vicomte accepts the dare, and dispatches himself to the country—where, however, he eventually sets his sights on another young woman instead.

She is the virtuous Madame de Tourvel (Michelle Pfeiffer), who wishes to be faithful to her husband. Certainly there is nothing overpoweringly attractive in the lecherous Vicomte, who is a little cadaverous and has a reputation as a cad. But the Vicomte persists, and he uses a weapon that sometimes works against the pure and the good: He presents himself as frankly evil, and thus inspires a spark of lust to stir within the woman herself. He plays on her curiosity about what it would be like to be a bad girl.

All this intrigue goes more or less according to plan, especially when the Marquise sics another young man on the unsuspecting Cecile, then uses that as an excuse to arrange for Cecile to visit the country home where, wouldn't you know, Valmont and Madame Tourvel are staying. The seduction of Cecile comes easily. But the seduction of Madame Tourvel, when it is finally arrived at, is a surprise for everyone, because it happens that Valmont and Tourvel actually do really fall in love.

This is too much for the Marquise; as her instrument, Valmont may make love to whomsoever he pleases, but he is not to *fall* in love with anyone. All of the pretend emotions of the game of seduction turn into the real emotions of the game of betrayal.

Dangerous Liaisons, based on Christopher Hampton's London and New York stage hit *Les Liaisons Dangereuses* (and on the scandalous 18th-century novel by Choderlos de Laclos), is a mannered, elegant film in which the languorous intrigues of the opening scenes set up the violent passions of the later ones. It is a film in which the surfaces are usually calm, and only the flash of an eye or a slightly raised voice betrays the most terrible struggles going on beneath.

It is played to perfection by Close and Malkovich in the central roles; their arch dialogues together turn into exhausting conversational games, tennis matches of the soul. The other key roles, played by Pfeiffer and Thurman, are trickier, because they involve characters who should not be entirely aware of what is really happening. Both actresses are well cast for their roles, and for Pfeiffer, in a year which saw her in such various assignments as *Married to the Mob* and *Tequila Sunrise*, the movie is more evidence of her versatility—she is good when she is innocent, and superb when she is guilty.

If there is anything lacking in the movie, it may be a certain gusto. The director, Stephen Frears, is so happy to make this a tragicomedy of manners that he sometimes turns away from obvious payoffs. I am not suggesting he should have turned the material toward the ribald, or gone for easy laughs, but there are times when he holds back and should have gone for the punch line. *Dangerous Liaisons* is an absorbing and seductive movie, but not a compelling one.

Dark Eyes ★ ★ ★ ½
NO MPAA RATING, 118 m., 1987

Marcello Mastroianni (Romano), Silvana Mangano (Elisa), Marthe Keller (Tina), Elena Sofonova (Anna), Pina Cei (Elisa's Mother), Vsevolod Larionov (Pavel). Directed by Nikita Mikhalkov and produced by Silvia D'Amico Bendico and Carlo Cucchi. Screenplay by Alexander Adabachian and Mikhalkov.

Some stories need to be told after they are over. We need to know that all the events are past and gone in order to feel the same nostalgia as the storyteller. When a story is happening "now," there is always the possibility of surprise and happiness. But when a story happened "then," and it is a love story, then even the happy moments feel bittersweet, and, of course, that is the whole point of the story.

Dark Eyes is a story told by a man who sits at a table in the lounge of an ocean liner, the bottle in front of him, the glass in his hand, his voice steady as if he has rehearsed these same facts many times before. He is a middle-aged man with sad eyes and a weary face. His listener is about the same age, but not so sad and not so weary. Neither one seems to much care about the ship's destination.

The man telling the story is Marcello Mas-troianni, the most complete of movie actors, his face never seeming composed for the screen but acting simply as a window for his words. He tells the stranger that once he was married, comfortably if not ecstatically, to a rich wife (Silvana Mangano). They were not in love, but they were content with one another. Then he went on a visit to a spa, and there he saw a young lady, and danced with her, and fell in love with her, and had one of those holiday romances that fade like postcards in the memory. After all, nothing could come of it; they were both married.

The problem with this romance, Mastroianni tells his listener, is that it did not fade. Back home again, he found he was still in love with the woman (Elena Sofonova). She grew stronger in his memory. He could not forget her. She was a Russian, and eventually he went to Russia in search of her, and found her, and they shared perfect love and vowed to divorce their spouses to marry each other. She went to tell her husband, and he returned to Italy to tell his wife, but at home he found his wife had lost all of her money, and his sense of loyalty was such that he could not leave her under those circumstances, and so . . .

Mastroianni continues with his story, but I will stop here, before all the twists and turns, the ironies, and the final heartbreak. *Dark Eyes* tells one of those stories where you think you know everything, but you do not, and at the end of the story you know that everyone is very unhappy, but you cannot see precisely what they should have done differently. The movie is based on stories by Chekhov, and has been directed by a Russian, Nikita Mikhalkov, who is not afraid of large romantic gestures and tragic coincidences. You realize after a while that it doesn't matter that Mastroianni can do nothing, that his tragedy is in the past; the telling of the story is the whole point, and he travels the world with his sad tale, telling it probably again and again, for the whole importance of his life has been reduced to his great loss.

This is a beautiful film, lavishly shot on location at Italian and Russian spas and in great houses. The nineteenth-century period is important, not simply because it recalls a time before telephones (which could have solved the whole tragedy), but because it recalls a state of mind before telephones, a time when people did not much believe in easy solutions. The movie is intriguing because of its moral complexity. After it's over, you find yourself asking hard questions about who did right and who did wrong, and you're confronted with the ironic possibility that maybe it didn't matter, that maybe everyone was doomed from the start.

The ending of this film is a real stunner. If you see *Dark Eyes*, ask yourself this question afterward: How would it have felt if the movie had provided the encounter we anticipate will be the last scene, but isn't? Would it have been simply corny? Or too heartbreaking to be endured?

Dawn of the Dead ★ ★ ★ ★
R, 126 m., 1979

With David Emge, Ken Foree, Scott H. Reiniger, and Gaylen Ross. Directed by George A. Romero and produced by Richard P. Rubenstein. Screenplay by Romero.

Dawn of the Dead is one of the best horror films ever made—and, as an inescapable result, one of the most horrifying. It is gruesome, sickening, disgusting, violent, brutal, and appalling. It is also (excuse me for a second while I find my other list) brilliantly crafted, funny, droll, and savagely merciless in its satiric view of the American consumer society. Nobody ever said art had to be in good taste.

It's about a mysterious plague that sweeps the nation, causing the recently dead to rise from their graves and roam the land, driven by an insatiable hunger for living flesh. No explanation is offered for this behavior—indeed, what explanation would suffice?—but there is a moment at which a survivor solemnly intones: "When there is no more room in hell, the dead will walk the Earth."

Who's that a quotation from? From George A. Romero, who wrote and directed *Dawn of the Dead* as a sequel to his *Night of the Living Dead*, which came out in 1968 and now qualifies as a cult classic. If you have seen *Night*, you will recall it as a terrifying horror film punctuated by such shocking images as zombies tearing human flesh from limbs. *Dawn* includes many more scenes like that, more graphic, more shocking, and in color. I am being rather blunt about this because there are many people who will *not* want to see this film. You know who you are. Why are you still reading?

Well . . . maybe because there's a little of the ghoulish voyeur in all of us. We like to be frightened. We like a good creepy thrill. It's just, we say, that we don't want a movie to go too far. What's too far? *The Exorcist? The Omen?* George Romero deliberately intends to go too far in *Dawn of the Dead*. He's dealing very consciously with the ways in which images can affect us, and if we sit through the film (many people cannot) we make some curious discoveries.

One is that the fates of the zombies, who are destroyed wholesale in all sorts of terrible ways, don't affect us so much after a while. They aren't being killed, after all: They're already dead. They're even a little comic, lurching about a shopping center and trying to plod up the down escalator. Romero teases us with these passages of humor. We relax, we laugh, we see the satire in it all, and then—*pow!* Another disembowelment, just when we were off guard.

His story opens in a chaotic television studio, where idiotic broadcasters are desperately transmitting inaccurate information (one hopes the Emergency Broadcast System will do a whole lot better). National Guard troops storm public housing, where zombies have been reported. There are ten minutes of unrelieved violence, and then the story settles down into the saga of four survivors who hijack a helicopter, land on the roof of a suburban shopping center, and barricade themselves inside against the zombies.

Their eventual fates are not as interesting as their behavior in the meantime; there is nothing quite like a plague of zombies to wonderfully focus your attention on what really matters to you. Romero has his own ideas, too, and the shopping center becomes a brilliant setting for a series of comic and satiric situations: Some low humor, some exquisitely sly.

But, even so, you may be asking, how can I defend this depraved trash? I do not defend it. I praise it. And it is not depraved, although some reviews have seen it that way. It is *about* depravity. If you can see beyond the immediate impact of Romero's imagery, if you can experience the film as being more than just its violent extremes, a most unsettling thought may occur to you: The zombies in *Dawn of the Dead* are not the ones who are depraved. They are only acting according to their natures, and, gore dripping from their jaws, are blameless.

The depravity is in the behavior of the healthy survivors, and the true immorality comes as two bands of human survivors fight each other for the shopping center: *Now* look who's fighting over the bones! But *Dawn* is even more complicated than that, because the survivors have courage, too, and

a certain nobility at times, and a sense of humor, and loneliness and dread, and are not altogether unlike ourselves. A-ha.

The Day After Trinity ★ ★ ★ ★
NO MPAA RATING, 88 m., 1980

A documentary produced and directed by Jon Else. Written by David Peoples, Janet Peoples, and Else.

There is a scene in *The Day After Trinity* showing the world's first atomic device being hoisted atop a steel frame tower that looks barely adequate to hold a windmill. The scene is not shot gracefully. The bomb looks like a giant steel basketball with some tubes and wires stuck onto it. In the background, the sky is a washed-out blue. In the next shot, the bomb is back on the ground again and a man is posing next to it, somewhat self-consciously. In 1945, the Russians would have killed for this footage.

On the sound track, the narrator reads sections of a personal diary kept by one of the scientists at Los Alamos, New Mexico, where the government ran its top-secret project to develop the atom bomb: *Gadget is in place . . . should we have the chaplain here?* It is all somewhat banal until, on reflection, it becomes emotionally shattering. The greatest achievement of *The Day After Trinity* is that it counts down those final days before nuclear weapons became a fact of our lives.

This is a documentary that develops more suspense than most of the thrillers I have seen. It includes photographs and film footage from the Los Alamos labaoratory, and it begins and ends with the story of J. Robert Oppenheimer, the brilliant scientist who was the "father of the atomic bomb" and then, a few years later, was branded as a security risk by Senator Joseph McCarthy. It includes newsreel footage of World War II, including the devastation of Hiroshima and Nagasaki, and more footage of Oppenheimer after the war and testifying before the McCarthy committee. And there are present-day interviews with some of the scientists who worked at Los Alamos.

All of this is gripping, especially the second thoughts of Oppenheimer and others about the wisdom of dropping the bomb. Of the wisdom of *developing* the bomb there seems to have been no doubt: The bomb was theoretically possible, it was technologically feasible, if we did not build it, the Russians would, and so we built it first, hurrah!

Oppenheimer's brother, Frank, remembers that Robert's initial reaction to the first nuclear explosion (the "Trinity" blast) was, "it worked!" It wasn't until after Hiroshima, he says, that it occurred to him that it killed people.

The most riveting sections of the film deal with the establishment of Los Alamos and the weeks and days leading up to the Trinity test. The New Mexico base was a jerry-built collection of temporary housing, muddy streets, 6,000 people, and paranoid secrecy. But it seems to have been a glorious time for the people who were there: It was like a summer camp for Ph.D.s, with Glenn Miller records playing on the jukebox and bright young nuclear whiz kids given the full resources of the government.

Those who were there on the day of Trinity remember that nobody really knew what would happen. One scientist took side bets that New Mexico would be incinerated. In the event, it was just a very big bang. A woman who was driving through the desert with her sister remembers that her sister saw the blast from hundreds of miles away; her sister was blind. Today, physicist Robert Wilson asks himself why he—why *they*—didn't just all walk away from the bomb after they saw what it could do. But of course they did not.

Day for Night ★ ★ ★ ★
PG, 116 m., 1974

Francois Truffaut (Ferrand), Jean-Pierre Aumont (Alexandre), Jacqueline Bisset (Julie), Jean-Pierre Leaud (Alphonse), Valentina Cortese (Séverine). Directed by Francois Truffaut and produced by Marcel Bébert. Screenplay by Truffaut, Jean-Louis Richard, and Suzanne Shiffman.

Movies about movies usually don't quite get things right. The film business comes out looking more romantic and glamorous (or more corrupt and decadent) than it really is, and none of the human feeling of a movie set is communicated. That is not the case with Francois Truffaut's funny and touching film, *Day for Night*, which is not only the best movie ever made about the movies but is also a great entertainment.

A movie company, especially if it's away from home on a location somewhere, is a family that's been thrown into close and sometimes desperate contact; strangers become friends and even intimates in a few weeks, and in a few more weeks they're scattered to the winds. The family is complicated by the insecurities and egos of the actors, and by the moviemaking process itself: We see the result, but we don't see the hours and days spent on special effects, on stunts, on making it snow or making it rain or making an allegedly trained cat walk from A to B. *Day for Night* is about all of these aspects of moviemaking; about the technical problems, the boredom between takes (a movie set is one of the most boring places on earth most of the time), and about the romances and intrigues. It's real; this is how a movie set really looks, feels, and smells. Truffaut's story involves a movie company on location in Nice. They're making a melodrama called *Meet Pamela*, of which we see enough to know it's doomed at the box office. But good or bad, the movie must be made; Truffaut, who plays the director in his own film, says at one point: "When I begin a film, I want to make a great film. Halfway through, I just hope to finish the film."

His cast includes a beautiful American actress (Jacqueline Bisset); an aging matinee idol (Jean-Pierre Aumont), and his former mistress, also past her prime (Valentina Cortese); the young, lovestruck male lead (Jean-Pierre Leaud), and the entire crew of script girls, camera operators, stunt men, and a henpecked production manager. (And if you have ever wondered what the key grip does in a movie, here's your chance to find out.) Truffaut sets half a dozen stories in motion, and follows them all so effortlessly it's almost as if we're gossiping with him about his colleagues. The movie set is a microcosm: there is a pregnancy and a death; a love affair ended, another begun, and a third almost but not quite destroyed; and new careers to be nourished and old careers to be preserved.

Truffaut was always a master of quiet comedy, and there are fine touches like the aging actress fortifying herself with booze and blaming her lack of memory on her makeup girl. Then there's the young male lead's ill-fated love for Jacqueline Bisset; she is happily married to a doctor, but unwisely extends her sympathy to the youth, who repays her by very nearly destroying her marriage as well as himself. And all the time there is the movie to be made: Truffaut gives us a hilarious session with the "trained" cat, and shows us without making a point of it how snow is produced on a set, how stunt drivers survive car crashes, and how third-floor balconies can exist without buildings below them.

What we see on the screen is nothing at all like what happens on the set—a truth the movie's title reflects. ("Day for night" is the technical term for "night" scenes shot in daylight with a special filter. The movie's original French title, *La Nuit Americaine*, is the French term for the same process—acknowledging their debt to Hollywood.)

The movie is just plain fun. Movie buffs will enjoy it like *Singin' in the Rain* (that perfect musical about the birth of talkies), but you don't have to be a movie buff to like it. Truffaut knows and loves the movies so much he's infectious; one of *Day for Night*'s best scenes is a dream in which the adult director remembers himself, as a little boy, slinking down a darkened street to steal a still from *Citizen Kane* from in front of a theater. We know who the little boy grew up to be, and that explains everything to us about how he feels now.

Day of the Dead ★ ½
R, 91 m., 1985

Lori Cardille (Sarah), Terry Alexander (John, the Pilot), Joseph Pilato (Rhodes), Richard Liberty (Dr. Logan), Howard Sherman (Bub, the Zombie). Directed by George A. Romero and produced by Richard P. Rubinstein. Screenplay by Romero.

The ghouls in *Day of the Dead* are marvels of special effects, with festoons of rotting flesh hanging from their purple limbs as they slouch toward the camera, moaning their sad songs. Truth to tell, they look a lot better than the ghouls in *Night of the Living Dead*, which was director George Romero's original ghoul film. His technology is improving; perhaps the recent emphasis on well-developed bodies (in *Perfect, Rambo,* etc.) has inspired a parallel improvement in dead bodies.

But the ghouls have another problem in *Day of the Dead:* They're upstaged by the characters who are supposed to be real human beings. You might assume that it would be impossible to steal a scene from a ghoul, especially one with blood dripping from his orifices, but you haven't seen the overacting in this movie. The characters shout their lines from beginning to end, their temples pound with anger, and they use distracting Jamaican and Irish accents, until we are so busy listening to their endless dialogue that we lose interest in the movie they occupy.

Maybe there's a reason for that. Maybe Romero, whose original movie was a genuine inspiration, hasn't figured out anything new to do with his ghouls. In his second ghoul film, the brilliant *Dawn of the Dead* (1979), he had them shuffling and moaning their way through a modern shopping mall, as Muzak droned in the background and terrified survivors took refuge in the Sears store. The effect was both frightening and satirical. The everyday location made the ghouls seem all the more horrible, and the shopping mall provided lots of comic props (as when several ghouls tried to crawl up the down escalator).

This time, though, Romero has centered the action in a visually dreary location—an underground storage cavern, one of those abandoned salt mines where they store financial records and the master prints of old movies. The ghouls have more or less overrun the surface of America, we gather, and down in the darkness a small team of scientists and military men are conducting experiments on a few captive ghoul guinea-pigs.

It's an interesting idea, especially if they had kept the semiseriousness of the earlier films. Instead, the chief researcher is a demented butcher with blood-stained clothes, whose idea of science is to teach a ghoul named Bub to operate a Sony Walkman. Meanwhile, the head of the military contingent (Joseph Pilato) turns into a violent little dictator who establishes martial law and threatens to end the experiments. His opponent is a spunky woman scientist (Lori Cardille), and as they shout angry accusations at each other, the real drama in the film gets lost.

In the earlier films, we really identified with the small cadre of surviving humans. They were seen as positive characters and we cared about them. This time, the humans are mostly unpleasant, violent, insane, or so noble that we can predict with utter certainty that they will survive. According to the mad scientist in *Day of the Dead*, the ghouls keep moving because of primitive impulses buried deep within their spinal columns—impulses that create the appearance of life long after consciousness and intelligence have departed. I hope the same fate doesn't befall Romero's ghoul movies. He should quit while he's ahead.

The Day of the Jackal ★ ★ ★ ★
PG, 150 m., 1973

Edward Fox (The Jackal), Terence Alexander (Lloyd), Michel Auclair (Colonel Rolland), Alan Badel (The Minister), Tony Britton (Inspector Thomas), Denis Carey (Casson), Olga Georges-Picot (Denise), Cyril Cusack (The Gunsmith). Directed by Fred Zinnemann and produced by John Woolf. Screenplay by Kenneth Ross.

Fred Zinnemann's *The Day of the Jackal* is one hell of an exciting movie. I wasn't prepared for how good it really is: it's not just a suspense classic, but a beautifully executed example of filmmaking. It's put together like a fine watch. The screenplay meticulously assembles an incredible array of material, and then Zinnemann choreographs it so that the story—complicated as it is—unfolds in almost documentary starkness.

The "jackal" of the title is the code name for a man who may (or may not) be a British citizen specializing in professional assassinations. He allegedly killed Trujillo of the Dominican Republic in 1961 and, now, two years later, he has been hired by a group of Frenchmen who want de Gaulle assassinated. His price is $500,000; he says, "and considering that I'm handing you France, I wouldn't call that expensive."

Zinnemann, working from Frederick Forsyth's bestseller, tells both sides of the story that unfolds during the summer of 1963. The jackal prepares two disguises and three identities, gets a legal passport by applying in the name of a child who died in 1931, and calls on European experts for his materials. An old gunsmith hand-makes a weird-looking lightweight rifle with silencer, sniper scope, and explosive bullets. A forger provides French identity papers and a driver's license (and comes to an unexpected end). And then the jackal enters France.

Meanwhile, the government has received information that an attempt will be made on de Gaulle's life. The general absolutely insists that he will make no changes in his public schedule, and that any attempt to prevent an assassination must be made in secret. The French police cooperate "unofficially" with the top police forces of other nations in attempting an apprehension. But they don't even know who the jackal is.

How can they stop him? The movie provides a fascinating record of police investigative work, which combines exhaustive checking with intuition. But the jackal is clever, too,

particularly when he's cornered. Some of the movie's finest moments come after the jackal's false identity is discovered and his license plates and description are distributed. He keeps running—and always convincingly; this isn't a movie about a killer with luck, but about one of uncommon intelligence and nerve.

Playing the jackal, Edward Fox is excellent. The movie doesn't provide much chance for a deep characterization, but he projects a most convincing persona. He's boyishly charming, impeccably groomed, possessed of an easy laugh, and casually ruthless. He will kill if there's the slightest need to. Fox's performance is crucial to the film, of course, and the way he carries it off is impressive.

The others on the case are uniformly excellent, especially Tony Britton as a harried police inspector and Cyril Cusack, in a nicely crafted little vignette, as the gunsmith. The movie's technical values (as is always the case with a Zinnemann film) are impeccable. The movie was filmed at great cost all over Europe, mostly on location, and it looks it. A production of this scope needs to appear absolutely convincing, and Zinnemann has mastered every detail—including the casting of a perfect de Gaulle look-alike.

The Day of the Jackal is two and a half hours long and seems over in about fifteen minutes. There are some words you hesitate to use in a review, because they sound so much like advertising copy, but in this case I can truthfully say that the movie is spellbinding.

Days of Heaven ★ ★ ★ ★
PG, 95 m., 1978

Richard Gere (Bill), Brooke Adams (Abby), Sam Shepard (The Farmer), Linda Manz (Linda), Robert Wilke (Foreman), Jackie Shultis (Linda's Friend), Stuart Margolin (Mill Foreman). Directed by Terence Malick and produced by Bert and Harold Schneider. Screenplay by Malick.

Can any description of Terence Malick's *Days of Heaven* quite evoke the sense of wonder this film inspires? It's about a handful of people who find themselves shipwrecked in the middle of the Texas Panhandle—grain country—sometime before World War I. They involve themselves in a tragic love triangle, but their secrets seem insignificant, almost pathetic, seen against the awesome size of their world. Our wonder is that they endure at all in the face of the implacable land.

The land is farmed by a sick young man

(Sam Shepard) who is widely believed to be on the edge of death. In the autumn, he and his foreman hire crews of itinerant laborers who ride out from the big cities on the tops of boxcars: swaggering, anonymous men who will follow the harvest north from Texas to Canada. Others pass through to entertain them and live off their brief periods of wage earning: aerial barnstormers, circus troupes, all specks on the great landscape.

We meet three people who set out together from the grime of Chicago, looking for harvest work: A strong young man (Richard Gere), his kid sister (Linda Manz), and the woman he lives with and also claims, for convenience, as his sister (Brooke Adams). They arrive at the farm of the sick young man, who falls in love with the older "sister."

Because they are so poor, because the farmer has a house, land, and money, the three keep quiet about his mistake and eventually the farmer and the "sister" marry. Her "brother"—her man—works on the farm and observes the marriage from a resentful, festering distance. The younger girl also observes, and the film's narration comes from her comments, deeply cynical, pathetically understated.

So goes the story of *Days of Heaven*, except that Malick's film doesn't really tell a story at all. It is an evocation of emptiness, loneliness, desolation, the slow accumulation of despair in a land too large for its inhabitants and blind to their dreams. Willa Cather wrote novels about such feelings—*The Lost Lady, Death Comes for the Archbishop,* the middle section of *The Professor's House*—and now Malick joins her company. This is a huge land we occupy. The first people to settle in it must have wondered if they could ever really possess it.

Malick's vision of the land, indeed, is so sweeping that an ordinary, human-scale "story" in the foreground would be a distraction. We get a series of scenes, like tableaux, as the characters involve themselves in their mutual tragedy. The visual compositions often place them against vast backdrops (this is one of the most beautifully photographed films ever made), but Malick finds terror, too, in extreme close-ups of grasshoppers, of a germinating seed, of the little secrets with which nature ultimately builds her infinite secret.

When it develops that the girl has really fallen in love with her new husband, that she is not a con artist but just another victim, we might expect, in another movie, all sorts of blame and analysis. A director not sure of this material could have talked it away. But Malick brings a solemnity to his revelations, as the farmer gradually discovers the deception, as the laborer discovers his loss, as the little sister loses what little childhood she had.

Days of Heaven is a unique achievement—I can't think of another film anything like it. It's serious, yes, very solemn, but not depressing. More than anything else, it wants to re-create its time and place, as if Malick believes the decisions of his characters (and maybe his very characters themselves) come out of the time and place, and are caused by them.

So many movies are jammed with people talking to each other all the time, people obsessed with the conviction they're saying something. The people of *Days of Heaven* are so overwhelmed by the sheer force of nature, by the weight of the land, the bounty of the harvest, the casual distraction of fire and plague, the sharp, involuntary impulses of their passions, that they hardly know what to say. When you look at it that way, who does?

Days of Thunder ★ ★ ★
PG-13, 106 m., 1990

Tom Cruise (Cole Trickle), Robert Duvall (Harry Hogge), Randy Quaid (Tim Daland), Nicole Kidman (Dr. Claire Lewicki), Cary Elwes (Russ Wheeler), Michael Rooker (Rowdy Burns), John C. Reilly (Buck Bretherton), Don Simpson (Aldo Benedetti), Donna Wilson (Darlene). Directed by Tony Scott and produced by Don Simpson and Jerry Bruckheimer. Screenplay by Robert Towne.

Days of Thunder is an entertaining example of what we might as well call the Tom Cruise Picture, since it assembles most of the same elements that worked in *Top Gun, The Color of Money,* and *Cocktail* and runs them through the formula once again. Parts of the plot are beginning to wear out their welcome, but the key ingredients are still effective. They include:

1. The Cruise Character, invariably a young and naive but naturally talented kid who could be the best, if ever he could tame his rambunctious spirit.

2. The Mentor, an older man who has done it himself and been there before and knows talent when he sees it, and who has faith in the kid even when the kid screws up because his free spirit has gotten the best of him.

3. The Superior Woman, usually older, taller, and more mature than the Cruise character, who functions as a Mentor for his spirit, while the male Mentor supervises his craft.

4. The Craft, which the gifted young man must master.

5. The Arena, in which the young man is tested.

6. The Arcana, consisting of the specialized knowledge and lore that the movie knows all about, and we get to learn.

7. The Trail, a journey to visit the principal places where the masters of the craft test one another.

8. The Proto-Enemy, the bad guy in the opening reels of the movie, who provides the hero with an opponent to practice on. At first the Cruise character and the Proto-Enemy dislike each other, but eventually through a baptism of fire they learn to love one another.

9. The Eventual Enemy, a *real* bad guy who turns up in the closing reels to provide the hero with a test of his skill, his learning ability, his love, his craft, and his knowledge of the Arena and the Arcana.

The archetypal Tom Cruise Movie is, of course, *Top Gun,* in which the young fighter pilot, a natural, was tutored by a once-great pilot and emotionally nurtured by an older female flight instructor before testing his wings against the hot dogs of his unit, in preparation for a final showdown against the Enemy. In *The Color of Money,* the young pool player, a natural, was tutored by a once-great pool hustler and emotionally nurtured by an older female who had been around the block a few times, in preparation for a two-part showdown with (a) his hated opponent on the professional pool circuit, and (b) his Mentor himself. In *Cocktail,* the young bartender, a natural, was tutored by an older bartender, before eventually meeting first an older female who taught him a thing or two, and then a younger but still more mature female who taught him how to forget them.

In *Days of Thunder,* all of these elements are present in an entertainment of great skill but predictable construction. The Craft is stock-car racing. The Mentor is played by Robert Duvall, as a veteran racing-team leader. The Superior Woman is a physician (Nicole Kidman), who is attracted to the raw energy of the hero but forces him to grow up by laying down the line of responsible behavior. The Arena is the auto-racing track, and the Arcana includes such lore as "slip-streaming," RPMs, tire temperature, and whether to pass on the outside or the inside. The Proto-Enemy is a driver named Rowdy (Michael Rooker), who challenges the hero to racing duels including one that winds them both up in the hospital. The Eventual Enemy (Cary Elwes) is a driver named Wheeler who would like to run the hero into the wall and kill him. And the Trail, of course, is the Southern stock-car circuit, ending in the holy city of Daytona.

Days of Thunder was directed by Tony Scott, the same man who started this whole cycle by directing *Top Gun,* and it shows the same mastery of the photography of fast machines. The movie's handicap is that auto racing is visually a boring sport unless you are standing close to the cars or they are crashing into each other. The rest consists of long shots of lots of anonymous cars dashing confusingly around the track, medium shots of two cars trying to pass one another, and closeups of drivers looking as if they were experiencing proctoscopy.

As *Days of Thunder* sees it, the principal strategy in stock-car racing consists of trying to sideswipe your opponent and push him into the wall, and Cruise's car scrapes the wall for easily half of the time it is on the track. Most of this racing footage is loud and fast enough to be exciting, however, and the off-track sequences are served by Robert Duvall's usual laconic, sensitive performance, Randy Quaid as a used-car dealer who has faith in the kid, and Michael Rooker as the perfect Proto-Enemy (he can look hateful and then turn it around with a smile). Nicole Kidman has little to do as the physician, and doesn't make much of an impression. And Tom Cruise is so efficiently packaged in this product that he plays the same role as a saint in a Mexican village's holy day procession: It's not what he does that makes him so special, it's the way he manifests everybody's faith in him.

The Dead ★ ★ ★
PG, 83 m., 1987

Anjelica Huston (Gretta), Donal McCann (Gabriel), Rachel Dowling (Lily), Dan O'Herlihy (Mr. Browne), Donal Donnelly (Freddy), Cathleen Delany (Aunt Julia), Helena Carroll (Aunt Kate), Ingrid Craigie (Mary Jane), Frank Patterson (Bartell D'Arcy). Directed by John Huston and produced by Wieland Schulz-Keil and Chris Sievernich. Screenplay by Tony Huston.

Better pass boldly into that other world, in the full glory of some passion, than fade and wither dismally with age. The words are from James Joyce's *The Dead,* sometimes called the greatest short story ever written in English. The thoughts belong to a middle-aged man, Gabriel Conroy, and when he thinks them he is lying next to his sleeping wife in a Dublin hotel room, and the snow is falling all over Ireland. He has spent a musical evening at the home of his aunts, Julia and Kate, in the company of the same old friends who gather every Christmas to sing the same songs and tell the old stories and cluck over the fact that poor Freddy Malins has turned up drunk again, to the embarrassment of his mother.

Most of the story is devoted to the party—who is there, and what happens, and what they say. But Joyce is somehow able to use words to suggest some great silence beneath the chatter, deeper feelings that go unexpressed in all the holiday cheer. The story ends as Gabriel and his wife, Gretta, ride across Dublin to their hotel, and she confesses to him that one of the songs reminded her of a boy who loved her when she was seventeen, a boy named Michael Furey, who was ill. When she made plans to go up to Dublin to convent school, he begged her not to go, and came and stood outside her window in the winter rain. A week later he was dead.

After Gretta tells the story, Gabriel realizes that there is a large part of his wife's life that he did not even suspect existed. She goes to sleep, and he lies beside her in the dark. Joyce writes: "Generous tears filled Gabriel's eyes. He had never felt like that himself toward any woman, but he knew that such a feeling must be love." He can see through the window that it is snowing, and he knows it is snowing all over Ireland, even on the grave where Michael Furey lies.

I have described so much of the Joyce story because I want to illustrate what a hard challenge John Huston set for himself when he decided to make a film of *The Dead.* It is easy enough to film all the details of the party, all the comings and goings, the toasts and the songs. But all of those scenes are there for only one reason: to establish the surface of a commonplace, satisfactory life, so that the closing moments of the story can shock us by showing what hidden depths of loneliness and passion can exist secretly in the hearts of people we think we know.

The key emotional moment in *The Dead* does not belong to Gretta, who still mourns for her dead young lover. It belongs to Gabriel, who weeps for the man his wife once loved, a man he never met or even heard of before tonight. To cry for a stranger is to shed tears for the human condition, to weep because in giving us consciousness, God also gave us the ability to know loss and to mourn it.

There is no way in the world that any filmmaker can reproduce the thoughts inside Gabriel's head at the end of *The Dead.* And that must have been something Huston knew when he decided to make this film. Then why did he make it anyway? I think I know the answer. He made it because he came of Irish blood and lived for many years in Ireland. He made it because the film would be written by his son, Tony, and would star his daughter, Anjelica. And he made it because he knew he was dying, and it would be his last film.

And there was one last reason, which can be glimpsed in the words I began with: "Better pass boldly into that other world, in the full glory of some passion, than fade and wither dismally with age." Huston was an old man when he died, but he had not withered dismally with age because he still had the courage and the imagination to attempt to make an impossible film of the greatest story that he had ever read. Look at Huston's *The Dead* and you will not see a successful film, but you will see a grand gesture, and you will see the best film that Huston could possibly have made. And now the snow falls upon every part of the lonely churchyard on the hill where John Huston lies buried.

Dead Calm ★ ★ ★
R, 97 m., 1989

Nicole Kidman (Rae Ingram), Sam Neill (John Ingram), Billy Zane (Hughie Warriner), Rod Mudlinar (Russell Bellows), Joshua Tilden (Danny), George Shevtsov (Doctor), Michael Long (Specialist Doctor). Directed by Phillip Noyce and produced by Terry Hayes, Doug Mitchell, and George Miller.

The key image of *Dead Calm* is of two ships drawing near each other in the middle of a vast, empty expanse of ocean. The emotions generated by this shot, near the beginning of the film, underlie everything that follows, making us acutely aware that help is not going to arrive from anywhere, that the built-in protections of civilization are irrelevant, and that the characters will have to settle their own destinies.

On board a sailing yacht are a married couple who hope the cruise will help them deal with the death of their son. On board the other ship—a sinking schooner—is a young man who seems to be the only survivor of a tragic incident of food poisoning. He jumps into a lifeboat and rows for his life toward the yacht, where he is taken aboard. The husband, curious, goes to inspect the schooner, leaving his wife alone with the castaway, who of course turns out to be a homicidal killer.

Almost the entire movie involves these three characters, in a violent game of psychological strategy. Sam Neill stars as the husband, who is stranded on the sinking ship when the killer sails away. Nicole Kidman is the wife, who has to outsmart and outfight the madman. And Billy Zane is the killer, wild-eyed and off-balance. The plot splits into two for most of the movie, with the woman on board the yacht with the killer, while her husband finds himself trapped in the hold of the sinking ship with the water rapidly rising above nose level. The counterpoint is effective.

A plot like this is probably impossible without two ancient movie traditions, the Talking Killer and the Undead Dead. Time and again in the movie, the story would be over if someone—anyone—simply pulled the trigger. There is a moment when the wife temporarily has the upper hand against this madman who had assaulted and beaten her and left her husband to drown, and what does she do? *She ties him up!* And with the knot in front, too—where he can get at it. Later in the film, after he appears to be dead, he reappears, of course, and has to be fought a second time.

And yet *Dead Calm* generates genuine tension because the story is so simple and the performances are so straightforward. This is not a gimmick film (unless you count the husband's method of escaping from the sinking ship), and Nicole Kidman and Billy Zane do generate real, palpable hatred in their scenes together.

Note: The film is based on a 1963 novel by Charles Williams, which inspired an ill-fated Orson Welles project that was suspended in 1970 and then abandoned in 1973 with the death of his leading man, Laurence Harvey. I haven't read the novel, but the story is worthy of a robust craftsman like John D. MacDonald—all except for the unnecessary prologue in the hospital, which he would have junked.

Dead Poets Society ★ ★
PG, 130 m., 1989

Robin Williams (John Keating), Robert Sean
Leonard (Neil Perry), Ethan Hawke (Todd
Anderson), Josh Charles (Knox Overstreet),
Gale Hansen (Charlie Dalton), Dylan Kussman
(Richard Cameron), Allelon Ruggiero (Steven
Meeks), James Waterston (Gerard Pitts).
Directed by Peter Weir and produced by
Steven Haft, Paul Junger Witt, and Tony
Thomas. Screenplay by Tom Schulman.

Peter Weir's *Dead Poets Society* is a collection of pious platitudes masquerading as a
courageous stand in favor of something—
doing your own thing, I think. It's about an
inspirational, unconventional English teacher and his students at "the best prep school
in America," and how he challenges them to
question conventional views by such techniques as standing on their desks. It is, of
course, inevitable that the brilliant teacher
will eventually be fired from the school, and
when his students stood on their desks to
protest his dismissal, I was so moved, I
wanted to throw up.

The film makes much noise about poetry,
and there are brief quotations from Ten-
nyson, Herrick, Whitman, and even Vachel
Lindsay, as well as a brave excursion into
prose that takes us as far as Thoreau's *Walden*. None of these writers are studied, however, in a spirit that would lend respect to
their language; they're simply plundered for
slogans to exhort the students toward more
personal freedom. At the end of a great
teacher's course in poetry, the students
would love poetry; at the end of this teacher's
semester, all they really love is the teacher.

The movie stars Robin Williams as the
mercurial John Keating, teacher of English
at the exclusive Welton Academy in Vermont. The performance is a delicate balancing act between restraint and schtick. For
much of the time, Williams does a good job
of playing an intelligent, quick-witted, well-
read young man. But then there are scenes in
which his stage persona punctures the character—as when he does impressions of Marlon Brando and John Wayne doing Shakespeare. There is also a curious lack of depth
to his character; compared to such other
great movie teachers as Miss Jean Brodie and
Professor Kingsfield, Keating is more of a
plot device than a human being.

The story in *Dead Poets Society* is also
old stuff, recycled out of the novel and movie

A Separate Peace and other stories in which
the good die young and the old simmer in
their neurotic and hateful repressions. The
key conflict in the movie is between Neil
(Robert Sean Leonard), a student who
dreams of being an actor, and his father
(Kurtwood Smith), a domineering parent
who orders his son to become a doctor, and
forbids him to go on stage. The father is a
strict, unyielding taskmaster, and the son,
lacking the will to defy him, kills himself.
His death would have had a greater impact
for me if it had seemed like a spontaneous
human cry of despair, rather than like a
meticulously written and photographed set
piece.

Other elements in the movie also seem to
have been chosen for their place in the
artificial jigsaw puzzle. A teen-age romance
between one of the Welton students and a
local girl is given so little screen time, so
arbitrarily, that it seems like a distraction.
And I squirmed through the meetings of the
"Dead Poets Society," a self-consciously
bohemian group of students who hold secret
meetings in the dead of night in a cave near
the campus.

The society was founded, we learn, by Mr.
Keating when he was an undergraduate, but
in its reincarnate form it never generates any
sense of mystery, rebellion, or daring. The
society's meetings have been badly written
and are dramatically shapeless, featuring a
dance-line to Lindsay's "The Congo" and
various attempts to impress girls with random lines of poetry. The movie is set in 1959,
but none of these would-be bohemians have
heard of Kerouac, Ginsberg, or indeed of the
beatnik movement at all.

One scene in particular indicates the distance between the movie's manipulative
instincts, and what it claims to be about.
When Mr. Keating is being railroaded by the
school administration (which makes him the
scapegoat for his student's suicide), one of
the students acts as a fink and tells the old
fogies what they want to hear. Later, confronted by his peers, he makes a hateful
speech of which not one word is plausible
except as an awkward attempt to supply him
with a villain's dialogue. Then one of the
other boys hits him in the jaw, to great
applause from the audience. The whole
scene is utterly false, and seems to exist only
so that the violence can resolve a situation
which the screenplay is otherwise unwilling
to handle.

Dead Poets Society is not the worst of

the countless recent movies about good kids
and hidebound, authoritarian older people.
It may, however, be the most shameless in its
attempt to pander to an adolescent audience.
The movie pays lip service to qualities and
values which, on the evidence of the screenplay itself, it is cheerfully willing to abandon.
If you are going to evoke Henry David Thoreau as the patron saint of your movie, then
you had better make a movie he would have
admired. Here is one of my favorite sentences from Thoreau's *Walden*, which I recommend for serious study by the authors of
this film: ". . . instead of studying how to
make it worth men's while to buy my baskets, I studied rather how to avoid the necessity of selling them." Think about it.

The Dead Pool ★ ★ ★ ½
R, 94 m., 1988

Clint Eastwood (Harry Callahan), Liam
Neeson (Peter Swan), Patricia Clarkson
(Samantha Walker), Evan Kim (Juan), David
Hunt (Harlan Rook). Directed by Buddy Van
Horn and produced by David Valdes.
Screenplay by Steve Sharon.

The little twitch comes and goes so fast it's
easy to miss. It's in the corner of Dirty
Harry's face, and it betrays the seething
anger hidden beneath his mask of calm. It's
not even anger, really, that seethes inside
there—but indignation that criminals are
going free while the San Francisco Police
Department devotes itself to public relations. What's interesting about the twitch is
that it comes at just the right moment, early
in the movie, and the audience is waiting for
it, and there's actually a cheer when they see
it.

Rarely can the mental states of a series
movie character have become more familiar
than those of Dirty Harry. *The Dead Pool* is
the fifth in the series, and most of the people
watching it will have seen the other four.
They know of Harry's impatience with
bureaucracy, and his willingness to go it
alone, one-on-one, with the criminals in his
path. Like the fans of a familiar opera, Dirty
Harry fans wait for the key moments.

After the twitch, we know that before long
there will be two more: the moment when
Det. Harry Callahan is called on the carpet in
his superior's office and given a severe dressing down, and the moment, not long after,
when he is suspended from active duty.

Unless my memory fails, Harry has solved all of his cases while on suspension.

The balancing act in a good Dirty Harry movie is between the familiar notes, which must remain the same every time, and the new angles in every new case. *The Dead Pool*, which is as good as the original *Dirty Harry*, has lots of new angles, and a lot of things to say, especially about horror films, television news, and the burden of being a celebrity.

The title comes from a macabre gambling game that is being played in San Francisco as the movie opens: A list of eight celebrities has been distributed, and people place bets on which of the eight will be the first to die. The winner takes the pool. And before long, of course, Harry Callahan's name is on the list.

One of the players of the game is Peter Swan (Liam Neeson), a monomaniacal British horror film director who is making a rock video in San Francisco. One of the names on the list is the drug-addicted rock star who is starring in the video. When the rock star is found dead, the director is naturally a prime suspect—but Harry thinks the plot runs deeper than that, and he is right.

In the course of his investigation, he crosses paths with Samantha Walker (Patricia Clarkson), an aggressive TV reporter who is constantly shoving her camera in Harry's face. One day Harry grabs her camera and throws it as far as he can, but in no time the two of them are having candlelit dinners and discussing the problems of fame—problems Harry has thought about much more deeply and interestingly than Samantha.

As the movie develops, we get point-of-view glimpses that clue us in to the fact that someone is killing the members of the Dead Pool and trying to frame the hapless Peter Swan. These shots arrive at some sort of climax in a brilliant and inspired scene in which Harry's car is pursued up and down the hills of San Francisco by another car that is filled with powerful plastic explosives. The gimmick is that the other car is a model, only about a foot long, and so the suspense is intermixed with a hilarious parody of the chase scene in *Bullitt*. (It is highly doubtful that such a small car could travel that fast, but what the hell.)

The best thing about *The Dead Pool* is the best thing about almost all of Clint Eastwood's movies—the film is smart, quick, and made with real wit. It's never just a crude action movie, bludgeoning us with violence. It's self-aware, it knows who Dirty Harry is and how we react to him, and it has fun with its intelligence. Also, of course, it bludgeons us with violence.

Dead Ringers ★ ★ ½
R, 115 m., 1988

Jeremy Irons (Mantle Twins), Genevieve Bujold (Claire Niveau), Heide Von Palleske (Mr. Weiler). Directed by David Cronenberg and produced by Marc Boyman. Written by Norman Snider and Cronenberg.

Twins seem a source of strange power to people who are not one. Part of it must be in our imaginations. We see a nod or a glance between one twin and another, and we imagine some kind of telepathic communication taking place, when in fact the whole transaction is probably just ordinary body language.

Twins themselves always seem to keep some private place for their twinship. They do not talk about it much. They begin sentences that somehow seem to go nowhere, as if it is not quite possible to put into words what this particular relationship means to them. Most of us, I imagine, would like to have a twin; there is something awesome in the thought.

Dead Ringers is the vulgar exploitation movie title given to David Cronenberg's film, which was originally and more poetically titled *Twins*. It stars Jeremy Irons in a dual role as both Beverly and Elliott Mantle, brilliant twins who grow up to be brilliant gynecologists. Beverly's name may be misleading; both twins are men, and they are unusually close, so much so that they routinely pretend to be each other.

The movie is not at all shy about exploiting the possibility that a woman going to see one of these gynecologists might end up being seen by the other. But that is only the beginning of their deception. We discover that Elliott has always been the dominant twin, and that it is his practice to seduce a woman and then turn her over to Beverly—without telling the woman, of course. "You'd still be a virgin if it weren't for me!" he cries.

A famous actress (Genevieve Bujold) comes to consult them about why she cannot have children. The answer, in this most gynecologically precise of movies, is that she has three openings to her uterus, and an ambitious sperm is likely to get caught in traffic at the intersection. Parts of the script seem lifted out of one of those women's magazine articles that treat the reproductive organs like a biological subway system.

Bujold begins a kinky love affair with Beverly, and shares not only her body but her drug habit. Then she discovers that she has been involved with both of the twins—and she lashes out at them. But who would win in a war like this? The girlfriend or the twins? She disappears from the movie after having planted the seeds for Beverly's destruction: The drugs seem to release the craziness that has always been a potential inside of him, and although his twin tries to cover for him, their lives eventually fly into pieces.

In one particularly gruesome sequence, Beverly invents some new surgical instruments that look like daydreams of the Marquis de Sade, and uses them in a bloody operation that looks like what you do to the turkey before the stuffing goes in. I saw the movie at the Toronto Film Festival with several women friends, who said it was harder for them to take than I, a man, could possibly imagine. But they were fascinated while it was on the screen. The secret may be that Cronenberg (director of *The Dead Zone* and *The Fly*) approaches his trashy material with the objectivity of a scientist; it is his detached, cold style that makes the material creepy instead of simply sensational.

Of course, everything depends on Jeremy Irons's performances as the twins. He is an intelligent, subtle actor, and he actually does succeed in making the two twins into substantially different people. In ways so understated we are sometimes not even quite aware of them, he makes it clear most of the time whether we are looking at Beverly or Elliott. He develops them separately, so that the chaos at the end really works.

Cronenberg is a master of special effects, as he demonstrated visibly in *The Fly* and as he demonstrates invisibly here. As everyone knows, when the same actor plays two characters in the same scene, one of the techniques used is the split screen. Clever viewers can usually spot the line—usually hidden in shadow—where one part of the picture ends and the other begins, but Cronenberg uses "moving splits" to fool them. Using computer technology, he can move the position of the split and the position of the camera at the same time, and he also sometimes drops in the split after one of the characters has just crossed the line where it will appear—so we think that space is "real." The result is that Irons does convincingly appear as two separate people, and not as trick photography.

The technical perfection of the film is not matched by its emotional content. The story could have used more of the Bujold character, who is sophisticated and worldly enough to understand the twins, but who is dropped when they begin to retreat into their private disintegration. *Dead Ringers* is a stylistic *tour de force*, but it's cold and creepy and centered on bleak despair. It's the kind of movie where you ask people how they liked it, and they say, "Well, it *was* well-made," and then they wince.

Dead of Winter ★ ★ ½
PG-13, 100 m., 1987

Mary Steenburgen (Katie McGovern), Roddy McDowall (Mr. Murray), Jan Rubes (Dr. Lewis), William Russ (Rob Sweeney), Ken Pogue (Officer Mullavy), Mark Malone (Roland). Directed by Arthur Penn and produced by John Bloomgarden and Marc Shmuger. Screenplay by Shmuger and Mark Malone.

Dead of Winter is one of those movies where you shout advice at the screen. The plot involves a young woman in mortal danger, and we can see how she can save herself, even if she can't.

It's easy to pick holes in movies like this, to find the inconsistencies and the oversights, and say the movie's no good because we're smarter than it is. But maybe that's exactly the point. Maybe the actual pleasure comes from the fun of being frustrated and full of free advice while the character marches to her doom.

The movie stars Mary Steenburgen as an out-of-work actress who is pleased to pass an audition and be summoned to an isolated country mansion for a screen test. She arrives in the middle of a howling blizzard, to meet her host, a meticulously polite old gentleman in a wheelchair, and his assistant, an obsequious, but sinister, Roddy McDowall.

What we know and she doesn't is that the two men need her because she's an exact double for a kidnap victim they've killed. They tell her she's needed as the double for an actress in a movie they're making, and she unknowingly studies the appearance and voice patterns of the dead woman, until she's good enough to read a script into a video camera. Of course, then they plan to kill her.

The plot is not really the point in a movie like this. Thriller plots are born to be manipulated and then forgotten. What counts is the architecture of the house, the exact locations of the one-way mirrors and the hidden staircases, the existence of a working telephone in the attic, the alarming moments when the heroine discovers that all is not as it seems. The plot is simply a device to get us from one heart-stopping moment to the next.

I must tread carefully, or I will give away important secrets. Let it be said that Miss Steenburgen functions in the time-honored tradition of damsels in distress, and does her share of screaming, running up and down stairs, and clawing her way up an icy hillside in a blizzard.

The evil doctor and his assistant are also well within movie tradition, but Jan Rubes and McDowall make the relationship more complex than usual; the older man seems to have some sort of subtle hold over the younger. McDowall is good in these blood-soaked roles, as he proved as the vampire-killer in *Fright Night*. He demonstrates the principle that a friendly villain is almost always more frightening than a threatening one.

For Steenburgen, there's a nice passage near the end where she tries to play a dual role; I won't say more. The movie itself is finally just an exercise in silliness—great effort to little avail—but the actors have fun with it, and the sets work, and there are one or two moments with perfect surprises.

And then, for the rest, there are the loopholes, such as (a) how many gas stations do you know that give away free goldfish in the winter—or give away anything at any time? Or (b) why couldn't Steenburgen look at the shoulder patches of the visiting cops to discover the name of the nearby town? Or (c) why can't the cops ever seem to put two and two together? And so on. Maybe they're not important. Maybe they come with the territory.

The Dead Zone ★ ★ ★ ½
R, 103 m., 1983

Christopher Walken (Johnny), Brooke Adams (Sarah), Herbert Lom (Dr. Weizak), Tom Skerritt (Sheriff), Martin Sheen (Candidate). Directed by David Cronenberg and produced by Debra Hill. Screenplay by Jeffrey Boam.

The Dead Zone does what only a good supernatural thriller can do: It makes us forget it is supernatural. Like *Rosemary's Baby* and *The Exorcist*, it tells its story so strongly through the lives of sympathetic, believable people that we not only forgive the gimmicks, we accept them. There is pathos in what happens to the Christopher Walken character in this movie and that pathos would never be felt if we didn't buy the movie's premise.

Walken plays a high school teacher whose life is happy (he's in love with Brooke Adams), until the night an accident puts him into a coma for five years. When he "returns," he has an extrasensory gift. He can touch people's hands and "know" what will happen to them. His first discovery is that he can foresee the future. His second is that he can change it. By seeing what "will" happen and trying to prevent it, he can bring about a different future. Of course, then he's left with the problem of explaining how he knew something "would have" happened, to people who can clearly see that it did not. Instead of ignoring that problem as a lesser movie might have, *The Dead Zone* builds its whole premise on it.

The movie is based on a novel by Stephen King and was directed by David Cronenberg, the Canadian who started with low-budget shockers *(The Brood, It Came From Within)* and worked up to big budgets *(Scanners)*. It's a happy collaboration. No other King novel has been better filmed (certainly not the dreadful *Cujo*), and Cronenberg, who knows how to handle terror, also knows how to create three-dimensional, fascinating characters.

In that he gets a lot of help from Walken, whose performance in this movie in a semi-reputable genre is the equal of his work in *The Deer Hunter*. Walken does such a good job of portraying Johnny Smith, the man with the strange gift, that we forget this is science fiction or fantasy or whatever, and just accept it as this guy's story.

The movie is filled with good performances: Adams, as the woman who marries someone else during Johnny's coma, but has a clear-eyed, unsentimental love for him at a crucial moment; Tom Skerritt, as the local sheriff who wants to enlist this psychic to solve a chain of murders; Herbert Lom as a sympathetic doctor; and Martin Sheen as a conniving populist politician. They all work together to make a movie that could have been just another scary thriller, and turn it into a believable thriller—which, of course, is even scarier.

Dear America: Letters Home From Vietnam ★ ★ ★ ★
PG-13, 86 m., 1988

Directed by Bill Couturie and produced by the Couturie Co. and Vietnam Veterans Ensemble Theater Company. Screenplay by Richard Dewhurst and Couturie.

Surf's up, and the Beach Boys are singing. American kids dive into the waves and come up wet and grinning, and there's a cooler of beer waiting under the palm trees. It looks like Vietnam is going to be a fun place. The opening scenes of *Dear America: Letters Home From Vietnam* are so carefree, so lighthearted, that it doesn't even seem strange that most of the soldiers look exactly like the kids they are—high school graduates drafted straight into war.

On the sound track, we hear the voices of these soldiers, in the words they wrote home. They speak of patriotism, of confidence, of new friendships. In their letters there is a sense of wonder at this new world they have found, a world so different from the American cities and towns they left behind. And then gradually the tone of their letters begins to change.

There have been several great movies about Vietnam. This is the one that completes the story, that has no plot except that thousands of young men went to a faraway country and had unspeakable experiences there, and many of them died or were wounded for life in body or soul. This movie is so powerful precisely because it is so simple—the words are the words of the soldiers themselves, and the images are taken from their own home movies, and from TV news footage of the war.

There are moments here that cannot be forgotten, and most of them are due to the hard work of the filmmaker, director Bill Couturie, who has not taken just any words and any old footage, but precisely the right words to go with the images. Couturie began with an anthology of letters written home by U.S. soldiers in Vietnam. Then he screened the *entire* archive of TV news footage shot by NBC-TV from 1967 to 1969—two million feet of film totaling 926 hours. He also gained access to footage from the Department of Defense, including previously classified film of action under fire. Much of the footage in this film has never been seen publicly before, and watching it, you know why.

What Couturie and his researchers have done is amazing. In many cases, they have matched up individual soldiers with their letters—we see them as we hear their words, and then we discover their fates. "I tell you truthfully I doubt if I'll come out of this alive," a private named Raymond Griffiths writes home to his girlfriend. "In my original squad, I'm the only one left unharmed." He died in action on the Fourth of July, 1966.

There are amateur 8-mm home movies here, of GIs clowning in front of the camera, and cracking beers, and cleaning their weapons. There are frightening firefights, and unflinching shots of men in the process of dying. And there are chilling scenes such as the one when General William Westmoreland greets the survivors from a bloodbath, and his words are the words of an automaton, with utterly no emotion in his voice as he "chats" with his troops. He is so false, it seems like a bad performance. If this footage had been shown on TV at the time, he might have been forced to resign.

The movie follows a chronology that roughly corresponds to a soldier's year in Vietnam. From the first days of swimming in the surf to the last exhausted days of fear and despair, it never looks away. And the words of the soldiers have the eloquence of simple truth. One soldier writes of the bravery of men who rescued their comrades under enemy fire. Another writes of a momentary hush in a tank battle on Christmas Eve, and of hearing someone begin to sing "Silent Night" and others joining in.

The words in the letters are read by some forty different actors and actresses, whose voices you can sometimes identify, until you stop thinking in those terms. The voices include Robert De Niro, Martin and Charlie Sheen, Kathleen Turner, Tom Berenger, Brian Dennehy, Howard Rollins, Jr., Sean Penn, Matt Dillon, Michael J. Fox. The music on the sound track is all from the period, and then, at the end of the movie, there is a heartbreaking flash-forward to the Vietnam War Memorial in Washington fifteen years later, and we hear Bruce Springsteen's "Born in the USA" as Ellen Burstyn reads a letter that the mother of a dead veteran left at the foot of the wall of names:

"Dear Bill, Today is February 13, 1984. I came to this black wall again to see and touch your name, William R. Stocks, and as I do I wonder if anyone ever stops to realize that next to your name, on this black wall, is your mother's heart. A heart broken fifteen years ago today, when you lost your life in Vietnam.

"They tell me the letters I write to you and leave here at this memorial are waking others up to the fact that there is still much pain left, after all these years, from the Vietnam War.

"This I know. I would rather have had you for twenty-one years, and all the pain that goes with losing you, than never to have had you at all. Mom."

Choose any film as the best movie ever made about Vietnam, and this is the other half of the same double feature. Francois Truffaut once wrote that it was impossible to make an "anti-war film," because any war film, no matter what its message, was sure to be exhilarating. He did not live to see this film.

Death in Venice ★ ★ ½
PG, 127 m., 1971

Dirk Bogarde (Aschenbach), Bjorn Andresen (Tadzio), Silvana Mangano (The Mother), Romolo Valli (Hotel Manager). Directed and produced by Luchino Visconti. Screenplay by Visconti and Nicola Badalucco.

I think the thing that disappoints me most about Luchino Visconti's *Death in Venice* is its lack of ambiguity. Visconti has chosen to abandon the subtleties of the Thomas Mann novel and present us with a straightforward story of homosexual love, and although that's his privilege, I think he has missed the greatness of Mann's work somewhere along the way. In the novel, Count Aschenbach goes to Venice at a certain season in his life, driven by a compulsion he does not fully understand and confronted by strange presences who somehow seem to be mocking or tempting him. Once settled in his grand hotel on the Lido, he becomes aware of a beautiful boy who is also visiting there with his family from Poland. His feelings toward this boy are terribly complicated, and to interpret them as a simple homosexual attraction is vulgar and simplistic. The boy represents, above all, an ideal of perfect physical beauty apart from sexuality; the irony is that this beauty stirs emotions in a man who (in the novel) has insisted on occupying the world of the intellect. The boy's youth and naturalness become a reproach to the older man's vanity and creative sterility.

Visconti undermines this contrast between beauty and the intellect by changing the Aschenbach character from a writer to a composer. He made the change, reportedly, because he decided that Mann had "really" based his character on Gustav Mahler, but so what? There are flashbacks where Aschenbach argues that beauty resides in the intellect, and a friend declares that beauty is a quality naturally possessed by beautiful things. Aschenbach's position could be held by a philosopher and scholar, but not (I imagine) by the composer of the romantic Mahler symphonies that are constantly present on the sound track.

Visconti also misses, or avoids, the subtlety of the novel's development of the relationship between the two characters. In the Mann version, the man can never really know what the boy thinks of him; they do not speak, and if the boy favors him sometimes with a look or a smile, he favors many others as well, because that is his nature. It is entirely possible, the way Mann tells the story, that the boy is totally unaware of any homosexual implication—and the man, indeed, may also be in love with an ideal rather than a person. No such possibility exists in the heavy-handed Visconti retelling. The boy's function in the film, which he performs at least two dozen times, is to self-consciously pose in front of the man, turn slowly, smile sweetly, and turn languorously away. This is almost literally the only physical characteristic the boy has in the movie; and Visconti lays on the turns, looks, and smiles with such a heavy hand that the boy could almost be accused of hustling.

By choosing to limit his story to this level, Visconti loses the philosophical content of the Thomas Mann work, and no amount of heavy-handed flashbacks can restore it. We see Aschenbach in discussions with colleagues, with his wife and child, and then at the child's funeral; we see him seemingly impotent in a bordello, and, unforgivably, Visconti even throws in a concert at which Aschenbach is booed, then comforted by his wife. Scenes in which the genius is assured that (someday!) his genius will be recognized went out, I thought, with *The Eddy Duchin Story.*

Visconti fails, then, to develop characters and relationships that matter. The failure is fatal to the movie's success; but the physical beauty of the film itself is overwhelming. The world of the Lido of sixty years ago has been re-created in painstaking detail. The fashions, the entertainments, the table settings reveal Visconti's compulsion for accuracy. The photography is almost the first I have seen that is fully worthy of the beauty of Venice; the pink-and-gray city rises from waters of a glasslike smoothness, so that the water and the quality of light itself seem to suggest the presence of the plague-bearing sirocco wind. The wind brings both plague and beauty, which is its function in the Mann novel, and Visconti's mastery of visual style almost succeeds in creating the very ideas and feelings that his heavy-handed narrative entirely misses.

Death Wish ★ ★ ★
R, 94 m., 1974

Charles Bronson (Paul Kersey), Hope Lange (Joanna Kersey), Vincent Gardenia (Frank Ochoa), Steve Keats (Jack Toby), William Redfield (Sam Kreutzer), Stuart Margolin (Ames), Jack Wallace (Policeman). Directed by Michael Winner and produced by Dino de Laurentiis. Screenplay by Wendell Mayes.

Death Wish is a quasifascist advertisement for urban vigilantes, done up as a slick and exciting action movie; we like it even while we're turned off by the message. It gives us Charles Bronson in a role that starts out by being somewhat out of character: He plays a liberal, an architect, a former conscientious objector. But he turns into the familiar Bronson man of action after his wife is murdered and his daughter reduced to catatonia by muggers.

His immediate reaction is one of simple grief. Then something happens which suggests a different kind of response. His office sends him to Arizona on a job, and he meets a land developer who's a gun nut. The man takes Bronson to his gun club, watches him squeeze off a few perfect practice rounds, and slips a present into his suitcase when he heads back to New York. It's a .32-caliber revolver.

Alone in his apartment, Bronson examines snapshots from his recent Hawaiian vacation with his wife. Then he examines the gun. He goes out into the night, is attacked by a mugger and shoots him dead. Then he goes home and throws up. But the taste for vengeance, once acquired, has a fascination of its own. And the last half of *Death Wish* is essentially a series of cat-and-mouse games, in which Bronson poses as a middle-aged citizen with a bag of groceries and then murders his attackers.

They are, by the way, everywhere. Director Michael Winner gives us a New York in the grip of a reign of terror; this doesn't look like 1974, but like one of those bloody future cities in science-fiction novels about anarchy in the twenty-first century. Literally every shadow holds a mugger; every subway train harbors a killer; the park is a breeding ground for crime. Urban paranoia is one thing, but *Death Wish* is another. If there were really that many muggers in New York, Bronson could hardly have survived long enough to father a daughter, let alone grieve her.

The movie has an eerie kind of fascination, even though its message is scary. Bronson and Winner have worked together on several films, and they've perfected the Bronson persona. He's a steely instrument of violence, with few words and fewer emotions. In *Death Wish* we get just about the definitive Bronson; rarely has a leading role contained fewer words or more violence.

And Winner directs with a cool precision. He's one of the most efficient directors of action and violence. His muggings and their surprise endings have a sort of inevitable rhythm to them; we're set up for each one almost like the gunfights in Westerns. There's never any question of injustice, because the crimes are attempted right there before our eyes. And then Bronson becomes judge and jury—and executioner.

That's what's scary about the film. It's propaganda for private gun ownership and a call to vigilante justice. Even the cops seem to see it that way; Bronson becomes a folk hero as the New York Vigilante, and the mugging rate drops fifty percent. So the police want to catch Bronson, not to prosecute him for murder, but to offer him a deal: Get out of town, stay out of town, and we'll forget this. Bronson accepts the deal, and in the movie's last scene we see him taking an imaginary bead on a couple of goons in Chicago.

Death Wish II   no stars
R, 89 m., 1982

Charles Bronson (Paul Kersey), Jill Ireland (Geri Nichols), Vincent Gardenia (Frank Ochoa), Anthony Franciosa (Commissioner), Robert F. Lyons (Fred). Directed by Michael Winner and produced by Menahem Golan and Yoram Globus. Screenplay by David Engleback.

You will have noticed that I've given a "no stars" rating for *Death Wish II,* starring Charles Bronson as an urban vigilante. A word of explanation. In my movie rating system, the most a movie can get is four stars (*My Dinner With André*) and the least is ordinarily half a star (even *The Beast Within* got a whole star). I award "no stars" only to movies that are artistically inept and morally repugnant. So *Death Wish II* joins such unsavory company as *Penitentiary II* and *I Spit on Your Grave*. And that, in a way, is a shame. I have a certain admiration for the screen presence of Charles Bronson. In his good roles, he can be lean, quiet, and efficient. He often co-stars with his wife, Jill Ireland, as he does in this movie, and she is a pleasant and capable actress. They were charming together in a little-seen movie named *From Noon to Three*.

This time, however, Bronson and Ireland and everyone else involved with *Death Wish II* create a great disappointment. Although the original *Death Wish* (1974) had its detractors, it was an effective movie that spoke directly to the law-and-order mentality of the Nixon-Ford era. It was directed with a nice slick polish by Michael Winner, and, on its own terms, it worked. *Death Wish II* is a disaster by comparison. It has the same director, Winner, but he directs the dialogue scenes as if the actors' shoes were nailed to the floor. It has two of the same stars—Bronson and New York cop Vincent Gardenia—but they seem shell-shocked by weariness in this film. It has the same plot (Bronson's loved ones are attacked, and he goes out into the streets to murder muggers). But while the first film convinced me of Bronson's need for vengeance, this one is just a series of dumb killings.

You will remember that *Death Wish* opened with home invaders killing Bronson's wife and raping his daughter. After Bronson used himself as bait to trap and kill nine New York City muggers, he became a folk hero. Gardenia, the cop, found out who he was, but decided not to arrest him. Bronson left town, and in this film, he's in Los Angeles. The film opens with his daughter being killed, and then Bronson hits the streets again. Ireland plays the woman he loves, and who suspects his guilty secret.

What's most shocking about *Death Wish II* is the lack of artistry and skill in the filmmaking. The movie is underwritten and desperately underplotted, so that its witless action scenes alternate with lobotomized dialogue passages. The movie doesn't contain an ounce of life. It slinks onto the screen and squirms for a while, and is over.

Death Wish 3 ★
R, 100 m., 1985

Charles Bronson (Paul Kersey), Ed Lauter (Captain Striker), Gavan O'Herlihy (Fraker), Martin Balsam (Bennett), Kirk Taylor (Giggler), Deborah Raffin (Kathryn). Directed by Michael Winner and produced by Menahem Golan and Yoram Globus. Screenplay by Michael Edmonds.

Death Wish 3 is a marginally better movie than the second part of this series; enough better to earn a one-star rating, instead of none. The action, direction, and special effects are all better than the last time around, which isn't saying much, since *Death Wish II* was so ineptly directed and edited that it was an insult even to audiences that were *looking* for a bad movie.

The plot is as before. Charles Bronson plays Paul Kersey, who was an architect in the original 1974 film, but has now apparently moved into a new career, as a professional vigilante. After knocking off several muggers in Kansas City and a few thieves in Chicago, he is back in New York at the beginning of this film, just in time to find an old friend dying after a vicious beating.

Kersey is arrested for the crime, but allowed back on the streets by the police captain (Ed Lauter), who offers a deal: Kersey can murder all the creeps he wants, if he keeps the cops informed. Kersey does not agree to this deal, but Lauter does not seem to notice. Indeed, by the end of the film, the two of them are stalking the mean streets side-by-side, like killers in the old West.

Bronson moves into a tenement building which seems to be in the middle of a vast burned-out wasteland, but which is still occupied by terrified old people. Among the tenants are an old watch repairman (Martin Balsam), who keeps a couple of machine guns in his closet, and an elderly Jewish couple who live on the first floor and make stuffed cabbage rolls while the creeps jump in through the window and toss their TV set outside. It is a little amazing that they still have a TV set when this movie opens, since the neighborhood has been under siege for weeks.

The neighborhood is ruled by a gang headed by Fraker (Gavan O'Herlihy), who wears a reverse Mohawk: He keeps his hair on the sides, but shaves down the middle, to make room for a gang symbol in warpaint. O'Herlihy looks a little like Richard Wid-

mark, and is quite satisfactory as a snarling, sadistic creep. He is also, of course, white. One of the hypocrisies practiced by the *Death Wish* movies is that they pretend to ignore racial tension in big cities. In their horrible new world, all of the gangs are integrated, so that the movies can't be called racist. I guess it's supposed to be heartwarming to see whites, blacks, and Latinos working side-by-side to rape, pillage, and murder.

Not quite so much equality applies to the victims, however. All of the good speaking roles go to white victims (especially Balsam). Two Latinos get to be minor supporting players (the wife is raped and murdered, the husband gets to sob and pound his fist on the table). The black victims are represented by an old lady who gets her purse snatched.

If it seems strange for me to be making a racial head-count like this, reflect that the filmmakers no doubt assigned races to their characters with equal cynicism. Since there is not a single character in this movie who *has* to belong to any particular race, *Death Wish 3* could have had Bronson protecting black citizens against black gang violence. That would reflect the reality of most big cities, but it would not, of course, have been as commercial as the integrated violence we get instead.

My only other observation has to be about Bronson himself. He looks very tired in this movie. In interviews, he has expressed his unhappiness with it. Despite the fact that he's the central character, he doesn't seem eager to leap in and take charge. And he probably says fewer words in *Death Wish 3* than any other major leading character since the introduction of sound. My guess is that he utters less than one hundred words in the whole movie. My hunch is he would have liked that number to be closer to zero.

Deathtrap ★ ★ ★
R, 116 m., 1982

Michael Caine (Sidney Bruhl), Christopher Reeve (Clifford Anderson), Dyan Cannon (Myra Bruhl), Irene Worth (Psychic). Directed by Sidney Lumet, produced by Burtt Harrisand. Screenplay by Jay Presson Allen.

Deathtrap is a wonderful windup fiction machine with a few modest ambitions: It wants to mislead us at every turn, confound all our expectations, and provide at least one moment when we levitate from our seats and come down screaming. It succeeds, more or less. It's a thriller that depends on all sorts of surprises for its effects, and you may continue reading in the confidence that I'll reveal none of them.

That doesn't leave me much to write about, however. Let's see. I can tell you something about how the movie begins. Michael Caine plays a very successful Broadway playwright whose latest mystery is a total flop. We see him at the outset, standing at the back of the house, a gloomy witness to a disastrous opening night. (It's a Broadway in-joke that the play he's watching is being performed on the stage set of *Deathtrap*.) Caine gets drunk and goes home to his farmhouse in Connecticut and sinks into despair. There is perhaps, however, some small shred of hope. In the mail the next day Caine receives a manuscript from a former student (Christopher Reeve). It is a new thriller, and Caine sees at once that it's a masterpiece. It could run for years and earn millions of dollars. As he talks with his wife (Dyan Cannon) about it, he slowly develops the idea that he could *steal* the play, kill Reeve, and produce the hit himself.

A plausible plan? Perhaps. Caine and Cannon invite Reeve to come for a visit to the country. They grill him, subtly, and discover that absolutely no one else knows he has written the play. The stage is set for murder, betrayal, and at least an hour and a half of surprises. The tables are turned so many times in this movie that you would think they were on wheels.

Anyway, that's all I'll say about the plot. It is fair to observe, however, that *Deathtrap* is a comic study of ancient and honorable human defects, including greed, envy, lust, pride, avarice, sloth, and falsehood. Interest in the movie depends on its surprises, but its delight grows basically out of the human characteristics of its performers. They do a very good job. Thrillers like this don't always bother to pay attention to the human nature of their characters (for example, the Agatha Christie omnibus whodunits, with their cardboard suspects). *Deathtrap*, however, provides a fascinating, quirky character in Sidney Bruhl, played by Caine, and two strong supporting performances in his goofy, screaming wife (Cannon, looking great) and his talented, devious student (Reeve, who has a light, handsome comic touch not a million miles removed from Cary Grant's). The dialogue is witty without being Neil Simonized. The sets are so good they're almost distracting (a windmill appears to operate in close association with the Bruhls' bed). The only distraction is a strange character played by Irene Worth—a next-door neighbor who's a busybody, snooping psychic who sniffs down false leads. We don't know why she's even in the play, until it's much too late.

Deathtrap is not a great film and will not live forever, but if you're an aficionado of whodunits and haven't seen this one, it'll be a treat. It's more fiendishly complicated than, for example, Caine's similar outing in *Sleuth*. It plays absolutely fair, more or less, and yet fools us every time, more or less. And perhaps its greatest gift is the sight of three lighthearted comic actors having a good time chewing on the dialogue, the scenery, and each other.

The Deer Hunter ★ ★ ★ ★
R, 183 m., 1978

Robert De Niro (Michael), John Cazale (Stan), John Savage (Steven), Christopher Walken (Nick), Meryl Streep (Linda), George Dzundza (John), Chuck Aspegren (Axel). Directed by Michael Cimino and produced by Barry Spikings, Michael Deeley, Cimino, and John Peverall. Screenplay by Deric Washburn.

Michael Cimino's *The Deer Hunter* is a three-hour movie in three major movements. It is a progression from a wedding to a funeral. It is the story of a group of friends. It is the record of how the war in Vietnam entered several lives and altered them terribly forever. It is not an anti-war film. It is not a pro-war film. It is one of the most emotionally shattering films ever made.

It begins with men at work, at the furnaces of the steel mills in a town somewhere in Ohio or Pennsylvania. The klaxon sounds, the shift is over, the men go down the road to a saloon for a beer. They sing "I Love You *Bay*-bee" along with the jukebox. It is still morning on the last day of their lives that will belong to them before Vietnam.

The movie takes its time with these opening scenes, with the steel mill and the saloon and especially with the wedding and the party in the American Legion Hall. It's important not simply that we come to know the characters, but that we feel absorbed into their lives, that the wedding rituals and rhythms feel like more than just ethnic details. They do.

The opening moment is lingered over; it's like the wedding celebration in *The Godfather*, but celebrated by hard-working people who have come to eat, dance, and drink a lot and wish luck to the newlyweds and to say good-bye to the three young men who have enlisted in the army. The party goes on long enough for everyone to get drunk who is ever going to, and then the newlyweds drive off and the rest of the friends go up into the mountains to shoot some deer. There is some Hemingwayesque talk about what it means to shoot deer: We are still at a point where shooting something is supposed to mean something.

Then Vietnam occupies the screen, suddenly, with a wall of noise, and the second movement of the film is about the experiences that three of the friends (Robert De Niro, John Savage, and Christopher Walken) have there. At the film's center comes one of the most horrifying sequences ever created in fiction, as the three are taken prisoner and forced to play Russian roulette while their captors gamble on who will, or will not, blow out his brains.

The game of Russian roulette becomes the organizing symbol of the film: Anything you can believe about the game, about its deliberately random violence, about how it touches the sanity of men forced to play it, will apply to the war as a whole. It is a brilliant symbol because, in the context of this story, it makes any ideological statement about the war superfluous.

The De Niro character is the one who somehow finds the strength to keep going and to keep Savage and Walken going. He survives the prison camp and helps the others. Then, finally home from Vietnam, he is surrounded by a silence we can never quite penetrate. He is touched vaguely by desire for the girl that more than one of them left behind, but does not act decisively. He is a "hero," greeted shyly, awkwardly, by the hometown people.

He delays for a long time going to the VA hospital to visit Savage, who has lost his legs. While he is there he learns that Walken is still in Vietnam. He had promised Walken—on a drunken moonlit night under a basketball hoop on a playlot, the night of the wedding—that he would never leave him in Vietnam. They were both thinking, romantically and naively, of the deaths of heroes, but now De Niro goes back in an altogether different context to retrieve the living Walken. The promise was adolescent stuff, but there is no adolescence left when De Niro finds Walken still in Saigon, playing Russian roulette professionally.

At about this point in a review it is customary to praise or criticize those parts of a film that seem deserving: the actors, the photography, the director's handling of the material. It should be said, I suppose, that *The Deer Hunter* is far from flawless, that there are moments when its characters do not behave convincingly, such as implausible details involving Walken's stay and fate in Vietnam, and unnecessary ambiguities in the De Niro character. It can also be said that the film contains greatly moving performances, and that it is the most impressing blending of "box office" and "art" in American movies since *Bonnie and Clyde*, *The Godfather*, and *Nashville*. All of those kinds of observations will become irrelevant as you experience the film: It gathers you up, it takes you along, it doesn't let up.

The Deer Hunter is said to be about many subjects: About male bonding, about mindless patriotism, about the dehumanizing effects of war, about Nixon's "silent majority." It is about any of those things that you choose, if you choose, but more than anything else it is a heartbreakingly effective fictional machine that evokes the agony of the Vietnam time.

If it is not overtly "anti-war," why should it be? What *The Deer Hunter* insists is that we not *forget* the war. It ends on a curious note: The singing of "God Bless America." I won't tell you how it arrives at that particular moment (the unfolding of the final passages should occur to you as events in life) but I do want to observe that the lyrics of "God Bless America" have never before seemed to me to contain such an infinity of possible meanings, some tragic, some unspeakably sad, some few still defiantly hopeful.

Defence of the Realm ★ ★ ★
PG, 94 m., 1987

Gabriel Byrne (Nick Mullen), Greta Scacchi (Nina Beckman), Denholm Elliott (Vernon Bayliss), Ian Bannen (Dennis Markham), Fulton Mackay (Victor Kingsbrook), Bill Paterson (Jack Macleod). Directed by David Drury and produced by Robin Douet and Lynda Myles. Screenplay by Martin Stellman.

Defence of the Realm is a newspaper thriller about a touchy investigation into British security matters. The story ends the way

many newspaper stories end—inconclusively—but the movie ends with a shocking event that suggests the British and their U.S. allies would do anything to defend the American nuclear presence in the U.K.

The movie stars Gabriel Byrne as a young, ambitious newspaper reporter who covers a scandal involving an MP who has the bad judgment to patronize the same call girl used by a KGB agent. Is he a security risk, or does he only seem to be one? Byrne's paper doesn't ask too many questions before putting the story on page one and forcing the politician's resignation.

But there's an older, more experienced hand at the newspaper—a veteran political reporter played by Denholm Elliott, that most dependable and believable of British character actors. He believes the MP may have been framed by people who wanted to silence his embarrassing questions in Parliament. Byrne half-listens to him, and halfway wants to go with the story just because it's so spicy. Upstairs on the executive floor, the proprietor of the paper likes the scandal because it increases circulation.

The film moves quickly and confidently into a net of intrigue, and the director, David Drury, does a good job of keeping us oriented even though the facts in the case remain deliberately confusing. In one especially effective scene, he shows Byrne pretending to be a policeman in order to get quotes from the wife of the disgraced MP; her simple, quiet dignity when she discovers the deception is a rebuke to him.

So is the dogged professionalism of the veteran reporter, who has an anonymous source who insists the MP is innocent. But then the old-timer dies suspiciously, and it's up to Byrne to decide whether there's a deeper story involved, or only a coincidence.

Defence of the Realm reminded me sometimes of *All the President's Men*, but this is a bleaker, more pessimistic movie, which assumes that a conspiracy can be covered up, and that the truth will not necessarily ever be found. The real target of the movie is the American nuclear presence in Britain, and the exciting framework of the newspaper story is an effective way to make a movie against nuclear arms without ever really addressing the point directly.

The acting is strong throughout, but Elliott is especially effective. What is it about this actor, who has been in so many different kinds of movies and seems to make each role special? You may remember him as the Tho-

reau-quoting father in *A Room With a View*, or as Ben Gazzara's lonely friend in *Saint Jack*. Here he is needed to suggest integrity and scruples, and does it almost simply by the way he looks.

Gabriel Byrne, a relative newcomer, is quietly effective as the reporter, and Greta Scacchi, as a woman who gets involved on both sides of the case, shows again that she can project the quality of knowing more than she reveals. *Defence of the Realm* ends on a bleak and cynical note—unless you count the somewhat contrived epilogue—and gets there with intelligence and a sharp, bitter edge.

Defending Your Life ★ ★ ★ ½
PG, 111 m., 1991
(See related Film Clip, p. 698.)

Albert Brooks (Daniel Miller), Meryl Streep (Julia), Rip Torn (Bob Diamond), Lee Grant (Lena Foster), Buck Henry (Dick Stanley). Directed by Albert Brooks and produced by Michael Grillo. Screenplay by Brooks.

A recent survey indicated that most Americans believe in heaven and hell, and of those who believe, the overwhelming majority expect to find themselves in heaven after they die. Since many of them obviously deserve to go to the other place, if only for owning cars with burglar alarms that go off in the middle of the night, a movie like *Defending Your Life* makes perfect sense.

It is Albert Brooks's notion in this film that after death we pass on to a sort of heavenly way station where we are given the opportunity to defend our actions during our most recent lifetime. The process is like an American courtroom, with a prosecutor, defense attorney, and judge, but the charges against us are never quite spelled out. The basic question seems to be, are we sure we did our best, given our opportunities?

In the movie, Brooks plays Dan Miller, a successful exec who takes delivery of a new BMW and plows it into a bus while trying to adjust the CD player. He awakens in a place named Judgment City, which resembles those blandly modern office and hotel complexes around big airports. He's given a room in a clean but spartan place that looks franchised by Motel 6.

At first, Dan is understandably dazed at finding himself dead, but the staff takes good care of him. He's dressed in a flowing gown, whisked around the property on a bus, and told he can eat all he wants in the cafeteria (where the food is delicious but contains no calories). Then he meets his genial, avuncular defense attorney (Rip Torn), and his hard-edged prosecutor (Lee Grant). It's time for the courtroom, in which we see flashbacks to Dan's life as he tries to explain himself.

This is a perfect story notion for Brooks, whose movies always involve his insecurities about himself, his relationships, and his material possessions (who can forget the moment in *Lost in America* when he mercilessly blasted his wife for gambling away their nest egg?). But his notion would finally have no place to go if Brooks didn't add a romantic subplot, in which he falls in love with another sojourner in Judgment City.

She is a sweet, open-faced, serene young woman named Julia and played by Meryl Streep, who is the only actress capable of providing the character's Streepian qualities. They fall into like with one another. Dan visits her hotel and is dismayed to discover that she has much better facilities than he does—Four Seasons instead of Motel 6—and he wonders if maybe your hotel assignment is a clue about how well you lived your past life. But nobody in Judgment City will give him a straight answer to a question like that.

The movie is funny in a warm, fuzzy way, and it has a splendidly satisfactory ending, which is unusual for an Albert Brooks film (his inspiration in his earlier films is bright but seems to wear thin toward the third act). The best thing about the movie, I think, is the notion of Judgment City itself. Doesn't it make sense that heaven, for each society, would be a place much like the earth that it knows? We're still stuck with images of angels playing harps, which worked fine for Renaissance painters. But isn't our modern world ready for images in which the angels look like Rotarians and CEOs?

Stanley Kubrick's *2001* ended with the astronaut leaving the solar system and finding himself, quite unexpectedly, in a spotless hotel room. The usual explanation for that scene is that a superior race from elsewhere in the universe had constructed this room for him as a place where he would feel at home, while they studied him—much as a zoo throws in some trees for the monkeys. The best joke in *Defending Your Life* is that heaven is run along the lines that would be recommended by a good MBA program.

The Delta Force ★ ★ ★
R, 129 m., 1985

Chuck Norris (Major McCoy), Lee Marvin (Colonel Alexander), Robert Forster (Abdul), Martin Balsam (Ben Kaplan), Joey Bishop (Harry Goldman), Lainie Kazan (Sylvia Goldman), George Kennedy (Father O'Malley), Hanna Schygulla (Ingrid), Bo Svenson (Captain). Directed by Menahem Golan and produced by Golan and Yoram Globus. Screenplay by James Bruner and Golan.

Some of the opening moments of *The Delta Force* had me ready to laugh. Here was a movie about an airplane hijacking, and who was on the passenger list? Why, George Kennedy, of course—fresh from four *Airport* movies and *Earthquake*—and Shelley Winters, going on her first vacation since the *Poseidon* sank. I thought this was going to be another hilarious disaster movie, but I was wrong. *The Delta Force* settles down into a well-made action film that tantalizes us with its parallels to real life.

The movie was inspired by the June 1985 hijacking of the TWA airplane and the hostage crisis after the passengers were held captive in Beirut. (In the movie, the airline is renamed ATW—real subtle.) Many of the moments in the film are drawn directly from life, as when an American serviceman is beaten to death by terrorists, and his body is dumped on the runway, or when a terrorist holds a gun to the head of the pilot during a press conference.

The docudrama approach gives an eerie conviction to the movie, although later, after Chuck Norris and Lee Marvin arrive on the scene, there's not much we would mistake for reality. The movie caters directly to our national revenge fantasies; in *The Delta Force*, the hijacking ends the way we might have wanted it to.

The story establishes the plane and its passengers, and then intercuts the hijacking with the movements of the Delta Force, a crack U.S. commando unit that specializes in antiterrorist missions. Delta is led by grizzled old Lee Marvin, and its best fighter is a hot dog played by Chuck Norris, who once again this time is depicted as a man who yearns only for retirement, but cannot resist the call to action, and arrives at the last moment in his trusty pickup truck. (If I were Chuck Norris's agent, I'd insist that his next movie include a new way of introducing him into the plot.)

There are a couple of hazards here that the movie has to face. The action inside the airplane has a tendency to degenerate into a retread of the old *Airport* movies, but director Menahem Golan wisely has his cast keep their acting fairly low-key. And the action involving Norris has a tendency to resemble his activities in *Missing in Action* and *Invasion USA*. Golan does nothing to fight this tendency—indeed, he relishes it, in scenes like the one where Norris drives his rocket-firing motorcycle right through the window of a terrorist hideout, and socks the bad guy on the jaw. This is the second movie in a row where Norris has possessed X-ray vision; in *Invasion USA* he drove his pickup into a department store to stop a terrorist attack. How does he know what's on the other side of the barriers he crashes through?

It's a funny thing about action movies. When they don't work, we have a lot of fun picking holes in them, like the fallacy of the hero's X-ray vision. When they do work, though, we forgive them their inconsistencies. *The Delta Force* works. It is taut and exciting and well-tuned to the personalities of Marvin and Norris, who work together here like a couple of laconic veterans of lots of tough jobs.

The movie also has the one other attribute that any good thriller needs: A first-rate performance by the actor playing the villain. As Abdul, the chief terrorist, an American actor named Robert Forster gives a frightening, good performance, intense and uncompromising. He makes the threat real, and keeps *The Delta Force* from becoming just an action comic book.

Desperate Hours ★ ★
R, 106 m., 1990

Mickey Rourke (Michael Bosworth), Anthony Hopkins (Tim Cornell), Mimi Rogers (Nora Cornell), Lindsay Crouse (Chandler), Kelly Lynch (Nancy Breyers), Elias Koteas (Wally Bosworth), Mike Nussbaum (Mr. Nelson). Directed by Michael Cimino and produced by Dino De Laurentiis and Cimino. Screenplay by Lawrence Konner, Mark Rosenthal, and Joseph Hayes.

Michael Cimino's *Desperate Hours* is an attempt to take a 1950s crime classic and remake it by turning up the heat, but Cimino has set the heat too high, and the result is an overwrought melodrama with dialogue even a *True Detective* editor would question. Cimino is not helped by the presence in his cast of Mickey Rourke and Anthony Hopkins, two splendid actors who should never be encouraged to go over the top, and by Lindsay Crouse's FBI agent, whose lines are so odd she seems to be speaking a language all her own.

The movie has been inspired by a 1955 film starring Humphrey Bogart and Fredric March, and by an earlier Broadway play, both by Joseph Hayes, and "inspired by real events," although a 1951 John Garfield film named *He Ran All the Way* is about the same sort of situation—a criminal hiding from the law by terrorizing an innocent family. Rourke plays Bosworth, a mad-dog killer with the ability to get his lawyer (Kelly Lynch) to smuggle a gun into court for him, after which he escapes, meets a couple of buddies, and selects a suburban house at random.

The house, which has just been sold, is occupied by a mother (Mimi Rogers), her teen-age daughter, and young son. Rogers has ended her marriage with Hopkins, a wealthy philanderer who now wants to come back home. "What is it you want from me?" he asks, in a pregnant early scene, and is told she wants, just once, someone she can trust. No points for guessing that later in this movie she will have to learn to trust him.

Rourke's getaway plan, which he hopes will eventually take him to Mexico, is confused as the movie starts and gets more muddled as he begins improvising on it. It is a version of the Idiot Plot (in which if everyone were not an idiot, the movie would soon be over). Although he reasonably needs to hide out for a while, there is little reason for him to enter an occupied house, take hostages, and involve himself in countless problems. No reason except that otherwise we wouldn't have a movie.

Rourke's two partners are his brother (Elias Koteas) and his boyhood friend (David Morse). They drive his getaway car and accompany him on the home invasion, but one is a loose cannon and the other has no nerve for the job. Neither one is necessary to the plot (things could have been simplified mightily by simply having Rourke steal a car—or pedal a bicycle to the suburbs, for all I care). Once they enter the house, the movie descends into a series of screamings and struggles, threats and promises, weeping and ultimatums, and would-be deals, most of them so overacted that the actors must have had difficulty keeping their faces straight.

And then there is Crouse, the FBI agent in charge. She picks a bitter confrontation with the local law, and doesn't help things much

by insulting and provoking every police officer in her way. After it's discovered that Rourke is in the house with the hostages, she insists on masterminding a complex "containment" scheme that I believe she alone, of all the people in the film or in the audience, is capable of understanding.

Marksmen climb trees, circle in helicopters, and set up roadblocks (although a teenage boyfriend roars right past in his sport-utility vehicle). But Rourke is not supposed to know he's surrounded. People come and go from the house (the daughter leaves with her boyfriend, to no purpose later explained in the film), but Rourke maintains an adequate quota of hostages, until finally we get the usual clichés involving the cops shouting through bullhorns, and so on.

Desperate Hours shows Cimino with more style than substance. Those shots of cars racing through the mountains are sure impressive, with the painted skies and the clouds of dust, and he must have liked the sweaty moments inside the house, too, but the movie is all style and flash. I never cared enough about the characters to become involved in the action, especially since this plot makes it clear fairly early on that it is going to follow the same parabola of all similar stories. It's a variation on an old movie theme, but not much of a variation, and on a very tired theme.

Desperately Seeking Susan ★ ★ ★
PG-13, 103 m., 1985

Rosanna Arquette (Roberta), Madonna (Susan), Aidan Quinn (Dez), Mark Blum (Gary), Robert Joy (Jim), Laurie Metcalf (Leslie). Directed by Susan Seidelman and produced by Sarah Pillsbury and Midge Sanford. Screenplay by Leora Barish.

Desperately Seeking Susan is a movie that begins with those three words, in a classified ad. A time and place are suggested where Susan can rendezvous with the person who is desperately seeking her. A bored housewife (Rosanna Arquette) sees the ad and becomes consumed with curiosity. Who is Susan and who is seeking her, and why? So Arquette turns up at the rendezvous, sees Susan (Madonna), and inadvertently becomes so involved in her world that for a while she even *becomes* Susan.

This sounds complicated, but, believe me, it's nothing compared to the complexities of this movie. *Desperately Seeking Susan* is a screwball comedy based on several cases of

mistaken identity. Susan, for example, is a punk drifter who is in a hotel room with a mobster the first time we see her. Shortly after, the mobster is killed and the mob hit man comes back looking for Susan, who may have been a witness. But meanwhile, Susan has sold the jacket that is her trademark, and the housewife has bought it, and then the housewife has banged her head and become a temporary amnesia victim, and there are people who see her jacket and think she's Susan.

But enough of the plot. I wouldn't even dream of trying to explain how Arquette ends up being sawed in half by a nightclub magician. The plot isn't the point, anyway; once you realize the movie is going to be a series of double-reverses, you relax and let them happen. The plot is so unpredictable that, in a way, it's predictable; that makes it the weakest part of the movie.

What I liked in *Desperately Seeking Susan* was the cheerful way it hopped around New York, introducing us to unforgettable characters, played by good actors. For example, Aidan Quinn plays a guy who thinks Arquette is Susan, his best friend's girl. He lets her spend the night, and inadvertently feeds her amnesia by suggesting that she *is* Susan. Laurie Metcalf plays Arquette's yuppie sister-in-law. Robert Joy plays Susan's desperately seeking lover. Peter Maloney is the broken-down magician. New York underground characters such as Richard Hell, Anne Carlisle, and Rockets Red Glare also surface briefly. The director is Susan Seidelman, whose previous film, *Smithereens*, was a similar excursion through the uncharted depths of New York.

Desperately Seeking Susan does not move with the self-confidence that its complicated plot requires. But it has its moments, and many of them involve the different kinds of special appeal that Arquette and Madonna are able to generate. They are very particular individuals, and in a dizzying plot they somehow succeed in creating specific, interesting characters.

Diamonds Are Forever ★ ★ ★
PG, 119 m., 1971

Sean Connery (James Bond), Jill St. John (Tiffany Case), Charles Gray (Blofeld), Lana Wood (Plenty O'Toole), Jimmy Dean (Willard Whyte), Bruce Cabot (Saxby), Bernard Lee (M), Desmond Llewelyn (Q). Directed by Guy Hamilton and produced by Albert R. Broccoli and Harry Saltzman.

The cultists like the early James Bond movies best, but I dunno. They may have been more tightly directed films, but they didn't understand the Bond mythos as fully as *Goldfinger* and *Diamonds Are Forever*. We see different movies for different reasons, and *Diamonds Are Forever* is great at doing the things we see a James Bond movie for.

Not the least of these is the presence of Sean Connery, who was born to the role: dry, unflappable (even while trapped in a coffin at a crematorium), with a mouth that does as many kinds of sly grins as there are lascivious possibilities in the universe. There's something about his detachment from danger that props up the whole Bond apparatus, insulating it from the total ridiculousness only an inch away.

In *Diamonds Are Forever*, for example, Bond finds himself driving a moon buggy (antennae wildly revolving and robot arms flapping) while being chased across a desert—never mind why. The buggy looks comical, but Connery does not; he is completely at home, as we know by now, with every form of transportation. Later, after outsmarting five Las Vegas squad cars in a lovely chase scene, he nonchalantly flips his Mustang up on two wheels to elude the sixth. But not a sign of a smile. There is an exhilaration in the way he does it, even more than in the stunt itself.

The plot of *Diamonds Are Forever* is as complicated as possible. That's necessary in order to have somebody left after nine dozen bad guys have been killed. It has been claimed that the plot is too complicated to describe, but I think I could if I wanted to. I can't imagine why anyone would want to, though. The point in a Bond adventure is the moment, the surface, what's happening now. The less time wasted on plot, the better.

Diary of a Mad Housewife ★ ★ ★
R, 95 m., 1970

Carrie Snodgress (Tina Balser), Richard Benjamin (Jonathan Balser), Frank Langella (George). Directed and produced by Frank Perry. Screenplay by Eleanor Perry.

Frank Perry's *Diary of a Mad Housewife* is about a long-suffering young woman who has somehow gotten herself married to the most supercilious dope in Manhattan. He's egotistical, cruel, insecure, immature, and bitchy. He sides with "his" children against his wife. He considers her a household drudge, good for housework during the day, and, maybe, a "little roll in de hay" at night. He humiliates her in public, and humiliates himself, too, by his shameless social-climbing. Does she hate him? Not exactly.

She's a masochistic type who sees her husband as, somehow, her fate in life. She enjoys martyrdom, I guess; I can't imagine any other reason why she'd put up with this monster she's married to. And that's at the base of our initial irritation with the film; she stays with this guy we can't stand, and so we have trouble admiring her. We even begin to doubt her sanity, until she falls into a love affair with a writer. And then *he* turns out to be such an egotistical, selfish, cruel type that we just about give up on her. She has what's known, I believe, as self-destructive tendencies. Not that she'd ever try suicide; that'd be too easy, and end the delight of suffering. What makes the movie work, however, is that it's played entirely from the housewife's point of view, and that the housewife is played brilliantly by Carrie Snodgress. We're irritated by the things the character puts up with, but Miss Snodgress is beautifully good at putting up with them.

Still, when you've finished watching this movie you start getting mad at Richard Benjamin. He overplays his character so much that he nearly destroys the role; nobody, but nobody, is that supercilious. Near the beginning of the movie there's a scene when the whole family is in an elevator, and Benjamin gives instructions to his wife about packing a suitcase. He describes everything in highly specific brand names, and with such precision that the dialogue passes beyond reality and becomes satire. You can see it as a caption under a *New Yorker* cartoon.

But then, then . . . you start thinking about the title and the point of view of the movie, and you realize this is indeed a diary; that we're getting the housewife's version of the story. So of course she seems noble and long-suffering, and of course he's a witless bastard—because that's the way she sees it. And of course his dialogue is extreme and hers isn't, because in her version of the story, she's sane, and he's not.

Dice Rules   no stars
NC-17, 87 m., 1991

A concert film featuring Andrew Dice Clay. Also featuring performances by "Noodles" Levenstein, Michael "Wheels" Parise, and "Hot Tub" Johnny West. Directed by Jay Dubin and produced by Fred Silverstein. Prologue written by Lenny Shulman, based on a story by Andrew Dice Clay. Concert material written by Clay.

Dice Rules is one of the most appalling movies I have ever seen. It could not be more damaging to the career of Andrew Dice Clay if it had been made as a documentary by someone who hated him. The fact that Clay apparently thinks this movie is worth seeing is revealing and sad, indicating that he not only lacks a sense of humor, but also ordinary human decency.

Andrew Dice Clay comes billed as a comedian, but does not get one laugh from me in the eighty-seven minutes of this film. I do not find it amusing to watch someone mock human affliction, and I don't find it funny, either, for him to use his fear of women as a subject for humor. Of course, any subject can theoretically be *made* funny, but just to stand and point is not the same thing as developing a humorous point of view.

An example: We have all known someone who has undergone a tracheotomy, having their voice box removed because of cancer. Sometimes these people are still able to speak through controlling the air stream in their throats, or by using small battery-powered devices that magnify their whispers. Andrew Dice Clay finds their speech funny, and mocks it in this film. I imagine that tracheotomy patients themselves use morbid humor as one way of dealing with their condition, but Clay is not using humor at all—he is simply pointing and making fun, like a playground bully.

He has many other targets: The handicapped. The ill. Minorities. Women. Homosexuals. Anyone, in fact, who is not exactly like Andrew Dice Clay is fair game for his cruel attacks. His material about women constitutes verbal rape, as far as I'm concerned. Using obscenity as punctuation, he describes women as essentially things to masturbate with.

I think his approach to women is based on fear of them. It is too painful and too consistent to be explained otherwise. Everything that he says about women is based on the kind of ignorant dirty jokes told by insecure teen-age boys among themselves, as they try to conceal their misinformation and bolster their courage by objectifying women into creatures who can be dismissed with the usual crude obscenities. Even then, if he were mocking or kidding this attitude, it could, perhaps, be funny. But not a single word in Clay's film indicates that he has been able to deal with the fact that women are living, thinking beings. He sees only their sexual organs, fears them, and must punish or conquer them to reassure himself.

Dice Rules was filmed in concert (what a word) at Madison Square Garden, which the comedian was able to fill two nights in a row. It is eerie, watching the shots of the audience. You never see anyone just plain laughing, as if they'd heard something that was funny. You see, instead, behavior more appropriate at a fascist rally, as his fans stick their fists in the air and chant his name as if he were making some kind of statement for them. Perhaps he is. Perhaps he is giving voice to their rage, fear, prejudice, and hatred. They seem to cheer him because he is getting away with expressing the sick thoughts they don't dare to say.

Comedians have long been a lightning rod for society, drawing down the dangers and grounding them. Some of the most brilliant comics of recent years—Lenny Bruce, Richard Pryor, George Carlin—have dealt with taboo words and concepts. But they bring insight and an attitude to them. They help us see how we regard them. They provide a form of therapy, of comic relief. Not Clay. Strutting and sneering, lacking the graceful timing of the great stand-up talents, reciting his words woodenly, he creates a portrait of the comedian as sociopath.

Crowds can be frightening. They have a way of impressing the low, base taste upon their members. Watching the way thousands of people in his audience could not think for themselves, could not find the courage to allow their ordinary feelings of decency and taste to prevail, I understood better how demagogues are possible.

Dick Tracy ★ ★ ★ ★
PG, 105 m., 1990

Warren Beatty (Dick Tracy), Al Pacino (Big Boy Caprice), Madonna (Breathless Mahoney), Glenne Headly (Tess Trueheart), Charlie Korsmo (Kid), Seymour Cassel (Sam Catchem), James Keane (Pat Patton), Charles Durning (Chief Brandon), Mandy Patinkin (88 Keys), Paul Sorvino (Lips Manlis), Dustin Hoffman (Mumbles), Dick Van Dyke (D.A. Fletcher). Directed and produced by Warren Beatty. Screenplay by Jim Cash and Jack Epps, Jr.

There was always something inbred about the *Dick Tracy* comic strip, some suggestion that all of its characters had been mutated by the same cosmic rays, and then locked together in a bizarre loony bin of crime. *Tracy* was the first comic strip I encountered after I outgrew funny animals, and what struck me was that the physical appearance of the characters always mirrored their souls, or occupations. They looked like what they were, and what you saw was what you got, from the square-jawed Tracy barking into his wrist radio, to Pruneface, Flattop, and the others.

Warren Beatty's production of *Dick Tracy* approaches the material with the same fetishistic glee I felt when I was reading the strip. The Tracy stories didn't depend really on plot—they were too spun-out for that—and of course they didn't depend on suspense—Tracy always won. What they were about was the interaction of these grotesque people, doomed by nature to wear their souls on their faces. We see this process at work in one of the film's first scenes, where a poker game is in progress, and everyone around the table looks like a sideshow attraction, from Little Face, whose features are at the middle of a sea of dissipation, to The Brow, always deep in shallow thought.

Another of the movie's opening shots establishes, with glorious excess, the Tracy universe. The camera begins on a window, and pulls back, and moves up until we see the skyline of the city, and then it seems to fly through the air, turning as it moves so that we sweep above an endless urban vista. Skyscrapers and bridges and tenements and elevated railways crowd each other all the way to the distant horizon, until we realize this is the grandest and most squalid city that ever was. It's more than a place. It's the distillation of the idea of City—of the vast, brooding, mysterious metropolis spreading in all directions forever, concealing millions of lives and secrets.

And then the camera moves in on one of those buildings, and as we see people again we realize that everything we have seen before—every skyscraper, every bridge—was created in a movie studio. *Dick Tracy* is a masterpiece of studio artificiality, of matte drawings and miniatures and optical effects. It creates a world that never could be. There is a scene where a giant locomotive roars down upon the fleeing figure of a small boy, and he jumps in front of it and we actually flinch. The whole fearsome train is actually a model and the running figure has been com-

bined with it in an optical process, but don't tell that to anyone watching the movie because they won't believe you.

Into this theater of the night comes striding the peculiar figure of a man in a yellow hat and a yellow raincoat—Dick Tracy. When Chester Gould first conceived him all those years ago, did it seem unlikely that a police detective would wear yellow? Maybe not, since Tracy didn't live in a city but in a comic strip, and the primary colors had to jump off the page. Beatty's decision to shoot *Dick Tracy* only in the seven basic colors of comic strips is a good one, because this is a movie about creatures of the imagination, about people who live in rooms where every table lamp looks like a Table Lamp and every picture on the wall represents only a Picture on the Wall. It was necessary for Tracy to wear the essence of hats and coat, and so of course they were yellow; anything less would have been too ordinary.

Tracy in the comics was always an enigma, a figure without emotion or complexity. Warren Beatty plays his Tracy as a slightly more human figure, a cop who does have a personality, however slight. To the degree that the human side of Tracy peeks through, I believe, the character is diminished; the critics who have described Tracy as too shallow have missed the entire point, which is that we are not talking about real people here, but about archetypes. Tracy should be as square as his jaw.

Surrounding him are the characters who provide the real meat of the movie, and the scene-stealer is Big Boy Caprice, played by Al Pacino with such grotesque energy that we seem to have stumbled on a criminal from Dickens. Consider the scene where Big Boy rehearses the chorus line in his nightclub. He dashes and darts behind the girls, pushing them, slapping them, acting more like a dog trainer than a choreographer. There is an edge of cruelty to his behavior, and later we see that some of his cruelty is directed toward himself. Unlike most of the villains of modern movies, he does not flaunt his evil, but is ashamed of it, and this Victorian trait makes him more interesting.

In the shadows around Big Boy are a gallery of other human grotesqueries—characters who have been named for their physical abnormalities, like Lips Manlis and Shoulders, or for other handicaps, like Mumbles (Dustin Hoffman), who talks so fast he cannot be heard. Because these characters are glimpsed rather quickly, their makeup can be more bizarre; the characters who are onscreen all the time look more normal, and among them are the two women in Tracy's life, the faithful Tess Trueheart (Glenne Headley) and the seductive Breathless Mahoney (Madonna).

Pop sociologists have made a specialty out of Madonnaology, claiming she changes images so quickly that she is always ahead of her audience, always on the cutting edge. Her very appearance in each new tour is a clue to her latest message about pop imagery, we're told. Her mistake in *Dick Tracy*, I think, is that she frankly reaches back to Marilyn Monroe and tries to make Breathless into a Monroe clone, right down to the lighting and costuming in some numbers, which seems inspired by Monroe in *Some Like It Hot*. It doesn't work. She's not Monroe and she's not Madonna, either. Breathless should have come out of a new place in her mind.

That's not a crucial flaw in the movie because Tracy himself is so bloodless that we barely believe he can be seduced. The deepest emotional attachment in the detective's life, indeed, is not even Tess Trueheart, but Kid (Charlie Korsmo), an orphan Tracy takes under his wing, and the movie's emotional high point is probably when Kid decides to call himself Dick Tracy, Jr.

Last summer's *Batman*, a movie I found disappointing, was at least a triumph of special effects—of set design and art direction. *Dick Tracy*, which is a sweeter, more optimistic movie, outdoes even *Batman* in the visual departments. This is a movie in which every frame contains some kind of artificial effect. An entire world has been built here, away from the daylight and the realism of ordinary city streets. And *Dick Tracy* also reflects the innocence of the comic strip that inspired it. Unlike the movie version of *Batman*, which hyped up the level of its violence to a degree that could have been truly disturbing to younger viewers, the PG-rated *Dick Tracy* contains no obscenity, no blood, and no "realistic" violence. It is one of the most original and visionary fantasies I've seen on a screen.

Die Hard ★ ★
R, 132 m., 1988

Bruce Willis (John McClane), Alan Rickman (Hans Gruber), Bonnie Bedelia (Holly McClane), Reginald Veljohnson (Sgt. Al Powell), Paul Gleason (Deputy Chief). Directed by John McTiernan and produced by Lawrence Gordon and Joel Silver. Screenplay by Jeb Stuart and Steven E. de Souza.

The idea has a certain allure to it: A cop is trapped inside a high-rise with a team of desperate terrorists. He is all that stands between them and their hostages. Give the terrorist leader brains and a personality, make one of the hostages the estranged wife of the cop, and you've got a movie.

The name of the movie is *Die Hard*, and it stars Bruce Willis in another one of those Hollywood action roles where the hero's shirt is ripped off in the first reel so you can see how much time he's been spending at the gym. He's a New York cop who has flown out to Los Angeles for Christmas, and we quickly learn that his marriage was put on hold after his wife (Bonnie Bedelia) left for the Coast to accept a great job offer. She is now Assistant to the President of the multinational Nakatomi Corp., and shortly before Willis makes his entrance at the office party, the terrorists strike.

They, too, are a multinational group, led by a German named Hans Gruber (Alan Rickman), who is well-dressed and has a neatly trimmed beard and talks like an intellectual and thinks he is superior to the riffraff he has to associate with. He has a plan that has been devised with clockwork precision, involving the theft of millions of dollars in negotiable bonds, and it is only after Willis starts causing trouble that he allows the situation to escalate beyond his original plans.

The terrorists are skilled and well-armed, and there are a lot of them. Willis's strategy involves keeping them off guard with lightning attacks from his hiding place, on an upper floor of the building that is still under construction. This plan involves the deployment of a great many stunts and special effects, as when Willis swings through a plate-glass window on the end of a fire hose, or when he drops plastic explosives down the elevator shaft of the building.

On a technical level, there's a lot to be said for *Die Hard*. It's when we get to some of the unnecessary adornments of the script that the movie shoots itself in the foot. Willis remains in constant radio contact with a police officer on the ground (Reginald Veljohnson), who tries to keep his morale up. But then the filmmakers introduce a gratuitous and unnecessary additional character, the deputy police chief (Paul Gleason), who doubts that the guy on the other end of the radio is really a New York cop at all.

As nearly as I can tell, the deputy chief is in the movie for only one purpose: to be consistently wrong at every step of the way, and to provide a phony counterpoint to Willis's progress. The character is so willfully useless, so dumb, so much a product of the Idiot Plot Syndrome, that all by himself he successfully undermines the last half of the movie. Thrillers like this need to be well-oiled machines with not a single wasted moment. Inappropriate and wrongheaded interruptions reveal the fragile nature of the plot and prevent it from working.

Without the deputy chief and all that he represents, *Die Hard* would have been a more than passable thriller. With him, it's a mess, and that's a shame, because the film does contain superior special effects, impressive stunt work and good performances, especially by Alan Rickman as the terrorist. Here's a suggestion for thriller-makers: You can't go wrong if all of the characters in your movie are at least as intelligent as most of the characters in your audience.

Die Hard 2: Die Harder ★ ★ ★ ½
R, 124 m., 1990

Bruce Willis (John McClane), Bonnie Bedelia (Holly McClane), William Atherton (Thornberg), Reginald Veljohnson (Al Powell), Franco Nero (Esperanza), William Sadler (Stuart), John Amos (Grant), Dennis Franz (Carmine Lorenzo). Directed by Renny Harlin and produced by Lawrence Gordon, Joel Silver, and Charles Gordon. Screenplay by Steven E. de Souza and Doug Richardson.

Die Hard 2, subtitled *Die Harder*, enters Bruce Willis in a decathlon of violence, and he places first in every event, including wrestling for guns, jumping onto conveyor belts, being ejected from cockpits, leaping onto the wings of moving airplanes, and fighting with the authorities. This is one of those thrillers like the *Indiana Jones* series that I categorize as Bruised Forearm Movies, because when the movie is over your forearm is black-and-blue from where your date has grabbed it during the moments of suspense.

Why is Bruce Willis so effective in a movie like this? Maybe because he combines a relatively athletic physique with the appearance and manner of everyman. The title of the movie describes the basic plot device: Here is a man who will not give up, who will not admit defeat, who doggedly carries on in the face of adversity. The dangers and tests he faces would daunt a James Bond, but for this open-faced cop with the receding hairline, there is no choice. After all: "My wife is on that plane!"

Again this time he plays a cop on vacation. He's in Washington's Dulles airport, waiting for his wife's flight to land, on a crowded evening during the Christmas season. And scheduled into the same airport at the same time is a military jet bringing a South American drug tyrant to justice. A skilled band of terrorists, led by a former CIA operative, plans to seize control of airport operations by electronically bypassing the control tower. They'll shut off the airport lights, leave dozens of planes circling overhead, and then cause one flight to crash as a warning. What they want is a fully fueled standby plane, ready to spirit the dictator to freedom.

Willis, who has a cop's practiced eye, spots one of the conspirators, follows him into a luggage handling area, and discovers that a plot is afoot. But he can't convince the chief of airport security (Dennis Franz), who resents an outside cop on his turf. After a killing and various other hints (including a plane crash), the security chief finally admits he may have a problem on his hands, but even then Willis's work is not over, and by the end of the movie he is single-handedly taking on whole planeloads of mercenaries in a fight to the finish.

Because *Die Hard 2* is so skillfully constructed and well-directed, it develops a momentum that carries it past several credibility gaps that might have capsized a lesser film. For example, how about the scene where the tower informs the circling airplanes that they'll be out of radio contact for a couple of hours and should just keep circling? Why can't those planes simply establish radio contact with other ground transmitters and be diverted to alternate airports? Because then Willis's wife (Bonnie Bedelia) wouldn't be up there in the sky and in mortal danger, that's why.

A more serious problem involves the whole rescue operation itself. When Noriega was taken captive and returned to the United States to stand trial, there was little serious effort to save him: At the end, he was a refugee in his own country, reduced to seeking asylum in the residence of a Vatican diplomat. Would anyone have the means, the money, and the will to mount such a vast and complicated terrorist operation simply to save one drug-connected dictator? Even if he does bear an uncanny resemblance to Fidel Castro? I doubt it.

But, on the other hand, I don't care. *Die Hard 2* is as unlikely as the Bond pictures and as much fun. It tells a story we can identify with, it has a lot of interesting supporting characters, it handles the action sequences with calm precision, and it has a couple of scenes that are worth writing home about.

One of those is a plane crash. Not everybody's favorite image, I'll grant you (and this is a feature that will be severely edited before it becomes an in-flight movie). Watching the plane burst into flames on a runway, I knew intellectually that I was watching special effects, probably a fairly large and detailed model photographed in slow motion. But no matter. The crash was scarily convincing.

Another shot, more fun, is harder to describe without giving away a plot point. But it involves placing the camera's eye hundreds of feet straight up in the air and then catapulting Willis up until his nose almost touches the lens before he begins to fall to earth again. Not only is this shot sensationally effective in terms of the story, but as a visual it is exhilarating: I love it when a director finds a new way to show me something.

The director of *Die Hard 2* is a Finn named Renny Harlin, whose other credits include *Nightmare on Elm Street 4* and the Andrew Dice Clay picture, *Ford Fairlane*. Like the Dutch-born Paul Verhoeven (*Robocop, Total Recall*), he has taken Hollywood commercial moviemaking, shaken it, and given it a new energy. Given the enormous success of the original *Die Hard* (a movie I didn't enjoy nearly as much as this one), producer Lawrence Gordon and his partners must have crossed their fingers before risking this sequel with a relatively untried director. But they did the right thing: This is a terrific entertainment.

Dim Sum ★ ★ ★
PG, 88 m., 1985

Laureen Chew (Geraldine Tam), Kim Chew (Mrs. Tam), Victor Wong (Uncle Tam), Ida F.O. Chung (Auntie Mary), Cora Miao (Julia), John Nishio (Richard). Directed by Wayne Wang and produced by Tom Sternberg, Wang, and Danny Yung. Screenplay by Terrel Seltzer.

Director Wayne Wang says his favorite image in *Dim Sum* is the sight of the shoes left outside the living-room door in the Tam household in San Francisco's Chinatown. They are Western shoes, taken off as the characters enter a home that is still run according to Chinese values by old Mrs. Tam, a sweet widow with a strong but quietly concealed will. After the success of *Chan Is Missing*, his first slice-of-life about Chinese-Americans, Wang was looking for another story, and when he saw some shoes left outside a Chinese home, he knew he had his viewpoint, and only had to create his characters.

He has created some unforgettable ones, including Mrs. Tam (Kim Chew), a sixtyish woman whose husband is dead and whose children have left home, all except for the youngest daughter; Geraldine Tam (Laureen Chew), the daughter, who says she wants to get married but feels she should stay with her mother, and Uncle Tam (Victor Wong), a jolly, worldly bartender who would marry Mrs. Tam if Geraldine would only get out of the way.

These three characters dance a subtle little emotional ballet during the film, as we gradually become aware of their true motives. Mrs. Tam is given to sadly shaking her head and bemoaning the fact that her daughter is thirty and still single, but there are clues that she enjoys the fact that Geraldine has stayed at home with her. That way, she will not have to deal with Uncle Tam, who, for that matter, may only be paying lip service to his desire to marry her. Meanwhile, Geraldine has a boyfriend in Los Angeles who has been waiting patiently to marry her, and perhaps Geraldine uses her mother as an excuse to avoid the idea of marriage.

What is remarkable is the way Wang deals with this complex set of emotions, in a movie that is essentially a comedy. Some of the scenes in *Dim Sum* are as quietly funny as anything I've seen, especially Mrs. Tam's birthday party, a long conversation she has over the back fence with a neighbor, and the way Uncle Tam effortlessly mixes his Chinese wisdom with the lessons he has learned as a bartender.

The movie is not heavily plotted, and that's good; a heavy hand would spoil this fragile material. Wang's camera enters quietly and observes as his characters lead their lives, trying to find a compromise between too much loneliness and too much risk. At the end, everyone is more or less happy, and more or less sad, and in this movie that is satisfactory.

Note: Although this is no doubt not what Wang had in mind, I couldn't help thinking, as I watched Dim Sum, *that the movie's characters and situations could be effortlessly spun off into a wonderful TV sitcom.*

Diner ★ ★ ★ ½
R, 110 m., 1982

Steve Guttenberg (Eddie), Daniel Stern (Shrevie), Mickey Rourke (Boogie), Kevin Bacon (Fenwick), Timothy Daly (Billy), Ellen Barkin (Beth). Directed by Barry Levinson and produced by Jerry Weintraub. Screenplay by Levinson.

Women are not strange, not threatening, not mysterious, unless you happen to be a man. Young men in particular seem to regard women with a combination of admiration, desire, and dread that is quite out of their control. This was especially true in the late 1950s, a decade during which the Playmate of the Month was more alien than E.T. is today. Women were such a puzzling phenomenon to 1950s young men that, after a date, the best way for males to restore their equilibrium was to regroup with the guys for the therapeutic consumption of cheeseburgers, greasy fries, black coffee, chocolate malteds, Lucky Strikes, and loud arguments about football teams and pop singers. *Diner* is a story about several such young men, who live in Baltimore. They share one awkward problem: They are growing up, painfully and awkwardly, at an age when they are supposed to have already grown up. Adolescence lasts longer for some people than society quite imagines. These guys are best friends for the time being, although in the fall they will go separate ways, to schools and jobs and even marriage, and it's possible they will never be this close again. They cling to one another for security, because out there in the real world, responsibility lurks, and responsibility is spelled *woman*. They have plans, but their plans are not as real as their dreams.

Diner is structured a lot like *American Graffiti* and Fellini's *I Vitelloni*. It's episodic, as the young men venture out for romantic and sexual adventures, practical jokes, drunken Friday evenings, and long mornings of hangovers and doubt. Some of the movie's situations seem quite implausible, but they all fit within the overall theme of fear of women. One bizarre sequence, for example, involves a young man who insists that his fiancée pass a tough quiz about pro football before he'll agree to marry her. He's serious: If she flunks, the wedding is off. This situation doesn't seem possible to me, but it's right symbolically, since what the man is really looking for in a wife is one of the guys—a woman who will agree to become an imitation man.

Another character, already married, is much more realistic. He has absolutely no communication with his wife and no way to develop any, since he sees her only as a "wife" and not as a friend, a companion, or even a fellow human being. Her great failure is an inability to regard his life with the proper reverence; when she gets his record collection out of alphabetical order, it's grounds for a fight. He's flabbergasted that she hasn't memorized the flip sides of all the Top 40 hits of 1958, but he never even suspects that he doesn't know what's inside her mind.

Diner is often a very funny movie, although I laughed most freely not at the sexual pranks but at the movie's accurate ear, as it reproduced dialogue with great comic accuracy. If the movie has a weakness, however, it's that it limits itself to the faithful reproduction of the speech, clothing, cars, and mores of the late 1950s, and never quite stretches to include the humanity of the characters. For all that I recognized and sympathized with these young men and their martyred wives, girlfriends, and sex symbols, I never quite believed that they were three-dimensional. It is, of course, a disturbing possibility that, to the degree these young men denied full personhood to women, they didn't *have* three-dimensional personalities.

Dirty Dancing ★
PG-13, 100 m., 1987

Jennifer Grey (Baby Houseman), Patrick Swayze (Johnny Castle), Jerry Orbach (Jake Houseman), Cynthia Rhodes (Penny Johnson), Jack Weston (Max Kellerman), Jane Brucker (Lisa Houseman), Kelly Bishop (Marjorie Houseman). Directed by Emile Ardolino and produced by Linda Gottlieb. Screenplay by Eleanor Bergstein.

Well, you gotta hand it to *Dirty Dancing* for one thing at least: It's got a great title. The title seemed to promise a guided tour into the anarchic practices of untrammeled teen-age lust, but the movie turns out to be a tired and relentlessly predictable story of love between kids from different backgrounds.

The movie takes place at a resort hotel that I guess is supposed to be in the Catskills. The hotel is run by Jack Weston, who wants to play matchmaker for his obnoxious nephew. When the Houseman family checks in, he immediately introduces this brat to Baby Houseman (Jennifer Grey), the daughter of Dr. Houseman, if you get the point. Baby doesn't like the brat, and she finds herself bored by the old people at the hotel. But from the cabins out back she hears the insistent beat of rock & roll, and when she sneaks a peek inside she finds the hotel staff engaged in an orgiastic dance sequence.

I use the word "sequence" advisedly. The actors playing the staff in this movie are such good dancers, and their dancing is so over-choreographed, that there's no question that these are just ordinary kids who can dance pretty well. Nope. It's pretty clear they're in a movie.

Baby falls in love with the best-looking dancer, a handsome jock named Johnny Castle (Patrick Swayze), who dances professionally in the hotel's show. At first, he doesn't pay her much attention, but then he kinda starts to like the kid, like in millions of other movies. Meanwhile, a waiter impregnates Swayze's partner, and when there's an emergency, Baby asks her father to help out. Her father (Jerry Orbach) assumes that Swayze was the father of the child, and so he is violently opposed to any romance between his Baby and this greasy jerk.

Of course, Swayze is not the father. There is no reason for Orbach to think so, except for the requirements of the movie's Idiot Plot, which obligates everyone to say exactly the wrong thing at the wrong time in order to protect the idiocy of his mistake. Meanwhile, the sick girl cannot dance in a big show at a nearby hotel, so Grey volunteers to take her place. And after some doubt, Swayze becomes her dance coach.

Can you figure out the rest of the plot? What's your best guess? Does Grey turn out to be a great dancer? Does Swayze fall in love with her? Do they dance together in front of everybody, while her father fumes and her mother keeps a cool head, and then does Orbach finally realize his mistake and accept the kid as his daughter's boyfriend? Are there stars in the sky?

The movie makes some kind of half-hearted attempt to rip off *West Side Story* by making the girl Jewish and the boy Italian—or Irish, I forget. It doesn't much matter, since the movie itself never, ever uses the word "Jewish" or says out loud what obviously is the main point of the plot: the family's opposition to a gentile boyfriend of low social status. I guess people who care about such things are supposed to be able to read between the lines, and the great unwashed masses of American moviegoers are condemned to think the old man doesn't like Swayze's dirty dancing.

This might have been a decent movie if it had allowed itself to be about anything. The performances are good. Swayze is a great dancer, and Grey, who is appealing, is also a great dancer. But the filmmakers rely so heavily on clichés, on stock characters in old situations, that it's as if they never really had any confidence in their performers.

This movie could have been about the subjects it pussyfoots around so coyly. It could have found a big scene a little more original than the heroine stepping in for the injured star. It could have made the obnoxious owner's nephew less of a one-dimensional S.O.B. But the movie plays like one long, sad compromise; it places packaging ahead of ambition. Where did I get that idea? I dunno. Maybe from the title.

Dirty Harry ★ ★ ★
R, 103 m., 1971

Clint Eastwood (Harry), Harry Guardino (Bressler), Reni Santoni (Chico), Andy Robinson (Killer), John Vernon (Mayor). Directed and produced by Don Siegel. Screenplay by Harry Julian Fink.

There is a book named *From Caligari to Hitler* that tries to penetrate the German national subconscious by analyzing German films between 1919 and the rise of the Nazis. I have my doubts about the critical approach (it gets cause and effect backwards), but if anybody is writing a book about the rise of fascism in America, they ought to have a look at *Dirty Harry*. The film is directed by Don Siegel, and like *Coogan's Bluff* it considers the role of a cop in society with lots of dynamite action and enough wry cynicism to keep the blood from getting too thick. It is photographed all over San Francisco, and is filled with good character actors.

The presence of Eastwood in an action role is enough to explain the movie's popularity, but when you see it you discover that the movie has a message with a vengeance. It is loosely based on 1970's headlines, and makes Eastwood a cop who is assigned to find a mysterious killer named Scorpio. The killer has kidnapped and killed various girls, he has tried to extract $200,000 ransom from the city, and in the film's climax he hijacks a school bus. The gimmick is that Eastwood is so filled with hatred for Scorpio that he violates the poor fiend's civil rights. While attempting to find out where a kidnapped girl is, for example, Eastwood gets no less than four amendments wrong. And so the city has to set Scorpio free—even though they have a murder weapon and a confession.

Eastwood doesn't care; he says to hell with the Bill of Rights and stalks out of the district attorney's office. But when Scorpio hijacks the school bus, it is Eastwood again, who is asked to be bag man and carry the ransom. This time he refuses. He wants Scorpio on his own. We've already seen him twisting Scorpio's broken arm ("I have a right to a lawyer!" Scorpio shouts), and soon we will see him kill Scorpio in cold blood. Then, in a thoughtful final scene, Eastwood takes his police badge and throws it into a gravel pit.

It is possible to see the movie as just another extension of Eastwood's basic screen character: He is always the quiet one with the painfully bottled-up capacity for violence, the savage forced to follow the rules of society. This time, by breaking loose, he did what he was always about to do in his earlier films. If that is all, then *Dirty Harry* is a very good example of the cops-and-killers genre, and Siegel proves once again that he understands the Eastwood mystique.

But wait a minute. The movie clearly and unmistakably gives us a character who understands the Bill of Rights, understands his legal responsibility as a police officer, and nevertheless takes retribution into his own hands. Sure, Scorpio is portrayed as the most vicious, perverted, warped monster we can imagine—but that's part of the same stacked deck. The movie's moral position is fascist. No doubt about it.

I think films are more often a mirror of society than an agent of change, and that when we blame the movies for the evils around us we are getting things backward. *Dirty Harry* is very effective at the level of a thriller. At another level, it uses the most potent star presence in American movies—Clint Eastwood—to lay things on the line. If there aren't mentalities like Dirty Harry's at loose in the land, then the movie is irrelevant. If there are, we should not blame the bearer of the bad news.

Dirty Rotten Scoundrels ★ ★ ★
PG, 110 m., 1988

Steve Martin (Freddy Benson), Michael Caine (Lawrence Jamieson), Glenne Headly (Janet Colgate), Anton Rodgers (Inspector Andre), Barbara Harris (Fanny Eubanks), Ian McDiarmid (Arthur), Dana Ivey (Mrs. Reed), Meagen Fay (Lady From Oklahoma). Directed by Frank Oz and produced by Bernard Williams. Screenplay by Dale Launer, Stanley Shapiro, and Paul Henning.

There's something about the very words "dirty rotten scoundrel" that makes being one OK. They evoke an earlier age of simpler evils, back before everyone was playing for keeps. And the movie *Dirty Rotten Scoundrels* evokes a more innocent time in the movies, too; it's a remake of the David Niven comedy *Bedtime Story* about a roguish Riviera con man bilking rich tourists out of more money than they needed in the first place.

The movie stars Michael Caine in the Niven role, as Lawrence Jamieson, a suave, aloof confidence man who seems so noble, so regal, so aloof, that gullible tourists from Nebraska have no difficulty believing he is a king in exile. Steve Martin plays Freddy Benson, a scruffy American who works the lower end of the scam ladder, accepting donations for his allegedly ailing grandmother.

They meet on a train, sort of, when Jamieson observes Benson pulling his crude routine on a tourist. When the slick European discovers that the gauche American is planning to locate in his own home territory—the wealthy Riviera resort town of Beaumont-sur-Mer—he decides to do anything possible to keep him out of town. Jamieson's theory is that bad crooks pollute the water for sophisticated con men like himself.

Freddy keeps turning up, however, like a bad penny, and finally Jamieson decides out of desperation that he must work with him. They do a couple of cons together, and then they make a wager of $50,000 on who will be the first to con a rich visiting American (Glenne Headley). So their pride is at stake—and a lot more than pride, it turns out.

The plot is mostly an excuse for a series of bizarre set pieces in which one con man tries to corner the other one in an outrageous trap. My favorite sequence came when Caine played an incredibly wealthy European aristocrat, and saddled Martin with the hapless role of Ruprecht, his brother. Ruprecht is so maladroit that he has to eat with a cork on the end of his fork, to prevent damage if he stabs himself in the eye. (For added protection, he also wears an eyepatch.)

The plot develops into a *Sting*-like series of cons within cons, as the two confidence men surpass themselves in their attempts to outsmart the surprisingly elusive Headly. Caine goes the high road, with visual and verbal humor. Martin does more pratfalls than in any of his movies since *The Jerk*, and he has one absolutely inspired scene in a jail cell. He knows the name of only one local citizen who might bail him out: Lawrence Jamieson. And as he tries to remember his name, his mind and body undergo the most fearsome contortions. Martin, who seems to be improvising the scene, tries to drag the missing name from his stubborn subconscious, one syllable at a time.

The plot of *Dirty Rotten Scoundrels* is not as complex as a movie like *The Sting*, and we can see some of the surprises as soon as they appear on the horizon. But the chemistry between Martin and Caine is fun, and Headly provides a resilient foil, as a woman who looks like a pushover but somehow never seems to topple.

The Discreet Charm of the Bourgeoisie
★ ★ ★ ★
PG, 100 m., 1972

Fernando Rey (Ambassador), Stephane Audran (Mrs. Senechal), Delphine Seyrig (Mrs. Thevenot), Bulle Ogier (Florence), Jean-Pierre Cassel (Senechal), Michel Piccoli (Secretary of State). Directed by Luis Bunuel and produced by Serge Silberman. Screenplay by Bunuel and Jean-Claude Carriere.

"The best explanation of this film is that, from the standpoint of pure reason, there is no explanation."—Bunuel's preface to *The Exterminating Angel*

There is never quite an explanation in the universe of Luis Bunuel. His characters slip in and out of each other's fantasies, driven by compulsions that are perhaps not even their own. Bunuel doesn't like characters who have free will; if they inhabit his films, they will do what he tells them. And his fancies are as unpredictable as they are likely to be embarrassing.

His theme is almost always entrapment. His characters cannot get loose. He places them in either literal or psychological bond-age, and forces them to watch with horror as he demonstrates the underlying evil of the universe. Bunuel is the most pessimistic of filmmakers, the most negative, certainly the most cynical. He is also the most obsessive, returning again and again to the same situations and predicaments; it's as if filmmaking, for him, is a grand tour of his favorite fetishes.

The Discreet Charm of the Bourgeoisie (which won the Oscar as 1972's best foreign film) has nothing new in it; but Bunuel admirers don't want anything new. They want the same old stuff in a different way, and Bunuel doesn't—perhaps cannot—disappoint them. The most interesting thing about *Discreet Charm* is the way he neatly reverses the situation in his *The Exterminating Angel* (1962).

In that film, one of my favorites, a group of dinner guests finds itself in an embarrassing predicament: After dinner, no one can leave the drawing room. There is nothing to prevent them; the door stands wide open. But, somehow, they simply . . . can't leave. They camp out on the floor for several days of gradually increasing barbarism, black magic, death, suicide, and visits from a bear and two sheep (which they capture and barbecue).

The film, as Bunuel noted in his opening title, makes no sense. Not that it needs to; it gives us an eerie feeling, and we look at his trapped characters with a mixture of pity and the notion that they got what was coming to them. In *The Discreet Charm of the Bourgeoisie*, Bunuel reverses the mirror; this time, his characters are forever sitting down to dinner—but they never eat.

The consummation of their feast is prevented by a series of disasters—some real, some dreams, some obviously contrived to feed some secret itch of Bunuel's. At first there is a simple misunderstanding; the guests have arrived on the wrong night. Later, at an inn, their appetites are spoiled when it develops that the owner has died and is laid out in the next room. Still later, there are interruptions from the army, the police . . . and the guests' own dreams. All of the fantasies of public embarrassment are here, including a scene in which the guests sit down to eat and suddenly find themselves on a stage in front of an audience.

The movie isn't about anything in particular, I suppose, although devoted symbol-mongers will be able to make something of the ambassador who is a cocaine smuggler and the bishop who gets off by hiring himself out as a gardener. Bunuel seems to have finally done away with plot and dedicated himself to filmmaking on the level of pure personal fantasy.

Since the form of a movie is so much more important than the content anyway, this decision gives Bunuel's immediately preceding films (*Tristana*, *Belle de Jour*) a feeling almost of relief. We are all so accustomed to following the narrative threads in a movie that we want to *make* a movie make "sense," even if it doesn't. But the greatest directors can carry us along breathlessly on the wings of their own imaginations, so that we don't ask questions; we simply have an experience. Ingmar Bergman's *Cries and Whispers* did that; now here comes old Bunuel to show that he can, too.

Diva ★ ★ ★ ★
R, 123 m., 1981

Wilhelmenia Wiggins Fernandez (Cynthia,) Frédéric Andrei (Jules), Richard Bohringer (Gorodish), Thay An Luu (Alba), Jacques Fabbri (Saporta), Chantal Deruaz (Nadia). Directed by Jean-Jacques Beineix and produced by Irene Silberman. Screenplay by Beineix and Jean Van Hamme.

The opening shots inform us with authority that *Diva* is the work of a director with an enormous gift for creating visual images. We meet a young Parisian mailman. His job is to deliver special-delivery letters on his motor scooter. His passion is opera, and, as *Diva* opens, he is secretly tape-recording a live performance by an American soprano. The camera sees this action in two ways. First, with camera movements that seem as lyrical as the operatic performance. Second, with almost surreptitious observations of the electronic eavesdropper at work. His face shows the intensity of a fanatic: He does not simply admire this woman, he adores her. There is a tear in his eye. The operatic performance takes on a greatness, in this scene, that is absolutely necessary if we're to share his passion. We do. And, doing so, we start to like this kid.

He is played by Frédéric Andrei, an actor I do not remember having seen before. But he could be Antoine Doinel, the subject of *The 400 Blows* and several other autobiographical films by Francois Truffaut. He has the same loony idealism, coexisting with a certain hard-headed realism about Paris. He lives and works there, he knows the streets, and yet he never quite believes he could get into trouble. *Diva* is the story of the trouble he gets into. It is one of the best thrillers of recent years but, more than that, it is a brilliant film, a visual extravaganza that announces the considerable gifts of its young director, Jean-Jacques Beineix. He has made a film that is about many things, but I think the real subject of *Diva* is the director's joy in making it. The movie is filled with so many small character touches, so many perfectly observed intimacies, so many visual inventions—from the sly to the grand—that the thriller plot is just a bonus. In a way, it doesn't really matter what this movie is about; Pauline Kael has compared Beineix to Orson Welles and, as Welles so often did, he has made a movie that is a feast to look at, regardless of its subject.

But to give the plot its due: *Diva* really gets under way when the young postman slips his tape into the saddlebag of his motor scooter. Two tape pirates from Hong Kong know that the tape is in his possession, and, since the American soprano has refused to ever allow any of her performances to be recorded, they want to steal the tape and use it to make a bootleg record. Meanwhile, in a totally unrelated development, a young prostitute tape-records accusations that the Paris chief of police is involved in an international white-slavery ring. The two cassette tapes get exchanged, and *Diva* is off to the races.

One of the movie's delights is the cast of characters it introduces. Andrei, who plays the hero, is a serious, plucky kid who's made his own accommodation with Paris. The diva herself, played by Wilhelmenia Wiggins Fernandez, comes into the postman's life after a most unexpected event (which I deliberately will not reveal, because the way in which it happens, and *what* happens, are enormously surprising). We meet others: A young Vietnamese girl who seems so blasé in the face of Paris that we wonder if anything truly excites her; a wealthy man-about-town who specializes in manipulating people for his own amusement; and a grab bag of criminals.

Most thrillers have a chase scene, and mostly they're predictable and boring. *Diva*'s chase scene deserves ranking with the all-time classics, *Raiders of the Lost Ark, The French Connection*, and *Bullitt*. The kid rides his motorcycle down into the Paris Metro system, and the chase leads on and off trains and up and down escalators. It's pure exhilaration, and Beineix almost seems to be doing

it just to show he knows how. A lot of the movie strikes that note: Here is a director taking audacious chances, doing wild and unpredictable things with his camera and actors, just to celebrate moviemaking.

There is a story behind his ecstasy. Jean-Jacques Beineix has been an assistant director for ten years. He has worked for directors ranging from Claude Berri to Jerry Lewis. But the job of an assistant director is not always romantic and challenging. Many days, he's a glorified traffic cop, shouting through a bullhorn for quiet on the set, and knocking on dressing room doors to tell the actors they're wanted. Day after day, year after year, the assistant director helps set up situations before the director takes control of them. The director gives the instructions, the assistant passes them on. Perhaps some assistants are always thinking of how *they* would do the shot. Here's one who finally got his chance.

Divine Madness ★ ★ ★ ½
R, 94 m., 1980

Bette Midler, with the Harlettes (Jocelyn Brown, Ula Hedwig, Diva Gray) and Irving Sudrow as the Head Usher. Directed and produced by Michael Ritchie. Written by Jerry Blatt, Bette Midler, and Bruce Vilanch.

Think of a concert film and you think of a camera bolted to the floor in front of the stage and shooting straight up into the singer's nostrils, which are half-concealed by the microphone. Those films are all right as recordings of song performances, but as cinema they stink. Some directors have broken out of the mold by making documentaries about the event of a concert; the best of those films is still Michael Wadleigh's *Woodstock* (1970).

Here Michael Ritchie, whose background is almost entirely in dramatic features (*Downhill Racer, The Candidate, The Bad News Bears*), tries a new approach. There are times in Ritchie's *Divine Madness* when he seems to be trying to turn a live Bette Midler stage concert into a Hollywood genre musical. He opens as if *Divine Madness* is going to be a traditional concert film—Bette charges on stage, the audience cheers, there's an electric performance feel. But from that beginning, Ritchie subtly moves into the material until there are times when we almost forget we're watching an actual concert performance.

Ritchie's first decision was to declare an

absolute ban on visible cameras. At no moment during *Divine Madness* do we see any cameras or any members of Ritchie's crew onstage, even though twenty cameras were used to shoot the performance. Ritchie and Midler used a week of rehearsal to choreograph the camera moves and time them to Midler's own abundant energy. So instead of looking beyond the performer and being distracted by cinematographers carrying hand-held cameras and sneaking around in their Adidas, we see only the stage, Midler, and her backup singers, the Harlettes. Ritchie also uses camera techniques that are rarely seen in concert films. There are, for example, crane shots in this movie—shots where the camera swoops up to look down on Midler or to circle down and toward her. That's especially effective during the Magic Lady sequence, in which Bette portrays a sort of dreamy bag lady on a park bench. This sequence comes closest to capturing the feel of a studio musical. That's not to say that *Divine Madness* loses the impact of a live concert performance. This movie is amazingly alive and involving, and Midler, who has become one of the great live performers, has an energy that steamrollers through an incredible variety of material.

When you think about *Divine Madness* after it's over, you realize what a wide range of material Midler covers. She does rock 'n' roll, she sings blues, she does a hilarious stand-up comedy routine, she plays characters (including a tacky show-lounge performer who enters in a motorized wheelchair outfitted with a palm tree), she stars in bizarre pageantry, and she wears costumes that Busby Berkeley would have found excessive. That's one reason *Divine Madness* doesn't drag: Midler changes pace so often that there's never too much of the same thing.

Is there a weakness in the film? I think there's one—a curious one. I don't think Ritchie intercuts enough close-up shots of the audience. That may seem like a curious objection, since I've already praised *Divine Madness* for sometimes feeling more like a movie musical than a concert documentary. But you can use people in an audience as characters. Richard Lester did in the original Beatles film, *A Hard Day's Night* (and who can ever forget that blond girl weeping and screaming?).

With a Midler concert, the audience is part of the show. Intercutting selected audience shots with the stage material could have set up a nice byplay in some of the numbers. But Ritchie keeps the audience mostly in long shot; it looks like a vast, amorphous mass out there in the dark. Since the film was actually edited together from three different concert performances, maybe he was concerned about matching audiences. But close-ups would have eliminated that problem.

No matter, though, really. Bette Midler is a wonderful performer with a high and infectious energy level and a split-second timing instinct that allows her to play with raunchy material instead of getting mired in it. She sings well, but she performs even better than she sings: She's giving a dramatic performance in music, and *Divine Madness* does a good job of communicating that performance without obscuring it in the distractions of most concert documentaries.

D.O.A. ★ ★ ★
R, 100 m., 1988

Dennis Quaid (Dexter Cornell), Meg Ryan (Sydney Fuller), Charlotte Rampling (Mrs. Fitzwaring), Daniel Stern (Hal Petersham), Jane Kaczmarek (Gail Cornell), Christopher Neame (Bernard), Robin Johnson (Cookie Fitzwaring), Rob Knepper (Nicholas Lang). Directed by Rocky Morton and Annabel Jankel and produced by Ian Sander and Laura Ziskin. Screenplay by Charles Edward Pogue.

Are we in the middle of something new here? Are thrillers abandoning supermen and embracing everyman? For a decade or more we've had the spectacle of the violent man of action, smashing everything that stands in his way. The only question was how long it would take him to kill everyone he didn't like. But lately, there's been a return of a quieter, more intriguing kind of thriller—in which ordinary people get caught up against their will in mysteries they don't understand.

D.O.A. is a movie like that, in which a college professor learns he has been poisoned, and has twenty-four hours to live—twenty-four hours to find his killer. Look at some other movies that came out at about the same time. In *Masquerade*, Meg Tilly plays a la-de-dah rich girl who falls blissfully in love, unaware that she is surrounded by a pack of vipers. *Frantic* stars Harrison Ford as an American doctor whose wife is kidnapped from their Paris hotel, all because of a baggage mix-up at the airport. In *The House on Carroll Street*, Kelly McGillis overhears a

conversation and is plunged into the midst of Nazi schemes.

What all of these movies have in common is that the hero is passive, and wants only to be left alone. But other people have other plans, and the hero is swept along by the tide. This is, of course, the classic definition of *film noir*, those 1940s thrillers in which ordinary people discovered the evil that lurked beneath the surface of society, and *D.O.A.* itself is inspired by a 1949 thriller starring Edmond O'Brien.

The plot is irresistible from the first frame onward. A man staggers into a police station to report a murder. A cop asks him who was murdered. "I was," he says. The man is a college English professor (Dennis Quaid), who has been told that his body contains a radioactive substance that will give him only twenty-four hours to live. During that time he must discover the identity of his killer, a problem made more complicated because he is being sought by the police on framed-up murder charges.

His search leads him into more bizarre corners than you would expect to find at the University of Texas at Austin, where the movie is set during the Christmas season. There are all sorts of suspects. The bright young student, for example, who commits suicide after Quaid delays in reading his novel. The jealous assistant professor who is enraged because Quaid has tenure and he does not. The mysterious mother of the dead student. Quaid's own ex-wife. And so on.

Although the plot follows the broad outlines of a 1940s whodunit, Charles Edward Pogue's screenplay adds a lot of campus atmosphere and academic intrigue. The Quaid character once published a brilliant first novel, we learn, and for a time was a promising writer, but he has produced nothing for four years. "They didn't kill me; I was dead already," he says at one point, equating, as only a writer could, death and writer's block. The whole story plays sly variations on the theme of "publish or perish."

It is required, of course, that the hero of a story like this fall in love along the way, in order to have company on his quest. Quaid's companion is a bright young student (Meg Ryan) who first flirts with him, then is frightened of him, and finally believes in him. Together, they travel a bloody road that leads from ancient family secrets to a deadly tar pit. The family with the secrets is headed by a mysterious widow (Charlotte Ram-

pling), who may have poisoned Quaid in revenge for her son's suicide. Then again, maybe not. Everything is settled in an ending that seems contrived and is the movie's weakest link.

D.O.A. is a witty and literate thriller, with a lot of irony to cut the violence. Quaid is convincing as the chain-smoking English professor, Meg Ryan is true-blue as the stalwart coed, and Rampling looks capable of keeping her victims alive just to toy with them. The film was directed by Rocky Morton and Annabel Jankel, who created Max Headroom. This is their first feature, showing an almost sensuous love for the shadows and secrets of *film noir*.

Dog Day Afternoon ★ ★ ★ ½
R, 120 m., 1975

Al Pacino (Sonny), Charles Durning (Moretti), James Broderick (FBI Man), John Cazale (Sal), Chris Sarandon (Leon), Judith Malina (Sonny's Mother). Directed by Sidney Lumet and produced by Martin Bregman and Martin Elfand. Screenplay by Frank Pierson.

There's a point midway in *Dog Day Afternoon* when a bank's head teller, held hostage by two very nervous stick-up men, is out in the street with a chance to escape. The cops tell her to run. But, no, she goes back inside the bank with the other tellers, proudly explaining, "My place is with my girls." What she means is that her place is at the center of live TV coverage inspired by the robbery. She's enjoying it.

Criminals become celebrities because their crimes provide fodder for the media. Many of the fashionable new crimes—hijacking, taking hostages—are committed primarily as publicity stunts. And a complex relationship grows up among the criminals, their victims, the police, and the press. Knowing they're on TV, hostages comb their hair and killers say the things they've learned on the evening news. That's the subject, in a way, of Sidney Lumet's pointed film. It's based on an actual bank robbery that took place in New York in the 1970s. And it seems to borrow, too, from that curious episode in Stockholm when hostages, barricaded in a bank vault with would-be robbers, began to identify with their captors. The presence of reporters and live TV cameras changed the nature of those events, helped to dictate them, made them into happenings with their own internal logic.

But Lumet's film is also a study of a fascinating character: Sonny, the bank robber who takes charge, played by Al Pacino as a compulsive and most complex man. He's street-smart, he fought in Vietnam, he's running the stick-up in order to get money for his homosexual lover to have a sex-change operation. He's also married to a chubby and shrill woman with three kids, and he has a terrifically possessive mother (the Freudianism gets a little thick at times). Sonny isn't explained or analyzed—just presented. He becomes one of the most interesting modern movie characters, ranking with Gene Hackman's eavesdropper in *The Conversation* and Jack Nicholson's Bobby Dupea in *Five Easy Pieces.*

Sonny and his zombie-like partner, Sal, hit the bank at closing time (a third confederate gets cold feet and leaves early). The stick-up is discovered, the bank is surrounded, the live TV mini-cams line up across the street, and Sonny is in the position, inadvertently, of having taken hostages. Sal (John Cazale) is very willing to shoot them, a factor in all that follows.

There are moments when *Dog Day Afternoon* comes dangerously close to the clichés of old Pat O'Brien gangster movies and the great Lenny Bruce routine inspired by them (the Irish cop shouts into his bullhorn "Come on out, Sonny, and nobody's gonna get hurt," and Sonny's mother pleads with him from the middle of the street). But Lumet is exploring the clichés, not just using them. And he has a good feel for the big-city crowd that's quickly drawn to the action. At first, Sonny is their hero, and he does a defiant dance in front of the bank, looking like a rock star playing to his fans. When it becomes known that Sonny's bisexual, the crowd turns against him. But within a short time (New York being New York), gay libbers turn up to cheer him on.

The movie has an irreverent, quirky sense of humor, and we get some notion of the times we live in when the bank starts getting obscene phone calls—and the giggling tellers breathe heavily into the receiver. There's also, in a film that's probably about fifteen minutes too long, an attempt to take a documentary look at the ways police and banks try to handle situations like this. And through it all there's that tantalizing attraction of instant celebrityhood, caught for an instant when a pizza deliveryman waves at the cameras and shouts, "Hey, I'm a star!"

Dominick and Eugene ★ ★ ★ ½
PG-13, 111 m., 1988

Tom Hulce (Dominick), Ray Liotta (Eugene), Jamie Lee Curtis (Jennifer), Robert Levine (Dr. Levinson), Todd Graff (Larry Higgins), Bill Cobbs (Jesse Johnson), Tommy Snelfire (Mickey), David Strathairn (Mickey's Father). Directed by Robert M. Young and produced by Marvin Minoff and Mike Farrell. Screenplay by Alvin Sargent and Corey Blechman.

Dominick was dropped on his head when he was young, and now he is a little "slow," but not so slow that he can't hold down a good job as a garbageman, and use his salary to send his brother through medical school. Eugene, the brother, is an overworked intern who is on duty long hours at a stretch, and hardly has time for a girlfriend, but does have time to love and care for Dominick. Their parents are dead, and the two brothers live upstairs over a deli in Philadelphia, where Dominick dreams of the day he'll be able to see Hulk Hogan in person.

This might possibly sound like one of those tearjerker plots that inspire you to start giggling halfway through (there is nothing quite so funny as melodramatic pathos). But *Dominick and Eugene* is a special movie, a movie that somehow negotiates its plot without becoming corny or ridiculous, and leaves us feeling surprisingly moved.

The film stars Tom Hulce in the crucial role of Dominick, a friendly, outgoing young man whose retardation has left him well able to function, but not always able to understand other people's motives. He is completely trusting, likes everyone, and expects everyone to like him, but it doesn't work that way with one of the stops on his garbage route. There's a young boy there named Mickey (Tommy Snelfire) who shares his love of comic books, and they trade back issues until Mickey's drunken father (David Strathairn) tells Dominick, "Stop hanging around my kid!"

Dominick's feelings are hurt. And there are other complications in his life. His brother, Eugene (Ray Liotta), turns up one day with a date (Jamie Lee Curtis), and Dominick fears that Eugene will run away and leave him. Larry (Todd Graff), the guy who works with him on the garbage truck, fills his head with bad ideas all the time, including the suggestion that Eugene may run away to Atlantic City and gamble away all of their money.

The director, Robert M. Young, regards this situation with an evenhanded point of view. We see Dominick's world through his own eyes, and then we see the world of Eugene at the hospital. Attention is paid to Eugene's relationship with Jamie Lee Curtis; they're both so busy, so ambitious, and so overworked as medical students that they seem to realize there is no place in their plans for each other. Sometimes Eugene grows frustrated with Dominick, and sometimes his temper explodes, but they have a loving relationship.

Then one day Dominick sees something. Little Mickey's drunken father mistreats him, and throws him down the basement steps, and as Dominick accidentally witnesses this act there is a long, painful close-up on his face and we realize he is remembering something. The way in which Tom Hulce projects his thoughts, in this scene and others, is surprisingly effective. His performance is a courageous one, completely uninhibited and without any fear of looking silly. Many actors protect themselves, refuse to go "too far," worry about their image; Hulce dedicates himself absolutely to this character.

I was also impressed by Ray Liotta's work as Dominick's brother. You may remember Liotta from *Something Wild*, where he was the mysterious, violent husband who turned up unexpectedly two-thirds of the way through. Liotta's ability to suggest an undercurrent of danger is present in this role, too, but channeled in a different direction. What comes out more strongly is his tenderness, his willingness to meet Tom Hulce's lack of inhibition and go with it. Jamie Lee Curtis has a fairly thankless role as an intelligent observer admitted into the family circle, but she is right for it, and projects a kind of fierce careerism that doesn't quite mask her emotions.

Dominick and Eugene is a message movie with several different messages, but it never feels like a messenger. In the way it shows the two brothers caring for each other, it captures a tenderness and intimacy that few love stories ever reach. It reminded me sometimes of *Midnight Cowboy*, another movie in which two men learned to take care of one another and make allowances for each other's weaknesses. The danger is that any description of the plot will make it sound so melodramatic that its genuine human qualities get overlooked. It's quite an experience.

Do the Right Thing ★ ★ ★ ★
R, 120 m., 1989

Danny Aiello (Sal), Ossie Davis (Da Mayor), Ruby Dee (Mother Sister), Richard Edson (Vito), Giancarlo Esposito (Buggin Out), Spike Lee (Mookie), Bill Nunn (Radio Raheem), John Turturro (Pino), Paul Benjamin (ML), Frankie Faison (Coconut Sid). Directed, produced, and written by Spike Lee.

Spike Lee's *Do the Right Thing* is the kind of film people find they have to talk about afterward. Some of them are bothered by it—they think it will cause trouble. Others feel the message is confused. Some find it too militant, others find it the work of a middle-class director who is trying to play street-smart. All of those reactions, I think, are simply different ways of avoiding the central fact of this film, which is that it comes closer to reflecting the current state of race relations in America than any other movie of our time.

Of course it is confused. Of course it wavers between middle-class values and street values. Of course it is not sure whether it believes in liberal pieties, or militancy. Of course some of the characters are sympathetic and others are hateful—and of course some of the likable characters do bad things. Isn't that the way it is in America today? Anyone who walks into this film expecting answers is a dreamer or a fool. But anyone who leaves the movie with more intolerance than they walked in with wasn't paying attention.

The movie takes place during one long, hot day in the Bedford-Stuyvesant neighborhood of Brooklyn. But this is not the typical urban cityscape we've seen in countless action movies about violence and guns and drugs. People live here. It's a neighborhood like those city neighborhoods in the urban movies of the Depression—people know each other, and accept each other, and although there are problems there is also a sense of community.

The neighborhood is black, but two of the businesses aren't. Sal's Famous Pizzeria has been on the same corner since before the neighborhood changed, and Sal (Danny Aiello) boasts that "these people have grown up on my pizza." And in a nearby storefront that had been boarded up for years, a Korean family has opened a fruit and vegetable stand. Nobody seems to quite know the

Koreans, but Sal and his sons are neighborhood fixtures—they know everybody, and everybody knows them.

Sal is a tough, no-nonsense guy who basically wants to get along and tend to business. One of his sons is a vocal racist—in private, of course. The other is more open toward blacks. Sal's ambassador to the community is a likable local youth named Mookie (Spike Lee), who delivers pizzas and also acts as a messenger of news and gossip. Mookie is good at his job, but his heart isn't in it; he knows there's no future in delivering pizzas.

We meet other people in the neighborhood. There's Da Mayor (Ossie Davis), a kind of everyman who knows everybody. Buggin' Out (Giancarlo Esposito), a vocal militant. Radio Raheem (Bill Nunn), whose boom box defines his life, and provides a musical cocoon to insulate him from the world. Mother Sister (Ruby Dee), who is sort of the neighborhood saint. And there's the local disk jockey, whose program provides a running commentary, and a retarded street person who wanders around selling photos of Martin Luther King and Malcolm X, and then there are three old guys on the corner who comment on developments, slowly and at length.

This looks like a good enough neighborhood—like the kind of urban stage the proletarian dramas of the 1930s liked to start with. And for a long time during *Do the Right Thing*, Spike Lee treats it like a backdrop for a Saroyanesque slice of life. But things are happening under the surface. Tensions are building. Old hurts are being remembered. And finally the movie explodes in racial violence.

The exact nature of that violence has been described in many of the articles about the film—including two I wrote after the movie's tumultuous premiere at the Cannes Film Festival—but in this review I think I will not outline the actual events. At Cannes, I walked into the movie cold, and its ending had a shattering effect precisely because I was not expecting it. I would like you to have the experience for yourself, and think about it for yourself. Since Spike Lee does not tell you what to think about it, and deliberately provides surprising twists for some of the characters, this movie is more open-ended than most. It requires you to decide what you think about it.

Do the Right Thing is not filled with brotherly love, but it is not filled with hate, either. It comes out of a weary urban cynicism that

has settled down around us in recent years. The good feelings and many of the hopes of the 1960s have evaporated, and today it would no longer be accurate to make a movie about how the races in America are all going to love one another. I wish we could see such love, but instead we have deepening class divisions in which the middle classes of all races flee from what's happening in the inner city, while a series of national administrations provides no hope for the poor. *Do the Right Thing* tells an honest, unsentimental story about those who are left behind.

It is a very well-made film, beautifully photographed by Ernest Dickerson, and well-acted by an ensemble cast. Danny Aiello has the pivotal role, as Sal, and he suggests all of the difficult nuances of his situation. In the movie's final scene, Sal's conversation with Mookie holds out little hope, but it holds out at least the possibility that something has been learned from the tragedy, and the way Aiello plays this scene is quietly brilliant. Lee's writing and direction are masterful throughout the movie; he knows exactly where he is taking us, and how to get there, but he holds his cards close to his heart, and so the movie is hard to predict, hard to anticipate. After we get to the end, however, we understand how, and why, everything has happened.

I believe that any good-hearted person, white or black, will come out of this movie with sympathy for all of the characters. Lee does not ask us to forgive them, or even to understand everything they do, but he wants us to identify with their fears and frustrations. *Do the Right Thing* doesn't ask its audiences to choose sides; it is scrupulously fair to both sides, in a story where it is our society itself which is not fair.

The Doors ★ ★ ½
R, 135 m., 1991

Val Kilmer (Jim Morrison), Frank Whaley (Robby Krieger), Kevin Dillon (John Densmore), Meg Ryan (Pamela Courson), Kyle MacLachlan (Ray Manzarek), Kathleen Quinlan (Journalist). Directed by Oliver Stone and produced by Bill Graham, Sasha Harari, and A. Kitman Ho. Screenplay by J. Randal Johnson and Stone.

F. Scott Fitzgerald wrote that the problem with American lives is that they have no second act. The problem with Jim Morrison's life was that it had no first and third. His childhood was lost in a mist of denial—he never quite forgave his father for being an admiral—and his maturity was interrupted by an early death, caused by his relentless campaign against his own mind and body. What he left behind was a protracted adolescence, during which he recorded some great rock 'n' roll.

If we can trust Oliver Stone's new biographical film, *The Doors*, life for Jim Morrison was like being trapped for months at a time in the party from hell. He wanders out of the sun's glare, a curly-haired Southern California beach boy with a cute pout and a notebook full of poetry. He picks up a beer, he smokes a joint, and then life goes on fast-forward as he gobbles up drugs and booze with both hands, while betraying his friends and making life miserable for anyone who loves him. By the age of twenty-seven he is dead. Watching the movie is like being stuck in a bar with an obnoxious drunk when you're not drinking.

The songs he left behind, it is true, are wonderful. Many of them are on the sound track of *The Doors*, which combines Morrison's original vocals and new vocals by Val Kilmer so seamlessly that there is never, not even for a moment, the sensation that Kilmer is not singing everything we hear. That illusion is strengthened by Kilmer's appearance. He looks so uncannily like Jim Morrison that we feel this is not a case of casting, but of possession.

The performance is the best thing in the movie—and since nearly every scene centers on Morrison, that is not small praise. Val Kilmer has always had a remarkable talent, which until now has been largely overlooked, but if you want to see why Stone thought he could be convincing as a rock star, look at *Top Secret!*, the *Airplane!*-style spoof of spy movies in which Kilmer plays Elvis Presley. Because of Kilmer, and because of extraordinary location work with countless convincing extras, the concert scenes in *The Doors* play with the authenticity of a documentary.

If the songs are timeless and the concert footage is convincing, however, the scenes from life are more painful than in any other backstage movie I can remember. The typical showbiz biopic describes a sort of parabola, in which the talented kid wins early fame, begins to self-destruct, hits bottom, and then makes his big comeback and goes on, of course, to have a movie made about him. Jim Morrison becomes a star very quickly, and then self-destructs as efficiently as he

can. It is not a pretty picture. He must have been one of those people with a constitutional inability to handle drugs or booze in any quantity. For him there is no moderation; he isn't seeking to get high, he's looking for oblivion.

He knows it. His poetry and lyrics—and a lot of the dialogue in the movie—glorify death. He's infatuated with it, mesmerized by death as the ultimate trip and as the ultimate loyalty test: If you love him, you will die with and/or for him. He's like Edgar Allen Poe on acid, crawling along the ledges outside hotel windows, or begging his lovers to stab him in the heart. This kind of narcissism has its source, of course, in self-loathing, and the early scenes of Jim preening and posturing before the camera like a male pinup eventually segue into scenes where he hides behind a beard and dark glasses, hibernating in hotel rooms on long, lonely binges.

Oliver Stone, who as a young man once tried to pitch an early version of this screenplay to Morrison himself, has a natural feel for the Los Angeles beach and rock scene in the years when The Doors were first establishing themselves as "the band from Venice." Morrison materializes on the beach like a young god from the sea, falls in love with a hippie chick (Meg Ryan), and reads his poetry, which as poetry is sophomoric, but translates easily into haunting song lyrics, helped by the mournful quality of his voice. Whatever else you can say about Morrison and The Doors, there is no denying their sound: Their records, especially "Light My Fire" and "L.A. Woman," have become a part of our shared consciousness.

Stone shows the band working out some early arrangements and playing early gigs at rock clubs on the Sunset Strip, and then, just as in life, Jim Morrison becomes a superstar at about the same time he becomes unreliable as a stage performer. He carries a bottle with him everywhere, gulping big slugs of booze as if it were pop. He uses drugs. They do not help his personality, and he becomes mean-spirited and autocratic to those who depend on him, and obnoxious to the public—except, of course, for those moments when lightning strikes and his underlying talent flashes out.

The band grows weary of him—of the missed dates, the no-shows, the late arrivals, and endless recording sessions in which a drunken or hungover Morrison indulges himself in expensive retakes. Keyboardist Ray Manzarek (Kyle MacLachlan), who first

told him he had potential as a singer, drifts into a kind of passive-aggressive trance, sitting stone-faced during Morrison's outbursts. Others threaten to quit. Listening to the final version of one of his best albums, Morrison tells the musicians, "That's not bad for a bunch of guys who weren't even talking to each other the day the album was recorded."

Prancing and preening onstage as a sex god, Morrison is bedeviled by impotence in real life; the drugs have done their work. In the movie's most extraordinary scene, he encounters an older rock journalist (Kathleen Quinlan) who is heavily into sadomasochism and the trappings of witchcraft, and who, through heroic measures including pain, ritual, and the mutual drinking of blood, succeeds in stimulating Morrison to the point where he actually achieves potency—although, if the movie is to be trusted, it was his last hurrah.

Quinlan's character is almost the only one able to break through the fog of Morrison's indulgences to create a distinctive screen persona for herself (the character is miles different from anything she has played before, and brilliantly conceived and executed). The other principals in Morrison's life, even his wife as played by Ryan, are supporting characters who drift in and out of focus during his long, sad binge.

The experience of watching *The Doors* is not always very pleasant. There are the songs, of course, and some electrifying concert moments, but mostly there is the mournful, self-pitying descent of this young man into selfish and boring stupor. Having seen this movie, I am not sad to have missed the opportunity to meet Jim Morrison, and I can think of few fates more painful than being part of his support system. The last hour of the film, in particular, is a dirge of wretched excess, of drunken would-be orgies and obnoxious behavior, of concerts in which the audiences waited for hours for the spectacle of Morrison stumbling onstage to fake a few songs or, notoriously, to expose himself.

In the end, Stone leaves a large question unanswered: How was Morrison able to leave the country after being sentenced to a jail term for public indecency? But leave he did, to die of an "apparent heart attack" in Paris, where he lies buried to this day, his tomb a mecca for his fans, who have spray-painted all of the neighboring tombs with exhortations and obscenities. Even in death, Jim Morrison is no fun to be around.

Down and Out in Beverly Hills
★ ★ ★ ★
R, 103 m., 1986

Nick Nolte (Jerry Baskin), Richard Dreyfuss (Dave Whiteman), Bette Midler (Barbara Whiteman), Little Richard (Orvis Goodnight), Tracy Nelson (Jenny Whiteman), Elizabeth Pena (Carmen). Directed and produced by Paul Mazursky. Screenplay by Mazursky and Leon Capetanos.

Buddy Hackett once said that the problem with Beverly Hills is, you go to sleep beside your pool one day and when you wake up you're seventy-five years old. *Down and Out in Beverly Hills* understands that statement inside-out.

It tells the story of a rich family that lives in the timeless comfort of a Beverly Hills mansion—in the kind of house where they use *Architectural Digest* for pornography. One day a bum wanders down the alley and into their backyard and tries to drown himself in their swimming pool. After he is saved, he changes their lives forever.

In its broad outlines, this story is borrowed from Jean Renoir's classic film *Boudu Saved from Drowning*. But this isn't just a remake. The director, Paul Mazursky, makes his whole film depend on the very close observation of his characters. Mazursky knows Beverly Hills (he lives there, on the quiet cloistered flatlands below Sunset Boulevard), and he knows the deceptions and compromises of upper-middle-class life (his credits include *An Unmarried Woman* and *Bob & Carol & Ted & Alice*). With great attention and affection, he shows us the lives that are disrupted by the arrival of the derelict—this seedy failure whose whole life is an affront to the consumer society.

The film's heroes are the Whitemans, Dave and Barbara (Richard Dreyfuss and Bette Midler), and the bum, Jerry Baskin. He is played by Nick Nolte as the kind of guy who didn't set out in life to be a failure, but just sort of drifted from one plateau down to the next, until finally he was spending most of his time talking to his dog.

It is, indeed, the dog's disappearance that inspires Nolte's suicide attempt, and it will be the Whitemans' own amazing dog, named Matisse, that gets some of the loudest laughs in the movie. Maybe Mazursky is trying to tell us something about the quality of human relationships in Beverly Hills.

The Dreyfuss character is a coat-hanger manufacturer. He didn't set out in life to be rich (one of his favorite conversational gambits involves his own good luck and assurances that it could have happened to you as easily as to him—nice if you are him, but not if you are you). Here he is, living in a manicured mansion, exploiting wetback labor, sleeping with the Mexican maid, driving a Rolls convertible, selling 900 million coat hangers to the Chinese, and yet, somehow, something is missing. And almost from the first moment he sets eyes on the Nolte character, he realizes what it is: the authenticity of poverty.

The movie has a quiet, offhand way of introducing us to the the rich man's milieu. We meet his wife, whose life involves long sessions with masseurs, yogis, and shrinks (even her dog has a doggie psychiatrist). We meet his daughter (Tracy Nelson), a sunny-faced, milk-fed child of prosperity. We meet the Whitemans' neighbor, played by Little Richard with an incongruous mixture of anger and affluence (he complains that he doesn't get full service from the police; when he reports prowlers, they don't send helicopters and attack dogs).

We meet Carmen (Elizabeth Pena), the maid, who greets her employer lustily in her servant's quarters, but who grows, during the movie, from a soap opera addict into a political radical. We also meet the extended family and friends of the Whitemans, each one a perfectly written vignette, right down to the dog's analyst.

Down and Out in Beverly Hills revolves around the fascination that Dreyfuss feels for Nolte's life of dissipation and idleness. He is drawn to the shiftless sloth like a moth to a flame. A bum's life seems to have more authenticity than his own pampered existence. And, indeed, perhaps the last unreachable frontier of the very rich, the one thing they cannot buy, is poverty. Dreyfuss spends a night down on the beach with Nolte and his bum friends, and there is a breathtaking moment at sundown when Nolte (who claims to be a failed actor) recites Shakespeare's lines beginning "What a piece of work is a man!"

Certain predictable things happen. Nolte not only becomes Dreyfuss's good buddy, but is enlisted by all of the women in the household—the wife, the daughter, and the maid—as a sex therapist. Dreyfuss will put up with almost anything, because he really likes this guy, and Nolte's best hold on them is the threat to leave. Mazursky makes the

most of that paradox, and gradually we see the buried theme of the movie emerging, and it is the power of friendship. What these people all really lacked, rich and poor, sane and crazy alike, was the power to really like other people.

The movie should get some kind of award for its casting. Dreyfuss, who has been so good in the past as a hyperactive overachiever, succeeds here in slightly deflecting that energy. He has the success, but is bedazzled by it, as if not quite trusting why great wealth should come to him for doing so little. He channels his energy, not into work, but into enthusiasms—and Nolte becomes his greatest enthusiasm.

For Bette Midler, Barbara Whiteman is the perfect character, all filled with the distractions of living up to her level of consumption. Nolte in some ways has the subtlest role to play, although when we first see it, it seems the broadest. His shiftless drifter has to metamorphose into a man who understands his hosts so deeply that he can play them like a piano.

The supporting roles are so well filled, one after another, that we almost feel we recognize the characters before they're introduced. And Mike, the dog, should get an honorary walk-on at the Oscars.

Perhaps I have made the movie sound too serious. Mazursky has a way of making comedies that are more intelligent and relevant than most of the serious films around; his last credit, for example, was the challenging *Moscow on the Hudson*. So let me just say that *Down and Out in Beverly Hills* made me laugh longer and louder than any film I've seen in a long time.

Down by Law ★ ★ ★
R, 95 m., 1986

Tom Waits (Zack), John Lurie (Jack), Roberto Benigni (Roberto), Nicoletta Braschi (Nicoletta), Ellen Barkin (Bobbie). Directed by Jim Jarmusch. Screenplay by Jarmusch.

It's a sad and beautiful world.
—Line of dialogue

Down by Law is a movie about cheap whiskey and black coffee, all-night drunks and lost jobs, and the bad times you can have with good-time girls. It tells the story of a pimp, an unemployed disc jockey, and a bewildered Italian tourist, and how they escape from jail together and wind up slogging through the Louisiana bayous looking for a decent place to have breakfast. It's like a collage made out of objects from old gangster movies, old blues songs, and old jailhouse stories. At the end, it's like that line of dialogue. It's a sad and beautiful world, someone says, and someone else should say, yeah, but so what?

The movie was directed by Jim Jarmusch. You may remember his *Stranger than Paradise* (1984), a deadpan black-and-white comedy in which three strangely assorted friends decided it was too cold in Cleveland in the winter, and went to Florida and lost all their money at the dog races. *Down by Law* has the same sort of feeling; it's about two people who choose to be losers and a third who has bought the American Dream.

The movie stars Tom Waits, whose sandpaper voice sounds like he's pushing his words through three layers of hangovers. The other two guys are played by John Lurie, who was the Hungarian-American poker player in *Stranger than Paradise*, and Roberto Benigni, a previously unknown Italian actor who resembles a cross between Father Guido Sarducci and Woody Allen. They meet in the same Louisiana jail cell through a series of misadventures in which two of the guys are framed and the third is severely misunderstood.

No cell is large enough to hold these three. Lurie and Waits hate each other, but hate is nothing compared to the emotions they feel for the Italian, who commits the unpardonable sin of being cheerful and constantly pleased with himself. Eventually the three prisoners escape, and the movie follows them through the swamps as they slog through every cliché Jarmusch can remember.

In notes accompanying the film, Jarmusch is at pains to explain that he never saw the Louisiana bayou country before he went to shoot a movie there. What he has seen are lots of movies, and *Down by Law* is an anthology of pulp images from the world of *film noir*. On the surface, it's grim and relentless, but there's a thread of humor running through everything, and that takes the curse off. We are never quite sure that Jarmusch intends us to take anything seriously, and there are times when the actors seem to be smiling to themselves as they growl through their lines.

Lurie is known from the previous film, and from his work as a musician. Tom Waits is a star playing himself. The discovery in the picture is the redoubtable Roberto Benigni, who has an irrepressible, infectious manner,

and is absolutely delighted to be himself. I don't know where he came from and I can't imagine what he's going to do next, but he could have a long comic career ahead of himself; he's like a show-off kid who gets you laughing and then starts laughing at himself, he's so funny, and then tries to top himself no matter what.

Down by Law is a true original that kind of grows on you. Maybe it goes on a little too long, and maybe it depends too much on its original inspiration—these three misfits and the oddballs they meet along the way—instead of trying to be about something. It doesn't have the inspired perfection of *Stranger than Paradise*, in which every shot seemed inevitable, but it's a good movie, and the more you know about movies the more you're likely to like it.

Dragnet ★ ★ ★
PG-13, 100 m., 1987

Dan Aykroyd (Friday), Tom Hanks (Pep Streebeck), Christopher Plummer (Whirley), Harry Morgan (Bill Gannon), Alexandra Paul (Connie Swail), Jack O'Halloran (Emil Muzz), Elizabeth Ashley (Jane Kirkpatrick), Dabney Coleman (Jerry Caesar). Directed by Tom Mankiewicz and produced by David Permut and Robert K. Weiss. Screenplay by Aykroyd, Alan Zweibel, and Mankiewicz.

From the loud, confident opening chords of the famous "Dragnet" theme music, I was filled with confidence that this 1987 *Dragnet* knew what it was doing. My confidence lasted several seconds. Then the original music segued into some kind of dreadful disco rap unmusic, and my heart sank. How could they? How could they possibly make a movie called *Dragnet* and think that *anything* had to be done to the music?

They make the same mistake at the end, over the closing titles. I guess it was some kind of a business deal, and they wanted to make a lot of money with the music video or something. Hollywood is so greedy these days. God forbid that whoever wrote the original "Dragnet" theme should make a dime, when it can be cloned and corrupted for profit.

In between, the movie's pretty good. To be more precise, it is great for an hour, good for about twenty-five munutes, and then heads doggedly for the Standard 1980s High Tech Hollywood Ending, which means an

expensive chase scene and a shoot-out. God, I'm tired of chases and shoot-outs.

The movie takes the basic ingredients of the "Dragnet" TV shows, kids them, and plugs them into a bizarre plot about a cult of Los Angeles pagans who hold weird satanic rites. Dan Aykroyd stars as Joe Friday, nephew of the original, and he was born to play this role, with his off-the-rack brown suit, his felt fedora, and his square jaw with the Chesterfield pasted into it. Tom Hanks is his partner, the nonconforming Detective Streebeck, game for anything but puzzled by Aykroyd's straight-arrow squareness.

There's a series of "pagan murders" in L.A. and the two cops get on the trail, which leads to a phony TV preacher, some highly placed creeps, and an absolutely hilarious pagan-rite scene, in which oddly assorted would-be pagans stomp around in thigh-high sheepskins, while the Virgin Connie Swail (Alexandra Paul) is prepared for a sacrifice.

That's what she's always called, the Virgin Connie Swail. Friday falls in love with her, and his heart beats so hard that he stays on the case even after Chief Gannon (the legendary Harry Morgan) lifts his badge. Among other familiar faces involved in the case is Jack O'Halloran, as Emil Muzz, the big killer (you may remember him as Moose Malloy in the Mitchum version of *Farewell, My Lovely*).

Aykroyd's performance is the centerpiece of the film. He must have practiced for hours, even days, to perfect the rapid-fire delivery he uses to rattle off polysyllabic utterances of impenetrable but kaleidoscopic complexity. Listening to him talk in this movie is a joy.

It's an open question, I think, how much they really wanted to kid the old "Dragnet" shows. Jack Webb's visual style was built around a series of deadpan close-ups and clipped one-liners, and there's a little of that in this movie, but they never make a real point of it or have a lot of fun with it. The visuals are a lot looser than Webb would have enjoyed. And the color photography, of course, is all wrong; this is a movie that begs to be in black-and-white.

Still, it's fun, a lot of the time. Several individual shots are hilarious, including a long shot in pantomime of the two partners trying to show Harry Morgan how the pagans did their dance. Hanks and Aykroyd have an easy, unforced chemistry, growing out of their laconic delivery and opposite personalities, and the movie is filled with nice supporting turns, especially from Elizabeth Ashley and Dabney Coleman, as crooked officials.

This would have been a great movie if they'd bothered to think of an ending for it. And used the original "Dragnet" theme. The end of the film cries out—*cries* out, mind you—for the simple, stark, authority of *dum-de-dum-dum*. I wanted to hear it so badly I walked out of the screening singing the notes out loud, to drown out the disco Drano from the screen.

The Draughtsman's Contract
★ ★ ★ ★
R, 103 m., 1983

Anthony Higgins (Mr. Neville), Janet Suzman (Mrs. Herbert), Anne Louise Lambert (Mrs. Talmann). Directed by Peter Greenaway and produced by David Payne. Screenplay by Greenaway.

What we have here is a tantalizing puzzle, wrapped in eroticism and presented with the utmost elegance. I have never seen a film quite like it. *The Draughtsman's Contract* seems to be telling us a very simple story in a very straightforward way, but after it's over you may need hours of discussion with your friends before you can be sure (if even then) exactly what happened.

The film takes place in 1694, in the English countryside. A rich lady (Janet Suzman) hires an itinerant artist to make twelve detailed drawings of her house. The artist (Anthony Higgins) strikes a hard bargain. In addition to his modest payment, he demands "the unrestricted freedom of her most intimate hospitality." Since the gentleman of the house is away on business, the lady agrees, and thus begins a pleasant regime divided between the easel and the boudoir.

All of this is told in the most precise way. All of the characters speak in complete, elegant, literary sentences. All of the camera strategies are formal and mannered. The movie advances with the grace and precision of a well-behaved novel. There is even a moment, perhaps, when we grow restless at the film's deliberate pace. But then, if we are sharp, we begin to realize that strange things are happening under our very noses.

The draughtsman demands perfection. There must be no change, from day to day, in the view he paints. He aims for complete realism. But little changes do creep in. A

window is left open. A ladder is found standing against a wall. There are things on the lawn that should not be on the lawn. The lady's daughter calls on the artist and suggests that a plot may be under way and that her father, the lord of the manor, may have been murdered. Furthermore, the artist may be about to be framed for the crime. As a payment for her friendship, the daughter demands the same payment in "intimate hospitality" as her mother. Now the artist is not only draughtsman but lover to mother and daughter *and* the possible object of a plot to frame him with murder.

There is more. There is a lot more, all allowed to unfold at the same deliberate pace. There is a mysterious statue in the garden. An eavesdropper. Misbehaved sheep. The raw materials of this story could have been fashioned into a bawdy romp like *Tom Jones*. But the director, Peter Greenaway, has made a canny choice. Instead of showing us everything, and explaining everything, he gives us the clues and allows us to draw our own conclusions. His movie is like a crossword puzzle for the senses.

The Dream Team ★ ★
PG-13, 113 m., 1989

Michael Keaton (Billy Caulfield), Christopher Lloyd (Henry Sikorsky), Peter Boyle (Jack McDermott), Stephen Furst (Albert Ianuzzi), Dennis Boutsikaris (Dr. Weitzman), Lorraine Bracco (Riley), Milo O'Shea (Dr. Newald), Philip Bosco (O'Malley), James Remar (Gianelli). Directed by Howard Zieff and produced by Christopher W. Knight. Screenplay by Jon Connolly and David Loucka.

Everybody's favorite scene in *One Flew Over the Cuckoo's Nest* is the one where the Jack Nicholson character takes his fellow mental patients on an unauthorized outing. *The Dream Team* starts with the inspiration of that scene and runs with it, telling the story of four patients who are taken by their psychiatrist to see a baseball game, and end up wandering the streets of New York after their minder is knocked unconscious.

This is not a bad starting place for a movie, but the filmmakers are unable to devise anything original for the patients to do once they've been set free, and so the movie immediately compromises its original inspiration and turns into another one of those lockstep-plot pictures where you are asked

to care about developments that are manufactured, false, and contrived.

The film's setup has a nice energy to it. We meet the Dream Team, one at a time. There's Billy (Michael Keaton), fast-talking, jazzed-up, and possibly violent; Henry (Christopher Lloyd), professorial and obsessive-compulsive; Jack (Peter Boyle), who has Messianic tendencies; and Albert (Stephen Furst), who doesn't talk to people. Separately, they're not able to function in society (although the Keaton character is no crazier than numbers of my friends). But together, they seem to forge a composite personality, each one contributing according to his abilities and taking according to his needs.

Dennis Boutsikaris plays the psychiatrist who has all four men in his encounter group, and it's his idea to take them all out for a day at the ballpark. They set out in the morning, high in spirits, but their troubles begin when Albert develops a desperate need to answer a call of nature. The doctor pulls into a gas station, Albert runs into an alley, the doctor follows, and inadvertently witnesses a murder. He's knocked senseless and later taken to a hospital, and the four patients are left to their own devices.

It's at this point that the movie takes a fatal turn toward the conventional. An ambitious, daring film would have seriously asked itself what might happen next. What experiences and adventures might these four men really have? And then it would follow them, together or separately, down the byways of city life as each encountered reality through his own special sieve.

The Dream Team is not ambitious and daring, unfortunately, and so it plugs us into a preassembled murder plot involving some bad cops. The unconscious doctor is taken to a hospital, where, as the only witness to the crime, he is obviously a man whose life is in danger. And then it all comes down to the bad guys versus the Dream Team, with the obligatory showdown in the hospital.

I despair when I see films like this. They must mean that the filmmakers have no faith in the curiosity and intelligence of the average filmgoer. Have we truly arrived at the point where the average movie does not dare to surprise, explore, and experiment? Are American movie audiences so hostile to anything out of the ordinary that a movie *must* follow the well-trod path of Identikit story lines and retread plots?

I ask because the people who made *The Dream Team* are not untalented. The director is Howard Zieff, whose credits include *Hearts of the West* and *Private Benjamin*, and who is capable of achieving a nice offbeat comic rhythm (even though in the second half of *Private Benjamin* he also went for the predictable). The actors are all capable of the kinds of sprung-rhythm craziness that would have been right for this movie; Keaton has the manic intensity, Lloyd (from *Back to the Future*) has the single-minded zeal, and Peter Boyle has a kind of deadpan earnestness that can be very funny. (Stephen Furst, as the patient who does not speak, could hardly have played his character any differently no matter what the plot.)

With this director and these actors, something could have been accomplished. But perhaps it's impossible to pitch a project that strays too far from the beaten path. Maybe movie executives no longer have the time or imagination to listen to something original. *The Dream Team* is essentially a formula picture filled with missed opportunities. The fact that it has several passages that really work, and that the actors create characters we can care about, only underlines the bankruptcy of its imagination.

Dreamchild ★ ★ ★
PG, 94 m., 1985

Coral Browne (Mrs. Hargreaves), Ian Holm (Reverend Dodgson), Peter Gallagher (Jack Dolan), Caris Corfman (Sally Mackeson), Nicola Cowper (Lucy), Jane Asher (Mrs. Liddell). Directed by Gavin Miller and produced by Rick McCallum and Kenith Trodd. Screenplay by Dennis Potter.

It probably comes as no surprise that the man who wrote *Alice's Adventures in Wonderland* was not an absolute paragon of normality. His biographers have recently revealed that the Rev. Charles Dodgson (who wrote under the pen name Lewis Carroll) had an obsession with young girls, which he satisfied through hundreds of photographic studies and through lots of chummy friendships and correspondence. *Dreamchild* deals with his obsession as a problem that he tried to resolve in basically healthy ways, but it does argue that the writing of *Alice* created lifelong problems for the girl who inspired it.

According to this movie, which is fiction inspired by fact, the original Alice was a girl named Alice Liddell. She suffered Dodgson's attentions for a time and allowed herself to be rowed up and down a river by

him one sunny afternoon, but she was more interested in playing with her friends than in having the original manuscript of *Alice* read to her. "But I wrote this just for you!" protests the anguished clergyman (played with a nice, quiet intensity by Ian Holm).

Dreamchild is not, in any event, a psychological case study. It's too much fun for that. The movie begins some seventy years after the book was published. The young girl, now eighty years old, is known as Mrs. Alice Hargreaves (Coral Browne) and is sailing for America to receive an honorary degree on the centennial of Dodgson's birth. She is accompanied by a young traveling companion named Lucy (Nicola Cowper), and on arrival in New York in 1932 she is surrounded by a mob of aggressive newspaper reporters. One of them (Peter Gallagher) succeeds in pushing his way into Mrs. Hargreaves's life and Lucy's heart.

What happens next is sort of sweet. As the reporter and Lucy gradually fall in love, Hargreaves at first is violently opposed to their relationship. She is, indeed, a rather unpleasant old lady—inflexible and dogmatic, with definite ideas about the proper conduct of young people.

But she is much more complex than we think, as we learn by sharing her private nightmares and fantasies. In her mind, the world of Alice's Wonderland still has a scary reality, and we see the original fantasy figures (the king and queen, the Cheshire cat, and so on) as grotesque caricatures designed not to delight a little girl, but to frighten her.

The movie uses these fantasy sequences as counterpoint for more realistic flashbacks in which we meet Dodgson, see Alice as a young girl, and begin to sense some of the pathetic extremes to which Dodgson went to satisfy his passion for her, which was platonic but nonetheless bothering. We begin to realize, as old Mrs. Hargreaves herself begins to realize, that her whole life has been shaped by things that happened seventy years before.

Dreamchild is a remarkable film in many ways, not least because it gives itself such freedom of style and subject matter. For example, all the creatures in Alice's fantasies appear as muppetlike creations done by Jim Henson and his Creature Shop, but they are not Muppets. The movie has some subtle points to make with them.

At the same time, *Dreamchild* is not unremittingly grim, and it is not just a case study. The newspaper world of New York in the

1930s is re-created with style and humor, and the love story between the two young people is handled with a lot of cheerful energy. *Dreamchild* is an ambitious movie that tries to do a lot of things, and does most of them surprisingly well.

Dressed to Kill ★ ★ ★
R, 105 m., 1980

Michael Caine (Dr. Elliott), Angie Dickinson (Kate Miller), Nancy Allen (Liz Blake), Keith Gordon (Peter Miller), Dennis Franz (Detective Marino), David Margulies (Dr. Levy). Directed by Brian De Palma and produced by George Litto. Screenplay by De Palma.

When Alfred Hitchcock died, the obituaries puzzled over the fact that Hitchcock had created the most distinctive and easily recognizable visual style of his generation—but hadn't had a great influence on younger filmmakers. The obvious exception is Brian De Palma, who deliberately set out to work in the Hitchcock tradition, and directed this Hitchcockian thriller that's stylish, intriguing, and very violent.

The ads for De Palma's *Dressed to Kill* describe him as "the master of the macabre," which is no more immodest, I suppose, than the ads that described Hitchcock as "the master of suspense." De Palma is not yet an artist of Hitchcock's stature, but he does earn the right to a comparison, especially after his deliberately Hitchcockian films *Sisters* and *Obsession*. He places his emphasis on the same things that obsessed Hitchcock: precise camera movements, meticulously selected visual details, characters seen as types rather than personalities, and violence as a sudden interruption of the most mundane situations.

He also has Hitchcock's delight in bizarre and unexpected plot twists, and the chief delight of the first and best hour of *Dressed to Kill* comes from the series of surprises he springs on us. Although other key characters are introduced, the central character in these early scenes is Kate Miller (Angie Dickinson), an attractive forty-fiveish Manhattan woman who has a severe case of unsatiated lust. De Palma opens with a deliberately shocking shower scene (homage to Hitch), and then follows the woman as her sexual fantasies become unexpectedly real during a lunchtime trip to the museum.

The museum sequence is absolutely brilliant, tracking Dickinson as she notices a tall, dark, and handsome stranger. She makes eye contact, breaks it, tries to attract the stranger's attention by dropping her glove, and then is tracked *by* the stranger. To her, and our, astonishment, this virtuoso scene (played entirely without dialogue) ends in a passionate sexual encounter in the back of a taxicab.

Later, she wakes up in the stranger's apartment, and De Palma shamelessly manipulates her, and us, by springing a series of plot surprises involving embarrassment and guilt: What would *you* do if you were a cheating wife and had just forgotten your wedding ring in a stranger's apartment? The plot now takes several totally unanticipated turns, and I, of course, would not dream of revealing them. Indeed, I'll be vague about the plot from now on, because De Palma's surprises are crucial to his effect.

The movie's other characters include Michael Caine, who's the psychiatrist of two of the characters in the film. Then there's Nancy Allen, who's wonderfully offbeat as a sweet Manhattan hooker who discovers a body and gets trapped in the investigation. And there's Keith Gordon: He's one of those teen-age scientific geniuses, and he invents brilliant gimmicks to investigate the crime.

Some people are going to object to certain plot details in *Dressed to Kill*, particularly the cavalier way it explains a homicidal maniac's behavior by lumping together transsexuality and schizophrenia. But I doubt that De Palma wants us to take his explanations very seriously; the pseudoscientific jargon used to "explain" the case reminds me of that terrible psychiatric explanation at the end of *Psycho*—a movie De Palma has been quoting from all along.

Dressed to Kill is an exercise in style, not narrative; it would rather look and feel like a thriller than make sense. Its plot has moments of ludicrous implausibility, it nearly bogs down at one point near the end and it cheats on us with the old "it was only a dream!" gimmick. But De Palma has so much fun with the conventions of the thriller that we forgive him and go along. And there are really nice touches in the performances: Dickinson's guilt-laden lust, Caine's analytical detachment, Allen's street-wise cool in life and death situations, Gordon's wiseguy kid. De Palma earns the title of master, all right . . . but Hitch remains the grand master.

The Dresser ★ ★ ★ ★
PG, 118 m., 1984

Albert Finney (Sir), Tom Courtenay (Norman), Edward Fox (Oxenby), Zena Walker (Her Ladyship). Directed and produced by Peter Yates. Screenplay by Ronald Harwood.

Much of mankind is divided into two categories, the enablers and the enabled. Both groups accept the same mythology, in which the enablers are self-sacrificing martyrs and the enabled are egomaniacs. But the roles are sometimes reversed; the stars are shaken by insecurities that are subtly encouraged by enablers who, in their heart of hearts, see themselves as the real stars. It's human nature. Ever hear the one about the guy who played the gravedigger in *Hamlet*? He was asked what the play was about, and he answered, "It's about this gravedigger . . ."

The Dresser is about a guy like that, named Norman. He has devoted the best years of his life to the service of an egomaniacal actor, who is called Sir even though there is some doubt he has ever been knighted. Sir is an actor-manager who runs his own traveling theatrical troupe, touring the provinces to offer a season of Shakespeare. One night he plays King Lear. The next night, Othello. The next, Richard III. Most nights he has to ask his dresser what role he is playing. Dressers in the British theater do a great deal more than dress their employers. In *The Dresser*, Norman is also Sir's confidant, morale booster, masseur, alter ego, and physician, nursing him through hangovers with medicinal amounts of brandy. Norman has been doing this job for years, and Sir is at the center of his life. Sir, however, takes Norman very much for granted, and it is this difference between them that provides the emotional tension.

The Dresser is a backstage movie, based on a backstage play, but the movie leaves the theater for a few wonderful additions to the play, as when Sir commands a train to stop, and the train does. Mostly, though, the action is in a little provincial theater, where tonight's play is *King Lear*, and Sir looks as if he had spent the last week rehearsing the storm scene. It is Norman's job to whip him into shape. Sir is seriously disoriented. He is so hung over, shaky, and confused that he can't even remember how the play begins—indeed, he starts putting on the makeup for *Othello*. There are other problems for Nor-

man to handle, such as Sir's relationships with his wife, his adoring stage manageress, and a young actress he is considering for Cordelia (she is slim, and would be easier to carry onstage). There are also an angry supporting player and a quaking old trouper who is being pressed into service as the Fool.

The minor characters are all well-drawn, but *The Dresser* is essentially the story of two people, and the movie has been well-cast to make the most of both of them; no wonder both actors won Oscar nominations. Norman is played by Tom Courtenay, who had the role on stage in London and New York and will also be remembered from all those British Angry Young Men films like *Billy Liar* and *Loneliness of the Long Distance Runner*. He is perfect for playing proud, resentful, self-doubting outsiders. Sir is played by Albert Finney, who manages to look far older than his forty-seven years and yet to create a physical bravura that's ideal for the role. When he shouts "Stop . . . that . . . train!" we are not too surprised when the train stops.

On the surface, the movie is a wonderful collection of theatrical lore, detail, and superstition (such as the belief that it is bad luck to say the name "Macbeth" aloud— safer to refer always to "the Scottish tragedy"). The physical details of makeup and costuming are dwelled on, and there is a great backstage moment when the primitive thunder machine is rattled to make a storm. Beneath those details, though, a human relationship arrives at a crisis point and is resolved, in a way. Sir and Norman come to the end of their long road together, and, as is the way with enablers and enabled, Norman finally understands the real nature of their relationship, while Sir, of course, can hardly be bothered. This is the best sort of drama, fascinating us on the surface with color and humor and esoteric detail, and then revealing the truth underneath.

Drive, He Said ★ ★ ★
R, 90 m., 1971

William Tepper (Hector), Karen Black (Olive), Michael Margotta (Gabriel), Bruce Dern (Coach Builion), Robert Towne (Richard), Harry Jaglom (Conrad). Directed by Jack Nicholson and produced by Steve Blauner and Nicholson. Screenplay by Jeremy Larner and Nicholson.

Jack Nicholson's *Drive, He Said* is a disorganized but occasionally brilliant movie about two college students and the world they, and we, inhabit. Their campus is a microcosm of the least reassuring aspects of contemporary America; the two overwhelming mental states are paranoia and compulsive competitiveness. Sufferers from both conditions are obsessed by the fear that something might be gaining on them. In *Drive, He Said*, the paranoic student is afraid of the draft, the System, and They, whoever They are. The other student is a star basketball player, or, as his friends tell him, "You stay after school to run around in your underwear." His fears are more general and vague and, therefore, more frightening.

The movie has a sort of jumpy, nervous rhythm, as if it were on speed, and sometimes that works but it's finally just distracting. The problem is that the stories of the two main characters don't mesh. They're roommates, to be sure, but that's a tenuous connection. And when the paranoid (Michael Margotta) has his three big adventures—freaking out at the draft physical, attacking a faculty wife, and freeing all the animals in a biology lab—the scenes feel like set pieces, unrelated to the movie.

The movie that surrounds them involves Hector (played with laconic charm by William Tepper), who plays basketball not because he's a jock but because he enjoys the self-testing that the game involves. By the time we meet him, he has become a star and a prime choice for the pro draft, but, well, somehow the whole thing is falling apart on him.

One of his problems is the faculty wife, played by Karen Black. He has been having an affair with her, but she breaks it off just as he discovers, uncomfortably, that he might be in love. And then it turns out she's pregnant. This is a real-life experience of the most unsettling sort, and makes it difficult for him to take basketball as seriously as his coach thinks he should.

The coach is an intense competitor who positively believes in all the values, moral and physical, that have been preached by all coaches since the dawn of time-outs. Bruce Dern's performance as the coach, by the way, is a small masterpiece of accurate observation.

The performances, indeed, are the best thing in the movie. Nicholson himself is a tremendously interesting screen actor, and he directs his actors to achieve a kind of intimacy and intensity that is genuinely rare.

But if Nicholson is good on the nuances, he's weak on the overall direction of his film. It doesn't hang together for us as a unified piece of work.

I have a notion he may have been trying for an effect similar to that in his three previous films as an actor (*Easy Rider, Five Easy Pieces*, and *Carnal Knowledge*), which were deliberately episodic and depended on the cumulative effect of the episodes for a structure that occurred to us only gradually. But the episodes refuse to come together in *Drive, He Said*, and what we're left with are some very good scenes in search of a home.

Driving Miss Daisy ★ ★ ★ ★
PG, 99 m., 1989

Morgan Freeman (Hoke Colburn), Jessica Tandy (Daisy Werthan), Dan Aykroyd (Boolie Werthan), Patti Lupone (Florine Werthan), Esther Rolle (Idella), Joann Havrilla (Miss McClatchey), William Hall, Jr. (Oscar), Alvin M. Sugarman (Dr. Well), Clarice F. Geigerman (Nonie). Directed by Bruce Beresford and produced by Richard D. Zanuck and Lili Fini Zanuck. Screenplay by Alfred Uhry.

Driving Miss Daisy is a film of great love and patience, telling a story that takes twenty-five years to unfold, exploring its characters as few films take the time to do. By the end of the film, we have traveled a long way with the two most important people in it—Miss Daisy Werthan, a proud old Southern lady, and Hoke Colburn, her chauffeur—and we have developed a real stake in their feelings.

The movie spans a quarter-century in the lives of its two characters, from 1948, when Miss Daisy's son decides it is time she stop driving herself and employ a chauffeur, to 1973, when two old people acknowledge the bond that has grown up between them. It is an immensely subtle film, in which hardly any of the most important information is carried in the dialogue, and in which body language, tone of voice, or the look in an eye can be the most important thing in a scene. After so many movies in which shallow and violent people deny their humanity and ours, what a lesson to see a film that looks into the heart.

The movie contains a performance nominated for an Academy Award by Morgan Freeman, as Hoke, and an Academy Award–winning role by Jessica Tandy, who at the age of eighty creates the best performance of her career as Miss Daisy. As the movie opens,

Miss Daisy still lives in proud self-sufficiency, with only her cook to help out, and she drives herself around in a big new 1948 Packard. One day she drives the Packard over the wall and into the neighbor's yard, and her son (Dan Aykroyd) lays down the law: It is time that she have a chauffeur.

She refuses. She needs no such thing. It is a nuisance to have servants in the house, anyway—they're like children, always underfoot. But her son hires a chauffeur anyway, and in their first interview he tells Hoke that it is up to him to convince Miss Daisy to let herself be driven. Thus commences a war of wills that continues, in one way or another, for twenty-five years, as two stubborn and proud old people learn to exist with one another.

Hoke's method is the employment of infinite patience, and Morgan Freeman's performance is a revelation, based on close observation and quiet nuance. Hoke is not obsequious. He is not ingratiating. He is very wise. His strategy is to express verbal agreement in such a way that actual agreement is withheld. If Miss Daisy does not want to be driven to the Piggly Wiggly, very well then, Hoke will not drive her. He will simply follow her in the car. The car by this time is a shiny new 1949 Hudson, and Hoke somehow defuses the situation by making the car itself the subject, rather than himself. It is a shame, he observes, that a fine new car like that is left sitting in the driveway. Not being used. It's good for a car to be driven. . . .

Eventually Miss Daisy agrees to be driven, and eventually, over the years, she and Hoke begin to learn about one another. Neither one is quick to reveal emotion. And although Miss Daisy prides herself on being a Southern Jewish liberal, she is not always very quick to see the connections between such things as an attack on her local synagogue and the Klan's attacks on black churches. Indeed, much of Hoke's relationship with her consists of helping her to see certain connections. When she goes to listen to a speech by Martin Luther King, for example, she has Hoke drive her—but although she has an extra ticket it never occurs to her to invite him to come inside. "Things have changed," she observes complacently in another scene, referring to race relations in the South, and he replies that they have not changed all *that* much.

"Is Morgan Freeman the greatest American actor?" Pauline Kael once asked, reviewing his performance as a steel-eyed pimp in

Street Smart (1987). It is when you compare that performance with his own in *Driving Miss Daisy* and another film, *Glory*, that you begin to understand why the question can be asked. The three performances have almost nothing in common; all three are works of the imagination in which Freeman creates three-dimensional characters that are completely convincing. In *Street Smart*, he created an aura of frightening violence. In *Lean on Me*, early in 1989, he was school principal Joe Clark, a man of unassailable self-confidence and bullheaded determination. In *Glory*, he was an ignorant grave digger who becomes a soldier in the Civil War. In *Miss Daisy*, he is so gentle, so perceptive, so patient, it is impossible to get a glimpse of those other characters.

It is a great performance, and matched by Miss Tandy's equally astonishing range, as she ages from a sprightly and alert widow in her sixties to an infirm old woman drifting in and out of senility in her nineties. Hers is one of the most complete portraits of the stages of old age I have ever seen in a film.

Driving Miss Daisy was directed by Bruce Beresford, an Australian whose sensibilities seem curiously in tune with the American South. His credits include the superb *Tender Mercies* and *Crimes of the Heart*, as well as the underrated and overlooked 1986 film about an aborigine teen-ager, *The Fringe Dwellers*. Working from a screenplay by Alfred Uhry, based on Uhry's play (and on Uhry's memories of a grandmother and a chauffeur in his own family), Beresford is able to move us, one small step at a time, into the hearts of his characters. He never steps wrong on his way to a luminous final scene in which we are invited to regard one of the most privileged mysteries of life: the moment when two people allow each other to see inside.

Drugstore Cowboy ★ ★ ★ ★
R, 100 m., 1989

Matt Dillon (Bob), Kelly Lynch (Diane), James Le Gros (Rick), Heather Graham (Nadine), Max Perlich (David), James Remar (Gentry), Grace Zabriskie (Bob's Mother), Beah Richards (Drug Counselor), William S. Burroughs (Tom the Priest). Directed by Gus Van Sant, Jr., and produced by Cary Brokaw. Screenplay by Van Sant and Daniel Yost.

Drugstore Cowboy is one of the best films in a long tradition of American outlaw road movies—a tradition that includes *Bonnie and Clyde, Easy Rider, Midnight Cowboy,* and *Badlands*. It is about criminals who do not intend to be particularly bad people, but whose lives run away with them. The heroes of these films always have a weakness, and in *Drugstore Cowboy* the weakness is drug abuse.

The movie stars Matt Dillon in one of the great recent American movie performances, as the leader of a pack of two young couples who are on the prowl in Washington and Oregon. It is 1971 and they are the rear guard of the love generation. They drift from one rented apartment or motel room to another, in an aimless migration in search of drugs. They will use almost anything, but their favorites are prescription drugs, and they have developed a smooth method of stealing them from drugstores.

We see them at work. The four enter a store separately. One of them creates a commotion—pretending to have a fit, let's say. Under cover of the confusion, Dillon sneaks behind the prescription counter and scoops up as many drugs as he can identify. What drugs they can't use, they sell. And when they aren't stealing or on the road, their lives fall into a listless routine of getting high, watching TV, smoking, talking, waiting.

Sex is not high on Dillon's list of enthusiasms. Like a lot of drug abusers, he is more turned on by drugs than sex—by the excitement of setting up a job, the fear during the actual stealing, and the payoff afterward when he gets high. He has apparently been with the same girlfriend (Kelly Lynch) since they were in high school, and at some point along the road they got married, but their eyes are turned toward drugs, not each other. They travel with a goofy sidekick (James Le Gros) and his girlfriend, a pathetic teen-age drifter (Heather Graham). Together, they're a family.

Strangely enough, it is the family feeling that makes *Drugstore Cowboy* so poignant and effective. This is not a movie about bad people, but about sick people. They stick together and try to help one another in the face of the increasing desperation of their lives. The movie is narrated by Dillon, whose flat voice doesn't try to dramatize the material; he could be telling his story at an AA meeting. He knows that it is sad, but he also knows that it is true, and he is not trying to glamorize it, simply trying to understand it.

There is humor in their lives—craziness almost always breeds humor—and there is also deeply buried hurt, as in the scene where the Dillon character goes to visit his mother (Grace Zabriskie). Up until this point in the movie we have seen him primarily through his own eyes and have grown to like him, a little, for the resourceful way he is trying to lead his team of losers. Then his mother refuses to let him into the house—not because she doesn't love him, but because she knows him too well and knows he will steal anything to get money for drugs. The way he has to stand there and accept this, and try to shrug it off, provides one of the most painful scenes in the movie.

Life falls into a rhythm of excitement and ennui. And their lives drift imperceptibly from bad to worse. There is a way in which desperate people can accept the conditions of their lives up to a point, and then there is the unmistakable day when that point has been passed. For this family, that day comes when the teen-age girl overdoses and they are stuck with a corpse in their room at a motel where a deputy sheriffs' convention is being held. It is a tribute to the sure hand of the director, Gus Van Sant, Jr., that this scene works through irony and desperation, instead of through the cheap laughs another director might have settled for.

Drugstore Cowboy is a story told with a threat of insane logic that makes it one of the most absorbing movies in a long time. It is a logic that many drug abusers would understand. It goes like this: I feel bad and drugs make me feel good, although they are also why I feel bad. But since they make me feel good now and bad later, I will worry about later when the time comes. Eventually, for the Dillon character, the time does come, and he tells his wife that he is heading back to Seattle to get into some kind of a program and try to kick drugs. He has the intelligence to see that things are out of control, that he can no longer make them hold together, that he has lost the fight and had better surrender before his corpse is somebody else's problem.

The movie then inserts a small supporting performance by William Burroughs that is like a guest appearance by Death. Sitting in a fleabag hotel room, playing a defrocked priest addicted to heroin, Burroughs talks to Dillon in a gallows voice about drugs. We sense two things about the character: that he should have died long ago, and that death would not have been unwelcome compared to his earthly purgatory. This cameo appearance has been criticized by some writers as the movie's single flaw. It's distracting to see Burroughs in a fiction film, they say. But with his skull shining through his eyes and his dry voice and his laugh like a smoker's cough, Burroughs creates a perfect moment. The Dillon character looks at him and sees one of the fates he is free to choose.

Like all truly great movies, *Drugstore Cowboy* is a joyous piece of work. I believe that the subject of a film does not determine whether it makes us feel happy or sad. I am unutterably depressed after seeing stupid comedies that insult my ingelligence, but I felt exhilarated after seeing *Drugstore Cowboy* because every person connected with this project is working at top form. It's a high-wire act of daring, in which this unlikely subject matter becomes the occasion for a film about sad people we come to care very deeply about.

At the end of the film, the Dillon character seems to have broken out of drugs. His wife is still on the road. "Are you crazy?" she asks him when he says he wants to kick his habit. She cannot imagine life without drugs. He can. That is the difference between them, and in painting that difference, this movie shows the distance between hope and despair.

A Dry White Season ★ ★ ★ ★
R, 106 m., 1989

Donald Sutherland (Ben du Toit), Janet Suzman (Susan), Zakes Mokae (Stanley), Jurgen Prochnow (Captain Stolz), Susan Sarandon (Melanie), Marlon Brando (McKenzie), Winston Ntshona (Gordon), Thoko Ntshinga (Emily). Directed by Euzhan Palcy and produced by Paula Weinstein. Screenplay by Colin Welland and Palcy.

When you are safe and well-off, and life has fallen into a soothing routine, there is a tendency to look the other way when trouble happens—especially if it hasn't happened to you. Say, for example, that you are a white schoolmaster in South Africa, and live in a comfortable suburban home with your wife and two children. Suppose your African gardener's son disappears one day. How do you feel? You feel sorry, of course, because you have humanitarian instincts. But what if it appears that the boy was the victim of police brutality and may be imprisoned illegally? What do you do then? In a country where the gardener has little hope of lodging an effec-

tive appeal, do you stick your neck out and help him?

That is the question posed to Ben du Toit (Donald Sutherland) in the opening passages of *A Dry White Season*. His answer is almost instinctive: "Best to let it go," he tells the gardener. "No doubt they'll see they made a mistake and release him. There's nothing to be done." This is a sensible answer, if the boy is not your son. But Gordon Ngubene (Winston Ntshona), the gardener, cannot accept it. With the help of an African lawyer, he tries to get some answers, to find out why and how his son disappeared. And it is not very long until Gordon has disappeared, too.

A Dry White Season is set in the 1970s, at the time when the schoolchildren of Soweto, an African township outside Johannesburg, held a series of protests. They wanted to be educated in English, not Afrikaans (a language spoken only in South Africa and mostly by whites). The protests resulted in the deaths of many marchers, but the government weathered the storm and clapped a lid on the possibility of a civil uprising, as it always has.

In 1989 we have arrived at another season of protest in South Africa, where, to the general amazement of almost everyone involved, peaceful antigovernment marches were permitted by the government in Cape Town and Johannesburg. As someone who has visited South Africa and studied for a year at the University of Cape Town, I wonder what the average American reader makes of the headlines. How does he picture South Africa? What does he think life is like there? Does he see these marches in the same context as American freedom marches? Does he ask how six million whites can get away with ruling twenty-four million Africans?

This film, based on a novel by Andre Brink, provides a series of bold images to go with the words and the concepts in the stories out of South Africa. Like *A World Apart* (1988), it is set mostly in the pleasant world of white suburbia, an easy commute from the skyscrapers of downtown (some Americans, I believe, still see South Africa in images from old Tarzan movies, and do not know the country is as modern and developed as any place in Europe or North America). We meet the schoolteacher, a decent and quiet man, a onetime Springbok sports hero, who finds it easy not to reflect overlong on the injustices of his society. He disapproves of injustice in principle, of course, but finds it prudent not to rock the boat.

Then disaster strikes into the life of the gardener, who also loves his family, and who also lives a settled family life, in a township outside the city. Jonathan, the gardener's son, is a clever lad, and the schoolteacher is helping him with a scholarship. Jonathan is arrested almost at random and jailed with many other demonstrators, and then a chain of events is set into motion that leads Ben du Toit into a fundamental difference with the entire structure of his society.

The movie follows him step by step as he sees things he can hardly believe, and begins to suspect the unthinkable—that the boy and his father have been ground up inside the justice system and spit out as "suicides." He meets with the African lawyer (Zakes Mokae) and with the gardener's wife (Thoko Ntshinga). He finds one catch-22 being piled on another. (After her husband is reported dead, the widow no longer has a legal right to stay in her house and must be deported to a "homeland" she has never seen, from where it will be impossible to lodge a legal protest.)

As a respected white man, the schoolteacher is allowed access to the system—until it becomes obvious that he is asking the wrong questions and adopting the wrong attitude. Then he is ostracized. He loses his job. Shots are fired through his windows. His wife (Janet Suzman, brittle and unforgiving) is furious that he has betrayed his family by appearing to be a "kaffir lover." His daughter finds him a disgrace. Only his young son seems to understand that he is wearily, doggedly, trying to do what is right.

A Dry White Season is a powerfully serious movie, but the director, Euzhan Palcy, provides a break in the middle, almost as Shakespeare used to bring on pantomime before returning to the deaths of kings. A famous South African lawyer, played by Marlon Brando, is brought in to lodge an appeal against the finding that one of the dead committed suicide. The Brando character knows the appeal is useless, that his courtroom appearance will be a charade, and yet he goes ahead with it anyway—using irony and sarcasm to make his points, even though the outcome is hopeless.

Brando, in his first movie appearance since 1980, has fun with the role in the way that Charles Laughton or Orson Welles would have approached it. He allows himself theatrical gestures, droll asides, astonished double takes. His scenes are not a star turn, but an effective performance in which we see a lawyer with a brilliant mind, who uses it cynically and comically because that is his form of protest.

At the center of the film, Donald Sutherland is perfectly cast and quietly effective as a man who will not be turned aside, who does not wish misfortune upon himself or his family, but cannot ignore what has happened to the family of his friend. Like *A World Apart* and *Cry Freedom*, the movie concentrates on a central character who is white (because the movie could not have been financed with a black hero), but *A Dry White Season* has much more of the South African black experience in it than the other two films.

It shows daily life in the townships, which are not slums but simply very poor places where determined people struggle to live decently. It hears the subtleties of voice when an intelligent African demeans himself before a white policeman, appearing humble to gain a hearing. It shows some of the details of police torture that were described in Joseph Lelyveld's *Move Your Shadow*, the most comprehensive recent book about South Africa. It provides mental images to go with the columns of text in the newspapers. American network TV coverage of South Africa all but ended when the government banned the cameras (proving that the South African government was absolutely right that the networks were interested only in sensational footage, and not in the story itself). Here are some pictures to go with the words.

Here is also an effective, emotional, angry, subtle movie. Euzhan Palcy, a gifted filmmaker, is a thirty-two-year-old from Martinique, whose first feature was the masterpiece about poor black Caribbean farm workers, *Sugar Cane Alley*. Here, with a larger budget and stars in the cast, she still has the same eye for character detail. This movie isn't just a plot trotted out to manipulate us, but the painful examination of one man's change of conscience. For years he has been blind, perhaps willingly. But once he sees, he cannot deny what he feels is right.

E

E.T.—The Extra-Terrestrial ★ ★ ★ ★
PG, 115 m., 1982

Henry Thomas (Elliott), Dee Wallace (Mary), Peter Coyote (Keys), Robert MacNaughton (Michael), Drew Barrymore (Gertie). Directed by Steven Spielberg and produced by Spielberg and Kathleen Kennedy. Screenplay by Melissa Mathison.

This movie made my heart glad. It is filled with innocence, hope, and good cheer. It is also wickedly funny and exciting as hell. *E.T.—The Extra-Terrestrial* is a movie like *The Wizard of Oz*, that you can grow up with and grow old with, and it won't let you down. It tells a story about friendship and love. Some people are a little baffled when they hear it described: It's about a relationship between a little boy and a creature from outer space that becomes his best friend. That makes it sound like a cross between *The Thing* and *National Velvet*. It works as science fiction, it's sometimes as scary as a monster movie, and at the end, when the lights go up, there's not a dry eye in the house.

E.T. is a movie of surprises, and I will not spoil any of them for you. But I can suggest some of the film's wonders. The movie takes place in and around a big American suburban development. The split-level houses march up and down the curved drives, carved out of hills that turn into forest a few blocks beyond the backyard. In this forest one night, a spaceship lands, and queer-looking little creatures hobble out of it and go snuffling through the night, looking for plant specimens, I guess. Humans arrive—authorities with flashlights and big stomping boots. They close in on the spaceship, and it is forced to take off and abandon one of its crew members. This forlorn little creature, the *E.T.* of the title, is left behind on Earth—

abandoned to a horrendous world of dogs, raccoons, automobile exhausts, and curious little boys.

The movie's hero is one particular little boy named Elliott. He is played by Henry Thomas in what has to be the best little boy performance I've ever seen in an American film. He doesn't come across as an over-coached professional kid; he's natural, defiant, easily touched, conniving, brave, and childlike. He just *knows* there's something living out there in the backyard, and he sits up all night with his flashlight, trying to coax the creature out of hiding with a nearly irresistible bait: Reese's Pieces. The creature, which looks a little like Snoopy but is very, very wise, approaches the boy. They become friends. The E.T. moves into the house, and the center section of the film is an endless invention on the theme of an extra-terrestrial's introduction to bedrooms, televisions, telephones, refrigerators, and six-packs of beer. The creature has the powers of telepathy and telekinesis, and one of the ways it communicates is to share its emotions with Elliott. That's how Elliott knows that the E.T. wants to go home.

And from here on out, I'd better not describe what happens. Let me just say that the movie has moments of sheer ingenuity, moments of high comedy, some scary moments, and a very sad sequence that has everybody blowing their noses.

What is especially wonderful about all of those moments is that Steven Spielberg, who made this film, creates them out of legitimate and fascinating plot developments. At every moment from its beginning to its end, *E.T.* is really *about* something. The story is quite a narrative accomplishment. It reveals facts about the E.T.'s nature; it develops the personalities of Elliott, his mother, brother, and sister; it involves the federal space agencies;

it touches on extra-terrestrial medicine, biology, and communication, and *still* it inspires genuine laughter and tears.

A lot of those achievements rest on the very peculiar shoulders of the E.T. itself. With its odd little walk, its high-pitched squeals of surprise, its tentative imitations of human speech, and its catlike but definitely alien purring, E.T. becomes one of the most intriguing fictional creatures I've ever seen on a screen. The E.T. is a triumph of special effects, certainly; the craftsmen who made this little being have extended the boundaries of their art. But it's also a triumph of imagination, because the filmmakers had to imagine E.T., had to see through its eyes, hear with its ears, and experience this world of ours through its utterly alien experience in order to make a creature so absolutely convincing. The word for what they exercised is empathy. *E.T.—The Extra-Terrestrial* is a reminder of what movies are for. Most movies are not for any one thing, of course. Some are to make us think, some to make us feel, some to take us away from our problems, some to help us examine them. What is enchanting about *E.T.* is that, in some measure, it does all of those things.

Earth Girls Are Easy ★ ★ ★
PG, 100 m., 1989

Geena Davis (Valerie), Jeff Goldblum (Mac), Jim Carrey (Wiploc), Damon Wayans (Zeebo), Julie Brown (Candy), Michael McKean (Woody), Charles Rocket (Ted), Larry Linville (Dr. Bob), Rick Overton (Dr. Rick). Directed by Julien Temple and produced by Tony Garnett. Screenplay by Julie Brown, Charlie Coffey, and Terrence E. McNally.

In my fantasies about visitors from outer

space, I always imagine them as strange and wondrous creatures that are eons ahead of us in intellectual and emotional development. But what if they are simply hot-shot space jockeys looking for a good time—like a bunch of Air Force fliers on a Saturday night? That is more or less the emotional level reached by the fur-covered aliens in *Earth Girls Are Easy*, a lighthearted and goofy musical comedy about a love affair between an extraterrestrial and a manicurist.

The manicurist is played by Geena Davis, in her first film appearance after she won the supporting actress Oscar for *The Accidental Tourist*. Although two movies could not possibly be more different, the characters played by Davis are actually somewhat similar: optimistic, openhearted, trusting women who can't help themselves when they see a guy in trouble.

As the movie opens, Valerie, the Davis character, is a manicurist in trouble. Her boyfriend (Charles Rocket) doesn't seem to be interested any longer. The boss at her beauty salon (Julie Brown) suggests a complete change of image, and makes her over into a platinum blonde. This does not work, since it turns out her boyfriend already has another woman on the hook. But the next day her love life begins to look up, when three aliens crash-land their spaceship in her swimming pool.

The aliens are nice guys, but hungry and clumsy and covered with fur. Valerie accidentally strands them on earth when she sinks their ship in her pool, and so to make it up to them she offers the most precious thing she can think of, a complete head-to-toe beauty makeover. The aliens emerge as three fairly good-looking guys (led by Jeff Goldblum), and after they all go out for a night on the town, romance blossoms between the Davis and Goldblum characters.

A lot of the humor in *Earth Girls Are Easy* depends on the ways the aliens misunderstand the everyday details of Earth culture. This is fairly familiar subject matter in the movies (as in *Starman* and *My Stepmother Is an Alien*), but *Earth Girls* peps it up by setting the movie in a day-glo, instantly disposable Southern California culture where even aliens *with* their fur would not attract a whole lot of attention.

The movie was directed by Julien Temple, who has had a considerable underground reputation ever since his cult Sex Pistols movie, *The Great Rock and Roll Swindle*, a decade earlier. His previous film was the strange, difficult *Absolute Beginners*, in which he shows a visual style that was willing to go to any length to make a point. Preparing for *Earth Girls*, he seems to have studied *Little Shop of Horrors* and the works of John Waters, and gives us a science fiction musical where the art direction is so flamboyant it should almost be billed along with the actors.

The movie's sense of fun is infectious, and saves the material when it starts to sag. Geena Davis is a manifestly happy young woman, and her joy of performance spills over into her character and inspires the actors around her, so that although the movie sometimes gets giggly it never gets distracted or loses its energy level. *Earth Girls Are Easy* is silly and predictable and as permanent as a feather in the wind, but I had fun watching it.

Easy Money ★ ★ ½
R, 95 m., 1983

Rodney Dangerfield (Monty Capuletti), Joe Pesci (Nicky Cerone), Geraldine Fitzgerald (Mrs. Monahan), Candy Azzara (Rose), Taylor Negron (Julio), Jennifer Jason Leigh (Allison). Directed by James Signorelli and produced by John Nicoletta. Screenplay by Dangerfield, Michael Enderl, P.J. O'Rourke, and Dennis Blair.

Easy Money is an off-balance and disjointed movie, but that's sort of okay, since it's about an off-balance and disjointed kinda guy. The credits call him Monty Capuletti, but he is clearly Rodney Dangerfield, gloriously playing himself as the nearest thing we are likely to get to W.C. Fields in this lifetime.

The movie's plot is simply a line to hang gags on. It stars Rodney as a baby photographer whose rich mother-in-law leaves him an inheritance of a $10 million department store. He can collect—but only if he stops drinking, gambling, smoking dope, running around late, and betting on the horses. This is a very tall order, but Rodney tries to fill it. The movie surrounds Dangerfield with a lot of good New York character actors, who populate the endless poker games and saloon scenes his life revolves around. There's also a very funny sequence involving his daughter's wedding to a Puerto Rican, an alliance that inspires a great backyard wedding party scene.

Because Rodney is Rodney, I laughed a lot during this movie. But I left it feeling curiously unsatisfied. I think maybe that was for two reasons: Because the movie introduces too many subplots that it never really deals with, and because Rodney isn't allowed to be hateful enough. First, the plot. I have the strangest feeling that *Easy Money* once had a much longer script than it has now. There are big scenes (like one where the Puerto Rican groom is sneaking into the bathroom) that end abruptly without a payoff or follow-through. There are whole sequences (like the department store's fashion show, based on Rodney's wardrobe) that seem to coexist uneasily with the rest of the movie. And the movie doesn't get enough comic mileage out of Rodney's attempt to quit drinking, smoking, and gambling (think of the fun you could have with Dangerfield attending an A.A. meeting).

Second, Rodney. I like him best when he's cynical and hard-edged. The Dangerfield of his concerts and records has been smoothed out for this movie, into a slightly more lovable guy. It looks like a masterstroke to make Rodney a baby photographer (think of W.C. Fields in that role), but not enough is done with it. He occasionally loses his temper at the little monsters, but he never seems to detest and despise them enough to be really funny. That's a problem. If you are a Rodney Dangerfield fan, it will not be insurmountable. If you are not a Dangerfield fan, of course, probably nothing on earth could induce you to go to this movie. The great Dangerfield movie, however, has still to be made. This one doesn't get quite enough respect.

Eating Raoul ★ ★
R, 87 m., 1983

Paul Bartel (Paul Bland), Mary Woronov (Mary Bland), Robert Beltran (Raoul). Directed by Paul Bartel. Screenplay by Bartel and Richard Blackburn.

Eating Raoul is one of the more deadpan black comedies I've seen: It tries to position itself somewhere between the bizarre and the banal, and most of the time, it succeeds. This has got to be the first low-key, laid-back comedy about murder, swingers' ads, and dominating women. Problem is, it's so laidback it eventually gets monotonous. If the style and pacing had been as outrageous as the subject matter, we might have had something really amazing here.

The movie's about a happily married couple, Paul and Mary Bland, who are victims of bad times. Paul gets fired from his job in the liquor store, and there's just not much work around for a dilettante with no skills. He's spent his last rent money when providence suggests a way for the Blands to support themselves. A lecherous swinger from the upstairs apartment tries to assault Mary, and Paul bops him over the head with the frying pan. The swinger dies, and the Blands overcome their horror long enough to check out his wallet. He's loaded.

What the movie does next is to present the most outrageous events in the most matter-of-fact manner. The Blands hit upon a scheme to take ads in swingers' tabloids, lure victims to their apartment, tap them over the head with the trusty skillet, and rob them. The only problem is disposing of their victims' bodies. That's where Raoul comes in. He's a locksmith who discovers the Blands' dirty little secret and offers to sell the bodies to a dog-food factory. All's well until Raoul becomes smitten with Mary. Then Paul grows jealous, especially when he discovers that Raoul has been stealing from them. The next step is perhaps suggested by the title of the movie, or perhaps not—I wouldn't want to give anything away.

The plot of *Eating Raoul* reminds me a little of *Motel Hell*, that truly ghastly movie about a farmer who kidnapped his motel customers, buried them in the garden up to their necks, force-fed them until they were plump, and then turned them into sausages. (His motto: "It takes lots of critters to make Farmer Vincent's fritters.") I liked *Motel Hell* more than *Eating Raoul*, however, because it had the courage of its execrable taste. *Eating Raoul*, on the other hand, wants to be an almost whimsical black comedy. It's got its tongue so firmly in cheek there's no room for Raoul. The movie's got some really funny stuff in it, and I liked a lot of it, and I wouldn't exactly advise not seeing it, but it doesn't quite go that last mile. It doesn't reach for the truly unacceptable excesses, the transcendent breaches of taste, that might have made it inspired instead of merely clever.

Educating Rita ★ ★
PG, 110 m., 1983

Michael Caine (Dr. Frank Bryant), Julie Walters (Rita). Directed and produced by Lewis Gilbert. Screenplay by Willy Russell.

If only I'd been able to believe they were actually reading the books, then everything else would have fallen into place. But I didn't believe it. And so *Educating Rita*, which might have been a charming human comedy, disintegrated into a forced march through a formula relationship. The movie stars Michael Caine as a British professor of literature and Julie Walters as the simple cockney girl who comes to him for tutorial lessons. She has problems: She is a working-class punk with an unimaginative husband. He has problems: He is a drunk whose only friends are cheating on him with each other. They have problems: Walters begins to idealize Caine, who then falls in love with her.

Perhaps it would be more accurate to say they both fall into love with the remake job they'd like to do on each other. Caine sees Walters as a fresh, honest, unspoiled intelligence. She sees him as a man who ought to sober up and return to his first love, writing poems. The idea of the curmudgeon and the cockney was not new when Bernard Shaw wrote *Pygmalion*, and it is not any newer in *Educating Rita*. But it could have been entertaining, if only I'd believed they were reading those books. They pass the books back and forth a lot. They sometimes read a line or two. There is a lot of talk about Blake this and Wordsworth that. But it's all magic. The books are like incantations that, used properly, will exorcise cockney accents and alcoholism. But the movie doesn't really believe that, so it departs from the stage play to bring in a lot of phony distractions.

The original *Educating Rita*, a long-running London stage hit by Willy Russell, had only the two characters. They were on the stage together for a long time, and by the end of the play we had shared in their developing relationship. Russell's movie rewrite has added mistresses, colleagues, husbands, in-laws, students, and a faculty committee, all unnecessary.

To the degree that *Educating Rita* does work, the credit goes to Michael Caine, who plays a man weary and kind, funny and self-hating. There is a real character there, just as there was in Caine's boozy diplomat in *Beyond the Limit*. In both movies, though, the characters are not well-served by the story. They're made to deliver speeches, take positions, and make decisions that are required by the plot, not by their own inner promptings. When Caine's professor, at the end of this movie, flies off to Australia to maybe sober up and maybe make a fresh start, it's a total cop-out—not by him, but by the screenplay. Maybe that's what happens when you start with an idealistic, challenging idea, and then cynically try to broaden its appeal.

Edward Scissorhands ★ ★
PG-13, 105 m., 1990

Johnny Depp (Edward Scissorhands), Winona Ryder (Kim), Dianne Wiest (Peg), Anthony Michael Hall (Jim), Kathy Baker (Joyce), Vincent Price (The Inventor), Alan Arkin (Bill). Directed by Tim Burton and produced by Denise Di Novi and Burton. Screenplay by Caroline Thompson.

The director, Tim Burton, wages valiant battle to show us new and wonderful things. In a Hollywood that placidly recycles the same old images, Burton uses special effects and visual tricks to create sights that have never been seen before. That is the good news. The disappointment is that Burton has not yet found the storytelling and character-building strength to go along with his pictorial flair.

That was true even of his *Batman*, which was the all-time box office champion, but could have been a better film, I believe, if there had been anyone in it to inspire our emotional commitment. Even comic characters can make us care. Unlike Richard Donner's original *Superman*, which actually had a heart beneath its special effects, Burton's *Batman* occupied a terrain in which every character was a grotesque of one sort or another, and all of their actions were inspired by shallow, melodramatic motivations.

That movie was stolen by a supporting character—Jack Nicholson's Joker—and now comes *Edward Scissorhands*, another inventive effort in which the hero is strangely remote and inaccessible. He is intended, I think, as an everyman, a universal figure like one of the silent movie clowns, who exists on a different plane from the people he meets in his adventures. One problem is that the other people are as weird, in their ways, as he is: Everyone in this film is stylized and peculiar, so he becomes another exhibit in the menagerie, instead of a commentary on it.

The movie takes place in an entirely artificial world, where a haunting gothic castle crouches on a mountaintop high above a storybook suburb, a goofy sitcom neighborhood where all of the houses are shades of pastels and all of the inhabitants seem to be emotional clones of the Jetsons. The warmest and most human resident of this suburb is the Avon lady (Dianne Wiest), who comes calling one day at the castle—not even its forbidding facade can deter her—and finds it occupied only by a lonely young man named Edward (Johnny Depp).

His story, told in a flashback, is a sad one. He was created by a mad inventor (Vincent Price), who was almost finished with his task when he died, leaving Edward with temporary scissors in place of real hands. One look at Edward and we see that scissors are inconvenient substitutes for fingers: His face is a mass of scars, and he tends to shred everything he tries to pick up.

The Avon lady isn't fazed. She bundles Edward into her car and drives him back down the mountain to join her family, which includes daughter Kim (Winona Ryder) and husband Bill (Alan Arkin). The neighbors in this suburb are insatiably curious, led by a nosy parker named Joyce (Kathy Baker). The movie then develops into a series of situations that seem inspired by silent comedy, as when Edward tries to pick up a pea.

Successful satire has to have a place to stand, and a target to aim at. The entire world of *Edward Scissorhands* is satire, and so Edward inhabits it, rather than taking aim at it. Even if he lived in a more hospitable world, however, it is hard to tell what satirical comment Edward would have to make, because the movie makes an abrupt switch in his character about two-thirds of the way through. Until then he's been a gentle, goofy soul, a quixotic outsider. Then Burton and his writer, Caroline Thompson, go on autopilot and paste in a standard Hollywood ending.

You know what that is. The hero and the villain meet, there is a deadly confrontation, and no prizes for guessing who wins. Except in pure action films, situations used to be solved by dialogue and plot developments. No more. Now someone is killed, and that's the solution, and the movie is over. In *Edward Scissorhands*, the villain is a neighborhood lout named Jim (Anthony Michael Hall), who doesn't like guys with scissors for hands and picks on Edward until finally there is a trumped-up fight to the finish up at the castle. This conclusion is so lame it's disheartening. Surely anyone clever enough to dream up Edward Scissorhands should be swift enough to think of a payoff that involves our imagination.

All of Burton's movies look great. *Pee-wee's Big Adventure* was an unalloyed visual delight, and so was *Beetlejuice*. And *Batman* gave us a Gotham City that was one of the most original and atmospheric places I've seen in the movies. But shouldn't there be something more? Some attempt to make the characters more than caricatures? All of the central characters in a Burton film—Pee-wee, the demon Betelgeuse, Batman, the Joker, or Edward Scissorhands—exist in personality vacuums; they're self-contained oddities with no connection to the real world. It's saying something about a director's work when the most well-rounded and socialized hero in any of his films is Pee-wee Herman.

Eight Men Out ★ ★
PG, 120 m., 1988

John Cusack (Buck Weaver), Don Harvey (Swede Risberg), John Mahoney (Kid Gleason), James Read (Lefty Williams), Michael Rooker (Chick Gandil), Charlie Sheen (Hap Felsch), David Strathairn (Eddie Cicotte), D.B. Sweeney ("Shoeless" Joe Jackson), John Sayles (Ring Lardner), Studs Terkel (Hugh Fullerton), Christopher Lloyd (Bill Burns), Clifton James (Charles Comiskey). Directed by John Sayles and produced by Sarah Pillsbury and Midge Sanford. Screenplay by Sayles.

Eight Men Out is an oddly unfocused movie, made of earth tones, sidelong glances, and elliptic conversations. It tells the story of how the stars of the 1919 Chicago White Sox team took payoffs from gamblers to throw the World Series, but if you are not already familiar with that story, you're unlikely to understand it after seeing this film. It's an insider's movie, a baseball expert's film that is hard for the untutored to follow.

Watching the movie, I gained a new appreciation for the old-fashioned Hollywood style of telling a story, in which, right near the beginning, we'd get a big close-up of each of the key characters, and somebody would call them by name or describe them. You know, something like, "See that fella over there? That's Shoeless Joe Jackson. He's one of the greatest fielders who ever lived, but they say he doesn't even know how to write his own name." By the half-hour mark in *Eight Men Out*, I had little idea who the individual players were, and I wasn't helped by the fact that many of the actors seemed to resemble each other. It was only days later, reading the press notes, that I realized that the character played by the movie's director, John Sayles, was supposed to be the great sportswriter Ring Lardner. He hangs out throughout the film with a buddy named Hugh Fullerton, who is played by Studs Terkel and was one of the sportswriters who uncovered the scandal—but how many people can be expected to know that today? On the evidence of the movie itself, Sayles and Terkel are playing a sort of Greek chorus, their heads bent toward each other as they exchange laconic asides on the action.

That's not a criticism of their performances—it was great to see Terkel chewing his cigar and looking as if he'd seen it all—but of the screenplay. If you're going to make a movie about a baseball scandal that happened before most of the audience was born, you'd better start by making it understandable, and then move on to considerations of art and drama.

Perhaps the problem is that Sayles, who wrote as well as directed the film, was so close to the material that he never decided what the focus of his story really was. Early in the film, we get a lot of vignettes designed to give us a flavor for professional baseball at the time, and they're intercut with short personal or domestic scenes in which the characters are established, not very clearly.

Then a villain emerges: Charles Comiskey, the "Old Roman," who owned the club and treated his players like slaves. When they won the pennant, he sent them flat champagne. If he promised a pitcher a $10,000 bonus for winning thirty games, he'd bench him after his twenty-ninth victory. The movie argues that there would have been no "Black Sox" scandal if Comiskey had shown the proper respect for the greatest baseball team of its era.

Well, maybe so. But then various big-time gamblers swim in and out of focus, making cash offers and arguing that everyone was going to be in on the deal. Are they villains, too, or only pirates? It's hard to believe they expected to get away with their audacious plan, especially given the way that Sayles presents the key plays in the World Series. The Sox players are so obviously throwing the game, with deliberate and not even subtle errors, that it's hard to imagine that anyone could have been fooled, even for a second.

Then there's a courtroom scene, which is less about baseball than about the standard clichés of all courtroom scenes. And the introduction of Judge Kenesaw Mountain Landis, who was signed up as the first baseball commissioner in an attempt by the owners to clean up the image of their sport. Although the Black Sox were found innocent in court, he banned them from big-league baseball all the same. His action was probably illegal, but it established a precedent that survived for many years, in which the government overlooked the way Major League Baseball has established a monopoly and was denying its player-employees their basic constitutional rights. All of this is true, but is it made clear in the movie? Not very.

84 Charing Cross Road ★ ★
PG, 99 m., 1987

Anne Bancroft (Helene Hanff), Anthony Hopkins (Frank Doel), Judi Dench (Nora Doel), Jean De Baer (Maxine Bellamy), Maurice Denham (George Martin). Directed by David Jones and produced by Geoffrey Helman. Screenplay by Hugh Whitemore.

Miss Fiske would have loved this movie. And I would have loved seeing it with her, through her eyes. I almost even loved it myself, because *84 Charing Cross Road* is a movie made for people who love London and books. The only problem is that the heroine doesn't get to London until it's too late, and nobody ever seems to read in this movie.

The film is based on a hit London and New York play, which was based on a best-selling book. Given the thin and unlikely subject matter, that's already a series of miracles. And yet there are people who are pushovers for this material. I should know. I read the book and I saw the play and now the movie, and I still don't think the basic idea is sound.

The story begins in the years right after World War II, when London was still gripped by food rationing and pocked by bomb craters. A New York woman (Anne Bancroft), who loves books but cannot afford expensive ones, sees an ad in *Saturday Review* for a London bookstore. She sends them her want list and is soon delighted to receive a package of used books—good readable editions, cheap. She begins a correspondence with the bookseller (Anthony Hopkins), and thus commences a relationship that lasts for years without the two people ever meeting each other.

There is not a lot of drama in this story. Most of the action takes place in the post office. The director, David Jones, does what he can. His previous film was Harold Pinter's *Betrayal*, which was a love story told

backward, beginning with the unhappy conclusion and ending with the lovers' first kiss. Now he has a love story in which the lovers do not meet. What can he look forward to next: autoeroticism?

Bancroft sends care packages of ham to postwar England. Hopkins sends precious editions of Boswell, Chesterton, and Cardinal Newman ("Dear John Henry," Bancroft calls him). Bancroft leads a lonely life in a New York apartment. Hopkins occupies a silent marriage in a London bedroom suburb. After many years, Hopkins dies and then Bancroft finally goes to London and visits the now-empty bookstore.

Sigh. Miss Fiske, whom you may remember from the first paragraph of this review, was the librarian at the Urbana Free Library when I was growing up. She instilled such a love of books in me that I still search used bookstores for the adventures of the Melendy Family by Elizabeth Enright; those were the first "real books" I read. Miss Fiske ran the book club and the Saturday morning puppet shows and the book fairs and the story readings. She never had to talk to me about the love of books because she simply exuded it and I absorbed it.

She would have loved this movie. Sitting next to her, I suspect, I would have loved it, too. But Miss Fiske is gone now, and I found it pretty slow going on my own. And for that matter, Miss Fiske had a sharp critical intelligence, and I suspect that after seeing this movie she would have nodded and said she enjoyed it, but then she might have added, "Why didn't that silly woman get on the boat and go to London ten years sooner and save herself all that postage?"

84 Charlie Mopic ★ ★ ★
R, 95 m., 1989

Jonathan Emerson (LT), Nicholas Cascone (Easy), Jason Tomlins (Pretty Boy), Christopher Burgard (Hammer), Glenn Morshower (Cracker), Richard Brooks (OD), Byron Thames (MoPic). Directed by Patrick Duncan and produced by Michael Nolin. Screenplay by Duncan.

Patrick Duncan's *84 Charlie Mopic* was directed by a veteran of combat in Vietnam, and Duncan is at such pains to provide us with the infantryman's point of view that he literally takes a 16mm camera along on a reconnaissance mission in the field. The premise of the movie is that a documentary

("mopic") is being made about a patrol—and all of the footage in the film is seen through a camera being carried along by a filmmaker assigned to the unit.

It's a style that makes the action feel immediate and unrehearsed; the other soldiers address the camera as if they're talking to the man who's carrying it, and the effect is that they're talking to us. The strength here is that the movie seems to happen as we watch it. The trade-off is that the director has less freedom to pick and choose his shots for dramatic effect; once he establishes the point of view, he's stuck with it.

The first-person point of view has rarely been used for an entire film (Robert Montgomery made the camera into a private eye in *Lady in the Lake*, and Orson Welles once wanted to film *Heart of Darkness* through the eyes of various protagonists including a bird), but Duncan's angle in *84 Charlie Mopic* is intriguing: By explaining the presence of the camera, he gives a realistic basis to the technique, instead of using it as pure style.

The story of *84 Charlie Mopic* is not original, nor was it meant to be. Anyone who has seen a fair number of war films will recognize the various types of characters in the platoon—the natural leader, the newcomer, the scared youngster—but what is original to this film is the sense of reality that Duncan is able to recapture. The types are familiar but what happens to them is not predictable, and the story takes the sudden, unexpected turns of real warfare rather than the manufactured developments of a Hollywood plot. As the patrol gets lost in the Central Highlands of Vietnam and finds itself in deeper and deeper trouble, we begin to feel the senselessness of their mission; their training helps them only to a point, and then they are in the hands of luck, or fate.

All of this is seen through the eyes of "MoPic," the cameraman, and what makes his subjective camera convincing is that he is not simply recording the action, but trying to make a documentary which can be used as a training film for other infantrymen. The six members of the reconnaissance unit are more or less experienced in the field, and they share their experience and lore with the camera; it's like giving a briefing to trainees. The film is filled with dozens of tiny details that only a field veteran like Duncan would know about—the danger of smoking, for example, when cigarettes can be smelled on the wind for hundreds of yards, and instantly identified as American tobacco. This kind of minutiae somehow adds up to more suspense than any number of mysterious shadows in the jungle.

The subjective camera is probably responsible for many of the weaknesses of *84 Charlie Mopic*, as well as its strengths. Duncan knows more about war than he knows about dramatic construction, and this shows in the way he builds the various relationships in the movie. There are a few too many speeches which are "overheard" by the camera—speeches that provide background information which the characters would probably not provide in quite that way. There are conflicts and tensions within the group, and sometimes we can feel them being created and manipulated by the script. If the genius of the movie is to show the unit through a camera, the movie's failure is to trust that approach enough. The development of the conflicts and character backgrounds should have been more subtle and offhand, as they might have been in real life.

Still, *84 Charlie Mopic* deserves a place by itself among the films about Vietnam. It is a brave and original attempt to record nothing more or less than the actual daily experience of a unit on patrol, drawn out of the memories of men who were there. I've never seen a combat movie that seemed this close to actual experience, to the kinds of hard lessons that soldiers are taught by their enemies. The filmmakers have earned their right to shoot with a subjective camera—because the eyes we are really seeing through are their own.

El Norte ★ ★ ★ ★
R, 141 m., 1983

Zaide Silvia Gutierrez (Rosa), David Villalpando (Enrique), Ernesto Gomez Cruz (Father), Alicia del Lago (Mother), Trinidad Silva (Monty). Directed by Gregory Nava and produced by Anna Thomas. Screenplay by Nava and Thomas.

From the very first moments of *El Norte*, we know that we are in the hands of a great movie. It tells a simple story in such a romantic and poetic way that we are touched, deeply and honestly, and we know we will remember the film for a long time. The movie tells the story of two young Guatemalans, a brother and sister named Rosa and Enrique, and of their long trek up through Mexico to *el Norte*—the United States. Their journey begins in a small village and ends in

Los Angeles, and their dream is the American Dream.

But *El Norte* takes place in the present, when we who are already Americans are not so eager for others to share our dream. Enrique and Rosa are not brave immigrants who could have been our forefathers, but two young people alive now, who look through the tattered pages of an old *Good Housekeeping* for their images of America. One of the most interesting things about the film is the way it acknowledges all of the political realities of Latin America and yet resists being a "political" film. It tells its story through the eyes of its heroes, and it is one of the rare films that grants Latin Americans full humanity. They are not condescended to, they are not made to symbolize something, they are not glorified, they are simply themselves.

The movie begins in the fields where Arturo, their father, is a *bracero*—a pair of arms. He goes to a meeting to protest working conditions and is killed. Their mother disappears. Enrique and Rosa, who are in their late teens, decide to leave their village and go to America. The first part of the film shows their life in Guatemala with some of the same beauty and magical imagery of Gabriel Garcia Marquez's *One Hundred Years of Solitude*. The middle section shows them going by bus and foot up through Mexico, which is as harsh on immigrants from the South as America is. At the border they try to hire a "coyote" to guide them across, and they finally end up crawling to the promised land through a rat-infested drainage tunnel.

The final section of the film takes place in Los Angeles, which they first see as a glittering carpet of lights, but which quickly becomes a cheap motel for day laborers, and a series of jobs in the illegal, shadow job market. Enrique becomes a waiter. Rosa becomes a maid. Because they are attractive, intelligent, and have a certain naive nerve, they succeed for a time, before the film's sad, poetic ending.

El Norte is a great film, one of 1983's best, for two different kinds of reasons. One is its stunning visual and musical power; the approach of the film is not quasi-documentary, but poetic, with fantastical images that show us the joyous hearts of these two people.

The second reason is that this is the first film to approach the subject of "undocumented workers" solely through *their* eyes. This is not one of those docu-dramas where we half-expect a test at the end, but a film

like *The Grapes of Wrath* that gets inside the hearts of its characters and lives with them.

The movie was directed by Gregory Nava and produced by Anna Thomas, who wrote it together. It's been described by *Variety* as the "first American independent epic," and it is indeed an epic film made entirely outside the studio system by two gifted filmmakers (their credits include *The Confessions of Amans*, which won a Gold Hugo at the Chicago Film Festival, and *The Haunting of M*, one of my favorite films from 1979). This time, with a larger budget and a first-rate cast, they have made their breakthrough into the first ranks of filmmaking.

The Electric Horseman ★ ★ ★
PG, 120 m., 1979

Robert Redford (Sonny), Jane Fonda (Hallie), Valerie Perrine (Charlotta), Willie Nelson (Wendell), John Saxon (Hunt Sears), Nicolas Coster (Fitzgerald). Directed by Sydney Pollack and produced by Ray Stark. Screenplay by Robert Garland.

The Electric Horseman is the kind of movie they used to make. It's an oddball love story about a guy and a girl and a prize racehorse, and it has a chase scene and some smooching and a happy ending. It could have starred Tracy and Hepburn, or Gable and Colbert, but it doesn't need to because this time it stars Robert Redford and Jane Fonda.

The movie almost willfully wants to be old-fashioned. It's got bad guys from a big corporation, and big kisses seen in silhouette in the sunset, and it works Fonda and Redford for all the star quality they've got. But *The Electric Horseman* doesn't try to be completely guileless. It has a bunch of contemporary themes and causes to dress up its basic situation—which is, let's face it, Girl meets Boy (and Horse). And although we are never for a moment in doubt about the happy ending, there *is* a certain basic suspense as Redford and Fonda head for the hills and the evil corporation follows by helicopter.

The movie begins with Redford in the process of downfall. He plays a former five-time national champion rodeo cowboy named Sonny, who has retired from competition and signed on as the spokesman for a cereal named "Ranch Breakfast." This is some cereal. It is fortified, we gather, not only with vitamins, minerals, and bran, but also with leather, nails, and sagebrush. Redford makes personal appearances on behalf of the cereal, wearing a garish electrified cowboy suit that plugs into the saddle of his horse. The cowboy outfit isn't the only thing that's lit up: Redford's drunk most of the time, and ignominiously falls off his horse during a half-time show.

Things come to a climax during a big Las Vegas convention sponsored by the conglomerate that owns Ranch Breakfast. Redford's supposed to ride onstage on a multimillion-dollar champion racehorse. But he has a run-in with the president of the conglomerate, discovers that the horse is drugged and on steroids, and decides to make his own personal gesture of defiance. He rides onstage, all right—and right offstage, too, and down the Vegas strip, and out into the desert.

Jane Fonda plays a TV newswoman who's covering the convention, and she does some clever detective work to figure out where Redford might be headed. And then the movie's more or less predictable: Fonda finds Redford, grows to share his indignation at how the horse has been treated, and trades her loyalty for exclusive rights to the story. It turns out to be a really big story, of course, as the conglomerate tries to track down its racehorse and the TV networks get in a race to find Redford.

If you spend much time scrutinizing the late show on television, some of this material might not sound dazzlingly original. The device of the famous runaway with a journalist in hot pursuit, for example, is straight out of It Happened One Night—and as Fonda calls her office from remote pay phones, we're reminded of Clark Gable in exactly the same situations. The notion of the last of the cowboys heading for the hills and being tracked by helicopters is also familiar; it's from Lonely Are the Brave, with Kirk Douglas, and some of the shots look hauntingly familiar.

The relationship between Fonda and Redford is also pretty basic stuff, in which the gruff outdoorsman and the perfect lady grow to respect each other while sharing the rigors of life on the run. Bogart and Hepburn made that relationship a classic in The African Queen, but Redford and Fonda have much the same chemistry. Remember that scene on the boat with Hepburn putting her chin in her hand and giving Bogart the old onceover? Fonda does that to Redford, and it's about as erotic as six of your average love scenes.

Both Redford and Fonda have identified themselves with a lot of the issues in this movie (which are—I have a list right here—the evils of corporate conglomeratism, the preservation of our wild lands, respect for animals, the phoniness of commercialism, the pack instinct of TV journalism, and nutritious breakfasts). But although this is a movie filled with messages, it's not a message movie. The characters and plot seem to tapdance past the serious stuff and concentrate on the human relationships.

If Electric Horseman has a flaw, it's that the movie's so warm and cozy it can hardly be electrifying. The director, Sydney Pollack, gives us solid entertainment, but he doesn't take chances and he probably didn't intend to. He's an ideal choice for orchestrating Redford and Fonda; he directed Fonda in They Shoot Horses, Don't They? and has made a subsidiary career out of directing Redford (in This Property is Condemned, Jeremiah Johnson, The Way We Were, and Three Days of the Condor). He has grown up with them, he respects the solidity of their screen personas, and he seems to understand (as the directors of Bogart, Hepburn, Gable, et al., did in the forties) that if you have the right Boy and the right Girl and the right story, about all you have to do is stay out of the way of the Horse.

The Elephant Man ★ ★
PG, 123 m., 1980

Anthony Hopkins (Frederick Treves), John Hurt (John Merrick), Anne Bancroft (Mrs. Kendal), John Gielgud (Carr Gomm). Directed by David Lynch and produced by Jonathan Sanger. Screenplay by Christopher DeVore, Eric Bergren, and Lynch.

The film of The Elephant Man is not based on the successful stage play of the same name, but they both draw their sources from the life of John Merrick, the original "elephant man," whose rare disease imprisoned him in a cruelly misformed body. Both the play and the movie adopt essentially the same point of view, that we are to honor Merrick because of the courage with which he faced his existence.

The Elephant Man forces me to question this position on two grounds: first, on the meaning of Merrick's life, and second, on the ways in which the film employs it. It is conventional to say that Merrick, so hideously misformed that he was exhibited as a sideshow attraction, was courageous. No doubt he was. But there is a distinction here that needs to be drawn, between the courage of a man who chooses to face hardship for a good purpose, and the courage of a man who is simply doing the best he can, under the circumstances.

Wilfrid Sheed, an American novelist who is crippled by polio, once discussed this distinction in a Newsweek essay. He is sick and tired, he wrote, of being praised for his "courage," when he did not choose to contract polio and has little choice but to deal with his handicaps as well as he can. True courage, he suggests, requires a degree of choice. Yet the whole structure of The Elephant Man is based on a life that is said to be courageous, not because of the hero's achievements, but simply because of the bad trick played on him by fate. In the film and the play (which are similar in many details), John Merrick learns to move in society, to have ladies in to tea, to attend the theater, and to build a scale model of a cathedral. Merrick may have had greater achievements in real life, but the film glosses them over. How, for example, did he learn to speak so well and eloquently? History tells us that the real Merrick's jaw was so misshapen that an operation was necessary just to allow him to talk. In the film, however, after a few snuffles to warm up, he quotes the Twenty-Third Psalm and Romeo and Juliet. This is pure sentimentalism.

The film could have chosen to develop the relationship between Merrick and his medical sponsor, Dr. Frederick Treves, along the lines of the bond between doctor and child in Truffaut's The Wild Child. It could have bluntly dealt with the degree of Merrick's inability to relate to ordinary society, as in Werner Herzog's Kaspar Hauser. Instead, it makes him noble and celebrates his nobility.

I kept asking myself what the film was really trying to say about the human condition as reflected by John Merrick, and I kept drawing blanks. The film's philosophy is this shallow: (1) Wow, the Elephant Man sure looked hideous, and (2) gosh, isn't it wonderful how he kept on in spite of everything? This last is in spite of a real possibility that John Merrick's death at twenty-seven might have been suicide.

The film's technical credits are adequate. John Hurt is very good as Merrick, somehow projecting a humanity past the disfiguring makeup, and Anthony Hopkins is correctly aloof and yet venal as the doctor. The direction, by David (Eraserhead) Lynch, is competent, although he gives us an inexcusable opening scene in which Merrick's mother is trampled or scared by elephants or raped—who knows?—and an equally idiotic closing scene in which Merrick becomes the Star Child from *2001*, or something.

Emmanuelle ★ ★ ★
x, 92 m., 1975

Sylvia Kristel (Emmanuelle), Alain Cuny (Mario), Marika Green (Bee), Daniel Sarky (Jean), Jeanne Colletin (Ariane), Christine Boisson (Marie-Ange). Directed by Just Jaeckin and produced by Yves Rousset-Rouard. Screenplay by Jean-Louis Richard.

Emmanuelle is a silly, classy, enjoyable erotic film that became an all-time box-office success in France. It's not remotely significant enough to deserve that honor, but in terms of its genre (soft-core skin flick) it's very well done: lushly photographed on location in Thailand, filled with attractive and intriguing people, and scored with brittle, teasing music. Now that hard-core porno has become passé, it's a relief to see a movie that drops the gynecology and returns to a certain amount of sexy sophistication.

There have been movies influenced by other movies, and directors influenced by other directors, but *Emmanuelle* may be the first movie influenced by magazine centerfolds. Its style of color photography seems directly ripped off from the centerfolds in *Penthouse*, including even the props and decor. Its characters (French diplomats and—especially—their women in Thailand) inhabit a world of wicker furniture, soft pastels, vaguely Victorian lingerie, backlighting, forests of potted plants, and lots of diaphanous draperies shifting in the breeze. It's a world totally devoid of any real content, of course, and Emmanuelle is right at home in it. She's the young, virginal wife of a diplomat, and has just flown out from Paris to rejoin him. Her husband refuses to be possessive, and indeed almost propels her into a dizzying series of sexual encounters that range from the merely kinky to the truly bizarre. In the midst of this erotic maelstrom, Emmanuelle somehow retains her innocence.

The director, Just Jaeckin, correctly understands that gymnastics and heavy breathing do not an erotic movie make, nor does excessive attention to gynecological detail. Carefully deployed clothing can,

indeed, be more erotic than plain nudity, and the decor in *Emmanuelle* also tends to get into the act. Jaeckin is a master of establishing situations; the seduction of Emmanuelle on the airplane, for example, is all the more effective because of its forbidden nature. And the encounter after the boxing match (Emmanuelle is the prize for the winning fighter and tenderly licks the sweat from his eyebrow) is given a rather startling voyeuristic touch (the spectators don't leave after the fight).

The movie's first hour or so is largely given over to lesbian situations, but then Emmanuelle comes under the influence of the wise old Mario (played by Alain Cuny, the French actor immortalized as Steiner, the intellectual who committed suicide in Fellini's *La Dolce Vita*). She is turned off at first by his age, but with age, she is assured, comes experience, and does it ever. Mario delivers himself of several profoundly meaningless generalizations about finding oneself through others and attaining true freedom, and then he introduces her to a series of photogenic situations. Mario's philosophy is frankly foolish, but Cuny delivers it with such solemn, obsessed conviction that the scenes become a parody, and *Emmanuelle*'s comic undertones are preserved.

What also makes the film work is the performance of Sylvia Kristel as Emmanuelle. She's a slender actress who isn't even the prettiest woman in the film, but she projects a certain vulnerability that makes several of the scenes work. The performers in most skin flicks seem so impervious to ordinary mortal failings, so blasé in the face of the most outrageous sexual invention, that finally they just become cartoon characters. Kristel actually seems to be present in the film, and as absorbed in its revelations as we are. It's a relief, during a time of cynicism in which sex is supposed to sell anything, to find a skin flick that's a lot better than it probably had to be.

Empire of the Sun ★ ★ ½
PG, 152 m., 1987

Christian Bale (Jim Graham), John Malkovich (Basie), Nigel Havers (Dr. Rawlins). Directed by Steven Spielberg and produced by Spielberg, Kathleen Kennedy, and Frank Marshall. Screenplay by Tom Stoppard.

Day and night, the boy dreams of flying. He knows the names of all the airplanes, and can

spot them by their silhouettes. When planes fly overhead in Shanghai in the last days before the war breaks out, they may be an ominous omen for his parents, but for him they are wondrous great machines, free of gravity, free to soar.

The boy's parents are wealthy British citizens who enjoy a life of great luxury in Shanghai, a life in which limousines hurry them through the crowded streets to business meetings and masquerade balls, and you hardly need notice the ordinary people in those streets. Sometimes the Chinese press too close to the car, sometimes they hold up traffic, but mostly they are simply invisible—until war breaks out, and the boy's whole world is shattered.

The most agonizing moment in Steven Spielberg's *Empire of the Sun* comes near the beginning, as the streets of Shanghai are filled with a panic-stricken mob, and the boy is separated from his parents as they flee to sanctuary. One moment his mother has him by the hand, and the next moment he has dropped his toy airplane and stooped to pick it up, and they are separated by five thousand frightened people, never to see each other again until the war is over.

The boy is lost, left behind, and finally placed in a Japanese prisoner of war camp. His story is based on the autobiographical novel by J.G. Ballard, who actually lived through a similar experience as an adolescent, but if Ballard had not written his novel, Spielberg might have been forced to, because the story is so close to his heart. Not only do we have the familiar Spielberg theme of a child searching for his parents, but we also have the motif of the magic above reality—the escape mechanism into a more perfect world, a world that may be represented by visitors from another planet, or time travel, or hidden treasure. This time, it is the world of the air, and airplanes.

Life on earth is not so enjoyable for the boy, whose name is Jim, and who is played by Christian Bale with a kind of grim poetry that suggests a young Tom Courtenay. There are no free passes for kids in the prison camp, and Jim soon finds a protector of sorts in Basie, an American prisoner played by John Malkovich with a laconic cynicism. Basie is a merchant seaman and born hustler, and his corner of the prison camp is a miraculous source for Hershey bars and other contraband (in his resourcefulness and capitalistic zeal, he's a reminder of the William Holden character in *Stalag 17*). Basie doesn't exactly play father to the kid; he permits him to exist in his sphere, and to survive.

Jim is a quick learner. Short, fast, and somewhat invisible because of his youth, he has the run of the camp. He knows all the shortcuts and all the scams, and steals to survive. He also dreams of airplanes, although as the months go by, he dreams less frequently of his parents and finally cannot quite even remember their faces. Spielberg portrays the prison camp as another of those typically Hollywood enclosures where the jailers embody cruel authority while somehow permitting the heroes to raise hell and have a relatively good time; like the adolescent in John Boorman's *Hope and Glory*, Jim in *Empire of the Sun* finds that young boys can even enjoy war, up to a point.

The movie is always interesting from a narrative point of view—Spielberg is a good storyteller with a good tale to tell. But it never really adds up to anything. What statement does Spielberg want to make about Jim, if any? That dreams are important? That survival is a virtue? The movie falls into the trap of so many war stories, and turns horror into nostalgia. The process is a familiar one. War experiences are brutal, painful, and tragic, but sometimes they call up the best in human beings, and after the war is over, the survivors eventually begin to yearn for that time when they surpassed themselves, when during better and worse they lived at their peak.

The movie is wonderfully staged and shot, and the prison camp looks and feels like a real place. But Spielberg allows the airplanes, the sun, and the magical yearning to get in his way. Jim has a relationship, at a distance, with a young Asian boy who lives outside the prison fence, and this friendship ends in a scene that is painfully calculated and manipulative. There is another moment, at about the same time in the film, where Jim creeps outside the camp by hiding in a drainage canal, and escapes capture and instant death not because of his wits, but because Spielberg forces a camera angle. And there is the inevitable moment when the boy is associated with a huge telephoto image of the sun, and we respond not to the shot, but to the memory that Spielberg loves huge celestial orbs so passionately that Jim isn't having a spontaneous moment, he's paying homage to the sun of *The Color Purple* and the moon of *E.T.*

The movie's general lack of direction leads to what seems like a series of possible endings; having little clear idea of where he was going, Spielberg isn't sure if he's arrived there. The movie's weakness is a lack of a strong narrative pull from beginning to end. The whole central section is basically just episodic daily prison life and the dreams of the boy. *Empire of the Sun* adds up to a promising idea, a well-seen production, and some interesting performances. But despite the emotional potential in the story, it didn't much move me. Maybe, like the kid, I decided that no world where you can play with airplanes can be all that bad.

Enemies, a Love Story ★ ★ ★ ½
R, 119 m., 1989

Ron Silver (Herman), Anjelica Huston (Tamara), Lena Olin (Masha), Margaret Sophie Stein (Yadwiga), Alan King (Rabbi Lembeck), Judith Malina (Masha's mother). Directed and produced by Paul Mazursky. Screenplay by Roger L. Simon and Mazursky.

Enemies, a Love Story is a movie about a man who ends up being married to three women at the same time, and it should not surprise you that he is not a happy man. He is not surprised. Happiness is not a part of his repertory.

His name is Herman, and there are times when he wonders why he is even alive. He was a Polish Jew during World War II, but he was saved from the camps and certain death because Yadwiga, his family's servant, hid him from the Nazis in the hayloft of a barn. Now it is 1949, and he is living in Coney Island with the woman, having married her and brought her to America after the war.

She is a good woman with a trusting heart, and she adores him. But he does not feel fulfilled by her, and he cheats on her with the zaftig and naughty Masha, his mistress, who lives in the Bronx. Yadwiga reminds him of the past, which cools his passion, and another problem is, she worships him so slavishly that making love with her is like attending devotions to himself.

With Masha it is different. She is a passionate woman, a Jew who also escaped the Nazis, but she doesn't live in the past, and they share a sexual obsession that helps them to exist only in the present—while they're making love, at any event. Masha knows about Yadwiga but doesn't much care. Then she gets pregnant. Herman wants to do the right thing and so he marries her.

This is complicated enough, but then Herman's true first wife, Tamara, unexpectedly turns up in New York. He had been told by eyewitnesses that she died in the camps. But they were wrong. She escaped to Russia and now here she is in New York, scaring the daylights out of poor Yadwiga when she turns up at their door. Yadwiga recognizes her instantly and assumes she is a ghost.

So, three wives. "In America," his first wife, Tamara, tells him, "they have a thing called a manager. That is what you need. I will be your manager, because you are incapable of making your decisions for yourself." She is absolutely correct. She knows him so well that when he first tells her he is married to Yadwiga, she immediately wants to know about the mistress she is sure he must also have.

Paul Mazursky's *Enemies, a Love Story*, based on the novel by Isaac Bashevis Singer, contains the clue to this story in its title. Who are the enemies? The women that Herman loves. Why are they his enemies? Because love presumes commitment, and Herman is not capable of commitment, is not even capable of forming a working faith in the future. Many others have suffered much more at the hands of the Nazis than he did—he was lucky, up there in his hayloft—but he has lived under the threat of death for so long that no relationship can have any meaning for him. As he scurries between his three women, desperately trying to keep all three happy or at least placated, what drives him is not love but guilt.

Guilt he understands. Love is the enemy. Singer is said to have based his novel on several similar stories about Jewish survivors of the Nazis who came to New York City to start over again. In the foreword to his novel, he writes, "The characters are not only Nazi victims, but victims of their own personalities and fates." And that is really the point he has to make: that these people, having been delivered more or less miraculously from death, are nevertheless left with the same character flaws and weaknesses they would have possessed if there had been no Nazis. In other words, they are still possessed of their full, fallible humanity.

Enemies, a Love Story is such an intriguing film because it refuses to be tamed, to settle down into a nice, comforting parable with a lesson to teach us. It is about the tumult of the heart, and Mazursky tells its story without compromise. There is no key to tell us how to feel. No easy laughs as Herman races from one woman to another, but no cheap pathos, either, at their fates. Indeed, this is not even a movie about how the women are victimized; each one receives more or less what her fate has dictated for her, and Herman, who suffers so grievously, is punished mostly by his own knowledge of what a rat he is.

The movie stars four actors in an ensemble that fits so well together that much can be shown without being said. Ron Silver is Herman, harried, desperate, making up lies on pay phones and always hushing one woman while reassuring another. Margaret Sophie Stein is Yadwiga, blond and blue-eyed and forever waxing the floor to make up for being totally intimidated by her husband. Lena Olin (she wore the bowler hat in *The Unbearable Lightness of Being*) is the carnal Masha, whose insouciance disguises a surprising grief. And Anjelica Huston is Tamara, the first wife, the wisest, not only because she knows Herman better than the others, but because she knows herself.

Enemies, a Love Story has been described here and there as a sad movie. That is a very limited view. Parts of it are very funny, as Herman tries to get away with his desperate juggling act. Parts are ironic. Parts, especially the scenes with Huston, are heartwarming in a strange way, because they show one human being accepting the weaknesses of another. Of course there is sadness in the story, and of course such a story cannot end happily. But reflect that these people are lucky to be alive at all, and their stories become almost triumphant. Because a person has survived a great evil does not make a great person—only a lucky one. And if you think Herman's not lucky, well, life's like that. You take your chances.

Everybody's All-American ★ ★
R, 122 m., 1988

Dennis Quaid (Gavin Grey), Jessica Lange (Babs Rogers Grey), Timothy Hutton ("Cake"), John Goodman (Ed Lawrence), Carl Lumbly (Narvel Blue), Raymond Baker (Bolling Kiely), Savannah Boucher (Darlene), Patricia Clarkson (Leslie). Directed by Taylor Hackford and produced by Hackford, Laura Ziskin, and Ian Sander. Screenplay by Tom Rickman.

F. Scott Fitzgerald said that American lives have no second acts. The problem with Gavin Grey's life is that it has four. When we first meet him, in the ecstasy of a championship season, he is a golden boy, "The Grey Ghost," one of the finest football players of the late 1950s, "unanimously twice chosen All-American." Twenty years later, he is a has-been old pro, a pitchman for artificial turf, and a partner in a sports bar and grill. Five years after that, the turf manufacturers have fired him, the restaurant has gone broke, his best buddy has been killed in a fight over gambling debts, and he is looking at his old game films at a class reunion.

Everybody's All-American represents the stories of a lot of great athletes who decline uneasily into the memories of middle age. For every Frank Gifford who finds a career on television, there are a hundred other old pros who do their play-by-plays night after night to a handful of strangers in a bar. As the old pro grows older, so do his listeners, until finally their memories of glorious youth are used as a club to fight off the young. "I've told those stories so many times," the Grey Ghost complains to his wife, "that I've almost forgot it was *me* who had those things happen to him. It seems like somebody else."

The Ghost is played, young and old, by Dennis Quaid, who does a good job of showing a man drifting into compromises. As a hotshot kid, the Ghost walks away from a man who wants to give him a free Chevy convertible. Later in life, after the pro career is over and the restaurant has gone broke, he becomes that man's partner in a restaurant venture—where he's expected to "show himself" and tell the same old stories to the drunks.

What is interesting about the movie is the way it shows the Ghost's gradual disintegration as the result of a series of rational decisions. What is there for an All-American to do, once he's hung up his cleats, and if he has no particular job training? His only skill is to get paid for being himself. The Ghost, however, has been followed through life by ghosts of his own.

One of them is his wife, Babs (Jessica Lange), a bubble-headed beauty queen who bears him four children and matures into a savvy businesswoman who supports the family. Another is Donnie (Timothy Hutton), a cousin who nurses a lifelong flame for Babs but succeeds in luring her away from the Ghost for only one passionate night. The third is Narvel Blue (Carl Lumbly), a black man who was probably as good a football player as the Ghost, but didn't get the chance to prove himself in the segregated South.

After a baptism in the civil rights movement, Blue goes into business instead, and becomes a fast food tycoon (ironically becoming Babs's employer).

Everybody's All-American follows these characters through twenty-five years with the single-mindedness of a John O'Hara. The Ghost's crew cut never changes, but Babs faithfully reflects every passing fashion of clothing and hairstyles, and Donnie, the cousin, has a different haircut every time he turns up in the movie, while his beards and moustaches come and go with bewildering variety. By the end of the film, we not only feel we know these people—we feel we know them too well, and would like to make some new friends.

The movie has too much incident, too much period detail, to support an essentially simple story. John Cheever took a few pages once to write a story about an aging athlete who used to get drunk at parties, line up the furniture, and hurdle it. *Everybody's All-American* tells the same story at such length that by the end even the characters seem to be tiring of their personalities. The relationship between Babs and Donnie, for example, is strung out in a long series of scenes which are all more or less the same, in which Donnie holds love in his heart and Babs stays faithful to the flawed but human Ghost.

One character who does bring life to the movie is Lawrence (John Goodman), a man-mountain who played center on the championship team, and later becomes the Ghost's partner in the restaurant. He gambles away all their savings before being killed by the mob, but while he's onstage he does a good job of reflecting the kind of good-ol'-boy camaraderie that the Ghost requires.

The rest of the movie consists of good performances stranded in scenes that repeat the same insights or lead nowhere. When Donnie doesn't go to Blue's aid in a civil rights riot, for example, he feels guilt ("He looked me straight in the eye. I should have helped him"). But this event is never followed up on, never referred to again, never given a payoff. There are lots of moments like that. *Everybody's All-American* is a good idea, well-acted, but the screenplay is so unfocused we never even really know if the movie is about the Ghost or Babs.

Evil Dead 2: Dead by Dawn ★ ★ ★
NO MPAA RATING, 96 m., 1987

Bruce Campbell (Ash), Sarah Berry (Annie), Dan Hicks (Jake), Kassie Wesley (Bobby Joe), Theodore Raimi (Henrietta). Directed by Sam Raimi and produced by Robert G. Tapert. Screenplay by Raimi and Scott Spiegel.

Evil Dead 2: Dead by Dawn is a comedy disguised as a blood-soaked shock-a-rama. It looks superficially like a routine horror movie, a vomitorium designed to separate callow teenagers from their lunch. But look a little closer and you'll realize that the movie is a fairly sophisticated satire. Level One viewers will say it's in bad taste. Level Two folks like ourselves will perceive that it is about bad taste.

The plot: Visitors to a cottage in the Michigan woods discover a rare copy of the *Book of the Dead* and accidentally invoke evil spirits. The spirits run amok, disemboweling and vivisecting their victims. The hero battles manfully with the dread supernatural forces, but he is no match for the unspeakably vile creatures in the basement, in the woods, and behind every door.

This story is told with wall-to-wall special effects. Skeletons dance in the moonlight. Heads spin on top of bodies. Hands go berserk and start attacking their owners. After they are chopped off, they have a life of their own. Heads are clamped into vises and squashed. Blood sprays all over everything. Guts spill. Slime spews. If nauseating images of horrific gore are not, as they say, your cup of tea, the odds are good you will not have a great time during this movie.

On the other hand, if you know it's all special effects, and if you've seen a lot of other movies and have a sense of humor, you might even have a great time seeing *Evil Dead 2*. I did—up to a point. The movie devours ideas at such a prodigious rate that it begins to repeat itself toward the end, but the first forty-five minutes have a kind of manic, inspired genius to them.

Consider, for example, the scene where the hero severs his hand from his body and the hand takes on a life of its own, attacking him. Leave out the blood and the gore and a few of the details, and this entire sequence builds like a tribute to the Three Stooges. Consider the scene where the hero attaches a chainsaw to what's left of his amputated arm. Disgusting, right? But the director, Sam Raimi, approaches it as a sly jab at *Taxi Driver*.

I'm not suggesting that *Evil Dead 2* is fun merely because you can spot the references to other movies. It is fun because (a) the violence and gore are carried to such an extreme that they stop being disgusting and become surrealistic; (b) the movie's timing aims for comedy, not shocks; and (c) the grubby, low-budget intensity of the film gives it a lovable quality that high-tech movies wouldn't have.

There is one shot in the film that is some kind of masterpiece. There is a force out there in the woods. We never see it, but we see things from its point of view. In one long and very complex unbroken point-of-view shot, this force roars through the woods, flattens everything, crashes through the cabin door, and roars through room after room with invincible savagery, chasing the hero until . . . but I wouldn't dream of giving away the joke.

Evil Under the Sun ★ ★ ★
PG, 102 m., 1982

Peter Ustinov (Hercule Poirot), Colin Blakely (Sir Horace Blatt), Jane Birkin (Christine Redfern), Nicholas Clay (Patrick Redfern), Maggie Smith (Daphne Castle), Roddy McDowall (Rex Brewster), Sylvia Miles (Myra Gardener), James Mason (Odell Gardener). Directed by Guy Hamilton and produced by John Brabourne and Richard Goodwin. Screenplay by Anthony Shaffer.

The delicious moments in an Agatha Christie film are supposed to come at the end, when the detective (in this case, the redoubtable Hercule Poirot) gathers everyone in the sitting room and toys with their guilt complexes before finally fingering the murderer. Well, there are delicious moments in the final fifteen minutes of *Evil Under the Sun*, but what I especially liked about this Christie were the opening scenes—the setup. They had a style and irreverence that reminded me curiously of *Beat the Devil*, with Bogart and Robert Morley chewing up the scenery. *Evil Under the Sun* is not, alas, as good as *Beat the Devil*, but it is the best of the recent group of Christie retreads (which include *Murder on the Orient Express*, *Death on the Nile*, and *The Mirror Crack'd*).

It begins in the usual way, with a corpse. It continues in obligatory fashion with the gathering of a large number of colorful and eccentric suspects in an out-of-the-way spot, which just happens to also be the destination of Hercule Poirot. It continues with the discovery of another corpse, with the liberal distribution of gigantic clues and with Poirot's lip-smacking summary of the evidence. It's the cast that makes *Evil* more fun than the previous manifestations of this identical plot. As Poirot, Peter Ustinov creates a wonderful mixture of the mentally polished and physically maladroit. He has a bit of business involving a dip in the sea that is so perfectly timed and acted it tells us everything we ever wanted to know about Poirot's appetite for exercise. He is so expansive, so beaming, so superior, in the opening scenes that he remains spiritually present throughout the film, even when he's not onscreen.

All of the rest of the cast are suspects. They include Maggie Smith, a former actress who now runs an elegant spa in the Adriatic Sea; Diana Rigg, as her jealous contemporary; Sylvia Miles and James Mason, as a rich couple who produce shows on Broadway; Jane Birkin and Nicholas Clay as a young couple constantly arguing over his roving eye; Colin Blakely as a rich knight who's been taken by a gold digger; Emily Hone as the young new wife; and Roddy McDowall as a bitchy gossip columnist who knows the dirt about everybody. The newly discovered corpse belongs to one of the above. The murderer is one (or more) of the above. Nothing else I could say about the crime would be fair.

I can observe, however, that one of the delights of the movies made from Agatha Christie novels is their almost complete lack of passion: They substitute wit and style. Nobody really cares who gets bumped off, and nobody really misses the departed. What's important is that all the right clues be distributed, so that Poirot and the audience can pick them up, mull them over, and discover the culprit. Perhaps, then, one of the reasons I liked *Evil Under the Sun* was that this time, when Ustinov paused in his summation (after verbally convicting everyone in the room), and it was clear he was about to finger the real killer, I guessed the killer's identity, and I was right. Well, half right. That's better than I usually do.

The Exorcist ★ ★ ★ ★
R, 121 m., 1973

Ellen Burstyn (Chris), Linda Blair (Regan), Jason Miller (Father Karras), Max von Sydow (Father Merrin), Kitty Winn (Sharon), Lee J. Cobb (Kinderman). Directed by William Friedkin and produced by William Peter Blatty. Screenplay by Blatty.

1973 began and ended with cries of pain. It began with Ingmar Bergman's *Cries and*

Whispers, and it closed with William Friedkin's *The Exorcist*. Both films are about the weather of the human soul, and no two films could be more different. Yet each in its own way forces us to look inside, to experience horror, to confront the reality of human suffering. The Bergman film is a humanist classic. The Friedkin film is an exploitation of the most fearsome resources of the cinema. That does not make it evil, but it does not make it noble, either.

The difference, maybe, is between great art and great craftsmanship. Bergman's exploration of the lines of love and conflict within the family of a woman dying of cancer was a film that asked important questions about faith and death, and was not afraid to admit there might not be any answers. Friedkin's film is about a twelve-year-old girl who either is suffering from a severe neurological disorder or—perhaps has been possessed by an evil spirit. Friedkin has the answers; the problem is that we doubt he believes them.

We don't necessarily believe them ourselves, but that hardly matters during the film's two hours. If movies are, among other things, opportunities for escapism, then *The Exorcist* is one of the most powerful ever made. Our objections, our questions, occur in an intellectual context after the movie has ended. During the movie there are no reservations, but only experiences. We feel shock, horror, nausea, fear, and some small measure of dogged hope.

Rarely do movies affect us so deeply. The first time I saw *Cries and Whispers*, I found myself shrinking down in my seat, somehow trying to escape from the implications of Bergman's story. *The Exorcist* also has that effect—but we're not escaping from Friedkin's implications, we're shrinking back from the direct emotional experience he's attacking us with. This movie doesn't rest on the screen; it's a frontal assault.

The story is well-known; it's adapted, more or less faithfully, by William Peter Blatty from his own bestseller. Many of the technical and theological details in his book are accurate. Most accurate of all is the reluctance of his Jesuit hero, Father Karras, to encourage the ritual of exorcism: "To do that," he says, "I'd have to send the girl back to the sixteenth century." Modern medicine has replaced devils with paranoia and schizophrenia, he explains. Medicine may have, but the movie hasn't. The last chapter of the novel never totally explained in detail the final events in the tortured girl's bedroom, but the movie's special effects in the closing scenes leave little doubt that an actual evil spirit was in that room, and that it transferred bodies. Is this fair? I guess so; in fiction the artist has poetic license.

It may be that the times we live in have prepared us for this movie. And Friedkin has admittedly given us a good one. I've always preferred a generic approach to film criticism; I ask myself how good a movie is of its type. *The Exorcist* is one of the best movies of its type ever made; it not only transcends the genre of terror, horror, and the supernatural, but it transcends such serious, ambitious efforts in the same direction as Roman Polanski's *Rosemary's Baby*. Carl Dreyer's *The Passion of Joan of Arc* is a greater film—but, of course, not nearly so willing to exploit the ways film can manipulate feeling.

The Exorcist does that with a vengeance. The film is a triumph of special effects. Never for a moment—not when the little girl is possessed by the most disgusting of spirits, not when the bed is banging and the furniture flying and the vomit is welling out— are we less than convinced. The film contains brutal shocks, almost indescribable obscenities. That it received an R rating and not the X is stupefying.

The performances are in every way appropriate to this movie made this way. Ellen Burstyn, as the possessed girl's mother, rings especially true; we feel her frustration when doctors and psychiatrists talk about lesions on the brain and she *knows* there's something deeper, more terrible, going on. Linda Blair, as the little girl, has obviously been put through an ordeal in this role, and puts us through one. Jason Miller, as the young Jesuit, is tortured, doubting, intelligent.

And the casting of Max von Sydow as the older Jesuit exorcist was inevitable; he has been through so many religious and metaphysical crises in Bergman's films that he almost seems to belong on a theological battlefield the way John Wayne belonged on a horse. There's a striking image early in the film that has the craggy von Sydow facing an ancient, evil statue; the image doesn't so much borrow from Bergman's famous chess game between von Sydow and Death (in *The Seventh Seal*) as extend the conflict and raise the odds.

I am not sure exactly what reasons people will have for seeing this movie; surely enjoyment won't be one, because what we get here aren't the delicious chills of a Vincent Price thriller, but raw and painful experience. Are people so numb they need movies of this intensity in order to feel anything at all? It's hard to say.

Even in the extremes of Friedkin's vision there is still a feeling that this is, after all, cinematic escapism and not a confrontation with real life. There is a fine line to be drawn there, and *The Exorcist* finds it and stays a millimeter on this side.

Experience Preferred . . . But Not Essential ★ ★ ★
PG, 77 m., 1983

Elizabeth Edmonds (Annie), Sue Wallace (Mavis), Geraldine Griffith (Doreen), Karen Meagher (Paula), Ron Bain (Mike), Alun Lewis (Hywel). Directed by Peter Duffell and produced by David Puttnam and Chris Griffin. Screenplay by June Roberts.

This movie is so slight and charming you're almost afraid to breathe during it, for fear of disturbing the spell. It's about ordinary people in an ordinary setting, but because the setting is a small resort hotel in Wales, and the time is the summer of 1962, there's also the strange feeling that we've entered another time and place, where some of the same rules apply, but by no means all of them.

The movie tells the story of a young woman named Annie (Elizabeth Edmonds) who comes to work for the summer in a hotel, and finds that she's entered a cozy little backstairs world with its own sets of loyalties and jealousies. All of the other waitresses at the hotel have all of their own stories, some funny, some sad, and Annie feels a little left out. "I'm the only one here without a past," she complains, but of course one of the reasons for spending your summer working in a hotel is to accumulate a past. The other women are suspicious of her because she's a student, but as the waitresses cram into the servants' quarters, three to a room and sometimes two to a bed, a sort of democracy sets in, and Annie is accepted.

The movie uses a wonderfully offhand style for filling us in on the characters. There's the gallant cook, who immediately takes a liking to Annie. And the redheaded bartender, who makes it a nightly habit to sleepwalk in the nude. And the conceited young waiter whose idea of a courtship is to belt his girl in the eye every once in a while. And the pretty hostess of the dining room, who owes her position and her private boudoir to the favors she supplies the hotel's owner. ("How did you get such a nice room?" Annie asks her, innocently.)

There's not much of a plot. Things just sort of happen. Young men and women work from dawn to dusk and then collapse into each other's arms, almost but not quite too exhausted for sex. And the sexual customs of the pre-Pill era take on a certain quaintness, and a certain desperation, as couples grimly try to walk the line between lust and prudence. *Experience Preferred* is charming precisely because of its inconsequential air. It's funny because it goes for whimsical little insights into human nature rather than for big, obvious jokes. It's charming because it doesn't force the charm.

Exposed ★ ★ ★ ½
R, 100 m., 1983

Nastassja Kinski (Elizabeth), Rudolph Nureyev (Daniel), Harvey Keitel (Rivas), Ian McShane (Miller), Bibi Andersson (Margaret), Pierre Clementi (Vic). Directed and produced by James Toback. Screenplay by Toback.

This movie contains moments so exhilarating they reawakened me to the infinite possibilities of movies. Yet this movie loses itself in its closing sequences and meanders through the details of a routine terrorist plot. Somewhere between its greatness and its wandering there must be a compromise, and I would strike it this way: *Exposed* contains the most exciting evidence I have seen so far that Nastassja Kinski is the next great female superstar. I do not say that she is a great actress; not yet, and perhaps not ever. I do not compare her with Meryl Streep or Kate Nelligan, Jill Clayburgh or Jessica Lange. I am not talking in those terms of professional accomplishment. I am talking about the mysterious, innate quality that some performers have to cast a special spell, to develop a relationship with the camera that you can call stardom or voodoo or magic, because its name doesn't really matter.

Kinski has it. There are moments in this film (two virtuoso scenes, in particular, and then many other small moments and parts of scenes) when she affects me in the same way that Marilyn Monroe must have affected her first viewers, in movies like *The Asphalt Jungle* or *All About Eve*. She was not yet a star and audiences did not even know her name, but there was a quality about her that could not be dismissed. Kinski has that quality. She has exhibited it before in better films,

such as *Tess*, and in ambitious, imperfect films such as *Cat People* and *One from the Heart*. Now here is *Exposed*, written and directed by James Toback, who in screenplays such as *The Gambler* and his brilliant, little-seen directing debut *Fingers*, has specialized in characters who live on the edge.

There are two sequences in *Exposed* where he pulls out all the stops. In one of them, Kinski (who plays a college dropout, lonely and sexually frustrated) dances all by herself in a nearly empty apartment. In another one, she meets a violinist (Rudolph Nureyev), they fall instantly into a consuming passion, and after he has tantalized her with a violin bow they make sudden, passionate love. The sheer quality of Kinski's abandon in these two scenes made me realize how many barriers can sometimes exist between a performance and an audience: Here there are none.

The movie is wonderful for its first hour or more. It follows Kinski through a brief, unhappy love affair with her professor (played by Toback), shows her moving to New York, has her discovered by a photographer and becoming a world-famous model (because she is Kinski, this is believable), and brings her up through the love affair with Nureyev. At this moment, *Exposed* seems poised on the brink of declaring itself one of the most riveting character portraits ever made.

And that is the moment where it falters, and loses itself in the details of a plot involving Harvey Keitel, as the leader of an underground terrorist cell in Paris. It's as if Toback didn't trust the strength of this character he had created (or, more likely, didn't know when he wrote his thriller that Kinski would bring the character so completely to life). The rest of the movie is okay, I suppose, in a somewhat familiar way. But its special quality is lost in plot details. Too bad. But if a movie can electrify me the way this one did, not once but twice and then some, I'm prepared to forgive it almost anything.

Extreme Prejudice ★ ★ ★
R, 104 m., 1987

Nick Nolte (Jack Benteen), Powers Boothe (Cash Bailey), Michael Ironside (Major Hackett), Maria Conchita Alonso (Sarita Cisneros), Rip Torn (Sheriff Pearson), Clancy Brown (Sergeant McRose). Directed by Walter Hill and produced by Buzz Feitshans. Screenplay by Deric Washburn.

The story elements in *Extreme Prejudice* are

so ancient they sound like ad copy: Two strong men, one good, one evil, battle each other for justice—and for the heart of the woman they both love. Walter Hill is the right director for this material. He specializes in male action movies where the characters are all a little taller, leaner, meaner, and more obscene than in real life.

Hill doesn't really try to avoid the clichés in a story like this. He simply turns up the juice. Like his *Southern Comfort*, *48 HRS*, and *The Warriors*, this is a movie that depends on style, not surprises. He doesn't want to make a different kind of movie; he wants to make a familiar story look better than we've seen it look recently. And yet there is a big surprise in *Extreme Prejudice* in the appearance and character of Nick Nolte.

When last seen, Nolte had successfully overcome his early pretty-boy image and turned into one of the shabbier ruins on the landscape of American leading men. His performance in *Teachers* needed a diagnosis, not a review. But then, about halfway through *Down and Out in Beverly Hills*, he underwent some kind of metamorphosis. He shaved off the beard and emerged as a weathered, older, more attractive actor; for the first time, I realized that he had the materials to become a big-league star like Cooper or Gable.

In *Extreme Prejudice*, he is working in the Cooper tradition. He is leaner than before, his face chiseled like some Western artifact, and he wears his Texas Ranger hat down on his forehead, so his eyes are always in shadow. He works the border, trying to control the drug trade, and at night he comes home exhausted to the bed of his girl (Maria Conchita Alonso).

She is restless with this arrangement. Her previous lover was Cash Bailey (Powers Boothe), once Nolte's best friend, now a drug baron who controls the flow across the border. Cash moves with impunity back and forth in a private helicopter and offers Alonso more than a Ranger's salary can buy. One day, she packs up and goes to live with him. Meanwhile, Nolte's territory is invaded by an unofficial, top-secret cadre of American combat veterans who apparently are working for a U.S. military covert operations team. Their mission remains murky (they screw up a mysterious bank heist), but they seem to be after Cash, too. That leads to the shoot-out at Cash's Mexican fortress, not to mention a lot of last-minute switching of sides and loyalties.

The specifics of the plot you can do without. You've seen this movie before, right down to the dozing guards who permit the enemy gunmen to walk right into the stronghold.

What makes the film good are Hill's style and the acting. Everything is cranked up about ten degrees. Nolte is quiet and tough, Boothe gives a great performance as a slimy drug merchant with some residual charm, and Alonso was born for her role as the passionate señorita trapped between two men who will kill for her.

The love triangle is sort of a broad, bloody version of *The Third Man*, where Orson Welles and Joseph Cotten were childhood friends who ended up on opposite sides of the law and in love with Alida Valli. The conflict in these triangles is always the same: The woman knows the bad guy is a slimy snake, but she loves him, anyway. That breaks the good guy's heart and leaves him free to kill his childhood buddy. Then you get the poignant ending.

Hill has made a lot of movies in the last fifteen years, and I guess it's too late to hope that he'll develop a real interest in his female characters. They're the pawns of his male buddies, and everything else boils down to the way the characters walk, the way they look at each other, the personal tics they develop, and the new ways the stunt men find for people to die. *Extreme Prejudice* offers a lot of technique, some strong acting, and the absolute confidence of a good director who knows what he wants to do and doesn't care if that limits him.

Eye of the Needle ★ ★ ★
R, 118 m., 1981

Donald Sutherland (Faber), Kate Nelligan (Lucy), Christopher Cazenove (David), Ian Bannen (Canter). Directed by Richard Marquand and produced by Stephen Friedman. Screenplay by Stanley Mann.

Eye of the Needle resembles nothing so much as one of those downbeat, plodding, quietly horrifying, and sometimes grimly funny war movies that used to be made by the British film industry, back when there was a British film industry. They used to star Stanley Baker or Trevor Howard. This one stars Donald Sutherland, as the kind of introverted psychopath who should inhabit only black-and-white movies, although the color here is sometimes gloomy enough to suffice.

I admired the movie. It is made with quiet competence, and will remind some viewers of the Alfred Hitchcock who made *The 39 Steps* and *Foreign Correspondent*. It is about a German spy, the "Needle," who dropped out of sight in Germany in 1938 and now inhabits a series of drab bed-sitting-rooms in England while he spies on the British war effort. He is known as the Needle because of his trademarked way of killing people by jabbing a stiletto into their rib cages. He kills with a singular lack of passion; this is Jack the Ripper crossed with J. Alfred Prufrock. As played by Sutherland, the Needle is a very lonely man. We are given hints to explain his isolation: He was raised by parents who did not love him, he was shipped off to boarding schools, he spent parts of his childhood in America, where he learned English. None of these experiences fully explains his ruthlessness, but then perhaps it is just a spy's job to be ruthless.

The plot is part espionage, part cliffhanger. The Needle discovers phony plywood "airplanes" intended to look, from the air, like Patton's invasion force—a ruse to throw off the Germans. His assignment is to personally deliver news of the actual Allied invasion plans to Hitler. This he intends to do with every fiber of his being, and yet we never get the feeling that the this man is a patriotic Nazi. He is more of a dogged functionary. In his attempts to rendezvous with a Nazi submarine, he's shipwrecked on an isolated island occupied only by a lighthouse-keeper and by a young married couple—a woman (Kate Nelligan), her legless husband (Christopher Cazenove), and their son. The last third of the movie turns into a bloody melodrama, as the Needle kills the husband and the lighthouse-keeper and threatens the woman, first in a psychological way and then with violence. But before the final standoff, he pretends to be merely a lost sailor. And the woman, frustrated by her husband's drunkenness and refusal to love, becomes attracted to the stranger. They make love. She grows fond of him. Does he grow fond of her? We can never be sure, but he tells her things he has told to no one else.

Some people will find the movie slow going. I preferred to think of it as deliberate. It is effective, I think, to develop a plot like this at a deliberate pace, instead of rushing headlong through it. That gives us time to meditate on the character of the Needle, and to ponder his very few, enigmatic references to his own behavior. We learn things

about him that he may not even know about himself, and that is why the film's final scene is so much more complex than it seems. "The war has come down to the two of us," Sutherland tells Nelligan, and in the final exchange of desperate looks between the man and the woman there is a whole universe left unspoken. The movie ends with Nelligan regarding a man who is either a treacherous spy or an unloved child, take your choice.

Eyewitness ★ ★ ★
R, 102 m., 1981

William Hurt (Daryll Deever), Sigourney Weaver (Tony Sokolow), Christopher Plummer (Joseph), James Woods (Aldo), Irene Worth (Mrs. Sokolow), Pamela Reed (Linda). Directed and produced by Peter Yates. Screenplay by Steve Tesich.

Somebody was explaining the difference between European and American movies to me the other day: European movies are about people, but American movies are about stories. It's an interesting idea, especially when it's applied to a thriller like *Eyewitness*, which is good precisely because it pays more attention to its people than its story. Does that make it European? Well, it was directed by Peter Yates, who is British but has directed some of the most "American" movies of the past decade, from *Bullitt* to *Breaking Away*. It is definitely set in America—from the bowels of a Manhattan boiler room to the newsroom of a TV station. But it's about such interesting, complicated, quirky, and sometimes funny people that it must at the least be mid-Atlantic.

The movie stars William Hurt as a janitor who stumbles across evidence that could lead to the solution of a murder investigation. But he doesn't go to the police with it because he's too complicated, too introspective, too distrustful of his own discovery . . . and, mostly, he's too much in love from afar with a TV news reporter (Sigourney Weaver). Maybe he can win her attention by giving her the scoop?

There are other complications. Sigourney Weaver is engaged to an Israeli agent (Christopher Plummer) who is involved in secret international negotiations to smuggle Jews out of the Soviet Union. His plan involves clandestine payments to a Vietnamese agent who got rich on the black market in Saigon and has now moved to Manhattan. The other characters include James Woods, as Hurt's eccentric and unpredictable fellow janitor, and Steven Hill and Morgan Freeman as a couple of cops who wearily track down leads in the case (their best line: "When Aldo was a little boy, he must have wanted to grow up to be a suspect").

The development and solution of the murder mystery are handled with professional dispatch by Yates and his writer, Steve Tesich (who also wrote *Breaking Away*). A final shoot-out in a midtown riding stable has a touch of Hitchcock to it; the old master always loved to mix violence with absolutely inappropriate settings. But what makes this movie so entertaining is the way Yates and Tesich and their characters play against our expectations.

Examples. Weaver is not only a TV newswoman, but also a part-time serious pianist and the unhappy daughter of her domineering parents. Hurt is not only a janitor but also a sensitive soul who can talk his way into Weaver's heart. Woods is not only a creepy janitor but also the enthusiastic promoter of a marriage between his sister and Hurt. Hurt and the sister (Pamela Reed) carry on the courtship because they are both too embarrassed to tell the other one they're not in love. Plummer is the most complicated character of all, and it's a very good question whether he's a villain. It all depends on how you view his own personal morality.

I've seen so many thrillers that, frankly, I don't always care how they turn out—unless they're really well-crafted. What I like about *Eyewitness* is that, although it *does* care how it turns out, it cares even more about the texture of the scenes leading to the denouement. There's not a scene in this movie that exists only to provide us with plot information. Every scene develops characters. And they're developed in such offbeat fidelity to the way people do behave that we get all the more involved in the mystery, just because, for once, we halfway believe it could really be happening.

F

F/X ★ ★ ★ ½
R, 108 m., 1985

Bryan Brown (Rollie Tyler), Cliff DeYoung (Lipton), Brian Dennehy (Lieutenant Leo McCarthy), Trey Wilson (Lieutenant Murdoch), Mason Adams (Mason), Martha Gehman (Andy), Diane Venora (Ellen), Jerry Orbach (DeFranco), Tim Gallin (Adams). Directed by Robert Mandel and produced by Dodi Fayed and Jack Wiener. Screenplay by Robert T. Megginson and Gregory Fleeman.

F/X is Hollywood shorthand for "effects," or special effects, the art form that creates bullet holes and gaping wounds, fake shotgun blasts, and severed limbs.

In the movie, Bryan Brown plays a special-effects man whose customized truck is a mobile effects lab. He can create his illusions almost anywhere, and is in big demand from the Hollywood studios. Then one day he gets an unusual request from the federal government. As part of their witness relocation and protection program, they want to fake the murder of an organized-crime leader. Their reasoning: If everybody thinks DeFranco is dead, nobody will try to kill him, and he will survive and be able to testify in court.

This premise is only the beginning of the movie's ingenuity. Like *Jagged Edge*, this is one of those tightly constructed plots in which the hero is almost the last person to find out anything. Who can he trust? Who is really on his side, who is lying to him, who is trying to kill him? One of the pleasures of *Jagged Edge* was that we could watch the central character, the lawyer played by Glenn Close, use all of her intelligence and intuition and still walk right into danger, because she could not believe that people could be such deceptive swine.

The same thing happens in *F/X*, and I will have to tread carefully to avoid giving away too much of the plot. Briefly, there are large, basic questions about who wants DeFranco, the underworld leader, killed, and who wants him alive. There are other fundamental questions about whether special effects have indeed been used, or whether he actually was killed. And there are great ominous possibilities that the special-effects man himself might be next on the hit list.

The movie moves quickly through a large gallery of players. At the center of everything is Rollie Tyler, the effects man, given a nice, laconic professionalism by Bryan Brown, whose Australian accent reminds us that he was not brought up to automatically trust the U.S. government in all matters.

The Broadway veteran Jerry Orbach plays DeFranco as an expensively barbered creep. Halfway through the movie, the dependable character actor Brian Dennehy turns up as a city cop not in on the scam. Cliff DeYoung is the slippery Lipton, mastermind of the federal scheme. Martha Gehman is Andy, the loyal assistant of the effects man, and Diane Venora is his doomed girlfriend.

I mention so many of these actors because, more than most thrillers that depend on tightly constructed plots, *F/X* also depends on good, well-observed performances. This movie takes a lot of delight in being more psychologically complex than it has to be. It contains fights and shoot-outs and big chase scenes, but they're all firmly centered on who the characters are and what they mean to one another. And by the end of the film when everything comes down to the events in a large, scary, and isolated mansion, the movie is able to use the personalities of the characters as part of the payoff.

Every year should bring a few good thrillers, to balance out all the failed and shallow attempts. The irony of *F/X*, which is a very good thriller indeed, is that it avoids the pitfall of so many thrillers; it doesn't degenerate into a mindless display of special effects. The effects in this film just happen to be the ways the hero has of expressing himself.

F/X 2: The Deadly Art of Illusion ★ ★
PG-13, 104 m., 1991

Bryan Brown (Rollie Tyler), Brian Dennehy (Leo McCarthy), Rachel Ticotin (Kim Brandon), Joanna Gleason (Liz Kennedy), Philip Bosco (Ray Silak), Kevin J. O'Connor (Matt Neely). Directed by Richard Franklin and produced by Jack Wiener and Dodi Fayed. Screenplay by Bill Condon.

There should be a special category for movies that are neither good nor bad, but simply excessive. A movie, for example, like *F/X 2: The Deadly Art of Illusion*. Here is a film with a plot I defy you to comprehend, characters who are constantly at the mercy of the filmmaker's bright ideas, and a level of reality that vibrates between the absurd and the hallucinatory. It's not every film, in other words, that includes both booby-trapped baked beans and a robotic clown piloting a helicopter.

The film is a sequel of sorts to *F/X*, a 1986 thriller that did fairly well at the box office and then went on to become one of the all-time top renters and grossers on home video. I can see why the original film did well on video, and why this one should, too. Home video is a medium that invites distractions, and *F/X* was the kind of film where you could casually glance at the screen, see something utterly amazing, and then look away again, secure in the knowledge that no crucial plot developments would escape you.

In *F/X 2*, all of the crucial plot developments have already escaped before the movie even begins. This is a film that defies synopsis. It stars, once again, the dependable and laconic Australian actor Bryan Brown, as a special effects genius. ("F/X" is movie shorthand for "effects".) He has retired from his original profession to devote time to his more advanced projects, including an invention of truly Tom Swiftian proportions: A suit you put on that registers all of your body movements and then duplicates them exactly with a robot.

That suit leads to the movie's single most incredible scene, in which a villain is trying to escape in a helicopter, and the helicopter pilot turns out to be, not a human being, but a robot. Below the helicopter in a boat, wearing the suit, Brown twists and gyrates so that the clown turns the helicopter trip into an insanely terrifying ride.

It's a clever scene, but ask yourself this question: If you were getting into a helicopter, especially with a fortune in loot under your arm, would you look to see who was piloting the helicopter? Or would you get in blindly, and wait until after takeoff to notice that the pilot . . . was Bluey the Clown?

I call movies like this "Hey, Waitaminut!" movies, because all during the film I'm repeating, "Hey! Wait a minute!" as the plot twists and turns in illogical and incomprehensible developments. Sometimes a Hey, Waitaminut movie can be fun, and sometimes this one is, but they can be frustrating, too.

The problem with F/X 2, I think, is that the movie has a more important agenda than telling a story. It wants to demonstrate wall-to-wall special effects, visual gags, scientific resourcefulness, and the ways that a supermarket can be turned into a minefield. Take the supermarket scene, for example. Brown and the bad guy are trapped inside along with Brown's girlfriend (Rachel Ticotin) and her child. Faced with an armed madman who wants to kill him, Brown uses resourcefulness, such as combining a display of baked beans and an aerosol can into a device that heats the cans of beans until they explode in the killer's face. Clever. Or, as a private eye in a 1940s movie might have said, too clever.

Brown and Ticotin both struggle bravely with the plot, which doesn't exactly slow down for character details, and Brian Dennehy is also back from the original film, as an old friend who becomes Brown's sidekick in the attempt to defeat their enemy, played with slimy conviction by the splendid character actor Philip Bosco.

F/X 2 is actually the kind of movie that rewards inattention. Sit quietly in the theater and watch it, and you will be driven to distraction by its inconsistencies and loopholes. But watch it on video, paying it half a mind, and you might actually find it entertaining. A little goes a long way.

The Fabulous Baker Boys ★ ★ ★ ¹/₂
R, 114 m., 1989

Jeff Bridges (Jack Baker), Michelle Pfeiffer (Susie Diamond), Beau Bridges (Frank Baker), Ellie Raab (Nina), Xander Berkeley (Lloyd), Jennifer Tilly (Monica), Dakin Matthews (Charlie), Ken Lerner (Ray), Albert Hall (Henry). Directed by Steve Kloves and produced by Paula Weinstein and Mark Rosenberg. Screenplay by Kloves.

There is a scene in *The Fabulous Baker Boys* where Michelle Pfeiffer, wearing a slinky red dress, uncurls on top of a piano while singing "Makin' Whoopee." The rest of the movie is also worth the price of admission. Pfeiffer stars in the film with Jeff and Beau Bridges, who play the halves of a cocktail lounge iano duet. Their act is growing relentlessly more hopeless when they decide to liven things up by hiring a girl singer. The singer is Pfeiffer. Things liven up.

The Fabulous Baker Boys is a new version of an old show-biz formula about the long-time partners whose relationship is threatened when one of them falls in love with the sexy new singer. *Young Man With a Horn* did a version of this material, and so have lots of other movies, but rarely with such intriguing casting and such a sure hand for the material. There's probably some autobiographical truth lurking beneath the rivalry of the Bridges brothers, old wounds from the twenty years they have both been working in the movies. And Pfeiffer quite simply has one of the roles of a lifetime as the high-priced call girl who wants to become a low-priced lounge singer.

The movie takes place in that shadowy area of show business where people make a living, even a fairly decent living, but they always seem to be marking time. Night after night, the Baker Boys sit down at their twin pianos in the lounges of fading Seattle supper clubs and pretentious motels, and go through an act they could do in their sleep. The audience, drunks in search of melancholy, doesn't even bother to listen.

The problem is, the fabulous Baker Boys are getting dated. They're doing tired material and arrangements that sound like elevator music. And the jobs aren't coming their way anymore. Deciding to add a singer to the act, they conduct a long series of auditions, during which they meet nearly every woman in town who should not consider a singing career. And then Pfeiffer walks in.

She's not an experienced singer. She doesn't quite know how to handle herself or her voice. But she has that ineffable vocal quality that causes people to listen because they might be missing something. And she looks like a million bucks. She's been a hooker, yes, but we know from a hundred other movies that she has a good heart and that the tough come-on is all an act.

Working with the girl singer, the Baker Boys begin to play real music again. This reopens an old wound. Jack Baker (Jeff Bridges) is, in fact, a brilliant jazz pianist, who has turned his back on the music he loves out of some twisted love-hate loyalty to his brother, Frank (Beau Bridges). Frank easily handles the business side of the partnership, and could easily go through the same hackneyed act night after night for years. So the girl inevitably comes between them. And Jack inevitably falls in love with her.

The Fabulous Baker Boys doesn't do anything very original, but what it does, it does wonderfully well. It was written and directed by a first-timer, Steve Kloves, and even though the screenplay depends on formulas, we begin to forget that; we begin to care about these people, especially when the relationship between the brothers turns inward and they start looking hard at what they both really need from life.

This is one of the movies they will use as a document years from now when they begin to trace the steps by which Michelle Pfeiffer became a great star. I cannot claim that I spotted her unique screen presence in her first movie, which, I think, was *Grease II*, but certainly by the time she made *Ladyhawke*, *Tequila Sunrise*, *Dangerous Liaisons*, and *Married to the Mob*, something was going on, and this is the movie of her flowering—not just as a beautiful woman, but as an actress with the ability to make you care about her, to make you feel what she feels.

All of those qualities are here in this movie, and so is the "Makin' Whoopee" number, which I can only praise by adding it to a short list: Whatever she's doing while she performs that song isn't merely singing—it's whatever Rita Hayworth did in *Gilda* and Marilyn Monroe did in *Some Like It Hot*, and I didn't want her to stop.

The Falcon and the Snowman
★ ★ ★ ★
R, 131 m., 1985

Timothy Hutton (Christopher Boyce), Sean Penn (Daulton Lee), Pat Hingle (Mr. Boyce), Joyce Van Patten (Mrs. Boyce), David Suchet (Alex), Boris Leskin (Mikhail). Directed by John Schlesinger and produced by Gabriel Katska and Schlesinger. Screenplay by Steven Saillian.

A few years ago there were stories in the papers about a couple of California kids who were caught selling government secrets to the Russians. The stories had an air of unreality about them. Here were a couple of middle-class young men from suburban backgrounds, who were prosecuted as spies and traitors and who hardly seemed to have it quite clear in their own minds how they had gotten into the spy business. One of the many strengths of *The Falcon and the Snowman* is that it succeeds, in an admirably matter-of-fact way, in showing us exactly how these two young men got in way over their heads. This is a movie about spies, but it is not a thriller in any routine sense of the word; it's just the meticulously observant record of how naiveté, inexperience, misplaced idealism, and greed led to one of the most peculiar cases of treason in American history.

The movie stars Timothy Hutton as Christopher Boyce, a seminarian who has a crisis of conscience, drops out of school, and ends up working almost by accident for a message-routing center of the CIA. Sean Penn is his best friend, Daulton Lee. Years ago, they were altar boys together, but in recent times their paths have diverged; while Boyce was studying for the priesthood, Lee was setting himself up as a drug dealer. By the time we meet them, Boyce is earnest and clean-cut, just the kind of young man the CIA might be looking for (it doesn't hurt that his father is a former FBI man). And Lee, with a mustache that makes him look like a failed creep, is a jumpy, paranoid drug dealer who is one step ahead of the law.

The whole caper begins so simply. Boyce, reading the messages he is paid to receive and forward, learns that the CIA is engaged in dirty tricks designed to influence elections in Australia. He is deeply offended to learn that his government would be interfering in the affairs of another state, and the more he thinks about it, the more he wants to do something. For example, supply the messages to the Russians. He doesn't want to be a Russian *spy*, you understand, just to bring this injustice to light. Lee has some contacts in Mexico, where he buys drugs. One day, in a deceptively casual conversation by the side of a backyard swimming pool, the two friends decide to go into partnership to sell the information to the Soviet Embassy in Mexico City. Lee takes the documents south and launches them both on an adventure that is a lark at first, and then a challenge, and finally just a very, very bad dream.

These two young men have one basic problem. They are amateurs. The Russians don't necessarily like that any better than the Americans would; indeed, even though the Russians are happy to have the secrets that are for sale, there is a definite sense in some scenes that the key Russian contact agent, played by David Suchet, is almost offended by the sloppy way Penn deals in espionage. The only thing Penn seems really serious about is the money.

The Falcon and the Snowman never steps wrong, but it is best when it deals with the relationship between the two young American spies. The movie was directed by John Schlesinger, an Englishman whose understanding of American characters was most unforgettably demonstrated in *Midnight Cowboy*, and I was reminded of Joe Buck and Ratso Rizzo from that movie as I watched this one. There is even a quiet, understated quote to link Ratso with the Penn character: a moment in a parking garage when Penn defies a car to pull in front of him, and we're reminded of Ratso crossing a Manhattan street and hurling the line "I'm *walking* here!" at a taxi that dares to cut him off. Instead of relying on traditional methods for creating the suspense in spy movies, this one uses the energy generated between the two very different characters, as the all-American Boyce gradually begins to understand that his partner is out of control. *The Falcon and the Snowman*, like most good movies, is not really about its plot but about its characters. These two young men could just as easily be selling stolen IBM programs to Apple, instead of CIA messages to the Russians; the point is that they begin with one set of motives and then the implacable real world supplies them with another, harder, more unforgiving set of realities.

Just as with *Midnight Cowboy*, it's hard to say who gives the better performance this time: Sean Penn, with his twitching intensity as he angles for respect from the Russians, or Timothy Hutton, the straight man, earnestly telling his girlfriend that she should remember he really loves her—"no matter what you may hear about me in a few days from now."

Fame ★ ★ ★ 1/2
R, 133 m., 1980

Eddie Barth (Angelo), Irene Cara (Coco), Lee Curreri (Bruno), Laura Dean (Lisa), Antonia Franceschi (Hilary), Boyd Gaines (Michael), Albert Hague (Shorofsky), Tresa Hughes (Mrs. Finsecker). Directed by Alan Parker and produced by David De Silva and Alan Marshall. Screenplay by Christopher Gore.

Mrs. Seward, the draconian rhetoric teacher who drilled literacy into generations of Urbana (Ill.) High School students, used to tell us we were having the best four years of our lives. We groaned. *Fame* is a movie that she might have enjoyed. It's about a dozen or so talented kids who enter New York's High School of the Performing Arts as freshmen and emerge four years later as future Freddie Prinzes and Benny Goodmans, Leonard Bernsteins and Mrs. Sewards.

Fame is a genuine treasure, moving and entertaining, a movie that understands being a teen-ager as well as *Breaking Away* did, but studies its characters in a completely different milieu. It's the other side of the coin: A big-city, aggressive, cranked-up movie to play against the quieter traditions of *Breaking Away*'s small Indiana college town. *Fame* is all New York City. It's populated by rich kids, ghetto kids, kids with real talent, and kids with mothers who think they have real talent. They all go into the hopper, into a high school of kids who are worked harder because they're "special"—even if they're secretly not so sure they're so special.

The movie has the kind of sensitivity to the real lives of real people that we don't get much in Hollywood productions anymore. Anyone who ever went to high school will recognize some of *Fame*'s characters: the quiet little girl who blossoms, the class genius who locks himself up in the basement with his electronic equipment, the kid who can't read but is a naturally gifted performer, the wiseass, the self-destructive type, the sexpot, the rich kid, and on and on. The cast has been recruited from New York's most talented young performers, some of them almost playing themselves. The teachers are familiar too: self-sacrificing, perfectionist, cranky, love-hate objects.

If the character types seem familiar, the movie's way of telling their stories is not. This isn't a movie that locks its characters into a conventional plot. Instead, it fragments the experiences of four years into dozens of vignettes, loosely organized into sections titled "The Auditions," "Freshman Year," and so on. We get to know the characters and their personalities gradually, as we see them in various situations. The effect is a little like high school itself; you come in as a total stranger and by the time you leave, the school has become your world.

If the kids in *Fame* are like high school kids anywhere, they're also different because they *are* talented, and the movie's at its best when it examines the special pressures on young people who are more talented than they are mature, experienced, or sure of themselves. The ghost that hovers over everyone in this school is a former graduate, Freddie Prinze, who had the talent but never figured out how to handle it.

The movie's director, Alan Parker, seems to have a knack for isolating just those moments in the lives of his characters when growth, challenge, and talent are all on the line at once. Where did he find his insights into talented young people? Probably while he was directing his first film, the wonderful *Bugsy Malone* (1976), which was a gangster musical with an all-kid cast. *Fame* is a perfect title for this movie; it establishes an ironic distance between where these kids are now and where they'd like to be someday, and then there's also the haunting suggestion that some of the ones who find fame will be able to handle it, and some will not.

Family Business ★ ★ ★
R, 73 m., 1989

Sean Connery (Jessie), Dustin Hoffman (Vito), Matthew Broderick (Adam), Rosana DeSoto (Elaine), Janet Carroll (Margie), Victoria Jackson (Christin), Bill McCutcheon (Doheny), Deborah Rush (Michele Dempsey), Marilyn Cooper (Rose), Salem Ludwig (Nat). Directed by Sidney Lumet and produced by Lawrence Gordon. Screenplay by Vincent Patrick.

What does Sidney Lumet's *Family Business* want to be? A caper movie, or a family drama? I ask because the movie seems to pursue both goals with equal success until about the three-quarter mark, and then leaves leftover details of the caper hanging disconcertingly in midair. I was distracted during the movie's important final scenes by a large unanswered question, which I'll get to later.

Good news first. The movie stars Sean Connery, Dustin Hoffman, and Matthew Broderick as three generations of the same family, all touched in one way or another by crime. Connery, the grandfather, is a Scotsman whose arrest record is as long as his arm. He lives by one of those macho criminal codes in which you haven't proven anything unless you've proven it with your fists, and as the movie opens he's in jail after getting in a bar brawl with an off-duty policeman.

Hoffman is Connery's son, half Scots and half Sicilian ("He'd be five inches taller with a Scots mother," Connery observes), and Broderick is Hoffman's son, half Jewish. The movie makes such a point of the hereditary makeup of the three men, I guess, because the caper involves breaking into a genetic-engineering laboratory and stealing some DNA research material. The idea for the caper comes from Broderick, a Westinghouse Scholar who has never been involved in crime before. Hoffman is adamantly opposed to it—he still bears the wounds of his childhood with a criminal father—but Connery is enthusiastic, and Hoffman finally decides to come along out of concern for the safety of his son.

All of the scenes establishing the characters and setting up the caper are joyful to watch, mostly because of the rich comic exaggerations of the Connery character, who makes such a contrast to his uptight son and all-American grandson. The caper itself is a disappointment (they have a key card and a security code, after all, so we're not talking brain surgery). The aftermath gets interesting when Broderick makes a stupid mistake and is collared by the cops—and Connery and Hoffman have to decide whether to turn themselves in to help the kid avoid a prison term.

It's going to be tricky explaining that big question that I think the movie leaves hanging. Without revealing too much, here goes. There is a crucial scene in which Connery corners the Chinese-American scientist who had originally hired them to steal the DNA material. The scientist tells him something which, if brought out in open court, would certainly lead to the whole case being seen in a different light. But the movie ignores this new material, and goes in another direction, leaving us patiently waiting for a big courtroom scene that never arrives. They should have either left the scientist out, or dealt with his information.

The closing scenes of the movie are a disappointment for more reasons than one. What happens to Connery is sudden, unprepared, and dramatically unsatisfactory. And then what happens between Hoffman and Broderick seems to belong in a different kind of movie. *Family Business* tries to play it down the middle, when it probably should have jumped in one direction or the other, toward a pure caper, or toward a family drama. The problem with capers and courtrooms is, once evidence is on the table, the audience can hardly think of anything else until it's disposed of.

Fanny and Alexander ★ ★ ★ ★
R, 197 m., 1983

Pernilla Allwin (Fanny Ekdahl), Bertil Guve (Alexander Ekdahl), Jan Malmsjö (Bishop Vergerus), Erland Josephson (Isak Jacobi), Kabi Laretei (Aunt Emma), Gunn Wallgren (Helena Ekdahl), Ewa Froling (Emilie Ekdahl), Gunnar Bjornstrand (Filip Landahl). Directed by Ingmar Bergman and produced by Jorn Donner. Screenplay by Bergman.

There was a time when Ingmar Bergman wanted to make films reflecting the whole of human experience. He asked the big questions about death, sex, and God, and he wasn't afraid of the big, dramatic image, either. Who else (except Woody Allen) has had the temerity to show a man playing chess with Death? Bergman was swinging for the fences in those deliberately big, important films. But he has discovered that a better way to encompass all human experience is to be specific about a small part of it and let the audience draw its own conclusions. In *The Seventh Seal* (1956), he portrayed Death as a symbolic grim reaper. But in *Cries and Whispers* (1973), by showing one particular woman dying painfully while her sisters and her maid stood by helplessly, he said infinitely more about death.

His film *Fanny and Alexander* is one of the most detailed and specific he's ever made, and therefore one of the most universal. It comes directly out of his experiences as a Swede in his mid-sixties who was born into a world of rigid religious belief, grew up in a world of war and turmoil, and is now old enough, wise enough, and resigned enough to develop a sort of philosophical mysticism about life. In its chronology, the film covers only a handful of years. But in its buried implications about life, I believe, it traces the development of Bergman's thought from his school days until the day before yesterday.

Fanny and Alexander is a long film that contains many characters and many events. Very simply: In a Swedish provincial town in the early years of this century, two children are growing up within the bosom of a large, jolly extended family. Their father dies and their mother remarries. Their new stepfather is a stern, authoritarian clergyman who means well but is absolutely incapable of understanding the feelings of others. Escape from his household leads them, by an indirect path, into the life of an old Jewish antique dealer whose life still has room for the mysticism and magic of an earlier time. Not everything is explained by the end of the film, but everything is reconciled.

Bergman has confessed that a great deal of the movie is autobiographical—if not literally, then in terms of its feelings. He had, for example, a father who was a strict clergyman. But it's too easy to assume the bishop in the movie represents only Bergman's father: Can he not also represent Bergman himself, who is seen within the circle of his collaborators as an authoritarian figure with a tendency to know what is right for everyone else? Bergman has hinted that there's a little of himself, indeed, in *all* the male characters in his movies. Looking for Bergman's autobiography in his characters is one thing. I think we also can see *Fanny and Alexander* as the autobiography of his career. The warm humanism of the early scenes reflects his own beginnings in naturalism. The stern aestheticism of the middle scenes reflects his own middle period, with its obsession with both philosophical and stylistic black-and-white. The last third of the film, like the last third of his career, admits that there are more things in heaven and on Earth than dreamed of in his philosophy.

Fanny and Alexander is a big, exciting, ambitious film—more of a beginning than, as Bergman claims, the summary of his career. If you've followed him on his long trek of discovery, this will feel like a film of resolution. If you're coming fresh to Bergman, it may, paradoxically, seem to burst with the sort of invention we associate with young first-time directors. It's a film for all seasons.

Fantasia ★ ★ ★ ★
G, 117 m., 1940

With Leopold Stokowski and the Philadelphia Orchestra. Narrative Introductions: Deems Taylor. Production Supervision: Ben Sharpsteen. Story Direction: Joe Grant and Dick Huemer. Musical Direction: Edward H. Plumb. Musical Film Editor: Stephen Csillag. Recording: William E. Garity, C.O. Slyfield, J.N.A. Hawkins.

Cartoon figures had hard edges before *Fantasia* was made in 1940, and many of them moved to rinky-tink music. Walt Disney did not invent animation, but he nurtured it into an art form that could hold its own against any "realistic" movie, and when he gathered his artists to create *Fantasia* he felt a restlessness, a desire to try something new.

The basic idea of the film had already been decided upon: take some of the most familiar compositions of classical music and illustrate them with animated drawings. Simply said. And some of the passages in the film would be in forms that were long familiar to the Disney artists. Mickey Mouse's adventures in "The Sorcerer's Apprentice" section, for example, placed him in a visual universe that was familiar to anyone who had ever seen Mickey in a cartoon.

But for other sections of the film, Disney wanted to try some new approaches. In their definitive 1981 book *Disney Animation*, studio artists Frank Thomas and Ollie Johnston remember the way Walt insisted on something new in the sequence where a fairy flies around the wood scattering fairy dust everywhere. Disney walked into a meeting, they recall, and saw a pastel drawing of a fairy. He liked it, especially its soft, luminescent quality. That's what he wanted in his film.

If there's one thing the book makes clear, it's that there's a lot more to animation than just drawing little animals and cartoon characters and having them hop around. The artists experimented for weeks with the fairy sequence, and eventually used a whole arsenal of techniques to get the desired effects: not only straightforward drawing and traditional animation, but also foreground and background matte paintings, gels, trick dissolves, multilayered paintings, and other special effects. The effortless magic of the sequence hardly suggests the painstaking work that went into it.

Throughout *Fantasia*, Disney pushes the edges of the envelope. And what makes this fiftieth anniversary re-release of the film special is the effort the studio has gone to in restoring the movie as it originally looked. *Fantasia* was the first movie released in stereophonic sound. Disney called his process "Fantasound," and used three speakers: one behind the screen and one on either side.

The original sound track, featuring Leopold Stokowski and the Philadelphia Orchestra, has been remastered, scrubbed, cleaned of hisses and pops, and now glows with its original warmth. "Fantasound" has also been restored in the version I saw, and is demonstrated in an opening sequence where Stokowski leads first one side of his orchestra, then the other, then the center, then all together, so that the audience can clearly hear the sources of the sound.

The picture looks better, too—cleaner and brighter. One surprising item of trivia about *Fantasia* is that this fiftieth anniversary release of the film is actually its first true national release. It was originally "roadshowed" in theaters equipped with special sound, and in later years was released piecemeal, here and there, always showing somewhere, never everywhere.

Purists will be pleased that the Disney people have also made the momentous decision to release the film in its original aspect ratio of 1:1.33—in other words, in a format about four feet wide for every three feet high. This is the format in which *Fantasia* and almost every other film made before 1953 was originally filmed in.

In several other re-releases of its classics, including such works as *Pinocchio* and *Snow White*, Disney cropped the top and bottom of the original artists' work in order to create the spurious illusion that the film was "widescreen." This proved nothing and was a form of desecration committed against drawings where everything had been carefully framed in the first place. It may seem like a small point to some people, but we're talking about film masterpieces here. Would anybody think it was all right to crop the side off a great painting just to make it match a newly fashioned shape? At last, with *Fantasia*, Disney has done the right thing.

Farewell, My Lovely ★ ★ ★ ★
R, 95 m., 1975

Robert Mitchum (Philip Marlowe), Charlotte Rampling (Velma), John Ireland (Lieutenant Nulty), Sylvia Miles (Mrs. Nulty), Jack O'Halloran (Moose Malloy), Anthony Zerbe (Brunette), Harry Dean Stanton (Billy Rolfe), Walter McGinn (Tommy Ray). Directed by Dick Richards and produced by George Pappas and Jerry Bruckheimer. Screenplay by David Zelag Goodman.

Los Angeles, 1941. A run-down street of seedy shop fronts and blinking neon signs. Music from a lonely horn. The camera pans up to a second-story window of a flophouse. In the window, his hat pushed back, his tie undone, Philip Marlowe lights another cigarette and waits for the cops to arrive. He is ready to tell his story.

These opening shots are so evocative of Raymond Chandler's immortal Marlowe, archetypical private eye, haunting the underbelly of Los Angeles, that if we're Chandler fans we hold our breath. Is the ambience going to be maintained, or will this be another campy rip-off? Half an hour into the movie, we relax. *Farewell, My Lovely* never steps wrong. It is, indeed, the most evocative of all the private-detective movies we have had in the last few years. It is not as great as Roman Polanski's *Chinatown*, which was concerned with larger subjects, but in the genre itself there hasn't been anything this good since Hollywood was doing Philip Marlowe the first time around. One reason is that Dick Richards, the director, takes his material and character absolutely seriously. He is not uneasy with it, as Robert Altman was when he had Elliott Gould flirt with seriousness in *The Long Goodbye*. Richards doesn't hedge his bet.

And neither does Robert Mitchum, in what becomes his definitive performance. Mitchum is one of the great screen presences. He was born to play the weary, cynical, doggedly romantic Marlowe. His voice and his face and the way he lights his cigarette are all exactly right, and seem totally effortless. That's his trademark. In a good Mitchum performance, we are never aware he is acting. And it is only when we measure the distances between his characters that we can see what he is doing. Mitchum is at home on the kinds of streets Philip Marlowe worked: streets of one-room furnished flats and pink stucco hotels, out-of-town newsstands and seedy bars, and always the drowsy commonness of the flat lands leading up to the baroque mansions in the hills and canyons.

Farewell, My Lovely gets all of this just right—Angelo Graham's art direction is a triumph—and then places Mitchum's Marlowe in the center of it and leads him through one of Chandler's tortuous plots. Although everything does finally tie together in this one (as it never did in Chandler's labyrinthine *The Big Sleep*), it doesn't matter that much. What's important is the gallery of characters Marlowe encounters, each grotesque and beautiful in his own way. The most touching is Moose Malloy, played by an ex-prizefighter named Jack O'Halloran. Moose towers over everyone in the film, both in stature and in the immensity of his need. Seven years ago he fell in love with a hooker named Velma and they were going to be married, but something went wrong during a bank job, and Moose took the rap. When he gets out of prison, he hires Marlowe to find his Velma.

Marlowe's quest for Velma, a faded memory from a hopeless love affair, leads him, as we might have known, into a case a lot larger and more important than he could have suspected. There is an odyssey through a lurid whorehouse and a killing in a ghetto bar, and a midnight rendezvous that ends in another death, and always there is Lieutenant Nulty, of the Los Angeles Police Department, trying to figure out why Marlowe winds up attached to so many dead bodies. Richards's approach, with screenplay by David Zelag Goodman, is to start the story at the end with Marlowe trying to explain things to Nulty and then flash back to the beginning and let Marlowe elaborate on the story voice-over. It is a strategy that is often distracting in movies. But not this time, because it borrows from Chandler's own first-person narrative. And it provides great one-liners, as when the elusive Velma (Charlotte Rampling) sizes Marlowe up and down and he says, "She threw me a look I caught in my hip pocket."

Farewell, My Lovely is a great entertainment and a celebration of Robert Mitchum's absolute originality. The day after you view it, you might find yourself quoting lines to friends, which is always the test in these cases, because most of the time private-eye stories have no meaning at all unless it is in the way their heroes behave in the face of the most unsettling revelations about human nature. This time Philip Marlowe behaves very well.

Farewell to the King ★ ★ ★
PG, 113 m., 1989

Nick Nolte (Learoyd), Nigel Havers (Botanist), Frank McRae (Tenga), Gerry Lopez (Gwai), Marilyn Tokuda (Yoo), Choy Chang Wing (Lian), James Fox (Ferguson). Directed by John Milius and produced by Albert S. Ruddy and Andre Morgan. Screenplay by Milius.

The opening image in *Farewell to the King* shows a man walking out on World War II. His lifeboat has been washed ashore on a tropical island somewhere in the Pacific, and while his fellow survivors are captured and executed by the Japanese, he plunges into the jungle, staggering and hallucinating, until he is found by a native tribe. When the movie rejoins his life three years later, he is the king of the tribe, and is trying to steer it clear of any contact with the war.

This image—of the white man deep in the jungle, ruling a tribe—must be a compelling one for John Milius, who wrote and directed *Farewell to the King*. In his screenplay for Francis Coppola's *Apocalypse Now*, Milius created a similar character for Marlon Brando. Learoyd, the character played by Nick Nolte in this film, is like Kurtz, the Brando character: He has gone both AWOL and native, and lives in a jungle fastness, catered to by a tribe that sees him as a sort of god.

There is probably a deep-seated personal impulse at work here. Does Milius imagine his characters shouldering the White Man's Burden, or does he see them escaping a corrupt civilization to live in an unspoiled natural society? With Kurtz, we never knew, but the Nolte character in *Farewell to the King* gladly embraces his new situation and wants to drop out of Western civilization if he can. At a key point in the film, he shows a visiting British officer a secret valley in the heart of the island, where a sort of Shangri-la has grown up, isolated from the corruptions of the outside. He feels it is his mission to protect this sacred place from the Japanese *and* the Allies.

It is tempting to consider the politics of this movie, which waver between benevolent despotism and anthropological zeal. But perhaps Milius really has no message. The spirit of the film seems closer to the work of Conrad or Melville than to contemporary politics: Here is an extraordinary man, the story says, who finds himself in an extraordinary situation and takes advantage of it. I was reminded a little of Van Wyk, the Dutchman in Conrad's *End of the Tether* who runs his corner of the Pacific more or less the way he wants to, and knows enough about his fellow Europeans to keep them at arm's length.

In a film like this, the central performance is crucial, and Nick Nolte is absorbed by the character. Just a few days before seeing *Farewell to the King* I saw Nolte as a painter—a manipulator and player in the New York art world—in the Martin Scorsese segment of *New York Stories*. Now here he was half-naked in the jungle, dandling an infant on his knee. The strength of Nolte as an actor is that he seemed to feel at home in both environments; he was an inhabitant, not a visitor.

The plot, based on a novel by Pierre Schoendoerffer, is much more predictable than the situation. Learoyd, the Nolte character, is a full-blown tribal king by the time we see him again, and the movie bypasses any attempt to show how he won that status, preferring instead to move ahead to a more conventional action scenario. British commandos, led by Nigel Havers, are parachuted onto the island to try to enlist the American and his tribesmen in the war against the Japanese. Learoyd wants nothing to do with them.

"You cannot turn your back on this war," Havers warns him, and sure enough, he is right. Milius then unfolds a more or less predictable series of action scenes in which Learoyd turns into a superhuman fighting machine, blasting countless foes to smithereens before finally announcing, "From this day forward, I will raise my hand against no man." This vow is less impressive than it might have been, since there are few enemies left alive to raise his hand against. And then there is a sequel revealing whether Learoyd realizes his dream of living apart from civilization.

What is most interesting about *Farewell to the King* is its impulse to tell this story at all. It could so easily have become ridiculous, or merely violent, but Milius keeps edging back toward the philosophy of his hero. Learoyd is given several speeches in which he explains why he believes what he believes, and the movie never becomes only an action film. There is a contradiction somewhere, I suppose, in the story of a pacifistic isolationist who kills in order to defend his vision, but what the heck, nobody's perfect.

Fast Times at Ridgemont High ★
R, 92 m., 1982

Sean Penn (Jeff Spicoli), Jennifer Jason Leigh (Stacy Hamilton), Judge Reinhold (Brad Hamilton), Robert Romanus (Mike Damone), Brian Backer (Rat Ratner), Phoebe Cates (Linda Barrett). Directed by Amy Heckerling and produced by Art Linson and Irving Azoff. Screenplay by Cameron Crowe.

How could they do this to Jennifer Jason Leigh? How could they put such a fresh and cheerful person into such a scuz-pit of a movie? Don't they know they have a star on their hands? I didn't even know who Leigh was when I walked into *Fast Times at Ridgemont High*, and yet I was completely won over by her. She contained so much life and light that she was a joy to behold. And then she and everybody else in this so-called comedy is invited to plunge into offensive vulgarity. Let me make myself clear. I am not against vulgarity as a subject for a movie comedy. Sometimes I treasure it, when it's used with inspiration, as in *The Producers* or *National Lampoon's Animal House*. But vulgarity is a very tricky thing to handle in a comedy; tone is everything, and the makers of *Fast Times at Ridgemont High* have an absolute gift for taking potentially funny situations and turning them into general embarrassment. They're tone-deaf.

The movie's another one of those adolescent sex romps, such as *Porky's* and *Animal House*, in which part of the humor comes from raunchy situations and dialogue. This movie is *so* raunchy, however, that the audience can't quite believe it. I went to a sneak preview thrown by a rock radio station, and the audience had come for a good time. But during a scene involving some extremely frank talk about certain popular methods of sexual behavior, even the rock fans were grossed out. There's a difference between raunchiness and gynecological detail.

The movie's cast struggles valiantly through all this dreck. Rarely have I seen so many attractive young performers invited to appear in so many unattractive scenes. Leigh, for example, plays a virginal young student at Ridgemont High. She's curious about sex, so the script immediately turns her into a promiscuous sex machine who will go to bed with anybody. And then her sexual experiences all turn out to have an unnecessary element of realism, so that we have to

see her humiliated, disappointed, and embarrassed. Whatever happened to upbeat sex? Whatever happened to love and lust and romance, and scenes where good-looking kids had a little joy and excitement in life, instead of all this grungy downbeat humiliation? Why does someone as pretty as Leigh have to have her nudity exploited in shots where the only point is to show her ill-at-ease?

If this movie had been directed by a man, I'd call it sexist. It was directed by a woman, Amy Heckerling—and it's sexist all the same. It clunks to a halt now and then for some heartfelt, badly handled material about pregnancy and abortion. I suppose that's Heckerling paying dues to some misconception of the women's movement. But for the most part this movie just exploits its performers by trying to walk a tightrope between comedy and sexploitation.

In addition to Leigh's work, however, there are some other good performances. Sean Penn is perfect as the pot-smoking space cadet who has been stoned since the third grade. Phoebe Cates is breathtaking as the more experienced girl who gives Leigh those distasteful lessons in love. Judge Reinhold has fun as a perennial fast-food cook who rebels against the silly uniforms he's supposed to wear. Ray Walston is suitably hateful as the dictatorial history teacher, Mr. Hand. But this movie could have been a *lot* more fun if it hadn't chosen to confuse embarrassment with humor. The unnecessary detail about sexual functions isn't funny, it's distasteful. Leigh looks so young, fresh, cheerful, and innocent that we don't laugh when she gets into unhappy scenes with men—we wince. The whole movie is a failure of taste, tone, and nerve—the waste of a good cast on erratic, offensive material that hasn't been thought through, or maybe even thought about.

Fat Man and Little Boy ★ ½
PG-13, 126 m., 1989

Paul Newman (Gen. Leslie R. Groves), Dwight Schultz (J. Robert Oppenheimer), Bonnie Bedelia (Kitty Oppenheimer), John Cusack (Michael Merriman), Laura Dern (Kathleen Robinson), Ron Frazier (Peer de Silva), John C. McGinley (Richard Schoenfield), Natasha Richardson (Jean Tatlock), Del Close (Worried Man). Directed by Roland Joffe and produced by Tony Garnett. Screenplay by Bruce Robinson and Joffe.

During the dark war days of 1942, the United States government gathered a group of the most brilliant scientists in the nation and sent them to live in the dust and mud of Los Alamos, New Mexico, where the army had hammered together a town for them overnight. Their mission on this top-secret base was to design and build an atomic bomb. They made an odd assembly, the intellectuals from Berkeley and Chicago, the refugees from Hitler, the tinkerers and craftsmen who were to physically construct the bomb, and all of their wives, children, lovers, pets, libraries, pianos, and eccentricities. To weld them together, the army assigned Gen. Leslie R. Groves, whose previous task had been to build the Pentagon.

Their endeavor was known as the Manhattan Project, and they were told they were in a race with Germany to build the first doomsday weapon. Germany surrendered before the bomb was finished, but it was used, of course, on Japan, and the shadow cast by its mushroom cloud still hovers over all of us today. *Fat Man and Little Boy* is a fiction based on the Manhattan Project, but it is thin and unfocused and hardly even suggests the enormous moral and practical questions that the scientists wrestled with, out there in the New Mexico desert.

The movie labors under an enormous handicap: A much better, more intelligent, and more exciting film has already been made about this same subject. It is *The Day After Trinity* (1980), a documentary by Jon Else that includes government footage from Los Alamos as well as interviews, then and now, with many of the men who worked on the bomb. In my review of *The Day After Trinity*, I wrote that it "delivers more suspense than most of the thrillers I have seen," and now that we have a fiction film to compare it to, that is even more clear.

The story of the birth of the bomb is one of high drama, but it was largely intellectual drama, as the scientists asked themselves, in conversations and nightmares, what terror they were unleashing on the earth. *Fat Man and Little Boy* reduces their debates to the childish level of Hollywood stereotyping, giving us a simplified personality conflict between General Groves (Paul Newman) and J. Robert Oppenheimer (Dwight Schultz), the scientific leader of the undertaking. Groves is portrayed as a saner, gentler version of George Patton—gruff, barking orders—and Oppenheimer is seen as a brilliant but unworldly intellectual. Since the

two men do not really violently disagree on anything, their conflict reduces itself to emotional speech-making, which, when carefully listened to, is not really about anything.

The Day After Trinity paints a picture of the community which grew up in Los Alamos, where the music of Glenn Miller and the popularity of the martini helped to break the tension after the day's work. *Fat Man and Little Boy* simplifies this, too, by showing the social life but not the tension. Most of the scientific details in the movie are reduced to scenes like the one where a young scientist (John Cusack) triggers an experiment, holds his breath, and then relaxes when the world does not vaporize. After work, the scientists attend cocktail parties which seem to exist only for the purpose of introducing minor characters, or they sit around holding earnest (but very brief) discussions that are so simplified by the screenplay that they sound like parodies.

The usual romantic subplots don't contribute much. Oppenheimer is seen torn between his left-wing, security-risk mistress (Natasha Richardson) and his adoring wife (Bonnie Bedelia), who essentially thinks he is the greatest man alive and deserves anything he wants. The Cusack character also has an adoring woman, a local nurse (Laura Dern) who whispers that she loves him as he dies of radiation poisoning. But the movie is cobbled together so ineptly that Cusack's death scene is intercut with the night of the first bomb test, and is so thoroughly upstaged that it never really ever gets the emotional reaction it deserves.

This movie, written by Bruce Robinson and the director, Roland Joffe, can't even steal successfully. In *The Day After Trinity*, there is gallows humor as a scientist remembers that he and his colleagues placed bets before the first atomic explosion on whether it would destroy the world or only New Mexico. They thought there was a real possibility the first nuclear explosion would rip the fabric of matter and expand wildly out of control. If *Fat Man and Little Boy* had simply recycled the dialogue and the incredibly exciting events of that day, it would have had an ending. Instead, Joffe is unable to deliver a climax even as the bomb explodes; he shows it reflected in the goggles of a character, and then cuts to what looks like special-effects footage of nuclear flames.

Much of the imagery in *Fat Man* is obviously inspired by the earlier documentary footage, including such details as what

the first bomb looked like, and how odd it was suspended in a tower in the desert. The look of the film is nevertheless all wrong; Vilmos Zsigmond's cinematography bathes everything in muted browns and golds and maroons so that New Mexico looks like outtakes from *The Godfather* when it should look stark and bright in the Southwest sunlight, and painted with bold O'Keeffe colors.

As for the performances, they are mostly hapless. Paul Newman is unable to generate any particular tone for his General Groves—no wonder, since the character has been written as a schoolmaster and scold—and Dwight Schultz's Oppenheimer lacks the quickness and fire of the real man, and seems curiously muted and befuddled. Many of the scientists at Los Alamos were young, it is true, but were they as young as the actors who play them here? Wearing their fedora hats and rimless glasses and smoking cigarettes, some of these actors look like high school kids playing adults in the class play.

Fatal Attraction ★ ★ ½
R, 120 m., 1987

Michael Douglas (Dan Gallagher), Glenn Close (Alex Forrest), Anne Archer (Beth Gallagher), Ellen Hamilton Latzen (Ellen), Stuart Pankin (Jimmy), Ellen Foley (Hildy), Fred Gwynne (Arthur). Directed by Adrian Lyne and produced by Stanley R. Jaffe and Sherry Lansing. Screenplay by James Dearden.

Fatal Attraction is a spellbinding psychological thriller, and could have been a great movie if the filmmakers had not thrown character and plausibility to the winds in the last act to give us their version of a grown-up *Friday the 13th.*

Because the good things in the movie, including the performances, are so very good, it's a shame that the film's potential for greatness was so blatantly compromised. The movie is so right for so long that you can almost feel the moment when the script goes "click" and sells out.

The story stars Michael Douglas as a lawyer who has been happily married for nine years, has a six-year-old daughter, loves his wife, and has no particular problems on the day when he meets an intriguing blonde (Glenn Close) at a business party. She makes it her business to get to know him, and one weekend when Douglas's wife and daughter are out of town visiting his in-laws, he invites the blonde out to dinner.

She finds him willing to be seduced, and they have wild, passionate sex. Their couplings take place in a freight elevator, on the kitchen sink, and, I think, in bed; the film was directed by Adrian *(9½ Weeks)* Lyne, whose ideas of love and genital acrobatics seem more or less equivalent.

Douglas has made it clear that he's a happily married man and that he sees their meeting as a one-night stand ("Two adults who saw an opportunity and took advantage of it"), but Close doesn't see it that way. The moment sex is over for her, capture begins, and she starts a series of demands on Douglas's time and attention.

He tells her to get lost. She grows pathological. She visits him at the office, calls him at home in the middle of the night, throws acid on his car, visits his wife under the pretext of buying their apartment. Desperate to keep his secret and preserve his happy marriage, Douglas tries to reason with her, threaten her, and even hide from her, but she is implacable. (And you should read no further if you plan to view the movie—or perhaps, come to think of it, you should.)

The early and middle passages of the movie are handled with convincing psychological realism; James Dearden's dialogue sounds absolutely right, especially the way he allows the Close character to bait her hook with honeyed come-ons and then set it with jealousy, possessiveness, and finally guilt (after she says, inevitably, that she is pregnant). With the exception of the silly sex scenes, *Fatal Attraction* never steps wrong until its third act—and then it steps very wrong.

First, let me suggest how I hoped the movie would continue. Having created a believable and interesting marriage between Michael Douglas and Anne Archer (who is wonderful as his wife), and having drawn Glenn Close as a terrifying and yet always plausible other woman, I hoped the film would continue to follow its psychological exploration through to the end.

I wanted, for example, to hear a good talk between Douglas and Archer, in which truth was told and the strength of the marriage was tested. I wanted to see more of the inner workings of Close's mind. I wanted to know more about how Douglas really felt about the situation; although he grows to hate Close, is he really completely indifferent to the knowledge that she carries his child?

The movie does not explore any of those avenues, although the filmmakers clearly have the intelligence to do so. Instead, the last third of the movie collapses into pathetic melodrama. The big scene of truth between Douglas and Archer is short-changed and feels unfinished. There is a pathetic sequence in which Close captures their daughter and scares her with a roller-coaster ride, while a frantic Archer gets in a car crash and breaks her arm. Give me a break.

And then there is the horror movie conclusion, complete with the unforgivable *Friday the 13th* cliché that the villain is never *really* dead. The conclusion, by the way, operates on the premise that Douglas cares absolutely nothing for his unborn child.

Fatal Attraction was produced by Stanley R. Jaffe and Sherry Lansing, and it seems to repeat a pattern for them. In 1984 they made *Firstborn*, with Teri Garr as a divorced mother who falls in love with Peter Weller as a man who is very wrong for her family. The first two-thirds of that film are also psychologically sound and dramatically fascinating, and then it degenerates into a canned formula of violence and an idiotic chase scene. Now they throw away the ending of *Fatal Attraction*. What's the matter here? Do they lack the courage to follow their convictions through to the end? They seem to have a knack for finding thoughtful, sensitive screenplays about interesting adults, and then adding gruesome Hollywood horror formulas to them. *Fatal Attraction* clearly had the potential to be a great movie. I walked out feeling cheated and betrayed.

Fellini's Roma ★ ★ ★ ★
R, 128 m., 1973

Featuring Peter Gonzales, Stefano Majore, Britta Barnes, Pia de Doses, Fiona Florence, Marno Maitland, Giovannoli Renato, Anna Magnani, Gore Vidal, and Federico Fellini. Directed by Federico Fellini. Screenplay by Bernardino Zapponi and Fellini.

Federico Fellini first included his name in the title of one of his movies with *Fellini Satyricon* (1969), and then for legal reasons: A quickie Italian version of the Satyricon was being palmed off in international film markets as the real thing. Once having savored the notion, however, Fellini found it a good one, and so we have *Fellini's Roma*, which was followed by *Fellini Casanova*.

The name in the title doesn't seem conceited or affected, as it might from another director (*Peckinpah's Albuquerque?*). This *is* Fellini's Rome and nobody else's, just as all of his films since *La Dolce Vita* have been autobiographical musings and confessions from the most personal—and the best—director of his time. Any connection with a real city on the map of Italy is libelous. Fellini's Rome gets its suburbs trimmed when he goes for a haircut.

The movie isn't a documentary, although sometimes he lets it look like one. It's a rambling essay, meant to feel like free association. There's a very slight narrative thread, about a young man named Fellini who leaves the little town of Rimini and comes to the great city and is overwhelmed by its pleasures of body and spirit. He moves into a mad boarding house that would make a movie all by itself; he dines with his neighbors in great outdoor feasts when the summer heat drives everyone into the piazzas; he attends a raucous vaudeville show and he visits his first whorehouse . . . and then his second.

This material, filmed with loving attention to period detail, exists by itself in the movie; there's no effort to link the naive young Fellini with the confident genius who appears elsewhere in the movie. It's as if Fellini, the consummate inventor of fantasies, didn't grow out of his young manhood—he created it from scratch.

The autobiographical material is worked in between pseudo-documentary scenes that contain some of the most brilliant images Fellini has ever devised. The movie opens with a monumental Roman traffic jam that, typically, becomes important because Fellini has deigned to photograph it. He swoops above it on a crane, directing his camera, his movie, and the traffic. A blinding rainstorm turns everything into a hellish apparition, and then there's a final shot, held just long enough to make its point, of the autos jammed around the Colosseum.

The image is both perfect and natural; as someone commented about Fellini's *8½*, his movies are filled with images, and they're all obvious. If Bergman is the great introvert of the movies, forever probing more and more deeply, Fellini is the joyous exponent of surfaces and excess, of letting more hang out than there is.

The obviousness of his images gives his movies a curious kind of clarity; he isn't reaching for things to say, but finding ways to say the same things more memorably. The decadence of Rome has been one of his favorite subjects throughout his career, and who could forget Anita Ekberg in the fountain, or the Mass procession at dawn, in *La Dolce Vita?*

But in *Roma*, he is even more direct, more stark: An expedition to inspect progress on the Rome subway system suddenly becomes transcendent when workmen break through to an underground crypt from pre-Christian times. The frescoes on the walls are so clear they might have been painted yesterday—until the air of the modern city touches them.

Rome, the eternal city, has historically been as carnal as it has been sacred. Fellini won't settle for one or the other; he uses scenes of carnality to symbolize a blessed state, and vice versa. Nothing could be more eternal, more patient, and more resigned than Fellini's use of a weary prostitute standing beside a highway outside Rome. She is tall, huge-bosomed, garishly made up, and her feet are tired. She stands among the broken stones of the Roman Empire, expecting nothing, hoping for nothing.

The prostitute, so often used as a symbol of fleeting moments and insubstantial experiences, becomes eternal; and the Church, always the symbol of the unchanging, the rock, becomes temporal. In his most audacious sequence, Fellini gives us an "ecclesiastical fashion show," with roller-skating priests, and nuns whose habits are made of blinking neon lights. What is unreal, and where is the real? Fellini doesn't know, and he seems to believe that Rome has never known. Rome has simply endured, waiting in the hope of someday finding out.

Fellini's Roma was attacked in some circles as an example of Fellini coasting on his genius. I find this point of view completely incomprehensible. Critics who would force Fellini back into traditional narrative films are missing the point; Fellini isn't just giving us a lot of flashy scenes, he's building a narrative that has a city for its protagonist instead of a single character.

The only sly thing is that the city isn't Rome—it's Fellini, disguised in bricks, mortar, and ruins. Fellini, who cannot find his way between the flesh and the spirit, who cannot find the connection between his youth and his greatness, and whose gift is to make movies where everything is obvious and nothing is simple. That was the dilemma that the Fellini character faced in *8½*, when he couldn't make sense of his life, and it's the dilemma we all face every day, isn't it?

Ferris Bueller's Day Off ★ ★ ★
PG-13, 103 m., 1986

Matthew Broderick (Ferris), Alan Ruck (Cameron Frye), Mia Sara (Sloane), Jeffrey Jones (Ed Rooney), Cindy Pickett (Mrs. Bueller), Jennifer Grey (Katie Bueller), Lyman Ward (Mr. Bueller), Edie McClurg (Secretary), Charlie Sheen (Young Punk). Directed by John Hughes and produced by Hughes and Tom Jacobson. Screenplay by Hughes.

Here is one of the most innocent movies in a long time, a sweet, warmhearted comedy about a kid who skips school so he can help his best friend win some self-respect. The therapy he has in mind includes a day's visit to Chicago, and after we've seen the Sears Tower and a parade down Dearborn Street, the Art Institute and the Board of Trade, architectural landmarks and lunch on Rush Street, and a game at Wrigley Field, we've got to concede that the city and state film offices have done their job. If *Ferris Bueller's Day Off* fails on every other level, at least it works as a travelogue.

It does, however, work on at least a few other levels. The movie stars Matthew Broderick as Ferris, a bright kid from the North Shore who fakes an illness so he can spend a day in town with his best friend, Cameron (Alan Ruck). At first, it seems as if skipping school is all he has in mind—especially after he talks Cameron into borrowing his dad's antique red Ferrari, a car the father loves more than Cameron himself.

The body of the movie is a lighthearted excursion through the Loop, including a German-American Day parade in which Ferris leaps aboard a float, grabs a microphone, and starts singing "Twist and Shout" while the polka band backs him up. The kids fake their way into a fancy restaurant for lunch, spend some time gawking at the masterpieces in the Art Institute, and then go out to Wrigley Field, where, of course, they are late and have to take left-field seats (the movie gets that detail right; it would be too much to hope that the kids could arrive in the third inning and find seats in the bleachers).

There is one great, dizzying moment when the kids visit the top of the Sears Tower and lean forward and press their foreheads against the glass, and look straight down at the tiny cars and little specks of life far below, and begin to talk about their lives. And that introduces, subtly, the buried theme of the movie, which is that Ferris wants to help

Cameron gain self-respect in the face of his father's materialism.

Ferris is, in fact, a bit of a preacher. "Life goes by so fast," he says, "that if you don't stop and look around, you might miss it." He's sensitive to the hurt inside his friend's heart, as Cameron explains how his dad has cherished and restored the red Ferrari and given it a place of honor in the house—a place denied to Cameron.

Ferris Bueller was directed by John Hughes, the philosopher of adolescence, whose credits include *Sixteen Candles*, *The Breakfast Club*, and *Pretty in Pink*. In all of his films, adults are strange, distant creatures, who love their teen-agers, but fail completely to understand them. That's the case here, all right: All of the adults, including a bumbling high school dean (Jeffrey Jones) are dim-witted and one-dimensional. And the movie's solutions to Cameron's problems are pretty simplistic. But the film's heart is in the right place, and *Ferris Bueller* is slight, whimsical, and sweet.

The Field ★
PG-13, 107 m., 1991

Richard Harris ("Bull" McCabe), Sean Bean (Tadgh McCabe), Brenda Fricker (Maggie McCabe), John Hurt ("Bird" O'Donnell), Malachy McCourt (Sergeant), Tom Berenger (The American). Directed by Jim Sheridan and produced by Noel Pearson. Screenplay by Sheridan.

The Field is a grim allegory of hard life on the land—a symbolic play transplanted uneasily to the greater realism of the film medium, where what we might accept on the stage now looks contrived and artificial. This was not a work that called out to be filmed. Once filmed, it calls out to be forgotten. But it will always have a footnote in cinematic history, because Richard Harris's work was nominated for an Academy Award in the best actor category.

Harris plays "Bull" McCabe, a weathered and bearded man of the soil, who has spent a lifetime tending a small field in his corner of Ireland. The time is the 1920s, but it could be the 1820s for all that life has changed in this soggy and overcast backwater, where the miserable McCabe and his retarded son, Tadgh, haul wicker baskets full of seaweed up the cruel cliffs and dump them on the field, as their fathers and the fathers of their fathers have done before them. Then a slick Irish-American (Tom Berenger) comes to town, smoking cigarettes and wearing a camel hair overcoat, and wants to buy the field, in order to strip-mine it, I think.

His arrival inevitably precipitates a crisis in the village, which can only be settled by rape, murder, and a public auction, accompanied by no end of wise epigrams by the wizened local inhabitants, who have been waiting a generation for their chance to mutter profound sayings about the land and the people who live on't. Harris growls and howls and looks like Lear as he wades about in the bitter sea and strides through the mud and peat, and there is no doubting this is a good performance, but in the service of a hopeless cause.

If I were watching this as a play, I might just be able to care about the field, if it were located far offstage. But the motion picture camera has an unforgiving way of photographing anything that is put before it, and so we can easily see that the McCabes, father and son and father's father and all, have been wasting their effort dragging that wet seaweed up the cliff to fertilize the field, because the village is surrounded by thousands of acres of prime pastureage. Tom Berenger is also on a fool's errand: Why does he need to strip the field when, if there is one thing the district has more of than fields, it is mineral rights, and if there is one thing it has no need of, it is gravel?

No, this play is not about the field, it is about eternal questions. Questions about (1) a man's right to the land, and (2) whether the owner should sell out to the highest bidder, and (3) whether the Irish in America have lost their respect for the land and its people, and forgotten the old ways. The answer to these questions, laid out here in dirge and lamentation, is that (1) if a man and his father and his father's father spend their lifetime dragging seaweed up a cliff and dumping it on the land, they have, by God, a right to that land, and (2) the owner should therefore sell it at a loss or give it away, and (3) yes.

Field of Dreams ★ ★ ★ ★
PG, 107 m., 1989

Kevin Costner (Ray Kinsella), Amy Madigan (Annie Kinsella), Gaby Hoffman (Karin Kinsella), Ray Liotta (Shoeless Joe Jackson), Timothy Busfield (Mark), James Earl Jones (Terence Mann), Burt Lancaster (Dr. "Moonlight" Graham), Frank Whaley (Archie Graham), Dwier Brown (John Kinsella). Directed by Phil Alden Robinson and produced by Lawrence Gordon and Charles Gordon. Screenplay by Robinson.

The farmer is standing in the middle of a cornfield when he hears the voice for the first time: "If you build it, he will come." He looks around and doesn't see anybody. The voice speaks again, soft and confidential: "If you build it, he will come." Sometimes you can get too much sun, out there in a hot Iowa cornfield in the middle of the season. But this isn't a case of sunstroke.

Up until the farmer (Kevin Costner) starts hearing voices, *Field of Dreams* is a completely sensible film about a young couple who want to run a family farm in Iowa. Ray and Annie Kinsella (Costner and Amy Madigan) have tested the fast track and had enough of it, and they enjoy sitting on the porch and listening to the grass grow. When the voice speaks for the first time, the farmer is baffled, and so was I: Could this be one of those religious pictures where a voice tells the humble farmer where to build the cathedral?

It's a religious picture, all right, but the religion is baseball. And when he doesn't understand the spoken message, Ray Kinsella is granted a vision of a baseball diamond, right there in his cornfield. If he builds it, the voice seems to promise, Joe Jackson will come and play on it—Shoeless Joe, who was a member of the infamous 1919 Black Sox team but protested until the day he died that he played the best he could.

As *Field of Dreams* developed this fantasy, I found myself being willingly drawn into it. Movies are often so timid these days, so afraid to take flights of the imagination, that there is something grand and brave about a movie where a voice tells a farmer to build a baseball diamond so that Shoeless Joe Jackson can materialize out of the cornfield and hit a few fly balls. This is the kind of movie Frank Capra might have directed and James Stewart might have starred in—a movie about dreams.

It is important not to tell too much about the plot. (I was grateful I knew nothing about the movie when I went to see it, but the ads gave away the Shoeless Joe angle.) Let it be said that Annie Kinsella supports her husband's vision, and that he finds it necessary to travel east to Boston so he can enlist the support of a famous writer (James Earl Jones) who has disappeared from sight, and north to Minnesota to talk to what remains of a doctor (Burt Lancaster) who never got the chance to play with the pros.

The movie sensibly never tries to make the slightest explanation for the strange events that happen after the diamond is constructed. There is, of course, the usual business about how the bank thinks the farmer has gone haywire and wants to foreclose on his mortgage (the Capra and Stewart movies always had evil bankers in them). But there is not a corny, stupid payoff at the end. Instead, the movie depends on a poetic vision to make its point.

The director, Phil Alden Robinson, and the writer, W.P. Kinsella, are dealing with stuff that's close to the heart (it can't be a coincidence that the author and the hero have the same last name). They love baseball, and they think it stands for an earlier, simpler time when professional sports were still games and not industries. There is a speech in this movie about baseball that is so simple and true that it is heartbreaking. And the whole attitude toward the players reflects that attitude. Why do they come back from the great beyond and materialize here in this cornfield? Not to make any kind of vast, earth-shattering statement, but simply to hit a few and field a few, and remind us of a good and innocent time.

It is very tricky to act in a movie like this; there is always the danger of seeming ridiculous. Kevin Costner and Amy Madigan create such a grounded, believable married couple that one of the themes of the movie is the way love means sharing your loved one's dreams. Jones and Lancaster create small, sharp character portraits—two older men who have taken the paths life offered them, but never forgotten what baseball represented to them in their youth.

Field of Dreams will not appeal to grinches and grouches and realists. It is a delicate movie, a fragile construction of one goofy fantasy after another. But it has the courage to be about exactly what it promises. "If you build it, he will come." And he does.

52 Pick-Up ★ ★ ★ ½
R, 111 m., 1986

Roy Scheider (Harry Mitchell), Ann-Margret (Barbara Mitchell), Vanity (Doreen), John Glover (Alan Raimy), Clarence Williams III (Bobby Shy), Lonny Chapman (Jim O'Boyle), Kelly Preston (Cini), Doug McClure (Mark Averson). Directed by John Frankenheimer and produced by Menahem Golan and Yorum Globus. Screenplay by Elmore Leonard and John Steppling.

The old golden-age Warner Brothers crime

dramas knew something that most modern movies have forgotten: Heroes are great, but a movie is only as good as its villain. John Frankenheimer's *52 Pick-Up* provides us with the best, most reprehensible villain of 1986, and uses his vile charm as the starting point for a surprisingly good film.

The villain's name is Raimy, and he is played by John Glover as a charming blackmailer with the looks of an aging British juvenile and a conscience with parts on order. He tries to pull a slick job on a rich businessman named Harry (Roy Scheider). He shows him videotapes of an affair Harry is having with a topless dancer. He wants $110,000.

Harry thinks it over, decides not to pay, and confesses everything to his wife, Barbara (Ann-Margret). She is very hurt, and in a scene of powerful understatement she says she had guessed the truth for a long time, but she just doesn't know why he had to tell her. Then Raimy turns up with another videotape. This one shows the topless dancer being murdered with Harry's gun.

This plot is not startlingly original (although there are some unexpected developments later in the film). What makes it special is the level at which it is told. The screenplay is based on an Elmore Leonard novel, and retains Leonard's gift for terse, colorful dialogue. It also isolates the key ingredient in Leonard's best novels, which is the sight of a marginal character being pushed far beyond his capacity to cope. In *52 Pick-Up*, there are actually three such characters, and by the end of the movie they are all desperately confused and frightened.

One is Raimy, a well-dressed sleazebag who makes porno movies and is capable of cold-blooded murder but caves in completely at the thought of his own destruction. One is Harry, an ordinary amoral businessman who rises to the challenge and figures out a way to outsmart his blackmailers by using their own character defects against them. The third is a sweaty little guy named Leo (Robert Trebor), who works for Raimy and went along with the crime but, holy God, never figured anyone was actually going to get hurt.

The problem with so many action adventures is that nobody in the movies ever seems scared enough. People are getting killed in every other scene, and they stay cool. If the movies were like real life and this kind of torture and murder were going on, everybody would be throwing up every five minutes—like they do in John D. MacDonald's novels.

52 Pick-Up creates that sense of hopelessness and desperation, and it does it with those three performances—three guys who are in way over their heads, and know it all too well.

There are three other good performances in the movie, by Ann-Margret, Vanity, and Clarence Williams III (as a black pimp who is a lot more experienced about violence and death than his cheerful white partners). Is it still necessary to be surprised when Ann-Margret is good in a role, as if she were still making *Viva Las Vegas*? She has grown into a dependable serious actress, and here she does a delicate job of finding the line between anger at what her husband has done and pride in how he is trying to fix it. Vanity has a smaller role, as a prostitute with crucial information, and she does what all good character actors can do—she gives us the sense that she's fresh from intriguing off-screen action.

The story of *52 Pick-Up* is basically revenge melodrama. No thriller fan is going to be very astonished by what happens. What matters is the energy level, and the density of detail in the performances. This is a well-crafted movie by a man who knows how to hook the audience with his story—it's John Frankenheimer's best work in years. And if we can sometimes predict what the characters will do, there's the fascination of seeing them behave like unique and often very weird individuals; they aren't clones. I have gotten to the point where the one thing I know about most thrillers is that I will not be thrilled. *52 Pick-Up* blind-sided me.

Firefox ★ ★ ★ ½
PG, 136 m., 1982

Clint Eastwood (Mitchell Gant), Freddie Jones (Kenneth Aubrey), David Huffman (Buckholz), Warren Clarke (Pavel Upenskoy), Ronald Lacey (Semelovsky), Kenneth Colley (Colonel Kontarsky), Stefan Schnabel (First Secretary). Directed and produced by Clint Eastwood. Screenplay by Alex Lasker and Wendell Wellman.

Clint Eastwood's *Firefox* is a slick, muscular thriller that combines espionage with science fiction. The movie works like a well-crafted machine, and it's *about* a well-crafted machine. The *Firefox* of the title is a top-secret Russian warplane capable of flying six times the speed of sound while remaining invisible on radar. Eastwood's mission, if he chooses to accept it: Infiltrate the Soviet Union disguised as a Las Vegas drug smuggler, and then steal the Firefox by flying it to the West.

This is one of those basic movie plots that can generate a lot of entertainment if it's handled properly. *Firefox* knows the territory. It complicates things slightly by making Eastwood a Vietnam veteran who is sometimes overcome by the hallucination that he's still in combat. The movie calls it Post-Combat Stress Syndrome. But the CIA man who recruits him explains that the government isn't much worried, because you don't have the syndrome while you're *in* combat, you see, but only afterward. Somebody ought to compile a textbook of psychology as practiced in movies.

Anyway, Eastwood trains for the mission, is disguised with a mustache and horn-rim glasses, and survives some uncomfortable moments at Moscow customs before he makes it into Russia. Then he makes contact with a confederation of spies and double agents who lead him to a Jewish dissident who is such a brilliant scientist that he is still being allowed to work on Firefox. Why does the dissident *want* to work on it? Because he knows how Eastwood could steal the plane. All of these scenes include obligatory shots, which are kind of fun to anticipate, if you're a fan of the Alistair Maclean–James Bond–"Mission: Impossible"-*Guns of Navarone* genre. The one indispensable scene is probably the Introduction of the MacGuffin. A MacGuffin, you will remember, was what Alfred Hitchcock called that element of the plot that everybody thinks is important. In this case, it's the Firefox, a long, sleek, cruel-looking machine that looks like a cross between a guided missile and a DeLorean. Eastwood and the camera circle it lovingly; this is the sexiest shot in a movie without a romantic subplot. The movie's climax involves Eastwood's attempt to fly this plane north to the Arctic Circle, make a refueling rendezvous, and then take it on home. His flight is intercut with comic opera scenes involving members of the Russian high command, who argue and bicker while looming over an illuminated map that casts an eerie underlight on their faces, making them look like ghouls from old E.C. comics.

Does Eastwood make it out in one piece? Does he bring along the plane? I wouldn't dream of giving away the plot. But I will say that the movie's climax is a sensational high-altitude dogfight between two different

Firefoxes, and that as Eastwood occupies the Firefox cockpit, surrounded by video screens and computer displays of flight patterns and missile trajectories, it looks as if Dirty Harry has died and gone to Atari heaven. The special effects are really pretty good in this movie. The planes looked surprisingly real to me, and the choreography of the dogfight was not only realistic but understandable. There's one sensational chase sequence that's an homage to *Star Wars*. Remember the *Star Wars* scene where the two ships chased each other between the towering walls of the city in space? Eastwood and his Russian pursuer rocket through a crevice between two ice cliffs, and it looks great even while we're realizing it's logically impossible. I guess that goes for the whole movie.

First Blood ★ ★ ★
R, 94 m., 1982

Sylvester Stallone (Rambo), Richard Crenna (Trautman), Brian Dennehy (Teasle), David Caruso (Mitch). Directed by Ted Kotcheff and produced by Buzz Feitshans. Screenplay by Michael Kozoll, William Sackheim, and Q. Moonblood.

Sylvester Stallone is one of the great physical actors in the movies, with a gift for throwing himself so fearlessly into an action scene that we can't understand why somebody doesn't *really* get hurt. When he explodes near the beginning of *First Blood*, hurling cops aside and breaking out of a jail with his fists and speed, it's such a convincing demonstration of physical strength and agility that we never question the scene's implausibility. In fact, although almost all of *First Blood* is implausible, because it's Stallone on the screen, we'll buy it.

What we can't buy in this movie is the message. It's handled in too heavy-handed a way. Stallone plays a returned Vietnam veteran, a Green Beret skilled in the art of jungle survival and fighting, and after a small-town police force sadistically mishandles him, he declares war on the cops. All of this is set up in scenes of great physical power and strength—and the central sections of the movie, with Stallone and the cops stalking each other through the forests of the Pacific Northwest, have a lot of authority. But then the movie comes down to a face-off between Stallone and his old Green Beret commander (Richard Crenna), and the screenplay gives

Stallone a long, impassioned speech to deliver, a speech in which he cries out against the injustices done to him and against the hippies who demonstrated at the airport when he returned from the war, etc. This is all old, familiar material from a dozen other films—clichés recycled as formula. Bruce Dern did it in *Coming Home* and William Devane in *Rolling Thunder*. Stallone is made to say things that would have much better been implied; Robert De Niro, in *Taxi Driver*, also plays a violent character who was obviously scarred by Vietnam, but the movie wisely never makes him talk about what happened to him. Some things are scarier and more emotionally moving when they're left unsaid.

So the ending doesn't work in *First Blood*. It doesn't necessarily work as action, either. By the end of the film, Stallone has taken on a whole town and has become a one-man army, laying siege to the police station and the hardware store and exploding the pumps at the gas station. This sort of spectacular conclusion has become so commonplace in action movies that I kind of wonder, sometimes, what it would be like to see one end with a whimper rather than a bang.

Until the last twenty or thirty minutes, however, *First Blood* is a very good movie, well-paced, and well-acted not only by Stallone (who invests an unlikely character with great authority) but also by Crenna and Brian Dennehy, as the police chief. The best scenes come as Stallone's on the run in the forest, using a hunting knife with a compass in the handle, and living off the land. At one point he's trapped on a cliffside by a police helicopter, and we really feel for this character who has been hunted down through no real fault of his own. We feel more deeply for him then, in fact, than we do later when he puts his grievances into words. Stallone creates the character and sells the situation with his presence itself. The screenplay should have stopped while it was ahead.

A Fish Called Wanda ★ ★ ★ ★
R, 108 m., 1988

John Cleese (Archie), Jamie Lee Curtis (Wanda), Kevin Kline (Otto), Michael Palin (Ken), Maria Aitken (Wendy), Tom Georgeson (George), Patricia Hayes (Mrs. Coady). Directed by Charles Crichton and produced by Michael Shamberg. Screenplay by Cleese and Crichton.

This may be a purely personal prejudice, but I do not often find big-scale physical humor very funny. When squad cars crash into each other and career out of control, as they do in nine out of ten modern Hollywood comedies, I stare at the screen in stupefied silence. What is the audience laughing at? The creative bankruptcy of filmmakers who have to turn to stunt experts when their own ideas run out?

I do, on the other hand, laugh loudly at comedies where eccentric people behave in obsessive and eccentric ways, and other, equally eccentric, people do everything they can to offend and upset the first batch. In *A Fish Called Wanda*, for example, a character played by Kevin Kline is very particular about one thing: "Don't you *ever* call me stupid!" He is then inevitably called stupid on a number of occasions, leading to the payoff when his girlfriend explains to him in great detail why and how he is stupid, and lists some of the stupid things he believes. ("The London Underground is not a political movement.")

I also like it when people have great and overwhelming passions—passions that rule their lives and are so outsized they seem like comic exaggerations—and then their passions are deliberately tweaked. In *A Fish Called Wanda*, for example, Michael Palin is desperately in love with a tank of tropical fish, and so Kevin Kline, who is equally desperate about discovering the whereabouts of some stolen jewels, eats the fish, one at a time, in an attempt to force Palin to talk. (The fact that Kline also stuffs French fries up Palin's nose gives the scene a nice sort of fish-and-chips symmetry.)

Another thing I like is when people are appealed to on the basis of their most gross and shameful instincts, and surrender immediately. When Jamie Lee Curtis wants to seduce an uptight British barrister, for example, she simply wears a low-cut dress and blinks her big eyes at him and tells him he is irresistible, and this illustrates a universal law of human nature, which is that every man, no matter how resistible, believes that when a woman in a low-cut dress tells him such things she must certainly be saying the truth.

Many of these things that I like come together in *A Fish Called Wanda*, which is the funniest movie I have seen in a long time; it goes on the list with *The Producers*, *This Is Spinal Tap*, and the early Inspector Clouseau movies.

One of its strengths is its mean-spiritedness. Hollywood may be able to make comedies about mean people (usually portrayed as the heroes), but only in England are the sins of vanity, greed, and lust treated with the comic richness they deserve. *A Fish Called Wanda* is sort of a mid-Atlantic production, with flawless teamwork between its two American stars (Curtis and Kline) and its British Monty Python veterans (Cleese and Palin). But it is not a compromise; this is essentially a late-1950s-style British comedy in which the Americans are employed to do and say all of the things that would be appalling to the British characters.

The movie was directed by Charles Crichton, who cowrote it with Cleese, and Crichton is a veteran of the legendary Ealing Studio, where he directed perhaps its best comedy, *The Lavender Hill Mob*. He understands why it is usually funnier to *not* say something, and let the audience know what is not being said, than to simply blurt it out and hope for a quick laugh. He is a specialist at providing his characters with venal, selfish, shameful traits, and then embarrassing them in public. And he is a master at the humiliating moment of public unmasking, as when Cleese the barrister, in court, accidentally calls Jamie Lee Curtis "darling."

The movie involves an odd, ill-matched team of jewel thieves led by Tom Georgeson, a weaselly thief who is locked up in prison along with the secret of the jewels. On the outside, Palin, Kline, and Curtis plot with and against each other, and a great deal depends on Curtis's attempts to seduce several key defense secrets out of Cleese.

The film has one hilarious sequence after another. For classic farce, nothing tops the scene in Cleese's study, where Cleese's wife almost interrupts Curtis in mid-seduction. Curtis and Kline are both behind the draperies while the mortified Cleese tries to explain a bottle of champagne and a silver locket. The timing in this scene is as good as anything since the Marx Brothers.

And then there is the matter of the three murdered dogs. One friend of mine said she wouldn't see *A Fish Called Wanda* because she heard that dogs die in it (she is never, of course, reluctant to attend movies where people die). I tried to explain to her that the death of a pet is, of course, a tragic thing. But when the object is to inspire a heart attack in a little old lady who is a key prosecution witness, and when her little darling is crushed by a falling safe, well, you've just got to make a few sacrifices in the name of comedy.

Fitzcarraldo ★ ★ ★ ★
PG, 157 m., 1982

Klaus Kinski (Fitzcarraldo), Claudia Cardinale (Molly), Jose Lewgoy (Don Aquilino), Miguel Angel Fuentes (Cholo). Directed by Werner Herzog. Screenplay by Herzog.

Werner Herzog's *Fitzcarraldo* is a movie in the great tradition of grandiose cinematic visions. Like Coppola's *Apocalypse Now* or Kubrick's *2001*, it is a quest film in which the hero's quest is scarcely more mad than the filmmaker's. Movies like this exist on a plane apart from ordinary films. There is a sense in which *Fitzcarraldo* is not altogether successful—it is too long, we could say, or too meandering—but it is still a film that I would not have missed for the world. The movie is the story of a dreamer named Brian Sweeney Fitzgerald, whose name has been simplified to "Fitzcarraldo" by the Indians and Spanish who inhabit his godforsaken corner of South America. He loves opera. He spends his days making a little money from an ice factory and his nights dreaming up new schemes. One of them, a plan to build a railroad across the continent, has already failed. Now he is ready with another: He seriously intends to build an opera house in the rain jungle, twelve hundred miles upstream from the civilized coast, and to bring Enrico Caruso there to sing an opera.

If his plan is mad, his method for carrying it out is madness of another dimension. Looking at the map, he becomes obsessed with the fact that a nearby river system offers access to hundreds of thousands of square miles of potential trading customers—if only a modern steamship could be introduced into that system. There is a point, he notices, where the other river is separated only by a thin finger of land from a river that already is navigated by boats. His inspiration: Drag a steamship across land to the other river, float it, set up a thriving trade, and use the profits to build the opera house—and then bring in Caruso! This scheme is so unlikely that perhaps we should not be surprised that Herzog's story is based on the case of a real Irish entrepreneur who tried to do exactly that.

The historical Irishman was at least wise enough to disassemble his boat before carting it across land. In Herzog's movie, however, Fitzcarraldo determines to drag the boat up one hill and down the other side in one piece. He enlists engineers to devise a system of blocks-and-pulleys that will do the trick, and he hires the local Indians to work the levers with their own muscle power. And it is here that we arrive at the thing about *Fitzcarraldo* that transcends all understanding: Werner Herzog determined to literally drag a real steamship up a real hill, using real tackle and hiring the local Indians! To produce the movie, he decided to do personally what even the original Fitzgerald never attempted.

Herzog finally settled on the right actor to play Fitzcarraldo, author of this plan: Klaus Kinski, the shock-haired German who starred in Herzog's *Aguirre, the Wrath of God* and *Nosferatu*, is back again to mastermind the effort. Kinski is perfectly cast. Herzog's original choice for the role was Jason Robards, who is also gifted at conveying a consuming passion, but Kinski, wild-eyed and ferocious, consumes the screen. There are other characters important to the story, especially Claudia Cardinale as the madam who loves Fitzcarraldo and helps finance his attempt, but without Kinski at the core it's doubtful this story would work.

The story of Herzog's own production is itself well-known, and has been told in Les Blank's *Burden of Dreams*, a brilliant documentary about the filming. It's possible that every moment of *Fitzcarraldo* is colored by our knowledge that Herzog was "really" doing the things we see Fitzcarraldo do. (The movie uses no special effects, no models, no opticals, no miniatures.) Perhaps we're even tempted to give the movie extra points because of Herzog's ordeal in the jungle. But *Fitzcarraldo* is not all sweat and madness. It contains great poetic images of the sort Herzog is famous for: An old phonograph playing a Caruso record on the deck of a boat spinning out of control into a rapids; Fitzcarraldo frantically oaring a little rowboat down a jungle river to be in time to hear an opera; and of course the immensely impressive sight of that actual steamship, resting halfway up a hillside.

Fitzcarraldo is not a perfect movie, and it never comes together into a unified statement. It *is* meandering, and it is slow and formless at times. Perhaps the conception was just too large for Herzog to shape. The movie does not approach perfection as *Aguirre* did. But as a document of a quest and a dream, and as the record of man's audacity and foolish, visionary heroism, there has never been another movie like it.

See also Burden of Dreams, *a documentary on the making of* Fitzcarraldo.

Five Easy Pieces ★ ★ ★ ★
R, 98 m., 1970

Jack Nicholson (Robert Dupea), Karen Black (Rayette), Susan Anspach (Catherine), Billy Green Bush (Elton), Helena Kallianiotes (Hitchhiker), Ralph Waite (Carl Dupea), William Challee (Nicholas Dupea), John Ryan (Spicer). Directed by Bob Rafelson and produced by Richard Wechsler and Rafelson. Screenplay by Adrien Joyce.

The title of *Five Easy Pieces* refers not to the women its hero makes along the road, for there are only three, but to a book of piano exercises he owned as a child. The film, one of the best American films, is about the distance between that boy, practicing to become a concert pianist, and the need he feels twenty years later to disguise himself as an oil-field rigger. When we sense the boy, tormented and insecure, trapped inside the adult man, *Five Easy Pieces* becomes a masterpiece of heartbreaking intensity.

At the outset, we meet only the man—played by Jack Nicholson with the same miraculous offhandedness that brought *Easy Rider* to life. He's an irresponsible roustabout, making his way through the oil fields, sleeping with a waitress (Karen Black) whose every daydreaming moment is filled with admiration for Miss Tammy Wynette. The man's name is Robert Eroica Dupea. He was named after Beethoven's Third Symphony and he spends his evenings bowling and his nights wearily agreeing that, yes, his girl sings "Stand By Your Man" just like Tammy.

In these first marvelous scenes, director Bob Rafelson calls our attention to the grimy life textures and the shabby hopes of these decent middle Americans. They live in a landscape of motels, highways, TV dinners, dust, and jealousy, and so do we all, but they seem to have nothing else. Dupea's friends are arrested at the mental and emotional level of about age seventeen; he isn't, but thinks or hopes he is.

Dupea discovers his girl is pregnant (his friend Elton breaks the news out in the field, suggesting maybe it would be good to marry her and settle down). He walks out on her in a rage, has a meaningless little affair with a slut from the bowling alley, and then discovers more or less by accident that his father is dying. His father, we discover, is a musical genius who moved his family to an island and tried to raise them as Socrates might have. Dupea feels himself to be the only failure.

The movie bares its heart in the scenes on the island, where Dupea makes an awkward effort to communicate with his dying father. The island is peopled with eccentrics, mostly Dupea's own family, but including a few strays. Among their number is a beautiful young girl who's come to the island to study piano with Dupea's supercilious brother. Dupea seduces this girl, who apparently suggests the early life he has abandoned. He does it by playing the piano; but when she says she's moved, he says he isn't—that he played better as a child and that the piece was easy anyway.

This is possibly the moment when his nerve fails and he condemns himself, consciously, to a life of self-defined failure. The movie ends, after several more scenes, on a note of ambiguity; he is either freeing himself from the waitress or, on the other hand, he is setting off on a journey even deeper into anonymity. It's impossible to say, and it doesn't matter much. What matters is the character during the time covered by the film: a time when Dupea tentatively reapproaches his past and then rejects it, not out of pride, but out of fear.

The movie is joyously alive to the road life of its hero. We follow him through bars and bowling alleys, motels and mobile homes, and we find him rebelling against lower-middle-class values even as he embraces them. In one magical scene, he leaps from his car in a traffic jam and starts playing the piano on the truck in front of him; the scene sounds forced, described this way, but Rafelson and Nicholson never force anything, and never have to. Robert Eroica Dupea is one of the most unforgettable characters in American movies.

The Five Heartbeats ★ ★ ★
R, 120 m., 1991

Robert Townsend (Duck), Michael Wright (Eddie), Leon (J.T.), Harry J. Lennix (Dresser), Tico Wells (Choirboy), Diahann Carroll (Eleanor Potter), Tressa Thomas (Duck's Baby Sister). Directed by Robert Townsend and produced by Loretha C. Jones. Screenplay by Townsend and Keenen Ivory Wayans.

Robert Townsend's *The Five Heartbeats* takes the notion of a musical biopic one step further than usual. His movie is not only the rags to riches story of a group of guys from the neighborhood who become big stars, but also the story of what happens to them next. Their ultimate destination is not simply stardom, which is fairly easy for them to attain, but maturity and happiness, which are a lot harder.

The Five Heartbeats are a singing group, loosely patterned on groups like the Dells and the Temptations. They start out singing for fun in living rooms and on street corners, they perform in local amateur nights, they gain an audience of friends and neighbors, and then they're spotted by a talent scout who wants two things—to make them stars, and to rip them off.

The broad outlines of this story are familiar from a lot of other showbiz biographies, maybe because this is more or less the way it happens with a lot of performers. What Townsend adds that's special is the way he sees each of the five group members as an individual with his own problems and destiny. This is not only a biography with music, but also a thoughtful look at the way five young men from a poor but nurturing black neighborhood find success and deal with it.

The screenplay, by Townsend and Keenen Ivory Wayans, begins some twenty-five or thirty years ago with a bunch of kids, two of them brothers, who are already very different individuals. There's Duck, the natural leader (Townsend), who has a cool head for the group's best interests. Eddie (Michael Wright), the lead singer, who has the biggest talent but also the biggest problems, including drugs. J.T. (Leon), Duck's brother, who is a ladies' man, incapable of settling down. Dresser (Harry J. Lennix), smooth and flashy. And Choirboy (Tico Wells), whose father is a minister who thinks jazz and rock 'n' roll are the work of the devil.

Townsend tells their stories in an interlocking series of episodes that's confusing at first—the opening twenty minutes or so are hard to follow—and then settles down, as if he's found his way. I doubt if the movie was shot in chronological order, but it certainly picks up confidence and power as it goes along, until by the end we really care about these guys, especially in a couple of scenes where they have to make decisions for a lifetime.

The big dramatic interest centers around Eddie, who has the real star power in the group, and whose ability to break out of a song and really let go has the fans in the front rows swooning. But Eddie is not simply the star; he's also the one with the most vulnerable ego, the biggest problems with self-regard, the almost inevitable attraction to drugs. He begins to screw up and miss dates, and eventually the group has to drop him—leading to a painful scene outside a club, where the Heartbeats are getting into their limo as Eddie comes stumbling up like a bum. Eddie's ultimate fate is the counterpoint for everything else in the movie.

The other characters are all sharply seen, in moments involving family and romance, pregnancies and heartbeaks, redemptions and breakthroughs. There is one obligatory scene showing racial prejudice against the group (they're touring the South when they're stopped by racist state troopers), and it seems a little tacked on, as if the only purpose of the Southern trip was to justify the scene; it's a retread from the much more effective similar scenes in *Bird*.

This is Townsend's first traditional feature film; his directorial debut, some four years ago, was *Hollywood Shuffle*, a series of comic sketches that parodied the clichéd ways Hollywood has used black characters in the movies. Most of those sketches were under ten minutes; this time, at feature length, Townsend shows a real talent, and, not surprisingly, an ability to avoid most clichés, to go for the human truth in his characters.

The Flamingo Kid ★ ★ ★ ½
PG-13, 100 m., 1984

Matt Dillon (Jeffrey Willis), Hector Elizondo (Arthur Willis), Molly McCarthy (Ruth Willis), Martha Gehman (Nikki Willis), Richard Crenna (Phil Brody), Jessica Walter (Phyllis Brody), Carole R. Davis (Joyce Brody). Directed by Garry Marshall and produced by Michael Phillips. Screenplay by Neal Marshall and Garry Marshall.

"When I was eighteen, my father was ignorant on a great many subjects," Mark Twain once said, "but by the time I was twenty-five, it was amazing the things the old man had learned." Here is a movie that condenses that process into one summer. The summer begins with a kid from a poor Brooklyn neighborhood taking a job as a cabana boy at a posh beach club out on Long Island. That's against the advice of his father, a plumber, who wants his son to get a job where he can learn about hard work. By the middle of the summer, the kid has started to idolize a

flashy car dealer who's the champion of the gin rummy tables. By Labor Day, he has found out more about the car dealer than he wanted to know. And he has come to love and understand his father in a new way.

The Flamingo Kid stars Matt Dillon as the teen-ager, Hector Elizondo as his father, and Richard Crenna as the car dealer. There are other characters—in particular, a bikinied goddess who helps Matt on life at the beach—but these are the three characters who stand at the heart of the story. Elizondo is a hard-working man who still remembers how to dream, but knows that life has few openings for dreamers. In some of the movie's most poetic passages, he reveals a lifelong obsession with ships, and the ways of harbor pilots. Crenna, on the other hand, is a man who firmly believes "You are what you wear," and values his status as the club's gin rummy champion as if it really meant something.

Dillon is a revelation in this movie. Perhaps because of his name, Matt Dillon has risked being confused with your average teen-age idol, the kind the pimple magazines put on their covers. Yet he has been an extraordinarily sensitive actor ever since his first appearance, in the unsung 1977 movie about alienated teen-agers, *Over the Edge*. In two movies based on novels by S.E. Hinton, *Tex* and *Rumble Fish*, he had the kind of clarity, the uncluttered relationship with the camera, that you see in only a handful of actors: He was a natural. He is here, too. His role in *The Flamingo Kid* could easily have been turned into an anthology of twitches and psychic anguish as he wrestles with the meaning of life. But Dillon has the kind of acting intelligence that allows him to play each scene for no more than that particular scene is really about; he's not trying to summarize the message in every speech. That gives him an ease, an ability to play the teenage hero as if every day were a whole summer long.

We fall into the rhythm of the beach club. Into the sunny days where all the members have lots of time to know and envy each other, and time is so plentiful that it can take hours for a nasty rumor to sweep through the cabanas. Dillon hurries from one member to another with drinks, towels, club sandwiches, messages. He feels acutely that he does not belong at this level of society—and when Richard Crenna takes notice of him, and even more when Crenna's daughter invites him home for dinner, Dillon feels that

he's cutting loose from the boring life back in Brooklyn. But this will be a summer of learning, and by autumn he will have learned how wise and loving his own father is, and how easy it is to be deceived by surfaces. Along the way to that lesson, *The Flamingo Kid* has a lot of fun (I hope I haven't made this social comedy sound dreary), and at the end it has a surprisingly emotional impact.

Flashback ★ ★ ★
R, 108 m., 1990

Dennis Hopper (Huey Walker), Kiefer Sutherland (John Buckner), Carol Kane (Maggie), Cliff De Young (Sheriff Hightower), Paul Dooley (Donald R. Stark), Richard Masur (Barry), Michael McKean (Hal), Kathleen York (Sparkle). Directed by Franco Amurri and produced by Marvin Worth. Screenplay by David Loughery.

I've heard people complaining recently that once you've seen the coming attractions trailer for a movie, you've seen the movie. That's the way I felt after seeing the trailer for Franco Amurri's *Flashback*, but the film itself is a pleasant surprise—deeper and more original than the formula that the trailer seemed to promise.

The movie stars Dennis Hopper as Huey Walker, once famous, now forgotten, who once got his picture on the cover of *Life* magazine as an "activist clown," but has now been in hiding for twenty years. Kiefer Sutherland is the straight-arrow young FBI man assigned to return him to Spokane for trial.

What was Huey Walker's crime? When Spiro T. Agnew was on whistle-stop through the Pacific Northwest in 1968, Walker uncoupled his railroad car—so when the train pulled out, Agnew was left waiting at the station. This was a gag good enough to make Walker a hero of the counterculture at the time, but now his time has long since passed, and he is just another sad drifter, moving along every time anyone begins to suspect his true identity.

Walker is finally betrayed to the FBI by an anonymous phone caller, and that's when John Buckner, the Sutherland character, is called into play. His job is to accompany the aging hippie as he goes back home to face the music. And, of course, the two men take the train. No points for correctly predicting that history will repeat itself.

Flashback seems to be settling down into a

combination of two recent movies, one good, one bad: *Midnight Run*, where Robert De Niro had to return Charles Grodin cross country, and *Rude Awakening*, where two aging 1960s hippies were dumped into 1989. But then, just when the movie seems content to settle into its formula, the screenplay by David Loughery gets inventive, instead.

Huey, played on a perfect note of spaced-out wackiness by Dennis Hopper, begins to play psychological games with Sutherland. He discovers the FBI man is only twenty-six years old, and begins to taunt him about his conservative appearance and rigidly correct opinions. Before long Sutherland has unwound enough to play a game of chess with his captive, and then Hopper convinces him he's slipped a tab of acid into his mineral water.

The FBI man begins to trip out, and the old hippie shaves his beard, cuts his hair, and changes places with him—so that when they arrive at an intermediate stop, it's Hopper who presents himself as the agent, and the zonked-out Sutherland who looks like the radical. This is all lots of fun, as Hopper and Sutherland develop an edgy back-and-forth rivalry, but it's also all predicted in the trailer. In fact, on the basis of the trailer, you'd predict that the movie would continue as a series of gags involving mistaken identity.

That's not what happens, and I'm reluctant to say what *does* happen, because the movie takes such an interesting U-turn into what develops into a halfway serious contrast between the values of the Summer of Love and the greed of the Me Decade. The movie sounds its new note at about the time Maggie, an unreformed 1960s hippie played by Carol Kane, enters into the picture. We learn some surprising things about Sutherland, Hopper begins to think some surprising thoughts about Maggie, and there are moments when *Flashback* is actually touching.

The best thing in the movie is the Hopper performance, which is quick and smart and oddly engaging. It's hard to play a character with charisma, since the charisma has to seem to come from the character and not from the actor, but Hopper does it here. He's convincing, and his dialogue actually sounds like the sorts of things an unrepentant hippie might say—not like the clichés someone might write for him. Credit is obviously due to the filmmakers, but Hopper puts the right spin on a difficult character, and makes the movie special. How long has it been since a movie gave us not only everything the trailer promised, but more?

Flashdance ★ ½
R, 96 m., 1983

Jennifer Beals (Alex), Michael Nouri (Nicky), Belinda Bauer (Katie Hurley), Lilia Skala (Hanna Long). Directed by Adrian Lyne and produced by Don Simpson and Jerry Bruckheimer. Screenplay by Tom Hedley and Joe Eszterhas.

I have a friend who has a simple test for a movie: Is this movie as interesting as the same things would be, happening in real life? A lot of movies aren't, and *Flashdance* sure isn't. If this movie had spent just a little more effort getting to know the heroine of its story, and a little less time trying to rip off *Saturday Night Fever*, it might have been a much better film.

My friend's simple test applies to this movie in another way: The movie is *not* as interesting as the real-life story of Jennifer Beals, the young actress who stars in it. Beals launched a career as a model (covers on *Town & Country* and *Vogue*) at the age of fifteen, after being discovered by Chicago photographer Victor Skrebneski. She enrolled in Yale, took some acting classes in New York, went to an audition, and won this role. The irony is that her story, simply and directly told, might have been a lot more interesting than the story of *Flashdance*, which is so loaded down with artificial screenplay contrivances and flashy production numbers that it's waterlogged. This is one of those movies that goes for a slice of life and ends up with three pies.

Jennifer Beals plays Alex, an eighteen-year-old who is a welder by day, *and* a go-go dancer by night, *and* dreams of being a ballet star, *and* falls in love with the Porsche-driving boss of the construction company. These are a lot of "character details" even if she *didn't* also have a saintly old woman as a mentor, a big slobbering dog as a friend, a bicycle she rides all over Pittsburgh, a loft the size of a sweatshop, a sister who ice skates, a grumpy old pop, *and* the ability to take off her bra without removing her sweatshirt. This poor kid is so busy performing the pieces of business supplied to her by the manic screenwriters that she never gets a chance to develop a character.

Meanwhile, the movie has a disconcerting way of getting sidetracked with big dance scenes. The heroine works in the most improbable working-class bar ever put on film, a joint named Mawby's that has a clientele out of Miller's Beer TV ads, stage lighting reminiscent of Vegas, go-go dancers who change their expensive costumes every night, *and* put on punk rock extravaganzas, *and* never take off all their clothes, *and* never get shouted at by the customers for not doing so.

Flashdance is like a movie that won a free ninety-minute shopping spree in the Hollywood supermarket. The director (Adrian Lyne, of the much better *Foxes*) and his collaborators race crazily down the aisles, grabbing a piece of *Saturday Night Fever*, a slice of *Urban Cowboy*, a quart of *Marty*, and a two-pound box of "Archie Bunker's Place." The result is great sound and flashdance, signifying nothing. But Jennifer Beals shouldn't feel bad. She is a natural talent, she is fresh and engaging here, and only needs to find an agent with a natural talent for turning down scripts.

Flatliners ★ ★ ★
R, 111 m., 1990

Kiefer Sutherland (Nelson), Julia Roberts (Rachel), Kevin Bacon (Labraccio), William Baldwin (Joe), Oliver Platt (Steckle), Kimberly Scott (Winnie Hicks), Joshua Rudoy (Billy Mahoney), Benjamin Mouton (Rachel's Father). Directed by Joel Schumacher and produced by Michael Douglas and Rick Bieber. Screenplay by Peter Filardi.

One of the things you learn in medical school, it is said, is how to think like God. No one can teach you that, but unless you somehow learn it, you'll never be comfortable looking people in the eye and telling them what their chances are. The characters in *Flatliners* are all medical students, and their egos are so healthy that during the course of the movie they engage in a competition to see who can look God himself in the eye.

Here's their plan. It starts with those stories about people who are pronounced dead but then are brought back to life—and how a lot of them report the same blissful afterlife experience. They talk about a tunnel of light, peaceful music, and the presence of loved ones welcoming them to the other side. And they talk about being outside their own bodies, looking down, conscious of the efforts to revive them but feeling detached, because death is so sweet.

The young heroes of *Flatliners* want to visit that land of light and music, and return to tell the story. So they devise a dangerous experiment in which, one after another, they'll deliberately create a condition of clinical death, sample the afterlife experience, and then be brought back to life by emergency measures. The audacity of this experiment is terrifying and intriguing, and let's face it: It's a great idea for a movie.

Flatliners was mostly shot in the neo-Gothic gloom of turn-of-the-century locations in and around the University of Chicago. Gargoyles and shadows and gloomy stained-glass windows surround the deadly experiments, as the students, urged on by ringleader Kiefer Sutherland, tamper with God's plans for them. One after another, they take what they hope is a round-trip into eternity. The risks are many: not only death, of course, but even expulsion from medical school.

What they find on the other side is not the proper business of a reviewer to reveal. How they come back, however, deserves some comment, because the movie engages in plot manipulation that is unworthy of the brilliance of its theme. Each student tries to one-up the others, to stay away a little longer, to go a little deeper into whatever is there. And so each resuscitation attempt is a little trickier. Eventually the movie falls into a disappointing pattern, in which we're supposed to once again hold our breath while yet another voyager balances between life and death. One resuscitation is suspenseful. Two are fine. More than two wear out their welcome.

The cast, talented young actors, inhabit the shadows with the right mixture of intensity, fear, and cockiness. In addition to Sutherland, there are Julia Roberts (her first role after *Pretty Woman*), Kevin Bacon, William Baldwin (Alec's brother), Oliver Platt, and Kimberly Scott. There were some hazards in this project—with the wrong note, they could easily look silly—and yet they take their chances and pull it off. *Flatliners* is an original, intelligent thriller, well-directed by Joel Schumacher. I only wish it had been restructured so we didn't need to go through the same crisis so many times.

Fletch ★ ★ ½
PG, 110 m., 1985

Chevy Chase (I.M. Fletcher), Joe Don Baker (Chief Karlin), Dana Wheeler-Nicholson (Gail Stanwyk), Richard Libertini (Walker), Tim Matheson (Alan Stanwyk), M. Emmet Walsh

(Dr. Dolan). Directed by Michael Ritchie and produced by Alan Greisman and Peter Douglas. Screenplay by Andrew Bergman.

Why did Chevy Chase want to play I.M. Fletcher, the laconic hero of Gregory McDonald's best-sellers? Was it because Chase saw a way to bring Fletch to life? Or was it because Chase thought Fletch was very much like himself? The problem with *Fletch* is that the central performance is an anthology of Chevy Chase mannerisms in search of a character. Other elements in the movie are pretty good: the supporting characters, the ingenious plot, the unexpected locations. But whenever the movie threatens to work, there's Chevy Chase with his monotone, deadpan cynicism, distancing himself from the material.

Fletch is not the first movie that Chase has undercut with his mannerisms, but it is the best one—since *Foul Play*, anyway. His problem as an actor is that he perfected a personal style on "Saturday Night Live" all those many years ago, and has never been able to work outside of it. The basic Chevy Chase personality functions well at the length of a TV sketch, when there's no time to create a new character, but in a movie it grows deadening. *Fletch* is filled with a series of extraordinary situations, and Chase seems to react to all of them with the same wry dubiousness. His character this time is an investigative reporter for a Los Angeles newspaper. Deep into an investigation of drug traffic on the city's beaches, Fletch is approached by a young man (Tim Matheson) with a simple proposition: He wants to be killed. The story is that Matheson is dying of cancer and wants to die violently so his family can qualify for enlarged insurance benefits, but Fletch doesn't buy it. Something's fishy, and Fletch pretends to take the job, while conducting his own investigation.

The case leads him to an extraordinary series of interesting characters; the film's director, Michael Ritchie, is good at sketching human originals, and we meet an aging farm couple in Utah, a manic editor, a no-nonsense police chief, a mysterious drug dealer, a slimy doctor, a beautiful wife, and a lot of mean dogs. Every one of the characters is played well, with the little details that Ritchie loves: The scene on a farmhouse porch in Utah is filled with such sly, quiet social satire that it could stand by itself. The movie's physical comedy is good, too. A scene where Fletch breaks into a realtor's

office—scaling a fence and outsmarting vicious attack dogs—is constructed so carefully out of comedy and violence that it's a little masterpiece of editing.

The problem is, Chase's performance tends to reduce all the scenes to the same level, at least as far as he's concerned. He projects such an inflexible mask of cool detachment, of ironic running commentary, that we're prevented from identifying with him. If he thinks this is all just a little too silly for words, what are we to think? If we're more involved in the action than he is, does that make us chumps? *Fletch* needed an actor more interested in playing the character than in playing himself.

Fletch Lives ★ ½
PG, 95 m., 1989

Chevy Chase (Fletch), Hal Holbrook (Ham Johnson), Julianne Phillips (Becky Culpepper), R. Lee Ermey (Jimmy Lee Farnsworth), Richard Libertini (Frank [Editor]), Randall "Tex" Cobb (Ben Dover), Cleavon Little (Calculus), Richard Belzer (Phil). Directed by Michael Ritchie and produced by Alan Greisman and Peter Douglas. Screenplay by Leon Capetanos.

Fletch Lives is one more dispirited slog through the rummage sale of movie clichés, at which we discover the following marked-down items: a wisecracking newspaper reporter, a crumbling Southern mansion, a genial small-town lawyer with eyes of steel, a TV evangelist, a jailhouse bully, a smart black FBI man who pretends to be stupid, a sexy young real-estate woman, an evil industrial polluter, and a cynical newspaper editor. I almost forgot the boring woman in the next seat in the airplane who won't stop talking. She's in here, too, not to mention a seductive Southern belle and a dozen Ku Klux Klansmen.

What's amazing is that people have the nerve, and find the strength, to make a movie involving these elements. If you were writing a screenplay, would you think a movie involving all of those pathetic clichés had the slightest chance of interesting anyone? Michael Ritchie, who directed this film, has made original work in the past (*Smile, Downhill Racer, The Candidate, Semi-Tough*). He also directed the original *Fletch* in 1985. How did Ritchie feel every morning as he marched forth to manipulate ingredients that had been exhausted by generations of filmmakers before him?

The key element in the movie is the presence of Chevy Chase in the title role as a wisecracking investigative reporter for a Los Angeles newspaper. Chase's assignment is to bring an angle, an edge, to plot materials that are otherwise completely without interest. And it's theoretically possible for that to happen; movies are bad not because of their subject matter, but because of how they approach it, what style they bring to it. But Chase is wrong for this material because of the pose of detachment and indifference that he brings to so many roles. He seems to be visiting the plot as a benevolent but indifferent outsider.

When Chevy Chase bothers to actually play a character, he can be very effective. But sometimes he seems to be covering himself, playing detached so that nobody can blame him if the comedy doesn't work. In this film he seems to have no emotions at all; consider the scene where he discovers that the woman he made love with has died during the night. Chase is at arm's-length from the plot, making little asides and whimsical commentaries while his hapless supporting cast does what it can with underwritten roles.

The movie has one or two good things in it. One of Chase's daydreams turns into a funny satire of the "Zippety-Doo-Dah" number in *Song of the South*. And R. Lee Ermey, the drill sergeant in *Full Metal Jacket*, brings presence to the role of a TV evangelist by playing him with a certain dignity, instead of using the standard approach to such roles and playing him as a hysterical clown. But other comic opportunities are blown; there is, for example, an expensive set of a Jim-and-Tammy-style religious theme park that doesn't generate a single laugh.

A mystery is concealed somewhere in the folds of the movie's plot, but one that will not surprise anyone who has seen half a dozen other mysteries. The identity of the bad guy can be deduced by applying the Law of Economy of Characters, which states that the mystery villain is always the only character in the plot who seems otherwise unnecessary. It admittedly takes a little more thought than usual to apply the law in this case, since so many of the characters seem unnecessary.

Fool for Love ★ ★ ★
R, 107 m., 1985

Sam Shepard (Eddie), Kim Basinger (May), Harry Dean Stanton (Old Man), Randy Quaid (Martin). Directed by Robert Altman and produced by Menahem Golan and Yoram Globus. Screenplay by Sam Shepard.

At the center of Sam Shepard's *Fool for Love* are two people whose hurts are so deep, whose angers are so real, that they can barely talk about what they really feel. That does not stop them from talking, on and on into the hurtful night, and eventually we can put together their stories, using what they have said, and especially what they have not said.

One of the characters is a blond slattern named May, whose natural beauty has been rearranged into a parody of the classic movie baby doll—Brigitte Bardot, say. The other character is named Eddie, and he is a cowboy who drives through the empty Texas reaches in the obligatory pickup truck with the obligatory rifle rack behind his head and the obligatory horse trailer behind. One night May is working behind the counter of a restaurant in a crumbling motel, and she sees Eddie's pickup coming down the road. She runs and hides. Standing in the shadows of the rundown motel is an older man (Harry Dean Stanton) who simply waits and watches.

Shepard's method is direct. He allows his characters to talk around what they're really thinking, and occasionally the talk escalates into brief, incisive bursts of action—even violence. Eventually we learn that the older man is the father of both Eddie and May, that they had different mothers, that the old man commuted between two families, and that Eddie and May eventually met under circumstances that were later determined to be incestuous.

These developments would provide the ingredients for a basic story of redneck passion, and there are times when *Fool for Love* wants to strike those very notes. We feel we might be looking at the characters in a story by William Faulkner or Erskine Caldwell, and the visual compositions look inspired by the lurid covers of 1940s paperback novels. The deliberately trashy surface, however, conceals deeper levels of feeling, and by the end of *Fool for Love* we have witnessed some sort of classic tragedy, set there in the Texas backlands.

Robert Altman's movie version of Shepard's play stars Shepard himself, in a strong performance as Eddie. But he doesn't dominate the story as much as you might think. The central performance in the movie is really Kim Basinger's, as May. Although she has played sexpots before—has indeed specialized in them—nothing prepared me for the dimensions she was able to find in this one. What's astonishing is that *Fool for Love* is essentially a male drama, told from a male point of view, and yet Basinger is able to suggest so much with her performance that she steals the center of the stage right away from the man who wrote the lines and is playing opposite her.

Part of her impact is probably because the director is Altman. Few other major directors are more interested in women, and in his films like *Thieves Like Us*, *Three Women*, and *Come Back to the 5 & Dime, Jimmy Dean, Jimmy Dean*, he has shown women in settings very similar to this one: unfulfilled women, conscious of the waste of their lives, living in backwaters where their primary pastime is to await the decisions of men.

Altman does a brilliant job of visualizing this particular backwater. From the opening aerial shots of the godforsaken motel, he creates a tangibly real, dusty, forlorn world. Some of his shots are so beautiful it's hard to figure how he obtained them: That ominous dark sky lowering over the motel, for example, looks almost like a painting. Altman is also up to some of the same visual tricks he used in *Jimmy Dean*, including the use of windows and mirrors to give us two planes of action at the same time. And he has a wonderfully subtle way of showing us the Harry Dean Stanton character in both the past and the present.

This is Altman's fourth movie in a row based on a play. It comes after *Jimmy Dean*, *Streamers*, and the extraordinary *Secret Honor*, about Richard Nixon (he has filmed three other plays for cable television). After a career as one of the most free-swinging of all modern movie directors (*M*A*S*H*, *McCabe and Mrs. Miller*, *Nashville*) it is interesting to see him embracing the discipline of a play script. Having made movies that were all over the map, he now inhabits interiors of rooms, and of people's minds. With *Fool for Love*, he has succeeded on two levels that seem opposed to each other. He has made a melodrama, almost a soap opera, in which the characters achieve a kind of nobility.

Footloose ★ ½
PG, 106 m., 1984

Kevin Bacon (Ren), Lori Singer (Ariel), John Lithgow (Reverend Moore). Directed by Herbert Ross and produced by Lewis J. Rachmil and Craig Zadan. Screenplay by Dean Pitchford.

Footloose is a seriously confused movie that tries to do three things, and does all of them badly. It wants to tell the story of a conflict in a town, it wants to introduce some flashy teen-age characters, and part of the time it wants to be a music video. It's possible that no movie with this many agendas *can* be good; maybe somebody should have decided, early on, exactly what the movie was supposed to be about. The film tells the story of a Chicago kid named Ren (Kevin Bacon), who has a fashionable haircut and likes to dance. He moves with his mother to a small town named Bomont, which is somewhere in the Midwest, although I seriously doubt a town like this exists anywhere outside of standard movie clichés. The old fuddies in Bomont have imposed a total ban on rock 'n' roll and dancing. The ban is led by an uptight preacher named Shaw Moore (John Lithgow), who is still grieving because he lost a child in a car wreck five years ago. To the Reverend Moore, dancing and rock lead to booze and drugs.

Ren falls in love with the preacher's daughter (Lori Singer). He also has the usual standard showdowns with the locals, including the high school bully. Ren decides what this town needs is a dance. His assignment, should he choose to accept it, is to (1) win the approval of the preacher and the town council to allow dancing, (2) beat up the bully, and (3) star in at least three segments of the movie that can be used as TV music videos. The basic conflict in this movie was not new when the *Beach Party* gang discovered it. Remember Annette and Frankie trying to persuade the old folks to let them hold a dance on the beach? If the movie had only relaxed and allowed itself to admit how silly the situation is, it could have been more fun. Instead, it gets bogged down in the peculiar personality of the preacher, who is played by Lithgow as a man of agonizing complexity.

Footloose makes one huge, inexplicable error with the Lithgow character. It sets him up as an unyielding reactionary, and then lets him change his mind 180 degrees without a word of explanation. In one scene, the preacher's daughter confronts her dad in church and announces she isn't a virgin (the movie never remembers to tell us whether she really is or not). The preacher turns livid, starts to scream, and then is interrupted by news that they're burning books down at the library. In the *very next scene*, the preacher is arguing against the book burners—and before long, without any meaningful transitional scenes, he has caved in to the idea of the dance. It's cheating to set up Lithgow as the enemy and then turn him into a friend without a word of explanation.

I mentioned the flashy teen-age characters. The one who gave me the most trouble was that preacher's daughter. She enjoys suicidal games of chicken, like balancing with her legs on the doors of a speeding car and a speeding truck while a speeding semi bears down on her. This trick is, of course, impossible to do in real life, and so it simultaneously makes her into an idiot and a stuntwoman. As for the music video scenes: On three different occasions, the movie switches gears and goes into prepackaged MTV-type production numbers, with the fancy photography and the flashy quick cuts. These scenes may play well on TV, but they break what little reality the story has, and expose *Footloose* as a collection of unrelated ingredients that someone thought would be exploitable.

For Keeps ★ ★ ★
PG-13, 98 m., 1988

Molly Ringwald (Darcy), Randall Batinkoff (Stan), Kenneth Mars (Mr. Bobrucz), Miriam Flynn (Mrs. Elliot), Conchata Ferrell (Mrs. Bobrucz), Sharon Brown (Lila), Jack Ong (Reverend Kim), Sean Frye (Wee Willy), Allison Roth (Ambrosia), Trevor Edmond (Ace). Directed by John G. Avildsen and produced by Jerry Belson and Walter Coblenz. Screenplay by Tim Kazurinsky and Denise DeClue.

The movies of Molly Ringwald have been responsible for a revolution in the way Hollywood regards teen-agers. Before Ringwald (and her mentor, John Hughes) there were horny teen-agers, dead teen-agers, teen-age vampires, and psychotic crack-ups. More recently teen-age movies have been working their way through some of the aspects of the normal lives of American teen-agers, and in *For Keeps*, Ringwald plays a popular high school senior who gets pregnant and gets married.

Because she is Ringwald, and because this is a movie, her experience of these adventures is probably a good deal more pleasant than the average American teen-age girl could look forward to. There is a line in the movie that could apply to the movie itself, when a high school teacher asks the very pregnant Ringwald to drop out of school and take night classes, because she's so popular that other girls might want to imitate her and get pregnant themselves.

If the movie lacks something, it is a sense of the real pain, shame, and suffering that someone like this high school senior might undergo with a pregnancy. She seems too sound, too well-adjusted, too resilient. And yet there is a certain bottom line of honesty in this movie, and if it is about the joy of young love, it is also about the pressures of young responsibility. (I hope impressionable teen-age viewers will devote careful attention to the scenes where Molly is stuck at home in her walk-up apartment while her young husband is out having a beer with his buddies.)

In the film, Ringwald and her boyfriend, played by Randall Batinkoff, begin to sleep together and almost immediately have to face the pregnancy. In a plot that centers around national holidays, she blurts out the news at Thanksgiving, and they decide to get married at Christmas. Both of these decisions are met with varying degrees of horror by their parents—by Miriam Flynn, as Ringwald's divorced and bitter mother, and by Kenneth Mars and Conchata Ferrell, as Batinkoff's loving, conventional parents.

The movie is perhaps a bit too willing to play Batinkoff's parents for laughs, and I could have done without a scene of a toppling Christmas tree. But the moments between Ringwald and Batinkoff are well-written and played with a quiet, touching sensitivity; we recognize elements of real life in their relationship.

The movie was written by Tim Kazurinsky and Denise DeClue, whose previous collaboration was the wonderful *About Last Night. . . .* That movie, based very loosely on a play by David Mamet, was about swinging singles in their twenties and thirties. This one, an original, has the same feel for plausible dialogue and the same knack for finding scenes that reveal personalities, instead of simply advancing the plot. Consider, for example, the sequence after the birth, when Ringwald suffers from post-partum depression; this is the sort of touching realism you wouldn't expect from a "teenage movie," and yet it lends weight and importance to the sequences that follow.

I also liked the way in which her husband was shown as unready to accept the responsibilities of marriage and fatherhood, and then the way the movie subtly suggests that Ringwald isn't ready, either—but as the woman, she's the one who gets stuck at home with the kid. All of this is made more dramatic because of a subplot about the husband's full-ride college scholarship, Ringwald's own college potential, and the lack of campus facilities for married freshmen.

The ending of the movie is too contrived, as all of the threads come together—marriage, parenthood, scholarships, family acceptance, college plans. And yet *For Keeps* is an intriguing movie that succeeds in creating believable characters, keeping them alive, and steering them more or less safely past the clichés that are inevitable with this kind of material. It's a movie with heart, and that compensates for a lot of the predictability. The one thing it lacks, perhaps, is a notice at the end advising teen-agers that for every young couple like this one, there are a thousand broken hearts.

For Queen and Country ★ ★
R, 105 m., 1989

Denzel Washington (Reuben), Dorian Healy (Fish), Amanda Redman (Stacey), Sean Chapman (Bob), Bruce Payne (Colin), Geff Francis (Lynford), George Baker (Kilcoyne). Directed by Martin Stellman and produced by Tim Bevan. Screenplay by Stellman and Trix Worrell.

He has fought for Great Britain in the streets of Belfast and on the muddy fields of the Falkland Islands, and he has seen his friends killed and maimed. So when the soldier returns to civilian life, he is not pleased to find that he is no longer considered a British citizen.

He is black, and was born in a former British colony. He came to London as a baby. He put his life on the line in the British army for nine years as a paratrooper. And now they tell him his passport is no good. That moment, in a government office, is the turning point in the life of Reuben, the returned soldier, played by Denzel Washington.

Until then, he has weathered the return to civilian life fairly well. Modern Britain is

often more blatantly racist than America, especially on the working-class level, but Reuben is a man who tries to put racism in its place, and indeed his best friend is a white man—a fellow paratrooper whose legs were blown off while Reuben watched. He can deal with racism on the personal level. But he takes his service in the army very seriously, and when Great Britain insults his patriotism by withholding his passport, he feels he has passed some sort of fundamental divide. The action strikes at the heart of his pride.

For Queen and Country follows this man for a few weeks after his return to civilian life, and to a black high-rise government tenement that is rife with crime, drugs, and disillusion. Reuben moves into an apartment with his books and clothes and military decorations, and starts looking for work, unsuccessfully. He is turned down in half a dozen different ways, most of them based on his race, and yet he is undiscouraged because he expects such treatment, and expects eventually to outsmart and outrun it, and succeed in spite of it.

But there is no job. And a local drug dealer, a white man he knows from the army, wants Reuben's help as a right-hand man, an intimidator and enforcer. Reuben wants nothing to do with drugs. But then his friend, the amputee, is faced with eviction, and one drug deal would provide enough money to secure the friend for months.

Up until about this point, *For Queen and Country* is absorbing and convincing. Then it starts to go wrong. It stops being the story of the daily life of this character, and starts plugging in the elements of a standard thriller plot. There is a villain—a sadistic policeman who is not for one instant believable as anything other than a convenience for the screenplay. There is a half-hearted love affair with a woman, who at first seems spontaneous and three-dimensional, but is then written out of the story on a technicality involving her dislike of guns. A complicated plot begins to evolve, based on a deeply hidden conspiracy between the police and the drug establishment. And Reuben is caught in the middle for no better reason, really, than that the plot requires it.

All of the manipulation and falseness of the concluding scenes are betrayed in the film's very last scene, which is so contrived it dramatizes how the film has gone wrong. That scene (which I will not reveal) illustrates what I like to call The Fallacy of the Predictable Tree (see Glossary entry). At the

end of *For Queen and Country*, a complex and unpredictable series of events ends with a character being in exactly the wrong place at the wrong time, and with another character already waiting there as if he foresaw it.

The scene reveals the trickery of the action passages in the movie. It's as if the filmmakers lost their faith in Reuben as a character, and felt they had to rescue themselves with interchangeable thriller elements taken right off the shelf, one size fits all. That's a shame. Denzel Washington creates the character as a convincing, sympathetic person (his performance came on the heels of his inspired work in *The Mighty Quinn*), and he deserves more than to have the character thrown away on a phoned-in plot.

For Your Eyes Only ★ ★
PG, 127 m., 1981

Roger Moore (James Bond), Carole Bouquet (Melina), Topol (Columbo), Julian Glover (Kristatos), Cassandra Harris (Lisl), Janet Brown (Prime Minister). Directed by John Glen and produced by Albert R. Broccoli. Screenplay by Richard Malbaum and Michael Wilson.

For Your Eyes Only is a competent James Bond thriller, well-crafted, a respectable product from the 007 production line. But it's no more than that. It doesn't have the special sly humor of the Sean Connery Bonds, of course, but also doesn't have the visual splendor of such Roger Moore Bonds as *The Spy Who Loved Me*, or special effects to equal *Moonraker*. And in this era of jolting, inspired visual effects from George Lucas and Steven Spielberg, it's just not quite in the same league. That will no doubt come as a shock to Producer Albert (Cubby) Broccoli, who has made the James Bond series his life's work.

Broccoli and his late partner, Harry Saltzman, all but invented the genre that Hollywood calls "event films" or "special effects films." The ingredients, which Bond popularized and others imitated, always included supervillains, sensational stunts, sex, absurd plots to destroy or rule the world, and, of course, a hero. The 007 epics held the patent on that formula in the late '60s and early '70s, but they are growing dated. *For Your Eyes Only* doesn't have any surprises. We've seen all the big scenes before, and when the villains turn out to be headquartered in an impregnable mountaintop fortress, we yawn. After *Where Eagles Dare* and *The Guns of Navarone* and the hollow Japanese volcano that Bond himself once infiltrated, let's face it: When you've seen one impregnable mountaintop fortress, you've seen 'em all.

The movie opens with James Bond trapped inside a remote-controlled helicopter being guided by a bald sadist in a wheelchair. After Bond triumphs, the incident is never referred to again. *This* movie involves the loss of the secret British code controlling submarine-based missiles. The Russians would like to have it. Bond's mission: Retrieve the control console from a ship sunk in the Aegean. The movie breaks down into a series of set pieces. Bond and his latest Bondgirl (long-haired, undemonstrative Carole Bouquet) dive in a mini-sub, engage in a complicated chase through the back roads of Greece, crawl through the sunken wreck in wet suits, are nearly drowned and blown up, etc. For variety, Bond and Bouquet are dragged behind a powerboat as shark bait, and then Bond scales the fortress mountain. A fortress guard spots Bond dangling from a rope thousands of feet in the air. What does he do? Does he just cut the rope? No, sir, the guard descends part way to tantalize Bond by letting him drop a little at a time. The rest is predictable.

In a movie of respectable craftsmanship and moderate pleasures, there's one obvious disappointment. The relationship between Roger Moore and Carole Bouquet is never worked out in an interesting way. Since the days when he was played by Sean Connery, agent 007 has always had a dry, quiet, humorous way with women. Roger Moore has risen to the same challenge, notably opposite Barbara Bach in *The Spy Who Loved Me*. But Moore and Bouquet have no real chemistry in *For Your Eyes Only*. There's none of that kidding byplay. It's too routine. The whole movie is too routine.

48 HRS ★ ★ ★ ½
R, 100 m., 1982

Nick Nolte (Cates), Eddie Murphy (Reggie), James Remar (Ganz), Sonny Landham (Billy Bear), Annette O'Toole (Elaine). Directed by Walter Hill and produced by Lawrence Gordon and Joel Silver. Screenplay by Roger Spottiswoode, Hill, Larry Gross, and Steven E. de Souza.

Sometimes an actor becomes a star in just one scene. Jack Nicholson did it in *Easy Rider*, wearing the football helmet on the back of the motorcycle. It happened to Faye Dunaway when she looked sleepily out of a screen window at Warren Beatty in *Bonnie and Clyde*. And in *48 HRS*, it happens to Eddie Murphy. His unforgettable scene comes about halfway through *48 HRS*. He plays a convict who has done thirty months for theft and still has six months to go—but he gets a forty-eight hour prison leave through the efforts of Nick Nolte, a hungover hot dog of a detective who's on the trail of some cop killers and figures Murphy can help. Murphy thinks there's a bartender who may have some information. The thing is, the bar is a redneck country joint, the kind where urban cowboys drink out of longneck bottles and salute the Confederate flag on the wall. Murphy has been jiving Nolte about how he can handle any situation. Nolte gives him a chance. And Murphy, impersonating a police officer, walks into that bar, takes command, totally intimidates everybody, and gets his information. It's a great scene—the mirror image of that scene in *The French Connection* where Gene Hackman, as Popeye Doyle, intimidated the black regulars in a Harlem bar.

Murphy has other good moments in this movie, and so does Nolte, who gives a wonderful performance as a cynical, irresponsible, and immature cop who's always telling lies to his girlfriend and sneaking a jolt of whiskey out of his personal flask. The two men start out suspicious of each other in this movie and work up to a warm dislike. But eventually, grudgingly, a kind of respect starts to grow.

The movie's story is nothing to write home about. It's pretty routine. What makes the movie special is how it's made. Nolte and Murphy are good, and their dialogue is good, too—quirky and funny. Character actor James Remar makes a really slimy killer, genuinely evil. Annette O'Toole gets third billing as Nolte's lover, but it's another one of those thankless women's roles. Not only could O'Toole have phoned it in—she does, spending most of her scenes on the telephone calling Nolte a no-good bum. The direction is by Walter Hill, who has never been any good at scenes involving women and doesn't improve this time. What he is good at is action, male camaraderie and atmosphere. His movies almost always feature at least one beautifully choreographed, unbelievably violent fight scene (remember Charles Bronson's bare-knuckle fight in *Hard Times?*), and the fight scene this time is exhausting.

Where Hill grows in this movie is in his ability to create characters. In a lot of his earlier movies *(The Warriors, The Driver, Long Riders, Southern Comfort)* he preferred men who were symbols, who represented things and so didn't have to be human. In *48 HRS*, Nolte and Murphy are human, vulnerable, and touching. Also mean, violent, and chauvinistic. It's that kind of movie.

Four Friends ★ ★ ★ ★
R, 114 m., 1981

Craig Wasson (Danilo Prozor), Jodi Thelen (Georgia Miles), Jim Metzler (Tom Donaldson), Michael Huddleston (David Levine), Reed Birney (Louie Carnahan), Julie Murray (Adrienne Carnahan), Miklos Simon (Mr. Prozor). Directed by Arthur Penn and produced by Penn and Gene Lasko. Screenplay by Steven Tesich.

Somewhere in the middle of *My Dinner with André*, Andre Gregory wonders aloud if it's not possible that the 1960s were the last decade when we were all truly alive—that since then we've sunk into a bemused state of self-hypnosis, placated by consumer goods and given the illusion of excitement by television. Walking out of *Four Friends*, I had some of the same thoughts. This movie brings the almost unbelievable contradictions of that decade into sharp relief, not as nostalgia or as a re-creation of times past, but as a reliving of all of the agony and freedom of the weirdest ten years any of us is likely to witness.

The movie is told in the form of a looseknit autobiography, somewhat inspired by the experiences of Steve Tesich, the son of Yugoslavian parents who moved to this country as a boy and lived in the neighborhoods of East Chicago, Indiana, that provide the film's locations. If the film is his emotional autobiography, it is also perhaps the intellectual autobiography of Arthur Penn, the film's director, whose *Bonnie and Clyde* was the best American film of the 1960s and whose *Alice's Restaurant* (1970) was an earlier examination of that wonderful and haunted time.

Their movie tells the stories of four friends. When we meet them, they're entering their senior year of high school. It is 1961. That is so long ago that nobody has yet heard of the Beatles. One of the friends is a young woman (Jodi Thelen), who imagines she is the reincarnation of Isadora Duncan, and who strikes attitudes and poses in an attempt to appear altogether too much of an artistic genius for East Chicago to contain.

The other three friends are male classmates. They all love the girl in one way or another, or perhaps it's just that they've never seen anyone like her before. In the ten years to follow, these four people will have lives that were not imaginable in 1961. They will have the opportunity to break out of the sedate conservatism of the Eisenhower era and into the decade of "alternative life-styles."

The movie is ambitious. It wants to take us on a tour of some of the things that happened in the 1960s, and some of the ways four midwestern kids might have responded to them. It also wants to be a meditation on love, and on how love changes during the course of a decade. When Thelen turns up at the bedroom window of her "real" true love (Craig Wasson) early in the movie and cheerfully offers to sleep with him, Wasson refuses, not only because he's a high school kid who's a little afraid of her—but also because he's too much in love with his idea of her to want to make it real. By the time they finally do come back together, years later, they've both been through bad scenes, through madness, drug abuse, and the trauma of the war in Vietnam. They have also grown up, some. The wonder is not that *Four Friends* covers so much ground, but that it makes many of its scenes so memorable that we learn more even about the supporting characters than we expect to.

There are individual scenes in this movie that are just right. One of them involves a crowd of kids walking home in the dusk after school. Another happens between Wasson and Miklos Simon, who plays his gruff, defensive Yugoslavian father, and who finally, painfully, breaks down and smiles after a poker-faced lifetime. A relationship between Wasson and a dying college classmate (Reed Birney) is well drawn, to remind us of undergraduate friendships based on idealism and mutual discovery. And the scene where Wasson and Thelen see each other after many years is handled tenderly and with just the right notes of irony.

Four Friends is a very good movie. Like *Breaking Away*, the story of growing up in Bloomington, Indiana (for which Tesich also wrote the original screenplay), this is a movie that remembers times past with such clarity that there are times it seems to be making it all up. Did we really say those things? Make those assumptions? Live on the edge of what seemed to be a society gone both free and mad at once? Some critics have said the people and events in this movie are not plausible.

I don't know if they're denying the movie's truth, or arguing that from a 1980s point of view the '60s were just a bad dream. Or a good one.

The Fourth Protocol ★ ★ ★ ½
R, 119 m., 1987

Michael Caine (John Preston), Pierce Brosnan (Petrofsky), Ned Beatty (Borisov), Joanna Cassidy (Vassilieva), Julian Glover (Brian Harcourt-Smith), Michael Gough (Sir Bernard Hemmings), Ray McAnally (General Karpov), Ian Richardson (Sir Nigel Irvine). Directed by John Mackenzie and produced by Timothy Burrill. Screenplay by Frederick Forsyth.

August 1987. I am writing this review in the Scottish Highlands, where the peace is broken only by the occasional low-level flyby of a jet fighter plane. I was walking yesterday along the banks of Loch Tummell, and I came to a lively waterfall that was tumbling through the woods. The birds were singing and the sun was doing its best to penetrate the mist, and then the sky was shattered by the arrogant roar of a warplane, swooping low over the hills, then gone in an instant.

The flights are part of a joint defense exercise by the United States and Royal Air Forces, and they fly on nearly every clear day. Folks up here don't like them much. It's like being subjected to a daily version of one of those moronic displays where the Blue Angels demonstrate how much noise they can make.

There are a lot of U.S. military bases on British soil, including the famous one at Greenham Common where anti-nuclear protesters have been camping out for years. If there were a nuclear accident at one of those bases, it would seriously undermine our welcome over here. The low-level training missions are no doubt important for security, but they have contributed to a good deal of grumbling among the citizens who live in their path. That grumbling, in a way, is what *The Fourth Protocol* is about.

The Fourth Protocol involves a Soviet plan to smuggle the elements for a nuclear device into Britain, assemble it, and detonate it right next to a U.S. base. The explosion would be so huge that its precise location would be obliterated, and it would look exactly like an American accident. Result: pressure for the Yankees to go home and a strategic victory for the Russians.

The key Russian operative is played by Pierce Brosnan, in what certainly is the best performance he has ever given, as a dark, brooding man with an outwardly cheerful disposition and a perfect British accent. The only person who seems capable of anticipating his plan, and stopping it, is Michael Caine as a British intelligence officer who is in political trouble with his bosses because he's too independent.

This is essentially the same character Caine played in the second movie role of his career, *The Ipcress File* (1965). This time, though, he's older, less cocksure, and more wily in getting his way. After his superiors take him off the case, he simply works on it in a different way. Eventually he puts the pieces together and realizes what the Soviets are up to, and then the movie becomes a race against time.

The Fourth Protocol is based on a novel by Frederick Forsyth, whose *Day of the Jackal* also made a terrific thriller. The stories have similar structures: The villain is as strongly drawn as the heroes, and there is a sympathetic woman character who loves the villain—unwisely, as it turns out. The woman in *The Fourth Protocol* is a Russian intelligence agent played by Joanna Cassidy, who does not work often enough in the movies but always is a strong, sure center for every scene. (Remember her in *Under Fire*, as the foreign correspondent caught between Nick Nolte and Gene Hackman?) This time she arrives with the key element Brosnan needs for his bomb, and if his treatment of her is unkind, consider what will happen to everyone within a forty-mile radius.

The Fourth Protocol is first-rate because it not only is a thriller, but it also pays attention to its characters and shows how their actions grow out of their personalities. Like Michael Caine's other 1987 British spy film, *The Whistle Blower*, it is effective not simply because it's a thriller but also because for long stretches it simply is a very absorbing drama.

The Fourth War ★ ★ ★
R, 95 m., 1990

Roy Scheider (Jack Knowles), Jurgen Prochnow (Valachev), Tim Reid (Lieutenant Colonel Clark), Lara Harris (Elena), Harry Dean Stanton (General Hackworth), Dale Dye (Sergeant Major), Bill MacDonald (M.P. Corporal). Directed by John Frankenheimer and produced by Wolf Schmidt. Screenplay by Stephen Peters.

I don't know when production began on John Frankenheimer's *The Fourth War*, but its timing is interesting: In period, it's the last Cold War movie, and in spirit, the first post–Cold War thriller. The suspense centers around whether someone will screw up detente. Some of the new geopolitical dialogue sounds a little strange to the ear, as when an American colonel stands near the border between West Germany and Czechoslovakia and fearlessly barks, "What we have here is primarily a public relations role!" No specific reference is made in the movie to the Gorbachev era, but it's clear that the primary purpose of the American border patrols is to avoid shooting themselves in the foot.

That prepares the canvas for the arrival of Col. Jack Knowles (Roy Scheider), who has been the army's loose cannon and maybe its loose screw ever since the war in Vietnam. Knowles has so many decorations you can't see his uniform, but he has never been known for his sound judgment in command positions. The army has posted him as far away from trouble as possible—Guam was a typical duty—but now he has finally been returned to a frontline command. It has something to do with how an old Vietnam buddy (Harry Dean Stanton) has faith that he's regained his senses.

The faith is premature. Knowles is a hothead and a lone wolf, and his war, as they like to say in the movie ads, is not over. It is his misfortune, and perhaps the misfortune of the entire planet, that he has been positioned on the Czech border exactly opposite an equally short-tempered Russian named Colonel Valachev (Jurgen Prochnow). On the first day of his new command, Knowles has to stand by impotently and watch as a would-be refugee is shot down within yards of freedom. Then Valachev hovers overhead in a Soviet helicopter and, in Knowles's words, "sticks his rockets in my face."

Nobody sticks his rockets in the face of Col. Jack Knowles, and before long Knowles is sneaking across the border on unauthorized solo missions to sabotage enemy installations and stick his own rockets, so to speak, in Valachev's face. Knowles's dangerous activities do not go unnoticed by his second in command (Tim Reid), and there are reprimands from Harry Dean Stanton back at division headquarters, but now Valachev has engaged himself in the dangerous game, and the two men refuse to back down. There are moments when the possibility of accidental war seems very real.

The Fourth War is essentially a psychological study of a man coming apart at the hinges. Knowles, played by Scheider, is an embittered, alcoholic loser who was a hero once, a long time ago and far away. Now appropriate conditions no longer exist for his kind of hot-dog heroism. Although the movie centers on well-made action scenes and contains a couple of tidy surprises, its strength comes from the portrait of this soldier on the edge. Scheider has a role not unlike Laurence Harvey's in Frankenheimer's masterpiece *The Manchurian Candidate*. He is a victim of his programming. He reacts to Soviet troops the way Harvey reacted to a hand of solitaire.

The supporting performances are where the movie's sanity resides. Tim Reid, as the second in command, plays the role as a textbook officer who knows he's on thin ice and does everything by the book. Stanton, as the general, has a long, angry speech in one scene, and as he slams his words into Scheider's silence, we're reminded of what a powerful actor he is.

Movies like *The Fourth War* are a reminder that Hollywood is running low on dependable villains. The Nazis were always reliable, but World War II ended forty-five years ago. Now the Cold War is winding down, and just when *Lethal Weapon 2* introduced South African diplomats as the bad guys, de Klerk came along to make that approach unpredictable. Drug dealers are wearing out their welcome. Bad cops are a cliché. Suggestions?

The Fox and the Hound ★ ★ ★
G, 83 m., 1981

With the voices of Pearl Bailey (Big Mama), Kurt Russell (Copper), Mickey Rooney (Tod), Sandy Duncan (Vixey), Pat Buttram (Chief), Jack Albertson (Slade). Directed by Art Stevens, Ted Berman, and Richard Rich and produced by Wolfgang Reitherman and Stevens. Screenplay by Larry Clemmons and others.

In all the old familiar ways, *The Fox and the Hound* looks like a traditional production from Walt Disney animators. It has cute little animals and wise old owls. It has a villain in the shape of a mountainous grizzly bear, and comic relief in a long-standing feud between a woodpecker and a caterpillar. And it has songs that contain such uncontroversial wishes as, "If only the world wouldn't get in the way . . . If only the world would let us

play." And yet, for all of its familiar qualities, this movie marks something of a departure for the Disney studio, and its movement is in an interesting direction. *The Fox and the Hound* is one of those relatively rare Disney animated features that contains a useful lesson for its younger audiences. It's not just cute animals and frightening adventures and a happy ending; it's also a rather thoughtful meditation on how society determines our behavior.

The movie is a fable about a small puppy named Copper and an orphaned fox named Tod. At the outset we sense something unusual—after the camera traces a gloomy path through the shadows of the forest, a mother fox and her baby come running terrified out of the woods, chased by hunters and hounds. Will the mother and child escape? They almost do. But then the mother hides her baby and sacrifices her life to draw attention away from him. This is the cruel world, without any magical cartoon escapes.

The little fox is taken under the wing, so to speak, by wise old Big Mama Owl, who arranges for the baby to be adopted by a kindly farm woman. It's at this point the puppy comes into the plot. Puppy and fox become great friends in their childhoods and pledge to be loyal to each other forevermore. But then the quickly growing hound is taken away to be trained as a hunter, and the next time the two friends meet, the hound is savagely trying to chase down the fox. After they are almost killed by the bear, there is a reconciliation of sorts. They realize (and perhaps the kids in the audience will realize, too) how quickly our better impulses can be drowned out by the noise of society. The message is not heavy-handed, nor does it need to be, because the lessons in the movie are so firmly illustrated by the lives of the animals.

Although *The Fox and the Hound* is the first Disney animated feature to have been made mostly by a newer generation of artists at the studio, the film's look still is in the tradition of *The Rescuers* (1977) and other Disney work in the 1970s. That means we don't get the painstaking, frame-by-frame animation of individual leaves and flowers and birds that made *Snow White* magical back when animator man-hours were cheaper. But we do get a lot of life and energy on the screen.

The star of the movie's sound track is Pearl Bailey as Big Mama Owl. She sings three songs, dispenses advice with a free hand, and struts around in the forest as a sort of feathered Ann Landers. The animators have done a wonderful job of giving their cartoon owl some of Pearlie Mae's personality traits, but the two leading characters (with Mickey Rooney as the fox and Kurt Russell as the hound) are more straightforward.

The bottom line, I suppose, is: Will kids like this movie? And the answer is, sure, I think so. It's a fast-moving, colorful story, and as I watched the animated images on the screen, I was suddenly reminded of a curious belief I held when I was a kid. I believed that cartoons looked more real than "live" features, because everything on the screen had sharper edges. I outgrew my notion, but I'm not sure that represents progress.

Foxes ★ ★ ★
R, 106 m., 1980

Jodie Foster (Jeanie), Scott Baio (Brad), Sally Kellerman (Mary), Randy Quaid (Jay), Lois Smith (Mrs. Axman), Adam Faith (Bryan), Cherie Currie (Annie), Marilyn Kagan (Madge), Kandice Stroh (Dierdre). Directed by Adrian Lyne and produced by David Puttnam and Gerald Ayres. Screenplay by Ayres.

God help us if many American teen-agers are like the ones in this movie—but God love *them*, for that matter, for surviving in the teen-age subculture of Los Angeles. *Foxes* is a movie about four teen-age girls who live in the San Fernando Valley, who come from broken or unhappy homes, who are surrounded by a teen-age subculture of sex, dope, booze, and rock and roll . . . and who aren't bad kids, not really.

They run in a pack, sleeping over at each other's homes, going to school together, hanging out together, forming a substitute family because home doesn't provide a traditional one. They form the fierce loyalties that all teen-agers depend upon—loyalties of friendship that run deeper than the instant romances and sudden crushes that are a dime a dozen. They live in a world where sixteen-year-old kids are somehow expected to live in adult society, make decisions about adult vices, and yet not be adult. That's what's scariest about *Foxes:* Our knowledge that alcohol, pot, and pills *are* available to teen-agers unwise enough to go looking for them, and that they can provide emotional over-

loads far beyond the ability of the kids to cope.

One of the kids in the movie does cope fairly well, though. She's Jeanie, played by Jodie Foster as a sort of teen-age mother hen, a young girl who's got problems of her own but is intelligent, balanced, and enough of a survivor to clearly see the mistakes the others are making. That doesn't mean she rejects her friends. She runs with the pack and she takes her chances, but she's not clearly doomed. And some of the others are.

The movie follows its four foxes through several days and several adventures. It's a loosely structured film, deliberately episodic to suggest the shapeless form of these teen-agers' typical days and nights. Things happen on impulse. Stuff comes up. Kids stay out all night, or run away, or get drunk, or get involved in what's supposed to be a civilized dinner party until it's crashed by a mob of greasers.

The subject of the movie is the way these events are seen so very differently by the kids and their parents. And at the heart of the movie is one particular, wonderful, and complicated parent-child relationship, between Jodie Foster and Sally Kellerman. They only have a few extended scenes together, but the material is written and acted with such sensitivity that we really understand the relationship. And we understand Kellerman, as an attractive woman in her thirties, divorced from a rock promoter, who is trying to raise a sixteen-year-old, attend college, and still have a love life of her own. Kellerman has a line that evokes whole lives, when she talks about "all those desperately lonely, divorced UCLA undergraduates."

The parallels here are obvious. The Kellerman character, we suspect, got swept up in the rock and drug subculture, got married too young, got pregnant immediately, and now, the mother of a sixteen-year-old, is *still* in the process of growing up herself. She doesn't want her kid to go through what she went through. But kids grow up so fast these days that, oddly enough, these two women are almost in the same boat.

Foxes is an ambitious movie, not an exploitation picture. It's a lot more serious, for example, than the hit *Little Darlings*. It contains the sounds and rhythms of real teen-age lives; it was written and directed after a lot of research, and is acted by kids who are to one degree or another playing themselves. The movie's rare attempt to provide a por-

trait of the way teen-agers really do live today in some suburban cultures.

Frances ★ ★ ★ ½
R, 139 m., 1983

Jessica Lange (Frances Farmer), Sam Shepard (Harry York), Bart Burns (Farmer). Directed by Graeme Clifford and produced by Jonathan Sanger. Screenplay by Eric Bergren, Christopher Devore, and Nicholas Kazan.

Graeme Clifford's *Frances* tells the story of a small-town girl who tasted the glory of Hollywood and the exhilaration of Broadway and then went on to lead a life during which everything went wrong. It is a tragedy without a villain, a sad story with no moral except that there, but for the grace of God, go we. The movie is about Frances Farmer, a beautiful and talented movie star from the 1930s and 1940s who had a streak of independence and a compulsion toward self-destruction, and who went about as high and about as low as it is possible to go in one lifetime. She came out of Seattle as a high school essay-contest winner and budding intellectual. She was talented and pretty enough to make her way fairly easily into show business, where she immediately gravitated to the left-wing precincts of the Group Theater and such landmark productions as Clifford Odets's *Waiting for Lefty.* She also became a movie star, and there was a time when her star shone so brightly that it seemed it would last forever.

It did not. She was a stubborn, opinionated star who fought with the studio system, defied the bosses, drank too much, took too many pills, and got into too much trouble. Her strong-willed mother stepped in to help her, and that's when Frances's troubles really began. The mother orchestrated a series of hospitalizations in bizarre mental institutions, where Frances Farmer was brutally mistreated and finally, horrifyingly, lobotomized. She ended her days as a vague, pleasant middle-age woman who did a talk show in Indianapolis and finally died of alcoholism.

Jessica Lange plays Frances Farmer in a performance that is so driven, that contains so many different facets of a complex personality, that we feel she has an intuitive understanding of this tragic woman. She is just as good when she portrays Farmer as an uncertain, appealing teen-ager from the Northwest as she is when she plays her much later, snarling at a hairdresser and screaming at her mother. All of those contradictions were inside Farmer, and if she had learned to hide or deal with some of them she might have lived a happier life.

The story of Frances Farmer makes a fascinating movie, if only because it's such a contrast to standard show-business biographies. They usually come in two speeds: rags to riches, or rags to riches to victim. *Frances* never really lays blame for the tragedy of Farmer's life. It presents a number of causes for Farmer's destruction. (A short list might include her combative personality, her shrewish mother, the studio system, betrayal by her lovers, alcoholism, drug abuse, psychiatric malpractice, and the predations of a mad lobotomist.) But the movie never comes right out and says what it believes "caused" Farmer's tragedy. That is good, I think, because no simple explanation will do for Farmer's life. The movie is told from her point of view, and from where she stood, she was surrounded. On one day she had one enemy, and on another day, another enemy. Always, of course, her worst enemy was herself. The movie doesn't let us off the hook by giving us someone to blame. Instead, it insists on being a bleak tragedy, and it argues that sometimes it is quite possible for everything to go wrong. Since most movies are at least optimistic enough to provide a *cause* for human tragedy, this one is sort of daring.

It is also well made by Clifford, whose credits as a film editor include such virtuoso work as *McCabe and Mrs. Miller* and *Don't Look Now*. In his debut as a director Clifford has made a period picture that wears its period so easily that we're not distracted by it, a movie that is bleak without being unwatchable.

There are a few problems with his structure, most of them centering around an incompletely explained friend of Farmer's, played by Sam Shepard as a guy who seems to drift into her life whenever the plot requires him. Kim Stanley plays Farmer's mother on a rather thankless note of shrillness, and the lobotomist in the picture seems to have wandered over from a nearby horror film. (He apparently gave the same impression in real life.) But Lange provides a strong emotional center for the film, and when it is over we're left with the feeling that Farmer never really got a chance to be who she should have been, or to do what she should have done. She had every gift she needed in life except for luck, useful friends, and an instinct for survival. She could have been one of the greatest movie stars of her time. As it is, when I was asked to name a few of Frances Farmer's best films, I had to admit that, offhand, I couldn't think of one.

Frantic ★ ★ ★
R, 115 m., 1988

Harrison Ford (Richard Walker), Emmanuelle Seigner (Michelle), Betty Buckley (Sondra Walker), John Mahoney (Embassy Official), Jimmie Ray Weeks (Embassy Security). Directed by Roman Polanski and produced by Thom Mount and Tim Hampton. Screenplay by Polanski and Gerard Brach.

The first thing I noticed were the tones of the voices, low, flat, and weary. Just like people should sound after the twelve-hour flight from San Francisco to Paris. They are happy to be in Paris, but would be happier to be in bed. This was where they spent their honeymoon, twenty years ago, and now Dr. Richard Walker and his wife, Sondra, have returned for a medical convention.

There is some confusion with the luggage; apparently she picked up the wrong bag at the airport. But everything else seems to be going perfectly when Walker steps into his hotel shower. The phone rings, his wife answers it and says something, but he can't hear her because the water is running. By the time he steps out of the shower, she has disappeared.

That's the setup for *Frantic*, Roman Polanski's thriller and a professional comeback for the director of *Rosemary's Baby* and *Chinatown*, who was previously reduced to serving as gun-for-hire on the dreary *Pirates*. Every scene of this film feels like a project from Polanski's heart—a film to prove he is still capable of generating the kind of suspense he became famous for. And every scene, on its own, seems to work. It is only the total of the scenes that is wrong; the movie goes on too long, adds too many elaborations, tacks on too many complications, until the lean and economical construction of the first hour begins to drift into self-parody.

The movie stars Harrison Ford as the visiting American doctor, who is unable to convince the hotel, police, and American Embassy officials that his wife (Betty Buckley) is truly missing. He tries to track her down on his own, with only a few clues. After finding a drunk who saw his wife being forced into a car, he opens the "wrong" suitcase she picked up at the airport and finds a phone number that may be a lead.

The movie then develops into a cat-and-mouse game played out in Paris nightclubs, airports, and parking garages. Along the way, Ford teams up with the young woman (Emmanuelle Seigner) who brought the suitcase into the country. She's a mercenary courier, who was hired to carry the suitcase, doesn't know what was in it, but wants the 10,000 francs she was promised.

I will not reveal any additional plot details. I will say, however, that the nature of the mystery becomes clear to the audience some time before it becomes clear to Ford, and that the movie begins to lose its tightly wound tension about the time the Seigner character enters the plot. Until then, it develops with chilling logic, one step at a time. After the doctor and the girl become partners, it falls into more conventional patterns. And the series of endings—one false climax after another—is too contrived to be exciting.

Still, to watch the opening sequences of *Frantic* is to be reminded of Polanski's talent. Here is one of the few modern masters of the thriller and the *film noir*, whose career in exile has drifted aimlessly. *Frantic* would have benefited from the coldhearted cutting of some scenes and the trimming of others (such as a dance sequence in a nightclub that continues until it is inexplicable). But perhaps Polanski was so happy to be back where he belonged, making a big-budget thriller with a big star, that he lost his objectivity. It's understandable. And even with its excesses, *Frantic* is a reminder of how absorbing a good thriller can be.

The French Lieutenant's Woman
★ ★ ★ ½
R, 124 m., 1981

Meryl Streep (Sarah and Anna), Jeremy Irons (Charles and Mike), Hilton McRae (Sam), Emily Morgan (Mary), Charlotte Mitchell (Mrs. Tranter), Lynsey Baxter (Ernestina). Directed by Karel Reisz and produced by Leon Clore. Screenplay by Harold Pinter.

Reading the last one hundred pages of John Fowles's *The French Lieutenant's Woman* is like being caught in a fictional labyrinth. We think we know where we stand in the story, and who the characters are and what possibilities are open to them, and then Fowles begins an astonishing series of surprises. He turns his story inside out, suggesting first one ending, then another, always in a way that forces us to rethink everything that has gone before. That complex structure was long thought to make Fowles's novel unfilmable. How could his fictional surprises, depending on the relationship between reader and omniscient narrator, be translated into the more literal nature of film? One of the directors who tried to lick *The French Lieutenant's Woman* was John Frankenheimer, who complained: "There is no way you can film the book. You can tell the same story in a movie, of course, but not in the same way. And how Fowles tells his story is what makes the book so good." That seemed to be the final verdict, until the British playwright Harold Pinter tackled the project.

Pinter's previous screenplays, such as *Accident* and *The Go-Between*, are known for a mastery of ambiguity, for a willingness to approach the audience on more than one level of reality, and what he and director Karel Reisz have done with their film, *The French Lieutenant's Woman*, is both simple and brilliant. They have frankly discarded the multi-layered fictional devices of John Fowles, and tried to create a new cinematic approach that will achieve the same ambiguity. Fowles made us stand at a distance from his two doomed lovers, Sarah and Charles. He told their story, of a passion that was forbidden by the full weight of Victorian convention, and then he invited us to stand back and view that passion in terms of facts and statistics about . . . well, Victorian passions in general. Pinter and Reisz create a similar distance in their movie by telling us two parallel stories. In one of them, Sarah Woodruff (Meryl Streep) still keeps her forlorn vigil for the French lieutenant who loved and abandoned her, and she still plays her intriguing cat-and-mouse game with the obsessed young man (Jeremy Irons) who must possess her.

In the other story, set in the present, two actors named Anna and Mike are playing Sarah and Charles. And Anna and Mike are also having a forbidden affair, albeit a more conventional one. For the length of the movie's shooting schedule, they are lovers offscreen as well as on. But eventually Mike will return to his family and Anna to her lover.

This is a device that works, I think. Frankenheimer was right in arguing that just *telling* the Victorian love story would leave you with . . . just a Victorian love story. The modern framing story places the Victorian lovers in ironic relief. Everything they say and do has another level of meaning, because we know the "real" relationship between the actors themselves. Reisz opens his film with a shot that boldly states his approach: We see Streep in costume for her role as Sarah, attended by a movie makeup woman. A clapboard marks the scene, and *then* Streep walks into the movie's re-creation of the British coastal village of Lyme Regis.

"It's only a movie," this shot informs us. But, of course, it's *all* only a movie, including the story about the modern actors. And this confusion of fact and fiction interlocks perfectly with the psychological games played in the Victorian story by Sarah Woodruff herself.

The French lieutenant's woman is one of the most intriguing characters in recent fiction. She is not only apparently the victim of Victorian sexism, but also (as Charles discovers) its manipulator and master. She cleverly uses the conventions that would limit her, as a means of obtaining personal freedom and power over men. At least that is one way to look at what she does. Readers of the novel will know there are others.

The French Lieutenant's Woman is a beautiful film to look at, and remarkably well-acted. Streep was showered with praise for her remarkable double performance, and she deserved it. She is offhandedly contemporary one moment, and then gloriously, theatrically Victorian the next. Opposite her, Jeremy Irons is authoritative and convincingly bedeviled as the man who is frustrated by both of Streep's characters. The movie's a challenge to our intelligence, takes delight in playing with our expectations, and has one other considerable achievement as well: It entertains admirers of Fowles's novel, but does not reveal the book's secrets. If you see the movie, the book will still surprise you, and that's as it should be.

Frenzy ★ ★ ★ ★
R, 116 m., 1972

Jon Finch (Richard Blaney), Barry Foster (Rusk), Barbara Leigh-Hunt (Brenda Blaney), Anna Massey (Babs Mulligan), Alec McCowen (Chief Inspector Oxford), Vivien Merchant (Mrs. Oxford). Directed by Alfred Hitchcock. Associate producer William Hill. Screenplay by Anthony Shaffer.

Alfred Hitchcock's *Frenzy* is a return to old forms by the master of suspense, whose newer forms have pleased movie critics but not his public. This is the kind of thriller Hitchcock was making in the 1940s, filled with macabre details, incongruous humor, and the desperation of a man convicted of a crime he didn't commit.

The only 1970s details are the violence and the nudity (both approached with a certain grisly abandon that has us imagining *Psycho* without the shower curtain). It's almost as if Hitchcock, at seventy-three, was consciously attempting to do once again what he did better than anyone else. His films since *Psycho* struck out into unfamiliar territory and even got him involved in the Cold War *(Tom Curtain)* and the fringes of fantasy *(The Birds)*. Here he's back at his old stand.

Frenzy, which allegedly has a loose connection with a real criminal case, involves us in the exploits of a murderer known as The Necktie Killer (Barry Foster). And involvement is the sensation we feel, I think, since we know his identity from the beginning and sometimes cannot help identifying with him. There is a scene, for example, in which he inadvertently gets himself trapped in the back of a potato truck with a sack containing the body of his latest victim. We know he is a slimy bastard, but somehow we're sweating along with him as he crawls through the potatoes trying to regain a bit of incriminating evidence. He is the killer but, as is frequently the case with Hitchcock, another man seems much more guilty. This is Richard Blaney (Jon Finch), an ex-RAF hero who is down on his luck and has just lost his job. Through a series of unhappy coincidences which I'd better not give away, he's caught red-handed with the evidence while the killer walks away.

Hitchcock sets his action in the crowded back alleys of Covent Garden, where fruit and vegetable vendors rub shoulders with prostitutes, third-rate gangsters, bookies, and barmaids. A lot of the action takes place in a pub, and somehow Hitchcock gets more feeling for the location into his films than he usually does. With a lot of Hitchcock, you have the impression every frame has been meticulously prepared. This time, the smell and tide of humanity slops over. (There is even one tide in the movie which does a little slopping over humanity itself—but never mind.)

It's delicious to watch Hitchcock using the camera. Not a shot is wasted, and there is one elaborate sequence in which the killer goes upstairs with his victim. The camera precedes them up the stairs, watches them go in a door, and then backs down the stairs, alone, and across the street to look at the outside of the house. This shot is not for a moment a gimmick; the melancholy of the withdrawing camera movement is one of the most touching effects in the film, despite the fact that no people inhabit it.

There's a lot of humor, too, including two hilarious gourmet meals served to the Chief Inspector (Alec McCowen) by his wife (Vivien Merchant). There is suspense, and local color ("It's been too long since the Christie murders; a good colorful crime spree is good for tourism") and, always, Hitchcock smacking his lips and rubbing his hands and delighting in his naughtiness.

The Freshman ★ ★ ★ ½
PG, 102 m., 1990

Marlon Brando (Carmine Sabatini), Matthew Broderick (Clark Kellogg), Bruno Kirby (Victor Ray), Penelope Ann Miller (Tina Sabatini), Frank Whaley (Steve Bushak), Jon Polito (Chuck Greenwald), Paul Benedict (Arthur Fleeber), Richard Gant (Lloyd Simpson). Directed by Andrew Bergman and produced by Mike Lobell. Screenplay by Bergman.

There have been a lot of movies where stars have repeated the triumphs of their past—but has any star ever done it more triumphantly than Marlon Brando does in *The Freshman*? He is doing a reprise here of his most popular character, Don Vito Corleone of *The Godfather,* and he does it with such wit, discipline, and seriousness that it's not a rip-off and it's not a cheap shot; it's a brilliant comic masterstroke.

The Brando character is named Carmine Sabatini this time, but in every other respect he's the Godfather. He looks like him, talks like him, and most of all has the easy air of great authority long exercised. In the film, he has a job for a young man who has just started in film school. He wants him to pick up a package at the freight terminal of the airport and deliver it to a certain address. Of course we're thinking it's drugs—that's what the young man assumes—but actually this delivery is of a most peculiar nature. It is a giant lizard.

The young man is played by Matthew Broderick. He has got off to an uncertain start in New York City after all of his possessions and money were stolen by a thief (Bruno Kirby) who met him in Grand Central Station and offered him a ride. Now he's in trouble at

New York University's film school, where the professor (Paul Benedict) doesn't want to hear excuses; he only wants to hear how all of his students have purchased his book. So when Kirby wanders by, Broderick chases him down the street, collars him, and demands his possessions back. Kirby offers him better than that. He offers him a job.

The job involves a trip to Little Italy and the cloistered world behind the anonymous shop front of a social club where Carmine Sabatini keeps his office. On the wall is a photograph of Mussolini, there for nostalgia's sake ("It is like you might have a photo of the Beatles," Sabatini explains to the young man). The job offer is made, and accepted (after the don symbolically crushes some nuts in his hand), and before Broderick realizes it he has been swept up into the embrace of this Mafia family.

Penelope Ann Miller plays the don's daughter, Tina. A man with a machine gun is posted above the entrance to their home. Over the fireplace is the *Mona Lisa.* It's not a copy, as Broderick assumes. "Remember when it was sent over here to tour all of the museums?" Miller asks. "It never went back." She pushes a button, and we hear Nat King Cole singing "Mona Lisa" on the stereo system.

The Freshman was written and directed by Andrew Bergman, an unconventional comedy talent whose credits include co-authoring the screenplay for *Blazing Saddles* and writing *The In-Laws.* What he has created in *The Freshman* is a comedy of the peculiar, the oblique, and the offbeat. Very little is predictable in *The Freshman*—not the job Broderick is asked to do, not the relationship he finds himself in, and certainly not the climactic scene in which some very rich people sit down to a strange banquet while Maximilian Schell acts as maitre d' and Bert Parks serenades them with a version of "Maggie's Farm" that is unlike any that has ever been performed before.

When Brando finished filming *The Freshman* last September, he attacked the movie in a notorious interview in the *Toronto Globe and Mail,* claiming it was trash and that he was retiring from acting. A few days later, he retracted his statements and conceded that the movie might be all right, after all. Who knows what his motives were for either statement? Who ever knows with Brando? The fact is that while he's on the screen, few actors have a more complete command of their work, and in *The Freshman* he walks a tightrope above the hazards of bad laughs.

Think how many ways this performance could have gone wrong. Think of the criticism Brando risked receiving, from those ready to attack him for cashing in on his most famous performance by reprising it for a comedy. Brando must have known the dangers, but he must have had confidence in himself, too—enough to go ahead anyway, and to win a considerable gamble.

The other actors, perhaps aware of the chances Brando was taking, seem a little in awe of him—which is as it should be. Broderick is fine in the central role as the earnest film student, and Bruno Kirby has a lot of fun as the fast-talking street kid who knows all the angles. And Bert Parks must have been saving up his ideas for this movie ever since they terminated him at the Miss America pageant. *The Freshman* plays like a celebration of a lot of talented people who have all decided to try to get away with something.

Friday the 13th, Part II ½ ★
R, 87 m., 1981*

Amy Steel (Ginny), John Furey (Paul), Adrienne King (Alice), Kirsten Baker (Terry). Directed and produced by Steve Miner. Screenplay by Ron Kurz.

I saw *Friday the 13th Part II* at the Virginia Theater, a former vaudeville house in my hometown of Champaign-Urbana, Illinois. The late show was half-filled with high school and college students, and as the lights went down I experienced a brief wave of nostalgia. In this very theater, on countless Friday nights, I'd gone with a date to the movies. My nostalgia lasted for the first two minutes of the movie.

The pretitle sequence showed one of the heroines of the original *Friday the 13th,* alone at home. She has nightmares, wakes up, undresses, is stalked by the camera, hears a noise in the kitchen. She tiptoes into the kitchen. Through the open window, a cat springs into the room. The audience screamed loudly and happily: It's fun to be scared. Then an unidentified man sunk an ice pick into the girl's brain, and, for me, the fun stopped.

The audience, however, carried on. It is a tradition to be loud during these movies, I guess. After a batch of young counselors turns up for training at a summer camp, a girl goes out walking alone at night. Everybody in the audience imitated hoot-owls and hyenas. Another girl went to her room and started to undress. Five guys sitting together started a chant: "We want boobs!"

The plot: In the original movie, a summer camp staff was wiped out by a demented woman whose son had been allowed to drown by incompetent camp counselors. At the end of that film, the mother was decapitated by the young woman who is killed with an ice pick at the beginning of *Part II*. The legend grows that the son, Jason, did *not* really drown, but survived, and lurks in the woods waiting to take his vengeance against the killer of his mother . . . and against camp counselors in general, I guess.

That sets up the film. The counselors are introduced, very briefly, and then some of them go into town for a beer and the rest stay at the camp to make out with each other. A mystery assailant prowls around the main cabin. We see only his shadow and his shoes. One by one, he picks off the kids. He sinks a machete into the brain of a kid in a wheelchair. He surprises a boy and a girl making love, and nails them to a bunk with a spear through both their bodies. When the other kids return to the camp, it's their turn. After almost everyone has been killed in a disgusting and violent way, one girl chews up the assailant with a chain saw, *after* which we discover the mummies in his cabin in the woods, *after* which he jumps through a window at the girl, etc.

This movie is a cross between the Mad Slasher and Dead Teen-ager genres; about two dozen movies a year feature a mad killer going berserk, and they're all about as bad as this one. Some have a little more plot, some have a little less. It doesn't matter.

Sinking into my seat in this movie theater from my childhood, I remembered the movie fantasies when I was a kid. They involved teen-agers who fell in love, made out with each other, customized their cars, listened to rock and roll, and were rebels without causes. Neither the kids in those movies nor the kids watching them would have understood a world view in which the primary function of teen-agers is to be hacked to death.

*This review will suffice for the *Friday the 13th* film of your choice.

The Friends of Eddie Coyle ★ ★ ★ ★
R, 102 m., 1973

Robert Mitchum (Eddie Coyle), Peter Boyle (Dillon), Richard Jordan (Dave Foley), Steven Keats (Jackie), Alex Rocco (Scalise), Joe Santos (Artie Van). Directed by Peter Yates and produced and written by Paul Monash.

Someone remarks of Eddie, about halfway through *The Friends of Eddie Coyle*, that for a two-bit hood, he has fingers in a lot of pies. Too many, as it turns out. Without ever rising to the top, Eddie has been employed in organized crime for most of his life. He's kind of a utility infielder, ready to trade in some hot guns, drive a hijacked truck, or generally make himself useful.

Eddie got the nickname "Fingers" some years ago after a gun deal. The buyers he supplied got caught. Their friends slammed Eddie's fingers in a drawer. He understood. There is a certain code without which it would be simply impossible to go on doing business.

But as the movie opens, Eddie is in trouble, and it looks like he'll have to break the code. He's facing a two-year stretch in New Hampshire, and he wants out of it. He doesn't want to leave his wife and kids and see them go on welfare. He is, at heart, just a small businessman; he deals in crime but is profoundly middle class. He thinks maybe he can make a deal with the state's attorney and have a few good words put in for him up in New Hampshire.

The movie is as simple as that. It's not a high-strung gangster film, it doesn't have a lot of overt excitement in it, and it doesn't go in for much violence. He gives us a man, invites our sympathy for him, and then watches almost sadly as his time runs out. And *The Friends of Eddie Coyle* works so well because Eddie is played by Robert Mitchum, and Mitchum has perhaps never been better.

He has always been one of our best screen actors: sardonic, masculine, quick-witted, but slow to reveal himself. He has never been in an absolutely great film; he doesn't have masterpieces behind him like Brando or Cary Grant. More than half his films have been conventional action melodramas, and it is a rare summer without at least one movie in which Mitchum wears a sombrero and lights bombs with his cigar. But give him a character and the room to develop it, and what he does is wonderful. Eddie Coyle is made for him: a weary middle-aged man, but tough and proud; a man who has been hurt too often in life not to respect pain; a man who will take chances to protect his own territory.

The movie is drawn from a knowledgeable novel by George V. Higgins, himself a state's attorney, and has been directed by one of the masters of this sort of thing, Peter Yates (*Robbery, Bullitt*). Paul Monash's screenplay

stays close to the real-life Massachusetts texture of the novel, and the dialogue sounds right. The story isn't developed in the usual movie way, with lots of importance being given to intricacies of plot; instead, Eddie's dilemma occurs to him as it occurs to us, and we watch him struggle with it.

If the movie has a flaw, it's that we don't really care that much about the bank robberies that are counterpointed with Eddie's situation. We're interested in him. We can get the bank robberies in any summer's caper picture. It's strange that a movie's interest should fall off during its action scenes. But this is Eddie Coyle's picture, and Mitchum's.

Fright Night ★ ★ ★
R, 106 m., 1985

Roddy McDowall (Peter Vincent), Chris Sarandon (Jerry, the Vampire), William Ragsdale (Charley), Amanda Bearse (Amy), Stephen Geoffreys (Evil Ed). Directed by Tom Holland and produced by Herb Jaffe. Screenplay by Holland.

The best line in *Fright Night* belongs to Roddy McDowall, who plays a broken-down old hambone actor who used to star in vampire movies. "The kids today," he complains, "don't have the patience for vampires. They want to see some mad slasher running around and chopping off heads." He's right. Vampires, who are doomed to live forever, have outlived their fashion. They've been replaced by guys in ski masks who hack their way through Dead Teen-ager Movies.

Fright Night is an attempt to correct that situation. It stars William Ragsdale as an impressionable teen-ager who becomes convinced that vampires have moved in next door. It doesn't take a detective to figure that out. The vampires almost flaunt their unholy natures, performing weird rites in front of open windows and disposing of the bodies of their victims in plastic garbage bags. They are safe in the knowledge that nobody believes in vampires anymore.

The kid calls the cops. The vampires have a plausible explanation for their activities. The kid claims there has to be a coffin somewhere down in the basement. The cops warn him to stop wasting their time. And then, when the vampires start getting really threatening, the kid has no place to turn—except to old Peter Vincent (McDowall), the former B-movie actor who has just been fired from his TV job as host of the local Creature Features.

McDowall knows all about vampires: How to detect them, how to repel them, how to kill them. He also knows all about being behind on the rent, being evicted, and being out of work. For 500 bucks, he agrees to have a go at the vampires, and that sets up the second half of *Fright Night*.

The first part of the movie is basically funny. The second half unleashes lots of spectacular special effects devised by Richard Edlund, the same man who created the effects for *Ghostbusters*. Since part of the fun with vampire movies is how bad the special effects usually are, Edlund has to walk a narrow line, and he does. He gives us satisfactory scenes of transformations and decompositions, and seems to know his way around vampires, but he doesn't overwhelm the action.

The center of the movie, however, is the Roddy McDowall character, whose name, Peter Vincent, is obviously supposed to remind us of Peter Cushing and Vincent Price. Throw in Christopher Lee, and you'd have a quorum. McDowall's performance is wickedly funny, and he must have enjoyed it, chewing the scenery on his horror movie TV program and then chewing real scenery down in the vampire's basement. *Fright Night* is not a distinguished movie, but it has a lot of fun being undistinguished.

The Fringe Dwellers ★ ★ ★ ½
PG-13, 98 m., 1987

Kristina Nehm (Trilby), Justine Saunders (Mollie), Bob Maza (Joe), Kylie Belling (Noonah), Denis Walker (Bartie), Ernie Dingo (Phil). Directed by Bruce Beresford and produced by Sue Milliken. Screenplay by Bruce and Rhoisin Beresford.

There always seem to be too many people in Trilby's home. She is a teen-age girl who lives in an aborigine shantytown in Australia, and who sometimes goes downtown to peer into the window of the travel agency and dream of Paris, London, and New York. At home, there are parents and brothers and sisters and uncles and aunts and cousins in a riotous, disorganized, and loving extended family. They all love Trilby, but she is a quiet child, proud and stubborn, determined that she will make something of her life.

Trilby's determination is the central story in *The Fringe Dwellers*, a gentle and powerful movie by Bruce Beresford, who made it between *Tender Mercies* and *Crimes of the Heart*. In all three films, he shows a strong instinct for people living on the outside of society, on their own terms, drawing strength when they can from the people who love them.

The Fringe Dwellers is probably the most interesting of the three, because it shows us a world we know little about: Aborigines in an uncertain relationship with white society in Australia. Trilby and her younger brother are both doing well in school. An older sister has a gift for nursing, and is well-regarded at the local hospital. But Trilby's parents belong to an earlier generation—their lives are still sometimes ordered by myths that go back to the traditional aborigine culture—and they are not, truth to tell, all that eager to embrace white society.

Trilby feels trapped by the communal life in the shantytown. She convinces her parents to buy a new home in a white housing development, even though they can hardly afford it. But all of the uncles and aunts and cousins and neighbors follow them there (her parents can't resist inviting them to move in), and she still doesn't have a room of her own.

The film unfolds in a series of brief episodes. Trilby and three other aborigines go into a soda shop and have to sit through rude stares and half-audible racist jokes from the white kids, which is bad, but then a white man assures everyone they have "a perfect right" to be there, and that's worse. "I don't want anyone speaking up for me," Trilby says.

In school, she slaps a white girl and is reprimanded. If she had been white, she tells her boyfriend, she would have been expelled: "They're going easy because they feel sorry for me." Through many small glimpses like this, we begin to know her as a young woman who wants to be judged entirely on her own.

The Fringe Dwellers is a movie filled with life and laughter, as well as hurtful silences. There is a remarkable scene between the mother and daughter in which some of the mother's heritage and wisdom is expressed. There are perhaps a dozen fringe characters, including an old cousin who feels his time has come to return to the Outback lands of his ancestors. And then there are the modern problems, as when Trilby gets pregnant.

Will the baby lock her into repeating the lifetime cycle of poverty? Here Beresford provides a mysterious, unexplained scene (which I will not reveal), which seems to answer that question with a much larger question. The scene, like a couple of others in the movie, seems to imply that aborigines really do have inherited psychic powers. This is a common theme in Australian films; stories may begin with racial prejudice as their subjects, but they tend to skew off into mystical speculations about the ancient traditions and metaphysical gifts of aborigines. These traditions and gifts may, for all I know, be real, but the function they play in the movies is the Australian equivalent of American truisms about how blacks have natural rhythm.

In *The Fringe Dwellers*, Trilby's life is touched by the supernatural—an old crone foretells the future in a disturbing scene—but it is controlled much more by Trilby's own determination. She is played by Kristina Nehm, in an extraordinary screen debut; this young actress is not only beautiful and graceful, but is able to express a great deal more than she says—which is the point. She is surrounded by wonderful performances, especially by Justine Saunders as her mother. And at the end of the movie, I found myself truly interested in what eventually would happen to her, and whether she would realize her dream. There aren't many movie characters I can really care about, but here is one.

Full Metal Jacket ★ ★ ½
R, 121 m., 1987

Matthew Modine (Private Joker), Arliss Howard (Cowboy), Vince D'Onofrio ("Gomer" Pyle), Dorian Harewood (Eightball), Lee Ermey (Sergeant Hartman), Adam Baldwin (Animal Mother), Kevyn Major Howard (Rafterman), Ed O'Ross (Lieutenant Touchdown). Directed and produced by Stanley Kubrick. Screenplay by Kubrick, Michael Herr, and Gustav Hasford.

Stanley Kubrick's *Full Metal Jacket* is more like a book of short stories than a novel. Many of the passages seem self-contained, and some of them are masterful, and others look like they came out of the bottom drawer. This is a stangely shapeless film from the man whose work usually imposes a ferociously consistent vision on his material.

The movie is about Vietnam, and was shot on stages and outdoor sets in England. To say it's one of the best-looking war movies ever made on sets and stages is not quite enough praise, after the awesome reality of *Platoon, Apocalypse Now,* and *The Deer Hunter.* The crucial last passages of the film too often look and feel like World War II films from Hollywood studios. We see the same sets from so many different angles that after the movie we could find our own way around Kubrick's Vietnam.

That would not be a problem if his material made the sets irrelevant. It does not, especially toward the end of the film. You can only watch so much footage of a man crouched behind a barrier, pinned down by sniper fire, before the situation turns into a cinematic cliché. We've been here before, in other war movies, and we keep waiting for Kubrick to spring a surprise, and he never does.

The opening passages of *Full Metal Jacket* promise much more than the film is finally able to deliver. They tell the story of a group of Marine grunts undergoing basic training on Parris Island, and the experience comes down to a confrontation between the Gunnery Sergeant (Lee Ermey) and a tubby misfit (Vince D'Onofrio) who is nicknamed Gomer Pyle. These are the two best performances in the movie, which never recovers after they leave the scene.

Ermey plays a character in the great tradition of movie drill instructors, but with great brio and amazingly creative obscenity. All situations in the Marines and in war seem to suggest sexual parallels for him, and one of the film's best moments has the recruits going to bed with their rifles and reciting a traditional U.S. Marine Corps love poem to them.

In scene after scene, the war/sex connection is reinforced, and it parallels the personal battle between Ermey and D'Onofrio, who at first fails all of the tasks in basic training, and then finds he has one skill; he is an expert marksman. It is likely that in a real boot camp D'Onofrio would have been thrown out after a week, but Kubrick's story requires him to stay, and so he does, until the final showdown between the two men.

In that showdown, and at several other times in the film, Kubrick indulges his favorite close-up, a shot of a man glowering up at the camera from beneath lowered brows. This was the trademark visual in *A Clockwork Orange,* and Jack Nicholson practiced it in *The Shining.* What does it mean? That Kubrick thinks it's an interesting angle from which to shoot the face, I think. In *Full Metal Jacket,* it promises exactly what finally happens, and spoils some of the suspense.

There is a surprise to come, however: The complete abandonment of the sexual metaphor once the troops are in Vietnam. The movie disintegrates into a series of self-contained set pieces, none of them quite satisfying. The scene in the press room, for example with the lecture on propaganda, seems to reflect some of the same spirit as *Dr. Strangelove.* But how does it connect with the curious scene of the Vietnamese prostitute—a scene with a riveting beginning but no middle or end? And how do either lead to the final shoot-out with a sniper?

Time and again in the film, we get great shots with no payoffs. In one elaborate setup, for example, Kubrick shows us a cameraman and a soundman being led by their shirttails as they pan down a line of exhausted Marines. At first the shot has power. Then the outcome is that several soldiers deliver neat one-liners, all in a row, all in their turns, all perfectly timed, and the effect is so contrived that the idea of actual battle is completely lost.

Kubrick seems to want to tell us the story of individual characters, to show how the war affected them, but it has been so long since he allowed spontaneous human nature into his films that he no longer knows how. After the departure of his two most memorable characters, the sergeant and the tubby kid, he is left with no characters (or actors) that we really care much about, and in a key scene at the end, when a Marine feels joy after finally killing someone, the payoff is diminished because we don't give a damn about the character.

The movie has great moments. Ermey's speech to his men about the great Marine marksmen of the past (Charles Whitman and Lee Harvey Oswald among them) is a masterpiece. The footage on the Parris Island obstacle course is powerful. But *Full Metal Jacket* is uncertain where to go, and the movie's climax, which Kubrick obviously intends to be a mighty moral revelation, seems phoned in from earlier war pictures. After what has already been said about "Vietnam" in the movies, *Full Metal Jacket* is too little and too late.

Full Moon on Blue Water ★ ★
R, 96 m., 1988

Gene Hackman (Floyd), Teri Garr (Louise), Burgess Meredith (The General), Elias Koteas (Jimmy), Kevin Cooney (Charlie), David Doty (Virgil), Gil Glasgow (Baytch), Becky Gelke

(Dorothy). Directed by Peter Masterson and produced by Lawrence Turman, David Foster, and John Turman. Screenplay by Bill Bozzone.

Full Moon on Blue Water is such a likable film in so many little ways that you want to forgive it for being so bad in so many big ones. The plot reads like overwrought Faulkner as rewritten by *Mad* magazine, but the characters are full of oats and the movie generates a zany charm. You can't believe much of it, but it keeps you waiting to see what will happen next.

The story takes place on an offshore Texas island, where Floyd (Gene Hackman) lives the life of a recluse in the bar he used to run with his wife. Business has fallen off to nothing in the year since his wife disappeared, mostly because Floyd spends his days and nights mourning her and playing the same faded old home movies over and over again.

He lives with his father-in-law (Burgess Meredith), who has Alzheimer's disease and uses a wheelchair. And he pays a mentally retarded local man named Jimmy (Elias Koteas) to look over the old codger, who is known as The General. From time to time, Floyd gets an offer on his property from the snakes in the local real-estate business, who know the shabby little island is ripe for a big tourist boom. But Floyd turns the offers down. He'd rather sit around and feel sorry for himself.

Enter Louise (Teri Garr), who must be responsible for the local job shortage since she has all the jobs herself. She drives the school bus, works part time for Floyd, and studies computers in night school. She's halfway in love with Floyd. She also knows that unless he gets off his butt in the next few months, he's going to lose his saloon because of nonpayment of taxes, and *then* where will he be?

Life has settled down to a routine. Jimmy wheels The General outdoors for some fresh air every day, and they enjoy a game where Jimmy pushes the wheelchair at full speed down a pier, putting on the brakes at the last possible moment before The General would hurtle to the rocks below. This seems to be a refreshing change of pace for both of them. Louise comes around occasionally to have a drink with Floyd and try to talk sense to him, but all he wants to do is watch those damn movies. His wife's been missing a year, and he still refuses to believe that she's dead.

As if this plot were not lurid enough

already, events reach three or four climaxes, none of which I will betray, except to say that the crisis involving Jimmy and The General, and another crisis involving Jimmy and a gun, do not inhabit the realm of the probable. This is one of those movies where the characters can't believe what's happening to them, and neither can you.

It must also be said, however, that *Full Moon on Blue Water* is not without its pleasures. Two of them are the performances by Gene Hackman and Teri Garr, who create an authenticity despite the ridiculous events they are called upon to experience. When Garr hauls off and lets Hackman know exactly what she thinks, what she feels, what she will do, and what she won't do—and what he'd damn well better say—the scene has an energy that's fun to watch. And there is a certain nobility in the way Hackman pines for his missing wife, perhaps because he puts just the slightest, most subtle spin on it, so you can see that his character is a little aware of his own absurdity.

What I cannot understand is why this genuinely interesting stuff is interrupted by the most bizarre melodramatic developments, including tragedies, resurrections, and visits from mainland villains who seem borrowed directly from nineteenth-century melodrama. *Full Moon on Blue Water* tries to exist on three or four different reality levels at the same time, when one would have been just fine.

Funny Farm ★ ★ ★ ½
PG, 98 m., 1988

Chevy Chase (Andy), Madolyn Smith (Elizabeth), Kevin O'Morrison (Sheriff Ledbetter), Joseph Maher (Michael Sinclair), Jack Gilpin (Bud Culbertson), Caris Corfman (Betsy Culbertson), William Severs (Newspaper Editor), Mike Starr (Crocker). Directed by George Roy Hill and produced by Robert L. Crawford. Screenplay by Jeffrey Boam.

Funny Farm is one of those small miracles that start out like a lot of other movies and then somehow find their own way, step after step, to an original comic vision. *Funny Farm* is funny, all right, but it's more than funny, it's likable. It enlists our sympathies with the characters even while cheerfully exploiting their faults. And at the end, I had a goofy grin on my face because the movie had won me over so completely I was even willing to accept the final gag about the two ducks.

The movie stars Chevy Chase and Madolyn Smith as a married couple who decide to move to a small New England town so he can write his novel and they can breathe the fresh country air and mow their own lawn. Chase has been a sportswriter for years, but now he figures that with the typewriter placed just exactly right next to the big open window on the second floor overlooking the lawn, conditions will be perfect for the creation of a bestseller.

Conditions are not perfect. The birds sing too loudly. The mailman speeds by in a cloud of dust hurling letters from the window of his pickup. There are snakes in the lake and a corpse buried in the garden and it costs twenty cents to make a call from the pay phone in the kitchen. And the townspeople, they discover, are drawn more from Stephen King than Norman Rockwell. By wintertime, Chase is withdrawn and bitter, drinking heavily, and sleeping past noon, while his wife has sold a children's novel about a city squirrel who moves to the country and has the same name as her husband.

None of this, I imagine, sounds as good as it plays. *Funny Farm* has a good screenplay by Jeffrey Boam, and yet in other hands it might have yielded only a routine movie. George Roy Hill, the director, makes it better than that because he finds the right tone and sticks to it—a sort of bemused wonder at the insanity of it all, in a movie that doesn't underline its gags or force its punch lines but just lets everything develop naturally. Notice, for example, the timing in the se-quence where the sheriff first comes to chat about the corpse in the garden.

Chevy Chase is not exactly playing a fresh kind of role here—his hero is a variation of the harassed husband he's been playing for years—but he has never been better in a movie. He has everything just right this time, and he plays the character without his usual repertory of witty asides and laconic one-liners. It's a performance, not an appearance. Madolyn Smith makes a good foil for him, although she isn't given enough to do in scenes of her own, and one scene in particular—a visit to an antique shop—felt suspiciously truncated.

The gallery of townspeople has to be seen to be believed. They are almost all mean-spirited, crafty, suspicious, and greedy, and happy to be just exactly who they are. The sheriff travels by taxi because he flunked his driving test, the lady who runs the antique shop seems to be selling nothing except her own precious and irreplaceable family heirlooms, and down at the local cafe, there's a competition to see who can eat the most stir-fried lamb testicles.

Funny Farm is kind of a loony, off-center comedy version of Hill's *The World According to Garp*, another movie about strange people in bizarre situations. *Garp* made too much of its significance, however, while the comedy in this film is light as a feather. The final sequence, in which the townspeople are bribed to act "normal," while Chase hands out Norman Rockwell covers from the *Saturday Evening Post* for them to admire, has a kind of inspired lunacy that is so fragile you almost don't want to laugh for fear of breaking the mood.

G

The Gambler ★ ★ ★
R, 111 m., 1974

James Caan (Axel), Paul Sorvino (Hips), Lauren Hutton (Billie), Morris Carnovsky (A.R. Lowenthal), Jacqueline Brooks (Naomi), Burt Young (Carmine). Directed by Karel Reisz and produced by Irwin Winkler and Robert Chartoff. Screenplay by James Toback.

"Jeez, Axel, I never seen such bad cards," Axel Freed's friend tells him consolingly. They're standing in the kitchen of a New York apartment, and gray dawn is seeping through the smoke. Axel has never seen such bad cards either. His disbelief that anyone could draw so many lousy poker hands in a row has led him finally $44,000 into debt. He doesn't have the money, but it's been a big-time game, and he has to find it somewhere or be in heavy trouble.

And that's how Karel Reisz's *The Gambler* begins: with a problem. The way Axel solves his problem is only fairly difficult. He borrows the money from his mother, who is a doctor. But then we discover that his problem is greater than his debt, because there is some final compulsion within him that won't let him pay back the money. He needs to lose, to feel risk, to place himself in danger. He needs to gamble away the forty-four grand on even more hopeless bets because in a way it isn't gambling that's his obsession—it's danger itself.

"I play in order to lose," he tells his bookie at one point. "That's what gets my juice going. If I only bet on the games I know, I could at least break even." But he doesn't want that. At one point, he's driven to bet money he doesn't really have on college basketball games picked almost at random out of the sports pages.

And yet Axel Freed is not simply a gambler, but a very complicated man in his mid-thirties who earns his living as a university literature teacher. He teaches Dostoyevski, William Carlos Williams, Thoreau. But he doesn't seem to teach their works so much as what he finds in them to justify his own obsessions. One of the students in his class has Axel figured out so completely that she always has the right answer, when he asks what Thoreau is saying, or what Dostoyevski is saying. They're saying, as Axel reads them, to take risks, to put the self on the line.

"Buffalo Bill's defunct," he says, quoting the e e cummings poem, and the death of the nineteenth-century age of heroes obsesses him. In that earlier age, he could have tested himself more directly. His grandfather came to America flat broke, fought and killed to establish himself, and still is a man of enormous vitality at the age of eighty. The old man is respectable now (he owns a chain of furniture stores), but the legend of his youth fascinates Axel, who recites it poetically at the eightieth-birthday party.

Axel finds nothing in 1974 to test himself against, however. He has to find his own dangers, to court and seduce them. And the ultimate risk in his life as a gambler is that behind his friendly bookies and betting cronies is the implacable presence of the Mafia, the guys who take his bets like him, but if he doesn't pay, there's nothing they can do. "It's out of my hands," his pal Hips explains. "A bad gambling debt has got to be taken care of." And that adds an additional dimension to *The Gambler*, which begins as a portrait of Axel Freed's personality, develops into the story of his world, and then pays off as a thriller. We become so absolutely contained by Axel's problems and dangers that they seem like our own. There's a scene where he soaks in the bathtub and listens to the last minutes of a basketball game, and

another scene where he sits in the stands and watches a basketball game he has tried to fix (while a couple of hit men watch him), and these scenes have a quality of tension almost impossible to sustain.

But Reisz sustains them, and makes them all the more real because he doesn't populate the rest of his movie with stock characters.

Axel Freed, as played by James Caan, is himself a totally convincing personality, and original. He doesn't derive from other gambling movies or even from other roles he's played.

And the people around him also are specific, original creations. His mother Naomi (Jacqueline Brooks) is a competent, independent person who gives him the money because she fears for his life, and yet understands that his problem is deeper than gambling. His grandfather, marvelously played by Morris Carnovsky, is able to imply by his behavior why he fascinates Axel so. The various bookies and collectors he comes across aren't Mafia stereotypes. They enforce more in sorrow than in anger. Only his girlfriend (Lauren Hutton) fails to seem very real. Here's still another demonstration of the inability of contemporary movies to give us three-dimensional women under thirty.

There's a scene in *The Gambler* that has James Caan on screen all by himself for two minutes, locked in a basement room, waiting to meet a Mafia boss who will arguably instruct that his legs be broken. In another movie, the scene could have seemed too long, too eventless.

But Reisz, Caan, and screenwriter James Toback have constructed the character and the movie so convincingly that the scene not only works, but works two ways: first as suspense, and then as character revelation. Because as we look into Axel Freed's caged eyes we see a person who is scared to death and yet stubbornly ready for this moment he has brought down upon himself.

Gandhi ★ ★ ★ ★
PG, 188 m., 1982

Ben Kingsley (Mahatma Gandhi), Candice Bergen (Margaret Bourke-White), Edward Fox (General Dyer), John Gielgud (Lord Irwin), Trevor Howard (Judge Broomfield), John Mills (The Viceroy) Martin Sheen (Walker), Rohini Hattangady (Kasturba Ghandi), Ian Charleson (Charlie Andrews), Athol Fugard (General Smuts). Directed and produced by Richard Attenborough. Screenplay by John Briley.

In the middle of this epic film there is a quiet, small scene that helps explain why *Gandhi* is such a remarkable experience. Mahatma Gandhi, at the height of his power and his fame, stands by the side of a lake with his wife of many years. Together, for the benefit of a visitor from the West, they reenact their marriage vows. They do it with solemnity, quiet warmth, and perhaps just a touch of shyness; they are simultaneously demonstrating an aspect of Indian culture and touching on something very personal to them both. At the end of the ceremony, Gandhi says, "We were thirteen at the time." He shrugs. The marriage had been arranged. Gandhi and his wife had not been in love, had not been old enough for love, and yet love had grown between them. But that is not really the point of the scene. The point, I think, comes in the quiet smile with which Gandhi says the words. At that moment we believe that he is fully and truly human, and at that moment, a turning point in the film, *Gandhi* declares that it is not only a historical record but a breathing, living document.

This is the sort of rare epic film that spans the decades, that uses the proverbial cast of thousands, and yet follows a human thread from beginning to end: *Gandhi* is no more overwhelmed by the scope of its production than was Gandhi overwhelmed by all the glory of the British Empire. The movie earns comparison with two classic works by David Lean, *Lawrence of Arabia* and *Dr. Zhivago*, in its ability to paint a strong human story on a very large canvas.

The movie is a labor of love by Sir Richard Attenborough, who struggled for years to get financing for his huge but "non-commercial" project. Various actors were considered over the years for the all-important title role, but the actor who was finally chosen, Ben

Kingsley, makes the role so completely his own that there is a genuine feeling that the spirit of Gandhi is on the screen. Kingsley's performance is powerful without being loud or histrionic; he is almost always quiet, observant, and soft-spoken on the screen, and yet his performance comes across with such might that we realize, afterward, that the sheer moral force of Gandhi must have been behind the words. Apart from all its other qualities, what makes this movie special is that it was obviously made by people who believed in it.

The movie begins in the early years of the century, in South Africa. Gandhi moved there from India in 1893, when he was twenty-three. He already had a law degree, but, degree or not, he was a target of South Africa's system of racial segregation, in which Indians (even though they are Caucasian, and thus should "qualify") are denied full citizenship and manhood. Gandhi's reaction to the system is, at first, almost naive; an early scene on a train doesn't quite work only because we can't believe the adult Gandhi would still be so ill-informed about the racial code of South Africa. But Gandhi's response sets the tone of the film. He is nonviolent but firm. He is sure where the right lies in every situation, and he will uphold it in total disregard for the possible consequences to himself.

Before long Gandhi is in India, a nation of hundreds of millions, ruled by a relative handful of British. They rule almost by divine right, shouldering the "white man's burden" even though they have not quite been requested to do so by the Indians. Gandhi realizes that Indians have been made into second-class citizens in their own country, and he begins a program of civil disobedience that is at first ignored by the British, then scorned, and finally, reluctantly, dealt with, sometimes by subterfuge, sometimes by brutality. Scenes in this central passage of the movie make it clear that nonviolent protests could contain a great deal of violence. There is a shattering scene in which wave after wave of Gandhi's followers march forward to be beaten to the ground by British clubs. Through it all, Gandhi maintains a certain detachment; he is convinced he is right, convinced that violence is not an answer, convinced that sheer moral example can free his nation—as it did. "You have been guests in our home long enough," he tells the British, "Now we would like for you to leave."

The movie is populated with many familiar faces, surrounding the newcomer Kingsley. Where would the British cinema be without its dependable, sturdy, absolutely authoritative generation of great character actors like Trevor Howard (as a British judge), John Mills (the British viceroy), John Gielgud, and Michael Hordern? There are also such younger actors as Ian Bannen, Edward Fox, Ian Charleson, and, from America, Martin Sheen as a reporter and Candice Bergen as the photographer Margaret Bourke-White.

Gandhi stands at the quiet center. And Ben Kingsley's performance finds the right note and stays with it. There are complexities here; *Gandhi* is not simply a moral story with a happy ending, and the tragedy of the bloodshed between the Hindu and Muslim populations of liberated India is addressed, as is the partition of India and Pakistan, which we can almost literally feel breaking Gandhi's heart.

I imagine that for many Americans, Mahatma Gandhi remains a dimly understood historical figure. I suspect a lot of us know he was a great Indian leader without quite knowing why and—such is our ignorance of Eastern history and culture—we may not fully realize that his movement did indeed liberate India, in one of the greatest political and economic victories of all time, achieved through nonviolent principles. What is important about this film is not that it serves as a history lesson (although it does) but that, at a time when the threat of nuclear holocaust hangs ominously in the air, it reminds us that we are, after all, human, and thus capable of the most extraordinary and wonderful achievements, simply through the use of our imagination, our will, and our sense of right.

The Garden of the Finzi-Continis
★ ★ ★ ★
R, 90 m., 1971

Dominique Sanda (Micol), Lino Capolicchio (Giorgio), Helmut Berger (Alberto), Fabrio Tesel (Malnate), Romolo Valli (Giorgio's Father). Directed by Vittorio de Sica and produced by Gianni Hecht Lucari. Screenplay by Ugo Pirro and Vittorio Bonicelli.

The Garden of the Finzi-Continis, as nearly as I can tell, is not an enclosed space but an enclosed state of mind. Eager for an afternoon of tennis, the young people ride into it on their bicycles one sunny Sunday afternoon. The Fascist government of Mussolini has declared the ordinary tennis clubs off limits for Italian Jews—but what does that matter, here behind these tall stone walls that have faithfully guarded the Finzi-Contini family for generations?

Micol, the daughter, welcomes her guests and gives some of them a little tour: That tree over there is said to be five hundred years old and might even have been planted by the Borgias. If it has stood for all those years in this garden, she seems to believe, what is there to worry about in the world outside?

She is a tall blond girl with a musical laugh and a way of turning away from a man just as he reveals himself to her. Giorgio, who has been helplessly in love with her since they were both children, deceives himself that she loves him. But she cannot quite love anyone, although she carries on an affair with a tall, athletic young man who is about to be drafted into the army. Giorgio's father says of the Finzi-Continis: "They're different. They don't even seem to be Jewish."

They're different because wealth and privilege and generations of intellectual and social position have bred them into a family as proud as it is vulnerable. The other Jews in the town react to Mussolini's edicts in various ways: Giorgio is enraged; his father is philosophical. But the Finzi-Continis hardly seem to know, or care, what is happening. They are above mere edicts; they chose to live behind their walls long before the Fascists said they must.

This is the situation as Vittorio de Sica sketches it for us at the outset of *The Garden of the Finzi-Continis*, which was a true surprise from a director who had seemed to lose his early genius. De Sica's previous two or three films (especially the disastrous *A Place for Lovers*) were embarrassments from the director of *Bicycle Thief* and *Shoeshine*.

But here he returned with a film that seems to owe little to his previous work. It is not neorealism; it is not a comic mixture of bawdiness and sophistication; it is most of all not the dreamy banality of his previous few films. In telling of the disintegration of the Jewish community in one smallish Italian town, de Sica merges his symbols with his story so that they evoke the meaning of the time.

It was a time in which many people had no idea what was really going on. Giorgio's younger brother, sent to France to study, finds out to his horror about the German concentration camps. There has been no word of them in Italy, of course. Italy in those final prewar years is painted by de Sica as a perpetual wait for something no one admitted would come: war and the persecution of the Jews.

The walled garden of the Finzi-Continis is his symbol for this waiting period. It seems to promise that nothing will change, and even the Jews who live in the village seem to cling to the apparent strength of the Finzi-Continis as assurance of their own power to survive.

In presenting the garden to us, de Sica uses an interesting visual strategy; he never completely orients us visually, and so we don't know its overall size and shape. Therefore, visually, we can't count on it: We don't know when it will give out. It's an uneasy feeling to be inside an undefined space, especially if you may need to hide or run, and that's exactly the feeling de Sica gets.

The ambiguity of the garden's space is matched by an understated sexual ambiguity. Nothing happens overtly, but de Sica uses looks and body language to suggest the complex varieties of sexual attractions among his characters. When Micol is discovered by Giorgio with her sleeping lover, she does a most interesting thing. She covers him, not herself, and stares at Giorgio until he goes away.

The thing is, you can't count on anything. And nothing permanent can be permitted to take place during this period of waiting. De Sica's film creates a feeling of nostalgia for a lost time and place, but it isn't the nostalgia of looking back. It's the nostalgia of the time itself, when people still inhabiting their world could sense it slipping away, and already missed what they had not yet lost.

Gates of Heaven ★ ★ ★ ★
NO MPAA RATING, 85 m, 1978

A documentary produced, directed, and written by Errol Morris.

There are many invitations to laughter during this remarkable documentary, but what *Gates of Heaven* finally made me feel was an aching poignancy about its subjects. They say you can make a great documentary about almost anything, if only you see it well enough and truly, and this film proves it. *Gates of Heaven*, which has no connection with the unfortunate *Heaven's Gate*, is a documentary about pet cemeteries and their owners. It was filmed in Southern Cali-

fornia, so of course we immediately anticipate a sardonic look at peculiarities of the Moonbeam State. But then *Gates of Heaven* grows ever so much more complicated and frightening, until at the end it is about such large issues as love, immortality, failure, and the dogged elusiveness of the American Dream.

The film was made by a California filmmaker named Errol Morris, and it has been the subject of notoriety because Werner Herzog, the West German director, promised to eat his shoe if Morris ever finished it. Morris did finish it, and at the film's premiere in Berkeley, Herzog indeed boiled and ate his shoe.

Gates of Heaven is so rich and thought-provoking, it achieves so much while seeming to strain so little, that it stays in your mind for tantalizing days. It opens with a monologue by a kind-looking, somewhat heavyset paraplegic, with a slight lisp that makes him sound like a kid. His name is Floyd McClure. Ever since his pet dog was run over years ago by a Model A Ford, he has dreamed of establishing a pet cemetery. The movie develops and follows his dream, showing the forlorn, bare patch of land where he founded his cemetery at the intersection of two superhighways. Then, with cunning drama, it gradually reveals that the cemetery went bankrupt and the remains of 450 animals had to be dug up. Various people contribute to the story: One of McClure's investors, a partner, two of the women whose pets were buried in his cemetery, and an unforgettable old woman named Florence Rasmussen, who starts on the subject of pets, and switches, with considerable fire, to her no-account son. Then the action shifts north to the Napa Valley, where a go-getter named Cal Harberts has absorbed what remained of McClure's dream (and the 450 dead pets) into his own pet cemetery, the Bubbling Well Pet Memorial Park. It is here that the movie grows heartbreaking, painting a portrait of a lifestyle that looks chillingly forlorn, and of the people who live it with relentless faith in positive thinking.

Harberts, a patriarch, runs his pet cemetery with two sons, Phil and Dan. Phil, the older one, has returned home after a period spent selling insurance in Salt Lake City. He speaks of having been overworked. Morris lets the camera stay on Phil as he solemnly explains his motivational techniques, and his method of impressing a new client by filling his office with salesmanship trophies. He has read all of Clement Stone's books on "Positive Mental Attitude," and has a framed picture of Stone on his wall. Phil looks neat, presentable, capable. He talks reassuringly of his positive approach to things, "mentally wise." Then we meet the younger brother, Dan, who composes songs and plays them on his guitar. In the late afternoon, when no one is at the pet cemetery, he hooks up his 100-watt speakers and blasts his songs all over the valley. He has a wispy mustache and looks like a hippie. The family hierarchy is clear. Cal, in the words of Phil, is "El Presidento." Then Dan comes next, because he has worked at the cemetery longer. Phil, the golden boy, the positive thinker, is maintaining his P.M.A. in the face of having had to leave an insurance business in Salt Lake City to return home as third in command at a pet cemetery.

The cemetery itself is bleak and barren, its markers informing us, "God is love; dog is god backwards." An American flag flies over the little graves. Floyd McClure tells us at the beginning of the film that pets are put on Earth for two reasons: to love and to be loved. At the end of this mysterious and great movie, we observe the people who guard and maintain their graves, and who themselves seem unloved and very lonely. One of the last images is of old Cal, the patriarch, wheeling past on his forklift, a collie-sized coffin in its grasp.

The Gauntlet ★ ★ ★
R, 111 m., 1977

Clint Eastwood (Ben Shockley), Sondra Locke (Gus Mally), Pat Hingle (Josephson), William Prince (Blakelock), Bill McKinney (Constable), Michael Cavanaugh (Feyderspiel). Directed by Clint Eastwood and produced by Robert Daley. Screenplay by Michael Butler and Dennis Shryack.

The Gauntlet is classic Clint Eastwood: fast, furious, and funny. It tells a cheerfully preposterous story with great energy and a lot of style, and nobody seems more at home in this sort of action movie than Eastwood. He plays a cop again this time, but not a supercop like Dirty Harry Callahan. He's a detective from Phoenix, and no hero: He drives up in front of police headquarters, opens his car door, and a whiskey bottle crashes to the street.

Eastwood hasn't compiled the most stellar record in the department, but somehow the police commissioner thinks he's the right man for the next assignment: Fly to Las Vegas, take custody of a hooker there, and bring her back to Phoenix to be a witness in an important court case. It sounds routine to Eastwood, until he flies to Vegas, takes custody, and discovers that the Mafia is quoting sixty-to-one odds against his witness leaving Nevada alive. Maybe, he begins to suspect, this isn't a totally typical witness . . . .

The witness (played by Sondra Locke) isn't a totally typical hooker, either. She's a college graduate, spunky, pleasant. She tells Eastwood he'd be wise to catch the next flight home, because there's a contract out on her. Eastwood's too stubborn. He's taken the assignment and he'll carry it out through hell and high water (which turn out to be just about the only two things he doesn't have to survive on this mission).

The return trip gets off to a slightly shaky start when they survive an auto bomb. Then, after Eastwood commandeers an ambulance, they're involved in a high-speed chase with three gunmen. They take refuge in Locke's house, which is promptly surrounded by dozens of police marksmen, who open fire, achieving overkill so completely that (in one of the movie's many mixtures of humor and violence), the house simply topples over. Still ahead of them are nights in the desert, an encounter with Hell's Angels, a fight on a moving freight train, a chase in which their motorcycle is pursued by a rifle marksman in a helicopter . . . and then the grand finale, in which Eastwood hijacks a passenger bus, armor-plates it, and drives himself and his witness through downtown Phoenix against a hail of machine-gun fire. You see what I mean about the plot's being cheerfully preposterous.

Eastwood directed himself again this time, and he's a good action craftsman (as The Outlaw Josey Wales demonstrated). He's also good at developing relationships; despite the movie's barrage of violence, there's a nice pacing as his cop and hooker slog through their ordeals and begin to like and respect one another. As in most Eastwood movies, by the way, the woman's role is a good one: Eastwood has such a macho image that maybe people haven't noticed that his female sidekicks (like Tyne Daly, Dirty Harry's partner in The Enforcer) have minds of their own and are never intended to be merely decorative.

The Gauntlet will no doubt be attacked in various quarters because of its violence, but it's a harmless, pop-art type of violence, often with a comic quality. The wall of gunfire during the final bus ride up the steps of the Hall of Justice, for example, is an extravaganza of sound and action during which, incredibly, no one is killed. Eastwood himself fires his pistol only twice: once at a door, and once at a gas tank.

George Stevens: A Filmmaker's Journey ★ ★ ★ 1/2
PG, 113 m., 1985

A documentary written, produced, and directed by George Stevens, Jr. Edited by Catherine Shields. Music by Carl Davis.

The last shot of Citizen Kane showed the dead tycoon's storerooms, vast spaces filled with the jumble of a lifetime. One of the early shots in this documentary about George Stevens has something of the same quality. We see the memorabilia of his long career: cowboy hats, leather-bound scripts, cans of film, albums of photographs, Oscars, diaries, belt buckles—everything with a story, and half the stories already forgotten.

The voice on the sound track is the filmmaker's son, telling us about his famous father. One of the things the father told him, one day when they were driving past the warehouse where all of these memories were stored, was, "That'll all be yours when I'm gone." As he rummaged through the souvenirs of his father's lifetime, he made some extraordinary discoveries: Not only the prints and scripts of such classics as Giant, A Place in the Sun, and Alice Adams, but also documentary footage of Stevens on the set of his movies, and rare color footage Stevens shot for himself while he was leading a newsreel unit during World War II.

More than most men, Stevens seems to have been concerned to leave behind a record of his career. He began in movies almost at the beginning, as an assistant on the early silent films, and his first work as a director was on the Laurel and Hardy films. We see some of his earliest footage, and then we begin to hear the voices of the people who knew him then, and worked with him: Old directors like Rouben Mamoulian and John Huston, stars like Katharine Hepburn and Warren Beatty, writers like Irwin Shaw. Hepburn gave Stevens his real start, rescuing him from grade B features and second-unit work because she was impressed by his enthusiasm for Alice Adams. It became his first prestigious production, but then there was a flood of others: the definitive Astaire-Rogers musical *Swing Time*, the audacious *Gunga Din*, and *Woman of the Year*, and Stevens began to build a reputation as a man who saw his own way through the standard scripts he was handed, freeing his actors so that *Gunga Din*, for example, became a high-spirited comic masterpiece instead of just another swashbuckler.

The film contains a lot of home movies and private documentary footage; Stevens shot the only color footage of the landing at Normandy, and we also see moments of Stevens at work, always quietly professional, thoughtful, not the flamboyant self-promoter so many other directors of his generation became. Stevens, more than anyone else, fashioned the image of James Dean. He directed some of Elizabeth Taylor's most memorable scenes. And he pressed on in the face of daunting odds to direct such movies as *The Greatest Story Ever Told*. Shooting in Utah, he was faced with the first snowstorms in a generation, and when he asked the cast and crew to pitch in and shovel snow, they respected him enough that they did it.

A Filmmaker's Journey is a film biography of a movie director, and it inevitably shares some of the conventions of the genre. We see the clips of great scenes, we hear the memories of old colleagues. Two things distinguish the film: The quiet professionalism with which the materials have been edited together, and the feeling that George Stevens, Jr., really is engaging in a rediscovery of his father through the making of this film. By the end of the film, we are less aware of George Stevens as a filmmaker than as a good and gifted man who happened to use movies as a means of expressing his gifts.

Getting It Right ★ ★ ★ ★
R, 102 m., 1989

Jesse Birdsall (Gavin Lamb), Helena Bonham Carter (Minerva Munday), Peter Cook (Mr. Adrian), John Gielgud (Sir Gordon Munday), Jane Horrocks (Jenny), Lynn Redgrave (Joan), Shirley Anne Field (Anne), Pat Heywood (Mrs. Lamb), Bryan Pringle (Mr. Lamb). Directed by Randal Kleiser and produced by Joanathan D. Krane and Kleiser. Screenplay by Elizabeth Jane Howard.

Getting It Right is a late-1980s version of all those driven, off-center London films like *Darling*, *Georgy Girl*, and *Morgan*—movies in which a wide-eyed innocent journeys

through the jungle of the eccentric, the depraved, and the blasé, protected only by a good heart and limitless naïveté.

The movie tells the story of Gavin Lamb, a hairdresser who shampoos the coiffures and the miseries of his ancient clients, and returns every night to the home of his parents—where his mother serves awesomely inedible dinners promptly at the stroke of six. Gavin is thirty-one and still a virgin, and his bedroom is a sanctuary where he keeps his precious collection of recorded music, meticulously arranged.

At first we can't get a reading on Gavin Lamb. He is pleasant, friendly, a little standoffish. Life doesn't seem to have happened to him yet. The character is played close to the vest by Jesse Birdsall, a young actor who manages to look thoroughly ordinary most of the time, and sublimely crafty the rest of the time. It's a performance a little like Dustin Hoffman's in *The Graduate*, where society is criticized by the character's very indifference to it.

One day Gavin is taken to a party that seems to be a last-gasp attempt to resurrect Swinging London. It's held in the spectacular penthouse of a garish divorcée (Lynn Redgrave), whose red wig and outlandish costumes look like a conscious attempt to keep people at arm's length. But she likes Gavin, and takes pity on him, and invites him to a secret inner sanctum in the vast apartment—the only room, apparently, where she feels free to take off her wig and be herself. Her secret identity turns out to be sweet and tender, and Gavin is started down the road toward losing his virginity and gaining his independence.

There is another woman at the party—a girl, really—who is dark and intense and small and determined. Her name is Minerva Munday (Helena Bonham Carter) and her father is fearsomely old and rich and eccentric (Sir John Gielgud has great relish with the role). Suddenly Gavin is catapulted out of his safe orbit of the hairdressing salon and life with Mum and Dad, and finds his romantic life more eventful than he could have dreamed.

Getting It Right is a character film, not a plot film, and so the point is not what happens, but who it happens to. The screenplay is by Elizabeth Jane Howard, based on her own novel, and it shows a novelist's instinct for character and dialogue. This is not one of those mechanically plotted forced marches through film school script formulas, but a

story that lives and breathes and gives the characters the freedom to surprise us.

Smaller roles, like Peter Cook's cameo as the owner of the hairdressing salon, are enriched with asides that suggest the entire character. And some of the characters sneak up on us—like Jenny (Jane Horrocks), who is Gavin's assistant at the salon. He has barely looked at her in two years, but now, emboldened by his late flowering, he looks at everyone in a new light, and Jenny begins to blossom.

Getting It Right was directed by Randal Kleiser, whose big hit film *Grease*, in 1978, has been followed by a career with no discernible pattern (can the same director have made *The Blue Lagoon*, *Flight of the Navigator*, and *Big Top Pee Wee?*).

With this film, however, Kleiser has gotten everything right; he is often dealing with the most delicate nuances, in which the whole point of some scenes depends on subtle reactions or small shifts of tone, and he doesn't step wrong. Look, for example, at his control of a scene where Gavin takes a date to a birthday party for a gay friend who breaks up with his lover right there on the spot; the scene is poignant, and yet still works as the comedy of embarrassment. There is a delicious delight seeing the film find its way into the lives of so many bright, lonely, mixed-up people. And *Getting It Right* does not box them into a plot, but allows them to be themselves.

Ghost ★ ★ ½
PG-13, 128 m., 1990

Patrick Swayze (Sam Wheat), Demi Moore (Molly Jensen), Whoopi Goldberg (Oda Mae Brown), Tony Goldwyn (Carl Brunner), Rick Aviles (Willie Lopez), Gail Boggs (Oda Mae's sister Louise), Armelia McQueen (Oda Mae's sister Clara), Vincent Schiavelli (Subway ghost). Directed by Jerry Zucker and produced by Lisa Weinstein. Screenplay by Bruce Joel Rubin.

The thing about ghost stories is that they usually have such limited imaginations. If a spirit were indeed able to exist in two realms at the same time—to occupy the spirit world while still involving itself in our designs here in the material universe—wouldn't it be aghast with glory and wonder? Wouldn't it transcend the pathetic little concerns of daily life? To put it another way: If you could live in the mind of God, would you still be telling your girlfriend she's wearing the T-shirt you spilled the margarita on?

Ghost is no worse an offender than most ghost movies, I suppose. It assumes that even after death we devote most of our attention to unfinished business here on earth, and that danger to a loved one is more important to a ghost than the infinity it now inhabits. Such ideas are a comfort to us. We like to picture our dear ones up there on a cloud, eternally "looking down" on us, so devoted that they would rather see what we're cooking for dinner than have a chat with Aristotle or Elvis.

In *Ghost*, Patrick Swayze plays an investment counselor who is killed by a mugger one night, but remains on the scene in his spirit form to observe, as his young girlfriend (Demi Moore) weeps and mourns and then attempts to piece her life together. Swayze has an important piece of information he needs to get to her: His death was not an act of random urban violence, but a contract murder. He was about to stumble across a multimillion-dollar computer theft by a sneaky colleague (Tony Goldwyn), and that's why he was murdered. Now Moore is in danger, too.

This plot takes place in the world of upscale Manhattan yuppies. Swayze and Moore inhabit a loft apartment so luxurious that he must be making a fortune at his job (or maybe she's doing well with her art pottery business). That's why, after Swayze's death, Moore doesn't believe it when a self-appointed psychic (Whoopi Goldberg) contacts her with messages from beyond the grave. What's amazing is that Goldberg really is able to hear every word Swayze says to her—even though she has no previous record of genuine psychic powers.

That's how we get around to the description of the T-shirt with the margarita stains. Swayze has to feed Goldberg so much personal information that Moore is forced to believe that the communications are genuine. This he does to a fault. One of the irritations of *Ghost* is that the Moore character is such a slow study. Over and over again, Goldberg tells her things only her boyfriend could possibly have known, and over and over again, Moore disbelieves her—she trusts the villain, instead. We are treading here on the edge of the Idiot Plot.

Ghost does, however, make a nice mixture of horror and humor, especially in the scenes involving Goldberg and her sisters (Gail Boggs and Armelia McQueen). The film's biggest

puzzlement involves the exact status of Swayze's spiritual sojourn in this world. Is he in heaven's holding pattern? Must he protect his girlfriend before he can ascend that tunnel of light into the sky? What about his ability to interact with the physical world? At first he walks right through everything, but later, after tutelage from his fellow dead, he learns simple parlor tricks—like picking up a penny—and, of course, by the end of the movie he is able to beat the hell out of the bad guy.

The movie's single best scene—one that does touch the poignancy of the human belief in life after death—comes when Swayze is able to take over Goldberg's body, to use her physical presence as an instrument for caressing the girlfriend that he loves. (In strict logic this should involve us seeing Goldberg kissing Moore, but, of course, the movie compromises and shows us Swayze holding her—too bad, because the logical version would actually have been more spiritual and moving.) Then there is the obligatory action climax, necessary in all mass-market entertainments these days, and a particularly ridiculous visitation from the demons of hell. *Ghost* contains some nice ideas, and occasionally, for whole moments at a time, succeeds in evoking the mysteries that it toys with.

Ghostbusters ★ ★ ★ ½
PG, 107 m., 1984

Bill Murray (Venkman), Dan Aykroyd (Stantz), Harold Ramis (Spengler), Sigourney Weaver (Dana), Ernie Hudson (Winston), Rick Moranis (Louis). Directed and produced by Ivan Reitman. Screenplay by Dan Aykroyd and Harold Ramis.

Ghostbusters is a head-on collision between two comic approaches that have rarely worked together very successfully. This time, they do. It's (1) a special-effects blockbuster, and (2) a sly dialogue movie, in which everybody talks to each other like smart graduate students who are in on the joke. In the movie's climactic scenes, an apocalyptic psychic mindquake is rocking Manhattan, and the experts talk like Bob and Ray.

This movie is an exception to the general rule that big special effects can wreck a comedy. Special effects require painstaking detail work. Comedy requires spontaneity and improvisation—or at least that's what it should feel like, no matter how much work has gone into it. In movies like Steven

Spielberg's *1941*, the awesome scale of the special effects dominated everything else; we couldn't laugh because we were holding our breath. Not this time. *Ghostbusters* has a lot of neat effects, some of them mind-boggling, others just quick little throwaways, as when a transparent green-slime monster gobbles up a mouthful of hot dogs. No matter what effects are being used, they're placed at the service of the actors; instead of feeling as if the characters have been carefully posed in front of special effects, we feel they're winging this adventure as they go along.

The movie stars Bill Murray, Dan Aykroyd, and Harold Ramis, three graduates of the Second City/*National Lampoon*/ "Saturday Night Live" tradition. They're funny, but they're not afraid to reveal that they're also quick-witted and intelligent; their dialogue puts nice little spins on American clichés, and it uses understatement, irony, in-jokes, vast cynicism, and cheerful goofiness. Rarely has a movie this expensive provided so many quotable lines.

The plot, such as it is, involves an epidemic of psychic nuisance reports in Manhattan. Murray, Ramis, and Aykroyd, defrocked parapsychologists whose university experiments have been exposed as pure boondoggle, create a company named Ghostbusters and offer to speed to the rescue like a supernatural version of the Orkin man. Business is bad until Sigourney Weaver notices that the eggs in her kitchen are frying themselves. Her next-door neighbor, Rick Moranis, notices horrifying monsters in the apartment hallways. They both apparently live in a building that serves as a conduit to the next world. The ghostbusters ride to the rescue, armed with nuclear-powered backpacks. There is a lot of talk about arcane details of psychic lore (most of which the ghostbusters are inventing on the spot), and then an earth-shaking showdown between good and evil, during which Manhattan is menaced by a monster that is twenty stories high, and about which I cannot say one more word without spoiling the movie's best visual moment.

Ghostbusters is one of those rare movies where the original, fragile comic vision has survived a multimillion-dollar production. It is not a complete vindication for big-budget comedies, since it's still true, as a general rule, that the more you spend, the fewer laughs you get. But it uses its money wisely, and when that, ahem, monster marches down a Manhattan avenue and climbs the side of a skyscraper . . . we're glad they spent the money for the special effects because it gets one of the biggest laughs in a long time.

The Girl in a Swing ★ ★ ½
R, 112 m., 1989

Meg Tilly (Karin), Rupert Frazer (Alan), Nicholas Le Prevost (Tony), Elspet Gray (Mrs. Desland), Lorna Heilbron (Flick), Claire Shepherd (Angela), Jean Boht (Mrs. Taswell), Sophie Tursfield (Deirdre), Lynsey Baxter (Barbara). Directed by Gordon Hessler and produced by Just Betzer. Screenplay by Hessler.

The Girl in a Swing is about the love of an ordinary Englishman for a mysterious, bizarre young woman he meets in Copenhagen—a dark-eyed beauty who falls instantly in love with him and seems to offer fulfillment of all his dreams. She's smart, sexy, beautiful, passionate, and she adores him. She is a woman so perfect that even the guy's mother likes her. But there is something wrong. Something in her past. Something way back in her past—all the way back, perhaps, to the birth of the human race. Can it be a coincidence that she invites him to bed one day while holding out an apple with one bite taken out of it?

The young woman is played by Meg Tilly in a performance so obsessed by the character's secrets that it is truly convincing. To the degree that the movie holds our interest—and it held mine for two hours, despite my growing frustration—it is because of Tilly, who is mesmerizing as she looks into the man's eyes and tells him what he dreams of. The man, played by Rupert Frazer, is one of those overgrown English adolescents whose reserve conceals a deep stream of romanticism. He meets the woman in Copenhagen when he needs a secretary, and soon she follows him to England and they are married—not in a church wedding, which she refuses, but during a holiday in Florida.

It is clear fairly early on that Karin, as the woman is called, has something deep and alarming in her nature. Some secret, or guilt, or power. There are little hints: a quick glimpse of a child, a veil over her past, the absence of any parents or relatives, her collapse at the communion rail. Whose child is it? Where does she come from? Why does she suddenly have those panic attacks? The music on the sound track reinforces the sense

of impending doom, and there are restless winds in the trees, and strange cries in the garden.

But life goes on. The man is an antique dealer specializing in porcelains, and one day at an auction Karin bids on an odd lot that astonishingly contains a statuette of a girl on a swing—a piece of legendary rarity that is worth more than $350,000. The man is overjoyed, and even happier when the impotence of his wedding night gives way to an unbridled sexuality. He makes love with Karin everywhere—even in the kitchen, and of course out in the yard on the swing.

She keeps wanting to tell him something. He keeps saying he doesn't want to know. I kept thinking, well, I *do* want to know, so shut up and let her talk. But the mystery remains veiled. And the strangest thing about this movie is that it remains veiled right up until the end. I was so mystified afterward that I even looked up the name "Karin" and all its variant spellings in my *Bullfinch's Mythology* and my *Brewer's Dictionary of Phrase and Fable*—determined to discover that Karin was a goddess, or a devil, or perhaps another name for Eve or Lillith.

No luck. Karin comes from "Katherine," although "Karen" is also a Tibeto-Burmese language. But you see to what lengths I was driven by the movie's insidiously impenetrable plot. And although I didn't want some kind of dumb climax in which Karin turned into a statue with snakes in her hair, I would have appreciated some kind of resolution to the story—instead of the confusion into which it eventually disappears.

If the movie is ultimately disappointing, it is not uninteresting. This is Meg Tilly's second role recently as a mesmerizing woman—after the underrated *Masquerade*—and she creates a genuinely original performance, a woman sometimes dreamy, sometimes intense, and always in pain. It's a performance so good it deserves a better movie.

Gloria ★ ★ ★
PG, 123 m., 1980

Gena Rowlands (Gloria Swenson), John Adames (Phil), Buck Henry (Jack), Julie Carmen (Jeri Dawn). Directed by John Cassavetes and produced by Sam Shaw. Screenplay by Cassavetes.

Well, it's a cute idea for a movie, and maybe that's why they've had this particular idea so often. You start with tough-talking, street-

wise gangster types, you hook them up with a little kid, you put them in fear of their lives, and then you milk the situation for poignancy, pathos, excitement, comedy, and anything else that turns up. It's the basic situation of *Little Miss Marker*, the Damon Runyon story that has been filmed three times. And now John Cassavetes tells it again in *Gloria*. The twists this time: The tough-talking gangster type is a woman, and the kid is Puerto Rican. Cassavetes has cast his wife, Gena Rowlands, in the title role, and it's an infectious performance—if infectious is the word to describe a chain-smoking dame who charges around town in her high heels, dragging a kid behind her.

The kid is also well cast. He's a youngster named John Adames who has dark hair and big eyes and a way of delivering his dialogue as if daring you to change one single word. Precisely because the material of this movie is so familiar, almost everything depends on the performances. And that's where Cassavetes saves the material and redeems the corniness of his story. Rowlands propels the action with such appealing nervous energy that we don't have the heart to stop and think how silly everything is.

The movie begins with a two-bit hoodlum (Buck Henry, an inexplicable casting choice) barricaded in an apartment with his Puerto Rican wife (Julie Carmen) and their kids. Men are going to come through the door at any moment with guns blazing. There's a knock on the door. It's Rowlands, as the neighbor, with the somehow inevitable name of Gloria Swenson. She wants to borrow sugar. She winds up with the kid. She doesn't want the kid. She doesn't like kids, she tells Henry: "Especially your kids." But the kid tags along. There's a shoot-out, the kid's family is dead, and things get even more complicated when it turns out that Henry gave his kid a notebook that has information in it the mob will kill to retrieve. That's the premise for the rest of the movie, which is a cat-and-mouse chase through the sleazier districts of New York and New Jersey.

Cassavetes has a nice eye for locale. There's a crummy flophouse where the clerk tells Rowlands, "Just pick a room. They're all open." There's a garishly decorated love nest that Rowlands occasionally occupies with a mobster. There are bus stations, back alleys, dimly lit hallways, and the kinds of bars that open at dawn and do most of their business by 9 A.M. (That provides one of the movie's best scenes. Gloria and the kid argue, Gloria tells the kid to split if that's the way he feels, and then she marches into the bar, orders a beer, lights a cigarette and says to the bartender: "Listen. There are reasons why I can't turn around and look . . . but is there a little kid heading in here?")

Cassavetes remains one of the most consistently interesting Hollywood mavericks. He makes money by acting, and immediately spends it producing his own films. Most of them are passionately indulgent of the actors, who sometimes repay his indulgence with inspired performances. Rowlands won an Oscar nomination for Cassavetes's *A Woman Under the Influence*. His next picture starred Ben Gazzara in *The Murder of a Chinese Bookie* (1978), which has become an unseen, lost film—better, if the truth be known, than *Gloria*, which is fun and engaging but slight. What saves this movie is Cassavetes's reliance on a tried-and-true plot construction. For once, his characters aren't all over the map in nonstop dialogue, as they were in *Husbands*, the talkathon he made in 1970 with Peter Falk, Gazzara, and himself. *Gloria* is tough, sweet, and goofy.

Glory ★ ★ ★ ¹/₂

R, 122 m., 1989
(See related Film Clip, p. 639.)

Matthew Broderick (Robert Gould Shaw), Denzel Washington (Trip), Cary Elwes (Cabot Forbes), Morgan Freeman (Rawlins), Jihmi Kennedy (Sharts), Andre Braugher (Searles), John Finn (Mulcahy). Directed by Edward Zwick and produced by Freddie Fields. Screenplay by Kevin Jarre.

The story goes that the author of *Glory*, Kevin Jarre, was walking across Boston Common one day when he noticed something about a Civil War memorial that he had never noticed before. Some of the soldiers in it were black. Although the American Civil War is often referred to as the war to free the slaves, it had never occurred to Jarre—or, apparently, to very many others—that blacks themselves fought in the war. The inspiration for *Glory* came to Jarre as he stood looking at the monument.

It tells the story of the 54th Regiment of the Massachusetts Volunteer Infantry, made up of black soldiers—some Northern freemen, some escaped slaves—and led by whites including Robert Gould Shaw, the son of Boston abolitionists. Although it was widely believed at the time that blacks would not

make good soldiers and would not submit to discipline under fire, the 54th figured in one of the bloodiest actions of the war, an uphill attack across muddy terrain against a Confederate fort in Charleston, South Carolina. The attack was almost suicidal, particularly given the battlefield strategies of the day, which involved disciplining troops to keep on marching into withering fire. The 54th suffered a bloodbath. But its members remained disciplined soldiers to the end, and their performance on that day—July 18, 1863—encouraged the North to recruit other blacks to its ranks, one hundred thousand in all, and may have been decisive in turning the tide of the war.

Glory tells the story of the 54th Regiment largely through the eyes of Robert Gould Shaw (Matthew Broderick), who in an early scene in the film is seen horrified and disoriented by the violence of the battlefield. Returned home to recover from wounds, he is recruited to lead a newly formed black regiment and takes the job even though his own enlightened abolitionist opinions still leave room for doubts about the capability of black troops.

It is up to the troops themselves to convince him they can fight—and along the way they also gently provide him with some insights into race and into human nature, a century before the flowering of the civil rights movement. Among the men who turn into the natural leaders of the 54th are Trip (Denzel Washington), an escaped slave, and John Rawlins (Morgan Freeman), first seen in the film as a grave digger who encounters the wounded Shaw on the field of battle.

These men are proud to be soldiers, proud to wear the uniform, and also too proud to accept the racism they see all around them, as when a decision is made to pay black troops less than white. Blacks march as far, bleed as much, and die as soon, they argue. Why should they be paid less for the same work?

Robert Gould Shaw and his second in command, Cabot Forbes (Cary Elwes), eventually see the logic in this argument and join their men in refusing their paychecks. That action is a turning point for the 54th, fusing the officers and men together into a fighting unit with mutual trust. But there are countless smaller scenes that do the same thing, including one in which Shaw is pointedly told by one of his men that when the war is over, nothing much will have changed: "You'll go back to your big house."

Glory has been directed by Edward Zwick, designed by Norman Garwood, and

photographed by Freddie Francis with enormous attention to period detail, as in such small touches as the shoes issued to the troops (they don't come in right and left, but get to be that way after you've worn them long enough). These little details lead up to larger ones, as when the children of poor black sharecroppers look on in wonder as black soldiers in uniform march past their homes. And everything in the film leads up to the final bloody battle scene, a suicidal march up a hill that accomplishes little in concrete military terms but is of incalculable symbolic importance.

Watching *Glory*, I had one recurring problem with the film. I didn't understand why it had to be told so often from the point of view of the 54th's white commanding officer. Why did we see the black troops through his eyes—instead of seeing him through theirs? To put it another way, why does the top billing in this movie go to a white actor? I ask, not to be perverse, but because I consider this primarily a story about a black experience and do not know why it has to be seen largely through white eyes. Perhaps one answer is that the significance of the 54th was the way in which it changed white perceptions of black soldiers (changed them slowly enough, to be sure, that the Vietnam War was the first in American history in which troops were not largely segregated). *Glory* is a strong and valuable film no matter whose eyes it is seen through. But there is still, I suspect, another and quite different film to be made from this same material.

The Go-Between ★ ★ ★ ¹/₂

PG, 116 m., 1971

Julie Christie (Marian), Alan Bates (Ted Burgess), Dominic Guard (Leo, as a Boy), Michael Gough (Mr. Maudsley). Directed by Joseph Losey and produced by John Heyman. Screenplay by Harold Pinter.

There was a time, fairly recent, when the British upper classes thought it was a shade embarrassing to have to work for a living. Boys from middle-class families might attend the same school as upper-class boys, but they were tarnished, somehow, by their parents' direct contact with money. Money was something that needed to pass through a few sets of intervening hands, to let the sweat dry, before it could be spent by the aristocracy.

In a famous essay about English boarding

schools, George Orwell delineated this delicate, cruel class distinction. He came from a white-collar family that made less than many blue-collar families, and yet had to present certain "standards" to the world. One of these was the necessity to send its children away to schools which, although they were shabby by Eton standards, were at least private. The children were the ones who suffered directly at the hands of class snobbism, of course, and sometimes their personalities were marked for life.

Joseph Losey's *The Go-Between* is about class distinction and its warping effect upon the life of one small boy. The story is set in the days before World War I, privileged days that seemed to stretch endlessly before the British upper class. The boy, Leo, comes to spend a summer holiday at the home of a rich friend. And he falls in hopeless schoolboy love with the friend's older sister (Julie Christie).

The sister is engaged to marry well, but she is in love with a roughshod tenant farmer (Alan Bates), and she enlists the boy to carry messages back and forth between them. The boy has only a shadowy notion at first about the significance of the messages, but during the summer he is sharply disillusioned about love, fidelity, and his own place in the great scheme of things.

Losey and his screenwriter, Harold Pinter, are terribly observant about small nuances of class. In the family's matriarch (Margaret Leighton) they give us a woman who seems to support the British class system all by herself, simply through her belief in it. They show a father and a fiancé who are aware of the girl's affair with the farmer, but do nothing about it. They are confident she will do the "right thing" in the end, and she does. "Why don't you marry Ted," the boy asks the young woman. "Because I can't," she replies. "Then why are you marrying Trimmington?" "Because I must."

She understands, and she is tough enough to endure. Indeed, at the end of the film she turns up years later as an old lady very much in the image of her mother. The victim is the boy, who is scarred sexually and emotionally by his summer experience. When we see him at the film's end, he is a sort of bloodless eunuch, called in to perform one last errand for the woman.

Losey's production is elegantly costumed and mounted and has the same eye for details of character that distinguished his two previous films with Pinter (*The Servant* and

Accident). One visual device is distracting, however, he keeps giving us short flash-forwards to the end of the film. On the one hand, this eventually gives the ending away. On the other, it imposes a ponderous significance on the events that go before, diluting their freshness.

If the film had been told in straight chronology followed by an epilogue, it would have been more effective. In fact, the epilogue could have been lost altogether with no trouble; everything that will become of this boy in his adult life is already there, by implication, at the end of his summer holiday.

The Godfather ★ ★ ★ ★
R, 171 m., 1972

Marlon Brando (Don Vito Corleone), Al Pacino (Michael Corleone), James Caan (Sonny Corleone), Robert Duvall (Tom Hagen), Richard Castellano (Clemenza). Directed by Francis Ford Coppola and produced by Albert S. Ruddy. Screenplay by Mario Puzo.

We know from Gay Talese's book *Honor Thy Father* that being a professional mobster isn't all sunshine and roses. More often, it's the boredom of stuffy rooms and a bad diet of carry-out food, punctuated by brief, terrible bursts of violence. This is exactly the feel of *The Godfather*, which brushes aside the flashy glamour of the traditional gangster picture and gives us what's left: fierce tribal loyalties, deadly little neighborhood quarrels in Brooklyn, and a form of vengeance to match every affront.

The remarkable thing about Mario Puzo's novel was the way it seemed to be told from the inside out; he didn't give us a world of international intrigue, but a private club as constricted as the seventh grade. Everybody knew everybody else and had a pretty shrewd hunch what they were up to.

The movie (based on a script labored over for some time by Puzo and then finally given form, I suspect, by director Francis Ford Coppola) gets the same feel. We tend to identify with Don Corleone's family not because we dig gang wars, but because we have been with them from the beginning, watching them wait for battle while sitting at the kitchen table and eating chow mein out of paper cartons.

The Godfather himself is not even the central character in the drama. That position

goes to the youngest, brightest son, Michael, who understands the nature of his father's position while revising his old-fashioned ways. The Godfather's role in the family enterprise is described by his name; he stands outside the next generation which will carry on and, hopefully, angle the family into legitimate enterprises.

Those who have read the novel may be surprised to find Michael at the center of the movie, instead of Don Corleone. In fact, this is simply an economical way for Coppola to get at the heart of the Puzo story, which dealt with the transfer of power within the family. Marlon Brando, who plays the Godfather as a shrewd, unbreakable old man, actually has the character lead in the movie; Al Pacino, with a brilliantly developed performance as Michael, is the lead.

But Brando's performance is a skillful throwaway, even though it earned him an Academy Award for best actor. His voice is wheezy and whispery, and his physical movements deliberately lack precision; the effect is of a man so accustomed to power that he no longer needs to remind others. Brando does look the part of old Don Corleone, mostly because of acting and partly because of the makeup, although he seems to have stuffed a little too much cotton into his jowls, making his lower face immobile.

The rest of the actors supply one example after another of inspired casting. Although *The Godfather* is a long, minutely detailed movie of some three hours, there naturally isn't time to go into the backgrounds and identities of such characters as Clemenza, the family lieutenant; Jack Woltz, the movie czar; Luca Brasi, the loyal professional killer; McCluskey, the crooked cop; and the rest. Coppola and producer Al Ruddy skirt this problem with understated typecasting. As the Irish cop, for example, they simply slide in Sterling Hayden and let the character go about his business. Richard Castellano is an unshakable Clemenza. John Marley makes a perfectly hateful Hollywood mogul (and, yes, he still wakes up to find he'll have to cancel his day at the races).

The success of *The Godfather* as a novel was largely due to a series of unforgettable scenes. Puzo is a good storyteller, but no great shakes as a writer. The movie gives almost everything in the novel except the gynecological repair job. It doesn't miss a single killing; it opens with the wedding of Don Corleone's daughter (and attendant upstairs activity); and there are the right number of auto bombs, double crosses, and garrotings.

Coppola has found a style and a visual look for all this material so *The Godfather* becomes something of a rarity: a really good movie squeezed from a bestseller. The decision to shoot everything in period decor (the middle and late 1940s) was crucial; if they'd tried to save money as they originally planned, by bringing everything up-to-date, the movie simply wouldn't have worked. But it's uncannily successful as a period piece, filled with sleek, bulging limousines and postwar fedoras. Coppola and his cinematographer, Gordon Willis, also do some interesting things with the color photography. The earlier scenes have a reddish-brown tint, slightly overexposed and feeling like nothing so much as a 1946 newspaper rotogravure supplement.

Although the movie is three hours long, it absorbs us so effectively it never has to hurry. There is something in the measured passage of time as Don Corleone hands over his reins of power that would have made a shorter, faster moving film unseemly. Even at this length, there are characters in relationships you can't quite understand unless you've read the novel. Or perhaps you can, just by the way the characters look at each other.

The Godfather, Part II ★ ★ ★
R, 200 m., 1974

Al Pacino (Michael), Robert Duvall (Tom Hagen), Diane Keaton (Kay), Robert De Niro (Don Vito Corleone), John Cazale (Fredo), Lee Strasberg (Hyman Roth), G.D. Spradlin (Senator Geary). Directed by Francis Ford Coppola and produced by Gray Frederickson and Fred Ross. Screenplay by Coppola and Mario Puzo.

Moving through the deep shadows and heavy glooms of his vast estate, Michael Corleone presides over the destruction of his own spirit in *The Godfather, Part II*. The character we recall from *The Godfather* as the best and brightest of Don Vito's sons, the one who went to college and enlisted in the Marines, grows into a cold and ruthless man, obsessed with power. The film's closing scenes give us first a memory of a long-ago family dinner, and then Michael at mid-life, cruel, closed, and lonely. He's clearly intended as a tragic figure.

The Corleone saga, as painted by Francis Ford Coppola and Mario Puzo in two films totaling nearly seven hours, has been a sort of success story in reverse. In a crazy way, *The Godfather* and its sequel belong in the same category with those other epics of immigrant achievement in America, *The Emigrants* and *The New Land*. The Corleone family worked hard, was ambitious, remembered friends, never forgave disloyalty, and started from humble beginnings to become the most powerful Mafia organization in the country. If it were not that the family business was crime, these films could be an inspiration for us all.

Coppola seems to hold a certain ambivalence toward his material. Don Vito Corleone as portrayed by Marlon Brando in *The Godfather* was a man of honor and dignity, and it was difficult not to sympathize with him, playing with his grandchild in the garden, at peace after a long lifetime of murder, extortion, and the rackets. What exactly were we supposed to think about him? How did Coppola feel toward the Godfather?

The Godfather, Part II moves both forward and backward in time from the events in *The Godfather*, in an attempt to resolve our feelings about the Corleones. In doing so, it provides for itself a structural weakness from which the film never recovers, but it does something even more disappointing: It reveals a certain simplicity in Coppola's notions of motivation and characterization that wasn't there in the elegant masterpiece of his earlier film.

He gives us, first of all, the opening chapters in Don Vito's life. His family is killed by a Mafia don in Sicily, he comes to America at the age of nine, he grows up (to be played by Robert De Niro), and edges into a career of crime, first as a penny-ante crook and then as a neighborhood arranger and power broker: a man, as the movie never tires of reminding us, of respect.

This story, of Don Vito's younger days, occupies perhaps a fourth of the film's 200 minutes. Coppola devotes the rest to Michael Corleone, who has taken over the family's business after his father's death, has pulled out of New York, and consolidated operations in Nevada, and has ambitions to expand in Florida and Cuba. Michael is played, again and brilliantly, by Al Pacino, and among the other familiar faces are Robert Duvall as Tom Hagen, the family's lawyer; Diane Keaton as Michael's increasingly despairing wife Kay; and John Cazale as the weak older brother Fredo.

Coppola handles a lot of this material very well. As in the earlier film, he reveals himself as a master of mood, atmosphere, and period. And his exposition is inventive and subtle. The film requires the intelligent participation of the viewer; as Michael attempts to discover who betrayed him and attempted his assassination, he tells different stories to different people, keeping his own counsel, and we have to think as he does so we can tell the truth from the lies.

Pacino is very good at suggesting the furies and passions that lie just beneath his character's controlled exterior. He gives us a Michael who took over the family with the intention of making it "legitimate" in five years, but who is drawn more and more deeply into a byzantine web of deceit and betrayal, all papered over with code words like respect, honor, and gratitude. By the film's end he has been abandoned by almost everyone except those who work for him and fear him, and he is a very lonely man.

But what was his sin? It was not, as we might have imagined or hoped, that he presided over a bloody enterprise of murder and destruction. No, Michael's fault seems to be pride. He has lost the common touch, the dignity he should have inherited from his father. And because he has misplaced his humanity he must suffer.

Coppola suggests this by contrast. His scenes about Don Vito's early life could almost be taken as a campaign biography, and in the most unfortunate flashbacks we're given the young Vito intervening on behalf of a poor widow who is being evicted from her apartment. The don seems more like a precinct captain than a gangster, and we're left with the unsettling impression that Coppola thinks things would have turned out all right for Michael if he'd had the old man's touch.

The flashbacks give Coppola the greatest difficulty in maintaining his pace and narrative force. The story of Michael, told chronologically and without the other material, would have had really substantial impact, but Coppola prevents our complete involvement by breaking the tension. The flashbacks to New York in the early 1900s have a different, a nostalgic tone, and the audience has to keep shifting gears. Coppola was reportedly advised by friends to forget the Don Vito material and stick with Michael, and that was good advice.

There's also some evidence in the film that Coppola never completely mastered the chaotic mass of material in his screenplay. Some scenes seem oddly pointless (why do we get almost no sense of Michael's actual dealings in Cuba, but lots of expensive footage about the night of Castro's takeover?), and others seem not completely explained (I am still not quite sure who really did order that attempted garroting in the Brooklyn saloon).

What we're left with, then, are a lot of good scenes and good performances set in the midst of a mass of undisciplined material and handicapped by plot construction that prevents the story from ever really building.

There is, for example, the brilliant audacity of the first communion party for Michael's son, which Coppola directs as counterpoint to the wedding scene that opened *The Godfather*. There is Lee Strasberg's two-edged performance as Hyman Roth, the boss of the Florida and Cuban operations; Strasberg gives us a soft-spoken, almost kindly old man, and then reveals his steel-hard interior. There is Coppola's use of sudden, brutal bursts of violence to punctuate the film's brooding progress. There is Pacino, suggesting everything, telling nothing.

But Coppola is unable to draw all this together and make it work on the level of simple, absorbing narrative. The stunning text of *The Godfather* is replaced in *Part II* with prologues, epilogues, footnotes, and good intentions.

The Godfather Part III ★ ★ ★ ½
R, 162 m., 1990

Al Pacino (Michael Corleone), Diane Keaton (Kay), Talia Shire (Connie), Andy Garcia (Vincent Mancini), Sofia Coppola (Mary Corleone), Eli Wallach (Don Altobello), Joe Mantegna (Joey Zasa). Directed and produced by Francis Ford Coppola. Screenplay by Mario Puzo and Coppola.

And so here we are back again now, in the rich, deep brown rooms inhabited by the Corleone family, the rooms filled with shadows and memories, and regretful decisions that people may have to die. We have been taught this world so well by Francis Ford Coppola that we enter it effortlessly; has there ever before been a film saga so seductive and compelling, so familiar to us that even after years we remember all of the names of the players? Here, for example, is a new character, introduced as "Sonny's illegitimate son," and, yes, we nod like cousins at a family reunion, yes, he *does* seem a lot like

Sonny. He's the same kind of hotheaded, trigger-happy lunatic.

The Godfather Part III continues the Corleone family history right down to the early 1980s, as the sins of the parents are visited upon the children. Despite every attempt to go legit, to become respectable, the past cannot be silenced. The family has amassed unimaginable wealth, and as the film opens Michael Corleone (Al Pacino) is being invested with a great honor by the church. Later that day, at a reception, his daughter announces a Corleone family gift to the church and the charities of Sicily, "a check in the amount of $100 million." But the Corleones are about to find, as others have throughout history, that money can't buy you love. Sure, you can do business with evil men inside the church, for all men are fallible and capable of sin. But God does not take payoffs.

Michael is older now, and walks with a stoop. He has a diabetic condition. He has spent the years since *The Godfather Part II* trying to move the family out of crime and into legitimate businesses. He has turned over a lot of the old family rackets to a new generation, to people like Joey Zasa (Joe Mantegna), who is not scrupulous about dealing dope, who is capable of making deals that would offend the fastidious Michael. It is Michael's dream, now that he senses his life is coming to a close, that he can move his family into the light.

But the past is seductive. Because Michael knows how to run a Mafia family, there is great pressure on him to do so. And throughout *Godfather III* we are aware of the essential tragedy of this man, the fact that the sins that stain his soul will not wash off—especially the sin of having ordered the death of his brother, Fredo. Michael is positioned in the story between two characters who could come from *King Lear*—his daughter, Mary (Sofia Coppola), whom he loves and wants to give his kingdom to, and Sonny's son, Vincent (Andy Garcia), who sees the death of his enemies as the answer to every question. Michael is torn between the futures represented by the two characters, between Mary, quiet and naive, and the hot-blooded Vincent. And when Vincent seduces Mary and makes her his own, Michael's plans begin to go wrong.

There is also Kay Corleone (Diane Keaton), of course, still the woman Michael loves and the mother of his children. He wants their son, Anthony, to join the family business. She defends his ambition to be an opera

singer. They face each other like skilled opponents. Perhaps she even still loves him, too, or would if she did not know him so well. She is the only person who can tell Michael what she really thinks, and in one of those dark, gloomy rooms she lets him know that it doesn't matter what grand order he is invested in by the church, he is at heart still a gangster. The best scenes in *Godfather III* are between these two, Michael and Kay, Pacino and Keaton, fiercely locked in a battle that began many years ago, at that wedding feast where Michael told Kay he was not part of his family business.

The plot of the movie, concocted by Coppola and Mario Puzo in a screenplay inspired by headlines, brings the Corleone family into the inner circles of corruption in the Vatican. Actual events—the untimely suddenness of John Paul I's death, the scandals at the Vatican Bank, the body of a Vatican banker found hanging from a London bridge—are cheerfully intertwined with the Corleone's fictional story, and it is suggested that the Vatican lost hundreds of millions in a fraud directed by the Mafia. We eavesdrop on corrupt Vatican officials, venal cardinals scheming in the vast Renaissance palaces that dwarf them, and we travel to Sicily so that Michael Corleone can consult with Don Tommasino, his trusted old friend, to discover who is plotting against him within the Mafia council.

They are so seductive, these Byzantine intrigues. Alliances are forged with a pragmatic decision, betrayed with sudden violence. Always there is someone in a corner, whispering even more devious advice. This trait of operatic plotting and betrayal is practiced beautifully by Connie Corleone (Talia Shire), Michael's sister, who has turned in middle age into a fierce, thin-faced woman in black, who stands in the deepest shadows, who schemes and lobbies for her favorites—especially for Vincent, whom she wants Michael to accept and embrace.

In the Godfather movies Coppola has made a world. Because we know it so intimately, because its rhythms and values are instantly recognizable to us, a film like *The Godfather Part III* probably works better than it should. If you stand back and look at it rationally, this is a confusing and disjointed film. It is said that Coppola was rewriting it as he went along, and indeed it lacks the confident forward sweep of a film that knows where it's going.

Some of the dialogue scenes, especially in the beginning, sound vaguely awkward; the answers do not fit the questions, and conversations seem to have been rewritten in the editing room. Other shots—long shots, into the light so we cannot see the characters' lips—look suspiciously like scenes that were filmed first and dubbed later. The whole ambitious final movement of the film—in which two separate intrigues are intercut with the progress of an opera being sung by Anthony—is intended to be suspenseful, but is so confusing we are not even sure which place (Sicily, Rome, London?) one of the intrigues is taking place in. The final scene of the movie, which is intended to echo Marlon Brando's famous death scene, is perfunctory and awkward.

And yet it's strange how the earlier movies fill in the gaps left by this one and answer the questions. It is, I suspect, not even possible to understand this film without knowing the first two, and yet, knowing them, *Part III* works better than it should, evokes the same sense of wasted greatness, of misdirected genius. Both Don Vito Corleone and Don Michael Corleone could have been great men. But they lacked that final shred of character that would have allowed them to break free from their own pasts. Or perhaps their tragedies were dictated by circumstances. Perhaps they were simply born into the wrong family.

The Gods Must Be Crazy ★ ★ ★
PG, 109 m., 1984

N!xau (Xixo), Marius Weyers (Andrew Steyn), Sandra Prinsloo (Kate Thompson), Louw Verwey (Sam Boga), James Uys (The Reverend). Directed and produced by Jamie Uys. Screenplay by Uys.

Here's a movie that begins with a Coke bottle falling from the heavens, and ends with a Jeep up in a tree. *The Gods Must Be Crazy* is a South African movie that arrived in Europe with little fanfare in 1982, broke box office records in Japan and South America and all over Europe, and even became a cult hit here in North America, where there has not been much of a demand for comedies from South Africa.

The film begins in the Kalahari Desert. A pilot in a private plane throws his empty Coke bottle out of the window. It lands near a Bushman who is on a hunting expedition. He has never seen anything like it before. He takes it back to his tribe, where it is put to dozens of uses: It becomes a musical instru-

ment, a patternmaker, a fire starter, a cooking utensil, and, most of all, an object of bitter controversy. Everybody in the tribe ends up fighting over the bottle, and so the Bushman, played by the Xhosa actor N!xau (the exclamation point represents a click), decides there is only one thing to do: He must return the bottle to the gods. This decision sends him on a long odyssey toward more settled lands on the edges of the desert, where the movie develops into a somewhat more conventional comedy.

We meet some of the new characters: A would-be schoolteacher, a goofy biologist, and an insurgent leader. They are all intent on their own lives and plans, but in one way or another, the Xhosa and his Coke bottle bring them together into unexpected combinations. And the director, Jamie Uys, has the patience to develop some really elaborate sight gags, which require a lot of preparation but pay off with big laughs—particularly the sequence with an indecisive, back-and-forth Jeep.

The star of the movie is N!xau, who is so forthright and cheerful and sensible that his very presence makes some of the gags pay off. In any slapstick comedy, the gags must rest on a solid basis of logic: It's not funny to watch people being ridiculous, but it is funny to watch people doing the next logical thing, and turning out to be ridiculous. N!xau, because he approaches Western society without preconceptions, and bases all of his actions on logical conclusions, brings into relief a lot of the little tics and assumptions of everyday life. I think that reveals the thought that went into this movie: It might be easy to make a farce about screwball happenings in the desert, but it's a lot harder to create a funny interaction between nature and human nature. This movie's a nice little treasure.

The Gods Must Be Crazy II ★ ★ ★
PG, 98 m., 1990

N!xau (Xixo), Lena Farugia (Dr. Ann Taylor), Hans Strydom (Dr. Stephen Marshall), Eiros (Xiri), Nadies (Xisa), Erick Bowen (Mateo), Treasure Tshabalala (Timi), Pierre Van Pletzen (George), Lourens Swanepoel (Brenner). Directed by Jamie Uys and produced by Boet Troskie. Screenplay by Uys.

I was looking at the laserdisk of *Mr. Hulot's Holiday* the other day—that wonderful Jacques Tati comedy about a whimsical fisherman who takes his holiday by the sea. And

I realized how much the movie's opening scenes benefitted from the character of his automobile, one of those ancient and obscure European models that was so small his head almost stuck out of the top of it like in a cartoon. *The Gods Must Be Crazy II* gets the same sort of effect with a quirky little airplane barely large enough to contain two passengers and a tank of gas.

The airplane isn't the only point of connection between the two movies. I do not mean to compare the great Tati with Jamie Uys, the director of both *The Gods Must Be Crazy* movies—that wouldn't be fair—but there's something of the same spirit in the work of the two men, and in these gloomy times it is welcome. Most movie humor these days springs from verbal or physical insult, ridicule, or unfunny "jokes" based on special effects and violence. The biggest laughs come when a character gets killed in an unexpected way.

Tati didn't work like that and neither does Uys. *The Gods Must Be Crazy II* is the work of a patient craftsman who gets his laughs out of the careful construction of elaborate physical and plot situations. Some of his buildups last for most of a movie, and his punch lines are usually inspired by character traits, not dumb gags. Uys's style sheds a sweet and gentle light on this new comedy, which is a sequel to the surprising international success—and, I think, a better film.

The location once again is an unspecified part of Southern Africa (Botswana, probably, but why are there Cuban troops on patrol?). The hero of the first film, Xixo (N!xau), is seen in the opening scenes with two of his children hunting on the veld. The children, a girl and her younger brother, get into big trouble when they climb into a water tank being pulled by the truck of game poachers. The truck drives off, separating them from their father and taking them steadily away from the area they know. Meanwhile, we meet two other characters, a scientist (Lena Farugia) and a naturalist and pilot (Hans Strydom).

The movie's method is to alternate scenes involving the children, the scientists, the poachers, and two soldiers—one local, one Cuban. What Uys does is weave all of these characters into a simple story about survival in the bush and depend upon the moment-to-moment charm of his situations rather than on heavy plotting.

The airplane is a sight to behold. Because I saw it fly in the movie, I assume such planes actually exist—but it's so tiny it looks like a joke, and at one point it actually takes off while the pilot is running along, holding it up to replace a broken wheel. Once the woman scientist and her pilot are marooned in the bush, the plane figures in a lot of gags—the plane becomes this movie's equivalent of the Jeep in the previous movie. Meanwhile, the misadventures of the kids become a cliff-hanger as Uys finds countless ways to develop their dilemma.

I read a news story recently that made an amazing claim: The video of *Lethal Weapon 2* is more popular among children, it said, than the video of *Batman.* This amazed me because I would have thought both movies were too dark, gloomy, and depressing for kids—that they'd be attracted to sunnier and more cheerful films. I guess I'm out of step, and today's kids are suffering from a malaise that prepares them for violent action pictures and revenge tragedies in which a masked hero atones for the mugging of his parents. But if you happen to know any kids who have not yet given up on life, who like happy movies better than grim and violent ones, they're likely to enjoy *The Gods Must Be Crazy II.* And so did I.

Godspell ★ ★ ★ ★
G, 102 m., 1973

Victor Garber (Jesus), David Haskell (John, Judas), Jerry Sroka (Jerry), Lynne Thigpen (Lynne), Katie Hanley (Katie), Robin Lamont (Robin), Gilmer McCormick (Gilmer), Joanne Jonas (Joanne), Merrell Jackson (Merrell), Jeffrey Mylett (Jeffrey). Directed by David Greene.

The thing about *Godspell* that caught my heart was its simplicity, its refusal to pretend to be anything more than it is. It's not a message for our times, or a movie to cash in on the Jesus movement, or even quite a youth movie. It's a series of stories and songs, like the Bible is, and it's told with the directness that simple stories need: with no tricks, no intellectual gadgets, and a lot of openness.

This was the quality that attracted me to the stage version. I had to be almost dragged to the play, because its subject matter sounded so depressingly contemporary. But after I finally got into the theater and sat down and let *Godspell* relax me, I found myself simply letting it happen. For a musical based on the Gospel according to St. Matthew, *Godspell* is strangly irreverent, wacky, and endearing.

The stage version has been opened up into a movie by taking the whole of New York as a set. Except for the scenes at the beginning and end—which show the city as a temple of mammon and a rat nest—the movie is populated only by its cast; we don't see anybody else, and the ten kids dance, sing, and act out parables in such unlikely places as the World Trade Center and a tugboat. This is a new use for New York, which looks unusually clean; even its tacky skyscrapers edge toward grandeur when the vast long shots engulf them.

Against this wilderness of steel and concrete, the characters come on like kids at a junior high reunion, clothed in comic book colors and bright tattered rags. Only two have names: Jesus, and a character who plays both John (who ushered Jesus into the Bible) and Judas (who hastened him out). The other eight characters, who seem to represent an on-the-spot gathering of disciples, are just themselves.

What's nice about the casting—which gives us all new faces—is that the characters don't look like professional stage youths. Remember *West Side Story,* where all the allegedly teen-age dancers looked like hardened theatrical professionals in greaser wigs? *Godspell*'s cast is not only young but is allowed to look like a collection of individuals. These could conceivably be real people, and their freshness helps put the material over even when it seems pretty obvious. For some blessed reason the director, David Greene, has resisted any temptation to make the movie visually fancy. With material of this sort, there must have been an impulse to go for TV-commercial trendiness, but Greene's style is unforced, and goes well with the movie's freshness and basic colors.

The movie characters, like the stage characters, are given little watercolor designs on their faces by Jesus. A girl gets a little yellow flower, a boy gets a tiny red star, and so on. It was necessary in the stage version to exaggerate this makeup to make it visible, but the movie underplays it and it was gentle and nice. It occurred to me, about an hour into the film, that maybe young people will pick up on this. Tattoos were big in the '70s—little butterflies and stars—so why not face-paint zigzags and pinwheels and flowers? Anything to brighten up this miserable world: Which is what *Godspell* is saying, anyway.

(Not yet available on videocassette.)

The Golden Child ★ ★ ★
PG-13, 94 m., 1986

Eddie Murphy (Chandler), Charlotte Lewis (Kee Nang), Charles Dance (Sardo), Victor Wong (Old Man), J.L. Reate (Golden Child), "Tex" Cobb (Til Randall), James Hong (Dr. Wong). Directed by Michael Ritchie and produced by Edward S. Feldman and Robert D. Wachs. Screenplay by Dennis Feldman.

There are a lot of moments to remember in *The Golden Child*, but the one I will treasure the longest happens when Eddie Murphy gets behind the wheel of a beat-up station wagon and is led by a sacred parrot to the lair of the devil.

Maybe you had to be there. The parrot, which has already made the round-trip between Tibet and Los Angeles twice, chirps merrily and flies off down a dusty road. Murphy leans down to look up at it through his windshield, and the way he looks at it is what started me laughing. There is just something about the tilt of his head that seems entirely appropriate for a man who is following a sacred parrot. Murphy is exactly right in that moment, but then he is exactly right all through this movie, which is utterly ridiculous and jolly good fun.

The advance rumors about *The Golden Child* were not encouraging. I heard Paramount feared it had a bomb on its hands, but what were they worried about? The preview audience laughed all through the movie. No wonder, because this film—insignificant and lightweight and monumentally silly—is entertaining from beginning to end. Although it contains the usual scatological language, the sex and violence are mild.

Murphy plays the hero, a professional searcher for lost children. After agents from hell kidnap a holy child from Tibet, Murphy is recruited to recover the child, find a magic dagger, defeat Satan's henchmen, beat up some Hell's Angels, pass several death-defying trials by fire, follow the sacred parrot, and fall in love with the beautiful heroine who must first be brought back from the dead. You know, the usual stuff.

The movie's opening shots should have had a subtitle flashing "Raiders Rip-off!" Hollywood must have a whole industry supplying temples and gongs to the spawn of Indiana Jones. But from the moment Murphy appears on the screen, he makes the movie all his own; the special effects are basically just comic props. Murphy slides through the picture with easy wisecracks and unflappable cool, like a hip Bob Hope.

A lot of the time, he seems to improvise his wise-ass one-liners—I haven't seen the script, and so I can't say for sure. What's amazing is that his dialogue always seems to fit. A lot of stand-up comedians throw off the pacing in a movie by going for improv at the wrong moments (Robin Williams is sometimes an example). Murphy usually seems to have the perfect reaction, even when he's shocked to catch a wise old seer picking his nose. Maybe the director, Michael Ritchie, deserves some of the credit for that; he let Williams wreck his *The Survivors* with inappropriate one-liners, but this time everything flows.

The movie's plot is an anthology of clichés from every Oriental swashbuckler in history; just off the top of my head I can remember a bottomless cavern, a 300-year-old woman with a dragon's tail, a child whose touch turns bad men into good ones, an evil spirit that turns into a serpent, several dozen temple guards, countless karate fights, secret rooms beneath the stores in Chinatown, and, of course, the preternaturally beautiful heroine.

Her name is Kee Nang, and she is played by Charlotte Lewis, the London schoolgirl who starred in Roman Polanski's *Pirates*. That movie won her an audience of dozens; this one will likely do a lot better. She is very beautiful, and since that is her role in this movie, she fulfills it flawlessly. She also does a good job of keeping a straight face while Murphy uses her as the subject of speculation, rejection, romance, and betrayal, and while she uses her effortless mastery of kung fu to protect him.

No silly swashbuckler is any better than its villain, and the leader of the evil forces is played by Charles Dance, last seen as Meryl Streep's coldly intellectual husband in *Plenty*. He, too, has to keep a straight face through this movie, in scenes such as the one where Murphy outsmarts him at airport customs and the scene where he turns into a rat. There's also good work from Victor Wong, who plays a wise old man in several different costumes and accents.

The Golden Child may not be the Eddie Murphy movie we were waiting for, but it will do. It is funnier, more assured and more tailored to Murphy than *Beverly Hills Cop* and it shows a side of his comic persona that I don't think has been much appreciated: his essential underlying sweetness. Murphy's

comedy is not based here on hurt and aggression, but on affection and an understanding that comes from seeing right through the other characters. His famous laugh is not aimed as a weapon at anybody, but is truly amused. He is perfectly suited to survive this cheerfully ridiculous movie, and even lend it a little charm.

Gone With the Wind ★ ★ ★ ★
NO MPAA RATING, 231 m., 1939
(re-released 1988)

Clark Gable (Rhett Butler), Vivien Leigh (Scarlett O'Hara), Leslie Howard (Ashley Wilkes), Olivia de Havilland (Melanie Hamilton), Hattie McDaniel (Mammy), Butterfly McQueen (Prissy). Directed by Victor Fleming and produced by David O. Selznick. Screenplay by Selznick and Sidney Howard.

How did *Gone With the Wind* look when it was first released? How green were the fields, how red was the soil? I was not there and cannot say. I saw the film in each of its three major theatrical revivals—in 1954, 1961, and 1967—and I have seen it on video. But when I looked at the new version produced by Turner Entertainment, I found that memory is a treacherous thing. This version looks terrific, but is it faithful to the original?

Gone With the Wind is fifty years old, and in preparation for its golden anniversary, a team of technicians has been working more than two years to restore it to its original quality. The challenge facing them is daunting. Simply to obtain a theatrical-quality print of *Gone With the Wind*, much work needed to be done. Prints of the film have gone through so many generations of copies since its 1939 premiere that the versions often seen by modern audiences are a pale shadow of the original glory. Colors have become washed out, the sound track has collected pops and hisses, and the contrast is sometimes so high that many small details are lost.

Yet earlier attempts to "modernize" the film over the years have often ended in catastrophe. The most misguided work on the film was done in 1967, when MGM decided to release it as a "wide-screen" movie. Simple mathematics will show why this was a tragic error. The original film was shot in the classic 1:1.33 ratio, which means that the picture was about four feet wide for every

three feet in height. By converting it into a wide-screen image, MGM was forced to chop at the top and bottom, and about a quarter of the original image was lost.

This loss was most apparent in spectacular scenes like the street-of-dying-men sequence in Atlanta, where Scarlett O'Hara wanders into the devastation of Sherman's siege of Atlanta and finds a street filled with the wounded. The camera pulls back and back, finally revealing hundreds of thousands of casualties, framed by a Confederate flag. But not in the 1967 version, where half of the original image was invisible.

When Ted Turner, the Atlanta cable king, bought MGM in 1986, the crown jewel in the package was *Gone With the Wind*. He ordered yet another "restored version" for the film's fiftieth anniversary, and this new version was shown on his TNT cable station before its release on video. Turner has become notorious in recent years for his colorized versions of many classic films—he savaged *Casablanca* with the vulgar treatment—but with *Gone With the Wind* his technicians faced a different challenge. Their assignment was to restore the color quality of a Technicolor film that had aged badly during five decades of wear and tear.

Gone With the Wind was filmed in three-strip Technicolor, a complex process that involved shooting three different negatives of the same scene, each recording one primary color (red, blue, and green). The three negatives were combined to produce the bright Technicolor look of many of the best color films of the 1940s and 1950s. But it was not a subtle process, and it was not used subtly; many Technicolor films were awash in bright, even gaudy, primary colors, and the process seemed most appropriate for musicals and costume pictures. More realistic films tended to be shot in black and white, and it was not until the 1960s—when black and white was denied to them—that many directors began to consciously exclude bright colors from color films, controlling the color palate instead of trying to get as much color as possible on the screen.

The ill-starred 1967 re-release version of *Gone With the Wind* was transferred by MGM to a new one-strip color process that has turned out, over the past twenty years, to age very badly. Films originally shot in the process, such as *The Graduate*, have faded quickly; bad prints have taken on the washed-out colors of old newspaper rotogravure sections. For their fiftieth anniversary re-release of the film, Turner technicians went back to the original three-strip master negatives of *Gone With the Wind*, which were stored at Eastman House in Rochester, New York. And there they found some problems. Although much of the film had survived intact, some sections had suffered shrinkage, so that the three strips were no longer perfectly aligned. Other scenes had gone out of focus in the middle or around the edges. Repair work was necessary, sometimes on a frame-by-frame basis.

But enough about technicalities. How does *Gone With the Wind* play after fifty years? It is still a great film, above all because it tells a great story. Scarlett O'Hara, willful, spoiled, scarred by poverty, remains an unforgettable screen heroine, and I was struck again this time by how strong Vivien Leigh's performance is—by how stubbornly she maintains her petulance in the face of common sense, and by how even her heroism is undermined by her character flaws.

The ending of the film still plays like a psychological test for the audience. What do you think we should really conclude? The next-to-last speech in the movie, Rhett Butler's "Frankly, my dear, I don't give a damn," is one many audience members have been waiting for; Scarlett gets her comeuppance at last. Then comes her speech about Tara, about how, after all, tomorrow is another day. Some members of the audience will read this as an affirmation of strength, others as a renewed self-delusion. (The most cynical will observe that Scarlett, like many another divorcée disappointed in love, has turned to real estate as a career.)

As I was watching the film, I was struck by the subtlety of the color in the restored version. I was not sure I altogether approved of it. My memories of *Gone With the Wind* are of a movie in bold, bright colors—the flames of the burning of Atlanta were bright red, as were the lips of the heroines. This fiftieth anniversary version has a more modern look to the color, with the brights somewhat muted and the flesh tones more true. Have the Turner technicians changed the look of the original or restored it? After all, I am not remembering the 1939 version, but later releases that were already suffering from the ravages of time.

An article by Richard May, who headed the restoration effort, addresses this issue obliquely: "(We) had to take into consideration how people 'thought' GWTW looked originally, together with how today's au-

dience, used to contemporary color styles in film and television, would react to any unusual color choices." He seems to be coming within a hair's-breadth here of admitting that his team "modernized" the color by toning down the brightness of the original three-strip Technicolor. I sensed a little of that—the flames of Atlanta, for example, now look more orange than red. But perhaps my memory deceives me. Twenty-two years after I last saw the movie on a large screen, I cannot be sure.

Turner supplied critics with video clips comparing several scenes in three versions—1954, 1967, and the new version—and in them the principal visible difference is that the new version has clearer, truer colors, and the print is not banged-up, faded, or scratched. *Gone With the Wind* looks like a new movie again, not a battered veteran of the revival wars. The restoration brings out visual details that have been lost through the generations—the shadowy backgrounds of candlelit rooms, for example—and makes the film effortlessly watchable by removing all the years of decay.

The film's sound track has been cleaned up considerably, thanks to the almost magical things that modern sound technicians can do. A lot of the surface noise—the quiet hissing on the video version—has been eliminated, and there are moments so clean that you can actually hear the squeaking of Clark Gable's shoes.

The bottom line is that this is a praiseworthy restoration, removing generations of grime and noise from one of the greatest of all Hollywood productions, and presenting it, crisp and clean, in its original aspect ratio. I would not have expected such a conscientious job from Ted Turner, who has expressed such zeal for the vandalism of black-and-white movies. But I must give credit where due.

The Goodbye Girl ★ ★ ★
PG, 110 m., 1977

Richard Dreyfuss (Elliott Garfield), Marsha Mason (Paula McFadden), Quinn Cummings (Lucy McFadden), Paul Benedict (Mark), Barbara Rhoades (Donna), Theresa Merritt (Mrs. Crosby). Directed by Herbert Ross and produced by Ray Stark. Screenplay by Neil Simon.

Neil Simon's *The Goodbye Girl* is a funny movie with its heart finally in the right place, but all sorts of unacknowledged complica-

tions lurk just beneath its polished surface. The surface is pure Simon, which means that it's a funny-sad-tough-warm story about basically nice people who are given just three snappy one-liners too many to be totally human. But this time Simon has slipped in some subtleties we might miss the first time around.

The story's about three people we can instantly identify with. There's the former actress (Marsha Mason) and her cute ten-year-old daughter (Quinn Cummings), and the would-be actor from Chicago (Richard Dreyfuss). Until the moment before the movie opens, Miss Mason has been living with another actor in an apartment on New York's Upper East Side, where apartments are harder to find than cabs, which are harder to find than plumbers who make house calls on Sunday (which is a Simon kind of progression).

Miss Mason and her daughter come home to find that her roommate, that rat, has jumped the boat. He leaves a note explaining that he's got a great role in the new Bertolucci picture in Europe—and lotsa luck, kid. That's bad enough. Worse is when she finds out that the apartment has been sublet to this actor from Chicago, who's paid three months' rent and, reasonably enough, expects to move in, especially since at the moment he's standing in the rain.

After the two of them shout at each other for a sufficient period of time, she does allow him to move in (he gets the smaller bedroom). And then we know the basic plot structure: Total warfare in the apartment will de-escalate into a guarded truce, followed by alternating forays of warmth and decency, until the kid acts as a catalyst and they fall in love.

Wonderful. Not so wonderful is the way the Marsha Mason character is written and acted. She's hardly ever sympathetic. Sure, she's been burned by a lot of guys—but she's so hard-edged you wonder how she met them in the first place. She sees the situation strictly in economic terms, consistently behaves as a bitch, and gives Dreyfuss no reason for getting to like her.

Dreyfuss, on the other hand, is great. Eccentric, yes, since Simon always gives his characters off-the-wall touches to make them human (he meditates, plays his guitar in the middle of the night, sleeps in the nude, eats health food, etc.). But he's a nice guy. He's trapped in this weird off-off-off-Broadway production of Shakespeare's *Richard III*, and the director is convinced Richard should be played as a gay (the scenes involving the production, performance, and reception of the play are the funniest in a movie since Mel Brooks staged *Springtime for Hitler*). He fears, rightly, that the play could be the end of his New York career, and his fears are played against the unsympathetic Mason character and her basically lovable daughter.

He finally wins the mother through her child ("Listen, I can't stand you, but you got a ten-year-old in there I'm nuts about . . ."). But why does he want to? Simon short-circuits the first scene in which Mason says a decent and warm word by having Dreyfuss fall asleep so he doesn't hear it. He never really provides the dialogue and situations we need to *like* the female character—and so, in a funny way, we *aren't* rooting for them to get together. When they do, though, the movie works best. The first hour is awkward at times and never quite involving, but some of the later scenes, especially a dinner on a rooftop and the way Dreyfuss receives the disastrous reviews of his play, are really fine. It's strange: We leave the movie having enjoyed its conclusion so much that we almost forgot our earlier reservations. But they were there, and they were real.

Good Morning, Vietnam ★ ★ ★ ★
R, 119 m., 1988

Robin Williams (Adrian Cronauer), Forest Whitaker (Edward Garlick), Tung Thanh Tran (Tuan), Chintara Sukapatana (Trinh), Bruno Kirby (Lieutenant Hauk), Robert Wuhl (Marty Lee Dreiwitz), J.T. Walsh (Sergeant Dickerson), Noble Willingham (General Taylor). Directed by Barry Levinson and produced by Mark Johnson and Larry Brezner. Screenplay by Mitch Markowitz.

Like most of the great stand-up comedians, Robin Williams has always kept a certain wall between himself and his audience. If you watch his concert videos, you see him trying on a bewildering series of accents and characters; he's a gifted chameleon who turns into whatever makes the audience laugh. But who is inside?

With George Carlin, Richard Pryor, Steve Martin, Billy Crystal, Eddie Murphy, we have an idea—or think we do. A lot of their humor depends on confessional autobiography. With Robin Williams, the wall remains impenetrable. Like Groucho Marx, he uses comedy as a strategy for personal concealment.

Williams's best movies (*Popeye, The World According to Garp, Moscow on the Hudson*) are the ones where he is given a well-written character to play, and held to the character by a strong director. In his other movies, you can see him trying to do his stand-up act on the screen, trying to use comedy to conceal not only himself from the audience—but even his character. The one-liners and ad-libs distance him from the material and from his fellow actors. Hey, he's only a visitor here.

What is inspired about *Good Morning, Vietnam*, which contains far and away the best work Williams has ever done in a movie, is that his own tactics are turned against him. The director, Barry Levinson, has created a character who *is* a stand-up comic—he's a fast-talking disc jockey on Armed Forces Radio during the Vietnam War, directing a non-stop monologue at the microphone. There is absolutely no biographical information about this character. We don't know where he comes from, what he did before the war, whether he's ever been married, what his dreams are, what he's afraid of. Everything in his world is reduced to material for his program.

Levinson used Mitch Markowitz's script as a starting point for a lot of Williams's monologues, and then let the comedian improvise. Then he put together the best parts of many different takes to create sequences that are undeniably dazzling and funny. Williams is a virtuoso.

But while he's assaulting the microphone, Levinson is doing something fairly subtle in the movie around him. He has populated *Good Morning, Vietnam* with a lot of character actors who are fairly complicated types, recognizably human, and with the aid of the script, they set a trap for Williams. His character is edged into a corner where he *must* have human emotions, or die.

The character (his name is Adrian Cronauer) resists. At one point his Jeep breaks down in the middle of the jungle in Viet Cong territory, and he starts using one-liners on the trees. He meets a Vietnamese girl he likes, and uses one-liners on her, too, in a genuine exercise in cynicism since she doesn't understand any of his humor. He runs afoul of top Army brass that doesn't approve of his anti-establishment tone on the radio, and he wisecracks at them, too, trying to insist that he's always on stage, that nothing is real, that the whole war is basically just material.

And then things happen. To impress the girl and her brother, he starts teaching an English-language class for the Vietnamese. He finds that he likes them. He witnesses (and barely survives) a particularly gruesome terrorist attack. He gets thrown off the radio. He meets some kids who are going into battle, and who admire him, and in their eyes he sees something that makes him start to take himself a little more seriously. By the end of the movie, Cronauer has turned into a better, deeper, wiser man than he was at the beginning; the movie is the story of his education.

I know there are other ways to read this material. *Good Morning, Vietnam* works as straight comedy, and it works as a Vietnamera *M*A*S*H*, and even the movie's love story has its own bittersweet integrity. But they used to tell us in writing class that if we wanted to know what a story was really about, we should look for what changed between the beginning and the end. In this movie, Cronauer changes. War wipes the grin off of his face. His humor becomes a humanitarian tool, not simply a way to keep him talking and us listening.

In a strange, subtle way, *Good Morning, Vietnam* is not so much about war as it is about stand-up comedy, about the need that compels people to get up in front of the room and try to make us laugh—to control us.

Why do comics do that? Because they need to have their power proven and vindicated. Why do they need that? Because they are the most insecure of earth's people (just listen to their language—they're gonna kill us, unless they die out there). How do you treat low self-esteem? By doing estimable things and then saying, hey, I did that! What happens to Cronauer in this movie? Exactly that. By the end of the film he doesn't wisecrack all the time because he doesn't need to. He no longer thinks he's the worthless (although bright, fast, and funny) sack of crap that got off the plane. In the early scenes of the movie, the character's eyes are opaque. By the end, you can see what he's thinking.

The Good Mother ★
R, 113 m., 1988

Diane Keaton (Anna), Liam Neeson (Leo), Jason Robards (Muth), Ralph Bellamy (Grandfather), Teresa Wright (Grandmother), James Naughton (Brian), Asia Vieira (Molly). Directed by Leonard Nimoy and produced by Arnold Glimcher. Screenplay by Michael Bortman.

The Good Mother is one of the most confused

and conflicted serious movies in a long time—a film that feels great passion about its subject matter, but has no idea what it wants to say, or how to say it. There are times when we groan, not at the wrongheadedness of the villains, but at the stupidity of the heroes. And other times when we wonder if anybody actually thought this story through and decided, for sure, what it was about.

Here is a film that has time for a long, nostalgic, bittersweet prologue about the heroine's childhood friendship with a rebellious aunt. But it does not have the time, nor the imagination, to show us the central episode the entire movie is about. We get New England moonlight and rowboats and summer cottages and people calling to each other across the water, and we even get the aunt's death by drowning, but none of this is necessary to the rest of the picture. And yet when a little girl and her mother's boyfriend are involved in the crucial event of the movie, the camera is elsewhere.

The movie stars Diane Keaton as Anna, a woman raising her young daughter by herself. She is divorced from her husband, who has moved to another city and remarried. Her rich grandparents offer her money for child care, but she wants to raise her daughter herself, even if it means taking a menial job as (literally) a bottle-washer. One day in the laundromat she meets an Irish sculptor named Leo (Liam Neeson), and they fall headlong into a passionate love affair. And one day she comes home to find her ex-husband (James Naughton), who announces he is taking custody of their daughter.

Why? We learn that little Molly spent the weekend with her daddy, and described some of her recent experiences. We have already seen one of these events: Anna and Leo are making love in the middle of the night when Molly wanders into their bedroom. They stop immediately. Molly climbs into bed and goes immediately to sleep. And then, according to later testimony, the two start making love again—"but while Molly was asleep." Oddly, during the scene itself it is not clear to us that they resume.

The second incident is more troubling. While Molly and Leo are home alone, Leo takes a shower. Molly, who has been reading a children's picture book on reproduction, walks into the bathroom and innocently asks Leo if she can touch his penis. Aware of Anna's belief in openness with her daughter, to give her no shame about nudity and sexuality, Leo permits her. These two incidents

form the basis of a custody battle alleging that Anna cannot provide a proper home for her daughter.

If you understand how the ex-husband is handled in the movie, you can begin to understand why the movie goes so wrong. He is used only as an evil, vindictive plot device. He appears out of thin air, makes a shrill and angry speech, and disappears with Molly. He appears again during the final court hearings, where his dialogue is so clipped he can hardly make himself clear. No effort is made to develop him into a three-dimensional person (this in a movie where Babe, the rebellious aunt, gets several long scenes of her own) and so he remains an inflexible caricature.

Why is this the wrong treatment? Because it underlines the way in which the movie wants to hammer home its anger. The story works only if the husband is a monster. We in the audience have normal human curiosity and want to know what's inside his heart. Is he motivated only by vindictiveness, or does he genuinely believe his daughter is at risk? Based on what his daughter told him, no doubt he was right to suspect Leo, the boyfriend. Or perhaps not. Why doesn't the movie (which has time for travelogue sequences in Harvard Square and street performers on the waterfront) give us the critical scene which would make clear what Leo did?

Of course I am aware that both missing scenes—the shower scene and what Molly told her father—would be enormously difficult to film with tact and taste. But that should have been the task of the tellers of this story. If the filmmakers don't know or don't care exactly what happened, then all the rest of the movie is just maudlin tearjerking. I tend to believe the version told by Leo, that he was following what he thought was Anna's philosophy about child-rearing. But there are fleeting moments when Anna does not know exactly what to believe, and they are fatal to the outcome of the film, because we have not seen what actually occurred.

There are, I think, two quite different ways in which The Good Mother fails, the first for a worthy reason, the second not. The director of the film, Leonard Nimoy, has said in interviews that he understands this story from the inside out, because he lives with a woman who has a small child. That experience may have helped him in the movie's quiet domestic scenes, which are well-handled, but it may also have made him rigidly unwilling to see the ex-husband as

anything more than a one-dimensional villain. The movie has no curiosity about the character, and seems eager to keep him offstage and deny him things to say. The inflexibility in this area leads to a courtroom climax which is stilted, unnatural, and unconvincing, because the film makes such unbending rules about what can be said, known, and understood.

The second way the film fails is in its use of Diane Keaton. Keaton has a warm and lovely smile, and can be engagingly abashed and confused as well as any actress now working. But we get so many smiles, so much charming confusion, in the scenes after she meets the sculptor that we begin to yearn for her to grow up. The movie doesn't discipline itself to tell the story it is about. Instead, the first third seems to be a sequel to *An Unmarried Woman*, in which we see what happened after the divorcée met the artist: Anna and Leo hang out in burger joints, go to rock concerts, visit his studio, read books to Molly, and disappear into a shapeless lyrical interlude until the ex-husband appears.

Other elements are also irritating. The courtroom sequence has all the elements of an Idiot Plot, in which the protagonists could solve their problems simply by repeating what everyone in the audience could prompt them to say. Did they, for example, make love in front of the child? No!—as we in the audience could clearly see. Why do they consistently say the wrong things in testifying? Because the rules of this movie require it to have an unhappy ending. Why is the judge so remote and unimaginative? Because he's from Central Casting. Only Jason Robards, playing Anna's attorney, creates a believable moment in the courtroom.

There is one scene in the movie that does work, in every way. That is when Anna visits her grandparents (Ralph Bellamy and Teresa Wright) to ask for money for a lawyer, and discovers the true nature of their relationship. This scene is powerfully acted by Wright and Bellamy, and succeeds, and is moving, and is so convincing that it shows up the contrivance and manipulation of the rest of the film. *The Good Mother* was made with the best of intentions, and the worst of screenplays.

GoodFellas ★ ★ ★ ★
R, 148 m., 1990

Robert De Niro (James Conway), Ray Liotta
(Henry Hill), Joe Pesci (Tommy DeVito),
Lorraine Bracco (Karen Hill), Paul Sorvino
(Paul Cicero), Frank Sivero (Frankie
Carbone), Catherine Scorsese (Tommy's
Mother). Directed by Martin Scorsese and
produced by Irwin Winkler. Screenplay by
Nicholas Pileggi and Scorsese.

There really are guys like this. I've seen
them in restaurants and I've met them on
movie sets, where they carefully explain that
they are retired and are acting as technical
consultants. They make their living as criminals, and often the service they provide is
that they will not hurt you if you pay them.
These days there is a certain guarded nostalgia for their brand of organized crime, because at least the mob would make a deal
with you for your life, and not just kill you
casually, out of impatience or a need for
drugs.

Martin Scorsese's *GoodFellas* is a movie
based on the true story of a mid-level professional criminal named Henry Hill, whose
only ambition, from childhood on, was to be
a member of the outfit. We see him with his
face at the window, looking across the street
at the neighborhood Mafiosi, who drove the
big cars and got the good-looking women
and never had to worry about the cops when
they decided to hold a party late at night.
One day the kid goes across the street and
volunteers to help out, and before long he's
selling stolen cigarettes at a factory gate and
not long after that the doorman at the Copacabana knows his name.

For many years, it was not a bad life. The
rewards were great. The only thing you could
complain about was the work. There is a
strange, confused evening in Hill's life when
some kidding around in a bar leads to a murder, and the guy who gets killed is a "made
man"—a man you do not touch lightly, because he has the mob behind him—and the
body needs to be hidden quickly, and then
later it needs to be moved, messily. This kind
of work is bothersome. It fills the soul with
guilt and the heart with dread, and before
long Henry Hill is walking around as if there's
a lead weight in his stomach.

But the movie takes its time to get to that
point, and I have never seen a crime movie
that seems so sure of its subject matter. There
must have been a lot of retired technical consultants hanging around. Henry Hill, who is
now an anonymous refugee within the federal government's witness protection program, told this life story to the journalist
Nicholas Pileggi, who put it into the bestseller *WiseGuy,* and now Pileggi and Scorsese
have written the screenplay, which also benefits from Scorsese's firsthand observations of
the Mafia while he was a kid with his face in
the window, watching the guys across the
street.

Scorsese is in love with the details of his
story, including the Mafia don who never,
ever talked on the telephone and held all of
his business meetings in the open air. Or the
way some guys with a body in the car trunk
will stop by to borrow a carving knife from
one of their mothers, who will feed them
pasta and believe them when they explain
that they got blood on their suits when their
car hit a deer. Everything in this movie rever-
berates with familiarity; the actors even inhabit the scenes as if nobody had to explain
anything to them.

GoodFellas is an epic on the scale of *The
Godfather,* and it uses its expansive running
time to develop a real feeling for the way a
lifetime develops almost by chance at first,
and then sets its fateful course. Because we
see mostly through the eyes of Henry Hill
(Ray Liotta), characters swim in and out of
focus; the character of Jimmy Conway (Robert De Niro), for example, is shadowy in the
earlier passages of the film and then takes on
a central importance. And then there's Tommy DeVito (Joe Pesci), always on the outside
looking in, glorying in his fleeting moments
of power, laughing too loudly, slapping backs
with too much familiarity, pursued by the
demon of a raging anger that can flash out of
control in a second. His final scene in this
movie is one of the greatest moments of sudden realization I have ever seen; the development, the buildup, and the payoff are handled by Scorsese with the skill of a great tra-
gedian.

GoodFellas isn't a myth-making movie, like
The Godfather. It's about ordinary people
who get trapped inside the hermetic world of
the mob, whose values get worn away because they never meet anyone to disagree
with them. One of the most interesting characters in the movie is Henry Hill's wife,
Karen (Lorraine Bracco), who is Jewish and
comes from outside his world. He's an outsider himself—he's half-Irish, half-Italian,
and so will never truly be allowed on the
inside—but she's so far outside that at first
she doesn't even realize what she's in for. She
doesn't even seem to know what Henry does
for a living, and when she finds out, she
doesn't want to deal with it. She is the co-
narrator of the film, as if it were a documentary, and she talks about how she never goes
anywhere or does anything except in the
company of other mob wives. Finally she
gets to the point where she's proud of her
husband for being willing to go out and steal
to support his family, instead of just sitting
around like a lot of guys.

The parabola of *GoodFellas* is from the era
of "good crimes," like stealing cigarettes and
booze and running prostitution and making
book, to bad crimes involving dope. The
godfather in the movie (Paul Sorvino) warns
Henry Hill about getting involved with dope,
but it's not because he disapproves of narcotics (like Brando's Don Corleone); it's because he seems to sense that dope will spell
trouble for the mob, will unleash street anarchy and bring in an undisciplined element.
What eventually happens is that Hill makes a
lot of money with cocaine but gets hooked on
it as well, and eventually spirals down into
the exhausted paranoia that proves to be his
undoing.

Throbbing beneath the surface of *Good-
Fellas,* providing the magnet that pulls the
plot along, are the great emotions in Hill's
makeup: a lust for recognition, a fear of powerlessness, and guilt. He loves it when the
headwaiters know his name, but he doesn't
really have the stuff to be a great villain—he
isn't brave or heartless enough—and so when
he does bad things, he feels bad afterward.
He begins to hate himself. And yet, he cannot hate the things he covets. He wants the
prizes, but he doesn't want to pay for the
tickets.

And it is there, on the crux of that paradox, that the movie becomes Scorsese's metaphor for so many modern lives. He doesn't
parallel the mob with corporations or turn it
into some kind of grotesque underworld version of yuppie culture. Nothing is that simple. He simply uses organized crime as an
arena for a story about a man who likes material things so much that he sells his own soul
to buy them—compromises his principles,
betrays his friends, abandons his family, and
finally even loses contact with himself. And
the horror of the film is that, at the end, the
man's principal regret is that he doesn't have
any more soul to sell.

The Goonies ★ ★ ★
PG, 114 m., 1985

Sean Astin (Mikey), Josh Brolin (Brand), Jeff Cohen (Chunk), Corey Feldman (Mouth), Kerri Green (Andy), Martha Plimpton (Stef), and Ke Huy Quan (Data). Directed by Richard Donner and produced by Donner and Harvey Bernhard. Executive producer, Steven Spielberg. Screenplay by Chris Columbus.

The Goonies is a smooth mixture of the usual ingredients from Steven Spielberg action movies, made special because of the high-energy performances of the kids who have the adventures. It's a fantastical story of buried pirate treasure, told with a slice-of-life approach that lets these kids use words Bogart didn't know in *Casablanca.* There used to be children's movies and adult movies. Now Spielberg has found an in-between niche, for young teen-agers who have fairly sophisticated tastes in horror. He supervises the formula and oversees the production, assigning the direction to stylish action veterans (this time, it's Richard Donner, of *Superman* and *Ladyhawke*).

Goonies, like *Gremlins*, walks a thin line between the cheerful and the gruesome, and the very scenes the adults might object to are the ones the kids will like the best: Spielberg is congratulating them on their ability to take the heavy-duty stuff. The movie begins with an assortment of engaging boys, including a smart kid, a kid with braces, a fat kid, an older brother, and an Asian kid whose clothing conceals numerous inventions. Along the way they pick up a couple of girls, whose function is to swap spit and get bats in their hair. The kids find an old treasure map and blunder into the hideout of a desperate gang of criminals—two brothers, led by a Ma Barker type. There is a third brother, a Quasimodish freak, who is kept chained down in the cellar, where he watches TV. The tunnels to the treasure begin under the hideout. The kids find the tunnels while fleeing from the bad guys, and then go looking for the treasure with the crooks on their tails. There are lots of special effects and among the set pieces are the same kinds of booby traps that Indiana Jones survived in *Raiders* (falling boulders, sharp spikes), and a toboggan ride on a water chute that will remind you of the runaway train in *The Temple of Doom.*

If the ingredients are familiar from Spielberg's high-powered action movies, the kids are inspired by *E. T.* The single most important line of dialogue in any Spielberg movie is probably the line in *E. T.* when one kid calls another kid "penis-breath." The dialogue hears and acknowledges the precocious way that kids incorporate vulgarity into their conversations, especially with each other; the line in *E. T.* created such a shock of recognition that the laughs swept away any objections.

This time, his kids say "shit" a lot, and it is a measure of Spielberg's insight that the word draws only a PG rating for the movie; Spielberg no doubt argues that most kids talk like that half the time, and he is right. His technique is to take his thirteen- and fourteen-year-olds and let them act a little older than their age. It's more refreshing than the old Disney technique, which was to take characters of all ages and have them behave as if they were twelve.

Another Spielberg trademark, faithfully achieved by Donner, is a breakneck narrative speed. More things happen in this movie than in six ordinary action films. There's not just a thrill a minute; there's a thrill, a laugh, a shock, and a special effect. The screenplay has all the kids talking all at once, all the time, and there were times, especially in the first reel, when I couldn't understand much of what they were saying. The movie needs to be played loud, and with extra treble.

During *Goonies*, I was often exhilarated by what was happening. Afterwards, I was less enthusiastic. The movie is totally manipulative, which would be okay, except it doesn't have the lift of a film like *E. T.* It has the high energy without the sweetness. It uses what it knows about kids to churn them up, while *E. T.* gave them things to think about, the values to enjoy. *The Goonies*, like *Gremlins*, shows that Spielberg and his directors are absolute masters of how to excite and involve an audience. *E. T.* was more like *Close Encounters;* it didn't simply want us to feel, but also to wonder, and to dream.

Gorillas in the Mist ★ ★ ★
PG-13, 130 m., 1988

Sigourney Weaver (Dian Fossey), Bryan Brown (Bob Campbell), Julie Harris (Roz Carr), John Omirah Miluwi (Sembagare), Iain Cuthbertson (Dr. Louis Leakey), Constantin Alexandrov (Van Vecten). Directed by Michael Apted and produced by Arnold Glimcher and Terence Clegg. Screenplay by Anna Hamilton Phelan.

Gorillas in the Mist tells us what Dian Fossey accomplished and what happened to her, but it doesn't tell us who she was, and at the end that's what we want to know. Here is a movie that has gone to great lengths to be technically accomplished—the shots of the apes are everything we could wish for—but the screenplay has been skimped on, and there is a person missing here somewhere. We leave feeling that when Fossey was buried in her beloved gle, the third act of the movie was buried there, too.

The film tells a life story that many people already know. Dian Fossey was a woman of average achievement and no particular scientific background, but she loved animals and she was deeply disturbed by reports that the mountain gorillas of central Africa were being threatened with extinction. With absolute determination, she convinced Louis Leakey, the guru of African anthropologists, to allow her to man a jungle camp and conduct a census of the gorillas. And over the years she grew into one of the great experts on these fearsome but manlike beasts, learning to imitate their behavior so well that they accepted her in their midst.

Fossey's work was featured in the *National Geographic* and on TV documentaries. She became a romantic figure, out there almost alone in the wild, protecting "her" gorillas against poachers who sold gorilla hands to be made into ashtrays. Then, in 1985, she was found murdered in her camp, and as more came to be known about her there were many likely suspects. Fossey had grown fanatical about her animals, had all but waged war against the pygmy tribes that were killing them. She had alienated the trappers who procured animals for zoos. And she had made powerful enemies in a government that needed all the foreign currency it could find—and made lots of money off of gorillas.

Who killed her? The movie does not say, and that's as it should be. This is not a whodunit. But why did she become the ferocious and antisocial recluse of her later years? Why did she prize her relationships with gorillas above those with humans? Why did she choose to stay in the jungle rather than to join the man she loved? I can imagine good answers to all of these questions—I think the fate of Dian Fossey was more or less inevitable, and admirable—but in the movie the transitions in her emotional state are made so abruptly that we become conscious of the story being told.

Fossey is played in the movie by Sigourney Weaver, who makes her passionate and private, and has an exquisite tenderness and tact in her delicate scenes with wild animals. It is impossible to imagine a more appropriate choice for the role. But she grows away from us as the movie reaches its conclusion. A woman we have come to know turns into a stranger, and even if that is what happened to Dian Fossey—even if she did pull a cocoon of obsession around her—we deserve to see that happening, and to understand it. The screenplay simply presents it as an accomplished fact.

There is also a rather canned feeling to the romance in the central scenes of the film, when a *National Geographic* photographer (Bryan Brown) turns up in the jungle, and the two people fall in love. He arrives, they become lovers, and then he tells her that he has an assignment on the other side of the world and he wants her to come along. He cannot, he says, stay in the jungle forever; he has a job to do. She tells him she will not leave, and that if he does, he need not ever return or ever write. Was this argument not inevitable from the moment they first met? Did the photographer expect this woman to leave? Did she expect him to stay? They never really talk with one another, and so we're not sure.

The movie's best scenes involve her gradual acceptance by the gorillas. Here it is hard to say who should get the most credit—those who photographed real animals in the jungle, or those who used special effects to create animals, and parts of animals, for particular shots. I imagine that some of the close-ups of a gorilla's hand clasping Weaver's were done with Rick Baker's special-effects creations. I imagine some of the gorillas in the jungle are real, and some are men inside gorilla suits. But the work is done so seamlessly that I could never be sure. Everything looked equally real to me, and the delicacy with which director Michael Apted developed the relationships between woman and beasts was deeply absorbing. There were moments when I felt a touch of awe. Those moments, which are genuine, make the movie worth seeing.

But what we are really dealing with here are two stories that do not fit together very easily. Do we care more about the public Dian Fossey or the private? Is her work more important or her madness? In these modern times we demand the whole life, we say we are realists and don't want the autobiogra-

phy cleaned up for a "screen version," but the result is a movie that is much more depressing and shapeless than it should be. The parabolas are wrong; Fossey's work fills us with joy, but her fate fills us with confusion and dismay. Perhaps an old-fashioned Hollywood cop-out would actually have been more satisfactory here, with Fossey against the bad guys and everyone assigned his role, and some kind of a happy ending. I left *Gorillas in the Mist* feeling cheated somehow, as if the story had no more insight into Dian Fossey than she apparently had into herself.

Gorky Park ★ ★ ★ ½
R, 128 m., 1983

William Hurt (Arkady Renko), Lee Marvin (Jack Osborne), Joanna Pacula (Irina), Brian Dennehy (Kirwell), Ian Bannen (Iamskoy). Directed by Michael Apted and produced by Gene Kirkwood and Howard W. Koch, Jr. Screenplay by Dennis Potter.

Mystery fans talk about the "police procedural," a crime novel that follows police work, step by meticulous step, from the opening of a case to its eventual resolution. The crimes aren't always solved, but then the solution isn't really the point. Instead, "procedurals" are a way to study human nature under stress, to see how a society works from the inside out and the bottom up. There are procedurals set all over the world, from Ed McBain's 87th Precinct on the East coast to the Martin Beck thrillers in Stockholm, but Martin Cruz Smith's *Gorky Park* was the first good police procedural set in Russia. It used the procedural approach to show us an honest cop under pressure, a system that functioned only through corruption, and a conflict between socialism and Russia's homegrown capitalism.

This is the movie of that book, and it has all of the same strengths. It begins with a shocking murder (three corpses found frozen in the snow with their faces and fingerprints removed). There are no clues. A police inspector named Renko (William Hurt) is assigned to the case, and makes it his personal crusade. He recruits a physical anthropologist to try to re-create the missing faces on the bodies. He prowls the black market, where deals are made in Western currency. He meets a beautiful young woman and a mysterious American businessman.

And he learns about the obsessive power of sable fur coats.

The investigation of the crime has a fascination of its own, but what makes *Gorky Park* really interesting is its views of Soviet cops, criminals, bureaucrats, and ordinary citizens. As Renko gets closer and closer to a solution to the case, his investigation leads him to powerful circles in the Soviet Union. And his heart, of course, leads him closer to the girl, who may have all of the necessary information but has been so warped by paranoia that she refuses to betray those she thinks are her friends.

The movie is directed with efficiency by Michael *(Coal Miner's Daughter)* Apted, who knows that pacing is indispensable to a procedural. Too long a pause for anything—romance, detail, speculation, explanation—and the spell is broken. He uses actors who are able to bring fully realized characters to the screen, so we don't have to stand around waiting for introductions. That involves a certain amount of typecasting. Lee Marvin, gravel-voiced, white-haired, expensively dressed, is perfect for the businessman. Joanna Pacula, a young Polish actress in her first Western role, is beautiful, vulnerable, wide-eyed, and fresh—and as an exile stranded in Paris when her Warsaw theater was closed by Poland's martial law, she doesn't have to fake her paranoia about the Soviet state.

William Hurt, as Renko, is probably the key to the picture. He makes this cop into a particular kind of person, cold, at times willfully blinded by duty, sublimating his feelings in his profession, until this case breaks him wide open. By the end of *Gorky Park*, we realize that it's not the solution that matters, but what the case itself forces the people to discover about themselves.

Great Balls of Fire ★ ★
PG-13, 108 m., 1989

Dennis Quaid (Jerry Lee Lewis), Winona Ryder (Myra Gale Lewis), John Doe (J.W. Brown), Stephen Tobolowsky (John Phillips), Trey Wilson (Sam Phillips), Alec Baldwin (Jimmy Swaggart), Steve Allen (Steve Allen), Lisa Blount (Lois Brown), Joshua Sheffield (Rusty Brown), Joe Bob Briggs (Dewey "Daddy-O" Phillips). Directed by Jim McBride and produced by Adam Fields. Screenplay by Jack Baran and McBride.

Jerry Lee Lewis has by all accounts led a

dark and driven life, shadowed by drugs, booze, violence, scandal, and the tragic ends of two of his several wives and one of his children. An accurate biopic about his life would belong on the same bill with *I'll Cry Tomorrow* or *The Rose*. But that picture wouldn't be much fun—as indeed great, long stretches of the life itself must not have been much fun—and so *Great Balls of Fire* gives us a Jerry Lee Lewis who has been sanitized, popularized, and lobotomized. Even then, the story ends in 1959—before most of the events for which "The Killer" became notorious.

This is a simpleminded rock 'n' roll history in which the pleasures are many and the troubles are few. Jerry Lee Lewis, played by Dennis Quaid as a grinning simpleton with a crazy streak and a manic piano style, climbs the same career ladder as many of the stars of musical biographies, but he does it with lightning speed.

As a kid, he eavesdrops on black rhythm and blues. Then we flash forward to Lewis pounding on the piano in the same style. Cut to a demo record that attracts the attention of Sam Phillips, the legendary head of Sun Records in Memphis. Cut to the record hitting the Top 40 charts. Cut to Lewis listening to a black band play "Whole Lotta Shakin' Goin' On." Cut to his version of the record being cheered by a rowdy bar crowd. Cut to stardom. In between, there are some meetings with Lewis's evangelist cousin, Jimmy Swaggart (Alec Baldwin), who warns him he must choose between heaven and hell. "Well, if I'm goin' to hell," Lewis says, "I'm gonna go playing the piano."

There must have been more to it than that, but not in this movie. In fact, that flash forward between the kid and the Killer jumps over a lot of ground, including Lewis's first two marriages. We rejoin his life just as he has moved in with his cousin, J.W. Brown, who joins his band as the bass player. And it's in Brown's house that Lewis meets young Myra Gale Brown (Winona Ryder), who became his bride at the age of thirteen (it is said she still believed in Santa Claus on her wedding night).

The makers of *Great Balls of Fire* say they had to choose between the legend and the facts in making Lewis's life, and they choose the legend. That means most of the events in the movie will come as no surprise to students of rock 'n' roll—especially not the scandal when the British press exposed the real age of Lewis's child bride. Those seeking insights into that marriage will be disappointed by this movie, however, which plays everything so obliquely that we have little idea of what the girl thinks of Lewis, and no idea of what he thinks of her.

I came out of *Great Balls of Fire*, indeed, with no idea of what Lewis thought of anything or anybody. As played by Quaid (perhaps accurately), the Killer comes across as monstrous, egocentric, shallow, irresponsible, selfish, and cold—and even his stage performances contain more anger than music. I've never seen a movie about anybody that probes so tentatively and apologetically into the subject's life, and still uncovers so many worms. If this is the legend, the facts must be inutterably depressing. Lewis has created the kind of legend that defiant drunks can clutch at like a straw—if he's still alive, I'm not so bad.

There is also the music. There are three great hits in the movie—"Whole Lotta Shakin' Goin' On," "Great Balls of Fire," and "Breathless"—and the rest is filler material like "High School Confidential." But Quaid does a good job of reproducing the Lewis stage persona, and the sound track piano and vocals are, as the end credits assure us, by "The Killer Himself." The director, Jim McBride, has some fun with a scene where the jubilant Lewis drives around Memphis in his new Olds 88 convertible and the whole town seems to be dancing to his record on the radio. (A matched scene, in which the same people shun him after his return from England, seems forced and false.)

This movie is the second collaboration between McBride and Quaid, who made the great *The Big Easy* together in 1987. It's easy to see from that film why it was thought that they could do justice to Jerry Lee Lewis. McBride has a natural feel for the South, and Quaid has the ability to play a charming, libidinous con man. But the script shies away from the dark side of Jerry Lee Lewis—from the long nights of a man who has been surrounded by violence and misery, and whose lifestyle has brought him near death more than once. It's a life that just doesn't fit into the clichés of a PG-13 rock 'n' roll biopic for summer release. An accurate movie could perhaps have been made about the real Jerry Lee Lewis, but it should have been directed by the Martin Scorsese of *Raging Bull*, and played by Robert De Niro in a foul mood with a killer hangover.

The Great Gatsby ★ ★ ½
PG, 146 m., 1974

Robert Redford (Gatsby), Mia Farrow (Daisy Buchanan), Bruce Dern (Tom Buchanan), Karen Black (Myrtle Wilson), Scott Wilson (George Wilson), Sam Waterston (Nick Carraway), Lois Chiles (Jordan Baker), Howard Da Silva (Meyer Wolfsheim), Robert Blossom (Mr. Gatz), Edward Herrmann (Klipspringer). Directed by Jack Clayton and produced by David Merrick. Screenplay by Francis Ford Coppola.

The Great Gatsby is a superficially beautiful hunk of a movie with nothing much in common with the spirit of F. Scott Fitzgerald's novel. I wonder what Fitzgerald, whose prose was so graceful, so elegantly controlled, would have made of it: of the willingness to spend so much time and energy on exterior effect while never penetrating to the souls of the characters. It would take about the same time to read Fitzgerald's novel as to view this movie—and that's what I'd recommend.

The movie is "faithful" to the novel with a vengeance—to what happens in the novel, that is, and not to the feel, mood, and spirit of it. Yet I've never thought the events in *The Great Gatsby* were that important to the novel's success; Fitzgerald, who came out of St. Paul to personify the romance of an age, was writing in a way about himself when he created Gatsby. The mundane Midwestern origins had been replaced by a new persona, by a flash and charisma that sometimes only concealed the despair underneath. For Fitzgerald, there was always something unattainable; and for Gatsby, it was Daisy Buchanan, the lost love of his youth, forever symbolized by that winking green beacon at the end of her dock.

The beacon and the other Fitzgerald symbols are in this movie version, but they communicate about as much as the great stone heads on Easter Island. They're memorials to a novel in which they had meaning. The art director and set decorator seem to have ripped whole pages out of Fitzgerald and gone to work to improve on his descriptions. Daisy and her husband, the ruthless millionaire Tom Buchanan, live almost drowning in whites, yellows, and ennui. Tom's mistress Myrtle and her husband, the shabby filling station owner George, live in a wasteland of ashes in Fitzgerald's novel; in the movie, they seem to have landed on the moon.

All of this unfeeling physical excess might have been overcome by performances. But the director, Jack Clayton, having assembled a promising cast, fails to exploit them very well. When the casting of Robert Redford as Jay Gatsby was announced, I objected because he didn't fit my notion of Gatsby: He was too substantial, too assured, even too handsome. I saw him as Tom Buchanan, and somebody else as Gatsby (Jack Nicholson, maybe, or Bruce Dern—who plays Tom). Having seen the movie, I think maybe I was wrong: Redford could have played Gatsby. I'm not even sure it's his fault he doesn't. The first time Clayton shows us Gatsby, it's a low-angle shot of a massive figure seen against the night sky and framed by marble: This isn't the romantic Gatsby on his doomed quest, it's Charles Foster Kane. A scene where Gatsby reaches out as if to snatch the green beacon in his hand is true to the book, but the movie's literal showing of it looks silly.

These hints of things to come lead up to two essential scenes in which Clayton fails to give us a Gatsby we care about. The first is the initial meeting between Gatsby and Nick (Gatsby wants Nick, his neighbor and Daisy's cousin, to invite her to tea so they can meet again). Redford is so inarticulate and formal in this scene with Nick that we laugh; it's the first time we hear him talk, and he's so mannered that the acting upstages the content of the scene. Doesn't that have to be Clayton's fault? We know Redford has range enough to have played the scene in several better ways. And then the actual reunion between Gatsby and Daisy—the moment on which the rest of the movie is going to depend—gives us Gatsby's toothpaste grin and Daisy's stunned reaction and holds both for so long that any tension reduces itself to the ridiculous. It doesn't even feel as if Gatsby's happy to see Daisy—more that he assumes she's overjoyed to see him.

The message of the novel, if I read it correctly, is that Gatsby, despite his dealings with gamblers and bootleggers, is a romantic, naive, and heroic product of the Midwest—and that his idealism is doomed in any confrontation with the reckless wealth of the Buchanans. This doesn't come through in the movie. When Nick, at his last meeting with Gatsby, tells him how much he admires him ("You're worth the whole crowd of them"), we frankly don't know why unless we've read the book. Oh, we're *told*, to be sure: The sound track contains narration by

Nick that is based pretty closely on his narration in the novel. But we don't feel. We've been distanced by the movie's overproduction. Even the actors seem somewhat cowed by the occasion; an exception is Bruce Dern, who just goes ahead and gives us a convincing Tom Buchanan. We don't have to be told the ways in which Tom is indifferent to human feeling, because we can sense them.

But we can't penetrate the mystery of Gatsby. Nor, to be honest, can we quite understand what's so special about Daisy Buchanan. Not as she's played by Mia Farrow, all squeaks and narcissism and empty sophistication. In the novel, Gatsby never understands that he is too good for Daisy. In the movie, we never understand why he thought she was good enough for him. And that's what's missing.

That, and one other small item: How could a screenplay that plundered Fitzgerald's novel so literally, that quoted so much of the narration and dialogue, have ended with a rinky-dink version of "Ain't We Got Fun" instead of the most famous last sentence of any novel of the century? Maybe because the movie doesn't ever come close to understanding it: "And so we beat on, boats against the current, borne back ceaselessly into the past."

The Great Mouse Detective ★ ★ ★
G, 102 m., 1986

Featuring the voices of Vincent Price, Barrie Ingham, Val Bettin, Susanne Pollatschek, Candy Candido, Diana Chesney, Evan Brenner, Alan Young, and Melissa Manchester. Directed by John Musker, Ron Clements, Dave Michener, and Bunny Mattison.

Philosophers have the notion of parallel universes—whole worlds that are right next to our own, but in a different dimension, so that we can't see them, even while our actions are mirrored with infinite variations. Movie animators have a similar notion, which is that human lives are mirrored on a smaller scale by the parallel lives of the little cartoon characters who live down there closer to the floor.

Near the beginning of *The Great Mouse Detective*, the camera moves through London, passing many of the familiar landmarks, before finally tilting down and moving in toward a little doorway down near to the ground. Inside there's a busy little mouse, a craftsman, hard at work. Like so

many domesticated cartoon animals, he is the very soul of bourgeois respectability (I always liked it in the "Tom & Jerry" cartoons when they showed the floor lamps and chintz-covered sofas inside the mouse holes).

Before long, however, a mysterious figure appears who disrupts this image of comfortable domesticity. And then *The Great Mouse Detective* launches its story, which depends on the conceit that London in those days housed not only a great human detective (Sherlock Holmes), but also a mouse who was every bit as good a detective.

The Sherlock Holmes legend is such a durable story that all sorts of filmmakers have adapted it to their own ends, styles, and genres. Just in recent years, we've seen Billy Wilder's *The Private Life of Sherlock Holmes*, Gene Wilder's *Sherlock Holmes' Younger Brother*, Nicholas Meyer's *The Seven Percent Solution*, and Steven Spielberg's *Young Sherlock Holmes*—which told the story of the schooldays of Sherlock and young Watson, surrounded by props and special effects borrowed from other Spielberg extravaganzas.

Here is the Disney version, told on a mouse scale in cartoon form, with a freedom and creativity of animation that reminded me of the earlier Disney feature-length cartoons. In recent decades, Disney and the other animators had started to cut corners; the old-style full animation of such classics as *Pinocchio* was simply too expensive to duplicate any more, with its endless man-hours of drawing. So we began to get backgrounds that didn't move, and actions that seemed recycled out of other actions. Now, however, computer animation has taken most of the drudgery and much of the expense out of animation, and the result is a movie like this, that looks more fully animated than anything in some thirty years.

The movie's story is the usual silliness about evil villains and abducted geniuses. Although the detective in the movie is not called Sherlock Holmes (or Sherlock Mouse, for that matter) he is obviously cut from the same cloth, right down to his ever-present pipe. And there is a Doctor Watson character, who befriends a bewildered waif in the street, and takes it to the great detective, who scents one of his greatest cases.

What's fun is the carefree way the animators swing through their story, using the freedom of the cartoon form to blend nineteenth-century realism with images that seem borrowed from more recent special-effects pictures. For a long time, I was down on the full-length animated efforts of Disney and others, because they didn't seem to reflect the same sense of magic and wonderment that the original animated classics always had. Who, for example, could ever equate *101 Dalmations* with *Snow White?* But now, maybe thanks to computers, animated movies are beginning to sparkle again.

The Great Muppet Caper ★ ★
G, 95 m., 1981

Charles Grodin (Nicky), Diana Rigg (Lady Holiday). With the Muppets and their performers: Jim Henson, Frank Oz, Dave Goetz, Jerry Holson, and Richard Hunt. Cameo appearances by Robert Morley, Peter Ustinov, and Jack Warden. Directed by Jim Henson and produced by Frank Oz. Screenplay by Tom Patchett, Jay Tarses, Jerry Juhl, and Jack Rose.

The Muppets are a wonderful creation, but they lose their special quality in *The Great Muppet Caper.* They behave like clones of other popular kiddie superstars—like the basic cartoon heroes they once seemed destined to replace. Jim Henson's original inspiration with the Muppets was to invest them with very real human qualities: Miss Piggy's vanity and insecurity, Kermit's insouciant inquisitiveness, Fozzie's fuzzy desire to be loved, and so on. Then he involved them in situations that revolved around their personalities, so that the kids who watched them could perhaps learn something about human nature. A lot of suspense during a Muppet story depended on how a particular Muppet would *feel* about something.

That was the approach of many of the Muppet TV episodes and of the original *The Muppet Movie* (1979). This time, though, Henson and his associates haven't developed a screenplay that pays attention to the Muppet personalities. Instead, they ship them to England and dump them into a caper plot, treating them every bit as much like a formula as James Bond. This won't do. We don't care about some dumb diamond the size of a baseball, and as Muppet fans we're probably also indifferent to Henson's ambition to satirize old movie genres.

When he gives us a Busby Berkeley-like water ballet starring Miss Piggy, our reaction is complex. We think (a) that kids in the audience won't know what is being satirized and (b) that Miss Piggy's fantasies have become less fun as they reveal less vulnerability. And as for Miss Piggy herself . . . I really hate to say this, but she's not nearly as appealing in *The Great Muppet Caper* as she's always been before. She is also alarmingly thinner. Are we witnessing the Hollywoodization of Miss Piggy? Is she perhaps beginning to believe her own publicity? She's less vulnerable this time, less touching, with fewer instantly recognizable human frailties.

The movie involves a Muppet expedition to London, a near-affair between Charles Grodin and Miss Piggy, and some missing jewels. It also features some cameo appearances by familiar stars, but Henson seems content that the stars are merely in his movie; he doesn't use them with comic imagination. Example: When the Muppets crash-land in the middle of a British pond, they're greeted by British Airways' TV spokesman Robert Morley. But Morley plays the scene absolutely straight. Here was a great chance to have fun with Morley's TV ads: He could have brusquely informed the Muppets that hotels were $400 a night, there were no theater tickets available, not a single rental car was to be had for miles around, and that, frankly, the British wished their American cousins would stay at home.

The lack of a cutting edge hurts this movie. It's too nice, too routine, too predictable, and too safe.

The Great Santini ★ ★ ★ ★
PG, 118 m., 1980

Robert Duvall (Bull Meechum), Blythe Danner (Lillian Meechum), Michael O'Keefe (Ben Meechum), Lisa Jane Persky (Mary Anne Meechum), Stan Shaw (Toomer Smalls), Theresa Merritt (Arrabelle Smalls). Directed by Lewis John Carlino and produced by Charles A. Pratt. Screenplay by Carlino.

Like almost all of my favorite films, *The Great Santini* is about people more than it's about a story. It's a study of several characters, most unforgettably the Great Santini himself—played by Robert Duvall. Despite his name, he is not a magician or an acrobat but a lieutenant colonel in the Marines with the real name of Bull Meechum. He sees himself as the Great Santini, an ace pilot, great Marine, heroic husband and father and, in general, a sterling man among men. His family is expected to go along with this— and to go along with him, as he's transferred to a duty camp in South Carolina in the early 1960s.

There are five other members of the Meechum family. His wife (Blythe Danner) is a sweet Southern girl who calls her kids "sugar" and understands her maverick husband with a love that is deep but unforgiving. His oldest son (Michael O'Keefe) is just turning eighteen and learning to stand up to a father who issues "direct orders," calls everyone "sports fan," and expects to be called "sir." There are two daughters and one more son, but the movie's main relationship is between the father and the oldest boy.

Santini, you understand, is one hell of a guy. All he understands is competition. He's a royal pain in the ass to his Marine superiors, because he's always pulling damn fool stunts and making a spectacle out of himself. But he's a great pilot and he's said to be a good leader (even though his first briefing session for the men under him in South Carolina leaves them totally bewildered). Santini wants to win at everything, even backyard basketball with his son.

But the son is learning to be his own man. And there's a subplot involving a friendship between O'Keefe and the intense actor Stan Shaw, who plays the son of the family's black maid. Marine kids grow up nowhere and everywhere, we learn, and in South Carolina these two kids go shrimping together, trade lore together, become friends. It's a nice relationship, although a little tangential to the main thrust of the movie.

It's Robert Duvall who really makes the movie live—Duvall and Blythe Danner in a stunning performance that nothing she's done before (in *1776, Hearts of the West,* etc.) prepares us for. Although *The Great Santini* is set about ten years before *Apocalypse Now,* Duvall is playing essentially the same character in both films—we remember his great scene in *Apocalypse,* shouting that napalm smells to him like victory, as he gives his gung-ho speeches in this movie.

Duvall and O'Keefe go hard at each other, in the father-son confrontation, and there's an especially painful scene where the father bounces a basketball off his son's head, egging him on. But this movie is essentially a comedy—a serious, tender one, like *Breaking Away,* which is also about a son getting to know his father.

There are wonderful little moments in the dialogue (as when the Great Santini's daughter wonders aloud if females are allowed full Meechum family status, or are only sort of one-celled Meechums). There are moments straight out of left field, as when Duvall and the family's new maid (the formidable Theresa Merritt) get into an impromptu shoulder-punching contest. There are moments so unpredictable and yet so natural they feel just like the spontaneity of life itself. And the movie's conclusion is the same way: sentimental without being corny, a tear-jerker with dignity.

The Great Santini is a movie to seek out and to treasure.

Green Card ★ ★ ★
PG-13, 108 m., 1991

Gerard Depardieu (George), Andie MacDowell (Bronte), Bebe Neuwirth (Lauren), Gregg Edelman (Phil), Robert Prosky (Bronte's lawyer), Jessie Keosian (Mrs. Bird). Directed and produced by Peter Weir. Screenplay by Weir.

Hollywood has, since time immemorial, defined the Meet Cute as a comic situation contrived entirely for the purpose of bringing a man and a woman together, after which they can work out their destinies for the remainder of the film. The classic Meet Cute involves the hero and heroine crashing into each other outside a department store, while all of their Christmas shopping falls to the ground. He helps her pick up her packages, they start to talk, and the rest is history—or formula comedy, anyway.

The package gambit is such a familiar Hollywood standby that *Green Card* has fun employing it as an alibi. The main characters—a Frenchman and an American woman who have to pretend their marriage is the real thing—solemnly explain to an immigration official that they met when they ran into each other, their packages fell to the ground, etc.

Actually the whole movie is a slightly more sophisticated application of the same formula. The Frenchman, played by Gerard Depardieu, needs a green card if he is to be able to stay in America. The woman, played by Andie MacDowell, needs a husband if she is to rent a desirable Manhattan apartment. They are introduced by a friend, they go through the fiction of a marriage ceremony, and then when immigration comes sniffing around, they have to put on a convincing show of really being married.

A movie like *Green Card* can supply two kinds of pleasures: those caused when it observes its formula, and those created when it violates it. The movie was written and directed by Peter Weir (*Dead Poets Society*, *Witness*), who constructs it lovingly according to sturdy old principles: The couple is at first indifferent to one another, then hostile, then in love, then in denial, and then, of course, they break up—right before they get together. All of these stops are observed, but, at the same time, Weir has added some nice touches, including the unconventional characters themselves.

Depardieu, the leading actor in France, here making his American debut, is a large, shaggy, untidy man who brings to every role a kind of effortless charm. He occupies a considerable psychic space on the screen. It is not hard to figure out his practical reasons for wanting to marry MacDowell. But her character has its work cut out: Would an attractive young woman, smart and with a great job, actually marry a stranger just to get an apartment? In Manhattan, this movie argues, the answer is yes—especially if the apartment incorporates a large solarium. We accept the marriage of convenience for the purposes of the plot, but the screenplay still has some explaining to do.

Weir is good with his actors and good, too, at putting a slight spin on some of the obligatory scenes. When Depardieu meets Mac-Dowell's parents, for example, the scene doesn't develop along standard lines of outrage and bluster. Instead, Conrad McLaren, as her father, grasps the situation instantly, and proves to be a good judge of character. I also liked the scene where Depardieu goes to a party and meets MacDowell's friends. Of course, they are snotty, and, of course, it is mentioned that Depardieu is a composer, and, of course, there is a piano there, and Depardieu is asked to play one of his compositions. But what happens then is perhaps the best scene in the movie.

Green Card is not blindingly brilliant, and is not an example of the very best work of the director who made *The Year of Living Dangerously* or the actor who starred in *Cyrano de Bergerac*. But it is a sound, entertaining work of craftsmanship, a love story between two people whose meet is not as cute as it might have been.

The Green Room ★ ★ ★
PG, 90 m., 1978

Francois Truffaut (Julien), Nathalie Baye (Cecelia). Directed by Francois Truffaut. Screenplay by Truffaut and Jean Gruault.

The films of Francois Truffaut seem divided into two categories, which I admire for completely different reasons. On one side are the films affirming life, films like *Small Change*, *Day for Night*, and *Stolen Kisses*. On the other side are the films involving his obsession with death, films like *The Bride Wore Black*, *Two English Girls*, and *The Story of Adele H.*

Truffaut's *The Green Room* most definitely belongs in the second category, and is in fact the closest he has come to suggesting that his own interest in death may be a morbid preoccupation. The film is based on one of the most death-obsessed stories in the English language, *The Altar of the Dead*, in which Henry James told the story of a man who worshiped the memory of his dead wife to the point of madness.

In the James story, and in the Truffaut film, the character arrives at a crisis when he falls in love with a woman who is undeniably still alive. How can the new love be reconciled with the adoration of the departed wife? The solution is appropriately macabre. The living woman is invited to join the man in worship at the altar of the dead—to become a fellow mourner.

That is the basic situation in James's version. What fascinates Truffaut about the story is where it leads from there, for the woman is obsessed with the dead, too, and has her own departed ones to worship. The man builds an altar, a shrine, photographs, and candles on every wall and in every corner, and he offers to admit the woman's dead to the shrine. But then he discovers that one of her dead is one of his old enemies—a man whose memory would desecrate his own dead. Thus his grief is betrayed as monstrously selfish.

Truffaut tells this story with necrophilic relish, and plays the leading role himself. Nathalie Baye, a young French actress who is usually unforced and natural, plays the woman, an equally obsessed person—but one who eventually wants to break away from the lure of the dead and admit love into her life again. To the man, of course, that is too much of a challenge. A perfect love can exist only with the dead, because it is always on the terms set down by the living.

The Green Room is, as you have intuited by now, a very somber and depressed film. But it is not depressing, because its characters are such grotesques, such caricatures, that we marvel at them instead of sympathizing. They carry their death obsessions so far that they almost exorcise them. Unlike the heroine of *Adele H.*, whose urge toward self-destruction was conceited, narcissistic, and a device to dramatize her own plight, the characters in *The Green Room* are so simple they are comic in a Dickensian sense; they exaggerate one attribute so absurdly that they lose all other human dimensions.

The Green Room should be seen by: admirers of Henry James, admirers of Truffaut, and admirers of crumbling old cemeteries where the tombs gape openly at passersby. As an admirer of all three of these subjects, no doubt I admired the film more than others might. I especially enjoyed the scene where the gates are bolted shut and Truffaut is locked among the graves overnight.

Gregory's Girl ★ ★ ★
PG, 93 m., 1982

Gordon John Sinclair (Gregory), Dee Hepburn (Dorothy), Chic Murray (Headmaster), Jake D'Arcy (Phil), Alex Norton (Alec), John Bott (Alistair). Directed by Bill Forsyth and produced by Clive Parsons and Davina Boling. Screenplay by Forsyth.

There was a little item in the paper not long ago that should have been front page news. It was about a survey reporting that physically handsome men were less successful in business, made less money, married younger, and had less "desirable" spouses than men of average or below-average looks. The sociologists who announced these conclusions speculated that the handsome guys tended to get sidetracked in high school, spending more time on social life and less time on studies; they tended to depend on their golden boy charm instead of plowing ahead through college; and they tended, because they were more sexually active at younger ages, to marry sooner and therefore to marry women who were looking for marriage rather than careers. On the average, therefore, the weird kid with acne who's president of Chem Club will do better in the long run than the prom king.

Bill Forsyth's *Gregory's Girl* is a charming, innocent, very funny little movie about the weird kid. It is set in Scotland, where the teen-agers are quieter, more civilized and more naive than, let's say, those in *The Class of 1984*. And it is about Gregory (Gordon John Sinclair), a gangling adolescent who has started to shoot up all of a sudden and finds he is hopelessly uncoordinated on the

soccer field. Gregory looks sort of like an immensely likable stork. He loses his place on the soccer team to another student who is a good deal faster and more coordinated. The other student happens to be a girl. Her name is Dorothy (Dee Hepburn), and Gregory instantly falls deeply in love with her. Nothing like this has ever hit him before, and romance becomes for him almost a physical illness. Dorothy is sweet to him, but distant, because she not only suspects Gregory's feelings but is way ahead of him in her analysis of the whole situation.

The movie takes place mostly in a pleasant suburb of Glasgow, where the kids hang about and trade endless speculation on the impossibility of being sixteen and happy at the same time. Gregory turns for romantic advice to his younger sister, who is much more interested in ice cream. His sister, in fact, is oblivious to boys, although one pays her an earnest compliment: "She's only ten, but she has the body of a woman of thirteen." Meanwhile, Gregory consoles his best friend, who is fifteen and a half and has never known love.

This movie is a reminder that we tend to forget a lot of things about adolescence. For example: That it is no use telling a teen-ager what his faults are, because he is painfully aware of every possible fault in the minutest detail; that boys are absolutely helpless in the throes of teen-age romance, whereas girls tend to retain at least some perspective; that it is an unwritten law of the universe that no sixteen-year-old ever falls instantly in love with the right person at the right time.

The movie has a lot of gentle, civilized fun with insights like that. And along the way, Gregory the stork is led on a wild goose chase with a swan at the end. The movie contains so much wisdom about being alive and teen-aged and vulnerable that maybe it would even be painful for a teen-ager to see it; it's not much help, when you're suffering from those feelings of low self-esteem and an absolutely hopeless crush, to realize that not only are you in pain and suffering an emotional turmoil, but you're not even unique. Maybe only grown-ups should see this movie. You know, people who have gotten over the pains of unrequited love (hollow laugh).

Gremlins ★ ★ ★
PG, 111 m., 1984

Hoyt Axton (Rand Peltzer), Zach Galligan (Billy), Phoebe Cates (Kate), Scott Brady

(Sheriff Frank), Polly Holliday (Mrs. Deagle). Directed by Joe Dante and produced by Michael Finnell. Executive producer Steven Spielberg. Screenplay by Chris Columbus.

Gremlins is a confrontation between Norman Rockwell's vision of Christmas and Hollywood's vision of the blood-sucking monkeys of voodoo island. It's fun. On the one hand, you have an idyllic American small town, with Burger Kings and Sears stores clustered merrily around the village square, and on the other hand you have a plague of reprehensible little beasties who behave like a rodent road company of Marlon Brando's motorcycle gang in *The Wild One*.

The whole movie is a sly series of send-ups, inspired by movie scenes so basic they reside permanently in our subconscious. The opening scene, for example, involves a visit to your basic Mysterious Little Shop in Chinatown, where, as we all know, the ordinary rules of the visible universe cease to operate and magic is a reality. Later on, after a kid's father buys him a cute little gremlin in Chinatown, we have a new version of your basic Puppy for Christmas Scene. Then there are such basic movie characters as the Zany Inventor, the Blustering Sheriff, the Clean-Cut Kid, the Cute Girlfriend, and, of course, the Old Bag.

The first half of the movie is the best. That's when we meet the little gremlins, which are unbearably cute and look like a cross between a Pekingese, Yoda from *Empire*, the Ewoks from *Jedi*, and kittens. They have impossibly big eyes, they're cuddly and friendly, and they would make ideal pets except for the fact that they hate bright lights, should not be allowed to get wet, and must never be fed after midnight. Well, of course, it's *always* after midnight; that's the tip-off that this isn't a retread of *E.T.* but comes from an older tradition, the fairy tale or magic story. And in the second half of the movie, after the gremlins have gotten wet, been fed after midnight, etc., they turn into truly hateful creatures that look like the monster in *Alien*.

The movie exploits every trick in the monster-movie book. We have scenes where monsters pop up in the foreground, and others where they stalk us in the background, and others when they drop into the frame and scare the Shinola out of everybody. And the movie itself turns nasty, especially in a scene involving a monster that gets slammed in a microwave oven, and another one where a wide-eyed teen-age girl (Phoebe Cates) explains why she hates Christmas. Her story is in the great tradition of 1950s sick jokes, and as for the microwave scene, I had a queasy feeling that before long we'd be reading newspaper stories about kids who went home and tried the same thing with the family cat.

Gremlins was hailed as another *E.T.* It's not. It's in a different tradition. At the level of Serious Film Criticism, it's a meditation on the myths in our movies: Christmas, families, monsters, retail stores, movies, boogeymen. At the level of Pop Moviegoing, it's a sophisticated, witty B movie, in which the monsters are devouring not only the defenseless town, but decades of defenseless clichés. But don't go if you still believe in Santa Claus.

Gremlins II ★ ★ ½
PG-13, 108 m., 1990

Zach Galligan (Billy Peltzer), Phoebe Cates (Kate Beringer), John Glover (Daniel Clamp), Robert Picardo (Forster), Haviland Morris (Marla), Robert Prosky (Grandpa Fred), Christopher Lee (Dr. Catheter), Leonard Maltin (Movie Policeman). Directed by Joe Dante and produced by Michael Finnell. Screenplay by Charlie Haas.

The first *Gremlins*, in 1984, was a meditation on movie myths—on Christmas, small towns, and things that will jump up and scare you. It was a superior B movie and a lot of fun. *Gremlins II* is a meditation on sequels, and like most sequels, it's a faded imitation of the original. Yes, it has some big laughs, and yes, some of the special effects are fun, but the movie has too many gremlins and not enough story line.

A word of background may be in order. You may recall from the original movie that gremlins are the mischievous alter egos of innocent, cuddly little creatures named Mogwais. They're cute and would make great pets, except for the two laws of gremlins, which are that they should never be fed after midnight, and should never, ever be allowed to get wet. When they're fed after midnight, they turn into horrible little monsters like the creature in *Alien*, and when they get wet, they multiply like sex-mad newts.

In the first movie, gremlins took over the small town of Kingston Falls, New York. In the sequel, the heroes of the first movie (Zach Galligan and Phoebe Cates) have moved to the big city, where they work for a zillionaire named Daniel Clamp (John Glover). Clamp, who seems to be a cross between Donald Trump and Ted Turner, if such a thing is possible, owns cable networks, financial concerns, and a giant automated tower so high that passing planes make a racket in his office. His corporate symbol, which supplies one of the biggest laughs in the movie, is a globe that has been flattened out by being clamped between the teeth of the letter C.

Clamp is now determined to evict the ancient owner of the little shop in Chinatown—the shop where the first Mogwais came from. Clamp wants to build a Chinatown trade center. But when his bulldozers roar over the little shop, a tiny creature escapes and ends up inside the Clamp Tower, where, of course, it is fed, gets wet, and turns into a marauding band of vicious gremlins.

At about this point, if not sooner, the movie abandons all pretense of telling a story and becomes a series of gags. Some of them are funny, some are near-misses, some fall flat, and who can debate what's funny, anyway? I enjoyed Christopher Lee's supporting role as the evil Dr. Catheter, who collects diseases and manipulates genes. And Robert Prosky does a nice job as Grandpa Fred, the host of one of Clamp's creature-feature programs. John Glover, who can play convincing villains as easily in a comedy as in a drama, has fun with Clamp.

But eventually the inspiration runs thin. We've seen the first movie. We know the gremlins will pop up when they're not expected, and look ugly, and scare everyone. And we know there will be a particularly gruesome scene (the microwave oven of the first movie meets its match this time in a paper shredder). We know that Galligan and Cates will try to convince everyone that the gremlins mean business. And we know that this movie exists essentially to cash in on the brand name of the original *Gremlins*.

The Grey Fox ★ ★ ★ ½
PG, 92 m., 1983

Richard Farnsworth (Bill Miner), Jackie Burroughs (Kate Flynn), Wayne Robson (Shorty), Ken Pogue (Jack Budd). Directed by Phillip Borsos and produced by Peter O'Brian. Screenplay by John Hunter.

Here's a lovely adventure: a movie about a stubborn, indomitable character who robs people because that's what he knows best. A man should work at his craft, shouldn't he? *The Grey Fox* tells the story of Bill Miner, a man who was thrown into prison in the heyday of the Old West, was kept behind bars for thirty-three years, and who finally emerged, confused but interested, into the twentieth century, where the movie begins in 1901. Bill Miner robbed stagecoaches. What's he supposed to do with a train? He's a whiskey old man, stubborn as a mule, and his pride hasn't grown any smaller during those years in jail. He heads for his sister's place to look for work and a roof over his head, but he doesn't get along with his brother-in-law and he also doesn't much like picking oysters for a living. He leaves. He hits the road, drifting aimlessly, a man without a mission—until the night in 1903 when he sees Edwin S. Porter's *The Great Train Robbery.* That famous movie is only eleven minutes long, but long enough to make everything absolutely clear to Miner, who realizes he has a new calling in life, as a train robber.

All of this could, of course, be an innocuous Disney movie, but it's well-written and directed, and what gives it zest and joy is the performance by Richard Farnsworth, who plays Miner. Maybe you'll recognize Farnsworth when you see him on the screen. Maybe not. His life has been one of those careers that makes you realize Hollywood is a company town, where you can make a living for years and never be a star. Farnsworth has been in more than three hundred movies. He was a stuntman for thirty years. He's had speaking roles in movies ranging from *The Cowboys* to *Resurrection*. He was even in "Roots" on TV. And yet there is absolutely no mention of his name in Leslie Halliwell's *Filmgoer's Companion.* Farnsworth is one of those unstudied, graceful, absolutely natural actors who has spent a lifetime behaving exactly as he feels. I think he is incapable of a false or a dishonest moment. He makes Miner so proud, so vulnerable, such a noble rascal, that the whole movie becomes just a little more complex because he's in it.

There's one scene where you can really see Farnsworth's gift for conviction. It's a love scene with a feminist lady photographer named Kate Flynn (Jackie Burroughs), who is touring the West to document its changing times. Bill and Kate are instantly attracted to one another. And their love scene together is a warm, amusing masterpiece of quiet affection. Miner doesn't deny his age; he triumphs with it. He's not handsome but he's damned attractive, and knows it. Kate Flynn can see that this man has six times the worth of an ordinary man, and adores him. The scene is a treasure, even when you don't know whether to laugh or cry.

The director, Phillip Borsos, is able to make this a human story and still keep it exciting as an action picture. And he gives it a certain documentary feel; *The Grey Fox* is apparently based, to some degree, on truth. That doesn't matter half as much as that Farnsworth bases his performance on how he sees the truth of Bill Miner.

Greystoke ★ ★ ★
PG, 129 m., 1984

Christopher Lambert (Tarzan), Ralph Richardson (Earl of Greystoke), Ian Holm (Captain D'Arnot), Andie MacDowell (Jane Porter). Directed by Hugh Hudson and produced by Hudson and Stanley S. Canter. Screenplay by P.H. Vazak and Michael Austin.

One of the most unforgettable mothers in the history of literature is named Kala, and she is an ape. Some people will immediately know that Kala is the great ape who adopted a shipwrecked orphan and raised him as her own, until he became Tarzan, Lord of the Apes. Other people will not know that, and for them, the movie *Greystoke* may be missing a certain resonance. I think it helps, in seeing this movie, to draw on a background of rainy Saturday afternoons when you were ten and had your nose buried in *Tarzan* books.

Greystoke, the Legend of Tarzan, Lord of the Apes is the most faithful film adaptation of the Tarzan legend ever made. That isn't saying much, because most of the forty or so Tarzan movies were laughable quickies with Tarzan trying not to be upstaged by cute chimps. *Greystoke* takes the legend seriously, and it's worthy of being taken seriously, I think, because the story of Tarzan has become one of the most durable of all the myths of the twentieth century. The obvious challenge for this movie is to convince an audience that it is actually looking at a little human baby being nurtured by wild animals. *Greystoke* passes that test. The movie combines footage of real animals with footage of human actors disguised by the special-effects makeup of Rick Baker, and I was hard-pressed to tell the difference. The movie has an extended opening sequence that takes place entirely in the jungle, without spoken dialogue, and that captures the central mystery of the Tarzan legend as well as anything I've ever seen.

Unfortunately, there's one other aspect of Tarzan that *Greystoke* doesn't capture as well. The Tarzan adventures were all inspired by the imagination of a pulp writer named Edgar Rice Burroughs, who was not a stylist or a philosopher but was certainly a great plotter and knew how to entangle Tarzan in cliff-hanging melodrama. *Greystoke* isn't melodrama and doesn't try to be, and I missed that. After the great early jungle scenes, it has the grown-up Tarzan (Christopher Lambert) being discovered by a Belgian explorer (Ian Holm) who returns him to his ancestral Scottish home, Greystoke Manor, where he meets his grandfather (Ralph Richardson) and also a young lady named Jane (Andie MacDowell). The movie has fun showing Tarzan's introduction to civilization; there's a spine-tingling moment when he growls into Jane's ear. The characters also are well-drawn, especially Ralph Richardson's Earl of Greystoke, who childishly slides down a staircase on a silver tray, and who has a touching death scene that was acted not long before Richardson himself died.

But where's the action? Shouldn't there be some sort of pulp subplot about the ant men, or the jewels of Opar, or a wild elephant on a rampage? *Greystoke* is the story of the legend of Tarzan, but it doesn't contain an adventure *involving* Tarzan. Who would have guessed there'd ever be a respectable Tarzan movie?

The Grifters ★ ★ ★ ★
R, 119 m., 1991
(See related Film Clip, p. 700.)

Anjelica Huston (Lily Dillon), John Cusack (Roy Dillon), Annette Bening (Myra Langtry), Pat Hingle (Bobo Justus), Henry Jones (Simms), J.T. Walsh (Cole), Charles Napier (Hebbing). Directed by Stephen Frears and produced by Martin Scorsese, Robert Harris, and James Painten. Screenplay by Donald E. Westlake.

Con men are more appealing than run-of-the-mill villains, who want to take your money because they are stronger or more dangerous than you are. Con men want to take it because they're smarter than you are. And there is hardly ever a con man who isn't likable, because, after all, if he can't win your confidence, how can he take your money?

Movies about con men are seductive because the audience is on both sides of the moral issues: We want to see justice done, of course, but at the same time we're intrigued by the audacity of this character who is trying to out-think his opposition.

You can see some of that seductiveness at work in David Mamet's *House of Games* (1987), where a woman psychologist grows fascinated by a con man and asks him to teach her some of the tricks of his trade. Does he ever. The con man is sweet and almost gentle as he devastates his victim. In a sense, he really does like her. In Stephen Frears's *The Grifters*, there aren't any outsiders to be seduced, because the three central characters are all confidence tricksters. So they seduce each other.

The movie is based on a 1950s novel, but it's set in the present day. There are a few details that don't translate very well—today's con man probably wouldn't stay in a colorful fleabag hotel, but in a downtown executive suite—but the underlying story is universal. It involves the archetypal triangle of the lover, the loved one, and the authority figure who would separate them. The lover is Roy Dillon (John Cusack), a con man in his twenties, who isn't very good and pulls mostly small-time cons. The loved one is Myra Langtry (Annette Bening), who looks young and sexy, but is probably older than she looks and certainly more dangerous than Roy realizes. And the authority figure is Roy's mother, Lily (Anjelica Huston), who has been pulling cons since a very early age and considers everyone a potential victim. That list would certainly include her son.

Myra has knocked around the country a good deal, working as a sexy decoy for big-time con operators. Lily has an arrangement with a major sports gambling operation and travels from one racetrack to another, placing large bets at the last minute to improve the odds. Roy isn't in their league. He's still pulling nickel-and-dime stuff like walking into a bar and getting change for a twenty dollar bill and then switching to a smaller bill. One day, a bartender catches him at it and beats him up so badly that he almost dies.

It's in his hospital room that the two women meet and unsheathe their claws. Roy doesn't realize it, but he's doomed right from the moment of their meeting, because, for each of these women, it is more important to win than to love, and poor, dumb, sentimental Roy doesn't play in that league. He loves too easily, perhaps, and the movie suggests Oedipal possibilities long before the shocking final confrontation.

The Grifters is the first American production by Stephen Frears, one of the best new British directors. His credit list is short but distinguished: *My Beautiful Laundrette, Prick Up Your Ears, Sammy and Rosie Get Laid,* and *Dangerous Liaisons.* All four films deal with labyrinths of passion, with characters deceiving others about the true nature of their loves. The story of *The Grifters* comes from a pulp novel by the recently rediscovered Jim Thompson, a poet of *film noir,* whose books exist in a world of cynicism and despair, where characters put up a big front but are being gnawed inside by fear, guilt, and low self-esteem. The screenplay is by another distinguished crime novelist, Donald Westlake, and, for once, here is a new movie that exudes the *film noir* spirit from its very pores, instead of just adding a few cosmetic touches to a modern chase-and-crash story.

The performances are all insidiously powerful. Cusack provides a sympathetic center for the film, as a kid with a burning ambition to be good at the con game, but with no particular talent and without the ruthlessness he will need. Anjelica Huston was an Academy Award nominee as his mother, who had this child when she was a teen-ager, and who has never fully accepted the fact that he is her son. And Annette Bening has some of that same combination of sexiness, danger, and vulnerability you could see in Gloria Grahame in movies like *The Big Heat* and *In a Lonely Place.*

One of the strengths of *The Grifters* is how everything adds up, and it all points toward the conclusion of the film, when all secrets will be revealed and all debts collected. This is a movie of plot, not episode. It's not just a series of things that happen to the characters, but a web, a maze of consequences; by the end, when Roy and his mother are facing each other in their last desperate confrontation, the full horror of their lives is laid bare.

Why do confidence operators do what they do? Why do they need to win our love and trust, and then betray us? In *The Grifters,* it's pretty clear that they're locked into an old pattern of trust and betrayal that goes back to childhood, and that they're trying to get even. Poor Roy. He thinks he wants to be a great con man, and all he really wants is to find just one person he can safely love, one person who isn't trying to con him.

Gross Anatomy ★ ★ ★
PG-13, 107 m., 1989

Matthew Modine (Joe Slovak), Daphne Zuniga (Laurie Rorbach), Christine Lahti (Rachel Woodruff), Todd Field (David Schreiner), John Scott Clough (Miles Reed), Alice Carter (Kim McCauley), Robert Desiderio (Dr. Banks), Zakes Mokae (Dr. Banumbra). Directed by Thom Eberhardt and produced by Howard Rosenman and Debra Hill. Screenplay by Ron Nyswaner and Mark Spragg.

Gross Anatomy contains scenes of laughter and scenes of romance, but the scenes that I identified with the most involved performance anxiety. This is a film that follows a group of students through their first year of medical school, and they seem to be taking an examination every ten minutes. The university atmosphere is reproduced with relentless accuracy, right down to the most subtle intonations in the voices of the professors setting the exams and asking the questions. And all of the dialogue has the ring of truth.

Watching the film, I began to ask myself what I was feeling. I was absorbed by the story, I cared about the characters, and yet I felt a growing unease, which I finally identified: The movie was reawakening fears that I thought I had buried years ago, those fears that the final exam was being held tomorrow and I'd never studied for the course, and I was going to fail miserably and humiliate myself and disappoint my family and flunk out of school and get drafted and die.

Because the movie gets that right, almost everything else in the plot seems to fall naturally into place. This is not a movie about medical school or medicine so much as it's a movie about being under relentless pressure. Early in their first semester, the students figure out they have to master about 3,500 pages of material a week, and attend lectures and anatomy laboratory, and somehow find time to eat and sleep. We can taste their exhaustion as they get up at five in the morning and march like zombies through one unrelenting day after another. Their lives are a race between total exhaustion and fear of failure.

There is one student, however, who seems unaffected by the pressure. He's Joe Slovak (Matthew Modine), a bright, cocky kid with a chip on his shoulder, who claims he doesn't care much about his future patients or anything else except making a lot of money. The only thing he takes seriously is his love for his lab partner (Daphne Zuniga), and she's almost too busy to have time for him.

Most of the classroom scenes take place in the anatomy laboratory, where the students dissect corpses with the most minute attention to detail, under the guidance of two doctors played by Zakes Mokae and Christine Lahti. He is a serene African who advises the students not to revise their exam papers, "because your first instincts are almost always right," and she is a stern, unforgiving administrator whose idea of an orientation lecture is to remind the students that medicine is the profession with the highest rates of alcoholism, drug addiction, divorce, and suicide.

Slovak, the Modine character, gets under her skin because he refuses to even pretend as if he cares. He's bright, he gets good grades, but he has an attitude about everything. He's sarcastic, and he insists on always getting the last word. He cares about the other members on his lab team (including not only Zuniga but also Todd Field as a worried loser, John Scott Clough as a compulsive perfectionist, and Alice Carter as an Asian woman determined to finish the year despite an unexpected pregnancy). But he doesn't care about sucking up to faculty members or playing campus politics.

Most of the major events in the movie can be anticipated, but they are played with a genuine grace. I especially admired the scene where Zuniga finally tells Modine, "All right, you've got me," and the one in which Lahti finally levels with her best student about her real hopes and fears. There is not much in this movie that hasn't been seen before, especially on TV medical shows, but the level of the direction, by Thom Eberhardt, gives the material more weight and importance, and the actors make their characters into particular people whose decisions begin to seem important to us.

The Guardian ★
R, 93 m., 1990

Jenny Seagrove (Camilla), Dwier Brown (Phil), Carey Lowell (Kate), Brad Hall (Ned Runcie), Miguel Ferrer (Ralph Hess), Natalia Nogulich (Molly Sheridan), Pamela Brull (Gail Krasno), Gary Swanson (Allan Sheridan). Directed by William Friedkin and produced by Joe Wizan. Screenplay by Stephen Volk, Dan Greenburg, and Friedkin.

Of the many threats to modern man documented in horror films—the slashers, the haunters, the body snatchers—the most innocent would seem to be the Druids. What, after all, can a Druid really do to you, apart from dropping fast-food wrappers on the lawn while worshiping your trees?

That's what I would have said, anyway, until I saw *The Guardian*, a movie about a baby-sitter whose goal is to capture babies and embed them in a vast and towering old sacred Druidical tree, which she apparently carts around with her from state to state and aeon to aeon.

The Druid, who is probably immortal but takes the human form of a foxy British governess, is played by Jenny Seagrove. Even the people who hire her observe that she's too pretty to be a governess. They are a Chicago couple (Dwier Brown and Carey Lowell) who move to Los Angeles after he gets a better job in the advertising business. A lot better: In Chicago they lived in a two-bedroom flat, but in L.A., despite the higher real estate prices, they're able to rent a house by a famous architect (Brad Hall), who even drops in personally to repair the doors. The house is right on the edge of one of those vast deep green forests that we all know are such a feature of Los Angeles topography.

The nanny brings good references with her, and has one of those British accents that costs a lot to acquire and maintain. She also knows a lot about children. She knows, for example, that after thirty days the "baby cells" in the bloodstream are replaced by grown-up cells. This seems to be particularly important to her.

Having established these facts, *The Guardian* then bolts headlong into the thickets of standard horror film clichés: ominous music, curtains blowing in the wind, empty baby cribs, dire warnings from strange women, manifestations of savage canines, and the lot. The architect comes to a gruesome end, the husband suspects the nanny's vile scheme, and about the only original touch in the movie is that, for the first time in horror film history, a chain saw is used against its intended target, a tree.

The Guardian was directed by William Friedkin, sometimes a great filmmaker (*The Exorcist, The French Connection, To Live and Die in L.A.*). His most recent previous film, based on a true crime case, was named *Rampage* and was not even properly released. I saw it and admired it. Now this. Maybe after years of banging his head against the system

Friedkin decided with *The Guardian* to make a frankly commercial exploitation film. On the level of special effects and photography and all that stuff, *The Guardian* is indeed well-made. But give us a break.

Guilty by Suspicion ★ ★ ★ ¹/₂
PG-13, 105 m., 1991

Robert De Niro (David Merrill), Annette Bening (Ruth), George Wendt (Bunny Baxter), Patricia Wettig (Dorothy Nolan), Sam Wanamaker (Felix Graff), Martin Scorsese (Joe Lesser). Directed by Irwin Winkler and produced by Arnon Milchan. Screenplay by Winkler.

Which should come first, your friend or your country? Honest people find they can take first one side and then the other—depending somewhat on which friend and which country. But for the people who were caught in the Hollywood witch-hunt beginning in the late 1940s, the decision meant, in many cases, betraying your ideals, or losing your job.

The House Un-American Activities Committee, convinced that Hollywood was a hotbed of subversion, held hearings into the alleged communist connections of many directors, writers, and actors. Many of them had been members of the Communist Party or its front groups, especially in the late 1930s, when Stalin's Russia was seen as an ally against fascism. Most of those who testified before HUAC admitted their own political activities (for that matter, membership in any political party was perfectly legal, then as now, protected by the Bill of Rights).

But HUAC wanted more than personal confessions. They wanted their witnesses to "name names," to list people they had seen at party meetings, or had heard were party members. Since this was hearsay evidence and the committee usually knew the names anyway, this process did not really further the campaign against subversion. It was a brutal process by which one group was offered public shame and humiliation at the hands of another.

The HUAC members, drunk with the power they had over the rich and famous, gloried in the publicity they got by quizzing big stars like John Garfield, playwrights like Arthur Miller and Lillian Hellman, and directors like Dalton Trumbo. The Hollywood studios fell right in line, blacklisting those people who would not "cooperate." So the classic debating question had become a night-

mare reality: Choose your friends or your country.

Few governmental agencies have been more "un-American" than HUAC, more opposed to what the nation stands for. But red-baiting gave it such publicity and clout that before long, a senator named McCarthy had seen the possibilities, and moved from Hollywood to the really big targets, waving a sheet of paper in the air and claiming it held the names of 500 highly placed communists in the federal government.

Guilty by Suspicion is a movie that tells the story of that time, a story that even today divides those who named names and those who did not. History has vindicated those who refused to betray their principles, but how would any of us have responded at the time—when to defy the committee meant virtual unemployment in show business?

The movie tells the story of a fictional director named David Merrill, played by Robert De Niro as a man who is not a fanatic or hero, but balks at betraying his friends before a group he has no respect for. As the film opens, Merrill has come back from Europe for a conference with Darryl F. Zanuck (Ben Piazza), head of 20th Century-Fox. He has heard things about the hearings, but thinks he won't be involved, because he's no subversive. Sure, he went to a couple of party meetings back in the 1930s, when it was commendable in Hollywood to embrace antifascist groups, but the party threw him out "for arguing too much, I think."

He finds that things are not going to go easily. The studio suggests he see a lawyer named Graff (played by Sam Wanamaker, himself a blacklist victim). The lawyer explains how everything can be handled behind closed doors. All he has to do is name some names, to "cooperate," and he'll be cleared to work on his new Fox project. If he doesn't cooperate, there will be public hearings, scandal, and no Fox project.

One of the names HUAC wants him to name is that of his friend Bunny (George Wendt), a writer. Merrill can't do that. He can't betray a friend that way. And so the Fox project is canceled and he drifts into a nightmare world where nobody will tell him exactly what the rules are, but he cannot find a job anywhere.

Merrill has been estranged from his wife (Annette Bening), but now, broke and needing encouragement, he moves back in with her and their son, sleeping on the couch. He makes a trip to New York, where old Broadway friends shun him when they discover he's blacklisted. He has to listen as Bunny, broken and in tears, confesses that now the committee wants him to name Merrill. And he is the witness to a suicide as a once-famous actress (Patricia Wettig) drives her car over a cliff, distraught by the blacklist.

Work, when it comes, is furtive. Another blacklisted director (Martin Scorsese) has decided to leave the country, and wants Merrill to finish editing his film. A sleazy B movie producer hires Merrill under a pseudonym to direct a Western, then fires him when the secret is discovered. Only the cowboy hero sticks up for him. (This scene, like many moments and much of the dialogue, is inspired by an actual event; Gary Cooper, no communist, balked at anyone being blackmailed into betraying his friends.) Finally the day comes when Merrill has to face HUAC in public hearings. He still cannot see himself as a fighter: "What the hell, maybe I'll talk. I'm tired of not working."

Guilty by Suspicion is not only a powerful statement against the blacklist, but also one of the best Hollywood movies I've seen. The filmmaker, Irwin Winkler, making his directing debut, has been an important producer for years (his credits, often with partner Robert Chartoff, include the *Rocky* pictures, *The Right Stuff, Raging Bull,* and Oscar nominee *GoodFellas*). He has a matter-of-fact approach to the business that feels much more authentic than the glitzy showbiz tinsel Hollywood usually dishes up. Notice, for example, the cool professionalism with which the two directors (played by De Niro and Scorsese) discuss how a sequence will be edited. Or the carefully measured dialogue with which the Zanuck character lays out the choices: Here is a man who has no regard for the blacklist, but also no desire to commit professional suicide.

Guilty by Suspicion is about a period that is now some forty years ago (although some blacklist members did not work again until the 1970s). But it teaches a lesson we are always in danger of forgetting: that the greatest service we can do our country is to be true to our conscience.

H

Hair ★ ★ ★ ★
R, 118 m., 1979

John Savage (Claude), Beverly D'Angelo (Sheila), Dorsey Wright (Hud), Cheryl Barnes (Hud's Fiancee), Treat Williams (Berger), Annie Golden (Jeannie), Don Dacus (Woof). Directed by Milos Forman and produced by Lester Persky and Michael Butler. Screenplay by Michael Weller.

I walked into *Hair* with the gravest doubts that this artifact of 1960s social shock would transfer to our current, sleepier times. In the 1960s we went to angry musicals; now we line up for *La Cage aux Folles*. My doubts disappeared with the surge and bold authority of the first musical statement: *This is the dawning of the Age of Aquarius!*

So maybe it isn't, really, and maybe the sun set on that particular age back around the time they pinched the Watergate burglars. But Milos Forman's *Hair* opens with such confidence and joy, moves so swiftly and sustains itself so well that I wonder why I had any doubts. *Hair* is, amazingly, not a period piece but a freshly conceived and staged memory of the tribulations of the mid-sixties.

It is also a terrific musical. The songs, of course, were good to begin with: The glory of "Hair" and "Let the Sun Shine In" and "Age of Aquarius" and the sly, silly warmth of "Black Boys/White Boys." But to the original music, the film version adds a story that works well with it, airy and open photography, and glorious choreography by Twyla Tharp.

I said I lost my doubts about *Hair* during "Age of Aquarius." To be more precise, they disappeared during Tharp's opening scene in Central Park, when the dancers were joined by the horses of mounted policemen. Anyone who can sit through that opening

dance sequence and not be thrilled should give up musicals.

The original play, you may recall, didn't exactly have what you could call much of a plot. The screenplay, by Michael Weller, remedies that, but not too much. Weller provides a framework structured around the experiences of a young Midwestern farmboy (John Savage) who takes the bus to Manhattan to be inducted into the army and makes instant friends with a family of hippies living in Central Park.

Savage is just right as the shy, introspective kid who feels suspicious of the hippies—and, indeed, of any alternative lifestyle. But he knows nobody else in New York, so he hangs around with these kids and suddenly a vision enters his life: a beautiful girl on horseback (Beverly D'Angelo), a debutante passing through Central Park and probably out of his life.

She comes from an incredibly wealthy family, he learns. They have nothing in common. But she's drawn, sort of, to the easy freedom of the hippies. And the leader of the hippies (Treat Williams, of *Jesus Christ Superstar*) leads them all in a high-spirited invasion of the girl's debutante party. It's one of the movie's best scenes, somehow finding a fresh way to handle the old cliché of the uninvited street people at a millionaire's party.

The movie also evokes the stylistic artifacts of the flower-power time. The love beads and vests and headbands and fringed jackets and all the other styles that were only yesterday, already look more dated than costumes from the 1940s. And it remembers the conflicts in lifestyles, mostly strikingly in scenes between the young black man (Dorsey Wright) who has joined the hippies, and the mother of his child (Cheryl Barnes), whom he left behind.

The movie's final sequences center on Savage's induction, leading to the hilarious "Black Boys/White Boys" number, an omnisexual showstopper. Twyla Tharp's choreography here is wonderfully happy and grin-inducing, as enlisted men rub legs under the table.

This number, like a lot of the movie, is loosely structured around the political attitudes of the Vietnam era, but the politics isn't heavy-handed. The movie's ideas are handled with grace and style. And it's interesting how it recalls *Hair*'s myths of the 1960s—especially the image of the youth culture as a repository, simultaneously, of ancient American values and the new values aborning in the Age of Aquarius.

That this time and spirit could be evoked so well and so naturally is a tribute to the director, Forman. His accomplishment is all the more remarkable when you reflect that when *Hair* first occupied a stage, the Russians were in the process of occupying Forman's native Czechoslovakia, and he was in the process of becoming a filmmaker without a country.

He has since, however, shown an uncanny feeling for the textures of American life, in his *Taking Off*, with its runaway children, in his *One Flew Over the Cuckoo's Nest*, and now in *Hair*. Maybe it's just as well that this version had to wait a decade to be filmed so Forman could be hired to do it. He brings life to the musical form in the same way that *West Side Story* did, the last time everyone was saying the movie musical was dead.

Hairspray ★ ★ ★

PG, 89 m., 1988

Ricki Lake (Tracy Turnblad), Shawn
Thompson (Corny Collins), Sonny Bono
(Franklin Von Tussle), Colleen Fitzpatrick
(Amber Von Tussle), Debbie Harry (Velma Von
Tussle), Divine (Edna and Arvin), Ruth Brown
(Maybell), Michael St. Gerard (Link Larkin),
Leslie Ann Powers (Penny), Jerry Stiller
(Wilbur Turnblad), Pia Zadora (Beatnik Girl).
Directed by John Waters and produced by
Rachel Talalay. Screenplay by Waters.

*"If you remember the sixties, you weren't
there."*—Dennis Hopper

Yeah, but those were the *late* sixties.
Everybody remembers the early sixties, that
season of innocence when a man could be
named Chubby Checker and still be a star.
The early sixties were before the Beatles,
LSD, Vietnam, and hippies. They were, in
fact, a lot like the late fifties, except that the
cars were not as stylish and people were joining the Peace Corps, and in every town large
enough to support a TV station there was a
version of "The Hop."

"The Hop" was the name of the show on
Channel 3 in Champaign-Urbana, Illinois,
where I grew up. It had other names in other
towns, but it always had the same format: A
studio full of pimply-faced teen-agers in ducktails and ponytails, pumping away to mainstream rock music under the benevolent supervision of the local clone of Dick Clark.

Everybody I knew watched "The Hop."
Nobody I knew ever appeared on it. Where
did they get these kids? Did they hire professional teen-agers from other towns? Nobody I
knew dressed as cool or danced as well as the
kids on "The Hop," and there was a sinking
feeling, on those long-ago afternoons in front
of the TV, that the parade had passed me by.

John Waters's *Hairspray* is a movie about
that time and those kids and the sinking feeling. It takes place in 1962 in Baltimore,
where a program known as "The Corny Collins Show" is at the center of many local
teen-age fantasies. The kids on Corny's show
are great dancers, with hair piled in grotesque mounds atop their unformed little
faces. They are "popular." They are on the
"Council," a quasi-democratic board of
teen-agers who advise Corny on matters of
music, and supervise auditions for kids who
want to be on the show.

One kid who hungers to be on the show is
Tracy (Ricki Lake), who is fat, but who can
dance better than Amber (Colleen Fitz-

patrick), who is not. Tracy dances in front of
her TV set and knows all the right moves,
and is tolerated in her fantasies by her parents,
who are played by Jerry Stiller and Divine.

The plot of the movie loosely involves
Ricki's attempts to win a talent show and win
a place on the Council, and the attempts that
are made to stop her by Amber and her
ambitious parents (Sonny Bono and Debbie
Harry). It is some kind of commentary on the
decivilizing eighties that Stiller and Divine
and Bono and Harry, who would have qualified as sideshow exhibits in the real sixties,
looked, in the context of this movie, like
plausible parents. The supporting cast includes various local weirdos, including Pia
Zadora as a "beatnik chick" (I quote from
the credits). If nothing else is worth the price
of renting this movie, perhaps you will be
persuaded by the prospect of Pia Zadora
reading from Allen Ginsberg's "Howl."

The movie carries a social message as sort
of a sideline: "The Corny Collins Show" is
racially segregated, and Ricki and her black
friends help to change that situation, gate-
crashing a Corny Collins night at the local
amusement park. But basically the movie is a
bubble-headed series of teen-age crises and
crushes, alternating with historically accurate choreography of such forgotten dances
as the Madison and the Roach.

The movie probably has the most to say to
people who were teen-agers in the early sixties—but they are, I suppose, the last people
likely to see this movie. It will also appeal to
today's teen-agers, who will find that every
generation has its own version of Corny Collins, and its own version of the Council,
designed to make you feel like a worthless
reject on the trash heap of teen-age history. If
there is a message in the movie, it is that John
Waters, who could never in a million years
have made the Council, did, after all, survive
to make the movie.

Half Moon Street ★ ★ ★

R, 90 m., 1986

Sigourney Weaver (Lauren Slaughter),
Michael Caine (Lord Bulbeck), Ram John
Holder (Lindsay Walker), Niall O'Brien
(Captain Twilley), Patrick Kavanagh (General
Newhouse), Nadim Sawalha (Karim Hatami),
Michael Elwyn (Tom Haldane). Directed by
Bob Swaim and produced by Geoffrey Reeve.
Screenplay by Swaim and Edward Behr.

I was reflecting, as the lights went down
before *Half Moon Street*, that I could not

recall a single bad performance by either of
the stars, Michael Caine and Sigourney
Weaver. Caine's record is all the more
remarkable because he has emerged untouched from some of the worst movies of the
last twenty years with his unshakable self-
confidence and quiet good humor. In a certain sense, it didn't even matter what *Half
Moon Street* was about, or whether it was
much good, because I was so curious to see
what Caine and Weaver would be like
together.

The movie stars Weaver as the wonderfully named Dr. Lauren Slaughter, an American academic who specializes in China and
works for a cold-war think tank in London.
She is tall, smart, calculating, and concerned
with her own advantage. When she writes an
article for the potty general who runs her
organization and it turns up in the *Spectator*
under his name, she doesn't go along with
the program: She lets him know he's a spineless pig. And when she reflects that she is
doing the work of her inferiors for starvation
wages, she takes action.

It happens this way: She meets a man at a
party, and he sends her a videotape documentary about a high-priced call-girl agency.
She looks at the tape, considers the possibilities, and goes to interview for a job. She
is completely open about the whole thing.
She entertains clients using her real name,
and when she is asked at an academic gathering what she does with her evenings, she
replies that she has dinner with rich men.

One night she recognizes one of her clients. He tries to introduce himself as Sam
Weller, but she has read her Dickens, smiles
at that, and calls him by his name—Lord
Bulbeck. He is a government spokesman on
defense in the House of Lords and a lonely
man who lives alone in a large house and says
he doesn't have the time to find sex and companionship through ordinary channels.

That's fine with her. They make love, start
talking, begin to like one another, and,
before long, they have crossed over that great
divide between asking each other what they
like in bed and asking each other how they
like their omelets. There is a certain instant
compatibility between them. They are both
friendly and outgoing people with something cold at their cores, and the device of
the escort agency rather suits them: It provides a
reason why they are in bed that does not
involve such complicated issues as love and
affection.

Dr. Slaughter meets other clients, including rich Middle Easterners who set her up in an expensive flat in Mayfair. She continues to work at the think tank, where she doesn't much mind that certain people know about her moonlighting. Bulbeck gets involved in tricky negotiations involving a Middle East peace settlement, and of course the Special Branch monitors all of his activities. It checks out Dr. Slaughter and eavesdrops on his private moments with her, and that is as it should be.

What makes *Half Moon Street* so intriguing up to this point is the literal and almost offhand honesty that grows between the Weaver and Caine characters. Their feelings are clear, their motives are clear, and with their eyes wide open they're falling in love.

This whole aspect of the movie is essentially the contribution of the director, Bob Swaim, and his co-writer, Edward Behr. In Paul Theroux's original novel, *Doctor Slaughter*, Lord Bulbeck was older and less amusing, and Dr. Slaughter was very alone in the world she had made for herself. The love that grows between the bright young woman and the gentle middle-aged man provides a subject that wasn't there in the Theroux version, and so it's sort of a shock when the plot reintroduces itself.

The plot has to do with Middle Eastern intrigues, spy rings, terrorists, and plans to sabotage Lord Bulbeck's peace initiative. And it leads to the movie's closing sequence, in which we lose the particular charms of the growing romance and find ourselves back in those familiar movie clichés where everything is settled with violence. God, it's boring to have to wait through an obligatory series of scenes until all of the right people have been killed and the movie can be over.

The last scene in *Half Moon Street* is particularly unconvincing, because for a long time this movie seemed so unorthodox that I expected a tough and realistic ending in which at least one of the wrong people would get killed. No such luck. And so I was right: The movie is interesting primarily because of the interaction between Weaver and Caine. Swaim deserves credit for the intelligence and wit of the first eighty or ninety minutes, but must also take the blame for the ending, which is a complete surrender to generic conventions.

Halloween ★ ★ ★ ★
R, 93 m., 1978

With Donald Pleasence, Jamie Lee Curtis, P.J. Soles, and Nancy Loomis. Directed by John Carpenter and produced by Irving Yablans. Screenplay by Carpenter and Debra Hill.

"I enjoy playing the audience like a piano."
—Alfred Hitchcock

So does John Carpenter. *Halloween* is an absolutely merciless thriller, a movie so violent and scary that, yes, I *would* compare it to *Psycho*. It's a terrifying and creepy film about what one of the characters calls Evil Personified. Right. And that leads us to the one small piece of plot I'm going to describe. There's this six-year-old kid who commits a murder right at the beginning of the movie, and is sent away, and is described by his psychiatrist as someone he spent eight years trying to help, and then the next seven years trying to keep locked up. But the guy escapes. And he returns on Halloween to the same town and the same street where he committed his first murder. And while the local babysitters telephone their boyfriends and watch *The Thing* on television, he goes back into action.

Period: That's all I'm going to describe, because *Halloween* is a visceral experience—we aren't seeing the movie, we're having it happen to us. It's frightening. Maybe you don't like movies that are *really* scary: Then don't see this one. Seeing it, I was reminded of the favorable review I gave a few years ago to *The Last House on the Left*, another really terrifying thriller. Readers wrote to ask how I could possibly support such a movie. But it wasn't that I was supporting it so much as that I was describing it: You don't want to be scared? Don't see it. Credit must be paid to filmmakers who make the effort to really frighten us, to make a good thriller when quite possibly a bad one might have made as much money. Hitchcock is acknowledged as a master of suspense; it's hypocrisy to disapprove of other directors in the same genre who want to scare us too.

It's easy to create violence on the screen, but it's hard to do it well. Carpenter is uncannily skilled, for example, at the use of foregrounds in his compositions, and everyone who likes thrillers knows that foregrounds are crucial: The camera establishes the situation, and then it pans to one side, and something unexpectedly looms up in the foreground. Usually it's a tree or a door or a bush. Not always. And it's interesting how he paints his victims. They're all ordinary, everyday people—nobody's supposed to be the star and have a big scene and win an Academy Award. The performances are all the more absorbing because of that; the movie's a slice of life that is carefully painted (in drab daylights and impenetrable night-times) before its human monster enters the scene.

We see movies for a lot of reasons. Sometimes we want to be amused. Sometimes we want to escape. Sometimes we want to laugh, or cry, or see sunsets. And sometimes we want to be scared. I'd like to be clear about this. If you don't want to have a really terrifying experience, don't see *Halloween*.

Halloween II ★ ★
R, 92 m., 1981

Jamie Lee Curtis (Laurie), Donald Pleasence (Sam Loomis), Charles Cyphers (Leigh Brackett), Dick Warlock (The Shape). Directed by Rich Rosenthal and produced by Debra Hill and John Carpenter. Written by Hill and Carpenter.

It's a little sad to witness a fall from greatness, and that's what we get in *Halloween II*. John Carpenter's original 1978 *Halloween* was one of the most effective horror films ever made, a scarifying fable of a mad-dog killer's progress through a small Illinois town on Halloween. That movie inspired countless imitations, each one worse than the last, until the sight of a woman's throat being slashed became ten times more common in the movies than the sight of a kiss.

Mad Slasher Movies, they were called, and they became a genre of their own, even inspiring a book of pseudoscholarship, *Splatter Movies*, by John McCarty. His definition of a Splatter Film is concise and disheartening, and bears quoting: "[They] aim not to scare their audiences, necessarily, nor to drive them to the edge of their seats in suspense, but to *mortify* them with scenes of explicit gore. In splatter movies, mutilation is indeed the message—many times the only one."

Halloween II fits this description precisely. It is not a horror film but a geek show. It is technically a sequel, but it doesn't even attempt to do justice to the original. Instead, it tries to outdo all the other violent *Halloween* rip-offs of the last several years. The movie does not have the artistry or the imagination of the original, but it does have new technology: For those like McCarty who keep records of such things, this movie has the first close-up I can remember of a hypodermic needle being inserted into an eyeball. We see that twice. It mortifies the viewer nicely, just as scenes in Splatter Movies are supposed to do. There are a few other moments of passable originality, as when the killer disfigures the face of a beautiful woman by plunging her repeatedly into the scalding water of a whirlpool bath. But for the most part, *Halloween II* is a retread of *Halloween* without that movie's craft, exquisite timing, and thorough understanding of horror.

The movie begins just where the last one left off—with some of the same footage, indeed. The mysterious, invincible killer (who escaped from an institution earlier that Halloween day) has just tried to kill Jamie Lee Curtis. But Donald Pleasence, a psychiatrist who has decided the killer is literally inhuman, fires six bullets at close range. The killer is down, but not out. As the first movie ended, his body had disappeared. As this one opens, he's on the prowl again, still shuffling after screaming women at the same maddening slow pace.

The plot of *Halloween II* absolutely depends, of course, on our old friend the Idiot Plot which requires that everyone in the movie behave at all times like an idiot. That's necessary because if anyone were to use common sense, the problem would be solved and the movie would be over. So Jamie Lee Curtis and other young women consistently run into traps where the killer can corner them. In the first film, Jamie Lee locked herself in an upstairs closet. This time, it's a basement boiler room. The movie's other idiotic masterstroke comes when Curtis and a young kid are hiding in a car parked outside, and the kid slumps forward and honks the horn, revealing his hiding place. Inspired. The killer keeps coming. He's relentless. So is the movie. It uses the standard horror formula: Cause a false alarm, get a laugh, and then spring violence on the audience. You know how it works. The heroine opens a creaking door into a dark room and peers inside. A hand claps her on the shoulder. The audience screams. But whaddya know, it's only the friendly teenage intern. Laughter. *Then* the killer strikes.

This can get monotonous. But since most of this movie takes place in a hospital, the killer has lots of props to work with. I've already mentioned the whirlpool bath and the needles. Another particularly nasty gimmick is the intravenous tube. The killer uses it to drain the blood from one of his victims. That's gruesome, but give the filmmakers credit. They use that gimmick to deliver the one scene I've been impatiently expecting for years and years in gore films: Finally, one of the characters kills himself by slipping on the wet blood and hitting his head on the floor. Sooner or later, it had to happen.

Halloween III ★ ½
R, 98 m., 1982

Tom Atkins (Dr. Challis), Stacey Nelkin (Ellie Grimbridge), Dan O'Herlihy (Conal Cochran), Ralph Strait (Buddy). Directed by Tommy Lee Wallace and produced by Debra Hill and John Carpenter. Screenplay by Wallace.

There are a lot of problems with *Halloween III*, but the most basic one is that I could never figure out what the villain wanted to accomplish if he got his way. His scheme is easy enough to figure: He wants to sell millions of Halloween masks to the nation's kiddies and then brainwash them to put them on at the same time, whereupon laser beams at the base of the neck will fry the tykes. Meanwhile, he runs a factory that turns out lifelike robots. What's his plan? Kill the kids and replace them with robots? Why?

A half-baked scheme like that feels right at home in *Halloween III*, which is a low-rent thriller from the first frame. This is one of those Identikit movies, assembled out of familiar parts from other, better movies. It begins at the end of *Halloween II*, when the monster was burned up in the hospital parking lot, but it's not still another retread of the invincible monster. In fact, the monster is forgotten, except for a lab technician who spends the whole movie sifting through his ashes. Instead, the plot follows the young daughter (Stacey Nelkin) of one of the victims, who ran a toy shop. She enlists the aid of a local doctor (Tom Atkins), and they retrace her father's steps back to an ominous toy factory run by Dan O'Herlihy. The factory has the whole town bugged and under surveillance, and the factory's guards are androids who crush their victims' heads with their hands.

Like a lot of horror movies in this age of self-conscious filmmaking, *Halloween III* is filled with references to other movies. The friendly motel owner in the company town, for example, is dressed as a dead ringer for Henry Fonda in *On Golden Pond*. The scene where the bugs and snakes crawl out of the crushed skull is a cross-reference, sort of, to *The Thing*—the last movie by John Carpenter, whose original *Halloween* was incomparably better than Parts II and III. But the funniest reference comes when the hero and heroine break into O'Herlihy's factory and are captured. Then the demented toymaker takes them on a tour of his facility, while explaining his diabolical scheme. He's got an obligatory underground mad scientist laboratory, and we know the approach by heart from all the James Bond movies: White-coated technicians scurry around with clipboards, while the boss arranges a demonstration of the weird method of killing that will soon be tried on our heroes. The funny part is that the underground lab is so cheesy. It consists of a few TV monitors on high-tech bookshelves and a papier-mâché mock-up of one of the stones from Stonehenge. (If you can figure out what Stonehenge has to do with this movie, you're smarter than anyone in it.) Next, there are lots of shots of the guy and girl running from O'Herlihy's henchmen. These are all obligatory shots where the man grabs the woman's hand and yanks her along, she of course being too dumb to run from danger on her own. (Cf. "Me-Push-Pull-You," in the Glossary.)

The one saving grace in *Halloween III* is Stacey Nelkin, who plays the heroine. She has one of those rich voices that makes you wish she had more to say and in a better role. But watch her, too, in the reaction shots: When she's not talking, she's listening. She has a kind of rapt, yet humorous, attention that I thought was really fetching. Too bad she plays her last scene without a head.

Hamlet ★ ★ ★ ½
PG, 120 m., 1990

Mel Gibson (Hamlet), Glenn Close (Gertrude), Alan Bates (Claudius), Paul Scofield (The Ghost), Ian Holm (Polonius), Helena Bonham-Carter (Ophelia), Stephen Dillane (Horatio). Directed by Franco Zeffirelli and produced by Dyson Lovell. Screenplay by Christopher De Vore and Zeffirelli.

I had a professor in college who knew everything there was to know about *Romeo and Juliet*. Maybe he knew too much. One day in class he said he would give anything to be able to read it again for the first time. I feel the same way about *Hamlet*. I know the play so well by now, have seen it in so many different styles and periods and modes of dress, that it's like listening to a singer doing an old standard. You know the lyrics, so the only possible surprises come from style and phrasing.

The style of Franco Zeffirelli's *Hamlet*, with Mel Gibson in the title role, is robust and physical and—don't take this the wrong way—upbeat. Gibson doesn't give us another Hamlet as Mope, a melancholy Dane lurking in shadows and bewailing his fate. We get the notion, indeed, that there was nothing fundamentally awry with Hamlet until everything went wrong in his life, until his father died and his mother married his uncle with unseemly haste. This is a prince who was healthy and happy and could have lived a long and active life if things had turned out differently.

Part of that approach may come from Zeffirelli, whose famous film version of *Romeo and Juliet* also played on the youth and attractiveness of its characters, who were bursting with life and romance until tragedy separated them. The approach may also come from Gibson himself, the most good-humored of contemporary stars, whose personal style is to deflect seriousness with a joke, and who doesn't easily descend into self-pity and morose masochism. He gives us a Hamlet who does his best to carry on, until he is overwhelmed by the sheer weight of events.

Zeffirelli sets his film in a spectacular location—a castle on an outcropping of the stark coast in northern Scotland, perched on top of a rock nearly surrounded by the sea. There is mud here, and rain and mist, and the characters sometimes seemed dragged down by the sheer weight of their clothing. This is a substantial world of real physical presence, fleshed out by an unusual number of extras; we have the feeling that this throne rules over real subjects, instead of existing only in Shakespeare's imagination.

Right at the outset, Zeffirelli and his collaborator on the shooting script, Christopher De Vore, take a liberty with *Hamlet*, by shifting some dialogue and adding a few words to create a scene that does not exist in the original: the wake of Hamlet's father, with Hamlet, Gertrude, and Claudius confronting each other over the coffin. In film terms, this scene makes the central problem of *Hamlet* perfectly clear and dramatically strengthens

everything that follows. It sets up not only Hamlet's anguish, but the real attraction between his mother and his uncle, which is seen in this version to be at least as sexual as it is political.

The cast is what is always called "distinguished," which usually, but not always, means "British," includes at least three actors who have played Hamlet themselves: Alan Bates, as Claudius; Paul Scofield, as the ghost of Hamlet's father; and Ian Holm, as Polonius. Holm is especially effective in the "to thine own self be true" speech, evoking memories of his great work as the track coach in *Chariots of Fire*, and I enjoyed Bates's strength of bluster and lust, as a man of action who will have what he desires and not bother himself with the sorts of questions that torture Hamlet.

The women of the play, Glenn Close, as Gertrude, and Helena Bonham-Carter, as Ophelia, are both well cast. Close, in particular, adds an element of true mothering that is sometimes absent from Gertrude. She loves her son and cares for him, and is not simply an unfaithful wife with a short memory. Indeed, there are subtle physical suggestions that she has loved her son too closely, too warmly, creating the buried incestuous feelings that are the real spring of Hamlet's actions. Why has she remarried with such haste? Perhaps simply so the kingdom's power vacuum will be filled; she seems a sensible sort, and indeed everyone in this version seems fairly normal, if only Hamlet could rid himself of his gnawing resentment and shameful desires long enough to see it.

Bonham-Carter is a small and darkly beautiful actress who is effective at seeming to respond to visions within herself. As Ophelia she has a most difficult role to play, because a character who has gone mad can have no further relationship with the other characters but must essentially become a soloist. All of her later scenes are with herself.

That leaves Hamlet and his best friend, Horatio (Stephen Dillane), as those who are not satisfied with the state of things in the kingdom, and Dillane, with his unforced natural acting, provides a good partner for Gibson. As everything leads to the final sword fight and all of its results, as Hamlet's natural good cheer gradually weakens under the weight of his thoughts, the movie proceeds logically through its emotions. We never feel, as we do sometimes with other productions, that events happen arbitrarily. Zeffirelli's great contribution in "popularizing" the play

has been to make it clear to the audience why events are unfolding as they are.

This *Hamlet* finally stands or falls on Mel Gibson's performance, and I think it will surprise some viewers with its strength and appeal. He has not been overawed by Shakespeare, has not fallen into a trap of taking this role too solemnly and lugubriously. He has observed the young man of the earlier and less troubled scenes, and started his performance from there, instead of letting every nuance be a foreshadow of what is to come. It's a strong, intelligent performance, filled with life, and it makes this into a surprisingly robust *Hamlet*.

The Handmaid's Tale ★ ★
R, 109 m., 1990

Natasha Richardson (Kate), Faye Dunaway (Serena Joy), Aidan Quinn (Nick), Elizabeth McGovern (Moira), Victoria Tennant (Aunt Lydia), Robert Duvall (Commander), Blanche Baker (Ofglen), Traci Lind (Ofwarren/Janine). Directed by Volker Schlondorff and produced by Daniel Wilson. Screenplay by Harold Pinter.

The subject of frogs came up the other night. Some of the people sitting around the table had read the stories about how frogs are dying off all over the world. Others thought we were making it up. On my bad days, I am half persuaded that mankind has already made some irreversible error in the management of this planet, and that the frogs are trying to tell us something. Science fiction specializes in such speculations, and *The Handmaid's Tale* is a fable set in "the recent future" when most of the women on Earth have become infertile.

A few have not. To keep track of them and assure that they do their duty for the state, they are rounded up and kept in indoctrination camps, where they are prepared for their role as mothers. A few of them are rebels, especially Kate (Natasha Richardson) and Moira (Elizabeth McGovern). Moira's motivation is particularly strong because she is a "gender traitor," i.e., a lesbian. They try to escape but are recaptured, and then Kate is assigned to the household of a party leader (Robert Duvall), his wife (Faye Dunaway), and their strapping young gardener (Aidan Quinn), who seems destined almost from his first appearance to play the role here that the gamekeeper played for Lady Chatterley.

The world inhabited by these people looks

more or less like our own. They live in suburban houses and drink whiskey in the den and plant flowers in the yard, and somewhere far away a war is raging, which they follow on television. The movie is a little vague about the conditions of the war and the society; this is not a political fable, like Orwell's *1984*, but a feminist one. The purpose is to isolate, exaggerate, and dramatize the ways in which women are the handmaidens of society in general and men in particular.

Childbearing is the movie's metaphor of choice. Children are seen as the rightful possession of a wealthy, powerful couple like Duvall and Dunaway, and of course adoption will not do; the male must father the child himself. The methods by which this takes place are perhaps intended as a satire on the ultimate reaches of the touch-me, feel-me movement; the legal wife (Dunaway) is present during conception as a sort of coach and spiritual godmother.

I am not sure exactly what the movie is saying here. Is it (a) that women are enslaved by their role as the bearers of children, or (b) that poor and powerless women are carrying an unfair share of the burden by having all the kids while the rich women enjoy life? The movie seems equally angry that women have to have children at all, and that it is hard for them to have children now that men have mucked up the planet with their greedy schemes.

For all its anger, *The Handmaid's Tale* is curiously muted. Natasha Richardson's passivity was effective in *Patty Hearst*, where it was required. Here it is a distraction; the role requires someone with a higher energy level—Sandra Bernhard, maybe. Duvall and Dunaway provide the best moments in the movie: he by showing the unconscious egotism of the male libido, she by showing that in all times and all weathers, some kinds of women will gauge their happiness by the degree to which their family's exterior appearance matches the values of society.

There is some melodrama here and there in the screenplay, which has been adapted by Harold Pinter from the Margaret Atwood novel. McGovern and Richardson plan and scheme, and of course Richardson and Quinn fall in love, or lust, and of course when Duvall's sperm goes down for the count, there is a friendly doctor to suggest a way in which the handmaid could get pregnant, even so. At the end of the movie we are conscious of large themes and deep thoughts, and of good intentions drifting out of focus.

Hannah and Her Sisters ★ ★ ★ ★
PG-13, 107 m., 1985

Woody Allen (Mickey), Michael Caine (Elliot), Mia Farrow (Hannah), Carrie Fisher (April), Barbara Hershey (Lee), Lloyd Nolan (Hannah's Father), Maureen O'Sullivan (Hannah's Mother), Daniel Stern (Dusty), Max von Sydow (Frederick), Dianne Wiest (Holly). Directed by Woody Allen and produced by Robert Greenhut. Screenplay by Allen.

Woody Allen's *Hannah and Her Sisters*, the best movie he has ever made, is organized like an episodic novel, with acute self-contained vignettes adding up to the big picture.

Each section begins with a title or quotation on the screen, white against black, making the movie feel like a stately progression through the lives of its characters. Then the structure is exploded, time and again, by the energy and the passion of those characters: an accountant in love with his wife's sister, a TV executive who fears he is going to die, a woman whose cocaine habit has made her life a tightrope of fear, an artist who pretends to be strong but depends pitifully on his girlfriend.

By the end of the movie, the section titles and quotations have made an ironic point: We try to organize our lives according to what we have read and learned and believed in, but our plans are lost in a tumult of emotion.

The movie spans two years in the lives of its large cast of characters—New Yorkers who labor in Manhattan's two sexiest industries, art and money. It begins and ends at family Thanksgiving dinners, with the dinner in the middle of the film acting as a turning point for several lives.

It is hard to say who the most important characters are, but my memory keeps returning to Elliot, the accountant played by Michael Caine, and Lee, the artist's girlfriend, played by Barbara Hershey. Elliot is married to Hannah (Mia Farrow), but has been blind-sided with a sudden passion for Lee. She lives in a loft with the tortured artist Frederick (Max von Sydow), who treats her like his child or his student. He is so isolated from ordinary human contact that she is actually his last remaining link with reality.

Lee and Hannah have a third sister, Holly (Dianne Wiest). They form parts of a whole. Hannah is the competent, nurturing one. Lee is the emotional, sensuous earth mother.

Holly is a bundle of tics and insecurities. When they meet for lunch and the camera circles them curiously, we sense that in some ways the movie knows them better than they will ever know themselves. And to talk about the movie that way is to suggest the presence of the most important two characters in the movie, whom I will describe as Woody Allen and Mickey.

Mickey is the character played by Allen; he is a neurotic TV executive who lives in constant fear of death or disease. He was married to Hannah at one time. Even after Hannah's marriage to Elliot, Mickey remains a member of the family, circling its security with a winsome yearning to belong.

The family itself centers on the three women's parents, played by Maureen O'Sullivan and Lloyd Nolan as an aging show-business couple who have spent decades in loving warfare over his cheating and her drinking and their mutual career decisions.

If Mickey is the character played by Woody Allen in the movie, Allen also provides another, second character in a more subtle way. The entire movie is told through his eyes and his sensibility; not Mickey's, but Allen's. From his earlier movies, especially *Annie Hall* and *Manhattan*, we have learned to recognize the tone of voice, the style of approach.

Allen approaches his material as a very bright, ironic, fussy, fearful outsider; his constant complaint is that it's all very well for these people to engage in their lives and plans and adulteries because they do not share his problem, which is that he sees through everything, and what he sees on the other side of everything is certain death and disappointment.

Allen's writing and directing style is so strong and assured in this film that the actual filmmaking itself becomes a narrative voice, just as we sense Henry James behind all of his novels, or William Faulkner and Iris Murdoch, behind theirs.

The movie is not a comedy, but it contains big laughs, and it is not a tragedy, although it could be if we thought about it long enough. It suggests that modern big-city lives are so busy, so distracted, so filled with ambition and complication that there isn't time to stop and absorb the meaning of things. Neither tragedy nor comedy can find a place to stand; there are too many other guests at the party.

And yet, on reflection, there is a tragedy buried in *Hannah and Her Sisters*, and that is the fact of Mickey's status as the perennial outsider. The others get on with their lives, but Mickey is stuck with his complaints. Not only is he certain there is no afterlife, he is very afraid that this life might also be a sham. How he ever married Hannah in the first place is a mystery; it must have been an intermediate step on his journey to his true role in life, as the ex-husband and hanger-on.

There is a scene in the movie where Michael Caine confronts Barbara Hershey and tells her that he loves her. She is stunned, does not know what to say, but does not categorically deny that she has feelings for him. After she leaves him, he stands alone on the street, ecstatic, his face glowing, saying "I've got my answer! I've got my answer!"

Underlying all of *Hannah and Her Sisters* is the envy of Mickey (and Woody) that anyone could actually be happy enough and lucky enough to make such a statement. And yet, by the end of the movie, in his own way, Mickey has his answer, too.

Hard Choices ★ ★ ★ ½
NO MPAA RATING, 90 m., 1986

Margaret Klenck (Laura), Gary McCleery (Bobby), John Seitz (Sheriff Johnson), John Sayles (Don), John Snyder (Ben), Martin Donovan (Josh). Directed by Rick King and produced by Robert Mickelson and Earle Mack. Screenplay by King.

Many movies start out strong and end in confusion and compromise. *Hard Choices* starts out like a predictable action picture, and grows and grows until at the end it astonishes us. It gives its characters a freedom very few movies are willing to relinquish—the freedom to surprise us by moving in unexpected directions. The movie develops in ways we anticipate, and then there is a startling turning point, a moment when one of the characters makes a radical decision and acts on it, and from that moment on, *Hard Choices* never lets go.

Any review of this film has to be a tightwire act. This isn't a case of "not giving away the ending," it's a case of preserving a crucial surprise so that it can strike you with the same impact it struck me with. The people who released this film cared so little about their surprise that they actually revealed it in film clips supplied to television reviewers. I'm not going to repeat that mistake, because at a time when a reasonably intelligent moviegoer can predict eighty percent of

what's going to happen in a movie, *Hard Choices* is a treasure.

The movie takes place in the backwoods of Tennessee, where Bobby (Gary McCleery), the hero, is a fifteen-year-old kid with good prospects for making something out of his life. His older brothers are into drugs and robberies. When they can't get the drugs they need, their insides fill up with a desperate vacuum, and they decide to rob a drugstore. They take their kid brother along. Everything goes wrong and a cop is killed and the three of them are caught and arrested, and the decision is made to try Bobby as an adult, for murder. There goes his life.

In jail, Bobby is not treated with the brutality that has become a cliché in movies like this. The local sheriff even has a sort of grudging sympathy for the kid. Meanwhile, a woman who works with juvenile offenders hears about his case; she travels to the small town and gets to know Bobby and becomes convinced that he did not want to go along on the robbery, did not pull the trigger, and was, in fact, an innocent bystander. The woman decides to do what she can to help Bobby.

This woman, played by Margaret Klenck, provides the central turning point in the movie. Until she appears, the story has developed along fairly routine lines. After she appears, there's nothing we can really count on. I don't want to say anything more about what actually happens in the movie, or what Klenck does. But look at her performance and you will see great screen action.

I've never seen Klenck before; I gather from the publicity material that she appeared for six years as Edwina Lewis on the TV soap opera "One Life to Live." What she does here is so deeply absorbing and yet so quiet that at first we don't even realize what's happening. She appears on screen wrapped in a cloak of conventionality. Everything is "normal" about her; how she looks, how she talks, how she behaves. And then, gradually, we realize that this woman is a true outsider, a person who works in the system but is not of the system, a person with an outlaw soul.

There are several other good performances in the movie, one by John Seitz, who turns the thankless role of the sheriff into a three-dimensional middle-aged guy with feelings; another by McCleery, as the kid, who has to survive a lot of tense and anguished scenes in the beginning before he can establish the interior rhythms of his character. One role is especially well-written: An intellectual, philosophical drug

dealer, played by John Sayles, who does not remind us of any drug dealer we've ever seen in a movie before.

Hard Choices is a sleeper. That means it doesn't have any stars and was made on a small budget and got haphazard distribution around the country and will never be heard of by most people. No wonder it has a low profile; it's intelligent, surprising, powerful, and true to itself, and that sure puts it outside the mainstream. It's a classic example of a movie waiting to be discovered on video.

Hardcore ★ ★ ★ ★
R, 106 m., 1979

George C. Scott (Jake VanDorn), Peter Boyle (Andy Mast), Season Hubley (Niki), Dick Sargent (Wes DeJong), Leonard Gaines (Ramada), David Nichols (Kurt), Gary Rand Graham (Tod), Larry Block (Burrows). Directed by Paul Schrader and produced by Buzz Feitshans. Screenplay by Schrader.

Hardcore is said to be the story of a father's search for a daughter who has disappeared into the underworld of pornography and prostitution. That does indeed describe its beginning and ending. But there are moments in between when it becomes something much more interesting: The story of a tentative, trusting human relationship between the father and the young prostitute he enlists in his search.

The man is played by George C. Scott, the girl by Season Hubley. They have moments in the movie when they talk, really talk, about what's important to them—and we're reminded of how much movie dialogue just repeats itself, movie after movie, year after year. There's a scene in *Hardcore* where the man (who is a strict Calvinist) and the prostitute (who began selling herself in her early teens) talk about sex, religion, and morality, and we're almost startled by the belief and simple poetry in their words.

This relationship, between two people with nothing in common, who meet at an intersection in a society where many have nothing in common, is at the heart of the movie, and makes it important. It is preceded and followed by another of those story ideas that Paul Schrader seems to generate so easily. His movies are about people with values, in conflict with society. He wrote *Taxi Driver* and *Rolling Thunder* and wrote and directed *Blue Collar*. All three are about people prepared to defend (with violence, if necessary) their steadfast beliefs.

The Scott character is a fundamentalist from Grand Rapids, Michigan—Schrader's own hometown. The opening scenes establish the family setting, at Christmas, with a fairly thick theological debate going on around the dinner table. (The small boy listening so solemnly, Schrader has said, can be taken for himself.) A few days later, Scott's daughter leaves home for a church rally in California. She never returns. Scott hires a private detective (Peter Boyle) to try to find her, and Boyle does find her—in an 8-millimeter porno movie. Can it be traced? Boyle says not: "Nobody made it. Nobody sold it. Nobody *sees* it. It doesn't exist."

But Scott vows to follow his daughter into the sexual underworld and bring her back. His efforts to trace her, through San Francisco and Los Angeles and San Diego, make *Hardcore* into a sneakily fascinating guided tour through massage parlors, whorehouses, and the world of porno movies. Schrader sometimes seems to be having it both ways, here: Scott is repelled by the sex scenes he explores, but is the movie?

That doesn't matter so much after he meets Niki (Season Hubley), who might know some people who might know where his daughter is. She is in many ways like all the other lost young girls who drift to California and disappear. But she has intelligence and a certain insight into why she does what she does, and so their talks together become occasions for mutual analysis.

She has a deep psychological need for a father figure, a need she thinks Scott can meet. She also has insights into Scott's own character, insights his life hasn't previously made clear to him. There's a scene near the waterfront in San Diego that perfectly illuminates both of their personalities, and we realize how rare it is for the movies to show us people who are speaking in real words about real things.

The movie's ending is a mess, a combination of cheap thrills, a chase, and a shootout, as if Schrader wasn't quite sure how to escape from the depths he found. The film's last ten minutes, in fact, are mostly action, the automatic resolution of the plot; the relationship between Scott and Hubley ends without being resolved, and in bringing his story to a "satisfactory" conclusion, Schrader doesn't speak to the deeper and more human themes he's introduced. Too

bad. But *Hardcore*, flawed and uneven, contains moments of pure revelation.

The Hard Way ★ ★ ★ ½
R, 111 m., 1991

Michael J. Fox (Nick Lang), James Woods (John Moss), Stephen Lang (Party Crasher), Annabella Sciorra (Susan), John Capodice (Grainy), Penny Marshall (Angie). Directed by John Badham and produced by William Sackheim and Rob Cohen. Screenplay by Daniel Pyne and Lem Dobbs.

There is nothing very remarkable about *The Hard Way*, except for its comic energy, but the energy of this movie is everything, reminding me of the wisecracking, hard-boiled, screwball comedies of the 1940s, back when they assumed the audience knew how to listen fast. You have to listen really fast during this movie, but what you get is an earful of James Woods in full flower, and Michael J. Fox so hyper he ventilates.

Woods plays the kind of role that, if they hadn't been able to hire him, they would have had to shut down the movie. Who else could play this rapid-fire, angry, violent, foul-mouthed, insecure, sneaky, and lying but lovable rascal? He's the toughest cop in New York, the kind who rams his police car into the back of a truck because he's late for a date. I have seen some James Woods movies I didn't enjoy, but it's hard to remember them—the names of few other actors give you more of a guarantee that you will not be bored and will possibly be electrified.

This time he plays John Moss, a homicide detective on the trail of the Party Crasher (Stephen Lang), a mass murderer who specializes in shooting his victims in the middle of discos, usually after inviting the police to attend. Moss almost catches the Crasher as the movie opens—there's a typical Woods scene that has him hanging onto the door of a speeding truck while the Crasher is at the wheel—but after he's nearly killed, his commander takes him off the case.

What's his new assignment? A Hollywood action star named Nick Lang (Michael J. Fox) wants more authenticity in his performances, and when he sees a clip of Woods in the TV news, he knows this is his man. He wants to move into the life of this cop, to follow him everywhere, to study his methods and mannerisms, to live in his apartment and see what makes him tick. He even gets to be friends with his girlfriend (Annabella Scior-

ra). Woods wants no part of this plan, and informs his commander in blunt and colorful language. The commander tells him it's an order.

This is essentially just another version of the reliable old cop partner movie, in which the veteran is assigned to take a rookie under his wing. But the filmmakers crank up the energy until the movie takes on a life of its own. The director, John Badham, knows how to make genre pictures; his credits include *Stakeout* and *WarGames*. The screenplay, by Daniel Pyne and Lem Dobbs, is clever and funny and provides Woods with some genuinely funny vulgarities. The stunts and action direction, the second unit work, and the special effects are all seamless and exciting—especially a climactic scene that manages to parody *North by Northwest* while substituting a billboard in Times Square for Mount Rushmore.

But mostly what we're talking about here is energy. There is a certain exhilarating, high-altitude buzz you get from actors who are working well at the limits of their ability, and I got it during *The Hard Way*. Faced with a plot that was potentially predictable, Woods and Fox seem to have agreed to crank up the voltage, to take the chance of playing every scene flat-out. They also take some chances with their images, or at least Fox does (Woods has always gloried in his role as a manic killer rat from speed city). The result is funny, fun, exciting and, when you look beneath the glossy surface, an example of professionals who know their crafts and enjoy doing them well.

Harlan County, U.S.A. ★ ★ ★ ★
PG, 103 m., 1976

A documentary directed and produced by Barbara Kopple.

One moment among many in *Harlan County, U.S.A.*: The striking miners are holding an all-day rally and picnic. A big tent has been pitched, and it's filled with people—some of them familiar to us by now, others new. There are speeches and songs and union battle cries, and then an old woman takes the microphone. The words she sings are familiar: *They say in Harlan County, there are no neutrals there. You'll either be a union man or a thug for Sheriff Blair.* And then the whole tent-full joins in the chorus: *Which side are you on?*

The woman who is leading the singing

wrote the song fifty years ago, during an earlier strike in the county the miners call "Bloody Harlan." And here it is 1973, in a county where the right of workers to organize has presumably long since been won, and the song is not being sung out of nostalgia. It is being sung by striking coal miners in Harlan County, where it still applies.

That's the most uncomfortable lesson we learn in Barbara Kopple's magnificent documentary: That there are still jobs for scabs and strike breakers, that union organizers still get shot at and sometimes get killed, and that in Harlan County, Kentucky, it still matters very much which side you're on. And so a song we know best from old Pete Seeger records suddenly proves itself still frighteningly relevant.

The movie, which won the 1976 Academy Award for best feature-length documentary, was shot over a period of eighteen months in eastern Kentucky, after the miners at the Brookside mine voted to join the United Mine Workers. The Duke Power Company refused to sign the UMW contract, fought the strike, and was fought in turn by the miners and—most particularly—their wives.

Barbara Kopple and her crew stayed in Harlan County during that entire time, living in the miners' homes and recording the day-by-day progress of the strike. It was a tumultuous period, especially since the mine workers' union itself was deep in the midst of the Tony Boyle-Jock Yablonsky affair. But what emerges from the film is not just a document of a strike, but an affecting, unforgettable portrait of a community.

The cameras go down into the mines to show us the work, which is backbreaking, dirty, and brutal. We get to meet many of the miners, and to notice a curious thing about the older ones: They tend to talk little, as if their attentions are turned inward to the source of the determination that takes them back down the mine every day. Their wives, on the other hand, seem born to lead strikes. The film shows them setting up committees, organizing picket lines, facing (and sometimes reciprocating) violence, and becoming eloquent orators.

Ms. Kopple is a feminist, and her work includes *Year of the Women*. In *Harlan County*, though, she doesn't seem to have gone looking for examples of capable, competent, strong women: They were simply inescapable. There are talents, energies, and intelligences revealed in this film that could, if we would tap them, transform legislatures

and bring wholesale quantities of common sense to public life. There are tacticians, strategists, and philosophers in *Harlan County, U.S.A.* who make the UMW theoreticians look tame—and the company spokesmen look callow and inane.

The movie is a great American document, but it's also entertaining; Kopple structures her material to provide tension, brief but vivid characterizations, and dramatic confrontations (including one incredibly charged moment when the sheriff attempts to lead a caravan of scabs past the picket line). There are gunshots in the film, and a death, and also many moments of simple warmth and laughter. The many union songs on the sound track provide a historical context, and also help Kopple achieve a fluid editing rhythm. And most of all there are the people in the film, those amazing people, so proud and self-reliant and brave.

Harlem Nights ★ ★
R, 100 m., 1989

Eddie Murphy (Quick), Richard Pryor (Sugar Ray), Redd Foxx (Bennie Wilson), Danny Aiello (Phil Cantone), Michael Lerner (Bugsy Calhoune), Della Reese (Vera), Berlinda Tolbert (Annie), Stan Shaw (Jack Jenkins), Jasmine Guy (Dominique La Rue), Vic Polizos (Richie Vento), Lela Rochon (Sunshine), Arsenio Hall (Crying Man). Directed by Eddie Murphy and produced by Robert D. Wachs and Mark Lipsky. Screenplay by Murphy.

Eddie Murphy's *Harlem Nights* is an uninspired cross between *The Cotton Club* and the characters of Damon Runyon, told in clichés so broad you keep waiting for it to poke fun at itself, but it never does. The movie stars Richard Pryor as a Harlem speakeasy owner and Murphy as his adopted son and plugs them into a plot involving the usual Mafia bosses, crooked cops, and sexy dames. There is not an original idea in the movie from one end to the other.

Or maybe, come to think of it, there is one: The movie is set in 1938 and has all the right cars and clothes for that era, but the dialogue is distractingly contemporary. Murphy and Pryor are famous for their liberal use of four-letter and twelve-letter words in their comedy monologues, but did Harlem dandies in the 1930s speak like stand-up comedians in the 1980s? I don't think so. There was an elegance in those days, a certain public standard of speech and behavior that a rich

black nightclub owner would have observed; he would have acted and spoken like a gentleman.

Murphy doesn't really seem interested in recreating the 1930s in an authentic way, however; like Madonna and the other stars in the recent and even more dreadful *Bloodhounds of Broadway*, he approaches his story more as a costume party in which everybody gets to look great while fumbling through a plot that has not been fresh since at least 1938.

The story: Pryor adopts Murphy after the lad does him a favor by shooting a tough guy who pulls a knife on him. Twenty-five years later, Pryor has prospered and is operating a Harlem nightclub that's pulling in $15,000 a week. That's when a white gangster named Bugsy Calhoune (Michael Lerner) gets interested. Working with a crooked cop (Danny Aiello) and a beautiful *femme fatale* (Jasmine Guy), Bugsy puts pressure on Pryor and Murphy to fork over $10,000 a week in protection money.

Things look bad. But then Pryor dreams up a scheme to invest a fortune with Bugsy's bookies for the upcoming title fight, which the black champion (Stan Shaw) is expected to win. By betting on the white fighter, they'll lead Bugsy to believe that they've paid the black champ to throw the fight—but then the black fighter will win, although not before Murphy and Pryor have stolen all the bet money from Bugsy's safes.

This sort of sting operation could have been made amusing in a movie with more wit and style, but Murphy, the director and writer, moves the plot so laboriously that even the actors seem to be waiting around for something to happen. And there are giveaway scenes that exist only for the purpose of explaining otherwise obscure plot points. The big payoff scene, in which the bad guys are lured to Pryor's house, is not even remotely believable. Meanwhile, the sexual intrigue in the movie unfolds in a particularly nasty way when Murphy and Guy make love—while each one has a pistol under the pillow and is prepared to shoot the other. Wasn't there any way to work a little romance and maybe a change of heart into this relationship, instead of having Murphy blow her brains out while she's still in bed with him?

Eddie Murphy is a talented and funny actor, but like all actors he needs good material to survive. His recent career has been a series of miscalculations in which Murphy's reputation has salvaged lousy material. I know that *Beverly Hills Cop II* and *Coming to America* have been among the all-time box-office best-sellers, but they were movies that hitched rides with Murphy's popularity and did not do justice to his talent. There is a time in the career of every superstar when he seems able to do no wrong. Sometimes that is the very moment when he is sowing the seeds of his downfall. Look at Burt Reynolds, who rode to the top of the charts in a series of dumb movies that destroyed his bankability. People may go to see Eddie Murphy once, twice, three, or even six times in disposable movies like *Harlem Nights*, but if he wants to realize his potential, he needs to work with a better writer and director than himself.

Harry and the Hendersons ★ ★
PG, 113 m,, 1987

John Lithgow (George), Melinda Dillon (Nancy), Margaret Langrick (Sarah), Joshua Rudoy (Ernie), Kevin Peter Hall (Harry), David Suchet (Jacques Lefleur), Lainie Kazan (Irene), Don Ameche (Dr. Wrightwood), M. Emmet Walsh (George, Sr.). Directed by William Dear and produced by Richard Vane and Dear. Screenplay by Dear, William E. Martin, and Ezra D. Rappaport.

Harry and the Hendersons doubtless will inspire a lot of comparisons to *E.T.*, if only because the story lines are similar: Typical American family takes a strange and exotic creature into its home and learns to love it, despite the havoc it wreaks. *Harry* contains a lot of the same elements as *E.T.*, and I enjoyed them, but it lacks one crucial element: awe.

No matter how lovable *E.T.* was, the little creature still possessed a certain mystery and majesty. To look into those wide-set eyes was to perceive a being that had seen a lot more than we had. The movie contained comedy, melodrama, and schmaltz, but it also was possessed of a rare spirit; there was an aura about *E.T.* that inspired a genuine sense of wonder.

Harry, the hero of *Harry and the Hendersons*, is a lovable creature, but he inspires condescension, not awe. He is a Bigfoot, a tall, shambling, hairy creature that the Henderson family adopts after they run him down with their family station wagon. At first he's a little scary, but before long it's clear all he wants is acceptance. And as he has been designed by Rick Baker, he doesn't

look menacing for more than a moment. He looks more like a big, friendly stuffed toy.

I have a friend who likes to introduce himself at parties with this line, which he claims he memorized off of a card stuck into a baked potato: "I've been tubbed, I've been rubbed, I've been scrubbed. I'm lovable, huggable, and eatable." Harry has many of the same qualities. After the Henderson family brings him home, he breaks up a lot of the furniture, the stairs, and the walls, but only because he's clumsy. His favorite pastime is watching TV.

There is a dumb subplot, really dumb, about a professional Bigfoot hunter (David Suchet) who dreams only of killing Harry. Suchet skulks about the neighborhood, hiding in bushes, brandishing his rifle and engaging in debates with an old scientist (Don Ameche) who once saw Bigfoot and now runs a Bigfoot souvenir stand. Another fairly unnecessary supporting character is the nosy neighbor, played by Lainie Kazan.

Indeed, much of this movie is unnecessary. That's because William Dear, the director and co-writer, apparently decided right at the start to make *Harry and the Hendersons* into a predigested sitcom instead of exploring the Bigfoot idea more thoughtfully. If we ever have wondered if Bigfeet exist, and how they survive, and what they think about, we won't learn the answers here: This movie's basic insight is that Bigfoot is a tall Cabbage Patch doll with hair.

Too bad. There are some nice moments in the movie, contributed by John Lithgow and Melinda Dillon, as the adult Hendersons, and by Ameche and Bigfoot. But they're offset by the obnoxious qualities of the Henderson kids (Margaret Langrick and Joshua Rudoy), who seem to be aiming for Drew Barrymore but hitting Dennis the Menace. Little kids probably will like this movie, especially if they haven't seen *E.T.*

Note: Rick Baker's effective Bigfoot costume is inhabited by an actor named Kevin Peter Hall, who thus joins the David Prowse Fan Club, named for the man inside the Darth Vader uniform.

Harry and Tonto ★ ★ ★ ★
PG, 115 m., 1974

Art Carney (Harry), Ellen Burstyn (Shirley), Chief Dan George (Indian), Geraldine Fitzgerald (Jessie). Directed and produced by Paul Mazursky. Screenplay by Mazursky and Josh Greenfield.

Paul Mazursky's *Harry and Tonto* tells the story of a feisty seventy-two-year-old who is carried forcibly from his New York apartment one step ahead of the wrecker's ball. He was happy with his life in the city (apart from the four muggings so far this year) and content to talk to his old cronies and to his cat, Tonto. But life without a home isn't easy. He goes for a while to live with his son on Long Island, where he's welcomed, sort of, into a household on the edge of insanity. One of his grandsons thinks the other one is crazy. The other won't respond because, you see, he has taken a vow of silence. Harry sizes up the situation, packs Tonto in a carrying case, and hits the road. The road becomes a strange and wonderful place for Harry, mostly because of his own resilient personality. He's played by Art Carney as a man of calm philosophy, gentle humor, and an acceptance of the ways people can be. He is also not a man in a hurry. When he can't carry Tonto onto an airplane, he takes the bus. When the bus can't wait for Tonto to relieve himself, he buys a used car and picks up hitchhikers.

One of them is a young girl who becomes his friend. She talks of her life, and he talks of his, including his long-ago romance with a member of the Isadora Duncan troupe. The last he'd heard of her, she was living in Peru, Indiana, as the wife of a pharmacist. The girl talks him into stopping in Indiana and looking the old woman up. And he does so, in a scene of rare warmth and tenderness. The woman, Jessie (played by Geraldine Fitzgerald), has a very shaky memory, but she does recall being a dancer, and in the calm of the recreation room at her nursing home, the old couple dances together one last time.

And then Harry's back on the road to Chicago, where he has a daughter who runs a bookstore. He spends a few days with her, walking on the beach and talking things over. His silent grandson has broken his vow and flown to Chicago to try to talk the old man into coming back to New York. But, no, Harry doesn't think he will. ("You're talking now?" he asks his grandson. "Garbo speaks," the kid shrugs.)

He heads vaguely westward. His young hitchhiker has fallen in love with his grandson, and they think they'll aim for a commune in Colorado. Harry gives them a lift because that's more or less where he's going, but he declines, just now, to join the commune. He gives them his car, hitches a ride with a Las Vegas hooker, is (to his vast surprise) seduced by her, has a good time in Vegas, and, alas, is arrested for having a few too many.

This leads to the film's most hilarious scene. Harry is tossed into a cell already occupied by an ancient Indian (Chief Dan George) who has been arrested for practicing medicine without a license. The two old men gravely discuss recent television shows and the problem of bursitis, and the chief cures Harry's aching shoulder in return for an electric blender. Chief Dan George is so solemn, so understated, with Mazursky's dialogue that the result is a great comic scene.

Harry and Tonto drift on West toward the Pacific, and we begin to get the sense that this hasn't been your ordinary road picture, but a sort of farewell voyage by a warm and good old man who is still, at seventy-two, capable of being thankful for the small astonishments offered by life. The achievement is partly Mazursky's, partly Carney's.

Mazursky has established himself as the master of a kind of cinema he calls "serious comedy"—movies that make us laugh and yet have a special attitude toward their material and American society. His earlier films have included *Bob & Carol & Ted & Alice* and the remarkable *Blume in Love*.

Art Carney has, of course, fashioned a distinguished career for himself on the stage after all those years as Norton on "The Honeymooners." Here, he flowers as a movie star. The performance is totally original, all his own, and worthy of the Academy Award it received. It's not easy to make comedies that work as drama, too. But Carney's acting is so perceptive that it helps this material succeed.

Havana ★ ★ ★
R, 145 m., 1990

Robert Redford (Jack Weil), Lena Olin (Bobby Duran), Alan Arkin (Joe Volpi), Raul Julia (Arturo Duran), Tomas Milian (Menocal), Daniel Davis (Marion Chigwell), Mark Rydell (Meyer Lansky), Richard Farnsworth (Professor). Directed by Sydney Pollack and produced by Pollack and Richard Roth. Screenplay by Judith Rascoe and David Rayfiel.

Sydney Pollack's *Havana*, which is a good movie, tells much the same story as *Casablanca*, which is a better movie. The difference between the two movies is instructive. *Casablanca* benefits from being part of our common mythology; lines from its dialogue have entered into our everyday speech, and Bogart and Bergman are remembered for that movie more than for any other. But look at it again and you will be surprised what a large role the supporting characters play. The very world of *Casablanca* is unthinkable without Paul Henreid, Claude Rains, Sydney Greenstreet, Peter Lorre, and, of course, Dooley Wilson.

Havana tells a similar story, of a man and a woman whose love is in conflict with the political dilemma of their times. It has a similar romantic triangle: The woman must choose between a good man who is politically correct, and a flawed man who seeks redemption through her. There are other parallels: The heroes of both films get a lot of their income from gambling, the actresses in both films are Swedish, gangsters control the world the characters live in. The most obvious difference between the two films—and this is the reason *Havana* is not better—is that *Casablanca* allows its key supporting character, the political idealist, to emerge more fully, and *Havana* sees him more as a backdrop to the stars.

Havana stars Robert Redford as Jack Weil, professional gambler come to Cuba in the waning days of the corrupt Batista regime, determined to find a high-stakes poker game and make a big score. He has a theory that high-rollers get reckless in times of political turmoil. Soon after he arrives in Havana—city of neon signs, garish casinos, corrupt officials and flashy Detroit convertibles—he meets Roberta Duran (Lena Olin), and of all of the gin rummy joints in the world, why did she have to walk into this one?

She is the wife of Arturo Duran (Raul Julia), a Communist with ties to Fidel Castro, who is up in the mountains, preaching revolution over a shortwave radio. Arturo is a good man. Jack Weil, on the other hand, is a cynical man, a manipulator who has played poker so long all his values can be expressed in a five-card hand. Their attraction is strongly physical, and when it appears that Arturo has been murdered by the police, she seeks consolation in Jack's arms. There is a moment when they plan to flee the country together and live happily in America. Then the political situation reaches a head, and Jack discovers that he may have values, after all.

There are so many parallels here with *Casablanca* that it's a wonder the screenplay, by Judith Rascoe and David Rayfiel, based on a story by Rascoe, doesn't credit the original 1942 screenplay. But the parallels don't make *Havana* a bad movie, and indeed there are powerful scenes here, as Redford and Olin make their characters complex and believable.

The central sequence of the film is one where Redford, foolhardy with love and idealism, drives his big Cadillac convertible out into the rebel-held countryside to look for Olin and try to save her from the coming storm. The sequence is implausible, and it's unlikely he could have survived that drive, but it's the kind of grand heroic gesture a story like this requires, and the scene they play together when they finally meet again is one of the best in the movie.

There are other good scenes, many of them involving Pollack's convincing, juicy re-creation of pre-Castro Havana (he filmed on sets and locations in the Dominican Republic). He peoples his Havana with bit players who embody some of the same seedy realism we remember from Greenstreet and Lorre in *Casablanca*. Guys like Joe Volpi (Alan Arkin), who runs the local casino for the Mafia; the secret police chief Menocal (Tomas Milian), who has two scenes of startling power; Marion Chigwell (Daniel Davis), the CIA spook who pretends to be a travel writer; and, borrowed from real life, mob boss Meyer Lansky (Mark Rydell), who washes a lot of his dirty linen in public in a foolhardy scene where he chews out the casino boss while Redford is listening.

All of these characters, drifting through the background, lend color and authenticity to the story. Often they add echoes from *Casablanca*, too, as when Menocal's residual humanity reminds us of the local police official, Claude Rains, in *Casablanca*, or when Chigwell's prissiness recalls the whining of Lorre, as the man who needed a stronger man to help him.

But the key figure in the supporting cast should be Arturo Duran, the idealistic revolutionary played by Raul Julia, and here the screenplay lets us down. Duran, like the resistance leader played by Henreid in *Casablanca*, comes from a sophisticated, wealthy background. He has cast his lot with the masses. His attraction for women is idealistic, rather than physical; women are attracted to his goodness. And it is essential that the movie convince us of this, or the ending will not work. *Havana* did not convince me.

Remember, for a moment, the great ending of *Casablanca*. Movie legend has it that the screenplay was being rewritten day by day, that Ingrid Bergman had no idea whether she would eventually end up with Bogart or Henreid. Perhaps, but of course the movie could only end one way, because if Bogart and Bergman had placed their love ahead of Henreid's anti-Nazi ideals, we could not have liked them, and they could not have faced each other. So it is essential that the Henreid character be seen in a strong, courageous light.

That doesn't happen with the Julia character in *Havana*. Somehow he fails to emerge, to convince, to move us. We know that he's on the right side, we know what "should" happen in the movie, and yet his dialogue and screen time aren't enough to do the trick. Perhaps the sheer psychic presence of Redford's starring role tended to diminish Julia's presence in the movie. Too bad. For the hero's sacrifice to have any meaning at the end, the reasons for it must be clear and convincing. And although our minds may understand why the characters do what they do in *Havana*, there's a way in which our hearts almost believe the lovers should have said the hell with it and jumped on that last plane to Las Vegas.

Heartbreakers ★ ★ ★ ½
R, 98 m, 1985

Peter Coyote (Arthur Blue), Nick Mancuso (Eli Kahn), Carole Laure (Liliane), Max Gail (King), Carol Wayne (Cathy), James Laurenson (Terry Ray), Jamie Rose (Libby), Kathryn Harrold (Cyd). Directed by Bobby Roth and produced by Bob Weis and Roth. Screenplay by Roth.

You can only play the field so long. Then you get stuck in it. You become a person so adept at avoiding commitment that it eventually becomes impossible for you to change your own rules, and so there you are, trapped in your precious freedom. Bobby Roth's *Heartbreakers* is about a group of people like that, a mixed bag of loners that includes a couple of artists, a businessman, a gallery owner, an aerobics instructor, and a model who specializes in telephone sex. During the course of a few weeks, their lives cross in ways that make it particularly hard for each one of them to deny his own unhappiness.

The movie stars Peter Coyote as an angry young artist and Nick Mancuso as his best friend, a businessman who is confused about women and a great many other things.

They've been pals for a long time, through good times and bad, but the one thing they've never been able to do is break down and talk about what they're really feeling. During the course of the film, they both fall in love with a beautiful young woman (Carole Laure) who works in an art gallery, and whose body is available but whose mind always seems to be somewhere else.

These three characters are in a movie populated with a lot of other interesting characters, the sort of mixed bag of people who find themselves thrown together in a big city like Los Angeles. Kathryn Harrold plays Coyote's longtime lover, who finally can't take his irresponsibility any longer and moves in with another artist (Max Gail), who is big and powerful but surprisingly gentle—his character is developed against type, in interesting ways. Jamie Rose plays an aerobics instructor who is attracted to Mancuso, but he is attracted to Laure, although not in a way that is likely to get him anywhere.

All of the threads of these lives seem to come together during one long night that Mancuso and Coyote spend with the busty, mid-thirties blonde who models for Coyote's kinky paintings. She is played by Carol Wayne, who had regular walk-ons on the Johnny Carson program until she drowned in Mexico not long after completing her work on this movie. Her performance is so good, so heartbreaking, if you will, that it pulls the whole movie together; her character's willingness to talk about what she really feels places the other characters in strong contrast.

When we first see her, she's an enigma at the edge of the screen—a seemingly dumb blonde who dresses up in leather to model for Coyote's strange, angry paintings. Later, the two men, adrift and unhappy about their respective love lives, end up in her apartment, and what begins as a *ménage à trois* ends up as her own startlingly direct confessional. She makes a frank assessment of her body, her appearance, her prospects. She talks about what she hoped for from life, and what she has received. There is an uncanny feeling that, to some degree, we are listening here to the real Carol Wayne, the real person beneath the image on the Carson show. It is one of the best movie scenes in a long time.

The rest of the movie is also very good, in the way it examines the complex relationships in its Los Angeles world of art, sex, and business, and in the way it shows how arid the Mancuso-Coyote buddy relationship

is. The people in this movie might seem glamorous if you glimpsed just a small corner of their lives. But *Heartbreakers* sees them whole, and mercilessly.

Heartbreak Hotel ★
PG-13, 102 m., 1988

David Keith (Elvis Presley), Tuesday Weld (Marie Wolfe), Charlie Schlatter (Johnny Wolfe), Angela Goethals (Pam Wolfe), Jacque Lynn Colton (Rosie Pantangellio), Chris Mulkey (Steve Ayres), Karen Landry (Irene), Tudor Sherrard (Paul Quinine), Paul Harkins (Brian Gasternick), Noel Derecki (Tony Vandelo). Directed by Chris Columbus and produced by Lynda Obst and Debra Hill. Screenplay by Columbus.

Heartbreak Hotel is a movie so bad in so many different and endearing ways that I'm damned if I don't feel genuine affection for it. We all know it's bad manners to talk during a movie, but every once in a while a film comes along that positively requires the viewers to shout helpful suggestions and lewd one-liners at the screen. *Heartbreak Hotel* is such a movie. All it needs to be perfect is a parallel sound track.

The film tells the story of an Ohio high school kid (Charlie Schlatter) back in 1972 who has his own rock & roll band. But the fuddy-duddies on the high school faculty don't like rock & roll, so they ban the band from the school talent show. Meanwhile, the kid has problems at home. His divorced mother (Tuesday Weld) is an alcoholic who sleeps with a guy who works at the junkyard. She's also a die-hard Elvis Presley fan. Things are not so great at home for Schlatter and his kid sister, who live upstairs over Mom's business, a fleabag motel. And things get worse when Weld is hospitalized after a traffic accident.

What to do? Well, Elvis himself is going to appear in Cleveland on Saturday night, and so Schlatter and the members of his band concoct a desperate plot to kidnap Presley and bring him home to cheer up Mom. How are they going to get him away from his cocoon of security guards? They come up with a brainstorm. Rosie, the local pizza cook, looks exactly like Elvis's beloved dead mother. So they'll give her a black wig, adjust her makeup, and convince Elvis that she has returned from the grave for one last visit with her son. Rosie, portrayed by Jacque Lynn Colton in a role the late Divine was born to play, sends Elvis flowers and lures him outside his hotel at 3 A.M., and then the high school kids chloroform him and whisk him away in a pink Cadillac.

Once Elvis enters the plot, the movie ascends new heights of silliness. Elvis, played in the film by David Keith (a good actor who doesn't look one bit like Elvis), is mad at first, of course. But then he begins to listen when this teen-age punk tells him he's lost his sense of danger and is playing it safe for his fans, who are mostly blue-haired old ladies. Elvis also sort of falls for Tuesday Weld, and he takes a special liking in his heart for her little daughter, Pam (Angela Goethals), who is afraid to sleep with the lights out. The tender bedside scenes between Elvis and the young girl are hard to watch with a straight face, especially if you've read Albert Goldman's muck-raking biography *Elvis*, with its revelations about the King's taste in pubescent adolescents.

I don't know what Chris Columbus, the writer and director of this film, had in mind when he made it. One of my fellow critics, emerging from the screening and wiping tears of incredulous laughter from his eyes, said maybe they were trying to make a Frank Capra film—*Mr. Presley Goes to Ohio*. Elvis gives Schlatter tips on picking up women, and holds lessons in pelvis-grinding before agreeing to make a guest appearance at the high school talent show. Any resemblance between this behavior and the real Presley exists only in the realm of fantasy.

And yet Elvis fans are a special lot, and will enjoy some of the small touches in the film, such as the name of Weld's motel (the Flaming Star) and the way the movie reproduces the famous jukebox dance and fight scene from one of Presley's aging classics. Some scenes are tongue-in-cheek send-ups of hoary old B-movie clichés, as when Elvis grabs a paintbrush and helps Weld redecorate her motel, or when he says a tearful good-bye at the airport before flying back to reality in his private jet (he reserves an especially fond pat on the head for the young daughter).

I never know how to deal with movies like *Heartbreak Hotel*. Sure, it's bad—awesomely bad, contrived, awkward, and filled with unintentional laughs. And yet I was not bored. The movie finds so many different approaches to its badness that it becomes endearing. The organizers of Golden Turkey film festivals have been complaining lately that they don't make truly great bad movies

anymore. *Heartbreak Hotel* is proof that the genre is not completely dead.

The Heartbreak Kid ★ ★ ★ ½
PG, 106 m., 1972

Charles Grodin (Lenny), Cybill Shepherd (Kelly), Jeannie Berlin (Lila), Eddie Albert (Mr. Corcoran), Audra Lindley (Mrs. Corcoran). Directed by Elaine May and produced by Edgar J. Scherick. Screenplay by Neil Simon.

We know as early as the wedding scene—which opens the film—that Elaine May's *The Heartbreak Kid* was directed with a sure feeling for how comedy can edge over into satire and then tragedy. Both of Lila's parents are determined to give her away. They flank her, each clutching an arm, and attempt to march down the aisle in their living room. But it won't do: The folding chairs are too close together.

The honeymoon which follows is, to put it mildly, a disaster. Lenny begins to tire of his new bride during the drive to Miami Beach. She smears egg salad all over her face while eating a sandwich. She sings the same songs over and over. Somewhat ominously, she has saved herself for her wedding night.

In Miami Beach, disaster strikes. Lila gets a terrific sunburn and is confined to the hotel room, immersed in lotion and pain. Lenny goes down to the beach alone, spreads out his towel, stretches out, and is confronted by his destiny. His destiny is named Kelly. She is a blond Nordic goddess from Minnesota, dedicated to twisting men around her little finger as a form of mild amusement. Lenny is thunderstruck with love and decides on the spot that he must divorce Lila, journey to Minnesota, and marry this creature.

That is the premise of *The Heartbreak Kid*, and maybe only Elaine May and the author of the screenplay, Neil Simon, could make such a hurtful situation funny, and still somewhat true. The movie is about how we do violence to each other with our egos—how everybody does, except for the poor nebbishes like Lila. She does violence only to egg salad. The movie has a way of making us laugh while it hurts, because it makes Lenny into such a blunt object of egotism, desire, and upward mobility.

But in a lot of ways the most interesting character in the movie is Kelly (as played by Cybill Shepherd). She's so inapproachably beautiful that, in a way, all she *can* do with men is tease and taunt them—they're too

hypnotized to treat her as if she were alive and accessible. She has a couple of husky athletes to carry her books, and a rich daddy who'd do anything for her (he's actually helpless when she smiles at him). And, inside, she hungers for love more, even, than Lenny.

Lenny is headed for heartbreak, all right, I don't think he really believes in the possibility of love—not for himself. He's into the acquisition of inaccessible goals; maybe the only reason he married Lila was because she *did* save herself. Now there are new peaks to climb. But Lenny's victories are so lonely; we see him at the movie's end, confronted with the fact that he would rather desire than possess.

Jeannie Berlin (Elaine May's daughter) is wonderful as Lila. She has enough acting confidence to be able to go too far and still make us believe; she can get away with smearing that egg salad around for several seconds after common sense says she should stop. Charles Grodin, as her husband, is good as a kind of Dustin Hoffman-as-over-achiever; in this role we can find the genesis of many of his later roles.

The movie doesn't constantly bow to Neil Simon's script (as most movie versions of his work do). Elaine May is willing to improvise, to indulge (and exploit) quirks in acting style, and to examine social hypocrisy with a kind of compulsive ferocity. It's a comedy, but there's more in it than that; it's a movie about the ways we pursue, possess, and consume each other as sad commodities.

Heartbreak Ridge ★ ★ ★
R, 130 m., 1986

Clint Eastwood (Highway), Marsha Mason (Aggie), Everett McGill (Major Powers), Moses Gunn (Sergeant Webster), Eileen Heckart (Little Mary), Bo Svenson (Roy Jennings), Mario Van Peebles (Stitch). Peter Koch (Swede). Directed and produced by Clint Eastwood. Screenplay by James Carabatsos.

Clint Eastwood's *Heartbreak Ridge* uses an absolutely standard plot, and makes it special with its energy, its colorful characters, and its almost poetic vulgarity. We have seen this story in a hundred other movies, where the combat-hardened veteran, facing retirement, gets one last assignment to train a platoon of green kids and lead them into battle. But Eastwood, as the producer, director, and star, caresses the material as if he didn't know B movies have gone out of style.

He plays a gunnery sergeant named Tom Highway, universally known as Gunney, a hard-drinking loser who has sacrificed everything—wife, family, friends, reputation—on the altar of the Corps. We meet him in a title sequence that seems directly inspired by *Dirty Harry*; he's in a drunk tank, smoking a cigar and telling tall tales, when a brawny giant attacks him. Eastwood hands his cigar to a bystander, creams the bully, and reaches for his cigar again (just as Dirty Harry finishes eating his hot dog after the opening shoot-out).

The opening scene promises his fans that *Heartbreak Ridge* will provide the violent Eastwood persona they have come to love. What's surprising is that Eastwood doesn't let Tom Highway stride through the picture beating up everybody in sight, and winning the war single-handedly. Instead, the movie is more of a tour through Highway's memories, a last hurrah for a combat veteran who won the Medal of Honor when he was a kid, and has been trying to lose it ever since.

Highway gets assigned to his old outfit, has a reunion with the veteran master sergeant he fought with in Korea, and is chewed out by the Annapolis grad (Everett McGill) who now heads the battalion and wants to run everything by the book. Highway is assigned to a platoon of misfits and malcontents, including a bright black kid (Mario Van Peebles), who wants to be a rock-and-roll singer, and a gigantic Swede (Peter Koch), who he is going to have to fight if he wants to win control of his new command.

There is also the reunion with his former wife (Marsha Mason), who couldn't take the weeks and months of waiting at home, watching the evening news for a glimpse of her husband in Vietnam. We can almost predict her dialogue; Highway was always more married to the Corps than he was to her.

The movie has a brisk, rough-and-tumble pace, with a knock-down fight every fifteen minutes or so. Highway may be over fifty, but of course he can still outfight any man alive, and there is one brutal scene in which he stands his ground and simply outtalks an opponent, his words as hard as his fists.

Nothing in *Heartbreak Ridge* is very subtle, and I wasn't surprised to learn that the shooting schedule lasted less than eight weeks—lightning speed for a movie including basic training and combat scenes. There is a certain raw energy in filmmaking at this pace, however; the actors swagger through their roles instead of chewing them, and there is never more subtlety than the plot can support.

It's easy to spot Eastwood, the director, as he cuts corners. The battalion only seems to support two platoons, for example, and its base seems limited to a few quonset huts. Even the climactic battle scenes are budget-basement: Highway leads his men into action on Grenada, where they liberate some medical students.

And yet *Heartbreak Ridge* has as much energy and color as any action picture of 1986, and it contains truly amazing dialogue. Some people may be offended by the scatological and ancestral generalities in Highway's speech, but I was mostly amused by his flights of verbal invention. (The U.S. Marine Corps intended to use this film at benefits for its "Toys for Tots" program, but withdrew its support after screening it, presumably because the characters talked too much like Marines.)

Heartbreak Ridge is Eastwood's thirteenth picture as a director, and by now he is a seasoned veteran behind the camera. He has starred in all but one of his films, and who knows Eastwood better? This time he makes himself look old, ragged, and scarred, with a lot of miles behind him. He uses harsh lighting to make his face into a fierce icon. He speaks in a low rasp. He seems to be aiming for the kind of scuzzy, fast-paced vitality of a low-budget Sam Fuller picture, and he gets it. *Heartbreak Ridge* doesn't aim as high as most current high-tech action movies, but it hits its target.

Heartburn ★ ★
R, 109 m., 1986

Meryl Streep (Rachel), Jack Nicholson (Mark), Jeff Daniels (Richard), Maureen Stapleton (Vera), Stockard Channing (Julie), Richard Masur (Arthur), Catherine O'Hara (Betty). Directed by Mike Nichols and produced by Nichols and Robert Greenhut. Screenplay by Nora Ephron.

Maybe Nora Ephron should have based her story on somebody else's marriage. That way, she could have provided the distance and perspective that good comedy needs. Instead, she based *Heartburn*—first her novel and now her screenplay—on her own marriage. And she apparently had too much anger to transform the facts into entertaining fiction. This is a bitter, sour movie about two people who are only marginally interesting.

The characters are Rachel, a New York writer, and Mark, a Washington political columnist. The originals for the characters are Ephron and Watergate journalist Carl Bernstein, whom she married and then divorced when she learned he was having affairs. In the movie, the characters are played by Meryl Streep and Jack Nicholson, and just by seeing their names on the marquee you'd figure the movie would have to be electrifying. But it's not. Here is the story of two people with no chemistry, played by two actors with great chemistry. The only way they can get into character is to play against the very things we like them for.

Streep seems dowdy and querulous. Nicholson seems to be a shallow creep. Their romance never seems real, never seems important and permanent. So when he starts fooling around, we don't feel the enormity of the offense. There's not much in their marriage for him to betray.

The story: Rachel meets Mark and it's love at first sight, but it's not the kind of loin-churning passion we felt when Nicholson met Kathleen Turner in *Prizzi's Honor*. It's more of a low-grade fever, something to be treated with aspirin—or marriage.

On her wedding day, Rachel takes to the bedroom of her father's apartment and refuses to emerge for hours. Her reluctance is touching at first, then comic, and finally annoying. After the ceremony, they move into a handyman special in Georgetown (affordable because it recently had a fire), and the joke is that the renovations to the house will last longer than their marriage.

There are scenes set in the thickets of Washington gossip, where Catherine O'Hara plays the reigning bitch goddess, and other scenes of domesticity, as when Nicholson wonders why the carpenters have not supplied a doorway from the kitchen to the rest of the house.

Here and there, we see glimpses of the greatness of both Nicholson and Streep, who on an ordinary day with a decent script can act circles around anybody. There's a scene in a maternity ward where Streep comes out of anesthesia and turns to see Nicholson standing there holding their baby. She asks if it's theirs, and the goofy grin on his face is a moment of pure joy.

There's another moment where they sing nursery rhymes to each other. And a moment when Nicholson sits by her bed and cries, because he knows that the flaw in his character will make it impossible for him to function responsibly as a husband and father.

Those moments are adrift in a sea of ennui. *Heartburn* is punctuated by scenes that feel like the director, Mike Nichols, is marking time. Was Bernstein's dislike for the project so great that the filmmakers prudently left out all of the really good stuff? If I were Bernstein, I would rather be portrayed as a colorful rake than as the hapless fall guy in this movie. If they're going to remember you at all, it's not going to be for being unmemorable.

Heartburn not only misses in its treatment of the two central characters, it also fails to give us a real sense of the New York-Washington media axis. The O'Hara character comes closest; I guess she's supposed to be a cross between celebrity reporter Barbara Howar and Washington gossip columnist Diana McLellan. She puts the right spin in her sly reports of the latest transgressions and infidelities.

But Nicholson never seems to be a Washington columnist. Most of the time, he doesn't have much to say. The Streep character is supposed to be some kind of a food writer, but what we totally miss is the manic desperation of the typical New York free-lancer. She seems too placid and laid back. She ought to be pitching projects and trying to get big advances.

When she wrote the screenplay, Ephron missed a bet by not writing in some scenes in which her character meets with a New York publisher and tries to pitch a comic novel in which she rips the lid off of her marriage to a famous journalist. If we're going to base a story on a real marriage, let's go all the way. After we've eviscerated the philandering husband, why stop before we get to the part where the ex-wife violates her own privacy and that of her children in a bid for revenge, the bestseller list and a sale to the movies? And what about the ex-husband's offer to sue? I had the strangest feeling that *Heartburn* ended just when it was starting to get interesting.

Heartland ★ ★ ★ ★
PG, 95 m., 1981

Conchata Ferrell (Elinore Randall), Rip Torn (Clyde Stewart), Barry Primus (Jack), Lilia Skala (Grandma), Megan Folsom (Jerrine). Directed by Richard Pearce and produced by Annick Smith, Michael Hausman, and Beth Ferris. Screenplay by Ferris.

Richard Pearce's *Heartland* is a big, robust, joyous movie about people who make other movie heroes look tentative. It takes place in 1910, out in the unsettled frontier lands of Wyoming, and it's about a determined young widow who packs up her daughter and moves out West to take a job as the housekeeper on a ranch. At first she is completely baffled by the rancher who has hired her ("I can't talk about anything with that man"), but in the end she marries him and digs in to fight an endless battle with the seasons, the land, and the banks.

A movie newcomer named Conchata Ferrell plays the widow, Elinore Randall. She's a big-boned, clear-eyed, wide-hipped woman of about thirty who makes us realize that most of the women in Westerns look as if they're about to collapse under the strain. She is extremely clear about her motivations. She gives a full day's work for a full day's pay, but she is tired of working for others, and would like to own her own land someday. She does not, however, speak endlessly about her beliefs and ambitions, because *Heartland* is a movie of few words. That is partly because of the character of Clyde Stewart (Rip Torn), the rancher she goes to work for. He hardly ever says anything. He is a hard man, a realist who knows that the undisciplined Western land can break his back. But he is not unkind, and in the scene where he finally proposes to marry her, his choice of words contains understated wit that makes us smile.

Everything in this movie affirms life. Perhaps that is why *Heartland* can also be so unblinking in its consideration of death. The American West was not settled by people who spent all their time baking peach cobbler and knitting samplers, and this movie contains several scenes that will shock some audiences because of their forthright realism. We see a pig slaughtered, a calf birthed, cattle skinned, and a half-dead horse left out in the blizzard because there is simply nothing to feed it.

All of *Heartland* is stunningly photographed on and around a Montana ranch. (The movie is based on the real life of a settler named Elinore Randall Stewart.) It contains countless small details of farming life, put in not for "atmosphere" but because they work better than dialogue to flesh out the characters. The desolation of the frontier is suggested in small vignettes, such as one involving a family that could get this far and no farther, and lives huddled inside a small wagon. Among the many scenes that delight

us with their freshness is one moment right after the wedding, when Ferrell realizes she got married wearing her apron and work boots, and another when she is about to give birth and her husband rides off into the storm to fetch the midwife from the next farm. We settle back here in anticipation of the obligatory scene in which the midwife arrives and immediately orders everyone to boil hot water, lots of it—but this time we're surprised. The husband returns alone; the midwife was not at her farm. Quiet little developments like that help expose the weight of cliché that holds down most Westerns.

In a movie filled with wonderful things, the very best thing in *Heartland* is Conchata Ferrell's voice. It is strong, confident, clear as a bell, and naturally musical. It is a fine instrument, bringing authenticity to every word it says. It puts this movie to a test, because we could not quite accept that voice saying words that sounded phony and contrived. In *Heartland*, we never have to.

Heart of Midnight ★ ★ ½
R, 96 m., 1989

Jennifer Jason Leigh (Carol Rivers), Peter Coyote (Sharpe/Larry), Gale Mayron (Sonny), Sam Schacht (Fletcher), Denise Dummont (Mariana), Frank Stallone (Ledray), Brenda Vaccaro (Carol's Mother). Directed by Matthew Chapman and produced by Andrew Gaty. Screenplay by Chapman.

Heart of Midnight is a horror film that descends into the depths of bizarre sexual behavior for no better reason than to see what it will find there. It finds a lot. The film opens with Carol, a troubled young woman, moving into Midnight, a shuttered nightclub willed to her by her uncle, a mysterious figure who has disappeared. She hopes to reopen the club as an elegant night spot, even though the street it's on looks like a war zone, populated mostly by layouts and sex fiends.

Carol, played by Jennifer Jason Leigh, has pluck. She hires some workmen and sets about remodeling the main room of the club, even while she wonders what lurks behind the locked doors in the red corridor upstairs. At nights, alone in the building, she is haunted by strange noises and unexplained events, and by nightmares left over from a troubled childhood. Then a bunch of keys mysteriously appears outside her room, and as she opens the locked doors she finds that she has inherited a brothel in which every room was decorated to cater to a different kinky taste.

She sets to work rehabilitating the club. Daytimes are filled with the ominous presence of the workmen, who devote themselves to using large power saws in order to make deafening noises whenever she tries to give instructions. Nights are filled with false alarms, and then by a rape attempt when some of the local louts break in. Her only comfort comes when a stranger (Peter Coyote) materializes in the club. He says he's the detective assigned to investigate the break-in. Well, maybe he is.

Flashbacks reveal that Carol has lived on the edge of insanity since childhood, has survived two nervous breakdowns, and believes that "making a go" of the club is her only hope of learning to cope with life. Besides, she tells Coyote, "I've always dreamed of running a sophisticated place, smoking cigarettes, leaning on the bar, firing the bartender if I don't like the way he operates." Coyote seems to be the only person in her life who believes she can achieve these dreams.

Heart of Midnight was written and directed by Matthew Chapman, whose previous film was the effective *Stranger's Kiss*. That one told the story of a director (Coyote) making a movie with mob money and falling in love with his leading lady, the mobster's girlfriend. Coyote lived, or lurked, in an aerie high up under the roof of the sound stage where he was working, and there also seem to be hiding spaces and hidden living quarters in the nightclub in *Midnight*. Maybe Chapman likes the idea of secret rooms and voyeurism.

A lot of secrets are unveiled before the end of *Heart of Midnight*, which it would be unfair to reveal, although I was intrigued by one character, a girl raised as a boy for reasons that the movie hints were thoroughly perverse. While such discoveries are indeed disturbing, much of *Heart of Midnight* is simply silliness, devoting itself to a series of false alarms in which strange noises mean nothing, and Carol is always having to calm herself after her imagination runs away with her.

Other moments, however, are more gruesome, and as the mystery deepens, we realize that Peter Coyote is gifted at acting friendly while projecting danger. Jennifer Jason Leigh is at the center of most of the scenes, looking young and vulnerable, and doing a fairly good job of not overplaying the melo-

drama. Chapman is a better director than he is a writer, and if the movie finally reveals itself as an overwrought shaggy-dog story, the visuals and the use of the Midnight nightclub set do show that Chapman has a gift for atmosphere and suspense. I am not sure he knows where he's going with this film, but he gets there in style.

Hearts of Darkness ★ ★ ★ ½
NO MPAA RATING, 97 m., 1991

Featuring Francis Ford Coppola, Eleanor Coppola, Martin Sheen, Marlon Brando, Dennis Hopper, and Robert Duvall. A documentary directed and written by Fax Bahr and George Hickenlooper, with footage and commentary by Eleanor Coppola.

The making of a film has never been documented with more penetration and truth than in *Hearts of Darkness*, which chronicles the agony and the ecstasy of Francis Ford Coppola's *Apocalypse Now*. That is because no other documentary has ever had access to materials that are normally off limits: shots that were never used, scenes that were abandoned, private arguments between the director and his actors, cries for help and confessions of despair, and even conversations between Coppola and his wife that she secretly tape-recorded.

The film strips Coppola bare of all defenses and yet reveals him as a great and brave filmmaker. It also reveals the ordeal he put his actors and crew through, on location in the Philippines, and what he endured at their hands. We see a drunken and bloodied Martin Sheen improvising a breakdown while the room is charged with the possibility that he will attack Coppola or his camera. Sheen being given first aid after a serious heart attack. Coppola screaming in outrage that Sheen's condition has been leaked to the trade papers and the news could pull the plug on the production: "Even if he dies, I don't want to hear anything but good news until it comes from me." Dennis Hopper, his mind adrift on drugs, unable to remember his lines and yet improvising brilliantly. Marlon Brando, at $1 million a week, turning up without preparation and engaging in endless debates with Coppola about his character. Brando beginning a scene, then wandering off while the camera is still running, and mumbling, ". . . and that's all the dialogue I can think of today."

Apocalypse Now premiered in 1979 at Cannes, shared the Palme d'Or, and went on to become one of the great mythic productions in film history. It told a story about Vietnam that was inspired by Joseph Conrad's great novella *Heart of Darkness*, about a journey up the Congo River in search of a man named Kurtz. In the film, Sheen commands a Navy patrol boat that penetrates a Vietnamese river in search of Colonel Kurtz (Brando), who has set himself up as the god of a tribe of jungle Indians.

Apocalypse Now is one of the greatest films ever made, and legends have grown up around it. Coppola, at a tumultuous press conference at Cannes in 1979, famously said, "My film is not about Vietnam. My film *is* Vietnam." He also confessed he did not think the ending worked. Now we see what he was talking about.

The script, written by John Milius and originally set to be directed by George Lucas, went through so many changes that finally Coppola was writing it as he shot it, and actors were improvising. The production was bedeviled by monsoons, destroyed sets, huge cost overruns, health problems, and logistical nightmares, as when the Philippine government of Ferdinand Marcos tried to rent Coppola the same helicopters it was using to fight rebels ten miles away. Brando put Coppola under enormous pressure by turning up without having read *Heart of Darkness* and refusing to be shot except in shadow.

And Coppola, in conversations he did not know were being recorded, shouted in despair to his wife, Eleanor: "I tell you from the bottom of my heart that I am making a bad film." And again, "We are all lost. I have no idea where to go with this."

Yet Coppola's vision somehow remained secure. Milius, flown to the Philippines by a desperate United Artists to try to bring sanity back to the script, remembers that he walked in prepared to convince Coppola that the war was lost and they had to salvage what they could. After ninety minutes, he says, "Francis had me convinced this would be the first film to win the Nobel Prize."

Hearts of Darkness, written and directed by Fax Bahr and George Hickenlooper, is based on documentary footage that Eleanor Coppola shot at the time, and on recent interviews with both Coppolas, plus Milius, Lucas, and actors Martin Sheen, Frederic Forrest, Robert Duvall, Dennis Hopper, Timothy Bottoms, and Larry Fishburne, who incredibly was only fourteen when he played one of the patrol boat crew. Eleanor's secret tape recordings were also made available, and the result is fascinating, harrowing film history. We feel for once we are witnessing the true story of how a movie got made. *See also* Burden of Dreams, *Les Blank's documentary about the no-less-legendary filming of Werner Herzog's Fitzcarraldo.*

Heat and Dust ★ ★ ★
R, 130 m., 1983

Julie Christie (Anne), Zakir Hussain (Inder Lal), Greta Scacchi (Olivia), Shashi Kapoor (The Nawab). Directed by James Ivory and produced by Ismail Merchant. Screenplay by Ruth Prawer Jhabvala.

Forster suggested in *A Passage to India* that the subcontinent would forever be beyond the understanding of Western minds, and that attempts to impose European ways upon it were bound to be futile and likely to be ridiculous. *Heat and Dust* makes the same argument by telling us two love stories, one set in the 1920s, the other set in the present day.

The heroine of the earlier love story is Olivia Rivers (Greta Scacchi), a free spirit whose independent ways do not fit in with the hidebound values of the British. Her husband demands that she conform, that she stay with the other British wives, share their values and interests, and keep India itself at arm's length. Olivia does not see it that way. She explores on her own. She becomes fascinated by India. Eventually she has an affair with the local Nawab (Shashi Kapoor), who is beguiling, attractive, cheerfully sophisticated, and possibly a murderer. When she becomes pregnant with his child, the whole fabric of British-Indian relationships is torn, because—depending on the point of view—*both* of the lovers have lowered themselves.

The second love story involves Olivia's great-niece, Anne (Julie Christie). Fascinated by hints about the long-ago family scandal, she follows Olivia's footsteps out to India and does her own exploring and has her own affair. There comes a moment in the movie when we realize, with a little shock, what the movie is really about. It's an effective scene; soon after Anne arrives at a decision about her own pregnancy, she visits the isolated cottage where the disgraced Olivia went to spend her confinement.

As Anne dreamily moves among the memories of the past, we realize that India and England, the East and the West, are not quite the issues here: that both women were made social outcasts from both societies in two different periods, simply because of biological facts. East is East and West is West, and never the twain shall meet—except possibly in a shared enthusiasm for sexist double standards.

Heat and Dust contains wonderful sights and sounds and textures. It is seductive, treating both of its love stories with seriousness; these are not romances, but decisions to dissent. It is fully at home in its times and places (the director, James Ivory, and the producer, Ismail Merchant, have spent twenty years making films about the British in India). And when it is over, we're a little surprised to find that it is angry, too. Angry that women of every class and every system, women British and Indian, women of the 1920s and of the 1980s, are always just not quite the same caste as men.

Heathers ★ ★ ¹/₂
R, 102 m., 1989

Winona Ryder (Veronica), Christian Slater (J.D.), Shannen Doherty (Heather Duke), Lisanne Falk (Heather McNamara), Kim Walker (Heather Chandler), Penelope Milford (Pauline), Glenn Shadix (Mr. Ripper). Directed by Michael Lehmann and produced by Denise Di Novi. Screenplay by Daniel Waters.

I approach *Heathers* as a traveler in an unknown country, one who does not speak the language or know the customs, and can judge the natives only by taking them at their word. The movie is a morbid comedy about peer pressure in high school, about teen-age suicide, and about the deadliness of cliques that not only exclude but also maim and kill. Life was simpler when I was in high school. "Teen-agers don't have any trouble with it," the film's director, Michael Lehmann, has said of the movie. "It's always adults that are shocked." This statement is intended, I assume, in praise of teen-agers. Adulthood could be defined as the process of learning to be shocked by things that do not shock teen-agers, but that is not a notion that has occurred to Mr. Lehmann.

In his film, the heroine is so appalled by the snobbish behavior of her friends that she joins in a plot to murder them and disguise the deaths as suicides. What sets *Heathers* apart from less intelligent teen-age movies is that it has a point of view toward this subject matter—a bleak, macabre, and bitingly satirical one. I imagine the film will indeed shock some adults with its cold-blooded treatment of death among the young, but after having weathered the eight-part *Friday the 13th* series and countless other Dead Teen-ager Movies, I have grown so hardened to the sight of adolescent movie corpses that this film seems only a little more cynical than most.

The title refers to a clique of four girls in an Ohio high school, three of them named Heather and the fourth (the good one) named Veronica. The girls form their own sadistic pecking order, make fun of socially unacceptable students, and carry out a reign of psychic terror. Veronica (Winona Ryder) is appalled by the behavior of her clique, but keeps her opinion to herself—until she falls in love with a rebel named J.D. (Christian Slater).

He rides a motorbike, wears leather, and stands completely outside the high school mainstream. And so, of course, Veronica keeps their affair a secret. It would destroy her social standing. When J.D. discovers her hidden loathing for the values of her friends, he suggests in a deceptively mild way that they devise a plot to murder Heather No. 1. Veronica goes along with his plan, probably because she doesn't take it very seriously. But when the first Heather is found dead—and the murder is successfully palmed off as a suicide—she is indeed shocked. She is not, however, so shocked that she breaks up with J.D., a smooth talker who seductively plays mind games with her.

The underlying dynamic in *Heathers* comes out of movies like *Bonnie and Clyde*, where the lovers back into crime almost absent-mindedly, using it as a backdrop for the truly important things in their lives. Another movie that comes to mind is *River's Edge*, based on the true story of a teen-ager who killed his girlfriend and then displayed her body to his friends, who did not inform authorities for three days.

Heathers applies, however, a completely different tone to its material. The movie is shot in bright colors and set in a featherweight high school environment in which dumb sight gags are allowed to coexist with the heavy stuff.

For a long time, we're not even sure of the point of view: Is this a black comedy about murder, or just a cynical morality play? The traveler in the foreign country is not sure, but he knows the film inspires thought, and has the ability to shock—two qualities that make it worth considering. Maybe it's true that teen-agers will understand it best. Maybe it's even true that they deserve to.

Heaven's Gate ½ ★
R, 220 m., 1981

Kris Kristofferson (Averill), Christopher Walken (Champion), John Hurt (Irvine), Sam Waterston (Canton), Brad Dourif (Eggleston), Isabelle Huppert (Ella), Joseph Cotten (Reverend Doctor), Jeff Bridges (John), Gordana Rashovich (Widow Kovach). Directed by Michael Cimino and produced by Joann Carelli. Screenplay by Cimino.

We begin with a fundamental question: Why is *Heaven's Gate* so painful and unpleasant to look at? I'm not referring to its content, but to its actual visual texture: This is one of the ugliest films I believe I have ever seen. Its director, Michael Cimino, opens his story at Harvard, continues it in Montana, and closes it aboard a ship. And yet a grim industrial pall hangs low over everything. There are clouds and billows of dirty yellow smoke in every shot that can possibly justify it, and when he runs out of smoke he gives us fog and such incredible amounts of dust that there are whole scenes where we can barely see anything. That's not enough. Cimino also shoots his picture in a maddening soft focus that makes the people and places in this movie sometimes almost impossible to *see*. And then he goes after the colors. There's not a single primary color in this movie, only dingy washed-out sepia tones.

I know, I know: He's trying to demystify the West, and all those other things hotshot directors try to do when they don't really want to make a Western. But this movie is a study in wretched excess. It is so smoky, so dusty, so foggy, so unfocused and so brownish yellow that you want to try Windex on the screen. A director is in deep trouble when we do not even enjoy the primary act of looking at his picture.

But Cimino's in deeper trouble still. *Heaven's Gate* has, of course, become a notorious picture, a boondoggle that cost something like $36 million and was yanked out of its New York opening run after the critics ran gagging from the theater. Its running time, at that point, was more than four hours. Perhaps length was the problem? Cimino went back to the editing room, while a United Art-

ists executive complained that the film had been "destroyed" by an unfairly negative review by *New York Times* critic Vincent Canby. Brother Canby was only doing his job. If the film was formless at four hours, it was insipid at 140 minutes. At either length it is so incompetently photographed and edited that there are times when we are not even sure which character we are looking at. Christopher Walken is in several of the initial Western scenes before he finally gets a close-up and we see who he is. John Hurt wanders through various scenes to no avail. Kris Kristofferson is the star of the movie, and is never allowed to generate enough character for us to miss him, should he disappear.

The opening scenes are set at Harvard (well, they were actually shot in England, but never mind). They show Kristofferson, Hurt, and other idealistic young men graduating in 1870 and setting off to civilize a nation. Kristofferson decides to go West, to help develop the territory. He explains this decision in a narration, and the movie might have benefited if he'd narrated the whole thing, explaining as he went along. Out West, as a lawman, he learns of a plot by the cattlebreeders' association to hire a private army and assassinate 125 newly arrived European immigrants who are, it is claimed, anarchists, killers, and thieves. Most of the movie will be about this plot, Kristofferson's attempts to stop it, Walken's involvement in it, and the involvement of both Kristofferson and Walken in the private life of a young Montana madam (Isabelle Huppert).

In a movie where nothing is handled well, the immigrants are handled very badly. Cimino sees them as a mob. They march onscreen, babble excitedly in foreign tongues, and rush off wildly in all directions. By the movie's end, we can identify only one of them for sure. She is the Widow Kovach, whose husband was shot dead near the beginning of the film. That makes her the emblem of the immigrants' suffering. Every time she steps forward out of the mob, somebody respectfully murmurs "Widow Kovach!" in the subtitles. While the foreigners are hanging onto Widow Kovach's every insight, the cattlemen are holding meetings in private clubs and offering to pay their mercenaries $5 a day plus expenses and $50 for every other foreigner shot or hung. I am sure of those terms because they are repeated endlessly throughout a movie that cares to make almost nothing else clear.

The ridiculous scenes are endless. Sam-

ples: Walken, surrounded by gunmen and trapped in a burning cabin, scribbles a farewell note in which he observes that he is trapped in the burning cabin, and then he signs his full name so that there will be no doubt who the note was from. Kristofferson, discovering Huppert being gang-raped by several men, leaps in with six-guns in both hands and shoots all the men, including those aboard Huppert, without injuring her. In a big battle scene, men make armored wagons out of logs and push them forward into the line of fire, even though anyone could ride around behind and shoot them. There is more. There is much more. It all adds up to a great deal less. This movie is $36 million thrown to the winds. It is the most scandalous cinematic waste I have ever seen, and remember, I've seen *Paint Your Wagon*.

Henry and June ★ ★ ★
NC-17, 134 m., 1990

Fred Ward (Henry Miller), Uma Thurman (June Miller), Maria de Medeiros (Anais Nin), Richard E. Grant (Hugo), Kevin Spacey (Osborn), Jean-Philippe Ecoffey (Eduardo). Directed by Philip Kaufman and produced by Peter Kaufman. Screenplay by Philip Kaufman and Rose Kaufman.

Henry Miller was the most notorious author of his generation, but unlike his predecessors in scandal like Lawrence and Joyce there was always some doubt about the quality of his writing. Yes, he was dirty, but was he very good? The irony about *Henry and June*, this odd film about Miller and his wife and the triangle they formed for a time with Anais Nin, is that circumstances force me to put the question in the opposite way: Yes, it's good, but is it very dirty?

This is the film that finally inspired the revision of the American movie ratings, and was the first film assigned to the new category of NC-17—admission limited to adults only. Why? Not because of its sexual content, I suspect, so much as because of the matter-of-fact way it accepts the unconventional sexual maneuvering of its three couples. Americans seem more comfortable with sex when it's lurid and thrill-soaked, as in the R-rated works of David Lynch. When adults are seen freely and calmly making unorthodox sexual decisions, we get all aflutter: Good heavens, they're taking this for granted!

Censors by their nature are happier with

sex when it is presented as sin, with red neon signs flickering through the slats on the window, and the music panting with passion. That shows the artists think their material is as excitingly immoral as the censors do. When an artist presents sexual material in an everyday manner, however, censors are offended, because that makes their jobs seem like less of a big deal. So they grow grave and perturbed, and we get the NC-17 rating when, for this film, an R would have been just fine.

What we have here is essentially a story of innocents abroad. Miller was the quintessential expatriate in that he never really felt at home anywhere except in America, and his restlessness in Paris, his astonishment at the sexual freedoms of the French, always seemed a little like the reaction of the proverbial farm boy in gay Paree. Read his books and you will find them dripping with the wonderful American qualities of enthusiasm, exaggeration, naivete, and envy. Read between the lines of his scenes of sexual descriptions, his breathless accounts of the exploits of his inexhaustible hero, and you will find a soldier boy writing home to his pals that they sure got a lot of loose wimmen in Paree.

Philip Kaufman's *Henry and June* is based loosely on a period in the 1930s when Miller fell into the orbit of Anais Nin, the great free spirit of her Parisian literary generation, the inexhaustable diarist who seldom had an unrecorded experience and who indeed, is seen here writing journal entries while between the sheets, if not literally while engaged in the acts she is recording.

Miller was in Paris with the intention of becoming a great author, pure and simple, and he rented a garret and filled it with the sound of typewriting and clouds of cigarette smoke, which is what all writers were then required to do. In between, he hung out in cafés and moved in bohemian circles and became an intellectual—which is the word for someone whose primary activity consists of describing his secondary activities.

Miller was married at the time to June, an American expected in Paris momentarily, but he had an affair, or sort of an affair, with Nin, and then when June arrived, she and Anais got along very well and Miller, for a time, formed the third part of the triangle. What they did in bed, doubly and triply, is depicted by Kaufman in scenes of wit and some restraint; this is not a "sex film," which is why the tarnished X-rating would have been so wrong for it.

Fred Ward is at the center of the film. He is an actor who specializes in being particularly American, and in films like *The Right Stuff, Uforia,* and *Miami Blues,* he has provided the kind of open-eyed, virile innocence that Miller projected in many of his books. If he does not always seem at home in *Henry and June,* perhaps it is because it is almost impossible to play a writer. Either you show him not writing, which misses the point, or you show him typing away furiously and racing into cafés with his manuscript, which makes him seem like some nutty kid you knew in high school.

June is played by Uma Thurman, from *Dangerous Liaisons,* as an enigma: How did she get to be so much cooler and more worldly than Miller, and what does she really think about her husband? Anais Nin is played by Maria De Medeiros, petite and large-eyed, absorbed in herself, a mystery, seeking material, it almost seems, as fodder for her journals. The three characters and their friends meet, talk, love, talk, argue, talk, are hurt, shift their loyalties, and in general seem to be test-driving new experiences. They lead the kinds of lives that make them seem very grown-up at the time, and very young later.

Henry and June is likely to be a little puzzling for those not familiar with Nin and Miller. It's hard to find the purpose of the film, not always easy to care about the characters, and what we learn about the written work of the two writers in the movie does not send us to a bookstore in search of volumes we have missed. And yet the film has a charm, the same charm that Miller had: The wide-eyed eagerness in the face of experience, the touching belief that in the physical we can find the spiritual.

Henry: Portrait of a Serial Killer
★ ★ ★ ¹/₂
NO MPAA RATING, 90 m., 1986

Michael Rooker (Henry), Tom Towles (Ottis), Tracy Arnold (His Sister). Directed by John McNaughton and produced by Waleed Ali. Screenplay by Richard Fire.

Filmed in 1986 and trapped in the movie rating system for three years, a movie named *Henry* finally came into wider view in the autumn of 1989. The story of a pathological mass murderer, it was told in such flat, unforgiving realism that it inspired angry debates after its screenings at film festivals and midnight cult screenings. Some viewers feel it is evil incarnate; others say it is superb filmmaking. The MPAA denied it an R rating (and said, indeed, that no possible cuts could qualify it for an R movie), so it was eventually released with no rating at all.

Henry was filmed during the winter of 1985–86 by a Chicago director named John McNaughton, on a budget of $125,000, using unknown actors from the free-wheeling Organic Theater Company. Loosely inspired by the confessions, since recanted, of a self-described mass murderer named Henry Lucas, the film uses a slice-of-life approach to create a docu-drama of chilling horror.

Unlike typical "slasher" movies, *Henry* does not employ humor, campy in-jokes, or a colorful antihero. Filmed in the gray slush and wet winter nights of Chicago's back alleys, honky-tonk bars, and drab apartments, it tells of a drifter who kills strangers, efficiently and without remorse. The movie contains scenes of heartless and shocking violence, committed by characters who seem to lack the ordinary feelings of common humanity.

Henry drifted in a cinematic no-man's-land after it was first seen publicly in a video version at the 1986 Chicago film festival. It played at midnight screenings in New York (where the *Village Voice*'s Elliott Stein called it one of the best American films of the year) but could not gain mass distribution without the R rating.

The title role in *Henry* is played with unrelenting power by Michael Rooker, who has since gone on to major Hollywood movies (he was the redneck who confronts Gene Hackman in *Mississippi Burning,* and the killer in *Sea of Love*). Organic Theater veteran Tom Towles plays the equally chilling role of Ottis, a casual friend who casually drifts into murder, and Tracy Arnold is Ottis's sister, a teen-age stripper who knows Henry killed his mother, and finds the fact intriguing.

In the film Henry becomes the roommate of Ottis, a parolee working in a gas station, and then the sister arrives from out of town and moves in. She is fascinated by Henry's stories of violence. Ottis, who may have a homosexual interest in Henry, eventually goes along with him in a series of brutal killings, including one where they pretend to have car trouble and then shoot a good samaritan, and another where they invade a home and videotape the murder of an entire family. The videotape scene appalls many viewers, but at least it shows *Henry* dealing honestly with its subject matter, instead of trying to sugar-coat violence as most "slasher" films do.

The director, McNaughton, is a onetime Chicago ad executive who dropped out for a few years to work in a traveling carnival, build sailboats in New Orleans, and tend bar in Homewood before getting into film by directing music videos. He raised the budget for *Henry* from Waleed Ali, a Chicago home-video executive, who wanted a horror film but was reportedly surprised when McNaughton gave him the real thing instead of an easy teen-age exploitation film. Ali's surprise has been reflected wherever the film has been shown.

At the Telluride festival, where I saw it in September 1989, some said the film was too violent and disgusting to be endured. Others said it was justified because of its uncompromising honesty in a world where most horror films cheapen death by trivializing it. The division seemed to be between those who felt the film did its job brilliantly, and those who felt its job should not have been done at all.

Henry V ★ ★ ★ ½
NO MPAA RATING, 138 m., 1989

Kenneth Branagh (Henry V), Derek Jacobi (Chorus), Emma Thompson (Katharine), Michael Maloney (Dauphin), Robbie Coltrane (Falstaff), Richard Briers (Bardolph), Judi Dench (Mistress Quickly), Alec McCowen (Ely), Ian Holm (Fleullen), Richard Innocent (Burgundy), Fabian Cartwright (Cambridge). Directed by Kenneth Branagh and produced by Stephen Evans. Screenplay by Branagh.

Shakespeare's *Henry V* is a favorite play of the British in times of national crisis, and in 1944, during the darkest days of World War II, Laurence Olivier directed and starred in it as a patriotic call to the barricades. Perhaps it is no coincidence that another hot-blooded Turk of the London stage, Kenneth Branagh, directed and starred in this new film version in 1989, as Britain stood poised uneasily on the banks of the new Europe, its toe dipped shyly into the waters of monetary union.

There is no more stirring summons to arms in all of literature than Henry's speech to his troops on St. Crispian's Day, ending with the lyrical "We few, we happy few, we band of brothers." To deliver this speech successfully is to pass the acid test for anyone daring to perform the role of Henry V in public, and as Kenneth Branagh, as Henry,

stood up on the dawn of the Battle of Agincourt and delivered the famous words, I was emotionally stirred even though I had heard them many times before. That is one mark of a great Shakespearean actor: to take the familiar and make it new.

Branagh is not yet thirty, and yet already the publicity machines are groaning to make him into the "new Olivier." Before his *Henry V,* he had made only one other movie (he was the sunburned young husband in *High Season*), but he has triumphed on the London stage in such talismanic roles as Jimmy Porter in Osborne's *Look Back in Anger* and his stock could not be higher. It was a risk to make this film, and it could have been a disastrous failure, but instead it is a success.

That it is not a triumph is because Branagh the director is not yet as good as Branagh the actor. He knows better how to play Henry V than how to get him on the screen, and his pacing could be improved. The film begins slowly, bogs down in the seemingly endless battle scenes, and then drags to its conclusion through Henry's endlessly protracted and coy courtship of Katharine.

Branagh himself seems to know that the opening sequences—involving a rebellion in the English court—are in trouble, and he attempts to speed them along with distractingly intrusive music, which only gets in the way of the words. Part of the problem is in Shakespeare, who dawdles with diplomatic matters before getting to the heart of his story. Olivier dealt with this problem in his 1944 film by facing it humorously. As the French ambassador and others squabble over boundaries and treaties, a frisky wind blows their documents around the stage. In Branagh, all is solemn and hard to follow.

One of the wonders of Shakespeare's prose is that, spoken by actors who understand the meaning of the words, it is almost as comprehensible today as when it was first written. In the Olivier film, the actors are better at making the words make sense, perhaps because, for Olivier, clarity of communication ranked above anything else in a performance. Branagh and his actors go for emotion or styles of delivery at the cost of clarity, and so the new *Henry V* is more appropriate for viewers familiar with the play; Olivier's version was literally intended for everyone.

And yet, these observations aside, Branagh has made quite a film here. His Henry V has a spectacular entrance, backlit and framed by huge palace doors, and is a king

from beginning to end (the youthful transgressions with Falstaff are firmly behind him). He is not a tall and dashing king—Branagh looks something like Jimmy Cagney—but he is a brave and stubborn one, and Branagh's direction wisely goes for realism in the battle scenes. They are not wars of words but of swords.

The famous British victory over the French at the Battle of Agincourt was Henry's and Medieval England's greatest triumph (although Shakespeare could not resist improving on the facts in the scene where Henry is informed of ten thousand French deaths as opposed to only twenty-nine on the English side). In the film, Branagh seems determined to account for every French death, and the battle wears on, steel against steel and horse against man, endlessly. There is too much of it—as if, having spent all the money for those extras and all those costumes, he wanted to get his money's worth. And yet, at the end, when the exhausted king confesses, "I know not if the day be ours or no," we share his exhaustion and his despair at bloodshed.

Branagh's approach depends on blood and thunder, as opposed to Olivier's insouciance. Even though Olivier made his film in the midst of a world war, it is probably true to say that we live in a more violent time today. Certainly our films are more violent, and in a sense Branagh is only keeping up with the state of the art when he soaks his battles in blood and mud. What happens as a result is that the scenes in court seem to exist on a different level of reality—especially the long scene of flirtation and proposal between Henry and Katharine, which ends the film. We have seen so much real blood that we have no patience for affected social gamesmanship, and the movie would probably play better if Henry had simply swept Katharine into his arms and forgotten the elaborate phrasemaking.

What works best in the film is the overall vision. Branagh is able to see himself as a king, and so we can see him as one. He schemes, he jests, and he deceives his soldiers during his famous tour of the field on the night before the battle. In victory he is humble, and in romance uncertain. Olivier, who was thirty-seven in 1944, wrote that Henry V was the kind of role he couldn't have played when he was younger: "When you are young, you are too bashful to play a hero; you debunk it." For Branagh, twenty-eight is old enough.

Her Alibi ½★
PG, 110 m., 1989

Tom Selleck (Phil Blackwood), Paulina Porizkova (Nina), William Daniels (Sam), James Farentino (Frank Polito), Hurd Hatfield (Troppa), Ronald Guttman ("Lucy" Comanescu), Tess Harper (Sally Blackwood). Directed by Bruce Beresford and produced by Keith Barish. Screenplay by Charles Peters.

You know a movie is in trouble when you start looking at your watch. You know it's in bad trouble when you start shaking your watch because you think it might have stopped. *Her Alibi* is a movie in the second category—endless, pointless, and ridiculous, right up to the final shot of the knife going through the cockroach. This movie is desperately bankrupt of imagination and wit, and Tom Selleck looks adrift in it.

He plays a detective novelist named Blackwood, who has run out of inspiration. So he goes to criminal court for fresh ideas, and there he falls instantly in love with Nina (Paulina Porizkova), a Romanian immigrant who is accused of murdering a young man with a pair of scissors. Blackwood disguises himself as a priest, smuggles himself into jail to meet Nina, and offers to supply her with an alibi: She can claim they were having an affair at his country home in Connecticut at the time of the crime.

These developments, and indeed the entire movie, are narrated by Blackwood in the language of a thriller novel he is writing as he goes along. One of the minor curiosities of the movie is why the Selleck character is such a bad writer. His prose is a turgid flow of cliché and stereotype, and when we catch a glimpse of his computer screen, we can't help noticing that he writes only in capital letters. Although the movie says he's rich because of a string of bestsellers, on the evidence, this is the kind of author whose manuscripts are returned with a form letter.

If the plot of his novel is half-witted, the plot of the movie is lame-brained. Blackwood and Nina move to Connecticut to make the alibi look good, and they're shadowed by a band of Romanian spies who make several murder attempts against them, including one in which they blow up Blackwood's house. The movie betrays its desperation by straying outside the confines of even this cookie-cutter plot for such irrelevant episodes as the one where Blackwood shoots himself in the bottom with an arrow, and is rushed to the hospital by Nina in one of those cut-and-dried scenes where the racing vehicle scares everyone else off the road before arriving safe and sound.

In a movie filled with groaningly bad moments, the worst is no doubt the dinner party at which Blackwood becomes convinced that Nina has poisoned him and everybody else at the table. Why does he think so? Because the cat is dead next to a bowl filled from the same casserole. We are treated to the sight of eight characters doing the dry heaves, and then another visit to the hospital, after which we learn it's all a false alarm and the cat was accidentally electrocuted in a neighbor's basement and returned by the solicitous neighbor to a resting place beside the suspicious bowl. Uh-huh.

The explanation for the whole story is equally arbitrary and senseless, and the big reconciliation scene between the two lovers is not helped by taking place at a clown's convention, with Selleck wearing a red rubber ball on his nose.

The Hidden ★ ★ ★
R, 98 m., 1987

Michael Nouri (Tom Beck), Kyle MacLachlan (Lloyd Gallagher), Ed O'Ross (Cliff Willis), Clu Gulager (Ed Flynn), Claudia Christian (Brenda Lee), Clarence Felder (John Masterson). Directed by Jack Sholder and produced by Robert Shaye. Screenplay by Bob Hunt.

The Hidden opens with a brutal bank robbery and a violent chase scene, and for a moment I thought I was in for another routine cop movie, but then I saw the funny look in the eyes of the bank robber, and I wasn't so sure. Here was a guy who seemed to be receiving secret transmissions. Aiming his car at a police barricade, he allowed a little smile to flicker on his lips, and when the cops aimed a hail of bullets at him, he took dozens of hits and yet still stayed on his feet and laughed at them.

Back at headquarters, Michael Nouri plays the cop assigned to the case. He wants to catch this guy, who has been responsible for an incredible string of violent crimes, but he's not so happy when an FBI man turns up and assigns himself to the case. The federal agent is played by Kyle MacLachlan, the clean-cut kid from *Blue Velvet*, and he looks just as clean-cut this time, but he, too, has a strange light in his eyes. Nouri discovers the key to this mystery about half an hour after we've figured it out for ourselves. Both the killer and the so-called FBI agent are from another planet. "Are we talking spaceman here?" Nouri asks, and we are.

The Hidden takes this situation and makes a surprisingly effective film out of it, a sleeper that talks like a thriller and walks like a thriller, but has more brains than the average thriller. It also has a sense of humor, and some subtle acting by MacLachlan, whose assignment is to play a character who is always just a beat out of step.

Jeff Bridges had a similar challenge in *Starman*, where he played an alien who cloned a human body and then tried to find his way around in it. MacLachlan takes a different approach, playing his alien with a certain strange reserve, as if he's trying the controls very lightly, afraid of going into a spin.

At first, Nouri naturally assumes this FBI guy is simply another weirdo. As he gradually begins to believe the story, his problem is to deal with his fellow cops, who don't believe in spacemen. Meanwhile, the killer moves from one host body to another, taking a guided tour of earth life-forms (his hosts include a dog and a stripper). The movie was directed by Jack Sholder, whose previous film was *A Nightmare on Elm Street, Part Two*. I don't know what I was expecting, but certainly not this original and efficient thriller.

Hidden Agenda ★ ★ ★
R, 108 m., 1990

Frances McDormand (Ingrid), Brian Cox (Kerrigan), Brad Dourif (Paul), Mai Zetterling (Moa). Directed by Ken Loach and produced by Eric Fellner. Screenplay by Jim Allen.

The tragedy of Northern Ireland is like a broken record. There was another incident just as this movie opened in the spring of 1991—the shooting death of young Fergal Caraher. The British authorities say he was shot while in a car trying to run a roadblock. Witnesses say he was shot without provocation. Thousands marched at his funeral. An investigation is promised.

Ken Loach's lacerating new film *Hidden Agenda* centers on an incident uncannily like the Caraher shooting. Two men in a car are shot without warning by British security forces. There is a great outcry. An investigation is promised. The movie, set in the recent past, is inspired by the Stalker Affair, in which a senior British police official, John Stalker, was assigned to investigate a killing by British security officials—and then suddenly removed from the investigation after uncovering evidence that the shooting was unjustified. That was a conclusion the Thatcher government could not tolerate.

Hidden Agenda is put together like a political thriller, like *Z* or *No Way Out*, but it adds a gritty everyday realism. The story is seen through the eyes of two Americans assigned to investigate charges that British security forces have sanctioned murder as a tactic in their struggle against Irish nationalism. The Americans (Frances McDormand and Brad Dourif) are members of a human rights group like Amnesty International, and are idealists out of their depth in the dangerous world they have entered. They become pawns in the political struggle when an IRA man slips a tape recording to them—an explosive tape with evidence that could not only lead to a murder conviction, but also suggest that a British right-wing group had run a "dirty tricks" campaign against national leaders.

Brian Cox plays the character based on Stalker. He's a career professional, a policeman who prides himself on ethical behavior, and he finds himself distinctly unwelcome in Northern Ireland. A senior Ulster policeman all but threatens him with death if he proceeds in his investigation, and tacitly concedes that the police have had to use illegal tactics to counter the terrorism of the IRA. But Cox persists, meeting with shadowy IRA figures in the back rooms of pubs and trying to get to the bottom of a killing that many powerful people would rather he forget.

The movie is set in everyday surroundings—hotel lobbies, car parks, pubs, and restaurants—and the participants are not the slick spies of Bond thrillers but ordinary, weatherbeaten people, often a little shabby. They have the look of weariness about them, as if the struggle has gone on too long and brought too much unhappiness. By contrast, the Ulster police official is all spit and polish, with a voice that's particularly grating when he tries to sound reasonable.

It quickly becomes apparent that the Amnesty investigators are in way over their heads, in a situation they do not understand, and that British security knows everything they're doing. It is also apparent that the corruption they are attempting to find extends all the way up to the highest levels of the British government. One of the most astonishing things about this film is the way it uses real names, dates, and places—charging a secret right wing group with attempting to bring down not only the Labour government of Harold Wilson, but the Conservative government of Edward Heath, which followed, and which the group found too soft for their taste. The implication is that Margaret Thatcher became prime minister at least partly through this group's efforts.

Hidden Agenda has understandably touched off a ferocious controversy in Great Britain. For Americans, it works more as a thriller than as political polemic, and indeed toward the end—when the dialogue threatens to overwhelm the action—the going gets thick. There is also the problem of that tape recording, which is seen as so important by everyone involved. Surely it could have been duplicated by the dozens and mailed all over the world? Questions like that are bothersome, and yet in its own terms and for much of the way, this is a superior thriller.

The Hidden Fortress ★ ★ ★ ★
NO MPAA RATING, 139 m., 1958

Toshiro Mifune (General Rokurota Makabe), Misa Uehara (Princess Yukihime), Takashi Shimura (General Nagakura), Susumu Fujita (General Tadokoro). Directed by Akira Kurosawa and produced by Kurosawa and Masumi Rumimoro. Screenplay by Kurosawa and Rumimoro.

The Hidden Fortress is grand, bold moviemaking—a Japanese adventure classic that combines elements of samurai films, Westerns, and myths of heroes and commoners. It does something else, too. It reveals many of the sources of the *Star Wars* movies so clearly that you can almost see R2D2, C3PO, and Princess Leia there on the screen. Now that we've had two sequels to *Star Wars*, how about this as a prologue?

The movie was made in 1958 by Akira Kurosawa, the greatest of Japanese directors, and it attracted a lot of attention at the time. It was the first Japanese movie in Cinemascope, it was one of the most expensive Japanese movies ever made, and it confirmed Kurosawa's role as a master of adventure epics. His *Seven Samurai* (1954) inspired Hollywood's *Magnificent Seven*, but it took George Lucas to use *The Hidden Fortress* as the starting point for the most popular American movies ever made.

The irony is that *The Hidden Fortress* has hardly been seen in this country. A much-shortened version had brief engagements in the early 1960s, but then it went out of release and the rights were allowed to lapse until late in 1983, when, for the first time, this uncut 139-minute version was brought to America. The best video version is the Criterion Collection's laserdisc, with a letter-boxed format so Kurosawa's entire widescreen compositions are visible.

The debt of the *Star Wars* pictures to Kurosawa is obvious almost from the opening shots, when two hapless Army underlings, one short, one tall, stagger through an empty landscape bemoaning their fates. Then the other story elements fall into place: a brave, outcast warrior general; a proud and fierce princess who is forced to disguise herself as a commoner; a feared military leader who first opposes the princess's cause but then supports it; a mysterious hidden fortress that must be captured, defended, or destroyed; and, of course, chases and sword-fights and appeals to tradition and history.

Does all of this sound more than vaguely familiar? Lucas gives full credit: He told Kurosawa he saw the movie in film school, never forgot it, and used the characters of the two foot soldiers as an inspiration for his two inseparable androids.

Kurosawa has made better movies, but never one more filled with humor and energy. His story isn't made into a dirge about honor and violence, but into a celebration of high spirits. The two foot soldiers enlist in the service of the general (Toshiro Mifune) without knowing who he is or that the woman accompanying him is their princess. They all conspire to move a wagonload of gold from one kingdom to another, concealing the gold inside sticks of firewood and hiding themselves in a procession to a firewood festival. There are close scrapes, double-crosses, cases of mistaken identity, and a thrilling lance-fight between Mifune and that other great Japanese star, Susumu Fujita. An overnight stop in a rowdy frontier town will remind you of the saloon planet in *Star Wars*.

There are also several breathtakingly great individual shots. One comes early in the film, when thousands of prisoners riot and run crazily down a long, sweeping flight of steps, overwhelming their captors. Another comes during the duel with lances, when the troops in the background are choreographed to mirror every move of the fight with their own body movements. And there's the firewood festival, with waves of celebrants dancing around the flames in a pagan dream. Seeing *The Hidden Fortress* is like visiting the wellspring of the Force.

High Anxiety ★ ★ ½
PG, 92 m., 1978

Mel Brooks (Dr. Thorndyke), Madeline Kahn (Victoria Brisbane), Cloris Leachman (Nurse Diesel), Harvey Korman (Dr. Montague), Ron Carey (Brophy), Howard Morris (Professor Lillolman), Murphy Dunne (Piano Player), Ira Miller (Psychiatrist). Directed and produced by Mel Brooks. Screenplay by Brooks, Ron Clark, Rudy DeLuca, and Barry Levinson.

One of the problems with Mel Brooks's *High Anxiety* is that it picks a tricky target: It's a spoof of the work of Alfred Hitchcock, but Hitchcock's films are often funny themselves. And satire works best when its target is self-important. It's easy for the *National Lampoon* to take on the *Reader's Digest*. But can you imagine a satire *of* the *National Lampoon?*

Almost all of Hitchcock's fifty-three or so films have their great moments of wit. And wit—the ability to share a sense of subtle fun with an audience—is not exactly Mel Brooks's strong point. He takes such key Hitchcock moments as the shower scene from *Psycho*, the climbing scene from *Vertigo*, and the shooting in *North by Northwest* and he clobbers them. It's not satire; it's overkill. Maybe it wasn't such a hot idea for Brooks to spoof Hitchcock in the first place. What he's done, though, is to go ahead and take the Hitchcock material, and almost bury his own comic talent in the attempt to fit things into his satirical formula. The best moments in *High Anxiety* come not when Brooks is being assaulted in the shower with a rolled-up newspaper, but when Brooks leaves Hitchcock altogether and does his own crazy, brilliant stuff.

Take, for example, a moment when dramatic music overwhelms the sound track while Brooks and his chauffeur are driving down a Los Angeles freeway. They look at each other, puzzled, and then we see the Los Angeles Symphony Orchestra performing in a bus in the next lane. Sure, he's pulled the same gag before (Count Basie turning up in the desert in *Blazing Saddles*), but it still works. Another Brooks specialty that works again this time is the casting of Cloris Leachman in variations of a neo-Nazi sadist. In *Young Frankenstein*, she was Frau Blucher,

whose very name made horses whinny with fright. Now she's Nurse Diesel, sinister presence at the Institute for the Very, *Very* Nervous, where Brooks has been hired as the new director. She has a closet full of whips and chains, and walks around as if her nurse's uniform covered a cast-iron corset. It's funny . . . but because it comes from Brooks and Leachman, not because it has much to do with Hitchcock.

Here's an example of why Hitchcock is so spoof-proof. At the end of *High Anxiety*, a victim dangles from the top of a tower for what seems like minutes on end, hanging at times by a single leg. Brooks is having fun with the way Hitchcock plays with his scenes of climactic violence. Fine. But remember Hitchcock's wonderful 1972 movie *Frenzy?* There's that strangling in it that goes on and on and on, played very straight, until we finally realize that Hitchcock is slyly giving us our money's worth by playing with the scene beyond all the possibilities of realism.

Brooks has made a specialty of movie satires: *Blazing Saddles, Young Frankenstein,* and *Silent Movie.* But they took on well-chosen targets. It's one thing to kid the self-conscious seriousness of a Western or a horror movie. It's another to take on a director of such sophistication that half the audience won't even get the in-jokes the other half is laughing at.

High Hopes ★ ★ ★ ★
NO MPAA RATING; 110 m., 1989

Philip Davis (Cyril), Ruth Sheen (Shirley), Edna Dore (Mrs. Bender), Philip Jackson (Martin), Heather Tobias (Valerie), Lesley Manville (Laetitia), David Bamber (Rupert). written and directed by Mike Leigh and produced by Simon Channing-Williams and Victor Glynn. Screenplay by Leigh.

The characters in *High Hopes* exist on either side of the great divide in Margaret Thatcher's England, between the new yuppies and the die-hard socialists.

Cyril and Shirley, quasi-hippie survivors of the 1970s, live in comfortable poverty in a small flat, supported by Cyril's earnings as a motorcycle messenger. Cyril's sister, Valerie, lives in an upscale home surrounded by Modern Conveniences with her husband, Martin, who sells used cars. In their language, their values, and the way they furnish their lives, each couple serves as a stereotype for their class: Cyril and Shirley are what

Tories think leftists are like, and Valerie and Martin stand for all the left hates most about Thatcherism.

Sometimes these two extremes literally live next door to each other. Cyril and Valerie's mother, a bitter, withdrawn old woman named Mrs. Bender, lives in solitude in the last council flat on a street that has otherwise been gentrified. Her next-door neighbors are two particularly frightening examples of the emerging social class the British call Hooray Henrys (and Henriettas). Paralyzed by their affected speech and gestures, they play out a grotesque parody of upper-class life in their own converted row house, which they like to forget was recently public housing for the poor.

All of these lives, and a few others, collide during the course of a few days in *High Hopes*, which was written and directed by Mike Leigh with the participation of the actors, who developed their scenes and dialogue in improvisational sessions. Leigh is a legendary figure in modern British theater, for his plays and television films that mercilessly dissect the British class system, using as their weapon the one emotion the British fear most, embarrassment.

Leigh has made only one other film, the brilliant *Bleak Moments*, some eighteen years ago. He cannot easily find financing for his films because, at the financing stage, they do not yet have scripts; he believes in developing the material as he goes along.

The backing for *High Hopes* came partly from Channel Four, the innovative alternative British TV channel, and with its money he has produced one of those rare films in which anger and amusement exist side by side—in which the funniest scenes are also the most painful ones.

Consider, for example, the dilemma of the old mother, Mrs. Bender, when she locks herself out of her council house. She naturally turns for help to her neighbors. But Rupert and Laetitia, who live next door, are upwardly mobile yuppies who treat the poor as a disease they hope not to catch. As the old woman stands helplessly at the foot of the steps, grasping her shopping cart, her chic neighbor supposes she must, after all, give her shelter, and says, "Hurry up, now. Chop, chop!"

Mrs. Bender calls her daughter, Valerie, who can hardly be bothered to come and help her, until she learns that her mother is actually inside the yuppie house next door. Then she's there in a flash, hoping to nose about and see what they've "done" with the place. Some of her dialogue almost draws blood, as when she looks into Rupert's leather-and-brass den and shouts, "Mum, look what they've done with your coal-hole!"

This sort of materialism and pride in possessions is far from the thoughts of Cyril and Shirley, the left-wing couple, who still sleep on a mattress on the floor and decorate their flat with posters and cacti. Lacking in ambition, they make enough from Cyril's messenger job to live on, and they smooth over the rough places with hashish. They are kind, and the movie opens with them taking a bewildered mental patient into their home; he has been wandering the streets of London, a victim of Thatcher's dismantled welfare state. (America and Britain are indeed cousins across the waters; we are reminded that the Reagan administration benevolently turned thousands of our own mentally ill out onto the streets.)

Most of the action in *High Hopes* centers around two set pieces, both involving the mother: the crisis of the lost keys, and then the mother's birthday party, which the hysterical Valerie stages as a parody of happy times. As the confused Mrs. Bender sits in bewilderment at the head of the table, her daughter shouts encouragement at her with a shrill desperation. The evening ends with a bitter quarrel between the daughter and her husband, while Cyril and Shirley pack the miserable old lady away home.

High Hopes is not a movie with a simple message; it's not left-wing propaganda in which all kindness resides with the Labourites and all selfishness with the Conservatives. Leigh shows us a London that exists beyond such easy distinctions, and it is possible he is almost as angry at Cyril and Shirley—laid-back, gentle, ineffectual potheads—as at the movie's cruel upward-strivers.

Much of the movie's concern seems to center around Shirley's desire to have a child, and Cyril's desire that they should not. Their conflict is not the familiar old one of whether or not to "bring" a child into "this world." It seems to center more around the core of Cyril's laziness. He cannot be bothered. Of course, he stands for all good things and opposes all bad ones, in principle—but in practice, it's simpler to light up a joint.

High Hopes is an alive and challenging film, one that throws our own assumptions and evasions back at us. Leigh sees his characters and their lifestyles so vividly, so mer-

cilessly, and with such a sharp satirical edge, that the movie achieves a neat trick: We start by laughing at the others, and end by feeling uncomfortable about ourselves.

High Season ★ ★ ★
R, 104 m., 1988

Jacqueline Bisset (Katherine), James Fox (Patrick), Irene Papas (Penelope), Paris Tselios (Yanni), Sebastian Shaw (Basil Sharp), Kenneth Branagh (Rick), Lesley Manville (Carol). Directed by Clare Peploe and produced by Clare Downs. Screenplay by Clare and Mark Peploe.

High Season reminds me a little of the neglected John Huston comedy *Beat the Devil*, with its assortment of eccentric exiles up to mischief far from home. The film takes place on the Greek island of Rhodes, where once a Colossus stood, but where now the most controversial sculpture is dedicated to the Unknown Tourist. For many years a celebrated British photographer (Jacqueline Bisset) has lived on the island with her daughter, and as the story opens, her past and future are both about to catch up with her.

She lives in a lazy white house in a small town that, until now, has not been discovered by the tourists. But now they have started to arrive in numbers, and that has created a schism in the most prominent local family. The son, Yanni (Paris Tselios) wants to turn the ancient family store into a T-shirt shop, while his mother (the immortal Irene Papas) wants to drive all tourists from the island—by force, if necessary.

Yanni has commissioned a trendy sculptor to create the monument to the Unknown Tourist. And because the sculptor is played by James Fox, we can all but relax, sure that something wickedly funny will come of all of this. The Fox brothers (James and Edward) are masters of a certain note of brave British dissipation. They play characters who are capable of doing fine things, if only they had the will. In this case, James Fox's arrival on the island precipitates a small crisis, since Bisset is his former wife.

Other newcomers also arrive; one of the great pleasures of a film like this is in the introduction of the new characters. We meet, for example, Basil Sharp (Sebastian Shaw), the legendary British art expert who is an old friend of Bisset's. He has come out to have a look at an invaluable Roman vase he

once gave her—and also to arrange a political defection. He confides in her that he has long been a Russian spy, and is preparing to meet Soviet agents and defect to Russia. (Sharp's character—and indeed his name—are obviously inspired by the scandal of Anthony Blunt, keeper of Her Majesty's picture collection until he was unmasked as a Soviet agent.)

Sharp's escape is with the approval of the British authorities, who feel they simply cannot deal with the scandal of another high-placed spy. Is it only coincidence that at the same time he arrives on the island, a famous international art dealer also turns up? And also a confused and forlorn young British couple? They have no place to stay until Papas unexpectedly rents them a room.

With all of the actors in place, the delights of the screenplay begin to unfold. The movie was directed by Clare Peploe and written by her and her brother, Mark, who were involved in such Michelangelo Antonioni projects as *The Passenger*. Nothing in their previous work would suggest they'd make a light-footed social satire like *High Season*, but the movie is completely assured as it juggles its characters and a labyrinthine plot involving the vase, the spy case, and the assorted old and new romances.

The best movies of this sort always include some sort of scene in which one or more of the decadent heroes voices regret at a misspent life. In *High Season*, Sebastian Shaw does a masterful job of looking back over his life of art, finance, and espionage, and his confessional scene with Bisset is one of the best pieces of work along that line I've ever seen.

I also enjoyed the playful way that the Peploes contrived a sequence involving a long, long night during which the precious vase and several hearts are tampered with. The ingeniousness with which they weave their tangled plot created real questions in my mind—which were resolved in one of those deeply satisfying endings in which everything has an answer and yet nobody turns out to have been quite blameless. *High Season* is an example of a rare species, the intelligent silly movie.

History of the World—Part I ★ ★
R, 90 m., 1981

Mel Brooks (Moses, Comicus, Torquemada, Jacques, Louis XVI), Dom DeLuise (Nero), Madeline Kahn (Empress Nympho), Harvey Korman (Count De Monet), Cloris Leachman (Madame Defarge), Ron Carey (Swiftus), Mary-Margaret Humes (Miriam). Directed and produced by Mel Brooks. Screenplay by Brooks.

Mel Brooks's movie *History of the World—Part I* is a rambling, undisciplined, sometimes embarrassing failure from one of the most gifted comic filmmakers around. What went wrong? Brooks never seems to have a clear idea of the rationale of his movie—so there's no confident narrative impetus to carry it along. His "history" framework doesn't have an approach or point of view; it's basically just a laundry-line for whatever gags he can hang on it.

What *is* this bizarre grab bag? Is it a parody of old Biblical, Roman, and French historical epics? Sometimes. Is it one-shot, comedy revue blackouts? Sometimes. Is it satire aimed at pompous targets? Sometimes. But most of the time it's basically just expensive sets sitting around waiting for Brooks to do something funny in front of them.

Brooks seems to rely on his own spontaneous comic genius in this film, and genius, even when you have it, is not something to be relied upon. He provides isolated moments that are indeed hilarious, moments that find an inspired image and zing us with it (as when a slave boogies through the streets of ancient Rome with a loud transistor radio glued to his ear). But as the movie creeps on, we realize that the inspirations are going to be rare, and that Brooks has not bothered to create a framework for the movie or to people it with characters. It's all just cardboard comic cutouts.

The film has another serious problem: It is in unfunny bad taste. That sounds strange coming from me. I've always enjoyed Brooks's ventures into taboo subject matter, and I still think his "Springtime for Hitler" from *The Producers* and the celebrated campfire scene in *Blazing Saddles* were hilarious. He seemed to be demonstrating that you could get away with almost anything in a movie, if you made it funny enough. (Told that *The Producers* was vulgar, he once responded loftily, "It rises *below* vulgarity.") But this time, the things he's trying to get

away with aren't funny. There is, for example, the movie's tiresome series of jokes about urination. There must be comic possibilities in the subject (and he finds one when he shows a Stone Age critic's method of reviewing a cave painting), but there is nothing inherently funny about urination, and Brooks proves it here, again and again.

There also is nothing inherently funny about Jews, Catholics, nuns, blacks, and gays. They can all conceivably provide the makings of comedy, of course, but in *History of the World* Brooks doesn't have the patience to introduce a character and then create a comic situation *about* him. He introduces the character and expects us to laugh at the character himself. Example: Instead of developing a comic situation around Orthodox Jews, he simply shows us some, complete with beards and hats, their heads stuck through a stockade, and expects us to laugh. But while we might laugh with Brooks at a comic situation, we have no reason to laugh *at* people just because of their appearance or religion.

The same thing goes wrong with Brooks's big production number in this movie, "The Inquisition," featuring a song-and-dance team of medieval monks, and a chorus line of nuns who splash in a pool, Busby Berkeley-style. We're supposed to laugh at the shocking juxtaposition of religious images and Hollywood corn. But Brooks never gives us an additional comic level, one where he's making funny points about the images. When he dresses up like a monk and then dances like Donald O'Connor, that's only funny for a second. If we knew anything about the monk as a comic character, the scene could build. Instead, it just continues.

History of the World—Part I was fairly expensive to produce, but it exists on the level of quick, disposable, television. It thumbs its nose at icons that have lost their taboo value for most of us, and between the occasional good laughs, we're a little embarrassed that the movie is so dumb and predictable. God knows Mel Brooks is straining for yuks up there on the screen, but he's like the life of the party who still has the lampshade on his head when everybody else is ready to go home.

Hollywood Shuffle ★ ★ ★
R, 82 m., 1987

Robert Townsend (Bobby Taylor), Anne-Marie Johnson (Lydia), Helen Martin (Grandmother), Starletta Dupois (Mother),

Craigus R. Johnson (Stevie), Domenick Irrera (Manvacum). Directed and produced by Robert Townsend. Screenplay by Townsend.

The story behind *Hollywood Shuffle* is more thrilling than anything on the screen. It's the story of Robert Townsend, young black actor from Chicago, talented, ambitious, who wins supporting roles in *Cooley High*, *Streets of Fire*, and *A Soldier's Story* but fails to gain stardom in a Hollywood where most roles for blacks are stereotypes and the rest go to people named Murphy, Pryor, and Glover.

In the ordinary course of events, Townsend would continue to make the weary rounds from one casting agent to another, auditioning for one forgettable role after another, paying the rent by waiting tables, until he was finally discovered or—more likely—quit the business and got a daytime job.

Townsend knew that routine as well as anyone, but he decided to break out of it. So he made his own movie. The saga of his production was well-publicized: He begged cinematographers for leftover film, borrowed every dollar he could find, talked cast and crew into working for deferred payments, and somehow made an expensive-looking movie for less than $100,000. Comparisons have been drawn to Spike Lee, another young black filmmaker who broke the rules and had his first hit with *She's Gotta Have It*.

It's a cliché that young novelists write their first novels about young novelists writing their first novels. Townsend's *Hollywood Shuffle* falls within this tradition. It is a movie about a young man much like Townsend, who makes the rounds, fights stereotypes, and dreams of the day when there will be a black Rambo.

The movie begins with Townsend working in a hot dog stand owned by a couple of negative thinkers who don't believe he can be successful as an actor. He defies their expectations and gets a job in a movie, but then he walks off the set; with his grandmother and his younger brother looking on, he just can't bring himself to mouth the street-talk clichés of his character, a gang member. This action inspires a series of fantasies in which Townsend sees himself in war movies, Westerns, and slice-of-life dramas, and even imagines a TV show in which two soul brothers are the feuding critics and give movies the finger as well as their thumbs.

There are a lot of good laughs in *Holly-*

wood Shuffle, and the movie certainly functions as a showcase for Townsend—who has a strong screen presence. The movie has its problems, however. Many of the skits run on too long after we've long since gotten the jokes. Some of the supporting performances are wooden and under-written. And many of the stereotypes Townsend protests against haven't been used in Hollywood movies in decades. His attacks on them will be the first time some viewers have seen the stereotypes at all.

I suspect many of these problems are the direct result of the movie's low budget, hurried shooting schedule, and limited supply of film. When one take of a scene was acceptable, Townsend must have been inclined to accept it, rather than to waste precious film stock in trying to make it better. Under the circumstances, *Hollywood Shuffle* is an artistic compromise but a logistical triumph, announcing the arrival of a talent whose next movie should really be something.

Home Alone ★ ★ ¹/₂
PG, 103 m., 1990

Macaulay Culkin (Kevin), Joe Pesci (Harry), Daniel Stern (Marv), John Heard (Peter), Roberts Blossom (Marley), Catherine O'Hara (Kate), John Candy (Gus Polinski). Directed by Chris Columbus and produced by John Hughes. Screenplay by Hughes.

Home Alone is a splendid movie title because it evokes all sorts of scary nostalgia. Being left home alone, when you were a kid, meant hearing strange noises and being afraid to look in the basement—but it also meant doing all the things that grown-ups would tell you to stop doing, if they were there. Things like staying up to watch Johnny Carson, eating all the ice cream, and sleeping in your parents' bed.

Home Alone is about an eight-year-old hero who does all of those things, but unfortunately, he also single-handedly stymies two house burglars by booby-trapping the house. And they're the kinds of traps that any eight-year-old could devise, if he had a budget of tens of thousands of dollars and the assistance of a crew of movie special effects people.

The movie's screenplay is by John Hughes, who sometimes shows a genius for remembering what it was like to be young. His best movies, like *Sixteen Candles, The Breakfast Club, Ferris Bueller's Day Off,* and *Planes,*

Trains and Automobiles, find a way to be funny while still staying somewhere within the boundaries of remote plausibility. This time, he strays so far from his premise that the movie suffers.

If *Home Alone* had limited itself to the things that might possibly happen to a forgotten eight-year-old, I think I would have liked it more. What I didn't enjoy was the subplot involving the burglars (Joe Pesci and Daniel Stern), who are immediately spotted by little Kevin (Macaulay Culkin), and made the targets of his cleverness.

The movie opens in the Chicago suburbs with a houseful of people on the eve of a big family Christmas vacation in Paris. There are relatives and kids everywhere, and when the family oversleeps and has to race to the airport, Kevin is somehow overlooked in the shuffle. When he wakes up later that morning, the house is empty. So he makes the best of it.

A real kid would probably be more frightened than this movie character, and would probably cry. He might also try calling someone, or asking a neighbor for help. But in the contrived world of this movie, the only neighbor is an old coot who is rumored to be the Snow Shovel Murderer, and the phone doesn't work. When Kevin's parents discover they've forgotten him, they find it impossible to get anyone to follow through on their panicked calls—for the simple reason that if anyone did so, the movie would be over.

The plot is so implausible that it makes it hard for us to really care about the plight of the kid. What works in the other direction, however, and almost carries the day, is the gifted performance by young Macaulay Culkin, as Kevin. Culkin is the little boy who co-starred with John Candy in *Uncle Buck,* and here he has to carry almost the whole movie. He has lots of challenging acting scenes, and he's up to them. I'm sure he got lots of help from director Chris Columbus, but he's got the stuff to begin with. He's such a confident and gifted little actor that I'd like to see him in a story I could care more about.

Home Alone isn't that story. When the burglars invade Kevin's home, they find themselves running a gamut of booby traps so elaborate they could have been concocted by Rube Goldberg—or by the berserk father in *Last House on the Left.* Because all plausibility is gone, we sit back, detached, to watch stunt men and special effects guys take over a movie that promised to be the kind of story audiences could identify with.

Home of the Brave ★ ★ ★ ¹/₂
NO MPAA RATING, 90 m., 1986

A concert documentary directed by Laurie Anderson and produced by Paula Mazur. Screenplay by Anderson.

Laurie Anderson once spoke, in a wondering voice, of the plight of human sperm: "Hundreds of thousands of tiny specks, all knowing exactly the same thing." Her performances are filled with insights like that. She doesn't make them to supply us with information, but to create a tone, an attitude. She is engulfed by the enormous mysteries of nature, and yet the human life around her seems more and more banal. Civilization is an assembly line to hell.

In retaliation, she weaves dream-images out of songs and symbols and electronic noises. She calls herself a "performance artist" rather than a musician. And although all musicians are performance artists, I think I know what she means. She does not give concerts. She attempts to create in her audiences a more open, wondering state of mind.

Home of the Brave is a ninety-minute documentary based on one of her performances. Large parts of it will be familiar to anyone who has seen her in person, but the film has a somewhat different feel than her live performances. As a backdrop to her music, Anderson uses a large rear-projection screen that sometimes relays messages made up of technological clichés and sometimes uses film loops to show the same images over and over.

The images have a hypnotic quality. Crudely drawn sheep jump over and over, again and again, or boats steam past a rusty bridge or—as she talks about the sperm—we see little tadpoles earnestly swimming upstream, one of them breaking away every once in a while for a loop-the-loop. The images are deliberately crude and machine-made. The film loops are so short that they announce themselves. We can see that the same images are being recycled in a circle, and the feeling is sort of poignant: All those sperm, all that effort, all for nothing.

In front of these images, the Laurie Anderson Band performs. With her short, spiky hair and her athletic grace, Anderson sometimes seems more like a craftsman than a singer. She moves in a kind of robot choreography, and she likes to seem deadpan. She takes the hand-held mike and wanders the stage, reciting parables and slices of bizarre information. She likes phrases such as "This just in . . . ,," as if she were at the anchor desk for the death of the world. She uses strange lighting effects to create instants of magic.

She was one of the first to use voice synthesizers, which lower the tone of her voice while maintaining the same speed of speech. The effect is sort of big-brotherish; she seems official, detached, a voice made from a machine, speaking words as objects. Behind her, the rhythms are seductive, statements made over and over until they lull us into her mind state.

There are times when Anderson seems like an anti-performance artist, times when she cuts off a song or interrupts a progression just as it is threatening to develop into melody and entertainment. But the effect is not dry and antiseptic, as it is with some ultramodern music. Every song has a soul of wit and an edge of rebellion.

It's strange. You can't put your finger on it, but after you see it, you have the feeling that your perception of things has been skewed slightly. Anderson is saying: We're surrounded by bankrupt images and music that is fascist noise, and they're pouncing away at us, trying to break us down, to kill the spark, but if we keep two things we will be able to survive and complete our journeys. Those two things are a sense of wonder and the ability to laugh back.

Honey, I Shrunk the Kids ★ ★
PG, 93 m., 1989

Rick Moranis (Wayne Szalinski), Matt Frewer (Big Russ Thompson), Marcia Strassman (Diane Szalinski), Kristine Sutherland (Mae Thompson), Thomas Brown (Little Russ Thompson), Jared Rushton (Ron Thompson), Amy O'Neill (Amy Szalinski), Robert Oliveri (Nick Szalinski). Directed by Joe Johnston and produced by Penney Finkelman Cox. Screenplay by Ed Naha and Tom Schulman.

I've been trying to figure out exactly what's missing in *Honey, I Shrunk the Kids*. The special effects are all there, nicely in place, and the production values are sound, but the movie is dead in the water. It tells an amazing and preposterous story, and it seems bored by it. It uses the same sorts of visual effects we remember from *The Incredible Shrinking Man*, but it lacks the same sense of fun.

The movie stars Rick Moranis as a suburban father who labors far into the night over a strange invention up in the attic. It's an "elec-tro-magnetic shrinking machine," which can, and does, reduce four of the neighborhood kids to microscopic size. They're smaller than ants, and get swept up and thrown out with the trash—setting up the central adventure of the movie, in which they try to survive in a backyard that has suddenly turned into a fearsome jungle.

The special effects used for these scenes are inventive and first-rate: We see blades of grass that tower over the tiny kids, a cigarette butt that looks like a glowing slag heap, and an ant so big that all four kids can ride on it. Two of the kids hold on for dear life during a crazy flight on the back of a bumble bee, which leaves them covered with pollen the size of softballs. When the sprinkler is turned on, the yard explodes into a treacherous mud swamp, and when a lawn mower gets loose, it sets up a terrifying vortex. And there's a battle between an ant and another insect (a miniature scorpion, I guess) that reminded me a little of the battle of the monsters in *King Kong*.

The technical expertise is there. But the story surrounding it is thin, slow, and lacking in inspiration. When the four neighborhood children disappear, the parents next door react in a kind of slow-motion daze. Meanwhile, Moranis realizes what has happened and starts searching the backyard, suspending himself in a harness and circling over the grass with a magnifying glass and searchlights. This should have been funny, but it's not, and we see the same process again and again.

All of the performances in the movie seem a little unfocused, as if the actors got exhausted waiting for the special effects and forgot their original inspiration. There should be chemistry between the four kids, but instead there are simply routine line readings. Moranis and his wife (Marcia Strassman) and the neighbors (Matt Frewer and Kristine Sutherland) are given so few recognizable emotions that they seem less involved in the story than the audience. And the pacing is slow. A whiz-bang, gee-whiz approach to the material might have helped.

The closing scenes are an example of the low energy level. One of the kids is about to be accidentally devoured in a spoonful of Cheerios. This scene could have been milked for suspense and malicious glee. Instead, it unfolds with lead-footed predictability. And James Horner's music, here and elsewhere in the film, is no help. It sounds surprisingly familiar, and seems to be a retread of the Nino Rota score for Fellini's *Amarcord*. In the Fellini movie, it worked.

Honkytonk Man ★ ★ ★
PG, 123 m., 1982

Clint Eastwood (Red Stovall), Kyle Eastwood (Whit), John McIntire (Grandpa), Alexa Kenin (Marlene), Verna Bloom (Emmy). Directed and produced by Clint Eastwood.

Clint Eastwood produced and directed *Honkytonk Man*, and stars in it as a Depression-era loser who drifts through the South with his young nephew, aiming eventually to get to Nashville and maybe get on the Grand Ol' Opry. The movie's credits say the screenplay is by Clancy Carlile, based on his own novel, but in speculating on what drew Eastwood to this project, I came across this entry in Ephraim Katz's *Film Encyclopedia*:

"Eastwood, Clint. Actor, director. Born on May 31, 1930, in San Francisco. A child of the Depression, he spent his early boyhood trailing a father who pumped gas along dusty roads all over the West Coast. . . ."

The entry goes on to list the usual odd jobs (logger, steel-furnace stoker) that all actors seem to hold down on their way to stardom, but I'd read enough to support my intuition that *Honkytonk Man* means a lot to Eastwood in ways that may not be immediately apparent. This is a sweet, whimsical, low-key movie, a movie that makes you feel good without pressing you too hard. It provides Eastwood with a screen character who is the complete opposite of the patented Eastwood tough guys and provides a role of nearly equal importance for his son, Kyle, as a serious, independent and utterly engaging young nephew named Whit. What happens to them on the road is not quite as important in this movie as what happens between them.

The movie starts with Eastwood drunk behind the wheel of a big 1930s touring car, knocking over the windmill on his latest return to the old homestead. He's sort of a Hank Williams type. His family has seen this act before. They put him to bed and hide the bottle. The next day, with an ominous cough, Eastwood talks about his dream of heading for Nashville and cashing in some old IOUs. He's a singer and a songwriter, luckless but not untalented, and he thinks he could make it onto the Opry. He wants to take the kid along. After some hesitation, the kid's mother (Verna Bloom) agrees, mostly because she hopes her son can ride herd on

Eastwood and keep him reasonably sober. She makes her son promise not to drink or fool around with women (thus putting her finger unerringly on one thing he did the night before, and another that he hopes to do as soon as possible). Old grandpa (John McIntire) also decides to go along for the ride; he's got some people in Tennessee he hasn't seen in forty years.

The road part of the picture is picaresque, photographed through a haze of romance and nostalgia, and spiced up with a visit to a gambling house and an encounter with a very individualistic young woman (Alexa Kenin) who also decides to join the traveling party. She has an amazing gift for couching the most ordinary sentiments in romantic prose. The movie's best scenes are the ones Eastwood plays in Nashville, during an audition at the Opry and, later, in a recording studio. He sings his songs with the kind of bone-weariness that doesn't hurt the right kind of country song, and there's a special moment in the studio when a supporting musician lends a hand. The movie turns out to be about realizing your dreams after all, which is sort of a surprise in a story where even the high points are only bittersweet.

This is a special movie. In making it, Eastwood was obviously moving away from his Dirty Harry image, but that's nothing new; his spectacular success in violent movies tends to distract us from his intriguing and challenging career as the director and star of such offbeat projects as *Bronco Billy* and *Play Misty For Me*. He seems to have a personal stake in this story, and we begin to feel it, too. Sometimes the simplest country songs are just telling the facts.

Hoosiers ★ ★ ★ ★
PG, 114 m., 1987

Gene Hackman (Norman Dale), Barbara Hershey (Myra Fleener), Dennis Hopper (Shooter), Sheb Wooley (Cletus), Fern Parsons (Opal Fleener), Chelcie Ross (George), Robert Swan (Rollin), Michael O'Guinne (Rooster). Directed by David Anspaugh and produced by Carter De Haven and Angelo Pizzo. Screenplay by Pizzo.

I was a sportswriter once for a couple of years in downstate Illinois. I covered mostly high school sports, and if I were a sportswriter again, I'd want to cover them again. There is a passion to high school sports that transcends anything that comes afterward; nothing in pro sports equals the intensity of a really important high school basketball game.

Hoosiers knows that. This is a movie about a tiny Indiana high school that sends a team all the way to the state basketball finals in the days when schools of all sizes played in the same tournaments and a David could slay a Goliath. The school in the movie is so small that it can barely field a team, especially after the best player decides to drop out. Can schools this small actually become state champs? Sure. That's what high school sports are all about.

Hoosiers is a comeback movie, but it's not simply about a comeback of this small team, the Hickory Huskers. It's also about the comeback of their coach, a mysterious middle-age guy named Norman Dale (Gene Hackman), who seems to be too old and too experienced to be coaching in an obscure backwater like Hickory.

And it's also the comeback story of Shooter, the town drunk (played by Dennis Hopper, whose supporting performance won an Oscar nomination). Everybody in this movie seems to be trying to start over in life, and, in a way, basketball is simply their excuse.

Hoosiers has the broad overall structure of most sports movies: It begins with the problem of a losing team, introduces the new coach, continues with the obligatory training sequences and personality clashes, arrives at the darkest hour, and then heads toward triumph. This story structure is almost as sacred to Hollywood as basketball is to Indiana.

What makes *Hoosiers* special is not its story, however, but its details and its characters. Angelo Pizzo, who wrote the original screenplay, knows small-town sports. He knows all about high school politics and how the school board and the parents' groups always think they know more about basketball than the coach does. He knows about gossip, scandal, and vengeance. And he knows a lot about human nature.

All of this knowledge, however, would be pointless without Hackman's great performance at the center of this movie. Hackman is gifted at combining likability with complexity—two qualities that usually don't go together in the movies. He projects all of the single-mindedness of any good coach, but then he contains other dimensions, and we learn about the scandal in his past that led him to this one-horse town. David Anspaugh's direction is good at suggesting

Hackman's complexity without belaboring it.

Hickory High School is where Hackman hopes to make his comeback, but he doesn't think only of himself. He meets Shooter (Hopper), the alcoholic father of one of his team members, and enlists him as an assistant coach with one stipulation: no more drinking. That doesn't work. In a way, Hackman knows it won't work, but by involving Shooter once again in the life of the community, he's giving him a reason to seek the kind of treatment that might help.

Hackman finds that he has another project on his hands, too: the rehabilitation of his heart. He falls in love with a teacher at the school (Barbara Hershey), and their relationship is interesting, as far as it goes, although it feels like key scenes have been cut out of the romance. Maybe another movie could have been made about them; this movie is about basketball.

The climax of the movie will come as no great surprise to anyone who has seen other sports movies. *Hoosiers* works a magic, however, in getting us to really care about the fate of the team and the people depending on it. In the way it combines sports with human nature, it reminded me of another wonderful Indiana sports movie, *Breaking Away*. It's a movie that is all heart.

Hope and Glory ★ ★ ★
PG-13, 118 m., 1987

Sebastian Rice Edwards (Bill), Geraldine Muir (Sue), Sarah Miles (Grace), David Hayman (Clive), Sammi Davis (Dawn), Derrick O'Connor (Mac), Susan Wooldridge (Molly), Jean-Marc Barr (Bruce), Ian Bannen (Grandfather). Directed, produced, and written by John Boorman.

Maybe there is something in the very nature of war, in the power of guns and bombs, that appeals to the imagination of little boys. Bombers and fighter planes and rockets and tanks are thrilling at that age when you are old enough to understand how they work, but too young to understand what they do. John Boorman's *Hope and Glory* is a film about that precise season in the life of a young British boy who grows up in a London suburb during the Second World War.

The boy (Sebastian Rice Edwards), probably meant to be Boorman himself, is bright and curious, and although he is sad when his dad goes away in uniform, there are certain consolations, such as the nightly German air raids that leave real pieces of shrapnel in the garden—some of them still hot from explosions, and all of them very collectible.

For his mother (Sarah Miles, in one of the best performances of her career), life is not so simple, but it has its consolations. Left to raise the family after her husband is drafted, she deals distractedly with rebellion in the ranks of her children, particularly from a teen-age daughter whose sexual awakening has been hastened by the arrival of Canadian troops who are training in the neighborhood.

Hope and Glory is first of all a painstaking re-creation of the period. All the cars and signs and clothes look right, and there are countless small references to wartime rationing, as when the older sister draws seams on her legs to make fake nylons. But after re-creating the period, Boorman also reconstructs the very feeling that was in the air.

The nightly routine of air raids quickly loses its novelty, and Miles has to shake her sleepyheads to get them out of bed and into the backyard bomb shelter. One night, they don't make it, and crouch in the hall closet as the bombs fall closer and closer. The next one, they whisper, will either hit them or not—but it misses, and hits the house of a mean old lady down the street, creating a great fire and drawing lots of exciting fire engines.

There is something almost perverse in the way Boorman defines his point of view. He is not concerned in this film about the tragedy of war, or the meaning of war, but only with the specific experience of war for a grade school boy. Drawing from his own autobiographical memories, he has not given the little boy in the movie any more insights than such a little boy should have. His approach is especially effective in a scene where the boy witnesses his sister making out with a soldier; he looks, and does not quite understand, and looks away, perhaps sensing that this is a chapter that has not yet opened for him.

Toward the end of the film, the locale changes; the family goes to stay in the country with Miles's grandparents, and existence there seems more idyllic than in the city. Probably this is the way Boorman remembers it; going to the country is not an escape from bombs, but a chance to float on the river and run in the pastures.

Wartime is always a time, on the domestic front, of personal upheaval. There is a quiet, touching subplot in *Hope and Glory* about a

choice Sarah Miles made when she got married. She married out of common sense, not out of love, and although she is still best friends with the man she loved, she is faithful to her absent husband. This situation leads to one of the film's best scenes, when the daughter confesses her love for a Canadian airman—and reveals that she is pregnant. The mother tells her daughter she must be true to her heart, and follow love wherever it leads, and we know that is exactly what she did not do.

Hope and Glory was an enormous success in England, where every frame must have its special memories for British audiences. Through American eyes, it is a more universal film, not so much about war as about memory. When we are young, what happens is not nearly as important as what we think happens. Perhaps that's true even when we are not so young.

The Hot Spot ★ ★ ★
R, 130 m., 1990
(See related Film Clip, p. 704.)

Don Johnson (Harry Madox), Virginia Madsen (Dolly Harshaw), Jennifer Connelly (Gloria Harper), Charles Martin Smith (Lon Gulik), William Sadler (Frank Sutton), Jerry Hardin (George Harshaw). Directed by Dennis Hopper and produced by Paul Lewis. Screenplay by Nona Tyson and Charles Williams.

A guy comes in from out of town. He doesn't have a past, at least not one he wants to talk about. He gets a job in a used car lot. It's one of those typical small towns from the movies of the 1940s and 1950s, the kind of backwater where the other guy on the job is a nerd, and the boss is a blowhard with a bum ticker—but the boss's wife is this great broad with blonde hair and big eyelashes and when she gets up in the morning, she puts on her negligee just when the other women in town are taking theirs off. Oh, and the bookkeeper at work is this innocent young girl who is intimidated, for mysterious reasons, by the vicious creep who lives in a shack outside of town.

I feel at home in movies like *The Hot Spot*. They come out of that vast universe formed by the historic meeting of B movies and the idea of *film noir*—films about the soft underbelly of the human conscience. There are certain conventions to be observed, and *The Hot Spot* knows them and observes them. The hero has to smoke and look laconic and

be trying to suppress something in his past. It helps if he drives a Studebaker. The boss's wife has to have learned all of her moves by studying old movies. The plot has to provide that the bad guys don't commit all of the crimes; the hero, for example, robs the bank.

Dennis Hopper, who directed *The Hot Spot*, grew up in the movies at a time when films like this were familiar—back in the days when there was time for luxuries like a supporting cast and a plot, back before high-tech violence and machine-gun editing came to dominate crime movies. As an actor, he was directed by *film noir* veterans like Nicholas Ray and Henry Hathaway. And maybe his sensibility is attuned to this kind of material, to the notion that an ordinary guy can stumble into some pretty strange stuff. The movie has been compared in some quarters to the work of David Lynch, but it's less self-hating and more stylistically exuberant.

The movie is all style and tone, and a lot of the tone is set by the performance of Virginia Madsen as Dolly Harshaw, the boss's wife. It's the kind of work that used to be done by Lana Turner or Barbara Stanwyck—the tough woman with the healthy sexual interest, who sizes a guy up and makes sure he knows what she likes in a man. Jennifer Connelly, as the innocent bookkeeper down at the office, is perfectly cast as her opposite. She's got the Teresa Wright role, the good girl who has been bruised by an uncaring world. Hopper regards both women with the visual imagination of a cheesecake photographer, which is kind of refreshing. Male superstars have come to dominate action movies so thoroughly that it's rare to find a movie with the time and inclination to linger on beautiful women.

The plot is silly, as such plots always are. It stars Don Johnson as Harry Madox, the stranger from out of town, and he figures out a way to steal money from the bank, and he also finds himself embroiled in violence when the creep in the shack outside of town starts messing with the young girl. And, of course, the boss's wife also has a connection to the creep, and the key to everything is in the shameful secrets of the past.

A film this simple can best be appreciated by a fairly sophisticated viewer, I think. Your average workaday moviegoer will relate to it on Level One and think it contains clichés and stereotypes. Only movie lovers who have marinated their imaginations in the great B movies from RKO and Republic will recognize *The Hot Spot* as a superior work in an old tradition—as a manipulation of story elements as mannered and deliberate, in its way, as variations on a theme for the piano.

Hotel Terminus ★ ★ ★
NO MPAA RATING, 267 m., 1988

A documentary directed by Marcel Ophuls and produced by Ophuls and Bernard Farrel. Edited by Albert Jurgenson and Catherine Zins.

Meandering through *Hotel Terminus*, I felt two sensations that do not ordinarily go together. One was a sense of outrage, and the other was the hypnotic rhythm of a repetitive process. The movie records a tireless search by Marcel Ophuls, a documentary filmmaker who went looking for anyone who could tell him about Klaus Barbie, the Nazi war criminal from France who became known as the "Butcher of Lyons." By the end of the film we know a lot about Barbie, and a lot about Ophuls.

Over and over during the course of the film, people protest that Ophuls is asking questions about things that happened "over 40 years ago." If that were true, it would not be a reason to avoid asking the questions. But it is not true. The whole point of the movie is that Klaus Barbie's war did not end with everyone else's, with the defeat of Nazi Germany.

Barbie was one of the lucky ones whose skills (mostly torture and interrogation) were useful to the postwar Allies in their fight against communism. So he was sheltered from charges of war crimes, used by various agencies (most notably the U.S. counterintelligence corps), and eventually provided with a new identity and resettled in South America—where he continued to practice his torturer's trade.

Barbie was eventually located and denounced by anti-Nazi groups, was extradited by Bolivia, stood trial in Germany, was convicted of war crimes including the sentencing of forty-one orphans to Nazi war camps, and is serving a life sentence. *Hotel Terminus* is not about his capture, trial, and conviction. It is about how people remember him.

Some remember what they want to remember, others remember what they cannot forget. In the film's most harrowing monologue, a woman describes how Barbie methodically tortured one particular prisoner—the woman's father. In other interviews, we learn that Barbie "made the Gestapo respectable" in Lyons by joining it, that he may have

betrayed various Resistance fighters, that he enjoyed hitting people, and also that he was a "nice" man, an intelligent man, and a man who was useful to the Allies after the war. As we listen to retired American intelligence agents describe how they used him, there is the impression that he was just the man they needed, a man not too squeamish to do the dirty jobs they were reluctant to do themselves.

Ophuls is a man with a highly developed sense of irony, and in editing more than 120 hours of interviews into a 267-minute film, he has often selected moments that are rich with self-contradiction. One man, for example, observes that his dog liked Barbie, "and you can't fool a dog." Of course you can fool a dog—and its owner. Other interview subjects are almost absurd as they do verbal handstands to avoid admitting what they almost certainly knew, did, and said.

I felt outrage as I viewed these scenes, and I noticed a curious thing within myself: At times I was more outraged at the "good citizens"—the retired American spies, the postwar officials—than I was at Barbie. This was because I accepted that Barbie was evil, but I did not want to accept that our side would leap to shelter him and work for him. It is easier when all the Nazis are Germans, but harder when we cannot isolate the evil of Nazism in the historical past, and have to accept that officials of several U.S. administrations and even the Vatican were willing to protect this man.

The other sensation I felt was the hypnotic rhythm of Ophuls's reporting process. Long films create a time of their own. Films like *Shoah*, *Little Dorrit*, and *Hotel Terminus* cut us loose from the expectation of a beginning, middle, and end, and leave us adrift for long periods in the center of the film with no shore in sight. Without a story structure to guide us, we become the accomplices of the director—his passengers. We go where he goes. Ophuls asks the same questions again and again, until we grow as angry as he does by the evasions of the answers. When he grows sarcastic (ridiculing one man who will not talk to him by interviewing the cabbages in his garden), it is a relief—we're fed up, too. By the end of *Hotel Terminus*, we have become absorbed somewhat into the filmmaking process; in a strange way, we have gone on the same quest as Ophuls.

Hotel Terminus is not a great film, like Ophuls's *The Sorrow and the Pity*, his masterful indictment of the French who collabo-

rated with the Nazis. It is almost deliberately a film in a minor key, a stubborn film, a gadfly's film, the film of a man who agrees with you that the Nazis were monsters, but adds that he hopes you won't mind if he clears up a few other details as well, such as the utter embarrassment of the postwar history of Klaus Barbie. *The Sorrow and the Pity* was the film of a man who held his audience spellbound. *Hotel Terminus* is the film of a man who continues the conversation after others would like to move on to more polite subjects. It is a stubborn, angry, nagging, sarcastic assault on good manners, and I am happy Ophuls was ill-tempered enough to make it.

Housekeeping ★ ★ ★ ★
PG, 117 m., 1988

Christine Lahti (Sylvie), Sara Walker (Ruth), Andrea Burchill (Lucille), Anne Pitoniak (Aunt Lily), Barbara Reese (Aunt Nona). Directed by Bill Forsyth and produced by Robert F. Colesberry. Screenplay by Forsyth.

In a land where the people are narrow and suspicious, where do they draw the line between madness and sweetness? Between those who are unable to conform to society's norm, and those who simply choose not to, because their dreamy private world is more alluring? That is one of the many questions asked, and not exactly answered, in Bill Forsyth's *Housekeeping*, which was one of the strangest and best films of 1988.

The movie, set some thirty or forty years ago in the Pacific Northwest, tells the story of two young girls who are taken on a sudden and puzzling motor trip by their mother to visit a relative. Soon after they arrive, their mother commits suicide, and before long her sister, their Aunt Sylvie, arrives in town to look after them.

Sylvie, who is played by Christine Lahti as a mixture of bemusement and wry reflection, is not an ordinary type of person. She likes to sit in the dusk so much that she never turns the lights on. She likes to go for long, meandering walks. She collects enormous piles of newspapers and hundreds of tin cans—carefully washing off their labels and then polishing them and arranging them in gleaming pyramids. She is nice to everyone and generally seems cheerful, but there is an enchantment about her that some people find suspicious.

Indeed, even her two young nieces are

divided. One finds her "funny," and the other loves her, and eventually the two sisters will take separate paths in life because they differ about Sylvie. At first, when they are younger, she simply represents reality to them. As they grow older and begin to attend high school, however, one of the girls wants to be "popular," and resents having a weird aunt at home, while the other girl draws herself into Sylvie's dream.

The townspeople are not evil, merely conventional and "concerned." Parties of church ladies visit, to see if they can "help." The sheriff eventually gets involved. But *Housekeeping* is not a realistic movie, not one of those disease-of-the-week docudramas with a tidy solution. It is funnier, more offbeat, and too enchanting to ever qualify on those terms.

The writer-director, Bill Forsyth, has made all of his previous films in Scotland (they make a list of whimsical, completely original comedies: *Gregory's Girl, Local Hero, Comfort and Joy, That Sinking Feeling*). For his first North American production, he began with a novel by Marilynne Robinson that embodies some of his own notions, such as that certain people grow so amused by their own conceits that they cannot be bothered to pay lip service to yours.

In Christine Lahti, he has found the right actress to embody this idea. Although she has been excellent in a number of realistic roles (she was Gary Gilmore's sister in *The Executioner's Song*, and Goldie Hawn's best friend in *Swing Shift*), there is something resolutely private about her, a sort of secret smile that is just right for Sylvie. The role requires her to find a delicate line; she must not seem too mad or willful, or the whole charm of the story will be lost. And although there are times in the film when she seems to be indifferent to her nieces, she never seems not to love them.

Forsyth has surrounded that love with some extraordinary images, which help to create the magical feeling of the film. The action takes place in a house near a lake that is crossed by a majestic, forbidding railroad bridge, and it is a local legend that one night decades ago, a passenger train slipped ever so lazily off the line and plunged down, down into the icy waters of the frozen lake. The notion of the passengers in their warm, well-lit carriages, plunging down to their final destination, is one that Forsyth somehow turns from a tragedy into a notion of doomed beauty. And the bridge becomes important at several moments in the film, especially the last one.

The pastoral setting of the film (in British Columbia) and the production design by Adrienne Atkinson are also evocative; it is important that the action takes place in a small, isolated community, in a place cut off from the world where whimsies can flourish and private notions can survive. At the end of the film, I was quietly astonished; I had seen a film that could perhaps be described as being about a madwoman, but I had seen a character who seemed closer to a mystic, or a saint.

House of Games ★ ★ ★
R, 102 m., 1987

Lindsay Crouse (Margaret Ford), Joe Mantegna (Mike), Mike Nussbaum (Joey), Lilia Skala (Dr. Littauer), J.T. Walsh (Businessman), Jack Wallace (Bartender). Directed by David Mamet and produced by Michael Hausman. Screenplay by Mamet.

This movie is awake. I have seen so many films that sleepwalk through the debris of old plots and secondhand ideas that it was a constant pleasure to watch *House of Games*, a movie about con men that succeeds not only in conning its viewers, but also in creating a series of characters who seem imprisoned by the need to con or be conned.

The film stars Lindsay Crouse as a psychiatrist who specializes in addictive behavior, possibly as a way of dealing with her own compulsions. One of her patients is a gambler who fears he will be murdered over a bad debt. Crouse walks through lonely night streets to the neon signs of the House of Games, a bar where she thinks she can find the gambler who has terrorized her client. She wants to talk him out of enforcing the debt.

The gambler (Joe Mantegna) has never heard anything like this before. But he offers her a deal: If she will help him fleece a high-roller Texan in a big-stakes poker game, he will tear up the marker. She does so. She also becomes fascinated by the back-room reality of these gamblers who have reduced life to a knowledge of the odds. She comes back the next day, looking for Mantegna. She tells him she wants to learn more about gamblers and con men, about the kind of man he is. By the end of this movie, does she ever.

House of Games was written and directed by David Mamet, the playwright *(Glengarry Glen Ross)* and screenwriter *(The Untouchables)*, and it is his directorial debut. Originally it was intended as a big-budget movie with an established director and major stars, but Mamet took the reins himself, cast his wife in the lead and old acting friends in the other important roles, and shot it on the rainy streets of Seattle. Usually the screenwriter is insane to think he can direct a movie. Not this time. *House of Games* never steps wrong from beginning to end.

The plotting is diabolical and impeccable, and I will not spoil the delight of its unfolding by mentioning the crucial details. What I can mention are the performances, the dialogue, and the setting. When Lindsay Crouse enters the House of Games, she enters a world occupied by characters who have known each other so long and so well, in so many different ways, that everything they say is a kind of shorthand. At first we don't fully realize that, and there is a strange savor to the words they use. They speak, of course, in Mamet's distinctive dialogue style, an almost musical rhythm of stopping, backing up, starting again, repeating, emphasizing, all the time with the hint of deeper meanings below the surfaces of the words. The leading actors, Joe Mantegna and Mike Nussbaum, have appeared in countless performances of Mamet plays over the years, and they know his dialogue the way other actors grow into Beckett or Shakespeare. They speak it as it is meant to be spoken, with a sort of aggressive, almost insulting, directness. Mantegna has a scene where he "reads" Lindsay Crouse—where he tells her about her "tells," those small giveaway looks and gestures that poker players use to read the minds of their opponents. The way he talks to her is so incisive and unadorned it is sexual.

These characters and others live in a city that looks, as the Seattle of *Trouble in Mind* did, like a place on a parallel time track. It is a modern American city, but like none we have quite seen before; it seems to have been modeled on the paintings of Edward Hopper, where lonely people wait in empty public places for their destinies to intercept them. Crouse is portrayed as an alien in this world, a successful, best-selling author who has never dreamed that men like this exist, and the movie is insidious in the way it shows her willingness to be corrupted.

There is in all of us a fascination for the inside dope, for the methods of the confidence game, for the secrets of a magic trick. But there is an eternal gulf between the shark and the mark, between the con man and his victim. And there is a code to protect the secrets. There are moments in *House of Games* when Mantegna instructs Crouse in the methods and lore of the con game, but inside every con is another one.

I met a woman once who was divorced from a professional magician. She hated this man with a passion. She used to appear with him in a baffling trick where they exchanged places, handcuffed and manacled, in a locked cabinet. I asked her how it was done. The divorce and her feelings meant nothing compared to her loyalty to the magic profession. She looked at me coldly and said, "The trick is told when the trick is sold." The ultimate question in *House of Games* is, who's buying?

The House on Carroll Street ★ ★ ★
PG, 101 m., 1988

Kelly McGillis (Emily), Jeff Daniels (Cochran), Mandy Patinkin (Salwen), Jessica Tandy (Miss Venable), Jonathan Hogan (Alan), Remak Ramsay (Senator Byington), Ken Welsh (Hackett), Christopher Rhode (Stefan). Directed and produced by Peter Yates. Screenplay by Walter Bernstein.

There is a kind of movie sequence which Alfred Hitchcock always did well, and which most later directors have chosen not to do at all. It involves the hero discovering information by being nosy. Little or no dialogue is used. Most of what the hero sees is in long-shot, and we can sometimes not quite make out all of the details. Half-heard words float on the air. What is being spied on is none of the hero's business, but he cannot resist the human need to be a spy, and neither can we.

The crucial developments in *The House on Carroll Street* are established with such a sequence, and so well is it handled that it casts a sort of spell over the movie. The time is the early 1950s, the height of McCarthyism. The heroine (Kelly McGillis) is a young woman who has just lost her job at a magazine, after refusing to testify before the House Un-American Activities Committee. Desperate for work, she takes a job reading aloud to an old lady. One afternoon, walking in the lady's garden, she sees some figures moving in the tall back windows of the house on the other side of the yard.

She is intrigued. She moves closer, hiding behind the branch of a tree. She overhears an argument. She can tell that something is wrong, but does not know what it could be.

Later, on the street, she sees a young man who was standing in the window. She tries to engage him in conversation, but he resists. Eventually, piecing together a clue here and a word there, she becomes convinced that the people in the house are smuggling Nazi war criminals into the United States, and that they have friends in high places.

There is more. Because the McGillis character is presumably a dangerous radical, she is being tailed by the FBI (there is a hint here of the opening scenes of *Notorious*). The important friends of the Nazis might want to smear her as a Commie, to confuse the trail. The Nazis begin to suspect what she knows. The old lady becomes a valuable ally. And in another echo from *Notorious*, she and one of the FBI men fall in love.

He's played by Jeff Daniels, that dependable, open-faced middle American from *Something Wild* and *Terms of Endearment*. Hey, maybe she is a Commie, but she sure is pretty. He is attracted to her, is disturbed when she is harassed by a search of her home, begins to trust her, and eventually becomes her ally in the fight against the Nazis and their protectors.

As thriller plots go, *The House on Carroll Street* is fairly old-fashioned, which is one of its merits. This is a movie where casting is important, and it works primarily because McGillis, like Ingrid Bergman in *Notorious*, seems absolutely trustworthy. She becomes the island of trust and sanity in the midst of deceit and treachery. The movie advances slowly enough for us to figure it out along with McGillis (or sometimes ahead of her), and there is a nice, ironic double-reverse in the fact that the government is following a good person who seems evil, and discovers evil people who seem good.

What is particularly welcome about the movie is that it's not high-tech. It not only takes place in the 1950s, but is happy there. We don't get the slam-bang cynicism of most characters in modern movies, and after a while I began to figure out why. This movie takes place so long ago that the characters in it have never had their imaginations boiled by full immersion in the thriller culture of recent decades. They're still sort of sweet and innocent, and believe everybody is basically good, and are shocked when they're wrong. Maybe that's the movie's ultimate twist.

House Party ★ ★ ★
R, 105 m., 1990

Christopher Reid (Kid), Christopher Martin (Play), Robin Harris (Pop), Tisha Campbell (Sidney), A.J. Johnson (Sharane), Martin Lawrence (Bilal), George Clinton (D.J.). Full Force: Stab, Zilla, and Pee Wee as played by The George Brothers: Paul Anthony, B. Fine, and Bowlegged Lou, respectively. Directed by Reginald Hudlin and produced by Warrington Hudlin. Screenplay by Reginald Hudlin.

House Party is first of all a musical, and best approached in that spirit. To call it a teen-age movie would confuse the characters with the subject. Yes, it's about a crowd of black teenagers who go to the same school and hang out together, and it's about their loves and rivalries, and a party one of the kids is having at his house. But the plot is an excuse to hang a musical on, and the movie is wall-to-wall with exuberant song and dance.

Original Hollywood musicals have fallen on hard times. The golden age is long gone, and now we get either retreads of Broadway shows or rock concert films. Only occasionally, in a film like *Saturday Night Fever, Dirty Dancing*, or even *The Little Mermaid*, do we get a film where the dramatic developments coexist with original and creative soundtrack music.

In the case of *House Party*, the musical is a canvas used by the director, Reginald Hudlin, to show us black teen-agers with a freshness and originality that's rare in modern movies. We hardly ever see black teen-agers at all in films, and when we do they're painted in images that are either negative and threatening or impossibly clean-cut. Hudlin's teen-agers are neither: They're normal, average kids with the universal desire to go to a party and dance.

The movie's hero is Kid (Christopher Reid), a bright goofball with a haircut that makes Eraserhead look like a marine. He lives with his father (Robin Harris), a gruff but lovable disciplinarian who doesn't want to seem unreasonable but does believe a kid should do his homework before partying at night. And when a kid gets in trouble, he should be grounded.

Kid doesn't want to be grounded. Like all teen-agers, he believes that life literally exists one day at a time, and that an opportunity missed today—especially an opportunity to meet the girlfriend of his dreams—is missed forevermore. He sneaks out of the house, leading to a long night of mild slapstick as he's chased by his father, by the police, and by three tough athletes from his school he has unwisely offended. The chases serve to punctuate the music and the dancing.

A lot of the energy in the movie comes from the natural, unaffected performance of Christopher Reid as the teen-ager who will do anything to get to that dance. He has an engaging, off-center rhythm that suggests he plans to think his way through life instead of making a frontal assault. In his encounters with the jocks from his high school, he tries to talk his way out of tight spots, and his seduction technique with girls is almost entirely verbal; he'll *convince* them they like him. To their credit, the girls, Sidney (Tisha Campbell) and Sharane (A.J. Johnson), look at times like they almost believe him. In matters of romance, teen-age boys can take themselves so dreadfully seriously that Kid must come as a change-of-pace.

House Party is a first feature for writer-director Reginald and producer Warrington Hudlin, brothers from East St. Louis, and is based on a shorter film Reginald made while a student at Harvard. Like his older contemporary Spike Lee, he is a black filmmaker who is concerned with his black characters on their own terms, and doesn't feel the need felt by an earlier generation of directors to relate his characters and plots to white society. His characters don't represent anything but themselves, and there are moments of refreshing honesty here, as when two teenage boys discuss the disadvantages of dating a girl from a project (one problem: her relatives always seem to be hanging around watching the TV).

There is a certain deadening way in which some critics have taken to evaluating recent films about blacks, in which points are given for positive image reinforcement, useful themes, and the promotion of middle-class values. To describe *House Party* in those terms would be unfair and would miss the whole point of the movie's energy and exuberance. It was refreshing for a change to see a story about young blacks that didn't revolve around social problems, thriller elements, drugs, or any particular form of seriousness. *House Party* is silly and high-spirited and not particularly significant, and that is just as it should be.

The Howling ★ ★
R, 91 m., 1981

Dee Wallace (Karen White), Patrick Macnee (Dr. Waggner), Kevin McCarthy (Fred), Slim Pickens (Sam), Dennis Dugan (Chris), Belina Balaski (Terry), John Carradine (Eric). Directed by Joe Dante and produced by Michael Pinell and Jack Conrad. Screenplay by John Sayles.

Now for America's favorite newspaper team, Uncle Roger and Little Jimmy. As we join them inside the Movie Lab, we hear . . .

(Whoo! Whoooo!)

I'm ol' Uncle Roger, and this is Little Jimmy!

(Arf! Barf!)

What's in the news today, Unca' Rog???

Well, Little Jimmy . . . new movie in town . . . name of The Howling.

(Whoooo! Chortle, chortle. Siren sound. Growwwwwl.)

What's it about???

Werewolves! Little Jimmy. Mean, nasty animals . . . story here . . . about a girl who went OUT ON A DATE . . . didn't know the guy too well . . . one thing led to another . . . the guy GROWS FANGS, Little Jimmy . . . starts dripping saliva all over her Gloria Vanderbilts.

(Whoooo!!)

Holy Alpo, Unca' Rog! What happened then!

Girl turns to the guy . . . doesn't know what to say . . . says, "GET YOUR HANDS OFF OF ME!" Werewolf . . . hardly listens. Doesn't SEEM TO HEAR!

Awful things can happen on a date, Unca' Rog.

Right, Little Jimmy. She said . . . she'd been out on dates with a wolf before . . . BUT NEVER A WEREWOLF!

What else happened?

(Pant, pant.)

Weird CALIFORNIA CULT, Little Jimmy. Up the coast from the big city. People . . . sitting around campfires . . . singing songs . . . getting their heads back together. One wanders off into the underbrush . . . NEVER SEEN AGAIN!

Holy lurking terrors!

Says here . . . this broad who was a TV ANCHORWOMAN. Investigating weird cults. Went into one of those adult movie arcades with the doors that lock from the inside . . . you know, Little Jimmy?

Two bits in the slot?

Right, Little Jimmy. Gets in there . . . locks the door . . . lights off . . . guy standing there in the dark . . . she wants to GET THE STORY. Guy says, "Turn around."

(Snaaaarrll!!!)

What happened then???

GUY'S A WEREWOLF! Cop comes in, blasts hell out of the private viewing booth . . . they take the body to the morgue . . . next day, the BODY IS MISSING! Says here . . . CLAW marks on the inside of the stainless steel door!

Holy Toledo Steel Works!

There's more. Broad follows the trail to the cult's summer camp . . . advice of her psychiatrist . . . turns out . . . WERE-WOLVES are running the camp. She's not just hearing things . . . the underbrush DOES have noises in it.

What next?

Guy says . . . tells her . . . says, "I want to give you a piece of my mind!"

Does he?

GIVES HER . . . a piece of his mind. Pulls it out and gives it to her. Nauseating. Research indicates . . . if you're bitten by a werewolf, so long, baby . . . you ARE a WEREWOLF. Legendary story . . . they come out only at night . . . NOT TRUE. Can come out anytime. Daytime not safe.

(Barf!)

Unca' Rog?

Yes, Little Jimmy?

What's the SCARIEST THING in this movie?

In the whole movie?

The MOST AWFUL THING in the whole movie, please, please, tell me, please?

All right . . . you asked for it . . . WORST thing . . . you've ever seen . . . MOST DISGUSTING SIGHT in the history of films . . . you don't believe what you're seeing . . . here it comes, Little Jimmy: Before your VERY EYES . . . this movie CHANGES INTO A DOG!

Holy White Fang!!! Is it worth seeing?

Yes, Little Jimmy, in a sense, it is. Ridiculous . . . yes. Comical at times . . . yes. Silliest film seen in some time by the Animals Movies Critics' Team. BUT . . . great special effects as men BECOME werewolves. WOMEN, too. Before your eyes. Done with . . . says here . . . HY-DRAULICS! Sensational!

Is it worth my money?

It sure is, Little Jimmy. Says here . . . worth your money, IF you get it two for one.

The Hunt for Red October ★ ★ ★ ½
PG, 134 m., 1990

Sean Connery (Marko Ramius), Alec Baldwin (Jack Ryan), Scott Glenn (Bart Mancuso), Sam Neill (Captain Borodin), James Earl Jones (Admiral Greer), Joss Ackland (Andrei Lysenko), Richard Jordan (Jeffrey Pelt), Peter Firth (Ivan Putin), Tim Curry (Dr. Petrov), Jeffrey Jones (Skip Tyler). Directed by John McTiernan and produced by Mace Neufeld. Screenplay by Larry Ferguson and Donald Stewart.

The movies have one sure way of involving us that never fails. They give us a character who is right when everybody else is wrong and then invite us to share his frustration as he tries to talk some sense into the blockheads. In *The Hunt for Red October*, that character is Jack Ryan, the intelligence man who believes he knows the real reason why a renegade Soviet skipper is trying to run away with a submarine.

The skipper's name is Ramius, and he is the most respected man in the Soviet underwater navy. He has trained most of the other captains in the fleet, and now he has been given the controls of an advanced new submarine named Red October—a sub that uses a revolutionary new drive and that is almost completely silent. American intelligence tracks the Red October as it leaves its Soviet shipyard, but then the sub seems to disappear—and, soon after, the entire Soviet navy mobilizes itself into a vast cat-and-mouse game in the North Atlantic.

The Soviets would like their American counterparts to believe that Ramius is a madman who wants to hide his sub off the American coast and aim its nuclear missiles at New York or Washington. They ask the U.S. Navy to help them track and destroy the Red October. But Ryan (Alec Baldwin) believes that would be a tragic mistake. He tells his superior, an admiral played by James Earl Jones, that Ramius is actually trying to defect and to bring his submarine along with him.

That is the setup for John McTiernan's film, as it was for Tom Clancy's best-selling novel, and in both cases it is also the starting point for a labyrinthine plot in which, half of the time, we have to guess at the hidden reasons for Ramius's actions. It is a tribute to the movie, which has much less time than Clancy did at book length, that it allows the plot its full complexity and yet is never less than clear to the audience.

Many military thrillers, especially those set in the Cold War period, rely on stereotyping and large, crude motivations to move their stories along. *The Hunt for Red October* has more fun by suggesting how easily men can go wrong, how false assumptions can seem seductive, and how enormous consequences can sometimes hang by slender threads. Ryan's knowledge of Ramius's personality, for example, upon which so much depends, is based almost entirely on one occasion when they dined at the same table. Everything else is simply a series of skilled hunches.

McTiernan, whose previous films were *Predator* and *Die Hard*, showed a sense of style and timing in those movies, but what he adds in *The Hunt for Red October* is something of the same detached intelligence that Clancy brought to the novel. Somehow we feel this is more than a thriller; it's an exercise in military and diplomatic strategy in which the players are all smart enough that we can't take their actions for granted.

The Hunt for Red October has more than a dozen important speaking roles, in addition to many more cast members who are crucial for a scene or two, and any film with a cast this large must depend to some extent on typecasting. We couldn't keep the characters straight any other way. What McTiernan does is to typecast without stereotyping. Sean Connery makes a convincing Ramius, and yet, with his barely concealed Scots accent, he is far from being a typical movie Soviet. Alec Baldwin, as the dogged intelligence officer, has the looks of a leading man, but he dials down his personality—he presents himself as a deck-bound bureaucrat who can't believe he has actually gotten himself into this field exercise. And Scott Glenn, as the commander of a U.S. submarine that finds itself within yards of the silent Red October, is leaner, younger, and has more edge than most of the standard movie skipper types.

The production design lends a lot to the movie's credibility. I'm told that the interiors of submarines in this movie look a good deal more high-tech and glossy than they do in real life—that there would be more grease around on a real sub—and yet, for the movie screen, these subs look properly impressive with their awesome displays of electronic gadgetry. The movie does not do as good a job of communicating the daily and hourly reality of submarine life as *Das Boot* did, but perhaps that's because we are not trapped and claustrophobic inside a sub for the whole movie. There are cutaways to the White House and CIA headquarters in Langley, to the Kremlin, and to the decks of ships at sea.

If there's one area where the movie is truly less than impressive, it's the underwater exterior shots. Using models of submarines, the filmmakers have attempted to give an impression of these behemoths maneuvering under the sea. But the outside of a submarine is not intrinsically photogenic, and what these shots most look like are large, gray, bloated whales seen through dishwater.

And yet that lapse doesn't much matter. *The Hunt for Red October* is a skillful, efficient film that involves us in the clever and deceptive game being played by Ramius and in the best efforts of those on both sides to figure out what he plans to do with his submarine—and how he plans to do it. The movie is constructed so we can figure that out along with everybody else, and that leaves a lot of surprises for the conclusion, which is quite satisfactorily suspenseful. There was only one question that bothered me throughout the movie. As one whose basic ideas about submarines come from Commander Edward Beach's classic *Run Silent, Run Deep*, in which the on-board oxygen supply was a source of constant concern, I kept asking myself if those Russian sailors should be smoking so much down there in the depths of the ocean.

I Love You to Death ★ ★ ★
R, 97 m., 1990

Kevin Kline (Joey), Tracey Ullman (Rosalie), Joan Plowright (Nadja), River Phoenix (Devo), William Hurt (Harlan), Keanu Reeves (Marlon), James Gannon (Lieutenant Schooner), Jack Kehler (Wiley). Directed by Lawrence Kasdan and produced by Jeffrey Lurie and Ron Moler. Screenplay by John Kostmayer.

I Love You to Death is like an acting class in which the students are presented with impossible situations and asked how they would handle them. The students in this case are accomplished actors—Kevin Kline, William Hurt, Tracey Ullman, and Joan Plowright, among others—but what was each one thinking in the scene where the dead man walks downstairs? How do you carry on a polite conversation with someone who has a bullet hole clean through him, but hasn't noticed? Particularly if you were involved in his attempted murder?

The movie's plot is so unlikely that of course it is based on fact. The story was in the news a couple of years ago, about how the wife of a pizzeria owner decided to kill her husband because he was cheating on her. After the murder attempt failed, the husband refused to press charges against his wife because he felt she had done the right thing. After all, he *was* guilty, wasn't he? My memory is hazy about what happened then. They lived happily ever after, most probably.

In the movie version, written by John Kostmayer and directed by Lawrence Kasdan, this story is developed into a domestic black comedy of droll and macabre dimensions. And it is told in a series of scenes in which most of the characters are either lying to each other, lying to themselves, or incapable of coherent thought. The few moments of

honesty and lucidity have a fascination all their own, since under those conditions the characters tend to become tongue-tied with embarrassment.

The result is an actor's dream, a film in which the truth of almost every scene has to be excavated out of the debris of social inhibition. I am not so sure this is a dream film for an audience, however; the moviegoer eager for plot and drama is likely to grow impatient and think nothing much is happening on the screen, when in fact volumes are happening inside the minds and consciences of the characters.

The movie begins with a happy day at the pizzeria in Tacoma, where Joey (Kevin Kline) and his wife Rosalie (Tracey Ullman) take care of business with the help of Devo (River Phoenix), who is very, very far out, but who occasionally focuses on the object of his devotion, Rosalie. Joey is a ladies' man. Cheerfully shouldering his kit of plumber's tools, he sallies forth daily to do "odd jobs" in the rental apartments the family owns—most of them occupied by willing females whose plumbing is in fine repair. It should be obvious to anyone that Joey is cheating, but Rosalie remains blissfully blind to the evidence. She trusts her Joey.

The moment of her awakening is a painful one. She feels betrayed and double-crossed. She confides in her mother (Joan Plowright), and they agree, without hesitation, that the death penalty is called for in this case. They dispatch the faithful Devo to a local pool hall, where two low-life drugheads (William Hurt and Keanu Reeves) are bent low over the pool table, for support. They agree to shoot Joey, for a price. Meanwhile, Rosalie and her mother have fed the philandering husband several helpings of spaghetti laced with three large bottles of sleeping pills.

The drugheads arrive, hold a confused

conference at the bedside, and shoot the slumbering victim. Then, while everyone is conferring downstairs, Joey appears, still alive. The movie's most difficult and intriguing scene now follows. It takes place almost entirely in the eyes of the actors, and in their pauses and silences, and is an exquisite exercise in guilty embarrassment. It is an almost impossible scene to pull off, but somehow they all accomplish it.

Another good thing about the movie is Tracey Ullman's low-key, plain-Jane approach to the wife. It's all the more effective because Kevin Kline has for some reason adopted a comic opera accent and mannerisms as the husband, and is hard to believe except in the scenes where he is almost dead. Ullman finds the stubborn vindictiveness inside her character, who is so sunny when she trusts her husband and so unforgiving when she discovers she was deceived. Joan Plowright might seem like an unlikely choice as the mother, but gets some of the movie's biggest laughs. William Hurt could have walked through the role of the spaced-out hit man, but takes the time to make the character believable and even, in a bleary way, complex.

Nothing in Lawrence Kasdan's previous career (*Body Heat, The Big Chill, Silverado, The Accidental Tourist*) seems like preparation for this film, but then what could? It is the first time Kasdan has directed from a screenplay he didn't write, and I assume he was attracted to it for the obvious reason—because it seemed all but impossible to do. I am not sure if the film is a success because I am not sure what it is trying to do. It founders in embarrassment, but not boringly.

I, Madman ★ ★ ★
R, 90 m., 1989

Jenny Wright (Virginia), Clayton Rohner (Richard), Randall William Cook (Malcolm), Stephanie Hodge (Mona), Michelle Jordan (Colette), Vance Valencia (Sergeant Navarro), Mary Baldwin (Librarian), Rafael Nazario (Hotel Clerk). Directed by Tibor Takacs and produced by Rafael Eisenman. Screenplay by David Chaskin.

She works in a used-book store and brings home lurid pulp thrillers to read at night, alone, while she's snuggled up on the sofa and a violent electrical storm is raging outside. She's reading one now, titled *Much of Madness, More of Sin*.

It's about a mad scientist who is rejected by the woman he loves. She doesn't like his facial features. He'll show her. He takes a scapel and removes his offending features, and comes calling on her with a hole where his face used to be.

This is some book. She turns a page. The lightning crackles outside. Something creaks in the hallway. The night is late and the single lamp leaves deep shadows in the room. And I'm thinking that I love movies that begin this way because they understand that horror movies can be fun. They don't have to be vomitoriums about mad slashers and dead teen-agers.

Tibor Takacs's *I, Madman* places its terrors where they belong, in the midst of everyday life. Virginia, the heroine (Jenny Wright), works days in the bookstore and would like to spend her evenings with her boyfriend, but he's a cop and always seems to be on a dope stakeout somewhere. So she reads. And the movie slips between reality and imagination—between the book she's reading and the things that really seem to be happening in her life.

The novel about the mad scientist is by a man named Malcolm Brand. We find out a little more about him than Virginia does. We learn, for example, that he lives in a fleabag hotel and conducts experiments in creating life. He wants to cross a monkey with a jackal and create a new race. His books may be autobiographical. And he may still be alive— or at least, alive in a sense. (Malcolm is played in the movie by special-effects man Randall William Cook, who designed the grotesque makeup and then convinced the director to let him wear it himself.)

Life goes on. There are strange visitors to the used-book store. In the streets outside, bizarre crimes are committed. Is Malcolm Brand killing people in order to steal their lips and noses so that he can stitch his own face back together again?

I, Madman contains the usual elements in a modern thriller, including the lonely woman, late at night, in danger. It gets the usual mileage out of the standard False Alarm scene, where the door creaks open and the heroine is terrified—but it's only her boyfriend. What's original about this movie is the fun it has with the thin line between reality and imagination, between what Virginia is reading and what is really happening.

Jenny Wright seems to enjoy the role, especially the parts where she curls up on the sofa and turns the pages while her eyes pop out of her head. Movies like this always have a scene where nobody will believe the heroine. She knows, she just *knows* that a madman is loose in the neighborhood—but everyone says it's only her hyperthyroid imagination.

Climaxes in thrillers have gotten pretty standard recently, involving chases and shoot-outs and a lot of blood. *I, Madman* has some surprises for her. There's that old trunk up in the attic of the used-book store—the one that turns out to be from the estate of the late Malcolm Brand. It has holes punched in the top, almost as if there's something inside that needs to breathe. Something with big teeth and very long arms.

I Never Promised You a Rose Garden ★ ★ ★
R, 90 m., 1977

Kathleen Quinlan (Deborah), Bibi Andersson (Dr. Fried), Ben Piazza (Mr. Blake), Lorraine Gary (Mrs. Blake), Michael McGuire (McPherson), Reni Santoni (Hobbs), Susan Tyrrell (Kitty), Robert Viharo (Anterrabae). Directed by Anthony Page and produced by Terence F. Deane, Daniel H. Blatt, and Michael Hausman. Screenplay by Gavin Lambert and Lewis John Carlino.

I'm becoming suspicious of movies that assure us mental illness can be cured if the victim "wants" to be cured, or assume that mental illness is not illness at all—because in an insane world the only sane people are the crazies. *I Never Promised You a Rose Garden* doesn't altogether avoid the first assumption, but it firmly rejects the second, and it gives us a heroine so convincingly real we finally believe perhaps she *could* cure herself.

The heroine is well known to the millions of readers of Joanne Greenberg's novel, which began as a cult paperback and became a durable bestseller. She is Deborah, sixteen, schizophrenic, child of an affluent home, but inhabitant of a personal fantasy. After a suicide attempt, she spends three years in a mental institution, coming close to self-destruction more than once, but finally surviving through her own efforts and those of a psychiatrist who really attempts to understand her.

We are given only sketchy information about what drove her to attempt suicide—her parents didn't understand her, she's filled with guilt because she believes she tried to kill a younger sister—but her fantasies are shown in much greater detail. As visualized in the film, they seem to be inspired by the paintings of Frank Frazetta: A race of muscular young people, clothed in furs and feathers, ride giant horses across the desert and want her to join them.

This alternative universe is so much more romantic and seductive than the real world, which for Deborah becomes Ward D of the mental institution. It's a women's ward, filled with the "worst" cases. Some of the patients do indeed seem to be totally within their private hells, but others (like the loud and often cheerful Kitty) have a reservoir of common sense. Deborah is wary, here, and often silent; she's properly afraid of the sinister male attendant Hobbs, but the turning point in her cure comes when she can admit of the other attendant, McPherson: "I like him. He treats me like I'm a real person." That touch of reality from outside is the first crack in the totality of her fantasies.

The psychiatrist is Dr. Fried, played by Bibi Andersson with sympathy and fortitude: She listens, encourages, supports, suggests, doesn't push. And over a period of three years Deborah is finally able to open herself to the world outside her dreams, to send her phantom gods galloping out into the desert without her.

I Never Promised You a Rose Garden has been compared, of course, to *One Flew Over the Cuckoo's Nest*, which first defied a kind of unwritten Hollywood superstition. That superstition was that movies about mental illness wouldn't succeed at the box office, that they were too depressing. *Cuckoo's Nest* wasn't filmed for years because of that taboo, and *Rose Garden* probably couldn't have been made if it hadn't been for *Cuckoo's Nest's* great success.

One big difference between the two movies is that R.P. McMurphy, in *Cuckoo*, was, in fact, sane. Deborah is not. *Cuckoo* celebrates McMurphy's cosmic sanity, and so has room for the dimensions of Jack Nicholson's manic performance. *Rose Garden* celebrates, instead, very small victories (and one of its most poignant moments comes when Deborah, burning herself with a cigarette, realizes with triumph that she actually feels pain—that her mind has let the reality in).

This is difficult material to bring to life, but a young actress named Kathleen Quinlan does it with heart and sensitivity. There were opportunities here for climbing the walls and chewing the scenery, I suppose, but her performance always finds the correct and convincing human note.

And it's the skill with which Miss Quinlan (and Bibi Andersson) follow that thread of characterization that makes the movie work. Otherwise, those desert fantasies and all those feathers and fur might have been fatally distracting. But because Deborah seems to regard them with a sober fatalism, we can almost accept them; and because she never expresses any emotions that don't seem to grow right out of the situations she finds herself in, we always accept her.

I Never Sang for My Father ★ ★ ★ ★
PG, 92 m., 1971

Melvyn Douglas (Tom), Gene Hackman (Gene), Dorothy Stickney (Margaret), Estelle Parsons (Alice, The Sister), Elizabeth Hubbard (Peggy). Directed and produced by Gilbert Cates. Screenplay by Robert Anderson.

At the beginning and again at the end of *I Never Sang for My Father*, we see a grainy snapshot of an old man and a middle-aged man, arms thrown about each other's shoulders, peering uncertainly into the camera as if they're not quite sure what drew them out into the sunshine to pose this day. And we hear Gene Hackman's voice: "Death ends a life. But it does not end a relationship." This film takes that simple fact and uses it to make a poignant and ultimately tragic statement about parents and children, life and death, and all the words that go unspoken. The man is played by Melvyn Douglas, and Hackman plays his son, and the film is about the fierce

love they bear for each other, and about their inability to communicate that love, or very much of anything else.

The story takes place at a time when the old man's life is ending, but he won't admit it, and when the younger man's life is about to permit a new beginning. The old man is eighty-one, and a long time ago he was the mayor and the school board president—one of the town's most important citizens. But now he has largely been forgotten, left to live a comfortable life in the rambling old family home. He lives there with his wife and his memories, and a fierce possessiveness for his son.

What he wants from the son is a show of devotion. He doesn't communicate with him; indeed, he spends a lot of time falling asleep in front of the television set. But he wants him there, almost as a hostage, because he has a hunger for affection left over from his own neglected childhood. The son tries to go through the motions. But his own wife died a year ago, and now, at forty-four, he has decided to marry a woman doctor who lives in California. This will mean leaving the hometown, and that would be heresy to his father.

The situation becomes urgent when the old man's wife dies. He seems to accept the death as an inconvenience, transferring his grief to memories of his own mother's death half a century before. But his dependence upon his son becomes almost total. His daughter (Estelle Parsons) comes home for the funeral; in a fit of rage, the old man had banished her for marrying a Jew. Now she explains to Hackman, with an objectivity that sounds cruel but springs from love, that an arrangement is going to have to be made about their father. He can't live in the big house by himself.

The trouble is, his pride makes him refuse to hire the housekeeper he could easily afford. He expects his son to watch over him. And Hackman has not gathered the courage to reveal his marriage plans. He goes to look at a couple of old people's homes, but he finds them depressing and he knows his father would never, ever, go to one. So there you have the son's dilemma. The father should not live alone. A nursing home seems impossible. For a moment, the children consider gaining power of attorney and insisting on a housekeeper. But then, in a scene of remarkable emotional impact, the son watches as his father finally breaks down and reveals his grief, and the son invites him to come and

live in California. But that, of course, is also unacceptable to the old man, whose pride will not allow him to admit that others could make his decisions, and whose stubbornness makes him insist on having everything his way, no matter what.

These bare bones of plot hardly give any hint of the power of this film. I've suggested something of what it's about, but almost nothing about the way the writing, the direction, and the performances come together to create one of the most unforgettably human films I can remember.

Robert Anderson's screenplay is from his autobiographical play, and it rings with truth. His dialogue is direct and revealing, without the "literary" touches or sophistication that could have sabotaged the characters. Eugene O'Neill was writing a different kind of dialogue for different purposes in *Long Day's Journey into Night*, a somewhat similar work that comes to mind. But for Anderson's story, which depends on everyday realism and would find symbolism dangerous, the unadorned dialogue is essential.

Gilbert Cates's direction also respects the fact that this is a movie not about visual style or any other fashionably cinematic self-consciousness. With the exception of an inappropriate song which sneaks onto the sound track near the film's beginning, Cates has directed solely to get those magnificent performances onto the screen as movingly as possible. Much of the film is just between the two of them and the characters seem to work so well because Douglas and Hackman respond to each other in every shot; the effect is not of acting, but as if the story were happening right now while we see it.

The film tells us that death ends a life, but not a relationship. That's true of all close and deep human relationships; when one person dies, the other continues long afterwards to wonder what could have been said between them, but wasn't.

I Never Sang for My Father has the courage to remain open-ended; the father dies, but the problems between father and son remain unresolved. That is really more tragic than the fact of death, because death is natural, but human nature cries out that parents and children should understand each other.

I Wanna Hold Your Hand ★ ★ ¹/₂
PG, 104 m., 1978

Nancy Allen (Pam), Bobby DiCicco (Tony), Marc McClure (Larry), Susan Kendall Newman (Janis), Theresa Saldana (Grace), Wendie Jo Sperber (Rosie), Will Jordan (Ed Sullivan). Directed by Robert Zemeckis and produced by Tamara Asseyev and Alex Rose. Screenplay by Zemeckis and Bob Gale.

I Wanna Hold Your Hand is a goofy, funny, slapstick movie about the day the Beatles invaded America—and especially about a bunch of kids who are determined to see them, no matter what. It's silly, it doesn't always make sense, but it's fun. And it has a nice anarchic touch: There is something inspired about the image of a crazed teenager scaling a television tower to knock the Beatles off the air, and having the ax blasted from his hand by a lightning bolt from that big Beatles fan in the sky.

The movie is put together sort of like *American Graffiti*: We meet the teen-age heroes as they jam into a record store to buy the first Beatles album, and then we follow them as they attempt literally anything to get past police lines and security guards and into the presence of the Beatles. Today's teenagers are likely to ask: Were kids *really* that crazy about the Beatles? Yes, today's teenagers . . . yes, they were.

But the movie's not a sociological document. It's a series of slapstick chases inspired, I suspect, by the Hollywood tradition of screwball comedies. Some of the scenes work, some don't, but the director, Robert Zemeckis, doesn't stop for breath. Many of the best moments star a kid named Bobby DiCicco, who bills himself as the world's foremost Beatles fan, and is capable of crashing through elevator doors and swinging like a crazed Tarzan from a cable above the heads of Ed Sullivan's audience.

There's also a pudgy girl (Wendie Jo Sperber) who suffers from the most agonizing torture a teen-ager can experience: knowing the answer to the question being asked on the radio that will win you two free tickets to the "Ed Sullivan Show," and *not being able to get to a telephone!* In her desperation to call in with the answers to tricky questions ("Who is both the youngest and the oldest Beatle?"*), she leaps from speeding cars and throws loose change at telephones like a maniac.

The movie does a fairly good job of remembering how people talked, looked, and dressed in 1964 (incredible as it may seem, guys had short hair and hardly anybody wore blue jeans). One funny scene has a long-haired Beatles fan being told by his obviously sadistic father that he can have two tickets to the Sullivan show—but only if he gets his hair cut. A point-of-view shot shows the barber leaning ominously over him . . . with a patch over one eye.

We never really see the Beatles in the film, but we do see kinescopes of their actual TV appearance (very well coordinated with the movements of doubles on the studio stage). And we hear more than a dozen Beatles songs, and even see what are supposed to be John's shoes. That's in the scene I liked best, in which one girl actually does get into the Beatles' empty suite at the Plaza, and orgiastically touches the glasses *they* drank from, and the chairs *they* sat in, the beds *they* rumpled and, my God, even the cigarette butts *they* left behind . . . .

*(*Answer: Ringo, the oldest in years but youngest in terms of service.)*

Iceman ★ ★ ★ ★
PG, 99 m., 1984

Timothy Hutton (Dr. Shephard), John Lone (Iceman), Lindsay Crouse (Dr. Diane Brady). Directed by Fred Schepisi and produced by Norman Jewison and Patrick Palmer. Screenplay by John Drimmer and Chip Proser.

Iceman begins in almost exactly the same way as both versions of *The Thing*, with a team of Arctic scientists chopping a frozen mammal out of the ice. But somehow we're more interested in this discovery because the frozen object isn't simply a gimmick at the beginning of a horror picture; it is presented with real curiosity and awe.

What is it? As a helicopter lifts the discovery aloft, we can glimpse its vague, shadowy outline through the block of forty-thousand-year-old ice. It seems almost to be a man, with its arms outstretched. If we remember Fellini's *La Dolce Vita*, we're reminded of its famous opening scene, as the helicopter flew above Rome with the statue of Christ. In both cases, a contrast is made between the technological gimmicks of man and an age-old mystery. In both cases, also, we're aware that we are in the hands of a master director. *Iceman* is by Fred Schepisi, the Australian who made *The Chant of Jimmy Blacksmith* and Willie Nelson's *Barbarosa*. Both of those movies were about men who lived entirely apart from modern society, according to rules of their own, rules that we eventually realized made perfect sense (to them, at least). Now Schepisi has taken that story idea as far as it will go.

The block of ice is thawed. As each drop of water trickles down a stainless-steel table to the floor, we feel a real excitement. We're about to discover something, just as we were when the apes found the monolith in *2001*. Inside the block of ice is a Neanderthal man, perfectly preserved, frozen in an instant with his hands pushing out and his mouth open in a prehistoric cry of protest. Such a discovery is at least theoretically possible; mastodons have been found in Russia, frozen so quickly in a sudden global catastrophe that the buttercups in their stomachs had still not been digested. Why not a man? Of course, the man's cell tissue would have been destroyed by the freezing process, right? Not according to *Iceman*, which advances an ingenious theory.

The scene in which the Neanderthal is brought back to life is one of those emergency room dramas we're familiar with from the TV medical shows, with medics pounding on the chest and administering electrical shocks. Then the movie leaves the familiar, and begins an intriguing journey into the past of the man. The Neanderthal (his name sounds like "Charlie") is placed in a controlled environment. Two scientists (Timothy Hutton and Lindsay Crouse) establish a relationship with him. Elementary communication is started—although here the movie makes a basic error in showing the scientists teaching Charlie to speak English, when of course they would want to learn his language instead.

The rest of the movie develops a theory about how Charlie was frozen and what he was looking for when that surprising event took place. There is also an argument between two branches of science: Those who are more interested in what they can learn from Charlie's body and those who want to understand his mind. This conflict seems to have been put in to generate suspense (certainly no responsible scientist, presented with a living Neanderthal man, would suggest any experiment that would endanger his life). But never mind; before it turns into conflict between good and evil, *Iceman* departs in an unexpected, mystical direction.

This movie is spellbinding storytelling. It

begins with such a simple premise and creates such a genuinely intriguing situation that we're not just entertained, we're drawn into the argument. What we feel about Charlie reflects what we feel about ourselves. And what he knows—that we've forgotten—illuminates the line between man the firebuilder, and man the stargazer. Think how much more interesting *The Thing* would have been if its frozen life form had been investigated rather than destroyed, and you have an idea of *Iceman*'s appeal.

The Idolmaker ★ ★ ★
PG, 117 m., 1980

Ray Sharkey (Vince Vacarri), Tovah Feldshuh (Brenda Roberts), Peter Gallagher (Caesare), Paul Land (Tommy Dee), Joe Pantoliano (Gino Pilate). Directed by Taylor Hackford and produced by Gene Kirkwood and Howard W. Koch, Jr. Screenplay by Edward Di Lorenzo.

At the core of *The Idolmaker*, making it a better film than it might otherwise have been, is the hungry, lonely ego of the movie's hero, Vince Vacarri. He has all the skills necessary to become a rock 'n' roll idol, especially in the late-1950s world of Top Forty payola and prefabricated stars. But he doesn't have the looks. He so desperately wants stardom, though, that he tries to have it vicariously, through the "idols" he painstakingly manufactures. Maybe that makes *The Idolmaker* sound more serious than it is, but it's that core of obsession in the Ray Sharkey performance that takes a movie that might have been routine and makes it interesting. This is not a dazzlingly original idea, but the movie understands its passions well enough to entertain us with them.

The "idolmaker" of the title is based, I understand, on the real-life character of Bob Marcucci (listed as the film's "technical adviser"). He is the Philadelphia Svengali who discovered, coached, and managed Frankie Avalon and Fabian, quarterbacking them to stardom. If this movie can be believed, he was a rock 'n' roll puppetmaster, supplying the lines, the songs, the delivery and—most importantly—the stage mannerisms and "look" of his personalities.

The movie moves the story to Brooklyn, and borrows heavily from the clichés of show-biz rags-to-riches movies: Not only is it lonely at the top in this movie . . . it's lonely at the bottom, too, for practice. The Sharkey character manufactures his first rock star (Paul Land) out of a little raw talent, an unshaped stage presence, and sheer energy. One of the movie's most engaging scenes shows Land at a high school record hop, doggedly pantomiming his first record while Sharkey, backstage, goes through the same motions.

Land does a good job of playing the movie's first rock singer—a spoiled, egotistical creation renamed "Tommy Dee." We can predict what will happen. He'll be pushed to the top by Sharkey, develop an inflated opinion of himself, and think he did it all alone. That's exactly what happens, but Land moves through these stages with a conviction that makes them seem fairly new, even while we're recognizing them.

Meanwhile, Sharkey has another discovery waiting in the wings. He spots a busboy (Peter Gallagher) in his brother's restaurant. The guy can't keep time, can't sing, and has one enormous hairy eyebrow all the way across his face. No problem: Sharkey pounds rhythm into him, grooms him, renames him Caesare and fast-talks him onto the movie's version of "American Bandstand." It turns out that this kid *does* have a natural rapport with the prepubescent girls in his audiences, and he's on his way.

None of this would work if *The Idolmaker* didn't have convincing actors playing the two rock singers. It does. Land and Gallagher can sing and move well enough to convince us they're plausible teen idols. They can also act well enough to modulate their stage performances—they start out terrible and work their way up to levels that Fabian himself must only have dreamed about. And the movie has fun with its production numbers. The songs are all standard late-fifties rock dreck (but newly composed for the movie), but the stage performances are a little sneaky. They're not as ridiculous as many of the late-fifties adolescent heroes actually were; they seem to owe a lot not only to Elvis (naturally) but also to such performers of a decade later as Mick Jagger.

All of this is not to say that *The Idolmaker* is a masterpiece. But it is a well-crafted movie that works, that entertains, and that pulls us through its pretty standard material with the magnetism of the Ray Sharkey performance. Because we sense his hungers, his isolations, and his compulsive needs, we buy scenes that might otherwise have been unworkable.

If Looks Could Kill ★ ★ ★
PG-13, 84 m., 1991

Richard Grieco (Michael Corben), Linda Hunt (Ilsa Grunt), Roger Rees (Augustus Steranko), Geraldine Hames (Vendetta Galente), Michael Sierry (Richardson), Gabrielle Anwar (Mariska). Directed by William Dear and produced by Craig Zadan and Neil Meron. Screenplay by Darren Star.

If Looks Could Kill is one of those zany capers that comes along occasionally to remind us of the pleasures of Wretched Excess. The movie tells a bizarre story about middle Americans trapped inside the Byzantine intrigues of Europe, and is perhaps the only film I can recall in which a mad economist traps an entire Detroit high school French class in an iron cage suspended above a cauldron of boiling gold.

At first, it appears the movie is only another one of those brain-damaged caper rip-offs in which boring people do stupid things at half the pace of real life. Then it turns on the supercharger and transforms itself into the kind of hallucinatory fable in which a tiny woman wears a golden whip around her neck, and uses it to reduce foreign ministers into lumps of placation.

The movie's hero is TV star Richard Grieco, who has the kind of sleek, dark looks that make you suspect he's wearing mascara when he's probably not. He plays a high school senior who has flunked his French class, but has a chance to make up the grade during the French Club's summer tour of Europe. The name of his character is Michael Corben—and that's an important detail, because on board the same flight to Europe is a superspy, also named Michael Corben, and when the real spy is killed, Grieco is mistaken for him. That leads to a labyrinthine plot tangle in which Grieco finally has to save all of Europe from the schemes of a mad politician (Roger Rees) who has a plan to convert the continent to a gold standard under which all of the coins will bear his likeness.

The plot is worthy of a James Bond villain, and indeed *If Looks Could Kill* plays like a head-on collision between Bond and Indiana Jones, if the primary goal of both of those heroes was transcendent silliness. The movie's endearing goofiness extends even to shooting the Paris scenes in Montreal, with a matte painting of the Eiffel Tower in the distance, and using a château in Quebec as Rees's headquarters for torture, gold-melting, and world domination.

It's all Grieco can do to keep up with the supporting cast, which seems to have been encouraged to unleash their latent skills for overacting. Linda Hunt has the most fun, as Rees's diminutive sidekick, enforcer, and torture mistress. There are also roles for a birdbrained French teacher, a seductive sexpot, and all the usual characters we'd expect to find at casinos, cabinet meetings, the first class sections of airplanes, and the dungeons of the perverse.

Did I enjoy the movie? My reactions were in a constant state of adjustment. I'm so accustomed to the badness of the movies in the spy-spoof genre that it took me a while to realize that William Dear and Darren Star, the director and writer, were sincerely trying to go over the top—that like the makers of such films as *In Like Flint, Invasion of the Bee Girls,* and the immortal *Infra-Man,* they indeed had an unholy light glinting in their eyes, and were making a subversive film rather than following a formula. By the time the château was in flames and the helicopter was chewing its way across the burning roof, I was ready to concede that, yes, I was enjoying it.

Imagine: John Lennon ★ ★ ★
R, 103 m., 1988

A documentary directed by Andrew Solt and produced by David L. Wolper and Solt. Written by Sam Egan and Solt. Narrated by John Lennon.

When John Lennon was killed on Dec. 8, 1980, he left behind some 200 hours of film and video footage, most of it never publicly seen, a lot of it in the category of home movies. The people who made *Imagine: John Lennon* had access to all of it, and so this is not a return visit to the familiar Beatles footage we've seen before in documentaries like *The Beatles Story.* Although *Imagine* begins in Lennon's childhood and of course includes the Beatles period, the emphasis is on the years after the Beatles broke up and he merged with Yoko Ono.

I use that word—merged—deliberately, because the movie portrays John and Yoko not so much as man and wife, business partners or artistic collaborators, but as two people who had spent so much time alone together on various planes of awareness that they had started to act as if they were one—like twins, or an old married couple. The effect is of a psychic barrier between John

and Yoko and the rest of the world; they're inside looking out.

Those final years were the end of a long journey for the restless boy from Liverpool who had a lonely, unsettled youth, who was raised by a beloved aunt, who was violent and moody and then burst forth into one of the greatest songwriters of modern times. Lennon was above all an artist—his music will live as long as songs are sung—but the Beatles made him into a cultural hero as well, a star who lived inside a bubble of wealth, fame, and adulation, and could rarely feel alone and off-guard. It was a form of heroism that led him to live in New York as if he were an ordinary person—insisting on walking the streets, going to movies, going to the park with his son, as if those freedoms were the right of anyone, even an ex-Beatle. That delusion was ended by Mark David Chapman.

Imagine is not an obituary, however, but a memory. What it remembers most clearly were those enchanted and befuddled days of hippies and flower power, be-ins and the love generation, when John and Yoko spent their honeymoon in bed together, holding press conferences to advise people to grow their hair and work for peace. The whole time comes rushing back in one long sequence where John and Yoko have a debate with Al Capp, the right-wing creator of "Li'l Abner," about the effectiveness of their "bedin." Capp is a performer, aware all the time that he's being filmed. In the face of his debating points, John seems bewildered and a little petulant.

The revealing moments in this exchange are there because they were filmed by outsiders, by documentarians who were trying to look through the lens and see what was happening. Other moments in the film are revealing precisely because they were *not* filmed self-consciously. They are the home movies, sometimes seemingly made by turning on the camera and sitting in front of it, sometimes perhaps made by John or Yoko or friends. In the sequence which opens the film and provides its framework, we see John at Tittenhurst, his country manor in England, in 1971, sitting at a piano, composing and singing. There is something so simple and pure about these images that they set the tone for the whole film.

At other times, however, the home movies are deceptive—they show less than they seem. When people film themselves, or each other, they are acutely aware of the camera,

and much of their behavior is self-conscious performance. It's the opposite of *cinéma vérité.* It's only when an unobtrusive, observant third party is holding the camera that we get a truly documentary vision. And the underlying problem with *Imagine* is that John and Yoko are holding the camera too much of the time— symbolically, anyway. The film shows the face they turned to the world, not the faces they turned to each other.

Much has been made of the fact that *Imagine* acts as a response to Albert Goldman's much-attacked biography of John Lennon, which paints him in his final years as an anorexic, drug-addicted puppet of Yoko Ono. In this movie, we were told, we would see him as a happy, healthy, productive family man. And there are shots that seem to show that person. But there are also moments when he does seem thin and ill, and times when he is clearly speaking from a drug-induced unreality. The film skirts so lightly over the touchy subject of John's decision to leave Yoko and live for a time with May Pang that, unless we know the story, we'd never understand it on the basis of this information.

Imagine was made with Yoko Ono's cooperation but without her imprimatur, and the result is the portrait of a man who was complex, sometimes confused, not always very happy, but a great artist all the same. Yoko Ono appears in the film not as his puppetmaster, but as his fellow-journeyer; whatever their reality, they shared it.

The most touching moments in the film come when it records direct testimony from those who knew Lennon the best. They look straight into the camera and speak simply and directly: his aunt Mimi; Cynthia Lennon, his first wife, and Julian Lennon, their son; Yoko Ono, and Sean Lennon, their son. They miss him, and perhaps we feel anger at Chapman for shooting him. But there is an extraordinary sequence in the film that almost seems to address that anger.

At Tittenhurst in 1971, a confused young drifter had been hanging around, in the delusion that Lennon's songs were messages to him. We see Lennon talking to the man, telling him he only writes for himself and for his friends and to make money and do a good job. He can't, he says, be everything to everybody. And then he tells the drifter he looks hungry, and invites him in for a meal. If you treat every confused drifter with that much humanity, you risk tragedy, as Lennon finally discovered. But his openness to the lonely and confused young man reveals, I think, the spirit of his greatest songs.

Immediate Family ★ ★
PG-13, 100 m., 1989

Glenn Close (Linda Spector), James Woods (Michael Spector), Mary Stuart Masterson (Lucy Moore), Kevin Dillon (Sam), Linda Darlow (Lawyer Susan Drew), Jane Greer (Michael's Mother), Jessica James (Bessie). Directed by Jonathan Kaplan and produced by Sarah Pillsbury and Midge Sanford. Screenplay by Barbara Benedek.

Haven't we seen this film before? *Immediate Family* is the story of a childless older couple who desperately wants to have a baby, and a young mother who is going to have a baby and doesn't know what to do about it. The story is right out of the headlines—too many headlines, and magazine articles, and TV docu-dramas, and talk shows, and even old movies, of which *The Babymaker* comes first to mind.

The key scenes in *Immediate Family* are so obligatory you could have written the screenplay yourself. Couple wants baby. Counselor puts them in touch with young mother. Young mother arrives, grows close to adoptive parents. Young father, a nice kid, also arrives. Older couple begins to feel like parents toward these two kids—a nice irony there. And then of course there is the inescapable moment when the young mother goes into labor, and there's a mad dash to the hospital and an obstinate nurse at the check-in counter, and then the mother gives birth while all the key characters stand around telling her when to breathe and when to push and how well she's doing, while she screams and sweats a lot.

The dash to the hospital and the delivery room scenes have become clichés by now, staples in the repertoire of every young actress, but let it be said that Mary Stuart Masterson is very good as the teen-age mother—she brings an unexpected resolve to the role, so we can see that the character might amount to something in life. The casting, indeed, is the only way in which *Immediate Family* transcends the predictable formula of its screenplay.

James Woods and Glenn Close, two of the best actors in the movies right now, play the adoptive couple, and Kevin Dillon, as the baby's father, finds an effective mixture of determination and uncertainty. Both of the

teen-age parents are good kids, we feel, but just not old enough to deal with the monumental arrival of a child in their lives. Woods is toned down from his other recent performances; he is the best actor in Hollywood at playing manics, crazies, hyperactive schemers, and intelligent con men, but here he simply plays a more or less normal husband with ordinary desires and passions. He and Close make a convincing couple.

And yet there is something lacking. I cared for all the characters, I was moved by the writing and acting in some of the key scenes—especially the ones involving the indecision of the young people when asked to part with their child—and yet the movie as a whole failed to really reach me. Was that because the material was simply too familiar? The subject matter of adoption, and "pre-birth agreements," and struggles for the possession of babies, is the fodder of talk shows these days, and having seen any number of tearful natural and adoptive mothers baring their souls on television, I found the characters in *Immediate Family* too familiar. (Like all characters on TV and in the movies, they never watch TV or go to the movies, and so are unaware that their lives are made of clichés.)

At about the same time I saw *Immediate Family*, I also saw *Look Who's Talking*, a lightweight comedy with John Travolta and Kirstie Alley and a baby with the voice of Bruce Willis. It also had the obligatory rush to the hospital, and the confused conversation with the stubborn admissions nurse, and the deep breathing and cries of encouragement in the delivery room. Its only ambition was to be a light comedy. *Immediate Family* wants to be a serious film, but *Look Who's Talking* is the better movie. It contains clichés, but knows they're clichés and has fun with them. And it does a more effective job of delivering charm and warmth than *Immediate Family* does at exploring deeper emotions. You can't measure movies on absolute scales, and the level of their achievement is often more important than the level of their ambition.

Impulse ★ ★ ★
R, 109 m., 1990

Theresa Russell (Lottie), Jeff Fahey (Stan), George Dzundza (Lt. Joe Morgan), Alan Rosenberg (Charley Katz), Nicholas Mele (Rossi), Eli Danker (Dimarjian), Charles McCaughan (Frank Munoff), Lynne Thigpen

(Dr. Gardner). Directed by Sondra Locke and produced by Albert S. Ruddy and Andre Morgan. Screenplay by John De Marco and Leigh Chapman.

Theresa Russell is an actress who likes characters who dance on the edge, who dare themselves to get into situations they'll have to think fast to escape from. The character she plays in *Impulse* seems at first to come out of the same mold as other recent female cops in the movies, but there's a twist to her—she's attracted to the dark impulses of the people she meets in her work, and she envies the sinners their freedom to sin. Sometimes it seems like the cops have to go home just when the fun is beginning.

Russell works for the vice squad as an undercover cop. She dresses in miniskirts and wears a lot of chains and works the bars and the sidewalks where the johns are. Her job is to guide them lustfully into the arms of the law, and when her backup support arrives to read the guy his rights, she's outta there.

The problem is, it's a dangerous and lonely job with a high frustration factor. Her boss on the force (George Dzundza) is a woman-hating creep who is mad at her because she broke up with him. His eyesight seems to be Pavlovian; when he sees a woman who looks like a hooker, he assumes she is a hooker—even if in fact she is an undercover cop. Yes, he likes it when Russell busts somebody. Sure, she's a good cop. But would she dress up that way if she were a nice girl?

Some nights the action gets a little dicey. Some nights she almost gets killed. Some nights adrenaline is pumping through her veins and she is expected to go quietly home and be a good girl until it's time to put on the push-up bra again. On one of those nights like that, tired and depressed, Russell goes into a bar and when a guy offers to buy her a drink, she accepts.

She knows what the score is. She's dressed like a hooker. He's dressed like a businessman with two hundred bucks in his pocket that he has just decided not to spend on flowers for his wife. But the thing is, she enjoys the power over men that this role gives her. All she has to do is wear the right blouse and smile the right way, and the brains of otherwise sensible men send Code Blue to their genitals. Just once, just tonight, with the warm coil of whiskey in her stomach, she decides to go back to the guy's place and maybe take the money and see what it's like.

It is here that the plot steps in. If *Impulse* had been a French movie, no doubt we would have continued to explore the twists and tastes of the woman's character, but in a Hollywood movie, personalities take second place to manipulation, and so we go on hold while the movie explains uninteresting details such as: The guy who picks her up is a criminal, and her colleagues on the force are working on his case, and it's all tied up with a lot of drug money, and so on.

And yet the movie gets interesting again, because of the corner Russell paints herself into. She makes some mistakes that become increasingly unwise and complicated, and the question is, can she think fast enough to stay ahead of some experienced cops who are likely to see straight through the whole tissue of lies at any moment?

Impulse is the second feature directed by Sondra Locke, whose first film, *Rat Boy*, quickly dropped from view. She seems to have learned a lot about directing since then. The movie is good to look at and painfully intense at times—not so much when the plot is squeezing in as when we're invited to identify with Russell when she's looking for trouble. You know the feeling? It's something you're not supposed to do, and you could get in trouble if you're caught, but you want to, and you're tired, and nobody loves you, and there's this seductive stirring inside you, and temptation has thrown an arm over your shoulder and is signaling the bartender with the other hand.

It's this impulse that makes the movie interesting and worth seeing. The other stuff—the relationship with Jeff Fahey as the good cop, the details of the criminal situation—are taken off the shelf, given a quick polish, and stuck in where they fit. Robert Bresson made a movie once named *Pickpocket*, about a man with a criminal personality. The movie followed the pickpocket and watched him, and that was enough. Would anybody in the audience have been seriously disappointed if *Impulse* had simply followed the Russell character? What if Locke hadn't felt the need to solve the plot and tie up the loose ends? What if nobody ever found out what Russell did and she was left to think about it? Isn't that what usually happens in life? And isn't it more fun, and more dangerous, that way?

In Country ★ ★ ★
R, 120 m., 1989

Bruce Willis (Emmett Smith), Emily Lloyd (Samantha Hughes), Joan Allen (Irene), Kevin Anderson (Lonnie), John Terry (Tom), Peggy Rea (Mamaw), Judith Ivey (Anita). Directed by Norman Jewison and produced by Jewison and Richard Roth. Screenplay by Frank Pierson and Cynthia Cidre.

Norman Jewison's *In Country* is constructed like a short story, not a novel. It sneaks up on us with a series of incidents from daily life—moments that don't seem to be leading anywhere in particular, until we're blindsided by the surprising emotional impact of the closing scene. It's not about conflict between characters, but about people in the process of learning about themselves.

The film's central character is a seventeen-year-old girl named Samantha (Emily Lloyd), who is living in the small town of Hopewell, Kentucky, with her uncle. He's a guy named Emmett (Bruce Willis), who fought in Vietnam and has spent the years since then wandering in sort of detached silence and watching a lot of television. Samantha's father was killed in Vietnam before she was born. Her mother (Joan Allen) has remarried.

In the course of the story, Sam is confronted by no less a question than the meaning of birth and parenthood. She wants to know more about her father, and finds some of his letters home. There are some old photographs, too, of a soldier barely older than she is now—a nineteen-year-old in a private's uniform. Sometimes she talks to the photograph, telling her father of some of the things he missed by being killed in Vietnam, things like listening to Springsteen.

Other events happen, connected to the notion of parents and children. Sam's own mother visits with her young daughter. One of Sam's friends gets pregnant and has to decide what to do. All of these events seem to circle the key questions in Sam's life: Who was her father, and what did his life and death mean? "Honey," her mother tells her in the movie's saddest line, "I married him four weeks before he left for the war. I was nineteen. I hardly even remember him."

Sam begins to wonder if her uncle Emmett, the Vietnam survivor, can provide the key to her questions. Emmett isn't the kind of stereotyped Vietnam veteran who has become a staple in action movies—the crazed nut case who runs amok with a machine gun. He has disappeared inside his own passivity, and seems content to let his life slip through his fingers. She tries to awaken him with questions and even through a dance the local people sponsor in "belated appreciation" for the boys who fought the war.

All of these episodes (and others involving Sam's grandparents) create emotional momentum without revealing where they're leading us. The movie is not constructed in the usual ways with clear milestones in the plot. It is only at the end, when Sam and Emmett and Sam's grandmother (Peggy Rea) go to visit the Vietnam Veterans Memorial in Washington, that we see what the movie has been leading up to. It's there, in a scene of amazing emotional impact, that Jewison releases all the emotional tension, all the sadness and bewilderment that has been piling up during the film.

In Country is based on the novel by Bobbie Ann Mason, and Jewison is faithful to its accumulation of small incidents involving ordinary people. It is the fact that the ending is so low-key that makes it work so well ("Let's go get us some of that barbecue," the grandmother suggests after they've finished their visit to the memorial). The film should almost list the Vietnam Memorial in its credits, it works so effectively as a focus for the emotion.

Emily Lloyd is astonishing in the film's leading role. A young actress from London with only two previous roles in her credits (*Wish You Were Here* and *Cookie*), she masters not only the Kentucky accent but the whole feeling of Sam—her gawkiness, her energy, the power of her curiosity. Bruce Willis has less-showy scenes (the character of Emmett is the opposite of every other character Willis has ever played), but he is well-cast, almost disappearing into the sad, silent survivor. The movie is like a time bomb. You sit there interested, absorbed, sometimes amused, sometimes moved, but wondering in the back of your mind what all of this is going to add up to. Then you find out.

In the Mood ★ ★ ★
PG-13, 98 m., 1987

Patrick Dempsey (Sonny Wisecarver), Talia Balsam (Judy), Beverly D'Angelo (Francine). Directed by Phil Alden Robinson and produced by Gary Adelson and Karen Mack. Screenplay by Robinson.

Sonny Wisecarver must have been some kinduva guy. When he was fifteen, he ran off with one older woman, and after they hauled him back and put him on probation, he ran off with another one. He made a lot of headlines back in 1944, after the tabloids named him "Woo Woo Wisecarver." What was the kid's secret?

Maybe it was just that he was so darn nice, and yet had a spark of rebellion that allowed him to see himself in ways that fifteen-year-olds ordinarily do not see themselves—for example, as the husband of a twenty-two-year-old with a couple of kids and a mean bastard of a common-law spouse at home.

As the movie opens, Sonny (Patrick Dempsey) is the captive of his dispirited parents, who occupy their home as if they had been sentenced to it. Across the street, there's music and fun, as Judy (Talia Balsam), the older woman, hosts a dance party every afternoon while her old man is away. Sonny drops in one day, and right away there's a spark between them. Before long they are friends, and then they are kissing, and then Sonny thinks up the plan for their escape to another state, where they are married.

There are a lot of headlines after they're brought back to California to face the law, but after he is sentenced to a youth camp, Sonny escapes and falls into the arms of another older woman (Beverly D'Angelo). She invites him for a cup of coffee. He resists, she smiles, there is another spark, and he's back in the headlines.

In order to make this movie at all, the right note had to be found. The Wisecarver story, which is based on fact, is filled with hazards for the wrong script. It could be distasteful, contrived, creepy. Phil Alden Robinson, who wrote and directed it, has made it charming by finding the essential sweetness in all of his characters. Sonny and his women run off together not out of unbridled lust, but because they are nice people in a cold world, and because it seemed like a good idea at the time.

A kid named Patrick Dempsey is the perfect choice to play Sonny. He's got the wise-cracking spirit of one of Neil Simon's autobiographical heroes, but he also has a certain saintly simplicity, a way of not seeing all the things that could go wrong. Talia Balsam, as his first love, does a wonderful job of revealing just enough of the hurt and suffering in her life, the hard knocks she has taken while still retaining a kind side. Beverly

D'Angelo, as the second woman, is a little older and a little wiser, and Woo Woo Wisecarver is already famous when she meets him, but she's also an innocent, and she can't understand why the newspapers and the courts would make such a big deal out of this nice kid.

The movie is comfortably set in its period, the mid-1940s of Roosevelt and rationing, Glenn Miller and Woody Herman, and a national hunger for headlines that were not about the war. The period is established without being allowed to overcome the picture, which finds a gentle offhand way to get its laughs; usually we're laughing, not at punch lines, but at human nature. The movie ends with a title card informing us that Sonny Wisecarver is alive and well and sends us his best regards, and that's sort of the ending the whole story was pointing to. The saga of Woo Woo Wisecarver was the best kind of sensational scandal, in which everybody got distracted from their problems and nobody really got hurt.

Indiana Jones and the Last Crusade
★ ★ ★ 1/2
PG-13, 125 m., 1989

Harrison Ford (Indiana Jones), Sean Connery (Dr. Henry Jones), Denholm Elliott (Marcus Brody), Alison Doody (Dr. Elsa Schneider), John Rhys-Davies (Sallah). Directed by Steven Spielberg and produced by Robert Watts. Screenplay by Jeffrey Boam.

There is a certain style of illustration that appeared in the boys' adventure magazines of the 1940s—in those innocent publications that have been replaced by magazines on punk lifestyles and movie monsters. The illustrations were always about the same. They showed a small group of swarthy men hovering over a treasure trove with greedy grins on their bearded faces, while in the foreground, two teen-age boys peered out from behind a rock in wonder and astonishment. The point of view was always over the boys' shoulders; the reader was invited to share this forbidden glimpse of the secret world of men.

Indiana Jones and the Last Crusade begins with just such a scene; Steven Spielberg must have been paging through his old issues of *Boys' Life* and *Thrilling Wonder Tales* down in the basement. As I watched it, I felt a real delight, because recent Hollywood escapist movies have become too jaded and cynical,

and they've lost the feeling that you can stumble over astounding adventures just by going on a hike with your Scout troop.

Spielberg lights the scene in the strong, basic colors of old pulp magazines, and of course when the swarthy men bend over their discovery, it seems to glow with a light of its own, which bathes their faces in a golden glow. This is the kind of moment that can actually justify a line like *It's mine! All mine!*—although Spielberg does not go so far.

One of the two kids behind the boulder is, of course, the young Indiana Jones. But he is discovered by explorers plundering an ancient treasure, and escapes just in the nick of time. The sequence ends as an adult claps a battered fedora down on Indiana's head, and then we flash forward to the era of World War II.

The opening sequence of this third Indiana Jones movie is the only one that seems truly original—or perhaps I should say, it recycles images from 1940s pulps and serials that Spielberg has not borrowed before. The rest of the movie will not come as a surprise to students of Indiana Jones, but then how could it? The Jones movies by now have defined a familiar world of death-defying stunts, virtuoso chases, dry humor, and the quest for impossible goals in unthinkable places.

When *Raiders of the Lost Ark* appeared, it defined a new energy level for adventure movies; it was a delirious breakthrough. But there was no way for Spielberg to top himself, and perhaps it is just as well that *Last Crusade* will indeed be Indy's last film. It would be too sad to see the series grow old and thin, like the James Bond movies.

Even in this third adventure, some of the key elements are recycled from *Raiders*. This time, Indy's quest is to find the Holy Grail, the cup Jesus Christ is said to have used at the Last Supper. (To drink from the cup is to have eternal youth.) The Holy Grail reminds us of the Ark of the Covenant in the first film, and in both cases the chase is joined by Nazi villains.

The new element this time is the way Spielberg fills in some of the past of the Jones character. We learn his real name (which I would not dream of revealing here), and we meet his father, Professor Henry Jones, who is played by Sean Connery on exactly the right note.

Like the fathers in classic boys' stories, Dr. Jones is not a parent so much as a grown-up ally, an older pal who lacks three dimensions because children are unable to see their parents in that complexity. I kept being reminded of the father in the Hardy Boys books, who shook his head and smiled at the exploits of his lovable tykes and only rarely "expressed concern" or "cautioned them sternly." Since the Hardy Boys were constantly involved, at a tender age, with an endless series of counterfeiters, car thieves, kidnap rings, Nazi spies, and jewel thieves, their father's detachment seemed either saintly or mad—and Connery has fun with some of the same elements.

Harrison Ford is Indiana Jones again this time, of course, and what he does seems so easy, so deadpan, yet few other actors could maintain a straight and a credible presence in the midst of such chaos. After young Indy discovers his life's mission in the early scenes, the central story takes place years later, when Professor Jones (the world's leading expert on the Grail) is kidnapped by desperados who are convinced he knows the secret of where it is now hidden.

He does. And Indy, working from his father's notebook, follows a trail from America to the watery catacombs beneath Venice, and then to the deserts of the Holy Land, where there is a sensational chase scene involving a gigantic Nazi armored tank. He is accompanied on his mission by Dr. Elsa Schneider (Alison Doody), a scientist he meets in Venice, but the character is a disappointment after the fire of Karen Allen in the first movie, and even the sultriness of Kate Capshaw in the second.

Spielberg devises several elaborate set pieces, of which I especially liked the rat-infested catacombs and sewers beneath Venice (I tried not to remember that Venice, by definition, has no catacombs). The art direction looks great in a scene involving a zeppelin, and an escape from the airship by airplane. And the great tank in the desert is a fearsome and convincing construction.

If there is just a shade of disappointment after seeing this movie, it has to be because we will never again have the shock of this material seeming new. *Raiders of the Lost Ark* now seems more than ever a turning point in the cinema of escapist entertainment, and there was really no way Spielberg could make it new all over again. What he has done is to take many of the same elements, and apply all of his craft and sense of fun to make them work yet once again. And they do.

Indiana Jones and the Temple of Doom ★ ★ ★ ★
PG, 118 m., 1984

Harrison Ford (Indiana Jones), Kate Capshaw (Willie Scott), Ke Huy Quan (Short Round), Amrish Puri (Mola Ram), Philip Stone (Captain Blumburtt), Roshan Seth (Chattar Lal). Directed by Steven Spielberg and produced by George Lucas. Screenplay by Willard Huyck and Gloria Katz.

Steven Spielberg's *Indiana Jones and the Temple of Doom* is one of the greatest Bruised Forearm Movies ever made. You know what a Bruised Forearm Movie is. That's the kind of movie where your date is always grabbing your forearm in a viselike grip, as unbearable excitement unfolds on the screen. After the movie is over, you've had a great time but your arm is black-and-blue for a week. This movie is one of the most relentlessly nonstop action pictures ever made, with a virtuoso series of climactic sequences that must last an hour and never stop for a second. It's a roller-coaster ride, a visual extravaganza, a technical triumph, and a whole lot of fun. And it's not simply a retread of *Raiders of the Lost Ark*, the first Indiana Jones movie. It works in a different way, and borrows from different traditions.

Raiders was inspired by Saturday afternoon serials. It was a series of cliff-hanging predicaments, strung out along the way as Indiana Jones traveled from San Francisco to Tibet, Egypt, and other romantic locales. It was an exotic road picture. *Indiana Jones* mostly takes place on one location, and belongs more to the great tradition of the Impregnable Fortress Impregnated. You know the kind of fortress I'm talking about. You see them all the time in James Bond pictures. They involve unbelievably bizarre hideaways, usually buried under the earth, beneath the sea, on the moon, or inside a volcano. They are ruled over by megalomaniac zealots who dream of conquest, and they're fueled by slave labor. Our first glimpse of an Impregnable Fortress is always the same: An ominous long shot, with Wagnerian music, as identically uniformed functionaries hurry about their appointed tasks.

The role of the hero in a movie like this is to enter the fortress, steal the prize, and get away in one piece. This task always involves great difficulty, horrendous surprises, unspeakable dangers, and a virtuoso chase sequence. The very last shots at the end of the sequence are obligatory: The fortress

must be destroyed. Hopefully, there will be great walls of flame and water, engulfing the bad guys as the heroes race to freedom, inches ahead of certain death.

But enough of intellectual film criticism. Let's get back to Indiana Jones. As *Temple of Doom* opens, Indiana is in a nightclub somewhere in Shanghai. Killers are after him. He escapes in the nick of time, taking along a beautiful nightclub floozy (Kate Capshaw), and accompanied by his trusty young sidekick, Short Round (Ke Huy Quan). Their getaway leads them into a series of adventures: A flight over the Himalayas, a breathtaking escape from a crashing plane, and a meeting with a village leader who begs Indiana to find and return the village's precious magic jewel—a stone which disappeared along with all of the village's children. Indiana is a plucky chap and agrees. Then there's a dinner in the palace of a sinister local lord. The dinner scene, by the way, also is lifted from James Bond, where it's an obligatory part of every adventure: James is always promised a sure death, but treated first to an elegant dinner with his host, who boasts of his power and takes inordinate pride in being a sophisticated host. After Indiana and Willie retire for the night, there's the movie's only slow sequence, in which such matters as love are discussed. (Make some popcorn.) Then the movie's second half opens with a breathtaking series of adventures involving the mines beneath the palace—mines that have been turned into a vision of hell.

The set design, art direction, special effects, and sound effects inside this underground Hades are among the most impressive achievements in the whole history of Raiders and Bond-style thrillers. As dozens of little kids work on chain gangs, the evil maharajah keeps them in slavery by using the sinister powers of the missing jewel and its two mates. Indiana and his friends look on in astonishment, and then Indiana attempts to steal back the jewel. Some of the film's great set pieces now take place: Human victims are lowered into a subterranean volcano in a steel cage, weird rituals are celebrated, and there is a chase scene involving the mine's miniature railway. This chase has to be seen to be believed. Spielberg has obviously studied Buster Keaton's *The General*, that silent classic that solved the obvious logistic problem of a chase on railway tracks (i.e., what to do about the fact that one train seemingly always has to be behind the other one). As Indiana and friends hurtle in the little out-of-control mine car, the pursuers are behind, ahead, above, below, and beside them, and the scene will wring you out and leave you breathless. *Indiana Jones and the Temple of Doom* makes no apologies for being exactly what it is: Exhilarating, manic, wildly imaginative escapism.

No apologies are necessary. This is the most cheerfully exciting, bizarre, goofy, romantic adventure movie since *Raiders*, and it is high praise to say that it's not so much a sequel as an equal. It's quite an experience. You stagger out with a silly grin—and a bruised forearm, of course.

Infra-Man ★ ★ ¹/₂
PG, 92 m., 1976

Li Hsiu-hsien, Wang Hsieh, Yuan Man-tzu, Terry Liu, Tsen Shu-yi, Huang Chien-lung, Lu Sheng. Directed by Hua Shan and produced by Rumme Shaw.

Within the first four mintues of *Infra-Man*, (a) a giant flying lizard attacks a school bus, (b) the Earth cracks open, (c) Hong Kong is destroyed by flames, (d) mountains disintegrate to reveal the forms of reptilian monsters with blinking yellow eyes, (e) the Professor announces that a twenty-million-year-old woman is unleashing the hibernating monsters upon civilization, (f) the Science Headquarters is shaken by a second quake, (g) the Mutants awake, and (h) the Professor, obviously shaken, informs a secret meeting of world leaders, "This situation is so bad that it is the worst that ever has been!"

No doubt about it: This is a case for Infra-Man. In his secret laboratory far beneath the Science Headquarters, the Professor explains to a brave volunteer: "We will wire your arms and legs with powerful transistors and death rays. You will be powered by a tiny nuclear reactor. Unfortunately, the operation will be very painful and you may die."

And so we're off and running, in the best movie of its kind since *Invasion of the Bee Girls*. I'm a pushover for monster movies anyway, but *Infra-Man* has it all: Horrendous octopus men, a gigantic beetle man with three eyes who sprays his victims with sticky cocoons, savage robots with coiled spring necks that can extend ten feet, a venomous little critter that looks like a hairy mutant footstool, elaborately staged karate fights, underground throne rooms, damsels in distress, exploding volcanoes, and a whip-cracking villainess named Princess Dragon Mom (Philip Wylie, please note).

The movie's totally, almost joyfully absurd, and a victim of John Carter's Syndrome. You remember J.C.S., based on the logical oversight in Edgar Rice Burrough's books about John Carter of Mars. After whole chapters of galloping across the Martian desert on his Martian steed and fighting off enemies in sword fights, John Carter finally says to hell with it, pulls out a ray gun, and fries everybody.

Same here. Gigantic mutant monsters with built-in death rays attack Infra-Man, who can hurl lightning bolts from the soles of his feet, and what do they do? They have a karate fight. After ten minutes of chopping and socking and doing acrobatic flips, THEN they zap each other.

No matter, *Intra-Man* contains terrific moments. In one cliff-hanging scene, for example, the Professor has Infra-Man wired up on the operating table when Science Headquarters is attacked by gigantic mutant arms. That's right, arms: no body, just arms. The arms squirm all over the headquarters, knocking off the power supply. The Professor shouts into his radio: "You have one minute to restore power before Infra-Man dies!"

His aide struggles toward a red power switch. He is knocked unconscious by an arm. Shot of a stopwatch ticking away the seconds. He regains consciousness, struggles some more. The arm attacks again. With ten seconds to go, soldiers burst into the room with a power saw and cut the arm in half. The switch is thrown and Infra-Man lives.

There are other good things. Lines like, "We are doing this for the children of the world." Or, "The clouds will cut off the sun and deprive Infra-Man of his power source." Or, "Drop the Earthling to her doom—she will melt at 3,000 degrees." The movie even looks good: It's a classy, slick production by the Shaw Brothers, the Hong Kong kung fu kings. When they stop making movies like *Infra-Man*, a little light will go out of the world.

Innerspace ★ ★ ★
PG, 120 m., 1987

Dennis Quaid (Tuck Pendleton), Martin Short (Jack Putter), Meg Ryan (Lydia Maxwell), Kevin McCarthy (Scrimshaw), Fiona Lewis (Dr. Canker), Vernon Wells (Mr. Igoe), Robert Picardo (The Cowboy). Directed by Joe Dante and produced by Michael Finnell. Screenplay by Jeffrey Boam and Chip Proser.

I would have loved to eavesdrop on the script conferences for *Innerspace*. Here is an absurd, unwieldy, overplotted movie that is nevertheless entertaining—and some of the fun comes from the way the plot keeps laying it on.

The movie stars Dennis Quaid as a daring but irresponsible test pilot who signs up for a bizarre mission: He will be placed inside a capsule, which will be reduced in size until it is smaller than a molecule, and then the capsule will be injected into a rabbit. (If the experiment is a success, future surgeons could operate from inside their patients' diseased organs.)

High-tech thieves want to steal the technology of Quaid's employers, and send a squad of hit men to steal the syringe that contains his capsule. A scientist flees with the syringe to a nearby shopping mall, where in desperation he plunges the needle into Martin Short, and injects Quaid's capsule where the sun don't shine.

Are you following this? Quaid uses a communications system to talk from within Short's head. At first Short thinks he's hearing things, but then Quaid tells him the whole story, and enlists Short's aid in a desperate effort to outwit the bad guys and restore Quaid to normal size before his oxygen runs out.

There are complications—a lot of them—mostly centering around Meg Ryan, as Quaid's estranged girlfriend. Short, with Quaid inside of him, has to convince Ryan of what's happening. And in the process, of course, he gets a crush on her—with Quaid eavesdropping on every word and heartbeat. It's a new twist on the old gag about the Siamese twin who wanted a moment alone with his girl.

This plot is not only unbelievable, but almost unworkable, especially when much is made of the intrigues of the villains. The complications grow so labyrinthine that the movie drags at times; it could have benefited from some fairly severe editing. And yet I liked *Innerspace* all the same, for the special effects and especially for the performances by Quaid and Short.

This was Short's comeback film after the unhappy experience of *The Three Amigos*. At last he shows what he can do in a film, realizing the promise of his peculiar but fascinating work on "Saturday Night Live." He gives us a little of his SNL schtick in a weird, off-balance dance, but basically he's playing a very confused straight man in this film, and he is always fun to watch.

Working inside Short in his tiny capsule, Quaid has a tougher role because he can't get physical. All of his actions have to be taken through the instrument of Short's body, and there are wonderful scenes where he uses rhetoric to inspire this nerd to act like a hero.

I wish I knew more about how they achieved the special effects. Some of the scenes inside the human bloodstream look like fairly straightforward, computer-generated animation. But there is a sequence involving the heart that has an uncanny reality to it, as if Quaid's capsule had been combined with actual footage of a beating heart, taken with miniaturized cameras.

Innerspace never quite knows whether to be a comedy or a thriller, and I never quite cared which way it went. The performances are so engaging and the effects are so enthusiastic that even when the movie runs long, it's only because it has too many ideas. In fact, it has one idea too many, leading to a howling logical error: When Quaid wants a drink, he asks Short to chug some Jack Daniel's—and then intercepts the booze on its way past the miniaturized capsule. But Quaid himself is as small as a molecule of the whiskey he wants to drink. I've felt that way myself some mornings.

NOTE: Then again, I'm not a molecular scientist. A couple of readers have written to point out that Quaid's ship is about the size of a blood cell, which would be millions of times larger than a molecule.

An Innocent Man ★ ½
R, 113 m., 1989

Tom Selleck (Jimmie Rainwood), F. Murray Abraham (Virgil Cane), Laila Robins (Kate Rainwood), David Rasche (Mike Parnell), Richard Young (Danny Scalise), Badja Djola (John Fitzgerald), Todd Graff (Robby), M.C. Gainey (Malcolm), Peter Van Norden (Peter Feldman), Bruce A. Young (Jingles). Directed by Peter Yates and produced by Ted Field and Robert W. Cort. Screenplay Larry Brothers.

An Innocent Man has all the elements to put us through an emotional wringer, but the movie never works up any enthusiasm for them. It's awfully relaxed for a crime movie. Tom Selleck may be one of the reasons; he's at his best when he plays light comedy and turns on the charm, but he seems miscast in this movie where he's fighting for his life

inside a vicious prison. There never seems to be anything truly at risk.

The film opens with scenes designed to show Selleck as a happy family man and a dedicated airline maintenance supervisor. They get the movie off to the wrong start by playing exactly like an airline ad. As Selleck tells one aircraft mechanic that there's no compromise on safety and diagnoses a tricky twisted cable for another, the music and the editing rhythm make the sequences feel like a TV commercial.

Once Selleck has been established as a plastic, one-dimensional symbol of innocence, the real plot starts. We meet a couple of crooked narcotics cops (David Rasche and Richard Young) who specialize in busting drug dealers, stealing their stash, and selling it back to the drug kingpin in the area. One day they get the wrong address and break down Selleck's door. He comes out of the shower with a hair dryer, they think he has a gun, and they shoot him. Then they realize their mistake and frame him. He refuses to cop a plea and gets six years in prison.

In prison, he learns the ropes fast. It's kill or be killed. A veteran convict (F. Murray Abraham) tells him that he has three choices: (1) Join the white racist Aryan Nation gang; (2) kill the vicious black convict who is picking on him; or (3) be sodomized by the blacks. Selleck would rather live and let live, but it doesn't work that way, and after he sees the gang-rape of another victim, he takes Abraham's advice and stabs the black convict to death. He has learned the movie's fascist lesson, which is that since society cannot be trusted to protect the individual, might makes right. The prison scenes are disquieting to watch, because the movie is too lightweight to accommodate the bloodthirsty race hatred of the prisoners. Racism as the subject of a serious movie is one thing. Racism exploited in an entertainment is another.

Three years pass. Out on parole, the hero tries to pick up the reins of his life again. But the crooked cops won't go away. They visit Selleck's home, insult his wife, and tell him that as a parole violator he's at their mercy. He remembers his prison lessons, and with the help of a black detective (Badja Djola) in the police internal-investigations unit, he sets up a situation in which their corrupt drug dealings are exposed and the final showdown develops. (As in all movies of this kind, the peaceful middle-class, middle-aged hero turns out to be an expert at leaping

into speeding cars, shooting at moving targets at night, and beating up young cops.)

This is the kind of simpleminded, dumb plot that could possibly be heated up into a good routine action picture. Instead, something goes seriously wrong with the tone. Nobody seems quite serious enough, especially not the two evil cops, who trade one-liners when they should be snarling. Laila Robins, as Selleck's wife, has several thankless scenes in which she pleads for his cause, and they feel like exactly what they are—obligatory cogs in the plot. At the center of the picture, Selleck is simply not wound up and tense enough. The role requires somebody like Mickey Rourke or Al Pacino, someone who can sweat bullets and go berserk with rage. The only performance in the movie that seems in tune is F. Murray Abraham's.

One of the problems is with the thin, assembly-line screenplay by Larry Brothers. It doesn't give the director, Peter Yates, the convincing stuff of real life to work with. There aren't many convincing moments of truth, and so we're painfully aware of the grinding plot. Yates is capable of making movies that feel exactly true (his credits include *Breaking Away* and *The Friends of Eddie Coyle*), but this time I didn't feel I was seeing a director's picture. Instead, I was seeing Selleck, a gifted light comedian, shoehorned into a role where he was never comfortable and rarely convincing. And I was watching a movie that takes ethical positions the producers would no doubt disagree with, if they had given them the slightest thought.

Insignificance ★ ★ ★
R, 110 m., 1985

Theresa Russell (The Actress), Tony Curtis (The Senator), Gary Busey (The Ballplayer), Michael Emil (The Professor), Will Sampson (Elevator Man). Directed by Nicolas Roeg and produced by Jeremy Thomas. Screenplay by Terry Johnson.

The premise is not too unlikely. Imagine that during one hot and steamy night in a New York City hotel room, the lives of these people crossed paths: Marilyn Monroe, Senator Joe McCarthy, Joe DiMaggio, and Albert Einstein. The key linking element is, of course, Monroe, a woman of such undefinable and ethereal appeal that her real life did indeed encompass such husbands as DiMaggio and Arthur Miller, such admirers as Norman Mailer and Laurence Olivier, such friends as Jack Kennedy and Robert Mitchum. Her address book, which disappeared mysteriously after she died, no doubt included names from such unexpected corners of America that DiMaggio, Einstein, and McCarthy would only have been starters.

But imagine, all the same, that long and steamy night and that hotel room, and you have the substance of *Insignificance*, which was first a play on the London stage and is now one of the last sorts of films I would have expected Nicolas Roeg to direct. Roeg is a master of baroque visuals and tangled plot lines. His *Don't Look Now* still has people trying to explain that Venetian dwarf in the red raincoat, and his credits include at least one good film, *Eureka*, that was not quite sure whether it was a dream.

Insignificance is a film in which almost all the audacity is contained by the premise—that these four most famous figures of the 1950s met during one long night. Grant Roeg that much, and he gives us a fairly realistic film most of the rest of the way. The characters are never actually given their real names in the film, but there seems to be little doubt who they're meant to be, especially when Einstein and Monroe work out the theory of relativity together, using a flashlight, a few simple props, and some almost perfect dialogue.

Monroe is played in the film by Theresa Russell, who is *still* only about twenty-six years old, and who already has appeared in such landmarks as *Straight Time*, *The Last Tycoon*, and *Bad Timing*. She doesn't really look very much like Monroe, but what does it matter? The blond hair and the red lips are there, and so is the manner, which has been imitated so often, and so badly, that the imitators prove that Monroe was a special case. Russell doesn't imitate. She builds her performance from the ground up, and it works to hold the movie together.

Tony Curtis has a lot of fun as the hard-drinking, paranoic senator. He has turned, in his middle years, into a glorious ham, willing to take the chance of appearing ridiculous in order to reach for the farther edges of a performance. His theories about the Russians in this film are little masterpieces of dialogue. Gary Busey is the ballplayer, stolid and not quite comprehending his famous wife, and Michael Emil is a wonderful Einstein, sweet and childlike, and closest of all of them to Monroe's own personality.

I am not quite sure, however, what the point of the movie is. It's more of an acting and writing tour de force than a statement on sports, politics, sex symbol, or relativity. It begins by imagining its remarkable meetings, and ends by having created them. It's all process, no outcome. I think in this case that's OK.

Interiors ★ ★ ★ ★
PG, 93 m., 1978

Kristin Griffith (Flyn), Mary Beth Hurt (Joey), Richard Jordan (Frederick), Diane Keaton (Renata), E.G. Marshall (Arthur), Geraldine Page (Eve), Maureen Stapleton (Pearl), Sam Waterston (Mike). Directed by Woody Allen and produced by Charles H. Joffe. Screenplay by Allen.

Yes, the opening *does* remind us of Bergman: The static shots, held for a moment's contemplation, of the rooms and possessions of a family. But then people enter the rooms, and their lives and voices have a particularly American animation; Woody Allen is right to say that his drama, *Interiors*, belongs more in the tradition of Eugene O'Neill than of Ingmar Bergman. But what's this? Here we have a *Woody Allen* film, and we're talking about O'Neill and Bergman and traditions and influences? Yes, and correctly. Allen, whose comedies have been among the cheerful tonics of recent years, is astonishingly assured in his first drama.

He gives us a time of crisis in a family, and develops it in counterpoint with the countless smaller joys and crises that are a family. He is very spare: Every scene counts, and the dialogue has the precision of a J.D. Salinger short story. There's nothing thrown in for effect unless the effect contributes specifically to the direction of the complete film.

Allen's central character is the family's mother, Eve, played by Geraldine Page as a heartbreaking showdown between total self-confidence in the past and catastrophic breakdown in the present. She is a designer, and her rooms are some, but not all, of the interiors of the title. She aims for a cool perfectionism in her rooms, for grays and greens and pale blues, for a look of irreproachable sterility. Her science and art is to know the correct place for a lamp, within a fraction of an inch.

She is married to a wealthy lawyer (E.G. Marshall). She has three daughters: A poet (Diane Keaton), a movie star (Kristin Griffith), and a searcher for meaningful occupation (Mary Beth Hurt). Keaton lives with an alcoholic would-be novelist (Richard Jordan). Hurt lives with a filmmaker (Sam Waterston). Marshall announces that he wants a trial separation from Page, and later introduces a woman he's met on a cruise and wants to marry (Maureen Stapleton).

There you have them, the eight people of this movie. Allen, who thought nothing in *Annie Hall* of producing Marshall McLuhan from behind a theater lobby display for a comic walk-on, isolates his characters in *Interiors* so thoroughly, we're reminded of O'Neill's family in *Long Day's Journey into Night*, coming and going in an old house with no access to any world outside.

There are hurts in this family that have been buried for years, and guilts that still hold it together. One daughter finally blurts out an accusation against her mother, who had thought herself so perfect and yet was as capable as anyone of pettiness and cruelty. We get the feeling, indeed, that this family has been together much too long, and that family life is not necessarily a blessing.

If there is a common wish shared by all the characters in the film, it's to live a life of their own. The father, defending to his daughters his decision to marry a woman they call a "vulgarian," argues not unreasonably that he's paid the bills and maintained the household for years—that now, in his early sixties, he's *earned* his right to some years of his own choosing.

The others have earned their rights, too, but each at the expense of the others. That is how each sees it, anyway. The same charge passes again and again around the family circle: That if the others had not been so demanding, or selfish, or jealous, or vindictive, then *this* person would have been set free to realize himself or herself.

Allen treats these themes in scenes that have an elegant economy of expression. The scene around the dinner table, for example, as the father announces his decision to leave, is handled in a way that etches the feelings of every member of the family, in just the right tones of anger, disbelief, or defiance. Scenes involving the daughters and their men suggest in different ways that the problems of this family will not end in this generation.

The funniest and saddest scene begins with the father's second marriage; Maureen Stapleton is wonderful as the "vulgarian," sweeping in with her red gown and finding Page's rooms "so gray. . . ." The dinner table conversation this time allows Allen to regard the Stapleton character with a mixture of tenderness and satire so delicately balanced, it's virtuoso.

The wonderment is that it's "serious." Yes, it is, but to be serious is not always to be good, and a movie both serious and bad is a great depression for everyone. *Interiors* becomes serious by intently observing complex adults as they fend and cope, blame and justify. Because it illuminates some of the ways we all act, it is serious but not depressing; when it's over, we may even find ourselves quietly cheered that Allen has seen so clearly how things can be.

Ironweed ★ ★ ★
R, 143 m., 1988

Jack Nicholson (Francis Phelan), Meryl Streep (Helen), Carroll Baker (Annie Phelan), Michael O'Keefe (Billy), Diane Venora (Peg), Fred Gwynne (Oscar Reo), Margaret Whitton (Katrina). Directed by Hector Babenco and produced by Keith Barish and Marcia Nasatir. Screenplay by William Kennedy.

At first the shape simply seems to be some old debris blown up against the side of a building, but then the shape stirs and we see that it is a man. At first we cannot quite make out his face, and when we can, and we see that the character is played by Jack Nicholson, there is a shock, for even in that first moment he seems to have been enveloped by the character. A little later in *Ironweed*, when we see Meryl Streep, there is a similar shock, not so much because of her appearance as because of her voice, which is an amalgam of high-class breeding and low-class usage.

Nicholson and Streep play drunks in *Ironweed*, and actors are said to like to play drunks, because it gives them an excuse for overacting, but there is not much visible "acting" in this movie; the actors are too good for that. Nicholson plays a man haunted by guilt from his past. He dropped and killed his baby son years ago, and has never forgiven himself. He left home soon after, and dropped like a stone until he hit the gutters of Albany, his hometown, where he still lives. Streep's guilt is less dramatic; she let herself down, or that is what she believes, for she does not understand that it is not her own fault she is a drunk.

Ironweed, directed by the Brazilian Hector Babenco, whose familiarity with the human sewers of Sao Paulo and Rio de Janeiro made *Pixote* one of the best films of 1981, is a movie of moods, locales, and voices. It is not much on plot, and even when something dramatic happens—when the Nicholson character returns home after many years to face his family—the scene is played for the silences as much as for the noises. It is probably a fault of the film that it contains so little drama; we quickly sense that hopelessness is a condition of this movie, that since alcoholism has been accepted as a fact of life, none of the other facts will be able to change. The movie generates little suspense and no relief.

And yet it is worth seeing as a chamber piece, an exercise in which two great actors expand their range and work together in great sympathy. Both Nicholson and Streep have moments as good as anything they have done. Nicholson's come in a graveyard scene at the beginning of the film, and in the long stretch after he returns to his home. Streep's come in a barroom fantasy scene, in which she sings as she remembers singing long ago, and in a confessional scene in a church where she tells the Virgin she is not a drunk, no matter what people say.

Nicholson's homecoming is all the more effective because Carroll Baker is so good as his wife, who has never remarried, who in her way does not blame him for what he has made of their lives, because he had his reasons. Baker was not nearly this impressive in her "first" career, many years ago, in movies ranging from *Baby Doll* to *The Carpetbaggers*. It may seem surprising to say that Baker holds the screen against Jack Nicholson, and yet she does.

The movie was shot mostly on location in upstate New York, and is set in the last years of the Depression. Its visual look is heightened realism, but Babenco also uses imaginary scenes, as he did in *Kiss of the Spider Woman*. As the drunk, hallucinatory Nicholson sees the face of a trolley driver he accidentally killed years ago, we begin to understand some of the chaos within his soaked brain.

Ironweed was released while *Barfly*, another movie about a Skid Row couple, was still playing around the country. Do the movies bear comparison? *Barfly*, with Mickey Rourke and Faye Dunaway, has more energy, more life and humor, and is more directly about advanced alcoholism. *Ironweed* carries a weight of memory and guilt, with drunkenness as a backdrop. I enjoyed *Barfly* more as a movie, but both films are well-acted. The difference is that in *Barfly* the characters scream a lot, and in *Ironweed* they listen a lot, to things we cannot hear.

Irreconcilable Differences ★ ★ ★ ¹/₂
PG, 112 m., 1984

Ryan O'Neal (Albert Brodsky), Shelley Long (Lucy Van Patten Brodsky), Drew Barrymore (Casey Brodsky), Sam Wanamaker (David Kessler), Allen Garfield (Phil Hanner), Hortensia Colorado (Maria Hernandez). Directed by Charles Shyer and produced by Arlene Sellers and Alex Winitsky. Screenplay by Nancy Meyers and Shyer.

The opening moments of *Irreconcilable Differences* are not promising. A lawyer is advising his client about divorce—and when we see the client, she turns out to be a little girl. Her plan is to divorce her parents, because they have (she stumbles over the word) ir . . . ir . . . rec . . . conci*lab*le differences. Right away, I was bracing myself for one of those smarmy movies about cute kids and mean parents. I could foresee the series this movie would inspire: "Kids' Court," with a different little plaintiff every week. It turns out that I was too cynical. *Irreconcilable Differences* is sometimes cute, and is about mean parents, but it also is one of the funnier and more intelligent movies of 1984, and if viewers can work their way past the ungainly title, they're likely to have a surprisingly good time.

The movie stars Drew Barrymore as the little girl. You may remember her from *E.T.*, when she hid E.T. in the closet with her stuffed animals. She has grown up just a little, but she still has that slight lisp and that air of preternaturally concentrated seriousness: She is the right actress for this role precisely because she approaches it with such grave calm. A kid trying to be funny would be a mistake. Her parents are played by Shelley Long of "Cheers," who is one of my favorite actresses, and Ryan O'Neal, who is not usually one of my favorite actors but is right for this role and good in it. They have a Meet-Cute while he is hitchhiking and she is returning her car to her tall, muscular boyfriend. It's love at first sight, even after Bink, the boyfriend, bursts into their motel room and figures out that his engagement is over.

O'Neal plans to be a great movie director. (His character seems inspired by Peter Bogdanovich, right down to the style of his glasses.) Long starts out to be a helpful wife and good mother, but then, after O'Neal's career hits the skids, she has great success as a writer. The point is that one parent or the other is always so busy, so successful, so much in demand, that the little girl gets overlooked. The only place she really feels loved and comfortable is when she goes home with the family's Mexican maid. So the kid sues for divorce. She wants to give the maid custody of herself. The parents are shocked. The media have a circus. The plot drifts dangerously toward a series of stagy confrontations, but avoids the obvious: This movie has been written with so much wit and imagination that even obligatory scenes have a certain freshness and style.

It also has a real edge, even a suggestion of bitterness, in its scenes about Hollywood. Although *Irreconcilable Differences* is a movie about family life, it's also a perceptive portrait of success and failure in Hollywood, with a good ear for the way people use the language of Leo Buscaglia to describe the behavior of Machiavelli.

The Drew Barrymore character sees right through all of this. She doesn't care about careers, she wants to be given a happy home and her minimum daily requirement of love, and, in a way, the movie is about how Hollywood (and American success in general) tends to cut adults off from the natural functions of parents. The theory is that kids will wait but a deal won't. Actually, it's just the opposite.

Ishtar ½★
PG-13, 105m., 1987

Warren Beatty (Lyle Rogers), Dustin Hoffman (Chuck Clarke), Isabelle Adjani (Shirra Assel), Charles Grodin (Jim Harrison). Directed by Elaine May and produced by Warren Beatty. Screenplay by May.

It's hard to play dumb. There's always the danger that a little fugitive intelligence will sneak out of a sideways glance and give the game away. The best that can be said for *Ishtar* is that Warren Beatty and Dustin Hoffman, two of the most intelligent actors of their generation, play dumb so successfully that on the basis of this film there's no evidence why they've made it in the movies.

Ishtar is a truly dreadful film, a lifeless, massive, lumbering exercise in failed comedy. Elaine May, the director, has mounted a multimillion-dollar expedition in search of a plot so thin that it could hardly support a five-

minute TV sketch. And Beatty and Hoffman, good soldiers marching along on the trip, look as if they've had all wit and thought beaten out of them. This movie is a long, dry slog. It's not funny, it's not smart, and it's interesting only in the way a traffic accident is interesting.

The plot involves the two stars as ninth-rate songwriters who dream of becoming Simon and Garfunkel. They perform bad songs badly before appalled audiences. Their agent gets them a gig in Morocco, and once they're in Northern Africa, they become involved in the political intrigues of the mythical nation of Ishtar. Isabelle Adjani plays the sexy rebel who leads them down the garden path, and dependable Charles Grodin supplies the movie's only laughs as the resident CIA man.

The movie cannot be said to have a plot. It exists more as a series of cumbersome set pieces, such as the long, pointless sequence in the desert that begins with jokes about blind camels and ends with Hoffman and Beatty firing machine guns at a helicopter. It probably is possible to find humor in blind camels and helicopter gunfights, but this movie leaves the question open.

As I was watching *Ishtar* something kept nagging at the back of my memory. I absorbed Hoffman and Beatty, their tired eyes, their hollow laughs, their palpable physical weariness as they marched through situations that were funny only by an act of faith. I kept thinking that I had seen these performances elsewhere, that the physical exhaustion, the vacant eyes, and the sagging limbs added up to a familiar acting style.

Then I remembered. The movie was reminding me of the works of Robert Bresson, the great, austere French director who had a profound suspicion of actors. He felt they were always trying to slip their own energy, their own asides, their own "acting" into his movies. So he rehearsed them tirelessly, fifty or sixty times for every shot, until they were past all thought and caring. And then, when they were zombies with the strength to do only what he required, and nothing more, he was satisfied.

That's what I got out of Beatty and Hoffman in *Ishtar*. There's no hint of Hoffman's wit and intelligence in *Tootsie*, no suggestion of Beatty's grace and good humor in *Heaven Can Wait*, no chemistry between two actors who should be enjoying the opportunity to act together. No life. I don't know if *Ishtar* was clearly a disaster right from the first, but

on the evidence of this film, I'd guess it quickly became a doomed project and that going to the set every morning was more like a sentence than an opportunity. It's said this movie cost more than $40 million. At some point, maybe they should have spun off a million each for Hoffman and Beatty, supplied them with their own personal camera crews and allowed them to use their spare time making documentaries about what they were going through.

I've Heard the Mermaids Singing
★ ★ ★ ½
NO MPAA RATING, 85 m., 1987

Sheila McCarthy (Polly Vandersma), Paule Baillargeon (Gabrielle St-Peres), Ann-Marie McDonald (Mary Joseph), John Evans (Warren), Brenda Kamino (Japanese waitress), Richard Monette (Critic). Directed by Patricia Rozema and produced by Rozema and Alexandra Raffe. Screenplay by Rozema.

"I have heard the mermaids singing, each to each. I do not think that they will sing to me."
                    —T.S. Eliot, "The Love Song of
                              J. Alfred Prufrock"

Don't we all know that feeling? That feeling that other people in other places are singing in the sunshine, but here in the shadows of our own miserable existence, the parade has passed us by. It is a key discovery of adult life that almost everyone else feels the same way, too, and that anyone who believes he's leading the parade is either stupid, mistaken, or a saint.

Polly (Sheila McCarthy), the heroine of *I've Heard the Mermaids Singing*, is a thirty-one-year-old Toronto woman who does not think the mermaids will sing to her. The most important thing in her life is photography, and sometimes she even dreams of the pictures she will take. But no one else has seen her work, and to all outward signs she is a winsome and lonely woman with few skills. Sometimes she gets office work through a temporary agency, but she isn't very good, and so it is with a certain amazement that she finds an employer who actually likes her.

The employer's name is Gabrielle (Paule Baillargeon), and she is an elegant French-Canadian woman who runs an art gallery in Toronto. Polly calls her "the Curator," and idolizes her. The Curator is able to overlook Polly's little lapses, such as turning letters into a sticky sea of correction fluid. And one night at a Japanese restaurant, she actually offers Polly a full-time job. Polly recalls that wonderful night, and other nights, on a homemade videotape that serves as the narration for the movie.

I've Heard the Mermaids Singing then develops into a much more subtle character study than the opening scenes might have prepared us for. Gabrielle, the Curator, reveals that her greatest regret in life is her inability to become a great painter; she sells the work of others, but she cannot paint. Polly asks to see some of her attempts, and is overwhelmed by them. But of course Polly has no confidence in her own taste, and so she smuggles one of the Curator's paintings into a show, where it is laboriously praised in impenetrable ArtSpeak by a hilarious caricature of a critic.

If the critic has validated the Curator's work, Polly thinks, maybe there is hope for her own photographs. So she sends them to Gabrielle anonymously, only to have them shot down as hopelessly inept. Her spirit is crushed. But there are more discoveries for her to make. She finds, for example, that Gabrielle has a lover, a woman named Mary, and that Mary, not Gabrielle, actually created the painting that the critic liked. It may be that the Curator lacks not only talent, but taste.

It is only gradually, while we're watching this movie, that we realize it is as much about Gabrielle as Polly, and that we are permitted to make discoveries about Gabrielle that Polly herself only dimly suspects. The movie was written and directed by Patricia Rozema, who uses a seemingly simple style to make some quiet but deep observations. What happens to Polly in the movie is easy to anticipate: She learns to trust in mermaids. What happens to Gabrielle is that she is closely observed and skillfully dissected.

When the movie is over, we leave thinking of Polly, and I have even read reviews in which the movie is treated entirely as Polly's story. That is partly because of Sheila McCarthy's extraordinary performance in the role; she has one of those faces that speaks volumes, and she is able to be sad without being depressing, funny without being a clown. She strikes just the right off-center note for the narration of the film; she must not seem too sure of herself, because the movie must not seem too sure of what it wants to say. It works by indirection, and Polly is actually only the instrument for the real story here, of a lonely and proud woman whose surfaces are flawless but whose sadness is deep.

If you see this movie and then have occasion to read "The Love Song of J. Alfred Prufrock," which contains lines that strike some readers with the force of a blow, reflect that the narrator of the poem is more like Gabrielle than Polly. More like the Curator, who has measured out her life in coffee spoons, who has seen the moment of her greatness flicker, who lacks the strength to force the moment to its crisis, who grows old. Polly is, I suspect, intended to be out there with the mermaids, neither stupid nor mistaken, but a saint.

J

Jacknife ★ ★ ★
R, 120 m., 1989

Robert De Niro (Megs), Kathy Baker (Martha), Ed Harris (Dave), Tom Isbell (Bobby). Directed by David Jones and produced by Robert Schaffel and Carol Baum. Screenplay by Stephen Metcalfe, based on his play *Strange Snow*.

There is a sense in which *Jacknife* is a continuation of *The Deer Hunter*, the 1978 movie in which a group of friends from a working-class town in Pennsylvania went off to fight the war in Vietnam. *Jacknife* begins some fifteen years after the war is over, and it takes place in a small town in Connecticut, but many of its shots and moods feel the same as in the earlier film, and the theme is the same, too: The idea that if your buddy gets left behind, you have to go back and get him.

The buddy who gets left behind this time is named Dave (Ed Harris). He doesn't get left behind in Vietnam, though. He gets left behind in the America that he has returned to. While other veterans return to jobs or families or education, Dave returns to a life that is empty except for the booze and the cigarettes that keep him company in lonely bars.

Dave lives with his sister, Martha (Kathy Baker). She is a schoolteacher in her thirties, and her life is on hold. Months pass into years in the house they inherited from their parents, where Martha's role is to put Dave's dinner on the table, do his laundry, change his sheets, give him money from time to time, and accept him exactly as he is. Her problem is, until Dave's life changes, hers cannot change, either. She is a classic case of an enabler; she's a one-woman support system allowing Dave to continue to drink and throw his life away.

The buddy who comes back to rescue Dave is named Megs (Robert De Niro). He doesn't have to come far—only across town. He turns up early one morning to remind Dave they have a date to go fishing together. It's a long-standing date, with a lot of significance to it, but we don't learn of the significance until later. Dave is in bed with a hangover, but Martha lets Megs in. He has never really noticed her before; maybe he's never even seen her. Now he likes what he sees.

Megs is their deliverance. If he is successful, he will be able to get Dave moving again, help him break out of the vicious cycle of booze-hangover-booze. And if Dave becomes self-supporting, Martha will be free. Free for Megs, maybe. What Megs represents is change, in a situation that has grown old with habit and stagnation.

There are not too many surprises in *Jacknife*, and not even the revelations in the flashbacks, the scenes showing what happened in the war, are really surprises. But this is not a movie of plot; it's a movie of character. It's about how these three people create a triangle of pain and possible healing. It's not a buddy movie, where the woman looks on while the two guys work things out. It's very much a triangle, in which a drunk has to learn to let go of his sister, a spinster has to learn to let go of her routine, and a loner has to learn to let go of his detachment from life.

All three performances are right for the characters. De Niro makes a good choice for Megs because of the reserve he brings to the role. This is a man not doing something he wants to do, but something he has to do. Harris, staring at his cigarette, sitting hour after hour at the end of the bar, is able to project an unhappiness and frustration so deep that when he explodes, as he sometimes does, we are almost relieved. And Baker's schoolteacher is not a drab wallflower who suddenly turns into a sexpot; she's a calm, competent woman who has gotten trapped in something that her guilt will not let her escape from.

Jacknife has some effective scenes that take place in a veterans' encounter group, where the lesson is that life goes on, and that today cannot be lived out in painful memories of the past. That's the same message Megs has for Dave. To a degree, this lesson is both familiar and predictable. *Jacknife* redeems it in the specifics of the performances. De Niro, Harris, and Baker seem to be oblivious to the "message" and lose themselves in the personalities of their characters. And so the movie works.

Jack's Back ★ ★ ★
R, 95 m., 1988

James Spader (John/Rick), Cynthia Gibb (Christine), Rod Loomis (Dr. Tannerson), Rex Ryon (Jack Pendler), Robert Picardo (Dr. Battera). Directed by Rowdy Herrington and produced by Tim Moore and Cassian Elwes. Screenplay by Herrington.

Exactly a century has passed since Jack the Ripper committed his monstrous crimes, and now a copycat killer is duplicating them—each murder one hundred years to the day after the Ripper's crime. This sounds depressingly like the premise for an exploitation film, and the title *Jack's Back* does nothing to encourage our hopes, but the surprising thing is that this is actually a good movie, with intriguing work by James Spader.

He plays two characters, twin brothers, one an earnest medical student, the other a rebel who has had some trouble with the law. Without revealing any more of the film's surprises, I can tell you that the good brother discovers one of the victims, and that the other brother eventually finds himself considered the police department's prime suspect for the murders. The movie develops into a thriller in which the second twin has to run from the police, clear his name, and somehow prevent the real killer from murdering the woman who has loved both twins.

All of this sounds contrived. Of course it is contrived. A movie like this is nothing without contrivance, and one of its pleasures is to watch the plot gimmicks as they twist inward upon themselves, revealing one level of surprise after another. By the end of the film we are more or less sure we understand everything that has happened, but even then there is one more surprise—and not the one you're no doubt expecting.

But apart from the pleasures of the plot, what makes *Jack's Back* worth seeing is the work of James Spader, a young actor who I believe has as much promise as anyone of his generation. He was the slick, detached drug dealer in *Less Than Zero*, projecting an easy charm that masked a cold contempt for his clients. And he has played villains in three other recent films: He was the guy who gave Charlie Sheen the insider tips in *Wall Street* and the nasty store employee in *Mannequin* and the ambitious yuppie who wanted Diane Keaton's job in *Baby Boom*. I don't have any statistics to prove this, but my notion is that actors who play villains early in their careers often turn out to have more interesting careers than those who always play the lead. They find more interesting places inside themselves, and they carry a hint of complexity and secretiveness even into heroic roles; look at Jack Nicholson, for example. *Jack's Back* is Spader's first chance to play a good guy, and he plays two of them—the good twin, and the bad twin who reveals positive qualities. It's the kind of dual role an actor loves because it allows him to do the same thing in two different ways.

Look carefully at a couple of the early scenes. There's a small moment in an emergency clinic when Spader comforts a wounded elderly woman, making the scene original and not a recycled docudrama—and then ending with a friendly, kidding one-liner that puts everything into context. And then notice later in the movie, when, as the other twin, Spader does a kind of leisurely dance around Cynthia Gibb, who is engaging and believable as the heroine. Does he like her? Does he frighten her? An actor who can make us ask those questions is doing his job.

Jack's Back was written and directed by Rowdy Herrington, who pays adequate homage to the requirements of the thriller, especially in a couple of truly shocking moments. But he's up to something more than a routine shock movie here. He's taken the trouble to make three-dimensional characters, and paused here and there to provide scenes that make the characters seem real and complicated, instead of just pawns in a movie formula.

Jacob's Ladder ★ ★ ★ ½
R, 115 m., 1990

Tim Robbins (Jacob), Elizabeth Pena (Jezzie), Danny Aiello (Louis), Matt Craven (Michael), Pruitt Taylor Vince (Paul), Jason Alexander (Geary). Direced by Adrian Lyne and produced by Alan Marshall. Screenplay by Bruce Joel Rubin.

This movie left me reeling with turmoil and confusion, with feelings of sadness and despair. Those are the notes it strives for. *Jacob's Ladder* enters into the hallucinations of a desperate mind, and lives there. It evokes a paranoid-schizophrenic state as effectively as any film I have ever seen. Despite an ending that is intended to be victorious, the movie is a thoroughly painful and depressing experience—but, it must be said, one that has been powerfully written, directed, and acted.

The story stars Tim Robbins, previously the pleasant young hero of such films as *Bull Durham*, as an American soldier in Vietnam who undergoes a shocking battle experience. The actual nature of the experience is withheld until the end of the film—and even then, we cannot be completely sure we know the truth—but it appears to send him back into civilian life as a psychological time bomb.

Years pass. He gains a doctoral degree, but does not use it. Instead, after a first marriage fails and a young son is killed in an accident, he goes to work for the post office, and starts to live with a woman he meets there. Then terrible things begin to happen to him. He is nearly run down by a subway train. Almost run over in the streets. Faceless demons pursue him. His doctor is killed in an automobile explosion. So is a friend.

He begins to suspect that he and his Vietnam friends were victims of some kind of misbegotten Army experiment. That day of their bloody battlefield experience, they all grew dizzy and their heads began to spin, and then he cannot remember what happened next. He was wounded, yes, and airlifted to a hospital—and what then? Flashbacks throughout the film follow his emergency treatment. But what is the secret of what happened? He gathers a group of fellow veterans, and they talk to a lawyer about representing them, but then the veterans and the lawyer back out.

I am ordinarily more than a little impatient with movies that deal with hallucinations, with dream states and delusions, because I feel artificially manipulated; the filmmakers are jerking my chain, and often it's a lazy substitute for the bother of constructing an intelligent screenplay. *Jacob's Ladder* is so well made, however, that I didn't feel impatient this time, because I didn't have the opportunity. The movie lives right on the raw edge of insanity and carries us along with it.

Coming out of the film, riding down in the elevator with some fellow critics, I got involved in a conversation about the underlying reality of the film. Was it all a flashback—or a flash-forward? What was real, and what was only in the hero's mind? Are even the apparently "real" sequences the product of his imagination? More than this I should not say, because the film should have the opportunity to toy with you as it toyed with us.

Making a chart of the real and the imagined is not the point of *Jacob's Ladder*, anyway. This movie is the portrait of a mental state, as Orson Welles's *The Trial* and Ken Russell's *Altered States* were. The screenplay is by Bruce Joel Rubin, who also wrote the completely different *Ghost*, and I've read an essay by him in which he talks about his original ideas for the film, and the way they were translated into visuals by the director, Adrian Lyne.

Judging by the essay, Lyne has done a good job of determining what could be translated, and what could be safely left behind. Rubin's original material, with its visions of demons and heaven and hell, has been replaced by the more frightening notion that paradise and the inferno are all about us here on earth, and that we participate in one or the other almost by choice.

The key performances in the film are by Robbins and Elizabeth Pena, who plays the woman he lives with. It's difficult to evaluate their work because the movie sets them the task of behaving in an utterly realistic, slice-of-life manner in many scenes (even some which are later revealed as hallucinations), and then coasting away into fearsome fantasy in other scenes. Pena achieves the difficult task here of creating a believable and even sympathetic woman, while, at the same time, suggesting dimensions which the hero can only guess at.

Most films tell stories. *Jacob's Ladder* undoubtedly contains a story, which can be extracted with a certain amount of thought. (Since the ending can be read in two different ways, however, the extraction process could result in two different stories.) That isn't the point. What *Jacob's Ladder* really wants to do is to evoke the feeling of a psychological state in the audience. We are intended to feel what the hero feels.

A lesser film would have ended with some dumb denouement in a courtroom, or some shoot-out with government security guys. This is a film about no less than life and death, and Jacob seems to stand at the midpoint of a ladder that reaches in two directions. Up to heaven, like the ladder that God put down for the biblical Jacob in Genesis. Or down to hell, in drug-induced hallucinations. This movie was not a pleasant experience, but it was exhilarating in the sense that I was able to observe filmmakers working at the edge of their abilities and inspirations. Not every movie has to be fun.

Jacques de Nantes ★ ★ ★ ½
NO MPAA RATING, 118 m., 1990

With Phillippe Maron, Edouard Joubeaud, Laurent Monnier, Brigitte de Villepoix, Daniel Dublet, and Jacques Demy. Directed by Agnes Varda. Screenplay by Varda, "after the memories of Jacques Demy."

In the spring of 1989 I went to visit Agnes Varda and Jacques Demy at their house in Paris. It was known that Demy was very ill. He had recently undergone surgery for a brain tumor, and yet Varda said that was the best reason why he should have company: "He needs people to keep him interested."

Their house was a strange, beautiful one. You entered through a door in the gate to the street, onto a long courtyard open to the sky, filled with trees and flowers, running from front to back, and on either side were two stories of rooms, each one opening onto the courtyard. One room was the kitchen. Another the library. One was the office for their film production company. One was for their son, Mathieu. A front room had been converted into a studio where Demy was painting.

We sat at a table in the courtyard and talked about the movies. Varda served pastries and tea. It rained just a little, a slow warm summer rain, but we were under a canopy and enjoyed it. It was a perfect afternoon snatched out of the jealous hands of time.

Varda and Demy, who together and separately had been making films for thirty years, began a new one in April 1990. It was about his childhood memories. If you have seen Demy's *The Umbrellas of Cherbourg*, a musical set in a garage and starring singing mechanics, among others, you may have guessed that Demy grew up as the son of an auto mechanic. That movie won all the awards—the prize at Cannes, the foreign language Oscar—and Demy made such others as *Lola* and *Donkey Skin*, often centering around the songs he remembered from his youth.

Meanwhile, Varda made films, too, often films based on her own life, such as *Daguerreotypes*, about the people who lived on their street in Paris, the rue Daguerre. She starred their son Mathieu in *Kung Fu Master* (1989), about a young boy's coming of age. This new film would be her film about Demy's memories.

"The film was shot exactly where Jacques Demy spent his childhood," Varda says, "in the garage of his father and in other places where, later, he was to film sequences." He wrote the storyline by telling his childhood memories to Agnes. But he refused to write the screenplay or dialogue because he wanted it to be her film. His health was failing through 1990, but he was able to visit the location, to appear in a few scenes, to see most of the rushes, before he died in October 1990.

And now here is *Jacques de Nantes*, a love film, a film a woman has made about the memories of the man she lived with for thirty-three years, as she has heard them told over the years or imagined them. The film uses three young actors to re-create the life of the French film director Jacques Demy from 1939, when he was eight, through the wartime years and his adolescence, to the years when he learns that he loves film and must be a director. It begins with a Punch and Judy show, which Demy saw and immediately imitated, making his own theater and figures out of cardboard. It continues as he goes to the movies, and is struck by their magic when he sees Walt Disney's *Snow White and the Seven Dwarfs*.

From the beginning, Demy knew he had to make his own films. He is given a cheap little toy projector and a worn-out old 8mm Chaplin short, which he views again and again,

until he muses, with the self-confidence of the born filmmaker, "I wish I could erase the film and make my own." And he does so, soaking the film in hot water and scraping off the images with a knife so that he can draw his own crude animated images directly on the film.

In a junk shop he finds a hand-wound camera and uses it to film his own stop-action animated stories, taking hours to move his cardboard puppets ever so slightly between every frame of film. He mails the exposed film off to the Pathe labs and waits breathlessly . . . and waits . . . and waits six full months until the developed film is returned, and he is crushed to discover that every frame is blank. "I have to learn about the f-stop," he says.

At last he gets a better camera. He films the screenplay in the instruction book that comes with the camera, casting his playmates, costuming them, ordering them around with the confidence of a born director. He goes all the time to the cinema. He tells his friends which directors are good and which cannot be depended on.

His father wants him to go to a trade school. He wants to go to the high school and become a film director. His father insists that he learn a trade. He spends hated months learning about a machine shop, while every free moment is spent in an attic room with his camera and his experiments. In a moment of betrayal, which Jacques Demy still remembered months before he died, his art teacher comes to visit his parents and agrees that the boy has talent, but advises against a career in film because "many are called but few are chosen."

But Jacques Demy was chosen. The film begins and ends with Demy on the beach, looking out at the sea, and then with close-ups of the grains of sand that run out through his fingers. It is not a sad film, however. It is a film about a boy lucky enough to discover how he wanted to spend his life, and able to spend it that way.

Jagged Edge ★ ★ ★ ½
R, 108 m., 1985

Glenn Close (Teddy Barnes), Jeff Bridges (Jack Forester), Peter Coyote (Thomas Krasny), Robert Loggia (Sam Ransom). Directed by Richard Marquand and produced by Martin Ransohoff. Screenplay by Joe Eszterhas.

Directors like to talk about playing the audience like a piano, about making movies that are efficient machines for assaulting our emotions. *Jagged Edge* is a movie like that, a murder thriller which dangles one clue after another before our eyes, daring us to decide who committed the murder. The machinery in this movie is so efficient that we don't know the answer until the very last shot— and I'll be getting back to that last shot in a moment.

The film stars Jeff Bridges as a powerful San Francisco publisher whose wife is brutally murdered in their isolated oceanside home. After an investigation reveals that he stood to inherit his wife's entire fortune, he is arrested and charged with the murder. Glenn Close plays his defense attorney. At first, she insists she has retired from courtroom cases, but then Bridges convinces her that he is innocent. And before long, she is also convinced that they are in love.

The Close character stands at the center of the film. Is she defending the man she loves against the unjust charges against him? Or is she defending a cold-blooded killer, who might murder her just as he murdered his wife? There are moments in *Jagged Edge* when each of these possibilities seems convincing, but most of the time we just don't know. There's a lot of evidence on both sides.

Close's courtroom opponent is the assistant D.A. (Peter Coyote). They worked together a few years ago on a case where, she believes, he concealed evidence in order to win a conviction. Is he concealing evidence this time? There comes a time when we think he may be. And by then the film's tension is so tightly wound that we, and Close, don't know what to believe.

Jagged Edge is supremely effective at what it sets out to do—toy with the audience. It's another effective thriller from Richard Marquand, who made *Eye of the Needle*. The performances are good and the plot is watertight, as a whodunit must be. I have only one quarrel with the film, but it's a fairly substantial one. The movie *only* wants to keep us guessing. The characters are developed only in ways intended to string us along. Any behavior is possible if it will further the plot. There's no sense of reality beneath the gleaming surface.

Even that would be all right, if the movie didn't reveal the identity of the real killer in the final shot. Here's my theory: In a movie which exists only to tantalize us with clues and deceptive evidence, we *shouldn't* find out who the killer was—because that should be what we're arguing about as we leave the theater. Once the killer is unmasked, his crime reflects on everything else we know about his character, and that's more realism than you really need in a well-oiled machine.

NOTE: As this movie went into wide release, a strange thing happened. People started to get confused about the identity of the real killer. Even though there is a close-up of his face, the shot is taken from such an oblique angle that some viewers were confused, and I got letters and phone calls suggesting at least three possible villians. I imagine a VCR freeze-frame will solve the mystery.

Jaws ★ ★ ★ ★
PG, 124 m., 1975

Roy Scheider (Brody), Robert Shaw (Quint), Richard Dreyfuss (Hooper), Lorraine Gary (Ellen Brody), Murray Hamilton (Mayor). Directed by Steven Spielberg and produced by Richard Zanuck and David Brown. Screenplay by Peter Benchley and Carl Gottlieb.

Steven Spielberg's *Jaws* is a sensationally effective action picture—a scary thriller that works all the better because it's populated with characters that have been developed into human beings we get to know and care about. It's a film that's as frightening as *The Exorcist*, and yet it's a nicer kind of fright, somehow more fun because we're being scared by an outdoor-adventure saga instead of by a brimstone-and-vomit devil.

The story, as I guess everyone knows by now, involves a series of attacks on swimmers by a great white shark, the response of the threatened resort island to its loss of tourist business, and, finally, the epic attempt by three men to track the shark and kill it. There are no doubt supposed to be all sorts of levels of meanings in such an archetypal story, but Spielberg wisely decides not to underline any of them. This is an action film content to stay entirely within the perimeters of its story, and none of the characters has to wade through speeches expounding on the significance of it all. Spielberg is very good, though, at presenting those characters in a way that makes them individuals. Before the three men get on that leaky old boat and go forth to do battle with what amounts to an elemental natural force, we know them well enough to be genuinely interested in the ways they'll respond. There's Brody (Roy Scheider), the police chief, who came to the island from New York looking, so he thought, for a change from the fears of the city. There's Quint (Robert Shaw), a caricature of the crusty old seafaring salt, who has a very particular personal reason for hating sharks. And there's Hooper (Richard Dreyfuss), the rich kid turned oceanographer, who knows best of all what a shark can do to a man, and yet is willing to get into the water with one.

All three performances are really fine. Scheider is the character most of us identify with. He's actually scared of the water, doesn't like to swim and, when he sees the giant shark swim past the boat for the first time, we believe him when he informs Quint, very sincerely, "We need a bigger boat." Shaw brings a degree of cheerful exaggeration to his role as Quint, stomping around like a cross between Captain Queeg and Captain Hook, and then delivering a compelling five-minute monologue about the time the *Indianapolis* went down and he was one of more than a thousand men in the water. By the time rescue came, two-thirds of them had been killed by sharks.

Probably the most inspired piece of casting in the movie is the use of Richard Dreyfuss as the oceanographer. He made this film soon after playing the driven, scheming, overwhelmingly ambitious title character in *The Apprenticeship of Duddy Kravitz*, and the nice kid, college-bound, in *American Graffiti*. Here he looks properly young, engaging, and scholarly, and introduces the technical material about sharks in a way that reinforces our elemental fear of them.

Which brings us to the shark itself. Some of the footage in the film is of an actual great white shark. The rest uses a mechanical shark patterned on the real thing. The illusion is complete. We see the shark close up, we look in its relentless eye, and it just plain feels like a shark. *Jaws* is a great adventure movie of the kind we don't get very often any more. It's clean-cut adventure, without the gratuitous violence of so many action pictures. It has the necessary amount of blood and guts to work—but none extra. And it's one hell of a good story, brilliantly told.

Jaws the Revenge   no stars
PG-13, 87 m., 1987

Lorraine Gary (Ellen Brody), Lance Guest (Michael), Mario Van Peebles (Jake), Karen Young (Carla), Michael Caine (Hoagie), Judith Barsi (Thea). Directed and produced by Joseph Sargent. Screenplay by Michael de Gusman.

Jaws the Revenge is not simply a bad movie, but also a stupid and incompetent one—a rip-off. And that's a surprise, because the film is the fourth in a series that has served Universal Pictures long and well, and the movie stars Lorraine Gary, the wife of the studio's chief executive officer. Wasn't there someone in charge of assuring that the film was at least a passable thriller, however bad? I guess not.

The plot centers on the character of Ellen Brody, who, you may recall, was the wife of the Roy Scheider character in the first and second *Jaws* movies. Now she is a widow, and her son has his dad's old job at the police department. The story opens at Christmas, as the son is eaten by a shark right off Martha's Vineyard, while a children's choir drowns out his screams with Christmas carols.

Mrs. Brody (Gary) flees in horror to the Bahamas, where her other son (Lance Guest) works as, you got it, a marine biologist. She pleads with him not to go into the water, but he argues that the great white shark has never been seen in warm waters. Not long after, the shark is seen, having made the trip from Martha's Vineyard to the Bahamas in three days.

Mrs. Brody, meanwhile, falls in love with a local pilot (Michael Caine), and there is a subplot about how her son is jealous of this new man in his mother's life. This jealousy, like every other plot device in the movie, is left unresolved at the end, but so what? The screenplay is simply a series of meaningless episodes of human behavior, punctuated by shark attacks.

Since we see so much of the shark in the movie, you'd think they would have built some good ones. They've had three earlier pictures for practice. But in some scenes the shark's skin looks like canvas with acne, and in others all we see is an obviously fake shark head with lots of teeth.

The shark models have so little movement that at times they seem to be supporting themselves on boats, instead of attacking

them. Up until the ludicrous final sequence of the movie, the scariest creature in the film is an eel.

What happens at the end? Ellen Brody has become convinced that the shark is following her. It wants revenge against her entire family. Her friends pooh-pooh the notion that a shark could identify, follow, or even care about one individual human being, but I am willing to grant the point, for the benefit of the plot. I believe that the shark wants revenge against Mrs. Brody. I do. I really do believe it. After all, her husband was one of the men who hunted this shark and killed it, blowing it to bits. And what shark wouldn't want revenge against the survivors of the men who killed it?

Here are some things, however, that I do not believe:

• That Mrs. Brody could be haunted by flashbacks to events where she was not present and that, in some cases, no survivors witnessed.

• That the movie would give us one shark attack as a dream sequence, have the hero wake up in a sweat, then give us a second shark attack, and then cut to the hero awake in bed, giving us the only thing worse than the old "it's only a dream" routine, which is the old "is it a dream or not?" routine.

• That Mrs. Brody would commandeer a boat and sail out alone into the ocean to sacrifice herself to the shark, so that the killing could end.

• That Caine's character could or would crash-land his airplane at sea so that he and two other men could swim to Mrs. Brody's rescue.

• That after being trapped in a sinking airplane by the shark and disappearing under the water, Caine could survive the attack, swim to the boat, and climb on board—not only completely unhurt but also wearing a shirt and pants that are not even wet.

• That the shark would stand on its tail in the water long enough for the boat to ram it.

• That the director, Joseph Sargent, would film this final climactic scene so incompetently that there is not even an establishing shot, so we have to figure out what happened on the basis of empirical evidence.

There is one other thing I can't believe about *Jaws the Revenge*, and that is that on March 30, 1987, Michael Caine passed up his chance to accept his Academy Award for *Hannah and Her Sisters* in person because of his commitment to this movie. Maybe he was thinking the same thing as the marine biolo-

gist in the movie, which is that if you don't go right back in the water after something terrible happens to you, you might be too afraid to ever go back again.

Jean de Florette ★ ★ ★ ½
PG, 121 m., 1987
(See also *Manon of the Spring*)

Gerard Depardieu (Jean de Florette), Yves Montand (Cesar Soubeyran), Daniel Auteuil (Ugolin), Elisabeth Depardieu (Aimee), Ernestine Mazurowna (Manon). Directed by Claude Berri and produced by Pierre Grunstein. Screenplay by Berri and Gerard Brach.

If you were to walk into the middle of *Jean de Florette*, you would see a scene that might mislead you.

In the middle of a drought, a farmer is desperate to borrow a mule to help haul water from a nearby spring. He asks his neighbor for the loan of the animal. The neighbor is filled with compassion and sympathy, but simply cannot do without his mule, which he needs in order to farm his own land and provide for his own family. As the neighbor rejects the request, his face is so filled with regret you'd have little doubt he is one of the best of men.

Actually, he is a thief. And what he is stealing is the joy, the hope, and even the future of the man who needs the mule. *Jean de Florette* is a merciless study in human nature, set in Provence in the 1920s. It's the story of how two provincial French farmers systematically destroy the happiness of a man who comes out from the city to till the land.

The man from the city is Jean de Florette, a hunchback tax collector played by Gerard Depardieu, that most dependable of French actors. When he inherits a little land in Provence, he is only too happy to pack up his loyal wife and beautiful child and move to the country for a new beginning. He wants to raise vegetables and rabbits on the land, which, according to the map, includes a freshwater spring.

His neighbors have other ideas. The old local farmer (Yves Montand) and his nephew (Daniel Auteuil) long have had their eyes on that land, and they realize if they can discourage the newcomer they can buy the land cheap. So they do what is necessary. They block the spring with concrete, conceal its location, and wait to see what happens.

At first, nothing much happens. There are

steady rains, the vegetables grow, and the rabbits multiply. Then comes the drought, and Depardieu is forced to bring water from a neighboring well, using his mule and his own strength, turning himself into a beast of burden. From morning to night he plods back and forth under the burning sun, and his wife helps when she can, but the burden is too much and the land surely will die. It is then that he asks for the loan of Auteuil's mule, and is turned down.

The director, Claude Berri, does not tell this story as a melodrama; all of the motives are laid out well in advance, and it is perfectly clear what is going to happen. The point of the film is not to create suspense, but to capture the relentlessness of human greed, the feeling that the land is so important the human spirit can be sacrificed to it.

To create this feeling, Berri stands well back with his camera. There are not a lot of highly charged close-ups, to turn the story into a series of phony high points. Instead, many of the shots are surrounded by the landscape and the sky, and there is one enormously dramatic set piece when the sky fills up with rain clouds, and the thunder roars and the rain seems about to come. And then, as Depardieu and his family run outside to feel it against their faces, the rain falls elsewhere and Depardieu shakes his fist at the heavens and asks God why he has been forsaken.

But God has not double-crossed him, his neighbors have. And the enormity of their crime is underlined by the deliberate pace of this film, which is the first installment of a two-part epic (the second part is *Manon of the Spring*). We realize here that human greed is patient, and can wait years for its reward. And meantime daily life goes on in Provence, and neighbors pass the time of day and regret that it is impossible to make a loan of a mule.

Jeremiah Johnson ★ ★ ★
PG, 108 m., 1972

Robert Redford (Jeremiah Johnson), Will Geer (Bear Claw), Stefan Gierasch (Del Gue), Allyn Ann McLerie (Crazy Woman), Delle Bolton (Swan), Charles Tyner (Robidoux). Directed by Sydney Pollack and produced by Joe Wizan. Screenplay by John Milius and Edward Anhalt.

If Thoreau had been a violent man, angry and unforgiving, *Jeremiah Johnson* might have been made from one of his books. Like *Walden*, it's the story of a man who goes alone into the wilderness to live by his hands and wits. It is good at showing us this man and the ways by which he survives; but not so good when it ventures into Indian myth and magic, and edges up to vast universal questions.

There's a sense in which movies like this should be rough-hewn and a little inarticulate. When a man makes up his mind to go into the mountains and say to hell with civilization, it's cheating a little to frame him against spectacular landscapes as if he were a particularly heroic tour guide. It may also be cheating to cast Robert Redford in the title role; he projects a kind of intellectual, winsome handsomeness that doesn't really belong in such a simple character.

Still, the movie does approach its subject with a certain dogged honesty; it agrees for the most part to coexist with the rhythms of the wilderness, and not go for big, phony climaxes (it is so studiously low-keyed, indeed, that it seems to end four or five times before it really does). The humor is direct and folksy, as when an old trapper asks Jeremiah if he can skin a grizzly. Jeremiah says he can, and so the trapper lures a grizzly into the cabin with Jeremiah, jumps out the back window and shouts, "Start skinnin'!"

The humor is direct, and so is the violence. Director Sydney Pollack approaches his scenes head-on. He doesn't deal in the choreography of violence, like Peckinpah, or the fetish of violence, like the Kubrick of *A Clockwork Orange*. Instead, his violent scenes are brutally short and forcible. Death occurs suddenly, and is absorbed by the emptiness of the mountain range.

The story follows Jeremiah as he makes a roughly circular journey through high mountain ranges and passes. He nearly starves the first winter, until the old trapper (Will Geer, looking like Father Christmas in his fur parka) has mercy on him. He forms brief friendships and partnerships with some of the other outcasts of the mountains; he has hostile encounters with Crow Indians and friendly ones with Flatheads; and as the result of a misunderstanding he finds himself married to the daughter of a Flathead chief. The marriage sets up the movie's most absorbing sequences. Jeremiah has earlier become a sort of guardian for a young boy, and now the three of them set up housekeeping. Pollack gets a kind of poetic documentary rhythm going as they clear a space, cut some trees, and build a cabin. Their long weeks of work are followed by a clumsy football game in which the three of them, so different from one another, show that they've become a family.

It is after this section of the movie that things begin to go a little wrong. Without telling you everything that happens (because that would remove the necessary shock value), I can say that Jeremiah runs up against a host of impenetrable wilderness mysteries, undying Indian blood feuds, and, yes, fate itself. In the end he becomes a mysterious and legendary figure, a man of the mountains, who is too symbolic to suit me.

Still, as the portrait of a man who turns his back on society, *Jeremiah Johnson* is a finely felt and beautiful film. And the scenery is particularly beautiful. I say that with a certain sense of pain; I made a vow never to praise a movie because "the scenery is beautiful." The scenery is always beautiful in movies. Liking a movie because of its beautiful scenery is like buying a car because its tires are round. And yet . . . the movie was shot on location in the national forests of Utah, and there are moments in it that make *Doctor Zhivago* look cramped for space.

The Jewel of the Nile ★ ★ ★
PG, 105 m., 1985

Michael Douglas (Jack Colton), Kathleen Turner (Joan Wilder), Danny DeVito (Ralph), Avner Eisenberg (Holy Man), Spiros Focas (Omar). Directed by Lewis Teague and produced by Michael Douglas. Screenplay by Mark Rosenthal and Lawrence Konner.

The Jewel of the Nile is more silliness in the tradition of *Romancing the Stone*, which in its turn was a funny action comedy inspired by the Indiana Jones epics. We walk into the theater expecting absolutely nothing of substance, and that's exactly what we get, served up with high style. The movie reassembles three key cast members—Michael Douglas, Kathleen Turner, and Danny DeVito—and goes on to a fourth inspired casting decision with the addition of Avner Eisenberg as a holy man of gentle goofiness.

Movie industry gossip had it that Kathleen Turner didn't particularly want to make this sequel, and that even Michael Douglas, who produces as well as stars, thought it might be best to quit while he was ahead. But the original contract specified a sequel, and it's to everybody's credit that *The Jewel of the Nile* is an ambitious and elaborate attempt to repeat the success of the first movie; it's not just a rip-off.

Even so, it lacks some of the pleasures of *Romancing*, especially the development of the romance between Douglas and Turner. This time, as the movie opens, they're old friends, unwinding in Cannes and reminiscing about the good times they had in South America. Perhaps sensing that there is nowhere to go with this essentially stable relationship, the movie plunges them almost immediately into Middle East intrigue.

A fabulously wealthy Arab (Spiros Focas) invites Turner to travel with him to his homeland, for reasons as vague as they are fascinating. Douglas temporarily drops out; after a manufactured spat, he decides he'd rather sail his boat through the Mediterranean. Turner is quickly involved in danger as the Arab reveals plans to usurp the role of a legendary holy man, and Douglas becomes an ally of the great spiritual leader, who is known as the Jewel of the Nile. (Danny DeVito is somewhat lost in all of this, and left for long stretches of the film to wander through the desert and suffer meaningless tortures in lieu of a clearly defined role.)

The Jewel of the Nile expends amazing resources on some of its scenes, including a gigantic spiritual meeting in the desert that is staged as a cross between a rock concert and the Nuremberg Rally. What makes the Middle Eastern stuff work, however, is the performance of Eisenberg, who is a true comic discovery. He has some of the same cynical innocence we sensed in the Harold Ramis character in *Ghostbusters:* he's very wise and very innocent. Some of his best moments involve his bewildering cross-cultural dialogue: he speaks in vast metaphysical concepts which are unexpectedly interrupted with 1985 slang and pop sociology.

Meanwhile, Douglas and Turner have fun with two of the broadest roles in recent memory. They fight, they make up, they wisecrack in the face of calamity. And they make an ideally matched comedy team. Just as Woody Allen and Diane Keaton always seem to be on the same wavelength in their comic dialogues, so do Douglas and Turner, in their own way, seem well matched. It seems clear that they like each other and are having fun during the parade of ludicrous situations in the movie, and their chemistry is sometimes more entertaining than the contrivances of the plot.

My favorite moment between them comes as they hang by their hands over a rat-pit, while acid gnaws away at the ropes which suspend them above certain doom. Sure, this scene owes something to *Raiders of the Lost Ark*. But what's new about it this time is the dialogue, the way they break down and confess they love each other and make marriage plans as death inexorably approaches. And then, when DeVito appears and might possibly save them, there is some business with a ladder that is followed by dialogue so perfectly timed that I laughed not so much in amusement as in delight at how well the mechanisms of the scene fell together.

For all of those pleasures, *The Jewel of the Nile* is a slight and lightweight entertainment. How could it be otherwise? And it is not quite the equal of *Romancing the Stone*. That's not a surprise. For what it is, though, it's fun. And for what it's worth, Douglas and Turner could keep on working in this tradition forever, giving us a 1980s version of the Crosby and Hope *Road* pictures. I guess they don't want to, though, and perhaps that's just as well. What I hope is that a casting director sees Avner Eisenberg for what he is, the most intriguing comedy discovery in a long time.

Jesus of Montreal ★ ★ ★ ½
R, 119 m., 1990

Lothaire Bluteau (Daniel Coloumbe), Catherine Wilkening (Mireille), Johanne-Marie Tremblay (Constance), Remy Girard (Martin), Robert Lepage (Rene), Gilles Pelletier (Father Leclerc), Yves Jacques (Richard Cardinal). Directed by Denys Arcand and produced by Roger Frappier and Roger Gendron. Screenplay by Arcand.

The Passion Play has been a success for more than forty years in the famous Montreal basilica, but the passage of time has made it seem old-fashioned, and modern audiences are growing restless. It's time for an overhaul. So the priest in charge hires some new actors—younger, more inventive—to stage a revised and updated version. And they make the mistake of taking their material literally.

The teachings of Christ, it has often been observed, would be radical and subversive if anyone ever took them literally. And they would be profoundly offensive to those who build their kingdoms in this world and not in the next. The actors who rewrite the Passion in *Jesus of Montreal* create a play that is good theater and perhaps even good theology, but it is not good public relations. And although audiences respond well and the reviews are good, the church authorities are reluctant to offend the establishment by presenting such an unorthodox reading of the sacred story. So they order the play to be toned down.

But by the time they act, a curious thing has happened to the actors. They have come to believe in their play; to be shaped by the roles they play. *Jesus of Montreal* does not try to force a parallel between the Passion of Christ and the experiences of these actors, and yet, certain similarities do appear, and Daniel (Lothaire Bluteau), the actor who plays Christ, discovers that his own life is taking on some of the aspects of Christ's. By the end of the film, we have arrived at a Crucifixion scene that actually plays as drama, and not simply as something which has been forced into the script.

Jesus of Montreal was written and directed by Denys Arcand, the best of the new generation of Quebec filmmakers. His previous film was *The Decline of the American Civilization*, in which a group of Montreal intellectuals gathered to prepare a meal and talk about the meanings of their lives; it was sort of a conversational version of *The Big Chill*. This film is much more passionate, and angrier. It suggests that most establishments, and especially the church, would be rocked to their foundations by the practical application of the maxims of Christ.

Many of the scenes have obvious parallels in the New Testament. In one, an actress from the troupe appears at an audition for a TV commercial and is asked to take off her clothes—not because nudity is required in the commercial, but more because the casting director wants to exercise his power. Arriving late at the audition, Daniel, the Christ figure, shouts out to his friend to leave her clothes on, and then, when the advertising people try to have him ejected, he goes into a rage, overturning lights and cameras. It is a version, of course, of Christ and the moneylenders in the temple.

Another way in which *Jesus of Montreal* parallels the life of Christ is in the way a community grows up around its central figure. Filled with a vision they believe in, nourished by the courage to carry on in the face of the authorities, these actors persist in presenting their play even in the face of religious and legal opposition. It's interesting the way Arcand makes this work as theology and drama at the same time; in a sense, *Jesus of Montreal* is a movie about the theater, not about religion.

Pay close attention to Lothaire Bluteau in

the title role. He is considered the most powerful actor to come out of Canada in years, with his emaciated good looks and his burning intensity, and he has received strong reviews for his stage work in London. He's an actor of the Mickey Rourke-Eric Roberts-James Woods school, consumed with fire, intense in his concentration, and he is just right for this role.

As for the film itself, I was surprised at how absorbed I became, even though, right from the beginning, I assumed I would see some kind of modern parallel of the Passion. Arcand doesn't force the parallels, and his screenplay is not simply an updated paraphrase of the New Testament. It's an original and uncompromising attempt to explore what really might happen if the spirit of Jesus were to walk among us in these timid and materialistic times.

Jo Jo Dancer, Your Life Is Calling
★ ★ ★
R, 97 m., 1986

Richard Pryor (Jo Jo), Debbie Allen (Michelle), Paula Kelly (Satin Doll), Billy Eckstine (Johnny Barnett), Art Evans (Arturo), J.J. Barry (Sal), Barbara Williams (Dawn), Carmen McRae (Grandmother), Diahnne Abbott (Mother), Scoey Mitchell (Father), E'Lon Cox (Little Jo Jo). Directed and produced by Richard Pryor. Screenplay by Rocco Urbisci, Paul Mooney, and Pryor.

Richard Pryor says that *Jo Jo Dancer, Your Life Is Calling* is not really his autobiography, and I believe him. But the movie is clearly inspired by the journey he has taken since that day in 1980 when he almost killed himself in a drug-related accident. There is pain in this movie, and truth, and also a lot of warmth and nostalgia. There is a certain incompleteness in the ending of the film, however; it seems to close without a third act. But Pryor has said there may be a sequel, and perhaps that's where the rest of the story will be told.

Jo Jo Dancer begins when its hero already is an entertainment superstar. We track him restlessly around his luxurious Hollywood home as he calls a drug dealer and sets up a party, all the time claiming that he's off drugs. He throws bottles and paraphernalia into the fireplace, screams to himself that he's gotta stop, and then decides to do cocaine one last time. The rest of the scene is borrowed from the headlines, as Jo Jo is raced into an emergency room with burns over most of his body.

He faces a turning point. Will he choose to live, or die? Jo Jo's alter ego separates from his body, looks down at the bandages, and says, "Jo Jo, what have you done to us this time?" And then the alter ego embarks on a trip back through Jo Jo's life and the memories that will die if the body dies.

We see little Jo Jo being raised in a small Ohio town, where his grandmother runs a whorehouse, and his mother is one of the girls. We see the affection he receives, but also the conflicting signals about sex, race, and booze. Later, after his mother has married, there is tension at home after Jo Jo announces that he thinks he could become a nightclub comedian. There are painful scenes of his first stumbling attempts to entertain an audience, and then the night when he talks back to a drunk and begins to find his own onstage voice.

This early show-business material supplies the most heartfelt material in the film, and some of its best characters, especially a stripper named Satin Doll (Paula Kelly), who befriends Jo Jo and gets him his first job. Backstage, we meet the boozy old emcee (Art Evans), and the veteran trouper (Billy Eckstine). There is a great sequence where Pryor, dressed in drag, pulls out a fake pistol and tries to bluff the club's Mafia owners into paying him his salary.

There's an abrupt transition from these early scenes, which seem bathed in a glow of nostalgia and gratitude, and later scenes in which Jo Jo starts to make it big and is introduced to the Beverly Hills cocaine scene. Along the way, there have been several wives, one too frightened to leave her hometown, one so mercenary she comes along only for the money, one white girl who likes cocaine too much. None of the relationships seems real, because Jo Jo doesn't seem real himself.

That's a point Pryor makes at the end of the film, in an onstage routine that represents his comeback nightclub act after he recovers from his accident. These passages are a reminder of *Richard Pryor Live on the Sunset Strip* and *Richard Pryor Here and Now,* his two post-cocaine concert films. He talks about always feeling that he didn't belong, always needing the instant confidence that came from booze and drugs, until finally they took away everything they had promised him.

The problem with the final onstage scene is that it's too self-contained. It doesn't take the dramatic chances that the rest of the movie is so willing to risk. It shows Pryor the performer, instead of continuing the story of Jo Jo the character. The structure of the movie leads us to a place where we expect some sort of redemption and re-evaluation from the character, but it's not there and we miss it. Maybe the sequel will show Jo Jo learning to live without drugs.

All the same, Pryor has taken some major risks in this movie. He has played straight and honest with his story, but he also has shown that he has a real gift as a director; the narrative scenes in the movie have a conviction and an interest that grow and hold us. This isn't a heartfelt amateur night, but a film by an artist whose art has become his life.

Joe Vs. the Volcano ★ ★ ★ 1/2
PG, 94 m., 1990

Tom Hanks (Joe), Meg Ryan (Patricia/Angelica/DeDe), Lloyd Bridges (Graynamore), Robert Stack (Dr. Ellison), Abe Vigoda (Chief of the Waponis), Dan Hedaya (Waturi), Barry McGovern (Luggage salesman), Ossie Davis (Marshall), Amanda Plummer (Dagmar). Directed by John Patrick Shanley and produced by Stephen Goldblatt. Screenplay by Shanley.

Gradually, through the opening scenes of *Joe Vs. the Volcano,* my heart began to quicken, until finally I realized a wondrous thing: I had not seen this movie before. Most movies, I have seen before. Most movies, you have seen before. Most movies are constructed out of bits and pieces of other movies, like little engines built from cinematic erector sets. But not *Joe Vs. the Volcano.* It is not an entirely successful movie, but it is new and fresh and not shy of taking chances, and the dialogue in it is actually worth listening to because it is written with wit and romance.

The movie announces its individuality in its opening shot, which is of a loathsome factory—a vast block of ugliness set down in the middle of a field of mud. Into this factory every morning trudge the broken spirits and unhealthy bodies of its employees, among them ashen-faced Joe (Tom Hanks), who has felt sick for years and believes the buzzing fluorescent tubes above his desk may be driving him mad.

The factory is a triumph of production design (by Bo Welch, who also designed *Beetlejuice*). It is a reminder that most movies these days are rigidly realistic in their settings, as if a law had been passed against flights of fancy like this factory that squats obscenely in the center of the screen. The entire movie breaks that law and allows fantasy back into the movies again. Like *Metropolis*, *The Wizard of Oz*, *Ghostbusters*, or *Batman*, this movie isn't content to photograph the existing world—it goes to the trouble of creating its own.

In the factory, Joe hunches in his little corner, quailing at the attacks of his boorish boss (Dan Hedaya) and hardly daring a peek at the office secretary (Meg Ryan), whose huge typewriter seems ready to crush her. He hates his job. Hates, hates, hates it. He barely has the strength to crawl out to a doctor's appointment, where he learns that a Brain Cloud is spreading between the hemispheres of his brain. He will feel terrific for four or five months, and then he will die.

The death sentence is a liberation. Joe quits his job and is almost immediately offered another one. A man named Graynamore (Lloyd Bridges) owns an island that is rich in a rare mineral. The island is inhabited by natives who must be placated. They need a human sacrifice for their volcano. Since Joe is going to die anyway, Graynamore reasons, why shouldn't he go out in style by leaping into the volcano?

Sounds good to Joe. And meanwhile the movie has been developing into a duet between whimsy and romance. The writer-director, John Patrick Shanley, is the same man who wrote Norman Jewison's wonderful *Moonstruck* and wrote the astonishingly bad *The January Man*. Now he is back on the track again. The best thing about his direction is his own dialogue. The characters in this movie speak as if they would like to say things that had not been said before, in words that had never been used in quite the same way.

En route to the island, Joe meets one of Graynamore's daughters and then the other. Both are also played by Meg Ryan, who has three different kinds of fun with her three characters: grungy, waspish, and delectable. They set sail for the South Seas. Everything leads to the moment when they stand on the lip of the fiery volcano, wondering whether they should risk fate by jumping in. Only in this movie could jumping into a volcano be considered risking fate, rather than certain death.

Joe Vs. the Volcano achieves a kind of magnificent goofiness. Tom Hanks and Meg Ryan are the right actors to inhabit it, because you can never catch them going for a gag that isn't there: They inhabit the logic of this bizarre world and play by its rules. Hanks is endearing in the title role because, in the midst of these astonishing sets and unbridled flights of fancy, he underplays. Like a Jacques Tati, he is an island of curiosity in a sea of mystery.

Some of the movie's sequences are so picaresque they do themselves in: The native tribe, for example, is a joke that Shanley is unable to pull off. What's strongest about the movie is that it actually does possess a philosophy, an idea about life. The idea is the same idea contained in *Moonstruck:* At night, in those corners of our minds we deny by day, magical things can happen in the moon shadows. And if they can't, (a) they should, and (b) we should always, in any event, act as if they can.

Johnny Dangerously ★ ★
PG-13, 90 m., 1984

Michael Keaton (Johnny), Joe Piscopo (Danny Vermin), Marilu Henner (Lil), Maureen Stapleton (Mom Kelly), Peter Boyle (Jocko), Griffin Dunne (D.A.), Glynnis O'Connor (Sally). Directed by Amy Heckerling and produced by Michael Hertzberg. Screenplay by Norman Steinberg, Bernie Kukoff, Harry Colomby, and Jeff Harris.

The opening scenes of *Johnny Dangerously* are so funny you just don't see how they can keep it up. And you're right: They can't. But they make a real try. The movie wants to do for gangster films what *Airplane!* did for *Airport*, and *Top Secret* did for spy movies. It has its work cut out; this formula consumes comic inspiration at an exhausting rate, and the gangster movie is not exactly an original target for satire. What distinguishes *Johnny Dangerously* from the other attempts in this direction is the caliber of the actors: This is a high-class cast, having fun with the material, and bringing a certain reality to some of the characters almost in spite of themselves.

Michael Keaton, from *Mr. Mom*, plays Johnny as a sweet, sort of gentle gangster who doesn't see any need to stir things up. His archenemy is Danny Vermin, played by Joe Piscopo, and there are a lot of other interesting characters around, including Marilu Henner as a sex bomb who spends some of her most intimate moments on top of a piano; Peter Boyle as an eminently reasonable mob patriarch, and Maureen Stapleton as Johnny's long-suffering mom.

The movie begins with the promise that it will grow into a great comedy. There's a title song out of left field, sung by Weird Al Yankovich, and then we see Johnny as a middle-aged pet-store owner, stamping prices on his animals using one of those tape labeling machines they use in grocery stores. A kid tries to shoplift, and that inspires Johnny to remember the days when he began his own career in crime. The flashback then develops more or less along standard gangster movie lines, with of course a comic twist on every cliché. It's a little dizzying trying to spot all of the cameo roles as they go by; everybody who wandered onto the 20th Century Fox lot must have been hired to walk through this movie. But what gradually occurs to us is that we aren't laughing as often; the movie keeps trying, but it runs out of steam.

Too bad. And especially too bad for Joe Piscopo, who is such an accomplished mimic that he once literally had me thinking I was watching Jerry Lewis on "Saturday Night Live." Since masters of disguise are a fixture in gangster movies, why didn't they let Piscopo play a most-wanted criminal who was desperately trying to alter his appearance, and kept running up against incompetent gangland plastic surgeons? He plays Danny Vermin well enough, but the role seems rather limiting.

Johnny Got His Gun ★ ★ ★ ★
R, 111 m., 1971

Timothy Bottoms (Joe Bonham), Kathy Fields (Kareen), Jason Robards (Joe's Father), Diane Varsi (Fourth Nurse), Donald Sutherland (Jesus Christ), Eduard Franz (General Tillery). Directed by Dalton Trumbo and produced by Bruce Campbell. Screenplay by Trumbo.

I've never much liked anti-war films. They've never much stopped war, for one thing. For another, they attract hushed and reverential praise which speaks of their universality and the urgency of their messages. Most anti-war films come so burdened with universality and urgency that the ads for them read like calls to sunrise services.

Dalton Trumbo's *Johnny Got His Gun* smelled like that kind of anti-war film. It came out of the Cannes Film Festival with three awards and a slightly pious aroma, as if it had been made for joyless Student Peace

Union types of thirty-five years ago. But it isn't like that at all. Trumbo has taken the most difficult sort of material—the story of a soldier who lost his arms, his legs, and most of his face in a World War I shell burst—and handled it, strange to say, in a way that's not so much anti-war as pro-life. Perhaps that's why I admire it. Instead of belaboring ironic points about the "war to end war," Trumbo remains stubbornly on the human level. He lets his ideology grow out of his characters, instead of imposing it from above. In this sense, his film resembles Joseph Losey's *King and Country* which also turned its back on the war in order to consider one ordinary, unremarkable soldier.

Trumbo's soldier is Joe Bonham (Timothy Bottoms), who comes from an American background that is clearly modeled on Trumbo's own. The boy works in a bakery, supports his mother and sisters after his father's death, is in love with an open-faced and sweet Irish girl, and enlists in the army because "it's the sort of thing a fellow ought to do, when his country is in trouble." Months later, he's sent on a patrol into no-man's land to bury a corpse that was offending a colonel's nose. A shell lands near him, and he wakes up in a hospital.

The army is convinced he has no conscious mind. They decide to keep him alive simply to learn from him. But he can think, and gradually the enormity of his injuries is revealed to him. He is literally the prisoner of his mind, for years, until he finds a way of communicating with a sympathetic nurse (Diane Varsi).

Trumbo uses flashbacks and fantasies to make Joe alive for us, while he exists in a living death. The most charming flashback is the first, when Joe and his girl kiss in her living room and are interrupted by her father. He's an old Wobbly who sends them both into the bedroom, and there is a love scene of such tenderness and beauty that its echoes resound through the entire film. Other scenes develop Joe's relationship with his father (Jason Robards) and with Jesus Christ (Donald Sutherland), whom he consults in fantasies. Christ really doesn't have much to suggest; he has no answers, in Joe's fantasies, because there are no answers.

The movie ends with no political solutions and without, in fact, even a political position. It simply states a case. Here was a patriotic young man who went off and was grievously wounded for no great reason, and whose conscious mind remains a horrible

indictment of the system that sent all the young men away to kill each other. The soldier's own answer to his situation seems like the only possible one. He wants them to put him in a sideshow, where, as a freak, he can cause people a moment's thought about war. If they won't do that, he wants them to kill him. The army won't do either, of course.

Johnny Handsome ★ ★ ★ ½
R, 100 m., 1989

Mickey Rourke (John Sedley), Ellen Barkin (Sunny Boyd), Elizabeth McGovern (Donna McCarty), Morgan Freeman (Lieutenant Drones), Forest Whitaker (Dr. Resher), Lance Henriksen (Rafe Garrett), Scott Wilson (Mikey Chalmette). Directed by Walter Hill and produced by Charles Roven. Screenplay by Ken Friedman.

"Film noir: *a motion picture with an often grim urban setting, photographed in somber tones and permeated by a feeling of disillusionment, pessimism, and despair.*"—Random House Dictionary

And, they might have added, you can't really get inside a *film noir* unless you are a romantic, a person who sees life in terms of the grand gesture and fate as a pair of dice. After I saw *Johnny Handsome*, I was unfortunate enough to encounter a couple of pragmatic modern nonromantic types, who assumed without even asking me that I had not approved of the movie. They were bright young things who found the movie filled with "stereotypes." I wish the professors who teach about stereotypes in undergraduate literature classes would remember to add that they are not necessarily a bad thing— that sometimes a film is better because it returns to its roots.

Johnny Handsome comes out of the *film noir* atmosphere of the 1940s, out of movies with dark streets and bitter laughter, with characters who live in cold-water flats and treat saloons as their living rooms. It is set in New Orleans, a city with a *film noir* soul, and it stars Mickey Rourke as a weary loser who has just about given up on himself. They call him "Johnny Handsome" because his face has been horribly disfigured since birth, and as the movie opens he and his best friend have been double-crossed by a couple of crooks who kill the friend, steal the loot, and leave Johnny to take the rap.

In jail, he's offered a deal if he'll identify his accomplices. He refuses, because it is the

underworld code that you do not rat on your associates, and also because he plans to kill them when he gets back on the street. But then an interesting thing happens to him. In the jail, a thoughtful surgeon (Forest Whitaker) suggests that plastic surgery could turn Johnny into a reasonably average-looking guy, and speech therapy could make him into a passable candidate for rehabilitation.

Johnny has nothing to lose and undergoes the surgery (which, true to the tradition of movies like this, is a snap). Out on parole, he goes straight with a job down on the docks. And he meets a girl (Elizabeth McGovern) who loves him. But Johnny has a problem: He has spent so many years walking around feeling distrustful and grotesque and unlovable that he has a hard time handling success. The movie presents him with a clear choice: He can go straight, keep his nose clean, and be happy with this woman. Or he can return to crime and carry out his revenge against the hoods who double-crossed him.

Because we live in a time of simple-minded action pictures, with audiences that are less adventurous than those of the 1940s and stars who like to look good at the end, there is the assumption that Johnny will take the direction of growth and happiness (not without some setbacks, of course). But Walter Hill, who directed this film, and Mickey Rourke, who seems to seek out difficult projects, would not have been interested in a simple modern approach. This is dark material, and they head for the shadows.

The movie is filled with real style. Matthew F. Leonetti, the cinematographer, finds a gritty loneliness in the seedy quarters of New Orleans, and the Ry Cooder music is a cross between the blues and a sob. The movie benefits from strong supporting performances by an unusually distinguished cast (also including Ellen Barkin as one of the double-crossers, and Morgan Freeman as a cop who can't wait for Johnny to fail). And Hill (who made *48 HRS* and *Streets of Fire*) directs with an almost rude disregard for modern Hollywood convention. This is a movie in the true tradition of *film noir*— which someone who didn't write a dictionary once described as a movie where an ordinary guy indulges the weak side of his character, and hell opens up beneath his feet.

The Journey of Natty Gann ★ ★ ★
PG, 101 m., 1985

Meredith Salenger (Natty Gann), John Cusack (Harry Slade), Ray Wise (Natty's Father). Directed by Jeremy Kagan and produced by Mike Lobell. Screenplay by Jeanne Rosenberg.

There is one sense in which I cannot stand any movie involving a child and an animal. I am acutely aware of the possibilities for manipulating the story in order to gain unearned emotional payoffs. There is another sense in which I cannot resist a story about a child and an animal—if it is done intelligently, bravely, and without cheap sentiment.

The Journey of Natty Gann falls into the second category. It begins with potentially lethal ingredients: A young girl is joined by a glorious wolf on a cross-country odyssey in search of her missing father. Along the way, she is befriended by another teen-age drifter, threatened by tough kids and railway cops, and faced with one setback after another. This is the sort of story that used to be routinely trashed by the Walt Disney people, who would turn it into sentimental melodrama. Amazingly, then, *The Journey of Natty Gann* is a Disney production, more evidence of the fresh winds blowing through the studio.

The movie stars Meredith Salenger, a solemn-faced newcomer, as Natty Gann, the young teen-age daughter of a Chicago working-class stiff (Ray Wise). The time is the Depression. Jobs are scarce and dollars are few. When Wise gets a chance at a good-paying lumberman's job in the Northwest, he decides to take it. The bus is pulling out, Natty is nowhere to be found, and he decides to leave her in the care of a boarding-house owner and send for her later.

It appears to Natty that he is never going to send for her, and the reformatory beckons. She hops on a freight train and heads west in a forlorn search for her father, and most of the movie concerns her adventures along the way. Her great moment comes when she is lost and alone in a rainstorm in a forest, and a wolf approaches her and, amazingly, curls up at her side. With the wolf as a companion, she is understandably protected from many of the dangers of the road, and she makes it out West and also makes a friend, Harry (John Cusack), another teen-ager riding the rails.

The film's photography is magnificent, as the girl, the boy, and the wolf make their way through the Rockies and into the Northwest. More to the point is the relationship between Natty and her wolf. The movie was written by Jeanne Rosenberg, co-author of *The Black Stallion*, and again this time there is a real, fundamental feeling for the reality of a relationship between a human and a beast. The wolf looks longingly into the forest, but stays by the girl's side, and there is a thrilling sequence in which both of them jump a freight train—a close call.

This is the kind of movie that younger teen-agers might like a lot, if they have not already been broken down by the corrupt cynicism of so many Hollywood "teen-age" movies. It is about dreams and fears and dangers, love and determination. And it does justice to those qualities.

Ju Dou ★ ★ ★ ½
NO MPAA RATING, 93 m., 1991

Gong Li (Ju Dou), Li Baotian (Yang Tianqing), Li Wei (Yang Jinshan), Zhang Yi (Yang Tianbai, infant), Zheng Jian (Yang Tianbai, youth). Directed by Zhang Yimou and produced by Zhang Wenze, Yasuyoshi Tokuma, and Hu Jian. Screenplay by Liu Heng.

Sex, it is said, is the only luxury with which the poor are as well supplied as the rich. But, within the rigid Chinese feudal society depicted by *Ju Dou*, that is not quite the case. The movie, which is set in the 1920s but might as well be set a century earlier, tells the story of a wealthy old textile man who marries a juicy young bride and hires a desperate young nephew and enslaves both of them with his cruel will.

The old man owns a factory where he dips bolts of cloth in great vats of bright dyes, and then hangs them on long poles to dry. The cloth is bold and brilliant, the colors of passion, but nothing to compare to the emotional tumult taking place beneath the old villain's roof. He is sadistic and impotent, and entertains himself by tormenting his bride while the nephew listens in the middle of the night. The nephew is too poor, of course, to afford a wife, and the bride too poor to take the husband of her choice. But one day she deliberately reveals herself to the young man, he is easily seduced, and they have a child, which she convinces the old man is his own.

The infant grows into a hateful, strong-willed little monster, while the old man grows older and eventually cripples himself in an accident. He has a cart built, in which he pushes himself around his domain, while the nephew and wife continue their affair. Their deception becomes even more dangerous when the child grows old enough to understand what is going on; ironically, he resembles the sour merchant more than the lusty young man who fathered him.

The ending of *Ju Dou* is as lurid and melodramatic as anything conceived by Edgar Allan Poe or filmed by Bunuel, and it exhibits justice completely untempered by mercy. But long before the gory finale, the Chinese censors had apparently already decided to suppress this film, which was directed by a young turk named Zhang Yimou. The film was suppressed in China, but went on the international festival circuit, and won a best director award at Cannes and the Gold Hugo at Chicago before becoming one of 1990's Oscar nominees in the foreign language category, over the official objections of the Chinese.

Why did the Chinese film establishment find *Ju Dou* so offensive? It is tempting for us to read it as a political parable, to see the old merchant as an example of the old order of Maoism, and the hateful little boy as a symbol of the Red Guard. But the Chinese might just as easily have been offended by the sexuality, which is frank for a Chinese film and for a puritanical society.

The film appealed to me for two reasons. First, because of its unabashed, lurid melodrama, in which the days are filled with scheming and the nights with passion and violence. Second, because of its visual beauty. When the Technicolor company abandoned its classic three-strip process for reproducing color on film, two of its factories were closed down, but the third was packed up and sold to China, and that is why the bright colors in the vats of the textile mill will remind you of a brilliance not seen in Hollywood films since the golden age of the MGM musicals. Not that this story would have been very easily set to music.

Julia and Julia ★ ★ ★
R, 98 m., 1988

Kathleen Turner (Julia), Gabriel Byrne (Paolo), Sting (Daniel), Gabriele Ferzetti (Paolo's Father), Angela Goodwin (Paolo's Mother), Lidia Broccolino (Carla), Alexander Van Wyk (Marco). Directed by Peter Del Monte and produced by Francesco Pinto and Gaetano Stucchi. Screenplay by Silvia Napolitano, Sandrea Petraglia, and Del Monte.

Julia and Julia tells one of those nightmare stories, like *The Trial*, where the hero is condemned to live in a world in which absolutely nothing can be counted on. The story unfolds as a series of surprises, and since even the first surprise is crucial to the plot, I frankly don't see any way to review the film without spoiling some of the effect. I will, however, carry on, but I advise you not to read any further if you plan to see the film.

The story begins on the wedding day of its heroine, Julia, who is played by Kathleen Turner as a sweet and rather moony young woman not at all like the smart, aggressive characters she usually creates. It is a beautiful day in Italy, in a sunlit garden where even the trees seem to bow in happiness, but a few hours later Julia and her new husband (Gabriel Byrne) are involved in a road accident, and Byrne is killed.

You see what I mean about not reading any further. Yet how can I review the film at all without discussing such details? And there are more to follow. Turner, an American, decides to stay in Italy. She moves into a small apartment across the street from the large flat that was to be her home. Time passes. One day something strange happens, which the movie shows but does not explain. She passes through some kind of dimension into a different time scheme, a parallel path in which things turned out differently, and her husband did not die, and they have a small boy.

The sequence in which she discovers this is wonderful. She goes to her little flat, which is occupied by a strange woman who insists she has always lived there. She sees lights in the large flat across the street, which she had always refused to sell. Trembling, she climbs the stairs to find Byrne at home with their son, and everyone treating her as if she had been with them all along and none of her tragic memories had ever taken place.

She is, of course, shattered. She does not know how this could have happened, and

there is no one she can discuss it with without appearing insane (although I kept wishing she wouldn't internalize everything). She is pathetically grateful to have her happiness back until one moment, completely without warning, when she is plunged back into her other, tragic lifetime. Then she is flipped back to happiness again, sort of like a pingpong ball of fate, and there is the complication of a lover (played by Sting), whom she apparently has taken in her "happy" lifetime. (The rule at the center of these paradoxes is that she always remembers all of the sad lifetime, but only remembers those parts of the happy one that we actually see her experiencing.)

What's going on here? Don't ask me—and don't ask the movie, either. Even the simplest explanation, of parallel time tracks, is one I've borrowed out of old science-fiction novels. *Julia and Julia* wisely declines to offer any explanation at all, preferring to stay completely within Julia's nightmares as she experiences them.

The construction of the story is ingenious and perverse, and has a kind of inner logic of its own, and if there is a flaw, it's that no woman could endure this kind of round-trip more than once, if that much, before being emotionally shattered. I was reminded of Kathleen Turner's work in *Peggy Sue Got Married*, in which she traveled back in time to her own adolescence; think how much more disturbing it would be to travel sideways into the happiness you thought you'd lost.

This is the kind of movie that proves unbearably frustrating to some people, who demand explanations and resent obscurity. I have seen so many movies in which absolutely everything could be predicted that I found *Julia and Julia* perversely entertaining.

NOTE: This movie wins a footnote in cinematic history as the first feature shot entirely in High-Definition Television and then transferred to film. How does it look? There are a few moments when quick movements seem to trail their shadows behind them, but in general, the quality is comparable to a 16-millimeter print blown up to 35-millimeter. Although the film lacks the sharpness and clarity of a true 35-millimeter print, the result is much better than any previous TV-to-film transfer I've seen.

Jungle Fever ★ ★ ★ ½
R, 132 m., 1991

Wesley Snipes (Flipper Purify), Annabella Sciorro (Angie Tucci), Spike Lee (Cyrus), Ossie Davis (Doctor Purify), Ruby Dee (Lucinda Purify), Samuel L. Jackson (Gator Purify), John Turturro (Paulie Carbone), Lonette McKee (Drew), Anthony Quinn (Mike). Directed, produced, and written by Spike Lee.

Jungle Fever is Spike Lee's term for unhealthy sexual attraction between the races—for relationships based on stereotypes. Too often, he believes, when blacks and whites go to bed with one another, they are motivated, not by love or affection, but by media-based myths about the sexual allure of the other race. Lee has explained this belief in countless interviews, and yet it remains the murkiest element in his new film, which is brilliant when it examines the people who surround his feverish couple, but uncertain when it comes to the lovers themselves.

The victims of *Jungle Fever* are Wesley Snipes, as Flipper, an affluent, married, successful architect, and Anabella Sciorro, as Angie, a temporary office worker. He is African-American; she is Italian-American. She comes to work in his Manhattan office one day, their eyes meet, and the fever starts. Their halting, tentative conversations expand into "working late," eating Chinese food from the takeaway, and finally having sex right there on top of the blueprints.

Because I have heard Lee discuss the film, I know he believes that the Snipes and Sciorro characters are blinded to other issues by each other's blackness and whiteness—that she is intrigued by the myth of black male prowess, that he is fascinated by the ideal of white female beauty. But, in fact, neither of these notions is really established in the film, which is least successful and focused in the scenes between its two principals. We never really believe the attraction they feel for one another, we never really understand their relationship, and their romance seems to be mostly an excuse for the other events in the movie to happen—the events that make the film special.

It's as if Lee himself, as a screenwriter, could see these characters only as stereotypes—could not, or would not, get inside of them. They lunge hungrily at one another, but his camera looks away from their passion, is already moving on to the real subjects of his film, which he finds in the communities that the two characters came from.

The black architect comes from a traditional, God-fearing Harlem family. His father (Ossie Davis) is a self-righteous former preacher called the Good Reverend Doctor by one and all. His mother (Ruby Dee) is loving and sensible. There is another son, Gator (Samuel L. Jackson), who is a crackhead, who has gone as far down as Flipper has gone up. Flipper is married to Drew (Lonette McKee), and he loves her, but that has nothing to do with the fever.

The office worker comes from an Italian-American family in Bensonhurst. Angie is engaged to Paulie (John Turturro), who works all day in the luncheonette owned by his father (Anthony Quinn), a hidebound old man who sits around upstairs praying to the photograph of his wife. When word gets back to the local communities about the new romance, it does not go over well. Flipper's wife is enraged and his father deeply offended (not least by the adultery), and all of Angie's relatives and friends react with shock.

But Lee does not leave it at that. He keeps burrowing, finding the truth beneath the pain, in dialogue of brutal honesty, as when Drew reveals her own deepest reasons for being hurt by her husband: She herself is half-white, has always suspected Flipper married her for her lighter skin color, now fears that color is also why he left her. And back in the luncheonette, inhabited by a stable of Italian-American regulars, the news

that Paulie's girl is dating a black man is received with anger and yet ambiguity by his friends, including one so swarthy that he himself has experienced rejection, yet is doubly racist as a result.

The mysteries and traps of pigmentation have always fascinated Lee, who told uncomfortable truths about them in his second film, *School Daze*, and again this time gives us a lot of frank talk. The best single scene in the movie comes as Drew and her friends sit around talking about black men, in hard truths ranging from sorrow and anger to humor. This scene was improvised over a period of two days by Lee and the actresses, who were asked to contribute their own deepest feelings on the subject.

Meanwhile, there is another story in *Jungle Fever*, the story of Gator, the brother who is a crackhead. Lee shows how drugs can split a family down the middle, so that while one brother is a white-collar success, another is trapped in a hell of addiction. The most harrowing sequence in the movie follows Flipper as he searches for Gator through the demonic sewers where crackheads gather—until finally there is a scene out of Dante, in a crackhouse where the moments of release are surrounded by a great bottomless pall of despair.

As in *Do the Right Thing*, Lee tells his larger story in terms of these many smaller stories—including a subtle development that takes place when the luncheonette operator

is told by Angie that she is dating a black man. The Turturro character takes this news surprisingly well, perhaps because he is not much in love with Angie himself, and has developed a soft spot for the sweet black woman who has a nice word for him every morning as she stops in for her coffee and Danish. When he tells the regulars he plans to ask her out, they beat him up almost as an automatic reflex, but he goes off to ring her doorbell anyway.

We sense that this relationship will probably not flower; she does not really see him as someone she can take seriously, and yet Lee seems to be suggesting that at least the Turturro character does not suffer from jungle fever—that he simply finds himself attracted to this woman, admires her, and wants to go out with her. If this relationship had been more fully developed, perhaps we could have contrasted it with the doomed love between Flipper and Angie.

But Lee seems least certain when it comes to the intricacies of the heart. *Jungle Fever* contains two sequences—the girl talk and the crackhouse visit—of amazing power. It contains humor and insight and canny psychology, strong performances, and the fearless discussion of things both races would rather not face. The one area where it is least certain is "jungle fever," which Lee uses as his starting point and then leaves behind as quickly as possible.

K

K-9 ★ ★
PG, 105 m., 1989

James Belushi (Dooley), Mel Harris (Tracy), Kevin Tighe (Lyman), Ed O'Neill (Brannigan), James Handy (Byers), Daniel Davis (Halstead), Marjorie Bransfield (Hostess), Jerry Lee (K-9, The Dog). Directed by Rod Daniel and produced by Lawrence Gordon and Charles Gordon. Screenplay by Steven Siegel and Scott Myers.

I talk to my cats a good deal, but only when nobody's around, and never with the thought that they can understand me. If the hero of *K-9* had adopted a similar approach to his dog, this might have been a better movie. Instead, we start with a standard drug movie and end up with so many monologues to the dog that the dialogue coach must have needed a pooper-scooper.

The film stars James Belushi as a San Diego narcotics detective who likes to work alone. He's your standard-issue eccentric loner, a guy who orders take-out pizzas to be delivered to his car during stakeouts, and then heats them up with his cigarette lighter. He's got the goods on a big drug dealer, and thinks he knows how to intercept a major dope delivery. When the dealer destroys Belushi's car with a helicopter attack, Belushi asks for a new car. His boss says he has to accept a partner. Belushi wants to work alone. He settles for the only partner he can stand, a police attack dog.

The movie up until this point has been such a relentlessly predictable collection of drug-movie clichés that the dog comes as a relief. Somewhere in Hollywood, they must have a data bank used by the authors of all thrillers involving drugs. How else can you explain the fact that these movies always feature (a) a helicopter attack, usually in the opening scenes; (b) a Mr. Big who dresses impeccably, speaks in civilized tones and is honored at charity events when he is not running drugs; (c) several vicious henchmen; (d) a large warehouse which is the setting for drug busts and shoot-outs; and (e) large fleets of very expensive cars with blacked-out windows.

If the crime elements in *K-9* are routine, the relationship between Belushi and the dog at least has the courage to be goofy. Although Belushi has a girlfriend in the movie (Mel Harris), he easily speaks three times as much dialogue to the dog than to the girl, and the dog responds by saving his life, chewing on several crooks, and cracking the case wide open by sniffing out the dope hidden in the cute little red Mercedes convertible.

All of this is more or less acceptable. What is not acceptable is the use of film editing and dog-training techniques to make it appear that the dog understands English and thinks in human terms. There is an almost unforgivable scene late in the film, in which the dog plays dead and Belushi delivers a eulogy, and the dog opens its eyes when Belushi's back is turned, but closes them real quick again when Belushi looks his way. Give me a break. And while you're at it, can someone pass a law against dogs who cover their eyes with their cute little paws when a sight is just too much for them?

Was I expecting a realistic movie about police dogs? Not really. Was I expecting a comedy? Not after the helicopter blew up the car. Was I expecting a tough police thriller? Belushi is capable of being as tough as anyone on the screen, but in this movie he's a lovable goofball. I guess what I'm saying is that everyone on the set must have really fallen in love with that dog, and they're probably right and it's probably a great pooch, but maybe they should have given a little more thought to the movie while they were at it.

Kagemusha ★ ★ ★ ★
PG, 160 m., 1980

Tatsuya Nakadai (Shingen and Kagemusha), Tsutomu Yamazaki (Nobukado), Kenichi Hagiwara (Katsuyori), Jinpachi Nezu (Bodyguard), Shuji Otaki (Fire General). Directed by Akira Kurosawa and produced by Kurosawa and Tomoyuki Tanaka. Screenplay by Kurosawa and Masato Ide.

Kagemusha, we learn, means "shadow warrior" in Japanese, and Akira Kurosawa's great film tells the story of a man who becomes the double, or shadow, of a great warrior. It also teaches the lesson that shadows or appearances are as important as reality, but that men cannot count on either shadows or reality.

Kagemusha is a samurai drama by the director who most successfully introduced the genre to the West (with such classics as *The Seven Samurai* and *Yojimbo*), and who, at the age of seventy, made an epic that dares to wonder what meaning the samurai code—or any human code—really has in the life of an individual man. His film is basically the story of one such man, a common thief who, because of his astonishing resemblance to the warlord Shingen, is chosen as Shingen's double. When Shingen is mortally wounded in battle, the great Takeda clan secretly replaces him with the double—so their enemies will not learn that Shingen is dead. Thus begins a period of three years during which the kagemusha is treated by everyone, even his son and his mistresses, as if he were the real Shingen. Only his closest advisers know the truth.

But he is not Lord Shingen. And so every scene is undercut with irony. It is important that both friends and enemies believe Shingen is alive; his appearance, or shadow, creates both the respect of his clan and the cau-

313

tion of his enemies. If he is unmasked, he is useless; as Shingen's double, he can send hundreds of men to be killed, and his own guards will willingly sacrifice their lives for him. But as himself, he is worthless, and when he *is* unmasked, he's banished into the wilderness.

What is Kurosawa saying here? I suspect the answer can be found in a contrast between two kinds of scenes. His film contains epic battle scenes of astonishing beauty and scope. And then there are the intimate scenes in the throne room, the bedroom, the castles, and battlefield camps. The great battle scenes glorify the samurai system. Armies of thousands of men throw themselves heedlessly at death, for the sake of pride. But the intimate scenes undermine that glorious tradition; as everyone holds their breath, Shingen's double is tested in meetings with his son, his mistresses, and his horse. They know him best of all. If they are not fooled, all of the panoply and battlefield courage is meaningless, because the Takeda clan has lost the leader who is their figurehead; the illusion that he exists creates the clan's reality.

Kurosawa made this film after a decade of personal travail. Although he is often considered the greatest living Japanese director, he was unable to find financial backing in Japan when he first tried to make *Kagemusha*. He made a smaller film, *Dodeskaden*, which was not successful. He tried to commit suicide, but failed. He was backed by the Russians and went to Siberia to make the beautiful *Dersu Uzala* (1976), about a man of the wilderness. But *Kagemusha* remained his obsession, and he was finally able to make it only when Hollywood directors Francis Ford Coppola and George Lucas helped him find U.S. financing.

The film he finally made is simple, bold, and colorful on the surface, but very thoughtful. Kurosawa seems to be saying that great human endeavors (in this case, samurai wars) depend entirely on large numbers of men sharing the same fantasies or beliefs. It is entirely unimportant, he seems to be suggesting, whether or not the beliefs are based on reality—all that matters is that men accept them. But when a belief is shattered, the result is confusion, destruction, and death. At the end of *Kagemusha*, for example, the son of the real Lord Shingen orders his troops into a suicidal charge, and their deaths are not only unnecessary but meaningless, because they are not on behalf of the sacred person of the warlord.

There are great images in this film: Of a breathless courier clattering down countless steps, of men passing in front of a blood-red sunset, of a dying horse on a battlefield. But Kurosawa's last image—of the dying kagemusha floating in the sea, swept by tidal currents past the fallen standard of the Takeda clan—summarizes everything: ideas and men are carried along heedlessly by the currents of time, and historical meaning *seems* to emerge when both happen to be swept in the same way at the same time.

The Karate Kid ★ ★ ★ ★
PG, 126 m., 1984

Ralph Macchio (Daniel), Noriyuki "Pat" Morita (Miyagi), Elisabeth Shue (Ali), Martin Kove (Kreese), William Zabka (Johnny). Directed by John G. Avildsen and produced by Jerry Weintraub. Written by Robert Mark Kamen.

I didn't want to see this movie. I took one look at the title and figured it was either (a) a sequel to *Toenails of Vengeance*, or (b) an adventure pitting Ricky Schroeder against the Megaloth Man. I was completely wrong. *The Karate Kid* was one of the nice surprises of 1984—an exciting, sweet-tempered, heartwarming story with one of the most interesting friendships in a long time. The friends come from different worlds. A kid named Daniel (Ralph Macchio) is a New Jersey teen-ager who moves with his mother to Los Angeles. An old guy named Miyagi (Pat Morita) is the Japanese janitor in their apartment building. When Daniel starts to date the former girlfriend of the toughest kid in the senior class, the kid starts pounding on Daniel's head on a regular basis. Daniel tries to fight back, but this is a Southern California kid, and so of course he has a black belt in karate. Enter Mr. Miyagi, who seems to be a harmless old eccentric with a curious hobby: He tries to catch flies with chopsticks. It turns out that Miyagi is a karate master, a student not only of karate fighting but of the total philosophy of the martial arts. He agrees to take Daniel as his student.

And then begins the wonderful center section of *The Karate Kid*, as the old man and the kid from Jersey become friends. Miyagi's system of karate instruction is offbeat, to say the least. He puts Daniel to work shining cars, painting fences, scrubbing the bottoms of pools. Daniel complains that he isn't

learning karate, he's acting as free labor. But there is a system to Mr. Miyagi's training.

The Karate Kid was directed by John G. Avildsen, who made *Rocky*. It ends with the same sort of climactic fight scene; Daniel faces his enemies in a championship karate tournament. But the heart of this movie isn't in the fight sequences, it's in the relationships. And in addition to Daniel's friendship with Miyagi, there's also a sweet romantic liaison with Ali (Elisabeth Shue), who is your standard girl from the right side of town and has the usual snobbish parents.

Macchio is an unusual, interesting choice for Daniel. He's not the basic handsome Hollywood teen-ager but a thin, tall, intense kid with a way of seeming to talk to himself. His delivery always sounds natural, even offhand; he never seems to be reading a line. He's a good, sound, interesting lead, but the movie really belongs to Pat Morita, an actor who has been around a long time (he was Arnold on "Happy Days") without ever having a role anywhere near this good. Morita makes Miyagi into an example of applied serenity. In a couple of scenes where he has to face down a hostile karate coach, Miyagi's words are so carefully chosen they don't give the other guy any excuse to get violent; Miyagi uses the language as carefully as his hands or arms to ward off blows and gain an advantage. It's refreshing to see a completely original character like this old man. *The Karate Kid* is a sleeper with a title that gives you the wrong idea: It's one of 1984's best movies.

The Karate Kid, Part III ★ ½
PG, 111 m., 1989

Ralph Macchio (Daniel), Noriyuki "Pat" Morita (Mr. Miyagi), Robyn Lively (Jessica), Thomas Ian Griffith (Terry), Sean Kanan (Mike Barnes), Jonathan Avildsen (Snake), Christopher Paul Ford (Dennis), Randee Heller (Lucille). Directed by John G. Avildsen and produced by Jerry Weintraub. Screenplay by Robert Mark Kamen.

I think I have the message by now. It was contained in *The Karate Kid* (1984), which was a wonderful movie, and then it was recycled in *The Karate Kid, Part II*. Now here we have *The Karate Kid, Part III*, and still the message is the same. This material is wearing out its welcome. I have mastered all of the lessons *The Karate Kid* movies have to teach, and all of the surprises they have to spring. I am also intimately familiar with the plot formula, so that nothing in this third film comes as the faintest surprise. Perhaps it is time, as Mr. Miyagi might say, to study something else.

The purpose of a sequel is allegedly to continue the original story, to tell us more about some characters we have already encountered. The problem with most movie sequels is that they don't continue the original story; they repeat it. They take the same conflicts, the same problems, and sometimes even the same dialogue, and they try to fool us into thinking we're seeing a new movie. *The Karate Kid, Part III* was made in 1989, but all of the original thinking on this movie took place five years ago. The same director, the same writer, and most of the same stars are back again—to do the same things.

In the first movie, we had the pleasure of meeting for the first time one of the genuinely interesting characters of recent movies, Mr. Miyagi, a Japanese-American janitor whose secret life included mastery of the practice and philosophy of karate, and who was a wise philosopher with a foolish love for restoring old cars. As he gradually revealed himself to Daniel, the "karate kid," we met him too, and it was a pleasure to guess his secrets and be taught some of his mysteries. That first movie had an attitude about karate and life.

The second film, which transferred part of the story to Okinawa, had interesting locales and a pretty girlfriend for the hero, but no new ideas about the plot—which involved Miyagi and his student being pushed so far by bad guys that they overcome their reluctance to fight. In this third film, Miyagi (Noriyuki "Pat" Morita) has been reduced to a standard element in a standard plot. And Daniel (Ralph Macchio) is no longer an interesting, quirky kid, but simply a series of predictable attitudes.

Terry, the villain (Thomas Ian Griffith), is one of those slicked-back wise guys with a squirmy smile who does hateful things because he's a hateful person (karate is his hobby; his real-life business is dumping toxic wastes). There's a little room left in the plot for the hapless Kreese (Martin L. Kove), who ran the corrupt karate school in the first movie. And then there's a new love interest named Jessica (Robyn Lively), who runs the pottery shop across the street from Mr. Miyagi's new bonsai store. And a new villain (Sean Kanan) whose job is simply to be violent, cruel, and hateful.

The plot: Terry is an old army buddy of Kreese's, whose school goes bankrupt after Miyagi and the kid win the big tournament. He finances a tournament challenge by the Kanan character, who convinces a reluctant Daniel to accept his challenge by trapping him at the bottom of a cliff and threatening the life of the cute potter. Mr. Miyagi counsels Daniel to retire from competition—but after the bad guys push him too far, he thrashes all of them and agrees to coach the kid for the tournament, with the usual results.

The only fresh element this time is Daniel's brief rebellion, when he is disloyal to Miyagi by accepting the scheming Terry as his coach. Formula movies like this are only as good as their villains, and I would have liked to know more about the weirdness that glows in their eyes, but the movie doesn't care—they're not in the movie as characters, but as little pop-up cartoon characters to further the plot.

The first movie made at least a bow in the direction of a nonviolent philosophy. No more. This movie depends as much on a violent showdown as *Rocky*—which had the same director, John G. Avildsen. It's hard to create original characters and give them interesting things to say, and Avildsen and writer Robert Mark Kamen have exhausted themselves with these particular characters. It's time to move on.

The Killing Fields ★ ★ ★ ★
R, 139 m., 1984

Sam Waterston (Sydney Schanberg), Dr. Haing S. Ngor (Dith Pran), John Malkovich (Al Rockoff), Craig T. Nelson (Military Attaché), Athol Fugard (Dr. Sundesval). Directed by Roland Joffe and produced by David Puttnam. Screenplay by Bruce Robinson.

There's a strange thing about stories based on what the movies insist on calling "real life." The haphazard chances of life, the unanticipated twists of fate, have a way of getting smoothed down into Hollywood formulas, so that what might once have happened to a real person begins to look more and more like what might once have happened to John Wayne. One of the risks taken by *The Killing Fields* is to cut loose from that tradition, to tell us a story that does not have a traditional Hollywood structure, and to trust that we'll find the characters so interesting that we won't miss the cliché. It is a risk that works, and that helps make this into a really affecting experience.

The "real life" story behind the movie is by now well-known. Sydney Schanberg, a correspondent for the *New York Times*, covered the invasion of Cambodia with the help of Dith Pran, a local journalist and translator. When the country fell to the communist Khmer Rouge, the lives of all foreigners were immediately at risk, and Schanberg got out along with most of his fellow Western correspondents. He offered Pran a chance to leave with him, but Pran elected to stay. And when the Khmer Rouge drew a bamboo curtain around Cambodia, Pran disappeared into a long silence. Back home in New York, Schanberg did what he could to discover information about his friend; for example, he wrote about four hundred letters to organizations like the Red Cross. But it was a futile exercise, and Schanberg had given up his friend for dead, when one day four years later word came that Pran was still alive and had made it across the border to a refugee camp. The two friends were reunited, in one of the rare happy endings that come out of a period of great suffering.

As a human story, this is a compelling one. As a Hollywood story, it obviously will not do because the last half of the movie is essentially Dith Pran's story, told from his point of view. Hollywood convention has it that the American should fight his way back into the occupied country (accompanied by renegade Green Berets and Hell's Angels, and Rambo, if possible), blast his way into a prison camp, and save his buddy. That was the formula for *Uncommon Valor* and *Missing in Action*, two box-office hits, and in *The Deer Hunter* one friend went back to Vietnam to rescue another. Sitting in New York writing letters is not quite heroism on the same scale. And yet, what else could Schanberg do? And, more to the point, what else could Dith Pran do, in the four years of his disappearance, but try to disguise his origins and his education, and pass as an illiterate peasant—one of the countless prisoners of Khmer Rouge work camps? By telling his story, and by respecting it, *The Killing Fields* becomes a film of an altogether higher order than the Hollywood revenge thrillers.

The movie begins in the early days of the journalistic coverage of Cambodia. We meet Schanberg (Sam Waterston) and Pran (played by Dr. Haing S. Ngor, whose own story is an uncanny parallel to his character's), and we sense the strong friendship and loyalty that they share. We also absorb the conditions in the country, where warehouses full of Coca-Cola are blown up by terrorists who know a symbolic target when they see one. Life is a routine of hanging out at cafes and restaurants and official briefings, punctuated by an occasional trip to the front, where the American view of things does not seem to be reflected by the suffering that the correspondents witness.

The whole atmosphere of this period is suggested most successfully by the character of an American photographer, played by John Malkovich as a cross between a dopehead and a hard-bitten newsman. He is not stirred to action very easily, and still less easily stirred to caring, but when an occasion rises (for example, the need to forge a passport for Pran), he reveals the depth of his feeling. As the Khmer Rouge victory becomes inevitable, there are scenes of incredible tension, especially one in which Dith Pran saves the lives of his friends by some desperate fast talking with the cadres of adolescent rebels who would just as soon shoot them. Then there is the confusion of the evacuation of the U.S. Embassy and a last glimpse of Dith Pran before he disappears for four years.

In a more conventional film, he would, of course, have really disappeared, and we would have followed the point of view of the Schanberg character. But this movie takes the chance of switching points of view in midstream, and the last half of the film belongs to Dith Pran, who sees his country turned into an insane parody of a one-party state, ruled by the Khmer Rouge with instant violence and a savage intolerance for any reminders of the French and American presence of the colonial era. Many of the best scenes in the film's second half are essentially played without dialogue, as Pran works in the fields, disguises his origins, and waits for his chance.

The film is a masterful achievement on all the technical levels—it does an especially good job of convincing us with its Asian locations—but the best moments are the human ones, the conversations, the exchanges of trust, the waiting around, the sudden fear, the quick bursts of violence, the desperation. At the center of many of those scenes is Dr. Haing S. Ngor, a non-actor who was recruited for the role from the ranks of Cambodian refugees in California, and who brings to it a simple sincerity that is absolutely convincing. Sam Waterston is effective in the somewhat thankless role of Sydney Schanberg, and among the carefully drawn vignettes are

Craig T. Nelson as a military attaché and Athol Fugard as Dr. Sundesval.

The American experience in Southeast Asia has given us a great film epic *(Apocalypse Now)* and a great drama *(The Deer Hunter)*. Here is the story told a little closer to the ground, of people who were not very important and not very powerful, who got caught up in events that were indifferent to them, but never stopped trying to do their best and their most courageous.

Kindergarten Cop ★ ★ ★
PG-13, 110 m., 1990

Arnold Schwarzenegger (Kimble), Penelope Ann Miller (Joyce), Pamela Reed (Phoebe), Linda Hunt (Miss Scholwski), Richard Tyson (Crisp), Carroll Baker (Eleanor Crisp). Directed by Ivan Reitman and produced by Reitman and Brian Grazer. Screenplay by Murray Salem, Herschel Weingrod, and Timothy Harris.

Kindergarten Cop is made up out of parts that shouldn't fit, but somehow they do, making a slick entertainment out of the improbable, the impossible, and Arnold Schwarzenegger. He plays a cop who finds himself teaching kindergarten as part of an undercover effort to locate a little boy and his mother. There is no way that Schwarzenegger can plausibly teach class, but that doesn't prevent him from finding warmhearted possibilities in the role—and it doesn't get in the way of several big laughs, either.

The movie opens with Arnold and his cop partner (Pamela Reed) on the trail of a vicious swine of a drug dealer and momma's boy, played with smarmy conviction by Richard Tyson. Tyson and his mother (Carroll Baker) are eager to discover the whereabouts of his ex-wife and their son. So is Arnold, because he dreams of nailing this creep, and also because he believes that the ex-wife may have $3 million of Tyson's drug earnings.

The trail leads to a storybook town in the Pacific Northwest, where Schwarzenegger and Reed believe the little boy is attending kindergarten. Reed used to be a schoolteacher, and so they convince the local school authorities to let her teach the kindergarten class—hoping to pick up clues, even though the little boy and his mother have changed their names. Then Reed gets food poisoning, and it's up to Arnold to face the screaming hordes of five-year-olds.

Kindergarten Cop was directed by Ivan Reitman, whose best work, like *Ghostbusters*,

shows an ability to mix the absurd with the dramatic, so that we're laughing as the suspense reaches its peak. That happens this time. The scenes involving Schwarzenegger and the kindergarten kids are the best things in the movie, not only because the kids say the darnedest things, but also because Arnold's strong point here is gentle comedy, often with himself as the foil.

Contrasting with the classroom stuff is a low-key little romance involving Arnold and one of the other teachers (Penelope Ann Miller), a parallel story involving the vicious drug dealer and his mom, who journey to the small town for the obligatory, but quite effective, violent climax. Reitman juggles the light stuff, the heartwarming scenes, the comedy, and the violence with endless invention, so that the movie doesn't seem to be shifting gears even when it is.

Movies like this are often no stronger than their villains, and Tyson and Baker make a scary and effective team. He's a spoiled-rotten mother's pet who has never grown up, and whose love for his son is basically narcissistic. She is a bitch on wheels. The other key performances are also effective, and it was interesting for me to observe, while seeing the movie in a large audience, what genuine affection the public has for Schwarzenegger. He has a way of turning situations to his advantage and creates an entertaining relationship with his young students in this movie.

Warning: This is not a film appropriate for young children. Despite the title and the ad campaign, which make it look like a sweet and jolly funfest, the movie contains images sure to be terrifying to grade-schoolers, such as a man setting the school on fire, small children kidnapped and terrorized, a father slapping his child, and so forth. In context and for mature viewers, the scenes have a purpose and the movie works. But it'll be nightmare time for young children who see it.

King Lear ★ ★ ★
PG, 138 m., 1972

Paul Scofield (King Lear), Irene Worth (Goneril), Jack MacGowran (Fool), Alan Webb (Gloucester), Cyril Cusack (Albany), Patrick Magee (Cornwall), Robert Lloyd (Edgar), Tom Fleming (Kent), Susan Engel (Regan), Annelise Gaboid (Cordelia). Directed by Peter Brook. Screenplay by Brook.

Peter Brook's *King Lear* occupies a barren kingdom frozen in the middle of a winter that chills souls even more than bodies. He is not his own master; he gives away his power and then discovers, with a childlike surprise, that he can no longer exercise it. Burdened by senility and a sense of overwhelming futility, he collapses gratefully into death.

It is important to describe him as Brook's Lear, because he is not Shakespeare's. *King Lear* is the most difficult of Shakespeare's plays to stage, the most complex and, to my mind, the greatest. There are immensities of feeling and meaning in it that Brook has not even touched. And for Shakespeare's difficulties of staging, he has substituted his own cinematic decorations.

This is not to say that his film is not a brave and interesting effort in its own right. Peter Brook is not constitutionally able to direct "screen versions" of someone else's work. The vision must be his own, even if that means Shakespeare finishes second; this is not so much a film of *King Lear* as a film about it, with Brook's critical analysis of the play suggesting his directorial strategy.

His approach was suggested by *Shakespeare Our Contemporary*, a controversial book by the Polish critic Jan Kott. In Kott's view, *King Lear* is a play about the total futility of things. The old man Lear stumbles ungracefully toward his death because, simply put, that's the way it goes for most of us. To search for meaning of philosophical consolation is to kid yourself.

I suppose every age has attempted to redefine Shakespeare in terms of its own preoccupations, and the Brook-Kott version of *Lear* is certainly fashionable and modern. But it gives us a film that severely limits Shakespeare's vision, and focuses our attention on his more nihilistic passages while ignoring or sabotaging the others.

There is a great deal of goodness in *King Lear*. There is the old king himself, "more sinned against than sinning," whose cruelties are the result of misplaced love. There is Cordelia, the most touchingly sincere heroine in all of Shakespeare. There is Edgar, totally devoted to the father who has disowned him, and Kent, who serves Lear out of love. And there are the moments when Lear shakes off his sense of doom and hurls taunts at the gods, or tells his beloved Cordelia that their suffering will pass and they will once again live like the songbirds and dabble in the gossip of the court. Lear even seems to die convinced that Cordelia lives; she does not, but his last conscious impulse is one of hope and faith. Perhaps that is Shakespeare's final thought: that the ability to

hope is what makes us human, even if, in fact, our hopes are futile.

This is a great humanistic assertion, and it has no place in the Peter Brook film. He omits or rearranges dialogue and scenes in order to make the evil daughters, Regan and Goneril, ambiguous in their villainy. He gives us a Cordelia who is not as perfect as she should be. He gives us a Lear who is only a figure of pity, not (as he was in Shakespeare) also sometimes a figure of greatness. He gives us a world so grim we might as well be dead.

Lear is played by Paul Scofield, whose beard and large, sad eyes make him look distractingly like the middle-aged Hemingway. Perhaps because of Brook's direction, Scofield's readings are often uninflected and exhausted. He reads Shakespeare's poetry the way Mark Twain said women use profanity: "They know the words, but not the music." The acting style suits Brook's ideas about the play, but leaves Lear diminished as a character.

Shakespeare's *Lear* survives in his play and will endure forever. Brook's *Lear* is a new conception, a rethinking, and a critical commentary on the play. It is interesting precisely because it contrasts so firmly with Shakespeare's universe; by deliberately omitting all faith and hope from Lear's kingdom, it paradoxically helps us to see how much is there.

The King of Comedy ★ ★ ★
PG, 101 m., 1983

Robert De Niro (Rupert Pupkin), Jerry Lewis (Jerry Langford), Diahnne Abbott (Rita), Sandra Bernhard (Masha), Ed Herlihy (Himself). Directed by Martin Scorsese. Screenplay by Paul Zimmerman.

Martin Scorsese's *The King of Comedy* is one of the most arid, painful, wounded movies I've ever seen. It's hard to believe Scorsese made it; instead of the big-city life, the violence and sexuality of his movies like *Taxi Driver* and *Mean Streets*, what we have here is an agonizing portrait of lonely, angry people with their emotions all tightly bottled up. This is a movie that seems ready to explode—but somehow it never does. That lack of release seriously disturbed me the first time I saw *The King of Comedy*. I kept straining forward, waiting for the movie to let loose, and it kept frustrating me. Maybe that was the idea. This is a movie about rejection, with a

hero who never admits that he has been rejected, and so there is neither comic nor tragic release—just the postponement of pain.

I left that first screening filled with dislike for the movie. Dislike, but not disinterest. Memories of *The King of Comedy* kept gnawing at me, and when people asked me what I thought about it, I said I wasn't sure. Then I saw the movie a second time, and it seemed to work better for me—maybe because I was able to watch without any expectations. I knew it wasn't an entertainment, I knew it didn't allow itself any emotional payoffs, I knew the ending was cynical and unsatisfying, and so, with *those* discoveries no longer to be made, I was free to simply watch what was on the screen.

What I saw the second time, better than the first, were the performances by Robert De Niro, Jerry Lewis, Diahnne Abbott, and Sandra Bernhard, who play the movie's most important characters. They must have been difficult performances to deliver, because there's almost no feedback in this movie. The actors can't bounce emotional energy off each other, because nobody *listens* in this film; everybody's just waiting for the other person to stop talking so they can start. And everybody's so emotionally isolated in this movie that they don't even seem able to guess what they're missing.

The movie stars De Niro, as Rupert Pupkin, a nerdish man in his thirties who fantasizes himself as a television star. He practices in his basement, holding condescending conversations with life-size cardboard cutouts of Liza Minnelli and Jerry Lewis. His dream is to get a stand-up comedy slot on the late-night talk show hosted by Lewis (whose name in the movie is Jerry Langford). The movie opens with Rupert's first meeting with Jerry; he barges into Jerry's limousine and is immediately on an obnoxious first-name basis. Jerry vaguely promises to check out Rupert's comedy routine, and the rest of the movie is devoted to Rupert's single-minded pursuit of fame. He arrives at Jerry's office, is politely brushed off, returns, is ejected, arrives at Jerry's country home with a "date" in tow, is ejected again, and finally decides to kidnap Jerry.

This *sounds* like an entertaining story, I suppose, but Scorsese doesn't direct a single scene for a payoff. The whole movie is an exercise in *cinema interruptus;* even a big scene in a bar, where Rupert triumphantly turns on the TV set to reveal himself on television, is deliberately edited to leave out the payoff shots—reaction shots of the amazed clientele. Scorsese doesn't want laughs in this movie, and he also doesn't want release. The whole movie is about the inability of the characters to get any kind of a positive response to their bids for recognition.

The King of Comedy is not, you may already have guessed, a fun movie. It is also not a bad movie. It is frustrating to watch, unpleasant to remember, and, in its own way, quite effective. It represents an enormous departure for Scorsese, whose movies teemed with life before he filmed this emotional desert, and whose camera used to prowl restlessly before he nailed it down this time. Scorsese and De Niro are the most creative, productive director/actor team in the movies right now, and the fact that they feel the freedom to make such an odd, stimulating, unsatisfying movie is good news, I guess. But *The King of Comedy* is the kind of film that makes you want to go and see a Scorsese movie.

The King of Marvin Gardens ★ ★ ★
R, 104 m., 1972

Jack Nicholson (David Staebler), Bruce Dern (Jason Staebler), Ellen Burstyn (Sally), Julia Anne Robinson (Jessica), Scatman Crothers (Lewis), Charles Levine (Grandfather). Directed and produced by Bob Rafelson. Screenplay by Jacob Brackman.

Bob Rafelson's *The King of Marvin Gardens* is a perversely satisfying movie—it works after going out of its way not to—and a very eccentric one. It backs into its real subject in much the same way that *Five Easy Pieces*, Rafelson's previous film, did. Only after it's over do some of its scenes and moments fall into place; for much of the way we've been disoriented and the story has been suspended somewhere in midair. As someone wrote about a totally dissimilar movie, Paul Morrissey's *Trash*, it's the kind of film you want to walk out of, and then when it's over you want to see it again.

The movie opens and closes with autobiographical monologues being delivered by an all-night talk jockey (Jack Nicholson) into the loneliness of the FM airwaves. He works in a darkened studio, stopping sometimes to search for words, and it's evident that his broadcasts tear something loose from deep inside. It's possible, indeed, that he says more on the radio (or into his tape recorder) in this movie than he ever gets around to say-

ing in the actual situations he finds himself in. He's tentative, unsure, private. His radio fantasies often involve his brother, Jason (Bruce Dern), who lives in Atlantic City, New Jersey, and does mysterious but glorious things there. After a long silence, Jason himself calls his brother and tells him to hustle down to Atlantic City because there are big deals cooking. They're going to buy an island near Hawaii and develop it into a resort. Sure.

Most of the movie takes place in Atlantic City, where the metaphor of a Monopoly game is employed a little too persistently, I thought. There's the Boardwalk, of course, and Marvin Gardens itself; but there are also Jason's attempts to buy a hotel, and the fact that he's in jail when we first meet him. This stuff is worked in quietly enough by Jacob Brackman's script, however, that it doesn't really distract.

Jason is living with a blonde on the far side of the hill (Ellen Burstyn) and her stepdaughter, a blonde coming up fast on this side (Julia Anne Robinson). A great deal of the movie is about the unacknowledged sexual competition between the two women, but this (like a few other things) becomes important only gradually. Most of the action seems to involve a disagreement between Jason, who turns out to be a minor hood, and the mysterious Lewis, who is the black rackets boss and moneyman in town. Jason's deals are based on reckless confidence in Lewis's money, and Lewis isn't going along.

Until the movie's end, when everything falls together with a really stunning force, Rafelson and Brackman seem to be going for a series of set-pieces. There is an unhappy lobster dinner with two Japanese investors reputed to have money; they wear their lobster-proof bibs happily, but don't come through. There's the matter of the older blonde marching into the hotel next door to take a bath ("Hell, you told me you *owned* the damn place," she says, then Jason explains the deal is still at the stage of "negotiations over language.")

And there is a truly fine scene, almost surrealistic, in which the stepmother concedes the sexual sweepstakes to her stepdaughter and throws all of her clothes and makeup apparatus into a bonfire on the beach. Even her false eyelashes. "They're made out of mink hairs, did you know that?" she says. "For twenty years I've been wearing animal hairs on my face."

The movie's performances are as good as

we've come to expect from the somewhat incestuous BBS Productions. Rafelson had directed three movies for the company before this one, and Nicholson had acted in three and directed one (*Drive, He Said*, in which Dern was wonderfully uptight and focused as the basketball coach). These people have worked together often enough that they have a kind of BBS feel for scenes, if you will; Nicholson and Dern work with each other as easily as any two actors. Ellen Burstyn succeeds in a difficult task; she has to make her performance striking enough to justify the movie's ending, but she can't push *too* far or we'll know too much, too soon.

For the rest, all I can say is that *The King of Marvin Gardens* is an original, individual, and often frustrating movie that takes a lot of chances and wins on about sixty percent of them. There are scenes (including a simulated Miss America pageant in a deserted hall and a horseback confrontation between Nicholson and Dern) that are hopelessly affected. There are others, including Dern's blurted-out declaration of his love for his brother, that are deeply affecting.

King of the Gypsies ★ ★ ★
R, 112 m., 1978

Sterling Hayden (King Zharko Stepanowicz), Shelley Winters (Queen Rachel), Susan Sarandon (Rose), Judd Hirsch (Groffo), Eric Roberts (Dave), Brooke Shields (Tita), Annette O'Toole (Persa). Directed by Frank Pierson and produced by Dino and Federico De Laurentiis. Screenplay by Pierson.

It's impossible to see *King of the Gypsies* and not to be reminded of *The Godfather*. The film stories have uncanny parallels, and that's all the more interesting because Peter Maas's book *King of the Gypsies* is based on fact: Reality is chasing fiction this time.

Both stories deal with grizzled, wise, and unshakably traditional old patriarchs. Both have sons who cannot quite fill their father's shoes. Instead of the still younger son in *The Godfather*, *King of the Gypsies* gives us a grandchild—but in both films this character is powerfully lured by the attractions of middle-class American affluence, he leaves the ethnic group to take a WASP girl as his lover, and he eventually does accept the responsibility of leading his clan.

The movies even feel rather the same, with their elegiac music, their ancient rituals, their stately processions of classic autos, their obsessions with the secrets of the clan. It must have taken a certain amount of courage for Frank Pierson, the screenwriter and director, to venture into territory already inhabited by cinematic landmarks, and yet he gets away with it: *King of the Gypsies* is poetic and violent and memorable, and it gives us the first authentic movie glimpse of American gypsy culture.

The story's about a transfer of power within the Stepanowicz family, gypsies living in the New York area. The old patriarch, the gypsy king, is dying (although Sterling Hayden plays the role with so much zest it's hard to believe that). The son (Judd Hirsch) is an alcoholic, a horse player, an unfit man to become king. But the grandson (Eric Roberts) is another story: He's smart, cunning, handsome, and ambitious. Unfortunately, he's also halfway assimilated into mainstream culture. He's not at all sure he even wants to be king of the gypsies.

He is sure, though, that his father is cruel and worthless, and that his mother (Susan Sarandon) should try to free herself from him. She doesn't; life outside the gypsy society is unthinkable to her. In one of the movie's central confrontations, she faces her son after having sold her daughter into marriage for $6,000 to pay her husband's gambling debts.

In *The Godfather*, Al Pacino was lured away from the Mafia clanship by the WASP attractions of Diane Keaton. In *King of the Gypsies*, Eric Roberts falls for Annette O'Toole. As an outsider, she presents a basic threat not only to the gypsy society but also to the continuity of the Stepanowicz family.

Peter Maas's original book revealed things that gypsies would no doubt much rather have kept secret. Frank Pierson explores some of those same secrets, but his film isn't just an exposé; it has a sense of life and humor, as when Sarandon takes her son into a jewelry store and trains him as a con man by having him swallow a diamond.

The movie is above all an elegy to a passing way of life, to a society of people who've endured and prevailed as outsiders in so different Western cultures. Gypsies have lived by choice outside the law, have been blamed no doubt for countless things they did not do, have preserved a fierce pride. *King of the Gypsies* suggests that gypsy culture may finally fall, not to laws and discrimination and persecution, but to that most insidious influence of all, the seductive middle-class way of life.

King of New York ★ ★
R, 103 m., 1990

Christopher Walken (Frank White), David Caruso (Dennis Gilley), Larry Fishburne (Jimmy Jump), Victor Argo (Roy Bishop), Wesley Snipes (Thomas Flannigan), Janet Julian (Jennifer Poe). Directed by Abel Ferrara and produced by Mary Kane. Screenplay by Nicholas St. John.

Abel Ferrara's *King of New York*, a gritty action movie about a New York drug kingpin, was a surprise entry in 1990's Telluride Film Festival, where tastes are usually loftier. Maybe the selection was intended to honor Ferrara as a stylist whose movies may look commercial, but feel as if the soul of an artist is stirring somewhere inside them. That was the case with his episodes for TV's "Crime Story" and for his film *China Girl*, the 1987 thriller that trapped two lovers, a Chinese-American girl and an Italian-American boy, in the battlefield between opposing gangs in New York's Little Italy and Chinatown. The movie was *Romeo and Juliet* recycled through *West Side Story* and the TV action series of your choice, but the look was something else—a garish, neon-lit *film noir* universe of warm lips, sleek hair, and desperate eyes.

Now comes *King of New York*, Ferrara's most expensive and ambitious picture to date, with borrowings from a different classic. Instead of *Romeo and Juliet*, this one recycles *Robin Hood*, with Christopher Walken as a New York drug kingpin who wants to use his profits to pay the budget of a hospital for poor people. The Walken character never quite gets around to explaining precisely how he plans to set up his financing, and I am not sure any money actually goes to the poor and the sick, but it's a good idea, anyway.

Walken glides through the movie with his usual polished and somehow sinister ease, a man supremely confident of his ability to succeed in an arena where most people end up dead. Part of his genius is to control a large gang of black drug dealers, whose fealty to him is hard to explain, although perhaps they enjoy attending business meetings in his suite at the Plaza Hotel. Eventually the empire breaks up, however, in double-crossings and reprisals, broken loyalties and stool pigeons, although it will take a viewer more clever than myself to explain exactly what happens in the fragmented labyrinth of the movie's plot.

All of Ferrara's movies make a point of interracial friendships and romance, and

Walken has at least two black girlfriends among his other sidekicks. (I do not write "at least" because I cannot remember the exact number, but because the relationships in this movie are so sketchy that it's hard to be sure.) Is there a point to be made here? No; Ferrara gives us a white leader of a black gang of drug dealers and scarcely seems to notice it.

The movie is much stronger in its particulars than in its overall drift. There are a couple of genuinely effective scenes, including one where the Walken character is accosted by muggers on the subway, shows them his gun, frightens them, then pulls out money and throws it to them, promising there's more where that came from and that they should simply "Ask for me at the Plaza." (The lack of a scene showing the muggers inquiring after Walken at the Plaza's front desk is one of the movie's more regrettable lapses.)

I am not sure that Walken is always sure exactly why his character behaves as he does (the screenplay has a cavalier way with details), but he has a way of slinking through the plot that's convincing. Walken is one of the few undeniably charismatic male villains of recent years; he can generate a snakelike charm that makes his worst characters the most memorable, and here he operates on pure style. No gaps in the film's logic, no inconsistencies in the plot, not even a decidedly peculiar ending can discourage him. He's somehow able to convince us that he knows why everything is happening, even if most of the other characters (not to mention the filmmakers) seem bewildered.

What Ferrara needs for his next film is a sound screenplay. He has gone about as far as a director can go on pure style, and he apparently isn't one of those filmmakers who can begin with a sketchy script and patch it up as he goes along. His effects are too good, his command of mood is too sure, for him to continue trying to bluff his way through half-written movies like this one. All it did was whet my appetite.

Kinjite: Forbidden Subjects ★
R, 97 m., 1989

Charles Bronson (Lieutenant Crowe), Perry Lopez (Eddie Rios), Juan Fernandez (Duke), Amy Hathaway (Rita Crowe), Peggy Lipton (Kathleen Crowe), James Pax (Hiroshi Hada), Kumiko Hayakawa (Fumiko Hada). Directed by F. Lee Thompson and produced by Pancho Kohner. Screenplay by Harold Nebenzal.

Charles Bronson has played so many avenging fathers in so many different movies in the past fifteen years that he seems almost to have settled into the role, as William Boyd eventually became Hopalong Cassidy. The moment we see Bronson, we want to know who's been messing with his family this time and how Bronson is going to exact his revenge. In *Kinjite*, an odd, well-made, and thoroughly unpleasant thriller, Bronson's character is a detective who is not simply protective of his young daughter, but has a hang-up about the way modern permissiveness is eroding traditional values.

The movie intercuts Bronson's uneasiness in America with the story of another family, in Japan. We meet a Japanese businessman (James Pax) who seems thoroughly respectable, but is capable of sliding his hand up the thigh of a young woman who is pressed up against him on the bus. He counts on inbred Japanese reticence to prevent the woman from making an outcry: She'll be too embarrassed to make a scene.

In Los Angeles, Bronson and his partner are engaged in a war against a sleazy pimp who specializes in kidnapping young girls and supplying them to rich, perverted businessmen. We learn that Bronson's hatred of this man borders on the deranged, and we also learn (in an awkward and embarrassing scene) that he is prejudiced against Asians.

With an inevitability born out of a thousand other plots, the Japanese businessman and his family are transferred to Los Angeles, where the businessman tries the same nasty trick on the bus—this time, of course, against Bronson's daughter (Amy Hathaway), who *does* raise an outcry. Bronson goes into a lather when he hears of this unspeakable deed, and mobilizes almost the entire vice squad in a search for the perpetrator. Meanwhile, in an irony we have been anticipating for many scenes, the Japanese businessman's grade school-age daughter is kidnapped by the pimp.

Now we have everything in place: Bronson hates the pimp even more than he hates Asians—but just wait until he finds out that the victim's father is the man who put his hand on Bronson's daughter's knee. (You'll apparently have to wait until the sequel; amazingly, although the daughter eventually recognizes her "accoster," there is no payoff for this laborious setup.)

Where do these plots come from? And does everybody keep a straight face at the script conferences? The story itself is lugubrious melodrama, but the details are truly nasty—especially a sequence in which the little girl is deflowered by the pimp and his two sidekicks. The literal details of this process are kept offscreen, but what we can imagine is so sad and so inhuman that the movie never recovers from it. Child molestation may be a subject for a sincere and serious movie, but not for a slick thriller. There is a breakdown of taste here.

Yet *Kinjite: Forbidden Subjects* is actually Bronson's most polished movie in a long time; it's slimy, but slick. After the inanities and ineptitudes of the later *Death Wish* movies, in which the directors often seemed to forget to film entire scenes, including the conclusions, here is a movie directed with some energy and style by the old war-horse J. Lee Thompson (whose credits range all the way from *The Guns of Navarone* down to *Death Wish IV*). Thompson has worked at least five previous times with Bronson, and so has producer Pancho Kohner, the son of Bronson's late agent. It's ironic that their best-made film is also their most distasteful.

A Kiss Before Dying ★ ★ ★
R, 93 m., 1991

Matt Dillon (Jonathan Corliss), Sean Young (Ellen/Dorothy Carlsson), Max von Sydow (Thor Carlsson), Diane Ladd (Mrs. Corliss), James Russo (Dan Corelli). Directed by James Dearden and produced by Robert Lawrence. Screenplay by Dearden.

Ambitious young men are almost always dangerous in the movies. They hunger, and brood, and dream, and they will allow nothing to stand in their way. They're a familiar type, almost always achieved by overacting: Asked to project resentment, hurt, and ambition, all at once, your average actor goes over the top. It is one of the strengths of James Dearden's *A Kiss Before Dying* that Matt Dillon is able to make his character self-contained, impassive, and so all the more dangerous.

Dillon plays Jonathan, a poor kid from the wrong side of the tracks, who as a child used to sit in his bedroom and gaze morosely at the endless freight trains rumbling past, all of them emblazoned with the logo of Carlsson Copper. One day, he apparently said to himself, those trains will be mine. We meet him next at the University of Pennsylvania, where he is dating Dorothy (Sean Young), one of two twin daughters of crusty old Thor Carlsson (Max von Sydow), a proud millionaire. And then the film springs a surprise on us, which I will not reveal—and even so, do not read any further unless you want to know that Dorothy is found dead, an apparent suicide.

Dorothy's twin is Ellen, also played by Sean Young, and soon she and Jonathan are in love. They both work in the same homeless rescue agency, picking up street kids and giving them counseling and a place to spend the night. But Jonathan doesn't see social work as a permanent career, and he ingratiates himself with the uncompromising old man, goes fishing with him, agrees with everything he says, and is eventually given a job in the family firm.

Ellen is in love, but she is obsessed with the notion that her twin did not commit suicide. There are all sorts of clues if you know where to look: For example, Dorothy was wearing new shoes, purchased just before she died. Is that the action of a suicidal person? And then there are the mysterious deaths of Dorothy's former friends and co-students. Did they know something? Are their deaths a coincidence?

Veteran filmgoers, familiar with the Rule of Economy of Characters, will have guessed that Jonathan, the Dillon character, is not in the film simply to stand by while Ellen finds the real killer. *A Kiss Before Dying* generates most of its suspense, in fact, by allowing us to know things about Jonathan that Ellen doesn't know. Dearden, the director, wrote *Fatal Attraction* and got substantial mileage out of the same idea—that a character is in mortal danger from a lover. In *Fatal Attraction* there was an additional twist, in that the audience was not quite so sure of the facts, but the strength of *A Kiss Before Dying* is that the Matt Dillon character is so private, so controlled by inner needs no one else in the film is allowed to see, that he is almost two persons, all by himself.

This is Matt Dillon's first film since *Drugstore Cowboy*, and demonstrates again that he is one of the best actors working in movies. He possesses the secret of not giving too much, of not trying so hard that we're distracted by his performance. Dillon was never trained as an actor, was a junior high school kid when he was cast in an unsung but powerful movie named *Over the Edge*, and has turned out to have a natural affinity with the camera. There was a brief period when his career was endangered by quasi-Teen Idol status, but he just kept working, choosing interesting roles and good directors, and today he and the slightly older Sean Penn are the best actors in their age group.

About Sean Young I am not quite so sure. In her best work like *The Boost* (1988), she is convincing—angry, obsessed, fearful. But here her character seems to know too much of the story; she has a detachment that's not appropriate, a way of seeming to know, as we do, what the real outcome is going to be. It undermines the concern we feel for her.

And yet *A Kiss Before Dying* works, in most of its scenes, because it is fueled by the need of the Dillon character. Dearden helps it work because he doesn't press his point. The film opens and closes with close-ups of Dillon as a small boy, looking at those trains going by, and Dillon is too good an actor to feel any need to improve on the emotions we associate with those wide little eyes.

Kiss of the Spider Woman ★ ★ ★ ¹/₂
R, 119 m., 1985

William Hurt (Luis Molina), Raul Julia (Valentin), Sonia Braga (Leni/Marta/Spider Woman), Jose Lewgoy (Warden). Directed by Hector Babenco and produced by David Weidman. Screenplay by Leonard Schrader.

Kiss of the Spider Woman tells one of those rare and entrancing stories where one thing seems to happen while another thing is really happening. There are passages in the movie that seem to be absolutely self-contained, and then a word or gesture will reveal that they have depths we can only guess. By the end of the film, what started out as a contest between two opposite personalities has expanded into a choice between two completely different attitudes toward life. And the choice is not sexual, although for a long time it seems so. It is between freedom and slavery.

The movie opens in a prison cell, somewhere in South America. A man is telling a story. The story is a lurid intrigue that seems pieced together from fragments and memories of countless old *film noir* melodramas— from those movies of the 1940s where the woman had lips that could kill, and the men were dying to kiss them. Only gradually does the reality of the film reveal itself: We are in a cramped, depressing prison cell, and the storyteller is a prisoner, trying to pass the days by escaping into fantasy.

His name is Luis. He is played by William Hurt as an affected homosexual, a window dresser who has been jailed for sex offenses. His cellmate is Valentin (Raul Julia), a bearded, macho political prisoner who has nothing but contempt for Luis's stories—not to mention his sexuality and his politics. But as Luis calmly explains, unless someone gives him a key to walk out of his prison, he will continue to escape in any way he can.

As he continues to weave his verbal movie plots, the movie uses fantasy scenes to depict them. There is a Nazi crime melodrama, and a thriller about a spider woman, and the woman in both of them is played by the same actress (Sonia Braga). Later in the film, she will also appear as Valentin's lover; reality and fantasy are by then thoroughly mixed.

What *Kiss of the Spider Woman* at first seems to be about is the changing nature of the relationship between two very different men who have been locked together in the same cell. They are opposites in every way. But they share the same experiences, day after day, and that gives them a common bond. Gradually, an affection grows between them, and we assume that the movie will be about the ways in which they learn to accept each other. Only gradually, mysteriously, do we realize that the movie is about a good deal more. Details of the plot are revealed so subtly and so surprisingly that I will say nothing more, except that the film does not lead in the directions we anticipate.

The performances are wonderful. The director, Hector Babenco, is a Brazilian, but he has directed his American stars in English without falling prey to the occasional loss of tone you sometimes hear as foreigners work in unfamiliar languages. William Hurt, who won the Academy Award and best actor award at Cannes for this film, creates a character utterly unlike anyone else he has ever played—a frankly theatrical character, exaggerated and mannered—and yet he never seems to be reaching for effects. Raul Julia, sweaty and physical in the early scenes, gradually reveals a poetry that makes the whole movie work. And Sonia Braga, called upon to satirize bad acting, makes a perfect spider woman.

Every decade seems to be dominated by the cinema of a different country (in addition to Hollywood, of course, a country of its own). In the 1950s it was Italy. In the 1960s, France. In the 1970s, Germany. In the 1980s, Brazil and Australia seem to be the centers of the most exciting work. Babenco's previous credits include the heartbreaking *Pixote* about a child growing up on the streets of San Paolo. *Kiss of the Spider Woman* is another film of insights and surprises.

Klute ★ ★ ★ ¹/₂
R, 114 m., 1971

Jane Fonda (Bree Daniel), Donald Sutherland (John Klute), Charles Cioffi (Frank Ligouri), Dorothy Tristan (Arlyn Page). Directed and produced by Alan J. Pakula. Screenplay by Andy K. and Dave Lewis.

What is it about Jane Fonda that makes her such a fascinating actress to watch? She has a sort of nervous intensity that keeps her so firmly locked into a film character that the character actually seems distracted by things that come up in the movie. You almost have the feeling, a couple of times in *Klute*, that the Fonda character had other plans and was just leaving the room when this (whatever it is) came up.

The movie is about a skilled, intelligent, cynical, and personally troubled New York call girl who does not, for once, have a heart of gold. She never feels anything when she's with a man, she tells her shrink, but she does experience a sense of professional pride when she's able to satisfy a client. And some of her clients have very complicated needs, which challenge the girl's imaginative acting ability. One old garment industry tycoon, for example, has spent all his life making clothes. But he fantasizes an idealistic sort of pre-World War I existence in Europe, in Vienna maybe, and the girl describes it to him in quiet, warm images while she disrobes. He never touches her.

The girl's name is Bree, and the movie should probably be titled *Bree* instead of *Klute*, because the Fonda character is at the center. John Klute (played by Donald Sutherland) is a policeman who has come to New York, free-lance, to try to settle a missing persons case. It appears that the missing man may still be alive, and may be the source of obscene letters and telephone calls Bree has been receiving. Bree initially refuses to talk to Klute, but she eventually does confide in him, mostly because she's frightened by midnight prowlers and wants his protection. The film examines their somewhat strange relationship, and at the same time functions on another level as a somewhat awkward thriller.

There are scary shots of the prowler, for example, and shots of hands gripping a mesh fence—shots that are not very satisfactory because the wrong point of view is established. One thing about a thriller is that the threat should always be seen from the point of view of the threatened. We don't like looking over the killer's shoulder at his victim; shots like that interfere with our desire to identify with the victim and be scared in a satisfactory way.

Klute doesn't scare us very satisfactorily, maybe because it's kind of schizo. The director is Alan Pakula, whose concern is all too much with plot, and it gets in the way of the unusual and interesting relationship between Bree and Klute. But how *do* you develop a relationship between a prostitute with hang-ups and a square suburban cop? *Klute* does it by making the cop into a person of restraint and dignity, a man who is genuinely concerned about this girl he's met. His attitude is what makes their love relationship so absorbing. Usually, in the movies, it's just assumed the lovers were drawn toward each other by magnetism or concealed springs or something.

The scenes between Fonda and Sutherland are very good, then, and Bree is further developed in scenes showing her trying to get out of the trade and into something straight. She takes acting lessons, she auditions to model for cosmetics ads. She talks to her shrink (in scenes that sound improvised and exhibit Fonda's undeniable intelligence).

Intelligence. I suppose that's the word. In *Klute* you don't have two attractive acting vacuums reciting speeches at each other. With Fonda and Sutherland, you have actors who understand and sympathize with their characters, and you have a vehicle worthy of that sort of intelligence. So the fact that the thriller stuff doesn't always work isn't so important.

Koyaanisqatsi ★ ★ ★
NO MPAA RATING, 87 m., 1983

Produced and directed by Godfrey Reggio.

ko·yaa·nis·qatsi, n. (Hopi). 1. crazy life. 2. life in turmoil. 3. life disintegrating. 4. life out of balance. 5. a state of life that calls for another way of living.

I give the definition because it is the key to the movie. Without it, you could make a sincere mistake. *Koyaanisqatsi* opens with magnificent images out of nature: great canyons and limitless deserts and a world without man. Through the use of speeded-up images, clouds climb the sides of mountains and speed across the sky, their shadows painting the landscape. Then the movie turns to images of smokestacks, factories, and expressways. There is an assumption on the part of the filmmaker, Godfrey Reggio, that we'll immediately get the message. And the message, I think, is that nature is wonderful, but that American civilization is a rotten despoiler that is creating a "crazy life."

But I am irreverent, and given to my own thoughts during the film. After I have admired its visionary photography (this is a beautiful movie) and fallen under the spell of its music (an original sound track by the distinguished composer Philip Glass), there is still time to think other thoughts, such as:

This film has one idea, a simplistic one. It contrasts the glory of nature with the mess made by man. But man *is* a messy beast, given to leaving reminders of his presence all over the surface of planet Earth. Although a Hopi word is used to evoke unspoiled nature, no Hopis are seen, and the contrast in the movie doesn't seem to be between American Indian society and Los Angeles expressways, but between expressways and a beautiful world *empty* of man. Thanks, but no thanks.

I had another problem. *All* of the images in this movie are beautiful, even the images of man despoiling the environment. The first shots of smokestacks are no doubt supposed to make us recoil in horror, but actually I thought they looked rather noble. The shots of the expressways are also two-edged. Given the clue in the title, we can consider them as an example of life out of control. *Or*—and here's the catch—we can marvel at the fast-action photography and reflect about all those people moving so quickly to their thousands of individual destinations. What a piece of work is a man! And what expressways he builds!

Koyaanisqatsi, then, is an invitation to knee-jerk environmentalism of the most sentimental kind. It is all images and music. There is no overt message except the obvious one (the Grand Canyon is prettier than Manhattan). It has been hailed as a vast and sorrowful vision, but to what end? If the people in all those cars on all those expressways are indeed living crazy lives, their problem is not the expressway (which is all that makes life in L.A. manageable) but perhaps social facts such as unemployment, crime, racism, drug abuse, and illiteracy—issues so complicated that a return to nature seems like an elitist joke at their expense. Having said that, let me add that *Koyaanisqatsi* is an impressive visual and listening experience, that Reggio and Glass have made wonderful pictures and sounds, and that this film is a curious throwback to the 1960s, when it would have been a short subject to be viewed through a marijuana haze. Far-out.

The Krays ★ ★ ★ ½
R, 119 m., 1990

Billie Whitelaw (Violet Kray), Gary Kemp (Ronald Kray), Martin Kemp (Reginald Kray), Susan Fleetwood (Rose), Charlotte Cornwell (May), Jimmy Jewel (Cannonball Lee). Directed by Peter Medak and produced by Dominic Anciano and Ray Burdis. Screenplay by Philip Ridley.

You meet kids like this in grade school sometimes. Kids who seem naturally mean-spirited and sadistic, who take pleasure in causing pain. When they twist your arm behind your back; they really are trying to break it. The strange thing about the schoolyard bully is that, nine times out of ten, he can put on an angelic face whenever he wants to. Comb his hair and put him in a tie, age him thirty years, and he'll look like a model citizen. Maybe he'll beat his wife or rough up his kids—maybe life is hell for his family—but he places great importance on seeming respectable.

The Krays is a movie about a couple of men like that. They were well-dressed, well-behaved, sleek, carefully groomed mother's boys who grew up to become the most sadistic criminals in the modern history of London. They ruled the East End, the Cockney neighborhoods stretching along the Thames beyond the Tower of London. But their fame spread far beyond the modest streets where they were born and lived, and by the end of their reign, they were regulars on the nightclub and show biz circuits. There is something about gangsters that interests a lot of people. It's probably related to the fascination of playing with fire.

Before the Kray twins, British crime was simply not down to the American standard. Neither the cops nor the robbers carried guns, and most crimes were done with cunning and stealth rather than by brute force. Criminals looked down on those who lacked the intelligence to figure out a nonviolent way to steal. But there were signs that urban violence was creeping across the Atlantic. In his famous essay "The Decline of the English Murder," George Orwell complained that the devious spouse-poisoners and acid-bath murderers of his youth had given way to a new generation of killers totally lacking in imagination, people who simply shot those they disliked, instead of plotting for years to squirrel their remains in a geranium bed.

Billie Whitelaw, who plays the twins' mother in *The Krays*, thinks maybe they learned some of their lessons through the study of Hollywood gangster movies. Certainly they were born with the pathology and innate sadism to be good students. The movie shows them observing the existing protection rackets in the East End and then muscling in and taking over by the simple expedient of being unimaginably more vicious than any of their competitors.

The violence in the movie is effective because it is matter-of-fact, business as usual. It's not the entertaining, even exhilarating fantasy-violence of a big-budget action picture, but the mean, low-key violence of a man who wants to hurt you so you'll pay him money. The most chilling scene in the movie is one where a former associate of the Krays has his mouth disfigured with a sharp knife, so quickly he hardly realizes he's being attacked.

The movie's visuals place the Krays in the dingy, drab world of the East End, of narrow streets crowded with tenements, of workingmen's cafés, of cinemas and bingo halls, pubs, and shabby nightclubs. But there is one haven of cheer and respectability—their home, which is ruled over by Violet, their loving mother, and also contains the less consequential figures of their father and Charlie, their brother. Violet will hear no evil of her boys, and it's something to see her straighten the ties and pat the cheeks of her glistening little killers.

The twins are played by brothers, Gary and Martin Kemp, as a sort of psychic double act. They share a secret wavelength, one on which Ronnie, who is truly pathological, uses subtle force to bring Reggie along with him. Whitelaw, who knew the Krays, believes that Reggie, without Ronnie, would have developed into an ordinary low-level criminal. It was Ronnie, with his deeper sickness, who turned the two of them into a fearsome unit.

The role of the mother is central to the film. She dotes, confides, encourages, loves, forgives. The twins continue to live at home at an age long after what seems appropriate,

and when Ronnie brings home a male lover, little notice is taken. Reggie moves out when he marries, but never seems far from home, and the gang's council meetings are held upstairs over the parlor.

The Krays was directed by Peter Medak, whose best previous film was *The Ruling Class* (1971), with Peter O'Toole as a British lord whose eccentricity shaded over into madness. This movie shares the sense of unspeakable secrets just beneath the surface. It's a gangster film by definition, but really it's a study of human pathology. Most people we meet in the course of a lifetime are basically good folks who want to live and let live. A few have something missing inside, maybe the ability to have any empathy for the feelings of others. To get what they want, they cause pain. Usually such people were mistreated as children, and are bullies to compensate for shame and low self-esteem. The strange thing about the Krays is that they were doted on as children, and their self-esteem seems robust and unquestioning. And they have such a nice mother.

Kung Fu Master ★ ★ ★
R, 80 m., 1989

Jane Birkin (Mary Jane), Mathieu Demy (Julien), Charlotte Gainsbourg (Lucy), Lou Doillon (Lou), Eva Simonet (The friend), Judy Campbell (The mother), David and Andrew Birkin (The father and brother). Directed and produced by Agnes Varda. Screenplay by Varda and Jane Birkin.

Agnes Varda's *Kung Fu Master* is a French film that tells the story of a love affair between a forty-year-old woman and a fourteen-year-old boy. The subject is disturbing, and yet Varda treats it with a rare sympathy and empathy, perhaps inspired by the fact that the boy in the film is played by her own son, Mathieu Demy. The movie was cowritten by Jane Birkin, an English actress who has lived in Paris for years and who plays the older woman—a woman who falls in love with the innocence and honesty of this young man.

Of course their relationship is doomed, and in a way, of course, they know that. It is wisely never made clear in the film exactly how far the relationship goes in a physical sense, but on the emotional side we can see that the boy is at first bold and audacious in his approach to the older woman, but then begins to tune out as his attention wanders.

A film like this cannot be described in

terms of its plot. Everything depends on the look in an eye, the tone of voice. Varda's true subject seems to be the way in which "pure" love, classical romanticism, can exist as an idea in a vacuum, but can survive in the real world only for a moment before practical considerations mercilessly wipe it out. There is a degree of deliberate daring in her choice of this subject matter. Like Louis Malle's *Murmur of the Heart* (1971), which dealt with incest, *Kung Fu Master* is on one level an experiment—to see if this shocking subject matter can be made palatable.

It can be, or at least it is here (one doubts if things would work out so smoothly in the real world). The film opens with a chance meeting between the woman and the boy at a birthday party for the woman's teen-age daughter. They meet on the stairs and talk. Nothing comes of it. They meet again and talk again, and then the boy makes a bold approach to her. She is shocked and amused—and intrigued. Gradually, surprising herself, she permits the relationship to continue.

Julien, the boy, is a loner who feels left out of his adolescent society. He spends a great deal of time riveted to Kung Fu Master, a video arcade game in a neighborhood café, where he has developed considerable skill at manipulating an animated karate master who must save a damsel in distress. His approach to Mary Jane, the woman, has the same directness. Although she is not ostensibly in distress, she is lonely and isolated, and for a time they fill each other's needs.

Mary Jane's daughter, of course, is offended and shocked by the entire episode. She can barely believe a woman of her mother's age has romantic feelings at all, let alone for a boy. One of the hardest scenes to believe is the one where the woman takes the boy to meet her family. It works only as wish-fulfillment. In the real world, the family and society in general would disapprove of this liaison—but the lovers try to hide from society. Picking up the boy at school, the woman plays the role of a responsible adult. And at one point they go off for a holiday on an island where the world is far away.

What redeems this movie and allows it to work is that it is about feelings, not actions. Varda draws an invisible line at physical frankness in the film, so there is never a moment when we feel embarrassment for the characters (or the actors). The film is really about the phenomenon of the romantic crush—about how another person can suddenly seem to embody an ideal for us, especially if that person is distant enough or different enough that we do not have to deal with his or her real-life situation.

The crush also involves projection, as we see ourselves in the other person. And here perhaps the woman sees her own innocent idealism in the boy, and the boy identifies with her somewhat dreamy isolation. Apart from the difference in their ages, they really are well-suited to one another, at least as long as they can dream and are not distracted by pragmatic reality.

Agnes Varda is one of the most individual and intriguing of contemporary French directors, in part because each of her films seems to satisfy a different need. Her previous film, the masterful *Vagabond*, was so different in tone from *Kung Fu Master* that it's hard to believe it comes from the same director. It told the story of an unhappy young woman who left her boring job for a carefree life on the road, and gradually sank, one small step at a time, down the scale of social acceptability until she became a vagrant. That film suggested that we may all be closer to the gutter than we think, if we lose our discipline and our support systems. This one suggests we may all be closer to our ideal but impossible love if we lose our fears.

L

L.A. Story ★ ★ ★ ★
PG-13, 95 m., 1991
(See related Film Clip, p. 715.)

Steve Martin (Harris), Victoria Tennant (Sara), Richard E. Grant (Roland), Marilu Henner (Trudi), Sarah Jessica Parker (SanDeE). Directed by Mick Jackson and produced by Daniel Melnick and Michael Rachmil. Screenplay by Steve Martin.

There are some big laughs in Steve Martin's *L.A. Story*, but also a certain delicacy of tone that is bewitching. Somehow the film evokes an elusive side of Los Angeles that isn't often seen in the movies. We know all about the weirdo Southern California lifestyle, the obsessions with food and physical appearance and lifestyle, and we know all the standard show biz types. We've seen movies about those subjects many times before (and, for that matter, Martin doesn't neglect them).

But there is also a bewitching Los Angeles, a city I glimpsed on my first visit there many years ago, where, after my team won in the Rose Bowl, I was driven up to Mulholland Drive and the whole city lay glittering beneath, and for a kid from downstate Illinois, there was something enchanting going on down there—there was the promise of not merely success and the fulfillment of lust, but even of happiness and the fulfillment of dreams.

None of that has much to do with the reality of the city, I am aware, and sometimes the dreams seem buried by car washes and minimalls, smog and traffic, and urban wretchedness. But *L.A. Story* is a lighthearted fantasy that asks us to just accept one small possibility, and promises us we may find contentment if we keep an open mind. That possibility is that a giant electrical traffic warning billboard might one day start sending personal messages to a TV weatherman, suggesting how he can make improvements in his life.

The weatherman is named Harris K. Telemacher (Martin), and he specializes in goofy weather reports that have little connection with actual climatic conditions. He makes enough money at his job to move in an affluent circle of beautiful people who seem prepared to sit in the sunshine ordering cappucino for the rest of their lives. Then Telemacher is fired, and discovers that his mistress (Marilu Henner) is having an affair, and with relief and a certain feeling of freedom he walks out of the relationship and takes stock of his life, inspired by the sentient highway sign. (He is not without his own difficulties in believing that the sign is on the level; the first time it talks to him, he looks around in paranoid despair, convinced he's on "Candid Camera.")

The sign urges him to telephone a number that's been given to him by a friendly Valley Girl in a clothing store, and before long he finds himself in an energetic relationship with SanDeE (Sarah Jessica Parker), who, like many Southern Californians, spells her name as if it were an explosion at the type foundry. SanDeE has a carefree and liberating air, but eventually Telemacher has to admit that the woman he's really attracted to is Sara (Victoria Tennant), a British journalist in town to do a story on L.A. lifestyles.

These stories of love provide the fragile narrative thread on which Martin (who wrote) and Mick Jackson (who directed) weave their spell. There are scenes that, in other hands, might have seemed obvious (for example, the daily routine of shooting at other drivers while racing down the freeway), but somehow there is a fanciful edge in the way they do it, a way they define all of their material with a certain whimsical tone.

The film is astonishing in the amount of material it contains. Martin has said he worked on the screenplay, on and off, for seven years, and you can sense that as the film unfolds. It isn't thin or superficial; there is an abundance of observation and invention here, and perhaps because the filmmakers know they have so much good material, there's never the feeling that anything is being punched up, or made to carry more than its share. I was reminded of the films of Jacques Tati, in which, calmly, serenely, an endless series of comic invention unfolds.

Steve Martin shows again in this film that he has found the right comic presence for the movies; the lack of subtlety in early films like *The Jerk* has now been replaced by a smoothness and unforced intelligence. The other cast members are basically in support of that character, although Sarah Jessica Parker has figured out a Valley Girl airhead right down to the ground. What you feel here, as you feel in the work of Tati and some of the comedians of the silent era, is that the whole film is the work of comedy—that it isn't about jokes, or a funny individual, but about creating a fictional world which is funny on its own terms.

La Bamba ★ ★ ★
PG-13, 108 m., 1987

Lou Diamond Phillips (Ritchie Valens), Esai Morales (Bob Morales), Rosana De Soto (Connie Valenzuela), Elizabeth Pena (Rosie Morales), Danielle von Zerneck (Donna Ludwig), Joe Pantoliano (Bob Keene). Directed by Luis Valdez and produced by Taylor Hackford and Bill Borden. Screenplay by Valdez.

La Bamba opens with a sequence that at first seems like a memory. Some teen-age boys are playing basketball in a school yard. Far overhead, a light plane drones through the sky.

The colors of this scene are all washed out, as in an old memory, and the voices sound far away. There is slow motion. Another airplane appears. The basketball game continues. We are lulled by the feeling of a slow summer afternoon. Then the two planes collide and fall into the school yard below.

Because *La Bamba* is the story of Ritchie Valens, we assume this is his memory. But he was not present when the planes fell, and the scene represents how he might have imagined it. One of his friends was killed that day. He always assumed that if he had been in the school yard, he would have been killed, too. That was why he never liked to take airplanes.

The scene itself is very effective. But I wonder if it is the right way to open *La Bamba*. Everyone who goes to the movie will know that Valens died in an airplane crash with Buddy Holly and the Big Bopper on February 3, 1959, the day the music died. The opening scene is followed by several other references to Valens's fear of flying, and the effect is to put the whole movie under a cloud, to weigh down every scene with the knowledge of impending death.

That robs *La Bamba* of a quality I think it could use: the sense of fun. This is a sincere, well-acted movie about the short life of a minor rock & roll star, and by the time it's over we almost have the feeling Valens would have been surprised not to have died in a crash.

He is played by Lou Diamond Phillips as a serious, introspective, intensely focused young man who wanted to play his music more than anything else in life. His dedication amounts almost to an obsession. He never seems to really let go.

Valens had only three hit songs. His public career lasted less than six months. He died before he was eighteen. There isn't a wealth of material to draw from as there was for *The Buddy Holly Story*. So Luis Valdez, the director, fleshes out the story with information about Valens's family, especially his hardworking, cheerful mother (Rosana De Soto) and his half brother (Esai Morales), who both supports him and resents him.

Valens's real surname was Valenzuela. He was a Mexican-American, raised for a time in migrant labor camps, and he idolized the older brother who would appear from time to time on a glamorous motorcycle. But he admired music more and began to sing wherever he could find work in Los Angeles in the late 1950s. After the family moved into the

city, and Valens got a girlfriend—a blond Anglo named Donna, whose parents didn't approve of Valens, inspiring "Donna," one of his hits. He had some of the usual adventures of growing up, and the movie makes much of a trip he and his brother took to Tijuana, where Valens was less interested in the girls than in the band (in the movie it is, of course, playing "La Bamba").

Once Valens is discovered by a minor record producer (Joe Pantoliano), his career goes surprisingly well. He records a song, it is a hit, he is invited by Alan Freed to appear in one of his pioneering rock & roll stage shows in Brooklyn and two other hits follow fairly quickly. Valens makes one crucial artistic decision: Although he doesn't speak Spanish, he insists on recording "La Bamba" in Spanish, using the irrefutable logic that if Nat King Cole could record in Spanish, he could, too.

Valens's last tour is handled in an almost perfunctory manner. We know how the movie will end, anyway. The Big Bopper circulates backstage, saying "Hello, baby!" to everyone he meets. Buddy Holly sings "Crying, Waiting, Hoping." They go out to the airport in a snowstorm, Holly flips a coin, and Valens calls heads and wins his place on the fated plane. Still to come, no doubt, is a movie about the Big Bopper. And why not one called *Rock & Roll Pilot* ("He Was at the Controls the Day the Music Died!")?

This is a good small movie, sweet and sentimental, about a kid who never really got a chance to show his stuff. The best things in it are the most unexpected things: the portraits of everyday life, of a loving mother, of a brother who loves and resents him, of a kid growing up and tasting fame and leaving everyone standing around at his funeral shocked that his life ended just as it seemed to be beginning.

La Cage aux Folles ★ ★ ★ ★
R, 91 m., 1979

Ugo Tognazzi (Renato), Michel Serrault (Zaza), Michel Galabru (Charrier), Claire Maurier (Simone), Remy Laurent (Laurent), Benny Luke (Jacob). Directed by Edouard Molinaro and produced by Marcello Danon. Screenplay by Francis Veber and Molinaro.

La Cage aux Folles are "birds of a feather," which are precisely and hilariously what do not flock together in this wonderful comedy from France. It's about the gay owner of a

scandalous nightclub in St. Tropez, his transvestite lover, and how the owner reacts after his son returns home one day and announces he's going to marry . . . a girl!

But that's not *really* what it's about: This is basically the first sitcom in drag, and the comic turns in the plot are achieved with such clockwork timing that sometimes we're laughing at what's funny and sometimes we're laughing at the movie's sheer comic invention. This is a great time at the movies.

The nightclub owner is played by Ugo Tognazzi, that grizzled Italian veteran of so many macho roles, and he has lived for twenty years with a drag queen (Michel Serrault) who stars in the club. They're like an old married couple, nostalgic and warm one minute, fighting like cats and dogs the next. Tognazzi sired the son all those years ago and has raised him with the help of "Auntie" Serrault and their live-in "maid," a wickedly funny black transvestite who has perhaps the movie's funniest moment.

Tognazzi and Serrault have trouble at first accepting the notion that their treasured young man is going to get married. They have more trouble, however, accepting the notion that the intended bride is the daughter of the Minister of Moral Standards—and that the in-laws are planning to come to dinner.

This dilemma inspires the film's hilarious middle section, in which Tognazzi's garishly bizarre apartment is severely redecorated in crucifixes and antiques, and Serrault is gently asked by the son if he'd mind being gone for the evening: "I told them my father was a Cultural Attaché; what'll they think when they find out he lives with a drag queen?"

Tognazzi, meanwhile, goes to visit the woman who bore his son two decades ago, to ask her to portray the mother for one night. She agrees. Too bad, because in the course of the uproariously funny dinner party, at least two reputed mothers are produced, one of them suspiciously hairy around the chest.

Describing a comedy is always a risky business; the bare plot outline is, of course, no hint as to how funny a film is, and to steal the jokes is a misdemeanor. What I can say, though, is that *La Cage aux Folles* gets the audience on its side with immediate ease; it never betrays our confidence; it astonishes us with the inspiration and logic it brings to ringing changes on the basic situation.

And it contains several classic sequences. The best is perhaps the one in which Tognazzi coaches Serrault on how to act "macho," an attribute that apparently consists of knowing how to butter your toast with manly firmness. There's also that extended dinner scene that begins with the Minister of Moral Standards discovering that . . . Greek boys . . . are doing . . . *something* . . . on his soup plate . . . and builds from there.

La Femme Nikita ★ ★ ★
R, 117 m., 1991

Anne Parillaud (Nikita), Jean-Hugues Anglade (Marc), Tcheky Karyo (Bob), Jeanne Moreau (Amande), Jean Reno (Nikita's Friend). Directed and produced by Luc Besson. Screenplay by Besson.

Here is a version of the Pygmalion legend for our own violent times—the story of a young woman who is transformed from a killer in the streets to a government assassin. *La Femme Nikita* is a smart, hard-edged psychoromantic thriller by the young French director Luc Besson (*Subway*), who follows a condemned woman as she exchanges one doom for another.

The woman is played by Anne Parillaud, who projects a feral hostility in the opening scenes, as she joins a crowd of drug-addled friends in holding up a drugstore. Cornered by the police, she takes advantage of a cop's momentary lapse of attention to grab his gun and shoot him point-blank in the face. She has no hope of escape; she is simply so antisocial and strung out that she doesn't care if she kills or dies.

The courts, of course, sentence her to death, but then a strange thing happens. Her death is faked, and she finds herself inside a secret government program that takes people with no hope and remakes them into programmed hit-men. She is given a new identity, new values, new skills. It doesn't happen overnight. Her controller, a tough spymaster, has to tame her like a circus animal; she is so filled with anger and violence that she will bite and kick him rather than listen gratefully now that he has spared her life. Finally, after three years, she is ready to graduate, to leave the secret training place and live an ordinary life in society until the government needs her.

It is then that she meets a simple, warm, humorous man—a check-out clerk in a grocery store. She likes him at first sight, takes him home, makes him her boyfriend, and begins to feel tenderness and trust, which for her are brand-new emotions. Then the inevitable government call comes. And the rest of the movie is about the ways in which she carries out her deadly assignment while still yearning to be true to the new emotion of love.

Parillaud is the right actress for this role. In the early scenes she barely seems aware she is a woman; she has lived rough in the streets with homeless drug addicts until all gentleness has been bleached from her soul. One of the movie's skills is the way it shows her slowly learning that she is a woman, and how to be a woman, and how to enjoy that. There is a short, touching scene with Jeanne Moreau, as an instructor in the government killing school, who seats Parillaud in front of a mirror and teaches her about makeup and grooming, hair care and eyeliner, and we see the grubby street waif turn into an attractive woman.

La Femme Nikita begins with the materials of a violent thriller, but transcends them with the story of the heroine's transformation. It is a surprisingly touching movie with the same kind of emotional arc as *Awakenings*; the character is in a trance of deprivation and poverty, neglect and drugs, until she is awakened by her violent act and its unexpected result. But, as she awakens to love and sweetness, to the touch of a man who knows nothing about her past, to questions of trust, she also awakens to a world in which, sooner or later, she will have to pay a price for her life and freedom.

La Lectrice ★ ★ ★ ★
R, 98 m., 1989

Miou-Miou (Constance/Marie), Christian Ruche (Jean/Philippe), Sylvie Laporte (Francoise), Michel Raskine (Agency Man), Brigitte Catillon (Eric's Mother/Jocelyn), Regis Royer (Eric), Simon Eine (Hospital Professor), Christian Blanc (Old Teacher). Directed by Michel Deville and produced by Rosalinde Deville. Screenplay by Rosalinde and Michel Deville.

Constance is in bed with her boyfriend when he asks her to read aloud to him. As she reads, she begins to imagine herself as the heroine of the story. The story Constance reads is about Marie, a young woman who needs employment and takes an ad in the paper, offering to read aloud to people. Marie finds that a surprising number of clients want to take advantage of her services— and, as she reads for them, she begins to enter into their lives.

This is the elegant, Chinese-box structure of Michel Deville's *La Lectrice*, and one of the pleasures of the film is the way Deville moves up and down through the various levels of the story, and then sideways through the sometimes devious motives of the clients who hire the reader. Only someone who loves to read would understand how one person can become another, can enter into the life of a person in a book. That is what happens in this movie.

Marie is played by Miou-Miou as a solemn woman who comes to care about her clients. There are several, each one with a different problem (and probably with a different "real" reason why he wants to be read aloud to). There is a young boy who has been gravely injured in an accident and fears for his potency. He wants Marie to read him passionate poetry—and he falls in love with her, identifying her with the poems. An old woman, once filled with fire and conviction, hires Marie to read to her, for one last time, the writers like Tolstoy and Marx who once inspired her. A busy mother hires Marie to read *Alice in Wonderland* to her small daughter. And a rich investor probably wants her to read him pornography, but is reluctant to say so, and so gets respectable erotica instead.

Each client's book reflects the nature of his or her fantasy, and Marie understands that immediately. As she reads to them, a curious process begins to take place. She becomes, in a way, the author of the books. The teen-ager idealizes her as a romantic. The old lady thinks she is an intellectual. The little girl sees her as a mother figure. And the businessman, of course, wants to sleep with her. What is intriguing is that Marie herself starts to identify with the books, and so is almost able to see herself as lover, confidante, mother, and prostitute.

La Lectrice is a movie in love with words— deliriously intoxicated by the stories and images in the pages that Marie reads. But making a movie about reading is like writing a symphony about looking at paintings: How do you make the leap from one medium to another? In Francois Truffaut's *Fahrenheit 451*, another film about the love of books, the final scene showed human beings who had "become" books in order to preserve their contents in an age of book-burning. One was *David Copperfield*, another was *Pride and Prejudice*, walking back and forth in the snow, reciting the words to themselves. In *La Lectrice*, the words become real in a different way—by having an actual effect. Because the love poems make the teen-ager amorous, because the eroticism arouses the businessman, the books become like magical talismans.

I hope I have not made *La Lectrice* sound too difficult or dryly intellectual. This is a sensuous film from beginning to end, a film that is all the more seductive because it teases the imagination. As the reader becomes the books she reads, we become the people she reads to. And so, in our imaginations, we see her in all her roles. In some scenes she is sweet, in others thoughtful, in others carnal. The film is a demonstration that we can rarely understand the secret minds of people, so therefore upon their exteriors we project our own fantasies. When the movie was over, I wanted to go out and find the novel by Raymond Jean that the screenplay is based on. I didn't want to read it. I wanted someone to read it to me.

Lady in White ★ ★ ★
PG-13, 112 m., 1988

Lukas Haas (Frankie), Len Cariou (Phil), Alex Rocco (Angelo), Katherine Helmond (Amanda), Jason Presson (Geno), Renata Vanni (Mama Assunta), Angelo Bertolini (Papa Charlie), Joelle Jacobi (Melissa), Jared Rushton (Donald), Gregory Levinson (Louie). Directed by Frank LaLoggia and produced by Andrew G. La Marca and LaLoggia. Screenplay by LaLoggia.

Lady in White tells a classic ghost story in such an everyday way that the ghost is almost believable, and the story is actually scarier than it might have been with a more gruesome approach. The film creates a run-of-the-mill small town, populates it with ordinary folks, gives us a bright grade-school kid as the hero, and then plunges into a tale of murder and revenge.

We have been this way before in countless other movies, but not often with so much style, atmosphere, and believable human nature. Frank LaLoggia, who wrote and directed *Lady in White*, knows that ghosts are more frightening when they appear in the midst of everyday life. He also knows that horror stories work best when they play by the rules of conventional morality and reality. The reason movies like the *Friday the 13th* efforts grow old and boring is they permit pure anarchy, in which anything can happen, and therefore, it's no use for us to hope, or care, about the characters.

This film's story stars Lukas Haas as

Frankie, an inquisitive kid with an active imagination who has a cruel trick played on him one night. Some other kids lure him into the school cloakroom and lock him in, and as the night grows darker and the moon rises, he realizes that no one knows where to look for him. Then an eerie thing happens. He sees a ghost, the ghost of a young girl about his age, who seems restless and tragic, as ghosts must—because why would they wander the earth unless a great injustice remained unsettled?

Frankie even speaks with the ghost, but then, not long after, the cloakroom has another visitor, a masked man who fishes down in the heating duct for something, and who almost kills Frankie, but finally lets him loose. Who is this strange man? Is he a ghost or a real human being? Students of the Law of Economy of Characters will figure out soon enough that the masked man is obviously the only character in the movie who has no other reason for being on the screen, but by then it's already too late to save Frankie from possible doom.

The peculiar thing about these goings-on, we discover, is that they really do exist on two levels: There is indeed a ghost in the movie, and also a real, live killer. And on a parallel track, there is the ghostly Lady in White who is said to wander the town at night, and also the weird Amanda (Katherine Helmond), a spinster whose home reminded me of that lonely closed room in *Great Expectations* where Miss Havisham kept her wedding cake.

All of these bizarre events are anchored in reality by the strong, commonsense performances of Lukas Haas, and by Alex Rocco as his father, and Len Cariou as a family friend. There are lots of small-town details in the movie, conversations that exist for no other reason than to establish the everyday reality against which the haunted events of the night take place. The movie does a good job of telling a very complicated story that accounts for the various ghosts and other midnight apparitions, and yet it is not shy when it comes to special effects and cliff-hanging endings.

It's kind of tricky, reviewing a movie like this. Almost nothing I can say will accurately reflect the tone of the film. I can write about ghosts and killers and strange old ladies, and I could be describing a much different film. But *Lady in White*, like most good films, depends more on style and tone than it does on story, and after a while, it's the whole insidious atmosphere of the film that begins

to envelop us. Like the best ghost stories of M.R. James and Oliver Onions, who were the best in their classic field, *Lady in White* is finally not really about being frightened by ghosts, but about feeling pity for them.

Lady Sings the Blues ★ ★ ★
R, 144 m., 1972

Diana Ross (Billie Holiday), Billy Dee Williams (Louis McKay), Richard Pryor (Piano Man), James Callahan (Reg Hanley), Paul Hampton (Harry), Virginia Capers (Mama Holiday). Directed by Sidney J. Furie and produced by Berry Gordy. Screenplay by Terence McCloy, Chris Clark, and Suzanne de Passa.

My first reaction when I learned that Diana Ross had been cast to play Billie Holiday was a quick and simple one: I didn't think she could do it. I knew she could sing, although not as well as Billie Holiday and certainly not in the same way, but I couldn't imagine Diana Ross reaching the emotional highs and lows of one of the more extreme public lives of our times. But the movie was financed by Motown, and Diana Ross was Motown's most cherished property, so maybe the casting made some kind of commercial sense. After all, Sal Mineo played Gene Krupa.

All of those thoughts were wiped out of my mind within the first three or four minutes of *Lady Sings the Blues*, and I was left with a feeling of complete confidence in a dramatic performance. This was one of the great performances of 1972.

And there is no building up to it. The opening scene is one of total and unrelieved anguish; Billie Holiday is locked into prison, destitute and nearly friendless, and desperately needing a fix of heroin. The high, lonely shriek which escapes from Ross in this scene is a call from the soul, and we know this isn't any "screen debut" by a Top 40 star; this is acting.

It was probably inevitable that the movie itself would follow the tried-and-true formula of most of the musical biographies of the last twenty years. The genre is well-established, and since most of the musicians they've made movies about have had unhappy privates lives, there's the problem of making downhill look like uphill, at least sometimes. This is usually handled (and it is again this time) by showing the performer hitting bottom, rebounding into the arms of friends, being nursed back to health, and making a spectacular comeback performance at Carnegie Hall, or at least the Palace. The formula is so firmly established that stars even seem to follow it consciously, and we're left with tantalizing possibilities: Did Judy Garland play the Palace for the last time to give the proper form to her biography? You gotta go out in triumph, no matter what happens before.

Lady Sings the Blues has most of the clichés we expect—but do we really mind clichés in a movie like this? I don't think so. There's the childhood poverty, the searching for love, the unhappy early sexual experiences, the first audition, the big break, the years of climbing to the top, the encounter with hard drugs, the fall, the comeback, the loyal lover . . . we know the scenes by heart.

What brings the movie alive is the performance that Diana Ross, and director Sidney J. Furie, bring to the scenes. As a gangly adolescent set out to work as a maid in a whorehouse, Ross somehow manages to look gangly and adolescent. When she is transformed into a great beauty later in the film, it IS a transformation, because she was brave enough, and good enough, to really look awful at first: "You got a long way to go," the madam tells her accurately, "before anybody gonna pay $2 for an hour of your time."

The movie is filled with many of the great Billie Holiday songs, and Ross handles them in an interesting way. She doesn't sing in her own style, and she never tries to imitate Holiday, but she sings somehow in the manner of Holiday. There is an uncanny echo, a suggestion, and yet the style is a tribute to Billie Holiday, not an impersonation. The songs do slow the movie down quite a bit, and it feels long at over two hours, but the Billie Holiday music is really the occasion, so I suppose I shouldn't complain.

The Land Before Time ★ ★ ★
G, 71 m., 1988

With the voices of: Pat Hingle (Narrator), Helen Shaver (Littlefoot's Mother), Gabriel Damon (Littlefoot), Candice Houston (Cera), Burke Barnes (Daddy Topps), Pat Hingle (Rooter), Judith Barsi (Ducky), Will Ryan (Petrie). Directed by Don Bluth and produced by Bluth, Gary Goldman, and John Pomeroy. Screenplay by Stu Krieger, based on a story by Judy Freudberg and Tony Geiss.

The love affair between small children and prehistoric dinosaurs is a phenomenon of the toy industry, which cannot manufacture brontosauruses and tyrannosaurus rexes fast enough to meet the demand. Kids love dinosaurs, I think, for the same reason they have always felt an emotional identification with movie creatures like Godzilla and Frankenstein's monster. Kids and monsters have lots in common: They are clumsy and are always knocking things over, they feel as if they cannot control themselves, they do not fit easily into the adult world, and they are usually misunderstood.

In *The Land Before Time* the filmmakers make a strategic error, I think, by making their dinosaurs into children. This destroys the distinction between the two species. The dinosaurs in this movie are just as human as the kitten in *Oliver & Co.*, the mouse in *An American Tail*, and all the animated dogs and rabbits and woodpeckers since time immemorial. One of the reasons kids like dinosaurs is that they are *not* human. They are deliciously alien.

I do not know what kind of movie could have been made from truly reptilian dinosaurs, but I'll bet it would have been interesting. The opening shots of *The Land Before Time*, before the dinosaurs start to speak English, have an eerie fascination. We see a tribe of brontosauruses roaming the parched land, looking for green leaves, which they call "tree stars." There are none to be found, because the climate has changed, and so these peaceful vegetarians head west, seeking a fabled green valley where they hope to find food. They are pursued by their enemies, the sharp-toothed, meat-eating tyrannosaurus rexes. The story is told through the eyes of Littlefoot, a baby brontosaurus who barely escapes being eaten in the first few minutes of the movie.

Littlefoot's saga is an adventure recycled directly out of other movies of this genre, and indeed I was not surprised to discover that the authors of the story also wrote *An American Tail*. Both films involve a childlike creature who is separated from its parents. In this film, Littlefoot's father is nowhere to be found, and his mother dies in an earthquake and the orphan has to undergo a long and perilous journey before finding happiness at the end. The perilous middle sections of both films are fairly rough, as natural forces and predators attempt to destroy the little hero, who joins up with the infants of four other dinosaur species to make his long trek. Both films could have been written by Jack London.

As a backdrop to the series of hazards, the visual look of *The Land Before Time* is apocalyptic. All but the last scenes take place in a blasted heath of red skies, parched land, withered trees, barren wastes, and thorn thickets. But the animation treats this wasteland gently, with little details such as the sparkling drops of water that fall from a leaf, or the ways in which the clumsy, childlike movements of the little creatures are lovingly created.

The Land Before Time does have some charming scenes to counterbalance its grim determinism. Director Don Bluth surpasses himself in a witty ballet in which several prehistoric birdlike creatures fight over a trove of cherries; the animation here is brilliant. There is also a sequence in which Littlefoot and several of his pals get stuck in a tar pit, and a moment at which a clumsy pterodactyl learns to fly. Bluth works in the time-honored Disney tradition, in which body movements are particularly convincing and the backgrounds are not simply static panoramas.

I guess I sort of liked the film, although I wonder why it couldn't have spent more time on natural history and the sense of discovery, and less time on tragedy.

Lassiter ★ ★ ★
R, 100 m., 1984

Tom Selleck (Lassiter), Jane Seymour (Sara), Lauren Hutton (Kari), Bob Hoskins (Becker). Directed by Roger Young and produced by Albert S. Ruddy. Screenplay by David Taylor.

Here's a basic rule about thrillers: Style is a lot more important than plot. What happens isn't nearly as important as how it happens and who it happens to—and if you doubt me, think back over to your favorite James Bond movies. *Lassiter* is a good example. Here's a movie with a plot spun out of thin air. That doesn't matter, though, because the movie is acted and directed with such style that we have fun slogging through the silliness. And part of the fun comes from watching Tom Selleck, the hero of "Magnum, P.I.," in a movie that does him justice. He was wasted in *High Road to China*, which looked like a *Raiders of the Lost Ark* rip-off with Selleck plugged into the Harrison Ford role. *Lassiter* is a movie that seems to have been made with Selleck in mind, and he delivers—he's clearly one of the few actors capable of making the leap from TV to the big screen.

The movie stars Selleck as Nick Lassiter,

an American thief in London on the eve of World War II. A hardheaded police inspector (Bob Hoskins) gets the goods on him and makes him a flat offer: Either Lassiter breaks into the German Embassy and steals $10 million in jewels, or he goes into the slammer. Lassiter goes for the jewels. That involves seducing the kinky, sadistic German countess (Lauren Hutton) who has the diamonds in her bedroom inside the well-guarded embassy. The movie misses a bet here: It spends a lot of time establishing the Hutton character (who has an unusual taste for blood), and we see her killing one of her bed partners. Yet when Lassiter finally goes to bed with her, the movie cuts to the morning after instead of showing how he survived the night. And there's no big final confrontation with the countess; at a crucial moment, Lassiter knocks her cold, and that's that.

Other characters are handled more carefully. We meet Lassiter's sweet girlfriend (Jane Seymour, looking more than ever like a perfect porcelain portrait); Hoskins, who played the mob boss in *The Long Good Friday;* and assorted creeps. Selleck occupies this world effortlessly. He is a big man, and yet he moves gracefully, wears a tuxedo well, makes charming small talk, doesn't seem to be straining himself during the fight scenes, and, in general, stands at the center of a lot of action as if he belonged there. He would make a good James Bond. *Lassiter* knows that, and knows that style and movement are a lot more important than making sense of everything. I squirm when the action stops in a thriller while the characters explain everything to one another; I think of those speeches as memos from the screenwriter to the director. *Lassiter* stops for nothing.

The Last Detail ★ ★ ★ ★
R, 104 m., 1974

Otis Young (Mulhall), Jack Nicholson (Buddusky), Randy Quaid (Meadows), Carol Kane (Prostitute), Michael Moriarty (Marine OD). Directed by Hal Ashby and produced by Gerald Ayres. Screenplay by Robert Towne.

Meadows is a big hulk of a kid who compulsively shoplifts candy bars and peanut butter sandwiches and eats them for consolation. He has been in the navy only long enough to get busted for stealing a charity box with forty bucks inside, for which he has been sentenced to eight years in the Portsmouth naval brig. Buddusky and Mulhall

are the two navy lifers assigned to transport him to Portsmouth, and *The Last Detail* is the story of how they travel there on a series of trains, buses, and drunks. It's a very good movie—and the best thing in it is Jack Nicholson's performance as Buddusky. Nicholson, always one of the most interesting of actors, does in *The Last Detail* what he did in *Easy Rider.* He creates a character so complete and so complex that we stop thinking about the movie and just watch to see what he'll do next.

What he tries to do is show the kid a good time. Now a good time, by Buddusky's standards, is not everybody's idea of a good time. It involves great volumes of time spent drinking great volumes of beer. It involves bitching about the system instead of doing something about it. But it also involves some small measure of human sympathy: Buddusky is personally affronted that the kid is going to be locked up for eight years before his life as a man has even begun.

Mulhall (Otis Young), the other member of this shore patrol, is a serious black man who has spent a lot of years working for his seniority and his retirement rights, and is not going to forfeit everything just by letting one dumb kid escape. But he goes along, within limits, and they take off the kid's handcuffs and try to give him some taste of life. They get him drunk in Washington and take him to a red-light house in New York—and the funny thing is, the kid goes along mostly to please them.

He might be described as a totally unformed youth. He's played superbly by Randy Quaid, who you might remember as the kid with the bottle in his sport-coat pocket in *The Last Picture Show*—the grinning kid in the corner who took Cybill Shepherd skinny-dipping in the next county. His character is the only one that changes in the movie. What happens is that he learns in a very tentative way to assert himself—even to value himself, and make a token protest against his fate.

The direction is by Hal Ashby. How good this movie really is can be gauged by comparing it to *Cinderella Liberty,* another navy movie based on a novel by the same author, Darryl Ponicsan. Both movies have similar world views, and the stories in both move somewhat relentlessly toward inevitable conclusions. But *Cinderella Liberty* just can't be believed, and in *The Last Detail,* we always have the sense that these people are plausible individuals: each limited in his own way, but

each somehow coping with life. The movie is ultimately pretty sad, but for most of the way it alternates between being poignant and being very funny. Nicholson plays comedy better than most comedians, because with him the humor seems to well up from the real experiences of his character.

The Last Emperor ★ ★ ★ ★
PG-13, 160 m., 1987

John Lone (Pu Yi, adult), Joan Chen (Wan Jung), Peter O'Toole (Reginald Johnston), Ying Ruocheng (Governor), Victor Wong (Chen Pao Shen), Dennis Dun (Big Li), Ryuichi Sakamoto (Amakasu), Maggie Han (Eastern Jewel). Directed by Bernardo Bertolucci and produced by Jeremy Thomas. Screenplay by Mark Peploe and Bertolucci.

The boy was three when he first sat on the Dragon Throne as emperor of China, and seven when he abdicated. He had barely reached what in the West is considered the age of reason, and already events beyond his control had shaped his life forever. Bernardo Bertolucci's *The Last Emperor* tells the story of this child, named Pu Yi, in an epic that uses the life of one man as a mirror that reflects China's passage from feudalism through revolution to its current identity crisis.

This is a strange epic because it is about an entirely passive character. We are accustomed to epics about heroes who act on their society—*Lawrence of Arabia, Gandhi*—but Pu Yi was born into a world that allowed him no initiative. The ironic joke was that he was emperor of nothing, for there was no power to go with his title, and throughout the movie he is seen as a pawn and victim, acted upon, exploited for the purposes of others, valued for what he wasn't rather than for what he was.

The movie reveals his powerlessness almost at once; scenes of his childhood in the Forbidden City are intercut with scenes from later in his life, when the Chinese communists had taken power, and he was seized and held in a re-education camp, where a party official spent a decade talking him through a personal transition from emperor to gardener—which was Pu Yi's last, and perhaps happiest, occupation.

But the process in the communist jail actually starts many years earlier, in one of the most poignant scenes in the film, when young Pu Yi is given a bicycle and excitedly pedals it around the Forbidden City until he reaches its gates to the outer world, and is stopped by his own guards. He is an emperor who cannot do the one thing any other little boy in China could do, which was to go out of his own house.

Bertolucci is able to make Pu Yi's imprisonment seem all the more ironic because this entire film was shot on location inside the People's Republic of China, and he was even given permission to film inside the Forbidden City—a vast medieval complex covering some 250 acres and containing 9,999 rooms (only heaven, the Chinese believed, had 10,000 rooms). It is probably unforgivably bourgeois to admire a film because of its locations, but in the case of *The Last Emperor*, the narrative cannot be separated from the awesome presence of the Forbidden City, and from Bertolucci's astonishing use of locations, authentic costumes, and thousands of extras to create the everyday reality of this strange little boy.

There is a scene early in the film when Pu Yi, seated on the Dragon Throne, attended by his minders and servants, grows restless, as small boys will do. He leaps impatiently from his seat and runs toward the door of the throne room, where at first a vast billowing drapery (a yellow one—the color reserved for only the emperor) obstructs the view. Then the curtain is blown aside, and we see an incredible sight, thousands of the emperor's minions, all of them traditionally costumed eunuchs, lined up in geometric precision as far as the eye can see, all of them kowtowing to the boy.

After he formally abdicates power in 1912, Pu Yi remains on the throne, a figurehead maintained in luxury for the convenience of the real rulers of China. A Scottish tutor named Reginald Johnston (Peter O'Toole) comes out to instruct him in the ways of Europe, and the youth (played in manhood by John Lone) becomes an anglophile, dreaming of "escaping" to Cambridge. Johnston advises him to escape instead into marriage, and he takes an empress (Joan Chen) and a concubine. In 1924, he is thrown out of the Forbidden City, and moves with his retinue back to his native Manchuria, then controlled by the Japanese. In a scene of great elegant irony, Bertolucci shows him in Western clothes, a cigarette in hand, leaning on a piano and crooning "Am I Blue?"

As World War II grows closer, Pu Yi grows increasingly irrelevant, except to the Jap-

anese, who set him up briefly as their puppet in Manchuria. His wife becomes an opium addict and begins a dalliance with a lesbian Japanese spy, his old tutor returns to England, he gives himself over to a life of depravity and drifting, and then everything changes for him when the communists take control of China and he is captured by Russians who turn him over to their new allies.

We might expect the communists to sentence Pu Yi to death (a fate he himself confidently expected), but instead there is the re-education process, complicated by the fact that this grown man has never done anything for himself and does not know how to tie his own shoes or turn off the tap after filling a glass with drinking water. When we see him at the end of the film, he is working as a gardener in Peking, and seems happy, and we assume that for him, at least, re-education was a success because it was essentially education in the first place, for a man whose whole life was directed toward making him impotent and irrelevant.

In Orson Welles's *Citizen Kane*, one of the tycoon's friends says, "I was there before the beginning—and now I'm here after the end." *The Last Emperor* ends with an extraordinary sequence, beyond the end, in which an elderly Pu Yi goes to visit the Forbidden City, which is now open to tourists. He sneaks past the velvet rope and climbs onto the Dragon Throne. Once that would have been a fatal offense. And the old man who was once the boy on that throne experiences a complex mixture of emotions. It is an inspired ending for the film, which never makes the mistake of having only one thing to say about the life of a man who embodied all the contradictions and paradoxes of twentieth-century China.

There aren't a lot of action scenes in *The Last Emperor*, and little enough intrigue (even the Japanese spy isn't subtle: "I'm a spy, and I don't care who knows it," she tells the empress on their first meeting). As in *Gandhi*, great historical changes take place during *The Last Emperor*, but, unlike Gandhi, the emperor has no influence on them. His life is a sad irony; his end is a bittersweet elegy. But it is precisely because so little "happens" in this epic that its vast and expensive production schedule is important. When we see those thousands of servants bowing to a little boy, for example, the image is effective precisely because the kowtowing means nothing to the boy, and the lives of the

servants have been dedicated to no useful purpose.

Everything involving the life of Pu Yi was a waste. Everything except one thing—the notion that a single human life could have infinite value. In its own way, the Dragon Throne argued that, making an emperor into a god in order to ennoble his subjects. And in its own way, the Chinese revolution argued the same thing by making him into a gardener.

Last Exit to Brooklyn ★ ★ ★ ½
R, 102 m., 1990

Stephen Lang (Harry Black), Jennifer Jason Leigh (Tralala), Burt Young (Big Joe), Peter Dobson (Vinnie), Jerry Orbach (Boyce), Stephen Baldwin (Sal), Alexis Arquette (Georgette), Zette (Regina), Ricki Lake (Donna). Directed by Uli Edel and produced by Bernd Eichinger. Screenplay by Desmond Nakano.

Love stories are about people who find love in happy times. Tragedies are about people who seek love in unhappy times. *Last Exit to Brooklyn* makes a point of taking place in the early 1950s, when all the escape routes had been cut off for its major characters. The union official cannot admit to being left wing. The strike leader cannot reveal he is homosexual. The father cannot express his love for his child, the prostitute cannot accept her love for the sailor, and the drag queen is not able to love himself. There isn't even any music to release these characters—rock 'n' roll is still in the future, and the pop ballads of the era mock the passions of everyday life. The characters drink and some of them do drugs, but they don't get high—they simply find the occasional release of oblivion.

The movie takes place in one of the gloomiest and most depressing urban settings I've seen in a movie. These streets aren't mean; they're unforgiving. Vast blank warehouse walls loom over the barren pavements, and vacant lots are filled with abandoned cars where mockeries of love take place. When Hubert Selby, Jr., wrote the book that inspired this movie twenty-five years ago, it was attacked in some quarters as pornographic, but it failed the essential test: It didn't arouse purient interest, only sadness and despair.

Why do I respond so strongly to movies like this—or *Barfly, Taxi Driver, The Cook,*

the Thief, His Wife and Her Lover, and Christiane F., which was the previous film by the
makers of Last Exit to Brooklyn? Most people
hate movies like this. I think perhaps it is because no attempt is being made to force the
characters and stories into comforting endings. The movies don't let me off the hook.
These are fellow human beings who suffer,
who are limited in their freedom to imagine
greater happiness for themselves, and yet in
their very misery they embody human striving. There is more of humanity in a prostitute trying to truly love, if only for a
moment, than in all of the slow-motion
romantic fantasies in the world.

The movie takes place in a Brooklyn
neighborhood torn by a bitter strike; most of
the men work at the factory and are unemployed by the dispute, but for Harry Black
(Stephen Lang), a worker who has been
hired to run the strike office, these are good
times. He has an expense account to stock
kegs of beer in the office, he has a telephone,
and best of all he has an excuse to spend long
hours away from the wife he does not love or
understand. He is a homosexual, and he
doesn't understand that, either, but strange
feelings fill him when the neighborhood
drag queen sashays by.

One of the striking workers is Big Joe
(Burt Young), whose daughter (Ricki Lake)
is pregnant. "She ain't pregnant—she's just
fat!" Big Joe insists even in the eighth
month, and yet when he discovers it is true,
he finds it his duty to beat up the responsible
boy—beat him up and then embrace him as a
future son-in-law and then beat him up some
more at the wedding. He accepts the boy as
his daughter's husband, and so the beatings
are not really intended as hostile acts, you
understand—just the price you have to pay in
pain for the freedom of sex.

Sex and pain are linked throughout the
movie. When Tralala (Jennifer Jason Leigh),
the local prostitute, lures the boys from the
Brooklyn Naval Yard into the vacant lots
where she works, it's not for sex—it's so
neighborhood guys can mug the young
draftees and roll them. Tralala gets beaten up
a lot, too, both physically and mentally. She
has been witness to so many loveless acts of
sex that her own body is a thing apart. "I've
got the best boobs in the West," she cries, as
if they were not a part of her but some kind of
award she won in a contest. When one sailor
takes her seriously and falls for her, she
moves into a Manhattan hotel with him for a
few days' mockery of a real relationship. He's

naive enough to believe it's love. She's almost
sad enough.

But love and sex do not connect in this
movie. When Harry Black, the strike leader,
finally admits he is gay and expresses his love
for the drag queen, he finds, as the sailor
does, that the person he loves cares only for
money. Eventually both Harry and Tralala
end up in vacant lots, brutally punished,
because of sex. The only difference is that
Harry is attacked because he tries to have
sex, and Tralala is punished through sex—
through a horrifying gang rape.

Is there any love in this movie? Yes, in a
sense. There is a rather simpleminded boy
who wanders through the film and idolizes
Tralala and yearns after her in a goofy way,
but she doesn't know what to do about him.
How do you explain to an admirer that his
love is misplaced—that really you don't
deserve it?

The performances are strong, true, and
not a little courageous. One of the best is by
Jerry Orbach (the mafioso brother in Crimes
and Misdemeanors), who plays a union leader.
At a time when McCarthyism is rampant and
strikes are seen as a symptom of communist
agitation, he tries to handle hotheads on both
sides, and there is the sense that he is successful partly because he sticks to business;
his personality doesn't have a sexual compo-
nent.

Last Exit to Brooklyn was banned as a book
and resulted in several obscenity cases in
both America and England. Remembering
the book and now looking at the movie, I
wonder what really upset people: Was it the
sex or just the lovelessness? The drugs or just
the despair? The violence, or its point-
lessness? Don't most books prosecuted for
sexual obscenity celebrate sex? This one
argues that it's not worth the trouble—that
you'll end up by breaking your heart.

Last House on the Left ★ ★ ★ ½
R, 82 m., 1972

David Hess (Krug), Ludy Gratham (Phyllis),
Sandra Cassell (Mari), Marc Sheffler (Junior),
Jeramie Rain (Sadie), Fred Lincoln (Weasel),
Gaylord St. James (Dr. Collingwood), Cynthia
Carr (Mrs. Collingwood). Directed by Wes
Craven and produced by Sean S.
Cunningham. Screenplay by Craven.

Last House on the Left is a tough, bitter little
sleeper of a movie that's about four times as

good as you'd expect. There is a moment of
such sheer and unexpected terror that it
beats anything in the heart-in-the-mouth
line since Alan Arkin jumped out of the
darkness at Audrey Hepburn in Wait Until
Dark.

I don't want to give the impression, however, that this is simply a good horror movie.
It's horrifying, all right, but in ways that
have nothing to do with the supernatural.
It's the story of two suburban girls who go
into the city for a rock concert, are kidnapped by a gang of sadistic escaped convicts
and their sluttish girlfriend, and are raped
and murdered. Then, in a coincidence even
the killers find extreme, the gang ends up
spending the night at the home of one of the
girls' parents.

The parents accidentally find out the
identities of the killers, because of a stolen
locket and some blood-stained clothing in
their baggage. Enraged, the father takes on
the gang single-handedly and murders them.
Does any of this sound familiar? Think for a
moment. Setting aside the modern details,
this is roughly the plot of Ingmar Bergman's
The Virgin Spring.

The story is also based on a true incident,
we're told at the beginning of the movie, but
I have my doubts; I think the producers may
simply be trying one of those "only the
names have been changed" capers. What
does come through in Last House on the Left
is a powerful narrative, told so directly and
strongly that the audience (mostly in the
mood for just another good old exploitation
film) was rocked back on its psychic heels.

Wes Craven's direction never lets us out
from under almost unbearable dramatic tension (except in some silly scenes involving a
couple of dumb cops, who overact and
seriously affect the plot's credibility). The
acting is unmannered and . . . natural, I
guess. There's no posturing. There's a good
ear for dialogue and nuance. And there is evil
in this movie. Not bloody escapism, or a
thrill a minute, but a fully developed sense of
the vicious natures of the killers. There is no
glory in this violence. And Craven has written in a young member of the gang (again
borrowed on Bergman's story) who sees the
horror as fully as the victims do. This movie
covers the same philosophical territory as
Sam Peckinpah's Straw Dogs, and is more
hard-nosed about it: Sure, a man's home is
his castle, but who wants to be left with nothing but a castle and a lifetime memory of horror?

The Last Metro ★ ★ ★
NO MPAA RATING, 133 m., 1980

Catherine Deneuve (Marion Steiner), Gerard Depardieu (Bernard Granger), Jean Poiret (Jean-Loup), Heinz Bennent (Lucas Steiner), Andrea Ferreol (Arlette), Paulette Dubost (Germaine), Jean-Louis Richard (Daxlat). Directed by Francois Truffaut. Screenplay by Truffaut, Suzanne Schiffman, and Jean-Claude Grumberg.

Francois Truffaut said he wanted to satisfy three old dreams by making *The Last Metro*. He wanted to take the camera backstage in a theater, to evoke the climate of the Nazi occupation of France, and to give Catherine Deneuve the role of a responsible woman. He has achieved the first and last dreams, but he doesn't evoke the occupation well enough to make *The Last Metro* more than a sentimental fantasy.

The film takes place backstage, and below-stage, at a theater in Paris. The theater's director is a German Jew (Heinz Bennent) who already has fled from Nazi Germany and now, with the occupation of Paris, goes into permanent hiding in the basement of his theater. Upstairs, his wife (Deneuve) spreads the rumor that he has fled to South America. Then she relays his instructions as the theater attempts to save itself from bankruptcy by presenting a new production.

There are many other characters in the movie, which at times resembles Truffaut's history of a film production in *Day for Night*. Gerard Depardieu plays the leading man for the new production. The supporting cast includes a young woman who will do anything for a job in the theater, an older woman of ambiguous sexuality, an avuncular stage manager, a gay director, and a powerful critic who is such an evil monster that he must surely have been inspired by a close Truffaut friend. Most of the movie's events take place within the walls of the theater; this is a backstage film, not a war film. We see the rehearsals under way, with Bennent downstairs listening through an air duct. There are the romantic intrigues among the cast members. There are occasional walk-throughs by Nazis. There are moments of great danger, somewhat marred by the fact that Truffaut does not resolve them realistically. And there is an unforgivably sentimental ending that ties up everything without solving anything.

The problem, I think, is that Truffaut sees

the Nazi presence in Paris simply as a plot device to create tension within his theatrical troupe. It is ever so much more dramatic if the show must go on despite raids, political directives, and an electrical blackout that requires the stagehands to power a generator by bicycle-power. It's all too cute. Nobody seems to *really* understand that there's a war on out there. And yet, within the unfortunate limitations that Truffaut sets for himself, he does deliver an entertaining movie. Catherine Deneuve is as beautiful as ever, and as enigmatic (it is typical of her performance that at the end we have to wait for the screenplay to tell us who she does, or does not, really love). Depardieu is gangly and sincere, a strong presence. Bennent, as the husband downstairs, is wan and courageous in the Paul Henreid role. And the most fascinating character in the cast is of course the villain, Daxlat, the pro-Nazi critic. He at least seems in touch with the true evil that the others, and Truffaut, see as backdrop.

The Last Picture Show ★ ★ ★ ★
R, 114 m., 1971

Timothy Bottoms (Sonny), Jeff Bridges (Duane), Cybill Shepherd (Jacy Farrow), Ben Johnson (Sam the Lion), Cloris Leachman (Ruth Popper), Ellen Burstyn (Lois Farrow), Eileen Brennan (Genevieve), Bill Thurman (Coach Popper). Directed by Peter Bogdanovich and produced by Bert Schneider and Stephen J. Friedman. Screenplay by Larry McMurtry and Bogdanovich.

There was something about going to the movies in the 1950s that will never be the same again. It was the decade of the last gasp of the great American movie-going habit, and before my eyes in the middle 1950s the Saturday kiddie matinee died a lingering death at the Princess Theater on Main Street in Urbana. For five or six years of my life (the years between when I was old enough to go alone, and when TV came to town) Saturday afternoon at the Princess was a descent into a dark magical cave that smelled of Jujubes, melted Dreamsicles, and Crisco in the popcorn machine. It was probably on one of those Saturday afternoons that I formed my first critical opinion, deciding vaguely that there was something about John Wayne that set him apart from ordinary cowboys. The Princess was jammed to the walls with kids every Saturday afternoon, as it had been for years, but then TV came to town and within

a year the Princess was no longer an institution. It survived into the early 1960s and then closed, to be reborn a few years later as the Cinema. The metallic taste of that word, cinema, explains what happened when you put it alongside the name "Princess."

Peter Bogdanovich's *The Last Picture Show* uses the closing of another theater on another Main Street as a motif to frame a great many things that happened to America in the early 1950s. The theater is the Royal, and along with the pool hall and the all-night cafe it supplies what little excitement and community survives in a little West Texas crossroads named Anarene.

All three are owned by Sam the Lion, who is just about the only self-sufficient and self-satisfied man in town. The others are infected by a general malaise, and engage in sexual infidelities partly to remind themselves they are alive. There isn't much else to do in Anarene, no dreams worth dreaming, no new faces, not even a football team that can tackle worth a damn. The nourishing myth of the Western (*Wagonmaster* and *Red River* are among the last offerings at the Royal) is being replaced by nervously hilarious TV programs out of the East, and defeated housewives are reassured they're part of the "Strike It Rich" audience with a heart of gold.

Against this background, we meet two high school seniors named Sonny and Duane, who are the co-captains of the shameful football squad. We learn next to nothing about their home lives, but we hardly notice the omission because their real lives are lived in a pickup truck and a used Mercury. That was the way it was in high school in the 1950s, and probably always will be: A car was a mobile refuge from adults, frustration, and boredom. When people in their thirties say today that sexual liberation is pale compared to a little prayerful groping in the front seat, they are onto something.

During the year of the film's action, the two boys more or less survive coming-of-age. They both fall in love with the school's only beauty, a calculating charmer named Jacy who twists every boy in town around her little finger before taking this skill away with her to Dallas. Sonny breaks up with his gum-chewing girlfriend and has an unresolved affair with the coach's wife, and Duane goes off to fight the Korean War. There are two deaths during the film's year, but no babies are born, and Bogdanovich's final pan shot along Main Street curiously seems to turn it from a real location (which it is) into a half-remembered backdrop from an old movie. *The Last Picture Show* is a great deal more complex than it might at first seem, and this shot suggests something of its buried structure. Every detail of clothing, behavior, background music, and decor is exactly right for 1951—but that still doesn't explain the movie's mystery.

Mike Nichols's *Carnal Knowledge* began with 1949, and yet felt modern. Bogdanovich has been infinitely more subtle in giving his film not only the decor of 1951, but the visual style of a movie that might have been shot in 1951. The montage of cutaway shots at the Christmas dance; the use of an insert of Sonny's foot on the accelerator; the lighting and black-and-white photography of real locations as if they were sets—everything forms a stylistic whole that works. It isn't just a matter of putting in Jo Stafford and Hank Williams.

The Last Picture Show has been described as an evocation of the classic Hollywood narrative film. It is more than that; it is a belated entry in that age—the best film of 1951, you might say. Using period songs and decor to create nostalgia is familiar enough, but to tunnel down to the visual level and get that right, too, and in a way that will affect audiences even if they aren't aware how, is one hell of a directing accomplishment. Movies create our dreams as well as reflect them, and when we lose the movies we lose the dreams. I wonder if Bogdanovich's film doesn't at last explain what it was that Pauline Kael, and a lot of the rest of us, lost at the movies.

Last Tango in Paris ★ ★ ★ ★
x, 127 m., 1972

Marlon Brando (Paul), Maria Schneider (Jeanne), Darling Legitimus (Concierge), Jean-Pierre Leaud (Tom). Directed by Bernardo Bertolucci and produced by Alberto Grimaldi. Screenplay by Bertolucci and Franco Arcalli.

Bernardo Bertolucci's *Last Tango in Paris* is one of the great emotional experiences of our time. It's a movie that exists so resolutely on the level of emotion, indeed, that possibly only Marlon Brando, of all living actors, could have played its lead. Who else can act so brutally and imply such vulnerability and need?

For the movie is about need; about the ter-rible hunger that its hero, Paul, feels for the touch of another human heart. He is a man whose whole existence has been reduced to a cry for help—and who has been so damaged by life that he can only express that cry in acts of crude sexuality.

Bertolucci begins with a story so simple (which is to say, so stripped of any clutter of plot) that there is little room in it for anything but the emotional crisis of his hero. The events that take place in the everyday world are remote to Paul, whose attention is absorbed by the gradual breaking of his heart. The girl, Jeanne, is not a friend and is hardly even a companion; it's just that because she happens to wander into his life, he uses her as an object of his grief.

The movie begins when Jeanne, who is about to be married, goes apartment-hunting and finds Paul in one of the apartments. It is a big, empty apartment, with a lot of sunlight but curiously little cheer. Paul rapes her, if rape is not too strong a word to describe an act so casually accepted by the girl. He tells her that they will continue to meet there, in the empty apartment, and she agrees.

Why does she agree? From her point of view—which is not a terribly perceptive one—why not? One of the several things this movie is about is how one person, who may be uncommitted and indifferent, nevertheless can at a certain moment become of great importance to another. One of the movie's strengths comes from the tragic imbalance between Paul's need and Jeanne's almost unthinking participation in it. Their difference is so great that it creates tremendous dramatic tension; more, indeed, than if both characters were filled with passion.

They do continue to meet, and at Paul's insistence they do not exchange names. What has come together in the apartment is almost an elemental force, not a connection of two beings with identities in society. Still, inevitably, the man and the girl do begin to learn about each other. What began, on the man's part, as totally depersonalized sex develops into a deeper relationship almost to spite him.

We learn about them. He is an American, living in Paris these last several years with a French wife who owned a hotel that is not quite a whorehouse. On the day the movie begins, the wife has committed suicide. We are never quite sure why, although by the time the movie is over we have a few depressing clues.

The girl is young, conscious of her beauty and the developing powers of her body, and is going to marry a young and fairly inane filmmaker. He is making a movie of their life together; a camera crew follows them around as he talks to her and kisses her—for herself or for the movie, she wonders.

The banality of her "real" life has thus set her up for the urgency of the completely artificial experience that has been commanded for her by Paul. She doesn't know his name, or anything about him, but when he has sex with her it is certainly real; there is a life in that empty room that her fiancé, with all of his *cinéma vérité*, is probably incapable of imagining.

She finds it difficult, too, because she is a child. A child, because she hasn't lived long enough and lost often enough to know yet what a heartbreaker the world can be. There are moments in the film when she does actually seem to look into Paul's soul and half-understand what she sees there, but she pulls back from it; pulls back, finally, all the way—and just when he had come to the point where he was willing to let life have one more chance with him.

A lot has been said about the sex in the film; in fact, *Last Tango in Paris* has become notorious because of its sex. There is a lot of sex in this film—more, probably, than in any other legitimate feature film ever made—but the sex isn't the point, it's only the medium of exchange. Paul has somehow been so brutalized by life that there are only a few ways he can still feel.

Sex is one of them, but only if it is debased and depraved—because he is so filled with guilt and self-hate that he chooses these most intimate of activities to hurt himself beyond all possibilities of mere thoughts and words. It is said in some quarters that the sex in the movie is debasing to the girl, but I don't think it is. She's almost a bystander, a witness at the scene of the accident. She hasn't suffered enough, experienced enough, to more than dimly guess at what Paul is doing to himself with her. But Paul knows, and so does Bertolucci; only an idiot would criticize this movie because the girl is so often naked but Paul never is. That's their relationship.

The movie may not contain Brando's greatest performance, but it certainly contains his most emotionally overwhelming scene. He comes back to the hotel and confronts his wife's dead body, laid out in a casket, and he speaks to her with words of absolute hatred—words which, as he says them, become one of the most moving speeches of love I can imagine.

As he weeps, as he attempts to remove her cosmetic death mask ("Look at you! You're a monument to your mother! You never wore makeup, never wore false eyelashes . . ."), he makes it absolutely clear why he is the best film actor of all time. He may be a bore, he may be a creep, he may act childish about the Academy Awards—but there is no one else who could have played that scene flat-out, no holds barred, the way he did, and make it work triumphantly.

The girl, Maria Schneider, doesn't seem to act her role so much as to exude it. On the basis of this movie, indeed, it's impossible to really say whether she can act or not. That's not her fault; Bertolucci directs her that way. He wants a character who ultimately does not quite understand the situation she finds herself in; she has to be that way, among other reasons, because the movie's ending absolutely depends on it. What happens to Paul at the end must seem, in some fundamental way, ridiculous. What the girl does at the end has to seem incomprehensible—not to us; to her.

What is the movie about? What does it all mean? It is about, and means, exactly the same things that Bergman's *Cries and Whispers* was about, and meant. That's to say that no amount of analysis can extract from either film a rational message. The whole point of both films is that there is a land in the human soul that's beyond the rational—beyond, even, words to describe it.

Faced with a passage across that land, men make various kinds of accommodations. Some ignore it; some try to avoid it through temporary distractions; some are lucky enough to have the inner resources for a successful journey. But of those who do not, some turn to the most highly charged resources of the body; lacking the mental strength to face crisis and death, they turn on the sexual mechanism, which can at least be depended upon to function, usually.

That's what the sex is about in this film (and in *Cries and Whispers*). It's not sex at all (and it's a million miles from intercourse). It's just a physical function of the soul's desperation. Paul in *Last Tango in Paris* has no difficulty in achieving an erection, but the gravest difficulty in achieving a life-affirming reason for one.

The Last Temptation of Christ
★ ★ ★ ★
R, 160 m., 1988

Willem Dafoe (Jesus), Harvey Keitel (Judas), Paul Greco (Zealot), Steven Shill (Centurion), Barbara Hershey (Mary Magdalene), Harry Dean Stanton (Paul), David Bowie (Pontius Pilate), Verna Bloom (Mary the Mother), Andre Gregory (John the Baptist). Directed by Martin Scorsese and produced by Barbara De Fina. Screenplay by Paul Schrader.

Christianity teaches that Jesus was both God and man. That he could be both at once is the central mystery of the Christian faith, and the subject of *The Last Temptation of Christ*. To be fully man, Jesus would have had to possess all of the weakness of man, to be prey to all of the temptations—for as man, he would have possessed God's most troublesome gift, free will. As the son of God, he would of course have inspired the most desperate wiles of Satan, and this is a film about how he experienced temptation and conquered it.

That, in itself, makes *The Last Temptation of Christ* sound like a serious and devout film, which it is. The astonishing controversy that has raged around this film is primarily the work of fundamentalists who have their own view of Christ and are offended by a film that they feel questions his divinity. But in the father's house are many mansions, and there is more than one way to consider the story of Christ—why else are there four Gospels? Among those who do not already have rigid views on the subject, this film is likely to inspire more serious thought on the nature of Jesus than any other ever made.

That is the irony about the attempts to suppress this film; it is a sincere, thoughtful investigation of the subject, made as a collaboration between the two American filmmakers who have been personally most attracted to serious films about sin, guilt, and redemption. Martin Scorsese, the director, has made more than half of his films about battles in the souls of his characters between grace and sin. Paul Schrader, the screenwriter, has written Scorsese's best films (*Taxi Driver, Raging Bull*) and directed his own films about men torn between their beliefs and their passions (*Hardcore*, with George C. Scott as a fundamentalist whose daughter plunges into the carnal underworld, and *Mishima*, about the Japanese writer who killed himself as a demonstration of his fanatic belief in tradition).

Scorsese and Schrader have not made a film that panders to the audience—as almost all Hollywood religious epics traditionally have. They have paid Christ the compliment of taking him and his message seriously, and have made a film that does not turn him into a garish, emasculated image from a religious postcard. Here he is flesh and blood, struggling, questioning, asking himself and his father which is the right way, and finally, after great suffering, earning the right to say, on the cross, "It is accomplished."

The critics of this film, many of whom did not see it, raised a sensational hue and cry about the final passages, in which Christ on the cross, in great pain, begins to hallucinate and imagines what his life would have been like if he had been free to live as an ordinary man. In his reverie, he marries Mary Magdalene, has children, grows old. But it is clear in the film that this hallucination is sent to him by Satan, at the time of his greatest weakness, to tempt him. And in the hallucination itself, in the film's most absorbing scene, an elderly Jesus is reproached by his aging Apostles for having abandoned his mission. Through this imaginary conversation, Jesus finds the strength to shake off his temptation and return to consciousness to accept his suffering, death, and resurrection.

During the hallucination, there is a very brief moment when he is seen making love with Magdalene. This scene is shot with such restraint and tact that it does not qualify in any way as a "sex scene," but instead is simply an illustration of marriage and the creation of children. Those offended by the film object to the very notion that Jesus could have, or even imagine having, sexual intercourse. But, of course, Christianity teaches that the union of man and wife is one of the fundamental reasons God created human beings, and to imagine that the son of God, as a man, could not encompass such thoughts within his intelligence is itself a kind of insult. Was he less than the rest of us? Was he not fully man?

There is biblical precedent for such temptations. We read of the forty days and nights during which Satan tempted Christ in the desert with visions of the joys that could be his if he renounced his father. In the film, which is clearly introduced as a fiction and not as an account based on the Bible, Satan tries yet once again at the moment of Christ's greatest weakness. I do not understand why this is offensive, especially since it is not presented in a sensational way.

I see that this entire review has been preoccupied with replying to the attacks of the film's critics, with discussing the issues, rather than with reviewing *The Last Temptation of Christ* as a motion picture. Perhaps that is an interesting proof of the film's worth. Here is a film that engaged me on the subject of Christ's dual nature, that caused me to think about the mystery of a being who could be both God and man. I cannot think of another film on a religious subject that has challenged me more fully. The film has offended those whose ideas about God and man it does not reflect. But then, so did Jesus.

The Late Show ★ ★ ★ ★
PG, 94 m., 1977

Art Carney (Ira Wells), Lily Tomlin (Margo), Bill Macy (Charlie Hatter), Eugene Roche (Ron Birdwell), Joanna Cassidy (Laura Birdwell), John Considine (Lamar), Howard Duff (Harry Regan), Ruth Nelson (Mrs. Schmidt). Directed by Robert Benton and produced by Robert Altman. Screenplay by Benton.

It's hard enough for a movie to sustain one tone, let alone half a dozen, but that's just what Robert Benton's *The Late Show* does. It's the story of a strangely touching relationship between two people. It's a violent crime melodrama. It's a comedy. It's a commentary on the private-eye genre, especially its 1940s manifestations. It's a study of the way older people do a balancing act between weariness and experience. It's a celebration of that uncharted continent, Lily Tomlin.

And most of all, it's a movie that dares a lot, pulls off most of it, and entertains us without insulting our intelligence. What's quietly astonishing is that all of it starts with a woman coming to a private eye about a missing cat. The woman is played by Lily Tomlin, who somehow provides scatterbrained eccentricism with a cutting edge. The cat has been missing a couple of days, and she's worried. The private eye is played by Art Carney, who has seen it all twice, when once would have been too much.

He takes the case maybe because he could use the money, maybe because he's intrigued by the client, maybe because he's bored, maybe because he's been taking cases so long it's second nature. He doesn't give a damn about the cat. But then, in a series of plot developments so labyrinthine we should be

taking notes, the missing cat leads to a mysterious robbery, a missing stamp collection, a fence with a house full of stolen goods, and a dead body that's in the . . .

But, no, I won't say where the body is, because the way Benton reveals it and then lets Lily Tomlin discover it (when all she was after was a Coke) is one of the movie's many pleasures. A friend of mine objected to the body, and to the movie's violence, as being unnecessary in a comedy. Well, *The Late Show* is a long way from being only a comedy, and the introductory shot of that body redeems any amount of gratuitous movie violence.

It's the case with most good detective fiction that the puzzle seems impossible to solve until the last chapter, when everything is made transparently clear. That's true here, with Art Carney providing a brilliant analysis of the connections and coincidences just when it's most irrelevant. But the plot's incidental to the movie's center, which has to do with Carney and Lily Tomlin.

You see, they're allowed to be people here. They're allowed to play characters who have no particular connection with clichés or stereotypes or characters who were successful in a box-office hit last year. Yes, Carney's a private eye, but a particular one: Overweight and wheezing, hard of hearing, given to comments that only obliquely refer to the problem at hand.

And Lily Tomlin . . . well, her character employs a form of reasoning that has nothing to do with logic but a lot to do with the good reasons we have for behaving as we do. An example. Art Carney pretends to be mortally ill (never mind why). He is not (never mind why). His ruse has saved their lives (never mind how). Lily Tomlin is not pleased: She could have had a heart attack! Does he think it's funny, playing with his own friend's *emotions* that way? Doesn't he have any *consideration*?

Benton's screenplay is filled with lines that perfectly define their moments (and belong so securely to the characters that they seem to come from them, as some of them probably did). The way in which Tomlin explains why today is the *pits*, for example. The way Carney wonders if it would kill her, for chrissakes, to wear a dress once in a while. The way Carney's sometime partner talks to himself before he dies. The way the fence offers a bribe of a stereo set.

The Late Show is one of three movies from the seventies that had their spiritual origins

in the classic private-eye films. The other two were Dick Richards's *Farewell, My Lovely* (in which Robert Mitchum demonstrated that he was born to play Philip Marlowe), and Robert Altman's *The Long Goodbye*, (in which Elliott Gould demonstrated that he was not).

Altman produced *The Late Show*, which is probably another way of saying he made it possible to be filmed, and Benton has brilliantly realized it. Maybe these three films about an all but extinct occupation are telling us something: That the more we become plastic and bland, the more we become fascinated by a strata in our cities we'd like to believe still exists, a society of loners and eccentrics, people brave and crazy and doomed, old private eyes and cat lovers. If they're OK, we're OK.

Lawrence of Arabia ★ ★ ★ ★
PG, 216 m., 1962 (re-released 1989)

Peter O'Toole (Lawrence), Alec Guinness (Prince Feisel), Anthony Quinn (Auda Abu Tayi), Jack Hawkins (General Allenby), Jose Ferrer (Turkish Bey), Omar Sharif (Sherif Ali), Anthony Quayle (Colonel Brighton), Claude Rains (Mr. Dryden), Arthur Kennedy (Jackson Bentley), Donald Wolfit (General Murray). Directed by David Lean and produced by Sam Spiegel. Screenplay by Robert Bolt. Restored director's cut produced and reconstructed by Robert A. Harris and Jim Painten.

What a bold, mad act of genius it was, to make *Lawrence of Arabia*, or even think that it could be made. In the words twenty-seven years later of one of its stars, Omar Sharif: "If you are the man with the money and somebody comes to you and says he wants to make a film that's four hours long, with no stars, and no women, and no love story, and not much action either, and he wants to spend a huge amount of money to go film it in the desert—what would you say?"

The impulse to make this movie was based, above all, on imagination. The story of Lawrence is not founded on violent battle scenes or cheap melodrama, but on David Lean's ability to imagine what it would look like to see a speck appear on the horizon of the desert, and slowly grow into a human being. He had to know how that would feel before he could convince himself that the project had a chance of being successful.

There is a moment in the film when the hero, a British eccentric named T.E. Lawrence, has survived a suicidal trek across the desert and is within reach of shelter and water—and he turns around and goes back to find a friend who has fallen behind. This sequence builds up to the shot in which the shimmering heat of the desert reluctantly yields the speck that becomes a man—a shot that is held for a long time before we can even begin to see the tiny figure. On television, this shot doesn't work at all—nothing can be seen. In a movie theater, looking at the stark clarity of a 70mm print, we lean forward and strain to bring a detail out of the waves of heat, and for a moment we experience some of the actual vastness of the desert and its unforgiving harshness.

By being able to imagine the sequence, the filmmakers were able to see why the movie would work. *Lawrence of Arabia* is not a simple biography or an adventure movie—although it contains both elements—but a movie that uses the desert as a stage for the flamboyance of a driven, quirky man. Although it is true that Lawrence was instrumental in enlisting the desert tribes on the British side in the 1914-17 campaign against the Turks, the movie suggests that he acted less out of patriotism than out of a need to reject conventional British society and identify with the wildness and theatricality of the Arabs.

T.E. Lawrence must be the strangest hero to ever stand at the center of an epic. To play him, Lean cast one of the strangest actors in recent movie history, Peter O'Toole, a lanky, almost clumsy man with a sculptured face and a speaking manner that hesitates between amusement and insolence. O'Toole's assignment was a delicate one. Although it was widely believed that Lawrence was a homosexual, a multimillion-dollar epic filmed in 1962 could not possibly be frank about that. And yet Lean and his writer, Robert Bolt, didn't simply cave in and rewrite Lawrence into a routine action hero.

Using O'Toole's peculiar speech and manner as their instrument, they created a character who combined charisma and craziness, who was so different from conventional military heroes that he could inspire the Arabs to follow him in that mad march across the desert. There is a moment in the movie when O'Toole, dressed in the flowing white robes of a desert sheik, does a victory dance on top of a captured Turkish train, and almost seems to be posing for fashion photos. This is a curious scene because it seems to flaunt gay stereotypes, and yet none of the other

characters in the movie seem to notice—nor do they take much notice of the two young desert urchins that Lawrence takes under his protection.

What Lean, Bolt, and O'Toole create is a sexually and socially unconventional man who is simply presented as what he is, without labels or comment. Could such a man rally the splintered desert tribes and win a war against the Turks? Lawrence did. But he did it partially with mirrors, the movie suggests; one of the key characters is an American journalist (Arthur Kennedy), obviously inspired by Lowell Thomas, who single-handedly retailed the Lawrence myth to the English-language press. The journalist admits he is looking for a hero to write about. Lawrence is happy to play the role. And only role-playing would have done the job; an ordinary military hero would have been too small-scale for this canvas.

For a movie that runs 216 minutes, plus intermission, *Lawrence of Arabia* is not dense with plot details. It is a spare movie with clean, uncluttered lines, and there is never a moment when we're in doubt about the logistical details of the various campaigns. Lawrence is able to unite various desert factions, the movie argues, because (1) he is so obviously an outsider that he cannot even understand, let alone take sides with, the various ancient rivalries; and (2) because he is able to show the Arabs that it is in their self-interest to join the war against the Turks. Along the way he makes allies of such desert leaders as Sherif Ali (Omar Sharif), Prince Feisel (Alec Guinness), and Auda Abu Tayi (Anthony Quinn) both by winning their respect and by appealing to their logic. The dialogue in these scenes is not complex, and sometimes Bolt makes it so spare it sounds like poetry.

I've noticed that when people remember *Lawrence of Arabia*, they don't talk about the details of the plot. They get a certain look in their eyes, as if they are remembering the whole experience, and have never quite been able to put it into words. Although it seems to be a traditional narrative film—like *The Bridge on the River Kwai*, which Lean made just before it, or *Doctor Zhivago*, which he made just after—it actually has more in common with essentially visual epics as Kubrick's *2001* or Eisenstein's *Alexander Nevsky*. It is spectacle and experience, and its ideas are about things you can see or feel, not things you can say. Much of its appeal is based on the fact that it does not contain a

complex story with a lot of dialogue; we remember the quiet, empty passage, the sun rising across the desert, the intricate lines traced by the wind in the sand.

Although it won the Academy Award as the year's best picture in 1962, *Lawrence of Arabia* would have soon been a lost memory if it had not been for two film restorers named Robert A. Harris and Jim Painten. They discovered the original negative in Columbia's vault, inside crushed and rusting film cans, and they also discovered about 35 minutes of footage that had been trimmed by distributors from Lean's final cut. To see it is to appreciate the subtlety of F.A. Young's desert cinematography—achieved despite blinding heat and the blowing sand, which worked its way into every camera. *Lawrence of Arabia* was one of the last films to be photographed in 70mm (as opposed to being blown up to 70mm from a 35mm negative). It is a great experience to see it as Lean intended it in 1962—and also a humbling one, to realize how the motion picture industry is losing the vision to make epic films like this, and settling for safe narrative formulas instead.

Lean on Me ★ ★ ½
PG-13, 104 m., 1989

Morgan Freeman (Joe Clark), Beverly Todd (Ms. Levias), Robert Guillaume (Dr. Napier), Alan North (Mayor Bottman), Lynne Thigpen (Leona Barrett), Robin Bartlett (Mrs. Elliott), Karen Malina White (Kaneesha Carter), Jermaine Hopkins (Thomas Sams). Directed by John G. Avildsen and produced by Norman Twain. Screenplay by Michael Schiffer.

Joe Clark is a real man who really did whip a New Jersey high school into shape. I know this because I have been told it a dozen times by people who think that explains the behavior of "Joe Clark," the hero of *Lean on Me*. But *Lean on Me* is not a documentary about the real Joe Clark. It is a fiction film about a character who is so troubled, obsessed, and angry that the film is never able to say quite what it thinks of him. After seeing the movie, neither are we.

Clark is played by Oscar nominee Morgan Freeman in a performance that is powerful and consistent and thus all the more troubling. Although he has taught in schools for more than twenty years, he has never really fit in anywhere. He has an unshakable belief in his own opinions, no interest in anyone else's, and a personality so abrasive it's no wonder his wife left him and he has only one friend. As an administrator, he shoots first and doesn't ask questions afterwards: He's sort of the Dirty Harry of the Paterson, N.J., educational system.

Lean on Me opens with a brief sequence showing Clark starting out at a well-run Eastside High in the 1960s, alienating his principal and being transferred out. It continues twenty years later, with Clark more or less happily teaching in a good school in a nice neighborhood. Then we get an updated look at Eastside High, which has become the town's deeply troubled, mostly minority high school, where violence, drug-dealing, and intimidation are facts of life, and little or no learning takes place. John Avildsen, the director, is so concerned to show us the hell of Eastside High that he goes overboard; the corridors look like a cross between a prison riot and a Hell's Angels rally.

There is obviously only one man capable of turning this situation around, and so "Crazy" Joe Clark is brought back to Eastside. His first act is to call an all-school assembly, gather all the druggies and troublemakers onstage, and expel them en masse. Then he begins to stalk the school corridors, enforcing his own reign of terror. He orders all the graffiti painted over. Fine. He orders everyone to learn the school song, on pain of expulsion. Sort of fine. He suspends a teacher for daring to stoop over and pick up a piece of scrap paper while Joe Clark was talking. Not fine. He insults a teacher in front of students, behaves in an erratic and irrational way, and conducts himself like an autocratic dictator. Bad.

This is a seriously troubled man. As the movie progresses, we wait for Joe Clark to undergo a personality change, to soften, to grow, to start learning to respect the right of other people to have an opinion. But with the exception of one half-hearted apology, Clark never does change. He is an arrogant bully, a martinet who demands instant, unquestioning obedience.

Yes, he does clean up Eastside High. And, yes, the students are able to pass a state proficiency exam, so that the school can remain under local control and not be taken over by the state. But we never see how this is done. *Stand and Deliver*, 1988's film about a dedicated Hispanic math teacher, was about a teaching and learning process. *Lean on Me* is about a disciplinary process. The movie's most bizarre scene has Clark onstage at a pre-exam pep rally, ranting and raving and leading the school song, as if the test were a football game. But you can't pass a test simply because your spirits are high. And I am not convinced that any kind of meaningful learning can take place under the reign of public humiliation enforced by Clark. Discipline is not the same thing as intimidation.

Is it true that tough schools need mad-dog teachers? One of the sneaky, uneasy feelings I got while watching *Lean on Me* is that the movie makes a subtle appeal to those who are afraid of unruly, loud, violent, black teenagers. As Joe Clark takes a baseball bat and begins to whip them into shape (at one point even physically fighting a student), the audience is cheered, not because education is being served, but because Clark is a combination of Dirty Harry and Billy Jack, enforcing the law on his own terms.

Lean on Me wants to be taken as a serious, even noble, film about an admirable man. And yet it never honestly *looks* at Joe Clark for what he really is—a grown-up example of the very troublemakers he hates so much, still unable even in adulthood to doubt his right to do what he wants, when he wants, as he wants. How can he teach when he's unteachable? His values have little to do with learning how to learn.

The Legend of Hell House ★ ★ ★ ½
PG, 94 m., 1973

Pamela Franklin (The Medium), Roddy McDowall (Fisher), Clive Revill (Barrett), Gayle Hunnicutt (Ann Barrett). Directed by John Hough and produced by Albert Fennell and Norman T. Herman. Screenplay by Richard Matheson.

It is, we are told, the Mount Everest of haunted houses. It has defied every attempt to understand or defeat it. Its windows were bricked up against the sun years ago by its evil master, Belasco, who presided over the depraved orgies inside. When the relatives of his guests had the house broken into by police, twenty-seven bodies were found, but never Belasco's. The party was over.

The only previous psychic expedition to probe the house's secrets ended with every one dead except one, Fisher, known to be the most powerful physical medium of his time. Now he is back with a spiritual medium and with a rational scientist, Barrett, who insists all paranormal phenomena have scientific explanations. It sounds good until the door slams shut behind them in Hell House.

The Legend of Hell House manages to be several things at once. It's a supernatural thriller; it's a shocker, with things leaping out of corners and hurling chandeliers; and it's an almost-convincing pseudoscientific study of psychic events.

The last was the trademark of the movie's author, Richard Matheson, who also wrote the book *Hell House* (which I liked more than *The Exorcist*). Matheson labored for years in the elusive territory between straight science fiction and the supernatural horror genre, developing a kind of novel in which vampires, ghouls, and the occult are treated as if they came under ordinary scientific classifications.

There was, for example, the Matheson classic *I Am Legend* (remade somewhat unhappily as *The Omega Man*, with Charlton Heston). In that one, a single normal man held hundreds of vampires (or were they werewolves?) at bay by figuring out the scientific reasons for old medieval antivampire measures like mirrors, crucifixes, and garlic. The Matheson novels of the 1950s and early 1960s anticipated pseudorealistic fantasy novels like *Rosemary's Baby* and *The Exorcist*.

And now here he is again with a tightly wound and really scary story, which has been directed by John Hough with a great deal of sympathy for the novel's spirit. A suitable Belasco House has been found, complete with library, upstairs bedrooms, and a chapel, which seems to be the source of all evil. The screenplay didn't have room (or perhaps couldn't find a visual equivalent?) for the steam room that suddenly filled with malevolent slime, but you can't have everything.

Roddy McDowall, looking like an owlishly haunted Andy Warhol, plays the sole survivor from the last team. Pamela Franklin is the young innocent who believes psychic events are God's manifestation on Earth. And Clive Revill and Gayle Hunnicutt, as husband and wife, move a large and curious machine into the manor.

He believes, you see, that there is no such thing as life after death, and that psychic happenings merely reflect electrical currents emanated by certain gifted persons. Belasco House is nothing but a vast psychic battery which has stored up the energies of all the evil people who lived and died there; his machine will ground the current and leave the house empty of energy. It all sounds promising, until the machine's dials begin to pick up energy emissions on their own . . . .

Less Than Zero ★ ★ ★ ★
R, 100 m., 1987

Andrew McCarthy (Clay), Jami Gertz (Blair), Robert Downey, Jr. (Julian), James Spader (Rip), Tony Bill (Bradford Easton), Nicholas Pryor (Benjamin Wells), Donna Mitchell (Elaine Easton), Michael Bowen (Hop), Sarah Buxton (Markie). Directed by Marek Kanievska and produced by Jon Avnet and Jordan Kerner. Screenplay by Harley Peyton.

George Carlin was once asked how cocaine made you feel, and he answered: "It makes you feel like having some more cocaine." That inescapable fact is at the bottom of *Less Than Zero*, a movie that knows cocaine inside out and paints a portrait of drug addiction that is all the more harrowing because it takes place in the Beverly Hills fast lane, in a world of wealth, sex, glamour, and helpless self-destruction.

The movie is about three very rich kids who graduate from the same high school. How rich? As a graduation present, the father of one of the kids sets him up in the recording industry. The character's name is Julian, and he is played by Robert Downey, Jr., as a slick, smart, charming young man who takes less than a year to lose everything. His best friend in high school was Clay, played by Andrew McCarthy. Clay, who wears a tie even in Southern California, goes off to an Ivy League university, leaving behind his girlfriend, Blair (Jami Gertz). By Thanksgiving, Downey and Gertz are sleeping together and doing cocaine together, and by Christmas, a terrified Gertz is calling McCarthy and begging him to come home and rescue Downey, who is in very big trouble.

The problem is, you cannot rescue someone who is addicted to drugs. You can lecture them, to no point, and plead with them, to no avail, but essentially, an outsider is powerless over someone else's addiction. Downey is clearly out of control and headed for bottom. He has lost the recording studio, spent all his money, made a half-hearted stab at a rehab center, gone back to using, and been banished from his home by his father, who practices tough love and tells him, "You can lead your life any way you want, but stay the hell out of mine."

The first hint of this movie's power comes during a Christmas party scene. McCarthy, back from the East, tries to talk to his old friend and his former girlfriend, but they're stoned, and talk too fast and too loud, almost mechanically, and have tiny attention spans. Later, Gertz begs McCarthy to help Downey—but what can he do? And then the movie's long middle section functions almost as a documentary of the Beverly Hills fast track, of private clubs that open at midnight, of expensive cars and smooth drug dealers and glamorous hangers-on, and the quiet desperation of a society of once-bright, once-attractive, once-promising young people who talk about a lot of things but essentially think only about cocaine.

The movie's three central performances are flawless: by Jami Gertz, as the frightened girl who witnesses the disintegration of her friend; by Andrew McCarthy, as the quiet, almost cold, witness from outside this group; and especially by Robert Downey, Jr., whose acting here is so real, so subtle, and so observant that it's scary.

His life in the film revolves around the will of a fourth character, his drug dealer (James Spader). He owes the dealer $50,000 and has no money and no prospects, and the most frightening thing about his situation is that the Spader character is actually fairly reasonable, as these characters go. "I'm not the problem," Spader tells McCarthy. "Julian is the problem." He has extended much more credit than he would usually permit, out of "friendship," but now Downey is at the end of the line.

The movie's last thirty minutes are like a kick in the gut, as Downey spirals through the ultimate results of his addiction. He appeals to his father, to his friends, and even to his dealer, and the fact is, he gets more help than perhaps he deserves. He makes firm resolutions to stop using, and vague plans to "get back into rehab," and his friends stand by him as much as they can. The movie's outcome reflects, more or less accurately, what awaits most cocaine addicts who do not get clean.

If this description of *Less Than Zero* makes it sound like a downbeat retread of *The Lost Weekend*, that's because I haven't described the movie's visual style. Director Marek Kanievska and cinematographer Ed Lachman have photographed Beverly Hills, Bel Air, and Palm Springs the way they look in high-priced fashion ads and slick TV commercials. The water in the pools is always an azure blue. The homes look like sets. The people look like models. The discos look like music videos. The whole movie looks brilliantly superficial, and so Downey's predicament is all the more poignant: He is surrounded by all of this, he is in it and of it, and he cannot have it. All he wants to have is a good time, but he is trapped in a paradox: Cocaine is the good time that takes itself away.

Lethal Weapon ★ ★ ★ ★
R, 110 m., 1987

Mel Gibson (Martin Riggs), Danny Glover (Roger Murtaugh), Gary Busey (Joshua), Mitchell Ryan (The General), Tom Atkins (Michael Hunsaker), Darlene Love (Trish Murtaugh), Traci Wolfe (Rianne Murtaugh). Directed by Richard Donner and produced by Donner and Joel Silver. Screenplay by Shane Black.

Lethal Weapon is another one of those Bruised Forearm Movies, like *Raiders of the Lost Ark*, a movie where you and your date grab each other's arm every four minutes and you end up black and blue and grinning from ear to ear. It's a buddy movie about two homicide cops who chase a gang of drug dealers all over Southern California, and the plot makes an amazing amount of sense, considering that the action hardly ever stops for it.

The cops are played by Danny Glover, as a homebody who has just celebrated his fiftieth birthday, and Mel Gibson, as a crazed, wild-eyed rebel who has developed a suicidal streak since his wife was killed in a car crash. In the space of less than forty-eight hours, they become partners, share a family dinner, kill several people, survive a shoot-out in the desert, battle with helicopters and machine guns, toss hand grenades, jump off buildings, rescue Glover's kidnapped daughter, drive cars through walls, endure torture by electric shock, have a few beers, and repair the engine on Glover's boat—not in that order.

The movie's so tightly wound up, it's like a rubber band ready to snap. Richard Donner, the director, throws action scenes at us like hardballs, and we don't know when to duck. All of the elements of this movie have been seen many times before—the chases, the explosions, the hostage negotiations—but this movie illustrates a favorite belief of mine, which is that the subject of a movie is much less important than its style. I'm a guy who is bored by shoot-outs and chase scenes. I've seen it all. But this movie thrilled me from beginning to end.

Part of that is because I cared about the characters. Glover has had important roles for several years (in movies as different as *Places in the Heart* and *The Color Purple*), but this movie makes him a star. His job is to supply the movie's center of gravity, while all the nuts and weirdos and victims whirl around him. He's a family man, concerned about those gray hairs he sees in the mirror, not interested in taking unnecessary chances.

Gibson is the perfect counterpoint, with his wild hair, his slob clothing, and his emotional misery. It's a running gag in the movie that Gibson is so suicidal he doesn't care if he lives or dies—and that gives him a definite advantage in showdown situations. That's what happens in a scene where Gibson is up on a rooftop trying to reason with a jumper. I won't spoil the scene; I'll just say the scene ends with one of the few genuinely unexpected surprises in any recent action film.

The supporting cast is strong, and has to be, to stand out in the midst of the mayhem. Gary Busey, slimmed down and bright of eye, makes an appropriately hateful killer. And Traci Wolfe, as Glover's good-looking daughter, is cute when she gets a teen-age crush on Gibson. But most of the attention focuses on Glover and Gibson, and they work easily together, as if they were having fun, their eccentric personal rhythms supplying a counterpoint to the movie's roar of violence.

Now about that matter of style. In a sense, a movie like *Lethal Weapon* isn't about violence at all. It's about movement and timing, the choreography of bodies and weapons in time and space. In lesser movies, the people stand there and shoot at each other and we're bored. In a movie with the energy of this one, we're exhilarated by the sheer freedom of movement; the violence becomes surrealistic and less important than the movie's underlying energy level.

Richard Donner has directed a lot of classy pictures. My favorites are *Inside Moves*, *Ladyhawke*, and the original *Superman*, which is still the best. This time he tops himself.

Lethal Weapon 2 ★ ★ ★ ¹/₂
R, 111 m., 1989

Mel Gibson (Martin Riggs), Danny Glover (Roger Murtaugh), Joe Pesci (Leo Getz), Joss Ackland (Arjen Rudd), Derrick O'Connor (Pieter Vorstedt), Patsy Kensit (Rika Van Den Haas), Darlene Love (Trish Murtaugh) Traci Wolfe (Rianne Murtaugh), Damon Hines (Nick Murtaugh), Ebonbie Smith (Carrie Murtaugh), Steve Kahan (Captain Murphy), Mary Ellen Trainor (Psychiatrist). Directed by Richard Donner and produced by Donner and Joel Silver. Screenplay by Jeffrey Boam.

Lethal Weapon 2 is that rarity, a sequel with most of the same qualities as the original. After anemic retreads like *Ghostbusters 2*, *Star Trek V,* and *The Karate Kid, Part III*, I walked into the movie with a certain dread—but this is a film with the same off-center invention and wild energy as the original.

The heroes once again are a couple of cops who form an odd couple: Riggs (Mel Gibson), who lives in a trailer by the beach and delights in making people think he's crazy, and Murtaugh (Danny Glover), a stolid middle-class family man with retirement plans. In the original *Lethal Weapon*, their relationship was the center of the film, and in the sequel they define it further—it's a balancing act between exasperation and trust.

But sequels do not live by repeating the same scenes and lessons as the films that inspired them. There has to be a new angle—and *Lethal Weapon 2* finds one in the creation of a band of diabolical villains. It's my contention that the James Bond films sink or swim on the quality of their villains, and that's true here, too: These aren't just violent bad guys, but particular characters, well-acted and malevolently conceived.

What Riggs and Murtaugh stumble over is a complex plot, never quite explained, by which South African diplomats are dealing illegally in gold and other contraband. It is unclear exactly what their plan is, but they are ruthless in its execution, led by Joss Ackland as a white-haired ambassador with steel eyes, and Derrick O'Connor as his lantern-jawed hitman.

Riggs and Murtaugh stumble onto their scheme through the help of the movie's most memorable character, a fast-talking pipsqueak named Leo (Joe Pesci). He's an accountant who has figured out a foolproof way to launder vast quantities of illegal drug money: half a billion dollars, he claims at one time. What's better, he's found a way to use the profits to obtain illegal income tax deductions.

"OK, OK, OK, OK," he says, with a wide chipmunk grin. "I like you guys, so I'll tell you how it's done." He's a government witness they're supposed to protect, but instead they drag him into the center of danger. And the movie is filled with invention as it devises clever forms for the danger to take.

There is, for example, the tricky situation Murtaugh finds himself in when it sits on the toilet and discovers that if he stands up, a bomb will explode. And the close call when Riggs's trailer is attacked by helicopter gunships. And the several astonishing chase scenes in the movie, which succeeded in entertaining me even though I am heartily sick of chase scenes in general.

The creation of the Leo Getz character is the movie's masterstroke; instead of recycling scenes in which the two partners fight with each other, *Lethal Weapon 2* provides a third character who can exasperate both men. Pesci, who was brilliant as the younger brother in *Raging Bull*, provides an entirely different kind of character here—ingratiating, slimy, self-deprecating, lovable. He gives us a counterpoint to the violence, and Gibson and Glover both have fun playing off of him.

Lethal Weapon 2 was directed by Richard Donner, who also made the first film and whose credits include the first, and best, *Superman* movie. Unlike a lot of directors specializing in high-tech action comedies, he doesn't seem exhausted or cynical. There's an alertness to his scenes, and a freshness to the dialogue by Jeffrey Boam. This doesn't seem like a sequel, but like a movie in which new discoveries are always possible.

Let's Spend the Night Together
★ ★ ¹/₂
PG, 94 m., 1983

Featuring The Rolling Stones. Directed by Hal Ashby and produced by Ronald L. Schwary.

It all comes down to the difference between a "concert film" and a documentary. *Let's Spend the Night Together* is essentially a concert film—a film recording an "ideal" Rolling Stones concert, put together out of footage shot at several outdoor and indoor Stones concerts. If that's what you want, enjoy this movie. I wanted more. I would have been interested in a film exploring the phenomenon of the Rolling Stones, who bill themselves as the greatest rock 'n' roll band in the world, and are certainly the most durable. I would have liked to know more about the staging of a modern rock concert, which is arguably the most sensually overpowering nonwartime spectacle in human history, and which may have been invented, in form and in its focus on a single charismatic individual, at Hitler's mass rallies. I would have liked to know more about Mick Jagger; how does it feel for an educated, literate, civilized man in his early forties, with a head for figures and a gift for contracts and negotiations, to strut with a codpiece before tens of thousands of screaming, drug-crazed fans?

Let's Spend the Night Together does not answer these questions—nor, to be fair, was it intended to. It is wall-to-wall music. The movie sells well in home video form; it's a cinematic Top Forty with Jagger and the Stones performing many of their best-known hits. But after a certain point it grows monotonous. At the beginning of the film I was caught up in the Stones' waves of sound energy, and fascinated by Jagger's exhilarating, limitless onstage energy. By the end of the film I was simply stunned, and not even "(Can't Get No) Satisfaction" could quite rouse me.

The movie was directed by Hal Ashby, a feature director whose credits include *Shampoo* and *The Last Detail.* It was reportedly photographed with twenty-one cameras, under the direction of cinematographers Caleb Deschanel and Gerald Feil. They've got a lot of good stuff on film, but they haven't broken any new ground. The best rock documentary is still *Woodstock* (1970), and the best concert film is probably Bette Midler's *Divine Madness* (1980). The Stones have been filmed more powerfully before, too, in *Gimme Shelter,* the stunning 1969 documentary of the Stones' Altamont concert, at which a man was killed.

The worst passages in *Let's Spend the Night Together* are the songs in which Ashby and his collaborators try to get seriously symbolic. There is, for example, a montage of images from a suffering world: starving children, a Buddhist monk immolating himself, the skeleton-like bodies of famine victims, decapitated heads of political prisoners, etc. The idea, I guess, is to provide visual counterpoint to the Stones' apocalyptic images. The effect is disgusting; this particular movie has not earned the right to exploit those real images.

The best passages involve Jagger, who is just about the whole show, with the exception of a truncated Keith Richards solo and a strange interlude during which would-be beauty queens invade the stage and dance along to "Honky Tonk Woman." Jagger is, as always, the arrogant hermaphrodite, strutting proudly before his fans and conducting the songs, the band, and the audience with his perfectly timed body movements. There is an exciting moment when he climbs down into the crowd and, carrying a hand-held mike, sings as he is lifted on a surge of security guards from one side of the auditorium to another.

It's fun, but it's about the only time we see the audience in this movie; Ashby apparently made a directorial decision to keep the audience in long-shot, making them into a collective, pulsating mass. But that limits his possibilities for setting up visual rhythms in his editing. In such landmark rock films as *A Hard Day's Night* (1964) and *Woodstock,* the audience provided not only counterpoint but also emotional feedback. *Let's Spend the Night Together* seems to have been pretty closely calculated as just simply the record of a performance, and if that's what you want, that's what you get.

Lianna ★ ★ ★ ½
R, 110 m., 1983

Linda Griffiths (Lianna), Jane Hallaren (Ruth), Jon DeVries (Dick), Jo Henderson (Sandy), John Sayles (Jerry). Directed by John Sayles. Produced by Jeffrey Nelson and Maggie Renzi. Screenplay by Sayles.

Movies are good at showing us people who make great changes in their lives, but not so good at showing us the consequences of those changes. It's easier to present the sudden dramatic revelation than to follow through into all the messy complications in everyday life. John Sayles's *Lianna,* the story of a woman who discovers in her early thirties that she is a lesbian, follows through. Instead of being the simple, dramatic story of a woman who "comes out," it is the complex, interesting story of what happens then.

The woman is named Lianna (Linda Griffiths). When she was an undergraduate, she fell in love with her teacher—a pattern she is about to repeat. Her husband is a film professor and the father of their two small children. He tends to treat her like one of the children, lecturing to the general audience at the dinner table as if his wife was about as bright as the kids. He is a boor. Lianna, unhappy, tries to change her life. She signs up for a night class in child psychology, and finds herself attracted to the professor, a woman who has a quick sense of humor and really seems to care about her students.

The woman, Ruth (Jane Hallaren), has been a lesbian for years, and is attracted to Lianna. But it is Lianna who makes the first, subtle moves, staying after class for a moment's chat, just as perhaps she did years ago with her husband. The two women become lovers fairly quickly, and although there are love scenes, the movie is not really about that side of their relationship. If *Personal Best* was an exploration of the physical aspects of lesbianism, *Lianna* explores the consequences. They are many. Lianna's husband throws her out and tries to block access to their children. Lianna's oldest friend, Sandy, is suddenly cold and distant. Ruth, a little surprised at the intensity of the affair, confesses that she has a long-standing relationship with another woman in another city. Lianna rents a room off-campus and begins a lifestyle that is free, yes, but also lonely and filled with guilt.

As *Lianna* looks into the large and small things that have changed in the life of its heroine, we become increasingly aware of the perception of the filmmaker, John Sayles, who wrote, directed, and edited. In this movie and his previous work, *Return of the Secaucus Seven,* he seems in touch with the kinds of changes that some Americans in their thirties are going through; his movies are cinematic versions of Gail Sheehey's *Passages.* He is attentive to what is said, what is worn, what attitudes are taken, what goes unsaid—and he is particularly interested, in both movies, in the ways that a generation raised to "do your own thing" now tries to decide when personal freedom ends and responsibility begins.

It's in that particular area that *Lianna* is a little shaky. It never quite dealt, I thought, with the issue of Lianna's two children. Although Lianna's lover is a child psychologist and Lianna herself seems to be a responsible and loving mother as the film opens, the kids are sort of left hanging. There are a couple of brief scenes with the kids, but no real resolution of the questions that a newly gay mother would have to answer. (Since the husband is presented as such a twerp, this absence of follow-through is doubly bothering.) Still, in many other scenes, including two in which Lianna has a subtly class-conscious affair with a woman in the armed services, *Lianna* is an intelligent, perceptive movie. And the performances, especially by Griffiths and Hallaren, are so specific that we're never looking at "lesbians"—only at people.

Licence to Kill ★ ★ ★ ½
PG-13, 135 m., 1989

Timothy Dalton (James Bond), Carey Lowell (Pam Bouvier), Robert Davi (Franz Sanchez), Talisa Soto (Lupe Lamora), Anthony Zerbe (Milton Krest), Frank McRae (Sharkey), Everett McGill (Killifer), Wayne Newton (Professor Joe Butcher), Benicio Del Toro (Dario), Anthony Starke (Truman-Lodge). Directed by John Glen and produced by Albert R. Broccoli and Michael G. Wilson. Screenplay by Wilson and Richard Maibaum.

The James Bond movies have by now taken on the discipline of a sonnet or a kabuki drama: Every film follows the same story outline so rigidly that we can predict almost to the minute such obligatory developments as (1) the introduction of the villain's specialized hit man; (2) the long shot which establishes the villain's incredibly luxurious secret hideout; (3) the villain's fatal invitation to Bond to spend the night; (4) the moment when the villain's mistress falls for Bond; (5) the series of explosions destroying the secret fortress; and (6) the final spectacular stunt sequence.

Connoisseurs evaluate the elements in a Bond picture as if they were movements in a symphony, or courses in a meal. There are few surprises, and the changes are evolutionary, so that the latest Bond picture is recognizable as a successor to the first, *Dr. No*, in 1962. Within this framework of tradition, *Licence to Kill* nevertheless manages to spring some interesting surprises. One is that the Bond character, as played now for the second time by Timothy Dalton, has become less of a British icon and more of an international action hero. The second is that the tempo has been picked up, possibly in response to the escalating pace of the Rambo and Indiana Jones movies. The third is that the villain has fairly modest aims for a change: He doesn't want to rule the world; he only wants to be a cocaine billionaire.

I've grown uneasy lately about the fashion of portraying drug smugglers in glamorous lifestyles; they're viewed with some of the same glamour as gangsters were in films of the 1930s. Sure they die in the end, but they have a lot of fun in the meantime. In *Licence to Kill*, however, the use of a drug kingpin named Sanchez (Robert Davi) and his

henchmen (Anthony Zerbe, Frank McRae) is apparently part of an attempt to update the whole series and make it feel more contemporary.

There are still, of course, the obligatory scenes. The film still begins with a sensationally unbelievable stunt sequence (Bond and friend lasso plane in midair, then parachute to a wedding ceremony). But then the action switches to the more-or-less recognizable modern world in and around Key West, Florida, where the British agent finds himself involved in an operation to capture Sanchez and cut his pipeline of cocaine.

Like all Bond villains, Sanchez has unlimited resources and a beautiful mistress. His operation uses an underwater shark-nabbing company as its cover, and keeps a few sharks on hand just so they can dine on federal agents. After Bond's friend, Felix Leiter, is mistreated by the bad guys, 007 begins a savage personal vendetta against Sanchez, which involves elaborate and violent stunt sequences in the air, on land, and underwater.

He is aided in his campaign by the beautiful Pam Bouvier (Carey Lowell), introduced as "Miss Kennedy, my executive secretary," and saved more than once by Sanchez's beautiful mistress, Lupe Lamora (Talisa Soto). Both women are as beautiful as the historical Bond standard, but more modern—more competent, intelligent, and capable, and not simply sex objects. This is no doubt part of the plan, announced before Dalton's first Bond picture, to de-emphasize the character's promiscuous sex life. Compared to his previous films, 007 is practically chaste this time.

My favorite moments in all the Bond pictures involve The Fallacy of the Talking Killer, in which the villain has Bond clearly in his power, and then, instead of killing him instantly, makes the mistake of talking just long enough for Bond to gather his wits and make a plan. The fallacy saves Bond's life two or three times in this movie—especially once when all that Davi has to do is slice his neck.

Licence to Kill ends, as all the Bond films do, with an extended chase and stunt sequence. This one involves some truly amazing stunt work, as three giant gasoline trucks speed down a twisting mountain road, while a helicopter and a light aircraft also join in the chase. There were moments when I was straining to spot the trickery, as a big semi rig spun along tilted to one side to miss a mis-

sile aimed by the bad guys. But the stunts all look convincing, and the effect of the closing sequence is exhilarating.

On the basis of this second performance as Bond, Timothy Dalton can have the role as long as he enjoys it. He makes an effective Bond—lacking Sean Connery's grace and humor and Roger Moore's suave self-mockery, but with a lean tension and a toughness that is possibly more contemporary. The major difference between Dalton and the earlier Bonds is that he seems to prefer action to sex. But then so do movie audiences, these days. *Licence to Kill* is one of the best of the recent Bonds.

Light of Day ★ ★ ★ ½
PG-13, 107 m., 1987

Michael J. Fox (Joe Rasnick), Gena Rowlands (Jeanette Rasnick), Joan Jett (Patti Rasnick), Jason Miller (Ben Rasnick), Michael McKean (Bu Montgomery), Thomas G. Waites (Smittie), Cherry Jones (Cindy). Directed by Paul Schrader and produced by Rob Cohen and Keith Barish. Screenplay by Schrader.

Early in *Light of Day*, a brother and sister go to their mother's birthday dinner at their parents' home. The atmosphere is charged with tension. At the table, the father sits silently in the calm before the storm. The mother begins to ask the blessing, and then her prayer turns into something more specific: She begins to ask God to forgive her daughter.

All hell breaks loose. The daughter runs from the table, and the brother follows her out of the house, trying to make peace. We can see that the two women are bitter enemies, although the mother probably would not see it that way; she uses prayer as a weapon, just as much as her daughter uses alienation and aggression.

This scene sets up the emotional conflict in *Light of Day*, which shows a family tearing itself apart despite the best efforts of the son, who wants to hold things together at almost any cost. This is a family drama, all right—but not one of those neat docudramas in which every character comes attached to a fashionable problem, and all the problems are solved in the same happy ending. The family in *Light of Day* is more like your average everyday unhappy family, in which the biggest problem is that some of the members quite simply hate each other.

Writer-director Paul Schrader tells his

story against a working-class background in Cleveland. The parents (Gena Rowlands and Jason Miller) have worked hard for their share of suburban respectability. The children (Michael J. Fox and Joan Jett) play every night in a rock band, and although Fox has a daytime job in a factory, Jett's life is on hold until the sun goes down; she says rock 'n' roll is the most important thing in the world, and she means it.

Because she means it, life is not very healthy for her little boy, a son born out of wedlock by a father she refuses to name. It is this child that has driven the wedge between mother and daughter. And soon it becomes the focus of her relationship with her brother. When their band goes on a tour—sometimes playing for no more than a few bucks and free drinks—the child is left in cheap motel rooms, and Fox doesn't approve of that. Jett, filled with anger and defiance, won't listen to his objections, and Fox stands by helplessly, trying to be all things to all people.

His family is clearly a matriarchy, a battleground between two strong women. The father, played by Miller as a sensitive wimp, has long since given up, and now Fox is trying to play the peacemaker, the responsible one, almost the parent. Fox obviously idolizes his sister (and, in a way, his mother), and so there are painful moments, very well acted, in which he hurts because he cannot help these people he loves.

The movie is subtle in its construction. Schrader doesn't telegraph his ending in the first half-hour, and indeed the movie's one fault is that it sometimes seems without a clear direction. At first the film seems to be a blue-collar story. Then a family drama. Then a rock 'n' roll movie. But then we see that the rock band is going nowhere, and the center of the story turns back to the family, after the mother becomes seriously ill. And it's the illness that provides the payoff, in strong and painful bedside scenes between Gena Rowlands, Fox, and Jett.

This mother may be sick, but she knows exactly what she's doing, and Rowlands's acting is powerfully, heartbreakingly effective. The mother uses love, truth, insight, and a measure of cynical calculation in an attempt to control what will happen to her family if she dies. She has always been a controller, and the possibility of death only inspires her to new efforts.

Light of Day is told like a short story by Henry James or Raymond Carver, in which the last few moments and the final words

throw everything else into focus. And there is so much pain and anger in the film's ending that we can speculate that this is the real material that Schrader only touched on in *Hardcore*, his 1979 film about a runaway daughter's rebellion against her strict fundamentalist family.

Light of Day arrived with an advance reputation as a rock 'n' roll film, and yet Joan Jett, the movie's one certified rocker, gives the most surprisingly good performance. In the bedside scene with Rowlands, she is acting in the big leagues; Rowlands is inspired and Jett rises to the same inspiration, and there's a rare, powerful chemistry. Fox, playing a weak, conciliatory character, is the right balance for these two strong women, and Miller, kept in the background in most of his scenes, has one searching speech in which he tries to explain what has happened to his family.

Schrader has been one of the most consistently interesting writers and directors of the last decade. Try to find the thread connecting his screenplays, such as *Taxi Driver* and *Raging Bull*, and his films as a director, such as *Blue Collar*, *Hardcore*, *American Gigolo*, *Cat People*, and *Mishima*, and what you come up with are wildly different characters with one thing in common: Their pasts keep them imprisoned, and shut them off from happiness in the present. Here is his most direct and painful statement of that theme.

Listen Up: The Lives of Quincy Jones
★ ★ ★ ½
PG-13, 111 m., 1990
(See related Film Clip, p. 708.)

With Quincy Jones and appearances by Ray Charles, Miles Davis, Billy Eckstine, Ella Fitzgerald, Herbie Hancock, Michael Jackson, Frank Sinatra, and Sarah Vaughan. Directed by Ellen Weissbrod and produced by Courtney Sale Ross.

There is a moment in *Listen Up: The Lives of Quincy Jones* where he pays a visit to the house on Chicago's South Side where he spent his earliest years. He remembers a lot of pain from those days, but it isn't connected to specific images until he sees and touches the scenes of his childhood. The texture of a hot-air register feels familiar to his hand, and suddenly memories come rushing back from more than fifty years earlier, and he walks through the house in a cloud of associations.

He did not spend a happy time here. His mother was mentally ill, and he remembers angers and rages and, most of all, the absence of a mother's love. On one of his birthdays, she threw his cake off the back porch. She was eventually sent away for care, and the family moved to Seattle—from an all-black to an all-white environment—and it was there that Jones picked up his first musical instrument, and was revealed as such a natural musician that he was playing with big bands when he was only fifteen.

The illness of Jones's mother was treatable ("It turned out what she really needed was only a lot of Vitamin B," he told me sadly in an interview), and eventually mother and family were reconciled. The past has been forgiven, but the scars are still there, and we learn in *Listen Up* of a man who feels his loss of a mother's love when he was young has made it all but impossible for him to trust women and have long-term relationships with them.

The yearning that he feels—a yearning from childhood that can never be answered, because the child itself no longer exists—has expressed itself in many ways in his life: in an outpouring of original songs. In musical scores for the movies, after Richard Brooks hired him for *In Cold Blood* and Jones became the first black composer to score for mainstream films. In his arrangements and the albums he has produced for musicians as varied as Ella Fitzgerald, Michael Jackson, Frank Sinatra, and Barbra Streisand. In thirty Grammy awards. In seven Oscar nominations. In his work as executive producer of *The Color Purple*.

Yet we learn in this film that the private Quincy Jones has not always been as happy as his smiling public image on talk shows and the Grammys. *Listen Up* is an extraordinarily frank story of a life that has also contained broken marriages, children who harbor some resentments, and health problems, including two harrowing brain surgeries and a nervous breakdown. The odds against both surgeries were one hundred to one, Jones mentions in the film, and the scar of one of them is still slightly visible above his right temple.

Listen Up is the stronger because of its honesty. This isn't a once-over-lightly PR job, but a movie about the peaks and valleys of a man's life. Director Ellen Weissbrod and producer Courtney Sale Ross have looked unblinkingly at the sad as well as the happy times, and some of the most poignant moments in the movie come as Jolie Jones, Quincy's oldest daughter, talks quietly about her father.

There are many other witnesses as well. People who never talk for documentaries talk for this one: Frank Sinatra, Ray Charles, the shy Michael Jackson (whose interview takes place partly in darkness). Because the filmmakers wanted to avoid the usual captions and subtitles of documentaries, each subject is asked to identify himself, and this leads to some humor, as when Ray Charles smiles that it's been a long time since anybody had to ask who he was.

The movie is constructed in an unusual kaleidoscopic way. Instead of moving ponderously from one subject to another, and following chronological order, the filmmakers organize their material more like a jazz composition. The interview subjects are like soloists improvising on a theme and, occasionally, stepping in to comment on someone else's observations. The result is not an orderly, routine documentary, but an original work that may be a little off-putting at first, but grows on you. By the end of this film, I felt I knew Quincy Jones better than I had ever expected to, and that now that I knew the bad things, I admired the good things even more.

Little Big Man ★ ★ ★
PG, 157 m., 1971

Dustin Hoffman (Jack Crabb), Faye Dunaway (Mrs. Pendrake), Martin Balsam (Merriweather), Richard Mulligan (General Custer), Chief Dan George (Old Lodge Skins), Jeff Corey (Wild Bill Hickok). Directed by Arthur Penn and produced by Stuart Millar. Screenplay by Calder Willingham.

Arthur Penn's *Little Big Man* is an endlessly entertaining attempt to spin an epic in the form of a yarn. It mostly works. When it doesn't—when there's a failure of tone or an overdrawn caricature—it regroups cheerfully and plunges ahead. We're disposed to go along; all good storytellers tell stretchers once in a while, and circle back to be sure we got the good p.. is.

It is the very folksiness of Penn's film that makes it, finally, such a perceptive and important statement about Indians, the West, and the American dream. There's no stridency, no preaching, no deep-voiced narrators making sure we got the point of the last massacre. All the events happened long

long ago, and they're related by a 121-year-old man who just wants to pass the story along. The yarn is the most flexible of story forms. Its teller can pause to repeat a point; he can hurry ahead ten years; he can forget an entire epoch in remembering the legend of a single man. He doesn't capture the history of a time, but its flavor. *Little Big Man* gives us the flavor of the Cheyenne nation before white men brought uncivilization to the West. Its hero, played by Dustin Hoffman, is no hero at all but merely a survivor.

Hoffman, or Little Big Man, gets around pretty well. He touches all the bases of the Western myth. He was brought West as a settler, raised as a Cheyenne, tried his hand at gunfighting and medicine shows, scouted for the cavalry, experimented with the hermit life, was married twice, survived Custer's Last Stand, and sat at the foot of an old man named Old Lodge Skins, who instructed him in the Cheyenne view of creation.

Old Lodge Skins, played by Chief Dan George with such serenity and conviction that an Academy Award was mentioned, doesn't preach the Cheyenne philosophy. It is part of him. It's all the more a part of him because Penn has allowed the Indians in the film to speak ordinary, idiomatic English. Most movie Indians have had to express themselves with an "um" at the end of every other word: "Swap-um wampum plenty soon," etc. The Indians in *Little Big Man* have dialogue reflecting the idiomatic richness of Indian tongues; when Old Lodge Skins simply refers to Cheyennes as "the Human Beings," the phrase is literal and meaningful and we don't laugh.

Despite Old Lodge Skins, however, Little Big Man doesn't make it as an Indian, or as a white man, either, or as anything else he tries. He looks, listens, remembers, and survives, which is his function. The protagonists in the film are two ideas of civilization: the Indian's and the white man's. Custer stages his bloody massacres and is massacred in turn, and we know that the Indians will eventually be destroyed as an organic community and shunted off to reservations. But the film's movement is circular, and so is its belief about Indians.

Penn has adopted the yarn form for a reason. All the characters who appear in the early stages of the film come back in the later stages, fulfilled. The preacher's wife returns as a prostitute. The medicine-quack, already lacking an arm, loses a leg (physician, heal

thyself). Wild Bill Hickok decays from a has-been to a freak show attraction. Custer fades from glory to madness. Only Old Lodge Skins makes it through to the end not merely intact, but improved.

His survival is reflected in the film's structure. Most films, especially ones with violence, have their climax at the end. Penn puts his near the center; it is Custer's massacre of an Indian village, and Little Big Man sees his Indian wife killed and his baby's head blown off. Penn can control violence as well as any American director (remember *Bonnie and Clyde* and *The Left Handed Gun*). He does here. The final massacre of Custer and his men is deliberately muted, so it doesn't distract from Old Lodge Skins's "death" scene.

But Custer stays dead, and Old Lodge Skins doesn't quite die ("I was afraid it would turn out this way"). So he leaves the place of death and invites Little Big Man home to have something to eat. Custer's civilization will eventually win, but Old Lodge Skins's will prevail. William Faulkner observed in his Nobel Prize speech that man will probably endure—but will he prevail? It's probably no accident that we don't smile when Old Lodge Skins explains the difference between Custer and the Human Beings.

Little Dorrit ★ ★ ★ ★
G, 357 m., 1988

Alec Guinness (William Dorrit), Sarah Pickering (Little Dorrit), Cyril Cusack (Frederick Dorrit), Amelda Brown (Fanny), Derek Jacobi (Arthur Clennam), Joan Greenwood (Mrs. Clennam), Roshan Seth (Mr. Pancks). Directed by Christine Edzard and produced by John Brabourne and Richard Goodwin. Screenplay by Edzard based on the novel by Charles Dickens.

I turned on the TV late one night, just in time to catch the closing moments of Truffaut's *Fahrenheit 451*. You remember the scene. In a world where the printed word has been forbidden, a little colony of book-lovers lives by the side of a lake in the woods. Each one has dedicated his life to memorizing the contents of one book. They walk slowly back and forth on paths through the snow, reciting the words over and over, and their voices form a litany of familiar passages.

Little Dorrit is like a film made in the same spirit. It is a six-hour epic, with 242 speaking roles, and yet it was crafted almost by hand.

The director, Christine Edzard, and the coproducer, her husband Richard Goodwin, live and work in a converted warehouse in London's dockland. When they are not making films, they manufacture dollhouses. They built the sets for this film inside their warehouse, they sewed all of the costumes on premises, they used their dollhouse skills to build miniature models which are combined with special effects to create a backdrop of Victorian London. And to their studio by the side of the Thames, they lured such actors as Alec Guinness, Derek Jacobi, Cyril Cusack, and Joan Greenwood to appear in a film that was made mostly out of the love of Charles Dickens.

I myself have spent some time in the company of Dickens. I read *Nicholas Nickleby* not long ago, and then *Our Mutual Friend*, and now here is this six-hour film version of *Little Dorrit*, which is so filled with characters, so rich in incident, that it has the expansive, luxurious feel of a Victorian novel. Dickens created worlds large enough that you could move around in them. He did not confine himself to the narrow focus of a few neurotic characters and their shell-shocked egos; he created worlds, in the closing words of *Little Dorrit*, where "the noisy and the eager, and the arrogant and the froward and the vain, fretted, and chafed, and made their usual uproar."

Little Dorrit opens with the information that the story will be told in two parts, the first through the eyes of Arthur Clennam, the second through the eyes of Little Dorrit. The two parts of the film contain many of the same scenes, seen from different points of view and remembered differently, so that half a line of throwaway dialogue in the first version may turn out, in the second version, to have been absolutely crucial. The use of two different points of view is not simply a conceit of the filmmakers, but creates a real romantic tension, because it is clear from the outset that Clennam and Little Dorrit are in love with each other—and neither one has any way of admitting that fact.

The film opens in Marshalsea Prison, where the heroine's father, William Dorrit (Alec Guinness) has been confined for twenty years for nonpayment of debt. Although her older sister despises the debtor's prison, Dorrit (Sarah Pickering) has grown to love it, as the only home she has ever known. On its stairs she received her education—learned to read and write, learned her English history in the form of stories told of

kings and queens. She is not too proud to be poor.

Near the beginning of the film, Dorrit goes to work in an old, gloomy house occupied by the grasping Mrs. Clennam (Joan Greenwood), who lives there with Flintwinch, her bitter steward (Max Wall). It is there that Dorrit first lays eyes on the old lady's son, Arthur (Derek Jacobi), who has plugged away honorably in life without getting much of anywhere. And it is there that Dorrit discovers the clue to an ancient inheritance that the mother is determined to keep from her son.

Arthur's first glimpse of Dorrit is only momentary. But he wants to know who that young girl was. He wants to know in a tentative, almost frightened voice that lets us know, immediately, that he has fallen irrevocably into love with her. But there are great barriers, of course. One of them is the difference in their ages—although that was not so big a problem in Victorian times, when poor young ladies were often married off for reasons of money rather than love. A greater problem is Dorrit's self-image. Since her father, who she dearly loves, lives in a debtor's prison, her place is at his side. The third problem, of course, is that Arthur and Dorrit can barely endure to be in the same room together, because they love each other so much and cannot admit it.

I saw *Little Dorrit* all in the same day. I think that is a good way to see it, although many people will want to split it into two different evenings. Very long films can create a life of their own. We lose our moorings. We don't know exactly where we stand within the narrative, and so we can't guess what will happen next. People appear and reappear, grow older and die, and we accept the rhythm of the story rather than requiring it to be speeded up.

This kind of timing imparts tremendous weight to the love story. During the course of the film, we ourselves come to love Little Dorrit and Arthur Clennam (who is a good man and a very lonely one). We see all their difficulties. We know all of their fears. We identify with all of their hesitations. When they are finally able to bring themselves to admit that they are in love, it is a joyous moment. And when old Dorrit comes to the time when he must die, Alec Guinness plays the scene with the kind of infinitely muted pathos that has you wiping your eyes even as you're admiring his acting craft.

Many good novels, it is said, begin with a

funeral and end with a wedding. *Little Dorrit* more or less travels that route, with another funeral at the end. It is never simply a love story, and it is not structured melodramatically. It is about the accumulation of incident. We are told that old Dorrit, the Guinness character, lives in the prison for twenty years. We begin to feel those years, as he sits in his chair by the window and we inventory the pathetically short list of his possessions. We see the hopelessness and waste of the Victorian debtor system, which Dickens helped to reform with novels such as this. But we also see the hope that could exist in a city where people lived cheek by jowl, rich by poor, everyone in sight of the street.

The Little Mermaid ★ ★ ★ ★
G, 82 m., 1989

With the voices of: Jodi Benson (Ariel), Kenneth Mars (Triton), Pat Carroll (Ursula), Buddy Hackett (Scuttle), Samuel E. Wright (Sebastian), Rene Auberjonois (Louis), Christopher Daniel Barnes (Eric), Jason Marin (Flounder), Edie McClurg (Carlotta), Ben Wright (Grimsby), Will Ryan (Seahorse). Directed by John Musker and Ron Clements and produced by Howard Ashman and Musker. Screenplay by Musker and Clements.

Walt Disney's *The Little Mermaid* is a jolly and inventive animated fantasy—a movie that's so creative and so much fun it deserves comparison with the best Disney work of the past. It's based on the Hans Christian Andersen tale about a mermaid who falls in love with a prince, but the Disney animators have added a gallery of new supporting characters, including an octopus named Ursula who is their most satisfying villainess since the witch in *Snow White*.

Watching *The Little Mermaid*, I began to feel that the magic of animation had been restored to us. After the early years of Walt Disney's pathfinding feature-length cartoons, we entered into a long dark age in which frame-by-frame animation was too expensive, and even the great Disney animation team began using shortcuts. Now computers have taken the busywork out of the high-priced hands of humans, who are free to realize even the most elaborate flights of imagination. And that's certainly what they do in this film.

The movie opens far beneath the sea, where the god Triton rules over his underwater kingdom. All obey his commands—except for his daughter, Ariel, a mermaid who dreams of far-off lands. One day Ariel makes a forbidden visit to the surface of the sea, and there she sees a human for the first time—a handsome young prince. She saves him from drowning, but he remembers nothing about the experience except for her voice, which he falls in love with. Triton is angry at Ariel's disobedience, but she can think of nothing but the prince, and eventually she strikes an unwise bargain with the evil Ursula, an octopus who can disguise herself in many different forms. Ursula will take away Ariel's tail and give her human legs so she can follow the prince onto the land—but in exchange Ariel must give up her haunting singing voice, and if the prince doesn't kiss her within three days, she will become Ursula's slave.

Two key elements in the storytelling make *The Little Mermaid* stand apart from lesser recent animated work. One is that Ariel is a fully realized female character who thinks and acts independently, even rebelliously, instead of hanging around passively while the fates decide her destiny. Because she's smart and thinks for herself, we have sympathy for her scheming. The second element involves the plot itself: It's tricky and clever, and involves some suspense as Ariel loses her voice and very nearly loses her prince to the diabolical Ursula (who assumes the form of a *femme fatale* and hijacks Ariel's beautiful voice).

As the plot thickens and the melodrama unwinds, the animators introduce a gallery of new characters who are instantly engaging. Ariel is accompanied most places, for example, by Sebastian, a crab with extraordinary wisdom, by Flounder, a fish who cannot always be counted upon, and by Scuttle, a busybody sea gull who looks and sounds a good deal like Buddy Hackett. They provide comic relief, especially in a sequence that mixes comedy and danger in the best Disney tradition, as Sebastian finds himself captured by a French chef who attempts to cook and serve the little blighter.

What's best about *The Little Mermaid* is the visual invention with which the adventures are drawn. There is a lightness and a freedom about the setting—from Triton's underwater throne room to storms at sea and Ursula's garden of captured souls (they look a little like the tourists buried in Farmer Vincent's backyard in *Motel Hell*). The colors are bright, the water sparkles with reflected light, and there is a sense that not a single frame has been compromised because of the cost of animation.

The songs are good, too. *The Little Mermaid* contains some of the best Disney music since the glory days. My favorite song is a laid-back reggae number named *Under the Sea*, sung by Samuel E. Wright in such a splendid blend of animation and music that I recommend it to the cable music channels. The movie was written and directed by John Musker and Ron Clements, who made the entertaining *The Great Mouse Detective* (1986), and the songs are by Alan Menken and the coproducer, Howard Ashman, who did *Little Shop of Horrors*.

Something seems to have broken free inside all of these men, and the animating directors they worked with: Here at last, once again, is the kind of liberating, original, joyful Disney animation that we remember from *Snow White*, *Pinocchio*, and the other first-generation classics. There has been a notion in recent years that animated films are only for kids. But why? The artistry of animation has a clarity and a force that can appeal to everyone, if only it isn't shackled to a dim-witted story. *The Little Mermaid* has music and laughter and visual delight for everyone.

Little Vera ★ ★ ★
R, 109 m., 1989

Natalya Negoda (Vera), Andrei Sokolov (Sergei), Ludmila Zaitzeva (Mother), Andrei Fomin (Andrei), Alexander Negreba (Viktor), Yuri Nazarov (Father), Alexandra Tabakova (Lena), Alexandra Linov (Mikhail). Directed by Vasily Pichul and produced by Gorky Film Studios. Screenplay by Maria Khmelik.

Little Vera comes advertised as the first Soviet film to deal frankly with youth rebellion, discontent with the system, and sex. Its star, Natalya Negoda, has gained a measure of fame by being the first Russian actress to appear nude in a fairly explicit sex scene. To help launch the film in America, she posed nude for *Playboy* and told her story to *People* magazine. The strangest thing about this process is that it has made a truly revolutionary Soviet film look like another one of those "one summer of happiness" sex romps from Scandinavia.

The strategy of selling a foreign film on its sexual content is tried and true, but *Little Vera* is not a sexy film, and its star is not the new Bardot or Loren. The sex in *Little Vera* is sweaty and passionate but not erotic, and the film's real fascination comes from its portrait of everyday life in the Soviet Union—life that contains few surprises, but has never before been shown with such frankness and honesty in a Russian film.

The film takes place in a provincial city where Vera, a restless teen-ager, lives in a cramped three-room apartment with her alcoholic father and her thoroughly disillusioned mother. A brother has moved to Moscow. Life in the family is a drab routine: The self-pitying, unemployed father gets up in the morning and starts to drink, and the mother and daughter plan their days around his rages and remorses. Not surprisingly, Vera seeks to escape from this life, and she leaves the apartment with relief, dressed in a miniskirt, to hang out with a group of nonconformist teen-agers who like to listen to rock 'n' roll and bait the authorities.

Among the scenes in *Little Vera* that we have not seen in a Soviet movie before is one where policemen with guard dogs break up a meeting of teen-agers. The film is frankly on the side of youth and against authority, and the cops are seen as repressive agents of a humorless system. Vera herself finds what cheer she can in the arms of Sergei, whom she has met at a dance. He is an "intellectual," a nonconformist, but it is hard for him to express his free spirit when he must move into Vera's flat with her warring parents. (The housing shortage in the USSR is actually one of the film's most important themes; none of the characters can count on a moment's privacy.)

Vera and Sergei share a few moments of happiness, including one ironic interlude on the beach where they pause in their lovemaking to discuss their goals, and Vera says: "In our country, we have but one goal—communism." This line, in all its sarcasm, has reportedly become as famous in the Soviet Union as "Plastics, Benjamin, plastics!" became after the release of *The Graduate* in this country.

Life in the cramped apartment becomes impossible. The drunken father fights with Sergei, who moves out, and Vera attempts suicide. Her brother, visiting from Moscow, screams in anguish over his impossible family situation, but what the film makes clear is that much of the unhappiness comes from a social system which has given people no clear tasks, few areas to exercise personal ambition, cramped living quarters, no privacy, and too much bootleg booze.

The irony is that *Little Vera* is being sold as a sex film. Eroticism in Soviet films reminds me of Dr. Johnson's famous line about a dog standing on its hind legs: "It is not done well, but one is surprised to find it done at all." What this film does express, strongly and clearly, is a deep discontent among Russians who have lived in an incompetently managed society for too long. The angers in this film are the same ones that have produced Mikhail Gorbachev. For an American, *Little Vera* confirms what we already knew: Life for the poor, the unemployed, and the alcoholic is as bad in Russia as it is here.

The Living Daylights ★ ★
PG, 130 m., 1987

Timothy Dalton (James Bond), Maryam d'Abo (Kara), Joe Don Baker (Whitaker), Art Malik (Kamran Shah), Jeroen Krabbe (Koskov), John Rhys-Davies (Pushkin). Directed by John Glen and produced by Albert R. Broccoli. Screenplay by Richard Maibaum and Michael G. Wilson.

The raw materials of the James Bond films are so familiar by now that the series can be revived only through an injection of humor. That is, unfortunately, the one area in which the new Bond, Timothy Dalton, seems to be deficient. He's a strong actor, he holds the screen well, he's good in the serious scenes, but he never quite seems to understand that it's all a joke.

The correct tone for the Bond films was established right at the start, with Sean Connery's quizzical eyebrows and sardonic smile. He understood that the Bond character was so preposterous that only lightheartedness could save him. The moment Bond began to act like a real man in a real world, all was lost. Roger Moore understood that, too, but I'm not sure Dalton does.

Dalton is rugged, dark, and saturnine, and speaks with a cool authority. We can halfway believe him in some of his scenes. And that's a problem, because the scenes are intended to be preposterous. The best Bond movies always seem to be putting us on, to be supplying the most implausible and dangerous stunts in order to assure us they can't possibly be real. But in *The Living Daylights*, there is a scene where Bond and his girlfriend escape danger by sliding down a snow-

covered mountain in a cello case, and damned if Dalton doesn't look as if he thinks it's just barely possible.

The plot is the usual grab-bag of recent headlines and exotic locales. Bond, who is assigned to help a renegade Russian general defect to the West, stumbles across a plot involving a crooked American arms dealer, the war in Afghanistan, and a plan to smuggle a half-billion dollars worth of opium. The story takes Bond from London to Prague, from mountains to deserts, from a chase down the slopes of Gibraltar, to a fight that takes place while Bond and his enemy are hanging out of an airplane. The usual stuff.

One thing that isn't usual in this movie is Bond's sex life. No doubt because of the AIDS epidemic, Bond is not his usual promiscuous self, and he goes to bed with only one, perhaps two, women in this whole film (it depends on whether you count the title sequence, where he parachutes onto the boat of a woman in a bikini). This sort of personal restraint is admirable, coming from Bond, but given his past sexual history surely it is the woman, not Bond, who is at risk.

The key female character is Kara (Maryam d'Abo), the Czech cellist, who gets involved in the plot with the Russian general, tries to work against Bond, and eventually falls in love with him. As the only "Bond girl" in the movie, d'Abo has her assignment cut out for her, and unfortunately she's not equal to it. She doesn't have the charisma or the mystique to hold the screen with Bond (or Dalton) and is the least interesting love interest in any Bond film.

There's another problem. The Bond films succeed or fail on the basis of their villains, and Joe Don Baker, as the arms-dealing Whitaker, is not one of the great Bond villains. He's a kooky, phony general who plays with toy soldiers and never seems truly diabolical. Without a great Bond girl, a great villain, or a hero with a sense of humor, *The Living Daylights* belongs somewhere on the lower rungs of the Bond ladder. But there are some nice stunts.

Local Hero ★ ★ ★ ★
PG, 112 m., 1983

Burt Lancaster (Happer), Peter Riegert (Mac), Peter Capaldi (Danny), Fulton McKay (Ben), Denis Lawson (Urquhart). Directed by Bill Forsyth and produced by David Puttnam. Screenplay by Forsyth.

Here is a small film to treasure; a loving, funny, understated portrait of a small Scottish town and its encounter with a giant oil company. The town is tucked away in a sparkling little bay, and is so small that everybody is well aware of everybody else's foibles. The oil company is run by an eccentric billionaire (Burt Lancaster) who would really rather have a comet named after him than own all the oil in the world. And what could have been a standard plot about conglomerates and ecology, etc., turns instead into a wicked study of human nature.

The movie opens in Houston, but quickly moves to the fishing village of Ferness. The oil company assigns an earnest young American (Peter Riegert) and a whimsical Scot (Peter Capaldi) to go to Ferness, and buy it up, lock, stock, and beachline, for a North Sea oil-refining complex. This is a simpler job than it appears, since a lot of the locals are all too willing to soak the oil company for its millions of dollars, sell the beach, and go in search of the bright lights of Edinburgh. But there are complications. One of them is old Ben, the cheerful philosopher who lives in a shack on the beach. It turns out that the beach has been the legal property of Ben's family for four centuries, ever since an ancestor did a favor for the king. And Ben doesn't want to sell: "Who'd look after the beach then? It would go to pieces in a short matter of time."

The local negotiations are handled by the innkeeper, Urquhart (Denis Lawson). He also is the accountant, and sort of the mayor, I guess, and is so much in love with his pretty wife that they're forever dashing upstairs for a quickie. Meanwhile, Riegert and Capaldi fall under the spell of the town, settle into its rhythms, become wrapped up in its intrigues, and, in general, are co-opted by a place whose charms are seductive.

What makes this material really work is the low-key approach of the writer-director, Bill Forsyth, who also made the charming *Gregory's Girl* and has the patience to let his characters gradually reveal themselves to the camera. He never hurries, and as a result, *Local Hero* never drags: Nothing is more absorbing than human personalities, developed with love and humor. Some of the payoffs in this film are sly and subtle, and others generate big laughs. Forsyth's big scenes are his little ones, including a heartfelt, whiskey-soaked talk between the American and the innkeeper, and a scene where the visitors walk on the beach and talk about the meaning of life. By the time Burt Lancaster reappears at the end of the film, to personally handle the negotiations with old Ben, *Local Hero* could hardly have anything but a happy ending. But it's a fairly close call.

Lone Wolf McQuade ★ ★ ★ ¹/₂
107 m., 1983

Chuck Norris (J.J. McQuade), David Carradine (Rawley), Barbara Carrera (Lola), Robert Beltran (Kayo Ramas), Sharon Farrell (Molly), Leon Isaac Kennedy (Jackson). Directed by Steve Carver.

To really understand *Lone Wolf McQuade*, you have to go back to those original spaghetti Westerns that made Clint Eastwood a star. They weren't great movies, and some critics attacked them for trashing the classic forms of the Western. But they had presence, style, and energy, and at the center of them they had a perfectly realized hero in Clint Eastwood. He was called The Man With No Name. He dealt violence with implacable fury. He stood at the middle of the maelstrom and remained untouched. And, in his own way, he was powerfully charismatic. Eastwood and Sergio Leone, his director, created a new kind of Western, pared down to its bare essentials of men and guns, horses and deserts, sweat and flies, and rotgut.

Now comes Chuck Norris. He's been in a series of karate and kung fu movies that were almost always better than average—but not a lot better than average. (The best of them was *Eye for an Eye*, directed by Steve Carver, who also directed *McQuade*.) The most you could say for a Chuck Norris film was that it did not have downright contempt for its action audiences; it tried to be better than the interchangeable chop-socky movies from Hong Kong, and Norris made an energetic, likable star. What Norris was really looking for in all those pictures, I guess, was the right character. Like Eastwood's Man With No Name, he needed a personality that would fit, that would contain his kung fu skills and allow him ways of expression not limited to flying fists and deadly elbows. That's what he's found in *Lone Wolf McQuade*.

This is an action movie. It makes no apology for that. But it's high-style action. Norris plays J.J. McQuade, a renegade modern-day Texas Ranger who walks alone, likes to work with machine guns, deals out justice on the spot, and hardly ever says much of anything. The movie surrounds him with a gallery of interesting characters, played by colorful stars: David Carradine is Rawley, the evil local criminal and karate master; Barbara Carrera is lovely, as usual, as Carradine's wife and Norris's mistress; Robert Beltran plays Kayo Ramas, Norris's Mexican-American sidekick; Leon Isaac Kennedy is the federal officer; grizzled L.Q. Jones lopes through a few scenes; and Sharon Farrell is counterpoint as Norris's former wife. All of these people are thrown together into a plot that is, of course, essentially meaningless. But the movie respects the plot, and keeps it moving, and a lot of excitement is generated.

Series characters always have one archetypal scene. With Eastwood, it was the time he killed three men with one bullet. Lone Wolf McQuade has a classic. He's shot. They think he's dead. They bury him in his supercharged, customized pickup truck. He comes to. Pours a beer over his head. Floors the accelerator and drives that mother right out of the grave. You get the idea.

The Lonely Guy ★ ¹/₂
R, 91 m., 1984

Steve Martin (Larry), Charles Grodin (Warren), Judith Ivey (Iris), Steve Lawrence (Jack), Robyn Douglass (Danielle), Dr. Joyce Brothers (Herself). Directed and produced by Arthur Hiller. Screenplay by Ed Weinberger and Stan Daniels.

I saw *The Lonely Guy* all by myself. It was one of those Saturday afternoons where the snow is coming down gray and mean, and you can't even get a decent recorded message on the answering machines of strangers.

There was a warm glow coming out of the windows of a tanning parlor. At a table in the window of a hot dog joint, three bums were laughing warmly, sharing a joke and a cup of coffee. I stuck my hands down deep into the pockets of my jeans and hunched my shoulders against the cold. I tried to force a smile to my frozen lips: Hey, I was going to the movies!

I walked up to the ticket booth of the Esquire theater and with a flourish presented my Plitt Theaters pass.

"What's this?" asked the ticket person.

"A pass to the Plitt Theaters," I said.

"I don't know," the person said. "I'll have to phone and check it out." I turned my back to the wind until the pass was verified, and then walked into the theater's priceless and irreplaceable Art Deco lobby, which cheered me somewhat.

"It's a shame they're tearing this theater down," said a young woman to her date, as they swept past me on their way to the street. I ordered a box of popcorn, and went into the theater.

"Good luck," an usher told me. "You're going to need it."

He was right. *The Lonely Guy* is the kind of movie that seems to have been made to play in empty theaters on overcast January afternoons. It stars Steve Martin, an actor who inspires in me the same feelings that fingernails on blackboards inspire in other people. He plays a lonely guy. His girl leaves him, and he keeps losing the phone number of the only girl in New York who will talk to him. This could have been fun, if the movie were only a little more upbeat about his loneliness. But it isn't. *The Lonely Guy* is a dreary slog through morose situations, made all the worse by Martin's deadpan delivery, his slightly off-balance sense of timing, and his ability to make you cringe with his self-debasing smarminess. In a movie crawling with bad scenes, the worst is probably the bedroom scene with Iris (Judith Ivey), the above-mentioned only girl in New York who will talk to him. She has never had an orgasm. He convinces her that she will have an orgasm every time he sneezes. She fakes it by screaming "gesundheit!"

The Lonely Guy is the kind of movie that inspires you to distract yourself by counting the commercial products visible on the screen, and speculating about whether their manufacturers paid fees to have them worked into the movie. I counted two Diet 7-Ups, two Tabs, and Steve Martin.

The Lonely Passion of Judith Hearne ★ ★ ★
R, 110 m., 1988

Maggie Smith (Judith Hearne), Bob Hoskins (James Madden), Wendy Hiller (Aunt D'Arcy), Marie Kean (Mrs. Rice), Ian McNeice (Bernard), Alan Devlin (Father Quigley), Rudi Davies (Mary). Directed by Jack Clayton and produced by Peter Nelson and Richard Johnson. Screenplay by Nelson.

The most intimate moment in *The Lonely Passion of Judith Hearne* is one played between the heroine and a bottle of whiskey. She retreats to her lonely room in a sad Dublin boardinghouse and locks the door, then runs to her closet and finds the bottle where it has been hidden away during all the recent days of happiness, waiting quietly until she would need it again. She pours the drink quickly, and then all is chaos once again in her life, as we sense it has been so many times before.

Maggie Smith brings precise body language to this scene. She does not play it eagerly, or desperately, but with well-rehearsed precision, showing us that for the alcoholic Miss Hearne, this is a ritual. Smith's goal in the scene is to show us, without telling us, that this is not the first time Judith Hearne has admitted despair. And as the whiskey takes hold and the lonely spinster begins to sing to herself, her boozy joy is all the more depressing because it comes from defeat, not victory.

The realities of Miss Hearne's life are made clear a little at a time. She is poor, but respectable. She lives in rooming houses. She has few friends, and the family she is closest to tolerates her out of pity. She gives piano lessons, and dreams that someday a white knight will come riding out of the mist—a man to sweep her off her feet and make everything right again. In this dream she is frequently disappointed, and then the bottle comes out of the closet and her downward spiral continues. Since the only apparent joy in her life comes from drunkenness, there is even the possibility that she sets up her own failures—to give herself an excuse to drink.

This time, though . . . this time may be different. As *The Lonely Passion of Judith Hearne* opens, she has moved into another boardinghouse, and at breakfast she meets the brother of the landlady. His name is James (Bob Hoskins), and he has just come back from spending many years in America. She thinks America must be a wonderful place, and before long she thinks James must be a wonderful person. He seems lonely, too, and after some shy verbal sparring they go to Mass together and to the picture show.

Eventually it becomes clear that James is interested in Judith primarily for the money he thinks she must have—money she might invest in his own dream of an American-style hot dog stand, to cater to all the Yankee tourists in Dublin. There is even talk of marriage between the two people, before Judith finally sees through to James's real motives. Then she gets drunk, of course, but that is not the end of the movie, only the midpoint, because then James must question his own motives.

We sense that this sort of scenario has repeated itself, in one version or another, for many years in Judith Hearne's life. But since James is, in some ways, her last chance, the cruelty of his betrayal hits her harder and almost destroys her. And her suffering leads up to a crucial scene in which she is at last able to tell James, and herself, the exact reality of her life. The movie implies that by seeing herself clearly, she can begin to mend.

For Maggie Smith, the movie is a triumph, a performance to compare with *The Prime of Miss Jean Brodie* of twenty years ago. Bob Hoskins is very good, too, but his character is less clearly seen, and it might have been wise for the screenplay to make his actual feelings for Judith Hearne more clear. The movie's ending is courageous and moving, I suppose, but since it deals more with Judith's fate than with her drinking, it rather evades the issue. Courage and clarity will not heal Judith unless they come after sobriety—without which, for her, even the best intentions will end with another ritualistic search for the bottle in the back of the closet.

The Long Good Friday ★ ★ ★ ★
R, 118 m., 1982

Bob Hoskins (Harold Shand), Helen Mirren (Victoria), Eddie Constantine (Charlie), Derek Thompson (Jeff), Bryan Marshall (Harris), Paul Freeman (Collin). Directed by John Mackenzie and produced by Barry Hanson. Screenplay by Barrie Keeffe.

Harold is as hard as a rock and he will crush you. He runs the London docks and he wants to put together the biggest real estate deal in Europe. He has Mafia money from America and the tacit cooperation of the London criminal organization. He's short, barrel-chested, with his thinning hair combed forward above a round face and teeth that always seem to be grinding. He cannot believe that in one weekend his whole world can come apart. Harold Shand is a hood, but he lives in a penthouse, anchors a world-class yacht in the Thames, has the love of an intelligent and tactful mistress, and talks obsessively about the ten years of peace he has helped negotiate in the London underground. Then a bomb blows up his Rolls Royce, killing his chauffeur. Another bomb demolishes the lovingly restored landmark pub he owns. A third bomb is found inside Harold's Mayfair casino, but fails to detonate. Who is after him? Who is his enemy?

And why has the enemy chosen this worst of all possible times to come after him—the Easter weekend when an American Mafioso is in town to consider investing millions in his real estate project?

The Long Good Friday, which is a masterful and very tough piece of filmmaking, eventually does answer these questions. But the point of the film isn't to analyze Harold Shand's problems. It's to present a portrait of this man. And I have rarely seen a movie character so completely alive. Shand is an evil, cruel, sadistic man. But he's a mass of contradictions, and there are times when we understand him so completely we almost feel affectionate. He's such a character, such an overcompensating Cockney, sensitive to the slightest affront, able to strike fear in the hearts of killers, but a pushover when his mistress raises her voice to him. Shand is played by a compact, muscular actor named Bob Hoskins, in the most-praised film performance of the year from England. Hoskins has the energy and the freshness of a younger Michael Caine, if not the good looks, of course. There are scenes where he hangs his enemies upside down from meat hooks and questions them about the bombings, and other scenes, moments later, where he solemnly kids with the neighborhood juvenile delinquents and tries to soft-talk the American out of his millions.

He's an operator. He's a con man who has muscled his way to the top by knowing exactly how things work and what buttons to push, and now here he is, impotent before this faceless enemy. *The Long Good Friday* tells his story in a rather indirect way, opening with a montage of seemingly unrelated events, held together by a hypnotic music theme. Everything is eventually explained. It's all a big misunderstanding, based on stupid decisions taken by Shand's underlings and misinterpreted by the IRA. But although we know the real story, and Harold Shand does, the IRA never does—and the movie's final shots are, quite simply, extraordinary close-ups, held for a long time, of Shand's ratlike face in close-up, as his eyes shift from side to side, and his mouth breaks into a terrified grin, and he realizes how it feels to get a dose of his own medicine. This movie is one amazing piece of work, not only for the Hoskins performance but also for the energy of the filmmaking, the power of the music, and, oddly enough, for the engaging quality of its sometimes very violent sense of humor.

The Long Goodbye ★ ★ ★
R, 112 m., 1973

Elliott Gould (Philip Marlowe), Nina van Pallandt (Eileen Wade), Sterling Hayden (Roger Wade), Mark Rydell (Marty Augustine), Henry Gibson (Dr. Verringer), David Arkin (Harry). Directed by Robert Altman and produced by Elliott Kastner. Screenplay by Leigh Brackett.

Robert Altman's *The Long Goodbye* attempts to do a very interesting thing. It tries to be all genre and no story, and it almost works. It makes no serious effort to reproduce the Raymond Chandler detective novel it's based on; instead, it just takes all the characters out of that novel and lets them stew together in something that feels like a private-eye movie.

The private eye is, I suppose, a fairly obsolete institution in our society. I'm not talking about the divorce case specialists and the missing persons guys; I'm thinking of the Chandler, Dashiell Hammett, Ross Mac-Donald kind of hired eye whose occupation takes him into glamorous danger and who subscribes to a weary private credo. The private eye as a fiction device was essentially a way to open doors; the best novels of Chandler and the others are simply hooks for a cynical morality.

Altman seems to understand this. He knows we don't care any more about the plot than he does; he agrees with Hitchcock that it doesn't even matter what the plot is about (as long as it's something). The important thing is the way the characters spar with each other. But Altman has added a twist: Instead of making his private eye into a cool, competent professional, he makes him into a 1950s anachronism. Philip Marlowe has been in a lot of movies, but never one in which he was more confused than he is in this one.

The story, or whatever you want to call it, involves a murder, a missing person, and an alcoholic writer with a bewitching blond wife. There are also some gangsters and a cat. The writer and his wife are played with really fine style by Sterling Hayden and Nina van Pallandt—who not only demonstrates that she can act, but also that a real woman is infinitely more interesting on the screen than some starlet beauty-school graduate who should be leading the pompon team.

The middle of this mess is inhabited by Elliott Gould, as the chain-smoking, mumbling, disorganized Marlowe. It's a good performance, particularly the virtuoso ten-minute stretch at the beginning of the movie when he goes out to buy food for his cat. Gould has enough of the paranoid in his acting style to really put over Altman's revised view of the private eye.

Altman doesn't string his scenes together to tell a taut story, but he directs each scene as if he were. There's an especially memorable scene involving Philip Marlowe and a gangster (played by Mark Rydell, who is usually a director). The gangster smacks his girlfriend with a pop bottle and then snarls at Marlowe: "Now that's someone I *love.* Think what could happen to you." The scene sounds rather grim in print, I know, but in the movie it has a kind of hard-boiled desperation to it. It feels like it belongs in a private eye's life and so does the whole movie—right up to the ending, which is really off the wall.

The Long Walk Home ★ ★ ★ ½
PG, 97 m., 1991
(See related Film Clip, p. 702.)

Sissy Spacek (Miriam Thompson), Whoopi Goldberg (Odessa Cotter), Dwight Schultz (Norman Thompson), Ving Rhames (Herbert Cotter), Dylan Baker (Tunker Thompson), Erika Alexander (Selma Cotter). Directed by Richard Pearce and produced by Howard W. Koch, Jr. and Dave Bell. Screenplay by John Cork.

The Long Walk Home tells the stories of two women and their families at a critical turning point in American history. One of the women is black, a maid in an affluent neighborhood, a hard-working woman who goes home after a long day and does all of the same jobs all over again for her family. The other woman is white, the wife of a successful businessman. She works, too. She doesn't have a paid job, but in 1955 in Montgomery, Alabama, it was full-time work to please a husband who thought a woman's place was in the home, and who had a great many other thoughts on the proper places of just about everybody in his narrow world.

These characters are confronted by a historic moment. One day in Montgomery, a black woman named Rosa Parks, who had worked hard and was tired, refused to stand up in the back of the segregated bus when there was an empty seat in the front. Her action, born out of a long weariness with the countless injustices of discrimination, inspired the Montgomery Bus Boycott, which was led by a young local preacher named Martin Luther King, Jr., and which grew into the civil rights movement.

For a woman like Odessa Cotter (Whoopi Goldberg), however, the eventual verdict of history could not have been easily guessed on the day she decided to join thousands of other Montgomery blacks in refusing to take the bus. She simply knew how she felt and acted on it, and started to walk to work every day. That meant getting up a couple of hours earlier in the morning, and getting home long after dark, and it meant blisters on her heels. It also meant inconvenience for her employer, Miriam Thompson (Sissy Spacek), who had a house to keep and a husband to feed, and who took her duties as a wife very solemnly—suppressing the obvious reality that he was a jerk.

Odessa is not eager for her employer to discover she is honoring the boycott—she doesn't want to risk losing her job—but one day Miriam finds out, and decides that she will give the maid a ride in her car a couple of days a week. This decision, of course, would enrage Miriam's husband, a self-satisfied bigot named Norman (Dwight Schultz), but Miriam doesn't tell him, and when he finds out, she defends her action as part of her job as a dutiful housewife.

In the meantime, she and her husband grow in different ways because of the boycott. Miriam is no activist, but she can see as a wife and a mother what the boycotting black women are going through, and begins to sympathize with them. Her husband is taken by a relative to a White Citizen's Council meeting, where rabble-rousers depict the boycotters as dangerous subversives (any true American would, of course, prefer to stand in the back of the bus than sit in the front—if he were black, that is).

The movie leads up to an inevitable confrontation between the white husband and wife, and to a climax of surprising power. But the general lines of the plot are not what make the movie special. We know going in more or less what will happen, both with the boycott and with these characters. What involved me was the way John Cork's screenplay did not simply paint the two women as emblems of a cause, but saw them as particular individuals who defined themselves largely through their roles as wives and mothers.

This movie would not have been made quite the same way ten or twenty years ago. The focus would have been on the liberalism of the white woman and the courage of the black woman, and most of the scenes would have involved the white family. *The Long Walk Home* takes the time to develop both families, to show that in addition to being heroic but abstract media images, the maids like Odessa were also individuals with all the usual human hopes and worries, not least of which was losing a job.

Because the movie does center some of its important scenes inside the black household, it's all the more surprising that it uses the gratuitous touch of a white "narrator"—apparently to reassure white audiences that the movie is "really" intended for them. The narrator is Spacek's teen-age daughter, who has no role of any importance in the movie and whose narration adds nothing except an unnecessary point of view. When she talks about her memories of "my mother," we want to know why Goldberg's daughter doesn't have equal time. She probably has more interesting memories.

That objection aside, *The Long Walk Home* is a powerful and affecting film, so well played by Goldberg and Spacek that we understand not just the politics of the time but the emotions as well. In a way, this movie takes up where *Driving Miss Daisy* leaves off. Both are about affluent white southern women who pride themselves on their humanitarian impulses, but who are brought to a greater understanding of racial discrimination—gently, tactfully, and firmly—by their black employees.

Miss Daisy and Miss Miriam are not revolutionaries. Neither are Hoke Colburn and Odessa Cotter. But the situation had gotten to the point where something had to be done, because people, after all, must be permitted fairness and dignity, and these two movies tell two small and not earth-shaking stories about ordinary people, black and white, who managed to talk and managed to listen, and made things a little better.

Longtime Companion ★ ★ ★ ½
R, 96 m., 1990

Stephen Caffrey (Fuzzy), Patrick Cassidy (Howard), Brian Cousins (Bob), Bruce Davison (David), John Dossett (Paul), Mark Lamos (Sean), Dermot Mulroney (John), Michael Schoeffling (Michael), Campbell Scott (Willy). Directed by Norman Rene and produced by Stan Wlodkowski. Screenplay by Craig Lucas.

"He is survived," the obituaries sometimes say, "by his longtime companion." The phrase is taken by everybody to mean "lover," but newspapers prefer the euphemism, and only in the age of AIDS have they even finally admitted that homosexuals do not live, or die, alone. Norman Rene's *Longtime Companion* is a film that begins on the day when an obscure story in the *New York Times* first mentions a disease that seems to be striking homosexual men, and it ends after AIDS has profoundly affected all their lives—mostly, but not entirely, for the worse.

That first small cloud on the horizon was a story about a "gay cancer" that doctors were reporting among some of their homosexual patients. Within a few months, the *Village Voice* was providing in-depth reporting on the "gay plague," which eventually was named AIDS. But at the beginning, the characters in the story have difficulty in believing that a disease could seem to single them out.

The movie has been written by Craig Lucas as a series of scenes, sometimes separated by months or years, in the lives of several ordinary homosexual men, and it is the very everyday quality of their lives—work and home, love and cooking, and weekends—that provides the bedrock for this film. The emphasis is on the notion of "longtime." During the course of the movie some characters will fall in love and others will break up, but most of them will be steadfast in their friendships, and they will stand by each other in a series of crises. Of course, others simply disappear when AIDS arrives to interfere with their personal priorities, but not everyone is a saint, and some of the events in this film require, or inspire, a quality of sainthood.

The movie is told in chronological order, so that at every moment we know as much as the characters do about AIDS. At first they can't believe it at all. Then they can't believe it could strike anyone they know—or themselves. Then they begin to ask themselves uneasy questions about less-than-prudent episodes in their lives: Are long-forgotten indiscretions about to come back and take a deadly toll? Is AIDS the revenge of the past?

When a friend gets sick, it is hard to ask what the matter is, easy to pretend it is "something else." A friend loses weight and inevitable questions arise. Lovers ask each other hard questions about fidelity and do not always get honest answers. One by one, over the period of years, the circle of friends grows smaller. Of course, many will survive, but there seems to be no sensible pattern in who is chosen, and no guarantee that a man will not care for his friend only to need help himself before long. Few films have done a better job of illustrating the virtue of "visiting the sick"—that cardinal act of mercy most neglected in an America that likes to let hospitals take care of that sort of hard work.

The central scene in the film—one of the most emotionally affecting scenes in any film on dying—involves Bruce Davison as the lover of a dying man. The struggle has been long and painful, but now it is almost over, and what Davison has to do is hold the hand of his friend and be with him when he dies. The fight has been so brave that it is hard to end it. "Let go," Davison whispers. "It's all right. You can let go now." The scene plays for a long, quiet time, and it is about the absolute finality of death, but it is also about why we are alive in the first place. Man is the only animal that knows it will die. This scene shows how that can be the source of courage and spiritual peace.

One of the particular strengths of *Longtime Companion* is that it does not identify its characters only through their sexual preferences. It would seem bizarre to watch a movie in which heterosexual men were defined only by the fact that they like to sleep with women—but many films about gays have made the opposite error and limited their characters as a result. *Longtime Companion* is about friendship and loyalty, about finding the courage to be helpful, and the humility to be helped.

Look Who's Talking ★ ★ ★
PG-13, 96 m., 1989

John Travolta (James), Kirstie Alley (Mollie), Olympia Dukakis (Rosie), George Segal (Albert), Abe Vigoda (Grandpa), Bruce Willis (Voice of Mikey). Mikey played at different ages by Jason Schaller, Jaryd Waterhouse, Jacob Haines, and Christopher Aydon. Directed by Amy Heckerling and produced by Jonathan D. Krane. Screenplay by Heckerling.

If I were sitting at home and watching TV, and I saw a commercial for this movie, I don't think I'd want to see it. For starters, I wouldn't want to see a movie where the thoughts of an infant were spoken aloud for it by Bruce Willis. Then I'd reflect that John Travolta had appeared in several disappointments recently and that Kirstie Alley's movies had not exactly set the world on fire.

As a movie critic, however, I am not permitted such thoughts—at least not officially—and so one afternoon not long ago I found myself feeling very good during a screening of *Look Who's Talking*. This fairly unlikely idea for a movie turns into a warm and lovable comedy—although I still don't think it needed the voice-overs from the baby.

The movie stars Kirstie Alley (best known as the bar manager from "Cheers") as an accountant who's having an affair with a boorish, self-centered businessman (George Segal). She gets pregnant, he double-crosses her, and suddenly she's a single mom. She encounters Travolta through one of those standard movie Meet Cutes, when she goes into labor and he's the taxi driver who races her to the hospital.

The rest of the movie, lightweight and warmhearted, is about how Travolta falls in love with both the mother and the child. It's easy to see what appeals to him: Alley glows with health and good cheer in this movie, and the baby (played by four different infants) is, I must confess, adorable. Reviewing a baby's "performance" in a movie is meaningless, since babies do what they do without paying much attention to their directors, but there are scenes in this movie (including one where Travolta waltzes around with the kid) where the filmmakers just plain lucked out and got some of the best baby-moments I've ever seen in a movie.

If the baby isn't predictable, the story is, right down to the moment when Travolta is the baby sitter while Alley goes out on a date with a fellow accountant. We've seen all this stuff before and, yep, they even throw in the obligatory toupee scene, where the baby lifts the rug off the poor guy's head.

But as a silly entertainment, *Look Who's Talking* is full of good feeling, and director Amy Heckerling (*Fast Times at Ridgemont High*) finds a light touch for her lightweight material. Travolta demonstrates, twelve years after *Saturday Night Fever*, that he is a warm and winning actor when he's not shoehorned into the wrong roles. And Kirstie Alley finds the kind of role she must have been looking for, a role that lets us see the person who was always there, beneath all those hours of TV images.

Looking for Mr. Goodbar ★ ★ ★
R, 136 m., 1977

Diane Keaton (Theresa), Tuesday Weld (Katherine), William Atherton (James), Richard Kiley (Mr. Dunn), Richard Gere (Tony), Alan Feinstein (Martin), Tom Berenger (Gary), Priscilla Pointer (Mrs. Dunn). Directed by Richard Brooks and produced by Freddie Fields. Screenplay by Brooks.

There's one crucial thing that *Looking for Mr. Goodbar* doesn't make clear: Just because you find Mr. Goodbar doesn't necessarily mean you were looking for him. The heroine of Judith Rossner's bestseller *was* looking. Theresa was turned on to a particular flavor of self-destructive sexual experience, one involving possible danger to herself, and she played a role in bringing about her own death.

In Richard Brooks's film version, that masochistic impulse isn't considered as openly. He gives us a Theresa who drinks too much, sleeps around too much, and takes too many drugs—but she seems more of a hedonist than a masochist. She's looking for a combination of good times, good sex, and a father figure, for psychological reasons the movie makes all too abundantly clear. But she isn't looking for danger, mistreatment, or death. Maybe Brooks thought audiences would find Rossner's masochistic heroine too hard to understand. He has rewritten the story, in any event, into a cautionary lesson: Promiscuous young women who frequent pick-up bars and go home with strangers are likely to get into trouble.

Brooks hasn't improved the story by changing its focus, and he's distracted from the heart of the narrative by several unnecessary scenes. Theresa's fantasies, for example, are handled in ways that annoy viewers more than they intrigue them. And her home life—its broadly painted Freudian details right out of soap operas—could have just simply been dropped.

But, all the same, Brooks hasn't directed a bad picture. *Looking for Mr. Goodbar* is very much worth seeing, particularly for the Diane Keaton performance. And it's not fair to praise her while damning Brooks (as so many critics have done). Brooks and Keaton must have worked together to create such a great performance; it's just a shame that it's surrounded by perhaps half an hour of material that only distracts.

The performance creates a character who

would have been unthinkable in the movies of thirty years ago: A young woman who spends her days teaching first grade to a classroom of deaf-mutes and her nights making herself available in singles bars. Women weren't allowed to be that complicated in the "women's pictures" that *Mr. Goodbar* has come such a long way from. They were ladies or they were tramps. Now they're allowed to be both, which has done wonders for the quality of the tramps you meet these days.

Diane Keaton suggests the motivation for her character almost independently from all those heavy-handed scenes in which her father stomps around the living room, and we get flashbacks of her tragic childhood. She suggests that Theresa is driven by a need to communicate on her own terms—and that those terms require her to have an advantage. She's great in a classroom of deaf-mutes, and great, too, with the men she picks up—men who are inarticulate because of insecurity, cultural short-changing, or too much booze. She delights in working people over verbally—in kidding them, mocking them, putting them down, playing games with them. On the physical level, though, she needs constant reassurance.

This Theresa is a different woman from the Judith Rossner character, but she's an interesting one. And Keaton plays her wonderfully, with a light touch you'd think would be impossible with this material. She's always moving. She choreographs every situation, and only eventually do we realize she's dancing out of the way. Her voice is liquid and funny, tossing off asides because they cut more deeply that way. The performance and the character are fully realized, even in this movie that finds room for so many loose ends and dead ends.

Then there's that ending that bothers me. On a New Year's Eve, she makes a fatal decision in choosing the next guy she's going to take home. *We* know she's made the wrong decision because Brooks abandons her point of view to show us a scene in which the guy is established as unbalanced and hostile. But she doesn't know that and gets killed because she doesn't. Her lack of knowledge is exactly the issue here: In the book, Theresa might have picked up the guy *because* she knew he'd be trouble.

What we get (and I quote from someone walking out of the screening ahead of me) is "another one of those movies that are supposed to be all filled with significance because the person gets killed at the end."

What we might have gotten is a movie about a character obsessed, and fascinated, by what the end might be. Even a movie about how she got to be that way.

Loose Cannons ★
R, 94 m., 1990

Gene Hackman (Mac), Dan Aykroyd (Ellis), Dom DeLuise (Gutterman), Ronny Cox (Smiley), Nancy Travis (Riva), Robert Prosky (Von Metz), Paul Koslo (Grimmer). Directed by Bob Clark and produced by Aaron Spelling and Alan Greisman. Screenplay by Richard Christian Matheson, Richard Matheson, and Clark.

Rarely has a movie been more appropriately named than *Loose Cannons*—although most of the cannons seem to have been below deck, where the writing and directing was done, instead of above the line with the stars. The movie is a bewildering collision between elements that don't fit, characters that don't work, and ideas that don't pay off—it's like the outtakes from a dozen other movies that were improved by the removal of these parts.

The film is jam-packed with all those little eccentric touches that are supposed to make the characters individual and end up making them look like they were written by a committee. Gene Hackman, for example, plays a cop who lives with his pet kitten in his station wagon—a late-1940s Ford wood-sided classic. Dan Aykroyd, assigned as his partner, is a mental patient with "multiple personality disorder," and speaks interchangably in the voices of Captain Kirk, Tweetie Pie, and Pee-wee Herman. Their quarry: a dangerous gang of neo-Nazis who possess a porno film of Adolph Hitler in the sack with the man who is about to become the new chancellor of West Germany.

The movie stinks from the spectacularly unfunny opening scene in which Hackman and another partner threaten to ticket a man for not wearing a condom. That's the kind of scene you'd expect in *Porky's*, which was also directed by Bob Clark; it's embarrassing to see a fine actor like Hackman wallow in this material. The tone is not elevated when Aykroyd climbs on board. He does a dozen different voices and tries to fake out his attackers in a violent S&M bar by the "diversionary tactic" of pretending to be both Sylvester and Tweetie Pie, but his schtick, which could possibly have provided one small payoff, is expected to do duty as comedy for the entire movie.

Dom DeLuise costars in the film, as a porno king who is negotiating to buy the rare Hitler footage, and there's a cameo by Robert Prosky, another fine actor, as the German politician who denies having known Hitler at all, let alone in the biblical sense. Indeed, there seems to be some kind of a logical plot slumbering down there in the buried levels of the script, although the surface action is so manic it hardly matters. The movie plays like one of those celebrity auctions in which stars donate their old books and shirts and publicity photos; certainly none of the stars in this enterprise have contributed anything of value.

As in so many other movies, an unspoken equation is implied in *Loose Cannons* between "German" and "Nazi," and it is assumed that underground Nazis still run Germany and are capable of putting their man into office. Will the statute of limitations ever run out on the German people, or will filmmakers feel free to label them as Nazis forever? No other ethnic or nationality group is so freely slandered without apology in respectable circles.

I'll bet this movie must have looked mouth-watering on paper. It has lots of sensational touches in it: a speedboat that rams into a warehouse, a chase scene in which the priceless Ford is destroyed, a gang of neo-Nazis who cruise the city streets firing a rocket launcher, and even a climax in which a man falls through the false ceiling of Grand Central Station and bounces on the floor far below (that's at least the second time I've seen that happen in a movie; is there a stuntman who specializes in it?).

Would-be screenwriters sometimes write me asking for advice. I usually have none to provide. Next time I think I'll suggest they study this movie. *Loose Cannons* is such an insane mess, such a wretched waste of time, that it proves almost any screenplay can be sold, produced, directed, acted in, and even released. There is hope, except for the rest of us.

Lost Angels ★ ★ ½
R, 118 m., 1989

Donald Sutherland (Dr. Charles Loftis), Adam Horovitz (Tim Doolan), Amy Locane (Cheryl Anderson), Don Bloomfield (Andy Doolan), Celia Weston (Felicia Marks), Graham Beckel (Richard Doolan). Directed by Hugh Hudson and produced by Howard Rosenman and Thomas Baer. Screenplay by Michael Weller.

The opening frames of *Lost Angels* explain the title. We see the words "Los Angeles" and then graffiti is used to add a "t" and cross out an "e." What we are seeing is the message of the movie: That in the affluent Los Angeles upper middle class, children are the lost angels—cast aside by parents who are dazzled by new jobs, more money, and second marriages.

The hero of the film is a taciturn, cynical seventeen-year-old named Tim Doolan (Adam Horovitz). As we meet him, he is being locked up in a privately run juvenile detention center by his mother and stepfather, who have lied to him about where he is going. In flashbacks, we see that this kid has gotten into a lot of trouble. He was with a girlfriend when she drove the family car into the swimming pool, and earlier he was in a gang fight and picked up a gun from the street that was used in the battle.

There is a sense in which this boy is indeed a delinquent, and another sense in which he is the victim of circumstances and very bad luck. (I kept thinking of the ending of *Angels With Dirty Faces*, in which Pat O'Brien says he became a priest and Jimmy Cagney became a mobster only because O'Brien could run faster from the cops.) Whether or not he's a "bad" kid, he's an angry and alienated one who at first needs to be strapped to a bed in a padded cell.

Enter the movie's hero, a psychiatrist named Loftis (Donald Sutherland). He is intelligent and empathetic, and begins to care about this kid. And then the movie explains the structure of the juvenile center, in which the youths grade themselves on levels one through four, on the basis of their progress. If *Lost Angels* has a surprise, it is that it makes this private detention center its real target. Most of the staff members are seen as timeservers with no real interest in the kids, and Sutherland scornfully dismisses the management, which is concerned only with a profitable bottom line: "When insurance paid for a year in a place like this, we said it took a year to help a kid. Now insurance pays for three months, and, presto, it takes three months to turn a kid around."

The movie's plot is a series of advances and setbacks for Tim, who is torn between the progress he makes on the inside, and the evil influence of his half-brother (Don Bloomfield) on the outside. The brother, a psychotic, tries to force Tim into shooting a gun into a crowd of teen-agers, and the tension in this scene is genuine and frightening.

Maybe some of Tim's misplaced family loyalty to his brother comes from a need to belong; the movie argues that all of its lost angels have been squeezed out of families, and Tim has a love affair with a deeply unhappy young woman whose mother clearly wishes to be rid of her.

Lost Angels avoids a lot of obvious clichés, treats its characters with dignity, and develops them as specific individuals. This is particularly true of the Sutherland character; we get a glimpse of his home life suggesting that he is more dedicated to the kids at the center than to his own family. The portrait of Tim Doolan is also interesting: Horovitz doesn't affect the glamorous moodiness of the usually Hollywood teen-age performance, but plays a truly withdrawn, bitter teen-ager whose real thoughts come out mostly in interior monologues.

All of these qualities make *Lost Angels*, which was directed by Hugh Hudson, into an intelligent, well-crafted picture. And yet while I was watching it, I remained strangely unmoved. There was a certain coldness and anger that had nothing to do with the characters, that was directed almost at life itself, that seemed to say the dedicated people were only fooling themselves.

This anger coexists uneasily with the unconvincing last scenes of the movie, in which we are expected to believe Tim makes a decision that nothing in the earlier scenes has prepared him for. Ending a downbeat movie with a happy ending is nothing new, but *Lost Angels* is so unremitting in its fundamental critique of an entire society that the optimistic ending seems almost like a cruel joke.

The Lost Boys ★ ★ ½
R, 97 m., 1987

Jason Patric (Michael), Corey Haim (Sam), Dianne Wiest (Lucy), Barnard Hughes (Grandpa), Ed Herrmann (Max), Kiefer Sutherland (David), Jami Gertz (Star), Corey Feldman (Edgar Frog), Jamison Newlander (Alan Frog). Directed by Joel Schumacher and produced by Harvey Bernhard. Screenplay by Janice Fischer, James Jeremias, and Jeffrey Boam.

The Lost Boys in this movie are vampires, teen-age vampires, and of course there is a lost girl, too, but why mention her? They hang from the ceiling of their lair, in the ruins of an old hotel, and at night they go out to cruise the boardwalk of Santa Clara, Mass Murder Capital of the World. When a new kid moves to town, the lost boys look threatening but the lost girl looks just great.

From this beginning, Joel Schumacher has devised an ambitious entertainment that starts out well but ends up selling its soul. There is a moment, early in this film, when it seems to have a handle on its characters and the after-dark teen-age world they inhabit. But the ending of the film is just another one of those by-the-numbers action climaxes, in which the movie is over when all the bad guys are dead. Has there been an action thriller recently in which the last twenty minutes weren't phoned in from the depository of bankrupt clichés?

The movie stars Jason Patric as Michael, a bright kid who moves to town with his widowed mother (Dianne Wiest) and little brother. Right away he meets a nice local man (Edward Herrmann), who comes calling on his mother. Before long he sees the great-looking girl (Jami Gertz), and not long after he sees the pack of lost boys, led by Kiefer Sutherland. The girl invites him to join them.

The Frog Brothers try to warn him. They're a couple of bright kids who run a comic-book store on the carnival boardwalk. They give him a couple of comic books about vampires, and offer their services if any vampires need to be killed, but Michael doesn't believe in vampires and doesn't make the connection until it's too late.

At about this point, the movie feels like it's going somewhere. But then the plot starts getting very complicated, with the adult romance between Wiest and Herrmann and the teen-age romance between Patric and Gertz, and the vampire intrigues of Sutherland. Because everything looks so good (the movie was photographed in rich dark colors by Michael Chapman), we almost give it the benefit of the doubt: The high quality of the photography and acting had me wondering if perhaps this wouldn't develop into a genuinely frightening and interesting vampire story. But no such luck. It is no longer a virtue in mainstream Hollywood to bring any genuine, unsettling imagination to a commercial movie.

If you really stop to think about it, a bunch of vampire teen-agers would be a terrible shame, a tragedy, a heartbreaking loss of innocence for them, let alone their victims. Am I silly to take them seriously? Maybe so. The movie doesn't. It lacks the sense of dread that creeps out from the pages of a novel like Anne Rice's *Interviews with the Vampire*, and substitutes instead the same old cornball, predictable action climax, everybody chasing everybody around with lots of screams and special-effects gore. Sometimes I think modern advances in special effects technology can be directly blamed for the collapse of original screenwriting.

There's some good stuff in the movie, including a cast that's good right down the line, and a willingness to have some fun with teen-age culture in the Mass Murder Capital. But when everything is all over there's nothing to leave with, no real horrors, no real dread, no real imagination. Just technique at the service of formula.

Lost in America ★ ★ ★ ★
R, 90 m., 1985

Albert Brooks (David Howard), Julie Hagerty (Linda Howard), Garry K. Marshall (Casino Boss), Art Frankel (Job Counselor). Directed by Albert Brooks and produced by Marty Katz. Screenplay by Brooks and Monica Johnson.

Every time I see a Winnebago motor home, I have the same fantasy as the hero of *Lost in America*. In my dream, I quit my job, sell everything I own, buy the Winnebago, and hit the open road. Where do I go? Look for me in the weather reports. I'll be parked by the side of a mountain stream, listening to Mozart on compact discs. All I'll need is a wok and a paperback.

In *Lost in America*, Albert Brooks plays an advertising executive in his thirties who realizes that dream. He leaves his job, talks his wife into quitting hers, and they point their Winnebago down that long, lonesome highway. This is not, however, a remake of *The Long, Long Trailer*. Brooks puts a different spin on things. For example, when movie characters leave their jobs, it's usually because they've been fired, they've decided to take an ethical stand, or the company has gone broke. Only in a movie by Brooks would the hero quit to protest a "lateral transfer" to New York. There's something intrinsically comic about that: He's taking a stand, all right, but it's a narcissistic one. He's quitting because he wants to stay in Los Angeles, he thinks he deserves to be named vice president, and he doesn't like the traffic in New York.

Lost in America is being called a yuppie comedy, but it's really about the much more universal subjects of greed, hedonism, and panic. What makes it so funny is how much we can identify with it. Brooks plays a character who is making a lot of money, but not enough; who lives in a big house, but is outgrowing it; who drives an expensive car, but not a Mercedes-Benz; who is a top executive, but not a vice president. In short, he is a desperate man, trapped by his own expectations.

On the morning of his last day at work, he puts everything on hold while he has a long, luxurious telephone conversation with a Mercedes dealer. Brooks has great telephone scenes in all of his movies, but this one perfectly captures the nuances of consumerism. He asks how much the car will cost—including *everything*. Dealer prep, license, sticker, add-ons, extras, *everything*. The dealer names a price.

"That's *everything?*" Brooks asks.

"Except leather," the dealer says.

"For what I'm paying, I don't get leather?" Brooks asks, aghast.

"You get Mercedes leather."

"*Mercedes* leather? What's that?"

"Thick vinyl."

This is the kind of world Brooks is up against. A few minutes later, he's called into the boss's office and told that he will not get the promotion he thinks he deserves. Instead, he's going to New York to handle the Ford account. Brooks quits, and a few scenes later, he and his wife (Julie Hagerty) are tooling the big Winnebago into Las Vegas. They have enough money, he conservatively estimates, to stay on the road for the rest of their lives. That's before she loses their nest egg at the roulette tables.

Lost in America doesn't tell a story so much as assemble a series of self-contained comic scenes, and the movie's next scene is probably the best one in the movie. Brooks the adman tries to talk a casino owner (Garry K. Marshall) into giving back the money. It doesn't work, but Brooks keeps pushing, trying to sell the casino on improving its image. ("I'm a high-paid advertising consultant. These are professional opinions you're getting.") There are other great scenes, as the desperate couple tries to find work to support themselves: An interview with an unemployment counselor, who listens, baffled, to Brooks explaining why he left a $100,000-a-year job because he couldn't

"find himself." And Brooks's wife introducing her new boss, a teen-age boy.

Lost in America has one strange flaw. It doesn't seem to come to a conclusion. It just sort of ends in midstream, as if the final scenes were never shot. I don't know if that's the actual case, but I do wish the movie had been longer and had arrived at some sort of final destination. What we do get, however, is observant and very funny. Brooks is especially good at hearing exactly how people talk, and how that reveals things about themselves. Take that line about "Mercedes leather." A lot of people would be very happy to sit on "Mercedes leather." But not a Mercedes owner, of course. How did Joni Mitchell put it? "Don't it always seem to go, that you don't know what you've got, till it's gone."

Louie Bluie ★ ★ ★ ½
NO MPAA RATING, 75 m., 1985

A documentary featuring Howard Armstrong and Ted Bogan. Directed and produced by Terry Zwigoff.

It was back in 1970 when the Earl called me up and said I should be at his bar on Monday night because he had something special, a band called Martin, Bogan, and the Armstrongs. "Don't ask any questions," he said. "Just be here." I was there, and I returned week after week for more than a year, along with a loyal cult who packed the place.

Martin, Bogan, and one of the Armstrongs were black men in their sixties and seventies (the other Armstrong, a son, played bass). They looked like a blues band, but they didn't play the blues, and in fact it was hard to figure out exactly what they did play. They did all the Mills Brothers standards, such as "Lazy River" and "Paper Doll," and they sang "Lady Be Good" and an unprintable version of "Sweet Georgia Brown." Howard Armstrong stood up and did fiddle solos on songs such as "Turkey in the Straw," and brought the house down.

Sixteen years later, those Monday sessions blur into a smoky series of hot summer nights when the sweet lyrics of Armstrong's fiddle danced above Martin's guitar and Bogan's mandolin, and they took turns on the vocals, including Martin's composition of "The Barnyard Dance" and Armstrong's pseudo-Hawaiian love songs. Toward the end of the evening, Ted Bogan would sing "Summertime" with such unadorned purity

that you knew, quite simply, that you would never, ever, hear that great song sung better by anyone, anywhere.

Martin, Bogan, and the Armstrongs stopped playing together in the mid-1970s, and a few years later the Earl of Old Town closed its doors. When I would run into Earl Pionke, I would ask him about them and he would have vague reports that they were in Detroit, or Tennessee. Then word came that Carl Martin, who always scowled the fiercest when he was singing the funniest lyrics, had died.

And that was the situation when I went to the 1985 Telluride Film Festival, up in the San Juan range of the Rockies, and there on Main Street I saw Howard Armstrong with his beret and all that hip jewelry around his neck, checking out the scene and giving free advice to Ted Bogan, who was nodding and not listening, just like he always did when Armstrong talked to him during the sets at the Earl.

The story of how they got to Telluride is an amazing one, and it explains the existence of *Louie Bluie*, an equally amazing music documentary film.

Terry Zwigoff, a music lover who went on to produce and direct *Louie Bluie*, was an avid collector of old jazz and blues recordings. He liked the sound on an old 1930s disc that was by somebody named Louie Bluie who never recorded before or since, and after years of searching he found out that Louie Bluie was Howard Armstrong, and his group, one of the first (and now one of the last) of the traditional black string bands, was still around.

Zwigoff tracked down Armstrong, who had moved to Detroit, and talked Armstrong and Bogan into appearing in a film, and *Louie Bluie* is that film, filled with music and life and humor, but also with an extraordinary portrait of Howard Armstrong, who is an artist, poet, composer, violin virtuoso, storyteller, and tireless womanizer (according to many of his stories).

The movie is loose and disjointed, and makes little effort to be a documentary about anything. Mostly, it just follows Armstrong around as he plays music with Bogan, visits his Tennessee childhood home, and philosophizes on music, love, and life. The film occasionally turns to the pages of the semi-pornographic journals Armstrong has kept through the years, filled with lurid cartoons and bawdy poems and his observations of life. Armstrong is a natural artist, and he remembers making his first colors out of dyes wrung out of crepe paper.

There is a lot of music in the movie, including some I could do without. (Armstrong likes his Hawaiian and German songs much better than I do.) There is also an enigma to consider: the relationship of Bogan and Armstrong, who have known each other and played together for almost seventy years, despite the fact that Armstrong is almost always on Bogan's case, and Bogan's eyes always seem to be looking for the nearest exit. *Louie Bluie* peers into the areas where nothing is certain, except that these people live and strive and laugh and make music. It is a wonderful film.

Love Letters ★ ★ ★ ½
R, 98 m., 1984

Jamie Lee Curtis (Anna), James Keach (Oliver), Amy Madigan (Wendy), Matt Clark (Mr. Winter). Directed by Amy Jones and produced by Roger Corman. Screenplay by Jones.

Love Letters teaches this lesson: Passion can exist between two people who know their relationship is wrong, but love cannot exist, because love demands to know that it is right. The movie stars Jamie Lee Curtis, in the best performance she has ever given, as Anna, a bright young woman who has an affair with a married man. She tries to make herself see their relationship as existing above conventional morality, but she can't, not after she sees the man's wife and kids.

The affair begins at a crossroads in her life. She's an announcer for a public radio station in San Francisco, and within a period of a few weeks her mother dies, and she gets a job offer from a larger station. She doesn't take the job, though, because something else happens. She meets a photographer (James Keach), who is a sensitive, intelligent, married man, and feels powerfully drawn to him. And she finds her mother's love letters, which reveal that her mother once had an affair. The old letters are used as a counterpoint to the events in the present. They're read on the sound track in the voice of the man who wrote them—a man we don't meet until the movie is almost over. They are letters about love, separation, loneliness, and loyalty. Anna learns to her astonishment that her mother continued the affair for years and years during her marriage, finally ending it

only because she had decided to stay with her husband.

We meet the husband, Anna's father. He is a self-pitying alcoholic who believes he was never good enough for Anna's mother, and who smothers Anna with neurotic demands. What happens then is fascinating, and the movie treats it with great intelligence. Anna is already attracted to the James Keach character. Now, reading the old love letters, she begins to develop a romantic idea about affairs. She hates her father, and so, perhaps, did her mother. Her mother cheated on her father—and so will she, by having an affair with Keach. She will become the same kind of noble, romantic outsider that the author of the love letters must have been.

All of this is handled with as much subtlety as Ingmar Bergman brought to similar situations in *Scenes from a Marriage*. This isn't a soap opera romance; it's an investigation into how we can intellectualize our way into situations where our passions are likely to take over. Anna and the photographer spend happy times together. They are "in love." Anna thinks she only wants an affair, but she grows possessive in spite of herself. And when she spies on Keach's family, she sees that his wife is a good woman and there is love in their home. Her life refuses to parallel the love letters.

Love Letters was written and directed by Amy Jones, whose previous credit was *The Slumber Party Massacre*. This is perhaps another case of a young filmmaker beginning with exploitation movies and finally getting the chance to do ambitious work. What she accomplishes here is wonderful. She creates a story of passion that is as absorbing as a thriller. She makes a movie of ideas that never, ever, seems to be just a message picture. And she gives Jamie Lee Curtis the best dramatic role of her career; this role, side-by-side with Curtis's inspired comic acting in *Trading Places*, shows her with a range we couldn't have guessed from all her horror pictures. *Love Letters* is one of those treasures that slips through once in a while: A movie that's as smart as we are, that never goes for cheap shots, that's about passion but never blinded by it.

Love Story ★ ★ ★ ★
PG, 100 m., 1970

Ali MacGraw (Jenny Cavilleri), Ryan O'Neal (Oliver Barrett IV), Ray Milland (Oliver Barrett III), John Marley (Phil Cavilleri). Directed by

Arthur Hiller and produced by Howard G. Minsky. Screenplay by Erich Segal.

I read *Love Story* one morning in about fourteen minutes flat, out of simple curiosity. I wanted to discover why five and a half million people had actually bought it. I wasn't successful. I was so put off by Erich Segal's writing style, in fact, that I hardly wanted to see the movie at all. Segal's prose style is so revoltingly coy—sort of a cross between a parody of Hemingway and the instructions on a soup can—that his story is fatally infected.

The fact is, however, that the film of *Love Story* is infinitely better than the book. I think it has something to do with the quiet taste of Arthur Hiller, its director, who has put in all the things that Segal thought he was being clever to leave out. Things like color, character, personality, detail, and background. The interesting thing is that Hiller has saved the movie without substantially changing anything in the book. Both the screenplay and the novel were written at the same time, I understand, and if you've read the book, you've essentially read the screenplay. Nothing much is changed except the last meeting between Oliver and his father; Hiller felt the movie should end with the boy alone, and he was right. Otherwise, he's used Segal's situations and dialogue throughout. But the Segal characters, on paper, were so devoid of any personality that they might actually have been transparent. Ali MacGraw and Ryan O'Neal, who play the lovers on film, bring them to life in a way the novel didn't even attempt. They do it simply by being there, and having personalities.

The story by now is so well-known that there's no point in summarizing it for you. I would like to consider, however, the implications of *Love Story* as a three-, four- or five-handkerchief movie, a movie that wants viewers to cry at the end. Is this an unworthy purpose? Does the movie become unworthy, as *Newsweek* thought it did, simply because it has been mechanically contrived to tell us a beautiful, tragic tale? I don't think so. There's nothing contemptible about being moved to joy by a musical, to terror by a thriller, to excitement by a Western. Why shouldn't we get a little misty during a story about young lovers separated by death?

Hiller earns our emotional response because of the way he's directed the movie. The Segal book was so patently contrived to force those tears, and moved toward that object with such humorless determination, that it must have actually disgusted a lot of readers. The movie is mostly about life, however, and not death. And because Hiller makes the lovers into individuals, of course we're moved by the film's conclusion. Why not?

Love Streams ★ ★ ★ ★
PG-13, 141 m., 1984

Gena Rowlands (Sarah Lawson), John Cassavetes (Robert Harmon), Diahnne Abbott (Susan), Seymour Cassel (Jack Lawson), Margaret Abbott (Margarita). Directed by John Cassavetes and produced by Menahem Golan and Yoram Globus. Screenplay by Ted Allan and Cassavetes.

John Cassavetes's *Love Streams* is the kind of movie where a woman brings home two horses, a goat, a duck, some chickens, a dog, and a parrot, and you don't have the feeling that the screenplay is going for cheap laughs. In fact, there's a tightening in your throat as you realize how desperate an act you're witnessing, and how unhappy a person is getting out of the taxi with all those animals. The menagerie scene occurs rather late in the film, after we've already locked into Cassavetes's method. This is a movie about mad people, and they are going to be acting in crazy ways, but the movie isn't going to let us off the hook by making them funny or picaresque or even symbolic (as in *King of Hearts*). They are, quite simply, desperate.

The brother, Robert (played by Cassavetes), is a writer who lives up in the Hollywood Hills in one of those houses that looks like *Architectural Digest* Visits a Motel. He writes trashy novels about bad women. A parade of hookers marches through his life; he gathers them by the taxi load, almost as a hobby, and dismisses them with lots of meaningless words about how he loves them, and how they're sweethearts and babies and dolls. The circular drive in front of his house is constantly filled with the cars of the lonely and the desperate. He is an alcoholic who stays up for two or three days at a stretch, as if terrified of missing one single unhappy moment. The sister, Sarah (Gena Rowlands), is as possessive as her brother is evasive. She is in the process of a messy divorce from her husband (Seymour Cassel), and her daughter is in flight from her. Rowlands thinks that maybe she can buy love: First she buys the animals, later she talks about buying her

brother a baby, because that's what he "needs."

At least Cassavetes and Rowlands can communicate. They share perfect trust, although it is the trust of two people in the same trap. There are other characters in the movie that Cassavetes talks at and around, but not with. They include a bemused young singer (Diahnne Abbott) who goes out with Cassavetes but looks at him as if he were capable of imploding, and a former wife (Michele Conway) who turns up one day on the doorstep with a small boy and tells him: "This is your son." The way Cassavetes handles this news is typical of the movie. The woman wonders if maybe he could baby sit for a weekend. He says he will. He brings the kid into the house, scares him away, chases him halfway down Laurel Canyon, brings him back, pours him a beer, has a heart-to-heart about "Women, Life and Marriage," and then asks the kid if he'd like to go to Vegas. Cut to Vegas. Cassavetes dumps the kid in a hotel room and goes out partying all night. He is incapable of any appropriate response to a situation requiring him to care about another human being. He fills his life with noise, hookers, emergencies, and booze to drown out the insistent whisper of duty.

The movie is exasperating, because we never know where we stand or what will happen next. I think that's one of its strengths: There's an exhilaration in this roller-coaster ride through scenes that come out of nowhere. This is not a docudrama or a little psychological playlet with a lesson to be learned. It is a raw, spontaneous life, and when we laugh (as in the scene where Cassavetes summons a doctor to the side of the unconscious Rowlands), we wince.

Viewers raised on trained and tame movies may be uncomfortable in the world of Cassavetes; his films are built around lots of talk and the waving of arms and the invoking of the gods. Cassavetes has been making these passionate personal movies for twenty-five years, ever since his *Shadows* helped create American underground movies. His titles include *Minnie and Moskowitz* (in which Rowlands and Cassel got married), *Faces*, *A Woman Under the Influence*, *The Killing of a Chinese Bookie*, *Gloria*, *Opening Night*, and *Husbands*. Sometimes (as in *Husbands*) the wild truth-telling approach evaporates into a lot of empty talk and play-acting. In *Love Streams*, it works.

Lucas ★ ★ ★ ★
PG-13, 99 m., 1985

Corey Haim (Lucas), Kerri Green (Maggie), Charlie Sheen (Cappie), Courtney Thorne-Smith (Alise), Guy Bond (Coach). Directed by David Seltzer and produced by Lawrence Gordon and David Nicksay. Screenplay by Seltzer.

The first loves of early adolescence are so powerful because they are not based on romance, but on ideals. When they are thirteen and fourteen, boys and girls do not fall in love with one another because of all the usual reasons that are celebrated in love songs; they fall in love because the other person is perfect. Not smart or popular or good-looking, but *perfect*, the embodiment of all good.

The very name of the loved one becomes a holy name, as you can see in *Lucas*, when the hero says, "Maggie. Is that short for Margaret?" And then hugs himself to find that it is, because he suddenly realizes that Margaret is the most wonderful name in all the world.

Everybody grows up, and sooner or later love becomes an experience that has limits and reasons. *Lucas* is a movie that takes place before that happens. It is about a very smart kid who looks a little too short and a little too young to be in high school, and when you tell him that, he nods and solemnly explains that he is "accelerated."

One summer day, while riding his bike through the leafy green of a suburb north of Chicago, he sees a red-haired girl practicing her tennis swing. He stops to speak to her, and before long they are fast friends who sit cross-legged in the grass, knees touching knees, and talk about things that begin with capital letters, like Life and Society and Art.

Lucas loves Maggie, but she is just a little older and more mature than he, and has her eye on a member of the football team. Lucas believes, of course, that the whole value system of football and cheerleaders and pep rallies is corrupt. Maggie says she agrees. But how can she argue when the football hero notices her, breaks up with his girlfriend, and asks her if he can have a kiss?

To describe this situation is to make *Lucas* sound like just one more film about teen-age romance. But it would be tragic if this film got lost in the shuffle of "teen-age movies." This is a movie that is as pure and true to the adolescent experience as Truffaut's *The 400*

Blows. It is true because it assumes all of its characters are intelligent, and do not want to hurt one another, and will refuse to go along with the stupid, painful conformity of high school.

The film centers around the character of Lucas, a skinny kid with glasses and a shock of unruly hair and a gift for trying to talk himself into situations where he doesn't belong. Lucas is played by Corey Haim, who was Sally Field's son in *Murphy's Romance*, and he does not give one of those cute little boy performances that get on your nerves. He creates one of the most three-dimensional, complicated, interesting characters of any age in any recent movie, and if he can continue to act this well he will never become a half-forgotten child star but will continue to grow into an important actor. He is that good.

But the film's other two major actors are just as effective. Kerri Green, who was in *The Goonies*, is so subtle and sensitive as Maggie that you realize she isn't just acting, she understands this character in her heart. As the football hero, Charlie Sheen in some ways has the most difficult role, because we're primed to see him in terms of clichés— the jock who comes along and wins the heart of the girl. Sheen doesn't play the character even remotely that way. It is a surprise to find that he loves Lucas, that he protects him from the goons at school, that although he has won Maggie away from Lucas, he cares very deeply about sparing the kid's feelings.

The last third of the movie revolves around a football game. So many films have ended with the "big match" or the "big game," that my heart started to sink when I saw the game being set up. Surely *Lucas* wasn't going to throw away all its great dialogue and inspired acting on another formula ending? Amazingly, the movie negotiates the football game without falling into predictability. Lucas finds himself in uniform and on the field under the most extraordinary circumstances, but they are plausible circumstances, and what happens then can hardly be predicted.

There are half a dozen scenes in the movie so well-done that they could make little short films of their own. They include: The time Lucas and Maggie listen to classical music and discuss her name; the scene between Maggie and the football hero in the high school's laundry room; the scene in which Lucas is humiliated at a school assembly, and turns the situation to his advantage; the way in which he takes the news that he will not be going to the dance with Maggie; and the very last scene in the whole movie, which is one of those moments of perfect vindication that makes you want to cry.

Lucas was written and directed by David Seltzer, who has obviously put his heart into the film. He has also used an enormous amount of sensibility. In a world where Hollywood has cheapened the teen-age years into predictable vulgarity, he has remembered how urgent, how innocent, and how idealistic those years can be. He has put values into this movie. It is about teen-agers who are learning how to be good to each other, to care, and not simply to be filled with egotism, lust, and selfishness—which is all most Hollywood movies think teen-agers can experience. *Lucas* is one of the year's best films.

M

M*A*S*H ★ ★ ★ ★
R, 116 m., 1970

Donald Sutherland (Hawkeye), Elliott Gould (Trapper John), Tom Skerritt (Duke), Sally Kellerman (Hot Lips Hoolihan), Robert Duvall (Major Burns), Jo Ann Pflug (Lieutenant Dish), Rene Auberjonois (Dago Red). Directed by Robert Altman and produced by Ingo Preminger. Screenplay by Ring Lardner, Jr.

One of the reasons *M*A*S*H* is so funny is that it's so desperate. It is set in a surgical hospital just behind the front lines in Korea, and it is drenched in blood. The surgeons work rapidly and with a gory detachment, sawing off legs and tying up arteries, and making their work possible by pretending they don't care. And when they are at last out of the operating tent, they devote their lives to remaining sane. The way they do that, in *M*A*S*H*, is to be almost metaphysically cruel. There is something about war that inspires practical jokes and the heroes (Donald Sutherland, Elliott Gould, and cronies) are inspired and utterly heartless. They sneak a microphone under the bed of Major "Hot Lips" Hoolihan, and broadcast her lovemaking to the entire camp. They drug a general and photograph him in a brothel.

We laugh, not because *M*A*S*H* is Sgt. Bilko for adults, but because it is so true to the unadmitted sadist in all of us. There is perhaps nothing so exquisite as achieving (as the country song has it) sweet mental revenge against someone we hate with particular dedication. And it is the flat-out, poker-faced hatred in *M*A*S*H* that makes it work. Most comedies want us to laugh at things that aren't really funny; in this one we laugh precisely because they're not funny. We laugh, that we may not cry.

But none of this philosophy comes close to the insane logic of *M*A*S*H*, which is achieved through a peculiar marriage of cinematography, acting, directing, and writing. The movie depends upon timing and tone to be funny. I had an opportunity to read the original script, and I found it uninteresting. It would have been a failure, if it had been directed like most comedies; but Ring Lardner, Jr., wrote it, I suspect, for exactly the approach Robert Altman used in his direction, and so the angle of a glance or the timing of a pause is funnier than any number of conventional gag lines. This is true, for example, in the football game between the surgeons and the general's team. The movie assumes, first of all, that we are intimate with the rules of football. We are. The game then becomes doubly funny, not just because the *M*A*S*H* boys have recruited a former pro as a ringer for their side, but because their victory depends upon legal cheating (how about a center-eligible play?). The audience's laughter is triumphant, because our guys have outsmarted the other guys. Another movie might have gone for purely physical humor in the scene (big guy walks over little guy, etc.) and blown it.

The performances have a lot to do with the movie's success. Elliott Gould and Donald Sutherland are two genuinely funny actors; they don't have to make themselves ridiculous to get a laugh. They're funny because their humor comes so directly from their personalities. They underplay everything (and Sutherland and Gould trying to downstage each other could eventually lead to complete paralysis).

Strangely enough, they're convincing as surgeons. During operations, covered with blood and gore, they mutter their way through running commentaries that sound totally professional. Sawing and hacking away at a parade of bodies, they should be driving us away, but they don't. We can take the unusually high gore-level in *M*A*S*H* because it is originally part of the movie's logic. If the surgeons didn't have to face the daily list of maimed and mutilated bodies, none of the rest of their lives would make any sense. When they are matter-of-factly cruel to "Hot Lips" Hoolihan, we cannot quite separate that from the matter-of-fact way they've got to put wounded bodies back together again. "Hot Lips," who is all Army professionalism and objectivity, is less human because the suffering doesn't reach her.

I think perhaps that's what the movie is about. Gould and Sutherland and the members of their merry band of pranksters are offended because the Army regulars don't feel deeply enough. "Hot Lips" is concerned with protocol, but not with war. And so the surgeons, dancing on the brink of crack-ups, dedicate themselves to making her *feel* something. Her façade offends them; no one could be unaffected by the work of this hospital, but she is. And so if they can crack her defenses and reduce her to their own level of dedicated cynicism, the number of suffering human beings in the camp will go up by one. And even if they fail, they can have a hell of a lot of fun trying. Also, of course, it's a distraction.

Macbeth ★ ★ ★ ★
R, 139 m., 1972

Jon Finch (Macbeth), Francesca Annis (Lady Macbeth), Martin Shaw (Banquo), Nicholas Selby (Duncan), John Stride (Ross), Stephen Chase (Malcolm), Paul Shelley (Donalbain), Terence Bayler (Macduff). Directed by Roman Polanski and produced by Andrew Braunsberg. Screenplay by Polanski and Kenneth Tynan.

We have all heard it a hundred times, Macbeth's despairing complaint about life: ". . . it is a tale told by an idiot, full of sound and fury, signifying nothing." But who has taken it more seriously than Roman Polanski, who tells his bloody masterpiece at precisely the level of the idiot's tale?

Macbeth always before seemed reasonable, dealing with a world in which wrongdoing was punished and logic demonstrated. Macbeth's character was not strong enough to stand up under the weight of the crime he committed, so he disintegrated into the fantasies of ignorant superstition, while his flimsy wife went mad.

It all seemed so clear. And at the proper moment, the forces of justice stepped forward, mocked the witches' prophecies which deluded poor Macbeth and set things right for the final curtain. There were, no doubt, those who thought the play was about how Malcolm became king of Scotland.

But in this film Polanski and his collaborator, Kenneth Tynan, place themselves at Macbeth's side and choose to share his point of view, and in their film there's no room at all for detachment. All those noble, tragic Macbeths—Orson Welles and Maurice Evans and the others—look like imposters now, and the king is revealed as a scared kid.

No effort has been made to make Macbeth a tragic figure, and his death moves us infinitely less than the murder of Macduff's young son. Polanski places us in a visual universe of rain and mist, of gray dawns and clammy dusks, and there is menace in the sound of hoofbeats but no cheer in the cry of trumpets. Even the heroic figure of Macduff has been tempered; now he is no longer the instrument of God's justice, but simply a man bent on workaday revenge. The movie ends with the simple fact that a job has been done: Macbeth got what was coming to him.

Polanski has imposed this vision on the film so effectively that even the banquet looks like a gang of highwaymen ready to wolf down stolen sheep. Everyone in the film seems to be pushed by circumstances; there is small feeling that the characters are motivated by ideas. They seem so ignorant at times that you wonder if they understand the wonderful dialogue Shakespeare has written for them. It's as if the play has been inhabited by Hell's Angels who are quick studies.

All of this, of course, makes Polanski's *Macbeth* more interesting than if he had done your ordinary, respectable, awe-stricken tiptoe around Shakespeare. This is an original film by an original film artist, and not an "interpretation." It should have been titled *Polanski's Macbeth*, just as we got *Fellini Satyricon*.

I might as well be honest and say it is impossible to watch certain scenes without thinking of the Charles Manson case. It is impossible to watch a film directed by Roman Polanski and not react on more than one level to such images as a baby being "untimely ripped from his mother's womb." Indeed, Polanski adds his own grim conclusion after Shakespeare's, with a final scene in which Malcolm, now crowned king, goes to consult the same witches who deceived Macbeth. Polanski's characters resemble Manson: They are anti-intellectual, witless, and driven by deep, shameful wells of lust and violence.

Why did Polanski choose to make *Macbeth*, and why this *Macbeth*? I have no way of guessing. This is certainly one of the most pessimistic films ever made, and there seems little doubt that Polanski intended his film to be full of sound and fury—which it is, to the brim—and to signify nothing.

It's at that level that Polanski is at his most adamant: The events that occur in the film must not be allowed to have significance. Polanski and Tynan take only small liberties with Shakespeare, and yet so successfully does Polanski orchestrate *Macbeth*'s visual content that we come out of the film with a horrified realization. We didn't identify with either Macbeth or Macduff in their final duel. We were just watching a sword-fight.

Mad Max Beyond Thunderdome
★ ★ ★ ★
R, 115 m., 1985

Mel Gibson (Mad Max), Tina Turner (Aunty Entity), Frank Thring (Collector), Angelo Rossitto (Master), Paul Larsson (Blaster), Angry Anderson (Ironbar). Directed and produced by George Miller. Co-directed by George Ogilvie. Screenplay by Miller and Terry Hayes.

It's not supposed to happen this way. Sequels are not supposed to be better than the movies that inspired them. The third movie in a series isn't supposed to create a world more complex, more visionary, and more entertaining than the first two. Sequels are supposed to be creative voids. But now here is *Mad Max Beyond Thunderdome*, not only the best of the three Mad Max movies, but one of the best films of 1985.

From its opening shot of a bizarre vehicle being pulled by camels through the desert, *Mad Max Three* places us more firmly within its apocalyptic postnuclear world than ever before. We are some years in the future; how many, it is hard to say, but so few years that the frames and sheet metal of 1985 automobiles are still being salvaged for makeshift new vehicles of bizarre design. And yet enough years that a new society is taking shape. The bombs have fallen, the world's petroleum supplies have been destroyed, and in the deserts of Australia, mankind has found a new set of rules and started on a new game.

The driver of the camels is Mad Max (Mel Gibson), former cop, now sort of a free-lance nomad. After his vehicle is stolen and he is left in the desert to die, he makes his way somehow to Bartertown, a quasi-Casablanca hammered together out of spare parts. Bartertown is where you go to buy, trade, or sell anything—or anybody. It is supervised by a Sydney Greenstreet-style fat man named the Collector (Frank Thring), and ruled by an imperious queen named Aunty Entity (Tina Turner).

And it is powered by an energy source that is, in its own way, a compelling argument against nuclear war: In chambers beneath Bartertown, countless pigs live and eat and defecate, and from their waste products, Turner's soldiers generate methane gas. This leads to some of the movie's most memorable moments, as Mad Max and others wade knee-deep in piggy-do.

Tina Turner herself lives far above the masses, in a birds'-nest throne room perched high overhead. And as Mad Max first visits Turner's sky palace, I began to realize how completely the director, George Miller, had imagined this future world. It has the crowding and the variety of a movie crossroads, but it also has a riot of hairstyles and costume design, as if these desperate creatures could pause from the daily struggle for survival only long enough to invent new punk fashions. After the clothes, the hair, the crowding, the incessant activity, the spendthrift way in which Miller fills his screen with throwaway details, Bartertown becomes much more than a movie set—it's an astounding address of the imagination, a place as real as Bogart's Casablanca or Orson Welles's Xanadu or the Vienna of *The Third Man*. That was even before the movie introduced me to Thunderdome, the arena for Bartertown's hand-to-hand battles to the death.

Thunderdome is the first really original movie idea about how to stage a fight since we got the first karate movies. The "dome" is a giant upside-down framework bowl. The spectators scurry up the sides of the bowl, and look down on the fighters. But the combatants are not limited to fighting on the floor of the arena. They are placed on harnesses with long elastic straps, so that they can leap from top to bottom and from side to side with great lethal bounds. Thunderdome is to fighting as three-dimensional chess is to a flat board. And the weapons available to the fighters are hung from the inside of the dome: Cleavers, broadaxes, sledge-hammers, the inevitable chainsaw.

It is into Thunderdome that Mad Max goes for his showdown with Aunty Entity's greatest warrior, and George Miller's most original creation, a character named Master-Blaster, who is actually two people. Blaster is a giant hulk of a man in an iron mask. Master is a dwarf who rides him like a chariot, standing in an iron harness above his shoulders. The fight between Mad Max and Master-Blaster is one of the great creative action scenes in the movies.

There is a lot more in *Mad Max Beyond Thunderdome*. The descent into the pig world, for example, and the visit to a sort of postwar hippie commune, and of course the inevitable final chase scene, involving car, train, truck, cycle, and incredible stunts. This is a movie that strains at the leash of the possible, a movie of great visionary wonders.

Madame Sousatzka ★ ★ ★ ★
PG-13, 120 m., 1988

Shirley MacLaine (Madame Sousatzka), Navin Chowdhry (Manek Sen), Peggy Ashcroft (Lady Emily), Shabana Azmi (Sushila), Twiggy (Jenny), Leigh Lawson (Ronnie Blum), Geoffrey Bayldon (Cordle), Lee Montague (Vincent Pick). Directed by John Schlesinger and produced by Robin Dalton. Screenplay by Ruth Prawer Jhabvala and Schlesinger, from the novel by Bernice Rubens.

The Indian boy comes every afternoon for piano lessons from Madame Sousatzka, who cannot disguise the love in her voice as she teaches him not only about music, but also about how to sit, how to breathe, how to hold his elbows, and how to think about his talent. Behind her, in the shadows of her musty London apartment, are the photographs of earlier students who were taught the same lessons before they went out into the world—where some of them became great pianists and others became just players of the piano.

Madame Sousatzka believes that this boy, Manek, can be a great pianist, a virtuoso—but we have no objective way to know if she is a great teacher of great musicians, or just a piano teacher who is deluding herself and the boy. That doesn't matter. *Madame Sousatzka* is not a one-level movie in which everything leads up to the cliché of the crucial first concert. This is not a movie about success or failure; it is a movie about soldiering on, about continuing to do your best, day after day, simply because you believe in yourself—no matter what anyone else thinks. Madame believes this sixteen-year-old boy can be a great pianist, and that she—no one else—is the person to guide him on the right path to his destiny.

Madame Sousatzka is a film about her efforts to protect the boy from all the pressures and temptations around him, while simultaneously shoring up the ruins of her own world. As played by Shirley MacLaine, in one of the best performances of her career, she is a faded, aging woman who possesses great stubbornness and conviction. Once, long ago, she failed in her own concert debut. Her own mother pushed her too fast, too soon, and she broke down in the middle of her debut concert and fled from the stage.

That humiliation is still in her nightmares, and still shapes her attitude toward her students. They must not be allowed to perform in public until they are ready. Unfortunately, Madame is hardly ever prepared to admit they are ready, and so sooner or later all of her pupils are forced to make a break with her. Their departures have made her career a series of heartbreaks, and populated the shelves of photographs in her apartment.

Manek, her latest student, is played by Navin Chowdhry as a teen-ager who apart from his talent is a fairly normal young man. He travels by skateboard despite Madame's explicit orders that he is not to endanger his hands, he enjoys playing the piano and yet is not obsessed by it, and he has a lively interest in the model (Twiggy) who lives upstairs in Madame's eccentric rooming house. His mother (Shabana Azmi) is divorced, and supports them by making gourmet Indian pastries for the food department of Harrod's.

She has an admirer, but Manek is jealous of her boyfriend, and wants to make his concert debut so that he—not some strange man—can support his mother. He is encouraged in his ambition by a predatory booking agent who overhears his playing and wants to use him immediately—creating a war of wills between Madame and her pupil.

Madame Sousatzka was directed by John Schlesinger, who plays it in a very particular kind of London household. The shabby rooming house is on a once-distinguished street that has now been targeted by realtors for gentrification. The house is owned by Lady Emily (Dame Peggy Ashcroft), a sweet-tempered old lady who lives in the basement and peacefully coexists with her tenants, who include Madame, the model, and Cordle (Geoffrey Bayldon), a decayed civil servant type with occasional, furtive homosexual adventures. Although the movie creates affection for the little community within the house, this is not a film about how the developers must be defeated—and you will be relieved to learn that the young pianist does not star in a benefit for Lady Emily.

The film is not about preserving the present, but about being prepared to change, and by the end of the film Lady Emily and Cordle have found that they can live quite comfortably in a little riverside flat, while Madame resolutely soldiers on in the house, undeterred by the noise and dirt of construction. But she has changed in a more important way, by being able to understand for the first time, a little anyway, why a student must eventually be allowed to go out into the world and take his chances.

MacLaine's approach to the role is interesting. She deliberately ages herself, and has put on weight for the role, so that there is relatively little of the familiar Shirley MacLaine to be seen on the screen. Even those traces soon disappear into the role of a woman who loves music, loves to teach, loves her students, and is crippled only by her traumatic failure on the stage. It might have embittered her, but it has not; she holds onto her students not out of resentment but out of pride, and fear.

The screenplay, by Ruth Prawer Jhabvala and Schlesinger, takes the time to be precise about teaching; we may feel by the end that we've had a few lessons ourselves. It is about discipline, about patience, about love of music. Manek tells Sousatzka at one point that when he goes on a stage, he will feel a small core of strength inside himself that she has given him. It is all, besides technique, that any teacher has to offer. *Madame Sousatzka* is an extraordinary movie that loves music and loves the people it is about, and has the patience to do justice to both.

Making Mr. Right ★ ★ ★ ½
PG-13, 98 m., 1987

John Malkovich (Jeff/Ulysses), Ann Magnuson (Frankie), Glenne Headly (Trish), Ben Masters (Steve), Laurie Metcalf (Sandy), Robert Trebor (Tuxedo Salesman). Directed by Susan Seidelman and produced by Mike Wise and Joel Tuber. Screenplay by Floyd Byars and Laurie Frank.

Making Mr. Right is about a scientist who invents a remarkably lifelike android in his own image and about an ad executive who begins to like the android more than the scientist. These raw materials easily could have been turned into a fairly dreary movie, but not this time. Instead, we get a smart, quick-witted, and genuinely funny movie.

A lot of the movie's smarts come from John Malkovich, who plays the dual role of the scientist and the android, and a newcomer named Ann Magnuson, who plays the account executive with a pert intelligence that reminded me of Susan Hayward or Gloria Grahame. Both actors see right through their roles, know what's funny and what's important, and are able to put a nice spin even on the obligatory scenes.

That's true, for example, during the sweet, tentative moments when the android begins to fall for the woman. Malkovich provides just the right amount of inept clumsiness for the android, which sometimes has trouble getting its mind-body coordination in line. Like Jeff Bridges in *Starman*, he's able to meet the tricky challenge of moving in an uncoordinated way without looking merely ridiculous.

Magnuson is fun, too, with her high heels and designer outfits, clipboards and speculative looks. She has an instantly combative relationship with the scientist who invented the android, and it's made trickier because as the android grows more human, the scientist subtly grows more robotic.

Making Mr. Right was directed by Susan Seidelman, whose previous credits are *Smithereens*, which I didn't much like, and *Desperately Seeking Susan*, which was much more assured. With this film, she hits her stride as a comedy director who would rather be

clever than obvious, who allows good actors such as Malkovich to go for quiet effects rather than broad, dumb clichés.

Another comedy depending on dual and mistaken identities is *The Secret of My Success*. Seeing the two movies is instructive because they take such different approaches to the challenge of identity. *Secret* has lots of moments when characters don't realize exactly who they're talking to, and it creates those moments out of the stupidity of the characters. In *Mr. Right*, there are scenes where the scientist and the android are mistaken for one another, and Seidelman uses the misunderstandings to make comic points about the personalities of her characters: They make wrong assumptions because of who they are, instead of because of how stupid they are. It makes all the difference in the world.

Seidelman also has fun populating the outskirts of her plot with good character actors, especially Robert Trebor as the tuxedo salesman. You may remember him as the smarmy, sweating porno store operator in *52 Pick-Up*. The distance between these two good performances is impressive.

At one point in *Making Mr. Right*, we see a theater marquee in the background advertising *The Parent Trap*. That was, of course, the movie where Hayley Mills played twins, thanks to trick photography. Malkovich is often seen onscreen with himself in this movie, but I never noticed any seams or glitches, and I was grateful to Seidelman for not providing any moments that were intended merely to exploit the trick.

Man of Iron ★ ★ ★ ★
NO MPAA RATING, 140 m., 1980

Jerzy Radziwilowicz (Tomczyk), Krystyna Janda (Agnieszka), Marian Opania (Winkiel), Lech Walesa (As himself). Directed by Andrzej Wajda. Screenplay by Aleksander Scibor-Rylski.

As a youth of thirteen, the Polish filmmaker Andrzej Wajda lived in a small town where he witnessed German troops lead thousands of Polish army officers to their deaths in concentration camps. As a young student after the war, he lived through the repressive Stalinist years. In the 1950s he made his first films, betraying a spirit that the Party ideologues found too individualistic for their taste. In a speech in 1981 at American University in Washington, D.C., he quoted from

"the best review I've ever had." It was from a confidential 1976 Polish censor's report:

. . . politically and ideologically he is not on our side. He has taken the position, often found among artists, of a "neutral judge" of history and today's times—believing that he has the right . . . to apply the gauge of humanism and morals to all the problems of the world and that he doesn't need Marxism nor any other philosophical-social system to do it.

Wajda is at it again, judging history, applying the gauge of humanism, not requiring Marxism, in *Man of Iron*, his extraordinary film about the birth of the Polish Solidarity labor movement. This film is a marriage between a fictional story and actual events, and Wajda took his cameras and his actors right into the firestorm of the Gdansk demonstrations to record the victorious Solidarity agreement at the Lenin Shipyard.

Wajda is in a strange position in Poland. He and Krystof Zanussi are the only two Polish directors still in Poland who have international reputations. He is honored all over the world, but at home the authorities are a little reluctant to give him his head; his films do not promote domestic tranquility.

Man of Iron, filmed during the tumultuous days of relative freedom when Solidarity seemed to hold all the cards, was permitted to be flown out of Warsaw during the closing days of the 1981 Cannes Film Festival, where it won the Grand Prize.

It's a sequel of sorts to Wajda's *Man of Marble* (1976), although you needn't have seen the earlier film, which was about a labor leader during the years of repressive policies in Poland. This film is about the same man's son, who is a Solidarity leader a few steps down in influence from Lech Walesa. Wajda follows his fictional characters into the center of real events (it's sometimes hard to tell where fiction ends and documentary begins), and he uses a broadcast newsman as an interviewer—a technique that allows his film to go places and ask questions that would be difficult to cover in "pure" fiction.

Exactly the same two techniques—the use of a character who is a journalist, and the juxtaposition of a fictional story with actual events—were used by Haskell Wexler in *Medium Cool*, the film about the 1968 Democratic convention demonstrations in Chicago. The approach leaves some ragged edges, but when you are filming at the cutting edge of history you can't stop for rewrites.

Wajda's film is not a polemic, however.

That humanist streak, complained of by the state censors, sneaks through even at the expense of the Solidarity politics he wants to celebrate. Wajda is an artist first, a reporter second or third, and not really a very good propagandist. And the best things in *Man of Iron* are the purely personal moments, the scenes where Wajda is concerned with the human dimensions of his characters rather than their ideological struggles.

Those dimensions come through most clearly in the character of Winkiel (Marian Opania), the alcoholic journalist who is sent by the party bosses in Warsaw to spy on Solidarity in the guise of a radio reporter. Winkiel had his own values once. Meeting the son of the old labor leader, he remembers the father. Arriving in Gdansk, Winkiel discovers to his horror that the area has been declared dry because of the troubles—he can't get booze. A party agent slips him a bottle of vodka, but Winkiel breaks it on the bathroom floor, and in a scene that will profoundly affect the way we understand his later actions, he desperately tries to soak up some of the vodka with a towel. He is a man whose spirit is broken, a man prepared to be a spy. The most moving of the several stories in *Man of Iron* concerns his gradual rediscovery of his old values, until he finally decides to side with the workers and to abandon his undercover role.

Man of Iron is a fascinating and courageous document—a film of dissent made because of, or in spite of, the upheaval in Poland.

In that speech in 1981, Wajda closed with these words: *Someone once asked me a naive question. It's a question often asked of very old writers: Do you feel that you've helped to make history? My answer is this. I don't know whether I helped make it. I know I didn't stand with my hands folded. I didn't look on indifferently as history was being made.*

The Man Who Would Be King
★ ★ ★ ★
PG, 129 m., 1975

Sean Connery (Daniel Dravot), Michael Caine (Peachy Carnahan), Christopher Plummer (Kipling), Saeed Jaffrey (Billy Fish), Shakira Caine (Roxanne). Directed by John Huston and produced by John Foreman. Screenplay by Huston and Gladys Hill.

John Huston's *The Man Who Would Be King* is swashbuckling adventure, pure and sim-

ple, from the hand of a master. It's unabashed and thrilling and fun. The movie invites comparison with the great action films like *Gunga Din* and *Mutiny on the Bounty*, and with Huston's own classic *The Treasure of the Sierra Madre:* We get strong characterizations, we get excitement, we even get to laugh every once in a while.

The action epics of the last twenty years seem to have lost their sense of humor; it's as if once the budget goes over five million dollars, directors think they have to be deadly serious. *Lawrence of Arabia* was a great movie, but introspective and solemn, and efforts such as *Doctor Zhivago* and *War and Peace* never dared to smile. Huston's movie isn't like that. It reflects his personality and his own best films; it's open, sweeping, and lusty—and we walk out feeling exhilarated.

Huston waited a long time to make this film, and its history is a Hollywood legend. He originally cast Bogart and Gable, but then Bogart died, and the project was shelved until 1975. Maybe it's just as well. We need movies like this more now than we did years ago, when Hollywood wasn't shy about straightforward action films. And Huston's eventual casting of Michael Caine and Sean Connery is exactly right.

They work together so well, they interact so easily and with such camaraderie, that watching them is a pleasure. They never allow themselves to be used merely as larger-than-life heroes, photographed against vast landscapes. Kipling's story, and Huston's interpretation of it, requires a lot more than that; it requires acting of a subtle and difficult sort, even if the sheer energy of the movie makes it look easy.

The two of them play former British soldiers who vow to march off into Afghanistan or somewhere and find a kingdom not yet touched by civilization. With their guns and training, they think they'll be able to take over pretty easily, manipulate the local high priests, and set themselves up as rulers. They tell their plan to an obscure colonial editor named Kipling (played very nicely by Christopher Plummer) and then they set off into the mountains. After the obligatory close calls, including an avalanche that somehow saves their lives, they find their lost land and it's just as they expected it would be.

The natives aren't too excited by their new rulers at first, but a lucky Masonic key chain saves the day—never mind how—and Connery finds himself worshiped as a deity. He even gets to like it, and condescends to

Caine, who remains a Cockney and unimpressed. The movie proceeds with impossible coincidences, untold riches, romances and betrayals, and heroic last words and—best of all—some genuinely witty scenes between Connery and Caine, and when it's over we haven't learned a single thing worth knowing and there's not even a moral, to speak of, but we've had fun. It's great that someone still has the gift of making movies like this; even Huston, after thirty years, must have wondered whether he still knew how.

The Man With Two Brains ★ ★
R, 91 m., 1983

Steve Martin (Dr. Hfuhruhurr), Kathleen Turner (Dolores), David Warner (Dr. Necessiter), Paul Benedict (Butler). Directed by Carl Reiner and produced by David V. Picker and William E. McEuen. Written by Reiner, Steve Martin, and George Gipe.

Steve Martin and Carl Reiner continue their tour of ancient movie genres with *The Man With Two Brains*, which does for Mad Scientist movies what *Dead Men Don't Wear Plaid* did for private eye pictures, which is to say, not very much. Some of the gags depend on a familiarity with classics like *Donovan's Brain, Bride of Frankenstein*—and even, in this case, Mel Brooks's *Young Frankenstein.* Other gags depend on Steve Martin's comic personality, as a guy whose elevator doesn't go all the way to the top floor. I've never found Steve Martin irresistibly funny. There's something stolid about his approach to humor, something deliberately half-paced and mannered that seems designed to be subtly irritating. I guess it's a tribute to *The Man With Two Brains* that I found myself laughing a fair amount of the time, despite my feelings about Martin. This is not a great comedy but it has scenes that don't know that.

Martin plays a brain surgeon named Dr. Michael Hfuhruhurr. The moment I heard the name I knew we were in trouble, and, sure enough, the movie never tires of making jokes based on his funny name. Since the First Law of Comedy should be *No funny names are funny unless they are used by W.C. Fields or Groucho Marx,* the name jokes are an exercise in futility. Hfuhruhurr has perfected something called the cranial screw-top method of brain surgery, and uses it to save the life of a beautiful young woman (Kathleen Turner) whom he's hit with his Mercedes. The woman, alas, turns out to be a gold digger. She seduces the gardener but refuses to have sex with Hfuhruhurr, who in his frustration falls in love with the brain of another young woman—a brain that has been pickled in a jar in the Vienna laboratory of the eccentric Dr. Necessiter (David Warner).

And so on. The movie uses the basic approach established by Brooks in *Young Frankenstein:* sight gags, cross-references, scatalogical puns, broad plotting, running gags, and so on. It filters its material through Martin's peculiar style, which is, I think, not light-footed enough. Martin is the kind of comedian who chews every line, lingering even on the throwaways.

Turner, seen in *Body Heat*, has a nice teasing quality as the hot-and-cold sexpot. David Warner (remember him from *Morgan* all those years ago?) makes a suitably cadaverous mad scientist. But the cast somehow seems underpopulated, and the characters are underdeveloped. That's one of the weaknesses of genre satires: The filmmakers depend on our knowledge of past characters as a substitute for creating new ones. And since comedy grows out of inappropriate behavior, and our notions of inappropriate behavior depend on what we know about people, the jokes all boil down to the fact that the characters in old Mad Scientist movies wouldn't behave like the characters in this one. So what?

The Manchurian Candidate ★ ★ ★ ★
PG-13, 126 m., 1962

Frank Sinatra (Bennett Marco), Laurence Harvey (Raymond Shaw), Janet Leigh (Rosie), Angela Lansbury (Raymond's Mother), Henry Silva (Chunjin), James Gregory (Senator John Iselin), Leslie Parrish (Jocie), John McGiver (Senator Thomas Jordan), Khigh Dhiegh (Yen Lo), James Edwards (Corporal Melvin). Directed by John Frankenheimer and produced by George Axelrod and Frankenheimer. Screenplay by Axelrod.

Here is a movie that was made more than twenty-five years ago, and it feels as if it were made yesterday. Not a moment of *The Manchurian Candidate* lacks edge and tension and a cynical spin—and what's even more surprising is how the film now plays as a political comedy, as well as a thriller. After being suppressed for a quarter of a century, after

becoming an unseen legend that never turned up on TV or on home video, John Frankenheimer's 1962 masterpiece now re-emerges as one of the best and brightest of modern American films.

The story is a matter of many levels, some of them frightening, some pointed with satirical barbs. In a riveting opening sequence, a group of American combat infantrymen are shown being brainwashed by a confident Chinese communist hypnotist, who has them so surely under his control that one man is ordered to strangle one of his buddies and shoot another in the head, and cheerfully complies.

Two members of the group get our special attention: the characters played by Frank Sinatra and Laurence Harvey. Harvey seems to be the main target of the Chinese scheme, which is to return him to American society as a war hero, and then allow him to lead a normal life until he is triggered by a buried hypnotic suggestion, and turned into an assassin completely brainwashed to take orders from his enemy controller. Harvey does indeed reenter society, where he is the son of a Republican dowager (Angela Lansbury), and the stepson of her husband (James Gregory). Gregory is a leading candidate for his party's presidential nomination, and more than that I choose not to reveal. Meanwhile, Sinatra also returns to civilian life, but he is haunted by nightmares in which he dimly recalls the terrifying details of the brainwashing. He contacts Harvey (who is not, we must remember, a conscious assassin, but merely a brainwashed victim). Sinatra also becomes central to a Pentagon investigation of a possible plot that affected all the members of his platoon—which disappeared on patrol and returned telling the same fabricated story.

Midway in his investigation, Sinatra meets and falls in love with a woman played by Janet Leigh, and their relationship provides the movie with what looks to me like a subtle, tantalizing suggestion of an additional level of intrigue. They meet in the parlor car of a train, where Sinatra, shaking, cannot light a cigarette and knocks over the table with his drink on it. Leigh follows him to the space between cars, lights a cigarette for him, and engages him in a very weird conversation, after which they fall in love and she quickly ditches her fiancé. What's going on here? My notion is that Sinatra's character is a Manchurian killer, too—one allowed to remember details of Harvey's brainwashing because that would make him seem more

credible. And Leigh? She is Sinatra's controller.

This possible scenario simply adds another level to a movie already rich in intrigue. The depths to which the Lansbury character will sink in this movie must be seen to be believed, and the actress generates a smothering "momism" that defines the type. By the end of the film, so many different people have used so many different strategies on Harvey's overtaxed brain that he is almost literally a zombie, unable to know what to believe, incapable of telling who can be trusted.

The Manchurian Candidate got glowing reviews when it was first released in 1962. (Pauline Kael wrote: "It may be the most sophisticated political satire ever made in Hollywood.") But then it was shelved in a dispute between United Artists and Sinatra. For more than twenty-five years, memories of *The Manchurian Candidate* have tantalized those who saw it at the time. Was it really as good as it seemed? It was.

Manhattan ★ ★ ★ ¹/₂
R, 96 m., 1979

Woody Allen (Isaac Davis), Diane Keaton (Mary Wilke), Michael Murphy (Yale), Mariel Hemingway (Tracy), Meryl Streep (Jill), Anne Byrne (Emily), Karen Ludwig (Connie), Michael O'Donoghue (Dennis). Directed by Woody Allen and produced by Charles H. Joffe. Screenplay by Allen and Marshall Brickman.

The overture is filled with brash confidence: Gershwin's "Rhapsody in Blue," played over powerful black-and-white visions of Manhattan and its skyline, and the mighty bridges leaping out to it from the provinces. The voice is filled with uncertainty and hesitation: "Chapter One. . . ."

The voice is Woody Allen's, of course, and we find ourselves laughing—actually laughing *already*—on the words "Chapter One," because the Allen character is so firmly established in our imaginations that we supply the rest of the joke ourselves. "Chapter One," yes, but Woody's the definitive vulnerable artist with giant dreams, and so of course he begins with confidence but will be mired in self-doubt long, long before Chapter Two.

A great deal of the success of Allen's *Manhattan* depends on how well he has established that Woody persona. Because we believe we know him (or the character he plays), we supply additional dimensions to the situations on the screen. A movie that might seem sketchily fleshed-out in other hands becomes a great deal more resonant in Allen's: This is a variation on a familiar theme.

And the Gershwin is a masterstroke. Woody Allen populates his film with people who are at odds with their own visions of themselves. They've been so sold, indeed, on the necessity of seeming true and grave and ethical that even their affairs, their deceptions, have to be discussed in terms of "values" and "meanings"—the dialogue in this film was learned in psychoanalysis. Their rationalizations double back upon themselves, and then, clear as a bell on the sound track, there are the Gershwin songs. "S'Wonderful" and "Embraceable You" and "Sweet and Low Down" and "I've Got a Crush on You" . . . written as if love were *simple*, for chrissakes, and you actually could "fall" in love when we all know it's more a matter of pulling yourself up, hand over hand, out of a pit of snapping emotions. In Allen's earlier films, middle-class society was usually the contrast to the Woody character's hang-ups and fantasies. This time, brilliantly, he sets his entire story in a "real" world—and uses the music as the counterpoint. No wonder it's deliberately loud and dominating; Gershwin is the second most important person in this film.

Allen's humor has always been based on the contrast between his character ("Woody," spectacled, anemic, a slob, incredibly bright and verbal, tortured by self-doubt) and his goals (writing a great novel, being like Bogart, winning the love of beautiful women). The fact that he thinks he can achieve his dreams (or that he *pretends* he thinks he can) makes him lovable. It is amazing, for example, how many women believe they are unique because they find Woody sexy.

What Allen does in *Manhattan* is to treat both the Woody character and the goals with more realism, and to deal with them in an urban social setting we can recognize. He was already doing this in *Annie Hall*, the comedy the critics said was "really" serious—as if comedy were not already serious enough. His earlier movies were made from farce, slapstick, stand-up verbal wit, satire, and the appeal of the Woody character. *Annie Hall* and *Manhattan* are made from his observations about the way we talk and

behave, and the fearsome distances between what we say and what we mean, and how we behave and how we mean to behave.

The story follows several characters through several affairs. Woody himself is twice-divorced as the movie opens—most recently from a lesbian who is writing a book that will tell all about their marriage. He is having an affair with a seventeen-year-old girl (Mariel Hemingway). His best friend, Yale (Michael Murphy), is married and is having an affair with a girl he met at a party (Diane Keaton). But Murphy has doubts about the relationship, and so subtly tries to shift Keaton to Allen, who in the meantime thinks he wants to ditch the seventeen-year-old. Inevitably, Woody and Keaton begin to fall in love, and their courtship is photographed against magnificent Manhattan backdrops. And once this is all set up, of course, it goes topsy-turvy.

The relationships aren't really the point of the movie: It's more about what people say during relationships—or, to put it more bluntly, it's about how people lie by technically telling the truth. *Manhattan* is one of the few movies that could survive a sound track of its dialogue; a lot of it, by Allen and Marshall Brickman, has the kind of convoluted intellectual cynicism of the early Nichols and May (and a lot of the rest of it consists of great one-liners).

Manhattan has been almost routinely praised by the New York critics as "better than *Annie Hall.*" I don't think so. I think it goes wrong in the very things the New York critics like the most—when, in the last forty-five minutes or so, Allen does a subtle turn on his material and gets serious about it. I'm most disturbed by the final scene between Woody and Mariel Hemingway. It's not really thought out; Allen hasn't found the line between the irony the scene needs and the sentiment he wants his character to feel. The later scenes involving the Michael Murphy character are also not as good as the early ones; the character is seen correctly for humor, but hasn't been developed completely enough to bear the burden of confession.

And yet this is a very good movie. Woody Allen is . . . Woody, sublimely. Diane Keaton gives us a fresh and nicely edged New York intellectual. And Mariel Hemingway deserves some kind of special award for what's in some ways the most difficult role in the film. It wouldn't do, you see, for the love scenes between Woody and Mariel to feel

awkward or to hint at cradle-snatching or an unhealthy interest on Woody's part in innocent young girls. But they don't feel that way: Hemingway's character has a certain grave intelligence, a quietly fierce pride, that, strangely enough, suggest that even at seventeen she's one Woody should be thinking of during Gershwin's "Someone to Watch Over Me."

NOTE: The video version of Manhattan *was released with black bands at the top and bottom to preserve the wide-screen composition of the film. This unusual decision reflects Allen's perfectionism—and provides an eye-opening demonstration of how much is lost when other widescreen formats are squeezed into the video frame.*

The Manhattan Project ★ ★ ★ ★
PG-13, 118 m., 1986

John Lithgow (John Mathewson), Christopher Collet (Paul Stephens), Cynthia Nixon (Jenny Anderman), Jill Eikenberry (Elizabeth Stephens). Directed by Marshall Brickman and produced by Brickman and Jennifer Ogden. Screenplay by Brickman and Thomas Baum.

The kid is really smart, but like a lot of smart kids he has learned to hide it, to lay back and observe and keep his thoughts to himself. When the new scientist arrives in town and starts to date the kid's mother, and then tries to make pals by taking the kid on a tour of the research lab where he works, the kid keeps his eyes open and his mouth shut. But he knows the lab is devoted to nuclear weapons research, and he's kind of insulted that the scientist would try to deceive him.

That's the setup for *The Manhattan Project*, a clever, funny, and very skillful thriller about how the kid builds his own atomic bomb. This is not, however, another one of those teen-age movies about bright kids and science projects. There have been some good movies in that genre—I liked *WarGames* and *Real Genius*—but this isn't really a teen-age movie at all, it's a thriller. And it's one of those thrillers that stays as close as possible to the everyday lives of convincing people, so that the movie's frightening aspects are convincing.

The kid is played by Christopher Collet. He is very, very smart. We know that not just because we are told so, but because the movie has lots of subtle, sometimes funny little ways of demonstrating it—as when the kid solves a puzzle in three seconds flat, just as we were trying to understand it.

The kid lives with his mother (Jill Eikenberry) in an upstate New York college town. John Lithgow plays the scientist who moves into the town and starts to date Eikenberry and makes friends with the kid. The movie is very sophisticated about the relationship between Collet and Lithgow. This isn't a case of the two men competing for the affections of the mother; indeed, there are times when these two bright, lonely males seem to have more in common with each other.

In particular, the Lithgow character isn't allowed to fall into clichés. He isn't a mad scientist, and he isn't a heartless intellectual: He's just a smart man trying to do his job well and still have some measure of simple human pleasure.

After Collet is given his tour of the "research center," he tells his girlfriend (Cynthia Nixon) that he's a little insulted that they thought they could fool him. He knows a bomb factory when he sees one. And so, to prove various things to various people, the kid figures out a way to sneak into the plant, steal some plutonium, and build his own nuclear bomb. He wants to enter it in a New York City science fair.

I love it when movies get very detailed about clever schemes for outsmarting people. *The Manhattan Project* invites us to figure out things along with Collet, as he uses his girlfriend as a decoy and outsmarts the security guards at the plant. Inside, he has it all figured out: how to baffle the automatic alarms, how to anticipate what the guards are going to do, how to get in and out without being detected.

The long closing sequence is probably too predictable, as Lithgow and the federal authorities try to convince the kid to take his bomb out of the science fair and allow them to disarm it before he vaporizes the city. Even here, the movie doesn't depend on ordinary thriller strategies; a lot depends not only on the relationship between the kid and the scientist, but on how they think alike and share some of the same goals.

The Manhattan Project was co-written and directed by Marshall Brickman, the sometime Woody Allen collaborator (*Annie Hall*, *Manhattan*) whose own films include *Lovesick* and *Simon*. This movie announces his arrival into the first ranks of skilled American directors. It's a *tour de force*, the way he combines everyday personality conflicts with

a funny, oddball style of seeing things, and wraps up the whole package into a tense and effective thriller. It's not often that one movie contains so many different kinds of pleasures.

Manon of the Spring ★ ★ ★
PG, 113 m., 1987
(See also *Jean de Florette*)

Yves Montand (Cesar Soubeyran), Daniel Auteuil (Ugolin), Emmanuelle Beart (Manon), Hippolyte Girardot (Schoolteacher), Elisabeth Depardieu (Aimee), Gabriel Bacquier (Victor). Directed by by Claude Berri and produced by Pierre Grunstein. Screenplay by Berri and Gerard Brach.

There is something to be said for a long story that unfolds with an inexorable justice. In recent movies, we've become accustomed to stories that explode into dozens of tiny, dim-witted pieces of action, all unrelated to each other. Cars hurtle through the air, victims are peppered with gunshot holes, heroes spit out clever one-liners, and at the end of it all, what are we left with? Our hands close on empty air.

Manon of the Spring, which is the conclusion of the story that began with *Jean de Florette*, is the opposite kind of movie. It moves with a majestic pacing over the affairs of four generations, demonstrating that the sins of the fathers are visited upon the children. Although *Manon* is self-contained and can be understood without having seen *Jean de Florette*, the full impact of this work depends on seeing the whole story, right from the beginning; only then does the ending have its full force.

In the first part of the story, as you may recall, a young hunchbacked man from Paris (Gerard Depardieu) came with his wife and daughter to farm some land he had inherited in a rural section of France. The locals did not greet him kindly, and one of the local patriarchs (Yves Montand) sabotaged his efforts by blocking the spring that fed his land. The young man worked morning to night to haul water for his goats and the rabbits he wished to raise, but in the end the effort killed him. Montand and his worthless nephew (Daniel Auteuil) were then able to buy the land cheaply.

Montand's plot against the hunchback was incredibly cruel, but the movie was at pains to explain that Montand was not gratuitously evil. His most important values

centered around the continuity of land and family, and in his mind, his plot against Depardieu was justified by the need to defend the land against an "outsider." As *Manon of the Spring* opens, some years later, the unmarried and childless Montand is encouraging his nephew to find a woman and marry, so the family name can be continued.

The nephew already has a bride in mind: the beautiful Manon (Emmanuelle Beart), daughter of the dead man, who tends goats on the mountainside and lives in poverty, although she has received a good education. Unfortunately for the nephew, he has a rival for her affections in the local schoolteacher. As the story unfolds, Manon discovers by accident that the nephew and his uncle blocked her father's spring—and when she accidentally discovers the source of the water for the whole village, she has her revenge by cutting off the water of those who killed her father.

All of this takes place with the implacable pace of a Greek tragedy. It sounds more melodramatic than it is, because the events themselves are not the issue here—the director, Claude Berri, has a larger point he wants to make, involving poetic justice on a scale that spans the generations. There are surprises at the end of this film that I do not choose to reveal, but they bring the whole story full circle, and Montand finally receives a punishment that is perfectly, even cruelly, suited to his crime.

Apart from its other qualities, *Manon of the Spring* announces the arrival of a strong and beautiful new actress from France in Emmanuelle Beart. Already seen in *Date With an Angel*, a comedy in which she supplied the only redeeming virtue, she is very effective in this central role, this time as a sort of avenging angel who punishes the old man and his nephew by giving them a glimpse of what could have been for them, had they not been so cruel.

The Marriage of Maria Braun
★ ★ ★ ★
R, 120 m., 1979

Hanna Schygulla (Maria Braun), Klaus Lowitsch (Hermann Braun), Ivan Desny (Oswald), Gottfried John (Willi), Gisela Uhlen (Mother), R.W. Fassbinder (Peddler). Directed and produced by Rainer Werner Fassbinder. Screenplay by Peter Marthescheimer and Pea Frohlicj.

Rainer Werner Fassbinder had been working his way toward this film for years, ever since he began his astonishingly prodigious output with his first awkward but powerful films in 1969. His films were always about sex, money, and death, and his method was often to explore those three subjects through spectacularly incompatible couples (an elderly cleaning woman and a young black worker, a James Dean look-alike and a thirteen-year-old girl, a rich gay about town and a simple-minded young sweepstakes winner).

Whatever his pairings and his cheerfully ironic conclusions, though, there was always another subject lurking in the background of his approximately thirty-three (!) features. He gave us what he saw as the rise and second fall of West Germany in the three postwar decades—considered in the context of the overwhelming American influence on his country.

With the masterful epic *The Marriage of Maria Braun*, he made his clearest and most cynical statement of the theme, and at the same time gave us a movie dripping with period detail, with the costumes and decor he was famous for, with the elegant decadence his characters will sell their souls for in a late-1940s economy without chic retail goods.

Fassbinder's film begins with a Germany torn by war and ends with a gas explosion and a soccer game. His ending may seem arbitrary to some, but in the context of West German society in the 1970s it may only be good reporting. His central character, Maria Braun, is played with great style and power by Hanna Schygulla, and Maria's odyssey from the war years to the consumer years provides the film's framework.

The film opens as Maria marries a young soldier, who then goes off to battle and presumably is killed. It follows her during a long period of mourning, which is punctuated by a little amateur hooking (of which her mother tacitly approves) and then by a tender and very carefully observed liaison with a large, strong, gentle black American soldier whom she really likes—we guess.

The soldier's accidental death, and her husband's return, are weathered by Maria with rather disturbing aplomb, but then we begin to see that Maria's ability to feel has been atrophied by the war, and her ability to be surprised has withered away. If war makes any plans absolutely meaningless, then why should one waste time analyzing coincidences?

Fassbinder has some rather bitter fun with what happens in the aftermath of the soldier's death (the lovestruck, or perhaps just shellshocked, husband voluntarily goes to prison, and Maria rises quickly in a multinational corporation). The movie is more realistic in its treatment of characters than Fassbinder sometimes is, but the events are as arbitrary as ever (and why not—events only have the meanings we assign to them, anyway).

The mini-apocalypse at the end is a perfect conclusion (an ending with "meaning" would have been obscene for this film) and then I think we are left, if we want it, with the sum of what Fassbinder has to say about the rebuilding of Germany: We got the stores opened again, but we don't know much about the customers yet.

The Marrying Man ★ ★ ★
R, 115 m., 1991

Kim Basinger (Vicki Anderson), Alec Baldwin (Charley Pearl), Robert Loggia (Lew Horner), Elisabeth Shue (Adele Horner), Armand Assante (Bugsy Siegel). Directed by Jerry Rees and produced by David Permut. Screenplay by Neil Simon.

They say *The Marrying Man* movie is based on a true story, involving the relationship of shoe tycoon Harry Karl and actress Marie "The Body" McDonald, two of the more colorful characters on the L.A.-Vegas circuit, circa 1950. They were married four times, it is said, even though she meanwhile carried on with mobster Bugsy Siegel. When Neil Simon heard the story he knew he had the makings of a comedy. What he didn't know is that the chemistry between his stars, Kim Basinger and Alec Baldwin, would make Karl and McDonald look like Ozzie and Harriet.

The saga of the filming of *The Marrying Man* is well known, having been chronicled in a steamy article in *Premiere* magazine which was, of course, denied by the agents of the stars. The magazine reported that Baldwin and Basinger fell deeply and passionately into love and lust, and that the filming of many a scene was delayed while they lingered in their mobile homes.

What cannot be denied is that they have chemistry on the screen. *The Marrying Man* is not a great comedy, but it is a living, breathing one that overcomes any problems connected with its filming to deliver a genuinely randy and scandalous love story, about two people who cannot live without one another, but keep trying to, anyway. There's more juice in the story than I usually expect from Neil Simon; the characters don't just trade one-liners, but get under each other's skins.

Baldwin plays Charlie Pearl, a sleek young Hollywood millionaire, who is engaged to the daughter (Elizabeth Shue) of a hot-headed studio chief (Robert Loggia). On the eve of his wedding, he goes to Vegas for a bachelor party, and in a sleazy gambling den outside of town he lays eyes, and soon everything else, on a sexy chanteuse named Vicki Anderson (Basinger). She describes herself as the property of Siegel (Armand Assante), and although Baldwin realizes it is certain death to flirt with the mobster's girl, he crawls in her bedroom window nevertheless and is cornered in *flagrante delicto* by Bugsy and his boys.

Bugsy is capable of surprises. Instead of ordering the execution of the two lovers, he orders them to be married ("I was about to dump her anyway"), and so they are, in a funny scene in one of those Vegas instant-wedding chapels. What they soon discover is that they're more in love with danger than with each other, and that leads to their first split.

But Baldwin is obsessed. So is Basinger. The movie is about lust, not love; about people who drive each other crazy, and can't help it. All of the rest of Simon's plot, energetically directed by Jerry Rees, is at the service of that fact. And the story is planted in a rich 1940s period atmosphere: the cars, the neon, the cigarettes, the brilliantine on the hair.

Simon, who has been around show business a long time, supplies his playboy with four buddies who are constantly getting him out of trouble, and, according to the press notes, these buddies are inspired by the young Sammy Cahn, Phil Silvers, Tony Martin, and Leo Durocher. They're standard wisecracking Simon supporting players, but a couple of the smaller roles are filled with real presence. Armand Assante, who looks and sounds different in every movie, is a sardonic and intelligent Bugsy Siegel, and Robert Loggia, as the studio boss, develops a towering rage that is impressive to behold. He screams so loudly you can't understand half the words, but you get the idea.

The Marrying Man is like those lightweight, atmospheric comedies of the postwar era, in which the chemistry between the stars covered up for a certain lack of logic, continuity, and polish. The movie has rough edges and a slapdash air about it, but somehow it works, perhaps because Basinger and Baldwin throw themselves with such abandon into their roles.

Chemistry is a strange phenomenon. Many critics found it lacking between Sean Connery and Michelle Pfeiffer in *The Russia House*, and between Robert Redford and Lena Olin in *Havana*. Both of those movies were made with far greater subtlety and skill than a humble item like *The Marrying Man*, but hardly anyone, I think, is likely to complain about the chemistry.

Mask ★ ★ ★ ½
PG-13, 120 m., 1985

Cher (Rusty Dennis), Eric Stoltz (Rocky Dennis), Sam Elliott (Gar), Estelle Getty (Evelyn), Richard Dysart (Abe), Laura Dern (Diana). Directed by Peter Bogdanovich and produced by Martin Starger. Screenplay by Anna Hamilton Phelan.

When we see him for the first time, it's a glimpse through his bedroom window, half-reflected in a mirror. A second later, we see him more clearly, this teen-age boy with the strange face. We are shocked for a second, until he starts to talk, and then, without effort, we accept him as a normal kid who has had an abnormal thing happen to him. The name of his disease is craniodiaphyseal dyaplasia, and it causes calcium deposits on his skull that force his face out of shape. "What's the matter?" he likes to ask. "You never seen anyone from the planet Vulcan before?"

The kid's name is Rocky Dennis, and his mother is named Rusty. She is not your normal mom, either. She rides with a motorcycle gang, abuses drugs, shacks up with gang members, and has no visible means of employment. But within about ten minutes, we know that she is the ideal mom for Rocky. That's in the scene where the school principal suggests that Rocky would be better off in a "special" school, and she tells the principal he is a jerk, her son is a good student with good grades, and here is the name of her lawyer.

Movies don't often grab us as quickly as *Mask* does. The story of Rocky and Rusty is absorbing from the very first, maybe because the movie doesn't waste a lot of time wringing its hands over Rocky's fate. *Mask* lands

on its feet, running. The director, Peter Bogdanovich, moves directly to the center of Rocky's life—his mother, his baseball cards, his cocky bravado, his growing awareness of girls. Bogdanovich handles *Mask* a lot differently than a made-for-TV movie would have, with TV's disease-of-the-week approach. This isn't the story of a disease, but the story of some people. And the most extraordinary person in the movie, surprisingly, is not Rocky, but his mother. Rusty Dennis is played by Cher as a complicated, angry, high-energy woman with a great capacity to love her son and encourage him to live as fully as he can. Rocky is a great kid, but because he succeeds so well at being a teenager, he is not a special case like, say, the Elephant Man. He is a kid with a handicap. It is a tribute to Eric Stoltz, who plays the role beneath the completely convincing makeup of Michael Westmore, that we accept him on his own terms.

Cher, on the other hand, makes Rusty Dennis into one of the most interesting movie characters in a long time. She is up front about her lifestyle, and when her son protests about her drinking and drugging, she tells him to butt out of her business. She rides with the motorcycle gang, but is growing unhappy with her promiscuity, and is relieved when the guy she really loves (Sam Elliott) comes back from a trip and moves in. She is also finally able to clean up her act, and stop drinking and using, after Rocky asks her to; she loves him that much.

Mask is based on a true story, and that doesn't come as a surprise: Hollywood wouldn't have the nerve to make a fictional tearjerker like this. The emotional peak of the movie comes during a summer that Rocky spends as an assistant at a camp for the blind. He falls in love with a blind teenager (Laura Dern), who feels his face and says he looks all right to her, and they have some of that special time together that only teen-agers can have: time when love doesn't mean sex so much as it means perfect agreement on the really important issues, like Truth and Beauty. Then the girl's parents come to pick her up, and their reaction to Rocky comes as a shock to us, a reminder of how completely we had accepted him.

Mask is a wonderful movie, a story of high spirits and hope and courage. It has some songs in it, by Bob Seger, and there was a lot of publicity about the fact that Peter Bogdanovich would rather the songs were by Bruce Springsteen. Let me put it this way:

This is a movie that doesn't depend on its sound track. It works because of the people it's about, not because of the music they listen to.

Masquerade ★ ★ ★
R, 91 m., 1988

Rob Lowe (Tim Whalan), Meg Tilly (Olivia Lawrence), Kim Cattrall (Brooke Morrison), Doug Savant (Mike McGill), John Glover (Tony Gateworth), Dana Delany (Anne Briscoe), Erik Holland (Chief of Police), Brian Davies (Granger Morrison), Barton Heyman (Tommy McGill), Bernie McInerney (Harland Fitzgerald). Directed by Bob Swaim and produced by Michael I. Levy. Screenplay by Dick Wolf.

"The problem with us," one of her relatives tells her, "is that we have too much money." They do. The whole family is rich, and now here is young Olivia, fresh out of school, single, an orphan, with a bank balance of $200 million. She's a target for every gold digger in the Hamptons. But even Olivia should not have to endure the way men treat her in *Masquerade*, which is a thriller in the shape of a Chinese puzzle box: Every time she solves one mystery, there's another one hidden inside it.

The movie's first mystery is Olivia herself, played by Meg Tilly in a very particular way that was slightly distracting at first, until I began to realize how well-chosen it was for the part. Tilly, who can be sharp-edged and observant, is a little dreamy this time. She talks in a breathy voice that seems filled with afterthoughts, and she comes across as innocent and passive.

Her character has not had an easy life. Her father died when she was twelve, and her mother has died just a few months before the story opens. She lives in a mansion in the Hamptons (one of her nine homes) with her mother's fourth husband, a drunken lout played with cheerful hatefulness by John Glover. She hates him, but there's no way to get him out of the house; he's protected by her mother's will.

Back home after school, Olivia drifts into a round of idle days and evenings filled with parties and dances. She runs into Mike (Doug Savant), the boy she promised to marry when she was twelve. He's now one of the local cops, forever on the other side of the divide between the rich and the poor. "Some dreams don't die," he tells her, but she tells him gently that it wasn't meant to be. Then one night at a dance she meets Tim (Rob Lowe), the handsome skipper of the racing sailboat owned by a local millionaire.

Tim has been sleeping with the millionaire's wife, but it's love at first sight when he sees Olivia. Before long they're holding hands on the beach and even committing the ultimate transgression: public fraternization between members and employees at the yacht club. Glover, the stepfather, is savage in his disapproval of the penniless sailor. He goes away for the weekend, the young couple sleep together in her house, Glover unexpectedly bursts in drunkenly, there is a struggle, and Tim shoots him dead.

That's what happens, all right, but what really happens is a lot more complicated. Because *Masquerade* depends so surely upon its many surprises, I won't reveal any more of the plot, except to say that Olivia tries to cover up for the man she loves, and Mike, the local cop, seems to go along with the cover-up for complicated motives going back to his original love for her.

If all of this sounds needlessly complicated (sort of a "Deathstyles of the Rich and Famous"), director Bob Swaim and writer Dick Wolf are sure-footed in their storytelling. One by one, the curtains of deception and intrigue are pulled back, and the most tantalizing thing about their method is that they always keep young Olivia in the dark. While evil currents swirl around her, while the people she trusts turn treacherous, she remains in a kind of innocent cocoon, gullible and deluded. That's why Meg Tilly's acting style is the right choice for the movie. Her dreaminess, which at first seems distracting, becomes an important part of the suspense, because while she drifts in her romantic reverie, a sweet smile on her face, we're mentally screaming at her to wake up and smell the coffee.

The other performances are mostly adequate. Rob Lowe is rather boxed in by the complicated things the plot does with his character, and Doug Savant goes through some interesting changes as the local cop. I was disappointed, though, by John Glover's evil stepfather. Glover was a superb villain in John Frankenheimer's *52 Pick-Up* (1986), suave and oily, but this time he overplays the drunk routine and lurches around the house so grotesquely that we fear more for his balance than Tilly's life.

This was Bob Swaim's third film, after the great *La Balance* and the intriguing *Half*

Moon Street. Like both of those films, it has its roots in the crime melodramas of the 1940s—when movies were about attractive victims, rather than attractive killers. The notion of placing a complete innocent at the center of the frame, and then surrounding her with menace, is a little old-fashioned, in a way; many recent films have preferred all-powerful heroes and heroines who destroy anyone who crosses them. But in Roman Polanski's *Frantic*, Peter Yates's *The House on Carroll Street*, and *Masquerade*, we see a rebirth of the innocent bystander.

Maurice ★ ★ ★
R, 140 m., 1987

James Wilby (Maurice), Hugh Grant (Clive), Rupert Graves (Scudder), Denholm Elliott (Dr. Barry), Simon Callow (Mr. Ducie), Billie Whitelaw (Mrs. Hall), Ben Kingsley (Lasker-Jones). Directed by James Ivory and produced by Ismail Merchant. Screenplay by Kit Hesketh-Harvey and Ivory.

Maurice tells the story of a young English homosexual who falls in love with two completely different men—and in their differences is the whole message of the movie, a message I do not agree with. Yet because the film is so well made and acted, because it captures its period so meticulously, I enjoyed it even in disagreement.

This is the first film from the team of James Ivory and Ismail Merchant since *A Room with a View*, and is based once again on a novel by E.M. Forster. Both books are about the gulf between idealistic romance and immediate physical passion, but otherwise they could not be more dissimilar. *Maurice*, written in 1913, was Forster's attempt to deal in fiction with his own homosexuality, and he suppressed the novel until after his death.

The story takes place in the years before World War I, when homosexuality was outlawed in Britain, and exposure meant disgrace and ruin. At Cambridge, two undergraduates become close friends, and then one day, in a moment of risk, one tells the other that he loves him.

The man declaring his love is Clive (Hugh Grant), an aristocrat who can look forward to a lifetime of wealth, privilege, and perhaps public office. The man he loves is Maurice (James Wilby), also well-born, who may go into the stock market. At first Maurice is shocked and repelled by what his friend says,

but later that night he climbs in the window to give him a quick, passionate kiss and whisper, "I love you."

From the first, their ideas about love are opposite. Clive is not much interested in the physical expression of love; he thinks it will "lower" them. His notions are more platonic and idealistic. Maurice, once he has been introduced to the idea of love between men, becomes a passionate romantic, and before long Clive, the pursuer, becomes the pursued.

Clive fears exposure and disgrace. He sees homosexuality as something to be battled and overcome, and he breaks off with Maurice to marry, assume his family responsibilities, and go into politics. At first Maurice is shattered, and there are tragicomic scenes in which he seeks help from a hypnotist and the family doctor. Then he has a physical encounter of astonishing passion with Scudder (Rupert Graves), the rough-hewn gamekeeper on Clive's estate, and eventually both men determine to risk everything, throw their reputations to the wind, and live together as lovers.

Merchant and Ivory tell this story in a film so handsome to look at and so intelligently acted that it is worth seeing just to regard the production. Scene after scene is perfectly created: a languorous afternoon floating on the river behind the Cambridge colleges; a desultory cricket game between masters and servants; the daily routine of college life; visits to country estates and town homes; the settings of the rooms. The supporting cast (Ben Kingsley, Simon Callow, Billie Whitelaw, Denholm Elliott) is unusually strong, and although some people might find Wilby unfocused in the title role, I thought he was making the right choices, portraying a man whose real thoughts were almost always elsewhere.

The problem in the movie is with the gulf between his romantic choices. His first great love, Clive, is a person with whom he has a great deal in common. They share minds as well as bodies. Scudder, the gamekeeper, is frankly portrayed as an unpolished working-class lad, handsome but simple. In the England of 1913, with its rigid class divisions, the two men would have had even less in common than the movie makes it seem, and the real reason their relationship is daring is not because of sexuality but because of class.

Apart from their sexuality, they have nothing of substance to talk about with each other in this movie. No matter how deep their love, I suspect that within a few weeks or months the British class system would have driven them apart.

In ignoring this reality, Forster and Ivory seem to be making the idealistic statement that love conquers all. Sometimes it does. Not usually. Physical sexuality is an important part of everyone, but, especially after the first passion has cooled, it is not the most important part. There comes a time when people need to simply talk to one another, to coexist as companions, and I doubt if that time could ever come between Maurice and Scudder.

By arguing that their decision to stay together was a good and courageous thing, *Maurice* seems to argue that the most important thing about them was their homosexuality. Perhaps in the dangerous atmosphere of homophobia in the England of seventy-five years ago, that might have seemed the case. But this film was made in 1987, and shares the same limited insight.

May Fools ★ ★ ★
R, 105 m., 1990

Michel Piccoli (Milou), Miou-Miou (Camille), Michel Duchaussoy (Georges), Dominique Blanc (Claire), Harriet Walter (Lily), Bruno Carette (Grimaldi), Francois Berleand (Daniel), Martine Gautier (Adele). Directed by Louis Malle and produced by Vincent Malle. Screenplay by Louis Malle and Jean-Claude Carriere.

A colleague of mine has a simple test for the worth of a movie. He asks himself, "Is this movie more interesting than a documentary of the same actors having a meal together?" Often the answer is "no." But how would the test apply to *May Fools*, a French movie which has a great many scenes in which the actors have meals together, and carry on the same sorts of conversations I imagine they might have in real life?

Many of the reviews of the film have criticized it on the basis of its plot and its message. I like it because of the time I got to spend with the characters as they dealt with family matters over a period of days. It was intrinsically interesting, not because of what it was about, but simply because of what it was.

The movie takes place in May of 1968, a month that has a special ring to the French ear. That was the month that the revolution

seemed poised to overthrow bourgeois society—the month the radicals shut down the Cannes Film Festival, the students occupied the streets of Paris, and rumors flew that De Gaulle was going to flee the country. I was in Paris during that time, and collected a few black-and-blue marks across the back of my legs, souvenirs of police truncheons when I made the mistake of trying to sightsee in the middle of a riot. For many Parisians, it appeared that society was up for grabs.

In the country, it was quieter, and *May Fools* takes place on a small farm that has been in the same family for generations. The matriarch, much loved and also feared, rules the household. Her children, some well into middle age, have moved away—all except for Milou (Michel Piccoli), a genial man who likes to go fishing and ride his bicycle and oversee the vineyards in a desultory sort of way.

One day, the mother drops dead. The family gathers for her funeral at the same moment in history when the radicals are trying to shut down French society. Among the survivors is Milou's daughter, Camille (Miou-Miou), who suggests the estate be divided into three and sold. Milou is shocked to think that the family's history would be so casually converted into cash, but the others point out that they have subsidized his idyllic existence in the country with their own hard work in the city.

Rumors of the outer world penetrate into the house, which is given over to a wake. One of the mourners is a sometime correspondent for *Le Monde*, who makes dire predictions about the future of France. Everyone seems to be on strike, and the mother cannot be properly buried because even the morticians are out. Most of the characters in the movie are solidly middle-class and conservative, but a few wayward rebels turn up, including a granddaughter who is a lesbian, and a passing truck driver who joins the wake as it turns gradually into a party.

Many meals are consumed. Some love affairs are considered, others consummated. A picnic is held on the grass, and for a second it seems that revolutionary fervor will inspire these people, half drunk on wine, to experiment with free love. But they are not quite ready for such a big step. Secrets are revealed, charges are traded, confessions are heard, and there are even a couple of small miracles, as the deceased seems to be not altogether dead.

May Fools was directed by Louis Malle

and written by Malle and that best of modern French screenwriters, Jean-Claude Carriere. It is a movie that is reluctant to announce its intentions. What *is* Malle trying to say here? The revolution comes to nothing, the family neither caves in nor rises to heroism, and the happiest person in the film is arguably the maid, Lily, who is unexpectedly included in the will.

I think perhaps Malle is gently trying to make a movie about imperfect but interesting people, the goodness of whose souls is tested by the coincidence of a public and private crisis at the same time. No great lessons are learned, no great statements made, but by the end of the film, we have spent some interesting time with these people and know them better. What more can you ask of any weekend in the country, or of any group of people? This is a movie that may be precisely as interesting as watching the actors having dinner with one another.

McCabe and Mrs. Miller ★ ★ ★ ★
R, 120 m., 1971

Warren Beatty (McCabe), Julie Christie (Mrs. Miller), Rene Auberjonois (Shehan), Hugh Millais (Butler), Michael Murphy (Sears), William Devane (Lawyer). Directed by Robert Altman and produced by David Foster and Mitchell Brower. Screenplay by Altman and Brian McKay.

McCabe rides into the town of Presbyterian Church under a lowering sky, dismounts, takes off his buffalo-hide coat, puts on his bowler hat, and mumbles something under his breath that we can't quite make out, but the tone of voice is clear enough. This time, he's not going to let the bastards grind him down. He steps off through the mud puddles to the only local saloon, throws a cloth on the table, and takes out a pack of cards, to start again. His plan is to build a whorehouse with a bathhouse out in back, and get rich. By the end of the movie, he will have been offered $6,250 for his holdings, and he will be sitting thoughtfully in a snowbank, dead, as if thinking it all over.

And yet Robert Altman's *McCabe and Mrs. Miller* doesn't depend on that final death for its meaning. It doesn't kill a character just to get a trendy existential feel about the meaninglessness of it all. No, McCabe doesn't find it meaningless at all, and once Mrs. Miller explains the mistake he made in his reasoning, he rides all the way into the next town to try to sell his holdings for half what he was asking, because he'd rather not die.

Death is very final in this Western, because the movie is about life. Most Westerns are about killing and getting killed, which means they're not about life and death at all. We spend a time in the life of a small frontier town, which grows up before our eyes out of raw, unpainted lumber and tubercular canvas tents. We get to know the town pretty well, because Altman has a gift for making movies that seem to eavesdrop on activity that would have been taking place anyway.

That was what happened in *M*A*S*H*, where a lot of time didn't have to be wasted in introducing the characters and explaining the relationships between them, because the characters already knew who they were and how they felt about each other. In a lot of movies, an actor appears on the screen and has no identity at all until somebody calls him "Smith" or "Slim," and then he's Smith or Slim. In *McCabe and Mrs. Miller*, Altman uses a tactfully unobtrusive camera, a distinctive conversational style of dialogue, and the fluid movements of his actors to give us people who are characters from the moment we see them; we have the sense that when they leave camera range they're still thinking, humming, scratching, chewing, and nodding to each other in the street.

McCabe and Mrs. Miller are an organic part of this community. We are aware, of course, that they're played by Warren Beatty and Julie Christie, but rarely have stars been used so completely for their talents rather than their fame. We don't ever think much about McCabe being Warren Beatty, and Mrs. Miller being Julie Christie; they're there along with everybody else in town, and the movie just happens to be about their lives.

Because the movie is about a period in the lives of several people (and not about a series of events that occur to one-dimensional characters), McCabe and Mrs. Miller change during the course of the story. Mrs. Miller is a tough Cockney madam who convinces McCabe that he needs a competent manager for his whorehouse: How would *he* ever know enough about managing women? He agrees, and she lives up to her promise, and they're well on their way to making enough money for her to get out of this dump of a mining town and back to San Francisco, where, she believes, a woman of her caliber belongs.

All of this happens in an indoor sort of a way, and by that I don't mean that the movie looks like it was shot on a sound stage. The outdoors is always there, and people are always coming in out of it and shaking the rain from their hats, and we see the trees whipping in the wind through the windows. But it's a wet autumn and then a cold winter, so people naturally congregate in saloons and grocery stores and whorehouses, and the climate forces a sense of community. Then the enforcers come to town: The suave, Scottish-accented Butler, who kills people who won't sell out to the Company, and his two sidekicks. One of them is slack-jawed and mean, and the other is a nervous blond kid with the bare makings of a mustache. On the suspension bridge that gets you across the river to the general store, he kills another kid—a rawboned, easygoing country kid with a friendly smile—and it is one of the most affecting and powerful deaths there ever has been in a Western.

The final hunt for McCabe takes place in almost deserted streets, because the church is burning down and everybody is out at the edge of town trying to save it. The church burns during a ghostly, heavy daylight snowstorm: fire and ice. And McCabe almost gets away. Mrs. Miller, who allowed him into her bed but always, except once, demanded five dollars for the privilege, caught on long before he did that the Company would rather kill him than up it up $2,000. She is down at the foot of town, in Chinatown, lost in an opium dream while the snow drifts against his body. *McCabe and Mrs. Miller* is like no other Western ever made.

Mean Streets ★ ★ ★ ★
R, 110 m., 1974

Robert De Niro (Johnny Boy), Harvey Keitel (Charlie). Directed by Martin Scorsese and produced by Jonathan T. Taplin. Screenplay by Scorsese and Mardik Martin.

Martin Scorsese's *Mean Streets* isn't so much a gangster movie as a perceptive, sympathetic, finally tragic story about how it is to grow up in a gangster environment. Its characters (like Scorsese himself) have grown up in New York's Little Italy, and they understand everything about that small slice of human society except how to survive in it. The two most important characters, Charlie and Johnny Boy, move through the Mafia environment almost because it's expected of them. Charlie is a Catholic with pathological guilt complexes, but because the mob is the family business, he never quite forces himself to make the connection between right and wrong and what he does. Not that he's very good at being a Mafioso: He's twenty-seven, but he still lives at home; he's a collector for his uncle's protection racket, but the collections don't bring in much. If he has any luck at all, he will be able to take over a bankrupt restaurant.

He is, at least fitfully, a realist. Johnny Boy, on the other hand, is a violent, uncontrolled product of romanticized notions of criminal street life. Little Italy is all around him, and yet he seems to have formed his style and borrowed half his vocabulary from the movies. He contains great and ugly passions, and can find no way to release them except in sudden violent bursts. Charlie is in love with Johnny Boy's sister, and he also feels a dogged sense of responsibility for Johnny Boy: He goes up on a roof one night when Johnny is shooting out streetlights and talks him down. At least Johnny releases his angers in overt ways. Charlie suppresses everything, and sometimes in desperation passes his hand through a flame and wonders about the fires of hell. He takes his Catholicism literally.

Scorsese places these characters in a perfectly realized world of boredom and small joys, sudden assaults, the possibility of death, and the certainty of mediocrity. He shot on location in Little Italy, where he was born and where he seems to know every nuance of architecture and personality, and his story isn't built like a conventional drama: It emerges from the daily lives of the characters. They hang out. They go to the movies. They eat, they drink, they get in sudden fights that end as quickly as a summer storm. Scorsese photographs them with fiercely driven visual style. We never have the sense of a scene being set up and then played out; his characters hurry to their dooms while the camera tries to keep pace. There's an improvisational feel even in scenes that we know, because of their structure, couldn't have been improvised.

Scorsese got the same feel in his first feature, *Who's That Knocking at My Door?* (1967). *Mean Streets* is a sequel, and Scorsese gives us the same leading actor (Harvey Keitel) to assure the continuity. In the earlier film, he was still on the edge of life, of sex, of violence. Now he has been plunged in, and he isn't equal to the experience. He's not tough enough to be a Mafia collector (and not strong enough to resist). Johnny Boy is played by Robert De Niro and it's a marvelous performance, filled with urgency and restless desperation.

The movie's scenes of violence are especially effective because of the way Scorsese stages them. We don't get spectacular effects and skillfully choreographed struggles. Instead, there's something realistically clumsy about the fights in this movie. A scene in a pool hall, in particular, is just right in the way it shows its characters fighting and yet mindful of their suits (possibly the only suits they have). The whole movie feels like life in New York; there are scenes in a sleazy nightclub, on fire escapes, and in bars, and they all feel as if Scorsese has been there.

Melvin and Howard ★ ★ ★ ½
R, 95 m., 1980

Paul Le Mat (Melvin Dummar), Jason Robards (Howard Hughes), Mary Steenburgen (Lynda Dummar), Pamela Reed (Bonnie Dummar), Michael J. Pollard (Little Red), Charles Napier (Man with Envelope), Robert Ridgely (TV Host), Melvin Dummar (Depot Counterman). Directed by Jonathan Demme and produced by Art Linson and Don Phillips. Screenplay by Bo Goldman.

Melvin Dummar is the man who claimed he gave a lift to a doddering old hitchhiker, loaned him a quarter, and was left $156 million in the hitchhiker's will. If he was telling the truth, the hitchhiker was Howard Hughes. But Jonathan Demme's wonderful comedy *Melvin and Howard* doesn't depend on whether the so-called Mormon Will was really written by Hughes. That hardly matters. This is the story of a life lived at the other end of the financial ladder from Hughes. It sees Dummar as the kind of American hero who is celebrated for being so extraordinarily ordinary.

For what, after all, constitutes heroism? And why shouldn't Dummar be considered a hero? We learn from this movie that he ventured single-handedly into the jungle of American consumerism, and lived. We see his major battles. Here's a guy who was married three times (twice to the same woman, the second time with the "Hawaiian War Chant" playing in an all-night Vegas chapel). He had three cars and a boat repossessed, he went from being Milkman of the Month to hauling his first wife off a go-go stage, he

loved his children, did not drink or smoke, and stood at the brink of losing his gas station franchise on the very day when a tall, blond stranger dropped what looked a lot like Hughes's last will and testament into his life.

The genius of *Melvin and Howard* is that it is about Melvin, not Howard. The film begins and ends with scenes involving the Hughes character, who is played by Jason Robards as a desert rat with fading memories of happiness. Dummar stops in the desert to answer a call of nature, finds Hughes lying in the sagebrush, gives him a ride in his pickup truck, and gets him to sing. For reasons of his own, Hughes sings "Bye, Bye Blackbird": *Got no one to love and understand me . . . oh, what hard-luck stories they all hand me.*

Robards is a chillingly effective Hughes. But this movie belongs to Paul Le Mat, as Dummar. Le Mat played the round-faced hot-rodder in *American Graffiti,* and Dummar is the kind of guy that character might have grown up to be. He is pleasant, genial, simple of speech, crafty of mind, always looking for an angle. He angles for Milkman of the Month, he plots to get his wife on a TV game show, he writes songs like "Santa's Souped-Up Sleigh," he plays the slots at Vegas and goes through his life asking only for a few small scores.

When he gets a big score—named the beneficiary of a $156 million will that seems to have been signed by Hughes—he hardly knows what to do. Long-lost relatives and new-found friends turn up by the dozens, and press conferences are held in front of his gas station. There is a court trial, but the movie never really addresses itself to the details of the Hughes will court case. It goes instead for the drama and for the effect on Dummar and his family.

This is a slice of American life. It shows the flip side of Gary Gilmore's Utah. It is a world of mobile homes, Pop Tarts, dust, kids, and dreams of glory. It's pretty clear how this movie got made. The producers started with the notion that the story of the mysterious Hughes will might make a good courtroom thriller. Well, maybe it would have. But my hunch is that when they met Dummar, they had the good sense to realize that they could get a better—and certainly a funnier—story out of what happened to him between the day he met Hughes and the day the will was discovered. Dummar is the kind of guy who thinks they oughta make a movie out of his life. This time, he was right.

Memories of Me ★ ★ ★ ½
PG 13, 103 m., 1988

Billy Crystal (Abbie), Alan King (Abe), JoBeth Williams (Lisa), David Ackroyd (Assistant Director), Phil Fondacaro (Bosco), Robert Pastorelli (Broccoli). Directed by Henry Winkler and produced by Alan King, Billy Crystal, and Michael Hertzberg. Screenplay by Eric Roth and Crystal.

Two of the most intriguing words in show business are "No—really!" They usually come right after a compliment, as in, "You're looking great! No—really!" The effect is of complete insincerity, since if the subject really *were* looking great, there wouldn't be any need to insist on it. This kind of double-reverse English, in which what is said is the opposite of what is meant, lies at the heart of Henry Winkler's *Memories of Me,* a comedy about a man who has never been able to talk seriously with his father. No—really.

Billy Crystal stars in the movie as Abbie, a high-powered New York surgeon who begins to take his life more seriously after he has a heart attack. He has been alienated for years from his father, Abe, a character who has become known as the King of the Extras out in Hollywood. Abbie has vague memories of Abe telling him bedtime stories, and then there is a great silence over many years. When he thinks of his father at all, Abbie thinks of him as an embarrassment. But now the heart attack has caused him to examine his life more closely, and so, almost against his will, he goes out West to visit his father.

The moment we see Abe, we recognize him. He's the life of the party, one of those ebullient types who keeps people at a distance while professing friendship. He slaps you on the back so he doesn't have to look in your eyes. Almost from the moment Abbie sees Abe, he's making plans to go back home to New York. But somehow, he stays. And eventually he begins to notice some disturbing things about his father. One day, for example, Abe is playing an extra in a daytime medical soap opera. He's a patient, and all he has to do is lie still and keep quiet. But he starts talking. Another day, dressed up like a big red lobster, he inexplicably starts reciting a speech from a play he was in years ago.

What's going on here? Alzheimer's? His son the doctor talks him into a complete medical examination, and the brain scan reveals a problem, "a little pimple on a blood vessel in the brain." Sometimes, Abe gets a little confused. He starts playing the wrong tapes. Someday, maybe tomorrow, maybe years from now, there could be much bigger trouble. Abe is dying.

But so what? Everybody is dying. That's Abe's approach to the problem. And the movie itself is not one of those depressing tear-jerker docudramas where everybody goes around describing symptoms. Most of the movie's scenes are upbeat, and some of them are hilarious, as Abbie and his fiancée (JoBeth Williams) follow Abe into the world of Hollywood extras. They have their own club, right off Hollywood Boulevard. They stick up for each other in times of trouble. They're always performing, always "on," and Abe is the leader of the pack.

The best moments in the movie involve tightly knit dialogue scenes between Alan King and Billy Crystal, who cowrote the movie. Their timing has the almost effortless music of two professionals who have spent their lifetimes learning how to put the right spin on a word. Much of it involves paradox, as when King observes that his wife was crazy: "That's why I divorced her."

"But," says Crystal, "she divorced you."

"See what I mean?"

Memories of Me is a surprise, a warm-hearted comedy that somehow creates believable characters without sacrificing big laughs. It is hard to imagine how two egos as secure as King's and Crystal's could have co-existed on the set—and indeed there are moments that feel like improvised one-upmanship—but Henry Winkler, the director, is able to find the strong story line from beginning to end, and so we do care when the film arrives at its touching conclusion. Crystal is very good in a role that must have been second nature to him; King, playing the more complicated character, is a genuine revelation. As the King of the Extras, he pulls off the neat trick of showing us why his son avoided him for so many years—and why he was wrong.

Memphis Belle ★ ★ ★
PG-13, 101 m., 1990

Matthew Modine (Dennis Dearborn), Eric Stoltz (Danny Daly), Tate Donovan (Luke Sinclair), D.B. Sweeney (Phil Rosenthal), Billy Zane (Val Kozlowski), Sean Astin (Richard "Rascal" Moore), Harry Connick, Jr. (Clay Busby). Directed by Michael Caton-Jones and produced by David Puttnam and Catherine Wyler. Screenplay by Monte Merrick.

Memphis Belle tells the story of the journey of several brave young Americans through an anthology of aviation movie clichés. Not a trick is missed—not even the faithful dog lifting its loyal head from the grass when a missing plane finds its way back to base. This movie is said to be based on a World War II documentary by William Wyler, but, in another sense, it is based on *The Battle of Britain, One of Our Aircraft Is Missing*, and countless other formula thrillers about the air war in Europe.

The task of the filmmakers is thankless. They have to introduce a dozen crew members of the Memphis Belle, and then somehow make them all memorable within the cramped confines of a plot where most of them have to wear oxygen masks most of the time. The movie begins while we see the young men playing football, and a voice-over narration names them and provides them with thumbnail character sketches. Then, later, we learn what assignments they have on board the Memphis Belle when the pilot holds a roll-call and they sign in, giving their names and battle stations.

The crew, we learn, has survived twenty-four bombing raids over Germany. One more, and they get to go home. The voice-over narration is by an Army Air Force P.R. man (John Lithgow), assigned to stage-manage the final raid for *Life* magazine. And given the fact that these man have flown twenty-four missions together, I hardly thought it necessary for them to introduce themselves by name to their pilot—but then the introductions were really for us, and the roll-call was an economical way to explain their various jobs—copilot, radioman, navigator, tail-gunner, bombardier, etc.

Michael Powell used exactly the same strategy to introduce the bomber crew members in his wartime drama *One of Our Aircraft Is Missing*, with the difference that he used a Wellington bomber, because his crew of six was easier for the audience to keep straight. He was right. The Flying Fortress used in *Memphis Belle* has such a large crew that the movie is fatally slowed as the screenplay works its way around and around the characters, trying to keep them all alive.

Each character is a different cliché: The cool and calculated captain, the jittery gunner and his practical-joking sidekick, the superstitious one, etc. On the ground, the characters are equally machine-made, from the taciturn commanding officer to the heartless general to the shameless flack. It would be safe to say there is not a single development in this movie that cannot accurately be predicted by any audience member familiar with the requirements of the genre.

And yet, despite everything I have said, I found *Memphis Belle* entertaining, almost in spite of my objections. That's because it exploits so fully the universal human tendency to identify with a group of people who are up in an airplane and may not be able to get down again. As the flak flies, as enemy fighters attack, as wings are shredded, as engines catch on fire and gun turrets are blown off, I found myself: (a) mentally ticking off the clichés, but (b) physically on the edge of my seat. It was a classic case of divided loyalties—the intelligence maintaining its distance while the emotions became engaged.

In a perverse sort of way, one of the appeals of *Memphis Belle* is in its adherence to dependable old clichés. This isn't a high-tech pinball machine like *Top Gun*, but a movie about people in a fairly primitive piston-engine aircraft. Their uniforms are not glossy aluminum underwear, but leather jackets and fur-lined helmets and wool sweaters. When petrol must be moved from one wing to another, by God, they crawl back to the pump handle and pump it themselves.

This human element in the experience of the *Memphis Belle* crew somehow compensates for a lack of human dimension in the characters. We can't really tell the crew members apart, and don't much care to, but we can identify with them. As they fly on their bombing mission, I reflected that such high-altitude bombing was seen at the time as inhuman. But at least the World War II flight crews flew their missions and took their chances. These days wars can be fought by pushing a button. It is somehow more fair when the combatants have to risk their lives to push the buttons.

Men of Respect ★
R, 113 m., 1991

John Turturro (Mike Battaglia), Katherine Borowitz (Ruthie Battaglia), Dennis Farina (Bankie Como), Peter Boyle (Duffy), Lilia Skala (Lucia), Steven Wright (Sterling), Rod Steiger (Charlie D'Amico). Directed by William Reilly and produced by Ephraim Horowitz. Screenplay by Reilly.

Men of Respect is a strange movie indeed; *Macbeth* done as a tragedy set inside the crime syndicate. All is darkness and offscreen rumblings, thunder and lightning, and a minor earthquake strikes New York as the characters plot and scheme against each other. At first the movie doesn't insist too much on the parallels with Shakespeare, but by the last half hour the Lady Macbeth character is wandering in the backyard with a flashlight and complaining about the spots in the linen of the family restaurant, while Macbeth is bragging, "All of these guys is of woman born. They can't do shit to me."

That is actually not such a terrible line, and indeed William Reilly's screenplay ("Adapted from *The Tragedy of Macbeth*, by William Shakespeare") has some nice dialogue, of which my favorite is when a mobster is talking about a colleague who has just been killed: "He's history. Tomorrow, he'll be geography." That got a laugh, and so did another scene, after the hero is told that he will not die until the stars fall from the sky. Then there is a fireworks exhibition, and one of the hero's sidekicks says, "Jeez! It looks just like stars, fallin' from the sky!"

The problem is that this movie is not intended as a comedy. Or maybe it is. Some of the moments have real wit, and yet the overall impression is of someone trying to drown the characters in the weight of guilt, blood, murder, and literary associations. The movie stars John Turturro as Mike Battaglia, a Mafioso who moves from the fringes of the outfit to center stage as the story progresses. One by one he wipes out his rivals, even stabbing a couple of them while they sleep, while his wife, Ruthie (Katherine Borowitz) eggs him on and gives him counsel.

The opening scene of the movie is incredibly dense with detail—it's as hard to follow as the setup for *Miller's Crossing*, with all the names and plot lines. But soon we begin to discern the guiding hand of the Bard, as Turturro and his friend stumble into the parlor of an old fortune-teller, who tells him essentially what the witches told Macbeth. What follows is a dark, murky version of some of the same kinds of scenes Scorsese did in *GoodFellas* and Demme in *Married to the Mob*, scenes in which middle-aged guys in suits pull guns on each other and grill steaks.

This leads to moments like the hero's horrendous dream scene, in which he imagines that two friends are plotting against him and will garrote and stab him while he's trying to decide between the hot dogs or the hamburgers they're charcoaling out in the backyard. It cannot be easy to act in material like this, and credit must be given to Turturro,

Borowitz, Dennis Farina, Peter Boyle, and others who actually do create effective and believable portraits even while the screenplay is marching them into brick walls.

Men of Respect was directed, as well as written, by Reilly, and it must be said of him that he has a distinctive touch, setting Turturro's headquarters down in a damp basement and shooting other scenes in alleys and restaurants and offices that seem to be in the grip of a citywide power failure. This is the darkest movie I've seen since *Eraserhead*, so filled with gloom and shadows that half the time it seems to be a play for voices. A lot of work went into it, and some good things are here and there. But the underlying inspiration for the film is a very, very bad idea.

Mephisto ★ ★ ★ ★
NO MPAA RATING, 135 m., 1981

Klaus Maria Brandauer (Henrik Hofgon), Krystyna Janda (Barbara Bruckner), Ildiko Bansagi (Nicolette Von Hiebuhr), Karin Boyd (Juliette Martens). Directed and produced by Istvan Szabo. Screenplay by Szabo and Peter Dobel.

There are times in *Mephisto* when the hero tries to explain himself by saying that he's only an actor, and he has that almost right. *All* he is, is an actor. It's not his fault that the Nazis have come to power, and that as a German-speaking actor he must choose between becoming a Nazi and being exiled into a foreign land without jobs for German actors. As long as he is acting, as long as he is not called upon to risk his real feelings, this man can act his way into the hearts of women, audiences, and the Nazi power structure. This is the story of a man who plays his life wearing masks, fearing that if the last mask is removed, he will have no face.

The actor is played by Klaus Maria Brandauer in one of the greatest movie performances I've ever seen. The character, Henrik, is not sympathetic, and yet we identify with him because he shares so many of our own weaknesses and fears. Henrik is not a very good actor or a very good human being, but he is good enough to get by in ordinary times. As the movie opens, he's a socialist, interested in all the most progressive new causes, and is even the proud lover of a black woman. By the end of the film, he has learned that his liberalism was a taste, not a conviction, and that he will do anything, flatter anybody, make any compromise, just to

hear applause, even though he knows the applause comes from fools.

Mephisto does an uncanny job of creating its period, of showing us Hamburg and Berlin from the 1920s to the 1940s. And I've never seen a movie that does a better job of showing the seductive Nazi practice of providing party members with theatrical costumes, titles, and pageantry. In this movie, not being a Nazi is like being at a black-tie ball in a brown corduroy suit. Hofgon, the actor, is drawn to this world like a magnet. From his ambitious beginnings in the provincial German theater, he works his way up into more important roles and laterally into more important society. All of his progress is based on lies. He marries a woman he does not love, because her father can do him some good. When the rise of the Nazis destroys his father-in-law's power, he leaves his wife. He continues all this time to maintain his affair with his black mistress. He has a modest, but undeniable, talent as an actor, but prostitutes it by playing his favorite role, Mephistopheles in *Faust*, not as he could but as he calculates he should.

The obvious parallel here is between the hero of this film and the figure of tragedy who sold his soul to the devil. But *Mephisto* doesn't depend upon easy parallels to make its point. This is a human story, and as the actor in this movie makes his way to the top of the Nazi propaganda structure and the bottom of his own soul, the movie is both merciless and understanding. This is a weak and shameful man, the film seems to say, but then it cautions us against throwing the first stone.

Mephisto is not a German but a Hungarian movie, directed by the talented Istvan Szabo, who has led his country's cinema from relative obscurity to its present position as one of the best and most innovative film industries in Europe. Szabo, in his way, has made a companion film to Fassbinder's *The Marriage of Maria Braun*. The Szabo film shows a man compromising his way to the top by lying to himself and everybody else, and throwing aside all moral standards. It ends as World War II is under way. The Fassbinder film begins after the destruction of the war, showing a woman clawing her way out of the rubble and repeating the same process of compromise, lies, and unquestioning materialism.

Both the man in the Szabo film and the woman in the Fassbinder film maintain one love affair all through everything, using their love (he for a black woman, she for a convict) as a sort of token contempt for a society whose corrupt values they otherwise completely accept. The fact that they *can* still love, of course, makes it impossible for them to quite deceive themselves. That is the price they pay for their deals with the devil.

Mermaids ★ ★ ★
PG-13, 110 m., 1990

Cher (Mrs. Flax), Bob Hoskins (Lou Landsky), Winona Ryder (Charlotte Flax), Michael Schoeffling (Joe), Christina Ricci (Kate Flax), Caroline McWilliams (Carrie). Directed by Richard Benjamin and produced by Lauren Lloyd, Wallis Nicita, and Patrick Palmer. Screenplay by June Roberts.

I had the feeling, watching *Mermaids*, that it was originally headed in another direction. The material is "funny" instead of funny, and we don't laugh so much as we squirm with recognition and sympathy. It's a story told by a teen-age girl whose mother avoids becoming known as the town tramp only because she changes towns so often. In the movies, eccentric parents can be palmed off as colorful originals. In life, especially to an adolescent, they can be excruciating embarrassments.

The mom in *Mermaids* goes by the name of Mrs. Flax, and is played by Cher. Not only played *by* Cher, but in an eerie sense, played *as* Cher, with perfect makeup and a flawless body that seems a bit much to hope for, given the character's lifestyle and diet. Mrs. Flax has a personality trait that leads her to seek doomed love affairs with hopeless men, and then move to another town when her life crashes down around her. Little attempt is made to present her as a plausible character; this is one of those movies sidetracked by the David Lynch Syndrome, in which characters exhibit a tacky trait of consumerism that is exaggerated out of all proportion (the meals served by Mrs. Flax, for example, consist entirely of artistic arrangements of "fun foods").

She has two daughters; a teen-ager, Charlotte (Winona Ryder), and a grade-schooler, Kate (Christina Ricci). As the movie opens, Kate is practicing her swimming, and will eventually see if she can match the world record for holding her breath underwater. That supplies one of the movie's many clues to the symbolism of its title, as well as suggesting the desperation Mrs. Flax inspires in

her children. The older daughter, Charlotte, has been driven nearly mad by her mother's incessant moves (eighteen by last count). She's never gone long to the same school, or made many friends, or experienced much normal life outside the hothouse of Mrs. Flax's fevered existence.

After yet another romantic disaster, the family moves again, to Massachusetts, where Charlotte makes friends with a young man named Joe (Michael Schoeffling), who has some kind of handyman job at a Roman Catholic convent that is just over the way. Charlotte is rather attracted to the nuns, to their quiet ways and cheerful encouragement, but she is more attracted to Joe, who perhaps possesses the secret of exactly what it is adults do when they're alone—what her mother does with all those men, for example.

This story is told by the director, Richard Benjamin, within a veritable thicket of art direction, which creates an odd world in which the realistic and the bizarre exist side by side. The movie makes a comparatively sedate companion piece for *Edward Scissorhands*, which also creates a fantasy universe out of exaggerated details of 1990-type popular culture. The central pop culture detail here is Cher, who, like Bette Midler in the somewhat similar *Stella*, does not entirely suffer her famous persona to disappear inside the role.

Her life begins to change, however, in Massachusetts, after she is discovered by Lou (Bob Hoskins), a husky salt-of-the-earth type, who sizes up the situation and decides that what Mrs. Flax and her daughters need is a transfusion of normalcy. He tries to contribute some balance to the family routine and has luck on the days when Mrs. Flax is not warring with him, while meanwhile a crisis develops in Charlotte's life: She is kissed by Joe, and becomes convinced she is pregnant.

It was here that I began to suspect that the movie may have lightened the vision it found in the original novel by Patty Dann. There are all sorts of gothic props around, including the monastery and a sinister river next to it, which suggest that terrible things could happen, but disasters are narrowly averted so that the movie can have one of those happy endings Hollywood likes so much right now. The plot of *Mermaids* seems to march toward that ending with great determination, looking neither right nor left at the way the events seem to impact on the lives of the characters.

And yet, perversely perhaps, I found this

an interesting movie. I didn't give a bean how it turned out, and I found a lot of it preposterous, but I enjoyed that quality. Why do we look at movies? To learn lessons and see life reflected back at us? Sometimes. But sometimes we simply sit there in the dark, stupefied by the spectacle. *Mermaids* is not exactly good, but it is not boring. Winona Ryder, in another of her alienated outsider roles, generates real charisma. And the movie is saying something about Cher as elusive as it is intriguing.

Metropolis ★ ★ ★ ★
NO MPAA RATING, 120 m., 1926, 1984 (Sound version)

Alfred Abel (Leader), Gustay Frohlich (His Son), Brigitte Helm (Maria), Rudolf Klein-Rogge (Rotwang), Heinrich George (Foreman). Directed by Fritz Lang. Screenplay by Lang and Thea Von Harbou. New sound track by Giorgio Moroder.

Fritz Lang's 1926 film *Metropolis* is one of the great achievements in the silent era, a work so audacious in its vision and so angry in its message that it is, if anything, more powerful today than when it was made. But it is rarely seen today; even in the era of insatiable home TV watching, silent films are condemned to the hinterlands of film societies and classrooms.

That is a great loss. Lang's movie is one of the great overwrought fantasies of German Expressionism, a story of a monstrous twenty-first-century city in which the workers labor like robots in their subterranean factories, while the privileged classes dance the night away, far above. The plot is broad melodrama: The son of the ruler of Metropolis visits the underground city and falls in love with a revolutionary named Maria, who makes impassioned speeches against the tyrants above. But the ruler orders a mad scientist to provide his new robot with Maria's face, creating a false Maria who will mislead the workers. Some of the individual scenes are amazing in their visual power, especially our first sight of the workers marching to their jobs, and a bizarre Art Deco factory wall where the humans are treated as parts of the machines. The movie was widely influential: The scene where the robot is turned into the false Maria was the inspiration for all the 1930s transformations of Frankenstein's monsters. Yet the original *Metropolis* is hardly known to today's filmgoers.

But now Giorgio Moroder, the composer of "Flashdance—What a Feeling" and the sound tracks for such movies as *Cat People*, has resurrected *Metropolis*, discovered or reconstructed some of its missing scenes, added some color tinting, and released it with a sound track of 1984 pop music. When this version of the movie was premiered at the 1984 Cannes Film Festival, it was sold primarily for its possibilities as a midnight cult film. In some sort of weird cultural inversion, Pat Benatar and Adam Ant would be used to sell Fritz Lang.

After you've seen the film with its new sound track, however, the notion seems almost sane. Silent films have always been accompanied by some sort of musical accompaniment—everything from orchestras to solo pianos. And in recent years such silent classics as *Napoleon* and *Peter Pan* have been resurrected with new scores. This is even the second time around for *Metropolis*, which was given a track of electronic music by the BBC in the 1970s. Moroder, however, has gone all the way and tarted up *Metropolis* with the same kinds of songs you'd expect to hear on MTV—he treats *Metropolis* like a music video. The film is too strong and original to be reduced to a formula, however; it absorbs the sound track, instead of being dominated by it, and the result is a film that works and a sound track that is an addition.

Some purists will not approve of Moroder's choice in music. Kevin Thomas of the *Los Angeles Times* was especially offended by the use of songs with words ("which sound especially silly because they're so painfully redundant"), but the words didn't bother me because, frankly, I didn't find myself listening to them. They are part of the background, and Fritz Lang's great film, so lovingly reconstructed, is the magnificent foreground.

Metropolitan ★ ★ ★ ½
PG-13, 98 m., 1990

Carolyn Farina (Audrey Rouget), Edward Clements (Tom Townsend), Christopher Eigeman (Nick Smith), Taylor Nichols (Charlie Black), Allison Rutledge-Parisi (Jane Clarke), Dylan Hundley (Sally Fowler), Isabel Gillies (Cynthia McLean), Bryan Leder (Fred Neff), Will Kempe (Rick von Sloneker), Elizabeth Thompson (Serena Slocum). Directed and produced by Whit Stillman. Screenplay by Stillman.

Metropolitan holds a mirror up to the lives and values of a group of New York preppies during the debutante season. They live in a world I dimly knew existed, but one as alien to me as if they belonged to a tribe in the Amazon. Yet their motives are universally recognizable: They want to be accepted, admired, and loved. They're teen-agers, many of them from wealthy homes, and they go to the right schools and want to be seen in the right places with the right people.

They are acutely aware that they are anachronisms. Even as they put on their tuxedos and venture out into the cold Christmas weather to attend debutante balls at the Plaza, they realize (in the words of the butler in Elaine May's *A New Leaf*) that they are carrying on in their own lifetimes a tradition that was dead before they were born.

They are, one of the kids says, the children of the UHB—the "urban haute bourgeoisie." They dress well and hold parties in the Park Avenue apartments of their parents, where they try to sound intellectual about Jane Austen and French socialists, and then play "truth games," like the one where you have to answer even the most embarrassing question with absolute veracity.

Into this tightly knit group comes a newcomer, Tom Townsend (Edward Clements), who lives on the West Side and wears a London Fog raincoat instead of a dark blue overcoat, and who says he doesn't believe in deb parties and the whole preppie value system. Nick (Christopher Eigeman), the most aware and cynical of the group, argues with him: "Deb parties are a way of getting invited to all of the best places and being supplied with food, drink, and companionship at very little cost to yourself. What could possibly be the matter with that?" Besides, Tom is told, there is a shortage of "escorts," and he'll actually be doing these poor girls a favor by coming along to their parties.

One of the girls develops an obvious crush on Tom, but he is oblivious to her; indeed, he seems to have an uncanny gift for thoughtless statements that hurt her feelings. He has a crush on the elusive Serena Slocum, once glimpsed at a dance, never forgotten. She has a reputation among the group members for being fast—probably not deserved—and another legendary character often talked about is the mysterious Rick von Sloneker (Will Kempe), said to have driven a girl to suicide.

These fabled people do eventually turn up in *Metropolitan*, but not before we've fallen into the seductive rhythms of the deb season—into bursts of hurt feelings or sudden crushes, punctuated by long, desultory conversations and deep confidences. The movie was written and directed by Whit Stillman, who, in his mid-thirties, is obviously still fascinated by the coming-of-age process he went through as a preppie. He has made a film F. Scott Fitzgerald might have been comfortable with, a film about people covering their own insecurities with a façade of social ease. And he has written wonderful dialogue, words in which the characters discuss ideas and feelings instead of simply marching through plot points as most Hollywood characters do.

Not very much happens in *Metropolitan*, and yet everything that happens is felt deeply, because the characters in this movie are still too young to have perfected their defenses against life. They care very much about what others think of them, their feelings are easily hurt, their love affairs are really forms of asking for acceptance.

It is strange how the romances of the teenage years retain a poignancy all through life—how a girl who turns you down when you're sixteen retains an aura in your memory even long after you, and she, have ceased to be who you were then. When I attended my high school reunion I discovered in the souvenir booklet assembled by the reunion committee that one of the girls in my class had a crush on me all those years ago. I would have given a great deal to have had that information at the time. This is a movie about people who are still living through that time, whose reunions and souvenir booklets are still ahead of them, along with their futures, and disappointments and pains that the whole world of debs and dances can scarcely prepare them for.

Miami Blues ★ ★
R, 97 m., 1990

Alec Baldwin (Fred Frenger), Fred Ward (Sgt. Hoke Moseley), Jennifer Jason Leigh (Susie Waggoner), Nora Dunn (Ellita Sanchez), Charles Napier (Sgt. Bill Henderson). Directed by George Armitage and produced by Jonathan Demme and Gary Goetzman. Screenplay by Armitage.

They're looking for the right tone in *Miami Blues*, and they don't find it very often, but when they do, you can see what they were looking for. The movie wants to be an off-center comedy, a lopsided cops-and-robbers movie where everybody has a few screws loose. But so much love is devoted to creating the wacko loonies in the cast that we're left with a set of personality profiles, not characters.

The film stars Alec Baldwin, fresh from *The Hunt for Red October*, as Fred Frenger, ex-con who has just arrived in Miami looking for a fresh start. He gets started off on the wrong foot. At the airport, he's approached by a Hare Krishna, and he bends the guy's finger back until it breaks. Not nice, especially since the cult member dies of shock.

Frenger is a thief, con man, and cheat. He is also incredibly reckless and will get himself into situations a dopey high-school kid would know enough to avoid. He wanders through the world looking for suitcases to steal, wallets to lift, identification papers he can use. Nothing much is planned, and most of his jobs depend on sheer blind luck. One piece of luck, sort of, is when he meets Susie, a hooker played by Jennifer Jason Leigh. She's a student at Dade Junior College, working her way through school, and she isn't very bright. In fact, she's so slow to catch on that conversation with her involves saying things and then explaining them, and then telling her it doesn't matter anyway.

Fred Ward is Sgt. Hoke Moseley, assigned to the case. His life is composed of equal parts of indigestion, alimony, and bureaucracy. Some simpleminded detective work leads him to Frenger. Fred and Susie, now living together, invite him to dinner and he stays gratefully, eating their chops and drinking their beer and belching cheerfully. He figures maybe Frenger broke the Hare Krishna's finger but didn't mean to kill him, and, truth to tell, he isn't very worked up over the case—not until Frenger visits his hotel room, beats him senseless, and steals his badge, gun, and false teeth. That's going too far.

Armed with identification as a cop, Frenger turns into a loose cannon, free-lancing all over town. He busts up robberies, steals from previous victims, flashes his badge, and takes advantage of that split second of doubt and guilt that's felt by the average citizen when anybody flashes a badge. And then the situation escalates as Frenger stupidly gets into more and more trouble, and Susie—who was never a very good hooker, but has convinced herself she could be a good wife—slowly realizes she is living with a very dangerous man.

The actors struggle manfully with their roles. Baldwin, who is good at playing intelligence, is not so good here at playing an ex-con with a screw loose. Fred Ward does a better job with the police sergeant; in movies like this and the underrated *Uforia*, he sits back and takes everything in and plays the cynic who will only really bother you if you really bother him. Jennifer Jason Leigh is another actress who has an easier time of playing smart (as she did in *Heart of Midnight*) than playing dumb. In *Miami Blues*, I think she plays too dumb—so dim that even the characters begin commenting on how she doesn't pick up on every little thing.

The movie was written and directed by George Armitage and produced by Jonathan Demme. Both are graduates of the Roger Corman low-budget exploitation assembly line of the 1960s, when Armitage directed *Private Duty Nurses* while Demme was writing *Angels Hard as They Come*. Demme has since gone on to develop his own idiosyncratic and likable directing style in movies like *Married to the Mob* and *Something Wild*. The problem is, Demme can do those movies but most people can't—and there are stretches where *Miami Blues* plays like a Demme film with sprung rhythm.

Micki & Maude ★ ★ ★ ★
PG-13, 115 m., 1984

Dudley Moore (Rob Salinger), Amy Irving (Maude Salinger), Ann Reinking (Micki Salinger), Richard Mulligan (Leo Brody), Lu Leonard (Nurse Verbeck). Directed by Blake Edwards and produced by Tony Adams. Screenplay by Jonathan Reynolds.

The key to the whole thing is Dudley Moore's absolutely and unquestioned sincerity. He loves both women. He would do anything to avoid hurting either woman. He wants to do the right thing but, more than that, he wants to do the kind thing. And that is how he ends up in a maternity ward with two wives who are both presenting him with baby children. If it were not for those good qualities in Moore's character, qualities this movie goes to great lengths to establish, *Micki & Maude* would run the risk of turning into tasteless and even cruel slapstick. After all, these are serious matters we're talking about. But the triumph of the movie is that it identifies so closely with Moore's desperation and his essentially sincere motivation that we understand the lengths to which he is driven. That makes the movie's inevitable climax even funnier.

As the movie opens, Moore is happily married to an assistant district attorney (Ann Reinking) who has no desire to have children. Children are, however, the only thing in life that Moore himself desires; apart from that one void, his life is full and happy. He works as a reporter for one of those TV magazine shows where weird people talk earnestly about their constitutional rights to be weird: For example, nudists defend their right to bear arms. Then he meets a special person, a cello player (Amy Irving) who has stepped in at the last moment to play a big concert. She thinks he has beautiful eyes, he smiles, it's love, and within a few weeks Moore and Irving are talking about how they'd like to have kids. Then Irving gets pregnant. Moore decides to do the only right thing, and divorce the wife he loves to marry the pregnant girlfriend that he also loves. But then his wife announces that she's pregnant, and Moore turns, in this crisis of conscience, to his best friend, a TV producer wonderfully played by Richard Mulligan. There is obviously only one thing he can do: become a bigamist.

Micki & Maude was directed by Blake Edwards, who also directed Moore in *10*, and who knows how to build a slapstick climax by one subtle development after another. There is, for example, the fact that Irving's father happens to be a professional wrestler, with a lot of friends who are even taller and meaner than he is. There is the problem that Moore's original in-laws happen to pass the church where he is having his second wedding. Edwards has a way of applying absolute logic to insane situations, so we learn, for example, that after Moore tells one wife he works days and the other one he works nights, his schedule works out in such a way that he begins to get too much sleep.

Dudley Moore is developing into one of the great movie comedians of his generation. *Micki & Maude* goes on the list with *10* and *Arthur* as screwball classics. Moore has another side as an actor, a sweeter, more serious side, that shows up in good movies like *Romantic Comedy* and bad ones like *Six Weeks*, but it's when he's in a screwball comedy, doing his specialty of absolutely sincere desperation, that he reaches genius. For example: The last twenty minutes of *Micki & Maude*, as the two pregnant women move inexorably forward on their collision course, represents a kind of filmmaking that is as hard to do as anything you'll ever see on a screen. The timing has to be flawless. So does the logic: One loose end, and the inevitability of a slapstick situation is undermined. Edwards and Moore are working at the top of their forms here, and the result is a pure, classic slapstick that makes *Micki & Maude* a real treasure.

Midnight Run ★ ★ ★ ½
R, 123 m., 1988

Robert De Niro (Jack Walsh), Charles Grodin (Jonathan Mardukas), Yaphet Kotto (Alonzo Mosely), John Ashton (Marvin Dorfler), Dennis Farina (Jimmy Serrano), Joe Pantoliano (Eddie Moscone), Richard Foronjy (Tony Darvo), Robert Miranda (Joey), Jack Kehoe (Jerry Geisler), Wendy Phillip (Gail). Produced and directed by Martin Brest. Screenplay by George Gallo.

Jack Walsh is a bounty hunter, a former cop who now works for bondsmen, bringing back clients who have tried to jump bail. Jonathan Mardukas is an accountant who embezzled millions of dollars from the mob in Vegas, and then jumped bail. Oddly enough, what these two men have most in common is the way they see themselves as more ethical than the system.

The two men are played in *Midnight Run* by Robert De Niro and Charles Grodin, an odd couple who spend most of the movie trying to survive a cross-country trip while the FBI is trying to capture them and the Mafia is trying to kill them. Along the way, of course, they discover that despite their opposite natures, they really do like and respect one another.

This sounds like a formula, and it is a formula. But *Midnight Run* is not a formula movie, because the writing and acting make these two characters into specific, quirky individuals whose relationship becomes more interesting even as the chase grows more predictable. Whoever cast De Niro and Grodin must have had a sixth sense for the chemistry they would have; they work together so smoothly, and with such an evident sense of fun, that even their silences are intriguing.

De Niro does not usually appear in movie comedies, and when he does, as in *Brazil*, it's usually in some sort of bizarre disguise. Here he proves to have comic timing of the best sort—the kind that allows dramatic scenes to develop amusing undertones while still working seriously on the surface. It's one thing to go openly for a laugh. It's harder to

do what he does, and allow the nature of the character to get the laughs, while the character himself never seems to be trying to be funny.

De Niro is often said to be the best movie actor of his generation. Grodin has been in the movies just about as long, has appeared in more different titles, and is of more or less the same generation, but has never received the recognition he deserves—maybe because he often plays a quiet, self-effacing everyman. In *Midnight Run*, where he is literally handcuffed to De Niro at times, he is every bit the master's equal, and in the crucial final scene, it is Grodin who finds the emotional truth that defines their relationship.

The movie develops that relationship during and between a series of virtuoso action sequences, after De Niro finds Grodin in New York and sets out to return him to Los Angeles. Grodin is afraid of flying, so the two men set out on a long cross-country odyssey that involves train trips, a shoot-out at the Chicago bus terminal, hitchhiking, riding the rails in boxcars, and being attacked by helicopters.

Their pursuers come in waves. The FBI is led by agent Alonzo Mosely (Yaphet Kotto), who is enraged because De Niro has stolen his FBI identification and is posing as a federal agent. The Mafia team is deployed by Jimmy Serrano (Dennis Farina), who grows increasingly enraged as his hit squads miss their targets.

And all the time, De Niro and Grodin feud with each other as Grodin schemes to escape. He knows that if he is ever returned to custody, the mob will have him killed in prison, and so his strategy is to convince De Niro he was only an embezzler in order to combat the mob. Oddly enough, this seems to be the truth, and fits in with De Niro's story—he's an ex-cop who left the force because of all the bureaucratic interference with his crusade against evil.

What *Midnight Run* does with these two characters is astonishing, because it's accomplished within the structure of a comic thriller. The director, Martin Brest, came to this project after *Beverly Hills Cop*, but if the action in the two films is comparable, the characters are a lot more interesting this time. It's rare for a thriller to end with a scene of genuinely moving intimacy, but this one does, and it earns it.

A Midsummer Night's Sex Comedy
★ ★
PG, 88 m., 1982

Woody Allen (Andrew), Mia Farrow (Ariel), Jose Ferrer (Leopold), Julie Hagerty (Dulcy), Tony Roberts (Maxwell), Mary Steenburgen (Adrian). Directed by Woody Allen and produced by Robert Greenhut. Screenplay by Allen.

The further north you go in summer, the longer the twilight lingers, until night is but a finger drawn between the dusk and the dawn. Such nights in northern climes are times of revelry, when lads and maids frolic in the underbrush to the pipes of Pan. Woody Allen's *A Midsummer Night's Sex Comedy* sneaks up rather suspiciously on this tradition; his men and women are rationalists, belong to such professions as finance, medicine, and psychiatry, and are nonchalant in the face of such modern inventions as flying bicycles. And yet here they all are, out in the country for the weekend. They gather at a little cottage somewhere in upstate New York, arriving by carriage or primitive auto, and in no time at all they are deeply unhappy about each other's sex lives. The host and hostess are Woody Allen and Mary Steenburgen. He is a stockbroker and she is his shy and sweet wife. The guests include Jose Ferrer, as an egotistical scientist, Mia Farrow, as his fiancée, Tony Roberts as a doctor, and Julie Hagerty as his abundantly sexed nurse.

During the course of their long weekend, many themes emerge, but the most common one is the enigma of male jealousy. Look at these three men, each one paired with the wonderful woman of his dreams. Allen, a part-time crackpot inventor, has a wife who loyally supports his experiments. Ferrer, an aging genius with a monstrous ego, has a beautiful young woman to hang on his arm. Roberts, an insatiable satyr, has a nubile nurse panting with desire. Are all three men happy and satiated? Not a chance. It is the most inevitable thing in the world that each man should be consumed with lust for one or more of the other women. It is not enough to have a bird in the hand; one must also have another bird in the bush. Or, as David Merrick once observed, "It is not enough for me to succeed. My enemies must fail."

From this simple and intriguing little situation, Woody Allen spins a rondelet of sexual intrigue and frustration. The basic developments: Allen pines away with the thought that he could once have made love to Farrow, but declined the chance. Ferrer conspires to meet Hagerty in the woods. Roberts attempts to seduce Farrow. And, through it all, Steenburgen steadfastly hopes for the best from everybody. To pass the time in between assignations and intrigues, the couples picnic, go for walks in the woods and express curiosity in Allen's latest inventions, which, in addition to the flying bicycle, include a metal sphere that can provide a magic lantern show that remembers the past and foresees the future.

This all sounds very charming and whimsical, and it is—almost paralyzingly so. *A Midsummer Night's Sex Comedy* is so low-key, so sweet and offhand and slight, there are times when it hardly even seems happy to be a movie. I am not quite sure what Allen had in mind when he conceived this material, but in addition to the echoes of Shakespeare and of Bergman's *Smiles of a Summer Night*, there are suggestions of John Cheever's Wapshots, Doctorow's *Ragtime*, and Jean Renoir films in which nice people do nice things to little avail. This is not a "Woody Allen film," then. It is not a brash comedy, it does not really contain the Woody Allen persona, and I guess Woody wanted it that way; he says he wants to try new things instead of giving people the same old stuff all the time. It is our misfortune that he arrived at that decision just after making *Annie Hall* and *Manhattan*, two wonderful films that brought his same old stuff to an exciting new plateau.

Now, with *Stardust Memories* and this film, he seems rudderless. I don't object to *A Midsummer Night's Sex Comedy* on grounds that it's different from his earlier films, but on the more fundamental ground that it's adrift. There doesn't seem to be a driving idea behind it, a confident tone to give us the sure notion that Allen knows what he wants to do here. It's a tip-off that the story is lacking in both sex and comedy. If the film seems at a loss to know where to turn next, the ending is particularly unsatisfactory. It involves a moment of fantasy or spirituality in which one of the movie's most rational characters dies and turns into a spirit of light, and bobs away on the twilight breeze. I don't object to the development itself, but to the way Allen handles it, so briefly and incompletely that it ends the film with what can only be described as a whimsical anticlimax.

There are nice small moments here and reflective, quiet performances, and a few laughs and smiles. But when we see Woody pedaling furiously to spin the helicopter blades of his flying bicycle, we're reminded of what we're missing. Woody doesn't have to be funny in every shot and he doesn't have to become another Mel Brooks, but he should allow himself to be funny when he feels like it, without apology, instead of receding into cuteness. I had the feeling during the film that Woody Allen was soft-pedaling his talent, was sitting on his comic gift, was trying to be somebody that he is not—and that, even if he were, would not be half as wonderful a piece of work as the real Woody Allen.

The Mighty Quinn ★ ★ ★ ★
R, 98 m., 1989

Denzel Washington (Xavier), James Fox (Elgin), Robert Townsend (Maubee), Mimi Rogers (Hadley), M. Emmet Walsh (Miller), Sheryl Lee Ralph (Lola), Art Evans (Jump), Esther Rolle (Ubu Pearl), Norman Beaton (Governor Chalk). Directed by Carl Schenkel and produced by Sandy Lieberson, Marion Hunt, and Ed Elbert. Screenplay by Hampton Fancher, based on the novel *Finding Maubee* by A.H.Z. Carr.

The Mighty Quinn is a spy thriller, a buddy movie, a musical, a comedy, and a picture that is wise about human nature. And yet with all of those qualities, it never seems to strain: This is a graceful, almost charmed, entertainment. It tells the story of a police chief on an island not unlike Jamaica, who gets caught in the middle when a wealthy developer is found murdered. Everyone seems to believe the chief's best friend, a no-account drifter named Maubee, committed the crime. Everyone but the chief and the chief's wife, who observes laconically, "Maubee is a lover, not a killer."

The film stars Denzel Washington, in one of those roles that creates a movie star overnight. You might have imagined that would have happened to Washington after he starred in *Cry Freedom*, as the South African hero Steven Biko. He got an Oscar nomination for that performance, but it didn't even begin to hint at his reserves of charm, sexiness, and offbeat humor. In an effortless way that reminds me of Robert Mitchum, Michael Caine, or Sean Connery in the best of the Bond pictures, he is able to be tough and gentle at the same time, able to play a hero and yet not take himself too seriously.

He plays Xavier Quinn, a local boy who once played barefoot with Maubee and got into the usual amount of trouble, but who grew up smart, went to America to be trained by the FBI, and has now returned as the police chief. The people of his district call him *The Mighty Quinn*, after the Bob Dylan song, and there is something both affectionate and ironic in the nickname. He knows everybody in town, knows their habits, and is on good terms even with the island governor (Norman Beaton), a cheerfully corrupt hack who only wants to keep the lid on things.

The murder is a great embarrassment. It is likely to discourage tourism, and perhaps there are more sinister reasons for sweeping the crime under the carpet and blaming Maubee. Quinn is the only one who wants to press an investigation, and it takes him into the decadent lives of the local establishment. He encounters Elgin, the suave local fixer (played by the elegant James Fox, that British specialist in the devious and the evasive). He is powerfully attracted to Elgin's restless wife (Mimi Rogers), and has a private encounter with her that is charged with eroticism precisely because he wants to resist her seductiveness.

Most troublesome of all, he encounters a shambling, overweight, genial American who wanders around with a camera and always seems to be in the wrong place at the right time. This character, Miller, is played by M. Emmet Walsh, one of Hollywood's greatest character actors, who in this movie seems to combine the Sydney Greenstreet and Peter Lorre roles: He is comic relief at first, sinister malevolence later.

As his investigation makes its way through this moral quicksand, Quinn also weathers trouble at home. His wife, Lola (Sheryl Lee Ralph), is rehearsing with a reggae trio and is just a shade too emasculating to make a man truly comfortable around her. A local beauty (Tyra Ferrell) wants to steal Quinn away from her. An old crone (Esther Rolle), who is the island's resident witch, makes prophecies of dire outcomes. And the carefree Maubee himself (played by Robert Townsend) turns up to taunt Quinn with his innocence.

This story, rich enough to fuel one of the great and complicated old Warner Bros. plots, is enriched still further by wall-to-wall music, including a lot of reggae and even a couple of appearances by Rita Marley. And the photography by Jacques Steyn is natural and amused, allowing us to ease into the company of these people instead of confronting us with them.

Denzel Washington is at the heart of the movie, and what he accomplishes is a lesson in movie acting. He has obligatory action scenes, yes, and confrontations that are more or less routine. He handles them easily. But watch the way he and Mimi Rogers play their subtle romantic encounter. The scene develops in three beats instead of two, so that the erotic tension builds. But coexisting with his macho side is a playfulness that allows him to come up behind a woman and dance his fingers along her bare arms, and sashay off again before she knows what has happened.

If Washington is the discovery in this movie, he is only one of its many wonderful qualities. I'd never heard of the director, Carl Schenkel, before, and I learned from the press releases only that he is Swiss and has directed a lot of commercials, but on the basis of this film, he's a natural. He is able in the moderate running time of 98 minutes to create a film that seems as rich and detailed as one much longer. He uses his Jamaican locations and interiors so easily that the movie seems to really inhabit its world, instead of merely being photographed in front of it. And the music helps; reggae somehow seems passionate, lilting, and comforting, all at once. *The Mighty Quinn* was one of 1989's best films.

The Milagro Beanfield War ★ ★ ½
R, 118 m., 1988

Ruben Blades (Sheriff Montoya), Richard Bradford (Ladd Devine), Sonia Braga (Ruby Archuleta), Julie Carmen (Nancy Mondragon), Chick Vennera (Joe Mondragon), Christopher Walken (Kyril Montana), John Heard (Charlie Bloom), Melanie Griffith (Flossie Devine), Carlos Riquelme (Amarante Cordova). Directed by Robert Redford and produced by Redford and Moctesuma Esparza. Screenplay by David Ward and John Nichols, based on the novel by Nichols.

One fine morning, Joe Mondragon gets mad and kicks at the gate on the irrigation ditch that runs past his dry field. Water flows into it, and he decides, just like that, to grow some beans in his field. Everybody in town knows the water belongs to a big land development corporation—but tensions are high between the outsiders and the longtime local Chicanos, and nobody is sure just how far

they should push this thing. For the sheriff, who sees everybody's point of view, it's an especially delicate balancing act.

Robert Redford's *The Milagro Beanfield War* opens with Joe Mondragon's small act of rebellion, and uses it to explore the dilemma of many regional cultures in the United States—pockets of language, custom, and heritage that are threatened with extinction by developers who want to turn everything into one homogenous mall/hotel/resort. His movie doesn't paint the situation in simple black-and-white terms; it's about how some of the locals support Mondragon's rebellion, a few oppose it, and still more are rather reluctant to get involved.

There is, for example, Ruby (Sonia Braga), the local garage owner, whose fiery temperament is perfectly suited to taking on the developers. She eggs on the local newspaper editor (John Heard), a onetime sixties Eastern radical who has cooled down in the desert and is not too eager to stir up trouble. She thinks he should run an editorial supporting Mondragon (Chick Vennera). Meanwhile, the owner of the development company (Richard Bradford) demands that Joe's water be shut off, and a vicious state police agent (Christopher Walken) seems ready to use force if necessary. The sheriff (Ruben Blades) shuttles from one side to the other, advising everyone to keep his cool.

The result is a wonderful fable, but the problem is, some of the people in the story know it's a fable and others do not. This causes an uncertainty that runs all through the film, making it hard to weigh some scenes against others. There are characters who seem to belong in an angry documentary—like Bradford, who wants to turn Milagro into a plush New Mexico resort town. And then there are characters who seem to come from a more fanciful time, like Mondragon, whose original rebellion is more impulsive than studied.

I'm not complaining about the characters who are clearly in the world of the spirit, like the old grandfather who has long conversations with his guardian angel. I'm speaking of the way the film shifts from one level of reality to another even within the same scene. When Walken loads his rifle and raises a posse and goes into the hills to try to shoot Joe Mondragon, that whole sequence somehow seems out of key with the colorful local old-timers and their magical legends. When the townspeople gather for a heated town meeting and cannot agree on a course of

action, that seems in contrast to a jolly later scene where they all gather to help Joe harvest his beans. The movie doesn't seem clear about its destination, and never quite arrives at one.

Maybe the problem is that Redford has tried to accomplish two incompatible things in one movie. He clearly loves the Spanish-Indian-Mexican culture of northern New Mexico, and his film opens on the note of a fable as the guardian angel does a dance through the sleeping town. But he is also very concerned with hard issues of land usage. There must be progress, but there should also be tradition, and the film is too fair-minded; it can see both sides of the question so clearly that its dramatic sympathies are confused.

And yet there is a lot of love and joy in *The Milagro Beanfield War*. Sonia Braga's performance is especially warm; she's all over town, hectoring the newspaper editor, gathering signatures on a petition, marveling that she knew all along that Joe Mondragon had it in him to do something wonderful. John Heard strikes an accurate note as the tired sixties radical who, in a way, just wants to retire in New Mexico like the people who will use the new resort. But another character, Herbie Platt (Daniel Stern) only muddies the situation. He is a New York anthropology student who comes to study the locals; at first, he does not share their "superstitions," but by the end of the film he is making a serious offering to one of their statues.

Did his offering help? In that case, will the locals prevail? Well, yes and no. The offering, and all of the folklore, religion, and magic, seem to have some power in Milagro. But the film seems to concede that the resort will eventually be built, and will even provide some employment. The film's final statement seems to be a vote of appreciation for these colorful Chicanos who have such wonderful customs, and a sigh of regret that their magic is not quite strong enough. I'm not sure audiences want that kind of ambiguity. If Redford had left out a few of the waffling, undecided characters and drawn his dramatic lines more strongly, the film might have been a lot more powerful.

Miles From Home ★ ★ ★
R, 113 m., 1988

Richard Gere (Frank Roberts), Kevin Anderson (Terry Roberts), Brian Dennehy (Frank, Sr.), Penelope Ann Miller (Sally), Helen Hunt (Jennifer), Judith Ivey (Frances), Laurie Metcalf (Exotic Dancer), John Malkovich (Reporter). Directed by Gary Sinise and produced by Frederick Zollo and Paul Kurta. Screenplay by Chris Gerolmo.

Miles From Home opens with what looks like old TV news footage, in snowy black and white, of big Cadillacs speeding down dusty roads past prosperous cornfields. Then we see the stocky man in the oversize suit climbing out of the limo, and we remember the event: This is the famous visit that Nikita Khrushchev paid to an average American farm in Iowa. On the front porch steps, he shakes hands with the farmer while the farmer's two small boys stand uneasily at attention, their hair slicked down flat with brilliantine.

That was thirty years ago. Now, as the film turns into color, a fierce rainstorm is sweeping the plains, and the farmer's two sons, grown to men, struggle to move a big combine before it can get stuck in the mud. The brothers are named Frank and Terry Roberts, and in the summer of 1987 they have a weather problem—ironically, in view of the drought of 1988, it is too much rainfall. Their corn is soaked and some of it is rotting. Their yield will be disappointing. On the walls of the farmhouse where they were born are plaques and clippings naming their father the Farmer of the Year. But this is not the first bad year the sons have had, and they will lose the farm to the bank.

Those are the opening scenes of *Miles From Home*, a movie about the farm crisis that is sometimes too contrived, but finally very moving as the story of an angry reaction to the squeeze on small farmers. The movie stars Richard Gere as the older, angrier brother, and Kevin Anderson as the younger, sweeter kid who is carried along by Gere's headlong rage.

There is a quiet scene near the front of the film that sets up a lot of things. The brothers are holding a yard sale to raise some cash. A thoughtless, pretty city girl (Penelope Ann Miller) stops by with a girlfriend and observes to Anderson, "People would have to be pretty desperate to try to sell junk like this." Then she realizes it is Anderson's farm. Her eyes fill with tears as she starts to apologize, but then there is a charged silence

between the two of them, as they realize they have fallen in love.

All right, so love at first sight is contrived and corny, an obvious plot device. Plots are as good as the actors who inhabit them, however, and Kevin Anderson and Penelope Ann Miller create a believable, warm chemistry here, one that will serve as the film's center when the Gere character flies out of control. That happens slowly, implacably, as Gere realizes he has failed the memory of his father and lost the farm. He blames himself, and there is a scene in a cemetery, Gere talking to his father's tombstone, before the furies inside of him break loose.

In an action that mirrors one of the key scenes in *Bonnie and Clyde*, he shoots out some of the windows of the farmhouse. Then he intimidates his kid brother to join him in a wilder plan to burn down the farmhouse and set the fields ablaze rather than see the farm fall into the hands of the bank. With the flames roaring against the sky, the two brothers set off on a doomed escape across the state of Iowa, where the symbolism of their act makes them folk heroes.

Many of the visuals in *Miles From Home* seem to echo compositions in Terence Malick's *Days of Heaven* (1978), one of Richard Gere's earliest films. But the story of the two fugitives becoming media heroes is a reminder of both *Bonnie and Clyde* and Malick's own earlier film, *Badlands*, with Martin Sheen and Sissy Spacek on the run. That film began with a murder; this one seems doomed at times to lead to one.

As Gere and Anderson use a series of stolen cars to move across the state, they meet a series of strange people—outsiders and rebels—who support them. There is a roadhouse stripper (Laurie Metcalf), and an entranced woman in a trailer park (Judith Ivey), and a lean reporter who wants to tell their story (John Malkovich). And there are all the people in the beer tent at a county fair, who know exactly who these two young men really are and protect them from the police.

With the exception of Gere, the cast of *Miles From Home* is largely populated with members and alumni of Chicago's Steppenwolf Theater. Malkovich, Ivey, and Metcalf are familiar faces in the movies, but this is only the second starring role for Kevin Anderson (after *Orphans*) and he is strong in it, especially in his scenes with Miller, in which he shares his growing fear that his brother is running wild, dangerously out of control.

The direction of the film is by another Steppenwolf member, Gary Sinise, who reflects the Steppenwolf tradition to go for broke emotionally. There are scenes in the film—like the first falling-in-love scene—that a filmmaker with less courage would have shot in a more understated style. Steppenwolf has always been in love with melodrama, and *Miles From Home* is, too.

Miller's Crossing ★ ★ ★
R, 115 m., 1990

Gabriel Byrne (Tom Reagan), Marcia Gay Harden (Verna), John Turturro (Bernie Bernbaum), Jon Polito (Johnny Caspar), J.E. Freeman (Eddie Dane), Albert Finney (Leo). Directed by Joel Coen and produced by Ethan Coen. Screenplay by Joel and Ethan Coen.

The room. I keep thinking about the room. The office from which Leo pulls the strings that control the city. Leo, played by Albert Finney, is a large, strong man in late middle-age, and he lacks confidence in only one area. He is not sure he can count on the love of Verna, the young dame he's fallen for. That causes him to hesitate when he knows that Verna's brother, Bernie, should be rubbed out. He doesn't want to lose Verna. And his hesitation brings the city's whole criminal framework crashing down in blood and violence.

But I think about the room. What a wonderful room. All steeped in dark shadows, with expensive antique oak furniture and leather chairs and brass fittings and vast spaces of flooring between the yellow pools of light. I would like to work in this room. A man could get something done in this room. And yet the room is a key to why *Miller's Crossing* is not quite as successful as it should be—why it seems like a movie that is constantly aware of itself, instead of a movie that gets on with business.

I do not really think that Leo would have such an office. I believe it is the kind of office that would be created by a good interior designer with contacts in England, and supplied to a rich lawyer. I am not sure a rackets boss in a big American city in 1929 would occupy such a space, even though it does set him off as a sinister presence among the shadows.

I am also not sure that the other characters in this movie would inhabit quite the same clothing, accents, haircuts, and dwellings as we see them in. This doesn't look like a gangster movie, it looks like a commercial intended to look like a gangster movie. Everything is too designed. That goes for the plot and the dialogue, too. The dialogue is well-written, but it is indeed written. We admire the prose rather than the message. People make threats, and we think about how elegantly the threats are worded.

Miller's Crossing comes from two traditions that sometimes overlap: the gangster movie of the 1930s and the *film noir* of the 1940s. It finds its characters in the first and its visual style in the second, but the visuals lack a certain stylish tackiness that *film noir* often had. They're in good taste. The plot is as simple as an old gangster movie, but it takes us a long time to figure that out, because the first thirty minutes of the film involve the characters in complicated dialogue where they talk about a lot of people we haven't met, and refer to a lot of possibilities we don't understand. It's the kind of movie you have to figure out in hindsight.

Don't get me wrong. There is a lot here to admire. Albert Finney is especially good as Leo, the crime boss, and Jon Polito was wonderful as Johnny Caspar, his rival, who keeps talking about "business ethics." One of the most interesting characters in the movie is Bernie Bernbaum (John Turturro), a two-timing bookie who pleads for his life in a monologue that he somehow keeps afloat long past any plausible dramatic length.

The pleasures of the film are largely technical. It is likely to be most appreciated by movielovers who will enjoy its resonance with films of the past. What it doesn't have is a narrative magnet to pull us through—a story line that makes us really care what happens, aside from the elegant, but mechanical, manipulations of the plot. The one human moment comes when Leo finds out Verna really can't be trusted. Even then, I was thinking about *Farewell, My Lovely*, where a big mug named Moose finds out the same thing about a dame named Velma.

Miracle Mile ★ ★ ★
R, 88 m., 1989

Anthony Edwards (Harry Washello), Mare Winningham (Julie Peters), John Agar (Ivan Peters), Lou Hancock (Lucy Peters), Mykel T. Williamson (Wilson), Kelly Minter (Charlotta), Kurt Fuller (Gerstead), Denise Crosby (Landa). Directed by Steve DeJarnatt. Produced by John Daly and Derek Gibson. Screenplay by DeJarnatt.

Miracle Mile has the logic of one of those nightmares in which you're sure something is terrible, hopeless, and dangerous, but you can't get anyone to listen to you—and besides, you have a sneaking suspicion that you might be mistaken. The film begins as a low-key boy-meets-girl story, and then a telephone is answered by the wrong person and everything goes horribly wrong. Much of the movie's diabolical effectiveness comes from the fact that it never reveals, until the very end, whether the nightmare is real, or only some sort of tragic misunderstanding.

The opening scenes are sunny and sweet. Harry (Anthony Edwards) and Julie (Mare Winningham) are two young people in Los Angeles who have what the movies like to call a Meet Cute; they like each other's looks, and begin to talk, and it's love at first sight, and so Harry makes a date to pick up Julie after she gets off work at the all-night coffee shop where she's a waitress. So far, so good, but then Harry oversleeps and wakes up in the middle of the night, confused and befuddled, and races down to the coffee shop, only to find that Julie has already left for home.

That's when the pay telephone rings in the booth outside the restaurant. Harry answers it, and hears some kind of panicky warning that he can barely understand. It's something about how nuclear missiles have been launched, and it's too late to recall them, and the Russians are involved, and the irrevocable events leading up to World War III have been set into motion. The guy on the other end of the line doesn't know who he's talking to; he thinks he called his father, and doesn't know he got the wrong number—and then there's the sound of gunfire, and Harry is told by a new voice to ignore everything he just heard.

Well, what *did* he hear? Was it a genuine call, or some sort of a practical joke? Did the guy on the other end really know what he was talking about? Or did Harry perhaps get everything out of context, and misunderstand it? This is the device through which the movie generates its suspense; we can never be sure that telephone call was genuine.

At first, Harry doesn't know what to do. And the inhabitants of the all-night diner aren't much help. One is a drunk, one is a drag queen, one is the hard-boiled short-order clerk, and then there's the impeccably groomed brunette at the counter who calmly takes out a portable phone, dials a secret number, and tells them all that things look bad—that an attack may be on the way. Is she crazy, or what?

The movie was written and directed by Steve DeJarnatt, who toys with our sense of reality by establishing a time limit early in the film; there's about an hour until the missiles arrive, if they're indeed arriving. What can be done in that time? Harry desperately tries to find Julie, the girl with whom he wants to share his last moments of life. He and the short-order clerk organize some kind of half-baked attempt to get out of town. Then there's a plan to use a helicopter pilot to airlift some of the characters out of the target zone. All of these disorganized plans are accompanied by confusion, bad communications, misunderstandings, accidents, and outbursts of violence—and the clock keeps ticking.

Miracle Mile reminded me a little, at times, of Martin Scorsese's *After Hours*. Both show a city at night, sleeping, dreaming, disoriented, while a character desperately tries to apply logic where it will not work. *Miracle Mile* is not as good as the Scorsese film, perhaps because its danger is an impersonal nuclear attack rather than the random craziness of late-night street people. But the effect is sometimes the same, and there is real terror in a scene where word of the possible attack begins to spread through the city, and there are riots in the streets. What the movie confirmed for me is something I've always suspected; that if there's ever an hour's warning that the nuclear missiles are on the way, thanks all the same, but I'd just as soon not know about it.

Misery ★ ★ ★
R, 104 m., 1990

James Caan (Paul Sheldon), Kathy Bates (Annie Wilkes), Richard Farnsworth (Buster), Frances Sternhagen (Virginia), Lauren Bacall (Marsha Sindell). Directed by Rob Reiner and produced by Andrew Scheinman and Reiner. Screenplay by William Goldman.

Stephen King has a modest, but undeniable genius for being able to find horror in everyday situations. My notion is that he starts with a germ of truth from his own life, and then takes it as far as he can into the macabre and the bizarre. Take *Misery*, for example, the story of a writer who finds himself the captive of his self-proclaimed "No. 1 fan." The hero has not finished a novel to her liking, and now she has him in her grip and he is writing under a particularly painful and violent deadline.

I can only imagine what some of the more peculiar fan letters of a writer like King must read like, and perhaps one of them even suggested this story. *Misery* involves a writer named Paul Sheldon (James Caan) who has been prostituting his talent for years with a series of romantic historical potboilers about a character named Misery, who after great triumphs and travails has finally been killed off. Having assassinated the character he had come to hate, Sheldon holes up in a Colorado lodge to write a "real" novel, and when he finishes it, he packs it into his car and heads down a mountain road in a blizzard, loses control of his car, and ends up injured and in a snowbank.

He might easily have died, but he's rescued by a brusque, resourceful woman named Annie Wilkes (Kathy Bates), who digs him out, takes him home, nurses him back to health, and then is outraged to learn he has killed off Misery. That simply will not do, and so she holds her invalid prisoner while he writes a sequel bringing Misery back to life.

The world thinks Sheldon is dead. We follow the search for his body, which involves his literary agent (Lauren Bacall), the local backwoods sheriff (Richard Farnsworth), and the sheriff's wife (Frances Sternhagen). They are essentially the only other actors in the movie, which develops mostly as a two-hander between Caan and Bates.

They make an intriguing team. Caan, who has been hyper in some of his recent performances, is controlled and even passive here, the disbelieving captive of a madwoman. Bates, who has the film's key role, is uncanny in her ability to switch, in an instant, from sweet solicitude to savage scorn. Some of the things Stephen King invents for her to do to the writer are so shocking that they could be a trap for an actor—an invitation to overact. But she somehow remains convincing inside her character's madness.

The material in *Misery* is so much Stephen King's own that it's a little surprising that a director like Rob Reiner would have been interested in making the film. Reiner has started with literary properties before—like King's *Stand by Me* and William Goldman's *The Princess Bride*—but his strength is in putting a personal stamp on his films (which also include the cross-country romance *The Sure Thing* and the fake documentary *This Is Spinal Tap*). What he does with *Misery* is essentially simply respectful—he "brings the story to the screen," as the saying goes.

It is a good story, a natural, and it grabs us. But just as there is almost no way to screw it up, so there's hardly any way to bring it above a certain level of inspiration. Many competent directors could have done what Reiner does here, and perhaps many other actors could have done what Caan does, although the Kathy Bates performance is trickier and more special. The result is good craftsmanship, and a movie that works. It does not illuminate, challenge, or inspire, but it works.

Mishima ★ ★ ★ ★
R, 121 m., 1985

Ken Ogato (Yukio Mishima), Mashayuki Shionoya (Morita), Hiroshi Mikami (First Cadet), Naoko Otani (Mother). Directed by Paul Schrader and produced by Mata Yamamoto and Tom Luddy. Screenplay by Paul and Leonard Schrader.

The Japanese author Yukio Mishima seems to have thought of his life as a work of art, and more than anyone since Hemingway he got other people to think of it that way, too. He was a brilliant self-promoter who not only wrote important novels and plays, but also cultivated the press, posed for beefcake photographs, and founded his own private army. He was an advocate of a return to medieval Japanese values, considered himself a samurai, and died on schedule and according to his own plan: After occupying an Army garrison with some of his soldiers, he disemboweled himself while being beheaded by a follower.

Mishima's life obviously supplies the materials for a sensationalistic film. Paul Schrader has not made one. Instead, his *Mishima* takes this most flamboyant of writers and translates his life into a carefully structured examination of three different Mishimas: Public, private, and literary.

The film begins with the public Mishima, a literary superstar who begins the last day of his life by ritualistically donning the uniform of his private army. From time to time during the film, we return to moments from that final day, as Mishima is jammed somewhat inelegantly into a tiny car and driven by his followers to an appointment with a Japanese general. The film ends with Mishima holding the general hostage, and winning the right to address the troops of the garrison (who must have been just as astonished as if Norman Mailer turned up at West Point). Although the film ends with Mishima's ritual suicide, it is not shown in the graphic detail that's popular in recent films; Schrader wisely realizes that too much blood would destroy the mood of his film and distract attention from the idea behind Mishima's death.

Mishima's last day is counterpointed with black-and-white sequences showing his childhood and adolescence, and with gloriously stylized color dramatizations of scenes from his novels, *Temple of the Golden Pavilion, Kyoko's House,* and *Runaway Horses.* The scenes from the novels were visualized by designer Eiko Ishioka, who seems to have been inspired by fantasy scenes from early Technicolor musicals. They don't summarize Mishima's novels so much as give us an idea about them; as we see the ritualistic aspects of his fantasies, we are seeing Japan through his eyes, as he wished it to be.

The black-and-white biographical sequences show a little boy growing up into a complicated man. Young Yukio, raised by his mother and his grandmother, was a lonely outcast with a painful stammer, and we can see in the insecurities of his youth impulses that led him to build his muscles, to leap for literary glory, and to wrap himself in the samurai ethic.

Mishima is a rather glorious project, in these days of pragmatic commercialism and rank cynicism in the movie industry. Although a sensationalized version of his life might have had potential at the box office (and although Schrader, author of *Taxi Driver,* director of *American Gigolo,* would have been quite capable of directing it), this is a much more ambitious and intellectual film.

It challenges us to think about Mishima, instead of simply observing the strange channels of his life. What did he prove, on the day when his life ended according to plan? That he was willing to pay the ultimate price to transform his life into an artistic statement—and also, perhaps, that some of his genius was madness. Was it worth it? Who can say who is not Mishima?

Miss Firecracker ★ ★ ★ ½
PG, 102 m., 1989

Holly Hunter (Carnelle Scott), Mary Steenburgen (Elaine Rutledge), Tim Robbins (Delmount Williams), Alfre Woodard (Popeye Jackson), Scott Glenn (Mac Sam), Veanne Cox (Tessy Mahoney), Ann Wedgeworth (Miss Blue), Trey Wilson (Benjamin Drapper), Amy Wright (Missy Mahoney), Kathleen Chalfant (Miss Lily). Directed by Thomas Schlamme and produced by Fred Berner. Screenplay by Beth Henley, based on her play *The Miss Firecracker Contest.*

At first I was thinking the beauty contest in *Miss Firecracker* was too impossibly cornball to be true, but then I remembered the county fair queens of my youth—teen-age girls made up to within an inch of their lives, and trotted out in their formal gowns to parade in the heat of an August afternoon, downwind from the hog judging, which always took place at about the same time. These contests were run by selfless volunteers, usually men of a certain age whose obsession with the rules and regulations helped them to sublimate their lust for the fairway beauties. The one thing I could sense, even as a kid covering the canned-goods competition for the local paper, was that these girls were desperate to prove something, and it had little to do with glamour.

In *Miss Firecracker*, the playwright Beth Henley has taken such a contest, the Fourth of July pageant in Yazoo City, Mississippi, and turned it into another of those Southern Gothic romances where mansions crumble and libidos boil, and young women weep bitter tears because their older sisters are prettier than they are. This is not new material, but Henley replaces some of the painful sincerity with a lighthearted goofiness that cheers things up, and the movie is performed with the kind of insight that could only have been achieved by actresses who once, for a moment however brief, dreamed of themselves stepping forward with a radiant smile to accept the crown and the roses.

The film stars Holly Hunter, fresh from *Broadcast News*, as Carnelle Scott, who was adopted by her cousins in the Williams family after becoming an orphan at eight. She is now somewhere in her twenties, works as a fish-gutter at the local catfish packing plant, and has earned the nickname of "Miss Hot Tamale" among the local swains. But she has never quite forgotten the glorious day in 1972 when her cousin Elaine (Mary Steenburgen) was named Miss Firecracker, and stepped forward in all her glory and a shocking red gown. This is the summer, Carnelle has vowed, when she will finally succeed her cousin as the Fourth of July queen.

The movie opens with an assembly of the key players. Carnelle's boy cousin, Delmount (Tim Robbins) has just arrived in town via freight train, and has a drunken plan to sell the crumbling Williams mansion to developers. Elaine has come home for a visit from Atlanta, where she lives with her husband; she is scheduled to deliver the keynote address at this year's pageant, "My Life as a Beauty." Meanwhile, Carnelle despairs

of getting Elaine to loan her the winning red dress, and turns in desperation to a local black seamstress named Popeye (Alfre Woodard), who has designed prize-winning costumes before—but for bullfrogs.

Carnelle is on her best behavior, turning a cold shoulder to the local boys in heat. She has determined to live down her image as a Hot Tamale, and finally amount to something. But then the carnival arrives in town for the Fourth of July, and she has a reunion with Mac Sam (Scott Glenn), the smooth-talking roustabout who has developed a taste for tamales over the years. Will she be able to preserve—or at least restore—her virtue? Will Elaine lend her the red dress? Will Delmount succeed in his scheme to sell the homestead out from under them? Will Popeye design a winning dress that does not make anyone think of bullfrogs?

Miss Firecracker is not so much concerned with the answers to these questions as with the asking of them. Every story like this has problems with the last act, in which all of the threads of plot have to be pulled together, but *Miss Firecracker* wisely spends most of its energy on character development, instead. Apart from Hunter and Steenburgen, who create a tight little ballet of cousinly "love" and jealousy, the most interesting characters in the movie are Delmount and Popeye—who behave in the most peculiar ways, and seem serenely unaware of it. They are both congenital outsiders, who sensibly cannot quite understand why anyone would want to be Miss Firecracker. Their difference is, Popeye wants to help Carnelle all she can, and Delmount affects a careless indifference. The performances by Tim Robbins (the young pitcher in *Bull Durham)* and Alfre Woodard (nominated for an Oscar for *Cross Creek)* are the hidden treasures of the movie.

The director and the cinematographer, Thomas Schlamme and Arthur Albert, surround the plot with a lot of local atmosphere—the movie was shot on location with the cooperation of everyone in Yazoo City, and I think we see most of them on the screen—and also with a sort of moony, romantic glow. Many of the scenes are set at night, when hearts can be bared with greater safety, and love can declare itself free from lust. What finally makes *Miss Firecracker* special is that it is not about who wins the contest, but about how all beauty contests are about the need to be loved, and about how silly a beauty contest can seem if somebody really loves you.

Missing ★ ★ ★
R, 122 m., 1982

Jack Lemmon (Ed Horman), Sissy Spacek (Beth Horman), Melanie Mayron (Terry Simon), John Shea (Charles Horman), Charles Cioffi (Capt. Tower), David Clennon (Consul Putnam). Directed by Constantin Costa-Gavras and produced by Edward and Mildred Lewis. Screenplay by Costa-Gavras and Donald Stewart.

Much has already been written about the bravery of *Missing*, which dares, we are told, to make a specific attack on American policies in Chile during and after the Allende regime. I wish the movie had been even braver—brave enough to risk a clear, unequivocal, uncompromised statement of its beliefs, instead of losing itself in a cluttered mishmash of stylistic excesses. This movie might have *really* been powerful, if it could have gotten out of its own way.

The story involves the disappearance in the early 1970s of a young American journalist in a country (not named) that is obviously intended to be Chile. The young man and his wife (played by John Shea and Sissy Spacek) have gone down there to live, write, and absorb the local color. But then a civil war breaks out, martial law is declared, troops roam the streets, and one day soldiers come and take the young man away. The movie is the record of the frustrating attempts by Spacek and her father-in-law (Jack Lemmon) to discover what happened to the missing man. It suggests that the young American might have been on some sort of informal hit list of left-wing foreign journalists, that he was taken away and killed, and that (this is the controversial part) American embassy officials knew about his fate and may even have been involved in approving his death.

If that was indeed the case, then it is a cause for great anger and dismay. And the best scenes in *Missing*—the ones that make this movie worth seeing despite its shortcomings—are the ones in which Spacek and Lemmon hack their way through a bureaucratic jungle in an attempt to get someone to make a simple statement of fact. Those scenes are masterful. The U.S. embassy officials are painted as dishonest weasels, shuffling papers, promising immediate action, and lying through their teeth. Lemmon and Spacek are about as good an example of Ordinary Americans as you can find in a movie, and their flat voices and stubborn determination and even their initial dislike for one another all ring exactly true. If *Missing* had started with the disappearance of the young man, and had followed Spacek and Lemmon in a straightforward narrative as they searched for him, this movie might have generated overwhelming tension and anger. But the movie never develops the power it should have had, because the director, Constantin Costa-Gavras, either lacked confidence in the strength of his story, or had too much confidence in his own stylistic virtuosity. He has achieved the unhappy feat of upstaging his own movie, losing it in a thicket of visual and editing stunts.

Let's begin with the most annoying example of his meddling. *Missing* contains scenes that take place before the young man disappears. We see his domestic happiness with his wife and friends, we see him reading from *The Little Prince* and making plans for the future. The fact that this material is in the movie suggests, at least, that the story is being told by an omniscient author, one who can also tell us, if he wishes to, what happened to the victim. But he does not. Costa-Gavras shows us all sorts of ominous warnings of approaching trouble (including a lot of loose talk by American military men who are not supposed to be in the country, but are, and all but claim credit for a coup). He shows us a tragic aftermath of martial law, guns in the streets, vigilante justice, and the chilling sight of row after row of dead young men, summarily executed by the new junta. But he does not show us what happened to make the film's hero disappear. Or, rather, he shows us several versions—visual fantasies in which the young husband is arrested at home by a lot of soldiers, or a few, and is taken away in this way or that. These versions are pegged to the unreliable eyewitness accounts of the people who live across the street. They dramatize an uncertain human fate in a time of upheaval, but they also distract fatally from the flow of the film.

By the time *Missing* begins its crucial last half-hour, a strange thing has happened. We care about this dead American, and his wife and father, almost *despite* the movie. The performances of Spacek and Lemmon carry us along through the movie's undisciplined stylistic displays. But at the end of the film, there isn't the instant discharge of anger we felt at the end of Costa-Gavras's great *Z* (1968), because the narrative juggernaut of that film has been traded in for what is basically just a fancy meditation on the nature of reality. Something happened to the missing young man (his story is based on real events). Somebody was guilty, and somebody was lying, and he was indeed killed. But *Missing* loses its way on the road to those conclusions, and at the end Lemmon and Spacek seem almost to mourn alone, while the crew is busy looking for its next shot.

The Mission ★ ★ ½
PG, 126 m., 1986

Robert De Niro (Mendoza), Jeremy Irons (Gabriel), Ray McAnally (Altamirano), Aidan Quinn (Felipe), Cherie Lunghi (Carlotta), Ronald Pickup (Hontar). Directed by Roland Joffe and produced by Fernando Ghia and David Puttnam. Screenplay by Robert Bolt.

The Mission feels exactly like one of those movies where you'd rather see the documentary about how the movie was made. You'd like to know why so many talented people went to such incredible lengths to make a difficult and beautiful movie—without any of them, on the basis of the available evidence, having the slightest notion of what the movie was about. There isn't a moment in *The Mission* that is not watchable, but the moments don't add up to a coherent narrative. At the end, we can sort of piece things together, but the movie has never really made us care.

The action takes place in South America, in the eighteenth century. Two great colonial forces are competing for the hearts and minds of the native Indians. On the one hand, there are the imperialist plunderers, who want to establish a trade in riches and slaves. On the other hand, there are the missionaries, who want to convert the Indians to Christ.

The central figure in the movie is Mendoza (Robert De Niro), who begins as the first kind of imperialist and ends as the second. Early in the film, he is a slave-trader, a man of the flesh, but after he kills his brother in a flash of anger, he yearns for redemption, and he gets it from the missionaries who assign him an agonizing penance: He must climb a cliff near a steep waterfall, dragging behind him a net filled with a heavy weight of armor. Again and again De Niro strives to scale the dangerous height, until finally all of the anger and sin is drained from him, and he becomes a missionary at a settlement run by Gabriel (Jeremy Irons).

The movie now develops its story through the device of letters which explain what happened to the mission settlement. The missionaries dream of a society in which Christian natives will live in harmony with the Spanish and Portuguese. But the colonial governors find this vision dangerous; they would rather enslave the Indians than convert them, and they issue orders for the mission to be destroyed. Irons and De Niro disagree on how to meet this threat: Irons believes in prayer and passive resistance, and De Niro believes in armed rebellion.

In the end, neither approach is effective, and the movie concludes in a confusing series of scenes in which badly choreographed battle sequences are intercut with Irons's final religious services. It is a measure of the film's disorganization that at the end, when it is crucial that we understand who the Indians are fighting, and how the battle is going, mere chaos takes over the screen, and the actors stagger out of clouds of smoke as if they're looking for directions.

The Mission was produced by David Puttnam and Roland Joffe, the same team that made the great film *The Killing Fields*. That film was fired by a pure, burning anger against a great injustice, and it had a dramatic center in the life and saga of Dith Pran, the Cambodian photographer who survived the occupation of his land and eventually lived to find freedom. Pran's story was a magnet that pulled us through the film. *The Mission* has no similar pull; indeed, it hardly seems to have a center, and feels like a massive, expensive film production that, once set in motion, kept going under its own momentum even though nobody involved had a clear idea of its final direction.

I suggested that no single shot in the movie is without interest. That is probably true. The locations are spectacular—especially a waterfall that supplies the great opening image of a crucified missionary floating to his doom. The actors are effective in their individual scenes. The mysterious atmosphere of the forest seeps into the story and lends it a certain mysticism. All that was needed to pull these elements together was a structure that would clearly define who the characters were, what they stood for, and why we should care about them. Unfortunately, that is all that is missing.

Mississippi Burning ★ ★ ★ ★
R, 127 m., 1988

Gene Hackman (Anderson), Willem Dafoe (Ward), Frances McDormand (Mrs. Pell), Brad Dourif (Deputy Pell), R. Lee Ermey (Mayor Tilman), Gailard Sartain (Sheriff Stuckey), Stephen Tobolowsky (Townley), Michael Rooker (Frank Bailey), Pruitt Taylor Vince (Lester Cowens), Badja Djola (Agent Monk), Kevin Dunn (Agent Bird). Directed by Alan Parker and produced by Frederick Zollo and Robert F. Colesberry. Screenplay by Chris Gerolmo.

Movies often take place in towns, but they rarely seem to live in them. Alan Parker's *Mississippi Burning* feels like a movie made from the inside out, a movie that knows the ways and people of its small Southern city so intimately that, having seen it, I know the place I'd go for a cup of coffee and the place I'd steer clear from. This acute sense of time and place—rural Mississippi, 1964—is the lifeblood of the film, which gets inside the passion of race relations in America, and was the best film of 1988.

The film is based on a true story, the disappearance of Chaney, Goodman, and Schwerner, three young civil rights workers who were part of a voter registration drive in Mississippi. When their murdered bodies were finally discovered, their corpses were irrefutable testimony against the officials who had complained that the whole case was a publicity stunt, dreamed up by Northern liberals and outside agitators. The case became one of the milestones, like the day Rosa Parks took her seat on the bus or the day Martin Luther King marched into Montgomery, on the long march toward racial justice in this country.

But *Mississippi Burning* is not a documentary, nor does it strain to present a story based on the facts. This movie is a gritty police drama, bloody, passionate, and sometimes surprisingly funny, about the efforts of two FBI men to lead an investigation into the disappearances. Few men could be more opposite than these two agents: Anderson (Gene Hackman), the good old boy who used to be a sheriff in a town a lot like this one, and Ward (Willem Dafoe), one of Bobby Kennedy's bright young men from the Justice Department. Anderson believes in keeping a low profile, hanging around the barber shop, sort of smelling out the likely perpetrators. Ward believes in a show of force, and calls in hundreds of federal agents and even the National Guard to search for the missing workers.

Anderson and Ward do not like each other very much. Both men feel they should be in charge of the operation. As they go their separate paths, we meet some of the people in the town: The mayor, a slick country-club type, who lectures against rabble-rousing outsiders. The sheriff, who thinks he can intimidate the FBI men. And Pell (Brad Dourif), a shifty-eyed deputy who has an alibi for the time the three men disappeared, and it's a good alibi—except why would he have an alibi so good, for precisely that time, unless he needed one?

The alibi depends on the word of Pell's wife (Frances McDormand), a woman who has taken a lot over the years from this self-hating racist, a man who needs a gun on his belt by day and a hood over his head by night just to gather the courage to stand and walk. Anderson, the Hackman character, singles her out immediately as the key to the case. He believes the sheriff's department delivered the three men over to the local klan, which murdered them. If he can get the wife to talk, the whole house of cards crashes down.

So he starts hanging around. Makes small talk. Shifts on his feet in her living room like a bashful boy. Lets his voice trail off, so that in the silence she can imagine that he was about to say what a pretty woman she still was. Anderson plays this woman like a piano. And she wants to be played. Because Gene Hackman is such a subtle actor, it takes us a while to realize that he has really fallen for her. He would like to rescue her from the scum she's married to, and wrap her up in his arms.

McDormand is wonderful in the role. She could have turned her role into a flashy showboat performance, but chose instead to show us a woman who had been raised and trained and beaten into accepting her man as her master, and who finally rejects that role simply because with her own eyes she can see that it's wrong to treat black people the way her husband does. The woman McDormand plays is quiet and shy and fearful, but in the moral decision she makes, she represents a generation that finally said, hey, what's going on here is simply not fair.

The relationship between the McDormand and Hackman characters is counterpoint to the main current of the film, which involves good police work, interrogations, searches and—mostly—hoping for tips.

There is reason to believe that the local black community has a good idea of who committed the murders, but the klan trashes and burns the home of one family with a son who might talk, and there is terror in the air in the black neighborhood.

Parker, the director, doesn't use melodrama to show how terrified the local blacks are of reprisals; he uses realism. We see what can happen to people who are not "good nigras." The Dafoe character approaches a black man in a segregated luncheonette and asks him questions. The black refuses to talk to him—and *still* gets beaten by the klan. Sometimes keeping your mouth shut can be sound common sense. Parker has dealt with intimidating bullies before in his work, most notably in *Midnight Express*, but what makes this film so particular is the way he understates the evil in it. There are no great villains and sadistic torturers in this film, only banal little racists with a vicious streak.

By the end of the film, the bodies have been found, the murderers have been identified, and the wheels of justice have started to grind. We knew the outcome of this case when we started watching. What we may have forgotten, or never known, is exactly what kinds of currents were in the air in 1964. The civil rights movement of the early 1960s was the finest hour of modern American history, because it was the painful hour in which we determined to improve ourselves, instead of others. We grew. The South grew, the whole nation grew more comfortable with the radical idea that all men were created equal and endowed with certain inalienable rights, among them life, liberty and the pursuit of happiness.

What *Mississippi Burning* evokes more clearly than anything else is how recently in our past those rights were routinely and *legally* denied to blacks, particularly in the South. In a time so recent that its cars are still on the road and its newspapers have not started to yellow, large parts of America were a police state in which the crime was to be black. Things are not great for blacks today, but at least official racism is no longer on the law books anywhere. And no other movie I've seen captures so forcefully the look, the feel, the very smell of racism. We can feel how sexy their hatred feels to the racists in this movie, how it replaces other entertainments, how it compensates for their sense of worthlessness. And we can feel something breaking free, the fresh air rushing in, when the back of that racism is broken.

Mister Johnson ★ ★ ★
PG-13, 101 m., 1991

Maynard Eziashi (Mister Johnson), Pierce Brosnan (Harry Rudbeck), Edward Woodward (Sargy Gollup), Beatie Edney (Celia Rudbeck). Directed by Bruce Beresford and produced by Michael Fitzgerald. Screenplay by William Boyd.

When the novelist Joyce Cary went out to Nigeria to join the British colonial civil service in 1913, there was no question in his mind, and in the minds of most British, that he was doing a good thing, representing the world's greatest democracy in an African backwater much in need of improvement. When Cary wrote *Mister Johnson*, the fourth of his African novels in 1939, some questions had begun to arise. The novel is about those questions.

Mister Johnson, directed by Bruce Beresford in his first film since *Driving Miss Daisy*, tells the story of an African civil servant, known to all as Mister Johnson, who works as a clerk in the office of the British district administrator. Mister Johnson, played by Maynard Eziashi in a performance of great humor, grace, and desperation, has adopted the values of Great Britain so enthusiastically that he even thinks of himself as British, and wears a white tropical suit and leather dress shoes even in the summer's fierce heat. He speaks of "our" standards and "our" institutions, and places his trust in his district officer while failing to understand that the purpose of British law in Nigeria is to protect the British and subdue Africans like himself.

He is a cheerful man, this Mister Johnson, hurrying through the district, flirting with the pretty girls, reprimanding laggards for not being up to his standards, and working efficiently for his boss, Harry Rudbeck (Pierce Brosnan). It is Brosnan's obsession to build a great road into the wilderness and connect his outpost with the capital. Perhaps he sees himself as a local version of an empire-builder of the earlier generation, Cecil Rhodes, who dreamed of an all-British route all the way from Cape Town to Cairo.

There is, alas, not enough money for the road, and it looks like work will have to be halted until Johnson suggests to Rudbeck that they juggle the books a little, robbing Peter to pay Paul, until the next year's budget comes through. Rudbeck agrees, but when the deception is discovered, of course,

it is Johnson who must be dismissed for the bookkeeping infraction.

Loss of his position and status is a serious blow for Mister Johnson, who has a good many debts to pay. But he soon finds another job, working as a clerk for Sargy Gollup (Edward Woodward), the hard-drinking British owner of the local general store. Gollup has a drunken love-hate relationship with Africans, who he sometimes beats "for their own good," and the desperate Mister Johnson agrees with him—partly because he has no other choice, but also because in his increasingly confused mind, he identifies with him.

There is obviously going to be a tragedy here somewhere, and it is equally obvious that it is Mister Johnson who is going to suffer, despite all of the glories of British justice which he so admires. There is a genuine sadness in the scenes where Johnson forgives Harry Rudbeck for the sentence he has to carry out, and even sympathizes with him and tries to cheer him up.

There is also, of course, a savage irony in the fact that Rudbeck knows Johnson got into trouble in the first place by taking the rap for him. One of the subtleties of the film is the way this is never quite spelled out—not even by Rudbeck to his wife, Celia (Beatie Edney). Rudbeck maintains silence about his own guilt even while outwardly continuing to be a humane and reasonable administrator, and the film's last scenes take on a terrible sadness because of this silence.

I have seen *Mister Johnson* two times, and both times I admired its sense of time and place, and the thoughtful performances of Eziashi, Brosnan, and Woodward. Beresford's screenwriter is the novelist William Boyd, whose own novels, especially *An Ice-Cream War*, are set in British East Africa a few decades later. What they are doing here is quiet and rather tricky. They're not banging the audience over the head with the injustice of what happens to Johnson, but trying to recreate a moment in colonial history when many people, both white and black, believed in the rhetoric of official idealism, even while it was rotting from within.

The result is a very subtle film, one where the ideas are sometimes in danger of being overwhelmed by the sheer exuberance of Eziashi's performance. After seeing the film, I found myself asking what it was really about—was there a message, or only a careful reconstruction of a moment in history? There is a message, I now believe, but so subdued that some viewers may leave the film think-

ing it has said the opposite of what Beresford and Boyd intended—that it mocks, rather than celebrates—the martyrdom of Mister Johnson. The movie, like the Cary novel, allows us to find its truth in our own way.

Mo' Better Blues ★ ★ ★
R, 129 m., 1990
(See related Film Clip, p. 712.)

Denzel Washington (Bleek Gilliam), Cynda Williams (Clarke Bentancourt), Joie Lee (Indigo Jones), Spike Lee (Giant), Wesley Snipes (Shadow Henderson), Giancarlo Esposito (Left Hand Lacey), Robin Harris (Butterbean Jones), Bill Nunn (Bottom Hammer), John Turturro (Moe Flatbush). Directed, produced, and written by Spike Lee.

Spike Lee's *Mo' Better Blues* is about a jazzman, but it's not really about jazz—it's about work, about being so wrapped up in your career that you don't have space for relationships, and you can't see where you're headed. It's a less passionate and angry film than Lee's previous work, *Do the Right Thing*, and less inspired, too. It's his fourth feature but suffers a little from the "second-novel syndrome," the pressure on an artist to follow up a great triumph. But it's a logical film to come at this point in Lee's career, since it's about the time and career pressures on a young artist.

The movie stars Denzel Washington as a trumpet player with the evocative name of Bleek. He leads a successful jazz group, but sometimes seems distracted and unhappy, maybe because he never really wanted to be a musician, maybe because he hasn't grown up enough to find himself. The movie gives us some insights into those possibilities in a prologue that shows Bleek as a young boy, growing up on a middle-class Brooklyn street, being forced by his mother to practice his trumpet while the neighborhood kids stand on the sidewalk and taunt him because he can't come out and play softball. "Let the boy be a boy," Bleek's father says, but the mother will have none of it. There won't be any softball until he finishes his scales.

We flash forward to Bleek as a successful jazzman. As played by Washington, he is handsome, assured, and a dedicated ladies' man. There are two women in his life: Clarke Bentancourt (Cynda Williams), as sleek as her name, a seductive songstress; and Indigo Downes (Joie Lee), sometimes as blue as her name, less glamorous but steadier and more emotionally healthy. Bleek desires both of them and has enough time for neither, and eventually gets himself into one of those situations where they both show up at the nightclub on the same evening wearing the same red dresses—identical gifts from Bleek.

The band is on the brink of breaking out big, but needs better leadership than it gets from Bleek and his childhood friend and manager, Giant (Spike Lee). Giant is a compulsive gambler who is hopelessly incompetent to guide anyone's career, but through some sort of perverse logic, Bleek is loyal to him instead of to the friends who would really help him. That leads into physical and professional tragedy.

The middle sections of the movie take place in a world of jazz clubs and dressing rooms, stage door entrances, bars, coffee shops, and apartments—urban New York at night. There is a lot of music in the film, provided both by Bill Lee's score and by the Bleek group, which has been dubbed by the Branford Marsalis Quartet. The music is sensuous big-city jazz from around midnight, swirling through cigarette smoke and perfume and the musty smell of a saloon, and it's good to listen to. On stage, Washington looks at home with his horn, and Wesley Snipes is also strong as Shadow, a saxophone player who likes to hog the solos.

Backstage in the dressing room, in scenes that feel improvised, the musicians argue about the band, its leadership, its direction, and even the romantic preferences of its members. One sideman has a white girlfriend, and the others argue the pros and cons of that until he tells them it's none of their business. In this film, as in Lee's three earlier films, questions involving race are a good deal more sophisticated and complicated than the simplistic formulas from earlier decades.

At the center of everything stands Bleek, who in some ways resembles the heroine of Lee's first film, She's Gotta Have It. That was about a woman who kept three guys on the line because she didn't want any one of them to feel he possessed her. This time, it's Bleek who tries to juggle the two women—but he's representing irresponsibility, not independence. And there's a suggestion of a theme from School Daze, in which Lee examined subtle value systems within the black community, based on the relative lightness of skin tone: Clarke has "whiter" features than Indigo, and that may go into Bleek's emotional quandary, too. Clarke represents a superficial ideal of beauty as portrayed in the media, even though the darker Indigo is clearly the woman he should choose.

Lee has said he doesn't do "push-button" movies, and indeed Mo' Better Blues completely avoids the central cliché in almost all musical biopics. After Bleek gets into real trouble and can't play for a year, he walks into a nightclub to make his comeback, and we settle back for the obligatory scene in which he makes his triumphant return. But that's not the way things work out.

Lee avoids the usual formulas in that scene only to surprise us again, with an epilogue which mirrors the prologue. This time, though, some years have passed, and it's Bleek's own son who is practicing the trumpet. The symmetry of this ending feels awkward, especially since there seems to be an act missing—how did Bleek get from where he was, to where he is in the final scene?

Mo' Better Blues is not a supremely confident film like Do the Right Thing, which never took a wrong step. There are scenes that seem incompletely thought-out, improvised dialogue that sounds more like improvisation than dialogue, and those strange narrative bookends at the top and bottom of the movie. But the film has a beauty, grace, and energy all the same. Washington has been seen mostly in heavy dramatic roles (Glory, Cry Freedom), and here, as in The Mighty Quinn, shows that he is gifted at comedy and romance. Cynda Williams, in her first film, is a luminous discovery; she has a presence that seems to occupy the screen by divine right. Joie Lee, in her most important role, isn't supposed to be as flashy, but succeeds in the challenge of drawing our sympathy away from the sexpot and toward the more substantial woman. And I liked Spike Lee's acting, too: He has a kind of off-center, driving energy that makes you into an accomplice even when he's marching straight for trouble. Mo' Better Blues is not a great film, but it's an interesting one, which is almost as rare.

The Moderns ★ ★ ★
NO MPAA RATING, 126 m., 1988

Keith Carradine (Nick Hart), Linda Fiorentino (Rachel Stone), John Lone (Bertnam Stone), Wallace Shawn (Oiseau), Genevieve Bujold (Libby Valentin), Geraldine Chaplin (Nathalie de Ville), Kevin J. O'Connor (Hemingway), Elsa Raven (Gertrude Stein), Ali Giron (Alice B. Toklas). Directed by Alan Rudolph and produced by Carolyn Pfeiffer from a screenplay by Rudolph and John Bradshaw.

When I was in college we used to do "source studies" for the plays of Shakespeare, reading the books that were allegedly in his library and trying to figure out where he got his ideas. The Moderns is sort of a source study for the Paris of Ernest Hemingway in the 1920s; it's a movie about the raw material he shaped into The Sun Also Rises and A Movable Feast, and it also includes raw material for books by Gertrude Stein, Malcolm Cowley, and Clifford Irving. My source studies were always ungainly, disorganized and filled with wild surmises ("Shakespeare was undoubtedly referring to . . .") and The Moderns is equally puerile, but more fun.

It takes place at that enchanted moment in Paris when the Lost Generation created itself and then proceeded to create, promote, fabricate, and publicize modern literature, art, music, and attitudes. It tells the stories of an American painter in exile, the woman he loved and lost, and the millionaire he lost her to. Important roles are also played by his unscrupulous art dealer, by a busy-body newspaperman on the English-language daily, and by Ernest Hemingway, Gertrude Stein, Alice B. Toklas, and others who are called by their real names even if the resemblance stops there.

The movie was directed and co-written by Alan Rudolph, who treats his Paris as something of a dream city; it's the same approach, but not the same look, as he used for the cities in Choose Me and Trouble in Mind— people drift in and out of each other's lives and conversations and eventually a plot develops, and it contains passion, greed, fear, envy, and lust, but hardly anybody ever raises a voice.

Keith Carradine stars as a starving artist who is stunned one day to see the woman he was married to (Linda Fiorentino) on the arm of a slick, sinister millionaire (John Lone). He still loves her. Maybe she still loves him. One thing's for sure. When he turns up unexpectedly in her bathroom, if she didn't still feel something for him, she wouldn't have invited him into the tub. Meanwhile, Carradine needs money badly, and his art dealer (Genevieve Bujold) offers him a secret commission to forge three famous paintings. When he discovers that the paintings are connected to John Lone, he agrees to do it—and from that decision springs most of the plot, such as it is.

Rudolph's Paris is a place where people wander into scenes, say a line or two, and leave. Ernest Hemingway (Kevin J. O'Connor) appears in the backgrounds of several scenes, sometimes reciting earlier versions of his famous lines, to see how they sound. He climbs into the ring for a boxing match with another expatriate, and we see a cross between his actual fight with F. Scott Fitzgerald and the fictional fisticuffs in *The Sun Also Rises*. There are other scenes where Gertrude Stein and Alice B. Toklas receive the expatriate community in their legendary apartment where the walls were covered by some of the most famous and priceless of all twentieth-century paintings, and other moments where minor characters say things that are immediately borrowed by their betters and turned into legend. Drifting around within earshot of everything is the gossip columnist for the *Paris Trib* (Wallace Shawn), who claims to have invented modernism while losing his own soul.

The Moderns is not a great movie and is fairly sloppy and unsatisfying, but I never found a moment of it uninteresting, maybe because I have always been so intrigued by the Paris of the Lost Generation that I found the cross-references fun to spot and sometimes amusing. If there is a flaw in the movie, it's that Rudolph didn't find a way to use even more of the famous one-liners of the Lost Generation, instead of getting so bogged down in his fake-art plot. We learn in *The Autobiography of Alice B. Toklas* that when Ezra Pound came to Paris, "Gertrude Stein liked him but did not find him amusing. She said he was a village explainer, excellent if you were a village, but if you were not, not." She could have been reviewing this movie.

Mommie Dearest ★
PG, 129 m., 1981

Faye Dunaway (Joan Crawford), Diana Scarwid (Christina, adult), Steve Forrest (Greg Savitt), Howard Da Silva (L.B. Mayer), Mara Hobel (Christina, child), Autanya Alda (Carol Ann). Directed by Frank Perry and produced by Frank Yablans. Screenplay by Yablans, Perry, Tracy Hotchner, and Robert Getchell.

I can't imagine who would want to subject themselves to this movie. *Mommie Dearest* is a painful experience that drones on endlessly, as Joan Crawford's relationship with her daughter, Christina, disintegrates from cruelty through jealousy into pathos. It is unremittingly depressing, not to any purpose of drama or entertainment, but just to depress. It left me feeling creepy. The movie was

inspired, of course, by a best-selling memoir in which adopted daughter Christina Crawford portrayed her movie-star mother as a grasping, sadistic, alcoholic wretch whose own insecurities and monstrous ego made life miserable for everyone around her. I have no idea if the book's portrait is an accurate one, but the movie is faithful to it in one key sense: It made life miserable for me.

Mommie Dearest repeats the same basic dramatic situation again and again. Baby Christina tries to do the right thing, tries to be a good girl, tries to please Mommie, but Mommie is a manic-depressive who alternates between brief triumphs and long savage tirades, infecting her daughter with resentment and guilt. In scene after scene, we are invited to watch as Joan Crawford screams at Christina, chops her hair with scissors, beats her with a wire coat hanger and, on an especially bad day, tackles her across an end table, hurls her to the carpet, bangs her head against the floor, and tries to choke her to death. Who wants to watch this?

This material is presented essentially as sensationalism. The movie makes no attempt to draw psychological insights from the life of its Joan Crawford—not even through the shorthand Freudianism much beloved by Hollywood. Mommie is a monster, that's all, and there's some mention of her unhappy childhood. Christina is a brave, smiling, pretty, long-suffering dope who might inspire more sympathy if she were not directed (in both her childhood and adult versions) to be distant and veiled.

The movie doesn't even make narrative sense. Success follows crisis without any pattern. At one moment, Joan is in triumph after winning the Oscar for *Mildred Pierce*. In the very next scene she goes so berserk we want to scrape her off the screen with a spatula. The scenes don't build, they just happen. Another example: After an especially ugly fight, Joan sends Christina to a convent school. There's a scene where the mother superior welcomes her and promises to reform her. One scene later, Christina checks out of the school, and the nun wishes her godspeed. No mention of what happened in the school, how it affected Christina, or whether the nun changed her opinion of the girl.

The movie also offers few insights into Crawford's relationships with others. There's a loyal housekeeper, but never a scene where Crawford speaks personally with her. There is

a lover and a third husband, both enigmas. Crawford's acting career is treated mostly in ellipses. The sets look absolutely great, Faye Dunaway's impersonation of Crawford is stunningly suggestive and convincing, and little Mara Hobel, as Baby Christina, handles several difficult moments very well. But to what end? *Mommie Dearest* is a movie that knows exactly how it wants to look, but has no idea what it wants to make us feel.

Mona Lisa ★ ★ ★ ★
R, 104 m., 1986

Bob Hoskins (George), Cathy Tyson (Simone), Michael Caine (Mortwell), Clarke Peters (Anderson), Kate Hardie (Cathy), Robbie Coltrane (Thomas). Directed by Neil Jordan and produced by Stephen Wooley and Patrick Cassavetti. Screenplay by Jordan and David Leland.

You can tell how much they will eventually like each other by how much they hate each other at first. His name is George. He's a short, fierce, bullet-headed foot-soldier in the London underworld, and he's just gotten out of prison. Her name is Simone. She's a tall, beautiful black woman who works as a high-priced call girl. George goes to Mortwell, who runs the mob, looking for a job. He is assigned to drive Simone around to expensive hotels and private homes and to wait for her while she conducts her business. He is also supposed to protect her if anything goes wrong.

At first he seems hopelessly unsuited to his job. He wears the wrong clothes, and stands out like a sore thumb in the lobbies of hotels like the Ritz. She can't believe she's been saddled with this misfit. He thinks she is stuck-up and cold, and puts on too many airs for a whore. They are at each other's throats day and night, fighting about everything, until eventually they realize they enjoy their arguments; they are entertained by one another.

That's the setup for *Mona Lisa*, a British film set in the tattered precincts of Soho, where vice lords run sordid clubs where bewildered provincial girls sell themselves to earn money for drugs. Simone now operates at a higher level in the sex business, but she never forgets where she started, and sometimes she orders George to cruise slowly in the big Rolls Royce, as she searches for a young girl who used to be her friend when they were on the streets together, and who is still the slave, she fears, of a sadistic pimp. These nighttime journeys are a contrast to her usual routine, which involves visiting wealthy bankers, decadent diplomats, and rich Middle Eastern investors who live on the most expensive streets of Hampstead. George drives her, argues with her, speculates about her, and falls in love with her. And when she asks him to help find the missing girl, he risks his life for her.

Mona Lisa stars Bob Hoskins as George. You may remember him as the ferocious little mob boss in *The Long Good Friday,* where he had it all fixed up to go respectable and then someone started blowing up his pubs. Hoskins is one of the very best new British actors, and this is a great performance—it won him the best actor award at the 1986 Cannes Film Festival. Simone is played by Cathy Tyson, and she is elegant and cool and yet able to project the pain that is always inside. The relationship of their characters in the film is interesting, because both people, for personal reasons, have developed a style that doesn't reveal very much. They have walls, and friendship means being able to see over someone else's wall while still keeping your own intact.

The third major character in the movie, and the third major performance, is by Michael Caine, as Mortwell, the vice boss. In the more than twenty years since I first saw Caine in a movie, I don't believe I've seen him in a bad performance more than once or twice. And I've rarely seen him doing the same thing, which is strange, since in one way or another he usually seems to look and talk like Michael Caine—and yet with subtle differences that are just right for the role. In *Mona Lisa,* he plays one of his most evil villains, a slimebag who trades in the lives and happiness of naive young girls, and he plays the character without apology and without exaggeration, as a businessman. That's why Mortwell is so creepy.

The movie plot reveals itself only gradually. At first *Mona Lisa* seems to be a character study, the story of George and Simone and how they operate within the call-girl industry. After we find out how important the missing girl is to Simone, however, the movie becomes a thriller, as George descends into gutters to try to find her and bring her back to Simone. The movie's ending is a little too neat for my taste. But in a movie like this, everything depends on atmosphere and character, and *Mona Lisa* knows exactly what it is doing.

Monsieur Hire ★ ★ ★ ★
PG-13, 88 m., 1990

Michel Blanc (Monsieur Hire), Sandrine Bonnaire (Alice), Luc Thuillier (Emile), Andre Wilms (Police Inspector). Directed by Patrice Leconte and produced by Philippe Carcassonne and Rene Cleitman. Screenplay by Leconte and Patrick DeWolf.

Monsieur Hire's life is organized with the extreme precision of a man who fears that any deviation from routine could destroy him. He lives alone in a neatly ordered room where everything has its place. He dresses carefully and conservatively and goes out every day to work by himself in a small office in the town, where he operates a mail-order business. He comes home to his dinner of a hard-boiled egg. He listens to the same piece of music over and over again. He speaks to people only to observe the formalities: "Good morning." "Nice day."

His sexual life is equally precise. Hour after hour, he stands in his darkened room, looking across the small courtyard of his building into the window of a young woman who lives directly opposite and one floor below. She never pulls her shades. He watches her dress, undress, read, eat, listen to the radio, make love. Hour after hour.

Another woman is found dead in the neighborhood—her body cast aside in an overgrown vacant lot. Who committed the crime? There are no suspects, but in this neighborhood a man like Monsieur Hire is always a suspect. He has no friends, no associations, no "life." The neighbors have marked him out as peculiar. To look at him you would think it was absurd that he could kill anyone. But suspicion begins to grow.

The story of Monsieur Hire was first told in a novel by Georges Simenon, that endlessly observant Belgian who wrote more than three hundred books, many of them works of genius. This is one of his best stories, a study of character and loneliness. Reading the book some years ago, I formed a picture of Hire in my mind, and seeing this movie I was startled to see how closely my notions matched the appearance of Michel Blanc, who plays the title role.

He is a solemn man with a fringe of black hair around a face that is more than merely pale; he seems to have been sprouted in a basement. He is reclusive, solemn, absorbed with his own thoughts. As he watches the woman across the courtyard, we can only imagine what he is thinking. Somehow the conventional sexual fantasies do not seem to fit him; perhaps he is thinking what a slattern she is, or what an angel.

The woman (Sandrine Bonnaire) has a boyfriend. He is cold, distant, and cruel, and he treats her badly. She does what he says. He does not make her happy, but certain women are attracted to cruel men. Did the boyfriend commit the murder? The movie is not really concerned with the solution to the crime—much less concerned than the Simenon novel. Indeed, when the police inspector turns up in the movie, we're not sure at first who he is. Maybe he's a family friend?

Monsieur Hire is so delicate that you almost hold your breath during the last half-hour. Events of grave subtlety are taking place. The heart of the movie involves two difficult questions: What exactly does the young woman think about Monsieur Hire, and what does he think that she thinks? Of course, the woman knows that Hire is always at his window, watching. She sees him one day, illuminated by lightning. Still she does nothing to conceal herself, and so from that moment on there is a kind of communication between them. Each knows the other is aware.

Monsieur Hire, so middle-aged and nondescript, is certainly not her "type." But is his adoration appealing to her? Is he the one man in the world who regards her simply as she is and finds her wonderful? Does he want nothing more from her than to worship? Does this make her grateful to him, in a sense, considering the mistreatment she gets from the boyfriend? Will she lie to save Hire? Will she lie to save the boyfriend?

The concluding passages of the movie have the weight of sad, inevitable tragedy to them. But nothing prepares us for the movie's extraordinary final shot, in which a swift action contains a momentary pause, a look that seems torn out of the very fabric of life itself. What does the look say? What is this woman trying to communicate? The director, Patrice Leconte, knows that to explain the look is to destroy the movie. *Monsieur Hire* is a film about conversations that are never held, desires that are never expressed, fantasies that are never realized, and murder.

Monty Python's Meaning of Life
★ ★ ¹/₂
R, 103 m., 1983

Written and starring: Graham Chapman, John Cleese, Terry Gilliam, Eric Idle, Terry Jones, and Michael Palin. Directed by Terry Jones and produced by John Goldstone.

Halfway through *Monty Python's Meaning of Life*, the thought struck me that One-Upmanship was a British discovery. You remember, of course, the book and movie *(School for Scoundrels)* inspired by Stephen Potter's theory of One-Upmanship, in which the goal of the practitioner was to One-Up his daily associates and, if possible, the world. A modern example:

Victim: I've just been reading Gabriel Garcia Marquez's *Chronicle of a Death Foretold* in *Vanity Fair* magazine.
One-Upman: Really? I'm afraid I missed it.
Victim: But Garcia Marquez is brilliant.
One-Upman: No doubt, dear fellow, but my subscription ran out in 1939.

I use this illustration as an approach to *Monty Python's Meaning of Life*, which is a movie that seems consumed with a desire to push us too far. This movie is so far beyond good taste, and so cheerfully beyond, that we almost feel we're being One-Upped if we allow ourselves to be offended. Take, for example, the scene featuring projectile vomiting. We don't get just a little vomit in the scene, as we saw in *The Exorcist*. No sir, we get gallons of vomit, streams of it, all a vile yellow color, sprayed all over everybody and everything in a formal dining room. The first reaction of the non-Upman is *"Yech!"* But I think the Python gang is working at another level. And, given the weakness of movie critics for discussing what "level" a movie "works" on, I find myself almost compelled to ask myself, "At what 'level' *does* the projectile vomiting 'work'?" And I think the Python One-Up reply would be, dear fellow, that it rises above vulgarity and stakes out territory in the surrealistic. Anyone who takes the vomiting literally has missed the joke; the scene isn't about vomiting, but about the lengths to which Python will go for a laugh.

There are other scenes in equally poor taste in this movie, which has a little something to offend everybody. And I mean *really* offend them: This isn't a Mel Brooks movie, with friendly little ethnic in-jokes. It's a barbed, uncompromising attack on generally observed community standards. Does the attack work? Only occasionally. The opening sequence of the film is one of its best, showing the overworked old clerks in an insurance company staging a mutiny. After they've gained control of their shabby old stone building, the movie does a brilliant turn into surrealism, the building becomes a ship, and the clerks weigh anchor and set sail against the fleets of modern high-rises, firing their filing cabinets like cannons. It's a wonderful sequence.

I also liked a scene set on a military parade ground, and a joke involving a tankful of fish, and a cheerfully unfair rugby match between two teams, one made up of twelve small schoolboys, the other with eighteen schoolmasters, all huge. Balanced against these bright moments is the goriest scene in Python history, showing a liver being removed from a transplant "volunteer" by brute force. There are also a lot of religious jokes, some straightforward sexism, and the above-mentioned vomiting sequence.

By admitting to being offended by some of the stuff in this movie, I've been One-Upped. By liking the funny stuff, I've been One-Upped again. ("But you liked the jokes that were in good taste? Jolly good!") But I'm a good loser, and I don't mind being One-Upped. In fact, let's say this is a tennis match, and the Pythons are the winners. Here, I'll hold down the net while they jump over to shake hands with me. Whoops!

Moon Over Parador ★ ★
PG-13, 127 m., 1988

Richard Dreyfuss (Jack Noah), Raul Julia (Roberto Strausmann), Sonia Braga (Madonna), Jonathan Winters (Ralph), Fernando Rey (Alejandro), Sammy Davis, Jr., (Himself), Michael Greene (Clint), Polly Holliday (Midge), Milton Goncalves (Carlo), Charo (Madame Loop). Produced and directed by Paul Mazursky. Screenplay by Leon Capetanos and Mazursky.

If an actor can become a national leader in America, then why not in Parador, a fictional country that seems to lie somewhere between Paraguay, Equador, and Carmen Miranda's memoirs? In Paul Mazursky's *Moon Over Parador*, Richard Dreyfuss explores that possibility, as a second-rate New York actor who is shooting a movie on location in Parador when the military dictator is finally killed by his imprudent lifestyle.

As it happens, Dreyfuss had been entertaining the dictator only days earlier with his own uncanny imitation of the leader's voice and mannerisms. Now the military attache who is the power behind the throne (Raul Julia) offers Dreyfuss the full-time job of impersonating the dead leader. He makes it clear that this is an offer Dreyfuss cannot refuse.

This is the promising premise of a disappointing comedy which unfortunately doesn't have nearly enough fun with it. Maybe the problem is that Mazursky spends too much time trying to get laughs out of Parador, and not enough time making fun of actors. Given the rich vein of satire which Mazursky and Dreyfuss explored together in their brilliant *Down and Out in Beverly Hills* (1986), I expected a sharper edge to this collaboration.

The nation of Parador seems recycled directly out of every comic cliché Hollywood has ever created about Latin America. The country is led by bemedaled buffoons, ruled by nepotism, tamed by a corrupt army, inhabited by seething mobs of chanting peasants, entertained by endless national holidays, and given solace by hot-blooded women who take their men neat. The woman in this story is played by Sonia Braga, as the mistress of the departed dictator and an Eva Peron who is somewhat beloved by many of the seething masses. She quickly realizes that her lover has been replaced, of course, but rather likes this vulnerable *New Yorker* who is trying to grow into his new job.

There is a current of warmth and sweetness at the heart of this film, and it is probably a bad idea. The Dreyfuss character is explored in terms of his personal development: Can he gain the self-confidence to take on this greatest challenge in his career, and also to accept the love of a beautiful woman? Well, of course he can, but not without a fair amount of bittersweet regret over the fact that such an idyllic existence cannot survive forever. The film is told in flashback, after Dreyfuss has returned to New York and started waiting in line at auditions again, and the nostalgic tone of his memories is exactly what's wrong with the film. His adventure shouldn't be a wonderful memory, but an up-for-grabs cliff-hanger.

I was also never quite convinced by his performance. It's a tricky matter, an actor playing an actor. Maybe there's an element of self-doubt in all actors that forces them to overplay that particular kind of role, more than any other. Actors don't let themselves off easily. Playing actors, they tend to lay it on thick, to show themselves as even more insecure and filled with self-loathing than probably is the case. If the Dreyfuss character in *Moon Over Parador* had been conceived on a more realistic basis, perhaps Mazursky and Dreyfuss could have had more fun exploring the true insecurities of the profession, instead of the stereotyped ones.

Sonia Braga is more than the equal of her role as the hot-blooded mistress, which has been played many times before, as she shows that she knows. Raul Julia has some nice moments as the military attache, convincing Dreyfuss he's equal to the impersonation by reading him the one thing no actor can resist hearing—his own good reviews. Jonathan Winters appears too briefly as the local CIA man, disguised as Jonathan Winters, and creates a character that could probably spin off into a sitcom. And Dreyfuss is good, too, but too human, and lacking in the wicked edge that might have put the movie over the top.

Moonlighting ★ ★ ★ ★
PG, 97 m., 1982

Jeremy Irons (Nowak), Eugene Lipinski (Banaszak), Jiri Stanislav (Wolski), Eugeniusz Haczkiewicz (Kudaj). Directed by Jerzy Skolimowski and produced by Mark Shivas and Skolimowski. Screenplay by Skolimowski.

Moonlighting is a wickedly pointed movie that takes a simple little story, tells it with humor and truth, and turns it into a knife in the side of the Polish government. In its own way, this response to the crushing of Solidarity is as powerful as Andrzej Wajda's *Man of Iron*. It also is more fun. The movie takes place in London, during the weeks just before and after the banning of the Solidarity movement in Poland. It begins, actually, in Warsaw, with a mystifying scene in which a group of plotters are scheming to smuggle some hardware past British customs. They're plotters, all right; their plot is to move into a small house in London and remodel it, knocking out walls, painting ceilings, making it into a showplace for the Polish government official who has purchased it. The official's plan is simplicity itself: By

bringing Polish workers to London on tourist visas, he can get the remodeling done for a fraction of what British workman would cost him. At the same time, the workers can earn good wages that they can take back to Poland and buy bicycles with. The only thing nobody counts on is the upheaval after Solidarity is crushed and travel to and from Poland is strictly regulated.

Jeremy Irons, of *The French Lieutenant's Woman*, plays the lead in the film. He's the only Polish workman who can speak English. Acting as foreman, he guides his team of men through the pitfalls of London and safely into the house they're going to remodel. He advises them to keep a low profile, while he ventures out to buy the groceries and (not incidentally) to read the newspapers. When he finds out about the crisis in Poland, he keeps it a secret from his comrades. The daily life of the renovation project falls into a pattern, which the film's director, Jerzy Skolimowski, intercuts with the adventures of his hero. Jeremy Irons begins to steal things: newspapers, bicycles, frozen turkeys. He concocts an elaborate scheme to defraud the local supermarket, and some of the movie's best scenes involve the subtle timing of his shoplifting scam, which involves the misrepresentation of cash-register receipts. He needs to steal food because he's running out of money, and he knows his group can't easily go home again. There's also a quietly hilarious, and slightly sad, episode involving a salesgirl in a blue-jeans store. Irons, pretending to be more naive than he is, tries to pick the girl up. She's having none of it.

Moonlighting invites all kinds of interpretations. You can take this simple story and set it against the events of the last two years, and see it as a kind of parable. Your interpretation is as good as mine. Is the house itself Poland, and the workmen Solidarity—rebuilding it from within, before an authoritarian outside force intervenes? Or is this movie about the heresy of substituting Western values (and jeans and turkeys) for a home-grown orientation? Or is it about the manipulation of the working classes by the intelligentsia? Or is it simply a frontal attack on the Communist Party bosses who live high off the hog while the workers are supposed to follow the rules?

Like all good parables, *Moonlighting* contains not one but many possibilities. What needs to be insisted upon, however, is how much *fun* this movie is. Skolimowski, a Pole

who has lived and worked in England for several years, began writing this film on the day that Solidarity was crushed, and he filmed it, on a small budget and with a small crew, in less than two months: He had it ready for the 1982 Cannes Film Festival where it was a major success. It's successful, I think, because it tells an interesting narrative in a straightforward way. Skolimowski is a natural storyteller. You can interpret and discuss *Moonlighting* all night. During the movie, you'll be more interested in whether Irons gets away with that frozen turkey.

Moonstruck ★ ★ ★ ★
PG, 100 m., 1987

Cher (Loretta Castorini), Nicolas Cage (Ronny Cammareri), Vincent Gardenia (Cosmo Castorini), Olympia Dukakis (Rose Castorini), Danny Aiello (Johnny Cammareri), Julie Bovasso (Rita Cappomaggi), John Mahoney (Perry), Louis Guss (Raymond Cappomaggi), Feodor Chaliapin (Old Man). Directed by Norman Jewison and produced by Patrick Palmer and Jewison. Screenplay by John Patrick Shanley.

"When the moon hits your eye, like a big-a pizza pie—that's amore!"—Dean Martin

The most enchanting quality about *Moonstruck* is the hardest to describe, and that is the movie's tone. Reviews of the movie tend to make it sound like a madcap ethnic comedy, and that it is. But there is something more here, a certain bittersweet yearning that comes across as ineffably romantic, and a certain magical quality that is reflected in the film's title.

The movie stars Cher, as an Italian-American widow in her late thirties, but she is not the only moonstruck one in the film. There is the moonlit night, for example, that her wise, cynical mother (Olympia Dukakis) goes out for dinner by herself, and meets a middle-aged university professor (John Mahoney) who specializes in seducing his young students, but who finds in this mature woman a certain undeniable sexuality. There is the furtive and yet somehow sweet affair that Cher's father (Vincent Gardenia) has been carrying on for years with the ripe, disillusioned Anita Gillette.

And at the heart of the story, there is Cher's astonishing discovery that she is still capable of love. As the movie opens, she becomes engaged to Mr. Johnny Cammareri (Danny Aiello), not so much out of love as out of weariness. But after he flies to Sicily to be at the bedside of his dying mother, she goes to talk to Mr. Johnny's estranged younger brother (Nicolas Cage), and is thunderstruck when they are drawn almost instantly into a passionate embrace.

Moonstruck was directed by Norman Jewison and written by John Patrick Shanley, and one of their accomplishments is to allow the film to be about all of these people (and several more, besides). This is an ensemble comedy, and a lot of the laughs grow out of the sense of family that Jewison and Shanley create; there are, for example, small hilarious moments involving the exasperation that Dukakis feels for her ancient father-in-law (Feodor Chaliapin), who lives upstairs with his dogs. (In the course of a family dinner, she volunteers: "Feed one more bite of my food to your dogs, old man, and I'll kick you 'til you're dead!").

As Cher's absent fiancé lingers at his mother's bedside, Cher and Cage grow even more desperately passionate, and Cher learns the secret of the hatred between the two brothers: One day Aiello made Cage look the wrong way at the wrong time, and he lost his hand in a bread-slicer. Now he wears an artificial hand, and carries an implacable grudge in his heart.

But grudges and vendettas and old wounds and hatreds are everywhere in this film. The mother knows, for example, that her husband is having an affair with another woman. She asks from the bottom of her heart why this should be so, and a friend replies, "Because he is afraid of dying." She sees at once that this is so. But does that cause her to sympathize with her husband? Hardly. One night he comes home. She asks where he has been. He replies, "Nowhere." She tells him she wants him to know one thing: "No matter where you go, or what you do—you're gonna die."

Some of these moments are so charged with tension they remind us of the great opening scenes of *Saturday Night Fever* (and the mother from that movie, Julie Bovasso, is on hand here as an aunt). But all of the passion is drained of its potential for hurt, somehow, by the influence of the moon, which has enchanted these people and protects them from the consequences of their frailties. Jewison captures some of the same qualities of Ingmar Bergman's *Smiles of a Summer Night*, in which nature itself conspires with lovers to bring about their happiness.

The movie is filled with fine perfor-

mances—by Cher, 1987's Best Actress Oscar winner, never funnier or more assured; by Olympia Dukakis (who was named Best Supporting Actress) and Vincent Gardenia, as her parents, whose love runs as deep as their exasperation; and by Nicolas Cage as the hapless, angry brother, who is so filled with hurts he has lost track of what caused them. In its warmth and in its enchantment, as well as in its laughs, this is a fine comedy.

The Morning After ★ ★ ★
R, 103 m., 1986

Jane Fonda (Alex), Jeff Bridges (Turner), Raul Julia (Manero), Diane Salinger (Isabel), Richard Foronjy (Sergeant Greenbaum), Geoffrey Scott (Bobby), Bruce Vilanch (Bartender). Directed by Sidney Lumet and produced by Bruce Gilbert. Screenplay by James Hicks.

If an ordinary person woke up in the morning feeling the way a drunk feels with a hangover, they'd call an ambulance and check themselves into the emergency room. I'm not talking about your average garden-variety office-party hangover. I'm thinking of one of those mornings when you pick up the phone and somebody says hello and you're stuck for an answer.

That's how Jane Fonda feels in the first scene of *The Morning After*. She crawls out of bed and looks in the mirror and sloshes some gin into a glass and wonders about the guy she woke up with. She wonders things like, who is he? She has apparently had a lot of mornings like this. She doesn't realize how bad things really are until she notices the guy has a knife stuck in his chest.

Did she kill him? She knows no cop is going to believe her story. She wanders back out into the blinding Los Angeles light, and in a shot from high overhead, she looks like a laboratory animal, trapped in some kind of a test.

This feels like the beginning of an extraordinary thriller. Unfortunately, *The Morning After* never lives up to its early promise—not as a thriller, anyway. The plot has some yawning gaps in it, and thriller plots should be watertight. But *The Morning After* is worth seeing anyway, because of the characters that it develops, and the performances of Fonda and Jeff Bridges in the two leads.

She plays an alcoholic actress who is long past her prime. He plays an ex-cop who happens to be repairing his car at the airport

parking lot when she tumbles into his backseat and pleads with him to get her away from there, fast. The mere presence of Jeff Bridges in this movie is sort of a tease; we remember him from *Jagged Edge*, when he was one of the prime suspects, and we wonder if it's a coincidence that he happens along this time.

Bridges lives in a Quonset hut, where he fixes things like toasters. This is all Fonda needs. She moves in the fast lane—her friends are bartenders and drag queens, and her estranged husband (Raul Julia) is the classiest hairdresser in Beverly Hills. What does she need with a small-appliance repairman? But Bridges is sure and steady, and she needs a friend. Of course it goes without saying that they fall in love.

The plot of *The Morning After* is not nearly as good as the everyday lives of these characters; indeed, I can imagine a movie which would leave out the murder and simply follow the natural human development of the relationship between Fonda and Bridges. The thriller stuff isn't necessary, but as long as they put it in, couldn't they have worked just a little harder and made it plausible? Why, for example, didn't the cops find the bloody sheets under Fonda's sink?

The whole murder plot gets such sloppy handling that maybe I shouldn't have been surprised by the big scene in which the identity of the murderer is revealed. I've seen a lot of revelations in a lot of murder movies, but rarely one as unsubtle as this one, where the plot secrets are simply blurted out in an unlikely speech. (Maybe I should be more grateful; I understand that this very scene—implausible and awkward as it is—was reshot because the original version was worse.)

It would be a mistake, however, to dismiss this movie just because the plot is so shaky. I think it's worth considering because of the performances. Fonda and Bridges are wonderful in the film, and their relationship, based on secrets and resentments and private agendas, gets really interesting. They feel good together, and they have some dialogue that seems more alive than most romantic talk in the movies.

I liked what they did with the characters, and I also liked what Sidney Lumet has done with the look of the movie. He creates a Los Angeles made out of great flat planes of cold pastels, and threatening sunlit open spaces. He pins the hungover Fonda on this canvas like a butterfly on the wall, and the visuals make the whole first hour of the movie much more threatening than it deserves to be. Too bad they couldn't have done something about the screenplay.

Mortal Thoughts ★ ★ ★
R, 104 m., 1991

Demi Moore (Cynthia Kellogg), Glenne Headly (Joyce Urbanski), Bruce Willis (James Urbanski), John Pankow (Arthur Kellogg), Harvey Keitel (Detective John Woods), Billie Neal (Linda Nealon), Frank Vincent (Dominic Marino), Karen Shallo (Gloria Urbanski). Directed by Alan Rudolph and produced by John Fiedler and Mark Tarlov. Screenplay by William Reilly and Claude Kerven.

There is a part of me that would sit at home all day reading true crime books and doing nothing else. I'm particularly attracted to stories set in the present, among ordinary people who would not think of themselves as criminals, but who one day commit a violent crime and think they can get away with it. The papers are filled with these stories, about jealous spouses and secret lovers, ancient grudges and fatal miscalculations, teen-age boyfriends and elderly recluses, usually with sex on their minds. When they are caught, as they almost always are, the perpetrators of these crimes turn into accomplished courtroom performers who begin to enjoy their overnight fame, to think of themselves as stars instead of defendants.

Alan Rudolph's *Mortal Thoughts* is a movie just like the true crime stories I enjoy the most. It's about two friends who work in the perfectly named Clip 'n' Dye Beauty Parlor in Bayonne, New Jersey. The owner, Joyce Urbanski (Glenne Headly) is married to Jim (Bruce Willis) an abusive lout of a husband who beats her, lies to her, and grabs money out of the cash register to go buy booze and drugs. Joyce's friend and business partner, Cynthia, is played by Demi Moore as a fascinated witness to the increasing violence in the Urbanski marriage. Her own marriage, to the boring but dedicated Arthur (John Pankow), seems to be just the opposite.

The two women engage in deadly but entertaining brinksmanship over the question of whether Jim, who everybody agrees is a reprehensible brute, should be murdered. Joyce is frequently overheard saying she'd like to knock her husband off, and on one occasion, she even fills the sugar bowl with rat poison and tells Cynthia all about it—and Cynthia has to run upstairs to save Jim's life.

She is thanked for her trouble by Jim's clumsy sexual advances and adolescent pawing.

Then one night, Jim and the two women go to a carnival, and Jim dies, or is murdered, and the women conspire to hide the body and cover up the death. We learn all of this a few days later, during a police interrogation being carried out by two detectives (Harvey Keitel and Billie Neal). They have the Demi Moore character in a small room, and are videotaping her as they lead her through the details of her crime.

There are a lot of unanswered questions, such as exactly how the husband was found dead, who found him, what happened then, and why. There is even another death to consider, although to discuss it would spoil a surprise for you, and indeed, this whole movie is an unfolding series of surprises and revelations. It begins as a case history, turns into a whodunit, and ends by trying to determine what was done, among other questions.

Like many crimes, the ones in this movie seem simple at first and only grow complicated the more you look at them. The screenplay, by William Reilly and Claude Kerven, is meticulously constructed so that the flashbacks during the testimony never reveal too much, and yet never seem to conceal anything. Nor is the screenplay simply ingenious; it is also very funny, in a mordant and blood-soaked way, as these two women scheme and figure and lie to the cops, to each other, and to themselves. There is a banality to their language and images that sets the correct tone.

The way Moore and Headly squirm to justify and defend themselves is deliciously fraudulent. Yet there is another level to *Mortal Thoughts* than either the guilt or innocence of the characters, or the wit with which Rudolph portrays their world. It is the level on which ordinary people cut themselves loose from ordinary morality, who commit crimes for their own convenience. Human life should be sacred, but we live in a world where people are killed simply to make life easier for their murderers. Maybe that's why the killers' alibis are often so pathetic, and their planning is so slipshod: If the murderers really took murder seriously, they'd take the time and trouble to get away with it.

Moscow on the Hudson ★ ★ ★ ★
R, 115 m., 1984

Robin Williams (Vladimir Ivanoff), Maria Conchita Alonso (Lucia Lombardo), Cleavant Derricks (Witherspoon), Alejandro Rey (Orlando Ramirez). Directed and produced by Paul Mazursky. Screenplay by Mazursky and Leon Capetanos.

Mike Royko likes to make fun of foreign-born taxi drivers. He uses a lot of phonetic spellings to show how funny dey speeka da Engleesh. Maybe he's missing out on some good conversations. Have you ever *talked* to a taxi driver from Iran or Pakistan or Africa? I have, and usually I hear a fascinating story about a man who has fled from poverty or persecution, who in some cases has left behind a thriving business, and who is starting out all over again in this country. I also usually get the name of a good restaurant.

I thought of some of those experiences while I was watching Paul Mazursky's *Moscow on the Hudson*, a wonderful movie about a man who defects to the United States. His name is Vladimir Ivanoff, he plays the saxophone in a Russian circus, and when the circus visits New York, he falls in love with the United States and defects by turning himself in to a security guard at Bloomingdale's. The Russian is played by Robin Williams, who disappears so completely into his quirky, lovable, complicated character that he's quite plausible as a Russian. The movie opens with his life in Moscow, a city of overcrowded apartments, bureaucratic red tape, long lines for consumer goods, secret pleasures like jazz records, and shortages so acute that toilet paper has turned into a currency of its own. The early scenes are eerily convincing, partly because Williams plays them in Russian. This isn't one of those movies where everybody somehow speaks English. The turning point of the movie occurs in Bloomingdale's, as so many turning points do, and Ivanoff makes two friends right there on the spot: Witherspoon, the black security guard (Cleavant Derricks) and Lucia, the Italian salesclerk (Maria Conchita Alonso).

They're a tip-off to an interesting casting decision by Mazursky, who populates his movie almost entirely with ethnic and racial minorities. In addition to the black and the Italian, there's a Korean taxi driver, a Cuban lawyer, a Chinese anchorwoman, all of them reminders that all of us, except for American

Indians, came from somewhere else. Ivanoff moves in with the security guard's family, which greatly resembles the one he left behind in Moscow, right down to the pious grandfather. He gets a job selling hot dogs from a pushcart, he works his way up to driving a limousine, and he falls in love with the salesclerk from Italy. That doesn't go so well. She dreams of marrying a "real American," and Ivanoff, even after he trims his beard, will not quite do.

Moscow on the Hudson is the kind of movie that Paul Mazursky does especially well. It's a comedy that finds most of its laughs in the close observations of human behavior, and that finds its story in a contemporary subject Mazursky has some thoughts about. In that, it's like his earlier films *An Unmarried Woman* (women's liberation), *Harry and Tonto* (growing old), *Blume in Love* (marriage in the age of doing your own thing), and *Bob & Carol & Ted & Alice* (encounter groups). It is also a rarity, a patriotic film that has a liberal, rather than a conservative, heart. It made me feel good to be an American, and good that Vladimir Ivanoff was going to be one, too.

The Mosquito Coast ★ ★
PG, 118 m., 1986

Harrison Ford (Allie Fox), Helen Mirren (Mother), River Phoenix (Charlie), Martha Plimpton (Emily), Andre Gregory (Mr. Spellgood), Butterfly McQueen (Ma Kennywock), Dick O'Neill (Tim Polski), Conrad Roberts (Mr. Haddy). Directed by Peter Weir and produced by Jerome Hellman. Screenplay by Paul Schrader.

Some kinds of bores you will tolerate, and other kinds you will not. *The Mosquito Coast* has the misfortune to be about the second kind of bore—about a man who is zealous in the pursuit of his obsessions long, *long* after they have ceased to interest anyone else.

The man's name is Allie Fox, and he is convinced that the American civilization is coming apart at the seams. Acting on his fears, Allie packs up his wife and children and moves them into the rain forests of Central America, where he plans to establish a new civilization. This man is not without intelligence; he has invented, for example, a new kind of machine for making ice, and nobody can say he is not handy with his hands. But he shares the common fault of many utopians; he wants to create a society

in which men will be free—but free only in the way he thinks they should be free.

Allie Fox is played in *The Mosquito Coast* by Harrison Ford, and it is one of the ironies of the movie that he does very good work. Ford gives us a character who has tunnel vision, who is uncaring toward his family or anyone else, who is totally lacking in a sense of humor, who is egocentric to the point of madness. It is a brilliant performance—so effective indeed, that we can hardly stand to spend two hours in the company of this consummate jerk.

There have been other madmen in other movies who tried to find their vision in these same rain forests. I think immediately of *Aguirre, the Wrath of God*, and *Fitzcarraldo*, two movies by Werner Herzog about crazed eccentrics who pressed on into the jungle, driven by their obsessions. Those movies were so much more watchable than *The Mosquito Coast* because they created characters (both played by Klaus Kinski) who were mad with a flamboyant, burning intensity. Allie Fox's madness is more of a drone, an unending complaint against the way things are. It is painful to watch him not because he is mad, but because he is boring—one of those nuts who will talk all night long without even checking to see if you're listening.

The movie is based on a novel by Paul Theroux, in which the narrator is Fox's teenage son, Charlie. Through Charlie's eyes, we gradually see the father turning from an idealist into an obsessive, and we also see Charlie becoming a man in the process of dealing with that change. In the movie, Charlie (River Phoenix) is still the narrator, but what he tells us on the sound track isn't reinforced by what we see on the screen; Charlie recedes into the family, and becomes just one more hapless victim to be dragged through the jungle by his father.

Another mysterious character in the movie is Mother (Helen Mirren), the wife, who stands by mutely and uncomplainingly while Allie Fox subjects her family to dangerous and pointless experiences. What does she feel? What does she really think? Apart from one welcome outburst, we never know. Mirren has said that the character was opposite to everything in her own nature, and that she played Mother by trying to become completely passive. Well, that's probably the only strategy that would have worked, but it leaves enormous questions about Mother's thoughts and fears—questions this movie is not prepared to answer.

The Mosquito Coast was directed by Peter Weir, an Australian who has made great films about the silences and mysteries of nature. In *Picnic at Hanging Rock*, he showed us a group of giggling schoolgirls on a day's outing, who are mysteriously lost somewhere within a vast prehistoric rock formation; the movie provided no answer to its mystery except for an awesome silence.

In that film and throughout his career, Weir has been able to capture the majesty of nature—and the production values in *The Mosquito Coast* are impressive, especially in a scene where a typhoon threatens to sweep away Ford's fragile settlement on a threatened beach.

The movie has been directed and acted so well, in fact, that almost all my questions have to do with the script: Why was the hero made so uncompromisingly hateful? The screenplay is by Paul Schrader, whose own movies (*Hardcore, Mishima*) and screenplays (*Taxi Driver*) are often about men obsessed with their own narrow range of vision. But Schrader's characters always have some measure of humanity that is lacking here.

Weir's previous movie was *Witness*, also with Harrison Ford, and also about a contrast between modern and utopian sensibilities. Ford played the cop who came to live with and understand an Amish farm community. He fell in love with a young woman whose father was rigid and uncompromising, so utterly sure of his own infallibility that he was heedless of the unhappiness he caused to others. *The Mosquito Coast*, unfortunately, is all about the father.

Motel Hell ★ ★ ★
R, 106 m., 1980

Rory Calhoun (Farmer Vincent), Paul Linke (Bruce Smith), Nancy Parsons (Ida Smith), Nina Axelrod (Terry), Wolfman Jack (Reverend Billy), Elaine Joyce (Edith Olson). Directed by Kevin Connor and produced by Steven-Charles Jaffe and Robert Jaffe. Screenplay by Jaffe and Jaffe.

Motel Hell satirizes a whole sub-basement genre of American movies that a lot of lucky people may never even have seen. I call them Sleazoid Movies; films that deliberately test our sensibilities, and our stomachs, by the subhuman and nauseating behavior of the characters on the screen. The genre includes *The Texas Chainsaw Massacre, The Hills*

Have Eyes, The Honeymoon Killers, Night of the Living Dead, and Last House on the Left.

These films are not to be confused with those of a neighboring genre, the Women in Danger films, which spew hatred of women. Sleazoid movies seem to exist on the edge of self-parody, and their ambition is to be to the cinema what the geek show is to the circus. They're not antiwoman, they're antitaste, and their characters sink into moronic, bestial savagery. They touch on the ultimate horror of people degraded into subhuman, animalistic behavior. Some of these films, I should add, are not without merit—although this isn't the place to launch into a defense of them.

What Motel Hell brings to this genre is the refreshing sound of laughter. This movie is disgusting, of course; it's impossible to satirize this material, I imagine, without presenting the subject matter you're satirizing. But Motel Hell is not nearly as gruesome as the films it satirizes, and it finds the right stylistic note for its central characters, who are simple, cheerful, smiling, earnest, and resourceful cannibals.

Motel Hell (the second "e" on the neon sign has gone out) is a ramshackle place that seems to be located in the same redneck backwoods where Russ Meyer's characters all live. It is operated by friendly Farmer Vincent (Rory Calhoun) and his sister (Nancy Parsons). The district is patrolled, none too adroitly, by a relative (Paul Linke), who is the sheriff, but sees nothing wrong with burying the victims of a motorcycle crash without benefit of investigation or autopsy.

That's just as well, because Farmer Vincent's specialty is burying people. He just doesn't wait until they're dead. He waylays unsuspecting travelers, knocks them unconscious, buries them up to their necks in his secret garden, fattens them up with cattle feed, and then slaughters them, smokes them in his smokehouse, and sells them as sausage at his roadside stand. His cheerful motto: "It takes all kinds of critters . . . to make Farmer Vincent's fritters."

All right now, of course this is disgusting. But hold on just a dagbone minute, as Farmer Vincent might say. It isn't simply the subject matter of Sleazoid Movies that makes them reprehensible, it's their low opinion of human nature, their acquiescence in the proposition that the world is essentially an evil place. Motel Hell, with Rory Calhoun looking like a Norman Rockwell model in his bib overalls, pushes this material so far in

such unlikely directions that, incredibly, it works as satire. A lot of horror movies used to work that way. We went to be scared, sure, but we also went to laugh, enjoying the delicious self-indulgence with which Vincent Price or Christopher Lee hammed it up. But horror movies stopped being funny. And now they're mostly just depressing, disgusting exercises in depravity.

Motel Hell is a welcome change-of-pace; it's to Chainsaw Massacre as Airplane! is to Airport. It has some great moments, including a duel fought with chainsaws, a hero swinging to the rescue on a meathook, and Farmer Vincent's dying confession of the shameful secret that he concealed for years. These moments illuminate the movie's basic and not very profound insight, which is that most of the sleazoids would be a lot more fun if they didn't take themselves with such gruesome solemnity.

Mountains of the Moon ★ ★ ★ ½
R, 135 m., 1990

Patrick Bergin (Richard Burton), Iain Glen (John Hanning Speke), Richard E. Grant (Oliphant), Fiona Shaw (Isabel), John Savident (Lord Murchison), James Villiers (Lord Oliphant), Adrian Rawlins (Edward). Directed by Bob Rafelson and produced by Daniel Melnick. Screenplay by William Harrison and Rafelson.

The astronauts of the nineteenth century were the explorers—those intrepid men, often British, who mounted expeditions from the club rooms of Pall Mall to the most exotic hinterlands of the world. When the astronauts came back from the moon, they told their stories to Life magazine. When the Victorians returned from their expeditions, they presented their findings in lectures before the Royal Geographical Society, and then they wrote their memoirs in large, leather-bound volumes. But make no mistake; they were some of the greatest celebrities of their age, the Robert Scotts and David Livingstones, and exploration was not only a rewarding but a democratic profession. Explorers did not need breeding or wealth to become famous—only luck and unholy determination.

Of all the British explorers of the nineteenth century, the most interesting is Richard Francis Burton (1821–90), who was also a linguist, a poet, and a pioneer of sexual studies who translated the Kama Sutra and

an unexpurgated version of The Arabian Nights into English. For his pains, he became thoroughly disrespectable, and on his death his wife burned his translation of The Perfumed Garden, a masterpiece of Arabic erotica he had been laboring over for fourteen years.

The black-magic practitioner Aleister Crowley, who was one of the few men of the time more disreputable than Burton, wrote in his Confessions that Victorians like Burton "seethed with impotent rage" at their doom, which was to live within the repressions and evasions of the Victorian period. If the Burtons were not banished altogether, their careers and lives were rewritten to give the age more proper heroes. A flamboyant original like Burton "was toned down into a famous traveler and translator," Crowley complained.

Now here is a movie to tone him up again. Bob Rafelson's Mountains of the Moon is centered on a series of expeditions led by Burton and John Hanning Speke, who marched for months through East Africa in their search for the source of the Nile. They were the first Europeans to set eyes on most of the lands they walked across, the first to see many African species of animals, birds, and insects, and the first to encounter tribal customs that had developed in an uninterrupted continuity since the birth of history. Burton was already famous for some of his other exploits, such as disguising himself as an Arab and slipping into the holy city of Mecca. Speke, a less dashing and more ambitious man, was not lacking in physical stamina but lacked Burton's fire. At first they were a good team. Later their differences destroyed them.

The movie is not one of those wide-screen epics that might have been directed by David Lean. It's wide screen, all right, and it's an epic, but it's a not a movie about adventure and action. It's an epic about the personalities of the men who endured incredible hardships because of their curiosity, egos, greed, or even because of their nobility. Rafelson (whose credits include Five Easy Pieces) fills his movie with unobtrusive period detail; he has not only the costumes and the settings right, but also the attitudes, as men in proper attire and an astonishing variety of facial hair crowd into the Geographical Society to hear lectures from the great explorers. These men look ancient and proper, but actually they are fans, and to them Richard Burton is a dashing hero—a man they envy because he has gotten out from under Victoria's skirts by thousands of dangerous miles.

To win their ovations, Burton and Speke were prepared to risk their lives in the unknown. We see their expeditions snaking across uncharted territories, where death by native attack was less of a threat than disease, famine, pestilence, or simply getting lost. When one expedition finally reaches a lake that may be a source of the Nile, Burton arrives carried on a stretcher, almost too sick to think. A diary by a member of Scott's expedition to the South Pole is titled *The Worst Journey in the World*. That could also be the diary of this expedition.

Back in London, Burton (Patrick Bergin) and Speke (Iain Glen) have a falling-out based on a lack of communication and a tragic misunderstanding. Speke takes credit for finding the source of the Nile; Burton is adamant that the evidence is not sufficient. An unscrupulous publisher tells Speke lies about Burton, and Speke acts on them, making unforgivable statements about his former friend. When he learns that they were lies—that Burton has the material to destroy him in a debate—he falls into despair. There is the suggestion, tantalizing and unresolved, that he may have been in love with Burton, a man whose sexual appetites seem to have been fueled as much by curiosity as by lust.

Mountains of the Moon is completely absorbing. It tells its story soberly and intelligently and with quiet style. It doesn't manufacture false thrills or phony excitement. It's the kind of movie that sends you away from the screen filled with curiosity to know more about this man Burton. Why, you ask yourself, has such an oversized character become almost forgotten? The movie is about the unquenchable compulsion of some men to see what is beyond the horizon, and about the hunger for glory. It is about stubbornness and pride. It is about a friendship that would have been infinitely less painful if the friends had not both been bullheaded and flawed. It is a tribute to this movie that, at the end, neither the filmmakers nor their audience have much interest in whether anyone found the source of the Nile.

Mr. and Mrs. Bridge ★ ★ ★ ★
PG-13, 127 m., 1991

Paul Newman (Walter Bridge), Joanne Woodward (India Bridge), Margaret Welsh (Carolyn Bridge), Kyra Sedgwick (Ruth Bridge), Blythe Danner (Grace Barron), Robert Sean Leonard (Douglas Bridge), Simon Callow (Dr. Alex Sauer). Directed by James Ivory and produced by Ismail Merchant. Screenplay by Ruth Prawer Jhabvala.

Mr. and Mrs. Bridge observes with great care and an almost frightening detachment the precise ways in which an emotionally paralyzed couple gets through life together. The movie is set in an affluent Kansas City neighborhood in the 1930s and 1940s. Manicured lawns surround generous white houses with green shutters, and inside the house of the Bridges lives a man who is absolutely sure he knows how life is best to be lived, but his knowledge is not bringing very much happiness to his family.

Mr. Bridge is a lawyer, played by Paul Newman in one of his most daring and self-effacing performances. Mrs. Bridge is a housewife, played by Joanne Woodward in a masterful observation of suppression and resignation. It is hard to say exactly what is the matter with Mr. Bridge—whether he is frightened of intimacy, or shy, or simply locked into his view of proper male behavior. Whatever his problem, it involves a subtle sort of psychological wife-beating, in which his wife is essentially his emotional captive. She can communicate with him only by following careful formulas involving what can be said, and how, and when.

Passion has perhaps never existed in this couple—not, at least, joyous passion. Even the first sexual experiences must have been largely physical, involving bodily functions more than personalities. Now life has settled into a routine. The children have nearly grown up, and are hardly known to their father. Their mother knows them better, but is afraid to reveal all she knows, or tell them all she wants to say. Mr. Bridge goes off to his office and does his job and associates in time-honored patterns of ritual with his fellow professional men, and Mrs. Bridge, "keeping house," reminds me of that woman that Stevie Smith wrote about—the woman out in the sea who seemed to be waving, but was not waving, but drowning.

The film is based on two novels by Evan S. Connell, adapted by another novelist, Ruth Prawer Jhabvala, for her longtime collaborators the director James Ivory and the producer Ismail Merchant. Their other work includes *A Room With a View* and *The Bostonians*, and it is not surprising that they were drawn to this carefully seen portrait of social behavior. The film does not have a plot in the ordinary sense of the word, perhaps because a plot would have appeared unseemly to Mr. Bridge; one does not, in his world, do this in order to have that happen. One exists as nearly as possible in the same admirable way, day after day.

Incidents happen. The Bridges have children who want to lead lives that do not correspond to the family values and timetable. They are absolutely forced to rebel in one way or another, because within the family there is no room for compromise. Mrs. Bridge has a friend (Blythe Danner) who is slowly cracking up; the alcoholism that is killing her is her only strategy for surviving. For Mrs. Bridge, this friend is an external sign of her own inner turmoil. Her own life is apparently ordered and serene, and seems placid and happy to the world, but in a way she is as desperate as her friend.

The movie is not heavy-handed. It does not present Mr. Bridge as a monster. He is as trapped in his world as everyone else. Very occasionally he permits himself the smallest of tight-lipped smiles, and once in a very long time, he will unbend a little. But essentially he is the captive of duty, and his duty as a professional white man in Kansas City in the late 1930s is to conform, to do what is expected, to present the proper appearances, and to beware of emotional extremes that could lead him to lose control.

Much is made of the excesses and silliness of the sixties, but it is because of that liberating decade that Mr. Bridge and his world will never quite exist again, and it is worth remembering that the young people of the 1960s were the children of parents who were often very much like the Bridges: parents who were playing out some ideal role of probity and respectability, and who were so wary of their own feelings that they disciplined their children for having feelings at all.

I hope I haven't made *Mr. and Mrs. Bridge* seem like a dreary or depressing film. Bad films are depressing. Good films, no matter what they're about, are exhilarating, and *Mr. and Mrs. Bridge* observes its characters with such attention and care that it is always absorbing. Most movies want us to care about what happens to the characters. This one simply wants us to care about them. The work of Woodward and Newman here is a classic example of a certain kind of acting, of studies of voice and behavior, of fleeting glances and subtle nuances of body language, of people who would almost rather drown than wave.

Mr. Destiny ★ ★
PG-13, 110 m., 1990

James Belushi (Larry Burrows), Linda Hamilton (Ellen Burrows), Michael Caine (Mike), Jon Lovitz (Clip Meltzer), Hart Bochner (Niles Pender), Bill McCutcheon (Leo Hansen), Rene Russo (Cindy Jo). Directed and produced by James Orr. Screenplay by Orr and Jim Cruikshank.

The plot of *Mr. Destiny* has been borrowed from unimpeachable sources. It's based on the same notion that worked in *It's a Wonderful Life*, and a century earlier in the story of Scrooge as retailed by Dickens in *A Christmas Carol*. It involves an ungrateful man being taken on a guided tour of his life, and seeing some of the other ways it could have turned out.

The tour guide can be a guardian angel, or perhaps the ghost of Christmas past, present, or future. This time it's a bartender, a genial soul in an obscure tavern in an unfamiliar part of town. A businessman named Larry (James Belushi) wanders into the bar after his car breaks down, and he's in a mood to grumble to the bartender about the way his life is turning out. It all started to go wrong, he moans, when he was the last man at bat in the final game of the state baseball championship, and he struck out. If only he had belted that last pitch out of the park, he believes, everything would have been different, and better.

The bartender listens and nods and pours him another drink, and because business is slow (Larry is the only customer this particular bar may ever have), he does the poor guy a favor. He puts his life on fast-reverse, lets him hit the winning run, and then shows him how things would have turned out. The bartender is probably God, I suppose. Michael Caine plays him like a guy who happens to be omnipotent and doesn't mind doing a favor for a stranger.

Because the story idea behind *Mr. Destiny* is so obviously a retread, I expected the movie to pay off with comedy, rather than trying to hook us one more time with the tried-and-true parable about the man who learns to be grateful for what he has. And Belushi does have three or four big laughs in the movie. In fact, he's very good as Larry— he's gentle, touching, and he makes a convincing everyman. But the movie is so low-

key, so muted and laid-back and slow-moving, that Belushi's contribution isn't enough. Someone should have picked up the tempo.

The story of Larry's life involves a man who becomes a mid-level executive at a company where his superior married the boss's daughter. Larry married a girl who consoled him after he struck out in the fatal championship game. In the alternative lifeline revealed to him, Larry marries the boss's daughter and becomes the boss, and his former superior is now his underling, and is married to the consoling girl. It sounds more complicated than it is.

Throughout *Mr. Destiny*, Larry remembers who he was in his "other" life, but everyone else thinks they're really in the alternative lifeline. That generates some funny situations, as when Larry realizes he is now married to the sexpot, or when he tries to convince his "real" wife that they were once married. Some of the poignancy here reminded me of *Chances Are*.

Linda Hamilton, of TV's "Beauty and the Beast," creates a lot of warmth and tenderness as Larry's once and future wife, and Rene Russo, who has big hair and a fetching way about her, has fun with the role of the boss's daughter. Michael Caine, of course, is flawless in a role that requires him to be civilized and look as if he knows more than anyone realizes.

But the movie is a slow march through foregone conclusions, and its curious passivity is underscored, if that is the word, by the quietest sound track I can remember. As someone who believes most movies have too much music on the sound track, I was surprised to find myself noticing how little music is in *Mr. Destiny*. David Newman's score is so understated; it is hushed. In the quiet, an innocent little fable grows, blossoms, and is harvested, to no great moment.

The Muppet Movie ★ ★ ★ ½
G, 94 m., 1979

Jim Henson (Kermit, Rowlf, Dr. Teeth, and Waldorf), Frank Oz (Miss Piggy, Fozzie Bear, Animal, and Sam), Jerry Nelson (Floyd Pepper, Crazy Harry, Robin the Frog, and Lew Zealand), Richard Hunt (Scooter, Statler, Janice, Sweetums, and Beaker), Dave Goelz (The Great Gonza, Zoot, and Dr. Bunsen Honeydew). Directed by James Frawley and produced by Jim Henson. Screenplay by Jerry Juhl and Jack Burns.

Jolson sang, Barrymore spoke, Garbo laughed, and now Kermit the Frog rides a bicycle. *The Muppet Movie* not only stars the Muppets but, for the first time, shows us their feet. And if you can figure out how they were able to show Kermit pedaling across the screen, then you are less a romantic than I am: I prefer to believe he did it himself.

He's pedaling on his way to Hollywood, and *The Muppet Movie* itself is one of those origin stories so beloved by comic books. We've learned how Spiderman came into his extraordinary powers, and now here are the earliest days of the Muppets.

Kermit, we learn, was born in a swamp. Well, maybe we coulda guessed it. And he was born with an ability somewhat unusual to frogs: a talent for playing the ukelele. We encounter him sitting on a log and singing one of the movie's several Paul Williams songs, and for just a second we wonder where Jim Henson is. That's because Kermit is quite clearly surrounded by water, and we can't for the life of us figure out where they hid the Muppeteer.

It turns out Henson was sitting in a watertight compartment and communicating with the rest of the crew via walkie-talkie, and that Kermit's hands on the ukelele were animated by remote control, and that all sorts of technology went into making the Muppets move, but after that first second we quit wondering: This is magic, after all, so who *wants* to know where Henson is?

Dom DeLuise, on the other hand, wants to know where Kermit is. DeLuise comes rowing through the swamp in a rowboat and hears Kermit's song and reveals himself to be a big Hollywood agent with a copy of *Variety* in his boat. And, wouldn't you know, *Variety* has an ad for singing frogs in it. So of course Kermit leaves his swamp behind and commences a cross-country odyssey to Hollywood to make his audition.

He makes his trip mostly in a late-1940s Studebaker, one of those models that looked like it was going in both directions simultaneously, and the trip would have been a happy one except for one thing: Kermit is pursued by an evil fast-food magnate (Charles Durning) who wants him to sign on as the trademark of a chain of French-fried frogs' legs restaurants. It is one of the movie's more poignant ironies that no sooner does Kermit obtain legs than humans find an unsavory use for them.

Durning and DeLuise are two of the several humans in the film. The format makes absolutely no distinction between the Muppets and other forms of life, so we meet such humans as Mel Brooks, Bob Hope, Carol Kane, Steve Martin, Richard Pryor, Telly Savalas, Orson Welles, and, in their last film appearance before their deaths, Edgar Bergen and Charlie McCarthy.

We also meet, of course, Miss Piggy, who falls instantly and incurably in love with Kermit. And we get to know all the Muppets better than we could on their television show. They turn out, somehow, to have many of the same emotions and motivations that we do. They are vain and hopeful, selfish and generous, complicated and true. They mirror ourselves, except that they're a little nicer.

The Muppets Take Manhattan ★ ★ ★
G, 94 m., 1984

With guest stars Dabney Coleman, Joan Rivers, Liza Minnelli, and John Landis. Directed by Frank Oz and produced by David Lazer. Written by Oz and Jim Henson.

Dear Kermit,

I hope you will take this in the right spirit. I know you've been tortured for some years now by an identity crisis, ever since you were discovered sitting on that log down in the swamp, strumming on your ukulele. Stardom happened almost overnight, and here you are in your third starring vehicle, *The Muppets Take Manhattan.* Yet you still don't know who you really are.

You are obviously not a frog. You have none of the attributes of a frog, except for your appearance and your name. In your first film, *The Muppet Movie,* you were sort of a greenish overgrown pop singer, an amphibian Frankie Avalon. In your second movie, *The Great Muppet Caper,* you were cast adrift in a plot that really belonged to the human guest stars. You basically had a supporting role, making the humans look good. Only in *The Muppets Take Manhattan,* your third film, do you really seem to come into your own. You take charge. You are the central figure in the plot, you do not allow yourself to get shouldered aside by Miss Piggy, and you seem thoroughly at home with the requirements of genre, stereotype, and cliché. In the 1940s, you would have been under contract to MGM.

The plot of your movie has been seen before. I doubt if that will come as news to you. *The Muppets Take Manhattan* is yet another retread of the reliable old formula in which somebody says "Hey, gang! Our senior class musical show is so good, I'll bet we could be stars on Broadway!" The fact that this plot is not original does not deter you, Kermit, nor should it. It's still a good plot.

I liked the scenes in which you persevered. I liked the way you went to New York and challenged the stubborn agents like Dabney Coleman, and upstaged Liza Minnelli in Sardi's. I especially liked the scenes where you supported yourself by waiting tables in a greasy spoon cafe with rats in the kitchen and a Greek owner who specialized in philosophical statements that didn't make any sense. I even liked Miss Piggy's scenes, especially her childhood memories. I gasped at the wedding scene, in which you finally married her. I refrained from speculating about your wedding night—and speculation is all your G-rated movie left me with.

In short, I liked just about everything about your movie. But what I liked best was your discovery of self. Kermit, you are no longer a frog with an identity crisis. You've found the right persona, old boy, and it will see you through a dozen more movies. It was clear to me from the moment you took your curtain call and basked in the spotlight. Kermit, this may come as a shock, but you're Mickey Rooney in a frog suit. Think about it. You're short. You're cute. You never say die. You keep smilin'. You have a philosophy for everything. You appear only in wholesome, G-rated movies. And sex bombs like Liza Minnelli only kiss you on the cheek.

One word of advice. Dump Miss Piggy. Stage a talent search for a Liza Minnelli Muppet. Mickey Rooney made a lot of movies with Liza's mother before you were hatched, Kermit, and now it's your turn. Move fast, kid, before you croak.

Murder on the Orient Express ★ ★ ★
PG, 128 m., 1974

Albert Finney (Hercule Poirot), Lauren Bacall (Mrs. Hubbard), Martin Balsam (Blanchi), Ingrid Bergman (Greta Ohlsson), Jacqueline Bisset (Countess Andrenyi), Jean-Pierre Cassel (Pierre Paul Michel), Sean Connery (Colonel Arbuthnot), John Gielgud (Beddoes), Wendy Hiller (Princess Dragomiroff), Anthony Perkins (Hector McQueen), Vanessa Redgrave (Mary Debenham), Richard Widmark (Ratchett), Rachel Roberts (Hildegarde Schmitt), Michael York (Count Andrenyi). Directed by Sidney Lumet and produced by John Brabourne and Richard Goodwin. Screenplay by Paul Deim.

There is a cry of alarm, some muffled French, a coming and a going in the corridor. Hercule Poirot, adjusting the devices that keep his hair slicked down and his mustache curled up, pauses for a moment in his train compartment. He lifts an eyebrow. He looks out into the hallway. He shrugs. The next morning, it's revealed that Ratchett, the hateful American millionaire, has been stabbed to death in his sleep. This is quite obviously a case for Poirot, the most famous detective in the world, and, over breakfast, he agrees to accept it. The list of suspects is long, but limited: It includes everybody on board the crack Orient Express, en route from Istanbul to Calais, and currently brought to a standstill by an avalanche of snow that has fallen across the track. Poirot arranges to begin a series of interviews and plunges himself (and the rest of us) into a net of intrigue so deep, so deceptive, and so labyrinthine that only Agatha Christie would have woven it. *Murder on the Orient Express* is a splendidly entertaining movie of the sort that isn't made any more: It's a classical whodunit, with all the clues planted and all of them visible, and it's peopled with a large and expensive collection of stars. Albert Finney, who plays Poirot, is the most impressive, largely because we can never for a moment be sure that he *is* Finney. His hair is slicked down to a patent-leather shine, his eyes have somehow become beady and suspicious, his French mustache is constantly quivering with alarm (real and pretended), and he scurries up and down the train like a paranoid crab. The performance is brilliant, and it's high comedy.

So the movie, although it's careful never to make its essentially comic intentions get in the way of Miss Christie's well-oiled mystery. This isn't a "thriller," because we're not thrilled, or scared—only amused. The murder itself has a certain antiseptic, ritualistic quality, and the investigation is an exercise in sophisticated cross-examination and sputters of indignation. What I liked best about this movie is its style, both the deliberately old-fashioned visual strategies used by director Sidney Lumet, and the cheerful overacting of the dozen or more suspects.

They form a suitably bizarre menagerie and at first glance have nothing in common with one another. Bear with me please, and I'll work my way through the all-stars: Lauren Bacall is a particularly obnoxious American, Ingrid Bergman is an African missionary, Michael York and Jacqueline Bisset are Hungarian royalty, Jean-Pierre Cassel is the conductor, Sean Connery is an English officer returning from India, Vanessa Redgrave is his constant companion, John Gielgud is a veddy, veddy proper man-servant to millionaire Richard Widmark, Wendy Hiller is an aloof Russian aristocrat, Anthony Perkins is Widmark's secretary, Rachel Roberts is a neo-Nazi ladies' maid, Martin Balsam is a director of the railroad line, and there are, believe it or not, others also under suspicion.

There are obviously big technical problems here: More than a dozen characters have to be introduced and kept alive, a very complicated plot has to be unraveled, and everything must take place within the claustrophobic confines of the railway car. Lumet overcomes his difficulties in great style, and we're never for a moment confused (except when we're supposed to be, which is most of the time).

There is hardly anything more I can tell you, or even hint, about the plot, except that nothing is as it seems (and you knew that already about a movie based on an Agatha Christie book). The movie provides a good time, high style, a loving salute to an earlier period of filmmaking, and an unexpected bonus: It ends with a very long scene in which Poirot asks everyone to be silent, please, while he explains his various theories of the case. He does so in great detail, and it's fun of a rather malicious sort watching a dozen high-priced stars keep their mouths shut and just listen while Finney masterfully dominates the scene.

Murphy's Romance ★ ★ ★
PG-13, 107 m., 1985

Sally Field (Emma Moriarty), James Garner (Murphy Jones), Brian Kerwin (Bobby Jack), Corey Haim (Jake), Dennis Burkley (Freeman Coverly), Georgann Johnson (Margaret). Directed by Martin Ritt and produced by Laura Ziskin. Screenplay by Harriet Frank, Jr., and Irving Ravetch.

From the moment Sally Field pilots her battered old pickup into town and parks her kid out at the farm and walks into James Garner's drugstore and they lay eyes on each other for the first time, it's pretty clear that they are going to have to fall in love with each other and get married. All you have to do is look at them to see that.

Murphy's Romance takes almost two hours to arrive at the conclusion that takes us two

minutes, but that doesn't mean this is a predictable movie. The whole point of this movie is how it looks at those characters, and listens to them, and allows them to live in a specific time and place. If they knew what we know, it would spoil all the fun, as they flirt and pout and spar and circle each other, and survive the sudden and unexpected appearance of Sally Field's no-good ex-husband.

His name is Bobby Jack, and Field describes him in a sentence: "How come you were never as good on your feet as you were between the sheets?" He's an immature, sweet-talking con man without a responsible bone in his body. He turns up one day, and moves in, and Field lets him stay because it means a lot to their son, Jake.

At first it appears that Bobby Jack's arrival is going to cause problems for the budding relationship between Emma and Murphy (Field and Garner). But Emma keeps on inviting Murphy to stay to dinner, and Murphy reads the situation correctly: Emma may be stuck with Bobby Jack, but she is stuck on Murphy.

Murphy is quite a guy. He figures he has a lot of knowledge about human nature, and he's not shy about sharing it. He doesn't take himself too seriously, but he likes to pretend that he does. He speaks thoughtfully, moves deliberately, and lets you know what a character he is by parking his mint-condition 1928 Studebaker out in front of his drugstore. Garner plays this character in more or less his usual acting style, but he has been given such quietly offbeat dialogue by the screenwriters, Harriet Frank, Jr., and Irving Ravetch, that he comes across as a true original.

Sally Field is also not particularly original in her approach to the character Emma, who is a close relative of other Field heroines: plucky, quietly sensible in the face of calamity. Originality is not called for in this performance, anyway; it would have been a mistake to turn into a colorful character, instead of letting her proceed at her own speed. In the movie's key series of scenes—where Bobby Jack makes his move and Emma sneezes at him and then a surprise visitor turns up from Tulsa—the movie is saved from melodrama only by Field's matter-of-fact ability to take things as they come.

Then comes the ending, which is one of the most carefully and lovingly written passages in any recent movie. Much depends on exactly what Emma and Murphy say to each

other, and how they say it, and what they don't say. The movie gets it all right.

Murphy's Romance was directed by Martin Ritt, who also directed Field's Oscar-winning performance in *Norma Rae* (and worked with her again in the less-than-successful *Back Roads*). Ritt specializes in movies about the rural South and Southwest (his credits also include *Sounder, Hud*, and *Conrack*), and one of the strengths of *Murphy's Romance* is the freedom he feels to simply pause, occasionally, and soak in the local color. Two examples: Listen carefully to the man who calls the bingo numbers, and the old man Murphy gives a lift to one day. They have particular voices and deliberate word choices, and they seem completely authentic. So, to a surprising degree, does the whole movie.

Music Box ★ ★
PG-13, 123 m., 1990

Jessica Lange (Ann Talbot), Armin Mueller-Stahl (Mike Laszlo), Frederic Forrest (Jack Burke), Donald Moffat (Harry Talbot), Lukas Haas (Mikey Talbot), Cheryl Lynn Bruce (Georgine Wheeler), Mari Torocsik (Magda Zoldan). Directed by Costa-Gavras and produced by Irwin Winkler. Screenplay by Joe Eszterhas.

There comes a moment in *Music Box* when several important photographs pop up, one after another, from the bowels of a music box—as if they were being ejected by a copying machine. It is intended as a dramatic moment, but it is all too neat, the clockwork machinery operating right on time for the requirements of the plot. The entire movie is like that. It is put together out of pieces taken off the shelf, and although it is about suffering, trust, and family love, it has no heart.

The movie stars Jessica Lange as a Chicago attorney whose father, an immigrant from Hungary, has led a blameless life for many years. He is loved by all who know him. Then investigators appear to accuse him of being a Nazi war criminal. They want to put him on trial for his crimes and deport him. The daughter, of course, is convinced of her father's innocence. It is all a mistake, some kind of insane bureaucratic nightmare, and she will defend him in court and prove that they have the wrong man.

Consider for a moment the possibilities in this plot. Is it possible that the movie could end with the old man found innocent? No, it is not. There is no market for a movie about Nazi-hunters bringing false charges against the innocent. So the man must be guilty. Either that or the plot must "really" be about something else—with the issue of guilt only a smoke screen. What I particularly disliked about *Music Box* is that it takes the easy way out. It is not about guilt or innocence; it is a courtroom thriller with all of the usual automatic devices like last-minute evidence and surprise witnesses.

This was the second movie in two years by the team of director Costa-Gavras, writer Joe Eszterhas, and producer Irwin Winkler. The previous one was *Betrayed*, the 1988 thriller starring Debra Winger as an FBI undercover agent who falls in love with a seemingly decent young man (Tom Berenger) and then discovers he belongs to a right-wing neo-Nazi group. At first she believes he cannot be guilty—he is too nice a man to believe those things. Then her life is endangered as she discovers that nice guys can decieve you.

Betrayed and *Music Box* are in many ways the same story: A decent liberal woman loves and trusts a man who may be a Nazi. In both cases, the Naziism is used only as a plot device, as a convenient way to make a man into a monster without having to spend much time convincing us of it. Neither movie is really about Naziism, but about the plot requirements of a thriller. But both movies use their moral righteousness in an attempt to seem more serious than they really are. Think back to *Jagged Edge*, the screenplay Eszterhas wrote just before *Betrayed*, and you will see the plot device more clearly: A young woman (Glenn Close) loves a man (Jeff Bridges) who may be a killer and may kill her. It is the same idea spun out in three different ways in three screenplays in a row.

What is most offensive about *Music Box* is that it makes no particular attempt to understand the personality of the old man who may have been a Nazi. As played, quite effectively, by Armin Mueller-Stahl, he is a decent, God-fearing man, respected in the community and loved by his family. He protests that communists have conspired to frame him because of his anticommunist past. The plot provides some reasons to believe this and other reasons not to. The final revelations all come out of the courtroom and not out of the old man's soul, because the movie has no time to really understand him. *Music Box* is a vehicle for the Jessica Lange character, and so the old man, who should be the central character if this movie took itself seriously, is only a pawn.

The Lange performance is very good—as strong as her work in *Frances*, for example, and yet Costa-Gavras and Eszterhas have let her down, too. They have put her into a thriller in which there can be no real suspense, and provided her with a lot of emotional scenes that we look at in a detached way because we have figured out the plot and her character has not. Nazis make convenient villians in the movies, because to call a man a Nazi is to save yourself any further trouble in establishing him as evil. The problem in a movie like this is that any intelligent audience member can run through the possibilities as I did above and see that unless it is going to be about careless mistakes by Nazi-hunters, the story has only one destination.

The Music Lovers ★ ★
R, 122 m., 1971

Richard Chamberlain (Tchaikovsky), Glenda Jackson (Nina Milukova), Max Adrian (Nicholas Rubenstein), Christopher Gable (Count Chiluvsky), Isabella Teleznska (Madame Von Meck). Directed and produced by Ken Russell. Screenplay by Melvyn Bragg.

Ken Russell's *The Music Lovers* is an involved and garish private fantasy which Russell, alas, presents to us as the life of Tchaikovsky. Poor Tchaikovsky. I know it is against the rules to complain that this or that detail may not be precisely accurate, or that Tchaikovsky may not have been dealt with in the fairest possible manner. I know, because I get letters from graduate students, that I must resolutely examine the film itself—or the "film itself" as they put it—and put aside considerations from real life. What difference does it matter whether Tchaikovsky actually existed as Russell portrays him—as long as Russell has made a good film?

Well, I suppose there's something to be said for that point of view, had Russell made a good film and not said it was about Tchaikovsky. But *The Music Lovers* is libelous not only to the composer but to his music. I am no composer, Lord knows, but I have a notion that even the greatest of composers must have spent most of their time hard at work composing. I doubt whether their great works came to them, full-blown, in moments of sexual, religious, political, or sporting ecstasy. I doubt whether any great work in any field of art "comes" to anybody. Great novels are not produced by automatic writing, so why should great symphonies be?

Russell apparently thinks they are. And so although his film is more visually daring and more sexually explicit than other biographies of composers, it rests on the same fallacious assumption: That a sunset, or a woman (or a man, in Tchaikovsky's case), or a famous naval victory, or something could inspire the composer to sit down and dash off a few inspired moments.

Lest you accuse me of exaggerating, let me just mention that Tchaikovsky's mental image, when the cannons roar in the "1812 Overture," is supposed to be a friend's head being blown off. Better we should have a movie in which Russell's image, during the same passage, is of his own head being blown off. We would save the head for last, of course, in order to deal with lesser extremities of the minor works.

The Music Lovers is totally irresponsible, then, as a film about, or inspired by, or parallel to, or bearing a vague resemblance to, Tchaikovsky, his life and times. It is not, however, a complete failure. Ken Russell is a most deviously baroque director, sucking us down with him into his ornate fantasies of decadent interior decoration, until every fringe on every curtain has a fringe of its own, and the characters have fringes, too, and the characters elbow their way through a grotesque jungle of candlesticks, potted plant stands, incense sticks, old champagne bottles, and gilt edges, and it is almost certain that something is happening in the movie. But what?

My Beautiful Laundrette ★ ★ ★
R, 93 m., 1986

Daniel Day Lewis (Johnny), Saeed Jaffrey (Nasser), Roshan Seth (Papa), Gordon Warnecke (Omar), Shirley Ann Field (Rachel), Rita Wolf (Tania). Directed by Stephen Frears and produced by Sarah Radclyffe and Tim Bevan. Screenplay by Hanif Kureishi.

When people told me they'd seen *My Beautiful Laundrette* and it was a good movie, I had a tendency to believe them, for who would dare to make a bad movie with such an uncommercial title? The launderette in question is a storefront operation in one of the seedier areas of London, and it is losing money when a rich Pakistani decides to entrust its management to his nephew. But this is not the saga of a launderette. It is the story of two kinds of outsiders in modern London.

The film opens with some uneventful days in the life of its hero, Omar, who is a young man in need of a job. His father is an alcoholic journalist, once important and successful, now never far from the gin bottle. His uncle Nasser is one of the more successful members of the Pakistani community in London, a businessman who owns a chain of parking garages and storefront retail shops. He enjoys success in British terms: He has a big house in the country, an expensive car, and a British mistress.

Because a man cannot stand by and see a member of his family fail for lack of opportunity, he gives Omar a job in a parking garage, and later turns the launderette over to him. He also suggests that Omar should get married, perhaps even to his own daughter.

There is some doubt, however, about whether Omar will ever get married. Earlier in the film, we have witnessed a strange scene. Omar and friends have been stopped by a gang of punk neo-fascist Paki-bashers, when Omar walks up fearlessly to their leader, Johnny, and greets him with affection. We discover that the two young men had been lovers, and before long Johnny abandons his gang to join with Omar in the operation of the launderette.

My Beautiful Laundrette refuses to commit its plot to any particular agenda, and I found that interesting. It's not about whether Johnny and Omar will remain lovers, and it's not about whether the launderette will be a success, and it's not about the drunken father or even about Nasser's daughter, who is so bored and desperate that during a cocktail party she goes outside and bares her breasts to Omar through the French doors: Anything to get away from the small talk.

The movie is not concerned with plot, but with giving us a feeling for the society its characters inhabit. Modern Britain is a study in contrasts, between rich and poor, between upper and lower classes, between native British and the various immigrant groups—some of which, like the Pakistanis, have started to prosper. To this mixture, the movie adds the conflict between straight and gay.

Their relationship encompasses some subtleties which the movie handles with great delicacy. Although Omar is a member of a non-white immigrant group and Johnny is Anglo-Saxon, the realities of their lives are that Omar will probably turn out to be more successful and prosperous than Johnny. He has the advantage of his uncle's capital, his family connections, and his own gift at business. Johnny is a true outsider with small prospects of success.

There is another outsider in the movie who shares his dilemma. She is Rachel, Nasser's British mistress. Nasser remains married to his Pakistani wife, and although the two women are more or less known to one another, he keeps them in separate compartments of his life. There is a moment, though, during the opening ceremonies at the launderette, when the two women are accidentally in the same room at the same time, and it results in an extraordinary speech by Rachel, who with pride and dignity defends her position as Nasser's mistress by describing herself as a woman who has never had a break in life, who has always had to ask for what she wanted, and who deserves some small measure of happiness, just like everybody else.

A movie like this lives or dies with its performances, and the actors in *My Beautiful Laundrette* are a fascinating group of unknowns, with one exception—Shirley Anne Field, who plays Rachel, and who may be familiar from *Saturday Night and Sunday Morning* and other British films.

The character of Johnny may cause you to blink, if you've seen the wonderful *A Room with a View;* he is played by Daniel Day Lewis, the same actor who in that film plays the heroine's affected fiancé Cecil. Seeing these two performances side by side is an affirmation of the miracle of acting: That one man could play these two opposites is astonishing.

Omar is played by Gordon Warnecke, an actor unknown to me, as a bright but passive youth who hasn't yet figured out the strategy by which he will approach the world. He is a blank slate, pleasant, agreeable, not readily showing the sorrows and angers that we figure ought to be inside there somewhere. The most expansive character in the movie is Nasser (Saeed Jaffrey), an engaging hedonist who doesn't see why everyone shouldn't enjoy life with the cynical good cheer he possesses.

The viewer is likely to go through a curious process while watching this film. At first there is unfamiliarity: Who are these people, and where do they come from, and what sort of society do they occupy in England? We get oriented fairly quickly, and understand the values that are at work. Then we begin to wonder what the movie is about. It is with some relief that we realize it isn't "about" anything; it's simply some weeks spent with some characters in a way that tells us more about some aspects of modern Britain than we've seen before.

I mentioned *A Room with a View* because of the link with Daniel Day Lewis. There is another link between the two films. They are both about the possibility of opening up views—of being able to see through a window out of your own life and into other possibilities. Both films argue that you have a choice. You can accept your class, social position, race, sexuality, or prejudices as absolutes, and live entirely inside them. Or you can look out the window, or maybe even walk out the door.

My Bodyguard ★ ★ ★ ½
PG, 97 m., 1980

Chris Makepeace (Clifford), Adam Baldwin (Linderman), Matt Dillon (Moody), Ruth Gordon (Gramma), Martin Mull (Mr. Peache), John Houseman (Dobbs), Paul Quandt (Carson), Craig Richard Nelson (Griffith). Directed by Tony Bill and produced by Don Devlin. Screenplay by Alan Ormsby.

There is a terrifying moment in adolescence when suddenly some of the kids are twice as big as the rest of the kids. It is terrifying for everybody: For the kids who are suddenly tall and gangling, and for the kids who are still small and are getting beat up all the time. *My Bodyguard* places that moment in a Chicago high school and gives us a kid who tries to think his way out of it.

The kid's name is Clifford. He has everything going against him. He's smart, he's new in the school, he's slightly built. As he's played by Chris Makepeace, he is also one of the most engaging teen-age characters I've seen in the movies in a long time. Too many movie teen-agers have been sex-crazed *(Little Darlings)*, animalistic food-fighters *(Meatballs)*, or hopelessly romanticized *(The Blue Lagoon)*. Clifford is basically just your normal, average kid.

He has just moved to Chicago with his family. His father (Martin Mull) is the new resident manager of the Ambassador East Hotel. His grandmother (Ruth Gordon) hangs out in the lobby and picks up old men in the bar. Life is great, backstage at a hotel (he gets his meals in the kitchen or sometimes in the Pump Room). But it's not so great at school. The movie sends Clifford to Lake View High School, where he's immediately shaken down for his lunch money.

The extortionist (Matt Dillon) is the kind of kid we all remember from high school. He's handsome in an oily way, he's going through a severe case of adolescent sadism, he's basically a coward. His threat is that unless Clifford pays protection money, he'll sic the dreaded Linderman on him.

Linderman (Adam Baldwin) is a school legend, a big, hulking kid who allegedly killed his brother, raped a teacher, hit a cop, you name it. The movie's inspiration is to have Clifford *think* his way out of his dilemma—neutralizing Linderman by hiring him as a bodyguard. This is genius, and there's a wonderful scene where Clifford springs Linderman on the rest of the kids.

Then the movie takes an interesting turn. Clifford and Linderman become friends, and we learn some of the unhappy facts of Linderman's life. It turns out Linderman isn't the Incredible Hulk after all—he's just another kid going through growing pains and some personal tragedy. This whole middle stretch is the best part of the movie, developing a friendship in a perceptive and gentle way that's almost shocking in comparison with the idiotic, violent teen-agers so many movies have given us.

The ending is predictable (it's a showdown between Linderman and another tough kid). And there are some distractions along the way from Clifford's family. Martin Mull makes an interesting hotel manager, whimsical and charming. But the movie gets off track when it follows Ruth Gordon through some of her adventures, including a romantic collision with a hotel executive played by John Houseman. These scenes just don't seem part of the same movie: The hotel stuff is sitcom, while the stuff in the high school is fresh and inventive.

That seems to apply to the performances, too. One of the strengths of *My Bodyguard* is in the casting of the younger performers—Chris Makepeace, Adam Baldwin, Matt Dillon. They look right for their parts, but, more to the point, they *feel* right. Dillon exudes creepiness, Makepeace is plausible while thinking on his feet, Linderman is convincingly vulnerable and confused, and there's another kid, the solemn-faced, wide-eyed Paul Quandt, who steals a couple of scenes with his absolute certainty that the worst is yet to come.

My Bodyguard is a small treasure, a movie about believable characters in an unusual situation. It doesn't pretend to be absolutely realistic, and the dynamics of its big city high school are simplified for the purposes of the story. But this movie is fun to watch because it touches memories that are shared by most of us, and because its young characters are recognizable individuals, and not simplified cartoon figures like so many movie teen-agers.

My Brilliant Career ★ ★ ★ ½
NO MPAA RATING, 101 m., 1980

Judy Davis (Sybylia Melvyn), Sam Neill (Harry Beecham), Wendy Hughes (Aunt Helen), Robert Grubb (Frank Hawden), Max Cullen (Mr. McSwat), Pat Kennedy (Aunt Gussie). Directed by Gillian Armstrong and produced by Margaret Fink. Screenplay by Eleanor Witcombe.

What magic is it that sometimes allows young girls in backward districts to guess that they need not play along with the general ideas about a "woman's role"? I ask because three of my favorite writers—and now a fourth—discovered, more or less by themselves, that the possibilities in their lives were unlimited.

Two of the writers are famous: Willa Cather, who wrote of independent young women in Nebraska and points west, and Doris Lessing, whose *Children of Violence* series chronicles the liberation of a young woman from Rhodesia. The other two writers are not so well known, but the parallels in their lives are so astonishing that I'd like to sketch them, briefly, before moving on to an extraordinary film, *My Brilliant Career*. Their names are Olive Schreiner and Miles Franklin. They both led isolated childhoods in the nineteenth century, in the backwaters of the British Empire. And they both wrote novels about those lives at a very early age.

Olive Schreiner was raised on a farm in the Orange Free State, in South Africa. She learned Afrikaans along with English, read the Bible daily, and in her mid-teens wrote a classic novel, *The Story of an African Farm*. It was about the awakening of the spirit of a teen-age girl (herself, obviously) who did not see why her life had to be so limited just because she was a woman. Schreiner's later life was spent in intellectual and feminist circles in London (and for a time she filled the challenging position of being Havelock Ellis's mistress).

The other writer is someone I've just learned about recently: Miles Franklin, born in 1879 in rural Australia and raised on an isolated country station in the outback. At the age of sixteen she wrote a novel about her experiences, *My Brilliant Career*. It was published six years later in Edinburgh. Like Schreiner, Franklin became a feminist, traveled abroad in her twenties (and came to Chicago, where she and Alice Henry organized the Women's Trade Union League).

The Story of an African Farm is an established literary classic. *My Brilliant Career*, on the other hand, was relatively forgotten until a group of Australian women filmmakers made it into this remarkable film. It tells the story of a restless, high-spirited young woman whose temperament just isn't suited to the leftover Victorian standards of Australian country districts in the 1890s.

Franklin's novel is successful as a movie primarily because of a brilliant casting discovery. Judy Davis, who plays the film's heroine, is so fresh, unique, irreverent, and winning that she makes this material live. She's a young actress from Perth, a sometime pop and jazz singer, who was reportedly the second choice for the film's lead; if that's so, it was a completely fortunate second choice.

My Brilliant Career could have been just another feminist film. The director, Gillian Armstrong, could have gone to great lengths to explain the thinking and motivations of her character—and bored us in the meantime. But she doesn't. Instead, she makes her points through Judy Davis's presence and personality.

This isn't a movie that ends with any final answers or conclusions. Instead, it's about a young woman in a painful and continuing process of indecision. She's not considered by her family to be an ideal young woman at all—she's too independent, untamed, unreconciled to a woman's role. She doesn't automatically swoon at the attentions of every young man in the district. She's red-haired, freckled, feisty.

These qualities do appeal, however, to one young neighboring man, a farmer who's of two minds about her: He finds her independence appealing, and yet he tends to share the prevailing view about proper behavior for women. Can he overcome his narrow view and accept her? He does propose marriage. Can she overcome her headstrong independence and accept him? That's the film's key question, and *My Brilliant Career* is wise in never quite answering it.

The film is beautiful to look at. It was filmed on location in the outback, in warm natural colors, and the costumes and settings meticulously establish the period. But Judy Davis's performance establishes it even more, because she creates a complicated character so naturally that we feel the conflicts instead of having to understand them intellectually. This is the best kind of movie of ideas, in which the movie supplies the people and emotions and *we* come up with the conclusions.

My Dinner with André ★ ★ ★ ★
NO MPAA RATING, 110 m., 1981

Wallace Shawn (Wally), André Gregory (André), Jean Lenauer (Waiter), Roy Butler (Bartender). Directed by Louis Malle and produced by George W. George and Beverly Karp. Screenplay by Shawn and Gregory.

The idea is astonishing in its audacity: a film of two friends talking, just simply talking—but with passion, wit, scandal, whimsy, vision, hope, and despair—for 110 minutes. It sounds at first like one of those underground films of the 1960s, in which great length and minimal content somehow interacted in the dope-addled brains of the audience to provide the impression of deep if somehow elusive profundity. *My Dinner with André* is not like that. It doesn't use all of those words as a stunt. They are alive on the screen, breathing, pulsing, reminding us of endless, impassioned conversations we've had with those few friends worth talking with for hours and hours. Underneath all the other fascinating things in this film beats the tide of friendship, of two people with a genuine interest in one another.

The two people are André Gregory and Wallace Shawn. Those are their real names, and also their names in the movie. I suppose they are playing themselves. As the film opens, Shawn travels across New York City to meet Gregory for dinner, and his thoughts provide us with background: His friend Gregory is a New York theater director, well-known into the 1970s, who dropped out for five years and traveled around the world. Now Gregory has returned, with wondrous tales of strange experiences. Shawn has spent the same years in New York, finding uncertain success as an author and playwright. They sit down for dinner in an elegant restaurant. We do not see the other customers. The bartender is a wraith in the background, the waiter is the sort of presence they were waiting for in *Waiting for Godot*. The friends order dinner, and then, as it is served and they eat and drink, they talk.

What conversation! André Gregory does most of the talking, and he is a spellbinding conversationalist, able to weave mental images not only out of his experiences, but also out of his ideas. He explains that he had become dissatisfied with life, restless, filled with anomie and discontent. He accepted an invitation to join an experimental theater group in Poland. It was *very* experimental, tending toward rituals in the woods under the full moon.

From Poland, he traveled around the world, meeting a series of people who were seriously and creatively exploring the ways in which they could experience the material world. They (and Gregory) literally believed in mind over matter, and as Gregory describes a monk who was able to stand his entire body weight on his fingertips, we visualize that man and in some strange way (so hypnotic is the tale) we share the experience.

One of the gifts of *My Dinner with André* is that we share so many of the experiences. Although most of the movie literally consists of two men talking, here's a strange thing: *We* do not spend the movie just passively listening to them talk. At first, director Louis Malle's sedate series of images (close-ups, two-shots, reaction shots) calls attention to itself, but as Gregory continues to talk, the very simplicity of the visual style renders it invisible. And like the listeners at the feet of a master storyteller, we find ourselves visualizing what Gregory describes, until this film is as filled with visual images as a radio play—*more* filled, perhaps, than a conventional feature film.

What Gregory and Shawn talk about is, quite simply, many of the things on our minds these days. We've passed through Tom Wolfe's Me Decade and find ourselves in a decade during which there will apparently be less for everybody. The two friends talk about inner journeys—not in the mystical, vague terms of magazines you don't want to be seen reading on the bus, but in terms of trying to live better lives, of learning to listen to what others are really saying, of breaking the shackles of conventional ideas about our bodies and allowing them to more fully sense the outer world.

The movie is not ponderous, annoyingly profound, or abstract. It is about living, and Gregory seems to have lived fully in his five years of dropping out. Shawn is the character who seems more like us. He listens, he nods eagerly, he is willing to learn, but—something holds him back. Pragmatic questions keep asking themselves. He can't buy Gregory's vision, not all the way. He'd like to, but this is a real world we have to live in, after all, and if we all danced with the druids in the forests of Poland, what would happen to the market for fortune cookies?

The film's end is beautiful and inexplicably moving. Shawn returns home by taxi through the midnight streets of New York. Having spent hours with Gregory on a wild conversational flight, he is now reminded of scenes from his childhood. In *that* store, his father bought him shoes. In that one, he bought ice cream with a girl friend. The utter simplicity of his memories acts to dramatize the fragility and great preciousness of life. He has learned his friend's lesson.

My Favorite Year ★ ★ ★ ½
PG, 92 m., 1982

Peter O'Toole (Alan Swann), Mark Linn-Baker (Benjy Stone), Jessica Harper (K.C. Downing), Joseph Bologna (King Kaiser), Lainie Kazan (Belle Corroca), Lou Jacobi (Uncle Morty). Directed by Richard Benjamin and produced by Michael Gruskoff. Screenplay by Norman Steinberg and Dennis Palumbo.

"Live? I can't go on *live!!* I'm a movie star—not an actor!"

Alan Swann is imploring them: Say it isn't so! He's an alcoholic British matinee idol, veteran of countless swashbuckling epics in which he faced fleets of pirates and waves of savage barbarians. Now he is being asked to accept the worst challenge of all: to appear on live television.

My Favorite Year is the story of an era when most television was live, and the great television stars were inventing the medium out of their own imaginations every Saturday night. The year is 1954. The program is "King Kaiser's Comedy Hour," obviously inspired by the old Sid Caesar and Imogene Coca programs. The British star, Alan Swann, is played by Peter O'Toole, but he could be Errol Flynn or John Barrymore or even O'Toole himself. The movie is told from the point of view of a young production assistant named Benjy (Mark Linn-Baker).

His job is to shadow the great Alan Swann, get him everything he wants except booze, keep him out of trouble, and deliver him intact to the studio in time for the broadcast. Along the way, Benjy adds a priority of his own, his continuing courtship of his would-be girlfriend, K.C. (Jessica Harper).

Through Benjy's eyes, we see Swann as the great man he was, as the pathetic drunk he is, and as the hero he could become—if he survives the live telecast. We also gain some understanding of King Kaiser (Joseph Bologna), who is a big, beefy, not-too-bright guy who has an absolutely accurate understanding of his own comic talent. Translated, that means he knows what will work. What will get a laugh. He has no taste, of course; when he offends a girl, he sends her steaks instead of flowers, and he sends a business associate a gift of tires. But he's a physical comedian with a gift for pumping the laughter out of this frail new medium, and he's backed up by a whole crew of talented writers.

Swann, meanwhile, is backed up only by memories of his greatness and fears of performing in front of a live audience. But as O'Toole plays this character, he becomes one of the great comic inventions of recent movies. Swann is a drunk, but he has an uncanny ability to pass from coma through courtliness to heroics without ever quite seeming to gain consciousness. A character like Swann could probably only be played by someone who is both a great actor and a great ham, and O'Toole is both.

My Favorite Year is not a perfect movie. I could have done without the entire romantic subplot between Benjy and K.C. But I liked the movie's ability to move from one unexpected comic situation to another. That produces one of the best scenes, when Benjy takes Swann home to Brooklyn to meet his mother and weird Uncle Morty (Lainie Kazan and Lou Jacobi in hilarious performances). There is, to be sure, a force running through the movie's disorganization, and that force is O'Toole's charisma. He is so completely charming, so doomed, so funny, and so pathetically invincible as Swann that this movie succeeds despite its occasional unnecessary scenes.

My Heroes Always Have Been Cowboys ★ ★
PG, 105 m., 1991

Scott Glenn (H.D. Dalton), Kate Capshaw (Jolie Meadows), Ben Johnson (Jesse Dalton), Balthazar Getty (Jud Meadows), Tess Harper (Cheryl Hornby), Gary Busey (Clint Hornby), Mickey Rooney (Junior). Directed by Stuart Rosenberg and produced by Martin Poll and E.K. Gaylord II. Screenplay by Joel Don Humphreys.

The elements of this movie are so familiar, so worn-out, that within a few minutes of the opening, we can predict with certainty almost everything that will happen. A rodeo cowboy is injured. He will mend. He comes back to his hometown, and finds that his father has been consigned to a nursing home. He will bust out the old curmudgeon. His sister and her husband want to sell the family land. He will prevent it. He meets a woman with a rebellious teen-ager. He will become the woman's lover and the boy's friend. And at the film's end, of course, he will get back into the rodeo ring and try to win enough money to solve all of his problems.

You don't have to be a genius to figure out this stuff. At a point about twenty-five minutes into the movie, the cowboy (Scott Glenn) walks out of a store and past a poster that advertises a $100,000 rodeo contest, and my little built-in movie computer immediately said *Rocky!* The movie had to end with a big bull-riding competition, or the poster would not have been there. So then I idly wondered what other reliable old elements would present themselves. Would the cowboy make his comeback despite an injury? Would the old man, the boy, and the girl turn up to cheer him on? Are there stars in the sky?

With a movie like this, after you've given up on the possibility of any originality, you sit back and look for nuggets of gold that may have been hidden here or there in a crevice of the screenplay. One thing I enjoyed throughout the movie was the work of Scott Glenn, an unsung but always interesting actor (*The Right Stuff, The River*), who plays the cowboy with a taciturn and weathered conviction. I also liked the unstudied sincerity of the great Ben Johnson, as his father (he was already playing this role twenty years ago, in *The Last Picture Show*). I liked the way old character actors like Dub Taylor turned up in a poker game, and it was fun to see Mickey Rooney again, although he should have turned the energy down a notch.

In more major roles, two actresses are given predictable dilemmas and thankless dialogue. Kate Capshaw is the divorced woman who catches Glenn's eye, and who then has to utter lines like "You've broken my heart once and I don't want it broken again," and Tess Harper, usually interesting, gets to play the angry sister. She's the one who wants to send the old man to the nursing home, and although at times she is reasonable ("The moment you mend you'll be out rodeoing again, and then who will look after him?"), too often she is simply let loose to be shrill and mean.

The most interesting element of the movie is the cantankerous old man, who is indeed impossible, and forgetful, and careless, and impossible to please. If they leave him in the nursing home he'll die, but if they let him live alone, he'll sooner or later kill himself or somebody else. So what should they do about him? Because this was the only question in the movie that had not already been answered in dozens of other films, I waited for the movie to attend to it. But, of course, room had to be made for the *Rocky* ending.

My Left Foot ★ ★ ★ ★
R, 103 m., 1989

Daniel Day-Lewis (Christy Brown), Brenda Fricker (Mrs. Brown), Alison Whelan (Sheila), Kirsten Sheridan (Sharon), Declan Croghan (Tom), Eanna MacLiam (Benny), Marie Conmee (Sadie), Cyril Cusack (Lord Castlewelland). Directed by Jim Sheridan and produced by Noel Pearson. Screenplay by Jim Sheridan and Shane Connaughton.

I am trying to imagine what it would be like to write this review with my left foot. Quite seriously. I imagine it would be a great nuisance—unless, of course, my left foot was the only part of my body over which I had control. If that were the case, I would thank God that there was still some avenue down which I could communicate with the world.

That is the story of Christy Brown, born in a large, poor, loving family in a Dublin slum and considered for the first ten years of his life to be hopelessly retarded. He was born with cerebral palsy, and his entire body was in revolt against him—all except for the left foot, with which one day he picked up a piece of chalk and wrote a word on the floor. Everyone was amazed except for Christy's mother, who had always believed he knew what was going on. She could see it in his eyes.

The story of Christy Brown is one of the great stories of human courage and determination. He belongs on the same list with Helen Keller—and yet it is hard to imagine Christy being good company for the saintly Miss Keller, since he was not a saint himself but a ribald, boozing, wickedly gifted Irishman who simply happened to be handicapped.

Jim Sheridan's *My Left Foot* is the story of Brown's life, based on his autobiography and on the memories of those who knew him. He was not an easy man to forget. Tiny and twisted, bearded and unkempt, he managed, despite his late start, to grow into a poet, a novelist, a painter, and a lyrical chronicler of his own life. Like many geniuses, he was not an easy man to live with, and the movie makes that clear in its brilliant opening scene.

Perhaps concerned that we will mistake *My Left Foot* for one of those pious TV docudramas, the movie begins in the middle of one of Brown's typical manipulations. He is backstage in the library of a great British country home, where he is soon to be brought out to be given an award. He has a pint of whisky hidden in his jacket pocket with a straw to allow him to sip it. But a hired nurse is watching him with a gimlet eye. Trying to get her out of the way for a second, he asks her for a light for his cigarette.

"But Mr. Brown," she says, "you know that smoking is not good for you."

"I didn't ask for a fucking psychological lecture," he replies. "I only asked for a fucking light."

It is the perfect opening scene because it breaks the ice. We know that it is all right to laugh with Christy and not to be intimidated by the great burden of his life. And as the movie develops, it is startling how much of it plays as comedy—startling unless we remember the universal Irish trait of black humor, in which the best laughter, the wicked laughter, is born out of hard times and bad luck.

My Left Foot charts Christy Brown's life from his earliest days until his greatest triumph, but the key scene in the movie may be one that takes place shortly after he is born. His father goes into the local pub to have a pint and consider the fact that his son has been born handicapped, and then he stubbornly makes the statement that no son of his will be sent to a "home." The decision to raise Christy as part of a large and loving family is probably what saved his life—for a man of such intelligence would have been destroyed by an institution. His brilliant mind, trapped inside his imperfect body, would have gone mad from calling for help.

Christy is played in the early scenes by Hugh O'Conor and from his teen-age years onward by Daniel Day-Lewis. The two actors fit Brown's life together into one seamless performance of astonishing beauty and strength. There is an early scene in which Christy's brothers and other neighbor kids are playing soccer in the street, and crippled Christy, playing goalie, defends the goal by deflecting the ball with his head. There is great laughter and cheering all around, but the heart of the scene is secure: This child is not being protected in some sort of cocoon of sympathy, but is being raised in the middle of life, hard knocks and all. This is reinforced in other scenes where Christy's siblings dump him in a barrow and wheel him around to their games.

As he watched and listened, the boy was making the observations that would inform his life work. His novel *Down All the Days* and his other writings see Dublin street life with a clarity that is only possible because he was raised right in the middle of it and yet was always an outsider. As a painter, he saw Dublin in the same way: as a stage upon which people did things he was intimately familiar with and yet would never do himself.

Christy's life as a man was not easy. He was willful and arrogant, and right from the first time he tasted whisky he knew there was at least one way to escape from the cage of his body. Like all men, he desired love, and there is a heartbreaking sequence in which he develops a crush on a teacher who works with him on speech therapy and loves Christy, but not in the romantic way that he imagines. Learning of her engagement, he creates a scene in a restaurant that in the power of its hurt and anger is almost unbearable.

He drank more. He was demanding. Like all bright people forced to depend on the kindness of others, he was filled with frustration. A woman did finally come into his life, a nurse who became his wife and loved him until the end, but by then happiness was conditional for Christy because he was an alcoholic. Since he could not obtain booze on his own—since it had to be brought to him and provided to him—there is the temptation to ask why his loved ones didn't simply shut him off. But of course that would have been a cruel exploitation of his weakness, and then too, Christy was a genius at instilling guilt.

My Left Foot is a great film for many reasons, but the most important is that it gives us such a complete picture of this man's life. It is not an inspirational movie, although it inspires. It is not a sympathetic movie, although it inspires sympathy. It is the story of a stubborn, difficult, blessed, and gifted man who was dealt a bad hand, who played it brilliantly, and who left us some good books, some good paintings, and the example of his courage. It must not have been easy.

My Stepmother Is an Alien ★ ★
PG-13, 108 m., 1988

Dan Aykroyd (Dr. Steve Mills), Kim Basinger (Celeste), Jon Lovitz (Ron Mills), Alyson Hannigan (Jessie Mills), Joseph Maher (Dr. Budlong), Seth Green (Fred Glass). Directed by Richard Benjamin and produced by Ronald Parker and Franklin R. Levy. Screenplay by Jerico and Herschel Weingrod, Timothy Harris, and Jonathan Reynolds.

What we have here is a goofy comic performance by Kim Basinger, weighed down by a turgid script and a decision to use Dan Aykroyd mostly as a straight man. Too bad. This is one of those movies where the credits list four writers, and most of the funny stuff is in between the lines. Basinger proves here, as she did in *Blind Date*, that she has a natural gift for slapstick, with a plastic face and a rubber body. She always makes a great package in a tight red dress, but this time she seems to be operating her body's controls with her elbows.

My Stepmother Is an Alien tells the story of an eccentric physicist (Aykroyd) who harnesses the power of lightning to send a beam to another galaxy. The response is a visit to Earth by a spaceship bearing Basinger as an alien who takes human form but never gets it quite right. She materializes on the beach, saunters into a party being given by Aykroyd's brother, and starts to nibble on the cigarette butts. Aykroyd falls in love with her, not because she looks sexy, but because she makes him laugh. I had much the same reaction.

But the screenplay never seems to realize the comic potential of the situation. The title suggests that the movie's point of view is taken from Aykroyd's thirteen-year-old daughter (Alyson Hannigan), and if the movie had been told from a teen-ager's perspective, it might have developed some real possibilities. Unfortunately, the role of the daughter is used mostly for negative scenes, in which she stands around and has hysterics because her dad won't believe her when she says she saw Basinger drinking battery fluid and plunging her hand into boiling water.

That's a missed opportunity, but even unhappier is the role of the scientist, played by Aykroyd, who seems to have been constructed out of spare parts. Everything involving the scientist in this movie seems to have been watered down from other movies. The film opens with one of those basic mad scientist scenes in which a violent thunderstorm rages, while everyone spins dials and screams at computer screens and lightning strikes the radar dish. Since the movie was directed by Richard Benjamin, who made *The Money Pit*, you'd expect him to go over the top in a scene like this, but basically, he relies on the special effects and chooses not to add a level of manic satire. What's left is kind of a bland updating of the opening of *The Bride of Frankenstein*.

Once the message is received and Basinger arrives on Earth, the film picks up. She has learned about humans by studying television shows from the 1950s, and so her dialogue sounds a little strange, but a woman who looks like Kim Basinger can go to a party on the beach and say almost anything and the men will nod approvingly and tell her she's made a good point. Her mission is to convince the Aykroyd character to repeat his experiment so that her home planet can be saved from some kind of gravity drain. But she doesn't expect him to fall in love with her, and that causes complications.

Basinger's gimmick in the movie is a purse that is able to manufacture such items as dresses and ID cards. It also contains a snake with an eyeball for a mouth, who is her traitorous sidekick. The purse is a key prop in the movie's best scene, where Aykroyd wants to kiss, and the purse projects movies on the wall behind him so that Basinger can copy her technique from old movies and other even stranger sources. Another big scene has Basinger serving breakfast to Aykroyd and his daughter, and filling the table with everything from the menu at the corner restaurant. This scene should have worked, but somehow it doesn't. It seems flat, and Benjamin can't find a way to give it a spin.

Dan Aykroyd is a solid presence in the movie, but he's the straight man, the earthling who likes to slave over a hot computer, and can't believe this woman really loves him. Basinger gets most of the good comic moments in the movie, and does with them what she can, but Benjamin and his writers seem to have run short of invention. Most of the plot developments are foregone conclusions, and most of the big set pieces (like a wedding) are handled routinely, without inspiration. *My Stepmother Is an Alien* is a great idea for a movie, but it seems to have stalled at the idea stage.

Mystery Train ★ ★ ★ ¹/₂
R, 110 m., 1990

Masatoshi Nagase (Jun), Youki Kudoh (Mitzuko), Screamin' Jay Hawkins (Night Clerk), Cinque Lee (Bellboy), Nicoletta Braschi (Luisa), Elizabeth Bracco (DeeDee), Joe Strummer (Johnny), Rick Aviles (Will Robinson), Steve Buscemi (Charlie). Directed by Jim Jarmusch and produced by Jim Stark. Screenplay by Jarmusch.

Mystery train. The two most evocative words in the language, suggesting streamliners into the night and strangers whose eyes meet in the club car as the train's rhythm creates an erotic reverie. But trains are no longer quite like that in America, and the opening shots of Jim Jarmusch's new film show two young Japanese tourists in a faded Amtrak coach, listening to their Walkmans as the train pulls through the outskirts of Memphis.

The girl is an Elvis fan. Her boyfriend believes Carl Perkins was the true father of rock 'n' roll. They have come to visit the shrines of Memphis: The Sun recording studios, for example, where rock 'n' roll was born.

In the hands of another director, this setup would lead directly into social satire, into a comic put-down of rock tourism with a sarcastic visit to Graceland as the kicker. But Jarmusch is not a satirist. He is a romantic who sees America as a foreigner might—as a strange, haunting country where the urban landscapes are painted by Edward Hopper and the all-night blues stations provide a sound track for a life.

The tourists arrive in Memphis, drag their luggage through the cavernous train station, and walk to the Sun studios, where a guide rattles off her spiel about Elvis and Carl

faster than an auctioneer could. Then they check into the Arcade Hotel, one of those fleabags that has grown exhausted waiting for the traveling salesmen who no longer come. This is a hotel out of a 1940s *film noir*, with neon signs and a linoleum lobby, and a night clerk who has seen it all and a bellboy whose eyes are so wide he might be seeing everything for the first time.

Other people will check into this hotel during the movie's long night of mystery. There is a woman who needs to spend the night somewhere before she flies away with the remains of her husband. She meets a woman who has just broken up with her boyfriend, and they decide to share a room for a night. Meanwhile, on the other side of town, some men are drinking too much and get into a disagreement, and drive off into the night in a pickup truck, and stick up a liquor store, and then they also head for the Arcade Hotel.

The sound track is from a local radio station, and Presley's version of "Blue Moon" is heard at one time or another during all three of these stories, providing a common link. An offscreen gunshot provides another link. And so does the ghost of Elvis, who seems to haunt the movie with his voice and his legend—and who appears to the woman whose husband has just died.

There is a strange appropriateness there. It is not her own husband who appears in the night, spectral and mysterious, but Elvis, and his legend seems to inspire the film. But this is not the Elvis of the supermarket tabloids, just as *Mystery Train* is not about dusty Amtrak coaches. The movie is about legends and people who believe in them. In fact it is the movie that believes most of all.

Jarmusch believes in an American landscape that existed before urban sprawl, before the sanitary sterility of the fast-food strips on the highways leading into town. His movies show us saloons where everybody knows each other, diners where the short-order cook is in charge, and vistas across railroad tracks to a hotel where transients are not only welcome, they are understood.

Mystery Train is Jarmusch's third film, after *Stranger than Paradise* and *Down by Law*. In all three there is the belief that America cannot be neatly packaged into safe and convenient marketing units, that there must be a life of the night for the drifters and the dropouts, the heroes of no fixed abode and no apparent place of employment. These are the people that songs like "Mystery Train" are about, and although in fact their lives may be flat and empty, in Jarmusch's imagination they are the real inhabitants of the city, especially after midnight.

Mystery Train is not a conventional narrative, and it is not how the story ends that is important, but how it continues. It is populated by dozens of small, well-observed moments of human behavior, such as the relationship between the night clerk (Screamin' Jay Hawkins) and the bellboy (Cinque Lee), or between the two teen-age Japanese tourists (Masatoshi Nagase and Youki Kudoh), whose entire image of American reality is formed out of popular culture.

The best thing about *Mystery Train* is that it takes you to an America you feel you ought to be able to find for yourself, if you only knew where to look. A place of people who are allowed to be characters, to be individuals, who do not have to graduate from Hamburger University to stand over a grill. The train is the perfect metaphor in this movie. It's not where it's been that's important, or even where it's going. It's the sound of that whistle as it finds its way through the night.

Mystic Pizza ★ ★ ★ ½
R, 104 m., 1988

Julia Roberts (Daisy Araujo), Annabeth Gish (Kat Araujo), Lili Taylor (Jojo Barboza), Vincent Phillip D'Onofrio (Bill Montijo), William R. Moses (Tim Travers), Adam Storke (Charles Gordon Winsor, Jr.), Conchata Ferrell (Leona Valsouano). Directed by Donald Petrie and produced by Mark Levinson. Screenplay by Amy Jones, Randy and Perry Howze, and Alfred Uhry.

There is a certain breathlessness about the summer after high school, which *Mystic Pizza* captures with an effortless charm. Childhood is officially behind. Adulthood is still a mystery, but one which it is now possible to begin solving. Romance still has the intensity of a teen-age crush, but for some teen-agers it also begins to require a certain idealism; the loved one must be not merely perfect, but good.

The movie takes place in a fishing town named Mystic, Conn., where many of the year-round people are Portuguese-American, and the summer people have names like Charles Gordon Winsor, Jr. It is about three girls who work in the Mystic Pizzeria, famous for the secret ingredients in its special sauce. Two of the girls are sisters, the third is their best friend, and the movie begins when the best friend walks away from the altar and leaves her fiancé standing there.

Her name is Jojo Barboza (Lili Taylor). She simply can't face marriage. She loves Bill (Vincent Phillip D'Onofrio), but she's not ready for a permanent commitment. Her problem is, like, he really turns her on, but he doesn't believe in sex until after marriage. Is she ready to marry him just to get him into bed? Not quite. Jojo doesn't plan to go on to college, and her dream is to someday inherit the secret pizza sauce from Leona (Conchata Ferrell), and run the pizzeria herself. Her friends are Daisy and Kat Araujo (Julia Roberts and Annabeth Gish), and one night they're drinking a few beers at a local hangout when Daisy sees Mr. Right walk in.

He's tall, preppy, cool, and able to almost hit three bull's-eyes on the dart board while drinking a shot of tequila before every dart. This may not seem like a skill that prepares him for life, but Daisy picks him up and before long they are more or less in love. He is a very rich kid named, of course, Charles Gordon Winsor, Jr. (Adam Storke), and he is in law school, he says, although actually he has been thrown out of law school for cheating, and that is why he can devote so much time to his dart game.

Kat, meanwhile, is baby-sitting for a thirty-year-old Yale graduate who is an architect rehabbing a local landmark. She's been accepted to Yale for the fall, and so they have that in common. Also reckless romanticism. His name is Tim (William R. Moses), his wife is in Europe, and Kat falls head over heels in idealism with him. They have long talks about Important Subjects, she impresses him with her intelligence, and she is so fresh and pretty that perhaps he is more easily impressed than he should be. She loves his baby, too. She projects herself into his life, declares him to be good and true, and tries not to think too much about his absent wife. Perhaps—she snatches at straws—they're going to be divorced.

Mystic Pizza takes these three couples and follows them through several months. Each romance turns into a hard lesson to be learned, but one of the nice qualities of this movie is how lightly it moves on its feet. It doesn't hammer its points home, it doesn't go for big, telegraphed scenes of heartbreak, and its single best scene is used to make a fairly subtle ethical point. The rich kid has brought the poor Portuguese-American girl home to have dinner with his family, and in the middle of the dinner the kid explodes at

an "insult" to his girl and attacks all of the relatives for being complacent, racist, stupid snobs. Then he pulls the tablecloth out from under all the dishes and storms out of the house, perhaps expecting to be followed by an adoring girl who admires him for sticking up for her.

But Daisy is not stupid, and she can read people better than Charles Gordon Winsor, Jr. She accuses him, accurately, of staging an embarrassing scene for his own self-aggrandizement, and concludes by telling him that he is not good enough for her. This twist on the scene—passing up the obvious docu-drama piety in order to make a more difficult point—is typical of what's best about this movie. The idea of three teen-age girls and their first posthigh school romances is a cliché, but *Mystic Pizza* does not treat it as one.

I have a feeling that *Mystic Pizza* may someday become known for the movie stars it showcased back before they became stars. All of the young actors in this movie have genuine gifts. Julia Roberts is a major beauty with a fierce energy, Annabeth Gish projects intelligence and stubbornness like a young Katharine Hepburn, and Lili Taylor, who is given what's intended as a more comic role, finds human comedy in her ongoing problems with the earnest and chaste Bill. It's fun to watch them work. Of the men, Vincent D'Onofrio, as Bill, has the best part to work with as he stubbornly explains how he doesn't believe in sex without a commitment. Moses and Storke have less to work with; their roles are constructed out of obligatory emotions, in a movie that is really about women.

There are nice performances around the edges of this movie, too, by Conchata Ferrell (from *Heartland*) as the pizza cook with the secret, and by Louis Turenne as the local television gourmet, who turns up one fateful day to review the famous pizza. *Mystic Pizza* does create the feeling of a small resort town and the people who live there and, amazingly, given the familiar nature of a lot of the material, it nearly always keeps us interested. That's because the characters are allowed to be smart, to react in unexpected ways, and to be more concerned with doing the right thing than with doing the expedient or even the lustful thing. The movie isn't really about three girls in love; it's about three girls discovering what their standards for love are going to be.

N

Nadine ★ ★ ½
PG, 83 m., 1987

Jeff Bridges (Vernon Hightower), Kim Basinger (Nadine Hightower), Rip Torn (Buford Pope), Gwen Verdon (Vera), Glenne Headly (Renee), Jerry Stiller (Raymond Escobar). Directed by Robert Benton and produced by Arlene Donovan. Screenplay by Benton.

As a general rule, you hardly can go wrong with a movie that uses a woman's first name as its title. Right away you know the film is going to showcase an actress playing a character who is indomitable, eccentric, stubborn, determined, and with a heart as big as all outdoors. Let's make a list: *Camille, Gilda, Julia, Sophie's Choice, Carrie, Norma Rae, Hello, Dolly!, Cleopatra.* (You hardly ever get a movie with a man's first name, probably because of some obscure, sexist impulse we will examine at a later date.)

Nadine is the latest entry in this tradition, a movie about a down-home Texas woman (Kim Basinger) who makes the mistake of posing for the wrong pictures for the wrong photographer. He was going to send them to his personal friend, Mr. Hugh M. Hefner, but now it looks like they may wind up on the back of a truck-stop poker deck, so she wants to get them back.

This involves enlisting her soon-to-be-ex-husband (Jeff Bridges) in a scheme to break into the photographer's office and grab the incriminating negatives. But first she has to pry him loose from the clutches of his current fiancée, the Pecan Queen. And then there's the problem of the dead body they stumble over in the photographer's studio. That's the setup for what looks like a screwball comedy, sounds like a screwball comedy, and is intended to be a screwball comedy, but is not, alas, very funny.

Basinger and Bridges make a nice team, fighting and making up and trying not to get killed after they're trapped in a conspiracy to get rich off of secret Texas state highway plans. The movie surrounds them with colorful character actors, gives them lots of down-home dialogue, and adds the usual number of chases and showdowns and scenes where they have to escape on a creaky ladder over a certain drop to their deaths. It would seem to have all the right ingredients.

And yet I didn't laugh very much watching this movie. There were a couple of genuinely funny moments, but they didn't build and the movie didn't redeem itself by making me very interested in the characters. I kept getting the idea I was looking at fabricated behavior that didn't have any foundation in real people that the filmmakers cared about.

You'd almost think, though, that Basinger and Bridges could pull it off no matter what. Although Basinger still somehow is dismissed as a sexy blonde (maybe because she is one), she is an actress of substantial talent and is right at home in Texas, as she showed in *Fool for Love*. Bridges is one of the most dependable Hollywood leading men, effortlessly likable, and they have a nice, easy chemistry together. But it doesn't add up to much.

Scene after scene just sort of sits there on the screen. The screenplay seems to be going through the motions. Stock supporting characters walk on, and they feel stock. They don't give the sense, as supporting characters should, of leading full lives just out of sight offscreen. Only Rip Torn, as one of the conspirators, seems convinced his character actually has a stake in the matters at hand.

This is the second movie Robert Benton has filmed in his home state of Texas; the other was *Places in the Heart*. He is obviously dealing with a lot of nostalgia here, and he has all the details right: the cars, the rhythm of the streets, the way rooms are furnished. What he doesn't have is much in the way of laughter. This is a curiously flat, unfinished, low-energy comedy, and what I liked the most was simply the ease with which Basinger and Bridges inhabited it.

The Naked Gun ★ ★ ★ ½
PG-13, 85 m., 1988

Leslie Nielsen (Lt. Frank Drebin), Priscilla Presley (Jane Spencer), Ricardo Montalban (Vincent Ludwig), George Kennedy (Capt. Hocken), O.J. Simpson (Nordberg), Nancy Marchand (L.A. Mayor), John Houseman (Driving Instructor), Reggie Jackson (Right-fielder). Directed by David Zucker and produced by Robert K. Weiss. Screenplay by Jerry Zucker, Jim Abrahams, and David Zucker.

Criticism quails in the face of *The Naked Gun*. The film is as transparent as a third-grader with a water gun, and yet it would be easier to review a new film by Ingmar Bergman, for there, at least would be themes to discuss and visual strategies to analyze. Reviewing *The Naked Gun*, on the other hand, is like reporting on a monologue by Rodney Dangerfield. You can get the words, but not the music.

The movie is as funny, let it be said, as any comedy of 1988, with the exception of *A Fish Called Wanda*. You laugh, and then you laugh at yourself for laughing. Some of the jokes are incredibly stupid. Most of them are dumber than that. And yet this is not simply a string of one-liners. There is a certain manic logic to the progression of the film, as the plot leads us from Yasser Arafat to Reggie Jackson, with a pause while Queen Elizabeth passes a hot dog to the person sitting on the other side of her at Dodger Stadium.

The movie stars Leslie Nielsen, star (it says here) of a thousand TV shows, as Lt. Frank Drebin, ace lawman who has been taken hostage at a summit conference of all of America's enemies. He frees himself and decks them with right crosses to the jaw, and makes a patriotic speech about the American Way. When he is returned by jet aircraft to American soil at last, the sun is shining, the band is playing, and the crowds are cheering—but they're not at the airport to greet him, they're there for Weird Al Yankovich.

And so on. *The Naked Gun* is the work of Zucker, Abrahams, and Zucker, the same firm that brought us *Airplane!* and the vastly underrated *Top Secret.* (In that one, a mortally wounded spy lay in a dark alley behind the Iron Curtain and handed a colleague an envelope that absolutely had to be postmarked no later than midnight. It was addressed to Publisher's Clearing House.)

These are the same guys behind the short-lived TV series "Police Squad," which has attained cult status on video, and *The Naked Gun* is in the same style of nonstop visual and spoken puns, interlaced with satire, slapstick, and scatalogical misunderstandings.

Do you even care about the plot? The critic knows his duty, and will press onward. Nielsen is soon investigating a fishy scam being masterminded by a criminal named Vincent Ludwig (played by Ricardo Montalban, who has said in publicity releases that he took the role for the money, and plans to buy a new Chrysler). Montalban's assistant is the sensuous Jane Spencer (Priscilla Presley, who has a light comic touch that works as a counterweight to the less subtle aspects of the movie, which are myriad).

Through complications too nonsensical to relate, Montalban's plans involve a plot to assassinate the Queen at a Dodgers home game, and Nielsen goes undercover—first posing as the opera star who sings "The Star-Spangled Banner," and then as the home-plate umpire. It's around here that Reggie Jackson shows up.

The wisdom of directing the assassination attempt at an actual public figure is questionable, but it must be said that the use of an Elizabeth look-alike inspires some very funny moments, most of them centering around the fact that she is appalled to be attending a baseball game.

Other famous walk-ons in the movie include not only Jackson but O.J. Simpson

and, in a very funny sequence, the late John Houseman—who plays a driving instructor who is unflappable in the face of disaster. *The Naked Gun* is an utterly goofy movie and a lot of fun, and don't let anyone tell you all the jokes before you watch it.

The Name of the Rose ★ ★ ½
R, 128 m., 1986

Sean Connery (William of Baskerville), F. Murray Abraham (Bernardo Gui), Christian Slater (Adso of Melk), Elya Baskin (Severinus), Feodor Chaliapin, Jr. (Jorge de Burgos), William Hickey (Ubertino de Casale), Michael Lonsdale (The Abbot). Directed by Jean-Jacques Annaud and produced by Berno Eichinger. Screenplay by Andrew Birkin, Gerard Brach, Howard Franklin, and Alain Godard.

In my imagination, there are two kinds of monks and two kinds of monasteries. The first kind of monastery is a robust community of men who work hard and pray hard and are bronzed by the sun and have a practical sense of humor. They have joined the life of prayer with the life of the hands. The second monastery is a shuttered series of gloomy passages and dank cells where jealous, mean-spirited little men scamper about playing politics. Their prayers are sanctimonious and their nights are long and resentful.

In the first few scenes of *The Name of the Rose*, we realize that this will be a movie about a contest between the two kinds of monks. Here comes the first one now, striding across the open fields of the Middle Ages, his heavy wool habit little protection against the cold winds, his young novice walking at his side. His name is William of Baskerville, and he is portrayed by Sean Connery, who plays him as the first modern man, as a scholar-monk who understands all of the lessons of the past but is able to see them in a wider context than the others of his time.

One day, William arrives at a vast monastery, which crouches with foreboding on top of a steep hill. At its base, starving peasants wrestle for scraps of food, which are thrown down from the monk's kitchens. At its pinnacle is a great tower that has been arranged as a labyrinth; you might find anything up there—except the way out.

A series of murders is taking place in the monastery. William has a reputation as something of an investigator, and soon after his arrival he is involved in trying to identify the causes of death and to find the murderer.

There are many suspects. Indeed, I cannot remember a single monk in this monastery who does not look like a suspect. The film has been cast to look like a cross between the grotesques of Fellini and the rat-faced devils scampering in the backgrounds of a tarot deck.

What we have here is the setup for a wonderful movie. What we get, unfortunately, is a very confused story, photographed in such murky gloom that sometimes it is hard to be sure exactly what is happening. William of Baskerville listens closely and nods wisely and pokes into out-of-the-way corners, and makes solemn pronouncements to his young novice. It is clear that he is onto something, but the screenplay is so loosely constructed that few connections are made between his conclusions and what happens next.

During the central sections of the film, the atmosphere threatens to overwhelm the action. *The Name of the Rose* was shot in a real monastery and on sets that look completely convincing, but unfortunately the film takes the "dark ages" literally and sets its events in such impenetrable gloom that sometimes it is almost impossible to see what is happening. The large cast of characters swims in and out of view while horrible events take place; a monk is found dead at the base of the tower, and another is drowned in a wine vat. William of Baskerville moves solemnly from one event to another, deliberately, wisely, but then the plot takes on a crazy rhythm of its own, as the Grand Inquisitor arrives to hold a trial and ancient secrets are discovered inside the labyrinth of the tower.

What this movie needs is a clear, spare, logical screenplay. It's all inspiration and no discipline. At a crucial moment in the film, William and his novice seem sure to be burned alive, and we have to deduce how they escaped because the movie doesn't tell us. There are so many good things in *The Name of the Rose*—the performances, the reconstruction of the period, the overall feeling of medieval times—that if the story had been able to really involve us, there would have been quite a movie here.

Nashville ★ ★ ★ ★
R, 159 m., 1975

Henry Gibson (Haven Hamilton), Ronee Blakley (Barbara Jean), Timothy Brown (Tommy Brown), Gwen Welles (Sueleen Gay), Michael Murphy (John Triplette), Shelley Duvall (L.A. Joan), Lily Tomlin

(Linnea Reese), Ned Beatty (Delbert Reese), Scott Glenn (Pfc. Glenn Kelly), Keith Carradine (Tom Frank), Geraldine Chaplin (Opal), Karen Black (Connie White), Barbara Harris (Albuquerque). Directed and produced by Robert Altman. Screenplay by Joan Tewkesbury.

Robert Altman's *Nashville*, which was the best American movie since *Bonnie and Clyde*, creates in the relationships of nearly two dozen characters a microcosm of who we were and what we were up to in the 1970s. It's a film about the losers and the winners, the drifters and the stars in Nashville, and the most complete expression yet of not only the genius but also the humanity of Altman, who sees people with his camera in such a way as to enlarge our own experience. Sure, it's only a movie. But after I saw it I felt more alive, I felt I understood more about people, I felt somehow wiser. It's that good a movie.

The movie doesn't have a star. It does not, indeed, even have a lead role. Instead, Altman creates a world, a community in which some people know each other and others don't, in which people are likely to meet before they understand the ways in which their lives are related. And he does it all so easily, or seems to, that watching *Nashville* is as easy as breathing and as hard to stop. Altman is the best natural filmmaker since Fellini.

One of the funny things about *Nashville* is that most of the characters never have entrances. They're just sort of there. At times, we're watching an important character and don't even know, yet, why he's important, but Altman's storytelling is so clear in his own mind, his mastery of this complex wealth of material is so complete, that we're never for a moment confused or even curious. We feel secure in his hands, and apart from anything else, *Nashville* is a virtuoso display of narrative mastery.

It concerns several days and nights in the lives of a very mixed bag of Nashville locals and visitors, all of whom, like the city itself, are obsessed with country music. Tennessee is in the midst of a presidential primary, and all over Nashville, there are the posters and sound trucks of a quasi-populist candidate, Hal Philip Walker, who seems like a cross between George Wallace and George McGovern. We never meet Walker, but we meet both his local organizer and a John Lindsay-type PR man. They're trying to round up country-western talent for a big benefit, and

their efforts provide a thread around which some of the story is loosely wound.

But there are many stories here, and in the way he sees their connections, Altman makes a subtle but shrewd comment about the ways in which we are all stuck in this thing together. There are the veteran country stars like Haven Hamilton (Henry Gibson), who wears gaudy white costumes, is self-conscious about his short stature, is painfully earnest about recording a painfully banal Bicentennial song, and who, down deep, is basically just a good old boy. There is the reigning queen of country music, Barbara Jean (Ronee Blakley), who returns in triumph to Nashville after treatment at a burn center in Atlanta for unspecified injuries incurred from a fire baton (she's met at the airport by a phalanx of girls from TIT—the Tennessee Institute of Twirling—only to collapse again). There is the corrupted, decadent rock star, played by Keith Carradine, who is so ruthless in his sexual aggression, so evil in his need to hurt women, that he telephones one woman while another is still just leaving his bed, in order to wound both of them.

But these characters are just examples of the people we meet in *Nashville*, not the leads. Everyone is more or less equal in this film, because Altman sees them all with a judicious and ultimately sympathetic eye. The film is filled with perfectly observed little moments: The star-struck young soldier keeping a silent vigil by the bedside of Barbara Jean; the campaign manager doing a double take when he discovers he's just shaken the hand of Elliott Gould ("a fairly well-known actor," Haven Hamilton explains, "and he used to be married to Barbra Streisand"); the awestruck BBC reporter describing America in breathless, hilarious hyperbole; the way a middle-aged mother of two deaf children (Lily Tomlin) shyly waits for an assignation with a rock singer; the birdbrained cheerfulness with which a young groupie (Shelley Duvall) comes to town to visit her dying aunt and never does see her, being distracted by every male over the age of sixteen that she meets.

The film circles around three motifs without, thankfully, ever feeling it has to make a definitive statement about any of them. Since they're all still very open subjects, that's just as well. What Altman does is suggest the ways in which we deal with them—really, in unrehearsed everyday life, not thematically, as in the movies. The motifs are success, women, and politics.

Success: It can be studied most fruitfully in the carefully observed pecking order of the country-and-western performers. There are ones at the top, so successful they can afford to be generous, expansive, well-liked. There are the younger ones in the middle, jockeying for position. There are what can only be described as the professional musicians at the bottom, playing thanklessly but well in the bars and clubs where the stars come to unwind after the show. And at the very bottom, there are those who aspire to be musicians but have no talent at all, like a waitress (Gwen Welles) who comes to sing at a smoker, is forced to strip, and, in one of the film's moments of heartbreaking truthfulness, disdainfully flings at the roomful of men the sweat socks she had stuffed into her brassiere.

Women: God, but Altman cares for them while seeing their predicament so clearly. The women in *Nashville* inhabit a world largely unaffected by the feminist revolution, as most women do. They are prized for their talent, for their beauty, for their services in bed, but not once in this movie for themselves. And yet Altman suggests their complexities in ways that movies rarely have done before. The Lily Tomlin character, in particular, forces us to consider her real human needs and impulses as she goes to meet the worthless rock singer (and we remember a luminous scene during which she and her deaf son discussed his swimming class). Part of the movie's method is to establish characters in one context and then place them in another, so that we can see how personality—indeed, basic identity itself—is constant but must sometimes be concealed for the sake of survival or even simple happiness.

Politics: I won't be giving very much away by revealing that there is an attempted assassination in *Nashville*. The assassin, a loner who takes a room in a boarding house, is clearly telegraphed by Altman. It's not Altman's style to surprise us with plot. He'd rather surprise us by revelations of character. At this late date after November 22, 1963, and all the other days of infamy, I wouldn't have thought it possible that a film could have anything new or very interesting to say on assassination, but *Nashville* does, and the film's closing minutes, with Barbara Harris finding herself, to her astonishment, onstage and singing, "It Don't Worry Me," are unforgettable and heartbreaking. *Nashville*, which seems so unstructured as it begins, reveals itself in this final sequence to have had a deep and very profound structure—but one of emotions, not ideas.

This is a film about America. It deals with our myths, our hungers, our ambitions, and our sense of self. It knows how we talk and how we behave, and it doesn't flatter us but it does love us.

Narrow Margin ★ ½
R, 97 m., 1990

Gene Hackman (Caulfield), Anne Archer (Hunnicut), James B. Sikking (Nelson), J.T. Walsh (Michael Tarlow), M. Emmet Walsh (Sergeant Dominick Benti), Susan Hogan (Kathryn Weller). Directed by Peter Hyams and produced by Jonathan A. Zimbert. Screenplay by Hyams.

Narrow Margin is a clumsy version of the Idiot Plot, dressed up as a high-gloss chase thriller. The Idiot Plot, as we know, is any plot that would be resolved in five minutes if everyone in the story were not an idiot. And rarely has there been a film in which more idiots make more mistakes than in this one.

The story involves Anne Archer as a woman who goes out on a blind date, and accidentally witnesses the man's murder by a mob killer, while the killer's boss—a crime kingpin—looks on. Archer is terrified that she will be the next victim, and immediately escapes to her secluded cabin in the Rockies, telling nobody except, of course, for her roommate who tells the police, who follow her there in a helicopter, and who are followed by another helicopter they fail to notice.

Gene Hackman plays the lawman on her trail. When the second helicopter starts spraying the cabin with machine-gun bullets, he leads her out the back window and into a waiting truck, so they can speed down the road while providing a target for more bullets. He eventually drives under the protection of tall trees, but soon he's out in the open again, as this chase sets a pattern for the movie by dragging on much too long.

Eventually the chase leads to a train station, and wouldn't you know that a train is just pulling in. It sits at this whistle-stop in the middle of the woods long enough for Hackman and Archer to buy tickets and talk an old couple out of their private compartment on the grounds that Archer is about to go into labor. Nobody asks (a) why a woman about to give birth would take a train ride instead of going to the hospital, or, more pointedly, (b) why she doesn't look remotely

pregnant (to fool the oldsters, she sticks her hands in the pockets of her sweater).

Hackman and Archer are followed onto the train by two or more killers, who have parked their helicopter nearby, I guess. What follows is an endless series of scenes in which killers and quarry follow each other up and down train corridors. The killers invariably make a habit of entering one end of a car and not seeing Hackman until he can duck out of sight at the other end. Then there is time for long, soul-searching talks at night, because as Hackman says, "They won't act until morning because they don't have to." Meanwhile, the train has turned into an express to Vancouver, shortly after stopping to pick up those folks in the middle of the woods.

As a connoisseur, I appreciated one scene where Hackman and Archer are safely hidden in a compartment, but he leaves to go to the diner for coffee and is found by the killers. And another scene where the bad guys try to bargain with him. And another scene where it is obvious to everyone but Hackman that the woman is not as innocent as she seems. And the scene where Hackman and Archer climb onto the top of a moving train, where the lawman, pushing sixty, runs up and down and engages a bad guy in hand-to-hand combat. And a scene where . . .

But never mind. I have more. How about the fact that there's not even a scene in which Hackman confronts the man who betrayed him? (It's handled over the telephone.) Or the way Hackman tells his backup to "meet me at the border," without saying *where* at the border? My favorite moment is when Hackman uses the oldest trick in Western lore to mislead the guys chasing him: He throws a pebble into the woods, and when they go that way, he goes this way. I thought Hopalong Cassidy had retired that particular ploy, but I guess not.

FILM FOOTNOTE. One of the newest clichés in the movies is the use of a black actor to play the obstructionist superior officer in a police drama. How many times have we seen the hero called on the carpet in the office of his superior, a black man, who orders him to stop hot-dogging around? This character is invariably wrong-headed and obtuse. Narrow Margin introduces a character like that, who then disappears except for mention in a phone call. In the bad old days, black actors were often cast in menial roles. Now they are cast as token superiors, but the stereotyping is just as relentless. What's the worse role, pushing a broom, or

being kicked upstairs? Why not let some of these actors into the mainstream of the plot?

The Nasty Girl ★ ★ ½
PG-13, 95 m., 1991

Lena Stolze (Sonic), Monika Baumgartner (Mother), Michael Gahr (Father), Fred Stillkrauth (Uncle), Elizabeth Bertram (Grandmother), Robert Giggenbach (Dr. Martin), Hans-Richard Muller (Juckenack). Directed and produced by Michael Verhoeven. Screenplay by Verhoeven.

Some people, you tell them to mind their own business, they do. Other people, you tell them the same thing, they get a curious kind of tingling sensation, and go leaping after other people's business like a retriever in a good mood. Sonic Rosenberger is the other kind of person, and *The Nasty Girl* is the story of what happened after the town fathers in her village in Bavaria told her not to go poking around in the archives to discover what went on during the Nazi era.

Before the authorities made what turned out to be that major miscalculation, Sonic was an unremarkable, if high-spirited, local schoolgirl, who had won an essay contest that provided her with a free trip to Paris. But then another contest came along, and Sonic thought maybe a hometown essay would win it. Something along the lines of "My Hometown in the Third Reich." The town fathers did not share her enthusiasm. The official line in her hometown was that the Nazis had not made much of an inroad there, but when she went to the village library to dig through old newspapers and archives, she found them closed to her, and she grew determined to discover what the city was trying to hide.

That's the story line of Michael Verhoeven's *The Nasty Girl*, titled after one of the less offensive names hurled at Sonic during her quest. The movie is based on the experiences of a real girl in a real town: Anja Rosmus, whose hometown of Passau did indeed have certain undeniable links with the Nazis. Hitler once lived there, in a house converted to a museum during the Third Reich, and Eichmann was married there. Over a period of ten years, Rosmus pursued her quest in the archives and in the courts, proving at one point that the editor of the local Catholic newspaper—who was hailed as a resistance hero—in fact wrote pro-Hitler editorials and even urged his readers to pray for the fuehrer.

These revelations did not make Rosmus popular in her hometown; she received anonymous phone threats, she was once beaten up by neo-Nazis, and her high school teacher, who she had married, left her after things began to heat up. All of these events are faithfully mirrored in the film, which has been made in a curiously lighthearted spirit and is not the dirge we might have expected. Lena Stolze, in the title role, is given to yodeling when she uncovers another piece of damning evidence, and her character in the movie has been compared by some critics to Nancy Drew.

It's the film's style that I object to. The story itself is fascinating, but the style seems to add another tone, a level of irony that is somehow confusing: Does Verhoeven see this as quite the cheery romp he pretends, or is there a sly edge to his method? As a rule, I welcome stylistic experiments—most movies are much too straightforward—but this time I'm not sure the movie's odd tone adds anything. Realism might have worked better.

The tone is most noticeable in the film's visual style, which uses obviously artificial sets and locations, and at times has its heroine walking in front of back-projected streets, or standing on pedestals in the embrace of local statues. She addresses the camera directly, as if she were conducting a Welcome Wagon introduction to the secrets of the Nazi past, and there are scenes where her opponents fume and bluster like the crooked banker in a Frank Capra comedy.

Perhaps in the original German the comic nuances come across more amusingly; perhaps we are missing subtleties in the subtitles. But as I watched the film, I found that the disparity between the subject and the style was so strange that it distracted from what the film was really about. Here is a story that cries out for a different kind of stylistic exaggeration—for the lurid melodrama of the late and lamented Fassbinder, perhaps, who would have also found humor in the panic of the local officials, but would have made it mordant rather than cheerful. There is a story to be told here, but somehow you have to see straight through the movie to find it.

National Lampoon's Animal House
★ ★ ★ ★
R, 109 m., 1978

John Belushi (Bluto), Tim Matheson (Otter), John Vernon (Dean Wormer), Verna Bloom (Mrs. Wormer), Thomas Hulce (Pinto), Cesare Danova (Mayor), Donald Sutherland (Jennings), Mary Louise Weller (Mandy), Stephen Furst (Flounder), Mark Metcalf (Neidermeier). Directed by John Landis and produced by Marry Simmons and Ivan Reitman. Screenplay by Harold Ramis, Douglas Kenney, and Chris Miller.

"What we need right now," Otter tells his fraternity brothers, "is a stupid, futile gesture on someone's part." And no fraternity on campus—on any campus—is better qualified to provide such a gesture than the Deltas. They have the title role in National Lampoon's Animal House, which remembers all the way back to 1962, when college was simpler, beer was cheaper, and girls were harder to seduce.

The movie is vulgar, raunchy, ribald, and occasionally scatological. It is also the funniest comedy since Mel Brooks made The Producers. Animal House is funny for some of the same reasons the National Lampoon is funny (and Second City and Saturday Night Live are funny): Because it finds some kind of precarious balance between insanity and accuracy, between cheerfully wretched excess and an ability to reproduce the most revealing nuances of human behavior.

In one sense there has never been a campus like this movie's Faber University, which was apparently founded by the lead pencil tycoon and has as its motto "Knowledge is Good." In another sense, Faber University is a microcosm of . . . I was going to say our society, but why get serious? Let someone else discuss the symbolism of Bluto's ability to crush a beer can against his forehead.

Bluto is, of course, the most animalistic of the Deltas. He's played by John Belushi, and the performance is all the more remarkable because Bluto has hardly any dialogue. He isn't a talker; he's an event. His best scenes are played in silence (as when he lasciviously scales a ladder to peek at a sorority pillow fight).

Bluto and his brothers are engaged in a holding action against civilization. They are in favor of beer, women, song, motorcycles, Playboy centerfolds, and making rude noises. They are opposed to studying, serious thought, the Dean, the regulations governing fraternities, and, most especially, the disgusting behavior of the Omegas—a house so respectable it has even given an ROTC commander to the world.

The movie was written by National Lampoon contributors (including Harold Ramis, who was in Second City at the same time Belushi was), and was directed by John Landis. It's like an end run around Hollywood's traditional notions of comedy. It's anarchic, messy, and filled with energy. It assaults us. Part of the movie's impact comes from its sheer level of manic energy: When beer kegs and Hell's Angels come bursting through the windows of the Delta House, the anarchy is infectious. But the movie's better made (and better acted) than we might at first realize. It takes skill to create this sort of comic pitch, and the movie's filled with characters that are sketched a little more absorbingly than they had to be, and acted with perception.

For example: Tim Matheson, as Otter, the ladies' man, achieves a kind of grace in his obsession. John Vernon, as the Dean of Students, has a blue-eyed, rulebook hatefulness that's inspired. Verna Bloom, as his dipsomaniacal wife, has just the right balance of cynicism and desperation. Donald Sutherland, a paranoic early sixties pothead, nods solemnly at sophomoric truisms and admits he's as bored by Milton as everyone else. And stalking through everything is Bluto, almost a natural force: He lusts, he thirsts, he consumes cafeterias full of food, and he pours an entire fifth of Jack Daniel's into his mouth, belches, and observes, "Thanks. I needed that."

He has, as I suggested, little dialogue. But it is telling. When the Delta House is kicked off campus and the Deltas are thrown out of school, he makes, in a moment of silence, a philosophical observation: "Seven years down the drain." What the situation requires, of course, is a stupid, futile gesture on someone's part.

National Lampoon's Christmas Vacation ★ ★
PG-13, 102 m., 1989

Chevy Chase (Clark Griswold), Beverly D'Angelo (Ellen Griswold), Johnny Galecki (Rusty), Juliette Lewis (Audrey), Randy Quaid (Cousin Eddie), Miriam Flynn (Eddie's wife), William Hickey (Uncle Lewis), Mae Questel (Aunt Bethany), E.G. Marshall (Art), Doris Roberts (Francis), John Randolph (Clark Sr.), Diane Ladd (Nora). Directed by Jeremiah S. Chechik and produced by John Hughes and Tom Jacobson. Screenplay by Hughes.

In the course of the three National Lampoon vacation movies, Clark Griswold has become an emblem for all that is sweetest and most ineffectual in the Hollywood husband. What he wishes for his family most desperately is that they have a good time. All he is able to deliver is chaos and hair-raising misadventures. His wife is at least loving and grateful, but his two children are thoroughly weary of his schemes and have lost all faith in his ability to deliver on his promises.

National Lampoon's Christmas Vacation, the third in the series, rings a small change on the formula. Instead of the Griswolds going on vacation, their relatives take vacations to visit them, and by Christmas Eve the Griswold household is vibrating with the pent-up anxieties and resentments of two sets of in-laws, a thoroughly wacko uncle and aunt, and a hillbilly cousin who seems to have traveled in his camper directly from Dogpatch.

None of these people are particularly good examples of the Christmas spirit. And the Griswsold children have grown sullen and ill-tempered, especially when Clark tries to enlist them in such projects as decorating the home with 125,000 light bulbs. Everything that can possibly go wrong will, of course, and that includes Griswold locking himself in the attic, falling off the roof, and being assaulted by the hillbilly cousin's ravenous hound.

There are long stretches in *National Lampoon's Christmas Vacation* when this almost works. The movie is curious in how close it comes to delivering on its material: Sequence after sequence seems to contain all the necessary material to be well on the way toward a payoff, and then it somehow doesn't work.

Chevy Chase, playing Clark Griswold once again, is lovable and dogged in his determination to provide an ideal Christmas for his family. Beverly D'Angelo, that sunny and underrated screen comedienne, is a loving wife. And Randy Quaid does what he can with the thankless role of Cousin Eddie, whose secret is that he and the family are actually living in that crappy old motor home, a shack on wheels, and don't have a dime to spend on Christmas. All of these actors do what they can, but the rhythm and pacing of the movie doesn't help them much.

I was disappointed, too, in how little was done with two sets of in-laws and the weirdo uncle and aunt. Maybe because there are simply too many characters for one movie, the in-laws are handled almost as a tour group to be shunted around in the backgrounds of shot after shot or lined up as a quartet to react to Clark's dilemmas. The in-laws are supposed to hate each other, but not much is done with this, and indeed they hardly emerge as individuals.

That's not the case with the peculiar old Uncle Lewis (William Hickey) and Aunt Bethany (Mae Questel), who are gothic caricatures. Hickey, best remembered as the Mafia godfather in *Prizzi's Honor*, has fun acting both benignly and malevolently peculiar, and Questel (Woody Allen's mother in *New York Stories*) is his match in every way.

And yet the parts don't fit. Maybe the movie's problem is with the director, Jeremiah S. Chechik, a first-timer at feature length, although he has won awards for his TV commercials. The screenplay was written by John Hughes, whose *Planes, Trains and Automobiles* was a masterful comedy about two travelers trying to find their way home for Thanksgiving. But with the Griswold saga, Hughes seems to set up sequences that Chechik isn't able to make pay off. You have the odd sensation, watching the movie, that it's straining to get off the ground but simply doesn't have the juice.

The Natural ★ ★
PG, 134 m., 1984

Robert Redford (Roy Hobbs), Robert Duvall (Max Mercy), Glenn Close (Iris Gaines), Kim Basinger (Memo Paris), Wilford Brimley (Pop Fisher), Barbara Hershey (Harriet Bird), Robert Prosky (The Judge), Richard Farnsworth (Red Blow). Directed by Barry Levinson and produced by Mark Johnson. Screenplay by Roger Towne and Phil Dusenberry.

Why didn't they make a baseball picture? Why did *The Natural* have to be turned into idolatry on behalf of Robert Redford? Why did a perfectly good story, filled with interesting people, have to be made into one man's ascension to the godlike, especially when no effort is made to give that ascension meaning? And were the most important people in the god-man's life kept mostly offscreen so they wouldn't upstage him?

Let's begin at the end of *The Natural*. Redford plays Roy Hobbs, a middle-aged ballplayer making his comeback. It's the last out of the last inning of the crucial play-off game, and everything depends on him. He's been in a slump. Can his childhood sweetheart, Iris Gaines (Glenn Close), snap him out of it? She sends him a note revealing that her child is his son. The fact that he has not already figured this out is incredible. But he is inspired by the revelation. He steps to the plate. He has been having some trouble with his stomach. Some trouble, all right. A stain of blood spreads on his baseball shirt. It's a pretty badly bleeding stomach when it bleeds right through the skin. Roy swats a homer that hits the lights, and they all explode into fireworks, showering fiery stars upon him as he makes the rounds. In the epilogue, Roy plays catch with Iris and their son—a son who has not been allowed a single onscreen word—and a woman whose role has been to sit in the stands, wreathed in ethereal light, and inspire him.

Come on, give us a break. The last shot is cheap and phony. Either he hits the homer and then dies, or his bleeding was just a false alarm. If the bleeding was a false alarm, then everything else in the movie was false, too. But I guess that doesn't matter, because *The Natural* gives every sign of a story that's been seriously meddled with. Redford has been placed so firmly in the foreground that the prime consideration is to show him in a noble light. The people in his life—baseball players, mistresses, gamblers, crooks, sportswriters—seem grateful to share the frame with him. In case we miss the point, Redford is consistently backlit to turn his golden hair into a saintly halo.

The Natural could have been a decent movie. One reason that it is not: Of all its characters, the only one we don't want to know more about is Roy Hobbs. I'd love to get to know Pop Fisher (Wilford Brimley), the cynical, old team manager. Robert Duvall, as the evil sportswriter, Max Mercy, has had his part cut so badly that we only know he's evil because he practically tells us. Richard Farnsworth, as a kindly coach, has a smile that's more genuine than anything else in the movie. But you have to look quick. And what's with Glenn Close? She's the childhood sweetheart who doesn't hear from Roy after an accident changes the course of his life. Then she turns up years later, and when she stands up in the bleachers she is surrounded by blinding light: "Our Lady of Extra Innings." In the few moments she's allowed alone with Roy, she strikes us as complicated, tender, and forgiving. But even the crucial fact of her life—that she has borne this man's son—is used as a plot gimmick. If *The Natural* were about human beings and not a demigod, Glenn Close and Robert Redford would have spoken together, in the same room, using real words, about their child. Not in this movie.

As for the baseball, the movie isn't even subtle. When a team is losing, it makes Little League errors. When it's winning, the hits are so accurate they even smash the bad guy's windows. There's not a second of real baseball strategy in the whole film. The message is: Baseball is purely and simply a matter of divine intervention. At about the 130-minute mark, I got the idea that God's only begotten son was playing right field for the New York team.

Navy Seals ★ ¹/₂
R, 113 m., 1990

Charlie Sheen (Hawkins), Michael Biehn (Curran), Joanne Whalley-Kilmer (Claire), Rick Rossovich (Leary), Cyril O'Reilly (Rexer), Bill Paxton (Dane), Dennis Haysbert (Graham), S. Epatha Merkerson (Jolena). Directed by Lewis Teague and produced by Brenda Feigen and Bernard Williams. Screenplay by Chuck Pfarrer and Gary Goldman.

Navy Seals is a throwback to that golden age of action movies in which six or seven guys could win the war. The same six or seven guys. Despite the fact that dozens or even hundreds or maybe thousands of men have been trained to do what these guys do, the Navy keeps on sending the same guys back again and again, mission after mission, from one end of the movie to another.

The movie tells the story of a tightly knit group of "Seals"—it's an acronym for Sea, Air, or Land—whose mission is to stage covert operations in the Middle East. Their method is almost always the same. They parachute into the water near their objective, or reach it by inflatable rubber rafts, and then they swim ashore, sneak through dark streets, and kill a lot of Arabs. They do this on four separate missions during the movie, which fails to answer one key question: Since every Seal mission is conducted while the guys are dripping wet, why don't they stand out more in a crowd, and why don't they ever catch cold?

The movie stars Charlie Sheen and Michael Biehn as Hawkins and Curran, lieutenants who are the co-leaders of the team, and the cast includes Dennis Haysbert as Graham, a marksman whose fiancée Jolena

(S. Epatha Merkerson) violates the No. 1 role of all war movies: Never, ever, say anything to tempt fate, because fate is most easily tempted. As the movie opens, Graham and Jolena are halfway down the aisle at their wedding ceremony when the beepers go off and the entire Seal team—the groom included—have to race out of the church and report for a secret mission. Jolena never does get married, but is steadfast in her love for Graham, and they have one of those tender love scenes that experienced watchers of war movies will instantly decode: It means they'll never see each other alive again.

The Seal missions are all more or less similar in movie terms, although the screenplay tries to tell them apart. They involve infiltrating Middle Eastern seaports in search of hostages, terrorist hideouts, and caches of stolen ground-to-air missiles. In some of their missions the Seals are assisted by intelligence provided by a half-Lebanese TV reporter (Joanne Whalley-Kilmer), who possesses secret information but has her ethical standards. ("I won't volunteer any information," she tells Curran. "But ask me what you want to know.")

The missions have a sameness about them. The Seals are all equipped with tiny radio transmitters so they can talk to each other at all times. This is an aid to the audience in scenes where we're not sure what's going on: By explaining the action to each other, the Seals explain it to us. Most of the raids involve sneaking up on Arab guards and killing them, although sometimes the Seals are surprised by guards who sneak up on them. All of the Arabs in the movie share the same puzzling tendency to talk first and shoot later. Even though they have the drop on the Seals they always shout out something, giving the Seals time to turn around and shoot them.

Although this movie was apparently shot with the cooperation of the Navy (still flush with the enlistments inspired by *Top Gun*), the Seals looked to me like a band of impulsive hotheads. The Sheen character is especially undisciplined, always looking for action, and he gets one of his pals killed by forcing a gunfight that wasn't necessary. But in other scenes the Seals blunder through the night, shoot what are presumably innocent civilians, get lost, allow terrorists and missiles to slip through their grasp, and create what in a more realistic movie would be a series of international incidents.

No matter. This is not a movie about Seals

or about politics. It is a movie about explosions and machine gun fire, lots and lots of both. You want to see cars exploding? Buildings going up in flames? Guys getting shot and falling off of high buildings? Guys with beards being shot by guys in camouflage? *Navy Seals* is the movie for you. I was about to evoke the name of John Wayne to help me describe the picture, but that wouldn't be fair. Even Wayne would have wanted a rewrite to add a few more IQ points to the mixture.

Neighbors ★ ★ ★
R, 90 m., 1981

John Belushi (Earl Keese), Kathryn Walker (Enid Keese), Cathy Moriarty (Ramona), Dan Aykroyd (Vic). Directed by John G. Avildsen and produced by Richard D. Zanuck and David Brown. Screenplay by Larry Gelbart.

If there's one quality that middle-class Americans have in common, it's a tendency to be rigidly polite in the face of absolutely unacceptable behavior. Confronted with obnoxious rudeness, we freeze up, we get a nervous little smile, we allow our eyes to focus on the middle distance, and we cannot believe this is happening to us. It's part of our desire to avoid a scene. We'd rather choke to death in a restaurant than break a plate to attract attention. *Neighbors* is about one such man, Earl Keese (John Belushi). He is a pleasant, low-key dumpling of a fellow. He lives an uneventful life with an uneventful wife (Kathryn Walker). Then the neighbors move in, and there goes the neighborhood. They are everything we dread in neighbors. They are loud. They are blatant freeloaders. The man (Dan Aykroyd) is gung-ho macho. The woman (Cathy Moriarty, from *Raging Bull*) is oversexed and underloved. They park some kind of customized truck on their front lawn. They invite themselves to dinner.

There are compensations. For example, the woman seems to be a nymphomaniac. That would be more of a compensation for Earl if he were not terrified of aggressive women. Earl has not the slightest notion of how to deal with these next-door maniacs, and his wife's no help: She puts on her best smile and tries to handle the situation as if everyone were playing by Emily Post's rules. The story of the Keeses and their weird neighbors was first told in Thomas Berger's novel. It was obviously a launching pad for a movie, but what sort of movie? The relationships among these neighbors depend almost entirely on the chemistry of casting: For example, obnoxious Richard Benjamin could have moved in next to meek Donald Sutherland. In *Neighbors*, however, we get Belushi and Aykroyd. I think it was brilliant casting, especially since they divided the roles somewhat against our expectations. Belushi, the most animalistic animal in *Animal House*, plays the mild-mannered Keese. And Aykroyd, who often plays straight-arrows, makes the new neighbor into a loud neo-fascist with a back slap that can kill.

The movie slides easily from its opening slices of life into a suburban nightmare. We know things are strange right at the start, when Aykroyd extorts money from Belushi to get a carry-out Italian dinner, and then secretly cooks the spaghetti right in his own kitchen. Belushi sneaks out into the night to spy on Aykroyd and catches him faking it with Ragu, but is too intimidated to say anything. The whole movie goes like that, with Belushi so intimidated that he hardly protests even when he finds himself sinking into quicksand.

Meanwhile, the women are making their own strange arrangements, especially after the Keeses's college-age daughter (Lauren-Marie Taylor) comes home from school and begins attracting Moriarty's attention. The movie operates as a satire of social expectations, using polite clichés as counterpoint to deadly insults (all delivered in pleasant conversational tones).

The first hour of *Neighbors* is probably more fun than the second, if only because the plot developments come as a series of surprises. After a while, the bizarre logic of the movie becomes more predictable. But *Neighbors* is a truly interesting comedy, an offbeat experiment in hallucinatory black humor. It grows on you.

Network ★ ★ ★ ★
R, 121 m., 1976

Faye Dunaway (Diana Christenson), William Holden (Alex Schumacher), Peter Finch (Howard Beale), Robert Duvall (Frank Hackett), Wesley Addy (Nelson Chaney), Ned Beatty (Arthur Jensen). Directed by Sidney Lumet and produced by Howard Gottfried. Screenplay by Paddy Chayefsky.

There's a moment near the beginning of *Network* that has us thinking this will be the definitive indictment of national television we've been promised. A veteran anchorman has been fired because he's over the hill and drinking too much and, even worse, because his ratings have gone down. He announces his firing on his program, observes that broadcasting has been his whole life, and adds that he plans to kill himself on the air in two weeks. We cut to the control room, where the directors and technicians are obsessed with getting into the network feed on time. There are commercials that have to be fit in, the anchorman has to finish at the right moment, the buttons have to be pushed, and the station break has to be timed correctly. Everything goes fine. "Uh," says somebody, "did you hear what Howard just said?" Apparently nobody else had.

They were all consumed with form, with being sure the commercials were played in the right order and that the segment was the correct length. What was happening—that a man has lost his career and was losing his mind—passed right by. It wasn't their job to listen to Howard, just as it wasn't his job to run the control board. And what *Network* seems to be telling us is that television itself is like that: An economic process in the blind pursuit of ratings and technical precision, in which excellence is as accidental as banality.

If the whole movie had stayed with this theme, we might have had a very bitter little classic here. As it is, we have a supremely well-acted, intelligent film that tries for too much, that attacks not only television but also most of the other ills of the 1970s. We are asked to laugh at, be moved by, or get angry about such a long list of subjects: Sexism and ageism and revolutionary ripoffs and upper-middle-class anomie and capitalist exploitation and Neilsen ratings and psychics and that perennial standby, the failure to communicate. Paddy Chayefsky's script isn't a bad one, but he finally loses control of it. There's just too much he wanted to say. By the movie's end, the anchorman is obviously totally insane and is being exploited by blindly ambitious programmers on the one hand and corrupt businessmen on the other, and the scale of evil is so vast we've lost track of the human values.

And yet, still, what a rich and interesting movie this is. Lumet's direction is so taut, that maybe we don't realize that it leaves some unfinished business. It attempts to deal with a brief, cheerless love affair between Holden and Dunaway, but doesn't really allow us to understand it. It attempts to suggest that multinational corporations are the only true contemporary government, but does so in a scene that slips too broadly into satire, so that we're not sure Chayefsky means it. It deals with Holden's relationship with his wife of twenty-five years, but inconclusively.

But then there are scenes in the movie that are absolutely chilling. We watch Peter Finch cracking up on the air, and we remind ourselves that *this* isn't satire, it was a style as long ago as Jack Paar. We can believe that audiences would tune in to a news program that's half happy talk and half freak show, because audiences *are* tuning in to programs like that. We can believe in the movie's "Ecumenical Liberation Army" because nothing along those lines will amaze us after Patty Hearst. And we can believe that the Faye Dunaway character could be totally cut off from her emotional and sexual roots, could be fanatically obsessed with her job, because jobs as competitive as hers almost require that. Twenty-five years ago, this movie would have seemed like a fantasy; now it's barely ahead of the facts.

So the movie's flawed. So it leaves us with loose ends and questions. That finally doesn't bother me, because what it does accomplish is done so well, is seen so sharply, is presented so unforgivingly, that *Network* will outlive a lot of tidier movies. And it won several Academy Awards, including those for Peter Finch, awarded posthumously as best actor; Chayevsky for his screenplay; Beatrice Straight, as best supporting actress; and Faye Dunaway, as best actress. Watch her closely as they're deciding what will finally have to be done about their controversial anchorman. The scene would be hard to believe—if she weren't in it.

Never Say Never Again ★ ★ ★ ½
PG, 137 m., 1983

Sean Connery (James Bond), Klaus Maria Brandauer (Largo), Max von Sydow (Blofeld), Barbara Carrera (Fatima Blush), Kim Basinger (Domino), Bernie Casey (Felix Leiter). Directed by Irwin Kershner and produced by Jack Schwartzman. Screenplay by Lorenzo Semple, Jr.

Ah, yes, James, it is good to have you back again. It is good to see the way you smile from under lowered eyebrows, and the way you bark commands in a sudden emergency, and it is good to see the way you look at women. Other secret agents may undress women with their eyes. You are more gallant. You undress them, and then thoughtfully dress them again. You are a rogue with the instincts of a gentleman.

It has been several years since Sean Connery hung it up as James Bond, several years since *Diamonds Are Forever*, and Connery's announcement that he would "never again" play special agent 007. What complex instincts caused him to have one more fling at the role, I cannot guess. Perhaps it was one morning in front of the mirror, as he pulled in his gut and reflected that he was in pretty damn fine shape for a man over fifty. And then, with a bow in the direction of his friend Roger Moore, who has made his own niche as a different kind of Bond, Sean Connery went back on assignment again.

The movie is called *Never Say Never Again*. The title has nothing to do with the movie—except why Connery made it—but never mind, nothing in this movie has much to do with anything else. It's another one of those Bond plots in which the basic ingredients are thrown together more or less in fancy. We begin with a threat (SPECTRE has stolen two nuclear missiles and is holding the world at ransom). We continue with Bond, his newest gadgets, his mission briefing. We meet the beautiful women who will figure in the plot (Barbara Carrera as terrorist Fatima Blush; Kim Basinger as the innocent mistress of the evil Largo). We meet the villains (Max von Sydow as Blofeld; Klaus Maria Brandauer as Largo). We visit exotic locations, we survive near-misses, and Bond spars with the evil woman and redeems the good one. All basic.

What makes *Never Say Never Again* more fun than most of the Bonds is more complex than that. For one thing, there's more of a human element in the movie, and it comes from Klaus Maria Brandauer, as Largo. Brandauer is a wonderful actor, and he chooses not to play the villain as a cliché. Instead, he brings a certain poignancy and charm to Largo, and since Connery always has been a particularly human James Bond, the emotional stakes are more convincing this time.

Sean Connery says he'll never make another James Bond movie, and maybe I believe him. But the fact that he made this one, so many years later, is one of those small show-business miracles. There was never a Beatles reunion. Bob Dylan and Joan Baez don't appear on the same stage anymore. But

here, by God, is Sean Connery as Sir James Bond. Good work, 007.

The Neverending Story ★ ★ ★
PG, 94 m., 1984

Barret Oliver (Bastian), Noah Hathaway (Atreyu), Tami Stronach (Empress), Moses Gunn (Cairon). Directed by Wolfgang Petersen and produced by Bernd Eichinger and Dieter Geissler. Screenplay by Petersen and Herman Weigel.

How's this for a threat? The kingdom of Fantasia is about to be wiped out, and the enemy isn't an evil wizard or a thermonuclear device, it's Nothingness. That's right, an inexorable wave of Nothingness is sweeping over the kingdom, destroying everything in its path. Were children's movies this nihilistic in the old days?

The only thing standing between Fantasia and Nothingness is the faith of a small boy named Bastian (Barret Oliver). He discovers the kingdom in a magical bookstore, and as he begins to read the adventure between the covers, it becomes so real that the people in the story know about Bastian. How could that be? Well, that's the very first question Bastian asks. This is a modern kid with quite a healthy amount of skepticism, but what can he do when he turns the page and the Child Empress (Tami Stronach) is begging him to give her a name so that Fantasia can be saved?

The idea of the story within a story is one of the nice touches in *The Neverending Story*. Another one is the idea of a child's faith being able to change the course of fate. Maybe not since the kids in the audience were asked to save Tinker Bell in *Peter Pan* has the outcome of a story been left so clearly up to a child's willingness to believe. There is a lot we have to believe in *The Neverending Story*, and that's the other great strength of this movie. It contains some of the more inventive special-effects work of a time when battles in outer space, etc., have grown routine. Look for example, at *The Last Starfighter*, where the special effects are competent but never original—all the visual concepts are ripped off from *Star Wars*—and then look at this movie, where an entirely new world has been created.

The world of Fantasia contains creatures inspired by Alice in Wonderland (a little man atop a racing snail), the Muppets (a cute dragon-dog that can fly), and probably B.C.

(a giant made of stone, who snacks on quartz and rumbles around on his granite tricycle). Many of the special effects involve sophisticated use of Muppet-like creatures (there are scenes that reminded me of *The Dark Crystal*). They are, in a way, more convincing than animation, because they exist in three dimensions and have the same depth as their human co-stars. And that illusion, in turn, helps reinforce the more conventional effects like animation, back projection, and so on. The world of this movie looks like a very particular place, and the art direction involved a lot of imagination. The movie's director, Wolfgang Petersen, is accustomed to creating worlds in small places; his last film, *Das Boot (The Boat)*, took place almost entirely within a submarine.

Within the world of Fantasia, a young hero (Noah Hathaway) is assigned to complete a hazardous quest, sneak past the dreaded portals of some stone amazons, and reach the Ivory Tower, where he will receive further instructions from the empress. In most movies, this quest would be told in a straightforward way, without the surrounding story about the other little boy who is reading the book. But *The Neverending Story* is *about* the unfolding of a story, and so the framing device of the kid hidden in his school attic, breathlessly turning the pages, is interesting. It lets kids know that the story isn't just somehow happening, that storytelling is a neverending act of the imagination.

New Jack City ★ ★ ★ ½
R, 97 m., 1991

Wesley Snipes (Nino Brown), Ice-T (Scotty Appleton), Chris Rock (Pookie), Judd Nelson (Nick Peretti), Mario Van Peebles (Detective Stone). Directed by Mario Van Peebles and produced by Doug McHenry and George Jackson. Screenplay by Thomas Lee Wright and Barry Michael Cooper.

There is a moment in *New Jack City* when Nino Brown, a character who has made millions by selling cocaine to poor blacks, relaxes in his suburban mansion. He has his own screening room and is viewing *Scarface*, the Al Pacino movie about a drug lord. Nino brags to his girlfriend that he will never make the mistakes the guy made in the movie—but as he stands in front of the screen, the image of Scarface's dead body is projected across his own.

In another movie, this moment might look

like simple cinematic tricksmanship. In *New Jack City*, it has a special impact, because this ambitious film aims to be a similar record of the rise and fall of a big drug business. The movie is being advertised (no doubt wisely) as a slam-bang action adventure, but in fact it's a serious, smart film with an impact that lingers after the lights go up.

The story involves the career of Nino (Wesley Snipes), a smart man with a certain genius for organization, as he ruthlessly takes over a Harlem apartment building and makes it the distribution headquarters for his cocaine business. He picks his lieutenants carefully, goes to elaborate lengths to enforce security, makes a lot of money, and seems invulnerable. He also surrounds himself with opulence and beauty. As played by Snipes, he has the threatening charisma of a great screen villain.

I've seen a lot of movies where the lifestyle of the drug lord looks seductive—until he's killed in the last reel, of course—but this isn't one of them. It's a character study of a bad man running an evil business, and by the end even his mistress is telling the cops she'll testify against him. The movie isn't a comic book that's been assembled out of the spare parts from other crime movies; it's an original, in-depth look at this world, written and directed with concern—apparently after a lot of research and inside information.

Against the clever Nino, the movie arrays some hard-edged street cops: Scotty (Ice-T) and Nick (Judd Nelson). They don't like each other, which is par for the formula, but the movie makes their rivalry intense and personal. Scotty is a genuinely interesting character, a cop who has been through cocaine himself and knows not only about addiction but about recovery. Nick is crazy and irresponsible, often on suspension, filled with hatred for drug dealers.

The buildup of the cop plot is done well, but is fairly standard stuff. What isn't standard is the payoff, as Nick rescues a young addict named Pookie (Chris Rock), who is so strung out on cocaine he can hardly lift his head. He gets the kid into a rehab center, lectures him on Narcotics Anonymous, and supports him through several NA meetings and a long recovery process. When Pookie is clean and sober, he wants to help the cop who helped him. Scotty has doubts, but reluctantly agrees to let Pookie infiltrate the crack house as an undercover spy.

This whole section of the movie takes on genuine urgency. That's partly because of

the performances (Ice-T and Chris Rock are effortlessly authentic and convincing), but also because of the direction by Mario Van Peebles and the screenplay by Thomas Lee Wright and Barry Michael Cooper. There is no sense that this movie wants to play it safe, to coast, to be a retread of all the other movies about cops and drugs. And Van Peebles takes chances to give his film an authentic and gritty feel: He shoots on location, he uses a lot of street slang, he allows his cast to sound like their street characters and not like guys from a TV cop show. This is the movie where he comes of age as a director.

The movie's ending involves the usual chase and shoot-out material, but it's more effective than usual, maybe because by then we know the characters and care about them, so their actions are not simply moves from an arcade game. By the end of the film, we have a painful but true portrait of the impact of drugs on this segment of the black community: We see how they're sold, how they're used, how they destroy, what they do to people.

Truffaut once said it was impossible to make an antiwar movie, because the war sequences would inevitably be exciting and get the audience involved on one side or the other. It is almost as difficult to make an antidrug movie, since the lifestyle and money of the drug dealers looks like fun, at least until they're killed. This movie pulls off that tricky achievement. Nino, who looks at the dead body of Scarface and laughs, does not get the last laugh.

New York, New York ★ ★ ★
PG, 163 m., 1977

Liza Minnelli (Francine Evans), Robert De Niro (Jimmy Doyle), Lionel Stander (Tony Harwell), Barry Primus (Paul Wilson), Mary Kay Place (Berenice), Georgie Auld (Frankie Harte). Directed by Martin Scorsese and produced by Irwin Winkler and Robert Chartoff. Screenplay by Earl Mac Rauch and Mardik Martin.

Martin Scorsese's *New York, New York* never pulls itself together into a coherent whole, but if we forgive the movie its confusions we're left with a good time. In other words: Abandon your expectations of an orderly plot, and you'll end up humming the title song. The movie's a vast, rambling, nostalgic expedition back into the big band era,

and a celebration of the considerable talents of Liza Minnelli and Robert De Niro.

She plays a sweet kid with a big voice who starts as a band vocalist and ends up as a movie star. He plays an immature, aggressive, very talented saxophone player whose social life centers around the saloon fights. A generation before Punk Rock, here's Punk Swing. They get married for reasons the movie never makes quite clear (oh, they're in love, all right, but he's so weird it's a miracle she'll have him). And then their marriage starts to disintegrate for reasons well hallowed in show-biz biographies: Her success, his insecurity, his drinking, their child.

De Niro comes on as certifiably loony from the start, and some of the movie's best scenes are counterpoint between his clowning and her rather touching acceptance of it. Maybe because he's really shy underneath, he likes to overact in social situations. He's egotistical, self-centered, inconsiderate, and all sorts of other things she should leave him because of, and there are times when the Minnelli character is so heroically patient that it's gotta be love. The movie doesn't really explore the nuances of their personalities, though; the characters are seen mostly by their surfaces, and they inhabit a cheerfully phony Hollywood back-lot New York. Scorsese, who knows how to shoot New York in California so it looks real (see *Mean Streets*), is going for a frankly movie feel with his sets and decors, and especially with his colors, which tend toward lurid rotogravure.

The look is right for the movie's musical scenes, and there are a lot of them: We start with a loving re-creation of V-J Day, with Tommy Dorsey's orchestra playing all the obligatory standards and De Niro trying with desperate zeal to pick up Minnelli. And then maybe half of the movie from then on will be music, mostly very good music (the movie's new songs deserve comparison with the old standards), and wonderfully performed. That Liza Minnelli has not been making an annual musical for the last decade is our loss; she's hauntingly good and so much more, well, human than Barbra Streisand.

It's a good thing the movie inhabits a familiar genre, though, because the fact that we've seen dozens of other musical biographies helps us fill in the gaps in this one. And there are a lot of them; the movie originally came in at something like four hours, and the cuts necessary to get it down to a more commercial length are responsible for a lot of confusion. The confusions, as I've suggested, can be forgiven because the movie has so many good things in it. And in the video version, to make amends, they've put back two musical numbers that weren't seen in the theater. But the ending is still puzzling. We've seen De Niro, totally unable to deal with the fact that he's become a father, tearfully (and amusingly) end their marriage right there in the maternity ward. Six years pass, there are Liza's great final production numbers, and then they have a backstage reunion after her night of triumph. Great, we're thinking, we've been here before, we relish the obligatory romantic reunion scene in the dressing room. But, no, he leaves. Then he calls her from a pay phone: He can't stand the people she's with, but would she like to sneak out, meet by the stage door, eat some Chinese food, and talk about themselves? Sure, she would. He waits outside the door. She approaches it from inside, pauses, sees no one there, and goes back to her dressing room. End of movie (with a nicely evocative night street scene). But did she change her mind and *decide* not to go out and meet him, or did she expect him to be waiting *inside* the door—and assume the cocky S.O.B. had stood her up again? This particular confusion is hard to forgive.

So the movie's flawed. It's not Scorsese's best work, or De Niro's (there are scenes in which his personality quirks and bizarre behavior make him seem uncannily like his Travis Bickle in Scorsese's *Taxi Driver*). Liza Minnelli's musical numbers are wondrous, as I've said, but the movie doesn't provide her with a character as fully understood as *Cabaret* did. So I guess we go to *New York, New York* to enjoy the good parts, and spend just a moment regretting the absence of a whole.

New York Stories
PG, 130 m., 1989

Produced by Jack Rollins and Charles H. Joffe.

Life Lessons ★ ★ ★ 1/2

Nick Nolte (Lionel Dobie), Rosanna Arquette (Paulette), Patrick O'Neal (Philip Fowler). Directed by Martin Scorsese and produced by Barbara DeFina from a screenplay by Richard Price.

Life Without Zoe ★ 1/2

Heather McComb (Zoe), Talia Shire (Charlotte), Giancarlo Giannini (Claudio), Don Novello (Hector the Butler). Directed by Francis Coppola from a screenplay by himself and Sofia Coppola. Produced by Fred Roos and Fred Fuchs.

Oedipus Wrecks ★ ★

Woody Allen (Sheldon), Mae Questel (Mother), Mia Farrow (Lisa), Marvin Chatinover (Psychiatrist). Directed by Woody Allen and produced by Robert Greenhut. Screenplay by Allen.

New York Stories is an anthology—a gathering of short films by Martin Scorsese, Francis Coppola, and Woody Allen, all three taking New York City as a backdrop, although the Scorsese and Allen films could have been set in many big cities. Anthologies were popular in the 1940s (*Trio, Quartet*) and in the 1960s (*Boccacio 70, Yesterday, Today and Tomorrow*), but have fallen on hard times recently, perhaps because, in an age of megaproductions, the movie industry is not interested in short stories.

Of the three films, the only really successful one is *Life Lessons*, the Scorsese story of a middle-aged painter and his young, discontented girlfriend. The Coppola, an updated version of the story of Eloise, the little girl who lived in the Plaza Hotel, is surprisingly thin and unfocused. And the Allen, about a fifty-year-old man still dominated by his mother, starts well but then takes a wrong turn about halfway through.

Although Scorsese's film begins before the director is identified, there's not a moment's doubt whose work it is. His restless nature is obvious from the first shots; Nestor Almendros's camera moves almost unceasingly throughout the film, and most of the cuts are on movement, so that we rarely get the feeling that there is anything still and contented in the soul of his hero.

This is a man named Lionel Dobie (Nick Nolte), a large, shaggy painter who works in a loft, weaving back and forth in front of his canvas like a boxer, painting to very loud rock & roll. He uses a garbage-can lid as a palate, and there is a voluptuous scene in which the camera follows his brush back and forth from paint to canvas. Dobie lives with a twenty-two-year-old woman (Rosanna Arquette), whose bedroom is perched on a balcony below the ceiling. She wants to leave

him, and in the long reaches of the night he looks up sometimes at her bedroom window like a middle-aged Romeo who has lost his Juliet.

Dobie is verbally clever but emotionally uncertain. In his attempts to keep the woman, he flatters her, makes promises of reform, explains that he can help her career, says he needs her. She has some canvasses of her own around the studio—anemic, unfocused, skeletal figures on muddy backgrounds—and she wants to know if she will ever be any good. But the one compromise Lionel Dobie cannot bring himself to make is to lie about the quality of a painting.

The film moves easily in the New York art world of dealers and openings, seeing and being seen. The girl has a crush on a young "performance artist," and Dobie takes her to his show, which consists of bad stand-up comedy and flashing searchlights in an abandoned subway station. Dobie's gesture is intended to show he understands her, but in fact he has contempt for the performer ("You sing, you dance, you act—what's performance art?"). And the girl, uncertain what she wants but certain that she must escape his smothering possessiveness, drifts away.

Life Lessons seems the longest of these short films because it has the greatest density, the most to say. It is not about love. It is about how the girl is first attracted by Dobie's power, then grows restless because there is no role in it for her, except as cheerleader and sex trophy. It is about how Dobie really does have deep loneliness and need, but that it does not require *this* woman to satisfy them; he is so needy, any woman will do. The movie never steps wrong until the final scene, which Scorsese continues for just a few lines too many. Dobie sees another young woman at a party. She admires him. His eyes light up. The scene could have ended there; everything else is where we came in.

Francis Coppola's *Life Without Zoe*, the middle of the three stories, stars Heather McComb as Zoe, a precocious little rich girl who lives in the Sherry-Netherland Hotel and attends a private school where her classmates include not only the richest boy in the world, but several of the runners-up. Zoe's father (Giancarlo Giannini) is a famous classical flautist, and her mother (Talia Shire) is in the fashion industry. Neither one is at home much, and Zoe's best friend is the hotel butler (Don Novello, in the most engaging performance in the movie).

Coppola's film is set in the present day, but treats New York as if this were still the 1940s, and spoiled little girls in expensive dresses could move easily around the city under the benevolent eyes of doormen and cops. The plot involves some silliness about a missing diamond earring and a birthday party for the rich boy, and Zoe's indifferent mother ends up as her closest friend, although the movie never explains how or why. The entire sketch seems without purpose, unless it is to show off the elaborate costumes and settings; nothing holds together on an emotional or plot level.

Woody Allen's *Oedipus Wrecks* is his first pure comedy since *Broadway Danny Rose* (1984), which will please those who don't like his serious films, but it is also his weakest film of any sort. The movie stars Allen as a fifty-year-old banker whose tiny, inalienable mother (Mae Questel) still dominates his life, embarrassing him by showing his baby pictures to strangers and turning up unannounced at his office.

The banker is engaged to a divorcée with three children (Mia Farrow), and this his mother doesn't understand. One day, under circumstances it would be unfair to reveal, the mother disappears (this disappearance, I might add, is a true comic inspiration—the high point of the film). The banker is at first troubled by her disappearance, but later learns that he can live with it. It's not as if she got sick or died. She just . . . disappeared.

The movie goes wrong, I think, from the moment the mother returns (once again, I will not reveal the details). If you see the film, ask yourself this question: Knowing what you know of New York, could this mother re-appear in this way and be received as the film shows her being received? Allen's mistake, I think, was to avoid dealing with the actual consequences that would result from such a startling manifestation. The last half of the film seems more odd and off-balance than funny. Perhaps it would have been better to build more satire into the mother's re-appearance, perhaps by having her come back like one of those miraculous holy images people are always seeing in screen doors, snowbanks, and the stains on their refrigerator doors.

9¹/₂ Weeks ★ ★ ★ ¹/₂
R, 113 m., 1985

Kim Basinger (Elizabeth), Mickey Rourke (John). Directed by Adrian Lyne and

produced by Anthony Rufus Isaacs and Zalman King. Screenplay by Patricia Knop, King, and Sarah Kernochan.

9¹/₂ Weeks arrived in a shroud of mystery and scandal, already notorious as the most explicitly sexual big-budget movie since *Last Tango in Paris*. I went expecting erotic brinksmanship (how far *will* its famous stars go in the name of their art?) and came away surprised by how thoughtful the movie is, how clearly it sees exactly what really happens between its characters.

That's not to say the movie isn't sexy. I suppose a project of this sort depends crucially on the chemistry between its actors, and Kim Basinger and Mickey Rourke develop an erotic tension in this movie that is convincing, complicated, and sensual.

In the film, they play strangers who meet one day in a Chinese grocery store in Manhattan—Elizabeth, the smart, pretty assistant in a Soho art gallery, and John, the smiling, enigmatic currency trader. Their first meeting is crucial to the entire film, and it is a quiet masterpiece of implication. She waits by a counter. Senses someone is standing behind her. Turns, and meets his eyes. He smiles. She turns away. Is obviously surprised by how much power was in their exchange of glances. She hesitates, turns back, meets his eyes again, almost boldly, and then turns away again. And a few minutes later looks at him very curiously as he walks away along the street.

They meet again, of course, and that is the beginning of their relationship, as chronicled first in a best-selling novel and now in this movie by Adrian Lyne, the director of *Flashdance*. It is clear from the start that they aren't going to follow an orthodox pattern of courtship and romance. He offers her, quite boldly, an experimental erotic relationship. The first time he touches her seriously, it is to tie a blindfold around her eyes. They advance into arenas of lovemaking often described in the letters column in *Penthouse* magazine, and Elizabeth, for the most part, is prepared to let John call all the shots. He wants to be in control, and as she surrenders to him, she abandons herself into dreamy erotic absent-mindedness.

John is nothing if not inventive. In one scene, he blindfolds her and feeds her all kinds of strange foods, sweet and sour, different textures, each one a surprise to her lips, and it's astonishing the way the movie makes this visual scene so tactile. John calls

her at unexpected times, orders her to unorthodox rendezvous, and as she follows his instructions they both seem to retreat more deeply into their obsession.

The movie contrasts their private life with the everyday world of her work: With the small talk and gossip of the art gallery, with a visit she pays to an old artist who lives like a hermit in the woods, with the intrigue as her ex-husband dates another woman in the gallery. This everyday material is an interesting strategy: It makes it clear that the private life of Elizabeth and John is a conscious game they're playing outside of the real world, and not just a fantasy in a movie where reality has been placed on hold.

Eventually, it is Elizabeth's hold on the real world that redeems the movie—makes it more than just a soft-core escapade—and sets up the thoughtful and surprising conclusion. So long as it is understood that she and John are engaged in a form of a game, and are conspiring in a sort of master-slave relationship for their mutual entertainment, Elizabeth has no serious objections. But as some of John's games grow more challenging to her own self-respect, she rebels. Does he want to engage her mind and body in an erotic sport, or does he really want to edge her closer to self-debasement? There are two times that Elizabeth draws the line, and a third time when she chooses her own independence and self-respect over what begins to look like his sickness.

That's what makes the movie fascinating: Not that it shows these two people entering a bizarre sexual relationship, but because it shows the woman deciding for herself what she will, and will not, agree to. At the end of *9¹/₂ Weeks*, there is an argument, not for sexual liberation, but for sexual responsibility.

I have a few problems with certain scenes in the film. There is a moment when John and Elizabeth run through the midnight streets of a dangerous area of Manhattan, chased by hostile people, and finally take refuge in a passageway where they make love in the rain. The scene owes more to improbable gymnastic events than to the actual capabilities of the human body.

There is another scene in which John and Elizabeth go into a harness shop, and John selects and purchases a whip, while the shop employees do double takes and Elizabeth stands wide-eyed, while he whooshes it through the air. There is no subsequent scene in which the whip is used. I do not argue that there should be; I only argue that in a movie like this, to buy a whip and not use it is like Camille coughing in the first reel and not dying in the last.

Any story like *9½ Weeks* risks becoming very ridiculous. The actors are taking a chance in appearing in it. Plots like this make audiences nervous, and if the movie doesn't walk a fine line between the plausible and the bizarre, it will only find the absurd. A lot of the success of *9½ Weeks* is because Rourke and Basinger made the characters and their relationship convincing.

Rourke's strategy is to never tell us too much. He cloaks himself in mystery, partly for her fascination, partly because his whole approach depends on his remaining a stranger. Basinger's strategy is equally effective, and more complicated. Physically, she looks sensuous and luscious; if you saw her in *Fool for Love*, you won't be surprised by the force of her appearance here. But if she'd just presented herself as the delectable object of all of these experiments, this would have been a modeling job, not an acting job.

In the early scenes, while she's at work in the gallery, she does a wonderful job of seeming distracted by this new relationship; her eyes cloud over and her attention strays. But one of the fascinations of the movie is the way her personality gradually emerges and finds strength, so that the ending of the film belongs completely to her.

The Hitcher, is also about a sadomasochistic relationship between a stronger personality and a weaker one. Because it lacks the honesty to declare what it is really about, and because it romanticizes the cruel acts of its characters, it left me feeling only disgust and disquiet. *9½ Weeks* is not only a better film, but a more humanistic one, in which it is argued that sexual experimentation is one thing, but the real human personality is something else, something incomparably deeper and more valuable—and more erotic.

1984 ★ ★ ★ ½
R, 117 m., 1984

John Hurt (Winston Smith), Richard Burton (O'Brien), Suzanna Hamilton (Julia), Cyril Cusack (Charrington), Gregor Fisher (Parsons). Directed by Michael Radford and produced by Simon Perry. Screenplay by Radford.

George Orwell made no secret of the fact that his novel *1984* was not really about the future but about the very time he wrote it in, the bleak years after World War II when England shivered in poverty and hunger. In a novel where passion is depicted as a crime, the greatest passion is expressed, not for sex, but for contraband strawberry jam, coffee, and chocolate. What Orwell feared, when he wrote his novel in 1948, was that Hitlerism, Stalinism, centralism, and conformity would catch hold and turn the world into a totalitarian prison camp. It is hard, looking around the globe, to say that he was altogether wrong.

Michael Radford's brilliant film of Orwell's vision does a good job of finding that line between the "future" world of 1984 and the grim postwar world in which Orwell wrote. The movie's 1984 is like a year arrived at through a time warp, an alternative reality that looks constructed out of old radio tubes and smashed office furniture. There is not a single prop in this movie that you couldn't buy in a junkyard, and yet the visual result is uncanny: Orwell's hero, Winston Smith, lives in a world of grim and crushing inhumanity, of bombed factories, bug-infested bedrooms, and citizens desperate for the most simple pleasures.

The film opens with Smith rewriting history: His task is to change obsolete government documents so that they reflect current reality. He methodically scratches out old headlines, obliterates the photographs of newly made "unpersons," and attends mass rallies at which the worship of Big Brother alternates with numbing reports of the endless world war that is still going on somewhere, involving somebody. Into Smith's world comes a girl, Julia, who slips him a note of stunning force. The note says, "I love you." Smith and Julia become revolutionaries by making love, walking in the countryside, and eating strawberry jam. Then Smith is summoned to the office of O'Brien, a high official of the "inner party," who seems to be a revolutionary too, and gives him the banned writings of an enemy of the state.

This story is, of course, well known. *1984* must be one of the most widely read novels of our time. What is remarkable about the movie is how completely it satisfied my feelings about the book; the movie looks, feels, and almost tastes and smells like Orwell's bleak and angry vision. John Hurt, with his scrawny body and lined and weary face, makes the perfect Winston Smith; and Richard Burton, looking so old and weary in this film that it is little wonder he died soon after finishing it, is the immensely cynical O'Brien, who feels close to people only while he is torturing them. Suzanna Hamilton is Julia, a fierce little war orphan whose rebellion is basically inspired by her hungers.

Radford's style in the movie is an interesting experiment. Like Chaplin in *Modern Times,* he uses passages of dialogue that are not meant to be understood—nonsense words and phrases, garbled as they are transmitted over Big Brother's primitive TV, and yet listened to no more or less urgently than the messages that say something. The 1954 film version of Orwell's novel turned it into a cautionary, simplistic science-fiction tale. This version penetrates much more deeply into the novel's heart of darkness.

Night of the Living Dead ★
R, 96 m., 1990

Tony Todd (Ben), Patricia Tallman (Barbara), Tom Towles (Harry), McKee Anderson (Helen), William Butler (Tom), Katie Finneran (Judy Rose). Directed by Tom Savini and produced by John A. Russo and Russ Streiner. Screenplay by George A. Romero.

In 1968 George Romero made a scruffy little low-budget horror film named *Night of the Living Dead,* and it was truly frightening. That was in the days before the MPAA rating system, and I saw it at a Saturday matinee filled with little kids who were so scared they were screaming and weeping. I noted their reaction in my review—I believed, then and now, that some films are simply not appropriate for children—but, at the same time, I had to admire the artistry of Romero's film. With grainy black and white photography, a handful of locations, and a cast of unknowns, he created a horrifyingly original vision that has been ripped off ever since—not least by Romero himself.

The "living dead" in the movie were ghouls who lurched about the landscape, their bodies decaying, their eyes blank, attempting to feed on human flesh. They had been dead, but their motor impulses and animal needs had somehow brought them back to a sickening parody of life, and now the only way to kill them was to destroy their brains. In the original film, the ghouls presided over a long night of terror, attacking seven normal people barricaded inside a farmhouse.

The creatures attacked again in Romero's *Dawn of the Dead* (1979), which was a superb horror film, and in his *Day of the Dead* (1985), which was not. Now they are back in a remake of the original film, which has been written by Romero but directed by Tom Savini, his longtime makeup expert. The remake is so close to the original that there is no reason to see both, unless you want to prove to yourself that black and white photography is indeed more effective than color for this material.

The film once again has a band of people barricaded inside a farmhouse. They desperately and endlessly nail boards, doorways, and tabletops across the windows; people spend more time hammering in this movie than doing anything else. The heroine (Patricia Tallman) is soon joined by the hero (Tony Todd), and then by a frightened young couple (William Butler and Katie Finneran). Eventually it's revealed that three more people are hiding in the cellar: a deranged husband (Tom Towles), his wife (McKee Anderson), and their unconscious daughter, who has been bitten by ghouls.

The discovery of the people in the basement leads to the movie's longest-running nonevent, a bitter fight between Towles and the others about whether they should all hide out in the basement or stay upstairs. Todd says no to the basement. Towles says yes, frothing at the mouth. They scream at each other in confrontations in which the overacting is so ludicrous it gets bad laughs. Towles is an actor who can indeed be chilling; he is unforgettable playing Ottis, the mass murderer's slack-jawed friend, in *Henry: Portrait of a Serial Killer*. But here, like all of the other actors, he is wasted on a film that confuses screaming with emotion.

Thanks for small gifts: I am grateful that Tallman's character eventually figures out something that has been abundantly obvious ever since the first *Living Dead* movie. The ghouls are very stupid and very slow. "You could just walk right past them!" she observes, looking out of the farmhouse. And so she does, for a while, until she is intercepted by a band of redneck hunters who are killing ghouls for sport. The ending of the movie, with its bonfire and tortured freeze-frame scenes, is apparently intended to suggest that we are really no better than the ghouls, a conclusion which, even based on the evidence of the characters in this movie, I have trouble in accepting.

Nine to Five ★ ★ ★
PG, 111 m., 1980

Jane Fonda (Judy Bernly), Lily Tomlin (Violet Newstead), Dolly Parton (Doralee Rhodes), Dabney Coleman (Franklin Hart, Jr.), Sterling Hayden (Tinsworthy), Elizabeth Wilson (Roz). Directed by Colin Higgins and produced by Bruce Gilbert. Screenplay by Higgins and Patricia Resnick.

Nine to Five is a good-hearted, simple-minded comedy that will win a place in film history, I suspect, primarily because it contains the movie debut of Dolly Parton. She is a natural-born movie star, a performer who holds our attention so easily that it's hard to believe it's her first film. The movie has some funny moments, and then it has some major ingredients that don't work, including some of its fantasy sequences. But then it also has Dolly Parton. And she contains so much energy, so much life and unstudied natural exuberance that watching her do anything in this movie is a pleasure. Because there have been so many Dolly Parton jokes (and doubtless will be so many more), I had better say that I'm not referring to her sex appeal or chest measurements. Indeed, she hardly seems to exist as a sexual being in the movie. She exists on another plane, as Monroe did: She is a center of life on the screen.

But excuse me for a moment while I regain my composure. *Nine to Five* itself is pleasant entertainment, and I liked it, despite its uneven qualities and a plot that's almost too preposterous for the material. The movie exists in the tradition of 1940s screwball comedies. It's about improbable events happening to people who are comic caricatures of their types, and, like those forties movies, it also has a dash of social commentary. The message has to do with women's liberation and, specifically, with the role of women in large corporate offices. Jane Fonda, Lily Tomlin, and Dolly Parton all work in the same office. Tomlin is the efficient office manager. Fonda is the newcomer, trying out her first job after a divorce. Parton is the boss's secretary, and everybody in the office thinks she's having an affair with the boss. So the other women won't speak to her.

The villain is the boss himself. Played by Dabney Coleman, he's a self-righteous prig with a great and sincere lust for Dolly Parton. She's having none of it. After the movie introduces a few social issues (day care, staggered work hours, equal pay, merit promo-

tion), the movie develops into a bizarre plot to kidnap Coleman in an attempt to win equal rights. He winds up swinging from the ceiling of his bedroom, attached by wires to a garage-door opener. Serves him right, the M.C.P. This whole kidnapping sequence moves so far toward unrestrained farce that it damages the movie's marginally plausible opening scenes. But perhaps we don't really care. We learn right away that this is deliberately a lightweight film, despite its superstructure of social significance. And, making the necessary concessions, we simply enjoy it.

What I enjoyed most, as you have already guessed, was Dolly Parton. Is she an actress? Yes, definitely, I'd say, although I am not at all sure how wide a range of roles she might be able to play. She's perfect for this one—which was, of course, custom-made for her. But watch her in the scenes where she's not speaking, where the action is elsewhere. She's always in character, always reacting, always generating so much energy we expect her to fly apart. There's a scene on a hospital bench, for example, where Tomlin is convinced she's poisoned the boss, and Fonda is consoling her. Watch Dolly. She's bouncing in and out, irrepressibly. What is involved here is probably something other than "acting." It has to do with what Bernard Shaw called the "life force," that dynamo of energy that some people seem to possess so bountifully. Dolly Parton simply seems to be having a great time, ready to sweep everyone else up in her enthusiasm, her concern, her energy. It's some show.

No Man's Land ★ ★ ★
R, 107 m., 1987

D.B. Sweeney (Benjy Taylor), Charlie Sheen (Ted Varrick), Lara Harris (Ann Varrick), Randy Quaid (Lieutenant Bracey), Bill Duke (Malcolm), R.D. Call (Frank Martin), Arlen Dean Snyder (Lieutenant Loos), M. Emmet Walsh (Captain Haun). Directed by Peter Werner and produced by Joseph Stern and Dick Wolf. Screenplay by Wolf.

The lieutenant wants the new patrolman to do undercover work for a couple of reasons: The kid knows all about Porsches, and he's so new on the force that he doesn't act like a cop. There are two things the lieutenant doesn't take into account: The kid really loves Porsches, and he doesn't think like a cop. By the end of *No Man's Land*, those two items have gotten everybody into a lot of trouble.

The young cop, played by D.B. Sweeney, is a fresh-faced rookie who spends all of his free time rebuilding old cars. The lieutenant wants him to infiltrate a Porsche dealership run by a rich kid (Charlie Sheen). The dealership seems to be a front for a car-theft and chop-shop operation, and the previous cop who infiltrated it has been murdered. The lieutenant is convinced that Sheen pulled the trigger.

Sweeney gets the job after he passes a couple of tests; he proves he knows all about repairing Porsches, and during a fast trip down the hairpin turns in the hills above Los Angeles, he proves to Sheen that he can drive one, too. You'd think that Sheen would be on the alert for another undercover cop, having just discovered one, but he trusts Sweeney and before long the two men have become friends.

It's a complicated friendship. Sweeney, from a working-class background, is impressed by Sheen's style and wealth, by the fancy discos and private clubs he hangs out in, and by the expensive cars he lets Sweeney drive. He is also impressed by Sheen's sister (Lara Harris), and after they fall in love, he becomes convinced that there's no way Sheen could have murdered a cop.

Randy Quaid, as the lieutenant, worries that his undercover guy is falling for a con job. "You're not going native, are you?" he asks. He's right; the kid hasn't been on the force long enough to develop good police instincts, and he falls under the influence of the charismatic Sheen. That leads him into a no man's land, halfway between the criminals and the law, and as he tries to do the right thing and juggle his conflicting loyalties, a tragic situation begins to develop.

No Man's Land is better than the average thriller because it is interested in these moral questions—in the way that money and beautiful women and fast cars look more exciting than good police work. The screenplay, by Dick Wolf, is subtle in the way it develops its temptations for Sweeney. He is seduced by Sheen's style and flash. And Sheen creates his character as a very complicated young man. True, he's rich, and doesn't need to steal and kill. But like the members of that Billionaire Boys' Club out in L.A., he is attracted to risk. And eventually he gets way in over his head.

The climax of the movie is fascinating in the way it uses a *really* corrupt cop to create a situation in which the two friends are faced with the consequences of their actions. By the end of the film, Sweeney and Sheen both possess all the facts, and in a way, they both understand all the facts. They think there must be a way they can work this thing out. But maybe there isn't. Like the *film noir* thrillers of the 1940s, *No Man's Land* is about ordinary people with flawed characters, who fall to temptation and pay for it.

The performances are very good, by Sheen (who played the narrator in *Platoon*), and especially by Sweeney, who at first seems lost in his role, until we realize that's the character he's playing. The director is Peter Werner, who creates a real sense of materialistic subculture in which $60,000 automobiles are the proof of personal worth (offered a chance to steal another expensive import, Sheen scornfully says, "I only steal Porsches"). The movie has lots of scenes of Sheen and Sweeney stealing cars, and it dwells on the details of their crimes, and the reckless way they risk capture. This is a movie about how money and excitement generate a seduction that can change personal values; it's better and deeper than you might expect.

No Mercy ★ ★ ★
R, 107 m., 1986

Richard Gere (Eddie Jillette), Kim Basinger (Michel Duval), Jeroen Krabbe (Losado), George Dzundza (Stemkowski), Joe Basaraba (Collins), William Atherton (Deneneux). Directed by Richard Pearce and produced by D. Constantine Conte. Screenplay by Jim Carabatsos.

I could go two ways. I could say that *No Mercy* is a dumb formula thriller, or I could go the other way, and talk about the movie's style and energy. I think I'll go the second way, because whatever this movie is, it's not boring. It doesn't take shortcuts and it delivers on its grimy, breathless action sequences.

The plot has the footprints of other movies all over it: A cop's partner is murdered. A beautiful blonde is involved. The cop follows the blonde to New Orleans, and discovers she belongs to a sleazy vice boss. He tries to arrest her, they become handcuffed to one another, he loses the key, the villain's goons try to kill them, and they escape into the bayou country with nothing more than her torn blouse standing between them and the alligators. Meanwhile, they're falling in love. So what do you want for six bucks?

It's easy to make fun of the plot, but what's a plot for? In a thriller like *No Mercy*, it exists for one simple reason, to provide the characters with something to do while they attempt to make themselves interesting. And the really remarkable thing about this movie is the genuine chemistry that is generated, not only between Richard Gere and Kim Basinger, who are on either end of the handcuffs, but also between both of them and the movie's two principal bad guys: An effete rich Southerner played by William Atherton, and a sadistic neo-Nazi vice lord, played by the Dutch actor Jeroen Krabbe.

Thrillers are often only as good as their villains. The Krabbe character seems seriously confused about time and place; I never understood what he was doing in the bayou with his Dr. Strangelove act, and I don't think his redneck followers did, either. But he makes a very satisfactory villain, especially after we learn that the Basinger character was heartlessly sold to him when she was only a child, and has been his slave ever since.

The Richard Gere character figures this out only belatedly. At first he thinks she's another one of this guy's hookers, used to lure his partner to his doom. But there is nothing like being handcuffed to Kim Basinger in the middle of a swamp to concentrate the mind, and eventually he can see that she is a victim. His realization comes at a delicately handled, understated turning point; he learns, almost by accident, that she has never learned to read, and we can see in his eyes that this touches him.

Gere is interesting all through the movie. As it happened, I'd just seen him again in *American Gigolo* a few days before I saw *No Mercy*, and so at first I was cross-referencing his standard mannerisms, like that way he struts across the screen. Then he sold me on the character, and I stopped thinking about Richard Gere and started caring about what was going to happen next.

With Basinger, that process was even easier. Although she fits all of the usual requirements for a movie sexpot, there is within her the genuine soul of an artist, and she throws herself into this role so convincingly that there is real pathos in her history. There is enough conviction in their relationship that it carries over even into the obligatory bloodbath that ends the film, and I found myself caring about them even while on another level I was running an inventory on the special effects.

The movie's climax, a shoot-out in a flophouse across the river from New Orleans, is an anthology of action clichés and a few fresher touches, such as the villain's ability to ram through walls. It's always a shame when a movie bothers to create interesting characters and then discards them in a high-tech climax. But up until then, *No Mercy* has been an above-average *film noir* and its creepy feeling for the backstreets of New Orleans and the sultry evil of its red-light suburbs got under my skin.

No Way Out ★ ★ ★ ★
R, 114 m., 1987

Kevin Costner (Tom Farrell), Gene Hackman (David Brice), Sean Young (Susan Atwell), Will Patton (Scott Pritchard), Howard Duff (Senator Duvall), George Dzundza (Sam Hesselman), Jason Bernard (Major Donovan), Iman (Nina Beka). Directed by Roger Donaldson and produced by Laura Ziskin and Robert Garland. Screenplay by Garland.

No Way Out is one of those thrillers like *Jagged Edge*, where the plot gives us a great deal of information, but the more we know, the less we understand. It's like a terrifying jigsaw puzzle. And because the story is so tightly wound and the performances are so good, I found myself really caring about the characters. That's the test of a good thriller: When you stop thinking about the mechanics of the plot and start caring about the people. The movie begins with the same basic situation that was always one of Alfred Hitchcock's favorites: An innocent man stands wrongly accused of a crime, and all the evidence seems to point right back to him. In *No Way Out*, there are a couple of neat twists. One is when the innocent man is placed in charge of the investigation of the crime.

The man is played by Kevin Costner in a performance I found a lot more complex and interesting than his work in *The Untouchables*. He plays a career Navy man who is assigned to the personal staff of the secretary of defense (Gene Hackman). Hackman and his devoted assistant (Will Patton) want Costner to handle some sensitive assignments for them involving the secretary's pet defense projects.

All of those details are handled in the first few minutes, and after the movie springs a

genuine erotic surprise. Costner goes to a diplomatic reception to meet Hackman. There is a beautiful young woman at the party. Their eyes meet. The chemistry is right. They leave almost immediately, and the woman throws herself at Costner in hungry passion.

They have an affair. The woman (Sean Young) is friendly, but mysterious, and eventually Costner finds out why: She is also Hackman's mistress. And that leads to the night when Hackman attacks her in a jealous rage, and she dies. Because Costner saw Hackman going into her apartment as he was leaving, he knows who committed the crime. But there are reasons why he cannot say what he knows. And then Patton determines to mastermind a cover-up and enlists Costner.

At about this point you may be thinking I have revealed too much of the plot. I haven't. *No Way Out* is truly labyrinthine and ingenious. The director, Roger Donaldson, sometimes uses two or three suspense-building devices at the same time, such as when a search of the Pentagon coincides with Costner's attempt to obtain evidence against Hackman, and the slow progress of a computer that may, or may not, enhance a photograph that could hang Costner.

A lot of what goes on in the film is psychological and not merely plot-driven. For example, there's the interesting performance of Patton, who says early on that he would willingly sacrifice his life for Hackman and who is later revealed to have more than one reason for his devotion. There's another good performance by George Dzundza (*The Deer Hunter*) as the wheelchair-bound Pentagon computer expert, trying to be a nice guy without ever really understanding what he's in the middle of.

The movie contains some of the ingredients I have declared myself tired of in recent thrillers, including a couple of chases. But here the chases do not exist simply on their own accord; they grow out of the logic of the plot. And as the plot moves on it grows more and more complex, until a final twist that some people will think is simply gratuitous but that does fit in with the overall logic.

Movies such as this are very hard to make. For proof, look at the wreckage of dozens of unsuccessful thrillers every year. *No Way Out* is a superior example of the genre, a film in which a simple situation grows more and more complex until it turns into a nightmare not only for the hero but also for everyone associated with him. At the same time, it

respects the audience's intelligence, gives us a great deal of information, trusts us to put it together, and makes the intellectual analysis of the situation one of the movie's great pleasures.

Norma Rae ★ ★ ★
PG, 114 m., 1979

Sally Field (Norma Rae), Ron Leibman (Reuben), Beau Bridges (Sonny), Pat Hingle (Father), Barbara Baxley (Mother), Gail Strickland (Bonnie). Directed by Martin Ritt and produced by Tamara Asseyev and Alex Rose. Screenplay by Irving Ravetch and Harriet Frank, Jr.

We're sometimes unfair to our movie actresses, and Sally Field's extraordinary performance in *Norma Rae* helps dramatize it. Most new actresses come up through television and its lame-brained sexist stereotyping. And most of the female TV stars have their moment of glory and then become unfairly categorized in our memories. Be honest: Didn't we think of Sally Field as the Flying Nun before this Oscar-winning performance?

For any actress, an opportunity to star on TV has to be great. But the opportunity to escape TV and appear in a challenging movie has to be a godsend. Jill Clayburgh got her chance with *An Unmarried Woman*. Here it's Sally Field's turn. And as the plain-spoken, spunky Southern textile worker in Martin Ritt's *Norma Rae*, she quite simply surpassed our expectations.

The performance is at the heart of the movie, because this isn't a film about labor unions or mill working conditions; it's about a woman of thirty-one learning to grow into her own potential.

She has a couple of kids—one out of wedlock, the other orphaned by a brawling father—and a few boyfriends here and there, and she's never taken much time to think about the value of her life. Like everyone in the town, she works in the textile mill, which has no union, pays minimum wages, has few benefits, and does little or nothing about brown lung disease.

Then a union organizer (Ron Leibman) from New York turns up in town. He finds precious little support, and almost none from Norma Rae; she's too absorbed in a whirlwind courtship and marriage with a local good ol' boy (Beau Bridges) who promises to bring his check home on Fridays and not chase around. She marries him, mostly out of affection and convenience.

But then the organizer begins to make a little sense to her. She grows less blind to the conditions at the mill. She gets angry when her father drops dead on an assembly line. She goes to a couple of meetings at which Leibman harangues his handful of recruits. She becomes a recruit herself, a volunteer organizer, and eventually it's taking up all of her time.

Her new husband complains—but both she and the movie tend to ignore him. The marriage, indeed, seems almost peripheral to the movie's central story, which is about the way she slowly opens her eyes to herself and her world. Leibman puts it simply: "You're too smart to do what you're doing to yourself."

She eventually agrees. And we're sort of set up for a situation where Norma Rae and the organizer fall in love with each other. But they don't; the movie is steadfast in its determination to show Norma Rae growing because of her own thought and will—not under the influence of yet another sexual liaison.

That's what makes the movie so special. It has all sorts of plot problems (especially involving the marriage), and there are scenes that don't quite fit together, and moments that don't sound right. But the character of Norma Rae is so deeply seen and realized, and played by Sally Field with such conviction, that we accept her in spite of our doubts about other things. In the tenth year of her acting career, Sally Field has made a remarkable debut.

North Dallas Forty ★ ★ ★ ½
R, 117 m., 1979

Nick Nolte (Phil Elliott), Mac Davis (Maxwell), Charles Durning (Coach Johnson), Dayle Haddon (Charlotte), Bo Svenson (Jo Bob), Steve Forrest (Conrad Hunter), G.D. Spradlin (B.A.), John Matuszak (O.W. Shaddock). Directed by Ted Kotcheff and produced by Frank Yablans. Screenplay by Yablans, Kotcheff, and Peter Gent.

North Dallas Forty is about pro football the way *Network* was about television. It's about the ways large and competitive institutions grind up people and spit them out. The guy who gets spit out in this movie is Phil Elliott, whose coach tells him he has the best hands in football, but a "bad attitude." Elliott is played by Nick Nolte in a muscular and com-

pelling performance: After this movie, people began to take Nolte seriously.

The movie is not really a sports film. It doesn't share the patented formula of the routine sports movie, in which everything depends on the bravura final match, or game, or race. The film does lead up to an important game, yes—North Dallas plays Chicago for a divisional championship—but by then we're so involved in the human drama that we almost don't care who wins.

The drama revolves around the Nolte character and his best friend, a quarterback played by Mac Davis. They play football very hard and very well. Off the field, they regard the business of football with a profound cynicism, and they assault themselves with boozing, drugs, all-night partying, and bleak thoughts about what they will do when the day comes when they finally cannot play any longer.

Characters in the movie talk, at times, about words like "play" and "game." Is professional football a game? Not according to John Matuszak, in real life an Oakland Raider, who in one of the movie's most electrifying scenes has a shouting match with a coach in the locker room. At *some* point, he screams, football for the players must be more than a business—must be a cause, a spirit. In the fourth quarter, when you're cold and hurt and exhausted, the game plan means nothing, but your desire means everything.

The North Dallas management doesn't quite see it that way. The owners and coaches are detached, scientific, quite prepared to see a player shoot up pain-killers and run the risk of permanently crippling himself. Nolte himself is prepared to do that. But the management doesn't like him. He's a wiseass. He has the wrong attitude. He's childish. Their ideal football player would be someone like the fearsome Jo Bob Priddy (Bo Svenson), who is not in fact as good a player as Nolte, but has a magnificently simpleminded "correct" attitude.

The pressures put Nolte in a vise: He loves playing, he cannot envision himself not playing, he even understands the management attitude if only they knew it. But age and wear and cynicism are closing in, and he finds himself, half astonished, in love with a woman. She represents a kind of settling down that football has given him license to avoid, and the movie uses the relationship as a counterpoint to a week of training and a climactic game.

The football scenes are brutally real; the locker room scenes are totally authentic. There are obscenities and violence and pain, and a clear view of how the "adults"—the coaches—manipulate their strong, fearsome, and intimidated employees. "*We're* not the team," Nolte shouts at the owner. "*You're* the team. We're only the equipment—like the jockstraps and the helmets."

The movie is funny at times, especially during the lecture meetings where the players, openly contemptuous, listen to such dim inspirational insights as that, if God had really meant all men to be equal, he wouldn't have called us the human "race." God, for example, clearly meant for North Dallas to be more equal than Chicago.

Those kinds of details, and the scenes of the players' agents and the parties and the practice sessions, have a convincing documentary feel. Holding it all together, making it work, forcing us to get involved, is the Nolte character. It's a tribute to this movie that we would probably care as much about Nolte if he were *not* a football player. What he's facing is common in so many parts of American society; in so many of the things we do and the jobs we have, at some ultimate level we are just simply part of somebody else's business.

Nosferatu ★ ★ ★ ★
R, 63 m., 1979

Klaus Kinski (Count Dracula), Isabelle Adjani (Lucy Harker), Bruno Ganz (Jonathan Harker). Directed, produced, and written by Werner Herzog.

Set aside for the moment the details of the Dracula story. They've lost their meaning. They've been run through a thousand vampire movies too many. It's as easy these days to play Dracula as Santa Claus. The suit comes with the job. The kids sit on your knee and you ask them what they want and this year they want blood.

Consider instead Count Dracula. He bears a terrible cross but he lives in a wonderful sphere. He comes backed by music of the masters and dresses in red and black, the colors De Sade found finally the most restful. Dracula's shame as he exchanges intimacies and elegant courtesies with you is that tonight or sometime soon he will need to drink your blood. What an embarrassing thing to know about someone else.

Werner Herzog's *Nosferatu* concerns itself with such knowledge. *Nosferatu*. A word for *the vampire.* English permits "vampire movies"—but a "nosferatu movie?" Say "vampire" and your lips must grin. The other word looks like sucking lemons. Perfect. There is nothing pleasant about Herzog's vampire, and this isn't a movie for Creature Feature fans. There are movies for people who like to yuk it up and make barfing sounds, God love 'em, while Christopher Lee lets the blood dribble down his chin, but they're not the audience for *Nosferatu.* This movie isn't even scary. It's so slow it's meditative at times, but it is the most evocative series of images centered around the idea of the vampire that I have ever seen—since F.W. Murnau's *Nosferatu,* which was made in 1922.

That is why we're wise to forget the details of the basic Dracula story. *Nosferatu* doesn't pay them heed. It is about the mood and *style* of vampirism, about the terrible seductive pity of it all. There is a beautiful passage early in the film showing the hero, Jonathan Harker, traveling from his home village to the castle of Dracula. The count has summoned him because he is considering the purchase of another home. Harker makes the journey by horse path. He enters into a high mountain pass filled with tenuous cloud layers that drift by a little too fast, as if God were sucking in his breath. The music is *not* your standard creepy Loony Tunes, but a fierce melody of exhilaration and dread. Deeper and deeper rides Harker into the cold gray flint of the peaks. Some will say this passage goes on too long and that nothing happens during it. I wish the whole movie were this empty.

Before long, we are regarding the count himself. He is played totally without ego by Klaus Kinski. The *count* has a monstrous ego, of course—it is Kinski who has none. There is never a moment when we sense this actor enjoying what a fine juicy cornpone role he has, with fangs and long sharp fingernails and a cape to swirl. No, Kinski has grown far too old inside to play Dracula like that: He makes his body and gaunt skull transparent, so the role can flicker through. Sit through *Nosferatu* twice, or three times. Cleanse yourself of the expectation that things will happen. Get with the flow. This movie works like an LP record: You can't love the music until you've heard the words so often they're sounds. It's in German with English subtitles. It would be just fine with no subtitles, dubbed into an unknown tongue. The need to know what

Dracula is saying at any given moment is a bourgeois affectation. Dracula is *always* saying, "I am speaking with you now as a meaningless courtesy in preface to the unspeakable event that we both know is going to take place between us sooner rather than later."

Not Without My Daughter ★ ★ ★
PG-13, 116 m., 1990

Sally Field (Betty), Alfred Molina (Moody), Sheila Rosenthal (Mahtob), Roshan Seth (Houssein), Sarah Badel (Nicole), Mony Rey (Ameh Bozorg), Georges Corraface (Mohsen). Directed by Brian Gilbert and produced by Harry J. Ufland and Mary Jane Ufland. Screenplay by David W. Rintels.

Here is a perplexing and frustrating film, which works with great skill to involve our emotions, while at the same time making moral and racial assertions that are deeply troubling. On one level, it tells a story that almost anyone can identify with—a mother deprived of her child and her freedom by the rigid rules of an unbending religion. On another level, it applies a harsh assortment of negative qualities to a group of people we found ourselves at war with.

The film stars Sally Field as Betty, an ordinary American mom in all respects but one—she has married an Iranian who is a doctor at the local hospital. They have a young daughter and a settled middle-class life, but beneath the surface all is not well. Her husband, Moody (Alfred Molina) suffers from racist taunts at the hospital, and grows homesick when he telephones to his family back in Iran. Finally, he suggests a visit to his homeland.

Betty is not so sure. She reads about unrest in Iran. She is not sure of her welcome. Moody promises her—on the Koran—that she has nothing to fear. But soon after they land in Iran, she is plunged into a frightening and alien world. As a woman, she is an occasion of sin. It is forbidden for her to reveal so much as a lock of hair in public. The other members of her husband's family make little effort to communicate with her—other than to give orders or repeat religious truths. They are interested in her only as the mother of her husband's child; her role, it appears, is to be the infidel mother of an Islamic daughter.

At first Moody is supportive. But as the time draws near for their return to America, he undergoes a personality change, becom-

ing angry and short with her, and finally admitting that they are not going back at all. He has lost his job at the hospital, and plans to stay in Iran. And as for Betty and their daughter? Why, they will stay, too. She is his wife and must obey him.

The movie then plunges us into a world of Islamic fundamentalism, which it depicts in shrill terms as one of men who beat their wives, of a religion that honors women by depriving them of what in the West would be considered basic human rights, of women who are willing or unwilling captives of their men. No attempt is made—deliberately, I assume—to explain the Muslim point of view, except in rigid sets of commands and rote statements. No Muslim character is painted in a favorable light; the local people who help the heroine are dissidents or outlaws. We are not even permitted to learn what they say, because the film declines to use subtitles to translate the considerable spoken dialogue of the Iranian characters. All is seen from the point of view of Betty, who is shown surrounded by harsh, cruel religious fanatics.

Islam is not a religion that reflects Western beliefs about human dignity. It seems to have little place for the concept of individual freedom—especially as it applies to women. The chilling death sentence pronounced against Salman Rushdie is an example of its regard for free speech, and Rushdie's attempts at compromise, as the price of buying his life, are understandable even while they are inutterably depressing. Yet, at the same time, we should stubbornly believe in a concept of fair play—even fair play for those who might not play fair with us. And *Not Without My Daughter* does not play fair with its Muslim characters. If a movie of such a vitriolic and spiteful nature were to be made in America about any other ethnic group, it would be denounced as racist and prejudiced. It is no excuse that some Muslims are our enemies. In a world that does not reflect our ideals, we must hold to them for ourselves.

Yet I recommend that the film be seen for two reasons. One reason is because of the undeniable dramatic strength of its structure and performances; it is impossible not to identify with this mother and her daughter, and Field is very effective as a brave, resourceful woman who is determined to free herself and her daughter from involuntary captivity.

The second reason is harder to explain. I think the movie should be seen because it is an invitation to thought. It can be viewed as simply a one-sided and bitter attack. But it also provides an opportunity for testing our own prejudices, our own sense of fairness. Must all movies be taken on their own terms, or do we retain the strength of mind to view them critically—to remain alert to prejudice and single-minded vitriol?

It is curious, in a way, that this movie is set in Iran. At the time its events take place— and at the time the film was made—Iran was our enemy and Iraq was our ally. Now times have changed, and Saddam Hussein, our so recent friend, is our enemy. Think of the box office possibilities if the movie had been set in Iraq! That would be right in keeping with the long sad human history of portraying enemies as godless, inhuman devils. But every soldier is somebody's child, and some, no doubt, hope to have children of their own, and movies fueled by hate are not part of the solution.

Nuns on the Run ★
PG-13, 92 m., 1990

Eric Idle (Brian Hope), Robbie Coltrane (Charlie McManus), Camille Coduri (Faith), Janet Suzman (Sister Superior), Doris Hare (Sister Mary of the Sacred Heart), Lila Kaye (Sister Mary of the Annunciation), Robert Patterson ("Case" Casey), Robert Morgan (Abbott). Directed by Jonathan Lynn and produced by Michael White. Screenplay by Lynn.

Why do filmmakers so often insist that nuns are funny? I'll bet there are some psychological reasons buried around here somewhere. Catholics who had unhappy experiences with nuns in school may be getting their revenge. Those who are not Catholic may be reacting to the universal tendency to think that other people's ceremonial costumes are hilarious. And a few people may be just plain frightened of nuns; making fun of them is their way of whistling in the dark.

If any of these psychological profiles fit, you may possibly find small moments of *Nuns on the Run* that are amusing. Your laughter may reveal more about you than about this particularly dreary film. I myself went to a Catholic school for eight years and had good experiences with a group of nuns who were dedicated teachers and kind women. I am not saying that in order to get all worked up and indignant about *Nuns on the Run*. I simply place it on the table as a fact and a possible explanation for why I found the movie inexplicable.

The film stars Eric Idle, of Monty Python, and Robbie Coltrane, of the British TV comedy troupe The Comic Strip, as a couple of gangsters who lose their taste for the trade. "In the old days, it wasn't like this," Idle complains after a bloody bank robbery. They didn't carry guns, nobody got hurt, everybody was happy. Now crime is more violent and they are older, and they want out. Unfortunately, their boss won't let them out. He's played by Robert Patterson, in a lean, scary performance, as the kind of criminal who has only two kinds of associates: current and dead.

During a shoot-out with a gang of Chinese drug czars, Idle and Coltrane fall into the possession of a large amount of money. Killers from both sides are in hot pursuit, so they dodge into a convent, slip into nuns' habits, and try to pass themselves off as sisters. And now we are into the movie's principal running gag, involving life behind the scenes in a nunnery.

We meet the cool Sister Superior (Janet Suzman) and the drunken sister who is an accountant (Lila Kaye) and the old curmudgeon (Doris Hare), and there is a subplot involving a waitress (Camille Coduri) who falls in love with Idle and ends up in the nuns' hospital, but never mind, you'll be too busy ticking off the other obligatory scenes, such as the alcoholic nun hiding a bottle in her habit or the shower scene with lots of young, nubile nuns running around naked. And, of course, there are jokes involving funny nun names.

The problem here is that very little of the material is intrinsically funny. It's funny only if you find nuns funny, or if the subject somehow seems daring or forbidden to you. The movie has the air of a gang of adolescent boys who think they're getting away with something—writing nasty words on the blackboard when sister's out of the room.

Watching *Nuns on the Run*, I had a fantasy. In my fantasy, the movie's first screening is over and the lights go up, and before the filmmakers can leave the room, Sister Superior comes in and says, "I want to know who did this." And nobody answers. And then she says that she has all day and that we're all going to sit right here in our seats until she gets the answer to her question. And finally Eric Idle breaks down and points to Robbie Coltrane and says, "He did, sister!" And Coltrane breaks into tears and says, "No, he did!" And then sister says she hopes that whoever did it has made a sincere act of contrition.

Nuts ★ ★
R, 115 m., 1987

Barbra Streisand (Claudia Draper), Richard Dreyfuss (Aaron Levinsky), Maureen Stapleton (Rose Kirk). Karl Malden (Arthur Kirk), Eli Wallach (Dr. Morrison), Robert Webber (Francis MacMillan), James Whitmore (Judge Murdoch). Directed by Martin Ritt and produced by Barbra Streisand. Screenplay by Tom Topor, Darryl Ponicsan, and Alvin Sargent.

If you were to meet this woman on the street, you wouldn't have much doubt she was nuts. She has that look in her eye, the one that suggests she can be reasonable one minute and lash out wildly the next. She is so filled with anger that the specific targets hardly matter; the whole world is her target.

Barbra Streisand does a good job of projecting that crazed wildness during the opening scenes of *Nuts*, but the problem is, the movie doesn't know where to go with it. This is not a movie like *One Flew Over the Cuckoo's Nest*, in which madness is seen as an antidote for regimentation. It aims lower, and accomplishes less. It's a courtroom drama, with all the conventional thrusts and parries of the legal system, and because the structure of the movie is so timid, Streisand's madness threatens to overwhelm it.

She plays a hooker who came from a conventional upper-middle-class home. We see her parents in the courtroom every day, and they're conventional, all right: They're played by Karl Malden and Maureen Stapleton as the picture of intelligent concern. Streisand has been charged with the death of one of her clients, and her parents are in league with a psychiatrist (Eli Wallach) who thinks she should be committed "for her own good."

What Streisand knows is that she's likely to spend more time locked up in a psychiatric ward than in jail. She claims she's innocent— she killed in self-defense—but even if she's found guilty, at least she will be given a finite sentence with definite provisions. If she's found incompetent to stand trial by reason of insanity, she could be put away indefinitely. And so she fights for the right to be tried.

Her parents hire an expensive lawyer, but she assaults him and he leaves the case. Then she gets a public defender (Richard Drey-fuss), and treats him with hostility until she sees that he's on her side. The judge (James Whitmore) moves the sanity hearing into a closed courtroom, which is the scene of one earth-shaking revelation after another, none of which really surprise us.

We sort of know, don't we, that because the character is a hooker and yet is played by Barbra Streisand, she will turn out to be good at heart. We know she may have killed her customer, but there had to be more to the story than that. And we have a pretty good hunch that Malden and Stapleton have more complicated stories than it would first appear. All of these hunches pan out. But the movie's revelations are told in such dreary, cliché, weather-beaten old movie terms that we hardly care.

The director, Martin Ritt, is not at the top of his form with this material. He uses the old gimmick of the Gradually Expanding Flashback. That's when we see just a flash of a past event, and then we see a little more, and eventually we see the whole event. Two different bathroom sequences are revealed in this way—one involving the Streisand character as a little girl, the other involving her bloody encounter with her victim.

Wouldn't you know that the childhood experiences are a perfect prediction of the night of murder? Isn't it almost inevitable that Malden, a stepfather, is also a child-molester? Doesn't Malden's $20 bill, slipped under the bathroom door, neatly foreshadow the way the john wants to pay her to take a bath? If all of psychiatry had been this simple, Freud wouldn't have been needed to devise it; the Brothers Grimm would have done.

As the courtroom drama slogs its weary way home, Streisand's authentic performance as a madwoman seems harder and harder to sustain. All the forces of do-good pop self-help are arrayed against her, pushing her character to become a reasonable, sweet, tragic victim. The problem is, the movie's opening scenes have been so wild and so unrestrained that the sanity hearing draws a wild card: It is quite possible, after all, that although this character was molested as a child, and although she killed in self-defense, she is *nevertheless* insane. *Nuts* is essentially just a futile exercise in courtroom clichés, surrounding a good performance that doesn't fit.

O

The Object of Beauty ★ ★ ★ ½
R, 97 m., 1991

John Malkovich (Jake), Andie MacDowell (Tina), Lolita Davidovich (Joan), Rudi Davies (Jenny), Joss Ackland (Mr. Mercer), Peter Riegert (Larry). Directed by Michael Lindsay-Hogg and produced by Jon S. Denny. Screenplay by Lindsay-Hogg.

Hiding from the hotel manager, slinking through the lobby like a hunted criminal, this is a man with a problem. His name is Jake and he lives in that world where money is made with money, but right now there is no money in his world. He put most of his funds into a cocoa deal in some Third World country where a revolution has stranded his cocoa on the docks and himself in a London hotel where he owes thousands of pounds and has not the slightest prospect of being able to pay.

Jake is played by John Malkovich as a man who maintains a cool, detached façade, no matter what. He lives with Tina (Andie MacDowell), an elegant beauty who once, briefly, was a model, and has now cast her lot with Jake, although they "are not, in the classic sense, man and wife," as they are careful to explain. For that matter, they do not, in the classic sense, live anywhere in particular; life for them has been an existence of drifting from one expensive hotel and city to another, while Jake does his business on the phone.

Now it has come down to this: Presenting an American Express card in a restaurant and then making the sign of the cross while the cashier checks the credit. Or taking the stairs rather than the elevator to avoid the hotel manager and his unctuous security chief. They literally do not have a dime. They want to be rich and famous, but in this hotel they are famous for not being rich. They have one asset to their name: A small

bronze head, sculpted by Henry Moore, that might be worth $50,000 or so. It is Tina's, given to her by her first husband (to whom she is still, in the classic sense, married).

Working in the hotel is a maid (Rudi Davies), who is deaf, and who lives in a basement hovel with her young brother, a loutish punk. She falls in love with the Moore figure because it speaks to her. One day, she slips it into her pocket. Meanwhile, in desperation, Jake has suggested to Tina that they sell the Moore to raise cash. "But I love my little head!" she pouts, and so they decide on an insurance scam to "steal" it and collect the money—only to discover that someone has gotten in ahead of them and already stolen it.

The Object of Beauty, which has been quietly, intelligently written and directed by Michael Lindsay-Hogg, is only about these financial problems on a surface level. What's underneath is really the ability of these people to learn to love and trust one another. The movie is too cool and witty to descend to obviously sloppy emotion, but in Jake and Tina we see two hedonistic drifters who have finally been forced to take stock of who they really are, separately and as a couple.

Jake is played by Malkovich as a man who would really rather die than be embarrassed in public, and who places so much trust in the way money protects him that when he runs out, he gallantly offers Tina her freedom. He can understand why she would want him for better but not for worse. And he would rather set her free than ask her to stand by him. We are given a brief but completely revealing glimpse into his character during a brief telephone call he makes to his parents—an alcoholic mother and a father he still calls "sir"—and in an instant we understand that he has been denied both affection and respect by his parents, and would do anything rather than admit inadequacy.

By the end of the film, the plot has been worked out to everyone's satisfaction, but the plot isn't really that important. What is important are the ways that people love one another—not only Jake and Tina, but the maid and her brother, and even the hotel manager and the security chief. And we meet two other important characters: Tina's first husband (Peter Riegert), who does not seem to have suffered very much upon losing her, and her best friend Joan (Lolita Davidovich), whom she should not, in the classic sense, trust.

Like a John Cheever short story or a sociological snapshot by Tom Wolfe, *The Object of Beauty* is about people who have been so defined by their lifestyles that without those styles they scarcely exist. Jake and Tina are not really married, do not really live anywhere, do not really work at anything. This whole episode is a blessing in disguise for them: They are, at last, really something, even if it is only broke.

Off Beat ★ ★ ★ ½
PG, 93 m., 1986

Judge Reinhold (Joe Gower), Meg Tilly (Rachel Wareham), Cleavant Derricks (Abe Washington), Joe Mantegna (Pete Peterson), Jacques D'Amboise (August), Amy Wright (Mary Ellen), John Turturro (Pepper), Harvey Keitel (Bank Robber), Julie Bovasso (Mrs. Wareham). Directed by Michael Dinner and produced by Joe Roth and Harry Ufland. Screenplay by Mark Medoff.

It's been a long time since I've found the characters in a comedy as sympathetic as they are in *Off Beat*. So many recent American comedies seem to hate their heroes, to want to make fun of them, but here is a movie about sweet, likable people who get into a funny situation and watch it grow funnier the more they try to escape from it. *Off Beat* is a movie with a sharp edge and more than a little hostility, but the overall feeling is sort of warm and romantic.

It's about this librarian named Joe (Judge Reinhold) who is going nowhere with his life. He puts on his roller skates and rolls back and forth in the stacks of the New York Public Library, feeding a conveyor belt with books for people he never sees. His promotion is blocked by the hateful Mr. Pepper (John Turturro), who is a Pee Wee Herman clone; his girlfriend has just left him, and he spends his evenings drowning his sorrows, drinking with his best friend, a black cop named Washington (Cleavant Derricks).

One day he screws up one of Washington's undercover assignments, and so he owes him one. And here is what Washington wants him to do: Having been assigned to audition for the dance line in a police department charity show, he wants Joe to go to the audition for him. Joe protests, but it's no use, and that's how he gets into the peculiar position of impersonating a police officer *and* a dancer, both at once.

The audition is not a happy event. Most of the cops are angry about having to be there. Joe figures he can flunk the audition, and that'll be that, but then his eyes meet the eyes of a high-spirited woman cop (Meg Tilly), and he decides to stick around. *Off Beat* will be the story of their love affair, cross-cut with such other matters as a bank robbery, backstage intrigue at the library, the hostility of the other cops, and the problems Joe walks into by wearing a police uniform around the streets of New York.

The movie has a more ingenious plot than is usually the case in modern comedies; it's not just a straight line from beginning to end, but a series of little character studies and quiet dialogue passages and small insights into human nature. Holding the elements together is the strong chemistry between Judge Reinhold (who was Eddie Murphy's partner in *Beverly Hills Cop*) and Meg Tilly (who won an Academy Award nomination for *Agnes of God*, but is ten or twenty times more interesting in this film). What's nice is that they approach each other out of vulnerability. There isn't that feeling you sometimes get with the big stars, that *of course* people are going to be attracted to them. They both seem a little flattered to be so much in love. It creates a good feeling.

But the movie isn't all sweetness. It contains one of the single most explosive and surprising comic moments of any movie in a long time, when a hostile cop delivers a brutal insult to Meg Tilly, and she responds appropriately. More than that I won't say, but the moment gets a laugh that grows out of shock, surprise, and the perfect timing of what happens.

Off Beat is filled with good character actors, bringing more dimensions to their characters than the roles might otherwise permit. Among them are Harvey Keitel as a bank robber, Julie Bovasso as Tilly's mother, and Joe Mantegna as a cop who hates ballet instructors.

At the center of everything, Reinhold and Tilly make a wonderful romantic couple. There is a real magic about the scene where they have a quiet dinner and then begin to dance. Reinhold became a star of sorts in *Beverly Hills Cop*, just by having a good role in a hit movie, but this time he carries the show, and gives promise of being around for a long time, probably in more of these Everyman roles that Jack Lemmon plays so well. Meg Tilly has been in wildly uneven movies over the years (and I was not one of the admirers of *Agnes of God*, her most prestigious film to date). This time, allowed to play a fairly tough and complicated character, she suddenly blossoms. She's never been more appealing.

Off Beat probably sounds contrived. The plot is filled with predictable devices and contrived meetings and wild coincidences, and elements that seem borrowed from other films. What's surprising is how original it all seems, maybe because the director, Michael Dinner, seems to really care for his characters.

An Officer and a Gentleman
★ ★ ★ ★
R, 126 m., 1982

Richard Gere (Zack Mayo), Debra Winger (Paula Pokrifki), Lou Gossett, Jr. (Sergeant Foley), David Keith (Sid Worley), Robert Loggia (Byron Mayo), Lisa Blount (Lynette), Lisa Eilbacher (Casey Seeger). Directed by Taylor Hackford and produced by Martin Elfand. Screenplay by Douglas Day Stewart.

An Officer and a Gentleman is the best movie about love that I've seen in a long time. Maybe that's because it's not about "love" as a Hollywood concept, but about love as growth, as learning to accept other people for who and what they are. There's romance in this movie, all right, and some unusually erotic sex, but what makes the film so special is that the sex and everything else is presented within the context of its characters finding out who they are, what they stand for—and what they will *not* stand for.

The movie takes place in and around a Naval Aviation Officer Candidate School in Washington state. Every thirteen weeks, a new group of young men and women come here to see if they can survive a grueling session of physical and academic training. If they pass, they graduate to flight school. About half fail. Across Puget Sound, the local young women hope for a chance to meet an eligible future officer. They dream of becoming officers' wives, and in some of their families, we learn, this dream has persisted for two generations.

After the first month of training, there is a Regimental Ball. The women turn out with hope in their hearts and are sized up by the candidates. A man and a woman (Richard Gere and Debra Winger) pair off. We know more about them than they know about one another. He is a loner and a loser, whose mother died when he was young and whose father is a drunk. She is the daughter of an officer candidate who loved and left her mother twenty years before. They dance, they talk, they begin to date, they fall in love. She would like to marry him, but she refuses to do what the other local girls are willing to do—get pregnant or fake pregnancy to trap a future officer. For his part, the man is afraid of commitment, afraid of love, incapable of admitting that he cares for someone. All he wants is a nice, simple affair, and a clean break at the end of OCS.

This love story is told in counterpoint with others. There's the parallel affair between another candidate and another local girl. She *is* willing to trap her man. His problem is, he really loves her. He's under the thumb of his family, but he's willing to do the right thing, if she'll give him the chance.

All of the off-base romances are backdrops for the main event, which is the training program. The candidates are under the supervision of a tough drill sergeant (Lou Gossett, Jr.) who has seen them come and seen them go and is absolutely uncompromising in his standards. There's a love-hate relationship between the sergeant and his trainees, especially the rebellious, resentful Gere. And Gossett does such a fine job of fine-tuning the line between his professional standards and his personal emotions that the performance deserves its Academy Award.

The movie's method is essentially to follow its characters through the thirteen weeks, watching them as they change and grow. That does wonders for the love stories, because by the end of the film we know these people well enough to care about their decisions and to have an opinion about what they should do. In the case of Gere and Winger, the romance is absolutely absorbing because it's so true to life, right down to the pride that causes these two to pretend they don't care for each other as much as they really do. When it looks as if Gere is going to throw it all away—is going to turn his back on a good woman who loves him, just because he's too insecure to deal with her love—the movie isn't just playing with emotions, it's being very perceptive about human behavior.

But maybe I'm being too analytical about why *An Officer and a Gentleman* is so good. This is a wonderful movie precisely because it's so willing to deal with matters of the heart. Love stories are among the rarest of movies these days (and when we finally get one, it's likely to involve an extra-terrestrial). Maybe they're rare because writers and filmmakers no longer believe they understand what goes on between modern men and women. *An Officer and a Gentleman* takes chances, takes the time to know and develop its characters, and by the time this movie's wonderful last scene comes along, we know exactly what's happening, and why, and it makes us very happy.

Oh, God! ★ ★ ★ ½
PG, 104 m., 1977

George Burns (God), John Denver (Jerry Landers), Teri Garr (Bonnie Landers), Donald Pleasence (Dr. Harmon), Ralph Bellamy (Sam Raven), William Daniels (George Summers), Paul Sorvino (Reverend Williams), Dinah Shore (Dinah). Directed by Carl Reiner and produced by Jerry Weintraub. Screenplay by Larry Gelbart.

Carl Reiner's *Oh, God!* is a treasure of a movie: A sly, civilized, quietly funny speculation on what might happen if God endeavored to present himself in the flesh yet once again to forgetful Man. He comes back this time looking and talking a great deal like George Burns, an improvement on his earlier cinematic incarnations. And as his contact on

Earth, he selects a common man—John Denver, to the manner born.

Part of the movie's charm is in the way it surprises us by treating its subject matter with affection and respect. I went expecting blasphemous jokes and cheap shots at religion, since serious subjects so rarely make it into comedies these days except as targets. But no: *Oh, God!* is lighthearted, satirical, and humorous and (that rarest of qualities) in good taste.

It also makes you feel good, in the way some of the Frank Capra comedies did. The John Denver character becomes a contemporary version of Mr. Smith, John Doe, Mr. Deeds, and those other Capra heroes who prevailed because they were decent, honest, and true. Once Denver gets over his initial astonishment at being selected as God's spokesman, he makes a good job of it, justifying God's faith in the common man, which he, after all, put into production.

God is careful, throughout the movie, to make his reasoning clear. Why did he pick Denver? "You're like the lady who's the millionth person across the bridge and gets to meet the governor. You're better than some people, and worse than others, but you came across the bridge at the right time." The message God wants to remind his creatures of is a simple one: That things *can* turn out all right, although they will not necessarily or automatically do so. That we have everything here on Earth that we need to bring a happy ending to our story. And that we should try being a little nicer to one another.

Carl Reiner's credits as a director include the immortal *Where's Poppa?* (1970), a masterpiece of comic bad taste. So there was reason to anticipate a showdown again this time between the sacred and the profane. As an idea, indeed, *Oh, God!* must have seemed almost impossibly supplied with ways to go wrong. But it doesn't. Reiner is superb at establishing the right tone for this very difficult material, and the casting of George Burns as God is an inspiration.

"I took this form," God explains, "because if I showed myself to you as I am, you wouldn't be able to comprehend me." He chose his form well. God, as Burns, recalls some of his miracles (the 1969 Mets), some of his mistakes (tobacco, giraffes, and avocados—"I made the seeds too big"), and some common misconceptions about himself ("To tell you the truth, I spent the first five days thinking and created everything on the sixth"). And he has such quiet authority,

such wonderfully understated humor, such presence. John Denver, too, is well-cast: Sincere, believable, with that face so open and goofy. They work with Reiner, and with Larry Gelbart's screenplay, to create a movie that takes a really risky comic gamble, and wins.

Oh, God! Book II ★ ★
PG, 94 m., 1980

George Burns (God), Louanne (Tracy), Suzanne Pleshette (Paula), David Birney (Don), John Louie (Shingo), Anthony Holland (Dr. Newell). Directed and produced by Gilbert Cates. Screenplay by John Greenfield, Hal Goldman, Fred S. Fox, Seaman Jacobs, and Melissa Miller.

Oh, God! Book II qualifies as a sequel only because of its title and the irreplaceable presence of George Burns in the title role. Otherwise, it seems to have lost faith in the film it's based on. It begins with the same great idea for a movie (what would happen if God personally came down to earth and got involved in the affairs of men?), but it winds up as a third-rate situation comedy, using its subject as a gimmick.

Neither of the *Oh, God!* movies is, of course, seriously religious; they create God as a sort of ancient Will Rogers on a Christmas card by Norman Rockwell, and then give him lots of cute lines and paradoxical comic insights. But the original film—with God appearing to a supermarket manager played by John Denver—did at least follow through on its basic premise. What if God really did turn up in the checkout line? How do you behave when God blows the whistle and challenges you to test his rules?

Oh, God! Book II doesn't seem willing to devote a whole movie to the same subject; it uses God as basically just a *deus ex machina*. He is, of course, enormously appealing, and George Burns is rich and understated in the role. But after he appears to a little girl named Tracy (played by a very little actress named Louanne), the movie uses him as a springboard for scenes involving the little girl, her parents, her school, her psychiatrist—everything except what we'd really enjoy—more scenes with God.

Tracy's basic problem, it appears, is that she can see God and talk with him, but nobody else can. Her parents and teachers think she's talking to herself. God asks her to organize an advertising campaign to promote his image on earth, and she comes up with a slogan ("Think God") which her little playmates plaster on every open space in town. But, meanwhile, a psychiatrist (Anthony Holland) determines that Tracy's got serious problems.

There are other sitcom-style distractions. Tracy's parents (Suzanne Pleshette and David Birney) are divorced. Tracy doesn't like her daddy's new girlfriend. The principal at school is a meanie. And so on. The movie's screenplay was written by no less than five collaborators, but they were so bankrupt of ideas that some scenes have a quiet desperation to them. For example: There's an awkward TV newscast staged in the movie, with Hugh Downs as the avuncular anchorman and none other than Dr. Joyce Brothers giving her opinion that little Tracy may, indeed, have seen God. It would be sad enough if the movie were using Downs and Brothers for laughs—but, God help us, they're brought in as authority figures.

There is, however, one additional small treasure in this movie, a supporting performance by Mari Gorman, who steals every scene she's in, playing Tracy's grade school teacher, Miss Hudson. She has a weird kind of off-balance walk and out-of-time speaking style that's infectious and funny. It's amazing that a movie so devoid of comic imagination would allow itself to play around with such an offbeat supporting performance. If Gorman had played, say, Tracy's mother—and if the rest of the movie had been equally willing to take chances with its approach—*Book II* could have been worth seeing.

Oh, God! You Devil ★ ★ ★ ½
PG, 96 m., 1984

George Burns (God and Harry), Ted Wass (Bobby Shelton), Roxanne Hart (Wendy), Ron Silver (Gary). Directed by Paul Bogart and produced by Robert M. Sherman. Screenplay by Andrew Bergman.

The *God* pictures are ideal for sequels; after all, the leading character has no beginning and no end. But sequels have a way of ripping off profitable ideas without anything new to say. They grow so dreary and pale that we forget why we liked the original picture in the first place. That's why *Oh, God! You Devil* is such a delight. Here is George Burns's third God movie, and not only does it have as much humor, warmth, and good cheer as the first—it actually has a better story. The story involves a young man who was placed under God's protection when he was a little baby; he had a fever,

and his father's prayers were answered. The kid has grown up into an unsuccessful musician, and one day while he's performing at some dumb wedding reception, he meets an unusual guest, one Harry O. Tophet, who is, of course, the devil. Harry makes the kid an offer he should, but does not, refuse, and before long the kid is the top rock superstar in the world.

Of course, there's a catch. He has to assume the identity of another musician—an existing superstar whose deal with the devil has just run out. And worst of all, he has to remember his previous life, including the wife he loved and the child they were expecting. This whole balancing act between success and loss is unexpectedly touching, and gives the movie a genuine human heart.

Meanwhile, the devil basks in his acquisition, and then God gets into the act when the rock star prays to be released from his deal with the devil.

It's here that we get what we've been waiting for all through the picture, the scenes where God and the devil, both played by George Burns, appear on the same screen. Dual appearances through trick photography are, of course, an old Hollywood standby, but what's fun here is the way Burns plays scenes with himself: This casting was made in heaven.

Oh, God! You Devil has two different kinds of successful elements. The Burns stuff is all superb, especially when the devil reflects whimsically about the evils he's unleashed upon the earth. But the other story—the story starring Ted Wass as the condemned rock star—has an authenticity of its own. Like Warren Beatty's *Heaven Can Wait*, it starts with a fantastical idea and then develops it along plausible human lines. For the first time in the God pictures, we care so much about the human characters that it really does make a difference what God does; it's not just a celestial vaudeville act.

Old Gringo ★ ★
R, 119 m., 1989

Jane Fonda (Harriet Winslow), Gregory Peck (Bitter), Jimmy Smits (Arroyo), Patricio Contreras (Col. Frutos Garcia), Jenny Gago (La Garduna), Gabriela Roel (La Luna), Sergio Calderon (Zacarias), Guillermo Rios (Monsalvo), Jim Metzler (Ron). Directed by Luis Puenzo and produced by Lois Bonfiglio. Screenplay by Aida Bortnik and Puenzo.

There is a potentially wonderful story at the heart of *Old Gringo*, but the movie never

finds it—the screenplay blasts away in every direction except the bull's eye. The movie is about a Yankee spinster (Jane Fonda), who decides one day in 1912 to break loose from her humdrum life by taking a job in Mexico as a governess. Once she arrives there, she is immediately caught in the middle of the Mexican Revolution. While buildings explode and bullets fly through the air, she has a passionate love affair with a revolutionary general and a meeting of minds with a great American author. The story ends in bloodshed, sadness, and nobility.

With just a slightly different slant, this could have been the plot outline for one of those paperback romance novels—the ones with the covers showing the heroine in the foreground, wide-eyed and heavingbosomed, while a swarthy young man with a mustache eyes her lustfully. But no, this is a serious enterprise, and the movie is based on a novel by the distinguished writer Carlos Fuentes. It's easy to imagine how the story attracted the filmmakers, but they spend too little time telling it, and too much time on aimless scenes of sound and fury.

The title comes from the identity of the old gringo in the movie, a weathered American (Gregory Peck) who walks fearlessly in the midst of battle because he has come to Mexico in search of death. Harriet Winslow, the Fonda character, encounters him soon after she arrives in Mexico, and gradually comes to love his stoic acceptance and sardonic wit. She does not realize until late in the film that he is, in fact, Ambrose Bierce, the bitter, elusive American author who disappeared in Mexico in 1913 or 1914.

The audience for this movie may never realize who the gringo is—because Bierce, I fear, is little known to most moviegoers, and the screenplay is almost willful in its refusal to explain who the man is or what he accomplished. Under the circumstances, Gregory Peck does a manful job of investing Bierce's shadow with character and idiosyncrasy, although Peck, so straightforward and stalwart, was a strange casting decision (I see Bierce as someone more like Harry Dean Stanton).

Most of the story revolves, however, not around the old gringo but the young gringa. It is startling how soon Harriet Winslow adjusts to the fact that she is no longer living in her mother's claustrophobic household. Perhaps a deep romantic streak was always present in her personality; she seems fated to end up in the arms of the handsome young revolutionary, General Arroyo (Jimmy Smits), and they embrace in the ruins of a mansion once occupied by the landowners who oppressed the local peasants. Fonda feels right in the role, but oddly enough (since she was one of the movie's producers), her character is given little to say—and many of her lines come in the form of an arch, self-consciously literary narration.

Old Gringo makes stabs at social commentary, as when Arroyo, occupying the mansion as his headquarters, begins to act more like a landowner than a revolutionary. But the film has a very thin story, and the director, Luis Puenzo, fills out the running time with expensively staged crowd scenes that run on too long. There is an endless battle, followed by another endless battle, followed by an endless dance, and so on, with hundreds of extras running through dust and dodging explosions while nothing much is actually happening.

What the movie lacks is a clear narrative line through from beginning to end. It's heavy on disconnected episodes, light on drama and storytelling. An occasional scene stands out—my favorite is the one where the old gringo and a local prostitute make a deal that respects their mutual standards—but despite all of its blood and death, the movie never generates much urgency.

Oliver & Co. ★ ★ ★
G, 73 m., 1988

With the voices of: Joey Lawrence (Oliver), Billy Joel (Dodger), Cheech Marin (Tito), Richard Mulligan (Einstein), Roscoe Lee Browne (Francis), Sheryl Lee Ralph (Rita), Dom Deluise (Fagin), Taurean Blacque (Roscoe), Carl Weintraub (Desoto), Robert Loggia (Sykes), Natalie Gregory (Jenny), William Glover (Winston), Bette Midler (Georgette). Directed by George Scribner. Inspired by Charles Dickens's *Oliver Twist*. Animation screenplay by Jim Cox, Timothy J. Disney, and James Mangold.

Walt Disney's *Oliver & Co.* is a safer version of *An American Tail*, with a kitten instead of a mouse trying to survive in the overwhelming streets of New York City. If children were disturbed, in *An American Tail*, by the hero's enforced separation from its parents, they may be relieved this time, since Oliver apparently has no parents and is on his own from a very early age. We see him for the first time in a cardboard box marked "Kittens

\$5," and later that night he is still there, even after having been marked down to "Free."

The kitten is swept out of its box by a torrential rainstorm, chased by savage dogs, finds refuge beneath the huge wheels of a truck, and is befriended the next day by a street-wise dog named Dodger (get it?). Together, they work a scam to steal some hot dogs from a vendor, but then the dog tries to make off with all of the wienies, and the kitten follows him back to a ramshackle houseboat where several dogs live with their owner, Fagin.

Fagin is a human who trains dogs to steal, just as the original Fagin in the Dickens story trained children to be pickpockets. That connection is about as close as *Oliver & Co.* gets to *Oliver Twist*, but since the connection is not insisted on and most smaller children will (alas) never have heard of Oliver Twist, I suppose it makes no difference.

The movie is filled with rousing action and chase scenes, and a properly menacing set of villains (the evil juice-loan vendor Sykes and his killer Dobermans). The animation, augmented by computers to do the detail work, is full-bodied and efficient, and if the street scenes still lack the kind of loving background detail and movement they had in the classic Disney movies, at least they contain an extraordinary number of subliminal plugs for Coca-Cola. Some of the action moments may be a little strong for younger kids (I'm not sure it was wise to demonstrate to them how a person can be strangled by being trapped by an automated car window). But the story is robust and muscular, the sentiments are not overdone, and the kitten is cute.

On Golden Pond ★ ★ ★ ★
PG, 109 m., 1981

Katharine Hepburn (Ethel Thayer), Henry Fonda (Norman Thayer, Jr.), Jane Fonda (Chelsea), Doug McKeon (Billy Ray), Dabney Coleman (Bill Ray). Directed by Mark Rydell and produced by Bruce Gilbert. Screenplay by Ernest Thompson.

Simple affection is so rare in the movies. Shyness and resentment are also seldom seen. Love is much talked-about, but how often do we really believe that the characters are in love and not simply in a pleasant state of lust and like? Fragile emotions are hard to portray in a movie, and the movies that reach for them are more daring, really, than movies

that bludgeon us with things like anger and revenge, which are easy to portray.

On Golden Pond is a treasure for many reasons, but the best one, I think, is that I could believe it. I could believe in its major characters and their relationships, and in the things they felt for one another, and there were moments when the movie was witness to human growth and change. I left the theater feeling good and warm, and with a certain resolve to try to mend my own relationships and learn to start listening better. All of those achievements are small miracles for any movie, but especially for this one, which began as a formula stage play and still contains situations and characters that are constructed completely out of cardboard.

The story of *On Golden Pond* begins with the arrival of an old, long-married couple (Henry Fonda and Katharine Hepburn) at the lakeside cottage where they have summered for many years. They know each other very well. Hepburn, of course, knows Fonda better than he knows her—or himself, for that matter. Fonda is a crotchety, grouchy old professor whose facade conceals a great deal of shyness, we suspect. Hepburn knows that. Before long, three more people turn up at the pond: Their daughter (Jane Fonda), her fiancé (Dabney Coleman), and his son (Doug McKeon).

That's the first act. In the second act, the conflicts are established. Jane Fonda feels that her father has never really given her her due—he wanted a son, or perhaps he never really understood how to be a father, anyway. Jane tells her parents that she's spending a month in Europe with Coleman, and, ah, would it be all right if they left the kid at the lake? Hepburn talks the old man into it. In the central passages of the movie, the old man and the kid grudgingly move toward some kind of communication and trust. There is a crisis involving a boating accident, and a resolution that brings everybody a lot closer to the realization that life is a precious and fragile thing. Through learning to relate to the young boy, old Fonda learns, belatedly, how to also trust his own daughter and communicate with her: The kid provides Henry with practice at how to be a father. There is eventually the sort of happy ending that some people cry through.

Viewed simply as a stage plot, *On Golden Pond* is so predictable we can almost hear the gears squeaking. Forty-five minutes into the movie, almost everyone in the audience can probably predict more or less what is going to happen to the characters, emotionally. And yet *On Golden Pond* transcends its predictability and the transparent role of the young boy, and becomes a film with passages of greatness.

This is because of the acting, first of all, but also because Ernest Thompson, who wrote such a formula play, has furnished it with several wonderful scenes. A conversation between old Henry Fonda and young Coleman is an early indication that this is going to be an unusual movie: A man who is forty-five asks a man who is eighty for permission to sleep in the same room with the man's daughter, and after the old man takes the question as an excuse for some cruel put-downs, the conversation takes an altogether unexpected twist into words of simple truth. That is a good scene. So are some of the conversations between Hepburn and Fonda. And so are some remarkable scenes involving the boating accident, in which there is no doubt that Hepburn, at her age, is doing some of her own stunts. It's at moments like this that stardom, acting ability, character, situation—and what the audience already knows about the actors—all come together into an irreplaceable combination.

As everybody knows, this is the first film in which Hepburn and the two Fondas have acted in any combination with one another. Some reviews actually seem to dismiss the casting as a stunt. I believe it adds immeasurably to the film's effect. If Hepburn and Henry Fonda are legends, seen in the twilight of their lives, and if we've heard that Jane and Henry have had some of the same problems offscreen that they have in this story—does that make the movie simple gossip? No, not if the movie deals honestly with the problems, as this one does. As people, they have apparently learned something about loving and caring that, as actors, they are able to communicate, even through the medium of this imperfect script. Watching the movie, I felt I was witnessing something rare and valuable.

On the Road Again ★ ★ ★
PG, 119 m., 1980

Willie Nelson (Buck), Dyan Cannon (Viv), Amy Irving (Lily), Slim Pickens (Garland), Joey Floyd (Jamie), Mickey Rooney, Jr. (Cotton). Directed by Jerry Schatzberg and produced by Sydney Pollack and Gene Taft. Screenplay by Carol Sobieski, William D. Wittliff, and John Binder.

The plot of Willie Nelson's *Honeysuckle Rose** is just a slight touch familiar, maybe because it's straight out of your basic country and western song. To wit: The hero, a veteran country singer still poised at the brink of stardom after twenty-five years on the road, won't listen to his wife's pleas that he leave the road and settle down with her and their son. Meanwhile, the band's guitarist, who is also the singer's best friend, retires. A replacement is needed, and the singer hires the best friend's daughter.

She is a shapely young lady who has had a crush on the singer since she was knee-high to a grasshopper. Once they go out on the road again, the singer and the best friend's daughter start sleeping with one another. This situation causes anguish for the singer, the daughter, the best friend, the wife, the son, and the band. But after going down to Mexico to slug back some tequila and think it over, the singer returns to his wife and the best friend's daughter wisely observes: "Anything that hurts this many people can't be right."

This story is totally predictable from the opening scenes of *Honeysuckle Rose*, which is a disappointment; the movie is sly and entertaining, but it could have been better. Still, it has its charms, and one is certainly the presence of Willie Nelson himself, making his starring debut at the age of forty-seven and not looking a day over sixty. He's grizzled, grinning, sweet-voiced and pleasant, and a very engaging actor. (He gave promise of that with a single one-liner in his screen debut in *The Electric Horseman*, expressing his poignant desire for the kind of girl who could suck the chrome off a trailer hitch.)

The movie also surrounds Nelson with an interesting cast: Dyan Cannon is wonderful as Willie's long-suffering wife, a sexy fortyish earth-woman with streaked hair and a wardrobe from L.L. Bean. She survives the test of her big scene, an archetypical C&W confrontation in which she charges onstage to denounce her husband and his new girlfriend.

Amy Irving is not quite so well-cast as the girlfriend; she has too many scenes in which she gazes adoringly at Willie—who, on the other hand, hardly ever gazes adoringly at her. Slim Pickens, who should be registered as a national historical place, is great as the best friend. And there is a hilarious bit part, a fatuous country singer, played by Mickey Rooney, Jr.

Mercifully, the movie doesn't drag out its

tale of heartbreak into a C&W soap opera. Instead, director Jerry Schatzberg *(Scarecrow)* uses an easy-going documentary style to show us life on the band bus, at a family reunion, and backstage at big concerts. All of these scenes are filled to overflowing with colors; this is one of the cheeriest, brightest looking movies I've ever seen, starting with Willie's own amazing costumes and including the spectrum at the concerts, reunions, picnics, etc. Half the movie seems to be shot during parties, and although we enjoy the texture and detail we sometimes wonder why so little seems to be happening.

The movie remains resolutely at the level of superficial cliché, resisting any temptation to make a serious statement about the character's hard-drinking, self-destructive lifestyle; this isn't a movie like *Payday*, in which Rip Torn re-created the last days of the dying Hank Williams. *Honeysuckle Rose* has the kind of problems that can be resolved with an onstage reconciliation in the last scene: Willie and Dyan singing a duet together and everybody knowing things will turn out all right.

If there's an edge of disappointment coming out of the movie, maybe it's inspired by that simplicity of approach to complicated problems. Willie Nelson has lived a long time, experienced a lot, and suffered a certain amount on his way to his current success, and my hunch is that he knows a lot more about his character's problems in this movie than he lets on. Maybe the idea was to film the legend and save the man for later.

*Retitled *On the Road Again* for TV and cassette.

Once Around ★ ★ ★ ½
R, 115 m., 1990

Richard Dreyfuss (Sam Sharpe), Holly Hunter (Renata Bella), Danny Aiello (Joe Bella), Laura San Giacomo (Jan Bella), Gena Rowlands (Marilyn Bella). Directed by Lasse Hallstrom and produced by Griffin Dunne and Amy Robinson. Screenplay by Malia Scotch Marmo.

Did I like *Once Around*? I'm not sure. Did it bore me? Not for a moment. Is it a good film? Not in any conventional way; it's too much of a mess for that, and yet, at the same time, it's not a stupid film and not without feeling. What we have here is the untidiness of life, and it hasn't been made neat and simple and subjected to a formula screenplay. It's as confusing, as unsatisfying, as frustrating, and as occasionally wonderful as a big, emotional, unruly family—which is what it's about. The family and a slick salesman named Sam who marries into it.

The family, the Bellas, are complicated and close-knit, ruled by a father (Danny Aiello) who is smart, affectionate, and wise about affairs of the heart, although not wise enough to deal with this new in-law. He and his wife (Gena Rowlands) have had a loving and successful marriage of thirty-four years, but their children seem to be having a harder time with love—especially Renata (Holly Hunter), who has been living with a guy who confesses he has no desire to marry her.

On the rebound, and with her own sister's marriage fresh in her mind, Hunter goes to the Caribbean to take a course on selling condominiums. The hero of the meeting is a supersalesman named Sam Sharpe (Richard Dreyfuss), who has allegedly sold countless condos for untold piles of money. She takes one look at him and decides, in her words, that one day they will be kissing on an altar in the sight of God. She moves the place-cards around to be sure of sitting next to him at lunch, and by the time lunch is over, they're holding hands.

But, hold on, it's not exactly that kind of story. This man, Sam Sharpe, is some piece of work. He has an unfailing touch for saying the wrong thing in the wrong way at the wrong time. All of his gestures are intended to be warm, kind, and generous, but he has the kind of style that grates the wrong way— he puts your teeth on edge while you're trying to smile back at him. And he is capable of the most amazingly vulgar expressions and offensive gestures, as when he orders belly dancers for birthday parties or insists, absolutely insists, on singing an obscure Lithuanian song at a party where that would be sensationally inappropriate.

We keep waiting for the other shoe to drop. What's the real story on this guy? Is he for real? Has he really sold all those condos? Can he be trusted? "We don't know a thing about him," Hunter's sister complains to their parents. And they don't. But we think we do—we think *Once Around* is going to fall into familiar screenplay modes, and that Sam will be unmasked as some kind of impostor.

The movie toys with our expectations, those and others. There is an ice-skating sequence in which we think we know exactly

what's going to happen, twice, and the movie manipulates our expectations shamelessly. The most effective scenes are studies of social embarrassment, in which we cringe at the way Sam brings everything down to his own level of phony-sincere smarminess. The family can't stand him.

But Holly Hunter sticks by him, and gets pregnant by him, and insists in one speech, "This is my adventure and nobody can take it away from me!" What does she see in this guy? Maybe by the end of the movie we can understand, even though the scene involving baptism and reunion is, to put it charitably, less than convincing.

The movie is essentially all about acting. Richard Dreyfuss creates a character here who is so difficult, so impossible, so offensive, that it is easy to dislike the personality and forget how good the performance is. But this is some of Dreyfuss's best and riskiest work—he's out there on the edge, with this suntanned, chain-smoking, larger-than-life case study. Holly Hunter brings to this role the same vulnerable intensity she had in *Broadcast News*, and something new, a certain mystery, so that we're not always sure just what she thinks about this unwieldy personality she's married to. Danny Aiello has delicate scenes to negotiate as the patriarch, and watch his face as he tells his daughter how he feels about her husband, or how he responds during key moments in family ceremonies.

One of the great strengths of the movie is its dialogue, which is literate and original without sounding "written." The screenplay is by Malia Scotch Marmo, the direction is by Lasse Hallstrom (*My Life as a Dog*), and I guess they had a lot to do with it. I'd be intrigued to learn how much input the producers, Amy Robinson and Griffin Dunne, had because in its underlying emotional rhythms this movie has a lot in common with *After Hours*, the Martin Scorsese film they produced in 1986. Both films create the sensation of accidents waiting to happen.

Watching the coming attractions trailer for *Once Around*, I observed to myself that it had not given me the slightest clue as to what this movie was about. Watching the movie, I have the same impression. It's an odd, eccentric, off-center study of some very strange human natures, and at every turn it confounds our expectations for them. It's untidy, unpredictable, and made me feel very uncomfortable at times. And it took me all the way through the process of writing this review to

discover a surprising thing about this movie, which is that I loved it.

Once Upon a Time in America
★ —short version
★ ★ ★ ★ —original version
R, 137 m., 227 m., 1984

Robert De Niro (Noodles), James Woods (Max), Elizabeth McGovern (Deborah), Treat Williams (Jimmy), Tuesday Weld (Carol), Burt Young (Joe). Directed by Sergio Leone and produced by Arnon Milchan. Screenplay by L. Benvenuti, P. De Bernardo, E. Medioli, F. Arcalli, F. Ferrini, Leone, and S. Kaminski.

This was a murdered movie, now brought back to life on cassette. Sergio Leone's *Once Upon a Time in America*, which in its intended 227-minute version is an epic poem of violence and greed, was chopped by ninety minutes for U.S. theatrical release into an incomprehensible mess without texture, timing, mood, or sense. The rest of the world saw the original film, which I saw at the Cannes Film Festival. In America, a tragic decision was made. When the full-length version (now available in cassette form) played at the 1984 Cannes Film Festival, I wrote:

"Is the film too long? Yes and no. Yes, in the sense that it takes real concentration to understand Leone's story construction, in which everything may or may not be an opium dream, a nightmare, a memory, or a flashback, and that we have to keep track of characters and relationships over fifty years. No, in the sense that the movie is compulsively and continuously watchable and that the audience did not stir or grow restless as the epic unfolded."

The movie tells the story of five decades in the lives of four gangsters from New York City—childhood friends who are merciless criminals almost from the first, but who have a special bond of loyalty to each other. When one of them breaks that bond, or thinks he does, he is haunted by guilt until late in his life, when he discovers that he was not the betrayer but the betrayed. Leone's original version tells this story in a complex series of flashbacks, memories, and dreams. The film opens with two scenes of terrifying violence, moves to an opium den where the Robert De Niro character is seeking to escape the consequences of his action, and then establishes its tone with a scene of great power: A ceaselessly ringing telephone, ringing forever in the conscience of a man who called the cops and betrayed his friends. The film moves back and forth in a tapestry of episodes, which all fit together into an emotional whole. There are times when we don't understand exactly what is happening, but never a time when we don't feel confidence in the film's narrative.

That version was not seen in American theaters, although it is now available on cassette. Instead, the whole structure of flashbacks was junked. The telephone rings once. The poetic transitions are gone. The movie has been wrenched into apparent chronological order, scenes have been thrown out by the handful, relationships are now inexplicable, and the audience is likely to spend much of its time in complete bewilderment. It is a great irony that this botched editing job was intended to "clarify" the film.

Here are some of the specific problems with the shortened version. A speakeasy scene comes before a newspaper headline announces that Prohibition has been ratified. Prohibition is then repealed, on what feels like the next day but must be six years later. Two gangsters talk about robbing a bank in front of a woman who has never been seen before in the film; they've removed the scene explaining who she is. A labor leader turns up, unexplained, and involves the gangsters in an inexplicable situation. He later sells out, but to whom? Men come to kill De Niro's girlfriend, a character we've hardly met, and we don't know if they come from the mob or the police. And here's a real howler: At the end of the shortened version, De Niro leaves a room he has never been before by walking through a secret panel in the wall. How did he know it was there? In the long version, he was told it was there. In the short version, his startling exit shows simple contempt for the audience.

Many of the film's most beautiful shots are missing from the short version, among them a bravura moment when a flash-forward is signaled by the unexpected appearance of a Frisbee, and another where the past becomes the present as the Beatles' "Yesterday" sneaks into the sound track. Relationships are truncated, scenes are squeezed of life, and I defy anyone to understand the plot of the short version. The original *Once Upon a Time in America* gets a four-star rating. The shorter version is a travesty.

One Flew Over the Cuckoo's Nest
★ ★ ★
R, 129 m., 1975

Jack Nicholson (R.P. McMurphy), Louise Fletcher (Nurse Ratched), Will Sampson (The Chief), William Redfield (Harding), Brad Dourif (Billy), Sydney Lassick (Cheswick), Scatman Crothers (Turkle), Dean R. Brooks (Dr. Spivey), Danny DeVito (Martini). Directed by Milos Forman and produced by Saul Zaentz and Michael Douglas. Screenplay by Lawrence Hauben and Bo Goldman.

Milos Forman's *One Flew Over the Cuckoo's Nest* is a film so good in so many of its parts that there's a temptation to forgive it when it goes wrong. But it does go wrong, insisting on making larger points than its story really should carry, so that at the end, the human qualities of the characters get lost in the significance of it all. And yet there are those moments of brilliance. If Forman was preaching a parable, the audience seemed in total agreement with it, and I found that a little depressing: It's a lot easier to make noble points about fighting the establishment, about refusing to surrender yourself to the system, than it is to closely observe the ways real people behave when they're placed in an environment like a mental institution.

That sort of observation, when it's allowed to happen, is what's best about *One Flew Over the Cuckoo's Nest*. We meet a classic outsider—R.P. McMurphy, a quintessentially sane convict sent to the institution as a punishment for troublemaking—whose charisma and gall allow him to break through to a group of patients who've mostly fallen into a drugged lethargy. Their passive existence is reinforced by the unsmiling, domineering Nurse Ratched, who lines them up for compulsory tranquilizers and then leads them through group therapy in a stupor.

McMurphy has no insights into the nature of mental illness, which is his blessing. He's an extroverted, life-loving force of nature who sees his fellow patients as teammates, and defines the game as the systematic defiance of Nurse Ratched and the system she personifies. In many of the best scenes in the film, this defiance takes the shape of spontaneous and even innocent little rebellions: During exercise period, the patients mill around aimlessly on a basketball court until McMurphy hilariously tries to get a game going.

He also makes bets and outrageous dares, and does some rudimentary political orga-

nizing. He needs the votes of ten patients, out of a possible eighteen, to get the ward schedule changed so they can all watch the World Series—and his victory is in overcoming the indifference the others feel not only toward the Series but toward existence itself. McMurphy is the life force, the will to prevail, set down in the midst of a community of the defeated. And he's personified and made totally credible by Jack Nicholson, in another of the remarkable performances that have made him the most interesting actor to emerge in the last two decades. Nicholson, manically trying to teach basketball to an Indian (Will Sampson) who hasn't even spoken in twelve years, sometimes succeeds in translating the meaning of the movie and Ken Kesey's novel into a series of direct, physical demonstrations.

That's when the movie works, and what it's best at. If Forman had stayed at that level—introducing his characters and making them real, and then seeing how they changed as they bounced off one another—*One Flew Over the Cuckoo's Nest* might have been a great film. It's a good one as it is, but we can see the machinery working. Take, for example, the all-night orgy that finally hands McMurphy over to his doom. He's smuggled booze and broads into the ward, and everyone gets drunk, and then the hapless Billy (Brad Dourif) is cheerfully bundled into a bedroom with a willing girl. Billy stutters so badly he can hardly talk, but he's engaging and intelligent, and we suspect his problems are not incurable. The next morning, as Nurse Ratched surveys the damage, Billy at first defies her (speaking without a stutter, which is too obvious) and then caves in when she threatens to tell his mother what he's done. Nurse Ratched and Billy's mother are old friends, you see (again, too obvious, pinning the rap on Freud and Mom). Billy commits suicide, and we're invited to stand around his pitiful corpse and see the injustice of it all—when all we've really seen is the plot forcing an implausible development out of unwilling subject matter.

Another scene that just doesn't work, because it's too heavily burdened with its purpose, occurs when McMurphy escapes, commandeers a school bus, and takes all the inmates of the ward on a fishing trip in a stolen boat. The scene causes an almost embarrassing break in the movie—it's Forman's first serious misstep—because it's an idealized fantasy in the midst of realism. By now, we've met the characters, we know them in the context of hospital politics, and when they're set down on the boat deck, they just don't belong there. The ward is the arena in which they'll win or lose, and it's not playing fair—to them, as characters—to give them a fishing trip.

Even as I'm making these observations, though, I can't get out of my mind the tumultuous response that *Cuckoo's Nest* received from its original audiences. Even the most obvious, necessary, and sobering scenes—as when McMurphy tries to strangle Nurse Ratched to death—were received, not seriously, but with sophomoric cheers and applause. Maybe that's the way to get the most out of the movie—see it as a simple-minded antiestablishment parable—but I hope not. I think there are long stretches of a very good film to be found in the midst of Forman's ultimate failure, and I hope they don't get drowned in the applause for the bad stuff that plays to the galleries.

One from the Heart ★ ★
PG, 98 m., 1982

Frederic Forrest (Hank), Teri Garr (Frannie), Raul Julia (Ray), Nastassja Kinski (Leila), Lainie Kazan (Maggie), Harry Dean Stanton (Moe). Directed by Francis Ford Coppola and produced by Bernard Gersten.

Arriving after two years of sound and fury, after all the news items on the financial pages and alarms and excursions in the movie trade press, Francis Ford Coppola's *One from the Heart* is an interesting production but not a good movie. From Coppola, the brilliant orchestrator of *Apocalypse Now* and the God-father films, it is a major disappointment. This must be the first movie in history to arrive with more publicity about its production techniques than about its stars. Everybody knows that Coppola used experimental video equipment to view and edit his movie, sealing himself into a trailer jammed with electronic gear so that he could see on TV what the camera operator was seeing through the lens. Of course the film itself was photographed on the same old celluloid that the movies have been using forever; Coppola used TV primarily as a device to speed up the process of viewing each shot and trying out various editing combinations. (Or, as an industry wisecrack had it, "He took an $8 million project and used the latest advances in video to bring it in for $23 million.")

If *One from the Heart* is the sort of film this process inspires, then Coppola should abandon it. But of course the process is neutral; films live or die according to an inner rhythm of their own. The most dismal thing about *One from the Heart* is that it lacks those rhythms. It is a ballet of graceful and complex camera movements occupying magnificent sets, and somehow the characters get lost in the process. There was never a moment in this film when I cared about what was happening to the people in it, and only one moment (a cameo by Allen Goorwitz as an irate restaurant owner) when I felt that an actor's spontaneity was able to sneak past Coppola's smothering style and into the audience.

The storyteller of *The Godfather* has become a technician here. There are chilling parallels between Coppola's obsessive control of this film and the character of Harry Caul, the wiretapper in Coppola's *The Conversation* (1974), who cared only about technical results and refused to let himself think about human consequences. Movies are a lot of different things, but most of the best ones are about people and for people, and *One from the Heart* pays little heed to the complexities of the human heart. Indeed, it seems almost on guard against the actors who occupy its carefully architectured scenes. They are hardly ever allowed to dominate. They are figures in a larger pattern, one that diminishes them, that sees them as part of the furniture. They aren't given many close-ups; they're often bathed in garish red glows or sickly blues and greens; they're placed in front of distractingly flamboyant sets or lost in badly choreographed crowds; and sometimes they're cut off in the middle of an emotion or a piece of business because the relentlessly programmed camera has business elsewhere.

I've neglected, in fact, to name the actors, or describe the characters they play. That's not so much of an oversight in a review of a film like this. The two main characters (Teri Garr and Frederic Forrest) inhabit a Las Vegas of disappointment, ennui, and glittering lights. For a brief time, they break out of their humdrum lives and meet new lovers (Raul Julia and Nastassja Kinski) who tease them with dreams and fantasies. The underlying story notion, I suppose, is that ordinary little people have a great night on the town, but the night and the town in Coppola's production so overwhelm them that they remain ordinary little people throughout.

There are small pleasures in this movie.

One is Harry Dean Stanton's walk-through as the seedy owner of a junkyard, although Coppola resists showing us Stanton's most effective tool, his expressive eyes. Kinski, as a circus tightrope walker, has a beauty much more mature than in *Tess* and a wonderful moment when she explains "to make a circus girl disappear, all you have to do is blink your eyes." Garr is winsome, but her role makes her thanklessly passive, and Forrest (the Oscar nominee from *The Rose*) is almost transparent here, he's given such a nebbish to play.

One-Trick Pony ★ ★ ★ ½
R, 98 m., 1980

Paul Simon (Jonah), Blair Brown (Marion), Rip Torn (Walter Fox), Joan Hackett (Lonnie Fox), Allen Goorwitz (Cal Van Damp), Mare Winningham (Modeena), Lou Reed (Steve), Harper Simon (Young Jonah). Directed by Robert M. Young and produced by Michael Tannen. Screenplay and original music by Paul Simon.

One-Trick Pony is a wonderful movie, an affectionate character study with a lot of good music in it, and it's being sold in all the wrong ways to Paul Simon "fans." True, you'll like it if you *are* a Paul Simon fan, but does Paul Simon have "fans" anymore? He has lots of admirers, people who follow his music—but they're not necessarily prepared to race out into the night to see this movie, as fans of, say, Bruce Springsteen might be willing to do. And that's sort of the point of *One-Trick Pony*, which tells the story of a folk singer who used to have a lot more fans than he does today.

It's ironic, the way the movie's ad campaign seemed to have exactly missed the point of the movie. Ironic, but not unusual. And never mind: This movie was one of a lousy film year's few good films, a work that knows exactly what it's like to be a musician on tour. Jonah, the character Paul Simon wrote and plays, is a person drawn from life. If you are or ever have been a regular at a marginal local folk club, you've seen singers like Jonah many times.

He was very big in the 1960s. He wrote one of the songs that became an anthem for that decade. His music was an anti-war rallying point. But the sixties are long ago. And Jonah has continued to perform more or less in the same vein. He still travels the country by van, working with a small band. He still writes and arranges his own songs. He is still very good, for that matter—but he's out of date. He plays smaller and smaller clubs, and back home, in New York, his wife and child are both growing up without him.

There is a point, this movie argues, when a singer like Jonah stops being a brave individualist and becomes merely a middle-aged man hanging onto an obsolete self-image. That's the opinion held by Jonah's wife (Blair Brown), who loves him but wants a divorce. Jonah is sort of willing to try a change. He begins to deal with a "hitmaker" (Rip Torn) who sets him up with an arranger (Lou Reed) who can almost guarantee a Top 40 sound.

The movie does an effortless job of teaching us this aspect of the music business. We hear various versions of one of Jonah's songs: first as it sounds in a small club, then as it sounds during a very nervous audition session, and finally as it is gruesomely transformed, violins and all, into a prepackaged "hit." During this period we begin to feel sympathy with a certain nobility in Jonah's character. *One-Trick Pony* never forces its points, but we begin to understand why his way might be preferable to success.

The movie is filled with interesting, sharply drawn characters. Allen Goorwitz is brilliant in a hateful role as an egotistical monster who controls radio playtime. Joan Hackett, as Torn's sexually adventurous wife, goes after Jonah in simple, lustful boredom, but ends up trying to be his friend, to explain the realities of the situation they find themselves in. Brown plays the singer's wife as a complex woman who, in her thirties, still knows and feels why she married this man, but wonders how long he has to prove his point before her life is sidetracked.

And Simon is very good in the central role. The movie has a lot of music in it that he sings well and with love, but it also contains some very tricky dramatic moments. Halfway through, we begin to realize that it's about a lot more things than an aging folk hero. It is also about the generation that was young and politically active in the 1960s and now has been overtaken by the narcissism of the most brutally selfish and consumer-oriented period in American history. Many children of the sixties have been, of course, willing converts to the new culture of the Cuisinart. Others stick to what they used to believe in. In Jonah's case, it's folk music. Everybody's case is different.

The Onion Field ★ ★ ★ ★
R, 126 m., 1979

John Savage (Karl Hettinger), James Woods (Greg Powell), Franklyn Seales (Jimmy Smith), Ted Danson (Ian Campbell), Ronny Cox (Pierce Brooks), David Huffman (Phil Halpin), Christopher Lloyd (Jailhouse Lawyer), Diane Hull (Helen Hettinger), Priscilla Pointer (Chrissie Campbell). Directed by Harold Becker and produced by Walter Coblenz. Screenplay by Joseph Wambaugh.

Since *The Onion Field* will inevitably inspire comparisons with *In Cold Blood*, we might as well begin with a basic one: Both the book and the film of *In Cold Blood* began with murder instead of ending with it.

The Onion Field does the same thing. It is also based on real events—the 1963 kidnappings of Los Angeles police officers Karl Hettinger and Ian Campbell, and the eventual cold-blooded murder of Campbell. And Joseph Wambaugh, who wrote the book and personally controlled the film production, didn't reorder the facts to give us a dramatic burst of gunfire at the end. Instead, he places the deadly event of the murder in an onion field at about where it should occur, midway between the criminal preparations that led up to it and the longest single criminal court case in California history, which lasted more than seven years.

For Wambaugh (himself a former policeman), the trial, too, was a crime—and the fact of Campbell's murder had to be considered in the context of the legal travesties that followed it. That attention to the larger context of the kidnap-killing is one thing that makes *The Onion Field* so much more than another cop drama. This movie is about people, about how they behave and why, and about how small accidents and miscalculations can place people in situations they never dreamed of. Life is a very fragile thing; *The Onion Field* knows that in its bones.

The film moves between two basic, completely dissimilar, sets of characters: the two police officers, and the two third-rate hoods who would eventually be convicted of the crime. The cops aren't seen in quite the same sharp focus as the criminals—perhaps because, until the night of the onion field, little they had done in their lives had prepared them for what would follow.

Campbell (Ted Danson), the one who is killed, is seen almost as a memory: a tall, good-looking, black-haired Scottish-American with an obsession for bagpipes. Hettinger (John Savage from *The Deer Hunter*) is seen at the beginning as a cheerful, open-faced young man who will only later, after the onion field, develop very deep hurts and complications.

The hoods are seen more clearly. There's Greg Powell (James Woods), a street-wise smartass with a quick line of talk and an ability to paint situations so other people see them his way. And then there's Jimmy Smith (Franklyn Seales), a disturbed, insecure young black who is a perfect recruit for Powell. They make a suitable team. Powell creates criminal scenarios out of his fantasies; Smith finds them real enough to follow; and in some convoluted way Powell then follows Smith into them.

The Onion Field makes these two characters startlingly convincing: It paints their manners, their speech, their environment, their indecisions in such a way that we can almost understand them as they blunder stupidly into their crimes.

It never quite captures the personality of Campbell, the man who will be killed, but in the aftermath of the killing it begins to develop disturbing insights into Hettinger, the survivor. In a dozen subtle ways he becomes an outcast in the department (he senses, perhaps correctly, that the other cops wonder how he could allow his partner to be killed). Eventually, punishing himself, seeking guilt, he becomes a shoplifter, and is caught and fired from the force. Savage's handling of a scene of near-suicide, late in the film, is so frightening we can hardly stand to watch it.

Those events take place as *The Onion Field* explores the bureaucratic nightmare of the criminal courts system. The case dragged on and on and on—Hettinger was called upon to testify in more than six different trials—and plea bargaining, delays, and continuances, and legal loopholes made the case into an impossible (and almost insoluble) tangle.

So there is a lot of ground for *The Onion Field* to cover. It covers it remarkably well, working both as a narrative and as Wambaugh's cry of protest against the complicated and maddening workings of the courts. The movie is actually a vindication for Wambaugh: He was so displeased with the Hollywood and TV treatments of his novels (especially *The Choirboys*) that he said he would never let this factual story be made into a movie unless he controlled the production.

He did, and he has made it into a strong and honorable film. His instinct in going with Harold Becker, a commercial director with little previous feature experience, was obviously a good one; the movie's craftsmanship is unobtrusive but fine. And the performances (especially James Woods's as Greg Powell) bring the characters into heartbreaking reality. This is a movie that, once seen, cannot be set aside.

Ordinary People ★ ★ ★ ★
R, 125 m., 1980

Donald Sutherland (Calvin), Mary Tyler Moore (Beth), Judd Hirsch (Berger), Timothy Hutton (Conrad), M. Emmet Walsh (Swim Coach), Elizabeth McGovern (Jeannine), Dinah Manoff (Karen). Directed by Robert Redford and produced by Ronald L. Schwary. Screenplay by Alvin Sargent.

Families can go along for years without ever facing the underlying problems in their relationships. But sometimes a tragedy can bring everything out in the open, all of a sudden and painfully, just when everyone's most vulnerable. Robert Redford's *Ordinary People* begins at a time like that for a family that loses its older son in a boating accident. That leaves three still living at home in a perfectly manicured suburban existence, and the movie is about how they finally have to deal with the ways they really feel about one another.

There's the surviving son, who always lived in his big brother's shadow, who tried to commit suicide after the accident, who has now just returned from a psychiatric hospital. There's the father, a successful Chicago attorney who has always taken the love of his family for granted. There's the wife, an expensively maintained, perfectly groomed, cheerful homemaker whom "everyone loves." The movie begins just as all of this is falling apart.

The movie's central problems circle almost fearfully around the complexities of love. The parents and their remaining child all "love" one another, of course. But the father's love for the son is sincere yet also inarticulate, almost shy. The son's love for his mother is blocked by his belief that she doesn't really love him—she only loved the dead brother. And the love between the two parents is one of those permanent facts that both take for granted and neither has ever really tested.

Ordinary People begins with this three-way emotional standoff and develops it through the autumn and winter of one year. And what I admire most about the film is that it really *does* develop its characters and the changes they go through. So many family dramas begin with a "problem" and then examine its social implications in that frustrating semifactual, docudrama format that's big on TV. *Ordinary People* isn't a docudrama; it's the story of these people and their situation, and it shows them doing what's most difficult to show in fiction—it shows them changing, learning, and growing.

At the center of the change is the surviving son, Conrad, played by a wonderfully natural young actor named Timothy Hutton. He is absolutely tortured as the film begins; his life is ruled by fear, low self-esteem, and the correct perception that he is not loved by his mother. He starts going to a psychiatrist (Judd Hirsch) after school. Things are hard for this kid. He blames himself for his brother's death. He's a semi-outcast at school because of his suicide attempt and hospitalization. He does have a few friends—a girl he met at the hospital, and another girl who stands behind him at choir practice and who would, in a normal year, naturally become his girlfriend. But there's so much turmoil at home.

The turmoil centers around the mother (Mary Tyler Moore, inspired casting for this particular role, in which the character masks her inner sterility behind a facade of cheerful suburban perfection). She does a wonderful job of running her house, which looks like it's out of the pages of *Better Homes and Gardens*. She's active in community affairs, she's an organizer, she's an ideal wife and mother—except that at some fundamental level she's selfish, she can't really give of herself, and she *has*, in fact, always loved the dead older son more. The father (Donald Sutherland) is one of those men who wants to do and feel the right things, in his own awkward way. The change he goes through during the movie is one of the saddest ones: Realizing his wife cannot truly care for others, he questions his own love for her for the first time in their marriage.

The sessions of psychiatric therapy are supposed to contain the moments of the film's most visible insights, I suppose. But even more effective, for me, were the scenes involving the kid and his two teen-age girlfriends. The girl from the hospital (Dinah Manoff) is cheerful, bright, but somehow

running from something. The girl from choir practice (Elizabeth McGovern) is straightforward, sympathetic, able to be honest. In trying to figure them out, Conrad gets help in figuring himself out.

Director Redford places all these events in a suburban world that is seen with an understated matter-of-factness. There are no cheap shots against suburban lifestyles or affluence or mannerisms: The problems of the people in this movie aren't caused by their milieu, but grow out of themselves. And, like it or not, the participants have to deal with them. That's what sets the film apart from the sophisticated suburban soap opera it could easily have become. Each character in this movie is given the dramatic opportunity to look inside himself, to question his *own* motives as well as the motives of others, and to try to improve his own ways of dealing with a troubled situation. Two of the characters do learn how to adjust; the third doesn't. It's not often we get characters who face those kinds of challenges on the screen, nor directors who seek them out. *Ordinary People* is an intelligent, perceptive, and deeply moving film.

Orphans ★ ★ ¹/₂
R, 115 m., 1987

Albert Finney (Harold), Matthew Modine (Treat), Kevin Anderson (Phillip), John Kellogg (Barney), Anthony Heald (Man in Park). Directed and produced by Alan J. Pakula and co-produced by Susan Solt. Screenplay by Lyle Kessler.

Orphans is a good play about behavior turned into a mediocre movie about nothing much at all. That is not intended as a criticism of the filmmakers, but simply as an observation about the nature of the material. Although it is possible to construct elaborate theories about this movie, you blink and they're gone. *Orphans* is not about a man who wants to be a father, or about boys who want to have a father, or about sublimated sexual desires, or the underlying bond between criminals and outcasts. It is about shouting and jumping around and posturing and eccentric behavior.

The movie stars Albert Finney as a Chicago gangster who travels to Newark with a briefcase full of negotiable bonds, and promptly gets drunk out of his mind in a tavern. He runs across Matthew Modine, a street punk, and instantly sentimentalizes him as a Dead-End Kid—perhaps out of some maudlin idea the gangster has of his own childhood. Finney gets even more drunk, and passes out, and wakes up tied to a chair. He has been kidnapped by Modine, who lives with his brother (Kevin Anderson) in a crumbling house in the middle of an urban wasteland.

Finney never loses his cool. He frees himself of his bonds and then, amazingly, does not take the opportunity to escape. Instead, he stays in the house, cleaning and painting it, and appoints himself to tutor the two brothers in the ways of the world. His task is to tame and domesticate Modine, who is too hot-tempered, and to free Anderson of self-imprisonment (the kid hasn't even been outdoors in years, because Modine has convinced him he's allergic to the outside world).

Modine has a stake in keeping his brother imprisoned. It gives him power and a godlike role in their small world. Finney works artfully, using object lessons, parables, and Q & A sessions, feeling his way, talking these kids into a new view of themselves. There is a lot of stage business for him to perform while he talks. He paints, does carpentry, plays with his gun, and watches while Anderson swings from the curtains and tumbles around the set like a monkey in a cage. Modine alternates between aggression and passivity; he takes a strong line at first, but eventually confesses his ignorance to the older man.

This sort of material is strong on the stage. You enter the same time and space as the actors; the lights go down, and the actors project great energy at the audience, which leaves feeling slightly more dangerous and alive than when it entered the room. It is a very satisfactory experience. Plays like Lyle Kessler's *Orphans* and Sam Shepard's *True West* (with its suite for pop-up toasters) can be considered as concerts for voices and movement. The playwright supplies the words and suggests the actions, and the actors cry and whisper, leap and crouch, fight and surrender, and reveal great hurts from their pasts. Along the way, it is important, of course, that they change, and that they discover some measure of the truth about themselves.

Actually, change and truth are the least important ingredients, because they are the most arbitrary and artificial—put in to make the behavior look like a real play. The actual physical and verbal behavior itself is the subject of the play. It is possible to construct

elaborate theories about the meaning of *Orphans*, but on the stage, the play works as an exercise in human vitality in which the actors test their instruments. On screen, where the impact of their actual physical presence is missing, the material is revealed as a series of contrivances.

Albert Finney, who does an excellent job of portraying Harold the gangster, probably realizes this. He saw the play in Chicago, brought it to London and performed it triumphantly on the stage. Of course a movie had to be made of it, and he was happy to play his role again, but when I talked to him about the film, he spoke of the play almost entirely in stage actor's words, in terms of the opportunities it gave him rather than in the statement it made. That's the right approach.

The theater works best when it places the audience in the same box of space and time as the actors and the material. Movies work best when they break out of the box, when they spring free from the physical constraints of space and time—even in such a simple matter as the way the camera's point of view is free to roam. The problem of filming a play is as old as the cinema itself, and *Orphans* doesn't solve it—not that this play *could* be successfully filmed. Pakula and his actors do their best, but "out there" feels as much like "offstage" at the end as at the beginning.

Out of Africa ★ ★ ★ ★
PG, 153 m., 1985

Meryl Streep (Karen), Robert Redford (Denys), Klaus Maria Brandauer (Bror), Michael Kitchen (Berkeley), Malick Bowens (Farah), Joseph Thiaka (Kamante), Stephen Kinyanjui (Kinyanjui), Michael Gough (Delamere), Suzanna Hamilton (Felicity). Directed and produced by Sydney Pollack. Screenplay by Kurt Luedtke.

Earlier, there was a moment when a lioness seemed about to attack, but did not. The baroness had been riding her horse on the veld, had dismounted, had lost her rifle when the horse bolted. Now the lioness seemed about to charge, when behind her a calm voice advised the baroness not to move one inch. "She'll go away," the voice said, and indeed the lioness did skulk away after satisfying its curiosity.

That scene sets up the central moment in Sydney Pollack's *Out of Africa*, which comes somewhat later in the film. The baroness is

on safari with the man who owned the cool voice, a big-game hunter named Denys. They happen upon a pride of lions. Once again, the man assumes charge. He will protect them. But then a lion unexpectedly charges from another direction, and it is up to the baroness to fell it, with one shot that must not miss, and does not. After the man and woman are safe, the man sees that the woman has bitten her lip in anxiety. He reaches out and touches the blood. Then they hold each other tightly.

If you can sense the passion in that scene, then you may share my enjoyment of *Out of Africa*, which is one of the great recent epic romances. The baroness is played by Meryl Streep. The hunter is Robert Redford. These are high-voltage stars, and when their chemistry is wrong for romances (as Streep's was for *Falling in Love*, and Redford's for *The Natural*), it is very wrong. This time, it is right.

The movie is based on the life and writings of Baroness Karen Blixen, a Danish woman who, despairing that she would be single forever, married her lover's brother, moved to Kenya in East Africa, ran a coffee plantation on the slopes of Kilimanjaro, and later, when the plantation was bankrupt and the dream was finished, wrote books about her experiences under the name Isak Dinesen.

Her books are glories—especially *Out of Africa* and *Seven Gothic Tales*—but they are not the entire inspiration for this movie. What we have here is an old-fashioned, intelligent, thoughtful love story, told with enough care and attention that we really get involved in the passions between the characters.

In addition to the people Streep and Redford play, there is a third major character, Bror, the man she marries, played by Klaus Maria Brandauer. He is a smiling, smooth-faced, enigmatic man, who likes her well enough, after his fashion, but never seems quite equal to her spirit. After he gives her syphilis and she returns to Denmark for treatment, she is just barely able to tolerate his behavior—after all, he did not ask to marry her—until a New Year's Eve when he flaunts his infidelity, and she asks him to move out.

He turns up once more, asking for money, after Redford has moved his things into the baroness's farmhouse. The two men have a classic exchange. Brandauer: "You should have asked permission." Redford: "I did. She said yes."

The movie takes place during that strange blip in history when the countries of East Africa—Kenya, Uganda, the Rhodesias—were attracting waves of European settlers discontented with life at home in the years around World War I. The best land available to them was in the so-called white highlands of Kenya, so high up the air was cooler and there were fewer insects, and some luck could be had with cattle and certain crops.

The settlers who lived there soon settled into a hard-drinking, high-living regime that has been documented in many books and novels; they were sort of "Dallas" crossed with *Mandingo*. The movie steers relatively clear of the social life, except for a scene where Streep is snubbed at the local club, a few other scenes in town, and an extraordinary moment when she goes down on her knees before the British governor to plead for land for the Africans who live on her bankrupt farm.

Before that moment, she has not seemed particularly interested in Africans, except for an old overseer who becomes a close friend (and this is not true to the spirit of her book, where Africans are of great importance to her). Instead, she is much more involved in the waves of passion that sweep over the veld, as Redford passes through her life like a comet on a trajectory of its own.

He wants to move "his things" in, but does not want to move himself in. He wants commitment, but personal freedom. His ambiguity toward her is something like his ambiguity toward the land, which he penetrates with truck and airplane, leading tours while all the time bemoaning the loss of the virgin veld. Because *Out of Africa* is intelligently written, directed, and acted, however, we do not see his behavior as simply willful and spoiled, but as part of the contradictions he needs to stay an individual in a land where white society is strictly regimented.

The Baroness Blixen needs no such shields; she embodies sufficient contradictions on her own. In a land where whites are foreigners, she is a foreign white. She writes and thinks instead of gossiping and drinking. She runs her own farm. She scorns local gossip. In this hunter, she finds a spirit equal to her own, which is eventually the undoing of their relationship.

Out of Africa is a great movie to look at, breathtakingly filmed on location. It is a movie with the courage to be about complex, sweeping emotions, and to use the star power

of its actors without apology. Sydney Pollack has worked with Redford before—notably in another big-sky epic, *Jeremiah Johnson*. He understands the special, somewhat fragile mystique of his star, who has a tendency to seem overprotective of his own image. In the wrong hands, Redford can look narcissistic. This time, he seems to have much to be narcissistic about.

Out of the Blue ★ ★ ★ ½
R, 94 m., 1982

Linda Manz (CeBe), Dennis Hopper (Don), Sharon Farrell (Kathy), Raymond Burr (Dr. Brean), Don Gordon (Charlie). Directed by Dennis Hopper and produced by Gary Jules Jouvenat. Screenplay by Leonard Yakir and Brenda Nielson.

Out of the Blue is one of the unsung treasures of independent films, a showcase for the maverick talents of two movie rebels: veteran actor Dennis Hopper, of *Easy Rider* and *Rebel Without a Cause*, and young, tough-talking Linda Manz, whose debut in *Days of Heaven* was so heartbreaking. Made in 1982, it never got a chance in commercial theaters. The movie is Hopper's comeback as a director. After the enormous international success of *Easy Rider* (1969) and the resounding thud of his next directorial effort, *Last Movie* (1971), he didn't direct again until this movie (he acted, in such films as *The American Friend* and *Apocalypse Now*). Originally hired just to act in *Out of the Blue*, he took over two weeks into production, rewrote the screenplay, found new locations and made this movie into a bitter, unforgettable poem about alienation.

Hopper is one of the movie's stars, playing an alcoholic truck driver whose semi-rig crashes into a school bus, kills children, and sends him to jail for six years. Manz plays his daughter, a leather-jacketed, punk teen-ager who combs her hair with shoe polish and does Elvis imitations. Her mother is played by Sharon Farrell as a small-town waitress who tries a reconciliation with Hopper when he gets out of prison but is undercut by her drug addiction. Manz is the centerpiece of the film. As she demonstrated in the magnificent pastoral romance *Days of Heaven*, she has a presence all her own. She's tough and hard-edged and yet vulnerable, and in this movie we can sometimes see the scared little kid beneath the punk bravado. She lives in a world of fantasy. All but barricaded into her

room, surrounded by posters of Elvis and other teen heroes, she practices her guitar (she isn't very good) and dresses up in her dad's leather jacket. He's a hero to her. She doesn't buy the story that he was responsible for the deaths of those kids. And when he finally gets out of prison, she has a father at last—but only for a few days.

Hopper's touch as a director is especially strong in a pathetic scene of reunion, including the family's day at the overcast, gloomy beach, and a "party" that turns into a violent brawl dominated by the Hopper character's drunken friend (Don Gordon). The movie escalates so relentlessly toward its violent, nihilistic conclusion that when it comes, we believe it. This is a very good movie that simply got overlooked. When it premiered at the 1980 Cannes Film Festival, it caused a considerable sensation, and Manz was mentioned as a front-runner for the best actress award. But back in North America, the film's Canadian backers had difficulties in making a distribution deal, and the film slipped through the cracks.

The Outlaw Josey Wales ★ ★ ★
PG, 135 m., 1976

Clint Eastwood (Josey), Chief Dan George (The Old Indian), Sondra Locke (The Girl), John Vernon (Fletcher). Directed by Clint Eastwood and produced by Robert Daley. Screenplay by Phil Kaufman.

Clint Eastwood's *The Outlaw Josey Wales* is a strange and daring Western that brings together two of the genre's usually incompatible story lines. On the one hand, it's about a loner, a man of action and few words, who turns his back on civilization and lights out for the Indian nations. On the other hand, it's about a group of people heading West who meet along the trail and cast their destinies together. What happens next is supposed to be against the rules in Westerns, as if *Jeremiah Johnson* were crossed with *Stagecoach*: Eastwood, the loner, becomes the group's leader and father figure.

We meet his character, Josey Wales, just after the Civil War. He's an unreconstructed Southerner, bitter about the atrocities he's witnessed, refusing to surrender. When Northern troops cold-bloodedly murder some of his comrades, he mows down the Yankees with a Gatling gun and becomes a fugitive. So far, we're on familiar ground; Eastwood plays essentially the same character he's been developing since the *Dollar Westerns*. He says little, keeps his face in the shadows, has an almost godlike personal invulnerability, and lives by a code we have to intuit because he'd die rather than explain it aloud.

But then this character begins to come across other drifters and refugees in the unsettled postwar West. The first is an old Indian, played by Chief Dan George with such wonderfully understated wit that there should have been an Oscar nomination around somewhere. "I myself never surrendered," he explains to Josey Wales. "But they got my horse, and *it* surrendered." George achieves the same magical effect here that he did in *Harry and Tonto*, trading Mixmasters for Indian medicine in a jail cell: He's funny and dignified at once. He joins up with the outlaw Eastwood, and their relationship is a reminder of all those great second bananas from the Westerns of the 1940s—the grizzled old characters played by Gabby Hayes and Smiley Burnette. But Chief Dan George brings an aura to his role that audiences seem to respond to viscerally. He has his problems (he's humiliated, as an Indian, that he's grown so old he can no longer sneak up behind people), but he has a humanity that's just there, glowing. He's as open with his personality as Josey Wales is closed; it's a nice match.

Various, and inexhaustible, bounty hunters are constantly on the outlaw's trail, despite the Eastwood ability (in this movie as before) to wipe out six, eight, ten bad guys before they can get off a shot. Eastwood keeps moving West, picking up along the way a young Indian girl and then the survivors of a Kansas family nearly wiped out on their quest for El Dorado. The relationships in the group are easily established or implied. There's not a lot of talking, but everybody understands each other.

Eastwood is such a taciturn and action-oriented performer that it's easy to overlook the fact that he directs many of his movies—and many of the best, most intelligent ones. Here, with the moody, gloomily beautiful, photography of Bruce Surtees, he creates a magnificent Western feeling.

Outrageous Fortune ★ ★
R, 96 m., 1987

Bette Midler (Sandy), Shelley Long (Lauren), Peter Coyote (Michael), Robert Prosky (Korzenowski), John Schuck (Atkins), George Carlin (Frank). Directed by Arthur Hiller and produced by Ted Field and Robert W. Cort. Screenplay by Leslie Dixon.

In an interview in the *New York Times*, Leslie Dixon, the author of the screenplay for *Outrageous Fortune*, revealed some of the secrets of being a successful writer for the movies. You have to read a lot of successful screenplays, she said, and be familiar with what's out there, what's selling at the studios. On the basis of this movie, she has done her job well; *Outrageous Fortune* is a combination of comedy and chase, billed by the producers as "the first genuine female buddy action comedy."

Unfortunately, the movie is so busy cross-pollinating its genres that it never pauses for the kind of thought that might have made it really special, instead of just fitfully funny. This is a movie that has its commercial concept written all over it; it's so painstakingly crafted as a product that the messy spontaneity of life is rarely allowed to interrupt.

The film stars Bette Midler and Shelley Long as two would-be acting students who discover they're both having an affair with the same fellow student. Midler plays a brassy, vulgar veteran of movies with names like *Ninja Vixens*, and Long is a Yale graduate who has deep ideas about "Art." The man they have in common is played by Peter Coyote, as a slick, mysterious Romeo who turns out, alas, to be involved in espionage.

I say "alas" because this movie goes wrong the moment it introduces its counterspy plot. You can almost hear the standard clichés slamming into place. Midler and Long discover that their drama teacher is a spy (Robert Prosky), that Coyote is in the class to spy on him, that there are people who want to kill them, and that it's up to them to chase all over the Western states and endure untold physical risks until the mystery is solved.

Take away the specific details, and this is the same premise that sabotaged *Jumpin' Jack Flash*, another "genuine" female action comedy. What happens is, the screenplay gets so wound up with the action that there's no time to explore the characters or let them be funny on their own terms. Midler has some very funny moments in *Outrageous Fortune*, but they're inspired by the personality she brings to the movie, not the one that Dixon's screenplay supplies for her. Long, who doesn't come packaged with a pre-existing comic persona, seems adrift most of the time.

My advice to Leslie Dixon would be:

After you've studied all those screenplays, ask yourself what's wrong with them, and you're likely to discover that they all begin with interesting characters and then march relentlessly into a series of clichés involving the CIA, the Russians, car chases, sinister plots, and colorful locations. Truly funny movies (here I include Midler's previous two films, *Down and Out in Beverly Hills* and *Ruthless People*) settle down in one location and explore their characters, finding humor in human nature instead of in a lot of expensive physical stunts.

Outrageous Fortune has a climax that must have been expensive and dangerous to film, but it's a waste of time. The plot requires Long to leap from one towering desert rock formation to another, while she's chased by the bad guys. The whole sequence breaks down for two reasons: (1) The stunt is so dangerous that it distracts from any latent comedy, and (2) we're so busy trying to spot when they're using the stunt doubles that we lose any remaining interest in the plot.

Overboard ★ ★ ★
PG, 113 m., 1987

Goldie Hawn (Joanna/Annie), Kurt Russell (Dean Proffit), Edward Herrmann (Grant Stayton III), Katherine Helmond (Edith Mintz), Michael Hagerty (Billy Pratt), Roddy McDowall (Andrew), Harvey Alan Miller (Dr. Korman). Directed by Garry Marshall and produced by Anthea Sylbert and Alexandra Rose. Screenplay by Leslie Dixon.

Overboard is one more twist on the old reliable story about the snob who learns how the other half lives. The formula is written in stone: The character is established as stuck-up, arrogant, and spoiled, and then something happens to bring reality crashing through the door. By the end of the movie, the hero has discovered humility, gratitude, and love.

The reason this formula has been around so long is that it's dependable, as Goldie Hawn cheerfully proves in *Overboard*. There is hardly a major development in this story that we can't predict thirty minutes in advance, but what does it matter when the performances are so much fun, and there are so many comic delights along the way? This is the kind of movie that not only could have been directed by Frank Capra or Preston Sturges, but may have been.

The movie stars Hawn as a rich, bitchy society lady who lives on a luxury yacht with her snotty husband (Edward Herrmann) and long-suffering butler (Roddy McDowall). When the yacht pulls into harbor for repairs, she hires a local carpenter (Kurt Russell) to remodel some of her closet space. Then she refuses to pay him because he didn't use cedar wood—and doesn't *everybody* know closets are constructed of cedar? In the disagreement that follows, she kicks Russell overboard and pitches in his tools after him.

Later that night, Goldie herself falls overboard, is struck by a garbage scow, and ends up in the local hospital with amnesia. Seeing her bedraggled photo on the TV news, Russell maps his revenge: He will claim Hawn as his own long-lost wife, and bring her down a notch or two by turning her into a domestic laborer and baby sitter for his four ill-behaved boys.

All together now, everybody, what happens next? Is there a scene of rebellion? And then a scene where Hawn shows how incompetent she is, even cleaning the windows with furniture polish? And a scene where Kurt and the boys play mean tricks on her? And a scene where she begins to change, just a little? And a scene where the boys get to like her? And a moment when she begins to feel she belongs with this family, and feels love and pride? And then a scene where her snotty husband turns up again? And a scene where she gets mad at Russell for having so cruelly deceived her?

If you cannot find each and every one of those scenes in *Overboard*, you're not even trying. The general outlines of this story—spoiled character is reformed by humbling experience—has even been followed before by Hawn herself in *Private Benjamin*. What makes *Overboard* special, however, is the genuine charm, wit, and warm energy that's generated by the entire cast and director Garry Marshall.

Hawn and Russell work well together, never overplaying scenes that could easily have self-destructed. The movie is filled with dozens of funny little moments, like the way McDowall arrives on time with the caviar and is bawled out for potentially being late. And the way Michael Hagerty, as Russell's best friend Billy, covers up when Hawn finds a pair of her own panties in Russell's truck and thinks they must belong to another woman ("I got lucky with one of them phone-for-sex gals").

If the ending of *Overboard* is reminiscent of *The African Queen*, maybe that's because the whole movie owes something to the Bogart-Hepburn relationship, in which a rude and crude man is civilized by a real lady. In *Overboard*, that development is cross-bred with the heartless bitch who is civilized by a real gentleman. It's kind of a nice process, and it makes a warm and funny movie.

P

Pacific Heights ★ ★

R, 107 m., 1990

Melanie Griffith (Patty Palmer), Matthew Modine (Drake Goodman), Michael Keaton (Carter Hayes), Mako (Toshio Watanabe), Nobu McCarthy (Mira Watanabe), Laurie Metcalf (Stephanie MacDonald), Dorian Harewood (Dennis Reed), Tippi Hedren (Florence Peters). Directed by John Schlesinger and produced by Scott Rudin and William Sackheim. Screenplay by Daniel Pyne.

Pacific Heights is a horror film for yuppies, in which the bad guy uses the ax to attack your three-flat, not you. It tells the story of a young couple who buy a Victorian home in San Francisco and are then attacked by the tenant from hell—a sinister man who moves in without authorization, never pays the rent, uses a jigsaw in the middle of the night, and breeds roaches which he dispatches on journeys to other parts of the building.

His strategy is to drive the couple into foreclosure and then pick up the property cheap, although exactly what financial steps this would entail is never explained. Maybe he's not so sure himself. Basically, he's a psycho who has been disowned by his family and gets his sick thrills by breaking up other happy households. And, as played with a certain effectiveness by Michael Keaton, he has that smarmy, ingratiating quality of the kind of guy whose smile makes your skin crawl.

The couple is played by Melanie Griffith and Matthew Modine, who fudge on their financial statement to buy the house, and then need every month's check from the two rental flats in order to keep up the payments. That's why it's so desperately important to them to evict Keaton and get possession of

the flat. Besides, what's he doing in there? He's moved in some kind of slack-jawed roommate, and the two of them hammer and saw all night long, until the nice Japanese-American couple in the rear flat are forced to move out (the tidal waves of cockroaches are another reason for leaving).

As a story idea, *Pacific Heights* has a certain appeal. The movie's problem is in its execution. I never much liked the young couple, or believed they liked one another, and I didn't get to see enough of Keaton in the early stages of the movie, because he was always behind a closed door. The rhythm of the movie is established early, and repeated until it gets predictable: Keaton commits an outrage, Modine starts to froth at the mouth, Griffith tries to restrain him, Modine goes too far, Keaton wins another victory.

The pattern escalates through all the usual clichés of the horror film, including several trips into the dark cellar and the dark garage. No obligatory moment is overlooked—no, not even the one where the strange noise in the cellar turns out to be the cat, or the one where the heroine realizes someone is sitting in the dark and looking at her. The most unbelievable scene has to be the one where Modine just happens to be in the crawl space under the Keaton apartment at the right time to overhear a conversation that explains everything to him.

There is one sequence that does work, and that's the one where Griffith figures out a way to get revenge on Keaton. I won't reveal her methods, but they're fun. What isn't fun is the movie's sprung pacing, which takes us on a leisurely tour of its horrors instead of socking us with them, and the way the plot alternates between slice-of-life realism and shameless manipulation. It would have been wise to choose a single tone early on, and stick to it.

In a way, *Pacific Heights* could stand comparison to *Rosemary's Baby*. Both films are about a young couple who are deeply concerned by events that seem to be happening in another flat in their building. The difference between the movies is instructive: Roman Polanski insinuates us into the gradually growing horror of his couple in *Rosemary's Baby*, while John Schlesinger, in *Pacific Heights*, seems concerned only with generating the most obvious shock effects.

There's not even the slightest attempt to present Keaton as a normal tenant who only slowly turns sinister. He's a monster from his first appearance—the Freddy Krueger of tenants. Maybe you can never really kill him, and we'll get *Pacific Heights* parts two, three, and four, with Keaton moving into gentrified neighborhoods from coast to coast.

The Package ★ ★ ★

R, 108 m., 1989

Gene Hackman (Johnny Gallagher), Joanna Cassidy (Eileen Gallagher), Tommy Lee Jones (Thomas Boyette), John Heard (Col. Glen Whitacre). Directed by Andrew Davis and produced by Beverly J. Camhe and Tobie Haggerty. Screenplay by John Bishop.

The Package is like one of those thrillers where you keep having to turn back to an earlier chapter to see if you missed something. It turns out you haven't. The movie's plot is so intricate that it seems there have to be loose ends, but there aren't any, and after it's over you rerun the events in your head, seeing at last how all the pieces fit together. Untangling the conspiracy is one of the story's pleasures.

The movie stars Gene Hackman in another one of those man-of-action roles he seems to play more convincingly than ever, now that he seems to be a little too old to be guys like this; both he and his characters seem to have the benefit of experience. He's the leader of a crack U.S. military unit in charge of security at an American-Soviet nuclear disarmament summit. When security seems to have been compromised and a carload of VIPs is ambushed, Hackman gets a lot of the blame. And he is rotated stateside, as the escort for a military prisoner (played with irony and menace by Tommy Lee Jones).

He has already picked up some hints that nothing—especially not the violent ambush—was quite as it seemed. And in a run-in before he leaves Europe, he encounters a specialist in undercover espionage (John Heard) who gives him the creeps. Hackman doesn't like spies. He doesn't think they're professional or quite honest, and the movie argues that he's right; we begin to witness small moments and snatches of conversation that suggest there's a conspiracy to undermine the peace talks—a conspiracy of spies from both sides. But by then Hackman is on a military aircraft to America with his prisoner.

And it is here, this early in the film, that the surprises start, as the plot turns in upon itself, giving us a series of people with shifting identities and allegiances. Who is the prisoner—really? When Hackman is attacked in the washroom of the airport in Washington and the prisoner is spirited away, was that an escape, a kidnapping, or part of the same plot? Attempting to track down reality in a bewildering maze of possibilities, Hackman calls on one person he knows he can trust: his former wife (Joanna Cassidy), who now outranks him in the military.

It would not be fair to reveal very much more of the plot. In fact, this plot really consists of its revelations. Like *The Manchurian Candidate*, it creates a world in which little is as it seems, and long-buried conspiracies eventually pay off. The Hackman character realizes he has stumbled over a remarkably subtle plan to assassinate a world leader during a visit to Chicago—but we know of the plan before he does, and one of the movie's pleasures is the way we are allowed to figure things out for ourselves, along with Hackman or a little ahead of him.

The Package is directed by Andrew Davis. It is his third film in a row to involve strong action heroes and labyrinthine conspiracies set in Chicago (the others were *Code of*

Silence, with Chuck Norris, and *Above the Law*, with Steven Seagal). Although shooting movies on location has been a Hollywood way of life for years, few directors get more out of a location than Davis. He doesn't seem to see cities as most other directors do; he contrives somehow to create a more convincing sense of actual places. By the time the moment for the would-be assassination has arrived, we have a good idea of the physical layout involved—the angles, the hiding places—but we also have an almost palpable sense of the city.

All three of Davis's movies have the same theme running just beneath the surface, one involving the loyalty of law-enforcement professionals to one another. He always has a character in his movies who is a veteran, street-smart cop with a strong sense of ethics, a man whose word can be absolutely counted on. And there's always a conspiracy somewhere else in the legal apparatus; all of Davis's movies involve diabolical schemes by top security people. What sets *The Package* apart from the earlier films is that there's less emphasis on violent action and more on the unfolding of the plot.

Hackman is very good in the leading role, but then Gene Hackman is so good, so often, that he sometimes seems like a natural force in danger of being taken for granted. What I noticed in this film was the way he made his character into a particular human being. There's not a lot to build on. The plot is so important, the pacing is so urgent, that the pure character moments are rare. So he works with his dialogue, finding ways to make it sound like his ingrained style of speech. There's never the sense he's reading dialogue; he has a habitual ease with the words, almost a weariness in the way he handles his business, that convinces us he's been doing his job for a long time.

I often complain that modern thrillers leave out the third act. There's the setup, the development, and then, instead of a payoff, we get a routine chase and shoot-out. *The Package* does end in a race against time, but Davis bases the race so firmly on who the characters are and what their goals are that it doesn't feel contrived. The whole movie, in fact, is smarter than most contemporary thrillers. It gives us credit for being able to figure things out, and it contains characters who are devilishly intelligent. Almost smart enough, we think for a while, to really pull this thing off.

Pale Rider ★ ★ ★
R, 113 m., 1985

Clint Eastwood (Preacher), Michael Moriarty (Hull Barret), Carrie Snodgress (Sarah Wheeler), Christopher Penn (Josh LaHood), Richard Dysart (Coy LaHood), Sydney Penny (Megan Wheeler), Richard Kiel (Club), Doug McGrath (Spider). Directed and produced by Clint Eastwood. Screenplay by Michael Butler and Dennis Shryack.

Clint Eastwood has become an actor whose moods and silences are so well-known that the slightest suggestion will do to convey an emotion. No actor is more aware of his own instrument, and Eastwood demonstrates that in *Pale Rider*, a film he dominates so completely that only later do we realize how little we really saw of him.

Instead of filling each scene with his own image and dialogue, Eastwood uses sleight of hand: We are shown his eyes, or a corner of his mouth, or his face in a shadow, or his figure with strong light behind it. He has few words. The other characters in the movie project their emotions upon him. He may indeed be the Pale Rider suggested in the title, whose name was death, but he may also be an avenging spirit, come back from the grave to confront the man who murdered him. One of the subtlest things in the movie is the way it plays with the possibility that Eastwood's character may be a ghost, or at least something other than an ordinary mortal.

Other things in the movie are not so subtle. In its broad outlines, *Pale Rider* is a traditional Western, with a story that has been told, in one form or another, a thousand times before. In a small California mining town, some independent miners have staked a claim to a promising lode. The town is ruled by a cabal of evil men, revolving around the local banker and the marshal, who is his hired gun. The banker would like to buy out the little miners, but, lacking that, he will use force to drive them off their land and claim it for his company.

Into this hotbed rides the lone figure of Eastwood, wearing a clerical collar and preferring to be called "Preacher." There are people here he seems to know from before. The marshal, for example, seems to be trying to remember where he has previously encountered this man. Eastwood moves in with the small miners, and becomes close with one group: a miner (Michael Moriarty) who lives with a woman (Carrie

Snodgress) and her daughter (Sydney Penny). He urges the miners to take a stand and defend their land, and agrees to help them. That sets the stage for a series of violent confrontations.

As the film's director, Eastwood has done some interesting things with his vision of the West. Instead of making the miners' shacks into early American antique exhibits, he shows them as small and sparse. The sources of light are almost all from the outside. Interiors are dark and gloomy, and the sun is blinding in its intensity. The Eastwood character himself is almost always backlit, so we have to strain to see him, and this strategy makes him more mysterious and fascinating than any dialogue could have.

There are some moments when the movie's myth-making becomes self-conscious. In one scene, for example, the marshal's gunmen enter a restaurant and empty their guns into the chair where Eastwood had been sitting moments before. He is no longer there; can't they see that? In the final shoot-out, the Preacher has a magical ability to dematerialize, confounding the bad guys, and one shot (of a hand with a gun emerging from a water trough) should have been eliminated—it spoils the logic of the scene. But *PaleRider* is, overall, a considerable achievement, a classic Western of style and excitement. Many of the greatest Westerns grew out of a director's profound understanding of the screen presence of his actors; consider, for example, John Ford's films with John Wayne and Henry Fonda. In *Pale Rider*, Clint Eastwood is the director, and having directed himself in nine previous films, he understands so well how he works on the screen that the movie has a resonance that probably was not even there in the screenplay.

The Paper Chase ★ ★ ★ ★
PG, 111 m., 1973

Timothy Bottoms (Hart), Lindsay Wagner (Susan), John Houseman (Kingsfield), Graham Beckel (Ford), Edward Herrmann (Anderson), Bob Lydiard (O'Connor). Directed by James Bridges and produced by Robert C. Thompson and Rodrick Paul. Screenplay by Bridges.

The Paper Chase is about an aggressive, very bright, terribly engaging first-year student at Harvard Law School. The movie respects its hero, respects the school, and most of all

respects the venerable Professor Kingsfield, tyrant of contract law.

Kingsfield is really the movie's central character, even though John Houseman gets supporting billing for the role. Everything centers around his absolute dictatorship in the classroom and his icy reserve at all other times. He's the kind of teacher who inspires total dread in his students, and at the same time a measure of hero worship; he doesn't just know contract law, he wrote the book.

Into his classroom every autumn come several dozen would-be Harvard law graduates, who fall into the categories we all remember from school: (a) the drones, who get everything right but will go forth to lead lives of impeccable mediocrity; (b) the truly intelligent, who will pass or fail entirely on the basis of whether they're able to put up with the crap; (c) those with photographic memories, who can remember everything but connect nothing; (d) the students whose dogged earnestness will somehow pull them through; and (e) the doomed.

One of each of these types is in the study group of Hart, the movie's hero, and the one who is truly intelligent. He's a graduate of the University of Minnesota and somewhat out of place among the Ivy League types, but he does well in class because he really cares about the law. He also cares about Kingsfield, to the degree that he breaks into the library archives to examine the master's very own undergraduate notes.

Hart is played by Timothy Bottoms, the star of *The Last Picture Show*. Bottoms is an awfully good actor, and so natural and unaffected that he shows up the mannerisms of actors like Dustin Hoffman or Jon Voight. Bottoms never seems to try; he's just there, complete and convincing. He falls in love, fatefully, with Susan (Lindsay Wagner), who turns out to be, even more fatefully, Kingsfield's daughter. Their relationship is a little hard to follow in the film; we aren't sure why she treats him the way she does—after all, she loves the guy—and the movie jerks abruptly in bringing them back together after a split-up.

But that isn't fatal because the fundamental relationship in the movie is between Hart and Kingsfield. The crusty old professor obviously appreciates the intelligence and independence of his prize student, but he hardly ever lets his affection show; there's a great scene in the classroom where he calls Hart forward, offers him a dime, and says:

"Call your mother and tell her you will never be a lawyer." Houseman is able to project subtleties of character even while appearing stiff and unrelenting; it's a performance of Academy Award quality, and resulted in an Oscar for Best Supporting Actor.

Lindsay Wagner, as the daughter, is also a surprise; she made her movie debut in the unfortunate *Two People*, which had Peter Fonda as a conscience-stricken Army deserter. She wasn't able to make much of an impression in that one, but *The Paper Chase* establishes her as an actress with class and the saving grace of humor.

What's best about the movie is that it considers interesting adults—young and old—in an intelligent manner. After it's over we almost feel relief; there are so many movies about clods reacting moronically to romantic and/or violent situations. But we hardly ever get movies about people who seem engaging enough to spend half an hour talking with (what would you say to Charles Bronson?). Here's one that works.

Paperhouse ★ ★ ★ ★
PG-13, 94 m., 1989

Charlotte Burke (Anna), Elliott Spiers (Marc), Glenne Headly (Kate), Ben Cross (Dad), Gemma Jones (Dr. Nichols). Directed by Bernard Rose and produced by Tim Bevan and Sarah Radclyffe. Screenplay by Matthew Jacobs, based on the novel *Marianne Dreams*, by Catherine Storr.

Paperhouse is a film in which every image has been distilled to the point of almost frightening simplicity. It's like a Bergman film, in which the clarity is almost overwhelming, and we realize how muddled and cluttered most movies are. This one has the stark landscapes and the obsessively circling story lines of a dream—which is, what it is.

The movie takes place during the illness of Anna (Charlotte Burke), a thirteen-year-old with a mysterious fever. One day in class, Anna draws a lonely house on a windswept cliff and puts a sad-faced little boy in the window. She is reprimanded by the teacher, runs away from the school, falls in a culvert, and is knocked unconscious.

And then she dreams of a "real" landscape just like the one in her drawing, with the very same house, and with a sad boy's face in an upper window. She asks him to come outside. He cannot, because his legs will not move, and because she has not drawn any stairs in the house.

Found by a search party, Anna is returned home, where her behavior is explained by the fever she has developed. The film alternates between Anna's sickroom and her dream landscape, and very few other characters are allowed into her confined world. Among them, however, are her mother (Glenne Headly) and her doctor (Gemma Jones), and there are flashbacks to her absent father (Ben Cross), who is the distant and ambiguous father figure of so many frightening children's stories.

The film develops a simple rhythm. Anna draws, dreams, and then revises her drawings. She sketches in a staircase for the young boy, whose name is Marc, and fills his room with toys. She adds a fruit tree and flowers to the garden. And then one day she discovers, to her astonishment, that her doctor has another patient—a boy named Marc, who faces paralysis, and about whom she is very concerned.

Paperhouse wisely never attempts to provide any kind of a rational explanation for its story, although we might care to guess that the doctor is sort of a psychic conduit allowing Anna and Marc to enter each other's dreams. Anna rebels briefly against the notion that she is someone playing God for Marc, but then accepts the responsibility of her drawings and her dreams.

Paperhouse is not in any sense simply a children's movie, even though its subject may seem to point it in that direction. It is a thoughtfully written, meticulously directed fantasy in which the actors play their roles with great seriousness. Watching it, I was engrossed in the development of the story, and found myself accepting the film's logic on its own terms.

The movie's director is Bernard Rose, a young Briton who had some success with music videos before this first feature. He carries some of the same visual inventiveness of the best music videos over into his images here, paring them down until only the essential elements are present, making them so spare that, like the figure of Death in Bergman's *Seventh Seal*, they seem too concrete to be fantasies.

I will not discuss the end of the movie, except to say that it surprised and pleased me. I don't know what I expected—some kind of conventional plot resolution, I suppose—but *Paperhouse* ends instead with a bittersweet surprise that is unexpected and

almost spiritual. This is not a movie to be measured and weighed and plumbed, but to be surrendered to.

Parenthood ★ ★ ★ ★
PG-13, 124 m., 1989

Steve Martin (Gil), Mary Steenburgen (Karen), Dianne Wiest (Helen), Jason Robards (Frank), Rick Moranis (Nathan), Tom Hulce (Larry), Martha Plimpton (Julie), Keanu Reeves (Tod). Directed by Ron Howard and produced by Brian Glazer. Screenplay by Lowell Ganz and Babaloo Mandel.

Ron Howard's *Parenthood* is a delicate balancing act between comedy and truth, a movie that contains a lot of laughter and yet is more concerned with character than punch lines. It's the best kind of comedy, where we recognize the truth of what's happening even while we're smiling, and where we eventually acknowledge that there is a truth in comedy that serious drama can never quite reach.

The movie is about a lot of parents and children—four generations, from an ancient matriarch to a three-year-old. Because almost everyone in this movie has both parents and children, almost everyone in the movie is both a child and a parent, and a lot of the film's strength comes from the way it sees each generation in reaction to its parents' notions of parenthood. The complexity of the movie—there are a dozen or more important characters—must have seemed daunting on the writing level, and yet the film's first strength is in the smart, nimble screenplay, which is also very wise.

Parenthood stars Steve Martin and Mary Steenburgen as the parents of three children, with another on the way. Life is not easy for them, although they are surrounded by all of the artifacts of middle-class suburbia, such as a nice home and new uniforms for the Little League team. Martin is engaged in warfare at the office, where he wants to be made a partner, and yet he resists spending too much time at work because he wants to be a good father—a better father than his father (Jason Robards), who was cold and distant.

We can see this for ourselves when we meet the Robards character. Or can we? Robards himself feels little love for his surviving parent, a mother of whom he snarls, "Yeah, she's still alive" at a family gathering. Robards has had four children, and we meet them all in the movie: characters played by

Martin, Dianne Wiest, Harley Kozak, and Tom Hulce.

The Hulce character, Robards's youngest child, is in his mid-twenties and is the family's black sheep (he is introduced with the line, "Whatever you do, don't lend him any money"). He is a compulsive gambler and liar, and yet Robards somehow keeps alive a flame of hope for him, and loves him and cares, and so you can see that parenthood has not been simple for him, either.

We learn these and other things in an indirect way; the screenplay, by Lowell Ganz and Babaloo Mandel, with input from director Ron Howard, never reveals an obvious plot line, but instead cuts between several different family situations.

With Martin and Steenburgen, we see an attempt being made to create a typical, wholesome American nuclear family—with Martin driven almost to exhaustion by his determination to be a "good pop." Dianne Wiest plays a divorced mother of two, who is bitter about her former husband, and weary but courageous in her determination to do her best by a strong-willed sixteen-year-old daughter (Martha Plimpton) and a secretive, distracted thirteen-year-old son (Leaf Phoenix).

Kozak plays a sensible mother whose husband (Rick Moranis) is insanely obsessed with his theories about tapping the genius within young children; he reads Kafka at bedtime to their daughter, not yet four, and proudly demonstrates that she can look at a group of paper dots and calculate their square root (the child is only human and later eats the dots). The Hulce character is the only one not yet married, and indeed, in his gambling and lying and dangerous brinksmanship he seems to have flown entirely out of the orbit of parenthood. Perhaps the best scene in the movie is the one between Robards and Hulce after the old man has decided to make one more sacrifice for his no-good son, and then the son betrays the trust because what he really wants is not help, but simply the freedom to keep on losing.

Howard, Ganz, and Mandel have fifteen children among them, I understand, and that is easy to believe. Even such standard scenes as the annual school play, with the parents beaming proudly from the audience and the kids dropping their lines onstage, is handled here with a new spin. There are many moments of accurate observation, as when kids of a certain age fall in love with terms for excrement, or when kids at a party refuse to have the good time that has been so expensively prepared for them.

What I enjoyed most about the movie was the way so many scenes were thought through to an additional level. Howard and his collaborators don't simply make a point, they make the point and then take another look at it from a new angle, finding a different kind of truth. There is a wonderful moment, for example, in which the old matriarch (Helen Shaw) makes a wise and pithy observation, and then goes out to get into the car. Her dialogue provides a strong exit line, and a lot of movies would have left it at that, but not *Parenthood*, which adds a twist: "If she's so smart," Martin observes, looking out the window, "why is she sitting in the neighbor's car?"

In a movie filled with good performances, I especially admired the work by Martin, Steenburgen, Wiest, and Robards. What we are seeing in their performances, I think, is acting enriched by having lived, having actually gone through some of the doubts and long nights and second thoughts that belong to their characters. For Ron Howard, the movie is a triumph of a different sort: Having emerged from a TV sitcom determined to become a director, he paid his dues with apprentice work like *Grand Theft Auto*, went on to box-office and critical success with *Splash* and *Cocoon*, and now has made a wonderful film that shows him as a filmmaker mature and secure enough to find truth in comedy, and comedy in truth, even though each hides in the other so successfully.

Parents ★ ★
R, 81 m., 1989

Randy Quaid (Nick Laemle), Mary Beth Hurt (Lily Laemle), Sandy Dennis (Millie Dew), Bryan Madorsky (Michael Laemle), Juno Mills-Cockell (Sheila Zellner), Kathryn Grody (Miss Baxter). Directed by Bob Balaban and produced by Bonnie Palef. Screenplay by Christopher Hawthorne.

Most children suspect that adults are capable of playing unspeakable tricks on them. One Sunday afternoon, my parents attempted to serve me "chicken," when I had every reason to believe that the presence of the "chicken" on my plate was ominously related to the disappearance of one of the rabbits from the hutch in the backyard of the Shaw family—a rabbit the Shaw boys and I had adopted as a special pet. To be sure, there was a war on,

and a lot of families were keeping rabbits or raising victory gardens, but as I looked at that pathetic little bunny drumstick, all floured and browned and crispy, I knew that I was being asked to become little more than a cannibal.

Parents is a movie about that feeling, about the conviction that after the kids are in bed and their lights are out, parents engage in weird rituals and unthinkable practices. What about those roars of laughter that come echoing down the hallway from the living room, for example: Are the grown-ups just having a good time, or are they holding their nightly planning session on how to play tricks on kids?

Parents takes place in the 1950s, an ideal decade for this material, and stars Bryan Madorsky as Michael, a solemn, owl-faced little boy whose life centers around one question: What are the "leftovers" left over from? Night after night, his parents place steaming shanks of meat, juicy red slabs of prime roast, on his plate. Where do they come from? "Leftovers," his mom says. But then his mom and dad wink at each other over the table and share a secret laugh, and little Michael knows in his bones that there is something fundamentally wrong with the menu.

Because it speaks to a terror that lurks deep within our memories, *Parents* has the potential to be a great horror film. But it never knows quite what to do with its inspiration. Is it a satire, a black comedy, or just plain horror? The right note is never found, and so the movie's scenes coexist uneasily with one another. There is, for example, the night that Michael creeps out of bed and discovers his parents engaged in some kind of bloody, savage rite on the living room floor. How does that fit with the sessions Michael has with the school psychiatrist, who is obviously crazier than any of her clients?

The director, Bob Balaban, has cast his movie well. Mary Beth Hurt plays the mom, a perky little thing with a '50s hairdo and clothes that come right out of the Simplicity pattern book. She's always in the kitchen doing things with enormous stainless steel knives. Dad is Randy Quaid, whose horn-rim glasses and business suits cannot disguise a certain predatory quality, especially when he leans over the table to skewer a big piece of "roast beef." The look of the movie, and the feel of the family's split-level '50s modern house, is all just right. But somehow there's no payoff.

Perhaps Balaban and his screenwriter, Christopher Hawthorne, should have declared themselves. Is this a horror movie? Or a psychological comedy about the secret fears of children? Some of the scenes stray so far into blood-soaked pathology that the others don't fit. The movie needs an organizing vision, a clear line through to the end, a feeling that the director is sure of the effect he wants to achieve. Satire of this sort is delicate, and Balaban has the same problem that Paul Bartel had in *Eating Raoul*, another comedy about cannibalism: The more a movie addresses itself to our secret terrors, the harder it has to work to be funny—because at some level, it is attempting to convince us to eat our pet rabbits.

Paris, Texas ★ ★ ★ ★
R, 145 m., 1984

Harry Dean Stanton (Travis), Nastassja Kinski (Jane), Hunter Carson (Their Son), Dean Stockwell (Walt), Aurore Clement (Anne), Bernhard Wicki (Dr. Ulmer). Directed by Wim Wenders and produced by Don Guest. Screenplay by Sam Shepard.

A man walks alone in the desert. He has no memory, no past, no future. He finds an isolated settlement where the doctor, another exile, a German, makes some calls. Eventually the man's brother comes to take him back home again. Before we think about this as the beginning of a story, let's think about it very specifically as the first twenty minutes of a movie. When I was watching *Paris, Texas* for the first time, my immediate reaction to the film's opening scenes was one of intrigue: I had no good guesses about where this movie was headed, and that, in itself, was exciting, because in this most pragmatic of times, even the best movies seem to be intended as predictable consumer products. If you see a lot of movies, you can sit there watching the screen and guessing what will happen next, and be right most of the time.

That's not the case with *Paris, Texas*. This is a defiantly individual film, about loss and loneliness and eccentricity. We haven't met the characters before in a dozen other films. To some people, that can be disconcerting; I've actually read reviews of *Paris, Texas* complaining because the man in the desert is German, and that another character is French. Is it written that the people in movies have to be Middle Americans, like refugees from a sitcom?

The characters in this movie come out of the imagination of Sam Shepard, the playwright of rage and alienation, and Wim Wenders, a West German director who often makes "road movies," in which lost men look for answers in the vastness of great American cities. The lost man is played this time by Harry Dean Stanton, the most forlorn and angry of all great American character actors. We never do find out what personal cataclysm led to his walk in the desert, but as his memory begins to return, we learn how much he has lost. He was married, once, and had a little boy. The boy has been raised in the last several years by Stanton's brother (Dean Stockwell) and sister-in-law (Aurore Clement). Stanton's young wife (Nastassja Kinski) seems to have disappeared entirely in the years of his exile. The little boy is played by Hunter Carson, in one of the least affected, most convincing juvenile performances in a long time. He is more or less a typical American kid, despite the strange adults in his life. He meets Stanton and accepts him as a second father, but of course he thinks of Stockwell and Clement as his family. Stanton has a mad dream of finding his wife and putting the pieces of his past back together again. He goes looking, and finds Kinski behind the one-way mirror of one of those sad sex emporiums where men pay to talk to women on the telephone.

Paris, Texas is more concerned with exploring emotions than with telling a story. This isn't a movie about missing persons, but about missing feelings. The images in the film show people framed by the vast, impersonal forms of modern architecture; the cities seem as empty as the desert did in the opening sequence. And yet this film is not the standard attack on American alienation. It seems fascinated by America, by our music, by the size of our cities, and a land so big that a man like the Stanton character might easily get misplaced. Stanton's name in the movie is Travis, and that reminds us not only of Travis McGee, the private eye who specialized in helping lost souls, but also of lots of American Westerns in which things were simpler, and you knew who your enemy was. It is a name out of American pop culture, and the movie is a reminder that all three of the great German New Wave directors—Herzog, Fassbinder, and Wenders—have been fascinated by American rock music, American fashions, American mythology.

This is Wenders's fourth film shot at least partly in America (the others were *Alice in the Cities*, *The American Friend*, and *Hammett*). It also bears traces of *Kings of the Road*, his German road movie in which two men meet by chance and travel for a time together, united by their mutual inability to love and understand women. But it is better than those movies—it's his best work so far—because it links the unforgettable images to a spare, perfectly heard American idiom. The Sam Shepard dialogue has a way of allowing characters to tell us almost nothing about themselves, except for their most banal beliefs and their deepest fears.

Paris, Texas is a movie with the kind of passion and willingness to experiment that was more common fifteen years ago than it is now. It has more links with films like *Five Easy Pieces* and *Easy Rider* and *Midnight Cowboy*, than with the slick arcade games that are the box-office winners of the 1980s. It is true, deep, and brilliant.

Pascali's Island ★ ★ ★
PG-13, 101 m., 1988

Ben Kingsley (Basil Pascali), Charles Dance (Anthony Bowles), Kevork Malikyan (Mardosian), George Murcell (Herr Gesing), Helen Mirren (Lydia Neuman), Nadim Sawalha (Pasha). Directed and written by James Dearden. Produced by Eric Fellner.

There is a bittersweet loneliness in the life of an exile that exerts a romantic appeal to many people. They see themselves as a mysterious figure on a Mediterranean island, seen by all, known to few, living a life of intense privacy in full view. The problem with such a life is that it cannot sustain trust; the very essence of exile is the belief that one can only really count on oneself.

Basil Pascali is a man with such a belief, and at the beginning of *Pascali's Island* we see him at his window, his pen in hand, looking out over the harbor where a stranger is being brought ashore. Pascali (Ben Kingsley) is a spy. The year is 1908, and he has been living on the Greek island of Simi for twenty years or more, faithfully filing his reports to the sultan of the Ottoman Empire. He cannot even remember when one of his reports was acknowledged, but his payment still arrives regularly, and so he mails out his reports just as faithfully.

Since there is every likelihood that no one ever reads a word he writes, why does he persevere? Perhaps it is because, in his exile, he has become a voyeur, feeding off the lives of others as a substitute for the sterility of his own. In the course of this movie, his lifelong practice will have disastrous results.

The stranger he sees being brought ashore is Anthony Bowles (Charles Dance), an Englishman who claims to be an archeologist. Like almost everyone in this forgotten corner of the world, however, he is probably lying about himself, and his motives can be assumed to be suspicious. He needs a translator for his work, and hires Pascali (who has been careful to put himself in the path of the job).

Another one of the exiles on the island is Lydia Neuman (Helen Mirren), a painter who drenches her pictures in the hot, blinding Mediterranean sun. Pascali has been in love with her for quite some time, from afar. He dares not draw closer because he is a spy (his official reason), and because he cannot abide sharing his privacy with anyone (his real reason). Yet he has cherished the notion that Lydia will someday be his own, and so it is with dismay that he realizes that the bluff, confident Bowles plans to romance her. Lydia is, however, something of a burnout case, and looks with bemusement on those who would love her.

Now we have the elements of the story: The voyeur who cannot trust, the adventurer who cannot be trusted, and the muse who cannot inspire. There are lots of others on the island, Turks, Greeks, Germans, all with more complicated motives than they admit. No one is quite as he seems on Simi. And then one day, in the midst of this, Bowles shockingly discovers something that is real, and that does mean what it seems to mean.

It is the perfect statue of a boy, a priceless, unblemished sculpture from ancient Greek times. Although Bowles is instantly transfixed by the worth and beauty of his find, what he cannot quite deal with is the fact that it is absolutely authentic. Such stark reality undercuts his personality, which is based on deception, on pretending to have more and to know more than he really does. How can such a man deal with the possession of the real thing?

Pascali's Island buries this question within a larger intrigue, as Pascali barters information to both sides and sets about an intrigue that ends in catastrophe. By the end of the film, everything has been lost, and the reason is that none of the characters knows how to deal with acceptance and success. At the heart of *Pascali's Island* is a deep irony: Its characters know how to mask failure, but not how to surrender it.

The movie was written and directed by James Dearden, who wrote *Fatal Attraction*, but it has almost nothing in common with that film. It is a mood piece, meditative, in which even the melodrama of the plot grows out of the flawed souls of the characters. Everything in a film like this depends on performance, and it is hard to imagine how it could have been better cast.

Ben Kingsley's performance is at the heart of everything, and he is a master at suggesting the passionate need and sadness that lurk just beneath a controlled, even cold, surface. Charles Dance, recently seen in *White Mischief* and *Plenty*, is cold, too, but with the easy surface charm of an Englishman who has spent most of his life trying to appear richer and more confident than he is. Helen Mirren plays a solitary woman painter at a time when such figures were rarely seen in the world, a woman who protects herself by seeming distracted, even slightly, charmingly, crazy. The conclusion of this movie, I suppose, is that all of these people get what they deserve, but that after all it is rather a shame.

A Passage to India ★ ★ ★ ★
PG, 160 m., 1984

Judy Davis (Adela Quested), Victor Banerjee (Dr. Aziz), Peggy Ashcroft (Mrs. Moore), Alec Guinness (Godbole) James Fox (Fielding), Nigel Havers (Ronny Heaslop). Directed by David Lean and produced by John Brabourne and Richard Goodwin. Screenplay by Lean.

"Only connect!"—E.M. Forster

That is the advice he gives us in *Howard's End*, and then, in *A Passage to India*, he creates a world in which there are no connections, where Indians and Englishmen speak the same language but do not understand each other, where it doesn't matter what you say in the famous Marabar Caves, since all that comes back is a hollow, mocking, echo. Forster's novel is one of the literary landmarks of this century, and now David Lean has made it into one of the greatest screen adaptations I have ever seen.

Great novels do not usually translate well to the screen. They are too filled with ambiguities, and movies have a way of making all their images seem like literal fact. *A Passage to India* is especially tricky, because the central event in the novel is something that happens offstage, or never happens at all—take your choice. On a hot, muggy day, the eager Dr. Aziz leads an expedition to the Marabar Caves. One by one, members of the party drop out, until finally only Miss Quested, from England, is left. And so the Indian man and the British woman climb the last path alone, at a time when England's rule of India was based on an ingrained, semiofficial racism, and some British, at least, nodded approvingly at Kipling's "East is East, and West is West, and never the twain shall meet."

In Forster's novel, it is never clear exactly what it was that happened to Miss Quested after she wandered alone into one of the caves. David Lean's film leaves that question equally open. But because he is dealing with a visual medium, he cannot make it a mystery where Dr. Aziz is at the time; if you are offstage in a novel, you can be anywhere, but if you are offstage in a movie, you are definitely not where the camera is looking. So in the film version we know, or think we know, that Dr. Aziz is innocent of the charges later brought against him—of the attempted rape of Miss Quested.

The charges and the trial fill the second half of Lean's *A Passage to India*. Lean brings us to that point by a series of perfectly modulated, quietly tension-filled scenes in which Miss Quested (Judy Davis) and the kindly Mrs. Moore (Peggy Ashcroft) sail to India, where Miss Quested is engaged to marry the priggish local British magistrate in a provincial backwater. Both women want to see the "real India"—a wish that is either completely lacking among the locals, or is manfully repressed. Mrs. Moore goes walking by a temple pool by moonlight, and meets the earnest young Dr. Aziz, who is captivated by her gentle kindness. Miss Quested wanders by accident into the ruins of another temple, populated by sensuous and erotic statuary, tumbled together, overgrown by vegetation.

Miss Quested's temple visit is not in Forster, but has been added by Lean (who wrote his own screenplay). It accomplishes just what it needed, suggesting that in Miss Quested the forces of sensuality and repression run a great deal more deeply than her sexually constipated fiancé is ever likely to suspect. Meanwhile, we meet some of the other local characters, including Dr. Godbole (Alec Guinness), who meets every crisis with perfect equanimity, and who believes that what will be, will be. This philosophy sounds like recycled fortune cookies but turns out, in the end, to have been the simple truth. We also meet Fielding (James Fox), one of those tall, lonely middle-aged Englishmen who hang about the edges of stories set in the Empire, waiting until their destiny commands them to take a firm stand.

Lean places these characters in one of the most beautiful canvases he has ever drawn (and this is the man who directed *Doctor Zhivago* and *Lawrence of Arabia*). He doesn't see the India of travel posters and lurid postcards, but the India of a Victorian watercolorist like Edward Lear, who placed enigmatic little human figures here and there in spectacular landscapes that never seemed to be quite finished. Lean makes India look like an amazing, beautiful place that an Englishman can never quite put his finger on—which is, of course, the lesson Miss Quested learns in the caves.

David Lean is a meticulous craftsman, famous for going to any lengths to make every shot look just the way he thinks it should. His actors here are encouraged to give sound, thoughtful, unflashy performances (Guinness strains at the bit), and his screenplay is a model of clarity: By the end of this movie we know these people so well, and understand them so thoroughly, that only the most reckless among us would want to go back and have a closer look at those caves.

Patton ★ ★ ★ ★
PG, 171 m., 1970

George C. Scott (Patton), Karl Malden (Bradley), Stephen Young (Captain Hansen), Michael Strong (General Carver), Karl Michel Vogler (Rommel), Michael Bates (Montgomery). Directed by Franklin J. Schaffner and produced by Frank McCarthy. Screenplay by Francis Ford Coppola and Edward H. North.

We have all of these things buried inside of us, waiting for a movie like *Patton* to release them. The reflex patriotism of World War II is still there, we discover, Vietnam has soured us on war, but not on that war. There is a small corner of our being that will always be thrilled by Patton's dash across Europe after the Germans, and we are still a little bit in admiration of heroes on his arrogant scale. And that is why, make no mistake, *Patton* is not an antiwar film. If I read one, I read half a dozen tortuous liberal rationalizations for this movie, written by people who liked it but felt guilty afterward. *Patton* is really against war, they said; by taking us almost inside the soul of the most fanatically military of all America's generals, *Patton* was supposed to fill us with distaste for militarism. It does not, of course. But neither is it a very hawklike movie. It is such an extraordinarily intelligent film, so sure of its purpose, that it makes war its medium but not its subject. It is not about war but about Patton at war, and it is one of the best screen biographies ever made.

Patton once said something to the effect that war was the supreme human activity because it forced men to operate at the ultimate limit of their abilities. This is not a very good justification for war, but it is a supreme test for men, and the action in *Patton* all takes place at the delicate balance point where the war meets the man. That was a basically brilliant idea in Francis Ford Coppola's original screenplay, but what makes it work so well in *Patton* is the performance of George C. Scott. He is absorbed into the role, and commands it. He is such a good actor that the movie doesn't have to explain a lot of things; we feel we know Patton and so we're sure of our footing. That's good, because it frees director Franklin J. Schaffner from a lot of cluttering props and plot lines. *Patton* is almost three hours long but it is a surprisingly uncomplicated movie, telling its story with clean, simple scenes and shots. Schaffner is at home here; one of the best things about his *Planet of the Apes* was the simplicity of style he found for it. If *Planet* had gotten complicated, we would have laughed at it.

The simplicity of *Patton* does not lead to any loss of subtlety; just the reverse. Because we are freed from those semiobligatory junk scenes that clutter up most war movies (the wife at home, the "human interest" drained from ethnic character actors, the battle scenes that are allowed to run too long because they cost so much) we can concentrate on the man, and we can even begin to believe we understand a warrior like this one. Because it's no good being hypocritical, I guess. Generals should be generals, and not lovable quasi-political figures like Ike or MacArthur. Patton's life was war (and how sad that really was) but he was honest enough to admit it, and the movie takes its stand on that point. And so although we deplore war we find ourselves respecting the movie; *Patton* is written and directed with integrity.

Beyond that, it's an awfully good movie, and one of its best features is the way it gets its laughs. There aren't any cheap laughs in *Patton*, but there are a lot of earned ones, all serving to flesh in our idea of this brilliant, obsessed man. And a lot of the humor is simply there, embodied in the Scott performance. It turns out *Patton* is exactly the war movie we didn't realize how much we wanted to see.

Patty Hearst ★ ★ ★
R, 108 m., 1988

Natasha Richardson (Patricia Hearst), William Forsythe (Teko), Ving Rhames (Cinque), Frances Fisher (Yolanda), Jodi Long (Wendy), Olivia Barash (Fahizah), Dana Delany (Gelina), Marek Johnson (Zoya), Kitty Swink (Gabi), Pete Kowanko (Cujo). Directed by Paul Schrader and produced by Marvin Worth. Screenplay by Nicholas Kazan. Based on the book *Every Secret Thing* by Patricia Campbell Hearst with Alvin Moscow.

I met Patty Hearst twice in the spring of 1988 at the Cannes Film Festival, once in a movie, and once in a restaurant. The effect was unsettling. In the movie, *Patty Hearst*, she was a quiet, desperate person, so lost in her ordeal that she had no clear idea of any of her motives. A person willing to hold up banks and brandish machine guns simply because of peer pressure from terrorists who had forced her to join their group. In person, she was a pleasant woman in her thirties, joking about how she was trying to trade *Patty Hearst* buttons for festival T-shirts.

I talked to her for a while, and then drifted over to the corner of the room, where I looked at her and tried to reconcile the two images, and finally realized that it was going to be impossible. Nothing in her previous life, and now nothing in her subsequent life, had any connection with the events that made Patty Hearst, at the age of nineteen, into the most famous fugitive in America.

Hearst was kidnapped by something called the Symbionese Liberation Army in 1974, and the case and its aftermath, including her famous legal ordeal, lasted until 1979. Even today, it is hard for people to place it—I saw an article mentioning Patty as a figure of the '60s—and I doubt if the case has gone into any American history textbooks, since what did it grow out of, where did it lead, what did it prove? It was all just a very odd footnote to history.

And yet the footnotes are sometimes where you find the human interest story. By what process could the heiress of America's most famous newspaper family, raised in a conventional upper-class Roman Catholic household and embracing most of the values of her parents, be transformed into the person we saw on TV in those days, brandishing a machine gun and shouting revolutionary slogans? Many children of privilege joined the "revolution," but Patty was kidnapped. What happened then?

That's the question director Paul Schrader wants to consider in this movie, and to answer it, he reconstructs the physical and mental ordeal that Hearst went through after her kidnapping. She is yanked out of a quiet evening at home with her boyfriend (Stephen Weed—how the names still have their resonance!), and thrown into the trunk of a car. Then she finds herself inside a darkened closet, where she is held for weeks, until the horizon of her world is limited to the moments when the door opens, and its population consists of half-heard voices.

The effect is to remove her entirely from everything she thought she could count on in life. When she is finally taken out of the closet and allowed to see her captors, she isn't angry, she's grateful to them for being allowed to look upon their faces. They have created a complete dependency, and from there it is only a matter of time until she identifies with the group and begins to share its aims. There is a powerful pressure, felt in all of us, to conform to what those around us consider to be proper behavior. Becoming a revolutionary might have been, for her, a form of good manners.

This is one of the oddest films Schrader has ever made. He is ordinarily a filmmaker of passion and kinetic energy, and this is a brooding and pale film, an introspective one that seems determined not to exploit the sensationalism of the case. Schrader is the favorite screenwriter of Martin Scorsese, for whom he wrote *Taxi Driver*, *Raging Bull*, and of course *The Last Temptation of Christ*. His own films are about guilt and passion, and they include *Cat People*, *American Gigolo*, and *Mishima*. When I heard that Schrader was going to film the Patty Hearst story, I thought I knew what to expect, but I was wrong.

The entire film centers on the remarkable performance by Natasha Richardson, as Patty. She convinces us she is Hearst, not by pressing the point, but by taking it for granted. She is quiet, a little sullen, not forthcoming. She tells people what they want to hear. During all of the tremendous excitement and passion of her ordeal, she hardly seems to be present; this is not a good time for her or a bad time, but a duty.

Schrader also avoids the temptation to make the SLA members into colorful firebrands. They come across as weak, sad people, so hidebound in ideology that they seem shellshocked. They are all passive personalities, under the will of the leader Cinque (Ving Rhames), who uses revolutionary rhetoric but has created in the SLA a community where no one is free. It's startling when Schrader re-enacts events we remember from TV (such as Patty's bank robbery), or uses actual TV news footage (of the firestorm that engulfed the SLA hideout). This whole story seemed so much more exciting from the outside.

Peeping Tom ★ ★ ★ ½
NO MPAA RATING, 109 m., 1960

Carl Boehm (Mark Lewis), Moira Shearer (Vivian), Anna Massey (Helen Stephens), Maxine Audley (Mrs. Stephens), Edmond Knight (Arthur Baden), Bartlet Mullins (Mr. Peters). Directed and produced by Michael Powell. Screenplay by Leo Marks.

In 1960, the year in which the psychic violence of Hitchcock's *Psycho* aroused such a storm, a film named *Peeping Tom* was premiered in London, was savaged by all the major British critics, brought the career of its director nearly to an end, and was then all but forgotten. The director was Michael Powell, whose credits included *The Thief of Bagdad* and *The Red Shoes*, and who was to make only four more very low-budget films after this one. He had worked with Hitchcock in the 1920s but apparently had not learned the master's gift of disguising abnormal criminal behavior as entertainment.

Peeping Tom has remained a legendary but unseen film ever since its release and burial (Susan Sontag uses it as a reference point in *On Photography*), and now it's in the process of rediscovery. It was first seen in America at 1978's Telluride Film Festival and then was purchased for U.S. release by a group backed by Martin (*Taxi Driver*) Scorsese. Now it's on video.

Perhaps the delay of more than twenty years works in the film's favor. Its story of a lonely voyeur's sadistic killings was horrifying in 1960, and Powell's visual strategy was to cloak the story in lurid rotogravure colors and deliberately banal settings—but now the film's dated clothing, mannerisms, and locations give it an additionally creepy flavor. We're given a man whose crimes are commit-

ted through, by, and because of cameras—and it's as if those crimes have been developing in the lab all these years.

The film stars the open-faced, blond actor Carl Boehm, whose regular Teutonic features and neatly combed-back hair give him the curious look of being too straight, too regular. And of course he's the opposite. He works as an assistant movie cameraman and then comes home to the boardinghouse that used to be his father's home. Upstairs, in seclusion, his sick obsession is to run films of his murder victims—women he has photographed as he killed them.

One day, by chance, he meets the girl who lives downstairs (Anna Massey). And here we have a classic Hitchcock situation, in which a possible victim is in constant danger, we know it, and she doesn't. The girl becomes his confidant, to a degree, and he spares her ("I never want to photograph *you!*") while committing another murder and hiding the body on the set of a movie.

Massey learns from him that his father had been a perverted psychologist who wanted to record Boehm's entire childhood on film—and who filmed and tape recorded his childish screams of fright. As a man, the killer's crimes are often elaborate re-enactments of his childhood terrors.

Is the film as disgusting as the British critics found it? Yes, but it is also very moving, a case study that could have been simply sadistic but emerges (especially because of the Boehm performance) as a tragic record of a destroyed life. Perhaps that's why *Peeping Tom* was so disturbing to its first viewers: It is *not* distanced into "entertainment" like *Psycho*, but remains unforgivingly as the story of horrible crimes seen straight-on.

Peggy Sue Got Married ★ ★ ★ ★
PG-13, 103 m., 1986

Kathleen Turner (Peggy Sue), Nicolas Cage (Charlie), Barry Miller (Richard), Catherine Hicks (Carol), Joan Allen (Maddie). Directed by Francis Ford Coppola and produced by Paul R. Gurian. Screenplay by Jerry Leightling and Arlene Sarner.

We walk like ghosts through the spaces of our adolescence. We've all done it. We stroll unseen across the high school football field. We go back to the drive-in restaurants where we all hung out, all those years ago. We walk into a drugstore for some aspirin, and the

magazine rack brings back a memory of sneaking a peek at a Playmate in 1959.

Certain times and places can re-create, with a headstrong rush, what it felt like to be seventeen years old—and we are sometimes more in touch with ourselves at that age than we are with the way we felt a year ago. Have you ever received a telephone message from somebody you were in love with when you were seventeen? And didn't it feel, for a second, as if it came from that long-ago teenager, and not from the adult who left it?

Peggy Sue Got Married is a lot of things—a human comedy, a nostalgic memory, a love story—but there are times when it is just plain creepy, because it awakens such vivid memories in us. It's about a woman who attends her twenty-fifth high school reunion, and passes out, and when she comes to it is 1958 and she inhabits her own teen-age body.

Those few details make the movie sound like *Back to the Future*, but give it some thought and you will see that *Peggy Sue* is not a clone, but a mirror image. In *Back to the Future*, the hero traveled backwards through time to meet his own parents when they were teen-agers. In *Peggy Sue* the heroine travels backwards to enter her own body as a teenager—and she enters it with her forty-two-year-old mind still intact.

What would you say, knowing what you know now, to the people you loved when you were seventeen? How would you feel if you picked up the telephone, and it was your grandmother's voice? Would you tell her she was going to die in another two years and three months? No, but you would know that, and wouldn't your heart leap into your throat, and wouldn't she wonder what was wrong with you, that you couldn't respond to her simple hello?

Peggy Sue Got Married provides moment after moment like that. It's like visiting a cemetery where all of the people are still alive. And yet it is a comedy. Frank Capra made comedies like this, in which the humor welled up out of a deep, even sentimental, drama of human emotions. There is a scene in the movie where the seventeen-year-old girl (with the mind of the forty-two-year-old woman) sits in the front seat of a car and necks with the teen-age boy that (she knows) she will marry and someday decide to divorce. Imagine kissing someone for the first time after you have already kissed them for the last time.

The movie stars Kathleen Turner, in a performance that must be seen to be believed. How does she play a seventeen-year-old? Not by trying to actually look seventeen, because the movie doesn't try to pull off that stunt (the convention is that the heroine looks adult to us, but like a teen-ager to the other characters). Turner, who is actually thirty-two, plays a teen-ager by making certain changes in her speech and movement: She talks more impetuously, not waiting for other people to reply, and she walks in that heedless teen-age way of those who have not yet stumbled often enough to step carefully. There is a moment when she throws herself down on her bed, and never mind what she looks like, it feels like a seventeen-year-old sprawled there. Her performance is a textbook study in body language; she knows that one of the symptoms of growing older is that you arrange your limbs more thoughtfully in repose.

The other important character in the movie is Charlie, her boyfriend and later her husband, played by Nicolas Cage. We meet him first as a local businessman in his early forties, and from the way he walks into a room you can tell he's the kind of man who inspires a lot of local gossip. He and his wife are separated and planning to divorce. When we see him again, he's the teen-age kid she's dating, and there are two delicate, wonderful scenes where she walks a tightrope, trying to relate to him as if she were a teen-ager, and as if she hadn't already shared his whole future.

That scene in the front seat of the car is a masterpiece of cross-purposes; she actually wants to go all the way, and he's shocked— shocked not so much by her desire, as by a girl having the temerity to talk and act that way in the 1950s. "Jeez," he says, after she makes her move, "that's a guy's line."

The movie was directed by Francis Coppola, who seems to have been in the right place at the right time. The *Peggy Sue* project got traded around from one actor and director to another (Turner's role was originally cast with Debra Winger, and Coppola was the third director on the project). After several years in which he has tried to make technical and production breakthroughs on his movies, experimenting with new film processes and new stylistic approaches with honorable but uneven results, this time Coppola apparently simply wanted to make a movie, and put some characters on the screen, and tell a story. He has, all right. This was one of the best movies of 1986.

Pelle the Conqueror ★ ★ ★ ½
NO MPAA RATING, 138 m., 1988

Max von Sydow (Lasse Karlsson), Pelle Hvenegaard (Pelle Karlsson), Erik Paaske (Manager), Kristina Tornqvists (Anna), Morten Jorgensen (Trainee), Axel Strobye (Mr. Kongstrup), Bjorn Granath (Erik). Written and directed by Bille August and produced by Per Holst. Based on the novel by Martin Anderson Nexo.

There were immigrants to American who thought the streets would be paved with gold. Lasse Karlsson, a middle-aged farmhand from Sweden, has more modest hopes as he sails with his young son to Denmark in the early years of this century. In Denmark, he says, they will drink coffee in bed on Sunday mornings, and eat roast pork with raisins for Sunday dinner. He cradles his son, Pelle, in his arms as their little passenger vessel noses into a small harbor, where disappointment sets in almost at once.

Almost everyone on the boat is a Swedish laborer, looking for work. Farmers have turned out to inspect them as if they were cattle. One by one, the men are hired, until finally only Lasse and Pelle are left. Nobody wants to hire Lasse (Max von Sydow). He is too old. He has a son. Half-drunk and defiant, he all but forces himself on the last of the farmers, a man named Kongstrup who has a shifty look about him. Lasse and Pelle sit in the farmer's cart as it passes through fields on its way to their futures.

Pelle the Conqueror uses this beginning, full of hope and dreams, in an interesting way. Through the seasons that follow during a long year on the Kongstrup farm, the vision somehow stays alive inside Pelle, even though life seems organized to disappoint him. The film begins with one hopeful immigration—Sweden to Denmark—and ends with another, Pelle's decision to take his chances in the larger world.

Life on the Kongstrup farm is defined by the land, the seasons, and the personalities of the people who live there. The Kongstrups themselves hardly appear for long stretches of time; they live in a big house set aside from the farm buildings, and Mrs. Kongstrup spends her days drinking brandy while her husband chases wenches. He has no shame, not even about the one unfortunate woman who appears at his front door from time to time, their child in her arms.

In the quarters where the laborers live, life

is defined by the sadism of the "Manager" (Erik Paaske), a bully who spots weaknesses in his men and exploits them. He is assisted in his cruelty by the "Trainee," a youth who takes particular pleasure in tormenting Pelle. The boy turns to his father for protection, but Lasse is too old and too weary to help. Eventually Pelle makes his own alliances for friendship and protection.

Pelle the Conqueror, which won the Grand Prix at the 1988 Cannes Film Festival, was directed by Bille August, whose previous film, *Twist and Shout*, was about teen-agers coming of age in the 1960s. In tone and sometimes in visuals, the movie resembles *The Emigrants* and *The New Land* (1974), Jan Troell's two-part epic about Scandinavians who settled in Minnesota. Both films star Max von Sydow, that mighty oak of Swedish cinema, who is unsurpassed at the difficult challenge of appearing not to act, of appearing to be simple and true even in scenes of great complexity.

The film is a richness of events. There are scenes of punishingly hard work in the fields, under the eye of the Manager. A challenge between the Manager and an independent-minded worker, with tragic results. The intrigue in the big house, where Mrs. Kongstrup exacts a particularly ironic revenge for her husband's philandering. The heartbreak of a beautiful local girl, who has fallen in love above her station.

The most touching sequence in the film involves a winter's romance between Lasse and a sailor's wife who lives in a cottage near the sea. Pelle is the first to meet the woman, whose husband has been missing for years and is presumed dead. He introduces his father to her, and the two people take a liking to one another that is practical as well as sentimental. There is a scene of great delicacy and sensible realism, in which they evaluate their resources and decide they should live together, and afterwards Lasse is able to suggest with a smile to his son that they might soon be having coffee in bed on Sundays after all.

Von Sydow's work in the film was honored with an Academy Award nomination, well-deserved, particularly after a distinguished career in which he stood at the center of many of Ingmar Bergman's greatest films (*The Virgin Spring, The Seventh Seal*). But there is not a bad performance in the movie, and the newcomer Pelle Hvenegaard never steps wrong in the title role (there is poetic justice in the fact that he was actually named after the novel which inspired this movie). It is Pelle, not Lasse, who is really at the center of the movie, which begins when he follows his father's dream, and ends as he realizes he must follow his own.

Performance ★ ★ ½
R, 105 m., 1970

James Fox (Charles), Mick Jagger (Turner), Anita Pallenberg (Pherber), Michele Breton (Lucy), Ann Sidney (Dana), John Bindon (Moody). Directed by Donald Cammell and Nicolas Roeg. Screenplay by Cammell.

Performance is a bizarre, disconnected attempt to link the inhabitants of two kinds of London underworlds: pop stars and gangsters. It isn't altogether successful, largely because it tries too hard and doesn't pace itself to let its effects sink in. But it does have a kind of frantic energy, and it introduced Mick Jagger in a role that reinforced his stage image without copying it. The movie is really about images anyway. On its most fundamental plot level, it's about a gangster (James Fox) who is trying to disguise himself so that he can slip out of England on a forged passport. He meets the Jagger character by accident when he takes a basement room in a boardinghouse.

Jagger is introduced as a top star of two or three years ago who has "retired" and hidden away to work on his memoirs or something. Mostly he seems to have submerged himself in a hedonistic existence with two girls, a variety of drugs, and a cloying assortment of Eastern artifacts. Almost every shot in his apartment is aimed past candles, incense, wall hangings, tapestries, and all that, and half the time we're even getting the Turkish rug reflected in the mirror.

This is not exactly the environment your everyday white-collar gangster feels at home in, but Fox plays a strange character who never feels at home anywhere. His workaday style is to beat and threaten potential "protection" customers. But despite his enthusiasm, he isn't really accepted even by the boss (every gangster has a boss) and his associates. So Jagger's little corner of London seems much like any other to him, affording a hideout until he can get the passport and fly to New York. Alas, Jagger doesn't see it that way, and over the course of a day or two, the gangster is sucked down into a psychedelic whirlpool with Jagger and the two girls. One of them feeds him a hallucinogenic mush-

room, after which the other dresses him in the unisex clothes they all wear, and then we get a lot of obligatory psychedelic photography showing the poor guy losing his identity, or his values, or in any event his inclination to escape.

The movie is so nervously edited that it doesn't stay around to develop the effects it introduces. That was a tendency with many semi-experimental British films of the early seventies; they were so concerned with reminding us they're movies that they don't do the work movies should. The first half of the movie is especially distracting. But after the gangster and the pop star meet, the editing and the story settle into a kind of consistency.

The surprise of the movie, and the reason to see it, is Mick Jagger's performance. It isn't simply good; it's a comment on his life and style. The ads emphasized his unisex appearance, and the role does so even more. When he slicks back his hair during a psychedelic fantasy, and seems to adopt the gangster's lifestyle, we're looking at acting insights of a very complex psychological order. Other than that, the movie is neither very good nor very bad. Interesting.

Permanent Record ★ ★ ★ ★
PG-13, 92 m., 1988

Alan Boyce (David Sinclair), Keanu Reeves (Chris Townsend), Michelle Meyrink (J.G.), Jennifer Rubin (Lauren), Pamela Gidley (Kim), Michael Elgart (Jake), Richard Bradford (Leo Verdell). Directed by Marisa Silver and produced by Frank Mancuso Jr. Screenplay by Jarre Fees, Alice Liddle, and Larry Ketron.

The opening shot of *Permanent Record* is ominous and disturbing, and we don't know why. In an unbroken movement, the camera tracks past a group of teen-agers who have parked their cars on a bluff overlooking the sea, and are hanging out casually, their friendship too evident to need explaining. There seems to be no "acting" in this shot, and yet it is superbly acted, because it feels so natural that we accept at once the idea that these kids have been close friends for a long time. Their afternoon on the bluff seems superficially happy, and yet there is a brooding quality to the shot, perhaps inspired by the lighting, or by the way the camera circles vertiginously above the sea below.

The following scenes unfold, it seems,

almost without plan. We meet a couple of kids who play in a rock band together, and try to sneak into a recording studio, and are thrown out, and arrive at school late. We meet the high school principal, a man who is enormously intriguing because he reveals so little, and yet still succeeds in revealing goodness. We meet the crowd that these two kids hang out with, and we attend some auditions for a school production of *The Pirates of Penzance*. We are impressed by the fact that these teen-agers are intelligent, thoughtful, and articulate; they come from a different planet than most movie teen-agers.

To describe the opening scenes makes them seem routine, and yet they captured my attention with an intensity I still do not understand. The underlying mystery of many good movies is the way they absorb us in apparently unremarkable details, while bad movies can lose us even with car crashes and explosions. Marisa Silver, who directed this film, and Frederick Elmes, who photographed it, have done something very subtle and strong here, have seen these students and their school in a way that inescapably prepares us for something, without revealing what it is.

The kids all hang out together, but one begins to attract our attention more than the others. He is David (Alan Boyce), an intense, dark-eyed musician who everyone knows is gifted. He leads the rock band, gives lessons to his fellow musicians, and is arranging the music for the production of *Pirates*. In a scene of inexplicable tension, he is told by the principal (Richard Bradford) that he's won a scholarship to a great music school. He tries to seem pleased, but complains that he is so busy—too busy. Bradford quietly reminds him the scholarship isn't until next year.

And then . . . but here I want to suggest that if you plan to see the film, you should read no further and permit yourself its surprises. I began watching this film knowing absolutely nothing about it, and this is the kind of film where that is an advantage. Let the movie unfold like life. Save the review until later.

I found myself impressed, most of all, by the subtlety with which Silver and her writers (Jarre Fees, Alice Liddle, and Larry Ketron) develop David's worsening crisis. This is not a young man made unhappy by the usual problems of TV docudramas. He doesn't use drugs, his girlfriend isn't pregnant, he isn't flunking out of school, and he doesn't have an unhappy home life. But it becomes clear, especially in retrospect, that there is no joy in his life, and we see that most clearly in the understated scene in the bedroom of the girl he sometimes sleeps with. Any other couple who do what they do together, she suggests, would be said to be going together. He nods.

There is something missing here. Some kind of connection with other people. Some exultation in his own gifts and talents. Giving guitar lessons to his friend Chris (Keanu Reeves), he is a little impatient; Chris does not strive hard enough for excellence. David, who is admired by everyone in his school, who is the one singled out by his friends for great success, has a deep sadness inside himself because he is not good enough. And that leads to the scene in which one moment he is on the side of that high bluff, and the next moment he is not.

The rest of the movie is about his friends—about the gulf he has left behind, and about their sorrow, and their rage at him. Again and again, Silver and her writers find authentic ways to portray emotions. We never feel manipulated, because the movie works too close to the heart. Perhaps the best scene in the whole film is the one where Chris, drunk, drives his car into David's yard and almost hits David's younger brother, and then, when David's father comes out on the lawn to shout angrily at him, Chris falls into his arms, weeping and shouting, "I should have stopped him." And the father holds him.

Life goes on. The school production is held. There is a dramatic moment in which David is eulogized, and there is also the sense that years from now his friends will sometimes remember him, be angry with him, and wonder what would have become of him. This is one of the year's best films, and one reason for its power is that it clearly knows what it wants to do, and how to do it. It is not a film about the causes of David's death, and it does not analyze or explain. It is a film about the event, and about the memory of the event. The performances, seemingly artless, are appropriate to the material, and I was especially impressed by the way Bradford suggested so many things about the principal while seeming to reveal so little.

Permanent Record is Marisa Silver's second feature, after the wonderful *Old Enough* (1984), which told the story of a friendship between two thirteen-year-old girls who were from opposite sides of the tracks but were on the same side of adolescence. In that film and this one, she shows that she has a rare gift for empathy, and that she can see right to the bottoms of things without adding a single gratuitous note.

Personal Best ★ ★ ★ ★
R, 124 m., 1982

Mariel Hemingway (Chris Cahill), Patrice Donnelly (Tory Skinner), Scott Glenn (Coach), Kenny Moore (Denny Stites). Directed and produced by Robert Towne. Screenplay by Towne.

Robert Towne's *Personal Best* tells the story of two women who are competitors for pentathlete berths on the 1980 U.S. Olympics team—the team that did not go to Moscow. The women are attracted to one another almost at first sight, and what begins as a tentative exploration develops into a love relationship. Then the romance gets mixed up with the ferocity of top-level sports competition.

What distinguishes *Personal Best* is that it creates *specific* characters—flesh-and-blood people with interesting personalities, people I cared about. *Personal Best* also seems knowledgeable about its two subjects, which are the weather of these women's hearts, and the world of Olympic sports competition.

It is a movie containing the spontaneity of life. It's about living, breathing, changeable people and because their relationships seems to be so deeply felt, so important to them, we're fascinated by what may happen next. The movie stars Mariel Hemingway and Patrice Donnelly as the two women track stars, Scott Glenn as their coach, and Kenny Moore as the Olympic swimmer who falls in love with Hemingway late in the film. These four people are so right for the roles it's almost scary; it makes us sense the difference between performances that are technically excellent and other performances, like these, that may sometimes be technically rough but always find the correct emotional note.

Mariel Hemingway plays a young, naive natural athlete. We sense that she always has been under the coaching thumb of her father, a perfectionist, and that her physical excellence has been won at the cost of emotional maturity. She knows everything about working out, and next to nothing about her heart, her sexuality, her own identity. She loses an important race at a preliminary meet, is sharply handled by the father, gets sick to her stomach, is obviously emotionally distraught.

Patrice Donnelly, as a more experienced athlete, tries to comfort the younger girl. In a dormitory room that night, they talk. Donnelly shares whatever wisdom she has about training and running and winning. They smoke a joint. They kid around. They arm wrestle. At this point, watching the film, I had an interesting experience. I did not already know that the characters in the film were homosexual, but I found myself thinking that the scene was so erotically charged that, "if Hollywood could be honest," it would develop into a love scene. Just then, it did! "This is scary," Donnelly says, and then she kisses Hemingway, who returns the kiss.

Personal Best is not simply about their romance, however, it is about any relationship in which the trust necessary for love is made to compete with the total egotism necessary for championship sports. *Can* two people love each other, and at the same time compete for the same berth on an Olympic team? Scott Glenn, the coach, doesn't think so. He accepts the fact of his two stars' homosexuality, but what bothers him is a suspicion that Donnelly may be using emotional black mail to undercut Hemingway's performance.

This is a very physical movie, one of the healthiest and sweatiest celebrations of physical exertion I can remember. There is a lot of nudity in the film—not only erotic nudity, although there is some of that, but also locker room and steam room nudity, and messing around nudity that has an unashamed, kidding freshness to it. One scene that shocks some viewers occurs between Mariel Hemingway and Kenny Moore, when he gets up to go to the bathroom and she decides to follow along; the scene is typical of the kind of unforced, natural spontaneity in the whole film. The characters in *Personal Best* seem to be free to have real feelings. It is filled with the uncertainties, risks, cares, and rewards of real life, and it considers its characters' hearts and minds, and sees their sexuality as an expression of their true feelings for each other.

Personal Services ★ ★ ★ 1/2
R, 97 m., 1987

Julie Walters (Christine Painter), Alec McCowen (Wing Commander Morton), Shirley Stelfox (Shirley), Danny Schiller (Dolly), Victoria Hardcastle (Rose), Tim Woodward (Timms). Directed by Terry Jones and produced by Tim Bevan. Screenplay by David Leland.

I'm writing this review in London, where the papers for the last few days have been filled with the scandal of the Conservative member of Parliament who had to resign his constituency after being convicted of spanking two male prostitutes who were younger than twenty-one, which is the age of consent for homosexual spankings in Britain. (Female prostitutes can legally be spanked once they are sixteen. There'll always be an England.)

This morning on the radio, they interviewed Cynthia Payne, who said she was shocked that this fine public servant had to have his reputation ruined: "What's wrong with wanting to slap somebody's bottom once in a while, so long as no harm is done? We all have our peculiarities, we just cover them up, that's all." She sounded just like all other housewives on the call-in show.

This was the same Cynthia Payne who has become something of a folk legend over here for operating what the tabloids called "the House of Cyn," a brothel catering to middle-age and elderly gentlemen with rather specialized tastes. Nicknamed the "Luncheon Voucher Madame" because she sometimes charged as little as you'd pay for a nice plate of sausages-and-mashed, Payne was acquitted on her latest round of charges and greeted outside the law court by a street full of her cheering supporters.

Payne has always insisted she did not engage in sex herself and did not supply sex to her clients. Instead, there were naughty fashion shows featuring lace undies, see-through nighties, and leather corsets. Also available were such specialties as charging men for the privilege of doing the housework and weeding her garden. Military men and successful businessmen were especially keen for the humiliation; it took their minds off their responsibilities.

Personal Services, by the Monty Python veteran Terry Jones, is an attempt to explore the peculiarly mercenary world of Payne. She is called "Christine Painter" in the movie but nevertheless is listed as an adviser and went to New York on a public relations tour. She began as a waitress who invested her savings in cheap flats and only got into the brothel-keeping business because hookers paid their rent on time.

As the movie tells it, Payne never really even intended to go into business; she just kept running across nice gentlemen who liked a bit of naughtiness once in a while. She preferred older gentlemen; they caused less

trouble and were more grateful. And, as she told the court, an evening at the "House of Cyn" simply involved having a few old friends over for a party. It was all very innocent; they preferred their crumpets with tea.

Personal Services is not a sensational movie, nor does it want to be. It is a study of banality, with flashes of genuine comedy, as when a retired war hero (Alec McCowen) takes the press on a tour of the House while singing the praises of transvestism.

The heroine is played by Julie Walters, seen in the Oscar-nominated title role of *Educating Rita* and she has it just right: the tight lips, polite reserve, the proper manner and bearing, all designed to keep passion and sex in different departments, where they belong.

The British law, on the other hand, comes across as more obsessed by sex than anyone at the madam's parties. Plainclothesmen infiltrate the goings-on and deliver breathless accounts of whips and leather knickers. Many of the clients are only too happy to go into the dock and testify to the underlying innocence of their particular hobbies, and by the end of the film there is the suggestion that the heroine probably will keep right on doing what she does best: having friends in for little parties. Which, as it turned out, was exactly what happened.

Physical Evidence ★ ★
R, 99 m., 1989

Burt Reynolds (Joe Paris), Theresa Russell (Jenny Hudson), Ned Beatty (James Nicks), Kay Lenz (Deborah Quinn), Ted McGinley (Kyle), Tom O'Brien (Matt Farley). Directed by Michael Crichton and produced by Martin Ransohoff. Screenplay by Bill Phillips.

You can often tell a movie that isn't really about anything because it has a sensational pre-title sequence. Like the Bond movies, which have popularized the PTS in modern times, they expend great amounts of effort and cleverness on the construction of a stunt gag that has little or no connection to the rest of the film. The idea, I guess, is that the writer or director has a great idea that doesn't seem to fit in anywhere, and so he starts his film with it. That way you've forgotten it before you get to the end and discover it was meaningless.

Physical Evidence begins with a man about to jump off a bridge, when he is accosted by another man. More than that I

will not tell (this movie has too few resources for me to squander any of them). After it appears that both of them may fall to their deaths, we get a sensational and unexpected development, and there is laughter in the audience from those members who are very easily amused.

Then we cut to the real story, which involves an ex-cop (Burt Reynolds) who wakes up with a hangover and blood on his shirt, and the evidence seems to suggest that he has committed a murder he cannot remember. This is not exactly an original beginning for a murder mystery (Cornell Woolrich opened a story the same way in 1936), but never mind, originality is not one of this film's goals.

The former cop turns out to have a history of violence, and when his blood type is found on the murder weapon, he's thrown in jail and things look bleak. Then he meets his attorney, a public defender who is, of course, an attractive woman (Theresa Russell). He doubts she can do the job. She's cocky and self-confident and thinks she can. And then, of course, they find themselves attracted to one another.

Physical Evidence was produced by Martin Ransohoff, who also produced the much better *Jagged Edge*. In that one, you will remember, the heroine, a lawyer, has to decide in a hurry whether she can trust the man she's defending. There's a little of that in this movie, too; Burt Reynolds is given a few moments when he projects some menace and mystery, just enough for us to suspect he may really have committed the crime. But then the plot doesn't follow through on that, and before long the story has settled into very familiar patterns.

The movie's basic idea is role-reversal in the Hepburn and Tracy mold, with Reynolds as the untamed ruffian and Russell as the no-nonsense lady who will love him only if he straightens out. This leads almost exactly where we anticipate it will, with all the plot threads coming together into suspense, danger, innocence, threat, and, of course, living happily ever after. The problem is that there is no chemistry at all between Reynolds and Russell; they stand near each other and speak words of emotion, but there's not much light in their eyes and they don't budge the needle on the romantic volt-meter.

That leaves only the usual prefabricated plot elements to plug in, such basic and obligatory scenes as the one where the heroine finds that her apartment has been broken into, or the one where the state's attorney offers to make a deal, or the one where the heroine gets threatened on a dark night, or the love scene that is followed by great menace. All of this stuff comes right out of the recycling bin, and *Physical Evidence* has not found a way to make it new.

Picnic at Hanging Rock ★ ★ ★ ½
PG, 110 m., 1980

Rachel Roberts (Miss Appleyard), Dominic Guard (Fitzhubert), Helen Morse (Dianne), Jacki Weaver (Minnie). Directed by Peter Weir and produced by James and Hal McElroy. Screenplay by Cliff Green.

Peter Weir's *Picnic at Hanging Rock* has something of the same sense of mystery and buried terror as Antonioni's *L'Aventura*—another film about a sudden and disquieting disappearance. But it's more lush and seductive than Antonioni's spare black-and-white images: Weir films an Australian landscape that could be prehistoric, that suggests that men have not come this way before . . . and that, quite possibly, they should not have come this time.

"This time" is 1900, when much of Australia remained unseen by European eyes, but when a staid and proper version of European culture had been established at such places as Appleyard College, presented here as a boarding school for proper young ladies. As is almost always the case in movies about proper boarding schools, an undercurrent of repressed sexuality runs through Appleyard, and especially through the person of its headmistress (Rachel Roberts).

We get a preliminary sense of that in the film's opening scenes, which show several of the young ladies preparing to spend the day picnicking at nearby Hanging Rock, a geological outcropping from time immemorial. And then there is the picnic itself, with the girls in their bonnets and parasols and immaculate white dresses, dappled in sunlight.

The film moves here at a deliberately lazy pace. The sun beats down, insects drone—and four of the young ladies, having climbed halfway up into the rock passages, are overcome by torpor. When they awake, three of them climb farther on, never to be seen again. The fourth, badly frightened, returns to the main group. A search is set into motion, and the local constable questions witnesses who saw the young girls later on in

the day, but the mystery of their disappearance remains unsolved.

It's that very inconclusiveness, linked with later scenes in which the cruel nature of the headmistress is developed, that make *Picnic at Hanging Rock* so haunting. What's going on here, we ask, knowing there is no possible answer and half-pleased by the enigma. The film opens itself to our interpretations: Is the disappearance a punishment, real or imagined, for the girls' stirring sexuality? Is it a rebuke from the ancient landscape against the brash inroads of civilization? Or is it, as it was in the famous Antonioni film, a statement of nihilism: These people have disappeared, so might we, it all matters nothing, life goes on meaninglessly.

Picnic at Hanging Rock of course subscribes to none of those readings or to any reading. I've heard its ending described as inconclusive (it is) and frustrating (ditto). But *why not?* Do we want a rational explanation? Arrest and trial for vagabond kidnappers? An autopsy revealing broken necks? Poisonous snakes named as the culprits? If this film *had* a rational and tidy conclusion, it would be a good deal less interesting. But as a tantalizing puzzle, a tease, a suggestion of forbidden answer just out of earshot, it works hypnotically and very nicely indeed.

Pink Cadillac ★
PG-13, 122 m., 1989

Clint Eastwood (Tommy Nowak), Bernadette Peters (Lou Ann McGuinn), Timothy Carhart (Roy McGuinn), Tiffany Gail Robinson and Angela Louise Robinson (McGuinn Baby), John Dennis Johnston (Waycross), Michael Des Barres (Alex). Directed by Buddy van Horn and produced by David Valdes. Screenplay by John Eskow.

Clint Eastwood plays a skip-tracer in *Pink Cadillac*, a free-lancer who works with bail bondsmen to return clients who have jumped bond. This is a profession more colorful in the movies than in life, I suspect, and Eastwood milks it for what it's worth, hiding behind a variety of disguises to trick his quarry. He runs a phony radio prize game, poses as a cop and a rodeo clown, and pretends to be a doorman at a Reno casino. This silliness might work in a movie like *Every Which Way But Loose*, but *Pink Cadillac* has a disturbing subplot about a secret army of

white racists—and so the comedy seems out of place.

In the film, Eastwood finds himself on the trail of a runaway mother (Bernadette Peters), whose lame-brained husband has been recruited by the white supremacists. She steals his 1959 Cadillac convertible for her getaway, little realizing that the right-wingers have hidden a quarter of a million dollars in bills under the convertible top. The woman is out on bail, and Eastwood is assigned to find her. But by the time he does, she's got the whole secret army on her tail. And of course, Eastwood and Peters fall in love.

This plot is sort of a cross between *Midnight Run*, with Robert De Niro as a bondsman becoming the friend of his quarry, and *Betrayed*, with Debra Winger as an undercover agent who falls in love with a white supremacist. There's little that's new in the material, and nobody seems to have asked whether the emotional charge of blatant racism belongs in a lightweight story like this—even if the racists are the villains.

There's another problem, and that's the idiotic behavior of most of the characters in the film. How can we take a thriller scene seriously when the characters don't? Observe, for example, a crucial moment when Eastwood gets the drop on the leader of the right-wing army and puts him and Peters in a car. "I'll drop you off a mile from the camp," he says—guaranteeing his getaway. But then what does he do? Drops him off about twenty-five yards down the road, putting himself back in danger.

Maybe I shouldn't be so hard on that scene. It's one of the few unpredictable moments in the movie. The whole progression of the romance between the skip-tracer and the woman has been seen many, many times before, and Eastwood and Peters do not seem to feel, or express, a convincing bond. The whole life and background of the Peters character is so artificial and manufactured, indeed, that it would be amazing if we did feel chemistry: This isn't a real woman, so how can she have real feelings?

What really bothered me, though, was that white supremacist army. I can imagine, and have seen, serious movies about outlaw racism in America. But to use a racist army as material for the villains in a light little action-comedy seems inappropriate. When the racist leader's dialogue ran down the usual litany of racist slurs and obscenities, I felt uncomfortable; in the times we live in, the offensiveness of such words should be observed, and they should not be used thoughtlessly.

Pixote ★ ★ ★ ★
R, 127 m., 1981

Fernando Ramos da Silva (Pixote), Marilla Pera (Sueli), Jorge Juliao (Lilica), Gilberto Moura (Dito). Directed by Hector Babenco and produced by Sylvia B. Naves. Screenplay by Babenco and Jorge Duran.

Kids love to play by the rules. They're great at memorizing them. They repeat them to one another like ancient commandments. They never pause to question them. For the kids in *Pixote*, the rules apply to their lives in the streets as thieves, beggars, and child prostitutes. These kids are only ten or twelve years old, and at the beginning of *Pixote* we learn that there are hundreds of thousands of them living in the streets of Rio and Sao Paolo, Brazil, where more than half the population is younger than eighteen.

Pixote is the story of one of those children, called Pixote because he is small and wide-eyed and solemn-faced and the name seems to fit. He is not a bad kid, but he lives in a fearsome environment, in which all crimes, even the most violent, are part of the daily routine. Some of the children who commit these crimes are too young to even fully understand the gravity of taking a human life. To them, a gun or a knife is a coveted possession, a prize captured from the adult world, and to use it is to gain in stature.

There is no attempt to reform these kids. They're rounded up from time to time, after a particularly well-publicized theft, mugging, or killing. They're thrown into corrupt reformatories that act as schools for crime. For all of them, the overwhelming fact of their society—the only *law* they finally understand—is that they are immune from the full force of the law until they are eighteen. They almost seem to interpret this as a license to steal, a license revoked on their eighteenth birthday, when real life begins.

Hector Babenco's film follows Pixote and several other street children through a crucial passage in their lives. They survive, they steal, they engage in innocent entertainments, they impassively observe the squalor around them, they pass through reformatory jails, they sit on the beach and dream of the future, and their lives lead up to a moment of unplanned, almost accidental violence.

Babenco shot his film on location, on the streets and inside the slum rooms of Brazil's big cities. He also cast it from among the street children themselves. Twenty-one homeless, parentless children play themselves, more or less, in this movie, and the leading character (Fernando Ramos da Silva) is an untrained, uneducated young orphan who succeeds, in this film, in creating a performance of utterly convincing realism. The film's other great performance is by Marilla Pera, as the prostitute who adopts him. (Pera won the National Society of Film Critics award for best actress for this performance; da Silva returned to the streets and was killed by police bullets in 1988.)

Babenco's filmmaking method, of casting actual people to play themselves, and then shooting on the locations where they live and work, has been used before, most successfully by the Italian neorealists. Such films as Vittorio De Sica's *Bicycle Thief* and *Shoeshine* were cast with non-actors and shot on location, and they captured a freshness and actuality that influenced the look and feel of subsequent mainstream films: After the neorealists, there was a movement in the studio films of the 1950s and 1960s toward performances, dialogue, and sets that reflected more of real life and less of the stylized Hollywood fantasies of the 1930s.

De Sica's story lines, however, were heavily, if simply, plotted, and his films drew clear conclusions about the social injustices suffered by his characters. *Pixote* is just as angry and committed as *Bicycle Thief*, but it has more of a documentary freedom. Even though it is loosely based on a novel, Babenco's film sometimes seems to be following characters no matter what they're inclined to do or say.

The one scene in the film that does seem planned is the last one, of a prostitute nursing a mournful child at her breast—and that scene, of course, is directly from John Steinbeck's *The Grapes of Wrath*, where even at the time it seemed contrived and too obviously symbolic.

The film otherwise moves with the very rhythms of life itself. It shows evil deeds (thefts, muggings, killings) that have no evil perpetrators; both criminal and target are victims. And it shows a society that perpetrates a class of child criminals because it is incapable of even really *seeing* them clearly, let alone helping to improve their lives. *Pixote* is one of the very best realistic dramas of modern cinema.

Places in the Heart ★ ★ ★
PG, 110 m., 1984

Sally Field (Edna Spaulding), John Malkovich (Mr. Will), Danny Glover (Mose), Lindsay Crouse (Margaret Lomax), Ed Harris (Wayne Lomax), Amy Madigan (Viola Kelsey). Directed by Robert Benton and produced by Arlene Donovan. Screenplay by Benton.

The places referred to in the title of Robert Benton's movie are, he has said, places that he holds sacred in his own heart: The small town in Texas where he grew up, various friends and relatives he remembers from those days, the little boy that he once was, and the things that happened or almost happened. His memories provide the material for a wonderful movie, and he has made it, but unfortunately he hasn't stopped at that. He has gone on to include too much. He tells a central story of great power, and then keeps leaving it to catch us up with minor characters we never care about.

The main story stars Sally Field as a sheriff's widow who learns from the banker that times are hard and she should sell her farm and maybe board her kids with somebody else. She refuses. She will keep the farm and keep the kids, thank you, although she's not sure just how that will work. Then a black hobo comes knocking at the back door, asking for food, and he sort of insists that he is just the man to plant her acreage in cotton and farm it. He knows all there is to know about cotton. Since Field has no choice, she takes the man at his word, and he plants the cotton. Meanwhile, the banker, trying to solve a family problem and maybe help her at the same time, brings around a blind relative named Mr. Will, who will be a paying boarder. The three adults and the two kids form a little family that pulls together to make that farm work—and that is the central story of *Places in the Heart*.

Unfortunately, there are other stories. We meet Field's sister (Lindsay Crouse), and her brother-in-law (Ed Harris), and the local woman (Amy Madigan) he's having an affair with. Their stories function as counterpoint to the drama on the farm, but who cares? We learn just enough about the other characters to suspect that there might be a movie in their stories—but not this one, please, when their adulteries and betrayals have nothing to do with the main story.

Places in the Heart is the kind of movie where people tend to dismiss the parts they don't like. I've seen some reviews where the story of Field and the farm is the only part of the movie the critics refer to, as if Crouse, Harris, and Madigan had slipped their minds. That's wishful thinking. The subplot is there, and it's an unnecessary distraction, and it robs the movie of a lot of the sheer narrative power it would have had otherwise. It also robs us of a chance to learn more about the relationships among Field, the black farmer (Danny Glover), and the blind boarder (John Malkovich). What a group of unforgettable characters! What do they talk about in their evenings at home? Do they ever get into politics or philosophy? This is Texas in the Depression: How do they think the neighbors like the idea of a black man helping a white woman farm her land? The movie spends so much time watching the hanky-panky at the dances in town that when the Ku Klux Klan suddenly turns up in the movie, it's like it dropped out of a tree.

The movie's last scene has caused a lot of comment. It is a dreamy, idealistic fantasy in which all the characters in the film—friends and enemies, wives and mistresses, living and dead, black and white—take communion together at a church service. This is a scene of great vision and power, but it's too strong for the movie it concludes. *Places in the Heart* can't support such an ending, because it hasn't led up to it with a narrative that was straight and well-aimed as an arrow. The story was on the farm and not in the town, and although the last scene tries to draw them together, you can't summarize things that have nothing in common.

Planes, Trains and Automobiles
★ ★ ★ ½
R, 93 m., 1987

Steve Martin (Neal Page), John Candy (Del Griffith). Directed and produced by John Hughes. Screenplay by Hughes.

The letters in the title of *Planes, Trains and Automobiles* roar across the screen like a streamliner, and the movie itself has the same confidence. The movie tells the story of two travelers who share a modest wish in life, to fly from LaGuardia to O'Hare on schedule, and it follows with complete logic the chain of events that leads them to share a soggy bed in a cheap motel in Wichita.

The travelers are played by Steve Martin and John Candy, Martin as the fastidious, anal-compulsive snob, and Candy as the big, unkempt shower-ring salesman with a weakness for telling long stories without punch lines. Both actors are perfectly cast, not so much because they are physically matched to their roles as because the movie is able to see past their differences to an essential sweetness they share.

The film was written and directed by John Hughes, who previously specialized in high-quality teen-age movies such as *Sixteen Candles* and *The Breakfast Club*. One hallmark of Hughes's work is his insistence that his characters have recognizable human qualities; he doesn't work with a cookie cutter, and the teen-age roles he wrote for Molly Ringwald, Emilio Estevez, Ally Sheedy, Matthew Broderick, and others helped transform Hollywood's idea of what a teen-age movie could be. Hughes's comedies always contain a serious undercurrent, attention to some sort of universal human dilemma that his screenplay helps to solve.

All of which may seem a million miles away from Steve Martin and John Candy, whom we left on that beer-soaked mattress in Kansas ("You should have known what would happen when you left a six-pack on a vibrating mattress," Martin complains). But *Planes, Trains and Automobiles* is a screwball comedy with a heart, and after the laughter is over, the film has generated a lot of good feeling.

The story opens in Manhattan a few days before Thanksgiving, when Candy grabs a taxi that Martin thought was his. The two men meet again at a departure lounge at LaGuardia, where their flight to Chicago has been delayed by bad weather. Martin immediately recognizes the other man as the SOB who got his cab, and inevitably, when they finally board the plane, he finds himself bumped out of first class and wedged into a center seat next to the ample Candy.

The flight eventually takes off, only to be diverted to Wichita, where Candy has enough connections through the shower-ring business to get them a room—one room with one bed. This is the beginning of a two-day nightmare for the fastidious Martin, who at one point screams at Candy that he snores and smokes, his socks smell, and his jokes aren't funny. How bad are Candy's jokes? Martin pulls out all the stops. He'd rather attend an insurance seminar than listen to one more of them. During Martin's long outburst, the camera holds on Candy's face, and we see that he is hurt, not offended. He only wants to please, to make friends, and, as usual, he has tried too hard.

Back at the Wichita airport the next morning, Martin tries to dump Candy, but fate has linked them together. Through a series of horrible misadventures on trains, buses, semi-trailer trucks, and automobiles, they end up on a highway somewhere in southern Illinois, trying to explain to a state trooper why they are driving a car that has not only crashed but burned.

There are a lot of big laughs in *Planes, Trains and Automobiles*, including the moment when the two men wake up cuddled together in the motel room, and immediately leap out of bed and begin to make macho talk about the latest Bears game. The movie's a terrific comedy, but it's more than that, because eventually Hughes gives the Martin and Candy characters some genuine depth. We begin to understand the dynamics of their relationship, and to see that although they may be opposites, they have more in common than they know. This is a funny movie, but also a surprisingly warm and sweet one.

Platoon ★ ★ ★ ★
R, 119 m., 1986

Tom Berenger (Barnes), Willem Dafoe (Sergeant Elias), Charlie Sheen (Chris), Forest Whitaker (Big Harold), Francesco Quinn (Raah), John C. McGinley (Sergeant O'Nill), Richard Edson (Sal), Kevin Dillon (Bunny). Directed by Oliver Stone and produced by Arnold Kopelson. Screenplay by Stone.

It was Francois Truffaut who said that it's not possible to make an anti-war movie, because all war movies, with their energy and sense of adventure, end up making combat look like fun. If Truffaut had lived to see *Platoon*, he might have wanted to modify his opinion. Here is a movie that regards combat from ground level, from the infantryman's point of view, and it does not make war look like fun.

The movie was written and directed by Oliver Stone, who fought in Vietnam and who has tried to make a movie about the war that is not fantasy, not legend, not metaphor, not message, but simply a memory of what it seemed like at the time to him.

The movie is narrated by a young soldier (Charlie Sheen) based on Stone himself; a middle-class college kid who volunteers for the war because he considers it his patriotic duty, and who is told, soon after he arrives in the combat zone, "You don't belong here." He believes it.

There are no false heroics in this movie, and no standard heroes; the narrator is quickly at the point of physical collapse, bedeviled by long marches, no sleep, ants, snakes, cuts, bruises, and constant, gnawing fear. In a scene near the beginning of the film, he is on guard duty when he clearly sees enemy troops approaching his position, and he freezes. He will only gradually, unknowingly, become an adequate soldier.

The movie is told in a style that rushes headlong into incidents. There is no carefully mapped plot to lead us from point to point, and instead, like the characters, we are usually disoriented. Anything is likely to happen, usually without warning. From the crowded canvas, large figures emerge: Barnes (Tom Berenger), the veteran sergeant with the scarred face, the survivor of so many hits that his men believe he cannot be killed; Elias (Willem Dafoe), another good fighter, but a man who tries to escape from the reality through drugs; Bunny (Kevin Dillon), the scared kid, who has become dangerous because that seems like a way to protect himself.

There is rarely a clear, unequivocal shot of an enemy soldier. They are wraiths, halfseen in the foliage, their presence scented on jungle paths, evidence of their passage unearthed in ammo dumps buried beneath villages. Instead, there is the clear sense of danger all around, and the presence of civilians who sometimes enrage the troops just by standing there and looking confused and helpless.

There is a scene in the movie that seems inspired by My Lai, although it does not develop into a massacre. As we share the suspicion that these villagers may, in fact, be harboring enemy forces, we share the fear that turns to anger, and we understand the anger that turns to violence.

Some of the men in *Platoon* have lost their bearings, are willing to kill almost anyone on the least pretext. Others still retain some measure of the morality of the situation. Since their own lives may also be at stake in their arguments, there is a great sense of danger when they disagree; we see Americans shooting other Americans, and we can understand why.

After seeing *Platoon*, I fell to wondering why Stone was able to make such an effective movie without falling into the trap Truffaut spoke about—how he made the movie riveting without making it exhilarating. Here's how I think he did it. He abandoned the choreography that is standard in almost all war movies. He abandoned any attempt to make it clear where the various forces were in relation to each other, so that we never know where "our" side stands and where "they" are. Instead of battle scenes in which lines are clearly drawn, his combat scenes involve 360 degrees. Any shot might be aimed at friend or enemy, and in the desperate rush of combat, many of his soldiers never have a clear idea of exactly who they are shooting at, or why.

Traditional movies impose a sense of order upon combat. Identifying with the soldiers, we feel that if we duck behind this tree or jump into this ditch, we will be safe from the fire that is coming from over there. In *Platoon*, there is the constant fear that any movement offers a fifty-fifty chance between a safe place or an exposed one. Stone sets up his shots to deny us the feeling that combat makes sense.

The Vietnam War is the central moral and political issue of the last quarter century for Americans. It has inspired some of the greatest recent American films: *Apocalyse Now*, *The Deer Hunter*, *Coming Home*, *The Killing Fields*. Now here is the film that, in a curious way, should have been made before any of the others. A film that says—as the Vietnam Memorial in Washington says—that before you can make any vast sweeping statements about Vietnam, you have to begin by understanding the bottom line, which is that a lot of people went over there and got killed, dead, and that is what the war meant for them.

Play It Again, Sam ★ ★ ★
PG, 85 m., 1972

Woody Allen (Allan), Diane Keaton (Linda), Tony Roberts (Dick), Jerry Lacy (Bogart), Susan Anspach (Nancy), Jennifer Salt (Sharon), Joy Bang (Julie), Viva (Jennifer). Directed by Herbert Ross and produced by Arthur P. Jacobs. Screenplay by Woody Allen.

Allan lives in an apartment furnished with movie trivia. He sleeps beneath a poster for *Across the Pacific*, shaves with *Casablanca* reflected in the mirror, and fries his eggs across from *The Big Sleep*. There is not a place in the apartment from which the names Mary Astor and Sydney Greenstreet cannot be read. He is a Humphrey Bogart fan. He is more than that. He is a Humphrey Bogart pupil.

Allan's wife moved out some weeks ago and is suing for divorce, so now there are only the two people living in the apartment: Allan and Bogie. Whenever Allan reaches a crisis in his life, Bogie appears. His snapbrim is pulled down low over his eyes, and the collar is turned up on his trench coat, and there is a gat in his pocket and a Chesterfield in his mug.

"Tell her your life has changed since you met her," Bogie advises. Allan turns toward the lovely brunette sitting next to him on the sofa. He turns back to Bogie. "She won't fall for that!" Allan says. "Oh no?" says Bogie. "Try it and see."

This is pretty high-class advice, but Allan is a mess around girls. He's your average, ordinary movie freak, perfectly at home in the dark cave of a revival theater, watching the airport scene from *Casablanca*. But get him away from the movies and he gets . . . nervous. His friends try to take him to the beach. "I hate the beach! I hate the sun!" he cries. "I'm pale and I'm redheaded! I don't tan—I stroke!"

You can see that he has problems, even with Bogie on his side. His friends, Linda and Dick, try to fix him up with girls, but he splashes himself with too much Canoe and then destroys his furniture during a seizure of nonchalance. After a while it begins to occur to him that he's in love with Linda, and she likes him, and Dick is always on the phone making real estate deals.

All of this is slightly less mad than your usual Woody Allen comedy, maybe because *Play It Again, Sam* is based on Woody's Broadway play, and with a play it's a little hard to work in material like a Howard Cosell play-by-play of an assassination in South America. Still, as comedies go, this is a very funny one. Woody Allen is one of those rare comedians who understands that humor can be based on pathos as well as sadism. While the high-pressure comics overwhelm us with aggressive humor, Woody is off in the bathroom somewhere being attacked by a hairdryer.

The notion of using a Bogart character is surprisingly successful. The Bogie imitation by Jerry Lacy is good, if not great, and the movie begins and ends with variations on that great *Casablanca* ending. That, and the movie's rather conventional Broadway plot structure, give it more coherence than the previous Woody Allen films, *Take the Money and Run* and *Bananas*. Maybe the movie has too much coherence, and the plot is too predictable; that's a weakness of films based on well-made Broadway plays. Still, that's hardly a serious complaint about something as funny as *Play It Again, Sam*.

Play Misty for Me ★ ★ ★ ★
R, 102 m., 1971

Clint Eastwood (Disc Jockey), Jessica Walter (Strange Woman), Donna Mills (Girlfriend), Don Siegel (Bartender). Directed by Clint Eastwood and produced by Robert Daley. Screenplay by Jo Heims and Dean Reisner.

The girl calls up every night at about the same time and asks the disc jockey to play "Misty" for her. Some nights he does. He's the all-night man on a small station in Carmel who plays records, reads poems, and hopes to make it someday in the big city. After work (and before work, for that matter) he drinks free at bars around town, places he sometimes mentions on the air. He had a steady girl for a while, but he's been free-lancing recently, and one night he picks up a girl in a bar. Or maybe she picks him up. She's the girl who likes "Misty." She is also mad. She insinuates herself into his life with a passionate jealousy, and we gradually come to understand that she is capable of violence. At the same time, the disc jockey's old love turns up in town, and he wants nothing more than to allow himself, finally, to quit playing the field and marry her. But the new girl doesn't see it that way. And she has this thing for knives.

Play Misty for Me is not the artistic equal of *Psycho*, but in the business of collecting an audience into the palm of its hand and then squeezing hard, it is supreme. It doesn't depend on a lot of surprises to maintain the suspense. There ARE some surprises, sure, but mostly the film's terror comes from the fact that the strange woman is capable of anything.

The movie was Clint Eastwood's debut as a director, and it was a good beginning. He must have learned a lot during seventeen years of working for other directors. In particular, he must have learned a lot from Don Siegel, who directed his previous four movies and has a bit part (the bartender) in this one. There is no wasted energy in *Play Misty for Me*. Everything contributes to the accumulation of terror, until even the ordi-nary, daytime scenes seem to have unspeakable things lurking beneath them.

In this connection, Eastwood succeeds in filming the first Semi-Obligatory Lyrical Interlude that works. The Semi-OLI, you'll recall, is the scene where the boy and girl walk in the meadow and there's a hit song on the sound track. In Eastwood's movie, he walks in the meadow with the girl, but the scene has been prepared so carefully that the meadow looks ominous. The grass looks muddy, the shadows are deep, the sky is gray, and there is a chill in the air. The whole visual style of the movie is strangely threatening.

The movie revolves around a character played with an unnerving effectiveness by Jessica Walter. She is something like flypaper; the more you struggle against her personality, the more tightly you're held. Clint Eastwood, in directing himself, shows that he understands his unique movie personality. He is strong but somehow passive, he possesses strength but keeps it coiled inside. And so the movie, by refusing to release any emotion at all until the very end, absolutely wrings us dry. There is no purpose to a suspense thriller, I suppose, except to involve us, scare us, to give us moments of vicarious terror. *Play Misty for Me* does that with an almost cruel efficiency.

Plenty ★ ★ ★ ½
R, 119 m., 1985

Meryl Streep (Susan), Charles Dance (Raymond), Tracey Ullman (Alice), John Gielgud (Darwin), Sting (Mick), Ian McKellen (Sir Andrew), Sam Neill (Lazar). Directed by Fred Schepisi and produced by Edward R. Pressman and Joseph Papp. Screenplay by David Hare.

At the end of World War II, a young woman stands on a hilltop in France and, as the sun bathes her in golden light, she says, "There will be days and days and days like this." That image provides the last shot in *Plenty*, which is the story of how very wrong she was.

The woman is Susan Traherne, a young English fighter in the French Resistance. She is not very seasoned and perhaps not very good at her job, but she stays alive behind enemy lines and she has a brief, poignant love affair with one of the men who parachuted down out of the night sky to fight the Germans.

The movie opens with her days in France. It follows her through the next fifteen or twenty years, and ends with that painful flashback to a day when she thought the future had nothing but good things for her. But nothing else in her life is ever as important, as ennobling or as much fun as the war. She is, perhaps, a little mad. She confesses at one point that she has a problem: "Sometimes I like to lose control."

The movie stars Meryl Streep as Susan and it is a performance of great subtlety; it is hard to play an unbalanced, neurotic, self-destructive woman, and do it with such gentleness and charm. Susan is often very pleasant to be around for the other characters in *Plenty*, and when she is letting herself lose control, she doesn't do it in the style of those patented movie mad scenes in which eyes roll and teeth are bared. She does it with an almost winsome urgency.

When she returns to England after the war, Susan makes friends almost at once. One of them is Alice (Tracey Ullman), a round-faced, grinning imp who seems born to the role of best pal. Another is Raymond (Charles Dance), a foreign-service officer who is at first fascinated by her free, Bohemian lifestyle, and then marries her and becomes her lifelong enabler, putting up a wall of patience and almost saintly tolerance around her outbursts.

It is hard to say exactly what it is that troubles Susan. At first, David Hare's screenplay leads us to her own interpretation: That after the glory and excitement of the war, after the heroism and romance, it is impossible for her to return to civilian life and suffer the boring conversations of polite society. Later, we begin to realize there is something a little willful, a little cruel, in the way she embarrasses her husband on important occasions, always seeking to say the wrong thing at the wrong time. Finally, we tend to agree with him when he explodes that she is cruel and brutish, and ungrateful to those who have put up with her.

But then there is an epilogue—a strange, furtive meeting with the boy, the parachutist, she made love with twenty years earlier. It is bathed in the cold, greenish-gray light of the saddest part of an autumn afternoon, and there is such desperation in the way they both realize that nothing will ever, ever touch them again the way the war did.

Plenty is finally not a statement about war, or foreign service, or the British middle class, but simply the story of this flawed woman who once lived intensely, and now feels that she is hardly living at all.

The performances in the movie supply one brilliant solo after another; most of the big moments come as characters dominate the scenes they are in. Streep creates a whole character around a woman who could have simply been a catalog of symptoms. Charles Dance has a thankless role, I suppose, as her long-suffering husband, but manages to suggest that he is decent as well as duped. Sting plays a nondescript young man who unsuccessfully attempts to father her child. John Gielgud has three brief scenes and steals them all.

The movie is written, acted, and directed (by Fred Schepisi) as a surface of literacy and brittle wit, beneath which lives the realization that life can sometimes be pointless and empty and sad—and that there can be days and days and days like that.

The Plot Against Harry ★ ★ ★ ½
NO MPAA RATING, 81 m., 1970

Martin Priest (Harry Plotnick), Ben Lang (Leo Perlmutter), Maxine Woods (Kay Plotnick), Henry Nemo (Max), Jacques Tylor (Jack Pomerance), Jean Leslie (Irene Pomerance), Ellen Herbert (Mae Klepper, Harry's sister), Sandra Kazan (Margie Skolnik, née Plotnick). Directed by Michael Roemer and produced by Michael and Robert Young. Screenplay by Roemer.

There is little joy in the life of Harry Plotnick. He is a low-level hoodlum, a banker for a numbers game in a New York neighborhood that was once Jewish but is now largely Hispanic and black—a neighborhood where he was once a big frog but is now without a pond. Is his numbers empire dissolving as part of a plot against him? Not really, but for Harry so many things are going wrong in so many different ways that life itself seems like a conspiracy aimed at him. Maybe everybody else got up earlier than he did today to attend a meeting on how they were all going to screw him.

As *The Plot Against Harry* opens, Harry (Martin Priest) has just been released after serving a short prison sentence. He is met by Max (Henry Nemo), his loyal chauffeur and bookkeeper, but as he returns to the old neighborhood he finds that he has to use a Chinese restaurant owner as an interpreter to even understand what his Spanish-speaking lieutenants are trying to say to him. Even

more ominously, the mob seems ready to turn over his numbers business to a black man.

Harry regards these developments from out of sad, tired eyes with large bags beneath them. He rarely smiles. Life has lost the ability to astonish him—until one day he almost has a traffic accident with a car that turns out to contain his ex-wife, his ex-brother-in-law, and a daughter he has never known. Life is amazing. He even has *another* daughter, he discovers, that he knew nothing about.

Now events begin to overtake Harry. He is plunged into a social whirl: One daughter is expecting, and the other is a lingerie model with a fiancé and wedding plans. His ex-brother-in-law (Ben Lang) owns a catering business and might want to take in a partner with some ready cash. His ex-wife is part of a respectable circle that includes an executive for the Heart Fund. Can Harry buy into this middle-class normality? Certainly he seems uncomfortable with the mob, where he is such small potatoes that when he testifies before a congressional crime commission, the members lose interest when they realize he knows almost nothing.

The Plot Against Harry is one of those comedies with a sprung rhythm, so that the jokes pay off by working against themselves. It's a film that makes its points through its observation of human nature, especially in such scenes as a charity benefit on a subway train and a wedding. The writer and director, Michael Roemer, doesn't build his payoffs by the boring formula of setup and punch line, but by gradually revealing the dilemma Harry finds himself in. Even the film's big moments (like the inspired scene where Harry passes out on camera at a telethon) get their laughs because of the deliberate steps by which Roemer paints the situation.

In a sense, this is filmmaking in the Robert Altman style: The camera plunges into the middle of a group of people who seem to carry on as if they're oblivious to it. They aren't playing to the camera, and the screenplay isn't aimed at the audience. Instead, the people seem strange, funny, and unique all on their own, and the audience is invited to share the filmmaker's delight as he discovers this.

The behind-the-scenes story of *The Plot Against Harry* is by now well-known. The movie was completed in 1970, but at the time, it was unable to find distribution—Hollywood didn't think it was funny. It waited on the shelf for twenty years, until

Roemer decided to transfer it to video to show to his children. The video technician started to laugh as he watched it. A curiosity stirred within Roemer: Could the movie possibly be good, after all? He submitted it to the Toronto, New York, and Park City film festivals, where audiences were enthusiastic, and then he won commercial distribution, two decades later.

That adds a certain poignancy to the whole enterprise. If you see the film, pay particular attention to the performances by Martin Priest as Harry and Ben Lang as the forever-smiling ex-brother-in-law. They have a genuinely intrinsically amusing quality. Priest has acted only occasionally in the last twenty years, and Lang not at all (he went back to his job as an auditor for the state). Would their careers have happened differently if this movie had been seen in 1970? Would the movie have been a hit then? Was it ahead of its time? (Altman's revolutionary *M*A*S*H* came out the same year.) Who can say? What can be said is that this time capsule from 1970 feels, in 1990, like a jolt of fresh air.

Police Academy   no stars
R, 97 m., 1984

Steve Guttenberg (Carey Mahoney), Kim Cattrall (Karen Thompson), G.W. Bailey (Lieutenant Harris), Bubba Smith (Moses Hightower), Georgina Spelvin (Hooker). Directed by Hugh Wilson and produced by Paul Maslansky. Screenplay by Neal Israel, Pat Proft, and Wilson.

Once upon a time there was a movie named *Airplane!* which had a clever notion: Wouldn't it be fun to satirize all of those *Airport* movies by combining their clichés into one gloriously confused mess, typecasting the movie with walking stereotypes, and going for every corny gag in the book? They were right. It was a great idea, and it made a very funny movie. It also inspired a dreary series of clones and rip-offs, including *Young Doctors in Love* and *Jekyll and Hyde—Together Again*. Now comes without any doubt the absolute pits of this genre, the least funny movie that could possibly have been inspired by *Airplane!* or any other movie.

It's really something. It's so bad, maybe you should pool your money and draw straws and send one of the guys off to rent it so that in the future, whenever you think you're sitting through a bad comedy, he could shake his head, and chuckle tolerantly, and explain that you don't know what bad is. This is the kind of movie where they'll bring a couple of characters onscreen and begin to set up a joke, and then, just when you realize you can predict exactly what's going to happen . . . not only doesn't it happen, but nothing happens—they just cut to some different characters! If there's anything worse than a punch line that doesn't work, it's a movie that doesn't even bother to put the punch lines in.

Among the many questions raised by *Police Academy*, the easiest is: What genre does this movie think it's satirizing? Are there any other movies about police academies? That hardly matters, since the academy in this movie resembles no police academy known to modern man, and seems, indeed, to be modeled after a cross between basic training and prep school. All of the trainee cops live on campus together, in big dorms. The head of the academy is sort of like the headmaster. The campus is green and leafy and peaceful and altogether unlike, I suspect, the training experience undergone by any real police officers.

In a movie this bad, one plot element is really idiotic. It involves the casting of Bubba Smith as a giant black recruit who only has to look at a guy, and his knees start to tremble. This is funny? Don't they know that in comedy, you need a twist—like, why not make Bubba Smith a pathological coward who's afraid of everybody? Now right there is one good idea more than you can find in this entire movie.

Poltergeist ★ ★ ★
PG, 114 m., 1982

Craig T. Nelson (Steve), Jo Beth Williams (Diane), Beatrice Straight (Dr. Lesh), Dominique Dunne (Dana), Oliver Robins (Robbie), Heather O'Rourke (Carol Anne). Directed by Tobe Hooper and produced by Steven Spielberg and Frank Marshall. Screenplay by Spielberg, Michael Grais, and Mark Victor.

Special effects in the movies have grown so skilled, sensational, and scary that they sometimes upstage the human actors. And they often cost a lot more. In *Poltergeist*, for example, the cast is made up of relatively unknown performers, but that's all right because the real stars are producer Steven

Spielberg *(Raiders of the Lost Ark)*, director Tobe Hooper *(The Texas Chainsaw Massacre)*, and their reputations for special effects and realistic violence. Their names on this horror film suggest that its technology will be impeccable. And they don't disappoint us. This is the movie *The Amityville Horror* dreamed of being. It begins with the same ingredients (a happy American family, living in a big, comfortable house). It provides similar warnings of doom (household objects move by themselves, the weather seems different around the house than anywhere else). And it ends with a similar apocalypse (spirits take total possession of the house, and terrorize the family). Even some of the special effects are quite similar, as when greasy goo begins to ooze around the edges of a doorjamb.

But *Poltergeist* is an effective thriller, not so much because of the special effects, as because Hooper and Spielberg have tried to see the movie's strange events through the eyes of the family members, instead of just standing back and letting the special effects overwhelm the cast along with the audience. The movie takes place in Spielberg's favorite terrain, the American suburb (also the locale of parts of *Close Encounters, Jaws,* and *E.T.*). The haunted house doesn't have seven gables, but it does have a two-car garage. It is occupied by a fairly normal family (two parents, three kids) and the movie begins on a somewhat hopeful note with the playing of "The Star Spangled Banner" as a TV station signs off.

The opening visuals, however, are somewhat ominous. They're an extreme close-up of a TV screen, filled with the usual patriotic images (Iwo Jima, the Lincoln Memorial). Why so close? We're almost being invited to look between the dots on the screen and see something else. And indeed, the family's youngest daughter, an open-faced, long-haired, innocent little cherub, begins to talk to the screen. She's in touch with the "TV people." Before long she disappears from this plane of existence and goes to live with the TV people, wherever they are. Weird events begin to happen in the house. An old tree behaves ominously. The swimming pool seems to have a mind of its own. And the villains are the same people who were the bad guys in Spielberg's *Jaws*—the real estate developers. This time, instead of encouraging people to go back into the water, they're building a subdivision on top of an old graveyard.

This is all ridiculous, but Hooper and Spielberg hold our interest by observing the everyday rituals of this family so closely that, since the family seems real, the weird events take on a certain credibility by association. That's during the first hour of the movie. Then all hell breaks loose, and the movie begins to operate on the same plane as *Alien* or *Altered States*, as a shocking special-effects sound-and-light show. A closet seems to exist in another dimension. The swimming pool is filled with grasping, despairing forms of the undead. The search for the missing little girl involves a professional psionics expert, and a lady dwarf who specializes in "cleaning" haunted homes. Nobody ever does decide whether a poltergeist really is involved in the events in the house, or who the poltergeist may be, but if that doesn't prevent them from naming the movie *Poltergeist* I guess it shouldn't keep us from enjoying it.

The Pope of Greenwich Village
★ ★ ★
R, 122 m., 1984

Eric Roberts (Paulie), Mickey Rourke (Charlie), Daryl Hannah (Diane), Geraldine Page (Mrs. Ritter), Kenneth McMillan (Barney), Tony Musante (Pete), Burt Young (Bedbug Eddie). Directed by Stuart Rosenberg and produced by Gene Kirkwood. Screenplay by Vincent Patrick.

Everybody is very ethnic in *The Pope of Greenwich Village*. They all wave their hands a lot, and hang out on street corners, and have uncles in the Mafia. They have such bonds of blood brotherhood, a cousin is closer than your mother is to you. And they've always got some kind of con game going on the side. Take Paulie, for example. He knows this racehorse that's selling for $15,000, only the joke is, this is a champion horse because it was sired with sperm stolen directly from the winner of the Belmont. Paulie explains about the horse while he has his mouth full of a hero sandwich that's a yard long. His cousin, Charlie, tells him he's crazy. That is a compliment in this family.

Paulie and Charlie have just been fired from their jobs at a restaurant for stealing from the management. Charlie is hard up. He can no longer support his girlfriend, a long-limbed, blond aerobics instructor who seems attracted to his exotic ethnic charm.

Paulie has the answer to their problems. He will buy the future champion racehorse with money from a juice loan and then pay off the loan by cracking a safe he has heard about. There is only one problem with this plan. The safe belongs to the Mafia godfather of Greenwich Village, and if he finds out who did it, not even Paulie's uncle in the Mafia can save them. Meanwhile, Charlie's girlfriend is pregnant, Paulie's car has been towed, a cop has killed himself falling down an elevator shaft, and on the sound track Frank Sinatra is singing "Summer Wind."

The Pope of Greenwich Village bills itself as a drama and is structured like a crime thriller, but I categorize it as basically a Behavior Movie. The real subject of the movie is the behavior of the characters, and the story is essentially an excuse for showboat performances. This movie is an actor's dream, and the actors involved are Eric Roberts, fresh from his triumph in *STAR 80*, as Paulie; Mickey Rourke, the hero of *Diner*, as Charlie; Daryl Hannah, right after her hit in *Splash*, as the aerobics instructor; and the usual supporting types like Tony Musante as the uncle, Burt Young—stuffing his face with pasta—as the godfather, and Geraldine Page as the tough-talking mother of the dead cop. Also, Kenneth McMillan has a well-acted key role as an old safecracker who gets caught in the middle of the whole deal.

There are times when *The Pope of Greenwich Village* seems to aspire to some great meaning, some insight into crime like *The Godfather* had. But the tip-off is the last shot, where the boys have a happy-go-lucky walk down the street and into a freeze-frame, while Sinatra is trotted out for his third encore. This movie is not really about anything except behavior, and the only human drama in it is the story of the safecracker and his family. That doesn't mean it's not worth seeing. The behavior is well-observed, although Eric Roberts has a tendency to go over the top in his mannered performance, and the last two scenes are highly unlikely. It's worth seeing for the acting, and it's got some good laughs in it, and New York is colorfully observed, but don't tell me this movie is about human nature, because it's not; it's about acting.

Popeye ★ ★ ★ ½
PG, 114 m., 1980

Robin Williams (Popeye), Shelley Duvall (Olive Oyl), Ray Walston (Poopdeck Pappy), Paul Dooley (Wimpy), Paul L. Smith (Bluto), Richard Libertini (Geezil). Directed by Robert Altman and produced by Robert Evans. Screenplay by Jules Feiffer.

One of Robert Altman's trademarks is the way he creates whole new worlds in his movies—worlds where we somehow don't believe that life ends at the edge of the screen, worlds in which the main characters are surrounded by other people plunging ahead at the business of living. That gift for populating new places is one of the richest treasures in *Popeye*, Altman's musical comedy. He takes one of the most artificial and limiting of art forms—the comic strip—and raises it to the level of high comedy and high spirits.

And yet *Popeye* nevertheless remains true to its origin on the comic page, and in those classic cartoons by Max Fleischer. A review of this film almost has to start with the work of Wolf Kroeger, the production designer, who created an astonishingly detailed and rich set on the movie's Malta locations. Most of the action takes place in a ramshackle fishing hamlet—"Sweethaven"—where the streets run at crazy angles up the hillsides, and the rooming houses and saloons lean together dangerously.

Sweethaven has been populated by actors who look, or are made to look, so much like their funny-page originals that it's hardly even jarring that they're *not* cartoons. Audiences immediately notice the immense forearms on Robin Williams, who plays Popeye; they're big, brawny, and completely convincing. But so is Williams's perpetual squint and his lopsided smile. Shelley Duvall, the star of so many other Altman films, is perfect here as Olive Oyl, the role she was born to play. She brings to Olive a certain . . . dignity, you might say. She's not lightly scorned, and although she may tear apart a room in an unsuccessful attempt to open the curtains, she is fearless in the face of her terrifying fiancé, Bluto. The list continues: Paul Smith (the torturer in *Midnight Express*) looks ferociously Bluto-like, and Paul Dooley (the father in *Breaking Away*) is a perfect Wimpy, forever curiously sniffing a hamburger with a connoisseur's fanatic passion. Even the little baby, Swee' Pea, played by Altman's grandson, Wesley Ivan Hurt, looks like typecasting.

But it's not enough that the characters and the locations look their parts. Altman has breathed life into this material, and he hasn't done it by pretending it's camp, either. He organizes a screenful of activity, so carefully choreographed that it's a delight, for example to watch the moves as the guests in Olive's rooming house make stabs at the plates of food on the table.

There are several set pieces. One involves Popeye's arrival at Sweethaven, another a stop on his lonely quest for his long-lost father. Another is the big wedding day for Bluto and Olive Oyl, with Olive among the missing and Bluto's temper growing until steam jets from his ears. There is the excursion to the amusement pier, and the melee at the dinner table, and the revelation of the true identity of a mysterious admiral, and the kidnapping of Swee' Pea, and then the kidnapping of Olive Oyl and her subsequent wrestling match with a savage octopus.

The movie's songs, by Harry Nilssen, fit into all of this quite effortlessly. Instead of having everything come to a halt for the musical set pieces, Altman stitches them into the fabric. Robin Williams sings Popeye's anthem, "I Yam What I Yam" with a growling old sea dog's stubbornness. Bluto's "I'm Mean" has an undeniable conviction, and so does Olive Oyl's song to Bluto, "He's Large." Shelley Duvall's performance as Olive Oyl also benefits from the amazingly ungainly walking style she brings to the movie.

Popeye, then, is lots of fun. It suggests that it *is* possible to take the broad strokes of a comic strip and turn them into sophisticated entertainment. What's needed is the right attitude toward the material. If Altman and his people had been the slightest bit condescending toward Popeye, the movie might have crash-landed. But it's clear that this movie has an affection for Popeye, and so much regard for the sailor man that it even bothers to reveal the real truth about his opinion of spinach.

Porky's ★ ½
R, 94 m., 1982

Dan Monahan (Pee Wee), Mark Herrier (Billy), Wyatt Knight (Tommy), Roger Wilson (Mickey), Kim Cattrall (Honeywell), Alex Karras (Sheriff), Susan Clark (Cherry Forever), Nancy Parsons (Ms. Balbricker). Directed by Bob Clark and produced by Don Carmody and Clark.

Porky's is another raunchy teen-age sex-and-food-fight movie. The whole genre seems fixated on the late 1950s and early 1960s, when the filmmakers, no doubt, were teen-agers. Do today's teen-agers really identify with jokes about locker rooms, Trojans, boobs, jockstraps, killer-dyke gym coaches, and barfing? Well, yes, probably they do. Teen-agers seem to occupy a time warp of eternally unchanging preoccupations. Hollywood originally entered that world with a certain innocence in the late 1950s with Pat Boone and beach party movies. That innocence is now long, long ago. Since *American Graffiti*, *National Lampoon's Animal House*, and *Meatballs*, the A.C.N.E.S. movie has turned cynical. You remember what A.C.N.E.S. stands for. It's an acronym for any movie about the dreaded Adolescent Character's Neurotic Eroticism Syndrome.

In *Porky's*, the male characters are neurotic about the usual three subjects: the size, experience, and health of their reproductive organs. The female characters, on the other hand, are seen almost entirely as an undiscovered species from a lost continent. They're whispered about, speculated about, spied upon, victimized, and, in general, feared. And it's not only Ms. Balbricker, the juggernaut gym coach, who's a heavy. All of the women in this movie are weird. One howls like a dog during sexual intercourse. Others lure unsuspecting horny teen-age boys into rooms with trapdoors, and dump them into alligator-infested waters.

In fact, the strangest thing about *Porky's* is how much it hates women. The only close friendships in the movie are between men. The movie even takes certain scenes that are usually clichés for female characters and assigns them to men. For example, you can hardly make a movie like this without a scene in which someone's caught nude in public. Remember Hot Lips in *M*A*S*H?* In *Porky's*, it's a kid named Pee Wee. He's caught with his pants down, chased into the woods, picked up by the cops, and deposited at the local drive-in hamburger stand, where he poses like September Morn.

Since the movie doesn't like women, its sex scenes all create fear and hostility, which prevents them from being funny (sex scenes *about* fear and hostility, on the other hand, can be very funny). Even in an easy scene like the one where the guys spy on the girls in the locker room, the director, Bob Clark, blows it. Peeping-tom scenes can be very funny (remember John Belushi on the ladder in *Animal House?*). Here, it's just smarmy.

There's one other problem. None of the male actors in this movie look, sound, or act like teen-agers. They all look like overgrown preppies at their fraternity pledge class's fifth reunion. Jokes based on embarrassment never work unless we can identify with the embarrassed character. Here, the actors all seem to be just acting.

I see that I have neglected to summarize the plot of *Porky's*. And I don't think I will. I don't feel like writing one more sentence (which is, to be sure, all it would take).

Postcards from the Edge ★ ★ ★
R, 101 m., 1990

Meryl Streep (Suzanne Vale), Shirley MacLaine (Doris Mann), Dennis Quaid (Jack Falkner), Gene Hackman (Lowell), Richard Dreyfuss (Dr. Frankenthal), Rob Reiner (Joe Pierce), CCH Pounder (Julie Marsden). Directed by Mike Nichols and produced by Nichols and John Calley. Screenplay by Carrie Fisher.

The practicing alcoholic is familiar with a gnawing feeling in the pit of the stomach—the guilt at letting other people down, the remorse at letting himself down. Criticism in any form is likely to be met with anger, because nothing you can tell him will make him feel worse than the things he tells himself.

In the opening scenes of *Postcards from the Edge*, a comedy based on Carrie Fisher's journey through addiction, this feeling is evoked so well that you begin to suffer along with the film's heroine, played by Meryl Streep. Then the movie forgets its original impulse and turns into a comedy of manners.

The story involves Suzanne, a young actress who has a more famous actress for her mother. The father, also famous, has been misplaced somewhere along the way. As the film opens, Suzanne has awakened in the bed of yet another boyfriend she does not quite remember meeting. Her life has become a confusion of blackouts, memory lapses, screw-ups on the set, and behavior that baffles even her. All that keeps her going on the set of a movie are the frequent visits to her dressing room in the company of a woman who sells her cocaine.

Meryl Streep plays this character with a kind of defiant sweetness that recalls the late Irene Dunne. She is not a bad person and she doesn't want to cause trouble for anybody, but her drug usage has befuddled her to the point where she's not much use. Her mother (Shirley MacLaine) is also a basket case—a maintenance alcoholic who is never far from her glass of chilled white wine. But because wine is socially acceptable and drugs are not, the mother is able to deny her problem while lecturing her daughter to the point of distraction. Meanwhile, MacLaine's latest husband sleeps most of the time, possibly as a way of avoiding his wife's voice.

Suzanne barely gets through her latest film. She is obviously on the edge of a crack-up, and after another misadventure she ends up in a rehab center, where her mother comes to visit and basks in the applause of her recovering fans. It's here that the movie takes the wrong turn, into a domestic show biz comedy that plays up the mother-daughter rivalry at the cost of its original subject, drugs in show business.

That's not to say I didn't enjoy Shirley MacLaine's performance in this movie; her role has been made too important, and yet I appreciated every moment of it, even a welcome home party at which mother and daughter perform songs that turn into a competition for the love of those present. MacLaine creates a glorious caricature of the aging star who has to put down her daughter to maintain her own ego.

Streep is very funny in the movie; she does a good job of catching the knife-edged throwaway lines that have become Carrie Fisher's specialty. And Nichols captures a certain kind of difficult reality in his scenes on movie sets, where the actress is pulled this way and that by people offering helpful advice. Everyone wants a piece of a star, even a falling one.

What's disappointing about the movie is that it never really delivers on the subject of recovery from addiction. There are some incomplete, dimly seen, unrealized scenes in the rehab center, and then desultory talk about offscreen AA meetings, but the film is preoccupied with gossip; we're encouraged to wonder how many parallels there are between the Streep and MacLaine characters and their originals, Fisher and Debbie Reynolds. Suzanne, the young actress, has some bad moments and then comes through as a trooper, and the movie almost seems to think her real problem is an inability to communicate with her mother.

Half the people in Hollywood seem to have gone through recovery from drugs and alcohol by now. And yet no one seems able to make a movie that's really about the subject.

Do they think it wouldn't be interesting? Any movie that cares deeply about itself—even a comedy—is interesting. It's the movies that lack the courage of their convictions, the ones that keep asking themselves what the audience wants, that go astray. *Postcards from the Edge* contains too much good writing and too many good performances to be a failure, but its heart is not in the right place.

Powwow Highway ★ ★ ★
R, 91 m., 1989

A Martinez (Buddy Red Bow), Gary Farmer (Philbert Bono), Amanda Wyss (Rabbit Layton), Joanelle Romero (Bonnie Red Bow). Directed by Jonathan Wacks and produced by Jan Wieringa. Screenplay by Janet Heaney and Jean Stawarz, based on the novel by David Seals.

Anyone who can name his 1964 Buick "Protector," and talk to it like a pony, has a philosophy we can learn from. Philbert Bono is the name of the philosopher. He is a member of the Northern Cheyenne tribe, and near the beginning of *Powwow Highway* he and a friend, Buddy Red Bow, set out to ride Protector from Lame Deer, Montana, to Sante Fe, New Mexico. They go by way of the Dakotas, because to Bono the best way to get to a place is not always the straightest way.

Powwow Highway is the story of their journey, and in one sense it's a road movie and a buddy movie, but in another sense it's a meditation on the way American Indians can understand the land in terms of space, not of time. Philbert Bono never states it in so many words, but it's clear that he doesn't think of a trip to Santa Fe in terms of hours or miles, but in terms of the places he must visit between here and there to make it into a journey and not simply the physical relocation of his body.

The movie supplies a plot in order to explain why the two Indians need to take their journey, but the plot is the least interesting element of the film. It involves a scheme against Buddy Red Bow, who is a tribal activist and opposes a phony land-rights grab that's being directed at some Indian territories. His sister is thrown into jail in Santa Fe, and he must go there to bail her out, and that will get him out of Montana at a crucial time. And so on.

The plot is not the point. What *Powwow Highway* does best is to create two unforgettable characters and give them some time together, and place them within a large network of their Indian friends, so that we get a sense of the way their community still shares and thrives. As Philbert points Protector east instead of south, as he visits friends and sacred Indian places along the road, he doesn't try to justify what he's doing. It comes from inside. And it comes, we sense, from a very old Indian way of looking at things. Buddy Red Bow is much more modern and impatient—he's Type A—but as their journey unfolds he can begin to see the sense of it.

The movie develops a certain magical intensity during the journey, and much of that comes from the chemistry between the two lead actors. Philbert is played by Gary Farmer, a tall, huge man with a long black mane of hair and a gentle disposition. He speaks softly and sees things with a blinding directness. Buddy Red Bow (A Martinez) is more "modern," more political, angrier. Their friendship has survived their differences.

The movie has been shot entirely on location, and the set decoration, I suspect, consists of whatever the camera found in its way. (If this is not so, it is a great tribute to the filmmakers who made it seem that way.) We visit trailer parks and dispossessed suburbs and pool halls and convenience stores, and we watch the dawn in more than one state, and we get the sense of life on the road in a way that is both modern (highways, traffic signals) and timeless (the oneness of the land and the journey). And although I have made this all sound important and mystical, *Powwow Highway* is at heart a comedy, and even a bit of a thriller, although the way they spring Buddy's sister from prison belongs to the comedy and not the thriller.

The movie is based on a novel by David Seals, which I have not read; the story resembles the tone in some of W.P. Kinsella's stories about North American Indians. In Buddy Red Bow it shows the somewhat fading anger of a man who was once a firebrand in the AIM organization (he has a concise, bitter speech about the programs "for" the Indians that will be an education for some viewers). In Philbert Bono it finds a supplement to that anger, in a man whose sheer, unshakable serenity is a political statement of its own.

One of the reasons we see movies is to meet people we have not met before. It will be a long time before I forget Gary Farmer, who disappears into the Philbert role so completely we almost think he *is* this simple, open-hearted man—until we learn he's an actor and teacher from near Toronto. It's one of the most wholly convincing performances I've seen.

Most of the people who view *Powwow Highway* will already have seen *Rain Man*. Will they notice how similar the movies are in structure? Philbert Bono does not have any sort of mental handicap, as the man with autism does in *Rain Man*, but he has a similar, absolutely direct, simplicity. Both characters state facts. They catalog the obvious. Deep beneath the simplicity of Philbert's statements is a serene profundity (we cannot be quite sure if anything lies at the bottom of the autistic's statements). In both movies the other man—younger, ambitious, impatient—learns from the older. Meanwhile, in both movies, the men become friends while they drive in ancient Buicks down the limitless highways of America.

Prancer ★ ★ ★
G, 103 m., 1989

Sam Elliott (John Riggs), Rebecca Harrell (Jessica Riggs), Cloris Leachman (Mrs. McFarland), Rutanya Alda (Aunt Sarah), John Joseph Duda (Steve Riggs), Abe Vigoda (Orel Benton), Michael Constantine (Store's Santa), Ariana Richards (Carol Wetherby), Mark Rolston (Butcher Drier), Boo (Prancer). Directed by John Hancock and produced by Raffaella De Laurentiis. Screenplay by Greg Taylor.

Every once in a while you meet a kid like Jessica, who is tough and resilient and yet hangs onto her dreams. She's a nine-year-old who still believes in Santa Claus and uses logic to defend her position: If there isn't a Santa then maybe there isn't a God, and if there isn't a God then there isn't a heaven, and, in that case, where did Jessica's mother go when she died?

Jessica lives with her dad and brother on a small farm outside of Three Oaks, Michigan. Her dad grows apples and is struggling to make ends meet. He may have to sell the tractor. "Will we have enough to eat?" she asks him. "Sure," he says. "We'll have apple sauce, apple juice, stewed apples, apple pie, baked apples. . . ." One day while she's walking down the main street on her way home from school, Jessica witnesses a disturbing accident: One of Santa's reindeers falls down from a holiday decoration strung up across the street. It's Prancer, the third in line.

Nobody seems to care much about the injured decoration, which is cleared from the road. But not long after, walking home alone through the frosty woods on a cold night, Jessica comes across a reindeer with an injured leg. It stands unafraid in a moonlit clearing and seems to be asking for help. Not long after, her dad comes along in his pickup, and then they both see the deer in the road. Her dad sees that it has a bad leg and wants to shoot it, but then the reindeer disappears. And when it turns up again in the barn, Jessica hides it in an outbuilding and brings it Christmas cookies to eat. She wants to nurse Prancer back to health and return him to Santa.

OK, I know, this sounds like a cloying fantasy designed to paralyze anyone over the age of nine, but not the way it's told by director John Hancock and writer Greg Taylor. They give the film an unsentimental, almost realistic edge by making the father (Sam Elliott) into a tough, no-nonsense farmer who's having trouble raising his kids alone and keeps laying down the law. And what really redeems the movie, taking it out of the category of kiddie picture and giving it a heart and gumption, is the performance by a young actress named Rebecca Harrell, as Jessica.

She's something. She has a troublemaker's look in her eye and a round pixie face that's filled with mischief. And she's smart—a plucky schemer who figures out things for herself and isn't afraid to act on her convictions. Her dialogue in the movie is fun to listen to because she talks like she thinks, and she's always working an angle. She believes ferociously that her reindeer is indeed Prancer, and to buy it a bag of oats she does housecleaning for the eccentric old lady (Cloris Leachman) who lives in the house on the hill.

Prancer is not filled with a lot of action. Only ordinary things happen, as when the local newspaper prints a letter that Jessica wrote to Santa, assuring him that Prancer would be back in good shape for Christmas duty (the headline, inevitably, is "Yes, Santa, there is a Virginia.") The reindeer is finally discovered, and Jessica's dad sells it to Mr. Drier, the local butcher. Of course Jessica is sure Prancer will end up as sausage meat, but, no, all Drier wants to do is exhibit the animal as a Christmas attraction.

The best thing about Prancer is that it doesn't insult anyone's intelligence. Smaller kids will identify with Jessica's fierce resolve to get Prancer back into action, and older viewers will appreciate the fact that the movie takes place in an approximation of the real world.

Predator ★ ★ ★
R, 105 m., 1987

Arnold Schwarzenegger (Dutch), Carl Weathers (Dillon), Elpidia Carrillo (Anna), Bill Duke (Mac), Jesse Ventura (Blain), Sonny Landham (Billy), Richard Chaves (Poncho), R.G. Armstrong (General Phillips), Shane Black (Hawkins), Kevin Peter Hall (Predator). Directed by John McTiernan and produced by Lawrence Gordon, Joel Silver, and John Davis. Screenplay by Jim and John Thomas.

Predator begins like Rambo and ends like Alien, and in today's Hollywood, that's creativity. Most movies are inspired by only one previous blockbuster.

The movie stars Arnold Schwarzenegger as the leader of a U.S. Army commando team that goes into the South American jungle on a political mission and ends up dueling with a killer from outer space. This is the kind of idea that is produced at the end of a ten-second brainstorming session, but if it's done well, who cares?

Predator is filmed very well. It's a slick, high-energy action picture that takes a lot of its strength from its steamy locations in Mexico. The heroes spend most of their time surrounded by an impenetrable jungle, a green wall of majestic vistas populated by all sorts of natural predators in addition to the alien. I've rarely seen a jungle look more beautiful, or more convincing; the location effect is on a par with Fitzcarraldo and The Emerald Forest.

As the film opens, Schwarzenegger and his comrades venture into this jungle in search of South American officials who have been kidnapped by terrorists. They track and locate the fugitives, and move in for the kill. But as they find the bodies of team members skinned and hanging from trees, they begin to realize they're up against more than terrorists.

The predator of the movie's title is a visitor from space; that's established in the opening scene. What it is doing in the jungle is never explained. The creature lives in the trees, even though it seems to be a giant biped much too heavy to swing from vines. When Schwarzenegger finally grapples with it, we discover it is wearing a space suit, and that inside the suit is a disgusting creature with a mouth surrounded by little pincers to shove in the food.

Such details are important, of course. Stan Winston, who designed the creature, has created a beast that is sufficiently disgusting to justify Schwarzenegger's loathing for it. And the action moves so quickly that we overlook questions such as (1) Why would an alien species go to all the effort to send a creature to Earth, just so that it could swing from trees and skin American soldiers? Or, (2) Why would a creature so technologically advanced need to bother with hand-to-hand combat, when it could just zap Arnold with a ray gun? Maybe the alien is a hunter who sees Earth as some kind of terrific vacation spot, and Schwarzenegger as big game worth traveling hundreds of light-years for. Theorists on extraterrestrial intelligence have debated for years what motivation it would take to inspire aliens to hurl themselves across the galaxy, and now we know. At one point in the movie, the creature removes its helmet so it can battle Arnold mano-a-mano, and I was cynical enough to assume that its motivation was not macho pride, but the desire to display Winston's special effects.

None of these logical questions are very important to the movie. Predator moves at a breakneck pace, it has strong and simple characterizations, it has good location photography and terrific special effects, and it supplies what it claims to supply: an effective action movie.

Students of trivia might want to note that the actor inside the predator costume is Kevin Peter Hall, who also occupies the Bigfoot costume in Harry and the Hendersons. This guy must really be a good sport.

Predator 2 ★ ★
R, 108 m., 1990

Kevin Peter Hall (The Predator), Danny Glover (Harrigan), Gary Busey (Keyes), Ruben Blades (Danny), Maria Conchita Alonso (Leona), Bill Paxton (Jerry). Directed by Stephen Hopkins and produced by Lawrence Gordon, Joel Silver, and John Davis. Screenplay by Jim Thomas and John Thomas.

Aliens are like dreams. We have bad ones when we're troubled. The creature who visits earth in *Predator* is a savage hunter that can make itself invisible, stalks from above, and eviscerates its human prey with savage skill. It is not related to the gentle beings who came to visit us in *Close Encounters of the Third Kind.*

Sometimes we seem to welcome visitors from outer space, sometimes we fear them. There is a universe of difference between E.T. and the creatures in *Alien*, between *The Thing* and Mr. Spock, between the austere intelligences that made the monoliths in *2001* and the devious chameleons in *The Hidden.*

The world of *Predator 2* is a fearful world, a Los Angeles in the year 1997 when gunfire rules the streets and cops shoot it out with drug dealers. During one confrontation, a strange event takes place. Five drug dealers, heavily armed and barricaded inside a building, are killed by some sort of visitor who is unarmed, who can throw a 160-pound man twenty feet in the air, and who leaves no trace.

What's going on here? That's what Danny Glover would like to know. He plays Harrigan, the toughest of street cops, and every time he gets a good lead in the case, he's warned away by a sneering federal agent (Gary Busey), who seems to have inside information. In the classic tradition of all cop movies, Glover takes to the streets on his own, a lone wolf heading for an eventual showdown with the predator.

We've seen this creature before, of course, when he made his entrance in the original *Predator* (1987). That movie starred Arnold Schwarzenegger as a commando in the jungle who was one of the first to encounter the predator after it arrived on earth. What was it here for? To stalk the planet and kill trophy animals. It was a hunter from the stars, and we were in season. The first movie was leavened with a certain humor (Arnold's one-liners), and also with the possibility that the alien would challenge our imagination in some way, and be more than just another special effects monster.

The predator did indeed have a certain fearsome beauty in the earlier film. No such luck this time. The movie blows its one chance to deal creatively with the alien culture, in a scene where Glover finds himself inside some kind of trophy room from outer space. What manner of creatures built this place, and what kind of civilization do they come from? Who knows? Who cares? It's no help that the predators can speak En-

glish, since the first word out of the creature's mouth is that vile twelve-letter street expression.

Since the predator is imaginary but the people who made this film are not, *Predator 2* speaks sadly of their own lack of curiosity and imagination. All they can give us in the way of an alien is a street mugger with intestines for a face, pincers around his mouth, and an Afro-style braided hairdo. (The creature in this movie is a work of subtle racism. Subliminal clues are slipped in to encourage us to subconsciously connect the menace with black males. One not-so-subtle scene has the predator threatening a Bernard Goetz-type on the subway. This time, the Goetz-type meets his match.)

The acting in the movie is applied hysteria. Danny Glover, so engaging as a different kind of cop in the *Lethal Weapon* movies, screams and sweats, swears, and climbs down tall buildings. He is assisted by a Latino woman, played by the wonderful Maria Conchita Alonso, whose idea of creating an identity for herself at headquarters is to grab a new guy by the cajones until he pleads for mercy. The dialogue is foul and clinical, and the special effects, while expensive, are not interesting.

But the film's greatest loss is of spirit. We live on a speck in a corner of a vast universe, and what makes us men is our ability to wonder about what's out there. Since we do not know, the fables we create serve only to inspire our dreams. *Predator 2* is a movie whose dreams are angry and ugly.

Presumed Innocent ★ ★ ★ ½
R, 128 m., 1990

Harrison Ford (Rusty Sabich), Brian Dennehy (Raymond Horgan), Raul Julia (Sandy Stern), Bonnie Bedelia (Barbara Sabich), Paul Winfield (Judge Larren Lyttle), Greta Scacchi (Carolyn Polhemus). Directed by Alan J. Pakula and produced by Sydney Pollack and Mark Rosenberg. Screenplay by Frank Pierson and Alan J. Pakula.

Presumed Innocent opens on a shot of a jury box in an empty courtroom, the shadows dark along the walls, the wood tones a deep oxblood, the whole room suggesting that they should abandon hope, those who enter here. On the sound track we hear Harrison Ford talking about his job as a prosecuting attorney, but as he speaks of the duty of the law to separate the guilty from the innocent,

there is little faith in his voice that the task can be done with any degree of certainty.

Presumed Innocent has at its core one of the most fundamental fears of civilized man—the fear of being found guilty of a crime one did not commit. That fear is at the heart of more than half of Hitchcock's films, and it is one reason they work for all kinds of audiences. Everybody knows that fear. This movie is based on a best-selling novel by Scott Turow that became notorious for its explicit sexual content—for the detail in which it examined shocking gynecological evidence—and yet the sex wouldn't have sold many copies without the fear. How do you defend yourself against a charge of rape when you were having an affair with the dead woman, and your fingerprints are on a glass in her apartment, and the phone records reveal that you called her earlier in the evening, and it would appear that your semen has been found at the scene of the crime?

That is the dilemma in which Rusty Sabich finds himself midway through *Presumed Innocent*. Sabich, played by Harrison Ford as a man whose flat voice masks great passions and terrors, plays an assistant state's attorney who is assigned to the murder of a young woman lawyer in his office. Her name was Carolyn Polhemus (Greta Scacchi), and she had the ability to mesmerize men, especially those who could do her some good. Among those men, we discover, was Rusty Sabich himself—and also his boss, State's Attorney Raymond Horgan (Brian Dennehy), who has assigned him to the case.

At first the investigation goes slowly, and then suddenly incriminating evidence surfaces, and the investigator finds himself named as the accused. The situation is made trickier because Dennehy faces an election in a few days. How does it look when the law and order candidate has a rapist and murderer on his own staff? The Ford character faces the complete collapse of his life as he knew it. Standing by him, but bitter because of his infidelity, is his wife, played by Bonnie Bedelia.

I will not provide a single hint in this review as to whether Ford is actually guilty. Everyone who has read the book will, of course, have a good idea of which way the story is likely to unfold, but the producers cleverly floated the notion that the film could turn out differently than the book. Even if you think you know what the solution is, the performances are so clever and the screenplay—by Frank Pierson and director Alan J. Pakula—is so subtle that it could well turn out that your expectations are wrong.

Pakula has made film versions of difficult books before; *Sophie's Choice* and *All the President's Men* are among his credits. This time, his challenge was to avoid getting bogged down in the marshes of circumstantial and forensic evidence, which make good reading but can expand into interminable movie dialogue. The adaptation of Turow's novel does a good job of presenting the evidence as needed, and no more than is needed, while allowing time for the characters to establish themselves.

The lead performance, by Harrison Ford, must have been a delicate balancing act, since at every point he must seem plausible both as a killer and as an innocent man. Ford's taciturn and undemonstrative acting style is well-suited to the challenge. Greta Scacchi is well-cast, too, as the heartless Carolyn Polhemus, so warm and yet so cold. The Bonnie Bedelia performance as the wife is another tricky challenge, since she, too, must be ambiguous throughout. And the supporting performances include Paul Winfield as a judge with hidden motives, Raul Julia as a defense attorney who can't get his client to stop acting like a lawyer, and Dennehy, expansive and yet with a wall of flint when it comes to saving his own skin.

Presumed Innocent is a very quiet movie, brooding and secretive, about people who are good at masking their emotions. The audience I was with watched it with a hush. Part of the quiet was due to the absorbing nature of the story, I suppose, but a lot of it may have been caused by people reflecting, as I always do during stories like this, that there—but for the grace of God—go we.

Pretty Baby ★ ★ ★
R, 109 m., 1978

Brooke Shields (Violet), Keith Carradine (Bellocq), Susan Sarandon (Hattie), Frances Faye (Nell), Antonio Fargas (Professor), Matthew Anton (Red Top), Diana Scarwid (Frieda). Directed and produced by Louis Malle. Screenplay by Polly Platt.

Louis Malle's *Pretty Baby* was a pleasant surprise: After all the controversy and scandal surrounding its production, it turned out to be a good-hearted, good-looking, quietly elegiac movie. That was a coup for Malle, who sometimes seemed to dare himself to

find acceptable ways of filming unacceptable subjects.

His subject this time is a twelve-year-old girl who is raised in the New Orleans brothel where her mother works. She plays in the garden, she rides a pony, she likes ragtime music, and one day she's auctioned off to the man who will deflower her. This is, of course, tragically perverted, but *Pretty Baby* itself is not a perverted film: It looks soberly, and with a good deal of compassion, at its period of history and the people who occupied it.

The pretty baby of the title is named Violet, and is played by Brooke Shields, as an extraordinarily beautiful child. Before anyone had seen *Pretty Baby*, Malle was being accused of exploiting that fact. But he's thoughtful and almost cautious in his approach: Given the film's subject matter and its obligatory sex scenes, Malle shows taste and restraint. And Shields really creates a character here; her subtlety and depth are astonishing.

Malle places her in an extraordinarily well-realized world, the Storyville section of New Orleans, circa 1917. The movie pays infinite attention to detail, and looks and feels accurate: We get to know the brothel so well, with its curving staircases and baroque furnishings, we almost feel we live there too. And we get to know the people, too, especially the strange and cynical brothel-keeper Madame Nell (Frances Faye), who observes at one point in her gravelly voice: "I am old. And I know one thing: Life is very long." An almost opaque line, but she invests it with infinite weariness.

She also keeps a well-run establishment, populated by hookers like Violet's mother Hattie (Susan Sarandon), who dreams of escaping from the life and eventually succeeds: She marries a prosperous businessman from St. Louis, and moves north. She wants to take her daughter with her, but Violet won't go: For her, this house *is* a home. Violet has in the meantime gained a protector and confidant: Bellocq (Keith Carradine), the silent, eccentric photographer. He seems at first to feel no passion at all, as he takes his infinite pains to arrange the lights and shadows in which he poses the prostitutes. There is, we feel, the possibility that he's asexual. But he does have a special feeling for Violet. And on the night she is auctioned off, there are two long, anguished close-ups: Of Bellocq, and of the house's black piano player (Antonio Fargas). Both of them

clearly feel the auction is an outrage. Neither one speaks out. They are both creatures of Storyville, and know how things are done.

After Hattie goes north, Violet stays in the house for a time, and then goes to live with Bellocq. Their relationship is, of course, a strange one, made more complicated by the fact that this experienced twelve-year-old prostitute is still just a little girl. One of the film's most heartbreaking scenes has Violet sitting under a tree, playing with her doll. She is pretending that the doll is herself and that she is her mother. There's such a curious mixture of resentment and envy in her game that we cringe.

Pretty Baby has been attacked in some quarters as child porn. It's not. It's an evocation of a time and a place and a sad chapter of Americana. The ragtime music and the blues that fill its sound track take on a deeper meaning, in the context of the story, and we are reminded that the artists who sang "Do You Know What It Means to Miss New Orleans?" knew very well, and perhaps for that reason missed it less than their listeners.

Pretty in Pink ★ ★ ★
PG-13, 96 m., 1985

Molly Ringwald (Andie Walsh), Harry Dean Stanton (Jack Walsh), Jon Cryer (Duckie Dale), Andrew McCarthy (Blane McDonoug), Annie Potts (Iona), James Spader (Steff McKee). Directed by Howard Deutch and produced by Lauren Shuler. Screenplay by John Hughes.

Although *Pretty in Pink* contains several scenes that are a great deal more dramatic, my favorite moments were the quietest ones, in which nothing was being said because a boy was trying to get up the courage to ask a girl out on a date, and she knew it, and he knew it, and still nothing was happening.

To be able to listen to such a silence is to understand the central dilemma of adolescence, which is that one's dreams are so much larger than one's confidence. *Pretty in Pink* is a movie that pays attention to such things. And although it is not a great movie, it contains some moments when the audience is likely to think, yes, being sixteen was exactly like that.

The movie stars Molly Ringwald as Andie Walsh, a poor girl from the wrong side of the tracks. Her mother bailed out of her life some years earlier, and she lives with her unemployed father (Harry Dean Stanton), whose first words after she wakes him one morning are, "Where am I?" Andie works in a record store in a downtown mall and wears fashions that seem thrown together by a collision between a Goodwill store and a 1950s revival.

Andie attends a high school where most of the kids are wealthy snobs, and she has a crush on a rich kid named Blane (Andrew McCarthy). Her best friends are Duckie (Jon Cryer), who is a case study of the kind of teen-age boy who thinks he can clown his way into a girl's heart, and Iona (Annie Potts), a thirtyish sprite who affects one radical hairstyle after another.

The movie's plot is old, old, old. It's about how the rich boy and the poor girl love each other, but the rich kid's friends are snobs, and the poor girl doesn't want anyone to know what a shabby home she lives in, and about how they do find true love after all. Since the basic truths in the movie apply to all teen-agers, rich and poor, I wish the filmmakers had found a new plot to go along with them. Perhaps they could have made the lovers come from different ethnic groups, which wouldn't have been all that original, either, but at least would have avoided one more recycling of ancient Horatio Alger stories.

There is one other major problem with the movie, and that involves the character of Steff McKee (James Spader), the effete, chain-smoking rich snot who is Blane's best friend. He has been turned down several times by Andie and now pretends to be appalled that Blane would want to go out with such a "mutant." His snobbery almost shipwrecks the romance. Steff does have one great line of dialogue: "Money really means nothing to me. Do you think I'd treat my parents' house this way if it did?" But, as played by Spader, he looks much too old to be a teen-ager, and his scenes play uneasily for that reason. He seems more like a sinister twenty-five-year-old still lurking in the high school corridors, the Ghost of Proms Past.

Those objections noted, *Pretty in Pink* is a heartwarming and mostly truthful movie, with some nice touches of humor. The movie was written by John Hughes, who repeats the basic situation of his *Sixteen Candles*, which also starred Molly Ringwald as a girl who had a crush on a senior boy, and whose best friend was the class geek. But Ringwald grows with every movie into an actress who can project poignancy and vulnerability without seeming corny or coy, and her scenes

here with Cryer and Potts have one moment of small truth after another.

The nicest surprise in the movie is the character created by Potts. The first time we see her, she's dressed in leather and chains, but the next time, she wears one of those beehive hairdos from the early 1960s. She is constantly experimenting with her "look," and when she finally settles on conservative good taste, the choice seems like her most radical so far.

Pretty in Pink is evidence, I suppose, that there must be a reason why certain old stories never seem to die. We know all the clichés, we can predict half of the developments. But at the end, when this boy and this girl, who are so obviously intended for one another, finally get together, there is great satisfaction. There also is the sense that Molly Ringwald just might have that subtle magic that will allow her, like young Elizabeth Taylor, to grow into an actress who will keep on breaking and mending boys' hearts for a long time.

Pretty Woman ★ ★ ★ ½
R, 119 m., 1990

Richard Gere (Edward Lewis), Julia Roberts (Vivian Ward), Ralph Bellamy (James Morse), Jason Alexander (Philip Stuckey), Laura San Giacomo (Kit De Luca), Alex Hyde-White (David Morse), Amy Yasbeck (Elizabeth Stuckey), Elinor Donahue (Bridget). Directed by Garry Marshall and produced by Arnon Milchan and Steven Reuther. Screenplay by J.F. Lawton.

Because *Pretty Woman* stars Richard Gere, Hollywood's most successful male sex symbol, and because it's about his character falling in love with a prostitute, it is astonishing that *Pretty Woman* is such an innocent movie—that it's the sweetest and most open-hearted love fable since *The Princess Bride.* Here is a movie that could have marched us down mean streets into the sinks of iniquity, and it glows with romance.

Oh, it seems to be constructed out of the stuff of realism, all right. It stars Gere as an out-of-town millionaire visiting Los Angeles, who borrows his friend's car and gets lost on Hollywood Boulevard. He asks a hooker for directions to his hotel. She offers to tell him, for five dollars. For ten, she'll guide him there.

He agrees. It is important to understand that he is looking for directions, not sex, and

that he has broken up—coldly and efficiently—with his current girlfriend only half an hour earlier in a terse telephone conversation. The girl gets into the car and it turns out that she knows a lot about cars, and this intrigues him. The result is that he invites her to join him in his hotel suite. But not for sex, of course, he says. But you still have to pay, of course, she says.

She is played by Julia Roberts (of *Mystic Pizza* and an Oscar-nominated role in *Steel Magnolias*) as a woman who is as smart as she is attractive, which makes her very smart. Like many prostitutes, she is able to perform the mental trick of standing outside of what she does, of detaching herself and believing that her real self is not involved. That's what *she* does. She overhears one of his telephone conversations and wants to know what *he* does.

He's a takeover artist. He buys companies, takes them apart, and sells the pieces for more than he paid for the whole. "But what about the people who work for those companies?" she wants to know. "People have nothing to do with it," he explains. "It's strictly business." "Oh," she says. "Then you do the same thing I do."

What is happening in these scenes is that the characters are emerging as believable, original, and sympathetic. Gere and Roberts work easily together; we sense that their characters not only like one another, but feel comfortable with one another. The catch is, neither one trusts the feeling of comfort. They've been hurt so often, they depend on a facade of cynical detachment. Everything is business. He offers her money to spend one week with him, she accepts, he buys her clothes, they have sex, and, of course (this being the movies), they fall in love.

They fall into a particularly romantic kind of love, the sort you hardly see in the movies these days—a love based on staying awake after the lights are out and confiding autobiographical secrets. This is the first Gere film containing more confession than nudity. During the day, the lovers try to recover their cold detachment, to maintain the distance between them. If the love story in *Pretty Woman* is inspired by *Cinderella,* the daytime scenes are *Pygmalion,* as the hotel manager (Hector Elizondo) takes a liking to his best customer's "niece," and tutors her on which fork to use at a formal dinner.

There is a subplot involving Gere's attempts to take over a corporation run by an aging millionaire (Ralph Bellamy)—a man whose lifework he is prepared to savage, even though he actually likes him. There are broad Freudian hints that Gere's entire career is a form of revenge against his father, and that Bellamy may be the father figure he is searching for. But he has an impulse to hurt what he loves, and there is one particularly painful scene in which Gere reveals to a friend that Roberts is a prostitute, and Roberts gains a certain insight by how hurtful that betrayal is.

I mentioned that the movie is sweet and innocent. It is; it protects its fragile love story in the midst of cynicism and compromise. The performances are critical for that purpose. Gere plays new notes here; his swagger is gone, and he's more tentative, proper, even shy. Roberts does an interesting thing; she gives her character an irrepressibly bouncy sense of humor, and then lets her spend the movie trying to repress it. Actresses who can do that *and* look great can have whatever they want in Hollywood.

The movie was directed by Garry Marshall (*The Flamingo Kid*), whose films betray an instinctive good nature, and it is about as warmhearted as a movie about two cold realists can possibly be. I understand that earlier versions of the screenplay were more hard-boiled and downbeat, and that Marshall underlined the romance when he came aboard as director. There could indeed be, I suppose, an entirely different movie made from the same material—a more realistic film, in which the cold, economic realities of the lives of both characters would make it unlikely they could stay together. And, for that matter, a final scene involving a limousine, a fire escape, and some flowers is awkward and feels tacked on. But by the end of the movie, I was happy to have it close as it does.

Prick Up Your Ears ★ ★ ★ ★
R, 111 m., 1987

Gary Oldman (Joe Orton), Alfred Molina (Kenneth Halliwell), Vanessa Redgrave (Peggy Ramsay), Wallace Shawn (John Lahr), Lindsay Duncan (Anthea Lahr), Julie Walters (Elsie Orton), James Grant (William Orton). Directed by Stephen Frears and produced by Andrew Brown. Screenplay by Alan Bennett.

For all of their years together, Joe Orton and Kenneth Halliwell lived in a cramped room in the north of London, up near the Angel tube stop where everything seems closer to hell. Even after Orton became famous, even after his plays were hits and he was winning awards and his picture was in the papers, he came home to the tiny hovel where Halliwell was waiting. One night he came home and Halliwell hammered him to death and killed himself.

Prick Up Your Ears is the story of Orton and Halliwell and the murder. They say that most murderers are known to their victims. They don't say that if you knew the victims as well as the murderer did, you might understand more about the murder, but doubtless that is sometimes the case. This movie opens with a brutal, senseless crime. By the time the movie is over, the crime is still brutal, but it is possible to comprehend.

When they met, Orton was seventeen, Halliwell was twenty-five, and they both wanted to be novelists. They were homosexuals, but sex never seemed to be at the heart of their relationship. They lived together, but Orton prowled the night streets for rough trade and Halliwell scolded him for taking too many chances. Orton was, by all accounts, a charming young man—liked by everybody, impish, rebellious, with a taste for danger. Halliwell, eight years older, was a stolid, lonely man who saw himself as Orton's teacher.

He taught him everything he could. Then Orton used what he'd learned to write plays that drew heavily on their life together. His big hits were *Loot* and *What the Butler Saw*, and both are still frequently performed. But when Orton won the *Evening Standard*'s award for the play of the year—an honor like the Pulitzer Prize—he didn't take Kenneth to the banquet; he took his agent.

Halliwell began to feel that he was receiving no recognition for what he saw as the sacrifice of his life. He dabbled in art and constructed collages out of thousands of pictures clipped from books and magazines. But his shows were in the lobbies of the theaters presenting Joe's plays, and people were patronizing to him. That began to drive him mad.

Prick Up Your Ears is based on the biography that John Lahr wrote about Orton, a biography that has become famous for discovering a private life so different from the image seen by the public.

Homosexuality was a crime in the 1960s in England, but Orton was heedless of the dangers. In fact, he seemed to enjoy danger. Perhaps that was why he kept Halliwell around, because he sensed the older man might explode. More likely, though, he kept him out of loyalty and indifference and didn't fully realize how much he was hurting him. One of the early scenes in the film shows Halliwell skulking at home, angry because Orton is late for dinner.

The movie is good at scenes like that. It has a touch for the wound beneath the skin, the hurt that we can feel better than the person who is inflicting it. The movie is told as sort of a flashback, with the Lahr character interviewing Orton's literary agent and then the movie spinning off into memories of its own.

The movie is not about homosexuality, which it treats in a matter-of-fact manner. It is really about a marriage between unequal partners. Halliwell was, in a way, like the loyal wife who slaves at ill-paid jobs to put her husband through medical school, only to have the man divorce her after he's successful because they have so little in common—he with his degree, she with dishwater hands.

The movie was written by Alan Bennett, a successful British playwright who understands Orton's craft. He bases one of his characters on Lahr (played by Wallace Shawn), apparently as an excuse to give Orton's literary agent (Vanessa Redgrave) someone to talk to. The device is awkward, but it allows Redgrave into the movie, and her performance is superb: aloof, cynical, wise, unforgiving.

The great performances in the movie are, of course, at its center. Gary Oldman plays Orton and Alfred Molina plays Halliwell, and these are two of the best performances of 1987. Oldman you may remember as Sid Vicious, the punk rock star in *Sid & Nancy*. There is no point of similarity between the two performances; like a few gifted actors, he is able to re-invent himself for every role. On the basis of these two movies, he is the best young British actor around. Molina has a more thankless role as he stands in the background, overlooked and misunderstood. But even as he whines we can understand his feelings, and by the end we are not very surprised by what he does.

The movie was directed by Stephen Frears, whose previous movie, *My Beautiful Laundrette*, also was about a homosexual relationship between two very different men: a Pakistani laundry operator and his working-class, neofascist boyfriend. Frears makes homosexuality an everyday thing in his movies, which are not about his characters' sexual orientation but about how their underlying personalities are projected onto their sexuality and all the other areas of their lives.

In the case of Orton and Halliwell, there is the sense that their deaths had been waiting for them right from the beginning. Their relationship was never healthy and never equal, and Halliwell, who was willing to sacrifice so much, would not sacrifice one thing: recognition for his sacrifice. If only Orton had taken him to that dinner, there might have been so many more opening nights.

Prime Cut ★ ★ ★
R, 86 m., 1972

Lee Marvin (Nick Devlin), Gene Hackman ("Mary Ann"), Angel Tompkins (Clarabelle), Gregory Walcott (Weenie), Sissy Spacek (Poppy), William Morey (Shay). Directed by Michael Ritchie and produced by Joe Wizan. Screenplay by Robert Dillon.

Prime Cut is a movie about an enforcer for the Chicago mob (Lee Marvin) who goes to Kansas City to collect a debt. So we expect a seamy journey into the guts of the city, right? But it doesn't quite work out like that. *Prime Cut* is very different from the usual gangster movie; it's put together almost like a comic strip, with all of the good and bad things that implies, and the Marvin character has more in common with superheroes than with mobsters.

We're almost on the familiar terrain of "Steve Canyon." All of the characters are caricatures, with nicknames and gimmicks to help us identify them. There's "Mary Ann" himself, a Kansas City dealer in prostitutes played by Gene Hackman. There's Weenie (Gregory Walcott), so-called because of his habit of carrying wieners around in his pocket—some of them made out of the ground-up bodies of his enemies. And there's Clarabelle (Angel Tompkins), who is Mary Ann's wife and lives in a luxurious houseboat with a mirror on the bedroom ceiling. Clearly, this is not the turf of Cagney and Bogart.

Prime Cut is a fantasy in which everything is very simple and usually takes place outdoors, and in which the characters act toward each other with great directness and brutality. It may owe a little to Hitchcock, as so many thrillers do. There's a scene at a county fair, for example, where Marvin and a young girl played by Sissy Spacek are trying to escape Hackman's gunmen. They do it all out in the open, casually walking in front of a grandstand in full view of thousands, so the gunmen can't shoot.

This is followed by the great wheat-field chase, in which Marvin and the girl are pursued by a giant reaper. A telephoto lens is used to give the impression that the giant reaper is almost literally on top of them, and every so often there's a cut to the obscene sight of the reaper dropping another bundle of wheat. Marvin and friend are saved when his chauffeur rams a limousine into the reaper—which digests it.

It's interesting to note that during the fairgrounds chase and the reaper chase, Marvin never lets go of the girl's hand (even though both could run faster if they weren't holding hands—and could even split up to avoid the reaper). This is a whammo visual signal of the movie's total male chauvinist orientation, which became clear much earlier during Gene Hackman's "cattle auction." The cattle, you see, are fresh, naked young girls, held in pens filled with straw. They have been raised in a special "orphanage," are certified to be virgin, and can be bought to stock your local bordello. Far-out.

Now you begin to see why *Prime Cut* is like a comic strip. It is broken up into several large set pieces (the introduction, the trip to Kansas City, Marvin's rescue of one of the orphan girls, a couple of love scenes, the fairgrounds, the reaper, and a gunfight). This structure is a lot less complex than those in the gangster movies we're used to, and makes *Prime Cut* seem larger than ordinary movie life. The colors are clearer, and the characters act and react only to each other's giant-sized images. It's fun, in a way.

Prince of the City ★ ★ ★ ★
R, 167 m., 1981

Treat Williams (Daniel Ciello), Jerry Orbach (Gus Levy), Richard Foronjy (Joe Marinaro), Don Billett (Bill Mayo), Jenny Marino (Dom Bando), Bob Balaban (Sentimassino), Lindsay Crouse (Carla Ciello). Directed by Sidney Lumet and produced by Burtt Harris. Screenplay by Jay Presson Allen and Lumet.

He will not rat on his partners. This is his bottom line. He will talk to investigators about all the other guys he knows things about. He will talk about how narcotics cops get involved in the narcotics traffic, how they buy information with drugs, how they string out addicts and use them as informers, how they keep some of the money and some of the drugs after big busts. He will tell what he knows about how the other cops do these things. But he will not talk about his partners in his own unit. This is his code, and, of course, he is going to have to break it.

That is the central situation of Sidney Lumet's *Prince of the City*. While you are watching it, it's a movie about cops, drugs, and New York City, in that order. After the film starts to turn itself over in your mind, it becomes a much deeper piece, a film about how difficult it is to go straight in a crooked world without hurting people you love.

Drugs are a rotten business. They corrupt everyone they come into contact with, because they set up needs so urgent that all other considerations are forgotten. For addicts, the need is for the drug itself. For others, the needs are more complex. The members of the special police drug unit in *Prince of the City*, for example, take on an envied departmental status because of their assignment. They have no hours, no beats, no uniforms. They are elite free-lancers, modern knights riding out into the drug underworld and establishing their own rules. They do not look at it this way, but their status depends on drugs. If there were no drugs and no addicts, there would be no narcs, no princes of the city. Of course, their jobs are also cold, dirty, lonely, dangerous, thankless, and never finished. That is the other side of the deal, and that helps explain why they will sometimes keep the money they confiscate in a drug bust. It's as if they're levying their own fines. It also explains why they sometimes supply informers with drugs: They know better than anyone how horrible the addict's life can be. "A junkie can break your heart," the hero of this movie says at one point, and by the movie's end we understand what he means.

The film is based on a book by Robert Daley about Bob Leuci, a New York cop who cooperated with a 1971 investigation of police corruption. In the movie, Leuci is called Ciello, and he is played by Treat Williams in a demanding and grueling performance. Williams is almost always on-screen, and almost always in situations of extreme stress, fatigue, and emotional turmoil. We see him coming apart before our eyes. He falls to pieces not simply because of his job, or because of his decision to testify, but because he is in an inexorable trap and he *will* sooner or later have to hurt his partners.

This is a movie that literally hinges on the issue of perjury. And Sidney Lumet and his co-writer, Jay Presson Allen, have a great deal of respect for the legal questions involved. There is a sustained scene in this movie that is one of the most spellbinding I can imagine, and it consists entirely of government lawyers debating whether a given situation justifies a charge of perjury. Rarely are ethical issues discussed in such detail in a movie, and hardly ever so effectively.

Prince of the City is a very good movie and, like some of its characters, it wants to break your heart. Maybe it will. It is about the ways in which a corrupt modern city makes it almost impossible for a man to be true to the law, his ideals, and his friends, all at the same time. The movie has no answers. Only horrible alternatives.

The Princess Bride ★ ★ ★ ½
PG, 98 m., 1987

Cary Elwes (Westley), Mandy Patinkin (Inigo Montoya), Chris Sarandon (Humperdinck), Christopher Guest (Count Rugen), Wallace Shawn (Vizzini), Andre the Giant (Fezzik), Fred Savage (Grandson), Robin Wright (Princess Bride), Peter Falk (Grandfather), Peter Cook (Clergyman), Billy Crystal (Miracle Max). Directed by Rob Reiner and produced by Andrew Scheinman and Reiner. Screenplay by William Goldman.

The Princess Bride begins as a story that a grandfather is reading out of a book. But already the movie has a spin on it, because the grandfather is played by Peter Falk, and in the distinctive quality of his voice we detect a certain edge; his voice seems to contain a measure of cynicism about fairy stories, a certain awareness that there are a lot more things in heaven and earth than have been dreamed of by the Brothers Grimm.

The story he tells is about a beautiful farm girl (Robin Wright) who scornfully orders around a farm boy (Cary Elwes) until the day when she realizes, thunderstruck, that she loves him. She wants to live happily ever after with him, but then he leaves, and is feared killed by pirates, and she is kidnapped and taken far away across the lost lands.

"Is this story going to have a lot of kissing in it?" Falk's grandson asks. Well, it's definitely going to have a lot of Screaming Eels. The moment the princess is taken away by agents of the evil Prince Humperdinck (Chris Sarandon), *The Princess Bride* reveals itself as a sly parody of sword and sorcery movies, a film that somehow manages to exist on two levels at once: While younger viewers will sit spellbound at the thrilling

events on the screen, adults, I think, will be laughing a lot.

In its own peculiar way, *The Princess Bride* resembles *This Is Spinal Tap*, an earlier film by the same director, Rob Reiner. Both films are funny not only because they contain comedy, but because Reiner does justice to the underlying form of his story. *Spinal Tap* looked and felt like a rock documentary—and *then* it was funny. *The Princess Bride* looks and feels like *Legend*, or any of those other quasi-heroic epic fantasies, and *then* it goes for the laughs.

Part of the secret is that Reiner never stays with the same laugh very long. There are a lot of people for his characters to meet as they make their long journey, and most of them are completely off the wall. There is, for example, a band of three brigands led by Wallace Shawn as a scheming little conniver, and including Andre the Giant as Fezzik the Giant, a crusher who may not necessarily have a heart of gold. It is Shawn who tosses the Princess Bride to the Screaming Eels, with great relish.

Another funny episode involves Mandy Patinkin as Inigo Montoya, heroic swordsman with a secret. And the funniest sequence in the film stars Billy Crystal and Carol Kane, both invisible behind makeup, as an ancient wizard and crone who specialize in bringing the dead back to life. (I hope I'm not giving anything away; you didn't expect the princess's loved one to stay dead indefinitely, did you?)

The Princess Bride was adapted by William Goldman from his own novel, which he says was inspired by a book he read as a child, but which seems to have been cheerfully transformed by his wicked adult imagination. It is filled with good-hearted fun, with performances by actors who seem to be smacking their lips, and by a certain true innocence that survives all of Reiner's satire. And also, it does have kissing in it.

Private Benjamin ★ ★ ★
R, 110 m., 1980

Goldie Hawn (Judy Benjamin), Eileen Brennan (Captain Lewis), Armand Assante (Henri Tremont), Robert Webber (Colonel Thornbush), Sam Wanamaker (Teddy Benjamin), Barbara Barrie (Harriet Benjamin), Harry Dean Stanton (Sergeant Ballard), Albert Brooks (Yale Goodman). Directed by Howard Zieff and written and produced by Nancy Meyers, Charles Shyer, and Harvey Miller.

Howard Zieff's *Private Benjamin* is an appealing, infectious comedy starring Goldie Hawn as Judy Benjamin, a Jewish-American princess, breathless with joy on the day of her second marriage. She has a real catch: He's named Yale, he's a professional man, he wants his study done in mushroom colors. Alas, he dies in the throes of passion on his wedding night (something his grieving mother discovers when Judy solemnly repeats his last words). And Judy goes into mourning.

What's she to do? She calls in to an all-night talk show and is promised a solution by another caller. The next day, we meet the guy with the answer. Played by Harry Dean Stanton, that wonderful character actor who could be Robert Mitchum's sneaky cousin, the guy turns out to be an Army recruiter. And he solemnly paints a picture of Army life that has Judy signing up. Her subsequent shocks of discovery provide the great laughs of the movie's best scenes. She solemnly explains to a captain (Eileen Brennan) that she *did* sign up with the Army, yes, but with another Army. Where, she asks, are the private condo living quarters the recruiter promised her? And surely the Army could have afforded some draperies? In no time at all, she's cleaning the latrines with her electric toothbrush.

This is an inspired idea for a movie comedy, and Goldie Hawn has a lot of fun with it. She finds just the right note for her performance, poised halfway between the avaricious and the slack-jawed, the calculating and the innocent. She makes some kind of impression on everyone she runs up against (or into), especially Robert Webber as the square-jawed Colonel Thornbush, commander of the Army's elite paratroop unit, the Thornbushers.

It's at about this point that the movie seems to lose its unique comic direction and turn into a more or less predictable combination of service comedy and romantic farce. After Judy's parents try to rescue her from the Army, she suddenly decides to stay and stick it out. She turns into a passable soldier. She almost inadvertently captures the entire Red team and makes them Blue prisoners of war during war games. And she is invited to join the Thornbushers by Colonel Thornbush himself (who turns out to have an alternative in mind if Judy doesn't want to jump at 13,000 feet).

Along the way, she meets a sexy and eligible French bachelor who's a gynecologist. After she blackmails Thornbush into sending her to Allied Army headquarters in Paris, she falls in love with the Frenchman (Armand Assante), and gets involved in Gallic romantic intrigues. It turns out that her would-be third husband is more interested in Sunday morning soccer games and cute little downstairs maids than in the kind of marriage Judy Benjamin was brought up to desire.

This stuff is occasionally funny, but it's kind of predictable. It turns *Private Benjamin* into areas that are too familiar: We've all seen the comic situations that grow out of the courtship with the Frenchman, and we'd really rather have seen more stuff of Private Benjamin in the Army. The movie would have been better off sticking with Goldie Hawn as a female Beetle Bailey and forgetting about the changes that allow her to find self-respect, deal with the Frenchman, etc. Still, *Private Benjamin* is refreshing and fun. Goldie Hawn, who is a true comic actress, makes an original, appealing character out of Judy Benjamin, and so the movie feels alive—not just an exercise in gags and situations.

Prizzi's Honor ★ ★ ★ ★
R, 129 m., 1985

Jack Nicholson (Charley Partanna), Kathleen Turner (Irene Walker), Anjelica Huston (Maerose), Robert Loggia (Eduardo Prizzi), John Randolph (Pop Partanna), William Hickey (Don Corrado Prizzi), Lee Richardson (Dominic). Directed by John Huston and produced by John Foreman. Screenplay by Richard Condon and Janet Roach.

John Huston's *Prizzi's Honor* marches like weird and gloomy clockwork to its relentless conclusion, and half of the time, we're laughing. This is the most bizarre comedy in many a month; a movie so dark, so cynical, and so funny that perhaps only Jack Nicholson and Kathleen Turner could have kept straight faces during the love scenes. They do. They play two professional Mafia killers who meet, fall in love, marry, and find out that the mob may not be big enough for both of them.

Nicholson plays Charley Partanna, a soldier in the proud Prizzi family, rulers of the East Coast, enforcers of criminal order. The godfather of the Prizzis, Don Corrado, is a mean little old man who looks like he has been freeze-dried by the lifelong ordeal of draining every ounce of humanity out of his wizened body. To Don Corrado (William Hickey), nothing is more important than the Prizzis' honor—not even another Prizzi. Charley Partanna is the Don's grandson. He has been

raised in this ethic, and accepts it. He kills without remorse. He follows orders. Only occasionally does he disobey the family's instructions, as when he broke his engagement with Maerose Prizzi (Anjelica Huston), his cousin. She then brought disgrace upon herself and, as the movie opens, is in the fourth year of self-imposed exile. But she is a Prizzi, and does not forget, or forgive.

The movie opens like *The Godfather*, at a wedding. Charley's eyes roam around the church. In the choir loft, he sees a beautiful blonde (Kathleen Turner). She looks like an angel. At the reception, he dances with her once, and then she disappears. Later that day, there is a mob killing. Determined to find out the name of the blond angel, Charley discovers even more—that she was the California hitman, brought in to do the job. He turns to Maerose for advice. She counsels him to go ahead: After all, it's good to have interests in common with your wife.

Charley flies to the coast, setting up a running gag as they establish a transcontinental commute. There is instant, electrifying chemistry between the two of them, and the odd thing is, it seems halfway plausible. They're opposites, but they attract. Nicholson plays his hood as a tough Brooklynite; he uses a stiff upper lip, like Bogart, and sounds simple and implacable. Turner, who is flowering as a wonderful comic actress, plays her Mafia killer like a bright, cheery hostess. She could be selling cosmetics.

What happens between them is best not explained here, since the unfolding of the plot is one of the movie's delights. The story is by Richard Condon, a novelist who delights in devious plot construction, and here he takes two absolutes—romantic love and the Prizzis' honor—and arranges a collision between them. Because all of the motivations are so direct and logical, the movie is able to make the most shocking decisions seem inevitable.

John Huston directed this film right after *Under the Volcano*, and what other director could have put those two back-to-back? It is one of his very best films, perhaps because he made it with friends; Condon is an old pal from Ireland, Anjelica Huston is, of course, his daughter, and Nicholson has long been Anjelica's lover. Together they have taken a strange plot, peopled it with carefully overwrought characters, and made *Prizzi's Honor* into a treasure.

Project X ★ ★ ★
PG, 115 m., 1987

Matthew Broderick (Jimmy), Helen Hunt (Teri), Bill Sadler (Dr. Carroll), Johnny Ray McGhee (Robertson), Jonathan Stark (Sergeant Krieger), Willie (Virgil). Directed by Jonathan Kaplan and produced by Walter F. Parkes and Lawrence Lasker. Screenplay by Stanley Weiser.

W.C. Fields hated to appear in the same scene with a baby, an animal, or a plunging neckline. He was afraid of being upstaged. Virgil, the gifted chimpanzee in *Project X*, does not quite upstage Matthew Broderick, but it's one of the strengths of this movie that he deserves co-star billing.

We meet Virgil, an African primate, as he's being shipped to America for a career at the University of Wisconsin's psychology department. As played by a charismatic chimp named Willie, he turns out to be a surprisingly clever little fellow, who picks up sign language from his trainer (Helen Hunt). Then his research project loses its funding, and Virgil is shipped off under mysterious circumstances to an Air Force base in Florida, where he will train on a flight simulator.

That's where Broderick comes in. He's a troublemaking would-be pilot who is assigned to the chimp project as punishment. Once there, he turns out to be naturally gifted at identifying with the animals, and after he discovers that Virgil speaks sign language, they develop a trusting relationship. Then Broderick discovers the secret purpose of the chimp research: First, the chimps are trained to operate flight simulators, and then they're exposed to lethal doses of radiation to find out how that might affect the performance of human pilots during a nuclear war.

There is a large logical flaw in this experiment, and, to give *Project X* fair credit, Broderick himself points it out: The difference between chimps and human pilots is that the humans would know they had been exposed to lethal radiation and that knowledge would affect their performance, but the chimps' behavior wouldn't be affected.

After the threat to Virgil's life is established, the movie turns into a thriller. Can Virgil be saved? Will Broderick destroy his career? What would happen if the chimps discovered that the experiment was designed to kill them? The last third of this movie contains so many surprises that it would be unfair for me to even hint at them.

Project X is not a great movie because its screenplay doesn't really try for greatness. It's content to be a well-made, intelligent entertainment aimed primarily, I imagine, at bright teen-agers. It works on that level. More complicated issues might have confused it. And if the movie had been forced to stay within the bounds of what a chimpanzee, even a smart one, can really do, we would have lost the story's climax, which is a lot of fun but completely implausible in the real world.

Psycho III ★ ★ ★
R, 93 m., 1986

Anthony Perkins (Norman Bates), Diana Scarwid (Maureen), Jeff Fahey (Duane), Roberta Maxwell (Tracy), Hugh Gillin (Sheriff Hunt), Lee Garlington (Myrna). Directed by Anthony Perkins and produced by Hilton A. Green. Screenplay by Charles Edward Pogue.

How well we remember Norman Bates. Tens of thousands of movie characters have come and gone since 1960, when he made his first appearance in *Psycho*, and yet he still remains so vivid in the memory, such a sharp image among all the others that have gone out of focus.

Most movies are disposable. *Psycho* supplied us with the furnishings for nightmares. "Dear Mr. Hitchcock," a mother wrote the master, "after seeing your movie my daughter is afraid to take a shower. What should I do?" Send her to the dry cleaners, Hitch advised her.

In *Psycho III*, there is one startling shot that completely understands Norman Bates. Up in the old gothic horror house on the hill, he has found a note from his mother, asking him to meet her in Cabin Number Twelve. We know that although his mother may have frequent conversations with him, she is in no condition to write him a note. Norman knows that, too. He stuffed her himself. As he walks down the steps and along the front of the Bates Motel toward his rendezvous, the camera tracks along with him, one unbroken shot, and his face is a twitching mask of fear.

The face belongs to Anthony Perkins, who is better than any other actor at reflecting the demons within. Although his facial expressions in the shot are not subtle, he isn't overacting; he projects such turmoil that we almost sympathize with him. And that is the real secret of Norman Bates, and one of the reasons that *Psycho III* works as a movie: Norman is not a mad-dog killer, a wholesale slasher like the amoral villains of the Dead Teen-ager Movies. He is at war with himself. He is divided. He, Norman Bates, wants to do the right thing, to be pleasant and quiet and pass without notice. But also inside of him is the voice of his mother, fiercely urging him to kill.

At the beginning of *Psycho III*, only a short time has passed since the end of *Psycho II*. In a nearby convent, a young novice (Diana Scarwid) blames herself when an older nun falls to her death. She runs out into the night, gets a ride with a sinister motorist (Jeff Fahey), and ends up at the Bates Motel. Fahey arrives there, too, and is hired as a night clerk. Other people also turn up: an investigative reporter who wants to do a story on Norman; a local woman who gets drunk and is picked up by Fahey; and finally a crowd of rowdies back for their high school reunion.

By the end of the movie, many of these people will be dead—and because this is a tragedy, not a horror story, some of the dead ones won't deserve it, and others will survive unfairly.

The movie was directed by Perkins, in his filmmaking debut. I was surprised by what a good job he does. Any movie named *Psycho III* is going to be compared to the Hitchcock original, but Perkins isn't an imitator. He has his own agenda. He has lived with Norman Bates all these years, and he has some ideas about him, and although the movie doesn't apologize for Norman, it does pity him. For the first time, I was able to see that the true horror in the *Psycho* movies isn't what Norman does—but the fact that he is compelled to do it.

There are a couple of scenes that remind us directly of Hitchcock, especially the scene where the local sheriff dips into the ice chest on a hot day, and doesn't notice that some of the cubes he's popping into his mouth have blood on them. Perkins permits himself a certain amount of that macabre humor, as when he talks about his hobby ("stuffing things") and when he analyzes his own case for the benefit of the visiting journalist. But the movie also pays its dues as a thriller, and there is one shocking scene that is as arbitrary, unexpected, tragic, and unfair as the shower scene in *Psycho*. Only one, but then one of those scenes is enough for any movie.

Punchline ★ ★
R, 123 m., 1988

Sally Field (Lilah Krytsick), Tom Hanks (Steven Gold), John Goodman (John Krytsick), Mark Rydell (Romeo), Kim Greist (Madeline Urie), Paul Mazursky (Arnold). Directed by David Seltzer and produced by Daniel Melnick and Michael Rachmil. Screenplay by Seltzer.

When did the laughs go out of stand-up comedy? When did stand-up comedians stop being humorists and start being "personalities" whose career moves follow a carefully defined trajectory, from local clubs to big clubs to "The Tonight Show" to cable to network to movie stardom? When did stand-ups start being bores?

Everybody knows that stand-up comics represent the unhappiest people in show business, and it is not by accident that their routines are filled with hostility toward the audience ("This'll kill ya") and masochistic self-pity ("I'm dying up here!"). Occasionally a comedian is able to make this funny, as Rodney Dangerfield, Jay Leno, and Garry Shandling do in their contrasting ways, but usually it is simply sick, a public display of ego and ambition unmatched by talent or imagination. If these guys want to perform so badly, why didn't they take accordion lessons?

This outburst is occasioned by *Punchline*, a pathetic movie into which a great deal of energy and talent has disappeared. The movie stars Sally Field as a housewife and mother who dreams of becoming a stand-up comedian, and Tom Hanks as a failed medical student who also wants to be a comic, and has had more experience than Field. They meet at a middle-level comedy club, where Field flops, Hanks succeeds, they become friends, and he tries to teach her the ropes while meanwhile her marriage is falling apart and her husband is threatening to take the kids and leave.

If this situation had been treated as slapstick, it might have worked. If it had been treated seriously, it also might have worked. But instead of taking the characters seriously, the movie makes the fatal mistake of taking stand-up seriously. And if you're gonna do that, you'd better have good material. It is a fact, sad but true, that none of the stand-up routines by Sally Field in this movie are any good—not the ones that are supposed to be bad, and not the ones that are supposed to be good, either. And Tom Hanks barely does better. The movie does not seem to know it is about two would-be comics who are both lacking in talent.

The structure of the film will be familiar to Sally Field fans. It shows her with lots of heart and pluck as she does what she knows is right. At the end, of course, she gets it both ways: She succeeds, while her husband and children cheer her on and learn to accept Mom's new obsession. But to get from the beginning to the end requires an awkward, unbelievable, and thankless about-face by her husband (John Goodman), who appears first as a monster and then as a nice guy. No attempt is made to explain this personality shift; it's simply dictated by the plot.

The best performance in the movie is by Mark Rydell, a movie director who moonlights as Romeo, the owner of the club where much of the action takes place. His character has the rhythms, the values, the presence, and the delivery to convince us he knows something about show business and stand-up comedy. Most of the other characters are babes in the woods.

The problem may be that the movie isn't nearly tough enough. It needs to be more hard-boiled, more merciless in its dissection of egos, more perceptive about the cut-throat nature of show business. Stand-up comedy is the nation's newest spectator sport, and any city worth its salt now has one or more comedy clubs, in which one "comic" after another is thrown to the wolves. What's really going on here? Is it really just a case of amateurs dreaming of getting into show biz? Or is it something deeper and sicker?

Comics used to be part of the act in show business—along with singers, dancers, tumblers, magicians, and anybody else Ed Sullivan could dredge up. But why a *whole evening* of nothing but comedy? Nobody wants to laugh that much. What's really going on is that the audience is judging the gall and self-confidence of would-be comics, who often fail and perhaps enjoy failing. It is some kind of masochistic rite that has little to do with humor, which is why when a comic makes it big, he immediately turns into a humanitarian statesman and starts volunteering for charity telethons. If you're born feeling guilty, and the audience has stopped giving you the rejection you know you so richly deserve, then you've got to find another way to feed your conscience. *Punchline* doesn't seem to know this, or much else about stand-up comedy.

The Purple Rose of Cairo ★ ★ ★ ★
PG, 87 m., 1985

Mia Farrow (Cecilia), Jeff Daniels (Tom Baxter/Gil Shepherd), Danny Aiello (Monk), Van Johnson (Larry), Alexander H. Cohen (Raoul Hirsh). Directed by Woody Allen and produced by Robert Greenhut. Screenplay by Allen.

About twenty minutes into Woody Allen's *The Purple Rose of Cairo*, an extraordinary event takes place. A young woman has been going to see the same movie over and over again, because of her infatuation with the movie's hero. From his vantage point up on the screen, the hero notices her out in the audience. He strikes up a conversation, she smiles and shyly responds, and he abruptly steps off the screen and into her life. No explanation is offered for this miraculous event, but then perhaps none is needed: Don't we spend our lives waiting for the same thing to happen to us in the movies?

Life, of course, is never as simple and dreamy as the movies, and so the hero's bold act has alarming consequences. The movie's other characters are still stranded up there on the screen, feeling angry and left out. The Hollywood studio is aghast that its characters would suddenly develop minds of their own. The actor who *played* the hero is particularly upset, because now there are two of him walking around, one wearing a pith helmet. Things are simple only in the lives of the hero and the woman, who convince themselves that they *can* simply walk off into the sunset, and get away with this thing.

The Purple Rose of Cairo is audacious and witty and has a lot of good laughs in it, but the best thing about the movie is the way Woody Allen uses it to toy with the very essence of reality and fantasy. The movie is so cheerful and open that it took me a day or two, after I'd seen it, to realize how deeply Allen has reached this time. If it is true, and I think it is, that most of the time we go to the movies in order to experience brief lives that are not our own, then Allen is demonstrating what a tricky self-deception we practice. Those movie lives consist of *only* what is on the screen, and if we start thinking that real life can be the same way, we are in for a cruel awakening.

The woman in the movie is played by Mia Farrow as a sweet, rather baffled small-town waitress whose big, shiftless lug of a husband bats her around. She is a good candidate for the magic of the movies. Up on the screen, sophisticated people have cocktails and plan trips down the Nile and are recognized by the doormen in nightclubs. The hero in the movie is played by Jeff Daniels (who was Debra Winger's husband in *Terms of Endearment*). He is a genial, open-faced smoothie with all the right moves, but he has a problem: He *only* knows what his character

knows in the movie, and his experience is literally limited to what happens to his character in the plot. This can cause problems. He's great at talking sweetly to a woman, and holding hands, and kissing—but just when the crucial moment arrives, the movie fades out, and therefore, alas, so does he.

Many of Allen's best moments come from exploring the paradox that the movie character knows nothing of real life. For example, he can drive a car, because he drives one in the movie, but he can't start a car, because he doesn't turn on the ignition in the movie. Mia Farrow thinks maybe they can work this out. They can learn from each other. He can learn real life, and she can learn the romance of the movies. The problem is, both of them are now living in real life, where studio moguls and angry actors and snoopy reporters are making their life miserable.

Allen's buried subject in *The Purple Rose of Cairo* is, I think, related to the subjects of his less successful movies, *Stardust Memories* (1980) and *Zelig* (1983). He is interested in the conflicts involving who you want to be, and who other people want you to be. *Stardust* was about a celebrity whose fame prevented people from relating to anything but his image. *Zelig*, the other side of the coin, was about a man whose anonymity was so profound that he could gain an identity only by absorbing one from the people around him. In *Purple Rose*, the movie hero has the first problem, and the woman in the audience has the second, and when they get together, they still don't make one whole person, just two sad halves.

Purple Rose is delightful from beginning to end, not only because of the clarity and charm with which Daniels and Farrow explore the problems of their characters, but also because the movie is so intelligent. It's not brainy or intellectual—no one in the whole movie speaks with more complexity than your average 1930s movie hero—but the movie is filled with wit and invention, and Allen trusts us to find the ironies, relish the contradictions, and figure things out for ourselves. While we do that, he makes us laugh and he makes us think, and when you get right down to it, forget about the fantasies; those are two of the most exciting things that could happen to anybody in a movie. The more you think about *The Purple Rose of Cairo*, and about the movies, and about why you go to the movies, the deeper the damned thing gets.

Q

Q ★ ★ ½
R, 92 m., 1982

Michael Moriarty (Quinn), Candy Clark (Girlfriend), David Carradine (Detective), Richard Roundtree (Detective), Ed Kovens (Crook). Directed by Larry Cohen and produced by Samuel Z. Arkoff. Screenplay by Cohen.

A few days after *Q* was screened at the Cannes Film Festival (under its original title, *The Winged Serpent*), the following conversation took place between Samuel Z. Arkoff, the film's producer, and Rex Reed, the critic:

Reed: Sam! I just saw *The Winged Serpent!* What a surprise! All that dreck—and right in the middle of it, a great Method performance by Michael Moriarty!
Arkoff: The dreck was my idea.

I believe him. Arkoff has been producing films for thirty years now, and even if he *was* honored with a retrospective at the Museum of Modern Art, his heart still lies with shots of a giant flying lizard attacking a woman in a bikini on top of a Manhattan skyscraper. He's just that kinda guy. There are, in fact, several shots in *Q* that owe their ancestry to Sam Arkoff. I am aware, of course, that Larry Cohen gets credit for having written and directed this movie, but where would Cohen or any other director be without the rich heritage of a quarter-century of American-International Pictures made by Sam Arkoff? Here are examples of the shots I have in mind:

• The camera looks straight down at terrified citizens fleeing from a menace. They run crazily across the street. Some run away from the camera, some toward it, so that you can't tell for sure where the menace is, and the shot can be intercut with shots of a menace approaching from any direction.

• The hero empties his machine gun into the giant serpent and turns away from a window to issue orders: "Everybody hold your positions!" Just then the serpent reappears behind him.

• There are False Serpent Alarms in which people get hit from behind by toy birds, chairs, and their boyfriends.

• David Carradine says, "He doesn't die easy."

You get the idea. *Q* is another silly monster movie. But think how long it's *been* since we had another silly monster movie. There was a time during the golden age of Sam Arkoff's career when there were lots of monster movies. Remember, for example, *Attack of the Crab Monsters, The Viking Women and the Sea Serpent, Creature from the Haunted Sea,* and *Wasp Woman.* But in the last few years Creature Features have been replaced by Dead Teen-ager Movies, and instead of awful special effects of a monster going berserk, we get worse shots of a homicidal maniac going berserk.

Q returns to the basic formula, in which a prehistoric creature terrorizes the city. In this case, the creature is a Quetzalcoatl, a mythical Aztec monster with wings *and* four claws. It apparently has been brought back into existence in connection with some shady human sacrifices at the Museum of Natural History (although this particular subplot is very muddled). It lives in a nest at the top of the Chrysler Building, lays eggs, and terrorizes helpless New Yorkers, who are not sure if this is a real monster or another crazy circulation stunt by Rupert Murdoch.

Rex Reed was right, though, about the Method performance by Michael Moriarty. In the middle of this exploitation movie, there's Moriarty, rolling his eyes, improvis-

ing dialogue, and acting creepy. He's fun to watch, especially in the scene where he names his terms for leading the cops to the lizard. The cast also includes David Carradine, Richard Roundtree, and Candy Clark, good actors all, but you have to be *awfully* good not to be upstaged by the death throes of a dying Quetzalcoatl.

Still to be answered: How did *one* Quetzalcoatl get pregnant?

Q & A ★ ★ ★ ½
R, 134 m., 1990

Nick Nolte (Mike Brennan), Timothy Hutton (Al Reilly), Armand Assante (Bobby Texador), Patrick O'Neal (Kevin Quinn), Lee Richardson (Leo Bloomenfeld), Luis Guzman (Luis Valentin), Charles Dutton (Sam Chapman), Jenny Lumet (Nancy Bosch), Leonard Cimino (Nick Petrone). Directed by Sidney Lumet and produced by Arnon Milchan and Burtt Harris. Screenplay by Lumet.

Sidney Lumet's *Q & A* is an excitingly well-crafted police movie, but he's a good director, and I think that was the easy part for him. What was hard—what the movie is really about—is the rough and careless way that cops and other tough guys throw around racial insults. I'm not talking about how they address their clients out in the streets; I'm talking about how they regard each other—the blacks and Irish and Jews and Hispanics and Italians and Slavics who make up their world. It is almost a badge of honor in certain circles to use, and ignore, racist verbal labels.

What does that kind of talk signify? Is it said in affection? Sometimes. Sometimes not. Is it said as a territorial thing—I'm Italian and you're not? Is it tribal, reminding everyone of loyalties that can be called on in times of trouble? At some level it's accepted—everyone in this movie uses racial and ethnic slang constantly—and yet, at another level, it is just what it sounds like, a kind of macho name-calling.

In Lumet's New York City, the streets are seen as dangerously near to spinning out of control. To the Irish-American chief of the homicide bureau (Patrick O'Neal), that means it is time to close ranks. It's a war out there, he believes, between the cops and the people who would destroy the city (by which he instinctively means blacks and Hispanics). When a legendary Irish street cop named Brennan (Nick Nolte) shoots a Puerto Rican in a slum doorway, O'Neal calls in a young assistant D.A. (Timothy Hutton) to head the investigation. But he briefs Hutton very specifically: "This is an open-and-shut case."

It is not. Hutton begins to suspect that Brennan may have committed murder. His investigation leads him into the lives of people in many different ethnic groups—and he is shocked one day when a Hispanic drug dealer (Armand Assante) walks in with a woman (Jenny Lumet) Hutton once dated and still loves.

He meets her privately and asks her to come back to him. She will not. He assumed she was Hispanic when they dated, and she will never forget the look in his eyes, she says, when he met her father for the first time and saw that he was black. Is it always there, the movie wonders, that instinctive racial discrimination that seems to be absorbed when we're young and has to be unlearned as part of the process of growing up and growing better?

The movie is about such questions, but in a subtle way, while the central story involves a web of treachery, bribery, and deceit. This is a movie with a large cast, and one of the ways Lumet deals with that is to use fine, experienced actors who almost exude the traits of their characters. There's Charles Dutton, as a hard-boiled black detective who explains that his real color is "blue"—"and when I was in the army, it was olive drab." There's Luis Guzman as his partner, a Puerto Rican detective who knows and accepts the realities of the streets but has his limits. There's Lee Richardson as an old Jewish lawyer who has high standards and gives wise counsel to Hutton—but is also finally part of the system. And Leonard Cimino has only a few small scenes as an ancient Mafia don, but he conveys the reality

of his power with ruthless and yet wryly humorous wisdom.

These people and others give us the sense that *Q & A* isn't just about a hermetically sealed plot, that its tendrils reach out into the whole hierarchy of law enforcement in a city like New York, and that the patterns seen here in the 34th Precinct are repeated in every other precinct and every other big American city. Nick Nolte's performance is central to that feeling. He knew Hutton's late father—a hero cop—and he also knows dirt on the father that he can use if he has to. It's fascinating to see the way he works on this kid. He's been screwing the system so long, he knows just what buttons to push.

One of the most interesting characters in the movie is Bobby Texador, the drug kingpin, played by Armand Assante in one of the best character performances of the year. I didn't recognize Assante at first behind the beard and the silken, poetic speech, but what I did recognize was an original character—not simply your standard movie drug dealer, but a man whose skills and cleverness had led him to success in his business and who was smart enough to want out (it's the rare drug millionaire—or any millionaire—with the imagination to have as much fun spending money as making it).

Lumet has made a lot of other movies about tough big-city types of one kind or another (*Dog Day Afternoon, Serpico, Network, Prince of the City, The Verdict*), but this is the one where he taps into the vibrating awareness of race which is almost always there when strangers of different races encounter each other in situations where one has authority and another doesn't. The law provides a context for how cops treat civilians, criminal or not, but does it also provide an arena where a racial contest for power in the city takes place? Can the law be color-blind when none of its instruments are? It is fascinating the way this movie works so well as a police thriller on one level, while on other levels it probes feelings we may keep secret even from ourselves.

Queen of Hearts ★ ★ ★ ½
NO MPAA RATING, 115 m., 1989

Ian Hawkes (Eddie), Vittorio Duse (Nonno), Joseph Long (Danilo), Anita Zagaria (Rosa), Eileen Way (Mama Sibilla), Vittorio Amandola (Barbaraccia), Tat Whalley (Beetle). Directed by Jon Amiel and produced by John Hardy. Screenplay by Toni Grisoni.

Queen of Hearts has the same sort of magical romanticism as *Moonstruck*, but in a more gentle key. It's the story of a big, loving Italian family that moves from Italy to London, where Papa wins enough at cards to open a little café. Eddie, the young son who is the hero of the story, grows up in the café, and eventually figures out a way to save it when an old family enemy follows them from Italy and tries to drive them into bankruptcy.

The movie tells this story mostly through Eddie's eyes. He's a smart eleven-year-old who doesn't miss much, although he believes all the family legends, even the one about how his parents fell in love and eloped. The movie opens with this legend as he imagines it: The mother engaged to be married to the horrible butcher Barbaraccia, the father spiriting her out of her parents' house, and loving couple pursued to the top of the local church tower and then leaping to their death—their lives saved when they land in a passing hay wagon.

In London, Eddie's father gets a job as a waiter and then takes advice from a talking pig, bets on the right cards, and wins the money to open the café. And then, as Eddie himself arrives on the scene, the family history grows a little more realistic. The café becomes the center of family life, especially after two of his grandparents arrive from Italy—his mother's mother, and his father's father. The old people hate each other, of course, but their hate is the sort that could almost be mistaken for affection.

Then disaster strikes, when the evil Barbaraccia also arrives from Italy, sets up a gambling shop in the neighborhood, and even pays Eddie's older brother to go to work for him. Will the family lose the café? Will Barbaraccia finally win his revenge? Will Eddie lose his best friend, Beetle, whose father runs the local bookie joint?

All of these questions are settled with the most buoyant charm and good cheer in *Queen of Hearts*, which is a truly happy movie and was directed by Jon Amiel, the British director of that brilliant but truly unhappy TV miniseries, "The Singing Detective." All the despair and bitterness seem to have drained out of Amiel during that project, leaving him nothing but sunshine and a touch of supernatural playfulness for *Queen of Hearts*.

The secret of the success of *Moonstruck*, I've always thought, was that the movie had a level above the realistic—a level at which coincidences were permitted, and people had grand romantic revelations, and dogs knew when to howl at the moon. *Queen of Hearts* has the same kind of freedom. Most of it is grounded in the real world, I suppose—but the real world as seen by a kid with a hyperactive imagination, who believes every one of his father's tall tales. Part of the fun of the movie comes because we know more than the kid. We know, for example, what bad trouble his family is in, and we know it's impossible that he could help them out. But he doesn't know that—and so he saves the day.

Queen of Hearts has no stars to help sell it, and may even lose some viewers who think it's an Italian movie and don't like subtitles (it's in English). I hope it weathers those problems, though, and begins to develop an audience. It's the kind of movie that grows on you, letting you in on the family jokes and involving you in the family feuds. By the end, you feel good, in a goofy way, and then when you think back over the movie you realize that under the fantasy and the humor there was also a fairly substantial story. A story about what it means to belong to a family.

Queens Logic ★ ★ ½
R, 116 m., 1991

Joe Mantegna (Al), John Malkovich (Eliot), Kevin Bacon (Dennis), Ken Olin (Ray), Tony Spiridakis (Vinny), Linda Fiorentino (Carla), Chloe Webb (Patricia), Tom Waits (Monte), Jamie Lee Curtis (Grace). Directed by Steve Rash and produced by Stuart Oken and Russ Smith. Screenplay by Tony Spiridakis.

Queens Logic begins as the characters are gathering in the New York borough of Queens for a bachelor party and a wedding, and over the next few days these events will be the occasion for various moments of truth and self-revelation, discovery and disappointment. Like such reunion movies as *Return of the Secaucus Seven* and *The Big Chill*, the plot gives the characters, who are now mostly in their thirties, an opportunity for a mid-life evaluation of how things are going and how they are likely to go.

We share their curiosity, but for at least the first thirty minutes of the movie we're curious about something else, as well: Who are these people, and what do they mean to one another? The screenplay by Tony Spiridakis introduces a large gallery of characters in no apparent order and then moves casually among their stories. Gradually we begin to know who the characters are and—vaguely, anyway—how they are related. And then,

almost insidiously, they grow more and more familiar, until by the end of the film we're beginning to really care what happens to them.

There's Al, the ringleader, played by Joe Mantegna, who is seen in a title sequence climbing a rope up the vast bridge that connects Queens with Manhattan. He has always been the madcap comedian, the party animal. He sells fish for a living, but his wife complains he's not a fishmonger, he's a lounge act. Al's partner is Eliot (John Malkovich), who is gay but does not act on that fact, preferring a life of celibate bachelorhood. Al's wife is Carla (Linda Fiorentino), feisty, proud, ready to move out if Al stays out all night one more time.

There are others: Ray and Patricia (Ken Olin and Chloe Webb), who are the couple getting married, maybe, and Dennis (Kevin Bacon), who has gone to Hollywood to make it in the music business but hasn't had any success as yet, and Monte (Tom Waits), who is about to drift away into his own world, but shows up for the weekend anyway. Much tension centers around the character of Ray, who is not really sure he wants to marry Patricia. Ray has had some success as a painter, and maybe, he thinks, she doesn't have the class to be an artist's wife. She is wiser than he is and tells him, in a key scene, that she is Queens and she will always be Queens and it isn't her, it's his own past he isn't proud of.

There are other good speeches and moments in the movie, which seems to have been built up out of a series of sketches rather than planned from the plot down. The center point of the movie is the rooftop garden where the bachelor party takes place, but the characters spin off from that location for fights at home, adventures in the streets, and Al's escapade with a strange young woman (Jamie Lee Curtis), who turns up at the party, on the prowl. At the end of a long night, many lessons have been learned, not least by Al when he attempts to make the same rope climb that once so impressed his friends.

How true is *Queens Logic* to Queens reality? I suspect the movie owes more to the tradition of the coming-of-middle-age films than it does to specific Queens details. (The overlooked 1989 film *True Love* is a more convincing examination of love and marriage in a New York neighborhood.) This is the kind of material actors love, because it gives them the opportunity to seem like nitty-gritty ordinary people, but a lot of the scenes seem written for punchlines rather than extracted

from life. Example: Al and Eliot hold a gun on their angry employees at the fishmarket while paying their wages.

What we're left with are some moments that do work, as when Jamie Lee Curtis boldly picks up Mantegna, or Malkovich is approached by a homosexual during the party and makes a speech that pretty clearly defines the choices he has made in life. Those scenes could have taken place anywhere, and when you compare *Queens Logic* to *True Love* or *Spike of Bensonhurst* or certainly *GoodFellas*, so could *Queens Logic*.

Quest for Fire ★ ★ ★ ½
R, 100 m., 1982

Everett McGill (Noah), Ron Perlman (Amoukar), Nameer El-Kadi (Gaw), Rae Dawn Chong (Ika). Directed by Jean-Jacques Annaud and produced by John Kemeny and Denis Heroux. Screenplay by Gerard Brach.

There are basically two ways to regard *Quest for Fire*. The movie is either (a) the moving story of how scattered tribes of very early men developed some of the traits that made them human, or (b) a laughable caveman picture in which a lot of lantern-jawed actors jump around in animal skins, snarling and swinging clubs at one another. During the movie's opening scenes, I found myself seeing it in the second way, as a borderline comedy. But then these characters and their quest began to grow on me, and by the time the movie was over I cared very much about how their lives would turn out.

Other viewers report some of the same confusion. The movie has been compared with such varied works of art as *2001: A Space Odyssey* and *Alley Oop*. The question, I suppose, is whether you can make your own leap of imagination into the world of the movie—whether you're willing to identify with these beetle-browed ancestors who made more important discoveries, in their way, than all of the Nobel laureates put together. I found I *was* willing, and I was a little surprised at how much affection the movie generated.

Quest for Fire was shot on rugged locations in Canada and Scotland and takes place at the dawn of man. It introduces us to a tribe of primitive men who guard their most precious possession, which is fire. They know how to tend it and how to use it, but not how to make it. And after a jealous tribe of less-advanced creatures attacks them and destroys their fire, three men set out on an odyssey to seek another tribe that possesses fire and to steal it from them. Along the way, there are terrifying adventures. A saber-toothed tiger chases the men up into a tree and keeps them there for days. On another occasion, the heroes are trapped between an unfriendly tribe of apes and a herd of mastodons. In each situation, the men realize that simply running away won't work; they can't run fast or far enough. And so they slowly and painfully figure out a solution to their dilemma. Climbing the tree, for example, is rather obvious, but their solution to the mastodon problem is a brave inspiration.

Eventually the men discover another tribe, a more advanced tribe that lives in primitive huts and knows how to make fire and has even developed arts (they decorate themselves with mud, and their clay pots have drawings of animals scratched on them). The leader of the wanderers lusts after one of the women of the new tribe, and after a strange initiation ceremony he has sex with her. Soon he will make one of his greatest discoveries: The difference between lust and love and how it leads to the difference between isolation—and loneliness.

Quest for Fire compresses prehistory quite radically, of course. It's a little much to expect that one man in one span of a few weeks could make the scientific, emotional, and tactical discoveries that take place in the movie. Our progress as a race must have been slower than that (although Loren Eiseley writes in his books of the amazing explosion of the size of the human brain in just a handful of generations). *Quest for Fire* isn't science, though, it's an imaginary re-creation of our past, and it uses history for inspiration, not as a data source. The only two technical advisers listed in the credits are, appropriately, a novelist and a scientific popularizer: Anthony Burgess created the special primitive languages in the film, and Desmond Morris choreographed the body language and gestures.

I suggested earlier that there's probably a temptation to laugh during *Quest for Fire*, especially during such touchy scenes as the one in which early woman teaches early man that it *wasn't* as good for her as it was for him. I smiled during those scenes. But, thinking over my response, I realize that I wasn't smiling at the movie, but at the behavior of the characters. Man is a comic beast. For all of our dignity, we are very simple in many of our wants and desires, and as we crawled out

of the primeval sludge and started our long trek toward civilization, there must have been many more moments of comedy than of nobility.

Quest for Fire cheerfully acknowledges that, and indeed some of its best scenes involve man's discovery of laughter. When one of the primitive tribesmen is hit on the head by a small falling stone, the woman from the other tribe laughs and laughs. Our heroes are puzzled: They haven't heard such a noise before. But it strikes some sort of deep chord, I guess, because later, one of the tribesmen deliberately drops a small stone on his friend's head, and then everybody laughs: The three men together with the woman who taught them laughter. That's human. The guy who got hit on the head is, of course, a little slow to join in the laughter, but finally he goes along with the joke. That's civilization.

Quick Change ★ ★ ★
R, 89 m., 1990
(See related Film Clip, p. 718.)

Bill Murray (Grimm), Geena Davis (Phyllis), Randy Quaid (Loomis), Jason Robards (Police Chief), Tony Shalhoub (Cab Driver), Steve Park (Grocery Cashier), Philip Bosco (Bus Driver), Stuart Rudin (Rider With Guitar). Directed by Howard Franklin and Bill Murray and produced by Robert Greenhut and Murray. Screenplay by Howard Franklin.

The clown rides on the subway, and few people notice. This is New York City. Notice the clown with his fright wig and his funny hat, and maybe he'll kill you. It's better not to notice. And *Quick Change* is a comedy based on things that people choose not to notice.

The clown is, in fact, a bank robber named Grimm, played by Bill Murray as a disgruntled city planner who has decided to pull off the perfect heist and get out of town. He has a couple of accomplices: Phyllis (Geena Davis), who is not really a criminal but admires Grimm for his daring, and Loomis (Randy Quaid), who accepted Grimm as his leader when they were both in the first grade and has never wavered in his devotion.

The way in which these three plan to stick up the bank is fairly ingenious, even in a world where almost all possible ways of robbing a bank have already been explored. Their plan involves actually inviting the police to surround the bank, where they have taken a group of hostages, and then pulling

off a deception based on disguises and mistaken assumptions. More I will not say.

The bank heist is the first act of the movie, and it's fun. Then the real movie starts, when Grimm and his accomplices attempt to get to the airport so they can hop on a flight to a faraway tropical destination. It is rarely easy to get to the airport from Manhattan, and sometimes, as they discover, it is impossible. Their trip turns into a long day's journey into nightmare, as they encounter manic cab drivers, grocery robberies in progress, and a bus driver (Philip Bosco), who deals with the chaos of the world around him by adhering to all of the rules, all of the time.

The Bosco character provides some of the funniest passages in the film. By rigidly establishing the conditions under which he will operate, he creates the kinds of problems that comedies thrive on. The desperately escaping bank robbers have to accept the inflexible rules of his logic to get anywhere—and when they do, it's not where they're going ("I didn't say the bus went to the airport. I said the bus went to *near* the airport").

Quick Change is a welcome film from Bill Murray, coming as it does after a career slump which produced the disappointing *Ghostbusters II* and the dreadful *Scrooged!* It has him back in the real world, which provides him with the kinds of comic possibilities he handles best. Murray, like the bus driver, often functions by bringing logic to bear on impenetrable stupidity. His pose is that he is smarter than the people around him, a master of lateral thinking who makes quiet little asides to highlight their obtuseness. He is quick, and needs a quick movie to function in.

Geena Davis remains an actress in the process of self-discovery, even after her Academy Award for *The Accidental Tourist*. She is beautiful, tall, sexy, and smart, and so there are no easy categories for her; every character is an original, and what makes her funny this time is a rather peculiar quirk: She finds intelligence sexy. The fact that Murray has the courage and imagination to pull off a complicated bank heist turns her on. Quaid, on the other hand, is a slavish follower whose laughs come from his dogged determination to do the right thing even if he doesn't know what it is.

Quick Change is a funny but not an inspired comedy. It has two directors—Howard Franklin and Bill Murray—and I wonder if that has anything to do with its inability to be more than just efficiently entertaining. Comedy is more individual than drama, I think, because it springs from one person's sense of the ridiculous. It's not a good idea to have two people standing around asking each other if they think something works.

With *Quick Change*, however, at least something works often enough that the movie announces Bill Murray is back and is funny again. He says he's going to be working more often now, and that's good news: The problem with becoming a major star is that everyone begins to take your career very seriously, and comedians more than anyone need to be able to say the hell with it, and mean it.

Quigley Down Under ★ ★ ½
PG-13, 120 m., 1990

Tom Selleck (Matthew Quigley), Laura San Giacomo (Crazy Cora), Alan Rickman (Elliot Marston), Chris Haywood (Major Ashley Pitt), Ron Haddrick (Grimmelman), Tony Bonner (Dobkin). Directed by Simon Wincer and produced by Stanley O'Toole and Alexandra Rose. Screenplay by John Hill.

Here is a Western much like many others, with the difference that it is the first new Western I've seen in a long time—since *Silverado* in 1985, I think, unless you count 1989's *Back to the Future, Part III*. A generation of moviegoers, now in their teens, have grown up never having seen a Western in a movie theater. Cowboy movies are too genteel, maybe, or the violence follows a code instead of being mindless, or maybe the kids today just can't see themselves riding horses.

Quigley Down Under stars Tom Selleck, an actor who with his height, authority, and natural ease might have been a major Western star in the old days, as an American sharpshooter who sails to Australia in search of work. A man named Marston (Alan Rickman) has advertised for a long-distance marksman, and Selleck is the best, able to hit targets so far away the camera can barely see them. Selleck is appalled, however, when he discovers that Marston wants to pay him to kill Aborigines. He throws the villain through the window, and starts a vendetta that only ends, of course, with an obligatory showdown in the corral.

One of the first people Quigley meets down under is Crazy Cora, played by Laura San Giacomo as a misplaced American with a tragic past that has driven her mad—but not so mad that Quigley cannot slowly fall in love with her. *sex, lies, and videotape* (1989) is the movie that made San Giacomo an overnight star, but this may be the movie that proves her staying power. She isn't just another pretty face and a great set of eyebrows. She has an authority, a depth of presence, that is attractive, and her voice is deep and musical. She and Selleck create a chemistry that is real enough, it's a shame the screenplay hardly notices it.

The film itself is not up to the contributions of its stars. A little more thought would have helped. From the quilting-bee music that plays during the fight scenes to the Fallacy of the Talking Killer, this is a movie that has been created by the numbers. The fallacy I refer to, of course, is the frequent mistake of allowing the bad guy to talk too long. He has his enemy trapped. There's no way out. All he has to do is plug him between the eyeballs and order lunch. But no. He talks. And talks. And sets up some kind of dumb test of manhood, which he is sure to fail. Because the conclusion of such a scene is a foregone conclusion, the F.T.K. almost always results in dead screen time.

Other elements in the film are more interesting. The use of the Aborigine characters, for example. The night San Giacomo must save a baby from the wild dogs. And Alan Rickman's performance as the villain. He has a polished grace that serves here to suggest evil dimensions just beneath the surface.

I also enjoyed, in a visceral way, the pleasures of seeing the visual beauties of a Western. The choreography of a gunfight in rocky foothills. The excitement of a chase on horseback. The ambushes and close calls and treks through the desert land. *Quigley Down Under* is a handsome film, well-acted, and it's a shame the filmmakers didn't spend a little more energy on making it smarter and more original.

R

Racing with the Moon ★ ★ ★ ½
PG, 108 m., 1984

Sean Penn (Hopper), Elizabeth McGovern (Caddie), Nicolas Cage (Nicky), Suzanne Adkinson (Sally), Julie Phillips (Alice). Directed by Richard Benjamin and produced by Alain Bernheim and John Kohn. Screenplay by Steven Kloves.

I'd like to start with a hypothetical question: How long has it been since you went to a movie that ended with the words "I love you"? For me, it had been a very long time, and one of the simpler pleasures of *Racing with the Moon* was to observe the movie marching inevitably toward those three words. A deeper pleasure was that the movie arrived there with grace and charm.

The story takes place in California in 1943, with the United States at war and teenagers volunteering for the service. We meet a couple of high school kids, Hopper and Nicky, who are pinspotters down at the bowling alley and otherwise spend their time cutting classes, shooting pool, hitching rides on trains, and talking about the meaning of life. We are reminded of Tom and Huck. One night Hopper goes to the movies. His eyes meet the girl who is selling him his ticket, and he is thunderstruck by her. Her name is Caddie. Nicky already has a girlfriend, a plump little blonde named Sally. Hopper starts a campaign to win Caddie's heart, by slipping her flowers anonymously and tracking her down in the high school library. It appears that Caddie is a rich kid who lives in the house on the hill. But she likes Hopper anyway, and he likes her, and *Racing with the Moon* turns into a love story.

So far, what we have here is a movie that could go in several different directions. It could be sappy, it could be great, it could be dripping with so much nostalgia that it would feel like a memory even while we were watching it. *Racing with the Moon* doesn't fall into the *Summer of '42* nostalgia trap, but tries to be honest with its romantic characters. The performers are probably the reason that approach works so well. The three leading actors are Sean Penn and Elizabeth McGovern, as the young lovers, and Nicolas Cage, as Penn's friend. It's a pleasure to watch them work.

Penn, in particular, shows a whole side we didn't see in movies like *Bad Boys* or, needless to say, *Fast Times at Ridgemont High*. He's somehow better-looking than before, and more relaxed and confident. He doesn't come across with a lot of distracting self-importance. He plays the kind of kid who uses a rough exterior—smoking and shooting pool—as a kind of cover-up for the intelligence and sensitivity underneath, and one of the movie's best quiet moments comes when he reveals how well he can play the piano. McGovern, who had such a sweet face and such a wicked charm as the mistress in *Ragtime*, seems younger here. She has a secret she keeps from Penn, but only because she loves him. The way she plays against him is fun to watch: She's not a flirt and she's not coy, but instead she's open with this kid and has fun teasing him; there's a scene where she sets him up for a date with her girlfriend, and it's written and choreographed so carefully that it takes you back to any soda fountain you may ever have inhabited. Cage is good, too, reckless and self-destructive and dreamy, and by the end of the movie we really have a feeling for their complex relationships with each other.

Racing with the Moon is a movie like *Valley Girl* or *Baby, It's You*, a movie that is interested in teen-agers and willing to listen to how they talk and to observe, with great tenderness, the fragility and importance of their first big loves. It's easy to end a movie with "I love you," but it's hard to get there honestly.

Radio Days ★ ★ ★
PG, 88 m., 1987

Mia Farrow (Sally White), Seth Green (Joe), Michael Tucker (Father), Josh Mostel (Abe), Tito Puente (Bandleader), Danny Aiello (Rocco), Diane Keaton (New Year's Singer), Wallace Shawn (Masked Avenger), Dianne Wiest (Bea). Directed by Woody Allen and produced by Robert Greenhut. Screenplay by Allen.

I can remember what happened to the Lone Ranger in 1949 better than I can remember what happened to me. His adventures struck deeply into my imagination in a way that my own did not, and as I write these words there is almost a physical intensity to my memories of listening to the radio. Television was never the same. Television shows happened in the TV set, but radio shows happened in my head.

That is one of the truths that Woody Allen evokes in *Radio Days*, his comedy about growing up in the 1940s. Another one is that glamor and celebrity meant something in those days. And for millions of people living in ordinary homes in ordinary neighborhoods, the radio brought images of beings who lived in a shimmering world of penthouses and nightclubs, in dressing rooms and boudoirs.

The hero of *Radio Days* is an ordinary person like that: an adolescent Jewish kid who grows up in Brooklyn in a house full of relatives and listens passionately to the radio. But the movie is not simply his story. It is also the story of 1940s radio itself, and it re-creates many of the legends that he remembers hearing.

For example, the story of the burglars who answered the phone in a house they were burgling and won the jackpot on "Name That Tune," and the prizes were delivered the next day to their bewildered victims. Or the embarrassing plight of the suave radio host who liked to play around and got locked on the roof of a nightclub with the cigarette girl. Or the way the macho heroes of radio adventure serials turned out, in real life, to be short little bald guys. (The one legend Allen leaves out is the scandal of the kiddie-show host who growled "That oughta hold the little bastards" into an open mike.)

Radio Days cuts back and forth between the adolescent hero's working-class neighborhood in Brooklyn and the glamorous radio world of Manhattan. And, like radio, it jumps easily from one level of reality to another. There are autobiographical memories of relatives and school, neighbors and friends, and then there are the glittering radio legends that seeped into these ordinary lives.

Allen is not concerned with creating a story with a beginning and an end, and his movie is more like a revue in which drama is followed by comedy and everything is tied together by music, by dozens of lush arrangements of the hit songs of the 1940s. He has always used popular music in his movies (remember the opening of *Manhattan?*), but never more than this time, where the muscular, romantic confidence of the big-band sound reinforces every memory with the romance of the era.

There are so many characters in *Radio Days*, and they are in so many separate vignettes, that it's hard to give a coherent description of the plot or plots. In form and even in mood, the movie it's closest to is Federico Fellini's *Amarcord*, which also was a memory of growing up—of family, religion, sex, local folk legends, scandalous developments, and intense romantic yearnings, underlined with wall-to-wall band music. In a way, both films have nostalgia itself as one of their subjects. What they evoke isn't the long-ago time itself, but the memory of it. There is something about it being past and gone and irretrievable that makes it more precious than it ever was at the time.

As part of this nostalgic feeling, Allen seems to have made a deliberate attempt to use as many of his former actors as possible. The movie is a roll call of casts from earlier films, from Mia Farrow and Diane Keaton to Tony Roberts, Danny Aiello, Dianne Wiest, Jeff Daniels, and Wallace Shawn. And viewers with good memories will notice there also are many actual radio veterans in the movie, such as Don Pardo and Kitty Carlisle, and the shadows of others, such as Bill Stern, whose inspirational parables about sports heroes are mercilessly satirized.

The one actor who is not visible is Allen. But his teen-age alter ego (Seth Green) provides a memory of young Allen in *Take the Money and Run*, and then there is Allen's own voice on the sound track, evoking those golden days of yesteryear. There also is the Allen irreverence in several moments of absolutely inspired comedy, such as a classroom show-and-tell session, or the time the young hero collects dimes for Israel and then spends them on a boxtop secret decoder ring and has to face the rabbi's wrath.

Radio Days is so ambitious and so audacious that it almost defies description. It's a kaleidoscope of dozens of characters, settings, and scenes—the most elaborate production Allen has ever made—and it's inexhaustible, spinning out one delight after another. Although there is no narrative thread from beginning to end, there is a buried emotional thread. Like music, the movie builds toward a climax we can't even guess is coming, and then Allen finds the perfect images for the last few minutes, for a bittersweet evocation of good-bye to all that.

His final moments are staged on a set representing a rooftop on Times Square, with a smoker puffing his cigarette on a Camel billboard, while in another direction a giant neon top hat is lifted and lowered. This set is so overblown and romantic, it's like the moment in *Amarcord* when all of the townspeople get into boats and go out to watch the great ocean liner go past, and we see that the liner is obviously a prop—a vast, artificial Christmas tree of shimmering lights and phony glory. Allen finds the same truth that Fellini did: What actually happens isn't nearly as important as how we remember it.

A Rage in Harlem ★ ★ ★
R, 98 m., 1991

Forest Whitaker (Jackson), Gregory Hines (Goldy), Robin Givens (Imabelle), Zakes Mokae (Big Kathy), Danny Glover (Easy Money), Badja Djola (Slim), Stack Pierce (Coffin Ed), George Wallace (Grave Digger), Screamin' Jay Hawkins (Himself). Directed by Bill Duke and produced by Stephen Woolley and Kerry Boyle. Screenplay by John Toles-Bey and Bobby Crawford.

A Rage in Harlem is a love story surrounded by a gangster movie, and the love story wins. The lovers are Forest Whitaker, as Jackson, a big, bashful, sweet, and innocent kid, and Robin Givens, as Imabelle, a smooth operator with a trunk full, instead of a heart full, of gold. It's the mid-1950s. She's stolen the gold from her criminal partners in Mississippi, and brought it up to New York in a trunk, pursued by various low-lifes from her previous existence. In Harlem, she's broke and homeless and isn't sure how to dispose of the gold, so she needs a fall guy. Some guy so naive and dumb she can move in and use him as a cover while she plans her next move. Jackson is the obvious victim. That's before they fall in love.

They meet at the annual Undertaker's Ball, where Jackson is surprised to find himself, because as a devout, church-going young man he has nothing to do with the types who hang around there—including Goldy (Gregory Hines), his street-smart brother. He is thunderstruck by his first sight of Imabelle, who ignores him until she realizes this is her ideal patsy. Then she asks him to dance ("It's easy. Just grab me and squeeze"), and he realizes she is the most beautiful and wonderful woman in the world.

He is not quite right. She reads him for an easy mark, and plans to use him as part of her plan to keep her hands on the gold. But then something strange happens. They go to his room, where she is blindsided by his innocence and sincerity—transformed by the pure sweetness of his love. For the first time in Imabelle's life, she's met a man who idealizes her, and the experience is almost too much for her. She struggles. She tries to remain true to her criminal ideals. But big, goofy, virginal Jackson looks at her adoringly, and her heart flutters.

The relationship between Jackson and Imabelle is at the heart of *A Rage in Harlem*, which is based on a novel by Chester Himes (1909–84), who specialized in atmospheric crime novels, and has walk-ons for two of his familiar characters: Grave Digger Jones and Coffin Ed Johnson, made famous in his *Cotton Comes to Harlem* (1965, filmed in 1970). It also has roles for a great many other characters, among them Easy Money (Danny Glover), a numbers boss; Big Kathy (Zakes

Mokae), a transvestite brothel keeper; and Slim (Badja Djola), a gang leader from the South who is Imabelle's former lover, and who knows about the gold.

Himes's novel is densely plotted, and so is the movie, as Easy Money schemes to get his hands on the gold, and Slim arrives from Mississippi with his own henchmen. Jackson is a babe in these woods, but Hines, as his con-man brother, uses his street connections to try to save them. Hines also tries to explain to his kid brother that Imabelle is a con artist, but the kid doesn't believe him, and, for once, he's right.

The movie has a nice period atmosphere, which is remarkable, since it was shot with Cincinnati doubling for Harlem, and it captures some of the texture of Himes's novel, his love of characters who use their wits to outsmart each other. What's best in the movie is the chemistry between Whitaker (who played the title role in *Bird*) and Givens, who is surprisingly effective in her first feature role. Their first love scene together—where the bashful kid awkwardly wins her heart—is sexier than any number of more explicit scenes. And their reunion at the end is just right.

Raggedy Man ★ ★ ★ 1/2
PG, 94 m., 1981

Sissy Spacek (Nita), Eric Roberts (Teddy), Sam Shepard (Bailey), R.G. Armstrong (Rigby). Directed by Jack Fisk and produced by Burt Weissbourd and William D. Wittliff. Screenplay by Wittliff.

Raggedy Man remembers the small-town years of World War II so exactly that, although not yet born when the war broke out, I found myself remembering things I didn't even know I knew. Things like the way kids zoomed around dusty backyards, making their arms into airplane wings and imitating the noises of dive bombers. Like the Andrews Sisters singing "Rum and Coca-Cola" on the radio. Like the absolutely correct detail of a plaster-of-paris plaque on the wall, with a child's hand print immortalized on it. Remember?

Sissy Spacek stars as the sole switchboard operator of a small-town telephone company somewhere in the wilds of Texas. She lives in a small white frame house with a slamming screen door, and tries to raise her two sons, who are almost too small to support such grown-up names as Henry and Harry. The

question of her husband is a mystery. Spacek hates her job, but she can't leave it: Mr. Rigby, the president of the telephone company, barks that this is wartime and her job is "frozen." Right, and she's frozen in it, until one day a young sailor (Eric Roberts) comes looking for a pay phone so he can call home. He's got a few days' leave, and has hitchhiked for hundreds of miles on the hopes of seeing his fiancée. The phone call reveals that she has taken up with a new beau. Roberts is crestfallen. Spacek kindly offers him some coffee. More or less, a little at a time, they fall in love.

These surface events of small-town life are wonderfully observed in *Raggedy Man*, which never pushes the romance between Spacek and Roberts too far: They remain decent, sensitive, courteous people, a little shy in the presence of large emotions. The town gossips about the woman taking up with the sailor, but people will gossip. (Nobody knows that better than the telephone operator!) Unfortunately, *Raggedy Man* has a whole additional level of plotting that is not nearly as rewarding as the events I've already described. There is, for example, the mystery of the "raggedy man" himself, a strange, scarecrow character who hangs about in the background of several scenes and has a disconcerting way of disappearing just when you want to get a closer look at him. There's also the matter of the town louts, who inhabit the beer hall and lust after the slim, young telephone operator.

These two plot strands lead up to a climactic ending that, quite frankly, I thought was unnecessary. Without giving away several secrets that the movie itself takes very seriously, I can say that *Raggedy Man* would have pleased me more if it had completely avoided its violent conclusion—and if the raggedy man himself had been left totally out of the story, the movie, and especially the symbolism.

Such regrets still leave my affection for this movie pretty much untouched. The Sissy Spacek performance is a small jewel: She has the words, the movements, the very tilt of her face, down just right. There's a scene where she puts music on the radio and dances with a broom, and another scene where she has a serious talk with her two little boys, and they're nearly perfect scenes. So is another one, where Roberts takes the two boys to a carnival. Roberts himself is a revelation: He is often overwrought in his acting; here, playing more quietly, he

expresses great reserve of tenderness and strength, and is very effective.

Raggedy Man was Sissy Spacek's first movie after she won the Academy Award for *Coal Miner's Daughter*, and the first movie directed by her husband, Jack Fisk. (She met him when he was the art director for her first starring movie, *Badlands*, back in 1973.) The movie was made with a lot of love and startlingly fresh memories of the early 1940s, and reminds us once again that Spacek is a treasure.

Raging Bull ★ ★ ★ ★
R, 119 m., 1980

Robert De Niro (Jake La Motta), Cathy Moriarty (Vickie La Motta), Joe Pesci (Joey), Frank Vincent (Salvy), Nicholas Colasanto (Tommy Como), Theresa Saldana (Lenore), Frank Adonis (Patsy), Mario Gallo (Mario). Directed by Martin Scorsese and produced by Irwin Winkler and Robert Chartoff. Screenplay by Paul Schrader and Mardik Martin.

Martin Scorsese's *Raging Bull* is a movie about brute force, anger, and grief. It is also, like several of Scorsese's other movies, about a man's inability to understand a woman except in terms of the only two roles he knows how to assign her: virgin or whore. There is no room inside the mind of the prizefighter in this movie for the notion that a woman might be a friend, a lover, or a partner. She is only, to begin with, an inaccessible sexual fantasy. And then, after he has possessed her, she becomes tarnished by sex. Insecure in his own manhood, the man becomes obsessed by jealousy—and releases his jealousy in violence.

It is a vicious circle. Freud called it the "madonna-whore complex." Groucho Marx put it somewhat differently: "I wouldn't belong to any club that would have me as a member." It amounts to a man having such low self-esteem that he (a) cannot respect a woman who would sleep with him, and (b) is convinced that, given the choice, she would rather be sleeping with someone else. I'm making a point of the way *Raging Bull* equates sexuality and violence because one of the criticisms of this movie is that we never really get to know the central character. I don't agree with that. I think Scorsese and Robert De Niro do a fearless job of showing us the precise feelings of their central character, the former boxing champion Jake La Motta.

It is true that the character never tells us

what he's feeling, that he is not introspective, that his dialogue is mostly limited to expressions of desire, fear, hatred, and jealousy. But these very limitations—these stone walls separating the character from the world of ordinary feelings—tell us all we need to know, especially when they're reflected back at him by the other people in his life. Especially his brother and his wife, Vickie.

Raging Bull is based, we are told, on the life of La Motta, who came out of the slums of the Bronx to become middleweight champion in the 1940s, who made and squandered millions of dollars, who became a pathetic stand-up comedian, and finally spent time in a prison for corrupting the morals of an underage girl. Is this the real La Motta? We cannot know for sure, though La Motta was closely involved with the production. What's perhaps more to the point is that Scorsese and his principal collaborators, actor Robert De Niro and screenwriter Paul Schrader, were attracted to this material. All three seem fascinated by the lives of tortured, violent, guilt-ridden characters; their previous three-way collaboration was the movie *Taxi Driver*.

Scorsese's very first film, *Who's That Knocking at My Door* (1967), starred Harvey Keitel as a kid from Little Italy who fell in love with a girl but could not handle the facts of her previous sexual experience. In its sequel, *Mean Streets* (1972), the same hang-up was explored, as it was in *Taxi Driver*, where the De Niro character's madonna-whore complex tortured him in sick relationships with an inaccessible, icy blonde, and with a young prostitute. Now the filmmakers have returned to the same ground, in a film deliberately intended to strip away everything but the raw surges of guilt, jealousy, and rage coursing through La Motta's extremely limited imagination.

Raging Bull remains close to its three basic elements: a man, a woman, and prizefighting. La Motta is portrayed as a punk kid, stubborn, strong, and narrow. He gets involved in boxing, and he is good at it. He gets married, but his wife seems almost an afterthought. Then one day he sees a girl at a municipal swimming pool and is transfixed by her. The girl is named Vickie, and she is played by Cathy Moriarty as an intriguing mixture of unstudied teen-ager, self-reliant survivor, and somewhat calculated slut.

La Motta wins and marries her. Then he becomes consumed by the conviction she is cheating on him. Scorsese finds a way to

visually suggest his jealousy: From La Motta's point of view, Vickie sometimes floats in slow motion toward another man. The technique fixes the moment in our minds; we share La Motta's exaggeration of an innocent event. And we share, too, the La Motta character's limited and tragic hang-ups. This man we see is not, I think, supposed to be any more subtle than he seems. He does not have additional "qualities" to share with us. He is an engine driven by his own rage. The equation between his prizefighting and his sexuality is inescapable, and we see the trap he's in: La Motta is the victim of base needs and instincts that, in his case, are not accompanied by the insights and maturity necessary for him to cope with them. The raging bull. The poor sap.

Ragtime ★ ★ ★ ½
PG, 156 m., 1981

Howard E. Rollins, Jr. (Coalhouse Walker), James Cagney (Rhinelander Waldo), Brad Dourif (Younger Brother), Mary Steenburgen (Mother), James Olson (Father), Elizabeth McGovern (Evelyn Nesbit), Kenneth McMillan (Willie Conklin), Pat O'Brien (Delmas), Mandy Patinkin (Tateh), Moses Gunn (Booker T. Washington). Directed by Milos Forman and produced by Dino De Laurentiis. Screenplay by Michael Weller.

Milos Forman apparently made a basic decision very early in his production of E.L. Doctorow's best-selling novel, *Ragtime*. He decided to set aside the book's kaleidoscopic jumble of people, places, and things, and concentrate on just one of the several narrative threads. Instead of telling dozens of stories, his film is mostly concerned with the story of Coalhouse Walker, Jr., a black piano player who insists that justice be done after he is insulted by some yahoo volunteer firemen.

Doctorow's novel was an inspired juggling act involving both actual and fictional characters, who sometimes met in imaginary scenes of good wit and imagery. The Coalhouse story was more or less equal with several others. A film faithful to the book would have had people walking in and out of each other's lives in an astonishing series of coincidences. That might have been a good film, too. It might have looked a little like Robert Altman's *Nashville* or *Buffalo Bill*, and indeed Altman was the first filmmaker signed to direct *Ragtime*. But we will never

see what Altman might have done, and Forman decided to do something different. He traces the ways in which Coalhouse Walker enters and affects the lives of an upstate New York family in the first decade of the century. The family lives in White Plains, New York, in a vast and airy old frame manor, and it consists of Father, Mother, and Younger Brother, with walk-ons by a grandfather and a young son.

For Younger Brother, the sirens of the big city call, in the form of an infatuation with the chorus girl Evelyn Nesbit (Elizabeth McGovern). That's before the saga of Coalhouse Walker alters his life. Coalhouse (in a superb performance by Howard E. Rollins, Jr.) meets the family by accident, or maybe by fate. A young black woman gives birth to Coalhouse's son, and then the family takes in both the woman and her son, hiring her as their maid. Coalhouse comes calling. He wants to marry the mother of his child. He has earned enough money. Everything's all set for the ceremony, when an event takes place that changes everything. The local volunteer firemen, enraged that a black man would own his own Model T, block the car's way in front of their station. They pile horse manure on the front seat. And Coalhouse, quite simply, cannot rest until he sees his car restored to him in its original condition.

The story develops quickly into a confrontation. Coalhouse barricades himself into New York's J. Pierpont Morgan Library, and issues a set of demands. The library is surrounded by police and guardsmen, led by Police Commissioner Rhinelander Waldo (the great James Cagney, out of retirement). Father (James Olson) gets drawn into negotiations, and Younger Brother (Brad Dourif) is actually one of Coalhouse's lieutenants, in blackface disguise. Meanwhile, Mother is running off with a bearded immigrant who started out making cutout silhouettes on the streets and is now one of the first film directors.

The story of *Ragtime*, then, is essentially the story of Coalhouse Walker, Jr. Forman, a Czechoslovakian with an unusually keen eye for American society—his credits include *One Flew Over the Cuckoo's Nest* and *Hair!*—has made a film about black pride and rage and . . . not *only* white racism, which we sort of expect, but also white liberalism.

The great achievement of *Ragtime* is in its performances, especially Rollins and the changes he goes through in this story, from youthful romantic love to an impassioned cry

"Lord, why did you fill me with such rage?" Olson, quiet and self-effacing, is subtly powerful as Father. Mary Steenburgen is clear-voiced, primly ethical Mother who springs a big surprise on everyone. Pat O'Brien has two great scenes as a corrupt, world-weary lawyer. Kenneth McMillan blusters and threatens as the racist fire chief. And when Cagney tells him "people tell me . . . you're slime," there is the resonance of movie legend in his voice.

Ragtime is a loving, beautifully mounted, graceful film that creates its characters with great clarity. We understand where everyone stands, and most of the time we even know why. Forman surrounds them with some of the other characters from the Doctorow novel (including Harry Houdini, Teddy Roosevelt, and Norman Mailer as the architect Sanford White), but in the film they're just atmosphere—window dressing. Forman's decision to stick with the story of Coalhouse is vindicated, because he tells it so well.

Raiders of the Lost Ark ★ ★ ★ ★
PG, 115 m., 1981

Harrison Ford (Indy), Ronald Lacey (Teht), John Rhys-Davies (Sallah), Karen Allen (Marion), Wolf Kahler (Dietrich). Directed by Steven Spielberg and produced by Frank Marshall. Executive producers, George Lucas and Howard Kazanjian. Screenplay by Lucas and Philip Kaufman.

Raiders of the Lost Ark is an out-of-body experience, a movie of glorious imagination and breakneck speed that grabs you in the first shot, hurtles you through a series of incredible adventures, and deposits you back in reality two hours later—breathless, dizzy, wrung-out, and with a silly grin on your face. This movie celebrates the stories we spent our adolescence searching for in the pulp adventure magazines, in the novels of Edgar Rice Burroughs, in comics—even in the movies. There used to be a magazine named *Thrilling Wonder Stories*, and every shot in *Raiders of the Lost Ark* looks like one of its covers. It's the kind of movie where the hero gets out of bed wondering what daring exploits and astonishing, cliff-hanging, death-defying threats he will have to survive in the next ten seconds.

It's actually more than a movie; it's a catalog of adventure. For locations, it ticks off the jungles of South America, the hinterlands of Tibet, the deserts of Egypt, a hidden submarine base, an isolated island, a forgotten tomb—no, make that *two* forgotten tombs—and an American anthropology classroom. For villains, it has sadistic Nazis, slimy gravediggers, drunken Sherpas, and scheming Frenchmen. For threats, it climaxes with the wrath of God, and leads up to that spectacular development by easy stages, with tarantulas, runaway boulders, hidden spears, falling rock slabs, burning airplanes, runaway trucks, sealed tombs, and snakes. Lots of snakes. For modes of conveyance, it looks like one of those old world's fair panoramas of transportation: It has horse carts, biplanes, motorcycles, submarines, ships, horse, trains, and trucks. No bicycles.

For heroes, it has Indiana Jones (Harrison Ford) and his former and future girlfriend, Marion (Karen Allen). She's the kind of girl . . . well, to make a long story short, when they first met ten years ago, Indiana deflowered her, and that made her so mad at men that she moved to the mountains of Tibet, opened a bar, and started nightly drinking contests with the Sherpas. She'll never forgive him, almost.

The time is 1936. Indy is an American anthropologist who learns that the Nazis think they've discovered the long-lost resting place of the Ark of the Covenant, the golden casket used by the ancient Hebrews to hold the Ten Commandments. Indy's mission: Beat the Nazis to the prize. He flies to Tibet, collects Marion and a priceless medallion that holds the secret of the Ark's location, and then tries to outsmart the Nazis. What is a little amazing about *Raiders of the Lost Ark* is that this plot somehow holds together and makes some sense, even though it functions primarily as a framework for the most incredible series of action and stunt set pieces I've ever seen in a movie. Indiana and Marion spend the entire film hanging by their fingernails—literally, at one point, over a pit of poisonous snakes.

They survive a series of gruesome and dreadful traps, pitfalls, double-crosses, ambushes, and fates worse than death (of which this movie suggests several). And Indiana engages in the best chase scene I've seen in a film. (I include, in second place, the chase from *The French Connection*, with *Bullitt* in third.) The chase involves a truck, three jeeps, a horse, a motorcycle, and an awesomely difficult stunt in which a character is required to make a 360-degree turn of the speeding truck. All of these spectacles are achieved with flawless movie technology brought to a combination of stunts, special visual effects, and sheer sweat. The makers of this film have covered similar ground before, if perhaps never so fluently; George Lucas, the executive producer, gave birth to the *Star Wars* movies, and Steven Spielberg, the director, made *Jaws* and *Close Encounters*. The rest of the all-star crew's work includes photography by veteran British cinematographer Douglas Slocombe, appropriately stirring and haunting music by *Star Wars* composer John Williams, sets by *Star Wars* production designer Norman Reynolds and art director Les Dilley, and countless wonderments by Richard Edlund, who supervised the visual effects.

Two things, however, make *Raiders of the Lost Ark* more than just a technological triumph: its sense of humor and the droll style of its characters. This is often a funny movie, but it doesn't get many of its laughs with dialogue and only a few with obvious gags (although the biggest laugh comes from the oldest and most obvious gag, involving a swordsman and a marksman). We find ourselves laughing in surprise, in relief, in incredulity at the movie's ability to pile one incident upon another in an inexhaustible series of inventions. And the personalities of the central characters are enormously winning. Harrison Ford, as Indy Jones, does not do a reprise of his *Star Wars* work. Instead he creates a taciturn, understated, stubborn character who might be the Humphrey Bogart of *The Treasure of the Sierra Madre* with his tongue in his cheek. He survives fires, crushings, shootings, burnings. He really hates snakes. Karen Allen plays the female lead with a resilient toughness that develops its own charm. She can handle herself in any situation. She *really* hates snakes.

Raiders of the Lost Ark is a swashbuckling adventure epic in the tradition of *Star Wars*, *Superman*, the James Bond pictures, and all the other multimillion-dollar special-effects extravaganzas. It wants only to entertain. It succeeds. Watch it with someone you know fairly well. There will be times during the film when it will be necessary to grab somebody.

The Rainbow ★ ★ ★ ½
R, 128 m., 1988

Dustin Hoffman (Raymond Babbitt), Tom Cruise (Charlie Babbitt), Valeria Golino (Susanna), Jerry Molen (Dr. Bruner), Jack Murdock (John Mooney), Michael D. Roberts (Vern), Ralph Seymour (Lenny), Lucinda Jenney (Iris), Bonnie Hunt (Sally Dibbs). Directed by Barry Levinson and produced by Mark Johnson. Screenplay by Ronald Bass and Barry Morrow.

Is it possible to have a relationship with an autistic person? Is it possible to have a relationship with a cat? I do not intend the comparison to be demeaning to the autistic; I am simply trying to get at something. I have useful relationships with both of my cats, and they are important to me. But I never know what the cats are thinking. That is precisely the situation that Charlie Babbitt (Tom Cruise) is faced with in *Rain Man*.

His brother, Raymond (Dustin Hoffman), is "high-level" autistic. He can carry on conversations, stick to a schedule, compile baseball statistics, memorize dinner menus, and become disturbed when anything upsets his routine. He can also count 246 spilled toothpicks in an instant, and calculate square roots in a flash. But what is he thinking?

There is a moment in *Rain Man* that crystallizes all the frustrations that Charlie feels about Raymond, a moment when he cries out, "I know there has to be somebody inside there!" But who? And where? *Rain Man* is so fascinating because it refuses to supply those questions with sentimental but unrealistic answers. This is not a movie like *Charly* in which there is a miracle cure.

Rain Man works so well within Raymond's limitations because it is a movie about limitations, particularly Charlie's own limited ability to love those in his life, or to see things from their point of view. As the film opens, we see Charlie frantically trying to juggle his way out of a crisis in his Los Angeles business, which seems to consist of selling expensive imported automobiles out of his hip pocket. He is driven, unhappy, a workaholic. One day he receives word that his father—a man with whom he has had no contact for years—has died back east. At the reading of the will, he learns that he has received a pittance (including a prized 1949 Buick Roadmaster), and that his father's $3 million fortune has gone into a trust.

Who is the trust for? Performing some amateur detective work, Charlie discovers with a shock that it goes to support an older brother he never knew he had—an autistic brother who has been institutionalized for years. Visiting Raymond at the home where he lives, Cruise finds a methodical, mechanical, flat-voiced middle-aged man who "definitely" knows things, such as that tapioca pudding is "definitely" on the menu, and that his favorite TV program is "definitely" about to come on the air.

Rain Man follows this discovery with a story line that is as old as the hills. Angry that he has been cut out of his share of the inheritance, Charlie takes Raymond out of the mental home and vows to bring him to live in California. But Raymond will not fly (he "definitely" recites the dates and fatalities of every airline's most recent crash). And so Charlie puts Raymond in the front seat of the 1949 Buick and they head out on a cross-country odyssey of discovery.

It is an old formula, but a serviceable one, using shots of the car against the sunset as punctuation. The two brothers meet genuine actual Americans on the road, of course, and have strange adventures, of course, and although we have seen this structure in dozens of other movies, it is new this time because for Raymond it is definitely not a voyage of discovery.

Everything changes in the movie except for Raymond. In a roadside diner somewhere along the way, he still stubbornly insists on the routines of the dining room in his mental institution: The maple syrup is definitely supposed to be on the table before the pancakes come. Charlie at first does not quite seem to accept the dimensions of Raymond's world, and grows frustrated at what looks like almost willful intractability. Eventually, toward the end of the journey, he finds that he loves his brother, and that love involves accepting him exactly as he is.

Rain Man is a project that Hoffman and Cruise have been determined to bring to the screen for a long time. Barry Levinson came on board after three previous directors signed off on this material. The problem, of course, was Raymond. If fiction is about change, then how can you make a movie about a man who cannot change, whose whole life is anchored and defended by routine? Few actors could get anywhere with this challenge, and fewer still could absorb and even entertain us with their performance, but Hoffman proves again that he almost seems to thrive on impossible acting challenges. "You want taller?" he says in the audition scene in *Tootsie*. "I can play taller. You want shorter? I can play shorter. You want a tomato?" And he can play autistic.

At the end of *Rain Man*, I felt a certain love for Raymond, the Hoffman character. I don't know quite how Hoffman got me to do it. He does not play cute, or lovable, or pathetic. He is matter-of-fact, straight down the middle, uninflected, unmoved, uncomprehending, in all of his scenes—except when his routine is disrupted, when he grows disturbed until it is restored. And yet I could believe that the Cruise character was beginning to love him, because that was how I felt, too. I loved him for what he was, not for what he was not, or could not be.

The changes in the movie all belong to Charlie, who begins the film as a me-first materialist, a would-be Trump without a line of credit. By the end of the film Charlie has learned how to pay attention, how to listen, and how to be at least a little patient some of the time. He does not undergo a spiritual transformation; he simply gets in touch with things that are more important than selling cars. He is aided in this process by his girl friend Susanna (Valeria Golino), a Latina who loves him but despairs of ever getting him off autopilot.

By the end of *Rain Man*, what have we learned? I think the film is about acceptance. Charlie Babbitt's first appearance in the movie has him wheeling and dealing in the face of imminent ruin, trying to control his life and the lives of others by blind, arrogant will-power. What Raymond teaches him is that he can relax, because try as he might, he will always be powerless over other people. They will do just about what they choose to do, no matter how loud Charlie Babbitt screams. Raymond has a lot he can teach Charlie about acceptance, even if it is the solitary thing he knows.

The Rainbow ★ ★ ★
R, 104 m., 1989

Sammi Davis (Ursula Brangwen), Paul McGann (Anton Skrebensky), Amanda Donohoe (Winifred Inger), Christopher Gable (Will Brangwen), David Hemmings (Uncle Henry), Glenda Jackson (Anna Brangwen), Dudley Sutton (MacAllister), Glenda McKay (Gudron Brangwen). Produced and directed by Ken Russell. Screenplay by Ken and Vivian Russell. Adapted from the novel by D.H. Lawrence.

Although much of D.H. Lawrence's original notoriety in Britain came from the sexual passion in his novels, what offended convention even more, I believe, was his belief that an artistic free spirit need not be concerned with hidebound ideas of social class. When he began to write, in the years before World War I, Britain was a nation of rigid social stratification. Everything depended on who your parents were, and what your accent was. The notion that one could break loose and fly was deeply revolutionary.

In *The Rainbow* and its sequel, *Women in Love,* Lawrence created two modern heroines who refused to have their lives defined by their class and their sex. They were defiant. They were artistic. They were not ashamed to have sexual feelings, just as men did. Although neither novel is even remotely pornographic in the current sense of the word, they were censored, banned, and pilloried when they were first published—attacked by men who feared that such ideas could lead anywhere, could lead even to women demanding the vote. At the time, Lawrence's *The Rainbow* was as controversial as his *Lady Chatterley's Lover.*

Ken Russell, the iconoclastic English director of such wildly different films as *Tommy, The Boyfriend,* and *The Lair of the White Worm,* first made his feature-length reputation with the brilliant *Women in Love,* released in 1969. Twenty years later, he is back with a film version of the first novel. The two films are linked by Glenda Jackson, who now plays the mother of the character she played in 1969.

The movie takes place in rural England around the time of the First World War, and centers on the story of Ursula Brangwen (Sammi Davis), daughter of an old-established and respectable farming family, who has no desire to march in step with the requirements of her family tradition. She is restless and inquisitive, and in Winifred, the local school teacher (Amanda Donohoe) she finds an older woman to model herself after.

Winifred is well-read, independent of mind, healthy of body. She is not married, and has become a schoolteacher because teaching and the stage were then two of the few professions in which a single woman could support herself. Her independence makes her a daily offense to the master of the school, one of those coarse male sadists Lawrence could draw so well. But to her students, she is a breath of freedom.

It is from Winifred that Ursula first learns that a woman's life need not be rigidly bound by social convention. They go for walks together and read books together, and Ursula falls in love with the older woman—not into sexual love, although that seems like a possibility, but into idealistic love. This woman becomes a symbol of Ursula's own quest.

But then things go wrong. We have already met Uncle Henry (David Hemmings), the strong-willed, complacent local mine owner. In his own way, he, too, is sexually liberated—although for him that means passing up conventional marriage for the pleasures of the flesh. Ursula is surprised and deeply shocked when Winifred marries Henry. This seems to her like a betrayal of their friendship, but for Winifred it is a hard, realistic choice; for a woman to have power in those days, she had to marry it.

There is also a man in Ursula's life—Anton Skrebensky (Paul McGann), something of a free spirit, who is attracted by Ursula's headstrong love of opinions and ideas. They fall in love, but then Ursula discovers that Anton is not as free as she thought. He talks easily and convincingly about the "woman question," and seems to support her convictions, but in the end he wants a conventional wife, someone whose will has been broken according to society's requirements.

The Rainbow sets this story against the pastoral beauty of the English countryside, but this is not a nostalgic costume drama, dripping with atmosphere. Russell has kept all of the hurt and anger of Lawrence's fiction. This is a movie that speaks to today, that could feel like an anthem to a young woman who feels that her spirit is not free.

Ken Russell is the most prolific of modern British directors, and the most uneven. Some of his films, like the recent *Gothic,* seem to have been composed and directed in a fit of mania. Others respect more traditional values, and in *The Rainbow* he has made a measured, thoughtful literary adaptation. He obviously believes Lawrence's message is as appropriate now as it was then, and he is right.

Raising Arizona ★ ½
PG-13, 103 m., 1987

Nicolas Cage (H.I.), Holly Hunter (Ed), Trey Wilson (Nathan Arizona, Sr.), John Goodman (Gale), William Forsythe (Evelle), Sam McMurray (Glen), Frances McDormand (Dot). Directed by Joel Coen and produced by Ethan Coen. Screenplay by Coen and Coen.

I have a problem with movies where everybody talks as if they were reading out of an old novel about a bunch of would-be colorful characters. They usually end up sounding silly. For every movie like *True Grit* that works with lines like "I was determined not to give them anything to chaff me about," there is a *Black Shield of Falworth,* with lines like "Yonder lies duh castle of my fadder."

Generally speaking, it's best to have your characters speak in strong but unaffected English, especially when your story is set in the present. Otherwise they'll end up distracting the hell out of everybody.

That's one of the problems with *Raising Arizona.* The movie is narrated by its hero, a man who specializes in robbing convenience stores, but it sounds as if he just graduated from the Rooster Cogburn School of Elocution. There are so many "far be it from me's" and "inasmuches" in his language that he could play Ebenezer Scrooge with the same vocabulary—and that's not what you expect from a two-bit thief who lives in an Arizona trailer park.

Maybe, of course, he just happens to talk that way. Even in this age of homogenized culture, a few people do retain distinctive and colorful speech patterns. That would be a good theory except that everyone in *Raising Arizona* talks funny. They all elevate their dialogue to an arch and artificial level that's distracting and unconvincing and slows down the progress of the film.

And what *Raising Arizona* needs more than anything else is more velocity. Here's a movie that stretches out every moment for more than it's worth, until even the moments of inspiration seem forced. Since the basic idea of the movie is a good one and there are talented people in the cast, what we have here is a film shot down by its own forced and mannered style.

The movie stars Nicolas Cage as the guy who sticks up all-night grocery stores, and Holly Hunter as the policewoman who falls in love with him while taking his mug shots. After he gets out of prison for what he hopes is the last time, they get married and set up their little home, and then discover that they cannot have children. Meanwhile, there have been stories in the paper about a local furniture czar, Nathan Arizona, whose wife took a fertility drug and had quints. Hunter convinces Cage that anybody with five kids is not going to miss one of them, and Cage steals into the Arizona home to kidnap one of the infants.

The movie has some fun with the bombastic Arizona (played like a used-car huckster by Trey Wilson), and it also contains some charming moments involving the photogenic child who has been cast as the kidnapping victim. But then there's a silly subplot about a couple of escaped cons, and an even more ridiculous development involving some kind of superhero Hell's Angel, who roars through town like a messenger from hell.

The movie cannot decide if it exists in the real world of trailer parks and 7-Elevens and Pampers, or in a fantasy world of characters from another dimension. It cannot decide if it is about real people, or comic exaggerations. It moves so uneasily from one level of reality to another that finally we're just baffled. Comedy often depends on frustrating the audience's expectations. But how can it work when we don't have a clue about what to expect—when the movie itself doesn't know what is possible and what is not?

Raising Arizona is the new work by the Coen brothers, Joel and Ethan, whose previous film was the superb thriller *Blood Simple*. That was a movie that pushed reality as far as it could go within the rigid confines of a well-made thriller. *Raising Arizona* needs the same kind of restraint. It's all over the map. If the same story had been told straight, as a comic slice of life, it might have really worked. I kept thinking of Jonathan Demme's *Melvin and Howard*, the film about the gas station owner and the billionaire, in which equally unlikely events happened but were very funny because they were allowed to be believable.

Rambo: First Blood Part II ★ ★ ★
R, 90 m., 1985

Sylvester Stallone (Rambo), Richard Crenna (Trautman), Charles Napier (Murdock), Steven Berkoff (Podovsky). Directed by George P. Cosmatos and produced by Buzz Feitshans. Screenplay by Stallone and James Cameron.

Rambo, subtitled *First Blood Part II* and continuing the adventures of Sylvester Stallone's one-man army, is two movies in one. First there's a hard-boiled, high-energy, violent action picture, which will probably find a large and enthusiastic audience. Lurking beneath the action is a political statement accusing the U.S. government of such base political motives that I was, quite simply,

astonished. *Rambo* is not left wing or right wing, but belongs to the paranoid wing of American politics, in which villains left and right crawl under the covers together and conspire to annihilate John Rambo.

If you saw the original *First Blood*, which was a big hit, you remember Rambo. He is a returned Vietnam hero, a superbly trained fighting machine who is considered by his superior officers to be the finest soldier they have ever seen. But Rambo becomes unhinged by civilian life, and by the insults which he believes society is heaping on men like himself, who risked their lives to fight the war. So Rambo reverts to his military training and turns into a one-man army dedicated to destroying the establishment that does not honor him.

At the end of *First Blood*, Rambo was captured after blowing up half a town and wiping out countless civilian and military authorities. If anyone had been keeping count, he would have qualified as the nation's most prolific mass killer. In the opening scenes of *Rambo*, he is breaking rocks on a chain gang when his old superior officer (Richard Crenna) arrives with a mission: Rambo is needed to parachute into Southeast Asia and scout out a suspected POW compound holding missing Americans. Any questions, Rambo? "Only one," he tells Crenna. "This time, do we get to win?"

His question places *Rambo* squarely within the revisionist genre of Vietnam movies, in which the war is refought with a happy ending. *Uncommon Valor*, the two *Missing in Action* movies, and this film are all about missions to free American MIAs and kill countless Asian soldiers. The basic assumption is that we lost the war because "the politicians" prevented men like Rambo from doing what they were trained to do. And indeed, again this time he has his hands tied: he's only supposed to take pictures, not engage in violence. Needless to say, if they only want pictures, they've picked the wrong mass murderer for the job.

Rambo's mission is outlined by a suspicious American intelligence officer (the square-jawed, rugged Charles Napier, a favorite of Russ Meyer *and* Jonathan Demme). Only after Rambo parachutes into the night does it become clear that Napier doesn't really want the mission to succeed. In logic so impenetrable that I would love to have somebody run it past me again, the movie argues that it would be politically embarrassing for American MIAs to be

found at this late date, and that therefore it would be best if Rambo's mission fails. If he *does* come back with photos, they'll be suppressed. In that case, I was wondering, why sponsor the mission in the first place—and especially with a loose cannon like Rambo? No matter; the movie turns into an efficient action picture, with Rambo wiping out legions of North Vietnamese and Russians with a variety of weapons, including explosive-tipped arrows. Back at headquarters, Napier does all he can to sabotage the mission, but it becomes clear that Rambo could have won the Vietnam war by himself, had he been unleashed, and everything leads to a big climax, a helicopter dogfight. The strange thing about *Rambo* is that it works despite its politics. Its conspiracy theory is so angry and so unlikely that we tend to ignore it, sit back, and enjoy the action.

Ran ★ ★ ★ ★
R, 160 m., 1985

Tatsuya Nakadai (Lord Hidetora), Akira Terao (Taro, Eldest Son), Jinpachi Nezu (Jiro, Second Son), Daisuke Ryn (Sahuro, Youngest Son), Mieko Harada (Lady Kaede, Taro's Wife), Yoshiko Miyazaki (Lady Sue, Jiro's Wife), Masayuki Yui (Tango, Hidetora's Servant), Peter (Kyoami, The Fool). Directed by Akira Kurosawa and produced by Serge Silberman and Masato Hara. Screenplay by Hideo Oquino, Masato Ide, and Kurosawa.

One of the early reviews of Akira Kurosawa's *Ran* said that he could not possibly have directed it at an earlier age. My first impression was to question that act of critical omnipotence. Who is to say Kurosawa couldn't have made this film at fifty or sixty, instead of at seventy-five, as he has? But then I thought longer about *Ran*, which is based on Shakespeare's *King Lear* and on a similar medieval samurai legend. And I thought about Laurence Olivier's Lear and about the *Lear* I recently saw starring Douglas Campbell and I realized that age is probably a prerequisite to fully understanding this character. Dustin Hoffman might be able to play Willy Loman by aging himself with makeup, but he will have to wait another twenty years to play Lear.

The character contains great paradoxes, but they are not the paradoxes of youth; they spring from long habit. Lear has the arrogance of great power, long held. He has wide knowledge of the world. Yet he is curiously innocent when it comes to his own children; he thinks they can do no wrong, can be trusted to carry out his plans. At the end, when his dreams have been broken, the character has the touching quality of a childlike innocence that can see breath on lips that are forever sealed, and can dream of an existence beyond the cruelties of man. Playing Lear is not a technical exercise. I wonder if a man can do it who has not had great disappointments and long dark nights of the soul.

Kurosawa has lived through those bad times. Here is one of the greatest directors of all time, out of fashion in his own country, suffering from depression, nearly blind. He prepared this film for ten years, drawing hundreds of sketches showing every shot, hardly expecting that the money would ever be found to allow him to make the film. But a deal was finally put together by Serge Silberman, the old French producer who backed the later films of Luis Bunuel (who could also have given us a distinctive Lear). Silberman risked his own money; this is the most expensive Japanese film ever made, and, yes, perhaps Kurosawa could not have made it until he was seventy-five.

The story is familiar. An old lord decides to retire from daily control of his kingdom, yet still keep all the trappings of his power. He will divide his kingdom in three parts among his children. In *Ran*, they are sons, not daughters. First, he requires a ritual statement of love. The youngest son cannot abide the hypocrisy, and stays silent. And so on.

The Japanese legend which Kurosawa draws from contains a famous illustration in which the old lord takes three arrows and demonstrates that when they are bundled, they cannot be broken, but taken one at a time, they are weak. He wishes his sons to remain allies, so they will be strong, but of course they begin to fight, and civil war breaks out as the old lord begins his forlorn journey from one castle to another, gradually being stripped of his soldiers, his pride, his sanity.

Nobody can film an epic battle scene like Kurosawa. He has already abundantly demonstrated that in *The Seven Samurai*, in *Yojimbo*, in *Kagemusha*. In *Ran*, the great bloody battles are counterpointed with scenes of a chamber quality, as deep hatreds and lusts are seen to grow behind the castle's walls.

King Lear is a play that centers obsessively around words expressing negatives. "Noth-

ing? Nothing will come of nothing!" "Never, never, never." "No, no, no, no, no." They express in deep anguish the king's realization that what has been taken apart will never be put together again, that his beloved child is dead and will breathe no more, that his pride and folly have put an end to his happiness. Kurosawa's film expresses that despair perhaps more deeply than a Western film might; the samurai costumes, the makeup inspired by Noh drama, give the story a freshness that removes it from all our earlier associations.

Ran is a great, glorious achievement. Kurosawa must often have associated himself with the old lord as he tried to put this film together, but in the end he has triumphed, and the image I have of him, at seventy-five, is of three arrows bundled together.

Re-Animator ★ ★ ★
NO MPAA RATING, 95 m., 1985

Jeffrey Combs (Herbert West), Bruce Abbott (Dan Cain), Barbara Crampton (Megan Halsey), David Gale (Dr. Carl Hill), Robert Sampson (Dean Halsey), Gerry Glack (Mace), Carolyn Purdy-Gordon (Dr. Harrod). Directed by Stuart Gordon and produced by Brian Yuzna. Screenplay by Dennis Paoli, William J. Morris, and Gordon.

One of the most boring experiences on Earth is a trash movie without the courage of its lack of convictions. If it only wants to be cynical, it becomes lifeless in every moment—a bad dream on the screen. One of the pleasures of the movies, however, is to find a movie that chooses a disreputable genre and then tries with all its might to transcend the genre, to go over the top into some kind of artistic vision, however weird.

Stuart Gordon's *Re-Animator* is a pleasure like that, a frankly gory horror movie that finds a rhythm and a style that make it work in a cockeyed, offbeat sort of way. It's charged up by the tension between the director's desire to make a good movie and his realization that few movies about mad scientists and dead body parts are ever likely to be very good. The temptation is to take a camp approach to the material, to mock it, as Paul Morrissey did in *Andy Warhol's Frankenstein*. Gordon resists that temptation, and creates a livid, bloody, deadpan exercise in the theater of the undead.

Seeing this movie at the Cannes Film Festival, I walked in with no particular expecta-

tions, except that I hoped *Re-Animator* would be better than the festival's run-of-the-mill exploitation films. I walked out somewhat surprised and reinvigorated (if not re-animated) by a movie that had the audience emitting taxi whistles and wild goat cries. In its own way, on its own terms, in its corrupt genre, this movie worked as well as any other movie in the festival.

I was reminded of Pauline Kael's sane observation: "The movies are so rarely great art, that if we can't appreciate great trash, there is little reason for us to go."

The movie's story involves . . . but why bother? In the ads, the hero was described as having a good head on his shoulders, and another one in the laboratory dish in front of him. That more or less captures the essence of *Re-Animator*. Driven by an insane desire to vindicate himself by creating living beings out of dead body parts, a scientist uses his intelligence to burrow more and more deeply into sheer madness.

Gordon's direction, and particularly his use of special effects, will come as no surprise to anyone who saw his famous *Warp* trilogy onstage. He borrows from the traditions of comic-book art and B-grade thrillers, using his special effects not as set pieces for us to study, but as dazzling throwaways as the action hurtles ahead. By the end of the film, we are keenly aware that nothing of consequence has happened, but so what? We have been assaulted by a lurid imagination, amazed by unspeakable sights, blind-sided by the movie's curiously dry sense of humor. I guess that's our money's worth.

Real Genius ★ ★ ★ ½
PG-13, 105 m., 1985

Val Kilmer (Chris Knight), William Atherton (Professor Hathaway), Gabe Jarret (Mitch), Michelle Meyrink (Jordan Cochran), Jonathan Gries (Laslo [recluse]), Robert Prescott (Kent Torokvei), Severn Darden (Dr. Meredith). Directed by Martha Coolidge and produced by Brian Grazer. Screenplay by Neal Israel, Pat Proft, and Peter Torokvei.

It is probably not true that all American college students have been lobotomized and pumped full of sex hormones, although most movies treat them that way. Some students are more like the ones we meet in *Real Genius*. They are smart but socially uncertain and relativity is easier for them to understand than what to say on a first date. This is the first movie in a long time that's set on a college campus where the students are supposed to be intelligent. The campus is apparently Cal Tech, and the students are the next generation of great physicists, the kind who will write papers proving that everything we know is wrong.

The movie involves the saga of Mitch (Gabe Jarret), a brilliant high school student whose Science Fair project has revised the theory of laser beam technology. He is personally recruited by Prof. Hathaway (William Atherton), a famous physics professor who wants the kid to work in his personal laboratory. Once on campus, the kid meets the legendary Chris Knight (Val Kilmer), who was the most brilliant freshman in history, and who is now a junior whose mind is beginning to be cluttered by mischief. The two students room together—and there seems to be a third person in the room, a strange, wraith-like bearded figure who disappears into the clothes closet, and doesn't seem to be there when the door is flung open.

The professor is running a scam. He has a Defense Department contract for a sophisticated laser device so accurate that it could incinerate a single man on earth from a base in orbit. The professor is using his students as slave labor to do most of the work on the project while ripping off the government grant to build himself a new house. The students, meanwhile, have no idea they're working on a weapons system, and are more interested in using laser beams to lead everyone to a "Tanning Invitational" they've set up by turning a lecture hall into a swimming pool.

Real Genius allows every one of its characters the freedom to be complicated and quirky and individual. That's especially true of Jordan (Michelle Meyrink), a hyperactive woman student who talks all the time and never sleeps and knits things without even thinking about it, and follows Mitch into the john because she's so busy explaining something that she doesn't even notice what he's doing. I could recognize students like this from my own undergraduate days. One of the most familiar types on campus (and one of the rarest in the movies) is the self-styled eccentric, who develops a complex of weird personality traits as a way of clearing space and defining himself.

Real Genius was directed by Martha Coolidge, who made *Valley Girl*, one of the best and most perceptive recent teen-age movies. What I like best about her is that she gives her characters the freedom to be themselves. They don't have to be John Belushi clones, or fraternity jocks, or dumb coeds. They can flourish in all of their infinite variety, as young people with a world of possibilities and a lot of strange, beautiful notions. *Real Genius* contains many pleasures, but one of the best is its conviction that the American campus contains life as we know it.

Red Heat ★ ★ ★
R, 106 m., 1988

Arnold Schwarzenegger (Ivan Danko), James Belushi (Art Ridzik), Peter Boyle (Lou Donnelly), Ed O'Ross (Viktor Rostavili), Larry Fishburne (Lt. Stobbs), Gina Gershon (Cat Manzetti), Marjorie Bransfield (Waitress). Directed by Walter Hill and produced by Hill and Gordon Carroll. Screenplay by Harry Kleiner, Hill, and Troy Kennedy Martin.

Red Heat is not the first movie about a couple of very different cops, and it will not be the last, but as the formula goes, this is a superior example. It's an action picture with a sense of humor and slyly comic performances by Arnold Schwarzenegger and James Belushi, and it's an example of slick professionalism.

Hollywood calls movies like this "high concept" pictures, because you can summarize the plot in a few words, and the words could go like this: Schwarzenegger plays a tough Russian cop who follows a criminal to Chicago and teams up with Belushi as a Chicago slob who knows more about clout than *glasnost*. Take that line and you have the movie. All you have to do is plug in a plot and some shoot-outs and chase scenes.

The man who directed and co-wrote *Red Heat* is Walter Hill, and he is a master at doing just that. Hill specializes in male buddy and action movies, and he more or less reinvented this genre with *48 Hours* and its pairing of Nick Nolte and Eddie Murphy. One of the nice things about *Red Heat* is that it doesn't rip off Hill's earlier picture (except for the basic concept, of course), and finds new things to say about an odd couple of law enforcement.

The Schwarzenegger character is a straight-arrow Russian cop, all business, muscular and tough. The Belushi character is the kind of cop who doesn't believe in busting his buns every second of every day, and who is capable of advising his Soviet comrade to lighten up. He is assigned to Schwarzenegger as sort of a guide and bodyguard, and together they stumble across the usual assortment of weirdos and conspiracies.

What actually happens in the plot is fairly unimportant in movies like this. Style is everything, and if there is a rapport between the two stars, then everything else falls into place. *Red Heat* works because Schwarzenegger and Belushi are both basically comic actors; Arnold's whole career is based on his ability to see the humor in apparently hard-boiled situations. That doesn't mean the actors stand around cracking one-liners, but that even the straight sequences are set-ups for later payoffs, and you get the quiet feeling that both actors are amused by the material.

The premise is that Schwarzenegger, nicknamed Iron Jaw, would rather die than bend, and that Belushi would rather bend than die. Confronted with the capitalistic excesses of Chicago, Schwarzenegger has some conventional Russian criticisms, and Belushi responds with dialogue that often sounds ad-libbed, even if it's not. The two of them both have to placate the hard-boiled captain (Peter Boyle), who issues stern warnings when they violate departmental procedure. At one point, Belushi is actually taken off the case, although that, of course, doesn't change any of his behavior. Boyle's role is the thankless one in the film; the stern chief is the oldest cliché in cop movies, with his obligatory lectures on protocol to tough cops who shift back and forth on their feet like guilty schoolboys.

The film is punctuated by violence, a great deal of violence, although most of it is exaggerated comic-book style instead of being truly gruesome. Walking that fine line is a speciality of Hill, who once simulated the sound of a fist on a chin by making tape recordings of pingpong paddles slapping leather sofas.

Reds ★ ★ ★ ½
PG, 200 m., 1981

Warren Beatty (John Reed), Diane Keaton (Louise Bryant), Edward Herrmann (Max Eastman), Jerzy Kosinski (Zinoviev), Jack Nicholson (Eugene O'Neill), Maureen Stapleton (Emma Goldman), Paul Sorvino (Louis Fraina), Gene Hackman (Pete Van Wherry). Directed and produced by Warren Beatty. Screenplay by Beatty and Trevor Griffiths.

The original John Reed was a dashing young man from Portland who knew a good story when he found one, and, when he found himself in the midst of the Bolshevik revolution, wrote a book called *Ten Days That Shook the World* and made himself a famous journalist. He never quite got it right again after that. He became embroiled in the American left-wing politics of the 1920s, participated in fights between factions of the Socialist Party and the new American Communist Party, and finally returned to Moscow on a series of noble fool's errands that led up, one way or another, to his death from tuberculosis and kidney failure in a Russian hospital. He is the only American buried within the Kremlin walls.

That is Reed's story in a nutshell. But if you look a little more deeply you find a man who was more than a political creature. He was also a man who wanted to be where the action was, a radical young intellectual who was in the middle of everything in the years after World War I, when Greenwich Village was in a creative ferment and American society seemed, for a brief moment, to be overturning itself. It is that personal, human John Reed that Warren Beatty's *Reds* takes as its subject, although there is a lot, and maybe too much, of the political John Reed as well. The movie never succeeds in convincing us that the feuds between the American socialist parties were much more than personality conflicts and ego-bruisings, so audiences can hardly be expected to care which faction is "the" American party of the left.

What audiences can, and possibly will, care about, however, is a traditional Hollywood romantic epic, a love story written on the canvas of history, as they used to say in the ads. And *Reds* provides that with glorious romanticism, surprising intelligence, and a consistent wit. It is the thinking man's *Doctor Zhivago*, told from the other side, of course. The love story stars Warren Beatty and Diane Keaton, who might seem just a tad unlikely as casting choices, but who are immediately engaging and then grow into solid, plausible people on the screen. Keaton is a particular surprise. I had somehow gotten into the habit of expecting her to be a touchy New Yorker, sweet, scared, and intellectual. Here, as a Portland dentist's wife who runs away with John Reed and eventually follows him halfway around the world, through blizzards and prisons and across icy steppes, she is just what she needs to be:

plucky, healthy, exasperated, loyal, and funny.

Beatty, as John Reed, is also surprising. I expected him to play Reed as a serious, noble, heroic man for all seasons, and so he does, sometimes. But there is in Warren Beatty's screen persona a persistent irony, a way of kidding his own seriousness, that takes the edge off a potentially pretentious character and makes him into one of God's fools. Beatty plays Reed but does not beatify him: He permits the silliness and boyishness to coexist with the self-conscious historical mission.

The action in the movie takes Reed to Russia and back again to Portland, and off again with Louise Bryant (Keaton), and then there is a lengthy pause in Greenwich Village and time enough for Louise to have a sad little love affair with the morosely alcoholic playwright Eugene O'Neill (Jack Nicholson). Then there are other missions to Moscow, and heated political debates in New York basements, and at one point I'm afraid I entirely lost track of exactly why Reed was running behind a horsecart in the middle of some forgotten battle in an obscure backwater of the Russian empire. The fact is, Reed's motivation from moment to moment is not the point of the picture. The point is that a revolution is happening, human societies are being swept aside, a new class is in control—or so it seems—and for an insatiably curious young man, that is exhilarating, and it is enough.

The heart of the film is in the relationship between Reed and Bryant. There is an interesting attempt to consider her problems as well as his. She leaves Portland because she is sick unto death of small talk. She wants to get involved in politics, in art, in what's happening: She is so inexorably drawn to Greenwich Village that if Reed had not taken her there, she might have gone on her own. If she was a radical in Portland, however, she is an Oregonian in the Village, and she cannot compete conversationally with such experienced fast-talkers as the anarchist Emma Goldman (Maureen Stapleton). In fact, no one seems to listen to her or pay much heed, except for sad Eugene O'Neill, who is brave enough to love her but not smart enough to keep it to himself. The ways in which she edges toward O'Neill, and then loyally returns to Reed, create an emotional density around her character that makes it really *mean* something when she and Reed embrace at last in a wonderful tear-jerking scene in the Russian train station.

The whole movie finally comes down to the fact that the characters matter to us. Beatty may be fascinated by the ins and outs of American left-wing politics sixty years ago, but he is not so idealistic as to believe an American mass audience can be inspired to care as deeply. So he gives us people. And they are seen here with such warmth and affection that we sense new dimensions not only in Beatty and Keaton, but especially in Nicholson. In *Reds*, understating his desire, apologizing for his passion, hanging around Louise, handing her a poem, throwing her out of his life, he is quieter but much more passionate than in the overwrought *The Postman Always Rings Twice*.

As for Beatty, *Reds* is his bravura turn. He got the idea, nurtured it for a decade, found the financing, wrote most of the script, produced, and directed and starred and still found enough artistic detachment to make his Reed into a flawed, fascinating enigma instead of a boring archetypal hero. I liked this movie. I felt a real fondness for it. It was quite a subject to spring on the capitalist Hollywood movie system, and maybe only Beatty could have raised $35 million to make a movie about a man who hated millionaires. I noticed, here at the end of the credits, a wonderful line that reads:

Copyright © MCMLXXXI Barclays Mercantile Industrial Finance Limited. John Reed would have loved that.

Repo Man ★ ★ ★
R, 92 m., 1984

Harry Dean Stanton (Bud), Emilio Estevez (Otto), Tracey Walter (Miller), Olivia Barash (Leila). Directed by Alex Cox and produced by Jonathan Wacks and Peter McCarthy. Screenplay by Cox.

Repo Man is one of those movies that slips through the cracks and gives us all a little weirdo fun. It is the first movie I know about that combines (1) punk teen-agers, (2) automobile repossessors, and (3) aliens from outer space. This is the kind of movie that baffles Hollywood, because it isn't made from any known formula and doesn't follow the rules. The movie begins with a mad scientist careening down a New Mexico road in his Chevy Malibu. He is stopped by a cop, who finds some really strange things happening in the car's trunk. Then the action moves to Los Angeles, where a punk kid (Emilio Estevez) is passing the time by going to dances and banging his head against other kids' heads, to demonstrate his affection.

The kid runs into a guy named Bud (Harry Dean Stanton), who is an auto repossessor. Bud tricks the kid into driving a repo car for him, and before long the kid is a full-time auto repossessor, learning the ropes. The ropes are pretty tough. Repo men, we learn, live their lives on the edge, operating under extreme tension that is caused partly by their working conditions and partly because as Stanton explains, "I've never known a repo man who didn't use a lot of speed." Harry Dean Stanton is one of the treasures of American movies. He has appeared in a lot of films without becoming a big star, but he has that total cynicism that brings jobs like repo into focus. In the movie, he and Estevez make a nice team; the beaten veteran and the cocky kid, and they cruise the streets looking for cars.

Meanwhile (and here I will be careful to respect some surprises in the story), the government is looking for that Chevy Malibu, because it is connected to the possibility that alien beings have visited the Earth. The feds put out a $10,000 reward for the car, which makes it the jackpot every repo man in L.A. is looking for. Hot on the trail of the car, Stanton and Estevez get into a duel with the famed Rodriguez brothers, known as the bandits of repo. All of this works very nicely, but what's best about *Repo Man* is its sly sense of humor. There are a lot of running gags in the movie, and the best of them involves generic food labels, of all things. (There is a moment involving some food in a refrigerator that gave me one of the biggest laughs I'd had at the movies in a long time.) The movie also has a special way of looking at Los Angeles, seeing it through Harry Dean Stanton's eyes as a wasteland of human ambitions where a few bucks can be made by the quick, the bitter, and the sly.

I saw *Repo Man* near the end of a busy stretch on the movie beat: Three days during which I saw more relentlessly bad movies than during any comparable period in memory. Most of those bad movies were so cynically constructed out of formula ideas and "commercial" ingredients that watching them was an ordeal. *Repo Man* comes out of left field, has no big stars, didn't cost much, takes chances, dares to be unconventional, is funny, and works. There is a lesson here.

The Rescuers Down Under ★ ★ ★
G, 76 m., 1990

With the voices of Bob Newhart (Bernard), Eva Gabor (Miss Bianca), John Candy (Wilbur), George C. Scott (McLeach), Tristan Rogers (Jake), Adam Ryen (Cody), and Wayne Robson (Frank). Directed by Hendel Butoy and Mike Gabriel and produced by Thomas Schumacher. Screenplay by Jim Cox, Karey Kirkpatrick, Byron Simpson, and Joe Ranft.

Animation can give us the glory of sights and experiences that are impossible in the real world, and one of those sights, in *The Rescuers Down Under*, is of a little boy clinging to the back of a soaring eagle. The flight sequence and many of the other action scenes in this new Disney animated feature create an exhiliration and freedom that's liberating. And the rest of the story is fun, too.

The movie marks a return for the tiny rescue squad of brave little mice, first seen in *The Rescuers* (1977). This time they're called to Australia after receiving word that an eagle and a little boy have been kidnapped by an evil poacher, McLeach (with the rasping voice of George C. Scott). Two intrepid rescuers, Bernard and Miss Bianca, with voices by Bob Newhart and Eva Gabor, fly down under on an airline run by, and consisting of, Wilbur the Albatross, whose voice is by John Candy.

Various flight sequences make up a lot of the movie—not only the soaring grace of the eagle, but also the seagull's flopping ineptitude. The animation in these action scenes, like those on Disney's wonderful *Little Mermaid* of 1989, is fully realized, convincing, and entertaining. After a few uncertain years in the 1970s and early 1980s, the Disney animators (assisted now by computers) are back in top form.

The movie's story pits the hero, a little boy named Cody, against the evil poacher McLeach. The villain roams the outback in a gigantic land craft that seems to be a combination of army amphibious vehicle and launching pad. His goal is to capture members of endangered species and sell them for profit—and when the kid tries to protect the eagle, McLeach captures him, too.

It's customary in Disney pictures for the major characters to have minor sidekicks, and there are some delightful new characters in this movie, including Jake, a kangaroo mouse; Joanna, a slithering goanna lizard who is McLeach's sidekick; and Frank, a frill-necked lizard who helps engineer a jailbreak. The good animals conspire against the bad ones and the poacher, as everything leads up to a cliff-hanging sequence in which the next generation of eagles is at stake.

There's one reservation I have about the movie. Why does the villain have to be so noticeably dark-complexioned compared to all of the other characters? Is Disney aware of the racially coded message it is sending? When I made that point to another critic, he argued that McLeach wasn't dark-skinned—he was simply always seen in shadow. Those shadows are cast by insensitivity to negative racial stereotyping.

Return of the Jedi ★ ★ ★ ★
PG, 133 m., 1983

Mark Hamill (Luke Skywalker), Harrison Ford (Han Solo), Carrie Fisher (Princess Leia), Billy Dee Williams (Lando Calrissian), Anthony Daniels (C-3PO), David Prowse (Darth Vader), James Earl Jones (Vader's Voice), Alec Guinness (Obi-Wan Kenobi). Directed by Richard Marquand and produced by Howard Kazanjian. Screenplay by Lawrence Kasdan and George Lucas.

Here is just one small moment in *Return of the Jedi*, a moment you could miss if you looked away from the screen, but a moment that helps explain the special magic of the Star Wars movies. Luke Skywalker is engaged in a ferocious battle in the dungeons beneath the throne room of the loathsome Jabba the Hutt. His adversary is a slimy, gruesome, reptilian monster made of warts and teeth. Things are looking bad when suddenly the monster is crushed beneath a falling door. And then (here is the small moment) there's a shot of the monster's keeper, a muscle-bound jailer, who rushes forward in tears. He is brokenhearted at the destruction of his pet. Everybody loves somebody.

It is that extra level of detail that makes the Star Wars pictures much more than just space operas. Other movies might approach the special effects. Other action pictures might approximate the sense of swashbuckling adventure. But in *Return of the Jedi*, as in *Star Wars* and *The Empire Strikes Back*, there's such a wonderful density to the canvas. Things are happening all over. They're pouring forth from imaginations so fertile that, yes, we do halfway believe in this crazy Galactic Empire long ago and far, far away.

Return of the Jedi is both a familiar movie and a new one. It concludes the stories of the major human characters in the saga, particularly Skywalker, Han Solo, Princess Leia, and Darth Vader. It revisits other characters who seem either more or less than human, including Ben (Obi-Wan Kenobi), Yoda, Chewbacca, and the beloved robots C-3PO and R2-D2. If George Lucas persists in his plan to make nine Star Wars movies, this will nevertheless be the last we'll see of Luke, Han, and Leia, although the robots will be present in all the films.

The story in the Star Wars movies is, however, only part of the film—and a less crucial element as time goes by. What *Jedi* is really giving us is a picaresque journey through the imagination, and an introduction to forms of life less mundane than our own. In *Jedi*, we encounter several unforgettable characters, including the evil Jabba the Hutt, who is a cross between a toad and the Cheshire cat; the lovable, cuddly Ewoks, the furry inhabitants of the "forest moon of Endor"; a fearsome desert monster made of sand and teeth; and hateful little ratlike creatures that scurry about the corners of the frame. And there is an admiral for the Alliance who looks like the missing link between Tyrannosaurus Rex and Charles de Gaulle.

One thing the Star Wars movies never do is waste a lot of time on introductions. Unlike a lot of special-effects and monster movies, where new creatures are introduced with laborious setups, *Jedi* immediately plunges its alien beasts into the thick of the action. Maybe that's why the film has such a sense of visual richness. Jabba's throne room, for example, is populated with several weird creatures, some of them only half-glimpsed in the corner of the frame. The camera in *Jedi* slides casually past forms of life that would provide the centerpiece for lesser movies.

The movie also has, of course, more of the amazing battles in outer space—the intergalactic video games that have been a trademark since *Star Wars*. And *Jedi* finds an interesting variation on that chase sequence in *Star Wars* where the space cruisers hurtled through the narrow canyons on the surface of the Death Star. This time, there's a breakneck chase through a forest, aboard airborne motorcycles. After several of the bad guys have run into trees and gotten creamed, you pause to ask yourself why they couldn't have simply flown *above* the treetops . . . but

never mind, it wouldn't have been as much fun that way.

And *Return of the Jedi* is fun, magnificent fun. The movie is a complete entertainment, a feast for the eyes and a delight for the fancy. It's a little amazing how Lucas and his associates keep topping themselves. From the point of view of simple moviemaking logistics, there is an awesome amount of work on the screen in *Jedi* (twice as many visual effects as *Star Wars* in the space battles, Lucas claims). The fact that the makers of *Jedi* are able to emerge intact from their task, having created a very special work of the imagination, is the sort of miracle that perhaps Obi-Wan would know something about.

Return of the Secaucus Seven ★ ★ ★
NO MPAA RATING, 110 m., 1981

Mark Arnott (Jeff), Gordon Clapp (Chip), Maggie Cousineau-Arndt (Frances), Adam Le Fevre (J.T.), Bruce MacDonald (Mike), Jean Passanante (Irene), John Sayles (Howie), Maggie Renzi (Katie). Directed and written by John Sayles. Produced by William Aydelott and Jeffrey Nelson.

A friend asked me what *Return of the Secaucus Seven* was about. "It's the story of your life," I said.

"*My* life?"

Well, and my life, too. Everybody's life who was younger once and demonstrated against one thing or another, and is older now and stumped for the moment by the curiosity that the most outspoken advocate of change in our society is Ronald Reagan. The movie tells the story of a group of friends who set out during the late 1960s to join the March on the Pentagon, and were arrested in Secaucus, New Jersey, on charges they still do not fully understand. So they didn't make it to the Pentagon, where their brain power might have made the difference in Abbie Hoffman's plan to levitate that building.

Those were strange times. Even Norman Mailer, in his *Armies of the Night*, reported that when the Yippies started to chant and meditate and try to levitate the Pentagon, he looked to see if it had started to rise: An unlikely event, of course, but one that a reporter would always kick himself for if he had missed it. Years have passed since those days. The original members of the Secaucus Seven have grown older now, can taste their

thirtieth birthdays, and as the movie opens have gathered for a weekend reunion in the country. The film tells the story of their weekend, as they take their measure and remember the 1960s.

The Sixties. A director once told me that he had been interviewed by a group of college editors, one of whom asked him, "Was drug usage really prevalent back in the 1960s?" He didn't know whether to laugh or cry. The Secaucus Seven has the same choice. They are never again going to be as young as they were, but they still remember their days of activism so sharply that they refuse to cut loose from them. These days, people still go through their thirtieth birthday crisis, all right, but they seem to hold it on their fortieth birthday.

The Secaucus Seven has grown slightly, with the addition of spouses, lovers, and even children. They gather to play basketball, sing songs, get drunk, fight, break up, and sleep together—or apart. In mood, the film resembles Alain Tanner's wonderful *Jonah Who Will Be 25 in the Year 2000*. Some of the Seven have become fairly successful: There are a congressional aide and a medical student. There is also a kid who is still trying to make it as a folk singer, an occupation that no longer pays very well even if he had the talent, which he does not. And another who has chosen to stay in the old hometown and pump gas.

John Sayles, who wrote and directed the movie, made it as a labor of love (and financed it by writing the screenplays for *Piranha* and *Alligator*, so he may still not quite have evened the scales). He alternates among the various couples and groupings and intrigues, and at first the movie is frankly confusing. We can't keep everybody straight, and there's too much explanation of who they all are and what they've all done. Before long, though, we have everyone sorted out. We know the relationships. And we grow quietly grateful that Sayles has chosen not to pack his weekend reunion with a series of dramatic confrontations and crises. There are no overdoses, suicides, or murders. Only the adjustments such a weekend would be expected to bring, and the inevitable bitterness when one couple has broken up, and the old and new lovers have to confront one another.

This is not a perfect film. Odds and ends stick out, and some scenes have a certain gracelessness. But it is an absorbing film that contains shrewd observations about human nature, and more than its share of humor. We leave with mixed feelings: We feel like we've ended that reunion, and at the same time we're relieved that we did not. It is easier to be young if your friends don't age on you.

Revenge ★ ★ ½
R, 124 m., 1990

Kevin Costner (Cochran), Anthony Quinn (Tibey), Madeleine Stowe (Miryea), Tomas Milian (Cesar), Joaquin Martinez (Mauro), James Gammon (Texan), Jesse Corti (Madero), Sally Kirkland (Rock Star). Directed by Tony Scott and produced by Hunt Lowry and Stanley Rubin. Screenplay by Jim Harrison and Jeffrey Fiskin.

Revenge plays like a showdown between its style and its story. It combines the slick, high-tension filmmaking fashion of today with the values and sexual stereotyping of yesterday. It's such a good job of salesmanship that you have to stop and remind yourself you don't want any. The old action pulp magazines liked strongly plotted stories in which women were viewed as the prizes in a male game, and *Revenge* is right in that tradition. It works like a country song: When your best friend steals your woman, you miss your friend more than your woman.

Revenge is set mostly in today's Mexico, where Anthony Quinn is a powerful, brutal millionaire who rules his own private empire. He's surrounded by killers and henchmen, but he lowers his guard to allow a friend into his inner circle—a former U.S. Air Force pilot (Kevin Costner) who once saved his life on a hunting trip. Costner knows that Quinn has an unsavory reputation, but he doesn't plan to get involved in Quinn's business. He's only on vacation.

That's before he sees Quinn's young wife, played by the beautiful Madeleine Stowe and first seen in a voyeuristic camera shot that starts at her ankles and climbs hand over hand up every wrinkle in her dress. Costner and Stowe fall in love at first sight, while Costner makes himself at home in Quinn's sprawling hacienda and goes on a hunting trip with him. All of these establishing scenes in the movie are effective—the director, Tony Scott, knows what he's doing—and we understand that the Quinn character has made a deliberate decision to lift his ruthless guard to allow this new friend inside.

Then elements of an Idiot Plot begin to appear. It is absolutely clear to us, but apparently not to Costner and Stowe, that Quinn

and his men know everything that goes on within miles of the house. Stowe makes compromising telephone calls that she should have known would be tapped, and then she and Costner have a rendezvous at the local airport. They might as well have taken out an ad in the paper.

There are, of course, the usual steamy sex scenes, at least one of which is not recommended in the front seat of Jeeps going more than thirty miles an hour, and then Quinn's men come bursting in, surprise the lovers, beat Costner to within an inch of his life, grab the faithless Stowe, and deliver her to a nearby bordello ("If you want to be a whore," Quinn explains, "you can be one for the rest of your life").

It's here that the movie betrays its true origins in the adolescent male values of 1940s pulp fiction. The woman is seen as merely a pawn in this contest between men. She is the property of the old lion, the young lion comes sniffing around, and then she's mauled and thrown aside so that the real story—the showdown between the males—can begin. This contest, which leaves not a single bloodsoaked possibility of violence unexplored, leads up to a sick sequence in which Quinn asks for an apology and receives one from Costner, who was his friend but offended him by sleeping with his wife. (No mention of an apology to the wife, who had her face laid open from lip to ear before being held captive in the red-light house.)

It's possible to respond to this material in more than one way. On the one hand, *Revenge* is a well-made movie, directed by Tony Scott with the eroticism he brought to *The Hunger* and the action gusto of his *Top Gun*. It contains the best Anthony Quinn performance in a long time—tough, subtle, convincing. The action scenes are well-handled, and we believe the attraction between Costner and Stowe, who play two very silly people who think they can put one over on Quinn.

All of that works. But still I didn't care about the outcome of the movie, because its values seemed too twisted. In a film like this it is helpful to believe that at least one of the characters is acting wisely and well, and *Revenge* has no righteous characters—they're all silly, stupid, or ruthless. Oddly enough, it's the Quinn character who comes closest to being attractive, because at least he is acting honestly (if by his own depraved values). By the end of the film I felt exhaustion, not exhilaration, because there is no triumph, only a numbed, bloody quiet.

Revenge of the Pink Panther ★ ★ ★
PG, 99 m., 1978

Peter Sellers (Clouseau), Herbert Lom (Dreyfus), Dyan Cannon (Simone), Robert Webber (Douvier), Burt Kwouk (Cato). Directed by Blake Edwards and produced by Tony Adams. Screenplay by Frank Walsman, Ron Clark, and Edwards.

In an uncertain world, Inspector Clouseau survives as an island of certainty. He is certain, first of all, of his genius as the greatest chief of detectives in all of history. He is just as certain of his skill as a deadly karate expert (although, in all their practice encounters, his faithful servant Cato reduces him to a trembling heap). Most poignant of all, he has absolute confidence in the disguises supplied to him by the trusted old family costume firm of Balls & Co.

But Clouseau's charm is in the absolute calm he maintains as his world crumbles about him. When everything has gone wrong, when the homes of innocent bystanders have been turned into smoking ruins, when Hong Kong has, alas, been blown off the map . . . Clouseau turns sharply to his colleagues and snaps, "What did you say?" Because, of course, criticism of his methods is unthinkable.

Clouseau's character was lovingly developed during the course of five movies in fifteen years by Peter Sellers, who played him, and Blake Edwards, who wrote and directed him. The inspector was not always quite the man he eventually became. (Which of us was?) He began, in the original *Pink Panther*, as a more-or-less standard comic Frenchman. It was only in the later films that he emerges as an absolute original, a crazed spirit set aside from mundane humanity, a nut without a country.

Revenge of the Pink Panther, which Sellers said was to be the inspector's last adventure (Edwards was not so sure), is quintessential Clouseau. He occupies the center of a maelstrom, confident that no one will notice him in his bizarre disguises, certain that no one could possibly suspect that the dwarfish figure in the corner, the one with the Toulouse-Lautrec costume and the Adidas running shoes, could possibly be Jacques Clouseau. He has reason for his confidence: The film opens with his funeral and burial, at which all France heaves a sigh of relief.

But Clouseau is not dead, merely sidetracked for a moment in his latest case in a showdown with the French Connection.

Someone is bringing contraband drugs into France from Hong Kong, and Clouseau, as he is the first to admit, is the man to stop them. He warms up in one of Edwards's most elaborate sight gags, an impossible series of misadventures that ends with the collapse of three floors of a house.

The movie is strongest in its sight gags. Edwards and Sellers seem to be returning to silent slapstick for their inspiration (although sound is, of course, useful when Clouseau mangles the language, speaking English as if it were very, very bad French). There are chases involving an ice cream wagon and bizarre miscalculations in the Chinese bordello that Cato has established in Clouseau's apartment. And then there are all of those disguises—especially the one in which Sellers appears as a sailor and a stuffed parrot is attached horizontally to the old salt's shoulder.

There is, alas, a plot here somewhere, although Edwards and Sellers take it with no more seriousness than in the preceding two Clouseau films (*Return of the Pink Panther* and *The Pink Panther Strikes Again*). Robert Webber plays a mafioso in charge of smuggling drugs into France, and Herbert Lom is, once again, the chief inspector who always winds up discovering Clouseau mangling the case.

Movies like this exist in the moment; like all true slapstick, they're cheerfully willing to do anything to make us laugh, and Edwards is not afraid of throwing in pratfalls, explosions, and people hurtling through the air, if that'll keep things moving. I like his spirit. And Sellers, of course, remains the essence of Clouseaudom. As he struggles with his unique pronunciation of "bomb" (it approximates "beaumbe"), we gradually realize, with him, that he would be incapable of making a bomb threat except by mail.

Reversal of Fortune ★ ★ ★ ★
R, 110 m., 1990
(See related Film Clip, p. 706.)

Glenn Close (Sunny von Bulow), Jeremy Irons (Claus von Bulow), Ron Silver (Alan M. Dershowitz), Annabella Sciorra (Carol), Uta Hagen (Maria), Fisher Stevens (David Marriott), Christine Baranski (Andrea Reynolds). Directed by Barbet Schroeder and produced by Edward R. Pressman and Oliver Stone. Screenplay by Nicholas Kazan.

I followed the investigative accounts of the von Bulow case with that special attention I always pay to the troubles of society people. With their advantages and connections, they have a better chance of being involved in a stimulating crime. Some of them, it is true, simply stab or shoot one another, but a few go to the trouble of using classic means—poisons and deceptions, subterfuge and wit. With all the lack of subtlety in modern murder, it is heartening to find that a few people still aspire to the perfect crime.

Having seen *Reversal of Fortune*, the story of Claus von Bulow's two trials on the charge of attempting to murder his wife, I am no closer than before to a clear idea of who did what, or why. That is the charm of the movie. Something terrible happened to Sunny von Bulow on that winter day eleven years ago, and nobody knows exactly what it was. The victim still lingers in a coma. Her husband was convicted of murder, but his conviction was overturned, and there is compelling suspicion that some of the evidence used against him was fishy.

And now we have this film, based on a book by Alan J. Dershowitz, the famous Harvard professor who conducted Claus von Bulow's appeal. It is a surprisingly entertaining film—funny, wicked, sharp-tongued, and devious. It does not solve the case, nor intend to. I am afraid it only intends to entertain. Because Sunny von Bulow does indeed lie in a coma, I felt at first a little guilty that I enjoyed the film so much. But I am in attendance as a critic, not a priest or prosecutor, and, like the other witnesses, I can only testify from my own experience.

The genius of *Reversal of Fortune* is that the story is narrated by Sunny from her sickbed. We hear her voice, wondering aloud at the chain of events caused by that day when she sank into her long sleep. She guides us through the details of the case. She reminisces about the first time she met Claus, about what she felt for him, about how their marriage progressed. She confesses herself as confused as anyone about what happened on her last day of consciousness. "You tell me," she says, and somehow this gives us permission to look at the film in a more genial mood.

The opening shot, taken from a helicopter, shows the great mansions of Newport, Rhode Island. They stand like sentinels at the edge of the sea, flaunting their wealth at the waves. In one of those mansions Sunny von Bulow lived with Claus and the children they had together or previously.

How could one not be entertained by living in such a place? And yet, Sunny seems to seek the escape of unconsciousness. She abuses pills and alcohol. After brief forays into the world, she retreats to her bed. She is not really present for her family; her mind is clouded, and her memory shaky. While her body goes through the motions of smoking and drinking and taking pills, her mind yawns and dozes.

One day she nearly dies, probably of an overdose, but is rescued in time. A year later, she is not so lucky, and by the time help is summoned she is in a coma. What happened? The maid says she was worried for hours before Claus would let her call for help. Claus says he thought she was sleeping; she had often slumbered deeply before. But how did she end up on the bathroom floor? And what about the insulin? Did Claus administer a fatal overdose? Whose insulin was it, anyway? And who found it?

The question of the insulin is what finally brings Alan Dershowitz into the appeal, after Claus is found guilty. The evidence was gathered by private investigators hired by Sunny's children, and then turned over to the authorities, and Dershowitz decides that the rich simply cannot be permitted to hire their own police and decide among themselves which evidence should be made available. It isn't fair. There are also questions about many other aspects of the case—so many that, if Claus is not innocent, there is at least no way to prove that he is guilty.

Reversal of Fortune is above all a triumph of tone. The director, Barbet Schroeder, and the writer, Nicholas Kazan, have not made a docu-drama or a sermon, but a film about personalities. The most extraordinary personality in the film is von Bulow's, as he is played by Jeremy Irons. He appears as a man with affections and bizarre mannerisms, a man who speaks as if he lifted his words from an arch drawing-room comedy, who smokes a cigarette as if hailing a taxi. Irons is able to suggest, subtly, that some of this over-the-top behavior is the result of fear. Von Bulow cannot modulate his tone, cannot find the right note, because beneath his facade he is quaking.

And yet he keeps up a brave front. That is one of the best qualities of the film, the way it shows him trying to brazen his way out of an impossible situation. If he wins, he keeps the fortune and the lifestyle. If he loses, he ends his life in jail. The man who can save him is Dershowitz, played by Ron Silver as a hyperkinetic showboat who surrounds himself with students and acolytes, possibly as a protection against the fear of silence. The law students plunge like beavers into their research, triumphantly emerging with new strategies for their leader, who does not like von Bulow much and doubts his innocence, but believes the case raises important legal points.

Glenn Close is important too, as Sunny. She appears in some flashbacks as well as narrating the film, and we see the things we need to notice: Her beauty and personality when she's got it together, and the vague lost confusion of her alcoholic and tranquilized daydreams. Without nudging us, the film shows us two things. First, why a man might finally be tempted to allow his wife to slip into the oblivion she seems so desperately to desire. Second, how she could have accidentally overdosed in any event.

What happened? Who knows. The movie's strength is its ability to tantalize, to turn the case this way and that, so that the light of evidence falls in one way and then another. You tell me.

Richard Pryor Here and Now
★ ★ ★ ★
R, 94 m., 1983

A documentary written and directed by Richard Pryor and produced by Bob Parkinson and Andy Friendly.

Is there anyone else in America who could have pulled off this film? *Richard Pryor Here and Now* is a documentary of one man talking. Pryor walks onto the stage of the Saenger Theater in New Orleans, establishes an immediate rapport with the audience, and away he goes. At the end of the movie we have been wrung out with laughter—and with a few other things, too, because Pryor is more than a comedian in this film: He's a social commentator and a man talking honestly about himself.

This is Pryor's third concert film. The first one, *Richard Pryor Live in Concert*, was made before he set himself on fire while freebasing cocaine. The second, *Richard Pryor Live on the Sunset Strip* (1982), recorded his first filmed concert after the accident, and included his description of Jim Brown's attempts to talk him out of drug use, and Pryor's own now-famous dialogue with cocaine. In *Here and Now*, filmed in August 1983 with Brown as executive producer,

Pryor firmly says he hasn't used drugs or alcohol for seven months. The arithmetic would seem to suggest that he hadn't stopped using everything when he made the second film, or that he had a relapse after his initial hospitalization. I mention that only because the Richard Pryor we see on screen in *Here and Now* has obviously found some kind of peace with himself that was lacking in the *Sunset Strip* film.

He can smile more easily. He doesn't have to reach for effects. He handles audience interruptions with grace and cool. He is the master of his instrument. And he takes bigger chances. Some of his material covers familiar ground—sex, booze, race, marriages. But all along he's showing his gift for populating the stage with a lot of different characters. He goes in and out of accents, body language, and characters, giving us confused drunks, defensive husbands, shrill wives, uptight WASPs, impenetrable Africans ("Everybody speaks English," one tells him in Zimbabwe, "but what language do you speak at *home?*"). And then at the end of his act, he goes into an extended characterization of a street black shooting heroin. In this character are humor and pain, self-deception and touching honesty, and the end of the sketch comes closer to tragedy than it does to comedy.

Pryor is a spokesman for our dreams and fears, the things we find funny and the things we're frightened of. He has assumed a role that has previously been filled by such comedians as Will Rogers, Lenny Bruce, Mort Sahl, and Woody Allen—all men who, as Rogers put it, talked about what they'd just seen in the papers. Pryor works off issues and subjects that are absolutely current, and he addresses them with a humor that is aimed so well, we duck. His story could have gone either way. He could have been killed in that wasteful accident. But he was not, and now, given a second chance, he is paying his dues.

Richard Pryor Live on the Sunset Strip
★ ★ ★ ★
R, 82 m., 1982

Directed by Joe Layton and produced by Richard Pryor.

At the beginning of this film, Richard Pryor is clearly nervous. He is back on a stage for the first time since he set himself on fire. That means he is working with the stand-up

comedian's greatest handicap, the audience's awareness of his vulnerability. Whatever else they do, comics must project utter confidence in their material, and when Pryor had his accident, he also had his whole hip image blown out from under him. So it's a shaky start. He begins by almost defiantly using the word "fuck" as an incantation, employing it not so much for shock value (does it still have any?) as for punctuation. His timing is a little off. He is not, at first, the supremely confident, cocky Richard Pryor of his earlier films. But as he gets rolling, as he populates the stage with a whole series of characters, we watch the emergence of a Richard Pryor who is older, wiser, and funnier than before. And the last fifty or sixty minutes of this film are extraordinary.

Richard Pryor Live on the Sunset Strip was filmed at the Hollywood Palladium, down at the unfashionable east end of that legendary street of rock clubs, restaurants, hookers and heroes, hot-pillow motels, and some of the most expensive real estate in the world. The movie opens with a montage of the strip's neon signs (including the Chateau Marmont, where John Belushi died). Then it cuts inside to the Palladium auditorium, and Pryor walks onstage and lays claim to being the most talented one-man stage show in existence right now.

His gift is to be funny and painfully self-analytical at the same time. Like Bill Cosby, he gets a lot of his material out of memories of growing up black in America. But he sees deeper than Cosby, and his vignettes capture small truths and build them into an attitude. In the brilliant middle sections of this film, he uses just his own voice and body to create little one-act plays, such as the one where he recalls working in a Mafia-owned nightclub in Ohio. In that one, his Italian-American-gangster accent is perfectly heard; in another skit, about the animals in Africa, he turns into a gifted physical comedian, getting laughs out of his impressions of the movements of gazelles, water buffaloes, and lions—and ending with a hilarious observation of the body language of two whites passing each other on the street in black Africa.

The whole middle passage of the film is that good. The last twenty minutes is one of the most remarkable marriages of comedy and truth I have ever seen. He talks with great honesty about his drug addiction, his accident, and how his life has changed since he stopped using drugs. He confesses that in the three weeks before his accident, he holed up alone in his room with his cocaine pipe, which talked to him in reassuring, seductive tones uncannily like Richard Nixon's. Then a friend, the actor Jim Brown, came to see him, and asked him flat-out, "Whatcha gonna do?" There was nothing he wanted to do but hide in drugs. What he finally did was set himself on fire.

I saw the film the same day that actor Shay Duffin opened his one-man evening with Brendan Behan at the Apollo Theater Center in Chicago. The papers that day carried the news that Belushi had overdosed. Behan, of course, killed himself with alcohol. Some day, inevitably, an actor will give us an evening with John Belushi. The dramatic structure is all there, for the Behans and Belushis: The genius, the laughter, and the doomed drive to self-destruction. Watching *Richard Pryor Live on the Sunset Strip*, a breathtaking performance by a man who came within a hair of killing himself with drugs, was like a gift, as if Pryor had come back from the dead to perform in his own one-man memory of himself. It is good we still have him. He is better than ever.

The Right Stuff ★ ★ ★ ★
PG, 193 m., 1983

Sam Shepard (Chuck Yeager), Ed Harris (John Glenn), Fred Ward (Gus Grissom), Dennis Quaid (Gordon Cooper), Scott Glenn (Alan Shepard), Barbara Hershey (Glennis Yeager), Mary Jo Deschanel (Annie Glenn), Pamela Reed (Trudy Cooper). Directed by Philip Kaufman and produced by Irwin Winkler and Robert Chartoff. Screenplay by Kaufman.

At the beginning of *The Right Stuff*, a cowboy reins in his horse and regards a strange sight in the middle of the desert: the X-1 rocket plane, built to break the sound barrier. At the end of the film, the seven Mercury astronauts are cheered in the Houston Astrodome at a Texas barbecue thrown by Lyndon B. Johnson. The contrast between those two images contains the message of *The Right Stuff*, I think, and the message is that Americans still have the right stuff, but we've changed our idea of what it is.

The original American heroes were loners. The cowboy is the perfect example. He was silhouetted against the horizon and he rode into town by himself and if he had a sidekick, the sidekick's job was to admire him. The new American heroes are team players. No wonder Westerns aren't made much anymore; cowboys don't play on teams. The cowboy at the beginning of *The Right Stuff* is Chuck Yeager, the legendary lone-wolf test pilot who survived the horrifying death rate among early test pilots (more than sixty were killed in a single month) and did fly the X-1 faster than the speed of sound. The movie begins with that victory, and then moves on another ten years to the day when the Russians sent up Sputnik, and the Eisenhower administration hustled to get back into the space race.

The astronauts who eventually rode the first Mercury capsules into space may not have been that much different from Chuck Yeager. As they're portrayed in the movie, anyway, Gus Grissom, Scott Carpenter, and Gordon Cooper seem to have some of the same stuff as Yeager. But the astronauts were more than pilots; they were a public-relations image, and the movie shows sincere, smooth-talking John Glenn becoming their unofficial spokesman. The X-1 flew in secrecy, but the Mercury flights were telecast, and we were entering a whole new era, the selling of space. There was a lot going on, and there's a lot going on in the movie, too. *The Right Stuff* is an adventure film, a special-effects film, a social commentary, and a satire. That the writer-director, Philip Kaufman, is able to get so much into a little more than three hours is impressive. That he also has organized this material into one of the best recent American movies is astonishing. *The Right Stuff* gives itself the freedom to move around in moods and styles, from a broadly based lampoon of government functionaries to Yeager's spare, taciturn manner and Glenn's wonderment at the sights outside his capsule window.

The Right Stuff has been a landmark movie in a lot of careers. It announces Kaufman's arrival in the ranks of major directors. It contains uniformly interesting performances by a whole list of unknown or little-known actors, including Ed Harris (Glenn), Scott Glenn (Alan Shepard), Fred Ward (Grissom), and Dennis Quaid (Cooper). It confirms the strong and sometimes almost mystical screen presence of playwright Sam Shepard, who played Yeager. And it joins a short list of recent American movies that might be called experimental epics: movies that have an ambitious reach through time and subject matter, that spend freely for locations or special effects, but that consider each scene as intently as an art film. *The*

Right Stuff goes on that list with *The God-father*, *Nashville*, *Apocalypse Now*, and maybe *Patton* and *Close Encounters*. It's a great film.

Risky Business ★ ★ ★ ★
R, 96 m., 1983

Tom Cruise (Joel), Rebecca De Mornay (Lana), Curtis Armstrong (Miles), Bronson Pinchot (Barry), Joe Pantoliano (Guido). Directed by Paul Brickman and produced by Joe Avnet and Steve Tisch. Screenplay by Brickman.

Risky Business is a movie about male adolescent guilt. In other words, it's a comedy. It's funny because it deals with subjects that are so touchy, so fraught with emotional pain, that unless we laugh there's hardly any way we can deal with them—especially if we are now, or ever were, a teen-age boy. The teenager in the movie is named Joel. His family lives in a suburb on Chicago's North Shore. It's the sort of family that has three cars: the family station wagon, Mom's car, and Dad's Porsche. As the movie opens, Mom and Dad are going off on vacation to a sun-drenched consumer paradise and their only son, Joel, is being left alone at home. It's a busy time in Joel's life. He's got college board exams, an interview with a Princeton admissions officer, and finals at high school.

It gets to be an even busier time after his parents leave. Joel gets involved in an ascending pyramid of trouble. He calls a number in one of those sex-contact magazines and meets a young hooker who moves into the house. He runs afoul of the girl's pimp. His mother's expensive Steuben egg is stolen. His dad's Porsche ends up in Lake Michigan. The family home turns into a brothel. He blows two finals. And so on. This description may make *Risky Business* sound like a predictable sitcom. It is not. It is one of the smartest, funniest, most perceptive satires in a long time. It not only invites comparison with *The Graduate*, it earns it. Here is a great comedy about teen-age sex.

The very best thing about the movie is its dialogue. Paul Brickman, who wrote and directed, has an ear so good that he knows what to leave out. This is one of those movies where a few words or a single line says everything that needs to be said, implies everything that needs to be implied, *and* gets a laugh. When the hooker tells the kid, "Oh, Joel, go to school. Learn something," the precise inflection of those words defines their relationship for the next three scenes.

The next best thing about the movie is the casting. Rebecca De Mornay somehow manages to take that thankless role, the hooker with a heart of gold, and turn it into a very specific character. She isn't all good and she isn't all clichés: she's a very complicated young woman with quirks and insecurities and a wayward ability to love. I became quietly astounded when I realized that this movie was going to create an original, *interesting* relationship involving a teen-ager and a hooker. The teen-age kid, in what will be called the Dustin Hoffman role, is played by Tom Cruise, who also knows how to imply a whole world by what he won't say, can't feel, and doesn't understand.

This is a movie of new faces and inspired insights and genuine laughs. It's hard to make a good movie and harder to make a good comedy and almost impossible to make a satire of such popular but mysterious obsessions as guilt, greed, lust, and secrecy. This movie knows what goes on behind the closed bathroom doors of the American dream.

Rita, Sue and Bob Too ★ ★ ★
R, 95 m., 1987

George Costigan (Bob), Siobhan Finneran (Rita), Michelle Holmes (Sue), Lesley Sharp (Michelle), Kulvinder Ghir (Aslam), Willie Ross (Sue's Father), Patti Nicholls (Sue's Mother), Paul Oldham (Lee). Directed by Alan Clarke and produced by Sandy Lieberson. Screenplay by Andrea Dunbar.

I've seen *Rita, Sue and Bob Too* twice, and the audiences were uneasy both times. They didn't seem sure exactly what to feel about this film. I'm not sure, either. The movie is a bleak, sardonic British comedy about the violation of a taboo: A married man in his thirties has affairs with two teen-age girls who are his baby-sitters. If this were a solemn TV docudrama with a psychiatrist to explain everything, we could relax. But it's an angry comedy, further complicated because both of the girls are so sassy and irreverent that it's hard to see them as victims.

The movie opens in a grim housing estate on the barren outskirts of a nondescript midlands city. One long shot establishes the scene: A drunk lurches into view, totters down the sidewalk, and disappears into a depressing brick building, and then a girl comes scurrying out, dressed for school, and runs down the street to meet her friend, whose front yard is occupied by a motorcycle gang.

The two girls are Rita and Sue. They are in their mid-teens but they already look worn by life, and yet they're filled with spirit. Rita (Siobhan Finneran) is more conventional, Sue (Michelle Holmes) is more likely to say things for shock effect, but they're peas in a pod. Like a lot of adolescent best friends, they can finish each other's sentences, and sometimes when the vibes are right they can even speak in unison.

That night they go to baby-sit at Bob and Michelle's home in a nearby suburb that is cosmetically more attractive than where Rita and Sue live, although perhaps there is just as much desperation behind the picture windows. There's a great scene of the two girls sitting side by side on a sofa, bouncing in time to a music video; we can see how young they really are, something that's not always very obvious.

Late at night, Bob brings his wife home and offers to drive the two girls home. Instead, they drive into the country, park overlooking the town, and have sex. Bob proposes the idea, they giggle, and then they get right to it, right there in the car. This is the scene that's hard to read. It is sordid, and Bob's behavior is certainly immoral, and yet the sex itself has a sort of low, bawdy humor to it, and the girls seem surprisingly casual about it.

To fortunate people with middle-class opportunities, the whole episode is likely to seem shocking. But the film means to shock, and the statement it makes is a political one. Rita and Sue come from utterly deprived homes, from the culture of poverty. Nothing is happening in their lives. Bob provides variety, someone to gossip and speculate about, and his demands are no more inconvenient for them than the casual, brutal promiscuity they see at home. The movie challenges us to disapprove of the conditions that produced Rita and Sue, rather than to take a safe, superficial stand against that rascal Bob.

But here I am lecturing, and the curious thing about *Rita, Sue and Bob Too* is that it does not lecture and contains no speeches. It is a comedy, if a sometimes depressing one, and the best thing in it is the irrepressible sauciness of the two girls. If this were an American film, it would be an R-rated sex romp without a brain in its head, another soft-core baby-sitter saga. But *Rita, Sue and Bob Too* is one of those recent small-scale British films that are more interested in human nature than in selling lots of tickets with lots of sex.

This is a movie about two tough, deprived girls from the worst part of town, and an irresponsible, feather-brained adult who thinks he's taking advantage of them when in fact they're a whole lot more worldly and cynical than he is. These aren't bad girls. They're totally without standards—after all, they haven't been taught any—but they have a sense of humor and high spirits, and this is one of those movies you talk about a lot afterward, because the motives of all the characters are so complicated that you're not absolutely sure just who came out ahead.

River's Edge ★ ★ ★ ½
R, 100 m., 1987

Crispin Glover (Layne), Dennis Hopper (Feck), Keanu Reeves (Matt), Ione Skye (Clarissa), Daniel Roebuck (Leitch Sampson), Joshua Miller (Tim), Roxana Zal (Maggie). Directed by Tim Hunter and produced by Sarah Pillsbury and Midge Sanford. Screenplay by Neal Jimenez.

I remember reading about the case at the time. A high school kid killed his girlfriend and left her body lying on the ground. Over the next few days, he brought some of his friends out to look at her body, and gradually word of the crime spread through his circle of friends. But for a long time, nobody called the cops.

A lot of op-ed articles were written to analyze this event, which was seen as symptomatic of a wider moral breakdown in our society. *River's Edge*, which is a horrifying fiction inspired by the case, offers no explanation and no message; it regards the crime in much the same way the kid's friends stood around looking at the body. The difference is that the film feels a horror that the teen-agers apparently did not.

This is the best analytical film about a crime since *The Onion Field* and *In Cold Blood*. Like those films, it poses these questions: Why do we need to be told this story? How is it useful to see limited and brutish people doing cruel and stupid things? I suppose there are two answers. One, because such things exist in the world and some of us are curious about them as we are curious in general about human nature. Two, because an artist is never merely a reporter and by seeing the tragedy through his eyes, he helps us to see it through ours.

River's Edge was directed by Tim Hunter, who made *Tex*, about ordinary teen-agers who found themselves faced with the choice of dealing drugs. In *River's Edge*—that choice has long since been made. These teenagers are alcoholics and drug abusers, including one whose mother is afraid he is stealing her marijuana and a twelve-year-old who blackmails the older kids for six-packs.

The central figure in the film is not the murderer, Sampson (Daniel Roebuck), a large, stolid youth who seems perpetually puzzled about why he does anything. It is Layne (Crispin Glover), a strung-out, mercurial rebel who always seems to be on speed and who takes it upon himself to help conceal the crime. When his girlfriend asks him, like, well, gee, she was our friend and all, so shouldn't we feel bad, or something, his answer is that the murderer "had his reasons." What were they? The victim was talking back.

Glover's performance is electric. He's like a young Eric Roberts, and he carries around a constant sense of danger. Eventually, we realize the danger is born of paranoia; he is reflecting it at us with his fear.

These kids form a clique that exists outside the mainstream in their high school. They hang around outside, smoking and sneering. In town, they have a friend named Feck (Dennis Hopper), a drug dealer who lives inside a locked house and once killed a woman himself, so he has something in common with the kid, you see? It is another of Hopper's possessed performances, done with sweat and the whites of his eyes.

River's Edge is not a film I will forget very soon. Its portrait of these adolescents is an exercise in despair. Not even old enough to legally order a beer, they already are destroyed by alcohol and drugs, abandoned by parents who also have lost hope. When the story of the dead girl first appeared in the papers, it seemed like a freak show, an aberration. *River's Edge* sets it in an ordinary town and makes it seem like just what the op-ed philosophers said: an emblem of breakdown. The girl's body eventually was discovered and buried. If you seek her monument, look around you.

The Road Warrior ★ ★ ★ ¹⁄₂
R, 97 m., 1982

Mel Gibson (Max), Bruce Spence (Gyro Captain), Vernon Wells (Wez), Emil Minty (Feral Kid), Virginia Hey (Warrior Woman). Directed by George Miller and produced by Byron Kennedy. Screenplay by Terry Hayes, Miller, and Brian Hannant.

The Road Warrior is a film of pure action, of kinetic energy organized around the barest possible bones of a plot. It has a vision of a violent future world, but it doesn't develop that vision with characters and dialogue. It would rather plunge headlong into one of the most relentlessly aggressive movies ever made. I walked out of *The Road Warrior* a little dizzy and with my ears still ringing from the roar of the sound track; I can't say I "enjoyed" the film, but I'll hardly forget it. The movie takes place at a point in the future when civilization has collapsed, anarchy and violence reign in the world, and roaming bands of marauders kill each other for the few remaining stores of gasoline. The vehicles of these future warriors are leftovers from the world we live in now. There are motorcycles and semi-trailer trucks and oil tankers that are familiar from the highways of 1982, but there are also bizarre customized racing cars, of which the most fearsome has two steel posts on its front to which enemies can be strapped (if the car crashes, the enemies are the first to die).

The road warriors of the title take their costumes and codes of conduct from a rummage sale of legends, myths, and genres: They look and act like Hell's Angels, samurai warriors, kamikaze pilots, street-gang members, cowboys, cops, and race drivers. They speak hardly at all; the movie's hero, Max, has perhaps two hundred words. Max is played by Mel Gibson, an Australian actor who starred in *Gallipoli*. Before that, he made *Mad Max* for the makers of *The Road Warrior*, and that film was a low-budget forerunner to this extravaganza of action and violence. Max's role in *The Road Warrior* is to behave something like a heroic cowboy might have in a classic Western. He happens upon a small band of people who are trying to protect their supplies of gasoline from the attacks of warriors who have them surrounded. Max volunteers to drive a tanker full of gasoline through the surrounding warriors and take it a few hundred miles to the coast, where they all hope to find safety.

After this premise is established with a great deal of symbolism, ritual, and violence (and so few words that sometimes we have to guess what's happening), the movie arrives at its true guts. The set piece in *The Road Warrior* is an unbelievably well-sustained chase sequence that lasts for the last third of the film, as Max and his semi-trailer run a gauntlet of everything the savages can throw at them.

The director of *The Road Warrior*, George Miller, compares this chase sequence to Buster Keaton's *The General*, and I can see what he means. Although *The General* is comedic, it's also very exciting, as Keaton, playing the engineer of a speeding locomotive, runs an endless series of variations on the basic possibilities of two trains and several sets of railroad tracks. In *The Road Warrior*, there is basically a truck and a road. The pursuers and defenders have various kinds of cars and trucks to chase or defend the main truck, and the whole chase proceeds at breakneck speed as quasi-gladiators leap through the air from one racing truck to another, more often than not being crushed beneath the wheels. The special effects and stunts in this movie are spectacular; *The Road Warrior* goes on a short list with *Bullitt*, *The French Connection*, and the truck chase in *Raiders of the Lost Ark* as among the great chase films of modern years.

What is the point of the movie? Everyone is free to interpret the action, I suppose, but I prefer to avoid thinking about the implications of gasoline shortages and the collapse of Western civilization, and to experience the movie instead as pure sensation. The filmmakers have imagined a fictional world. It operates according to its special rules and values, and we experience it. The experience is frightening, sometimes disgusting, and (if the truth be told) exhilarating. This is very skillful filmmaking, and *The Road Warrior* is a movie like no other.

Road House ★ ★ ¹⁄₂
R, 107 m., 1989

Patrick Swayze (Dalton), Kelly Lynch (Doc), Sam Elliott (Wade Garrett), Ben Gazzara (Brad Wesley), Marshall Teague (Jimmy), Julie Michaels (Denise), Red West (Red Webster). Directed by Rowdy Herrington and produced by Joel Silver. Screenplay by David Lee Henry and Hilary Henkin.

The guiding spirit of *Road House* can be glimpsed in one particular scene, which is set in the trophy room of an evil sadist who holds a helpless town in his iron grasp. His hunting trophies include not only the usual deer and elk and antelopes, but also orangutans, llamas, and a matched set of tropical monkeys. This guy went hunting in the zoo.

We are expected to believe that the sadist financed these hunting expeditions by shaking down the businessmen in a town which, on the visible evidence, contains a bar, a general store, a Ford dealership, and two residences. *Road House* is the kind of movie which leaves reality so far behind that you have to cave in and accept it on its own terms.

Was it intended as a parody? I have no idea, but I laughed more during this movie than during any of the so-called comedies I saw during the same week. Consider, for example, the movie's hero, a bar-room bouncer name Dalton and played by Patrick Swayze (last seen in *Dirty Dancing*). Here is a man known as the best bouncer in the business—and the business must pay well, since he owns a Mercedes convertible. But he is not simply your average tough guy. He has a Ph.D. in philosophy from New York University, and is capable of deep insights into his trade, such as, "In a fight, nobody wins."

Dalton is summoned to a small Missouri town where the Double Deuce, the local nightclub, is terrorized nightly by the local goons and louts. His assignment: Bring peace to the bar, so the owner can remodel and expand. His enemies: The hired guns of Brad Wesley (Ben Gazzara), the extortionist with the exotic trophy room. (Everyone in this movie has names out of a Western—not only Dalton and Brad Wesley, but also such characters as Wade Garrett, Doc, Emmet, and Cody. Doc is a girl, but never mind.)

Dalton wades into the fray on opening night and finds himself in the middle of a fight in which the furnishings of the Double Deuce are reduced to matchsticks. Wounded by a knife cut, he goes to the hospital, where the gash is sewn closed by Doc (Kelly Lynch), a beautiful blonde who is impressed by Dalton's doctorate in philosophy and his ability to withstand pain.

In no time at all, Dalton and Doc are making love on the porch roof outside Dalton's rented room—a roof that can clearly be seen by the evil Brad Wesley, who once entertained his own hopes of becoming Doc's lover. (These two houses, on either side of a river, seem to be the only homes in town, and most of what goes on in each house seems to be staged for the benefit of the other.)

Dalton sees he needs help to clean up the bar. So he calls in his best friend, Wade Garrett (Sam Elliott), who is the second-best bar-room bouncer in the world. (Note to cable TV operators: The world finals of bouncing might pull in decent ratings.) This upsets Brad Wesley no end, since his income depends on maintaining an iron rule of terror over the local townspeople.

Road House is said to be based on that actual case in Missouri where the local bad guy, universally hated by everyone in town, was murdered in broad daylight—and no one in town seems to have seen a thing. If that is the genesis for the story, everything else in it seems to have come from a cheerful willingness to go over the top in every way possible.

This is the first movie in a long time to use the line, "Prepare to die!" And how long has it been since the same movie contained (a) a dash into an exploding building to save an occupant; (b) a rock & roll band protected by a plexiglass shield; (c) goons who line up for instructions and call the bad guy "boss;" (d) a lecture on the fine points of bouncing; (e) a sexy woman doctor who goes all the way on the first date; and (e) random quotations from the great Western philosophers?

This movie is so top-heavy with plot, it can even afford to ignore some obvious possibilities. For example, Swayze's rented room is on a ranching spread across the river from Gazzara, and Gazzara is so busy with his other villainous duties that he doesn't have time for the standard subplot in which he wants to run the rancher off the land so he can build a subdivision. Of course, in a town with two residences, there may not be much pent-up housing demand.

Robin Hood: Prince of Thieves ★ ★
PG-13, 138 m., 1991

Kevin Costner (Robin Hood), Morgan Freeman (Azeem), Christian Slater (Will Scarlett), Alan Rickman (Sheriff of Nottingham), Mary Elizabeth Mastrantonio (Maid Marian), Nick Brimble (Little John). Directed by Kevin Reynolds and produced by John Watson, Pen Densham, and Richard Lewis. Screenplay by Densham and John Watson.

Robin Hood: Prince of Thieves is a murky, unfocused, violent, and depressing version of the classic story, with little of the light-heartedness and romance we expect from Robin Hood. It's shot mostly at night or in gloomy forests, beneath overcasts or by

flickering firelight or in gloomy dungeons, which is all very well for the atmosphere, but makes the action scenes almost impossible to follow.

Among the movie's many problems: Kevin Costner plays a tortured, thoughtful Robin Hood, totally lacking in the joy of living that we associate with the character. The romance between Robin and Maid Marian (Mary Elizabeth Mastrantonio) seems inspired more by necessity than by desire, as if both of them had read the book and knew they were required to fall in love with one another. The most colorful character is the villain, the Sheriff of Nottingham (Alan Rickman), but both the character and the performance are inappropriate for this film. And the amount of gore is appalling in a film that will presumably be aimed at a family market.

To begin with the gore: The movie begins with a hand being chopped off, and continues with various amputations, gorings, stabbings, burnings, floggings, hangings (a small boy is one of the intended hanging victims), explosions, and falls from great heights, before reaching a climax of sorts as the Sheriff of Nottingham attempts to rape Maid Marian, and has just succeeded in spreading her legs (a graphic floor-level shot here) before Robin Hood comes swinging in through the window to save her.

Then there is the general moral climate of the movie, in which all of the priests are seen as corrupt or drunken swine, and the sheriff consults an old crone in a dungeon who foretells the future by reading blood and chicken bones. The leading cleric of Nottingham is a turncoat and a liar, who marries Marian to the sheriff against her will while the castle is under siege. You know we have entered a shaky liturgical era when Friar Tuck is the most religious person in the film.

The movie casts Robin Hood as sort of a populist guerilla, a Che Guevera with bow and arrow, who lives with his followers in Sherwood Forest and intercepts the king's mail by using tunnels and camouflaged hiding-places under the forest floor, Viet Cong style. His best friend and right-hand man is a Moor (Morgan Freeman), who he has brought back from the Holy Land after saving his life in prison. His biggest disciplinary problem is a young hothead (Christian Slater), who is so obviously bursting with a secret he desires to share that it's amazing Robin is able to wait almost until the end of the movie before learning it.

Much has been said about Kevin Costner's British accent, or lack of same, in advance publicity about the movie. Neither the accent nor the lack of same bothered me in the slightest. What bothered me was that the filmmakers never found the right tone for Costner to use, no matter what his accent. He isn't joyous, or robust, or comical, or heroic, but more of a thoughtful, civilized, socially responsible Robin Hood, sort of a nonpartisan saint who wants to preserve the kingdom for the absent Richard the Lionhearted. Costner plays Robin Hood as if he were Alan Alda.

Alan Rickman, in complete contrast, plays the Sheriff as if he were David Letterman: He's a wicked, droll, sly, witty master of the put-down and one-liners, who rolls his eyes in exasperation when Robin comes bursting in to interrupt the rape. Rickman's performance has nothing to do with anything else in the movie, and indeed seems to proceed from a uniquely personal set of assumptions about what century, universe, etc., the story is set in, but at least when Rickman appears on the screen we perk up, because we know we'll be entertained, at whatever cost to the story.

The only major player who finds the right tone and voice for all of his scenes is Morgan Freeman, as the Moor, who finds humor when it is needed, courage when it is required, and somehow even survives being given a running joke that has to be carefully nurtured from one end of the movie to the other. Mary Elizabeth Mastrantonio does what she can with Marian, but must have been confused when the screenplay gave her a thoughtful, independent woman in the earlier scenes, and then turned her into a clichéd damsel in distress at the end.

The costumes look as if they have things growing in them. The treehouses in Sherwood Forest permit Robin and his men to engage in a key battle scene that looks like a cross between *Tarzan* and the savage tribesmen at the end of *Apocalypse Now*. (This battle deserves greater analysis. In it, hired Celtic mercenaries attack Robin's band and are all but destroyed, after which they only then use their fire catapults, and all but destroy Robin's side, after which, for the later assault on the castle, Robin hardly seems to have lost a man.) The music is your standard rum-dummy-dum false epic dirge kind of stuff. The editing is desperate. The most depressing thing about the movie is that children will watch it expecting to have a good time.

RoboCop ★ ★ ★
R, 103 m., 1987

Peter Weller (Murphy/RoboCop), Nancy Allen (Lewis), Daniel O'Herlihy (The Old Man), Ronny Cox (Jones), Kurtwood Smith (Clarence), Miguel Ferrer (Morton), Robert DoQui (Sergeant Reed). Directed by Paul Verhoeven and produced by Arne Schmidt. Screenplay by Edward Neumeier and Michael Miner.

There is a moment early in *RoboCop* when a robot runs amok. It has been programmed to warn a criminal to drop his gun, and then to shoot him if he does not comply. The robot, an ugly and ungainly machine, is wheeled into a board meeting of the company that hopes to make millions by retailing it. A junior executive is chosen to pull a gun on the machine. The warning is issued. The exec drops his gun. The robot repeats the warning, counts to five, and shoots the guy dead.

This is a very funny scene. (Whether it was even funnier before the MPAA Code and Ratings Administration requested trims in it is, I suppose, a moot point.) It is funny in the same way that the assembly line in Chaplin's *Modern Times* is funny—because there is something hilarious about logic applied to a situation where it is not relevant.

Because the scene surprises us in a movie that seemed to be developing into a serious thriller, it puts us off guard. We're no longer quite sure where *RoboCop* is going, and that's one of the movie's best qualities.

The film takes place at an unspecified time in the future, in Detroit, a city where gang terror rules. There has been a series of brutal cop killings. A big corporation wants to market the robot cops to stamp out crime, but the demonstrator model is obviously not up to the job.

A junior scientist thinks he knows a better way to make a policeman, by combining robotics with a human brain. And he gets his chance when a hero cop (Peter Weller) is killed in the line of duty. Well, not quite killed. Something remains, and around that human core the first "robocop" is constructed—a half-man, half-machine that operates with perfect logic except for the shreds of human spontaneity and intuition that may be lurking somewhere in the background of its memory.

Nancy Allen co-stars in the movie as a woman cop who was Weller's partner before he was shot. She recognizes something familiar about the robocop, and eventually realizes what it is: Inside that suit of steel, it's her old partner, Weller. It actually shouldn't have taken her long to figure it out, since Weller's original nose, mouth, chin, and jaw are visible. His inventor apparently agrees with Batman and Robin that if you can't see the eyes of someone you know, you'll never recognize them.

The broad outline of the plot develops along more or less standard thriller lines. But this is not a standard thriller. The director is Paul Verhoeven, the gifted Dutch filmmaker whose earlier credits include *Soldier of Orange* and *The Fourth Man*. His movies are not easily categorized. There is comedy in this movie, even slapstick comedy. There is romance. There is a certain amount of philosophy, centering on the question, What is a man? And there is pointed social satire, too, as RoboCop takes on some of the attributes and some of the popular following of a Bernard Goetz.

Oddly enough, a lot of RoboCop's personality is expressed by his voice, which is a mechanical monotone. Machines and robots have spoken like this for years in the movies, and now life is beginning to copy them; I was in the Atlanta airport, boarding the shuttle train to the terminal, and the train started talking to me just like RoboCop, in an uninflected monotone. ("Your-attention-please the-doors-are-about-to-close.")

I laughed. No one else did. Since the recorded message could obviously have been recorded in a normal human voice, the purpose of the robotic audio style was clear: to make the commands seem to emanate from a pre-programmed authority that could not be appealed to. In *RoboCop*, Verhoeven and Weller get a lot of mileage out of the conflict between that utterly assured voice and the increasingly confused being behind it.

Considering that he spends much of the movie hidden behind one kind of makeup device or another, Weller does an impressive job of creating sympathy for his character. He is more "human," indeed, when he is RoboCop than earlier in the movie, when he's an ordinary human being. His plight is appealing, and Nancy Allen is effective as the determined partner who wants to find out what really happened to him.

Most thriller and special-effects movies come right off the assembly line. You can call out every development in advance, and usually be right. *RoboCop* is a thriller with a difference.

RoboCop II ★ ★
R, 117 m., 1990

Peter Weller (Murphy/RoboCop), Tom
Noonan (Cain), Willard Pugh (Mayor Kuzak),
Belinda Bauer (Dr. Faxx), Nancy Allen (Anne
Lewis), Daniel O'Herlihy (Old Man), Felton
Perry (Johnson), Robert Do Qui (Sergeant
Reed), Gabriel Damon (Hob). Directed by
Irvin Kershner and produced by Jon Davison.
Screenplay by Frank Miller and Walon Green.

RoboCop II is a bizarre mixture of violence
and humor. It's a film with a split personality, giving us gruesome scenes and then
moving on as if they didn't really mean anything. This is a movie where one scene features a tycoon announcing plans to "take
Detroit private," and another scene has
RoboCop snatching the brains of his enemy
out of their artificial skull and pounding
them into the pavement. The movie's technique is to alternate the laughs and the gore,
so that right after the brains get smashed,
there's a line of funny dialogue.

Apart from anything else, the very idea of
RoboCop is funny: There's a human tendency to be amused by anything that seems
to be intelligent, but is actually governed by
laws of behavior it doesn't understand.
That's why we like plastic teeth that chatter
when we wind them up, and stupid pet
tricks. RoboCop is a creature like that: An
incredibly expensive, complicated piece of
machinery and computer circuits that
stomps around Detroit making all of the
wrong decisions.

The story this time begins at a moment
when Detroit is in even worse shape than it
was at the end of the last movie. There's a
citywide police strike, in protest of pay cuts
masterminded by the evil Omni Consumer
Products conglomerate, a giant corporation
that wants to replace cops with RoboCops
and take over Detroit in the process. OCP is
run by the Old Man (Daniel O'Herlihy), a
tycoon whose vision would make Mike Mil-
ken envious: He'll force the city into bankruptcy, take over at a bargain price, and strip
it of its assets.

This plot doesn't really have much to do
with the central confrontation in *RoboCop
II*, which is between Cain (Tom Noonan),
the inventor of a popular new drug, and the
forces of justice as represented by RoboCop
(Peter Weller). Cain's sidekicks include a
violent, foul-mouthed young boy (Gabriel
Damon), who looks to be about twelve years

old but kills people without remorse, swears
like Eddie Murphy, and eventually takes
over the drug business. I hesitate to suggest
the vicious little tyke has been shoehorned
into this R-rated movie so that the kiddies
will have someone to identify with when they
see it on video, but stranger things have happened.

The movie's screenplay is a confusion of
half-baked and unfinished ideas. The most
distracting loose end is the suggestion that
Murphy, the cop whose organic matter has
been recycled into RoboCop, may still be
human after all. He acts as if he is—driving
past his house to look longingly at his wife—
but then they reprogram him to acknowledge that he is only a machine. The way he
says that makes us suspect that he's trying to
fool his programmers, but then the whole
plot thread is dropped and we never find out
if he's really human or not.

Then there's the question of who makes a
good RoboCop. After the initial success of
the original model, one prototype RoboCop
after another self-destructs. They get suicidal, according to scientists in the movie,
because they lack a strong sense of duty.
That's why the character Murphy made such
a good RoboCop. Since each RoboCop costs
untold millions to develop, the corporation
can't waste money on unpromising material.

So okay, then: Why do they decide to turn
Cain, the drug dealer, into a robot? He's
completely whacked out on chemicals all of
the time, but they steal his brain and stick it
in a big, mean robot for no better reason, I
suppose, than so RoboCop and the new monster can slug it out in the finale. (The bad
robot has a head that looks like a Nazi
helmet; did its inventors know they were
manufacturing a villain?)

The concluding passages of the movie
expend untold thousands of machine-gun
bullets, most of them fired at the bad robot
despite the fact that it's manifestly impervious to bullets. The vicious little tyke gets a
tender deathbed scene, no doubt out of def-
erence to his tender years. The tycoon and
his strategists plan to blame everything on a
woman scientist, but the movie ends before
they can. And we never find out if RoboCop
has true human feelings or not.

In fact, we see relatively little of RoboCop
in this movie, perhaps because Peter Weller
rebelled against the inhuman ordeal of wearing that heavy metal suit any longer than necessary. What we do see are lots of violence
and action, lots of dialogue between minor

characters that never pays off, and lots of
humorous TV ads for the world of the future.
The ads are funny—especially the one that
opens the movie. I didn't much like *Robo-
Cop II* (the use of that killer child is beneath
contempt), but I've gotta hand it to them:
It's strange how funny it is, for a movie so
bad. Or how bad, for a movie so funny.

Rocky ★ ★ ★ ★
PG, 119 m., 1976

Sylvester Stallone (Rocky), Talia Shire
(Adrian), Burt Young (Paulie), Carl Weathers
(Apollo Creed), Burgess Meredith (Mickey),
Frank Stallone (Timekeeper). Directed by
John Avildsen and produced by Robert
Chartoff and Irwin Winkler. Screenplay by
Sylvester Stallone.

She sits, tearful and crumpled, in a corner of
her little bedroom. Her brother has torn
apart the living room with a baseball bat.
Rocky, the guy she has fallen in love with,
comes into the room.

"Do you want a roommate?" she asks
shyly, almost whispering.

"Absolutely," says Rocky.

Which is exactly what he should say, and
how he should say it, and why *Rocky* is such
an immensely involving movie. Its story,
about a punk club fighter from the back
streets of Philly who gets a crack at the world
championship, has been told a hundred
times before. A description of it would sound
like a cliché from beginning to end. But
Rocky isn't about a story, it's about a hero.
And it's inhabited with supreme confidence
by a star.

His name is Sylvester Stallone, and, yes,
in 1976 he did remind me of the young Marlon Brando. How many actors have come and
gone and been forgotten who were supposed
to be the "new Brando," while Brando
endured? And yet in *Rocky* he provides shiv-
ers of recognition reaching back to *A Streetcar Named Desire*. He's tough, he's tender, he
talks in a growl, and hides behind cruelty
and is a champion at heart. "I coulda been a
contender," Brando says in *On the Waterfront*. This movie takes up from there.

It inhabits a curiously deserted Philadelphia: There aren't any cars parked on the
slum street where Rocky lives or the slightest
sign that anyone else lives there. His world is
a small one. By day, he works as an enforcer
for a small-time juice man, offering to break
a man's thumbs over a matter of $70 ("I'll

bandage it!" cries the guy. "It'll *look* broke"). In his spare time, he works out at Mickey's gym. He coulda been good, but he smokes and drinks beer and screws around. And yet there's a secret life behind his facade. He is awkwardly in love with a painfully shy girl (Talia Shire) who works in the corner pet shop. He has a couple of turtles at home, named Cuff and Link, and a goldfish named Moby Dick. After he wins forty bucks one night for taking a terrible battering in the ring, he comes home and tells the turtles: "If you guys could sing and dance, I wouldn't have to go through this crap." When the girl asks him why he boxes, he explains: "Because I can't sing and dance."

The movie ventures into fantasy when the world heavyweight champion (Carl Weathers, as a character with a certain similarity to Muhammad Ali) decides to schedule a New Year's Eve bout with a total unknown—to prove that America is still a land of opportunity. Rocky gets picked because of his nickname, the Italian Stallion; the champ likes the racial contrast. And even *here* the movie looks like a genre fight picture from the 1940s, right down to the plucky little gymnasium manager (Burgess Meredith) who puts Rocky through training, and right down to the lonely morning ritual of rising at four, drinking six raw eggs, and going out to do roadwork. What makes the movie extraordinary is that it doesn't try to surprise us with an original plot, with twists and complications; it wants to involve us on an elemental, a sometimes savage, level. It's about heroism and realizing your potential, about taking your best shot and sticking by your girl. It sounds not only clichéd but corny—and yet it's not, not a bit, because it really does work on those levels. It involves us emotionally, it makes us commit ourselves: We find, maybe to our surprise after remaining detached during so many movies, that this time we *care*.

The credit for that has to be passed around. A lot of it goes to Stallone when he wrote this story and then peddled it around Hollywood for years before he could sell it. He must have known it would work because he could see himself in the role, could imagine the conviction he's bringing to it, and I can't think of another actor who could quite have pulled off this performance. There's that exhilarating moment when Stallone, in training, runs up the steps of Philadelphia's art museum, leaps into the air, shakes his fist

at the city, and you know he's sending a message to the whole movie industry.

The director is John Avildsen, who made *Joe* and then another movie about a loser who tried to find the resources to start again, *Save the Tiger*. Avildsen correctly isolates Rocky in his urban environment, because this movie shouldn't have a documentary feel, with people hanging out of every window: It's a legend, it's about little people, but it's bigger than life, and you have to set them apart visually so you can isolate them morally.

And then there's Talia Shire, as the girl (she was the hapless sister of the Corleone boys in *The Godfather*). When she hesitates before kissing Rocky for the first time, it's a moment so poignant it's like no other. And Burt Young as her brother—defeated and resentful, loyal and bitter, caring about people enough to hurt them just to draw attention to his grief. There's all that, and then there's the fight that ends the film. By now, everyone knows who wins, but the scenes before the fight set us up for it so completely, so emotionally, that when it's over we've had it. We're drained.

Rocky II ★ ★ ★
PG, 119 m., 1979

Sylvester Stallone (Rocky Balboa), Talia Shire (Adrian), Burt Young (Paulie), Carl Weathers (Apollo Creed), Burgess Meredith (Mickey), Tony Burton (Apollo's Trainer). Directed by Sylvester Stallone and produced by Irwin Winkler and Robert Chartoff. Screenplay by Stallone.

Rocky II isn't the movie the first *Rocky* was—what could equal that original burst of vitality?—but it's a well-crafted sequel with a lot of the same appeal, and with a climactic fight scene that's sensationally effective. 1979 was a year of sequels and prequels and remakes, and, as they go, this is one of the best.

That's because it's legitimately a sequel: It continues the story and further develops the characters, instead of just ripping off a successful formula. At the end of *Rocky* we wanted to know what came next, and now we do. That's a lot different from something like *Beyond the Poseidon Adventure*, which essentially just repeats the original movie.

Rocky II begins exactly where the first movie ended, with Rocky Balboa's once-in-a-million shot at the heavyweight title. Sylvester Stallone, who directed this time as

well as writing and starring, is wise to quote from that fight footage. It's a reminder of the extraordinary impact of *Rocky*, which took a tired old Hollywood genre and brilliantly rediscovered its strength.

Stallone then gives us a scene that speaks directly to our memories of the first movie. After their mutual battering, both Rocky and heavyweight champ Apollo Creed are hospitalized. And in the middle of the night Rocky opens Apollo's door and says, "Apollo? You awake?" Yeah. "Can I ask you somethin'?" Yeah. "Did you give me your best shot?" Yeah, I did. "Thank you."

Rocky's life changes dramatically, of course, after his moral victory in the fight. He's badgered by agents who want him to endorse products and do TV commercials (and he does at least one, holding a club and wearing a leopard skin and standing in a cage to endorse a men's after-shave). One of the first things he does, of course, is to marry his girlfriend Adrian (Talia Shire). They buy a car and a house. And Rocky looks around for a job.

His problem is that he can't fight again. Doctor's orders: He suffered damage to his eyes, and another fight could lead to blindness. But Rocky Balboa can't really *do* anything but fight. After a couple of menial jobs, he goes back to the gym run by his trainer, Mickey (played by Burgess Meredith in a jolly, scenery-chewing performance). These scenes—interlaced with Adrian's pregnancy and the birth of their son, Rocky, Jr. (with an astonishing head of hair)—head up to a sustained stretch of soap opera. Adrian goes into a coma. Rocky goes into a depression. Apollo Creed, driven by the need to clear his reputation, taunts Rocky for another fight in newspaper ads.

This is all pretty obvious stuff, and if it were handled with less care we might be tempted to laugh at the clichés. But Stallone as a writer has a way of getting away with things. He tells stories that are simple, basic, and human; he doesn't apologize for them, and he plays them with a conviction that makes them work.

He is also interesting as a director. The first *Rocky* was directed by John Avildsen, who placed it in a Philadelphia landscape deliberately kept barren of people who didn't figure in the story. The streets were empty, and the result was curiously effective: The characters gained a mythic stature because they were kept in relief and not marched through crowds of extras.

Stallone uses that same approach in *Rocky II*. But he also introduces an element of highly personal humor that first surfaced in *Paradise Alley* (1978), which he also wrote and directed. He likes characters who are offbeat and cheerfully grotesque. He likes scenes that are allowed to drift from realism into comic exaggeration. He likes to view life at an angle.

Paradise Alley gave us three heroic, crazy, goofy brothers, and scenes like the one in which the organ grinder's monkey is kept captive in the bathroom. *Rocky II* has fun with the wedding scene, with the absurd TV commercials, and especially with the night of the big fight. Instead of going for conventional devices to build the tension, Stallone cuts between drama and comedy, between the mounting excitement inside the fight arena and Rocky's leisurely progress through the city. Apollo Creed is sweating it out in his dressing room, but Rocky Balboa's stopping off at a parish hall for a quick blessing from the priest.

Then comes the fight scene. I wouldn't dream, of course, of telling you who wins. But the scene itself is terrific action footage, and Stallone's occasional use of slow motion seems to work here; in *Paradise Alley*'s closing fight, it was distracting and excessive. *Rocky II* tells the story crisply and with style, and keeps us hooked even during the soap opera stuff.

But almost any sequel to an enormous hit movie has this problem: We are already familiar with the qualities that made the original extraordinary. *Rocky* introduced us to this strange, eccentric, funny-talking, big lug from Philly who had turtles named Cuff and Link and a dog named Butkus, and was in love with the shy girl who worked at the pet store. It showed us Rocky's one-time shot at the big time. It established a fictional world that was fresh.

Rocky II can't do those things. It doesn't have the advantage of novelty. If you liked *Rocky*, you'll certainly want to see *Rocky II*. But the impact just can't be quite the same. Maybe that's why it's so good to have the fight scene at the end: It has such sheer animal intensity that it's got us cheering, just like the first time around.

Rocky IV ★ ★
PG, 90 m., 1986

Sylvester Stallone (Rocky Balboa), Talia Shire (Adrian), Burt Young (Paulie), Carl Weathers (Apollo Creed), Brigitte Nielsen (Ludmilla), Dolph Lundgren (Drago), Tony Burton (Duke), James Brown (Godfather of Soul). Directed by Sylvester Stallone and produced by Irwin Winkler and Robert Chartoff. Screenplay by Stallone.

The *Rocky* series is finally losing its legs. It's been a long run, one hit movie after another, but *Rocky IV* is a last gasp, a film so predictable that viewing it is like watching one of those old sitcoms where the characters never change and the same situations turn up again and again. Even Sylvester Stallone seems to be getting tired of the series; as the writer and director, as well as the star, he puts himself through the same old paces.

The movie begins with footage from Rocky's big fight with Mr. T. Then we meet Drago (Dolph Lundgren), a six-foot-four, 261-pound Russian fighting machine. Then it's time for a quick roll call of all the regular characters who pop up in every installment.

There's a bizarre birthday party for Paulie (Burt Young), Rocky's brother-in-law, who gets a robot for his present (the robot, by the way, can understand statements and respond spontaneously, suggesting that Rocky's suppliers have licked the problem of artificial intelligence). Maybe Paulie needs the robot for company; he has apparently made no friends during nine years as the champ's in-law, and only three people attend his party.

There's the obligatory romantic scene between Rocky and his wife Adrian (Talia Shire), who seem to have lost all passion during nine years of marriage, and are content to be worshippers at the shrine of their ideal love. There's a walk-on for Rocky, Jr., a couple of scenes with old pal Apollo Creed, and then it's time for the big fight scenes and the final freeze-frame.

It's tempting to forget how good the original *Rocky* was, back in 1976. It was a fresh, wonderful film, and we met some real people—quirky, lovable characters—on the way to the final fight scene. Rocky Balboa had a distinctive way of expressing himself, a love of colorful language that set him apart from the clichés of his characters. The people around him were genuine originals.

The next two Rocky pictures lost some of those qualities, but were still superior entertainments. Maybe it was inevitable that Rocky himself came to dominate his movies, while the others were reduced to perfunctory walk-ons. Maybe Rocky's opponents had to grow more and more bizarre, as the human and vulnerable Apollo Creed gave way to Mr. T's antics. But now, with *Rocky IV*, almost all of the human emotions have been drained out of the series, and what's left is technology. Stallone assembles and photographs two fight scenes (the first always a loss, the second always a victory), and links them together with perfunctory drama. Even the colorful dialogue is missing this time, replaced with endless, unnecessary songs on the sound track; half the time, we seem to be watching MTV.

Rocky IV has many moments that are not believable. My favorite is the moment when Rocky faces Drago in the ring in Moscow, and the all-Russian crowd starts chanting "Rocky! Rocky!" Sure. Uh-huh. You bet. My next favorite moment is when Drago demonstrates that he has four times the punching strength and glove velocity of any other fighter who has ever lived. By my reckoning, and considering how violent a heavyweight punch is anyway, that should be enough to decapitate Rocky. The third most awkward moment is a grotesque exhibition match between Drago and Apollo Creed, who meet on a Las Vegas stage where Creed's warm-up consists of an appearance with soul singer James Brown. This single scene sets some kind of a record: It represents almost everything that the original 1976 Rocky Balboa would have found repellent.

Drago makes more of a James Bond villain than a Rocky-style character. He's tall, blond, taciturn, and hateful. He lets his wife (Brigitte Nielsen) do almost all of the talking on his behalf, and yet, interestingly, he and his wife do not have a single intimate scene together. Their most personal moments seem to occur at press conferences. Why couldn't (a) Drago do his own talking, or (b) Drago not require a wife in the movie? Could the answer be that Brigitte Nielsen was Stallone's wife?

Rocky IV is movie-making by the numbers. Even the climactic fight scene isn't as exciting as it should be, maybe because we know with a certainty born of long experience how it will turn out. Stallone says this will be the last Rocky movie. He should have taken Rocky Marciano as an example, and retired undefeated.

Rocky V ★ ★
PG-13, 104 m., 1990

Sylvester Stallone (Rocky), Talia Shire (Adrian), Burt Young (Paulie), Sage Stallone (Rocky, Jr.), Burgess Meredith (Mickey), Tommy Morrison (Tommy), Richard Gant (George W. Duke). Directed by John G. Avildsen and produced by Irwin Winkler and Robert Chartoff. Screenplay by Sylvester Stallone.

Rocky V arrives advertised as the last of the Rocky pictures, and I hope that's true, because the series has run out of steam. You can only make the same movie so many times, and Sylvester Stallone has now discovered how many times that is when it comes to Rocky Balboa. This film's interest is generated mostly by the good will we've built up over the last fourteen years for Rocky, Adrian, Uncle Paulie, and the others. Like a tired fighter, *Rocky V* doesn't have the stuff to go the distance.

The key element in each episode of a movie series is the villain. Consider the James Bond pictures. The bad guy is the only major character who changes. We know *Rocky V* is in trouble when one of the major villains doesn't even appear in the movie; he's an accountant who remains offscreen, never seen, while he strips the Balboa family of its assets.

The movie labors to explain how that happened. Dumb old Uncle Paulie (Burt Young), who has even taken to concealing his booze in a pair of binoculars, got Rocky to sign a power of attorney before he went off to Russia for the big fight in *Rocky IV*. The accountant used the document to steal or mortgage all of Rocky's assets, and so the champ, retiring undefeated, is broke.

You'd think that a celebrity like Rocky Balboa could drum up some dough making TV commercials or sponsoring a line of exercise apparel (even despite that old conviction for beating up the loan shark). But no. It's straight to the poorhouse for the Balboas, who watch while their home and its contents are auctioned off, right down to Rocky Junior's motorbike. Then they move back into a tiny row house in the old neighborhood, where schoolyard bullies steal Rocky Junior's jacket.

Rocky could solve everything with another multimillion-dollar fight, but the doctors tell him he has brain damage. So he reopens the old gym and starts training youngsters,

including Tommy Gunn (Tommy Morrison), an up-and-comer. Enter the scheming George Washington Duke (Richard Gant), a fight promoter who steals Tommy Gunn away from Balboa and sets up a title bout, all as part of a scheme to force Rocky out of retirement. We already know from the coming attractions and the TV ads that this leads to a street fight, during which all concern for Rocky's brain damage is put temporarily on hold. (His eyesight, by the way, seems to have recovered since it was threatened in *Rocky II*.)

Tommy Morrison is an actual boxer, but the surprise is, he can act. He holds his own in the dialogue scenes, but the screenplay never really makes him into a bad guy; he's a naive victim of the promoter's manipulations. That means that the Rocky-Tommy showdown lacks a little edge, since it's based more on pride than hate.

The original *Rocky*, which came out long, long ago, in 1976, made Sylvester Stallone a star, and that stardom has been the real subject of the next four movies. *Rocky II* (1979) was at least a legitimate sequel, and created the appealing character of Apollo Creed. But the later Rocky movies have been low on inspiration and eager to repeat the same formula, in which everything leads up to a climactic fight scene and a triumphant fade-out. Stallone is smart enough that he could have made this series into a meditation on sports celebrity in America, but that theme has always been at the edge of the stories; the formula occupies center ring.

If Rocky himself seems to be running on autopilot, that's also the case for the other series characters. Talia Shire, as the long-suffering wife Adrian, is once again limited to lamentations for her wounded husband, and Burt Young, as Paulie, burps and belches and chews on his cigar. Stallone's son, Sage, proves himself a solid little actor as Rocky Junior, and there is a reprise for Burgess Meredith, as Rocky's late trainer, Mickey. He turns up as a cross between a ghost and a memory.

Will Stallone stick to his resolution to make this the last Rocky movie? Maybe—or perhaps it will simply be the last movie in which Rocky personally fights. After all, Rocky Junior wins a big fight on the schoolyard and gets his jacket back, and the kid has a nice right hand. The movie closes with a nostalgic visit by father and son to the Rocky statue in front of the Philadelphia Art Museum, and there is just the slightest hint that

maybe Junior will want to carry on the family name. Meanwhile, Rocky is free to pursue other interests: "All the times I've come up here," he confides, "I never knew before that this building has pictures inside."

The Rocky Horror Picture Show
★ ★ ¹/₂
R, 105 m., 1975

Tim Curry (Dr. Frank N. Furter), Susan Sarandon (Janet), Barry Bostwick (Brad), Richard O'Brien (Riff Raff). Directed by Dick Sharman and produced by Michael White. Screenplay by Sharman and Richard O'Brien.

The Rocky Horror Picture Show is not so much a movie as more of a long-running social phenomenon. When the film was first released in 1975 it was ignored by pretty much everyone, including the future fanatics who would eventually count the hundreds of times they'd seen it. *Rocky Horror* opened, closed, and would have been forgotten had it not been for the inspiration of a low-level 20th Century-Fox executive who talked his superiors into testing it as a midnight cult movie.

The rest is history. At its peak in the early 1980s, *Rocky Horror* was playing on weekend midnights all over the world, and loyal fans were lined up for hours in advance out in front of the theater, dressed in the costumes of the major characters. There were jolly reunions of Janets and Brads, the All-American couple played in the movie by Susan Sarandon and Barry Bostwick, conspiratorial knots of Dr. Frank N. Furters, the mad transvestite scientist played by Tim Curry, and clumps of Riff Raffs—he was the hunchback butler played by Richard O'Brien, who also wrote the songs.

Inside the theater, the fans put on a better show than anything on the screen. They knew the film by heart, chanted all of the lines in unison, sang along with the songs, did dances on stage, added their own unprintable additions to the screenplay, and went through a lot of props like toilet paper and water pistols. They also formed a sort of weird extended family. They met every week, exchanged ritual greetings, celebrated each other's birthdays and other major holidays, and even dated and married and gave birth to a new generation of *Rocky Horror* cultists.

It was a strange exhibitor-audience relationship, because the regulars were essentially buying tickets so they could attend their own show.

The *Rocky Horror* midnight cult still survives, in a muted form (how long into middle age, after all, can one really continue to dress up like a Transylvanian transsexual?). But as the cult slowly fades in the moonglow, Fox has taken the long-delayed step of releasing the movie on home video. There are likely to be two results: (1) A brief epidemic of *Rocky Horror* costume parties, and (2) disillusionment with the movie itself. The whole thing about *Rocky Horror* was that the movie played as a backdrop to the stage show by the fans.

As for the movie itself, it's no better than it ever was. Viewed on video simply as a movie, without the midnight sideshow, it's cheerful and silly, and kind of sweet, and forgettable.

Roger & Me ★ ★ ★ ★
R, 100 m., 1989

A documentary directed, produced, and written by Michael Moore.

The peculiar genius of *Roger & Me* is not that it's a funny film or an angry film, or even a film with a point to make—although it is all three of those things. It connects because it's a revenge comedy, a film in which the stinkers get their comeuppance at last. It generates the same kind of laughter that Jack Nicholson inspired in that immortal scene where he told the waitress what she could do with the chicken salad. It allows the audience to share in the delicious sensation of getting even.

The movie was made by Michael Moore, a native of Flint, Michigan, the birthplace of General Motors. As GM closed eleven plants in Flint and laid off some thirty-three thousand workers, Moore got mad—and this is his response. But it's not a dreary documentary about hard times in the rust belt. It's a stinging comedy that sticks in the knife of satire and twists.

The ostensible subject of the film is the attempt by Moore to get an interview with Roger Smith, chairman of General Motors. We know right away that this is one interview that is unlikely to take place. Moore, a ramshackle man-mountain who fancies baseball caps and overflowing Hush Puppies, wanders through the film like a babe in toyland. He's the kind of guy who gets in an elevator in GM headquarters in Detroit and is surprised when the button for the top floor—Smith's office—doesn't light up when it's pressed. The closest he gets to Smith is a slick, oily GM public relations man who explains why the layoffs are regrettable but necessary. (It goes without saying that the spokesman himself is eventually laid off.)

Denied access to Smith, *Roger & Me* pokes around elsewhere in Flint. It follows a deputy sheriff on his rounds as he evicts unemployed auto workers. It covers a Flint Pride parade that marches depressingly past the boarded-up store windows of downtown. It listens to enthusiastic spokesmen for Auto World, an indoor amusement park where Flint citizens can visit a replica of their downtown as it used to look before the boards went up. It listens as a civic booster boasts that Flint's new Hyatt Hotel has escalators and "big plants" in the lobby—just like the Hyatts in Atlanta and Chicago. The hotel and amusement park are supposed to create a tourism industry for Flint, but the biggest convention booked into the hotel is the state Scrabble tournament, and when Auto World goes out of business, the rueful Chamber of Commerce-type speculates that asking people to come to Flint for Auto World "is sort of like asking them to come to Alaska for Exxon World."

Many celebrities wander through the film, brought to Flint by big fees to cheer people up. Anita Bryant sings, Pat Boone suggests that the unemployed workers might become Amway distributors, and Ronald Reagan has pizza with the jobless, but forgets to pick up the check.

Meanwhile, some resourceful victims fight back. A woman advertises "Bunnies as Pets or Rabbits as Meat." Jobless auto workers hire themselves out as living statues who stand around in costume at a *Great Gatsby* charity benefit. Some local industries even improve—there's need for a new jail, for example. And the local socialites hold a charity ball in the jail the night before it opens for business. They have a lot of fun wearing riot helmets and banging each other over the head with police batons.

Roger & Me does have a message to deliver—a message about corporate newspeak and the ways in which profits really are more important to big American corporations than the lives of their workers. The movie is a counterattack against the amoral pragmatism of modern management theory, against the sickness of the *In Search of Excellence* mentality.

Michael Moore has struck a nerve with this movie. There are many Americans, I think, who have not lost the ability to think and speak in plain English—to say what they mean. These people were driven mad by the 1980s, in which a new kind of bureaucratese was spawned by Ronald Reagan and his soulmates—a new manner of speech by which it became possible to "address the problem" while saying nothing and yet somehow conveying optimism.

Roger Smith and General Motors are good at that kind of talk. *Roger & Me* undercuts it with blunt contradictions. In the movie's single most haunting image, Smith addresses a GM Christmas television hookup, reading from *A Christmas Carol* while Moore shows deputies evicting a jobless GM worker and throwing his Christmas tree in the gutter. A spokesman for GM has attacked this scene as "manipulative." It certainly is. But Smith's treacly Christmas ceremony is manipulative, too, and so is the whole corporate doublespeak that justifies his bottom-line heartlessness. The genius of *Roger & Me* is that it understands the image-manipulating machinery of corporate public relations and fights back with the same cynicism and cleverness. The wonder is that the movie is both so angry and so funny. We knew revenge was sweet. What the movie demonstrates is that it is also hilarious—for the avenged.

Romancing the Stone ★ ★ ★
PG, 106 m., 1984

Michael Douglas (Jack Colton), Kathleen Turner (Joan Wilder), Danny DeVito (Thug), Alfonso Arau (Juan), Manuel Ojeda (Zolo). Directed by Robert Zemeckis and produced by Michael Douglas. Screenplay by Diane Thomas.

It may have an awkward title, but *Romancing the Stone* is a silly, high-spirited chase picture that takes us, as they say, from the canyons of Manhattan to the steaming jungles of South America. The movie's about a New York woman who writes romantic thrillers in which the hungry lips of lovers devour each other as the sun sinks over the dead bodies of their enemies. Then she gets involved in a real-life thriller, which is filled with cliffhanging predicaments just like the ones she writes about. The writer, played by Kathleen Turner, uses her novels as a form of escape. Throbbing loins may melt together on her pages, but not in her life. Then she gets a desperate message from her sister in South America: Unless she flies to Cartagena with a treasure map showing the location of a priceless green jewel, her sister will be killed.

What follows is an adventure that will remind a lot of people of *Raiders of the Lost Ark*, but it will be a pleasant memory. After all the *Raiders* rip-offs, it's fun to find an adventure film that deserves the comparison, that has the same spirit and sense of humor. Turner lands in Colombia, and almost instantly becomes part of the plans of a whole lineup of desperadoes. There are the local police, the local thugs, the local mountain bandits, and the local hero, a guy named Jack Colton, who is played by Michael Douglas.

Movies like this work best if they have original inspirations about the ways in which the heroes can die. I rather liked the pit full of snarling alligators, for example. They also work well if the villains are colorful, desperate, and easy to tell apart. They are. Danny DeVito, from TV's "Taxi," plays a Peter Lorre type, complete with a white tropical suit and a hat that keeps getting trampled in the mud. He's a gangster from up north, determined to follow Turner to the jewel. There's also a suave local paramilitary hero named Zolo (Manuel Ojeda), who wears a French Foreign Legion cap and lusts after not only Turner's treasure map but all of her other treasures. And Alfonso Arau plays a rural bandito who turns out to have memorized all of Turner's thrillers.

Movies like this have a tendency to turn into a long series of scenes where the man grabs the woman by the hand and leads her away from danger at a desperate run. I always hate scenes like that. Why can't the woman run by herself? Don't they both have a better chance if the guy doesn't have to always be dragging her? What we're really seeing is leftover sexism from the days when women were portrayed as hapless victims. *Romancing the Stone* doesn't have too many scenes like that. It begins by being entirely about the woman, and although Douglas takes charge after they meet, that's basically because he knows the local territory. Their relationship is on an equal footing, and so is their love affair. We get the feeling they really care about each other, and so the romance isn't just a distraction from the action.

A Room with a View ★ ★ ★ ★
PG-13, 110 m., 1985

Maggie Smith (Charlotte Bartlett), Helena Bonham Carter (Lucy Honeychurch), Denholm Elliott (Mr. Emerson), Julian Sands (George Emerson), Daniel Day Lewis (Cecil Vyse), Simon Callow (Reverend Beebe), Judi Dench (Miss Lavish), Rosemary Leach (Mrs. Honeychurch). Directed by James Ivory and produced by Ismail Merchant. Screenplay by Ruth Prawer Jhabvala.

My favorite character in *A Room with a View* is George Emerson, the earnest, passionate young man whose heart beats fiercely with love for Lucy Honeychurch. She is a most respectable young woman from a good family, who has been taken to Italy on the grand tour, with a lady companion, Miss Bartlett. Lucy meets George and his father in their *pensione*. A few days later, while standing in the middle of a waving field of grass, the sun bathing the landscape in a yellow joy, she is kissed by George Emerson, most unexpectedly. He does not ask her permission. He does not begin with small talk. He takes her and kisses her, and for him, something "great and important" has happened between them.

Lucy Honeychurch is not so sure. She catches her breath, and Miss Bartlett appears on top of a hill and summons her back to tea, and a few months later, in England, Lucy announces her engagement to Cecil Vyse, who is a prig. Cecil is the sort of man who would never play tennis, who wears a *pince-nez*, who oils his hair, and who thinks that girls are nice because they like to listen to him read aloud. Cecil does not have many clues as to what else girls might be nice for.

Meanwhile, George Emerson and his father—who is an idealist, a dreamer, and a follower of Thoreau—take a cottage in the neighborhood. And one day George kisses Lucy again. He then delivers himself of an astonishing speech, in which he explains that love exists between them. (Not love but Love—you can hear the capital letter in his voice.) Lucy must not marry Cecil, he explains, for Cecil does not understand women and will never understand Lucy, and wants her only for an ornament. George, on the other hand, wants her as his partner in the great adventure of life.

George does not have many big scenes, other than those two. The rest of the time, he keeps a low profile and says little. But his function is clear: He is the source of passion in a society that is otherwise tightly bound up in convention, timidity, and dryness. He is the man to break the chains, to say what he thinks, to free Lucy's spirit. And that he does, with great energy and efficiency. George is my favorite character because he is such a strange bird, so intense, so filled with conviction, so convinced of Lucy's worth.

A Room with a View is the story of George and Lucy, but it is also an attack on the British class system. In the opening scenes of the movie, Lucy and Miss Bartlett have been given a room in the Italian *pensione* that does not have a view. Dear old Mr. Emerson insists that the women take his rooms, which have a view. By the end of the film, George will have offered Lucy a view out of the room of her own life. She has been living a suffocating, proper existence—and he will open the window for her. That's what's exhilarating about the film, that it is not only about perplexing and eccentric characters, it's about how they can change their lives.

The movie has been adapted from the E.M. Forster novel by three filmmakers who have specialized recently in film adaptations of literary works: Director James Ivory, producer Ismail Merchant, and screenwriter Ruth Prawer Jhabvala. Their other recent credits include *The Bostonians*, *The Europeans*, and *Heat and Dust*. This is the best film they have ever made.

It is an intellectual film, but intellectual about emotions: it encourages us to think about how we feel, instead of simply acting on our feelings. It shows us a young woman, Lucy Honeychurch, who is about to marry the wrong man—not because of her passion, but because of her lack of thought. Only think about your passion, the movie argues, and you will throw over Cecil and marry George. Usually thought and passion are opposed in the movies; this time it's entertaining to find them on the same side.

The story moves at a deliberate pace, with occasionally dramatic interruptions for great passion. The dialogue is stately and abstract, except when all of a sudden it turns direct and honest. The performances are perfectly balanced between the heart and the mind. At the center of everything stands Lucy, who is played by Helena Bonham Carter, that dark-browed, stubborn little girl from *Lady Jane*. Maggie Smith is wonderfully dotty as her companion. Denholm Elliott, the most dependable of all British character actors, steals scene after scene as George's free-thinking father ("Leave me my portrait of Thoreau," he insists, as they are moving from their cottage). Julian Sands is the intense young George and Daniel Day Lewis creates a foppish masterpiece in his performance as Cecil; give him a monocle and a butterfly, and he could be on the cover of the *New Yorker.*

A Room with a View enjoys its storytelling so much that I enjoyed the very process of it; the story moved slowly, it seemed, for the same reason you try to make ice cream last—because it's so good.

Rosalie Goes Shopping ★ ★ ★
PG, 94 m., 1990

Marianne Sägebrecht (Rosalie Greenspace), Brad Davis (Ray Greenspace), Judge Reinhold (Priest), Erika Blumberger and Willy Harlander (Rosalie's parents), Alex Winter (Schatzi), Patricia Zehentmayr (Barbara), John Hawkes (Schnucki). Directed by Percy Adlon and produced by Percy and Eleonore Adlon. Screenplay by Percy and Eleonore Adlon and Christopher Doherty.

Most movies have a dominant quality, and in *Rosalie Goes Shopping* that sought-after quality is Reassurance. The movie is about a woman who reassuringly provides her family with all the best things in life, and reassuringly lies to the banks and the credit-card companies that she will be able to pay for them, and reassuringly assures herself that she is a splendid wife and a wonderful mother and an exemplary human being.

Sometimes, to be sure, she has her infinitesimal little moments of doubt, and when they spring up, she goes to confession, where her parish priest listens in wonder to her tale of scams, con games, and check kitings. He gives the best advice he can, and she leaves him trying to reassure himself that he belongs in the priesthood. How does a priest feel when a penitent seems more positive about her sins than he does about her redemption?

The whole movie takes place somewhere in rural Arkansas, where Rosalie (Marianne Sägebrecht), a plump German woman with a beatific smile, has settled down with her husband to raise a large and increasingly affluent family. The husband (Brad Davis), is a crop-dusting pilot who presumably wooed and won Rosalie during a tour of duty with the air force in Germany. Now he is confronted by a wife who is a delight and a

puzzlement to him. She showers the benefits of the consumer society on their family, she walks around the house in a cocoon of serenity, and yet, and yet—the question must be asked: Where does the money come from?

The answer is that the money comes from thin air. I have a friend who was once a credit-card swindler, and the way he explains it, the credit-card companies are almost pathetically happy to send you their cards and let you use them, and not as swift as they ought to be to figure out who isn't paying. When you use one card to pay another, and combine that with the judicious use of check-floating strategies and a home equity loan on a home with no equity in it, you can live pretty well in the short run. And, of course, you should never even think in the long run.

Rosalie Goes Shopping is the third movie directed by Percy Adlon and starring Sägebrecht, whose previous collaborations include *Sugarbaby* and *Bagdad Cafe.* She is an unlikely looking movie star, plump and angelic and somewhere around forty, but it cannot be denied that she has a particular screen quality: She glows. It is an innocent, benevolent glow. She is happy with herself, pleased to make others happy, and she lets tomorrow take care of itself.

The movie doesn't tell her story as a financial thriller, with lots of dates and times and bank balances. Adlon is more concerned with the meaning of what she does. She sees comfort and plenty all around her, she wants it for her family, and she finds that people will sell it to her on credit, time, and plastic. So what's the point of saving up first? Live it up now and let your ship come in tomorrow!

The family has its doubts. At least some of the children seem to suspect uneasily that Mom may be living in a dream world, and Davis would be worried, too, if he thought about such things. Certainly Rosalie's parents grow concerned when they visit from Germany and see children being raised with lax discipline, a household being run on credit—and their own return tickets being sold to raise a little emergency cash.

Rosalie Goes Shopping records the mood of a large part of society—of those people in the TV commercials and sometimes in real life, who measure their happiness by material possessions, brand names, and the latest models of the newest gizmos. Rosalie occupies the center of the film almost in a daze; she's a juggler who can keep all her balls in the air only if she stays half-hypnotized by their rhythm. Call her attention to any-

thing—especially her current net worth—and the whole act would come crashing to the earth.

The Rose ★ ★ ★
R, 134 m., 1979

Bette Midler (Rose), Alan Bates (Rudge), Frederic Forrest (Dyer), Harry Dean Stanton (Billy Ray), Barry Primus (Dennis), David Keith (Mal). Directed by Mark Rydell and produced by Martin Worth and Aaron Russo. Screenplay by Bill Kerby and Bo Goldman.

If *The Rose* accomplished nothing else, it would deserve praise for frustrating our national desire to turn the deaths of celebrities into entertainment events. It has gotten to the point in recent years where a popular singer can hardly hope to make it without being dead, and the hot thing for Hollywood lawyers is to put together a portfolio of superstar estates.

The Elvis Industry, balanced precariously between idolatry and necrophilia, is particularly depressing, but count our dead heroes: Jim Croce, Jimi Hendrix, Jim Morrison, Buddy Holly, Otis Redding, Janis Joplin . . . and there was that stir several years ago when yearning Beatles fans tried to bury Paul McCartney the better to praise him.

The girl rock-and-roll singer portrayed by Bette Midler in *The Rose* is officially not Janis Joplin, of course; Midler and director Mark Rydell say they drew from lots of sources, and the movie shows that they did. But the popular conception is that Bette's playing Janis, and audiences are going to *The Rose* to get the lowdown on her and Bobby McGee. The reaction after the movie is over is fascinating: It's a downer, some people complain. Too depressing. You see how fickle we are with our fads. We want movies celebrating the early deaths of our heroes—but they shouldn't be too glum. It's on record that Joplin went to her doom speeded by drugs and Southern Comfort, but maybe what the fans want now is a remake of *Heaven Can Wait*, with Warren Beatty greeting her in heaven.

The Rose is not that movie, and fans hoping to chuckle along at good ol' Rose as she self-destructs will be disappointed. This movie about the pressures of rock stardom and its road tours is told from the inside in two ways: Midler and the filmmakers know what it's like because they've been there, and the movie also concentrates on staying mostly inside the Rose character's head.

Rose, in the movie, is a junkie, a drunk, dependent on uppers, downers, and levelers (she is also, I should probably add, capable of having a good time, able to belt out some terrific performances, and not totally wasted until the end). The movie suggests some of the reasons for her shotgun addictions, but most people use drugs and booze, of course, not because of the personality and behavioral "reasons" so beloved by the social help experts but—quite simply—because they got addicted, and now can't stop. Telling someone he can beat a habit once he understands "why" he's using something is as cruel as telling a man with a broken leg that he can walk if he understands his bone structure.

The Rose seems to understand this. It is intelligent on the subject of addictions, and its insights are reflected in an interesting stylistic strategy. People on booze or certain drugs develop a tunnel vision in dealing with their environment: They focus on what's important to them at a given moment, and screen out the distractions.

The Rose handles its locations and supporting characters in that way, from Rose's point of view, so that cast members swim in and out of focus and we're seduced into Rose's state of mind. That makes the movie's gradual descent from good times into disquiet, pity, doom, and silence an especially effective one.

But some people say they don't like it, it's depressing. One is tempted to wonder what they expected (how do you base a comedy on Janis Joplin?), but maybe it's not their fault. We've been so brainwashed by the Elvis Industry and its lesser clones that we expect dead stars to come in a nice-smelling package. Used to be fans just identified with their heroes. Now they want the final word.

'Round Midnight ★ ★ ★ ★
R, 130 m., 1986

Dexter Gordon (Dale Turner), Francois Cluzet (Francis Borier), Gabrielle Haker (Berangere), Sandra Reaves-Phillips (Buttercup), Lonette McKee (Darcey Leigh), Christine Pascal (Sylvie), Herbie Hancock (Eddie Wayne), Martin Scorsese (Goodley). Directed by Bertrand Tavernier and produced by Irwin Winkler. Screenplay by David Rayfiel and Tavernier.

In Dexter Gordon's voice in this movie there is a quality that at first sounds like a great weariness. As I listened more carefully, however, I realized that there were other notes also present.

Here is a man (I speak of the character, not the actor) who has gone too far and seen too much, and who knows that in one way or another his death is near. Yet he is not impatient with those who still have long to live; he takes what remains of his precious time to speak carefully with them. And when he speaks of the world around him, it is with a quiet amazement that he is still there to see it.

I mention Gordon's voice because it plays the same notes as the music in this film. As with all great musicians, the notes that come from within are the same as the feelings that come from within. I believe that musicians who use breath to play their instruments—those who play the various horns—arrive sooner or later at a point where they play and speak in the same voice. Dexter Gordon makes it easy to hear that; the music that comes from his saxophone is sad and tender, and so are his words.

In *'Round Midnight*, he plays a man named Dale Turner, an American jazzman who goes to Paris in 1959 to play at a club called the Blue Note. Turner is about sixty, an alcoholic and drug abuser whose pattern has been to pull things together for a while, and then let them slide. Each slide is closer to death. He is on the wagon in Paris, watched over by a ferocious landlady and a vigilant club owner, who want him sober so he can get his job done. In the smoky little club every night, he plays the new music of Monk and Bird, the standards of Gershwin and Porter, and songs that come up spontaneously while they are being played.

Outside in the rain one night, a young Frenchman stands by a window, listening to the music, not caring if he gets wet. He believes Dale Turner is the greatest sax player in the world, but he doesn't have enough money to go inside to hear him. One night he follows the old man out of the club, and is able to see without very much trouble that Dale needs help. So he offers it.

Dale Turner is the most hopeless kind of alcoholic, the kind who tries to stay dry by depending on his own willpower and the enforcement of others. Sooner or later his willpower will advise him to drink, and sooner or later the others will not be there, so sooner or later he will be drunk. The young Frenchman senses this, and also senses the overwhelming loneliness of Dale's life, and invites him home for food and talk.

That seemingly very slight gesture—a fan trying to help the man he admires—is the heart of *'Round Midnight*. This is not a heavily plotted movie, one of these musical biographies that are weighted down with omens and light on music. It is about a few months in a man's life, and about his music. It has more jazz in it than any other fiction film ever made, and it is probably better jazz; it makes its best points with music, not words.

Dexter Gordon plays the central role with an eerie magnetism. He is a musician, not an actor, and yet no actor could have given this performance, with its dignity, its wisdom, and its pain. He speaks slowly, carefully considering, really making his words mean something, and so even commonplace sentences ("Francois, this is a lovely town you have here") are really meant. He calls everyone "Lady" in the movie, and doesn't explain it, and doesn't need to.

The music was recorded live. The director, Bertrand Tavernier, believes that in earlier jazz films, the audience could sense that the actors were not really playing; that you could see in their eyes that they were not listening to the other musicians onstage with them. In *'Round Midnight*, the music happens as we hear it, played by Gordon, Herbie Hancock on piano, and such others as Freddie Hubbard, Bobby Hutcherson, Ron Carter, and Billy Higgins, with Lonette McKee on vocals. You do not need to know a lot about jazz to appreciate what is going on, because in a certain sense this movie teaches you everything about jazz that you really need to know.

There are side-stories: Dale's old loves, new possibilities, painful memories, battle with drink, and his suicidal decision to return to New York (where he is awaited by a slick agent and a patient, fatalistic heroin dealer). They all add up to the story of the end of a life. The story needs a song, and the movie has the song, *'Round Midnight*.

Roxanne ★ ★ ★ ½
PG, 107 m., 1987

Steve Martin (C.D. Bales), Daryl Hannah (Roxanne), Rick Rossovich (Chris), Shelley Duvall (Dixie), John Kapelos (Chuck), Fred Willard (Mayor Deebs), Michael J. Pollard (Andy). Directed by Fred Schepisi and produced by Michael Rachmil and Daniel Melnick. Screenplay by Steve Martin.

Roxanne is a gentle, whimsical comedy starring Steve Martin as a man who knows he has the love of the whole town, because he is such a nice guy, but fears he will never have the love of a woman, because his nose is too big. His nose is pretty big, all right; he doesn't sniff wine, he inhales it.

The movie is based on *Cyrano de Bergerac*, a play that was written in 1890 but still strikes some kind of universal note, maybe because for all of us there is some attribute or appendage we secretly fear people will ridicule. Inside every adult is a second-grader still terrified of being laughed at.

In *Roxanne*, the famous nose belongs to C.D. Bales, a small-town fire chief, who daydreams of a time when the local citizens will have enough confidence in his department to actually call it when there's a fire.

In despair at the incompetence of his firemen, he hires a firefighting expert (Rick Rossovich) to train them. The expert arrives in town almost simultaneously with a tall, beautiful blonde (Daryl Hannah), who is an astronomer in search of an elusive comet.

Both men fall instantly in love with the woman. At first she has eyes for Rossovich, who is tall, dark, and handsome. But he is totally incapable of talking to a woman about anything but her body, and after he grosses her out, who can she turn to except Martin, the gentle, intelligent, poetic fire chief?

Martin is afraid to declare his love. He thinks she'll laugh at his nose. He assumes the role of a coach, prompting Rossovich, writing love letters for him, giving him advice. In the movie's funniest scene, Martin radios dialogue to Rossovich, who wears a hat with earflaps to conceal the earphone.

What makes *Roxanne* so wonderful is not this fairly straightforward comedy, however, but the way the movie creates a certain ineffable spirit. Martin plays a man with a smile on his face and a broken heart inside—a man who laughs that he may not cry. He has learned to turn his handicap into comedy, and when a man insults him in a bar, he counterattacks with twenty more insults, all of them funnier than the original. He knows how to deal with his nose, but he has never learned how to feel about it.

Hannah provides a sweet, gentle foil to the romantic fantasies of Martin and Rossovich. She has come to their small town because the air is clear and she can get a good view of the comet with her telescope. She isn't really looking for romance, and although she thinks Rossovich is cute, she's turned off by lines about her body. She likes his letters, though, and when she finds out the letters are really from Martin, she is able to accept him for his heart and not for his nose, which is the whole point, so to speak, of *Cyrano*.

All of the corners of this movie have been filled with small, funny moments. Michael J. Pollard, the getaway driver in *Bonnie and Clyde* twenty years ago, is back as a weird little fireman. Fred Willard is the pompous local mayor. Shelley Duvall, as the owner of the local cafe, does double-takes at the strangeness of ordinary life. And Martin proceeds manfully ahead, rescuing cats from trees, helping strangers, fighting fires, and trying to still the beating of his heart.

Runaway Train ★ ★ ★ ★
R, 111 m., 1985

Jon Voight (Manny), Eric Roberts (Buck), Rebecca De Mornay (Sara), Kyle T. Heffner (Frank Barstow), John P. Ryan (Ranken), Kenneth McMillan (Eddie). Directed by Andrei Konchalovsky and produced by Menahem Golan and Yoram Globus. Screenplay by Djordje Milicevic, Paul Zindel, and Edward Bunker.

The great adventure movies have all been stories of character, not just tales of action. One of the great losses in the movies of recent years has been that sense of real character: One-dimensional people insert themselves into chases and explosions, and the mindless spectacle on the screen is supposed to replace the presence of plausible human beings.

Runaway Train is a reminder that the great adventures are great because they happen to people we care about. That was true of *The African Queen*, and of *Stagecoach*, and of *The Seven Samurai*, three movies that would otherwise seem to have little in common. And it is also true of this tale of two desperate convicts on board a train that is hurtling through the snows of Alaska.

The movie stars Jon Voight and Eric Roberts, who were both nominated for Oscars. They are two actors with dramatically different styles. Voight is always internalized and moody; Roberts has a collection of verbal and physical tics that are usually irritating, and are sometimes meant to be. Here they are both correctly cast, as two convicts in a maximum-security prison in Alaska, who escape through a drain tunnel and then blunder onto the train that takes them on their hellbound mission.

Voight plays Manny, a convict who is so distrusted by the warden that his cell doors have been welded shut for three years. "He's not a human being—he's an animal," the warden says, and this is not just stock dialogue, but the thesis on which the whole movie will rest. Roberts is Buck, a trusty who works for the prison laundry. The warden is Ranken (John P. Ryan), and he has a personal grudge against Manny. In fact, he releases him from solitary in the wicked hope that Manny will try to escape—he's done it before—and that will give Ranken license to kill him.

The opening passages are intense, but somewhat routine; they're out of the basic kit of prison movie clichés. Then the two convicts escape, and stumble by luck into one of the back cabs of a train that consists of four locomotives linked together. The train starts, the engineer suddenly collapses with a heart attack, and the movie's epic journey has begun.

Runaway Train is based on an original screenplay by the Japanese master Akira Kurosawa, whose best movies use the actors as a means of studying character. After some rewriting, *Runaway Train* was directed by Andrei Konchalovsky, the emigré Russian who figures so memorably (under a pseudonym) as Shirley MacLaine's lover in her bestseller *Dancing in the Light*. He has given the story the kind of wildness and passion it requires; this isn't a high-tech Hollywood adventure movie, but a raw saga that works close to the floor.

Once the train has started to move, the movie follows three threads. One involves the three people on the train (the two men discover after a while that a woman crew member, played by Rebecca De Mornay, is also on board, and also powerless to stop the engines). The second thread involves the railway dispatchers, who quarrel over a computer system that may possibly have the ability to clear the tracks ahead of the runaway. The third involves the ferocious determination of Ranken, the warden, to track the train by helicopter, and kill the men inside. Those elements might be enough to make *Runaway Train* a superior action movie. What makes it more than that is the dynamic inside the cab of the train. Voight is seen as a man who is intelligent enough to realize how desperate the situation is—because he has been caught not just in a physical trap, but also in a psychological one. In an impassioned speech that may be the best single scene he has ever played, he tries to explain to Roberts how limited their choices are in life. He uses a story of a man with a broom to create a parable about the impossibility of living as a free man.

The Roberts character does not quite understand the story. He is a wild man of limited intelligence, and prison life has made him dangerous—he acts without regard for the consequences. When these two men are joined by a woman, it is not just a plot gimmick; her role as an outsider gives them an audience and a mirror.

The action sequences in the movie are stunning. Frequently, in recent movies, I've seen truly spectacular stunts and not been much excited, because I knew they were stunts. All I could appreciate was their smoothness of execution. In *Runaway Train*, as the characters try to climb along the sides of the ice-covered locomotive, as the train crashes through barriers and other trains, as men dangle from helicopters and try to kill the convicts, there is such a raw, uncluttered desperation in the feats that they put slick Hollywood stunts to shame.

The ending of the movie is astonishing in its emotional impact. I will not describe it. All I will say is that Konchalovsky has found the perfect visual image to express the ideas in his film. Instead of a speech, we get a picture, and the picture says everything that needs to be said. Afterwards, just as the screen goes dark, there are a couple of lines from Shakespeare that may resonate more deeply the more you think about the Voight character. This was one of the year's best.

Running on Empty ★ ★ ★ ★
PG-13, 113 m., 1988

Christine Lahti (Annie Pope), River Phoenix (Danny Pope), Judd Hirsch (Arthur Pope), Jonas Abry (Harry Pope), Martha Plimpton (Lorna Phillips), Ed Crowley (Mr. Phillips), L.M. (Kit) Carson (Gus Winant), Steven Hill (Mr. Patterson), Augusta Dabney (Mrs. Patterson), David Margulies (Dr. Jonah Reiff). Directed by Sidney Lumet. Produced by Amy Robinson and Griffin Dunne. Screenplay by Naomi Foner.

How do you explain it to your children, when you take the family dog and put it out into the street, and say that it will surely find a home—and then you drive out of town, forever? That's what happens in an early scene of *Running on Empty*, and the most chilling thing about it is that the children take it

fairly well. They've abandoned family dogs before. And they've left town a lot of times.

The movie is about the Popes, a married couple who have been underground since the 1960s, and about their children—especially Danny, who is a senior in high school and has never known any other kind of lifestyle. The Popes were involved with radical politics, and they blew up a building, and there was a janitor inside who they didn't know would be there. They've been on the run ever since, changing towns, changing names, learning how to find jobs that don't attract attention, learning to keep the kids home on the day they take the school picture.

But it's a funny thing about the past. The more you run from it, the more it's in your thoughts. And now time is catching up with this family. What, for example, is Danny (River Phoenix) going to do? He is a gifted piano player, and through one of his teachers he gets a scholarship to Juilliard. But he can't claim it unless he produces his high school transcripts—which are scattered back along his trail in many towns under many different names.

Arthur Pope (Judd Hirsch) has taken a hard line for years, and he's not ready to change it now. He believes that the family must stay together, must protect itself against the world. He's built a fortress mentality, and Danny shares it. He knows that if he comes clean and enters the school, he cannot see his family again; he'll have an FBI tail every moment. His mother, Annie (Christine Lahti), feels as if her heart will break. She has been running a long time, and she doesn't regret the sacrifices she made, but she can't bear the thought that Danny will have to sacrifice his future, just as she lost hers.

Life, in the short run, goes on. Danny makes a girlfriend (Martha Plimpton), whose father is the music teacher. They share secrets, but Danny cannot share his deepest one. This is the first time he's had a girlfriend, the first time he's allowed anyone to grow this close, and he has to learn a neat trick, the trick of learning to trust without being trustworthy. Plimpton knows something is wrong, but she doesn't know what.

The family has survived every crisis that came from the outside, every close call with the FBI, every question from a pushy neighbor. But this is a threat that's unanswerable, because it comes from within: It is no longer possible for these people to avoid questioning the very foundations on which they have

built their lives. And that questioning leads to the movie's emotional high point, when the Lahti character calls up her father (Steven Hill), and arranges to meet him for lunch. Long ago, she broke his heart. She disappeared from his life for years. Now she wants her parents to take Danny so that he can go to music school. She will lose her son, just as her father lost her. It's ironic, and it's very sad, and by the end of the scene we have been through a wringer.

The movie was directed by Sidney Lumet, who made a movie called *Daniel* three years ago, inspired by the children of the Rosenbergs, who were charged with spying for the Russians. That film never quite came clear on what it thought about the Rosenbergs—not about whether they were guilty or innocent, but whether they were good or bad. They were seen through so many political and historical filters that we never knew who we were looking at. *Running on Empty* doesn't make that mistake. These are people who have made a choice and are living with the consequences, and during the course of the film they will have to re-evaluate their decisions.

The family is not really political at all. Politics, ironically, have been left far behind—that kind of involvement would blow the cover of the Pope family. The film is a painful, enormously moving drama in which a choice must be made between sticking together, or breaking up and maybe fulfilling a long-delayed potential. The parents never fulfilled whatever potential they had because of their life underground. Now are they justified in asking their son to abandon his own future? And how will they do that? Push him out of the car and drive away, and trust that he will find a home, just as the dog did?

Lumet is one of the best directors at work today, and his skill here is in the way he takes a melodramatic plot and makes it real by making it specific. All of the supporting characters are convincing, especially Plimpton and her father (Ed Crowley). There is a chilling walk-on by L.M. (Kit) Carson as a radical friend from the old days. And there are great performances in the central roles. River Phoenix essentially carries the story; it's about him. Lahti and Hill have that shattering scene together. And Lahti and Hirsch, huddled together in bed, fearfully realizing that they may have come to a crossroads, are touching; we see how they've depended on each other. This was one of the best films of 1988.

Running Scared ★ ★ ★
R, 107 m., 1986

Gregory Hines (Ray), Billy Crystal (Danny), Darlanne Fluegel (Anna), Tracy Reed (Maryann), Joe Pantoliano (Snake), Steven Bauer (Frank), Jonathan Gries (Tony), Dan Hedaya (Captain Logan). Directed by Peter Hyams and produced by David Foster and Lawrence Turman. Screenplay by Gary Devore and Jimmy Huston.

Running Scared is yet another movie about street-smart cops who are best buddies, wisecracking their way through one hair-raising situation after another. This genre is so overpopulated that it hardly seems like we need one more example, and yet *Running Scared* transcends its dreary roots and turns out to be a lot of fun. Most of the fun comes from the relationship between the two cops, who are played by Gregory Hines and Billy Crystal as if they were both successfully stealing the picture.

The movie takes place in the middle of a cold, gray Chicago winter, which is made all the colder and grayer by the hilariously inept use of fake movie snow. Considering how many vertical surfaces are plastered with "snow" in this movie, while the ground remains clear, Chicago must be the only city in which the snow falls from Oak Park instead of from the sky.

Slogging through the grim, mean alleyways, Hines and Crystal stumble across a major drug ring. Their good luck starts with an encounter with Snake (Joe Pantoliano), a two-bit hood who has $50,000 in his briefcase. They want to arrest Pantoliano but don't have anything to charge him with. So, in a brilliant scene, they convince Pantoliano to request arrest: Crystal loudly tells the neighborhood hoods that Pantoliano is carrying fifty grand and requests them to keep an eye out for suspicious perpetrators.

The movie unfolds in the usual ways. A criminal mastermind vows to kill the two cops, a commanding officer bawls them out and orders them to go on vacation, and a couple of friendly women warm the winter nights. As stories go, nothing in *Running Scared* is very original.

But Crystal and Hines (and the screenplay by Gary Devore and Jimmy Huston) don't need a plot because they have so much good dialogue and such a great screen relationship. The intelligence and wit flowing between them are so palpable you can almost

see them, and there are so many throw-away lines that even the bit players get some good ones.

The movie was directed by Peter Hyams, who can claim the distinction of using two spectacular locations: There is a chase on the El tracks and an acrobatic shoot-out inside the State of Illinois Center. The original twist with the El chase is that the chase vehicles are cars, not trains. Crystal and Hines pursue a Cadillac limo in their Yellow Cab.

It sounds like a great chase, but it's curiously anticlimactic, maybe because we get mostly point-of-view shots from the two cars. I kept waiting for at least one shot from ground level, showing bystanders doing double-takes as a Yellow Cab zooms past on the El. But the shot is missing—an oversight for which the chase coordinator should be punished by being made to work on the next three *Cannonball Run* movies.

The State of Illinois Center sequence is something else. Hines lowers himself on a window-washer's rig down through the vast rotunda from the ceiling while firing a machine gun and we reflect that the true test of architecture is its versatility. But even here, oddly enough, the action pales just a little because it is so conventional to end a movie like this with a spectacular shoot-out. I liked the smaller-scale scenes the best, the ones where Hines and Crystal were doing their stuff.

The Russia House ★ ★
R, 123 m., 1990

Sean Connery (Barley), Michelle Pfeiffer (Katya), Roy Scheider (Russell), James Fox (Ned), John Mahoney (Brady), Michael Kitchen (Clive), Klaus Maria Brandauer (Dante). Directed by Fred Schepisi and produced by Paul Maslansky and Schepisi. Screenplay by Tom Stoppard.

It takes a lot of patience to watch *Russia House*, but it takes even more patience to be a character in the movie. To judge by this film, the life of a cold war spy consists of sitting for endless hours in soundproof rooms with people you do not particularly like, waiting for something to happen. Sort of like being a movie critic.

The top-level spies in this film are apparently hooked into some kind of high-tech electronics network that allows them to know at all times what their people in the field are doing. But the people are often not

doing very much, and so my mind wandered, speculating what it would be like to sit for hours in cynical world-weariness, drinking coffee or sherry in book-lined rooms, waiting for something to happen so you can make a suitably jaundiced comment about it.

The film, like John Le Carré's novel, takes place in a world where *glasnost* is eroding the old certainties about the cold war. It tells the story of a small-time, alcoholic London book publisher named Barley (Sean Connery), who is sent a manuscript by a beautiful Russian woman he claims never to have met. The manuscript is intercepted by British intelligence, which pays a visit to Barley in the Lisbon flat where he often repairs for drinking bouts, and they quiz him about the book and the girl until in exasperation he agrees to go to Moscow and follow up on the transaction.

The key questions are, who wrote the manuscript, and why? It appears to be a highly technical work calling into question the quality of the Soviet Union's defense weaponry. Is it true? False? Does the author know what he is talking about? All of these questions are debated at length before and after Barley's trip, during which he actually meets the mystery woman who passed the manuscript to the West.

Her name is Katya, she is played by Michelle Pfeiffer, and she is, in Barley's words, "seriously beautiful." Yes, of course she is. This is a movie, after all. But she is also the one woman to strike a spark of hope and romance in old Barley's breast, to make him believe that after all these decades of boozing and self-contempt and weary cynicism, he can dare to hope and love. He tells her these things, in more or less those words, and then the plot deepens because the manuscript comes from a scientist (Klaus Maria Brandauer) who might also feel some of the same things about her.

And so what develops is one of those infinitely gentle, sad Le Carré plots in which men who have worked too long within the mole-tunnels of intelligence come out into the sunlight and stand, blinking and disoriented, in the glare of beauty, romance, truth, and fresh air. All of which needs to be talked about a great deal, especially by men who have been spies too long, and cannot unlearn their old habits. These include the Americans (Roy Scheider and John Mahoney) who take over the case from the impotent British.

The movie has been perfectly cast. Having read the book, I knew that Barley would have to be Sean Connery or perhaps Michael Caine (John Hurt would have been good, but is not a box office name). Michelle Pfeiffer makes a splendid Katya, with her hair pulled back to accentuate her vaguely Slavic cheekbones. Klaus Maria Brandauer, of course, gets all substantial male Russian and Eastern European roles these days, with his sleek and slightly sinister intelligence. And James Fox, as Ned, the Brit master spy, provides that precise note of cold British analytical reserve that is required.

So all is in place for an effective movie, except for a screenplay in which anything happens. The director, Fred Schepisi, obtained the playwright Tom Stoppard to make Le Carré's novel into a film, but what it has been made into is sort of a filmed dramatic reading, with endless variations of shots in which middle-aged men stand around saying Le Carré's dialogue.

What's good are the few emotional moments that break out of the weary spy formula: Connery, declaring his love for Pfeiffer, or the British and Americans getting on each other's nerves. But these flashes of energy are isolated inside a screenplay that is static and boring, that drones on lifelessly through the Le Carré universe, like some kind of space probe that continues to send back random information long after its mission has been accomplished.

Ruthless People ★ ★ ★ ½
R, 93 m., 1986

Danny DeVito (Sam Stone), Bette Midler (Barbara Stone), Judge Reinhold (Ken Kessler), Helen Slater (Sandy Kessler), Anita Morris (Carol). Directed by Jim Abrahams, David Zucker, and Jerry Zucker and produced by Michael Peyser. Screenplay by Dale Launer.

It is hard to play a lovable villain, and Danny DeVito does it so easily. His eyes narrow, his voice deepens, and he speaks with great earnestness and sincerity about his selfish schemes and vile designs. *Ruthless People* opens as DeVito is having lunch with his mistress, and we can see that this is a man filled with passion. In this case, the passion is hatred for his wife and for all that she stands for, and for all that her rich father stands for, and even for all that her poodle stands for.

DeVito is the mainspring of *Ruthless People*, the engine of murderous intensity right at the center. His passion is so palpable that it adds weight to all the other performances in the movie. If we can believe he really wants to kill his wife, then we can believe he would not pay the ransom if she were kidnapped, which is the movie's comic premise.

It is, indeed, a pleasure to watch his face as he receives the first call from the kidnappers and they threaten to kill his wife if he doesn't follow every single one of their instructions to the letter. As he agrees to their stipulations, one after another, a wondrous calm spreads over his face, and the scene builds to a perfect climax.

The wife is played by Bette Midler, who makes her first entrance kicking and screaming inside a burlap bag. She has been kidnapped by Judge Reinhold and Helen Slater, who want to get even with DeVito, a clothing manufacturer who has ripped off their designs. It's a juicy role for Midler, a first cousin to the airhead housewife she played in *Down and Out in Beverly Hills*, and she milks it for all it's worth, turning into an exercise freak while being held captive in a basement.

The movie doesn't depend on just the one inspiration—the husband who doesn't want to ransom his wife. It has lots of other ideas and characters that fit together like a clockwork mechanism. We have the mistress (Anita Morris) and her boyfriend (Bill Pullman), who is not playing with a full deck. And then there are the police chief (William G. Schilling), who backs himself into an embarrassing situation, and a mad slasher (J.E. Freeman), who picks the wrong victim when he comes after Midler.

The movie is slapstick with a deft character touch here and there. It's hard to keep all the characters and plot lines alive at once, but *Ruthless People* does it, and at the end I felt grateful for its goofiness.

The discovery in the movie is DeVito. After seeing him on television's "Taxi" and here and there in character roles, I began to notice how good he was in *Romancing the Stone*. Then came his great performance in *Wise Guys*, opposite Joe Piscopo, and now this second virtuoso performance in a row.

He is, of course, very short, but there's a funny thing about his stature: It seems to be a fact of his body, not his mind or personality. In close-ups and whenever he speaks, he has so much force that he can easily command his scenes. He never seems to be compensating; he seems to be holding back. Like British actor Bob Hoskins, who is also shorter than most of the people in most of his scenes, he has a way of making the taller people around him seem unsure of what to do with their legs.

DeVito is a great joy to watch in this movie, as the turns of the plot catch him in one dilemma and then another. First he wants the kidnappers to kill his wife. Then, when he is charged with faking her kidnapping, he wants to ransom her. All along, there's a running gag as he negotiates the ransom price, and Midler has a great moment when she learns that her husband is trying to buy her back—at a discount. *Ruthless People* is made out of good performances, a script of diabolical ingenuity, and a whole lot of silliness.

S

Saint Jack ★ ★ ★ ★
R, 112 m., 1979

Ben Gazzara (Jack Flowers), Denholm Elliott (William Leigh), James Villiers (Frogget), Joss Ackland (Yardley), Rodney Bewes (Smale), Peter Bogdanovich (Schuman), Monika Subramaniam (Monika), George Lazenby (Senator). Directed by Peter Bogdanovich and produced by Roger Corman. Screenplay by Howard Sackler, Paul Theroux, and Bogdanovich.

Sometimes a character in a movie inhabits his world so freely, so easily, that he creates it for us as well. Ben Gazzara does that in *Saint Jack*, as an American exile in Singapore who finds himself employed at the trade of pimp. He sticks his cigar in his mouth and walks through the crowded streets in his flowered sport shirts, he knows everyone, he knows all the angles—but this isn't a smart-aleck performance, something borrowed from Damon Runyon. It's a performance that paints the character with a surprising tenderness and sadness, with a wisdom that does not blame people for what they do, and thus is cheerfully willing to charge them for doing it.

The character, Jack Flowers, is out of a book by Paul Theroux, who took a nonfiction look at this same territory in *The Great Railway Bazaar*, one of the best modern books of travel. The film is by Peter Bogdanovich, and what a revelation it is, coming after three expensive flops.

Bogdanovich, who began so surely in *The Last Picture Show*, seemed to lose feeling and tone as his projects became more bloated. But here everything is right again, even his decision to organize the narrative into an hour of atmosphere and then an hour of payoff.

Everything. Not many films are this good at taking an exotic location like Singapore and a life with the peculiarities of Jack Flowers's, and treating them with such casual familiarity that we really feel Jack lives there—knows it inside out. The movie's complex without being complicated. Its story line is a narrative as straight as *Casablanca*'s (with which it has some kinship), but its details teem with life.

We meet the scheming Chinese traders Jack sometimes works for; the forlorn and drunken British exiles who inhabit "clubs" of small hopes and old jokes; the whores who do not have hearts of gold or minds at all; the odd Ceylonese girl who is Jack's match in cynicism, but not his better.

And we meet William Leigh, another remarkable fictional creation. Leigh is a British citizen out from Hong Kong on business, who looks up Jack Flowers because Jack can arrange things. To Jack's well-concealed surprise, William Leigh doesn't want a prostitute. He wants some talk, a drink, some advice about a hotel room. Jack never really gets to know Leigh, but a bond forms between them because Leigh is *decent*, is that rare thing, a good man.

Denholm Elliott, usually seen here in third-rate British horror films, has the role, and triumphs in it. It is a subtle triumph; the movie doesn't give Leigh noble speeches or indeed much of anything revealing to say, but Elliott exudes a kind of cheery British self-pride, mixed with fears of death, that communicates as clearly as a bell.

Jack Flowers, meanwhile, runs into trouble. Singapore hoodlums are jealous of the success of his brothel, so they kidnap him and tattoo insulting names on his arms (altogether a more diabolical and satisfactory form of gangland revenge than the concrete overcoat). Jack has the tattoos redecorated into flowers, as William Leigh gets drunk with him. Then, his Singapore business opportunities at an end, he signs up with an American CIA type (Bogdanovich) to run an Army brothel near a rest and recreation center.

One of the joys of this movie is seeing how cleanly and surely Bogdanovich employs the two levels of his plot. One level is Jack's story, and leads up to an attempted blackmailing scene that's beautifully sustained. The other level is the level of William Leigh, whose life is so different from Jack's, and yet whose soul makes sense to him. The levels come together in a conclusion that is inevitable, quietly noble, wonderfully satisfactory.

All of this works so well because Bogdanovich, assisted by a superb script and art direction, shows us Jack Flowers's world so confidently—and because Ben Gazzara makes Jack so special. It's not just a surprise that Gazzara could find the notes and tones to make *Saint Jack* live. He has been a good actor for a long time. What's surprising, given the difficulties of this character, is that anyone could.

Salaam Bombay! ★ ★ ★ ★
NO MPAA RATING. 113 m., 1988

Shafiq Syed (Krishna/Chaipau), Sarfuddin Qurrassi (Koyla), Raju Barnad (Keera), Raghubir Yadav (Chillum), Aneeta Kanwar (Rekha), Nana Patekar (Baba), Hansa Vithal (Manju), Mohanraj Babu (Salim), Chandrashekhar Naidu (Chungal). Produced and directed by Mira Nair. Screenplay by Sooni Taraporevala.

The history of the making of *Salaam Bombay!* is almost as interesting as the film itself. The filmmakers gathered a group of the street children of Bombay and talked with them about their experiences, visiting the streets and train stations, bazaars and red-light districts where many of them lived. Out of these interviews emerged a screenplay that was a composite of several lives. Then many of the children were enlisted for weeks in a daily workshop, not to teach them "acting" (for that they already knew from hundreds of overacted Indian film melodramas), but to teach them how to behave naturally in front of the camera.

Out of those workshops a cast gradually emerged, and it was clear almost from the start that the star was an eleven-year-old street child named Shafiq Syed, whose history was unknown, but who proved to be such a natural filmmaker that he sometimes reminded the directors of errors in continuity. Using Syed and shooting on actual locations in Bombay, director Mira Nair has been able to make a film that has the everyday, unforced reality of documentary, and yet the emotional power of great drama. *Salaam Bombay!* is one of the best films of 1988.

Shafiq Syed plays its hero, a boy named Chaipau who works for a traveling circus. One day he is sent on an errand—to get some cigarettes from a neighboring village—and when he returns, the circus has packed up and disappeared. He goes to a nearby village and takes a train to Bombay, following some half-formed plan to return to his native village and his mother, who perhaps sold him to the circus. But Chaipau cannot read or write, and he is not quite sure where his village is, or perhaps even what it is named, and he disappears naturally into the ranks of thousands of children who live, and die, on the streets of Bombay.

These streets are without doubt a cruel and dreadful place, but as Nair sees them, they are not entirely without hope. Her Bombay seems to have a kinship with one of the Victorian slums of Dickens, who portrayed a society in which even the lowest classes had identity and a role to play. In that respect, *Salaam Bombay!* is quite different from *Pixote*, the 1981 film about Brazilian street children. Although the two films obviously have much in common, the children of *Pixote* exist in an anarchic and savage world, while those in *Salaam Bombay!* share a community, however humble.

Chaipau is an intelligent boy, stubborn and wily, and he finds a job as a runner for a man who runs a tea stall in the street. Chaipau's job is to race up flights of tenement stairs with trays of tea, and in the tenements he finds a world of poverty, sweatshops, prostitution, and drug dealing. One of the

friends he makes is a pathetic sixteen-year-old girl who was sold or kidnapped away from her native village, and is being held captive by a rapacious madam who plans to sell her virginity to the highest bidder. The other characters in the neighborhood include a hopeless drunk and addict who befriends the children as best he can.

One of the subplots of the film involves the relationship between a drug dealer and the prostitute who is his common-law wife. She lives for her child, and exists in daily fear that the child will be taken from her because of the life she leads. Nair treats this woman with such sensitivity that we feel great sympathy for her when the child is threatened, and this illustrates one of the underlying beliefs of *Salaam Bombay!*—that the street life, however hard, is preferable to what happens to people once they are identified by the law and become the victims of official institutions.

It is remarkable how well Nair creates this street world and tells us its rules without seeming to force her story. One of her secrets is location shooting; not a single scene in this movie was shot on a set or in a studio, and some of the scenes—including a funeral procession—were shot with hidden cameras to capture the unrehearsed behavior of the spectators.

It is a well-known truism of filmmaking that color photography tends to make locations look better than they are; we lose the smells and the suffering, and see the bright colors and the sunlight. That happens here, I think; the very act of photographing this society has probably tended to romanticize it somewhat. And yet there are moments that remain raw and painful, as when Chaipau drops his street-smart facade for a second and we see the lonely little boy behind it.

One of the questions asked, but not answered, by the film is what should be done about these children. At one point, Chaipau and some friends are rounded up by the police and herded into a large institution that combines the worst features of an orphanage and a prison, but that doesn't seem to be the answer, and we are left with the troubling impression that in Bombay, at any event, the children seem to fare better on the streets. There they have an identity and a measure of hope. Of course, in the best of possible worlds, something would be "done" about them, but *Salaam Bombay!* takes place far from such a world, and the movie is about children doing the best they can for themselves.

Salvador ★ ★ ★
R, 125 m., 1986

James Woods (Richard Boyle), James Belushi (Dr. Rock), Michael Murphy (Ambassador Kelly), John Savage (John Cassady), Elepedia Carrillo (Maria), Tony Plana (Major Max), Colby Chester (Jack Morgan), Cynthia Gibb (Cathy Moore). Directed by Oliver Stone and produced by Gerald Green and Stone. Screenplay by Stone and Richard Boyle.

Given the headlines, you might perhaps think *Salvador* was a controversial movie about America's role in Central America, but actually it's a throwback to a different kind of picture, to the Hunter Thompson story *Where the Buffalo Roam*, where hard-living journalists hit the road in a showdown between a scoop and an overdose. The movie has an undercurrent of seriousness, and it is not happy about the chaos which we are helping to subsidize, but basically it's a character study—a portrait of a couple of burnt-out free-lancers trying to keep their heads above the water.

The movie stars James Woods, that master of nervous paranoia, as a foreign correspondent who has hit bottom. He's drinking, drugging, unemployed, living off past glories. When all hell breaks loose in Central America, he figures it's a good story, since he still has some contacts down there. So he enlists his best friend, a spaced-out disc jockey (James Belushi), and they load up with beer and drive their jalopy down through Mexico to where the action is.

The heart of the movie is in their relationship, and I kept being reminded of another Hunter Thompson saga, his book *Fear and Loathing in Las Vegas*, where the journalist and his lawyer drove their car through the desert, where drug-induced dragons seemed to swoop at them out of the sky. *Salvador* is a movie about real events as seen through the eyes of characters who have set themselves adrift from reality. That's what makes it so interesting.

Once they're at their destination, Woods and Belushi start looking up Woods's old contacts, who include a neofascist general, several bartenders, and an old girlfriend. Woods makes a stab at being a correspondent—he's always on long distance to New York, trying to get credentials from a reputable news-gathering agency—while Belushi settles into the local routine of bars and loose women.

A plot of sorts emerges, along with the usual characters we expect in a story like this—the American generals and embassy spokesmen and CIA types. Woods and Belushi hurry off recklessly in all directions, keep finding themselves surrounded by the wrong people, and escape with their lives only because Woods is such a con artist.

And he is. This is the sort of role James Woods was born to play, with his glibness, his wary eyes, and the endless cigarettes. There is an utter cynicism just beneath the surface of his character, the cynicism of a journalist who has traveled so far, seen so much, and used so many chemicals that every story is just a new version of how everybody gets screwed. That's why there is a special interest in the love affair in this movie, between Woods and Elepedia Carrillo, as the local woman Maria, the woman he truly loves but who lives by a code of Catholicism and respectability—a code that seems constantly in danger of being overwhelmed by events.

The central scene in the movie is possibly the one where Woods goes to confession. He has decided to marry the woman, in order to get her out of the country before all hell breaks loose. She insists on a church wedding. And so we get an extraordinary close-up of Woods's face as he talks with the priest, and tries to make some sort of a bargain between Catholic requirements and his own total ignorance of conventional morality.

Meanwhile, we meet some of the other people on the scene, including John Savage, as a great war photographer, and Michael Murphy, as the American ambassador, a tortured liberal who speaks of peace and freedom while the CIA goes about its usual business right under his nose. The subplot involving the Savage character is not very successful. I can see what they're doing, trying to set him up as a dedicated photojournalist who will risk his life for a great picture, but when he finally does come to his personal turning point, it's for a photo even the audience knows isn't great: A shot of an airplane swooping out of the sky. Without context, it could be any airplane, flying out of any sky.

Salvador is long and disjointed, and tries to tell too many stories for its length. A scene where Woods debates policy with the American officials sounds tacked-on, as if the director and co-writer, Oliver Stone, was afraid of not making his point. But the heart of the movie is fascinating. And the heart consists of Woods and Belushi, two losers set adrift in a world they never made, trying to play games by everybody else's rules.

Sammy and Rosie Get Laid ★ ★ ★ ½
R, 97 m., 1987

Shashi Kapoor (Rafi), Frances Barber (Rosie), Claire Bloom (Alice), Ayub Khan Din (Sammy), Roland Gift (Danny), Wendy Gazelle (Anna), Suzette Llewellyn (Vivia), Meera Syal (Rani). Directed by Stephen Frears and produced by Tim Bevan and Sarah Radclyffe. Screenplay by Hanif Kureishi.

London is not entirely made up of Westminster Abbey, the Tower, the Zoo, and bobbies on bicycles, two by two. It is also made up of the homeless in a cardboard city, under Royal Festival Hall. And of squatters living in rows of houses that seem to belong to nobody. And of people like Sammy and Rosie, living unconventional lives that they seem to improvise day by day.

Rosie is British. Sammy is from India or Pakistan—it's deliberately never made quite clear—where his father is a controversial political leader. Sammy and Rosie live in a comfortable house on a nice street that seems to be on the edge of a war zone. Anarchic mobs seem to hover just out of view. Sammy and Rosie have conventional left-wing political views, and a circle of friends that spans several races and sexes. To some degree, they are upwardly mobile. Then one day, Sammy's father (played by the famous Indian actor Shashi Kapoor) comes to visit.

He is a large, genial man who seems to genuinely love people. But as the taxi brings him from the airport, we cannot fail to notice that the driver wears a bloody headband and has an empty eye socket. The father fails to notice, however, perhaps because in his country the unfortunate are less visible, or perhaps because the cabbie is a ghostly vision that will return to haunt him throughout the movie.

We meet other people in this strange new London. A black, for example, who seems to move freely among several groups as a spokesman for the homeless and a prophet of doom. He helps guide the bewildered father home through the dangerous streets, and then seems to casually move in as a member of the family circle. There are other friends, sexually and politically liberated, who seem to have more freedom than they are happy with. And occasionally that bloody and bandaged figure that seems to haunt the edges of the frame.

Sammy and Rosie Get Laid tells the story of all of these people in a film that is far from hopeful about the future of London. It sees the city as a bulwark of privilege against the homeless, a city in which racism is bad, but class divisions are worse and more harmful, and in which real estate values are routinely considered more important than human lives and plans. In this world, Sammy and Rosie do get laid—by each other, by various friends, and (the movie implies) by the system itself. In one scene that many critics have not applauded, the screen splits in three, horizontally, to show the outcome of a wild party. The sex is desperately cheerless, a metaphor for their lives.

The film was directed by Stephen Frears, whose last film, *My Beautiful Laundrette*, was an international success. It told the story of outsiders who banded together in an unlikely cause: Two gays—an Asian and a white neo-Nazi—became lovers and then partners in running a launderette that was financed by the Asian's rich, property-owning uncle.

In *Sammy and Rosie Get Laid*, there is also the sense that interracial love, once considered some kind of social breakthrough, is not going to change anything fundamental when all races are oppressed by the same economic system (the movie begins with the voice of Margaret Thatcher, praising prosperity while we see people living rough in an urban wasteland).

We learn that Kapoor, the father, was a great admirer of London when he studied there, before returning home to preside over a totalitarian regime. He has fond memories of the parks, walking by the Thames, going to plays at the Royal Court, and falling in love with an elegant British woman (Claire Bloom). Now, during his visit, he tries to recreate some of the magic he remembers. While gangs roam the streets, he revisits some of his favorite places, and spends some heartbreaking time with Bloom, who has never married and who still, in some ways, loves him. The conversations they have are the emotional heart of the film, for what Kapoor is trying to believe is that his romanticism and sentimentality can exist completely apart from his politics.

It doesn't work that way, and that seems to be Frears's argument throughout the film. *Sammy and Rosie Get Laid* is a frontal attack on the favorite fantasies of anglophiles and the British themselves, who see the magical facade of London and ignore the inequalities and social crimes that are right underneath their noses. This will be a difficult film for anyone not fairly familiar with the city and its people; it doesn't have the universal comic undertones of *My Beautiful Laundrette*. It is about specific people and the specific hell they inhabit—a hell that is probably meant to be somewhat prophetic, since not all of the horrors in this film exist (yet) in London. For people who love London and yet are thoughtful about it, this film is indispensable.

Santa Sangre ★ ★ ★ ★
R, 124 m., 1990

Axel Jodorowsky (Fenix), Sabrina Dennison (Alma), Guy Stockwell (Orgo), Blanca Guerra (Concha), Thelma Tixou (Tattooed Woman), Adan Jodorowsky (Fenix, eight years), Faviola Elenka Tapia (Alma, seven years), Jesus Juarez (Aladin). Directed by Alejandro Jodorowsky and produced by Claudio Argento. Screenplay by Jodorowsky, Robert Leoni, and Argento.

Santa Sangre is a throwback to the golden age, to the days when filmmakers had bold individual visions and were not timidly trying to duplicate the latest mass-market formulas. This is a movie like none I have seen before, a wild kaleidoscope of images and outrages, a collision between Freud and Fellini. It contains blood and glory, saints and circuses, and unspeakable secrets of the night. And it is all wrapped up in a flamboyant parade of bold, odd, striking imagery, with Alejandro Jodorowsky as the ringmaster.

Those who were going to the movies in the early 1970s will remember the name. Jodorowsky is the perennial artist in exile who made *El Topo*, that gory cult classic that has since disappeared from view, trapped in a legal battle. Then he made *The Holy Mountain*, another phantasmagoric collection of strange visions, and in recent years he has written a series of fantasy comic books which are best-sellers in France and Mexico. Now he is back with a film that grabs you with its opening frames and shakes you for two hours with the outrageous excesses of his imagination.

The film takes place in Mexico, where the hero, Fenix, travels with his father's circus.

His father is a tattooed strongman, and his mother is an aerialist who hangs high above the center ring, suspended from the long locks of her hair. She is also a mystic who leads a cult of women who worship a saint without arms—a woman whose arms were severed from her body during an attack by a man. The blood of this saint is *santa sangre*, holy blood, collected in a pool in a church which the authorities want to bulldoze.

The church is pulled down in the opening moments of the movie, while horrendous events take place under the big top. While the mother is suspended from her hair high in the air, she sees her husband sneak out with the tattooed lady—and she tracks them down to their place of sin, kills her, and maims her husband with acid before he cuts off her arms and then kills himself.

Or is that what actually happened? The young son, who witnesses these deeds, is discovered years later in an insane asylum, sitting up in a tree, refusing all forms of human communication. Then he receives a visitor—his mother, come to deliver him from his madness. When he re-enters the outer world, he encounters Alma, the deaf-mute girl who was his childhood friend, and who has now grown into a grave, calm young woman. And he embarks on a journey that leads into the most impenetrable thickets of Freudian and Jungian symbology.

Fenix's mother, still without arms, makes him her psychological slave. He must always walk and sit behind her, his arms thrust through the sleeves of her dresses, so that his hands do her bidding. Together they perform in a nightclub act—she sitting at the piano, he playing. But is this really happening, or is it his delusion?

Jodorowsky hardly pauses to consider such questions, so urgent is his headlong rush to confront us with more spectacle. I will never forget one sequence in the movie, the elephant's burial, where the circus marches in mournful procession behind the grotesquely large coffin of the dead animal. It is tipped over the side into a garbage dump, where the coffin is pounced upon and ripped open by starving scavengers. Another powerful image comes in a graveyard, where the spirits of female victims rise up out of their graves to confront their tormentor. And there is the strange, gentle, almost hallucinatory passage where Fenix joins his fellow inmates in a trip into town; Jodorowsky uses mongoloid children in this sequence, his actors communicating with them with

warmth and body contact in a scene that treads delicately between fiction and documentary.

If Jodorowsky has influences—in addition to the psychologists he plunders for complexes—they are Fellini and Bunuel. Federico Fellini, with his love for grotesque and special people and his circuses and parades, and Luis Bunuel, with his delight in depravity and secret perversion, his conviction that respectability was the disguise of furtive self-indulgence. *Santa Sangre* is a movie in which the inner chambers of the soul are laid bare, in which desires become visible and walk into the room and challenge the yearner to possess them.

When I go to the movies, one of my strongest desires is to be shown something new. I want to go to new places, meet new people, have new experiences. When I see Hollywood formulas mindlessly repeated, a little something dies inside of me: I have lost two hours to boors who insist on telling me stories I have heard before. Jodorowsky is not boring. The privilege of making a film is too precious to him, for him to want to make a conventional one. It has been eighteen years since his last work, and all of that time the frustration and inspiration must have been building. Now comes this release, in a rush of energy and creative joy.

Saturday Night Fever ★ ★ ★ ½
R, 118 m., 1977

John Travolta (Tony Manero), Karen Gorney (Stephanie), Barry Miller (Bobby C), Joseph Cail (Joey), Paul Paps (Double J), Donna Pescow (Annette). Directed by John Badham and produced by Robert Stigwood. Screenplay by Norman Wexler.

Each night I ask the stars up above:
Why must I be a teen-ager in love?
　　　　　　　—Dion and the Belmonts

Saturday Night Fever is an especially hard-edged case and a very good movie. It's about a bunch of Brooklyn kids who aren't exactly delinquents but are fearsomely tough and cynical and raise a lot of hell on Saturday nights. They live for Saturday night, in fact: They hang their gold chains around their necks and put on the new shirts they bought with their Friday paychecks, and they head for a place called Disco 2001, and they take pills and drink and, as Leo Sayer put it, dance the night away. Occasionally they go out to the parking lot for a session in the back seat with a girl.

John Travolta is the center of the crowd: He's Tony Manero, the best dancer, the best looker, the guy with the most confidence. His life is just as screwed up as everyone else's, but they don't know that, and they tell him: "You know somethin', Tony? You always seem to be in control."

He is not. He works all week at a paint and hardware store and comes home to a family that worships his older brother, who is a priest. The family's sketched briefly right at the beginning in a dinner scene which, like the whole movie, is able to walk the tightrope between what's funny and what's pathetic.

We meet Tony's friends and the girls that hang around them, and we are reminded that feminism has not yet conquered Brooklyn. Some of the girls, especially a spunky little number named Annette (Donna Pescow), worship Tony. He dances with Annette because she's a good dancer, but he tries to keep her at arm's length otherwise. He's caught in a sexist vise: Because he likes her, he doesn't want to sleep with her, because then how could he respect her? The female world is divided, he explains, between nice girls and tramps. She accepts his reasoning and makes her choice.

The Brooklyn we see in *Saturday Night Fever* reminds us a lot of New York's Little Italy as Martin Scorsese saw it in *Who's That Knocking at My Door?* and *Mean Streets*. The characters are similar: They have few aims or ambitions and little hope of breaking out to the larger world of success—a world symbolized for them by Manhattan, and the Brooklyn Bridge reaching out powerfully toward it. But *Saturday Night Fever* isn't as serious as the Scorsese films. It does, after all, have almost wall-to-wall music in it (mostly by the Bee Gees, but including even "Disco Duck"). And there are the funny scenes (like the one where Travolta shouts at his father: "You hit my hair!") to balance the tragic and self-destructive ones.

There's also a hint of *Rocky,* whose poster Travolta's character has on his bedroom wall. Travolta meets a Brooklyn girl (Karen Gorney) who's made it in Manhattan, sort of, as a secretary. She comes back to Brooklyn to dance, and they team up to enter a $500 disco contest. They win it, too, but not before winning has become meaningless to Travolta. Their relationship is interesting because Travolta sees Miss Gorney not so much as a girl (although he thinks she's beau-

tiful) but as an example of how *he* might escape Brooklyn.

The movie's musical and dancing sequences are dazzling. Travolta and Miss Gorney are great together, and Travolta does one solo (in an unbroken shot) that the audiences cheered for. The movie was directed by John Badham (*The Bingo Long Traveling All-Stars*), and his camera occupies the dance floor so well that we really do understand the lure of the disco world, for all of the emptiness and cruelty the characters find there.

Say Amen, Somebody ★ ★ ★ ★
G, 100 m., 1983

Featuring Willie May Ford Smith, Thomas A. Dorsey, Sallie Martin, the Barrett Sisters, Edward and Edgar O'Neal, and Zella Jackson Price. Directed by George Nierenberg and produced by George and Karen Nierenberg.

Say Amen, Somebody is one of the most joyful movies I've ever seen. It is also one of the best musicals and one of the most interesting documentaries. And it's a terrific good time. The movie is about gospel music, and it's filled with gospel music. It's sung by some of the pioneers of modern gospel, who are now in their seventies and eighties, and it's sung by some of the rising younger stars, and it's sung by choirs of kids. It's sung in churches and around the dining room table; with orchestras and a capella; by an old man named Thomas A. Dorsey in front of thousands of people; and by Dorsey standing all by himself in his own backyard. The music in *Say Amen, Somebody* is as exciting and uplifting as any music I've ever heard on film.

The people in this movie are something, too. The filmmaker, a young New Yorker named George T. Nierenberg, starts by introducing us to two pioneers of modern gospel: Mother Willie May Ford Smith, who is seventy-nine, and Professor Dorsey, who is eighty-three. She was one of the first gospel soloists; he is known as the Father of Gospel Music. The film opens at tributes to the two of them—Mother Smith in a St. Louis church, Dorsey at a Houston convention— and then Nierenberg cuts back and forth between their memories, their families, their music, and the music sung in tribute to them by younger performers.

That keeps the movie from seeming too

much like the wrong kind of documentary— the kind that feels like an educational film and is filled with boring lists of dates and places. *Say Amen, Somebody* never stops moving, and even the dates and places are open to controversy (there's a hilarious sequence in which Dorsey and Mother Smith disagree very pointedly over exactly which of them convened the first gospel convention).

What's amazing in all of the musical sequences is the quality of the sound. A lot of documentaries use "available sound," picked up by microphones more appropriate for the television news. This movie's concerts are miked by up to eight microphones, and the Dolby system is used to produce full stereo sound that really rocks. Run it through your stereo speakers, and play it loud.

Willie May Ford Smith comes across in this movie as an extraordinary woman, spiritual, filled with love and power. Dorsey and his longtime business manager, Sallie Martin, come across at first as a little crusty, but then there's a remarkable scene where they sing along, softly, with one of Dorsey's old records. By the end of the film, when the ailing Dorsey insists on walking under his own steam to the front of the gospel convention in Houston, and leading the delegates in a hymn, we have come to see his strength and humanity. Just in case Smith and Dorsey seem too noble, the film uses a lot of mighty soul music as a counterpoint, particularly in the scenes shot during a tribute to Mother Smith at a St. Louis Baptist church. We see Delois Barrett Campbell and the Barrett Sisters, a Chicago-based trio who have enormous musical energy; the O'Neal Twins, Edward and Edgar, whose "Jesus Dropped the Charges" is a show-stopper; Zella Jackson Price, a younger singer who turns to Mother Smith for advice; the Interfaith Choir; and lots of other singers.

Say Amen, Somebody is the kind of movie that isn't made very often, because it takes an unusual combination of skills. The filmmaker has to be able to identify and find his subjects, win their confidence, follow them around, and then also find the technical skill to really capture what makes them special. Nierenberg's achievement here is a masterpiece of research, diligence, and direction. But his work would be meaningless if the movie didn't convey the spirit of the people in it, and *Say Amen, Somebody* does that with great and mighty joy. This is a great experience.

Say Anything ★ ★ ★ ★
PG-13, 103 m., 1989

John Cusack (Lloyd Dobler), Ione Skye (Diane Court), John Mahoney (James Court), Lili Taylor (Corey Flood), Amy Brooks (D.C.), Pamela Segall (Rebecca), Jason Gould (Mike Cameron), Loren Dean (Joe). Directed by Cameron Crowe and produced by Polly Platt. Screenplay by Crowe.

She is the class brain, and so, of course, no one can see that she is truly beautiful—no one except for the sort of weird kid who wants to devote his life to kick-boxing, and who likes her because of her brains. He calls her up and asks her out. She says no. He keeps talking. She says yes. And after their first date, she tells her father she likes him because he is utterly straightforward and dependable. He is a goofy teen-ager with absolutely no career prospects, but she senses that she can trust him as an anchor.

She discusses him so openly with her father because they have made a pact: They can say anything to one another. When her parents got divorced, she chose to live with her father because of this trust, because of the openness that he encourages. Her father's love for her is equalled by his respect. And she sees him as a good man, who works long hours running a nursing home because he wants to help people.

Honesty is at the core of *Say Anything*, but dishonesty is there, too, and the movie is the story of how the young woman is able to weather a terrible storm and be stronger and better afterward. This was one of the best films of 1989—a film that is really about something, that cares deeply about the issues it contains—and yet it also works wonderfully as a funny, warmhearted romantic comedy.

The young woman, Diane, is played by Ione Skye as a straight-A student with a scholarship to a school in England. She is one of the class beauties, but doesn't date much because she intimidates boys. The boy who finally asks her out is Lloyd (John Cusack), and he dates her not only out of hormonal urging, but because he admires her. Her father (John Mahoney) is a caring, trusting parent who will do anything he can to encourage his daughter—but his secret is that he has done too much. They find that out when IRS agents come knocking on the door with charges of criminal tax evasion.

The movie treats Diane's two relationships with equal seriousness. This is not one of those movies where the father is a dim-witted, middle-aged buffoon with no insights into real life, and it is also not one of those movies where the young man is obviously the hero. Everyone in this film is complicated, and has problems, and is willing to work at life and try to make it better.

The romance between Diane and Lloyd is intelligent and filled with that special curiosity that happens when two young people find each other not only attractive but interesting—when they sense they might actually be able to learn something useful from the other person. Lloyd has no career plans, no educational plans, no plans except to become a champion kick-boxer, and then, after he meets Diane, to support her because she is worthy of his dedication. In the way they trust each other and learn to depend on each other, their relationship reminded me of the equally complex teen-age love story between River Phoenix and Martha Plimpton in *Running on Empty*.

What's unique to this movie is how sure-footed it is in presenting the ordinary everyday lives and rituals of kids in their late teens. The parties, the conversations, and the value systems seem real and carefully observed; these teen-agers are not simply empty-headed *Animal House* retreads; the movie pays them the compliment of seeing them as actual people with opinions and futures.

Cameron Crowe, who wrote and directed the film, develops its underlying ideas with a precise subtlety. This is not a melodrama about two kids who fall in love and a parent who gets in trouble with the IRS. It considers the story as if it were actually happening, with all the uncertainties of real life. When Diane goes to confront a government agent, and tells him that he is harassing her father who is a good man, Crowe allows the scene to develop so that we can see more than one possibility; he even cares enough to give the IRS agent—a minor character—three dimensions.

I was also surprised to find that the movie had a third act and a concluding scene that really concluded something. Today's standard movie script contains a setup, some development, and then some kind of violent or comic cataclysm that is intended to pass for a resolution. *Say Anything* follows all the threads of its story through to the end; we're interested in what happens to the characters, and so is the movie.

The performances are perfectly suited to the characters. Ione Skye—who was a model before she was an actress—successfully creates the kind of teen-age girl who is overlooked in high school because she doesn't have the surface glitz of the cheerleaders, but who emerges at the tenth class reunion as a world-class beauty. John Cusack, a unique, quirky actor with great individuality, turns in a fast-talking, intensely felt performance that is completely original; he is so good here that if you haven't seen him in *The Sure Thing* or *Eight Men Out*, you might imagine he is simply playing himself. But his performance is a complete and brilliant invention. And John Mahoney (Olympia Dukakis's sad-eyed would-be swain in *Moonstruck*) finds the right note for a father who cares, and loves, and deceives both himself and his daughter, and tries to rationalize his behavior *because* he cares and loves.

Say Anything is one of those rare movies that has something to teach us about life. It doesn't have a "lesson" or a "message," but it observes its moral choices so carefully that it helps us see our own. That such intelligence could be contained in a movie that is simultaneously so funny and so entertaining is some kind of a miracle.

Scandal ★ ★ ★ ★
R, 112 m., 1989

John Hurt (Stephen Ward), Joanne Whalley-Kilmer (Christine Keeler), Bridget Fonda (Mandy Rice-Davies), Ian McKellen (John Profumo), Leslie Phillips (Lord Astor), Britt Ekland (Mariella Novotny), Daniel Massey (Mervyn Griffith-Jones), Roland Gift (Johnnie Edgecombe), Jean Alexander (Mrs. Keeler). Directed by Michael Caton-Jones and produced by Stephen Woolley. Screenplay by Michael Thomas.

All Stephen Ward ever really wanted to do in life was to move in the right circles, with the right friends, and be left in peace and quiet. His strategy for gaining admission to the world of British society was unorthodox, but not unkind. He found young women with promise but no prospects, and then he groomed them, coached them, took them to the right places, and introduced them to his important friends.

He was, in a sense, the Henry Higgins of his time, and his most successful Eliza Doolittle was a poor but pretty girl he discovered in a strip show. Her name was

Christine Keeler, and he lovingly transformed her into a desirable companion for cabinet members, diplomats, and the aristocracy. His only miscalculation was to allow her to sleep with the British defense minister and a Russian military attache during the same period. That was a mistake that brought down a government, and cost Ward his life.

Scandal tells the story of Stephen Ward with a great deal of sympathy for his motives, and a great deal of anger against the British establishment. Although Ward was convicted of living off the earnings of a prostitute—a decision handed down after he committed suicide in the middle of his trial— the film argues that he never accepted any meaningful sums of money from anybody, and his only real motive, a rather touching one, was to do a favor for both the girls and his famous friends. If his method for doing that—arranging illicit sexual relationships— was unconventional or unsavory, let it be noted that none of the participants on either side of the bargain made the slightest complaint until they found their faces on the front pages of the newspapers.

The facts of the Ward affair are part of modern British history. Christine Keeler and her friend, Mandy Rice-Davies, moved in circles that included some of the most famous and powerful men of their time. After one of them, Defense Minister John Profumo, admitted that he had lied to Parliament about his involvement with Keeler, he was forced to resign, and eventually the widening scandal brought down the Conservative government of Harold Macmillan. The movie *Scandal* argues that a scapegoat had to be found to contain the outrage—and Ward, a harmless and gentle osteopath, was the victim. So efficiently and ruthlessly did the establishment circle its wagons to defend itself that even now, twenty-five years later, attempts to make *Scandal* as a TV miniseries were blocked in England, and it has finally appeared as a movie—as a political melodrama that is also an unexpectedly touching love story between almost the only two major players in the episode who never slept with one another, Ward and Keeler.

The movie's strength is that it is surprisingly wise about the complexities of the human heart. Although the newspapers scorned Keeler's claim that she and Ward were simply "close friends," the movie argues that that was quite possible, and true: She felt gratitude for his decision to pluck her from obscurity and groom her for a kind of stardom, and she believed, if she did not fully understand, that his only reward was in seeing his creation pass, respected and unquestioned, in the highest circles. Since England is one of the most class-conscious nations on earth, this sort of transfer in social strata has a powerful hold on the national imagination (cf. the Ascot scene in *My Fair Lady*, with Eliza testing her upper-class accent).

The movie stars John Hurt in one of the best performances of his career as Ward, the chain-smoking, shabbily genteel doctor, who lives in a coach house with Keeler but spends his weekends as the guest of such friends as Lord Astor, who gave him the key to a guest cottage on his estate. In an early scene, Hurt's eyes light up as he sees a pretty girl walking down the street, and somehow Hurt is able to make us understand that he feels, not lust, but simply a deep and genuine appreciation for how wonderful a pretty girl can look on a fine spring day.

Christine Keeler is played by Joanne Whalley-Kilmer, an actress previously unknown to me, and she walks a fine line with great confidence, seeming neither innocent nor sluttish, but more of a smart, ambitious, and essentially honest young woman who finds that it is no more unpleasant to sleep with rich and important men than with her poor and obscure boyfriend. Mandy Rice-Davies (Bridget Fonda) is a different type of woman, more calculating, more cynical, and probably more intelligent, and perhaps it is no accident that Rice-Davies has gone on to a certain success in business and society during the last twenty-five years, while Keeler has returned to a form of the anonymity from which Ward tried to rescue her.

Some of the most evocative scenes in the movie involve backstage moments between the two women, when they casually discuss their lovers, plan their lives, and pay the most painstaking attention to their faces. These women apply themselves more voluptuously to their makeup than to any of the men in their lives.

The movie, written by Michael Thomas and directed by Michael Caton-Jones, has the feeling of having been made from the inside. It moves effortlessly through the mine fields of British government and society, capturing such nuances as the way in which Lord Astor summons Ward to his club to inform him, shame-facedly, that the scandal has forced him to ask for the return of the key to his cottage. Always circling outside the walls of this inner sanctum are the rabble of the British gutter press—and even as a fellow newspaperman, I am willing to describe them in that way, because there is a certain level of decency in news-gathering which they seem never to have glimpsed.

Scandal is a sad story about human nature, which understands why people sometimes sleep in the wrong beds, and takes note that this is understood privately, but not publicly. When the light of day shines on these affairs, lives are destroyed. The saddest moment in the movie comes in the final courtroom scene, when Keeler is called as a witness and is mercilessly battered by the prosecutor until finally Ward stands up in the defendant's box and cries out, "That is not fair!" That is the cry of this movie.

Scarecrow ★ ★ ★
R, 112 m., 1973

Gene Hackman (Max), Al Pacino (Lion), Dorothy Tristan (Coley), Ann Wedgeworth (Frenchy). Directed by Jerry Schatzberg and produced by Robert M. Sherman. Screenplay by Garry Michael White.

Max has been in the slammer and Lionel has been away at sea. Max has been sending his prison wages back to a savings and loan in Pittsburgh, and Lionel has been sending his to a wife in Detroit and a child he's never seen. They hitch up on the Coast and hit the road with a dream of their own car wash with real nylon brushes.

It's a trip we've taken before. We took it in *Of Mice and Men*, when there was a nice little farm at the end of the rainbow; we took it in *Easy Rider*, with the drug dealers who wanted to retire in Florida; we took it, most recognizably, in *Midnight Cowboy*, where the goal was those Florida orange groves.

Movies like *Scarecrow* (which shared the 1973 grand prize at Cannes) depend upon a couple of conventions. One is that we know more about the lower-middle-class characters than they know about themselves. The other is that we accept the easy rhythm of a picaresque journey without depending too much on plot. *Scarecrow* doesn't quite make it on either count, but it is a well-acted movie and for long stretches we're hoping it will work.

The performers are Gene Hackman and Al Pacino, two of the most gifted of contemporary actors, and the dialogue and locations (on the road, in taverns, at lunch counters, on a prison farm) strike a nicely realistic low key. But then director Jerry Schatzberg and his writer, Garry Michael White, commit the first of several mistakes: They tell us what the title means. The moment we hear the philosophy behind the scarecrow (he doesn't scare the crows; he makes them laugh) we begin to suspect these characters are too conscious of their symbolic roles, and we're right.

There's another problem, too. Schatzberg, a celebrated photographer, has teamed up with Vilmos Zsigmond (*McCabe and Mrs. Miller*) to produce a movie so obsessed with its visual look that it suffers dramatically. The movie is annoyingly lighted; we constantly seem to be peering through fog at the characters. In a scene or two, this could be nice. At almost two hours, it's an affectation. So is Schatzberg's willingness to allow shots to continue at length; an opening conversation at a lunch counter runs maybe three or four minutes. It's a virtuoso piece of acting by Hackman and Pacino, but after a while the shot calls attention to itself and away from them.

Still, there are fine moments, as there would have to be with Hackman and Pacino. There's a scene in a bar when a would-be fight turns into a comic striptease by Hackman. There's a bittersweet interlude with Max's sister and her girlfriend. And there are times of just rambling, as the two friends depend on each other in a big and lonely world. It's too bad everything is brought together to a big, smashing, dramatic crisis at the end; *Scarecrow* somehow should have drifted out on a lower key.

Scarface ★ ★ ★ ★
R, 170 m., 1983

Al Pacino (Tony Montana), Steven Bauer (Manny Ray), Michelle Pfeiffer (Elvira), Mary Elizabeth Mastrantonio (Gina), Robert Loggia (Frank Lopez). Directed by Brian De Palma and produced by Martin Bregman. Screenplay by Oliver Stone.

The interesting thing is the way Tony Montana stays in the memory, taking on the dimensions of a real, tortured person. Most thrillers use interchangeable characters, and most gangster movies are more interested in action than personality, but *Scarface* is one of those special movies, like *The Godfather*, that

is willing to take a flawed, evil man and allow him to be human. Maybe it's no coincidence that Montana is played by Al Pacino, the same actor who played Michael Corleone. Montana is a punk from Cuba. The opening scene of the movie informs us that when Cuban refugees were allowed to come to America in 1981, Fidel Castro had his own little private revenge and cleaned out his prison cells, sending us criminals along with his weary and huddled masses. We see Montana trying to bluff his way through an interrogation by U.S. federal agents, and that's basically what he'll do for the whole movie: bluff. He has no real character and no real courage, although for a short time cocaine gives him the illusion of both.

Scarface takes its title from the 1932 Howard Hawks movie, which was inspired by the career of Al Capone. That Hawks film was the most violent gangster film of its time, and this 1983 film by Brian De Palma also has been surrounded by a controversy over its violence, but in both movies the violence grows out of the lives of the characters; it isn't used for thrills but for a sort of harrowing lesson about self-destruction. Both movies are about the rise and fall of a gangster, and they both make much of the hero's neurotic obsession with his sister, but the 1983 *Scarface* isn't a remake, and it owes more to *The Godfather* than to Hawks.

That's because it sees its criminal so clearly as a person with a popular product to sell, working in a society that wants to buy. In the old days it was booze. For the Corleones, it was gambling and prostitution. Now it's cocaine. The message for the dealer remains the same: Only a fool gets hooked on his own goods. For Tony Montana, the choices seem simple at first. He can work hard, be honest, and make a humble wage as a dishwasher. Or he can work for organized crime, make himself more vicious than his competitors and get the big cars, the beautiful women, and the boot-licking attention from nightclub doormen. He doesn't wash many dishes.

As Montana works his way into the south Florida illegal drug trade, the movie observes him with almost anthropological detachment. This isn't one of those movies where the characters all come with labels attached ("boss," "lieutenant," "hit man") and behave exactly as we expect them to. De Palma and his writer, Oliver Stone, have created a gallery of specific individuals and one of the fascinations of the movie is that we

aren't watching crime-movie clichés, we're watching people who are criminals.

Al Pacino does not make Montana into a sympathetic character, but he does make him into somebody we can identify with, in a horrified way, if only because of his perfectly understandable motivations. Wouldn't we all like to be rich and powerful, have desirable sex partners, live in a mansion, be catered to by faithful servants—and hardly have to work? Well, yeah, now that you mention it. Dealing drugs offers the possibility of such a lifestyle, but it also involves selling your soul. Montana gets it all and he loses it all. That's predictable. What is original about this movie is the attention it gives to how little Montana enjoys it while he has it. Two scenes are truly pathetic; in one of them, he sits in a nightclub with his blond mistress and his faithful sidekick, and he's so wiped out on cocaine that the only emotions he can really feel are impatience and boredom. In the other one, trying for a desperate transfusion of energy, he plunges his face into a pile of cocaine and inhales as if he were a drowning man.

Scarface understands this criminal personality, with its links between laziness and ruthlessness, grandiosity and low self-esteem, pipe dreams and a chronic inability to be happy. It's also an exciting crime picture, in the tradition of the 1932 movie. And, like the Godfather movies, it's a gallery of wonderful supporting performances: Steven Bauer as a sidekick, Michelle Pfeiffer as a woman whose need for drugs leads her from one wrong lover to another, Robert Loggia as a mob boss who isn't quite vicious enough, and Mary Elizabeth Mastrantonio, as Pacino's kid sister who wants the right to self-destruct in the manner of her own choosing. These are the people Tony Montana deserves in his life, and *Scarface* is a wonderful portrait of a real louse.

Scenes from a Mall ★
R, 87 m., 1991

Bette Midler (Deborah), Woody Allen (Nick), Bill Irwin (Mime), Daren Firestone (Sam), Rebecca Nickels (Jennifer), Paul Mazursky (Dr. Hans Clava). Directed and produced by Paul Mazursky. Screenplay by Roger L. Simon and Mazursky.

There is a theory about film directing which teaches that every shot is wasted that does not further the story. When details are added to make things "interesting" or "colorful," they only distract from the forward progress of the narrative, and bore us. For example, I tell you, "A guy is on a lonely road in cold weather, trying to get his car started." What do you want to know? What he does to get his car started, right? Now what if I say, "A balding, middle-aged appliance salesman is on Alaska Route 47, trying to get his Ford Victoria started when it's forty-seven below zero." More interesting, or less?

Less, I'd say, because the additional detail was not crucial for the thrust of my story. And what if I added lots of other touches, like giving him a bumper sticker that says "The more I know men, the more I trust dogs." Better, or worse? In a mediocre film with nothing to say, the details might provide momentary flashes of distraction. But the pure story line would be lost: The guy against the elements and a stubborn machine. When a movie seems overflowing with interesting, colorful details, that is often a sign of desperation—a way of saying, if the picture's no good, get a gaudier frame.

These remarks are inspired by Paul Mazursky's *Scenes from a Mall*, a movie that stars Woody Allen and Bette Midler, and is very bad indeed. Ever since seeing the film I've been trying to figure out what went wrong. This is a movie I've been looking forward to since it was first announced. How could Mazursky, whose work includes *An Unmarried Woman*, *Down and Out in Beverly Hills*, and *Enemies, a Love Story*, possibly make a bad movie starring Woody Allen and Bette Midler? Isn't the combination of director and cast so good that the movie has to work?

And yet the movie doesn't work, except for a short time at the beginning, when we are meeting the characters. They're affluent professionals who have just packed the kids off to camp and are now embarking on a shopping trip to the local mall. There are some laughs in these opening scenes, but more importantly, interest is generated: We learn enough about these people to become curious. Even if they're not stranded in the Arctic, even if they're only celebrating their sixteenth wedding anniversary, that's enough, and we wait patiently to see where the day will lead them.

Where it leads them, alas, is into a fog of arbitrary storytelling and desperate gimmicks, sudden revelations and unmotivated mood swings, in a movie that seems to have been written without having been thought about very much. The screenplay—by Roger L. Simon, with Mazursky—creates big gestures for its characters because it doesn't know them well enough to give them small gestures.

The entire drama, lock, stock, and barrel, takes place inside the mall. All of the fights, all of the reconciliations. This leads to a mechanical and increasingly desperate search for new locations, such as a sushi bar, a champagne-and-caviar lounge, many different shops, and escalators, lots of escalators.

Why so many colorful things in the background? Why so many dreary reaction shots of people being shocked by the behavior of Allen and Midler? Why so many fancy trick shots in mirrors and up and down escalators and through windows and augmented by elaborate pictorial props? It's a desperate search to insert pictorial interest into a frame that everyone must have known was lacking dramatic interest.

And then there's the matter of the mime, played by Bill Irwin in a performance that must go immediately into the hall of shame for supporting actors. Everywhere Allen and Midler go, they're shadowed by this obnoxious mime, who has been hired by the mall to entertain the customers, but has a face and manner that inspires immediate dislike. Irwin's performance distracts from, and diminishes, everything else on the screen. The mime is so repellent that he spoils even a scene that should have raised a cheer from viewers—when Allen socks him in the jaw. This is a scene you wouldn't think could miss, since everyone in the audience has been wanting to take out this SOB for an hour, but somehow the timing doesn't deliver the laugh, and the too-long-held reaction gives the whole moment the charm of fingernails on a blackboard.

How could *Scenes from a Mall* have been repaired? Only at the screenplay level, before filming began. Allen and Midler struggle heroically with their characters, but there is nothing in this story for us to believe. Every moment feels arbitrary. Nothing flows from genuine human feelings. The mime mimics and mocks the characters, but in the strongly negative feelings he inspires, perhaps he also mocks the hopes of the filmmakers, by dramatizing in a visible way how much the film has been tricked up with gimmicks to disguise the absence of real care for real characters.

Scenes from a Marriage ★ ★ ★ ★
PG, 168 m., 1974

Liv Ullmann (Marianne), Erland Josephson (Johan), Bibi Andersson (Katarina), Jan Malmslo (Peter). Directed and written by Ingmar Bergman.

They have reached a truce which they call happiness. When we first meet them, they're being interviewed for some sort of newspaper article, and they agree that after ten years of marriage, they're a truly happy couple. The husband, Johan, is most sure: He is successful in his work, in love with his wife, the father of two daughters, liked by his friends, considered on all sides to be a decent chap. His wife, Marianne, listens more tentatively. When it is her turn, she says she is happy, too, although in her work she would like to move in the direction of—but then she's interrupted for a photograph. We are never quite sure what she might have said, had she been allowed to speak as long as her husband. And, truth to tell, he doesn't seem to care much himself. Although theirs is, of course, a perfect marriage.

And so begins one of the truest, most luminous love stories ever made, Ingmar Bergman's *Scenes from a Marriage*. The marriage of Johan and Marianne will disintegrate soon after the film begins, but their love will not. They will fight and curse each other, and it will be a wicked divorce, but in some fundamental way they have touched, really touched, and the memory of that touching will be something to hold to all of their days.

Bergman has been working for years with the theme of communication between two people. At one time, he referred to it as "the agony of the couple." And who can forget the terrible recriminations and psychic bloodshed of the couples in *Winter Light* or *The Passion of Anna*? And here he seems finally to have resolved his crisis.

The years that preceded the making of this film saw a remarkable conciliation going on within the work of this great artist. In *Cries and Whispers*, he was at last able to face the fact of death in a world where God seemed silent. And now, in this almost heartbreaking masterpiece, he has dealt with his fear that all men are, indeed, islands. The film (168 minutes, skillfully and without distraction edited down from six, fifty-minute Swedish television programs) took him four months to make, he has said, but a lifetime to experience.

His married couple are Swedish upper-middle-class. He is a professor, she is a lawyer specializing in family problems (for which, read divorce). They have two daughters, who remain offscreen. They are intelligent, independent. She truly believes their marriage is a happy one (although she doesn't much enjoy sex). One evening, he comes to their summer cottage and confesses that he has gone and fallen in love with someone else. There is nothing to be done about it. He must leave her.

The way in which his wife reacts to this information displays the almost infinite range of Liv Ullmann, who is a beautiful soul and a gifted performer. Her husband (Erland Josephson) has left her literally without an alternative ("You have shut me out. How can I help us?") and still she loves him. She fears that he will bring unhappiness upon himself.

But he does leave, and the film's form is a sometimes harsh, sometimes gentle, ultimately romantic (in an adult and realistic way) view of the stages of this relationship. At first, their sexual attraction for each other remains, even though they bitterly resent each other because of mutual hurts and recriminations. The frustrations they feel about themselves are taken out on each other. At one point, he beats her and weeps for himself, and we've never seen such despair on the screen. But the passage of time dulls the immediate hurt and the feeling of betrayal. And at last, they are able to meet as fond friends and even to make love, as if visiting an old home they'd once been cozy in.

They drift apart, they marry other people (who also remain offscreen), they meet from time to time.

Ten years after the film has opened, they find themselves in Stockholm while both their spouses are out of the country, and, as a nostalgic lark, decide to spend a weekend in their old summer cottage. But it's haunted with memories, and they go to a cottage nearby.

In the last section of the film (subtitled "In the Middle of the Night in a Dark House"), Marianne awakens screaming with a nightmare, and Johan holds her.

And this is twenty years after they were married, and ten years after they were divorced, and they are in middle age now but in the night still fond and frightened lovers holding on for reassurance.

And that is what Bergman has been able to accept, the source of his reconciliation: Beyond love, beyond marriage, beyond the selfishness that destroys love, beyond the centrifugal force that sends egos whirling away from each other and prevents enduring relationships—beyond all these things, there still remains what we know of each other, that we care about each other, that in twenty years these people have touched and known so deeply that they still remember, and still need.

Marianne and Johan are only married for the first part of this film, but the rest of it is also scenes from their marriage.

School Daze ★ ★ ★ ½
R, 114 m., 1988

Larry Fishburne (Dap Dunlap), Giancarlo Esposito (Julian Eaves), Tisha Campbell (Jane Toussaint), Kyme (Rachel Meadows), Joe Seneca (President McPherson), Branford Marsalis (Jordan), Spike Lee (Half-Pint). Directed, produced, and written by Spike Lee.

Spike Lee's *School Daze* is the first movie in a long time where the black characters seem to be relating to one another, instead of to a hypothetical white audience. His *She's Gotta Have It* was another, and then you have to go back to films like *Sweet Sweetback's Baadasssss Song* in 1970. Although the film has big structural problems and leaves a lot of loose ends, there was never a moment when it didn't absorb me, because I felt as if I was watching the characters talk to one another instead of to me.

Most good movies are voyeuristic—we feel as if we're getting a glimpse of other people's lives—but most movies about blacks have lacked that quality. They seem acutely aware of white audiences, white value systems, and the white Hollywood establishment. They interpret rather than reveal, and even in attacking mainstream white society (as Eddie Murphy does in the *Beverly Hills Cop* movies), they pay homage to it in a backhanded way. *School Daze* couldn't care less.

What's surprising is that its revolutionary approach is found in a daffy story about undergraduates at an all-black university. The movie is basically a comedy, with some serious scenes that don't always quite seem to fit. (It begins with a demonstration against the school's investments in South Africa, but doesn't remember to resolve that subject.) It deals with divisions within the student body—between Greeks and independents, and between political activists and kids who just want to get good grades.

And with utter frankness it addresses two subjects that are taboo in most "black movies"—complexion and hair. Lee divides the women on his campus into two groups, the lighter-skinned girls of the Gamma Ray sorority, with their straightened and longer hair, and the darker-skinned independents, with shorter hair or Afros. These two groups call each other the "Wannabes" and the "Jigaboos," and in a brilliant and startling song-and-dance sequence called "Straight and Nappy," they express their feelings for each other. Lee's choice of a musical production number to consider these emotionally charged subjects is an inspiration; there is possibly no way the same feelings could be expressed in spoken dialogue without great awkwardness and pain.

The division within the movie is dramatized by two characters—Dap Dunlap (Larry Fishburne), the intellectual activist and leader of demonstrations against the conservative administration; and Half-Pint (Spike Lee), the undersized kid who dreams of being initiated into the school's most popular fraternity. The two characters play cousins, and it is a sign of the movie's subtle appreciation of campus values that Fishburne, the revolutionary who rejects fraternities, quietly goes to the president of the chapter to put in a good word for his cousin.

In its own way, *School Daze* confronts a lot of issues that aren't talked about in the movies these days, not only issues of skin color and hair, but also the emergence of a black middle class, the purpose of all-black universities in an integrated society, and the sometimes sexist treatment of black women by black men. In one of the movie's most uncompromising sequences, a black fraternity pledge-master expresses concern that Half-Pint is still a virgin (none of the brothers in this house should be virgins), and he supplies his own girlfriend (Tisha Campbell) to initiate the freshman. She actually goes through with it, tearfully, and although the scene was so painful it was difficult to watch, I later reflected that Lee played it for the pain, not for the kind of smutty comedy we might expect in a movie about undergraduates.

Although there was a brief age of "black exploitation movies" in the 1970s, there have never been very many good American movies about the varieties of the black experience. Black superstars like Eddie Murphy and Richard Pryor are essentially playing to (and with) white audiences, and serious dramas about blacks, even strong ones like *The Color Purple*, are so loaded with nobility and message that they feel like secular sermons. Now here is Spike Lee with a slight, disorganized comedy named *School Daze*, and he just sort of assumes a completely black orientation for his film. There is not a single white person in it. All of the characters, good and bad, are black, and all of the characters' references are to each other.

In *Shoot to Kill*, a 1988 Sidney Poitier film, no mention at all is made of his race until a scene where he jumps up and down and scares away a bear. Then he says, "People here act like they've never seen a black man before." The line got a big laugh from the sneak preview audience I saw it with, but when you analyze it, it was an aside pitched straight at the audience. There are no asides in *School Daze*, and no self-conscious references to blackness. The result is an entertaining comedy, but also much more than that. There is no doubt in my mind but that *School Daze*, in its own way, is one of the most honest and revealing movies I've ever seen about modern middle-class black life in America.

Scrooged ★
PG-13, 101 m., 1988

Bill Murray (Frank Cross), Karen Allen (Claire Phillips), Alfre Woodard (Grace Cooley), David Johansen (Cabby/Christmas Past), Carol Kane (Sugar Plum Fairy/Christmas Present), Bobcat Goldthwait (Eliot Loudermilk), Robert Mitchum (Preston Rhinelander), Nicholas Phillips (Calvin Cooley), John Forsythe (Lew Hayward), John Glover (Brice Cummings), Mabel King (Gramma), Brian Doyle-Murray (Father in 1958), John Murray (Brother James), Michael J. Pollard (Herman). Directed by Richard Donner and produced by Donner and Art Linson. Screenplay by Mitch Glazer and Michael O'Donoghue.

Scrooged is one of the most disquieting, unsettling films to come along in quite some time. It was obviously intended as a comedy, but there is little comic about it, and indeed the movie's overriding emotion seems to be pain and anger. This entire production seems to be in dire need of visits from all of the ghosts of Christmas.

The movie stars Bill Murray as Frank Cross, a tormented TV network president who is approaching the Christmas season in a foul mood. He has cut himself off from everybody who loves him, he delights in criticizing and humiliating his colleagues, and he leads a lonely life, sitting in his high-rise office watching TV and pouring down vodka. His idea of an effective promotional ad is one that scares viewers into watching. His next production will be a multimillion-dollar live Christmas Eve performance of *Scrooge*, and we follow him through the wreckage of his life as he attempts to wreck the TV show, as well.

Cross is a thoroughly miserable wretch, played by Bill Murray in a thoroughly miserable mood. What seems to be missing is the lightness and good cheer that lurk beneath the surface of most Murray performances. He's often gruff in his movies, but in a way that lets you know he's just kidding. This time, he doesn't seem to be kidding, and his ill humor affects the chemistry of scene after scene, introducing a kind of undertow. When he shouts at people, he doesn't add a little spin of self-mocking exaggeration so that we know to laugh. He seems to be really shouting. And the other actors look as if they feel really shouted at.

During the course of the movie, the TV executive experiences his own version of the events that haunted Ebenezer Scrooge in Charles Dickens's *A Christmas Carol*. Frank Cross is visited by the ghosts of Christmas past, present, and future, and shown how miserable he really is, and how unhappy he has made everyone else. The Bob Cratchit of his story is his long-suffering secretary Grace Cooley (Alfre Woodard) whose son, the Tiny Tim character, is old enough to speak but has never opened his mouth. Cross gives the secretary a bath towel for Christmas, but when he is taken by a ghost to look in through the window of her household, he realizes how much happiness is missing from his life.

Meanwhile, there is trouble for Cross on the professional front. The chief executive officer of the network (Robert Mitchum) has lost confidence in him and brought in a brash outsider (John Glover) to "lend a hand." Cross fears that his job is threatened, especially since the Mitchum character seems to have gone off the deep end ("Do you realize," he asks his underling, "that there is increasing evidence that dogs and cats watch television?").

The fear of job loss and the lessons from the Christmas ghosts result in a moral trans-formation for Cross, and in the final scenes of the movie the repentant TV executive barges onto the set of the live production of *Scrooge* and testifies to his change of heart. This sequence is the strangest in the film. The words are there, but the heart is lacking. Bill Murray stands center stage and rants and raves about the spirit of Christmas, but it's not an inspiring speech and certainly not a funny one. It sounds more desperate than anything else, and it continues at embarrassing length. It looks like an onscreen breakdown. Finally he demands a miracle, and his secretary's little tyke is dragged forward to demonstrate that he can actually speak at last. Then the entire cast and crew line up behind Murray to sing of Christmas cheer, and I can't remember when I've seen anything along these lines that was more forced and depressing.

What went wrong here? I have no idea. The chemistry must have been bad from the start. Or perhaps the material was simply intractable. One problem is that Murray frequently interjects one-liners that are at right angles to the material, blocking the flow of the story. We get the impression, at those moments, that he is seeking to distance himself from the film, but a story like this works only if it seems to believe in itself. You can't bad-mouth *A Christmas Carol* all the way through and then expect us to believe the good cheer at the end.

Sea of Love ★ ★ ★
R, 113 m., 1989

Al Pacino (Frank Keller), Ellen Barkin (Helen Cruger), John Goodman (Sherman Touhey), Michael Rooker (Terry). Directed by Harold Becker and produced by Martin Bregman and Louis A. Stroller. Screenplay by Richard Price.

Sea of Love tells an ingeniously constructed story that depends for its suspense on the same question posed by *Jagged Edge* and *Fatal Attraction:* What happens when you fall in love with a person who may be quite prepared to murder you? The movie stars Al Pacino, looking older and a little lined, but more convincing than in most of his other recent roles, as a homicide detective who is assigned to a messy murder case. The victim is a male who has been shot in his own bed, and the killer, it appears, was a woman.

Tracking down leads, Pacino crosses paths with another detective (John Goodman) who is handling a similar case. They discover that both of their victims had placed rhyming ads in one of those singles magazines where people advertise for partners. Lacking any other clues, Pacino has a brainstorm: Why don't he and Goodman place an ad of their own and then date all the women who answer it? By getting the women's fingerprints on wine glasses, the cops may be able to discover the murderer.

This notion leads to one of the movie's better sequences, as Pacino devotes half an hour apiece to assembly-line dates with a series of lonely hearts, while Goodman plays the waiter at his table. Then something unexpected happens. There is chemistry between Pacino and one of the women (Ellen Barkin), and although it is unprofessional and possibly dangerous, he sees her again and they find themselves powerfully attracted to one another.

The movie uses this attraction to set a frankly manipulative plot into motion. Is Barkin, in fact, the killer? Various hints are dropped; various clues are planted. Pacino is meanwhile portrayed as so seriously disturbed within himself that he would almost prefer to die at this woman's hands than surrender his love. (The situation has an uncanny parallel with Glenn Close's feelings for Jeff Bridges in *Jagged Edge*.)

The pure plot elements in *Sea of Love* work well enough until the very end of the movie, I suppose, when the solution turns out to be a red herring. But what impressed me most in the film was the personal chemistry between Pacino and Barkin. There can be little doubt, at this point, that Barkin is one of the most intense and passionately convincing actresses now at work in the American movies. Her performance in *The Big Easy* (1987) was Oscar caliber, and again this time, she seems to cross some kind of acting threshold. When she roughly embraces Pacino and then stalks around the room like a tigress in heat before returning to her quarry, there is an energy that almost derails the movie.

For Pacino, *Sea of Love* is a reminder of the strong presence he established in street roles in the 1970s before he drifted away into an unfocused stardom in too many softer roles. This time he seems sharp, edgy, complicated, and authentic. Goodman (who plays Roseanne Barr's husband on TV) makes a good partner for him, especially in the scenes where he stands by helplessly while his friend apparently chooses to be in love with a murderess.

Movies like this need to work on two levels. The human elements should feel right,

and the initial complications of the plot should not be shortchanged at the end. I think the ending of *Sea of Love* cheats by bringing in a character from left field at the last moment. Part of the fun in a movie like this is guessing the identity of the killer, and part of the problem with *Sea of Love* is that the audience is not really played fair with. Technically, I suppose, the plot can be justified. But I felt cheated. I had good feelings for the characters and their relationship, but I walked out feeling that the plot had played fast and loose with the rules of whodunits.

Secret Honor ★ ★ ★ ★
NO MPAA RATING, 90 m., 1984

Philip Baker Hall (Nixon). Directed and produced by Robert Altman. Screenplay by Donald Freed and Arnold M. Stone.

The most tantalizing images in Woodward and Bernstein's *The Final Days* were those stories of a drunken Richard M. Nixon, falling to his knees in the White House, embarrassing Henry Kissinger with a display of self-pity and pathos. Was the book accurate? Even Kissinger said he had no idea who the authors' sources were (heh, heh). But as Watergate fades into history, and as revisionist historians begin to suggest that Nixon might after all have been a great president—apart from the scandals, of course—our curiosity remains. What were the real secrets of this most complex president? Robert Altman's *Secret Honor*, which is one of the most scathing, lacerating and brilliant movies of 1984, attempts to answer our questions. The film is a work of fiction. An actor is employed to impersonate Nixon. But all of the names and many of the facts are real, and the film gives us the uncanny sensation that we are watching a man in the act of exposing his soul.

The action takes place in Nixon's private office, at some point after his resignation. The shelves are lined with books, and with a four-screen video monitor for the security system. The desk top is weighted down with brass and gold. From the walls, portraits peer down. Eisenhower, Lincoln, Washington, Woodrow Wilson, Kissinger. Nixon begins by fiddling with his tape recorder; there is a little joke in the fact that he doesn't know quite how to run it. Then he begins to talk. He talks for ninety minutes. That bare description may make *Secret Honor* sound like *My Dinner with André*, but rarely have I seen ninety more compelling minutes on the

screen. Nixon is portrayed by Philip Baker Hall, an actor previously unknown to me, with such savage intensity, such passion, such venom, such scandal, that we cannot turn away. Hall looks a little like the real Nixon; he could be a cousin, and he sounds a little like him. That's close enough. This is not an impersonation, it's a performance.

What Nixon the character has to say may or may not be true. He makes shocking revelations. Watergate was staged to draw attention away from more serious, even treasonous, activities. Kissinger was on the payroll of the Shah of Iran, and supplied the Shah with young boys during his visits to New York. Marilyn Monroe was indeed murdered by the CIA, and so on. These speculations are interwoven with stories we recognize as part of the official Nixon biography: the letter to his mother, signed "Your faithful dog, Richard"; the feeling about his family and his humble beginnings; his hatred for the Eastern Establishment, which he feels has scorned him.

Truth and fiction mix together into a tapestry of life. We get the sensation of a man pouring out all of his secrets after a lifetime of repression. His sentences rush out, disorganized, disconnected, under tremendous pressure, interrupted by four-letter words that serve almost as punctuation. After a while the specific details don't matter so much; what we are hearing is a scream of a brilliant, gifted man who is tortured by the notion that fate might have made him a loser.

A strange thing happened to me as I watched this film. I knew it was fiction. I didn't approach it in the spirit of learning the "truth about Nixon." But as a movie, it created a deeper truth, an artistic truth, and after *Secret Honor* was over, you know what? I had a deeper sympathy for Richard Nixon than I have ever had before.

See No Evil, Hear No Evil ★ ½
R, 103 m., 1989

Richard Pryor (Wally), Gene Wilder (Dave), Joan Severance (Eve), Kevin Spacey (Kirgo), Alan North (Braddock), Anthony Zerbe (Sutherland), Louis Giambalvo (Gatlin), Kirsten Childs (Adele). Directed by Arthur Hiller and produced by Marvin Worth. Screenplay by Earl Barret, Arne Sultan, Eliot Wald, Andrew Kurtzman, and Gene Wilder.

See No Evil, Hear No Evil has one good idea, introduces it in the opening scenes, and then surrenders to the requirements of the Hollywood assembly line. There is nothing so disheartening for a moviegoer as the realization that a movie has not tried—that the filmmakers have chosen to reassemble tired and worn-out spare parts from a hundred other movies rather than imagine something new.

The good idea: Richard Pryor plays a character who is blind, and Gene Wilder plays a character who is deaf, and once they become friends they make a great team. The possibilities for visual comedy with this idea are seemingly endless, but the movie chooses instead to plug the characters into a dumb plot about industrial espionage.

Wilder runs a newsstand, a customer drops a gold coin into his coin tray, and the coin turns out to be a disguised microchip worth millions, so of course that means that an assortment of villains have to threaten the heroes from one end of the movie to the other. The only other character in the movie of any interest is Joan Severance, a tall and classic beauty who is a suspect in the murder of a man connected with the chip. She's great to look at—a not inconsiderable element in a movie like this—and she has a nice, dry sense of humor that reminds you of the intelligence of a Kathleen Turner. But she is not enough to redeem the stock company of goons and heavies who have been written in as her companions.

The movie doesn't seem to have had the impulse to experiment with its central idea. Think what a great physical comedian like Jacques Tati or Buster Keaton could have done with this notion—or never mind, Hollywood has forgotten how to aim that high. But think of the sight gags, the double-takes, and subtle little touches you could find in everyday life if two buddies, one deaf, one blind, teamed up together. This movie's idea of exploiting that inspiration is to have Wilder stand behind Pryor during a fistfight and tell him where to throw the punches. (This misses the point, since Wilder, who can see, could throw the punches himself.)

In addition to its recycled plot, the movie has another almost fatal problem: Both of its heroes are nice guys. Wilder and Pryor both play loving, sensitive, kind, and gentle souls, and that would be wonderful in life, but a movie needs some edge to it. I doubt if Gene Wilder has it in him to play a mean-spirited, vindictive character, but Pryor used to be able to call on that other side. He became a movie star by being a wise-guy. In recent years, however, he seems to have locked himself into a series of sweet roles in which the cutting edge of his personality remains concealed.

What if the movie had made the relationship between its two guys one of necessity, not of friendship? What if they hated each other, yet still had to work as a team? That's an old formula, too—used successfully by Robert De Niro and Charles Grodin in *Midnight Run*—but it would have generated some tension. Instead, all we get are two really nice guys and some cardboard computer crooks.

See You in the Morning ★ ★ ¹/₂
PG-13, 115 m., 1989

Jeff Bridges (Larry), Alice Krige (Beth), Farrah Fawcett (Jo), Drew Barrymore (Cathy), Lukas Haas (Petey), David Dukes (Peter), Frances Sternhagen (Neenie), George Hearn (Martin), Theodore Bikel (Bronie), Linda Lavin (Sidney). Directed by Alan J. Pakula and produced by Pakula and Susan Solt. Screenplay by Pakula.

At about the midway point in *See You in the Morning*, there is a scene set in a group therapy session—one of those groups where all the statements seem to begin with the words, "The trouble with you is. . . ." The women in the group have trouble with men, and the men have trouble with women, and the issue is usually Trust, although it can also be Dependence or even Childhood Loss. The fears expressed during this group seem to radiate out into the rest of the screenplay, infecting a relatively simple story with psychological jargon.

Perhaps that is the point. The hero of the story is Larry Livingstone (Jeff Bridges), a psychiatrist. He is the very model of a modern, sensitive male, who is able to see both sides of every issue so thoroughly that he even discusses his own mistakes with a certain bemused wonder. At the outset of the movie, he is married to a model (Farrah Fawcett) and lives happily, it would seem, with her and their two children. Then she says they need to have a talk. She wants a divorce.

We meet another family, the Goodwins, also with two children. He is a concert pianist who is faced with the paralysis of one of his hands. She has devoted her life to supporting him. One day his hand betrays him in the middle of a concert, and two years later, we learn, he kills himself. Both this death and the divorce proceedings of the Livingstones are kept offscreen, while the film flashes forward three years to a meeting between Bridges, as the psychiatrist, and Beth, the pianist's widow (Alice Krige).

They fall in love. Well, of course they do. They're both in need, both lonely, and as he walks her home through the rain they discover, as people always do in the movies, that getting wet together is one of the most romantic things that can happen to you. There is a marriage, and then the movie settles in for the long haul, to consider Larry's problems as the new stepfather of Beth's kids, Cathy (Drew Barrymore) and Petey (Lukas Haas).

Cathy seems more or less normal. Petey has a habit of practicing his cello far into the night, "as if," his mother says, "he feels that he somehow caused his father's death by not practicing enough." When Beth is sent to Russia to photograph a concert tour, Larry is left with the two kids, and tries his best to understand them and relate to them in an intelligent and sensitive way. Of course he fails, intelligently and sensitively. And when Beth and Larry get that worked through, Larry's first mother-in-law grows ill and dies. Alone with his first wife in a northern cottage, he grows foolishly nostalgic for what they once had together, and attempts to have it again, but is betrayed by his equipage.

Of course his near miss must be confessed immediately to Beth, but in terms so abstract and analytical that he seems to be diagnosing, not castigating himself. And in the treatment of that scene I finally began to discover that I had been through enough therapy. If a movie is going to alternate between simple human spontaneity and tortured self-analysis, then it had better have a point of view toward one or the other. To use them as a sort of sweet-and-sour of the soul is unbearably frustrating.

What almost redeems *See You in the Morning* are the performances. Jeff Bridges is completely at home in the central role, seeming relaxed around the children and convincingly decent in his relationships with the women. Alice Krige is a good choice for his second wife; she has a way of conveying absolute good faith, and so it is painful to see her confronted with the dialogue in the big confession scene, where at a crucial turning point everything she is given to say sounds false.

The movie was written and directed by Alan J. Pakula, and is, like Blake Edwards's *That's Life*, one of those unsparing movies of experience and analysis in which it is the audience that is not spared. The screenplay is so scrupulous, so fair, so enlightened, and so intelligent that real people have trouble shouldering it aside so they can share messy human emotions. Nothing is ever quite this neat. (And the film's level of taste is so high that a closing scene, involving a couple of cops, seems even more contrived and idiotic than it is.)

I liked the people in *See You in the Morning*. I just wish they felt free to like themselves more. Actually, I don't really know if that's true. It's just that after listening to them for almost two hours, I find myself thinking in phrases like that. Phrases about liking themselves more. Maybe I'm only saying that. Possibly I have a resentment against them. It's hard to be sure. I'll see you in the morning.

September ★ ★ ★ ½
PG, 82 m., 1987

Denholm Elliott (Howard), Dianne Wiest (Stephanie), Mia Farrow (Lane), Elaine Stritch (Diane), Sam Waterston (Peter), Jack Warden (Lloyd), Ira Wheeler (Mr. Raines), Jane Cecil (Mrs. Raines), Rosemary Murphy (Mrs. Mason). Directed by Woody Allen and produced by Robert Greenhut. Screenplay by Allen.

If you could take all of the different combinations of love won and love lost from many different periods in your life and join them all together for a weekend in the country, the weekend might turn out a little like *September*. Some of the guests at your party might be older or younger than you are, or smarter or more vulnerable, or of a different sex. But when you looked closely at their romantic strivings, you would recognize yourself, because there are, after all, only so many ways to be in love with the wrong person at the wrong time.

There are six major characters in the movie, each and every one of them hungry to be loved and taken care of. And everyone in the movie loves somebody—but usually not the person who loves him. The entire weekend comes down to a series of little emotional tangos, in which the characters move restlessly from room to room, trying to arrange to be alone with the object of their love—and away from the person obsessed with them.

The dominant person in the household is Diane, the middle-aged but still charismatic

movie star. Played by Elaine Stritch, she is a woman who has lived a great deal, compromised too often, and become what is known as a "survivor," which is to say, a person you are surprised is still functioning. She has been married several times, currently to Lloyd (Jack Warden), an industrialist who is no doubt proud to have won this woman who was a sex symbol when they were both much younger. (By the same token, if Marilyn Monroe were still alive today, how many men over forty would not still feel some nostalgic erotic stirring if they found themselves alone in the room with her?)

Diane has come out to the family's country place to join her fortyish daughter, Lane (Mia Farrow), who has been living there for some time, recovering from a breakdown. For several months, Lane's close companion has been Howard (Denholm Elliott), the quiet, self-effacing neighbor. Lane has allowed Howard to grow close to her, but actually she feels passion only for Peter (Sam Waterston), the writer who has taken a place nearby for the summer. Peter has rather encouraged her. But this weekend, Lane has invited Stephanie (Dianne Wiest), her closest friend, to the country. And now Peter has conceived an enormous passion for Stephanie.

So, Howard loves Lane, who loves Peter, who loves Stephanie, who is thinking of breaking up with her husband. And Lloyd loves his memories of Diane, who looks in the mirror and still finds much to love in herself. And meanwhile there is a horrible family secret lurking beneath the pleasant conversations of the mother and the daughter—a secret that will burst out later in the film, in a moment of anger.

What is Allen up to here? The structure of his story is all too neat to make a messy, psychologically complicated modern movie. In the neat pairings of couples and non-couples, Allen almost seems to be making a modern-dress Elizabethan comedy. And that may be his point. When we fall in love, we are always so wound up in the absolute uniqueness of ourselves and our loved one, in the feeling that nothing like this has ever happened before, that we cannot see how the same old patterns repeat themselves. To turn toward one person, we must turn away from another. If the person we turn to is not interested, we are left stranded, which is the way all but the luckiest of us probably feel most of the time.

Allen has made so many comedies that it is easy to insist that he make nothing else.

Actually, he is as acute an author of serious dialogue as anyone now making movies, and in *September*, most of the real action goes on in the word choices. By the precise words that they do or don't use, his characters are able to convey exactly how much of what they say is sincere, and how much is polite. Listening to Farrow gently speak to Elliott, for example, anyone but Elliott would know instantly that she does not and never will love him. Listening to Waterston talk to Farrow, anyone but Farrow would know that he does not and never will love her.

How is it that the Farrow character is perceptive enough to know what words to say to Elliott, but not sensitive enough to hear the same words when they are being said to her? That is the whole mystery of this film. We can clearly see the people we are not in love with, but when we look at the people we love, we see only what we choose to see, and hear only what we can stand to hear. *September* is the first movie in a long time that has been able to listen that closely.

The Serpent and the Rainbow ★ ★ ★
R, 98 m., 1988

Bill Pullman (Dennis Alan), Cathy Tyson (Marielle Celine), Zakes Mokae (Dargent Peytraud), Paul Winfield (Lucien Celine), Brent Jennings (Mozart), Conrad Roberts (Christophe), Badja Djola (Gaston). Directed by Wes Craven and produced by David Ladd and Doug Claybourne. Screenplay by Richard Maxwell and A.R. Simoun.

The Serpent and the Rainbow was inspired by a book by Wade Davis, a Harvard scientist who investigated the voodoo society of Haiti and identified two of the drugs used for "zombification"—drugs that lower the metabolic rate of their victims so much that they appear dead and are buried, only to be dug up later and revived.

Resurrected zombies apparently appear somewhat lobotomized, a not unreasonable result of being turned into the living dead and buried alive. Although Davis himself did not become a zombie—at least not more so than any other doctoral candidate—his adventures inspired this thriller in which a Harvard researcher, played by Bill Pullman, ventures into the heart of voodoo and witnesses strange and gruesome realities.

In the movie, Pullman plays a cross between William Hurt and Indiana Jones: he's a tall, good-looking, sensitive intellectual who is called upon to wrestle leopards, battle corpses, confront an evil voodoo leader, and eventually be buried alive along with a deadly spider that makes itself cozy on his paralyzed eyeball.

Pullman's mission in going to Haiti is to isolate the active ingredient in secret voodoo powder, so that it can perhaps be used as an anesthetic. His contact in Haiti is the beautiful Marielle Celine, played by Cathy Tyson in her first role since *Mona Lisa*. She runs a people's clinic, as the sexy heroines in these movies always do. Other local experts include Paul Winfield, as a well-connected local leader, and Brent Jennings, as a man named Mozart who knows all of the secrets in the secret ingredients.

In most voodoo movies, voodoo itself is taken only as a backdrop, a gimmick. This movie seems to know something about voodoo (it knows more than I do, anyway), and treats it seriously as a religion, a way of life, and an occult circle that does possess secrets unexplored by modern medicine. One of the most convincing elements in the movie is the way the more "modern" Haitians nevertheless regard voodoo as something not to be taken lightly. As Pullman slowly enters the voodoo society, penetrating first one level of concealment and then another, we get the sensation—unusual in a horror film—that his discoveries are genuine.

The movie was shot on location in Haiti and the Dominican Republic, and unlike most voodoo movies, it attempts to look and sound realistic—even including TV clips of the overthrow and flight of the dictator "Baby Doc" Duvalier. The visual look of the movie is stunning; there's never the sense of sets, of costumes, of hired extras, but more of a feeling of a camera moving past real people in real places. Even the obviously contrived scenes, including some of the hallucinations and voodoo fantasies, have an air of solid plausibility to them.

The film was directed by Wes Craven, a master of horror, whose credits include *Last House on the Left*, *Swamp Thing*, and the original *A Nightmare on Elm Street*. Craven will never advance in the Hollywood establishment until he embraces more respectable projects, and yet he has a sure touch for horror and the macabre, and *The Serpent and the Rainbow* is uncanny in the way it takes the most lurid images and makes them plausible.

The Seventh Sign ★ ★
R, 94 m., 1988

Demi Moore (Abby Quinn), Michael Biehn (Russell Quinn), Jurgen Prochnow (The Boarder), Peter Friedman (Lucci), Manny Jacobs (Avi), John Taylor (Jimmy). Directed by Carl Schultz and produced by Ted Field and Robert W. Cort. Screenplay by W.W. Wicket and George Kaplan.

The Seventh Sign begins with portents of the Apocalypse. The rivers run with blood, the sea boils, the desert freezes, the birds fall from the sky, the earth shakes, and things are not so hot out on the beach in California either. A strange man with burning eyes has just rented the little apartment upstairs over the garage in the backyard of Demi Moore's house, and she finds ancient Hebrew manuscripts in his desk—in a secret code.

This is the kind of movie where I tend to settle back and relax. I actually enjoy thrillers about biblical prophecies and the second coming and the Antichrist. After the sheer anarchy unleashed upon Hollywood by the slice-and-dice movies, it's actually comforting to know that these characters play by the rules. They believe in good and evil, and they act as if individual human beings can have an influence on the outcome of events. Compared to the *Friday the 13th* world view, *The Seventh Sign* is positively sanguine.

Like *Rosemary's Baby*, *The Exorcist*, and the *Omen* movies, this one places its supernatural events within a framework that at first seems everyday and sane. There is an art to this process. You show characters going about the mundane events of their routine daily lives, but on the sound track you play far-off Gregorian chants, so it's clear that the forces of evil are marshaling their troops offscreen.

Demi Moore has the central role, as a woman who has lost one child during pregnancy and is now fearful of losing another. The story begins in the last two months of her pregnancy, with her husband (Michael Biehn) lending moral support while her doctor shows her the fetus on a television screen. There's a lot of talk, of course, about the quantity of her amniotic fluid. Why is it that movies about the forces of darkness always place such an emphasis on details of the female reproductive process? Ever since Charles Grodin played the gynecologist in *Rosemary's Baby*, you can't see one of these movies without learning something about pregnancy.

But I digress. Moore is strong and clear in the movie's central role, and proves once again (after *About Last Night . . .*) that she has a genuine charisma, an aura of intelligence and resolve, reinforced by her throaty voice. I was not sure at first, however, that she was the correct choice for this movie. I thought she was perhaps too strong, and that the role required more of a screamer. Not so. By the end of the film, she is called upon to save the planet and all living things upon it, and so she needs that strength.

She provides a strong center to the film, but the rest of it, alas, is all over the map. I am not even sure I completely understood all of the details. What connection was there, for example, between the Hebrew code letters with their wax seals, and the dread events that followed every time one was opened? What were those flashbacks to Roman times? Who was that strange priest that traveled around the globe checking out the frozen deserts and bloody rivers? And on whose side was the boarder over the garage?

By the end of the movie, I was fairly certain of the answers to most of those questions, but the body of the film seemed almost deliberately confused and obscure, to no purpose. Why not explain the priest's actual mission, instead of saving it for a denouement at the last minute? Wouldn't that have been more interesting? And why is it that only the characters in the movie seem to be aware that things are going to hell and the Apocalypse is at hand? To be sure, CNN has nonstop bulletins about the weird events taking place in the world, but nobody in the street seems much affected. In fact, the movie's two earthquakes are not commented on by anyone—not even the leading characters.

And then there is the problem of the ending of the movie. I have to go at this very delicately, so as not to give too much away. But if you see the film, ask yourself this: When the baby reaches out his hand toward the mother's face, why doesn't he simply touch it? If you see what I mean.

sex, lies, and videotape ★ ★ ★ ½
R, 104 m., 1989

James Spader (Graham), Andie MacDowell (Ann), Peter Gallagher (John), Laura San Giacomo (Cynthia), Ron Vawter (Therapist), Steven Brill (Barfly), Alexandra Root (Girl on Tape), Earl T. Taylor (Landlord). Directed by Steven Soderbergh and produced by Robert Newmyer and John Hardy. Screenplay by Soderbergh.

I have a friend who says golf is not only better than sex but lasts longer. The argument in *sex, lies, and videotape* is that conversation is also better than sex—more intimate, more voluptuous—and that with our minds we can do things to each other that make sex, that swapping of sweat and sentiment, seem merely troublesome. Of course this argument is all a mind game, and sex itself, sweat and all, is the prize for the winner. That's what makes the conversation so erotic.

The movie takes place in Baton Rouge, Louisiana, and it tells the story of four people in their early thirties whose sex lives are seriously confused. One is a lawyer named John (Peter Gallagher), who is married to Ann (Andie MacDowell) but no longer sleeps with her. Early in the film, we hear her telling her psychiatrist that this is no big problem; sex is really overrated, she thinks, compared to the larger issues such as how the earth is running out of places to dispose of its garbage. Her husband does not, however, think sex is overrated, and is conducting a passionate affair with his wife's sister, Cynthia (Laura San Giacomo), who is an artist and who has always resented the goody-goody Ann.

An old friend turns up in town. His name is Graham (James Spader), and he was John's college roommate. Nobody seems quite clear what he has been doing in the years since college, but he's one of those types you don't ask questions about things like that, because you have the feeling you don't want to know the answers. He's dangerous, not in a physical way, but through his insinuating intelligence, which seems to see through people.

He moves in. Makes himself at home. One day he has lunch with Ann, and they begin to flirt with their conversation, turning each other on with words carefully chosen to occupy the treacherous ground between eroticism and a proposition. She says she doesn't think much of sex, but then he tells her something that gets her interested: He confesses that he is impotent. It is, I think, a fundamental fact of the human ego in the sexually active years that most women believe they can end a man's impotence, just as most men believe they are heaven's answer to a woman's frigidity. If this were true, impotence and frigidity would not exist, but if hope did not spring eternal, not much else would spring either.

The early stages of *sex, lies, and videotape* are a languorous, but intriguing, setup for the tumult that follows. The adultery be-

tween John and Cynthia has the usual consequences and creates the usual accusations of betrayal, but the movie (and, I think, the audience) is more interested in Graham's sexual pastimes. Unable to satisfy himself in the usual ways, he videotapes the sexual fantasies of women and then watches them. This is a form of sexual assault; he has power not over their bodies but over their minds, over their secrets, and I suspect that the most erotic sentence in his vocabulary is "She's actually telling me this stuff!"

Ann is horrified by Graham's hobby, and fascinated, and before long the two of them are in front of his camera in a scene of remarkable subtlety and power, both discovering that, for them, sex is only the beginning of their mysteries. This scene, and indeed the whole movie, would not work unless the direction and acting were precisely right (this is the kind of movie where a slightly wrong tone could lead to a very bad laugh), but Spader and MacDowell do not step wrong. Indeed, Spader's performance throughout the film is a kind of risk-taking; can you imagine the challenge an actor faces in taking the kind of character I have described and making him not only intriguing but seductive? Spader has the kind of sexual ambiguity of the young Brando or Dean; he seems to suggest that if he bypasses the usual sexual approaches it is because he has something more interesting up, or down, his sleeve.

The story of *sex, lies, and videotape* is by now part of movie folklore: how Soderbergh, at twenty-nine, wrote the screenplay in eight days during a trip to Los Angeles, how the film was made for $1.8 million, how it won the Palme d'Or at the 1989 Cannes Film Festival, as well as the best actor prize for Spader. I am not sure it is as good as the Cannes jury apparently found it; it has more intelligence than heart, and is more clever than enlightening. But it is never boring, and there are moments when it reminds us of how sexy the movies used to be, back before they could show everything, and thus had to think about nothing.

Shaft ★ ★ ½
R, 98 m., 1971

Richard Roundtree (Shaft), Moses Gunn (Boss), Gwenn Mitchell (Ellie), Christopher St. John (Militant). Directed by Gordon Parks and produced by Joel Freeman. Screenplay by Ernest Tidyman and John D.F. Black.

Gordon Parks's *Shaft* gave us the first really convincing black private eye. Movies about private detectives have always been among my favorites—they seem to be better than most other formula movies—and John Shaft, as played by Richard Roundtree, belongs in the honorable tradition of Philip Marlowe, Sam Spade, Lew Archer, and company. He belongs because, like them, he keeps no regular company. Private eyes (in the movies, anyway) are loners in a way that defines the word. They live in dingy walk-up offices, sipping bourbon from the office bottles and waiting for the phone to ring.

These may all be clichés, but, hell, a private-eye movie without clichés wouldn't be worth the price of admission. We don't go to Westerns to see cowboys riding ostriches. The strength of Parks's movie is his willingness to let his hero fully inhabit the private-eye genre, with all of its obligatory violence, blood, obscenity, and plot gimmicks. The weakness of *Shaft*, I suspect, is that Parks is not very eager to inhabit that world along with his hero.

Gordon Parks was the first black director to make a major studio film, and his *The Learning Tree* (1969) was a deeply felt, lyrically beautiful film that was, maybe, just too simple and honest to be commercial. It didn't find a large audience, and I suspect that Parks turned next to *Shaft* for commercial survival.

The nice thing about *Shaft* is that it savors the private-eye genre, and takes special delight in wringing new twists out of the traditional relationship between the private eye and the boys down at homicide. The story covers some of the same ground as *Cotton Comes to Harlem*, but in a different way. Shaft is brought in by a Harlem rackets boss (Moses Gunn) whose traditional slice of power is being threatened by the Mafia. They don't want a partnership anymore, so they kidnap the boss's daughter. Shaft's job is to get her back.

His adventures along the way include a thoroughly unpleasant encounter with a white pick-up, who is insulted because all black exploitation movies have to insult at least one white pick-up (and why not? Fair is fair). The climax involves a complicated plan with Shaft and his allies swinging from ropes and using firehoses to accomplish with five people in five minutes what could have been done with one, in one. Parks isn't especially good at action direction, but the heart of a private-eye movie is in the mood scenes, anyway, and he supplies a scene in a bar and another one with the Harlem rackets boss that are very nice.

Shakedown ★ ★ ★
R, 105 m., 1988

Peter Weller (Roland Dalton), Sam Elliott (Richie Marks), Patricia Charbonneau (Susan Cantrell), Antonio Fargas (Nicky Carr), Blanche Baker (Gail Feinberger), Tom Waits (Officer Kelly). Directed by James Glickenhaus and produced by J. Boyce Harman, Jr. Screenplay by Glickenhaus.

If they ever stopped to collect the dead bodies in a movie like *Shakedown*, the hero would have to play a coroner. But a movie like this never looks back, and *Shakedown* is very definitely a movie like this. It's an assembly of sensational moments, strung together by a plot that provides the excuses for amazing stunts, and not much else. But then not much else is needed.

Imagine this. A private jet airplane is taking off from LaGuardia. A public defender and a tough plainclothesman are chasing it down the runway in a Porsche. At the last moment, the cop leaps from the car and grabs one of the wheels of the plane. As the plane gains altitude, he shoots a bullet through an engine, forcing the pilot to turn back. Then, as the plane approaches the runway for an emergency landing, he slips a hand grenade into the wheel well and falls into the water below. The grenade explodes, making it look like the plane crashed, while the cop swims to safety and is hauled ashore by his buddy, the defender.

You like it? Then you'll also like the scene where they're racing to the courthouse and a construction crane accidentally snags their car and lifts it over a mob and onto the courthouse steps. Or the scene where the cop gets in a fight on the roller coaster, is thrown out, uses his bare hands to pull the car's power supply loose, and then lets go, saving himself as the powerless roller coaster rockets off the tracks.

Movies like *Shakedown* are what they are. They represent a tremendous amount of craftsmanship and skill, and a fair degree of courage on the part of the stunt people who make it look real. They also require strong, unsubtle but convincing performances by the actors; too much psychological realism in a movie like this can allow the real world to distract from the thrills. And they require a

director who takes no hostages, who knows how to sustain a headlong momentum, who is compelled to make the plot hurtle ahead with no regard for logic or nuance.

Shakedown was directed by James Glickenhaus, who has produced such earlier, mostly unsung, action dramas as *The Exterminator*, *The Soldier*, and *The Protector* (near the beginning of the picture, his disheveled plainclothesman snoozes through a screening of *The Soldier* in a Times Square fleapit). Those films did not gather a great deal of attention, but with *Shakedown* Glickenhaus will now be recognized as another of the manic breed of young hotshots who will do anything to stage a sensational stunt.

The stars of the movie are Peter Weller, who segues from *RoboCop* to this role as a determined public defender, and Sam Elliott, Cher's aging hippie lover in *Mask*, as the plainclothes cop. Their relationship is perhaps inspired by similar teams in *48 HRS* and *Lethal Weapon*, but the stunts and firefights in this movie are so overwhelming that something has to give, and the relationship is the first thing Glickenhaus can do without.

The plot: A crooked cop tries to stick up a drug dealer in Central Park, and is shot dead. The drug dealer is brought to trial, but Weller becomes convinced that he didn't fire first, and that the incident is the tip of an iceberg of corruption in the police department. His friend Elliott becomes convinced of the same thing, and together they work inside and outside the law to help the defendant beat a murder rap, and expose other corrupt cops. Weller has some nice moments in the courtroom, although his legal style is so informal and disorganized that it's hard to believe, and Patricia Charbonneau (from *Desert Hearts*) has a nice supporting role as the opposing assistant D.A. who is also, of course, his former and future lover.

The movie has everything. There's a subplot about Weller's rich fiancée, and another one about a secret tape recording of the murder, and even some funny moments when Weller and Elliott try to top each other in absolute cynicism. But the movie is basically action and stunts, a high-tech sideshow of explosives, hurtling automobiles, shattering glass, and impossible feats. It is what it is.

Sharky's Machine ★ ★ ★
R, 119 m., 1981

Burt Reynolds (Sharky), Rachel Ward (Dominoe), Vittorio Gassman (Victor), Brian

Keith (Papa), Charles Durning (Frisco). Directed by Burt Reynolds and produced by Hank Moonjean. Screenplay by Gerald Di Pago.

Sharky's Machine contains all of the ingredients of a tough, violent, cynical big-city cop movie, but what makes it intriguing is the way the Burt Reynolds character plays against those conventions. His name is Sharky. As the movie opens, he's an undercover narcotics cop. He blows a big case and is demoted to the vice squad—which is a bawdy, brawling, vocal gang of misfits who act like a cross between "Hill Street Blues" and a Joseph Wambaugh nightmare.

Sharky is not happy in vice. He is, in fact, not happy anywhere, not until a young woman named Dominoe enters his life. She is a hooker. She also seems to be involved with some snaky big-money characters, and so Sharky places her under twenty-four hour surveillance. That involves moving several cops, telescopes, cameras, and bugging devices into the high-rise opposite her apartment. The cops set up housekeeping and settle down for a long wait. And it's here that the movie begins to really involve us. Reynolds, as Sharky, falls in love with the woman. It is a voyeuristic love, involving spying and eavesdropping, and Sharky is not a voyeur—so it is particularly painful for him to witness the woman's sexual involvement with others.

The central scenes of the movie, involving the call girl's private life and the probing eyes of Sharky, could easily have become tawdry—could have disintegrated into a peep show. That doesn't happen, partly because Reynolds (who also directed the film) doesn't provide cheap displays of flesh, but also because the call girl is played by British actress Rachel Ward, who brings poignancy and restraint to the role. She plays a hooker who's not a tramp. She has a husky voice and an astonishing body, but there's an innocence in her manner. Later, we discover that she has been in virtual bondage to her pimp since she was an infant. She knows no other life. This is a setup of sorts, a device in the plot to allow the female lead to be both prostitute and victim, but it clarifies the relationship between Reynolds and Ward. And when they fall in love, as they inevitably do, it provides some leftover innocence to be celebrated.

Reynolds surrounds this central relationship with a lot of cops, known as Sharky's Machine. They are played by actors who have played a lot of other cops in a lot of other movies—Brian Keith, Charles Durning—and by Bernie Casey, who is playing his first cop but does it with special grace. There's a long scene in the film, reportedly improvised, in which Casey tells Reynolds what it felt like, the first time he was shot. We are reminded that cops in the movies hardly ever talk about being shot.

Sharky's Machine has a lot of plot, most of it inspired by the original novel by William Diehl. Maybe it has too much plot for a movie that Reynolds has referred to as *Dirty Harry Goes to Atlanta*. But this is an ambitious film; it's as if something inside Reynolds was chafing at the insipid roles he was playing in one car-chase movie after another. He doesn't walk through this movie, and he doesn't allow himself the cozy little touches that break the mood while they're letting the audience know how much fun Burt is having.

The result of his ambition and restraint is a movie much more interesting than most cop thrillers. *Sharky's Machine* does have a lot of action, including an extended, exhausting, brutal shoot-out at the end. But it also has the special qualities of the relationship between Reynolds and Ward (more fully developed than the camaraderie between Reynolds and Catherine Deneuve, as another hooker in another thriller, *Hustle*, in 1974). As a director, Reynolds allows himself a few excesses (one howler is the dramatic cut from a sex scene to the phallic glory of the Peachtree Plaza Hotel). But he's put a lot of his ambition in this movie, and it reminds us that there is a fine actor within the star of *Cannonball Run*.

She-Devil ★ ★ ★
PG-13, 99 m., 1989

Meryl Streep (Mary Fisher), Roseanne Barr (Ruth), Ed Begley, Jr. (Bob), Linda Hunt (Hooper), Sylvia Miles (Mrs. Fisher), Elisebeth Peters (Nicolette Patchett), Robin Leach (Himself), Sally Jessy Raphael (Herself). Directed by Susan Seidelman and produced by Jonathan Brett and Seidelman. Screenplay by Barry Strugatz and Mark R. Burns.

There must have been moments on the set of *She-Devil* when Roseanne Barr went into her dressing room and locked the door and asked herself what she was doing there, costarring in a movie with the immortal Meryl Streep. We're in on the amazement, because Barr has

done such a thorough job of documenting her life in comedy routines, in confessional interviews, in her book, and on talk shows. Here is a woman who only a few years ago couldn't have gotten an autograph from Meryl Streep, let alone stolen a scene from her.

There's a delicious element of sweet revenge in Roseanne Barr's entire career. Here is the woman who proves for all of us that we could be TV stars and stand-up comics, if only we got a couple of breaks—because we've sure got more on the ball than the morons who *are* making it in show biz. And that sense of realized revenge is an undercurrent throughout *She-Devil*, which works both on a fictional level and as a real-life demonstration that Barr and Streep are indeed right there in the same movie.

If Barr is correctly cast, so is Meryl Streep, who has always had a rich vein of comedy bubbling through her personal life—few people are merrier during interviews—but who has dedicated her career to playing serious or even tragic women, most of them with accents. Here she's given a juicy role to sink her teeth into: Mary Fisher, the best-selling romance novelist who seems to be what would happen if the genes of Barbara Cartland, Jackie Collins, and Danielle Steel were combined in the same trash compactor. It's a role that calls out for broad, fearless interpretation, and Streep has a lot of fun with it.

Roseanne Barr's character is named Ruth, and she's a fat, plain suburban housewife with a mole under her lower lip that looks like a surgically implanted raisin. She is married, none too securely, to an accountant named Bob (Ed Begley, Jr.), who dreams of moving up in the ranks of his profession by becoming an accountant to the stars. Fate grants his wish. He meets Mary Fisher during an incident involving a spilled drink at a charity benefit, and one thing leads to another so rapidly that he cruelly drops off his wife at home before ending up in bed with the lustful novelist.

The heart of the movie involves the revenge Ruth takes out on her husband and Mary Fisher—revenge so thorough and methodical that she even takes time to jot down the areas of her husband's life she wants to destroy: first, his home. Then his family, career, and freedom, in that order. Bob has accused her of being a she-devil, and she is more than willing to play the role. She will haunt the faithless bastard until he

wishes he had never heard of accounting, much less of Mary Fisher.

She-Devil was directed by Susan Seidelman, whose credits include *Desperately Seeking Susan*, the underrated *Making Mr. Right*, and the recent *Cookie*. She has a sure touch for off-center humor, the kind that works not because of setups and punch lines, but because of the screwy logic her characters bring to their dilemmas. In the middle passages of this movie, she goes for broad comic strokes, especially in the way she portrays the gauche lifestyle of Mary Fisher, whose home looks like a Holiday Inn's wet dream. Streep, as Fisher, has erected a glamorous fictional facade around the mundane actual facts of her life, and it is with grim precision that Barr's character pulls it to pieces.

When Zsa Zsa Gabor's treacherous schoolmate added ten years to the actress's official age by producing that old school yearbook not long ago, I felt a twinge of sympathy for Zsa Zsa. If there is no honor among women lying about their ages, then what is sacred? But the Mary Fisher character in *She-Devil* is such a vain and snobbish woman that we can take a sadistic delight in Barr's most devilish scheme, which is to disguise herself as a nurse, locate the novelist's feisty mother (Sylvia Miles) in an old-folks' home, and produce her to the press along with a detailed history of Fisher's true past.

Begley, that tall, vaguely handsome, and subtly bewildered actor from "St. Elsewhere," is the fulcrum for a lot of humor. His character requires him to operate consistently from the basest motives: lust, greed, and envy. He projects these emotions so effortlessly, I hope they're grooming him for the Donald Trump story. Willing to betray his wife on a moment's notice but yet more interested in Fisher's body and fame than in the inner character she presumably possesses, he is a shallow and utterly worthless man, until the she-devil teaches him a lesson.

Debut movies are traditionally tricky for TV stars. For every Pee-wee Herman who finds the perfect movie vehicle, there's a Henry Winkler who doesn't. Roseanne Barr could presumably have made an easy, predictable, and dumb comedy at any point in the last couple of years. Instead, she took her chances with an ambitious project—a real movie. It pays off, in that Barr demonstrates that there is a core of reality inside her TV persona, a core of identifiable human feelings like jealousy and pride, and they provide a sound foundation for her comic acting.

The proof of it is that, on the basis of this movie, Meryl Streep didn't have to retire to her own dressing room to ask herself what she was doing in a movie with Roseanne Barr.

The Sheltering Sky ★ ★
R, 137 m., 1991

Debra Winger (Kit Moresby), John Malkovich (Port Moresby), Campbell Scott (George Tunner), Jill Bennett (Mrs. Lyle), Timothy Spall (Eric Lyle), Eric Vu-An (Belquassim), Paul Bowles (Narrator). Directed by Bernardo Bertolucci and produced by Jeremy Thomas. Screenplay by Mark Peploe and Bertolucci.

In the aftermath of World War II, three youngish Americans arrive in Tangiers in search of new experiences. They describe themselves as travelers, not tourists. They intend to immerse themselves in the Northern African culture and climate, to taste the exotic and judge the forbidden for themselves. Two of them—Port and Kit Moresby—are a married couple, writers, intellectuals, who have remained together for some ten years, even though there are large unsettled areas between them. The third is their friend, George Tunner, who is along, more or less, as a lark.

They seek the exotic, and they find it. Dazed by the brightness of the desert sun, seduced by the darkness of the labyrinth of the city's streets, confronted by a society where every sensual excess is available more or less on demand, they lose their roots as housebroken Americans. They are intoxicated by freedom, but instead of liberating their creative juices, so that they can write those novels that are penned up inside, they grow restless and dissatisfied—with themselves, with each other.

Port and Kit are obviously losing their moorings. Tunner is curious about the exact nature of their relationship—there are scenes subtly suggesting he may have an erotic curiosity about both of them—and concerned that they are losing their way. They fall in with the local expatriate community, particularly with the unspeakable Lyles, mother and son, who claim to be writing a travel book but seem more obsessed by their own Freudian tangles.

The city grows restrictive to the Moresbys. The desert beckons, and they are seduced by its purity, beauty, and harshness, much as another traveler, T.E. Lawrence,

once was. They venture out into its wildness. Port sickens and dies, and Kit is rescued—or so it seems at the time—by a passing Arab, who makes her his concubine. By now the sun is so hot, the light so harsh, the shadows so deep, and the bizarre so real that Kit has hardly any hold left on reality.

This story sounds, in its outline, lurid and melodramatic enough to furnish almost any movie with a sufficiency of plot. Indeed, the press releases for *The Sheltering Sky* promise something of the sort: ". . . the intimate proximity of doomed lovers . . . the scale of their passion juxtaposed against the vastness of the Sahara Desert," etc. But in another sense, nothing of great importance happens in the plot of this story; all of the big changes take place in the minds of the characters.

It is my handicap, perhaps, that I've read Paul Bowles's novel, *The Sheltering Sky*, which inspired this movie. It makes it difficult for me to see Bernardo Bertolucci's film in a fresh light, to judge it on the basis of what it is, rather than what it is not. The book is so complete, so deep, and so self-contained that it shuts the movie out. Bertolucci shows us the outsides and the surfaces, and a person seeing this movie without having read the book might fairly ask what it is about.

It is not about travelers and doomed lovers and juxtapositions, that's for sure. It is about educated, bookish, somewhat jaded American intellectuals being confronted by an immensity of experience that they cannot read or understand. Here is civilization up against the unanswerable indifference of nature.

Two narratives that resemble *The Sheltering Sky* are *A Passage to India* and *Picnic at Hanging Rock*—both of them stories about conventional Europeans who find themselves lost in the overwhelming mystery of ancient continents. *Hanging Rock* is a geological outcropping in Australia into which the picnickers disappear, never to return. The tourists in *A Passage to India* enter the Marabar Caves, where no matter what word you shout into the emptiness, the echo is always a hollow, meaningless sound. The desert serves the same function in *The Sheltering Sky*. It is simply there. The people who live in it have come to some kind of mystical understanding with it, but these "travelers" venture into it at their own hazard.

Bertolucci has done almost everything right in this movie except to communicate the theme. His leading actors are John Malkovich, as Port, and Debra Winger, as Kit, and they strike just the right notes—smart,

jaded, tired, knowing each other too well, not that thrilled about everything they know. His cinematographer, Vittorio Storaro, makes the desert as alive as Freddie Francis did for David Lean in *Lawrence of Arabia*. His location photography is always authentic and convincing, right down to the flies on the skins of the actors. It is all here, and yet at the end, thinking of the film, I was left with the impression of my fingers closing on air.

She's Having a Baby ★ ★
PG-13, 106 m., 1988

Kevin Bacon (Jake Briggs), Elizabeth McGovern (Kristy), Alec Baldwin (Davis), William Windom (Kristy's Father), Cathryn Damon (Kristy's Mother), James Ray (Jake's Father), Holland Taylor (Jake's Mother), Isabel Lorca (The Girl). Directed, produced, and written by John Hughes.

She's Having a Baby begins with the simplest and most moving of stories, and interrupts it with an amazing assortment of gimmicks. It is some kind of tribute to the strength of the story, and the warmth of the performances by Kevin Bacon and Elizabeth McGovern, that the movie somehow manages almost to work, in spite of the adornments.

The story begins on their wedding day, which Bacon faces with deep misgivings. Although he fell in love with McGovern literally at first sight, he is reluctant to surrender his freedom and take up the responsibilities of adulthood. But it's too late to back out, and before long the young couple have settled into a shoebox condo, and Bacon has conned his way into a low-level job with a Chicago advertising agency.

Years pass. The couple moves into what Bacon describes as "a mortgage with three bedrooms." They settle into a version of suburban conformity, although Bacon still grows restless with his neighbor's endless debates on rival brands of lawn mowers. The parents on both sides of the family begin to drop loud hints that they would appreciate a grandchild. Bacon is not ready for the awesome responsibilities of parenthood. But then it develops that he has a deficient sperm count (caused, we learn, by tight underwear raising the temperature of his groin above ideal sperm weather), and he joins McGovern in a determined effort to conceive a child. (Their resulting love scene must be the first copulation on film that is accompanied by the song "Workin' on the Chain Gang.")

Other aspects of their lives drift in and out of view. Alec Baldwin, the best friend, visits Chicago from time to time, makes a pass at McGovern, is rejected ("It's not happening in this lifetime," she explains), remains a friend. The routine at the ad agency begins to tell on Bacon, who has, of course, aspirations of becoming a novelist. And there are the erotic temptations of a strange, beautiful girl, who appears to Bacon in a disco, in the ad agency, and in his dreams, offering an alternative to his quiet yuppie lifestyle. But then come pregnancy, childbirth, and fatherhood, and he realizes that the age-old values are the best ones.

All of this sounds completely straightforward, and a logical development for the filmmaker, John Hughes, who has been charting the progress of teen-agers in a series of good films, including *Sixteen Candles*, *The Breakfast Club*, and *Ferris Bueller's Day Off*. But something strange got into Hughes this time.

The progression of his ordinary story is interrupted by some extraordinary flights of fancy. There are fantasy sequences, imaginary conversations, and a ballet for suburban husbands and their lawn mowers. Bacon narrates the film, and other characters also get into the act, including the preacher who marries them and incorporates all the duties of the perfect yuppie husband into the wedding vows. On their own, these bizarre touches are sometimes amusing (the choreography of the suite for lawn mowers would make a good TV commercial). But why are they in this story? What additional dimension do they contribute? Mostly they seem merely cute and clever distractions, not part of the story, not adding to it, not necessary.

The last sequence in the movie, where Bacon waits and worries while his wife undergoes a difficult labor, is the most effective. It is honest and strong and has genuine emotional strength. It suggests what a better movie this might have been if the whole story had been told in the same straightforward style, freed of Hughes's flourishes and gimmicks. The good parts of *She's Having a Baby* make the rest of it feel like a missed opportunity.

She's Out of Control   no stars
PG, 97 m., 1989

Tony Danza (Doug Simpson), Ami Dolenz (Katie Simpson), Catherine Hicks (Janet Pearson), Wallace Shawn (Mr. Fishbinder), Dick O'Neill (Mr. Pearson), Laura Mooney (Bonnie Simpson), Derek McGrath (Jeff). Directed by Stan Dragoti and produced by Stephen Deutsch. Screenplay by Seth Winston and Michael J. Nathanson.

What planet did the makers of this film come from? What assumptions do they have about the purpose and quality of life? I ask because *She's Out of Control* is simultaneously so bizarre and so banal that it's a first: The first movie fabricated entirely from sitcom clichés and plastic lifestyles, without reference to any known plane of reality.

The film stars Tony Danza as Doug, a divorced dad with an unhealthy obsession about the dating behavior of his teen-age daughter, Katie (Ami Dolenz). He wants to keep her forever trapped in an asexual, prepubescent hinterland, but then Doug's fiancée, Janet (Catherine Hicks), takes the kid for a complete beauty makeover: hair, makeup, wardrobe, and attitude. And the next time Doug sees his daughter, she's descending the staircase looking like she stepped out of one of those soft-core perfume ads.

Doug spends a lot of time looking at his daughter. He sees her so specifically as a sexual creature, and is so obsessed by what he sees, that in another movie his attention would probably seem perverse. The character he plays in this movie is so dim-witted and lacking in psychological insight, however, that his behavior is not so much perverse as slack-jawed.

There are a couple of minute subplots in the movie, one involving the romance between Doug and Janet, and the other one involving Katie's influence on her kid sister, Bonnie (Laura Mooney). But the heart of this movie is the father's unsuccessful attempts to enforce curfews, dictate behavior, and curtail the emotional development of his daughter.

The scene that sets up this obsession is a sick one—the sicker the more you think about it. Doug takes the family to the beach, and then stares in horrified fascination as Katie comes running out of the surf in her one-piece bathing suit, her breasts bouncing in slow motion like outtakes from a TV jiggle show.

The problem with this scene is that Doug seems to regard his daughter not in parental terms but in sexual ones. The movie does not possess a shred of healthy insight into the process by which people mature; it sees ado-

lescent girls as commodities to be protected from predatory males.

The French director Jean-Luc Godard once said that the way to criticize a movie is to make another movie. By a happy coincidence, just such a movie opened on the same day as *She's Out of Control*. It was called *Say Anything*, and it is healthy, sensitive, and true about a relationship between a father, his daughter, and her boyfriend. It is a movie about personal standards, about learning to trust, about growing up healthy and sane. The people who made *She's Out of Control* could learn a lot from it.

Shirley Valentine ★
R, 108 m., 1989

Pauline Collins (Shirley Valentine), Tom Conti (Costas Caldes), Julia McKenzie (Gillian), Alison Steadman (Jane), Joanna Lumley (Marjorie), Bernard Hill (Joe), Gillian Kearney (Young Shirley). Directed and produced by Lewis Gilbert. Screenplay by Willy Russell.

I have heard a great deal about how fine, how fetching and captivating, Pauline Collins was in the one-woman stage version of *Shirley Valentine*. I didn't see the play, but I have a feeling the reports may be right; this is the kind of story that might work as a tour-deforce, with one actor populating the stage with her imagination, as Collins is said to do.

Unfortunately, the film of *Shirley Valentine* takes a completely different approach by "opening up" the story into a realistic drama of appalling banality. There were moments during the movie when I cringed at the manipulative dialogue, as the heroine recited warmed-over philosophy and inane one-liners when she should have been allowed to speak for herself.

The story involves one Shirley Valentine, British provincial housewife and lonely soul who spends a great deal of time talking to her kitchen walls and other inanimate objects. She is meant to be plucky and brave in her monologues, but since she often includes us in her solitude by talking directly to the camera, I had trouble believing she was all that desperate. Shirley's husband is a kind but remote figure; her marriage is cheerless; she feels life slipping from her grasp.

Then one day an old girlfriend wins a trip for two to Greece, and asks Shirley to come along. This is a bigger dare than she has accepted for years, and she is sure her husband will never approve, but finally she flies off to Greece, because just once in her life (if I remember correctly) she wants to see the sun set over a foreign sea. Or words to that effect. Many of the sentiments in this film seem recycled directly from greeting cards.

In no time at all her friend is having an affair with a strange man on the other side of the island of Mykonos, and Shirley drifts, lonely as a cloud, through restaurants and hotel lobbies and plazas and beachfronts until she catches the eye of a handsome waiter (Tom Conti), who asks her to go for a ride on a boat. He protests that he does not harbor lust for her, but of course he does, and of course she hopes he does, and before long they are up to their necks in the Mediterranean, and we are up to our necks, too.

It is little wonder that a British actor, Conti, was hired to play the Greek waiter. No self-respecting Greek actor would want this role, which is cobbled together out of every Hellenic Lover cliché of the last several decades. He is poetic and gentle, tender and passionate, and he has a big black moustache, and of course he is not faithful, but what the heck—she will never forget the love-drenched moments they have spent together.

Shirley Valentine was directed by Lewis Gilbert from a script by Willy Russell, based on his stage play, but they have not solved the problem of how to tell the story. Some scenes take place while we watch them. Some take place while Shirley watches them along with us. Some consist of Shirley talking directly to us or to the wall or the sky or something. Most of the scenes fly straight in the face of common sense, as when we are supposed to cheer because Shirley, jilted by her Greek lover, finds happiness anyway as a waitress in his restaurant.

If there is a shred of plausibility in the film, it comes from Bernard Hill's performance as Shirley Valentine's husband. He isn't a bad bloke, just a tired and indifferent one, and when he follows his wife to Greece at the end of the film, there are a few moments so truthful that they show up the artifice of the rest.

Shoah ★ ★ ★ ★

NO MPAA RATING, 563 m. on five cassettes, 1986

A documentary directed and produced by Claude Lanzmann.

For more than nine hours I sat and watched a film named *Shoah*, and when it was over, I sat for a while longer and simply stared into space, trying to understand my emotions. I had seen a memory of the most debased chapter in human history. But I had also seen a film that affirmed life so passionately that I did not know where to turn with my confused feelings. There is no proper response to this film. It is an enormous fact, a 563-minute howl of pain and anger in the face of genocide. It is one of the noblest films ever made.

The film's title is a Hebrew word for chaos or annihilation—for the Holocaust. The film is a documentary, but it does not contain images from the 1940s. There are no old newsreel shots, no interviews with the survivors of the death camps, no coverage of the war crimes trials. All of the movie was photographed in the last five or six years by a man named Claude Lanzmann, who went looking for eyewitnesses to Hitler's "Final Solution." He is surprisingly successful in finding people who were there, who saw and heard what went on. Some of them, a tiny handful, are Jewish survivors of the camps. The rest are mostly old people, German and Polish, some who worked in the camps, others who were in a position to observe what happened.

They talk and talk. *Shoah* is a torrent of words, and yet the overwhelming impression, when it is over, is one of silence. Lanzmann intercuts two kinds of images. He shows the faces of his witnesses. And then he uses quiet pastoral scenes of the places where the deaths took place. Steam engines move massively through the Polish countryside, down the same tracks where trains took countless Jews, gypsies, Poles, homosexuals, and other so-called undesirables to their deaths. Cameras pan silently across pastures, while we learn that underneath the tranquility are mass graves. Sometimes the image is of a group of people, gathered in a doorway, or in front of a church, or in a restaurant kitchen.

Lanzmann is a patient interrogator. We see him in the corners of some of his shots, a tall, lanky man, informally dressed, chain-smoking. He wants to know the details. He doesn't ask large, profound questions about the meaning of the extermination of millions of people. He asks little questions. In one of the most chilling sequences in the film, he talks to Abraham Bomba, today a barber in Tel Aviv. Bomba was one of the Jewish barbers ordered to cut off the hair of Jewish women before they were killed in Treblinka.

His assignment suggests the shattering question: How can a woman's hair be worth more than her life? But Lanzmann does not ask overwhelming and unanswerable questions like this. These are the sorts of questions he asks:

You cut with what? With scissors?
There were no mirrors?
You said there were about sixteen barbers?
You cut the hair of how many women in one batch?

The barber tries to answer. As he talks, he has a customer in his chair, and he snips at the customer's hair almost obsessively, making tiny movements with his scissors, as if trying to use the haircut as a way to avoid the questions. Their conversation finally arrives at this exchange, after he says he cannot talk any more:

A. I can't. It's too horrible. Please.
Q. *We have to do it. You know it.*
A. I won't be able to do it.
Q. *You have to do it. I know it's very hard. I know and I apologize.*
A. Don't make me go on, please.
Q. *Please. We must go on.*

Lanzmann is cruel, but he is correct. He must go on. It is necessary to make this record before all of those who were witnesses to the Holocaust have died.

His methods in obtaining the interviews were sometimes underhanded. He uses a concealed television camera to record the faces of some of the old Nazi officials whom he interviews, and we look over the shoulders of the TV technicians in a van parked outside the buildings where they live. We see the old men nonchalantly pulling down charts from the wall to explain the layout of a death camp, and we hear their voices, and at one point when a Nazi asks for reassurance that the conversation is private, Lanzmann provides it. He will go to any length to obtain this testimony.

He does not, however, make any attempt to arrange his material into a chronology, an objective, factual record of how the "Final Solution" began, continued, and was finally terminated by the end of the war. He uses a more poetic, mosaic approach, moving according to rhythms only he understands among the only three kinds of faces we see in this film: survivors, murderers, and bystanders. As their testimony is intercut with the scenes of train tracks, steam engines, abandoned buildings, and empty fields, we are left with enough time to think our own thoughts, to meditate, to wonder.

This is a long movie but not a slow one, and in its words it creates something of the same phenomenon I experienced while watching *My Dinner with André*. The words themselves create images in the imagination, as they might in a radio play. Consider the images summoned by these words, spoken by Filip Muller, a Czech Jew assigned to work at the doors of the gas chambers, a man who survived five waves of liquidations at Auschwitz:

A. You see, once the gas was poured in, it worked like this: It rose from the ground upwards. And in the terrible struggle that followed—because it was a struggle—the lights were switched off in the gas chambers. It was dark, no one could see, so the strongest people tried to climb higher. Because they probably realized that the higher they got, the more air there was. They could breathe better. That caused the struggle. Secondly, most people tried to push their way to the door. It was psychological; they knew where the door was; maybe they could force their way out. It was instinctive, a death struggle. Which is why children and weaker people and the aged always wound up at the bottom. The strongest were on top. Because in the death struggle, a father didn't realize his son lay beneath him.

Q. *And when the doors were opened?*

A. They fell out. People fell out like blocks of stone, like rocks falling out of a truck.

The images evoked by his words are inutterably painful. What is remarkable, on reflection, is that Muller is describing a struggle that neither he nor anyone else now alive ever saw. I realized, at the end of his words, that a fundamental change had taken place in the way I personally visualized the gas chambers. Always before, in reading about them or hearing about them, my point of view was outside, looking in. Muller put me inside.

That is what this whole movie does, and it is probably the most important thing it does. It changes our point of view about the Holocaust. After nine hours of *Shoah*, the Holocaust is no longer a subject, a chapter of history, a phenomenon. It is an environment. It is around us. Ordinary people speak in ordinary voices of days that had become ordinary to them. A railroad engineer who drove the trains to Treblinka is asked if he could hear the screams of the people in the cars behind his locomotive:

A. Obviously, since the locomotive was next to the cars. They screamed, asked for water. The screams from the cars closest to the locomotives could be heard very well.

Q. *Can one get used to that?*

A. No, it was extremely distressing. He knew the people behind him were human, like him. The Germans gave him and the other workers vodka to drink. Without drinking, they couldn't have done it.

Some of the strangest passages in the film are the interviews with the officials who were running the camps and making the "Final Solution" work smoothly and efficiently. None of them, at least by their testimony, seem to have witnessed the whole picture. They only participated in a small part of it, doing their little jobs in their little corners. If they are to be believed, they didn't personally kill anybody, they just did small portions of larger tasks, and somehow all of the tasks, when added up and completed, resulted in people dying. Here is the man who scheduled the trains that took the Jews to die:

Q. *You never saw a train?*

A. No, never. We had so much work, I never left my desk. We worked day and night.

And here is a man who lived 150 feet from a church where Jews were rounded up, held, and then marched into gas vans for the trip to the crematoriums:

Q. *Did you see the gas vans?*

A. No—yes, from the outside. They shuttled back and forth. I never looked inside; I didn't see Jews.

What is so important about *Shoah* is that the voices are heard of people who did see, who did understand, who did comprehend, who were there, who know that the Holocaust happened, who tell us with their voices and with their eyes that genocide occurred in our time, in our civilization.

There is a tendency while watching *Shoah* to try to put a distance between yourself and the events on the screen. These things happened, after all, forty or forty-five years ago. Most of those now alive have been born since the events happened. Then, while I was watching the film, came a chilling moment. A name flashed on the screen in the subtitles, the name of one of the commandants at Treblinka death camp. At first I thought the name was "Ebert"—my name. Then I realized it was "Eberl." I felt a moment of relief, and then a moment of intense introspection as I realized that it made no difference what the subtitle said. The message of this film (if we believe in the brotherhood of man) is that these crimes were committed by people like us, against people like us.

But there is an even deeper message as well, and it is contained in the testimony of Filip Muller, the Jew who stood at the door of a crematorium and watched as the victims walked in to die. One day some of the victims, Czech Jews, began to sing. They sang two songs: "The Hatikvah," and the Czech national anthem. They affirmed that they were Jews and that they were Czechs. They denied Hitler, who would have them be one but not the other. Muller speaks:

That was happening to my countrymen, and I realized that my life had become meaningless. (His eyes fill with tears.) Why go on living? For what? So I went into the gas chamber with them, resolved to die. With them. Suddenly, some who recognized me came up to me. . . . A small group of women approached. They looked at me and said, right there in the gas chamber . . .

Q. *You were inside the gas chamber?*

A. Yes. One of them said: "So you want to die. But that's senseless. Your death won't give us back our lives. That's no way. You must get out of here alive, you must bear witness to our suffering and to the injustice done to us."

And that is the final message of this extraordinary film. It is not a documentary, not journalism, not propaganda, not political. It is an act of witness. In it, Claude Lanzmann celebrates the priceless gift that sets man apart from animals and makes us human, and gives us hope: the ability for one generation to tell the next what it has learned.

A Shock to the System ★ ★ ★
R, 89 m., 1990

Michael Caine (Graham Marshall), Elizabeth McGovern (Stella Anderson), Peter Riegert (Robert Benham), Swoosie Kurtz (Leslie Marshall), Will Patton (Lieutenant Laker), Jenny Wright (Melanie O'Connor), John McMartin (George Brewster), Barbara Baxley (Lillian). Directed by Jan Egleson and produced by Patrick McCormick. Screenplay by Andrew Klavan.

It's the voice that does it. The flat Michael Caine delivery that always seems to imply there are more angles than meet the eye. Caine plays the narrator and hero of *A Shock to the System*, and as he dryly describes his progress up the corporate ladder and his steps toward a refurbished love life, we realize that this is the voice of a man who thinks he can get away with murder, and may be right.

In the movie, Caine is Graham Marshall, next in line to head the department in the big New York ad agency where he works. But then a smarmy pest of a younger man (Peter Riegert) gets the job. Meanwhile, Caine's life on the home front is an unendurable round of boredom and domestic psychological torture, engineered by his wife (Swoosie Kurtz). One day while he is down in the basement replacing a fuse, Caine gets a nasty electrical shock, and it starts him to thinking.

A Shock to the System is the story of how Caine methodically eliminates the barriers to his professional success and personal pleasure. To say more would be to spoil some of the fun. The movie toys with us as it shows Caine almost getting caught, as it plants clues we're sure somebody will find, and as it introduces the character of a genial Connecticut police detective (Will Patton) who persists in asking uncomfortable questions. Will the cop or anybody else figure out what Caine is doing? By cleverly manipulating the conventions of the crime movie, director Jan Egleson and writer Andrew Klavan lead us up one garden path and down another.

Michael Caine is a splendid movie actor, a consummate professional who is fun to watch in any film because there is always a layer of irony and fun right there below the surface. That makes him especially entertaining as a villain; his charm makes his sins seem permissible, or at least understandable. He rarely plays villains we hate. More often, we want him to get away with his sins. Since the sins he commits in *A Shock to the System* are wicked ones, that sets up a nice tension inside the movie. We see things from his point of view, we are invited to identify with him, and yet when the Connecticut detective comes calling, we think it's about time.

The movie is filled with sneaky personalities and office traitors; it's *Crimes and Misdemeanors* crossed with *Wall Street*. Riegert is especially effective as the underling who becomes an insufferable overling. Swoosie Kurtz has fun with the whining housewife who can't leave well enough—or, indeed, anything—alone. And there is a nice performance by Elizabeth McGovern as the office colleague who provides a sympathetic shoulder for Caine to cry, and breathe, upon.

They have a scene together that's a small masterpiece, one everyone can recognize

from real life, where the two office workers meet at the nearby bar and find that they are in complete agreement that they are right and good and brilliant and unappreciated, and that everyone else is full of it. There's some delicate comic acting here: Caine with his fragile male ego so easily bruised, and McGovern with psychic bandages, and eyes that say "there, there."

Movies have been growing depressingly nice lately, and *A Shock to the System* is a refreshing change of pace. It isn't a nice movie. There once was a time when movies were allowed to be embittered, dark, and brooding, and when evil was occasionally allowed to have a momentary victory. Now the conventional movie ends with a cheerleading scene. But *A Shock to the System* confounds our expectations and keeps us intrigued, because there's no way to know, not even in the very last moments, exactly which way the plot is going to fall.

Shoot the Moon ★ ★ ★ ½
R, 124 m., 1982

Albert Finney (George Dunlap), Diane Keaton (Faith Dunlap), Karen Allen (Sandy), Peter Weller (Frank), Dana Hill (Sherry). Directed by Alan Parker and produced by Alan Marshall. Screenplay by Bo Goldman.

Alan Parker's *Shoot the Moon* is a film that sometimes keeps its painful secrets even from itself. It opens with a shot of a man in agony. In another room, his wife, surrounded by four noisy daughters, dresses for a dinner that evening at which the man will be honored. The man has to pull himself together. His voice is choking with tears, he telephones the woman he loves and tells her how hard it will be to get through the evening without her. Then he puts on his rumpled tuxedo and marches out to do battle. As we watch this scene, we assume that the movie will answer several of the questions it raises, such as: What went wrong in the marriage? Why is the man in such agony? What is the nature of his love for the other woman? One of the surprises in *Shoot the Moon* is that none of these questions is ever quite answered, and we are asked to fill in the gaps ourselves.

That is not necessarily a flaw in the film. *Shoot the Moon* is not the historical record of this marriage, but the emotional history. It starts with what should be a happy marriage. A writer of books (Albert Finney) lives with his beautiful, funky wife (Diane Keaton) and

their four rambunctious daughters in a converted farmhouse somewhere in Marin County, California. Their house is one of those warm battle zones filled with books, miscellaneous furniture, and the paraphernalia for vast projects half-completed. We learn that the marriage has gone disastrously wrong. That the man is determined to stalk out and be with his new woman. That the wife, after a period of anger and mourning, is prepared to react to this decision by almost deliberately having an affair with the loutish but well-meaning young man who comes to build a tennis court. That the husband and wife still harbor fugitive feelings of love and passion for another.

We never really learn how the marriage went wrong. There is the usual talk about how one partner was not given the room to grow, or the other did not have enough "space"—concepts that love would render meaningless, but that divorce makes into savagely defended positions. We also learn just a tantalizing little about the two new lovers. Albert Finney's new woman (Karen Allen) is so cynical about their relationship in one scene that we wonder if their affair will soon end (we never learn). Diane Keaton's new man (Peter Weller) is so emotionally stiff, closed-off, that we don't know for a long time whether Keaton really likes him, or simply desires him sexually and wants to use him to spite her husband.

Does it matter that the movie doesn't want to provide insights in these areas? I think it does. When Ingmar Bergman covered similar grounds in his *Scenes from a Marriage*, he provided us with enough concrete information about the issues in the marriage that it was possible for us to discuss the relationship afterward, taking sides, seeing both points of view. After *Shoot the Moon*, we don't discuss the relationship, we discuss our questions about it. And yet this is sometimes an extraordinary movie. Despite its flaws, despite its gaps, despite two key scenes that are dreadfully wrong, *Shoot the Moon* contains a raw emotional power of the sort we rarely see in domestic dramas.

The film's basic conflict is within Albert Finney's mind. He can no longer stay with his wife, he must leave and be with the other woman, and yet he still wants to own the family and possessions he has left behind. He doesn't want his ex-wife dating other men. He wants to observe the birthday of an eldest daughter (Dana Hill) who hates him and resents his behavior. He remodeled the house with his own hands, and cannot bear to see another man working on it. In one scene of heartbreaking power, he breaks into his own house and finds himself beating his daughter because he loves her so much and she will not love him.

In scenes like that (and in the quiet scenes where Hill asks, "Why did Daddy leave us?" and Keaton answers, "I don't think he left you; I think he left me"), *Shoot the Moon* is a great film. In scenes like the one where they fight in a restaurant, or argue in court, it ranges from the miscalculated to the disastrous. *Shoot the Moon* is a rare, good film, and yet, afterward, most of my thoughts were about how it might have been better. It is frustrating to feel that the filmmakers knew their characters intimately, but chose to reveal them only in part.

Shoot to Kill ★ ★ ★
R, 100 m., 1988

Sidney Poitier (Warren Stantin), Tom Berenger (Jonathan Knox), Kirstie Alley (Sarah), Clancy Brown (Steve), Richard Masur (Norman), Andrew Robinson (Harvey), Kevin Scannell (Ben). Directed by Roger Spottiswoode and produced by Ron Silverman and Daniel Petrie, Jr. Screenplay by Harv Zimmel, Michael Burton, and Petrie.

Shoot to Kill is yet another example, rather late in the day, of the buddy movie, that most dependable genre from the early 1970s. The formula still works. Two characters who have nothing in common are linked together on a dangerous mission, and after a lot of close calls they survive, prevail, and become buddies. The movie got more than the usual amount of attention because it marked Sidney Poitier's return to acting after ten years behind the camera. He didn't win any awards for this performance, but it was nice to have him back.

Poitier plays Warren Stantin, an FBI agent who holds himself personally responsible after a kidnapper kills two hostages and escapes into the Pacific Northwest. The killer (Clancy Brown) is a sneering sadist who joins up with a group of sportsmen who plan to trek into the wilderness on a fishing trip. His plan: Kill them and force their guide to lead him through the wilderness to the Canadian border.

The guide is played by Kirstie Alley from the TV show "Cheers," in a robust display of pink cheeks and deep breathing. She leads her charges into the woods. Her boyfriend (Tom Berenger, seen in *Platoon*) is at a base station, and Poitier tries to convince Berenger to lead him after the fugitive. Of course, the mountain man doesn't believe the city slicker can keep up on a tough cross-country hike that includes some rock climbing, and, of course, Poitier is determined to prove himself.

Have we seen this before? I think so. The route passes along a standard wilderness obstacle course, including a terrifying rope bridge over a chasm far below. Alley leads her group across, but then Brown sabotages the bridge, and Berenger nearly falls to his death before Poitier comes to his rescue. Later, it's Berenger's turn to save Poitier's life, and gradually the two men come to respect one another.

There are just a few teeny-weeny holes in this plot. For example: Why would the FBI let one agent go out as Poitier does, on a hunch? Why does another FBI agent spill the beans over the radio, since the quarry would likely be listening? Why walk for arduous miles across a grueling landscape when it might be easier to hitch a ride? Why put us through the whole cross-country trek when, at the end, the payoff comes not in the mountains but at sea?

Only a churl would ask such questions. *Shoot to Kill* is a genre movie in which the specifics hardly matter. Only the formula is important: Two guys team up, conquer great difficulties, and become friends. And at that level, *Shoot to Kill* works like an efficient machine. Poitier and Berenger create a nice give-and-take chemistry, and there are some funny gags, mostly involving the city slicker's uneasiness around horses. The device of cutting back and forth between Kirstie Alley's group and their pursuers keeps the buddy formula from growing too oppressive. And the action scene at the end is effective, although I question whether a gun can fire underwater. *Shoot to Kill* is fast-food moviemaking: quick, satisfying, and transient. Now let's see Poitier in something more challenging.

The Shootist ★ ★ ★ ½
PG, 100 m., 1976

John Wayne (The Shootist), Lauren Bacall (The Widow), James Stewart (The Doctor), Ron Howard (The Son), Harry Morgan (The Sheriff), John Carradine (The Undertaker), Hugh O'Brian (The Gambler), Richard Boone (The Gunman). Directed by Don Siegel and produced by M.J. Frankovich and William Seif. Screenplay by Miles Hood.

The old man was around for a long time. When he played the fresh-faced Ringo Kid in *Stagecoach*, back in 1939, he was already thirty-two years old. And I didn't believe it either until I'd counted the credits twice—but *Stagecoach* was his sixtieth film. John Wayne grew, role by role, into the most mythic presence in American movies. Some of the roles were pretty bad ones, but maybe at the time we didn't know that. Maybe at the time we were ten or twelve years old, and it was a Saturday afternoon, and what we registered was that Wayne was up there on the screen, squinting into the sun, making decisions, ready for action. For my generation, while presidents came and went, John Wayne merely grew a little more thoughtful.

He rides onscreen in *The Shootist* afraid that he is dying. Not afraid he'll be killed, but afraid he's dying, which is the last thing we anticipated a John Wayne character would do of his own accord. It is 1901: He has outlived his century. A sawbones in the next state has given him the bad news and now he wants to hear it from the lips of Doc Hostetler, who nursed him back to health after a violent afternoon twenty years ago. And so he rides, the Shootist, into a Carson City to which the Old West has become an embarrassment. The streets are still wide enough to turn a mule train in, but now an abashed little horse trolley runs down the middle of them, and electricity's going to put the horse out of business next year. The pain is way down deep in his back, and he rides on a red velvet cushion he stole out of a whorehouse. It doesn't do a damn bit of good. Hostetler hems and haws and comes out with it: cancer. Two months to live, six weeks, maybe less. In the meantime he can do what he wants. After a while he won't feel like doing much.

In his time, the Shootist shot a lot of men dead. Out at the livery stable, burnt into the leather of his saddle, they find his name: J.B. Books. His arrival in Carson City immediately becomes news. Hostetler steers him over to a boarding house run by the Widow Rogers, who shows him a two-dollar room. It'll do fine. Books settles down to die. But all these gunfighters had the same problem: People weren't content to let them die in bed, because they made too good a trophy.

So there is a tricky dilemma: To die with

some measure of dignity, and to avoid being shot in the meantime. As the film opens, Books has eight days. You will be surprised with what gentleness and humanity he lives them, before the inevitable gunfire at the end. And unless you have already discovered that John Wayne is an actor as well as a movie star, you will be surprised by the dimensions he provides for J.B. Books.

The movie isn't a bit sentimental. Everybody in town wants the bastard dead, except for the Widow Rogers and her son, Gillom. Even Doc Hostetler, who knows what people can go through toward the end of these illnesses, stops Books at the door and advises him point-blank not to wait around and see how things will eventually feel. The Sheriff is almost cheerful at the prospect of Books's approaching end. The Undertaker offers a free funeral, free tombstone, free casket, free flowers, even two mourners thrown in at no extra charge. "You son of a bitch," Books says, "you aim to do to me what they did with John Wesley Hardin. Lay me out and parade every damn fool in the state past me at a dollar a head, half price for children, and then stuff me in a gunny sack and shovel me under." He is correct.

Still, eight days are enough to establish the beginnings of human contact. The Widow Rogers is appalled at first to have a killer as her paying guest, but an affection and respect grows up between them. Her kid, Gillom, contracts a case of hero worship even while trying to swindle the Shootist out of his horse. And Wayne, as Books, occupies the substantial center of the film. He vows to read a newspaper through from front to back before he dies. He sends his Sunday-go-to-meeting clothes out to the cleaners. And he challenges three old Carson City enemies to meet him in the saloon at eleven o'clock Monday morning.

It's here that the movie doesn't quite work. We hardly know the three enemies. We don't know why they'd oblige the Shootist's wish to die in a gunfight. We understand his reasoning, but not theirs. And the movie's final scene, in which Gillom Rogers symbolically steps into the Shootist's boots, is just a little too neat to be real. Westerns probably have to end along these lines with confrontations and gunfire and heroism, but *The Shootist* will be remembered for the quieter scenes that came before.

The cast is excellent because it understands the material, and sympathizes with it: James Stewart, as the doctor, and Lauren Bacall, as the widow, play scenes with Wayne that absolutely make us forget we're watching a movie. Gaunt old John Carradine has been an undertaker all his life; finally they cast him as one. Don Siegel's direction reveals a sensitivity we didn't suspect after films like *Dirty Harry*. And observe the way John Wayne says "Good day, Mrs. Rogers" to Lauren Bacall for the last time.

Shy People ★ ★ ★ ★
R, 120 m., 1988

Jill Clayburgh (Diana), Barbara Hershey (Ruth), Martha Plimpton (Grace), Merritt Butrick (Mike), John Philbin (Tommy), Don Swayze (Mark), Pruitt Taylor Vince (Paul), Mare Winningham (Candy). Directed by Andrei Konchalovsky and produced by Menahem Golan and Yoram Globus. Screenplay by Gerard Brach, Konchalovsky, and Marjorie David.

Two great early shots define the two worlds of *Shy People*. The first is circular, the second straight ahead.

The film's opening shot circles at a vertiginous height above Manhattan, showing the canyons of skyscrapers with people scurrying below like ants. The camera moves through a complete circle, finally coming to rest inside a high-rise apartment where a restless teen-ager and her distracted mother have no idea what to do about each other.

The second shot, a few minutes later in the film, is also taken from a height; we are above a speedboat that drones relentlessly into the heart of the Louisiana bayou country. This shot, inexplicably thrilling, is like scenes from adventure books we read when we were kids. We feel a quickening of excitement as the boat penetrates the unknown.

The two shots define the two women who are at the heart of the film. Jill Clayburgh plays a shallow, sophisticated Manhattan magazine writer, who convinces her bosses at *Cosmopolitan* to let her write about her family roots. And Barbara Hershey plays Clayburgh's long-lost distant cousin, who lives in isolation in a crumbling, mossy home in the heart of the bayou. The movie is essentially about the differences between these women, about family blood ties, and about the transparent membrane between life and death.

Shy People is one of the great visionary films of recent years, a film that shakes off the petty distractions of safe Hollywood entertainments and develops a large vision.

It is about revenge and hatred, about mothers and sons, about loneliness. It suggests that family ties are the most important bonds in the world, and by the end of the film, Clayburgh will discover that Hershey is closer to her "dead" husband than most city-dwellers are to anybody.

Yet the film is not without a wicked streak of humor. Clayburgh invites her precocious daughter (Martha Plimpton) to accompany her into the Louisiana backwaters, where the adolescent girl meets Hershey's ill-assorted sons. One is literally locked in an out-building when the New Yorkers arrive, another is light in the head, and still another is disowned and never mentioned, because he dared to move out of the bayou and open a nightclub in town. As the girl flirts with her cousins, and the women warily spar with each other, and the darkness of the swamp closes in.

Shy People was directed by Andrei Konchalovsky, the Russian emigre whose other English-language movies include *Runaway Train* and *Duet for One*. Because he is an outsider, he is not so self-conscious about using American images that an American director might be frightened away from. The world of *Shy People* is the world of Erskine Caldwell's *Tobacco Road*, or Faulkner's Snopes family, of Al Capp and Russ Meyer. Hershey and her family are not small, timid people, but caricatures, and it's to Hershey's credit that she is able to play the role to the hilt and yet still make it real.

There are great sequences in the film, including one extraordinary night in which Clayburgh is lost in the swamp, is up to her neck in the fetid waters, and sees, or thinks she sees, the ghost of Hershey's dead husband.

There is a barroom fight in which the wrathful Hershey wades into her son's nightclub with a gun. Most extraordinary of all, there are spooky, quiet moments in which the mosquitoes drone in the sleepy heat of midday, while the two women pore over old photograph albums.

Sid & Nancy ★ ★ ★ ★
R, 111 m., 1986

Gary Oldman (Sid Vicious), Chloe Webb (Nancy Spungen), Drew Schofield (Johnny Rotten), David Hayman (Malcolm McLaren), Debby Bishop (Phoebe), Jude Alderson (Ma Vicious). Directed by Alex Cox and produced by Eric Fellner. Screenplay by Cox and Abbe Wool.

His real name was John Simon Ritchie, and his father was a trombone player who left before he was born. His mother wore her hair long and went to all the hippie festivals with the little boy at her side. They lived in London's East End, within the culture of poverty and drugs. When he was fifteen, Ritchie dropped out of school. When he was seventeen, he was one of the most famous people in England, although by then he was known as Sid Vicious of the notorious Sex Pistols.

What did he respond to when the American girl, Nancy Spungen, came into his life? She was a groupie from New York, but she was also an authority figure who pushed him to try harder, complained when he was not given his due, and plotted to get him better deals and wider exposure. If she had not bled to death that night in New York, she might have made Vicious really amount to something, someday.

The astonishing thing about *Sid & Nancy* is the amount of subtle information it gives us about their relationship, given the fact that the surface of the movie is all tumult and violence, pain and confusion. This movie doesn't take the easy way out and cast these two lovers as Romeo and Juliet, misunderstood waifs. It sees beneath their leather and chains, their torn T-shirts and steel-toed boots, to a basically conventional relationship between an ambitious woman and a man who was still a boy.

They needed each other. Spungen needed someone to mother, and Vicious, according to his friends, needed self-esteem and was immensely proud that he had an American girlfriend. They were meant for each other, but by the end it was all just ashes and bewilderment, because they were so strung out on drugs that whole days would slip by unnoticed. In their fantasies of doomed romance, they planned to go out together in a suicide pact, but by the end they were too sick to even go out together for a pizza.

By now, everybody knows that Vicious woke up one morning in New York's Chelsea Hotel to find Spungen's dead body. He was booked on suspicion of murder, released on bail, and two months later was dead of a drug overdose. The available evidence strongly suggests that he did not stab Spungen to death, but that she died of one of those untidy accidents that befall drug abusers. A human being is a dangerous thing to let loose in a room with itself, when it cannot think.

There were some good times earlier in their story, but on the evidence of this movie there were not many. By the time Spungen met Vicious in London in the mid-1970s, the Sex Pistols were the most infamous punk rock band in the world. But they were in the position of Gandhi in that apocryphal story where he sees the mob run past and races to get in front of his followers. The punk conceit was a total rejection of conventional society; their credo was the line by Johnny Rotten, the Pistols' lead singer: "Got a problem and the problem is you." For the Pistols to stay in front of that mob, they had to be meaner, more violent, more negative than their followers. How did it feel to stand on a bandstand and make angry music while your fans stood face to face, banging heads until unconsciousness came?

Sid & Nancy suggests that Vicious never lived long enough to really get his feet on the ground, to figure out where he stood and where his center was. He was handed great fame and a certain amount of power and money, and indirectly told that his success depended on staying fucked up. This is a big assignment for a kid who would otherwise be unemployable. Vicious did his best, fighting and vomiting and kicking his way through his brief days and long nights, until Spungen brought him a measure of relief. Some nights she was someone to hold, and other nights she was someone to hold onto. What difference did it make?

Sid & Nancy makes these observations with such complexity, such vividness, and such tenderness that at the end of the film a curious thing happens. You do not weep for Vicious, or Spungen, but maybe you weep for all of us, that we have been placed in a world where it is possible for people to make themselves so unhappy. Vicious was not a hero, just a guy who got himself into a situation he couldn't handle. But to thousands of London kids, he represented an affront to a society that offered no jobs, no training, no education, and no entry into the world of opportunity. If life offers you nothing, the least you can offer it is the finger.

Performances like the ones in this film go beyond movie acting and into some kind of evocation of real lives. Vicious is played by Gary Oldman and Spungen is played by Chloe Webb, and there isn't even a brief period at the top of the movie where we have to get used to them. They are these people, driven and relentless.

The movie was directed by Alex Cox, who made *Repo Man* a couple of years ago, and

here he announces himself as a great director. He and his actors pull off the neat trick of creating a movie full of noise and fury, and telling a meticulous story right in the middle of it.

But why should anyone care about a movie about two scabrous vulgarians? Because the subject of a really good movie is sometimes not that important. It's the acting, writing, and direction that count. If a movie can illuminate the lives of other people who share this planet with us and show us not only how different they are but, how even so, they share the same dreams and hurts, then it deserves to be called great. If you have an open mind, it is possibly true that the less you care about Sid Vicious, the more you will admire this movie.

Sidewalk Stories ★ ★ ★ ½
R, 97 m., 1989

Charles Lane (Artist), Nicole Alysia (Child), Sandye Wilson (Young Woman), Darnell Williams (Father), Trula Hoosier (Mother), Michael Baskin (Doorman), George Riddick (Street Partner). Directed, produced, and written by Charles Lane.

Charles Lane's film *Sidewalk Stories* is a silent movie shot in black and white. If you are absolutely sure you wouldn't want to see a silent, black-and-white movie, read no further. There is no help for you here.

What I want to evoke is the different consciousness created by watching a silent film. Sitting in the dark, viewing *Sidewalk Stories*, I became aware that somehow my attention had been heightened and I was looking at the screen with more intensity than would usually be the case. Why was this? I think perhaps the silent format inspires us to participate more directly in the movie. A sound film comes to us, approaches us—indeed, it sometimes assaults us—from the screen. But a silent film stays up there on the glowing wall, and we rise up to meet it. We take our imagination and join it with the imagination of the filmmaker.

That's what happened to me during *Sidewalk Stories*. Another interesting thing also happened. Watching this movie photographed in New York City in 1989, I found myself being set free from a lot of my stereotypes and preconceptions about the big city by the fact that the film was silent. In a sound film, the characters usually represent themselves. In a silent film, they represent a type.

They stand for others like themselves, which is one reason silent films are more universal than talkies.

In sound movies set in modern cities, for example, we are likely to assume that street people are violent, disturbed, and antisocial. *Sidewalk Stories* opens with a long, elaborate tracking shot past a row of sidewalk entertainers—jugglers, pavement artists, magicians, three-card-monte shills—and because the film is silent we do not assume they are all clones of Travis Bickle. They seem gentler, more universal characters, like people we would meet in a film by Chaplin. That's a strange assumption, since the movie is set in an area of present-day Greenwich Village where drug dealers and other vermin are always present, and yet the silent film somehow mythologizes the characters.

The shot ends on a shot of the Artist (played by Charles Lane himself). He is a small, determined black man who has set up his easel and hopes to persuade pedestrians to pay him to draw them. Right next to his spot on the pavement is another artist, a tall, broad bully who also wants this turf. He pushes the Artist to the ground. The Artist gets up. He pushes him over again. The Artist gets up again. He pushes him over a third time. The Artist begins to get up, thinks better of it, and pushes himself back down to the ground—saving the bully trouble.

This is, almost movement for movement, a comic bit of business from Charlie Chaplin. It's as if Lane is starting his film by acknowledging that debt. Then he moves on. As the story develops, the Artist befriends the mother of a small girl, and after an altercation in an alley involving the mother and the girl's father, the Artist finds to his consternation that he has been left with the little girl—and it's up to him to protect her.

In a sound movie, he would go to a social agency. In a silent movie, of course, he takes her home with him—home to the rude little room where he is a squatter in the ruins of a church marked for demolition. And he begins to figure out how to care for the little orphan. (The child is played perfectly by Lane's own daughter, Nicole Alysia, and her naturalness is one of the strengths of the movie.) The domestic details, right down to the box of cornflakes, all provide comic possibilities. And when it turns out that the child's crayon scrawls are snapped up as "modern art," the movie takes a wicked turn.

The movie's story develops as a melodrama in which the Artist is befriended by a successful businesswoman (Sandye Wilson), threatened by thugs, and eventually is able to restore the child to her rightful mother (Trula Hoosier). Along the way there are the kinds of confrontations between rich and poor that Chaplin liked to explore, including a scene where the businesswoman invites the Artist and the child to her high-rise apartment, but the doorman doesn't want to let them in. Lane is endlessly inventive in the ways he finds to create humorous situations and tell his story through images, and the sound-track music, by Marc Marder, reinforces everything that happens. The movie, at ninety-seven minutes, seems shorter.

I have a quarrel with one thing Lane does. At the end of the film, the camera lingers in a public place where some of the homeless have congregated. They're panhandlers, asking the passing public for change, and gradually, slowly, we begin to be able to hear their voices on the sound track: "Remember the homeless!" "Can you spare a quarter?" The sound in this sequence was not necessary. Lane's whole movie has already made the points that he now reinforces with spoken dialogue. It violates the magic of silence. But up until then, *Sidewalk Stories* weaves a spell as powerful as it is entertaining.

The Silence of the Lambs ★ ★ ★ ½
R, 116 m., 1991

Jodie Foster (Clarice Starling), Anthony Hopkins (Dr. Hannibal Lecter), Scott Glenn (Jack Crawford), Anthony Heald (Dr. Frederick Chilton), Ted Levine (Jamie Gum), Kasi Lemmons (Ardelia Mapp). Directed by Jonathan Demme and produced by Edward Saxon, Kenneth Utt, and Ron Bozman. Screenplay by Ted Tally.

It has been a good long while since I have felt the presence of Evil so manifestly demonstrated as in the first appearance of Anthony Hopkins in *The Silence of the Lambs*. He stands perfectly still in the middle of his cell floor, arms at his sides, and we sense instantly that he is not standing at attention; he is standing at rest—like a savage animal confident of the brutality coiled up inside him. His speaking voice has the precision of a man so arrogant he can barely be bothered to address the sloppy intelligence of the ordinary person. The effect of this scene is so powerful that it underlies all the rest of the movie, lending terror to scenes that do not even involve him.

Like all great entrances in the movies, his is carefully prepared. We learn that his character, Dr. Hannibal Lecter, is both a brilliant psychiatrist and a mass murderer, known as "Hannibal the Cannibal" because he eats his victims. He is already behind bars (and unbreakable Plexiglas) when the movie opens, and, indeed, *The Silence of the Lambs* is about the search for another mass murderer, named "Buffalo Bill," who skins his victims. Operating on the theory that it takes one to know one, the FBI agent in charge of the case (Scott Glenn) thinks Lecter might be able to provide useful clues in the search for Buffalo Bill. But Lecter toys with most of his inquisitors, or dismisses them, and so the agent hits on the idea of sending in an untried young female trainee (Jodie Foster). Perhaps she will appeal to the monster.

The notion of the beauty and the beast is, of course, central to horror stories, but watching *The Silence of the Lambs* for the second time, I began to wonder if the author of the original novel, Thomas Harris, had started the project by jotting down a list of the great universal phobias and dreads. Here is a movie involving not only cannibalism and the skinning of people, but also kidnapping, being trapped in the bottom of a well, decomposing corpses, large insects, being lost in the dark, being tracked by someone you cannot see, not being able to get people to believe you, creatures who jump from the shadows, people who know your deepest secrets, doors that slam shut behind you, beheadings, bizarre sexual perversions, and being a short woman in an elevator full of tall men.

If the movie were not so well made, indeed, it would be ludicrous. Material like this invites filmmakers to take chances, and punishes them mercilessly when they fail. That's especially true when the movie is based on best-selling material a lot of people are familiar with (*The Silence of the Lambs* was preceded by Harris's *Red Dragon*, about Hannibal Lecter, which was also made into a film, *Manhunter*).

The director, Jonathan Demme, is no doubt aware of the hazards, but does not hesitate to take chances. His first scene with Hopkins could have gone over the top, and in the hands of a lesser actor almost certainly would have. But Hopkins is in the great British tradition of actors who internalize instead of overacting, and his Hannibal Lecter has certain endearing parallels with his famous London stage performance in *Pravda*, where he played a press baron not unlike Rupert Murdoch. There are moments when Hopkins, as Lecter, goes berserk, but Demme wisely lets a little of this go a long way, so that the lasting impression is of his evil intelligence.

Jodie Foster is inevitably upstaged by Hopkins's rich and gruesome creation, but her steadiness and pluck are at the heart of the movie. Some interesting aspects have been provided for her character: She is "one generation up from white trash," as Lecter correctly guesses, she tries to disguise her hillbilly accent, and she has to muster up all of her courage to order a roomful of lascivious lawmen out of an autopsy room. The movie has an undercurrent of unwelcome male attention toward her character; rarely in a movie have I been made more aware of the subtle sexual pressures men put upon women with their eyes.

Against these qualities, the weak points of the movie are probably not very important, but there are some. The details of Foster's final showdown with Buffalo Bill are scarcely believable. Unless you look closely, you may miss the details of how Lecter deceives his pursuers in one grisly scene. The very last scene in the film is hard to follow. But against these flaws are balanced true suspense, unblinking horror, and an Anthony Hopkins performance that is likely to be referred to for many years when horror movies are discussed.

Silent Movie ★ ★ ★ ★
PG, 88 m., 1976

Mel Brooks (Mel Funn), Marty Feldman (Marty Eggs), Dom DeLuise (Dom Bell), Bernadette Peters (Vilma Kaplan), Sid Caesar (Studio Chief), Harold Gould (Engulf), Ron Carey (Devour), Henny Youngman (Fly-in-Soup Man). Directed by Mel Brooks and produced by Michael Hertzorg. Screenplay by Brooks, Ron Clark, Rudy DeLuca, and Barry Levinson.

There's a moment very early in *Silent Movie* (before the opening credits, in fact) when Mel Brooks, Marty Feldman, and Dom DeLuise are tooling through Los Angeles in a tiny sports car. They pass a pregnant lady at a bus stop. "That's a very pregnant lady!" Brooks says (on a title card, of course, since this is a silent movie). "Let's give her a lift!"

The lady gets into the back of the car, which tilts back onto its rear wheels. Mel drives off with the front wheels in the air.

This is far from being the funniest scene in a very funny movie, but it helps to illustrate my point, which is that Mel Brooks will do anything for a laugh. Anything. He has no shame. He's an anarchist; his movies inhabit a universe in which everything is possible and the outrageous is probable, and *Silent Movie*, where Brooks has taken a considerably stylistic risk and pulled it off triumphantly, made me laugh a lot. On the Brooks-Laff-O-Meter, I laughed more than in *Young Frankenstein* and about as much as in *Blazing Saddles*, although not, I confess, as much as in *The Producers*.

Silent Movie is not only funny, it's fun. It's clear at almost every moment that the filmmakers had a ball making it. It's set in contemporary Hollywood, where Big Pictures Studio ("If it's a big picture, we've made it") teeters on the edge of bankruptcy and a takeover from the giant Engulf and Devour conglomerate. Enter Mel Funn (Brooks), a once-talented director whose career was cut short by drunkenness, who vows to save the studio by convincing Hollywood's biggest stars to make a silent movie. This is a situation that gives rise to a lot of inside jokes (I wonder whether executives at Gulf and Western, which took over Paramount, will notice any parallels), but the thing about Brooks's inside jokes is that their outsides are funny, too.

The intrepid gang of Mel, Dom, and Marty set out to woo the superstars, materializing in the shower of one (who counts his hands, puzzled, and finds he has eight) and plucking another out of a nightclub audience. (There are several "actual" stars in the movie, but it would be spoiling the fun to name them.) Everything's done amid an encyclopedia of sight gags, old and new, borrowed and with a fly in their soup. There are gags that don't work and stretches of up to a minute, I suppose, when we don't laugh—but even then we're smiling because of Brooks's manic desire to entertain. There's a story about the days, years ago, when Brooks was a writer for Sid Caesar and Caesar would march into the writers' office, pick up their desks, brandish them and shout *"funnier!"* I think the lesson rubbed off.

In a movie filled with great scenes, these moments are classics: The battle with the Coke machine. The behavior with the horse on the merry-go-round. The nightclub

scene. The dramatic reaction of Engulf and Devour's board of directors to the photo of sexpot Vilma Kaplan. The fly in the soup. The Pong game in the intensive-care unit. The . . . but space is limited: Perhaps I should mention, though, that the movie isn't really silent. It's filled with wall-to-wall music, sound effects, explosions, whistles, and crashes and, yes, one word.

Silent Running ★ ★ ★ ★
G, 90 m., 1972

Bruce Dern (Lowell), Cliff Potts (Wolf), Ron Rivkin (Barker), Jesse Vint (Keenan), Mark Persons, Steven Brown, Cheryl Sparks, Larry Wisenhunt (Drones). Directed by Douglas Trumbull and produced by Michael Gruskoff. Screenplay by Deric Washburn, Mike Cimino, and Steve Bochco.

In the not very distant future, man has at last finished with Earth. The mountains are leveled and the valleys filled in, and there are no growing plants left to mess things up. Everything is nice and sterile, and man's global housekeeping has achieved total defoliation. Out around the rings of Saturn, a few lonely spaceships keep their vigil. They're interplanetary greenhouses, pointed always toward the sun. Inside their acres and acres of forests, protected by geodesic domes that gather the sunlight, the surviving plants and small animals of Earth grow. There are squirrels and rabbits and moonlit nights when the wind does actually seem to breathe in the trees: a ghostly reminder of the dead forests of Earth.

The keeper of one of these greenhouses, Freeman Lowell, loves the plants and animals with a not terribly acute intelligence. *Silent Running* is his story. In an earlier day, he might have been a forest ranger and happily spent the winter all alone in a tower, spotting forest fires. Now he is millions of miles from Earth, but his thoughts are filled with weedings and prunings, fertilizer and the artificial rainfall.

One day the word comes from Earth: Destroy the greenhouses and return. Lowell cannot bring himself to do this, and so he destroys his fellow crew members instead. Then he hijacks his spaceship and directs it out into the deep galactic night. All of this is told with simplicity and a quiet ecological concern, and it makes *Silent Running* a movie out of the ordinary—especially if you like science fiction.

The director is Douglas Trumbull, a Canadian who designed many of the special effects for Stanley Kubrick's *2001*. Trumbull also did the computers and the underground laboratory for *The Andromeda Strain,* and is one of the best science-fiction special-effects men. *Silent Running,* which has deep space effects every bit the equal of those in *2001,* also introduces him as an intelligent, if not sensational, director.

The weight of the movie falls on the shoulders of Bruce Dern, who plays the only man in sight during most of the picture. His only companions are Huey, Louie, and Dewey, who are small and uncannily human robots who help with the gardening. They're OK with a trowel but no good at playing poker, as their human boss discovers during a period of boredom.

Dern is a very good, subtle actor, who was about the best thing in Jack Nicholson's directing debut, *Drive, He Said.* Dern played a basketball coach as a man obsessed with the notion of winning—and the deep-space ecologist this time is a quieter variation on the theme.

Silent Running isn't, in the last analysis, a very profound movie, nor does it try to be. (If it had, it could have been a pretentious disaster.) It is about a basically uncomplicated man faced with an awesome, but uncomplicated, situation. Given a choice between the lives of his companions and the lives of Earth's last surviving firs and pines, oaks and elms, and creepers and cantaloupes, he decides for the growing things. After all, there are plenty of men. His problem is that, after a while, he begins to miss them.

Silkwood ★ ★ ★ ★
R, 128 m., 1983

Meryl Streep (Karen Silkwood), Kurt Russell (Drew Stephens), Cher (Dolly Pelliker), Craig T. Nelson (Winston). Directed by Mike Nichols and produced by Nichols and Michael Hausman. Screenplay by Nora Ephron and Alice Arlen.

When the Karen Silkwood story was first being talked about as a movie project, I pictured it as an angry political exposé, maybe *The China Syndrome, Part 2.* There'd be the noble, young nuclear worker, the evil conglomerate, and, looming overhead, the death's-head of a mushroom cloud. That could have been a good movie, but predict-

able. Mike Nichols's *Silkwood* is not predictable. That's because he's not telling the story of a conspiracy, he's telling the story of a human life. There are villains in his story, but none with motives we can't understand. After Karen is dead and the movie is over, we realize this is a lot more movie than perhaps we were expecting.

Silkwood is the story of some American workers. They happen to work in a Kerr-McGee nuclear plant in Oklahoma, making plutonium fuel rods for nuclear reactors. But they could just as easily be working in a Southern textile mill (there are echoes of *Norma Rae*), or on an assembly line, or for a metropolitan public school district. The movie isn't about plutonium, it's about the American working class. Its villains aren't monsters; they're organization men, labor union hotshots, and people afraid of losing their jobs. As the movie opens, Karen Silkwood fits naturally into this world, and the movie is the story of how she begins to stand out, how she becomes an individual, thinks for herself, and is punished for her freedom. Silkwood is played by Meryl Streep, in another of her great performances, and there's a tiny detail in the first moments of the movie that reveals how completely Streep has thought through the role. Silkwood walks into the factory, punches her time card, automatically looks at her own wristwatch, and then shakes her wrist: It's a self-winding watch, I guess. That little shake of the wrist is an actor's choice. There are a lot of them in this movie, all almost as invisible as the first one; little by little, Streep and her coactors build characters so convincing that we become witnesses instead of merely viewers.

The nuclear plant in the film is behind on an important contract. People are working overtime and corners are being cut. A series of small incidents convinces Karen Silkwood that the compromises are dangerous, that the health of the workers is being needlessly risked, and that the company is turning its back on the falsification of safety and workmanship tests. She approaches the union. The union sees some publicity in her complaints. She gets a free trip to Washington—her first airplane ride. She meets with some union officials who are much more concerned with publicity than with working conditions, and she has a little affair with one of them. She's no angel. At home in Oklahoma, domestic life resembles a revolving door, with her boyfriend (Kurt Russell)

packing up and leaving, and her friend (Cher), a lesbian, inviting a beautician to move in. It's a little amazing that established movie stars like Streep, Russell, and Cher could disappear so completely into the everyday lives of these characters.

The real Karen Silkwood died in a mysterious automobile accident. She was on her way to deliver some documents to a *New York Times* reporter when her car left the road. Was the accident caused in some way? Was she murdered? The movie doesn't say. Nor does it point suspicion only toward the company. At the end there were a lot of people mad at Karen Silkwood. *Silkwood* is the story of an ordinary woman, hard-working and passionate, funny and screwed-up, who made those people mad simply because she told the truth as she saw it and did what she thought was right.

Silverado ★ ★ ★ ½
PG-13, 132 m., 1985

Kevin Kline (Paden), Scott Glenn (Emmett), Kevin Costner (Jake), Danny Glover (Mal), Linda Hunt (Stella), Jeff Goldblum (Slick), Brian Dennehy (Sheriff Cobb), Rosanna Arquette (Hannah), John Cleese (Sheriff Langston). Directed and produced by Lawrence Kasdan. Screenplay by Lawrence Kasdan and Mark Kasdan.

Walking home after the second Western was over at the Princess Theater, we'd play the roles we had seen on the screen. We were seven or eight years old at the time, but we didn't have the slightest difficulty in identifying with the cowboys in the movies. All of their motives were transparently clear to us—except, possibly, why anyone would want to kiss a girl when he could be practicing his lasso tricks instead.

The Westerns I remember from those days have been filtered through a golden haze of time, but the one thing I am sure I remember correctly is that they were fun. They were high-spirited, joyous, anarchic movies in which overgrown adolescents jumped on their horses and whooped and waved their hats in the air, and rode as fast as the wind to the next town and to the next adventure.

Silverado is a Western like that. I mean the comparison to be praise. This movie is more sophisticated and complicated than the Westerns of my childhood, and it is certainly better looking and better acted. But it has the same spirit; it awards itself the carefree freedom of the Western myth itself—the myth of a nation "endlessly realizing Westward," as Robert Frost had it, with limitless miles of prairie and desert and mountain, interrupted only occasionally enough for a dozen men to shoot at each other without all of them necessarily getting hit.

Silverado is the work of Lawrence Kasdan, the man who wrote *Raiders of the Lost Ark*, and it has some of the same reckless brilliance about it. It's the story of four cowboys who join up together, ride into town, refuse to knuckle under to the corrupt sheriff, and end up fighting for justice. This is a story, you will agree, that has been told before. What distinguishes Kasdan's telling of it is the style and energy he brings to the project.

The cowboys include a sweet-faced young man who hopes to make his fortune (Kevin Kline), a black man who vows to avenge his father's murder (Danny Glover), a taciturn loner (Scott Glenn) who gets restless when he's not a long way from civilization, and his goofy brother (Kevin Costner). They meet along the way, after Glenn saves Kline from death in the desert, and together they help Costner escape from jail. Joining up with Glover, they ride on into the next town, Silverado, which is dominated by a slick sheriff (Brian Dennehy) and a gambling saloon run by a formidably competent little woman named Stella (Linda Hunt, in a scene-stealing performance).

I will not tell you too much of what happens next, but then perhaps I do not need to. If you are familiar with the Western, you will be familiar with this one. What may seem a little strange is that, if there is any nostalgia connected to this film, it will be found in our hearts and not in the characters on the screen. Too many Westerns in the last fifteen years have been elegies to a dead past, played out by actors remembering the cowboy roles of their youth (remember, if you can, the last Westerns of Robert Mitchum, William Holden, Randolph Scott, John Wayne, Joel McCrea, Kirk Douglas). *Silverado* contains a group of talented young actors (Scott Glenn, the oldest, is in his forties), and this is not their last Western but, in many cases, their first. The movie is set at the time when the West was still being opened up, when there was still opportunity there, and when the bad guys were still so unsophisticated they could fall for a dumb trick like getting trapped in a box canyon.

What does it prove, this movie about a bunch of cowboys held together by honor,

this movie about bartender philosophers, evil sheriffs, and young pioneer women with lines like "My beauty will pass someday, but the land will only grow more beautiful." What does it prove? That the Western myth is most at home in a setting of innocence, that *Silverado* understands that, and that somewhere in our hearts there may still be memories of little boys and girls who chose up sides for who got to be the good guys on the long walk home.

Sing ★ ★ ★
PG-13, 99 m., 1989

Lorraine Bracco (Miss Lombardo), Peter Dobson (Dominic), Jessica Steen (Hannah), Louise Lasser (Rosie), George DiCenzo (Mr. Marowitz), Patti LaBelle (Mrs. DeVere). Directed Richard Baskin and produced by Craig Zadan. Screenplay by Dean Pitchford.

The roots of *Sing* can be found firmly planted in the clichés of the past, in all those Rooney and Garland pictures where they rented the old barn and put on a show, or in the Beach Party movies where they held a rock 'n' roll benefit to rescue the teen center. This time, a Brooklyn high school is going to be closed, and the school board has refused permission for the students to hold their traditional spring talent show.

No reason is given for the ban on the show, but, of course, none is needed. It is necessary for the show to be prohibited in order for the students to defy the ban and put it on anyway. If there is one absolutely obligatory shot in a movie of this sort, it's the one where the evil fuddy-duddy comes bursting into the back of the auditorium and demands that the show be halted—only to be squelched by a triumphant song-and-dance number.

Since absolutely everything in *Sing* is completely predictable, I was surprised how much I enjoyed the movie. It's a victory of style over substance, and its energy owes a lot to Lorraine Bracco and Patti LaBelle, who play two of the teachers in the high school. Both of these women are absolute individuals, and the confidence with which they present themselves has a lot to do with the movie's whole tone.

Bracco is a thin, intense brunette with a Brooklyn accent and a face full of character and humor. She's wry and tough, and she has a key scene early in the movie where she stares down a tough kid who tries to assault her and offers him a choice: Go along with my program, or go to jail. The power of this

scene carries over to the whole movie, really, giving the material a weight it might not have had otherwise.

LaBelle, the rock legend from Philadelphia, is not given much of a character to play; there are times when she almost seems to be appearing as a guest star. But there's a song-and-dance sequence where she takes the stage and shows the kids how it's done, and the scene is a showstopper, like the Pee-wee Herman sequence in *Back to the Beach*: The plot goes on hold, and the movie simply has a great time for five minutes.

The plot, as I said, has been seen before. We know, of course, that there must be a romance, preferably between a good girl and a bad boy she can redeem. The girl is played by Jessica Steen, as a good-hearted senior who has nothing to do with the local hoods like Peter Dobson. Both kids have family problems. Steen's mother (Louise Lasser) is a widow who moans constantly over the ordeal of running the family diner. Dobson's brother is a small-time thief who takes the kid along on robberies—including, of course, Lasser's diner.

The plot questions are equally predictable: Will the bad kid repudiate his brother, win the respect of the girl, and dance in the big musical? Will the girl convince her mother that life is worth living? Will the teachers and their principal succeed in defying the board of education? Will the show go on? Are there stars in the sky? Sometimes it's fun watching the setups for scenes you know will follow. For example, when the girl gives her mother tickets to the show, and the mother turns them down, saying she's too busy to attend. What do you want to bet that at a key moment, the mother will turn up in the back of the auditorium and exchange a heartfelt nod of forgiveness with her daughter on the stage?

I'm of two minds about genre pictures like this one. On the one hand, I'd prefer something I hadn't seen before. On the other hand, because the plot has been phoned in, I'm free to observe the performances. And Lorraine Bracco was a particular pleasure. In this film and two others (*Someone to Watch Over Me* and *Dream Team*), she has emerged as one of those rare actors who has obvious and tangible integrity on the screen; she can sell dialogue even as tired as the lines in this script, because she puts her own spin on them. High school talent shows always end with somebody being thrust into the spotlight of stardom. In *Sing*, it's the teacher.

Sisters ★ ★ ★
R, 93 m., 1973

Margot Kidder (Danielle Breton), Jennifer Salt (Grace Collier), Charles Durning (Joseph Larch), Bill Finley (Emil Breton), Lisle Wilson (Philip Woode). Directed by Brian De Palma and produced by Edward R. Pressman. Screenplay by De Palma and Louisa Rose.

Brian De Palma's *Sisters* was made more or less consciously as an homage to Alfred Hitchcock, but it has a life of its own and it's a neat little mystery picture. The opening is pure Hitchcock. The movie begins with events so commonplace they're almost trivial, and the horror of the situation is revealed only gradually. A lithe fashion model and a young newspaperman meet on a quiz show (it's called "Peeping Tom" and asks the question, what would *you* do if you were inadvertently made voyeur-for-a-day?). She wins a set of stainless steel cutlery, he wins dinner for two at a supper club, and they decide they like each other.

After a few brushes with a mysterious stranger who may or may not be her former husband, the young couple spend the night together and in the morning he is brutally knifed to death. And, no, I haven't given away too much of the plot. Because there are a few complications. For example, the girl is half of a famous set of Siamese twins. She's the nice one, but her sister isn't—not at all.

Then there's the crusading young girl newspaper reporter, kind of a women's lib Lois Lane, who lives across the courtyard and witnesses the crime (à la *Rear Window*). She calls the police, but they resent a recent series of exposés she's written. And when they visit the so-called murder apartment they find no blood, no body, no signs of a crime; only the sweet young fashion model.

I don't suppose I can reveal another line of the plot without spoiling some of De Palma's nice surprises. But the movie works not so much because of the twists and turns and complications as because of the performances. In a movie industry filled with young actresses who look great but can't act so well (especially when they've got to play intelligent characters), De Palma has cast two of the exceptions: Margot Kidder and Jennifer Salt.

Both of them are really fine, but Jennifer Salt is the bigger surprise because she's so convincing as the tough, stubborn, doggedly persistent outsider. It's a classic Hitchcock role. She's totally uninvolved and innocent, and in possession of information no one will believe. She can't doubt the evidence of her own eyes, but the cops mistrust her, the body's gone—and the killer knows who and where she is.

De Palma directs with a nice feeling for the incongruous. There is, for example, Ms. Salt's delightful suburban mother (Mary Davenport), who wishes sometimes her daughter would stop writing those newspaper columns and settle down in a nice, comfortable marriage. There's the mysterious stranger (Bill Finley), who looks like an extraterrestrial crossed with a Cold War spy. And there is even the other sister, the other Siamese twin, about whom perhaps the less said the better.

Sixteen Candles ★ ★ ★
PG, 93 m., 1984

Molly Ringwald (Samantha Baker), Anthony Michael Hall (The Geek), Michael Schoeffling (Jake Ryan), Gedde Watanabe (Long Duk Dong), Paul Dooley (Jim Baker). Directed by John Hughes and produced by Hilton A. Green. Screenplay by Hughes.

Sixteen Candles is a sweet and funny movie about two of the worst things that can happen to a girl on her sixteenth birthday: (1) Her grandparents shrieking "Look! She's finally got her boobies!" and (2) her entire family completely and totally forgetting that it's even her birthday. The day goes downhill from there, because of (3) her sister's wedding to a stupid lunkhead, (4) her crush on the best-looking guy in the senior class, and (5) the long, involved story about how a freshman boy named the Geek managed to get possession of a pair of her panties and sell looks at them for a dollar each to all the guys in the locker room.

If *Sixteen Candles* begins to sound a little like an adolescent raunch movie, maybe it's because I haven't suggested the style in which it's acted and directed. This is a fresh and cheerful movie with a goofy sense of humor and a good ear for how teen-agers talk. It doesn't hate its characters or condescend to them, the way a lot of teen-age movies do; instead, it goes for human comedy and finds it in the everyday lives of the kids in its story.

The movie stars Molly Ringwald as Samantha, a bright-eyed teen-ager who pulls off the difficult trick of playing a character who takes everything too seriously—without ever taking herself too seriously. The movie's told mostly from her point of view, and it's like *Valley Girl*—it's about young kids who think a lot about sex, but who are shy and inexperienced and unsure and touchingly committed to concepts like True Love. She has a crush on a senior boy named Jake (Michael Schoeffling), who looks like Matt Dillon, of course, and doesn't even know she's alive. Meanwhile, the Geek (Anthony Michael Hall) is in love with her. Also, there are complications involving Jake's stuck-up girlfriend, Samantha's impossible grandparents, various older and younger brothers and sisters, and a foreign exchange student named Long Duk Dong, who apparently has come to this country to major in partying.

Sixteen Candles contains most of the scenes that are obligatory in teen-age movies: The dance, the makeout session, the party that turns into a free-for-all. But writer and director John Hughes doesn't treat them as subjects for exploitation; he *listens* to these kids. For example, on the night of the dance, Samantha ends up in the shop room with the Geek. They're sitting in the front seat of an old car. The Geek acts as if he's sex-mad. Samantha tells him to get lost. Then, in a real departure for this kind of movie, they really start to talk, and it turns out they're both lonely, insecure, and in need of a good friend.

There are a lot of effective performances in this movie, including Paul Dooley as Samantha's harried father, Blanche Baker as the zonked-out older sister, Hall as the Geek, and Gedde Watanabe as the exchange student (he elevates his role from a potentially offensive stereotype to high comedy). Ringwald provides a perfect center for the story, and her reaction in the first scene with her grandmother is just about worth the price of admission.

Skin Deep ★ ★ ★
R, 102 m., 1989

John Ritter (Zach), Vincent Gardenia (Barney), Alyson Reed (Alex), Joel Brooks (Jake), Julianne Phillips (Molly), Chelsea Field (Amy), Peter Donat (Sparky), Don Gordon (Curt). Directed by Blake Edwards and produced by Tony Adams. Screenplay by Edwards.

Blake Edwards, who directed *Skin Deep*, is like a magician who distracts you with his rapid-fire patter and his sexy assistant while he's switching the rabbits behind his back. The movie is the ultimately serious story of a man who bottoms out on those two vices of the moment, drinking and womanizing. But this is the only serious movie I can think of that contains a ballet for glow-in-the-dark condoms.

The hero of the story is a novelist named Zach (John Ritter), whose life is coming apart at the seams. He's got writer's block. He can't stop chasing every pretty girl who comes along. His wife is leaving him. His agent is dying. He gets arrested for drunk driving about twice a week. His house has burned to the ground. The opening scene is an indication of his desperation: His mistress catches him in bed with her hairdresser, and then his wife walks in on all three of them.

Zach's fundamental problem is alcoholism. He's one of those drunks whose evenings develop in stages. Early on, he can be charming and seductive to women. A little later, he knows how to play Cole Porter on the piano. In the morning, he is likely to wake up in his bartender's guest room, having thrown up in the aquarium, stuck the dog to the ceiling with Super Glue, and wrapped himself in toilet paper because he was cold.

Although Zach's situation is desperate, Edwards approaches him with the detachment and maniacal glee of a sardonic jokester. Zach is a pathetic case, but the movie is wicked and lighthearted as it follows his misadventures with a parade of bedable women. One of them is a massive body-builder. Another likes to pour lighter fluid on his piano and set it afire. In the scene I will undoubtedly remember the longest, he goes to bed with a rock star's girlfriend, who suggests he wear one of the star's condoms—an iridescent glow-in-the-dark model that leads to two of the strangest and funniest scenes Edwards has ever filmed.

If this character seems a little familiar, that's because we've met him before in films by Blake Edwards. He has a lot in common with the Dudley Moore characters in *10* and *Micki & Maude*, the Burt Reynolds character in *The Man Who Loved Women*, and the Jack Lemmon character in *That's Life*. All of these men were in love with sensible, intelligent, dependable, responsible, beautiful women, usually their wives—and yet were driven by lust into the arms of transient conquests, and by alcoholism into the hands of understanding bartenders.

Indeed, the role of best friend and confidant is more important in all of these films than the roles of any of the women except for the one character starts with. Who could forget Brian Dennehy as the bartender Moore poured his troubles out to in *10*? Or Richard Mulligan, the boss who helped Moore weather the pressures of bigamy in *Micki & Maude*? The John Ritter character in *Skin Deep* is so desperate, he needs two confessors: not only a bartender (Vincent Gardenia) but also a psychiatrist (Michael Kidd).

And yet what can they tell him? That he drinks too much? His alcoholism is visible to everyone in his life, but not to him, and (as Louis Armstrong once said about jazz) there's some folks that, if they don't know, you can't tell 'em. Ritter drinks and complains and suffers and moans and makes a public spectacle of himself and can't write and becomes impotent and considers suicide and thinks he has all of these problems, and finally it takes the shrink to say: "Do you know what I tell alcoholics who want me to help them? First, stop drinking."

This is sound advice, and drunks would save millions in therapy dollars if all psychiatrists were as realistic. But *Skin Deep* is not a *Clean and Sober* set in Malibu. It's a curious hybrid of the serious and the profane, of desperation and farce. The women in the movie all have something in common—they're interesting, opinionated individuals. That goes without saying; bimbos would be turned off by the Ritter character on first sighting, but these women make the mistake of staying around long enough to discover that he is complex and charming, and that gets them into a lot of trouble, since he grows steadily more complex and less charming the more he drinks.

Ritter's performance in *Skin Deep* is a transitional role; he has more depth here, more dimension, than he's shown before, and he is able to handle the trickiest part of playing a drunk in a movie, which is to understand that you are both the clown and the straight man. You're not only the fool, you're the foil that lets other people seem funny. The daring thing Edwards does in *Skin Deep* is to try to combine two entirely different tones within the same film. This is a smart, sensitive film that knows a lot about human nature, and it also has sequences that are deliberately designed to outrage. Look at the ground Edwards covers in that scene where his hero goes to dinner with his ex-wife, ex-mother-in-law, ex-stepson, and the stepson's girlfriend. There's wit, rudeness, satire, lust, and pathos, all effortlessly rolled up together. *Skin Deep* is sort of a filmmaker's triathlon, and if Edwards doesn't set any new records, at least he enters every event.

Slaves of New York ½ ★
R, 125 m., 1989

Bernadette Peters (Eleanor), Adam Coleman Howard (Stash Stotz), Nick Corri (Marley Mantello), Charles McCaughan (Sherman McVittie), Madeleine Potter (Daria), Chris Sarandon (Victor Okrent), Mary Beth Hurt (Ginger), Mercedes Ruehl (Samantha). Directed by James Ivory and produced by Ismail Merchant and Gary Hendler. Screenplay by Tama Janowitz.

I detest *Slaves of New York* so much that I distrust my own opinion. Maybe it's not simply a bad movie. Maybe it takes some kind of special knack, some species of sly genius, to make me react so strongly. I pause. I leaf through my memories of the film. I try to analyze what I really feel.

OK. I feel calmer now. The first thing I feel is a genuine dislike for the people in this film—the ambitious climbers on the lower rungs of the ladder in the New York art world. I dislike them because they are stupid and have occupied my time with boring conversation. It is more than that. They are not simply stupid. They *value* stupidity. They aim their conversations below the level of their actual intelligence because they fear to appear uncool by saying anything interesting. By always being bored, they can never be passé. No wonder Andy Warhol wanted to film this material.

The second thing I feel is that their entire act is a hypocritical sham. They want to succeed so much they can not only taste it, they can choke on it. And it doesn't matter what they succeed at. They move through a world of art, fashion, photography, and design, but the actual disciplines and psychic rewards of this world are not interesting to them. They want to use art as a way of obtaining success, which is more important to them than art will ever be.

The heroine of the movie is a young woman who designs hats. They are truly hideous hats, designed to bring embarrassment and ridicule to those who wear them, but never mind what the hats look like. The important thing is, how does the designer herself feel about her hats? I have no idea. She never permits herself to react to them, to care for them, to be proud of them. She looks at them as if they were her fingernail clippings—once a part of her, but not important, and now no longer even attached.

Her boyfriend manufactures paintings he does not love. Other people in her life also play at the extrusion of art, in the hopes that their work will sell, and they will find a gallery to represent them, and that eventually they will be able to afford a really nice apartment in New York City. The title, *Slaves of New York*, is explained by its author, Tama Janowitz, to mean that life in New York is basically a matter of becoming successful enough to have a nice apartment, and that if you do not have one, you move in with someone who does and become that person's slave. The whole idea is to eventually get your own apartment and have slaves of your own.

I have a suspicion that, to some degree, Janowitz is right, and the slave/apartment syndrome does operate in New York. That would certainly explain a great deal of the bad art that's around. Watching the film, I remembered a conversation I had with the actor John Malkovich about the way off-Broadway theater was dying in New York while thriving in the provinces. "To have off-Broadway," he said, "you have to have starving actors. And to have starving actors, you have to have a place for them to starve. New York is too expensive for that. You can't afford to starve there anymore."

There was once a time, in decades not too long ago, when life for a young artist consisted of living in a threadbare apartment while trying to create great art, instead of trying to live in a great apartment while creating threadbare art.

Sleeper ★ ★ ★ ½
PG, 88 m., 1973

Woody Allen (Miles Monroe), Diane Keaton (Luna), John Beck (Erno), Marya Small (Dr. Nero). Directed by Woody Allen and produced by Jack Grossberg. Screenplay by Allen and Marshall Brickman.

So how would you feel if your name was Miles Monroe and you ran the Happy Carrot Health Food Store in Greenwich Village and you went into St. Vincent's Hospital for a minor operation one morning and woke up two hundred years in the future? And America had become a police state? And the

underground wanted to use you because you were the only person alive without an identification number?

What Woody Allen does is scream bloody murder and claim to be a coward: "I'm even beaten up by Quakers." But life becomes a grim struggle, etc., and Woody finds himself at battle with the thought police.

If the plot sounds slightly insane, recollect that one Allen movie began with Howard Cosell doing a play-by-play of an assassination, and another had Woody slapping Listerine under his arms and squirting Right Guard into his mouth before a big date.

Sleeper establishes Woody Allen as the best comic director and actor in America, a distinction that would mean more if there were more comedies being made. Without making a count, I'd guess that a dozen action movies get made for every comedy, which says more about our taste than our comedians. Mel Brooks only seems to get geared up every three years or so, but Allen is prolific as well as funny.

He gives us moments in *Sleeper* that are as good as anything since the silent films of Buster Keaton. There is, for example, a scene where a futuristic instant pudding erupts from a mixing bowl and threatens to fill the kitchen; Woody beats it down with a broom. The scene is part of a long sequence in which he has to pretend to be a robot house servant; he lurches about and buzzes and finally tears up the robot assembly line (in a scene like something from *Modern Times*). Protesting all the way, Allen eventually penetrates into the inner circles of the underground and the government, and discovers the terrible truth about the nation's dictator, known as The Leader.

Nine months earlier, The Leader's home had burned down leaving nothing of The Leader but his nose. Through great medical innovation, the nose has been kept alive ever since, and the plan is to use genetic engineering to grow, or clone, The Leader's body back onto the nose. Inevitably, Allen is mistaken as the chief surgeon.

Whether the movie's Leader bears any relationship to the nation's current chief executive is a secret that only Woody Allen knows; he does not, however, go to many pains to keep it.

There's also a funny satirical scene in which Allen, as a genuine relic of 1973, is asked to identify such artifacts as General de Gaulle, a *Playboy* centerfold, and a Howard Cosell broadcast ("When people committed

great crimes, they were forced to watch that.").

Sleeper is the closest Allen has come to classic slapstick-and-chase comedy, and he's good at it. His earlier films depended more on plot (except for *Everything You Always Wanted to Know about Sex*).

And sometimes he had a tendency to get a little sentimental as in *Take the Money and Run*, which opened with a hilarious documentary style biography of its hero, but then got bogged down in a love story that Allen apparently took seriously. (There was even a slow-motion Semi-Obligatory Lyrical Interlude in which Allen and his girl ran through the park and he didn't even seize the opportunity to satirize a Salem commercial.)

This time, though, he moves at breakneck speed and will risk anything, especially the plot, for a gag. Things move so fast we don't even get around to wondering how, in the middle of the movie, Allen got into the Miss America contest . . . and won.

Sleeping with the Enemy ★ ½
R, 98 m., 1991

Julia Roberts (Sara/Laura), Patrick Bergin (Martin), Kevin Anderson (Ben), Elizabeth Lawrence (Chloe), Kyle Secor (Fleishman), Claudette Nevins (Dr. Rissner). Directed by Joseph Ruben and produced by Leonard Goldberg. Screenplay by Ronald Bass.

Because the opening scenes of *Sleeping with the Enemy* are so powerful, the rest of the movie is all the more disappointing. The film begins as an unyielding look at a battered wife, and ends as another one of those thrillers where the villain toys with his victim and the audience. There are good performances all through the movie, but the filmmakers don't keep faith with their actors.

This is the first major film after *Pretty Woman* for Julia Roberts, who plays the young wife of a millionaire investment counselor. Presumably they have a place in town somewhere, but all of their domestic scenes together are spent in their luxurious summer home at the beach, where the husband (Patrick Bergin) institutes a reign of psychological and physical terror.

He's one of those men who sees his wife as both possession and servant. She's attractive to show off at parties, but at home he lashes out at her if the towels aren't perfectly straightened in the bathroom, or the canned goods aren't lined up on the shelves with military precision. She is allowed no will of her own, and when he strikes her for the first time, that has a brutal impact on the audience. Bergin is very good as the anal-retentive tyrant, and the film seems poised to make some sort of effective dramatic statement.

But no. *Sleeping with the Enemy* is a slasher movie in disguise, an up-market version of the old exploitation formula where the victim can run, but she can't hide. Roberts fakes her own death by drowning and tries to disappear into a new lifestyle far away in Iowa, but, of course, Bergin tracks her down, with no small thanks to several hamhanded plot developments so obvious that she might just as well have mailed him a change-of-address card.

There are some well-handled scenes in Iowa, including the gradual steps by which she learns to trust her next-door neighbor, a drama teacher played warmly and effectively by Kevin Anderson. But the director, Joseph Ruben, and the writer, Ronald Bass, seem determined to force this potentially special material into the mold of horror formulas. Ruben's 1987 film *The Stepfather* received high praise in some quarters for its portrait of a soft-spoken, clear-eyed man who specialized in marrying women with children and then killing them and looting their assets. It was an exploitation film trying to transcend its genre. This time, with a first-rate cast and a larger budget, Ruben seems to be moving in the opposite direction.

I found myself watching the film in sinking spirits. The opening scenes on the beach were effective and held my attention. Then the middle passages of the movie, where Bergin discovers the deception and comes looking for Roberts, began to disillusion me. The one thing a viewer should never do, during scenes like this, is question the plot logic. And yet I kept having questions, such as: (1) If the wedding ring is still in the bottom of the toilet, does that mean the toilet hadn't been used for weeks? and (2) How did the woman in the YWCA class get Bergin's number at work? and (3) How did Roberts pay her mother's nursing home bill in the six months after she told her husband the mother was dead? and (4) How did Bergin know where Roberts lived before she led him there? and (5) How is it possible, in a small house, for a man to avoid discovery while slinking around rearranging all of the towels and canned goods, with perfect timing? and (6) Why would he bother, anyway?

That last one is a real good question. From the point of view of Roberts and the viewer, Bergin is a monster whose domestic neatness is his trademark. But would Bergin himself, concerned with trying to track and kill, take the time to rearrange the kitchen shelves? There is only one reason for him to do that: So Roberts can discover that the shelves are rearranged, and the movie can provide us with a cheap little shock. But hold on. Put yourself in her shoes. You're alone in a house and terrified that you may have been tracked by your husband, a pathological madman. What do you do? Check out the kitchen shelves?

And then, of course, there's the obligatory scene at the end where it turns out a dead man isn't dead after all. After *Carrie* and *Halloween*, where this gimmick worked, and after the countless dreary times since then when it has reappeared with clockwork monotony, isn't it time for a new twist on the gimmick? *Sleeping with the Enemy* is a movie that briefly seems to have greatness in its grasp, and goes straight for the mundane.

Sleuth ★ ★ ★ ★
PG, 138 m., 1972

Laurence Olivier (Andrew Wyke), Michael Caine (Milo Tindle), Alec Cawthorne (Inspector Doppler), Eve Channing (Marguerite), John Matthews (Sergeant Talvant), Teddy Martin (Constable Higgs). Directed by Joseph L. Mankiewicz and produced by Morton Gottleib. Screenplay by Anthony Shaffer.

We come upon Andrew Wyke, the mystery writer, in an appropriate setting. He's in the middle of his vast garden, which is filled with shrubbery planted to form a maze. There is no way into, or out of, the maze—unless you know the secret. The better we come to know Andrew Wyke, the more this seems like the kind of garden he would have.

Wyke is a game-player. His enormous Tudor country manor is filled with games, robots, performing dolls, dart boards, and chess tables. He also plays games with people. One day poor Milo Tindle comes for a meeting with him. Milo is everything Wyke detests: only half-British, with the wrong accent, and "brand-new country gentleman clothes."

But Milo and Andrew's wife have fallen in love, and they plan to marry. So Andrew has a little scheme he wants to float. He is will-ing—indeed, happy—to give up his wife, but only if he can be sure she'll stay gone. He wants to be sure Milo can support her, and he suggests that Milo steal the Wyke family jewels and pawn them in Amsterdam. Then Milo will have a small fortune, and Andrew can collect the insurance.

Up to this point, everything in *Sleuth* seems so matter-of-fact that there's no hint how complicated things will get later on. But they do get complicated, and deadly, and reality begins to seem like a terribly fragile commodity. Andrew and Milo play games of such labyrinthine ferociousness that they eventually seem to forget all about Andrew's wife (and his mistress) and to be totally absorbed with stalking each other in a macabre game of cat and mouse.

Sleuth, a totally engrossing entertainment, is funny and scary by turns, and always superbly theatrical. It's the kind of mystery we keep saying they don't make anymore, but sometimes they do, and the British seem to write them better than anyone. The movie is based on the long-running play by Anthony Shaffer, who also wrote Alfred Hitchcock's *Frenzy*. Both films have in common a nice flair for dialogue and a delicate counterpoint between the ironic and the gruesome.

What really makes the movie come alive—what makes it work better than the play, really—are the lead performances by Sir Laurence Olivier, Michael Caine, and Alec Cawthorne. Olivier plays the wealthy mystery writer Andrew Wyke as a true-blue British eccentric: His head, like his house, is cluttered with ornate artifacts largely without function. The hero of his detective stories, the wonderfully named St. John Lord Merridewe, is equally dotty. Olivier is clearly having fun in the role, and he throws in all kinds of accents, asides, and nutty pieces of business. Michael Caine, who might seem an unlikely candidate to play Milo Tindle, turns out to be a very good one. He manages somehow to seem smaller and less assured than Olivier (even while he towers over Sir Laurence). And he is strangely touching as he dresses up in an absurd clown's costume to steal the jewels. Inspector Doppler, the kindly old investigator who suspects that Andrew has murdered Milo, is played by Alec Cawthorne, a veteran stage actor making his movie debut.

It's difficult to say more about *Sleuth* without giving away its plot—which in this case would be a capital offense. Let me just mention that the play makes a remarkably easy transition to the screen because of director Joseph L. Mankiewicz's willingness to respect its timing and dialogue, instead of trying to jazz it up cinematically. And, despite the fact that most of the movie takes place indoors, we never get the sense of visual limitations because Ken Adams's set designs give us such an incredible multitude of things to look at (and through) in the mansion.

Small Change ★ ★ ★ ★
PG, 104 m., 1976

Geory Desmouceaux (Patrick), Philippe Goldman (Julien), Christine Pelle (Madame), Jean-François Stevenin and Chantal Mercier (The Teachers). Directed by François Truffaut. Screenplay by Truffaut and Suzanne Schiffman.

There's a moment in François Truffaut's *Small Change* that remembers childhood so well we don't know whether to laugh or cry. It takes place in a classroom a few minutes before the bell at the end of the school day. The class cutup is called on. He doesn't have the answer (he never does), but as he stands up his eyes stray to a large clock outside the window. The hand stands at twenty-eight minutes past the hour. Click: twenty-nine minutes. He stalls, he grins, the teacher repeats the question. Click: thirty past, and the class bell rings. The kid breaks out in a triumphant grin as he joins the stampede from the room.

This moment, like so many in Truffaut's magical film, has to be seen to be appreciated. He re-creates childhood, and yet he sees it objectively, too: He remembers not only the funny moments but the painful ones. The agony of a first crush. The ordeal of being the only kid in class so poor he has to wear the same sweater every day. The painful earnestness that goes into the recitation of a dirty joke that neither the teller nor the listeners quite understand.

Truffaut has been over some of this ground before. His first feature, *The 400 Blows*, told the painful story of a Paris adolescent caught between his warring parents and his own better nature. In *Small Change* he returns to similar material in a sunnier mood. He tells the stories of several kids in a French provincial town, and of their parents and teachers. His method is episodic; only gradually do we begin to recognize faces, to pick the central

characters out from the rest. He correctly remembers that childhood itself is episodic: Each day seems separate from any other, each new experience is sharply etched, and important discoveries and revelations become great events surrounded by a void. It's the accumulation of all those separate moments that create, at last, a person.

"Children exist in a state of grace," he has a character say at one point. "They pass untouched through dangers that would destroy an adult." There are several such hazards in *Small Change*. The most audacious—Truffaut at his best—involves a two-year-old child, a kitten, and an open window on the tenth floor. Truffaut milks this situation almost shamelessly before finally giving us the happiest of denouements. And he exhibits at the same time his mastery of film; the scene is timed and played to exist exactly at the border between comedy and tragedy, and from one moment to the next we don't know how we should feel. He's got the audience in his hand.

That's true, too, in a scene involving a little girl who has been made to stay at home as a punishment. She takes her father's battery-powered megaphone and announces indignantly to the neighbors around the courtyard that she is hungry, that her parents have gone out to a restaurant without her, and that she has been abandoned. The neighbors lower her food in a basket: Chicken and fruit but not, after all, a bottle of red wine one of the neighborhood kids wanted to put in.

In the midst of these comic episodes, a more serious story is developed. It's about the kid who lives in a shack outside of town. He's abused by his parents, he lives by his wits, he steals to eat. His mistreatment is finally found out by his teachers, and leads to a concluding speech by one of them that's probably unnecessary but expresses Truffaut's thinking all the same: "If kids had the vote," the teacher declares, "the world would be a better and safer place."

Smash Palace ★ ★ ★ ★
R, 100 m., 1982

Bruno Lawrence (Al Shaw), Anna Jemison (Jacqui Shaw), Greer Robson (Georgie Shaw), Keith Aberdeen (Ray Foley), Des Kelly (Tiny). Directed and produced by Roger Donaldson. Screenplay by Donaldson, Peter Hansard, and Bruno Lawrence.

Step by step, this powerful movie takes a

man from perfect happiness into a personal hell. By the end of the film, the man is behaving irrationally, but here's the frightening thing: Because we've followed him every step of the way, we have to admit he's behaving as we ourselves might, in the same circumstances. The man in *Smash Palace* is Al Shaw, a Grand Prix driver who leaves the racing circuit to take over his father's auto garage in New Zealand. Played by Bruno Lawrence, Al is a straight-talking, direct man who enjoys working with his hands and takes a vast delight in the affections of his wife and the love of his small daughter. It's a long way from the Grand Prix to repairing transmissions, but he's happy with his work and content to raise a family in peace and quiet. His wife (Anna Jemison) is not so content. She wanted him to leave the racing circuit before he was killed, but now, in the quiet backwaters of New Zealand, she is going quietly stir-crazy. She begins an affair with a local cop (Keith Aberdeen) and finally tells her husband she's leaving him. She's moving into town.

Her decision starts him on a series of wrong moves that may seem logical, one by one, but which eventually add up in the minds of others to a simple conclusion: He has lost his reason. He is jealous—of course. He holds a great fury against his wife and the cop. But, much more important, he misses his daughter. He wants custody. But because he acts in ways that are violent and frightening to his wife (and because her lover is on the police force, which must respond to the domestic emergencies he creates), he works himself into a Catch-22: The more he does to take back his daughter, the closer he is to losing her. Finally, he kidnaps her. He takes her out into the woods where they live together for a time in isolation and happiness. It's an idyll that can't last. But *Smash Palace* doesn't lead up to the inevitable violent conclusion we might expect. All along the way, this film prefers the unexpected turns of actual human behavior to the predictable plot developments we might have expected, and, at the end, there's another turn, a fascinating one.

Smash Palace is one of 1982's best films, an examination of much the same ground as *Shoot the Moon*, but a better film, because it has the patience to explore the ways in which people can become consumed by anger (*Shoot the Moon* contented itself with the outward symptoms). One of the reasons the movie works so well is the performances, which are all the stronger because they come from actors we have not seen before. Bruno Lawrence, bald-headed, wiry, tough, and surprisingly tender, is just right as the man who loses his family. Anna Jemison has a difficult assignment as his wife: We're on his side, and yet we see the logic of her moves. Keith Aberdeen is properly tentative as the other man; he feels love and lust, and yet is not unaware of the unhappiness he is causing. And there's a guy named Des Kelly who plays Tiny, an employee at the Smash Palace who looks on, and sees all, and wishes he knew what to do.

The movie was directed by a young filmmaker named Roger Donaldson, who, in a sense, *is* the New Zealand film industry. He has produced six features for New Zealand television, and his first feature film, *Sleeping Dogs*, starred Warren Oates in a horrifying and plausible fantasy about the American occupation of New Zealand. Now comes this film, so emotionally wise and observant that we learn from it why people sometimes make the front pages with guns in their hands and try to explain that it's all because of love. Love, yes, but also the terrible frustration of trying to control events, to make people do what you want them to do, what you "know" would make them happy—no matter what they think. The hero of *Smash Palace* does not act wisely, but if we are honest, it's hard to see where we might have acted differently.

Smooth Talk ★ ★ ★ ½
PG-13, 92 m., 1986

Laura Dern (Connie), Treat Williams (Arnold Friend), Mary Kay Place (Katherine), Elizabeth Berridge (June), Levon Helm (Harry), Sarah Inglis (Jill). Directed by Joyce Chopra and produced by Martin Rosen. Music by James Taylor. Screenplay by Tom Cole.

There is a certain kind of teen-ager who always seems to be waiting for something. Others live in the moment, but these waiting ones seem to be the victims of time. It stretches before them in long, empty hours. You can look at them and almost literally see the need in their eyes. It is a need to be someone else, somewhere else.

Connie, the heroine in *Smooth Talk*, is a girl like that. She is about fifteen years old, tall, blonde, unformed. At least that is the vision of her we receive the first time we see her. Then there is a transformation scene. She leaves her house, dressed like a teen-ager

on the way to a ballgame, and meets her friends at the mall. They go into the ladies' room and apply makeup and mascara and stuff their jackets into their bags, and when they emerge they look like the runners-up in the Madonna lookalike contest. Sexy beyond their own knowledge, they parade through the mall, attracting attention they do not know how to handle. There is a risky, reckless bounce in their step; they are still waiting, but now they seem to know what they are waiting for.

Appearances deceive. Emotionally, Connie is younger than she looks. At home, she suffers because her mother clearly prefers her older sister. She suffers, too, from the well-meaning idiocy of her father, who talks in vague terms of "finally having a home of our own," as if this were Connie's goal, too, and she would always be fifteen and always coming home to it. She looks at her father as if he were speaking a foreign language. He looks at her as if he were seeing someone else. Connie is played by Laura Dern, an actress who seems perfectly suited to this role; she is a chameleon who looks twelve in one shot, eighteen in the next, and is able to suggest the depth of her unhappiness by the way she tries to seem cheerful.

The first hour of *Smooth Talk* is deceptive. Nothing much seems to happen. Connie and her friends hang out. Connie fights with her parents. Connie waits through the long, endless afternoons of summer. This is the setup for the second half of the movie, which is an astonishing denouement.

Because *Smooth Talk* depends so completely on surprise, it is hard to know how to write about it. Many will be shocked by the movie's ending, and would want to be warned. Others will see it as a modern morality tale, a Grimm story for the late twentieth century, a time when evil seems more banal and seductive than it should. I will walk lightly around the ending without revealing it.

Smooth Talk is based on a short story by Joyce Carol Oates, who so often finds the materials of classic tragedy in the lives of everyday people. Although the movie is shocking, it is not sensational in the way it might have been—if it had been handled as a horror story, say, instead of as a morality play. Oates's story, adapted by Tom Cole and directed by Joyce Chopra, is about a young girl who is surrounded by sexuality, who is curious about it, who flirts dangerously in the wrong places, and who not only learns

her lesson, but grows up, all at once, into a different person than she was.

What happens is that a boy (Treat Williams) sees her at the drive-in. He says his name is Arnold Friend, and that he wants to be *her* friend. Everything about this guy is all wrong. He is nowhere near being as young as he says. There is a bad look in his eye. He pals around with another guy, who doesn't say anything, and doesn't need to, because one look at him and you realize he is missing important parts.

Connie walks around in her shorts and halter top, and Arnold Friend watches her. He makes a pass at her, and she puts him off with the kind of cute flirtation that would work with another kid, but Arnold just looks at her—looks through her—and a chill wind seems to blow. One Sunday when Connie is left at home alone and the family is all hours away, Arnold Friend comes to visit. He does not physically rape her. What he does is much worse than that. He talks to her in a way that forever brings an end to her innocence.

Smooth Talk is not a "teen-age movie." It is not, despite its plot, a horror film. It is a study in deviant psychology, and in the power that one person can have over another, especially if they push in the direction where the other person is already headed. The movie is almost uncanny in its self-assurance, in the way it knows that the first hour, where "nothing" happens, is necessary if the payoff is to be tragic, instead of merely sensational. The movie is also uncanny in what it does with its last three shots. I watched them, and could not believe so much could be implied so simply. Leave the movie before it's over, and you miss almost everything, because what Connie does at the very end of the film is necessary. It makes *Smooth Talk* the story of the process of life, instead of just a sad episode.

Soapdish ★ ★ ★ ½
PG-13, 92 m., 1991

Sally Field (Celeste Talbert), Kevin Kline (Jeffrey Anderson), Robert Downey, Jr. (David Barnes), Cathy Moriarty (Montana Moorehead), Whoopi Goldberg (Rose Schwartz), Elisabeth Shue (Lori Craven), Carrie Fisher (Betsy Faye Sharon), Garry Marshall (Edmund Edwards), Teri Hatcher (Ariel Maloney). Directed by Michael Hoffman and produced by Alan Greisman and Aaron Spelling. Screenplay by Robert Harling and Andrew Bergman.

Soapdish is *Network* crossed with *Beyond the Valley of the Dolls*, a soap opera about a soap opera, with a plot that churns together sex, scandal, jealousy, secrets from the past, television in-jokes, and the supreme sacrifice of becoming a brain donor. It's the funniest movie since *The Freshman*, and was written by the same man, Andrew Bergman, this time with the collaboration of Robert Harling and the screwball timing of director Michael Hoffman.

The movie takes place onstage and backstage at one of those long-running daytime soaps with endless plot twists and an almost acrobatic ability to combine sex with the headlines. The current plot line involves the homeless in Jamaica, neurosurgeons, lascivious nurses, and a mute girl in a bathing suit who turns out to be a long-lost daughter, and miraculously regains her power of speech, but contracts a rare condition that will cause her brain to explode within a few days unless her mother agrees to a brain transplant, to be undertaken on the bar of a Jamaican resort, as the surgeon mutters, "I've operated under worse conditions."

The plot, as I have briefly sketched it (and believe me, I've left out most of it), intertwines shocking events that are happening to the characters with equally shocking events affecting the actors in the soap. It literally defies description. And yet the actors somehow hold it together with gifted farcical acting, which involves playing everything completely seriously—especially the completely goofy parts.

Sally Field stars as "America's Sweetheart," the beloved and famous long-running heroine of the soap, who is now the victim of a conspiracy involving the predatory Montana Moorehead (Cathy Moriarty), a blond sex bomb who promises the show's callow young producer (Robert Downey, Jr.) a roll in the hay if he will write Field out of the part.

Field's interests are defended by her best friend and longtime head writer (Whoopi Goldberg), who can't believe Downey wants to resurrect a character who was beheaded in an old episode, but will now be miraculously restored to life. The character was played by Field's long-ago flame (Kevin Kline), who is now reduced to appearing in *Death of a Salesman* in a Florida dinner theater.

The movie knows a lot about television, and has fun with such characters as the network boss (Garry Marshall) and the producer, who is played by Downey as a shameless liar who will blame anything on anybody just to protect his position on the show. Then there is a surprise subplot involving a balloon messenger girl (Elisabeth Shue), who wrangles a bit part as one of the Jamaican homeless, only to suddenly find herself playing a leading role, both on camera and behind it.

This is the kind of movie that is a balancing act, really. If it doesn't work, it fails spectacularly, but it does work, and it succeeds in making its plot clear even though the basic story device is unending confusion. The bravura scenes are distributed nicely among the cast (Kline in front of a senile dinner theater audience, Goldberg and Field artificially staging a scene in a mall to inspire autograph hounds, Moriarty seducing Downey with promises of unimaginable sexual license, if only he writes Field out of the show). Even a TelePrompTer is funny for a scene.

Of the filmmakers, the one best known to me is Andrew Bergman, who wrote and directed *The Freshman* and wrote the hilarious *The In-Laws*. His inventions are like a juggling act, in which three or four plots are kept simultaneously in the air, while the connections between the characters grow increasingly bizarre. Since all of the characters in *Soapdish* are shamelessly venal and banal (the big motivations are lust, greed, jealousy, and vanity), the movie has the purity of a Marx Brothers comedy. Also some of the anarchy.

A Soldier's Story ★ ★ ½
PG, 99 m., 1984

Howard E. Rollins, Jr. (Captain Davenport), Adolph Caesar (Sergeant Waters), Art Evans (Private Wilkie), David Alan Grier (Corporal Cobb), David Harris (Private Smalls), Denzel Washington (Private Peterson), Patti LaBelle (Big Mary). Directed by Norman Jewison and produced by Jewison, Ronald L. Schwary, and Patrick Palmer. Screenplay by Charles Fuller.

A Soldier's Story is one of those movies that's about less than you might think. It begins with the murder of a black sergeant, who is shot near an Army base in Louisiana in 1944. Suspicion immediately points to the local whites, who are not too happy about all these blacks stationed in their branch of the deep South. An Army lawyer, a captain, is sent from Washington to handle the investigation, and he turns out to be black, too—the first black officer anyone in the movie has ever seen. As he conducts his investigation, we get to meet some of the important characters on the base, from black privates to the white officers who brag about their experiences at "commanding Negroes." Each time the captain conducts an interview, we get a flashback to another version of the events leading up to the murder. And eventually, we find out who committed the crime.

As a storytelling device, this mechanism is excruciating. The problem is in the time structure. If an investigation begins at the present moment and proceeds, suspense can build. But if the truth is going to emerge from a series of flashbacks, then obviously the movie knows who did it, and is withholding the information from us, using it as a hook to get us to sit through all of its other points. *A Soldier's Story* is not really a murder mystery, then. What is it? I guess it's supposed to be a docudrama. A great deal of the plot revolves around the character of the dead man, Sergeant Waters (Adolph Caesar), who is a scrappy little veteran of World War I, and believes that blacks should always behave so as to favorably impress whites and reflect credit upon their race. He is filled with self-hate, and takes it out on the black men under him who are not acting the way he thinks they should.

This fact is gradually revealed in a series of interviews conducted by the lawyer, Captain Davenport, who is played by Howard E. Rollins, Jr. And what a disappointing performance it is, coming from the same actor who won an Academy Award nomination for *Ragtime*. He invests his character with little humanity; he tries to seem dispassionate, curbed, correct, just a little more noble than anyone else in the picture. The result is such a laid-back performance that the lawyer seems less interested in solving the case than in keeping his cool (the murdered Sergeant Waters would have been proud of him).

The movie ends with a handshake between Davenport and one of the white officers who has made life hard for him. This is a more ironic ending than was perhaps intended, because *A Soldier's Story* was directed by Norman Jewison, the director who ended *In the Heat of the Night* with Sidney Poitier and Rod Steiger shaking hands. The ending worked in 1967, but in 1984 I think we expect a little more. Did this movie have to be so lockstep, so trapped by its mechanical plot, so limited by a murder mystery? What the movie has to say is so pale and limited that, ironically, the most interesting character in the movie is the victim—that black racist sergeant. At least he has fire and life and, misguided as he is, at least he's vital.

Some Kind of Wonderful ★ ★ ★
PG-13, 95 m., 1987

Eric Stoltz (Keith Nelson), Mary Stuart Masterson (Drummer Girl), Craig Sheffer (Hardy Jenns), Lea Thompson (Amanda Jones), John Ashton (Mr. Nelson), Elias Koteas (Skinhead). Directed by Howard Deutch and produced by John Hughes. Screenplay by Hughes.

Most movies are not about people. Most movies are about things, and in the category of things I include those movie stars who have become such icons that "they," rather than their characters, perform the adventures in movies.

Hardly ever do we get an American movie about adults who are attempting to know themselves better, live better lives, get along more happily with the people around them. Most American movies are about the giving and receiving of violent pain. That's why I look forward to John Hughes's films about American teen-agers. His films are almost always about the problems of growing up and becoming a more complete person.

Some Kind of Wonderful, which Hughes wrote and produced, and which Howard Deutch directed, is a movie like that. It's not a great movie. It progresses slowly at times and it uses some fairly standard characters. But it is not about whether the hero will get the girl. It is about whether the hero *should* get the girl, and when was the last time you saw a movie that even knew that could be the question?

The film stars Eric Stoltz as Keith, a pleasantly shaggy young man who is an outsider at his high school. He would rather be an artist than fit in with the crowd, and his best friend is another outsider, a tomboy (Mary Stuart Masterson). Keith has a crush on Amanda Jones (Lea Thompson), who is the school sexpot. She goes steady with a stuck-up rich kid.

Here we have all the ingredients, I suppose, for another standard John Hughes teen-ager film. But Hughes always gives his characters the right to be real, and by the end of *Some Kind of Wonderful*, I felt a lot of empathy for these kids.

The Thompson character, for example, is not just a distant, unattainable symbol, but a young woman with feelings. The tomboy doesn't just pine from afar, but helps Keith in his campaign to win a date with this girl of his dreams. And in the final sequence, in which the tomboy acts as chauffeur on the dream date, the dialogue isn't about sex; it's about learning to be true to yourself and not fall for the way people are packaged. By the movie's end, all the characters have learned something about themselves.

I guess I'm making this sound like a film they should show in sociology class. *Some Kind of Wonderful* is a worthwhile film, all right, but it's also entertaining—especially in the scenes between Stoltz and John Ashton, who plays his father. Ashton wants his kid to go to college; the kid would rather devote the energy to his artwork. This disagreement doesn't quite degenerate into a shouting match, and by the end of the film the two are able to have a surprisingly civilized fight about it.

All of the actors in this story are appealing, but my favorite was Masterson as the tomboy whose love is totally overlooked by this guy who thinks he knows all about her. There's something a little masochistic about the way she volunteers to chauffeur him on his big date, but something sweet, too, in the way she cares for him. She has a lot of tricky scenes in which she has to look one way and feel another way, and she's good at them.

Some Kind of Wonderful is yet another film in which Hughes and his team show a special ability to make an entertaining movie about teen-agers which is also about life, about insecurity, about rejection, about learning to grow. As somebody who sees almost all the new movies, I sometimes have the peculiar feeling that the kids in Hughes's movies are more grown up than the adults in most of the other ones.

Someone to Watch Over Me ★ ★
R, 106 m., 1987

Tom Berenger (Mike Keegan), Mimi Rogers (Claire Gregory), Lorraine Bracco (Ellie Keegan), Jerry Orbach (Lieutenant Garber), John Rubinstein (Neil Steinhart), Andreas Katsulas (Joey Venza). Directed by Ridley Scott and produced by Thierry de Ganay and Harold Schneider. Screenplay by Howard Franklin.

"High Concept" is a Hollywood expression for a movie story idea that can be summarized in one sentence, such as, "Detroit street cop goes to Beverly Hills." The phrase is a little misleading, since such movies are almost always low in the ambition of their conception, and sometimes so short-sighted that they cannot see the flaws in their own formulas.

Take *Someone to Watch Over Me* as an example. The story of this movie can be summarized in this sentence: "Detective from working-class background falls in love with society beauty." If you have read that sentence and are a reasonably experienced moviegoer, is there anything I can add that would surprise you?

Would you, for example, be surprised to find that the beauty needs a police bodyguard because her life is in danger after she has witnessed a murder? Would you be amazed to learn that the cop assigned to the night shift is young and handsome? That the murderer is vile and sadistic? That the beauty's lover is rich but distant? That the cop's wife is feisty and determined? That the cop's boss threatens to fire him for screwing around with this dame? That the movie's set decorator has supplied the society woman with a Manhattan apartment so lavish that even Donald Trump would need roller skates?

You would not, I suspect, be very surprised. That's the problem with High Concept movies. Once you master the concept, there's nothing left for the movie—except, of course, for the obligatory sequence of the cop tracking the killer through the darkened apartment, which is the high-rise equivalent of the chase scene. Movies like this are on automatic pilot. Unless we are very young, very naive, or hopelessly lusting after one of the stars, there is little to interest us aside from interior decorating hints. And yet, *Someone to Watch Over Me* does contain one element of extraordinary interest. That is the character of the cop's wife, played by Lorraine Bracco with great force and imagination. The character is a cliché: the good-looking but not glamorous woman who has spent the last ten years being married to this guy, cooking his breakfast, and bearing his child. At first she trusts her husband with this beautiful society woman. Then she gets suspicious. The movie's best scene has her playing tough, asking him to level with her.

In an earlier, more literate and inventive age, Hollywood would have known that *this* was the heart of the story. The society woman would have been cast as the brazen hussy—

Joan Crawford, maybe—and the wife would have been cast as the heroine. Audiences would have been titillated by the seductive aura of the other woman, and there would have been a scene in which the cop skated dangerously close to the edge. But then there would have been one of those delicious scenes where the rich bitch gets her comeuppance.

In today's Hollywood, money and status are so much a religion that it is obligatory, I guess, for the cop to fall for the rich woman. He does in this movie. The cop is played by Tom Berenger, the socialite is played by Mimi Rogers, and their coupling has all the excitement of an arranged marriage. The movie's high-tech sex scenes are done with all the cinematic technical support the director, Ridley Scott, can muster, but they're dead, because they contain only sex, not passion.

Needless to say, there are no sex scenes in the film between Berenger and Bracco—between the man and wife. They get a tearful reconciliation, and that's that. There is something fundamentally wrong about a script in which the hero sleeps with the wrong woman. I am not talking here in moral terms, but in story terms. The makers of this film got so carried away by their High Concept that they missed the point of the whole story. That rich broad really does have a great kitchen, though.

Something Wild ★ ★ ★ ½
R, 106 m., 1986

Jeff Daniels (Charlie Driggs), Melanie Griffith (Lulu Hankel), Ray Liotta (Ray Sinclair), Margaret Colin (Irene), Jack Gilpin (Larry Dillman), Su Tissue (Peggy Dillman). Directed and produced by Jonathan Demme. Screenplay by E. Max Frye.

She has his number. She looks him straight in the eye and tells him he's the kind of guy who sometimes walks out on a check in a restaurant, just for the secret little sexual charge he gets out of it. He squirms and tries to deny it, but she knows. He's supposed to get right back to the office, but she suggests a little ride around town, and the next thing he knows, he's handcuffed to the bed in a sleazy motel and she's holding the phone up to his mouth so he can lie to his boss.

The opening sequence of Jonathan Demme's *Something Wild* is filled with such a headlong erotic charge that it's hard to see

how he can sustain it, and, in fact, he can't. After an hour or so of exuberant sexual comedy, the movie settles down into a slightly more conventional groove, and we can begin to guess what's coming next. It's still a good movie; it's just not as inspired as those risky opening scenes where Demme closes his eyes and steps on the gas.

The movie stars Jeff Daniels as Charlie, a superficially conventional businessman whose heart is easily stirred by boldness in women, and Melanie Griffith as Lulu, an alcoholic sex machine with a very creative imagination. Daniels plays some of the same notes here that he used in *Terms of Endearment*, where he was the sound, dependable, serious husband and father who liked to fool around with cute coeds. He looks like he was born to wear a suit and a tie, but he has that naughty look in his eye. Griffith's performance is based not so much on eroticism as on recklessness: She is able to convince us (and Daniels) that she is capable of doing almost anything, especially if she thinks it might frighten him.

Even while they're standing on the sidewalk in front of that restaurant and she's pretending to accuse him of theft, there's a charge between them. The casting is crucial in a movie like this; there has to be some kind of animal compatibility between the man and the woman or it doesn't matter how good the dialogue is.

Once they've made their connection, Daniels willingly goes along for the ride. After a while she even takes his handcuffs off, although he sort of liked the idea of having lunch in a restaurant with the cuffs dangling from one of his wrists. They drive down the East Coast from New York to Tallahassee, while she steals money from cash registers and he sinks into the waking reverie of the sexually drained.

There's a wonderful scene where she takes him home to meet her mother, introducing him as her husband: "See, Mama? Just the kind of man you said I should marry." Her mother greets them, feeds them, welcomes them and then lets Daniels learn that she knows exactly what's going on: "You look out for that girl." I was reminded of Bonnie's mother in *Bonnie and Clyde*, who saw so clearly through the romance to the death that was approaching.

At Griffith's high school reunion, Daniels runs into the last person he wants to see, the accountant from his office. And Griffith runs into the last person she wants to see, her

husband, who is fresh out of prison. He follows them, takes them captive, and forces them to join him on a crime spree. And Daniels realizes that he must fight, not only for the woman he has started to love, but for his life. It's here that the movie begins to feel more conventional, even though a newcomer named Ray Liotta is mesmerizing as the evil husband with vengeance on his mind. We have seen stories before that are more or less like this one, and it becomes easier to foresee the movie's ending. After the freedom and anarchy of the opening and middle scenes, the closing passages feel like a reduction of tension.

But *Something Wild* is quite a movie. Demme is a master of finding the bizarre in the ordinary. Remember his *Melvin and Howard* and the topless dancer who had a cast on her arm? If he had conceived this movie as a "madcap comedy," it probably wouldn't have worked. The accomplishment of Demme and the writer, E. Max Frye, is to think their characters through before the very first scene. They know all about Charlie and Lulu, and so what happens after the meeting outside that restaurant is almost inevitable, given who they are and how they look at each other. This is one of those rare movies where the plot seems surprised at what the characters do.

Sometimes a Great Notion ★ ★ ★
PG, 114 m., 1971

Paul Newman (Hank), Henry Fonda (Henry), Michael Sarrazin (Dan), Lee Remick (Hank's Wife). Directed by Paul Newman and produced by John Foreman. Screenplay by John Gay.

Paul Newman's *Sometimes a Great Notion* tells sort of an old-fashioned story about prideful clans carving empires out of the wilderness. The characters seem a little familiar, too. Take the three most important. Henry Fonda is the proud old patriarch, Paul Newman is the son who stays at home but makes up his own mind, and Michael Sarrazin is the kid brother who comes back to the land with all sorts of half-baked notions and scores to settle. So far, the relationships remind us of *Hud*.

But then Newman starts tunneling under the material, coming up with all sorts of things we didn't quite expect, and along the way he proves himself (as he did with *Rachel, Rachel*) as a director of sympathy and a sort of lyrical restraint. He rarely pushes scenes to their obvious conclusions, he avoids melodrama, and by the end of *Sometimes a Great Notion*, we somehow come to know the Stamper family better than we expected to.

The story takes place during a timber strike in the Northwest. The local merchants (especially the neurotic fellow who runs the movie theater and the dry cleaners) are going broke because money has dried up. The striking timber workers idly hang around the union office. But the Stamper family continues to work in defiance of the strike, and despite the fact that Fonda has broken half the bones on his left side in an accident.

Sarrazin, Newman's half-brother by Fonda's second wife, comes home to help—and also to mope, to get over a bummer of a year, and to suggest to Newman's wife (Lee Remick) that maybe she should clear out from the obsessed Stamper clan. There are a lot of things left fairly unclear, though; I'm not quite sure what was on Remick's mind during most of the movie. The character is left wavering, and we don't fully understand her relationship to her husband. Newman shortchanges what you might call the indoor scenes in order to give us the lumber business.

The best scene in the film takes place during a day of work. The Stamper men seem terribly small as they bring enormous trees crashing to the ground, wrap chains around them, and load them on trucks with big, musclebound machines. The direction of this scene is superb; the reality and the danger of the huge logs are caught in a way that defines the men and their job better than any dialogue could.

Another scene that reveals Newman's insight as a director takes place at a lumbermen's picnic. Some of the strikers invite some of the Stampers to a game of touch football. The game develops into a brawl, of course, but in an interesting way; instead of going for a hard-action approach to the scene, Newman shoots it in a sort of twilight, bittersweet style. All through the film, he avoids making the strikers into heavies and their hatred for the Stampers seem melodramatic. Instead, they're clumsy, resentful enemies, and when they try to sabotage a Stamper lumber raft, they only wind up drifting out to sea—and having to be rescued by the Stampers.

The movie doesn't seem very sure of what it thinks about the Fonda character's fierce and stubborn pride. The character himself believes all that matters is getting up for another day, and working, and eating, and

sleeping, and getting on with life. Another character, a brother-in-law, played by Oscar nominee Richard Jaeckel, has been "saved" at the local fundamentalist church and has a sort of sweet simplicity that seems out of place—until the scene where he dies. He dies in a way that is truly filled with grace and humor, and the scene is one of the several things in *Sometimes a Great Notion* that make it worth seeing, even if its overall design is murky.

Songwriter ★ ★ ★ ½
R, 94 m., 1985

Willie Nelson (Doc Jenkins), Kris Kristofferson (Blackie Buck), Melinda Dillon (Honey Carder), Rip Torn (Dino McLeish), Lesley Ann Warren (Gilda), Richard Sarafian (Rocky Rodeo). Directed by Alan Rudolph and produced by Sydney Pollack. Screenplay by Matthew Leonetti.

Songwriter is one of those movies that grows on you. It doesn't have a big point to prove, and it isn't all locked into the requirements of its plot. It's about spending some time with some country musicians who are not much crazier than most country musicians, and are probably nicer than some. It also has a lot of good music.

The movie stars Willie Nelson as a country songwriter named Doc Jenkins, who has a real bad head for business. One day he gets fast-talked into selling control of his company to a slick operator named Rocky Rodeo (Richard Sarafian). Homeless and betrayed, he turns for support to his best friend, a country music star named Blackie (Kris Kristofferson). Blackie, meanwhile, is being promoted by a sleazy manager named Dino (Rip Torn) who has somewhere found a neurotic young singer named Gilda (Lesley Ann Warren). In an early scene that lets us know this movie is not going to be routine, Blackie tries to foist Gilda off on an audience that has paid to see Blackie, and when the audience rebels, Blackie grabs the mike and starts advising them to commit anatomical impossibilities upon themselves.

During the course of some days and nights on the road and back home in Austin, Doc comes up with a clever scheme. Instead of writing any more songs for the despised Dino, he'll write his songs under a pseudonym, and give them to Gilda to record. Blackie will include Gilda on his next tour, and Dino will get screwed. This seems like a good idea to everybody, especially Gilda,

who has a tricky drinking problem and thinks she might be falling in love with Doc.

The movie unwinds casually, introducing us to the other people in the lives of these characters. The most important is Doc's former wife (Melinda Dillon), and the best scene in the movie is where Doc visits her and the kids, and is shy and sweet and tremendously moving. Another good scene is one where Gilda invites Doc into her bed, and he tries to be gentle and tactful in explaining that he doesn't think that's a good idea. Willie Nelson is the key to both of those scenes, and it's interesting how subtle his acting is. Unlike a lot of concert stars whose moves tend to be too large for the intimacy of a movie, Nelson is a gifted, understated actor. Watch the expression on his face as he turns down Gilda; not many actors can say as much with their eyes.

Songwriter was directed by Alan Rudolph, who also made *Choose Me*. Rudolph's teacher was Robert Altman, and, like Altman, he specializes in offbeat rhythms of a group of characters in an unpredictable situation. We never have a clear idea of where *Songwriter* is headed; is it about Doc's love for his first wife, or Gilda's self-destruction, or Rocky Rodeo's con games? It's good that we don't know, because then we don't know what to expect next, and the movie can surprise us.

Both Rudolph and Altman also specialize in unlikely combinations of actors; Kris Kristofferson and Nelson don't, at first, seem to belong in the same movie with Warren, Torn, and Dillon, but watch them work together. One of Torn's great unsung roles was in *Payday*, the movie based on the last days of Hank Williams, Sr. This time, he's like the same character a little further down the road, a little more spaced out. Kristofferson is basically the straight man, the hero's best friend. Nelson sings less and acts more than we expected. And Lesley Ann Warren's performance is endlessly inventive: She takes the fairly standard character of a kooky would-be singer, and makes her into a touching, unforgettable creation.

Sophie's Choice ★ ★ ★ ★
R, 157 m., 1982

Meryl Streep (Sophie), Kevin Kline (Nathan), Peter MacNicol (Stingo), Greta Turken (Leslie Lapidus), Gunther Maria Halmer (Rudolf Hoess). Directed by Alan J. Pakula and produced by Pakula and Keith Barish. Screenplay by Pakula.

Sometimes when you've read the novel, it gets in the way of the images on the screen. You keep remembering how you imagined things. That didn't happen with me during *Sophie's Choice*, because the movie is so perfectly cast and well-imagined that it just takes over and happens to you. It's quite an experience.

The movie stars Meryl Streep as Sophie, a Polish-Catholic woman, who was caught by the Nazis with a contraband ham, was sentenced to a concentration camp, lost her two children there, and then was somehow spared to immigrate to Brooklyn, U.S.A., and to the arms of an eccentric charmer named Nathan. Sophie and Nathan move into an old boardinghouse, and the rooms just below them are taken by Stingo, a jug-eared kid from the South who wants to be a great novelist. As the two lovers play out their doomed, romantic destiny, Stingo falls in love with several things: with his image of himself as a writer, with his idealized vision of Sophie and Nathan's romance, and, inevitably, with Sophie herself.

The movie, like the book, is told with two narrators. One is Stingo, who remembers these people from that summer in Brooklyn, and who also remembers himself at that much earlier age. The other narrator, contained within Stingo's story, is Sophie herself, who remembers what happened to her during World War II, and shares her memories with Stingo in a long confessional. Both the book and the movie have long central flashbacks, and neither the book nor the movie is damaged by those diversions, because Sophie's story is so indispensable to Stingo's own growth, from an adolescent dreamer to an artist who can begin to understand human suffering. The book and movie have something else in common. Despite the fact that Sophie's story, her choices, and her fate are all sad, sad stories, there is a lot of exuberance and joy in the telling of them. *Sophie's Choice* begins as a young Southerner's odyssey to the unimaginable North—to that strange land celebrated by his hero, Thomas Wolfe, who took the all-night train to New York with its riches, its women, and its romance. Stingo is absolutely entranced by this plump blond Polish woman who moves so winningly into his life, and by her intense, brilliant, mad lover.

We almost don't notice, at first, as Stingo's odyssey into adulthood is replaced, in the film, by Sophie's journey back into the painful memories of her past. The movie be-

comes an act of discovery, as the naive young American, his mind filled with notions of love, death, and honor, becomes the friend of a woman who has seen so much hate, death, and dishonor that the only way she can continue is by blotting out the past, and drinking and loving her way into temporary oblivion. It's basically a three-character movie, and the casting, as I suggested, is just right. Meryl Streep is a wonder as Sophie. She does not quite look or sound or feel like the Meryl Streep we have seen before in *The Deer Hunter* or *Manhattan* or *The French Lieutenant's Woman*. There is something juicier about her this time; she is merrier and sexier, more playful and cheerful in the scenes before she begins to tell Stingo the truth about her past. Streep plays the Brooklyn scenes with an enchanting Polish-American accent (she has the first accent I've ever wanted to hug), and she plays the flashbacks in subtitled German and Polish. There is hardly an emotion that Streep doesn't touch in this movie, and yet we're never aware of her straining. This is one of the most astonishing and yet one of the most unaffected and natural performances I can imagine.

Kevin Kline plays Nathan, the crazy romantic who convinces everyone he's on the brink of finding the cure for polio and who wavers uncertainly between anger and manic exhilaration. Peter MacNicol is Stingo, the kid who is left at the end to tell the story. Kline, MacNicol, and Streep make such good friends in this movie—despite all the suffering they go through—that we really do believe the kid when he refuses to act on an unhappy revelation, insisting, "These are my *friends*. I love them!"

Sophie's Choice is a fine, absorbing, wonderfully acted, heartbreaking movie. It is about three people who are faced with a series of choices, some frivolous, some tragic. As they flounder in the bewilderment of being human in an age of madness, they become our friends, and we love them.

Sounder ★ ★ ★ ★
G, 105 m., 1972

Cicely Tyson (Rebecca Morgan), Paul Winfield (Nathan Lee Morgan), Kevin Hooks (David Lee Morgan), Carmen Mathews (Mrs. Boatwright), Taj Mahal (Ike), James Best (Sheriff Young), Janet MacLachlan (Camille, the Teacher), Sylvia "Kuumba" Williams (Harriet). Directed by Martin Ritt and produced by Robert B. Radnitz. Screenplay by John Alonzo.

Sounder is a story simply told and universally moving. It is one of the most compassionate and truthful of movies, and there's not a level where it doesn't succeed completely. It's one of those rare films that can communicate fully to a child of nine or ten, and yet contains depths and subtleties to engross any adult. The story is so simple because it involves, not so much what people do, but how they change and grow. Not a lot happens on the action level, but there's tremendous psychological movement in *Sounder*, and hardly ever do movies create characters who are so full and real, and relationships that are so loving.

The movie is set in rural Louisiana in about 1933, and involves a black sharecropper family. The boy, David Lee, is twelve or thirteen years old, just the right age to delight in the night-time raccoon hunts he goes on with his father and their hound, Sounder. The hunts are not recreation but necessity. There is no food and no money, and at last, the father steals a ham in desperation. He's sentenced to a year at hard labor, and it's up to the mother and the children (two of them too small to be much help) to get the crop in. They do. "We'll do it, because we have to do it," the mother says.

The boy sets out to find the labor camp where his father is being held. He never does, but he comes across a black school where the teacher talks to him of some of the accomplishments of blacks in America. He decides that he would like to attend her school; by special dispensation, he had been attending a segregated school near his home as sort of a back-row, second-class student.

He returns home, the father returns home, and there is a heartbreaking moment when, for the boy, no school in the world could take him away from this family that loves him. He runs away, filled with angry tears, but his father comes after him and talks to him simply and bluntly: "You lose some of the time what you go after, but you lose all of the time what you don't go after."

The father has a totally realistic understanding of the trap that Southern society set for black sharecroppers, and he is determined to see his son break out of that trap, or else. The scene between the father (Paul Winfield) and the son (Kevin Hooks) is one of the greatest celebrations of the bond between parents and children that I have ever seen in a movie. But it is only one of the scenes like that in *Sounder*.

The mother is played by Cicely Tyson, and

it is a wonder to see the subtleties in her performance. We have seen her with her family, and we know her strength and intelligence. Then we see her dealing with the white power structure, and her behavior toward it is in a style born of cynicism and necessity. She will say what they want to hear in order to get what she wants to get.

The story is about love, loss, anger, and hope. That's all, and it's enough; not many movies deal with even one of those subjects with any honesty or power. Hope is probably the emotion evoked most by *Sounder*—the hope of the parents that the school will free their bright and capable son from the dead end of sharecropping; the hope of the teacher, who is representative of the Southern growth of black pride and black studies; and, of course, the boy's hope.

The movie was attacked in a few quarters because of this orientation. It is merely "liberal," some of its critics say. It isn't realistic, it's deceiving. I don't think so. I think it has to be taken as a story about one black family and its struggle. It is, I suppose, a "liberal" film, and that has come to be a bad word in these times when liberalism is supposed to stand for compromise—for good intentions but no action. This movie stands for a lot more than that, and we live in such illiberal times that *Sounder* comes as a reminder of former dreams. It's not surprising that the boy in the movie reminded Mrs. Coretta Scott King of her husband.

This is a film for the family to see. That doesn't mean it's a children's film. The producer, Robert B. Radnitz, has specialized in authentic and serious family films (*A Dog of Flanders*, *The Other Side of the Mountain*). The director, Martin Ritt, is one of the best American filmmakers (his credits include *Hud*, *The Molly Maguires*, and *The Great White Hope*), and he has made *Sounder* as a serious and ambitious undertaking. There is no condescension in it, no simplification. The relationship between the man and wife is so completely realized on a mature level that it comes as a shock; we'd forgotten that authentic grown-ups can be portrayed in films. We'd thought, for a moment, that to be a movie adult you had to drive a fast car, be surrounded by sexy dames, and pack an arsenal. *Sounder* proves it isn't so.

Southern Comfort ★ ★ ★
R, 106 m., 1981

Keith Carradine (Spencer), Powers Boothe (Hardin), Fred Ward (Reece), Franklyn Seales (Simms), T.K. Carter (Cribbs), Lewis Smith (Stuckey). Directed by Walter Hill and produced by David Giler. Screenplay by Michael Kane, Hill, and Giler.

Southern Comfort is a well-made film, but it suffers from a certain predictability. I suspect the predictability is part of the movie's point. The film is set in the Cajun country of Louisiana, in 1973, and it follows the fortunes of a National Guard unit that gets lost in the bayous and stumbles into a metaphor for America's involvement in Vietnam.

The movie's approach is direct, and its symbolism is all right there on the surface. From the moment we discover that the guardsmen are firing blanks in their rifles, we somehow know that the movie's going to be about their impotence in a land where they do not belong. And as the weekend soldiers are relentlessly hunted down and massacred by the local Cajuns (who are intimately familiar with the bayou), we think of the uselessness of American technology against the Viet Cong.

The guardsmen are clearly strangers in a strange land, and they make fatal blunders right at the outset. They cut the nets of a Cajun fisherman, they "borrow" three Cajun boats, and they mock the Cajuns by firing blank machine-gun rounds at them. The Cajuns are not amused. By the film's end, guardsmen will have been shot dead, impaled, hung, drowned in quicksand, and attacked by savage dogs. And all the time they try to protect themselves with a parody of military discipline, while they splash in circles and rescue helicopters roar uselessly overhead. All this action is shown with great effect in *Southern Comfort*. The movie portrays the bayous as a world of dangerous beauty. Greens and yellows and browns shimmer in the sunlight, and rare birds call to one another, and the Cajuns slip noiselessly behind trees while the guardsmen wander about making fools and targets of themselves. *Southern Comfort* is a film of drum-tight professionalism.

It is also, unfortunately, so committed to its allegorical vision that it never really comes alive as a story about people. That is the major weakness of its director, the talented young Walter Hill, whose credits include

The Warriors, *The Driver*, and *The Long Riders*. He knows how to make a movie look great, and how to fill it with energy and style. But I suspect he is uncertain about the human dimensions of his characters. And to cover that up, he makes them into larger-than-life stick figures, into symbolic units who stand for everything except themselves. That tendency was carried to its extreme in *The Driver*, a thriller in which the characters were given titles (the Driver, the Girl) rather than names. It was also Hill's approach in *The Warriors*, which translated New York gang warfare into the terms of Greek myth. His approach bothered me so much in *The Warriors* that I overlooked, I now believe, some of the real qualities of that film. It bothers me again in *Southern Comfort*.

Who *are* these men? Of the Cajuns we learn nothing: They are invisible assassins. Of the guardsmen, however, we learn little more. One is swollen with authority. One intends to look out for himself. One is weak, one is strong, and only the man played by Keith Carradine seems somewhat balanced and sane. Once we get the psychological labels straight, there are no further surprises. And once we understand the structure of the movie (guardsmen slog through bayous, get picked off one by one), the only remaining question is whether any of them will finally survive.

That's the weakness of the storytelling. The strength of the movie is in its look, in its superb use of its locations, and in Hill's mastery of action sequences that could have been repetitive. The action is also good: The actors are given little scope to play with in their characters, but they do succeed in creating plausible weekend soldiers. "We are the Guard!" they chant, and we believe them. And there is one moment of inspired irony, when they are lost, cold, wet, hungry, and in mortal fear of their lives, and one guy asks, "Why don't we call in the National Guard?"

Spartacus ★ ★ ★
PG-13, 187 m., 1960

Kirk Douglas (Spartacus), Laurence Olivier (Crassus), Jean Simmons (Varinia), Charles Laughton (Gracchus), Peter Ustinov (Batiatus), John Gavin (Julius Caesar), Tony Curtis (Antoninus), Woody Strode (Black Gladiator). Directed by Stanley Kubrick and produced by Edward Lewis. Screenplay by Dalton Trumbo.

At the time of its first release in 1960, *Spartacus* was hailed as the first intellectual epic since the silent days—the first Roman or Biblical saga to deal with ideas as well as spectacle. Even the ending was daring. The crucified hero is denied a conventional victory, and has to be consoled with the hope that his ideas will survive.

Seen three decades later in a lovingly restored version, *Spartacus* still plays like an extraordinary epic, and its intellectual strength is still there. But other elements of the film are dated. The most courageous thing about it, from today's standards, is that it closes without an obligatory happy ending, and an audience that has watched for 187 minutes doesn't get a tidy, mindless conclusion.

The film tells the story of the Roman slave Spartacus (Kirk Douglas), who toils for the Roman Empire while dreaming, the narrator assures us, "of the death of slavery—which would not come until 2,000 years later." He is sentenced to death after biting a Roman guard, but spared by Peter Ustinov, as Batiatus, a broker of gladiators. Spartacus is trained in the arts of combat at Batiatus's gladiatorial academy, where one day two powerful men arrive from Rome, one with his wife, the other with his fiancée. The spoiled women ask to be entertained by the sight of two fights to the death, and Spartacus is matched with a skilled black gladiator (Woody Strode), who spares him and is killed.

The notion of being forced to fight for the entertainment of spoiled women enrages Spartacus, who leads a slave revolt that eventually spreads over half of Italy. Leading his men into battle against weak and badly-led Roman legions, Spartacus stands on the brink of victory, before his troops are finally caught between two armies and outnumbered.

All of this takes place against a backdrop of Roman decadence, and we become familiar with the backstage power plays of the Senate, where Crassus (Laurence Olivier) hopes to become a dictator at the expense of the more permissive and gentler old man Gracchus (Charles Laughton). There are also sexual intrigues; Gracchus is a womanizer, and Crassus a bisexual, who is attracted to a handsome young slave (Tony Curtis), but is also driven by the desire to win the love of the slave woman Varinia (Jean Simmons), who is the wife of Spartacus.

The movie was inspired by a best-seller by Howard Fast, and adapted to the screen by the blacklisted writer Dalton Trumbo. Kirk Douglas, executive producer of the film, effectively broke the blacklist by giving Trumbo screen credit instead of making him hide behind a pseudonym. The direction is by the thirty-one-year-old Stanley Kubrick, who realizes the ideas of Douglas, Fast, and Trumbo, but cannot be said to add much of his own distinctive style to the film.

I've seen *Spartacus* three times now—in 1960, 1967, and 1991. Two things stand up best over the years: the power of the battle spectacles, and the strength of certain of the performances, especially Olivier's fire, Douglas's strength, and Laughton's mild amusement at the foibles of humankind. The most entertaining performance in the movie, consistently funny, is by Ustinov, who upstages everybody when he is onscreen (he won an Oscar). Some of the supporting performances now seem dated and the line readings stilted; dialogue like "How will I ever be able to thank you?" delivered by a senator placed in charge of a legion, gets a bad laugh.

All historical films share the danger that their costumes and hairstyles will age badly. *Spartacus* stands at a divide between earlier epics, where the female characters tended to look like models for hairdressing salons, and later epics that placed more emphasis on historical accuracy. But the hairstyles of the visiting Roman women at the gladiatorial school are laughable, and even Jean Simmons looks too made up and coiffed at times.

Balancing against those dated elements are some that were ahead of their time, including a muted but sophisticated understanding of sexual motivation. Olivier's character becomes more complex in this revival than it was at the time, because of the restoration of a key scene, cut by censors, in which he and Tony Curtis share a bath together, and he confesses, "I like both oysters and snails," leaving little doubt where either is to be found, as far as he is concerned. That brings his desire for Jean Simmons into focus: He wants her not merely to possess her, but as a form of victory over Spartacus.

The film has been restored by Robert A. Harris, the same man who brought *Lawrence of Arabia* back to its original glory, and Harris has done a good job. The full 187 minutes of screen time has been pieced back together from various shorter release versions; the color has been renewed by going back to the original materials and restoring them; the

sound track is in six-track Dolby, and the 70mm, wide-screen picture reminds us of when movies filled our entire field of vision.

One aspect of the sound track is distracting: In the early days of stereo, movies such as *Spartacus* used the left track for characters on the left side of the screen, and the right track for those on the right, and then switched for the reverse shot—a disorienting auditory experience for the audience. Today's approach in surround sound puts the voices on the center channel and the effects on the side, a better approach.

Perhaps the most interesting element of *Spartacus* is its buried political assumptions. The movie is about revolution, and clearly reflects the decadence of the parasitical upper classes and the superior moral fiber of the slaves. But at the end, Spartacus, like Jesus, dies on the cross. In the final scene, his wife stands beneath him and holds up their child, saying "He will live as a free man, Spartacus." Yes, but the baby's freedom was granted him not as its right, but because of the benevolence of the softhearted old Gracchus. Today, that wouldn't be good enough.

The Spider's Stratagem ★ ★ ★
PG, 100 m., 1973

Giulio Brogi (Athos Magnani), Alida Valli (Draifa), Tino Scotti (Costa), Pippo Campanini (Gaibazzi). Directed by Bernardo Bertolucci and produced by Giovani Bertolucci. Screenplay by Bernardo Bertolucci.

Thirty years before, Athos Magnani was a great man, a popular hero, and the leading anti-fascist in the district. But then he was killed, and time has stood still for his little town ever since. It is filled with "old men, madmen, and mad old men," and even though Athos is thirty years dead, he is still the most vital presence in the community.

One day a young man gets off the train for a visit in the village. He is Athos Magnani, Jr., and he looks exactly like his father—so much so, indeed, that his father's mistress attempts to substitute him and begin life all over again in the late 1930s. The son wants to find the killer of his father, in a way. In another way, *The Spider's Stratagem* isn't about a search for a killer, or the truth from the past, or anything else, except a question of human identity: What's more important, who we are, or who people think we are?

The movie is by Bernardo Bertolucci, who

later made *Last Tango in Paris*. It's a movie with a beautiful cinematic grace, a way of establishing atmosphere and furthering plot without a lot of talking. We learn all we need to know about the relationship between the father, the son, and the town, in one group of opening shots. The boy stops on "Via Athos Magnani"—a street named for his father—and then approaches the square where his father's statue stands. Bertolucci lines up the deep-focus shot so that it begins with the son completely blocking out the statue. Then, as he walks through the square, the statue completely obscures the son.

He's on a strange sort of quest. He doesn't seem to really care much who killed his father (if you'll forgive me for not taking the plot at quite face value). In a way, he is his own father, or his father's alter-ego. Magnani was the only vital life force in the district, and the district defined itself by his energy. Even the fascist brownshirts gained stature and dignity because Magnani opposed them, and Bertolucci demonstrates this with a great scene at an outdoor dance. The brownshirts order the band leader to play the fascist anthem. All dancing stops, and everyone looks at Magnani to see what he'll do. Coolly, elegantly, he selects the most beautiful girl and begins to dance with her.

But this is, alas, the last waltz in town, because before long Magnani is shot during a concert. The events leading up to his death, and the identity of his killers, remain very murky. Three fellow anti-fascists claim to have done it, in order to (a) punish Magnani for squealing to the police, and (b) provide the district with a genuine martyr. But did they really? It's hard to say.

The Spider's Stratagem is not, as you've probably gathered, a mass-audience movie. It will have most appeal to people sensitive to Bertolucci's audacious use of camera movements and colors; Pauline Kael said a long time ago that, of all directors influenced by Godard, Bertolucci has been the only one to extend Godard's way of looking, instead of just copying. *The Spider's Stratagem* documents that, and is better to look at than analyze.

Spike of Bensonhurst ★ ★ ★
R, 101 m., 1988

Sasha Mitchell (Spike Fumo), Ernest Borgnine (Baldo), Anne DeSalvo (Sylvia), Sylvia Miles (Congresswoman), Talisa Soto (India), Geraldine Smith (Helen Fumo),

Antonia Rey (Bandana's Mother), Rick Aviles (Bandana), Maria Pitillo (Angel), Karen Shallo (Blondie), Chris Anthony Young (Carmine). Directed by Paul Morrissey and produced by David Weisman and Nelson Lyon. Screenplay by Alan Bowne and Morrissey.

Movies imitate life, life imitates movies. Travolta played Tony Manero in *Saturday Night Fever*, Stallone played Rocky Balboa in *Rocky*, and now here is Spike Fumo, a cocky kid from Brooklyn who fools around with the wrong girls, and wants to be a boxer. Where did he come from? Out of those earlier movies, I'll bet, just like American gangsters in the 1930s learned how to dress and talk by studying Cagney and Raft.

Spike is a thoroughly irresponsible, completely likable character—a kid like everybody knows, who gets away with murder while his friends wait with fascination for a comeuppance that never comes. He lives in an Italian section of Brooklyn, where he boxes out of the local gym and has eyes for a cute blonde who happens to be the daughter of the neighborhood Mafia boss. The boss doesn't want Spike hanging around his daughter. The daughter is being saved for the snotty son of the local Congresswoman. But the problem is, she loves Spike.

That's the setup for Paul Morrissey's *Spike of Bensonhurst*, which is not the best comedy ever made but has energy and local color and a charismatic lead performance by Sasha Mitchell, as Spike. When he gets an unmistakable signal from the mob boss (Ernest Borgnine) that he should leave the neighborhood right away, he goes to live in a nearby Puerto Rican neighborhood with Bandana (Rick Aviles), a friend of his who is also a boxer. And there he falls in love with Bandana's sister, the beautiful, raven-haired India (Talisa Soto). This is the kind of guy that song was written about—the one where if he's not with the one he loves, he loves the one he's with.

The comedy in this movie is generated mostly out of broad racial stereotypes, and I know people who were offended by it; one person told me the film was nothing but an extended racist slur against Italians and Puerto Ricans. This is a hard call. I do not think the filmmakers or the actors had any racist intents. I think they were inspired more by the ethnic humor of TV sitcoms and movies like *Saturday Night Fever*. And because offense was not intended, perhaps none should be taken. When Bandana's

mother says she's pleased to meet a kid with Mafia connections because it's a way to move up in the world, is this racism? Or irony? Or sarcasm on her part? The fact that we have to guess makes it funny.

For a movie about a hero who gets both of his girlfriends pregnant, this is a chaste film. Spike never even kisses the beautiful India, although she has her lips parted in expectation at one moment, while we lean forward in our seats. When we learn she's pregnant, we're thunderstruck, because we're still waiting for that first kiss. Talisa Soto, who plays India, is a famous model who photographs, let it be said, as the most beautiful woman in the movies since Daphne Zuniga. She is gorgeous, but, alas, she cannot act.

Morrissey should have worked with her, showing her how to move more naturally, how not to always look as if she were waiting for a late train. And dialogue coaches might have helped with her speaking voice, which is uninflected and passionless, lacking energy and personality. If she wants to act, and is willing to study hard, there is little she cannot have, because she already has the one thing most movie actors never obtain, an electricity with the camera.

The second half of the movie is not as funny as the first, but there are several big scenes that pay off nicely, especially a wedding party paid for by the Congresswoman (Sylvia Miles), with Borgnine as the guest of honor. *Spike of Bensonhurst* contains Borgnine's funniest performance in a long time; the character is suited to his larger-than-life acting style, and he has a nice comic rapport with Anne DeSalvo, as his wife. The domestic arrangements of a middle-class Mafia household are examined here as hilariously as in *Married to the Mob*, and if we do not care much about the final fight by the time it comes, well, neither do the fighters.

Splash ★ 1/2
PG, 111 m., 1984

Tom Hanks (Allen), Daryl Hannah (Madison), Eugene Levy (Walter), John Candy (Freddie). Directed by Ron Howard and produced by Brian Grazer. Screenplay by Lowell Ganz, Babaloo Mandel, and Bruce Jay Friedman.

There is a funny movie lurking at the edges of *Splash*, and sometimes it even sneaks on screen and makes us smile. It's too bad the relentlessly conventional minds that made this movie couldn't have made the leap from sitcom to comedy. They must have thought they had such a great idea (Manhattan bachelor falls in love with mermaid) that they couldn't fail. But great ideas are a dime a dozen. *Splash* tells the story of a young man who is twice saved from drowning by a beautiful young mermaid. She falls in love with him and follows him to Manhattan, where he is a fruit and vegetable wholesaler. He falls in love with her. She can, it appears, metamorphose from a mermaid into a human; she has a tail when she's wet, but it turns into legs when she's dry. There are a lot of jokes about her total ignorance about all the ways of civilization. She walks naked onto Ellis Island, for example, and eats lobsters—shell and all.

All right. Now that's the situation. But the situation isn't going to be enough. We need some characters here. The mermaid is just fine. As played by the lovely Daryl Hannah, she is young and healthy and touchingly naive. But what about the guy who falls in love with her? It's here that the movie makes its catastrophic casting mistake. You see, they figured they have a comedy as long as the girl has a tail, and a romance whenever she has legs. So they gave her a romantic leading man when they should have given her a lonely guy who could swim. The leading man is Tom Hanks. He is conventionally handsome and passably appealing, and he would do in a secondary role. He'd be great, for example, as the straight-arrow brother. Instead, they make him the mermaid's lover, and they cast John Candy as the brother.

You remember Candy from SCTV. He is the large, shambling, Charles Laughton-type who has such a natural charisma that he's funny just standing there. They should have made Candy the lover, and Hanks the brother. Then we'd be on the side of this big lunk who suddenly has a mermaid drop into his life and has to explain her to his creepy, swinging-singles brother. Plus, there's the sweet touch that this transcendently sexy mermaid has fallen for the tubby loser with the heart of lust, and not for his slick brother. See what I mean? Instead, they go the other way. John Candy is not used much in the movie, Tom Hanks comes across as a standard young male lead, and they have to concoct a meaningless and boring subplot in order to make the movie long enough. Don't they know in Hollywood that once all the geniuses think they've finished with the screenplay, you just gotta rotate everything 180 degrees and you got a movie?

The Spy Who Loved Me ★ ★ ★ ½
PG, 125 m., 1977

Roger Moore (James Bond), Barbara Bach (Anya Amasova), Curt Jurgens (Stromberg), Richard Kiel (Jaws), Caroline Munro (Naomi), Bernard Lee (M), Desmond Llewelyn (Q), Lois Maxwell (Miss Moneypenny). Directed by Lewis Gilbert and produced by Albert R. Broccoli. Screenplay by Christopher Wood and Richard Maibaum.

The best of the James Bond adventures have always depended on cheerfully silly violence, and *The Spy Who Loved Me* is one of the best. It's heartening to see there's life in the old series yet. The first 007 caper was released in 1962, and here's Bond back once again with his beautiful girls, his lethal gadgets, and that tuxedo that never seems to wear out no matter how many mountains he climbs or deserts he treks in it.

There have been a lot of obituaries for the 1960s recently, but, no, Virginia, the sixties will never die, not so long as there is another twenty million dollars somewhere in the world to film another James Bond thriller. Bond lives in that yesterday we can vaguely remember: in a world of conspicuous consumption, fast cars, unliberated women, bizarre weapons, man-eating creatures of land, air, and sea, archvillains with German accents, and a British Empire upon which the sun has not yet set, although it's getting rather dusky out. The Bond universe is an anachronism, but one we've grown fond of, and *The Spy Who Loved Me* celebrates it with abundant energy. There was a time there, during some of the middle Bonds, when the series seemed to be losing its nerve, to be apologizing for its excesses. But not this time: *The Spy Who Loved Me* is gloriously ridiculous from beginning to end, and that's as it should be.

The stories in a lot of the Bond movies bear only the most tenuous relationship to the original fantasies of Ian Fleming, and that's especially true here. The plot involves a villain named Stromberg, who has a plan to capture nuclear submarines and use them to start World War III, after which he will rule the Earth from his undersea headquarters. British Agent 007 (Roger Moore) is assigned to trace the missing British sub, and Soviet Agent XXX (Barbara Bach) is after the Russian sub.

The chase leads to all sorts of places: Cairo, the pyramids, the desert, Sardinia.

And it features the best would-be Bond-killer since the immortal Odd Job in *Goldfinger*; Stromberg's hired assassin, named Jaws (Richard Kiel) stands seven-feet-two-inches tall, has hands about the size of the Sears catalog, and sharp steel teeth that can chomp through wood and steel, attacking sharks and foreign agents.

It's in the showdowns with Jaws that the movie has a lot of its fun. Jaws can tear apart vans, kill a shark one-on-one, hurl Bond through the air with ease, but he keeps getting almost killed—and one of the movie's standing jokes is his incredible power of survival. Agents 007 and XXX, meanwhile, make their way through incredible difficulties to the one obligatory scene in every Bond movie—the scene involving a gigantic indoor set where the destruction of the world is being plotted and enemy troops dressed in matching jumpsuits scurry about on catwalks high up under the ceiling.

The movie is jammed with special effects. It contains, in fact, almost as many spectacular stunts and effects as *Star Wars*, although their terrestrial locale may make them seem more routine. There's a car that turns into a submarine, and a tanker that turns into a sub-snatcher, and all sorts of guided missiles and instruments of oceanic warfare and spectacular explosions, and of course the underwater headquarters of the evil Stromberg, with its hungry sharks lurking at the bottom of the elevator shaft. *The Spy Who Loved Me* is in the tradition of the best Bonds: thrilling, sexy, ridiculous, gimmicky, violent, and, what all the Bonds are supposed to be, preposterous escapist fun.

Stakeout ★ ★ ★
R, 115 m., 1987

Richard Dreyfuss (Chris Lecce), Emilio Estevez (Bill Reimers), Madeleine Stowe (Maria McGuire), Aidan Quinn (Stick), Dan Lauria (Phil Coldshank), Forest Whitaker (Jack Pismo), Ian Tracey (Caylor Reese). Directed by John Badham and produced by Jim Kouf and Cathleen Summers. Screenplay by Kouf.

Richard Dreyfuss has always had a certain cockiness about him. He carries himself like a high-school basketball guard, ready to fake you out and go for the basket. And he talks the same way, often with a little smile to let you know there's an edge to his thinking, an angle. He had that way about him in *The*

Apprenticeship of Duddy Kravitz, and he has it still. It keeps me watching him even during the slow passages of his movies; there's always the feeling that what you see is not necessarily all you get.

Dreyfuss and his style are the two best things in *Stakeout*, a movie that consists of a good idea surrounded by a bad one. The good idea is the film's basic premise: Two cops stake out a good-looking woman whose ex-boyfriend is a dangerous escaped convict. During the long, weary hours while they're watching her, one of the cops falls in love. He finds a way to move into her life, leaving his partner stuck across the street with the binoculars.

That's the good idea, further fleshed out with the notion that Dreyfuss and his partner (Emilio Estevez) alternate shifts with two other cops who don't much like them. What would happen if the other cops saw Dreyfuss waking up in bed with the suspect?

The movie's bad idea is that this comic notion needs to be surrounded by a violent thriller. The opening scenes of the film are abrupt and bloody, as the dangerous convict (Aidan Quinn) escapes from prison and heads toward a showdown with Dreyfuss and Estevez. The closing scenes are another bad idea, still one more of those routine Hollywood chases and shoot-outs, with a fight on a boat for good measure.

The two parts of the movie don't go together. The violence is out of keeping with the humor. The humor can't develop in a context of brutality. And yet there's a long central stretch in the movie when things do work, when the courtship between Dreyfuss and the suspect (Madeleine Stowe) gets interesting. Dreyfuss poses as a telephone repairman, bugs her phones, falls in love with her, and eventually begins conducting his investigation from her bedroom. Estevez is stuck with the essentially thankless role of the guy who has to wait across the street and react to everything, but his reactions provide a lot of the movie's humor.

I liked the relationship between Dreyfuss and Stowe, who plays a headstrong Latino, but I might have liked it more if they had cast a funnier actress in the role—maybe Maria Conchita Alonso. Since it's likely that the director, John Badham, tested Alonso for this role, I wonder why he didn't cast her. Perhaps because she has an irrepressible good humor about her, and always seems to be amused by everything; she has the same sort of extra angle that Dreyfuss delivers. Maybe

Badham was afraid that good humor would work against the violence of his opening and closing scenes.

But all that's speculation. All I can say is *Stakeout* is an example of a movie that would have been a lot better if the filmmakers had been prepared to trust the human dimensions of their characters—to follow these people where their personalities led. Instead, Badham takes out an insurance policy by adding the assembly-line violence.

What is it? Has mainstream Hollywood so lost touch with simple human nature that you can't have a cop movie without everyone being blown away?

Stand and Deliver ★ ★ ½
PG-13, 106 m., 1988

Edward James Olmos (Jaime Escalante), Lou Diamond Phillips (Angel), Rosana De Soto (Fabiola Escalante), Andy Garcia (Ramirez), Virginia Paris (Chairwoman Ortega), Carmen Argenziano (Principal Molina). Directed by Ramon Menendez and produced by Tom Musca. Screenplay by Menendez and Musca.

There were moments in *Stand and Deliver* that moved me very deeply, and other moments so artificial and contrived that I wanted to edit them out, right then and there. The result is a film that makes a brave, bold statement about an unexpected subject—but that lacks the full emotional power it really should have.

Stand and Deliver tells the story of a high school mathematics teacher who takes a class of losers and potential dropouts and transforms them, in the course of one school year, into kids who have learned so much that eighteen of them are able to pass a tough college-credit calculus exam at the end of the year—an exam so hard that only two percent of students nationwide can pass it, although everyone in this class does.

The story is based on fact, on the life of Jaime Escalante, an actual East Los Angeles man who left a higher-paying job in business to return to education and prove something. What he proved is that motivation and hard work can rewrite the destinies of kids that society might be willing to write off.

Escalante, played in the film by Edward James Olmos, faces a disheartening challenge on the first day of school. His class is undisciplined, unmotivated, and rebellious. He doesn't confront them; he outflanks them. Adopting a weird sideways shuffle and

a strange habit of talking to himself, he strikes them at first as simply bizarre; they stop making noise because they want to hear what foolish thing he'll say next.

Then he starts teaching, using examples out of the everyday lives of his students, making them think things out for themselves, announcing that the "punishment" for not working hard in class is to be banished from the class—a class most of the kids would rather be out of, anyway. The kids themselves are amazed that this strategy works, and more amazed still to find that they're expected to do thirty hours of homework a week, and come in on Saturday mornings for extra classes.

All of this material is fine and strong. Not so fascinating, however, are the vignettes of student life outside the school. Some of these scenes are important to the story—as when we discover why it is so hard for some of the kids to find time for their homework—but others, including a high school romance, are simply marking time.

I was also disturbed by the cloudiness of the screenplay in the movie's most crucial scene. After the eighteen kids have taken, and passed, the exam, their test scores are questioned by the Educational Testing Service for two reasons: (1) It seems extremely unlikely that all of these kids could pass the exam without cheating, and (2) they all suspiciously made some of the same mistakes.

Because we have been though the movie and the experience with the kids, we know they were not cheating. But the ETS authorities cannot be blamed for their suspicions. What the screenplay needed, I think, was at least one speech in simple, clear dialogue, explaining what I assume to be true: The kids all made the same mistake because their teacher made that mistake in teaching them. There is a scene in the movie that seems to suggest this possibility; the teacher comes up with an assertion that everyone in the classroom tells him is wrong, but he won't back down. However, that scene ends without making it clear whether the teacher was wrong, and the later scene never explains the similar wrong answers. This adds unnecessary cloudiness to no purpose.

Other things in the movie may bother some viewers more than they did me. The Olmos performance takes a lot of chances. He is so mannered in his stooped shuffle and his sideways manner of expressing himself, that perhaps he should have toned it down once he'd made his point. The kids in his class, on the other hand, do a good job of avoiding the usual high school clichés—especially Lou Diamond Phillips, who, in a wonderful scene, explains why he needs two sets of textbooks—one to keep at school and the other to keep at home, since it would never do for his street friends to see him carrying books.

The last shot of *Stand and Deliver* puts some astonishing statistics on the screen, indicating that in every year since 1982 (the year of the story), even more students from this East L.A. high school have passed the difficult ETS exam. That is a dramatic story, and this is a worthy movie for telling it. I only wish I hadn't been reminded, so often, that the movie was making it feel just a little better than life.

Stanley & Iris ★ ★ ½
PG-13, 104 m., 1990

Jane Fonda (Iris King), Robert De Niro (Stanley Cox), Swoosie Kurtz (Sharon), Martha Plimpton (Kelly), Harley Cross (Richard), Jamey Sheridan (Joe), Feodor Chaliapin (Leonides Cox), Zohra Lampert (Elaine), Loretta Devine (Bertha). Directed by Martin Ritt and produced by Arlene Sellers and Alex Winitsky. Screenplay by Harriet Frank, Jr., and Irving Ravetch.

Once when I was much younger and was taking the Panama Limited to Chicago, I sat in the dining car across from a man who had a problem. On the railroads of those days, you had to write out your own order on a guest check and hand it to the waiter. The man licked his pencil and studied the menu. When the waiter came, the man simply pointed to me and said, "I'll have what he's having." Since he didn't know what I was having, it took me some time to figure this out, and then suddenly the answer came to me: This was a man who couldn't read and write.

Stanley & Iris provides some insight into the lives of people with that dilemma. If we are to believe the movie, they cannot tell aspirin bottles from Sudafed, or deal with claim checks when they leave their shoes to be resoled, or get a driver's license, or grow up into independent adults. When we first see Stanley (Robert De Niro) in this movie, he is taking a bus, and a little later he gives Iris (Jane Fonda) a ride on his bicycle. Eventually he gets fired from his job in a company cafeteria because the boss discovers that he is illiterate and reasons, not unfairly, that he

might put rat poison into the soup one day instead of salt.

I did not know whether to believe all of Stanley's problems in the movie, because I know that any smart person with a handicap soon figures out a way around it: putting the claim check in a special part of the billfold, for example, or looking for a skull-and-crossbones on the poison, or grabbing all six little plastic bottles on the shelf in the company commissary and saying, "We got everything here. What do you want?" What I did believe was that Stanley felt cut off from ordinary life, just as a traveler in another land might feel strange to find that all of the street signs were in a language completely foreign to him.

For Stanley, the foreign land is his hometown, where he lives with his father—a traveling salesman who never kept the kid in one school long enough for him to learn anything. After Stanley encounters Iris (the Meet Cute happens after a purse-snatcher grabs her bag on a bus), he gets the first chance in his life to make up for lost time—to learn to read and write, even in his forties. This involves some courage and some love.

The relationship between Stanley and Iris, between De Niro and Fonda, is the nicest and most believable thing in this movie. Both of them create gentle, complex characters—De Niro an introspective tinkerer who makes inventions in the garage that doubles as his home, and Fonda as a widow who works on the assembly line down at the bakery. I read a review of this movie that complained that Fonda's voice and bearing were too classy to belong to a bakery worker; the reviewer obviously doesn't know that a lot of classy people end up in jobs they hate because they want to feed their families.

What was strange about this movie was that I believed almost all of it—except for the scenes dealing with illiteracy, its alleged subject. The director, Martin Ritt, and his screenwriters, Harriet Frank, Jr., and Irving Ravetch, create a real sense of time and place, and people it with believable characters, but they have not found a way to make illiteracy real. Three or four small examples are supposed to suggest the nature of De Niro's problem, and they do, but the actual scenes in which Fonda tries to teach him to read and write are the least convincing scenes in the movie. And there is at least one puzzling continuity gap, in which he temporarily seems to read better than he should, and then later goes back to reading poorly again.

That makes illiteracy into the movie's gimmick instead of its subject. This isn't really a story about reading and writing, but about love. And on that level it works nicely, as Fonda and De Niro grow closer to one another, and De Niro finds some acceptance in Fonda's extended family (hard times have forced her to take in a sister and brother-in-law, and to deal with the pregnancy of a daughter). True to the ancient laws of movie structure, the two lovers must hit emotional bottom and separate before they can come back together again and love one another, but we accept such conventions. It's the awkwardness of the reading scenes—as Stanley learns to make his letters, for example—that stands out.

Stanley & Iris has its heart in the right place, and it has some good acting and a superb job by Ritt of creating the look and feel of a small town. But the theme feels shoehorned in and doesn't fit. I know this sounds cynical, and that everyone involved with the movie probably felt very deeply about its theme, but here is a movie that is about more than it needs to be about.

STAR 80 ★ ★ ★ ★
R, 102 m., 1983

Mariel Hemingway (Dorothy Stratten), Eric Roberts (Paul Snider), Cliff Robertson (Hugh Hefner), Carroll Baker (Dorothy's Mother), Roger Rees (Aram Nicholas). Directed by Bob Fosse and produced by Wolfgang Glattes and Kenneth Utt. Screenplay by Fosse.

Bob Fosse dresses all in black and makes films about the demonic undercurrents in our lives. Look at his credits: *Cabaret, Lenny, All That Jazz,* and now *STAR 80.* Although his Broadway musicals have been upbeat entertainment, he seems to see the movie camera as a device for peering into our shames and secrets. *STAR 80* is his most despairing film. After the Nazi decadence of *Cabaret,* after the drug abuse and self-destruction in *Lenny,* and the death-obsessed hero of *All That Jazz,* here is a movie that begins with violent death and burrows deeper. There were times when I could hardly keep my eyes on the screen, and a moment near the end when I seriously asked myself if I wanted to continue watching.

And yet I think this is an important movie. Devastating, violent, hopeless, and important, because it holds a mirror up to a part of the world we live in, and helps us see it more clearly. In particular, it examines the connection between fame and obscurity, between those who have a moment of praise and notoriety, and those who see themselves as condemned to stand always at the edge of the spotlight. Like Martin Scorsese's *Taxi Driver*, it is a movie about being an outsider and about going crazy with the pain of rejection.

The movie tells the story of two young people from Vancouver. One of them was Dorothy Stratten, a shy, pretty blonde who thought her hands and feet were too big, who couldn't understand why anyone would value her, and who was close enough to some sort of idealized North American fantasy that she became the 1979 Playmate of the Year. The other was Paul Snider, a Vancouver small-timer who worked as a salesman, con man, and part-time pimp. When Paul saw Dorothy behind the counter of a hamburger stand, he knew she was his ticket to the big time. Dorothy resisted his compliments at first, but he was so relentless in his adoration that she surrendered to his fantasies. Paul masterminded Dorothy's rise. He arranged the photo session that attracted the eye of *Playboy*'s talent scouts. He bought her dresses and flowers. He pushed her into the limelight and then edged into it next to her. But then she went to Los Angeles and found the real stardust, the flattery of the Playboy Mansion, the attentions of young men whose sports cars were bought with their own money, while Paul's was bought with hers.

Paul had a vanity license plate made: STAR 80. But Dorothy had moved out of his world, had been given a taste of a larger world that, frankly, Paul didn't have the class to appreciate. She fell in love with a movie director. She went out of town on location. She and Paul drifted apart, and he went mad with jealousy and resentment. On August 14, 1980, Dorothy went back to the shabby little North Hollywood bungalow they had rented together, and Paul murdered her.

STAR 80 begins with the murder. Everything else is in flashback, and, therefore, the film has no really happy scenes. Dorothy's triumphs are all stained with our knowledge of what will happen. Every time she smiles, it's poignant. We know Paul will go berserk and kill her, and so we can see from the beginning that he's unbalanced. Fosse knows his material is relentlessly depressing, and so he doesn't try for moments of relief. Although we enter the world of *Playboy* and see Dorothy partying in the mansion and

posing in nude modeling sessions, although the whole movie is concerned with aspects of sex, there is never an erotic moment. Fosse keeps his distance, regarding Dorothy more as a case study than as a fantasy. That makes Mariel Hemingway's performance as Dorothy all the more powerful. She has been remade into the sleek, glossy Playmate image, but she still has the adolescent directness and naiveté that she used so well in *Manhattan* and *Personal Best*. She's a big kid. Her eyes open wide when she gets to Los Angeles, and she's impressed by the attention she's receiving. The character she plays is simple, uncomplicated, shallow, and so trusting that she never does realize how dangerous Paul is.

The other performances in the movie are equally strong. Eric Roberts as Paul even succeeds in persuading us to accept him as a suffering human being rather than as a hateful killer. Like Robert De Niro as Travis Bickle in *Taxi Driver*, he fills his role with so much reality that we feel horror, but not blame. Carroll Baker, as Dorothy's mother, is heartbreakingly incapable of connecting in any meaningful way with her daughter.

What is the point of *STAR 80?* I'm not sure, just as I wasn't sure of the points of *In Cold Blood* or *Lacombe, Lucien* or "The Executioner's Song." There is no redemption in the movie, no catharsis. It unblinkingly looks at the short life of a simple, pretty girl, and the tortured man who made her into something he couldn't have, and then killed her for it. The movie seems to be saying: These things happen. After it was over, I felt bad for Dorothy Stratten. In fact, for everybody.

A Star Is Born ★ ★ ★ ★
PG, 175 m., 1954 (1983)

Judy Garland, James Mason, Jack Carson, Tommy Noonan, Charles Bickford. Directed by George Cukor.

A Star Is Born hasn't merely been restored. It has been rediscovered. George Cukor's 1954 movie, which starred James Mason and Judy Garland in the story of Hollywood lives destroyed by alcoholism, always has been considered one of the great tear-jerking Hollywood melodramas, populated with bravura performances. But has it ever been praised for its purely cinematic qualities? I don't think so, and yet it showed Cukor's mastery not only of the big effects, but also of

subtle lighting and exquisite compositions. It's an irony, but if Warner Brothers hadn't chopped twenty-seven minutes out of the movie in 1954 and tried to throw them away, the whole movie never would have been rereleased in its current form. It is very good to have the missing footage back, of course, but it's even better to have the whole movie back again, a landmark of Hollywood melodrama.

Although this version is exactly as long as Cukor's final cut in 1954, it doesn't have quite all the footage. Two major production numbers and a charming little scene in a drive-in restaurant were rediscovered by film historian Ron Haver (after months of detective work). Haver also found the movie's complete stereo sound track, but about seven minutes of the visual footage seem to be gone forever—and so this restoration uses an effective montage of music, dialogue, and production stills to bridge the gaps. Seeing this version of the movie makes it clear what major surgery was performed by Warner Brothers. The studio chopped out an entire Judy Garland musical number, "Here's What I'm Here For," filled with fire and energy. That's wonderful to have back again, but the other major restored sequence is almost indispensable to the film.

It's a scene from fairly early in the film. The alcoholic movie star (Mason) has convinced the young band vocalist (Garland) to risk everything and try for a movie career. With his support, she's on the brink of stardom. She's recording a song with a studio orchestra, and afterward she rests on a staircase with Mason. He proposes marriage. She says he drinks too much. He promises to reform. Neither one realizes that their whole conversation is being recorded by an eavesdropping overhead mike. Then, as a joke by the director, the proposal is played back for all the musicians to hear—and Garland accepts. By taking out that proposal scene, Warner Brothers had a movie that skipped unconvincingly from Garland's movie debut to her elopement with Mason. The earlier missing footage—the scenes represented by the still photos—also represented important bridging material, covering an uncertain period during which Garland thinks Mason has forgotten about her. Without those scenes, the movie skips directly from Garland's early hopes to her first day at the studio, with no period of uncertainty.

The missing scenes are good to have back again. But the movie's central scenes are even better to see again. There is an absolutely brilliantly lit and directed scene in a darkened nightclub, with Garland singing while the camera prowls silently among the musicians' instruments; it's one of the best examples of composition I've ever seen. And near the end of the movie, there's Garland's big, bravura scene, in which she interrupts a big production number for a heart-rending dressing-room conversation with her studio chief (Charles Bickford). And then, of course, there is Mason's sad, lonely walk into the sea, and the movie's unforgettable closing line: "Good evening, everyone. This is Mrs. Norman Maine."

A Star Is Born is one of the rare films that successfully integrate music with drama; it's not exactly a musical, but it has more music than most musicals. It's also not exactly a serious drama—it's too broad and predictable for that—but it's the sort of exaggerated, wide-gauge melodrama that Rainer Werner Fassbinder would experiment with twenty years later; a movie in which larger-than-life characters are used to help us see the melodramatic clichés that we do, indeed, sometimes pattern our own lives after.

I was lucky enough to visit George Cukor at his Hollywood home in December of 1981. He said he had never seen the butchered version of *A Star Is Born* and never would. "If they wanted it shorter," he said, "I could have sweated out twenty-five minutes here and there, and nobody would have missed them. Instead, they took an ax to the movie." George Cukor died on the evening before he was to see a rough version of this restored print. That is sad, but then Cukor, of course, knew what his original movie looked like. Now the rest of us can know, too.

Star Trek: The Motion Picture ★ ★ ★
G, 132 m., 1979

William Shatner (Kirk), Leonard Nimoy (Spock), DeForest Kelley ("Bones" McCoy), James Doohan (Scotty), George Takei (Sulu), Walter Koenig (Chekov). Directed by Robert Wise and produced by Gene Roddenberry. Screenplay by Harold Livingston.

Two things occurred to me as I watched *Star Trek:*

• The producers have succeeded at great expense in creating a toy for the eyes. This movie is fun to watch.

• Epic science-fiction stories, with their

cosmic themes and fast truths about the nature of mankind, somehow work best when the actors are unknown to us. The presence of the *Star Trek* characters and actors—who have become so familiar to us on television—tends in a strange way to undermine this movie. The audience walks in with a possessive, even patronizing attitude toward Kirk and Spock and Bones, and that interferes with the creation of the "sense of wonder" that science fiction is all about.

Let's begin with the toy for the eyes. The *Star Trek* movie is fairly predictable in its plot. We more or less expected that two of the frequent ingredients in the television episodes would be here, and they are: a confrontation between Starship *Enterprise* and some sort of alien entity, and a conclusion in which basic human values are affirmed in a hostile universe. In *Star Trek: The Motion Picture*, the alien entity is an unimaginably vast alien spaceship from somewhere out at the edge of the galaxy. The movie opens as it's discovered racing directly toward Earth, and it seems to be hostile. Where has it come from, and what does it want?

The Starship *Enterprise*, elaborately rebuilt, is assigned to go out to intercept it, with Admiral Kirk, of course, in charge. And scenes dealing with the *Enterprise* and the other ship will make up most of the movie—if the special effects aren't good, the movie's not going to work. But they are good, as, indeed, they should be: The first special-effects team on this movie was fired, and the film's release was delayed a year while these new effects were devised and photographed. (The effects get better, by the way, as the movie progresses. The alien ship looks great but the spaceports and futuristic cities near the film's beginning loom fairly phony.)

The *Enterprise*, perhaps deliberately, looks a lot like other spaceships we've seen in *2001, Silent Running, Star Wars,* and *Alien.* Kubrick's space odyssey set a visual style for the genre that still seems to be serviceable. But the look of the other spaceship in *Star Trek* is more awesome and original. It seems to reach indefinitely in all directions, the *Enterprise* is a mere speck inside of it, and the contents of the alien vessel include images of the stars and planets it has passed en route, as well as enormous rooms or spaces that seem to be states of a computer-mind. This is terrific stuff.

But now we get to the human level (or the half-human level, in the case of Mr. Spock).

The characters in this movie are part of our cultural folklore; the *Star Trek* television episodes have been rerun time and time again. Trekkies may be unhappy with me for saying this, but there are ways in which our familiarity with the series works against the effectiveness of this movie. On the one hand we have incomprehensible alien forces and a plot that reaches out to the edge of the galaxy. On the other hand, confronting these vast forces, we have television pop heroes. It's great to enjoy the in-jokes involving the relationships of the *Enterprise* crew members and it's great that Trekkies can pick up references meant for them, but the extreme familiarity of the Star Trek characters somehow tends to break the illusion in the big scenes involving the alien ship.

Such reservations aside, *Star Trek: The Motion Picture* is probably about as good as we could have expected. It lacks the dazzling brilliance and originality of *2001* (which was an extraordinary one-of-a-kind film). But on its own terms it's a very well-made piece of work, with an interesting premise. The alien spaceship turns out to come from a mechanical or computer civilization, one produced by artificial intelligence and yet poignantly "human" in the sense that it has come all this way to seek out the secrets of its own origins, as we might.

There is, I suspect, a sense in which you can be too sophisticated for your own good when you see a movie like this. Some of the early reviews seemed pretty blasé, as if the critics didn't allow themselves to relish the film before racing out to pigeonhole it. My inclination, as I slid down in my seat and the stereo sound surrounded me, was to relax and let the movie give me a good time. I did and it did.

Star Trek II: The Wrath of Khan
★ ★ ★
PG, 113 m., 1982

William Shatner (Kirk), Leonard Nimoy (Spock), Ricardo Montalban (Khan), DeForest Kelley ("Bones" McCoy), Kirstie Alley (Lieutenant Saavik). Directed by Nicholas Meyer and produced by Robert Sallin. Screenplay by Jack B. Sowards.

The peculiar thing about Spock is that, being half human and half Vulcan and therefore possessing about half the usual quota of human emotions, he consistently, if dispassionately, behaves as if he possessed very heroic human emotions indeed. He makes a choice in *Star Trek II* that would be made only by a hero, a fool, or a Vulcan. And when he makes his decision, the movie rises to one of its best scenes, because the *Star Trek* stories have always been best when they centered around their characters. Although I liked the special effects in the first movie, they were probably not the point; fans of the TV series wanted to see their favorite characters again, and *Trek II* understood that desire and acted on it.

Time has passed since the last episode. Kirk has retired to an administrative post. Spock is commanding the *Enterprise*, with a lot of new faces in the crew. The ship is on a mission concerning the Genesis device, a new invention which, if I understand it correctly, is capable of seeding a barren planet with luxuriant life. A sister ship, the USS *Reliant*, is scouting for lifeless planets and finds one that seems to be dead, but its instruments pick up a small speck of life. Crew members investigate, and find the planet inhabited by an outlaw named Khan, who was exiled there years ago by Kirk, and has brooded of vengeance ever since.

Khan is played as a cauldron of resentment by Ricardo Montalban, and his performance is so strong that he helps illustrate a general principle involving not only *Star Trek* but *Star Wars* and all the epic serials, especially the James Bond movies: Each film is only as good as its villain. Since the heroes and the gimmicks tend to repeat from film to film, only a great villain can transform a good try into a triumph. In a curious way, Khan captures our sympathy, even though he is an evil man who introduces loathesome creatures into the ear canals of two *Enterprise* crew members. Montalban doesn't overact. He plays the character as a man of deeply wounded pride, whose bond of hatred with Admiral Kirk is stronger even than his traditional villain's desire to rule the universe.

There is a battle in outer space in this movie, a particularly inept one that owes more to "Captain Video" than to state-of-the-art special effects. I always love it when they give us spaceships capable of leaping across the universe, and then arm them with weapons so puny that a direct hit merely blows up a few control boards and knocks people off their feet. Somehow, though, I don't much care if the battles aren't that amazing, because the story doesn't depend on them. It's about a sacrifice made by Spock, and it draws on the sentiment and

audience identification developed over the years by the TV series.

Perhaps because of that bond, and the sense that an episode may be over but the *Enterprise* will carry on, the movie doesn't feel that it needs an ending in a conventional sense. The film closes with the usual *Star Trek* end narration, all about the ship's mission and its quest, and we are obviously being set up for a sequel. You could almost argue that the last few minutes of *Trek II* are a trailer for *Trek III*, but, no, that wouldn't be in the spirit of the *Enterprise*, would it?

Star Trek III: The Search for Spock
★ ★ ★
PG, 105 m., 1984

William Shatner (Kirk), DeForest Kelley ("Bones" McCoy), James Doohan (Scotty), Walter Koenig (Chekov), George Takei (Sulu), Nichell Nichols (Uhura), Mark Lenard (Sarek), Leonard Nimoy (Spock). Directed by Leonard Nimoy and produced by Harve Bennett. Screenplay by Bennett.

Read no further if you don't want to know whether Mr. Spock is alive at the end of *Star Trek III: The Search for Spock*. But, if you, like me, somehow had the notion that there was a 100 percent chance that they would find Spock (if only so he would be available for *Star Trek IV*), then you will be relieved to learn that his rediscovery and rebirth pay due homage to the complexities of the Vulcan civilization. By the end of this movie, all Mr. Spock has to do is raise one of those famous eyebrows, and the audience cheers.

This is a good but not great *Star Trek* movie, a sort of compromise between the first two. The first film was a *Star Wars* road company that depended on special effects. The second movie, the best one so far, remembered what made the *Star Trek* TV series so special: not its special effects, not its space opera gimmicks, but its use of science fiction as a platform for programs about human nature and the limitations of intelligence. *Star Trek III* looks for a balance between the first two movies. It has some of the philosophizing and some of the space opera, and there is an extended special-effects scene on the exploding planet Genesis that's the latest word in fistfights on the crumbling edges of fiery volcanoes.

There is also a great-looking enemy spaceship that resembles a predatory bird in flight (although why ships in the vacuum of space

require wings is still, of course, a question *Star Trek* prefers not to answer).* The ship is commanded by the fairly slow-witted Klingon warrior Kruge (played by Christopher Lloyd of "Taxi"), who falls for a neat little double cross that is audacious in its simplicity. The movie's plot involves a loyal attempt by the Enterprise crew to return to the planet Genesis in an attempt to reunite Spock's body and spirit. The alien spaceship is in the same sector, attempting to steal the secret of Genesis, a weapon from the last movie that begins by bringing life to dead planets and goes on from there. The showdown between the Klingons and the Enterprise crew resembles, at times, one of those Westerns where first Bart had the draw on Hoppy and then Hoppy had the draw on Bart, but the struggle to the death between Kirk and Kruge takes place against such a great apocalyptic background that we forgive all.

The best thing the *Star Trek* movies have going for them is our familiarity with the TV series. That makes for a sort of storytelling shorthand. At no point during this film, for example, is it ever explained that Vulcans are creatures of logic, not emotion—although we have to know that in order to understand most of the ending. It's not necessary. These characters are under our skins. They resonate, and a thin role in a given story is reinforced by stronger roles in a dozen others. That's sort of reassuring, as (a fanfare, please) the adventure continues.

*Leonard Nimoy sent me a helpful explanation: "The Klingon Bird of Prey has wings for the same reason that our own space shuttle does. It can land in an earth-like atmosphere."

Star Trek IV: The Voyage Home
★ ★ ★ ¹/₂
PG, 119 m., 1986

William Shatner (Admiral Kirk), Leonard Nimoy (Mr. Spock), DeForest Kelley (McCoy), Catherine Hicks (Gillian Taylor), Robert Ellenstein (Federation President), Brock Peters (Cartwright), John Schuck (Klingon Ambassador), Jane Wyatt (Spock's Mother). Directed by Leonard Nimoy and produced by Harve Bennett. Screenplay by Steve Meerson, Peter Krikes, Bennett, and Nicholas Meyer.

When they finished writing the script for *Star Trek IV*, they must have had a lot of silly grins on their faces. This is easily the most absurd of the *Star Trek* stories—and yet, oddly enough, it is also the best, the funniest, and the most enjoyable in simple human terms. I'm relieved that nothing like restraint or common sense stood in their way.

The movie opens with some leftover business from the previous movie, including the Klingon ambassador's protests before the Federation Council; these scenes have very little to do with what the rest of the movie is about, and yet they provide a certain reassurance (like James Bond's ritual flirtation with Miss Moneypenny) that the series remembers that it has a history.

Meanwhile, the crew of the Starship *Enterprise* is still marooned on a faraway planet with the Klingon starship* they commandeered in *Star Trek III*. They vote to return home aboard the alien vessel, but on the way they encounter a strange deep-space probe. It is sending out signals in an unknown language which, when deciphered, turns out to be the song of the humpback whale.

It's at about this point that the script conferences must have really taken off. See if you can follow this: The *Enterprise* crew determines that the probe is zeroing in on earth, and that if no humpback songs are picked up in response, the planet may well be destroyed. Therefore, the crew's mission becomes clear: Since humpback whales are extinct in the twenty-third century, they must journey back through time to the twentieth century, obtain some humpback whales, and return with them to the future—thus saving earth. After they thought up this notion, I hope the writers lit up cigars.

No matter how unlikely the story is, it supplies what is probably the best of the *Star Trek* movies so far, directed with calm professionalism by Leonard Nimoy. What happens is that the *Enterprise* crew land their Klingon starship in San Francisco's Golden Gate Park, surround it with an invisibility shield, and fan out through the Bay Area looking for humpback whales and a ready source of cheap nuclear power.

What makes their search entertaining is that we already know the crew members so well. The cast's easy interaction is unique among movies, because it hasn't been learned in a few weeks of rehearsal or shooting; this is the twentieth anniversary year of "Star Trek," and most of these actors have been working together for most of their professional lives. These characters *know* one another.

An example: Admiral Kirk (William Shatner) and Mr. Spock (Leonard Nimoy) visit a Sea World-type operation, where two humpback whales are held in captivity. Catherine Hicks, as the marine biologist in charge, plans to release the whales, and the Trek crew needs to learn her plans so they can recapture the whales and transport them three centuries into the future.

Naturally, this requires the two men to ask Hicks out to dinner. She asks if they like Italian food, and Kirk and Spock do a delightful little verbal ballet based on the running gag that Spock, as a Vulcan, cannot tell a lie. Find another space opera in which verbal counterpoint creates humor.

The plots of the previous Trek movies have centered around dramatic villains, such as Khan, the dreaded genius played by Ricardo Montalban in *Star Trek II*. This time, the villains are faceless: The international whale hunters who continue to pursue and massacre whales despite clear indications that they will drive these noble mammals from the face of the earth. "To hunt a race to extinction is not logical," Spock calmly observes, but we see shocking footage of whalers who are doing just that.

Instead of providing a single human villain as counterpoint, *Star Trek IV* provides a heroine, in Hicks. She is obviously moved by the plight of the whales, and although at first she not unreasonably doubts Kirk's story that he comes from the twenty-third century, eventually she enlists in the cause and even insists on returning to the future with them, since of course, without humpback whales, the twenty-third century also lacks humpback whale experts.

There are some major action sequences in the movie, but they aren't the high points; the *Star Trek* saga has always depended more on human interaction and thoughtful, cause-oriented plots. What happens in San Francisco is much more interesting than what happens in outer space, and this movie, which might seem to have an unlikely and ungainly plot, is actually the most elegant and satisfying *Star Trek* film so far.

Leonard Nimoy, we've got you now.

In Star Trek III, *the Klingon starship was in the shape of a vast, evil bird of prey—inspiring me to ask, in my review of that film, why a starship needed wings to operate in interstellar space. After all, the* Enterprise *certainly didn't have wings.*

You wrote me a helpful note, explaining that the Klingon vessel needed wings because it operated in planetary atmospheres.

All right, except in Star Trek IV, *when the* Enterprise *crew commandeers the Klingon ship and uses it to travel through time, there is a scene in Golden Gate Park where the ship levitates vertically from the grass. If it can conquer gravity, then once again, I ask, why does it have wings?*

Your answer, please?

"It doesn't conquer gravity," he told me soon after the movie opened. "It uses vertical take-off technology, like the Harrier jets in the Royal Air Force."

Oh.

Star Trek V: The Final Frontier ★ ★
PG, 108 m., 1989

William Shatner (Admiral James T. Kirk), Leonard Nimoy (Mr. Spock), DeForest Kelley (Dr. Leonard McCoy), James Doohan (Montgomery Scott), Walter Koenig (Pavel Chekov), Nichell Nichols (Commander Uhura), George Takei (Sulu). Directed by William Shatner and produced by Harve Bennett. Screenplay by David Loughery.

There was a moment in *Star Trek V*—only one, and a brief one, but a genuine one—when I felt the promise of awe. The Starship *Enterprise* was indeed going where no man had gone before, through the fabled Great Barrier which represents the end, or perhaps the beginning, of the finite universe. What would lie beyond? Would it be an endless void, or a black hole, or some kind of singularity of space and time that would turn the voyagers inside out and deposit them in another universe? Or would the barrier even reveal, as one of the characters believes, the place where life began? The place called by the name of Eden and countless other words?

As the *Enterprise* approached the Barrier, I found my attention gathering. The movie had been slow and boring until then, with an interminable, utterly inconsequential first act, and a plot that seemed to exist in a space-time singularity all its own. But now, at last, the fifth *Star Trek* movie seemed to be remembering what was best about the fictional world of *Star Trek*: Those moments when man and his ideas are challenged by the limitless possibilities of creation.

As I've said, my awe was real. It was also brief. Once the *Enterprise* crew members (and the Vulcan who was holding them hostage) had landed on the world beyond the

Barrier, the possibilities of God or Eden or whatever quickly disintegrated into an anticlimactic special-effects show with a touch of *The Wizard of Oz* thrown in for good measure. I do not want to give away important elements in the plot, but after you've seen the movie, ask yourself these questions:

(1) How was it known that the voyagers would go beyond the Barrier? (2) What was the motivation behind what they found there? (3) How was it known that they would come to stand at exactly the point where the stone pillars came up from the earth? (4) In a version of a question asked by Kirk, why would any entity capable of staging such a show need its own starship? and (5) Is the Great Barrier indeed real, or simply a deceptive stage setting for what was found behind it? (What I'm really complaining about, I think, is that *Star Trek V* allows itself enormous latitude in the logic beneath its plot. If the Barrier is real, what exactly are we to make of the use to which it is put?)

Before we get to ask those questions, *Star Trek V* spends much of its time meandering through some of the goofiest scenes in the entire series. The movie opens with the taking of three hostages on a desert planet, who have been captured for the sole purpose of luring Admiral Kirk and his starship to the planet, so that the ship can be commandeered for the voyage through the Barrier. I have explained these plot details in one sentence. The movie takes endless scenes, during which the key crew members of the *Enterprise* need to be summoned back to their ship in the middle of a shore leave. And that process, in turn, requires interminable scenes of Kirk, Spock, and Bones on a camping trip in Yosemite, during which they attempt to sing "Row, row, row your boat" and nearly succeed in sinking the entire movie. If there is a sillier and more awkwardly written scene in the entire *Star Trek* saga than this one, I've missed it.

After the pointless opening scenes, the movie begins to develop a plot of sorts, but it is so confused and inadequately explained that there are times when we simply give up and wait for what's next. That was particularly the case during the inexplicable closing scenes, where the humans and the Klingons seem to join sides after an off-camera speech by a former Klingon leader who had been put out to pasture. Since this leader is identified as having been badly treated by the Klingons in his retirement, how did he suddenly regain the authority to negotiate a truce? And, for that matter, do we really *want* to see the mighty Klingons reduced to the status of guests at a cocktail party?

One of the trademarks of the *Star Trek* saga has been the way the supporting characters are kept alive in little subplots. In *Star Trek V,* the *Enterprise* starts its voyage while the ship is suffering a series of mechanical failures, and that involves countless brief scenes in which Scotty, the chief engineer, emerges from beneath a piece of equipment, brandishes his wrench, and says he'll have things fixed in a moment. Two or three of these scenes might have been enough.

Another irritation is the way in which we meet apparently major characters, including those played by David Warner, Laurence Luckinbill, and Cynthia Gouw, who are introduced with fanfares of dialogue and then never developed or given anything to do. The entire movie seems crowded with loose ends, overlooked developments, and forgotten characters, and there are little snatches of dialogue where some of these minor characters seem to be soldiering on in their original subplots as if unaware that they've been cut from the movie.

Star Trek V is pretty much of a mess—a movie that betrays all the signs of having gone into production at a point where the script doctoring should have begun in earnest. There is no clear line from the beginning of the movie to the end, not much danger, no characters to really care about, little suspense, uninteresting or incomprehensible villains, and a great deal of small-talk and pointless dead ends. Of all of the *Star Trek* movies, this is the worst.

Star Wars ★ ★ ★ ★
PG, 121 m., 1977*

Mark Hamill (Luke Skywalker), Carrie Fisher (Princess Leia), Harrison Ford (Han Solo), Alec Guinness (Obi-Wan Kenobi), David Prowse (Darth Vader), James Earl Jones (Vader's Voice), Kenny Baker (R2D2), Anthony Daniels (C3PO). Directed by George Lucas and produced by Gary Kurtz. Screenplay by Lucas.

Every once in a while I have what I think of as an out-of-the-body experience at a movie. When the ESP people use a phrase like that, they're referring to the sensation of the mind actually leaving the body and spiriting itself off to China or Peoria or a galaxy far, far away. When I use the phrase, I simply mean that my imagination has forgotten it is actually present in a movie theater and thinks it's up there on the screen. In a curious sense, the events in the movie seem real, and I seem to be a part of them.

Star Wars works like that. My list of other out-of-the-body films is a short and odd one, ranging from the artistry of *Bonnie and Clyde* or *Cries and Whispers* to the slick commercialism of *Jaws* and the brutal strength of *Taxi Driver.* On whatever level (sometimes I'm not at all sure) they engage me so immediately and powerfully that I lose my detachment, my analytical reserve. The movie's *happening,* and it's happening to me.

What makes the *Star Wars* experience unique, though, is that it happens on such an innocent and often funny level. It's usually violence that draws me so deeply into a movie—violence ranging from the psychological torment of a Bergman character to the mindless crunch of a shark's jaws. Maybe movies that scare us find the most direct route to our imaginations. But there's hardly any violence at all in *Star Wars* (and even then it's presented as essentially bloodless swashbuckling). Instead, there's entertainment so direct and simple that all of the complications of the modern movie seem to vaporize.

Star Wars is a fairy tale, a fantasy, a legend, finding its roots in some of our most popular fictions. The golden robot, lion-faced space pilot, and insecure little computer on wheels must have been suggested by the Tin Man, the Cowardly Lion, and the Scarecrow in *The Wizard of Oz.* The journey from one end of the galaxy to another is out of countless thousands of space operas. The hardware is from *Flash Gordon* out of *2001,* the chivalry is from *Robin Hood,* the heroes are from Westerns and the villains are a cross between Nazis and sorcerers. *Star Wars* taps the pulp fantasies buried in our memories, and because it's done so brilliantly, it reactivates old thrills, fears, and exhilarations we thought we'd abandoned when we read our last copy of *Amazing Stories.*

The movie works so well for several reasons, and they don't all have to do with the spectacular special effects. The effects *are* good, yes, but great effects have been used in such movies as *Silent Running* and *Logan's Run* without setting all-time box-office records. No, I think the key to *Star Wars* is more basic than that.

The movie relies on the strength of pure narrative, in the most basic storytelling form known to man, the Journey. All of the best tales we remember from our childhoods had to do with heroes setting out to travel down roads filled with danger, and hoping to find treasure or heroism at the journey's end. In *Star Wars*, George Lucas takes this simple and powerful framework into outer space, and that is an inspired thing to do, because we no longer have maps on Earth that warn, "Here there be dragons." We can't fall off the edge of the map, as Columbus could, and we can't hope to find new continents of prehistoric monsters or lost tribes ruled by immortal goddesses. Not on Earth, anyway, but anything is possible in space, and Lucas goes right ahead and shows us very nearly everything. We get involved quickly, because the characters in *Star Wars* are so strongly and simply drawn and have so many small foibles and large, futile hopes for us to identify with. And then Lucas does an interesting thing. As he sends his heroes off to cross the universe and do battle with the Forces of Darth Vader, the evil Empire, and the awesome Death Star, he gives us lots of special effects, yes—ships passing into hyperspace, alien planets, an infinity of stars—but we also get a wealth of strange living creatures, and Lucas correctly guesses that they'll be more interesting for us than all the intergalactic hardware.

The most fascinating single scene, for me, was the one set in the bizarre saloon on the planet Tatooine. As that incredible collection of extraterrestrial alcoholics and bug-eyed martini drinkers lined up at the bar, and as Lucas so slyly let them exhibit characteristics that were universally human, I found myself feeling a combination of admiration and delight. *Star Wars* had placed me in the presence of really magical movie invention: Here, all mixed together, were whimsy and fantasy, simple wonderment and quietly sophisticated storytelling.

When Stanley Kubrick was making *2001* in the late 1960s, he threw everything he had into the special effects depicting outer space, but he finally decided not to show any aliens at all—because they were impossible to visualize, he thought. But they weren't at all, as *Star Wars* demonstrates, and the movie's delight in the possibilities of alien life forms is at least as much fun as its conflicts between the space cruisers of the Empire and the Rebels.

And perhaps that helps to explain the movie's one weakness, which is that the final assault on the Death Star is allowed to go on too long. Maybe, having invested so much money and sweat in his special effects, Lucas couldn't bear to see them trimmed. But the magic of *Star Wars* is only dramatized by the special effects; the movie's heart is in its endearingly human (and non-human) people.

*See review of *The Hidden Fortress*, p. 271, which inspired Lucas.

Stardust Memories ★ ★
PG, 89 m., 1980

Woody Allen (Sandy), Charlotte Rampling (Dori), Jessica Harper (Violinist), Marie-Christine Barrault (Frenchwoman). Directed by Woody Allen and produced by Robert Greenhut. Screenplay by Allen.

Woody Allen's *Stardust Memories* is a deliberate homage to *8½*, the 1963 film in which Federico Fellini chronicled several days in the life of a filmmaker who had no idea where to turn next. The major difference between the two films is that Fellini's movie was *about* a director bankrupt of new ideas, while Allen's is a movie *by* a director with no new ideas. I know that sounds harsh, especially when applied to one of the few American directors who can be counted on for freshness and intelligence, but *Stardust Memories* is an incomplete, unsatisfying film.

The movie begins by acknowledging its sources of visual inspiration. We see a claustrophobic Allen trapped in a railroad car (that's from the opening of *8½*, with Marcello Mastroianni trapped in an auto), and the harsh black-and-white lighting and the ticking of a clock on the sound track give us a cross-reference to the nightmare that opens Ingmar Bergman's *Wild Strawberries*. Are these the exact scenes Allen had in mind? Probably, but no matter; he clearly intends *Stardust Memories* to be his *8½*, and it develops as a portrait of the artist's complaints.

Most of the action of the film centers around two subjects. The first is a weekend film seminar (obviously patterned after Judith Crist's weekends at Tarrytown, N.Y.), to which the Allen character has been invited. The second subject is a very familiar one, Allen's stormy relationships with women. The subjects blend into the basic complaint of the Woody Allen persona we have come to know and love, and can be summarized briefly: If I'm so famous and brilliant and everybody loves me, then why doesn't anybody *in particular* love me?

At the film seminar, the Allen character is constantly besieged by groupies. They come in all styles: pathetic young girls who want to sleep with him, fans who want his autograph, weekend culture vultures, and people who spend all their time at one event promoting the next one they're attending. Allen makes his point early, by shooting these unfortunate creatures in close-up with a wide-angle lens that makes them all look like Martians with big noses. They add up to a nightmare, a nonstop invasion of privacy, a shrill chorus of people whose praise for the artist is really a call for attention.

Fine, except what *else* does Allen have to say about them? Nothing. In the Fellini film, the director-hero was surrounded by sycophants, business associates, would-be collaborators, wives, mistresses, old friends, all of whom made calls on his humanity. In the Allen picture, there's no depth, no personal context: They're only making calls on his time. What's more, the Fellini character was at least trying to create something, to harass his badgered brain into some feeble act of thought. But the Allen character expresses only impotence, despair, uncertainty, discouragement. All through the film, Allen keeps talking about diseases, catastrophes, bad luck that befalls even the most successful. Yes, but that's what artists are for: to hurl their imagination, joy, and conviction into the silent maw. Sorry if I got a little carried away. *Stardust Memories* inspires that kind of frustration, though, because it's the first Woody Allen film in which impotence has become the situation rather than the problem. This is a movie about a guy who has given up. His relationships with women illustrate that; after the marvelous and complex women in *Annie Hall* and *Manhattan*, in *Stardust Memories* we get a series of enigmas and we never really feel that Allen is connecting with them. These women don't represent failed relationships, they represent walk-throughs.

Woody Allen has always loved jazz and the great mainstream American popular music. There's a lot of it in *Stardust Memories*, but it doesn't amplify or illustrate the scene this time—it steals them. There's a scene where Allen remembers a wonderful spring morning spent with a former love (Charlotte Rampling), and how he looked up in his apartment to see her there, and for a moment felt that life was perfect. As Allen shows that moment, Louis Armstrong sings "Stardust" on the sound track, and something happens that should not be allowed to happen. We find our attention almost entirely on Armstrong's wonderfully loose jazz phrasing.

Stardust Memories is a disappointment. It needs some larger idea, some sort of organizing force, to pull together all these scenes of bitching and moaning, and make them lead somewhere.

Starman ★ ★ ★
PG, 112 m., 1984

Jeff Bridges (Starman), Karen Allen (Jenny Hayden), Charles Martin Smith (Mark Shermin), Richard Jaeckel (George Fox). Directed by John Carpenter and produced by Larry J. Franco. Screenplay by Bruce A. Evans and Raynold Gideon.

Starman begins by reminding us of Voyager, that little spacecraft that is even now speeding beyond the solar system. Remember Carl Sagan on the "Tonight" show, explaining to Johnny about all the messages that were on board, in case someday an alien race found this postcard from Earth? Voyager carried greetings in all of the tongues of man, and there is something inevitable about the scene, early in *Starman*, when we get an extraterrestrial visitor who has studied them carefully, and is able to say "hello" a hundred different ways.

The starman of the title is a ball of glowing light. He, or it, has traveled to Earth in response to the invitation from Voyager, but of course the Air Force treats the spacecraft as a possible invader and shoots missiles at it. Knocked off course, the starman lands in rural Wisconsin, where it becomes the identical clone of a dead house painter. The painter's widow (Karen Allen) is stunned when she sees this creature from beyond the grave. It is even more difficult when she realizes this is not her husband, but something infinitely different that just happens to look exactly like her husband. The visitor is very smart, but has a lot to learn, and at first it controls its human host body with a lot of awkward lurching. Meanwhile, government officials led by Richard Jaeckel are seeking the extraterrestrial for "security" reasons, and scientist Charles Martin Smith hopes to get there first and record the historic moment of man's first meeting with a race from another world.

All of this seems like a setup for a science-fiction movie, but what's interesting is the way the director, John Carpenter, makes a U-turn and treats *Starman* as a road movie. The visitor (played by Jeff Bridges) forces Allen to start driving in the direction of the Great Meteor Crater, where he has a rendezvous with his ride home. And as the two characters spend time together as refugees from the search parties, they begin to communicate, and the woman's initial hostility turns into respect and finally into love. This is a wonderfully sweet process, especially as Allen and Bridges go about it. *Starman* contains the potential to be a very silly movie, but the two actors have so much sympathy for their characters that the movie, advertised as space fiction, turns into one of 1984's more touching love stories. Meanwhile, Carpenter provides many of the standard scenes from earlier road movies, including a stop in a roadside diner where the alien's uncertain behavior draws attention. And there's an interlude in Vegas where the extraterrestrial tries to outsmart the slots.

The most interesting thing about *Starman* is probably Bridges's approach to playing a creature from another world. The character grows gradually more human as the film moves along, but he is never completely without glitches: His head movements are birdlike, his step is a little uncertain, he speaks as if there were just a millisecond's delay between brain and tongue. Actors sometimes try to change their appearance; Bridges does something trickier, and tries to convince us that Jeff Bridges is not inhabited by himself. I think he succeeds, and that *Starman* makes Voyager seem like a good investment.

State of Grace ★ ★ ★ ½
R, 134 m., 1990

Sean Penn (Terry), Ed Harris (Frankie), Gary Oldman (Jackie), Robin Wright (Kathleen), John Turturro (Nick), Burgess Meredith (Finn). Directed by Phil Joanou and produced by Ned Dowd, Randy Ostrow, and Ron Rotholz. Screenplay by Dennis McIntyre.

State of Grace is not quite sure which is worse—murder, or yuppies moving into the neighborhood. That's one of its charms. The movie is so sincere and confused in its values that it mirrors the goofy loyalties and violent pathology of its characters. They're low-level Irish-American gangsters who operate in the Hell's Kitchen area of New York City, west of Times Square, and one measure of their success as gangsters is the fact that rising rents are forcing them out of the neighborhood.

The movie opens with a reunion. Terry (Sean Penn), who used to live in the neighborhood, has been on the road for a few years. Now he's back in town, and embracing his best friend Jackie (Gary Oldman) in one of the sleazy saloons where gangsters and winos seem to be the only customers.

Crime in this neighborhood is a family affair. The Irish gang is led by Jackie's older brother Frankie (Ed Harris), who has moved to the suburbs and calls the shots from his middle-class house on a tree-lined street, far from the drug deals that pay his mortgage. The two brothers have a sister named Kathleen (Robin Wright), who has also tried to get out of the neighborhood—she works as a clerk in an uptown hotel. But she and Terry used to be in love, and so, of course, Fate is going to have a hand in what happens next.

Since a great deal of what happens in *State of Grace* depends on an important secret that is not revealed until the second half of the movie, I will have to tread gingerly around some of the details. But the most interesting aspect of the movie is right up front: The confused notion by Jackie that he is, in some way, protecting the neighborhood by committing crimes there. Although the gang's main business seems to be selling drugs, Frankie is willing to pull some jobs simply as a civic service. For example, he takes Terry along one night when he burns down a construction office on a site that will soon be a yuppie apartment building.

Frankie is probably crazy, or maybe his mind has been completely addled by the drugs and booze he has channeled through it. His idea of making arson into fun is to pour the gasoline between himself and the door, and then see if he can run through it without killing himself. He also likes to hold target practice up on the roof. And he is capable of shocking, cold-blooded killing, as he shows in one of the movie's most surprising scenes, a reconciliation with the Mafia that has an unexpected ending.

Gary Oldman's performance in the movie is the best thing about it. Sean Penn is just as good an actor, but he has the lead, and there's not as much he can do with it. He has to be sane and tortured and conflicted, and battle with his opposing emotions. All standard screenplay stuff. Oldman's character is more pure. He acts only on the basis of his instincts and prejudices, or out of vengeance and fear. His character doesn't have to do the fancy footwork.

There are moments in the film that are

absolutely chilling—as when Ed Harris, who wanted to be at arm's length from the crimes committed for his profit—finds that he has to personally kill someone he loves. But the movie's plot paradoxically gets less and less original, the more complicated it becomes. At the outset, when it seems concerned only with the behavior of its characters, it's original and challenging. Then it turns into a story filled with familiar elements, and by the end everything is happening by the numbers.

What's best about *State of Grace* is what's unique to it—the twisted vision of the Oldman character, who lives in a world of evil and betrayal and has somehow thought himself around to the notion that he is doing the right thing.

Stay Hungry ★ ★ ★
R, 102 m., 1976

Jeff Bridges (Craig Blake), Sally Field (Mary Tate), Arnold Schwarzenegger (Joe Santo), R.G. Armstrong (Thor Erickson), Robert Englund (Franklin), Helena Kallianiotes (Anita), Roger E. Mosley (Newton), Woodrow Parfrey (Uncle Albert), Scatman Crothers (William). Directed by Bob Rafelson and produced by Harold Schneider and Rafelson. Screenplay by Charles Gaines and Rafelson.

Bob Rafelson's *Stay Hungry* is ungainly and confused at times—it stretches its seams a little too much—but it's a breath of fresh air—a quirky, funny, oddball movie about the most unlikely characters ever to be trapped in the same plot. Jeff Bridges plays the lead, an Alabama blueblood of uncounted generations of aristocracy. He's involved in a real estate deal that involves convincing a gymnasium owner to sell his property so a high-rise can go up. Bridges visits the gym, becomes fascinated by the earnest body-builders and fierce female karate instructors and sort of forgets to do anything about the deal. And one of the body-builders (the former Mr. Universe, Arnold Schwarzenegger, who likes to work out in a rubber Batman suit) introduces him to a sweet young thing he can't help falling in love with.

The girl is played by Sally Field, and she's a simple country type who doesn't exactly fit in with Bridges's genteel cousins; she attends a family party dressed in something that looks mail-ordered from Frederick's of Hollywood. Bridges begins to get letters from his Uncle Albert, who points out that this newfound interest in muscle-building and

girls without any breeding is going to qualify him as the family's first black sheep since the cousin who moved to Puerto Rico and opened a goat farm. Meanwhile, the would-be real estate investors turn out to be mob types with a penchant for sending guys around to wreck the air conditioning.

The movie doesn't concern itself very much with plot; like Rafelson's *Five Easy Pieces* and the underrated *The King of Marvin Gardens*, it introduces us to sharply defined, rather odd characters and then lets them mix it up. The movie is episodic, and some of the episodes are brilliant. Among the best is a scene in which the aged family retainer (Scatman Crothers) announces his resignation and his intention of taking a suit of armor with him, another in which several dozen body-builders race through the startled streets of Birmingham, a harrowing fight scene in a gym in which people throw weights at each other, and a tables-turned situation in which a hooker is forcibly given a massage.

Schwarzenegger, in his first dramatic role, turns in an interesting performance as Bridges's newfound buddy. He works out incessantly, speaks in an Austrian accent, and then turns out to be the lead fiddler in a blue-grass band (people in Rafelson movies are always revealing unsuspected musical abilities).

One of the best things about *Stay Hungry* is that we have almost no idea where it's going; it's as free-form as *Nashville* and Rafelson is cheerfully willing to pause here and there for set pieces like the woman's karate class and the eventual Mr. Universe competition (in which the muscled competitors, back-lit, rise slowly onto a revolving stage in a moment reminiscent of the sunrise in *2001*). When the movie's over, we're still not sure why it was made (maybe it's a subtle comment on Southern class structure—very subtle), but we've had fun and so, it appears, has Rafelson.

Staying Alive ★
PG, 96 m., 1983

John Travolta (Tony Manero), Cynthia Rhodes (Jackie), Finola Hughes (Laura), Julie Bovasso (Mother). Directed by Sylvester Stallone and produced by Robert Stigwood. Screenplay by Stallone and Norman Wexler.

Staying Alive is a big disappointment. This sequel to the gutsy, electric *Saturday Night Fever* is a slick, cinematic jukebox, a series of self-contained song-and-dance sequences

that could be cut apart and played forever on MTV. Like *Flashdance*, it isn't really a movie at all, but an endless series of musical interludes between dramatic scenes that aren't there. It's not even as good as *Flashdance*, but it may appeal to the same audience; it's a Walkman for the eyes.

The movie has an extremely simple plot. Extremely. Six years have passed since Tony Manero (John Travolta) gazed longingly at the lights of Manhattan at the end of *Saturday Night Fever*. Now he lives in a fleabag Manhattan hotel, works as a waiter and a dance instructor, and dates a young dancer (Cynthia Rhodes) with the patience of a saint. He's still a woman-chaser. But he meets a long-haired British dancer (Finola Hughes) who's his match. She's a queen bitch who takes him to bed and jilts him. Meanwhile, he gets a job as a dancer in her new show and when her lead dancer falters, Tony gets the job. Does this all sound familiar?

The movie was co-authored and directed by Sylvester Stallone, and is the first bad movie he's made. He remembers all the moves from his Rocky plots, but he leaves out the heart—and, even worse, he leaves out the characters. Everybody in *Staying Alive* is Identikit. The characters are clichés, their lives clichés, and God knows their dialogue is clichés. The big musical climaxes are interrupted only long enough for people to shout prepackaged emotional counter-charges at each other. There is little attempt to approximate human speech. Like the Rocky movies, *Staying Alive* ends with a big, visually explosive climax. It is so ludicrous it has to be seen to be believed. It's opening night on Broadway. Tony Manero not only dances like a hero, he survives a production number of fire, ice, smoke, flashing lights, and laser beams, throws in an improvised solo—and ends triumphantly by holding Finola Hughes above his head with one arm, like a quarry he has tracked and killed. The musical he is allegedly starring in is something called *Satan's Alley*, but it's so laughably gauche it should have been called *Springtime for Tony*. Stallone makes little effort to convince us we're watching a real stage presentation; there are camera effects the audience could never see, montages that create impossible physical moves, and—most inexplicably of all—a vocal track, even though nobody on stage is singing. It's a mess. Travolta's big dance number looks like a high-tech TV auto commercial that got sick to its stomach.

What I really missed in *Staying Alive* was the sense of reality in *Saturday Night Fever*—the sense that Tony came from someplace and was somebody particular. There's no old neighborhood, no vulgar showdowns with his family (he *apologizes* to his mother for his "attitude"!), and no Brooklyn eccentricity. Tony's world has been cloned into a backstage musical. And not a good one.

Still, the movie has one great moment. A victorious Tony says "I want to strut!" and struts across Times Square while the Bee Gees sing "Stayin' Alive." That could have been the first shot of a great movie. It's the last shot of this one.

Staying Together ★ ★
R, 91 m., 1989

Sean Astin (Duncan McDermott), Stockard Channing (Nancy Trainer), Melinda Dillon (Eileen McDermott), Jim Haynie (Jake McDermott), Levon Helm (Denny Stockton), Dinah Manoff (Lois Cook), Dermot Mulroney (Kit McDermott), Tim Quill (Brian McDermott), Keith Szarabajka (Kevin Burley). Directed by Lee Grant and produced by Joseph Feury. Screenplay by Monte Merrick.

Staying Together is a relentless slice of life about good-hearted people with real-life problems; it's the kind of movie that's so homespun and genuine and caring that you wonder if these characters have ever seen any movies or watched any television: Do they know their lives are clichés?

The film tells the story of the hard-working McDermott family, who live in a small and friendly Southern town. Dad has been supporting his clan for years by running a chicken restaurant down by the lake. Mom is usually bustling around at home in the kitchen, asking her three unruly sons for a head count for dinner. The sons are lovable tykes who drink together, smoke pot together, and do just about everything together except for tomcatting around, of which they do a great deal separately.

I guess making the sons into irrepressible substance abusers is the movie's concession to reality. When it's breakfast time in the morning, for example, Mom (Melinda Dillon) tells the oldest son that the clan has precisely five minutes to get downstairs to the kitchen table. It's like a scene out of *Cheaper by the Dozen*. But then the eldest jumps out his bedroom window and jogs around town to find the middle brother (in bed with a girl who's engaged to someone else) and the youngest (sleeping it off on a park bench in front of the police station, covered in his own vomit). And gol-darn, wouldn't you know those rascally tykes all make it to the table just in time?

Material like this cries out to be satirized. Unfortunately, director Lee Grant and writer Monte Merrick take it seriously. They have some issues they're discussing here. For example, the rich developers from the big city want to buy the chicken restaurant. It's on prime real estate next to the scenic lake. (They're not real bright developers; they want to replace it with a franchise chicken restaurant, when the site cries out for a slab of ugly condos.) The McDermott brothers don't want to sell; all three of them love the restaurant and presumably want to work in it for the rest of their lives.

But Dad McDermott (Jim Haynie) is ready to sell. He's sick of chickens. Hates 'em. Never wants to see another one in his life. He dreams of a happy retirement, fishing and hunting and never seeing another chicken as long as he lives. Of course, it's dangerous to make talk like that in the movies. Talk about the happy twilight years stretching out in front of you, and you're tempting fate. And so we arrive at the crisis in the movie, which we can spot coming down the road for about sixteen miles before the characters can.

If there's anything worse than a predictable family crisis in a heartwarming, homespun small-town drama, it's the obligatory rebuilding process that takes place afterward—as the brothers shoulder responsibility, Mom demonstrates her courage, and everybody marries the right people after telling off the wrong ones. Take out the boozing and the wenching, and *Staying Together* has all the ingredients to be one of Frank Capra's lesser films.

Steel Magnolias ★ ★ ★
PG, 118 m., 1989

Sally Field (M'Lynn Eatenton), Dolly Parton (Truvy Jones), Shirley MacLaine (Ouiser Boudreaux), Daryl Hannah (Annelle Dupuy Desoto), Olympia Dukakis (Claree Belcher), Julia Roberts (Shelby Eatenton Latcherie), Tom Skerritt (Drum Eatenton), Sam Shepard (Spud Jones), Dylan McDermott (Jackson Latcherie), Kevin J. O'Connor (Sammy Desoto). Directed by Herbert Ross and produced by Ray Stark. Screenplay by Robert Harling.

Steel Magnolias is essentially a series of comic one-liners leading up to a teary tragedy, but let it be said that the one-liners are mostly funny and the tragedy deserves most, but not all, of the tears. The movie takes place down in Louisiana during what is said to be the 1980s and involves a tightly knit group of women friends whose husbands (being absent, depressed, or dead) leave them lots of time to gossip at the beauty parlor.

Gossip is what they do best, and one of the characters even appropriates Alice Roosevelt Longworth's immortal line, "If you have something bad to say about somebody . . . sit down right here beside me!" What the women treasure most is anyone with a "past," and when the gawky new girl at the beauty parlor confesses that she "thinks" she is married, they draw closer and hold their breath.

The beauty shop is operated by Dolly Parton in still another reminder that she is one of the sunniest and most natural of actresses. Into her hands, at the beginning of the movie, comes a young bride-to-be (Julia Roberts), who almost faints when she sees herself in the mirror. It's not shock, it's diabetes, but a glass of orange juice brings her around. Parton has just hired a new girl (Daryl Hannah), who does her best with the mother of the bride (Sally Field). Dropping in to exchange insights are Shirley MacLaine, as the richest and meanest woman in town, and Olympia Dukakis, whose character has lost her husband but has a potbellied suitor on the horizon.

These six women are the steel magnolias of the title, Southern belles who are dippy on the outside but strong enough inside to survive any challenge, of which in this film there are many. At first we are not aware of impending tragedy, however, because the movie sticks so successfully to its comic dialogue. I doubt if any six real women could be funny and sarcastic so consistently (every line is an epigram), but I love the way these women talk, especially when Dukakis observes, "What separates us from the animals is our ability to accessorize."

The men do not amount to much in this movie. Tom Skerritt, as the father of the bride, spends much of his time trying to chase pigeons from his trees and the rest of his time grinning benevolently. Sam Shepard, as Parton's husband, lays abed in depression many days and then gets a job on an offshore oil rig that keeps him away for a week at a spell. Dylan McDermott, who is going to marry the bride, is a pleasant non-entity who gets upstaged, or lost track of entirely, at the key events in his life. And then there is the hapless Kevin J. O'Connor, whose seduction of Shirley MacLaine has progressed to the point where she will actually wink at him in church.

No, this is a woman's picture. And the women in it cook and sew and mend and drive each other around town. They fight and make up and hug each other and cry. They get their hair done. And when tragedy strikes and there is a death in their little group, they have the strength to grieve and the character to smile through their tears.

The big scene in the movie is a brief, heartbreaking monologue by Sally Field, who asks God the question that is often uppermost in all our minds: "Why?" The way she asks it, and the words she uses, are tremendously effective, and, yes, we are moved. I heard some snuffling and the blowing of noses. But then the tears are followed by a great big laugh that is very funny but is right on the brink of being a cheap dramatic trick, and we're reminded that *Steel Magnolias*, for all its pretensions, is closer to *Miss Firecracker* than to *Terms of Endearment*.

The movie was written by Robert Harling, based on his own play, and has been directed by Herbert Ross, who choreographs wonderfully entertaining performances from all the women in his cast—especially MacLaine as the town nut case who lurches around in overalls, towed by a big ugly dog. The principal pleasure of the movie is in the ensemble work of the actresses, as they trade one-liners and zingers and stick together and dish the dirt. *Steel Magnolias* is willing to sacrifice its overall impact for individual moments of humor, and while that leaves us without much to take home, you've got to hand it to them: The moments work.

Stella ★ ★ ★ ¹/₂
PG-13, 106 m., 1990

Bette Midler (Stella Claire), John Goodman (Ed Munn), Trini Alvarado (Jenny Claire), Stephen Collins (Stephen Dallas), Marsha Mason (Janice Morrison), Eileen Brennan (Mrs. Wilkerson), Linda Hart (Debbie Whitman), Ben Stiller (Jim Uptegrove). Directed by John Erman and produced by Samuel Goldwyn, Jr. Screenplay by Robert Getchell.

Stella is the kind of movie they used to call a tearjerker, and we might as well go ahead and still call it that, because all around me at the sneak preview people were blowing their noses and sort of softly catching their breath—you know, the way you do when you're having a great time. It tells a story that is predictable from beginning to end, except that who would have predicted this old story still had so much life in it, or that the actors would fill it with such warmth and sentiment? *Stella* may be corny, but it's got a great big heart.

The basic plot elements are more or less the same as the last time this story was filmed, starring Barbara Stanwyck, in 1937. A poor but plucky mother has a daughter out of wedlock, proudly refuses financial aid from the rich man who is the father, and raises the girl on her own. Mother and daughter love each other, but the day comes when the mother—a former barmaid now selling cosmetics door to door—realizes that the father and his sophisticated fiancée can give the girl (now of college age) the advantages she needs. So the mother gives away her daughter—all but drives her away—and the ending is pure melodrama.

"Audiences came to sneer and stayed to weep," film historian Leslie Halliwell said of the 1937 version. They're likely to do the same thing this time. Every charge you can make against this movie is probably true—it's cornball, manipulative, unlikely, sentimental, and shameless. But once the lights go down and the performances begin, none of those things really matter, because this *Stella* has a quality that many more sophisticated films lack: It makes us really care about its characters.

Bette Midler and Trini Alvarado play the mother and daughter as well as I can imagine them being played, with style and life. They don't put on long faces and march through the gloom. Midler must have played around with a lot of walks and a lot of accents—she must have experimented with attitudes and personal styles—before she hit on the right note for Stella. She's a tough broad who, as the movie opens in 1969, tends bar for a living and has even been known to climb up on the bar when they play "The Stripper" on the jukebox. She's not educated, but she's smart and funny, and has a determined, independent attitude toward life.

The bar is a working-class, shot-and-beer joint. One night a slick customer comes in wearing a cashmere sweater and a nice smile. He likes the way she has fun when she

dances. Against her better judgment, they have an affair, she gets pregnant, he halfway offers to marry her, she says nothing doing, and the rest of the movie is about how she raises the kid, named Jenny, on her own. The father (Stephen Collins) stays in the picture, however, because he comes to love his daughter. So does his fiancée (Marsha Mason). And there is the steady guy in Stella's life, a bartender named Ed (John Goodman) who is a pal, not a lover, and sticks with her through her problems while piling up a lot of his own.

The movie, directed by John Erman and written by Robert Getchell, doesn't miss a single opportunity to generate emotion from its story. There's the girl's sixteenth birthday party, where nobody comes. The lonely Christmas Eve. The crush that Jenny gets on a sincere young preppy, and the way her mother embarrasses her by dancing with the waiter at a posh Florida resort. What *Stella* proves is that no scene is really hackneyed or predictable unless the people making the movie think of it that way. Midler and Alvarado put so much belief into their scenes, so much unforced affection and life, that only an embittered grinch could refuse to be touched.

In an odd sort of way, some of the same notes in *Stella* were played, not so well, in Midler's previous tearjerker, *Beaches* (1988). That one was more sophisticated and cool and knowledgeable, and not half as effective. There are scenes here of great difficulty which Midler plays wonderfully; the scene, for example, where she goes to Marsha Mason's office to ask if Jenny can come to live with Mason and Collins. She believes the time has come to let Jenny take advantage of her father's culture and position, even if that means she loses her daughter: "I'm not gonna let nothing stand in the way of my Jenny," she says. She learns that Mason, the chic publishing executive, comes from a poor, rural background. She asks about Mason's sisters. Are they successful? Are they happy? Mason's face shows they are not. "I knew it," Midler says. "They didn't get out."

Although the story in *Stella* is what manipulates the audience, the style is what makes the movie glow. Midler's Stella shows quiet flashes of the Midler stage persona, especially when she puts people down, and in moderation, the flashes work. So does the movie's refusal to allow Stella to live in self-pity. She sheds some tears, yes, but in her own mind she has achieved a series of victories in bearing a daughter, preserving her own self-esteem, and launching Jenny into the great world. *Stella* is the kind of movie that works you over and leaves you feeling good, unless you absolutely steel yourself against it. Rent it to sneer. Watch it to weep.

The Stepfather ★ ★ ½
R, 95 m., 1987

Terry O'Quinn (The Stepfather), Jill Schoelen (Stephanie Maine), Shelley Hack (Susan Blake), Charles Lanyer (Dr. Bondurant), Stephen Shellen (Ogilvie), Robyn Stevan (Karen). Directed by Joseph Ruben and produced by Jay Benson. Screenplay by Donald E. Westlake.

He's one of those guys with a bland smile and a voice so nice and sweet that right away you know he's twisted. He has a knack for convincing women to marry him, but children see him with clearer eyes, and know there's something wrong. There sure is. Battling inside of him are two conflicting obsessions: The desire to be the perfect father of a model family, and a towering rage that turns him into a killer.

The Stepfather tells his story in a blood-soaked thriller that is uneven but haunting. While I was watching the film, I was distracted by elements of the Idiot Plot Syndrome—moments when only an idiot would have made such obvious mistakes. Now, remembering the film, what I recall most clearly is the central performance by Terry O'Quinn.

He is a journeyman actor from TV and many movies, usually in supporting roles, and you may or may not recognize him. What's clear at once is that he is a strong actor, and given this leading role he brings all kinds of creepy dimensions to it. He has the thankless assignment of showing us a completely hateful, repellent character—and he approaches the task as an exercise in cloying middle-class good manners.

The stepfather seems to be such a nice man. So understanding. So accommodating. He always marries into families with children—providing a strong shoulder for a widow to lean on. He's handy around the house. He likes to spend time in his basement workshop, where sometimes the pressure builds up so intensely that he has to smash things.

He's obsessed with a vision of the perfect family. He wants each of his families to be perfect. When they disappoint him, as every family eventually will, he starts shopping around for his next family and his next identity. When he has that lined up, he murders this family.

The Stepfather is very effective in presenting that character. Unfortunately, it places him inside a plot that has too many distracting loose ends and oversights, avoidable errors and Idiot Plot mistakes. Why did the movie have to be a thriller at all? Why not simply a character study?

There were box-office considerations, I suppose, and yet the thriller aspects of the film are the least satisfying. It's distracting to watch a movie and know that a movie character is doing something that makes no sense—and is doing it only so that the plot can move on to its next chapter.

Like many movies that study psychopathic killers (*Badlands*, *In Cold Blood*, even *Black Widow*), this film seems to have no larger purpose than simply to show us the killer. Because the murderer is mentally ill, because he is not killing out of any motive that we can understand, the film is simply an exercise in despair; a portrait of a tragic man.

Violence itself seems to sell, even when it's divorced from any context. Maybe that's what the filmmakers were thinking. What often happens, though, is that in an otherwise flawed film there are a couple of things that are wonderful. *The Stepfather* has one wonderful element: Terry O'Quinn's performance.

Stevie ★ ★ ★ ★
NO MPAA RATING, 102 m., 1981

Glenda Jackson (Stevie Smith), Mona Washbourne (Her Aunt), Alec McCowen (Freddie), Trevor Howard (The Man). Directed and produced by Robert Enders. Screenplay by Hugh Whitemore.

Stevie Smith came across a newspaper clipping one day that told of a man who drowned within a few hundred yards off the shore. The people on the beach saw him waving, and they waved back. The truth, as Stevie expressed it in a famous poem, was the man's problem was just like her own:

I was much too far out all my life
And not waving, but drowning.

In those lines, Stevie Smith made an image of her own life, and it is an image that Glenda Jackson's film *Stevie* expresses with clarity, wit, and love.

Stevie Smith was a British poet of considerable reputation, who died in 1971 at the age of sixty-nine. She spent almost all of her life living in a small home in the London suburb of Palmers Green, where she moved as a child. She worked every day in an office in the city, until her growing reputation as a poet allowed her to take an early retirement. She lived with an old maid aunt, and eventually she became an old maid herself. We watch this process as it is punctuated by a marriage proposal, by a visit to Buckingham Palace for tea with the queen, by a half-hearted suicide attempt. Every night, there was definitely a glass or two or more of sherry, or sometimes gin.

To the world, she must have appeared to be an exemplary example of a talented English eccentric. Her poems were irreverent, sharply satirical, and laconic. She was capable of writing one day:

The Englishwoman is so refined
She has no bosom and no behind.

And on another day, writing about death:

I have a friend
At the end
of the world.
His name is a breath
Of fresh air.

She was not waving, but drowning. The film *Stevie* captures this laconic despair, but it also does a great deal more. It gives us a very particular portrait of a woman's life. The movie is based on a play by Hugh Whitemore, and it contains one of Glenda Jackson's greatest performances. She knows this character well. She played Stevie on the London stage and on a BBC radio production before making this film. She does what great actors can do: She takes a character who might seem uninteresting, and makes us care deeply about the uneventful days of her life.

Although *Stevie* is totally dominated by Jackson's performance, it is not a one-character film by any means. The veteran British actress Mona Washbourne provides a magnificent performance as Stevie's maiden aunt, who is a little dotty and a little giggly and very loving, who likes her glass of sherry and wears flowered print dresses that Stevie says look like a seed catalog illustration titled "They All Came Up." Alec McCowen plays Freddie, the not-so-young man who comes calling, and whose proposal Stevie rejects. And the wonderful Trevor Howard has an ambiguous part as "the man." On one level, "the man" is just someone she met at a literary party and conned into giving her rides to poetry readings. At another level, especially when he is seen by himself, telling us about Stevie and reading some of her lines, he is the understanding, forgiving father figure Stevie never had.

Movies like *Stevie* run the risk of looking like photographs of stage plays, but *Stevie* somehow never feels that way. Even though it uses the artifices of the stage (including remarks addressed by Glenda Jackson directly to the audience), and even though a lot of its dialogue is poetry, *Stevie* always feels as if it occupies this woman's life. She is the poet, we are her confidantes, and it is a privilege to get to know her. I have perhaps given the impression that *Stevie* is grim and depressing. It is not at all. It is very sad at times, of course, but there are other times of good humor and barbed wit, when she's not drowning, but waving.

Stop Making Sense ★ ★ ★ ½
NO MPAA RATING, 88 m., 1984

With the Talking Heads: David Byrne, Chris Frantz, Jerry Harrison, and Tina Weymouth. Guest musicians: Edna Holt, Lynn Mabry, Steve Scales, Alex Weir, and Bernie Worrell. Directed by Jonathan Demme and produced by Gary Goetzman.

The overwelming impression throughout *Stop Making Sense* is of enormous energy, of life being lived at a joyous high. And it's not the frenetic, jangled-nerves energy of a rock band that's wired; it's the high spirits and good health we associate with artists like Bruce Springsteen. There are a lot of reasons to see concert films, but the only ones that usually get mentioned are the music and the cinematography. This time the actual physical impact of the film is just as exhilarating: Watching the Talking Heads in concert is a little like rock 'n' roll crossed with "Jane Fonda's Workout." The movie was shot during two live performances of the Talking Heads, a New York rock band that centers on the remarkable talent of its lead singer, David Byrne. Like David Bowie, his stage presence shows the influence of mime, and some of his best effects in *Stop Making Sense* are achieved with outsize costumes and

hand-held lights that create shadow plays on the screen behind him.

Given all the showmanship that will develop later during the film, the opening sequences are a low-key, almost anticoncert throwaway. Byrne walks on a bare stage with a ghetto-blaster in his hand, puts it down on the stage, turns it on and sings along with "Psycho Killer." Eventually he is joined onstage by Tina Weymouth on bass. Then stagehands wander out from the wings and begin to assemble a platform for drummer Chris Frantz. Gear is moved into place. Electrical cables are attached. The backup singers, Edna Holt and Lynn Mabry, appear. And the concert inexorably picks up tempo.

The music of the Talking Heads draws from many sources, in addition to traditional rock 'n' roll. You can hear the echoes, in Byrne's voice, of one of his heroes, country singer Hank Williams. In the music itself, there are elements of reggae and of gospel, especially in the driving repetitions of single phrases that end some of the songs. What is particularly delightful is that the Talking Heads *are* musical: For people who have passed over that invisible divide into the age group when rock sounds like noise, the Heads will sound like music.

The film is good to look at. The director is Jonathan Demme *(Melvin and Howard)*, making his first concert film, and essentially using the visuals of the Talking Heads rather than creating his own. Instead of the standard phony cutaways to the audience (phony because, nine times out of ten, the audience members are not actually reacting to the moment in the music that we're hearing), Demme keeps his cameras trained on the stage. And when Byrne and company use the stage-level lights to create a shadow play behind them, the result is surprisingly more effective than you might imagine: It's a live show with elements of *Metropolis*.

But the film's peak moments come through Byrne's simple physical presence. He jogs in place with his sidemen; he runs around the stage; he seems so happy to be alive and making music. Like Springsteen and Prince, he serves as a reminder of how sour and weary and strung-out many rock bands have become. Starting with Mick Jagger, rock concerts have become, for the performers, as much sporting events as musical and theatrical performances. *Stop Making Sense* understands that with great exuberance.

Stormy Monday ★ ★ ★ ½
R, 93 m., 1988

Melanie Griffith (Kate), Tommy Lee Jones (Cosmo), Sting (Finney), Sean Bean (Brendan). Directed by Mike Figgis and produced by Nigel Stafford-Clark. Screenplay by Figgis.

"Why is it," someone was asking the other day, "that you movie critics spend all of your time talking about the story, and never talk about the visual qualities of a film—which are, after all, what *make* it a film?" Good question. Maybe it's because we work in words, and stories are told in words, and it's harder to use words to paint pictures. But it might be worth a try.

Stormy Monday is about the way light falls on wet pavement stones, and about how a neon sign glows in a darkened doorway. It is about the attitudes that men strike when they feel in control of a situation, and the way their shoulders slump when someone else takes power. It is about smoking. It is about cleavage. It is about the look on a man's face when someone is about to deliberately break his arm, and he knows it. And about the look on a woman's face when she is waiting for a man she thinks she loves; he is late, and she fears it is because he is dead.

Stormy Monday is also about symbols. It takes place mostly near the seedy waterfront of Newcastle, where a crooked Texas millionaire is trying to run a nightclub owner out of business, so he can redevelop the area with laundered money. But now we're back to the story again. You see how easy it is to slip. The movie uses a lot of symbols of America: The flag, stretched large and bold behind a podium. Baton-twirlers. A curiously frightening old man with a sinister smile, who struts in front of the baton twirlers, his shoulders thrown back, tipping his hat to the crowd. A car—big, fast, and red. Bourbon whiskey. Marlboros and cigars.

It is also about lonely furnished rooms, and rain, and standing in the window at night looking out into the street, and signaling for someone across a crowded nightclub floor, and about saxophones, which are the instrument of the night. It is about the flat, masked expressions on the faces of bodyguards, and about the face of a man who is consumed by anger. And it is about kissing, and about the look in a woman's eyes when she is about to kiss a man for the first time. And it is about high heels, and cleavage. I believe I already mentioned cleavage. Some images reoccur more naturally than others.

The movie is not all images. It is also about sounds. About the breathy, rich, and yet uncertain tone of Melanie Griffith's voice, which makes her sound as if she's been around the track too many times, and yet is still able to believe in love. And the flat, angry voice of Tommy Lee Jones, who never seems to raise his voice, or need to. And about the innocence in the voice of Sean Bean, an earnest young man who only wants a job, and gets trapped in a bloodbath. And about the voice of Sting, who looks Jones in the eye and talks as flat and angry as he does, until Jones's shoulders slump. And about saxophones, the sound of the night.

It is also about the sound of a deliberately discordant performance of "The Star Spangled Banner," and about explosions and gunfire and squealing tires, and about modern jazz from Krakow. It is about the sound of ice cubes in a glass, and smoke being exhaled, and bones being broken. It is about the sound of a marching band, and about the voice of a disc jockey who wants to sound American and doesn't know when to stop. And about how a woman tells a man, "I get off work at midnight." And how she looks when she says that. And how he looks.

So there's your review.

Story of Women ★ ★ ½
R, 110 m., 1990

Isabelle Huppert (Marie), Francois Cluzet (Paul), Marie Trintignant (Lulu/Lucille), Nils Tavernier (Lucien), Aurore Gauvin (Mouche 1), Lolita Chammah (Mouche 2), Guillaume Foutrier (Pierrot 1), Nicolas Foutrier (Pierrot 2). Directed by Claude Chabrol and produced by Marin Karmitz. Screenplay by Colo Tavernier O'Hagan and Chabrol.

It is the unique ability of Isabelle Huppert to betray almost nothing to the camera, when she chooses to. Some of the best moments in her performances come when she regards the camera as if daring us to guess what she is thinking. This quality is indispensable to the character she plays in Claude Chabrol's *Story of Women*, because the story is based on the mystery of what she really thinks and feels.

The movie begins in 1941, in wartime France. She plays Marie, a poor woman with a drunken nobody of a husband. The lives of herself and her two small children are wretched. One day she barges into a neigh-

bor's apartment and finds the woman trying to perform an abortion upon herself. Marie knows a little about abortions—more than the neighbor, anyway—and assists her, using a different method. The abortion is successful and the woman gives her a present—a record player. Listening to the music on the player, Marie reflects that a clever woman need not be trapped by poverty.

The provincial French society around her looks thoroughly corrupt. Although a brave resistance is fighting somewhere, for many people the Nazi occupation has ushered in an era of collaboration and black-marketeering. Many of the men have gone off to take wartime jobs or even to fight for the Nazis. Most women, struggling to hold their families together in the face of poverty and the rationing of food and all consumer goods, have no desire for more babies. Yet wartime brings many pregnancies, some of them the result of liaisons while a woman's husband is far away. There is money to be made in abortion.

Marie is the kind of person who reacts so directly to events that you can never say she has a plan. She stumbles into being an abortionist for two reasons: there is a demand, and she can use the money. She moves into a better apartment. There is more food for her children. As nearly as we can tell, she never gives a moment's thought to whether what she is doing is right or wrong. It is illegal, but she doesn't give that a moment's thought, either.

One day she meets a former girlfriend who seems to be doing well. The woman is a prostitute. Marie is unconcerned. It is worth remembering that in many societies, until fairly recent decades, the only ways a lower-class woman could support herself economically were as a servant, a laborer, a religious, an actress, or a prostitute. Marie agrees to take care of any friends of the friend who may become pregnant. Clients materialize at her door. She moves into a still larger place, begins to buy some luxuries for herself and rents extra rooms to prostitutes.

Her husband is a problem. He makes no money and is generally useless, but he has his male pride, and Marie has no remaining sexual interest in him—she has taken a young collaborator as her lover. So she pays the maid to have an affair with her husband. We begin to see her pattern. She does what is necessary to save herself trouble and keep her income out of jeopardy.

Eventually the notoriety of her activities catches up with her, and she is arrested and

taken to Paris for a wartime show trial. Now her eyes are as blank as they were before. What does she feel? Guilt? Fear? Does she understand it will be necessary for the occupation government to make an example of her?

Claude Chabrol is one of the most prolific of active directors; he has made more than forty films, of a very wide range of quality, from masterpieces (*Le Boucher, This Man Must Die*) to whodunits and steamy melodramas. He is at his best where sex and crime intersect, and he is most fascinated by criminals who do not seem to relate emotionally to their own crimes (study the character of the murderer in *Le Boucher*). Huppert is the perfect actress for him.

The story he tells here, of an actual woman named Marie Latour, is well-known in France, where she was one of the last three women to receive the death penalty. The Latour case obviously fascinates Chabrol, perhaps because he does not know what her true motivations were. She began in poverty and was able to thrive and flourish under the Nazi occupation. She bought furs and kept a lover. She was not a "liberated woman" in any sense, and did not see her role as an abortionist as a brave or necessary one, but simply as a profitable and even inevitable route to a larger income. Nor did the government really see her as a criminal; the prosecution in the film is shown as devoid of moral outrage, but obsessed by the need to "set an example." The whole episode seems to have unfolded without anyone really feeling much of anything—anyone except, of course, for the family of a desperate mother of six who dies after one of Marie's abortions. Today the collaborationist government is reviled in France, abortion is legal and paid for by the government, and Marie Latour is dead. What is Chabrol's message? He does not say. His film is as opaque as his character. *Story of Women* is a morality play without a conclusion. We have to make up our own minds. Most movies on themes like this instruct us about how to think by portraying its characters as good or bad and casting them to seem attractive or otherwise. Chabrol does not make it so easy.

Straight Time ★ ★ ★ ½
R, 114 m., 1978

Dustin Hoffman (Max Dembo), Theresa Russell (Jenny Mercer), Harry Dean Stanton (Jerry Schue), Gary Busey (Willy Darin),

M. Emmet Walsh (Earl Frank), Sandy Baron (Manny). Directed by Ulu Grosbard and produced by Stanley Beck and Tim Zinnemann. Screenplay by Alvin Sargent, Edward Bunker, and Jeffrey Boam.

Straight Time is a great sleeper, a film good enough that we wonder why we didn't hear more about it. So does Dustin Hoffman, who sued Warner Brothers for what he considered the mishandling of the picture. He may have had a point; his performance here as Max Dembo, ex-con turned thief, is one of his very best.

Max gets out of prison determined to go straight. It's not easy. Under the conditions of his parole, for example, he can't take a job that involves the handling of money. But a girl in an employment office does find him a job, at a can company. And when he asks her out to dinner, she accepts. He also finds a room he can afford to rent, and so he's doing fairly well. He's on the road to personal rehabilitation, as his parole officer might put it. The parole officer (M. Emmet Walsh) is not, however, very good at the rehabilitation game. He's mean-spirited, suspicious, and sadistic, all behind a large, cynical smile. He busts Max on suspicion of drug use, causing him to lose his job—and that's enough for Max, who returns to the trade he knows best, theft.

Straight Time is based on a novel by an ex-con, and it feels authentic. What especially absorbs us is the way the movie projects the feeling of being a thief—the compulsion, the addiction, the rush of adrenaline, the fear. It's also good at explaining why this guy would be attractive to a girl, and especially the girl at the employment office.

She's played by Theresa Russell, who does a good job of projecting her feelings. She doesn't talk a lot, but she listens well, and she's drawn to the mysteries in Max's character. He wants to keep her out of his jobs but not out of his life, and she is eventually willing to settle for his terms.

Max pulls several jobs. He sticks up a grocery, for example, and then a pawnshop, where he gets the shotgun that will be useful in his stick-ups of a bank and a jewelry store. He enlists old buddies as his accomplices, and Harry Dean Stanton is especially good as an ex-con who almost succeeds in going straight. Stanton's got it all together: A house, a swimming pool, hamburgers grilled on the patio . . . but he can't resist the urgency of Max Dembo's sales pitch.

The robberies themselves have the same sense of manic desperation we felt in *Dog Day Afternoon*. And they have something else, as well: They project the feeling that Max Dembo, without admitting it even to himself, *wants* to get caught again. He lingers. He dawdles. His partner is calling out the number of seconds that have elapsed, as part of their plan to get out before the cops arrive. But Max Dembo isn't listening. Maybe that's part of the emotional payoff he needs, stretching a job to its last second, walking out the back door as the cops come in the front, taunting society while at the same time almost begging for punishment.

Hoffman's performance reminds me of his Ratso Rizzo in *Midnight Cowboy*, especially in his ways of telling the world to go to hell. Ratso was far gone on his own personal death trip, of course, and Max Dembo has whole moments when he rathers enjoys life. But they're similar in their moves, their choices. They belong outside society because it doesn't dare have places for them. Maybe *that's* what turns the girl on; maybe she has a sheltering instinct.

Straight Time exists so close to the drabness and desperation of its story that it might turn some people off. Hoffman must have known that; this is such a personal project that after he bought the original novel he planned to direct it himself before deciding, instead, on the Broadway and sometime movie director Ulu Grosbard. But Hoffman and Grosbard don't change details just to make their movie more palatable. Instead, they stick with Max Dembo, figuring him out, following his impulses, until those oddly disturbing final photographs—his mug shots—with the eyes suggesting that somehow this particular human being was *always* doomed.

Stranger than Paradise ★ ★ ★ ★
R, 90 m., 1984

John Lurie (Willie), Eszter Balint (Eva), Richard Edson (Eddie), Cecillia Stark (Aunt Lottie), Danny Rosen (Billy), Rammellzee (Man with Money), Tom Decillo (Airline Agent). Directed by Jim Jarmusch and produced by Sara Driver. Screenplay by Jarmusch.

Stranger than Paradise is filmed in a series of uninterrupted shots; the picture fades in, we watch the scene, and when the scene is over, there's a fade to black. Then comes the next fade-in. This is not a gim-mick, but a visual equivalent of the film's deadpan characters, who take a lot to get excited.

The movie's hero is Willie (John Lurie), who arrived on these shores from Hungary about ten years ago, and has spent the intervening decade perfecting his New York accent and trying to make nothing out of himself. He lives in an apartment where the linoleum is the highlight. On a good day, he'll sleep late, hang out, play a little poker. His cousin Eva arrives from Budapest. This is the last thing he needs, a sixteen-year-old girl who needs a place to stay. She hates him, too. But she has to kill some time before she goes to Cleveland to live with her aunt Lottie. She has good taste in American music, but not according to him. Willie's friend, Eddie, comes over occasionally and eyeballs Eva. Nothing much happens. She leaves for Cleveland.

The screen is filled with large letters: ONE YEAR LATER. This in itself is funny, that we'd get such a momentous time cue in a movie where who even knows what day it is. Eddie and Willie get in some trouble over a poker game and Eddie suddenly remembers Willie's cousin in Cleveland. They go to see her. It is cold in Cleveland. Eva has bought the American Dream and is working in a fast-food outlet. They all go to look at the lake, which is frozen. Aunt Lottie turns out to make Clara Peller look like Dame Peggy Ashcroft. The guys say to hell with it and head for Florida. Then they come back and get Eva and take her along with them. They have a postcard that makes Florida look like paradise, but they wind up living at one of those hotels where the permanent guests live in the woodwork. Everything goes sour. Eva wants to go back to Hungary. The guys lose all their money at the dog races. Creeps start hanging around. It will take a miracle to give this movie an upbeat ending. There is a miracle.

Stranger than Paradise is a treasure from one end to the other. I saw it for the first time at the 1984 Cannes Film Festival, where it was having its first public showing. Half the people in the theater probably didn't speak English, but that didn't stop them from giving the movie a standing ovation, and it eventually won the Camera d'Or prize for the best first film. It is like no other film you've seen, and yet you feel right at home in it. It seems to be going nowhere, and knows every step it wants to make. It is a constant, almost kaleidoscopic experience of discovery, and we try to figure out what the film is up to and it just keeps moving steadfastly ahead, fade in, fade out, fade in, fade out, making a mountain out of a molehill.

Strapless ★ ★ ★
R, 103 m., 1990

Blair Brown (Lillian Hempel), Bruno Ganz (Raymond Forbes), Hugh Laurie (Colin), Billy Roch (Gerry), Camille Coduri (Mrs. Clark), Gary O'Brien (Mr. Clark), Bridget Fonda (Amy Hempel), Spencer Leigh (Hus), Alan Howard (Mr. Cooper), Suzanne Burden (Romaine Salmon). Directed by David Hare and produced by Rick McCallum. Screenplay by Hare.

The most romantic passage in any relationship, I sometimes think, is just before you start beginning to know the other person. That person still remains an intriguing mystery, so you can project your desires and fantasies onto him or her: that person potentially represents everything you've been searching for. The other person, of course, is equally free to project fantasies upon your screen, and at some point in this process, the two people agree that they were destined for each other. Then the painful and difficult process of getting to know the other person begins, and destiny takes a holiday.

The opening scenes of David Hare's *Strapless* are poised at precisely such a moment in the relationship of two strangers: Lillian, an American nurse who has worked for several years in London, and Raymond, a mysterious stranger she meets while on holiday. They encounter each other in a church. Each is clearly intrigued. Raymond is the kind of man who seems able to anticipate just what a woman wants to hear, and to say it just before she knows she needs to hear it. Lillian, an independent and lonely woman, finds herself saying things she thought she'd never say again.

Back in London, life goes on. Lillian (Blair Brown) is involved in labor activities at the hospital, where the nursing staff opposes budget cuts by the Thatcher regime. At home, her life is complicated by the arrival of Amy, a younger sister (Bridget Fonda), who sleeps with a succession of boyfriends and makes vague plans to support herself as a dress designer. One day Amy tells Lillian she is pregnant and plans to have the baby—primarily, it would seem, in order to experience the wonders of going through natural childbirth while listening to Mozart.

Lillian is appalled by the irresponsibility of Amy's life, but she is also burdened by the responsibilities of her own; as the head of the strike committee, she spends long hours nursing and then additional hours in negotiations, and as an American she sometimes feels she is an outsider no matter what she does. Then Raymond (Bruno Ganz, the sad angel in *Wings of Desire*) comes back into her life. He has a home in London, it would seem. An expensive little house that is decorated in impeccable taste and filled with the most exquisite personal possessions.

Everything about Raymond speaks of money and taste. But who is he, really, and where does he come from? How does he make his money? Can Lillian trust him? These are questions that fade in the flame of their passion, but they need to be answered, and Raymond is clearly incapable of answering them. He is, in fact, incapable of any commitment at all, and the viewer begins to suspect that he is addicted to only the early stages of a relationship. He likes the intrigue of seduction, but not the messiness of love.

Strapless was written and directed by the playwright David Hare (*Plenty, A Map of the World*), who includes one perfect scene that explains Raymond without explaining him. I will not diminish the pleasure of the scene by describing it, except to say that it provides us with a glimpse of Raymond's past that makes us feel a particular sympathy for him, as we do for any wounded creature.

The title of the movie is referred to in a scene where the two sisters and some other women try on strapless gowns that Amy has designed, and Amy says, "They shouldn't stay up, but they do." Presumably David Hare is trying the same trick with the whole movie, suspending his characters and plot in the air without benefit of the usual structural supports. That works with the relationship between Raymond and Lillian, which must be an enigma in order to work at all. But the movie falters badly in its subplot about labor unions and industrial relations—it's as if Hare wanted to work some social commentary into a story that has no room for it.

Streamers ★ ★ ★ ★
R, 118 m., 1984

Matthew Modine (Billy), Michael Wright (Carlyle), Mitchell Lichtenstein (Richie), David Alan Grier (Roger), Guy Boyd (Rooney), George Dzundza (Cokes). Directed by Robert Altman and produced by Altman and Nick H. Mileti. Screenplay by David Rabe.

Robert Altman's *Streamers* is one of the most intense and intimate dramas I've ever seen on film. It's based on the play by David Rabe, about young soldiers waiting around a barracks for their orders to go to Vietnam. Most directors, faced with a play that takes place on one set, find ways to "open it up" and add new locations. Altman has moved in the opposite direction, taking advantage of the one-room set to tighten the play until it squeezes like a vise. Watching this film is such a demanding experience that both times I've seen it, it has been too much for some viewers, and they've left. Those who stay, who survive the difficult passages of violence, will find at the end of the film a conclusion that is so poetic and moving it succeeds in placing the tragedy in perspective.

It is the era of Vietnam. In a barracks somewhere, three young men wait for their orders. They are Billy, who is white and middle-class; Roger, who is black and middle-class; and Richie, a dreamy young man who likes to tease the others with hints that he is a homosexual. The only other occupants of the barracks are two drunken master sergeants, Rooney and Cokes, who are best friends and who are stumbling through idiotic revelry in an attempt to drown the realization that Cokes has leukemia. Into this little world comes Carlyle, an angry young black man who is gay, and whose conversations with Richie will lead the others into anger and denial before the situation finally explodes.

There are some surprises, but the developments in *Streamers* flow so naturally out of the material that its surprises should be left intact. A lot can be said, however, about the acting, Altman's direction, and Rabe's writing. I didn't see this play on stage and don't know how it worked there, but Altman is so completely the visual master of this material that we're drawn into that barracks room and into its rhythms of boredom, drunkenness, and passion.

The actors are all unknown to me, except for George Dzundza, who plays Cokes. They are all so natural that the dialogue has an eerie double quality: We know it's written dialogue because it has a poetry and a drama unlikely in life, but Rabe's ear is so accurate it sounds real, and the performers make it so convincing there's never a false note. The two key performances are by Mitchell Lichtenstein, as Richie, and Michael Wright, as Carlyle. Richie is indeed homosexual, as we realize long before his barracks mates are willing to acknowledge it. He likes to tease the others with insinuations that they may be gay, too. Billy boasts that he is straight, but he protests too much. Roger tries to be a peacekeeper. Then Carlyle wanders in from another unit. He is drunk and angry, collapses, sleeps it off, blearily looks around, figures out Richie, and tries to make a connection.

But there is a lot more going on here than sexual competition. *Streamers* uses both sex and race as foreground subjects while the movie's real subject, war, hovers in the background and in several extraordinary monologues—one about snakes, one about a battle, and one about the realities of parachuting. As the veteran master sergeants make their drunken way through the movie, they drop these hard realities into the lives of the unseasoned kids. And when anger turns to violence and a tragedy occurs, it is up to one of the fat old guys (Dzundza) to deliver a monologue that is one of the most revealing, intimate, honest, and moving speeches I've ever heard.

Street Smart ★ ★ ★
R, 97 m., 1987

Christopher Reeve (Jonathan Fisher), Mimi Rogers (Alison Parker), Morgan Freeman (Fast Black), Kathy Baker (Punchy). Directed by Jerry Schatzberg and produced by Menahem Golan and Yoram Globus. Screenplay by David Freeman.

Sometimes you run across a movie that's far from perfect and yet it contains things that are so good they take your breath away. *Street Smart* is a movie like that—a clever thriller with a lot of unbelievable scenes and a sappy ending, but two wonderful performances.

The performances are by Morgan Freeman, as a Times Square pimp, and by Kathy Baker, as one of the hookers he controls. They play their characters as well as I can imagine them being played. Freeman has the flashier role—as a smart, very tough man who can be charming or intimidating—whatever's needed. Baker is a small-town girl who has been a hooker for years, who lives by the rules of the street but still has feelings.

Surrounding their performances is a plot that would have been interesting if it had been handled more realistically. Christopher Reeve plays a magazine reporter who concocts a completely fictional story about a colorful pimp. After the story is published and creates a sensation, the district attorney becomes convinced that the subject of the story is really the Freeman character—who is on trial for murder. He subpoenas Reeve's notes, but of course there aren't any.

From this promising beginning, *Street Smart* takes its story in two different directions. On one hand, we get a satirical view of the New York publishing and television industries, with André Gregory as the cynical magazine publisher and Reeve as an overnight journalism star who is instantly hired as a TV street reporter. On the other hand, we get Reeve trying to cover his tracks by going back and doing the reporting he should have done in the first place.

This second story—which involves Freeman and Baker—is much more interesting than the first. The pimp quickly figures out Reeve's problem and offers him a deal: He'll agree that he was the subject of the fictional story if Reeve provides him with an alibi. Reeve refuses. Freeman turns dangerous and violent: He's facing a life sentence and, for him, this isn't a matter of ethics but of his life.

The second hour of *Street Smart* almost seems to be scenes from two different movies. Freeman's dialogue is particularly good, as he analyzes Reeve's motives, talks about people who condescend to him, and terrorizes Baker for becoming Reeve's friend. There is one powerful, frightening scene where he threatens her with scissors; the power on the screen reminded me of vintage De Niro or Pacino.

Many of the street scenes have the uncanny feeling of real life, closely observed. For example, look at the scene where Freeman and his sidekick take Reeve for a tour of the streets in their Cadillac. When Freeman decides to discipline one of his girls, he squeezes her into the front seat, too, so Reeve is forced to confront reality up close, and maybe get blood on his suit. The staging of this scene—four people all in the front seat—is what makes it work.

The movie's other story, the one involving the magazine and TV news, is sort of silly. It's impossible to believe Reeve would so quickly become a TV newsman, difficult to believe most of the stories he reports, and incredible that Baker somehow always knows exactly where, in all of Manhattan,

Reeve is going to be doing his next remote TV report.

The end of the movie is also a disappointment. It's yet another shoot-out. Screenwriters have grown so lazy in recent years that it's almost too much to ask them to resolve a plot on human terms. The last reel of most thrillers now involves the obligatory death of the villain, as if death were a solution. Since we know that's how the movie will end, the last reel is a loss—a waste of the movie's own time. And in *Street Smart* where Freeman creates such an unforgettable villain, I really resented it when he wasn't given the chance to participate in his own fate.

As a film school exercise, would-be screenwriters should be required to rewrite thrillers like this, with real human endings instead of the out of the standard sequence: chase, shoot-out, death, fade out. When an actor like Freeman goes to the trouble of creating a great character, the film should go to the trouble of providing him with a final scene.

Streetwise ★ ★ ★ ★
R, 92 m., 1985

Directed by Martin Bell and produced by Cheryl McCall. Reported by Mary Ellen Mark.

The mother is being frank about her daughter. She says she knows the girl is working as a prostitute, but she figures "it's just a phase she's going through." Her daughter is about fifteen years old. That is not the most harrowing moment in *Streetwise*, a heartbreaking documentary about the street children of Seattle. There are worse moments, for example the one where a street kid tries to talk to her mother about the fact that her stepfather "was fooling around . . . doing perverted things with me" when she was a baby. "Yes," says the mother philosophically, "but now he's stopped."

The subject of runaway, abducted, and abandoned children has received a lot of attention in the news, but never anything remotely like *Streetwise*, which enters into the lives of these underage survivors as they fight for life and love on the streets of Seattle. The movie was inspired by a *Life* magazine article on a group of the kids, who, at an age when other kids are in school, are learning to be hookers, thieves, con men, pushers, and junkies. Now comes this movie, which contains extraordinary everyday footage, which the filmmakers obtained by spending months hanging out with the kids, until they gained their trust and their cameras became accepted.

The street kids lead horrifying lives, but sometimes there are moments of acceptance and happiness. They cling to each other. They relate uneasily with a social worker who seems philosophically resigned to the facts of street life. They try to dodge the cops. They live in an abandoned hotel, get money by begging and prostitution, eat by raiding the dumpsters behind restaurants. They even have a system for marking garbage so they don't eat food that's too old.

What is amazing is that some of these kids are still in touch with their parents. One girl shrugs that her mother is off to the woods for a weekend: "I've always known she don't love me or shit. So OK." She hugs herself. Another girl tries to talk to her mother, who says, "Be quiet. I'm drinking." A kid named DeWayne goes to visit his father in prison and gets a long lecture about smoking, drinking, and taking drugs, and a pie-in-the-sky speech about how they're going to open a thrift shop when the old man gets out of prison. The next time we see DeWayne, it is at his funeral; he hanged himself in a jail cell.

You walk out of *Streetwise* realizing that these aren't bad kids. They are resourceful, tough, and true to their own standards. They break the law, but then how many legal ways are there for fourteen-year-olds to support themselves? They talk about their parents in a matter-of-fact way that, we suspect, covers up great wounds, as when one girl says she's never met her natural father— "unless maybe I dated him once."

Streetwise is surprising for the frankness of the material it contains. How did the filmmakers get these people to say these things, to allow the cameras into their lives? We see moments of intimacy, of violence, of pain. The answer, I suspect, is that a lot of these kids were so starving for attention and affection that by offering both, the filmmakers were able to get whatever they wanted. Some of the scenes are possibly staged, in the sense that the characters are aware they are in a movie, but none of the scenes are false or contrived. These are children living rough in an American city, and you would blame their parents if you didn't see that the parents are just as alienated and hopeless, and that before long these kids will be damaged parents, too.

Stripes ★ ★ ★ ¹/₂
R, 105 m., 1981

Bill Murray (John), Harold Ramis (Russell), Warren Oates (Sergeant Hulka), P.J. Soles (Stella), Sean Young (Louise), John Candy (Ox). Directed by Ivan Reitman and produced by Reitman and Dan Goldberg. Screenplay by Goldberg, Len Blum, and Harold Ramis.

Stripes is an anarchic slob movie, a celebration of all that is irreverent, reckless, foolhardy, undisciplined, and occasionally scatological. It's a lot of fun. It comes from some of the same people involved in *National Lampoon's Animal House*, and could have been titled *National Lampoon's Animal Army* with little loss of accuracy. As a comedy about a couple of misfits who find themselves in the U.S. Army's basic training program, it obviously resembles Goldie Hawn's *Private Benjamin*. But it doesn't duplicate that wonderful movie; they could play on the same double feature. *Stripes* has the added advantage of being a whole movie about the Army, rather than half a movie (*Private Benjamin* got sidetracked with Hawn's love affair).

The movie is not only a triumph for its stars (Bill Murray and Harold Ramis) and its director (Ivan Reitman), but a sort of vindication. To explain: Reitman directed, and Murray starred in, the enormously successful *Meatballs*, which was an entertaining enough comedy but awfully ragged. No wonder. It was shot on a shoestring with Canadian tax-shelter money. What Murray and Reitman prove this time is that, given a decent budget, they can do superior work—certainly superior to *Meatballs*, for starters. For Harold Ramis, who plays Murray's grave-eyed, flat-voiced, terminally detached partner in *Stripes*, this is a chance, at last, to come out from behind the camera. Ramis and Murray are both former Second City actors, but in Hollywood, Ramis has been typecast as a writer *(Animal House, Meatballs, Caddyshack)*, maybe because he sometimes looks too goofy for Hollywood's unimaginative tastes.

In *Stripes*, Murray and Ramis make a wonderful team. Their big strength is restraint. Given the tendency of movies like this to degenerate into undisciplined slapstick, they wisely choose to play their characters as understated, laid-back anarchists. Murray enlists in the Army in a what-the-hell mood after his girlfriend throws him out, and Ramis enlists because one stupid gesture deserves another. They're older than the usual Army recruit, less easily impressed with gung-ho propaganda, and quietly amazed at their drill instructor, Sergeant Hulka, who is played by Warren Oates with tough-as-nails insanity.

The movie has especially good writing in several scenes. My favorite comes near the beginning, during a session when recruits in the new platoon get to know one another. One obviously psycho draftee, who looks like Robert De Niro, quietly announces that if his fellow soldiers touch him, touch his stuff, or interfere in any way with his person or his privacy, he will quite simply be forced to kill them. Sergeant Hulka replies: "Lighten up!"

The movie's plot follows basic training, more or less, during its first hour. Then a romance enters. Murray and Ramis meet a couple of cute young military policewomen (P.J. Soles and Sean Young), and they happily violate every rule in the book. One funny scene: Murray and Soles sneak into the kitchen of the base commander's house and do unprecedented things with kitchen utensils.

It's an unwritten law of these movies that the last half hour has to involve some kind of spectacular development. In *Animal House*, it was the homecoming parade. In *Stripes*, the climax involves the Army's latest secret weapon, which is a computerized, armored, nuclear weapons carrier disguised as a recreational vehicle. Murray's platoon is assigned to go to Europe and test it. Murray, Ramis, and their girls decide to test it during a weekend holiday swing through the Alps. After they inadvertently cross the Iron Curtain, all hell breaks loose.

Stripes is a complete success on its intended level—it's great, irreverent entertainment—but it was successful, too, as a breakthrough for Ramis, Reitman, and Murray, on their way to *Ghostbusters*. Comedy is one of the hardest film genres to work in. Nobody knows all its secrets, not even Woody Allen and Mel Brooks. Here's a comedy from people who know some of the secrets most of the time.

Stroszek ★ ★ ★ ★
NO MPAA RATING, 108 m., 1978

Bruno S. (Stroszek), Eva Mattes (Eva), Clement Scheitz (Scheitz), Wilhelm von Homburg (Pimp), Burkhard Dreist (Pimp), Clayton Szlapinski (Scheitz's Nephew), Ely Rodriguez (Indian). Directed, produced, and written by Werner Herzog.

Werner Herzog has subtitled *Stroszek* as "a ballad," and so it is: It's like one of those bluegrass nonsense ballads in which impossible adventures are described in every verse, and the chorus reminds us that life gets teedjus, don't it? But because Herzog has one of the most original imaginations of anyone now making movies, *Stroszek* is a haunting and hilarious ballad at the same time, an almost unbelievable mixture of lunacy, comedy, tragedy, and the simply human.

Consider. He gives us three main characters who are best friends, despite the fact that they're improbable as people and impossible as friends. There's Stroszek himself, just released from prison in Germany. He's a simple soul who plays the piano and the accordion and never quite understands why people behave as they do. There's Eva, a dim but pleasant Berlin prostitute. And there's old Scheitz, a goofy soul in his seventies who has been invited to live with his nephew in upstate Wisconsin.

This mixture is further complicated by the fact that Stroszek is played by Bruno S., the same actor Herzog used in *Kaspar Hauser.* Bruno S. is a mental patient, described by Herzog as schizophrenic, and it's a good question whether he's "acting" in this movie or simply exercising a crafty survival instinct. No matter: He comes across as saintly, sensitive, and very strange.

The three friends meet when Eva's two pimps beat her up and throw her out. She comes to live with Stroszek. The pimps (evil hoods right out of a Fassbinder gangster movie) later visit Stroszek and Eva and beat them both up, leaving Stroszek kneeling on his beloved piano with a school bell balanced on his derriere.

It is clearly time to leave Berlin, and old Scheitz has the answer: Visit his relatives in America. The nephew lives on a Wisconsin farm in an incredibly barren landscape, but to the Germans it's the American Dream. They buy an enormous mobile home, seventy feet long and fully furnished, and install a color TV in it. Eva gets a job as a waitress, and turns some tricks on the side at the truck stop. Stroszek works as a mechanic, sort of. Old Scheitz wanders about testing the "animal magnetism" of fence posts.

The Wisconsin scenes are among the weirdest I've ever seen in a movie: Notice, for example, the visit Stroszek and Eva get from that supercilious little twerp from the bank, who wants to repossess their TV set and who never seems to understand that

nothing he says is understood. Or notice the brisk precision with which an auctioneer disposes of the mobile home, which is then carted away, all seventy feet of it, leaving the bewildered Stroszek looking at the empty landscape it has left behind.

Stroszek gets most hypnotically bizarre as it goes along, because we understand more of the assumptions of the movie. One of them is possibly that Kaspar Hauser might have become Stroszek, had he lived for another century and studied diligently. (Hauser, you might remember, was the "wild child" kept imprisoned in the dark for nineteen years, never taught to speak, and then dumped in a village square.)

The film's closing scenes are wonderfully funny and sad, at once. Stroszek and Scheitz rob a barber shop, and then Stroszek buys a frozen turkey, and then there is an amusement park with a chicken that will not stop dancing (and a policeman reporting "The dancing chicken won't stop"), and a wrecker driving in a circle with no one at the wheel, and an Indian chief looking on impassively, and somehow Herzog has made a statement about America here that is as loony and utterly original as any ever made.

Sudden Impact ★ ★ ★
R, 117 m., 1983

Clint Eastwood (Harry Callahan), Sondra Locke (Jennifer Spencer), Pat Hingle (Chief Jannings), Bradford Dillman (Captain Briggs). Directed and produced by Clint Eastwood. Screenplay by Joseph C. Stinson.

Most of what you hear about pop art and pop culture is pure hype. But there comes a moment about halfway through *Sudden Impact*, a Dirty Harry movie, when you realize that Harry has achieved some kind of legitimate pop status, as the purest distillation in the movies of the spirit of vengeance. To all those cowboy movies we saw in our youth, all those TV westerns and cop dramas and war movies, Dirty Harry has brought a great simplification: A big man, a big gun, a bad guy, and instant justice.

We learned early to cheer when John Wayne shot the bad guys. We cheered when the cavalry turned up, or the Yanks, or the SWAT team. What Eastwood's Dirty Harry movies do is very simple. They reduce the screen time between those cheers to the absolute minimum. *Sudden Impact* is a Dirty

Harry movie with only the good parts left in. All the slow stuff, such as character, motivation, atmosphere, and plot, has been pared to exactly the minimum necessary to hold together the violence. This movie has been edited with the economy of a thirty-second commercial. As a result, it's a great audience picture. It's not plausible, it doesn't make much sense, it has a cardboard villain and, for that matter, a hero who exists more as a set of functions (grin, fight, chase, kill) than as a human being. But none of those are valid objections. *Sudden Impact* is more like a music video; it consists only of setups and payoffs, its big scenes are self-contained, it's filled with kinetic energy, and it has a short attention span. That last is very important, because if anyone were really keeping track of what Callahan does in this movie, Harry would be removed from the streets after his third or fourth killing. Dirty Harry movies are like Roadrunner cartoons; the moment a body is dead, it is forgotten, and nobody stands around to dispose of the corpses.

The movie's basically a revenge tragedy. A young woman (Sondra Locke) and her sister are sexually attacked at a carnival by a group of quasi-human bullies. The sister goes nuts, and Locke vows vengeance. One by one, she tracks down the rapists, and murders them by shooting them in the genitals and forehead. Dirty Harry gets assigned to the case, and the rest is a series of violent confrontations. Occasionally there's comic relief, in the form of Harry's meetings with his superiors, and his grim-jawed putdowns of anyone who crosses his path. ("Suck fish heads," he helpfully advises one man.)

If the movie has a weakness, it's the plot. Because I'm not sure the plot is relevant to the success of the film, I'm not sure that's a weakness. The whole business of Locke's revenge is so mechanically established and carried out that it's automatic, and because she has a "good" motive for her murders, she doesn't make an interesting villain. If Eastwood could create a villain as single-minded, violent, economically chiseled, and unremittingly efficient as Dirty Harry Callahan, then we'd be onto something.

Sunday Bloody Sunday ★ ★ ★ ★
R, 110 m., 1971

Glenda Jackson (Alex Greville), Peter Finch (Dr. Daniel Hirsh), Murray Head (Bob Elkin), Peggy Ashcroft (Mrs. Greville), Tony Britton (Businessman), Maurice Denham (Mr. Greville). Directed by John Schlesinger and produced by Joseph Janni. Screenplay by Penelope Gilliatt.

The official East Coast line on John Schlesinger's *Sunday Bloody Sunday* was that it is civilized. That judgment was enlisted to carry the critical defense of the movie; and, indeed, how can the decent critic be against a civilized movie about civilized people? My notion, all the same, is that *Sunday Bloody Sunday* is about people who suffer from psychic amputation, not civility, and that this film is not an affirmation but a tragedy.

The story involves three people in a rather novel love triangle: A London doctor in his forties, a divorced woman in her thirties, and the young man they are both in love with. The doctor and the woman know about each other (the young man makes no attempt to keep secrets) but don't seem particularly concerned; they have both made an accommodation in order to have some love instead of none at all.

The screenplay by Penelope Gilliatt takes us through eight or nine days in their lives, while the young man prepares to leave for New York. Both of his lovers will miss him—and he will miss *them*, after his fashion—but he has decided to go, and between them, they don't have enough pull on him to make him want to stay. So the two love affairs approach their ends, while the lovers go about a melancholy daily existence in London.

Both the doctor and the woman are involved in helping people, he by a kind and intelligent approach to his patients, she through working in an employment agency. The boy, on the other hand, seems exclusively preoccupied with the commercial prospects in America for his sculpture (he does things with glass tubes, liquids, and electricity). He isn't concerned with whether his stuff is any good, but whether it will sell to Americans. He doesn't seem to feel very deeply about anything, in fact. He is kind enough and open enough, but there is no dimension to him, as there is to his lovers.

It is with the two older characters that we get to the core of the movie. In a world where everyone loses eventually, they are still survivors. They survive by accommodating themselves to life as it must be lived. The doctor, for example, is not at all personally disturbed by his homosexuality, and yet he doesn't reveal it to his close-knit Jewish family; maintaining relations-as-usual with them is another way for him to survive. The woman tells us late in the film, "Some people believe something is better than nothing, but I'm beginning to believe that nothing can be better than something." Well, maybe so, but we get to know her well enough to suspect that she will settle for something, not nothing, again the next time.

The glory of *Sunday Bloody Sunday* is supposed to be the intelligent, sophisticated—civilized!—way in which these two people gracefully accept the loss of a love they had shared. Well, they *are* graceful as hell about it, and there is a positive glut of being philosophical about the inevitable. But that didn't make me feel better for them, or about them, the way it was supposed to; I felt pity for them. I insist that they would *not* have been so bloody civilized if either one had felt really deeply about the boy. The fact that they were willing to share him is perhaps a clue: They shared him not because they were willing to settle for half, but because they were afraid to try for all. The three-sided arrangement was, in part, a guarantee that no one would get in so deep that being "civilized" wouldn't be protection enough against hurt.

The acting is flawless. Peter Finch is the doctor, Glenda Jackson the woman, and Murray Head the young man. They are good to begin with and then just right for Gilliatt's screenplay and Schlesinger's direction. They are set down in a very real and sad London (seen mostly in cold twilights), and surrounded by supporting actors who resonate in a way that fills in all the dimensions of the characters. I think *Sunday Bloody Sunday* is a masterpiece, but I don't think it's about what everybody else seems to think it's about. This is not a movie about the loss of love, but about its absence.

Superman ★ ★ ★ ★
PG, 144 m., 1978

Christopher Reeve (Superman/Clark Kent), Marlon Brando (Jor-El), Gene Hackman (Lex Luthor), Margot Kidder (Lois Lane), Ned Beatty (Otis), Jackie Cooper (Perry White), Glenn Ford (Jonathan Kent), Trevor Howard (First Elder), Valerie Perrine (Miss Teschmacher). Directed by Richard Donner and produced by Pierre Spengler. Screenplay by Mario Puzo, David Newman, Leslie Newman, and Robert Benton.

Superman is a pure delight, a wondrous combination of all the old-fashioned things we never really get tired of: adventure and romance, heroes and villains, earthshaking special effects, and—you know what else? Wit. That surprised me more than anything: That this big-budget epic, which was half a decade making its way to the screen, would turn out to have an intelligent sense of humor about itself.

The wit, to be sure, is a little slow in revealing itself. The film's opening scenes combine great intergalactic special effects with ponderous acting and dialogue—most of it from Marlon Brando, who, as Superman's father, sends the kid to Earth in a spaceship that barely survives the destruction of the planet Krypton. Brando was allegedly paid $3 million for his role, or, judging by his dialogue, $500,000 a cliché. After Superbaby survives his space flight and lands in a Midwestern wheat field, however, the movie gets down to earth, too. And it has the surprising ability to have *fun* with its special effects. That's surprising because special effects on this vast scale (falling airliners, derailing passenger trains, subterranean dungeons, cracks in the earth, volcanic eruptions, dams bursting) are so expensive and difficult that it takes a special kind of courage to kid them a little—instead of regarding them with awe, as in the witless *Earthquake.*

The audience finds itself pleasantly surprised, and taken a little off guard; the movie's tremendously exciting in a comic book sort of way (kids will go ape for it), but at the same time it has a sly sophistication, a kidding insight into the material, that makes it, amazingly, a refreshingly offbeat comedy.

Most of the humor centers, of course, around one of the central icons of American popular culture, Superman (who, and I quote from our common memory of hundreds of comic books and radio and TV shows, in his dual identity as Clark Kent is a mild-mannered reporter for the *Daily Planet*). The producers held a worldwide talent search for an actor to play Superman, and although "talent searches" are usually 100 percent horsefeathers, this time, for once, they actually found the right guy.

He is Christopher Reeve. He *looks* like the Superman in the comic books (a fate I would not wish on anybody), but he's also an engaging actor, open and funny in his big love scene with Lois Lane, and then correctly awesome in his showdown with the archvillain Lex Luthor. Reeve sells the role; wrong casting here would have sunk everything.

And there would have been a lot to sink. *Superman* may have been expensive, all right, but the money's there on the screen. The screenplay was obviously written without the slightest concern for how much it might cost. After Clark Kent goes to work for the *Daily Planet* (and we meet old favorites Perry White, Lois Lane, and Jimmy Olsen), there's a nonstop series of disasters just for openers: Poor Lois finds herself dangling from one seatbelt after her helicopter crashes high atop the Daily Planet Building; Air Force One is struck by lightning and loses an engine; a thief climbs up a building using suction cups, and so on. Superman resolves his emergencies with, well, tact and good manners. He's modest about his abilities. Snaps a salute to the president. Says he's for "truth, justice, and the American Way." And, of course, falls in love with Lois Lane.

She's played by Margot Kidder, and their relationship is subtly, funnily wicked. She lives in a typical girl reporter's apartment (you know, a penthouse high atop a Metropolis skyscraper), and Superman zooms down to offer an exclusive interview and a free flight over Metropolis. Supposing *you're* a girl reporter, and Superman turns up. What would you ask him? So does she.

Meanwhile, the evil Lex Luthor (Gene Hackman) is planning an apocalyptic scheme to destroy the entire West Coast, plus Hackensack, New Jersey. He knows Superman's weak point: the deadly substance Kryptonite. He also knows that Superman cannot see through lead (Lois Lane, alas, forgets). Luthor lives in a subterranean pad that's a comic inspiration: A half-flooded, subterranean train station. Superman drills through the earth for a visit.

But enough of the plot. The movie works so well because of its wit and its special effects. A word more about each. The movie begins with the tremendous advantage that almost everyone in the audience knows the Superman saga from youth. There aren't a lot of explanations needed; that's brilliantly demonstrated in the first scene where Superman tries to change in a phone booth. Christopher Reeve can be allowed to smile, to permit himself a double entendre, to kid himself.

And then the special effects. They're as good in their way as any you've seen, and they come thick and fast. When the screenplay calls for Luthor to create an earthquake and for Superman to try to stop it, the movie doesn't give us a falling bridge or two, it gives us the San Andreas Fault cracking open. No half measures for Superman. The movie is, in fact, a triumph of imagination over both the difficulties of technology and the inhibitions of money. *Superman* wasn't easy to bring to the screen, but the filmmakers kept at it until they had it right.

Superman II ★ ★ ★ ★
PG, 127 m., 1981

Christopher Reeve (Superman/Clark Kent), Gene Hackman (Lex Luthor), Ned Beatty (Otis), Margot Kidder (Lois Lane), Terence Stamp (General Zod), Jackie Cooper (Perry White), Sarah Douglas (Ursa), Jack O'Halloran (Non), Valerie Perrine (Eve). Directed by Richard Lester and produced by Alexander and Ilya Salkind and Pierre Spengler. Screenplay by Mario Puzo, David Newman, and Leslie Newman.

I thought the original *Superman* was terrific entertainment—and so I was a little startled to discover that I liked *Superman II* even more. Perhaps the secret of the sequel is that it has more faith in Superman. Before the original *Superman* was released in 1978, the producers knew he could carry a speeding locomotive, all right—but could he carry a movie? They weren't sure, and since they were investing millions of dollars in the project, they didn't want to rest a whole movie on the broad shoulders of their unknown star, Christopher Reeve. So they began *Superman* ponderously, on the planet Krypton, with the presence of Marlon Brando as a sort of totem to convince audiences that this movie was big league. They told us of Superman's origins with a solemnity more befitting a

god. They were very serious and very symbolic, and it wasn't until Superman came to Earth that the movie really caught fire. *Then*, half an hour or more into its length, it started giving us what we came for: Superman flying around with his red cape, saving mankind.

Superman II begins in midstream, and never looks back (aside from a brief recap of the first movie). In many ways, it's a repeat of the last ninety minutes of the first film. It has the same key characters, including archvillain Lex Luthor. It continues the love story of Lois Lane and Superman, not to mention the strange relationship of Lois and Clark Kent. It features the return of three villains from Krypton, who when last seen were trapped in a one-dimensional plane of light and cast adrift in space. And it continues those remarkable special effects.

From his earliest days in a comic book, Superman always has been an urban hero. He lived in a universe that was defined by screaming banner headlines and vast symbolic acts, and *Superman II* catches that flavor perfectly with its use of famous landmarks like the Eiffel Tower, the Empire State Building, Niagara Falls, and the Coca-Cola sign in Times Square. He was a pop hero in a pop world, and like Mickey Mouse and the original Coke trademark, he became an instantly recognizable trademark.

That's why the special effects in both *Superman* movies are so crucial. It is a great deal simpler to show a rocket ship against the backdrop of outer space than to show Kryptonian villains hurling a city bus through the air in midtown Manhattan. But the feeling of actuality makes Superman's exploits more fun. It brings the fantastic into our everyday lives; it delights in showing us the reaction of the man on the street to Superman's latest stunt. In the movie, as in the comic book, ordinary citizens seem to spend their days glued to the sidewalk, gazing skyward, and shouting things like "Superman is dead!" or "Superman has saved the world!"

In *Superman II* he saves large portions of the world, all right, but what he preserves most of all is the element of humanity within him. The *Superman* movies made a basic decision to give Superman and his alter ego, Clark Kent, more human feelings than the character originally possessed. So *Superman II* has a lot of fun developing his odd dual relationship with Lois Lane. At long, long last, Lois and Superman make love in this movie (after champagne, but discreetly off-screen in Superman's ice palace). But Lois and Clark Kent also spend the night together in highly compromised circumstances, in a Niagara Falls honeymoon haven. And the movie has fun with another one of those ultimate tests that Lois was always throwing at Clark to make him admit he was really Superman. Lois bets her life on it this time, hurling herself into the rapids below Niagara Falls. Either Clark can turn into Superman and save her—or she'll drown. And what then? All I can say is, Clark does *not* turn into Superman.

This scene has a lot of humor in it, and the whole film has more smiles and laughs than the first one. Maybe that's because of a change in directors. Richard Donner, who made the first *Superman* film and did a brilliant job of establishing a basic look for the series, was followed this time by Richard Lester *(A Hard Day's Night, The Three Musketeers)*, and this is some of Lester's best work. He permits satire to make its way into the film more easily. He has a lot of fun with Gene Hackman, as the still-scheming, thinskinned, egomaniacal Lex Luthor. And he draws out Christopher Reeve, whose performance in the title role is sly, knowing, and yet still appropriately square. This movie's most intriguing insight is that Superman's disguise as Clark Kent isn't a matter of looks as much as of mental attitude: Clark is disguised not by his glasses but by his ordinariness. Beneath his meek exterior, of course, is concealed a superhero. And, the movie subtly hints, isn't that the case with us all?

Superman III ★ ★ ½
PG, 125 m., 1983

Christopher Reeve (Superman/Clark Kent), Richard Pryor (Gus Gorman), Annette O'Toole (Lana Lang), Robert Vaughn (Ross Webster). Directed by Richard Lester and produced by Alexander Salkind. Screenplay by David and Leslie Newman.

Superman III is the kind of movie I feared the original *Superman* would be. It's a cinematic comic book, shallow, silly, filled with stunts and action, without much human interest. What's amazing is that the first two *Superman* movies avoided that description, creating a fantasy with a certain charm. They could have been manipulative special-effects movies, but they were a great deal more. With this third one, maybe they've finally run out of inspiration.

The big news about *Superman III* is, of

course, the presence of Richard Pryor in the cast. But Pryor isn't used very well here. He never really emerges as a person we care about. His character and the whole movie seem assembled out of prefabricated pieces. The first two films were too, in a way, but real care was taken with the dialogue, and we could occasionally halfway believe that real people had gotten themselves into this world of fantasy. Not this time. *Superman III* drops most of the threads of the first two movies—including Lois Lane's increasingly complex love affair with Clark Kent and Superman—and goes for the action. There's no real sense of what Superman, or Clark, ever really feels. The running gag about the hero's double identity isn't really exploited this time. The sheer amazingness of Superman isn't explored; the movie and the people in it take this incredible creature for granted. After the bird and the plane, it's "Superman" when it should be SUPERMAN!

The plot involves the usual scheme to control the Earth. The villain this time is Robert Vaughn, as a mad billionaire who wants to use satellites to control the Earth's crops and become even richer. He directs his satellites and weapons systems by computer, and that's how he hooks up with Pryor, as a brilliant, but befuddled, computer programmer. Superman, meanwhile, has a couple of things on his mind. After Lois Lane leaves to go on vacation at the beginning of the movie (in a particularly awkward scene), Clark goes home to his Smallville High School reunion, and has a love affair with Lana Lang (Annette O'Toole). It's sweet, but it's not half as interesting as the Ice Castle footage with Lois Lane in *Superman II*. Then Superman gets zapped with some ersatz Kryptonite and turns into a meanie, which is good for some laughs (as a practical joke, he straightens the Leaning Tower of Pisa).

All of this is sort of fun, and the special effects are sometimes very good, but there's no real sense of wonder in this film—no moments like the scene in *Superman* where California threatened to fall into the sea and Superman turned back time to save humanity. After that, who cares about Robert Vaughn's satellites? Or Richard Pryor's dilemma? Pryor can be a wicked, anarchic comic actor, and that presence would have been welcome here. Instead, like the rest of *Superman III*, he's kind of innocuous.

Superstar: The Life and Times of Andy Warhol ★ ★ ★
NO MPAA RATING, 87 m., 1991

A documentary with interviews given by Andy Warhol and featuring commentary by Holly Woodlawn, Dennis Hopper, Grace Jones, Ultra Violet, Viva, David Hockney, and Roy Lichtenstein. Directed, produced, and written by Chuck Workman.

The one thing everyone knows about Andy Warhol is that he once said that, in the future, everyone would be famous for fifteen minutes. This is the sort of news people like to hear. Warhol himself was a grand master of publicity, remaking himself into one of the most famous people in the world by always presenting the same face—an unchanging blank bored cipher—which he turned faithfully upon more people at more parties than anyone else in the history of New York City.

He was the master of the nonconversation, the nonreply, the verbal put down. Legions of journalists turned up to interview him, and, of course, he was always willing to be interviewed, but he never *said* anything. "Yes." "No." "I don't know." Those answers were his faithful servants, and when the desperate interviewer supplied an answer or a theory of his own, Warhol would nod and say, "That's right." Or maybe simply "yes." Sometimes, if it could not be avoided, "no."

His management of the media was, of course, an exercise in passive aggression. The more he seemed not to care, the more he intrigued people. The less he sought publicity, the more of it he attracted. And, of course, there was a method to his vagueness. He worked tirelessly to put himself into places where he could experience indifference; he never missed an opportunity to be bored.

The result of his lifelong image-construction is that there is precious little of Andy Warhol onscreen in Chuck Workman's *Superstar: The Life and Times of Andy Warhol*. And there is not a single moment of personal revelation; a single frame of film in which Andy lets his guard down. He is a pale, blank, monosyllabic, unresponsive presence, and yet the strange thing is, the film succeeds despite that. And it succeeds on his terms, by making us pay attention to him without revealing any of his secrets.

Or perhaps we learn a few. There is a priceless moment when his relatives from back in Pennsylvania say they were surprised to discover how much he was like them. Put that moment beside those in which such famous people as Dennis Hopper or David Hockney talk about Warhol, and you will discover that he was like *them*, too. Perhaps he was the original inspiration for Woody Allen's *Zelig*, the man who couldn't help taking on the coloration and characteristics of everyone he met.

If Warhol himself was a cipher, his work was a trumpet blast of aggressive self-confidence. His soup cans and Mao portraits, his wallpaper and movies and silkscreen prints, became part of the visual image of his time. He came to fame in the 1960s, but survived that decade and continued to be important after the work of many of his contemporaries had been revealed as fads and passing fancies. To view *Superstar* is to be reminded of how pervasively his view saturated our visual universe, how omnipresent he was.

"He was a pointer," Dennis Hopper says in the film. "He did what Marcel Duchamp said an artist should do. He pointed at things, and then we could see them." He pointed first at the Campbell's soup cans and the Coca-Cola trademark, and called them Pop Art, but then he started pointing at people and just by his pointing made them "superstars." What he did was reveal that there is little difference between the famous and the obscure, except that the famous are better known.

The movie has a strangely ingratiating quality to it. Workman (the man who does the compilation documentaries for the Oscar cast) is content to let his subject gradually reveal itself. He collects witnesses and bits of old films and TV interviews, clips from Warhol movies and speculations by his friends and family. And finally what we are left with is an artist whose greatest art was his attitude. Not just the blank passivity he served up to the public, but also what I would make bold to describe as his enthusiasm. He saw, he pointed, we saw. If he had been talkative, it might not have worked.

The Sure Thing ★ ★ ★ ½
PG-13, 94 m., 1985

John Cusack (Walter Gibson), Daphne Zuniga (Alison Bradbury), Anthony Edwards (Lance), Boyd Gaines (Jason), Tim Robbins (Gary Cooper), Lisa Jane Persky (Mary Ann Webster), Viveca Lindfors (Professor), Nicollette Sheridan (Sure Thing). Directed by Rob Reiner and produced by Roger Birn-baum. Screenplay by Steven Bloom and Jonathan Roberts.

The love story is one of Hollywood's missing genres. The movie industry seems better at teen-age movies like *Porky's*, with its sleazy shower scenes, than with screenplays that involve any sort of thought about the love lives of its characters. That's why *The Sure Thing* is a small miracle. Although the hero of this movie is promised by his buddy that he'll be fixed up with a "guaranteed sure thing," the film is not about the sure thing but about how this kid falls genuinely and touchingly into love.

The movie's love story begins in an Eastern college classroom. Walter Gibson (John Cusack) walks into his English class and falls immediately into love with Alison Bradbury (Daphne Zuniga), who is smart and good-looking and not one of your brainless movie broads. He asks her out, but succeeds, of course, in acting like a total nerd, and she invites him to get out of her life. End of act one. In act two, Walter plans to spend his Christmas vacation in Los Angeles, where his buddy says the Sure Thing is eagerly awaiting his arrival. Alison also plans to go to L.A., to visit her fiancé, who is studying to be a boring middle-class vegetable. They both sign up for rides, and, of course, they both wind up in the back seat of the same car. At first they don't talk. Then they start to fight. Then they are ditched at the side of the road and have to hitchhike to L.A. together.

I know this is an obvious movie ploy. I know, in fact, that what will happen next is completely predictable: They'll fight, they'll share experiences, they'll suffer together, and eventually they'll fall in love. I know all of these things, and yet I don't care. I don't care because love is always a cliché anyway, and the only thing that makes it endlessly fascinating is that the players are always changing. These two particular characters, Walter and Alison, played by these two gifted young actors, Cusack and Zuniga, make *The Sure Thing* into a special love story.

One of the unique things about the movie is that the characters show a normal shyness about sex. Most movie teen-agers seem to be valedictorians from the Masters & Johnson Institute. They're born knowing more about sex than Rhett Butler would have been able to teach Scarlett O'Hara. They are also, of course, not shy, not insecure, not modest, and occasionally not human. Walter and Alison are closer to real teen-agers, with real doubts and hesitations and uncertainties. The other surprising thing about the film is that it successfully avoids an obligatory sex scene with the Sure Thing (Nicollette Sheridan, in a thankless role). This film is so revolutionary, it believes sex should be accompanied by respect and love! By the end of the movie, when Walter and Alison finally do kiss, it means something. It means more, in fact, than any movie kiss in a long time, because it takes place between two people we've gotten to know and who have gotten to know each other.

Suspect ★ ★ ½
R, 118 m., 1987

Cher (Kathleen Riley), Dennis Quaid (Eddie Sanger), Liam Neeson (Carl Wayne Anderson), John Mahoney (Judge Helms), Joe Mantegna (Charlie Stella), Philip Bosco (Paul Gray). Directed by Peter Yates and produced by Daniel A. Sherkow. Screenplay by Eric Roth.

Art films can play all the games they want. But if you're going to make a film in a commercial genre, then I think you have to play by the rules of that genre. In the case of a courtroom whodunit, that means you can't produce the guilty man out of left field, with no clues and no preparation. The audience has to have a fair chance to figure things out. *Suspect* is a well-made thriller, but it was spoiled for me by an extraordinary closing scene where Cher, as the defense attorney, solves the case with all the logic of a magician pulling a rabbit out of a hat.

The plot involves the murder of a Washington legal secretary. A Skid Row bum is arrested for the murder, and Cher is the public defender assigned to his case. He is a deaf-mute who has lost all trust in society, but Cher penetrates his defenses and becomes convinced he is innocent. In that case, who committed the murder?

A key clue is provided in the first scene of the movie, which shows a Supreme Court justice committing suicide. Other clues appear from time to time, especially after one of the jurors on the case decides to take things into his own hands. He's played by Dennis Quaid, as a lobbyist who is summoned for jury duty and becomes convinced the defendant didn't commit the crime. He conducts his own private investigation, and feeds clues to Cher.

She's afraid of jury-tampering charges (although this seems more like a case of lawyer-tampering). But things get really sticky when Cher and Quaid fall in love. I liked their scenes together, and I admired their performances. Indeed, I found a lot to like in this movie, which was directed by Peter Yates with particular attention to the texture of the lives of his characters.

One of the movie's themes is that all the characters are homeless—not just the bum, but also the lobbyist, the public defender, and everyone else we meet. They have places that they live in, that they use to sleep at night, but they do not have a "home" and they do not have loved ones around them. Their loneliness is underlined in one of the movie's most quietly effective scenes, where Quaid sleeps with a congresswoman, and it's a toss-up whether he's doing it out of ambition, politics, or need.

The movie develops its case with the kind of logic I enjoy in a whodunit. We meet the suspects, we evaluate the clues, and then (after the obligatory woman-in-danger sequence with a knife-wielding assailant chasing Cher through shadowy corridors) there's the big showdown in court. That's where the movie goes wrong. Cher stands up and rattles off a long, complicated speech in which the real murderer is revealed—and I began to develop a real case of resentment, because the murderer is a complete dark horse. That's not fair. It's as if an Agatha Christie novel evaluated six suspects in a British country house, and then in the last chapter we discover that the killer was a guy from next door.

Swamp Thing ★ ★ ★
R, 102 m., 1982

Louis Jourdan (Arcane), Adrienne Barbeau (Alice), Ray Wise (Dr. Holland), Dick Durock (Swamp Thing), David Hess (Ferret), Nicholas Worth (Brung). Directed by Wes Craven and produced by Benjamin Melniker and Michael Uslan. Screenplay by Craven.

Swamp Thing had already won my heart *before* its moment of greatness, but when that moment came, I knew I'd discovered another one of those movies that fall somewhere between buried treasures and guilty pleasures. The moment comes after Dr. Alec Holland, brilliant scientist, is attacked by thugs, is splashed with his own secret formula, catches on fire, leaps into the swamp, and turns into Swamp Thing when the formula interacts with his body and the vegetation in the swamp. Crawling back onto dry

land, Swamp Thing is not recognized by his former girlfriend, the beautiful Alice Cable (Adrienne Barbeau). But after the thugs fill him with machine-gun bullets and hack off his left arm, Alice asks, "Does it hurt?" and Swamp Thing replies, "Only when I laugh."

That was the movie's moment of greatness. There are others that come close, as when Swamp Thing, dripping with moss and looking like a bug-eyed spinach soufflé, says "There is great beauty in the swamp . . . if you know where to look." And when the evil villain (Louis Jourdan) drinks the secret formula and confidently waits for it to transform him into a powerful genius, he discovers that the formula doesn't so much *change* you, as develop what is already latent within you. Therefore, once a horse's ass, *always* a horse's ass.

This is one of those movies like *Infra-Man* or *Invasion of the Bee Girls:* an off-the-wall, eccentric, peculiar movie fueled by the demented obsessions of its makers. *Swamp Thing* first saw the light of day, so to speak, as a hero in a celebrated series of DC Comics. The movie version was written and directed by Wes Craven, who made *Last House on the Left*, a movie I persist in admiring even in the face of universal repugnance. Craven also made *The Hills Have Eyes*, which even I found decadent, and the made-for-NBC movie *Stranger in Our House*, with Linda Blair. This time, with *Swamp Thing*, he betrays a certain gentleness and poetry along with the gore; in fact, this movie is a lot less violent than many others in the same genre. Craven's inspiration seems to come from James Whale's classic *Bride of Frankenstein* (1935), and he pays tribute in scenes where his swamp monster sniffs a flower, admires a young girl's beauty from afar, and looks sadly at a photograph in a locket. *Swamp Thing* doesn't stop there; it also contains an exact visual quote from Russ Meyer's *Lorna*, and a scene in which the jailer in a dungeon cheerfully quotes the title of a Werner Herzog film: "It's every man for himself, and God against all!"

Will you like this film? Yes, probably, if you like monster and horror movies. The movie occupies familiar ground, but it has a freshness and winsome humor to fit it, and Craven moves confidently through the three related genres he's stealing from (monster movies, mad scientist movies, and transformation movies—in which people turn into strange beings). There's beauty in this movie, if you know where to look for it.

Swann in Love ★ ★ ★
R, 110 m., 1984

Jeremy Irons (Charles Swann), Ornella Muti (Odette de Crecy), Alain Delon (Baron de Charlus), Fanny Ardant (Duchesse de Guermantes), Marie-Christine Barrault (Madame Verdurin). Directed by Volker Schlondorff and produced by Nicole Stephane. Written by Peter Brook, Jean-Claude Carriere, and Marie-Helene Estienne.

All of the reviews I've read of Volker Schlondorff's *Swann in Love* treat it like a classroom assignment. The movie is described as a version of one of the stories that make up *Remembrance of Things Past*, the epic novel by Marcel Proust, and then the exercise becomes almost academic: "Compare and contrast Proust and Schlondorff, with particular attention to the difference between fiction and the film." Imagine instead, that this is not a film based on a novel, but a new film from an original screenplay. It will immediately seem more lively and accessible. Because not one person in a hundred who sees the film will have read Proust, this is a sensible approach; it does away with the nagging feeling that one should really curl up with those twelve volumes before going to the theater.

Schlondorff's *Swann in Love*—as opposed to Proust's—is the story of a pale young man who goes one day to visit a prostitute, and is actually indifferent to her until she stands him up. Then he becomes obsessed. She is not the right woman for him, but her very wrongness becomes fascinating. Because she is vulgar, because she lies, because she toys with his affection, and most particularly because she lets him smell the orchid in her bodice, she becomes the most important person in the world to him, and he throws his life and reputation at her feet. Proper society, of course, disapproves of his affair—and talks of nothing else. In the elegant salons where ladies and gentlemen gather, Swann is not welcome if he brings along his Odette, but because he cannot be happy without her, this is no punishment. In the most humiliating scenes in the movie, he abjectly follows her through the night, knocks on a door he hopes is hers, and stands in her boudoir while she nonchalantly disrobes and dresses for an appointment with another man.

Casting is everything in a film like this. Jeremy Irons is perfect as Charles Swann, pale, deep-eyed, feverish with passion. This was his third movie (after *The French Lieu-*

tenant's Woman and Betrayal) in which love seemed necessary to his nature. We can believe his passion. As Odette, Schlondorff has cast Ornella Muti, who has a sort of languorous bemusement that is maddening: We wonder if she is even capable of understanding that the man before her is mad with love and desire, and then we realize, of course, that her very *inability* to care is what creates her fatal attraction. *Swann in Love* is a stylish, period love story, surrounding its central characters with still other pathetic seekers of perfection (Alain Delon is wonderful as a gloomy homosexual who pursues an idealized form of misery). Yet at the film's end, we've probably learned nothing except that lovers were as silly in 1875 as they are now. Sillier, perhaps; they had more time.

Sweet Liberty ★ ★ ½
PG, 107 m., 1986

Alan Alda (Michael Burgess), Michael Caine (Elliott James), Michelle Pfeiffer (Faith Healy), Bob Hoskins (Stanley Gould), Lise Hilboldt (Gretchen Carlsen), Lillian Gish (Cecelia Burgess), Saul Rubinek (Bo Hodges). Directed by Alan Alda and produced by Martin Bregman. Screenplay by Alda.

Sweet Liberty tells the story of a Hollywood movie company that arrives in a small Southeastern college town to shoot a film about the Revolutionary War. It also tells three or four other stories, and that is the problem: The movie wants to juggle a lot of characters all at once, but it keeps dropping the most interesting ones.

The movie stars Alan Alda as the local history professor who sold his book to the movies. He didn't exactly expect them to turn it into a scholarly documentary, but he is shocked to see it rewritten into a seamy tale of lust, betrayal, intrigue, and violence. He makes a liaison with the screenwriter (Bob Hoskins), who tutors him in cynicism, and together they try to change some of the worst parts.

Meanwhile, the small town itself is turning into a seamy hotbed of lust, betrayal, and intrigue. Alda has been dating another faculty member (Lise Hilboldt), but then he falls instantly in love with the movie's sexy leading lady (Michelle Pfeiffer). That's sort of all right, because Hilboldt has a fling with the leading man (Michael Caine). And there are subplots involving the director, the local extras, and even Alda's ancient mother (por-

trayed by the legendary Lillian Gish, who, old as the character is, still plays below her age).

These are a lot of story strands to keep straight, and *Sweet Liberty* doesn't always succeed. I was left with the impression there was more material than the time to deal with it, and I especially wanted to see more of that excellent comic actor, Michael Caine. His character, a shameless philanderer with a streak of poetry in his soul, is so promising that it's a shame he's onscreen so infrequently.

Alda wrote and directed the movie, as well as starred in it, and he has some nice touches. I liked the scene in which Caine covered up the unexpected arrival of his wife by taking everybody on a roller-coaster ride. And I liked the next scene, too, where they walk drunkenly through the town late at night, talking about those great romantic truths which always seem so elusive in the morning.

Alda's best-written character in the movie is probably Faith Healy, the sexy actress played by Michelle Pfeiffer—and her performance uses some wonderfully subtle touches, as she moves back and forth between her historical character and her distinctly more cynical modern one. It's here that the movie comes closest to its theme, which is (I think) the ways that adults can deceive themselves even while thinking they are perfectly aware of all their motives.

The Lillian Gish character is a distraction. Her obsession with an old boyfriend is intriguing enough, however, maybe this particular story should have been lifted completely out of *Sweet Liberty* and made into a movie of its own. There's a great scene where Alda and Hilboldt go to visit the old boyfriend, whose wife complains that the old lady has made their life miserable. It's such a strong scene that, paradoxically, it doesn't belong in this movie; its tone is wrong for the other stuff.

Sweet Liberty will probably play better on TV and video than it did at the theater, where its episodic structure will be more at home, and it won't be so obvious how all of the little set pieces don't hang together. Like most movies about movies, it is not very realistic. It's unlikely a big-budget historical movie would use such shabby painted backdrops, and completely impossible for the climactic scene (a sabotaged battle) to unfold the way it does. Few movies have had the patience to show moviemaking the way it really is (Truffaut's *Day for Night* came fairly close),

but there are times here when the onscreen director (Saul Rubinek) doesn't even seem convinced of his own authenticity.

Sweetie ★ ★ ★ ½
R, 100 m., 1990

Genevieve Lemon (Sweetie), Karen Colston (Kay), Tom Lycos (Louis), Jon Darling (Gordon), Dorothy Barry (Flo), Michael Lake (Bob), Andre Pataczek (Clayton). Directed Jane Campion and produced by John Maynard. Screenplay by Gerard Lee and Campion.

Curious experience, this movie. The first time I saw it, at the 1989 Cannes Film Festival, I didn't know what to make of it. I doubted if I "liked" it, and yet it was certainly a work of talent. There was something there. I didn't *feel* much from it, though; the experience seemed primarily cerebral. Then six months later I saw *Sweetie* a second time, and suddenly there it all was, laid out in blood and passion on the screen, the emotional turmoil of a family's life. Maybe the second time I found the heart of the movie, and the first time I had been distracted by the substance.

The film takes place in Australia, in the present, in a world that has been carefully art-directed to make the commonplace look a little strange. It has been directed by Jane Campion, a short-film maker, and photographed by Sally Bongers, whose compositions and color sense give everything a sensation of heightened reality, or unreality. The acting style edges toward parody, the material is unforgiving of Australian middle-class life in the boondocks, and then, pow!— Sweetie waltzes onto the screen.

We have already met the rest of her family, including her sister, Kay (Karen Colston), who tries to lead a relatively normal life, and her parents, Flo and Bob, who do lead relatively normal lives by the device of denying their bizarre family reality. Then Sweetie (Genevieve Lemon) comes back into their lives—Sweetie, the spoiled daughter whose cute, childish antics have persisted right on up to the onset of middle age.

It becomes clear that Sweetie has always terrorized this family. In the early days (suggested in flashbacks), Dad spoiled Sweetie and told her what a wonderful little girl she was, and Sweetie, the monster, took his approval as an assignment to hold center stage in all family events and terrorize those who would not pay attention to her. In more recent years, grown obese, obnoxious, and more obviously unbalanced, Sweetie has drifted in and out of their lives. Her return is like a family disease that has gone out of remission.

There are scenes in this movie that are perfect set pieces. One of them is the "lunch meeting" held by Dad and Sweetie's "manager," a stoned zombie who slips beneath the table in the midst of negotiations. Another is Sweetie's refusal to come down from the tree. Still another, funny and horrifying at the same time, is Sweetie's demonstration of what a clever girl she is. Look! She can stand on a straight chair and make it tilt so that she rides it back down without falling off or breaking anything! We can guess how often this terrorized family has been forced to applaud this stunt of stultifying banality.

Sweetie is not, however, a family drama or a docu-drama of any conventional sort. It looks and feels too strange for that, and there are too many deft touches in the dialogue and sly looks out of the side of the camera's lens. It is a story with a realistic origin, told with a fresh and bold eye. "In most films," Campion says, "what people are doing is trying to pretend the shots aren't there." Campion and Bongers don't do that. All of their shots are there. Look at the way the little boy in the next yard is presented by the camera. Observe the look of the family's house and yard. And the feral way Sweetie hides under her blanket and barks at her father. How the movie is seen is part of the experience.

In my reviews, I try never to discuss whether "you," whoever you are, will enjoy a movie or not. I do not know you and would not presume to guess your tastes. I imagine most people will have a hard time with *Sweetie*, simply because I did the first time. But this movie is real, it's the genuine article, and it's there on the screen in all of its defiant strangeness. Most movies slide right through our minds without hitting anything. This one screams and shouts every step of the way.

Swimming to Cambodia ★ ★ ★
NO MPAA RATING, 87 m., 1987

Written by and starring Spalding Gray.
Directed and produced by Jonathan Demme.

Spalding Gray is an actor who had a small role in *The Killing Fields* (the assistant to the American ambassador), and in this movie he talks about that performance and other matters. He sits at a table—a glass of water and a micro-

phone before him, a couple of maps behind him—and talks and talks. Because he is a good talker, and because he has something to say, this curious idea for a movie actually works.

Swimming to Cambodia is based on a one-man, two-evening stage performance that Gray polished and took on tour a couple of years ago. It has been edited down to less than two hours and directed by Jonathan Demme with an unobtrusive authority. There are subtle light and music cues, a few sound effects such as fluttering helicopter blades, and, for the rest, there is Gray's face and his voice.

His monologue begins with his auditions for the role in *The Killing Fields*, the film that told the story of a friendship between a *New York Times* correspondent and his Cambodian assistant. The assistant, Dith Pran, was played by Haing S. Ngor, who won an Academy Award for his performance. Gray won no awards for his work in the movie and indeed is a minor character whose few scenes are shown in the course of his monologue.

What he had, during the course of the shooting in Thailand, was a great deal of spare time. He seems to have used this time to investigate not only the fleshpots of Bangkok, but also the untold story of the genocide that was practiced by the fanatic Khmer Rouge on their Cambodian countrymen. He recounts in great and gory detail all of his findings, from the infamous "banana show" in a local nightclub to the disappearance of millions of Cambodians in the greatest mass murder of modern history.

He is a spellbinding storyteller, and as he speaks, something occurs that might be called the "radio phenomenon." This is the same effect that was created in *My Dinner with André* (1981), another movie in which the characters simply sit and talk. Although we are essentially only seeing a face on a screen, we are picturing the story's events in our minds; it's like listening to a radio play.

Gray is not afraid to be dramatic. His voice races quickly through a litany of images, his arms wave, his eyes flash. Then sometimes he is quiet, contemplative. This is a monologue that has been polished during many hundreds of hours on the stage, and although he makes it sound fresh, he is so familiar with it that he can gallop through a tricky passage with the confidence of an auctioneer. Like a good preacher, some of his power comes from the sheer virtuosity of his speech.

Gray's theater performance, and now this

film, have been praised in many quarters, but in the *New Yorker* review, Pauline Kael was not amused. She admired Demme's direction and even Gray's presence, but asked aloud if it had occurred to him that he was exploiting the genocide in Cambodia for his own aggrandizement. This is a serious charge, particularly since Gray did not, of course, personally witness anything at all in Southeast Asia except some strip shows, some local scenery, and the filming of part of *The Killing Fields*. His material about the war is all hearsay.

I respect what Kael is getting at, but I ask myself this question: Would it have been more worthy for Gray to talk about the strippers and the moviemaking while ignoring the fact that *The Killing Fields* was inspired, indirectly, by the deaths of those millions of people? There is a fine line to be drawn here, and I am not sure where it falls.

Of course, *Swimming to Cambodia* is, on some level, self-aggrandizement. All actors might enjoy the thought of a feature film devoted entirely to their face and their voice, but few would have the nerve to go ahead with one. On the other hand, literally all possible subjects are exploited whenever they are turned into fiction. All war movies, for example, take the suffering and deaths of untold victims and use them as the setting for a fictional story about a few idealized characters. Is *Swimming to Cambodia* any more exploitive than *The Deer Hunter*, *Platoon*, or for that matter, *Paths of Glory* or *All Quiet on the Western Front*?

None of us can directly experience more than we actually see and hear. Everything else is hearsay. All we really know, for sure, is what happened to us. There's that story about the actor hired to play the gravedigger in *Hamlet*. Asked what the play was about, he replied, "It's about this gravedigger, who meets a prince. . . ."

Swimming to Cambodia is about this actor, who meets a war.

Switch ★ ★ ½
R, 104 m., 1991

Ellen Barkin (Steve "Amanda" Brooks), Jimmy Smits (Walter), JoBeth Williams (Margo), Lorraine Bracco (Sheila), Tony Roberts (Arnold), Perry King (Steve [the man]). Directed by Blake Edwards and produced by Tony Adams. Screenplay by Edwards.

We hear all the time on the talk shows from men who believe they are women trapped inside a man's body, but what about a man trapped inside a woman's body—against his will? That's the peculiar experience undergone by the hero, or heroine, of Blake Edwards's *Switch*, who begins the film as a male advertising executive named Steve and ends it as a female executive named Amanda, who is doing Steve's job rather better than Steve ever did.

The character is played briefly at the beginning of the film by Perry King, as a male chauvinist pig who is so despised by the women in his life that some of them would like to kill him. Steve does indeed die, and goes on to the next realm, where he is informed that his behavior on Earth toward women has been so despicable that he will spend eternity in hell.

Is there any chance of an appeal? Only one. He will be sent back to Earth to search for one woman who loves him. If he can find such a person, he has a possibility of reprieve. There is a catch. He will return to Earth as a woman to see what it feels like. Steve is caught up in some kind of magical heavenly process, and wakes up the next morning as Ellen Barkin—who plays the lead for the rest of the film, in a performance of true comic invention.

Barkin has always been an aggressive, self-confident actress with a touch of the masculine in her behavior. Remember her great scene in *Sea of Love*, where she pinned Al Pacino against the wall and had her way with him? Playing a man trapped inside her own body, she has fun with every possibility in the role—from peering in astonishment down the front of her blouse to staggering around the office in high heels.

Switch was written and directed by Blake Edwards, and it reflects two of his favorite themes: androgyny and finding yourself in another person's shoes. His 1982 comedy *Victor/Victoria* starred Julie Andrews as a woman playing a man playing a woman. Now here is a film where the man must play the woman for the rest of his or her life. Steve, who takes the name of Amanda, doesn't much enjoy the experience. But he—or shall we say "she" from now on—certainly does learn to see things from a new point of view.

One of her problems is to convince the other people in her life that this is really Steve inside this good-looking female body. The first to learn is one of Steve's former lovers,

Margo (JoBeth Williams), who is blackmailed into loaning clothes and providing makeup tips. Another person who has a great deal of trouble accepting the new reality is Walter (Jimmy Smits), who was Steve's best friend when Steve was a man. And then there are new friends to make, including the millionaire perfume executive Sheila (Lorraine Bracco), who is a lesbian powerfully attracted to Amanda.

Switch has an intriguing premise and a terrific performance by Barkin. But it fails to really deliver on its promise, and I think the ways in which it deals with Walter and Sheila are crucial. Steve has always really liked Walter. So does Amanda. The two of them get drunk together, and Amanda is able to convince Walter that she is "really" Steve, but even despite that they find themselves attracted to each other. What do they do now? Would it be homosexuality if they made love, even though Steve is now Amanda? And what about the beautiful, sexy Sheila, who falls for Amanda? Would it be cheating for Steve to take advantage of that situation?

Blake Edwards glories in questions like that, and his work has always been full of double-reverse paradoxes. But here I think he loses his nerve. He slips out of the implications of the affair with Walter by creating a convenient alcoholic blackout, and eludes the implications of Sheila by whipping up the lame excuse that, as a homophobe, Steve cannot be attracted to Sheila because she is a lesbian. This ignores the tendency of men—especially chauvinist pigs like Steve was—to find lesbianism sexy.

If Edwards had somehow found a way to really grapple with the implications of his story—if he had pushed to see how far he could go—*Switch* might have been a truly revolutionary comedy, on the order of *Tootsie*, but more sexually frank. Unfortunately, he seems determined to make everything palatable to the sensibilities of the kinds of people who probably wouldn't attend this kind of movie in the first place—and, in the process, he takes a daring idea and plays it safe. Too safe.

Switching Channels ★ ★ ★
PG-13, 105 m., 1988

Kathleen Turner (Christy Colleran), Burt Reynolds (John L. Sullivan IV), Christopher Reeve (Blaine Bingham), Ned Beatty (Roy Ridnitz), Henry Gibson (Ike Roscoe), George Newbern (Siegenthaler), Al Waxman

(Berger), Ken James (Warden Terwilliger), Barry Flatman (Zaks), Ted Simonett (Tillinger). Directed by Ted Kotcheff and produced by Martin Ransohoff. Screenplay by Jonathan Reynolds.

Newspapers once had editions all day long, and reporters were forever feeding rewritemen a new angle for the replate. The front-page headlines changed from edition to edition, to make the news seem forever breathlessly new. Now that kind of continuing update is left to television; ever notice how Headline News updates the breaking stories while repeating the feature stuff over and over again?

The Front Page is, of course, a comedy about newspapers—the most famous newspaper comedy ever written. It was conceived in the hothouse of the Chicago newspaper world in the 1920s, when a dozen reporters were chasing every story, and there were new editions all day long. Those were the days when a "scoop" meant you stole a story right out from under the other guy's nose. These days, an "exclusive" is more likely to mean you outbid the opposition for the serial rights to a TV star's steamy confessions.

So maybe it's only appropriate that the latest remake of *The Front Page* involves, not newspapers, but a TV cable news operation. Ben Hecht and Charles MacArthur, who wrote the classic play, might even approve; they abandoned Chicago for Hollywood, where remakes were routine and the 1931 screen version of *The Front Page* was updated nine years later in *His Girl Friday* by simply making one of the boys in the press room into a girl.

The Front Page was filmed again by Billy Wilder in 1974, with Jack Lemmon and Walter Matthau, and now here is Ted Kotcheff's 1988 version, titled *Switching Channels* and starring Burt Reynolds, Kathleen Turner, and Christopher Reeve. It's not as good as *His Girl Friday*, but it's comparable with the others.

Turner plays a hard-driving TV news reporter who seems willing, in the opening credits, to go anywhere and do anything as long as the videotape is rolling. Reynolds is her ex-husband and current boss, the managing editor of the cable news operation. And on a long-overdue vacation, Turner falls in love with Christopher Reeve, a New York millionaire. She decides to quit TV, marry Reeve, and move to New York, but hold on a minute—a famous criminal is scheduled to be executed at midnight, and Reynolds will do anything to keep his star reporter on the story.

This is more or less the same premise as the first three versions, allowing for the adjustments that have to be made when the star reporter is a woman (as Rosalind Russell was in the 1940 edition). Christopher Reeve's role has been greatly expanded (the fiancé was mostly offstage in the earlier versions), and I'm not sure that's a good thing; too much time is wasted while Reynolds and Reeve insult each other while the news is put on hold.

But Kathleen Turner has perfect timing as the long-suffering anchor, and she and Reynolds work up a nice sweat and some good chemistry in their relationship, which seems to be based on a few good memories and a whole lot of one-liners. The Reeve character is unnecessary much of the time, but Reeve has fun with it anyway, with his floppy tailored suits, his newly blond hair, and his willingness to accommodate the obviously derailed Turner.

The details of the update don't much matter, either. This time the convicted man is hidden inside a Xerox machine instead of a roll-top desk, but the basic mechanics of the original Hecht-MacArthur story are still sound, and *Switching Channels* is true to the obsessive-compulsive hostility that is the fuel for all good reporters.

There is, however, one major lapse that should not go unreported. As everyone who has ever seen the play knows, it ends with the most famous closing line in American theatrical history: "The son of a bitch stole my watch!" The first two movie versions couldn't get away with that language, but the 1974 version did, and now here it is 1988, and *Switching Channels* has the temerity to leave the line out altogether (even though Reynolds steals Reeve's expensive pen, in what looks like a setup). If the ghosts of Hecht and MacArthur see this movie, may they haunt the filmmakers, their spectral voices complaining, "The sons of bitches didn't steal our greatest line!"

T

Talk Radio ★ ★ ★ ★
R, 110 m., 1988

Eric Bogosian (Barry), Ellen Greene (Ellen), Leslie Hope (Laura), John C. McGinley (Stu), Alec Baldwin (Dan), John Pankow (Dietz), Michael Wincott (Kent), Linda Atkinson (Sheila Fleming). Directed by Oliver Stone and produced by Edward R. Pressman and A. Kitman Ho. Screenplay by Eric Bogosian and Stone.

Alan Berg was a Denver talk radio host who was murdered on June 18, 1984. He was a goofy-looking bird, with a thin face and a bristly white beard that hid the ravages of teen-age acne. He wore reading glasses perched far down on his nose, and he dressed in unlikely combinations of checks and stripes and garments that looked left over from the 1950s. When the members of a lunatic right-wing group gunned him down in the driveway of his home, they could not have mistaken him for anybody else.

I met Berg three or four times. The first time I was going to be on his radio show; I listened to it as I drove from Boulder to Denver. He was chewing out some hapless housewife whose brain was a reservoir of prejudice against anyone who was the slightest bit different from her. Berg was telling her that no one in their right mind would want to be anything like her at all.

Why were you so hard on that lady? I asked him when we were on the air.

"She was asking for it. Why would she call up and feed me all those straight lines if she didn't want me to tell her how stupid she was?"

Cruel, perhaps, but quite possibly correct. Berg was the top radio personality in Denver because he told people exactly what he thought of them. It was unusual to hear somebody on the radio who was not tailoring his words to the sensibilities of his audience. Talking with Berg off the air, I found that he was a man who had been through a lot, including the loss of a law practice in Chicago because of alcoholism. Now he was sober and successful, but I had the feeling that he was grateful every morning for somehow having pulled out of his crash dive. I liked him. When I learned that he had been murdered, my first reaction was disbelief that anyone could have taken him that seriously. Jeez, didn't they know he was just another poor bastard trying to earn a living?

Oliver Stone's film Talk Radio is inspired by the murder of Alan Berg, but it is not based on his life. Berg was older, calmer, and more amused by life than Barry Champlain, the tortured talk radio host in the movie. Berg was also not self-destructive or suicidal, and Champlain is both. When he is mailed a suspicious box in a plain brown wrapper, he puts it next to the microphone. When he gets a call from the man who mailed the box, and the man hints that it contains a bomb, Champlain opens it on the air. When another caller rants and raves incoherently about Champlain's beliefs and calls him a coward, Champlain asks him to come over to the radio station—and invites the man, a disheveled, wild-eyed street person, to come into the studio.

Champlain works in a studio in a Texas high-rise, surrounded by other high-rises. I was aware all during the movie of the thousands of windows with a view into his studio. When the man who sent the box says, "I can see you have it," I cringed, because I imagined someone with a sniper-scope. But Barry Champlain, played with rasping, aggressive sarcasm by Eric Bogosian, simply doesn't care. He is gambling with his life in the same self-hating way as people who get drunk and point a speedboat into the blackness of a storm.

Talk Radio is directed by Stone with a claustrophobic intensity. The camera rarely leaves the radio studio—and then it's only for brief flashbacks into the hero's troubled personal life, or for a personal appearance he makes at a basketball game where some of the fans seem to have crawled out from under their rocks for the purpose of acting weirdly toward him. Most of the movie takes place during the long nights of the radio program, and the movie's beginnings as a stage play are evident when several key characters—including Champlain's former wife—turn up on the scene to bare their hearts to him.

Even so, the movie doesn't feel as boxed-in as many filmed plays do, perhaps because radio itself is such an intimate, claustrophobic medium. It's not over there in the TV set; it's inside your head. In a sense we become listeners of "The Barry Champlain Show," and as he pushes his listeners more and more insistently, egging them on, we begin to feel how some of the people out there in the night could go over the edge. Talk Radio is based on a play that Bogosian wrote and starred in, and it was the right decision to star him in the movie, too, instead of some famous star. He feels this material from the inside out, and makes the character convincing. That's especially true during a virtuoso, unsettling closing monologue in which we think the camera is circling Bogosian—until we realize the camera and the actor are still, and the backgrounds are circling.

Alan Berg is more famous in death than life. His memory haunts many people, even those who never heard him on the radio, because his death could be read as a message: Be cautious, be prudent, be bland, never push anybody, never say what you really think, offer yourself as a hostage to the weirdos even before they make the first move. These days, a lot of people are opposed to the newfound popularity of "trash television," and no doubt they are right and the hosts of these shows are shameless controversy-mongers. But at least they are not intimidated. Of what use is freedom of speech to those who fear to offend?

The Tall Guy ★ ★ ★ ½
R, 90 m., 1990

Jeff Goldblum (Dexter King), Emma Thompson (Kate Lemon), Rowan Atkinson (Ron Anderson), Emil Wolk (Cyprus Charlie), Geraldine James (Carmen), Kim Thomson (Cheryl). Directed by Mel Smith and produced by Paul Webster. Screenplay by Richard Curtis.

The Tall Guy is a sweet, whimsical, and surprisingly intelligent comedy about an American actor in London, who falls in love with a nurse and finds that he has to treasure the gift of romance and not take it for granted. The tall guy is played by Jeff Goldblum, whose character wanders through the movie in need of a haircut and a shot of self-confidence. The nurse is Emma Thompson, and she is trim and organized—one of those women with the disconcerting practice of telling you exactly what they think, just when you were trying to find a cowardly way to weasel it out of them.

The movie is narrated by Goldblum's character, whose name is Dexter, and who has spent five years as "the tall guy" in a two-man show starring the rude and obnoxious short comedian Ron Anderson (Rowan Atkinson). Anderson hogs the spotlight so much that the audience hardly even realizes there's a stooge in the cast. Dexter, meanwhile, bicycles home to his rented room in the flat of a nymphomaniac, whose lovers paddle nakedly through the kitchen at odd hours in search of a glass of water.

One day Dexter finds himself at the hospital, and is riven by a thunderbolt of love for the nurse, whose name is Kate Lemon, although his mind insists on remembering her as Kate Tampon. Desperate to ask her for a date, he signs up for a series of inoculations for a fictitious trip to Morocco, and eventually she does go out with him, and up to her room with him, and they roll passionately across oranges and stale Wheetabix cubes and are in love.

All of this would not in itself make *The Tall Guy* worth seeing, despite the charm of

Thompson and the drollery of Goldblum, if it were not for the direction by Mel Smith and the script by Richard Curtis, who assume that their audience has a certain level of intelligence and information. That makes the movie more fun even for those viewers who do not always know what they are referring to.

For example: The typical Hollywood script assumes that its audience was born yesterday and knows nothing. There are no topical references to anyone or anything. Events occurring more than ten years previously are tacitly assumed not to have happened at all. Even the names of small cities are replaced with the names of larger ones, to avoid giving offense. References to the names of authors, poets, painters, or presidents are left out if at all possible, although sports figures are very occasionally allowed to slip in. No character is now, or ever has been, a member of any political party.

I get so weary of movies that assume I, and my fellow viewers, know nothing. Plots that involve a rudimentary introduction of good and bad guys, and the elimination of the second by the first, not without difficulty. Characters who never talk about anything real—anything, indeed, other than the plot. The last third of *The Tall Guy* turns into a hilarious send-up of the modern musical, when Dexter somehow gets cast in a musical version of *The Elephant Man*. This production, called *Elephant!*, must be the funniest deliberately bad play in a movie since Mel Brooks's "Springtime for Hitler" in *The Producers*. Thank God they didn't decide no one in the audience had ever heard of the Elephant Man (most people are assumed to have heard of Hitler).

Near the end of this movie, Kate, the girlfriend, accuses Dexter of having an affair with a young actress. How does she know this? Not because she stumbles across Polaroids they took of each other in their knickers. No, she figures it out because, at a cast party, Dexter fills the other woman's glass with champagne, which she allows him to do without acknowledgment. Taking someone for granted like that is a sure sign, Kate says, that they are lovers. She is right, of course, and this movie is right about a great many things, one of them being that there is a market for comedy among people who were not born yesterday.

Tampopo ★ ★ ★ ★
NO MPAA RATING, 117 m., 1987

Tsutomu Yamazaki (Ooro), Nobuko Miyamoto (Tampopo [Dandelion]), Koji Miyamoto (Man in White Suit), Ken Watanabe (Gun), Rikiya Yasuoka (Pisken), Kinzo Sakura (Shohei). Directed by Juzo Itami and produced by Juzo Itami, Yasushi Tamaoki, and Seigo Hosogoe. Screenplay by Itami.

Tampopo is one of those utterly original movies that seems to exist in no known category. Like the French comedies of Jacques Tati, it's a bemused meditation on human nature, in which one humorous situation flows into another off-handedly, as if life were a series of smiles.

As it opens, the film looks like some sort of Japanese satire of Clint Eastwood's spaghetti Westerns. The hero is Ooro (Tsutomu Yamazaki), a lone rider with a quizzical smile on his face, who rides a semi instead of a horse. Along with some friends, he stages a search for the perfect noodle restaurant, and cannot find it. Then he meets Tampopo (Nobuko Miyamoto), a sweet young woman who has her heart in the right place, but not her noodles.

The movie then turns into the fairly freestyle story of the efforts by Tampopo and her protector to research the perfect noodle and open the perfect noodle restaurant. Like most movies about single-minded obsessions, this one quickly becomes very funny. It might seem that American audiences would know little and care less about the search for the perfect Japanese noodle, but because the movie is so consumed and detailed, so completely submerged in "noodleology," it takes on a kind of weird logic of its own.

Consider, for example, the *tour de force* of a scene near the beginning of the movie, where a noodle master explains the correct ritual for eating a bowl of noodle soup. He explains every ingredient. How to cut it, how to cook it, how to address it, how to think of it, how to regard it, how to approach it, how to smell it, how to eat it, how to thank it, how to remember it. It's a kind of gastronomic religion, and director Juzo Itami languishes in creating a scene that makes noodles in this movie more interesting than sex and violence in many another.

The movie is constructed as a series of episodes along the route to the perfect noodle restaurant. Some of the scenes hardly even seem to apply, but are hilarious anyway—the treatment, for example, of a man who dies in the pursuit of the perfect bowl of noodles. *Tampopo* doesn't limit itself to satirizing one genre of Hollywood film, either; although the central image is of an Eastwood-style hero on an ultimate quest, there are all sorts of other sly little satirical asides, including one so perfectly aimed that even to describe it would take away some of the fun.

Humor, it is said, is universal. Most times it is not. The humor that travels best, I sometimes think, is not "universal" humor at all, but humor that grows so specifically out of one culture that it reaches other cultures almost by seeming to ignore them. The best British comedies were the very specifically British films like *The Lavender Hill Mob* and *School for Scoundrels*. The best Italian comedies were local products like *Seduced and Abandoned*. The funniest French films were by Tati, who seemed totally absorbed in himself. And this very, very Japanese movie, which seems to make no effort to communicate to other cultures, is universally funny almost for that reason. Who cannot identify with the search for the perfect noodle? Certainly any American can, in the land of sweet corn festivals, bake-offs, and contests for the world's best chili.

Tango and Cash ★
R, 98 m., 1989

Sylvester Stallone (Tango), Kurt Russell (Cash), Teri Hatcher (Kiki), Jack Palance (Yves Perret), Brion James (Courier/Requin), James Hong (Quan), Marc Alaimo (Lopez), Michael J. Pollard (Owen). Directed by Andrei Konchalovsky and produced by Jon Peters and Peter Guber. Screenplay by Randy Feldman.

Tango and Cash is a brainless, exhausted example of the buddy action picture, that wheezy old format where a couple of hotshot cops team up to destroy an army of bad guys. The chief innovation in this version is the ratio of action to dialogue, which must be around 9-to-1 (in favor of personal injury and against people talking to one another). The best thing I can think of to say about the film is that it makes absolutely no difference whether you walk in at the beginning or at any other point. The whole thing is a big, noisy, vulgar loop.

The stars are Sylvester Stallone and Kurt Russell, as Tango and Cash, respectively. Tango dresses in expensive suits and takes calls from his broker. Cash dresses in sweatshirts that have the necks ripped out of them. Who rips the necks out of all those movie sweatshirts, anyway? The boys are known as the two top narcs in L.A., and when they get together, the drug kingpins duck for cover. Excuse me if that sentence reads like a line from an ad. The screenplay for this movie sounds like lines from an ad.

Beloved old Jack Palance is the other star of the movie, as the wonderfully named Yves Perret, a drug kingpin. No one has ever looked less like an Yves Perret than Jack Palance. He controls a billion-dollar cocaine empire, but he still commits the Fallacy of the Talking Killer, defined as that movie cliché where the killer, instead of killing, talks too much and gives the good guys time to act. Palance does most of the talking in the movie. He wants Tango and Cash killed, but not *simply* killed, you see: No, they have to die according to his own specific scenario, which is so complicated and time-consuming, alas, that it gives them time to kill him. (Is that giving away the ending? Who cares? If this movie ended with Palance killing Stallone and Russell, now *that* would be news.)

One of the wondrous things about *Tango and Cash* was that I knew with an awful certainty it would be bad right from the opening seconds. The screen goes black and we hear Stallone saying, "All right, let's do it," and then the sound track bursts forth with that unspeakably grotesque action-movie music they manufacture these days out of percussion and synthesizer—the music that sounds like they're beating the hell out of a leather sofa filled with muffled cymbals while a keyboard screams for help in the next room. Since Stallone was speaking in his own voice about the movie, the pretitle statement was a clue that the movie was not about the characters, but about itself. About the deal. About Stallone the loner making his first buddy movie.

There are a lot of special effects in this movie. Explosions. Chases. Bodies hurtling through the air. In one scene, Tango and Cash slide to freedom down an electric wire. How? Cash goes first. He puts his belt in his mouth, leaps through the air, and grabs the cable in both hands. Holding on with his left hand, he uses the right hand to take the belt from his mouth and whip it over the cable. Then he grabs the other end of the belt with the left hand and slides down the wire. Will someone tell me why he did not fall during the time when neither hand was hanging onto the wire?

If you have the answer to that one, how about this one? Early in the film, Stallone stands in the middle of a highway and levels his gun at the driver of a tanker truck owned by the bad guys. The driver sees he is going to get shot and slams on the brakes. Slams them on so hard, in fact, that the driver and his partner are hurled through the windshield of the truck! Has anyone ever seen a truck brake that quickly? The scene sure is a compelling argument for buckling up.

The movie's attempts at characterization are pathetic. The Palance character is given a couple of mice to play with and an obsolete twelve-screen TV console to look at. Russell is allowed to fall in love with Stallone's sister, who is a go-go dancer and whose primary purpose in the movie, of course, is to be held hostage at the climax. There are the usual crooked FBI guys and ugly criminal henchmen. Of the film's sparse dialogue, my favorite line is when Russell is hit by a bullet and Stallone asks him if he was hurt bad. Russell replies, "Naw. Clean exit."

Tap ★ ★ ★
PG-13, 111 m., 1989

Gregory Hines (Max Washington), Suzzanne Douglas (Amy), Sammy Davis, Jr. (Little Mo), Savion Glover (Louis), Joe Morton (Nicky), Dick Anthony Williams (Francis). Characters based on themselves: Sandman Sims, Bunny Briggs, Steve Condos, Jimmy Slyde, Pat Rico, Arthur Duncan, and Harold Nicholas. Directed by Nick Castle and produced by Gary Adelson and Richard Vane. Screenplay by Castle.

Imagine how Bruce Springsteen would feel if rock & roll lost its popularity overnight, and you'd know, I guess, how the great tap dancers felt in the early 1950s. One day, tap dancing was enormously popular (I can remember half the kids in my grade school class taking lessons at Thelma Lee Ritter's Dance Studio, up above the Princess Theater on Main Street in Urbana, Illinois). The next day, it was passé—blown away by rock. And there was another cruel blow for many of the tap stars, who were black: As the civil rights movement gained strength, tap dancing itself was seen as projecting the wrong image of black people.

Tap stars Gregory Hines as Max Washington, the son of one of the greatest tap dancers—a man who is a great dancer himself, but has thrown away his heritage to lead a life of crime. Now he is out of prison and on the streets again, and his old associates want him to pull a big-time jewel heist. But upstairs over Sonny's, the shabby dance club his father used to run on Times Square, people who love him have other plans for him.

The club is run by Little Mo (Sammy Davis, Jr.). His daughter, Amy (Suzzanne Douglas) runs a tap academy on the second floor, and upstairs on the third floor there's a sort of retirement home for Mo and seven of his pals, old tap dancers. Little Mo dreams that there could be a fusion of tap and rock, and that Sonny's is just the place to launch it. He wants Max to lead the way.

What we have here, then, is the outline for a fairly standard musical plot. Will Max steal the jewels or return to his dancing heritage? Will Little Mo be able to teach him to dream again? And, of course, will Max and Amy fall in love? They were lovers once before, but now there is coldness between them, because Max has grown hard and cynical. And he grows even more bitter when he's insulted by the director of a Broadway show who doesn't know beans about tap dancing.

The parts of this plot seem recycled out of old musicals, all right, but the spirit of the film is fresh and the characters are convincing. Gregory Hines has been dancing professionally since he was a juvenile in the 1950s, but he's better known as an actor, and here he has a role that challenges him on both levels. He has a way of being strong, and being subtle about it. Sammy Davis, Jr., has never had a juicier role in a movie, and for once he isn't playing himself—he's playing the opposite of glitter and glitz, and his sincerity is believable. And the discovery of the movie is Suzzanne Douglas, who can dance and act and looks beautiful on the screen. Her chemistry with Hines is real, and that makes her somewhat predictable role more interesting.

And then there are those old guys who live upstairs. The movie has cast the roles with legendary tap-dance veterans: Sandman Sims, Bunny Briggs, Steve Condos, Jimmy Slyde, Pat Rico, Arthur Duncan, and Harold Nicholas. There is a scene where the youngster is unwise enough to suggest that they've lost their legs, and they accept the challenge with enthusiasm, each one putting on a show of his best stuff. This scene, like the whole movie, is lighted and photographed by director Nick Castle and cinematographer David Gribble to create a kind of warm, shadowy, nostalgic feeling; we see the old times as if through a veil of good memories.

The weakness of *Tap*, as I've suggested, is that almost everything that happens in the movie is borrowed, more or less frankly, from old movie lore. In a way, that's also a strength: This is a musical about musicals, as well as being a tap-dance movie about tap dancers. This film about the decline of tap is, itself, a form of resurrection.

Taps ★ ★ ★
PG, 126 m., 1981

George C. Scott (General Bache), Timothy Hutton (Brian Moreland), Ronny Cox (Colonel Kerby), Sean Penn (Alex), Tom Cruise (David). Directed by Harold Becker and produced by Stanley R. Jaffe and Howard B. Jaffe. Screenplay by Darryl Ponicsan and Robert Mark Kamen.

Taps is a meditation on two subjects for which some adolescents have a great capacity: idealism and authoritarianism. It takes place in a realistic setting (it was shot on location at Valley Forge Military Academy), but it is not intended as a realistic film. There are all sorts of clues, including the pointed absence of all but one of the academy's adult faculty members, to indicate that *Taps*, like the emotionally similar *Lord of the Flies*, is using its realistic texture as a setting for a fantasy about human nature.

The film begins with an emotionally stirring commencement exercise at Bunker Hill Military Academy (as the school is called in the film). Sousa marches fill the air, the cadets march around the parade ground looking gloriously proud of themselves, and the reviewing stand is dominated by the legendary old General Harlan Bache, the academy's commander. Bache is played by George C. Scott, and it is probably no accident that his performance in this movie echoes his title role in *Patton* (1970): He is an iron-willed and yet incurably romantic professional soldier.

We soon meet the leading upperclassman, Brian Moreland (Timothy Hutton). He has been selected to lead the cadet corps next year. In one of the most important evenings of his life, he is granted the great privilege of having dinner with old General Bache and sipping some of the old man's brandy. Soon after, however, this whole network of discipline, glory, and tradition is destroyed when it's revealed that the school's pigheaded trustees intend to sell the school and its land to some condominium developers (it is almost worth the price of admission to hear Scott pronounce "condominiums"). Bache is removed from the scene, in a dramatic development I will not reveal. And then Moreland, the cadet commander, takes inventory of the school's supplies of weapons and decides to lead the student body in making a stand for it. They'll take over the school in a military occupation, bar the gates, mount machine guns, and guard posts, and issue a set of demands designed to save the school.

The central passages of *Taps* are devoted to this scheme. The students barricade themselves in the school grounds, the police and National Guard surround the school, and a standoff develops. Meanwhile, within the student body, tensions develop between those kids who are unstable and a little too violent, and those who would secretly rather be on the outside looking in. Hutton, as Moreland, does a lot of learning and soul-searching as he tries to hold his mad scheme together.

There are obviously various problems of plot (such as: Where are the other faculty members? Why are the outside authorities both so stupid and so uncompromising? Why would the trustees have no appreciation of the school's tradition? Why would the grade-school-age cadets be issued live ammunition?, etc.). These questions do not really matter. *Taps* is basically a character study, a portrait of the personalities engaged in the showdown. And, like *Lord of the Flies*, it observes that adolescent males can easily translate the idealistic lessons they have been taught into a rationale for acting in ways that are rigid, dogmatic, and self-justifying.

Taps works as an uncommonly engrossing story, primarily because the performances are so well done. All of the cadet roles are wellacted, not only by seasoned actors like Hutton (who won an Academy Award for *Ordinary People*) but even by the very young kids who struggle with guns and realities much too large for them. By the film's end, we share their love for their school, we despair at the situation they have gotten themselves into, and we are emotionally involved in the outcome. After the film, there are some ideas to think about, involving the implications when might and right are on the same side—and when they are not.

Tarzan, the Ape Man ★ ★ ½
R, 112 m., 1981

Bo Derek (Jane), Richard Harris (Parker), John Phillip Law (Holt), Miles O'Keeffe (Tarzan), Akushula Seleyah (Africa), Steven Strong (Ivory King). Directed and photographed by John Derek and produced by Bo Derek. Screenplay by Tom Rowe and Gary Goddard.

Tarzan, the Ape Man is *The Blue Lagoon* with elephants. Of course it's completely ridiculous, but at the same time it has a certain disarming charm. Sure, it's easy to groan at the secondhand "plot." It's easy to laugh at the clichés and mourn the demotion of Tarzan, who started out in the movies as king of the jungle and now gets fourth billing behind a schoolgirl, an anthropologist, and a wimp. And yet when Tarzan beats his chest and screams and swings to the rescue on a vine, there is something primal happening on the screen. And when Jane and three loyal chimpanzees tenderly bathe the body of the unconscious ape-man, we're getting very close to the reasons why we watch movies, and why there will always be a few movies to reawaken the child within us.

This Bo Derek version of the "Tarzan" legend is allegedly a remake of the MGM version of 1932, starring Johnnie Weissmuller and Maureen O'Sullivan. Not in that version or in any of the others, however, did Hollywood honestly address the central mystery of the Tarzan story, which is—what, exactly, *was* the intimate relationship between Tarzan and Jane? Were they lovers? Friends? Neighbors? Business partners? They presumably made love in order to produce Boy, but the reproduction took place far, far off-screen. I always thought there was something just a little peculiar about the behavior of Weissmuller, Lex Barker, Gordon Scott, and other movie Tarzans. There they were, all alone in the jungle with the beautiful Jane, and what did they do? Swing around on vines and talk to the animals. If I'd wanted *Dr. Doolittle*, I would have seen *Dr. Doolittle*.

This 1981 version is nothing if not willing to satisfy our curiosity about sex life in the rain forest. Bo Derek (who stars and produced) and her husband John (who directed and photographed) are frankly interested only in the relationship between Tarzan and Jane. The whole movie is a setup for several steamy scenes of confrontation between the savage, muscular jungle man and the petite

young girl with eyes as wide as her shoulders. When Tarzan and Jane first meet, the movie all but abandons its plot in favor of foreplay. This is not a movie to waste time on ivory-smuggling, Nazis, cities of gold, antmen, slave girls, lost safaris, or any of the countless other plot devices Edgar Rice Burroughs used as substitutes for interpersonal relationships. It gets right down to business.

The movie opens with a vow by Bo Derek's scientist father (Richard Harris) to lead an expedition to plunder the jungle of its secrets. His real mission: To capture the legendary ape-man Tarzan and bring him back to his club—stuffed and mounted, if possible. Harris takes Bo along on his expedition, which also includes John Phillip Law in the role of the wimp assistant. Law has hardly anything to say, and is always the guy who's looking the other way when Tarzan kidnaps Jane. After a series of routine shots of the jungle march, Tarzan *does* meet Jane and finds himself powerfully attracted to her. Harris is of course insane with jealousy: "Do you know what he *really* wants?" he asks Jane. She hopes so.

Tarzan kidnaps Jane, and then the movie boringly intercuts the jealous father searching for the curious girl. Harris's role in this movie is as hapless as Jason Robards's role in *The Lone Ranger*. Nobody cares about him, his dialogue is overwrought and underwritten, and every time Tarzan and Jane are poised to jump into the bullrushes, the movie cuts back to Harris, slogging through the jungle and cursing the ape-man.

The story line was ridiculous to begin with, but it goes berserk by the time of the movie's incomprehensible climax in a village of mud worshippers. They capture Derek, smear her with paint, and prepare her for some sort of unspeakable sacrifice before Tarzan gallops to the rescue with a herd of elephants. Those friendly elephants are, of course, part of the Tarzan legend. Tarzan speaks Elephant, and there's always that great moment when he needs help, and the elephants hear his screams and perk up their ears. I've always thought it would be dangerous to ask Tarzan for help unless you really wanted it. Say you had a small problem like a missing gourd or a stolen spear, and Tarzan arrived at your village with a herd of elephants to fix things. You'd get your gourd back, maybe, but you'd be cleaning up for weeks.

But never mind. This movie's scenes between Bo Derek, as Jane, and Miles

O'Keeffe, as a Tarzan who never speaks a word, show them as complete sexual innocents, fascinated by the wonderment of each other's bodies. Jane's expression as she looks at the unconscious Tarzan is entrancing. Her unabashed curiosity about him is sexier than any number of steamy sex scenes would have been. Although some of Bo Derek's nude scenes have reportedly been cut from the movie at the insistence of the spoilsport Edgar Rice Burroughs estate, the remaining nude footage is remarkably free of prurience. The Tarzan-Jane scenes strike a blow for noble savages, for innocent lust, for animal magnetism, and, indeed, for soft-core porn, which is ever so much sexier than the hard-core variety. If you do not agree with me, you will probably think Bo's banana scene is ridiculous. I prefer to think it was inevitable.

Taxi Blues ★ ★ ★
NO MPAA RATING, 110 m., 1991

Pyotr Mamonov (Liosha [Jazzman]), Piotr Zaitchenko (Schlikov [Taximan]), Vladimir Kachpour (Old Netchiporenko), Natalia Koliakanova (Christina), Hal Singer (Himself), Elena Satonova (Nina). Directed by Pavel Lounguine and produced by Marin Karmitz. Screenplay by Lounguine.

The bleak and passionate Russian film *Taxi Blues* is one of those movies that seems to exist in two ways at once: It tells a central story, while at the same time telling us another story with the elements around the edge of the frame. The first story involves an obsessive relationship between a hard-headed taxi driver and an irresponsible jazz musician. The other material provides an offhand, casual, and therefore, doubly interesting view of daily life in today's Moscow.

The film begins as a taxi driver, completely at home in the mean streets and familiar with all the angles on the black market, picks up a carload of drunken musicians for a night on the town. One by one they disappear, until finally the last one, a saxophonist named Liosha, stiffs him for a steep seventy-ruble fare. The driver, named Schlikov, does not take this passively. He haunts the jazzman's usual hangouts until he corners him, and then holds his precious saxophone hostage while forcing the man to work out the fare with manual labor.

But there is more than simply bill-collecting going on here. The musician is Jewish, and the taxi driver is casually anti-Semitic, although open-minded enough to be surprised about some of the things he learns about Jews ("They drink like Russians!" he says admiringly of Liosha, who, in fact, drinks like an alcoholic). There is another conflict in the film, between the image of the stalwart, muscular, working-class driver and the thin, tired-eyed musician, who live in completely different worlds. The driver sees the musician as a parasite, the musician sees the driver as a drone, and yet somehow they work out an uneasy arrangement that borders on friendship.

What brings them together is mutual dependency, and it's there that the second level of the movie—the everyday life—comes into play. We see the makeshift sleeping quarters of the driver, who covers every square inch of his small room with posters extolling the women and creature comforts of the West. We see the jazz clubs and speakeasies where Moscow bohemians cluster together for mutual support. And we understand such relationships as the one between the driver and his girlfriend, who works in a meat-packing plant and is therefore invaluable as a black market connection.

The movie is an example of the kind of long-repressed truth-telling that seems to be welling up in today's unsettled Soviet Union, which in the midst of its troubles is experiencing great ferment in the arts. *Taxi Blues* has nothing to do with any official Soviet view of what a film should show, or tell, or be, and everything to do with the Western notion of the movie director as an impassioned witness to his society.

The filmmaker is a forty-one-year-old Soviet Jew named Pavel Lounguine, who was a scriptwriter for years before making a chance contact with a Paris producer who cofinanced this film. Like many films that come from passion, it has been an unexpected commercial and critical hit; it won the best director award at the Cannes Film Festival in 1990, and is a box office winner in Russia and throughout Western Europe.

It is clear from the energy in the story that Lounguine has been waiting a long time to get his hands on the camera, and his point of view swoops and soars through Moscow like a bird released from its cage. If the story is sometimes hard to take—neither one of the protagonists is very pleasant to be around—the anger and passion of the director are exhilarating. And the film is also interesting just for the objective information it displays.

Without mental pictures of a place, we fall back on postcards: Red Square, the Kremlin, Lenin's tomb. Now I will also remember the taxi driver's room, and the lust in the eyes of everyone lucky enough to gaze upon a black market steak.

Taxi Driver ★ ★ ★ ★
R, 112 m., 1976

Robert De Niro (Travis Bickle), Jodie Foster (Iris), Albert Brooks (Tom), Harvey Keitel (Sport), Leonard Harris (Palantine), Peter Boyle (Wizard), Cybill Shepherd (Betsy). Directed by Martin Scorsese and produced by Michael Phillips and Julia Phillips. Screenplay by Paul Schrader.

Taxi Driver shouldn't be taken as a New York film; it's not about a city but about the weathers of a man's soul, and out of all New York he selects just those elements that feed and reinforce his obsessions. The man is Travis Bickle, ex-Marine, veteran of Vietnam, composer of dutiful anniversary notes to his parents, taxi driver, killer. The movie rarely strays very far from the personal, highly subjective way in which he sees the city and lets it wound him.

It's a place, first of all, populated with women he cannot have: Unobtainable blond women who might find him attractive for a moment, who might join him for a cup of coffee, but who eventually will have to shake their heads and sigh, "Oh, Travis!" because they find him . . . well, he's going crazy, but the word they use is "strange." And then, even more cruelly, the city seems filled with men who *can* have these women—men ranging from cloddish political hacks to street-corner pimps who, nevertheless, have in common the mysterious ability to approach a woman without getting everything wrong.

Travis could in theory look for fares anywhere in the city, but he's constantly drawn back to 42nd Street, to Times Square and the whores, street freaks, and porno houses. It's here that an ugly kind of sex comes closest to the surface—the sex of buying, selling, and using people. Travis isn't into that, he hates it, but Times Square feeds his anger. His sexual frustration is channeled into a hatred for the creeps he obsessively observes. He tries to break the cycle—or maybe he just sets himself up to fail again. He sees a beautiful blonde working in the storefront office of a presidential candidate. She goes out with him a couple of times, but the second time he

takes her to a hard-core film and she walks out in disgust and won't have any more to do with him. All the same, he calls her for another date, and it's here that we get close to the heart of the movie. The director, Martin Scorsese, gives us a shot of Travis on a pay telephone—and then, as the girl is turning him down, the camera slowly dollies to the right and looks down a long, empty hallway. Pauline Kael's review called this shot—which calls attention to itself—a lapse during which Scorsese was maybe borrowing from Antonioni. Scorsese calls this shot the most important one in the film.

Why? Because, he says, it's as if we can't bear to watch Travis feel the pain of being rejected. This is interesting, because later, when Travis goes on a killing rampage, the camera goes so far as to adopt slow motion so we can see the horror in greater detail. That Scorsese finds the rejection more painful than the murders is fascinating, because it helps to explain Travis Bickle, and perhaps it goes some way toward explaining one kind of urban violence. Travis has been shut out so systematically, so often, from a piece of the action that eventually he has to hit back somehow.

Taxi Driver is a brilliant nightmare and like all nightmares it doesn't tell us half of what we want to know. We're not told where Travis comes from, what his specific problems are, whether his ugly scar came from Vietnam—because this isn't a case study, but a portrait of some days in his life. There's a moment at a political rally when Travis, in dark glasses, smiles in a strange way that reminds us of those photos of Bremer just before he shot Wallace. The moment tells us nothing, and everything: We don't know the specifics of Travis's complaint, but in a chilling way we know what we need to know of him. The film's a masterpiece of suggestive characterization; Scorsese's style selects details that evoke emotions, and that's the effect he wants. The performances are odd and compelling: He goes for moments from his actors, rather than slowly developed characters. It's as if the required emotions were written in the margins of their scripts: Give me anger—fear—dread. Robert De Niro, as Travis Bickle, is as good as Brando at suggesting emotions even while veiling them from us (and in many of his close-ups, Scorsese uses almost subliminal slow motion to draw out the revelations). Cybill Shepherd, as the blond goddess, is correctly cast, for once, as a glacier slowly receding toward humanity. And there's Jodie Foster, chillingly cast as a twelve-year-old prostitute whom Travis wants to "save." Harvey Keitel, a veteran of all of Scorsese's films (he was the violent maniac in *Alice Doesn't Live Here Anymore)* is the pimp who controls her, and he's got the right kind of toughness that's all bluff.

These people are seen almost in flashes, as if darkness threatens to close over them altogether. *Taxi Driver* is a hell, from the opening shot of a cab emerging from stygian clouds of steam to the climactic killing scene in which the camera finally looks straight down. Scorsese wanted to look away from Travis's rejection; we almost want to look away from his life. But he's there, all right, and he's suffering.

A Taxing Woman ★ ★
NO MPAA RATING, 127 m., 1988

Nobuko Miyamoto (Ryoko Itakura), Tsutomu Yamazaki (Hideki Gondo), Masahiko Tsugawa (Asst. Inspector), Hideo Murota (Hotel President), Shuji Otaki (Tax Office Manager), Daisuke Yamashita (Taro Gondo). Directed by Juzo Itami and produced by Yasushi Tamaoki and Seigo Hosogoe. Screenplay by Itami.

In three movies in only two years, all of them directed after he reached the age of fifty, Juzo Itami has established himself as one of the wittiest and most merciless of Japanese satirists, the brightest talent produced by his country's cinema since Oshima.

His biggest success in this country was with 1987's *Tampopo,* a droll comedy in which a truck driver rode into town like the Man With No Name and befriended a forlorn woman whose restaurant was failing because her noodles were not good enough. The trucker and the cook spied on her competitors to discover the secret of perfect noodles, while meanwhile Itami intercut their adventures with brief scenes mercilessly satirizing Japanese customs and foibles.

Tampopo was his second movie; before it he made *The Funeral,* which scrutinized Japanese ways of death, and now he has made *A Taxing Woman,* about the country's preoccupation with taxes and money. Considering that sex is an undercurrent in all of his films, Itami has now made films about the four obsessions of modern life: death, food, money, and eros.

Tampopo was a gem of a film, starring Nobuko Miyamoto, Itami's wife, as the would-be noodle mistress. *A Taxing Woman* stars her once again, as a pleasant, low-key, relentless tax inspector who lives only to catch cheats at their schemes. Since Itami apparently believes that all Japanese cheat on their taxes in one way or another, Miyamoto has an endless task—and she never considers herself off the job.

Consider, for example, how she stumbles across the case that will transform her career. By accident, she happens into a Tokyo "love hotel," a hot-pillow operation where the turnover seems so quick that she estimates every room must be occupied more than once a night. Yet she finds that the owner of the hotel, a gangster/investor played by Hideo Murota, is reporting an income far below her estimates. So she launches a zealous one-woman campaign to bring him to justice.

A Taxing Woman is not really about her investigation, however. It is about the strange bond that grows up between these two people—the shy bureaucrat and the flamboyant gangster. They do not fall in love, not exactly. Instead, they begin to see in each other's eyes a respect for the same thing—for cleverness, for the creation and solving of mysteries, and especially, for money.

The hotel owner begins to enjoy the tax inspector because she is perhaps the only person in the world who is as interested in his financial manipulations as he is. And she begins to enjoy him because he has given her a bigger challenge than anybody else. Perhaps, however, "enjoy" is the wrong word; they play against each other like seasoned poker adversaries.

All of this should work like clockwork, and sometimes it does, but I found *A Taxing Woman* a disappointment after the lean economy of *Tampopo.* The movie sometimes seems shapeless, overlong and meandering, and there are stretches when nothing much seems to happen. The movie is less like an essay than like a series of disconnected observations; in approaching his subject from many angles, Itami fails to find the one that he needs.

Yet there are reasons to see the movie anyway, and one of them is its portrait of everyday Japanese life. There are ways in which modern Japanese society seems on the same track as American society, and other ways in which it seems totally impenetrable. The tax system in Japan will seem familiar to any American viewer, and so will the actions of the gangster and the "taxing woman." But I was baffled, and intrigued, by the ways that accounting procedures seemed to function as a metaphor for sexuality. I yearned for the simplicity of noodles.

Teenage Mutant Ninja Turtles ★ ★ ¹/₂
PG, 93 m., 1990

Judith Hoag (April O'Neil), Elias Koteas (Casey Jones), Josh Pais (Raphael), Michelan Sisti (Michelangelo), Leif Tilden (Donatello), David Forman (Leonardo), Michael Turney (Danny Pennington), Toshishiro Obata (Tatsu). Directed by Steve Barron and produced by Kim Dawson, Simon Fields, and David Chan. Screenplay by Todd W. Langen and Bobby Herbeck.

Anyone unfortunate enough to have a Nintendo device in the house will be familiar with the Teenage Mutant Ninja Turtles, who star in one of the most insidiously addictive Nintendo games. The turtles live in the subways beneath Manhattan, where, exposed to radiation, they have grown into teen-age-sized, intelligent creatures and absorbed such items from the culture as surfer jargon.

On the Nintendo screen, the turtles leap, spin, cartwheel, and eat pizza. Everything they do is accompanied by the same maddening music, which plays over and over again until it drills itself into the tooth of your mind. There are said to be many levels to the video game, but I succeeded in penetrating only to the second before I realized I had to abandon Ninja Turtles that instant or risk permanent psychic damage.

Now comes *Teenage Mutant Ninja Turtles,* the movie. I did not walk into the screening with a light step and a heart that sang. For that matter, I did not walk out afterward with my spirits renewed. But this movie is nowhere near as bad as it might have been and is probably the best possible Teenage Mutant Ninja Turtle movie.

It supplies, in other words, more or less what Turtle fans will expect: The Ninja Turtles, subways, pizzas, villains, a rudimentary plot, and an explanation of how the Turtles met their Zen master, a wise old rodent.

Having not followed every detail of the film's production with great interest, I was surprised to discover it's a live-action film. I expected animation—a spin-off of the weekday afternoon Turtle cartoon show. But no. These are actual human beings for the most part, including stuntmen inside the life-size

Turtle suits (certain other characters have been created artifically by the Jim Henson folks).

The plot? Do you care? It involves a TV news reporter and her friends, a teen-age crime wave, a secret society named The Foot, and a learning experience for the Turtles as they grow and adapt and become braver warriors with more character. And there are flashbacks to give us the back-story about how their rodent teacher came by his knowledge.

The most interesting part of the film for a non–Teenage Mutant Ninja Turtle fan is the production design—the sewers and the city streets above them. Roy Forge Smith is the designer, and seems inspired by a low-rent vision of *Batman* or maybe *Metropolis*. The city looks like a grungy back-lot version of shabby *film noir*, and the sewers are like medieval dungeons. It's a very dark film, and one wonders, after seeing it, if young Turtle fans are being denied the brightness and bounciness of an earlier generation of kiddie films.

Concerns have been expressed about the Turtles recently on two subjects: the level of violence and the presence in some Turtle stories of characters that may imply negative racial stereotypes. There is no racism in the film version, and the violence is fairly routine, as these things go—stylized and not very graphic.

"Turtle," by the way, is a very funny word.

Teenage Mutant Ninja Turtles II: The Secret of the Ooze ★
PG, 88 m., 1991

Paige Turco (April O'Neil), David Warner (Professor Jordan Perry), Michelan Sisti (Michelangelo), Leif Tilden (Donatello), Kenn Troum (Raphael), Mark Caso (Leonardo). Directed by Michael Pressman and produced by Thomas K. Gray, Kim Dawson, and David Chan. Screenplay by Todd W. Langen.

I bent over backward to be fair to the first movie about the Teenage Mutant Ninja Turtles. It was, I wrote, "probably the best possible Teenage Mutant Ninja Turtle movie." Now we have the sequel, subtitled *The Secret of the Ooze*. I may not get what I want, but I get what I deserve.

Once again, here are the four superhero turtles, their friends Keno and April, their enemy the Shredder, his buddies the Foot Gang, and the maddening Turtle theme

music, which sounds like a berserk merry-go-round. There is also a mad scientist, necessary to explain additional details about how the turtles got that way.

Kids like the turtles. A national survey reported that ninety-five percent of grade school teachers could trace aggressive, antisocial classroom behavior to the Ninja Turtles—high praise. As someone who was raised on Superman, Batman, Spiderman, and Wonder Woman, I think the kids are getting the short end of the stick. What kind of a superhero is a reptile who lives in sewers, is led by a rat, eats cold pizza, and is the product of radioactive waste? Is this some kind of a cosmic joke on the kids, robbing them of their birthright, a sense of wonder? Or is it simply an emblem of our drab and dreary times?

One disturbing thing about the turtles is that they look essentially the same. All that differentiates them, in the Nintendo game that gave them birth, are their weapons. It's as if the whole sum of a character's personality is expressed by the way he does violence. The turtles are an example of the hazards of individuality. They hang out together, act together, fight together, and have a dim collective IQ that expresses itself in phrases like "Cowabunga, dude."

This is the way insecure teen-age boys sometimes talk in a group, as a way of creating solidarity, masking fears of inadequacy, and forming a collective personality that is stupider than any individual member of it. The way you attain status in the group is by using violence to defend it against outsiders.

I liked the older superheroes better. The ones that stood out from a crowd, had their own opinions, were not afraid of ridicule, and symbolized a future of truth and justice. Spiderman and Superman represented democratic values. Today's kids are learning from the Turtles that the world is a sinkhole of radioactive waste, that it's more reassuring to huddle together in sewers than take your chances competing at street level, and that individuality is dangerous. Cowabunga.

Tell Them Willie Boy Is Here ★ ★ ★ 1/2
PG, 96 m., 1970

Robert Redford (Cooper), Katharine Ross (Lola), Robert Blake (Willie Boy), Susan Clark (Liz). Directed by Abraham Polonsky and produced by Philip A. Waxman. Screenplay by Polonsky.

Abraham Polonsky's *Tell Them Willie Boy Is Here* is a simple, direct, almost stark retelling of an event that took place in 1909. It's about Willie Boy, a Paiute Indian whose personal fight for freedom was elevated by the press into an Indian uprising against President William Howard Taft. It is also about white racism and Indian pride, and it is no ordinary Western. It marked the resumption of the directorial career of Polonsky, interrupted twenty years earlier by the House Committee on Un-American Activities during the Hollywood witchhunt. Before he was blacklisted in 1950, Polonsky had written Robert Rossen's *Body and Soul* and directed John Garfield in the classic *Force of Evil*.

Polonsky, who also wrote *Willie Boy*, is at pains to tell his story without gimmicks. It's about how Willie Boy (Robert Blake) comes back to the reservation to marry the girl he loves, Lola (Katharine Ross). But her father forbids them to see each other. In a confrontation, Willie Boy kills the father in self-defense and then goes on the run with Lola. The Indians accept the event as "marriage by capture," forced upon Willie Boy because, as he tells Lola, "I've asked for you the white man's way, and I'm through asking." But Lola, it turns out, was a favorite of the reservation superintendent (Susan Clark), a proper Bostonian who wanted her to be a teacher. At the superintendent's insistence, the sheriff (Robert Redford) gets up a posse and goes after the couple.

Almost all the movie is concerned with the chase, which takes place at a time when President Taft is visiting the area. The president's visit has drawn dozens of newspaper reporters to town, and they sensationalize Willie Boy's case. When Willie Boy accidentally kills one of the members of the posse, an instant "uprising" is born in the papers. Redford wants to forget the whole thing: "It's Indian business, and besides, this posse couldn't catch a dog in the street." But the publicity forces him to keep after Willie Boy, until a final personal confrontation.

Redford gets top billing, and is very good as the sheriff. He has a natural feel for acting in movies; he makes small gestures do the work of large ones, and he can convey a lot of meaning without spelling it out in dialogue. But the film's real star is Robert Blake, who played one of the killers in *In Cold Blood*. Blake is all gristle and nerve and pride, and gained his greatest fame as TV's Baretta.

The movie is paced more slowly than we'd expect for a Western, but then it's not really a

Western at all, but a study of personality. There aren't a lot of action scenes and shoot-outs; this is essentially an essay on the stereotypes by which white men have attempted to justify their theft of the Indian lands and independence. *Tell Them Willie Boy Is Here* works powerfully on that level, and it is impossible to see it without thinking that the same sort of exploitation still goes on today.

10 ★ ★ ★ ★
R, 123 m., 1979

Dudley Moore (George), Julie Andrews (Sam), Bo Derek (Jenny), Robert Webber (Hugh), Dee Wallace (Mary Lewis), Sam Jones (David), Brian Dennehy (Bartender). Directed by Blake Edwards and produced by Edwards and Tony Adams. Screenplay by Edwards.

Blake Edwards's *10* is perhaps the first comedy about terminal yearning. Like all great comedies, it deals with emotions very close to our hearts: In this case, the unutterable poignance of a man's desire for a woman he cannot have. The woman, of course, must be unbelievably desirable (and the hero of *10*, on a scale of 1 to 10, gives this particular woman an 11). It helps, too, if the man is short, forty-two years old, and filled with inchoate longings.

You remember inchoate longings. They used to stalk the pages of novels by Thomas Wolfe, back in the years before the Me Generation and the cult of instant gratification. There used to be a time, incredibly, when you couldn't have something *just because you wanted it*—*10* remembers that time. Its hero, Dudley Moore, begins *10* as a man who seems to have more or less what any man could desire. He is a successful composer. His girlfriend is Julie Andrews. He has a great house up in the hills, he drives a Rolls-Royce, he has cable TV with remote tuning.

But then one day, driving his Rolls down Santa Monica Boulevard, he is visited by a vision. She is a preternaturally beautiful young woman in the next car. She turns to regard him, and he is instantly, helplessly, in love. She turns away. She must be about her business. She is dressed in a bridal gown and is on her way to the church to be married.

He follows her. He is stung by a bee in the church. He has six cavities painfully filled by her father, who is a dentist. Groggy from pain pills and brandy, he finds himself aboard an airplane flying to Mexico—where,

amazingly, he winds up at the same resort as his ideal woman (and, of course, her husband—one of the vacuous beach-boy types with a smile fit for a Jockey T-shirts model).

Blake Edwards's screenplay now plunges into some slightly more serious waters, where we will not follow. What we're struck with, in *10*, is the uncanny way its humor gets laughs by touching on emotions and yearnings that are very real for us. We identify with the characters in this movie: Their predicaments are funny, yes—but then ours would be, too, if they weren't our own.

The central treasure in the film is the performance by Dudley Moore. There must have been times when Moore wondered if he'd *ever* get the girl. In *10*, he does. He also brings his character such life and dimension that *10* is a lot more than a comedy: It's a study in the follies of human nature.

The girl (the one who scores 11) is played by Bo Derek. She is so desirable, such a pure and cheerful embodiment of carnal perfection, that we're in there with Dudley Moore every step of the way, even when he's slogging it out to Ravel's interminable "Bolero." Julie Andrews has a small but delightful role as the sensible mistress, and the movie also has warm performances by Robert Webber, as Moore's vulnerable gay friend, and by Brian Dennehy, as a particularly understanding bartender in Mexico.

10 is not only one of the best films Blake Edwards has ever made, but was something of a turning point in his career: The previous decade he had alternated between successful Pink Panther movies and non-Panther flops like *The Tamarind Seed*, *The Wild Rovers*, and *The Carey Treatment*. Did he have another good straight movie in him? Yes, as a matter of fact, he did.

Tender Mercies ★ ★ ★
PG, 93 m., 1983

Robert Duvall (Mac Sledge), Tess Harper (Rosa Lee), Betty Buckley (Dixie), Wilford Brimley (Harry), Ellen Barkin (Sue Anne), Allan Hubbard (Sonny). Directed by Bruce Beresford and produced by Philip S. Hobel. Screenplay by Horton Foote.

Tender Mercies visits some fairly familiar movie territory, and achieves some quietly touching effects. The movie's about the rhythms of a small Texas town, and about the struggle of a has-been country singer to regain his self-respect. It might remind you

of parts of *The Last Picture Show* and *Honkytonk Man*, with a little bit of *Payday* thrown in (that was the movie starring Rip Torn, based on the last days of the dying Hank Williams, Sr.). This time, the broken-down country singer is named Mac Sledge. He's at the end of his personal road. He was once a big star and a hero to young musicians around the Southwest, but as his final act opens he's sitting in a fleabag motel outside a small Texas town, drinking himself to death, and fighting for the bottle with another guy he hardly even knows.

When he wakes up on the floor the next morning, the other guy is gone and Sledge is hung over, broke, and without prospects. He throws himself on the mercy of the young widow who runs the motel: He'll work for his room and board. She agrees to that, and throws in $2 an hour, but says he can't drink while he's at the motel. He agrees, and that is the day his life turns around and he begins the rebuilding process.

Tender Mercies tells the story of the relationship between the singer and the young widow in a quiet, subtle way; this isn't one of those movies that spells everything out. The key to the movie's tone is in the performance by Robert Duvall as Sledge. Duvall plays him as a bone-weary, seedy, essentially very simple man who needs some values to hold onto. The widow can provide those, and can also provide the stability of a home and family (she has a young son, whose father was killed in Vietnam). What the Duvall character wants to do, essentially, is keep a low profile, work hard, not drink, and forget about the glories of country singing. It's hard for him to remain invisible, though, after the local paper prints a story and the members of a local band start dropping around for advice. There are more complications: Sledge's ex-wife is still touring as a country singer, and would like to turn his eighteen-year-old daughter against him.

What's interesting about *Tender Mercies* is the way it refuses to approach this material as soap opera *or* as drama. The movie's told more like one of those quiet, sly *New Yorker* stories where the big emotional moments sneak up on you, and the effects are achieved indirectly. Sometimes this movie smiles (as in a scene of a double baptism). Sometimes it simply sits there and talks straight (as in a touching speech by Sledge on the meaning of life). Sometimes its low budget allows the seams to show (as in the unconvincing concert scene involving Sledge's wife). But mostly it just lets these stories happen, lets them get to know these people, and see them dealing with life. Some of them get better, and some of them get worse. It's like a country song.

Tequila Sunrise ★ ★ 1/2
R, 120 m., 1988

Mel Gibson (Dale McKussic), Kurt Russell (Nick Frescia), Michelle Pfeiffer (Jo Ann), Raul Julia (Escalante), J.T. Walsh (Maguire), Arliss Howard (Lindroff), Ann Magnuson (Shaleen). Directed by Robert Towne and produced by Thom Mount. Screenplay by Towne.

In the mind of Robert Towne there must be many crannies, many hidden pathways to the same conclusions. In considering a problem he must ponder first this, then that possibility, projecting scenarios on the screen of his imagination. I doubt if he's the kind of guy you'd ask for the shortest way to Studio City.

In his movies, the plots turn and twist upon themselves. Nothing is as it seems. No character can be taken at face value. We learn more about the characters when they're not on the screen than when they are. And even when we think we've got everything nailed down, he pulls another rabbit out of his hat, showing us what fools we were to trust the magician.

His most famous credit is the screenplay for *Chinatown*, a film so labyrinthine that it is difficult to explain precisely what happened in it, even after you've just seen it. *Tequila Sunrise*, written and directed by Towne, contains so many devious plot developments that at times we miss what's on the screen because we're still trying to figure out what the previous scene was revealing.

The movie stars Mel Gibson as Dale McKussic, the nicest drug dealer you'd ever want to know. He lives on the beach with a young son that he adores, and the greatest fear in his life is that he'll lose custody to his ex-wife. Why will he lose custody? Because he's a drug dealer? No, because he isn't a drug dealer—he has retired, and his wife is mad at him because the money is no longer rolling in. Only in Southern California would you lose custody because you'd stopped selling drugs.

But no matter. McKussic seems to have survived a long career as a narcotics distributor without doing any permanent psy-

chic harm to himself. He's not cruel, he's not mean, he's not strung out on drugs, and when he falls in love with a girl he's too shy to tell her. The central question in the movie, however, is whether he's really left his past behind.

His best pal and worst enemy doesn't think so. This is Nick Frescia (Kurt Russell), head of the sheriff's drug detail and an old high-school running-mate of McKussic. Frescia learns from a federal agent (J.T. Walsh) that a big drug shipment is coming to town, personally escorted by the Mexican drug kingpin Escalante (Raul Julia). Escalante and McKussic have been close friends for years. Will McKussic try to score one more deal?

The personal and professional tension between the two old pals is complicated because they are both in love with the same woman—Jo Ann Vallenari (Michelle Pfeiffer), who runs the Italian restaurant they hang out in. The most intriguing triangle in the movie involves, not the drug people, but this three-way romantic tug of war. Jo Ann likes both men. Which one will she choose? The lawman who seems to deceive her? Or the outlaw who plays straight?

As we descend into the somewhat murky depths of Towne's screenplay, these and other questions confound us. *Tequila Sunrise* weaves a tangled web, and there are times when we are not sure what is happening, or why. There are even moments when the chronology itself seems confused, when characters seem to know things they could not be aware of, when other characters arrive at places they should not have known about.

Towne is a gifted writer, and he has created some interesting people here. The Gibson character is especially intriguing because he presents such a mystery; even at the end of the movie, we're not quite sure whether he had really retired from the drug business, or not. But there are times when the movie seems to be complicated simply for the purpose of puzzlement, when additional layers of confusion are added as a sort of exercise having nothing to do with the plot. And the central surprise in the movie—the one big amazing revelation that stuns everybody—is so unlikely that you start scratching your head. *Tequila Sunrise* is an intriguing movie with interesting characters, but it might have worked better if it had found a cleaner narrative line from beginning through to end. It's hard to surrender yourself to a film that seems to be toying with you.

Terminator 2: Judgment Day
★ ★ ★ 1/2
R, 135 m., 1991

Arnold Schwarzenegger (The Terminator), Linda Hamilton (Sarah Connor), Edward Furlong (John Connor), Robert Patrick (T-1000), Earl Boen (Dr. Silberman), Joe Morton (Miles Dyson). Directed and produced by James Cameron. Screenplay by Cameron and William Wisher.

In *Terminator 2: Judgment Day*, the future once again comes hunting to kill John Connor. Even though the world after the nuclear holocaust of 1997 is ruled by machines, a single man can still make a difference—and that man is Connor, who is a youngster as the movie opens, but is destined to grow up into the leader of the human resistance movement against the cyborgs.

You will recall from the original *The Terminator* (1984), or perhaps you will not, that the first Terminator, played by Arnold Schwarzenegger, was sent back from the future to kill Connor's mother (Linda Hamilton). That mission failed, and the young man was born, and so, now, in *Terminator 2*, two Terminators journey back from the future: a good one, played by Schwarzenegger, who is assigned to protect young Connor, and a bad one, played by Robert Patrick, whose mission is to destroy him. (Terminators, by the way, look like humans but are made of high-tech materials and have computer brains; the bad one, named T-1000, was apparently named after his great-grandfather, a Toshiba laptop.) You'd think those machines of the future would realize their mission is futile; that since Connor is manifestly the leader of the human resistance, their mission to kill him obviously must fail. But such paradoxes are ignored by *Terminator 2*, which overlooks an even larger one: If indeed, in the last scene of the film, the computer chips necessary to invent Terminators are all destroyed, then there couldn't have been any Terminators—so how come they exist in the first place? Science fiction has had fun toying with such paradoxes for generations, but *Terminator 2* takes the prudent course of simply ignoring them and centering its action in the present, where young John Connor (Eddie Furlong) is a wild street kid, being raised in a foster home because his birth mother (Hamilton) is a prisoner in a mental hospital. They think she's crazy, of course, because she keeps trying to warn mankind about the approaching nuclear disaster.

From the opening chase scene—in which young Connor, on a fast motorcycle, outruns T-1000, at the wheel of a semi—*Terminator 2* develops a close relationship between the young boy and the good Terminator. Before long young Connor even discovers that Schwarzenegger is programmed to follow his instructions, and so he orders the awesome machine to stop killing people. The result is a neat twist on the tradition of the Schwarzenegger special effects film; this time, instead of corpses littering the screen, the Arnold character shoots to maim or frighten. It's fun for a kid, having his own pet Terminator, and that's one of the inspirations in the screenplay by director James Cameron and William Wisher—Schwarzenegger becomes a father figure for young Connor. Another intriguing screenplay idea is to develop the Terminator's lack of emotions; like Mr. Spock in *Star Trek*, he does not understand why humans cry.

Schwarzenegger's genius as a movie star is to find roles that build on, rather than undermine, his physical and vocal characteristics. Here he becomes the straight man in a human drama—and in a human comedy, too, as the kid tells him to lighten up and stop talking like a computer. After the kid's mother escapes from the mental home, the threesome works together to defeat T-1000, while at the same time creating an unlikely but effective family unit.

While that's happening on the story level, the movie surpasses itself with special effects. There are the usual car chases, explosions, and fight scenes, of course, all well done, but what people will remember is the way the movie envisions T-1000. This cyborg is made out of a newly invented liquid metal that makes him all but invincible. Shoot a hole in him, and you can see right through him, but the sides of the hole run together again, and he's repaired and ready for action. In one grotesque scene, his entire body is twisted into a bizarre sculpture, but it recombines, and in another scene, he is frozen with liquid nitrogen and shattered into a million pieces, but when the pieces melt they flow together and he's as good as new. These scenes involve ingenious creative work by Industrial Light & Magic, the George Lucas special-effects shop. The basic idea for T-1000 was first tried out by ILM in *The Abyss* (1990), where an undersea station was invaded by a creature with a body made entirely out of water. The trick is to create a computer simulation of the movement desired,

and then use a computer paintbox program to give it surface color and texture—in this case, the appearance of liquid mercury. The computer images are then combined with the live action; T-1000 turns from shiny liquid into a human being through a dissolve from the effect to the actor. All of that work would simply be an exercise if the character itself were not effective, but T-1000, as played by Patrick, is a splendid villain, with compact good looks and a bland expression. His most fearsome quality is his implacability; no matter what you do to him, he doesn't get disturbed and he doesn't get discouraged. He just pulls himself together and keeps on coming.

The key element in any action picture, I think, is a good villain. *Terminator 2* has one, along with an intriguing hero, a fierce heroine, and a young boy who is played by Furlong with guts and energy. The movie responds to criticisms of excessive movie violence by tempering the Terminator's blood lust, but nobody, I think, will complain it doesn't have enough action.

Terms of Endearment ★ ★ ★ ★
PG, 129 m., 1983

Debra Winger (Emma Horton), Shirley MacLaine (Aurora Greenway), Jack Nicholson (Breedlove), Jeff Daniels (Flap Horton), Danny DeVito (Vernon), John Lithgow (Sam Burns). Directed, produced, and written by James L. Brooks.

When families get together to remember their times together, the conversation has a way of moving easily from the tragedies to the funny things. You'll mention someone who has passed away, and there'll be a moment of silence, and then somebody will grin and be reminded of some goofy story. Life always has an unhappy ending, but you can have a lot of fun along the way, and everything doesn't have to be dripping in deep significance.

The most remarkable achievement of *Terms of Endearment*, which is filled with great achievements, is its ability to find the balance between the funny and the sad, between moments of deep truth and other moments of high ridiculousness. A lesser movie would have had trouble moving between the extremes that are visited by this film, but because *Terms of Endearment* under-

stands its characters and loves them, we never have a moment's doubt: What happens next is supposed to happen, because life's like that. *Terms of Endearment* feels as much like life as any movie I can think of. At the same time, it's a triumph of show business, with its high comic style, its flair for bittersweet melodrama, and its star turns for the actors. Maybe the best thing about this movie is the way it combines those two different kinds of filmmaking. This is a movie with bold emotional scenes and big laughs, and at the same time it's so firmly in control of its tone that we believe we are seeing real people.

The movie's about two remarkable women, and their relationships with each other and with the men in their lives. The mother is played by Shirley MacLaine. She's a widow who lives in Houston and hasn't dated a man since her husband died. Maybe she's redirected her sexual desires into the backyard, where her garden has grown so large and elaborate that she either will have to find a man pretty quickly or move to a house with a bigger yard. Her daughter, played by Debra Winger, is one of those people who seems to have been blessed with a sense of life and joy. She marries a guy named Flap who teaches English in a series of Midwestern colleges; she rears three kids and puts up with Flap, who has an eye for coeds.

Back in Houston, her mother finally goes out on a date with the swinging bachelor (Jack Nicholson) who has lived next door for years. He's a hard-drinking, girl-chasing former astronaut with a grin that hints of unspeakable lusts. MacLaine, a lady who surrounds herself with frills and flowers, is appalled by this animalistic man and then touched by him.

There are a couple of other bittersweet relationships in the film. Both mother and daughter have timid, mild-mannered male admirers: MacLaine is followed everywhere by Vernon (Danny DeVito), who asks only to be allowed to gaze upon her, and Winger has a tender, little affair with a banker.

The years pass. Children grow up into adolescence, Flap gets a job as head of the department in Nebraska, the astronaut turns out to have genuine human possibilities of becoming quasi-civilized, and mother and daughter grow into a warmer and deeper relationship. All of this is told in a series of perfectly written, acted, and directed scenes that flow as effortlessly as a perfect day, and then something happens that is totally unexpected, and changes everything. I don't want to suggest what happens. It flows so naturally that it should be allowed to take place.

This is a wonderful film. There isn't a thing that I would change, and I was exhilarated by the freedom it gives itself to move from the high comedy of Nicholson's best moments to the acting of Debra Winger in the closing scenes. She outdoes herself. It's a great performance. And yet it's not a "performance." There are scenes that have such a casual gaiety that acting seems to have nothing to do with it. She doesn't reach for effects, and neither does the film, because it's all right there.

Tess ★ ★ ★ ★
PG, 180 m., 1980

Nastassja Kinski (Tess), Peter Firth (Angel Clare), Leigh Lawson (Alec d'Urberville), Rosemary Martin (Mrs. Durbeyfield), Sylvia Coleridge (Mrs. d'Urberville), John Collin (John Durbeyfield), Tony Church (Parson), Brigid Erin Bates (Girl in Meadow). Directed by Roman Polanski and produced by Claude Berri. Screenplay by Gerard Brach, Polanski, and John Brownjohn.

Roman Polanski's *Tess* is a love song with a tragic ending—the best kind of love song of all, just so long as it's not about ourselves. He tells the story of a beautiful young girl, innocent but not without intelligence, and the way she is gradually destroyed by the exercise of the male ego. The story is all the more touching because it is not an unrelenting descent into gloom, as it might have been in other hands, but a life lived in occasional sight of love and happiness. Tess is forever just on the brink of getting the peace she deserves.

The movie is based on a novel by Thomas Hardy, but Polanski never permits his film to become a Classics Illustrated; this isn't a devout rendering of a literary masterpiece, but a film that lives and breathes and has a quick sympathy for its heroine. Nastassja Kinski is just right for the title role. She has the youth, the freshness, and the naiveté of a Tess, and none of the practiced mannerisms of an actress engaged to "interpret" the role. That's good because Tess is a character who should stick out like a sore thumb in many scenes, and Kinski's occasional shy awkwardness is just right for the story of a girl

who attempts to move up in social class on sheer bravado.

The story involves a young girl who will be the victim, the prey, and sometimes the lover of many men, without ever quite understanding what it is that those men want of her. The first man in her life is her father, a drunken farmer named John Durbeyfield, who discovers from the local parson that he is related to the noble local family of d'Urbervilles. The farmer and his wife immediately send their beautiful daughter, Tess, off to confront the d'Urbervilles and perhaps win a position in their household.

Tess is almost immediately seduced by a rakish cousin. She becomes pregnant, and her child dies soon after it is born. She never tells the cousin. But later, after she falls in love with the son of a local minister and marries him, she confesses her past. This is too much for her new husband to bear; he "married down" because he was attracted to Tess's humble origins. But he is not prepared to accept the reality of her past. He leaves on a bizarre mission to South America. Tess, meanwhile, descends to rough manual labor for a few pennies an hour. She is eventually reunited with her cousin (who is not a complete bastard, and complains that he should have been informed of her pregnancy). She becomes his lover. Then the wayward husband returns, and the physical and psychic contest for Tess ends in tragedy.

As a plot, these events would be right at home in any soap opera. But what happens in Polanski's *Tess* is less important than how Tess feels about it, how we feel about it, and how successfully Polanski is able to locate those events in a specific place and time. His movie is set in England, but was actually photographed in France. It is a beautifully visualized period piece that surrounds Tess with the attitudes of her time—attitudes that explain how restricted her behavior must be, and how society views her genuine human emotions as inappropriate. This is a wonderful film; the kind of exploration of doomed young sexuality that, like *Elvira Madigan*, makes us agree that the lovers should never grow old.

Testament ★ ★ ★ ★
PG, 90 m., 1983

Jane Alexander (Carol Wetherly), William Devane (Tom Wetherly), Ross Harris (Brad), Roxana Zal (Mary Liz), Lukas Haas (Scottie), Philip Anglim (Hollis), Leon Ames (Henry

Abhart), Rebecca De Mornay (Mother with Baby). Directed by Lynne Littman and produced by Jonathan Bernstein and Littman. Screenplay by John Sacret Young.

Testament may be the first movie in a long time that will make you cry. It made me cry. And seeing it again for a second time, knowing everything that would happen, anticipating each scene before it came, I was affected just as deeply. But the second time I was able to see more clearly that the movie is more than just a devastating experience, that it has a message with a certain hope.

The film is about a suburban American family, and what happens to that family after a nuclear war. It is not a science-fiction movie, and it doesn't have any special effects, and there are no big scenes of buildings blowing over or people disintegrating. We never see a mushroom cloud. We never even know who started the war. Instead, *Testament* is a tragedy about manners: It asks how we might act toward one another, how our values might stand up in the face of an overwhelming catastrophe.

The movie begins with one of those typical families right out of TV commercials. The father (William Devane) is a physical-fitness nut. The mother (Jane Alexander) is loving, funny, and a little harried. The kids include a daughter who practices the piano, a son who races his dad up hills on their ten-speed bikes, and a little boy who guards the "treasure" in the bottom drawer of his chest. The movie follows these people long enough for us to know them, to appreciate their personalities, their good and weak points, and then one sunny afternoon the war starts.

Most of the film is about what happens then. Anarchy does not break out. There is some looting, but it is limited. For the most part, the people in the small northern California town stick together and try to do the best that they can. There are meetings in the church. There are public-health measures. A beloved community leader (Leon Ames, of TV's "Life with Father" many years ago) is a ham-radio operator, and makes contact with a few other places. A decision is made to go ahead with the grade-school play. Life goes on . . . but death invades it, as radiation poisoning begins to take a toll, first on the babies, then on the children, until finally the cemetery is filled and the bodies have to be burned on a pyre.

The movie finds dozens of small details to suggest existence after the bomb. All the kids, for example, take the batteries out of their toys and computer games, and turn them in for emergency use. Gasoline is rationed, and then runs out. The survivors have no garbage collection, no electricity, and, worst of all, no word from elsewhere. The sky gradually grows darker, suggesting realistically that a nuclear war would finally kill us all by raising great clouds of dust that would choke the Earth's vegetation.

In the midst of this devastation, Jane Alexander, as the mother, tries to preserve love and decency. She stands by her children, watches as they grow in response to the challenges, cherishes them as she sees all her dreams for them disappear. It is a great performance, the heart of the film. In fact, Alexander's performance makes the film possible to watch without unbearable heartbreak, because she is brave and decent in the face of horror. And the last scene, in which she expresses such small optimism as is still possible, is one of the most powerful movie scenes I've ever seen.

Tex ★ ★ ★ ★
PG, 103 m., 1982

Matt Dillon (Tex), Jim Metzler (Mason), Meg Tilly (Jamie), Bill McKinney (Pop), Frances Lee McCain (Mrs. Johnson), Ben Johnson (Cole Collins). Directed by Tim Hunter and produced by Ron Miller. Screenplay by Charlie Haas and Hunter.

There is a shock of recognition almost from the beginning of *Tex*, because we're listening to the sound of American voices in an authentically American world, the world of teen-age boys trying to figure things out and make the right decisions. The voices sound right but may be a little unfamiliar, because adolescents on television are often made to talk in pseudo-hip sitcom nonspeak. Here in *Tex* are the clear voices of two young men who are worthy of attention. Their names are Tex and Mason. They're brothers, one about eighteen, the other fourteen and a half. They live by themselves in a rundown house on some land outside a rural suburb of Tulsa. Their father is a rodeo cowboy who hardly ever stops in at home and forgets to send money for weeks at a time. These two kids are raising themselves and doing a pretty good job of it.

The movie tells the story of a couple of weeks in their lives. These are the kinds of weeks when things can go either well or badly—and if they go badly, we sense, Tex could get his whole life off to the wrong start. The brothers are broke. Mason sells their horses to raise money to buy food and get the gas turned back on. That makes Tex angry and sad; he's a kid looking for trouble.

We meet the other people in their world. There's the rich family down the road, dominated by a stern father who makes his teenagers toe a strict line. His kids are just as unpredictable as anyone else's, but he doesn't believe that. He believes their two undisciplined friends, Tex and Mason, are leading them into trouble and practically dragging them to late-night beer parties. There's another complication. His daughter and Tex are beginning to fall in love.

There's another friend, a local kid who got a girl pregnant, married her, and moved to Tulsa to start a family. He's dealing drugs. Mason knows this intuitively and surely, and knows the kid is heading for trouble. Tex knows it, too, but there comes a time in this story when Tex just doesn't give a damn, and when the drug dealer happens to be there, Tex accepts a ride into Tulsa with him. Tex doesn't do drugs himself, but he gets into a very scary situation with another dealer, and there's a harrowing scene in which Tex wavers just at the brink of getting into serious trouble.

There is more to this movie's story, but the important thing about it isn't what happens, but how it happens. The movie is so accurately acted, especially by Jim Metzler as Mason and Matt Dillon as Tex, that we care more about the characters than about the plot. We can see them learning and growing, and when they have a heart-to-heart talk about "going all the way," we hear authentic teen-agers speaking, not kids who seem to have been raised at Beverly Hills cocktail parties.

Tex is based on a famous novel by S.E. Hinton, who has had two of her other novels filmed by Francis Ford Coppola. She knows a great deal about adolescents, and her work is unaffected by sentimentality and easy romance. It's authentic. But the backgrounds of the two filmmakers are also interesting. Tim Hunter and Charles Haas bought the book and wrote the screenplay, and Hunter directed. Their previous collaboration was a little movie named *Over the Edge*, about teen-agers who feel cornered and persecuted by the rigid middle-class rules of a cardboard Denver suburb. That movie, a small masterpiece containing Matt Dillon's first movie appearance, never got a fair chance in theaters. Now here are Hunter and Haas again, still remembering what it's like to be young, still getting the dialogue and the attitudes, the hang-ups and the dreams, exactly right.

The Texas Chainsaw Massacre ★ ★
R, 87 m., 1974

Paul A. Partain (Frankle), Marilyn Burns (Debbie), Teri McMinn (Other Girl). Directed and produced by Tobe Hooper. Screenplay by Kim Henkel and Hooper.

Now here's a grisly little item. *The Texas Chainsaw Massacre* is as violent and gruesome and blood-soaked as the title promises—a real Grand Guignol of a movie. It's also without any apparent purpose, unless the creation of disgust and fright is a purpose. And yet in its own way, the movie is some kind of weird, off-the-wall achievement. I can't imagine why anyone would want to make a movie like this, and yet it's well-made, well-acted, and all too effective.

The movie's based on factual material, according to the narration that opens it. For all I know, that's true, although I can't recall having heard of these particular crimes, and the distributor provides no documentation. Not that it matters. A true crime movie like Richard Brooks's *In Cold Blood*, which studies the personalities and compulsions of two killers, dealt directly with documented material and was all the more effective for that. But *The Texas Chainsaw Massacre* could have been made up from whole cloth without any apparent difference. No motivation, no background, no speculation on causes is evident anywhere in the film. It's simply an exercise in terror.

It takes place in an isolated area of Texas, which five young people (one of them in a wheelchair) are driving through in their camper van. They pick up a weirdo hitchhiker who carries his charms and magic potions around his neck and who giggles insanely while he cuts himself on the hand and then slices at the paraplegic. They get rid of him, so they think.

But then they take a side trip to a haunted-looking old house, which some of them had been raised in. The two girls laugh as they clamber through the litter on the floor, but one of the guys notices some strange totems and charms which should give him warning. They don't. He and his girlfriend set off for the old swimming hole, find it dried up, and then see a farmhouse nearby. The guy goes to ask about borrowing some gasoline and disappears inside.

His girl gets tired of waiting for him, knocks on the door, and disappears inside, too. A lot of people are going to be disappearing into this house, and its insides are a masterpiece of set decoration and the creation of mood. We see the innocent victims being clubbed on the hand, hung from meat hooks, and gone after with the chain saw.

We see rooms full of strange altars made from human bones, and rooms filled with chicken feathers and charms and weird relics. And gradually we realize that the house is inhabited by a demented family of retarded murderers and grave robbers. When they get fresh victims, they carve them up with great delight. What they do with the bodies is a little obscure, but, uh, they run a barbecue stand down by the road.

One way or another, all the kids get killed by the maniac waving the chain saw—except one girl, who undergoes a night of panic and torture, who escapes not once but twice, who leaps through no fewer than two windows, and who screams endlessly. All of this material, as you can imagine, is scary and unpalatable. But the movie is good technically and with its special effects, and we have to give it grudging admiration on that level, despite all the waving of the chain saw.

There is, for example, an effective montage of quick cuts of the last girl's screaming face and popping eyeballs. There are bizarrely effective performances by the demented family (one of them, of course, turns out to be the hitchhiker, and Grandfather looks like Dustin Hoffman in *Little Big Man*). What we're left with, though, is an effective production in the service of an unnecessary movie.

Horror and exploitation films almost always turn a profit if they're brought in at the right price. So they provide a good starting place for ambitious would-be filmmakers who can't get more conventional projects off the ground. *The Texas Chainsaw Massacre* belongs in a select company (with *Night of the Living Dead* and *Last House on the Left*) of films that are really a lot better than the genre requires. Not, however, that you'd necessarily enjoy seeing it.

Texasville ★ ★ ★ ½
R, 123 m., 1990

Jeff Bridges (Duane Jackson), Cybill Shepherd (Jacy Farrow), Annie Potts (Karla Jackson), Timothy Bottoms (Sonny Crawford), Cloris Leachman (Ruth Popper), Randy Quaid (Lester Marlow), Eileen Brennan (Genevieve). Directed by Peter Bogdanovich and produced by Barry Spikings and Bogdanovich. Screenplay by Bogdanovich.

The Royal Theater still stands on Main Street in Anarene, Texas, but it has been closed for more than thirty years now and the paint is peeling away from its weatherbeaten sign. In the course of *Texasville*, Peter Bogdanovich's camera pauses for just a second to regard it, and to my surprise I remembered the name of Sam the Lion. He was the man who used to own the Royal, back before television came along and forced small-town movie theaters out of business.

Sam the Lion and the other characters in Bogdanovich's *The Last Picture Show* (1971) remain somehow fresh in the memory, even though it's been years since I saw the movie. The simple, stark black-and-white images of that great film have the poignancy of pictures from your high school days—of earlier, simpler times.

Now comes Bogdanovich's *Texasville*, an almost unprecedented reunion of many of the same people, on both sides of the camera. It is, in a sense, like a high school reunion, taking people we last saw in 1951 and continuing their histories in the early 1980s. The story is again by Larry McMurtry, who wrote a sequel to his earlier novel. The screenplay and direction are again by Bogdanovich, who in 1971 was at the dawn of his career and now needs this project as a comeback. Most of the stars are back, too, including Cybill Shepherd, Jeff Bridges, Timothy Bottoms, Randy Quaid, Cloris Leachman, and Eileen Brennan (although Ben Johnson, who was perhaps the best thing in the earlier film, and along with Leachman won an Oscar for his work, isn't here because Sam the Lion is dead).

The location is the same, too: a small Texas town where everybody knows everybody, and they all seem to be having affairs, and everybody knows all about it. In 1951, Sonny, the Bottoms character, had an affair with the coach's wife, and both Sonny and Duane (Bridges) were in love with Jacy (Shepherd), the town's cool and inaccessible

beauty. Then Duane went off to fight the war in Korea, and Jacy moved to Dallas, and now, as we resume the story, it's Duane's son who is sleeping with half the women in town. Sonny is the town mayor and runs the convenience store, but he gets confused some days and doesn't seem quite sure what's going on around him. And Duane is married to Karla (Annie Potts) and has met his match.

Then Jacy comes back to town. Everybody knows the news at once, of course, and speculation flies. She wound up in Italy, apparently, and had some kind of a minor career as an actress in B-movies, but now she's divorced and has just lost a child, and has come back home to gather herself. Shepherd makes her entrance in the movie by emerging, dripping wet, from the waters of a lake and startling Duane, who is floating in his boat. And we're reminded that in the earlier film she looked great in a bathing suit, too—so perfect she inflamed the fantasies and desires of a generation of young men in Anarene.

The difference between then and now, between *The Last Picture Show* and *Texasville*, is between nostalgia and human comedy, between a film that wanted to be bittersweet and one that also wants to be raucous. Things are simply not as *serious* in Anarene as they used to be. Adulteries are not tragedies, but material for gossip. The kids of some thirty years earlier have not grown up into adults like Sam the Lion, but into middle-aged adolescents. Dreams are hardly ever spoken of at all. And yet underneath somewhere there is still the heartbeat of the old values.

The Last Picture Show was lean and hardbitten, and Bogdanovich said he didn't want to shoot it in color because that would "prettify" it. *Texasville* is in color, probably on the studio's uncompromising insistence, and it suffers by comparison; the color makes things seem jollier and more picturesque, and takes the edge off the real suffering that's going on here. And still all the same, there are shadows and sorrows in Anarene, and one of the things that's touching is the way the town has informally and tacitly agreed to overlook some of Sonny's problems and help him out when they can.

In 1951, Jacy was content to be the center of male attention, to be a tease and a flirt. Now that three decades have passed, she sees things a little differently, and one of the unexpected developments in this film is the way she makes friends with Karla, Duane's wife, and they get to be so thick that actual rumors get started. Duane, meanwhile, has his own problems in the romantic area, not to mention trying to deal with his son's, and one of the most common attitudes in this movie is lethargy in the face of overwhelming developments. The town motto could be, "What you gonna do?"

Bogdanovich brings some of the story threads together in a long sequence built around the Anarene centennial celebration, and there is a parade in which Jacy gets to wave from a float decorated with the tactless legend, "Homecoming Queen Through the Ages." There are also some moments of heartfelt emotion, confession, and tragedy, and the oil crisis and other international events occasionally hover on the horizon, but in general the town seems to be preoccupied as ever with its own personalities and memories, as if it were sitting for its portrait.

Is *Texasville* as good as *The Last Picture Show?* No, because the previous picture was complete, and this one seems to lack a genuine reason for existence. Jacy does indeed return to town, but, once there, she seems to fall easily into the general aimlessness, and the citizens of Anarene seem so accepting of human nature that they have given up having any dreams or expectations for it. There has to be more to life than screwing around. Well, doesn't there?

And yet in a subtle way, *Texasville* is making the same point as the previous film: That the last picture show has closed, and that the dreams of the old West, the dreams in movies like *Red River* (which was the last movie that played at the Royal), have been forgotten, and now under these wide Texas skies people lower their eyes to smaller concerns and lives without vision. During the Centennial celebration, one of the living exhibits is labeled "County's Oldest Inhabitant." I wonder what Sam the Lion would have thought about that.

That's Dancing! ★ ★ ★
PG, 105 m., 1985

With hosts Mikhail Baryshnikov, Ray Bolger, Sammy Davis, Jr., Gene Kelly, and Liza Minnelli. Directed by Jack Haley, Jr., and produced by David Niven, Jr., and Haley. Screenplay by Haley.

There is a sense in which it is impossible to dislike *That's Dancing!* and another sense in which movies like this—made by splicing together all the "good parts" —are irritating

and sort of unfair to the original films. Given the choice of seeing *Singin' in the Rain* again or spending the same amount of time looking at scenes from *Singin'* and maybe sixty other films, I'd rather see the real movie all the way through. But *That's Dancing!* is not setting an either-or test for us; what it basically wants to do is entertain us with a lot of good dance scenes from a lot of good, and bad, movies, and that is such a harmless ambition that I guess we can accept it.

The movie has been put together by Jack Haley, Jr., and David Niven, Jr., and it recycles Haley's formula in *That's Entertainment!* (1974), the original slice-and-dice anthology from Hollywood's golden ages. There also has been a *That's Entertainment II* (or "too," I seem to recall), and the law of diminishing returns is beginning to apply. Sooner or later, we'll get *That's All, Folks!* In the first movie, for example, we got Gene Kelly's immortal title dance number from *Singin' in the Rain;* in the first movie, we got Donald O'Connor's equally immortal "Make 'em Laugh" sequence; and that leaves Kelly and O'Connor's only somewhat immortal "Moses Supposes" number for this film. Pretty soon we're going to be getting *That's What's Left of Entertainment!*

That's Dancing! shares with the earlier movies an irritating compulsion to masquerade as a documentary, which it isn't. The tone is set by Kelly's opening generalizations about the universality of dance, etc., while we see *National Geographic* outtakes of dancing around the world: tribes in Africa, hula skirts in Hawaii, polkas, geisha girls, and so on. Kelly is later spelled by such other dance analysts as Liza Minnelli, Ray Bolger, Mikhail Baryshnikov, and Sammy Davis, Jr., all of whom can dance with a great deal more ease than they can recite pseudo-profundities.

There is, however, a lot of good dancing in this movie, including rare silent footage of Isadora Duncan. We see Busby Berkeley's meticulously choreographed dance geometries, the infinite style of Fred Astaire, the brassy joy of Ginger Rogers, the pizazz of Cyd Charisse and Eleanor Powell, a charming duet between Bill "Bojangles" Robinson and Shirley Temple, and a dazzling display by the Nicholas Brothers, who were the inspiration for the dance team played by the Hines brothers in *Cotton Club.* The movie is up-to-date, with John Travolta from *Saturday Night Fever* and footage from breakdance movies, *Flashdance,* and Michael Jackson's *Thriller.* But perhaps its most pleasing single moment is a little soft-shoe by

Jimmy Cagney, who was perhaps not the technical equal of Astaire, but was certainly on the same sublime plane when it came to communicating sheer joy.

One of the insights offered in the narration of *That's Dancing!* is that Astaire was responsible for the theory that you should see the entire body of the dancer in most of the shots in a dance scene, and that the scene should be shown in unbroken shots, as much as possible, to preserve the continuity of the dancer's relationship with space and time. That's the kind of seemingly obvious statement that contains a lot of half-baked conclusions. True, you have to see the dancer's whole body to appreciate what he's doing (look at the disastrous choreography in Travolta's *Stayin' Alive,* which inspired Ginger Rogers to call it a dance film—"from the waist up"). But you also need the cutaways to show the faces of the dancers, and the chemistry between them, as when Astaire and Rogers have their enchanted dancing lesson in *Swing Time.* True, shooting the whole thing in one unbroken take preserves the integrity of the visual record—but what about the sensational dance sequences in *Flashdance* that were achieved by literally cutting between different dancers, all doing their own specialty? All that really matters is the end result.

What conclusions can be drawn from the movie's survey of sixty years of dancing on screen? I can think of one, sort of obvious and sort of depressing: Style has gone out of style. New dancers in recent dance movies are in superb physical shape and do amazing things on the screen, but they do not have the magical personal style of an Astaire or a Kelly. They're technicians. And there's another thing: They don't really dance together. A lot of them are soloists, or two soloists sharing the same floor. When Astaire and Rogers danced together, they danced *together.* And that is maybe what dancing is finally all about.

That's Entertainment! ★ ★ ★ ★
G, 132 m., 1974

Selected scenes from MGM musicals between 1929 and 1958, introduced by Frank Sinatra, Fred Astaire, Gene Kelly, Mickey Rooney, Liza Minnelli, Elizabeth Taylor, James Stewart, Donald O'Connor, and others. Written, produced, and directed by Jack Haley, Jr.

It used to be said that the trickiest thing about a musical was to figure out a way for the characters to break gracefully into song. Maybe that was all wrong. Maybe the hardest thing was for them to stop, once the singing had started. That's my notion after seeing *That's Entertainment!*, a magical tour through the greatest musicals produced by the king of Hollywood studios, Metro-Goldwyn-Mayer.

This isn't just a compilation film, with lots of highlights strung together. Those kinds of movies quickly repeat themselves. *That's Entertainment!* is more of a documentary and a eulogy. A documentary of a time that began in 1929 and seemed to end only yesterday, and a eulogy for an art form that will never be again.

Hollywood will continue to make musicals, of course (although, curiously enough, the form never has been very popular overseas). But there will never be musicals like this again, because there won't be the budgets, there won't be the sense of joyous abandon, there won't be so many stars in the same place all at once, and—most of all—there won't be the notion that a musical has to be "important."

The various segments of the film are introduced and narrated by MGM stars of the past (Fred Astaire, Gene Kelly), superstars like Frank Sinatra and Elizabeth Taylor, offspring like Liza Minnelli, and even a ringer like Bing Crosby (he was a Paramount star, but never mind). They seem to share a real feeling of nostalgia for MGM, which, in its heyday, was not only a studio, but also a benevolent and protective organization ruled by the paternal Louis B. Mayer. Liza Minnelli sounds at times as if she's narrating a visit to her mother's old high school. The movie avoids the trap of being too worshipful in the face of all this greatness. It's not afraid to kid; we see Clark Gable looking ill at ease as he pretends to enjoy singing and dancing, and we see a hilarious montage of Judy Garland and Mickey Rooney ringing endless changes to the theme, "I know—we'll fix up the old barn and put on a show!"

And then there are the glorious, unforgettable moments from the great musicals. My favorite musical has always been *Singin' in the Rain*, the 1952 comedy about Hollywood's traumatic switch to talkies. *That's Entertainment!* opens with a montage of musicals (neatly surveying three decades of film progress), and later returns to the two most unforgettable numbers in the film:

Gene Kelly sloshing through puddles while singing the title song, and Donald O'Connor in his amazing "Make 'em Laugh," in which he leaps up walls, takes pratfalls, and dives through a set.

There are other great moments: The closing ballet from *An American in Paris;* Nelson Eddy and Jeanette MacDonald being hilariously serious in *Rose Marie;* Astaire and Ginger Rogers, so light-footed they seem to float; Gene Kelly's incredible acrobatics as he does his own stunts, swinging from rooftop to rooftop; William Warfield singing "Old Man River" in *Showboat;* Judy Garland singing "You Made Me Love You" to a montage of stills of Clark Gable; Garland, again, with "Get Happy" (and a vignette of little Liza's first movie appearance, aged about three); the acrobatic woodchopper's scene from *Seven Brides for Seven Brothers;* and even Esther Williams rising from the deep.

The movie's fun from beginning to end. It's not camp, and it's not nostalgia: It's a celebration of a time and place in American movie history when everything came together to make a new art form.

Thelma & Louise ★ ★ ★ ½
R, 128 m., 1991

Susan Sarandon (Louise), Geena Davis (Thelma), Harvey Keitel (Hal), Michael Madsen (Jimmy), Christopher McDonald (Darryl), Stephen Tobolowsky (Max), Brad Pitt (J.D.). Directed by Ridley Scott and produced by Scott and Mimi Polk. Screenplay by Callie Khouri.

Thelma & Louise is in the expansive, visionary tradition of the American road picture. It celebrates the myth of two carefree souls piling into a 1956 T-Bird and driving out of town to have some fun and raise some hell. We know the road better than that, however, and we know the toll it exacts: Before their journey is done, these characters will have undergone a rite of passage, and will have discovered themselves.

What sets *Thelma & Louise* aside from the great central tradition of the road picture—a tradition roomy enough to accommodate *Easy Rider, Bonnie and Clyde, Badlands, Midnight Run,* and *Rainman*—is that the heroes are women this time: working-class girlfriends from a small Arkansas town, one a waitress, the other a housewife, both probably ready to describe themselves as utterly

ordinary, both containing unexpected resources.

We meet them on days that help to explain why they'd like to get away for the weekend. Thelma (Geena Davis) is married to a man puffed up with self-importance as the district sales manager of a rug company. He sees his wife as a lower order of life, to be tolerated so long as she keeps her household duties straight and is patient with his tantrums. Louise (Susan Sarandon) waits tables in a coffee shop and is involved with a musician who is never ever going to be ready to settle down, no matter how much she kids herself.

So the girls hit the road for a weekend (Thelma is so frightened of her husband she leaves him a note rather than tell him). They're almost looking to get into trouble, in a way; they wind up in a saloon not too many miles down the road, and Thelma, a wild woman after a couple of margaritas, begins to get caught up in lust after a couple of dances with an urban cowboy.

That leads, as such flirtations sometimes tragically do, to an attempted rape in the parking lot. And after Louise comes to her friend's rescue, there is a sudden, violent event that ends with the man's death. And the two women hit the road for real. They are convinced that no one would ever believe their story—that the only answer for them is to run, and to hide.

Now comes what in a more ordinary picture would be the predictable stuff: the car running down lonely country roads in front of a blood-red sunset, that kind of thing, with a lot of country music on the sound track. *Thelma & Louise* does indeed contain its share of rural visual extravaganza and lost railroad blues, but it has a heart, too. Sarandon and Davis find in Callie Khouri's script the materials for two plausible, convincing, lovable characters. And as actors they work together like a high-wire team, walking across even the most hazardous scenes without putting a foot wrong.

They have adventures along the way, some sweet, some tragic, including a meeting with a shifty but sexy young man named J.D. (Brad Pitt), who is able, like the dead saloon cowboy, to exploit Thelma's sexual hungers, left untouched by the rug salesman. They also meet old men with deep lines on their faces, and harbingers of doom, and state troopers, and all the other inhabitants of the road.

Of course, they become the targets of a manhunt. Of course, every cop in a six-state area would like to bag them. But back home in Arkansas there's one cop (Harvey Keitel) who has empathy for them, who sees how they dug themselves into this hole and are now about to get buried in it. He tries to reason with them. To "keep the situation from snowballing." But it takes on a peculiar momentum of its own, especially as Thelma and Louise begin to grow intoxicated with the scent of their own freedom—and with the discovery that they possess undreamed-of resources and capabilities.

Thelma & Louise was directed by Ridley Scott, from Britain, whose previous credits (*Blade Runner, Black Rain, Legend*) show complete technical mastery, but are sometimes not very interested in psychological questions. This film shows a great sympathy for human comedy, however, and it's intriguing the way he helps us to understand what's going on inside the hearts of these two women—why they need to do what they do.

I would have rated the movie at four stars, instead of three and a half, except for one shot: the last shot before the titles begin. This is the catharsis shot, the payoff, the moment when Thelma and Louise arrive at the truth that their whole journey has been pointed toward, and Scott and his editor, Thom Noble, botch it. It's a freeze frame that fades to white, which is fine, except it does so with unseemly haste, followed immediately by a vulgar carnival of distractions: flashbacks to the jolly faces of the two women, the roll of the end credits, an upbeat country song.

It's unsettling to get involved in a movie that takes 128 minutes to bring you to a payoff that the filmmakers seem to fear. If Scott and Noble had let the last shot run an additional seven to ten seconds, and then held the fade to white for a decent interval, they would have gotten the payoff they deserved. Can one shot make that big of a difference? This one does.

Thelonious Monk: Straight, No Chaser
★ ★ ★ ½
PG-13, 88 m., 1989

Thelonious Monk Quartet: Charlie Rouse, tenor saxophone; Larry Gales, bass; Ben Riley, drums. Thelonious Monk Octet: Charlie Rouse, tenor saxophone; Phil Woods, alto saxophone; Johnny Griffin, tenor saxophone; Ray Copeland, trumpet; Jimmy Cleveland, trombone; Larry Gales, bass; Ben Riley, drums. Duo piano performance by Tommy Flanagan and Barry Harris. Narration by Samuel E. Wright. Directed by Charlotte Zwerin and produced by Zwerin and Bruce Ricker.

Right before I sat down to write this review, I put on the 1956 album *Brilliant Corners* by Thelonious Monk. If you are not very familiar with Monk, you may not recognize the title. But if you have ever found yourself in a bar with a good jukebox, you will recognize the music. The title song is a happy one, but it is not mood that carries the stamp of Monk; it is authority. He played the piano as if he knew exactly what every note should mean and be and had known it for a long time.

That is why *Thelonious Monk: Straight, No Chaser* is vaguely disturbing right from the opening scenes. We can sense there is something wrong here, and unless we know the life history of Monk, we don't know what it is. The music is great, free-spirited, and liberating, but in the person of Monk there is a shadow of some kind, a vagueness, a disinclination to connect. The movie never does put a name to Monk's condition, but by the end of the film enough people who loved him have made enough references to it that we know what we need to know: He went gradually and rather stoically mad.

The last years of his life, we learn, were spent sitting quietly in the room of a friend. He did not play jazz anymore, but when friends would come over to play, they knew he could still listen because he would leave the door of his room open. The mental illness, whatever it was, must have begun many years earlier. There is a shot in this movie of Monk in an airport somewhere, turning around and around in the same place, engrossed in this repetition as if it were some kind of meditation. And throughout the movie, when Monk talks, it seems to be in a kind of code, and when he looks at the camera, he doesn't quite look at the camera.

This is a new movie, but the footage of Monk in it is more than twenty years old, shot for German television by Christian Blackwood in 1967 and 1968. Two decades passed before the by-now-forgotten footage was mentioned by Blackwood to Bruce Ricker, whose *Last of the Blue Devils* (1980) was a landmark documentary about Kansas City jazz. Using the Blackwood footage of Monk as their foundation, Ricker and documentarian Charlotte Zwerin began tracking down the survivors who knew Monk best: his son; his tenor sax player, Charles Rouse; his manager; his road manager; and Baroness Nica de Koenigswarter, who appeared in Monk's life at about the time his wife was near exhaustion with the effort of dealing with him, and seems to have shared both the effort and the man with her.

They all seem to remember more or less the same man; there are not a lot of different versions of Monk in this movie. He was, they agree, a musical genius, and of course history has proven them right. He could see the clear line through to the end of a composition that baffled other people, and his squiggles on a piece of paper, interpreted by Monk as if anybody should have been able to understand them, often turned out to be immortal works of jazz. He gathered other geniuses around him—John Coltrane was a member of his Blue Note band in the late 1950s—and he traveled, recorded, played, composed, jammed, inspired, and produced music that changed forever the way modern jazz sounds.

At the same time, he drifted into himself. His reveries must have become seductively comfortable to him. At some point he withdrew and wasn't there anymore for his friends. He was locked inside. The movie doesn't go into detail about this gradual process, and for that, in a way, I am grateful, because his music puts us in our own mood for reverie, not diagnosis. I had heard the music before. What the film gave me was an opportunity to see Thelonious Monk creating some of it and, just as important, an opportunity to see how those who knew him loved him.

Therese ★ ★ ★ ½
NO MPAA RATING, 90 m., 1987

Catherine Mouchet (Therese), Aurore Prieto (Celine), Silvie Habault (Pauline), Ghislane Mona (Marie), Helene Alexandridis (Lucie), Jean Pelegri (Father), Armand Meppiel (The Pope). Directed by Alain Cavalier and produced by Maurice Bernart. Screenplay by Cavalier and Camille De Casabianca.

Therese is such a strong, pure, apparently simple movie that there's a temptation to let it carry us along. We don't want to ask questions. And yet at the end of this movie there are so many unanswered questions that we realize the movie is one long question: What was the secret of Therese Martin's joy?

She was known as the "Little Flower of Jesus." As a girl, she wanted to enter the strict cloisters of the Carmelite nuns, and when she was refused permission she went all the way to the Pope to finally obtain it. Inside the walls, she struck everyone with the openness and sweetness of her disposition, and after she died in 1897 she became famous through the publication of her journal. She was canonized in 1925.

The movie centers itself around the depth of her passionate love affair with Jesus. The nuns are figuratively wed to Christ in the ceremony which admits them to the order, and in Therese's case she seems to have taken the wedding not only seriously but literally. In a way, *Therese* is the story of a girl who dies on her honeymoon.

The story is told with stark visual simplicity by Alain Cavalier, who shoots against plain backdrops and includes only those costumes or props that are needed to make sense of a scene. His real visual subject is the human face. And after Therese is admitted to the closed convent, where a vow of silence is usually enforced, the faces themselves seem to speak.

We become familiar with the other nuns. With an old, old woman of great saintliness. With a wise mother superior. With a young nun who has a crush on Therese. And with Therese herself, who is played by Catherine Mouchet with a kind of transparent, low-key ecstasy. There is a real sense of the community of the convent. In one of the movie's best scenes, a man comes from outside to bring gifts of food to the nuns, who cover their faces and flutter around him like blinded birds.

Therese is not like any other biographical film of a saint—or of anyone else. It makes a bold attempt to penetrate to the mystery of Therese's sainthood, and yet it isn't propaganda for the church and it doesn't necessarily even approve of her choice of a vocation. Perhaps the local bishop was right, in saying Therese was too young for the strenuous life of the convent. Perhaps her devotion to Jesus was indeed, as Andrew Sarris wrote in his review of the film, "displaced sexuality and transsubstantiated fetishism."

This movie is so deep and so subtle that we cannot ever be sure just what the filmmaker thinks about Therese. That's one of the reasons I found it so disturbing and provoking. What Cavalier gives us is a portrait of the externals of sainthood, and just those internals that can be glimpsed and guessed through the eyes of a gifted actress. He makes no statement about his material. After we've seen the movie, we ask ourselves what

it was that motivated Therese, and whether perhaps it was good even though it violates modern notions, and we also ask ourselves why she was so happy. We would not be happy living her life. But then we are not saints.

They Shoot Horses, Don't They?
★ ★ ★ ★
PG, 123 m., 1970

Jane Fonda (Gloria), Michael Sarrazin (Robert), Susannah York (Alice), Gig Young (Rocky), Red Buttons (Sailor), Bonnie Bedelia (Ruby), Severn Darden (Cecil). Directed by Sydney Pollack and produced by Irwin Winkler and Robert Chartoff. Screenplay by James Poe and Robert E. Thompson.

Erase the forced smiles from the desperate faces, and what the dance marathons of the 1930s came down to was fairly simple. A roomful of human beings went around and around within four walls for weeks at a time without sleep, populating a circus for others who paid to see them. At the end, those who didn't collapse or drop dead won cash prizes that were good money during the Depression. And the Depression, in an oblique sort of way, was the reason for it all. The marathons offered money to the winners and distraction to everyone else. To be sure, some of the marathons got pretty grim. Contestants tried to dance their way through illnesses and pregnancies, through lice and hallucinations, and the sight of them doing it was part of the show. Beyond the hit tunes and the crepe paper and the free pig as a door prize, there was an elementary sadism in the appeal of the marathons.

Among American spectator sports, they rank with stock-car racing. There was always that delicious possibility, you see, that somebody would die. Or freak out. Or stand helplessly while his partner collapsed and he lost the investment of thousands of hours of his life.

They Shoot Horses, Don't They? is a masterful re-creation of the marathon era for audiences that are mostly unfamiliar with it. In addition to everything else it does, *Horses* holds our attention because it tells us something we didn't know about human nature and American society. It tells us a lot more than that, of course, but because it works on this fundamental level as well it is one of the best American movies of the 1970s. It is so good as a movie, indeed, that it doesn't have to bother with explaining the things in my

first two paragraphs; they are all there (and that's where I found them), but they are completely incorporated into the structure of the film.

Director Sydney Pollack has built a ballroom and filled it with characters. They come from nowhere, really; Michael Sarrazin is photographed as if he has walked into the ballroom directly from the sea. The characters seem to have no histories, no alternate lives; they exist only within the walls of the ballroom and during the ticking of the official clock. Pollack has simplified the universe. He has got everything in life boiled down to this silly contest; and what he tells us has more to do with lives than contests.

Sarrazin meets Jane Fonda, and they became partners almost absent-mindedly; he wasn't even planning on entering a marathon. There are other contestants, particularly Red Buttons and Bonnie Bedelia in splendid supporting performances, and they are whipped around the floor by the false enthusiasm of Gig Young, the master of ceremonies. "Yowzza! Yowzza!" he chants, and all the while he regards the contestants with the peculiarly disinterested curiosity of an exhausted god.

There are not a lot of laughs in *Horses*, because Pollack has directed from the point of view of the contestants. They are bitter beyond any hope of release. The movie's delicately timed pacing and Pollack's visual style work almost stealthily to involve us; we begin to feel the physical weariness and spiritual desperation of the characters.

The movie begins on a note of alienation and spirals down from there. *Horses* provides us no cheap release at the end; and the ending, precisely because it is so obvious, is all the more effective. We knew it was coming. Even the title gave it away. And when it comes, it is effective not because it is a surprise but because it is inevitable. As inevitable as death.

The performances are perfectly matched to Pollack's grim vision. Jane Fonda is hard, unbreakable, filled with hate and fear. Sarrazin can do nothing, really, but stand there and pity her; no one, not even during the Depression, should have to feel so without hope. Red Buttons, as the sailor who's a veteran of other marathons and cheerfully teaches everybody the ropes, reminds us that the great character actor from *Sayonara* still exists, and that comedians are somehow the best in certain tragic roles.

And that's what the movie comes down to, maybe. The characters are comedians trapped in tragic roles. They signed up for the three square meals a day and the crack at the $1,500 prize, and they can stop (after all) whenever they want to. But somehow they can't stop, and as the hundreds and thousands of hours of weariness and futility begin to accumulate, the great dance marathon begins to look more and more like life.

Thief ★ ★ ★ ¹/₂
R, 126 m., 1981

James Caan (Frank), Tuesday Weld (Jessie), Willie Nelson (Okla), James Belushi (Barry), Robert Prosky (Leo), Tom Signorelli (Attaglia), John Santucci (Urizzi), Tom Erhart (Judge). Directed by Michael Mann and produced by Jerry Bruckheimer and Ronnie Caan. Screenplay by Mann.

Michael Mann's *Thief* is a film of style, substance, and violently felt emotion, all wrapped up in one of the most intelligent thrillers I've seen. It's one of those films where you feel the authority right away: This movie knows its characters, knows its story, and knows exactly how it wants to tell us about them. At a time when thrillers have been devalued by the routine repetition of the same dumb chases, sex scenes, and gun fights, *Thief* is completely out of the ordinary.

The movie stars James Caan as a man who says he was "raised by the state" and spent eleven years in prison. As the movie opens, he's been free four years, and lives in Chicago. He is a highly skilled professional thief—a trade he learned behind bars from Okla (Willie Nelson), a master thief. The film's opening sequence establishes Caan's expertise as he cracks a safe with a portable drill. Caan sees himself as a completely independent loner. But we see him differently, as a lonely, unloved kid who is hiding out inside an adult body. He's a loner who desperately needs to belong to somebody. He trusts his partner (James Belushi), but that's not enough. He decides, on an almost abstract intellectual level, to fall in love with a cashier (Tuesday Weld), and in one of the movie's best scenes he tells this woman, who is essentially a stranger, all about his life in prison and his plans for the future. She takes his hand and accepts him.

But there is another person who comes into his life: Leo, the master criminal, the fence who sets up heists and hires people to pull them. Leo, in a wonderfully complex performance by the sad-faced Robert Prosky, knows how to enlist Caan: "Let me be your father," he says. "I'll take care of everything." He does. He even supplies Caan and Weld with an illegally obtained baby boy when they're turned down at the adoption agency. But once the thief goes with Leo, his life gets complicated. The cops seem to be on his case. His phone is bugged. Everybody knows his business. The movie leads up to one final caper, a $4 million diamond heist in Los Angeles, and then it ends in a series of double crosses and a rain of violence.

This movie works so well for several reasons. One is that *Thief* is able to convince us that it knows its subject, knows about the methods and criminal personalities of its characters. Another is that it's well cast: Every important performance in this movie successfully creates a plausible person, instead of the stock-company supporting characters we might have expected. And the film moves at a taut pace, creating tension and anxiety through very effective photography and a wound-up, pulsing score by Tangerine Dream.

If *Thief* has a weak point, it is probably in the handling of the Willie Nelson character. Nelson is set up well: He became Caan's father-figure in prison, Caan loves him more than anybody, and when he goes to visit him in prison they have a conversation that is subtly written to lead by an indirect route to Nelson's understated revelation that he is dying and does not want to die behind bars. This scene is so strong that it sets us up for big things: We expect Willie to get out, get involved in the plot, and be instrumental in the climax. That doesn't happen. There is a very nice courtroom scene, during which you'll have to pay close attention to catch on to the subverbal and illegal conversation conducted between the judge and the lawyer. But then the Nelson character quickly disappears from the movie, and we're surprised and a little disappointed. Willie has played the character so well that we wanted more. But, then, I suppose it is a good thing when a movie creates characters we feel that strongly about, and *Thief* is populated with them. It's a thriller with plausible people in it. How rare.

Thieves Like Us ★ ★ ★ ¹/₂
R, 123 m., 1974

Keith Carradine (Bowie), Shelley Duvall (Keechie), John Schuck (Chicamaw), Bert Remsen (T-Dub), Louise Fletcher (Mattie), Ann Latham (Luie). Directed by Robert Altman and produced by Jerry Bick. Screenplay by Calder Willingham, Joan Tewkesbury, and Altman.

Like so much of his work, Robert Altman's *Thieves Like Us* has to be approached with a certain amount of imagination. Some movies are content to offer us escapist experiences and hope we'll be satisfied. But you can't sink back and simply absorb an Altman film; he's as concerned with style as subject, and his preoccupation isn't with story or character, but with how he's showing us his tale. That's the case with *Thieves Like Us*, which no doubt has all sorts of weaknesses in character and plot, but which manages a visual strategy so perfectly controlled that we get an uncanny feel for this time and this place. The movie is about a gang of fairly dumb bank robbers, and about how the youngest of them falls in love with a girl, and about how they stick up some banks and listen to the radio and drink Coke and eventually get shot at.

The outline suggests *Bonnie and Clyde*, but *Thieves Like Us* resembles it only in the most general terms of period and setting. The characters are totally different; Bonnie and Clyde were anti-heroes, but this gang of Altman's has no heroism at all. Just a kind of plodding simplicity, punctuated by some of them with violence, and by the boy with a kind of wondering love. They play out their sad little destinies against two backdrops: One is the pastoral feeling of the Southern countryside, and the other is an exactly observed series of interior scenes that recapture just what it was like to drowse through a slow, hot summer Sunday afternoon, with the radio in the background and the kids playing at pretending to do Daddy's job. If Daddy's a bank robber, so what?

The radio is constantly on in the background of *Thieves Like Us*, but it's not used as a source of music as it was in *American Graffiti* or *Mean Streets*. The old shows we hear are not supposed to be heard by Altman's characters; they're like theme music, to be repeated in the film when the same situations occur. "Gangbusters" plays when they rob a bank, for example, even though the bank would have been closed before "Gangbusters" came on. That's OK, because the radio isn't supposed to be realistic; it's Altman's wry, elegiac comment on the distance between radio fantasy and this dusty, slow-witted reality.

At the heart of the movie is a lovely relationship between the young couple, played by Keith Carradine and Shelley Duvall. They've both been in Altman movies before (just about everybody in view here is in his stock company), and it's easy to see why he likes them so. They don't look like movie stars. They share a kind of rangy grace, an ability to project shyness and uncertainty. There's a scene in bed that captures this; it's a two-shot with Keith in the foreground and Shelley, on her back, eyes to the ceiling, slowly exhaling little plumes of smoke. Nothing is said. The radio plays. Somehow we know just how this quiet, warm moment feels.

The movie's fault is that Altman, having found the perfect means for realizing his story visually, did not spend enough thought, perhaps, on the story itself. *Thieves Like Us* is not another *Bonnie and Clyde*, and yet it does end in a similar way, with a shootout. And by this time, we've seen too many movies that have borrowed that structure; that have counted on the bloody conclusion to lend significance to what went before. In *Thieves Like Us*, there just wasn't that much significance, and I don't think there's meant to be. These are small people in a weary time, robbing banks because that's their occupation, getting shot because that's the law's occupation.

Altman's comment on the people and time is carried out through the way he observes them; if you try to understand his intention by analyzing the story, you won't get far. Audiences have always been so plot-oriented that it's possible they'll just go ahead and think this is a bad movie, without pausing to reflect on its scene after scene of poignant observation. Altman may not tell a story better than any one, but he sees one with great clarity and tenderness.

The Thin Blue Line ★ ★ ★ ½
NO MPAA RATING, 101 m., 1988

A film directed by Errol Morris and produced by Mark Lipson.

One dark night in 1976, a Dallas police officer named Robert Wood was shot dead by someone inside a car he had stopped for a minor traffic violation. The man who was convicted of that murder, a young drifter named Randall Adams was, when this film was released in the summer of 1988, in the eleventh year of a life sentence. The chief witness against him, David Harris, had been sentenced to death for another murder. In the tense last moments of *The Thin Blue Line*, David Harris confesses to the murder of Officer Wood. Those moments were the result of a thirty-month investigation by Errol Morris, one of America's strangest and most brilliant documentary filmmakers, who sometimes jokes that he is not a "producer-director" but a "detective-director." Morris originally went to Texas to do a documentary on Dr. James Grigson, a Dallas psychiatrist nicknamed "Doctor Death" because in countless capital murder cases over fifteen years, he has invariably predicted that the defendants deserved the death penalty because they were sociopaths who would certainly kill again. While researching Grigson, Morris interviewed Randall Adams, a young man who had no criminal record until the Wood case.

"Adams told me he was innocent," Morris told me at the Toronto Film Festival, "but everybody in prison tells you they are innocent. It was only after I met David Harris that I began to suspect that the wrong man had been convicted of murder."

Although *The Thin Blue Line* assembles an almost unassailable case for Adams and against Harris, it is not a conventional documentary—not a feature-length version of one of those "60 Minutes" segments in which innocent men are rescued from Death Row. Although he makes documentaries, Errol Morris is much more interested in the spaces between the facts than with the facts themselves. He is fascinated by strange people, by odd word choices and manners of speech, by the way that certain symbols or beliefs can become fetishes with the power to rule human lives.

Morris's first film was *Gates of Heaven* (1978), which I believe is one of the greatest films ever made. Ostensibly a documentary about two pet cemeteries in Northern California and the people who owned them, it is in fact one of the most profound, and funniest, films ever made about such subjects as life and death, success and failure, dreams and disappointments, and the role that pet animals play in our loneliness. Although *Gates of Heaven* has never failed to fascinate

and amaze the approximately fifty audiences I have seen it with, it has never reached large numbers of people because of its subject matter; people quite simply think they don't want to see a movie about pet cemeteries, and only enthusiastic word-of-mouth has kept the movie alive (it is only recently available on home video).

Morris's next film, about the strange and wonderful people he found in and around a small southern town, was called *Vernon, Florida*. It played on PBS in 1981. In the years which followed, although he has worked on several projects, there was no new Morris film until *The Thin Blue Line*. For a time in the early 1980s, he supported himself as a private detective. Then the case of Randall Adams began to obsess him, and the result is a film that takes its viewers back to the events on the night when Robert Wood was shot dead.

Morris has assembled many of the key witnesses in the case, including Randall Adams, who seems passive and defeated about the fate that deposited him in a life sentence for murder, and David Harris, who talks wonderingly about the fact that a person's whole life can be changed because he happens to be in the wrong place at the wrong time.

"Is Randall Adams an innocent man?" Morris asks Harris.

"I'm sure he is."

"How can you be sure?"

"Because I'm the one that knows."

Morris's visual style in *The Thin Blue Line* is unlike any conventional documentary approach. Although his interviews are shot straight on, head and shoulders, there is a way his camera has of framing his subjects so that we look at them very carefully, learning as much by what we see as by what we hear.

In addition to the interviews, Morris uses staged reconstructions of the murder of Officer Wood—the car without headlights, the pursuit by the police vehicle, the approach of Wood, the behavior of his fellow officer, even the lazy, slow-motion whirl of a drive-in milkshake that flies through the air and falls to earth soon after Robert Wood's bullet-ridden body.

Morris also uses other kinds of images. There are scenes from *Swinging Cheerleaders*, the film that Adams and Harris saw together in a drive-in before the murder. (Harris said they saw the last show; Morris has discovered there was no late show on the night in question.) There are also close-ups of physical evidence, of places, of clocks visualizing the impossible chronology of some of the testimony. We see family photographs that reconstruct moments in David Harris's troubled childhood. We see guns, empty streets, newspaper headlines, all-night food stores.

The use of this footage is repetitive and rhythmic, and underlined by the cold, frightening, original music score by Philip Glass. The result is a movie that is documentary and drama, investigation and reverie, a meditation on the fact that Randall Adams was plucked from the center of his life and locked up forever for a crime that no reasonable person could seriously believe he committed.

Footnote 1989: As a result of this film, the case against Adams was reopened, his conviction set aside, and he was released from prison.

The Thing ★ ★ ½
R, 108 m., 1982

Kurt Russell (MacReady), Wilford Brimley (Blair), T.K. Carter (Nauls), David Clennon (Palmer), Keith David (Childs), Richard Dysart (Dr. Copper). Directed by John Carpenter and produced by David Foster and Lawrence Turman. Screenplay by Bill Lancaster.

A spaceship crash-lands on Earth countless years ago and is buried under Antarctic ice. It has a creature on board. Modern scientists dig up the creature, thaw it out, and discover too late that it still lives—and has the power to imitate all life-forms. Its desire to live and expand is insatiable. It begins to assume the identities of the scientists at an isolated Antarctic research station. The crucial question becomes: Who is real, and who is the Thing? The original story was called *Who Goes There?* It was written by John W. Campbell, Jr., in the late 1930s, and it provided such a strong and scary story that it inspired at least four movie versions before this one: The original *The Thing* in 1952, *Invasion of the Body Snatchers* in 1956 and 1978, *Alien* in 1979, and now John Carpenter's 1982 remake, again called *The Thing.*

I mention the previous incarnations of *The Thing* not to demonstrate my mastery of *The Filmgoer's Companion,* but to suggest the many possible approaches to this material. The two 1950s versions, especially *Body Snatchers,* were seen at the time as fables based on McCarthyism; communists, like victims of the Thing, looked, sounded, and acted like your best friend, but they were infected with a deadly secret. *Alien,* set on a spaceship but using the same premise, paid less attention to the "Who Goes There?" idea and more to the special effects: Remember that wicked little creature that tore its way out of the astronaut's stomach? Now comes this elaborate version by John Carpenter, a master of suspense *(Halloween).* His *Thing* depends on its special effects, which are among the most elaborate, nauseating, and horrifying sights yet achieved by Hollywood's new generation of visual magicians. There are times when we seem to be sticking our heads right down into the bloody, stinking maw of the unknown, as the Thing transforms itself into creatures with the body parts of dogs, men, lobsters, and spiders, all wrapped up in gooey intestines.

The Thing is a great barf-bag movie, all right, but is it any good? I found it disappointing, for two reasons: the superficial characterizations and the implausible behavior of the scientists on that icy outpost. Characters have never been Carpenter's strong point; he says he likes his movies to create emotions in his audiences, and I guess he'd rather see us jump six inches than get involved in the personalities of his characters. This time, though, despite some roughed-out typecasting and a few reliable stereotypes (the drunk, the psycho, the hero), he has populated his ice station with people whose primary purpose in life is to get jumped on from behind. The few scenes that develop characterizations are overwhelmed by the scenes in which the men are just set-ups for an attack by the Thing.

That leads us to the second problem, plausibility. We know that the Thing likes to wait until a character is alone, and then pounce, digest, and imitate him—by the time you see Doc again, is he still Doc, or is he the Thing? Well, the obvious defense against this problem is a watertight buddy system, but, time and time again, Carpenter allows his characters to wander off alone and come back with silly grins on their faces, until we've lost count of who may have been infected, and who hasn't. That takes the fun away.

The Thing is basically, then, just a geek show, a gross-out movie in which teen-agers can dare one another to watch the screen. There's nothing wrong with that; I like being scared and I *was* scared by many scenes in *The Thing.* But it seems clear that Carpenter made his choice early on to concentrate on the special effects and the technology and to allow the story and people to become secondary. Because this material has been done before, and better, especially in the original *The Thing* and in *Alien,* there's no need to see this version unless you are interested in what the Thing might look like while starting from anonymous greasy organs extruding giant crab legs and transmuting itself into a dog. Amazingly, I'll bet that thousands, if not millions, of moviegoers *are* interested in seeing just that.

Things Change ★ ★ ★
PG, 105 m., 1988

Don Ameche (Gino), Joe Mantegna (Jerry), Robert Prosky (Joseph Vincent), J.J. Johnston (Frankie), Ricky Jay (Mr. Silver), Mike Nussbaum (Mr. Green), Jack Wallace (Repair Shop Owner), Dan Conway (Butler). Directed by David Mamet and produced by Michael Hausman. Screenplay by Mamet and Shel Silverstein.

Things Change is a neat little exercise in wit and deception in which an old Italian-American shoeshine man convinces the Mafia boss of Lake Tahoe that he is the man *behind* the man behind the man. His secret is to have no secret. He answers every question truthfully. He does most of his talking about how to get a perfect shoeshine. By the end of the film, we have witnessed a con so perfect that the people pulling it didn't even want to pull a con.

The movie was directed by David Mamet, who wrote it with Shel Silverstein. Coming after the diabolical trickery of *House of Games* (1987), it confirms Mamet's gift for leading us through truly bewildering plots. What makes his movies so entertaining is that the characters are bewildered, not the audience, which is usually the case with sloppier screenwriters. He makes us co-conspirators.

His story is based on a series of accidents, coincidences, and misunderstandings. It begins when Gino, the old Chicago shoeshine man (Don Ameche), is escorted from his shop and taken into the presence of a local crime chief (Mike Nussbaum) and asked to confess to a murder. If Gino agrees, he will be back on the street in three years and the mob will give him his dream—a fishing boat of his own in Sicily.

First he refuses. Then he changes his mind. The dialogue in this scene is pure Mamet, the repetition of ordinary phrases that take on sinister meanings. Describing the murder of a man in the street, a mobster punctuates each paragraph with the line, "This is public knowledge," before finally coming to his point: "What I am now about to tell you is not public knowledge." When I write it down, it doesn't sound funny. When you hear it, you laugh. It is Mamet's gift to know how words work aloud.

Gino is assigned to Jerry, a younger Mafioso (Joe Mantegna), whose job is to guard him over the weekend until he can confess on Monday. The two men retire to a hotel room, where Jerry grows restless, says the hell with it, and decides to take the old guy to Tahoe for the weekend. In Nevada, Jerry is spotted by a chauffeur as a guy from the Chicago mob, and Gino is immediately assumed to be very important. No one has ever seen him before—but that's just proof of how important he is. Of course, they get the suite with the sunken tub, free of charge, plus unlimited credit in the casino.

Mamet and Silverstein now unspin a labyrinthine plot in which half-truths and assumptions follow one after another until Gino is in the presence of the local Mafia boss (Robert Prosky). The don has invited Gino and Jerry to his mountain estate for two reasons: to embrace them if they are the real thing, and to kill them if they are not. In a scene involving exquisite timing and painfully drawn-out silences, the boss tries to get answers without seeming to ask questions, and Gino tries to answer without saying anything. There is not a word or a glance or a moment of body language that feels wrong in this scene—and the scene is the crux of the movie.

More complications follow, which I will leave for you to discover. The chief delight in the movie is the joining of comedy and menace: The Mantegna character is keenly aware that one wrong step will result in instant death, but the Ameche character is able to save them both by simply being himself. There is a moment when Ameche and Prosky sit against a wall in the sun, two old men with their shoes off, and we sense that the local guy would almost rather not know that his visitor is not a Mafia don, because he plays the part so well.

I've been looking at a lot of *films noir* lately—those stylish black-and-white crime movies from the 1940s in which evil was found to lurk just below the surfaces of ordinary American lives. *Things Change* is a film in which the surface is evil and goodness

lurks beneath. The strangest thing about the film is the way the bond between the Ameche and Prosky characters seems to redeem the Nevada boss, to convince him if only for an afternoon that the real reason he got into crime was to demonstrate his loyalty to his friends.

If there is a flaw in the movie, it is Mamet's deliberation. A clever movie should always be quicker than its audience, and here there are moments when we have time to see ahead into the plot. Mamet has a genuine gift for movie direction—his films are not just illustrations of his dialogue, but have an energy of their own—but timing is the area where he needs to tinker. His dialogue for the stage is written in such a way that an actor reading it is almost forced to time it the way Mamet imagined it. His characters punctuate their sentences by repeating the same words and phrases for emphasis. But in the movies, words exist in a different kind of time than on the stage, and Mamet tends to play around and find what works for his dialogue.

The performances here are all wonderful, especially Ameche's. Working in the midst of a cast that is otherwise entirely drawn from the Mamet stock company, he finds just the right note of bewilderment and cleverness. The character is never other than a confused old Italian shoeshine man, and yet time and again he saves himself by somehow finding the right thing to say. Joe Mantegna, as his keeper, walks a fine line between desperation and comedy—and isn't afraid to go broader in scenes where he pantomimes what Ameche should be saying and doing. And Robert Prosky, his face a mask of jovial cunning, is touching in the way he wants to believe in this stranger who is so apparently phony. *Things Change* is a delicate balance of things that don't easily go together: farce, wit, violence, and heart. Here they do.

36 Fillette ★ ★ ★ ½
NO MPAA RATING; 92 m., 1989

Delphine Zentout (Lili), Etienne Chicot (Maurice), Olivier Parniere (Bertrand), Jean-Pierre Leaud (Boris Golovine), Berta Dominuez D. (Anne-Marie), Jean-Francois Stevenin (The Father), Diane Bellego (Georgia). Directed by Catherine Breillat and produced by Emmanuel Schlumberger and Valerie Seydoux. Screenplay by Breillat.

36 Fillette follows a few crucial days in the

life of Lili, a fourteen-year-old French girl whose body is ripe and whose soul is troubled by an unhappy home life. One night during a miserable family vacation at a tacky resort, she talks her older brother into taking her to a disco, and there she begins a series of risky flirtations with older men.

The first man she encounters fancies himself to be a playboy, but he is in fact a middle-aged salesman who is still locked into his adolescent dream of picking up girls in his convertible. After he picks up Lili, he finds he is in for more than he bargained for. She is not a victim but a tough little cookie who tantalizes him all night long, until finally he gives up, protesting that at his age he simply lacks the stamina for an extended chase. When I first saw him I was prepared to scorn him as an irresponsible adult taking advantage of an inexperienced girl, but by this point in the evening I could see the rueful humor in his situation.

Drifting on through the dreary resort where she finds herself, Lili (Delphine Zentout) encounters a man who is said to be a famous French personality of some sort—and indeed, he is played by a famous actor, Jean-Pierre Leaud, who long ago in Truffaut's *The 400 Blows* (1959) portrayed the same kind of angry, alienated adolescent who now confronts him. He listens to her intently, looks at her quizzically, and gives her some weary advice. No doubt his advice is correct, but she is too young to understand it, and must make her own mistakes.

The next day is another day of unhappiness with her parents, who mostly seem to drink, sleep, and fight. She is alienated and isolated, and she decides it is "miserable" to be a virgin, so she sets out to flirt with danger, not quite knowing what she is looking for, or if she really wants it. She dresses boldly and goes out to hitchhike into town, and again crosses paths with the tired, alcoholic playboy (Etienne Chicot). He leads an exhausted night life in gloomy discos, and decides he doesn't want to have anything to do with her because she is underage. But she taunts him with her flamboyant dress and voluptuous body, and then dances away when he begins to respond. Eventually they fall into some kind of tacit friendship, based on a mutual desperation they recognize in each other.

At first we are prepared to blame the man for taking advantage of a vulnerable teenager. But that is not the subject of this particular film, which the director, Catherine

Breillat, says is somewhat autobiographical. *36 Fillette* (the title is a French bra size) is a film told from Lili's point of view, and the middle-aged man is almost a prop; at this moment in her life, any man would have done, since she is not sure what she's looking for anyway.

We have caught her at a moment when her unhappiness has coincided with her sudden discovery of her sexuality and the power she can have over men. With a boldness born of anger and naïveté, heedless of danger, she sets out to manipulate this man. Her psychological motivations are hinted at in a scene where her father is uncaring, but this is a film of observation, not analysis.

The key scene in the film is a long, meticulously observed emotional fencing match in the man's hotel room, during which they both sense, perhaps, that despite the gulf between them they share the same loneliness and unhappiness with themselves. This is a great scene, and its whole delicate existence depends on the performance by Delphine Zentout, a sixteen-year-old in her acting debut. She gives a brave and convincing performance.

The movie is controversial because of the difference in age between the two lovers, and because of the girl's blatant, if naive, sexuality. But Breillat has made a film far more complex than it might seem. This film depicts the sort of situation one should deplore, but the film is so specifically about two particular people that it slips away from convention and just quietly goes its own way.

This Is Elvis ★ ★ ★ ½
PG, 88 m., 1981

Voices: Elvis (Ral Donner), Joe Esposito (Joe Esposito), Linda Thompson (Linda Thompson), Priscilla Presley (Lisha Sweetnam). Directed, produced, and written by Malcolm Leo and Andrew Solt. Featuring documentary footage of Elvis Presley.

This Is Elvis is the extraordinary record of a man who simultaneously became a great star and was destroyed by alcohol and drug addiction. What is most striking about its documentary footage is that we can almost always see both things happening at once. There is hardly a time when Elvis doesn't appear to be under the influence of mind-altering chemicals, and never a time, not even when he is only weeks from death, when he doesn't possess his special charisma. The

movie's lesson is brutal, sad, and inescapable: Elvis Presley was a man who gave joy to a great many people but felt very little of his own, because he became addicted and stayed addicted until the day it killed him.

This movie does not, however, intend to be a documentary about Presley's drug usage. It just turns out that way, because Presley's life turned out that way. The film is a re-creation of his life and image, and uses documentary footage from a wide variety of sources, including Presley's own professionally made home movies. Not all the footage is even really of Presley. Some early childhood scenes are fiction, with a young actor playing Elvis. They don't work, but they're soon over. A few other scenes are also faked, including one shot following Presley into his home on the night he died, and another showing him rushing to his mother's sickbed (the double is an Elvis imitator named Johnny Harra). But the faked footage adds up to only about 10 percent of the movie, and is helpful in maintaining continuity.

The rest of the film's footage is extraordinary, and about half of it has never been seen anywhere. This film isn't just a compilation of old Elvis documentaries. The filmmakers got permission from Presley's manager, Colonel Tom Parker, to use Presley's own private film archives and to shoot inside Graceland, his mansion. They include footage that was not even suspected to exist, including scenes from a birthday party Elvis had in Germany when he was still in the Army (we see a very young Priscilla at the party), scenes of Elvis's parents moving into Graceland, scenes with Elvis clowning around with buddies, and shots taken inside his limousine very near the end, when he was drunk and drugged and obviously very ill. There are also sequences during which we frankly wonder if he will be able to make it onto the stage.

The documentary also includes some of Presley's key television appearances, including his first guest appearances on the old "Dorsey Brothers Bandstand" and the "Ed Sullivan Show" (with Ed assuring America that Elvis was "a real decent, fine boy . . . Elvis, you're thoroughly all right"). There is newsreel footage of Elvis getting out of the Army (and, significantly, observing "it was so cold some nights we had to take bennies to stay awake"). There is an old kinescope, long thought to be lost, of a TV special hosted by Frank Sinatra to welcome Elvis back to civil-

ian life (and in his duet with Sinatra, Presley is confused and apparently under the influence of tranquilizers).

The young Elvis in this movie is an entertainer of incredible energy and charisma. The charisma stays, but somewhere along the way we notice a change in his behavior, a draining away of cheerfulness, a dreadful secret scourge. And in the film's final scenes, Presley is shockingly ill: He's bloated, his skin is splotchy, he's shaking and dripping with sweat, and, in one very painful sequence shot during a concert, he cannot remember the words to his songs. But he pushes through anyway, and his final renditions of "My Way" and "Are You Lonesome Tonight?" are beautiful and absolutely heartbreaking. He may have lost his mind, but he never lost his voice or his heart.

Elvis Presley should, of course, still be alive. The film interviews his former bodyguards about his drinking and drug usage, and they argue convincingly that they could not stop him from doing what he was determined to do. But an addict, of course, has only two choices, no matter how he might deceive himself that he has many. He can either continue to use, or he can ask for help.

The irony in Presley's case is that his own doctor was apparently the source of most of his drugs. Could Elvis have stopped? Sure. Would he have been alive today? Probably. But he was never able to admit his addiction and find the will to seek help. And he was surrounded by foot-kissers and yes-men. This movie shows the disintegration and death of a talented man who backed himself into a corner. He did it his way.

This Is Spinal Tap ★ ★ ★ ★
R, 87 m., 1984

Rob Reiner (Marty DiBergi), Michael McKean (David St. Hubbins), Christopher Guest (Nigel Tufnel), Harry Shearer (Derek Smalls). Directed by Rob Reiner and produced by Karen Murphy. Screenplay by Christopher Guest, Michael McKean, Harry Shearer, and Reiner.

The children born at Woodstock are preparing for the junior prom, and rock 'n' roll is still here to stay. Rock musicians never die, they just fade away, and *This Is Spinal Tap* is a movie about a British rock group that is rocketing to the bottom of the charts.

The movie looks like a documentary filmed during the death throes of a British rock band named Spinal Tap. It is, in fact, a satire. The rock group does not really exist, but the best thing about this film is that it could. The music, the staging, the special effects, the backstage feuding, and the pseudo-profound philosophizing are right out of a hundred other rock groups and a dozen other documentaries about rock.

The group is in the middle of an American tour. The tour is not going well. Spinal Tap was once able to fill giant arenas, but its audiences have grown smaller and smaller, and concert dates are evaporating as the bad news gets around. No wonder. Spinal Tap is a bad rock 'n' roll band. It is derivative, obvious, phony, and pretentious, and it surrounds itself with whatever images seem commercial at the moment (a giant death's-head on stage, for one). The movie is absolutely inspired in the subtle way it establishes Spinal Tap's badness. The satire has a deft, wicked touch. Spinal Tap is not that much worse than, not that much different from, some successful rock bands. A few breaks here or there, a successful album, and they could be back in business. (Proof of that: A sound-track album, "Smell the Glove," is getting lots of air play with cuts like "Sex Farm.")

The documentary is narrated by its director, Marty DiBergi, played by Rob Reiner, the director of the real movie. He explains that he was first attracted to the band by its unusual loudness. He follows them on tour, asking profound questions that inspire deep, meaningless answers, and his cameras watch as the group comes unglued. One of the band members brings in a girlfriend from England. She feuds with the group's manager. Bookings are canceled. The record company doesn't like the cover for the group's new album. One disastrous booking takes Spinal Tap to a dance in a hangar on a military base. The movie is brilliant at telling its story through things that happen in the background and at the edges of the picture: By the end of the film, we know as much about the personalities and conflicts of the band members as if the movie had been straightforward narrative.

There are a lot of great visual jokes, which I don't want to spoil—especially the climax of the band's Stonehenge production number, or another number that involves them being reborn from womblike stage props. There also are moments of inspired satire aimed at previous styles in rock films, as when we get glimpses of Spinal Tap in its ear-

lier incarnations (the band started as sort of a folk group, plunged into the flower-people generation, and was a little late getting into heavy metal, satanism, and punk).

This Is Spinal Tap assumes that audiences will get most of the jokes. I think that's right. "Entertainment Tonight" and music TV and Barbara Walters specials have made show-business trade talk into national gossip, and one of the greatest pleasures of the movie is that it doesn't explain everything. It simply, slyly, destroys one level of rock pomposity after another.

Three Men and a Baby ★ ★ ★
PG, 99 m., 1987

Tom Selleck (Peter), Steve Guttenberg (Michael), Ted Danson (Jack), Nancy Travis (Sylvia), Margaret Colin (Rebecca). Directed by Leonard Nimoy and produced by Ted Field and Robert W. Cort. Screenplay by James Orr and Jim Cruickshank.

Three Men and a Baby begins with too many characters and too much plot, and fifteen minutes into the film, I was growing restless. It spends a lot of time describing the lifestyles of three bachelors—Tom Selleck, Steve Guttenberg, and Ted Danson—who share a luxury apartment and play host to a never-ending stream of girlfriends. We meet too many of the girlfriends and too many of their friends, and then it's the morning after Selleck's big birthday bash, and on the doorstep outside their apartment is a bassinette containing a little baby named Mary. From that point on, the movie finds its rhythm, and it works.

The baby was apparently fathered by Danson, an actor who has just left to spend ten weeks shooting a film in Turkey. Selleck and Guttenberg contemplate the little bundle with dread, and Selleck's confusion is not helped when he goes to the market to buy baby food and gets a lot of advice about babies from a helpful clerk. ("You mean you don't even know how *old* your baby is?" she asks incredulously.)

Shortly after comes one of the funniest scenes in a long time, as Selleck and Guttenberg, an architect and a cartoonist, try to change Mary's diapers. The basic situation may sound familiar and even overworked, but the way they act it and the way Leonard Nimoy directs it, it builds from one big laugh to another.

The movie never steps wrong as long as it

focuses on the developing love between the two big men and the tiny baby. At first they're baffled by this little bundle that only eats, sleeps, cries, and makes poo-poo—lots and lots of poo-poo. "The book says to feed the baby every two hours," Selleck complains, "but do you count from when you start, or when you finish? It takes me two hours to get her to eat, and by the time she's done, it's time to start again, so that I'm feeding her all of the time."

Those scenes are the heart of the movie. Unfortunately, there is also a completely unnecessary subplot to distract from the good stuff. *Three Men and a Baby* is a faithful reworking of a French film from a few years ago, in which the basic plot device was that "packages" were left with the bachelors on the same day—a baby and a fortune in heroin—along with the message that "the package" would be picked up a few days later.

The plot allows them to know nothing about the heroin, so they think the "package" is the baby, and that leads to a misunderstanding with some vicious drug dealers. Learning that an American remake of the French movie was being planned, I assumed that the drug angle would be the first thing written out of the script. To begin with, it's completely unnecessary; the fact that the baby is left on the doorstep is all the story needs to get under way, and the central story is so funny and heartwarming that drugs are a downer.

But, no, Leonard Nimoy and writers James Orr and Jim Cruickshank have remade the entire French movie, drugs and all, leading to a badly staged and distracting confrontation between the heroes and the dealers in a mid-town construction site. Why bother with all the exhausted apparatus of crime and violence, recycled out of TV crime shows, when the story of the men and the baby is so compelling?

Luckily, there's enough of the domestic comedy to make the movie work despite its crasser instincts. And one of the big surprises in the movie is Tom Selleck's wonderful performance as the bachelor architect. After playing action heroes on TV and in the movies, he now reveals himself to be a light comedian in the Cary Grant tradition—a big, handsome guy with tenderness and vulnerability. When he looks at baby Mary with love in his eyes, you can see it there, and it doesn't feel like acting.

Because of Selleck and his co-stars (including twin baby girls Lisa and Michelle

Blair), the movie becomes a heartwarming entertainment. There are, however, a couple of glitches at the end. When Mary's mother turns up, the men allow her to leave with the baby without even asking the obvious question on the mind of everyone in the audience: How could she have abandoned the baby in the first place? Another problem is that Selleck isn't the only one who doesn't know how old Mary is. If you follow the various dates mentioned in the script, the filmmakers also haven't a clue. But by the time the movie reaches its predictable but comfortable ending, who cares?

Three Men and a Little Lady ★ ★
PG, 100 m., 1990

Tom Selleck (Peter), Steve Guttenberg (Michael), Ted Danson (Jack), Nancy Travis (Sylvia), Robin Weisman (Mary), Christopher Cazenove (Edward), Leona Shaw (Miss Lomax). Directed by Emile Ardolino and produced by Ted Field and Robert W. Cort. Screenplay by Charlie Lie Peters.

Of course, the story has always been preposterous—the three yuppie bachelors living happily under one roof with the woman who has borne the child of one of them, but loves another. It was preposterous in the original French comedy where the story was first used, and it was preposterous in the 1987 remake, *Three Men and a Baby*, but it didn't seriously start to bother me until this sequel, *Three Men and a Little Lady*. How far can you stretch this conceit before it snaps?

The baby, you will recall, was fathered by the Ted Danson character, an actor who shared a luxurious bachelor pad with two other guys, Tom Selleck as an architect and Steve Guttenberg as a cartoonist. One morning after a wild party, they looked outside their door, and found a bassinet with a helpless baby inside—little Mary, who had been left by her mother, Nancy Travis. The story of why a mother would seem to abandon her infant took up far, far too much screen time in the original movie, and involved a breakdown in communications and a ludicrous subplot about drug dealers. But never mind. The baby was there, and the three bachelors, of course, fell immediately in love with it.

Many of the charms of the first movie were based on the simple pleasure of seeing a warm actor like Tom Selleck handle the little child. There was the celebrated turkey-baster scene. And all of the jokes about poo-

poo. And the happy ending. But now time has moved on, and little Mary's mother has started to think she ought to get married and provide a proper father for her child. Danson is obviously too irresponsible a choice, and besides, she doesn't love him. She does love Selleck, who loves her but is too dense to pick up all the obvious signals she's sending out, and so in a fit of pique she agrees to marry a loathsome British stage director (Christopher Cazenove).

The mechanics of the plot now take over. Mother and child move to England, where the director inhabits a stately country home. The bachelors, tiring of the wild parties and gin rummy games which they hold in an apartment that looks uncannily like a movie set, fly away to attend the wedding. Then it turns out the Brit is a reprehensible liar, and it's up to Selleck and Danson to save the day with a dashing motorcycle chase and a devious disguise.

The only bright spot amid these dreary machinations is the appearance of a hilarious supporting performance by Leona Shaw as the headmistress of the unspeakable girls' school where the creep plans to send the infant Mary. This woman believes Selleck is in love with her, and that leads to some funny misunderstandings. Most of the laughs come from the physical humor in Shaw's performance: She gives the impression of being constantly on the borderline of uncontrollable lust, and her bodily movements resemble someone trying to give themselves a massage from deep inside their own body.

She's funny, and there is a nice deception involving Danson, but really, do we care? The situation in *Three Men and a Little Lady* is so unbelievable that it works best when it's farce, and worst when it's heart-drenching sentiment. The story is more and more beginning to resemble a sitcom on its last legs, when every possible variation has been wrung out of a premise that was thin to begin with.

3 Women ★ ★ ★ ★
PG, 125 m., 1977

Sissy Spacek (Pinky), Shelley Duvall (Millie), Janice Rule (Willie), Robert Fortier (Edgar), Ruth Nelson (Mrs. Rose), John Cromwell (Mr. Rose), Craig Richard Nelson (Dr. Maas), Maysie Hoy (Doris). Directed, produced, and written by Robert Altman.

Robert Altman's *3 Women* is, on the one

hand, a straightforward portrait of life in a godforsaken California desert community, and, on the other, a mysterious exploration of human personalities. Its specifics are so real you can almost touch them, and its conclusion so surreal we can supply our own.

The community exists somewhere in Southern California, that uncharted continent of discontent and restlessness. Some of its people have put themselves down in a place that contains, so far as we can see, a spa where old people take an arthritis cure, a Western-style bar with a shooting range out back, and a singles residential motel with a swimming pool that has the most unsettling murals on its bottom.

Into this outpost one day comes Pinky (Sissy Spacek), a child-woman so naive, so open, so willing to have enthusiasm, that in another century she might have been a saint, a strange one. She takes a job at the spa and is instructed in her duties by Millie (Shelley Duvall), who is fascinated by the incorrect belief that the men in town are hot for her. Millie recruits Pinky as a roommate in the motel.

This whole stretch of the film—the first hour—is a funny, satirical, and sometimes sad study of the community and its people, who have almost all failed at something else, somewhere else. The dominant male is Edgar (Robert Fortier), a onetime stuntman, now a boozer with a beer bottle permanently in his hand. He's married to Willie (Janice Rule), who never speaks, and is pregnant, and is painting the murals. It's all terrifically new to Pinky: Drinking a beer (which she does as if just discovering the principle of a glass), or moving into Millie's apartment (which she solemnly declares to be the most beautiful place she's ever seen).

Then the film arrives at its center point, one of masked sexual horror. Millie comes home with Edgar and throws Pinky out of their bedroom, and Pinky tries to commit suicide by jumping into the pool. She survives, but as she recovers the film moves from realism to a strange, haunted psychological landscape in which, somehow, Pinky and Millie exchange personalities. *3 Women* isn't Altman out of Freud via *Psychology Today*, and so the movie mercifully doesn't attempt to explain what's happened in logical terms (*any* explanation would be disappointing, I think, compared to the continuing mystery). Somehow we *feel* what's happened, though, even if we can't explain it in so many words.

The movie's been compared to Bergman's *Persona*, another film in which women seem to share personalities, and maybe *Persona*, also so mysterious when we first see it, helps point the way. But I believe Altman has provided his own signposts, in two important scenes, one at the beginning, one at the end, that mirror one another. Millie, teaching Pinky how to exercise the old folks' legs in the hot baths, places Pinky's feet on her stomach and moves them back and forth, just as Pinky sees the apparition of two twins on the other side of the pool.

Later, when the older woman, Willie, is in labor, Millie places her legs in the same way and moves them in the same way, trying to assist the delivery. But the baby is stillborn, and so are the male-female connections in this small society. And so the women symbolically give birth to each other, around and around in a circle, just as (Altman himself suggests) the end of the picture could be seen as the moment just before its beginning.

The movie's story came to Altman during a dream, he's said, and he provides it with a dreamlike tone. The plot connections, which sometimes make little literal sense, do seem to connect emotionally, viscerally, as all things do in dreams. To act in a story like this must be a great deal more difficult than performing straightforward narrative, but Spacek and Duvall go through their changes so well that it's eerie, and unforgettable. So is the film.

Throw Momma from the Train ★ ★
PG-13, 87 m., 1987

Danny DeVito (Owen), Billy Crystal (Larry), Kim Greist (Beth), Anne Ramsey (Momma), Kate Mulgrew (Margaret), Branford Marsalis (Lester). Directed by Danny DeVito and produced by Larry Brezner. Screenplay by Stu Silver.

Movies borrow from other movies all the time, but few have the honesty to admit it. Danny DeVito is nothing if not an honest man. He not only borrows the plot device from Alfred Hitchcock's *Strangers on a Train* for his comedy *Throw Momma from the Train*, but he even has one of his characters actually go to the movies and study the relevant scene from Hitchcock's 1951 classic.

The character (played by DeVito himself) sits in the dark of a revival house and gazes moonily up at the screen, where Robert Walker is smoothly explaining to Farley Granger how two strangers can commit two perfect murders. Each one commits the *other* man's murder, while preparing an airtight alibi for his "own." Since the prime suspect will have an unshakable alibi and the killer cannot be linked to the crime by any possible motive, the police will be stymied.

This seems like a wonderful idea to DeVito, whose character is a little light in the head. He wants to murder his mother, who is a cross between a bag lady and a boxing instructor, and he has the ideal partner in crime: Billy Crystal, his creative-writing instructor at the local community college. Crystal is angry because his ex-wife has ripped off a book he wrote, and turned it into a bestseller. "I wish she was dead!" he cries one day at the school cafeteria, and DeVito takes him at his word.

Most of the movie centers on the relationship between DeVito and Crystal, who are complete opposites—the genial, smiling, round little man, and the distracted intellectual. DeVito is the kind of man who (in one of the movie's best moments) can calmly discuss murder and then interrupt himself to exclaim, "Look! Cows!" as they pass a billboard advertising a dairy.

This relationship produces a fair number of laughs, but *Throw Momma from the Train* is not as funny as it might have been, maybe because the script lacks the maniacal tension that the material requires. For a relatively short movie (eighty-seven minutes) it seems too heavy on plot, with all sorts of comings and goings and explanations and misunderstandings, all of which are not really necessary. In his study of Hitchcock, DeVito should have absorbed the Master's theory of the MacGuffin, defined as whatever it is that everybody is concerned about. Hitchcock believed that most movies spent too much time on the MacGuffin, and not enough time on how the characters felt about the MacGuffin. The plot in *Throw Momma from the Train* is top-heavy, but the movie doesn't make as much as it could from its weird characters.

What about Momma, for example? As played by Anne Ramsey in one of the most thankless portrayals since Dick Durdock played Swamp Thing, she is a true monster: A shambling wreck of a woman who talks as if her mouth is full of marbles, and bitterly castigates her son for minor infractions. In fantasies perhaps inspired by *Where's Poppa?* DeVito imagines himself slipping lye into his mother's soft drink, or driving a scissors into her ear. But where did this woman come from, and what makes her tick? If her relationship with her son is exclusively barbaric, how did it get that way? By leaving out complexities and guilt, DeVito probably missed some good comic opportunities.

Billy Crystal, a good actor, is also underutilized by Stu Silver's thin screenplay. An early writer's block scene goes on forever; he's stuck on the words "The night was . . ." and tries countless combinations (wet, dry, humid) without ever (a) stumbling on the old dependable "It was a dark and stormy night . . ." or (b) finding any business funnier than throwing crumpled sheets of typing paper into the wastebasket. Blocked writers don't do that anymore. They work on computers, not typewriters, and when they're blocked, they play computer games like "Leather Goddesses of Phobos."

No matter. *Throw Momma from the Train* is a series of missed opportunities and unexploited situations, a movie that wants to have genuine nastiness at its heart, but never quite works up the energy or the nerve to be truly heartless. Paradoxically, its best scenes are the ones of gentle whimsy. The scene, for example, in which DeVito shows Crystal his coin collection, which is made up, not of valuable coins, but of "important" ones, like the penny he got in change the day his dad took him to the zoo. Maybe at some point during the rewrites, they should have just forgotten about Momma and Hitchcock, and started all over again with that scene.

THX 1138 ★ ★ ★
PG, 88 m., 1971

Robert Duvall (THX 1138), Donald Pleasence (SEN 5241), Don Pedro Colley (SRT), Maggie McOmie (LUH 3417). Directed by George Lucas and produced by Lawrence Sturhahn. Screenplay by Lucas and Walter Murch.

The brave new world of the American Zoetrope studio began in the late 1960s in San Francisco. Francis Ford Coppola, a young director of promise, persuaded Warner Bros. to help finance and distribute a group of features by the bright new filmmakers he'd gathered around him. Coppola had just finished a successful mainstream production for Warners', *Finian's Rainbow*, and his proposal sounded good in that era of youth films, bike films, trip films, and other high hopes.

The youth film and the others turned out

to be lost causes, however, and as the American film industry moved back to traditional narrative pictures, not many of the proposed American Zoetrope films were made, and even fewer ever opened. Warner Bros., having decided to drop the San Francisco experiment, didn't back the surviving features very enthusiastically. The greatest casualty was George Lucas's *THX 1138*, a science-fiction parable set in the twenty-fifth century and displaying remarkable visual mastery.

The movie's strength is not in its story but in its unsettling and weirdly effective visual and sound style. The story is standard sci-fi stuff: Five centuries in the future, mankind inhabits vast underground cities which are programmed by computers and policed by robots. The citizens are force-fed drugs to inhibit their passions, but THX 1138 (Robert Duvall) and his mate LUH 3417 (Maggie McOmie) cut down on their drug rations and discover that they have sexual appetites. Worse still, they are in love.

What follows is a battle against the centralized computer system, a few episodes of outsmarting the dumb robot policemen, and a chase scene. None of this is very original, and the whole business of Love versus State is out of Orwell and countless lesser writers. But Lucas doesn't seem to have been very concerned with his plot, anyway. His film was inspired by a student film he did at UCLA, which won the National Student Film Festival in 1968. The student work was sort of a dry run for this one, exploring ways of creating inexpensive but totally convincing special effects for a futuristic society. The experiment was a success; the subterranean laboratories, apartments, and corridors in *THX 1138* have a blinding, white porcelain sameness, and the characters seem to inhabit the future's most spectacular and sanitary bathroom fixtures.

The sound effects add to the illusion of a distant and different society. The dialogue seems half-heard, half-forgotten; people talk in a bemused way, as if the drugs had made them indifferent. Their words are suspended in a muted, echoing atmosphere in which only the computer-programmed recorded announcements seem confident. And the featureless whiteness of this universe stretches away into infinity (especially in the effective scene involving a prison with no walls—how can you escape from a prison that is simply an empty void?). *THX 1138* suffers somewhat from its simple story line, but as a

work of visual imagination it's special, and as haunting as parts of *2001*, *Silent Running*, and *The Andromeda Strain*.

Ticket to Heaven ★ ★ ★ ½
R, 107 m., 1981

Nick Mancuso (David), Saul Rubinek (Larry), Meg Foster (Ingrid), Kim Cattrall (Ruthie), R.H. Thomson (Linc Strunk), Jennifer Dale (Lisa). Directed by Ralph L. Thomas and produced by Vivienne Lebosh.

Ticket to Heaven is about a young man who enters the all-encompassing world of a religious cult. What makes the movie absolutely spellbinding is that it shows us not only how he is recruited into the group, but how *anyone* could be indoctrinated into one of the many cults in America today. This is a movie that has done its research, and it is made with such artistry that we share the experience of the young man.

His name is David. He is played by Nick Mancuso, a powerful young actor, as an independent type who flies from Toronto to San Francisco to discover what has happened to a friend who joined up with the cult. He is welcomed to their communal residence, joins in a meal and some singing, and is asked if he'd like to spend the weekend at a retreat on the group's farm. He would. By the end of the weekend, he is a cult member. Can it happen that fast? I've read stories claiming that some cults need only seventy-two hours to convert almost anyone to their way. The best and the brightest make the best recruits, they say. The movie shows the three techniques used to indoctrinate new members: (1) low-calorie, low-protein diets; (2) sleep deprivation; (3) "love-bombing," which involves constant positive reinforcement, the chanting of slogans and great care *never* to allow the recruit to be alone for a moment.

Although *Ticket to Heaven* does not mention any existing cult by name, it is based on a series of newspaper articles about a former Moonie. The techniques in the film could, I suppose, be used by anybody. What makes the film so interesting is that it's not just a docudrama, not just a sensationalist exposé, but a fully realized drama that involves us on the human level as well as with its documentary material. There are scenes that are absolutely harrowing: an overhead shot of David trying to take a walk by himself and being "joined" by jolly friends; a scene where he

guiltily bolts down a forbidden hamburger; a scene where another cult member whispers one sentence that sounds to us, as much as to David, like shocking heresy. By that point in the film, we actually understand why David has become so zombie-like and unquestioning. We have shared his experience.

The final scenes in the film involve a deprogramming attempt. They are not as absorbing as what went before, if only because they involve an effort of the intellect, instead of an assault on the very personality itself. I've seen *Ticket to Heaven* three times, and at first I thought the film's ending was "weaker" than the rest. Now I wonder. What cults offer is freedom from the personality. They remove from your shoulders the burden of being you. That is a very seductive offer: why else do people also seek freedom from self through drugs, alcohol, and even jogging? As David is seduced into the cult's womb, we also submit vicariously to the experience. We understand its appeal. At the end, as David's reason is appealed to, as his intellect is reawakened, as he is asked to once again take up the burden of being himself, he resists—and maybe we do, too.

Tie Me Up! Tie Me Down! ★ ★
NO MPAA RATING, 100 m., 1990

Victoria Abril (Marina), Antonio Banderas (Ricky), Francisco Rabal (Maximo Espejo), Loles Leon (Lola), Julieta Serrano (Alma), Maria Barranco (Berta). Directed by Pedro Almodovar and produced by El Deseo. Screenplay by Almodovar.

"To know me is to love me."

This cliché is popular for a reason, because most of us, I imagine, believe deep in our hearts that if anyone truly got to know us, they'd truly get to love us—or at least know why we're the way we are. The problem in life, maybe the central problem, is that so few people ever seem to have sufficient curiosity to do the job on us that we know we deserve.

Pedro Almodovar's *Tie Me Up! Tie Me Down!* is a movie about a disturbed young man who decides to give an actress that opportunity. Her name is Marina, his name is Ricky. She is a bad actress with a background in pornography, but to Ricky she is a perfect angel, and that is why he kidnaps her and ties her to the bed while he attempts to convince her to love him.

This story has been told before, and better, in movies like William Wyler's *The Collector*, but Almodovar tries to bring a certain style to it by making it an unsprung comedy. We occasionally get the sense that both characters *know* they're in a movie—that the whole thing is about role-playing, and the actress never really takes her kidnapping very seriously.

That playfulness gets the movie off at least one hook; the material isn't as disturbing as it might have been, because we have the sense that this isn't a real "kidnapping," especially after the woman begins to assist in her own captivity. Does she enjoy being someone's possession? There is certainly a lot of security in being tied up and cared for, and you don't find yourself with a lot of tough decisions to make. In a perverse sense, it is always the captive who is in control, always the masochist who gets what he desires.

If Almodovar had gone further in this direction—if he had explored the paradoxes of this sort of sexual captivity—we might have had something here, maybe a dark comedy to remind us of something by his Spanish countryman, Luis Bunuel. But the movie is too flighty and uncentered, and it allows actual violence to break the spell when false alarms would have sufficed. It's most entertaining in the quiet times in between the big moments—the little scenes where Marina begins to understand Ricky just a little.

Almodovar is a director with an enormous following around the world, but movies like *Tie Me Up! Tie Me Down!* leave me feeling increasingly left out. His previous film was the widely praised *Women on the Verge of a Nervous Breakdown*, a movie I had a curious relationship with. I saw it once, and had no discernible reaction at all. It did not engage my attention for even a scene, and at the end, I had trouble even remembering it. So I went to see it again, and the same thing happened.

That doesn't mean the film contained nothing; what it means, I think, is that Almodovar's polarities are so perfectly lined up in opposition to my own that it is quite possible for one of his movies to shoot right through my brain without striking a single cell. I seek an explanation for this phenomenon not in film criticism, but in the behavior of subatomic particles.

With *Tie Me Up! Tie Me Down!* I was at least left with a memory of the film, but I am not sure this is progress for Almodovar.

Tightrope ★ ★ ★ 1/2
R, 114 m., 1984

Clint Eastwood (Wes Block), Genevieve Bujold (Beryl Thibodeaux), Dan Hedaya (Detective Molinari), Alison Eastwood (Amanda Block), Jennifer Beck (Penny Block). Directed by Richard Tuggle and produced by Clint Eastwood and Fritz Manes. Screenplay by Tuggle.

Most modern police thrillers are simpleminded manipulations of chases, violence, pop psychology, and characters painted in broad stereotypes. *Tightrope* contains all four of those ingredients, to be sure, but it also contains so much more that it's a throwback to the great cop movies of the 1940s—when the hero wrestled with his conscience as much as with the killer.

The movie stars Clint Eastwood as a New Orleans homicide detective who is as different as possible from Dirty Harry Callahan. The guy's name is Wes Block. His wife has recently left him, and he lives at home with his two young daughters and several dogs. He is a good but flawed cop, with a peculiar hang-up: He likes to make love to women while they are handcuffed. The movie suggests this is because he feels deeply threatened by women (a good guess, I'd say). Detective Block is well-known to most of the kinkier prostitutes in the French Quarter, but his superiors don't know that when they assign him to a big case: A mad strangler, apparently an ex-cop, is killing hookers in the Quarter. Block's problem is that he cannot easily enter this world as a policeman after having entered it often as a client. His other problem is that when he walks into that world, all of his old urges return.

The police work in *Tightrope* is more or less standard: The interviews of suspects, the paperwork, the scenes where his superiors chew him out for not making more progress on the case. What makes *Tightrope* better than just another police movie are the scenes between Eastwood and the women he encounters. Some of them are hookers. Some are victims. One of them, played by Genevieve Bujold, is a feminist who teaches women's self-defense classes. Block has always been attracted to flashy, gaudy women, like the Quarter's more bizarre prostitutes. We do not know why his wife left him, and we are given no notions of what she was like, but right away we figure that Bujold isn't his type. She's in her mid-thirties, uses

no makeup, wears sweat shirts a lot, and isn't easily impressed by cops. But somehow a friendship does begin. And it becomes the counterpoint for the cop's investigation, as he goes deeper into the messy underworld of the crimes—and as more of the evidence seems to suggest that he should be one of the suspects. It's interesting that the movie gives Eastwood two challenges: To solve the murders, and to find a way out of his own hang-ups and back into an emotional state where he can trust a strong woman.

Tightrope may appeal to the Dirty Harry fans, with its sex and violence. But it's a lot more ambitious than the Harry movies, and the relationship between Eastwood and Bujold is more interesting than most recent male-female relationships in the movies, for three reasons: (1) There is something at risk in it, on both sides; (2) it's a learning process, in which Eastwood is the one who must change; (3) it pays off dramatically at the end, when their developing relationship fits into the climax of the investigation. Think how unusual it is for a major male star to appear in a commercial cop picture in which the plot hinges on his ability to accept and respect a woman. Apart from the other good things in *Tightrope*, I admire it for taking chances; Clint Eastwood can get rich making Dirty Harry movies, but he continues to change and experiment, and that makes him the most interesting of the box-office megastars.

Time Bandits ★ ★ ★
PG, 98 m., 1981

Craig Warnock (Kevin), John Cleese (Robin Hood), Sean Connery (Agamemnon), Shelley Duvall (Pansy), Ian Holm (Napoleon), Ralph Richardson (Supreme Being). The Dwarfs: David Rappaport (Randall), Kenny Baker (Fidget), Jack Purvis (Wally), Mike Edmonds (Og), Malcolm Dixon (Strutter), Tiny Ross (Vermin). Directed and produced by Terry Gilliam. Screenplay by Michael Palin and Gilliam.

First reactions while viewing *Time Bandits:* It's amazingly well-produced. The historic locations are jammed with character and detail. This is the only live-action movie I've seen that literally looks like pages out of *Heavy Metal* magazine, with kings and swordsmen and wide-eyed little boys and fearsome beasts. *But* the movie's repetitive, monotonous in the midst of all this activity.

Basically, it's just a kid and six dwarfs racing breathlessly through one set piece after another, shouting at one another. I walked out of the screening in an unsettled state of mind. When the lights go up, I'm usually fairly certain whether or not I've seen a good movie. But my reaction to *Time Bandits* was ambiguous. I had great admiration for what was physically placed on the screen; this movie is worth seeing just to *watch*. But I was disappointed by the breathless way the dramatic scenes were handled and by a breakneck pace that undermined the most important element of comedy, which is timing.

Time Bandits is the expensive fantasy by Terry Gilliam, one of the resident geniuses of Monty Python's Flying Circus. It is *not* a Monty Python film. It begins with a little boy who goes up to bed one night and is astonished, as we all would be, when a horseman gallops through his bedroom wall and he is in the middle of a pitched battle. Before long, the little kid has joined up with a band of six intrepid dwarfs, and they've embarked on an odyssey through history. The dwarfs, it appears, have gained possession of a map that gives the location of several holes in time—holes they can pop through in order to drop in on the adventures of Robin Hood, Napoleon, and King Agamemnon, and to sail on the *Titanic*'s maiden voyage.

As a plot gimmick, this sets up *Time Bandits* for a series of comic set pieces as in Mel Brooks's *History of the World—Part I*. But *Time Bandits* isn't revue-style comedy. It's more of a whimsical, fantastic excursion through all those times and places, and all of its events are seen through the wondering eyes of a child. That's where the superb art direction comes in—inspired work by production designer Milly Burns and costume designer Jim Acheson. I've rarely, if ever, seen a live-action movie that looks more like an artist's conception. And yet, admiring all of these good things (and I might also mention several of the performances), I nevertheless left the screening with muted enthusiasm. The movie was somehow all on the same breathless, nonstop emotional level, like an overlong Keystone Kops chase. It didn't pause to savor its delights, except right near the end, when Sir Ralph Richardson lingered lovingly over a walk-on as the Supreme Being. I had to sort things out. And I was helped enormously in that process by the review of *Time Bandits* by Stanley Kauffmann in *The New Republic*. He de-

scribes the film, unblinkingly, as a "children's movie." Of course.

There have been so many elaborate big-budget fantasies in recent years, from *Raiders* to *Superman* to *Clash of the Titans*, that we've come to assume that elaborate costume fantasies are aimed at the average eighteen-year-old filmgoer who is trying to recapture his adolescence. These movies have a level of (limited) sophistication and wickedness that is missing in *Time Bandits*. But perhaps *Time Bandits* does work best as just simply a movie for kids. I ran it through my mind that way, wondering how a kid would respond to the costumes, the panoply, the explosions, the horses and heroic figures, and, of course, the breathless, nonstop pacing. And I decided that a kid would like it just fine. I'm not sure that's what Gilliam had in mind, but it allows me to recommend the movie—with reservations, but also with admiration.

A Time of Destiny ★ ★ ★ ½
PG-13, 118 m., 1988

William Hurt (Martin), Timothy Hutton (Jack), Melissa Leo (Josie), Stockard Channing (Margaret), Megan Follows (Irene), Francisco Rabal (Jorge). Directed by Gregory Nava and produced by Anna Thomas. Screenplay by Nava and Thomas.

A Time of Destiny is a film of strong, pure emotions, of which the most powerful are love, hate, and jealousy. It is not a film about timid little people peeking out of their small lives, but about characters whose motives are so large they are operatic, and whose faults are so ancient they are biblical. Any criticism of this film on the basis of implausibility completely misses the point.

The movie tells the story of a proud, flawed family, and the outsider who marries into it. The sickness of the family flows from the father, a proud Basque immigrant who has found success in California in the years before World War II, but still rules his life and family by old-world paternalism. As the movie opens, one of his sons is dead, another son is all but disowned, and all of his love and possessiveness are focused on his middle daughter. When she elopes to get married, his rage and jealousy are towering.

The old man is played by Francisco Rabal as a survivor with a fierce stubbornness. He knows he is right, and one of the things he is right about is this—few men, if any, are good enough for his daughter. She is played by

Melissa Leo as a girl caught halfway between modern America and the values of her childhood. And the man she elopes with, one rainy night, is played by Timothy Hutton as the kind of straight-arrow American who seems commonplace against this convoluted family's deep passions.

If jealousy is a family disease, the old man is the carrier, but his son is the victim. He is also an enigma. Played by William Hurt as a man who seems, at first glance, confident and competent, he is actually on the edge of emotional collapse. His father has no use for him because of his history of failure—failure, we suspect, inspired by the father's inability to make room inside the family for more than one strong man. The Hurt character has grown up into a man filled with grandiose notions of family tradition and pride, and they are all a fantasy, because his father considers him worthless and has written him out of the will.

This convoluted family situation sets the stage for *A Time of Destiny*, which is a melodramatic romance in which the images all seem a little larger and clearer than life. The movie was directed by Gregory Nava and produced by Anna Thomas, who together cowrote the screenplay; they are the team who made *El Norte* five years earlier, and their gift is for passionate, headlong narrative. In this film, the opening scenes are literally explosive; there is a spectacular point-of-view shot of a shell flying through a cannon barrel and down upon a straggling line of Yankee soldiers in Italy, and then we see two of the soldiers, tired beyond exhaustion, pledge to each other to somehow survive the madness.

The soldiers are Hutton and Hurt, and in a flashback we find that this pledge is not as simple as it seems. Hutton and Leo conduct a courtship in the face of her father's disapproval, and everything leads up to a rainswept night when they elope, are married, and then are tracked down to their hotel by the father, in a towering rage. He demands that she return with him or lose his love. She agrees, promising Hutton that they will eventually be together. The old man and his daughter drive out into the dangerous night, Hutton pursues in his car, there is an accident, and the old man dies.

For William Hurt, this is a long-awaited moment. He is simultaneously freed of his father's persecution and given a stage on which to pretend to inherit his father's crown. Hutton (who has never met Hurt and does not know what he looks like) goes off to fight the war; Hurt arranges to join the same Army group, and he vows to murder Hutton to avenge the death of his father. But during a dark and confused night of hand-to-hand fighting, the two men instead save each other's lives. That should set the stage for a reconciliation, but instead, Hurt gradually reveals the true depths of the wound inside his soul.

You see what I mean when I call the movie operatic. It glories in brooding vengeance, fatal flaws of character, coincidence, and deep morality. Its plot is so labyrinthine that it constitutes the movie's major weakness; can we follow this convoluted emotional journey? Its passions are so large that they are a challenge to actors trained in a realistic tradition, but Hurt, who has the most difficult passages, rises to the occasion with one of the strangest and most effective performances he has given. A great deal hinges on one scene that he plays before a mirror, as various aspects of his personality fight for control, and the way he plays this scene is further evidence of his power as an actor. He does not overact, and yet he is not afraid of pulling out all the stops, of taking the risk of making himself look silly. Many actors would have protected themselves by pulling back during this scene. Not William Hurt.

Even the title of *A Time of Destiny* reflects the film's vision. It is a movie about fate in an age that does not believe in fate; its plot is nineteenth-century, without apology, and it is not timid or compromised. As I watched the film, I grew increasingly grateful for the chances it was taking. This same story could have been ground in the mill of psychological realism and come out as oatmeal. But Nava and Thomas have chosen a more difficult and risky approach, and the result is muscular and brave.

The Times of Harvey Milk ★ ★ ★ ½
NO MPAA RATING, 87 m., 1985

A documentary by Robert Epstein and Richard Schmiechen, narrated by Harvey Fierstein.

Harvey Milk must have been a great guy. You get the sense watching this documentary about his brief public career that he could appreciate the absurdities of life and enjoy a good laugh at his own expense. He was also serious enough and angry enough about the political issues in his life that he eventually ran for the San Francisco Board of Supervisors and became California's first openly homosexual public official. That victory may have cost him his life.

The Times of Harvey Milk describes the lives and deaths of Milk and Mayor George Moscone, who both were shot dead in 1978 by Dan White, one of Milk's fellow supervisors. It also describes the political and social climate in San Francisco, which during the 1960s and 1970s began to attract growing numbers of gays because of its traditionally permissive attitude. Milk was one of those gays, and in old photographs we see him in his long-haired beatnik and hippie days before he eventually shaved off the beard and opened a camera store in the Castro District. It was from the Castro that Milk ran for office and was defeated three times before finally winning in the same election that placed the first Chinese-American, the first black woman, and the first avowed feminist on the board. Milk was a master at self-promotion, and the movie includes vintage TV news footage showing him campaigning on such issues as "doggy-do," and stepping, with perfect timing, into a strategically placed pile of same at the climax of the interview.

There is a lot of footage of Milk, Moscone, and White (who disapproved of homosexuals but was naive enough to once suggest that the issue be settled by a softball game between his ward and Milk's ward). It is intercut with later interviews with many of Milk's friends, including a veteran leftist who admits that he was prejudiced against gays for a long time, until he met Milk and began to understand the political issues involved. There is a Chinese-American who parallels his own radicalization with Milk's. And there is immensely moving, emotional footage of the two demonstrations inspired by the deaths of Milk and Moscone: a silent, candlelight parade of forty-five-thousand people on the night of their deaths, and an angry night of rioting when White got what was perceived as a lenient sentence.

"If Dan White had only killed George Moscone, he would have gone up for life," one person says in the film. "But he killed a gay, and so they let him off easy." This is not necessarily the case, and the weakest element in *The Times of Harvey Milk* is its willingness to let Milk's friends second-guess the jury, and impugn the jurors' motives.

Many people who observed White's trial believe that White got a light sentence, not because of antigay sentiment, but because of incompetent prosecution. Some of the jurors were presumably available to the filmmakers, and the decision not to let them speak for themselves—to depend instead on the interpretation of Milk's friends and associates—is a serious bias. That objection aside, this is an enormously absorbing film, for the light it sheds on a decade in the life of a great American city and on the lives of Milk and Moscone, who made it a better, and certainly a more interesting, place to live.

Tin Men ★ ★ ★
R, 109 m., 1987

Richard Dreyfuss (BB), Danny DeVito (Tilley), Barbara Hershey (Nora), John Mahoney (Moe), Jackie Gayle (Sam), Stanley Brock (Gil), Seymour Cassel (Cheese), Bruno Kirby (Mouse). Directed by Barry Levinson and produced by Mark Johnson. Screenplay by Levinson.

They tool up to work in those bloated '50s Cadillacs from back in the days when you knew a Cadillac was the best car on the road because it was the biggest car on the road. They park their Caddys and hang around the diner, drinking coffee and killing time, talking about the citizens they've defrauded and the TV shows they're gonna watch tonight. They're tin men. They sell aluminum siding. One day, BB (Richard Dreyfuss) takes delivery on his new Caddy, and backs it out of the showroom and into the path of a Caddy owned by Tilley (Danny DeVito). Sheet metal is crunched and words are exchanged. They become mortal enemies. They hurl insults and threats at one another, and for weeks afterward they plot and scheme to wreak vengeance for the dents in the fenders of their phallic symbols.

The feud between BB and Tilley is the centerpiece of *Tin Men*, a loosely organized series of events in the lives of some middle-aged and fairly desperate Baltimore salesmen, circa 1958. These guys are worried because the law is closing in, a commission is holding hearings on their high-pressure sales techniques, and they're afraid they'll lose their jobs.

Meanwhile, they carry on in the only ways they know. They use the "loss leader" scam ("After your house becomes the neighborhood showplace, we'll give you a cut when your neighbors sign up for siding"), the *Life* magazine scam ("We need a picture of your house for a layout on how ugly houses are before the aluminum siding is added"), and the sudden breakdown scam (My buddy didn't mean to make you that offer. He hasn't been quite right lately. But I'll tell you what I will do"). And then they meet after work to trade lies and philosophies.

BB figures out a way to really get even with Tilley. He'll seduce his wife (Barbara Hershey). Two things go wrong with this plan. First, Tilley hates his wife and is happy to get rid of her. Second, BB falls in love. That is a high price to pay for a dented fender.

Tin Men was written and directed by Barry Levinson in a style similar to his inspired 1982 comedy, *Diner*. That was a movie about a crowd of teen-age buddies who were mystified by sex, life, ambition, and especially women. They were trying to grow up at an age when they were already supposed to be grown-up. The median age of the characters in *Tin Men* is probably forty-five, but they're still growing up too, and they're still mystified by sex, life, ambition, and women—by everything but Cadillacs.

Like *Diner*, Levinson's new movie uses a series of scenes strung together with the diner as home base. There, in a window booth, pouring sugar into their coffee, the salesmen discuss the bafflements of life. "This show 'Bonanza' is about a fifty-year-old father and his three forty-seven-year-old sons," one of the guys says. "What kind of a show is that?" That line is delivered by Jackie Gayle, who has a lot of the movie's funniest moments, maybe because the Dreyfuss and DeVito characters have serious undertones.

Why do BB and Tilley hate each other so much? Because they hate themselves so much. Why's that? Because they're secretly ashamed to be con men, and their Cadillacs impart a respectability they don't really feel. So if you dent their fenders, you question the very depths of their identities.

Because *Tin Men* is based on fundamental truth, it is able to be funny even in some of its quieter moments. The good jokes always hurt a little. This movie isn't slapstick and it's not a farce; it's the kind of comedy the guy was thinking about when he wrote, "We laugh, that we may not cry."

To Be or Not To Be ★ ★ ★
R, 108 m., 1983

Mel Brooks (Bronski), Anne Bancroft (Anna Bronski), Tim Matheson (Lieutenant Sobinski), Charles Durning (Colonel Erhardt), Jose Ferrer (Professor Siletski). Directed by Alan Johnson and produced by Mel Brooks. Screenplay by Thomas Meehan and Ronny Graham.

It's an old gag, the one about the actor who is always interrupted in the middle of Hamlet's soliloquy by a guy in the third row who has to go to the john and loudly excuses himself all the way to the end of the row. But I can't think of a better Hamlet for this particular gag than Mel Brooks. "That is the QUESTION!" he bellows, as the guy screws up his timing, his delivery, his concentration. And the punch line is that the guy is actually going backstage to have a quick assignation with the actor's wife.

Mel Brooks loves show business and has worked it into a lot of his movies, most unforgettably in *The Producers*. He also loves musicals and has worked musical numbers into the most unlikely moments in his movies. (Remember Frankenstein's monster doing the soft-shoe?) In *To Be or Not To Be*, Brooks combines a backstage musical with a wartime romance and comes up with an eclectic comedy that races off into several directions, sometimes successfully.

The movie costars Brooks and his wife, Anne Bancroft, working together for the first time on screen as Frederick and (Anna) Bronski, the impresarios of a brave little theatrical troupe in Warsaw on the brink of war. (Anna) Bronski, whose name is in parentheses because her husband has such a big ego, is a femme fatale with an eye for the handsome young servicemen that worship her nightly in the theater. Bronski is an all-over-the-map guy who does Hamlet's soliloquy and stars in a revue called *Naughty Nazis* in the same night and on the same stage. Then the Nazis march into Poland. What can a humble troupe of actors do to stop them? "Nothing!" Bronski declares—but then the troupe gets involved in an elaborate masquerade, pretending to be real Nazis in order to throw Hitler's men off-course and prevent the success of the German plans.

When *To Be or Not To Be* was originally made, by Ernst Lubitsch in 1942, the Nazis *were* in Poland, which gave a certain poignancy to every funny line. Lubitsch's stars

were Jack Benny and Carole Lombard, both specialists in underplaying. Brooks and Bancroft go in the opposite direction, cheerfully allowing farce, slapstick, pratfalls, and puns into the story, until the whole movie seems strung together like one of the revues in Bronski's theater.

The supporting players, given license to overact, have fun. Charles Durning plays a rigid but peculiarly confused Nazi colonel, and Tim Matheson is the young aviator who excuses himself loudly and sneaks backstage to meet Bancroft. The veteran actor Jose Ferrer plays Professor Siletski, a two-faced collaborator.

It will probably always be impossible for Brooks to remain entirely within the dramatic logic of any story, and here he gives himself a lot of freedom with lines like "Sondheim! Send in the clowns!" But *To Be or Not To Be* works as well as a story as any Brooks film since *Young Frankenstein*, and darned if there isn't a little sentiment involved as the impresario and his wife, after years of marriage, surprise each other by actually falling in love.

To Live and Die in L.A. ★ ★ ★ ★
R, 110 m., 1985

William L. Petersen (Richard Chance), Willem Dafoe (Eric Masters), John Pankow (John Vukovich), Debra Feuer (Bianca Torres), John Turturro (Carl Cody), Darlanne Fluegel (Ruth Lanier), Dean Stockwell (Bob Grimes), Robert Downey (Thomas Bateman). Directed by William Friedkin and produced by Irving H. Levin. Screenplay by Gerald Petievich and Friedkin.

In the hierarchy of great movie chase sequences, the recent landmarks include the chases under the Brooklyn elevated tracks in *The French Connection*, down the hills of San Francisco in *Bullitt*, and through the Paris Metro in *Diva*. Those chases were not only thrilling in their own right, but they reflected the essence of the cities where they took place. Now comes William Friedkin, director of *The French Connection*, with a movie that contains a second chase that belongs on that short list. The movie is set in Los Angeles, and so of course the chase centers around the freeway system.

To Live and Die in L.A. is a law enforcement movie, sort of. It's about Secret Service agents who are on the trail of a counterfeiter who has eluded the law for years, and who flaunts his success. At one point, when undercover agents are negotiating a deal with the counterfeiter in his expensive health club, he boasts, "I've been coming to this gym three times a week for five years. I'm an easy guy to find. People know they can trust me."

Meanwhile, he's asking for a down payment on a sale of bogus bills, and the down payment is larger than the Secret Service can authorize. So, Richard Chance (William L. Petersen), the hot-dog special agent who's the hero of the movie, sets up a dangerous plan to steal the advance money from another crook, and uses it to buy the bogus paper and bust the counterfeiter.

Neat. The whole plot is neat, revolving around a few central emotions—friendship, loyalty, arrogance, anger. By the time the great chase sequence arrives, it isn't just a novelty, tacked onto a movie where it doesn't fit. It's part of the plot. The Secret Service agents bungle *their* crime, the cops come in pursuit, and the chase unfolds in a long, dazzling ballet of timing, speed, and imagination.

The great chases are rarely just chases. They involve some kind of additional element—an unexpected vehicle, an unusual challenge, a strange setting. The car-train chase in *The French Connection* was a masterstroke. In *Diva*, the courier rode his motor scooter into one subway station and out another, bouncing up and down the stairs. Or think of John Ford's sustained stagecoach chase in *Stagecoach*, or the way Buster Keaton orchestrated *The General* so that trains chased each other through a railway system.

The masterstroke in *To Live and Die in L.A.* is that the chase isn't just on a freeway. It goes *the wrong way* down the freeway. I don't know how Friedkin choreographed this scene and I don't want to know. It probably took a lot of money and a lot of drivers. All I know is that there are high-angle shots during the chase during which you can look a long way ahead and see hundreds of cars across four lanes, all heading for the escape car which is aimed at them, full-speed. It is an amazing sequence.

The rest of the movie is also first-rate. The direction is the key. Friedkin has made some good movies (*The French Connection, The Exorcist, Sorcerer*) and some bad ones (*Cruising, Deal of the Century*). This is his comeback, showing the depth and skill of the early pictures. The central performance is by William L. Petersen, a Chicago stage actor

who comes across as tough, wiry, and smart. He has some of the qualities of a Steve McQueen, with more complexity. Another strong performance in the movie is by Willem Dafoe, as the counterfeiter, cool and professional as he discusses the realities of his business.

I like movies which teach me about something, movies which have researched their subject and contain a lot of information, casually contained in between the big dramatic scenes. *To Live and Die in L.A.* seems to know a lot about counterfeiting, and also about the interior policies of the Secret Service. The film isn't just about cops and robbers, but about two systems of doing business, and how one of the systems finds a way to change itself in order to defeat the other. That's interesting. So is the chase.

To Sleep with Anger ★ ★ ½
PG, 102 m., 1990

Danny Glover (Harry), Mary Alice (Suzie), Paul Butler (Gideon), Richard Brooks (Babe Brother), Carl Lumbly (Junior), Vonetta McGee (Pat). Directed by Charles Burnett and produced by Caldecot Chubb, Thomas S. Byrnes, and Darin Scott. Screenplay by Burnett.

At some point in every child's life a stranger comes to the door and stands there, mysterious and threatening, until a light is turned on or a name is called out, and the stranger is revealed as a friend. That ominous moment of mystery—the dark outline, the knocking at the door from the great terrifying world—connects with an archetypal fear we all grow up sharing. Rare is the person who welcomes unexpected visitors.

Yet there are rules to be followed. When the visitor turns out to be a relative from far away, a man not seen in quite a while, the door must be opened, drinks must be poured, food set upon the table. And if the visitor expansively makes himself at home and puts his shoes on the furniture and calls people by their familiar names when he is not exactly familiar with them, why, then, courtesy demands that the hosts put up with a good deal of that kind of behavior.

And if the stranger does not leave? If he announces that he might stay for a day or two, and receives a hesitant agreement, and then stays for a week or two, and shows no sign of leaving? What then? At what point do the obligations of host and the loyalty to fam-

ily wear thin? At what point is the relative shown the door?

Charles Burnett's *To Sleep with Anger* is a subtle kind of horror movie in which the unwelcome visitor is not a slasher or a cartoon character, but a soft-spoken relative from down South, getting on a bit in years, well-dressed, seemingly courteous. The tension in the movie is created as he stays and stays, until he is clearly unwelcome and yet no one can figure out a way to get rid of him. And the horror element comes as it begins to dawn on us, and the characters in the movie, that this man is some sort of emissary of evil. Perhaps not Satan precisely, but familiar with the neighborhood.

The visitor is named Harry. That is a familiar name for the devil, probably inspired by the devil's love of harrying people. That's what Harry does. He gets under their skins. He knows old secrets and refers to them after everybody has stopped talking about them for decades. He remembers shameful things people have done in their pasts. He ferrets out their present weaknesses and mocks them. He makes demands he knows are unreasonable. He brings a plague of anger and sadness down upon the house, and the family—a happy, prosperous black family that has long since settled in California—becomes divided and sick; the father even takes to his bed and lapses into a coma.

Harry is played in the movie by Danny Glover, who usually plays the most pleasant of men; he is the easygoing member of the team in the *Lethal Weapon* movies. Here his very pleasantness makes him more sinister. His good manners turn oily, somehow, and the others begin to clear a space around him, physically and in conversation. Glover is an actor of considerable presence, and here he lets us know his character is from hell, and hardly has to raise his voice.

Around him, the family members begin to turn unhappy. A younger brother grows weak and without direction. The father is ill. The mother is morose over what is happening in her household. Unwelcome visitors turn up to play cards and drink. Eventually, like in every other horror movie, something must be done to destroy the monster.

The film's only flaw is that the "eventually" is too long in coming. The movie seemed well-done but too long when I saw it at the Sundance Film Festival. It has been trimmed, but still plays too slowly. What should be brooding comes across as too deliberate. The reality of Harry's invasion and its effect on the family is still developed by Burnett after he has made his point. What should be a coiled film, exploding at the end, is one where the final act releases our impatience rather than our tension. There are some good things in this movie, and too much time in between them.

Tommy ★ ★ ★
PG, 108 m., 1975

Ann-Margret (Nora Walker), Oliver Reed (Frank Hobbs), Roger Daltrey (Tommy), Elton John (Pinball Wizard), Eric Clapton (Preacher), Keith Moon (Uncle Ernie), Jack Nicholson (Specialist), Tina Turner (Acid Queen). The Who: Pete Townshend, John Entwhistle, Daltrey, and Moon. Directed by Ken Russell and produced by Robert Stigwood and Russell. Screenplay by Russell.

Ken Russell's *Tommy* is a case of glorious overkill—a big, brassy, vulgar overproduction that works because it never stops for a breath or a second thought. It's got confidence. It's a blast of wall-to-wall music for almost two hours, and its quietest moment is a Moog-synthesized belch from Oliver Reed that sounds like the Carlsbad Caverns throwing up. There's not the slightest hint of moderation or restraint in the movie, and there shouldn't be. This is Ken Russell giving a Bronx cheer to the most pretentious of the late 1960s rock operas, turning it into a clothesline on which he strings a series of bizarre, manic production numbers. Sit down in front, slide back in your seat, and let it assault you.

The movie's purpose and achievement would be hard to figure out on the basis of what its makers say about it. Pete Townshend, who wrote the original album for The Who, says *Tommy* is an attack on the hypocrisy of organized religion. Ken Russell, who's made a specialty of films about musicians (Tchaikovsky, Mahler, and Liszt), says *Tommy* is the greatest work of art the twentieth century has produced. He was almost certainly misquoted. What he meant to say was that it was a heaven-sent opportunity for him to exercise his gift for going too far, for creating three-ring cinematic circuses with kinky sideshows.

The message of *Tommy*, if any, is contained mostly in the last thirty minutes (of which we could have done without about fifteen). By then the hero (who started out in life as a blind deaf-mute) has become the pinball superstar of all time, even though he can't

see the machine. Stardom brings him a fortune, he becomes the leader of a quasireligious cult, regains his senses, and gets his own Tommy T-shirt. But then things get out of hand. Tommy is on the level, but the people around him begin to commercialize on his fame in order to peddle T-shirts, record albums, and other artifacts. Tommy's enraged fans turn on him and what they perceive as his hypocrisy. How the makers of the film feel about this commercialization can be gauged by the prominence with which the end titles inform us that the sound-track album is available on Polydor Records. To make money on a rock opera attacking those who would make money on a rock opera: that was the brave moral stand taken by *Tommy*.

But none of this matters, because Russell correctly doesn't give a damn about the material he started with, greatest art work of the century or not, and he just goes ahead and gives us one glorious excess after another. He is aided by his performers, especially Ann-Margret, who is simply great as Tommy's mother. She has one number that begins in an all-white bedroom with her sexy red dress slit up the side to about the collarbone, and ends with her slithering through several hundred pounds of baked beans. It's that kind of movie.

Tommy's odyssey through life is punctuated by encounters with all sorts of weird folks, of whom the most seductive is Tina Turner as the Acid Queen. The scene begins with Tina as the hooker upstairs from the strip parlor operated by Tommy's wicked stepfather, and ends with a psychedelic stainless steel mummy with acid in its veins. This scene is the occasion for Tommy's first smile, as well it might be.

Then there's the great pinball tournament, which is the movie's best single scene: a pulsating, orgiastic turn-on edited with the precision of a machine gun burst. Elton John, wearing skyscraper shoes, is the defending pinball champion. Tommy is the challenger. Russell cuts between the crowds, the arena, and a dizzying series of close-ups of the games (at times, we almost seem to be inside the pinball machines), and the effect is exhilarating and exhausting.

Tootsie ★ ★ ★ ★
PG, 116 m., 1982

Dustin Hoffman (Michael), Jessica Lange (Julie), Charles Durning (Les Nichols), Teri Garr (Sandy), Bill Murray (Roommate), Dabney Coleman (Ron), Doris Belack (Rita), Sydney Pollack (Agent). Directed by Sydney Pollack and produced by Dick Richards. Screenplay by Larry Gelbart.

One of the most endearing things about *Tootsie*, a movie in which Dustin Hoffman plays a middle-aged actress, is that the actress is able to carry most of her own scenes as herself— even if she weren't being played by Hoffman. *Tootsie* works as a story, not as a gimmick. It also works as a lot of other things. *Tootsie* is the kind of Movie with a capital M that they used to make in the 1940s, when they weren't afraid to mix up absurdity with seriousness, social comment with farce, and a little heartfelt tenderness right in there with the laughs. This movie gets you coming and going.

Hoffman stars as Michael Dorsey, a character maybe not unlike Hoffman himself in his younger days. Michael is a New York actor: bright, aggressive, talented—and unemployable. "You mean *nobody in New York* wants to hire me?" he asks his agent, incredulously. "I'd go farther than that, Michael," his agent says. "Nobody in Hollywood wants to hire you, either." Michael has a bad reputation for taking stands, throwing tantrums, and interpreting roles differently than the director. How to get work? He goes with a friend (Teri Garr) to an audition for a soap opera. The character is a middle-aged woman hospital administrator. When his friend doesn't get the job, Michael goes home, thinks, decides to dare, and dresses himself as a woman. And, improvising brilliantly, he gets the role.

That leads to *Tootsie's* central question: Can a fortyish New York actor find health, happiness, and romance as a fortyish New York actress? Dustin Hoffman is actually fairly plausible as "Dorothy," the actress. If his voice isn't quite right, a Southern accent allows it to squeak by. The wig and the glasses are a little too much, true, but in an uncanny way the woman played by Hoffman looks like certain actual women who look like drag queens. Dorothy might have trouble passing in Evanston, but in Manhattan, nobody gives her a second look.

Tootsie might have been content to limit itself to the complications of New York life in drag; it could have been *Victor/Victoria Visits Elaine's.* But the movie's a little more ambitious than that. Michael Dorsey finds to his interest and amusement that Dorothy begins to take on a life of her own. She's a liberated eccentric, a woman who seems sort of odd and funny at first, but grows on you and wins your admiration by standing up for what's right. One of the things that bothers Dorothy is the way the soap opera's chauvinist director (Dabney Coleman) mistreats and insults the attractive young actress (Jessica Lange) who plays Julie, a nurse on the show. Dorothy and Julie become friends and finally close confidantes. Dorothy's problem, however, is that the man inside her is gradually growing uncontrollably in love with Julie. There are other complications. Julie's father (Charles Durning), a gruff, friendly, no-nonsense sort, lonely but sweet, falls in love with Dorothy. Michael hardly knows how to deal with all of this, and his roommate (Bill Murray) isn't much help. Surveying Dorothy in one of her new outfits, he observes dryly, "Don't play hard to get."

Tootsie has a lot of fun with its plot complications; we get almost every possible variation on the theme of mistaken sexual identities. The movie also manages to make some lighthearted but well-aimed observations about sexism. It *also* pokes satirical fun at soap operas, New York show-business agents, and the Manhattan social pecking-order. *And* it turns out to be a touching love story, after all—so touching that you may be surprised how moved you are at the conclusion of this comedy.

Too Beautiful for You ★ ★ ★ ½
R, 91 m., 1990

Gerard Depardieu (Bernard), Josiane Balasko (Colette), Carole Bouquet (Florence), Roland Blanche (Marcello), Francois Cluzet (Pascal), Didier Benureau (Leonce), Philippe Loffredo (Tanguy), Sylvie Orcier (Marie-Catherine). Directed, produced, and written by Bertrand Blier.

Lust occurs between bodies. Love occurs between personalities. Because we see the outsides of others but know the thoughts of ourselves, this truth causes a great deal of unhappiness and misunderstanding. And that is the subject of *Too Beautiful for You*, the story of a man who has a beautiful wife and yet falls in love with his dumpy secretary.

She isn't much to look at—so you might say, unless you saw the dreaminess in her eyes after she has been brought to passion. She wears fuzzy sweaters that she pulls down over the skirts that cling to her generous hips. She knows little about the cosmetic arts. Her hair style is sensible—which means that after you wash it and dry it, it looks washed and dried. The moment he lays eyes on her, he is thunderstruck. Her presence speaks to something deep and elemental inside of him. He cannot tear his eyes away from her.

His name is Bernard. He is played by Gerard Depardieu, that superb French actor who always seems afraid to break something. Her name is Colette. She is played by Josiane Balasko with such an honesty that you understand why anyone would love her. The wife, the woman who fulfills all standards of modern fashionable beauty, is played by Carole Bouquet, who in other films has shown herself to be warm and comical, but in this film is just what she's supposed to be—a woman whose beauty is no match for a woman who can touch a man's heart.

In *Too Beautiful for You*, Bertrand Blier tells the story of these people in a curious way that takes a little getting used to. He opens with strong, stark images of passion, and then allows some of the characters to talk directly to the audience, and then uses fantasy scenes in which we see what it would be like if the fears of adulterers were ever made real. In the most startling of the fantasies, the wife addresses a dinner party at which Colette is present and tells her friends that she knows they have always hated her because she was too beautiful.

The opening scene of the movie takes place in Bernard's automobile dealership. Colette is the new secretary. Through the glass walls of the offices, he can see her sitting in her cubicle. Their eyes meet, and then they exchange one of those groin-wrenching moments of instantaneous passion that only the movies can do justice to (I was reminded of the way Gene Tierney stared rudely and speechlessly at a man on a train in *Leave Her to Heaven*). He turns away from the strength of it. He cannot hear her, but she talks to him: "Please turn around and look at me."

The day comes to an end. They cannot get each other out of their thoughts. All day long, she has spoken to him—but only we could hear her—in terms of such tenderness and understanding that we want to hug her. She leaves to go to the bus stop. He runs after her. He has missed her. No—here she is! They look in each other's eyes and all is known between them, and all is lost.

This is grown-up love, not the silly adolescent posturing of Hollywood sex symbols. It is love beyond sex, beyond attraction, beyond lust. It is the love of need, the love that says, I am a puzzle and you are the solution. The rest of the movie's story circles around the great fact of this love.

Depardieu is one of the most endlessly fascinating actors of our time. He works constantly, in roles of such variety that to list them is astonishing: He was the hunchbacked farmer in *Jean de Florette*, and the sculptor Rodin in *Camille Claudel*, and the imposter in *The Return of Martin Guerre*. Here he plays just an ordinary man—one of the most difficult roles in the movies. He makes his passion believable because he never overacts it, and because the movie conveys it mostly through the eyes of the actress, Balasko. She sees that she is loved. Bouquet, in the movie's most difficult role, has to accept defeat of a sort: She is beautiful, but that has not been enough. People envy her and she knows she is not to be envied.

Somebody was asking the other day what the difference was between French and American films. American films are about plots, I said, and French films are about people. You can usually tell where a plot is heading, but a person, now—a person will fool you.

Top Gun ★ ★ ½
PG, 109 m., 1986

Tom Cruise (Maverick), Kelly McGillis (Charlie), Val Kilmer (Iceman), Tom Skerritt (Viper), Anthony Edwards (Goose). Directed by Tony Scott and produced by Don Simpson and Jerry Bruckheimer. Screenplay by Jim Cash and Jack Epps, Jr.

In the opening moments of *Top Gun*, a skilled Navy pilot flies upside down about four feet above a Russian-built MiG and snaps a Polaroid picture of the enemy pilot. Then he flips him the finger and peels off.

It's a hot-dog stunt, but it makes the pilot (Tom Cruise) famous within the small circle of Navy personnel who are cleared to receive information about close encounters with enemy aircraft. And the pilot, whose code name is Maverick, is selected for the Navy's elite flying school, which is dedicated to the dying art of aerial dogfights. The best graduate from each class at the school is known as "Top Gun."

And there, I think, you have the basic materials of this movie, except, of course, for three more obligatory ingredients in all movies about brave young pilots: (1) the girl, (2) the mystery of the heroic father, and (3) the rivalry with another pilot. It turns out that Maverick's dad was a brilliant Navy jet pilot during the Vietnam era, until he and his plane disappeared in unexplained circumstances. And it also turns out that one of the instructors at the flying school is a pretty young blonde (Kelly McGillis) who wants to know a lot more about how Maverick snapped that other pilot's picture.

Top Gun settles fairly quickly into alternating ground and air scenes, and the simplest way to sum it up is to declare the air scenes brilliant and the earthbound scenes grimly predictable. This movie comes in two parts: It knows exactly what to do with special effects, but doesn't have a clue as to how two people in love might act and talk and think.

Aerial scenes always present a special challenge in a movie. There's the danger that the audience will become spatially disoriented. We're used to seeing things within a frame that respects left and right, up and down, but the fighter pilot lives in a world of 360-degree turns. The remarkable achievement in *Top Gun* is that it presents seven or eight aerial encounters that are so well choreographed that we can actually follow them most of the time, and the movie gives us a good secondhand sense of what it might be like to be in a dogfight.

The movie's first and last sequences involve encounters with enemy planes. Although the planes are MiGs, the movie provides no nationalities for their pilots. We're told the battles take place over the Indian Ocean, and that's it. All of the sequences in between take place at Top Gun school, where Maverick quickly gets locked into a personal duel with another brilliant pilot, Iceman (Val Kilmer). In one sequence after another, the sound track trembles as the sleek planes pursue each other through the clouds, and, yeah, it's exciting. But the love story between Cruise and McGillis is a washout.

It's pale and unconvincing compared with the chemistry between Cruise and Rebecca De Mornay in *Risky Business*, and between McGillis and Harrison Ford in *Witness*—not to mention between Richard Gere and Debra

Winger in *An Officer and a Gentleman*, which obviously inspired *Top Gun*. Cruise and McGillis spend a lot of time squinting uneasily at each other and exchanging words as if they were weapons, and when they finally get physical, they look like the stars of one of those sexy perfume ads. There's no flesh and blood here, which is remarkable, given the almost palpable physical presence McGillis had in *Witness*.

In its other ground scenes, the movie seems content to recycle clichés and conventions out of countless other war movies. Wouldn't you know, for example, that Maverick's commanding officer is the only man who knows what happened to the kid's father in Vietnam? And are we surprised when Maverick's best friend dies in his arms? Is there any suspense as Maverick undergoes his obligatory crisis of conscience, wondering whether he can ever fly again?

Movies like *Top Gun* are hard to review because the good parts are so good and the bad parts are so relentless. The dogfights are absolutely the best since Clint Eastwood's electrifying aerial scenes in *Firefox*. But look out for the scenes where the people talk to one another.

Top Secret! ★ ★ ★ ½
R, 90 m., 1984

Val Kilmer (Nick Rivers), Lucy Gutteridge (Hillary), Omar Sharif (Cedric), Peter Cushing (Bookseller). Directed by Jim Abrahams, David Zucker, and Jerry Zucker and produced by Jon Davison and Hunt Lowry. Written by Abrahams, Zucker and Zucker, with Martyn Burke.

I have a friend who claims he only laughed real loud on five occasions during *Top Secret!* I laughed that much in the first ten minutes. It all depends on your sense of humor. My friend claims that I have a cornpone sense of humor, because of my origins deep in central Illinois. I admit that is true. As a Gemini, however, I contain multitudes, and I also have a highly sophisticated, sharply intellectual sense of humor. Get me in the right mood, and I can laugh all over the map. That's why I liked *Top Secret!* This movie will cheerfully go for a laugh wherever one is even remotely likely to be found. It has political jokes and boob jokes, dog poop jokes, and ballet jokes. It makes fun of two completely different Hollywood genres: the spy

movie and the Elvis Presley musical. It contains a political refugee who fled America by balloon during the Carter administration, a member of the French underground named Escargot, and Omar Sharif inside a compacted automobile.

To describe the plot would be an exercise in futility. This movie has no plot. It does not need a plot. One does not attend movies like *Top Secret!* in order to follow the story line. I think you can figure that out right away, in the opening sequence, which is devoted to the sport of "skeet surfin'" and has beach boys on surfboards firing at clay targets. Instead of a plot, it has a funny young actor named Val Kilmer as the hero, a 1950s-style American rock 'n' roller who is sent on a concert tour behind the Iron Curtain, and manages to reduce East Germany to a shambles while never missing a word of "Tutti Frutti" (he never even stumbles during *a-wop-bop-a-doo bop, a bop-bam-boom*).

The movie is physical humor, sight gags, puns, double meanings, satire, weird choreography, scatological outrages, and inanity. One particular sequence, however, is such an original example of specifically cinematic humor that I'd like to discuss it at length. (Do not read further if you don't like to understand jokes before laughing at them.) The sequence involves a visit by the hero to a Swedish bookshop. Never mind why he goes there. The scene depends for its inspiration on this observation: People who run tape recorders backward often say that English, played backward, sounds like Swedish (especially, of course, to people who do not speak Swedish). What *Top Secret!* does is to film an entire scene and play it backward, so that the dialogue sounds Swedish, and then translate it into English subtitles. This is funny enough at the beginning, but it becomes inspired at the end, when the scene finally gives itself away.

There are other wonderful moments. The dance sequence in the East Berlin nightclub develops into something Groucho Marx would have been proud of. The malt shop musical number demolishes a whole tradition of Elvis Presley numbers. And how the ballerina makes her exit in *Swan Lake* will, I feel confident, be discussed for years wherever codpieces are sold.

Topaz ★ ★ ★ ½
PG, 124 m., 1970

Frederick Stafford (Andre Deverauz), Dany Robin (Nicole, His Wife), John Vernon (Rico Parra), Karin Dor (Juanita), Michel Piccoli (Jacques Granville), Philippe Noiret (Henri Jarre), John Forsythe (Nordstrom). Directed by Alfred Hitchcock. Screenplay by Samuel Taylor.

In some ways *Topaz* is a perfectly typical Alfred Hitchcock movie, but in other ways it's something new and rather unexpected from the master. The Hitchcock style is still there, all right: The action in incongruous places, the montages showing cause and effect, the sinister qualities of everyday objects, the tightly programmed editing style. That's all there and, even if you don't notice it, it works the old Hitchcock tricks on you and you're scared when he wants you to be. But what's new in *Topaz* is Hitchcock's choice of a field of action. He goes much wider this time, using three groups of protagonists instead of one or two central characters, and his subject is nothing less than the spy systems of the Cold War.

Hitchcock claimed, and he was probably telling the truth, that he really didn't care what his movies were about. He approached them scientifically, manipulating his actors to produce the desired effects in the audience. He liked to get suspense when he wanted it; he liked to play an audience like a piano. In most of his movies, then, he ignored the "real" world and made no attempt to show things as they might really happen. He shut everybody into a Hitchcock universe and tried to trap you in it, too.

So his basic theme was usually the same: An innocent man, wrongly accused, is placed in a position where he must clear himself before he is overtaken by either the bad guys or the law. This theme is terribly useful for getting viewers involved and perhaps (psychology aside) that's why Hitchcock likes it. But in *Topaz*, he made one of his occasional excursions into other areas, and this time he went farther afield than he ever did in *Foreign Correspondent* or *The 39 Steps* or *The Birds*.

Properly speaking, *Topaz* doesn't have a hero, although it has two or three characters who function that way occasionally. It doesn't have a hero because it doesn't have a moral point of view; Hitchcock deals with an American-French-Cuban spy network at the time of the Cuban missile crisis, and yet his focus is so firmly on the spies as professionals that we hardly get the feeling we should be for the French or against the Cubans. The plot is complex, with a lot of characters left over from the mediocre Leon Uris novel. The action moves from Washington to New York to Havana to Paris as two spy networks conspire to get information on the missile crisis to either Washington or Moscow. The movie begins with a good chase scene in Denmark, where a high-ranking Russian has defected. It's not a *Bullitt*-type chase with lots of speed and fast cutting, but one of those Hitchcock chases where everyone's forced to walk slowly and act naturally and smile a lot, nervously. The Americans finally get the Russian back to Washington where he reveals information about the Cuban missiles and also about a security leak in Paris.

Hitchcock does a good job of re-creating that far-off time, 1963. There is a fascinating sequence in Harlem where the Cuban UN delegation (remember?) had taken over the Theresa Hotel. The idea is to get some papers to photograph them. Hitchcock uses a remarkable actor, Roscoe Lee Browne, as a black journalist who saunters in and breezes out again with the secrets. Browne's scenes are the most delightful in the movie; for the most part, Hitchcock allowed his actors to remain so wooden they all look alike.

There is then some hanky-panky in Cuba, including the most protracted tearful-death scene in years (the beautiful Karin Dor done in by blue-eyed, sinister John Vernon). And then the action switches to Paris for the complicated conclusion. The interesting thing about that conclusion, by the way, is that Hitchcock goes out on a downbeat. There's no climax, no chase; just the sordid working-out of a messy game of spying. It's a nice, quiet ending, very much in keeping with the film, and *Topaz* is good Hitchcock. When you see it, wait for that scene where Michel Piccoli urges Philippe Noiret to hurry up and drink his cognac, and you tell me if you believe Piccoli expects a visitor.

Torch Song Trilogy ★ ★ ★ ½
R, 120 m., 1988

Harvey Fierstein (Arnold), Anne Bancroft (Ma), Matthew Broderick (Alan), Brian Kerwin (Ed), Karen Young (Laurel), Eddie Castrodad (David), Ken Page (Murray), Charles Pierce (Bertha Venation), Axel Vera (Marina Del Rey). Directed by Paul Bogart and produced by Howard Gottfried. Screenplay by Harvey Fierstein.

Torch Song Trilogy opens with a close-up of Arnold, the hero, looking his very worst. He's backstage at the drag club where he works as a female impersonator, and he's halfway into his makeup. You can see every facial flaw—of the male face underneath and the female face he's applying to the surface. Cigarette smoke drifts through the shot. You can almost smell the cold cream. He's talking about his life as a homosexual, and there are moments when his voice catches with emotion. We're touched that he's revealing himself so honestly. But then, of course, he breaks the spell with a throwaway one-liner.

He breaks a lot of spells that way. This is a man who has used sarcasm and self-satire to build a wall around himself. One of the earliest scenes in the movie is a flashback to childhood, when his mother surprises him on the floor of her closet playing dress-up with her high heels and her makeup. It is obvious that dressing like a woman is important to him, but later he turns that part of himself into a parody, as a drag queen who laughs first so that the joke is never on him.

Torch Song Trilogy is basically a movie about a man who slowly becomes more comfortable with himself. As written and performed by Harvey Fierstein as a long-running stage hit, it was seen as a sort of nostalgic visit to the problems gays had in the years before the horror of AIDS. The movie has more or less the same focus, but because it's a movie, it becomes more intimate and intense. It's about a man who was born gay, and has known about himself from an early age, and has accepted his homosexuality more easily than certain other facets of himself—such as his fear of loneliness, his painful insecurity about his appearance, and his almost paralyzing shyness. Homosexuality is not his problem—it is the arena for his problems.

I'm glad they let Fierstein star in the movie himself. There might have been a temptation to go out and hire some established, bankable star who could win points for his courage in playing a gay (compare Richard Burton and Rex Harrison in *Staircase*). That would have been phony from the outset, but it would also have denied us a look at this extraordinary individual with the deep, raspy voice, and the exaggerated double takes, and the face that looks handsome from some angles, goofy from others, and ravaged when he has a hangover. I have not seen anyone quite like Harvey Fierstein in the movies before, and the fact that he is a specific individual gives this material a charm and weight it might have lacked if an interchangeable actor had played the role.

The movie is told in three major parts, with some moments in between. Arnold falls in love with Ed, a bisexual man (Brian Kerwin) who is not sure of his sexuality and certainly not sure of Arnold. Arnold loses Ed. Arnold falls in love with Alan (Matthew Broderick), and they love each other and try to build a life together. Alan is killed by gay-bashers. Devastated, Arnold falls into a deep depression, which is mostly offscreen; in the last part of the film, he is friends again with Ed, and he has adopted a gay teen-ager and sounds exactly like his mother when he talks to the kid.

Written down starkly like that, the movie almost sounds like a formula of love and loss. But *Torch Song Trilogy* is seen in a lot of specific scenes, in moments like the one where Arnold wakes up before Ed in the morning, dashes into the bathroom to make himself look as good as possible, and then jumps back into bed a second before the alarm goes off. Or the moments in the alley outside the nightclub, where Arnold's friend Bertha (Charles Pierce), also a drag queen, provides a few words of advice that come from a lifetime of experience. Or the painful scene in a gay bar where Arnold is so shy he can hardly bring himself to respond to Ed. A person emerges from these moments.

There are some passages that don't work very well. The whole business of the adopted son feels unconvincing and tacked-on, and Eddie Castrodad plays the teen-ager like the precocious host of his own party. Another awkward scene involves a weekend in the country, with Arnold and Alan visiting Ed and his bride (Karen Young). Ed and Alan wind up in the hayloft (of all places), but I was never sure what the point of their infidelity was supposed to be.

The movie's ending is a powerful, painful confrontation between Arnold and his mother (Anne Bancroft). I've had reservations about Bancroft in some of her recent performances because she tends to go over the top, but here there is no reason to hold back. She is the demonstrative, emotional mother of a son who shares many of the same mannerisms, and I believed her in the role. I also believed Arnold when he finally told her exactly what he thought about his sexuality and her

attitude toward it, and when he said, "There are two things I demand from the people in my life: love and respect." He could have been speaking for anybody.

Total Recall ★ ★ ★ ½
R, 110 m., 1990

Arnold Schwarzenegger (Quaid), Rachel Ticotin (Melina), Sharon Stone (Lori), Ronny Cox (Cohaagen), Michael Ironside (Richter), Marshall Bell (George/Kuato), Michael Champion (Helm), Mel Johnson, Jr. (Benny), Roy Brocksmith (Dr. Edgemar). Directed by Paul Verhoeven and produced by Buzz Feitshans and Ronald Shusett. Screenplay by Shusett, Dan O'Bannon, and Gary Goldman.

There may be people who overlook the Arnold Schwarzenegger performance in *Total Recall*—who think he isn't really acting. But the performance is one of the reasons the movie works so well. He isn't a superman this time, although he fights like one. He's a confused and frightened innocent, a man betrayed by the structure of reality itself. And in his vulnerability, he opens the way for *Total Recall* to be more than simply an action, violence, and special-effects extravaganza.

There is a lot of action and violence in the movie, and almost every shot seems to embody some sort of special effect. This is one of the most complex and visually interesting science-fiction movies in a long time. But the plot, based on a story by the great sci-fi writer Philip K. Dick, centers on an intriguing idea: What would happen if you could be supplied with memories? If your entire "past," right up until this moment, could be plugged into your brain, replacing the experiences you had really lived through?

That's what seems to happen to Quaid, the Schwarzenegger character in *Total Recall*, although at times neither he nor we can be quite sure. We meet him in a future world where he lives in a comfortable apartment with his loving blond wife and goes off to work every day at a construction job. His life seems idyllic, but he keeps having these dreams about Mars—dreams that finally inspire him to sign up with a strange kind of travel agency that provides you with the memory of a vacation instead of a real one.

What they do is strap you into a machine and beam the memories into your mind, so that it seems utterly convincing to you that you've been to Mars and done some dan-

gerous spying there and fallen in love with the brunette of your specifications (Quaid specifies she be "athletic, sleazy, and demure"). Before long, sure enough, Quaid seems to be on Mars, involved in some secret-spy stuff, and in the arms of his custom-ordered brunette (Rachel Ticotin).

But is this a packaged memory or a real experience? The movie toys tantalizingly with the possibilities, especially in a scene where a convincing doctor and Quaid's own wife (Sharon Stone) "appear" in his dream to try to talk him down from it. Meanwhile, the plot—dream or not—unfolds. Mars is in the midst of a revolutionary war between the forces of Cohaagen, a mercenary captain of industry (Ronny Cox), and a small band of rebels. There is a mystery involving a gigantic reactor that was apparently built by aliens on Mars a million years ago and has been uncovered during mining operations. And can the brunette trust Quaid—even though he doesn't remember that they were once lovers?

Total Recall moves back and forth between various versions and levels of reality, while at the same time filling its screen with a future world rich with details. The red planet Mars is created in glorious visual splendor, and the inside of the Mars station looks like a cross between Times Square and a submarine. Strange creatures pop up, including mutants, weird three-breasted strippers, and a team of hit men led by Richter (Michael Ironside), Cohaagen's most vicious lieutenant.

The movie is wall-to-wall with violence, much of it augmented by special effects. Even in this future world, people haven't been able to improve on the machine gun as a weapon of murder, even though you'd imagine that firearms of all kinds would be outlawed inside an airtight dome. There are indeed several sequences in which characters are sucked outside when the air seal is broken, but that doesn't stop the movie's villains from demonstrating the one inevitable fact of movie marksmanship: Bad guys never hit their target, and good guys never miss.

Not that it makes the slightest difference, but the science in this movie is laughable throughout. Much is made, for example, of a scene where characters find themselves outside on Mars and immediately begin to expand, their eyes popping and their faces swelling. As Arthur C. Clarke has written in an essay about his *2001*, a man would not explode even in the total vacuum of deep space. (What's even more unlikely is that after the alien reactors are started and quickly provide Mars with an atmosphere, the endangered characters are spared from explosion.)

Such quibbles—and pages could be filled with them—are largely irrelevant to *Total Recall*, which is a marriage between swashbuckling space opera and the ideas of the original Philip Dick story. The movie was directed by Paul Verhoeven, whose credits range from *The Fourth Man* to *RoboCop*, and he is skilled at creating sympathy for characters even within the overwhelming hardware of a story like this. That's where Schwarzenegger is such a help. He could have stalked and glowered through this movie and become a figure of fun, but instead, by allowing himself to seem confused and vulnerable, he provides a sympathetic center for all the high-tech spectacle.

Tough Guys Don't Dance ★ ★ ½
R, 109 m., 1987

Ryan O'Neal (Tim Madden), Isabella Rossellini (Madeleine), Debra Sandlund (Patty Lareine), Wings Hauser (Regency), John Bedford Lloyd (Wardley Meeks III), Lawrence Tierney (Dougy Madden), Frances Fisher (Jessica Pond), Penn Jillette (Big Stoop). Directed by Norman Mailer and produced by Tom Luddy. Screenplay by Mailer.

Norman Mailer's *Tough Guys Don't Dance* has the form of a thriller, and an impressive content of sex and violence, but beneath that is a strange nostalgia that seems to have nothing to do with anything else. The nostalgia is for Provincetown, seen in a cold winter season with the weathered gray houses against a pink and purple sky, the gulls' cries lonely in the twilight. This place is so deeply seen that the people in the movie sometimes seem like ghosts, occupying it for a time.

That is the deepest level. Above it is the practical plot level of severed heads, missing persons, alcoholic blackouts, and dirty business to be done. The film's hero is Tim Madden (Ryan O'Neal), a writer in a slow season, whose past begins to catch up with him. He has spent a good many years drinking too much, smoking too much pot, sleeping with the wrong women, and not sleeping with the right ones. Now he has made some people mad at him, and one day he discovers a severed head in the place where he hides his stash.

I will not reveal the owner of the head for two reasons: First, because it would be unfair to reveal the plot, and second, because although I have read the novel and seen the movie and even visited the location while the filming was under way, I cannot remember whose head it was. There is a press release here from the distributors that I could easily consult for the name, but that would be cheating: It says something about this film that the women, played by such memorable actresses as Isabella Rossellini, the blond newcomer Debra Sandlund, and the intriguing Frances Fisher, play characters not nearly as memorable as themselves.

Something comes back to me now. The Sandlund character, Patty Lareine, is a hillbilly once married to a preacher. The O'Neal character and his then-girlfriend met them through a singles ad and engaged in a weekend of sexual abandon, which led in a complicated way to the more recent events, after Patty Lareine left the preacher to marry the hero's rich friend from prep school, Wardley Meeks III, who now appears on the scene after a crisis of identity.

This is as confusing as *The Big Sleep*. The characters come and go, in the past and the present, and their severed heads appear and disappear, and it is almost as if Mailer himself does not much care to take inventory. The film's center of gravity is in Tim Madden's befuddled and paranoid head, and much depends on a night he cannot remember, a night when he gained a tattoo and perhaps committed a murder.

He drinks, and makes cautious inquiries, and tries to determine from people's actions what they think he did. The local police chief calls him in, for reasons not entirely clear. The inventory of heads in his stash changes from one, to two, to none. He can hardly bear to look to see whose heads they are. He cannot understand who knows the location of his stash, and the identities of women from his past, and even more so, who would want to kill them. Then there is the question of the strange couple from California, who turned up in the local inn shopping for real estate, and drank with him, and who disappeared, their car abandoned, after the night he cannot remember.

In the middle of this morass, the film's best character appears: Dougy Madden (Lawrence Tierney), father of the O'Neal character, a tough old bartender and fighter who always seemed to the son more authentic and courageous than he could ever possibly

be. Now Dougy is dying of cancer, but is still man enough to put the bodies—there are more of them by this point—into a boat and row them out to sea and sink them beyond the reach of gulls and police. The relationship between the father and son is the best thing in the movie.

I wonder if Mailer even cared about the details of his thriller. Few people who see the film only once will be able to accurately describe just what happens in it at a plot level. I suspect he used his thriller, with its lurid sex and blood-soaked bodies, as a lure to convince his backers to let him direct the movie, and that his attention was really on the father-son relationship and on Provincetown itself, which becomes as important as what happens in it. The photography, under the "supervision" of John Bailey, is stunning and evocative of a time and place, and O'Neal occupies it like a man on a last, sad visit.

What is strange is that *Tough Guys Don't Dance* leaves me with such vivid memories of its times and places, its feelings and weathers, and yet leaves me so completely indifferent to its plot. Watching the film, I laughed a good deal; many of the situations play like comedy. Remembering it, it seems elegiac, but in a way that has nothing to do with the deaths in the plot. Something else seems to die and be mourned, something to do with Dougy and the cold flats of the sand at twilight.

Track 29 ★ ★ ★
R, 90 m., 1988

Theresa Russell (Linda Henry), Gary Oldman (Martin), Christopher Lloyd (Henry), Colleen Camp (Arlanda), Sandra Bernhard (Nurse Stein), Seymour Cassel (Dr. Bernard Fairmont). Directed by Nicolas Roeg and produced by Rick McCallum. Screenplay by Dennis Potter.

Somebody asked me if I liked this movie, and I had to answer that I did not, but then I realized once again what an inadequate word "like" is. The reason I didn't like *Track 29* is that the film is unlikable—perhaps deliberately so. But that doesn't make it a bad film, and it probably makes it a more interesting one. Like many of the strange, convoluted works of Nicolas Roeg (*Don't Look Now*, *Bad Timing*, *Eureka*, *Insignificance*), it is bad-tempered, kinky, and misogynistic. But not every film is required to massage us with pleasure. Some are allowed to be abrasive and frustrating, and make us think.

The title of *Track 29* comes from the lyrics of "Chattanooga Choo-Choo," and the film's heroine is a mad woman married to a surgeon (Christopher Lloyd) who collects model trains. He has a great layout down in the basement—lots of track and a terrific collection of rolling stock—and when he's not playing with his trains, he's attending fanatic conventions of model railroaders, or being spanked in his office by a helpful nurse who wears rubber gloves (Sandra Bernhard). Although much is made of this man's obsessions, and he attends a model railroad convention which is a piece of social satire in the spirit of *Dr. Strangelove*, this character is essentially unimportant—he's window dressing. All of his pastimes are used to keep him elsewhere while the film's main event unfolds in the mind of his wife.

Her name is Linda (Theresa Russell), and she lives in a nice house that seems to have been slammed down at random in the middle of an industrial park. She drinks a lot, and has daydreams about sex, and hangs out at the hamburger shop with her best pal. One day a strange young man materializes in the town—literally. We see him appear out of thin air. This man is named Martin, and he is played by Gary Oldman as an emotional monster who amuses himself by pulling her strings. Linda meets Martin down at the hamburger stand, and before long he's back at the house, slyly insinuating himself into her delusions.

There are flashbacks to help explain this person. Linda was raped, it appears, during a visit to a carnival when she was sixteen. As we look at a memory of this event, we can vaguely see that the rapist appears to be Martin—but Martin unchanged, looking the same as he does today. And then there is talk that Linda had a child after that event, but gave the child up for adoption, and now bitterly regrets losing it. Martin now tries to present himself as that child, rediscovered after all these years. Also as lover, father-figure, baby, and tormentor.

Although Martin usually seems real enough in *Track 29* (he occupies a volume of space and casts a shadow, just like Roger Rabbit), we eventually realize that he exists entirely inside Linda's imagination. He is the star player in her madness, and when he grows destructive around the house, there is the possibility that she created him to mask her own desire to destroy her husband's

obsessions. There is much craziness in this movie, many emotional outbursts, a few puzzled moments of disoriented peace, and, digging away at everything, the taunts and teasings of young Martin.

This performance by Gary Oldman is another strong example of acting to put beside his work in *Sid & Nancy* and *Prick Up Your Ears*. He makes Martin into an insinuating, dirty-minded little bugger who accuses Linda of the most shocking things, and then smirks at her reactions. Theresa Russell, who has survived the convoluted terrain of many of Nicolas Roeg's movies (he is her husband), seems at home in this twisted landscape, and the two actors work their characters up into an orgy of mutual laceration. Meanwhile, the other stuff—the model railroading and the rubber gloves—provides the sideshow. The movie was written by Dennis Potter, the author of *Pennies from Heaven* and *The Singing Detective*, and reflects his jaundiced view of the possibility of happiness.

Look at it this way. Most of the time we go to the movies hoping to be amused, and often we are disappointed. *Track 29* does not offer amusement, but it promises confusion, frustration, weirdness, and the bizarre. You probably won't like it. But it won't disappoint you.

Trading Places ★ ★ ★ ½
R, 106 m., 1983

Dan Aykroyd (Louis Winthorpe III), Eddie Murphy (Billy Ray Valentine), Ralph Bellamy (Randolph Duke), Don Ameche (Mortimer Duke), Denholm Elliott (Coleman), Jamie Lee Curtis (Ophelia), Jim Belushi (King Kong). Directed by John Landis and produced by Aaron Russo. Screenplay by Timothy Harris and Herschel Weingrod.

Trading Places resembles *Tootsie* and, for that matter, some of the classic Frank Capra and Preston Sturges comedies: It wants to be funny, but it also wants to tell us something about human nature and there are whole stretches when we forget it's a comedy and get involved in the story. And it's a great idea for a story: A white preppy snot and a black street hustler trade places, and learn new skills they never dreamed existed.

This isn't exactly a new idea for a story (Mark Twain's *The Prince and the Pauper* comes to mind). But like a lot of stories, it depends less on plot than on character, and

the characters in *Trading Places* are wonderful comic inventions. Eddie Murphy plays Billy Ray Valentine, the con man who makes his first appearance as a blind, legless veteran. Dan Aykroyd is Louis Winthorpe III, the stuck-up commodities broker. And, in a masterstroke of casting, those aging veterans Ralph Bellamy and Don Ameche are cast as the Duke brothers, incalculably rich men who compete by making little wagers involving human lives.

One day a particularly tempting wager occurs to them. Aykroyd has had Murphy arrested for stealing his briefcase. It's an unfair charge and Murphy is innocent, but Murphy is black and had the misfortune to bump into Aykroyd in front of a snobby club. To Mortimer Duke (Ameche), a believer that environment counts for more than heredity, this is a golden opportunity to test his theory. He bets his brother that if Aykroyd and Murphy were to change places, the black street kid would soon be just as good at calling the shots in the commodity markets as the white Ivy Leaguer ever was. Because the Dukes are rich, they can make almost anything happen. They strip Aykroyd of everything—his job, his home, his butler, his fiancée, his limousine, his self-respect. They give Murphy what they've taken from Aykroyd. And the rest of the movie follows the fortunes of the two changelings as they painfully adjust to their new lives, and get involved in a commodities scam the Duke brothers are trying to pull off.

This is good comedy. It's especially good because it doesn't stop with sitcom manipulations of its idea, and it doesn't go only for the obvious points about racial prejudice in America. Instead, it develops the quirks and peculiarities of its characters, so that they're funny because of who they are. This takes a whole additional level of writing on top of the plot-manipulation we usually get in popular comedies, and it takes good direction, too.

But what's most visible in the movie is the engaging acting. Murphy and Aykroyd are perfect foils for each other in *Trading Places*, because they're both capable of being so specifically eccentric that we're never just looking at a "black" and a "white" (that would make the comedy unworkable). They both play characters with a lot of native intelligence to go along with their prejudices, peculiarities, and personal styles. It's fun to watch them thinking. The supporting cast has also been given detailed attention, instead of being assigned to stand around as stereotypes. Jamie Lee Curtis plays a hooker with a heart of gold and a lot of T-bills; Ameche and Bellamy have a lot of fun with the Duke brothers; and Denholm Elliott successfully plays butler to both Aykroyd and Murphy, which is a stretch. The movie's invention extends all the way to the climactic scenes, which involve, not the usual manic chase, but a commodities scam, a New Year's Eve party on a train, and a gay gorilla.

Tribute ★ ★ ★
PG, 123 m., 1981

Jack Lemmon (Scottie Templeton), Robby Benson (Jud Templeton), Lee Remick (Maggie Stratton), Colleen Dewhurst (Gladys Petrelli), John Marley (Lou Daniels), Kim Cattrall (Sally Haines). Directed by Bob Clark and produced by Joel B. Michaels and Garth H. Drabinski. Screenplay by Bernard Slade.

I am aware that *Tribute* hauls out some of the oldest Broadway clichés in the book, that it shamelessly exploits its melodramatic elements, and that it is not a movie so much as a filmed stage play. And yet if I were to review it just on those grounds, I would be less than honest. In the abstract, *Tribute* may not be a very good film at all. But in its particulars, and in the way they affected me, it is a touching experience.

It's supposed to be cheating to make an admission like that. I myself believe that it is a film's form, more than its message, that makes it great. And yet *Tribute* is not a visually distinguished film. It has been directed, by Bob Clark, as a straightforward job of work. There are long sequences that are obviously just filmed scenes from Bernard Slade's original stage play. Yet the characters transcend these limitations and become people that we care about.

The film is mostly Jack Lemmon's, and he deserved his seventh Academy Award nomination for his performance as Scottie Templeton, the movie's hero. We all know somebody like Scottie—if we are not, God forbid, a little like Scottie ourselves. He's a wisecracking, popular guy with hundreds of deeply intimate passing acquaintances. He also has a few friends. One of them is his business partner (John Marley) and another is his ex-wife (Lee Remick). They love him and stand by him, but he can't allow himself to reveal how much that means to him. He is also hurt by his relationship with his son

(Robby Benson), who has the usual collection of post-adolescent grudges against his father. All of these relationships suddenly become much more important when Scottie discovers he is dying. The movie begins at about that point in Scottie's life, and examines how the fact of approaching death changes all of Scottie's ways of dealing with the living.

His son comes home to visit for a few weeks. His ex-wife returns to New York for a college reunion and stays to become involved in the crisis. The friend, Marley, acts as counsel and adjudicator. Other characters pass through, including a young woman (Kim Cattrall) who Scottie thinks would be ideal for his son (after all, she'd previously been ideal for Scottie himself). Veteran playgoers can already predict the obligatory scenes growing out of this situation. Scottie will be brave at first, then angry, then depressed, then willing to reach out to his son, and finally reconciled to his fate. Scottie's friends will rally around. His son will learn to love the old man. Everybody will become more human and sensitive, and the possibility of death will provide an occasion for a celebration of life. Et cetera.

What's amazing is that when these predictable situations appear, the movie makes them work. A great deal of the credit for that belongs to Lemmon and Benson. They are both actors with a familiar schtick by now: Benson trembling with emotions, Lemmon fast-talking his way into sincerity. In *Tribute*, though, the movie's characters are so close to the basic strengths of Lemmon and Benson that everything seems to work.

Take Lemmon, for example. Another actor, playing Scottie Templeton, might simply seem to be saying funny lines, alternating with bittersweet insights. Lemmon makes us believe that they're not lines; they're the way this guy talks. The big emotional changes take place underneath the surface wisecracks, making them all the more poignant. Robby Benson sometimes comes across as too vulnerable, almost affected in his sensitivity. Here, he's good, too: Examine the early scene where his father asks what the hell's going on, and Benson begins, "Let me try to explain about that . . ." with touching formality.

Maybe your reaction to *Tribute* will depend on your state of mind. I know people who say they "saw through it," dismissing it as merely a well-made play. I know others, myself included, who were really touched by

it. Perhaps the film works better because it's *willing* to be a bittersweet soap opera. Life itself, after all, is rarely a great directorial achievement, but almost always seems to work on the melodramatic level.

The Trip to Bountiful ★ ★ ★ ½
PG, 106 m., 1985

Geraldine Page (Mrs. Watts), John Heard (Ludie Watts), Carlin Glynn (Jessie Mae), Richard Bradford (Sheriff), Rebecca De Mornay (Thelma). Directed by Peter Masterson and produced by Sterling Van Wagenen and Horton Foote. Screenplay by Foote.

The thing that saves this movie from sentimentality is that the heroine is a little ornery. She's not just a sweet and gentle little old lady. She's a big old lady, with a streak of stubbornness. And just because she's right doesn't mean she's always all that nice. When *The Trip to Bountiful* tells us that she wants to leave her miserable life in the city and pay one last visit to her childhood country home, somehow we know that the movie won't be over when she hears the birds singing in the trees.

The movie stars the redoubtable Geraldine Page in her Academy Award-winning role as Mrs. Watts, a country woman who has come to live in a cramped city apartment with her son and daughter-in-law. The apartment isn't big enough for two women. They're always on each other's nerves.

The wife, Jessie Mae (Carlin Glynn), doesn't like Mrs. Watts singing her hymns around the house. Mrs. Watts's strategy is more subtle: She tries to appear long-suffering, a martyr, and she is much given to throwing herself on the couch and pulling a comforter over her head to muffle her sobs.

Both of these women have a pretty good case against each other, but it's Mrs. Watts we sympathize with. She hates life in the city, she knows it's choking her to death, and she wants to pay one final visit to Bountiful, the little town where she was born. So she goes to the train station, but the milk train doesn't stop in Bountiful anymore. So she goes to the bus station and buys a ticket to the nearest large town. This is in Texas in 1947. Because her son and daughter-in-law have gone to the train station to head her off (she's tried to escape before), she makes her getaway.

The whole middle section of the movie is the best, as she meets another traveler on the bus, a young woman named Thelma (Rebecca De Mornay). They sit next to each other during the long, drowsy trip, and they exchange memories and confidences. Thelma is, in a way, only an excuse to give Mrs. Watts someone to talk to, so that we can eavesdrop. Yet De Mornay makes the character so interesting, so young and open-faced, that the relationship between these two women becomes the heart of the movie. Even the ending itself doesn't quite live up to it.

The Trip to Bountiful has a quiet, understated feel for the small towns of its time. The little rural bus station, with its clerk drowsing under a lonely lamp bulb, looks just right, and so do the midnight streets outside. And when the sheriff arrives, alerted to look for a runaway old lady, it's perfect the way he and the ticket agent size up the situation and let Mrs. Watts have her last look at her childhood home.

Then her family arrives: her son Ludie (John Heard) and his wife Jessie Mae. Ludie really has his work cut out with these two women. Both of them live at a time when many women lived their lives through their men, and there is not enough room inside Ludie's simple, desperate soul for both of these women. Yet there is a moment of poetry as she sits on the porch of the old farmhouse and talks about how she almost expected to see her own parents come walking through the door, just as if all those years had never passed, just as if her own lifetime was a dream, and she was still a young girl again.

The Trip to Bountiful was written by Horton Foote, who based it on his own stage play. This is Foote's second recent slice of life from Texas: *Tender Mercies*, the wonderful movie starring Robert Duvall as an alcoholic country singer, was also written by him. You can see that *Bountiful* was based on a play—it falls fairly obviously into three acts—but the rhythms and dialogue come out of unstudied real life. And Geraldine Page inhabits the central role with authority and vinegar. The movie surprises us: It's not really about conflict between the generations, but about the impossibility of really understanding that you are even a member of an older generation, that decades have gone by.

Geraldine Page, who somehow always manages to have a hint of girlishness in her performances, who always seems to be up to something roguish and not ever quite ready to cave in to age, finds just the right notes in the final scenes to tell her son something he

might never be able to understand: Someday he will be old, too, and he won't be able to believe it either.

Tron ★ ★ ★ ★
PG, 96 m., 1982

Jeff Bridges (Flynn/Clu), Bruce Boxleitner (Alan/Tron), David Warner (Dillinger/Sark), Cindy Morgan (Lora/Yori), Barnard Hughes (Gibbs/Dumont), Dan Shor (Ram). Directed by Steven Lisberger and produced by Donald Kushner. Screenplay by Lisberger.

The interior of a computer is a fine and private place, but none, I fear, do there embrace, except in *Tron*, a dazzling movie from Walt Disney in which computers have been used to make themselves romantic and glamorous. Here's a technological sound-and-light show that is sensational and brainy, stylish, and fun.

The movie addresses itself without apology to the computer generation, embracing the imagery of those arcade video games that parents fear are rotting the minds of their children. If you've never played Pac-Man or Space Invaders or the Tron game itself, you probably are not quite ready to see this movie, which begins with an evil bureaucrat stealing computer programs to make himself look good, and then enters the very mind of a computer itself to engage the villain, the hero, and several highly programmable bystanders in a war of the wills that is governed by the rules of both video games and computer programs.

The villain is a man named Dillinger (David Warner). The hero is a bright kid named Flynn (Jeff Bridges) who created the original programs for five great new video games, including the wonderfully named "Space Paranoia." Dillinger stole Flynn's plans and covered his tracks in the computer. Flynn believes that if he can track down the original program, he can prove Dillinger is a thief. To prevent that, Dillinger uses the very latest computer technology to break Flynn down into a matrix of logical points and insert him *into* the computer, and at that point *Tron* leaves any narrative or visual universe we have ever seen before in a movie and charts its own rather wonderful path.

In an age of amazing special effects, *Tron* is a state-of-the-art movie. It generates not just one imaginary computer universe, but a multitude of them. Using computers as their tools, the Disney filmmakers literally have

been able to imagine any fictional landscape, and then have it, through an animated computer program. And they integrate their human actors and the wholly imaginary worlds of Tron so cleverly that I never, ever, got the sensation that I was watching some actor standing in front of, or in the middle of, special effects. The characters *inhabit* this world. And what a world it is! Video gamesmen race each other at blinding speed, hurtling up and down computer grids while the movie shakes with the overkill of Dolby stereo (justified, for once). The characters sneak around the computer's logic guardian terminals, clamber up the sides of memory displays, talk their way past the guardians of forbidden programs, hitch a ride on a power beam, and succeed in entering the mind of the very Master Control Program itself, disabling it with an electronic Frisbee. This is all a whole lot of fun. *Tron* has been conceived and written with a knowledge of computers that it mercifully assumes the audience shares. That doesn't mean we *do* share it, but that we're bright enough to pick it up, and don't have to sit through long, boring explanations of it.

There is one additional observation I have to make about *Tron*, and I don't really want it to sound like a criticism: This is an almost wholly technological movie. Although it's populated by actors who are engaging (Bridges, Cindy Morgan) or sinister (Warner), it is not really a movie about human nature. Like *Star Wars* or *The Empire Strikes Back*, but much more so, this movie is a machine to dazzle and delight us. It is not a human-interest adventure in any generally accepted way. That's all right, of course. It's brilliant at what it does, and in a technical way maybe it's breaking ground for a generation of movies in which computer-generated universes will be the background for mind-generated stories about emotion-generated personalities. All things are possible.

Troop Beverly Hills ★ ★
PG, 105 m., 1989

Shelley Long (Phyllis Nefler), Craig T. Nelson (Freddy Nefler), Betty Thomas (Velda Plendor), Mary Gross (Annie Herman), Stephanie Beacham (Vicki Sprantz), Audra Lindley (Frances Temple), Edd Byrnes (Ross Coleman), Ami Foster (Claire Sprantz). Directed by Jeff Kanew and produced by Ava Ostern Fries. Screenplay by Pamela Norris and Margaret Grieco Oberman.

Troop Beverly Hills is a comedy about the world's richest scouting troop, eight little girls led by den mother Shelley Long, who dresses in a designer uniform and helps the girls roast marshmallows in front of a fireplace in a bungalow at the Beverly Hills Hotel. The girls arrive at den meetings in chauffeured limousines, consume caviar on their picnics, and sell cookies at Spago and Jane Fonda's Workout.

If this movie had been a satire, it could have been deadly. Unfortunately, the story turns out to have a heart of gold. Instead of being a merciless evisceration of the lifestyles of the rich, it's a little morality play in which Shelley Long transforms herself into a warm and useful person. Nobody within a mile of this project seems to have possessed an ounce of irony.

The film opens with Long on a shopping spree. She arrives home with the Rolls convertible piled high with expensive purchases, which she's bought in order to punish her husband (Craig T. Nelson), who wants a divorce. "You were once smart and promising and funny," he tells her, "and I couldn't wait to see what you have made of that promise. What you have become—is a compulsive shopper." She's hurt. And when her daughter's Wilderness Girls troop needs a leader, she volunteers.

If *Troop Beverly Hills* had been directed by Paul Mazursky, Robert Altman, or any other director with a sardonic glint in his eye, this plot would have been the setup for a satirical field day. And, indeed, there are a few mild jabs in the direction of satire, as when one little girl tells a ghost story in which there are scary noises in the foyer and then in the maid's room.

But the movie doesn't have the imagination to make Shelley Long and her troop members the target of real satire; Long once again plays a character who is good at heart, when in fact she'd be perfect for a movie that savaged her goody-goody image. It is left to "Hill Street Blues" veteran Betty Thomas to play the villain—the bitter, vindictive supervisor of the Wilderness Girls, who is jealous of Long and wants to sabotage her. All of Thomas's scenes are constructed of painfully mean-spirited dialogue; she isn't given the opportunity to create a character we could enjoy seeing put down. There are so many missed opportunities in the film that we could make another movie out of them.

There's a sequence, for example, in which the parents of the little rich girls are introduced; we meet millionaires, boxing champions, a dictator, and an out-of-work actor (Edd Byrnes) whose little girl tries to cheer him up. Nothing is done with these characters. There are also lots of scenes shot on "actual Beverly Hills locations," such as Rodeo Drive and the Spago restaurant, but the movie seems happy to be there, and doesn't have a wicked or satirical thought in its head. There are countless celebrities in cameo roles (Pia Zadora, Robin Leach, Cheech Marin, Annette Funicello, Kareem Abdul-Jabbar, Dr. Joyce Brothers, Frankie Avalon), but apparently we are supposed to laugh merely with the delight of seeing them; no comic point is ever made.

The underlying problem with *Troop Beverly Hills* is that the movie does not think Beverly Hills is funny. It sees nothing wrong with devout materialism. It has no sense of the ridiculous. A movie like Mazursky's *Down and Out in Beverly Hills* has more pointed satire and hard-edged social observation in its opening sixty seconds than *Troop Beverly Hills* ever aspires to. If you want to see a movie in which a spoiled rich woman becomes noble through her experiences as a scoutmaster, here's your chance. I have a sneaking suspicion that Jeff Kanew, who directed the film, and Pamela Norris and Margaret Grieco Oberman, who wrote it, thought they were making a satire. But what they have made is more of a sitting duck for satire.

Trouble in Mind ★ ★ ★ ★
R, 111 m., 1985

Kris Kristofferson (Hawk), Keith Carradine (Coop), Lori Singer (Georgia), Genevieve Bujold (Wanda), Joe Morton (Solo), Divine (Hilly Blue), George Kirby (Detective). Directed by Alan Rudolph and produced by Carolyn Pfeiffer and David Blocker. Screenplay by Rudolph.

Here is a movie that takes place within our memories of the movies. The characters and the mysteries and especially the doomed romances are all generated by old films, by remembered worlds of lurid neon signs and deserted areas down by the docks, of sad cafes where losers linger over a cup of coffee, and lonely rooms where the light bulb is a man's only friend. This is a world for which the saxophone was invented, a world in which the American Motors Javelin was a popular car.

The movie begins with a man being released from prison, of course, and he is dressed in black and has a beard and wears a hat, of course, and is named Hawk, of course, and the first place he goes when he arrives in town is Wanda's Cafe, where Wanda keeps a few rooms upstairs for her old lovers to mend their broken dreams.

The cafe is on a worn-out old brick street down at the wrong end of Rain City. It's the kind of place that doesn't need to advertise, because its customers are drawn there by their fates. One day a young couple turn up in a broken-down camper. The kid is named Coop, and he knows he always gets into trouble when he comes to the city, but he needs to make some money to support his little family. His girlfriend is named Georgia, and she looks way young to have a baby, but there it is, bawling in her arms. She's a blonde with a look in her eyes that makes the Hawk's heart soar.

Coop falls into partnership with the wrong man, a black man named Solo who sits in a back booth at Wanda's Cafe and recites poems about anger and hopelessness. Before long, Coop and Solo are involved in a life of crime, and Hawk is telling Georgia she's living with a loser.

Wanda stands behind the counter and watches all this happen with eyes that have seen a thousand plans go wrong. She hires Georgia as a waitress. That turns Hawk into a regular customer. Wanda knows Hawk is in love with Georgia, because Wanda and Hawk used to be in love with each other, and once you learn to hear that note in a man's voice, you hear it even when he's not singing to you.

Coop and Solo are trying to sell some hot wristwatches. Hilly Blue doesn't like that. Hilly is the boss of the local rackets, and lives in a house that is furnished like the Museum of Modern Art. The best way to describe Hilly Blue is to say that if Sydney Greenstreet could have reproduced by parthenogenesis after radioactive damage to his chromosomes, Hilly would have been the issue.

Trouble in Mind is not a comedy, but it knows that it is funny. It is not a fantasy, and yet strange troops patrol the streets of Rain City, and as many people speak Korean as English. It does not take place in the 1940s, but its characters dress and talk and live as if it did. Could this movie have been made if there had never been any movies starring Richard Widmark, Jack Palance, or Robert Mitchum? Yes, but it wouldn't have had any style.

To really get inside the spirit of *Trouble in Mind*, it would probably help to see *Choose Me* first. Both films are the work of Alan Rudolph, who is creating a visual world as distinctive as Fellini's and as cheerful as Edward Hopper's. He does an interesting thing. He combines his stylistic excesses with a lot of emotional sincerity, so that we believe these characters are really serious about their hopes, and dreams, even if they do seem to inhabit a world of imagination. Look at it this way. In Woody Allen's *The Purple Rose of Cairo*, a character stepped out of a movie and off the screen and into the life of a woman in the audience. If that had happened in *Trouble in Mind*, the woman would have asked the character why he even bothered.

Sometimes the names of movie actors evoke so many associations that further description is not necessary. Let's see. Hawk is played by Kris Kristofferson. Coop is Keith Carradine. Wanda is Genevieve Bujold. Hilly Blue is the transvestite Divine, but he is not in drag this time, allegedly. Mix them together, light them with neon reds and greens, and add a blond child-woman (Lori Singer) and a black gangster (Joe Morton) whose shades are his warmest feature, and perhaps you can begin to understand why they call it Rain City.

True Believer ★ ★ ★

R, 103 m., 1989

James Woods (Eddie Dodd), Robert Downey, Jr. (Roger Baron), Margaret Colin (Kitty Greer), Yuji Okumoto (Shu Kai Kim), Kurtwood Smith (Robert Reynard), Tom Bower (Cecil Skell), Miguel Fernandes (Art Esparza), John Snyder (Chucky Loeder), Misan Kim (Mrs. Kim). Directed by Joseph Ruben and produced by Walter F. Parkes and Lawrence Lasker. Screenplay by Wesley Strick.

Let us now consider the case of James Woods, a name on that brief list of actors whose presence more or less guarantees that a film will be interesting. Woods works a lot. In the 1988-89 season he made *Cop*, about a dangerously out of control homicide detective, *The Boost*, about a salesman who gets swept away in the Los Angeles fast lane, and now *True Believer*, about a radical lawyer from the 1960s who has recently specialized in defending drug dealers.

The characters in these movies are not all the same man, although they all share some of Woods's high-energy restlessness. The high-flier in *The Boost*, for example, is not nearly as intelligent as Eddie Dodd, the fast-talking lawyer in *True Believer*. And yet both characters are hypnotically watchable because Woods talks fast and is always thinking, and his performances assume that the audience can listen and think as quickly as he can.

Does Woods tinker with the scripts he gets, or are they written with him in mind? In *True Believer*, he bursts into his walk-up office in Greenwich Village, says hello to his secretary, asks "What is this thing?" about a weird piece of sculpture standing in a corner, and disappears before he can get the answer. The moment has no purpose in the larger context of the movie, and yet it establishes the character, and it implies that this lawyer leads a larger life, with other concerns, that began before the movie and will continue after it's over.

Woods loves to pepper his roles with throwaways like that. It lends tension and texture even to plots that might seem standard in other hands. And the story in *True Believer* is a fairly routine version of the urban paranoia thriller, in which killers walk the streets because of corruption and compromise in high places. As the movie begins, Eddie Dodd is a burned-out pothead who represents drug dealers because they pay well, and usually in cash. He defends his practice by describing himself as being on the cutting edge of civil liberties law, no matter that all his clients are guilty.

Then a young man walks into his life: Roger Baron (Robert Downey, Jr.), an idealistic lawyer who has read all about Eddie's great cases in the sixties and wants to sit at his feet and learn. Baron soon learns he's the unpaid assistant of a cynic. But then a Korean woman walks into the office with a plea to Eddie: Her son has been in prison for eight years for a murder he did not commit. Eddie's instincts cry out to avoid the case, but the kid acts as his conscience, and before long both men are up to their necks in a dangerous investigation.

The case involves lots of flaws in the original trial: unreliable eyewitnesses, time discrepancies, conflicts of interest. In other hands, this material might seem familiar, but Woods puts a spin on it, an intensity that makes it feel important—to him, and therefore to us. And in the obligatory courtroom showdown that ends the film, Woods is able to find new ways to handle all of those old clichés about the surprise witnesses and the dramatic last-minute revelations.

Watching the film, I was not particularly impressed by Robert Downey, Jr., as the idealistic young law graduate. He seemed sort of indistinct, and I wondered why. Downey gave one of the best performances of recent years in *Less Than Zero*, as a self-destructing drug abuser. What was missing here? A few days after seeing *True Believer*, I saw Downey again in *Chances Are*, where he carries the movie effortlessly and with grace. Seeing that second fine performance, I began to get an angle on Woods: He's the kind of actor who has such high voltage, who's so wound up, that maybe a younger actor tends to defer. We've all had that feeling of being in a conversation with someone else who has seized the advantage and is keeping it. Maybe working with Woods gives you the same feeling; it takes an improvisational veteran like James Belushi, Woods's costar in *Salvador*, to match his pace.

If you run James Woods's best performances through your memory—the ones I've mentioned and *The Onion Field*, *Against All Odds*, and *Once Upon a Time in America*—you see a certain pattern emerging. Woods doesn't like dumb movies, and he doesn't like to play dumb characters. In the season of the Idiot Plot (the plot that doesn't work unless everyone in it is an idiot), Woods makes movies in which the audience has to be on its toes to keep up with him. It's quite an act, and when I see Woods on the screen in the first shot of a movie, I sort of smile to myself because I know that something strange and offbeat and maybe even inspired is about to happen.

True Colors ★ ★

R, 112 m., 1991

John Cusack (Peter Burton), James Spader (Tim Garrity), Imogen Stubbs (Diana Stiles), Mandy Patinkin (John Palmeri), Richard Widmark (Senator Stiles). Directed by Herbert Ross and produced by Ross and Laurence Mark. Screenplay by Kevin Wade.

True Colors has ambition. It wants to be an *All the King's Men* or *The Candidate* for the 1990s, a film to show how unprincipled ambition can lead a young man to the very top of politics, and then cast him down again. The new twist this time is that the young man comes from humble origins, and betrays the rich aristocrat who has been his friend. Usually it's the other way around.

The movie otherwise follows a predictable formula, but occasionally overcomes it through the skill of its acting, which redeems several scenes that seem to have been constructed out of durable Victorian novels. The key actors are John Cusack and James Spader, two of the best of their generation, playing this time against type: Cusack is often a hero, and Spader is usually a villain.

The movie begins with a Meet Cute on the first day of law school, when the two men have a fender-bender that's Cusack's fault. This scene and the one that follows it are so contrived—so entirely at the service of the plot—that it's all the actors can do to soldier through them, but later it gets worse, as it is revealed that Cusack has anglicized his name and fabricated his background in order to move in more elevated circles. These revelations are made in dialogue so tortured it belongs in a soap opera.

The movie was produced by Lawrence Mark and written by Kevin Wade, the same team who made *Working Girl*. Apparently since then they've had a change of heart, or a reversal of class consciousness. This year's model of the Working Class Hero gets to the top, not through pluck and determination, but through greed, naked ambition, and an apparently inbred moral weakness. The movie actually seems to imply that many of the Cusack character's flaws can be traced back to the fact that he did not have Spader's advantages of birth, wealth, and education.

No matter. Cusack is a rotter through and through, a fact that is instantly apparent to everyone in his life except those the screenplay strikes temporarily blind. Early in the story, Spader is engaged to the daughter (Imogen Stubbs) of a powerful senator (Richard Widmark), and invites Cusack to the senator's home for a Christmas party. In no time at all Cusack has angled himself onto the Senator's staff and into the daughter's bed, and the two men go on a ski holiday together, where Cusack confesses his infidelity, providing a lame excuse for the two of them to have a ludicrous fight on skis.

Spader rises above this disappointment, and many others (he volunteers to be the best man at the wedding between Cusack and Stubbs). He even succeeds in blinding himself, for a time, to the unwholesome relationship between Cusack and Mandy Patinkin, as a local real estate developer with mob connections. But then Cusack goes too far,

blackmailing Widmark with inside information, and Spader finally fights back.

It's so unlikely that Cusack would fall for what Spader does, however, that we are left with a film in which it's amazing nobody sees through the Cusack character for the first ninety minutes, and through the Spader character for the next thirty. *True Colors* requires more than the willing suspension of disbelief; it demands a willful abandonment of incredulity.

True Confessions ★ ★ ★
R, 110 m., 1981

Robert De Niro (Des Spellacy), Robert Duvall (Tom Spellacy), Charles Durning (Jack Amsterdam), Ed Flanders (Dan T. Campion), Burgess Meredith (Seamus Fargo). Directed by Ulu Grosbard and produced by Irwin Winkler and Robert Chartoff. Screenplay by John Gregory Dunne and Joan Didion.

True Confessions contains scenes that are just about as good as scenes can be. Then why does the movie leave us disoriented and disappointed, and why does the ending fail dismally? Perhaps because the attentions of the filmmakers were concentrated so fiercely on individual moments that nobody ever stood back to ask what the story was about. It's frustrating to sit through a movie filled with clues and leads and motivations, only to discover at the end that the filmmakers can't be bothered with finishing the story.

The film is about two brothers, one a priest, the other a cop. In a nice insight in casting, Robert De Niro plays the priest and Robert Duvall plays the cop; offhand, we'd expect it to be the other way around, but Duvall is just right, seedy and wall-faced, as the cop, and after a scene or two we begin to accept De Niro as a priest (although he seems too young for a monsignor).

The brothers live in Los Angeles in 1948. It is a Los Angeles more or less familiar from dozens of other movies, especially *Chinatown* and the Robert Mitchum *Farewell, My Lovely*—a small town, really, where the grafters and the power brokers know each other (and in some cases are each other). The movie's plot is complicated on the surface but simple underneath. It centers around a creep named Amsterdam (Charles Durning), a construction tycoon who got his start as a pimp. Both brothers have had dealings with the man. When Duvall was a vice cop, he helped handle the protection for

Amsterdam's whorehouses. Now De Niro, the cardinal's right-hand man, oversees the building projects of the Los Angeles archdiocese. And Amsterdam gets most of the contracts for new schools and hospitals, even though his operation is tainted with scandal.

It's tainted with more than that after the dead body of a young woman is found in a field, cut in two. Duvall's investigation leads to a madam who once took a rap for him, long ago, and to a sleazy L.A. porno filmmaker. Eventually, certain clues point all the way back to Amsterdam. Try to follow this closely: Amsterdam met the girl through a business associate, who met her as a hitchhiker. When he first gave her a lift in his car, De Niro was another passenger. The movie makes a great deal of the fact that the monsignor once shared a car with the "virgin tramp," as the newspapers label the victim. But so what? One of the maddening things about *True Confessions* is that it's shot through with such paranoia that innocent coincidences take on the same weight as evil conspiracies.

The movie's emotional center is in the cop character. He's painted as a man who's not above taking a bribe. But at the same time he has a moral code that's stiffer than his brother's. (The monsignor, for example, isn't above rigging a church raffle so that a city councilman's daughter will win the new car.) What begins to eat away at Duvall is that this Amsterdam, honored as the Catholic Layman of the Year, is a grafter and former pimp. Did he also murder the girl? Duvall frankly doesn't care: The guy is such slime he should be arrested for the crime just on general principles.

True Confessions spends a lot of effort in laying the groundwork for its complex plot, but then it refuses to ever settle things. Instead, there are inane prologues and epilogues showing the two brothers years later, their hair gray, as they sigh philosophically over impending death and shake their heads at the irony and tragedy of it all—whatever it all was.

Since this isn't a thriller, we are invited, I guess, to take it as a cynical meditation on the corruptibility of man. Joan Didion and John Gregory Dunne, who based the screenplay on his novel, see the social institutions in their story as just hiding places for hypocrites and weary, defeated men. But they never follow through on their insights. The movie has, for example, a major subplot involving an old priest (Burgess Meredith) who is being put out to pasture. The priest is evidently a symbol of something, especially since the young De Niro gets the dirty job of firing him. But the movie never comes to terms with this story; it just leaves it sitting there.

At the end of *True Confessions*, we're just sitting there, too. We have been introduced to clearly drawn and well-acted characters, we've entered a period in time that is carefully reconstructed, we've seen moments between men and women that are wonderfully well-observed. But we haven't seen a film that cares to be about anything in particular, to state its case or draw its lines, or be much more than a skilled exercise in style.

True Love ★ ★ ★
R, 104 m., 1989

Annabella Sciorra (Donna), Ron Eldard (Michael), Aida Turturro (Grace), Roger Rignack (Dom), Star Jasper (J.C.), Michael J. Wolfe (Brian), Kelly Cinnante (Yvonne), Rick Shapiro (Kevin). Directed by Nancy Savoca and produced by Richard Guay and Shelly Houis. Screenplay by Savoca and Guay.

True Love plunges into the middle of the preparations for a marriage, and shows us a man and woman being swept toward matrimony by a tide of relatives, friends, traditions, and plans—even though they probably shouldn't get married at all. It's a comedy about uneasiness; nearly everyone in the film knows, in one way or another, that the marriage is a bad idea, but once events are set into motion, nothing can stop them. Even as the bride is on her way to the church, her father is assuring her it's not too late to back out—but to hell with your life, how can you disappoint your friends?

The movie is a fiction film that looks and sometimes feels like a documentary. The director, Nancy Savoca, who cowrote the screenplay with Richard Guay, uses a mobile camera to give us the impression we're in the middle of one of those *cinéma vérité* documentaries where life goes on regardless of the filmmakers. We're there at the family conference, and at the heartfelt confessions over kitchen tables, and in the saloons where the groom-to-be hangs out with his buddies. Although the movie has been carefully constructed, it creates the feeling of improvisation and spontaneity—a lot of scenes unfold like a movie by John Cassavetes, where the events seem to be happening while we watch

them, and the camera seems to be present by a lucky chance.

The film stars Annabella Sciorra as Donna, bride-to-be at the center of a large Italian-American family in New York, and Ron Eldard as Michael, her fiancé. They've been engaged for a long time, their friends see them as a couple, and on every side there are pressures urging them toward the altar. There seems to be something about matrimony that brings out a profoundly conservative side in all of the friends and family members of a would-be couple; marriage is held up as an inevitable goal, and there is so much institutional pressure in favor of it that a couple can hold out only so long.

There is a sense in *True Love* that the marriage preparations lead to the marriage almost through the sheer force of momentum. A hall has to be hired. A menu has to be selected (with mashed potatoes dyed to match the color of the bridesmaids' dresses). Family and friends swarm about the two stars of the event until they hardly have time to communicate with each other.

But they do talk. And gradually, as we listen, we begin to realize that *True Love* is deeper than it first seemed. The movie begins as a comedy of wedding preparations and lifestyles, but as it goes along and we get to know Donna and Michael better, we begin to suspect that these people should never get married. That Michael is an immature alcoholic, and that in some ways Donna knows it, but lacks the determination to call off the ceremony.

The key moment in the movie comes at the banquet after the wedding, and it takes place in the women's room, where Donna has fled, weeping, after Michael has informed her that he plans to go out drinking with his buddies instead of spending the wedding night with her. The chilling thing about his decision is that he doesn't seem to fully realize just how bizarre it is. He justifies it as "just one last night out with the guys," not realizing that he should already have had that night—that this, of all nights, should be his first with his wife.

Michael is a little dense in these matters, anyway. As played by Ron Eldard, he's one of those good-looking, superficially nice young men who has gotten a free ride from friends and family despite the handicap of never having had an interesting thought in his life. All of his opinions are secondhand, most of his remarks are clichés. Marriage is something he sees in terms of something he "ought" to

do, rather than as a personal commitment. Even the movie's love scenes seem learned out of movies.

Donna, as played by Sciorra in the movie's central and best performance, is a wiser woman, and one who probably doesn't want to get married at all. But the institution sweeps her along. The idea of marriage and the urging of her friends are so overwhelming to her that she chooses to disregard the clear evidence of Michael's immaturity. Because all of the other wedding arrangements have been made, she is able to overlook the most important one: the choice of a suitable husband.

At the end of *True Love*, I was left with the clear impression that this marriage wouldn't last long. But it is the genius of the movie that it almost sweeps the audience along with everyone else in cheering the couple toward the altar. This is a subtle movie that invites us to read between the lines. It suggests that a lot of couples may be married to marriage rather than to each other.

True Stories ★ ★ ★ ½
PG-13, 88 m., 1986

John Goodman (Louis Fyne), Swoosie Kurtz (Laziest Woman), Spalding Gray (Earl Culver), Alix Elias (Cute Woman), Annie McEnroe (Kay Culver), Pops Staples (Mr. Tucker), Jo Harvey Allen (Lying Woman), David Byrne (Narrator). Directed by David Byrne and produced by Gary Kurfirst. Screenplay by Stephen Tobolowsky, Beth Henley, and Byrne.

There are more than fifty sets of twins in David Byrne's *True Stories*, I learned by studying the press notes, and perhaps we should pause here for a moment to meditate upon that fact. A hundred twins are not going to make or break a movie, and the average audience is not going to notice more than a fraction of them.

But, consider the state of mind of the person who decided the film should *have* fifty sets of twins.

That person undoubtedly is Byrne. What was he thinking of? My hunch is that he was thinking about the movie's voodoo: the magical things that go on beneath the surface of the work of art, lending it an aura that seeps up into the visible parts. Any movie made by actors and technicians who know that the director has hired fifty sets of twins is going to be a movie made by people who think the director is a very strange man. And that will affect their work. Even the ordinary moments in *True Stories* seem a little odd, as if the actors are trying to humor the weirdo they're working for.

Byrne says the movie was influenced by true stories he read in the papers, and he has published a book of some of those stories he has collected. They range from the mundane (the happily married couple who have not spoken to one another for fifteen years) to the cosmic (the Universal Product Code on grocery items is the advance sign of the coming of the Antichrist).

In *True Stories*, Byrne visits a mythical Texas town named Virgil in which everyone is a little strange and some people are downright unique. Try to imagine Virgil as being populated by everyone who went stir-crazy in Lake Wobegon.

Byrne narrates his film and is the host for the tour of Virgil. He is a thin, quiet, withdrawn figure with a voice so flat that you have to listen to the pauses to figure out when the sentences end. He drives a new red convertible and wears Saturday night cowboy clothes. He takes us to Virgil just as it's about to celebrate "150 Years of Specialness."

There is no real plot here, just wonderment. We meet a woman too lazy to get out of bed, and a man who advertises for a wife but says she must be prepared to accept his teddy-bear figure. We meet the lying woman, who confides shocking inside scandal on many of the most important events of the last twenty-five years. She knows because she was there. We meet civic leaders and marching bands, we visit an old man who casts spells and foretells the future, and we meet a preacher who in one unbroken sentence leaps from the death of Elvis Presley to the fact that we always run out of Kleenex and toilet paper at the same time. The studio went nuts trying to figure out how to sell this film. They came down hard on the angle that it had a lot of music by the Talking Heads, the avant-garde rock group that Byrne founded and leads. It does have a lot of music in it, and that will appeal to the viewers who have made *Stop Making Sense*, the Talking Heads concert film, a hit.

But this is not a musical. It's a bold attempt to paint a bizarre American landscape. This movie does what some painters try to do: It recasts ordinary images into strange new shapes. There is hardly a moment in *True Stories* that doesn't seem everyday to anyone who has grown up in Middle America, and not a moment that doesn't seem haunted with secrets, evasions, loneliness, depravity, or hidden joy—sometimes all at once. This is almost like a science-fiction movie: Everyone on screen looks so normal and behaves so oddly, they could be pod people.

The photography is an important element of the film. The movie was shot by Ed Lachman, who has become a brand name for people interested in offbeat directors. He was the guy who followed Werner Herzog to the slopes of a volcano that was about to erupt to film *La Soufriere*, and he has worked for Wim Wenders, Shirley Clarke, Bernardo Bertolucci, Jean-Luc Godard, and Tina Turner.

This time, he finds a new look: His landscapes and city scenes are like those old postcards in which everything seems slightly skewed. His buildings look like parodies of buildings. His people are seen against indoor landscapes of the objects they own—so many objects they seem about to be buried.

And then Byrne orchestrates all of this in the most deadpan way. If you walk in looking for payoffs, you're going to be disappointed. This movie doesn't start here and go there, and the closest thing it has to a story is the quest of the shy bachelor (John Goodman) for a wife. Will he marry the woman who never leaves her bed? If he does, where will the ceremony take place? It's the kind of courtship where, when you know the woman well enough, you ask her if she'd like to get *out* of bed. You see how one thing leads to another?

Truly, Madly, Deeply ★ ★ ★
NO MPAA RATING, 89 m., 1991

Juliet Stevenson (Nina), Alan Rickman (Jamie), Bill Paterson (Sandy), Michael Maloney (Mark), Jenny Howe (Burge). Directed by Anthony Minghella and produced by Robert Cooper. Screenplay by Minghella.

For some time now I have been complaining about movies in which people return from the afterlife. My complaint is always the same: If the afterlife is as miraculous as we expect it to be, why would anyone want to return? I have my answer. They come back to watch movies on video. This is a relief. I would not want to contemplate going through eternity without occasionally being able to put *Five Easy Pieces* on the VCR.

My information about the afterlife comes from Anthony Minghella's *Truly, Madly, Deeply*, a truly odd film, maddening, occasionally deeply moving. It opens as the story of a woman consumed by grief. Her man has died and she misses him, and his absence is like an open wound. Then he returns. He steps back into her life from beyond the grave and folds her in his arms, and the passion with which she greets him is joyous to behold. He is back, he explains, because he did not die "properly." He got caught in some kind of reality warp, I guess, between life and death, and the upshot of it is, he's back. Oh, he's dead. But he's here.

The woman is played by Juliet Stevenson, as one of those intelligent but vulnerable women like Nathalie Baye plays in French films. The man is Alan Rickman, who you will look at on the screen and know you have seen somewhere, and rattle your memory all during the movie without making the connection that he was the villain in *Die Hard*.

He was a cello player in life, and now he is one in death, and he and Stevenson hang around the house all day, making ga-ga eyes. For various reasons she has to keep his return secret from her friends, who cannot understand why she has bounced back from profound depression into a state of giddy happiness.

All of these passages of the movie are convincing, in a strange way: This is sort of a *Ghost* for grown-ups. Then the movie takes a turn toward the really odd, as various new pals of the man return from the next world to join him. This eventually leads Juliet Stevenson to deliver one of the most memorable lines of dialogue of this or any year: "I can't believe I have a bunch of dead people watching videos in my living room."

I do not want to reveal the turns the plot takes then. I will mention, however, the character played by Michael Maloney, who ventures into Stevenson's life and falls in love with her and makes her choose between this world and the next. His character is truly goofy, and charming, and in his own indirect way he leads the movie toward some truths that are, the more you think about them, really pretty profound.

Truth or Dare ★ ★ ★ ½
R, 118 m., 1991

A documentary featuring Madonna on her 1990 Blond Ambition tour. Directed by Alek Keshishian and produced by Sigurjon Sighvatsson, Steve Golin, and Madonna.

Lawsuits have been filed over moments considerably less shocking than the ones Madonna cheerfully allows to be included in *Truth or Dare*, the new documentary about her 1990 Blond Ambition tour of Japan, the United States, and Europe. This is a backstage documentary with a vengeance, an authorized invasion of privacy in which the camera follows Madonna even during intimate moments with her family and childish sex games with her backup dancers.

Although the movie seems happiest when it is retailing potential scandal, its heart is not in sex but in business, and the central value in the film is the work ethic. Madonna schedules herself for a punishing international tour of one-night stands and then delivers with a clockwork determination, explaining to a family member in Detroit that she can't go out to party because she has to conserve her strength.

Night after night the exhausting show goes on, taking on aspects of a crusade for the cast members. Ironically—given Madonna's onstage use of sacrilege as a prop—every show is preceded by a prayer session, everyone holding hands while Madonna asks God's help and recites a daily list of problems. And when her dancers have personal problems, they come to her as a counselor and mother figure.

She seems to like it that way, and halfway through the film I was even wondering if she deliberately chose insecure dancers with dependent personalities because she enjoyed playing mother to them. Madonna has kept her act fresh by adopting a long series of public star personas, yet backstage, people don't relate to her as a star, but as the boss. Her charisma comes not through glitter but through power, and there is never any doubt exactly who is in charge. We get the feeling that if show biz ever loses its appeal for her, she could be successful in business or even politics: She's a hard-headed organizer, a taskmaster, disciplined and clear-headed.

The movie follows the Blond Ambition tour from its soggy beginnings in Japan's rainy season, through a series of one-night stands across the world. There are the Los Angeles concerts with all of the celebrities backstage (Kevin Costner tells her the concert was "neat," and she sticks a finger down her throat). Detroit, her hometown, where she assures her father that she can indeed get him tickets for the show. Toronto, where the police threaten to arrest her for public masturbation ("What do they mean, masturba-

tion?" "When you grab your crotch"). Then she tours Italy and Spain, inviting guys she has crushes on to parties, only to discover they're married or gay.

At one point in the film, talking about how lonely it is at the top, she's asked if she ever knew true love, and she answers sadly, "Sean. Sean." But she never says another word about her former husband Sean Penn. In the opening scenes she is glimpsed briefly with boyfriend Warren Beatty, but then he disappears, unmentioned, after making what sounded to me like fairly sensible observations (he complains that, for Madonna, if it doesn't happen on camera it hardly happens at all).

The organizing subject of the whole film is work. We learn a lot about how hard Madonna works, about her methods for working with her dancers and her backstage support team, about how brutally hard it is to do a world concert tour. Unlike most rock documentaries, the real heart of this film is backstage, and the onstage musical segments, while effectively produced, seem obligatory—they're not the reason she wanted to make this film. Why is work so important to her? Maybe there's a hint in the many scenes where she takes a motherly interest in the personal lives of her dancers, and even joins them between the sheets for innocent, bored, adolescent sex games. Madonna, who has had such success portraying a series of sexual roles and personalities, seems asexual on a personal level. A voyeur rather than a participant. Control and power are more interesting to her than intimacy. When she manipulates the minds of a stadium full of fans, that's exciting. It's not the same working with one person at a time.

Tucker: The Man and His Dream
★ ★ ¹/₂
PG, 110 m., 1988

Jeff Bridges (Preston Tucker), Joan Allen (Vera), Martin Landau (Abe), Frederic Forrest (Eddie), Mako (Jimmy), Elias Koteas (Alex), Christian Slater (Junior), Nina Siemaszko (Marilyn Lee), Anders Johnson (Johnny), Corky Nemec (Noble). Directed by Francis Ford Coppola and produced by Fred Roos and Fred Fuchs. Screenplay by Arnold Schulman and David Seidler.

The car itself is the star of this movie, the low-slung bullet-nose that looks like a discreet cross-breeding of the postwar Stud-

ebaker and the Batmobile. And the most amazing fact about the Tucker automobile is that Preston Tucker did actually succeed in building fifty of them, just as he said he would, before he was shot down by the Big Three from Detroit and their hired guns in Washington.

Would automotive history have been different if Tucker had been spared to put his dream into mass production? Probably not; the Tucker would probably have thrived for a few late-1940s years and then joined the long, slow parade to oblivion of the Hudson, the Kaiser, the Nash, the Studebaker, the Packard, the Willys, and all the other makes that your dad always warned that you couldn't get parts for.

And yet Francis Ford Coppola's film is not so much about the car as about the man, and it is with the man that he fails to deliver. *Tucker: The Man and His Dream* paints us a Preston Tucker who is a genial, incurably optimistic dreamer, a man who gathers a small band around him and inspires them to build a great car, and yet all the time lacks an ounce of common sense or any notion of the real odds against him. And since the movie never really deals with that—never really comes to grips with Tucker's character—it begins as a saga but ends in whimsy.

Tucker is played in the film by Jeff Bridges, with a big, broad smile and a knack for finding hope even in the ash heaps of his dreams. He lives in the center of a large, cheerful family, with a wife (Joan Allen) and a brood of kids who seem cloned directly from those late-1940s radio sitcoms where somebody was always banging in through the screen door and announcing that he smelled fresh apple pie.

Tucker made his fortune during World War II by inventing and manufacturing the Tucker turret for Air Corps bombers. Now he thinks the American public is ready for a truly modern automobile—one with great design and good mileage and safety features like pop-out windshields and seat belts. His master touch is a third headlight in the middle of the front grille, which will turn in the same direction as the steering wheel. But Detroit doesn't much like the idea of seat belts—they might give the public the idea that cars aren't safe—and they don't like the idea of Tucker, either.

Tucker applies for the use of a war-surplus manufacturing plant on the Southwest Side of Chicago, and gets it. He and his team throw together a prototype automobile out of spare parts scavenged in a junkyard. He's a master at personal publicity, floats a stock issue to raise money, sets up his assembly line, and starts racing against a deadline for introducing his first model.

But it's about here that the movie really loses its grip. We are never given any real insights into what makes Tucker tick; we see him from the outside, like the public, and he's all bluff and charm and sideshow pep talks. The problems of the assembly line are also painted without any details. Some guys wrestle some sheet metal in place, some other guys get covered with grease, Tucker and his assistants look at some plans, and presto, there are gleaming new Tuckers on display. There is no sense here that the movie gives any serious attention to the process.

The worst scene in the movie is the most crucial, the scene where Tucker is scheduled to unveil his new beauty to the assembled American automobile press. We get a passage that's too long and too confused, a comedy of errors as the workmen try to push the big car up a ramp while a fire starts backstage, and meanwhile, Tucker stands in front of the curtain bamboozling the press and calling for tunes from the big brass band. A little of this would have made the point; Coppola pushes it to distraction.

It is difficult, by the way, to avoid the notion that, in Preston Tucker, Francis Coppola sees a version of himself. Coppola says he has been fascinated by the Tucker legend ever since he first saw a Tucker car in the late forties, and he has owned his own rare collector's model during the ten years he's been trying to get this dream film off the ground. Many details are the same between the automaker and the filmmaker: the loyal wife, the big family, the close-knit group of friends who pitch in at all hours, the grandiose schemes, the true genius, the peculiar knack of confusing the public with unnecessary explanations, and in particular the ability to hold a launching—or a premiere—in the worst possible way. Coppola is known for holding "secret" previews that the press somehow gate-crashes, leading to premature and hostile reviews. And he is known for fiascos like his ill-advised decision to publicly announce that he was having "problems" with the ending of *Apocalypse Now,* allowing self-doubt to cast an unnecessary shadow on his masterpiece.

The parallels between Coppola and Tucker are so obvious that it's surprising

Coppola didn't observe one more: He has been as protective of Tucker's private life as he rightly is of his own. *Tucker* does not probe the inner recesses of Preston Tucker, is not curious about what really makes him tick, does not find any weaknesses, and blames his problems not on his own knack for self-destruction, but on the workings of a conspiracy. And it makes the press into a convenient and hostile villain. This won't do. If we're offered a movie named *Tucker: The Man and His Dream,* we leave feeling cheated if we only get the dream.

Tune in Tomorrow . . . ★ ★ ¹/₂
PG-13, 108 m., 1990

Barbara Hershey (Aunt Julia), Keanu Reeves (Martin Loader), Peter Falk (Pedro Carmichael), Bill McCutcheon (Puddler), Patricia Clarkson (Aunt Olga), Richard Portnow (Uncle Luke). Directed by Jon Amiel and produced by John Fiedler and Mark Tarlov. Screenplay by William Boyd.

The trouble begins with the Albanians. Not with real Albanians, but with the fictional Albanians who are libeled at every possible moment in *Tune in Tomorrow* . . . . They provide a running joke on a radio soap opera being written in the early 1950s for a New Orleans station. The author of the soap is Pedro Carmichael (Peter Falk), a man who has apparently had some bad experiences with Albanians in the past, and who allows the dialogue of his radio characters to take sudden and unprovoked detours into the most outrageous attacks on Albanians in general, and Albanian milkmaids in particular.

Tune in Tomorrow . . . is based on *Aunt Julia and the Scriptwriter,* a novel by Mario Vargas Llosa, a onetime Peruvian presidential candidate, whose original hero was obsessed by resentments against Bolivians. I am not completely sure, but I imagine that outrageous attacks on Bolivians would be funnier in Peru than attacks on Albanians are to American audiences. Maybe *Tune in Tomorrow* . . . should have made them Canadians. We are all familiar with the unspeakable practices of Canadian milkmaids.

The rest of the novel translates fairly easily from Peru to New Orleans, since it is the sort of comic fantasy that could essentially be set anywhere there is a radio station. The film stars Falk as an itinerant radio writer who invents outrageous plots and then peoples

them with the folks he observes around him—stealing not only their personalities, but also their dialogue.

In the film, Keanu Reeves is Falk's student, a bright and willing young man who wants to learn the radio game, and Barbara Hershey is Reeves's aunt, who has moved to New Orleans to add a new chapter to her unhappy experiences with men. In no time at all, Reeves is in love with Hershey, and their dialogue, which has to be heard to be believed, is soon heard all over town, because Falk eavesdrops and steals their lines word-for-word.

The movie has been directed by Jon Amiel (who made *The Singing Detective* and the wonderful *Queen of Hearts,* the movie about an Italian family in London). He likes to push the edges of the envelope of plausibility, to fool around with what's real and what isn't. In *Queen of Hearts,* supernatural events took place side-by-side with natural ones, and in this movie the story cuts back and forth between Falk's soap opera and the characters who are in it.

That creates a story-within-a-story. Elizabeth McGovern plays a robust ingenue whose marriage is the obsessive concern of a large and peculiar family, played by John Larroquette, Buck Henry, Peter Gallagher, and others. Falk's script delights in leading them up to such unspeakable topics as incest and then letting them speak about them, and the film's method is to cut back and forth between this other story and the equally lurid adventures of the "real" heroes.

The joke is the same as in Woody Allen's *Radio Days,* where Wallace Shawn (of *My Dinner with André*) played the Masked Avenger, a radio hero who sounded ferocious on the air but looked, in person, exactly like Shawn. Here the actors are workaday radio personalities, shouldering up to the mike with their scripts, but to the radio listeners of New Orleans they are gorgeous romantic figures.

Some of the movie's best laughs come when the jaws of the listeners drop open with shock and amazement at some of Falk's more outrageous fantasies. Nobody seems to know quite how to react to his blatantly unprincipled attacks on the Albanians, however, and indeed the movie's uncertain comic tone is a problem all through the story. Sometimes we laugh easily, sometimes uncertainly, and sometimes we just look at the screen and wonder why anyone thought *that* was funny. The Albanians are part of the problem, although perhaps not when the film plays in Turkey.

The Turning Point ★ ★ ★ ½
PG, 119 m., 1977

Anne Bancroft (Emma), Shirley MacLaine (Deedee), Mikhail Baryshnikov (Yuri), Leslie Browne (Emilia), Tom Skerritt (Wayne), Martha Scott (Adelaide). Directed by Herbert Ross and produced by Ross and Arthur Laurents. Screenplay by Laurents.

Perfect movies are very rare, and very easy to write about. Imperfect movies are harder to write about, and the hardest reviews of all are of movies like *The Turning Point* that are touched with greatness and yet keep losing their way. The good things in it are *so* good that you cherish them, and there's the temptation to forgive the lapses.

So let's start with the good. The movie's the story of an old friendship between a great ballerina (Anne Bancroft) and a ballerina (Shirley MacLaine) who might have been great but will never really know for sure. Twenty years have passed since they were both young dancers, and now Miss Bancroft performs in Miss MacLaine's hometown and their friendship reasserts itself. Miss MacLaine's daughter is a promising young ballerina—she already has professional experience—and Miss Bancroft arranges for her to join her company.

As Miss MacLaine accompanies her daughter to New York, three themes assert themselves: Miss MacLaine's jealousy, smoldering for twenty years; Miss Bancroft's fear of approaching age and yet her desire to see the young girl succeed; the self-doubt both women have about the choices they made of careers or marriage. These are adult themes, and *The Turning Point* handles them thoughtfully.

It also gives us a love story or two. Miss MacLaine's daughter falls in love with the ballet company's superstar (Mikhail Baryshnikov, typecast). And during the long summer of the movie's action, Miss MacLaine has to deal not only with her own feelings but with her daughter's. We're dealing here with soap opera stuff, but never in a soap opera way. *The Turning Point* confronts its big emotional moments directly and simply, and maybe that's why they affect us so much.

The straightforward dramatic sections of the movie, then, are very well written and acted; Miss Bancroft and Miss MacLaine are particularly good, and then there are sensitive supporting performances by Tom Skerritt, as Miss MacLaine's husband, and by Leslie Browne, the talented young dancer who plays their daughter. When people say they loved *The Turning Point*, they're probably thinking about moments like the one when Miss Bancroft pushes the reluctant and sick young girl back onto the stage, or when the two older women go aside at a party and finally say all the things they've bottled up, or when Miss MacLaine is so touchingly mystified by how she should react to the news of her daughter's first affair.

Those moments are good enough to make the movie. And, of course, there's also a lot of dancing in the film; Baryshnikov is a wonder, and the film's director, Herbert Ross, is a choreographer who knows how to see dance through his camera. But it's during the ballet sequences that the film breaks down, because Ross can photograph the dances so much better than he can work them into his film.

This has been a juicy, realistic, achingly human movie for most of its length, dealing with age and jealousy, love and the cruel demands of great art. So we feel real disappointment when Ross breaks the mood and the flow. He does that most unforgivingly in a sequence where Miss Browne has a triumph onstage, and Ross cuts away to close-ups of Miss MacLaine and Miss Bancroft watching her—while prophetic dialogue from earlier in the film is repeated in flashback on the sound track. Unforgivable. And the movie's climactic dance scenes—the evening at ballet, punctuated by the hoary old gimmick of a hand turning the pages of a program—are fun for ballet fans, yes, but they land with a thud in the middle of the movie's emotional drama.

To sort out my feelings: *The Turning Point*'s story is handled with real care and touches us. The movie's dance sequences are virtuoso in themselves. But the pieces don't match, and Ross doesn't help by encumbering the dance material with ungainly story devices from the 1930s. You watch this film about a woman wondering if she could have been a great dancer, and you find yourself wondering if it could have been a great film.

Turtle Diary ★ ★ ★ ½
PG-13, 97 m., 1985

Ben Kingsley (William Snow), Glenda Jackson (Neaera Duncan), Michael Gambon (George Fairbairn), Eleanor Bron (Miss Neap), Harriet Walter (Harriet). Directed by John Irvin and produced by Peter Snell. Screenplay by Harold Pinter.

I saw this scene once in the London Zoo. It happened in the gloom of an insect house. Two men stood stooped over, side by side, their hands clasped behind their backs, peering through a glass into the chamber where a rare spider lived. Their faces were bathed in the low red light coming from the enclosure.

As they watched the spider, I watched them, until at last the spider did whatever it was they had been waiting for it to do. Then they stood up, looked briefly at each other, exchanged a matter-of-fact nod, and went their separate ways. London has always seemed to me to be a city of hobbyists and fanatics, experts in obscure specialities. But this moment stands out in particular, as a spider and two voyeurs shared one of the spider's most intimate moments.

Turtle Diary, the quiet, sly, and immensely amusing film from a screenplay by Harold Pinter, begins with two more such devotees. They are obsessed by giant sea turtles. They peek through the glass as the turtles lazily wheel around and around their cramped space in a tank at the London Zoo. They meet again, by chance, in a bookshop way over on the other side of the city, where the man (Ben Kingsley) is a clerk, and the woman (Glenda Jackson) has come to buy a book on turtles. They gradually become aware that they are seeing each other frequently at the turtle house, and then they discover that each has approached the turtles' keeper with the same question: What would it take to steal those giant turtles and set them free in the sea?

Turtle Diary is about a scheme by Kingsley, Jackson, and the zoo curator to do just that. But it is about a great many other things, as well. It is about the strange boarding house where Kingsley lives in company with a jolly landlady, a moody spinster, and a Turk who never cleans up the kitchen after himself. It is about the flat where Jackson lives, alone with her pet water beetle and about the man across the landing who knows a great deal about snails. And it is about the young woman who works with Kingsley in the bookshop, and lusts after him.

In a movie filled with wonderful, small sequences, I think my favorite begins when Kingsley suddenly turns to the young woman and says, out of the clear sky, "That's a pretty dress." In the next scene they are in a pub, in the next scene a restaurant. And if you want to observe the mastery of screen acting, watch the way Kingsley keeps a poker face while discussing his sex life with the woman, and then watch the way he allows himself to smile.

Ben Kingsley's smile, so warm and mysterious, is the sun that shines all through *Turtle Diary*. This is not a predictable movie, and it does not have a predictable structure (it does not even begin to end with the climax of the turtle caper). It is about peculiar people who somewhere find the impulses to do things that make them very happy.

If this movie had been made in America, I fear, it would have turned into a burlesque, with highway cops chasing turtles down the Santa Monica Freeway. *Turtle Diary* could only have been written, directed, and acted in the country where I saw those two strangers wait with such infinite patience for the spider to do its thing.

28 Up ★ ★ ★ ★
NO MPAA RATING, 136 m., 1985

Featuring Tony Walker, Bruce Balden, Suzanne Dewey, Nicholas Hitchon, Peter Davies, Paul Kligerman, John Brisby, Andrew Brackfield, Charles Furneaux, Neil Hughes, Jackie Bassett, Lynn Johnson, Susan Sullivan, and Simon Basterfield. Directed by Michael Apted and produced by Margaret Bottomley and Apted.

The child is father of the man.
—William Wordsworth

Somewhere at home are photographs taken when I was a child. A solemn, round-faced little boy gazes out at the camera, and as I look at him I know in my mind that he is me and I am him, but the idea has no reality. I cannot understand the connection, and as I think more deeply about the mystery of the passage of time, I feel a sense of awe.

Watching Michael Apted's documentary *28 Up*, I had that feeling again and again, the awe that time does pass, and that the same individual does pass through it, grows from a child to an adult, becoming someone new over the passage of years, but still containing some of the same atoms and molecules and fears and gifts that were stored in the child.

This film began in 1964 as a documentary for British television. The assignment for Michael Apted was to interview several seven-year-olds from different British social classes, races, backgrounds, and parts of the country, simply talking with them about what they found important or interesting about their lives. Seven years later, when the subjects were fourteen, Apted tracked them down and interviewed them again. He repeated the process when they were twenty-one, and again when they were twenty-eight, and this film moves back and forth within that material, looking at the same people when they were children, teen-agers, young adults, and now warily approaching their thirties.

We have always known that the motion picture is a time machine. John Wayne is dead, but the angle of his smile and the squint in his eye will be as familiar to our children as it is to us. Orson Welles is dead, but a hundred years from now the moment will still live when the cat rubs against his shoe in *The Third Man*, and then the light from the window catches his sardonic grin. What is remarkable about *28 Up* is not, however, that the same individuals have been captured at four different moments in their lives. We quickly grow accustomed to that. What is awesome is that we can see so clearly how the seven-year-old became the adolescent, how the teen-ager became the young man or woman, how the adult still contains the seeds of the child.

One sequence follows the lives of three upper-class boys who come from the right families and go to all the right schools. One of the boys is a snot, right from the beginning, and by the time he is twenty-one he is a bit of a reactionary prig. We are not surprised when he declines to be interviewed at twenty-eight; we could see it coming. We are curious, though, about whether he will check back in at thirty-five, perhaps having outlived some of his self-importance. Another little boy is a winsome loner at seven. At fourteen, he is a dreamy idealist, at twenty-one he is defiant but discontented, and at twenty-eight—in the most unforgettable passage in the film—he is an outcast, a drifter who moves around Great Britain from place to place, sometimes living in a shabby house trailer, still a little puzzled by how he seems to have missed the boat, to never have connected with his society.

There is another little boy who dreams of growing up to be a jockey, and who is a stable

boy at fourteen, and does get to be a jockey, briefly, and now drives a cab and finds in his job some of the same personal independence and freedom of movement that he once thought jockeys had. There is a determined young Cockney who is found, years later, happily married and living in Australia and doing well in the building trades. There is a young woman who at twenty-one was clearly an emotional mess, a vague, defiant, bitter, and unhappy person. At twenty-eight, married and with a family, she is a happy and self-assured young woman; the transformation is almost unbelievable.

As the film follows its subjects through the first halves of their lives, our thoughts are divided. We are fascinated by the personal progressions we see on the screen. We are distracted by wonderment about the mystery of the human personality. If we can see so clearly how these children become these adults—was it just as obvious in our own cases? Do we, even now, contain within us our own personal destinies for the next seven years? Is change possible? Is the scenario already written?

I was intending to write that certain groups would be particularly interested in this movie. Teachers, for example, would hardly be able to see *28 Up* without looking at their students in a different, more curious light. Poets and playwrights would learn from this film. So would psychiatrists. But then I realized that *28 Up* is not a film by or for experts. It is superb journalism, showing us these people passing through stages of their lives in such a way that we are challenged to look at our own lives. It is as thought-provoking as any documentary I've ever seen.

I look forward to the next edition of this film, when its subjects are thirty-five. I have hope for some, fear for others. It is almost scary to realize this film has given me a fair chance of predicting what lies ahead for these strangers. I almost understand the motives of those who chose to drop out of the experiment.

Twice in a Lifetime ★ ★ ★ ½
R, 117 m., 1985

Gene Hackman (Harry), Ann-Margret (Audrey), Ellen Burstyn (Kate), Amy Madigan (Sonny), Ally Sheedy (Helen), Stephen Lang (Keith), Darrell Larson (Jerry), Brian Dennehy (Nick). Directed and produced by Bud Yorkin. Screenplay by Colin Welland.

Everyday American life is so rare in the movies these days that some of the pleasures of *Twice in a Lifetime* are very simple ones, like seeing a family around a dinner table, or watching a kid sister prepare for her wedding day. The rhythms of life and the normal patterns of speech seemed almost unfamiliar, after all the high-tech thrillers and teen-age idiot films I've seen. This film was so sensible, perceptive, and grown-up that I almost looked for the subtitles.

The film stars Gene Hackman as a working man whose marriage is happy in all the official ways, and dead in the personal ways. His wife (Ellen Burstyn) has centered her life entirely around her home and her family to such an extent that on Hackman's birthday she doesn't even want to go out with him. She tells him to go down to the corner tavern and enjoy himself. And she means it. There is a lot missing in this marriage.

At the saloon, Hackman meets the new barmaid (Ann-Margret) and begins a wary process of falling in love with her. He eventually decides to leave his wife and move in with this woman, and this decision causes upheaval throughout his family. His wife is devastated. But the angriest family member is his oldest daughter (Amy Madigan), who bitterly resents the way he's dumping them—especially when her kid sister (Ally Sheedy) is about to get married.

Twice in a Lifetime stacks its cards very carefully. One of the strengths of the movie is that it allows us to see so many points of view. Hackman has not simply dumped his wife for a sex bomb: the Ann-Margret character has been around the block a few times and operates from a center of quiet realism. It is possibly true that the life and growth has gone out of his marriage. Perhaps he deserves another chance—although the movie is too hasty to assume that his wife does, too, if only she knew it.

The most complicated and interesting character in the movie is Amy Madigan's angry daughter. She's mad about more than the broken marriage. Her husband is out of work, and in her late twenties she feels somewhat trapped by her marriage and children. A lot of her hopes have gone into her kid sister. She wants her to go to college and make a future for herself, but Ally Sheedy is rushing into her own early marriage, blinded by young love.

Madigan acts as the contact point between the various parts of the story: loving her sister, exasperated by her, standing by her

mom, resentfully excluding her father. It's quite an assignment, and as she tries to balance all those demands we see one of the most complex movie characters in a long time (have you noticed how many recent movies assign their characters one mood and think that's enough?).

The Gene Hackman and Ann-Margret characters are complex, too. They are attracted not by lust but by the promise of a new life. They both feel that when they get up in the morning there's nothing to look forward to all day. This movie knows one of the differences between young love and middle-aged love: Kids often are motivated by romance, but people in their forties and fifties sometimes are inspired by the most romantic notion of all—idealism, and the notion that they have found a mate for their minds.

The least-defined character in *Twice in a Lifetime* is the wife, played by Burstyn. Her husband has made his decision and left her to make hers. At first she is simply lost. Eventually she starts picking up the pieces, and she gets a job in the local beauty parlor. She even gets a new hairdo (in one of the movies' most durable clichés). By the end of the film she has started to realize that she, too, was trapped by the marriage. But there is the slightest feeling that her realization owes more to the convenience of the screenplay than to her own growth.

The movie does not have a conventional happy ending. Life will go on, and people will strive, and new routines will replace old ones. The movie has no villains and few heroes. But it has given us several remarkable scenes, especially two confrontations between Madigan and Hackman, one in a bar, the other at a wedding rehearsal, in which the movie shows how much children expect from their parents, and how little the parents often have to give. Growing up is learning that parents are fallible. The people who find that hardest to learn are parents.

Twilight Zone—the Movie

Prologue and Segment 1. Written and directed by John Landis. Starring Dan Aykroyd, Albert Brooks, Vic Morrow, and Doug McGrath. ★ ★
Segment 2. Directed by Steven Spielberg. Written by George Johnson. Starring Scatman Crothers. ★ ¹/₂
Segment 3. Directed by Joe Dante. Written by Richard Matheson. Starring Kathleen Quinlan, Jeremy Light, and Kevin McCarthy. ★ ★ ★ ¹/₂
Segment 4. Directed by George Miller. Written by Richard Matheson. Starring John Lithgow and Abbe Lane. ★ ★ ★ ¹/₂
PG, 101 m., 1983

Produced by Steven Spielberg and inspired by the television series created by Rod Serling.

Every year at Oscar time, somebody comes up with the bright idea of making the Academy Awards into a fair fight. Instead of making the voters choose among five widely different performances, they say, they ought to have five actors playing the same scene. That way you'd really be able to see who was best. It's an impractical idea, but *Twilight Zone—the Movie* does almost the same thing. It takes four stories that are typical of the basic approach of the great "Twilight Zone" TV series, and has four different directors try their hand at recapturing Rod Serling's "wondrous land whose boundaries are that of imagination." And the surprising thing is, the two superstar directors are thoroughly routed by two less-known directors whose previous credits have been horror and action pictures.

The superstars are John *(Blues Brothers)* Landis and Steven *(E.T.)* Spielberg. The relative newcomers are Joe Dante, whose *The Howling* was not my favorite werewolf movie, and George Miller, whose *The Road Warrior* is some kind of a manic classic. Spielberg, who produced the whole project, perhaps sensed that he and Landis had the weakest results, since he assembled the stories in an ascending order of excitement. *Twilight Zone* starts slow, almost grinds to a halt, and then has a fast comeback.

Landis directed the first episode, which stars Vic Morrow in the story of a bigot who is transported back in time to Nazi Germany and Vietnam and forced to swallow his own racist medicine. This segment is predictable, once we know the premise, and Landis does nothing to surprise us. Because we know that

Morrow was killed in a helicopter accident during the filming of the segment, an additional pall hangs over the whole story.

Spielberg's segment is next. It stars Scatman Crothers as a mysterious old man who turns up at an old folks' home one day and literally gives the residents what they think they want; to be young again. The easily anticipated lesson is that one lifetime is enough. Spielberg's visual style in this segment is so convoluted and shadowy that the action is hard to follow; the master of clearcut, sharp-edged visuals is trying something that doesn't work.

But then comes Joe Dante's weird, offbeat segment about a traveler (Kathleen Quinlan) who strays off the beaten path and accepts an offer of hospitality from a fresh-faced young kid who looks healthy and harmless. Once Quinlan is inside the roadside farmhouse where the kid lives, however, she's in another dimension—a bizarre world telepathically projected by the boy's imagination. The kid loves video games and TV cartoons, and he's trapped a whole group of adults in his private fantasies. The art direction in this segment is especially good at giving the house interior a wonderland quality.

George Miller's fourth segment stars John Lithgow in a remake of a famous "Twilight Zone" TV story in which a nervous air traveler sees (or imagines that he sees) a little green man hacking away at the engine of his airplane. But there *couldn't* be a little green man out there—could there? The beauty of *Twilight Zone—the Movie* is the same as the secret of the TV series: It takes ordinary people in ordinary situations and then zaps them with "next stop—the Twilight Zone!"

Twins ★ ★ ★
PG, 107 m., 1988

Arnold Schwarzenegger (Julius Benedict), Danny DeVito (Vincent Benedict), Kelly Preston (Marnie Mason), Chloe Webb (Linda Mason), Bonnie Bartlett (Mary Ann Benedict), Hugh O'Brian (Granger). Directed and produced by Ivan Reitman. Screenplay by William Davies, William Osborne, Timothy Harris, and Herschel Weingrod.

When he is shown into the orphanage where his twin brother spent his childhood, Julius Benedict is able to point out the very bed where his brother must have slept. "That's amazing," a nun says. "How did you know?" Julius smiles. "Hit vas seem-pull," he says.

"Hit is zah bed by zah fire eggstinguisher. The zame one I would haf chozun. In zah event of fire, he could grab zah eggstinguisher and zave all of zah roar-phans."

The accent belongs to Arnold Schwarzenegger, who has long had a gift of comedy, but has seldom had a comedy to exercise it in. In *Twins*, teamed up in several different ways with Danny DeVito, he gets the movie off to a funny start. The movie begins with Schwarzenegger as the unpaid assistant of a scientist who lives on an island somewhere between Bora Bora and Australia. Discovering that he has a twin brother he has never known about, Arnold commandeers an inflatable dinghy and starts rowing for the nearest airport.

Meanwhile, back in the States, DeVito is in trouble. He's a professional con man who also does amateur cons in his spare time. His sideline is stealing luxury cars at the airport and selling them to chop shops, and about the time Arnold is arriving in America, DeVito is thrown into jail with hundreds of dollars of unpaid parking tickets. Arnold tracks him down in a jail cell, and tells him of their secret past. The diminutive DeVito, of course, does not believe this muscular Teuton is his twin. Few would. But if Schwarzenegger has bail money, DeVito is prepared to play along with him.

Good comedies often have central ideals that are transparently simple. *Twins* is an example. When the movie opened, there were giant billboards all over the United States showing DeVito's picture with the block letters "Schwarzenegger" underneath, and vice versa. It's a brilliant sell, and a clever idea—but the reason it works so well in the movie is that both Schwarzenegger and DeVito have genuinely tender sides to their natures. You know the movie is a running gag, but somehow there's a sweetness in their relationship that makes the plot seem less manipulated.

The explanation for their twinship is that both men were the result of a eugenics experiment in which the sperm from six different fathers was combined into a kind of natal milkshake and administered to their mother. The men represented brains, brawn, and other attributes, and the woman was as nearly perfect as possible. But the experiment misfired and produced, not one perfect baby, but twins.

"Your brother got all of the good stuff," DeVito is told years afterward, when he finally confronts the mastermind behind the bizarre experiment. "You got the leftovers." That's why Schwarzenegger is an awesome physical specimen who speaks six languages and is a brilliant scientist, and why DeVito is a small-time hustler who manages to steal the wrong cars. For example, a late-model Cadillac that just happens to have a trunk containing industrial contraband worth millions.

When I saw the plot turning toward the contraband, I began to grow apprehensive. And when the movie introduced a murderous industrial spy, my heart sank. I thought I could foresee yet another Hollywood movie in which the third act was jettisoned in favor of a shoot-out and a chase. In the event, however, director Ivan Reitman soft-pedals the subplot involving the stolen goods, and actually manages to supply the movie with a real ending involving thought, dialogue, and other elements that recently have tended to disappear in the last twenty-five minutes of Hollywood entertainments.

The movie supplies both men with love interests—DeVito with a long-suffering girlfriend (Chloe Webb, from *Sid & Nancy*), and Schwarzenegger with Kelly Preston, who plays a hilarious love scene with him on the floor of a motel room. Why the floor? Because that's where Arnold prefers to sleep. The movie claims that the Schwarzenegger character is a virgin, and there is a certain justification for that; the filmmakers claim that this is actually Arnold's first love scene, in fourteen years of stardom.

Schwarzenegger's gift for comedy was apparent in his very first film, the documentary *Pumping Iron* (1974), and in his first feature, Bob Rafelson's *Stay Hungry*, two years later. But it has had precious little use since then in a series of high-voltage action pictures, even though Schwarzenegger always finds a way to introduce comic dialogue or some sort of self-deprecating humor even in the most violent films. This time, given comedy from beginning to end, he handles it with ease. DeVito's performance is equally assured, but less surprisingly, since we already knew he could cover this ground. *Twins* is not a great comedy—it's not up there with Reitman's *Ghostbusters*, and DeVito is not as funny as he was in *Ruthless People* and *Wise Guys*—but it is an engaging entertainment with some big laughs and a sort of warm goofiness.

Two English Girls ★ ★ ★ ★
R, 108 m., 1972

Jean-Pierre Leaud (Claude), Kika Markham (Anne Brown), Stacey Tendeter (Muriel Brown), Sylvia Marriott (Mrs. Brown), Marie Mansart (Madame Roc), Phillipe Leotard (Diurka), Mark Peterson (Mr. Flint), Irene Tunc (Ruta). Directed by François Truffaut and produced by Claude Miler. Screenplay by Truffaut and Jean Gruault.

It's wonderful how offhand François Truffaut's best films feel. There doesn't seem to be any great effort being made; he doesn't push for his effects, but lets them flower naturally from the simplicities of his stories. His film, *Two English Girls*, is very much like that. Because he doesn't strain for an emotional tone, he can cover a larger range than the one-note movies. Here he is discreet, even while filming the most explicit scenes he's ever done; he handles sadness gently; he is charming and funny even while he tells us a story that is finally tragic.

The story is from the second novel by Henri-Pierre Roche, who began writing at the age of seventy-four and whose first novel, *Jules and Jim*, provided the inspiration for nearly everyone's favorite Truffaut film. The two novels (and the two films) are variations on the same theme: What a terrible complex emotional experience it is to have to share love.

We would say that both stories involve romantic triangles, but Roche seems to see them more simply (and poignantly) as the shared dilemmas of people caught helplessly in their situations. Nobody sets out deliberately to involve himself in a triangular relationship—not when the love involved is real. It hurts too much.

Truffaut introduces us to Claude, a young French art critic, and then introduces him to Anne Brown, an English girl visiting in Paris. They form a friendship, and the girl invites him to come and visit her mother and sister in Wales. During the visit, he falls in love (or thinks he does) with the sister, Muriel. They want to marry, but they both have poor health, and it is decided to put off the marriage for a year. Claude returns to Paris, where Anne follows after a while, and then they fall into a sexual relationship that passes for a time as love. The virgin Muriel, meanwhile, remains passionately in love with Claude and nearly has an emotional breakdown when she learns that he no longer plans to marry her.

The story, as it unfolds, is involved but never untrue. Love itself is an elusive prize that passes among them; it is their doom that whenever two of them are together, it is the third who possesses love. The film relates love and loss so closely that we almost forgive Claude for his infidelities and stubbornness. Perversely, he wants to be apart from Muriel (and later Anne) so that he can desire all the more.

If *Two English Girls* resembles *Jules and Jim* in theme, it has an unmistakable stylistic relationship to Truffaut's little-seen masterpiece of 1970, *The Wild Child*. Both films used diaries, journals, and a spoken narration in order to separate us from the immediate experience of the stories. Truffaut wants us to feel that we're being told a fable, a sad winter's tale, that is all the more touching because these events happened long ago and love is trapped irretrievably in the past.

His visual strategy for creating this feeling is another favorite device from *The Wild Child*: the iris shot. (Put simply, this is the use of a slowly contracting circle to bring a shot to an end, instead of a fade or a cut). The iris isolates one element in the picture, somehow making it feel alone and vulnerable—and past. The film is photographed in a low-keyed color, and the sound recording is also a little muted; this isn't a film for emotional highs, we sense, because it's far and away too late for these lost love opportunities to be regained.

The one scene that violates this tone is as necessary as it is effective; when Muriel finally makes love with Claude we feel the terrible force of her passion, pent up for so many years, and then the camera pans to the blood-stained sheet and goes out of focus. Put in so many words, this probably sounds crude and obvious; in fact, this is almost the only red in the film, and is Truffaut's perfect visual metaphor for the fact that these three people have created a lot of their own unhappiness by avoiding or deflecting the consequences of their emotional feelings.

Jules and Jim was a young man's film (Truffaut was twenty-eight when he made it). *Two English Girls* is the film of a man some ten or twelve years down the road; it is still playful and winsome, but it realizes more fully the consequences of an opportunity lost. The final scene shows Claude, fifteen years later, wandering in the garden where he used to walk with Anne and Muriel. There are English children playing there, and he thinks to ask one of them, "Are you Muriel Brown's daughter?" But he doesn't, because . . . well, because.

The Two Jakes ★ ★ ★ ½
R, 128 m., 1990
(See also *Chinatown;* related Film Clip, p. 720.)

Jack Nicholson (Jake Gittes), Harvey Keitel (Jake Berman), Meg Tilly (Kitty Berman), Madeleine Stowe (Lillian Bodine), Eli Wallach (Cotton Weingerger), Ruben Blades (Mickey Nice), Frederic Forrest (Chuck Newty), David Keith (Loach, Jr.), Richard Farnsworth (Earl Rawley), Tracey Walter (Tyrone Otley). Directed by Jack Nicholson and produced by Robert Evans and Harold Schneider. Screenplay by Robert Towne.

Here at long last is Jack Nicholson's *The Two Jakes*, seven years in the trade papers, center of prolonged teeth-gnashing at Paramount Pictures, and it turns out to be such a focused and concentrated film that every scene falls into place like clockwork; there's no feeling that it was a problem picture. It's not a thriller and it's not a whodunit, although it contains thriller elements and at the end we do find out whodunit. It's an exquisite short story about a mood, and a time, and a couple of guys who are blindsided by love.

The movie takes place in postwar Los Angeles—the 1940s of the baby boom and housing subdivisions—instead of the 1930s city where *Chinatown* was set. It's not such a romantic city anymore. And private eyes like J.J. Gittes (Jack Nicholson) are a little more worn by time and care. The Gittes of *Chinatown* was the spiritual brother of Philip Marlowe. But now it is after the war, and Gittes has moved out of the two-room suite into a building of his own. He heads a staff of investigators. He belongs to a country club and has a fiancée and has put on some weight. One of these days he's going to stop calling himself an investigator altogether, and become a security consultant.

But he still handles some of the old kinds of cases. The cases where the outraged husband bursts into the motel room and finds his wife locked in the arms of a priapic adulterer, and then the investigator leaps in with a camera and takes photos that will look bad in divorce court. He knows, Gittes tells us in the film's opening narration, that he shouldn't get involved in messy situations like that anymore. He's outgrown them.

They're beneath him. But sometimes he still takes the jobs.

That's how he meets the other Jake—Jake Berman (Harvey Keitel), a property developer who thinks his wife (Meg Tilly) is fooling around with his partner. So Gittes tutors Berman on how to act when he bursts in through the door, and what to say, and then they stake out a motel where the evil act is confidently expected to take place. But Berman doesn't follow the script. A gun appears from somewhere, and the partner is shot, and the partner's wife (Madeleine Stowe) thinks that maybe it wasn't a case of adultery at all. Maybe it was cold-blooded murder, and Berman intended to kill his partner so that he and his wife could collect the partner's share of the property development. That might make Gittes accessory to murder.

So far, what we have here is the kind of plot that any private eye movie might have been proud of. But *The Two Jakes* uses the plot only as an occasion for the deeper and more brooding things it has to say. Everyone connected with this movie seems to have gone through the private eye genre and come out on the other side. The screenplay is by Robert Towne, who at one stage in the project's troubled history was going to direct it. He has not simply assembled some characters from his *Chinatown*, added some new ones, and thrown them into a plot. This movie is written with meticulous care, to show how good and evil are never as simple as they seem, and to demonstrate that even the motives of a villain may emerge from a goodness of heart.

Jack Nicholson has directed the film, and Vilmos Zsigmond has photographed it, in the same spirit. This isn't a film where we ricochet from one startling revelation to another. Instead, the progress of the story is into the deeper recesses of the motives of the characters. We learn that Gittes, fiancée and all, is still deeply hurt by the murder of the Faye Dunaway character in *Chinatown*; he will never be over her. We learn that the property being developed by Berman has been visited before by Gittes, in that long-ago time. We learn that love, pure love, is a motive sufficient to justify horrifying actions. And we learn that when the past has been important enough to us, it will never quite leave us alone.

The movie is very dark, filled with shadows and secrets and half-heard voices, and scratchy revelations on a clandestine tape recording. Out in the valley where the development is being built, the sunshine is harsh and casts black shadows, and the land is cruel—the characters are shaken by earthquakes which reveal that the land rests uneasily on a dangerous pool of natural gas.

The performances are dark and gloomy, too, especially Nicholson's. He tones down his characteristic ebullience and makes Gittes older and wiser and more easily disillusioned. And he never even talks about the loss which hangs heavily on his heart; we have to infer it from the way his friends and employees tiptoe around it. Right from his first meeting with the Keitel character, when he notices they are wearing the same two-tone shoes, he feels a curious kinship with him, and that leads to a key final confrontation which I will not reveal. And he feels something, too, for the Meg Tilly character, who has been deeply hurt in her past and is afraid to express herself. She is like a bird with a broken wing.

The point of *The Two Jakes* is that love and loss are more important than the mechanical distribution of guilt and justice. When Nicholson and Keitel, as the two Jakes, have their final exchange of revelations, it is such a good scene because the normal considerations of a crime movie are placed on hold. The movie is really about the values which people have, and about the things that mean more to them than life and freedom. It's a deep movie, and a thoughtful one, and when it's over you can't easily put it out of your mind.

2001: A Space Odyssey ★ ★ ★ ★
G, 141 m., 1968

Keir Dullea (Bowman), Gary Lockwood (Poole), William Sylvester (Dr. Heywood Floyd), Daniel Richter (Moonwatcher), Douglas Rain (HAL 9000 [Voice]), Leonard Rossiter (Smyslov), Margaret Tyzack (Elena), Robert Beatty (Halvorsen), Sean Sullivan (Michaels), Frank Miller (Mission Controller). Directed and produced by Stanley Kubrick. Screenplay by Kubrick and Arthur C. Clarke.

It was e.e. cummings, the poet, who said he'd rather learn from one bird how to sing than teach ten thousand stars how not to dance. I imagine cummings would not have enjoyed Stanley Kubrick's *2001: A Space Odyssey*, in which stars dance but birds do not sing. The fascinating thing about this film is that it fails on the human level but succeeds magnificently on a cosmic scale.

Kubrick's universe, and the spaceships he constructed to explore it, are simply out of scale with human concerns. The ships are perfect, impersonal machines which venture from one planet to another, and if men are tucked away somewhere inside them, then they get there, too. But the achievement belongs to the machine. And Kubrick's actors seem to sense this; they are lifelike but without emotion, like figures in a wax museum. Yet the machines are necessary because man himself is so helpless in the face of the universe.

Kubrick begins his film with a sequence in which one tribe of apes discovers how splendid it is to be able to hit the members of another tribe over the head. Thus do man's ancestors become tool-using animals. At the same time, a strange monolith appears on Earth. Until this moment in the film, we have seen only natural shapes: earth and sky and arms and legs. The shock of the monolith's straight edges and square corners among the weathered rocks is one of the most effective moments in the film. Here, you see, is perfection. The apes circle it warily, reaching out to touch, then jerking away. In a million years, man will reach for the stars with the same tentative motion.

Who put the monolith there? Kubrick never answers, for which I suppose we must be thankful. The action advances to the year 2001, when explorers on the moon find another of the monoliths. This one beams signals toward Jupiter. And man, confident of his machines, brashly follows the trail.

Only at this point does a plot develop. The ship is manned by two pilots, Keir Dullea and Gary Lockwood. Three scientists are put on board in suspended animation to conserve supplies. The pilots grow suspicious of the computer, "HAL," which runs the ship. But they behave so strangely—talking in monotones like characters from "Dragnet"—that we're hardly interested.

There is hardly any character development in the plot, then, and as a result little suspense. What remains fascinating is the fanatic care with which Kubrick has built his machines and achieved his special effects. There is not a single moment, in this long film, when the audience can see through the props. The stars look like stars and outer space is bold and bleak.

Some of Kubrick's effects have been criticized as tedious. Perhaps they are, but I can understand his motives. If his space vehicles move with agonizing precision, wouldn't we have laughed if they'd zipped around like props on *Captain Video*? This is how it would really be, you find yourself believing.

In any event, all the machines and computers are forgotten in the astonishing last half-hour of this film, and man somehow comes back into his own. Another monolith is found beyond Jupiter, pointing to the stars. It apparently draws the spaceship into a universe where time and space are twisted.

What Kubrick is saying, in the final sequence, apparently, is that man will eventually outgrow his machines, or be drawn beyond them by some cosmic awareness. He will then become a child again, but a child of an infinitely more advanced, more ancient race, just as apes once became, to their own dismay, the infant stage of man.

And the monoliths? Just road markers, I suppose, each one pointing to a destination so awesome that the traveler cannot imagine it without being transfigured. Or as cummings wrote on another occasion, "Listen—there's a hell of a good universe next door; let's go."

NOTE: This movie is best viewed in the letterboxed version, which preserves the widescreen compositions.

2010 ★ ★ ★
PG, 157 m., 1984

Roy Scheider (Heywood Floyd), John Lithgow (Curnow), Helen Mirren (Kirbuk), Bob Balaban (Chandra), Keir Dullea (Bowman), Douglas Rain (HAL 9000). Directed and produced by Peter Hyams. Screenplay by Hyams. Based on a novel by Arthur C. Clarke.

All those years ago, when *2001: A Space Odyssey* was first released, I began my review with a few lines from a poem by e.e. cummings:

I'd rather learn from one bird how to sing than teach ten thousand stars how not to dance.

That was my response to the people who said they couldn't understand *2001*, that it made no sense and that it was one long exercise in self-indulgence by Stanley Kubrick, who had sent a man to the stars, only to abandon him inside some sort of extraterrestrial hotel room. I felt that the poetry of *2001* was precisely in its mystery, and that to explain everything was to ruin everything—like the little boy who cut open his drum to see what made it bang.

2001 came out in the late 1960s, that legendary time when yuppies were still hippies, and they went to see the movie a dozen times and slipped up to the front of the theater and lay flat on their backs on the floor, so that the sound-and-light trip in the second half of the movie could wash over them and they could stagger to the exits and whisper "far out" to one another in quiet ecstasy. Now comes *2010*, a continuation of the Kubrick film, directed by Peter Hyams, whose background is in more pragmatic projects such as *Outland*, the Sean Connery space station thriller. The story is by Arthur C. Clarke (who, truth to tell, I always have suspected was a little bewildered by what Kubrick did to his original ideas). *2010* is very much a 1980s movie. It doesn't match the poetry and the mystery of the original film, but it does continue the story, and it offers sound, pragmatic explanations for many of the strange and visionary things in *2001* that had us arguing endlessly through the nights of 1968.

This is, in short, a movie that tries to teach ten thousand stars how not to dance. There were times when I almost wanted to cover my ears. Did I really want to know (a) why HAL 9000 disobeyed Dave's orders? or (b) the real reason for the Discovery's original mission? or (c) what the monoliths were trying to tell us? Not exactly. And yet we live in a most practical time, and they say every decade gets the movies it deserves. What we get in *2010* is not an artistic triumph, but it is a triumph of hardware, of special effects, of slick, exciting filmmaking. This is a movie that owes more to George Lucas than to Stanley Kubrick, more to *Star Wars* than to *Also Sprach Zarathustra*. It has an ending that is infuriating, not only in its simplicity, but in its inadequacy to fulfill the sense of anticipation, the sense of wonder we felt at the end of *2001*.

And yet the truth must be told: This is a good movie. Once we've drawn our lines, once we've made it absolutely clear that *2001* continues to stand absolutely alone as one of the greatest movies ever made, once we have freed *2010* of the comparisons with Kubrick's masterpiece, what we are left with is a good-looking, sharp-edged, entertaining, exciting space opera—a superior film of the *Star Trek* genre.

Because *2010* depends so much upon its story, it would be unfair to describe more

than the essentials: A joint Soviet-American expedition sets out for the moons of Jupiter to investigate the fate of the Discovery, its crew, and its on-board computer HAL 9000. There is tension on board between the American leader (Roy Scheider) and the Soviet captain (Helen Mirren), and it's made worse because back on Earth, the superpowers are on the brink of nuclear war over Central America. If Kubrick sometimes seemed to be making a bloodless movie with faceless characters, Hyams pays a great deal of attention to story and personality. But only one of the best moments in his movie grows out of character (the touching scene where a Soviet and an American hold onto each other for dear life during a terrifying crisis). The other great moments are special-effects achievements: a space walk threatened by vertigo, the awesome presence of Jupiter, and a spectacular flight through the planet's upper atmosphere.

It is possible that *no* conclusion to *2010* could be altogether satisfying, especially to anyone who still remembers the puzzling, awesome simplicity of the Star Child turning to regard us at the end of *2001*. This sequel has its work cut out for it. And the screenplay compounds the difficulty by repeatedly informing us that "something wonderful" is about to happen. After we've been told several times about that wonderful prospect, we're ready for something *really* wonderful, and we don't get it. We get a disappointingly mundane conclusion worthy of a 1950s sci-fi movie, not a sequel to *2001*. I, for one, was disappointed that the monoliths would deign to communicate with men at all—let alone that they would use English, or send their messages via a video screen, like the latest generation of cable news.

So. You have to make some distinctions in your mind. In one category, *2001: A Space Odyssey* remains inviolate, one of the handful of true film masterpieces. In a more temporal sphere, *2010* qualifies as superior entertainment, a movie more at home with technique than poetry, with character than with mystery, a movie that explains too much and leaves too little to our sense of wonderment, but a good movie all the same. If I nevertheless sound less than ecstatic, maybe it's because the grave eyes of the *2001* Star Child still haunt me, with their promise that perhaps someday man would learn to teach ten thousand stars how to sing.

U

Uforia ★ ★ ★ ★
PG, 100 m., 1985

Cindy Williams (Arlene), Harry Dean Stanton (Brother Bud), Fred Ward (Sheldon), Alan Beckwith (Brother Roy), Beverly Hope Atkinson (Naomi), Harry Carey, Jr. (George Martin), Diane Diefendorf (Delores), Robert Gray (Emile). Directed by John Binder and produced by Gordon Wolf. Screenplay by Binder.

I've always wanted to know one of those women you read about in the *National Enquirer,* those intense Midwestern housewives who are sucked up into flying saucers and flown to Mars, where they have their measurements taken, and are told they will be contacted again real soon. It's not that I want to hear about the trip to Mars. I'd just enjoy having her around the house, all filled with a sense of mystery and purpose.

Uforia is a great and goofy comedy about a woman just like that. Her name is Arlene, and she works as a supermarket checker in a backwater town in the Southwest. She reads all the UFO publications and believes every word, and knows in her heart that They are coming. But the movie is not really about whether They come or not. It's about how waiting for Them can give you something wonderful to think about, to pass the time of those dreary, dusty days.

The movie has two other characters who get involved in Arlene's dream. One of them is named Sheldon, and he is the kind of good ol' boy who drives through the desert in a big ol' convertible, with the car on cruise control and his feet propped up on the dashboard and a can of beer in his hand.

The other one is named Brother Bud, a phony faith-healer who conducts revival services in a tent outside of town. When Sheldon sees Arlene at the supermarket, he falls in love, and before long he has settled down, sort of, in her mobile home. Sheldon and Brother Bud are brothers, and Sheldon hires on with Bud to portray a guy whose sick leg gets healed every night. Meanwhile, Arlene's faith grows that the UFO will arrive at any moment.

This is one of those movies where you walk in not expecting much, and then something great happens, and you laugh, and you start paying more attention, and then you realize that a lot of great things are happening, that this is one of those rare movies that really has it. *Uforia* is not just another witless Hollywood laugh machine, but a movie with intelligence and a sly, sardonic style of humor. You don't have to shut down half of your brain in order to endure it.

The casting is just perfect. Cindy Williams is the cornerstone, as Arlene, a woman whose hopes and dreams are too big for the small corner of the Earth she has been given to occupy. She doesn't know what to do when she meets Sheldon (played by Fred Ward, from *Remo Williams* and *The Right Stuff*). She likes this guy and she hasn't had a man in a long time. But, then again, she always gets her heart "broke" when she falls for a guy, and so she prays for guidance and starts on the tequila.

Ward gives a wicked performance as the good ol' boy Sheldon. He's Smokey and the Bandit with brains. He has a couple of double takes in this movie that are worth the price of a ticket. And he's not a male chauvinist pig, although everything in his background probably points him in that direction. He doesn't see Arlene as a conquest, but as just the lady he's been looking for. He gets a little tired of the flying-saucer stuff, however.

Harry Dean Stanton plays Brother Bud. This is exactly the kind of role Stanton has been complaining that he's tired of: the weary, alcoholic con man with the jolly cynicism. Yet they keep casting him in these roles, and in *Uforia* you can see why: Nobody does a better job. He has an assistant in the movie, a junior evangelist named Brother Roy (Alan Beckwith), whose face shines with conviction and who is always bathed in wonderment and glory. The quiet, offhand way Stanton deals with him is one of the movie's many treasures.

Uforia didn't have a lot of money and a big ad campaign behind it. It doesn't have big stars, unless you are the kind of movie lover for whom the names Cindy Williams, Harry Dean Stanton, and Fred Ward guarantee a movie will at least be interesting.

Like *Repo Man* and *Turtle Diary* and *Hannah and Her Sisters,* it is willing to go for originality in a world that prizes the entertainment assembly line. I was hugging myself during this movie, because it had so many moments that were just right.

The Unbearable Lightness of Being
★ ★ ★ ★
R, 172 m., 1988

Daniel Day Lewis (Tomas), Juliette Binoche (Tereza), Lena Olin (Sabina), Derek de Lint (Franz), Erland Josephson (The Ambassador), Pavel Landovsky (Pavel), Donald Moffat (Chief Surgeon), Daniel Olbrychski (Interior Ministry Official), Stellan Skarsgard (The Engineer), Tomek Bork (Jiri). Directed by Philip Kaufman and produced by Saul Zaentz. Screenplay by Jean-Claude Carriere.

In the title of Philip Kaufman's *The Unbearable Lightness of Being,* the crucial word is "unbearable." The film tells the story of a young surgeon who attempts to float above the mundane world of personal responsibility and commitment, to practice a sex life that has no traffic with the heart, to escape untouched from the world of sensual pleasure while retaining his privacy and his loneliness. By the end of the story, this freedom has become too great a load for him to bear.

The surgeon's name is Tomas, and he lives in Prague; we meet him in the blessed days before the Russian invasion of 1968. He has an understanding with a woman named Sabina, a painter whose goal is the same as his own—to have a physical relationship without an emotional one. The two lovers believe they have much in common, since they share the same attitude toward their couplings, but actually their genitals have more in common than they do. That is not to say they don't enjoy great sex; they do, and in great detail, in this most erotic serious film since *Last Tango in Paris*.

One day the doctor goes to the country, and while waiting in a provincial train station, his eyes fall upon the young waitress Tereza. He orders a brandy. Their eyes meet. They go for a little walk after she gets off of work, and it is clear there is something special between them. He returns to Prague. One day she appears in the city and knocks at his door. She has come to be with him. Against all of his principles, he allows her to spend the night, and then to move in. He has betrayed his own code of lightness, or freedom.

The film tells the love story of Tomas and Tereza in the context of the events of 1968, and there are shots that place the characters in the middle of the riots against the Russian invaders. Tereza becomes a photographer, and tries to smuggle pictures of the uprising out of the country. Finally, the two lovers leave Prague for Geneva, where Sabina has already gone—and then Tomas resumes his sexual relationship with Sabina because his philosophy, of course, is that sex has nothing to do with love.

Crushed by his decision, Tereza attempts her own experiment with free love, but it does not work because her heart is not built that way. Sabina, meanwhile, meets a professor named Franz who falls in love with her so urgently that he decides to leave his wife. Can she accept this love? Or is she even more committed to "lightness of being" than Tomas, who tutored her in the philosophy? In the middle of Sabina's indecision, Tereza appears at her door with a camera. She has been asked to take some shots for a fashion magazine and needs someone to pose nude.

Sabina agrees, and the two women photograph each other in a scene so carefully choreographed that it becomes a ballet of eroticism.

By this point in the movie, a curious thing had happened to me as a viewer. I had begun to appreciate some of the life rhythms of the characters. Most films move so quickly and are so dependent on plot that they are about events, not lives. *The Unbearable Lightness of Being* carries the feeling of deep nostalgia, of a time no longer present, when these people did these things and hoped for happiness, and were caught up in events beyond their control.

Kaufman achieves this effect almost without seeming to try. At first his film seems to be almost exclusively about sex, but then we notice in countless individual shots and camera decisions that he does not allow his camera to become a voyeur. There is a lot of nudity in the film, but no pornographic documentary quality; the camera does not linger, or move for the best view, or relish the spectacle of nudity. The result is some of the most poignant, almost sad, sex scenes I have ever seen—sensuous, yes, but bittersweet.

The casting has a lot to do with this haunting quality. Daniel Day Lewis plays Tomas with a sort of detachment that is supposed to come from the character's distaste for commitment. He has a lean, intellectual look, and is not a voluptuary. For him, sex seems like a form of physical meditation, rather than an activity with another person. Lena Olin, as Sabina, has a lush, voluptuous body, big-breasted and tactile, but she inhabits it so comfortably that the movie never seems to dwell on it or exploit it. It is a fact of nature. Juliette Binoche, as Tereza, is almost ethereal in her beauty and innocence, and her attempt to reconcile her love with her lover's detachment is probably the heart of the movie.

The film is based on the novel by the Czech novelist Milan Kundera, whose works all seem to consider eroticism with a certain wistfulness, as if to say that while his characters were making love, they were sometimes distracted from the essentially tragic nature of their existence. That is the case here. Kaufman, whose previous films have included *The Right Stuff* and a remake of *Invasion of the Body Snatchers*, has never done anything remotely like this before, but his experiment is a success in tone; he has made a movie in which reality is asked to coexist with a world of pure sensuality, and almost, for a moment, seems to agree.

The film will be noticed primarily for its eroticism. Although major films and filmmakers considered sex with great frankness and freedom in the early and mid-seventies, films in the last decade have been more adolescent, more plot- and action-oriented. Catering to audiences of adolescents, who are comfortable with sex only when it is seen in cartoon form, Hollywood has also not been comfortable with the complications of adult sexuality—the good and the bad. What is remarkable about *The Unbearable Lightness of Being*, however, is not the sexual content itself, but the way Kaufman has been able to use it as an avenue for a complex story, one of nostalgia, loss, idealism, and romance.

Uncle Buck ★ ½
PG, 100 m., 1989

John Candy (Uncle Buck), Jean Kelly (Tia Russell), Gaby Hoffman (Maizy Russell), Macaulay Culkin (Miles Russell), Amy Madigan (Chanice Kobolowski), Elaine Bromka (Cindy Russell), Garrett M. Brown (Bob Russell), Laurie Metcalf (Marcie Dahlgren-Frost). Directed by John Hughes and produced by Hughes and Tom Jacobson. Screenplay by Hughes.

Uncle Buck attempts to tell a heartwarming story through a series of uncomfortable and unpleasant scenes; it's a tug-of-war between its ambitions and its methods. It stars John Candy as the title character, a big-hearted softy who has been drifting through life as an unemployed horse-racing fan. Buck's brother Bob calls one night with an emergency: Bob's father-in-law has had a heart attack, and they need someone to house-sit and watch the kids for a few days.

Buck agrees, and arrives a few hours later, driving a big gas hog that leaves billowing clouds of exhaust fumes in its wake. (It's often a sign of desperation in a movie when a character is given a funny car, and *Uncle Buck* is no exception.) At his brother's expensive home in the northern suburbs of Chicago, he finds three kids uneasily waiting for him: A cute little boy and girl, and a glowering fifteen-year-old (Jean Kelly) who resents him just as she resents, apparently, every facet of her existence.

The parents hurry off to Indianapolis to clear the way for the predictable plot in which shabby old Uncle Buck tries his best to be a good parent, and eventually wins the love of all of the kids, although not without some hard times in between. Although Buck attempts to project serenity around the house, he has heavy matters weighing on him, not least his relationship with his girlfriend (Amy Madigan), who owns a tire store and is fed up with Buck's wayward life plan.

What happens in *Uncle Buck* is not hard to anticipate, but what's surprising is how many wrong notes are sounded by the story, written and directed by John Hughes. Often it's a matter of tone. The rebellious teen-ager is too angry sometimes, too sharp to be sympathetic. A promiscuous neighbor (Laurie Metcalf), who comes over to make a play for Uncle Buck, is such a caricature that she doesn't amuse, she repels. In one particularly uncomfortable scene, Uncle Buck confronts a grade-school teacher and flips her a quarter ("to go downtown and have a rat gnaw that growth off of your face"). The scene is handled with such a mean spirit that any possible humorous effect is lost, and we simply feel bad afterward.

We also feel uneasy, most of the time, while Uncle Buck attempts to deal with the fifteen-year-old girl's relationship with her boyfriend. Buck delivers one long speech in which he offers to shave the lad's kneecaps with an ax, and a little later he comes after him with a power drill, and then locks him in a car trunk. Sure, the kid is no good, but these scenes seem borrowed from some black comedy from a bloodier universe than good old Buck seems to inhabit.

Many of the elements in *Uncle Buck* represent familiar territory for John Hughes, who often deals with teen-agers and almost always shoots in the Chicago suburbs. Perhaps the title character in *Uncle Buck* was inspired by the hapless, lovable character played by Candy in Hughes's 1987 comedy, *Planes, Trains and Automobiles;* this could be a glimpse of the same man's life when he's not on the road. But Hughes is usually the master of the right note, the right line of dialogue, and this time there's an uncomfortable undercurrent in the material. The movie is filled with good intentions and good feelings, but they seem to conceal another side of Uncle Buck—a side that makes the movie feel creepy and subtly unwholesome.

Under Fire ★ ★ ★ ½
R, 128 m., 1983

Nick Nolte (Russell Price), Gene Hackman (Alex Grazier), Joanna Cassidy (Claire), Ed Harris (Oates). Directed by Roger Spottiswoode and produced by Jonathan Taplin. Screenplay by Ron Shelton and Clayton Frohman.

This is the kind of movie that almost always feels phony, but *Under Fire* feels real. It's about American journalists covering guerrilla warfare in Central America, and so right away we expect to see Hollywood stars transplanted to the phony jungles of one of those movie nations with made-up names. Instead, we see Hollywood stars who create characters so convincing we forget they're stars. And the movie names names: It's set in Nicaragua, in 1979, during the fall of the Somoza regime, period.

We meet three journalists who are there to get the story. This is not the first small war they've covered, and indeed we've already seen them packing up and leaving Africa. Now they've got a new story. Nick Nolte is Price, a photographer. Gene Hackman is Grazier, a TV reporter who dreams of becoming an anchorman. Joanna Cassidy is a radio reporter. During the course of the story, Cassidy will fall out of love with Hackman and into love with Nolte. These things happen under deadline pressure. Hackman cares, but not enough to affect his friendship with both of them.

The story is simply told, since *Under Fire* depends more upon moments and atmosphere than on a manufactured plot. During a lull in the action, Hackman heads back for New York and Nolte determines to get an interview with the elusive leader of the guerrillas. He doesn't get an interview, but he begins to develop a sympathy for the rebel cause. He commits the journalistic sin of taking sides, and it leads him, eventually, to a much greater sin: faking a photograph to help the guerrilla forces. That is, of course, wrong. But *Under Fire* shows us a war in which morality is hard to define and harder to practice. One of the key supporting characters in the movie is a mysterious American named Oates (played by Ed Harris). Is he CIA? Apparently. He's always in the thick of the dirty work, however, and if his conscience doesn't bother him, Nolte excuses himself for not taking an ethical stand. There are, in fact, a lot of ethical stands not

taken in this movie. It could almost have been written by Graham Greene; it exists in that half-world between exhaustion and exhilaration, between love and cynicism, between covering the war and getting yourself killed. This is tricky ground, and the wrong performances could have made it ridiculous (cf. Richard Gere's sleek sexual athlete in *Beyond the Limit*). The actors in *Under Fire* never step wrong.

Nolte is great to watch as the seedy photographer with the beer gut. Hackman never really convinced me that he could be an anchorman, but he did a better thing. He convinced me that he thought he could be one. Joanna Cassidy takes a role that could have been dismissed as "the girl" and fills it out as a fascinating, textured adult. *Under Fire* surrounds these performances with a vivid sense of place and becomes, somewhat surprisingly, a serious and moving film.

Under the Volcano ★ ★ ★ ★
R, 109 m., 1984

Albert Finney (Geoffrey Firmin), Jacqueline Bisset (Yvonne Firmin), Anthony Andrews (Hugh Firmin), Ignacio Lopez Tarso (Dr. Vigil), Katy Jurado (Senora Gregoria). Directed by John Huston and produced by Michael Fitzgerald. Screenplay by Guy Gallo.

The consul drinks. He has been drinking for so many years that he has arrived at that peculiar stage in alcoholism where he no longer drinks to get high or to get drunk. He drinks simply to hold himself together and continue to function. He has a muddled theory that he can even "drink himself sober," by which he means that he can sometimes find a lucid window through the fog of his life. *Under the Volcano* is the story of the last day in his drinking.

He lives in Cuernavaca, Mexico, in the years just before World War II. He is not really the British consul anymore: he was only a vice consul, anyway, and now that has been stripped from him, and he simply drinks. He has a few friends and a few acquaintances, and his long days are spent in a drunk's neverending occupation, monitoring his own condition. On this morning, for example, he had a bit too much and passed out in the road. One of those things. Earlier, or later, sometime in there, he had stumbled into a church and prayed for the return of his wife, who had left him. Now he sits on his veranda talking with his half-brother. He turns his head. His wife is standing in the doorway. He turns back. It cannot be her. He looks again. She is still there. Turns away. It cannot be. Looks again. A hallucination. But it persists, and eventually he is forced to admit that his wife has indeed returned, in answer to his prayers.

He drinks. He passes out. He wakes. The three of them set off on a bus journey. A peasant is found dead on a roadside. Later, in a bar, there is an unpleasantness with a whore. Still later, the day ends in a ditch. The consul's day is seen largely through his point of view, and the remarkable thing about *Under the Volcano* is that it doesn't resort to any of the usual tricks that movies use when they portray drunks. There are no trick shots to show hallucinations. No spinning cameras. No games with focus. Instead, the drunkenness in this film is supplied by the remarkably controlled performance of Albert Finney as the consul. He gives the best drunk performance I've ever seen in a film. He doesn't overact, or go for pathos, or pretend to be a character. His focus is on communication. He wants, he desperately desires, to penetrate the alcoholic fog and speak clearly from his heart to those around him. His words come out with a peculiar intensity of focus, as if every one had to be pulled out of the small hidden core of sobriety deep inside his confusion.

The movie is based on the great novel by Malcolm Lowry, who used this day in the life of a drunk as a clothesline on which to hang several themes, including the political disintegration of Mexico in the face of the rising tide of Nazism. John Huston, the surefooted old veteran who directed the film, wisely leaves out the symbols and implications and subtexts and just gives us the man. Lowry's novel was really about alcoholism, anyway; the other materials were not so much subjects as they were attempts by the hero to focus on something between his ears.

The movie belongs to Finney, but mention must be made of Jacqueline Bisset as his wife and Anthony Andrews as his half-brother. Their treatment of the consul is interesting. They understand him well. They love him (and, we gather, each other). They realize nothing can be done for him. Why do they stay with him? For love, maybe, or loyalty, but also perhaps because they respect the great effort he makes to continue to function, to "carry on," in the face of his disabling illness. Huston, I think, is interested in the same aspect of the story, that within every

drunk is a man with self-respect trying to get free.

An Unmarried Woman ★ ★ ★ ★
R, 124 m., 1978

Jill Clayburgh (Erica), Alan Bates (Saul), Michael Murphy (Martin), Lisa Lucas (Patti), Cliff Gorman (Charlie), Pat Quinn (Sue), Kelly Bishop (Elaine), Linda Miller (Jeannette), Andrew Duncan (Bob), Penelope Russianoff (Tanya). Directed by Paul Mazursky and produced by Mazursky and Tony Ray. Screenplay by Mazursky.

It is, Erica thinks, a happy marriage, although perhaps she doesn't think about it much. It's *there*. Her husband is a stockbroker, she works in an art gallery, their daughter is in a private high school, they live in a high-rise and jog along the East River. In the morning there is "Swan Lake" on the FM radio, and the last sight at night is of the closing stock prices on the TV screen. Had she bargained for more?

One day, though, swiftly and cruelly, it all comes to an end: Her husband breaks down in phony tears on the street and confesses he's in love with another woman. A younger woman. And so her happy marriage is over. At home, consumed by anger, grief, and uncertainty, she studies her face in the mirror. It is a good face in its middle thirties, and right now it looks plain scared.

So end the first, crucial passages of Paul Mazursky's *An Unmarried Woman*. They are crucial because we have to understand how *completely* Erica was a married woman if we're to join her on the journey back to being single again. It's a journey that Mazursky makes into one of the funniest, truest, sometimes most heartbreaking movies I've ever seen. And so much of what's best is because of Jill Clayburgh, whose performance is, quite simply, luminous.

We know that almost from the beginning. There's a moment of silence in the morning, right after Erica's husband and daughter have left the house. "Swan Lake" is playing. She's still in bed. She's just made love. She speaks from her imagination: "The ballet world was thrilled last night. . . ." And then she slips out of bed and dances around the living room in her T-shirt and panties, because she's so happy, so alive . . . and at that moment the movie's got us. We're in this thing with Erica to the end.

The going is sometimes pretty rough,

especially when she's trying to make sense out of things after her husband (Michael Murphy) leaves her. She gets a lot of support and encouragement from her three best girl friends, and some of the movie's very best scenes take place when they meet for long lunches with lots of white wine, or lie around on long Sunday mornings paging through the *Times* and idly wondering why *their* lives don't seem to contain the style of a Bette Davis or a Katharine Hepburn. And then there are the scenes when she talks things over with her daughter (Lisa Lucas), who's one of those bright, precocious teen-agers who uses understatement and cynicism to conceal how easily she can still be hurt.

After Erica gets over the period where she drinks too much and cries too much and screams at her daughter when she doesn't mean to, she goes to a woman psychiatrist, who explains that men are the problem, yes, but they are not quite yet the enemy. And so Erica, who hasn't slept with any man but her husband for seventeen years, finds herself having lunch in Chinese restaurants with boors who shout orders at waiters and try to kiss her in the back seat of a cab. There's also the self-styled stud (Cliff Gorman) who's been hanging around the art gallery, and she finally does go up to his place—warily, gingerly, but she has to find a way sometime of beginning her life again.

And then one day a British artist is hanging a show at the gallery, and he asks her if she doesn't think one side of the painting is a little low, and she says she thinks the *whole* painting is too low, and he doesn't even seem to have noticed her as he says, "Let's discuss it over lunch." They fall in love. Oh, yes, gloriously, in that kind of love that involves not only great sex but walking down empty streets at dawn, and talking about each other's childhood. The painter is played by Alan Bates, who is cast, well and true, as a man who is perfectly right for her and perfectly wrong for her, both at the same time.

An Unmarried Woman plays true with all three of its major movements: The marriage, the being single, the falling in love. Mazursky's films have considered the grave and funny business of sex before (most memorably in *Bob & Carol & Ted & Alice* and *Blume in Love*). But he's never before been this successful at really dealing with the complexities and following them through. I wouldn't want to tell you too much about the movie's conclusion, but believe this much: It's honest and it's *right*, because Mazursky and Jill

Clayburgh care too much about Erica to dismiss her with a conventional happy ending.

Clayburgh takes chances in this movie. She's out on an emotional limb. She's letting us see and experience things that many actresses simply couldn't reveal. Mazursky takes chances, too. He wants *An Unmarried Woman* to be true, for starters: We have to believe at every moment that life itself is being considered here. But the movie has to be funny, too. He won't settle for less than the truth *and* the humor, and the wonder of *An Unmarried Woman* is that he gets it. I've been reviewing movies for a long time now without ever feeling the need to use dumb lines like "You'll laugh—you'll cry." But I did cry, and I did laugh.

The Untouchables ★ ★ ½
R, 127 m., 1987

Kevin Costner (Eliot Ness), Robert De Niro (Al Capone), Sean Connery (Jimmy Malone), Andy Garcia (George Stone), Charles Martin Smith (Oscar Wallace). Directed by Brian De Palma and produced by Art Linson. Screenplay by David Mamet.

There is a moment in *The Untouchables* when a mobster doesn't want to talk to the law. He's just been captured by federal agents up at the Canadian border, while trying to run some booze down to Chicago for Capone. One of the guy's pals has been shot dead, out on the porch. He doesn't know his partner is dead.

Sean Connery walks outside, grabs the corpse, props it up against a wall, says he's gonna shoot the guy if he doesn't talk—and then puts a bullet into him and drops him. Inside the cabin, the other mobster decides to talk.

It's a moment of quick, brutal improvisation, and it has an energy that's lacking during most of *The Untouchables*. Here is a movie about an era when law enforcement resembled gang warfare, but the movie seems more interested in the era than in the war. *The Untouchables* has great costumes, great sets, great cars, great guns, great locations, and a few shots that absolutely capture the Prohibition Era. But it does not have a great script, great performances, or great direction.

The script is by David Mamet, the playwright, but it could have been by anybody. It doesn't have the Mamet touch, the conversational rhythms that carry a meaning beyond words. It also lacks any particular point of view about the material, and, in fact, lacks the dynamic tension of many gangster movies written by less talented writers. Everything seems cut and dried, twice-told, preordained.

The performances are another disappointment. The star of the movie is Kevin Costner, as Eliot Ness, the straight-arrow federal agent who vows a personal struggle against the Capone mob. Costner is fine for the role, but it's a thankless one, giving him little to do other than act grim and incorrigible. The script doesn't give him, and he doesn't provide, any of the little twists and turns of character that might have made Ness into an individual.

But the big disappointment is Robert De Niro's Al Capone. All of the movie's Capone segments seem cut off from the rest of the story; they're like regal set pieces, dropped in from time to time. De Niro comes on screen with great dramatic and musical flourish, strikes an attitude, says a line, and that's basically the whole idea. There isn't a glimmer of a notion of what made this man tick, this Al Capone who was such an organizational genius that he founded an industry and became a millionaire while he was still a young man.

The best performance in the movie is by Sean Connery, as a Scottish-American cop who signs on as Ness's right-hand man and seems, inexplicably, to know everything about the mob and its liquor business. Connery brings a human element to his character; he seems to have had an existence apart from the legend of the Untouchables, and when he's onscreen we can believe, briefly, that the 1920s were inhabited by people, not caricatures.

What's good about the movie is the physical production itself. There's a shot of the canyon of LaSalle Street, all decked out with 1920s cars and extras, that's sensational. And a lot of other nice touches, like Capone's hotel headquarters, or the courtroom where his trial is held. But even the good use of sets and locations is undermined by Brian De Palma's curiously lead-footed direction—curious, because he is usually the most nimble and energetic of directors.

Look, for example, at an early scene where Ness and his men are staking out a gang headquarters, and Ness spots a nosy photographer snooping around. The editing is so clumsy we can't understand why the mob doesn't see Ness and the photographer.

(And the photographer himself stays around for the whole picture as an implausible distraction, who is somehow always able to turn up whenever he's needed.)

The 1920s were already a legend by the 1930s, when Warner Brothers turned them into the gangster movie industry. Directors have been struggling ever since to invest them with life, and free them from clichés. The best film about the era remains the uncut original version of Sergio Leone's *Once Upon a Time In America*. De Palma's *The Untouchables*, like the TV series that inspired it, depends more on clichés than on artistic invention.

Up the Sandbox ★ ★ ★
R, 98 m., 1973

Barbra Streisand (Marjorie), David Selby (Paul), Ariana Heller (Elizabeth), Jacobo Morales (Fidel Castro), Carol White (Miss Spittlemeister). Directed by Irvin Kershner and produced by Robert Chartoff and Irwin Winkler. Screenplay by Paul Zindel.

It's a little hard to make a movie about a woman's liberation when the woman in question is happy with her life, in love with her husband, and looking forward to having her third child. Such a woman somehow doesn't seem to be your typical *MS* subscriber.

I'm dealing in stereotypes, of course, but so does *Up the Sandbox*—sometimes. This is a Barbra Streisand movie, and so we know the central character won't (can't) be stereotyped; nothing even remotely like Streisand has existed in movies before. But the movie's other characters stray dangerously close to becoming case histories for Gloria Steinem.

Streisand plays Marjorie, a woman who once wrote a term paper so brilliant that her old professor still remembers it. She doesn't; she's set aside plans for an academic career and devotes herself to loving her husband, raising her children, and maintaining a New York apartment that even Erma Bombeck would describe as a mess.

Marjorie's husband is a professor at Columbia, and of course he's brilliant and engaged in "important" work and is fascinating to young women at cocktail parties—particularly, Marjorie observes, young women with low-cut dresses. This causes her some concern, and so do the erratic guerrilla raids staged on her apartment by her mother. Marjorie's mother is a spokesman for all that women's lib is against: She wants Marjorie to move to the suburbs, play cards, engage in housekeeping competition with the other women in the block, and, in general, degenerate gracefully into the zombie-like state of housewives who are attracted to detergents (but nothing else) by sex appeal.

Marjorie retaliates with a series of fantasies which sometimes work, in terms of the movie, and sometimes fail terribly. The best ones are inspired. Director Irvin Kershner (who directed the best party scene of 1971 in his comedy masterpiece *Loving*), gives us another party that is horrifying in its realism.

It's the thirty-third anniversary for Marjorie's mom and dad, and Mom seizes on her after-dinner speech as the proper occasion to (1) urge Marjorie to surrender to the suburbs and (2) announce that Marjorie is preggers. Marjorie's fantasy is to the point. She mashes her mother's face into the anniversary cake and then they wrestle under the table while a tipsy cousin shoots the action for a home movie.

Scenes like this work as fierce, funny satire; but some of the other fantasies (particularly a visit to an African tribe where the women carry the spears and the men wash the dishes) are a waste of effort. Considerable effort; the cast went to Africa to film them, and perhaps they cost so much money Kershner was reluctant to cut them out.

No matter; Streisand herself is really fine in *Up the Sandbox*, which was more or less her first straight role (depending on how you took *On a Clear Day You Can See Forever*). She does not give us a liberated woman, or even a woman working in some organized way toward liberation. Instead, she gives us a woman who feels free to be herself, no matter what anyone thinks. This is a kind of woman, come to think of it, who is rare in American movies; female intelligence on the screen still

actually seems quietly revolutionary, which is a sad truth but one *Up the Sandbox* does nothing to further.

Used Cars ★ ★
R, 113 m., 1980

Kurt Russell (Rudy Russo), Jack Warden (The Fuchs Brothers), Gerrit Graham (Jeff), Frank McRae (Jim), Deborah Harmon (Barbara Fuchs). Directed by Robert Zemeckis and produced by Bob Gale. Screenplay by Zemeckis and Gale.

I wonder where the idea got started that it's intrinsically funny to see cars crashing into each other. It's not. It is also not *more* funny when there are dozens or hundreds of cars; the delicate timing you need for comedy is lost when a scene becomes a logistical demonstration. When it comes to cars in movies, more is less—a lesson *Used Cars* does not demonstrate.

When the movie isn't manipulating cars, it does have its good moments. It involves an ancient family feud between two brothers who own competing used car lots across the street from each other. The brothers, both played by Jack Warden, have been treated differently by fate: One is rich and successful; the other is on his last legs, like the cars on his lot. Warden does a good enough job in the dual role, but I always wonder why dual roles seem like a good idea in the first place. If you want two brothers, why not cast two brothers, and accentuate their differences? Why cast one actor and settle for one tour de force instead of two undistracting performances?

Anyway, the movie's plot thickens when it appears that the rich brother will run the poor brother out of business. The plot, in fact, does more than thicken, it congeals.

There are so many different characters and story lines in the movie that it's hard to keep everything straight, and harder still to care.

The great comedies almost always have very simple story structures, upon which complex gags can be elaborated. Remember, for example, Buster Keaton's *The General*, in which magnificent complexities were developed out of a story that essentially amounted to Keaton driving a locomotive from point A to point B and back again. *Used Cars* makes the fatal error of achieving the reverse effect: Simple gags are generated out of bafflingly complex situations.

Meanwhile, back at the used car lot . . . Kurt Russell plays a used car salesman who hopes to save the failing business in order to raise money for his political campaign. Gerrit Graham has some funny moments as a superstitious, sex-mad salesman. Deborah Harmon is the long-lost daughter of the less successful brother; her surprise reappearance gives him an heir just when he needs one the most.

Used Cars was written, directed, and produced by the team of Bob Zemeckis and Bob Gale, two young filmmakers who seem to be higher on kinetic energy than on structure and comedic instinct. Their first collaboration, which I really enjoyed, was *I Wanna Hold Your Hand*, a fantasy about the Beatles' first concert in New York. Their next collaboration was the screenplay for Steven Spielberg's unsuccessful *1941*. Next came *Used Cars*. The second and third projects, in particular, are filled with too many ideas, relationships, and situations—with plot overkill. And they seem to share the notion that if something is big enough and expensive enough, it will also be funny enough.

V

Vagabond ★ ★ ★ ★
NO MPAA RATING, 105 m., 1986

Sandrine Bonnaire (Mona), Macha Meril (Madame Lanier), Stephane Friess (Jean-Pierre), Laurence Cortadellas (Elaine), Marthe Jarnias (Tante Lydie), Yolande Moreau (Yolande), Joel Fosse (Paulo). Directed by Agnes Varda. Screenplay by Varda.

The opening shot moves in ever so slowly across the bleak fields of a French winter landscape. Two trees stand starkly outlined at the top of a hill. There is no joy here. As the camera moves closer, we see in the bottom of a ditch the blue and frozen body of a young woman. A field hand discovers her and sets up a cry. Soon the authorities are there with their clipboards, recording those things which can be known, such as the height and weight and eye color of the corpse, and wondering about all the things which cannot be known, such as her name and why she came to be dead in the bottom of a ditch.

Then we hear Agnes Varda's voice on the sound track, telling us that she became absorbed by the mystery of this young stranger's last months on earth and sought the testimony of those people who had known her. *Vagabond*, however, is the story of a woman who could not be known. And although there are many people who can step forward and say they spoke with the young woman, sheltered her, gave her food and drink, shared cigarettes and even sex with her, there is no one to say that they knew her.

Vagabond tries to feel like a documentary, a series of flashbacks to certain days in the last months of the girl's life. Actually, it is all fiction. And, like all good fiction, it is able to imply much more than it knows. From bits and pieces of information that the girl spreads out among the people that she meets,

we learn that she was born of middle-class parents, that she took secretarial training, that she worked in an office but hated it, that eventually she went on the road, carrying her possessions and a tent in a knapsack on her back, begging food and shelter, sometimes doing a little work for a little money.

She looks ordinary enough, with her wide, pleasant face and her quiet smile. People talk about how bad she smells, but we cannot know about that. She rolls her own cigarettes and sometimes prefers them to food. Sometimes in a cafe, when she is given a few francs, she spends them on the jukebox instead of on bread.

Only gradually do we realize that she contains a great passivity. When a goat herder and his wife take her in, feed her and give her a small trailer to spend the winter in, she does not embrace the opportunity to help them in their work. She sits inside the trailer, staring blankly ahead. She is utterly devoid of ambition. She has gone on the road, not to make her fortune, but to drop out completely from all striving.

It is hard to read her signals. Sometimes she seems to be content, opening the flap of her tent and staring out, half-blinded, at the brightness of the morning sun. She stops for a few days in a chateau and laughs with the old countess who lives there as they get drunk on the countess's brandy and the old lady complains that her son is only waiting for her to die. She seems to respond briefly to a woman professor, an agronomist who takes her along in the car as she inspects a plague among the plane trees. But is she really warming up to these people, or only providing them with a mirror that reflects their own need to touch somebody?

One of the most painful subtleties of this film is the way we see the girl's defenses finally fall. One day after another, almost

without seeming to, she sinks lower and lower. The life of the vagabond becomes the life of the outcast, and then the outcast becomes the abandoned. Finally, the abandoned becomes an animal, muddy and unkempt, disoriented, at the bottom, no longer bewildered, frightened, amazed at how low she has fallen. Finally she cries, and we remember how young and defenseless she is, under that tough skin.

What a film this is. Like so many of the greatest films, it tells us a very specific story, strong and unadorned, about a very particular person. Because it is so much her own story and does not seem to symbolize anything—because the director has no parables, only information—it is only many days after the end of the film that we reflect that the story of the vagabond could also be the story of our lives. For how many have truly known us, although many have shared our time.

Valley Girl ★ ★ ★
R, 95 m., 1983

Nicolas Cage (Randy), Deborah Foreman (Julie), Elizabeth Dailey (Loryn), Michael Bowen (Tommy), Colleen Camp (Mom), Frederic Forrest (Dad). Directed by Martha Coolidge and produced by Wayne Crawford and Andrew Lane. Screenplay by Crawford and Lane.

Disgruntled and weary after slogging through Sex-Mad Teen-ager Movies, I came upon *Valley Girl* with low expectations. What can you expect from a genre inspired by *Porky's?* But this movie is a little treasure, a funny, sexy, appealing story of a Valley Girl's heartbreaking decision: Should she stick with her boring jock boyfriend, or take a chance on a punk from Hollywood? Having seen many Sex-Mad Teen-ager Movies in which a typical slice of teen-ager life consisted of seducing your teacher, being seduced by your best friend's mom, or driving off to Tijuana in search of hookers, I found *Valley Girl* to be surprisingly convincing in its portrait of kids in love. These *are* kids. They're uncertain about sex, their hearts send out confusing signals, and they're slaves to peer pressure.

The movie stars Deborah Foreman as Julie, a bright, cute high school girl who is in the process of breaking up with her blond jock boyfriend (Michael Bowen). He's gorgeous to look at, but he's boring and conceited and he does the one thing that drives all teen-age girls mad: He sits down next to them in a burger joint and casually helps himself to their lunch. One night at a party, Julie meets Randy (Nicolas Cage). He's a lanky, kind of goofy-looking kid with an appealing, crooked smile. He's also a punk from across the hills in Hollywood. Julie likes him. He makes her laugh. He's tender. It's awesome. She falls in love. And then her friends start working her over with all sorts of dire predictions, such as that she'll be "totally dropped" if she goes out with this grotty punk. Caving in to peer pressure, Julie agrees to go to the prom with the jock. And then there's the big climax where the punk gets his girl.

One of the nicest things about this movie is that it allows its kids to be intelligent, thoughtful, and self-analytical. Another thing is that it allows the *parents* to be modern parents. Have you ever stopped to think how *dated* all the parents in teen-ager movies are? They seem to have been caught in a time warp with Dagwood and Blondie. In *Valley Girl*, the parents (Frederic Forrest and Colleen Camp) are former hippies from the Woodstock generation, now running a health food restaurant and a little puzzled by their daughter's preppy friends. It's a perfect touch.

And here's one more nice thing about *Valley Girl*. Maybe because it was directed by a woman, Martha Coolidge, this is one of the rare teen-ager movies that doesn't try to get laughs by insulting and embarrassing teen-age girls. Everybody's in the same boat in this movie—boys and girls—and they're all trying to do the right thing and still have a good time. It may be the last thing you'd expect from a movie named *Valley Girl*, but the kids in this movie are human.

Valmont ★ ★ ★ ½
R, 140 m., 1989

Colin Firth (Valmont), Annette Bening (Merteuil), Meg Tilly (Tourvel), Fairuza Balk (Cecile), Sian Phillips (Madame De Volanges), Jeffrey Jones (Gercourt), Henry Thomas (Danceny), Fabia Drake (Madame De Rosemonde). Directed by Milos Forman and produced by Paul Rassam and Michael Hausman. Screenplay by Jean-Claude Carriere.

Valmont was the second film within twelve months based on the same story about sexual intrigue in eighteenth-century France. It was directed by Milos Forman, a Czech now living in America. The earlier version, *Dangerous Liaisons*, was directed by Stephen Frears, who is British. What we are given here is a delicious opportunity to compare the same material as filtered through two different national temperaments, and on the basis of this film, each lives up to its reputation: The British director's film is more cool and cerebral, while the Czech director's film is more sensuous and voluptuous.

The bare events in the two films are more or less the same. The Marquise de Merteuil, a widow of a certain age, amuses herself by setting up sexual intrigues among her acquaintances. She has a lover, Gercourt, who rejects her because he plans to marry Cecile, a young virgin. The widow enlists a close friend, Valmont, who is a complete cad, to seduce Cecile—thus depriving Gercourt of the girl's innocence. The friend goes to a country home to seduce the virgin, but immediately falls under the spell of Madame de Tourvel, a breathtaking young married woman who is visiting there at the same time. Events play themselves out with utter depravity until the evil plans of the schemers are undermined by the one thing they had not anticipated: the appearance of true love.

There are no doubt countless tones and shadings with which to tell this story, but Forman and Frears have found such different approaches that their two films could be seen on the same double bill with little redundancy except in the names of the characters. It is possible that Frears is more faithful to the spirit of the scandalous classic by Choderlos de Laclos, whose book has been banned and praised for two hundred years. The story is about an age when love was less prized than status or money, when families routinely married their innocent young

daughters off to decrepit leeches with a title or a fortune. In that society, one of the great pleasures for the wicked was manipulating the lives of the naive—and the Marquise de Merteuil is shown as an intellectual sadist whose greatest sexual pleasures came from preventing other people from attaining theirs.

The Frears version, which was released late in 1988, contained a great deal of talk and an occasional homage to a magnificently powdered bosom. Now here is *Valmont*, the Forman version, in which—it cannot be denied—many of the characters would actually rather make love than talk about it.

The casting of the two movies betrays the sentiments of their directors. For the elegant Glenn Close, who played the Marquise in 1988, we now get the saucy Annette Bening. For the detached and ironical John Malkovich, as Valmont, we get the sometimes charming Colin Firth, whose feelings seem closer to the surface. For the almost ethereal Uma Thurman, who played the young virgin, there is the delightful Fairuza Balk, who seems closer to Shakespeare's Juliet than to de Laclos's innocent little Cecile. Only the character of Madame de Tourvel, the dreamy married woman, is cast in a similar fashion in the two films; Michelle Pfeiffer (1988) and Meg Tilly (1989) may differ in many ways, but they are alike in their ability to project a sexual curiosity that gnaws at their marriage vows.

Milos Forman is one of the most successful directors of our time (his credits include two Academy Award winners, *One Flew Over the Cuckoo's Nest* and *Amadeus*). In *Valmont*, he has mounted a beautiful period production that uses locations, sets, settings, and costumes to create a world so seductive that sexual intrigue seems to drip from the ceilings and collect in the corners in little pools of psychic lust. His characters not only think of little but sex, they do little except sleep with one another or talk about it. If there is a flaw in Colin Firth's Valmont, it's that the character seems to enjoy sex so much that it is difficult to imagine him possessing the discipline to use it as a weapon.

The most affecting passages in the film involve two sets of lovers: Valmont and Madame de Tourvel, of course, and then the innocent Cecile and Danceny (Henry Thomas), her young harp teacher. Although Cecile has been promised to the loathsome Gercourt (Jeffrey Jones), it is in the clear young eyes of Danceny that she sees her love reflected, and they leave each other romantic notes hidden in the wrappings of the harp. He is her Romeo.

De Tourvel, as played by Tilly, is less naive. She is a married woman, she understands her depraved society, and she knows full well that Valmont is a sexual brigand who will love her and leave her. He even tells her so himself. Her problem is, the more she thinks about it, the more she would like to be loved, even to be left. She enters into a liaison in that spirit, but then finds to her own surprise that she actually cares for him—and there is an affecting scene in which she waits in the rain outside his house, humiliating herself because she will not be sent away until she sees him.

If *Dangerous Liaisons* was a movie to stimulate the mind, *Valmont* is more compelling for the emotions. I admired the earlier movie, but I watched it as if I were watching creatures in a human zoo, observing their behavior with my own detached amusement. In *Valmont*, I found myself falling into the same trap that de Laclos set for his characters—I found myself beginning to care about these people. I even wanted them to be happy, which was more than they wanted for each other. The frightening thing about the film is that at the end, after all the hearts have been broken and all the cynical compromises have been made, I could see how many of these characters would be able to make their adjustments and be happy, even surrounded by the wreckage of their ideals. It is always a little disturbing to see people sell out at a profit. Maybe that's what the film wants us to discover.

The Vanishing ★ ★ ★ ½
NO MPAA RATING, 100 m., 1991

Johanna Ter Steege (Saskia), Gene Bervoets (Rex), Bernard-Pierre Donnadieu (Raymond Lemorne). Directed by George Sluizer and produced by Sluizer and Anne Lordon. Screenplay by Tim Krabbé and Sluizer.

One of the most intriguing things about *The Vanishing* is the film's unusual structure, which builds suspense even while it seems to be telling us almost everything we want to know. The movie is a thriller based on a domestic tragedy—on a wife who inexplicably vanishes into thin air, and of her husband's three-year search for information about what happened to her. Almost from the beginning of the film, we know more

than the husband does, and yet the more we know, the more we wonder and fear.

The film opens on a clear bright summer's day, as a Dutch couple drives down the expressway for a cycling holiday in France. They've had a little domestic quarrel, nothing important, but now they are happy again as they stop at a roadside gas station for gas and refreshments. They throw around a Frisbee. They bury a couple of coins to mark the spot forever. The wife goes back to the station to buy beer and soft drinks, and she never returns. She disappears.

At first the husband cannot believe what has happened. He leaves a note on their car and goes looking for her. He can even see, in the background, the bright dot of her red hair in an idle Polaroid he snapped while waiting for her. Where did she go? The question becomes an obsession with him, even years later after he has lost hope of finding her alive. He simply needs to know.

Now at this point I must be cautious about what I write, because I don't want to spoil the film. Let it be said that we know from fairly early on who is responsible for the disappearance. He is a pleasant family man with a round, open face, and he seems mostly pleased with himself. We do not know how he abducted her, or what happened to her then, although there are clues. On the surface, he does not seem to be an evil man. He certainly doesn't fit the profile of a killer. But there is something twisted there, and we learn more about it as we learn more about his life story.

The husband has advertised all over France and Holland for his wife. He can think of nothing else—even though he is in a new relationship with a woman who tries to understand the obsession. The abductor, of course, has seen the advertisements. He is not without sympathy for this man. And so the final scenes unfold.

The Vanishing is a thriller, but in a different way than most thrillers. It is a thriller about knowledge—about what the characters know about the disappearance, and what they know about themselves. The movie was directed by George Sluizer, based on a screenplay he did with Tim Krabbé, which in turn was based on Krabbé's novel *The Golden Egg*. Together they have constructed a psychological jigsaw puzzle, a plot that makes you realize how simplistic many suspense films really are. The movie advances in a tantalizing fashion, supplying information obliquely, suggesting as much as

it tells, and everything leads up to a climax that is as horrifying as it is probably inevitable.

The Verdict ★ ★ ★ ★
R, 122 m., 1982

Paul Newman (Frank Galvin), Charlotte Rampling (Laura Fischer), Jack Warden (Mickey Morrissey), James Mason (Ed Concannon), Milo O'Shea (Judge Hoyle), Edward Binns (Bishop Brophy), Julie Bovasso (Maureen Rooney), Lindsay Crouse (Kaitlin Costello). Directed by Sidney Lumet and produced by Richard Zanuck and David Brown. Screenplay by David Mamet.

There is a moment in *The Verdict* when Paul Newman walks into a room and shuts the door and trembles with anxiety and with the inner scream that people should *get off his back*. No one who has ever been seriously hung over or needed a drink will fail to recognize the moment. It is the key to his character in *The Verdict*, a movie about a drinking alcoholic who tries to pull himself together for one last step at salvaging his self-esteem.

Newman plays Frank Galvin, a Boston lawyer who has had his problems over the years—a lost job, a messy divorce, a disbarment hearing, all of them traceable in one way or another to his alcoholism. He has a "drinking problem," as an attorney for the archdiocese delicately phrases it. That means that he makes an occasional guest appearance at his office and spends the rest of his day playing pinball and drinking beer, and his evening drinking Irish whiskey and looking to see if there isn't at least one last lonely woman in the world who will buy his version of himself in preference to the facts. Galvin's pal, a lawyer named Mickey Morrissey (Jack Warden) has drummed up a little work for him: An open-and-shut malpractice suit against a Catholic hospital in Boston where a young woman was carelessly turned into a vegetable because of a medical oversight. The deal is pretty simple. Galvin can expect to settle out-of-court and pocket a third of the settlement—enough to drink on for what little future he is likely to enjoy.

But Galvin makes the mistake of going to see the young victim in a hospital, where she is alive but in a coma. And something snaps inside of him. He determines to try this case, by God, and to prove that the doctors who took her mind away from her were guilty of incompetence and dishonesty. In Galvin's mind, bringing this case to court is one and the same thing with regaining his self-respect—with emerging from his own alcoholic coma. Galvin's redemption takes place within the framework of a courtroom thriller. The screenplay by David Mamet is a wonder of good dialogue, strongly seen characters, and a structure that pays off in the big courtroom scene—as the genre requires. As a courtroom drama, *The Verdict* is superior work. But the director and the star of this film, Sidney Lumet and Paul Newman, seem to be going for something more; *The Verdict* is more a character study than a thriller, and the buried suspense in this movie is more about Galvin's own life than about his latest case.

Frank Galvin provides Newman with the occasion for one of his great performances. This is the first movie in which Newman has looked a little old, a little tired. There are moments when his face sags and his eyes seem terribly weary, and we can look ahead clearly to the old men he will be playing in ten years' time. Newman always has been an interesting actor, but sometimes his resiliency, his youthful vitality, have obscured his performances; he has a tendency to always look great, and that is not always what the role calls for. This time, he gives us old, bone-tired, hung over, trembling (and heroic) Frank Galvin, and we buy it lock, stock, and shot glass.

The movie is populated with finely tuned supporting performances (many of them by British or Irish actors, playing Bostonians not at all badly). Jack Warden is the old law partner; Charlotte Rampling is the woman, also an alcoholic, with whom Galvin unwisely falls in love; James Mason is the ace lawyer for the archdiocese; Milo O'Shea is the politically connected judge; Wesley Addy provides just the right presence as one of the accused doctors. The performances, the dialogue, and the plot all work together like a rare machine.

But it's that Newman performance that stays in the mind. Some reviewers have found *The Verdict* a little slow-moving, maybe because it doesn't always hum along on the thriller level. But if you bring empathy to the movie, if you allow yourself to think about what Frank Galvin is going through, there's not a moment of this movie that's not absorbing. *The Verdict* has a lot of truth in it, right down to a great final scene in which Newman, still drinking, finds that if you wash it down with booze, victory tastes just like defeat.

Vice Versa ★ ★ ★ ½
PG, 97 m., 1988

Judge Reinhold (Marshall), Fred Savage (Charlie), Corinne Bohrer (Sam), Swoosie Kurtz (Tina), Jane Kaczmarek (Robyn), David Proval (Turk), William Prince (Avery), Gloria Gifford (Marcie), Beverly Archer (Mrs. Luttrell), Harry Murphy (Larry). Directed by Brian Gilbert and produced by Dick Clement and Ian La Frenais. Screenplay by Clement and La Frenais.

Who would have guessed it? Who would have been able to predict that the plot of one of 1987's worst movies could produce one of 1988's most endearing comedies? Here at last is proof that the right actors can make anything funny, or perhaps it is proof that the wrong actors cannot. The name of the movie is *Vice Versa*, and when they made it in 1987 it was called *Like Father, Like Son*. The screenplays for the two movies are amazingly similar, through a rare Hollywood coincidence. But what a difference there is in the movies.

It was, I must admit, with lagging step and a heavy heart that I made my way to see *Vice Versa*. I had sincerely disliked *Like Father, Like Son*, which starred Dudley Moore and Kirk Cameron in the story of a father and son whose minds magically enter each other's bodies, forcing them to trade identities. Now here was *Vice Versa*, which stars Judge Reinhold and Fred Savage in the story of a father and son whose minds magically enter each other's bodies, forcing them to trade identities. If the material was bad when it was fresh, how could it be good when it was familiar?

My state of mind lasted for perhaps the first five minutes of the movie. Then I was laughing too hard to care. I suppose film students of the future will want to analyze the differences between the two treatments of similar material, to see how Reinhold and Savage and director Brian Gilbert and writers Dick Clement and Ian La Frenais got it right when the 1987 team got it all wrong. I would prefer to think maybe it was a matter of style.

Reinhold plays a Chicago department store executive, divorced, hard-working, upward-bound in his organization. Savage plays his eleven-year-old son, who comes to stay for a few weeks while his mother is on vacation. At one point, while they are both touching an ancient gold-trimmed Tibetan skull, they are unwise enough to wish that they could be each other. Through a mysterious, magical process that need not concern us, Reinhold and Savage are suddenly consumed in a searing bolt of light, and their personalities are transferred. That puts a little boy into a man's body and, as the title suggests, vice versa.

The movie's plot situations are fairly predictable. The kid goes to the department store in his dad's body, plays with the drums in the musical instrument section, acts like a kid with his secretary, and behaves strangely at a board meeting. Meanwhile, his dad, in a kid's body, goes to school in a limousine, barks orders into the phone, finishes exams in three minutes, and talks back to the teachers. In a couple of the best scenes, the kid (as his dad) visits his grade school teacher, and gets even with the bullies who have been tormenting him. And the dad (as his son) tells his girlfriend things he lacked the courage to say when he was an adult.

All of this is fun and well-done, but it is simply plotting. What makes *Vice Versa* so wonderful is the way Reinhold and Savage are able to convince us that each body is inhabited by the other character. They are masters of body language. Notice, for example, the scene where Reinhold demolishes the fifth-grade bullies and then, when he thinks no one is watching him, swings his arm through the air in a joyous boilermaker. Look, too, at the restless and immature way he suggests that a child would inhabit an adult body; children haven't yet had their spirits broken to make them sit still all the time.

Savage, as the adult inside the kid, is equally good at moving with quiet confidence, even impatience, and ordering people around, and expecting to be obeyed. After he calls a limousine and it lets him out in front of the department store, he strides inside and a doorman asks the chauffeur, "Is he famous?" "He's about to be," the chauffeur says, "because I'm gonna kill him."

Vice Versa is a treasure of a movie, in which the performances hold the key. It's a movie that finds its humor in many small moments of truth and accurate observation, and if there is even a certain gentle knowledge of human nature in this film, you know what? That is not necessarily wrong for a comedy, not even in the cynical weathers that surround us.

Victor/Victoria ★ ★ ★
R, 133 m., 1982

Julie Andrews (Victor/Victoria), James Garner (King), Robert Preston (Toddy), Lesley Ann Warren (Norma), Alex Karras (Squash), John Rhys-Davies (Cassell). Directed by Blake Edwards and produced by Edwards and Tony Adams.

I've always felt this way about female impersonators: They may not be as pretty as women, or sing as well, or wear a dress as well, but you've got to hand it to them; they sure look great and sing pretty—for men. There are no doubt, of course, female impersonators who practice their art so skillfully that they cannot be told apart from real women—but that, of course, misses the point. A drag queen should be maybe 90 percent convincing as a woman, tops, so you can applaud while still knowing it's an act.

Insights like these are crucial to Blake Edwards's *Victor/Victoria*, in which Julie Andrews plays a woman playing a man playing a woman. It's a complicated challenge. If she just comes out as Julie Andrews, then of course she looks just like a woman, because she is one. So when she comes onstage as "Victoria," said to be "Victor" but really (we know) actually Victoria, she has to be an ever-so-slightly imperfect woman, to sell the premise that she's a man. Whether she succeeds is the source of a lot of comedy in this movie, which is a lighthearted meditation on how ridiculous we can sometimes become when we take sex too seriously.

The movie is made in the spirit of classic movie sex farces, and is in fact based on one (a 1933 German film named *Viktor und Viktoria*, which I haven't seen). Its more recent inspiration is probably *La Cage Aux Folles*, an enormous success that gave Hollywood courage to try this offbeat material. In the movie, Andrews is a starving singer, out of work, down to her last franc, when she meets a charming old fraud named Toddy, who is gay, and who is played by Robert Preston in the spirit of Ethel Mertz on "I Love Lucy." Preston is kind, friendly, plucky, and comes up with the most outrageous schemes to solve problems that wouldn't be half so complicated if he weren't on the case. In this case, he has a brainstorm: Since there's no market for girl singers, but a constant demand for female impersonators, why shouldn't Andrews assume a false identity and pretend to be a drag queen? "But they'll know I'm not a man!" she wails. "Of course!" Preston says triumphantly.

The plot thickens when James Garner, as a Chicago nightclub operator, wanders into Victor/Victoria's nightclub act and falls in love with him/her. Garner refuses to believe that lovely creature is a man. He's right, but if Andrews admits it, she's out of work. Meanwhile, Garner's blond girlfriend (Lesley Ann Warren) is consumed by jealousy, and intrigue grows between Preston and Alex Karras, who plays Garner's bodyguard. Edwards develops this situation as farce, with lots of gags depending on split-second timing and characters being in the wrong hotel rooms at the right time. He also throws in several nightclub brawls, which aren't very funny, but which don't much matter. What makes the material work is not only the fact that it is funny (which it is), but that it's about likable people.

The three most difficult roles belong to Preston, Garner, and Karras, who must walk a tightrope of uncertain sexual identity without even appearing to condescend to their material. They never do. Because they all seem to be people first and genders second, they see the humor in their bewildering situation as quickly as anyone, and their cheerful ability to rise to a series of implausible occasions makes *Victor/Victoria* not only a funny movie, but, unexpectedly, a warm and friendly one.

Vincent ★ ★ ★ ★
NO MPAA RATING, 99 m., 1989

A documentary written and directed by Paul Cox and produced by Tony Llewellyn-Jones. Words by Vincent Van Gogh, read by John Hurt.

"How rich art is! If only one can remember what one has seen."—Vincent Van Gogh, in a letter to his brother

"Dear Theo," the letters always began, and there were more than 750 of them, written by Vincent Van Gogh to his brother, Theo. The painter spoke of his life, his finances, his health, his prospects, his opinions of the art world—but most of all he spoke about his paintings, and about the discoveries he was making. To read the letters while looking at the paintings (as you can do if you have the book *Vincent by Himself*) is like having Van Gogh take you by the hand and lead you through an exhibit of his work.

Few other painters have left such a moving and honest personal correspondence.

If you only read the letters and look at the works, however, you will miss something—the look of the everyday world that Van Gogh was transforming into his paintings. What Paul Cox has done in *Vincent*—which is the best film about a painter I have ever seen—is to take his camera to some of the places Van Gogh painted, and to re-create some of the others in his imagination. This is not, however, one of those idiotic "art appreciation" films in which we see the windmill and then we see the painting of the windmill; Cox knows too much about art to be that simplistic. Instead, he adopts the role of a disciple of the painter, a man who wants to stand in the same places and see the same things as a simple act of love toward Van Gogh's work.

All of the words on the sound track are from Vincent's letters to Theo, read by the British actor John Hurt. On the screen, we see landscapes such as Van Gogh might have seen, and we visit some of the places where he painted. But there are fictionalized, created sequences as well: scenes of farmers in their fields, or peasants walking down country lanes, or shadows sweeping across fields of sunflowers. And there is a magical sequence in which the people in a room go about their daily business until they arrange themselves, seemingly by accident, into a reproduction of a painting.

Sometimes Cox makes no effort to photograph specific things that Van Gogh might have seen or been influenced by. Instead, his camera visits woods and fields, and watches birds and flowers, and meanders down alleyways populated with people who seem to harbor some of the weariness and fear of so many of Van Gogh's models. The words continue over these images as well, creating the illusion that the painter is narrating the film himself.

The best parts of the film are the most specific. Cox uses close-ups to show the smallest details of some of the paintings, while the narration describes the painter's technical discoveries and experiments. There are times when we almost seem to be looking at the very brushstroke that Van Gogh is describing in a letter. These moments create a sense of the specific. We aren't looking at stars in the sky, or fields of flowers, or a portrait of the artist; we're looking at frozen moments in time when Van Gogh's brush moved just such a way in response to his feeling and his craft. The strokes seem enormous, on the big movie screen, and they call our attention to the detail, to the way that Van Gogh's paintings were not about their subjects but about the way he saw his subjects.

So much of the popular image of Van Gogh is crude and inaccurate, fed by the notion that he was "mad," fueled by the fact that he cut off his ear. There is an entirely different Vincent here, a poetic, thoughtful man who confides everything to his brother, who is not mad so much as completely open to the full range of his experience, including those parts that most of us prudently suppress. *Vincent* is the most romantic and yet the most sensible documentary about a painter I can imagine.

Vincent & Theo ★ ★ ★ ½
PG-13, 138 m., 1990
(See related Film Clip, p. 695.)

Tim Roth (Vincent van Gogh), Paul Rhys (Theo van Gogh), Johanna Ter Steege (Jo Bonger), Wladimir Yordanoff (Paul Gauguin), Jean-Pierre Cassel (Dr. Paul Gachet). Directed by Robert Altman and produced by Ludi Boeken. Screenplay by Julian Mitchell.

How to portray the artist at work? Directors through the years have shown them sporadically applying paint to canvas, but for the most part the artist's task in the movies is to drink wine, argue by candlelight, and spend a good deal of time in unheated studios with undressed models. The big dramatic scenes involve confrontations with those who do not understand his genius: His dealers, his lovers, his public, and his creditors.

Only occasionally does a film come along where we get the sensation that actual creation is taking place before our eyes. That happens when the filmmakers are also in the art of creating, and transfer their inspiration to the characters in a sort of artistic ventriloquism. *Camille Claudel* (1989) had that feeling, as Isabella Adjani grubbed about in a ditch, digging up clay for her sculptures. And now here is Robert Altman's *Vincent & Theo*, another film that generates the feeling that we are in the presence of a man in the act of creation.

True art is made as if God were a lot of little cottage industries. Artists take up shapeless raw material—paint or clay, or a blank sheet of paper—and transform it into something wonderful that never existed before. This is such a joyous activity that I am at a loss to understand how an artist could ever be unhappy, and yet so many are. Perhaps, like God, they grieve when man ignores their handiwork.

Vincent van Gogh was one of the unhappiest of artists. Some medical experts now believe it was because he suffered from a maddening ear disease. *Vincent & Theo* does not attempt a diagnosis. It simply regards the fact that van Gogh, whose paintings most people today instinctively love from the first moment they see them, suffered all of his life from overwhelming rejection. He did not paint because he wanted to; he painted because he had to. He did not develop a style; he painted in the only way he could. During his lifetime he sold only one painting. How would you feel, if you worked a lifetime to create beautiful things for people to look at, and they turned their backs and chose to look at ugly things instead? And if you saw your brother sacrifice himself to support your lonely work?

Altman's approach in *Vincent & Theo* is a very immediate, intimate one. He would rather show us things happening than provide themes and explanations. He is most concerned with the relationship that made the art possible, the way in which Theo, the younger brother, essentially became Vincent's parent and patron. We meet van Gogh (Tim Roth) and his brother (Paul Rhys) in the middle of their relationship, we hear them fight and see them through the thickets of exasperation, and at the end we realize that it took two obsessives to create the work of Vincent van Gogh: The brother who painted it, and the brother who believed that to support the painting was the most important thing he could possibly do with his lifetime.

The movie takes place inside and outside the claustrophobic art world of Paris in the late nineteenth century, where the two Dutch brothers try to make their mark. Theo is a passable art dealer, skilled at selling safe paintings to cautious people, and he is lucky in finding employers who sympathize with his more radical tastes and eventually give him the opportunity to strike out on his own. Even then, given free rein, he is unable to sell his brother's work. And Vincent lives in a series of barren rooms and small houses, writing continuously to his brother (the apparent subject is art, but the buried subject is usually money).

There is the sense that Vincent had no knowledge of the way people normally behave toward one another. At some point in his childhood, he failed to decipher that code. Consider the scene where the prostitute (Jip Wijngaarden) comes to pose for him. She is cold and hungry, and the only support of her daughter. Vincent asks her to come and live with him. She explains her needs. He agrees to them. His need is to have someone to paint, and everything else—the expense, the distraction, the responsibility, and certainly the subject of sex—never occurs to him.

His painting is such a direct expression of his mood, indeed, that ordinary human speech often seems unnecessary. He is the rare artist who truly does speak through his work, and Altman dramatizes that in a remarkable scene in a field of sunflowers, where, as van Gogh paints, Altman's camera darts restlessly, aggressively, at the flowers, turning them from passive subjects into an alien hostile environment. The film is able to see the sunflowers as Altman believed van Gogh saw them. To make a sunflower stand for anything other than itself is a neat trick, and Altman accomplishes it in his own way, as van Gogh did in his.

The details of van Gogh's life are here. The infamous ear episode. The fights with Theo. The death. *Vincent & Theo* follows the trajectory of a biopic more faithfully than we might have expected, given Altman as the director. This is a more classically constructed film than much of his work, and although Altman says it's that way because he had to follow the chronology of a man's life, I think the reason is more complex: That van Gogh's personality was so fractured and tortured that the movie needed to be stable and secure, as a frame for it.

Vision Quest ★ ★ ★ ½
R, 108 m., 1985

Matthew Modine (Louden Swain), Linda Fiorentino (Carla), Michael Schoeffling (Kuch), Ronny Cox (Louden's Dad), Harold Sylvester (Tanneran), Charles Hallahan (Coach), R.H. Thomson (Kevin), J.C. Quinn (Elmo), Frank Jasper (Shute). Directed by Harold Becker and produced by Jon Peters and Peter Guber. Screenplay by Darryl Ponicsan.

We think we know the story pretty well already: Young wrestler has two dreams: (a) to win the state championship, and (b) to win the love of a girl. The defending state champion is a man-mountain who carries telephone poles to the top of stadiums. The girl is an independent drifter who is twenty years old and doesn't take the hero seriously. By the end of the movie, the only suspense is whether it will end with a victory in bed or in the ring. Although *Vision Quest* sticks pretty close to that outline, it is nevertheless a movie with some nice surprises, mostly because it takes the time to create some interesting characters. The movie's hero, Louden Swain, is probably the closest thing to a standard movie character, but Matthew Modine plays him with such an ingratiating freshness that he makes the character quirky and interesting, almost in spite of the script.

The other people in the movie are all real originals. They include Louden's father (Ronny Cox), who has lost the family farm and his wife, but still retains the respect of his son; Louden's best pal (Michael Schoeffling), who bills himself as a "half-Indian spiritual adviser"; a black history teacher (Harold Sylvester) who cares about Louden and listens to him; an alcoholic short-order cook (J.C. Quinn) who works in the kitchen of the hotel where Louden's a bellboy, and a wrestling coach (Charles Hallahan) who has mixed feelings about Louden's drive to get down to the 168-pound class so he can wrestle the toughest wrestler in the state. All of those characters are written, directed, and acted just a little differently than we might expect; they have small roles, but they don't think small thoughts.

And then there is the movie's most original creation, the twenty-year-old drifter, Carla (Linda Fiorentino). Without having met the actress, it's impossible for me to speculate on how much of Carla is original work and how much is Fiorentino's personality. What comes across, though, is a woman who is enigmatic without being egotistical, detached without being cold, self-reliant without being suspicious. She has a way of talking—kind of deliberately objective—that makes you listen to everything she says.

All of these people live in Spokane, which looks sort of wet and dark in many scenes, and feels like a place that prizes individuality. Instead of silhouetting the Modine character against the city and a lot of humble supporting roles, and turning him into a Rocky of wrestlers, the movie takes time to place the character in the city and in the lives of the other people. We begin to value his relationships, and it really means something when the short-order cook puts on a clean shirt and goes to the big wrestling meet.

The movie's plot doesn't really equal its characters. After the Rocky movies and *Breaking Away* and *The Karate Kid* and a dozen other movies with essentially the same last scene, it's hard to care about the outcome of the big fight, or race, or match, because, let's face it, we know the hero's going to win. Just once, why couldn't they give us characters as interesting as the ones in *Vision Quest*, in a movie where they'd be set free from the same tired old plot and allowed to live?

Visions of Eight ★ ★ ★
NO MPAA RATING, 110 m., 1973

Segments directed by Milos Forman, Arthur Penn, Kon Ichikawa, Claude Lelouch, John Schlesinger, Mai Zetterling, Juri Ozerov, and Michael Pfleghar. Produced by Stan Marguiles.

The idea sounded like a great one at the time: Eight important directors would be given their own budgets and camera crews and dispatched to Munich to record their personal visions of the 1972 Olympics. What nobody could have anticipated, perhaps, is how similar many of those visions would be. Too often during *Visions of Eight* the Olympic events are reduced to slow-motion ballets that finally just repeat themselves.

There is, I suppose, some interest in Kon Ichikawa's slow-motion replay of the 100-meter dash; the world's fastest men are slowed down to grotesque life-sized robots with pumping cheeks and contorted faces, and we get a feeling for the event's special agony. But the sequence is held too long; and so is Arthur Penn's segment on pole vaulting. We get jump after jump in slow motion, but all of that footage doesn't tell us as much about the vaulters as one single shot, near the end, where Penn shows us a competitor meticulously removing an invisible piece of lint from his hand grip.

There are other small touches that make the film worth seeing. In Claude Lelouch's segment on the losers, for example, there's an astonishing display of bad sportsmanship from a defeated boxer who refuses to leave the ring. For three or four minutes caught in a single take, he expresses his contempt for the decision and his outrage at the crowd (which generously boos him).

There's another kind of losing, too. In Mai Zetterling's segment, we see a massive weightlifter as he nervously circles the weights, and we can almost taste his apprehension. We've seen other competitors lift this bar (which takes five men to carry from the stage), and we know how heavy it is. So does he. He circles the stage, breathing deeply, trying to psych himself into the lift. He approaches the bar, grabs it, backs away. Circles some more. Just looking at him, we sense he can't lift it. He approaches the bar again, heaves, gets it a foot off the ground, then throws it back down again with disgust and walks off the stage. In a moment like that, we begin to understand something of the difficulties of the weightlifter.

The movie's still, beautiful center is occupied by the fawnlike Soviet gymnast Ludmilla Tourischeva. She's in Michael Pfleghar's segment on the women in the Olympics, and he shows us her entire routine on the uneven parallel bars. It is an exercise of grace made possible through superb athletic skill, and he wisely refuses to gimmick it up with cuts or slow motion. (Surely, as a general rule, the beauty of the Olympic events is that they take place in real time; slowing down Tourischeva's gymnastics would have missed the point.)

The most successful segment was directed by John Schlesinger, who considers the twenty-six-mile marathon race from the points of view of one of the British competitors. We see the runner in his home in the north of England, getting up every morning to run ten miles to and from work. Some days he runs home for lunch. On Saturdays he does a complete marathon course. We get a real feel for the loneliness of the long-distance runner as we see him running on dreary country roads during an overcast morning.

Then Schlesinger shows the runner at the Olympics, and in a stunning use of imagination, he gives us dream-like sequences designed to suggest what goes through the mind of the marathon runner: Memories of the long morning runs, thoughts of his family, wordless awareness of his surroundings. Schlesinger intercuts this footage with rather superficial coverage of the murdered Israelis.

His is the only segment to refer to the tragedy, and at first he doesn't really seem to have anything coherent to say. But then he pulls his images together in his last few minutes; as Avery Brundage is making his closing speech as if the whole Olympic pageantry hadn't already turned to ashes with the murders, a final dogged marathon runner, hours behind the rest, stubbornly runs into the stadium and crosses the finish line. That's it, Schlesinger seems to be saying:

The dignity of this loser, still loyal to his sport, eclipses the electric scoreboards and the official blazers.

Vixen ★ ★ ★
x, 68 m., 1969

Erica Gavin (Vixen), Harrison Page (Niles), Garth Pillsbury (Tom), Michael O'Donnell (O'Banlon), Vincent Wallace (Janet), Robert Aiken (Dave), Jon Evans (Jud). Directed and produced by Russ Meyer. Screenplay by Robert Rudelson.

Some time ago it might have been necessary to devise all sorts of defenses for Russ Meyer's *Vixen*, finding hidden symbolism and all that. But I see no reason why we can't be honest: *Vixen* was the best film of its day in that uniquely American genre, the skin-flick.

It is also a celebration of zestful direction and photography, and a lot of the time it's very funny. In a field filled with cheap, dreary productions, Meyer is the best crafts-man and the only artist. He has developed a directing style so open, direct, and good-humored that it dominates his material; what a relief it was to hear laughter during a skin-flick, instead of the dead silence that usually envelops their cheerless audiences.

Vixen is not only a good skin-flick, but a merciless put-on of the whole genre. As Terry Southern demonstrated with his novel *Candy*, you can't satirize pornography with-out writing it. The movie version of *Candy* failed because it lacked the courage to find itself ridiculous; how can a put-on take itself seriously? *Vixen*, on the other hand, catalogs the basic variations in skin-flick plots and ticks them off one after another.

It's done with such droll dialogue and high humor that even the most torrid scenes somehow manage to get outside themselves; instead of placing his hero and heroine in the shower and grinding away in the panting style of his imitators, Meyer takes the basic shower scene, writes it with hilariously mal-aprop dialogue ("We decided to stop doing this when we were twelve," Vixen's brother protests), and intercuts it with a scene out-side in which a red-bearded Irish Commu-nist makes a speech to a black draft dodger.

Meyer is also heavy on the redeeming social value department. His characters de-bate communism, Cuban Marxism, Vietnam, draft-dodging, civil rights, and airplane hijacking, deciding in favor of civil rights and against the others.

The story line is barely strong enough to hold the scenes together; it involves a bush pilot and his wife (Vixen, portrayed admira-bly by Erica Gavin) who take another couple on a fishing weekend in Canada. Also pres-ent are Vixen's brother and his black friend, a draft evader protesting what he believes is a racist war. The Irish Marxist wanders in later from somewhere. There is also a Royal Cana-dian Mounted Policeman who wanders off somewhere.

At the time the movie was released, "re-deeming social value" was a key line of defense against charges that a movie was por-nographic. Meyer's inspiration was to put all of the redeeming speeches at the end. "The audience will know," he once said, "that when the characters get on the airplane, the good parts are over." Sound advice.

W

Walkabout ★ ★ ★ ★
PG, 95 m., 1971

Jenny Agutter (The Girl), Lucien John (Brother), David Gumpilil (Aborigine), John Mellon (Father). Directed by Nicolas Roeg and produced by Si Litvinoff. Screenplay by Edward Bond.

It is possible to consider *Walkabout* entirely as the story it seems to be: The story of a fourteen-year-old girl and her little brother, who are abandoned in the Australian outback and then saved through the natural skills of a young aborigine boy. It is simpler and easier to consider it on that level, too, because *Walkabout* is a superb work of storytelling and its material is effortlessly fascinating. There's also a tendency (unfortunate, probably) to read *Walkabout* as a catch-all of symbols and metaphors, in which the Noble Savage and his natural life are tested and found superior to civilization and cities. The movie does, indeed, make this comparison several times. Hundreds of miles from help, the girl turns on her portable radio to hear a philosopher observe: "It is now possible to state that 'that is' is." Well, this isn't exactly helpful, and so we laugh. And more adolescent viewers may have to stifle a sigh and a tear when the girl is seen, at the movie's end, married to a cloddish office clerk and nostalgically remembering her idyllic days in the desert.

The contrast between civilization and man's more natural states is well-drawn in the movie, and will interest serious-minded younger people (just as, at the level of pure story, *Walkabout* will probably fascinate kids). But I don't think it's fruitful to draw all the parallels and then piously conclude that we would all be better off far from the city, sipping water from the ground, and spearing kangaroos for lunch. That sort of comparison doesn't really get you anywhere and leaves you with a movie that doesn't tell you more than you already knew. I think there's more than that to *Walkabout*. And I'm going to have a hard time expressing that additional dimension for you, because it doesn't quite exist in the universe of words. Even in these days of film experiments, most movies have their centers in the worlds of plots and characters. But *Walkabout* . . .

Well, to begin with, the film was directed and photographed by Nicolas Roeg, the cinematographer of *Petulia* and many other British films. Roeg's first stab at direction was as co-director of *Performance*. This was his first work as an individual. I persisted in seeing *Performance* on the level of its perfectly silly plot, and on that level it was a wretched movie indeed. People told me I should forget the plot and simply enjoy the movie itself, but I have a built-in resistance to that notion, usually. Perhaps I should have listened. Because Roeg's *Walkabout* is a very rare example of that kind of movie, in which the "civilized" characters and the aborigine exist in a wilderness that isn't really a wilderness but more of an indefinite place for the story to be told. Roeg's desert in *Walkabout* is like Beckett's stage for *Waiting for Godot*. That is, it's nowhere in particular, and everywhere.

Roeg's photography reinforces this notion. He is careful to keep us at a distance from the physical sufferings of his characters. To be sure, they have blisters and parched lips, but he pulls up well short of the usual clichés of suffering in the desert. And his cinematography (and John Barry's otherworldly music) make the desert seem a mystical place, a place for visions. So that the whole film becomes mystical, a dream, and the suicides which frame it set the boundaries of reality. Within them, what happens between the boy and the girl, and the boy and the little brother, is not merely "communication" or "survival" or "cooperation," but the same kind of life-enhancement that you imagine people feel when they go into the woods and eat berries and bring the full focus of their intelligence to bear on the problem of coexisting with nature.

Wall Street ★ ★ ★ ½
R, 125 m., 1987

Charlie Sheen (Bud Fox), Michael Douglas (Gordon Gekko), Daryl Hannah (Darien Taylor), Martin Sheen (Carl Fox), Terence Stamp (Sir Larry), Hal Holbrook (Lou Mannheim), Sean Young (Kate Gekko), James Spader (Roger Barnes), Saul Rubinek (Harold Salt), Sylvia Miles (Realtor). Directed by Oliver Stone and produced by Edward R. Pressman. Screenplay by Stanley Weiser and Stone.

How much is enough? the kid keeps asking the millionaire stock trader. How much money do you want? How much would you be satisfied with? The trader seems to be thinking hard, but the answer is, he just doesn't know. He's not even sure how to think about the question. He spends all day trying to make as much money as he possibly can, and he cheerfully bends and breaks the law to make even more millions, but somehow the concept of "enough" eludes him. Like all gamblers, he is perhaps not even really interested in money, but in the action. Money is just the way to keep score.

The millionaire is a predator, a corporate raider, a Wall Street shark. His name is Gordon Gekko, the name no doubt inspired by the lizard that feeds on insects and sheds its tail when trapped. Played by Michael Douglas in Oliver Stone's *Wall Street*, he paces relentlessly behind the desk in his skyscraper office, lighting cigarettes, stabbing them out, checking stock prices on a bank of computers, barking buy and sell orders into a speaker phone. In his personal life, he has everything he could possibly want—wife, family, estate, pool, limousine, priceless art objects—and they are all just additional entries on the scoreboard. He likes to win.

The kid is a broker for a big Wall Street firm. He works the phones, soliciting new clients, offering secondhand advice, buying and selling and dreaming. "Just once I'd like to be on *that* side," he says, fiercely looking at the telephone a client has just used to stick him with a $7,000 loss. Gekko is his hero. He wants to sell him stock, get into his circle, be like he is. Every day for thirty-nine days, he calls Gekko's office for an appointment. On the fortieth day, Gekko's birthday, he appears with a box of Havana cigars from Davidoff's in London, and Gekko grants him an audience.

Maybe Gekko sees something he recognizes. The kid, named Bud Fox (Charlie Sheen), comes from a working-class family. His father (Martin Sheen) is an aircraft mechanic and union leader. Gekko went to a cheap university himself. Desperate to impress Gekko, young Fox passes along some inside information he got from his father. Gekko makes some money on the deal and opens an account with Fox. He also asks him to obtain more insider information, and to spy on a competitor. Fox protests that he is being asked to do something illegal. Perhaps "protests" is too strong a word—he "observes."

Gekko knows his man. Fox is so hungry to make a killing, he will do anything. Gekko promises him perks—*big* perks—and they arrive on schedule. One of them is a tall blond interior designer (Daryl Hannah), who decorates Fox's expensive new high-rise apartment. The movie's stylistic approach is rigorous: We are never allowed to luxuriate in the splendor of these new surroundings. The apartment is never quite seen, never relaxed in. When the girl comes to share Fox's bed, they are seen momentarily, in silhouette. Sex and possessions are secondary to trading, to the action. Ask any gambler.

Stone's *Wall Street* is a radical critique of the capitalist trading mentality, and it obviously comes at a time when the financial community is especially vulnerable. The movie argues that most small investors are dupes, and that the big market killings are made by men like Gekko, who swoop in and snap whole companies out from under the noses of their stockholders. What the Gekkos do is immoral and illegal, but they use a little litany to excuse themselves: "Nobody gets hurt." "Everybody's doing it." "There's something in this deal for everybody." "Who knows except us?"

The movie has a traditional plot structure: The hungry kid is impressed by the successful older man, seduced by him, betrayed by him, and then tries to turn the tables. The actual details of the plot are not so important as the changes we see in the characters. Few men in recent movies have been colder and more ruthless than Gekko, or more convincing. Charlie Sheen is, by comparison, a babe in the woods; I would have preferred a young actor who seemed more rapacious, like James Spader, who has a supporting role in the movie. If the film has a flaw, it is that Sheen never seems quite relentless enough to move in Gekko's circle.

Stone's most impressive achievement in this film is to allow all the financial wheeling and dealing to seem complicated and convincing, and yet always have it make sense. The movie can be followed by anybody, because the details of stock manipulation are all filtered through transparent layers of greed. Most of the time we know what's going on. All of the time, we know why.

Although Gekko's law-breaking would of course be opposed by most people on Wall Street, his larger value system would be applauded. The trick is to make his kind of money without breaking the law. Financiers who can do that, like Donald Trump, are mentioned as possible presidential candidates, and in his autobiography Trump states, quite simply, that money no longer interests him very much. He is more motivated by the challenge of a deal, and by the desire to win. His frankness is refreshing, but the key to reading that statement is to see that it considers only money, on the one hand, and winning, on the other. No mention is made about creating goods and services, or manufacturing things, or investing in a physical plant, or contributing to the infrastructure.

What's intriguing about *Wall Street*—what may cause the most discussion—is that the movie's real target isn't Wall Street criminals who break the law. Stone's target is the value system that places profits and wealth and the Deal above any other consideration. His film is an attack on an atmosphere of financial competitiveness so ferocious that ethics are simply irrelevant, and the laws are sort of like the referee in pro wrestling, part of the show.

The War of the Roses ★ ★ ★
R, 117 m., 1989

Michael Douglas (Oliver Rose), Kathleen Turner (Barbara Rose), Danny DeVito (Gavin D'Amato), Marianne Sägebrecht (Susan), Sean Astin (Josh at seventeen), Heather Fairfield (Carolyn at seventeen), G.D. Spradlin (Harry Thurmont). Directed by Danny DeVito and produced by James L. Brooks. Screenplay by Michael Leeson.

The first and last shots of *The War of the Roses* show us a divorce attorney with a tragic tale to tell. He informs a client that there will be no charge. "I get paid $425 an hour to talk to people," he says, "and so when I offer to tell you something for free, I advise you to listen carefully." He wants to tell the story of a couple of clients of his, Oliver and Barbara Rose, who were happy, and then got involved in a divorce and were never happy again.

The attorney is played by Danny DeVito, who also directed *The War of the Roses*, and although I usually dislike devices in which a narrator thinks back over the progress of a long, cautionary tale, this time I think it works. It works because we must never be allowed to believe, even for a moment, that Oliver and Barbara are going to get away with their happiness. The lawyer's lesson is that happiness has nothing to do with it, anyway. He doubts that any marriage is destined to be happy (of course, as a divorce lawyer, he has a particular slant on the subject). His lesson is more brutal: Divorce is survivable. If only the Roses had listened.

The movie stars Michael Douglas and Kathleen Turner as the doomed Roses, and although both actors also teamed with DeVito in *Romancing the Stone*, no two movies could be more dissimilar. *The War of the Roses* is a black, angry, bitter, unrelenting comedy, a war between the sexes that makes James Thurber's work on the same subject look almost resigned by comparison.

And yet the Roses fell so naturally and easily into love in those first sunny days so long ago. They met at an auction, bidding on the same cheap figurine, and by evening they were in each other's arms. ("If this relationship lasts," Barbara muses, "this will have been the most romantic moment of my life. If it doesn't, I'm a complete slut.")

He went into law. She went into house-keeping. They were both great at their work. Oliver made a lot of money, and Barbara spent a lot of money, buying, furnishing, and decorating a house that looks like just about the best home money can buy. Meanwhile, a couple of children, one of each sex, grow up and leave home, and then Barbara decides she wants something more in life than the curatorship of her own domestic museum. One day she sells a pound of her famous liver pâté to a friend and realizes that she holds in her hand the first money she has actually earned for herself in seventeen years. It feels good. She asks for a divorce. She wants to keep the house.

That is the beginning of the war. There have been battles of the sexes before in the movies—between Spencer Tracy and Kath-arine Hepburn, between George C. Scott and Faye Dunaway, between Mickey and Minnie—but never one this vicious. I wonder if the movie doesn't go over the top. The war between the Roses begins in the lawyer's office and escalates into a violent, bloody conflict that finally finds them both bar-ricaded inside their house beautiful, doing battle with the very symbols of their mar-riage—the figurines, the gourmet kitchen range, the chandelier.

There are a great many funny moments in *The War of the Roses*, including one in which Turner (playing an ex-gymnast) springs to her feet from a prone position on her lawyer's floor in one lithe movement, and another in which Douglas makes absolutely certain that the fish she is serving for dinner will have that fishy smell. But the movie treads a dan-gerous line. There are times when its ferocity threatens to break through the boundaries of comedy—to become so unremitting we find we cannot laugh.

It's to the credit of DeVito and his costars that they were willing to go that far, but maybe it shows more courage than wisdom. This is an odd, strange movie, and the only one I can remember in which the moral is, "Rather than see a divorce lawyer, be gener-ous—generous to the point of night sweats."

WarGames ★ ★ ★ ★
PG, 110 m., 1983

Matthew Broderick (David), Dabney Coleman (McKittrick), John Wood (Falken), Ally Sheedy (Jennifer), Barry Corbin (General Beringer). Directed by John Badham and produced by Harold Schneider. Screenplay by Lawrence Lasker and Walter F. Parkes.

Sooner or later, a self-satisfied, sublimely confident computer is going to blow us all off the face of the planet. That is the message of *WarGames*, a scary and intelligent thriller that is one of the best films of 1983. The movie stars Matthew Broderick as a bright high school senior who spends a lot of time locked in his bedroom with his home com-puter. He speaks computerese well enough to dial by telephone into the computer at his school and change grades. But he's ready for bigger game. He reads about a toy company that's introducing a new computer game. He programs his computer for a random search of telephone numbers in the company's area code, looking for a number that answers with a computer tone. Eventually, he connects with a computer. Unfortunately, the com-puter he connects with does not belong to a toy company. It belongs to the Defense Department, and its mission is to coordinate early warning systems and nuclear deter-rents in the case of World War III. The kid challenges the computer to play a game called "Global Thermonuclear Warfare," and it cheerfully agrees.

As a premise for a thriller, this is a master-stroke. The movie, however, could easily go wrong by bogging us down in impenetrable computerese, or by ignoring the technical details altogether and giving us a *Fail Safe* retread. *WarGames* makes neither mistake. It convinces us that it knows computers, and it makes its knowledge into an amazingly entertaining thriller. (Note: I do not claim the movie is *accurate* about computers—only convincing.) I've described only the opening gambits of the plot, and I will reveal no more. It's too much fun watching the story unwind. Another one of the pleasures of the movie is the way it takes cardboard charac-ters and fleshes them out. Two in particular: the civilian chief of the U.S. computer oper-ation, played by Dabney Coleman as a man who has his own little weakness for simple logic, and the Air Force general in charge of the war room, played by Barry Corbin as a military man who argues that men, not com-

puters, should make the final nuclear deci-sions.

WarGames was directed by John Badham, best known for *Saturday Night Fever* and *Blue Thunder*, a thriller that I found consider-ably less convincing on the technical level. There's not a scene here where Badham doesn't seem to know what he's doing, weav-ing a complex web of computerese, person-alities, and puzzles; the movie absorbs us on emotional and intellectual levels at the same time. And the ending, a moment of blinding and yet utterly elementary insight, is won-derful.

We Think the World of You ★ ★ ★
PG, 91 m., 1989

Alan Bates (Frank), Gary Oldman (Johnny), Frances Barber (Megan), Liz Smith (Millie), Max Wall (Tom), Kerry Wise (Rita). Directed by Colin Gregg and produced by Tomasso Jandelli. Screenplay by Hugh Stoddart.

Here is a movie about one love that dares not speak its name, and another that can only bark. It and *Le Chat* are the only films I can think of about the common human practice of projecting emotions onto animals—of making a dog or a cat stand for another per-son, and treating the animal the way one would like to treat the human.

We Think the World of You stars Alan Bates as Frank, a lonely middle-aged man who has been in love for a long time with Johnny, a younger married man (Gary Oldman). This love has brought him nothing but frustration and loneliness. The time is the early 1950s in Britain, where homosexuality was a crime and arrest would have instantly destroyed Frank's modest civil-service career. But homosexuality was also not widely perceived or understood in those days, and so Frank occupies a strange, undefined position in Johnny's life, as a "friend" who gives finan-cial support to Johnny's wife and child, and also to Johnny's mother, who used to be Frank's maid.

The implication is that Frank was first attracted to Johnny years earlier, that their relationship has never been very honest on either side, and that Johnny has tried to have it both ways—marrying and having a child, while still stringing Frank along for his financial support. But there are complicat-ing factors, such as Johnny's choice of a par-ticularly unpleasant and overbearing wife (Frances Barber), and his penchant for committing crimes and getting sent to prison, where he is free of both his lover and his wife.

Soon after the film opens, Johnny is in prison and Frank is desperate for visiting privileges. But neither Johnny's wife nor his mother will carry a message into the prison for him. Frank's life turns into a humiliating round of self-abasing visits to these monstrous people, who know well enough why he cares about Johnny, but will not admit it.

They lie to themselves, but then this entire film is about lies. The central lie involves the fact of homosexuality. Frank is gay but cannot admit it. Johnny is at least bisexual, but uninterested in confronting that fact. His wife and mother are happy to have Frank's money while snickering behind his back. But there is one completely honest creature in the movie, and that is Evie, Johnny's German shepherd.

When Johnny goes to prison, the dog is kept locked up inside the house or in a small pen. Frank begins to fret about its wellbeing. It is a fine animal, healthy and high-spirited, and it needs to run in the fresh air to keep its sanity. Locked up, it begins to grow mean, morose, and sick, and when it snarls, it is beaten. There is a parallel here, of course, with Johnny, who like his dog is being kept locked up.

Frank begins to obsess about the dog. He wants to take it for walks. He worries that it will die of imprisonment. He tries to send messages into jail to Johnny, begging for custody of the dog, but of course the stupid people who have the dog do not deliver the messages, and eventually the whole story comes down to the way Frank projects his love onto the dog, and all the others conspire to keep the dog away from him.

We Think the World of You requires us to pay attention, since the characters are usually not talking about the things they really care for, or saying what they really mean. It is not a particularly "entertaining" film in the usual sense, because so much of Frank's life is sad, boring, or frustrating. But this is a film that rewards attention. It is wise and perceptive about human nature, and it sees how all of us long for love and freedom, and how the undeserved, unrequited love of an animal is sometimes so much more meaningful than the crabbed, grudging, selfish terms that are often laid down by human beings.

The Weavers: Wasn't That a Time!
★ ★ ★ ★
PG, 78 m., 1982

Featuring Lee Hays, Ronnie Gilbert, Fred Hellerman, and Pete Seeger. Directed by Jim Brown and produced by Brown, George Stoney, and Harold Leventhal.

Here is one of the most joyous musical documentaries in a long time, a celebration of the music and the singers that made up the Weavers. There are, I suppose, a lot of people who don't know who the Weavers were, but for a time in the fifties they were the top pop quartet in America, and for twenty years their recordings were a key influence on modern American folk music.

The owners of old Weavers record albums treasure them. I have four or five, and when things get depressing and the sky turns overcast and grim, I like to play one of them. There's just something magical about the joy with which the Weavers sing "Goodnight, Irene" or "Kisses Sweeter than Wine" or "The Sloop John B." or "This Land is Your Land."

The Weavers reached their popular peak in the fifties, with a string of Top Ten hits, which also included "On Top of Old Smokey," "Tzena, Tzena," and "If I Had a Hammer" (which was written by the Weavers, and not, as many people believe, by Bob Dylan). The height of their popularity unfortunately coincided with the height of McCarthyism, and the Weavers, all of them longtime left-wing activists, were blacklisted. They couldn't get jobs on television or in nightclubs, and their records were banned.

For several years in the late fifties, the group existed primarily on records. And the artists went their separate ways: Ronnie Gilbert into theater, Fred Hellerman into San Franciso-area media projects, Pete Seeger into a successful solo concert career, and Lee Hays into semi-retirement on his New England farm.

There were many calls for a Weavers reunion (in some circles, an event more fervently desired than the Beatles reunion). And in May of 1980, Lee Hays himself convened such a reunion, inviting the other Weavers and their families and friends to a picnic on his farm. As they sat around and sang and played, the idea of a public reunion began to take shape, and on November 28 and 29 of 1980, they held one last historic concert at Carnegie Hall.

The Weavers: Wasn't That a Time! is not simply a concert film, however, but a documentary about the Weavers. The director, Jim Brown, was a neighbor of Hays, and grew to admire the old man who kept on singing after his legs were amputated for diabetes and his heart needed a pacemaker.

Brown's film begins with the picnic at Hays's farm, flashes back to newsreel and archive footage of the Weavers in their prime, and then concludes with the concert in Carnegie Hall. It is impossible not to feel a lump in your throat as the Weavers gather once again on stage, and it's hard not to tap your feet when they start to sing.

Seeing this film is a wonderful experience. I'd recommend it wholeheartedly to those who don't know about the Weavers. I imagine that Weavers fans won't need any encouragement.

A Wedding ★ ★ ★ ½
PG, 125 m., 1978

Desi Arnaz, Jr. (Dino Corelli), Carol Burnett (Tulip Brenner), Geraldine Chaplin (Rita Billingsley), Howard Duff (Dr. Meecham), Mia Farrow (Buffy Brenner), Vittorio Gassman (Luigi Corelli), Lillian Gish (Nettie Sloan), Lauren Hutton (Photographer), Viveca Lindfors (Ingrid Hellstrom), Pat McCormick (MacKenzie Goddard), Dina Merrill (Antoinette Goddard), Nina Van Pallandt (Regina Corelli). Directed and produced by Robert Altman. Screenplay by John Considine, Patricia Resnick, Allan Nicholls, and Altman.

The two families in Robert Altman's *A Wedding* live right there in the closets with their skeletons. They present a cheerful facade to the outer world, of old Lake Forest money on the one hand and new Southern money on the other. But just beneath the surface there are jealousies and greeds and hates, and the random dirty tricks of fate.

Altman plunges gleefully into this wealth of material; there are forty-eight characters in his movie, give or take a few, and by the film's end we know them all. We may not know them *well*—at weddings there are always unidentified cousins over in the corner—but we can place them, and chart the lines of power and passion that run among them. And some of them are drawn as well as Altman has drawn anyone.

That's because *A Wedding* is a lot deeper and more ambitious than we might at first expect. It begins in comedy, it moves into realms of social observation, it descends into personal revelations that are sometimes tragic, sometimes comic . . . and then it ends in a way that turns everything back upon itself. The more you think about what Altman's done, the more impressive his accomplishment becomes.

A Wedding aims to upset our expectations. It takes our society's most fertile source of clichés and stereotypes—a society wedding—and then chisels away at it with maniacal and sometimes savage satire. Nobody gets away: not the bride and groom, so seemingly "ideal;" not the loving parents on either side; not the relatives, with their little dramas that are no doubt played out on every family occasion; and not even the staff of wedding coordinators, chefs, photographers, musicians, and other accomplices.

Altman begins in solemnity and ceremony, with the high Episcopalian wedding. Desi Arnaz, Jr., and Amy Stryker, as the wedding couple, are all but lost in the chaos: The bishop fumbles his lines, a camera crew maneuvers awkwardly behind the palms, and, meanwhile, back at the mansion, the groom's grandmother (Lillian Gish) drops dead of anticipated mortification.

Her death is concealed when the wedding party returns to the mansion: Concealed from the family and from the single guest who turns up for the magnificently catered affair. Altman introduces us almost effortlessly to the house jammed with people; his compositions allow characters to be established in the backgrounds while the plot is being pushed ahead in the foreground, so it's as if we're wandering around the house like everyone else.

There are any number of subplots. The parents of the groom are Nina Van Pallandt, whose drug habit is ministered to by the family doctor, and Vittorio Gassman, an Italian who seems to have sinister associations in his past. The bride's parents are Carol Burnett, all sweetness and convention until—gasp!—she's wooed by one of the guests, and Paul Dooley, vulgar, hard-drinking, with a tad too much affection for his youngest daughter (Mia Farrow).

Farrow, it develops, is pregnant—by her sister's new husband, perhaps, or (it develops) by any other member of his class at military school. Other characters reveal themselves as drunks, unreconstructed Communists, secret weepers, fountains of jealousy,

reservoirs of lust, or advocates of diverse sexual proclivities.

This is the sort of material that easily lends itself to farce, and, when it does, Altman cheerfully follows. But he leads in other directions, as well. He moves so slyly from one note to another that when Pat McCormick attempts a clumsy seduction of Carol Burnett, we're moved simultaneously by comedy and pathos. And there are scenes of extraordinary emotional complexity, as when a singalong is organized in the basement dining room, or when Nina Van Pallandt tearfully and defiantly reviews the terms under which she's lived her marriage.

Like Altman's other movies with lots of characters (M*A*S*H, McCabe and Mrs. Miller, the incomparable Nashville), A Wedding doesn't fit easily into established feature film categories. For some viewers, it won't satisfy; it doesn't set up situations and then resolve them in standard ways. It's got all the disorganization and contradictions of life— and then Altman almost mystically gives everything a deeper meaning by the catastrophic surprise he springs on us near the end.

Weeds ★ ★ ★
R, 115 m., 1987

Nick Nolte (Lee Umstetter), Lane Smith (Claude), William Forsythe (Burt), John Toles-Bey (Navarro), Joe Mantegna (Carmine), Ernie Hudson (Bagdad), Mark Rolston (Dave), J.J. Johnson (Lazarus), Rita Taggart (Lillian). Directed by John Hancock and produced by Bill Badalato. Screenplay by Dorothy Tristan and Hancock.

Weeds tells a story as old as the movies—the rags-to-riches saga of a troupe of theatrical amateurs who bring their show to Broadway—but it tells it with such a distinctive style, such a curious mixture of pathos and offhand wit, that it works for one more time. There's never a moment when there's much doubt about the outcome, but the movie gets there by a series of small delights and surprises.

The movie opens with the hero trying to kill himself in prison. He throws himself over a railing, but breaks only his arms. Then he tries to hang himself. No luck. He's in for life, with no possibility of parole, and so in desperation he does something that's even harder for him than suicide: He checks a book out of the prison library.

The prisoner's name is Lee Umstetter, played by Nick Nolte with a certain weathered weariness and a way of hanging his head to one side and walking crooked. He's a lifer with a broken spirit, until the books put ideas in his head and he writes a play in prison. He decides to produce it, and the auditions provide a scene that's a small masterpiece, as one convict sings "The Impossible Dream" and another one recites "Eeny Meeny Miney Moe," which is the only poem he knows, and not a good one for prison recitals.

The play is a success, and a warmhearted middle-aged drama critic (Rita Taggart) falls in love with Nolte and tries to convince the governor to commute his sentence. The rest of the movie involves Nolte's attempts to round up his old prison friends, reassemble the troupe on the outside, and take the show on the road. First stop, San Francisco. Then Iowa, Illinois, and Broadway. The opening night off-Broadway supplies an example of how the movie finds surprises in familiar themes. We see a famed drama critic, drenched by a rainstorm, arriving late and trying to compose himself for the opening curtain. Will he be able to be objective? The movie gets such a big laugh with his arrival that we hardly care. The opening night party at Sardi's has more surprises, and the scene is stolen by Anne Ramsey, as Nolte's ramshackle but lovable mother. And there's another great moment, done with body language and a perfect double-take, when Nolte is so overjoyed he tries to kiss Ernie Hudson, one of his fellow actors, on the lips.

The troupe develops into a tight-knit band, played by Nolte, Hudson, Lane Smith, William Forsythe, John Toles-Bey, Mark Rolston, and J.J. Johnson, with Joe Mantegna as a professional New York actor who joins them midstream and seems baffled by what kind of situation he's walked into. There is a real sense of community in their little group, which communicates itself even if the play they are performing does not. It's usually the case with plays-within-movies that the plays seem less than convincing, although in this movie there's a reason for that.

Unfortunately, the whole prison sequence at the end of the film is also less than convincing, and so are the recycled '60s leftist panaceas that pass, in that sequence, as electrifying truth-telling. It's all a little too pat. Weeds is a movie that is best when it observes small moments of human truth, and at its worst when it tries to inflate them into large moments.

Weekend at Bernie's ★
PG-13, 99 m., 1989

Andrew McCarthy (Larry Wilson), Jonathan Silverman (Richard Parker), Catherine Mary Stewart (Gwen Saunders), Terry Kiser (Bernie Lomax), Catherine Parks (Tina). Directed Ted Kotcheff and produced by Victor Drai. Screenplay by Robert Klane.

Weekend at Bernie's makes two mistakes: It gives us a joke that isn't very funny, and it expects the joke to carry an entire movie. It's a decision that leads to some long, dreary sequences and a certain desperation on the part of the actors.

The movie tells the story of two interchangeable, unremarkable young men (played by Andrew McCarthy and Jonathan Silverman) who work for an insurance company. They discover that someone is stealing from the company, and take their discoveries to Bernie, their boss (Terry Kiser), who is, in fact, the thief. He invites them to his summer home on an island, where he plans to have them killed. But first someone kills Bernie.

The young executives are frightened and don't know what to do. They prop Bernie on a couch in the living room, and just then a floating party of weekend drunks drifts in— and nobody notices that Bernie is dead. This leads to a macabre weekend in which the hapless Bernie is carted around everywhere, apparently alive. He visits the beach and even goes boating, all as part of a desperate plot by the two heroes to conceal his death until they can find out who's trying to kill them.

Movies centering on dead bodies are rarely very funny—which would be a truism if so many directors didn't try to make them. The most famous example is Alfred Hitchcock's *The Trouble with Harry,* one of his less successful movies, but Blake Edwards did pull off the idea in *S.O.B.,* a movie in which a dead man is able, briefly, to play an important role.

Why don't dead characters work? The temptation is to say that we find them in bad taste—that the idea is too gruesome to be funny. But comedy is often founded on bad taste and the offensive. I think the problem is more obvious. They don't work because they require the other characters to be so stupid.

In *Weekend at Bernie's,* for example, it should be immediately obvious to several people that Bernie is dead. In order for them not to notice, they must be incredibly dense. Their behavior in not noticing is so idiotic that we can't take them seriously or care about what they do.

One answer might be to limit Bernie's exposure more severely—to show him just a little, at a distance, so that someone could plausibly be fooled by his appearance. To make his dead body a key element of the plot, but not the central one. In this movie, however, there are scenes in which characters actally wrap an arm around Bernie and hold business conversations with him. We can't believe they could be so unobservant.

To prove my point, one of the scenes that does work is successful because Bernie is kept offscreen. That's the one where his New York mistress (Catherine Parks) goes into a bedroom where Bernie's body awaits her, while the two heroes look at each other in consternation. When she emerges, she says Bernie has "never been better."

What happened behind the closed door? The joke works because we don't know.

A Week's Vacation ★ ★ ★ ½
NO MPAA RATING, 102 m., 1980

Nathalie Baye (Laurence Cuers), Gerard Lanvin (Pierre). Directed by Bertrand Tavernier. Screenplay by Tavernier, Colo Tavernier, and Marie-Francoise Hans.

It's nothing special, just an overcast day in Lyons when everybody's going to work just as usual. A car pulls out of the stream of traffic, and a young woman gets out. Her name is Laurence, she is a schoolteacher, and this day she does not feel like teaching school. It is more than that: She cannot. There is no particular crisis. A great tragedy has not descended on her life. In fact, things are going fairly well. She is thirty-one years old, she lives with her boyfriend, she has been teaching at the same school for ten years. It is simply that large and inarticulate emotions are welling up inside her, and she is desperately unhappy. She goes to see her doctor, and he prescribes a week's vacation.

A Week's Vacation is as simple, and as complicated, as that. It was directed by Bertrand Tavernier, the gifted French filmmaker who has made his hometown of Lyons the locale for some of his best work, including *The Clockmaker* (1974). That movie was based on a novel by Georges Simenon, and *A Week's*

Vacation could well have been; it has the same matter-of-fact fascination with the great depths and unexpected secrets in the lives of people who outwardly seem ordinary. *A Week's Vacation* follows the schoolteacher, played by Nathalie Baye, as she spends her week of freedom wandering without a plan through her city, her past, and her sexuality. She meets a friendly café owner and talks to him. She goes out to the country to visit her father, who is so old he has surely discovered the answer to the puzzle of life, but it has made him speechless. Returning to the city, she has an embarrassing encounter. The café owner, mistaking her friendliness for sexual interest, tries to kiss her. She was not thinking along those lines. As they both try to free themselves from the awkward situation, as he damns himself for being such a fool, there comes a turning point in her week's vacation: It seems to me that this foolish encounter, this mundane sexual pass based on mistaken assumptions, is the catalyst she needs to get back into life again.

What is best about Tavernier is his feeling for the ordinary currents of everyday life. He creates such empathy between his audiences and his characters that when they fall into a reverie, we have no difficulty imagining their thoughts. In *A Week's Vacation,* he has taken the occasional feeling we all have that we just can't go on any longer, not because of sadness or illness or tragedy, but simply because we have forgotten why we set out in the first place on this journey of life. And he has shown us the answer. The key is in that funny, embarrassing, fumbling little attempt at a kiss: We keep on plugging away because we never know when someone might decide to kiss us, and, better still, because it's so interesting to see how we'll react.

Weird Science ★ ★ ★ ½
PG-13, 94 m., 1985

Anthony Michael Hall (Gary), Kelly LeBrock (Lisa), Ilan Mitchell-Smith (Wyatt), Bill Paxton (Chet), Suzanne Snyder (Deb), Judie Aronson (Hilly). Directed by John Hughes and produced by Joel Silver. Screenplay by Hughes.

Weird Science combines two great traditions in popular entertainment: Inflamed male teen-age fantasies and Frankenstein's monster. Then it crosses them with a new myth, of the teen-age computer geniuses who lock themselves in their bedrooms, hunch over their computer keyboards, and write programs that can change the universe.

In the movie's opening scenes, a couple of bright kids write a program with their specifications for a perfect woman. They feed in centerfolds and magazine covers, measurements and parameters. Then, for additional brain power, they tap into a giant government computer. And at exactly that instant, lightning strikes (just as it did in *The Bride of Frankenstein*), and out of the mix of bytes and kilowatts steps . . . a perfect woman.

She is played by Kelly LeBrock in the movie, and she has full, sensuous lips, and a throaty English accent, and a lot of style. She is a little more than the kids had bargained on. For one thing, she isn't an idealized Playmate, all staples and no brains, but an intelligent, sensitive woman who sees right through these teen-age boys and tries to do them some good.

That's why *Weird Science* is funnier, and a little deeper, than the predictable story it might have been. The movie is the third success in a row for John Hughes, a director who specializes in films about how teen-agers really talk and think. His two earlier films were *Sixteen Candles* and *The Breakfast Club*, and they both featured a young actor named Anthony Michael Hall, who is the co-star of *Weird Science*.

Hall was the geek in *Sixteen Candles* and the intellectual in *Breakfast Club*, and I like John Hughes's definition of a geek: "A geek is a guy who has everything going for him, but he's just too young. By contrast, a nerd will be a nerd all of his life." Hall talks fast, with a sprung rhythm that lets you feel you can hear him thinking. He has the ordinary lusts of a teen-age boy, but once he invents this perfect woman, he is quick to catch on to the advantages: For example, your status in high school is sure to change dramatically if a gorgeous model thinks you're the max.

Hughes's earlier teen-age films depended mostly on character and dialogue (which was fine). This one has a lot of special effects, including some reverse photography that plays tricks with time. But the center of the film is the simple, almost elementary insight that fantasies can be hazardous: You've got to be careful what you ask for, because you might get it. Kelly LeBrock is wonderful as the fantasy woman, because she plays the character, not for sex, but for warmth and an almost motherly affection for these two kids. "All you have to do is command me," she says at one point. "You created me. You are

my master." It could be soft porn, but the way she says it, her voice has a wink.

Welcome Home ★ ★
R, 96 m., 1989

Kris Kristofferson (Jake), JoBeth Williams (Sarah), Sam Waterston (Woody), Brian Keith (Harry), Thomas Wilson Brown (Tyler), Trey Wilson (Colonel Barnes), J.J. (Dwayne), Kieu Chinh (Leang). Directed by Franklin J. Schaffner and produced by Martin Ransohoff. Screenplay by Maggie Kleinman.

Welcome Home opens in 1988 with a sick man being brought to a refugee camp somewhere on the Cambodia-Vietnam border. His name is Lt. Jake Robins (Kris Kristofferson), was in the U.S. Air Force, and he was shot down seventeen years ago. There are some bones in a grave back home in America that are supposed to be his, and his name is engraved on the Vietnam Veterans' Memorial, but he is very much alive. And when he is returned to the United States, he is very embarrassing to the military—because it raises the question of how many other Americans might still be over there in the jungle, as prisoners or by choice.

Robins was not a deserter. He was a prisoner, then he escaped, and then the situation was so tense that the jungle was the safest place to hide. He stayed there and found an Asian wife (Kieu Chinh) and had two children. But now, feverish and hallucinating, he is returned to America without this family. He's treated in a military hospital, cross-examined by an intelligence officer, and then returned to civilian life with the promise that he will keep a low profile.

He goes to see his dad (Brian Keith). He discovers that the woman he married before he left for the war (JoBeth Williams) had a child after he was gone—that he has a seventeen-year-old son. He goes one day to try to catch a glimpse of the son and is seen instead by the wife, and then wounds open up again that had been almost healed. Most of *Welcome Home* is about the fact that Robins is an embarrassment and an inconvenience, because surely once a man is dead and the grieving is over, he should not turn up alive and confuse everyone.

The strength of the movie is that this situation is fully and intelligently discussed by all the characters in the story. No one is made into an easy villain, and nothing is done for

simply melodramatic reasons. The other man in the family—the second husband, played by Sam Waterston—is seen as a sensitive person of almost superhuman forbearance who refuses to be jealous or wounded and keeps his own counsel while trying to help the others discover what they really feel. Much of the turmoil centers on the son (Thomas Wilson Brown), who never knew his father, loves his stepfather, and sees this bearded stranger as a threat to the security of his family.

Kristofferson, who indeed looks as if he has been inhabiting refugee camps, plays the returning veteran as a man of great weariness, determination, and tact (he keeps apologizing for having returned after so many years to disturb a happy family). His obsession is with finding his Asian wife and their children, who were separated from him at the refugee camp, and the emotional weather gets a little stormy when it appears that he may be falling back in love with the JoBeth Williams character.

The movie's intelligence cannot be faulted, but its energy level can be. There is a certain sad, tired, low-key undertow to the film that prevents it from really delivering its emotional content. *Welcome Home* is the last work of its director, Franklin J. Schaffner, whose best film was *Patton*, and who died before the film's release. Perhaps if he had lived to see the film through post-production, he would have tightened it a little or chosen takes that punched up important passages. As it is, the movie sort of rests there on the screen. You can admire it, but you can't feel it as strongly as the material seems to deserve.

Still, there are some fine moments. One of them occurs when Kristofferson's father returns unexpectedly to find his son and his son's first wife in a compromising situation. Another is when Waterston lays it on the line with his character's stepson, telling him to stop worshiping the shrine of medals and photos on his dresser and start celebrating the miracle that brought his dad back alive. The movie's strongest scene should be its very last one (which I will not reveal), but it comes off pale and predictable. I left *Welcome Home* feeling it had the materials to be a great movie, but not the energy.

Welcome Home, Roxy Carmichael
★ ★
PG-13, 98 m., 1990

Winona Ryder (Dinky Bossetti), Jeff Daniels
(Denton Webb), Laila Robins (Guidance
Counselor), Thomas Wilson Brown
(Boyfriend), Frances Fisher (Rochelle Bossetti),
Graham Beckel (Les Bossetti). Directed by Jim
Abrahams and produced by Penney Finkelman
Cox. Screenplay by Karen Leigh Hopkins.

Welcome Home, Roxy Carmichael contains
one small treasure: A perceptive and particular performance by Winona Ryder in the role
of a high school outcast. Her work is surrounded by a screenplay so flat-footed that
much of our time is spent waiting impatiently for foregone conclusions.

Ryder plays Dinky Bossetti, the brightest
girl in the high school. The other kids
have cast her in the role of an outsider, and
she plays the role with some determination,
dressing herself entirely in black, confronting people with unwavering stares, and locking herself into her room. She has a secret life
down by the river near her small Ohio hometown; she's turned an abandoned boat into
an ark where she cares for a menagerie of animals—dogs, goats, pigs, turtles—who all
seem to coexist happily between her visits.

The town is agog because the famous Roxy
Carmichael, who lived there fifteen years
ago, is about to return. The movie never
quite makes clear exactly what Roxy did to
achieve fame (she's a movie star, maybe, or a
singer) but now, on the dawn of her return,
her home has been turned into a shrine and
the local population is preparing for a big
welcome-home dance.

Dinky Bossetti, who has been adopted, is
convinced Roxy is her real mother. That
would mean her real father is Denton Webb
(Jeff Daniels), a local landscaper who once
had an affair with Roxy. Other people involved in her fate include her adoptive parents Rochelle and Les (Frances Fisher and
Graham Beckel), who want to cart her away
to a home for problem children, and her sometime boyfriend (Thomas Wilson Brown), who
likes her but wishes she'd get her act together.

There's enough material here for several
movies, but none of them turn into this one.
It's especially distracting the way the story
cuts to Roxy Carmichael (seen from the neck
down) preparing for her big visit; these shots
suggest an approach that never develops. I
also doubted that the landscaper would have

such an instant rapport with Dinky, that the
landscaper's wife would pick such a contrived fight with him, and that the movie's
realistic soul-searching could coexist in the
same movie's broad and corny humor.

The two relationships that do work are
between Dinky and her boyfriend, and
between Dinky and the guidance counselor
(Laila Robins), who sees through her facade
and really cares for her. These characters give
Dinky an opportunity to reveal a touching and
vulnerable personality—which, combined with
her intelligence, makes her as likeable and
special as the teen-age couple in the wonderful *Say Anything*. Too bad these insights
weren't developed more. Instead, the movie
sinks into contrived plot manipulation.

We're No Angels ★ ★ ★
PG-13, 101 m., 1990

Robert De Niro (Ned/Father Reilly), Sean
Penn (Jim/Father Brown), Demi Moore
(Molly), Hoyt Axton (Father Levesque),
Bruno Kirby (Deputy), Ray McAnally (The
Warden), James Russo (Bobby), Wallace
Shawn (The Translator). Directed by Neil
Jordan and produced by Art Linson.
Screenplay by David Mamet.

Robert De Niro and Sean Penn have two of
the best faces in the movies—screwed up,
sideways faces with a lot of mischief in the
eyes. *We're No Angels* is a movie made for
those faces, and one of the pleasures of
watching the film is to see them looking sidelong at each other as they try to figure a way
out of the complicated mess they're in. The
movie has a lot of other good stuff to look at
(including dramatic period locations in a
small Canadian town) and to listen to (dialogue by David Mamet), but I can think of
no other recent movie in which so much of
the pleasure lies in watching the expressions
on the faces of the actors—especially when
they're reacting, not talking.

The movie is set in the 1930s and stars De
Niro and Penn as a couple of convicts who
are doing hard time in a prison that looks like
it was hammered together out of Sing Sing,
the Bastille, and the underworld in *Mad Max
Beyond Thunderdome*. This is a great, evil,
venal prison, populated by vindictive killers
and sadistic guards, and when De Niro and
Penn escape from it, freedom is like a splash
of cold air in their faces: They go tumbling
down snowy slopes in a desolate forest wil-

derness, until they get a lift from an old lady
and end up in a small border town.

Their objective: To cross the bridge that
spans the river between the U.S. and Canada.
Their problem: They have been mistaken for
two priests and have been given shelter in the
local monastery. Their solution: To go along
with the gag and pretend to be priests, even
though anyone in his right mind could plainly
see they're fugitives from a 1930s prison movie.

Mamet and Neil Jordan, who directed the
movie, wisely remember the most important
thing about any mistaken-identity comedy:
The fact that someone's identity is mistaken
is not always funny even the first time and
rarely thereafter. Movies that depend on mistaken identities for their laughs are among
the slowest, dreariest slogs through cinema.
What's important is that the heroes be funny
no matter who people think they are—and
that the other characters be funny even despite the mistakes they're making.

Most of the characters in *We're No Angels*
pass that test, especially the crew at the local
monastery (Hoyt Axton as the prior, Ken Bu-
hay as a foreign bishop who insists on saying
grace, and Wallace Shawn as the bishop's translator). Demi Moore has an important supporting role as a local woman with a child who is
attracted to De Niro, but because no comic spin
was put on her character, her scenes don't add
much. They provide, in fact, a serious undercurrent that the movie doesn't necessarily need.

These days a lot of movies are shot on location, but I've rarely seen a location used
more effectively than in *We're No Angels*,
where the small town of Mission, in British
Columbia, has been dressed to match the
Depression era. The town, the surrounding
peaks, the river, and the waterfall provide a
genuine sense of place. De Niro and Penn
are both essentially serious dramatic actors,
and maybe the reality of the location gave
them such a solid grounding that they felt
they had permission for the necessary goofiness.

Wetherby ★ ★ ★ ★
R, 118 m., 1985

Vanessa Redgrave (Jean Travers), Ian Holm
(Stanley Pilborough), Judi Dench (Marcia
Pilborough), Marjorie Yates (Verity
Braithwaite), Tim McInnerny (John Morgan),
Suzanna Hamilton (Karen Creasy), Joely
Richardson (Young Jean). Directed by David
Hare and produced by Simon Relph.
Screenplay by Hare.

A man kills himself among strangers. They never knew who he was, and they do not know why he chose to die. A man dying among strangers is like a tree falling unobserved in the forest. Death, especially suicide, requires resonance from those who knew the living person before it can be assigned its proper meaning. That is why *Wetherby* is such a haunting film, because it dares to suggest that the death of the stranger is important to everyone it touches—because it forces them to decide how alive they really are.

The movie begins with a woman who is living a sort of dead life. Her name is Jean Travers (played by Vanessa Redgrave); she was once in love with a young man who went off to fight the war and was killed. He was not killed gloriously, but stupidly, while getting involved in someone else's drunken quarrel, but he was dead all the same. As the movie opens, Jean has been teaching school in the small town of Wetherby, where her life is on hold. She doesn't walk around in a state of depression, she does have friends, she is a good teacher, but she is not engaged in life because she put all of her passion into the boy who died so many years ago.

One night she throws a small dinner party. Everyone drinks wine and sits around late, talking. One of the men at the table, John Morgan, sits mute all evening and finally makes a short speech about pain and love and honesty that sounds as if every word were written with his own bitter tears. The next day, John Morgan comes back to Jean's house, sits down for a cup of tea, and kills himself. A funny thing comes out in the investigation: John Morgan was not known to any of the people at the dinner party. Apparently he invited himself.

The film moves from this beginning into an examination of the people who were touched by the death. In addition to Jean, there are the Pilboroughs (Ian Holm and Judi Dench), the local constable (Tom Wilkinson), and a young woman (Suzanna Hamilton) who knew the dead man. Some small suspense develops for a while when it appears that Jean spent some time upstairs with John Morgan during the evening of her party—but that, and many other things, seem to be dead ends.

The movie flashes back into events in Jean's youth, and she is played as a young girl by Joely Richardson, Redgrave's daughter. There is an innocence and tenderness in those early scenes, as young Jean and her

boyfriend kiss and neck and make promises, and as Jean gradually realizes that she is looking forward to marriage but he is much more excited by the prospect of putting on a uniform and going overseas. He goes overseas, and in some ways this movie is about the fact that Jean has become a middle-aged woman still waiting for him to come back.

Wetherby was written and directed by David Hare, who also wrote the film *Plenty.* Both films are about women who were never able to fully live their lives after what happened to them during the War. I admire both films, but I found *Wetherby* more moving, because the heroine of *Plenty* was essentially a disturbed woman using her war memories as a crutch, and Jean Travers is a whole and healthy woman who only needs to give herself the permission to live. I left the movie thinking that was the lesson she learned from John Morgan. Hoping so, anyway.

The Whales of August ★ ★ ★
NO MPAA RATING, 90 m., 1987

Bette Davis (Libby Strong), Lillian Gish (Sarah Webber), Vincent Price (Mr. Maranov), Ann Sothern (Tisha Doughty), Harry Carey, Jr. (Joshua), Frank Grimes (Mr. Beckwith), Mary Steenburgen (Young Sarah). Directed by Lindsay Anderson and produced by Carolyn Pfeiffer and Mike Kaplan. Screenplay by David Berry.

The two old women have been at war for years, until they have become beloved enemies. Now death is near for both of them—not today or tomorrow or perhaps even this year, but before long. For decades, since they were children, they have returned to this old cottage on an island off the coast of Maine, where in August it has been their custom to watch at twilight as the whales pass on their journeys to wherever it is that whales go. Although they make plans for the future and argue over whether they should install a new picture window, there is the sense that this will be their last summer in the cottage.

That is the story. As stories go, it is conventional enough, but in *The Whales of August,* as in grand opera, the story is only the occasion for the performances. This film stars Lillian Gish and Bette Davis, and to cast those two actresses as the leads of the same movie is to make their very presences more important than anything else. This is not their fault, nor do they use it as the occasion for self-conscious acting, for any inap-

propriate drawing of attention to themselves. It is just a fact.

Lillian Gish, who was born in 1896, was the star of D.W. Griffith's *The Birth of a Nation* (1915), the first great narrative film. She appeared in some 150 movies before and since. Bette Davis, who was born in 1908, was one of the great movie queens of Hollywood's golden age. Together they make this movie into the kind of project that filmmakers dream about but are rarely about to arrange. They are supported in the film by two other actors who bring a lot of memories onscreen with them: Vincent Price and Ann Sothern.

The film mostly takes place during the course of one day, which ends in a birthday dinner party and a good deal of truth. It begins with Gish and Davis gingerly talking around many of the issues that have divided them for years—and some of the issues, we feel, are not nearly so important to them as the simple satisfaction of being right, of prevailing in a personality struggle that has continued since childhood. Gish is the older sister, but in slightly better health. Davis, whose character is blind, has the blind person's love of order and continuity, as a way of finding her way around not only a familiar house but a familiar life.

Nothing of great moment happens during the day, but many small moments occur. One of them, the most touching, is Gish's quiet "private time" with the memory of her late husband. She speaks to him in a monologue that is not only moving but surprisingly passionate. Another special moment occurs when the two sisters walk out on the lawn to look for the whales, which only Gish can see. And I liked the subtle verbal gamesmanship that was the real subject of most of their conversations.

Many of the crucial moments in the movie play mostly in close-up, and I could not help meditating on these famous faces as I watched them. At her great age, Gish still sometimes looks girlish, capable of teasing and practical jokes, but the moment when she lets her hair down in front of the portrait of her dead husband is a revelation, because it contains a genuine erotic content, a sense of memory of her character's romance with this man. Davis contains surprises, too. In so many of the roles in the third act of her career, her face was a painted mask of makeup—not out of vanity, but because she was often cast as a painted madwoman or harpy. Here, devoid of much makeup, her features emerge with strength and a kind of peace that is no longer denying age. Both women, in other words, are beautiful.

Against such competition, supporting actors have their work cut out. Ann Sothern is sensible and cheery as a neighbor woman, who has shared the lives of these sisters for many years and accepts them. She is sort of a peacemaker, whose life lacks the complexity that the sisters' long struggle has created. The other major character in the film is the old aristocrat, down on his luck, played by Vincent Price with a self-deprecating humor that creates dignity out of thin air. Mr. Maranov, his character, was once a "real" member of European nobility, but now has no money and no prospects, and depends on the kindness of strangers. His previous sponsor has died, and now he is searching for someone else to support him. He knows this, and everyone else knows it, and yet he still retains a certain nobility, even as a beggar. It is an interesting character.

The movie was directed by Lindsay Anderson, whose previous films have been nothing at all like this one, to put it mildly. After *This Sporting Life*, *If*, *O Lucky Man*, and *Britannia Hospital*, here is a quiet film of a conventional story, a star vehicle designed to show everyone to advantage. This is not one of Anderson's great films, but he succeeds at the assignment he has set himself. There is a story that during the filming of *The Whales of August*, Anderson told Miss Gish one day that she had just performed wonderfully in a close-up. "She should," Miss Davis declared. "She invented them."

When Harry Met Sally . . . ★ ★ ★
R, 95 m., 1989

Billy Crystal (Harry Burns), Meg Ryan (Sally Albright), Carrie Fisher (Marie), Bruno Kirby (Jess), Steven Ford (Joe), Lisa Jane Persky (Alice), Michelle Nicastro (Amanda). Directed by Rob Reiner and produced by Reiner and Andrew Scheinman. Screenplay by Nora Ephron.

When Harry Met Sally . . . is a love story with a form as old as the movies and dialogue as new as this month's issue of *Vanity Fair*. It's about two people who could be characters in a Woody Allen movie if they weren't so sunny, and about how it takes them thirteen years to fall in love. We're with them, or maybe a little ahead of them, every step of the way.

Harry meets Sally for the first time at the University of Chicago in the spring of 1977, when they team up to share the driving for a trip to New York. Both plan to start their careers in the city—she as a journalist, he as a labor organizer. Presumably they are both successful, since they live in those apartments that only people in the movies can afford, but their professional lives are entirely offscreen. We see them only at those intervals when they see each other.

They meet, for example, three years later, at LaGuardia. She's with a new boyfriend. They meet a few years after that, when they're both in relationships, and a few years after that, when her boyfriend has left and his wife wants a divorce. They keep on meeting until they realize that they like one another and they become friends, even though on their very first cross-country trip Harry warned Sally that true friendship is impossible between a man and a woman because the issue of sex always gets in the way.

The movie apparently believes that—and it also suggests that the best way to get rid of sex as an issue is to get married, since married people always seem too tired for sex. That and other theories about sex and relationships are tested as if Harry and Sally were a proving grounds for *Cosmopolitan*, until finally, tired of fighting, they admit that they do love one another after all.

The movie was written by Nora Ephron, and could be a prequel to her novel and screenplay *Heartburn*, which starred Jack Nicholson and Meryl Streep in the story of a marriage and divorce. But this marriage seems headed for happier times, maybe because most of the big fights are out of the way before love is even declared. Harry is played by Billy Crystal and Sally is Meg Ryan, and they make a good movie couple because both actors are able to suggest genuine warmth and tenderness. This isn't a romance of passion, although passion is present, but one that becomes possible only because the two people have grown up together, have matured until they can finally see clearly what they really want in a partner.

Ephron's dialogue represents the way people would like to be able to talk. It's witty and epigrammatic, and there are lots of lines to quote when you're telling friends about the movie. The dialogue would defeat many actors, but Crystal and Ryan help it to work; their characters seem smart and quick enough to almost be this witty. It's only occasionally that the humor is paid for at the expense of credibility—as in a hilarious but

unconvincing scene where Sally sits in a crowded restaurant and demonstrates how to fake an orgasm. I laughed, but somehow I didn't think Sally, or any woman, would really do that.

When Harry Met Sally . . . was directed by Rob Reiner, the onetime Meathead of "All in the Family," whose credits now qualify him as one of Hollywood's very best directors of comedy (his films include *The Sure Thing*, *Stand by Me*, *This is Spinal Tap*, and *The Princess Bride*—each film completely different from the others, each one successful on its own terms). This film is probably his most conventional, in terms of structure and the way it fulfills our expectations, but what makes it special, apart from the Ephron screenplay, is the chemistry between Crystal and Ryan.

She is an open-faced, bright-eyed blonde; he's a gentle, skinny man with a lot of smart one-liners. What they both have (to repeat) is warmth. Crystal demonstrated that quality in his previous film, the underrated *Memories of Me*, and it's here again this time, in scenes when he visibly softens when he sees that he has hurt her. He is one of the rare actors who can make an apology on the screen and convince us he means it. Ryan (from *Innerspace* and *D.O.A.*) has a difficult assignment—she spends most of the movie convincing Harry, and herself, that there's nothing between them—and she has to let us see that there is something, after all.

Harry and Sally are aided, and sometimes hindered, in their romance by the efforts of their two best friends (Carrie Fisher and Bruno Kirby), who meet on a blind date arranged by Harry and Sally to provide possible partners for Sally and Harry. They're the kind of people who don't make it hard for themselves, who realize they like each other, accept that fact, and act on it. Harry and Sally are tougher customers. They fight happiness every step of the way, until it finally wears them down.

Where the Heart Is ★ ½
R, 94 m., 1990

Dabney Coleman (Stewart McBain), Uma Thurman (Daphne), Joanna Cassidy (Jean), Crispin Glover (Lionel), Suzy Amis (Chloe), Christopher Plummer (Homeless Man), David Hewlett (Jimmy), Maury Chaykin (Harry), Dylan Walsh (Tom), Ken Pogue (Hamilton), Sheila Kelley (Sheryl). Directed and produced by John Boorman. Screenplay by Telsche Boorman and John Boorman.

Where the Heart Is was originally set to be filmed in London, according to a press release about the film. Then the studio suggested that director John Boorman transpose the story to New York, which he did. Perhaps that was the initial mistake right there—taking a story that might have been believable with British characters and removing it to a city where it's not an easy fit.

The story stars Dabney Coleman as a man who makes his living by tearing down buildings. He has his sights set on a Brooklyn landmark named the Dutch Building, which looks to him like an eyesore but to preservation groups like an irreplaceable piece of architectural history. The preservationists win, and Coleman is stuck with the building. Meanwhile, he is also saddled with a houseful of grown children who would rather soak up free room and board than go out into the world and pay their own way. Coleman sees a way to kill two birds with one stone by ordering his children out of his house and into the Dutch Building.

Am I crazy in not seeing this as a New York story? I can picture it in London, taking place right down the street from where the property speculators had their eyes on the boarding house where Madame Sousatzka gave her lessons. But Brooklyn somehow seems like a tougher and less forgiving environment, especially in this movie's neighborhood, where hookers parade the streets, the homeless are everywhere, and three lazy rich kids would turn into instant targets.

The movie's screenplay was written by director John Boorman and his daughter, Telsche, and it shows signs of leftover Britishness, especially in the way it sees street people and neighborhood characters as essentially benevolent and colorful. So they may be, in the films of Frank Capra, but by failing to create a convincing reality for their city neighborhood, the filmmakers reveal it for what it is, a set. (Appearances can be deceiving: One of the ways the movie created a kinder, gentler Brooklyn was by shooting most of the film on location in Toronto.)

In British movies like *Getting It Right* or *A Fish Called Wanda*, we meet characters who are all more or less eccentrics and grotesques (in the Sherwood Anderson sense of the word—grotesque because one attribute of their personality has been magnified out of all proportion). In Britain, such peculiarities are prized; in this country people have less time or will to develop themselves into collectors' items. Although we have our share of

human oddities, they do not operate with the smugness of a British eccentric who is absolutely delighted to be himself.

That's one of the problems with the Dabney Coleman character: He seems too much like a plausible demolition contractor and not enough like the kind of preposterous buffoon whose set ideas about the world could create comedy. He blusters early in the film about the demonstrators who want to save the Dutch Building. But his British counterpart would be outraged by the mere existence of such people. Lurking beneath every would-be eccentric in this film is an essentially reasonable person.

That's the case with a character like Chloe (Suzy Amis), one of Coleman's daughters, whose art combines the body-painting of friends with the backgrounds of famous paintings, so that the friends seem to be part of the paintings. The paintings, created for the film by the artist Timma Woollard, are beautiful and interesting, but Chloe seems more like a promising young artist on the way up than the obsessed goofy genius we might have been amused by. Another character, a fashion designer named Lionel (Crispin Glover), moves into the Dutch Building while readying his latest collection; once again, he seems too plausible to be funny. And such characters as the daughter Daphne (Uma Thurman) are so completely normal that we sense comic opportunities being lost on every side.

Where the Heart Is is essentially a fable set in the wrong city. Its story doesn't fit in New York or seem correctly placed in 1990; it's not quick-witted or street-smart enough. It seems to exist in some movie never-land where characters do what they're supposed to do, for essentially good reasons, and the happy ending comes when everybody sees the light. There are some awfully nice people in the cast. They ought to go back to wherever they came from. They'll be happier there.

Who Framed Roger Rabbit ★ ★ ★ ★
PG, 103 m., 1988

Bob Hoskins (Eddie Valiant), Christopher Lloyd (Judge Doom), Joanna Cassidy (Dolores), Charles Fleischer (Roger's voice), Stubby Kaye (Marvin Acme). Directed by Robert Zemeckis and produced by Robert Watts and Frank Marshall. Screenplay by Jeffrey Price and Peter S. Seaman.

I stopped off at a hot dog stand before the screening of *Who Framed Roger Rabbit*, and ran into a couple of the other local movie critics. They said they were going to the same screening. I asked them what they'd heard about the film. They said they were going to see it for the second time in two days. That's the kind of word of mouth that money can't buy.

And *Who Framed Roger Rabbit* is the kind of movie that gets made once in a blue moon, because it represents an immense challenge to the filmmakers: They have to make a good movie while inventing new technology at the same time. Like *2001, Close Encounters*, and *E.T.*, this movie is not only a great entertainment, but a breakthrough in craftsmanship—the first film to convincingly combine real actors and animated cartoon characters in the same space in the same time and make it look real.

I've never seen anything like it before. Roger Rabbit and his cartoon comrades cast real shadows. They shake the hands and grab the coats and rattle the teeth of real actors. They change size and dimension and perspective as they move through a scene, and the camera isn't locked down in one place to make it easy, either—the camera in this movie moves around like it's in a 1940s thriller, and the cartoon characters look three-dimensional and seem to be occupying real space.

In a way, what you feel when you see a movie like this is more than appreciation. It's gratitude. You know how easy it is to make dumb, no-brainer action movies, and how incredibly hard it is to make a movie like this, where every minute of screen time can take days or weeks of work by the animators. You're glad they went to the trouble. The movie is a collaboration between the Disney studio and Steven Spielberg, the direction is by Robert (*Back to the Future*) Zemeckis, and the animation is by Raymond Williams. They made this a labor of love.

How did they do it? First they plotted every scene, shot by shot, so they knew where the live actors would be, and where the animated characters would be. Then they shot the live action, forcing actors like Bob Hoskins, the star, to imagine himself in a world also inhabited by cartoons (or "Toons," as the movie calls them). Then they laboriously went through the movie frame by frame, drawing in the cartoon characters. This is not a computer job. Real, living animators did this by hand, and the effort shows in moments like the zowie zoom shots where the camera hurtles at Roger Rabbit and then careens away, with the rabbit changing size and perspective in every frame.

But I'm making the movie sound like homework for a movie class. *Who Framed Roger Rabbit* is sheer, enchanted entertainment from the first frame to the last—a joyous, giddy, goofy celebration of the kind of fun you can have with a movie camera. The film takes place in Hollywood in 1947, in a world where humans and Toons exist side by side. The Toons in the movie include not only new characters like Roger Rabbit and his wife, the improbably pneumatic Jessica, but also established cartoon stars like Bugs Bunny, Betty Boop, Dumbo, Mickey Mouse, and both of the great ducks, Donald and Daffy (they do an act together as a piano duo).

The Toons live in Toontown, a completely animated world where the climax of the movie takes place, but most of the time they hang out in a version of Hollywood that looks like it was borrowed from a 1940s private-eye movie. The plot revolves around the murder of a movie tycoon, and when Roger Rabbit is framed for the murder, private eye Hoskins gets caught in the middle of the action. As plots go, this one will be familiar to anyone who has ever seen a hard-boiled '40s crime movie—except, of course, for the Toons.

The movie is funny, but it's more than funny, it's exhilarating. It opens with what looks like a standard studio cartoon (Mother goes shopping and leaves Roger Rabbit to baby-sit her little brat, who immediately starts causing trouble). This cartoon itself, seen apart from the movie, is a masterpiece; I can't remember the last time I laughed so hard at an animated short. But then, when a stunt goes wrong and the cartoon "baby" stalks off the set and lights a cigar and tells the human director to go to hell, we know we're in a new and special universe.

The movie is filled with throwaway gags, inside jokes, one-liners, and little pokes at the screen images of its cartoon characters. It is also oddly convincing, not only because of the craft of the filmmakers, but also because Hoskins and the other live actors have found the right note for their interaction with the Toons. Instead of overreacting or playing up their emotions cartoon-style, Hoskins and the others adopt a flat, realistic, matter-of-fact posture toward the Toons. They act as if they've been talking to animated rabbits for years.

One tricky question is raised by a movie like this: Is it for kids, or adults, or both? I think it's intended as a universal entertainment, like *E.T.* or *The Wizard of Oz*, aimed at all audiences. But I have a sneaky hunch that adults will appreciate it even more than kids, because they'll have a better appreciation of how difficult it was to make, and how effortlessly it succeeds. Kids will love it too—but instead of being amazed at how they got the rabbits in with the humans, they'll be wondering what adults are doing walking around inside a cartoon.

The Whistle Blower ★ ★ ★ ½
PG, 100 m., 1987

Michael Caine (Frank Jones), James Fox (Lord), Nigel Havers (Bob Jones), Felicity Dean (Cynthia Goodburn), John Gielgud (Sir Adrian Chappel), Kenneth Colley (Bill Pickett), Gordon Jackson (Bruce). Directed by Simon Langton and produced by Geoffrey Reeve. Screenplay by Julian Bond.

The Whistle Blower is about the British spy establishment, but at first it doesn't feel at all like a spy movie. It begins as the quiet account of the daily life of a middle-aged man who has set up in the office equipment business and who almost welcomes his anonymity. He was once in intelligence, he was once at the center of important matters, but now he has put all that behind him.

The man is played by Michael Caine, with a quiet self-effacement that is very convincing. He is mild and soft-spoken, and it is clear that to some extent he is living his life through the life of his son, whom he loves very much. The son is a likable, disorganized, untidy, very serious young man who is in love with an older woman with children.

Caine is not sure this is the right relationship, but in his performance there are a few quiet, crucial moments when he seems to do nothing—he just sort of stands there in a shot, regarding those around him—and you can feel his hope that his son will be happy.

Caine is such a good actor that he doesn't overplay those moments or indeed seem to play them at all. Yet they underlie the whole film. We begin by understanding that Caine has placed action behind him, we identify with his new emotional calm, we sense his love for his son and that prepares us for everything that follows.

It is important that I not reveal, however, too much of what follows. *The Whistle Blower* is not a conventional spy thriller, but it does depend upon surprises and unexpected revelations of character, and they grow naturally out of the story. In general terms, I can say that Caine's son becomes a pawn in an intelligence game with much higher stakes and that what Caine eventually comes to understand is that little people such as himself and his son are expendable in the view of the entrenched establishment that rules the country.

Like another British thriller, *Defence of the Realm*, this movie uses the British spy apparatus as a way of dramatizing the class distinctions that still exist in Britain. The Caine character is in reaction against the feeling that nothing—not God, not the throne, not patriotism, certainly not security considerations—is as important as defending a network of privilege. The crucial moment in the film comes when Caine accuses a traitor of letting innocent people die, just so that he can continue to have tea with the queen. The steps by which Caine arrives at this speech are what the movie is about.

The Whistle Blower was hardly ahead of the headlines in Britain. The Spycatcher controversy had the country in an uproar against the action of five bewigged Law Lords, solemnly forbidding the press from printing details from a book that was a worldwide bestseller. The book alleges, of course, that a head of British intelligence was a Soviet mole from the start, the same assumption *The Whistle Blower* is founded on.

Despite a few obligatory scenes of threats and violence, most of the action in the movie takes place within the mind of the Caine character. Having taken his leave of Hollywood with the truly dreadful *Jaws the Revenge*, Caine returned to England in three quite different performances: this one, the slimy Soho mob boss in *Mona Lisa*, and the maverick spy who tries to prevent a nuclear explosion in *The Fourth Protocol*. The three performances are completely different, and yet it is hard to see what Caine does differently in them. He has the same dry, flat inflection, the sometimes masked face, the way of seeming to stand completely impassively until action is called for, the sense of enormous reserves of strength and anger banked inside. Yet in *Mona Lisa* he is a villain, in this film he is a decent, angry man, and in *The Fourth Protocol* he is more of an action hero.

It all seems to come from inside. The one

thing you will rarely catch Caine doing in a movie is seeming to go for an effect. Maybe that's why he achieves them so consistently; the screen is a magnifying glass that rarely forgives excess.

What's especially nice about *The Whistle Blower* is that it never quite lets plot become more important than character. Like a novel by Graham Greene, it isn't really about what happens, but about how the events feel to the characters and how they change them. There is a scene in this movie, a quiet walk and talk between father and son, that is as touching a portrait of parenthood as any I can remember.

White Fang ★ ★ ★
PG, 104 m., 1991

Klaus Maria Brandauer (Alex), Ethan Hawke (Jack), Seymour Cassel (Skunker), Susan Hogan (Belinda), James Remar (Beauty), Bill Mosely (Luke). Directed by Randal Kleiser and produced by Marykay Powell. Screenplay by Jeanne Rosenberg, Nick Thiel, and David Fallon.

Jack London's great novel *White Fang*, which held me in its spell when I was ten and again thirty years later, is the story of a dog, and the dog's journey through many kinds of human habitations, under many kinds of masters. Much of that story can be glimpsed in this new film of *White Fang*, although not so distinctly, because the movie is the story of a boy and not a dog.

The boy's name is Jack (Ethan Hawke), and he has come out to the Yukon in 1898 to prospect his dad's claim in the great Gold Rush. He meets up with a couple of prospectors (Klaus Maria Brandauer and Seymour Cassel), and they travel by dogsled into the wilderness of the Arctic winter. Their adventures are intercut with the early days of White Fang, a wolf with some dog blood, whose mother is killed when he is a pup. White Fang is captured by Indians, then traded to men who train him for dog fights, and then finally comes into the possession of Jack, who takes him along when he goes to live at the claim.

The London novel was intended as a comparison of dogs and men, in which most men came up short. In the book, the dog eventually becomes the property of a mining engineer, who takes it back to a sunny retirement in California. The Disney version, of course, transmutes the adult into Jack the

teen-ager, and ends with a joyous reunion of man and beast after the human decides not to go to California after all, but heed the call of the wild. Jack has good reason to stick with White Fang, who by the end of the film has saved him from being eaten by a bear and killed by thieving claim jumpers.

We are agreed then, that the movie makes no serious claim to be a version of the Jack London novel. (That project would be mostly about dogs, and require patience on the order of the 1989 film, *The Bear*, which took a year to film because each of the animal movements had to be separately photographed. Fans of *The Bear* will be pleased that its star, Bart, makes a guest appearance here.) *White Fang* is, however, a superior entertainment on its own terms, a story of pluck and survival at a time when men poured into the Yukon dreaming of riches, and found mostly disease and death.

The movie is magnificently photographed on location. The performances are authentic and understated, and Brandauer makes a convincing veteran prospector, part hard-bitten, part dreamer. As the boy, Ethan Hawke is properly callow at the beginning and properly matured at the end, although it's all he can do to carry off the final joyous reunion with the dog. And the dog itself (played by Jed) is a fine-looking, intelligent animal so good at displaying its fangs that I actually believed it could scare off a bear.

Movies like this are an antidote to the violent and defeatist thrillers a lot of younger moviegoers seem to be hooked on. It's an adventure, it's exciting, it stirs the imagination, and there are scenes of terrific suspense—as when Jack ventures out on that thin ice, or gets cornered by the bear. Like *The Black Stallion*, *Never Cry Wolf*, and *Crusoe*, it's a film that holds the natural world in wonder and awe. And it might even inspire someone to read the novels of Jack London, who was such a good writer he could tell a story that I fell in love with when I was ten years old and much harder to please than I am now.

White Hunter, Black Heart ★ ★ ★
PG, 112 m., 1990

Clint Eastwood (John Wilson), Jeff Fahey (Pete Verrill), Charlotte Cornwell (Miss Wilding), Norman Lumsden (Butler George), George Dzundza (Paul Landers), Edward Tudor Pole (Reissar), Marisa Berenson (Kay Gibson). Directed and produced by Clint

Eastwood. Screenplay by Peter Viertel, James Bridges, and Burt Kennedy.

Film directors have to be a little like God, convinced that they have the correct answer to every question, and the responsibility to impose their opinion on everyone around them. Nice-guy directors—those praised for listening to their colleagues, keeping an open mind, and encouraging their actors to improvise—rarely make great movies. Great directors are routinely described as mean sons of bitches, but there is awe in the voices describing them.

John Huston was not, by most accounts, a nice guy. He ran roughshod over marriages, friendships, and responsibilities, he had a habit of losing interest in a project halfway through, and he indulged his passions for horses, drink, gambling, and women as if he had the divine right to be supplied endlessly with same. In his last years, crippled by emphysema, he nevertheless did present his daughter Anjelica with the role of her career in *Prizzi's Honor*, and he grew closer to his other children, helping their careers while he somehow struggled through the making of *The Dead*—a brave film he correctly predicted would be his last.

Huston was a legend, larger than life, and his best films were about men something like himself. The actor who mirrored Huston the best was Humphrey Bogart, in *The Maltese Falcon*, *Treasure of the Sierra Madre*, and *The African Queen*, and it is Huston's making of the *Queen* that supplied Clint Eastwood with the subject for *White Hunter, Black Heart*.

The original screenplay for *The African Queen* was adapted from C.S. Forester's novel by James Agee, a hard-drinking, hard-smoking writer, who Huston expected to drink all night with him, be his tennis partner in the morning, and his collaborator in the afternoon. This regimen probably hastened the heart attack that brought an end to Agee's work on the *Queen*, and when Huston went to Africa with Bogart and Katharine Hepburn to film the movie, he took along a young writer named Peter Viertel, who did the final version of the screenplay.

Viertel was a privileged observer to what has become one of the legendary location shoots of Hollywood history, and his novel from the mid-1950s, *White Hunter, Black Heart*, was obviously based on the experience. It did not paint a flattering portrait of "John Wilson," the Huston character, who was more concerned with shooting an elephant than shooting a movie. After he finished the novel, Viertel told me, he sent it to Huston, who—to give him his due—said he enjoyed it and did nothing to prevent its publication. Huston was not a hypocrite and did not pretend to be other than he was.

Now comes Clint Eastwood to produce and direct the long-delayed film of Viertel's book, and to star as John Huston, familiar accent and all. It must have taken some nerve for Eastwood to tackle this project. It is hard enough for a famous movie actor to disappear into a character who is not himself—but almost impossible for him to disappear into another famous character, into someone equally legendary and familiar.

In the early scenes of *White Hunter, Black Heart*, Eastwood fans are likely to be distracted to hear Huston's words and vocal mannerisms in Eastwood's mouth, and to see Huston's swagger and physical bravado. Then the performance takes over, and the movie turns into a thoughtful film about the conflicts inside an artist. Huston emerges as a strong-willed, intelligent man who, nevertheless, places his own desires above his ideals, who rails at Hollywood's dishonesty and yet is not above keeping an expensive film on hold while he abandons his location to go elephant shooting.

Why does he want so badly to shoot an elephant? Perhaps because he has not shot one before. Perhaps to prove he is brave. Perhaps to give the elephant the privilege of being shot by John Huston. The obsession wraps itself around his evasions and self-justifications until the character's motive is hardly important; he is selfish enough that he will do it simply because he wants to.

There is a lot more to *White Hunter, Black Heart* than this description suggests. I especially enjoyed the verbal fencing matches between Eastwood and George Dzundza, as his producer, and his confidences and confessions to Jeff Fahey, in the Viertel role. But what it comes down to is a man who puts his career on hold and keeps his colleagues waiting while he indulges in his own determined ego-gratification.

Why did Eastwood make this movie? At one time I thought it was an attack on the Hollywood where he has functioned as a particularly successful outsider. Now I wonder if it isn't also intended as a contrast to some of the action heroes he's played in other movies. The Eastwood hero almost always does what he damn well pleases. Here is a movie about a man who does what he pleases, but it doesn't make him a hero.

White Mischief ★ ★ ★
R, 100 m., 1988

Sarah Miles (Alice), Joss Ackland (Broughton), John Hurt (Colville), Greta Scacchi (Diana), Charles Dance (Erroll), Susan Fleetwood (Gwladys), Alan Dobie (Harragin), Hugh Grant (Hugh), Jacqueline Pearce (Idina), Catherine Neilson (June), Trevor Howard (Soames). Directed by Michael Radford. Produced by Simon Perry. Screenplay by Radford and Jonathan Gems, based on the book by James Fox.

In the years between the first and second world wars, the more affluent British settlers in Kenya developed a lifestyle that became famous for its luxury and scandalous for its decadence. In their so-called Happy Valley, on the slopes of the Aberdare mountains, where the climate was close to home, they built their ranches and villages, made a lot of money, and tried to ignore the war clouds gathering over Europe. Some of them worked hard and most of them partied hard, and as war grew closer their detachment seemed more and more of a scandal.

Then, on the eve of war, the settlement was rocked by a murder that is still one of the most famous crimes of the British Empire, the crime at the center of *White Mischief*. An older rancher, Sir Henry Jock Broughton (Joss Ackland) had returned from a trip to England with a wild young bride named Diana (Greta Scacchi). She had married for money, a fact Jock had few illusions about, but what he did not expect was that she would so quickly flaunt her cynicism in the colony. She fell under the power of the handsome young Earl of Erroll (Charles Dance), a shameless womanizer, and their affair scandalized the colony until the day of January 24, 1941, when the Earl was found shot dead in his car, not far from an exclusive club where he had last been seen with Diana.

Jock Broughton was charged with the murder, but eventually was acquitted, and the case remains officially unsolved to this day. The one survivor who might have been sure about the identity of the killer, Diana Broughton, died a few years ago. But the case lives on in British memory, partly because it occurred in a colony that was living in luxury while the homeland itself was enduring the Battle of Britain and the terrors of World War II.

White Mischief is an elegant, almost luxurious, retelling of the story of Jock, Diana, and the earl, filmed on location in Kenya at great expense, and forming a sort of companion piece to *Out of Africa*, which takes place in East Africa at the beginning of the same era but among much different sorts of people. In the movie, the period is lovingly restored—the clothes, the cars, the rambling architecture, the lifestyle that could not conceive that Kenya would ever be independent, and was scarcely able to even see racism, much less decry it. Happy Valley is seen as a society of narcissists, in love with their own beauty and idle charm, and existing primarily to drink and to gossip.

In this society, Jock is a figure of some dignity at first. Erect and proud in middle age, he is Establishment through and through. But he makes the mistake of falling in love with the beautiful young Diana, and he makes another mistake, too—he goes broke. Diana is carefree as the wind, and hardly even wants to hurt Jock's feelings. She is simply too selfish and irresponsible to think much about them. When the Earl of Erroll sees the opportunity for an entertaining affair, both he and Diana make the mistake of underestimating Jock—of pushing him too far, too publicly.

The film was directed by Michael Radford (who also made the recent version of *1984*), and he goes for atmosphere rather than plot. I think that is the right decision. A languorous scene at a party gradually trails down into a lazy, low-key orgy, and the tone is just right: These people are almost too comfortable to be perverted. Radford is especially good at finding the tensions in a party scene, where various couples are changing partners and not everybody likes it, but nobody misses it.

One of the keys to the movie's re-creation of Happy Valley is in the large supporting cast, including John Hurt as a rough-hewn local farmer who is also in love with Diana; Sarah Miles as a promiscuous local woman whose affairs feed the gossip mills; and the late Trevor Howard, in his last performance, as a local landowner who tries to give Jock some good advice. All of these people come together to create a genuinely interesting period piece, in which nobody is quite sure who shot the Earl of Erroll, but most people would agree he had it coming to him.

White Palace ★ ★ ★ ½
R, 103 m., 1990

Susan Sarandon (Nora Baker), James Spader (Max Baron), Jason Alexander (Neil), Kathy Bates (Rosemary), Eileen Brennan (Judy), Spiros Focas (George), Jeremy Piven (Kahn). Directed by Luis Mandoki and produced by Mark Rosenberg, Amy Robinson, and Griffin Dunne. Screenplay by Ted Tally and Alvin Sargent.

"I'm forty-three years old," she tells him. "On my next birthday I'm going to be forty-four."

"I'm twenty-seven," he says.

They look at each other, and then they fall into each other's arms, in a spontaneous expression of sexual passion. The moment gets a laugh, because we like it when movie characters allow their emotions to overcome them. But the underlying issue is more serious. This couple isn't "appropriate" for each other. A lot of people are made uncomfortable by May-December romances, especially when it's the woman who's the older party.

White Palace was billed as a Cinderella story like *Pretty Woman.* But there are some differences. This time, it's not a rich executive falling in love with a gorgeous hooker, but a young ad executive falling for an older woman who's a waitress down at the local hamburger joint. Also, there's some doubt about who stands to benefit most from the relationship: The young man, who is uptight and distant, or the older woman, who knows how to be honest and is also (as a song on the sound track reminds us) at her sexual prime.

The executive, played by James Spader, is told several times by women in the movie that he has beautiful eyes and is really good-looking. Neither the compliments nor much of anything else seem to reach him. He's shut down emotionally since his young wife was killed in an auto accident. The woman, played by Susan Sarandon, lives in a dump and hangs out in smoky bars after work, but she can reach him—first with sex, and then with an overall attraction that he finds mesmerizing.

But the movie isn't really about that attraction. It's a film on the subject of appropriateness. Spader is fascinated by this woman and wants to be with her, but he also feels it necessary to hide her from his upper-middle-class Jewish circle of family and friends. They would disapprove, he guesses, because of her background, her age, and her religion. So he lies and evades and avoids taking her to a friend's wedding, and when he finally does break down and take her to a family dinner, it's a disaster. That's partly because a few of the women at the party resent her—they see Spader as a prime catch to be matched with an appropriate single woman, not thrown away on a short-order waitress. But part of the blame is Sarandon's, too: She drinks too much and causes an unnecessary confrontation at the dinner table.

Why? Because she found out Spader was lying to her—that he didn't really want to invite her to the dinner, until she forced him into it. From that point the movie follows time-honored lines; she flees, he follows, etc. But before it falls into formula, *White Palace* has raised interesting questions about those romances that fall outside of socially approved formulas.

It is the easiest thing in the world to slide comfortably into an "appropriate" relationship with a partner who conforms with the tastes and prejudices of your social circle. Yet many people, nevertheless, find themselves in nonconformist relationships, and my guess is that the depth of feeling in those relationships is often greater. If your partner does not match society's definition of the sort of person you should be in love with, then presumably he or she fills some deeper need—in the words of a famous British beer ad, refreshes the parts others cannot reach.

That's the dilemma faced by Spader in *White Palace.* He has never met a woman who reaches him more deeply than Sarandon does. Not even his wife. Is it love? He doesn't know. It's need. It's compulsion. Yet she exists so far outside his social circle he doesn't want to let her in. He lives in an expensive apartment. She lives in a ramshackle house where, one day, her electricity is shut off. ("Isn't it a hoot being poor?" she asks.) The strength of the movie is when it deals with the subject of a nonconforming relationship. The best moments involve verbal bolts of lightning—comic insights that blindside us.

But the weakness of the film is when it falls into the same sappy romantic clichés as countless other love stories. The final scene in the movie, for example, is such a loathsome version of such an idiotic cliché that I couldn't believe my eyes. And yet there's a lot that's good in *White Palace,* involving the heart as well as the mind.

Wild at Heart ★ ★ ½
R, 126 m., 1990

Nicolas Cage (Sailor Ripley), Laura Dern (Lula Pace Fortune), Diane Ladd (Mariette Fortune), Willem Dafoe (Bobby Peru), Isabella Rossellini (Perdita Durango), Harry Dean Stanton (Johnnie Farragut), Crispin Glover (Dell), Grace Zabriskie (Juana). Directed by David Lynch and produced by Monty Montgomery, Steve Golin, and Joni Sighvatsson. Screenplay by Lynch.

There is something inside of me that resists the films of David Lynch. I am aware of it, I admit to it, but I cannot think my way around it. I sit and watch his films and am aware of his energy, his visual flair, his flashes of wit. But as the movie rolls along, something grows inside of me—an indignation, an unwillingness, a resistance. At the end of both *Blue Velvet* and *Wild at Heart,* I felt angry, as if a clever con man had tried to put one over on me.

My taste is in the minority. *Blue Velvet* (1986) was hailed as one of the best films of the decade. Lynch's "Twin Peaks" was a cult hit on television. Now comes *Wild at Heart,* which won the Palme d'Or at the 1990 Cannes Film Festival, to great cheers and many boos, some of the latter from me. I do not think this is the best film that played at Cannes that year (what about Depardieu in *Cyrano?*) and I do not even, in fact, think it is a very good film. There is something repulsive and manipulative about it, and even its best scenes have the flavor of a kid in the school yard, trying to show you pictures you don't feel like looking at.

The movie is lurid melodrama, soap opera, exploitation, put-on, and self-satire. It deals in several scenes of particularly offensive violence, and tries to excuse them by juvenile humor: It's all a joke, you see, and so if the violence offends you, you didn't get the joke. Well, violence in itself doesn't offend me. But *Wild at Heart* doesn't have the nerve to just be violent, it has to build in its excuses.

Take, for example, an opening scene where the hero (Nicolas Cage) is attacked by a black man on a staircase at a party. The man is a killer hired by the evil mother (Diane Ladd) of Cage's girlfriend (Laura Dern). He pulls a knife on Cage, whose character is the local version of Elvis Presley crossed with James Dean and Tab Hunter. Cage disarms him, and then smashes him to a pulp, viciously and with great thoroughness, taking the man's hair in his hand and pounding his skull violently against the marble floor until the bones crack and blood spatters and the man is dead. Then Cage staggers to his feet, steadies himself on the handrail, lights a cigarette, and glares up from beneath lowered brows, gasping for breath, the cigarette dangling from his lip.

Some people laugh when they see this scene. They like the way the look is overplayed—Cage looks like a villain in a silent movie. I didn't laugh. I saw the payoff as Lynch's attempt to defuse the violence—to excuse a racially charged scene of unapologetic malevolence. There are other such scenes in the movie. The scene, for example, when the clerk gets his hand blown off with a shotgun, and crawls around on the floor looking for it, talking about how they can sew hands back on these days. Lynch cuts to a dog running from the building with the bloody hand in its mouth. This shot is lifted from Kurosawa's *Yojimbo*, but not many people in the audience will read it as an homage.

And then there's the scene where the villain (Willem Dafoe) blows off his own head with a shotgun, and the head flies through the air and bounces along on the ground. This was the scene that got to the MPAA's film rating board, which threatened *Wild at Heart* with an X. But the movie qualifies for an R rating by adding a little gunsmoke to the shot, so that you can't see the head coming off quite so clearly.

The violence aside, *Wild at Heart* also exercises the consistent streak of misogyny in Lynch's work. He has a particular knack for humiliating women in his films, and this time the primary target is Diane Ladd, as Mariette Fortune, the town seductress and vamp. The way this woman is photographed, the things she is given to do, and the dialogue she has to pronounce are equally painful to witness. Not even Hitchcock was ever this cruel to an actress. Laura Dern is Ladd's real-life daughter, and in the movie she, too, is subjected to the usual humiliations. Ever since I witnessed the humiliation of Isabella Rossellini in *Blue Velvet*, I've wondered if there is an element in Lynch's art that goes beyond filmmaking; a personal factor in which he uses his power as a director to portray women in a particularly hurtful and offensive light.

All of these wounds and maimings are told within the framework of a parody, in which Dern and Cage are young lovers on the run

from unspeakable secrets in the past, and the vengeance of Dern's mother and her hired goons. It's a road picture with a 1950s T-Bird convertible as the chariot, and lots of throwaway gags about Cage's snakeskin jacket, his "personal symbol of individuality." Cage does a conscious imitation of Presley in all of his dialogue, and even bursts into song a couple of times, delivering "Love Me Tender" from the hood of the car in the big climax.

I've seen the movie twice now. I liked it less the second time. Take away the surprises and you can see the method more clearly. Like *Blue Velvet*, this is a film without the courage to declare its own darkest fantasies. Lynch wraps his violence in humor, not as a style, but as a strategy. Luis Bunuel, the late and gifted Spanish surrealist, made films as cheerfully perverted and decadent as anything Lynch has ever dreamed of, but he had the courage to declare himself. Lynch seems to be doing a Bunuel script with a Jerry Lewis rewrite. He is a good director, yes. If he ever goes ahead and makes a film about what's really on his mind, instead of hiding behind sophomoric humor and the cop-out of "parody," he may realize the early promise of his *Eraserhead*. But he likes the box office prizes that go along with his pop satires, and so he makes dishonest movies like this one. Understand that it's not the violence I mind. It's the sneaky excuses.

Wild Orchid ★
R, 103 m., 1990

Mickey Rourke (Wheeler), Jacqueline Bisset (Claudia), Carre Otis (Emily), Assumpta Serna (Hanna), Bruce Greenwood (Jerome), Oleg Vidov (Otto), Milton Goncalves (Flavio). Directed by Zalman King and produced by Mark Damon and Tony Anthony. Screenplay by Patricia Louisianna Knop and King.

We engage in a conspiracy of silence about erotic movies. We discuss their plots, their characters, the truthfulness of their worlds. We never discuss whether or not they arouse us—whether we're turned on. Critics are the worst offenders, occupying some Olympian peak above the field of battle, pretending that the film in question failed to engage their intelligence when what we want to know is whether it engaged their libido.

Wild Orchid is an erotic film, plain and simple. It cannot be read in any other way. There is no other purpose for its existence.

Its story is absurd, and even its locale was chosen primarily for its travelogue value; this movie no more needs to take place in Brazil than in Kansas, which the heroine leaves in the opening scene.

And yet none of that is relevant. What is relevant is that I did not find the movie erotic. It tells the story of a virginal young woman (Carre Otis) who is hired as an international lawyer, leaves on the next flight for Rio de Janeiro, and there meets a man and woman (Mickey Rourke and Jacqueline Bisset) locked in a contest of psychological control. By the end of the film Otis will have been mentally savaged and physically ravished by Rourke and others, at first against her will, I guess, although she puts up what only her mother would consider a struggle.

Details in the opening scene almost invite us to snicker. Can we believe that Otis, who looks about eighteen, has graduated from law school, mastered three or four languages, and spent eighteen months with "a major Chicago law firm" before being hired on the spot by a top New York firm, which puts her on the next plane to Brazil? Hardly, since in the few scenes where she is required to talk like a lawyer, she speaks like someone who is none too confident she has memorized the words correctly. Can we believe that Bisset is an international negotiator who wants to buy valuable beachfront property from Rourke? That Rourke is a street kid from Philadelphia who bought his first house at sixteen, fixed it up, sold it at a profit, and is now one of the world's wealthiest men?

Well, we can almost believe it about the Rourke character (what's hard to accept is that anyone so rich would still be making money by actually doing things—like buying hotels—instead of simply ripping off the less wealthy through cleverness in the financial markets). But what I couldn't believe was the chemistry between Rourke and Otis, whose passion is supposed to shake the earth but seemed more like an obligation imposed on them by their genitals.

Rourke has had chemistry before. Who can forget his relationship with Kim Basinger in *9½ Weeks*? That he doesn't have it here is largely because Carre Otis, beautiful and appealing as she is, brings little conviction to her role. It is hard for us to believe her character exists—but apparently almost impossible for her.

The screenplay by Patricia Louisianna Knop and Zalman King, and the direction by King, strain for a psychological complexity that simply isn't there. Rourke is a man who cannot feel, they tell us, and so he lives through others—by arranging for Otis to have an affair with a strange man, for example. His untouchability has driven Bisset mad, which is why she "sent" Otis to Rourke in the first place—to see if he is incapable of loving all women or only Bisset. Without the sex, this could be a Henry James novel (if it had been written by Henry James, of course).

I have seen, however, movies nearly as unbelievable than *Wild Orchid* which nevertheless stirred me at an erotic level (the original *Emmanuelle* was one, and *9½ Weeks* was another). Apparently the lesson to be learned here is that sexuality itself is not enough, nor is nudity or passion. What is required is at least some notion that the personalities of the characters are really connecting. Unless they find each other sexy, why should we?

Willie and Phil ★ ★ ★
R, 116 m., 1980

Michael Ontkean (Willie), Margot Kidder (Jeannette), Ray Sharkey (Phil), Jan Miner (Mrs. Kaufman), Tom Brennan (Mr. Kaufman), Julie Bovasso (Mrs. D'Amico), Louis Guss (Mr. D'Amico), Kathleen Maguire (Mrs. Sutherland). Directed and written by Paul Mazursky and produced by Mazursky and Tony Ray.

Willie and Phil meet after a screening of Truffaut's *Jules and Jim*, which is a movie about two good friends and how they both fall in love with the same woman, who becomes the third good friend. Shortly after they see the movie, in Greenwich Village in 1970, Willie and Phil meet Jeannette, and then the three of them spend the 1970s working out their own version of a triangle.

If Paul Mazursky's *Willie and Phil* is supposed to be a psychologically plausible telling of this story, then it doesn't work. The movie gives away its own game right at the beginning, with the reference to *Jules and Jim*. These aren't real people in this movie; they're characters. They don't inhabit life, they inhabit Mazursky's screenplay—which takes them on a guided tour of the cults, fads, human potential movements, and alternative lifestyles of the decade during which zucchini replaced Faulkner as the most popular subject on campus.

But I don't think *Willie and Phil* was intended to work on a realistic level, or that we're intended to believe that Willie, Phil,

and Jeannette are making free choices throughout the movie. In a subtle, understated sort of way, Mazursky is giving us a movie that hovers between a satirical revue and a series of lifestyle vignettes. The characters in his movie are almost exhausted by the end of the decade (weren't we all?). Not only have they experimented with various combinations of commitments to one another, but they've also tried out most of the popular 1970s belief systems.

Willie (Michael Ontkean) is a high school teacher as the movie opens, but he wants to be more, to feel deeply, to think on more exalted levels, and his journey through the decade takes him into radicalism, back to the earth, and all the way to India for lessons in meditation. Phil (Ray Sharkey) says he wants love and security, but he holds himself at arm's length from Jeannette and other possible sources of love. Unable to communicate, he channels all of his energy into making it in the communications industries. Jeannette (Margot Kidder) . . . well, what does she want? To love, to be loved, to be possessed, to be free, to commit, but not to be trapped, to . . . have kids? A career? Willie? Phil?

I think Mazursky's suggesting something interesting about the 1970s. It was a decade without a consuming passion, without an overall subject or tone. Every decade from the 1920s to the 1960s had an overriding theme, at least in our collective national imagination, but in the 1970s we went on life-style shopping trips, searching for an impossible combination of life choices that would be morally good, politically correct, personally entertaining, and outperform the market—all at once.

And what were we left with in the 1980s? Confusion, vague apprehension, lack of faith in belief systems, EPA mileage estimates, megavitamins as the last blameless conspicuous consumption, and, echoing somewhere in the back of our minds, Peggy Lee singing "Is That All There Is?" How'd we get stuck? Why'd we wind up with a sense of impending doom when we tried every possible superficial substitute for profound change? Mazursky finds this note and strikes it in *Willie and Phil*, and that's what's best about his movie.

But like the decade itself, *Willie and Phil* is not completely substantial or satisfying. What redeems it, curiously, are the scenes involving Willie's Jewish parents, Phil's Italian parents, and Jeannette's Southern mother. Their scenes are reactions to what's

happening to their kids in the 1970s, and they work like field trips from other decades. The parents observe, try to understand, are baffled, react with resentment, anger, love, confusion. I loved it when the Italian mother, trying to figure out how Jeannette was going to sleep with her boyfriend in the house of her ex-husband while the ex-husband bunked downstairs and the parents took the guest room, got up, said it was all just too complicated for her, and left for the airport. That's sort of the motif for this movie.

Willie Wonka and the Chocolate Factory ★ ★ ★ ★
G, 98 m., 1971

Gene Wilder (Willie Wonka), Jack Albertson (Grandpa Joe), Peter Ostrum (Charlie), Michael Bollner (Augustus Gloop), Aubrey Wood (Mr. Bill), Gunter Meissner (Mr. Slugwork). Directed by Mel Stuart and produced by Stan Margulies and David L. Wolper. Screenplay by Roald Dahl.

Kids are not stupid. They are among the sharpest, cleverest, most eagle-eyed creatures on God's Earth, and very little escapes their notice. You may not have observed that your neighbor is still using his snow tires in mid-July, but every four-year-old on the block has, and kids pay the same attention to detail when they go to the movies. They don't miss a thing, and they have an instinctive contempt for shoddy and shabby work. I make this observation because nine out of ten children's movies are stupid, witless, and display contempt for their audiences, and that's why kids hate them. Is that all parents want from kids' movies? That they not have anything bad in them? Shouldn't they have something good in them—some life, imagination, fantasy, inventiveness, something to tickle the imagination? If a movie isn't going to do your kids any good, why let them watch it? Just to kill a Saturday afternoon? That shows a subtle kind of contempt for a child's mind, I think.

All of this is preface to a simple statement: *Willie Wonka and the Chocolate Factory* is probably the best film of its sort since *The Wizard of Oz*. It is everything that family movies usually claim to be, but aren't: Delightful, funny, scary, exciting, and, most of all, a genuine work of imagination. *Willie Wonka* is such a surely and wonderfully spun fantasy that it works on all kinds of minds, and it is fascinating because, like all classic fantasy, it is fascinated with itself.

It's based on the well-known Roald Dahl children's book, and it was financed by the Quaker Oats Company as an experiment in providing high-quality family entertainment. It succeeds. It doesn't cut corners and go for cheap shortcuts like Disney. It provides a first-rate cast (Gene Wilder as the compulsively distrustful chocolate manufacturer, Jack Albertson as the game old grandfather), a first-rate production, and—I keep coming back to this—genuine imagination.

The story, like all good fantasies, is about a picaresque journey. Willie Wonka is the world's greatest chocolate manufacturer, and he distributes five golden passes good for a trip through his factory and a lifetime supply of chocolate. Each pass goes to a kid, who may bring an adult along, and our hero Charlie (a poor but honest newsboy who supports four grandparents and his mother) wins the last one.

The other four kids are hateful in one way or another, and come to dreadful ends. One falls into the chocolate lake and is whisked into the bowels of the factory. He shouldn't have been a pig. Another is vain enough to try Wonka's new teleportation invention, and winds up six inches tall—but the taffy-pulling machine will soon have him back to size, right? If these fates seem a little gruesome to you, reflect that all great children's tales are a little gruesome, from the Brothers Grimm to Alice to Snow White, and certainly not excluding Mother Goose. Kids are not sugar and spice, not very often, and they appreciate the poetic justice when a bad kid gets what's coming to him.

Willow ★ ★ ½
PG, 126 m., 1988

Val Kilmer (Madmartigan), Joanne Whalley (Sorsha), Warwick Davis (Willow), Jean Marsh (Queen Bavmorda), Patricia Hayes (Raziel), Billy Barty (High Aldwin), Pat Roach (Kael), Gavan O'Herlihy (Airk). Directed by Ron Howard and produced by George Lucas. Screenplay by Bob Dolman.

A producer and a pharaoh find a baby on a raft on the Nile. "What an ugly kid," the pharaoh says. "That's funny," says the producer. "He looked great in the rushes."—Old movie joke

Willow is a fearsomely ambitious movie, but it is not fearsome, and it is not wondrous, and it is about a journey too far down a road

too well-traveled by other movies. It's a fantasy about the quest of a lovable little person and his heroic newfound friend to return a lost baby to where it belongs, and to outsmart a wicked queen and kill a two-headed dragon in the process. In other words, standard stuff.

What was supposed to make *Willow* special was the quality of the production. This is a sword-and-sorcery epic produced by George Lucas, whose *Star Wars* portrayed the same kind of material in the future, and directed by Ron Howard, whose human touch made *Cocoon* one of the best recent science-fiction movies. The special effects are by Lucas's company, Industrial Light and Magic, which has set the standard in such matters. The budget was umpteen million dollars, and Hollywood was hoping that the Force was definitely with this film.

Alas, even the largest budgets and the most meticulous special effects are only dead weight unless they have a story to make them move. And at the story level, *Willow* is turgid and relentlessly predictable. Not much really happens, and when it does, its pace is slowed by special-effects set pieces that run on too long and seem to be recycled out of earlier movies.

The story. Willow, citizen of the Nelwyns, a race of little people, is chosen by his community to take a baby to a far-off crossroads where it can be found by its people, the Daikinis. The baby was carried to Willow's land on a crude raft that was swept along by river waters, but what Willow does not know is that the baby was placed on the raft by its desperate mother. That was to save it from a decree of death dealt out to all girl-children by Bavmorda, the vicious queen and sorceress, who fears her successor has been born. So already we have the story of Moses, cross-pollinated with *Snow White and the Seven Dwarfs*. Lucas has a reputation as a student of old legends and folklore, but there is a thin line between that and simply being a student of old movies.

One of the crucial problems in *Willow* is that we are going to be seeing so much of this baby. It is dragged from one end of the known world to the other, usually with a plucky smile on its face, and whenever something interesting happens, we get an appropriate reaction shot from the baby. Hey, I like kids, but even Baby Leroy couldn't have saved this character.

Willow (Warwick Davis) sets off with the baby in arms, and at the crossroads he meets

Madmartigan (Val Kilmer), a warrior who has been imprisoned in a cage. Madmartigan convinces Willow to free him, using much too much dialogue in the process, and then they team up to continue their quest, which leads eventually to Bavmorda's fortress, guarded by a two-headed, fire-breathing dragon.

So, OK, the dragon is well done. All of the special effects are competent, but they do not breathe with the fire of life because they are not motivated by a strong story we really care about. The characters in *Willow* are shallow and unexciting, the story is a plod through recycled legend, and therefore, even the battle with the dragon is a foregone conclusion. There can be no true suspense in a movie where even the characters seem to be inspired by other movies.

Willow is certainly not a breakthrough film to a mass audience—but is it at least a successful children's picture? I dunno. Its pacing is too deliberate, and it doesn't have a light heart. That's revealed in the handling of some *really* little characters named the Brownies, represented by a couple of men who are about nine inches tall and fight all the time. Maybe Lucas thought these guys would work like R2D2 and C3PO did in *Star Wars*. But they have no depth, no personalities, no dimension; they're simply an irritant at the edge of the frame. Touches like that will only confuse kids, who know that good dreams do not have to be clever, or consistent, or expensive, but that they should never, ever make you want to wake up.

Wings of Desire ★ ★ ★ ★
NO MPAA RATING, 130 m., 1988

Bruno Ganz (Damiel), Solveig Dommartin (Marion), Otto Sander (Cassiel), Curt Bois (Homer), Peter Falk (Himself). Directed by Wim Wenders and written by Wenders and Peter Handke.

In notes that he wrote after directing *Wings of Desire*, Wim Wenders reflected that it would be terrible to be an angel: "To live for an eternity and to be present all the time. To live with the essence of things—not to be able to raise a cup of coffee and drink it, or really touch somebody." In his film, this dilemma becomes the everyday reality of two angels, who move through Berlin observing people, listening, reflecting, caring. They can see and hear, but are cut off from the senses of touch, taste, and smell. Human life appears to them as if it were a movie.

The angels look like two ordinary men, with weary and kind faces. They can move through the air free of gravity, but in all other respects they appear to the camera to be just as present as the human characters in a scene. Their role is a little unclear. They watch. They listen. Sometimes, when they are moved by the plight of a human they care about, they are able to stand close to that person and somehow exude a sense of caring or love, which seems to be vaguely perceived by the human, to whom it can provide a moment of hope or release.

The angel we are most concerned with in the film is Damiel, played by Bruno Ganz, that everyman of German actors whose face is expressive because it is so lived-in, so tired. He moves slowly through the city, hearing snatches of conversation, seeing moments of lives, keenly aware of his existence as a perpetual outsider. One day he comes across Marion (Solveig Dommartin), a trapeze artist, and is moved by her sadness. He helps her in the ways that he can, but eventually he realizes that he does not want to end her suffering so much as to share it.

That is the problem with being an angel. He can live forever, but in a sense, he can never live. To an angel, a being who exists in eternity, human lives must seem to be over in a brief flash of time, in a wink of history, and yet during our brief span, at least humans are really alive—to grow, to learn, to love, to suffer, to drink a cup of coffee, while an angel can only imagine the warmth of the cup, the aroma of the coffee, the taste, the feel.

Damiel determines to renounce immortality and accept human life with all its transience and pain. And in that act of renunciation, he makes one of the most poignant and romantic of gestures. He is accepting the limitations not only of his loved one, but of life itself.

Wings of Desire was directed by Wenders (whose credits include *Paris, Texas* and *The American Friend*), and cowritten by Wenders and Peter Handke, the German novelist who also wrote and directed *The Left-Handed Woman*. They are not interested in making some kind of soft-hearted, sentimental Hollywood story in which harps play and everybody feels good afterward.

Their film is set in divided Berlin, most insubstantial of cities because its future always seems deferred. Most of the film is shot in black and white, the correct medium for this story, because color would be too realistic to reflect the tone of their fable. Many of the best moments in the film have no particular dramatic purpose, but are concerned only with showing us what it is like to be forever an observer. Ganz walks quietly across empty bridges. He looks into vacant windows. He sits in a library and watches people as they read. He is there, and he is not there. The sterility of his existence almost makes us understand the choice of Lucifer in renouncing heaven in order to be plunged into hell, where at least he could suffer, and therefore, feel.

This is the kind of film that needs to be seen in a meditative frame of mind. It doesn't much matter what happens in the story, but it does matter how well we are able to empathize with it, how successfully we are able to enter into the state of mind of an angel. Leaving the movie, I reflected that sometimes we are bored by life, and feel as if nothing exciting is happening. But if we had spent eternity as an angel, observing life without feeling it, and then were plunged into a human body with its physical senses, think what a roar and flood of sensations would overwhelm us! It would be almost too much to bear. It would be everyday life.

Winter of Our Dreams ★ ★ ★
R, 89 m., 1983

Judy Davis (Lou), Bryan Brown (Rob), Cathy Downes (Gretel), Baz Luhrmann (Pete). Directed by John Duigan and produced by Richard Mason. Screenplay by Duigan.

Rob runs a bookstore and lives in one of those houses where the bedrooms hang under the eaves; one false move and you dash your brains out onto the living room floor below. Lou is a prostitute who lives on the streets. They both once had a friend named Lisa, back in the late 1960s when they were all part of the Australian protest movement. Now Lisa has been murdered, and Lou, searching for a meaning in her life or death, runs into Rob again. She thinks he's a trick. He thinks she's an interesting, complicated person who deserves his attention. I think she's closer to the mark.

This is the setup for *Winter of Our Dreams*, an Australian film starring two popular Australian new wave actors, Judy Davis (of *My Brilliant Career*) and Bryan Brown (of *Breaker Morant* and TV's "A Town Like Alice"). Davis brought a kind of wiry, feisty intelligence to *My Brilliant Career*, playing an Australian farm woman who rather felt she would do things her own way. She's wonderful this time, in a completely different role as an insecure, distrustful, skinny street waif. It's Brown who is the trouble. Maybe it's the performance, maybe it's the character, or maybe it's Brown, but I've rarely seen a more closed-off person on the screen. When the story calls for him to reach out to Davis, we feel he's holding his nose. Sometimes there are movies where the leading actors cannot stand one another (Ken Wahl said he was only able to kiss Bette Midler in *Jinxed!* by thinking of his dog), and maybe Brown just couldn't express the feelings that were in the script. But I was never really convinced that he cared for Davis.

That's less of a handicap later in the movie, however, when the Brown character is *required* to draw back from any involvement with this pathetic street kid. The relationships in *Winter of Our Dreams* are very tangled—maybe too tangled. Brown's character has been married for six years to Gretel (Cathy Downes), a handsome, smart woman who has a lover. They have an open marriage, and there's no objection when Brown brings Davis home for the night. Davis, taking this all in, can't understand it. Trying to learn how to feel again, she can't understand why anyone would deliberately trivialize his feelings. The key passages in the film involve Brown's discovery that Davis is a heroin junkie, and then her tortured period of drug withdrawal. They are both pretending to care for one another, and after Davis gets straight maybe Brown will become her lover, while his wife disappears into the woodwork. That is not, however, even remotely in the cards, and there's a painful scene during a party at Brown's house, where Davis realizes that Brown is *very* married, open marriage or not.

There seem to be two movements in *Winter of Our Dreams*. One is Davis's movement away from the cynicism and despair of prostitution, and back toward an ability to care for another person. The other is Brown's initial concern for this girl, and then his retreat back into his shell. Davis performs her movement magnificently. Brown didn't win my sympathy for a moment. What just barely saves this film is the fact that we're not *supposed* to like the Brown character. As for Davis, she's a wonder.

Wired ★ ½
R, 112 m., 1989

Michael Chiklis (John Belushi), Ray Sharkey (Angel Valesquez), J.T. Walsh (Bob Woodward), Patti D'Arbanville (Cathy Smith), Lucinda Jenny (Judy Belushi), Alex Rocco (Arnie Fromson), Gary Groomes (Dan Aykroyd), Jere Burns (Lou), Clyde Kusatsu (Coroner). Directed by Larry Peerce and produced by Edward S. Feldman. Screenplay by Earl Mac Rauch.

You know the spirit of John Belushi is in trouble when the second and third billings in his life story go to an angel and a reporter from the *Washington Post*. And you know the movie is in trouble when both of those characters are used as devices to tell the story. In *Wired*, the angel visits the morgue where Belushi's body is being held, and leads the comedian's ghost through a series of flashbacks. Meanwhile, the reporter is busy interviewing survivors and witnesses to Belushi's sensational self-destruction.

The reporter in the movie is named Bob Woodward, and is apparently intended to represent the real Woodward doing research for his best-selling book about Belushi. The angel is named Valesquez. The reporting scenes are supposed to be realistic, and the angel's guided tour is a fantasy, and yet I kept hoping that Woodward would cross paths with the angel and get himself a *real* exclusive. There could even be a bit part for Ben Bradlee, sending Woodward a telegram: *"Forget Belushi—interview angel."*

The story of the life and death of John Belushi is a labyrinth of fact and conjecture, rumor and gossip and secondhand memories, and it is further complicated by the enormous gulf between the comedian and actor who made so many people laugh, and the human being who made himself so very unhappy. Maybe there was no way to make a good movie out of this material, not yet, when everyone remembers Belushi and any actor who attempts to play him is sure to suffer by comparison. *Wired* is in some ways a sincere attempt to deal with the material, but it is such an ungainly and hapless movie, so stupidly written, so awkwardly directed and acted, that it never gets off the ground.

There should be, at some point in a movie like this, a moment when we have the illusion that we are seeing the real John Belushi, that we are eavesdropping on the facts of his life. That moment never comes. I was always aware that an actor (Michael Chiklis) was before me on the screen, and that *Wired* was an ungainly fictional construction. The saddest moments were the ones in which Chiklis attempted to recreate some of Belushi's famous characters and routines. He never gives us a living Belushi, and so why should we care about the movie's dead Belushi?

One of the problems of the movie is also a problem with Woodward's book. Neither one has the slightest insight into the dynamics and reality of alcoholism and drug addiction. Woodward has said that he was attracted to the story of John Belushi because, although both of them came out of the same high school in Wheaton, Illinois, they were such opposites. They remain opposites. The movie's strategy is to sketch Belushi's rise to fame and then to contrast it with the downward spiral of his drug addiction. But why do people drink and use drugs to excess? The movie is relentless in parroting the tired old show biz cliché about the "pressures of stardom," as if 98 percent of those pressures, in Belushi's case, did not come from his addiction itself.

In the year before this movie, there was a series of uncommonly intelligent movies about addiction (*Clean and Sober* and *The Boost*, in particular). They are movies made from the inside, as it were, by people who understand alcoholism and drug addiction. *Wired* sees Belushi's problems in a lurid light through an outsider's sensationalist frame of reference. It is hardly more sophisticated on the subject of Belushi's disease than *Reefer Madness*. Indeed, it doesn't even think Belushi had a disease—it prefers to see him as a tortured soul wallowing in excess. For those who knew him, the reason why John Belushi took drugs was simplicity itself: He was addicted to them. The answer, if he were to save himself, was to stop using them and look for help to stay stopped. Such simplicities are beyond this movie.

Is there any reason to see it? Not for the Belushi material; you can see that firsthand from his own movies and his "Saturday Night Live" performances. To learn about his problems? The movie fails to understand them. To watch the performances? There is not a convincing imitation of a known performer in the entire movie. John Belushi made millions of people laugh and broke the hearts of those who loved him, and there is little in this film to explain how, or why, he did either of those things.

Wise Guys ★ ★ ★ ½
R, 92 m., 1986

Danny DeVito (Harry Valentini), Joe Piscopo (Moe Dickstein), Harvey Keitel (Bobby DiLea), Ray Sharkey (Marco), Dan Hedaya (Tony Castelo), Captain Lou Albano (Fixer), Julie Bovasso (Lil Dickstein), Patti LuPone (Wanda Valentini). Directed by Brian DePalma and produced by Aaron Russo. Screenplay by George Gallo.

Wise Guys tells the story of Harry and Moe, two low-level hoodlums who become the toys of the Mafia gods. They're just ordinary guys, working stiffs who live next door to each other in houses tucked under a New Jersey expressway. They dream of the day when they'll be assigned to really important jobs, like shaking down widows. But when the godfather holds his morning staff meetings in the back booth of his favorite restaurant, these guys get humiliated: Their job is to pick up the boss's laundry.

The two friends are played by Joe Piscopo, as Moe Dickstein, and Danny DeVito, as Harry Valentini. They move with easy familiarity through the world of the mob; sometimes the little guys get the best view. They all know so much, in fact, that when they screw up, when they do something that is very, very bad, they don't even have to be told they're dead. It goes without saying.

Here's what they do. They go to the track with Fixer, the mob's chief enforcer (played by Captain Lou Albano, the gigantic professional wrestler). Their assignment is to place a bet for Tony, the boss (Dan Hedaya). DeVito gets to thinking, which is always dangerous. The boss has been betting on the wrong horses for weeks. They could be heroes by placing the money on the nose of the horse that DeVito knows will win. Better still, they could get rich by betting on the winning horse and then letting Fixer and the boss believe the money was lost.

This is a great plan, except unfortunately, this is the one day that the boss's horse comes in first, and so DeVito and Piscopo have lost the boss hundreds of thousands of dollars. This is bad. It is so bad that DeVito is plunged into a lobster tank at the restaurant, and Piscopo is suspended over a pit full of attack dogs. Then the boss thinks up their *real* punishment: He will secretly assign each one of them to kill the other one. It's here that the movie really gets rolling. The two wise guys hit the road, looking for safety, looking for a mob elder statesman who can bargain for their safety. And we begin to realize that the movie is filled with an inexhaustible supply of great character actors, that we are going to meet a lot of people in this story, and they are all going to be memorable.

In New Jersey, there was Hedaya as the boss, clean-shaven and slick, and Albano as Fixer, in one of the year's great supporting roles. Then, in Atlantic City, we meet the casino manager Bobby DiLea, played by the great Harvey Keitel. He doesn't want anyone to get killed in his casino, and once Harry and Moe check into the penthouse suite (using Fixer's stolen credit card), he knows he is going to have to be very lucky to keep that from happening. Very lucky, or very weird.

Wise Guys is an abundant movie, filled with ideas and gags and great characters. It never runs dry. It never has the desperation of so many gangster comedies, which seem to be marching over the same tired ground. This movie was made with joy, and you can feel it in the sense of all the actors working at the top of their form.

The movie was directed by Brian DePalma, who specializes in movies about crime and whose credits include *Scarface*, *Body Double*, and *Dressed to Kill*. I admired all those movies—indeed, I think DePalma is one of the best stylists at work right now—but I wouldn't have suspected that he had this comedy in him. His early credits include such problematic comedies as *Hi, Mom!* (which was one of Robert De Niro's first movie jobs), but here's this polished, confident comedy that never seems to step wrong.

A lot of the credit goes to Piscopo and DeVito, who develop an instant, easy camaraderie. I really did feel that they care for each other. I liked the way DeVito waved his arms and demanded attention, and the way Piscopo played his slightly slower, sweeter, dumber pal. DeVito has been good in other recent movies (such as *Romancing the Stone*), but this is the first time he's been at the top of the cast, and really free to show his stuff. He is inspired: This could be a new beginning for his career. Piscopo, from "Saturday Night Live," has worked less in the movies, and has always seemed in search of a character. Here he finds one.

And then there's that gallery of supporting performances. Albano is so fearsome as Fixer that I found myself laughing at a time I don't think I was supposed to be funny: There's a reference to "Mrs. Fixer." Keitel is

suave and sinister as the casino boss, always staying within character, playing it straight, not going for laughs, and so getting more of them.

Laughter doesn't come out of formula, or stupidity, or the manipulation of things that worked before in other films. It comes out of characters and performances, out of people who have some measure of reality, and whose dilemmas we can share. *Wise Guys* is broad and farcical, but there's not a moment when Moe and Harry stop being lovable, and even sort of believable.

Wish You Were Here ★ ★ ★ ¹/₂
R, 92 m., 1987

Emily Lloyd (Lynda), Tom Bell (Eric), Jesse Birdsall (Dave), Geoffrey Durham (Harry Figgis), Pat Heywood (Aunt Millie), Geoffrey Hutchings (Hubert). Directed by David Leland and produced by Sarah Radclyffe. Screenplay by Leland.

Her mother's dead, her father's a drunk, and inside of her beats a spirit that is free and true. But this is a working-class neighborhood of an English provincial town in 1951, when a girl such as Lynda was expected to know her place, to apologize by her very manner for having come from humble origins, and done little to distinguish herself. Lynda isn't made that way. The boys like to look at Betty Grable's legs in the cinema, so Lynda flashes her knickers on the beach. What's to lose?

Wish You Were Here tells the story of an adolescent girl with a spirit that refuses to be crushed, but who has few ways to express herself. Her father absolutely fails to comprehend her. An aunt sees her as a bad girl, a problem girl. The lads of the town see her as a tramp and a possible good time. There is no one in the town to understand her high spirits and good nature, except, perhaps, for the little old lady who plays piano in the tea room and applauds her the day she tells a customer to shove it.

Wish You Were Here is a comedy with an angry undertone, a story of a free-spirited girl who holds a grudge against a time when such girls were a threat to society, to the interlocking forces of sexism and convention that conspired to break their spirits. Because the film sometimes doesn't know whether to laugh or cry, it's always interesting: We see a girl whistling on her way to possible tragedy.

The movie was written and directed by

David Leland. You may have seen or heard about *Personal Services*, an earlier movie he wrote. It was based on the story of a notorious British madam named Cynthia Payne, who ran a house of ill repute for old-age pensioners and retired military men with kinky tastes.

Although *Wish You Were Here* never makes the connection, it is based on stories that Payne told Leland about her childhood, when sex was something nobody talked about and sexual initiation was accompanied by ignorance, fear, and psychic trauma. Payne could never quite see what the fuss was about—still can't, if the latest headlines about her are correct. Her approach was completely amoral: If sex is something they want and you can supply, and you can benefit as much as, or more than, they can, then where's the problem?

The answer is, of course, that there can be endless problems, especially to a girl so essentially innocent and vulnerable as Lynda in this movie. After she gets a job at the bus station, her boss walks in to catch her flashing her legs for the appreciative bus drivers. A young local lad fancies himself a Don Juan, and gets her into bed, only to appear in the bedroom door in a silk dressing gown, smoking a cigarette in a holder, and doing his Ronald Colman imitation (which is, as it turns out, his idea of sex).

"Do you fancy me?" he asks. "Not half as much as you fancy yourself," she says, and the night ends with her still largely ignorant about the facts of life. But her schooling resumes at the hands of a middle-aged projectionist at the local theater, who understands the mechanics of sex and totally lacks any understanding of human nature—hers, or his own.

Under the circumstances, it is hard for Lynda to keep smiling, to think positive in the face of a general conspiracy to treat sex as filthy and herself as worthless. The last shot of the movie will strike some people as hopeless and misleading romanticism; I prefer to see it as optimism in the face of despair.

The key to this movie is the performance by sixteen-year-old Emily Lloyd as Lynda. The screenplay could have gone a dozen different ways, depending on who was cast in the role. Lloyd is so fresh, so filled with fun and rebellion, that she carries us past the tricky parts on the strength of personality alone. It's one of the great debut roles for a young actress. I was reminded of a cross between Julie Christie in *Darling* and Rita Tushingham in *A Taste of Honey*. It'll be interesting to see what the future holds for her. More than it did for Lynda, I imagine, and for Cynthia Payne.

The Witches ★ ★ ★
PG, 92 m., 1990

Anjelica Huston (Miss Ernst/Grand High Witch), Mai Zetterling (Helga), Jasen Fisher (Luke), Rowna Atkinson (Mr. Stringer), Bill Paterson (Mr. Jenkins), Brenda Blethyn (Mrs. Jenkins), Charles Potter (Bruno Jenkins), Anne Lambton (Woman in Black). Directed by Nicolas Roeg and produced by Mark Shivas. Screenplay by Allan Scott.

The best children's stories are the scariest ones, because to kids they seem most likely to contain the truth. A lot of stories end with everybody living happily ever after, but they're boring stories unless there seems to be a good chance that unspeakable dangers must be survived on the way to the ending. Roald Dahl's children's stories always seem to know that truth, and the best thing about Nicolas Roeg's film of Dahl's book *The Witches* is its dark vision—this is not only a movie about kids who are changed into mice, it's a movie where one of the mice gets its tail chopped off.

The film opens on an ominous note in Norway, with Luke (Jasen Fisher) being told stories about witches by his old grandmother (Mai Zetterling). They're real, she says, and they walk among us. But you can spot them if you get a good look at them, because they have square feet. They're also bald and have pointy noses, but the important thing is they're not imaginary. The grandmother has even heard tell of a Grand High Witch, who rules all of the others, and is the most terrible of all.

Tragedy strikes. Luke's parents are killed in a car crash. He travels with his grandmother to England on family business, and they end up in a seaside hotel which is hosting a convention of the Society for the Prevention of Cruelty to Children. Somehow when you see the head of the society, Miss Ernst (Anjelica Huston), you don't feel good about your chances of having cruelty prevented to you if you're a child.

Huston, whose energy dominates the film, dresses like a vampire vamp with stiletto heels, a tight black dress, a severe hairstyle, and blazing red lipstick. Roeg often photographs her using lenses which make her leer into the camera, and she's

always towering over everybody, especially little boys like Luke. Wandering through the labyrinthine hallways of the old hotel, Luke stumbles upon a private meeting one day, and discovers to his horror that the Society is actually a convention of witches—and that Huston, the fabled Grand High Witch, has plans to turn all of the children in England into mice.

Luke is, of course, discovered while eavesdropping, and becomes the first child forced to drink a secret potion and become a mouse. And it's here that the genius of the late Jim Henson comes into play, as his special effects team creates a world in which gigantic pieces of furniture tower over the little boy-mouse and some of his friends, as they try to survive cats and extermination and save the children of England.

Some of the sequences are predictable from other movies about people who shrink to microscopic size. Others are fresh, including the way Luke is finally able to convince his grandmother he is her grandson and not a mouse. Lucky for him she believes in witches already. The movie turns into a race against time, good against evil, and Roeg doesn't spare his young audiences the sinister implications of the plot.

This is the first so-called children's movie from Nicolas Roeg, that most unorthodox of directors, whose credits include *Don't Look Now*, *Track 29*, *Eureka*, and *Insignificance*. He almost always expresses a twisted, sinister sensuality in his films, and in this one that sensibility expresses itself in his willingness to let the child-mice face some of the real dangers of their predicament. The result is that the movie might be too intense for smaller viewers (although some of them these days seem hardened to anything). But *The Witches* is an intriguing movie, ambitious and inventive, and almost worth seeing just for Anjelica Huston's obvious delight in playing a completely uncompromised villainess.

The Witches of Eastwick ★ ★ ★ ½
R, 125 m., 1987

Jack Nicholson (Daryl), Cher (Alexandra), Susan Sarandon (Jane), Michelle Pfeiffer (Sukie), Veronica Cartwright (Felicia), Richard Jenkins (Clyde), Keith Jochim (Walter). Directed by George Miller and produced by Neil Canton, Peter Guber, and Jon Peters. Screenplay by Michael Christofer.

It's all done with the ambidextrous eyebrows. Jack Nicholson can elevate either brow singly to express his intention of getting away with murder, and he can elevate them in unison to reflect his delight when he has done so. In the annals of body language, his may be a small skill, but it's a crucial one, because it makes us conspirators with Nicholson; he's sharing his raffish delight with us.

He does that a lot in *The Witches of Eastwick*, in which he plays the devil: a role he was born to fill. He finds himself in Eastwick, a sedate New England village, after being invoked by three bored housewives who have not found what they are looking for in the local male population. Nicholson is exactly what they are looking for, by definition, because he can be all things to all people.

He buys the big mansion on the edge of town, moves in, and starts cooking. Nobody knows where he came from or what his story is, and he's certainly an oddball: Look at those floppy, ungainly clothes, or remember the time he began to snore, deafeningly, at the village concert. But the three women who summoned him aren't complaining, because he's giving each one of them just what she wants.

The women are played in the movie by Cher, Michelle Pfeiffer, and Susan Sarandon, and they have a delicious good time with their roles. These women need to be good at double takes, because they're always getting into situations that require them. When they're together, talking up a storm, they have the kind of unconscious verbal timing that makes comedy out of ordinary speech. We laugh not only because they say funny things but because they give everyday things just a slight twist of irony.

But it's Nicholson's show. There is a scene where he dresses in satin pajamas and sprawls full length on a bed, twisting and stretching sinuously in full enjoyment of his sensuality. It is one of the funniest moments of physical humor he has ever committed. There is another sequence in which he presides over a diabolical celebration in his mansion, orchestrating unspeakable acts and realizing unconscious fantasies. In the hands of another actor it might look ridiculous, but Nicholson seems perfectly at home with the bizarre.

The Witches of Eastwick is based on the John Updike novel, which must have presented a mine field for George Miller, the director. Fantasies usually play better on the page than on the screen, because in the imagination they don't seem as ridiculous as they sometimes do when they've been reduced to actual images. There are moments in *The Witches of Eastwick* that stretch uncomfortably for effects—the movie's climax is overdone, for example—and yet a lot of the time this movie plays like a plausible story about implausible people. The performances sell it. And the eyebrows.

Withnail & I ★ ★ ★ ★
R, 104 m., 1987

Richard E. Grant (Withnail), Paul McGann (Marwood), Richard Griffiths (Monty), Ralph Brown (Danny), Michael Elphick (Jake), Daragh O'Malley (Irishman), Michael Wardle (Isaac Parkin), Una Brandon-Jones (Mrs. Parkin). Directed by Bruce Robinson and produced by Paul M. Heller. Screenplay by Robinson.

Withnail & I takes place in England at the end of the Swinging Sixties. Two would-be actors live in squalor and poverty in a mean little flat in a wretched section of London. They are cold, desperate, broke, and hung over. They dream of glory but lurk about in the corners of pubs to keep warm.

One of them is Withnail, who is tall, craggy, and utterly cynical. He affects a kind of weary bitterness. The other is Marwood, younger, more optimistic, more impressionable. Their situation is desperate. "Something has to happen," Withnail says, "or I'm going to crack."

Then he has an inspiration: His rich and eccentric Uncle Monty has some sort of a place in the country. They'll talk him into lending it to them, and perhaps the change of scenery will give them the courage to carry on. The scene that begins when they appear at the door of Monty's London mansion is sly and droll, filled with hazardous currents and undertows as Monty takes a fancy to young Marwood. He agrees to lend them his country place.

The country is bitter, cold, angry, and hostile. Neighbors will not talk to them. Farmers will not sell them firewood. Their wives will not part with eggs or milk. Huddled over a wretched blaze made of Uncle Monty's furniture, Withnail and Marwood contemplate a bleak prospect: They have no food, fuel, money, or (worst of all) drink.

Outside the door, the idyllic countryside is roamed by randy bulls.

Then Uncle Monty arrives unexpectedly and sets himself on a determined romantic pursuit of young Marwood, who wants nothing to do with him. Withnail confesses that he told his uncle that Marwood was gay, "because otherwise how would we have gotten the cottage?" Uncle Monty is, however, not only gay but also rich and fat, and the erotic tension in the cottage is interrupted by large and leisurely meals.

The performances make the movie, and Richard Griffiths is wonderful as Uncle Monty: overfed, burbling with second-hand eloquence, yet with a cold intelligence lurking behind his bloodshot eyes. It's the best supporting performance in a British movie since Denholm Elliott in *A Room with a View*. Withnail and Marwood, played by Richard E. Grant and Paul McGann, are like Rosencrantz and Gildenstern: They know all their lines but are uncertain about which direction the play is taking.

Withnail & I is a comedy, but a grimly serious one. Nothing is played for laughs. The humor arises from poverty, desperation, and bone-numbing cold. It is not the portrait of two colorful, lovable characters, but of two comrades in emotional shipwreck. The movie is rigorously dyspeptic, and that's why I liked it: It doesn't go for the easy laughs or sentimentalized poverty, but finds its humor in the unforgiving study of selfish human nature.

Without a Trace ★ ★ ★ ½
PG, 119 m., 1983

Kate Nelligan (Susan Selky), Judd Hirsch (Menetti), David Dukes (Graham Selky), Stockard Channing (Jocelyn). Directed and produced by Stanley Jaffe. Screenplay by Beth Gutcheon.

"A woman's bravery and a police detective's relentless search for her missing son provide the elements of suspenseful human drama in Without a Trace."

—Press release

They have it exactly wrong. The press release describes what might have happened to this story if it had been turned into one of those TV docudramas where every emotion is predictably computed. What makes *Without a Trace* interesting is that it's *not* predictable, because it goes with the ebbs and flows of imperfect human beings. It's not about a

woman's bravery but about her intelligence and vulnerability. It's not about a detective's relentless search, but about routine police work, made up of realism and hunches.

Without a Trace opens with a sequence that is very painful, since we know from the movie's title what's about to happen. A young mother (Kate Nelligan), who lives alone with her first-grader, gets him up, gets him his breakfast, scolds him for feeding his breakfast to the dog, tells him he's a good boy, and sends him off to school. He's almost seven—sort of young to walk alone to school, but it's only two blocks and there's a crossing guard. Nelligan goes off to school herself. She's an English professor at Columbia University. She comes home and waits for her child. He's late. She makes a call. He never arrived at the school. She calls the police and a search begins at once, but her son has apparently disappeared into thin air. There are door-to-door canvasses, helicopter searches, anonymous phone calls, predictions by psychics, and a neighborhood campaign to put "missing" posters in store windows. But there is no little boy.

One of the unexpected things about *Without a Trace* is that it's not really about the police search for the child. Instead, it's about what happens to people when tragedy turns into open-ended frustration. The mother waits and waits. The detective in charge of the case (Judd Hirsch) follows up leads and does all the things a competent cop is supposed to do. The city lends its resources and pays for an expensive investigation. But everything leads to nothing.

The central passages of the film are the best, as Nelligan plays an intelligent, civilized woman fighting to keep control. She feels rage, yes, but she is a rational person and she tries to behave reasonably. Underneath, she is deeply grieving. It takes her best friend (Stockard Channing) to suggest, after several months, that perhaps it is time to give up and admit that the little boy must be dead. It's time to let go of the past and rebuild her own life. Nelligan rejects that reasoning. And the movie remains neutral. What *is* the right answer: Should she accept what looks like the inevitable, or should she continue to hope? Nelligan's performance grows immensely subtle at this point. We can almost read her mind, and what we are reading is a battle between instinct and intelligence, between common sense and a mother's love.

Then a "suspect" is arrested—a gay sadomasochist. The circumstantial evidence against him is overwhelming. But Nelligan refuses to be bullied into agreement by a police department eager to close its books on the case. She becomes convinced that the man is innocent. And *Without a Trace*, which could so easily have been just another police drama, grows into a thought-provoking movie about how we behave, and why. It asks hard questions. It also has its moments of joy, but it earns every one of them.

Without You I'm Nothing ★ ★ ★
R, 89 m., 1990

Sandra Bernhard (Herself), John Doe (Himself), Steve Antin (Himself), Lu Leonard (Sandra's Manager), Ken Foree (Emcee), Cynthia Bailey (Roxanne); Female backup singers: Grace Broughton, Kimberli Williams, Axel Vera, Estuardo M. Volty; Male backup singers: Kevin Dorsey, Arnold McCuller, Oren Waters. Directed by John Boskovich and produced by Jonathan D. Krane. Screenplay by Sandra Bernhard and Boskovich.

You're a very special audience tonight. No, really!

Rock stars rarely talk to their audiences except in throwaway lines. There is a godlike detachment about them. In nightclubs, Vegas lounges, and the "entertainment rooms" of resort hotels, however, performers are talking all the time. They're relating to their audience with a mixture of confession, autobiography, and facile sincerity. The typical act in such a place is the same night after night and year after year, and interchangeable with other acts. It's canned; it's been fixed. Remember the Fabulous Baker Boys. And yet there is a great emphasis on insisting that *tonight* is different. That *this* audience is really very special. No, really!

Sandra Bernhard's *Without You I'm Nothing* seems to be set in lounge act hell. She plays a series of cabaret artists doomed to appear night after night before a completely indifferent audience. In this version of hell, time runs together, and so do the acts—so that at times she's doing Nina Simone, or borscht belt, or Burt Bacharach, or a set designed for a gay bar.

Some reviews of the film have suggested she "imitates" Simone or Streisand or Diana Ross. Nothing could be further from the truth. Bernhard is actually working in the ancient nightclub tradition of "emulation," in which obscure performers try to wrap the mantle of greatness around themselves. Having no hits of their own, they draw applause by singing the greatest hits of other people. The deep irony is that when applause comes, it is usually for the original, not the copy; the Vegas lounge singer does "Strangers in the Night," and the audience applauds for Sinatra.

All of this takes its toll in self-esteem, and although some lounge singers are happy people who enjoy entertaining, many are wrapped in bitterness and boredom as they sing to rooms full of indifferent strangers. They tell the audience it's "really special" tonight because it isn't special—it's the same as last night. They say "I love ya" but they mean "If you loved me but I know you don't." Their patter is based on wishes, not realities. And that is the essential insight of *Without You I'm Nothing*. It is a heart-rending, merciless assault on the phoniness of entertainment rhetoric.

Early in the film, there is a scene in Sandra Bernhard's dressing room. She prepares herself for the performance and addresses the camera directly, telling us how beautiful she is, how desirous. Although I have found Bernhard intriguing ever since I first saw her as one of Jerry Lewis's kidnappers in *The King of Comedy*, she is not, in fact, beautiful in the conventional sense. Her features are too angular and her mouth too angry for the current norm (although, for my taste, her face would wear better in the long run than a conventional cover girl's, because it would be more interesting). The point of the movie is, however, that she believes herself beautiful and seductive and irresistible, and she insists that we feel the same way. There is naked aggression here, the resentment that is usually buried in lounge act patter.

She goes onstage and her strange show begins. It is not really an act but a fantasy about a series of acts, in which she adopts wigs, makeup, and disguises to show that she can "be" anybody—or that there is no real person there. Her patter and songs are intercut with mysterious appearances by a beautiful black woman (Cynthia Bailey), who wanders through the film and leaves a rude message at the end. This woman is explained as her "alter ego," which is really no explanation at all. Bernhard is joined onstage by backup singers—some of them transvestites, according to the movie's credits, so maybe they prove the point that anybody can be anything. Nightclub announcements are made in extreme close-up, showing only a woman's beautiful lipsticked lips—perhaps in contrast to Bernhard's own less lovely mouth.

Bernhard sings. She does standup. She does autobiographical material about her childhood. She is angry, she is sad, she defies us to like her. And occasionally she unleashes her stage ego—telling us the things many performers probably yearn to say, which is that they are beautiful, they are gifted, they can do anything and be anybody. The audience looks on in boredom and begins to drift away, and in response her act grows more and more insistent, until in a shocking finale she drapes herself in the American flag and then removes it to reveal herself almost nude. It's as if she's saying she will do anything to hold our attention. That no secret is too private, no revelation too shaming.

It's an uneasy experience, sitting through this film. Parts of it are funny, parts of it are moving, and parts of it are uncomfortable and off-putting. It's not a jolly night out at the movies. My first reaction, frankly, was that I wasn't enjoying myself. Then I analyzed that feeling. This is not, after all, a "concert film" that wants only to entertain. It is about concert films, and about show business. It is about vanity and narcissism, performers and audiences, self-love and self-hate. And it may be about the only lounge act in history that you'll be able to remember a month later.

Witness ★ ★ ★ ★
R, 120 m., 1985

Harrison Ford (John Book), Kelly McGillis (Rachel), Josef Sommer (Schaeffer), Lukas Haas (Samuel), Alexander Godunov (Daniel Hochleitner). Directed by Peter Weir and produced by Edward S. Feldman. Screenplay by Earl Wallace.

Witness comes billed as a thriller, but it's so much more than a thriller that I wish they hadn't even used the word "murder" in the ads. This is, first of all, an electrifying and poignant love story. Then it is a movie about the choices we make in life and the choices that other people make for us. Only then is it a thriller—one that Alfred Hitchcock would have been proud to make.

The movie's first act sets up the plot, leaving it a lot of time to deal with the characters and learn about them. The film begins on an Amish settlement in Pennsylvania, where for two hundred years a self-sufficient religious community has proudly held onto the ways of their ancestors. The Amish are deeply suspicious of outsiders and stubbornly dedicated to their rural lifestyle, with its horses and carriages, its communal barn-raisings, its gas lanterns instead of electricity, hooks instead of buttons.

An Amish man dies. His widow and young son leave on a train journey. In the train station in Philadelphia, the little boy witnesses a murder. Harrison Ford plays the tough big-city detective who gets assigned to the case. He stages lineups, hoping the kid can spot the murderer. He shows the kid mug shots. Then it turns out that the police department itself is implicated in the killing. Ford is nearly murdered in an ambush. His life, and the lives of the widow and her son, are in immediate danger. He manages to drive them all back to the Amish lands of Pennsylvania before collapsing from loss of blood.

And it's at this point, really, that the movie begins. Up until the return to Amish country, *Witness* has been a slick, superior thriller. Now it turns into an intelligent and perceptive love story. It's not one of those romances where the man and woman fall into each other's arms because their hormones are programmed that way. It's about two independent, complicated people who begin to love each other because they have shared danger, they work well together, they respect each other—*and* because their physical attraction for each other is so strong it almost becomes another character in the movie.

Witness was directed by Peter Weir, the gifted Australian director of *The Year of Living Dangerously.* He has a strong and sure feeling for places, for the land, for the way that people build their self-regard by the way they do their work.

In the whole middle section of this movie, he shows the man from the city and the simple Amish woman within the context of the Amish community. It is masterful filmmaking. The thriller elements alone would command our attention. The love story by itself would be exciting. The ways of life in the Amish community are so well-observed that they have a documentary feel. But all three elements work together so well that something organic is happening here; we're *inside* this story.

Harrison Ford has never given a better performance in a movie. Kelly McGillis, the young actress who plays the Amish widow, has a kind of luminous simplicity about her;

it is refreshing and even subtly erotic to see a woman who doesn't subscribe to all the standard man-woman programmed responses of modern society.

The love that begins to grow between them is not made out of clichés; the cultural gulf that separates them is at least as important to both of them as the feelings they have. When they finally kiss, it is a glorious, sensuous moment, because this kiss is a sharing of trust and passion, not just another plug-in element from your standard kit of movie images.

We have been getting so many pallid, bloodless little movies—mostly recycled teenage exploitation films made by ambitious young stylists without a thought in their heads—that *Witness* is like a fresh new day. It is a movie about adults, whose lives have dignity and whose choices matter to them. And it is also one hell of a thriller.

The Wiz ★ ★ ★
G, 133 m., 1978

Diana Ross (Dorothy), Michael Jackson (Scarecrow), Nipsey Russell (Tinman), Ted Ross (Lion), Mabel King (Evillene), Theresa Merritt (Aunt Em), Thelma Carpenter (Miss One), Lena Horne (Glinda the Good), Richard Pryor (The Wiz). Directed by Sidney Lumet and produced by Rob Cohen. Screenplay by Joel Schumacher.

Magical tornadoes can strike down anywhere, I guess, and spin you off to the land of Oz. On that wonderfully logical premise, the classic *Wizard of Oz* was transformed into a Broadway musical named *The Wiz,* and then the most expensive movie musical ever made. Is the movie a match for the 1939 Judy Garland version? Well, no, it's not—what movie could be?—but as a new approach to the same material, it's slick and energetic and fun.

The Wiz is set in present-day New York City, and finds its locations in fanciful sets suggesting Harlem, Coney Island, school playgrounds, the subway system, and a sweatshop. Our heroine, Dorothy, has been transformed from a Kansas teen-ager to a twenty-four-year-old black schoolteacher. And Diana Ross wears the same simple white frock for the entire film and projects a wide-eyed innocence that kind of grows on you.

Some churlish souls suggested, however, that *The Wiz* strains our credibility too much. That a twenty-four-year-old school-

teacher should be too sophisticated to consort with cowardly lions and scarecrows and men made out of tin. Pay no attention: Critics like that wouldn't know a yellow brick road if they saw one.

The Wiz asks for our suspension of disbelief and earns it (after a slow start) in that great shot of Dorothy and the Scarecrow dancing across a yellow brick bridge toward the towers of Manhattan. Up until then the going has been a little awkward. We don't really understand why Dorothy's such a mope at her aunt's dinner party—and, after she and her dog Toto are whirled away by a snowstorm, the scene in the playground really drags. Lots of graffiti people, drawn on the walls, come to life and dance about like a Broadway chorus line (which, of course, they are), and then Dorothy finally finds her first yellow brick.

It's good that the Scarecrow is the first traveling companion she meets; Michael Jackson fills the role with humor and warmth. Nipsey Russell is fine as the Tinman, too, but Ted Ross sort of disappears into his lion's costume, done in by the makeup man. We can't see enough of him to get to know him.

There are lots of good scenes in the Emerald City. A dance sequence, for example, where The Wiz calls the shots and everybody instantly changes their clothes to stay in fashion. A run-in with a roller coaster. The scenes in the subway, where Dorothy and her friends are chased by enormous, menacing trash bins that snap their jaws ferociously. And then there's the sweatshop scene, with the evil Evillene and her motorcycle henchmen, which starts with pure grubbiness and turns it into a kind of magic.

Finally, at the very end of the journey, there's Richard Pryor as The Wiz, coward at heart, filled with doubts, hiding behind the electronic gadgets he uses to enslave the Emerald City and keep Evillene at bay. The songs get a little sticky about here—all sorts of unthrilling messages about how you can achieve anything if only you believe—but Diana Ross knows how to sell them, and she has a virtuoso solo in a totally darkened frame that reminds us of Barbra Streisand's closing number in *Funny Lady.*

The movie has great moments and a lot of life, sensational special effects and costumes—and Ross, Jackson, and Russell. Why *doesn't* it involve us as deeply as *The Wizard of Oz?* Maybe because it hedges its bets by wanting to be sophisticated *and* universal, childlike *and* knowing, appealing to both a mass audience and to media insiders. *The Wizard of Oz* went flat-out for the heart of its story; there are times when *The Wiz* has just a touch too much calculation.

The Wizard ★
PG, 100 m., 1989

Luke Edwards (Jimmy), Vincent Leahr (Tate), Wendy Phillips (Christine), Dea McAllister (Counselor), Sam McMurray (Bateman), Beau Bridges (Sam), Fred Savage (Corey), Christian Slater (Nick), Will Seltzer (Putnam), Jenny Lewis (Haley). Directed by Todd Holland and produced by David Chisholm and Ken Topolsky. Screenplay by Chisholm.

The Wizard is one of those movies that provokes the Hey, Wait a Minute Syndrome—you know, the kind where you keep saying things like, "Hey, wait a minute—how could a nine-year-old boy walk miles along a desert highway without being noticed?" Or "Wait a minute—do you mean to say a trucker wouldn't even stop if he saw two little kids coasting down an interstate highway on a skateboard?" Or, "Wait a minute—do businessmen on their lunch hours really gamble on video games with little kids?" Or "Wait a minute—could three little kids (for their ranks have swelled by now) really make it from Utah to Los Angeles without anything terrible happening to them?"

But wait a minute. I know, I know, *The Wizard* is only a silly Christmas kiddie movie, and we aren't supposed to ask questions like that. But we must. In an age when child abduction is the subject of half the TV docudramas and all the milk cartons, how are we supposed to blind ourselves to the central fact of this movie, which is that a thirteen-year-old boy and his nine-year-old brother, accompanied part of the way by a thirteen-year-old girl, manage to walk, hitchhike, and con themselves all the way from Utah to the National Video Game Championships in L.A.?

The movie is filled with shots of these little kids walking down highways, and hitching rides, and walking into bars and video parlors and Reno gambling casinos, and there wasn't a moment when I didn't question the sanity of the film and fear for their safety. It was only after the three kids arrived safely at the championships that I began to question the ethics of the film, which is,

among other things, a thinly disguised commercial for Nintendo video games and the Universal studio tour.

For, make no mistake, it is Nintendo games that these kids are expert on, and a lot of them are mentioned by name in the movie, along with lots of shots of the Nintendo trademark and various Nintendo game screens in action. And the movie's big chase scene is backstage at the Universal tour, where King Kong and a lot of complicated machinery cause various kinds of problems.

The plot of the movie involves the little kid's desire to walk to California (for reasons which, when they are finally revealed, make you want to cringe). His brother decides to help him do it, and along the way the kid reveals a talent at video games that not only allows them to support themselves, but suggests the goal of the world championship and its fifty-thousand-dollar first prize. Those are only the headlines; a full plot description would make this movie sound like a nasty pile-up down at the screenplay factory.

The Wizard is the kind of movie where every adult role is hapless, but the adults are rarely as plumb imbecilic as they are this time. The movie's hero, played by young Fred Savage, kidnaps his younger half-brother from an institution and helps him realize his dream of going to California—and the kids are chased by Savage's father (Beau Bridges) as well as an older brother and an evil man who tracks down missing kids for a living.

This leads to various idiotic scenes in which the father and the child-chaser ram into each other's vehicles and other examples of heart-rending goofiness in which the older brother complains that he can't communicate with his father. There is also another subplot involving the little kid's real mother and her current husband, and yet *another* villain in the shape of a mean little Nintendo expert.

Who was this movie intended for? No one above the age of reason will be able to abide it. Of those below that age, the studio may have targeted kids who are Nintendo fans—but here the problem is that the movie doesn't have much Nintendo in it and some of that is wrong (when it's announced, for example, that the third level of Teenage Mutant Ninja Turtles has been reached, the movie screen clearly shows the first level). *The Wizard* is finally just a cynical exploitation film with a lot of commercial plugs in it, and it is so insanely overwritten and ineptly

directed that it will disappoint just about everybody and serve them right for going in the first place.

A Woman Under the Influence
★ ★ ★ ★
R, 155 m., 1974

Peter Falk (Nick Longhetti), Gena Rowlands (Mabel Longhetti), Katherine Cassavetes (Mama Longhetti), Lady Rowlands (Martha Mortensen), Fred Draper (George Mortensen). Directed by John Cassavetes and produced by Sam Shaw. Screenplay by Cassavetes.

John Cassavetes's *A Woman Under the Influence* gives us a woman whose influences only gradually reveal themselves. And as they do, they give us insight not only into one specific, brilliantly created, woman, but into some of the problems of surviving in a society where very few people are free to be themselves. The woman is Mabel Longhetti, wife and mother and (in some very small, shy, and faraway corner) herself. Her husband, Nick, is the head of a construction gang and a gregarious type with an expansive nature; he's likely to bring his whole crew home at 7 A.M. for a spaghetti dinner.

Mabel isn't gregarious, but she tries. She tries too hard, and that's her problem. She desperately wants to please her husband, and when they're alone, she does. They get along, and they do love one another. But when people are around, she gets a little wacky. The mannerisms, the strange personal little ways she has of expressing herself, get out of scale. She's not sure how to act, because she's not sure who she is. "I'll be whatever you want me to be," she tells Nick, and he tells her to be herself. But who is that?

The film takes place before and after six months she spends in a mental institution. Her husband has her committed, reluctantly, after she begins to crack up. There have been some indications that she's in trouble. She behaves strangely when some neighbor children are brought over to stay for a while with her own, and the neighbor is afraid to leave his kids because of the way she's acting. But what, exactly, is "strange"? Well she's insecure, hyper, manic. She laughs too much and pushes too hard. She's not good with other people around. So her husband does what he thinks he has to do and commits her. But what about him? What kind of a guy is he? It's here that *A Woman Under the Influence* gets to be complicated, involved, and fascinating—a revelation. Because if Mabel is disturbed, then so is he. He's as crazy as she is, maybe more so. But because he's a man and has channels for his craziness, he stays at home and she gets sent away.

Their ways with kids, for example, are revealing. She feels insecure around them. She's not confident enough to be a mother, and almost wants to be another kid. But the father, when he takes over the responsibility of raising them, yanks them out of school in the middle of the day and drags them, bewildered, to the seashore for the most depressing, compulsory day at the beach we can imagine. And then on the way home, he lets them share a six-pack with him. If Mabel wants to be one of the kids, Nick wants them to be three of the boys.

I don't suppose (although I'm not sure) that real families like this exist, and I don't think Cassavetes wants us to take the film as a literal record. The characters are larger than life (although not less convincing because of that), and their loves and rages, their fights and moments of tenderness, exist at exhausting levels of emotion.

Nick, as played by Peter Falk, shouts and storms and is always on. Mabel (Gena Rowlands, who won an Oscar nomination), seems so touchingly vulnerable to every kind of influence around her that we don't want to tap her, because she might fall apart. Because their personalities are so open, so visible, we see what might be hidden in a quieter, tidier film: that Nick no less than Mabel is trapped in a society where people are assigned roles, duties, and even personalities that have little to do with what they really think and who they really are. This is where Cassavetes is strongest as a writer and filmmaker: at creating specific characters and then sticking with them through long, painful, uncompromising scenes until we know them well enough to read them, to predict what they'll do next, and even to begin to understand why.

Mabel and Nick and their relatives and friends are fully realized, convincing, fictional creations, even though Cassavetes does sometimes deliberately push them into extreme situations. There's a scene, for example, where Nick goes almost berserk in throwing a party for Mabel, who's due home from the institution, then tells all the non-family guests to leave immediately and then berates the family, and Mabel, and himself, in a painful confrontation around the dining room table. The scene's just too extreme to take literally. But as psychodrama, or whatever you want to call it, it abandons any niceties or evasions and deals directly with what the characters are really thinking.

There's also the scenes of great quiet comedy, as when one of Nick's co-workers somehow dumps his entire plate of spaghetti into his lap and the others battle between decorous table manners and their desire to laugh. There's Gena Rowlands's incredible command of her physical acting resources to communicate what Mabel feels at times when she's too unsure or intimidated to say. There's Falk, in a performance totally unlike his Columbo, creating this character who's so tender, so much in love, and so screwed up. I have a friend who said, after seeing *A Woman Under the Influence*, that she was so affected, she didn't know whether to cry or throw up. Well, sometimes that's the choice life presents you with—along with the laughs.

Woodstock ★ ★ ★ ★
R, 180 m., 1970

Featuring Richie Havens, Joan Baez, Joe Cocker, Santana, The Who, Sha-Na-Na, Ten Years After, John Sebastian, Crosby, Stills & Nash, Country Joe and The Fish, Arlo Guthrie, Sly and the Family Stone, and Jimi Hendrix. Directed by Michael Wadleigh and produced by Bob Maurice.

Defense Attorney: "Where do you live?"
Abbie Hoffman: "I live in Woodstock nation."
Defense Attorney: "Will you tell the court and the jury where it is?"
Abbie Hoffman: "Yes, it is a nation of alienated young people. We carry it around with us as a state of mind, in the same way the Sioux Indians carry the Sioux nation with them. . . ."

Michael Wadleigh's *Woodstock* is an archaeological study of that nation, which existed for three days in 1969. Because of this movie, the Woodstock state of mind now has its own history, folklore, myth. In terms of evoking the style and feel of a mass historical event, *Woodstock* may be the best documentary ever made in America. But don't see it for that reason; see it because it is so good to see.

It has a lot of music in it, photographed in an incredible intimacy with the performers, but it's not by any means only a rock-music movie. It's a documentary about the highs and lows of a society that formed itself briefly at Woodstock before moving on. It covers that civilization completely, showing how the musicians sang to it and the Hog Farm fed it and the Port-O-San man provided it with toilet facilities.

And it shows how 400,000 young people formed the third largest city in New York State, and ran it for a weekend with no violence, in a spirit of informal cooperation. The spirit survived even though Woodstock was declared a "disaster area," and a thunderstorm soaked everyone to the skin, and the food ran out. The remarkable thing about Wadleigh's film is that it succeeds so completely in making us feel how it must have been to be there. It does that to the limits that a movie can.

Woodstock does what all good documentaries do. It is a bringer of news. It reports, it shows, it records, and it interprets. It gives us maybe sixty percent music and forty percent on the people who were there, and that is a good ratio, I think. The music is very much part of the event, especially since Wadleigh and his editors have allowed each performer's set to grow and build and double back on itself without interference. That is what rock music in concert is all about, as I understand it. Rock on records is another matter, usually, but in the free form of a concert like Woodstock, the whole point is that the performers and their audience are into a back-and-forth thing from which a totally new performance can emerge.

We get that feeling from Jimi Hendrix when he improvises a guitar arrangement of "The Star Spangled Banner," rockets bursting in air and all. We get it from Country Joe, poker-faced, leading the crowd through the anti-Vietnam "I Feel Like I'm Fixin' to Die Rag." We get it in the raunchy 1950s vulgarity of Sha-Na-Na doing a tightly choreographed version of "At the Hop." And we get it so strongly that some kind of strange sensation inhabits our spine, when Joe Cocker and everybody else in the whole Woodstock nation sings "With a Little Help from My Friends."

This sort of participation can happen at a live concert, and often enough it does. But it is hard to get on film, harder than it looks. It is captured in *Woodstock*, maybe because Wadleigh's crew understood the music better and had the resources to shoot 120 miles of film with sixteen cameras. This gave them miles and hours of film to throw away, but it also gave them a choice when they got into the editing room. They weren't stuck with one camera pointed at one performer; they could cut to reaction shots, to multiple images, to simultaneous close-ups when two members of a band did a mutual improvisation.

And of course they always had the option of remaining simple, even shy, when the material called for it. One of the most moving moments of the film, for me, is Joan Baez singing the old Wobbly song "Joe Hill," and then rapping about her husband David, and then putting down the guitar and singing "Swing Low, Sweet Chariot," with that voice which is surely the purest and sweetest of our generation. Wadleigh and company had the integrity to let her just sing it. No tricks. No fancy camera angles. Just Joan Baez all alone on a pitch-black screen.

But then when the occasion warrants it, they let everything hang out. When Santana gets to their intricate rhythm thing, Wadleigh goes to a triple-screen and frames the drummer with two bongo players. All in synchronized sound (which is not anywhere near as easy as it sounds under outdoor concert conditions). And the editing rhythm follows the tense, driving Santana lead. The thing about this movie, somehow, is that the people who made it were right there, right on top of what the performers were doing.

Watch, for example, the way Richie Havens is handled. He is supposed to be more or less a folk singer—a powerful one, but still within the realm of folk and not rock. So you would think maybe he'd seem slightly less there than the hard-rock people? Not at all, because Wadleigh's crew went after the power in Havens's performance, and when they got it they stuck so close to it visually that in his second song, "Freedom," we get moved by folk in the way we ordinarily expect to be moved by rock.

We see Havens backstage, tired, even a little down. Then he starts singing, and we don't see his face again, but his thumb on the guitar strings, punishing them. And then (in an unbroken shot) down to his foot in a sandal, pounding with the beat, and then the fingers, and then the foot, and only then the face, and now this is a totally transformed Richie Havens, and we are so close to him, we see he doesn't have any upper teeth. Not that it matters; but we don't usually get that close to anybody in a movie.

Moving along with the music, paralleling it sometimes on a split screen, are the more traditionally documentary aspects of *Woodstock*. There are the townspeople, split between those who are mean and ordinary and closed off, and those like the man who says, "Kids are hungry, you gotta feed 'em. Right?" And the farmer who made his land available. And kids skinny-dipping, and turning on, and eating and sleeping.

Wadleigh never forces this material. His movie is curiously objective, in fact. Not neutral; he's clearly with the kids. But objective; showing what's there without getting himself in the way, so that the experience comes through directly.

With all that film to choose from in the editing room, he was able to give us dozens of tiny unrehearsed moments that sum up the Woodstock feeling. The skinny-dipping, for example, is free and unself-conscious, and we can see that. But how good it is to see that kid sitting on a stump in the water and turning to the camera and saying, "Man, a year ago I never would have believed this was the way to swim. But, man, this *is* the way to swim."

What you're left with finally, though, are the people. I almost said the "kids," but that wouldn't include the friendly chief of police, or the farmer, or Hugh Romney from the Hog Farm ("Folks, we're planning breakfast in bed for 400,000 people"), or the Port-O-San man, or the townspeople who took carloads of food to the park.

Wadleigh and his team have recorded all the levels. The children. The dogs (who were allowed to run loose in this nation). The freaks and the straights. The people of religion (Swami Gi and three nuns giving the peace sign). The cops (eating Popsicles). The Army (dropping blankets, food, and flowers from helicopters). *Woodstock* is a beautiful, complete, moving, ultimately great film, and now that many years have come to pass and the Woodstock generation is attacked for being just as uptight as all the rest of the generations, it's good to have this movie around to show that, just for a weekend anyway, that wasn't altogether the case.

Working Girl ★ ★ ★ ★
R, 116 m., 1988

Melanie Griffith (Tess McGill), Harrison Ford (Jack Trainer), Sigourney Weaver (Katharine Parker), Alec Baldwin (Mick Dugan), Joan Cusack (Cyn), Philip Bosco (Oren Trask), Nora Dunn (Ginny), Olympia Dukakis (Personnel Director). Directed by Mike Nichols and produced by Douglas Wick. Screenplay by Kevin Wade.

The problem with working your way up the ladder of life is that sometimes you can't get there from here. People look at you and make a judgment call, and then, try as you might, you're only spinning your wheels. That's how Tess McGill feels in the opening scenes of *Working Girl*. She is intelligent and aggressive, and she has a lot of good ideas about how to make money in the big leagues of high finance. But she is a secretary. A secretary with too much hair. A secretary who rides the Staten Island ferry to work. A secretary who started talking like a little girl because it was cute when she was eleven and is still talking the same way, except now she is thirty. There is no way anybody is ever going to take her seriously.

One day, Tess (Melanie Griffith) gets a new boss at the mergers and acquisitions firm where she works. The boss (Sigourney Weaver) is a woman of almost exactly Tess's age, but with a different set of accessories. For example, she talks in a low, modulated voice, and wears more businesslike clothes, and has serious hair. "If you want to get ahead in business," Tess muses, "you've got to have serious hair." She gets along fine with her boss until the boss goes on a skiing holiday and breaks her leg and ends up in traction for six weeks. Then Tess goes into her boss's computer, and finds that the boss was about to steal one of Tess's brilliant suggestions and claim it as her own.

This makes her fighting mad, and so she begins an elaborate deception in which she masquerades as an executive at the firm, and figures out a way to meet a guy named Jack Trainer (Harrison Ford), who is the right guy at another firm to make the deal happen. She meets Trainer at a party and gets drunk and ends up in bed with him, even though she *explained* to him, "I have a head for business and a bod for sin." Will he ever take her seriously now? Yes, it turns out he will, because he likes her, and because he thinks her idea really is pretty brilliant.

That's the setup for *Working Girl*, which is one of those entertainments where you laugh a lot along the way, and then you end up on the edge of your seat. Structurally, the film has some parallels with *The Graduate*, Nichols's 1967 classic—including a climactic scene where an important ceremony is interrupted by the wrong person bursting in through the door. But this movie is the other side of the coin. *The Graduate* was about a young man who did not want to make money in plastics. *Working Girl* is about a young woman who very definitely wants to make money in mergers.

This is Melanie Griffith's movie in the same way that *The Graduate* belonged to Dustin Hoffman. She was not an obvious casting choice, but she is the right one, and in an odd way her two most famous previous roles, in *Body Double* and *Something Wild*, work for her. Because we may remember her from those sex-drenched roles, there is a way in which both Griffith and her character are both trying to get respectable—to assimilate everything that goes along with "serious hair."

Supporting roles are crucial in movies like this. The Sigourney Weaver role is a thankless one—she plays the pill who gets humiliated at the end—and yet it is an interesting assignment for an actor with Weaver's imagination. From her first frame on the screen, she has to say all the right things while subtly suggesting that she may not mean any of them. If she is subtle, so is Harrison Ford, an actor whose steadiness goes along with a sort of ruminating passion; when he's in love with a woman, he doesn't grab her, he just seems to ponder her a lot. Weaver and Ford provide the indispensable frame within which the Griffith character can be seen to change.

The plot of *Working Girl* is put together like clockwork. It carries you along while you're watching it, but reconstruct it later and you'll see the craftsmanship. The Kevin Wade screenplay is sort of underhanded, the way it diverts us with laughs and with a melodramatic subplot involving Griffith's former boyfriend, while all the time it's winding up for the suspenseful climax. By the time we get to the last scenes, the movie plays like a thriller, and that's all the more effective because we weren't exactly bracing for that. *Working Girl* is Mike Nichols returning to the top of his form, and Melanie Griffith finding hers.

Working Girls ★ ★ ★

NO MPAA RATING, 90 m., 1987

Louise Smith (Molly), Ellen McElduff (Lucy), Amanda Goodwin (Dawn), Marusia Zach (Gina), Janne Peters (April), Helen Nicholas (Mary). Directed by Lizzie Borden and produced by Borden and Andi Gladstone. Screenplay by Borden and Sandra Kay.

There is, I imagine, somewhere in the mind of every man who goes to a prostitute the fantasy that he is somehow unique; that the woman has never met anyone quite like him before, and that, although her other clients may be "johns," he is an individual.

Working Girls both supports and destroys that illusion. The prostitutes in this movie may, indeed, never have met anyone quite like certain clients before, but that is not necessarily a compliment. What makes each man different is the nature of his fantasy life, the specific scenario he is seeking from a prostitute. What makes each man the same is that there are only so many fantasies, and so many ways to fulfill them, and, for the working girls, only so many hours in a day.

Working Girls takes place during one day in a Manhattan bordello. The routine is well-established. The guys call in, the "phone girl" makes an appointment or a sales pitch, the women pass the time with idle small talk and gossip, and occasionally something truly exciting happens—such as when the phones are put on hold and the madam has a temper tantrum.

One by one, the guys come in through the door, each one burdened with the weight of his uniqueness. "How's everything?" one of the hookers asks a client. "Terrific," he says. "We have a new secretary at the office." "Yeah, it's been pretty busy around here," the girl says. "I can imagine," the guy says.

Some of the johns have really wild scenarios going on in their heads. One of them, for example, wants a hooker to enact a situation in which she is blind and only sexual intercourse with the guy can make her see again.

Others are into more kinky situations, but the bottom line is always the same: What goes on in bed between the hooker and the john is simply the occasion for the man to replay old and deep needs that have been in place for years. The woman is relatively unimportant, because she is not the fantasy but more like the supporting cast.

Working Girls has a lot of fascinating stuff in it, but most of it has to do with management and capitalism, not sex. We learn a great deal about clean towels, birth control, disease prevention, and never putting the phones on hold. We also learn a lot of euphemisms: For example, "Make sure the client is completely comfortable before you take any money." In other words, make sure the guy is naked, because then you know he's not a cop.

The movie is told largely through the eyes of Molly (Louise Smith), a lesbian whose lover doesn't know what she does for a living. After Molly arrives at work (on her ten-speed bike), we meet the other girls, some of them naive, some of them middle-age and weary, all of them bereft of illusions about men.

Sometimes, however, something touching happens in the sessions behind the closed doors. There are fugitive moments of tenderness, quiet passages of communication. It is a cliché that prostitutes are really selling companionship, not sex, and *Working Girls* seems to support that notion. What is remarkable is not that the girls are cynical and hardened, but that they have retained as much gentleness and empathy as they have. Like workers in more respectable professions such as psychiatry, medicine, and the ministry, they seem to have the ability to care, if only for a short time, about some of their clients, and to be nice to them. By the end of this movie, you wonder where they find not only the patience, but also the strength.

Working Girls is not a slick and dramatic movie. There are moments that seem forced and amateurish, and the overall structure of the story is fairly predictable. What the movie does have, though, is the feeling of real life being observed accurately. I was moved less by the movie's conscious attempts at artistry than by its unadorned honesty: The director, Lizzie Borden, has created characters who seem close to life, and her movie helps explain why the world's oldest profession is, despite everything, a profession.

The World According to Garp ★ ★ ★

R, 126 m., 1982

Robin Williams (Garp), Mary Beth Hurt (Helen Holm), Glenn Close (Jenny Fields), John Lithgow (Roberta), Hume Cronyn (Mr. Fields), Jessica Tandy (Mrs. Fields), Swoosie Kurtz (Hooker), Amanda Plummer (Ellen James). Directed by George Roy Hill and produced by Hill and Robert L. Crawford. Screenplay by Steve Tesich.

John Irving's best-selling novel, *The World According to Garp*, was cruel, annoying, and smug. I kept wanting to give it to my cats. But it was wonderfully well-written and was probably intended to inspire some of those negative reactions in the reader. The movie version of *Garp*, however, left me entertained but unmoved, and perhaps the movie's basic failing is that it did not inspire me to walk out on it. Something has to be wrong with a film that can take material as intractable as *Garp* and make it palatable.

Like a lot of movie versions of novels, the film of *Garp* has not reinterpreted the material in its own terms. Indeed, it doesn't interpret it at all. It simply reproduces many of the characters and events in the novel, as if the point in bringing *Garp* to the screen was to provide a visual aid for the novel's readers. With the book we at least know how we feel during the saga of Garp's unlikely life; the movie lives entirely within its moments, keeping us entirely inside a series of self-contained scenes.

The story of Garp is by now part of best-selling folklore. We know that Garp's mother was an eccentric nurse, a cross between a saint and a nuisance, and that Garp was fathered in a military hospital atop the unconscious body of a brain-damaged technical sergeant. That's how much use Garp's mother, Jenny Fields, had for men. The movie, like the book, follows Garp from this anticlimactic beginning through a lifetime during which he is constantly overshadowed by his mother, surrounded by other strange women and women-surrogates, and asks for himself, his wife and children only uneventful peace and a small measure of happiness.

A great deal happens, however, to disturb the peace and prevent the happiness. Garp is accident-prone, and sadness and disaster surround him. Assassinations, bizarre airplane crashes, and auto mishaps are part of his daily routine. His universe seems to have been wound backward.

The movie's method in regarding the nihilism of his life is a simple one. It alternates two kinds of scenes: those in which very strange people do very strange things while pretending to be sane, and those in which all of the dreams of those people, and Garp, are shattered in instants of violence and tragedy.

What are we to think of these people and the events in their lives? The novel *The World According to Garp* was (I *think*) a tragicomic counterpoint between the collapse of middle-class family values and the rise of random violence in our society. A protest against that violence provides the most memorable image in the book, the creation of the Ellen James Society, a group of women who cut out their tongues in protest against what happened to Ellen James, who had her tongue cut out by a man. The bizarre behavior of the people in the novel, particularly Garp's mother and the members of the Ellen Jamesians, is a cross between activism and insanity, and there is the clear suggestion that without such behavior to hold them together, all of these people would be unable to cope at all and would sign themselves into the nearest institution. As a vision of modern American life, *Garp* is bleak, but it has something to say.

The movie, however, seems to believe that the book's characters and events are somehow real, or, to put it another way, that the *point* of the book is to describe these colorful characters and their unlikely behavior, just as Melville described the cannibals in *Typee*. Although Robin Williams plays Garp as a relatively plausible, sometimes ordinary person, the movie never seems bothered by the jarring contrast between his cheerful pluckiness and the anarchy around him.

That created the following dilemma for me. While I watched *Garp*, I enjoyed it. I thought the acting was unconventional and absorbing (especially by Williams, by Glenn Close as his mother, and by John Lithgow as a transsexual). I thought the visualization of the events, by director George Roy Hill, was fresh and consistently interesting. But when the movie was over, my immediate response was not at all what it should have been. All I could find to ask myself was: What the hell was *that* all about?

A World Apart ★ ★ ★ ★
PG, 112 m., 1988

Barbara Hershey (Diana Roth), Jodhi May (Molly Roth), Jeroen Krabbe (Gus Roth), Carolyn Clayton-Cragg (Miriam Roth), Linda Mvusi (Elsie). Directed by Chris Menges and produced by Sarah Radclyffe. Screenplay by Shawn Slovo.

A World Apart was written by a woman who grew up in South Africa in the 1960s, while her parents were involved in the antiapartheid movement, and it is very much a daughter's story; even though her parents were brave and dedicated, their child still nurses a sense of resentment because she did not get all of the attention she felt she deserved. *A World Apart* is both political and personal—a view of a revolutionary as the middle-class mother of a normal thirteen-year-old girl.

The girl's name is Molly (Jodhi May), and the film opens with episodes from her typical childhood in an affluent white South African community. She takes ballet lessons, she is picked up after class in a big American convertible piloted by her friend's mother, she attends the usual birthday parties, and splashes in a neighbor's swimming pool. The only thing unusual about her life is that some of her parents' friends are black—and in white South Africa in 1963, that is very unusual indeed.

Her parents are the Roths, Diana and Gus, and they are involved in a lot of activities she knows nothing about. One night her father comes to say goodbye to her, and the next day he is gone, having fled the country one step ahead of arrest on charges of communist subversion. Her mother stays behind, works for an anti-government newspaper, and moves in left-wing circles. A law is passed authorizing the government to detain anyone for up to ninety days on suspicion of subversive activities, and Diana Roth (Barbara Hershey) is one of the first to be detained.

We see this detention in two ways. Through the eyes of the mother, it is a terrifying form of torture, in which she is separated from her family and given no certain future to look forward to. She is interrogated daily by a government official who tries to ingratiate himself with her as kind of a good guy—he falls a little in love with her—but she adopts a stoic mask of determined resistance.

Hershey's own mother steps in to take care of the family during the period. For Molly, everything in her life turns out to have changed. Her best friend, for example, is suddenly cold toward her. She isn't invited to any more birthday or pool parties. Her parents are criminals and so she is somehow a criminal and a pariah, too. Meanwhile, on another front, the brother of the family's maid dies in the hands of the police, and political turmoil begins to simmer.

From a certain point of view, there is an irony here. Why should we care that a thirteen-year-old is not invited to swimming parties, when millions of black South Africans are denied elementary civil rights? From another point of view, *A World Apart* is stronger because it chooses to deal with the smaller details of specific lives. Unlike *Cry Freedom*, which was painted on such a large canvas that subtlety was lost, *A World Apart* is about the specific ways in which individual lives are affected by a legal system in which one's rights depend on one's race.

I spent a year in South Africa, in 1965, at

the University of Cape Town, and I have often been disturbed by the ways in which so many fictional depictions of the country seem unable to communicate what it is like to live there. For most people of all races in South Africa, most days are fairly routine, devoted to the various activities of family and work, getting and spending and caring, that are the bedrock of lives everywhere. The country is not some sort of permanent political passion play. It is possible to fall into a workable, even comfortable, routine. It is by showing the placid surface of everyday life that *A World Apart* is able to dramatize how close beneath that surface the police state resides. For those who do not rock the boat, South Africa can be a very pleasant place to live.

Diana Roth rocks the boat, and through her daughter's eyes we see the result of that action. As played by Barbara Hershey, Roth is not an ideal mother, although she is a dutiful one; there is a certain hardness in her, an edge of anger that focuses on injustice and sometimes overlooks the needs of her family in what seem to be the more urgent needs of society. This is another fine, strong performance by Hershey, who has emerged in recent years as one of our best actresses.

Jodhi May, as young Molly, is equally impressive, and in many ways this is her movie. The screenplay (by Shawn Slovo, based on her own memories) gives May much to work with, but the ways in which her eyes express hurt and rejection are all her own. (Hershey, May, and Linda Mvusi, who plays the family's maid, shared the best actress award at the 1988 Cannes Film Festival.)

A World Apart has moments of almost unbearable hurt. One of them is at the moment when Hershey thinks her imprisonment is over, and is wrong. Another is when young Molly discovers the truth of a friend's rejection. Another, very powerful, is at the funeral of the murdered black man—a scene smaller, but more powerful, than the similar scene in *Cry Freedom*. The film is the first directorial work by Chris Menges, the cinematographer of *The Killing Fields* and *The Mission*. It is strong, angry, and troubling.

Y,Z

The Year of Living Dangerously
★ ★ ★ ★
PG, 114 m., 1983

Mel Gibson (Guy Hamilton), Linda Hunt (Billy Kwan), Sigourney Weaver (Jill Bryant), Michael Murphy (Pete Curtis), Noel Ferrier (Wally O'Sullivan), Bill Kerr (Colonel Henderson). Directed by Peter Weir and produced by Jim McElroy. Screenplay by David Williamson, Weir, and C.J. Koch.

The Year of Living Dangerously achieves one of the best re-creations of an exotic locale I've ever seen in a movie. It takes us to Indonesia in the middle 1960s, a time when the Sukarno regime was shaky and the war in Vietnam was just heating up. It moves us into the life of a foreign correspondent, a radio reporter from Australia who has just arrived in Jakarta, and who thrives in an atmosphere heady with danger. How is this atmosphere created by Peter Weir, the director? He plunges into it headfirst. He doesn't pause for travelogue shots. He thrusts us immediately into the middle of the action—into a community of expatriates, journalists, and embassy people who hang out in the same bars, restaurants, and clubs, and speculate hungrily on the possibility that Sukarno might be deposed. That would be a really big story, a corrective for their vague feelings of being stuck in a backwater.

Guy Hamilton, the journalist (Mel Gibson), is a lanky, Kennedyesque, chain-smoking young man who has a fix on excitement. He doesn't know the ropes in Indonesia, but he learns them quickly enough, from a dwarfish character named Billy Kwan. Billy is half-Oriental and half-European, and knows everybody and can tell you where all the bodies are buried. He has a warm smile and a way of encouraging you to do your best, and if you sometimes suspect he has

unorthodox political connections—well, he hasn't crossed you yet. In all the diplomatic receptions he's a familiar sight in his gaudy tropical shirts. *The Year of Living Dangerously* follows Guy and Billy as they become friends, and something more than friends; they begin to share a common humanity and respect. Billy gets Guy a good interview with the local Communist Party chief. He even introduces Guy to Jill Bryant (Sigourney Weaver), a British attaché with two weeks left on her tour. As the revolution creeps closer, as the stories get bigger, Guy and Jill become lovers and Billy, who once proposed to Jill, begins to feel pushed aside.

This sounds, no doubt, like a foreign correspondent plot from the 1940s. It is not. *The Year of Living Dangerously* is a wonderfully complex film about personalities more than events, and we really share the feeling of living in that place, at that time. It does for Indonesia what Bogdanovich's *Saint Jack* did for Singapore. The direction is masterful; Weir (whose credits include *Picnic at Hanging Rock*) is as good with quiet little scenes (like Billy's visit to a dying child) as big, violent ones (like a thrilling attempt by Guy and Billy to film a riot).

The performances of the movie are a good fit with Weir's direction, and his casting of the Billy Kwan character is a key to how the film works. Billy, so small and mercurial, likable and complicated and exotic, makes Indonesia seem more foreign and intriguing than any number of standard travelogue shots possibly could. That means that when the travelogue shots *do* come (and they do, breathtakingly, when Gibson makes a trip into the countryside), they're not just scenery; they do their work for the film because Weir has so convincingly placed us in Indonesia. Billy Kwan is played, astonishingly, by a woman—Linda Hunt, a New York stage

actress who enters the role so fully that it never occurs to us that she is not a man. This is what great acting is, a magical transformation of one person into another. Mel Gibson (of *The Road Warrior*) is just right as a basically conventional guy with an obsessive streak of risk-taking. Sigourney Weaver has a less interesting role but is always an interesting actress. This is a wonderfully absorbing film.

Yentl ★ ★ ★ ½
PG, 134 m., 1983

Barbra Streisand (Yentl), Mandy Patinkin (Avigdor), Amy Irving (Hadass), Nehemiah Persoff (Papa). Directed and produced by Barbra Streisand. Screenplay by Jack Rosenthal and Streisand.

To give you a notion of the special magic of *Yentl*, I'd like to start with the following complicated situation:

Yentl, a young Jewish girl, wants to be a scholar. But girls are not permitted to study books. So she disguises herself as a boy, and is accepted by a community of scholars. She falls in love with one of them. He thinks she is a boy. He is in love with a local girl. The girl's father will not let him marry her. So he convinces Yentl to marry his girlfriend, so that at least he can visit the two people he cares for most deeply. (The girlfriend, remember this, thinks Yentl is a boy.) Yentl and the girl are wed. At first Yentl manages to disguise her true sex. But eventually she realizes that she must reveal the truth. That is the central situation in *Yentl*. And when the critical moment came when Yentl had to decide what to do, I was quietly astonished to realize that I did not have the slightest idea how this situation was going to turn out, and that I really cared about it.

I was astonished because, quite frankly, I expected *Yentl* to be some kind of schmaltzy formula romance in which Yentl's "secret identity" was sort of a running gag. You know, like one of those plot points they use for Broadway musicals where the audience is really there to hear the songs and see the costumes. But *Yentl* takes its masquerade seriously, it treats its romances with the respect due to genuine emotion, and its performances are so good that, yes, I really did care.

Yentl is Barbra Streisand's dream movie. She had been trying to make it for ten years, ever since she bought the rights to the Isaac Bashevis Singer story it's based on. Hollywood told her she was crazy. Hollywood was right—on the irrefutable logical ground that a woman in her forties can hardly be expected to be convincing as a seventeen-year-old boy. Streisand persisted. She worked on this movie four years, as producer, director, cowriter, and star. And she has pulled it off with great style and heart. She doesn't really look like a seventeen-year-old boy in this movie, that's true. We have to sort of suspend our disbelief a little. But she *does* look seventeen, and that's without a lot of trick lighting and funny filters on the lens, too. And she sings like an angel.

Yentl is a movie with a great middle. The beginning is too heavy-handed in establishing the customs against women scholars (an itinerant book salesman actually shouts, "Serious books for men . . . picture books for women"). And the ending, with Yentl sailing off for America, seemed like a cheat; I missed the final scene between Yentl and her "bride." But the middle 100 minutes of the movie are charming and moving and surprisingly interesting. A lot of the charm comes from the cheerful high energy of the actors, not only Streisand (who gives her best performance) but also Mandy Patinkin, as her long-suffering roommate, and Amy Irving, as the girl Patinkin loves and Streisand marries.

There are, obviously, a lot of tricky scenes involving this triangle, but the movie handles them all with taste, tact, and humor. It's pretty obvious what strategy Streisand and her collaborators used in approaching the scenes where Yentl pretends to be a boy. They began by asking what the scene would mean if she *were* a male, and then they simply played it that way, allowing the ironic emotional commentaries to make themselves.

There was speculation from Hollywood that *Yentl* would be "too Jewish" for middle-American audiences. I don't think so. Like all great fables, it grows out of a particular time and place, but it takes its strength from universal sorts of feelings. At one time or another, almost everyone has wanted to do something and been told they couldn't, and almost everyone has loved the wrong person for the right reason. That's the emotional ground that *Yentl* covers, and it always has its heart in the right place.

Young Einstein ★
PG, 91 m., 1989

Yahoo Serious (Young Einstein), Odile Le Clezio (Marie Curie), John Howard (Preston Preston), Pee Wee Wilson (Mr. Einstein), Su Cruickshank (Mrs. Einstein). Directed by Yahoo Serious and produced by Serious, Warwick Ross, and David Roach. Screenplay by Serious and Roach.

Young Einstein is a one-joke movie, and I didn't laugh much the first time. It seems to take place in an alternate universe, a place in time and space where an unsung genius named Albert Einstein was born on the obscure island of Tasmania and grew up in Australia instead of Europe. Of course, this means that his major discoveries have to do with beer, rather than relativity, and his big breakthrough comes when he finds a way to apply the Law of Relativity to the problem of carbonation.

Young Einstein is played in the movie by Yahoo Serious, an actor whose very name violates a law discovered by me, the First Law of Funny Names ("In a movie, the use of funny names is a certain sign of desperation"). For Serious, the making of this movie was a miracle of sorts, and I want to give him his due: He received his first inspiration while on a trip through the Brazilian rain forests, where he saw an Indian wearing an Albert Einstein T-shirt, and (Eureka! I suppose) began to ask himself how things might have worked out if Einstein had been born in another time and place.

By moving Einstein to Australia, he was able to set up comic situations that appeal to the vast and inexhaustable fascination the Australians have about their own isolation and gawky charm, but the jokes don't travel very well, and *Young Einstein* eventually reveals itself as the same formula, repeated again and again.

The formula: The boy genius is presented with a mundane problem (flat beer), and solves it by applying a solution that will revolutionize man's view of the universe he inhabits. Onlookers are slow to recognize the genius of the solution, but villians stand ready to capitalize on it, until a lucky chance saves the day.

His genius reaches out into other fields, as when he invents the electric guitar by turning a bass viol on its side, or when he invents the atomic bomb when a beer-making experiment runs out of control. Many of these scenes involve payoffs in which gigantic explosions destroy outhouses, after which Yahoo Serious appears unharmed but covered in soot. If Serious had discovered post-Keystone film comedy in the course of his research, this would have been a better movie.

The whole construction of the film depends on deliberate anachronisms—as when Young Einstein invents rock 'n' roll music, and indeed sings the song "Rock 'n' Roll Music" some years before it, or rock 'n' roll, came on the scene. Is this funny? I don't think so. I think it's the sort of thing that sounds funny when you're writing a script, but one burst of laughter over a keyboard doesn't translate into the audience buying a whole sequence in the film.

I was also unmoved by his great love affair with Marie Curie, whom he meets while on a train in the outback. Why is it funny that this character is named Marie Curie? What does it say to mass film audiences, who do not know enough about Madame Curie to find any cross-references funny (not that the movie makes any)? One payoff after another falls flat, while we imagine Serious and his colleagues at script conferences, rocking with laughter at what they fancy is their cleverness.

Young Einstein won a great deal of attention in Australia, where Yahoo Serious became the biggest homegrown star since Paul Hogan, and the saga of how he got this movie made—as the director, coproducer, and cowriter as well as star—is intriguing enough to make a movie of its own. Discovering the Law of Relativity is relatively easy, compared to getting a feature film made when you're an unknown with no money.

Young Frankenstein ★ ★ ★ ★
PG, 108 m., 1974

Gene Wilder (Dr. Frankenstein), Peter Boyle (His Monster), Madeline Kahn (Elizabeth), Cloris Leachman (Frau Blucher), Gene Hackman (Blind Man), Teri Garr (Inga). Directed by Mel Brooks and produced by Michael Gruskoff. Screenplay by Gene Wilder and Brooks.

The moment, when it comes, has the inevitability of comic genius. Young Victor Frankenstein, grandson of the count who started it all, returns by rail to his ancestral home. As the train pulls into the station, he spots a kid on the platform, lowers the window, and asks: "Pardon me, boy; is this the Transylvania station?" It is, and director Mel Brooks is home with *Young Frankenstein*, his most disciplined and visually inventive film (it also happens to be very funny). Victor is a professor in a New York medical school, trying to live down the family name and giving hilarious demonstrations of the difference between voluntary and involuntary reflexes. He stabs himself in the process, dismisses the class, and is visited by an ancient family retainer with his grandfather's will.

Frankenstein quickly returns to Transylvania and the old ancestral castle, where he is awaited by the faithful houseboy Igor, the voluptuous lab assistant Inga, and the mysterious housekeeper Frau Blucher, whose very name causes horses to rear in fright. The young man had always rejected his grandfather's medical experiments as impossible, but he changes his mind after he discovers a book entitled *How I Did It* by Victor Frankenstein. Now all that's involved is a little grave-robbing and a trip to the handy local Brain Depository, and the Frankenstein family is back in business.

In his two best comedies, before this, *The Producers* and *Blazing Saddles*, Brooks revealed a rare comic anarchy. His movies weren't just funny, they were aggressive and subversive, making us laugh even when we really should have been offended. (Explaining this process, Brooks once loftily declared, "My movies rise below vulgarity.") *Young Frankenstein* is as funny as we expect a Mel Brooks comedy to be, but it's more than that: It shows artistic growth and a more sure-handed control of the material by a director who once seemed willing to do literally anything for a laugh. It's more confident and less breathless.

That's partly because the very genre he's satirizing gives him a strong narrative he can play against. Brooks's targets are James Whale's *Frankenstein* (1931) and *Bride of Frankenstein* (1935), the first the most influential and the second probably the best of the 1930s Hollywood horror movies. Brooks uses carefully controlled black-and-white photography that catches the feel of the earlier films. He uses old-fashioned visual devices and obvious special effects (the train ride is a study in manufactured studio scenes). He adjusts the music to the right degree of squeakiness. And he even rented the original *Frankenstein* laboratory, with its zaps of electricity, high-voltage special effects, and elevator platform to intercept lightning bolts.

So the movie is a send-up of a style and not just of the material (as Paul Morrissey's dreadful *Andy Warhol's Frankenstein*). It looks right, which makes it funnier. And then, paradoxically, it works on a couple of levels: first as comedy, and then as a weirdly touching story in its own right. A lot of the credit for that goes to the performances of Gene Wilder, as young Frankenstein, and Peter Boyle as the monster. They act broadly when it's required, but they also contribute tremendous subtlety and control. Boyle somehow manages to be hilarious and pathetic at the same time.

There are set pieces in the movie that deserve comparison with the most famous scenes in *The Producers*. Demonstrating that he has civilized his monster, for example, Frankenstein and the creature do a soft-shoe number in black tie and tails. Wandering in the woods, the monster comes across a poor, blind monk (Gene Hackman, very good) who offers hospitality and winds up scalding, burning, and frightening the poor creature half to death.

There are also the obligatory town meetings, lynch mobs, police investigations, laboratory experiments, love scenes, and a cheerfully ribald preoccupation with a key area of the monster's stitched-together anatomy. From its opening title (which manages to satirize *Frankenstein* and *Citizen Kane* at the same time) to its closing, uh, refrain, *Young Frankenstein* is not only a Mel Brooks movie but also a loving commentary on our love-hate affairs with monsters. This time, the monster even gets to have a little love-hate affair of his own.

Young Sherlock Holmes ★ ★ ★
PG-13, 109 m., 1985

Nicholas Rowe (Holmes), Alan Cox (Watson), Sophie Ward (Elizabeth), Anthony Higgins (Rathe), Susan Fleetwood (Mrs. Dribb), Freddie Jones (Cragwitch), Nigel Stock (Waxflatter). Directed by Barry Levinson and produced by Mark Johnson. Executive producer, Steven Spielberg. Screenplay by Chris Columbus.

It really does make sense, once you've overcome the novelty of the idea, that Sherlock Holmes and John H. Watson originally met while at school. Their friendship is the sort of immature bond that can best be forged between adolescents, based on Watson's hero worship and Holmes's need for an admiring audience. There has always been something of the eternal teen-ager about Holmes and Watson, especially in their love of gadgets and mysteries and technical intricacies, and their complete bafflement when faced with such complex subjects as human nature, for example, or women.

Young Sherlock Holmes suggests that Holmes and Watson met in their middle teens, at an English public school, and that Holmes solved his first case at about the same time. This theory involves a rewriting of their historic first meeting, but the movie suggests that it set a pattern for many more meetings to come: Watson blunders into the orbit of the supercilious Holmes, who casually inspects him and uses a few elementary clues to tell him everything about himself.

The school they attend is one of those havens of eccentricity that have been celebrated in English fiction since time immemorial. It is run by Rathe (Anthony Higgins), a bright young man, but it is also inhabited by old professor Waxflatter (Nigel Stock), a retired don who hopes to invent the first airplane, and who regularly launches unsuccessful flights from the tops of the school buildings.

Holmes and Watson look, as schoolboys, like younger versions of the men they would someday become. Holmes (Nicholas Rowe) is tall, slender, and taciturn, and Watson (Alan Cox) is short and round and nearsighted. Watson is in every sense the new boy, always available to run an errand for the adored Holmes, to provide a cheering section, and to chronicle the great man's adventures.

The plot of *Young Sherlock Holmes* seems

constructed out of odds and ends of several stories by Arthur Conan Doyle. For unknown reasons, several men with no apparent connection to one another die under mysterious circumstances. To Watson's amazement, Holmes finds the missing connection, determines that they have died while hallucinating, identifies the hallucinatory drug and its means of attack, and arrives at a likely suspect.

If these story elements seem typical of Conan Doyle, there is also a lot in this movie that can be traced directly to the work of Steven Spielberg, the executive producer. The teen-age heroes, for example, are not only inspired by Holmes and Watson, but are cousins of the young characters in *The Goonies*. The fascination with lighter-than-air flight leads to a closing scene that reminded me of *E. T.* And the villain's secret temple, with its ritual of human sacrifice, was not unlike scenes in both Indiana Jones movies.

It also doesn't take a Sherlock Holmes to identify the one element of *Young Sherlock Holmes* that definitely doesn't fit; that's the character of Elizabeth, a fetching young girl played by Sophie Ward. She is the granddaughter of the mad inventor, and also lives at the school, and we are asked to believe that young Holmes has had a schoolboy crush on her. I personally do not believe that Sherlock Holmes, the great investigator, ever even began to penetrate the mystery of women, but the movie just barely gets away with the character of Elizabeth by having Holmes swear there will never be another woman for him, for the rest of his life.

The elaborate special effects also seem a little out of place in a Sherlock Holmes movie, although I'm willing to forgive them because they were fun. The traditional world of Holmes (in the movies, anyway) has been limited to fogbound streets, speeding carriages, smoky sitting rooms, and the homes and laboratories of suspects. In this film, we get a series of hallucinations that are represented by fancy special effects, and then there's the pseudo-Egyptian temple of doom at the end.

The effects were supplied by Industrial Light & Magic, the George Lucas brain trust, and the best one is a computer-animated stained-glass window that fights a duel with Holmes. I liked the effect, but I would have liked it more if, at the end of the movie, Holmes had drawn Watson aside, and, using a few elementary observations on the apparent movement of the stained glass, had deduced the eventual invention of computers.

Zelig ★ ★ ★
PG, 79 m., 1983

Woody Allen (Leonard Zelig), Mia Farrow (Dr. Fletcher). Interviews: Susan Sontag, Irving Howe, Saul Bellow, Bricktop, Bruno Bettelheim, Professor John Morton Blum. Directed by Woody Allen. Produced by Robert Greenhut. Screenplay by Allen.

Woody Allen's *Zelig* represents an intriguing idea for a movie, and it has been made with great ingenuity and technical brilliance. That's almost enough. In fact, if *Zelig* were only about an hour long, it would be enough, but the unwritten code of feature films requires that it be longer, and finally there is just so much Zelig that we say enough, already.

The movie is a fake documentary, a film that claims to tell the story of Leonard Zelig, a once-famous American who suffered from a most curious disease: He was a human chameleon. He was so eager to please, so loath to give offense, so willing to blend right in, that perhaps some change took place at a cellular level, and Zelig began to take on the social, intellectual, and even physical characteristics of people that he spent time with. Put him with a psychiatrist, and he began to discuss complexes. Put him next to a Chinese man, and he began to look Oriental. This ability to fit right in propelled Zelig, we are told, to the heights of fame in the earlier decades of this century. He hobnobbed with presidents, was honored by ticker-tape parades, and his case was debated by learned societies. *Zelig* at first seems to be simply the documentary record of Zelig's case, but then another level begins to sneak in.

We are introduced (always through the documentary means of newsreel film, still photos, old radio broadcasts, and narration) to one Dr. Eudora Fletcher, who is a psychiatrist. She takes Zelig as a patient, and eventually they fall in love (we can see it happening, by implication, in documentary footage that apparently concerns other matters). The best thing about *Zelig*, apart from its technical accomplishment, is the way Woody Allen develops the human story of his hero; we get a portrait of a life and a poignant dilemma, peeking out from behind the documentary façade. The technical approach of *Zelig* has been experimented with before, most memorably in the fictional *March of Time* newsreel that introduced *Citizen Kane*. In that movie, we saw Charles Foster Kane apparently standing on balconies with Hitler and talking with Mussolini. In *Zelig*, the actors (Woody Allen, Mia Farrow, and dozens more) are so successfully integrated into old footage that we give up trying to tell the real from the fictional.

Zelig is a technical success, and it is also a success as a statement: Allen has a lot to say here about the nature of celebrity, science, and the American melting pot. He has also made an essay about film itself; the way that *Zelig*'s documentary material goes at right angles to its human story makes us think about the line between documentary and poetic "truth."

But the problem is, all of those achievements are easily accomplished at less length than the movie takes. The basic visual approach is clear from the first frames, and although it continues to impress us, it ceases after a while to amaze us. The emerging of Zelig's personality is intriguing, but the documentary framework allows it to emerge only so far, and no farther. We're left wanting more of Zelig and less of the movie's method; the movie is a technical masterpiece, but in artistic and comic terms, only pretty good.

Film Clips

Woody Allen

New York, December 19, 1990—Woody Allen found the first ticklings of inspiration for *Alice*, his new movie, by getting a sty in his eye. One of those annoying little bumps by the tear ducts. That was why he went to the acupuncturist. And then the incident began to grow in his imagination, flowering and folding in upon itself, and finally it became a story about Mia Farrow as a rich New York trophy wife who is compelled to evaluate every aspect of her life after a strange old man in Chinatown gives her special herbs for her tea.

"When you get a sty they're very annoying," Allen was explaining to me the other afternoon. We were sitting in a corner of his living room on Fifth Avenue, and the winter sun was hanging low over Central Park. He sounded like someone for whom the very memory of a sty was painful.

"They're not fatal, but you have to have them lanced, and it's a very unpleasant thing, and when you get one, you tend to get a wave of them. I tried everything, and then someone told me that she was seeing this tremendous acupuncturist downtown at this dingy little place. He was giving her herbs every week in little bags, and I noticed she'd go into the kitchen sometimes and pour these things together and drink them before going out to dinner, and I figured, gee, this guy's making a fortune!

"A friend of mine went down there and said all these rich women come in to see this man. They think it's for their skin, their hair, and their youth, and I was completely skeptical about it. I thought it was a total fraud. And she said, 'Why don't you try and have him cure your sties? You've been going to a Western doctor now for years, and you still keep getting them. Give this guy a chance.'

"I said, 'I'll bet you anything that there's no chance in the world that this guy can ever cure my sties. I think this guy's a total fraud.' But I said I would see him just to prove he was a fraud. So he came over to this apartment, and he read my pulse to diagnose me, which was just nonsense I thought, and told me to stop eating shellfish, and then he said, 'The way I think you can get rid of them is with a cat's whisker.'"

Woody looked up at the ceiling, as if appealing to reason and sanity. "He kept saying, 'Whisker of cat, whisker of cat! I take care of this with whisker of cat!' I was totally skeptical. The next week the guy came back with his niece and a little silver box, and in it were these little cat's whiskers. She held my arms down, and he got over me, and he started manipulating a cat's whisker in the tear duct, and I'm thinking if this works, it's going to be the miracle of all time."

But, of course, we are inhabitants of the New Age, and so we know how the story ended. The agnostic Woody was completely and miraculously cured, and has not had a sty in his eye ever since. Right?

"It didn't work at all. It was a totally meaningless thing, and when I told my eye doctor about it, he said, 'Jeez, don't let this guy poke cat's whiskers in your tear ducts because it's not going to help you any, and it could create a problem.' The guy was totally fraudulent, but it stayed with me, because it was such a funny story. The guy was here, my friends were here, and they were laughing hysterically, but to the best of my knowledge he still runs an incredibly thriving business in a dive in Chinatown, and rich women still go up the rickety stairs to see him."

And he is probably famous as the guy that Woody Allen always uses.

Woody laughed. "I don't think he needs it."

In a lot of your movies, I said, you like to write in wise people who are supposed to have the answers. Shrinks or rabbis or priests or philosophers. Even magicians.

"It doesn't hurt. Everybody, including me, is always searching for something, but nobody ever helps you—that's the problem."

He thought for a moment about the meaning of the Chinese acupuncturist and magician.

"One could make the case," he said, "that in a certain sense what he does isn't that different from a psychoanalytic experience. You wish your analyst could perform magic, but he can't, so in a very slow, tedious way you start to find out about yourself, and this takes years, if it happens at all, and finally you change your life. In the movie, she goes and she gets a very fast, much more colorful version of it, but she's really doing the same thing, working with her creative impulses, her dreams, past memories of relationships. I didn't intend it that way when I wrote the movie, but now I can see that possibility."

And in *Alice*, which is a whimsical comedy with an undercurrent as dark as dread, after the mysterious magician does help the Mia Farrow character, her life is never the same again. The film opens with a virtuoso scene at break-neck pace, establishing Alice as the rich and pampered wife of an incredibly wealthy investment professional—a cool, detached man (played by William Hurt) who deflects all possible arguments with vague reassurances and slippery compliments. They live in a hermetic womb of creature comfort, with a cook who buys only free-range chickens, and a nanny who attends to the children so efficiently that the parents barely even need to talk to the little darlings.

One day, after sixteen years of marriage, like a thunderbolt, the notion of an affair strikes Alice. Dropping her kids off at private school, she drops a book on the stair. A dark, handsome stranger (Joe Mantegna) returns it to her, and soon she can think of no one else. She's so worked up, she develops back pains, and so she has the limousine drive her down to Chinatown, where the fabled Dr. Yang (Keye Luke) occupies a shadowy office filled with strange props, like a revolving pinwheel that hypnotizes her.

He thinks her problem is not her back, but her marriage. He supplies Alice with various herbs and potions that liberate her so completely that for the rest of the movie she's on an inspection tour of her own life, re-evaluating her husband, her mother, her sister, her purpose for living. At times she even flies above the spires of Manhattan, held safely by the ghost of a former lover—or is that a dream, inspired by the herbs Dr. Yang asked her to burn in a teacup?

The world of *Alice* is the world of wealthy New York, of men who make money and women who spend it with skill and grace. It is a New York of elegant brownstones, exclusive high-rises, private schools, expensive shops, and little private parks with quaint benches lining the paths. The end credits thank Cartier, Ben Kahn, Valentino, and the New York Zoological Society. The musical score is lush with Erroll Garner, Paul Weston, and those romantic big-band arrangements Jackie Gleason was famous for. This is a New York that exists only in ads in *Architectural Digest* and *Town & Country*, and in this movie.

"It's the rich New York," Allen said. "If you have as much money as these people did, you can live pretty well. If you live on upper Fifth Avenue or Park Avenue, and you shop on Madison, and you have all the charge accounts, and you have a car and a driver, and nannies, and maids, and you live in a building that's heavily door-manned, and you know the city well enough so that you eat at Le Cirque and the Russian Tea Room, and you know certain parts of the park that are beautiful and quite safe—you can live a perfectly fine life. But if you're not in that fortunate group, then you have to take public transportation, and you've got to be in neighborhoods that aren't safe, and your hours are not your own, so you've got to travel in traffic, and in the park where it's not so safe . . . and it's not so good. What's killing the city is that it has no middle class."

That other New York, of the people who have to take public transportation, is nowhere on display in *Alice*, at least not until the very end, when Alice seeks spiritual inspiration in a most unlikely quarter. At the beginning, she is a woman so elevated above the daily inconveniences of life that she hardly has responsibilities even to her children—except to bear them, of course, as a gesture to her husband. You have to listen carefully to even catch her speaking to the children, who are ignored most of the time and are backdrops the rest of the time.

"That's a phenomenon that I have observed," Allen said. "Not with Mia, because she's the opposite, but I've seen it when I used to go pick up my kid from school. I'd see nannies doing everything. I'm not blaming the parents necessarily, because probably a number of them are working, but it is an amazing thing how people delegate that responsibility."

Allen himself became a parent only in his fifties—he and Farrow adopted one child and conceived another—and these days he gets up early, at five, so he can be across the park to her apartment by six to spend time with the kids before they go to school and go to work. And in the afternoon, after his clarinet practice, he's there for dinner and story time. "They are the absolutely central fact of my life," he said, shaking his head wonderingly, this man who never saw himself as a father.

But Alice, I said, only goes to the school to pick up her kids because she wants to run into this guy she has a crush on. Otherwise she wouldn't even be there.

"Yeah. You see that frequently at the schools. The nannies do it all. I'll take the kids to school, and it will be a dreary, cold winter morning, and it will be some nannies and a half a dozen mothers, and I'll be surrounded by all these floor-length mink coats. They're from around the corner on Fifth Avenue, with no makeup on, almost with their hair in curlers, wearing whatever house clothes they threw on, with their floor-length mink coats thrown on top, to take the kid to school. It looks like a little mink farm."

Although many of Allen's movies use Judaism as either a background or a comic foil, the religion of choice in *Alice* is Catholicism. The character was raised as a Catholic, went through a "religious phase," and now considers herself culturally Catholic, but nonpracticing. This arouses the considerable amusement of Dr. Yang, who makes a couple of jokes at her expense, but it also inspires a fantasy scene in which Alice revisits her childhood home and finds a priest and a confessional installed in the front yard.

"Mia has had a very Catholic background," Allen said, "and I drew on some of it for the screenplay. She was going to be a nun for a long time. Mother Teresa has been a major icon in her life. She was raised Catholic, and it was always interesting to me to hear about it. I've always been interested in the aesthetics of Catholicism. It's such a lovely religion to an outsider from an aesthetic point of view. Remember, I was contemplating becoming Catholic in

Hannah and Her Sisters, because it's so filled with beauty and ritual. I got that all from Mia. When she was a little girl she used to pray with her arms outstretched so it would be more uncomfortable.

"I remember when I was very young, I went on a trip to a monastery outside of Washington. It was very quiet and peaceful. There were very few people there. Just the thought that the monks would wake up in the morning, and they would tread those paths, and they were not afraid of dying, and they didn't want anything—I loved that. It was a stoic life. They had no great desires. They just trod, and sat, and thought, and prayed. I guess there were ones like Mendel, who wanted to fool around with pea pods and cross-pollinate and do their little hobbies. It is seductive; there is no question. But on the surface, I don't believe in any of this."

You've often said, when life is over, it's over.

"It certainly seems that way."

And yet you're afraid to sleep in a graveyard, or spend the night in a haunted castle. Why should *your* life be over for good, when all of these other lucky people get to be ghosts and hang around to frighten you?

"You just can't know for sure. So, while I'm totally skeptical, and I believe that, of course, you can walk under a ladder, and there's nothing more to life than what you see, there's always that element of doubt. When I go to Mia's house in Connecticut, it's not that I'm afraid that two guys are gonna pull up like Dick and Perry in *In Cold Blood*. It's more that I'm gonna see two eyes at the window, or I'm going to be walking along the shore, and a hand is going to come up out of the lake. Or if I'm home alone, and the city is very black, and it's a big house, eleven rooms, and you hear a little noise, and you get a slightly creepy feeling. It isn't that a mugger is in the house. That's not frightening. That you can deal with. If it's a mugger you can scream, pick up the phone, pick up the fireplace poker. It's that there might be . . . something else."

And because there might be something else, we should lead good lives.

"Well, we should not waste time. That's what I was always told as a child: Don't waste time! And so I have this movie coming out, and I'm shooting another one right now, and I'm working on the screenplay for the next one, and I would enjoy nothing more than writing and directing a really good detective movie, because I'd enjoy that more than anything, but I never will—because I would be afraid of wasting my time."

Robert Altman

Chicago, November 13, 1990—You always know with a Robert Altman film that you'll get some kind of nudge, a dig in the ribs to wake you up and make you think differently. In the days when he was riding high with *M★A★S★H* and *Nashville*, and now in these latter days when his ec-

centricity isn't fashionable, that hasn't changed. When you ask him why he's working in Paris or on Broadway or cable TV, Altman always grins and says, "I fiddle on the corner where they throw the coins." It's one of his favorite expressions. But he fiddles where he damn well pleases.

I came of age as a movie critic in the 1970s, a decade when Altman's brilliance and whimsy seemed right at home, and once a year or so I could look forward to a new flight of Altman's fancy. He made hit films like *M★A★S★H* and *McCabe and Mrs. Miller*, and his *Nashville* is considered one of the best films of the decade, but I also came to love the strange excursions into his private visions, movies like *3 Women* (1977), with Shelley Duvall and Sissy Spacek as denizens of a desert condo who exchange personalities. I picked that one as the best film of the year, but it was such a puzzlement to audiences that it's still not even on home video.

Altman simply did not care whether a project was commercial. He cared only if the project intrigued him. In the 1970s that was permissible, because a lot of people in Hollywood thought the same way. Then the wind shifted and blew Bob out of town. It wasn't that Altman's pictures lost money. Indeed, *Popeye* (1980), his last big-budget film, made a lot of money for Paramount. It was that a timid production executive couldn't look at an Altman project and make any sense out of it. His films didn't sound like other films, and they didn't rip off the hit pictures of the moment. They were originals. So how could the executive know if they'd make money or not?

Predictability is the big thing in Hollywood these days. Movies are products like soap or shampoo, and the audience has been trained to attend pictures that can be described in a sentence or two. And so Altman has gone his own way in the last decade, with projects like the Broadway play *Come Back to the 5 & Dime, Jimmy Dean, Jimmy Dean* (1982), which he made into a film that made Cher plausible as a movie actress. Or *Fool for Love* (1985), from the Sam Shepard play, with Shepard and Kim Basinger as strangers in the night in a Texas road stop. That one made Basinger plausible as a serious actress. Or *Streamers* (1984) the play, and then the film about buried tensions in an Army barracks. Or *Secret Honor* (1984), the brilliant one-man film that starred Philip Baker Hall in a long night's monologue by Richard M. Nixon. And there was *Tanner*, the made-for-cable project that starred Michael Murphy as a candidate in the 1988 presidential election.

And now here is *Vincent and Theo*, Robert Altman's first film for the 1990s, proving once again that this is a natural filmmaker, that what he does is always of interest, and that he is still cheerfully out of step. The movie tells the story of the intertwined lives of the painter Vincent van Gogh and his brother Theo, who had to deal together with the fact that although Vincent might be a genius, the world disagreed, and only one of his paintings was sold in his lifetime.

The movie industry doesn't have time anymore for movies like this. They're too busy mapping out the $100 million grosses. *Vincent and Theo* has received Altman's best reviews in more than ten years, and yet his strategy for the picture places an emphasis on survival: "I think the film has to go into theaters where it can sit through Christmas and find its audience," he told me recently. "It's going to be a word-of-mouth audience, because you know they're not going to spend a lot of money advertising it. It's going to have to survive on critics, and awards, and that sort of thing, creating a rumble that people will pick up on. It's going to be a difficult trip, and I don't know what's going to happen."

He shrugs. We talked a couple of times, at this year's Toronto and Chicago film festivals, where *Vincent and Theo* premiered to enthusiastic audiences, and then the movie was launched, somewhat to his surprise, with a two-page advertising spread in the Sunday *New York Times*—the distributors having apparently gathered that they had something worth spending money on after all.

But the current truths in Hollywood are such that Altman's basic dilemma remains: Nobody wants to invest in a movie that doesn't seem to reflect a sure-fire formula.

"Today's marketing thing is so uncomplicated," he said. "They're not looking for anything different. They're looking for another hit like last year's hit. There's very little chance for breakthroughs, I think, unless they happen right at the beginning—like *sex, lies, and videotape*, which got its kickoff at the Cannes festival. It couldn't have made it from a standing start in America. Things are so sad in the movie business right now. Everybody wants to make a blockbuster. They look at *Pretty Woman* and *Ghost*, and for the next year every movie's going to be about a prostitute who's a ghost."

He grinned. "It's astonishing how fast the studios respond to the market. At the beginning of the summer, *Dick Tracy*, *Die Hard*, and *Total Recall* were going to be monster hits, and the studios were all going to make more movies just like them, and suddenly, just this quick, *Pretty Woman* and *Ghost* are the biggest hits, and everybody's talking about ghosts. They think the audience wants stuff that's sentimental and romantic."

Are the big action pictures dead, and is romantic comedy back in?

"I figured it all out," Altman said. "You have to have ghosts because you have to have sex without risk. You can't get AIDS from a ghost. It's as simple as that."

Altman has a prostitute in his picture, too, a forlorn creature who comes one day to pose for Vincent, who asks her to stay with him. But why? He is not interested in sex with her, or apparently with anybody, but perhaps he feels some elementary need for companionship. *Vincent and Theo* is above all a portrait of loneliness, of a tortured man who made paintings of great power—working not out of technique or theory, but out of need and compulsion.

The film stars Tim Roth and Paul Rhys, actors better known in Britain than here, in the title roles. Roth has been in several movies—most recently *The Cook, the Thief, His Wife and Her Lover*—and Rhys was in the marathon film version of *Little Dorrit*, but most of their work has been on the London stage. As Vincent and Theo, they create realistic performances in a movie that is much more linear and traditional than most of Altman's work.

"I think it kind of had to be more traditional," Altman mused, "because it's a guy's life. There are certain things you have to pay attention to. For instance, I couldn't leave the ear thing out. I couldn't leave out his death. The newness in the story mostly comes from Theo. Most people don't know that much about him."

With the exception of *McCabe*, Altman's films have all taken place in modern times, with contemporary stories and characters. It's surprising to find him making a period autobiography in a more subdued style.

"I'd been dealing with the idea for five or six years," he said. "I know a lot of painters, and I'm interested in art. I don't feel I've ever seen the subject of artists done right in a movie. I flirted for a long time on doing a film about Jackson Pollack, and then I gave that up. Then I was actually working on a project where I was going to get five or six writers to write a short story that had to do with art. I would shuffle those and do a *Nashville* structure. Of course, I could never get that going.

"Then *Vincent and Theo* came to me, and my first response was—no, I don't want to do it. I don't like these kinds of films. I don't like films about famous people. But I was building this hero in my mind, and when I see a hero, I feel compelled to claim him. I went into it not knowing what kind of film I was going to make, but I clearly knew what kind of film I *wasn't* going to make."

There are two notable films about Vincent: the Kirk Douglas biopic *Lust for Life*, directed by Vincent Minnelli, and *Vincent*, a hauntingly beautiful film by Paul Cox directed in 1988, which drew on Vincent's letters and lingered on close-up details of his work. Altman wasn't interested in remaking either one of them.

"I'd seen *Lust for Life* years before," Altman said. "I didn't see it again, although we showed it to the props and wardrobe people to look at the things we didn't want to do. The Paul Cox film I didn't see. I purposely did not. I wanted to begin with a clean slate."

Altman also avoided getting bogged down in theories about the nature of van Gogh's illness, including a recent medical hypothesis that van Gogh was not insane at all, but cut off his ear and eventually killed himself because of a maddening ear disease. Tim Roth's performance is able to suggest Vincent's increasing madness and depression, and Altman is content to leave it at that. This isn't one of those movies that feels compelled to write in potted psychological theories.

The progress of Vincent's unhappiness is charted in the

very fabric of the film itself. There is a brilliant sequence near the very end, for example, where Vincent stands in the middle of a sunflower field and paints, and the camera darts here and there among the sunflowers, making them seem strangely ominous. Not flowers, but a malevolent presence. The scene reminded me of Martin Scorsese's sequence in *New York Stories*, where his camera darts back and forth from the palette to the canvas, following the movements of the painter. But in *Vincent and Theo*, the camera seems to copy the artist's eye, not his hand, and the sunflowers seem to be looking right back at him. Finally van Gogh dips his brush in his black paint, and puts in bold, hostile blackbirds, flying low over the sunny field. Messengers of despair and death. It was his last completed painting before his suicide.

"The flowers look like an audience," Altman says. "We never had anything in the script about that scene, and, in fact, there's no evidence that he painted the blackbird painting while standing out in the sunflowers. He did most of his painting inside. But where we were making the film, it was a twenty-minute drive every morning to where our headquarters were, and we'd pass these god-damned sunflowers every day, and I was just fascinated by them. The shoot was not easy, conditions were not very good, the cast and crew lived in summer cottages, that sort of thing, and I came in one morning and they said, 'We've got a problem; the set isn't ready,' and I said let's go out and shoot in the field. And we did just that. It's one of the key scenes in the movie."

You're living in Paris now?

"My office has been in New York for over fifteen years. But I was in Paris for about six years. I'm out of there now, except for doing *Tanner* here in 1988. I still have a car in Paris, but that's because it's held hostage by the Paris customs with red tape."

Why did you go to Paris? Could we romantically call it a period of exile?

"Because I work," he said, and I knew what he would say next. "I fiddle on the corner where they throw the coins."

That quote, I said, is in that big new book about you. I was referring to *Robert Altman: Jumping Off the Cliff*, by Patrick McGilligan (St. Martin's Press), which I discovered I admired a great deal more than Altman did.

"Don't talk about that book."

I liked it.

"I didn't. I think it was kind of hypocritical. In the first place, I resent it because when the guy called me about doing it I told him I'm in the middle of my career, and I don't want to have a book written about me like I'm dead. I've done some of the best work I've done since that book, and it's such a goddamned big book, it's not like it's some little study."

Would you be happier if it were little?

"I'd be happier if it hadn't been done. I just don't think

it's accurate. There's a story in there that some guy told him, and I'm sure the guy who told him thought it was true. I mean if you and I talked about a dinner that we had at Cannes on a certain night, we can tell two entirely different stories, both as we remembered it. This story has me one time down and out and feeling very low in Paris, and walking in the streets in the rain, and I see Orson Welles, who is my idol, and go chasing after Welles, and just as I got up to him, Orson Welles disappears into the revolving door of a hotel."

A big revolving door?

"That's exactly what I said. First of all, Welles couldn't get into a revolving door! I mean, I liked his work, but *Citizen Kane* is not the definitive film for me. I just never had a big adulation thing for him. I may have seen him in the rain, but I sure didn't chase him down the street and then despair. Those kinds of things come from someone else's imagination, and I think when you talk to people about other people, there comes a distortion that isn't even consistent. If you have one person's version of another person, you can allow for the personal filter, but when you take part of it here and part of it there, well, I couldn't see anything recognizable, truthfully recognizable, in the center of it. I mean, it wasn't even salaciously interesting."

Meanwhile, Altman soldiers on. His next film, he says, will be based on a group of short stories by Raymond Carver, an author who knew the drinking world very well, and wrote about it during the last ten years of his life, after he stopped drinking. Carver died in 1988.

"I read all of his stories in March, coming back from Europe on the plane," Altman said. "I thought it would be interesting to take several of the stories and interconnect them, move back and forth between various story lines— the same technique we used in *Nashville*. We started out with fourteen at one time, and we dropped it to eleven or maybe nine, and sometimes I'll just use a piece of a story. There might be an incidental character in one of the stories who becomes the main character in another of the stories. They're really all just personal stories. He was an alcoholic, and it's all about losers, and they're painful as hell. I've just literally finished the script last week. I've been working all summer on it. I have financing from Europe and need a little American financing, and if I can get it, we'll go. Not that American financing is that easy to get."

It's harder for you than in Europe?

"My problem has always been that films are made to serve an existing market. Everybody's geared toward selling to that market that already exists. It's set up. I don't do that well. I don't know how to do it. If I had to do a film like *Lethal Weapon*, I'd oversleep. I wouldn't get to work on time. I'd get bored with it. I think it's fine that *Lethal Weapon* and those things are made, but I think there should be room for me, too. I know there is, because every breakthrough film, every film that's changed the market, is always a film that nobody wanted to make—somebody's personal view. But it ain't easy. How did that song in *Popeye* go? It ain't easy being me."

Albert Brooks

Los Angeles, April 3, 1991—This is a very small anecdote, but maybe it will lead somewhere. I went to interview Albert Brooks out at his office at Warner Bros. We were going to talk about *Defending Your Life*, his new comedy about a man who discovers the afterlife is a place named Judgment City, and you go on trial there. We had a good talk.

As I was getting up to go, Brooks said, "Look at these funny coffee mugs the studio sent over."

He had four or five of them on a shelf, cups shaped like the Warner cartoon heroes.

"Here," he said. "Have one. I want you to have one."

He pressed Elmer Fudd into my hands. No, that's OK, I said.

"Take one. What is this, a bribe? They're worth ten cents apiece. Twenty-five cents, tops."

You know, I said, looking at the shelf, I've never really been a fan of Elmer Fudd. My hero has always been Daffy Duck.

Brooks took the Daffy Duck mug from the shelf.

"Here, take it," he said. "I want you to have it. Really."

I could tell from the subtle intonation in his voice exactly what had happened. He had given me Elmer Fudd because he didn't like Elmer Fudd, either. He liked Daffy Duck. I had taken his favorite mug.

No, you keep Daffy, I said. I'll bet it's your favorite.

"Come on, come on," he said. "Take Daffy Duck. Take the one you want."

I tried to put Daffy back on the shelf. He pressed Daffy into my hands. I left with Daffy, but I would have bet a hundred bucks that the moment I was out of his office, Brooks had his secretary call Warners to see if they could send another Daffy Duck over.

Now what is the moral of this anecdote? It is that things like this keep happening to Albert Brooks, and he is intensely alert to them, and they form the foundation of his humor. He has made four movie comedies in the last decade, and they have all been based on a character, played by himself, who dreads embarrassment and desperately wants to do the right thing, and is filled with fear that he will be found out, and who uses appeasement as a tactic.

In this case, he feared that he would be found wanting in generosity. The ceramic mugs were not worth much in dollar terms, but he tried to give away the one he didn't like and got caught, and ended up giving away his favorite. That is one interpretation. Another is that this whole reality was created in my mind, and he didn't give a damn whether he was left with Daffy or Elmer. But—here is the crucial part—his persona inspired my fantasy. That's even worse:

the possibility that people think this way about him even if it isn't true.

You are losing patience with this whole line of reasoning. You wonder what it has to do with *Defending Your Life*. I will tell you. The stories in all of Albert Brooks's movies are generated by his deep-seated compulsion to be good, and his equally deep fear that he will be found wanting. That's why his comedy is so distinctive: It doesn't come out of the manipulation of comic formulas, it comes out of emotions he really feels.

You think I'm making this all up? Try sitting and talking to Albert Brooks for an afternoon. His whole conversational style consists of holding his motives up to the light and scrutinizing them. He never ever once even for a second asks if you think his movie is funny. He wants you to know his motives are pure, that he worked hard, that he took pains so that you would not be disappointed. I find this characteristic both honorable and endearing, although on the other hand, I would not want to sit next to Brooks on a three-day bus ride.

Defending Your Life is his most mature, thought-out comedy because it springs directly from his own daily, even hourly, examinations of conscience. The movie is about a guy named Dan Miller, played by Brooks, who drives his new car head-on into a bus, and finds himself in a heavenly holding area where there's a courtroom, a prosecutor, a defense attorney, a judge, and a big screen where you can view episodes from your past. You have to defend yourself, or you'll be sent right back to Earth for another lifetime.

"The funny part of the movie, to me," Brooks said, "is the idea that Earth is *not* the place you want to be. All the other afterlife movies are about people trying to return to Earth, revisit their friends and families. This is a movie about wanting to leave the Earth completely behind."

In the movie, Judgment City is like a big retirement resort with trams that shuttle the residents back and forth between their hotels and tennis courts. The Brooks character is given a clean, well-lighted room with a bare minimum of luxury; Tom Bodett would price it at about $26 dollars a day, some locations a little more, a few less. Brooks is content until he meets a beautiful woman played by Meryl Streep and visits her hotel, which looks like a fairly expensive Hyatt. Do his accommodations reflect the moral quality of the life he has just finished leading?

"There are so many things that are hinted at," Brooks said. "Rip Torn (who plays the defense attorney) asks me, 'Did you ever give to charity? It's not a good or a bad thing, I'm just asking.' I keep getting all these little hints that I didn't do quite as well as I should have. I ask him why I'm in this particular hotel, and not one of the nicer ones. 'I don't know, don't worry about it. It's not a good or bad thing.'

"Should I just give up then, since obviously in Judgment City they don't think I'm ready for the two-room suite? What I was really overcoming was fear. What this movie says, in its simplest form, is that it's not too late. A lot of people including myself have said, oh man, it's gone bad for this long, forget it! The only hopeful concept to me in life is that if you decide to get off your ass, it just might count. I'm not promising you anything, but you may not have to go back to first grade. Give it a try. See what happens."

He was as solemn as if this were a theological discussion. "I'm happy to throw this idea out there. If some people think it's stupid, if some people think it's real, at least it's another idea in the fire now. This isn't another recycled heaven from another movie. There are no clouds in this movie, I'm proud of that."

Not even fake clouds in the special effects scenes?

"No! And for the money we paid, they were going to throw it in! 'You sure you don't want some clouds?' Nah, that's OK."

Diane Keaton made a movie called *Heaven* in 1986 that consisted of a lot of people talking about their notion of heaven. Their ideas were intercut with clips from movies about heaven, including that great image of David Niven arriving in the afterlife in *A Matter of Life and Death*, and seeing the residents gazing down upon him from gigantic round galleries in the sky. Many of us were raised with the notion that our departed loved ones spent most of their time up there "looking down on us," even though the catechism suggests that their time is more profitably occupied with gazing upon the perfection of God. What no one has ever suggested, before Albert Brooks, is that heaven is like an efficient corporate personnel processing center.

"People ask me, do you believe in this?" Brooks said. "Here's my answer. I think if there were a lottery about what the next world is like, I'd bet on this. A computer works by discarding all the wrong answers, and the remaining one is right. I approached the afterlife the same way. All I've ever seen in movies are clouds, and wings, and harps, and angels, and I said damn it! It's gotta be *something*, but why is it that?"

One of the biggest box office hits of the last year was *Ghost*, in which Patrick Swayze was so concerned about seeing justice done on Earth that he actually took lessons on how to rematerialize his corporal body. That would never happen in a Brooks movie.

"Movies like *Ghost*, movies that suggest that people come back to help you, those are pretty much the predominate images of the afterlife. *A Guy Named Joe*, (remade by Steven Spielberg as *Always*) and those movies. It's a nice thought. It's a tender thought. I lost my father at an early age, and I'm sure he's with me in spirit, but I've never seen him, so I couldn't write about it honestly, and so I guess I've looked around for years thinking well, what clues do we have?

"So I thought, let's say our world didn't come from nothing. Let's just say it came from something. And if this is how it works, then maybe heaven works the same way.

Then, if you want to know how heaven would process newly arrived visitors, all you have to do is figure out the most practical way to do it on Earth.

"And what would they be looking for, in the new arrivals? I looked for the one thing that bonds us all, and I think that all human beings are afraid of something. We're afraid. If it's a tiger on the bank of the Euphrates, or it's a tank in the Persian Gulf, or if it's going on 'Saturday Night Live.' I don't know what it is, but our hearts pound, and I always thought in my own life about all the stuff that I could do if I could conquer fear. So, maybe they're testing us to see how well we have learned to handle fear.

"To me, the one thing we're all going to do is leave here, and isn't it remarkable over the course of cinema, how few stories there are about it! The Buddhists believe that existence is a wheel, and if you are condemned to hell, you just are kept at work, pushing the wheel on Earth. But if you are fortunate enough, you're plucked from the wheel, and then you, in fact, have escaped."

How he visualized Judgment City, he said, is sort of an eerie story: "I had a tape recorder beside me, and I must have driven 300 miles without knowing I went a foot. I swear to God I went to this place, Judgment City. I mean I drove safely, but I was walking down these streets, I was smelling the clean air. The next thing I know, I drove into a 7-Eleven and said, where am I? And I was in Bakersfield."

Brooks's previous movies have all had fairly small budgets. There was *Real Life* (1979), the spoof on a *cinema verité* documentary like *An American Family*. And *Modern Romance* (1981), about the impossibility of transcending your flaws to build a good relationship. And *Lost in America* (1985), about a couple who risked everything for their freedom, and then gambled away their nest egg on the first night in Vegas.

Between his filmmaking jobs, Brooks has worked as an actor, most notably in *Taxi Driver*, *Private Benjamin*, and *Broadcast News*, where his character started sweating uncontrollably when he got his chance at an anchor job. Now comes *Defending Your Life*, which is a big-budget movie for Brooks, over $20 million, with an expensive star like Meryl Streep and lots of special effects. Did he feel strange having all of these resources at the disposal of his notions about heaven?

"Let's say somebody throws you in small movie jail," he said. "You can only make $3 million movies. Well, I still wouldn't want to give up this subject. We could have shot it in this office. I could have had Rip sitting at that desk, and this could have been the waiting room, and you could rent a hotel room and do the movie."

But he was glad he had the extra money, he said, because that gave him the freedom to make Judgment City look real, right down to the giant, sinister trams that whisked people to and fro, and which he rented from the Universal Studios Tour for a great deal of money. And also right down to the long shots of Judgment City, which are special effects, although they don't look it. And right down to Meryl Streep.

"Working with her is like being a fast-ball pitcher," he said. "You get it back as hard as you throw it. How she came to be in the movie is, I'm close friends with Carrie Fisher, and Carrie asked me to her house for dinner, and Meryl was there, and what I saw was this person that I had never seen before. I thought of Meryl Streep as almost an untouchable, and I saw the most natural, hanging-out person I ever saw. I thought, that's the woman in the movie! Even when we were filming, some people had their doubts. Because they think of *Sophie's Choice*. Well, this is Sophie's other choice."

The other American filmmaker who resembles Albert Brooks, at least in the way that he writes and directs his own films, and often deals with his own neuroses, is Woody Allen. But when I mentioned his name, Brooks got analytical.

"I'll tell you something. It is getting to be a harder world to make movies that gross $5 million in than it used to be. Woody, bless his heart, had a running start at it, and had about thirteen under his belt before the world changed, and then at least they could say, well, we've made thirteen, so let's keep going, but the company he's working for (Orion) is now having hard times, so I think he's going to have a little trouble.

"I think there's going to come a time when there will be a pretty tragic meeting. I'd like to be a fly on the wall. A meeting where some schmuck says to Woody Allen, 'Well, what's it about?' I mean, Woody Allen has had unprecedented freedom, no audience testing, no anything. He doesn't even have to give them a title.

"I had to go out and raise my money, and that took a year of work, and a very unrewarding year's work, because you don't get a single laugh, and nobody compliments you. No one even knows what you're doing. You're just out there in hotels."

He thought about that for a moment, and sighed, and offered me a coffee mug made in the image and likeness of Elmer Fudd.

John Cusack

Chicago, January 15, 1991—Jim Thompson has been dead for fifteen years now, and he never got much notice when he was alive, but all of his books are in print again—with covers showing the broads with low necklines, the desperate guys with their cigarettes and three-day beards, and always in the foreground the bottle of booze.

"It's a doomed world, isn't it?" asks John Cusack. "A godless universe. It says so right in the book."

There is something peculiarly American about the stories written by Thompson and the other masters of the dregs of crime, writers like James M. Cain, Fredric Brown,

Raymond Chandler, and Howard Browne. They write of wounded men on the fringes, living out of hot-sheet hotels and having their hearts broken, again and again, by women with flaming hair and no principles. Maybe it is the loss of innocence that is so American; a European wouldn't fall for dames like these.

Cusack's new movie is named *The Grifters*, and it is one of the best films of 1991, the story of a young man who thinks he is an expert at playing the confidence game—until he runs into two women who really are experts, who destroy every illusion he ever had that he could count on someone or love someone. One of the women is his girlfriend. The other woman is his mother. It's that kind of world.

The movie is the first U.S. work by the British director Stephen Frears (*My Beautiful Laundrette*, *Prick Up Your Ears*), and perhaps because he was telling an American story for the first time, he gravitated toward Thompson's novel—which is quintessentially American and may even have given the word "grifter" to the language.

A grifter is one who grifts, and drifts, and in this story Cusack plays a guy whose grifts are pretty far down on the totem pole. He specializes in giving bartenders a ten dollar bill and getting change for a twenty. And for that grift he is beaten up so badly one night that he thinks he might die. The lesson is, if they're going to hurt you that much, be sure it's for something worth having.

In the movie, Cusack meets Myra, a good-looking woman (Annette Bening) who cannot possibly be as young as she seems. She's been around, working with the best con artists in Texas and Oklahoma. She's beautiful and she seems to love him, and he's weak and in pain, and what man alive could face that combination and not fall in love? And then there is another woman, who comes to visit him in the hospital: his mother (Anjelica Huston), who is in the con game, too. She had him when she was very young, and never related to him as a mother should, because she loved money more. She works for the mob now, moving around the country to the big tracks, laying down bets to even up the odds.

When the two women meet for the first time, there is an instant dislike, a spitting, clawing hostility they don't bother to conceal. A man might be forgiven for feeling complimented when two women compete for him, but the sinister secret of *The Grifters* is that they aren't competing for his affection; they're fighting for the right to use him. It's all a con.

If the movie had been made twenty-five or thirty years ago, when Thompson wrote his book, Hollywood would have required some major changes, particularly in an uncomfortable end scene where Huston toys mercilessly with her son's male feelings. And some of the violence would have been toned down.

"It's pretty harsh," Cusack said one afternoon a while ago, after we'd seen the premiere of the movie at the

Toronto Film Festival. "What's interesting about the movie is that everyone comes out stunned by the violence, but it's really not that explicitly violent. It's psychologically violent. If you look at a scene like that last scene between my character and his mother, and then you look at the death kills of a *Predator* or *Total Recall*, well, there's massive hyper-violence everywhere. But *The Grifters* has some choice scenes where it really crosses the boundary, not so much with physical violence as with how the characters know what will *really* hurt. I think it's really disturbing. The first time I saw it, I was disturbed."

The characters hurt each other, I said. There aren't too many innocent bystanders who get wounded in this film.

Cusack smiled. "That's what the guy says: 'Anybody can whip a fool—fools were made to be whipped. But to take another pro, somebody who has his eye on you, to take your partner, *that's* a score.'"

He was quoting Thompson by heart—Thompson, the obscure pulp writer whose novels appeared in trashy paperbacks from struggling publishers, who wrote for the movies but never made big bucks, the man who is more successful now than when he was alive, whose novels have been made into Peckinpah's *The Getaway* and Tavernier's *Coup de Torchon*, and into three current movies: *After Dark, My Sweet*, *The Kill-Off*, and this one.

To help himself with the special idiom of Thompson, Frears hired a man who had walked some of the same dark streets in his fiction; the screenplay is by Donald West-lake, the celebrated mystery writer. "We were always referring back to Thompson's book as this kind of dark little bible," Cusack said. "It's just a raunchy little paperback, and it just seems so cheap, but it's so loaded. We kept going back to the book, and looking for bits that we liked, descriptive paragraphs to explain a scene."

Talking to Cusack, I wondered why he seemed to fit so naturally into this world of failed 1950s grifters, whose very cons seem touchingly old-fashioned in these modern times when the really capable con men all go into the financial world, where the rewards are larger.

"These stories are kind of about America, I think," he said. "I love *film noir*. They're classic films. They're about twisted, complicated people who are fascinating to watch and fascinating to play. There's a certain kind of detachment that comes with a survival instinct. Roy, the guy I play in *The Grifters*, is a guy who had a very bleak life. His mother had him at thirteen, and then when she was seventeen or eighteen and he was four or five, they were trapped in a small Texas town somewhere, and she was ready to do anything to get out.

"They had a horrible life together, and she was very cruel to him. So he's got all of this anger pent up that he will not address, and also all of his lust for his mother, so I think the only time Roy's really happy is when he's grifting. That's the closest he'll come to peace, is when he's taking back, getting back. The rest of the time, it's maintaining a façade. He's got a job, a house, a relationship with his neighbors, a relationship with his mother and his lover, and none of them mean anything. They're all hollow."

One strange aspect of the movie is that the male lead, the Cusack character, is essentially the passive victim of the women. He's not macho. The women of *film noir* can occasionally be as evil as the men—remember the games that Jane Greer played with Robert Mitchum in *Out of the Past*, or Barbara Stanwyck's manipulation of Fred Mac-Murray in *Double Indemnity*, or Kathleen Turner destroying William Hurt in *Body Heat*—but in recent years that kind of predatory woman has gone out of style in the movies. In *The Grifters*, they're back. These women are deadly and unprincipled, and Cusack's young man is out of his depth with them.

"The toughest person on the bill is clearly Lilly, Anjelica's character," Cusack said. "The only person who could bring Lilly down would be Roy, and the only person who could bring Roy down would be Lilly, and neither of them buy into Myra."

Cusack, saying these things in the long afternoon of a hotel bar, seems to undergo a transition himself. He is one of the best actors of his generation, and yet in a way one of the most surprising. He began his career playing a series of vulnerable teen-agers, and yet in person he's physically imposing and much taller than you would think—two or three inches over six feet. Perhaps because he has played uncertain kids in some of his best roles, such as *The Sure Thing* and *Say Anything*, it's easier to think of him as smaller, younger, and more defenseless than he is. Even in *The Grifters*, he doesn't seem that tall, perhaps because he plays many scenes opposite the tall Anjelica Huston. But here, in person, he is not only taller but more serious, more thoughtful, than you might expect, and in his face you can see an echo of the greatest of all *film noir* actors, Robert Mitchum.

He got into acting more or less by accident. He is a member of a large, gifted family (sister Joan and brother Bill are actors, sister Ann is a singer; only sister Susie has so far stayed free of show business).

"Our parents more or less just kind of wanted us to pursue our passions," Cusack said. "Whatever they would have been, they would have helped light the fire. They are very liberal, artistic people, but they didn't force us into acting. They let us find our own ways."

How did you actually get started?

"I grew up in Evanston and lived in Chicago for a long time, in Old Town and Wrigleyville. I did three films when I was in high school. The first was *Class*, with Rob Lowe. I had a supporting role in that. For nine weeks, instead of going to my junior year in high school, I went to a movie set with Jacqueline Bisset. Not bad. I was loving life, just loving it. The second movie was John Hughes's *Sixteen Candles*, with Molly Ringwald, and then I did this little film called *Grandview USA*, and then I was cast by Rob

Reiner for *The Sure Thing*, so—three supporting roles, and then I got a lead role, and I've been doing leads ever since."

He has never, however, turned into a Hollywood celebrity or had anything to do, however remotely, with Brat Pack types. His favorite kind of evening is spent in Chicago, after a Cubs game, having a few beers with friends and relatives at a hangout like O'Rourke's at Halstead and North, where he has been seen to tend bar himself from time to time.

"Yeah, it's a great place. It's always a place where I can go and not have to talk about my films. I can go hang out, and nobody really gives a damn if I'm an actor."

You don't go for the movie star thing?

"It seems really hollow to me. It feels very pretentious. It's nothing you can really get anything from. You bust your ass to do a good job on a film, and you want people whose opinions you respect to like what you do, but you can't get anything out of playing the star game. I don't walk around talking about my life and spouting my philosophy to people I don't know. I mean, if I get to know them, I'll talk for hours. I guess I like a lower-key scene."

But look. You're still in your early twenties and you're a movie star and it gives you a certain amount of power and recognition, and isn't it only human to enjoy that once in a while?

"Yeah, it is." He grinned, and lost about ten years. "Like if I walk in really happy, and at the top of my game, and strut a little bit, a lot of times the star thing starts to happen, but if you walk in and are unassuming, the same people might not recognize you. You can just sort of shut yourself off if you want."

Whoopi Goldberg

Chicago, March 6, 1991—Whoopi Goldberg has collected many words of wisdom over the years. She makes it her practice to go to all those Hollywood fund-raisers with an autograph book, and she sidles up to the heroes of her youth and asks them for advice.

"Jessica Tandy told me, 'Listen to this. Take the work. People will tell you you're overexposed, but you only get better when you take the work.' Jimmy Stewart told me you have to be the big actor in little movies and the little actor in big movies, that's how you get better. Burt Lancaster said, 'Listen kid, this is a bitch of a business. You're gonna be OK. Tell the truth, hit your marks, do your job, and if it's you on the screen, then fight for it. They're going to say terrible things about you, but no one will ever be able to say that you didn't shoot for the very best you're capable of.' "

Goldberg curled up in the corner of a sofa and lit a Marlboro and smiled. "I talk to everybody at those Happy Birthday salutes to Hollywood. That's why I do them. I bring my autograph book, and I corner people, and I talk to them."

With responses like that, maybe you ought to have a talk show.

"If I was doing a talk show," she said, "I would do the kind of show that comes on just once a month, with amazing guests. I'd like to do three first ladies, Lady Bird Johnson—the Bird, who I adore—Betty Ford, and Rosalyn Carter. I would like to say to the Bird, 'Now listen, we've read all these books about what happened. How did you stay with this guy?' She was really, I think, the balls behind the man after awhile. He was my favorite president, because you knew where he stood. You scratch my back, I'll scratch yours."

We were having this conversation one afternoon last September at the Toronto Film Festival, after a screening of *The Long Walk Home*, a movie that is just now going into national release. It's the story of the 1955 Montgomery bus boycott, told through the eyes of Goldberg, as a maid, and Sissy Spacek, as her employer. But we were also talking about *Ghost*, which had come out not long before, and was already at the top of all the money charts.

It's the No. 1 hit, I said wonderingly.

"I know. It just cracks me up."

I don't know where Whoopi Goldberg was the day they announced the Oscar nominations, and I don't know how she reacted, but when they read her name for her supporting work in *Ghost*, my guess is that she laughed long and loudly. In my fantasy she laughed because she was delighted, of course, but also because of the irony of the whole thing: She was nominated for a role the filmmakers agonized for months over giving her, at a time when her screen career was allegedly in the toilet. It may also have occurred to her, as it did to me, that the Oscar nomination came for the kind of work she has done many times before in the movies—while the Academy overlooked her inspired and truly wonderful performance in *The Long Walk Home*.

In the movie, Spacek and her husband (Dwight Schultz) lead a comfortable middle-class life in Montgomery, made easier by the labors of their cook and maid. Then Rosa Parks refuses to move to the back of the segregated bus, and that leads to a bus boycott. For the maid, Goldberg, it also means a long walk to and from work every day. Spacek's husband, a white supremacist, thinks that serves her right. But Spacek secretly begins to provide her maid with a ride some days of the week, and that experience opens her eyes to a few of the realities of her society.

One of the qualities that makes the movie special is that the family lives of both women are treated by the story. A few years ago, the movie would have been told through the eyes of the Spacek character, and the Goldberg character's reality would have been defined mostly in terms of her work as a maid who undergoes heroic suffering. In *The Long Walk Home* we learn, however, that Goldberg has a husband and children, makes a good home for them, and has a whole existence little guessed at by her employer.

"That was one of the areas where I had to take Burt

Lancaster's advice and fight, because it was me on the screen," Goldberg said. "When they were talking about scenes they thought they might be able to lose, and two of the scenes were my family scenes, I lived up to my reputation and went ape crap. But they're in there."

One of the things I didn't like, I said, was the gratuitous narration by the young daughter of the Spacek character, who has no real role on the screen. She appears on the sound track, telling her memories of what her mother went through at that time. The narration is obviously not necessary, and seems to exist only to reassure white viewers that the movie is told from their point of view.

"I couldn't agree more," Goldberg said. "It bugged the hell out of me. Why couldn't the narrator have been my kid, or no kid? Why couldn't the story stand on its own? I didn't understand why they put it in there. Maybe they wanted to show how brave the white woman was in the face of all of this. But the black woman was brave, too.

"The thing that saved us is the fact that my family comes off as a real family. My husband works. He's a working man, and he's got some anger, but it's not 'we-gonna-get-you-Whitey' anger. It's about how people had to behave. People have told me it's a very restrained performance. It's restrained because that's what those women had to do. They were mad, but they had to work to support their families."

There's a scene where the white in-laws talk with incredible rudeness right in front of your character, as you're serving them dinner, and when you get down to the bottom of the driveway with the cook you say, "She damn near got a plate full of food right upside her head."

Goldberg grinned. "Yeah. You know, it was a big thrill to sit down and see this thing. I'm just really proud of it. I could say all kinds of stuff, little nit-picky stuff, but it's not necessary. People will take from it what they take, but I really am glad, thrilled actually, that it is as equal as it is in showing the two families, because, boy, it could have gone the complete other way."

Now about Goldberg's other role, the one that won the Oscar nomination. We didn't really discuss it much; the occasion for our talk was *The Long Walk Home*. But we did discuss Oscar possibilities, and, for me, that Montgomery maid was a sure bet. I was wrong—maybe because the movie wasn't seen by nearly as many people as *Ghost*.

What's disappointing is that Goldberg's role in *Ghost* is the sort of thing she has done before in several films. Her character, a psychic who starts picking up vibes from a dead young man and acts as his conduit to his girlfriend, is well-played, warm, and funny. But it isn't new. And it helps illustrate one of Goldberg's big professional frustrations: the type-casting that prevents her from being considered for certain kinds of roles.

"There are roles I am never considered for. Meryl Streep roles, let's say. Why not? I really wanted to do *Ironweed*,

for example, because the Depression era in this country was one of the best for multiracial people, because everybody was poor. Everybody lived in the tents, and under buildings, and under gratings, together. It is a frustrating thing that I was not considered for that role. Or a lot of roles that could be played by a black woman, except they never think that way. Or male roles. I would love to play a male role.

"I have the strangest time to get cast in anything. *Ghost* was the same thing. Six months I had to wait for them to decide they had seen everybody possible. Why not? What limits me? I'm black? Oh, am I black? What will I be when you shoot me? I could be from England. It took MTV to tell us that there are black people in England! It took Fassbinder with his black actors to tell us there are black people in Germany. Sad to say, but over the last five years, I have come to the realization that I am black, and somehow that's supposed to hinder me.

"It's not that Meryl takes my roles. Sigourney doesn't take my roles. It's that I'm not allowed in the door to read for the things. I feel that I could have played the Glenn Close role in *Fatal Attraction*. It would have been interesting. Maybe not the same, but interesting."

But then they would have felt they had to explain the interracial relationship.

"All right, then, why can't I have a relationship with a Warren Beatty, or a Jack Nicholson? I think acting-wise I'm up for it, but I'm plodding along, and I just keep hoping for the best. Sean Connery has always been the epitome of a man to me, I'd love to play opposite him. People say, 'But he's the one who says it's OK to pop a woman every once in a while,' and I say, 'Yeah, well, he'd pop me once, and that would be it. It'd break his arms.'

"But why can't this kind of casting be considered? There was an article in the paper that showed artists that have played other ethnic groups, like Yul Brynner and Brando, and they were wonderful in these parts. Then somebody said to me, 'Do you think that Olivier should have played Othello? He's called the greatest Othello that ever lived!'

"And I asked, how many black actors got the opportunity? How do we know he was the greatest? It wasn't like there was a large group of people offered the role, and he happened to get it because he was the best. All actors should be able to play all roles, that's the magic. But the opportunities are not there."

Actually, I said, your very name is an attempt to fly in the face of preconceptions.

"I can't tell you how many people have said, 'So where did the name Goldberg come from?' And I say it came from my mom. That it was my grandmother's mother's mother's maiden name. And they say, 'But you know it's a Jewish name.' And I say, 'Well, I'm a Jewish girl, with a Catholic upbringing.' And they go, 'Oh, really?' It's just so odd, you're not allowed to just be an actor. You have to be in some category. They have to be able to look at you and tell you what roles you can play."

It's true that Goldberg wasn't in an enormous box office hit between her first movie, *The Color Purple*, and *Ghost*. But in her case the theatrical box office figures don't tell the whole story. Ask the guy behind the counter at the video store and you'll discover that for some reason she is a superstar on home video. *Entertainment Weekly* recently singled her out in that category, reporting, for example, that her *Jumpin' Jack Flash* sold 6.9 million theatrical tickets (itself not so bad), but has been rented on video more than nineteen million times.

Why is that? Maybe it's because Whoopi Goldberg sort of grows on you. She doesn't have conventional beauty, she doesn't play conventional roles, but there is always a presence there, and usually it's interesting. She's not like everyone else on the screen. Just by persisting, by being herself and yet playing roles that the conventional wisdom says she's wrong for, she may be helping to expand the ranges of a lot of actors. At first, Hollywood treated her like an alien from outer space: She played one-of-a-kind characters who had few real relationships with anybody.

"It's a very old argument, that I look wrong for certain roles," she said. "It has a lot to do with people's personal stuff. I worked with Sam Elliott in a film called *Fatal Beauty*, and one of the initial talks that I had with the director after the contracts were signed was about this scene that was a really great love scene. I don't have the body to take my clothes off, but you know, it had hands to faces, and kisses, and all that romantic stuff that you always want when you find the right guy.

"It's the right stuff, and the director said to me, 'Well, you know this character is somewhat based on me, and frankly, I don't see him seeing anything attractive about you.' So I just kind of took a deep breath, and said, 'Well, maybe he had many years of drugs, and he just doesn't know any better, and his brain is half fried.'"

Sam Elliott did have a sort of love interest with you in *Fatal Beauty*, I said.

"Yeah, they couldn't get around it."

He kissed you.

"Yes, and I gave him a peck and a hug, but there was no deep sort of Mickey Rourke kissing going on. I've had two kisses in my career. That, and also, of course, my hair has bothered people for many years. Finally Euzhan Palcy and Milli Vanilli came along, and they decided maybe braids were OK. I've even worn a dress or two recently, and now people suspect that there may be something interesting under there, and I guess I'm growing into my face, or they're just getting used to me, and so they're finally sort of talking to me about women's roles. *The Long Walk Home* is the first movie where I have a family and a love interest who even kisses me. It's wild."

She lit another cigarette, and blew out smoke, and sighed.

"All I really want to do is just keep acting, and some of it will stink, and some of it will be really good, and maybe when I'm eighty-five and presenting an Oscar like Bette Davis did, I can look back and say, 'It was OK; I did all right.'

"You know what Bette Davis told me? She told me, 'Fuck 'em! Fuck 'em!' That's what she said to me. 'They told me I couldn't do this and I couldn't do that, and fuck you, I told them! So Whoopi, fuck 'em!' That's what she told me, and she was right."

Dennis Hopper

Chicago, October 17, 1990—Truffaut once said that it was impossible to pay attention to a film shot in the house where you were born because you'd always be noticing that they wallpapered the bedroom. I knew I was in for the same sort of problem in the opening scene of *The Hot Spot*, Dennis Hopper's new thriller. The film was made in 1990, but its psychic center is 1957, and Don Johnson, who plays a mysterious stranger from out of town, roars onto the screen in a 1957 Studebaker Golden Hawk.

This is the only car I have ever loved. In 1957, when I was a kid working in a sporting goods store after high school, I'd go next door to the Studebaker dealer and just stand there and look at the car. I felt awe. In *Rain Man*, Tom Cruise and Dustin Hoffman are driving down the highway in that old Buick, and they pass a '57 Hawk going in the opposite direction, and Hoffman, the autistic with the steel-trap memory, correctly identifies it. And I shouted out, *Yes!*

Now, here is a movie where the hero drives a '57 Golden Hawk through the entire picture. And here is Dennis Hopper, talking to me about his movie, telling me the screenplay was originally written for Robert Mitchum back in the 1960s. Somehow it's almost as well that Mitchum didn't make the film. A movie containing both Mitchum, the central icon of *film noir*, *and* the Golden Hawk, the most beautiful American production sports car since the war, would have encompassed more than any one film could safely contain. It would have been perfect. I could have stopped going to the movies.

Hopper was up at the Toronto Film Festival for the premiere of his movie, and I walked into the room and asked him flat out why Don Johnson was driving the '57 Hawk.

It was a question he did not sound surprised to hear. "Because I like the car," he said. "I think it's the best-looking car ever made. It was designed by Raymond Loewy, the same guy that designed the Coke bottle. It's the greatest-looking car ever made. It really is.

"Why it's in the movie is, I put it in. The movie is based on a book called *Hell Hath No Fury*, written by Charles Williams in 1951. The screenplay was written in 1961 for Robert Mitchum, also by Williams. If you look at the movie, it will appear that it takes place in the present day, because Johnson is a used-car salesman and he's selling recent cars. But I didn't really change anything, because I didn't want to. At heart it's a *film noir* from the 1940s or 1950s. I put them all in 1940s-looking clothes. I figured, in a small town in Texas, not a whole hell of a lot has really changed, you know?"

The movie is one of those exercises in style, sex, and shadows that was familiar in the postwar years, before high-tech violence came along and took all of the fun out of sin. It's a sultry melodrama starring Johnson as a man without a past. He drives into town (in the '57 Hawk) and gets a job in a used-car lot by selling a car to a customer even before he's met the guy who owns the lot. The owner is a slow-thinking fleshapoid with a bum ticker who lives in a big house up on the hill, where his young and reckless wife (Virginia Madsen) is bored, bored, bored by her endless routine: get up, slip into a negligee, drink and smoke all day. She needs a real man. The first time she looks at Johnson, she's like a butcher trying to decide where to make the first cut on a side of prime beef.

Down at the used-car lot, Johnson also catches the attention of another girl (Jennifer Connelly), a shy, virginal kid with soft brown hair that floats down to her shoulders and big brown eyes that blink ever so slowly at the concept of lust. Johnson's partner at the lot is another salesman (Charles Martin Smith), who somehow senses that Johnson will flash through this job like a meteor on his way to better things—or death.

The plot involves all the great old *noir* concepts like an evil man who lives in a shack outside of town and knows a dread secret out of the virginal girl's past, and has on occasion been the lover of the bored car dealer's wife. It also involves a plan to commit the perfect crime by sticking up a bank in broad daylight. And it includes a lot of scenes where women look yearningly at the hero through plate glass windows, and seem ready to come right through the glass after him and bleed to death if that's what it takes.

Virginia Madsen drives an old car, too, I observed. A '58 Cadillac.

"Yeah, right," Hopper said, "and there's a scene that's not in the picture—I hated to but I had to cut it out; the movie was running four hours—a scene where he first comes into town, and they drive past each other and slow down and look at each other's cars, and she flicks her cigarette at him and drives off, and he almost runs into a truck that's backing out."

Madsen plays the Lana Turner type.

"Yeah, exactly. Lana Turner is just what I had in mind. Of all the young actresses, she's the only one who has that kind of style. That forties movie star kind of quality. She has it. And Jennifer Connelly, the young girl, she has a different style. It's almost invisible acting. She doesn't push, but she's there. I hate to compare her to Montgomery Clift, but it's there, that simplicity."

Hopper is holding court now, enjoying the sound of his words. He has the air of a man who has triumphed over great adversity, as indeed he has. He is eight years clean and sober after hitting a bottom so hard that he actually spent some time locked up in the proverbial rubber room. We've talked about that before. Since then he has enjoyed a career renaissance that leaves you almost breathless, wondering what he might have accomplished if he *hadn't* spent those years of oblivion.

His first career—his first lifetime, really—was as an actor of alienation in movies like *Rebel Without a Cause* (1955). He played the kid in a lot of Westerns (how many people know he was in *Gunfight at the O.K. Corral* and *True Grit?*). In 1968 he single-handedly ushered in the whole era of low-budget "youth pictures" with the great success of *Easy Rider*. He was here and there in the 1970s, often playing the spaced-out character he had become, in movies like Coppola's *Apocalypse Now* and Henry Jaglom's *Tracks*. Then came the lost years, followed by his comeback in 1983 as the director of *Out of the Blue*. As an actor, he has been unceasingly busy, starring in movies like *Blue Velvet*, *Hoosiers*, *River's Edge*, *Black Widow*, and the recent *Flashback*, in which he played a 1960s survivor. His career as a director resumed with *Colors*, the 1988 Sean Penn cop drama, and now here is *The Hot Spot*. And that's not all. *People* magazine likes to run cover lines like, "He's back with a new film, a new wife, and a new baby!" And in Hopper's case, that's true.

Anyone who grew up as Hopper did, in the late 1940s and 1950s, knows the feeling of a *film noir* inside out. The key element in many of those movies, I think, is the tension between the bland middle Americans in the supporting roles and the potential for evil in the leading characters. In a time when everyone conformed, the man who was willing to break the rules was sensed as a danger, even if he never acted on his impulse.

Perhaps Hopper thought he could find that old *film noir* innocence if he set his film in the little town of Taylor, Texas. To a degree, he does. To another degree, he simply pretends it is still 1951 and the values are all the same, no matter how new the cars are that Don Johnson is selling.

"Orion Pictures brought me this project to see if I might be interested in directing it," Hopper said. "I read the script, and I thought, yeah, I can make a movie out of this. I gave it to Paul Lewis, my partner, who works with me on everything. We've been together since *Easy Rider*. He read it and told me there was a 1961 script based on the same book, and it was a much better script then. I said, 'Don't tell me better script. This is a go project. I can make a good movie out of this.' He said, 'Well, OK, but I'm telling you there's a better script.'

"It turned out Paul had broken the script down for Mitchum in 1961. He knew all about the project, but it was never made. And when they rewrote and updated the script last year, they decided they would take this guy with no past and do the one thing they should never have tried to do, and that is to give him a history. There's a flashback where we learn the reason he robs the bank is because when he was a kid the bad banker came and took the farm away from the father. Well, finally Paul got me to read the original 1961 script, and he was right. It was better. So we decided to talk Orion into junking the new script and doing the old script while we were already actually on location."

So what we have here, in a sense, is a movie in a time warp: A 1961 *film noir* for Robert Mitchum, made in 1990 with Don Johnson. Not that Don Johnson on his best day will ever be a match for Robert Mitchum, but, of course, on the other hand we do have the bonus of the '57 Hawk. And Virginia Madsen could have held her own against any *film noir* heroine in the book.

Hopper's direction is clean and economical in the movie, most of the time, and then he breaks out occasionally into tricky moments with light and shadow.

"I do very simple sorts of things," he said. "My films are all shot at eye level. I have one scene where the camera goes up at the car lot, but it's like a joke thing. It rises up when he's proving he can sell a car. Usually it's all eye-level stuff. There's no tricky, fun, or weird shots or stuff. I'm not doing Orson Welles. I keep it simple. The only thing I do that most directors don't do is, I use the stead-icam a lot so the cameraman can walk around and follow the action. I do masters, close-ups, over-the-shoulders, and it's simple style. I'm back with John Ford and Huston and Hawks—and Hathaway; I learned a lot from Hath-away when I was acting in *The Sons of Katie Elder*."

That's a nice shot, I said, from inside the cabin. While the violence is taking place, we see headlights through two different windows, lighting the acting first one way and then another.

"I work things out at the moment. I block the scene, and then I become the camera, and I move all through the scene, and then I show the steadicam guy my movements. I'm a very visual person. I also walk through all the actors' parts. I just feel on my feet how it can be shot."

Are you still basically an actor, or are you becoming more of a director?

"The ideal would be to direct a movie and then act in a movie, back and forth, but that's pretty difficult. I love acting. I really love it. It's really relatively easy for me now, even the most complex roles, but directing is a lot of work. In the fear of not being allowed to direct, I will probably push the acting away, because right now I really want to direct. I feel that I've wasted so much time, that I should have made more films."

"I was looking out of the plane on the way here today thinking. I was thinking I had no life or any memory really until now. I mean it's amazing, and every day it gets better. But there's always this fear of not being able to make the films, not being able to do the work, because it's inherent in the profession that maybe you're not going to be able to work anymore. I don't think anybody, no mat-ter how successful they get, ever loses that fear. If you've ever had a period of time where you weren't allowed to direct—maybe because you were doing drugs and alcohol, but you didn't know that was their reason—then the fear is always with you."

Jeremy Irons

Chicago, October 11, 1990—It is one of the oddest perfor-mances of recent years, an exercise in mannered behavior that has the audience snickering with disbelief before they realize it's all right to laugh because, in a way, it's sup-posed to be funny. The performance is by Jeremy Irons in *Reversal of Fortune*, where he plays Claus von Bulow, a man accused of attempting to murder his wife.

As von Bulow, Irons strikes poses that would seem affected in a Noel Coward drawing room. He holds his cigarette as if it were being smoked by someone else. His dialogue sometimes seems to have been written by P.G. Wodehouse. The astonishing thing is that this strange performance not only works, it succeeds so well that it provides an avenue into this perverse material. Having read about the von Bu-low case for more than a decade, having followed Claus's progress through two sensational trials, having read the periodic updates on his wife, Sunny—who is still alive in an irreversible coma—I would have said the story of this case was unfilmable. I would have been wrong.

Reversal of Fortune is a balancing act of such varied skills that it's hard to know which one to start with. It is, first of all, fairly close to the facts in the case. It is based on a book written by the famous Harvard law professor Alan Dersho-witz after he successfully defended von Bulow on appeal. It offers fair approximations of the principal characters. Irons gives us a man who feels like the von Bulow we know from the media. Ron Silver gets so close to Dershowitz that when I met the professor himself I was struck by the resemblance.

And in the performance of Glenn Close, as Sunny, the movie finds a way to make this material bearable. If the entire film took place with Sunny as an offscreen, mute, accusing figure, it would be a very depressing experience. But the film's director, Barbet Schroeder, and his writer, Nicholas Kazan, have found a solution: The entire movie is narrated by Sunny, who, in describing the day she was found in a coma, finds herself as baffled as everyone else by the mystery of what really happened. "You tell me," she invites us, setting a tone for the movie that allows it to move through a remarkable range of moods and materials with surprising ease.

"A comedy laced with rat poison," Tom Luddy of the Telluride Film Festival wrote in his note when the movie premiered there over the Labor Day weekend. It is indeed a comedy, but such an odd one that even the distributor, Warner Bros., seemed unsure of what note to strike in its coming attractions trailer. Is this an exposé, a denouncement, an accusation, a real-life crime thriller, a legal procedural, or what?

A week after seeing the movie at Telluride, I sat down with Jeremy Irons at another film festival, Toronto, to talk about *Reversal of Fortune*. The buzz had already started; here was a performance, a lot of people were saying, that would win an Academy Award nomination. And here was a film that would win box office success for director Barbet Schroeder, whose previous works have been either art house hits or movies like *Barfly* that generated a lot of enthusiasm but limited receipts.

"Isn't it strange how things come together?" Irons asked me. "How does that happen? I'm thrilled the movie's being received so well, because I perceived it as being difficult to sell. It was a very loose script. I knew that I had to get some comedy into Claus, because he has it about him, a sort of wicked black humor, and I needed it for the balance of the character."

Sitting in a hotel suite, sipping a beer, Irons seemed like the intelligent, soft-spoken character he has played in a lot of movies—films such as *The French Lieutenant's Woman*, *Betrayal*, and the TV miniseries "Brideshead Revisited." From his work in the dual role as twin gynecologists in *Dead Ringers*, we know he's capable of suggesting a buried malevolence, but his Claus von Bulow is a real leap—a leap into an affected British-European accent, a theatrical personal style, a hint of the possibility of evil even in the midst of wounded innocence.

It's that ability to seem plausibly guilty and innocent at the same time that makes his performance, and the movie, intriguing, because *Reversal of Fortune* does not finally say whether it thinks von Bulow is a wife-poisoner or simply a suspicious bystander. "I think some people will be irritated that the film doesn't come to an obvious conclusion," Irons said, "but I love that. I think it would be a far lesser film if it painted one clear side or the other at the end."

Instead, it ends with a scene that Schroeder was still testing at Telluride. Von Bulow walks into a newsstand to buy some cigarettes, is recognized by the woman behind the counter, and asks her for "a small vial of insulin, please." Her face registers shock. She knows this man has been accused of giving his wife an overdose of insulin. "Only kidding," he says. The same note is struck constantly through the movie; von Bulow seems to enjoy tantalizing people with the possibility of his guilt.

"I'm not sure Claus still enjoys his celebrity as a possible wife murderer," Irons said. "I think he did when it was a real currency in New York. I think in London it's slightly tarnished currency."

He smiled that wan Jeremy Irons smile, and shrugged, as if to suggest that a man cannot, after all, expect to go on dining out indefinitely on the celebrity of having been tried for attempting to poison his wife.

You are not, I said, the first person I would have thought of to play this man. Why did they think of you, and how did you react when you were offered the role?

"Apparently, they wanted an Englishman. I suggested to them they use Klaus Maria Brandauer or Robert Duvall. Claus himself had already suggested Duvall. I think they felt that so much of Claus was an Englishman, that they had to get one to play him. Claus considers himself an Englishman, with an English reserve and a Scandinavian coldness, so that's why they thought of me, I suppose. I thought it was curious casting. I think a lot of his Englishness is a put-on, actually."

Did you meet him or study tapes of his voice?

"I didn't think it would be useful to meet him. To start with, I felt so unlike him physically, that at the beginning I thought I was a dreadful idea for a casting choice. But strangely, when we got the hair right and all of that, I thought it just might be possible. I knew that if I met Claus he wouldn't tell me anything I really needed to know. He wouldn't tell me the truth, and even if he did, I wouldn't be able to discern if it was the truth. And I didn't want to feel the need to play an impersonation. That's not what I do. I'm not very good at impersonations. I wanted to get a distilled essence of him. I thought meeting him would be too big an event in my mind.

"I did watch his interviews with Barbara Walters. She did two big ones, and Donahue did a big one. I watched those, and I talked to people who knew him quite well, and began to get a feeling for him."

The feeling was for von Bulow as a singularly odd man, a man who would seem to the average American moviegoer to have come from Mars. Irons gives him such an off-center spin that watching the performance would be absorbing no matter what the movie was about. He does something else, too, and it's the mark of a good actor. Many of von Bulow's scenes are with Silver, playing Dershowitz, and in those scenes, Irons makes von Bulow seem especially affected, for a good reason: He is frightened to death. In one extraordinary moment at their first meeting, he actually tells Dershowitz he has "the greatest respect for members of the Jewish race."

"Everybody thought it was too much when I did it, when I played that scene," Irons said. "I certainly was worried that I might have gone too far. I thought it was too loud, for one thing. But I had to think of it from his point of view. I think he was frightened. He was pleading for his freedom. He might go to jail for the rest of his life, so he needs this man. He's very concerned as to whether Dershowitz will take on the case. The stakes are terribly high for him, and I think we tend to forget this when talking about it."

Yet it is beyond him to beg or plead.

"Yes. We see a man who, when he makes that horrendous remark about admiring Jews, really means that as a way to connect with Dershowitz, and, of course, it comes out all wrong, and it's taken all wrong. He is constantly concerned with making a correct appearance, and sometimes he has no real idea, outside of his own little world, of what a correct appearance might be."

A lot of people were annoyed, I said, by Barbet Schroeder's previous film, *Barfly*, because they thought Mickey Rourke's performance went over the top. Schroeder doesn't seem to believe that every performance has to be a naturalistic slice of life. Von Bulow is an odd person. You created an odd eccentric man, but made me feel he was real. He's not like anyone else you've played. How did you come to that oddness?

"He was made up from different elements. The voice came embarrassingly late into the picture. It felt right about a third of the way through, and it wasn't until then that I knew what I was after. The accent is not accurate to Claus, because he actually speaks better English than that. But it's certainly right for my Claus.

"About the mannerisms. At times he uses that theatrical gravity, that ponderousness, for effect. You see people at dinner tables, who like to be the center of attention; they draw it out, especially if they have a secret, if people want to know something. They use that and concentrate on that sometimes to cover themselves. You often see people speaking slowly to make sure they haven't left themselves open by what they say.

"In other words, Claus gives the impression of a man who perhaps is not saying the absolute truth, for whatever his reasons. He is an elegant man. He likes to think of himself as an aristocrat. He's not, but he is a great snob."

Irons smiled and reached again for his beer. "I mustn't talk about him," he said. "I promised I wouldn't talk about him. I can justify everything he does. I know why he's doing it. I know what he's thinking while he does it. But I'm not him, and I don't know the real truth.

"I fell into that trap very badly in an early interview with a German magazine. It appeared that I was talking about Claus, and it was written as though I was talking about him, and I had never met him. I don't know him. I was talking about myself, about 'my' Claus. He set me right about a few things, and obviously it concerned him, and I thought—he's right. I don't see why this man should have to put up with this. You know, of having his friends send him articles about what some lunatic actor has been pontificating about him. Most journalists will write as if I am pronouncing myself Claus von Bulow rather than talking about my character, which unfortunately has the same name.

"My argument has always been that Claus is a victim. Claus is the one who has to live with all that publicity, all that finger-pointing, and now—still—all the uncertainty about his guilt or innocence. He's as much or more a victim than Sunny."

In the film, in flashback scenes, Glenn Close portrays Sunny as a woman so adrift in tranquilizers and alcohol that she has only a tenuous hold on reality and spends much of her time in bed. There is an eerie dinner scene where the others eat a normal meal while she smokes a cigarette and picks at an ice cream sundae. The film gives the impression that she would have died sooner or later by accident or by her own hand.

"I think it's a shame that we don't see her a little bit more," Irons said. "A lot of people who knew her said she wasn't like that. I thought, well, of course she wasn't like that when she was out among people, because Claus got her home pretty fast. So they remembered her as charismatic and pretty."

Were there any problems portraying a living person from a legal point of view?

"No, because we based the film very closely on the Dershowitz book, and we knew the book was all right legally. If we wanted to deviate from the book at all, then yes, we had to tread most carefully. One of the witnesses in the case got ahold of a copy of the book before it was printed and sold that copy to the stepchildren, and the stepchildren called and said they'd sue if it was published. Dershowitz said he'd sue them for receiving stolen goods if they did, and that's as far as it went."

You don't sue Alan Dershowitz lightly, do you?

"I don't think so. I mean, he was saying with gusto today at a press conference that he felt it was a frame-up by the children, and one of the journalists said, 'You're not afraid they're going to sue?' He said, 'I'd be delighted to be sued, because then we'd get to the bottom of this case.'"

Quincy Jones

Toronto, September 19, 1990—To see the film is to watch a man who remembers pain with every cell of his body. A man whose mother's erratic behavior put scars on his childhood (he still remembers her throwing his birthday cake off the back porch when he was six) and who has been through three marriages and two brain surgeries and a complete emotional shutdown. The odds against the success of each surgery were 100-to-1. What does that make the odds on two of them?

Quincy Jones hasn't added up the numbers. He knows they're pretty high. Yes, Quincy Jones, the musician you thought was blessed with success and luck. Quincy, the man everybody likes, the first black musician to crack the Hollywood studios as a composer of scores, the man who wrote the music for *The Color Purple* and has produced and arranged albums for Sinatra and Streisand and Michael Jackson, and who wrote "We Are the World." Quincy Jones, it turns out, has been through fifty-seven years that many people would not have survived, and some days it is still touch and go.

Quincy Jones—it also turns out—is a brave and honest man who allowed two women to make a documentary about him that tells a lot of truths another man might have wanted to conceal. The name of the movie is *Listen Up: The Lives of Quincy Jones*, and at its premiere here at the Toronto Film Festival, the audience walked in expecting a musical biography and walked out having seen the joys and sorrows of a man's soul.

"I can hardly even watch the film," Jones told me one afternoon over lunch. "It's so painful I will have to watch it ten or twenty more times just to get over the impact enough so I can start looking at the filmmaking, looking at it technically."

Listen Up, which was directed by Ellen Weissbrod and produced by Courtney Sale Ross, is the kind of project that might easily have gone in a different, safer direction. Ross is the wife of Time/Warner chairman Steve Ross, which helps to explain why people as camera-shy as Streisand, Jackson, Sinatra, Ella Fitzgerald, and Miles Davis agreed to talk about their friend. But she and Weissbrod are not concerned with making a tame film of publicity and tribute. *Listen Up* hops around like a bebop composition, weaving an intricate editing pattern out of thousands of brief sound bites, as faces and revelations swim in and out of focus. At first we wonder if the film really has a structure. Then we see that it does, a musical structure, a composition where each note is someone's memory.

The life story that emerges is of a man who was born on Chicago's South Side, whose mother was institutionalized when he was six, who moved to Seattle, picked up a French horn when he was twelve, and by the age of fifteen was playing professionally with some of the top jazz musicians of the day.

A prodigy, yes? But also a driven man who confesses he has never been any good at relationships with women, who set his sights on Hollywood and became the first black composer to break through the studio's color bar, who won every award and set every record and conquered the music industry, who has survived intact what looked like certain death from blood clots in his brain, and who at fifty-seven is just now thinking he might be moving into a period of serenity with himself. Not everybody in *Listen Up* always speaks well of Quincy Jones. You can hear the hurt in the voice of one of his daughters, who is the film's principal witness. One of the other witnesses who does not speak well is Jones himself.

"A lot of discoveries I've made, I probably wouldn't have made them if it hadn't been for the film," he said, leaning back, looking healthy and confident and not like the sometimes fearful man in the movie. "I wouldn't have gone back to my childhood home that I haven't seen in fifty years and remembered some things I thought I'd forgotten. That's heavy. There's a lot that has worked in my life—that I already knew—but this movie was a revelation of what makes me cry. It's really hard for me to watch this because of some of the emotions."

I'd been told by Courtney Ross that the visit to his home triggered memories that Jones had repressed since childhood, when he could not understand why his mother acted so strangely and did not seem to love him.

How does a kid deal with that? I asked him. All that he knows is his mother has thrown away his birthday cake. It doesn't have a thing to do with mental illness.

"Right. It doesn't. And the tragic thing is, the doctors say now that she could have been cured with vitamin B. It's that simple. She was a beautiful woman. She's eighty-seven now. She speaks eight languages. She can write a letter that can take your skin off. It's unbelievable. She takes mine off a lot. She types 160 words a minute. She sent to me the New Testament for Christmas that she re-typed herself. So, I guess that's a happy ending, because we got to know each other, and it's a close relationship."

When did that relationship begin to re-form?

"When I was fifteen. But then I resisted it for fifteen or twenty more years."

She was better by then?

"Yes, and she came out to Seattle to try and find us. In her mind we were still seven or eight years old. She just could never really handle the reality of it. She still talks to me sometimes as if I'm seven or eight years old. She's quite a character. I remember when we went up to the closing of the Goodwill Games. She told us all, 'I've got a great idea! I think you should all have your penises amputated, because you've all had enough sex.' That went over really well."

He was able to laugh, but in the movie he says that those early experiences—the unreasoning denial of a mother's love—caused him to mistrust women all of his life, and led to the breakup of his marriages and his reputation as a dedicated but not very happy ladies' man. What gave him direction, what gave him a key to possible happiness, was the day he picked up his first musical instrument.

"It was 1945. I must have been twelve years old. The world started to open up like a telephoto lens. I played all the brass instruments—I remember going all the way from sousaphone to the tuba, because the school had a marching band. We were lucky in Seattle because we had the chance to be so eclectic. We used to play from seven to ten P.M. at white tennis clubs—'To Each His Own,' songs like that—and then we'd play for the black clubs, rhythm and blues, and then we'd go play be-bop at 3 A.M. in the red light district around the Elk's Club, and then at school we'd be playing 'Pomp and Circumstance' and a little bit of Copeland or whatever."

Somebody in the film says, "Pop? Doesn't that mean white music?"

Jones laughed. "Miles. It could only be Miles. Miles is great. I'm sitting here looking at this film, and it's not about any doubts about anything musical. There's Bobby Tucker who grabbed me at fourteen and put me with Billie Holiday, at fifteen with Billy Eckstein and Clark Terry and Ray Charles. I mean, these are the people I played with. Their own interpretation is a little shaky, too, like when they can't remember if I was a good trumpet player or not. If I played with Lionel Hampton and Dizzy Gillespie I couldn't have played that bad, or I wouldn't have been playing with them."

What would you have done if music hadn't come into your life?

"Been waiting in the alley someplace and selling dope. It's all about energy—energy that's either focused or misdirected. I think about that a lot, because I was on that borderline. Coming from Chicago you can't help it. We were doing everything, and a police car was at our house every weekend. We'd go in the Army camp, and steal parts for machine guns because we used to like to play war out in the woods, and we'd have thirty-caliber water-cooled machine guns out there in the woods, chopping down trees. Remember, it was the middle of World War II, and that was a real gung-ho war, and I was a paper boy, so I could go through the barbed wire fence and steal those parts. It could have gone either way."

Somebody in the movie talks about teen-age years when you and your friends were twenty seconds from a prison sentence.

"That happens in most communities with situations like that. You're idle. You don't have the opportunity to do anything, so the creative energy goes wherever. I feel the same way about the choices kids have to make today between degrees and a very comfortable living selling dope. It's a serious choice, between getting a master's degree so you can carry bags at the airport, or you're out there at eleven years old and you're making $1,800 a day with dope and supporting your family. It's a real serious social-political trick bag out there. I could have gone either way."

But maybe if you hadn't gone into music the energy would have gone into something else, into business or education . . . .

"No, I would have ended up in prison. Here's what you really have to remember, and this is what opened up my eyes when I had to go back to the old neighborhood for this film. I came out of the biggest ghetto in the United States at ten years old, watching teachers getting killed and teen-agers getting killed every day, and then I moved to an all-white city, Seattle city schools, and in the curriculum, it's as though no black people exist. There were no blacks on TV, and on the radio they had Amos and Andy, but they were played by whites, so you didn't exist! It's an incredible feeling to discover you're a nonentity."

But there were blacks in music.

"That's probably one of the things that attracted me about it. Seattle was a hot spot during the war; all the action was there, and I'd see these well-groomed, intelligent, proud, black musicians with all the great bands. The discipline was there, and they had a sense of pride and dignity about them. Everybody looks for a way to find their self-esteem. So I knew that was what I had to do. There was no MTV then, and kids making $60 million dollars by the time they're twenty-five. Our heroes were Charlie Parker and Dizzy and Miles.

"Before then, I really wondered, where did I belong? I used to play hookey and go watch movies when I was twelve years old, and I knew the sounds of the musical scores from each studio. I knew Alfred Newman's sound from Fox; I could feel Victor Young from Paramount; I could feel the style and the musical editorial policy. But how could I ever compose for the movies? I never thought I'd ever get a shot because I'd see these long four-syllable names on the scores. When they did give the blacks a chance, they'd put them in self-contained scenes that could be cut out when the movie played in the South."

And yet, *Listen Up* is a film, I said, about a man who not only composed for the movies, but eventually felt he had outgrown that and went on to bigger challenges.

"The first thing I thought when I saw the film was, it's not too late to make up for all the screwups I've made. Especially with my kids. I have to make a deal now with my grandson, because he could make me a great-grandfather now. He's sixteen. Great-grandfather, give me a break!"

The movie is a little vague on some of the domestic details in Jones's life; we know he is divorced from Peggy Lipton because that is the stuff of everyday publicity, now that she's starring on "Twin Peaks," but the specific biographical details in the film are handled impressionistically. When we see an overhead shot of all of his children posing for a birthday picture for him, we realize that we're not sure who all of these people are or what marriages they come from. *Listen Up* is not a factual record; it's improvisational, and at the end you feel you know the truth about some of Jones's relationships, but not the facts.

That's also the case with the coverage of his two brain operations after an aneurysm nearly killed him. Did I hear a voice on the sound track, I asked, say that the odds on your operation were 100-to-1?

"Uh-huh. I was really surprised when I woke up."

What did you start doing differently after your operation?

"The first thing I started doing was hugging a lot." He smiled. "You know that old cliché about your life flashing in front of you? Well, it really does. It's like it's exhausting your whole memory. All these things are flying by. I remember when I first felt the pain of the aneurysm, all these things just came out. A lot of it was about realizing you'd never have a chance to tell people how you really felt about them. That's terrifying. And not being able to realize your dreams. It put the biological clock on a different wake-up time. You start to think about what difference you can make being here.

"When you get to be fifty, you start dealing with the countdown, and you can deal with it in a positive way or a negative way. I try to deal with it in a positive way, saying I don't have time to waste on making another album with somebody I don't like. You try to make this little life to be this great gift."

It's strange, I said, that Quincy Jones would wonder what difference he could make. And yet in the movie there are comments about a period only five years ago when you had a breakdown and found you couldn't work at all.

"That was 1985 and into 1986. I was finishing *The Color Purple*, and starting to work on Michael Jackson's *Bad*. I was doing a lot of those gigs where you raise the money, and you get honored and everything. So, a doctor came up to me one day and told me I was in big trouble. I asked him what he was talking about. He said he could see the signs in my eyes that I had adrenal syndrome. I didn't know what the hell that meant, although the end of *The Color Purple* had been very difficult. He said, 'What's happened is, your adrenal gland has shrunk to the size of a pea, and it should look like a walnut.' It's the domino theory after that. All the other glands start to shut down, and you get irritability, sleeplessness, lack of appetite, you're spiraling. Eventually you turn on the people you love, and you turn on yourself."

Jones's voice grew quieter as he remembered. "He just laid it out. He said half the cure was psychological—I had to live a Robinson Crusoe life with no time demands for a while. And so Brando told me to go to his island in the South Pacific, and I grabbed my bag of about thirteen books that I thought could help me find the truth—you know, *The Rays of Dawn*, *The Road Less Traveled*, the Bible—and I sat on the beach."

And it worked?

Jones smiled. "At the end, I was in worse shape than ever before. I thought I was insane. It was a van Gogh situation. Then I came back, and everything fell apart, my marriage and everything. Then, with the help of a doctor, my senses came back, because they had been gone. One night everything came back, my sexuality, everything just came right back."

So what is the answer?

"I do meditation. I do prayer, and I've investigated almost every religion since I was twelve years old. Dianetics back when I was fifteen, just curious about it. Buddhism and Judaism, everything else. You see what a business religion is, and that you don't need a middle man. That's what I've discovered. I don't need a middle man anymore. I've got God's private number."

David Lean: In Memoriam

On the day I went to visit David Lean's set of *Ryan's Daughter* in Dingle, Ireland, in 1969, the sun was shining and it reflected a dazzling light off the sands of the beach. The next day it started to rain, and within a week Robert Mitchum made his famous observation, "We've shot for one day and we're eight days behind schedule." Months later, Lean eventually took cast and crew members all the way to Natal in South Africa to match the sunny beach. He could, of course, have started over again and shot the beach

scene with an overcast, but an overcast wasn't what he had in mind. He wanted sun, even in Ireland, even in March.

Perfectionism was not simply a quality in the work of David Lean, who died in England on April 16, 1991, at the age of eighty-three. It was a fetish. He was a man in no hurry to make a movie. He would wait years, if necessary, before be began a project, and he was most content in the stages before and after the actual shooting. He would polish a screenplay forever, and then, after the final shot, would disappear into the editing room for half a year or more.

As he grew older he worked more and more deliberately. Five years passed between *The Bridge on the River Kwai* (1957) and *Lawrence of Arabia* (1962). Three years later he made *Dr. Zhivago*. He shot *Ryan's Daughter* in 1969, released it in 1970, and then, stung by its negative critical reception, waited fifteen years before he made *A Passage to India* (1984). Seven years later, at the time of his death, he was preparing a film of Joseph Conrad's *Nostromo*.

Not all of that long dry spell between 1970 and 1985 was entirely his making, to be sure. More than half of that time was spent working with Robert Bolt, his writing partner, on a screenplay for *Mutiny on the Bounty*, which Lean planned as a very expensive two-part epic to be produced by Dino de Laurentiis. When de Laurentiis pulled the plug on the project (and eventually made a scaled-down, shorter version called *The Bounty* with another director), Lean was bitter and depressed, and perhaps some of that emotion carried over into *A Passage to India*. The central image of that film was a cave in India that absorbed all words shouted into its darkness and echoed back only an empty "boom."

Lean began in the British cinema in 1934 as an editor, and in the years before his films grew to epic length and scope, he directed a series of tight, bright, pointed black and white dramas that helped define British postwar moviemaking. Among his key credits in that period were *Blithe Spirit* and *Brief Encounter*, both in 1945; *Great Expectations* (1946); *Oliver Twist* (1948); the underrated *Breaking the Sound Barrier* (1954); *Hobson's Choice* (1954); and the Katharine Hepburn romantic comedy *Summertime* (1955).

His editing was a model of craftsmanship. The American director Martin Scorsese remembers his own days at the New York University film school, where students were given the shots in the opening graveyard sequence of *Great Expectations* and asked to re-edit them. A generation of students gave it their best, learning in the process that Lean had put them together in the best possible way.

Although the epic film has always been an important part of film history, Lean's own epics came toward the end of the period when they were most fashionable. *Lawrence of Arabia* in 1962 was the kind of film that today's moviegoers think of when they think of epics, yet it came ten years after the Hollywood epic's heyday. It was different in another way, too: While Hollywood liked excess and bravado, lots of big stars and fast action, Lean's *Lawrence* starred an unknown (Peter O'Toole), was a thoughtful psychological study, and had the courage to leave the camera to stare unblinkingly at an empty expanse of desert until, finally, the audience could see what a character saw, a faraway rider on a camel.

Lawrence of Arabia made O'Toole into a star, and images from the movie became a permanent part of film history. But the movie itself was almost lost. Shot in wide-screen and 70mm, it was shortened, re-edited, and then chopped down the sides to squeeze into the narrow shaped box of a television tube. Meanwhile, the priceless original 70mm print was cast into the jumbled vaults of Columbia Pictures, only to be rescued in 1989 by a historic restoration process. At the banquet for Lean in Hollywood on the occasion of the film's official revival, Bob Harris, who restored the film, held up one of the steel cans the film was found in. It was crushed and rusted, and the film inside was creased and torn. But *Lawrence*, restored to its original glory, thrilled a new generation of filmgoers.

Dr. Zhivago was another 70mm wide-screen epic, and it was characteristic of Lean that at a time when television and home video became crucial to a film's profits, he made films you just about had to see in a theater. One of the great images of *Zhivago* was of a train, seen from miles away, moving across a limitless snow field. On the big screen it was a thrilling image, but on the tube all you saw was a dot surrounded by whiteness.

Was *Ryan's Daughter*, his next film, as bad as most critics thought, or did it simply come at the wrong time? Its old-fashioned story of love and passion in Ireland in the 1920s was not fashionable in 1970 among filmgoers raised on *Easy Rider*, *2001*, and *Bonnie and Clyde*. When Lean's characters made love, his camera panned to a lake where dandelion seeds drifted onto the surface of the water, and audiences snickered.

Lean, a proud man, heard those snickers and at one low point said he would never work again. Then came *The Bounty* debacle, followed by the triumph of *A Passage to India*, an intelligent adaptation of the E.M. Forster novel about British colonials at sea in the mysteries of India.

In May of 1988, at the Cannes Film Festival, the British held a dinner in honor of (by then) Sir David Lean. There was a little reception for him beforehand on a private yacht, and what was striking was the way he stood out from the crowd: tall, imposing, with facial features so large they looked sculpted as a test for a statue of a hero. He was close to eighty, but still robust and aggressive, filled with plans. What he wanted to make, he said, was a film based on Conrad's *Nostromo*, the story of a nineteenth-century anticolonial rebellion in South America. In microcosm in Conrad's novel, he thought, were the beginnings of all the issues of twentieth-century politics.

The *Nostromo* project moved majestically ahead until last year when Lean seemed poised to start shooting. Because of his age, the insurance companies insisted a back-up director be hired to stand by in case Lean could not continue. *Variety* announced that Arthur Penn (*Bonnie and Clyde*) had agreed to backstop Lean, partly because he wanted to see the film get made. But it was not to be. From a location scouting trip, Lean returned ill to England last winter, never to return.

What will history's verdict be on his lifework? His critics are represented by David Thomson, who, in his influential *Biographical Dictionary of Film*, writes of Lean as "relentlessly middlebrow," with "no consuming passion for making films," stating "commonplace meanings and feelings." Well, it is true Lean was not a rebel. He was one who perfected film language rather than reinventing it.

But to go back in the memory to Miss Havisham's wedding cake in *Great Expectations*, or the look of sorrow on Trevor Howard's face in *Brief Encounters*, to the glory of Lawrence in the desert, and the unflappable transplanted Englishness of Dame Peggy Ashcroft in *A Passage to India*, is to remember a director whose visual imagination was towering, and who made the movies big just when the industry was trying to make them little.

Spike Lee

Chicago, July 25, 1990—Spike Lee's *Mo' Better Blues* begins and ends with scenes of a young boy practicing the trumpet when he would rather be outside playing softball with his friends. The boy at the beginning of the movie grows up to be a professional musician, played by Denzel Washington. The boy at the end is Washington's son. It's a tidy, circular, reassuring structure for a movie, but what happens in between is not reassuring.

The movie stars Washington as a jazz musician, a trumpet player who cannot bring himself to commit to either one of the two women in his life. He does make one commitment, however, a tragically mistaken one, to his manager—a compulsive gambler played by Spike Lee himself. The manager gets into serious trouble with professional gamblers, the trumpet player gets caught up in the trouble, and in a moment of violence his professional career is brought to an end.

Although the ads for *Mo' Better Blues* make it look like a comedy, it's a complicated film in which the comedy and everything else serves a deeper purpose. Bleek Gilliam, the jazzman played by Washington, has a lot of similarities with the heroine of Lee's first film, *She's Gotta Have It*, who kept a lot of men on the line and never let any of them feel he owned her heart. The difference between the two films is the difference between independence and irresponsibility—between a person not ready to settle down, and one constitutionally incapable of settling down.

If the movie is not a comedy, it's also not the other kind of film it resembles, a musical biography. The rules of the genre of musical biography have been sacred for decades, and *Mo' Better Blues* violates most of them. For one thing, it doesn't chronicle the hero's slow rise to stardom; Bleek is already established as a top jazz player when the movie flashes forward from his childhood to his career. For another, the movie avoids the classic cliché of the musical biography, the Big Comeback. After Bleek's lip is injured and he can't play for a year, he walks back into a club one night and we're ready for that obligatory scene where he tries, falters, and then finally triumphs. It's a standard in every musical biopic. But not this one.

"I just don't make that type of film," Lee was telling me one day last week. "I don't make the type of film where you just connect the dots."

What he did make in *Mo' Better Blues*, is simply a drama about the life of a man. There's a lot of music in the film, much of it performed by the Branford Marsalis Quartet, but it's not a biopic and it's not a jazz film; it's a story about how some men need to get badly shaken up before they understand what's really important to them.

"We wanted to use music in the film," Lee said, "but at the same time it's not necessarily a music film. I cannot risk that with a $10 million budget. There aren't enough jazz people out there to keep the film in the theaters. Universal Pictures kept throwing the grosses for *Round Midnight* and *Bird* in our faces, and asking, 'Why should we give you X amount of dollars, when these films don't make anything and you're making a jazz film?' It was only after they saw the dailies that they said, 'Let's not use that word—jazz. Let's sell this as a romantic film. Let's sell Denzel.'"

That was all right with Lee, because he wanted to sell Denzel Washington in the first place. "I wrote the film for Denzel," he said, beginning a litany of praise that made him sound like the agent he plays in the movie. "This film was tailor-made for him. He is star quality. Women love him. He has sex appeal. He has magnetism. He has 'it.' He's handsome. Plus he can act on top of all that. So I think he's a full package. Denzel has a large female following, yet at the same time, I don't think he's ever really had the role where he could utilize all his strengths. He's never really had the leading romantic role."

Although Washington is a major Hollywood star after his work in *Glory* and *Cry Freedom* and on TV's "St. Elsewhere," the only previous film role that gave him a chance to play romantic comedy was last year's *The Mighty Quinn*, a lilting movie set in the Caribbean and combining reggae and a murder investigation. I thought it was one of the year's best films. But it didn't do much business, maybe because it was released poorly by a studio in financial turmoil, maybe because to the mainstream American movie audience reggae is even less commercial than jazz.

In *Mo' Better Blues*, his character's attention is divided between the beautiful jazz soloist and seductress, Clarke Bentancourt, and the more loyal but less glamorous longtime girlfriend, Indigo Downes. It would not oversimplify the plot to say Bleek is constantly in the process of betraying one woman in other to lie to the other, and it

is only at the end, after he hits bottom, that he realizes which woman he should stay with and why.

"There's no way in the world," Lee said, "that he would have ended up with Indigo without him taking that fall. He might have been a greater musician, but he would have been very lonely and unhappy."

Indigo is played by Lee's sister, Joie Lee, who has appeared in all of Spike's films, and was most memorable in *Do the Right Thing* as Lee's sister. Bentancourt is played by a Chicagoan named Cynda Williams, a first-time film actress who is not only a great beauty but also an assured actress and singer who smolders in her love scenes with Washington, even though they reportedly got off on the wrong foot during rehearsals and never recovered.

Lee thinks Williams will become a star on the basis of this film. "When I wrote this film, I always figured Clarke would be a girl who came to New York from the Midwest, trying to be a star," Lee said, "and we came to Chicago to cast the role. No luck. Cynda was living in New York at the time, having moved from Chicago six months earlier, and one day while we were casting, she just walked into the office. She didn't get the role right away. We brought her back six more times, and the final time with Denzel. I wanted Denzel to have some input into it, since he had to be intimate with this person, and she got the role. I think that she's the biggest discovery ever for me. That song she sings at the end of the movie, 'Harlem Blues,' that is her own voice. For me, she's almost a reincarnation of Dorothy Dandridge. She can sing, she can act, she can dance, and she's very beautiful."

I was reading in the paper, I said, that she and Denzel didn't get along so well.

Lee laughed. "I saw that. I'll tell you a story. We were in rehearsal, and Cynda every now and then wanted to make a suggestion, and Denzel told her that she was a newcomer and should just be quiet and listen. Later on he apologized to her, but after that Cynda was kind of cool toward him. But you don't see that on the screen at all." He smiled. "They're both good actors. It's easier to do a love scene with somebody you like, than somebody that you hate. That's for sure."

We were talking during a quick visit Lee made to Chicago in the middle of one of his typically action-packed weeks. He is not only one of the hottest feature directors in the country right now, but also one of the most recognizable—on the basis of his supporting roles in the TV commercials he directs starring Michael Jordan. At thirty-three, he is rich and famous, but busy—too busy—and sometimes, he said, his grandmother tells him he's working too hard.

"The part that I like about success is, I get to go into the locker room after the game," Lee said. "I get to have great seats at games. I don't have to worry about money. I have financial stability, and I am able to do a lot of things for other people, especially my family. But the most important thing is, I'm doing what makes me happy, making films. Nothing makes me happier than making movies. Ninety-nine percent of the people in this world go to their grave having worked at a job that they hated. So, I'm really fortunate."

But you're also really busy.

"You wouldn't believe. We start shooting my next movie, *Jungle Fever*, less than five weeks from now. *Mo' Better Blues* opens August 3. Last week we had a press junket for it. Monday night is the premiere. Sunday, I'm opening up a new store that's selling all the memorabilia from my movies. Yesterday I was in Vermont shooting my eighth commercial this year. I'm doing the Levi's 501 campaign. I've got to shoot another commercial at Lincoln Center on Friday night. Next week, I'm shooting three commercials with Michael Jordan for Nike. I'm the guest editor of *Spin* magazine for October. And we're casting *Jungle Fever* and we start shooting August 20, and we'll be shooting until November 2, and we'll be working seven days a week just to get it finished in time for the Cannes Film Festival next May. Then also, of course, basketball season begins in November. My grandmother thinks I might have a heart attack or something."

This movie, I said, all of the stuff about domesticity and raising a little trumpet player on a tree-lined street in Brooklyn and finding the right girl. Is it a message that you're getting ready to slow down and maybe even get married?

"Well, I'm thirty-three, and one day I definitely hope to get married. I don't have any prospects. I've got *Jungle Fever* to shoot, and after that hopefully I'll be directing *The Autobiography of Malcolm X* . . . so maybe after the next two films . . . ."

Your third project down the road would be marriage.

"Yeah. That'll be a project."

So it's in preproduction right now?

He grinned. "No, it's the planning stage. It's not even in preproduction yet."

I knew that Spike Lee's father, Bill, who composes the scores for his films, was a musician, and I wondered if there was any autobiography in the opening and closing scenes of *Mo' Better Blues*, where the Bleek character is made to practice his scales, but later turns into a more lenient parent himself.

"That's not me at the beginning," Lee said, "because I did not want to be a musician, and my parents, luckily, did not press me and my brothers and sisters to be musicians. My mother was the disciplinarian in the family. She didn't want to do that, but she had to assume that role because my father, well, whatever you wanted to do, he would just say it was OK. You wanted to jump off the Brooklyn Bridge, it was OK with him. He was a great father, but his way of discipline was to have none. My mother knew better, and she had to be the disciplinarian, and therefore, growing up, we liked my father better than

my mother. She was the heavy, but she had to take that role, or we'd have had no parental supervision at all."

What kind of parent will you turn out to be?

"I think I'm going to try and find that balance between the two, because I don't want to stamp them out, but at the same time, I want my children to be obedient, because when I tell them to do something, I want it done, no questions asked. But I'm not going to be a tyrant. I'm looking forward to having a family. I don't know when it's gonna be, but I'm looking forward to it. I think if anybody looks at this film and knows me, you can see that in this film."

One place you cannot see Spike Lee in *Mo' Better Blues* is in the character he plays, Giant, who was Bleek's childhood friend and is kept on as his manager long after he has outlived any usefulness and has become a danger.

"Giant is the most pitiful character I've ever played," Lee said. "He's pathetic. He's a compulsive gambler. He's an addict. He's sick. He has a good heart, but he's a terrible manager, and because of his sickness, he ends up costing Bleek his career as a musician."

You're a famous basketball fan. Do you bet on the games?

"No way. I hate losing money."

So the character isn't drawn from you?

"I've never even known a compulsive gambler. This character is based on Pete Rose. When I was writing the script, Rose was in the headlines every day. So that's where Giant comes from. But people ask me, when am I going to play a hero in one of my films? All of the characters I play are misfits. But I don't have a problem with that. I find it more interesting to play characters like that. I don't have to build myself up in my films. I'll be the supporting character; it's more fun. In *She's Gotta Have It*, the would-be lover, that was my funniest role. In *School Daze*, there was Half-Pint, who was really pathetic, who wanted to be loved so much that he would do anything just to be liked. He was spineless till the end of the movie, when he saw how stupid and ignorant he'd been. And Mookie, in *Do the Right Thing*, Mookie's a person who sits on the fence throughout the entire movie until the tragedy of seeing his best friend murdered by the police makes him act, makes him take a stand. And now Giant. Which do you like best?"

Mookie.

"Yeah. Mookie. But I'm not acting in my films to build up my ego. The reason why I act in my films, is because it's easier to get my films made with me in them. There will come a time, hopefully soon, where I won't have to be in my films to get them made or to get the kind of money I want."

I'd like to see a movie of yours where you're the star.

"I don't know if I could actually carry a whole film the way Denzel does. That's a lot of work. Plus, it would really distract from my directing if I was in front of the camera the whole movie. I don't really want to be a leading man. I don't think I'm really an actor. I think the little I do, I do well, and I get out of the way and let the real actors take over. I would never do theater, because you can fake it in a film, but you can't fake it on stage. I would never get on stage and do theater, never."

Maybe Lee's uncertainty about playing the lead explains some of the autobiographical threads in the film, since he admits that some of the problems of the Washington character are drawn from his own life.

"I'm not going to try and hide the fact that there are similarities between Bleek and myself. I think that I'm in all my films. I think I'm more driven than Bleek is. At the same time, I think that I realize you can have a balance between your career and the rest of your life, where Bleek doesn't. He thinks it has to be all his music, all his trumpet, and everything else has to be secondary. His flaw is in his loyalty to Giant, his childhood friend, who is the world's worst manager.

"I have loyalty, but I will not let loyalty jeopardize my career. There are plenty of people who worked with me on She's Gotta Have It, who no longer work with me because they were not able to raise the level of their work. So they had to go. Some of them were dear friends, but they had to go, because they'll drag you down with them. Giant has a good heart, but he's a dangerous person, because people like that, you go right down with them."

This is a movie, I said, about an artist who finds that he can no longer practice his art. What would you do if that ever happened to you?

"You mean if I couldn't direct anymore? Hmmm. I would try to produce films. If I couldn't do that, I'd be involved in films some way. What injury would I have to get? Hit by a truck?"

Or make a string of box office flops.

"Don't say that! I guess I'd just have to go out and raise the money myself, like I did with She's Gotta Have It. I'd still make films."

You couldn't be stopped by not having access to the big studios?

"No. If Hollywood didn't want to finance my films, I'd look for financing elsewhere. You can do a lot of work outside of Hollywood, outside the major studios."

You are constantly being described, I said, as America's leading "black director." How do you react to that qualifying adjective?

"What does it mean? It means I'm a black director. I'm not going to spend one iota of energy denying the fact that I'm a black director. I think it's useless. I think if you're a black person in this country, no matter how high the level of success you achieve, you're always going to be considered black. There's no getting around it. It's always going to be like that, no matter what. So why fight it? I'm not saying it's fair, but it's always going to be like that. I know why it's done, but I can't kick and scream about it. It's a waste of my time."

Why is it done?

"Because black people are not thought of as equals, so,

therefore, you have a qualifying word like the 'black' director. Like 'How does it feel to be the first black quarterback in the Super Bowl?' Doug Williams was asked that question two million times. I liked his answer. He said, 'I'm a quarterback. I'm here to play the game.'"

Steve Martin

Chicago, January 30, 1991—In a review published in 1984, I wrote that Steve Martin was "an actor who inspires in me the same feelings that fingernails on blackboards inspire in other people." This judgment, sincerely made at the time, was just a tad premature. In a review published later that same year, I was astonished to find that I genuinely admired his work in *All of Me*. And in the years since then, I have also appreciated his work in such movies as *Roxanne, Planes, Trains and Automobiles*, and *Parenthood*—not to mention two films that hardly any critics liked, *Dirty Rotten Scoundrels* and *My Blue Heaven*.

I am not even sure, in fact, that Steve Martin himself much enjoyed *My Blue Heaven*, but by then the fingers had long since stopped screeching for me. After his early films like *The Jerk, Pennies From Heaven, The Lonely Guy*, and *Dead Men Don't Wear Plaid*, I wrote about "his ability to make you cringe with his self-abasing smarminess." Recently I have been looking forward to his films with the kind of anticipation I reserve for something involving Woody Allen or Dustin Hoffman. And now here is his latest film, *L.A. Story*, based on his own screenplay and suffused with a comic brilliance. All right, then—either I was wrong, or Martin is no longer self-abasingly smarmy.

Interviewing Steve Martin the other day, I didn't know quite how to introduce the phenomenon of my changing reactions ("Why do you think it is, Steve, that your performances no longer remind me of fingernails on blackboards?"). I did sort of gently nudge my way into the subject by casually mentioning that I "didn't like" much of his early work (no mention of fingernails) and that since *All of Me* I had liked his work more and more.

Martin resisted the masochistic tendency of many actors who agree—or claim to agree—with all negative assessments of their work. He didn't disclaim his pre-1984 film career, and when pressed, even claimed he would like to play a character like the Jerk again—an all-joke comedy like *The Naked Gun*. But he did seem to think it was possible that his work had improved about the same time I began to admire it more.

"I think in those early films," he said, "I was still finding my way, still trying to figure out what kind of films to make, and I believed that the kind of films I should make, with the exception of *Pennies From Heaven*, should be extensions of what I was doing on stage. The same kind of character, more or less. And then, right around *All of Me*, I dropped that and saw that movies were very different from just doing some crazy jokes. I think in the early films, there are moments that are pretty funny, but the stories are always sort of weak. I wish they'd worked a little better. But I think there's something in each one of them that's a little daring. I really can't evaluate them that well, because it's me."

One of the things that has become obvious, I said, is that you've turned out to be quite a good actor. In a straight role like *Parenthood*, for example.

"Well, I learned a lot when I did *Pennies From Heaven*, and I enjoy going underneath something. I enjoy getting serious. It's really the same intensity as comedy, only it's the underside of it. I feel better about my work now. I feel that I'm just waiting to do something, all I need are the right words."

When you're making a film, is there a moment when something clicks, and you think, this is really going to work?

"Yes. On every film. Of course, the moment is not always correct."

There is a certain inverted logic at work there, and Martin's wife, actress Victoria Tennant, believes his humor begins with the fact that he studied philosophy in university. Martin himself thinks it may go back even further: "I remember being twelve years old, and my dream was going to work and wearing a suit." Martin was wearing a suit the other day, a perfectly cut, deep blue suit with a white shirt and a tie that was cheerful but not impudent. And he had gone to work. He is on the road promoting *L.A. Story*, which in two hours says more funny things about Los Angeles than most films say in a lifetime.

"Another thing is that his humor is never cruel," Victoria Tennant says. "He's never mean or sarcastic. There's always a sweetness in his work." She is not only Martin's wife but also his costar in the movie, where she plays a British newspaper reporter who is assigned to do a story on Los Angeles lifestyles and falls in love with a wild and crazy TV weatherman, played by Martin.

She is quite correct about *L.A. Story*, which is a delicate balancing act involving fantasy, slapstick, romance, satire, unbridled exaggeration, and social commentary. It's amazing how the movie finds its way through such a wide variety of material while always maintaining a certain gentle tone. Martin, who took years to write the original screenplay, is like those screen comedians of the past—Buster Keaton and Jacques Tati come to mind—who did not depend on violence, embarrassment, and the put-down for their laughs, and instead just simply put genuinely funny things on the screen.

Example of a funny thing: A Southern California pedestrian crossing sign that lights up and says, *"Uh, like don't walk."*

Another example: Two polite lines waiting at an automated banking terminal, one of people withdrawing money, the other of hold-up men.

A third: The Martin character telephones for a dinner reservation, and is subjected to a detailed background and credit check by the restaurant owner.

"Some of the things in the movie come from my own personal observations over the years," Martin said. "The freeway sign certainly. They have these enormous computerized electric signs on the freeways in Los Angeles that theoretically tell you how the traffic is up ahead. Fine, except they're never turned on. I've only seen them on once in the last fifteen years. In the movie, you have one that actually tells you what to do with your life."

The sign in the movie seems to have a personal relationship with the Martin character. It poses him riddles, gives him advice, and offers him predictions about the future. The first time it starts sending messages to him, he looks around suspiciously: "I just know I'm being filmed right now," he mutters darkly. But he is not. The sign is somehow supernaturally inspired to encourage him to become a better person and fall in love with the right woman.

"The movie is like a Rorschach test for how you feel about L.A.," he said. "I think people who live in L.A. will see it as very friendly to L.A., and the people who don't live in L.A. and want to think of L.A. as this disgusting place, might interpret it as that."

Martin himself seems to have an ambiguous relationship to the city. He has lived all of his life there and he loves it, he says, but what he likes most about it is his own home:

"You know, L.A. is only where you live, because otherwise it's just a sprawling mass of everything, and I think if you live in L.A., you get a little network of places you go and people you see, and when you leave town you do miss those places and your friends."

L.A. Story is a movie about a man who could almost be described in those words. Martin's weatherman has been dating the same woman (Marilu Henner) for such a long time that he has almost reached the point when he can predict when she will be finished dressing and ready to go to a party. He has had the same job at the same television station so long he's a fixture, a weatherman for whom the weather is only an excuse for stand-up comedy.

And then everything changes when he discovers she's been having an affair, and that liberates him to move out—frees him to be ready for the advice of the roadside electric sign, which encourages him to go out on a date with SanDeE (Sarah Jessica Parker), a hippy dippy airhead he meets in a clothing store, and who, like many Los Angelenos, spells her name as if it were an eye chart. Later, when he is ready for a more meaningful affair, the sign steers him toward the Victoria Tennant character.

All of this is done with a charm impossible to describe, a certain whimsical, lighthearted romantic goofiness that weaves a spell over the film. In one sense, Martin's screenplay is as insubstantial as a feather, but in another way, it is as well-constructed as any script in recent memory. Movies don't get to be this charming and fanciful by accident.

"I started writing it about seven years ago," Martin said,

"before I even started writing *Roxanne*, and then I put it in a drawer, because it's the kind of thing that's very scary to think of ever being made into a movie. You're risking a lot. I'd think, no, I can't do this, then I'd get encouraged again, and I'd pick it up and do it."

Is it the sort of thing, I asked, that you can't just sit at the keyboard and be inspired to write—the kind of material that has to accumulate in its own time?

"Yes, I think so, because a lot of the ideas for the movie occurred to me in little bits. I'd make a note and put it away. In this movie, every scene has to have an angle because the story itself is a sort of regular love story. So there's always something going on behind the action. I always had to think of a place, or an idea, or an attitude, or something that lifts the scene up a little.

"Like, for example, the gravedigger scene with Rick Moranis, which has fun with *Hamlet*. All the scene really achieves, on the story level, is to make the man and the woman interested in each other. But having Rick as the gravedigger gets this other thing happening too, at the same time, rather than just having the characters standing on the sidewalk. Or like the scene outside the automated teller machine. You're killing two birds with one stone. You're showing a little bit of the relationship between myself and the young girl, SanDeE, and yet you're also getting this gag going on at the same time."

Did you start right out with the notion of a communicating billboard?

"No, that only came within the last year and a half or two."

And yet that was really the organizing principle, wasn't it?

"Yeah. It shows you how drastically things can change. The original draft had me leaving L.A. and ending up in Turkey, because I wanted something that was just the opposite of L.A. Turkey didn't make it into the final draft. I never got out of L.A."

L.A. Story is such an original and particular movie, I said, that it must have been almost impossible to pitch in a meeting with studio executives. Is this kind of project tough to sell or to get financed?

"A little tougher, yeah. I have a feeling a lot of studios wanted to make it, but they didn't want to pay for it. They wanted it to be very cheap. As it turns out, the movie was very cheap by today's standards, but it couldn't be *that* cheap; it needed some class to it. I think it's a risky film. At least, it was seen as risky when we were pitching it. I don't know if it seems so risky now, when you can see what we had in mind. It's like *Roxanne* was a very risky film, at least in my head, before we started rolling, but then when it opened people said well, it's OK, I had a good time, I enjoyed it, it's OK to tell my friends to go."

It has seemed strange to me, I said, that the ideas that lead to the worst movies always seem to get financed the most quickly, and the ones that lead to the best movies always seem to have some kind of tangled web of production difficulties behind them.

Martin grimaced. "I think the seemingly worst ideas I've ever had have been the best, and the ideas that I think are naturals just don't work. I don't know why. I guess you just don't put your heart and soul into it somehow."

Give me an example.

"Well, *Roxanne*, which was a very problematical idea—setting Cyrano in modern times—did $42 million, which was considered a hit for a very small movie like that, and *Three Amigos*, which was meant to be this sort of big blockbuster movie, maybe did $42 million, too, which was a disappointment."

Another unexpected thing about *L.A. Story* is that it wasn't directed by a proven Hollywood veteran, but by Mick Jackson, previously unknown in Los Angeles.

"Victoria found him," Martin said, "and showed me a tape of a miniseries he did in England called 'A Very British Coup,' which was the best thing I ever saw, I mean, I just couldn't believe it! It was exactly the feel I was looking for for the movie. I knew it couldn't just be three cameras, medium-shot, close-up-type shot. There had to be some style, and he delivered it."

I liked the look of the movie. The translucent night sky, for example, which seems to sparkle with stars and the moon.

"Yeah, and see, I never would have thought of that. That's what the director and the cinematographer do. They used time-lapse photography. I mean, here's a guy who's been making movies for twenty-five years, and no one had ever heard of him."

One of the things I noticed, talking with Martin, was that although he makes his living as a comic actor, he didn't seem to say or do anything that was intended to be particularly funny. Many comedians are on all the time—are desperate for the instant feedback and reassurance of laughter. I wondered if Martin's reserved, laid-back conversational style was a reaction to his early image as a wild and crazy guy.

"Maybe, and it may be why I don't go out so much. Sometimes you see people laughing at something you said that maybe isn't that funny, and you realize, this is not an honest relationship here. It may make you tend to stick with your friends, because you do want to be relaxed. I don't do my act in private. I used to do it on stage, and that's when I did it. Of course, that all originated from my real life, so what I was now, or then, I just don't know . . . ."

What's interesting though, is when people have a great success at a very early age, they often turn into great bores who repeat their schticks for the rest of their lives, who in every single social encounter are still doing something that worked for them for about six months in the fifties. How do you cut loose from that?

"I just have a different mindset than that," he said. "I

don't like to look back, and I'm always worried about the next thing rather than resting on the laurels or the degradations of the last thing. I've also known about that type that you described, and I want to be cautious with it. I don't want to end up like that. Like when I finally retire, I just want to go away so no one has to listen to me."

He thought for a moment. "I never thought much about success early on," he said. "I only thought about being a comedian—or just being in show business, is really more accurate. I developed my act, and only in my late twenties, when I'd really done it a long time and had gotten better at it, and *had* an act, did I think—'Gee, the future looks really bleak! If something doesn't happen, I'll be doing this in nightclubs for the rest of my life.' And just about that time, my movie career started to happen. Then I worried about being a flash-in-the-pan, because the star ascended very quickly. So that was my next worry, and now that I don't have to worry about being a flash-in-the-pan, I have to worry about being an old bore."

You don't have any need to be reinforced every ten seconds with approval?

"About once a year is good."

Bill Murray

Chicago, July 3, 1990—Bill Murray dribbled into the hotel suite and sank the basketball in a chair in the corner. He was wearing your average after-school jock's uniform of jeans, a T-shirt, and designer running shoes, and he said he needed a shave. He disappeared into the bathroom and then stuck his face out again, covered with lather, and asked, "How do you plan to explain your one-star review of *Scrooged?*"

I was hoping it wouldn't come up, I said.

"It wasn't that bad," Murray said. "It had some good stuff in it. Watch it on video and you'll see."

It just didn't work for me, I said.

"I thought maybe you had some inside information, you know, about an unhappy set or something," he said.

No, I said, it just didn't seem that funny. Did you have some disagreements with the director?

"Only a few," he said. "Every single minute of the day. That could have been a really, really great movie. The script was so good. There's maybe one take in the final cut movie that is mine. We made it so fast, it was like doing a movie live. He kept telling me to do things louder, louder, louder. I think he was deaf."

That was then; this is now. Murray has a new movie named *Quick Change*, and he likes it a lot better than *Scrooged*. What worries him a little, though, is that in a summer dominated by high-tech exercises in violence and action, a comedy might not be able to hold its own.

"This movie doesn't have any violence in it," he said. "Six months ago that didn't bother me at all, and it really doesn't bother me now, either. But people are saying things

like, 'This is a gentle movie.' I don't think it's gentle at all. I think it's weird and funny. I think it's as strange as anything. It's about New York, and it's weird, but it isn't violent.

"There's an audience that talks to the screen, a screaming audience that likes the violence, and there's a bonding that goes on in that group. There's a moment they've got to have, where they get to watch something horrible happen, and they get to enjoy it without actually having to do it or be a victim to it. I've seen that coming for a few years. I remember the first time I saw a violent movie that was supposed to be a comedy. There was a scene where somebody just got five 9mm slugs in their chest, and they sort of slid down a mirror, and there was this blood on the mirror, and I thought, wait a second, this isn't comedy. This is something different.

"Or look at some of the movies that did well first time out, like *Die Hard*, *48 HRS*, or *RoboCop*. They were all kind of funny, even though there was violence in them. Although I haven't seen any of the sequels yet, I can tell they're a lot more violent than the originals."

He thought for a moment, drumming his fingers on the table. "Or maybe it's just the sequel business itself," he said. "I made a sequel (*Ghostbusters II*), and it's hard, it's really hard to make a sequel, no matter how sincere you are, how much you want to try. Somehow the directors take over from the writers and the comedians, and the thing ends up being a lot more action than comedy. Action is a lot easier to direct than comedy."

It's also easier to advertise. The TV ads give away some of the good parts, like Bruce Willis jumping onto the wing of a plane, or Arnold Schwarzenegger's face splitting up into slices. It's hard to sell a comedy that way, since comedies depend more on situations and characters than on single sensational moments. That's why Murray would be happier if the fate of a movie wasn't determined so quickly these days by the box office box score.

"It used to be," he said, "that if a movie opened up and did a couple of million on its opening weekend, that was a big deal. It's not like that anymore. They do these big TV buys now. They spend so much money, it's really scary. We're going to spend $3 million on Monday. It's like an army invasion. And when the movies open, all the papers print charts showing which movie grossed the most that weekend. I don't know why, because in theory only a couple of studios are going to profit from releasing that kind of information. And I don't know why they print it—if they think it's news, or they think it makes people interested in movies."

Bill Murray's own movie will be that kind of news a week from now. In a summer when the studios have laid claim to weekends as if they were gangs defining their turf, Warner Bros. hopes it has the biggest summer comedy. *Quick Change* stars Murray as a bank robber who disguises himself as a clown and stages a complicated heist, only to experience the most extraordinary troubles in getting to the airport. Geena Davis and Randy Quaid costar as his partners in crime, and along the way they meet a gallery of character actors in weird supporting roles.

The movie is basically split into two parts: (1) the opening bank robbery, in which the New York police become thoroughly confused over who is a robber and who is a hostage, and (2) the attempts by the three robbers to get to Kennedy and board their getaway flight to Fiji. Along the way they meet such characters as an anal retentive bus driver (Philip Bosco), who believes in running a tight bus. There's also a run-in with some Mafia types, and a wild ride with a crazed cab driver.

The movie's opening scene discovers Murray, dressed as a Bozo look-alike, riding to work on the subway. Inside the bank, he seems to have a plan firmly in mind, even though he does what he can to make the guards—and the police who quickly surround the block—think he's a loony. His plan involves a series of disguises, but what I wanted to know was, is a major star taking a chance when he plays all of his opening scenes in clown makeup?

"You do kind of worry," Murray said, "because you wonder if they're going to know who you are. You could be so disguised they can't recognize you. We tried to let the face come through, so I could use my facial expressions. We didn't want to make it such a mask that I couldn't react."

Murray's face is recognizable, sort of, beneath the greasepaint, but what comes through more obviously is his manner: the laconic, wise-cracking character with the ironic asides and one-liners. That kind of dialogue has been a Murray trademark right from the start, in the early 1970s, when he and John Belushi were regulars in the same Second City company. Belushi was always the more physical comedian, and perhaps that helped Murray develop his own persona, that of the detached observer who stands in the midst of chaos and maintains his wry point of view.

"The reason so many Second City people have been successful is really simple," Murray said. "At the heart of it is the idea that if you make the other actors look good, you'll look good. It works sort of like the idea of life after death. If you live an exemplary life, trying to make someone else look good, you'll look good. It's true. It really does work. It braces you up when you're out there with that fear of death, which is really the difference between the Second City actors and the others.

"If you go to actor's class, you don't really die, because there's never really an audience. But if you work for Second City, there's an audience, and you die in the improv set five times out of nine. So, once you get over your fear of dying, nothing else ever really scares you. And 'Saturday Night Live' was as tough as Second City. Once you get through those, making movies is a joke.

"On a movie they'll say, all right, we're only going to have three minutes to get this coat off and get you in the other shirt. And I just start laughing. Three minutes? In three minutes I can take off a shirt, put on a wig, a hat, a fat stomach, an enormous raincoat, galoshes, soak my head, take a shower, and be covered with soap and walk out and talk in another language. It's nothing!"

He grinned. "People don't know how hard those jobs were. The National Lampoon show that we did on Broadway was hard, too. It was like crowd control theater. It was a brawl every single night, and they were going to take the stage if you didn't. It was really an ugly audience. It's what biker bars are all about. So those three jobs really prepare you. And then, since 'SNL' always had a guest host, there was the tradition of service, of trying to cover for this poor sap, whoever he was. Between dress rehearsal and airtime, they'd be so terrified, they'd be almost weeping in the dressing room. It was a zoo, that show. We'd have the Chinese acrobats of Taiwan, we'd have Jim Nabors, we'd have dog acts, singers, fire-breathers, Argentinian gauchos, there was everything."

One of the sad things about Belushi's death, I said, was that ever since then, people have eulogized that period instead of enjoying it. They forget how much fun "SNL" was.

"People deny they lived in the 1960s," Murray said. "Did you ever see that *Newsweek* piece? That big 1960s piece where people said, 'This is what I was in the 1960s, and I hate myself for it. I hated what I was. I was disgusting. I was wild and really horrible.' How really sad. And looking back at 'SNL,' people like to say we were all into heavy drugs and stuff. Well, yeah, anybody who wants to work a 125-hour week could come around and see how well you could do it on drugs. The only drugs involved were the kind required to keep you in one place for twelve hours at a time, so you'd work."

After the Second City and "SNL" days, Murray became a movie star almost overnight, with a couple of low-budget but funny quickies named *Meatballs* (1979) and *Stripes* (1981). He did a famous job of scene-stealing in *Tootsie* (1982), in an unbilled performance as Dustin Hoffman's roommate. And he starred in *Ghostbusters* (1984), still the best-selling movie comedy of all time.

But in the six years since *Ghostbusters*, Murray's career has drifted from the sincere but unsuccessful drama *The Razor's Edge* to the unfunny *Scrooged* to the less funny *Ghostbusters II*. His funniest work during the period was a guest-starring role as a dental patient in *Little Shop of Horrors*.

Why didn't he make more pictures after the original *Ghostbusters*?

"Well, basically I thought that *Ghostbusters* was the biggest thing that would ever happen to me. It was such a big phenomenon that I felt slightly radioactive. So I just moved away for a while. I lived in Europe for six months or so, and I was supposed to do a movie when I came back, and when I came back and I saw the script that I was supposed to do, I didn't want to do it. And that put me a whole season behind, and then I went through a kind of funny thing. There are actual moviemaking seasons, you know, and the three weeks before every season I would get twenty phone calls a day from people wanting to do a movie, and there would be this incredible amount of pressure. On Friday I'd get like thirty phone calls, and then on Monday no one would call, and I'd look in the paper, and someone else was doing the movie because I didn't say yes."

So you're back on schedule now?

"I don't ever want to take that much time off again. I don't want to be somebody with twenty-five movies in development, because then there are always twenty-four people who hate you. It's good to just keep working. I should have kept writing all that time, because when you take time off, it takes you all that much more time to get back up to speed."

He got up and went over to the sideboard and opened a beer.

"One of my gripes about movies," he said, "is that people take them so seriously, and the money-making aspects are so brutal. I've been lucky; I've had movies that made a lot of money, so I don't feel like I have to kill every time out. I don't want that pressure. I don't need it. It's not right. Look at Warren Beatty—the guy's having a nervous breakdown. I think he's really doing great, but the opening weekend *Dick Tracy* only made $21 million, and so what did he do? He was on every television show including the Home Shoppers Network for the next seventy-two hours, hyping the box office. And this was with a 'success.'"

Jack Nicholson

New York, August 1, 1990—And so here it is at last, *The Two Jakes*, one of the best-known "troubled productions" in recent Hollywood history. This is the *Chinatown* sequel that was canceled within days of its scheduled start date, that languished in limbo for years on the Paramount production schedule, and that finally got made only because Jack Nicholson, its star, said he would direct it, too.

"After all, not that many movies actually get on the set, ready to shoot, and then have the plug pulled," Nicholson was reflecting the other day. "But we were on schedule and on budget from the beginning when I took this job on. The bad publicity started again when I finished shooting. The studio said they'd like to have the picture by Christmas. I said, well, look, I know how long things take. This movie can't be really ready until March 30, unless we get a miracle."

But that would have been in the middle of the distractions of the Oscar publicity—not a good release date. And then came the launch of the summer blockbuster season—no wisdom in going up against Schwarzenegger—and so here is *The Two Jakes* in the middle of August 1990, right on schedule from Nicholson's point of view, but nine months late if you listen to the industry gossips.

It's strange how the buzz gets started on a movie. You hear it's been delayed, and delayed again, and finally a little dark cloud begins to form over it, and you figure there must be something wrong with it. Then gossips say the studio is "hiding" it, as if it would play only in Mozambique, on cable.

The surprising thing when you see *The Two Jakes* is that the movie itself bears no signs of being troubled. It unfolds with a self-confidence bordering on inevitability, and maintains the same tone, mood, and voice from beginning to end—a kind of dark, despairing postwar gloom in which all good intentions get corrupted by the compromises of the past.

The movie stars Nicholson as, once again, J.J. Gittes, who in *Chinatown* was a 1930s private eye with a certain cynical gleam that might have been inspired by the novels of Raymond Chandler. Now it is after the war, and a lot of things have changed, among them Gittes. He is more prosperous now (he works out of the Art Deco splendors of the Gittes Building), heavier-set, more cynical, a member of the country club, a man who actually has a fiancée. None of these things would have been possible for the Gittes of *Chinatown*, and you form the notion that before long he will abandon the private eye racket altogether and start renting security guards to big corporations.

The story involves the suspicions of a property developer (Harvey Keitel) that his wife (Meg Tilly) is having an affair with his partner. Nicholson, as Gittes, helps stage-manage one of those scenes where the outraged husband breaks down the door just as the adulterers are adultering—but what Nicholson doesn't count on is that Keitel has a gun and shoots his partner dead. After details of their partnership become public, the whole event begins to look a little like murder, with Nicholson as an accessory.

Watching the movie, I was impressed by how all the parts seemed to flow together like a tragic short novel, and not like a formula whodunit. That would be because of Robert Towne's original screenplay, I supposed—Towne, the man who wrote *Chinatown* and was the original director on *The Two Jakes* before the plug got pulled the first time. And yet I had heard about enormous changes at the last minute on the script. If that were true, why did it play so smoothly?

"Bob had this script ready, and he has the next one already written, too—*Chinatown* was always going to be a trilogy," Nicholson said. "We went through a tremendous amount of threshing of the material, but most of the rewriting was inside the scenes. There weren't many added scenes, or big additions, or eliminations of characters—because with a mystery, you can't displace the clues. You've got to keep the information coming pretty much in the tempo that it was written in.

"The main change was I shot the original ending, and it

simply didn't work. It read brilliantly, but it didn't play in the picture, and pictures have a life of their own. I like to shoot the opening the first day, and the ending the second day, because if it works, you know what you're shooting for, and if it doesn't, you've got plenty of time to adjust. In this picture, you've got a suicide, which seems to be the end, and then you've still got more to do, so getting that to work was the main part of the rewrite."

We were having this conversation in Nicholson's suite at the Carlyle, the one on the twenty-ninth floor he always stays in, with the view in three directions over the towers of New York. He was talking more like a writer than an actor, which is natural, since he started as a writer and was about to quit acting altogether when the surprise success of *Easy Rider* (1969) gave him new hope for his prospects in front of the camera.

He was doing some interviews, he said, because, frankly, he thought the picture could use a little help on its launch.

"I've shown the movie only to a few friends. One of them is an ex-Chicago cop named Elmer Valentine, who's a friend of mine. He used to work Wrigley Field. He said, 'Maybe it's because I'm an ex-cop, but I gotta have a bad guy in the picture.' That is as negative a response as I've gotten to date."

Without revealing important plot details, it's hard to explain why Valentine thought the picture needed a bad guy. Isn't the killer the bad guy—or, if not the killer, his victim?

"Everybody's doing something in quotes in this movie," Nicholson said. "They're bad, but are they bad? With Harvey's character, when you see why he's done what he did, it's almost the equivalent in a suspense picture of pulling the cat out of the bag.

"I don't know how the audience will take it. If you're telling a story where uncertainty is a part of the design, one of the things that you have to do is inform the audience that it's all right to not know. That's why my character does a running narration in the film. Just having ol' Uncle Jack as a tour guide accomplished something I wasn't able to do by the many other things I tried to do as a director.

"Part of what's said in this movie is what's not said. It's felt in the details of the postwar period. I wanted to do a stop in time. This was the beginning of the postatomic age. It was the end of melody in music. My generation brought percussion and rock 'n' roll to high school in the fifties. It's a big risk, trying to make a movie that includes elements like that, and you do need support with it."

Nicholson was explaining these matters in his usual tone of voice, which is almost hypnotic, the way he includes you in those low-pitched but resonant confidences. I realized, listening to him, that one of his gifts as an actor is the ability to convince a listener he's letting him in on something that should remain strictly between the two of them. Sitting at the other end of a sofa, he concentrates so fully on the interviewer that when the interviewer leans toward the coffee table to pick up a glass, Nicholson leans, too—and then leans back in unison when the movement is completed. Is this an idiosyncrasy or an exercise learned in acting class, this intensity in the way he mirrors the movements of his conversational partner?

Nicholson is one of the most intellectual of Hollywood stars, and he has had an almost uncanny good taste in selecting material. Not all of his movies are big financial successes, but can you name one that was an embarrassment or was made simply for money? Nicholson can, and does:

"I think I learned my lesson with *On a Clear Day You Can See Forever*, which I made between the finishing and the release of *Easy Rider*. I was married. I didn't have any money. I needed the money. Plus I loved Vincente Minnelli, but I did that movie primarily for money, and felt no compunction about it. Working on *Head*, which I wrote, and *Easy Rider*, which we all worked on together, I experienced a little more of my own self-expression in the movies. It was an elixir I hadn't fully appreciated until suddenly now I was working on *On a Clear Day*, and there were problems on the picture, crazy decisions, until I thought I was regressing back to the earliest days of my career.

"If I had money problems I would have done movies for money, just like anybody else, but I haven't had to do that. So, I've never had to make any career decisions other than to take the most creative job that was available to me. Granted, I knew *The Godfather* was going to make a lot of money when I turned it down for *King of Marvin Gardens*, but I felt an Italian should play that part. I could have played it in spades. Michael Corleone. That book, you can't make a bad movie out of that book. Whoever you are. I felt the same way about *Lonesome Dove*. This is one area where the actors really vibrate ahead of everybody else. Actors know material."

And if you look at the films in his career, Nicholson knows material better than most actors. One of the constants running through the list of his films is how many of them seemed unlikely or impossible at the outset. Films, for example, like *Five Easy Pieces*, *One Flew Over the Cuckoo's Nest*, *Terms of Endearment*, *Prizzi's Honor*, *The Shining*, and *The Witches of Eastwick* must have seemed daunting to filmmakers and actors looking only for commercial prospects. But by betting right on them, Nicholson has compiled a filmography since 1968 that is more consistently good, with fewer obvious clinkers on it, than any other actor of his generation. The films before 1968—like *Cry Baby Killer* and the original *Little Shop of Horrors*—belong to a period in which he labored in the vineyards of exploitation and exercised almost no control over his career.

The way he protects his control these days, he said, is by resisting typecasting, not only in the roles he plays, but in the private image he projects.

"One of the reasons I never, ever do television interviews is, if you don't resist, they'll make you into their favorite Jack. They think they know you. You've got to fight that, or the orifice through which you can express yourself becomes narrower and narrower. I'm a person who is very aware of this, maybe because I worked for a long while before I had any say in what I did exactly. But I was consciously aware, in the choices that I made, of protecting this quality of my job—of not getting restricted to, 'Oh, he's this,' and 'Oh, he's that.' I may be this and I may be that, and I may find a way to be something else, too. I can do Shakespeare, for example, but nobody wants to see me do it. So I have to put that quality into *The Witches of Eastwick* or *The Shining*, movies that have a Shakespearean quality."

He smiled, as if he were savoring a victory over absent forces. "I had very sincere aesthetic reasons, for example, for doing *Batman*," he said. "I'd been asked about many similar projects. But when I talked with Tim Burton about *Batman*, I knew we'd both started out in the animation department. I told him, 'Remember it's dark. Just like basketball, it's night comedy.' He approached it with no condescension. So did I. I always knew you could bring Nietzsche to the Joker."

What about directing? I asked. *The Two Jakes* is Nicholson's third film as a director, after *Drive, He Said* (1970) and *Goin' South* (1978), and seems to imply a directorial commitment about once a decade.

"I had intended to direct a little more frequently than this," he said, "and maybe I will be now. I don't know. *Drive, He Said* was not a particularly big success. You'll be glad to know I got my first overage check on *Goin' South* a couple of months ago, so that goes off the list of movies which did not exceed my guarantee, of which there are very few. But I'm not interested in directing just any old movie, just to have a job title. I'd be perfectly content to rest my case on the three movies I've directed. I'm very proud of them. I would have done more directing, it's just that *The Two Jakes* has been hung up for seven years."

Nicholson didn't look as if he were too disturbed by that. He looked, in fact, amused, and he somehow got onto the subject of his improvised dances in the movies, of which there are several, not only the obvious ones like in *The Witches of Eastwick* and as the Joker in *Batman*, but the less obvious ones like when he dances around the room while making love in *Five Easy Pieces*.

"You know I'm the greatest improvisational dancer in the movies," he said, half seriously. "Fred Astaire was a dear friend to me. His movies don't get old. You can look at Fred Astaire movies just like you can look at the Mona Lisa. I watched him rehearse his walk when I first went to the Oscars. He practiced his walk up to the podium. For forty-five minutes he rehearsed. Pocket or no pocket? Left arm or right arm? This is what produces effortlessness.

"And he showed me another thing. I know how exhausting electric light is from working in it. That's one of the reasons I've worn shades all my life. At the Oscars one year, I'm sitting next to Astaire, we're dishing with Sammy Davis, and there are sixty-seven arc lamps pointing in the faces of the people on stage. No wonder people say such goofy things at the Oscars. The lights drive them crazy. Astaire is up for best supporting actor. The category is always first. They announce it, and no Fred Astaire. He put on his sunglasses the second he didn't win. My point is, if Fred Astaire can wear his sunglasses indoors at the Oscars, I can wear my sunglasses indoors at the Oscars. And anywhere else."

Martin Ritt: In Memoriam

He was a large, genial, thoughtful man who was not quite your picture of a big-time Hollywood director. For one thing, he wore a jumpsuit everywhere he went. He had a closet full of them in different colors and fabrics, and there was even a black-and-white "formal" jumpsuit that he wore with a bow tie to the Academy Awards. He said he didn't like to waste time every morning deciding what to wear for the rest of the day. He had better things to think about.

Martin Ritt, who died December 8, 1990, at seventy-six, had a lot of better things to think about, and more than most directors, he wanted us to think about them, too. His films almost always explored social issues close to his heart.

He made comedies and thrillers and melodramas, but his surest touch was for movies about little people who went up against the system. *Norma Rae* was probably his most representative film, starring Sally Field as a half-literate Southern textile worker who was raising a couple of kids and working for the minimum wage in a textile mill, and who surprised herself by becoming a union organizer.

Many people remember *Norma Rae*, which won Sally Field her first Academy Award, but how many know that it was directed by Martin Ritt? How many, for that matter, would recognize that the same filmmaker was responsible for such films as *Sounder*, *Hud*, *The Great White Hope*, *Edge of the City*, *The Long Hot Summer*, *Hombre*, *Conrack*, *The Front*, *Cross Creek*, and *Murphy's Romance*?

In an age of auteurs who wore their name above the title, of first-time directors hailed as geniuses, Martin Ritt worked for thirty-four years to make sound, perceptive pictures about people. Although the official biographies had his age at seventy when he died, the family said he was seventy-six, and that meant he was forty-two when he directed his first feature film, the *film noir* classic *Edge of the City*, in 1956. That's old for a Hollywood director to get started, and maybe it explains why he didn't make any mass-market entertainments designed to open in 1,600 theaters on Friday and be forgotten in six months. He made movies by and about adults.

Maybe that was one of the reasons actors liked to work with him so much. He gave them grown-up, intelligent roles to fit their personalities. He was responsible for seeing through Sally Field's goody-goody image and redirecting her entire career with *Norma Rae*. And remember also the bone weariness of Richard Burton in *The Spy Who Came in From the Cold*, as a disillusioned spy who had to pretend to be even more disillusioned than he was. Or the ferocious populist spirit of the coal miners in *The Molly Maguires*, the first major movie to show that Sean Connery had resources beyond those of James Bond. Or recall the simple humanity of James Garner in *Murphy's Romance*, as the small-town chemist who thinks love has passed him by, but is wrong.

Ritt was the key director in Paul Newman's career, shaping the way we and other directors were to see him, as early as *The Long Hot Summer* (1958). He also directed Newman in *Hud* (1963), which may have been the actor's best movie, and in *The Outrage* (1964) and *Hombre* (1967).

Oscars fell thickly to actors, cinematographers, and writers who worked with him—especially the husband-and-wife screenplay team of Harriett Frank, Jr., and Irving Ravetch, who wrote many of his movies—but Ritt himself was nominated only one time, for *Hud*. Somehow it did not seem that he made "director's pictures," and he encouraged that view: "As far as 'a Martin Ritt production' is concerned," he told the film historian Leslie Halliwell, "I wouldn't embarrass myself to take that credit. What about the Ravetches? They wrote it. What about the actors who appeared in it? If I ever write one, direct it, and appear in it, then you can call it a Martin Ritt production."

But how many films could have been more personally felt than *Sounder* (1972), a film whose characters seemingly had nothing in common with Ritt? It starred Paul Winfield and Cicely Tyson as poor sharecroppers in Mississippi in 1933, and looked through the eyes of their son when the father is taken away to a work camp for stealing a ham to feed his family. The boy runs away to find the camp and never does, but he does find a schoolteacher who encourages him to come to her school and study. And when both the father and the son return home, they have a talk that is one of the great moments in recent movies. He is so happy to be with his father that he never wants to leave home, but his father doesn't want him to stay locked in the same poverty that has trapped him, and explains, "You lose some of the time what you go after, but you lose all of the time what you don't go after."

The movie was dismissed in some quarters as "liberal," which has become a two-edged word, implying convictions without action. But to make someone feel is to act upon him, and *Sounder* made millions of people feel in such a way that surely their actions were subtly influenced over the years. That was the point with a Ritt film. He didn't pound you over the head with a lot of political rhetoric. He simply let you know how he felt, in a way that was hard to disagree with.

The film that came most directly out of his own experience was possibly *The Front* (1976), starring Woody Allen and Zero Mostel in the story of an insignificant little man who allowed his name to be signed to screenplays written by a blacklisted writer. Ritt knew the blacklist experience at first hand. Born of immigrant parents on the Lower East Side of New York, he got into show business through the Group Theater. He was an actor to begin with, in plays like Clifford Odets's *Golden Boy*, and then he directed a lot of live television—much of it involving social issues—before he was blacklisted in 1952 for past association with communist groups. That lasted five years, while he supported himself as an acting teacher, and then, at forty-two, he began his life's work with *Edge of the City*, which was based on one of his TV dramas. You may have seen it on the late show, the knife-edged melodrama starring Sidney Poitier as a longshoreman, John Cassavetes as an Army deserter, and Jack Warden as a crooked union man.

I saw Martin Ritt for the last time in January 1989 at the Sundance Film Festival in Utah. His film, *Stanley and Iris*, starring Robert De Niro as an illiterate man and Jane Fonda as the woman who falls in love with him and teaches him to read and write, had been selected for the opening night of the festival. Backstage before the event, he looked tired and hemmed in, but when he came onstage to say a few words, his personality came booming forth, not in self-praise, but with the hope that everyone would enjoy the picture and maybe think a little about some of the questions it raised. For Marty Ritt, that was a worthy enough ambition to inspire a life's career.

Billie Whitelaw

Chicago, October 31, 1990—London had never seen anything quite like the brothers Kray, the sadistic twins who ran a protection empire and palled around with café society. They became celebrities of a sort. British professional criminals followed a more genteel tradition until the Krays came along in the 1950s and early 1960s. You might have gotten bashed on the head or even, after great provocation, shot dead, but until the Krays, it was unlikely anyone would pull out a sword and redecorate your face.

The Krays got a reputation for performing their sickest crimes themselves, and then turning up, immaculately dressed, at the posh nightclubs. The British tabloids made an industry out of them, but what nobody could quite believe was that they really did go back home every night to the humble East End semi-detached home they shared with their Cockney mom.

The genius of *The Krays*, Peter Medak's new film about the most notorious villains of modern British crime, is that the movie is not simply a catalog of stabbings, garrotings, and bloodletting. It goes deeper than into the twisted pathology of twins whose faces would light up with joy when their Mom told them they looked just like proper gentlemen.

Reggie and Ronnie, their names were. Ronnie was the instigator, the one who got off on killing, and Reggie was the weaker one who killed only once, under Ronnie's insistent pressure, but at the time there was nothing to choose between them: They were the two most feared men in the East End. And their mother, Violet, was treated very, very nicely, wherever she went.

"She was the most important love interest in their lives," Billie Whitelaw was musing one afternoon after the movie's North American premiere. Whitelaw is the distinguished British actress who is known as the foremost interpreter of the works of Samuel Beckett, and she plays mother Kray in the movie. It's quite a performance. "Violet was just as well-known as the twins," she said, "but for different reasons. She was a classic East End mother figure. And the whole focus of the movie is domestic. Violet and her boys. There's a most horrific film to be made about the Krays, because what Peter Medak has done is just the tip of the iceberg of the atrocities they committed. If you wanted to make a gory horror movie out of the Krays, it's all there to make. But Peter has actually made a domestic film about a mother and her two sons."

In *The Krays*, Violet cheerfully rules her husband, her other son, Charlie, and all the neighbors and relatives. She's a forcible, opinionated, strong-willed woman who knows when she holds her twins for the first time that they're destined to be special. As children they were mean and violent, and forged a strange bond of twinship that distrusted the rest of the world—except for Violet. She could see no evil in them. She doted even on their "business," which all London knew was extortion.

In the film, the Krays are played by brothers, Gary and Martin Kemp, whose sleek good looks seem right at home in expensive suits and polished shoes. Their performances suggest an eerie quality to the twins—the notion that they are never entirely offstage, that everything they say is for effect, sometimes ironic effect, and that they are never more dangerous than when their oily politeness is on display.

Whitelaw knew the twins at the height of their powers. "I was working at the Theatre Workshop with Joan Littlewood," Whitelaw remembered, "and they were around then. They actually offered Joan protection, but I think it was a courteous, nice protection. They loved theatricals."

And yet the protection they were offering, I said, was basically protection against themselves.

"I suppose so, yes. But they always wanted to be considered gentlemen. That was very important to them. They behaved with great courtesy. Their brother, Charlie, who I know quite well, the oldest one, always behaved with enormous courtesy. And a number of the old gang members who were around when we shot the film were extremely polite on the set. They very much wanted to be considered gentlemen, and in their own way, they are, sending flowers, doing this, doing that, standing up when a lady comes into the room."

You've been quoted, I said, as telling Charlie you didn't know if you could get Violet quite right; you didn't know if you could do her justice in terms of how warm she was, and what a good mother she was.

"I know that these three boys were besotted with their mother," Whitelaw said. "They all three of them loved her. In fact, everyone I've spoken to who knew Violet Kray loved her. I was talking to Charlie about her very early on, in fact, and whenever I started to talk in detail about Violet, tears would come to his eyes. Even her brother loved her, and that's unusual, isn't it? For siblings to love one another, and I didn't know if I could be that lovable."

Yet she gave birth to the most feared and violent London criminals of their time, twins who brought professional street violence to a city where the policemen didn't carry guns.

Whitelaw smiled. "They always claimed that they only slashed, beat up, and tortured their own—the gangs with which they were constantly warring. It has been said if the Krays were around today, that they would clean up the drug scene, that they would have it under control. But perhaps the price would be too high to pay."

We were talking in Whitelaw's hotel suite in Toronto, where the film had just played in the film festival. It arrived on this continent having set box office records in England, where the Krays are still serving the long prison sentences that brought an end to their empire.

The film is the biggest hit Whitelaw has been in. She does most of her work on the stage, and her best-known films are probably *No Love for Johnnie* (1961), as the wife of ambitious politician Peter Finch, and *Charlie Bubbles* (1968), for which she won a British Film Award as the wife of philandering football fan Albert Finney. The central fact of her career has been her long association with the work of Samuel Beckett, the late great exiled Irish playwright, who chose her as the key interpreter of his work.

For Medak, the director, the film is a career high. The Hungarian-born filmmaker, long in Britain, is best known for *The Ruling Class* (1971), starring Peter O'Toole as a very, very strange aristocrat, but his career in recent years has included such unexpected material as *The Changeling* and *Zorro, the Gay Blade*.

The film works so well, I think, because it creates such a disturbing tension between the evil done by the Krays and the love they basked in at home. Whitelaw's concern that she could not make Violet lovable enough is significant; how could a woman that lovable have produced—and doted on—the Krays?

"Perhaps love is blind," she said. "Actually blind. I mean, I love my children to bits. I do, and I would fight tooth and nail like a tigress for my children. But a lot of mothers love their sons, and they don't turn out to be psychopathic torturers. I was astonished when I saw the film at how angry I seemed to get, at how often I lost my temper, and I think it was because, as an actress, the way my love was coming out was in fiercely protecting those boys."

Do you have any theories about whether her love may have led them in the wrong direction—or were they simply bad seeds?

"I've always thought the fact that they were twins had something to do with it. And the fact that one of the twins was a psychopath had a hell of a lot to do with it. There's no question that both of those boys are very bright. If Reggie had been just one little chicken to come out of that egg, instead of two, I think he would have gone through the usual East End working class pilfering—the bit of wheeling and dealing that goes on in all working class areas—but he would have gone through that, and come out the other side. But Ronnie is a psychopath. And because of that, he had enormous influence on Reggie.

"It's sad," she said, "if you are going to feel sad about these men at all, that Ronnie, who was the one who instigated all these things, is kept in a hospital. He's kept under sedation, so he's quite happy. He's getting happy pills all the time, and he's allowed to see people, within reason, whenever he wants to, and he sits in a room, and they have coffee and talk. But Reggie, who was the sane one, who was put in an ordinary hard-core prison situation, is now the one who is acutely depressed. He is the one who now has great emotional and mental problems."

And Violet sleeps beneath a huge marble stone that says, "Mother."

My New List of the Ten Greatest Films of All Time

If I must make a list of the ten greatest films of all time, my first vow is to make the list for myself, not for anybody else. I am sure than Eisenstein's *Battleship Potemkin* is a great film, but it's not going on my list simply so I can impress people. Nor will I avoid *Casablanca* simply because it's so popular; I love it all the same.

If I have a criteria for choosing the greatest films, it's an emotional one. These are films that moved me deeply in one way or another. The cinema is the greatest art form ever conceived for generating emotions in its audience. That's what it does best. (If you argue instead for dance or music, drama or painting, I will reply that the cinema incorporates all of these arts.)

Cinema is not very good, on the other hand, at intellectual, philosophical, or political argument. That's where the Marxists were wrong. If a movie changes your vote or your mind, it does so by appealing to your emotions, not your reason. And so my greatest films must be films that had me sitting transfixed before the screen, involved, committed, and feeling.

Therefore, alphabetically:

• *Casablanca.* After seeing this film many times, I think I finally understand why I love it so much. It's not because of the romance, or the humor, or the intrigue, although those elements are masterful. It's because it makes me proud of the characters. These are not heroes—not except for Paul Heinreid's resistance fighter, who in some ways is the most predictable character in the film. These are realists, pragmatists, survivors: Humphrey Bogart's Rick Blaine, who sticks his neck out for nobody, and Claude Rain's police inspector, who follows rules and tries to stay out of trouble. At the end of the film, when they rise to heroism, it is so moving because heroism is not in their makeup. Their better nature simply informs them what they must do.

The sheer beauty of the film is also compelling. The black-and-white close-ups of Ingrid Bergman, the most bravely vulnerable woman in movie history. Bogart with his cigarette and his bottle. Greenstreet and Lorre. Dooley Wilson at the piano, looking up with pain when he sees Bergman enter the room. The shadows. "As Time Goes By."

• *Citizen Kane.* I have just seen it again, a shot at a time, analyzing it frame-by-frame out at the University of Colorado at Boulder. We took ten hours and really *looked* at this film, which is routinely named the best film of all time, almost by default, in list after list. Maybe it is. It's some movie. It tells of all the seasons of a man's life, shows his weaknesses and hurts, surrounds him with witnesses who remember him but do not know how to explain him. It ends its search for "Rosebud," his dying word, with a final image that explains everything and nothing, and although some critics say the image is superficial, I say it is very deep indeed, because it illustrates the way that human happiness and pain are not found in big ideas but in the little victories or defeats of childhood.

Few films are more complex, or show more breathtaking skill at moving from one level to another. Orson Welles, with his radio background, was able to segue from one scene to another using sound as his connecting link. In one sustained stretch, he covers twenty years between "Merry Christmas" and "A very happy New Year." The piano playing of Kane's young friend Susan leads into their relationship, his applause leads into his campaign, where applause is the bridge again to a political rally that leads to his downfall, when his relationship with Susan is unmasked. We get a three-part miniseries in five minutes.

• *Floating Weeds.* I do not expect many readers to have heard of this film, or of Yasujiro Ozu, who directed it, but this Japanese master, who lived from 1903 to 1963 and whose prolific career bridged the silent and sound eras, saw things through his films in a way that no one else saw. Audiences never stop to think, when they go to the movies, *how* they understand what a close-up is, or a reaction shot. They learned that language in childhood, and it was codified and popularized by D.W. Griffith, whose films were copied everywhere in the world—except in Japan, where for a time a distinctively different visual style seemed to be developing. Ozu fashioned his style by himself, and never changed it, and to see his films is to be inside a completely alternative cinematic language.

Floating Weeds, like many of his films, is deceptively simple. It tells of a troupe of traveling actors who return to an isolated village where their leader left a woman behind many years ago—and, we discover, he also left a son. Ozu

727

weaves an atmosphere of peaceful tranquility, of music and processions and leisurely conversations, and then explodes his emotional secrets, which cause people to discover their true natures. It is all done with hypnotic visual beauty. After years of being available only in a shabby, beaten-up version usually known as *Drifting Weeds*, this film has now been re-released in superb videotape and Laserdisc editions.

• *Gates of Heaven.* This film, not to be confused in any way with *Heaven's Gate* (or with *Gates of Hell*, for that matter) is a bottomless mystery to me, infinitely fascinating. Made in the late 1970s by Errol Morris, it would appear to be a documentary about some people involved in a couple of pet cemeteries in northern California. Oh, it's factual enough: The people in this film really exist, and so does the pet cemetery. But Morris is not concerned with his apparent subject. He has made a film about life and death, pride and shame, deception and betrayal, and the stubborn quirkiness of human nature.

He points his camera at his subjects and lets them talk. But he points it for hours on end, patiently, until finally they use the language in ways that reveal their most hidden parts. I am moved by the son who speaks of success but cannot grasp it, the old man whose childhood pet was killed, the cocky guy who runs the rendering plant, the woman who speaks of her dead pet and says, "There's your dog, and your dog's dead. But there has to be something that made it move. Isn't there?" In those words is the central question of every religion. And then, in the extraordinary centerpiece of the film, there is the old woman, Florence Rasmussen, sitting in the doorway of her home, delivering a spontaneous monologue that Faulkner would have killed to have written.

• *La Dolce Vita.* Fellini's 1960 film has grown passé in some circles, I'm afraid, but I love it more than ever. Forget about its message, about the "sweet life" along Rome's Via Veneto, or about the contrasts between the sacred and the profane. Simply look at Fellini's ballet of movement and sound, the graceful way he choreographs the camera, the way the actors move. He never made a more "Felliniesque" film, or a better one.

Then sneak up on the subject from inside. Forget what made this film trendy and scandalous more than thirty years ago; ask what it really says. It is about a man (Marcello Mastroianni in his definitive performance) driven to distraction by his hunger for love, and driven to despair by his complete inability to be able to love. He seeks love from the neurosis of his fiancée, through the fleshy carnality of a movie goddess, from prostitutes and princesses. He seeks it in miracles and drunkenness, at night and at dawn. He thinks he can glimpse it in the life of his friend Steiner, who has a wife and children and a home where music is played and poetry read. But Steiner is as despairing as he is. And finally Marcello gives up and sells out and at dawn sees a pale young girl who wants to remind him of the novel he meant to write someday, but he is hung over and cannot hear her shouting across the waves, and so the message is lost.

• *Notorious.* I do not have the secret of Alfred Hitchcock and neither, I am convinced, does anyone else. He made movies that do not date, that fascinate and amuse, that everybody enjoys and that shout out in every frame that they are by Hitchcock. In the world of film he was known simply as The Master. But what was he the Master of? What was his philosophy, his belief, his message? It appears that he had none. His purpose was simply to pluck the strings of human emotion—to play the audience, he said, like a piano. Hitchcock was always hidden behind the genre of the suspense film, but as you see his movies again and again, the greatness stays after the suspense becomes familiar. He made pure movies.

Notorious is my favorite Hitchcock, a pairing of Cary Grant and Ingrid Bergman, with Claude Rains the tragic third corner of the triangle. Because she loves Grant, she agrees to seduce Rains, a Nazi spy. Grant takes her act of pure love as a tawdry thing, proving she is a notorious woman. And when Bergman is being poisoned, he misreads her confusion as drunkenness. While the hero plays a rat, however, the villain (Rains) becomes an object of sympathy. He does love this woman. He would throw over all of Nazi Germany for her, probably—if he were not under the spell of his domineering mother, who pulls his strings until they choke him.

• *Raging Bull.* Ten years ago, Martin Scorsese's *Taxi Driver* was on my list of the ten best films. I think *Raging Bull* addresses some of the same obsessions, and is a deeper and more confident film. Scorsese used the same actor, Robert De Niro, and the same screenwriter, Paul Schrader, for both films, and they have the same buried themes: a man's jealousy about a woman, made painful by his own impotence, and expressed through violence.

Someday if you want to see movie acting as good as any ever put on the screen, look at a scene two-thirds of the way through *Raging Bull*. It takes place in the living room of Jake LaMotta, the boxing champion played by De Niro. He is fiddling with a TV set. His wife comes in, says hello, kisses his brother, and goes upstairs. This begins to bother LaMotta. He begins to quiz his brother (Joe Pesci). The brother says he don't know nothin'. De Niro says maybe he doesn't *know* what he knows. The way the dialogue expresses the inner twisting logic of his jealousy is insidious. De Niro keeps talking, and Pesci tries to run but can't hide. And step by step, word by word, we witness a man helpless to stop himself from destroying everyone who loves him.

- **The Third Man.** This movie is on the altar of my love for the cinema. I saw it for the first time in a little fleabox of a theater on the Left Bank in Paris, in 1962, during my first $5-a-day trip to Europe. It was so sad, so beautiful, so romantic that it became at once a part of my own memories—as if it had happened to me. There is infinite poignancy in the love that the failed writer Holly Martins (Joseph Cotten) feels for the woman (Alida Valli) who loves the "dead" Harry Lime (Orson Welles). Harry treats her horribly, but she loves her idea of him, and neither he nor Holly can ever change that.

Apart from the story, look at the visuals! The tense conversation on the giant Ferris wheel. The giant, looming shadows at night. The carnivorous faces of people seen in the bombed-out streets of postwar Vienna, where the movie was shot on location. The chase through the sewers. And of course the moment when the cat rubs against a shoe in a doorway, and Orson Welles makes the most dramatic entrance in the history of the cinema. All done to the music of a single zither.

- **28 Up.** I have very particular reasons for including this film, which is the least-familiar title on my list but one which I defy anyone to watch without fascination. No other film I have ever seen does a better job of illustrating the mysterious and haunting way in which the cinema bridges time. The movies themselves play with time, condensing days or years into minutes or hours. Then going to old movies defies time, because we see and hear people who are now dead, sounding and looking exactly the same. Then the movies toy with our personal time, when we revisit them, by re-creating for us precisely the same experience we had before.

Then look what Michael Apted does with time in this documentary, which he began more than thirty years ago. He made a movie called *7 Up* for British television. It was about a group of British seven-year-olds, their dreams, fears, ambitions, families, prospects. Fair enough. Then,

seven years later, he made *14 Up*, revisiting them. Then came *21 Up* and, in 1985, *28 Up*, and next year, just in time for the *Sight & Sound* list, will come *35 Up*. And so the film will continue to grow . . . 42 . . . 49 . . . 56 . . . 63 . . . until Apted or his subjects are dead.

The miracle of the film is that it shows us that the seeds of the man are indeed in the child. In a sense, the destinies of all of these people can be guessed in their eyes, the first time we see them. Some do better than we expect, some worse, one seems completely bewildered. But the secret and mystery of human personality is there from the first. This ongoing film is an experiment unlike anything else in film history.

- **2001: A Space Odyssey.** Film can take us where we cannot go. It can also take our minds outside their shells, and this film by Stanley Kubrick is one of the great visionary experiences in the cinema. Yes, it was a landmark of special effects, so convincing that years later the astronauts, faced with the reality of outer space, compared it to *2001*. But it was also a landmark of non-narrative, poetic filmmaking, in which the connections were made by images, not dialogue or plot.

An ape learns to use a bone as a weapon, and this tool, flung into the air, transforms itself into a spaceship—the tool that will free us from the bondage of this planet. And then the spaceship takes man on a voyage into the interior of what may be the mind of another species.

The debates about the "meaning" of this film still go on. Surely the whole point of the film is that it is beyond meaning, that it takes its character to a place he is so incapable of understanding that a special room—sort of a hotel room—has to be prepared for him there, so that he will not go mad. The movie lyrically and brutally challenges us to break out of the illusion that everyday mundane concerns are what must preoccupy us. It argues that surely man did not learn to think and dream, only to deaden himself with provincialism and selfishness. *2001* is a spiritual experience. But then all good movies are.

The Fiftieth Anniversary of *Citizen Kane*

Fifty years ago last year, Orson Welles had made what would eventually become known as the greatest movie of all time. But he was having trouble getting it released.

Citizen Kane told the story of a press tycoon whose arrogance had alienated him from everyone who loved him, and who had died alone inside his vast Gothic castle in Florida. To many observers, Charles Foster Kane bore an uncanny resemblance to William Randolph Hearst, the aging press tycoon who lived in San Simeon, his famous California castle. And to Hearst's underlings, *Citizen Kane* was so unflattering to their boss that they banned all mention of it from the Hearst papers, radio stations, and wire services. For good measure, they also banned all mention of every other movie from the same studio, RKO Radio Pictures.

During one extraordinary moment in the negotiations leading up to the release of *Citizen Kane*, the very existence of the film itself was in doubt. Terrified by the possibility of an anti-Hollywood campaign by the Hearst press, a group of industry leaders, lead by MGM's Louis B. Mayer, offered RKO a cash settlement to simply destroy the film. It would have covered RKO's costs and added a small profit. But by then Welles had already sneak-previewed the movie to so many powerful opinion-makers that it was too late to sweep it under the rug.

Citizen Kane never did get a proper national release, however. It could not play in the major theaters in many cities, because they were block-booked by the big studios, which boycotted it. It could not be advertised in the influential Hearst papers (the ads referred only to a mysterious "New Screen Attraction"). And although the film was instantly hailed by many critics, John O'Hara in *Newsweek* and Bosley Crowther in the *New York Times* among them, it won only one Academy Award—which Welles shared with Herman Mankiewicz, for the screenplay.

The legend of *Citizen Kane* and Orson Welles was, in the next half century, to become one of the central myths of Hollywood: How a boy genius in his mid-twenties was given a completely free rein to make exactly the movie he wanted to make, and how in response he made the greatest movie of all time, only to see both the film and his own career chewed up and spat out by the venal, small-minded Hollywood establishment. Welles became the great outsider hero of cinema, central to the French auteur critics,

championed by independent filmmakers, cited by anyone who wants to make an argument for film art over film commerce.

And now it is fifty years later and Welles is dead and so are many of the other bright-eyed young people in his Mercury Theater troupe who went West to make a movie. But the legend of *Citizen Kane* lives on. It is routinely voted the greatest film of all time, most notably in the international polls by the British film magazine *Sight & Sound* in 1962, 1972, and 1982. And in 1991 a bright, sparkling new restored print of *Citizen Kane* was restored on tapes and discs.

There is a certain irony in the national release of this revival, since *Citizen Kane* is now owned by Ted Turner, an international media baron with certain similarities to both Hearst and Kane. All three men came from humble origins, got their first broken-down media property cheap, had a vision of a new mass audience, and became famous millionaires who settled down with actresses.

Turner says he has the time to watch only three or four movies a year, but I'll bet *Citizen Kane* is among them. And perhaps he notices parallels with his own career: how his undoubted achievements and great successes are sometimes undermined by a failure of taste. Kane's great downfall came because he fell in love with a humble shopgirl and became determined to turn her into a great opera singer, despite her lack of talent. The Achilles' heel in Turner's career came when he fell in love with a sleazy technical innovation named colorization, and became determined to turn black-and-white movies into ersatz color movies, despite the outraged protests of film lovers everywhere. Yes, the Ted Turner who has made the beautiful, lovingly restored new print of *Citizen Kane* is the very same man who also wanted to colorize Welles's masterpiece.

"Make me one promise," Welles told his friend Henry Jaglom a few weeks before his death. "Keep Ted Turner and his goddamned Crayolas away from my movie." In the event, it was a document fifty years old that kept Turner's crayons away from *Kane*. Welles's original contract with RKO, hailed at the time as the most extraordinary contract any studio had ever given any filmmaker, guaranteed Welles's absolute control over every aspect of the production—including its color, or lack of same.

And so the new print that went into theatrical release

around the country looked substantially the same as when the movie had its premiere in 1941. For many filmgoers, that was a revelation. More than most films, *Citizen Kane* must be seen in a 35mm theatrical print to be appreciated.

I've seen *Kane* at least fifty times on 16mm, videotape, and Laserdisc. I have gone through it a scene at a time, using a stop-frame film analyzer, at least twenty-five times in various film classes and at festivals. Yet I've seen it in 35mm only twice: In 1956, when it had its first major re-release and I was in junior high school, and in 1978, when a new print was shown at the Chicago Film Festival.

From my 1956 viewing, I remember only the overwhelming total impression of the film, which in its visual sweep and the sheer audacity of its imagination outclassed all the small-minded entertainments I was used to seeing at the movies. From the 1978 viewing, I remember how the brightness and detail of the 35mm print opened up the corners and revealed the shadows of the great film.

Citizen Kane makes great use of darkness and shadow. Welles, working with the gifted cinematographer Gregg Toland, wanted to show a man's life that was filled to bursting with possessions, power, associates, wealth, and mystery. He created a gloomy, dark visual style for the picture, which in 35mm reveals every nook and cranny to contain a treasure or a hint. And because of Toland's famous deep-focus photography, the frame is filled from front to back as well as from left to right.

The first apartment of Kane's mistress, for example, contains the paperweight he drops much later when he dies. It's on a table with other odds and ends. The famous warehouse shot at the end of the film includes a portrait of young Charlie Kane with his parents. You can see those details easily in 35mm, but not so easily in the 16mm prints of the movie, or even in the superb Laserdisc issued by the Criterion Collection. If you've only seen the movie on broadcast television or in a beaten-up 16mm classroom print, you may be amazed at the additional details visible in 35mm.

The story of the making of *Citizen Kane* is by now one of the central legends of movie lore. Many books have been written about the film, most notably *The Citizen Kane Book* (Little, Brown) by Pauline Kael, with her famous essay "Raising Kane," which argues that the contribution of writer Herman Mankiewicz to the production has been underappreciated. Robert Carringer, a Welles expert at the University of Illinois, has published *The Making of Citizen Kane* (California), with much analysis of visual strategies and production details. And Harlan Lebo's new *Citizen Kane: The Fiftieth Anniversary Album* (Doubleday) includes many inside details from interviews with the participants. (Example: Welles gashed his left hand in the scene where he tears apart Susan's apartment, and pulls it out of camera view in the close-up where he picks up the paperweight.)

Recently, at the University of Colorado, I went through *Citizen Kane* once again, with a 16mm film analyzer, joined by several hundred students, faculty, and townspeople. We sat in the dark, and audience members called out "Stop!" when there was something they wanted to discuss. Scene by scene and sometimes shot by shot we looked at the performances, the photography, the special effects.

In preparing for this fiftieth-anniversary salute to "Kane," I reread all of the books once again. There is much disagreement about many of the facts. You can read that Hearst did personally see *Citizen Kane*, or that he did not. That Hearst, if he did see the film, was offended by it, or actually rather enjoyed it. That Welles took credit for the work of his associates, or that he inspired them to surpass all their earlier achievements.

Reading the many accounts of *Citizen Kane* is a little like seeing the movie: The witnesses all have opinions, but often they disagree, and sometimes they simply throw up their hands in exasperation. And the movie stands there before them, a towering achievement that cannot be explained yet cannot be ignored. Fifty years later, it is as fresh, as provoking, as entertaining, as funny, as sad, as brilliant, as it ever was. Many agree it is the greatest film of all time. Those who differ cannot seem to agree on their candidate.

A Viewer's Guide to *Citizen Kane*

• **"Rosebud."** The most famous word in the history of cinema. It explains everything, and nothing. Who, for that matter, actually *heard* Charles Foster Kane say it before he died? The butler says, late in the film, that he did. But Kane seems to be alone when he dies, and the reflection on the shard of glass from the broken paperweight shows the nurse entering the room.

Gossip has it that the screenwriter, Herman Mankiewicz, used "rosebud" as an inside joke, because as a friend of Hearst's mistress, Marion Davies, he knew "rosebud" was the old man's pet name for the most intimate part of her anatomy.

• **Deep Focus.** Everyone knows that Orson Welles and his cinematographer, Gregg Toland, used deep focus in *Kane*. But what is deep focus, and were they using it for the first time? The term refers to a strategy of lighting, composition, and lens choice that allows everything in the frame, from the front to the back, to be in focus at the same time. With the lighting and lenses available in 1941, this was just becoming possible, and Toland had experimented with the technique in John Ford's *The Long Voyage Home* a few years earlier.

In most movies, the key elements in the frame are in focus, and those closer or further away may not be. When everything is in focus, the filmmakers must give a lot more thought to how they direct the viewer's attention, first here and then there. What the French call *mise-en-scène*—the movement within the frame—becomes more important.

• **Optical Illusions.** Deep focus is especially tricky because movies are two-dimensional, and so you need visual guideposts to determine the true scale of a scene. Toland used this fact as a way to fool the audience's eye on two delightful occasions in the film.

One comes when Kane is signing away control of his empire in Thatcher's office. Behind him on the wall are windows that look of normal size and height. Then Kane starts to walk into the background of the shot, and we realize with surprise that the windows are huge, and their lower sills are more than six feet above the floor. As Kane stands under them, he is dwarfed—which is the intent, since he has just lost great power. Later in the film, Kane

walks over to stand in front of the great fireplace in Xanadu, and we realize it, too, is much larger than it first seemed.

• **Visible Ceilings.** In almost all movies before *Citizen Kane*, you couldn't see the ceilings in rooms because there weren't any. That's where they put the lights and microphones. Welles wanted to use a lot of low-angle shots that would look up toward ceilings, and so Toland devised a strategy of cloth ceilings that looked real but were not. The microphones were hidden immediately above the ceilings, which in many shots are noticeably low.

• **Matte Drawings.** These are drawings by artists that are used to create elements that aren't really there. Often they are combined with "real" foregrounds. The opening and closing shots of Kane's great castle, Xanadu, are examples. No exterior set was ever built for the structure. Instead, artists drew it, and used lights behind it to suggest Kane's bedroom window. "Real" foreground details such as Kane's lagoon and private zoo were added.

• **Invisible Wipes.** A "wipe" is a visual effect that wipes one image off the screen while wiping another into view. Invisible wipes disguise themselves as something else on the screen that seems to be moving, so you aren't aware of the effect. They are useful in "wiping" from full-scale sets to miniature sets.

For example: One of the most famous shots in *Kane* shows Susan Alexander's opera debut, when, as she starts to sing, the camera moves straight up to a catwalk high above the stage, and one stagehand turns to another and eloquently reviews her performance by holding his nose. Only the stage and the stagehands on the catwalk are real. The middle portion of this seemingly unbroken shot is a miniature, built in the RKO model workshop. The model is invisibly wiped in by the stage curtains, as we move up past them, and wiped out by a wooden beam right below the catwalk. Another example: In Walter Thatcher's library, the statue of Thatcher is a drawing, and as the camera pans down it wipes out the drawing as it wipes in the set of the library.

• **Invisible Furniture Moving.** In the early scene in the Kanes' cabin in Colorado, the camera tracks back from a window to a table where Kane's mother is being asked to sign a paper. The camera tracks right through where the table would be, after which it is slipped into place before we can see it. But a hat on the table is still trembling from the move. After she signs the paper, the camera pulls up and follows her as she walks back toward the window. If you look sharply, you can see that she's walking right through where the table was a moment before.

• **The Neatest Flash-Forward in *Kane*.** Between Thatcher's words "Merry Christmas" and ". . . a very Happy New Year," two decades pass.

• **From Model to Reality.** As the camera swoops above the night club and through the skylight to discover Susan Alexander Kane sitting forlornly at a table, it goes from a model of the nightclub roof to a real set. The switch is concealed, the first time, by a lightning flash. The second time we go to the nightclub, it's done with a dissolve.

• **Crowd Scenes.** There aren't any in *Citizen Kane*. It only looks like there are. In the opening newsreel, stock footage of a political rally is intercut with a low-angle shot showing one man speaking on behalf of Kane. Sound effects make it sound like he's at a big outdoor rally. Later, Kane himself addresses a gigantic indoor rally. Kane and the other actors on the stage are real. The audience is a miniature, with flickering lights to suggest movement.

• **Slight Factual Discrepancies.** In the opening newsreel, Xanadu is described as being "on the desert coast of Florida." But Florida does not have a desert coast, as you can plainly see during the picnic scene, where footage from an earlier RKO prehistoric adventure was back-projected behind the actors, and if you look closely, that seems to be a pterodactyl flapping its wings.

• **The Luce Connection.** Although *Citizen Kane* was widely seen as an attack on William Randolph Hearst, it was also aimed at Henry R. Luce and his concept of faceless group journalism, as then practiced at his *Time* magazine and "March of Time" newsreels. The opening "News on the March" segment is a deliberate parody of the Luce newsreel, and the reason you can never see the faces of any of the journalists is that Welles and Mankiewicz were kidding the anonymity of Luce's writers and editors.

• **An Extra with a Future.** Alan Ladd can be glimpsed

in the opening newsreel sequence, and again in the closing warehouse scene.

• **The Most Thankless Job on the Movie.** It went to William Alland, who plays Mr. Thompson, the journalist assigned to track down the meaning of "Rosebud." He is always seen from behind, or in backlit profile. You can never see his face. At the movie's world premiere, Alland told the audience he would turn his back so they could recognize him more easily.

• **The Brothel Scene.** It couldn't be filmed. In the original screenplay, after Kane hires away the staff of the *Chronicle*, he takes them to a brothel. The Production Code office wouldn't allow that. So the scene, slightly changed, takes place in the *Inquirer* newsroom, still with the dancing girls.

• **The Eyeless Cockatoo.** Yes, you can see right through the eyeball of the shrieking cocatoo, in the scene before the big fight between Kane and Susan. It's a mistake.

• **The Most Evocative Shot in the Movie.** There are many candidates. My choice is the shot showing an infinity of Kanes reflected in mirrors as he walks past.

• **The Best Speech in *Kane*.** My favorite is delivered by Mr. Bernstein (Everett Sloane), when he is talking about the magic of memory with the inquiring reporter:
"A fellow will remember a lot of things you wouldn't think he'd remember. You take me. One day, back in 1896, I was crossing over to Jersey on the ferry, and as we pulled out, there was another ferry pulling in, and on it there was a girl waiting to get off. A white dress she had on. She was carrying a white parasol. I only saw her for one second. She didn't see me at all, but I'll bet a month hasn't gone by since that I haven't thought of that girl."

• **Genuine Modesty.** In the movie's credits, Welles allowed his director's credit and Toland's cinematography credit to appear on the same card—an unprecedented gesture that indicated how grateful Welles was.

• **False Modesty.** In the unique end credits, the members of the Mercury Company are introduced and seen in brief moments from the movie. Then smaller parts are handled with a single card containing many names. The final credit down at the bottom, in small type, says simply:
Kane . . . . Orson Welles

Why *GoodFellas* Was the Best Film of 1990

For two days after I saw Martin Scorsese's film, *Good-Fellas*, the mood of the characters lingered within me, refusing to leave. It was a mood of guilt and regret, of quick stupid decisions leading to wasted lifetimes, of loyalty turned into betrayal. Yet at the same time there was an element of furtive nostalgia, for bad times that shouldn't be missed, but were.

Most films, even great ones, evaporate like mist once you've returned to the real world; they leave memories behind, but their reality fades fairly quickly. Not this film, which shows America's finest filmmaker at the peak of his form. No better film has ever been made about organized crime—not even *The Godfather*, although the two works are not really comparable.

GoodFellas is a memoir of life in the Mafia, narrated in the first person by Henry Hill (Ray Liotta), an Irish-Italian kid whose only ambition, from his earliest teens, was to be a "wise guy," a Mafioso. There is also narration by Karen, the Jewish girl (Lorraine Bracco) who married him, and who discovered that her entire social life was suddenly inside the Mafia; mob wives never went anywhere or talked to anyone who was not part of that world, and eventually, she says, the values of the Mafia came to seem like normal values. She was even proud of her husband for not lying around the house all day, for having the energy and daring to go out and steal for a living.

There is a real Henry Hill, who disappeared into the anonymity of the federal government's witness protection program, and who over a period of four years told everything he knew about the mob to the reporter Nicholas Pileggi, whose *WiseGuy* was a best-seller. The screenplay by Pileggi and Scorsese distills those memories into a fiction that sometimes plays like a documentary, that contains so much information and feeling about the Mafia that finally it creates the same claustrophobic feeling Hill's wife talks about: the feeling that the mob world is the real world.

Scorsese is the right director—the only director—for this material. He knows it inside-out. The great formative experience of his life was growing up in New York's Little Italy as an outsider who observed everything—an asthmatic kid who couldn't play sports, whose health was too bad to allow him to lead a normal childhood, who was often overlooked but never missed a thing.

There is a passage early in the film in which young Henry Hill looks out the window of his family's apartment and observes with awe and envy the swagger of the low-level wiseguys in the social club across the street, impressed by the fact that they got girls, drove hot cars, had money, that the cops never gave them tickets, that even when their loud parties lasted all night, nobody ever called the police. That was the life he wanted to lead, the film's narrator tells us. The memory may come from Hill and may be in Pileggi's book, but the memory is also Scorsese's, and in the twenty-three years I have known him, we have never had a conversation that did not touch at some point on that central image in his vision of himself—of the kid in the window, watching the neighborhood gangsters.

Like *The Godfather*, Scorsese's *GoodFellas* is a long movie, with the space and leisure to expand and explore its themes. It isn't about any particular plot; it's about what it felt like to be in the Mafia—the good times and the bad times. At first they were mostly good times, and there is an astonishing camera movement in which the point of view follows Henry and Karen on one of their first dates, to the Copacabana night club. There are people waiting in line at the door, but Henry takes her in through the service entrance, past the security guards and the off-duty waiters, down a corridor, through the kitchen, through the service area and out into the front of the club, where a table is literally lifted into the air and placed in front of all the others so that the young couple can be in the first row for the floor show. This is power.

Karen doesn't know yet exactly what Henry does. She finds out. The method of the movie is a slow expansion through levels of the Mafia, with characters introduced casually and some of them not really developed until later in the story. We meet the don Paul Cicero (Paul Sorvino), and Jim (Jimmy the Gent) Conway (Robert De Niro), a man who steals for the sheer love of stealing, and Tommy DeVito (Joe Pesci), a likable guy except that his fearsome temper can explode in a second, with fatal consequences. We follow them through thirty years, at first through years of unchallenged power, then through years of decline (but they have their own kitchen in prison, and boxes of thick steaks and crates of wine), and then into betrayal and decay.

At some point the whole wonderful romance of the Mafia goes sour for Henry Hill, and that moment is when he and Jimmy and Tommy have to bury a man whom Tommy kicked almost to death in a fit of pointless rage. First they have to finish killing him (they stop at Tommy's mother's house to borrow a knife, and she feeds them dinner), then they bury him, then later they have to dig him up again. The worst part is, their victim was a "made" guy, a Mafioso who is supposed to be immune. So they are in deep, deep trouble, and this is not how Henry Hill thought it was going to be when he started out on his life's journey.

From the first shot of his first feature, *Who's That Knocking at My Door* (1967), Scorsese has loved to use popular music as a counterpoint to the dramatic moments in his films. He doesn't simply compile a sound track of golden oldies; he finds the precise sound to underline every moment, and in *GoodFellas* the popular music helps to explain the transition from early days when Henry sells stolen cigarettes to guys at a factory gate, through to the frenetic later days when he's selling cocaine in disobedience to Paul Cicero's orders, and using so much of it himself that life has become a paranoid labyrinth.

In all of his work, which has included arguably the best film of the 1970s (*Taxi Driver*) and of the 1980s (*Raging Bull*), Scorsese has never done a more compelling job of getting inside someone's head as he does in one of the concluding passages of *GoodFellas*, in which he follows one day in the life of Henry Hill, as he tries to do a cocaine deal, cook dinner for his family, placate his mistress, and deal with the suspicion that he's being followed.

This is the sequence that imprinted me so deeply with the mood of the film. It's not a straightforward narrative passage, and it has little to do with plot; it's about the feeling of walls closing in, and the guilty feeling that the walls are deserved. The counterpoint is a sense of duty, of compulsion; the drug deal must be made, but the kid brother must also be picked up, and the sauce must be stirred, and meanwhile Henry's life is careening wildly out of control.

Actors have a way of doing their best work—the work that lets us see them clearly—in a Scorsese film. Robert De Niro emerged as the best actor of his generation in *Taxi Driver*. Joe Pesci, playing De Niro's brother in *Raging Bull*, created a performance of comparable complexity. Both De Niro and Pesci are here in *GoodFellas*, essentially playing major and very challenging supporting roles to Ray Liotta and Lorraine Bracco, who establish themselves here as clearly two of our best new movie actors. Liotta was Melanie Griffith's late-arriving, disturbingly dangerous husband in *Something Wild*, and here he creates the emotional center for a movie that is not about the experience of being a Mafioso, but about the *feeling*. Bracco was the cop's wife from out in the suburbs in *Someone to Watch Over Me*, a film in which her scenes were so effective that it was with a real sense of loss that we returned to the main story. The sense of their marriage is at the heart of this film, especially in a shot where he clings to her, exhausted. They have made their lifetime commitment, and it was to the wrong life.

Many of Scorsese's best films have been poems about guilt. Think of *Mean Streets*, with the Harvey Keitel character tortured by his sexual longings, or *After Hours*, with the Griffin Dunne character involved in an accidental death and finally hunted down in the streets by a misinformed mob, or think of *The Last Temptation of Christ*, in which even Christ is permitted to doubt.

GoodFellas is about guilt more than anything else. But it is not a straightforward morality play, in which good is established and guilt is the appropriate reaction toward evil. No, the hero of this film feels guilty for not upholding the Mafia code—guilty of the sin of betrayal. And his punishment is banishment, into the witness protection program, where nobody has a name and the headwaiter certainly doesn't know it.

What finally got to me after seeing this film—what makes it a great film—is that I understood Henry Hill's feelings. Just as his wife Karen grew so completely absorbed by the Mafia inner life that its values became her own, so did the film weave a seductive spell. It is almost possible to think, sometimes, of the characters as really being good fellows. Their camaraderie is so strong, their loyalty so unquestioned. But the laughter is strained and forced at times, and sometimes it's an effort to enjoy the party, and eventually the whole mythology comes crashing down, and then the guilt—the real guilt, the guilt a Catholic like Scorsese understands intimately—is not that they did sinful things, but that they want to do them again.

The Case Against David Lynch

CANNES, France—The jury at 1990's Cannes Film Festival celebrated David Lynch's film *Wild at Heart* with its highest award, the Palme d'Or, an honor that has gone in the past to Rossellini, Coppola, Kurosawa, and Bergman. Does this place Lynch in the pantheon of great directors, and did it certify his artistic achievement at the very moment when the TV soap opera "Twin Peaks" was proving his popular appeal?

I think not. I think both successes are symptomatic of a despair among moviegoers and TV watchers, a loathing of trash that runs so deep it has turned inward against itself. Sick at their hearts of the "entertainment" they have grown addicted to and fearsome of trying anything new, Lynch's audiences have embraced his work because he reflects their feelings—he hates the movies, too.

Wild at Heart is a cinematic act of self-mutilation, a film that mocks itself. Show biz executives have a cynical shorthand formula for commercial success: sex, drugs, and rock 'n' roll. Lynch's work is exclusively concerned with these three elements, but in an angry, self-hating way; he shoves our nose in it. We want sex? He'll give us undreamed-of perversity. We want drugs? Dennis Hopper, in *Blue Velvet*, will inhale a substance so forbidden that no one has even been able to figure out what it is. We want rock 'n' roll? The Nicolas Cage character in *Wild at Heart* talks and walks like Elvis and even sings two of his songs.

If Lynch were merely providing us with these commodities, he would be only an exploitation filmmaker. But he is not a minor talent; he is a gifted director with a strong sense of style. If he allowed himself a more positive vision—if he dared to believe in people—he could be a great film artist. But he is infected with self-doubt and cynicism, and he believes the worst of his audiences, so he makes films inspired by his despair.

In form, *Wild at Heart* is a road picture about two young people on the run. Played by Nicolas Cage and Laura Dern, they are fleeing from hired killers who have been set on Cage's trail by Dern's mother (Diane Ladd). Their big Detroit convertible sails across the desolate American plains past truck stops and rusting gas stations, and violence follows them.

Lynch tells this story with his customary hyperbole. Everything is taken past satire to extreme distortion—which is supposed to be funny, or at least make people laugh. The movie opens with a black man being savagely beaten to death by Cage, who, after he splashes the man's brains against a concrete wall, lights a cigarette and glowers up at the camera. The audience at Cannes laughed. Why? Not because it was funny. Perhaps because they, and Lynch, could congratulate each other that they spotted the cinematic cliché—that they knew Lynch was taking the edge off of violence by letting us in on the gag.

The structure of *Wild at Heart* proceeds from gothic melodrama. There is a horrible murder by burning that is constantly flashed back to, and a deadly secret that must be kept hidden, and then there is the episodic structure of the road movie, which includes bizarre characters encountered along the way.

The adventures of the young couple are punctuated by extreme violence; in one scene, the brain matter of a killer (Willem Dafoe) is blasted into the sky by a shotgun and plops back to earth in front of the camera. In another, a clerk loses his hand in a bloody shoot-out, and we see him and a friend crawling on the floor, covered with blood, assuring each other that doctors can "sew these things back on in a minute"—but they are too late, because then we see a dog happily trotting out the door with the hand in its mouth.

When *Wild at Heart* played at Cannes, these sensational moments were greeted with laughter, cheers, and booing in about equal proportions. They're obviously intended as rabble-rousing moments; no director since Alfred Hitchcock has been more obsessed than Lynch with inspiring and controlling audience emotion. Sitting in the audience, I wanted to cheer, I wanted to be exhilarated, I wanted to enjoy the movie with its energy and its bright visual images, but I could not. Underneath the flash, it was simply too sad; to applaud it would be like cheering a drunken clown while knowing he really was an alcoholic.

The dominant feeling I took with me from *Wild at Heart* was despair. David Lynch is a gifted filmmaker who, for one reason or another, has backed himself into a corner of satirical self-mockery and feels trapped there. He may tell himself that his movies are commentaries on popular culture, but actually they *are* pop culture—there is no ironic distance, no personal angle, just the willingness to go over the top and give the mob even more of what it wants.

At the press conference after the screening, actress

Diane Ladd, who is Laura Dern's mother, was asked how she felt about her daughter's many and protracted scenes of sex and violence. She murmured the usual things about letting one's daughter go her own way, and then she added, looking at Lynch, "Besides . . . you don't second-guess Michelangelo."

But that is precisely the trouble. Someone should. Everyone, even Lynch himself, now apparently accepts the myth that he is a great artist of the cinema, and the applause has stilled his ability to criticize his own work.

Apart from its other dubious qualities, *Wild at Heart* is too long, slow-moving, and soporific (in between the moments of sensation). And it is certainly not original. At the risk of inviting scorn from Lynch's critical admirers, I would like to point out that the entire style—visual, editing, and narrative—of *Wild at Heart* has been inspired by such Russ Meyer films as *Faster Pussycat—Kill! Kill!*,

SuperVixens, Cherry, Harry and Raquel, and, yes, *Beyond the Valley of the Dolls*, for which I wrote the screenplay. Russ Meyer invented the cinema of David Lynch twenty-five years ago, and did it sincerely and cheerfully with robust good humor, not with Lynch's sneaky stylistic apologies.

The criticism of art is a curious thing, and its practitioners almost always hail the copy as the original. Critics who are probably not even familiar with Russ Meyer now find Lynch's *Wild at Heart* original, when it is actually reactionary. The parallels between Meyer's work and *Wild at Heart* are so many and so obvious that you'd imagine they'd be hard to miss. But Lynch comes wreathed in the victor's garlands from Cannes, and so of course this must be art, and no one observes that Michelangelo has no clothes.

Violence and American Pie

More than anything else, the American movie audience loves violence. This is a fact of life. Comedies are fun and everybody approves of family films, but if a Hollywood studio wants to pull down a surefire $20 million weekend, what it takes is blood and gore, gunfire and car chases, and new twists on sadistic mayhem.

Some people consider the Fourth of July holiday the most typical of all American holidays (I prefer Thanksgiving, but realize I am hopelessly idealistic). In backyards and city parks and on beaches from coast to coast, we observe our national birthday with loud bangs and explosions and thunderous whistling rockets that send showers of fire floating through the sky. At the end of the day the nation is minus a few eyes and fingers, but what a small price to pay for so much noise!

Fireworks, alas, are only tolerated around the Fourth. The rest of the year, we indulge our passion for mayhem by going to the movies. In the summer of 1990, for example, millions of moviegoers thrilled to *RoboCop II*, a mediocre movie distinguished by:

• A twelve-year-old boy who uses all of the usual four-letter words and kills people with machine guns.

• An operation in which a man's brain is taken from his skull in gory detail. First a saw is used to cut through the bone, then the top of the brain is popped off by a surgeon who stands holding it, so we can get a good look.

• The brain is installed in a killer robot, which engages in a fight to the death with the "good" RoboCop, who eventually can kill it only by tearing open the mechanical braincase, pulling out the living gray matter, and smashing it on the pavement.

RoboCop II is not one of the great violent movies, but it will do for the audiences who have worked their way through *Total Recall*. Then there is *Die Hard II*, which is relatively restrained in its violence—apart from the villain who is squashed on a conveyor belt and another who is sucked into the jet engine of a Boeing 747 and sprayed all over the side of the plane. Another summer offering, *Dick Tracy*, did surprisingly well, considering it contained no four-letter words and no realistic violence. In the summer of 1990, *that* was risky filmmaking.

Critics such as myself, paid to evaluate the new movies, fall back on a generic approach. We are more likely to approve of movies that supply violence with humor and style. I enjoyed *Total Recall*, for example, for such reasons as the movie's visionary special effects, its cleverness, and the strength of Arnold Schwarzenegger's performance. I appreciated the good character performances and exciting story of *Die Hard II*. I disliked *RoboCop II* because of its messy plot, stupid characters, and the truly shocking spectacle of that foul-mouthed little villain (is nothing sacred?).

Some violent movies can be exhilirating. I've enjoyed the Lethal Weapon, Mad Max, and Indiana Jones movies. When I get letters from readers protesting a movie I've recommended, however, it is almost never a mass-market Hollywood bloodbath. I doubt if I get a single letter questioning my recommendation of *Total Recall*, but there was a stack on the desk from people who were appalled by *The Cook, the Thief, His Wife and Her Lover*.

That's partly because the people going to see *The Cook* are mostly art-film lovers, not hardened to the conventional levels of violence on the screen. It's also because the violence in *The Cook* has a psychological realism that's lacking in mass-market gore. There's a certain lack of reality about what happens to the victims in *RoboCop II*. They're ducks in a shooting gallery, and after they're dead the movie has no further interest in them.

The mainstream movie audience is not interested in movies like *The Cook*, which uses violence because it *wants* to disturb the audience. The big-time violent films work by making the violence abstract and human lives meaningless. Characters are introduced for no other reason than so they can experience sensational deaths. They're picked off as casually as the little computerized villains in Nintendo games. The *fact* of the loss of life, which used to be shocking in the movies, is now no longer even noted. It is the *manner* that counts.

It is routine for editorial writers to be pious about this bloodshed on the screen, and for citizens' groups to decry the violence. But nobody is listening. There is still a censorious lobby against sex in America, but violence is a lost cause. It provides the very building blocks of our national entertainment machine. The movies and television could not exist without relying on stories about people killing each other. Many teen-agers will not sit still for anything else. Violent movies do not have to be as carefully written, as intelligently constructed, or as lovingly photographed as other kinds. They can be assembled out of elaborate stunt sequences, and in many cases the stunt and explosion and car chase experts are consulted on a shot-by-shot basis.

I see all the movies, and so I am a little hardened. Like the typical moviegoer, I can distance myself from this stuff. When the guy went into the jet engine, I wasn't particularly appalled; I could see it coming from the set-up earlier in the scene. It was inevitable. When they pounded the living brain matter against the sidewalk in *RoboCop II*, I was appalled, however. Hadn't seen *that* before.

And when they let the little kid use all those four-letter words, it seemed to me that they'd broken an unwritten rule. They'd violated a taste barrier that even the most cynical of Hollywood movies had respected up until then—

the notion that kids are supposed to be protected from the vile ugliness of life. But what the heck! Kids see these movies on video anyway, don't they? Might as well give them someone to identify with.

When I was a teen-ager, we went to the movies to see how adults lived. Now kids go to the movies to see how they die. Is Hollywood creating this universe of blood and doom? No, it's supplying a product for which there is a great national affection. And our anarchy is being unleashed on the rest of the world. Is there an answer? Of course there is—an obvious one. We must gather the children and womenfolk and the wise books of our civilization, and go to the caves in the wilderness, and wait there for the coming of a gentler age.

In Praise of Marlon Brando

In *The Freshman*, Marlon Brando goes ice-skating. Simply ice-skating, his vast bulk gliding over the ice with his partner, the actress who plays his daughter. He guides her gently and with grace, until they pull up at the rail. I have seen the film twice, and both times some members of the audience have applauded.

Why? Because it is thrilling to see a man in his sixties ice-skate? Because one does not expect it of Brando? Because he seems too heavy to be so graceful? None of the obvious answers seem to apply. Perhaps we should look earlier in the movie, to a scene where he offers a job to a young film school student, played by Matthew Broderick. In this scene, Brando offers him something else first: a chestnut. Broderick declines. Brando offers the bowl again, using a peculiar movement of his hand and wrist, sort of a looseness, a carelessness. It is a subtle moment of body language that manages to suggest that Brando has more chestnuts where these came from, that he has given away many chestnuts in his time, that he expects his gift to be accepted.

The young man takes a chestnut. A little later in the scene, to punctuate a moment of dialogue, Brando takes a nut himself, and crushes it in one large hand. But have I told you who he looks like in this scene—apart from Marlon Brando, of course? He resembles in every nuance of face, voice, and gesture the most popular character he has ever played in a movie, Don Corleone, from *The Godfather*.

Other actors satirize themselves, and we are embarrassed for them. Old movie tough-guys like George Raft used to turn up on TV, ripping off their own famous lines, and it was humiliating. But when Brando plays Don Corleone in *The Freshman* (and make no mistake—he is intended as the Godfather, in every detail of the performance) it is not an embarrassment—it is a triumph, because Brando is still *playing* him, still acting, every moment, in character.

That is why the audience applauds, I think, when Brando ice-skates: Because Don Corleone is on the ice as well, the actor and his most famous character brought together in an image as unexpected as it is effective. And when Brando offers the chestnut to Broderick, there is suspense in the scene because Brando brings a palpable power to the gesture.

Watching *The Freshman*, I found myself amazed by how overwhelming Brando's performance was. I see dozens of movies every month and am a somewhat hardened observer, and yet when Brando was on the screen my eyes and my complete attention were absorbed by him. Why was I so fascinated by this large man, dressed entirely in black, moving in and out of a shadow behind a desk on a platform in a social club in Little Italy? Was it the voice? The face? The concentration?

No. It was the authority. By one means or another, Marlon Brando has learned, over the years, to dominate a scene more completely than any other living actor. He is not performing, he is there. He is a fact. And behind the fact are the shadows of our memories of all of his other performances: of a threatening young man on a motorcycle in *The Wild One*, of Stanley Kowalski in a torn T-shirt in *A Streetcar Named Desire*, of a longshoreman who could have been a contender in *On the Waterfront*, of Sky Masterson in *Guys and Dolls*, of Don Corleone toppling to his death in a tomato patch, of a lonely man dancing in *Last Tango in Paris*, of a death's head in the darkness in *Apocalypse Now*.

Brando is said to be the greatest movie actor of his time. Other actors have been described in the same way: Jack Nicholson, Robert De Niro, Gerard Depardieu. Brando is certainly the most *legendary* movie actor of his time, the one who carries the most psychic presence to the screen. For a decade, between *The Formula* (1980) and *A Dry White Season* (1989), he was absent from the screen altogether, as if his performances were like chestnuts, and he had given us the gift of many of them, had more than he could use, and had grown careless of them.

But in *A Dry White Season*, as a liberal lawyer who knows his arguments mean nothing in a South African court, he was able to convey irony as a weapon, to ask questions that carried their own answers, to bring victory (in his opinion) out of defeat (in the opinion of the court). Now comes this strange performance in *The Freshman*, where he does something we would have bet he would never do—where he plays Don Corleone in a comedy.

How was he convinced to do it? How did Andrew Bergman, the director, and Michael Lobell, the producer, present the idea to him? Wouldn't you simply assume that he would turn it down flat? Indeed there was a scandal when Brando was filming *The Freshman* in Toronto, and told a

Canadian reporter that the film was no good and that he would probably quit acting forever after he completed it. A few weeks later he gave another interview, saying he was misunderstood and retracting his review of the movie—which is, in fact, very good and in which he gives a performance that makes you wonder how wit can seem so deep.

I wonder if Brando took this role in the first place out of a certain contempt for his own past, out of a willingness to satirize Don Corleone. He has always been ambivalent about his triumphs; remember that when he won an Academy Award for Corleone he sent the mysterious Sacheen Littlefeather to reject it? In preparing for *The Freshman*, I imagine he invented most of his own bits of actor's business—and in the moment when he offers the nuts there is a deliberate echo of a scene in *The Formula*, when he offers M&Ms to a visitor. There is a lot in *The Freshman* to evoke echoes from the past, including a throwaway line, half-swallowed, which if completed might have turned out to be "I could have been a contender," and another moment, the last, when he walks away from the camera like the Little Tramp grown big.

What am I getting at here? I realize I am finding such large portents in such small gestures that I run the risk of seeming to satirize film criticism, just as Brando teases *The Godfather*. You can only go so far with parallels between M&Ms and chestnuts. And yet I am serious. As I watched *The Freshman*, I grew amazed at how directly the Brando performance was affecting me, at how important, how authoritative he seemed on the screen. I asked myself what he was doing, and how.

Maybe silence and stillness have something to do with it. Today's movies are shrill and up-front, and they assault our eyes and ears. Performances are filled with histrionics. Now here is Brando, an actor whose great tool in these later performances is immobility and mystery. We have to come to him. He makes us wait. Each line is thought about before it is pronounced. He comes reluctantly out of shadow. He will not be hurried. He must be paid attention to. He does not court our approval, he is not eager to please, he does not care if we like him. And so we hang on every word.

The Black New Wave

CANNES, France—The French New Wave was a rebirth of French films in the early 1960s, and the German New Wave represented the same process in Germany in the 1970s. Now black American filmmakers are developing a new stylistic and personal vision that reached critical mass at the Cannes Film Festival. In May of 1991, here in the incongruous setting of the French Riviera, far from the urban settings of most of their films, the black New Wave came of age.

The "nouvelle vogue" in France began in the late fifties with a trickle of films that seemed to speak in a different voice, with more freshness and confidence, than those around them. By the early sixties, it was a flood. The same process seems to be taking place thirty years later with a new wave of American films by and about black people.

The black New Wave was predicted by the arrival of Spike Lee on the scene in 1986. His *She's Gotta Have It*, which premiered here in the Director's Fortnight of the Cannes Film Festival, was a break with the two central paths of black-oriented films of earlier years: It was neither a self-conscious socially responsible film, bearing a liberal message, nor was it an exploitation film, using sex and violence as its currency.

Even more importantly—and this is the key element in the black New Wave—it was a film that considered the African-American experience in its own terms, instead of filtering it through implied white values, or tailoring it for white audiences. Lee's film was about a black woman who had the personal and sexual independence more often associated with men, and was delighted by the ways that the men in her life were confounded by that.

As a film critic who had seen virtually every "black film" of the past twenty years, I felt at once I was seeing something new here: a film made not only by blacks, and about blacks, but for blacks. So many of the other black films seemed to be trying to force themselves into white mainstream categories. As a white viewer, I found Lee's approach incomparably more interesting than those tortured "crossover" films that seemed to be translated into an idiom that didn't belong anywhere.

In the late eighties, Lee consolidated his approach. There was *School Daze*, a zany and yet dead-serious musical comedy set on campus of a black university, and frankly confronting the issue of skin pigmentation in a story involving lighter and darker skinned African-Americans. This was a taboo subject among black filmmakers until Lee's films; perhaps it was thought to be impolitic to mention the subject when whites were listening. But *School Daze* was not made in reference to whites; all of its characters and conflicts involved black characters.

Lee's *Do the Right Thing* (1989), the most important American film of recent years, did confront black-white relationships, in its famous story of a black New York neighborhood and an Italian-American pizzeria owner who is still in business there. The movie's characters said out loud what people in such situations really do say and think, and it ended in violence, with the death of a young black man and the burning of the pizzeria. Yet it was a film of hope, because it was based not on hatred, but on empathy. I wrote at the time, and still believe, that it was impossible for any open-minded viewer of either race to leave the movie without more empathy for the members of the other race.

That is the key to Lee's work, and one of the central facts of the black New Wave which his films have inspired. He has moved on beyond the ritual charges of racism, beyond the image of wronged and angry black characters, to a new plateau of sophistication on which there is room for good and bad characters of all races, on which racism is seen not as a knee-jerk response to skin color, but as a failure of empathy—a failure of the ability to imagine the other person's point of view.

Spike Lee is sometimes perceived in popular journalistic shorthand as an angry young man. He is not. Yes, he feels anger, but it does not define him. He is the most open-minded of filmmakers, as illustrated by his latest film, *Jungle Fever*, in which two of the most sympathetic characters happen to be whites. The film also illustrates the way he allows his black characters the freedom to be all kinds of people—good, bad, intelligent, stupid—instead of limiting themselves to the approved Hollywood black categories of earlier years.

Look at the black family in *Jungle Fever*: an architect (Wesley Snipes), his brother, a crackhead (Samuel L. Jackson), their parents, the sanctimonious Reverend Doctor (Ossie Davis), and his long-suffering wife (Ruby Dee). Lee is not constrained by categories. He does not fall into the easy trap of making the Davis character a conventionally good older man, but shows him blinded and limited by his self-righteousness. And by creating two brothers whose walks in life have been radically different, he is able to dramatize the way many black American families bridge the gap between poverty and the new professional and middle classes. The best scene in the film shows the architect, with his briefcase and Brooks Brothers suit, descending into the hell of a crack house in search of his brother.

Spike Lee is the director whose arrival heralded the black New Wave, as Goddard and Truffaut launched the new wave in France, and Fassbinder and Herzog gave rebirth to the German cinema. But at the Cannes festival this year the African-American presence was so strong that the trade papers ran headlines about "black power on the Riviera," and every Paris and London newspaper wrote about the phenomenon.

On one night, for example, there were two big post-screening parties in town, both for films by black Americans. In a nightclub up in town, rap artist Ice Cube performed in a disco jam-packed with people celebrating the premiere of *Boyz N the Hood*, the extraordinary new film by twenty-three-year-old John Singleton. Down on the beach, there was a celebration for Bill Duke's *A Rage in Harlem*, a romantic comedy based on one of the books of Harlem crime novelist Chester Himes.

At the *Boyz* party, I found myself sitting next to Frank Price, president of Columbia Pictures and the man who gave Singleton, then twenty-two and still in film school, the green light to write and direct the film.

"When John came in and started to talk about his ideas," Price said, "I was reminded of another kid who walked into my office once—Steven Spielberg." Singleton wanted to make a film about a bright black kid who grows up in South Central Los Angeles, who lives in the middle of gang violence and the other usual ghetto problems, who is surrounded by ways to go wrong, but who is raised by a father who takes his responsibilities seriously. The movie, which played out of competition in a category called "Un Certain Regard," was by general agreement the most talked-about and well-liked film at Cannes this year, and Price seemed pleased with himself for having placed a wise bet on Singleton.

The *Rage in Harlem* party, down at the beach, was besieged by so many paparazzi it was almost impossible to get in. I was glad I'd had a chance to talk to some of the guests more quietly, a couple of nights earlier, in one of those endless Cannes conversations at La Pizza, down by the harbor, which stays open all night. At the table were Bill Duke, an actor and TV director who was making his film debut with *A Rage in Harlem*, his leading actress Robin Givens, and Duke's agent, Hillard Elkins. We were talking about the new kind of American black cinema that seems to be emerging.

A Rage in Harlem is an example: a comedy and a love story, with a wide variety of characters, all of them black, and a freedom to portray a complete range of behavior without playing to an unseen, hypothetical white audience. One problem Duke said he was frustrated by, as an actor, is the pious Hollywood reluctance to cast blacks in negative roles: "We can't get those good roles as villains because they're afraid of offending us." The prime role of Dr. Hannibal Lecter in *The Silence of the Lambs*, for example, was fiercely competed for by two gifted actors—Morgan Freeman and Lou Gossett—but liberal Hollywood's wisdom was that a black shouldn't be seen in such a negative light. So the role, and a certain Oscar nomination, went to Anthony Hopkins.

One of the freedoms of the black New Wave is to be able to create black villains, such as Danny Glover's "Easy Money" in *A Rage in Harlem*, or Samuel L. Jackson's crackhead in *Jungle Fever*—a character so shattered he terrorizes his own mother, in a performance so strong it won the Cannes prize for best supporting actor.

Lee, Singleton, and Duke were all at Cannes, but back home in the U.S., no less than nineteen films directed by African-Americans were set for release between then and year's end. "That's more than in the previous decade," Lee said during a Cannes panel discussion, exaggerating, but not by much. Already in 1991, Mario Van Peebles's *New Jack City* has emerged as a genuine box office and critical success, with grosses of around $45 million and praise for the strong performance of Wesley Snipes as a murderous drug kingpin. Now here was Snipes again, in *Jungle Fever*, as a white-collar architect, showing the growing range of roles available to the top black actors.

Other movies, such as the low-budget, surprisingly strong *Straight Out of Brooklyn*, the *Diner*-style coming-of-age movie *Hangin' With the Homeboys*, and Robert Townsend's *Five Heartbeats*, about a five-man singing group, are also in the mix. Some of them make it, like *New Jack City*. Some don't: Audiences revealed little desire to see *Five Heartbeats*. Yet the secret financial weapon of many black films is their above-average performance in the video rental and sales markets. Before she made *Ghost*, for example, Whoopi Goldberg starred in several box-office flops. Producers kept hiring her because her films all made money in video. Even *The Telephone*, a film she personally disliked and which hardly opened theatrically, was a top video moneymaker.

In looking at theatrical receipts, however, you still hear the key word "crossover" in any discussion of black-oriented films. Will a film cross over and attract white filmgoers, or will it play mostly to blacks? Recent experience seems to indicate that the less a film consciously tries to cross over, the more luck it is likely to have. White audiences are tired of lectures and message pictures about racism, or themes toned down to make them more palatable. But many are interested in the black American experience itself. They won't pay for preachy parables, but when directors focus on realistic black characters and their lives, there is a white audience out there for them.

The proof in that seems to be *Boyz N the Hood*, which has the potential for the kind of success enjoyed in earlier years by *Stand By Me, Diner, Mean Streets, The Last Picture Show, American Graffiti*, and all the other movies about strong-willed young people on the brink of manhood. One night late in the festival, I went out to dinner with Singleton and we talked about the possible career paths for a twenty-three-year-old with a hit picture. He mentioned two directors as his examples: Spike Lee and Steven Spielberg. He said he likes pictures that made people laugh, and made them cry.

And that's it, really. Movies are not an appropriate medium for political and intellectual messages. The written word is best for those. Movies make you feel. If it is possible to generalize about black-oriented films of ear-lier years, it was that too many second thoughts went into them. The people who financed, produced, distributed, and made them were too concerned with "proper" images, with messages, with ideological correctness, with crossing over.

The black New Wave takes its tone from Lee, who is as happy to offend blacks as whites, who allows his characters the freedom to be flawed and relieves them of the obligation to be exemplary. Lee's films are about emotion, and about universal desires and needs. They are not self-conscious. They are not rewritten to respond to the feelings, real or imagined, of white viewers. Each of the previous "new waves" in film history has given voice to the generation disenfranchised by the film establishment that came before it. The black New Wave breathes that same free air.

The Liberation of *Thelma & Louise*

Chicago, June 11, 1991—Women all over the country are going to see *Thelma & Louise* with a rare enthusiasm, despite Hollywood's conventional wisdom that men make most of the moviegoing decisions. To understand how they're connecting with the movie, look at an afternoon screening in a theater like Chicago's 900 N. Michigan complex, in the basement of Bloomingdale's. The largely female crowd isn't made up of teen-agers, but more mature generations—married women, professionals, older women, visitors to the city. They love this movie. They cheer it, they get teary-eyed, and they bring their friends to see it.

In *Thelma & Louise*, maybe they're getting the same kind of charge that men got more than twenty years ago with *Easy Rider* or *Butch Cassidy and the Sundance Kid*. This at last is a female version of the genres that defined the late sixties: the road movie, the buddy picture, the outlaw against society. Was there an unwritten law that only men could star in those formulas? Not according to *Thelma & Louise*.

When I saw the movie, about seven weeks ago, I reacted to it strongly. It had the kind of passion and energy I remembered from the rebel movies of the late sixties and early seventies. My only major criticism of the film was the complaint of someone who really loved it: I thought the very last shot, the freeze-frame and fade-out of their T-bird in mid-air should have been held longer so that its meaning could sink in and provide a more complete catharsis. The movie fades out with unseemly haste, and then cuts immediately to music, flashbacks, and the end credits, all to distract us from what modern Hollywood dreads the most, an unhappy ending.

The people in the audience don't think of that ending as unhappy, and, of course it isn't. It's a victory for Thelma and Louise, an existential shout of defiance. Their final act is directed not only at pigs like that truck driver who wriggles his tongue at them, but even at paternalistic do-gooders like the cop who wants to save them. They are shouting into the maw of the universe that men are no longer going to make their decisions for them.

Some critics have found *Thelma & Louise* dated, a throwback to the sixties. I don't think it's dated; I think it's simply overdue. The antiestablishment films of the 1966–76 period were typically about men who told society

to go screw itself. Along the way, sometimes, a few women were allowed into the stories, mostly to provide the heroes with carnal relief, sympathy, and admiration. Does anybody remember the women in *Easy Rider*? What was the importance, exactly, of Katharine Ross in *Butch Cassidy*?

The sixties are long over now. But, hold on—did they ever occur for women? Who, exactly, was liberated during that liberating decade? Judging by the women of all ages who relate so strongly to *Thelma & Louise*, there is still a real hunger for all of the basic elements of those classic movies of rebellion against society, but translated this time into women's terms. The original screenplay by Callie Khouri was written in response, she says, to countless movies in which men were the free agents and women were decorations or sidekicks. It was time for the women to get the last word, for a change.

Consider what happens in *Thelma & Louise*. A drunken rapist gets blown away. A slimebag truck driver, who harasses the heroines with his obscene sideshow, gets his truck blown to smithereens. A husband who is smugly indifferent to the needs and voice of his wife finds out he has no idea who he was married to. A lot of cops get outsmarted and made into fools. And the women get the last word.

One critic complained sanctimoniously that if there was a movie where men did to women what *Thelma & Louise* do to men, there'd be protests of outrage. Excuse me? Men have been making victims out of women in hundreds of movies for years. It's an old story in our society: Oppressive behavior is permitted from the oppressor class, but becomes offensive if practiced by the formerly oppressed. Besides, *Thelma & Louise* isn't a realistic portrait of behavior, anyway; it's a parable. You can tell that by the spare, empty landscape the women drive through, by the visceral American symbolism of their T-bird convertible, and by the gallery of male stereotypes they encounter on the road.

One of the most mysteriously beautiful scenes in the entire film, for me, is the one where Susan Sarandon encounters an old, old man with a deeply weather-lined face, who gazes out impassively into the landscape. She hunkers down next to him for a long time, just looking at him. He does not seem to notice. Finally she gives him all of her jewelry in return for his hat. What's going on here?

What does this trade represent? The way I see it, she is gazing with consuming curiosity at a man who has been a man for a long time, and wondering what made him that way, and why. He is as alien to her, staring out into the distance, as the statues on Easter Island are to us, and seems to have been gazing at the horizon nearly as long. She gives away her jewels—traditional men's presents to women—in return for his hat, a traditional man's present to himself, as if to put on his knowledge.

All of the men in this movie are equally inscrutable to the women. Freud is said to have asked, "Woman! What does she want? Great God almighty, what does she want?" To which *Thelma & Louise* would seem to reply, "Man! We know what he wants. But, great God almighty, is that all he wants? Isn't there any more to him than that?"

Geena Davis's big scene in the movie is one in which she discovers that, for some men, there really isn't any more than that. After the two women are on the road, she meets a young stud, an attractive outlaw who satisfies her sexually for the first time in her life. She walks around moony-faced for a scene or two, delighted by what she has discovered about her body, only to find out that a man can give that kind of pleasure and *still* not give a damn about her. She trusted him because he was a good lover, and he knew that and took advantage of it.

In rebel movies of this nature—especially the ground-breaking ones—audiences shout with delight because they see taboos being broken, words said aloud for the first time, forbidden thoughts finally expressed. Peter Fonda flips the bird to the redneck in *Easy Rider*, and Jack Nicholson tells the waitress exactly how he wants his toast in *Five Easy Pieces*, and the audience cheers because its frustrations are being released. But today's women are still frustrated, and movies have not been a release for them.

The feminist revolution has taken place too largely in whining books and magazine articles and encounter groups, in attenuated novels of complaint, and sad dirges by masochistic folksingers. It hasn't benefitted from the kind of release that a good popular movie can provide, when society is taken by the throat and shaken. It is not enough for a female character to negotiate a moral victory, as she usually does in movies with a feminist angle. Women audiences are hungry for female characters who *get away* with something, like the guys always seem to. When that gasoline tanker goes up in flames, it's vengeance, but it's also outlaw behavior that women characters rarely get away with in the movies.

Women don't want to see men killed meaninglessly, as so many men seem to enjoy seeing random violence in "their" movies, but they do want to see revenge, when it's deserved. And *Thelma & Louise* is a revenge tragedy wrapped in humor, discovery, and rebellion. There have been a lot of movies in which women acted "like" men, but usually the characters seemed like men in drag—Shelley Winters with a cigar and a machine gun, or Angie Dickinson as a cop. In *Thelma & Louise*, we are seeing actual everyday women—a housewife and a waitress—taste the heady freedoms that the movies usually reserve for Clint Eastwood, Jack Nicholson, or Robert Redford.

The film was directed by Ridley Scott. Surprise has been expressed within the movie business that Scott could make a movie about people; he's supposed to be a special-effects expert. But look at his *Blade Runner* and you will see some of the same sensibility expressed here. That movie contained a creature played by Sean Young, called a "replicant," who looked and moved and felt and talked like a real woman, but was a robot. Except . . . she felt she had a right to be alive, to be treated like a real human being. *Thelma & Louise* is about the liberation of two replicants.

Not long ago I found myself discussing *Thelma & Louise* on the Oprah Winfrey program. "It's a female buddy movie," I said, meaning that as praise. "It isn't either," a woman in the audience replied. "It's about sisterhood!" She got a rousing burst of applause. I wanted to ask her what the difference was between buddyhood and sisterhood, and then I realized something: That was the whole point.

Costner Is Not the Bad Guy in *Robin Hood*'s Failure

June 18, 1991—And so all of a sudden Kevin Costner is a schmuck. The hero of last March, the smiling young man holding the golden Academy Award, has overnight become the target of nearly unanimous critical pans because he dared to appear in a bad movie named *Robin Hood*. The actor whose social conscience was applauded after *Dances With Wolves* has been transformed into a tiresome preacher. The man whose vision led to the Oscar for best picture of the year has now become, in the words of one critic, an actor who swings on a rope as if he's afraid he'll fall off.

I didn't admire *Robin Hood, Prince of Thieves* either. I thought it was dreary, murky, too violent, and lacking in magic. I could not see the need for an attempted rape involving Maid Marian—especially not a rape with the camera right down there on the floor for the point-of-view shot when her legs are forced apart. I still do not quite understand how a legend so filled with enchantment and lighthearted heroism could be transformed into a movie only marginally more upbeat than *The Doors*.

And yet that doesn't make Costner a bad guy. He is an actor in an unsuccessful movie, not a criminal, and some of the sarcasm leveled at this film seems almost personal, as if the critics had been forced to sit through dreck from Costner for years and years. Out in Hollywood, Warner Bros. is chortling over the movie's opening grosses—$25 million on the first weekend—and believes *Robin Hood* has the potential to do well at the box office, despite the reviews. Executives claim they weren't surprised: The movie tested well, and if preview audiences loved it, then the bad press is more of a backlash against Costner than a fair assessment of the movie.

It could be a little of both. *Robin Hood, Prince of Thieves* is not a good movie—it drags, it's photographed in such gloom we can hardly see it, and the performances of the actors hit such divergent notes we almost seem to be channel-surfing. Movie preview audiences notoriously have short memories, and most of them may never have seen the Errol Flynn *Robin Hood*, let alone Sean Connery and Audrey Hepburn in *Robin and Marian*. I guess if they say they like the movie, they're telling the truth.

The nation's critics, on the other hand, have seldom been more unanimous in panning a film. Even the "good" reviews, like *USA Today*'s three-star rating, were filled with grumblings and complaints. Were the critics simply reporting the facts as they saw them? Or was there indeed some sort of backlash taking place, an impulse to put Costner back in his place now that he's won his Oscar?

Many of the reviews said Costner's act was growing tiresome; the critics were referring to his liberalism, his sensitivity, his political correctness (*Robin Hood* contains a feminist Marian and a heroic black sidekick). They complained that he was too thoughtful and intellectual as Robin Hood, and didn't have enough fun with the role. He couldn't win. He was attacked for attempting a British accent, for abandoning it, and for talking in a voice that was too soft no matter which accent he used. And in the cruelest barb of all, his costar, Alan Rickman, was credited with stealing the movie even while being blamed for acting in another style altogether.

Some of these criticisms are valid. But that doesn't mean Kevin Costner is a bad actor or a bad man, and indeed I think the failure of *Robin Hood* can largely be attributed to two Hollywood practices that have victimized many actors: Miscasting, and rushing the production schedule.

First, miscasting: Kevin Costner is simply not the right actor to play Robin Hood. By all reports, that was his own opinion for a long time, and he turned down this movie repeatedly. What finally got him into it was the hiring of his friend, Kevin Reynolds, as the director—Reynolds, who directed him in *Fandango* when he was still getting established, and who did a virtuoso job as the second unit director on the buffalo hunt sequence in *Dances With Wolves*. Perhaps Costner thought that Reynolds, having transformed the buffalo scene, would perform similar magic in Sherwood Forest.

Why was Costner thought to be appropriate casting for *Robin Hood*? Maybe because his agent, like all agents, thought that by definition his client was right for any desirable role. Maybe because the screenplay was being slanted toward a "modern" point of view that reflected some of Costner's concerns. No doubt because after *The Untouchables*, *Field of Dreams*, *Bull Durham*, and the buzz on *Dances With Wolves*, he was seen as an authentic movie hero. Many of the reviews compared him with Gary Cooper, and maybe nobody stopped to consider that Cooper would have made a lousy Robin Hood.

In any event, Costner was seriously miscast. All of us are born with certain attributes and skills—with notes we can play and other notes we can't reach. Costner, who has had perfect pitch in many of his roles (who else could have pulled off *Field of Dreams?*) simply does not have a swash-buckling, extroverted action hero in his repertory. A less subtle, more physical actor like Kurt Russell, Dennis Quaid, or Patrick Swayze might have been more appropriate.

While pondering the mysteries of casting, consider the surprise cameo by Sean Connery in the movie. It gets a shout of joy from the audience—the most relaxed and sincere cheer in the whole film. Maybe that's because by his very presence Connery suggests the kind of acting note that is appropriate in any film with *Robin Hood* in its title. Connery is the kind of actor whose presence suggests he can get away with murder. Costner, by nature, is more of a Hamlet—a man at home with doubts and moral dilemmas.

If there had been more time to consider and prepare the movie, perhaps Costner or his advisers would have arrived at this realization themselves, and found a graceful way to exit. But *Robin Hood, Prince of Thieves* was engaged in a race to the box office with another *Robin Hood* project, and there was no time for second thoughts. Costner started shooting almost immediately after finishing *Dances With Wolves*, with no rehearsal time, no time for screen-testing his look or listening to his accent, no time to try different approaches to the role. Given no time to prepare, Costner found himself playing Robin Hood as a character a great deal like Costner—modest, friendly, accommodating, sincere, and a little doubtful. Those are not qualities Robin Hood should have anything to do with.

Not long ago, in Hollywood, I was talking with an actor who told me, "Paramount wants me to do something in a couple of months." What, I asked? "They don't know. They say they'll come up with something." That is an attitude symptomatic of the second Hollywood practice that may have hurt *Robin Hood*—rushing the production schedule.

Was the screenplay ever really finished? Was it written to have a tone and a consistent approach, or was it cobbled to meet the demands of second-guessers? Were rewrites being done on a daily basis, and basic concepts being argued even as the movie was being shot? That's what has been reported. Everyone who has seen the movie—Costner included—has agreed that Alan Rickman, as the Sheriff of Nottingham, seems to be appearing in a different movie than anyone else in the cast. (To add to the irony, it is a more entertaining movie.) How did that happen? How did Costner get lines of stolid, plodding nobility, while Rickman was written as a hip, bitchy villain who would have been at home in *Batman*?

We've all heard the story of *Dances With Wolves*, about how the screenplay was turned down by five major studios before one finally took a chance on it. The advantage to that process was that the screenplay was *finished* by the time it went into production: Everybody could read it and see what was there. With *Robin Hood, Prince of Thieves*, the concept and the casting apparently blinded everyone to the truth that there was no movie there. No reason, even a crass commercial one, why this movie had to be made at this time.

And now the movie has been released and whether it sinks or swims, it will be marked down as a failure for Kevin Costner. The swan has been turned into an ugly duckling. There is a tendency to blame the most visible and highly paid participant in any movie for whatever goes wrong with it, but in this case perhaps Costner was simply at the end of a chain of errors and miscalculations.

I do not think he has become a bad actor overnight. I have not grown tired of him. I still like what he does. Nothing in *Robin Hood* diminishes my admiration for his talents. I gave the movie a negative review because it was a bad movie. That doesn't make Costner a bad guy.

Will Hollywood learn a lesson from this film? Will it stop rushing half-baked projects into production in order to meet deadlines with disaster? I doubt it. But I think it will be a long while before Kevin Costner allows himself to be bamboozled into another one of these flim-flams.

How to Attend a Film Festival

Yes, you can attend a film festival. Not just the one in your hometown, but even the glittering events in Venice, Berlin, and Toronto. Almost all film festivals are open to the public, a fact the public does not always realize. For movie fans, the combination of a film festival and a holiday destination make an attractive package—going to the movies gets you in off the slopes or the beaches and allows you to meet fellow movie buffs instead of boring ordinary people.

The Cannes Festival, held in the middle of May every year, is of course the largest and most famous in the world, but also one of the most difficult to get credentials for. It's essentially a trade fair. Don't even think of going unless you have connections. Other festivals, however, actively encourage people who aren't in the business. Of the big ones I've attended, my favorites are Montreal in August and Toronto in September, which are the two big "destination" festivals in North America. Both are particularly eager to accommodate visitors, and offer ticket and hotel packages.

The Telluride festival over the Labor Day weekend, the Sundance (Park City) festival in January and Mill Valley in October are smaller fests dedicated to the discovery of offbeat and independent films. And the Hawaii festival, in late November and early December, has an aloha spirit all its own.

Most of the big-city festivals in the U.S. cater mostly to people who live in the cities themselves, and attract fewer out-of-town visitors than the Canadian festivals. The big five are New York, Chicago, Los Angeles, San Francisco, and Seattle. The smaller U.S. festivals, like Denver, Cleveland, Dallas, Houston, Philadelphia, and Miami, likewise, are mostly aimed at locals.

Overseas, the Edinburgh Film Festival is part of the amazing explosion of festivals that takes over the town for most of the month of August. The movies have to compete with theater, classical music, dance, books, and a fringe theater festival that attracts more than five hundred companies. The Venice Film Festival, in late summer, is an opportunity to visit the beautiful city and sample the Bellinis at the Hotel Excelsior and the gossip at the Lion Bar.

After Cannes, the most important European festival is either Venice or Berlin, but many smaller festivals, such as San Sebastian, Cambridge, and Deauville, have created niches for themselves. (Deauville, in September, is dedicated to American movies and always has a few big Hollywood stars hanging around.) Most of the countries of Eastern Europe have festivals that actively recruit Western visitors.

There are also smaller regional film festivals in many American cities, and specialized festivals devoted to science fiction and fantasy, animation, and documentaries. Dusty and Joan Cohl, founders of the Toronto festival, even launched a Floating Film Festival with the Florida-based Holland-American lines in 1991, and plan to sail again the first week of February 1992.

Here's where to write for information on some of the key festivals, arranged alphabetically, as compiled with the research assistance of Monica Eng and with information from *Variety*, the show biz bible:

Baltimore. March.
c/o Museum of Art, Baltimore, MD 21218.

Berlin. Early February.
Budapester Str. 50, D-1000, West Berlin 30, West Germany.

Brussels. Late January.
Place Madou 8, Bte. 5, Brussels, Belgium.

Cambridge. July.
P.O. Box 17, Cambridge CB2 3PF England.

Cannes. Mid-May.
71 rue du Faubourg St. Honore, 75008 Paris, France.

Chicago. October.
415 N. Dearborn, Chicago, IL 60610.

Cleveland. April.
6200 SOM Center Road, C20, Cleveland, OH 44139.

Cork. October.
c/o Triskel Arts Center, Tobin Street, Cork, Ireland.

Dallas. USA Film Festival, Box 3105, Dallas, TX 75275.

Deauville (American Cinema).
Early September.
33 Ave. MacMahon, 75017 Paris, France.

Denver. Mid-October.
Box 17508, Denver, CO 80217.

Edinburgh. August.
Film House, 88 Lothian Road, Edinburgh, EH3 9BZ, Scotland.

Gdansk (Polish Film Festival).
September.
Piwna 22, P.O. Box Nr. 192, 80–831
Gdansk, Poland.

Hawaii (Films of Asia-Pacific).
Late November, early December.
c/o East-West Center, 1777 East-
West Road, Honolulu, HI 96848.

Houston.   Late April.
Box 56566, Houston, TX 77256.

Jerusalem.   June.
P.O. Box 8561, Jerusalem 91083,
Israel.

Los Angeles.   April.
AFI Festivals, 2021 N. Western
Ave., Los Angeles, CA 90027.

London.   November.
National Film Theater, South Bank,
London SE1, England.

Melbourne.   Mid-June.
G.P.O. Box 2760 Ee, Melbourne,
Victoria 3001, Australia.

Miami.   Early February.
7600 Red Road, Suite 307, Miami
FL 33143.

Mill Valley.   Early October.
80 Lomita Drive, #20, Mill Valley,
CA 94941.

Montreal.   Late August, early
September.
1455 rue de Maisonneuve Ouest,
Montreal, Quebec H3G 1M8,
Canada.

Moscow.   July.
Sovinfest, 10 Khokhlovsky Per-
eulok, 109028 Moscow, USSR.

New York.   Mid-September.
Film Society of Lincoln Center, 140
W. 65th St., New York, NY 10023.

Palm Springs (Comedy).
Mid-January.
401 S. Pavilion Way, Box 1786,
Palm Springs, CA 92263.

Philadelphia (Philafilm).   July.
121 N. Broad St., Suite 618,
Philadelphia, PA 19101.

San Francisco.   Early May.
San Francisco Film Society, 1650
Fillmore St., San Francisco, CA
94115.

San Sebastian.   September.
Apartado Correos 397, Box 397,
20080 San Sebastian, Spain.

Seattle.   May.
801 E. Pine St., Seattle, WA 98122.

Sundance (Park City, Utah).
Third week in January.
c/o Sundance Institute, 19 Exchange
Pl., Salt Lake City, UT 84111.

Sydney.   Mid-June.
P.O. Box 25, Glebe, N.S.W. 2037,
Australia.

Telluride, Colorado.
Labor Day weekend.
c/o National Film Preserve, Box
B1156, Hanover, NH 03755.

Tokyo.   September.
No. 3, Asano Daisan Bldg., 2-4-19
Ginza Chou-ku, Tokyo 104, Japan.

Toronto (Festival of Festivals).
Early September.
69 Yorkville, Suite 205, Toronto,
ON. M5R 1B8, Canada.

Vancouver.   Mid to late
September.
303–788 Beatty St., Vancouver, BC
V6B 2M1, Canada.

Venice.   Early September.
CA. Giustinian, San Marco, 30124
Venice, Italy.

A Movie Lover's Source List

Where can I find this movie?

Every year I receive letters from readers of the *Companion* who complain they can't find many titles in their local video stores. Although many communities have stores that take pride in the range of their stock, other video stores practice a hit-oriented philosophy and stock multiple copies of the latest hits instead of extending their range a little.

It is possible, however, to rent or buy virtually every one of the thousands of movies on tape and laserdisc. Updated and expanded for 1992, here is a list of companies that rent or sell videos by mail. Many of them have toll-free 800 numbers and accept credit cards over the phone. Most of them issue catalogs, and a few of the catalogs are particularly informative.

Barr Digital. 2507 186th Ave. NE, Redmond, WA 98052. Laserdisc and technology experts who publish *BD Notebook* , a literate and detailed newsletter for serious laserdisc collectors. It's free if you purchase discs through Barr; otherwise it's $1 an issue and more than worth it. 1-800-274-7002. Fax 206-746-3536.

Complete Guide to Special Interest Videos. This massive six-hundred-page reference is a labor of love by James R. Spencer, who catalogs some seventy-five hundred videos in such categories as cars, business, computers, cooking, fishing, home improvement, travel, music, photography, language, and how-to. You can order through the catalog or use it to obtain videos through your local deal-er. It's $14.95 from James Robert Publishing, 3535 East Inland Empire Blvd., Ontario, CA 91764. 1-800-383-8811.

Facets Video. 1517 W. Fullerton, Chicago, IL 60614. The nation's leading specialists in foreign, classic, documentary, and independent films, plus a wide range of American films. Quality is a criterion; Facets does not stock potboilers. Their literate catalog ($4) has the page size of a tabloid newspaper, runs 242 pages, lists thousands of titles, including even obscure underground films. There are also smaller catalogs on foreign videos, of which they have the best stock in the nation, including some videos they produce themselves. They rent by mail every title in the catalog and sell many of them (VHS only; no Beta or discs). 1-800-331-6197, or in Illinois, 312-281-9075.

Home Film Festival. P.O. Box 2032, Scranton, PA 18501-9952. The original rent-by-mail people, with a large selection of titles that rent at $5 for one, $9 for two, $13 for three (plus shipping), and can be kept for three days. They ship to you via UPS; you mail tapes back by U.S. mail, in return packaging that is included. HFF gives a ten percent discount on purchases. For the 130-page catalog, call 1-800-258-3456, or, in Philadelphia, 1-800-633-3456.

J. & R. Frogg. 19126 Haynes St., #6, Reseda, CA 19335. This mail-order laserdisc dealer is hailed by reader Dan Buchan of Dickinson College for pricing many Criterion Collection titles at twenty-five percent off. (818-342-7886)

Ken Crane's LaserDisk. 14260 Beach Blvd., Westminster, CA 92683. Claims to stock all available laserdiscs, gives a ten percent discount, ships free via UPS. Issues periodic sixty-page catalogs, sometimes has special sale titles. 1-800-624-3078, or, in California, 1-800-626-1768.

The Knowledge Collection. c/o Video School House, 167 Central Ave., Pacific Grove, CA 93950. Specialists in "nontheatrical" videos, with 7,000 titles. Their 450-page catalog ($9.95) lists no less than 225 exercise and fitness videos, 175 cooking videos, lots of painting and sketching lessons, computer tutorials, foreign languages, hobbies, popular and classical music, and other titles ranging from *The Complete Guide to Beekeeping* to *The Man Who Skied Down Everest*. They rent by mail and sell. 1-800-345-1441.

Laser. c/o Stephen McGouldrick, 420 4th Ave., Beth, PA 18018. A newsletter specializing in the history and lore of movies on laserdisc, including the earliest days of the laser medium. McGouldrick is especially interested in the differences between various film-to-video transfers, inclusion of "lost" footage, etc. For a sample copy, call 215-758-9934 (from 9 P.M. to 11 A.M. and on Sundays, he says).

Laser Advantage. 1490 Lafayette St., Suite 305, Denver, CO 80218. Publishes a quarterly catalog including some hard-to-get discs by specialty distributors, plus discounts on overstocks. 1-303-894-8704.

Laser Disk Newsletter. Suite 428, 496 Hudson St., New York, NY 10014. A publication for fanatics about sound and picture quality, edited and published by Douglas Pratt, who seems to inspect every new disc a frame at a time. Comprehensive reviews, heavy on the technical specs, of most new laserdiscs. Pratt only reviews and does not sell. $3 for a sample copy or $35 a year.

Laser Scene. A monthly for Laservision enthusiasts edited by Scott A. Hughes, includes industry news and gossip, coverage of pricing policies, reviews, and essays on such topics as letterboxing, plus a guide to new releases. $25 a year from 386 Noe St., San Francisco, CA 94114.

Loonic Video. 2022 Taraval St., Suite 6427, San Francisco, CA 94116. Specialists in rare, unusual, and cult films, from the silents to today. Titles on the cover include *I Used My Body for Blackmail* and *Screaming Skull*; titles inside include priceless old Bob & Ray television shows, cartoons, vintage late late shows. All tapes are $15.95. 1-415-526-8070.

Metro Golden Memories. 5425 W. Addison St., Chicago, IL 60641. Specialists in rare movies and tapes of classic television shows; their $1 catalog includes old features, silents, serials, and such TV shows as "Amos 'n' Andy," "The Avengers," "Ozzie and Harriett," and just about any other vintage series. 1-312-736-4133.

Movies Unlimited. 6738 Castor Ave., Philadelphia, PA 19149. Their catalog is enormous; the 1988 edition was telephone-book-sized at 626 pages, cost $7.95 plus $2 shipping, and claimed to list over 20,000 titles, including VHS, Beta, and laserdiscs. Regular updates are issued during the year. Sales only. Orders at 1-800-523-0823,

or to order a catalog call the customer service line at 1-800-722-8398.

The Perfect Vision. This is a unique quarterly magazine, written by and for video and audio fanatics. No other publication has more exacting standards, and it's a must for operators of high-end home entertainment systems. Each issue contains some 150 tightly packed pages of articles about movies and video, technical, and artistic controversies, and reviews of new equipment. $6 an issue, $22 a year. Box 357, Sea Cliff, NY 11579, or order by credit card at 1-800-222-3201.

Picture Start. 221 E. Cullerton, 6th Floor, Chicago, IL 60616. Not a video source but a 16mm film rental company offering more than 750 independent, experimental, animated, documentary, and underground films, plus traveling programs of festival winners. Useful as a source of short subjects for a film society. The 120-page catalog is descriptive and illustrated. 312-326-6233; fax 312-326-6181.

Proud To Be . . . This is a mail-order company specializing in black-oriented videos. They publish a catalog and *The Collector's Corner* newsletter and have movies by and about blacks in such categories as children's films, sports, opera, theater, dance, comedy, gospel, reggae, and educational documentaries, as well as many features. One Kendall Square, Building 600, Suite 125, Cambridge, MA 02139; 1-617-868-8965.

Quality Comics and Video Store. Specializes in offbeat, cult, and B-grade materials, and describes itself as "a full-service cultural cesspool." They rent and sell by mail, and the catalog is seventy-five cents from 20 Division St., Somerville, NJ 08876; 1-201-526-3221.

Sight & Sound Laser Disks. 1275 Main St., Route 117, Waltham, MA 02154. In Japan, more people watch laserdiscs than tapes, and the quality

of some Japanese discs is legendary. This company imports Japanese pressings that are not available in America (most in the original language plus Japanese subtitles). American discs are also in stock. "The owners are dedicated in a way that true artists are dedicated," writes *MHC* reader Charles Thomas of Cambridge, Mass. Catalogs are issued periodically. 1-617-894-8633.

TLA Video. 521 S. Fourth, Philadelphia, PA 19147. Prides itself on a wide-ranging selection including many foreign films and independent features. The 178-page catalog ($2) includes helpful, knowledgeable thumbnail descriptions indicating that the TLA folks have viewed most of the videos themselves, which is likely, since they also run the Roxy Screening Room, a Philly repertory house. 1-215-922-3838, or 1-215-564-3838.

Video-Ink. This is a monthly newsletter about movies newly released on video, with lots of supporting information. For each film, there's a review, a "who's who" of previous credits by members of the cast, a "critic's consensus" of ten or so critics, a point score, plus cast and credits. No ads. Edited and largely written by Donald V. Hess and Frederick T. Mensch. $30 yearly from Video-Ink, Box 990, Kenosha, WI 53141. Credit cards or sample issues: 414-654-7727.

Viewfinders. P.O. Box 1665, Evanston, IL 60204. Publishes a 72-page *Catalog of Uncommon Video* including animation, art, ballet, classical music, documentaries, jazz, nature, and opera, and Beta is represented on many titles. 1-800-342-3342; in Illinois 312-869-0600.

Wok Talk. 85 River St., Suite 5, Waltham, MA 02154–8304. Imports new laserdiscs from Japan, including many titles not available in the U.S., and publishes a catalog of discs from overseas. Also stocks U.S. discs, at discounts. 1-617-894-8633.

Glossary of Movie Terms

This year's Glossary of Movie Terms has been much expanded and improved by the helpful contributions of many readers. Once again, it attempts to identify and label those clichés and inevitable developments that become wearying with familiarity to the faithful movie lover. Your suggestions for improvements will be welcomed for the next edition, and may be sent in c/o the publishers.

Ali MacGraw's Disease. Movie illness in which only symptom is that the sufferer grows more beautiful as death approaches.

Ark Movie. Dependable genre in which a mixed bag of characters are trapped on a colorful mode of transportation. Examples: *Airport* (airplane), *The Poseidon Adventure* (ocean liner), *Marooned* (space satellite), *The Cassandra Crossing* (train), *Aliens* (outer space), *The Hindenberg* (dirigible), *The Taking of Pelham One Two Three* (subway train), *The Abyss* (undersea station), and of course the best of them all, *Stagecoach*.

Baked Potato People. The nice, good, sweet little people who form a chorus in the hero's background, especially during any movie set in a mental home. Cf. *The Dream Team, Crazy People.* The lesson is always the same: It's the real world that's crazy, and the crazy people who speak real truth. (Inspired by a sign seen on a baked potato in a steak house: "I've been tubbed, I've been rubbed, I've been scrubbed. I'm lovable, huggable, and eatable!")

Balloon Rule. Good movies rarely contain a hot-air balloon. Most egregious recent use of a hot-air balloon: *Men Don't Leave*, where the heroine is cured of clinical depression by a ride in one. (Readers keep writing in with exceptions to this rule, including *Witness*, but the general principle still applies.)

Barroom Bum Slide. Most bar fights in the movies end with the loser being pushed so hard he slides halfway down the bar. In real life, this is impossible. (Douglas W. Topham, Woodland Hills, CA)

Beginning, The. Word used in the titles of sequels to movies in which everyone was killed at the end of the original movie, making an ordinary sequel impossible. Explains to knowledgeable filmgoers that the movie will concern, for example, what happened in the Amityville house before the Lutzes moved in. Other examples: The First Chapter, The Early Days, etc.

Body Switch Movie. The brain of one character somehow finds itself in the body of another. Requires actors to confront an actor's nightmare, i.e., acting as if they were another actor.

Box Rule. Beware movies advertised with a row of little boxes across the bottom, each one showing the face of a different international star and the name of a character (i.e., "Curt Jurgens as the Commandant"). Example: Most films made from Agatha Christie novels.

Brotman's Law. "If nothing has happened by the end of the first reel, nothing is going to happen." (Named for Chicago movie exhibitor Oscar Brotman.)

Camel, Slow-Moving. All camels in Middle Eastern thrillers are crossing the road for the sole purpose of slowing down a pursuit vehicle.

Caring Blanket Tuck-In. Effective in conveying the soft heart of an otherwise unappealing character. Cf. James Woods in *Cop*. Also used in scenes involving the hero, usually as a setup for a scene in which tucked-in child suddenly finds itself in great danger. Cf. Glenn Ford in *The Big Heat*. (Tony Whitehouse, Verbier, Switzerland)

Chase-and-Crash Scenes. Replaces the third act or any other form of plot resolution in the modern thriller. After the hero has left dozens of burning cars and trucks behind him, we never see emergency vehicles responding to the carnage. Despite working under a Wrong-Headed Commanding Officer, (q.v.), the hero cop is never called on the carpet because yesterday he drove his squad car through the walls of several warehouses.

Classic Car Rule. Whenever a beautiful classic car—usually the prized possession of an unsympathetic father—is introduced at the beginning of a film, that car will be wrecked by the end of it. (See *Risky Business, Ferris Bueller's Day Off, Coupe de Ville*, etc.)

CLIDVIC (Climb from Despair to Victory). Formula for *Rocky* and all the *Rocky* rip-offs. Breaks plot into three parts: (1) Defeat and despair; (2) Rigorous training, usually shown in the form of would-be MTV videos; (3) Victory, preferably ending in freeze-frame of triumphant hero.

Climbing Villain. Villains being chased at the end of a movie inevitably disregard all common sense and begin climbing up something—a staircase, a church tower, a mountain—thereby trapping themselves at the top. (Whitehouse)

Cole Rule, The. No movie made since 1977 containing a character with the first name "Cole" has been any good. (Exception: *Days of Thunder*, which was good but not all that good.)

Dead Teen-ager Movie. Generic term for any movie primarily concerned with killing teen-agers, without regard for logic, plot, performance, humor, etc. Often imitated, never worse than in the *Friday the 13th* sequels. Requires complete loss of common sense on the part of the characters. Sample dialogue: "All of our friends have been found horribly mutilated. It is midnight and we are miles from help. Hey, let's take off our clothes, walk through the dark woods, and go skinny-dipping!"

Deadly Change of Heart. When the cold heart of a villain softens and he turns into a good guy, the plot will quickly require him to be killed, usually after maudlin final words.

Detour Rule. In any thriller, it is an absolute certainty that every road detour sign is a subterfuge to kidnap the occupants of a car. Cf. Camel, Slow-Moving, "Hay Wagon!," etc.

Docudrama. TV term for extended-length program which stars a disease or social problem and costars performers willing to give interviews on how they experienced personal growth through their dramatic contact with same.

Doomed Crop-duster. Every crop-dusting plane in the history of the movies has crashed. (The famous scene in *North by Northwest* does not disprove this rule, because the plane was only masquerading as a crop-duster.)

Fallacy of the Predictable Tree. The logical error committed every time the good guy is able to predict exactly what the bad guy is going to do. For example, in *First Blood*, law enforcement officials are searching the woods for John Rambo. A cop pauses under a tree. Rambo drops on him. Question: Out of all the trees in the forest, how did Rambo know which one the guy would pause under?

Fallacy of the Talking Killer. The villain wants to kill the hero. He has him cornered at gunpoint. All he has to do is pull the trigger. But he always talks first. He explains the hero's mistakes to him. Jeers. Laughs. And gives the hero time to think his way out of the situation, or to be rescued by his buddy. Cf. most James Bond movies. (Gene Siskel)

Falling Villain. Suggested by reader Steve Dargitz of Ann Arbor, Mich., perhaps in response to the Glossary entry on the Climbing Villain (q.v.). The rule states that the villain must fall from a great height, and crash if possible through a glass canopy before landing on an automobile.

Far-off Rattle Movies. Movies in which the climactic scene is shot in a deserted warehouse, where far-off rattles punctuate the silence.

Feedback Rule. Every time anyone uses a microphone in a movie, it feeds back. (Arden J. Cooper, Warren, MI)

First Law of Funny Names. No names are funny unless used by W.C.

Fields or Groucho Marx. Funny names, in general, are a sign of desperation at the screenplay level. See "Dr. Hfuhruhurr" in *The Man with Two Brains*.

First Rule of Repetition of Names. When the same names are repeated in a movie more than four times a minute for more than three minutes in a row, the audience breaks out into sarcastic laughter, and some of the ruder members are likely to start shouting "Kirsty!" and "Tiffany!" at the screen. Cf. *Hellbound: Hellraiser II*.

Floating Luggage. In every scene where actors carry luggage, the luggage is obviously empty. They attempt, with pained expressions on their faces, to pretend the bags are heavy, and yet they can flick them around like feathers. (Tom Kirkpatrick)

"Food Fight!" Dialogue which replaced "Westward ho!" as American movies ended the long frontier trek and began to look inward for sources of inspiration.

"Fruit Cart!" An expletive used by knowledgeable film buffs during any chase scene involving a foreign or ethnic locale, reflecting their certainty that a fruit cart will be overturned during the chase, and an angry peddler will run into the middle of the street to shake his fist at the hero's departing vehicle.

(Of all the definitions in the glossary, this has become the most popular. It has been gratifying to be part of an audience where people unknown to me have cried out "Fruit cart!" at appropriate moments. The movie *Ski Patrol* even contained a "Siskel and Ebert Fruit Cart.")

Generation Squeeze. New Hollywood genre that tries to bridge the generation gap by creating movies which will appeal to teen-agers at the box office and to adults at the video rental counter. Typical plot device:

An adult becomes a teen-ager, or vice versa. Cf. *Like Father, Like Son*; *Hiding Out*; *Peggy Sue Got Married*; *Vice Versa*; *18 Again*; *Big*. Also sometimes masquerades as a movie apparently about adults, but with young actors in the "adult" roles. Cf. *No Man's Land, The Big Town*.

Hand-in-Hand Rule. In many Hollywood action pictures, the woman characters are incapable of fleeing from danger unless dragged by a strong man, who takes the woman's hand and pulls her along meekly behind him. This convention is so strong it appears even in films where it makes no sense, such as *Sheena*, in which a jungle-woman who has ruled the savage beasts since infancy is pulled along by a TV anchorman fresh off the plane.

"Hay Wagon!" Rural version of "Fruit Cart!" (q.v.). At the beginning of chase scenes through colorful ethnic locales, knowledgeable film buffs anticipate the inevitable scene in which the speeding sports car will get stuck on a narrow country lane behind a wagon overloaded with hay.

Hey! Cody! Rule. Bad guy has drop on good guy. Can pull trigger and kill him. Inevitably shouts "Hey! Cody!" (fill in name of good guy), after which good guy whirls, sees him, and shoots him first.

Hollywood Car. Looks like a normal automobile, but backfires after being purchased from used car lot by movie heroine who is starting out again in life and is on her own this time.

Hollywood Cop Car. Driven by the slovenly member of the team in all police versions of the Opposites in Collision plot (q.v.) Always unspeakably filthy, dented, rusty, and containing all of the cop's possessions in the back seat, as well as several weeks' worth of fast-food wrappers. Usually, but not necessarily, some kind of distinctive make or model (Gremlin, old Ford woody wagon, beat-up Caddy convertible, 4x4 van, etc.).

Hollywood Hospital. Where people go to die. Victim checks in, doesn't check out, because screen time is too valuable for characters to go into the hospital only to recover a few scenes later. Dialogue clue: When any seemingly able-bodied character uses the word "doctor," especially in a telephone conversation not intended to be overheard, he/she will be dead before the end of the film. (Siskel)

Horny Teen-ager Movie. Any film primarily concerned with teen-age sexual hungers, usually male. Replaced, to a degree, by Dead Teen-ager Movies (q.v.), but always popular with middle-aged movie executives, who like to explain to their seventeen-year-old starlets why the logic of the dramatic situation and the teachings of Strasberg require them to remove their brassieres. Cf. *Blame It on Rio, She's Out of Control*.

Idiot Plot. Any plot containing problems which would be solved instantly if all of the characters were not idiots. (Originally defined by Damon Knight.)

Impregnable Fortress Impregnated. Indispensable scene in all James Bond movies and many other action pictures, especially war films. The IFI sequence begins early in the picture, with long shots of a faraway fortress and Wagnerian music on the sound track. Eventually the hero gains entry to the fortress, which is inevitably manned by technological clones in designer uniforms. Sequence ends with destruction of fortress, as clones futilely attempt to save their marvelous machines. See *The Guns of Navarone*, etc.

Inevitable Sister. In any movie where the heroine catches her boyfriend dancing in public with another woman, and makes a big scene, the other woman invariably turns out to be the boyfriend's sister. Cf. *Mystic Pizza*, etc. (Stuart Cleland)

Intelligence. In most movies, "all that separates us from the apes." In *Sheena, Queen of the Jungle*, what we have in common with them.

Kookalouris. Name for a large sheet of cardboard or plywood with holes in it, which is moved back and forth in front of a light to illuminate a character's face with moving light patterns. Popular in the 1930s; back in style again with the movies of Steven Spielberg, who uses a kookalouris with underlighting to show faces that seem to be illuminated by reflections from pots of gold, buckets of diamonds, pools of fire, pirate maps, and radioactive kidneys.

Land Boom Rule. In any movie where there is a cocktail party featuring a chart, map, or model of a new real estate development, a wealthy property developer will be found dead inside an expensive automobile.

Law of Economy of Characters. Movie budgets make it impossible for any film to contain unnecessary characters. Therefore, all characters in a movie are necessary to the story— even those who do not seem to be. Sophisticated viewers can use this Law to deduce the identity of a person being kept secret by the movie's plot: This "mystery" person is always the only character in the movie who seems otherwise extraneous. Cf. the friendly neighbor in *The Lady in White*. (See also Unmotivated Close-up.)

Law of Inevitable Immersion. Whenever characters are near a body of water, the chances are great that one of them will jump, fall, or be pushed into it. If this does occur, it is inevitable that the other character(s) will also jump, fall, or be pushed in. See *Sullivan's Travels* (swimming pool), *La Dolce Vita* (Roman fountain), *Tom Jones* (pond), *A Room with a View* (rural stream), *Summertime* (Grand Canal), etc. (Cleland)

Lenny Rule. Named for the gentle giant in Steinbeck's *Of Mice and Men*, this rule dictates that if a film character is of less than normal intelligence or ability, he or she will inadvertently get into serious trouble during the film. (Cleland)

Long-Haired Woman Seen from Behind. When approached by hero, inevitably turns out to be a man.

Mad Slasher Movies. Movies starring a mad-dog killer who runs amok, slashing all of the other characters. The killer is frequently masked (as in *Halloween* and *Friday the 13th*), not because a serious actor would be ashamed to be seen in the role, but because then no actor at all is required; the only skills necessary are the ability to wear a mask and wield a machete. For additional reading, see *Splatter Movies*, by John ("mutilation is the message") McCarty.

Mirror Gimmick. Tired old cinematographic trick in which we think we are seeing a character, but then the camera pans and we realize we were only looking in a mirror. (Cooper)

Murphy's Law. In movies made before 1985, any character named "Murphy" was a cop, a priest, a drunk, a tough guy, or all of the above. *Murphy's Romance* was the first to break with this rule. Prior to TV's "Murphy Brown," all Murphys were male. Any character named Murphy will sooner or later be shown in a saloon or drinking heavily. (Robert F. Murphy, Providence, RI)

Myopia Rule. Little girls who wear glasses in the movies always tell the truth. Little boys who wear glasses in the movies always lie. (Siskel)

Myth of the Seemingly Ordinary Day. The day begins like any other, with a man getting up, having breakfast, reading the paper, leaving the house, etc. His activities are so uneventful they are boring. That is the tip-off. No genuine ordinary day can be allowed to be boring in a movie. Only seemingly ordinary days—which inevitably lead up to a shocking scene of violence, which punctuates the seeming ordinariness.

Nah Reflex. Character sees someone but can't believe his eyes, so shakes his head and says "Nah." Inevitably it is the person it couldn't be. (John Weckmueller, Menomonee, Wis.)

Near Miss Kiss. The hero and heroine are about to kiss. Their lips are a quarter of an inch apart—but then they're interrupted. (Topham)

Noble Savage Syndrome. Thrown into the company of a native tribe of any description, the protagonist discovers the true meaning of life and sees through the sham of modern civilization. Wisdom and sensitivity are inevitably possessed by any race, class, age group, or ethnic or religious minority that has been misunderstood. Such movies seem well intentioned at first glance, but replace one stereotype for another; the natives seem noble, but never real. They may be starving, but if they're noble and have a few good songs, why worry? (Murphy)

Odd Couple Formula. Seemingly incompatible characters are linked to each other in a plot which depends on their differences for its comic and dramatic interest. Cf. *Tango and Cash*, *Homer and Eddie*, *Lethal Weapon*, *Loose Cannons*. Essential that one member of each team be a slob, as revealed by presence of fast-food wrappers in back seat of his Hollywood Cop Car (q.v.).

Odds on Edge Rule. The odds that a car in real life will be able to travel any appreciable distance balanced on two wheels: 1 in 7 million. The odds that this will happen during a chase scene in a movie: 1 in 43.

Oops, Sorry! Rule. Character sees person from behind on street, thinks it is someone he knows, runs up and confronts person, inevitably to discover it is someone else. (Dan Saunders, Oakland, CA)

Principle of Evil Marksmanship. The bad guys are always lousy shots in the movies. Three villains with Uzis will go after the villain, spraying thousands of rounds that miss him, after which he picks them off with a handgun. (Jim Murphy)

Principle of Pedestrian Pathology. Whenever a character on foot is being pursued by one in a car, the pedestrian inevitably makes the mistake of running down the middle of the street, instead of ducking down a narrow alley, into a building, behind a telephone pole, etc. All that saves such pedestrians is the fact that in such scenes the character on foot can always outrun the car. (Cleland)

Rising Sidewalk. No female character in an action film can flee more than fifty feet before falling flat on her face. Someone then has to go back and help her up, while the monster/villain/enemy gains ground. (James Portanova, Fresh Meadows, NY)

Seeing-Eye Man. Function performed by most men in Hollywood feature films. Involves a series of shots in which (1) the man sees something, (2) he points it out to the woman, (3) she then sees it too, often nodding in agreement, gratitude, amusement, or relief. (First identified by Linda Williams.)

Semi-Obligatory Lyrical Interlude (Semi-OLI). Scene in which soft focus and slow motion are used while a would-be hit song is performed on the sound track and the lovers run through a pastoral setting.

Common from the mid-1960s to the mid-1970s; replaced in 1980s with the Semi-Obligatory Music Video (q.v.).

Semi-Obligatory Music Video (Semi-OMV). Three-minute sequence within otherwise ordinary narrative structure, in which a song is played at top volume while movie characters experience spasms of hyperkinetic behavior and stick their faces into the camera lens. If a band is seen, the Semi-OMV is inevitably distinguished by the director's inability to find a fresh cinematic approach to the challenge of filming a slack-jawed drummer.

Sequel. A filmed deal.

Seven Minute Rule. In the age of the seven-minute attention span (inspired by the average length between TV comemrcials), action movies aimed at teen-agers are constructed out of several seven-minute segments. At the end of each segment, another teen-ager is dead. When all the teen-agers are dead (or, if you arrived in the middle, when the same dead teen-ager turns up twice), the movie is over.

Short Time Syndrome. Applies to prison, war, or police movies, where the hero only has a few more days until he is free, his tour is over, or he can retire with full pension. Whenever such a character makes the mistake of mentioning his remaining time ("Three days and I'm outta here!") he will die before the end of that time.

Stanton-Walsh Rule. No movie featuring either Harry Dean Stanton or M. Emmet Walsh in a supporting role can be altogether bad. An exception was *Chatahoochee* (1990), starring Walsh. Stanton's record is still intact. (Reader Matthew J. Carson of Wallingford, PA, writes in to argue that Michael J. Pollard should be included in this rule, but Carson's de-

fense of Pollard in *Tango and Cash* is less than convincing.)

Still Out There Somewhere. Obligatory phrase in Dead Teen-Ager and Mad Slasher Movies, where it is triggered by the words, "The body was never found. They say he/she is. . ."

Sturgeon's Law. "Ninety percent of everything is crap." (First formulated in the 1950s by the science fiction author Theodore Sturgeon; quoted here because it so manifestly applies to motion pictures.)

Third Hand. Invisible appendage used by Rambo in *Rambo*, in the scene where he hides from the enemy by completely plastering himself inside a mud bank. Since it is impossible to cover yourself with mud without at least one hand free to do the job, Rambo must have had a third, invisible, hand. This explains a lot about the movie.

Tijuana. In modern Horny Teenager Movies, performs the same symbolic function as California did for the Beatniks, Marrakech did for the hippies, and Paris did for the Lost Generation.

Turtle Effect. Once knocked down, a character just lies there as if unable to get up. Cf. Sigourney Weaver in *Alien*. (Portanova)

Undead Dead. In horror movies, whenever the killer is killed, he is never dead. This rule is as old as the movies, but was given its modern shape in *Halloween* (1978) when the killer arose from apparent destruction to jump up behind Jamie Lee Curtis. Since then, all of the Dead Teen-ager Movies, most of the Bond pictures, and many other thrillers have used a false climax, in which the villain is killed—only to spring up for a final threat. In an ordinary thriller, the cliché of the Undead Dead is part of the game—but its use in *Fatal Attraction* was unforgivable.

Unmotivated Close-up. A character is given a close-up in a scene where there seems to be no reason for it. This is an infallible tip-off that this character is more significant than at first appears, and is most likely the killer. See the lingering close-up of the undercover KGB agent near the beginning of *The Hunt for Red October*. (Cleland)

Unsilenced Revolver. Despite dozens of movies which think otherwise, a revolver cannot be silenced, because the sound escapes, not from the barrel where they fit the silencer, but from the gap between the frame and the cylinder. Only closed-breech weapons, like pistols with magazines in the grip, can be silenced—unless you wrap them in a pillow. (Dawson E. Rambo, Las Vegas)

"Wait Right Here!" Rule. One character, usually male, tells another character, usually female, to "Wait right here. Do *not* follow me into the warehouse, cave, house, etc." The woman inevitably does so, is captured, and must be rescued. Often inspires the line "I thought I told you to wait outside." (Donna A. Higgins, Prairie du Chien, WI)

We're Alive! Let's Kiss! Inevitable conclusion to any scene in which hero and heroine take cover from gunfire by diving side-by-side into a ditch, and find themselves in each other's arms, usually for the first time. Cf. *High Road to China*.

Wedding Cake Rule. In any movie comedy involving a wedding, the cake will be destroyed. (Weckmueller)

Wet. In Hollywood story conferences, suggested alternative to nude, as in: "If she won't take off her clothes, can we wet her down?" Suggested by Harry Cohn's remark about swimming star Esther Williams: "Dry, she ain't much. Wet, she's a star."

Wrong-headed Commanding Officer. In modern police movies, the commanding officer exists solely for the purpose of taking the hero off the case, calling him on the carpet, issuing dire warnings, asking him to hand over his badge and gun, etc. Cf. the Dirty Harry series, *Blue Steel*, etc. (Whitehouse)

Wunza Movie. Any film using a plot which can be summarized by saying "One's a . . . ." For example, "One's a cop. One's an actor." Or "One's a saint. One's a sinner." (David King, Los Angeles)

X-ray Driver. In many thrillers, the hero crashes his car or truck through the window or wall of a building at the precise time and place to allow him to rescue a victim or kill the bad guys. How can he see through the walls to know exactly where his car will emerge? Why doesn't he ever drive into a load-bearing beam?

Youngblood Rule. No movie with a hero named "Youngblood" has ever been any good. Cf. *Youngblood Hawke*, *Youngblood*, etc.

Z. Pronounced "zed" in British movies, something most American audiences do not know.

Four-Star Reviews

About Last Night. . .
Accidental Tourist, The
After Hours
After the Rehearsal
Alex in Wonderland
Alice Doesn't Live Here Anymore
Amadeus
Amarcord
American Graffiti
Another Woman
Apocalypse Now
Au Revoir les Enfants
Autumn Sonata
Awakenings

Badlands
Bang the Drum Slowly
Barfly
Being There
Best Boy
Betrayal
Big Easy, The
Birdy
Black Stallion, The
Blood Simple
Blow Out
Blue Collar
Blume in Love
Born on the Fourth of July
Bounty, The
Breaking Away
Bring Me the Head of Alfredo
   Garcia
Broadcast News
Burden of Dreams
Bye Bye Brazil

California Split
Carmen (ballet)
Carmen (opera)
Chariots of Fire
China Syndrome
Chinatown
Chocolat
Chuck Berry Hail! Hail! Rock 'n'
   Roll

Claire's Knee
Close Encounters of the Third
   Kind: The Special Edition
Color Purple, The
Coming Home
Conversation, The
Cook, the Thief, His Wife and Her
   Lover, The
Cotton Club, The
Cries and Whispers

Dance With a Stranger
Dances With Wolves
Dawn of the Dead
Day After Trinity, The
Day for Night
Day of the Jackal, The
Days of Heaven
Dear America: Letters Home From
   Vietnam
Deer Hunter, The
Dick Tracy
Discreet Charm of the Bourgeoisie,
   The
Diva
Do the Right Thing
Down and Out in Beverly Hills
Draughtsman's Contract, The
Dresser, The
Driving Miss Daisy
Drugstore Cowboy
Dry White Season, A

E.T.—The Extra-Terrestrial
El Norte
Exorcist, The

Falcon and the Snowman, The
Fanny and Alexander
Fantasia
Farewell, My Lovely
Fellini's Roma
Field of Dreams
Fish Called Wanda, A
Fitzcarraldo
Five Easy Pieces

Four Friends
Frenzy
Friends of Eddie Coyle, The

Gambler, The
Gandhi
Garden of the Finzi-Continis, The
Gates of Heaven
Getting It Right
Godfather, The
Godspell
Gone With the Wind
GoodFellas
Good Morning, Vietnam
Great Santini, The
Grifters, The

Hair
Halloween
Hannah and Her Sisters
Hardcore
Harlan County, U.S.A.
Harry and Tonto
Heartland
Hidden Fortress, The
High Hopes
Hoosiers
Housekeeping
House of Games

I Never Sang for My Father
Iceman
Indiana Jones and the Temple of
   Doom
Interiors

Jaws
Johnny Got His Gun

Kagemusha
Karate Kid, The
Killing Fields, The

L.A. Story
La Cage aux Folles
La Lectrice
Last Detail, The
Last Emperor, The

Last Picture Show, The
Last Tango in Paris
Last Temptation of Christ, The
Late Show, The
Lawrence of Arabia
Less Than Zero
Lethal Weapon
Little Big Man
Little Dorrit
Little Mermaid, The
Local Hero
Long Good Friday, The
Lost in America
Love Story
Love Streams
Lucas

M*A*S*H
Macbeth
Mad Max Beyond Thunderdome
Madame Sousatzka
Man of Iron
Man Who Would Be King, The
Manchurian Candidate, The
Manhattan Project, The
Manon of the Spring
Marriage of Maria Braun, The
McCabe and Mrs. Miller
Mean Streets
Mephisto
Metropolis
Micki & Maude
Mighty Quinn, The
Mishima
Mississippi Burning
Mona Lisa
Monsieur Hire
Moonlighting
Moonstruck
Moscow on the Hudson
Mr. and Mrs. Bridge
My Dinner with André
My Left Foot

Nashville
National Lampoon's Animal House
Network
No Way Out
Nosferatu

Officer and a Gentleman, An
On Golden Pond
Once Upon a Time in America
Onion Field, The
Ordinary People
Out of Africa

Paper Chase, The
Paperhouse
Parenthood
Paris, Texas
Passage to India, A
Patton
Peggy Sue Got Married
Permanent Record
Personal Best
Pixote
Platoon
Play Misty for Me
Prick Up Your Ears
Prince of the City
Prizzi's Honor
Purple Rose of Cairo, The

Radio Days
Raging Bull
Raiders of the Lost Ark
Ran
Return of the Jedi
Reversal of Fortune
Richard Pryor Here and Now
Richard Pryor Live on the Sunset
   Strip
Right Stuff, The
Risky Business
Rocky
Roger & Me
Room with a View, A
'Round Midnight
Runaway Train
Running on Empty

Saint Jack
Salaam Bombay!
Santa Sangre
Say Amen, Somebody
Say Anything
Scandal
Scarface
Scenes from a Marriage
Secret Honor
Shoah
Shy People
Sid & Nancy
Silent Movie
Silent Running
Silkwood
Sleuth
Small Change
Smash Palace
Sophie's Choice
Sounder

STAR 80
Star Is Born, A
Star Wars
Stevie
Stranger than Paradise
Streamers
Streetwise
Stroszek
Sunday Bloody Sunday
Superman
Superman II

Talk Radio
Tampopo
Taxi Driver
10
Terms of Endearment
Tess
Testament
Tex
That's Entertainment!
They Shoot Horses, Don't They?
This Is Spinal Tap
3 Women
To Live and Die in L.A.
Tootsie
Tron
Trouble in Mind
28 Up
Two English Girls
2001: A Space Odyssey

Uforia
Unbearable Lightness of Being, The
Under the Volcano
Unmarried Woman, An

Vagabond
Verdict, The
Vincent

Walkabout
WarGames
Weavers, The: Wasn't That a Time!
Wetherby
Who Framed Roger Rabbit
Willie Wonka and the Chocolate
   Factory
Wings of Desire
Withnail & I
Witness
Woman Under the Influence, A
Woodstock
Working Girl
World Apart, A

Year of Living Dangerously
Young Frankenstein

Reviews Appearing in Previous Editions

Agnes of God ★ (1989 ed.)
All Night Long ★ ★ (1986 ed.)
. . . All the Marbles ★ ★ (1986 ed.)
Alligator ★ (1990 ed.)
Amityville II: The Possession ★ ★ (1988 ed.)
Any Which Way You Can ★ ★ (1988 ed.)
Asylum ★ ★ (1991 ed.)
Awakening, The ★ (1986 ed.)
Baby . . . The Secret of the Lost Legend ★ (1987 ed.)
Back Roads ★ ★ (1987 ed.)
Bad Dreams ¹/₂★ (1990 ed.)
Best Little Whorehouse in Texas, The ★ ★ (1991 ed.)
Beyond the Limit ★ ★¹/₂ (1989 ed.)
Beyond Therapy ★ (1988 ed.)
Big Brawl, The ★¹/₂ (1986 ed.)
Big Foot ¹/₂★ (1990 ed.)
Black Cauldron, The ★ ★ ★¹/₂ (1987 ed.)
Black Stallion Returns, The ★ ★¹/₂ (1986 ed.)
Black Widow ★ ★¹/₂ (1991 ed.)
Blame It on Rio ★ (1987 ed.)
Blind Date ★ ★¹/₂ (1988 ed.)
Blue Lagoon, The ¹/₂★ (1991 ed.)
Brainstorm ★ ★ (1986 ed.)
Breathless ★ ★¹/₂ (1989 ed.)
Brewster's Millions ★ (1988 ed.)
Brighton Beach Memoirs ★ ★ (1989 ed.)
Brubaker ★ ★¹/₂ (1991 ed.)
Burglar ★ (1989 ed.)
Butley ★ ★ ★ (1987 ed.)
Caligula no stars (1990 ed.)
Cannery Row ★ ★¹/₂ (1987 ed.)
Cannonball Run, The ¹/₂★ (1991 ed.)
Cannonball Run II ¹/₂★ (1988 ed.)
Cat's Eye ★ ★ ★ (1986 ed.)
Caveman ★¹/₂ (1986 ed.)
City Heat ¹/₂★ (1991 ed.)
City of Women ★ ★¹/₂ (1991 ed.)
Clan of the Cave Bear ★¹/₂ (1989 ed.)
Coca-Cola Kid, The ★ ★ ★ (1987 ed.)

Company of Wolves, The ★ ★ ★ (1987 ed.)
Compromising Positions ★ ★ (1987 ed.)
Cowboys, The ★ ★¹/₂ (1991 ed.)
Creator ★ ★¹/₂ (1987 ed.)
Cross My Heart ★ ★¹/₂ (1989 ed.)
Curse of the Pink Panther ★¹/₂ (1986 ed.)
Daniel ★ ★¹/₂ (1987 ed.)
Dark Crystal, The ★ ★¹/₂ (1991 ed.)
Date with an Angel ★ (1989 ed.)
D.C. Cab ★ ★ (1988 ed.)
Desert Hearts ★ ★¹/₂ (1988 ed.)
Dogs of War, The ★ ★ ★ (1988 ed.)
Dragonslayer ★ ★ ★ (1989 ed.)
Dreamscape ★ ★ ★ (1989 ed.)
Dune ★ (1988 ed.)
Eddie and the Cruisers ★ ★ (1987 ed.)
Electric Dreams ★ ★ ★¹/₂ (1989 ed.)
Eleni ★ ★ ★ (1987 ed.)
Emerald Forest, The ★ ★ (1988 ed.)
Endless Love ★ ★ (1991 ed.)
Enemy Mine ★ ★¹/₂ (1988 ed.)
Escape from New York ★ ★¹/₂ (1988 ed.)
Eureka ★ ★ ★ (1986 ed.)
Excalibur ★ ★¹/₂ (1987 ed.)
Explorers ★ ★ (1987 ed.)
Exterminator, The no stars (1990 ed.)
Extremities ★ (1989 ed.)
Fade to Black ★ ★¹/₂ (1991 ed.)
Falling in Love ★ ★ (1987 ed.)
Fiendish Plot of Dr. Fu Manchu, The ★ (1986 ed.)
Final Conflict, The ★ ★ ★ (1987 ed.)
Final Countdown, The ★ ★ (1988 ed.)
Firestarter ★ ★ (1987 ed.)
First Deadly Sin, The ★ ★ ★ (1986 ed.)
Firstborn ★ ★ (1987 ed.)
Flash Gordon ★ ★¹/₂ (1988 ed.)
Flash of Green, A ★ ★ ★ (1987 ed.)
Fog, The ★ ★ (1988 ed.)
Formula, The ★ ★ (1987 ed.)
Fort Apache, The Bronx ★ ★ (1987 ed.)
Fraternity Vacation ★ (1990 ed.)

Ghost Story ★ ★ ★ (1989 ed.)
Ginger and Fred ★ ★ (1988 ed.)
Give My Regards to Broad Street ★ (1986 ed.)
Godzilla 1985 ★ (1988 ed.)
Gotcha! ★ ★ (1986 ed.)
Hardly Working no stars (1986 ed.)
Harold and Maude ★¹/₂ (1991 ed.)
Harry & Son ★ (1986 ed.)
Heart Beat ★ ★¹/₂ (1991 ed.)
Hearse, The ¹/₂★ (1986 ed.)
Heat ★ ★ (1988 ed.)
Heaven ★ ★ (1990 ed.)
Heaven Help Us ★ ★¹/₂ (1989 ed.)
Heavenly Kid, The ★ (1987 ed.)
Hell Night ★ (1986 ed.)
Hellbound: Hellraiser II ¹/₂★ (1990 ed.)
Hero and the Terror ★ ★ (1991 ed.)
High Road to China ★ ★ (1987 ed.)
Hitcher, The no stars (1990 ed.)
Home and the World, The ★ ★ ★ (1987 ed.)
Howling II ★ (1987 ed.)
Hunger, The ★¹/₂ (1991 ed.)
I Spit on Your Grave no stars (1990 ed.)
Incredible Shrinking Woman, The ★ ★¹/₂ (1991 ed.)
Into the Night ★ (1987 ed.)
Invasion USA ¹/₂★ (1989 ed.)
Jazz Singer, The ★ (1987 ed.)
Julia ★ ★¹/₂ (1988 ed.)
Jumpin' Jack Flash ★ ★ (1990 ed.)
Just Between Friends ★¹/₂ (1987 ed.)
Kerouac ★ ★¹/₂ (1987 ed.)
King David ★ (1987 ed.)
Lair of the White Worm, The ★ ★ (1991 ed.)
Last Dragon, The ★ ★¹/₂ (1991 ed.)
Last Flight of Noah's Ark, The ¹/₂★ (1986 ed.)
Last Starfighter, The ★ ★¹/₂ (1991 ed.)
Legend ★ ★ (1989 ed.)
Like Father, Like Son ★ (1991 ed.)

Little Darlings ★ ★ (1987 ed.)
Little Drummer Girl, The ★ ★ (1991 ed.)
Little Nikita ★ 1/2 (1991 ed.)
Lonely Lady, The 1/2 ★ (1988 ed.)
Lords of Discipline, The ★ ★ (1991 ed.)
Lovesick ★ ★ ★ (1989 ed.)
Lust in the Dust ★ ★ (1990 ed.)
Making Love ★ ★ (1988 ed.)
Man Who Loved Women, The ★ ★ (1988 ed.)
Mannequin 1/2 ★ (1990 ed.)
Marie ★ ★ ★ (1987 ed.)
Max Dugan Returns ★ ★ 1/2 (1986 ed.)
Maxie 1/2 ★ (1987 ed.)
Men Don't Leave ★ ★ (1991 ed.)
Merry Christmas, Mr. Lawrence ★ ★ 1/2 (1991 ed.)
Money Pit, The ★ (1991 ed.)
Monsignor ★ (1987 ed.)
Mother's Day **no stars** (1991 ed.)
Mr. Mom ★ ★ (1987 ed.)
My Tutor ★ ★ ★ (1986 ed.)
Nightmare on Elm Street 3, A: Dream Warriors ★ 1/2 (1990 ed.)
Nobody's Fool ★ ★ (1991 ed.)
Nomads ★ 1/2 (1987 ed.)
Nothing in Common ★ ★ 1/2 (1988 ed.)
On the Edge ★ ★ ★ 1/2 (1989 ed.)
On the Right Track ★ ★ 1/2 (1986 ed.)
One Magic Christmas ★ ★ (1987 ed.)
$1,000,000 Duck ★ (1987 ed.)
Only When I Laugh ★ (1987 ed.)
Paternity ★ ★ (1986 ed.)
Pennies from Heaven ★ ★ (1988 ed.)
Perfect ★ 1/2 (1987 ed.)
Pirates of Penzance, The ★ ★ (1986 ed.)
Possession of Joel Delaney, The ★ ★ (1991 ed.)
Postman Always Rings Twice, The ★ ★ 1/2 (1991 ed.)

Power ★ ★ 1/2 (1988 ed.)
Protocol ★ ★ 1/2 (1987 ed.)
Psycho II ★ ★ 1/2 (1991 ed.)
Pumping Iron II: The Women ★ ★ ★ 1/2 (1988 ed.)
Purple Hearts 1/2 ★ (1987 ed.)
Quicksilver ★ ★ (1987 ed.)
Raise the Titanic ★ ★ 1/2 (1986 ed.)
Razor's Edge, The ★ ★ 1/2 (1988 ed.)
Red Sonja ★ 1/2 (1987 ed.)
Return of the Living Dead ★ ★ ★ (1987 ed.)
Return to Oz ★ ★ (1987 ed.)
Revenge of the Nerds II ★ 1/2 (1990 ed.)
Rhinestone ★ (1987 ed.)
Rich and Famous ★ ★ 1/2 (1987 ed.)
River, The ★ ★ (1991 ed.)
St. Elmo's Fire ★ 1/2 (1987 ed.)
Santa Claus: The Movie ★ ★ 1/2 (1987 ed.)
Scene of the Crime ★ ★ 1/2 (1988 ed.)
Secret of My Success, The ★ 1/2 (1989 ed.)
Secret of NIMH, The ★ ★ ★ (1986 ed.)
Seems Like Old Times ★ ★ (1986 ed.)
Sheena, Queen of the Jungle ★ (1990 ed.)
Shooting Party, The ★ ★ ★ (1987 ed.)
Slugger's Wife, The ★ ★ (1986 ed.)
Smokey and the Bandit II ★ (1986 ed.)
Soldier of Orange ★ ★ ★ 1/2 (1986 ed.)
Somewhere in Time ★ ★ (1988 ed.)
Soul Man ★ (1989 ed.)
Spaceballs ★ ★ 1/2 (1991 ed.)
Spring Break ★ (1988 ed.)
Stephen King's Silver Bullet ★ ★ ★ (1988 ed.)
Sting II, The ★ ★ (1986 ed.)
Stir Crazy ★ ★ (1987 ed.)
Streets of Fire ★ ★ ★ (1988 ed.)
Stripper ★ ★ ★ (1987 ed.)
Stroker Ace ★ 1/2 (1986 ed.)

Stuff, The ★ 1/2 (1987 ed.)
Stunt Man, The ★ ★ (1988 ed.)
Summer of '42 ★ ★ 1/2 (1987 ed.)
Supergirl ★ ★ (1988 ed.)
Surrender ★ ★ (1989 ed.)
Survivors, The ★ 1/2 (1991 ed.)
Sweet Dreams ★ ★ (1988 ed.)
Swing Shift ★ ★ ★ (1988 ed.)
Sylvester ★ ★ ★ (1988 ed.)
Table for Five ★ 1/2 (1986 ed.)
Teachers ★ ★ (1986 ed.)
Teen Wolf Too 1/2 ★ (1989 ed.)
Terror Train ★ (1986 ed.)
That Was Then . . . This Is Now ★ ★ (1987 ed.)
They Call Me Bruce ★ ★ (1986 ed.)
Tiger's Tale, A ★ ★ (1989 ed.)
Tin Drum, The ★ ★ (1988 ed.)
Tough Enough ★ ★ ★ (1986 ed.)
Turk 182! ★ (1987 ed.)
Two of a Kind 1/2 ★ (1986 ed.)
Until September 1/2 ★ (1987 ed.)
Up the Creek ★ ★ ★ (1989 ed.)
Videodrome ★ 1/2 (1988 ed.)
Violets Are Blue ★ ★ ★ (1987 ed.)
War Party ★ (1991 ed.)
Watcher in the Woods, The ★ ★ (1986 ed.)
Where the Boys Are '84 1/2 ★ (1987 ed.)
Where the Buffalo Roam ★ ★ (1991 ed.)
Where the Green Ants Dream ★ ★ ★ (1988 ed.)
White Nights ★ ★ (1988 ed.)
Wildcats ★ 1/2 (1990 ed.)
Willard ★ ★ (1991 ed.)
Xanadu ★ ★ (1988 ed.)
Year of the Quiet Sun ★ ★ ★ ★ (1987 ed.)
Youngblood ★ ★ (1987 ed.)
Young Doctors in Love ★ ★ (1991 ed.)
Zabriskie Point ★ ★ (1991 ed.)
Zorro, the Gay Blade ★ ★ (1991 ed.)

Index

Titles with asterisks are on Roger Ebert's ten-best list for the year in which they opened.

Titles with asterisks are on Roger Ebert's ten-best list for the year in which they opened.

Titles with asterisks are on Roger Ebert's ten-best list for the year in which they opened.

Titles with asterisks are on Roger Ebert's ten-best list for the year in which they opened.

Titles with asterisks are on Roger Ebert's ten-best list for the year in which they opened.

Titles with asterisks are on Roger Ebert's ten-best list for the year in which they opened.

Titles with asterisks are on Roger Ebert's ten-best list for the year in which they opened.

Titles with asterisks are on Roger Ebert's ten-best list for the year in which they opened.

Titles with asterisks are on Roger Ebert's ten-best list for the year in which they opened.

Titles with asterisks are on Roger Ebert's ten-best list for the year in which they opened.

Titles with asterisks are on Roger Ebert's ten-best list for the year in which they opened.

Titles with asterisks are on Roger Ebert's ten-best list for the year in which they opened.

Titles with asterisks are on Roger Ebert's ten-best list for the year in which they opened.

Titles with asterisks are on Roger Ebert's ten-best list for the year in which they opened.

Titles with asterisks are on Roger Ebert's ten-best list for the year in which they opened.

Titles with asterisks are on Roger Ebert's ten-best list for the year in which they opened.

Titles with asterisks are on Roger Ebert's ten-best list for the year in which they opened.

Titles with asterisks are on Roger Ebert's ten-best list for the year in which they opened.

Titles with asterisks are on Roger Ebert's ten-best list for the year in which they opened.

Titles with asterisks are on Roger Ebert's ten-best list for the year in which they opened.

Titles with asterisks are on Roger Ebert's ten-best list for the year in which they opened.

Titles with asterisks are on Roger Ebert's ten-best list for the year in which they opened.

Titles with asterisks are on Roger Ebert's ten-best list for the year in which they opened.

Titles with asterisks are on Roger Ebert's ten-best list for the year in which they opened.

Titles with asterisks are on Roger Ebert's ten-best list for the year in which they opened.

Titles with asterisks are on Roger Ebert's ten-best list for the year in which they opened.

Titles with asterisks are on Roger Ebert's ten-best list for the year in which they opened.

Titles with asterisks are on Roger Ebert's ten-best list for the year in which they opened.

Titles with asterisks are on Roger Ebert's ten-best list for the year in which they opened.

Titles with asterisks are on Roger Ebert's ten-best list for the year in which they opened.

Titles with asterisks are on Roger Ebert's ten-best list for the year in which they opened.

Titles with asterisks are on Roger Ebert's ten-best list for the year in which they opened.

Titles with asterisks are on Roger Ebert's ten-best list for the year in which they opened.

Titles with asterisks are on Roger Ebert's ten-best list for the year in which they opened.

Titles with asterisks are on Roger Ebert's ten-best list for the year in which they opened.

Titles with asterisks are on Roger Ebert's ten-best list for the year in which they opened.

Titles with asterisks are on Roger Ebert's ten-best list for the year in which they opened.

Titles with asterisks are on Roger Ebert's ten-best list for the year in which they opened.

Titles with asterisks are on Roger Ebert's ten-best list for the year in which they opened.

Titles with asterisks are on Roger Ebert's ten-best list for the year in which they opened.

Titles with asterisks are on Roger Ebert's ten-best list for the year in which they opened.